W9-BKB-164

CONTENTS

The arrow symbol (→) used in this book indicates that additional information can be found in *Harper's Bible Dictionary* in the article(s) named following the arrow; for example (→ Corinth) or (→ Samuel; Saul).

HARPER'S BIBLE COMMENTARY

Harper's Bible Commentary

GENERAL EDITOR

James L. Mays

ASSOCIATE EDITORS

Joseph Blenkinsopp
Jon D. Levenson
Wayne A. Meeks
Carol A. Newsom
David L. Petersen

With the Society of Biblical Literature

1817

Harper & Row, Publishers, San Francisco

Cambridge, Hagerstown, New York, Philadelphia, Washington
London, Mexico City, São Paulo, Singapore, Sydney

Publication Staff

Senior Editor:
John B. Shopp
Associate Editor:
Kandace Hawkinson
Chief Copyeditor:
Ann Moru
Copyediting Coordinator:
Dorian Gossy
Copyeditors:
Jean Blomquist, Phil Harnden, Virginia Rich
Proofreading Coordinator:
Janet Reed
Proofreaders:
Arla Ertz, Kathy Lee, Jean Mann, Annelise Zamula, Beverly Zegarski
Editorial Assistant:
Hilary M. Vartanian
Photo Researcher:
Lindsay Kefauver
Design:
Design Office Bruce Kortebein, Leigh McLellan
Typesetter:
Auto-Graphics, Inc.
Text Printer and Binder:
The Haddon Craftsmen
Cartographer and Color Maps Printer:
Hammond, Inc.
Jacket Printer:
The Longacre Press, Inc.
Color Photographs Printer:
New England Book Components, Inc.

Library of Congress Cataloging-in-Publication Data

Harper's Bible commentary.

   Bibliographies.
   Includes index.
   1. Bible—Commentaries.   I. Mays, James Luther.   II. Harper & Row.   III. Society of Biblical Literature.
BS491.2.H37   1988   220.7   88-45148
ISBN 0-06-065541-0

88   89   90   91   92   10   9   8   7   6   5   4   3   2   1

CONTRIBUTORS

Elizabeth Achtemeier, Ph.D.
Adjunct Professor of Bible and Homiletics
Union Theological Seminary in Virginia
Richmond, Virginia
Zephaniah

Paul J. Achtemeier, Th.D.
Jackson Professor of Biblical Interpretation
Union Theological Seminary in Virginia
Richmond, Virginia
1 Peter

Peter R. Ackroyd, Ph.D.
Professor Emeritus, Old Testament Studies
University of London
London, England
Haggai

Harold W. Attridge, Ph.D.
Professor of New Testament
University of Notre Dame
Notre Dame, Indiana
Hebrews

David E. Aune, Ph.D.
Professor of Religious Studies
Saint Xavier College
Chicago, Illinois
*The Bible and the Literature of Antiquity:
The Greco-Roman Period, Revelation*

William Baird, Ph.D.
Professor of New Testament
Brite Divinity School
Texas Christian University
Fort Worth, Texas
Galatians

James Barr, Th.D.
Regius Professor of Hebrew
Oxford University
Oxford, England
The Bible and Its Communities

John Barton, D. Phil.
Lecturer in Theology (Old Testament)
St. Cross College
Oxford University
Oxford, England
Reading and Interpreting the Bible

Richard J. Bauckham, Ph.D.
Reader in the History of Christian Thought
University of Manchester
Manchester, England
2 Peter, Jude

J. Christiaan Beker, Ph.D.
Professor of New Testament Theology
Princeton Theological Seminary
Princeton, New Jersey
Colossians

Theodore A. Bergren, Ph.D.
University of Pennsylvania
Philadelphia, Pennsylvania
2 Esdras

Adele Berlin, Ph.D.
Professor of Hebrew
University of Maryland
College Park, Maryland
Ruth

Roger S. Boraas, Ph.D.
Professor of Religion
Upsala College
East Orange, New Jersey
Consultant for Maps

Roddy L. Braun, Th.D.
Pastor
Our Savior Lutheran Church
Arlington, Virginia
1 Chronicles, 2 Chronicles

Duane L. Christensen, Th.D.
Professor of Old Testament Languages and
Literature
American Baptist Seminary of the West and
Graduate Theological Union
Berkeley, California
Nahum

Richard J. Clifford, Ph.D.
Dean and Professor of Old Testament
Weston School of Theology
Cambridge, Massachusetts
Isaiah 40–66

David J. A. Clines, M.A.
Professor of Biblical Studies
University of Sheffield
Sheffield, England
*Introduction to the Biblical Story: Genesis–
Esther, Esther, The Additions to Esther*

Robert L. Cohn, Ph.D.
Philip and Muriel Berman Scholar in
Jewish Studies
Lafayette College
Easton, Pennsylvania
1 Samuel

John J. Collins, Ph.D.
Professor of Hebrew Bible and Judaica
University of Notre Dame
Notre Dame, Indiana
Introduction to the Apocrypha,
3 Maccabees

Fred B. Craddock, Ph.D.
Bandy Professor of Preaching and New
Testament
Candler School of Theology
Emory University
Atlanta, Georgia
Luke

James L. Crenshaw, Ph.D.
Professor of Old Testament
The Divinity School
Duke University
Durham, North Carolina
Ecclesiastes, Sirach

R. Alan Culpepper, Ph.D.
James Buchanan Harrison Professor of New
Testament Interpretation
Southern Baptist Theological Seminary
Louisville, Kentucky
1, 2, 3 John

Nils A. Dahl, Dr. Theol.
Buckingham Professor Emeritus of New
Testament Criticism and Interpretation
Yale University
New Haven, Connecticut
Ephesians

John R. Donahue, S.J., Ph.D.
Professor of New Testament
Jesuit School of Theology at Berkeley and
Graduate Theological Union
Berkeley, California
Mark

Robert Doran, Th.D.
Associate Professor in Religion
Amherst College
Amherst, Massachusetts
The Additions to Daniel

Eldon Jay Epp, Ph.D.
Harkness Professor of Biblical Literature
Case Western Reserve University
Cleveland, Ohio
Biblical Literature in Its Historical Context:
The Apocrypha and the New Testament

J. Cheryl Exum, Ph.D.
Associate Professor, Department of Theology
Boston College
Chestnut Hill, Massachusetts
Judges

Marcia Falk, Ph.D.
Visiting Associate Professor of Religious
Studies
Stanford University
Palo Alto, California
Song of Songs

Elisabeth Schüssler Fiorenza, Dr. Theol.
The Krister Stendahl Professor of New
Testament
Harvard University
Cambridge, Massachusetts
1 Corinthians

Michael Fishbane, Ph.D.
Samuel Lane Professor of Jewish Religious
History and Social Ethics
Brandeis University
Waltham, Massachusetts
The Bible and Its Interpreters: Jewish
Biblical Interpretation

Michael H. Floyd, Ph.D.
Professor of Old Testament
Episcopal Theological Seminary of the
Southwest
Austin, Texas
Obadiah

Carole R. Fontaine, Ph.D.
Associate Professor of Old Testament
Andover-Newton Theological School
Newton Centre, Massachusetts
Proverbs

Terence E. Fretheim, Th.D.
Professor of Old Testament
Luther Northwestern Theological Seminary
St. Paul, Minnesota
Jonah

Reginald H. Fuller, S.T.D.
Professor Emeritus
Virginia Theological Seminary
Alexandria, Virginia
Matthew

Victor Paul Furnish, Ph.D.
University Distinguished Professor of New
Testament
Perkins School of Theology
Southern Methodist University
Dallas, Texas
2 Corinthians

Edwin M. Good, Ph.D.
Professor of Religious Studies
Stanford University
Palo Alto, California
Job

Norman K. Gottwald, Ph.D.
W. W. White Professor of Biblical Studies
New York Theological Seminary
New York, New York
Lamentations

David M. Gunn, Ph.D.
Professor of Old Testament
Columbia Theological Seminary
Decatur, Georgia
2 Samuel

Paul D. Hanson, Ph.D.
Florence Corliss Lamont Professor of
Divinity
Harvard University
Cambridge, Massachusetts
Malachi

Daniel J. Harrington, S.J., Ph.D.
Professor of New Testament
Weston School of Theology
Cambridge, Massachusetts
*Baruch, Letter of Jeremiah, Prayer of
Manasseh, Psalm 151*

John H. Hayes, Ph.D.
Professor of Old Testament
Candler School of Theology
Emory University
Atlanta, Georgia
Leviticus

Ronald F. Hock, Ph.D.
Associate Professor of Religion
University of Southern California
Los Angeles, California
Philippians

Carl R. Holladay, Ph.D.
Associate Professor of New Testament and
Associate Dean
Candler School of Theology
Emory University
Atlanta, Georgia
Acts

Robert Jewett, Dr. Theol.
Harry R. Kendall Professor of New
Testament Interpretation
Garrett-Evangelical Theological Seminary
Evanston, Illinois
Introduction to the Pauline Letters

Luke Timothy Johnson, Ph.D.
Associate Professor of Religious Studies
Indiana University
Bloomington, Indiana
James

Ralph W. Klein, Th.D.
Christ Seminary-Seminex Professor of Old
Testament
Lutheran School of Theology at Chicago
Chicago, Illinois
Ezra, Nehemiah, 1 Esdras

John S. Kselman, Ph.D.
Associate Professor of Old Testament
Weston School of Theology
Cambridge, Massachusetts
Genesis

James L. Kugel, Ph.D.
Professor of Near Eastern Languages
Harvard University
Cambridge, Massachusetts
Introduction to Psalms and Wisdom

Burke O. Long, Ph.D.
Professor of Religion
Bowdoin College
Brunswick, Maine
2 Kings

W. Eugene March, Ph.D.
A. B. Rhodes Professor of Old Testament
Louisville Presbyterian Theological
Seminary
Louisville, Kentucky
Micah

Ralph P. Martin, Ph.D.
Professor of New Testament and Director of
Graduate Studies Program
Fuller Theological Seminary
Pasadena, California
1, 2 Timothy and Titus

S. Dean McBride, Jr., Ph.D.
Professor of Old Testament Interpretation
Union Theological Seminary in Virginia
Richmond, Virginia
*Biblical Literature in Its Historical Context:
The Old Testament*

P. Kyle McCarter, Jr., Ph.D.
W. F. Albright Professor of Biblical and
Ancient Near Eastern Studies
Johns Hopkins University
Baltimore, Maryland
Exodus, 1 Kings

Roy F. Melugin, Ph.D.
Cloud Professor of Religion
Austin College
Sherman, Texas
Amos

Paul W. Meyer, Th.D.
Helen H. P. Manson Professor of New
Testament Literature and Exegesis
Princeton Theological Seminary
Princeton, New Jersey
Romans

Richard D. Nelson, Ph.D.
Professor of Old Testament
Lutheran Theological Seminary
Gettysburg, Pennsylvania
Deuteronomy

George W. E. Nickelsburg, Th.D.
Professor of New Testament and Early
Judaism
University of Iowa
Iowa City, Iowa
Tobit

Dennis T. Olson, Ph.D.
Assistant Professor of Old Testament
Princeton Theological Seminary
Princeton, New Jersey
Numbers

Thomas W. Overholt, Ph.D.
Professor of Religious Studies
University of Wisconsin, Stevens Point
Stevens Point, Wisconsin
Jeremiah

Pheme Perkins, Ph.D.
Professor of Theology (New Testament)
Boston College
Chestnut Hill, Massachusetts
*1 Thessalonians, 2 Thessalonians,
Introduction to the General Letters to the
Churches*

Norman R. Petersen, Ph.D.
Washington Gladden Professor of Religion
Williams College
Williamstown, Massachusetts
*Introduction to the Gospels and Acts,
Philemon*

Walter E. Rast, Ph.D.
Professor, Department of Theology
Valparaiso University
Valparaiso, Indiana
Joshua

James M. Reese, S.T.D.
Associate Professor, Department of Theology
St. John's University
Jamaica, New York
Wisdom of Solomon

J. J. M. Roberts, Ph.D.
W. H. Green Professor of Old Testament
Literature
Princeton Theological Seminary
Princeton, New Jersey
*The Bible and the Literature of Antiquity:
The Ancient Near East*

Lawrence H. Schiffman, Ph.D.
Professor of Hebrew and Judaic Studies
New York University
New York, New York
1 Maccabees, 2 Maccabees

Luis Alonso Schökel, Dr. S. S.
Professor of Old Testament Theology
Pontificio Istituto Biblico
Rome, Italy
Judith

Gerald T. Sheppard, Ph.D.
Associate Professor of Old Testament
Emmanuel College of Victoria University in
the University of Toronto
Isaiah 1–39

D. Moody Smith, Ph.D.
George Washington Ivey Professor of New
Testament
The Divinity School, Duke University
Durham, North Carolina
John

Michael F. Stone, Ph.D.
Professor of Armenian Studies
Hebrew University of Jerusalem
Jerusalem, Israel
2 Esdras

Stanley K. Stowers, Ph.D.
Associate Professor of Religious Studies
Brown University
Providence, Rhode Island
4 Maccabees

Carroll Stuhlmueller, C.P., S.S.D.
Professor of Old Testament Studies
Catholic Theological Union at Chicago
Chicago, Illinois
Psalms

Marvin A. Sweeney, Ph.D.
Assistant Professor of Religious Studies
University of Miami
Coral Gables, Florida
Habakkuk

W. Sibley Towner, Ph.D.
The Reverend Archibald McFadyen
Professor of Biblical Interpretation
Union Theological Seminary in Virginia
Richmond, Virginia
Daniel

Gene M. Tucker, Ph.D.
Professor of Old Testament
Candler School of Theology
Emory University
Atlanta, Georgia
Hosea

J. William Whedbee, Ph.D.
Nancy M. Lyon Professor of Biblical History
and Literature
Pomona College
Claremont, California
Joel

Robert L. Wilken, Ph.D.
William R. Kenan, Jr., Professor of the
History of Christianity
University of Virginia
Charlottesville, Virginia
*The Bible and Its Interpreters: Christian
Biblical Interpretation*

Robert R. Wilson, Ph.D.
Professor of Old Testament and Religious
Studies
Yale University
New Haven, Connecticut
Ezekiel

SHORT ESSAYS

Gk.	Greek	Dt.	Deuteronomic
Heb.	Hebrew	Dtr.	Deuteronomistic historian
Lat.	Latin	DSS	Dead Sea Scrolls
		LXX	Septuagint
ASV	American Standard Version	MT	Masoretic Text
JB	Jerusalem Bible	NT	New Testament
JPS	New Jewish Translation/	OT	Old Testament
	Jewish Publication Society	Vg.	Vulgate
KJV	King James Version		
NAB	New American Bible	chap(s).	chapter(s)
NASB	New American Standard Bible	col(s).	column(s)
NEB	New English Bible	fol(s).	folio(s)
NIV	New International Version	ms(s).	manuscript(s)
NJB	New Jerusalem Bible	n(n).	note(s)
RSV	Revised Standard Version	pl(s).	plate(s)
TEV	Today's English Version	p(p).	page(s)
		v(v).	verse(s)
→	Further information can be	vol(s).	volume(s)
	found in *Harper's Bible*	vs(s).	version(s)
	Dictionary under the article(s)		
	listed.		

BOOKS OF THE BIBLE (WITH APOCRYPHA)

Old Testament

Gen.	Genesis	Eccles.	Ecclesiastes
Exod.	Exodus	Song of Sg.	Song of Songs
Lev.	Leviticus	Isa.	Isaiah
Num.	Numbers	Jer.	Jeremiah
Deut.	Deuteronomy	Lam.	Lamentations
Josh.	Joshua	Ezek.	Ezekiel
Judg.	Judges	Dan.	Daniel
Ruth	Ruth	Hos.	Hosea
1 Sam.	1 Samuel	Joel	Joel
2 Sam.	2 Samuel	Amos	Amos
1 Kings	1 Kings	Obad.	Obadiah
2 Kings	2 Kings	Jon.	Jonah
1 Chron.	1 Chronicles	Mic.	Micah
2 Chron.	2 Chronicles	Nah.	Nahum
Ezra	Ezra	Hab.	Habakkuk
Neh.	Nehemiah	Zeph.	Zephaniah
Esther	Esther	Hag.	Haggai
Job	Job	Zech.	Zechariah
Ps. (Pss.)	Psalms	Mal.	Malachi
Prov.	Proverbs		

Apocrypha

1 Esd.	1 Esdras	Add. to Dan.	Additions to Daniel
2 Esd.	2 Esdras	Song of Three	Song of the
Tob.	Tobit	Youths	Three Youths
Jth.	Judith	Sus.	Susanna
Add. to Esther	Additions to Esther	Bel and Dragon	Bel and the Dragon
Wisd. of Sol.	Wisdom of Solomon	Pr. of Man.	Prayer of Manasseh
Sir.	Sirach	1 Macc.	1 Maccabees
Bar.	Baruch	2 Macc.	2 Maccabees
Let. Jer.	Letter of Jeremiah	3 Macc.	3 Maccabees
		4 Macc.	4 Maccabees
		Ps. 151	Psalm 151

New Testament

Matt.	Matthew	1 Tim.	1 Timothy
Mark	Mark	2 Tim.	2 Timothy
Luke	Luke	Titus	Titus
John	John	Philem.	Philemon
Acts	Acts of the Apostles	Heb.	Hebrews
Rom.	Romans	James	James
1 Cor.	1 Corinthians	1 Pet.	1 Peter
2 Cor.	2 Corinthians	2 Pet.	2 Peter
Gal.	Galatians	1 John	1 John
Eph.	Ephesians	2 John	2 John
Phil.	Philippians	3 John	3 John
Col.	Colossians	Jude	Jude
1 Thess.	1 Thessalonians	Rev.	Revelation
2 Thess.	2 Thessalonians		

PSEUDEPIGRAPHA AND EARLY PATRISTIC BOOKS

Adam and Eve	Books of Adam and Eve	Gos. Naass.	Gospel of the Naassenes
2–3 Apoc. Bar.	Syriac, Greek Apocalypse of Baruch	Gos. Pet.	Gospel of Peter
		Gos. Thom.	Gospel of Thomas
Apoc. Mos.	Apocalypse of Moses	Prot. Jas.	Protevangelium of James
As. Mos.	Assumption of Moses	1–2 Clem.	1–2 Clement
4 Bar.	4 Baruch (Expansions of Jeremiah)	Did.	Didache
		Diogn.	Diognetus
1–2–3 Enoch	Ethiopic, Slavonic, Hebrew Enoch	Herm. Man.	Hermas, Mandate
Jos. Asen.	Joseph and Aseneth	Sim.	Similitude
Jub.	Jubilees	Vis.	Vision
Let. Arist.	Letter of Aristeas	Ign. Eph.	Ignatius, Letter to the Ephesians
Mart. Isa.	Martyrdom of Isaiah	Magn.	Ignatius, Letter to the Magnesians
Odes Sol.	Odes of Solomon		
Pss. Sol.	Psalms of Solomon	Phld.	Ignatius, Letter to the Philadelphians
Sib. Or.	Sibylline Oracles		
T. 12 Patr.	Testaments of the Twelve Patriarchs	Pol.	Ignatius, Letter to Polycarp
		Rom.	Ignatius, Letter to the Romans
T. Levi	Testament of Levi	Smyrn.	Ignatius, Letter to the Smyrnaeans
T. Benj.	Testament of Benjamin, etc.		
Acts Pil.	Acts of Pilate	Trall.	Ignatius, Letter to the Trallians
Apoc. Abr.	Apocalypse of Abraham		
Apoc. Elij.	Apocalypse of Elijah	Let. Barn.	Letter of Barnabas
Apoc. Pet.	Apocalypse of Peter	Mart. Pol.	Martyrdom of Polycarp
Apoc. Zeph.	Apocalypse of Zephaniah	Pol. Phil.	Polycarp, Letter to the Philippians
Gos. Eb.	Gospel of the Ebionites		
Gos. Eg.	Gospel of the Egyptians	Bib. Ant.	Ps.-Philo, Biblical Antiquities
Gos. Heb.	Gospel of the Hebrews		

DEAD SEA SCROLLS AND RELATED TEXTS

CD	Cairo (Genizah text of the) Damascus (Document)
Hev	Naḥal Ḥever texts
Mas	Masada texts
Mird	Khirbet Mird texts
Mur	Wadi Murabba'at texts
p.	Pesher (commentary)
Q	Qumran
QL	Qumran literature
1Q, 2Q, 3Q, etc.	Numbered caves of Qumran, yielding written material; followed by abbreviation of biblical book or other writing
1QapGen	Genesis Apocryphon of Qumran Cave 1
1QH	Hôdāyôt (Thanksgiving Hymns) from Qumran Cave 1

1QpHab	*Pesher on Habakkuk* from Qumran Cave 1
1QIsa[a,b]	First or second copy of *Isaiah* from Qumran Cave 1
1QM	*Milḥāmāh* (*War Scroll*)
1QS	*Serek hayyaḥad* (*Rule of the Community, Manual of Discipline*)
1QSa	Appendix A (*Rule of the Congregation*) to 1QS
1QSb	Appendix B (*Blessings*) to 1QS
3Q15	Copper Scroll from Qumran Cave 3
4QBibHam	*Words of the Heavenly Luminaries* from Qumran Cave 4
4QFlor	*Florilegium* (or *Eschatological Midrashim*) from Qumran Cave 4
4QJudg	Text of *Judges* from Qumran Cave 4
4QMess ar	Aramaic "Messianic" text from Qumran Cave 4
4QPhyl	*Phylacteries* from Qumran Cave 4
4QPsAp[a]	*Apocryphal psalms* from Qumran Cave 4
4QPBless	*Patriarchal Blessings* from Qumran Cave 4
4QPseudoDan	Pseudo-Daniel from Qumran Cave 4
4QPrNab	*Prayer of Nabonidus* from Qumran Cave 4
4QSam[a]	First copy of *Samuel* from Qumran Cave 4
4QShirShab	*Song of the Sabbath Sacrifice* from Qumran Cave 4
4QTestim	*Testamonia* text from Qumran Cave 4
4QTLevi	*Testament of Levi* from Qumran Cave 4
4Q380–381	Fragments of Extra-canonical psalms from Qumran Cave 4
4Q510–511	Manuscript fragment from Qumran Cave 4
11QtgJob	*Targum of Job* from Qumran Cave 11
11QMelch	Melchizedek text from Qumran Cave 11
11QPs[a]	*Psalms Scroll* from Qumran Cave 11
11QTemple	*Temple Scroll* from Qumran Cave 11

TARGUMIC MATERIAL

Tg. Onq.	*Targum Onqelos*	Tg. Neof.	*Targum Neofiti 1*
Tg. Neb.	*Targum of the Prophets*	Tg. Ps.-J.	*Targum Pseudo-Jonathan*
Tg. Ket.	*Targum of the Writings*	Tg. Yer. I	*Targum Yerušalmi I*
Frg. Tg.	*Fragmentary Targum*	Tg. Yer. II	*Targum Yerušalmi II*
Sam. Tg.	*Samaritan Targum*	Yem. Tg.	*Yemenite Targum*
Tg. Isa.	*Targum of Isaiah*	Tg. Esth. I,	*First or Second Targum of*
Pal. Tgs.	*Palestinian Targums*	II	*Esther*

MISHNAIC AND RELATED LITERATURE

m.	Mishnah	Ker.	Keritot
t.	Tosepta	Ketub.	Ketubot
b.	Babylonian Talmud	Kil.	Kil'ayim
y.	Jerusalem (Palestinian) Talmud	Ma'aś.	Ma'aśerot
'Abod. Zar.	'Aboda Zara	Ma'as. Š.	Ma'aśer Šeni
'Abot	'Abot	Mak.	Makkot
'Arak.	'Arakin	Makš.	Makširin (= Mašqin)
B. Bat.	Baba Batra	Meg.	Megilla
Bek.	Bekorot	Me'il.	Me'ila
Ber.	Berakot	Menaḥ.	Menaḥot
Beṣa	Beṣa (= Yom Ṭo)	Mid.	Middot
Bik.	Bikkurim	Miqw.	Miqwa'ot
B. Mes.	Baba Meṣi'a	Mo'ed	Mo'ed
B. Qam.	Baba Qamma	Mo'ed Qaṭ.	Mo'ed Qaṭan
Dem.	Demai	Našim	Našim
'Ed.	'Eduyyot	Nazir	Nazir
'Erub.	'Erubin	Ned.	Nedarim
Giṭ.	Giṭin	Neg.	Nega'im
Ḥag.	Ḥagiga	Nez.	Neziqin
Ḥal.	Ḥalla	Nid.	Niddah
Hor.	Horayot	Ohol.	Oholot
Ḥul.	Ḥullin	'Or.	'Orla
Kelim	Kelim	Para	Para

Pe'a	Pe'a	Ta'an.	Ta'anit
Pesaḥ.	Pesaḥim	Tamid	Tamid
Qidd.	Qiddušin	Tem.	Temura
Qinnim	Qinnim	Ter.	Terumot
Qod.	Qodašin	Tohar.	Toharot
Roš. Haš.	Roš Haššana	T. Yom	Tebul Yom
Šabb.	Šabbat	'Uq.	'Uqṣin
Sanh.	Sanhedrin	Yad.	Yadayim
Šeb.	Šebi'it	Yebam.	Yebamot
Šebu.	Šebu'ot	Yoma	Yoma (= Kippurim)
Šeqal.	Šeqalim	Zabim	Zabim
Soṭa	Soṭa	Zebaḥ	Zebaḥim
Sukk.	Sukka	Zer.	Zera'im

OTHER RABBINIC WORKS

'Abot R. Nat.	'Abot de Rabbi Nathan	Pesiq. R.	Pesiqta Rabbati
'Ag. Ber.	'Aggadat Berešit	Pesiq. Rab Kah.	Pesiqta de Rab Kahana
Bab.	Babylonian	Pirqe R. El.	Pirqe Rabbi Eleizer
Bar.	Baraita	Rab.	Rabbah (following
Der. Er. Rab.	Derek Ereṣ Rabba		abbreviation for biblical
Der. Er. Zuṭ.	Derek Ereṣ Zuṭa		book: Gen. Rab. [with
Gem.	Gemara		periods] = Genesis
Kalla	Kalla		Rabbah)
Mek.	Mekilta	Sem.	Semaḥot
Midr.	Midraš; cited with usual	Sipra	Sipra
	abbreviation for biblical	Sipre	Sipre
	book; but Midr. Qoh. =	Sop.	Soperim
	Midraš Qohelet	S. 'Olam Rab.	Seder 'Olam Rabbah
Pal.	Palestinian	Talm.	Talmud
		Yal.	Yalquṭ

NAG HAMMADI TRACTATES

Acts Pet. 12 Apost.	Acts of Peter and the Twelve Apostles	Marsanes	Marsanes
Apost.	Apostles	Melch.	Melchizedek
Allogenes	Allogenes	Norea	Thought of Norea
Ap. Jas.	Apocryphon of James	On Bap. A	On Baptism A
Ap. John.	Apocryphon of John	On Bap. B	On Baptism B
Apoc. Adam	Apocalypse of Adam	On Bap. C	On Baptism C
1 Apoc. Jas.	First Apocalypse of James	On Euch. A	On the Eucharist A
2 Apoc. Jas.	Second Apocalypse of James	On Euch. B	On the Eucharist B
		Orig. World	On the Origin of the World
Apoc. Paul	Apocalypse of Paul	Paraph. Shem	Paraphrase of Shem
Apoc. Pet.	Apocalypse of Peter	Pr. Paul	Prayer of the Apostle Paul
Asclepius	Asclepius 21–29	Pr. Thanks.	Prayer of Thanksgiving
Auth. Teach.	Authoritative Teaching	Sent. Sextus	Sentences of Sextus
Dial. Sav.	Dialogue of the Savior	Soph. Jes. Chr.	Sophia of Jesus Christ
Disc. 8–9	Discourse on the Eighth and Ninth	Steles Seth	Three Steles of Seth
		Teach. Silv.	Teachings of Silvanus
Ep. Pet. Phil.	Letter of Peter to Philip	Testim. Truth	Testimony of Truth
Eugnostos	Eugnostos the Blessed	Thom. Cont.	Book of Thomas the Contender
Exeg. Soul	Exegesis on the Soul		
Gos. Eg.	Gospel of the Egyptians	Thund.	Thunder, Perfect Mind
Gos. Phil.	Gospel of Philip	Treat. Res.	Treatise on Resurrection
Gos. Thom.	Gospel of Thomas	Treat. Seth	Second Treatise of the Great Seth
Gos. Truth	Gospel of Truth		
Great Pow.	Concept of our Great Power	Tri. Trac.	Tripartite Tractate
Hyp. Arch.	Hypostatis of the Archons	Trim. Prot.	Trimorphic Protennoia
Hypsiph.	Hypsiphrone	Val. Exp.	A Valentinian Exposition
Interp. Know.	Interpretation of Knowledge	Zost.	Zostrianos

PREFACE

JAMES L. MAYS

THE BIBLE DEMANDS commentary because of its importance and character. It contains the sacred Scriptures of Judaism and Christianity and the primal literature of our culture; its significance for religion and culture calls for perennial work to interpret its texts in every generation. The books collected in the Bible were written in three different languages, in a succession of cultures, across centuries of time. To understand them, we need to call upon all the resources which the new knowledge available in our time can provide about their languages, cultures, and thought.

In this Commentary the members of the Society of Biblical Literature together with Harper & Row, Publishers, have undertaken to respond to that demand. The Commentary is designed to make the best current scholarship available to general audiences for reading and studying the books of the Bible. The contributors are all specialists in their subjects, but they use a style and vocabulary that will make their scholarship accessible to all who seek help in understanding the Bible. The general public, students, and teachers will all find in this Commentary a kind of interpretive writing that, on the one hand, does justice to the demands of the Bible for serious scholarship and, on the other, speaks to all who seek to use the Bible with discernment.

Like *Harper's Bible Dictionary*, this Commentary is the result of a cooperative effort between the Society of Biblical Literature and Harper & Row. The Society of Biblical Literature has assumed responsibility for the conception and content of the Commentary. As the major association of biblical scholars in North America, the Society has been able to enlist a panel of contributors from North America and abroad particularly qualified to write on the subjects assigned them. Harper & Row has brought to the project its outstanding experience and competence in designing and publishing resources for biblical study. The result is a volume of the highest usefulness and quality.

Harper's Bible Commentary and *Harper's Bible Dictionary* are companion volumes. They have been planned and written to complement each other. The Dictionary deals with the Bible in terms of subjects, the Commentary in terms of books. Of course each volume stands on its own, is complete in itself, and can be used independently, but one enriches and extends the resources available in the other. Used together, Commentary and Dictionary compose a little library for biblical study that is unique in comprehensiveness and usefulness for such a compact set.

The contributors were selected because of their recognized competence in the interpretation of the particular subjects and literature on which they have written. The contributors are diverse as a group, coming from the two major religious traditions that have the Bible as their heritage. Their contributions to the Commentary are composed to put their learning to work to interpret the biblical books as documents of the times in which the books were written. The editors have not sought to impose artificial uniformity on the contributors. The positions and approaches presented in this volume represent the mainstream of scholarship typical of the Society of Biblical Literature; eccentric and improbable positions are avoided. The individual commentaries and articles, however, do express the learning and judgment of their authors as scholars.

As a result, the volume includes a rich diversity of biblical scholarship. Those who use this Commentary encounter the variety that characterizes the continuing work of scholarship on the Bible rather than the single approach of one school of interpretation.

How the Commentary Is Organized. The focus of the Commentary is on the books of the Bible. The commentary on a particular book offers an interpretation based primarily on the book's structure and language. Behind many of the biblical books is a long history of development. Scholarly interpretation works in light of the history of a book's composition, but here the concern is not primarily with the history of the formation of the book. The goal rather is to help readers understand and appreciate the books as documents of the religious communities in which they arose.

The Commentary introduces and interprets all of the Hebrew Scriptures, the books of the Apocrypha, and those in the New Testament. It thus covers the biblical canons of Judaism, Catholicism, Eastern Orthodoxy, and Protestantism. The order of the books is that of the Revised Standard Version. To the traditional list of books that make up the Apocrypha have been added 3 Maccabees, 4 Maccabees, and Psalm 151 because of their importance as literature and the regard in which they are held by the Eastern Orthodox churches.

The Commentary introduces the books of the Bible in three ways. A set of general articles in the Introduction deals with matters that concern the entire Bible (e.g., "Reading and Interpreting the Bible"). A second series of articles introduces the parts of the Bible in which the books show a similarity and have a relationship to each other (e.g., "Introduction to the Biblical Story: Genesis–Esther"). Then there are the commentaries on the individual books. This plan provides readers with three approaches for study: to the Bible as a whole, to the major divisions of its literature, and to the particular books. By reversing the order and combining the approaches, one book of the Bible can be put in successively broader contexts. For instance, the book of Amos can be studied in detail in the commentary "Amos." Then it can be read in its relation to other prophetic books in "Introduction to the Prophetic Books." And finally, it can be read in the context of prophecy's historical course in Israel and the ancient Near East in "Biblical Literature in Its Historical Context: The Old Testament."

General Articles. The general articles in the Introduction are comprehensive and integrative. Their number has been kept to a minimum to avoid separating related matters into the subjects of many short treatments. Instead, subjects are held together so that readers can learn about them in their connectedness. For instance, rather than having one article on the history of Israel and others treating the historical setting of the Hebrew Scriptures, this Commentary provides one article that shows how the Hebrew Scriptures emerged in the course of Israel's unfolding history, thus holding the history of the people and the origin of its sacred literature together. Each of the general articles explores a relationship of the biblical literature that is crucial for its understanding and appreciation. The relation of the Bible to contemporary readers is discussed in "Reading and Interpreting the Bible." One article on "Biblical Literature in Its Historical Context" describes the relation between biblical literature and the history of Israel, early Judaism and the beginnings of Christianity. "The Bible and the Literature of Antiquity" explores the relation between the biblical genres and books and the literature of the cultures and nations in whose midst Israel existed and Judaism and Christianity emerged. The Bible has from the time of its earliest forms never been without interpreters; "The Bible and Its Interpreters" shows how these interpreters, by their methods and conclusions, created a variegated tradition of how the Bible is to be understood. Finally, the Bible has different forms for different religious communities, so the last article in the Introduction tells how and why the various canons of Judaism, Catholicism, and Protestantism arose.

Part Introductory Articles. The articles of the second type, which stand at the beginning of the parts into which the Commentary divides the Bible, offer further introductory help. There are special articles introducing the narrative books of the Hebrew Scriptures, the Psalms and the books of wisdom literature, the books of the Prophets, the apocryphal books, the Gospels and Acts, and the books written in the form of letters. These special articles are also comprehensive and integrative in purpose. They discuss in one place the common characteristics and roles of books that have a similarity and relationship. This arrangement helps readers see a book as part of a larger group of literature to which it belongs. It relieves the necessity for a repeated treatment of the same matters in the introductions to particular books. The location of these articles at the beginning of the parts of the Commentary identifies the introductory discussion that is relevant to the following books.

Commentaries on Individual Books. The commentaries on the individual books of the Bible provide an introduction, section-by-section comment on the book, and a bibliography.

The introductions furnish the information and orientation needed for reading each book. Because biblical books are so different, the task of particular introductions differs, but, generally, the introduction describes the literary character and form of the book, locates it in the historical, social, and religious settings in which it was composed, and assesses its role and significance for the community in which it appeared.

The parts, sections, and units into which the text is divided for comment display the structure of the book's contents. These divisions assist in reading and studying the book in light of its own order and arrangement. The headings of the divisions make a running outline of that book of the Bible. Comment on these divisions does not proceed verse by verse, nor is it composed of a series of unrelated explanations of details in the text. Rather, it takes the form of integrated exposition that interprets the unit under discussion as a whole and so gives users a coherent commentary to accompany the reading of that book of the Bible. From time to time, short essays develop topics of particular importance. The aim has been to provide an understandable explanatory guide that may be read alongside the text.

This Commentary is compatible with the major contemporary English translations of the Bible rather than being bound to one. This volume may be used profitably with any of them. The commentators on the individual books often cite one or another of the current English versions where a particular translation helps clarify meaning, but the commentaries are based on the Hebrew, Aramaic, and Greek texts of the Bible. All translations appearing in the volume in quotation marks are those of the commentator unless otherwise identified. Where the original language of the text is cited, a general phonetic system of transliteration is used so that readers may read and pronounce the words, and a translation or explanation always stands immediately beside the transliteration.

A system of reference is used in the articles and commentaries to assist in using *Harper's Bible Dictionary* as a companion. Where the Dictionary contains further and more detailed information about people and places, topics and terms, methods and judgments, readers are alerted by the use of the arrow symbol (→), e.g., (→Corinth) or (→Samuel; Saul).

Historical dates are identified by the use of the designations B.C. and A.D. because these abbreviations are the most widely used and recognized. They are employed here as historical conventions and are not to be interpreted as confessional statements. Dates for persons and events may be found to vary within the Commentary and in comparison to the Dictionary. Such variations, usually small, express the differing best judgments of scholars about matters subject only to estimates of probability.

This volume is the work of many. The development of its plan, the selection of its writers, and the editorial oversight of its content were carried out by the five associate editors whose excellence and assiduousness as a team are surely unmatched. The general editor of the Dictionary assisted with advice and counsel. Some eighty-two contributors gave their assignments a place of priority in the midst of commitments already made. Professors Kent H. Richards and Gene M. Tucker, as officers of the Society of Biblical Literature, gave the project support and encouragement from its inception. From the publisher's side, John B. Shopp and Kandace Hawkinson provided the knowledge, skills, and collegial cordiality indispensable to such a project. Mrs. Robert M. Lumpkin cared for administrative and coordinating tasks with an interest that never flagged.

The work of writing and publication having been done, it remains for readers to take up the work and enjoy the reward of answering the Bible's demand for understanding. The scholars of the Society of Biblical Literature offer this Commentary in hope that it will be found useful in that venture.

INTRODUCTION

סכום הפסוקים פּרשׁלטפר

וֹאֵלֶּה שְׁמוֹת בְּנֵי
יִשְׂרָאֵל הַבָּאִים

READING AND INTERPRETING THE BIBLE

JOHN BARTON

"So Philip ran to him, and heard him reading Isaiah the prophet, and asked, 'Do you understand what you are reading?' And he said, 'How can I, unless someone guides me?'" (Acts 8:30–31).

In this conversation between Philip and the Ethiopian official we have the only justification for commentaries on the books of the Bible: these books are not always easy to understand without help. For most Jewish and Christian readers the books of the Bible seem more in need of commentaries than other books for two reasons. First, they are of unique importance from a religious point of view. To understand them correctly is not just a question of satisfying intellectual curiosity; it has a religious significance. Second, they are very old books, much older than any other books most modern people ever read. This means that there is much in them that is bound to be obscure without a certain amount of background information. Good translations can be a great help in bridging the gap between modern readers and these ancient texts, but translation cannot bear the whole weight of the explanation needed if the Bible is to be properly understood.

But the Bible's uniqueness can easily obscure the fact that understanding any piece of writing, religious or secular, modern or ancient, is a far from simple matter. Reading and interpreting *any* book is a complicated and subtle process. It is just that when we read straightforward texts written by our own contemporaries we do not notice the complications, because we have grown used to them—just as we do not think about the grammar of our own native language. Reading and interpreting the Bible is only a special case of a general problem, the problem of how one human being understands words written by another. The study of this problem is sometimes called hermeneutics (→ Hermeneutics). Three processes are involved in reading and interpreting any book: understanding, exposition, and application.

Previous page: The beginning of Exodus in Hebrew; detail of a manuscript page from the *British Museum Codex of the Pentateuch* (ca. A.D. 950), one of the most important Masoretic manuscripts of the first five books of the Hebrew Bible.

UNDERSTANDING

To understand the Bible we must first, as with any book, understand the words it is composed of: that is, we must either know the biblical languages (→ Hebrew; Aramaic; Greek, New Testament) or have access to good translations (→ English Bible, The; Texts, Versions, Manuscripts, Editions). On one level a commentary can be useful in explaining obscure words or technical terms (e.g., "ephod," "teraphim," "elder," "covenant") or unraveling complex and ambiguous or obscure sentences (e.g., Rom. 3:9).

But it is also necessary to understand what kind of book we are reading, and this is a literary, not just a linguistic, matter. To understand the Psalms, for example, we have to realize that they are poems and hymns, and that we should not read them as though they were statements of doctrine. To understand the writings of Paul it is essential to know that they are letters, written to a particular set of readers whose problems and questions the writer was dealing with. One of the difficulties for modern readers is that sometimes we do not know exactly what kind of works biblical books are. Thus, it is hard to know how far the narrative books such as Samuel, Chronicles, or Acts are to be understood as similar to what we call history or to what we call legend, folktale, or even fiction. An important part of the task of biblical criticism is therefore to classify the books of the Bible into different types or genres and thus to help modern readers understand the intentions of the writers (→ Biblical Criticism).

Even in reading modern books this need to classify is familiar to us. We do not read a "whodunit" with the same expectations as we do a romantic novel; we do not read laws as if they were poems, or political speeches as if they were encyclopedia articles. But as soon as we try to classify the books in the Bible we notice a feature common in ancient literature but much rarer today: many biblical books are composite. They are not the work of a single author but seem to be put together from fragmentary earlier works. Sometimes this means that they are in effect anthologies (Psalms, Proverbs), sometimes that they have gone through a number of editions before reaching their present form. Understanding books such as Genesis or the Gospel of Matthew demands the ability to trace their growth through a number of stages (→ Sources of the Pentateuch; Gospel, Gospels). At some of these stages editors may have incorporated small units of material that originated not in writing at all but in oral tradition (→ Oral Materials, Sources, and Traditions). These small units are classified and studied by form criticism (→ Form Criticism). The earlier stages through which these units in their turn may have developed before they were fixed in writing can sometimes be reconstructed. To understand a biblical book fully is thus a three-dimensional undertaking involving earlier stages in the text's growth as well as its present, finished form.

To say that we have understood a book implies that we have a grasp of the book's *meaning*. In most of our everyday reading, we assume that the meaning of a piece of writing is what its author intended. This is unproblematic with material like personal letters, newspaper reports, and most nonfiction, where known authors have written to communicate their thoughts and enable us to reproduce them in our own minds. But matters are not quite so simple with the Bible.

First, and most obviously, composite writings do not have an "author" in the same sense that most modern books do. We need to speak instead of the intentions of the many individuals or groups who were responsible for the various stages in the book's growth: the worshipers in the Temple who composed and used the psalms, early preachers proclaiming the gospel by telling and retelling stories and sayings of Jesus, and so on. Where the final form of a composite biblical book is concerned, we have to speak of the intentions of the "editor," or "redactor," rather than of the "author." Nevertheless, this editor's intentions can sometimes be discerned from the way material has been arranged. In the last thirty years biblical scholars have spent much effort in trying to understand the minds of redactors and have used the term *redaction criticism* to describe this task (→ Redaction Criticism).

A second, more complex question arises with the kinds of writing we call "literature." Novels and poems often seem to have a life of their own: a fresh "reading" of a great tragedy, like a fresh interpretation of a great symphony, can sometimes go beyond anything the author consciously intended and yet can strike us as true to what he or she wrote. One of the things that makes the Bible special even for many people who are not religious believers is that it is a great literary classic, with the power, like that of the greatest works of literature, to stimulate fresh interpretations. Some biblical scholars would say that the "meaning" a new interpretation finds in it is just as legitimate as the meaning intended by those who first wrote or compiled it. They would argue that the text of the Bible as it now stands has a certain priority over hypothetical earlier stages, so that what readers should be trying to understand is not the intention of the writer or compiler but a meaning that inheres in the words of the text itself (sometimes called a "text-immanent" meaning). This tendency can be seen in the works of some modern literary critics who have studied the Bible. Others who feel that the task of readers is to understand the final form of the biblical text have religious rather than literary reasons for this belief. The Bible as it stands, they argue, not the fragments from which it was composed, is the Bible that Jews and Christians have received. Its "author" is the believing community that (under God) accepted this particular version as canonical.

EXPOSITION

The test of understanding is exposition. Having grasped what a text means, one's next step is to state its meaning in one's own words. Of course our restatement of the meaning can never be a substitute for the original words of the Bible. If it could, we could replace the Bible with our own handbooks of biblical thought. But unless we can find words of our own that will express at least partially what we have understood, our understanding is mute. Exposition involves two elements: contextualization and systematization.

Contextualization

In expounding a text we have to begin by explaining the context within which it makes sense. This does not mean merely the place within a longer work where a given passage belongs, but the whole cultural and historical setting of the text. Just as we ourselves cannot understand a piece of writing without knowing something of the culture from which it derives, so it is impossible to explain the book to others without sketching for them the background against which it is to be read. Any good commentary will include information about the place and time at which a book (or the parts of which it is composed) was written and will explain customs and ways of thought in it that are unfamiliar to modern readers. Thus, in expounding many OT stories one will need to explain family and tribal customs, geographical settings, and aspects of language and idiom. In NT exposition it is often necessary to describe the society of the Mediterranean world in the first century of our era and to explain Jewish customs of the time.

One reason biblical exposition has to be done anew in each generation is that what is familiar and what unfamiliar changes with cultural change in our own society. We need to explain many of the cultural assumptions of NT times—for example, about the world of spirits—precisely because they are no longer ours. Other features of NT thought, however, that seemed so alien as to need explanation, or indeed apology, a century ago are now once again part of the common currency of modern thought. An example is the common first-century belief that the end of the present world-order is at hand. This struck many nineteenth-century readers of the Bible as an extremely alien and remote idea, but the concerns of a nuclear age have put it back on our own intellectual map.

For some biblical scholars the contextualization of biblical books is always an exercise in "cultural relativism." It means pointing out to modern readers that the world of the Bible is not their world, thus distancing readers from the text. It is undoubtedly good for modern believers to realize that the Bible comes from a culture that is radically different from our own, and so not to make too ready an equation of its concerns with ours. Biblical criticism helps to guard against naïveté in assuming that the Bible has answers to all our questions and that everything in it can be simply read as if it were written for our situation.

On the other hand, there is continuity as well as discontinuity between human cultures, and much of the skill of biblical exposition lies in discerning where the Bible's concerns and ours are and where they are not the same. One of the major programs of biblical interpretation this century has been that of Rudolf Bultmann (1884–1976), whose key idea, "demythologization," depends crucially on this distinction. Bultmann stressed that many of the Bible's modes of expression presupposed a system of thought that he called "mythological" (heaven as a physical place, the world as full of angels and demons, sickness as divine punishment for sin). But the whole purpose of pointing this out in biblical exposition was to clear the ground for readers to grasp the central truths of biblical faith, which transcend cultural relativity— the direct address of God to the individual and his call for response in faith. Thus for Bultmann contextualization was not a way of relegating the Bible to the status of an antique but precisely of liberating it from being treated as such.

Systematization

In trying to understand any piece of writing there is always a strong drive toward finding coherence and unity in it. As we have seen, there are times when this drive is frustrated in reading the Bible, and then readers are forced to the conclusion that the text is really fragmentary or composite. But even in these cases redaction criticism looks for some unity of purpose that editors may have imposed on the text, despite its fragmentary character. And although the Bible is clearly not a literary unity in the way that a single work by a single author is a unity, it does derive from a religious tradition with common roots and a recognizable common flavor. One major task of biblical exposition is to lay bare the underlying system of beliefs, presuppositions, and experiences that unite the biblical books and enable us to speak of a "biblical faith."

One of the chief manifestations of this systematizing drive in twentieth-century biblical study has been the production of books on biblical theology (→ Theology, New Testament; Theology, Old Testament). The aim of biblical theology has been to articulate the common themes running through the whole Bible and to expound individual books and sections in accordance with them. Though most scholars who have written such works would agree that the Bible does not form a single, completely unified work, their attempts to locate particular guiding threads can be a great help to readers finding their way through this varied literature. Such themes as "covenant," "saving history," and "promise and fulfillment" provide focal points that help one to make sense of the whole.

Again, such aids to exposition have to be reforged for each new generation of readers, not because the Bible itself changes, but because the questions readers put to the text change. In principle there are many different ways in which one could do justice to the underlying thematic unity of the Bible, and it is legitimate to allow our own most pressing concerns to shape the investigation. However, the aim in such exposition is always to let the Bible itself act as a control on what is said about it, so that appeal to the text, not to the interpreter's needs or concerns, remains the final appeal. Contextualization and systematization act as checks on each other, to ensure that the interpreter expounds the Bible in a way that does equal justice to the givenness of the text and to the interests and concerns of readers. (Recent challenges to this way of seeing the interpreter's task are discussed below.)

APPLICATION

It is obvious that understanding and exposition are needed in reading any book, but application may seem uniquely a feature of reading the Bible or, at least, religious literature. It is, after all, possible to read a book with merely "academic" interest, that is, without any concern for applying its message in one's own life.

In fact, however, there are other kinds of writing than simply religious literature where application is a concern. Laws, for example, exist principally to be applied, and there is a long tradition of legal hermeneutics concerned with such questions as how the meaning of an ambiguous law is to be settled and whether or not one should attend to the original intentions of those who framed it. Much traditional Jewish exposition of Scripture has been a kind of legal hermeneutic, having the practical application of the biblical text to ethical life as its major concern (→ Law; Halakah).

But quite apart from this narrow sense of the word "application," all reading of texts is in a broader sense just as concerned with application as with understanding and exposition. We read books because we expect to "get something out" of them; we expect to benefit in some way from what we read. The kind of benefit we look for naturally depends on the kind of book we are reading. Just as it is a mistake in understanding to look for factual information in a lyric poem or spiritual enlightenment in a computer manual, so it may also be called a mistake in application—it is an attempt to use the text for an inappropriate purpose. But application of some kind is nearly always in our minds when we read.

In the case of the Bible, exposition tends to pass over almost unnoticed into application. When we expound the text in a way that takes account of our own concerns as well as those of its authors, we are trying to find ways of making it as fruitful in our own context as it was in its original context. Bultmann's demythologization program, already mentioned, is a clear case of exposition serving application. Most scholars who have written on the theology of the Bible have had it as their further aim to make the Bible come alive in the modern religious context by showing that its underlying system of thought and faith can be applied today. What was true then, they have believed, can still be true now.

An alternative possibility, if one is seeking to "apply" the Bible, lies in exploring the potential religious importance of some of those earlier stages in the development of the biblical text that source, form, and redaction criticism have illuminated. Biblical criticism has enabled scholars to rediscover the process by which the religious faith of ancient Israel and of the early church was transmitted, to reconstruct the history within which it took shape and the individuals and groups who formed it. It is quite possible to regard any of these as theologically significant in its own right. Thus someone might want to say that the prophet Isaiah himself had something to say that is of great application today, even though, strictly speaking, what he taught is not identical with the message that appears in his name in the Bible, since the book called Isaiah is something of a compendium of prophecies from many different periods, many of them not by Isaiah himself. Or again, we may think that the character of God was revealed in the fact that Israel, his chosen nation, was in reality small and politically insignificant, even though the Bible's own presentation suggests that it was an important power. Or again, it may be said that Christians today can learn how best to preach the gospel by following the example of those early preachers who (according to form critics) freely retold and readapted the story of Jesus to the needs of their audience—rather than by imitating the fixity of form the Gospels eventually achieved. Strictly speaking, these are not applications of the Bible but of hypotheses arrived at through research into the origins of the Bible. The theological ideas they represent are not so much biblical ideas as ideas prompted by the study of the Bible.

Because the Bible is the foundation document for both Judaism and Christianity, people will have quite varied ways of finding spiritual value in it, and if some of these are not strictly ways of applying the Bible itself but ways of applying insights reached by studying the Bible, that only demonstrates how enormously fruitful a book the Bible is. Like other great classics of literature and religion, it can stimulate an endless diversity of new thoughts and ideas.

CRITICAL AND PRECRITICAL INTERPRETATION

The account of reading and interpreting the Bible given so far describes the way in which most serious students of the Bible have seen their task since the European Enlightenment of the eighteenth century. Understanding, exposition, and application have been presented as three successive phases in interpreting the Bible, indeed, any piece of writing. The order cannot be reversed. We cannot apply a text until we have expounded it, that is, stated its meaning, and we cannot state its meaning until we have understood it. Consequently it is incorrect to try to apply a biblical text until we have discovered its meaning by paying attention to its original context. It is equally incorrect to think that we can discover its context without first grasping the type of text it is.

This methodical way of proceeding is usually called a "critical" approach and is distinguished from the "precritical" style of interpretation—really a large number of different styles—that can be found in early Jewish biblical exposition, in the Christian fathers, in medieval biblical commentaries, and in the work of the Reformers. For a "critical" reading, the most important thing about the text is its literary character: what kind of work it is, how it came to be written, what the intentions of its author(s) were, what purpose it was meant to serve. Only when these things have been established can any further progress be made. Thus, until we know whether a book in the Bible was written to convey factual information or not, we cannot form any opinion on the truth of statements contained in it. If a book is a piece of fiction, then statements it appears to make about the past are not meant seriously as fact and should not be treated as such. It is because most scholars now think, for example, that the book of Jonah is a piece of conscious fiction that they regard questions about the possibility of Jonah's having survived being swallowed by the great fish as pointless—there never was such a fish, and no one ever meant to affirm that there was.

This is not the way people saw the Bible before the rise of critical scholarship. Traditionally, the most important fact about the Bible, which determined the whole way it was read and interpreted, was its status as divine revelation. Since the Bible is inspired by God, it was held to follow that it would always be possible to apply it in every fresh situation, and complex methods were devised to ensure that it would be interpreted correctly. Instead of the order understanding–exposition–application, precritical interpretation tended to favor the order application–exposition–understanding. The text was not read for itself and for its natural meaning but only in the process of applying it. It was then expounded in accordance with the application it was believed to have, and this exposition provided the basis on which readers understood it.

When the Bible is approached in this way, one effect is that it becomes extremely difficult for any reader to notice when its plain sense contradicts what the religious community believes to be true. Indeed, in both Judaism and Christianity many of the methods of interpretation developed in the course of time were expressly designed to avoid any possible clash between what the Bible might be understood to mean and the beliefs and practices current among its readers. Judaism has long had a primary concern with "legal" applications of the Bible: the Bible has been important primarily as a source of instruction in living as an observant Jew. Much energy was expended in the rabbinical schools of medieval Europe in reconciling conflicting regulations in the Pentateuch or Torah and in interpreting the rest of the Hebrew Bible (the Prophets and Writings) so that they too could be read in relation to the Law and so that they did not appear to differ from the Torah itself in the rules they laid down (→ Torah). Precritical Christian interpretations were less interested in ethical questions—though where these arose there was a similar desire to reconcile one text with another—and showed a greater concern for the predictive, prophetic aspect of OT texts and the doctrinal implications of the NT. The methods used to ensure that the Bible spoke with a single voice on doctrinal matters were very similar, however, to the Jewish methods.

A particular characteristic of medieval Christian exegesis was its allegorical style. Many biblical texts—especially those whose surface meaning is obscure, trivial, or seemingly indecent—were interpreted as having a figurative meaning, so that they convey, through a kind of code, deeper truths about God, the spiritual life, or the church. The context of passages was often entirely disregarded in this way of reading the Bible, and a religious significance was assigned to individual verses, sentences, or even words.

Allegorical interpretation and the attribution of hidden meanings to obscure passages are no longer practiced in the biblical exposition of mainstream Christian churches, though they survive in small sects, some extreme fundamentalist groups, and in the liturgical use of the Bible. The last case, however, is not so much a case of scriptural *interpretation* as of the use of scriptural texts for their literary and evocative power, regardless of their original meaning. Churches that continue to use Scripture in this way generally do not retain the allegorical approach when using the Bible in theological discussion. The resulting discord between the use of Scripture in liturgy and in doctrine is a source of difficulty in those Christian traditions for which public worship is the primary context in which believers encounter the Bible.

"POSTCRITICAL" INTERPRETATION

By no means everyone believes that the triumph of the critical approach to the Bible has been a blessing. Though few would probably wish or feel able to return to precritical methods, recent biblical study has shown a widespread desire to move beyond what is felt to be the excessively "historical" orientation of critical approaches. We have already noted that some scholars consider a concern for the earlier stages in the growth of biblical books to be misplaced, stressing the primacy of the "final form" of a book as the object of study.

Canonical Criticism

Among those who favor this line of approach, some are motivated partly by dissatisfaction with many traditional works on biblical theology. Typically, a "New Testament theology" is a description not of the theological contents of the NT (read as if it were a single, continuous work) but of the development of religious thought in the early church during the period for which the NT simply happens to be our best or only witness (roughly the first century of our era). "Canonical critics" feel that, though this is an entirely legitimate subject for study, it is not, strictly speaking, the theology *of the New Testament,* which is a religious classic in its own right, irrespective of its potential usefulness to the historian of Christian origins. It would be perfectly possible to treat the NT as a literary work and to analyze the theological ideas that it conveys if read, as it were, two-dimensionally—with a deliberate lack of interest in its historical and cultural context. Some tentative studies along these lines are now being written. In some ways the results resemble the sorts of theological systems that used to be derived from the Bible before critical questions began to be asked. It is too early to say whether this "canonical" approach will come to command general assent.

Structuralism

In the 1960s and 1970s structuralist critics in France and North America became interested in the Bible, and many studies were written that subjected the biblical text to the procedures of structural analysis. Structuralist interpretations pay great attention to the articulation of the text and the way in which its parts cohere to form a whole—generally with a deliberate disregard for questions about the text's historical origins. Thus features that critical readers see as evidence that the biblical books are composite (such as apparently pointless repetition of trivial detail or dislocations in thought or syntax) are treated by structuralists as part of the data that the interpreter ought to integrate into a coherent reading of the text, rather than as a problem, and they are often seen as charged with a great deal of meaning. Structuralist interpretations make no claims about the original meaning of the text but simply propose a creative and interesting reading that readers are asked to consider on its own merits.

Folktale and other essentially oral genres of literature have proved particularly congenial material for structural analysis, and since some of the Bible (especially the narrative portions of the OT and the Gospels) has some similarity to folktale and may well reflect a lengthy oral transmission, interesting results have been achieved.

Reader-Response Criticism

Recently some critics have begun to argue that the meaning of a piece of writing lies neither in the author's intentions nor within the words of the text itself but in the interplay between the text and the reader. Reading, in other words, should be seen as a creative activity, on the analogy of musical performance. Whereas traditional criticism, as we have seen, requires the interpreter to allow the text to exercise control over the interpretation, in reader-response criticism the creative role of the reader is regarded as entirely legitimate.

Everyone acknowledges that readers bring particular questions, assumptions, and interests to the books they read; as argued above, it is because each generation asks different questions that the exposition of texts is never a completed process but is an activity that has to be carried out anew in every age. But traditional criticism has set itself the goal of achieving as much objectivity as possible. Critics have tried to become conscious of their own interests and prejudices to prevent these from distorting their critical judgment and have insisted on applying texts only *after* they have been expounded with as much objectivity as possible. In reader-response criticism prejudgment or "preunderstanding" (German Vorverständnis) is regarded as a necessary tool in interpretation, and objectivity in the traditional sense is seen as not only impossible but also undesirable. The reader is an active partner in dialogue with the text, and an assumption of neutrality is only self-deception. Reader-response criticism has contributed to the interpretation of biblical texts that seem inherently to call for a response of commitment on the reader's part, such as some of the parables. It is not yet clear whether it will prove able to deal as effectively with other genres within the Bible.

"Committed" Interpretation

The idea that reading is a dialogue between text and reader can be seen in a slightly different way by taking these thoughts about "preunderstanding" somewhat further. One particularly powerful presupposition of most traditional study of the Bible, whether critical or precritical, has been that the reader's job is to understand the text intellectually. Bible study has usually been a branch of academic study, and modern biblical scholarship in particular is clearly understood by most of those engaged in it as a branch of the study of literature, which in its turn is part of the humanities or liberal arts studied in universities. The Bible thus belongs, in this way of seeing it, to the university curriculum. Some Christians, especially those engaged in difficult pastoral work in contexts far removed from the centers of intellectual life, feel that this is such a false context for the study of the Bible as to call in question any interpretations that might be arrived at through it. They point out that university-based biblical scholars are far more remote from the sort of people who wrote the Bible than are many of the poor and dispossessed in today's world, and they claim that the Bible can be properly understood only by those who have a prior commitment to the Bible's own values—especially what liberation theology calls its "preferential option" for the poor. They suggest that a commitment to various political and social concerns, such as the liberation of the poor or the cause of feminism, can function as fruitful "preunderstandings" to help unlock truths in the Bible that have been suppressed by scholars claiming to work "objectively" (but actually betraying a commitment to the political status quo). The stories of the Exodus and the books of the prophets have been especially important for critics of this persuasion, since they show that the God of the Bible sides with the oppressed against their oppressors. There is a strong sense that the Bible needs to be taken out of the hands of academic scholars and given back to ordinary believers, to live and work by.

PERSONAL BIBLE READING

Even a brief survey of the issues that biblical interpretation raises may make the Bible seem remote from the experience of ordinary persons whose main motive for reading the Bible is personal religious faith. It is important to realize that nearly all the methods and hypotheses about the Bible developed by specialists have arisen from experiences of reading the Bible that began from the very same religious motives as those of ordinary Jewish or Christian Bible readers. With most precritical interpretation, however complicated, this is apparent in the concern to make the Bible's message conform with religious orthodoxy. Critical study does not begin with an opposition in principle to this approach but simply with a concern to read the text for itself and to let the Bible be the arbiter of its own meaning. This concern was in its origins related to the Protestant insistence that the Bible must not be interpreted by the church in defiance of its natural sense but must be heard in its own right. Thus critical study of the Bible is not in itself a secularizing approach but has religious roots, even though it can be practiced without religious commitment.

Ordinary readers are free to accept or reject the particular interpretations that biblical scholars offer in commentaries by testing them out against the words of the text itself, which are there for all to read. With the exception of scholars who support the "committed" styles of interpretation just discussed, biblical specialists regard unprejudiced readers as the best judge of the interpretations they put forward. Commentaries are never a substitute for the text itself; they are meant to send readers back to the text with clearer eyes, to explore its riches for themselves.

Bibliography

Armerding, C. E. *The Old Testament and Criticism.* Grand Rapids, MI: Eerdmans, 1983.

Barr, J. *The Bible in the Modern World.* London: SCM, 1973.

_____. *Holy Scripture: Canon, Authority, Criticism.* Philadelphia: Westminster, 1983.

Barton, J. *Reading the Old Testament: Method in Biblical Study.* Philadelphia: Westminster, 1984.

Stuhlmacher, P. *Historical Criticism and Theological Interpretation of Scripture.* Philadelphia: Fortress, 1977.

BIBLICAL LITERATURE IN ITS
HISTORICAL CONTEXT:
THE OLD TESTAMENT

S. DEAN McBRIDE, JR.

INTRODUCTION

The Hebrew Bible insists that ancient Israel was forged on the anvil of history for a singular purpose: to be an enduring witness among the world's nations to the beneficent sovereignty and providence of the God who had fashioned it. This sublime consciousness of corporate vocation is expressed most fully in the books of the Pentateuch and Prophets, which together provide a more or less continuous account of Israel's antecedents, its formation as the covenant people of God, and its national history from the time a homeland was acquired at the end of the Bronze Age through the restoration of a Judean state in the earlier Persian period. The third division of the Jewish canon, the Writings, enriches this account not only by supplementing the historical narrative, but by preserving vivid literary testimony to ways in which psalmists and sages contributed to Israel's sense that divine providence embraced every aspect of its own life and of all creaturely existence.

Study of the intricate relationships between the literature comprising this canonical legacy and the history to which it bears witness has in large measure shaped the agenda of modern biblical scholarship.

FORMATION OF THE PEOPLE
"ISRAEL"

Civilization was already old in the Near East when Israel appeared on the scene of history. Over the course of the fourth and third millennia B.C., literate cultures had flourished, and in some cases died or grown moribund, in Mesopotamia (→ Accad; Babylon; Mitanni; Sumer), Anatolia (→ Hittites), Syria (→ Ebla; Mari; Ras-Shamra), and of course Egypt. Israel was at least an indirect heir to intellectual achievements of most of these predecessors, and in the traditions of Genesis it traced back its own lineage among them. Yet when biblical sources describe the events that indelibly fixed Israel's peculiar character, they focus on a religious drama, recalling how a warrior deity, Yahweh, created a people distinct from all others, nurtured it in wilderness isolation, and granted it through conquest arable land in which to dwell. Israel thus knew itself to be both continuous with and radically separate from other peoples; this contributes to the difficulty of reconstructing the formative stages of its political development.

Palestine During the Transition from Late Bronze to Early Iron Ages (ca. 1250–1100 B.C.)

Israel's proximate origins, as distinct from the antecedent histories of the groups that comprised it, must be sought in the turmoil of late Bronze Age politics, which effectively destroyed both the Hittite and Egyptian empires in greater Syro-Palestine. Upheavals of the thirteenth century B.C. were followed in the first half of the twelfth by gradual consolidation of regional powers.

According to biblical sources, all of these regional powers figured prominently as peers and competitors in the history of Israel's own political formation. The earliest extrabiblical evidence to establish a specifically Israelite presence among them is a remarkable reference in the victory stele of Pharaoh Merneptah, now dated to 1207 B.C. The text records Merneptah's claim to have reasserted hegemony over the southern district of Egypt's former province of Canaan—by defeating several city-states and wholly obliterating the population of "Israel." The very mention of Israel by Merneptah suggests that it was able to muster a significant force against him, but secure evidence is still wanting to determine how much earlier an entity by this name may have been present in Canaan, where it came from, and the extent of its initial occupation. However, because neither the fourteenth-century B.C. Amarna letters nor campaign reports of Merneptah's immediate pharaonic predecessors refer to such a population, it is likely that "Israel" only emerged in Canaan toward the end of the thirteenth century.

Merneptah's campaign may well have dealt severe blows to Canaanite city-states and "Is-

14

rael" alike in central Palestine, so that the twelfth century became a period of recovery and extended struggle for dominance among them. But Israelite clans and tribes can be associated with the numerous new agricultural settlements that appear in the central Palestinian highlands during the initial phase of the Iron Age.

Traditions of the Israelite League

The oldest literary compositions preserved in the Hebrew Bible are poetic works dating probably to the latter half of the twelfth century B.C. that celebrate triumphs of Yahweh, Israel's God, over historical adversaries. The lyric poem in Exod. 15:1–18 (cf. v. 21) may be likened to a national anthem, serving both to preserve and to shape popular memory of formative experiences. While the anthem is imbued with an intense patriotic consciousness, the corporate unity it evokes is Yahweh's "people" rather than "Israel." Throughout, hymnic praise of Yahweh—as ancestral deity and, especially, preeminent divine warrior—is juxtaposed with terse narrative elements: God's victory over Pharaoh and Egypt's chariot forces at the Sea of Reeds (→Red Sea); God's guidance of those delivered from the Egyptian foe to a haven in the wilderness; the trepidation felt by political leaders of Philistia, Transjordan, and Canaan when word reaches them of Yahweh's deeds; and, finally, implantation of the newly created people of God in the Palestinian highlands, thereby establishing a sacral kingdom over which Yahweh is to rule forever.

The victory ode in Judges 5, ascribed to the prophetess Deborah and the military commander Barak, provides a sharper portrait of early Israel's social composition. An objective political entity "Israel" is expressly in view here; it is exalted alongside "Yahweh, Israel's God," whose timely intervention has enabled a volunteer army of Israelites to prevail in battle near Megiddo against a coalition of Canaanite kings.

These archaic poems, together with similar sources dating to the following century (e.g., the hymnically framed tribal blessings in Deut. 33), sketch a reasonably coherent picture of an emergent community joined by religious traditions as well as common political interests. Available evidence warrants several interrelated conclusions regarding the character and significance of this early Israelite league or confederation.

The alliance of tribes had military capability and purpose. When occasion demanded, "Israel" could muster a militia. Whether defensive or offensive, the league wars were considered to be Yahweh's wars, because God not only sanctioned them but participated as warrior in them.

The tribes understood themselves to form an extended family, joined together in covenant with Yahweh to whom they owed ultimate political allegiance (Deut. 33:3–5; cf. 6:4–5; Josh. 24:1–27). The concept of Yahweh's kingship over Israel and the related ideology of sacral warfare had ritual expression, no doubt in irregular tribal conclaves to prepare for battle but more importantly in periodic pilgrimage festivals held at various regional shrines (esp. Gilgal, Bethel, Shechem, and Shiloh). Such occasions for celebrating Yahweh's providential deeds and gifts to Israel were the settings in which a national epic began to emerge.

Except for extraordinary circumstances (cf. Judg. 19–21), judicial authority, like military leadership, was exercised at the levels of clan and tribe rather than league. In sacral affairs, however, professionalism took hold early on in the form of clerical "families" or guilds serving at major regional sanctuaries who traced their lineages to notable priestly ancestors, Moses and Aaron in particular (cf. Judg. 18:30; 20:26–28; and 1 Sam. 1–3). These guilds became increasingly important channels for transmission of Yahwistic ethos and league traditions (cf. Deut. 33:6–11). For example, legislation preserved in the Book of the Covenant (Exod. 21–23) may represent the tradition of covenantal law transmitted by the Shiloh circle of Mosaic priests (cf. Deut. 33:6–11).

STATEHOOD AND EMPIRE
(ca. 1000–922 B.C.)

After more than a century of securing a homeland, early Israel sought to stabilize a polity and to interact with and become more like other successful nations round about it. This did not inevitably mean the demise of the Yahwistic league and its ideals. The tribal confederation had shaped a communal identity—"Israel," the people of Yahweh—and this endured; but the alliance had yet to build a political structure able to promote internal justice and pursue advantageous relations with its neighbors. Efforts to do so brought rapid social change and greatly expanded cultural horizons, along with strong opposition from traditionalists.

Monarchical Governance and the Kingdom of Yahweh

By the middle of the eleventh century B.C., parts of greater Israel had begun to experiment with monarchy in several guises. Some of the figures with the title "judge" (Heb. *shofet*) were patricians who at least acted like petty kings (Judg. 10:3–5; 12:8–15). After leading Israel to victory against Midianite raiders, Gideon turned down an offer to become its "king" (Heb. *melek*), a status that one of his sons, Abimelech, actively sought and gained over the city of Shechem (Judg. 8:22–23; 9:1–6). But it was Saul, a Benjaminite, who created the first royal house and the territorial state of Israel. His accomplishments should not be underestimated. Yet in all respects, Saul's achievement was overshadowed by that of David, an erstwhile Saulide commander who in the span of several decades transformed Israel into an imperial power.

After his breach with Saul, David established a petty kingdom of his own in the southeastern corner of the Judean highlands. Despite nominal vassalage to the Philistines, he enlarged his own dominion and, about the time of Saul's death (ca. 1000 B.C.), became independent monarch of a Judean territorial state, with Hebron as his capital. A period of intermittent warfare between David's forces and the reduced kingdom of Israel ended with the assassination of Ishbosheth, Saul's son and successor. Elders of the old tribal league assembled in Hebron where they enacted a covenant establishing David as Israel's king. In a series of bold moves, David consolidated and vastly expanded his rule: he used his personal troops to conquer the Jebusite city of Jerusalem, making it his new capital; he established friendly relations with Phoenician Tyre; he led Israel's militia to victory against the Philistine coalition, reducing it to vassal status; and in subsequent years he waged successful wars against the Transjordanian kingdoms of Ammon, Edom, and Moab as well as the Aramean city-states of Syria to the north and the Amalekites to the south. Thus the regional powers that in the twelfth century B.C. had replaced pharaonic rule over Syro-Palestine were, by the mid-tenth, once again linked through military conquest and treaty. In effect, David restored an imperium to the whole of Egypt's former province of Canaan.

The impact of all this on Israelite religion must have been profound. David's conquests were also Yahweh's, so Yahweh too ruled an empire; its religious center was the pavilion erected by David on Jerusalem's acropolis to enshrine the Ark, an object symbolic of divine presence during the earlier period of the league (2 Sam. 6; cf. Ps. 132). In another important move, David reorganized the old priestly guilds of Israel and Judah into a unified "levitical" clergy, which officiated at the central sanctuary in Jerusalem but was also deployed widely in greater Israel to oversee civil and sacral affairs alike (cf. 1 Chron. 26:29–32).

Later years of David's reign were troubled by civil strife and bitter struggles among his sons to gain succession to the imperial throne. Solomon emerged victorious and dealt severely with those who had opposed him. He reorganized the administration of united Israel, rebuilt cities to defend it, exploited the economic resources of both kingdom and empire, and vigorously promoted international trade. He expended some of the new wealth to construct a monumental Temple for Yahweh, of Canaanite-Phoenician design, thus replacing the Davidic tent-shrine with a far more conspicuous and permanent symbol of divine presence. He also built in the eastern environs of Jerusalem lesser shrines for the deities of states subject to and allied with him, no doubt symbolizing thereby that just as he was ruler of nations so Yahweh was sovereign among national gods. For traditionalists, especially in the north, the question was whether either Yahwism or "Israel" could survive Solomon's splendidly cosmopolitan achievements.

Israelite Literature of the Early Monarchical Period

Israel's culture had been literate from the outset, but under monarchy the written word grew in importance and with it the scribal profession. The literary accumulation that was to culminate in the Hebrew Bible seems also to have begun in the golden age of empire.

David himself had renown in Israel as a balladeer and poet. Apart from the numerous psalms ascribed to him, Scripture preserves several works of poetry that most likely exhibit his personal imprint (2 Sam. 1:19–27; 3:33–34; 23:1–7). The internationalism studiously cultivated by Solomon's regime provides a likely setting for the beginnings of Israelite literary wisdom, whose basic genres and motifs are well attested in sapiential works of other Near Eastern monarchical societies. Whether any of the collections of proverbial lore bearing Solomon's name in the book of Proverbs actually derive from him or his immediate courtly circle is debatable (cf. Prov. 25:1; 1 Kings 4:29–34). The other two biblical books associated with him—Song of Songs and Ecclesiastes—belong to a considerably later period.

Much of the evidence used by scholars to reconstruct the early history of the Jerusalem cult—(cult is used here in its more general sense to mean a system of worship)—and its liturgy is derived from the book of Psalms. Although the Psalter itself is a postexilic anthology and precise dating of individual psalms is notoriously difficult, typologically early hymns and prayers that celebrate Yahweh's enthronement and sovereignty over the nations and glorify Zion and its king (e.g., Pss. 2; 18; 29; 68; 72; 93) may be taken to represent the oldest traditions of the Temple cult in Jerusalem.

Criticism has also discerned literary deposits from the early monarchical period embedded within the sixth-century B.C. historiographical works of the Pentateuch and Former Prophets (1–2 Samuel, 1–2 Kings). Because this old material has been supplemented and in some parts extensively reworked by authors responsible for the later forms of the literature, much is uncertain regarding its original extent and character. Most critics have taken the view that the deposits represent a number of originally self-contained compositions, possibly written or compiled from oral traditions by scribes attached to the courts of David and Solomon. Typically posited are the following discrete sources or documents: the so-called Yahwist narrative (J) underlying or incorporated into the pentateuchal books of Genesis, Exodus, and Numbers; an "Ark narrative" (attested principally in 1 Sam. 4–6) that recounts the story of the Ark's capture and return during the early period of the wars between the Israelite league and the Philistines; the account of David's rise to power (comprising most of 1 Sam. 16–2 Sam. 5); and the brilliantly crafted narrative that traces the threads of court intrigue, blood vengeance, and conspiracy that have their denouement in Solomon's accession to the throne of David (2 Sam. 9–20; 1 Kings 1–2). Yet none of these narratives seems complete in itself, and there are features of style, theme, and theology common to all of them. Thus it is possible that they represent not independent works but only the most conspicuous parts of a comprehensive national epic—crafted from earlier Israelite sources and popular Near Eastern traditions during the Solomonic era—that traced, as it were, a history of human civilization, from primeval times and the rise of nations through the origins and exaltation of Israel, culminating with accounts of the transcendent achievements of David and Solomon.

FROM DIVIDED MONARCHY TO EXILE
(922–586 B.C.)

Rebellion abroad and growing unrest in the north of Israel itself tarnished Solomon's splendor even before his long reign had ended. During the next four centuries there were few occasions for realistic hope that the golden age of empire could be recovered. And yet the legacy of David and Solomon, like that of the Israelite league before them, was never lost. Israel had begun its historical pilgrimage learning itself to be the people of Yahweh; it had explored a new form of this identity in the dazzling era of United Kingdom and empire. The ideals and limitations of both of these Israels endured not merely as treasured memories but as models to be reexamined and reinterpreted in the light of subsequent events.

The Royal Houses of Israel and Judah

While Judah became a more or less integral part of Israel under David, it kept its own identity, so that Solomon had in effect worn a double crown. Soon after his death (ca. 925), representatives of the Israelite tribes convened again, this time at Shechem in the heartland of the original league, to reconsider and nullify their oath of allegiance to the house of David. Instead of Rehoboam, Solomon's defiant heir, they elected to royal office one of their own, Jeroboam, an Ephraimite. The rupture between the kingdoms proved to be permanent, and the torn fabric of a united Israel, Yahweh's people, was almost irreparable.

Jeroboam reestablished under royal auspices the Israelite sanctuaries of Bethel and Dan, where the old Yahwistic iconography of the bull replaced the cherubim of Solomon's Temple. Provincialization of the national religion may have served Jeroboam's immediate purposes but it seems also to have contributed to the continuing instability of the northern state. Under Omri, Ahab, and their two dynastic successors, Israel did become a major power in Syro-Palestine and Samaria became a cosmopolitan center rivaling Solomon's Jerusalem. But the biblical record describes this as an era of growing apostasy from Yahwism and its traditional values.

National resurgence of Assyria in the mid-ninth century B.C., under Shalmaneser III (858–824), and the waxing and waning of its imperial power throughout the following two centuries dramatically affected the political fortunes of Israel and other Syro-Palestinian states. Under the rule of Tiglath-pileser III (745–727) Assyria's empire expanded to include virtually all Syro-Palestine as well as Mesopotamia and eastern Anatolia. Israel's rapid decline during this period was punctuated by a series of coups and futile efforts, in alliance with other states, first to resist and then to rebel against Assyrian sovereignty. When the last Israelite ruler, Hoshea, began to reign in 732, his reduced kingdom consisted only of Samaria and its immediate environs. Yet he took Tiglath-pileser's death as occasion for another rebellion. The brutal response came a few years later, in 722–720, when the forces of Shalmaneser V (727–722) and his successor, Sargon II (722–705), besieged and destroyed Samaria, deported its surviving population, and moved in settlers from other parts of the Assyrian Empire.

Later History of the Judean Monarchy

During Ahaz's reign, Judah too became an Assyrian vassal (ca. 730 B.C.), but refrained from joining in the rebellions that brought Israel's downfall. However the next Davidic dynast,

17

Hezekiah, was a zealous nationalist who systematically prepared for revolt. In addition to conspiring with other states, Hezekiah welcomed refugee settlers from the northern tribes into Judah; he encouraged them to identify with his realm by instigating major religious and political reforms aimed at restoring preeminence to Jerusalem's Temple as the center of an all-Israelite Yahwism. Consistent with this, he seems to have reorganized the Yahwistic clergy on the model of David's levitical priesthood. Jerusalem's own defenses were extended and strengthened. When Sargon died and Sennacherib (705–681 B.C.) acceded to the Assyrian throne, revolts flared up throughout the empire; Hezekiah began his with an assault on Philistine coastal cities whose rulers remained loyal to Assyria. Sennacherib retaliated in 701, securing the Phoenician coast and easily defeating Hezekiah's Philistine allies; Assyrian troops laid siege to Judean fortresses. Hezekiah capitulated, but Jerusalem itself was spared when Sennacherib's forces withdrew.

Assyria remained strong through the reigns of Esarhaddon (680–669 B.C.) and Ashurbanipal (668–627 B.C.), but the empire declined rapidly thereafter. The capital city of Ashur was taken by the Medes in 614, and they, together with the Babylonians, conquered Nineveh and other Assyrian strongholds two years later.

In the first half of the seventh century B.C. Hezekiah's successors, Manasseh and Amon, reintroduced non-Yahwistic cults and practices into Judah. Amon was assassinated (640), and Judean forces secured the throne for his son, Josiah, who was only eight at the time. In the years following Ashurbanipal's death, when Assyria lost hold on its empire, Josiah seems to have made a bold bid to restore Davidic rule over territories of the former United Kingdom of Israel and Judah. Like Hezekiah a century before him, he purged Jerusalem and Judah of alien cults, and restricted sacrificial worship of Yahweh to Zion's Temple. But he also desecrated the altar of Bethel to the north of greater Judah and destroyed shrines throughout the Assyrian province of Samaria. The most celebrated events occurred in the eighteenth year of his reign (622 B.C.) when a document called "the book of the law [Heb. torah]" (2 Kings 22:8), or "the book of the covenant [Heb. berit]" (2 Kings 23:2) was recovered from the Temple archives. Convinced of the document's constitutional import, Josiah read it aloud before a plenary assembly of Judah's citizens, and he and they together entered into covenant with Yahweh to observe faithfully all of its stipulations. But if Josiah aspired to restore the Davidic kingdoms, it was not to be. In 609 B.C. he was slain in battle, attempting to halt at the pass of Megiddo a contingent of Egyptian troops, commanded by Pharaoh Neco II, which was marching north in a futile attempt to save the remnants of Assyria's army from final destruction at Haran.

Josiah's son, Jehoahaz (Shallum), reigned for only three months. He was deposed by Pharaoh Neco, who enthroned Jehoahaz's older brother, Jehoiakim (Eliakim), as an Egyptian vassal. But Egypt's renewed claims on Syro-Palestine collapsed after Neco's forces were defeated by Babylon, under Nebuchadnezzar, at Carchemish in 605 B.C. Jehoiakim became vassal to Babylon, only to rebel several years later. It was his newly enthroned son, Jehoiachin (Jeconiah/Coniah), who suffered the consequences. In 598, Nebuchadnezzar's army took Jerusalem and looted its coffers; Jehoiachin, along with many of Jerusalem's elite, was deported to Babylon where he spent the rest of his life in exile. His uncle, Zedekiah (Mattaniah), was appointed to remain in Jerusalem as surrogate vassal-ruler. In league with Egypt, he too rebelled. Nebuchadnezzar's army returned and after a prolonged siege conquered the city in 587–586, reducing it, including the despoiled Solomonic Temple, to rubble. Leading priests, other officials, and Zedekiah's own sons were executed; Zedekiah was blinded, then led into exile together with other survivors. Although decimated, Judah was not depopulated. North of the ruined capital, the Babylonians established a provincial garrison, Mizpah, which served as a residence for Gedaliah, a member of a prominent family of Judean scribes, who was appointed to remain as governor. His overtures to Judah's remnant population, to lay down arms and begin rebuilding a stable society under Babylonian auspices, had some success, until he was assassinated by a band of die-hard rebels. Fearing Babylonian retaliation, some remaining Judeans fled to Egypt, taking the prophet Jeremiah with them.

Prophecy and Kingship

Most of the phenomena typical of Israelite prophetism are now closely paralleled in literary sources from other ancient Near Eastern cultures. Under various titles, prophets functioned as spiritually sensitive channels through whom gods could convey visions and oracles to human audiences. Not surprisingly, kings figure most prominently among those to whom such divine communications are addressed in extant sources (e.g., letters from Mari, an ancient city of the upper Euphrates River area). In biblical traditions, the correlation be-

Opposite: Assyrian king Tiglath-pileser III and his attendants; detail of a mural from the palace at Til Barsib, eighth century B.C..

19

tween prophetism and monarchy is particularly close.

Israelite prophecy thus acquired a special institutional significance: prophets were seen as having central responsibility in defining the intersection between divine and human politics. They were more than inspired advisers to kings, because they were empowered to speak and act on behalf of Yahweh, Israel's preeminent sovereign.

This institutional understanding of prophecy seems to have developed especially in the Northern Kingdom during the ninth century B.C. The review of Omride rule and its demise gives unusual prominence to prophetical figures (1 Kings 16–2 Kings 10). Moreover, there are thematic links between this material and so-called Elohistic (E) narrative segments embedded in the Pentateuch. The old national epic drafted by Solomon's scribes (represented in the Pentateuch by the "J" narrative) may have been reworked and expanded in the court of Jehu to justify the consolidation of his reign as a return to pristine covenantal Yahwism.

A century later, a new flowering of Israelite prophetism occurred. Spoken words of at least some prophets were committed to writing, the better to preserve their testimony to God's involvement in affairs of the world. Around these early collections of prophetical traditions grew the canonical books of the Latter Prophets (Isaiah to Malachi).

Literary witnesses to eighth-century B.C. prophecy exhibit many similarities of genre and message but also significant differences in perspective, theological theme, and emotional tone. In the preserved visions and speeches of Amos, a Judean who addressed the elite of the Northern Kingdom during the heyday of Jeroboam II's reign (ca. 750 B.C.), it is outrage at Israel's perversion of social justice, abuse of prosperity, and religious hypocrisy that predominates. Hosea, a northerner, seems to have prophesied during the era of frantic royal politics that preceded the nation's total collapse. His message, like Amos's, knows the certainty of divine judgment, but the depth of God's compassion means that there is always prospect of restoration beyond punishment. Materials in the anthological books of Isaiah and Micah that can be assigned to the late eighth century B.C. portray Yahweh, the divine warrior of old, as majestically enthroned above the fray of human history and yet acting diligently as judge to guide its course toward fulfillment of a master plan that includes vindication of Zion and the Davidic dynasty.

The Covenantal Legacy of Israel

Israelites who found refuge in Judah after the destruction of Samaria brought a rich legacy

with them: their version of the national epic; traditions of prophecy, hymnody, and wisdom; and, above all, their memory that long before divine election of Zion a pact had been made in the wilderness between Yahweh and Hebrew refugees from Egyptian oppression. If the ethos of the Israelite league had faded in monarchical Judah, Hezekiah's policies were midwife to its rebirth. His reforms enabled Jerusalem to nurture visions of Mount Horeb as well as Zion, to celebrate Moses, model liberator and lawgiver, as well as David, archetypal builder of Yahweh's empire among the nations.

The most enduring achievement of Hezekiah's reign is probably the "Torah of Moses" preserved in the book of Deuteronomy (chaps. 4–28); its earliest form may have been drafted by levitical officials of Hezekiah's reorganized clergy, which included priests of Mosaic lineage (cf. Deut. 10:8–9; 18:1–8; 33:4–5, 8–11). An edition of the national epic may have been written in Hezekiah's court, not only updating the old Solomonic version but enlarging it with traditions brought from the north. That Hezekiah's scribes endeavored to preserve a literary heritage of wisdom is indicated by Prov. 25:1; perhaps the archaic poetical drama of Job (whose familiar themes are as pertinent to the crises of the later eighth century B.C. as to those of the early sixth) is the work of this same circle.

The revitalization of Israelite nationalism and Yahwistic religion initiated under Hezekiah seems to have suffered a serious setback during the reigns of his successors, until the era of the Josian reforms at the end of the seventh century B.C. At this time, apparently, the Deuteronomic Torah was brought out of the Temple archives and made the law of the land. Josiah's scribes were probably responsible for the penultimate form of the outer framework of Deuteronomy (chaps. 1–3, 29–34), which served as an introduction to their edition of the following books of Joshua, Judges, Samuel, and Kings. This "Deuteronomic" (or "early Deuteronomistic") version of the national epic thus traced the history of the covenant people, "all Israel," from the time of its formation under Moses' leadership in the wilderness through its ostensible reconstitution under Josiah, when the Mosaic law once again became the polity of the nation (cf. 2 Kings 23:24–25). Obviously, there was still a final chapter of monarchical history to be tragically lived and then written in exile.

Literary reflections of the Josian period and its aftermath can also be discerned elsewhere in Scripture. The oldest stratum of the so-called Priestly pentateuchal laws—specifically the Holiness Code represented mainly in Leviticus 17–26—appears to be the work of Josiah's Aaronitic clergy, drafted in part as a corrective to the levitical program promulgated in the Deuteronomic Torah. The Yahwistic nationalism generated by Josiah's religious reforms and political policies is attested in the books of Zephaniah and Nahum, the latter celebrating Nineveh's fall in 612 B.C. The somber dialogue of Habakkuk reflects a slightly later period, after Josiah's death and about the time of the battle of Carchemish (605 B.C.). However, the fullest witnesses to the final decades of the kingdom of Judah and the beginning of the Exile are found in the books of Jeremiah and Ezekiel.

Jeremiah belonged to a family of levitical priests that traced its lineage back through the old Shiloh clergy to Moses; his prophecy consistently reflects this ancestral heritage as it was most forcefully expressed in the traditions of Deuteronomic covenantal Yahwism. In Jeremiah's view, the demise of the Judean state, like that of monarchical Israel before it, was the inevitable result of God's people having wantonly violated the covenant obligations upon which their corporate existence depended. Ezekiel, on the other hand, was a priest of Zadokite lineage who was taken into exile with the deportation of 597 B.C. While influence of Deuteronomic covenantal themes and language can be discerned in the work ascribed to him, his theological perspective, with its reciprocal emphases on divine glory and ritual purity, indicates closest affiliation with the Priestly circle responsible for the Holiness Code.

The greatest achievement of Judean prophecy was to envision a future beyond judgment, sustaining the faithful, whether they lived in distant exile or in sight of the Temple's ruins; but for the while, the appropriate liturgical response to disaster was mourning and prayerful petition (Lamentations; Pss. 44, 74, 79, 137; 1 Kings 8:22–53).

THE AGE OF RESTORATION
(538–432 B.C.)

Throughout the six centuries of Israelite and Judean history preceding the Exile, the entire eastern Mediterranean world had been a seething cauldron of political violence. A degree of international calm, especially in Syro-Palestine, was effected by the more tolerant policies of early Achaemenid rulers. The scattered remnants of "Israel" not only benefited from these policies in the short term but brought them to eloquent intellectual expression, at once preserving their own spiritual heritage while making a lasting contribution to human civilization.

Reconstruction and Reform

After his spectacular victories in Asia Minor Cyrus "the Great" of Persia defeated the forces of Babylon in 539 B.C. and established hegemony over its exhausted empire. He cultivated an image of himself as divinely chosen liberator of captive peoples and restorer of the sanctuaries of their gods. In accord with this program (outlined in the text of the "Cyrus Cylinder") he issued an edict in 538, claiming that "Yahweh, God of Heaven" had granted him sovereignty over all the world's kingdoms and had charged him to rebuild the Jerusalem Temple. Judeans were urged to return to their homeland and carry out the mandate (Ezra 1:2–4; cf. 6:3–5; 2 Chron. 36:22–23). Sheshbazzar (Shenazzar), a member of the Judean royal family, was appointed to serve as Jerusalem's governor. He and those who returned with him may have laid foundations for a new Temple (Ezra 1:7–11; 5:13–16; cf. 1 Chron. 3:18).

Early in the reign of Darius (522–486 B.C.) another group of Judeans reached Jerusalem and, despite some initial interference from officials of the Syrian satrapy, secured a renewal of Cyrus's mandate; construction of the Temple was resumed in 520 and completed in 515 (Ezra 5–6).

The biblical account of this era and the rest of the Persian period is laconic, focusing narrowly on the restoration of the Temple cultus and emphasizing that every stage of the work had the active support of the Persian crown. Major attention is given to the efforts of Ezra and Nehemiah.

The date of Ezra's journey from Babylon to Jerusalem, leading back another party of exiles, is disputed, but an earlier setting in the reign of Xerxes I (486–464 B.C.) or Artaxerxes I (464–423 B.C.) is preferable, if only because the authority granted to Ezra in matters pertaining to both Persian and traditional Mosaic law (Ezra 7:11–26) is most easily understood to be a direct outgrowth of policies initiated by Darius. Ezra, the "scribe," seems to have been a prominent legal scholar within the continuing Judean community of Babylonia, who served as adviser to the Persian crown on matters affecting especially the Jerusalem Temple. Thus he was not simply leader of yet another phase of the return but was sent to Jerusalem as a royal ambassador, empowered to finish the work of reconstituting the Temple cult in accord with ancient Yahwistic tradition and to establish judicial procedures relevant to the Temple's status as an imperial institution (Ezra 7:21–26; cf. 6:8–10).

Jerusalem's consolidation as a Persian provincial center is credited to Nehemiah. While serving as "cupbearer" to Artaxerxes I in Susa (Neh. 1:11) he solicited and received from the king a term appointment as "governor" (Neh. 5:14) in order to rebuild Jerusalem's fortifications. Once the city wall had been repaired (ca. 445 B.C.), Nehemiah used the rest of his initial term as governor and a second some years later to implement important economic, political, and religious reforms; these measures were consistent with Persian imperial interests but they also enforced provisions of the polity that Ezra had previously established.

Israelite Theology in the Setting of Exile

The Deuteronomistic History in its completed form is an early exilic attempt (ca. 560 B.C.) to take stock of what had happened to all Israel and why. The final segment of the work (2 Kings 23:26–25:30) narrates the rapid decline and fall of monarchical Judah, ending with notice of King Jehoichin's release from Babylonian prison. Conspicuous is the segment's introductory claim that Manasseh's gross acts of apostasy had sealed Judah's fate (2 Kings 23:26–27; cf. 21:10–15). Other exilic supplements to the work spread blame for national disaster more widely, declaring the whole people culpable for breach of covenant (e.g., Deut. 28:64–68; 29:20–28; Josh. 23:11–16). If painful awareness of retributive justice is the dominant theme of such passages, a deeper perception of divine providence is adumbrated in the theological discourse of Deut. 4:1–40. Here dispersal of Israel from the land is just recompense but emphatically not the end of the covenant relationship, for Yahweh is not only "divine retributor" but the "compassionate deity" who never abrogates promises made in the past (Deut. 4:24, 31). Moreover, the degradation of exile among the nations becomes occasion for Israel to discover new profundity in its own unique historical experience: Yahweh, the God who created Israel in unparalleled fashion, who gave it the wisdom of Torah through Moses, and who remains forever with it in victory and defeat, is the sole sovereign of the cosmos (Deut. 4:5–8, 32–40).

This insight came to even more eloquent expression in the growth of Isaian tradition that critics designate "Second Isaiah" (Isa. 40–55), a work composed at the time of Cyrus's edict of 538 B.C. The poet envisioned a courtroom drama of cosmic scope, involving a plenary assembly of the world's nations, in which Yahweh is at once presiding judge and defendant. While the case focuses on Israel's experiences, and above all the ruin of Zion (cf. Isa. 34:8; 40:2; 49:14–26; 51:17–23; 52:1–10), the crucial issue is whether universal sovereignty is exercised by Yahweh or the putative gods of nations that have prevailed over the covenant people. The trial unveils wondrous things about which Israel is called to give witness (40:27–31; 43:8–13; cf. 2:1–5): Yahweh alone is God, creator and lord of history, whose justice is manifest in Zion's humiliation and imminent restoration; Cyrus is God's anointed and through his conquests the rule of Yahweh is being extended to the nations; and, most astonishing of all, the destiny of the covenant people —God's chosen "servant," personified also as Zion, trampled down and despised by the nations—is to become a prophetical light to the nations, instructing them in the ways of true justice revealed through Torah (42:1–9, 18–25; 51:4–8).

The grand vision of Second Isaiah foresaw a glorious future for those who immigrated with Sheshbazzar to Jerusalem, but it offered little guidance on what to do once they got there. The first generations of the return had to deal with formidable obstacles, not the least of which were created by divergent views among them regarding who was to comprise the new Israel, how it was to be governed, and what it should strive to become. Largely in consideration of such issues, the later works included in the Hebrew Bible were written and the Scriptural canon itself began to take shape.

Prophetic Vision and Mosaic Constitution

Biblical sources agree that the crux of the restoration was the reestablishment of Jerusalem as cultic center of Yahwism. At the same time, prophetical texts dating to the early Persian period show that some within the restoration community had considerably broader goals in view. The final chapters of the Isaian anthology (Isa. 56–66), often designated "Third Isaiah," understand the promised exaltation of Zion to include a full ingathering of the Israelite Diaspora (Isa. 60:4; 65:1–12; 66:18–21) and even incorporation of gentile converts into the community of the new Israel (Isa. 56:3–8). Obadiah, Joel, Ezekiel 38–39, and Zechariah 9–14 exhibit a more militant stance toward the nations, envisioning Yahweh's imminent kingdom to involve a revival of Israelite nationalism. These differences of perspective bear upon the final stages in the literary formation of biblical Torah, "Law."

In addition to contents of the Pentateuch, there is another corpus in the Hebrew Bible identified as Torah, specifically the "Torah of the Temple" (Ezek. 43:12) preserved within the elaborate vision report of Ezekiel 40–48. The entire report, dated to the year 573 B.C. but certainly supplemented during the initial phase of the Persian period, lays out under the prophetical authority of Ezekiel a restoration program that is both grandly idealistic and decidedly more concrete than the vision of Second Isaiah.

It includes a revelational blueprint—with specific measurements and description of materials and decor—for rebuilding the Temple complex. Various factors suggest that this text was the charter under which the Jerusalem Temple was reconstructed as an imperial shrine in the first years of the reign of Darius I. At least the initial phase of the work was completed under the direction of Zerubbabel and Jeshua, leader of the Zadokite clergy, and with the prophetical support of Haggai and Zechariah.

However, the Torah ascribed to Ezekiel did not long remain the official polity of the Judean community. The prophecy of Malachi, probably dating to the early fifth century B.C., provides insight into why and with what it was replaced. Zadokite exclusivism is attacked as a perversion of God's "covenant" with all the families of Levi (Mal. 2:1–9), while the community as a whole is indicted for abandoning its ancient covenantal commitments as set forth in the Torah of Moses (Mal. 3:1–12; cf. 4:4). The issue was definitively resolved some years later, when Ezra reached Jerusalem with a royal commission to establish and implement "the Law [Aramaic data'] of the God of Heaven" (Ezra 7:11–26).

Although critics continue to debate the matter, in all likelihood the Pentateuch in its completed form preserves the literary traditions of divine "Law" or Torah that Ezra brought with him to Jerusalem. His reforms and those of Nehemiah somewhat later presuppose juridical interpretations of a constitutional document that included the Mosaic Torah of Deuteronomy but also ritual ordinances preserved in the "Priestly" (P) edition of Genesis through Numbers. The latter is a remarkable work of theological history writing, apparently crafted by Judean clergy in Babylonia, which restructured and extensively supplemented the initial segments of the Israelite national epic of late monarchical times. "P" preserves older traditions of covenantal law (esp. the Decalogue, the Book of the Covenant, and the Holiness Code), but emphasis is placed on revelation of the design of a portable sanctuary, the "tabernacle" (Heb. mishkan), along with its attendant institutions and rites. When, under the close supervision of Moses and Aaron, Israel carries out the divine instructions, it is transformed from a tribal assembly into an articulated cultic community, a human temple as it were, both serving and sustained by the sovereign God who tabernacles in its midst.

The Pentateuch is thus a sacral archive designed to include both the Deuteronomic corpus of Mosaic law and the "Priestly" history of Israel's formation as the unique people of God. What provides coherence to this archive is less a matter of its broad narrative integrity than of the claim that it preserves authoritative record of Moses' work. In short, neither the visionary program of Ezekiel 40–48 nor any other prophetical testimony could replace or supersede what God had revealed to Israel through Moses (cf. Deut. 34:10–12).

ISRAEL AMONG THE NATIONS

Ezra and Nehemiah successfully reformed the Judean community around Temple worship and Mosaic Torah. If alternative visions of Israel's destiny were left unresolved, they had been relativized.

The Judean Commonwealth During the Later Persian and Early Hellenistic Periods (432–164 B.C.)

Governors who followed Nehemiah seem to have kept the province of Judah relatively prosperous and secure, even though Achaemenid rule grew increasingly weaker through the first half of the fourth century B.C. When the Macedonian forces of Alexander III shattered the Persian Empire altogether in 334–332 B.C., Jerusalem neither gave resistance to the conquerors nor, apparently, experienced any immediate change in circumstances.

After Alexander's death in 323 B.C., control of the Near Eastern territories he had conquered passed to two of his generals. Seleucus ruled Babylonia and most of Syria, while Ptolemy claimed Egypt, building Alexandria as his capital. Jerusalem's position as cultic and judicial center of Judea seems largely to have been unaffected by Ptolemaic policies.

A second and politically tumultuous phase of the Hellenistic period began for Judea when the Seleucids gained control over the whole of Syro-Palestine at the beginning of the second century B.C. Although Antiochus III (223–187 B.C.) was magnanimous in victory, recognizing Jerusalem's autonomy in religious affairs, the kingdom inherited by his successor, Seleucus IV (187–175 B.C.), was in financial disarray and threatened externally on every major front. International events had once again conspired to put Palestine at the center of a world locked in conflict.

After Antiochus IV Epiphanes (175–163 B.C.) ascended to the Seleucid throne, Judea experienced a series of convulsions that provoked anew questions of "Israel's" true identity and its destiny among the nations. Antiochus took an interventionist stance toward Judean affairs, perhaps above all because he coveted the Temple's pecuniary resources but also, in the interest of unifying his realm, to support those among the Judean aristocracy who wanted isolated, conservative Jerusalem to catch up with the Hellenistic cultural revolution that had already engulfed other urban centers of Syro-Palestine. Antiochus resorted to force when Judean society, already polarized into Hellenist and traditionalist parties, was torn apart by strife over the high-priestly office. Seleucid troops brutally enforced a decree banning traditional practices of Yahwism. The Temple became a shrine of the realm, where divine Antiochus was venerated alongside the imperial deity, Zeus Olympios, whose altar was raised in the forecourt.

When the zealots of Hellenistic nationalism controlling Jerusalem tried to uproot Yahwism from the Judean countryside and to enforce observance of the imperial cult, they soon met vigorous resistance. Insurgent groups of varying political and religious persuasions coalesced under the leadership of the Hasmonean priestly family of Mattathias and his five sons, the third of whom—Judah, called the "hammer" (Maccabeus)—proved to be a brilliant guerrilla strategist. The Hasmonean army reclaimed most of Jerusalem itself in 164 B.C. The Temple precincts were purged of pagan accoutrements, repairs were made, and a loyal priesthood was restored to office; the sacrificial altar in the forecourt was rebuilt according to provisions of the Mosaic Torah and consecrated to Yahweh alone (1 Macc. 4:36–58). While this era of violent political strife had not yet completed its course, the flames rekindled on the altar and in the lamps of the Temple became a new memorial to the ancient concept of Israel as the liberated people of God. (This period overlaps with the period in which books of the Apocrypha took shape, and its story is continued and told in more detail in another article; see "Biblical Literature in Its Historical Context: The Apocrypha and the New Testament.")

Torah and Prophets

Although modern scholars have generally viewed the Exile as the major turning point in ancient Israel's religious and political history, the canonical sources—or, if one prefers, those who designed the canon of the Hebrew Bible—identify the era of Ezra and Nehemiah as decisive, because it was then that a normative social order, supported by an expansive synthesis of Yahwistic traditions, was achieved. The crux of this synthesis is, of course, the pentateuchal Torah of Moses, understood to be the sufficient though not exclusive revelation of God's sovereign design of the cosmos, with the sanctuary people, Israel, forming its human center in the midst of the nations.

Mosaic Torah undergirded the role of Tem-

ple worship and clergy in mediating divine blessing to all humanity (Num. 6:22–27; cf. Gen. 1:28; 12:1–3; 22:15–19), but its import for Israel's religious thought was by no means limited to sacerdotal concerns. At the broadest social level, affecting Diaspora Judaism as well as the Temple community, provisions of the Torah encouraged a piety fully embracing both love of God and love of neighbor. To live in accord with the mandate of Torah involved study, prayer, and communal worship but also diligent observance of covenantal demands to pursue public well-being, justice, and human rights.

In large extent, the synthesis that formed around commitment to the preeminent revelation of Torah was able to absorb Yahwistic prophetism and its varied literary traditions. This occurred conceptually in a twofold development based on the pentateuchal claim that Moses had been Israel's "prophet" par excellence (Deut. 34:10–12): his promulgation of Torah became the measure of truth by which all subsequent prophetical revelations were to be assessed and interpreted (cf. Num. 12:1–8; Deut. 18:15–22; 30:11–14); and prophecy itself was broadened to include gifts of the spirit, especially "inspired" leadership, in the model and legitimate succession of Moses (cf. Num. 11:16–29; Deut. 34:9; Sir. 44:1–3; 46:1). The Deuteronomistic History of Israel from conquest to exile came to be included in the canonical division "Prophets" because it witnessed both to activities of Moses' prophetical successors (e.g., 1 Sam. 3:19–20; 1 Kings 11:29–39; 2 Kings 17:13) and, above all, to the perduring prophetic authority of Mosaic Torah itself in the life of Israel (e.g., Josh. 1:2–8; 1 Kings 2:1–4; 2 Kings 23:24–25; cf. Deut. 31:28–32:47; Ezra 9:10–15). Similarly, works included in the literary corpus of Isaiah through Malachi supplement and extend the record of authentic Israelite prophecy through the restoration period; but they were also read and interpreted as testimony that Torah disclosed the trustworthy plan of God's continuing rule over Israel and, in the fullness of time, all the world's nations (e.g., Isa. 2:3; 51:7; Jer. 31:33; Mal. 4:1–6; cf. Jonah).

The Writings

As the name itself indicates, the canonical division "Writings" (Heb. ketubim) is a miscellany of Israelite literature. Individual works in this collection differ widely in literary genre, content, and provenance. Although most of them were composed before or during the restoration era, some—notably Esther and Ecclesiastes—probably belong to the end of the fourth century B.C. or the beginning of the third; the book of Daniel in its completed form is even later, dating to the time of Antiochus' assault on traditional Yahwism (ca. 165 B.C.). Yet the diversity of the Writings exemplifies the scope of the late restoration synthesis.

A comprehensive historiographical presentation of the synthesis is found in the work of the so-called Chronicler, which at least in its composite edition dates to the end of the fifth century B.C. and comprises the books of 1 and 2 Chronicles together with their narrative sequel in Ezra and Nehemiah (cf. also 1 Esdras). Drawing extensively on the Deuteronomistic narrative, the central part of the work selectively reviews monarchical history, stressing that through the inspired efforts of David and the continued patronage of his loyal dynastic successors the people "Israel" was institutionally formed around the Jerusalem Temple worship (cf. esp. 1 Chron. 16–17; 22–29; 2 Chron. 2–7; 30–35); yet Israel's sacral constitution, fidelity to which was the sine qua non of its existence, remained the Torah mediated through Moses and reaffirmed by subsequent prophetical messengers (e.g., 1 Chron. 22:12–13; 2 Chron. 8:12–13; 36:15–16). The account of the restoration itself in the books of Ezra and Nehemiah completes the work, confirming the centrality of both Temple worship and pentateuchal Torah in Israel's corporate life while committing Israel's future among the nations to the intricacies of divine providence.

The hymnic compositions preserved in the canonical book of Psalms, most of which derive from pre-exilic times, provide ample witness to the continuity of liturgical tradition between the communities that worshiped at the First and Second Temples (cf. Ps. 126). However, some of the postexilic additions to the corpus (esp. Pss. 1; 19; 37; 111–12; 119) are particularly noteworthy because they attest the full development of a piety centered on Torah.

Integration of Israel's sapiential lore with other Yahwistic traditions was a natural development, which had begun during monarchical times if not before. But a more inclusive agenda for the pursuit of wisdom emerged in the Persian period and accounts in large measure for the continuing intellectual creativity of postexilic Judaism, especially in its confrontation with Hellenistic culture. The most compelling factor in setting this agenda was the conviction that Mosaic Torah, complemented by subsequent prophetic revelations, not only laid out the peculiar covenantal norms of Israelite life but disclosed the perennial scheme of divine rule over all space and time. If Yahweh alone was sovereign "God of Heaven," as restoration theology insisted, then all genuine knowledge —whether imparted through Scripture or gleaned from observation of historical process, the phenomenal universe, and the manifold data of human experience—should ultimately coalesce into a unitary theological design (cf.

Sir. 1:1–20; 24; 39; 43). Given the epistemological breadth of this agenda, it is possible to understand inclusion in the Writings not only of Proverbs and Job but also of such ostensibly "humanistic" works as Song of Songs and the didactic novellas of Ruth and Esther. However the books of Ecclesiastes and Daniel offer the most conspicuous canonical witnesses to the scope of sapiential thought in postexilic Judaism.

Ecclesiastes (Qohelet) contains the purported memoirs of an anonymous "sage." The memoirs stress the futility of every effort to secure on human terms a meaningful existence. Particularly in light of the narrator's epilogue (Eccles. 12:9–14), the book can more readily be interpreted as a response to the pretensions of Hellenistic rationalism than as a critique of traditional Yahwism. Reverence for God through observance of Torah's stipulations remains the supreme human wisdom (cf. esp. Eccles. 3:12–14; 8:12–13; 12:13–14).

Throughout the narratives and vision reports that comprise the book of Daniel, the chief protagonist is a sage whose life and learning variously model the inspiration attributed to Israel's former prophets and kings (cf. 2 Sam. 23:1–7; 1 Kings 3:5–14; Sir. 24:33–34). The core of the narratives (Dan. 1–6) validate trust in Yahweh's universal sovereignty and providence: through fidelity to the demands of Torah and diligent exercise of God-given wisdom, the faithful may not only withstand the pressures of an alien cultural environment but triumph over them (e.g., Dan. 1:17–20; 2:20–23; 47–49; 6:25–28; cf. Deut. 4:2–8). In their received form, the narratives anticipate the vision reports (Dan. 7–12; cf. 2:36–45), which reflect the era of Antiochene persecutions. The message to the faithful remains essentially the same in the visions, even though it is more urgent here and appears in the elaborate guise of mythological symbolism and "apocalyptic" scenario.

When one recalls Pharaoh Merneptah's claim to have obliterated "Israel" and the celebration of Yahweh's kingship in Exodus 15, there is a remarkable symmetry between the beginning of ancient Israel's history and the latest witness to divine providence preserved in the literature of the Hebrew Bible.

Bibliography

Ben-Sasson, H. H., ed. *A History of the Jewish People.* Cambridge, MA: Harvard University Press, 1976.

Blenkinsopp, J. *A History of Prophecy in Israel.* Philadelphia: Westminster, 1983.

Bright, J. *A History of Israel.* 3d ed. Philadelphia: Westminster, 1981.

25

Cross, F. M. *Canaanite Myth and Hebrew Epic: Essays in the History of the Religion of Israel.* Cambridge, MA: Harvard University Press, 1973.

Hanson, P. D. *The People Called: The Growth of Community in the Bible.* San Francisco: Harper & Row, 1986.

Hayes, J. H., and J. M. Miller, eds. *Israelite and Judaean History.* Philadelphia: Westminster, 1977.

Knight, D. A., and G. M. Tucker, eds. *The Hebrew Bible and Its Modern Interpreters.* Philadelphia: Fortress, 1985.

BIBLICAL LITERATURE IN ITS HISTORICAL CONTEXT: THE APOCRYPHA AND THE NEW TESTAMENT

E L D O N   J.   E P P

Biblical literature, like other literature, cannot be fully understood apart from its historical and cultural context. Each of the writings that became part of the Apocrypha and the NT originated within a set of real-life circumstances. For some writings these can be rather easily discovered and described with considerable specificity, while the situation out of which other writings emerged may never be clearly known. To the extent possible, specific circumstances must be sought for each separate writing, but this general introduction seeks mainly to sketch the broad historical context in which and out of which the large body of apocryphal and NT writings arose.

Traditionally, many Christians of past generations—and ultra-conservative Christians even today—have been taught that there were "four hundred silent years" between the OT and the NT, an assertion made on the incorrect assumption that the latest book of the OT was written around 400 B.C., that the earliest NT books were written when Christianity originated, and that the Jewish people produced no literature in the intervening period while, presumably, they passively awaited the expected Messiah. Such a perception, of course, is completely wrong, for neither were there four hundred years between the OT and NT (rather, about two hundred years), nor were they by any means silent or passive years. Indeed, it was during these two centuries prior to Christianity, as well as the one or two centuries following, that both the apocryphal and related writings and the NT books themselves were produced.

The term "Apocrypha" refers to about fifteen books or parts of books that were not included in the Hebrew canon but, with an exception or two, were contained in the Greek OT. Another group of related works, known as the Pseudepigrapha, comprises some sixty-five writings by Jews and Christians, though probably none of them was part of a Jewish or Christian canon of Scripture (→ Apocrypha, Old Testament; Pseudepigrapha).

What was the historical, cultural, and social climate that produced this vast quantity and wide variety of religious works? A consideration of the various periods of Jewish history will provide a convenient framework for discovering the answer.

THE BABYLONIAN (587–539 B.C.) AND PERSIAN (539–333 B.C.) PERIODS

Following Nebuchadnezzar's destruction of Jerusalem in 587 B.C. and the Exile of the Jewish people that accompanied it, the Jews were open to foreign influences as never before. These extraneous influences continued in the Persian period, which began when Cyrus II conquered the Babylonians in 539 B.C. His lenient policies toward conquered peoples permitted the Jews—within limits—to develop their own life, culture, and religion, including the rebuilding of the Temple between 520 and 515 B.C. in the reign of Darius I. Persian rule, of course, permitted the migration of Jewish exiles from Babylonia where, in the absence of the Temple, the study and authority of Torah had assumed the central place in the Jewish religion.

Although none of the apocryphal or pseudepigraphical books was written during these periods, many claim to be written then or find their setting in these times. For example, the Letter of Jeremiah was probably written in the fourth century B.C.; 1 Esdras; Baruch; Tobit; Song of the Three Youths, Susanna, and Bel and the Dragon (three additions to Daniel); Judith; and The Additions to Esther are all works written actually in the second century B.C. or thereabouts. Others, notably the apocalyptic writings, contain ideas or motifs that influenced the Jews during their exile in Babylonia or Persia, for example, the procedure of periodizing history that is found in much apocalyptic literature. 2 Esdras (= 4 Ezra) is such an apocalypse, completed about A.D. 200.

THE HELLENISTIC PERIOD (333–63 B.C.)

Alexander and His Successors

Alexander the Great became king of Macedon and leader of the Hellenic League of Greek states upon the assassination of his father, Philip II, in 336 B.C. He adopted his father's determination to master the Persian Empire and to spread Greek culture throughout the known world. Only ten years were required to achieve this incomparable goal, including Alexander's defeat of Darius III at Issus in 333, his liberation of Egypt in 332 and the building of the city of Alexandria, and his march north through Syro-Palestine and then eastward to Babylon and to the Persian capital, Susa, and finally to India. Alexander died in Babylon in 323 at the age of thirty-three. Perhaps no one before or after so significantly changed the course of world history, for Alexander opened the East to Greek culture and brought into the "known world" a unity of Greek language and culture. The environment thus created (and carried forward by the Romans) was that in which both Judaism and Christianity were to thrive—in spite of the difficulties and persecutions that were to intervene periodically.

Alexander's early death, however, left the new empire without clearly delineated leadership, and forty years of struggles among his generals and other successors (the Diadochi) led finally in 281 B.C. to two dynasties: that of Egypt and Coele Syria (including Palestine) under Ptolemy and that of northern Syria, Babylon, and Asia Minor under Seleucus. A substantial period of peace prevailed in Palestine, until the Seleucid ruler Antiochus III defeated the Ptolemaic forces in 198 B.C. and took control of Coele Syria, bringing Palestine also under Seleucid rule. The dire effects of this change began to be obvious when Antiochus IV (Epiphanes) proclaimed himself king in 175 B.C. His eagerness to embrace and enhance hellenizing ways of life, including the athletics of the gymnasium and other urban and progressive Hellenistic cultural activities, created difficult choices and deep tensions in the Jewish community of Judea and Jerusalem. In fact, struggles over the high-priesthood in Jerusalem soon were based on pro-Greek versus orthodox Jewish views, and intrigue was the order of the day.

The hellenizing practices of Antiochus IV were not, at least in the beginning, intended to displace Torah as a way of life for pious Jews, but the increased mingling with Gentiles and the rising peer pressure heightened the intra-Jewish tensions. Then in 169 B.C. Antiochus IV committed hostile acts against the Jews, plundering the Temple, and in 167 he ordered a pagan altar to Zeus Olympios to be erected on the altar of sacrifice, thus defiling the Temple. This is the "abomination of desolation" referred to in Dan. 11:31; 12:11; 1 Macc. 1:54; and Mark 13:14. This desecration, along with Antiochus' proscription of the central features of Jewish religion (sacrifices, festivals, circumcision, and reading of Torah), instigated the Maccabean or Hasmonean revolt against the Hellenistic powers in 168 B.C. These events are described, with embellishments and sometimes in legendary form, in 1 and 2 Maccabees, and also in the writings of the first-century Jewish historian Josephus. 1 Maccabees attempts to defend the Hasmonean high-priestly dynasty by tracing its achievements in stopping the persecution, reinstating Torah, and winning for Israel a period of religious and political independence. Originally composed in Hebrew, it is preserved in Greek and was written between 104 and 63 B.C. 2 Maccabees emphasizes the hellenizing of Jerusalem, with vivid depictions of atrocities and heroism. It is a condensation of a five-volume work by an otherwise unknown Jason of Cyrene and was written in Greek after 110 B.C. The Wisdom of Jesus the Son of Sirach (Ecclesiasticus) was written about 180 B.C. and depicts Jewish society just before the Maccabean revolt.

The Maccabean Revolt (168–142 B.C.)

Mattathias, a priest at Modein (seventeen miles northwest of Jerusalem), not only refused to comply with Syrian orders to offer improper sacrifice, but he killed a Jew about to do so, as well as a Syrian officer. Fleeing to the wilderness with his five sons and followers, Mattathias determined to secure religious freedom for Judea. They were joined for a time by the "Pious" (Hasidim), who opposed hellenization (and from whom the Pharisees seem to have sprung). Early in the movement, they made a wrenching decision to fight on the Sabbath, and when Mattathias died in 166 B.C., leadership fell to his third son, Judas (known as Judas Maccabeus, "the hammer"), who successfully fought the Seleucid forces and reclaimed and rededicated the Temple in 164 B.C. His successes were aided by the divisions and diversions of the Syrians, but the triumph of Judas was of extraordinary significance and is still celebrated among Jews on Hanukkah (→ Dedication, Feast of).

This achievement of religious liberty, however, was not sufficient for Judas, and the campaign soon became a nationalistic movement for political freedom as well. In 162 B.C. Demetrius I assumed Seleucid control and defeated the army of Judas at Elasa, near Jerusalem, in 160, where Judas was killed. Jonathan, Judas's younger brother, succeeded him as head of the

Hasmonean house (160–143 B.C.), and was able to make peace with the Syrians for a five-year period (157–152), during which his influence increased. Rivalry between Demetrius I and a pretender, Alexander Balas, further enhanced Jonathan's position by the alternate courting of his favor. In the process, the Hellenizers in the Jewish community—against whom both Judas and Jonathan had fought—lost their Syrian support. Balas appointed Jonathan high priest in 152 B.C., and from that point until 63 B.C. religious, political, and military authority all rested in one person (the various successors) in the Hasmonean family. Soon Demetrius I met Balas in battle (150 B.C.) and was killed; in 145 B.C., however, Demetrius II (Nicator), Demetrius' son and successor, defeated Balas and assumed the Syrian throne. Intra-Seleucid power struggles found Jonathan supporting and being supported by Demetrius II and then by Tryphon, Demetrius' rival, one of Balas's generals. Jonathan, however, was finally betrayed and soon murdered by Tryphon in 143 B.C., and his brother Simon, the only surviving son of Mattathias, was chosen to head the Hasmoneans.

Political Independence for the Jewish Nation (142–63 B.C.)

Simon achieved what both Judas and Jonathan had sought: complete political independence from Syria. This was granted by Demetrius II in 142 B.C. and lasted—through troubled times—until 63 B.C. when the Romans took control. In 134, however, Simon and two of his sons were murdered by Ptolemy, Simon's ambitious son-in-law. His surviving son, John Hyrcanus, became high priest and ruled for thirty years. In 109 B.C. he became the first Jewish ruler to mint his own coins, which were inscribed, "John the High Priest and the Community of the Jews." Although their origins are obscure, at this time the Pharisees and Sadducees were well established and prominently mentioned. Hyrcanus sided with the Sadducees, apparently in face of Pharisaic criticism of Hasmoneans holding the high-priesthood. He died in 104 B.C.

Following an ignominious year of rule by his eldest son, Aristobulus I (104–103 B.C.), the latter's brother Alexander Jannaeus became high priest and also officially claimed the title of king. A ruthless warmonger, he enlarged an already extensive kingdom so that it equaled the ancient kingdoms of David and Solomon. His infamous atrocity—crucifying eight hundred opposing Pharisees and killing their families—is the first use by a Jewish ruler of this Roman form of execution, an event that seems to be recalled in the Qumran commentary on Nahum. Upon his death, his widow, Salome Alexan-

dra, became queen (76–67 B.C.). Excluded by Torah—as a woman—from the high-priesthood, she appointed her elder son, Hyrcanus II, to that office. During her reign, the Pharisees gained substantial influence, and the Sadducees declined correspondingly.

Upon Alexandra's death in 67, Hyrcanus II briefly became king but was forced to relinquish power to his younger brother, Aristobulus II, who ruled from 67 to 63 B.C. After Pompey defeated Aristobulus and took Jerusalem in 63—and entered the Temple's Holy of Holies—he reinstated Hyrcanus as high priest, naming him "ethnarch" ("ruler of the people"). The title "king" was no longer used, and Hyrcanus, who reported directly to the Roman governor, now in actuality was merely a high priest over a religious community—and a rather small one, since it now included only Judea, Galilee, Idumea, and Perea. The rule of the Hasmonean house, therefore, came to an end, and once again the Jewish nation was under foreign domination.

The Psalms of Solomon, written about mid-first century B.C., obviously refer to the events of Pompey's conquest, lamenting the desecration of the Temple and looking forward to better times in a Messianic future.

ROMAN PERIOD (63 B.C.–A.D. 135)

Hyrcanus II continued as high priest and was reconfirmed in the position by Gabinus, governor of Syria, and again in 47 B.C. by Julius Caesar. Caesar also made Antipater procurator of Judea, and he, in turn, constituted his son Herod as governor of Galilee. After Antipater's assassination in 43 B.C., Herod was named governor of Coele Syria and then tetrarch of Galilee, while Antipater's other son, Phasael, became tetrarch of southern Judea. They supported and were supported by Antony, who ruled the eastern part of the Roman territory. Antigonus, the son of Aristobulus II, supported the Parthians, and—by their support in return—ruled as high priest and king of the Jews from 40 to 37 B.C. (issuing coins inscribed "King Antigonus" and "Mattathias the High Priest"). He assumed the high-priesthood after having Hyrcanus' ears cut off—since a mutilated person could not hold that office.

Thus, Antigonus and Herod alone remained as rivals. Herod cleverly allied himself with the Romans, and in 40 B.C. the Senate named him king of the Jews, though he had yet to claim his territory from the Parthians. With Roman help, he captured Jerusalem in 37 B.C. and then actually assumed his office. With the execution of Antigonus, the last power struggle of the Hasmoneans had been put down, and Herod ruled from 37 to 4 B.C.

Herod the Great (37–4 B.C.)

Under the emperor Octavian (Augustus), Rome was generally peaceful, and Herod enjoyed the benefits of this favorable situation. Civil war did break out between Octavian and Antony, which Octavian won at the Battle of Actium in 31 B.C., marking the beginning of the Roman Empire. Herod, a nominal Jew but culturally a Greek and politically a Roman, tried to please all his subjects, attempting to be a Jew to the Jews and a Greek to the Gentiles. He rebuilt and enlarged the Temple, though the power of the Sanhedrin, the Jewish high council, diminished under his rule. His attitude toward the Pharisees, however, was positive, but they were cautious toward Herod; even though he avoided offending Jewish religious scruples, pious Jews in general despised the calculating and ruthless king. These characteristics were more clearly seen when Herod provided for the succession of power by arranging the deaths of three of his sons and calling for the division of his kingdom into three parts, each headed by other sons: Archelaus over Judea, Samaria, and Idumea; Antipas over Galilee and Perea; Philip over the northern, Transjordanian regions. Augustus confirmed these arrangements, in spite of Jewish petitions to Rome to abolish Herodian rule. A year or two before Herod's reign ended, John the Baptist and Jesus of Nazareth were born.

The Herodians (4 B.C.–A.D. 39)

Archelaus, with the title ethnarch ("ruler of a nation," which suggested he was in line to be king), controlled Judea, Samaria, and Idumea only ten years—until A.D. 6—when he was exiled by Rome after a joint complaint to Augustus by his otherwise divided subjects, the Jews and Samaritans. His brief reign was marked by brutality and capriciousness, and he was succeeded by Roman governors.

Herod Antipas, as tetrarch ("ruler of a fourth"), controlled Galilee and Perea until 39. This was the home territory of John the Baptist and Jesus, and events involving Antipas' second wife, Herodias, and their daughter, Salome, as well as the death of John the Baptist, are narrated in the Gospels. Antipas was a builder, and the city of Tiberias was his proud creation. The first three decades of his rule were calm, but the last decade much less so, and power struggles led finally to his deposition in 39 by Gaius Caligula.

In contrast to his brothers, Philip, also named tetrarch, controlled his largely non-Jewish territory justly and efficiently until his death in 34. During his regime, the city of Caesarea Philippi was enlarged and modernized.

Philip left no heirs, and his kingdom was placed under the Roman province of Syria from 34 to 37. Then his brother-in-law Agrippa, a grandson of Herod, was named king by the new emperor Gaius Caligula in 37. In 39, Caligula exiled Herod Antipas to Gaul and gave his territories to Agrippa. Upon Caligula's assassination in 41, the new emperor, Claudius, gave Agrippa I both consular rank and the territories of Judea and Samaria, making Agrippa's kingdom coterminous with the former kingdom of Herod. The Wisdom of Solomon may have been written by a Jew in Caligula's time, when the Jewish people were suffering under the Romans (→ Agrippa I; Herod).

Judea Under Roman Procurators (A.D. 6–41)

When Judea became a Roman province after the exile of Archelaus, it fell under the direct control of the emperor Augustus, who appointed Quirinius as governor, with headquarters at Antioch. In A.D. 6 or 7, a census, as a basis for tax assessment, was carried out under his authority. This seems to be the "enrollment" referred to in Luke 2:1–3, though serious chronological problems arise when this link is made (→ Enrollment; Quirinius, P. Sulpicius).

Procurators, stationed at Caesarea by the Sea, followed up on Quirinius' tax registration. They supervised tax collection (the term "procurator" means "financial agent"), had soldiers at their command, and had the power of capital punishment.

With the consent of Quirinius and under the procurators, the Sanhedrin was restored as a kind of parliament. Annas, as high priest, was the leader of this body from 6 to 15 and unofficially thereafter until his death in 35. Caiaphas, his son-in-law, was high priest from 18 to 36; then Jonathan, Annas's son, in 36–37; then Ananias from 48–58; and another son of Annas, Ananus II, in 62.

Under Augustus, procurators served terms of about three years (Coponius, 6–9; Ambibulus, 9–12; and Rufus, 12–15), but Tiberius (emperor from 14–37) instituted longer terms, and Gratus served 15–26, followed by Pontius Pilate, 26–36. The trial and death of Jesus, of course, occurred during Pilate's term, though again the dating of these events varies from 27 to 33. Pilate, whose contemporaries considered him corrupt and savage, was deposed in 36 by the Syrian legate, Vitellius, who appointed Marcellus temporarily. When Tiberius was succeeded by Caligula (emperor from 37–41), the latter appointed Marullus as procurator (37–41 —though it is possible that Marcellus and Marullus are the same person).

30

Agrippa I (A.D. 41–44) and the Last Roman Procurators (A.D. 44–66)

Like his grandfather, Herod the Great, Agrippa represented himself to the Jews as a devout Jew, but as a Hellenist to those outside Judaism. During his brief reign, James the son of Zebedee was executed (Acts 12:1–3), perhaps in 42. Agrippa died in 44. Claudius (41–54) renewed the procurators in 44, as follows (though now including not only Judea and Samaria, but Galilee as well): Fadus (44–46); Alexander (46–48), who was a nephew of the Jewish scholar Philo of Alexandria; Cumanus (48–52), whose soldiers perpetrated anti-Jewish acts, leading to riots and slaughter; and Felix (52–60), during whose rule Paul was arrested, eventually to be tried before the emperor in Rome.

In 54 Nero became emperor, ruling until 68. Three procurators governed the Jewish territory during this period: Festus (60; perhaps 60–62), also mentioned in Acts; Albinus (62–64); and Florus (64–66). During these procuratorships, especially the last few, Jewish-Roman relationships deteriorated and open revolt was inevitable.

The First Jewish Revolt (A.D. 66–70)

Many events prepared the way for the Jewish revolt in 66, such as the execution of two Zealots under the procurator Alexander, the Jewish riots and civil war under Cumanus, the greed and plundering of Florus, and even the devastating fire in Rome in 64, which occasioned the disintegration of Nero's power and furthered unrest throughout the empire. Some wanted to blame Nero himself for the fire—an unlikely charge—while Nero sought to blame foreigners. Jews were not a likely target, however, for a Jewish section of the city was also burned and the empress Poppea had protected the Jews since her intervention for them against Festus. But Poppea died in 65, and the increasing Jewish nationalism and especially the revolutionary Sicarii and Zealot movements led to the Jewish-Roman conflict in 66. At the same time, Christians in Rome were blamed for the Roman fire and were severely persecuted by Nero around 65, though this was a local and limited persecution. Thereafter Jews and Christians—who generally had been considered a single group by the Romans—were seen as distinct groups.

The financial demands of Florus, who extracted a large sum from the Temple treasury in 66, which precipitated an anti-Roman demonstration and a bloody military raid, was followed by the Temple officials' decision to suspend the daily sacrifices offered on behalf of the emperor (and all Romans). This action placed the Jewish nation officially in rebellion against Rome, for it violated a treaty with Rome; at the same time, a Jewish revolutionary force secured the surrender of the Roman garrison at Masada, but then massacred the Roman soldiers. Before the year 68 ended, Jerusalem was entirely controlled by the Jews, that is, by the Zealots, with whom the pro-Roman Jews also united, and the government was again under a succession of high priests.

Factions developed in Jerusalem; beside the Zealots, John of Gischala led a group, as did Simon bar Giora. These groups fought one another, as well as taking vengeance on the moderates who wanted peace with Rome. In 67, Nero placed the general Vespasian in charge of the problem, and he gathered numerous troops, including those of his son Titus from Egypt, and moved toward Jerusalem. City after city fell, first those of Galilee and then, in 68, those of Perea and in the countryside of Judea, including the Qumran community, which produced the Dead Sea Scrolls. According to the historian Eusebius, it was at this time that the Jerusalem Christians fled to Pella. Nero died in 68, causing Vespasian to pause in the Jerusalem campaign, though he resumed it in 69, when only Masada, Jerusalem, and two other cities remained under Jewish control. In the meantime, during 68 and 69, three emperors had been installed and had become victims of murder or suicide. Vespasian became emperor in 69, to rule until 79, and he put the Jewish war in the hands of his son, Titus. Jerusalem fell in autumn of 70; the Temple went up in flames as Titus entered the Holy of Holies to snatch its trophies, and survivors were executed, enslaved, or used as forced labor in the mines. The Temple tax, formerly used to support the Temple activities, was ordered by Vespasian to be used in support of the temple of Jupiter Capitolinus in Rome, and Judea became an imperial province. The capture of Masada followed, perhaps in 74, under Flavius Silva.

Judaism had to be reorganized outside of Jerusalem and in the absence of the Temple. This was accomplished, with Vespasian's approval, at Jamnia under Rabbi Johanan ben Zakkai, a Pharisee, who reopened the schools and established a new council to replace the Sanhedrin. In contrast to the latter, which was under the control of the Sadducees (who had dominated the Temple priesthood), the council now consisted entirely of scribes or lawyers—men learned in Torah. The high-priesthood, apparently, had ended. The synagogue, now a widespread and flourishing institution, facilitated the practice and growth of Judaism. This scholarly form of Judaism was permitted to prosper under the Flavian dynasty (Vespasian, 69–79; Titus, 79–81; and Domitian, 81–96).

Titus proved to be a tolerant and even generous emperor but died of sickness after a short reign. Domitian, Titus's brother (both were sons of Vespasian), was judged negatively by history primarily because of his actions at the end of his reign, but his conduct in office was actually more along the lines of his father's. He had positive concerns for Roman religion, morality, and society in general, aiming to improve the middle class; this was done to the disadvantage of the upper class and created senatorial opposition. In 89 and following, aristocrats and philosophers were terrorized, and in 93 the senatorial party and more philosophers were castigated. Finally, in 95–96, Domitian heightened his own position in the Roman ruler cult and notable Romans were persecuted for lack of attention to it. Some of these were charged with atheism (rejecting the state gods) and others with blasphemy (rejecting Roman majesty). The same charge could have been made against Jews and Christians, though there is no evidence to suggest persecution or suppression of Judaism; rather, as noted earlier, it flourished under the Flavians. Domitian's involvement in the Roman religious trials, however, led him to be portrayed as a tyrant, and this period may be reflected in the *Apocalypse of Ezra* and in the Revelation of John (at least, the latter is often interpreted against the background of Domitian's reign).

Persecution of Christians had occurred locally under Nero in 65, but Vespasian was seen as tolerant by early Christian writers, and there is no suggestion of persecution by Titus, or by Domitian during the first twelve years of his rule (81–92). 1 Clement (written about 95) reports, however, that the church at Rome was severely persecuted about 94. Then in 96 Domitian was murdered, and Nerva ruled from 96 to 98.

All of the books of the NT were written during the period from the reign of Claudius (41–54) to that of Trajan (98–117), that is, between about A.D. 50 to 115, though the dates of very few NT writings are certain and many are disputed.

The Last Jewish Revolt (A.D. 132–35)

Nerva was succeeded by Trajan (98–117), and a second unsuccessful Jewish revolt may have broken out in 115–17 (the evidence is slight). During Hadrian's reign (117–38) the final Jewish revolt was led by Simon Ben Kosiba, later known as Simon Bar Kochba ("Son of a Star"), beginning in 131–32 and ending in 135.

It may have been precipitated by Hadrian's construction of a shrine to Jupiter on the Temple site or by a prohibition of circumcision, or both, but the struggle was successful in that a Jewish state was established and existed for three years. But in 135 Bar Kochba was killed, and Jerusalem, renamed Aelia Capitolina, became a Roman colony from which Jews were excluded (except for a ritual wailing once a year), and temples of Jupiter and Hadrian were constructed on the Temple grounds.

CONCLUSION

The foregoing sketch has been limited largely to the geographical area we now call Israel, but ever since the Exile—and especially in the Greek and Roman periods—Jews were to be found nearly everywhere in the ancient world. Christianity also moved quickly from its Jewish matrix into a Hellenistic milieu, becoming virtually a gentile religion within a generation of its beginnings and penetrating every portion of the Roman world. The full portrayal of the complicated histories of early Judaism and Christianity occupies thousands of books and articles, but the brief narrative offered here provides a basis and a point of departure for those important and fascinating epochs of human history.

Bibliography

Horsley, R. A., and J. S. Hanson. *Bandits, Prophets, and Messiahs: Popular Movements in the Time of Jesus.* Minneapolis, MN: Winston, 1985.

Koester, H. *Introduction to the New Testament.* 2 vols. Philadelphia: Fortress, 1982.

Leaney, A. R. C. *The Jewish and Christian World 200 B.C. to A.D. 200.* New York: Cambridge University Press, 1984.

McCullough, W. S. *The History and Literature of the Palestinian Jews from Cyrus to Herod, 550 B.C. to 4 B.C.* Toronto: University of Toronto Press, 1975.

Nickelsburg, G. W. E. *Jewish Literature Between the Bible and the Mishnah: A Historical and Literary Introduction.* Philadelphia: Fortress, 1981.

Reicke, B. *The New Testament Era: The World of the Bible from 500 B.C. to A.D. 100.* Philadelphia: Fortress, 1968.

Rhoads, D. M. *Israel in Revolution: 6–74 C.E.: A Political History Based on the Writings of Josephus.* Philadelphia: Fortress, 1976.

THE BIBLE AND THE LITERATURE OF ANTIQUITY: THE ANCIENT NEAR EAST

J. J. M. ROBERTS

INTRODUCTION

Scholars have always been aware that the biblical literature resembled in some respects other ancient literature, and even precritical commentators made comparisons between the biblical and extrabiblical literature. Until Napoleon's campaign in Egypt, however, the earliest extensive sources available for comparison were the classical sources in Greek and Latin. Champollion's decipherment of Egyptian hieroglyphics in 1823, the decipherment of Akkadian in the 1850s, and the subsequent discovery and decipherment of Sumerian, Hittite, Ugaritic, and an increasing number of early West Semitic inscriptions have radically changed this situation. This recovery of the ancient Near Eastern literature contemporary with and even a millennium older than the earliest OT writings has provided an important new framework within which to study OT literature.

A perusal of the collection of ancient Near Eastern texts translated into English in the third edition of *Ancient Near Eastern Texts* (J. B. Pritchard, ed.), though it is by no means complete, can give one some idea of the scope and significance of this body of ancient literature. The value of ancient Near Eastern literature for the interpretation of the OT is profound, and that value is immediately apparent when one studies OT law, psalmody, or wisdom literature.

LAW AND COVENANT

In addition to numerous legal formulations scattered throughout the Pentateuch, the OT contains three major bodies of law: the so-called Book of the Covenant (Exod. 21:1–23:33), the Holiness Code (Lev. 17–26), and the Deuteronomic Law Code (Deut. 12–26). Prior to V. Scheil's publication of the stele of Hammurabi's law code in 1902, the study of these biblical collections was carried out in what one could well call a cultural vacuum. As late as 1861 an important German commentator in his treatment of the goring ox law (Exod. 21:28–36) could claim that of all ancient peoples only Israel had a law that held owners responsible if their animals killed or injured another person. The reason for this difference, he claimed, was because no other people had recognized that humans were made in the image of God.

Such a claim would be impossible for a responsible contemporary critic, because the cultural vacuum has been filled. The modern student of OT law has several major collections of cuneiform law with which to compare the biblical material. There are the Sumerian laws of Ur Nammu and Lipit Ishtar, the Old Babylonian laws of Eshnunna and Hammurabi, the Middle Assyrian laws from Asshur, the Hittite law code, and a small collection of Late Babylonian laws. Apart from the Late Babylonian collection, all these collections are prior in date to the period of composition of the biblical collections of law. Not only are these collections of cuneiform law older than the legal collections in the OT, comparative study shows that they constitute particular embodiments of a common law tradition that, for all its local and temporal variations, was basically shared throughout the region of Mesopotamia, Syria, and Palestine. The formal similarity between these written collections suggests that the act of making such written collections had itself become, probably under strong Mesopotamian influence, part of this widespread legal tradition.

To return to the goring ox law, far from the value placed on human life in this law being unique to the biblical material, a comparison with Eshnunna laws 53–55 and Hammurabi laws 250–52 shows that the biblical law is just a slightly different formulation of a much older law embodying the same legal principle. The slight differences in formulation do not suggest any superior evaluation of human life. Moreover, a comparative study of these laws demonstrates that the respect for human life reflected in the biblical law is not dependent on the theological doctrine of creation in the image of God. Respect for human life was part of the legal tradition in the Near East and in Israel well before the formulation of the doctrine of the image of God in Genesis 1. Its author has simply undergirded received ethical and legal mores with theological reflection.

Such theological elaboration of the received ethical and legal mores is paradigmatic for the whole development of biblical law. Very little in biblical law is unique to Israel. Even the Ten Commandments, delivered to the Israelites at Mount Sinai/Horeb by the voice of Yahweh, contain little that would not have been acknowledged everywhere else in the Near East. Apart from the limitation of worship to the one God, the prohibition of images, and perhaps the observance of the Sabbath, these commands simply embody in a very pithy formulation the ethical standards common in the region. As we know from Mesopotamian sources, other religious communities had their own sacred days of abstention from work, so the only significant elements of uniqueness in the Ten Commandments are closely tied to the monotheistic thrust of Israelite religion. Even the biblical laws concerning the Sabbatical and Jubilee years (Exod. 23:11; Lev. 25; Deut. 15:1–4), long considered utopian and unenforceable, may have their roots in much earlier Mesopotamian legal tradition. Throughout the Old Babylonian period the Babylonian government issued periodic *mesharum*-edicts (Akkadian) at fairly regular intervals cancelling debts and otherwise easing the economic plight of the impoverished elements of Babylonian society. The Israelite Sabbatical Year, which seems to have the same purpose and recurs at about the same interval, appears to be an Israelite adaptation of this *mesharum*-edict tradition. The Jubilee Year probably represents a later easing of the Sabbatical Year requirements by lengthening the period between such attempts at economic redress.

In the light of this older legal tradition, the role of Moses as lawgiver must be reevaluated. His work must be seen as in some sense analogous to that of Hammurabi. Neither was primarily engaged in the formulation of brand-new laws. Both were responsible for a new collection, revision, and necessary updating of laws already current in the legal tradition of the people or the region.

On the other hand, Moses appears to have placed Israelite law in a new religious context. While the gods, and particularly Shamash, the god of justice, appear as the ultimate source and guarantors of Mesopotamian law, the revision and promulgation of particular collections is primarily the work of the king. Divine revelation of the individual commandments is not stressed, and the concept of the commandments as the stipulations of a covenant between the gods and the people is simply unknown in Mesopotamia. In Israel, on the contrary, not only the major collections of law, but almost all laws are considered stipulations in the covenant that Yahweh graciously entered into with Israel under the mediatorship of Moses. As a part of God's covenant they were given to Moses by direct revelation from God. The tensions, con-

tradictions, and redundancies in the biblical legal material give ample evidence of later revisions and additions just as one finds such revisions in earlier Mesopotamian law. But while a new Mesopotamian ruler could issue a new collection of law in his own name, there was tremendous pressure in Israel to attribute all law, no matter how late, to Moses. Divine sanction for the law was more secure if the laws were seen as a part of the covenant stipulations God revealed to Moses on the sacred mountain.

Covenant, then, is an important ingredient in Israel's concept of law. The Bible speaks of God's covenant with Noah, with Abraham, with David and his house, with particular priestly families, and of the covenant with Israel given at Sinai or Horeb, but the search for ancient Near Eastern analogues has not produced any clear examples of a covenant between a god and his people or even a very convincing example of a covenant between a god and his chosen king. On the contrary, the evidence suggests that Israel adapted political language dealing with contractual relations between human parties to describe the religio-political relationship between God and his people or between God and his chosen representatives. The study of ancient Near Eastern political treaties of various types, however, has been very fruitful for a clearer understanding of Israelite covenant theology. Despite the ongoing debate and many unresolved questions, few would deny that the careful study of the many political treaties from the ancient Near East has aided in the understanding of Israelite covenant theology, especially as it is formulated in Deuteronomy. The study of royal grants given by Babylonian and Assyrian kings to chosen officials to reward meritorious service to the crown has also proven fruitful in providing a possible political model for the Davidic type covenant.

Because Israelite law was set within the context of covenant and obedience to it was seen as the appropriate religious response to Yahweh's gracious deeds on behalf of Israel, the content of that law came to include specifically religious and ritual obligations, and in the course of time some of the legal collections were elaborated in a hortatory style. The ancient Near Eastern law codes have nothing that would correspond to the ritual demands found in the Book of the Covenant (Exod. 23:14–19), much less to the detailed laws for the various kinds of sacrifice legislated in the book of Leviticus. For parallels to this type of ritual instruction, one must turn from the ancient law codes to the Hittite instruction texts or to the Akkadian, Egyptian, Hittite, and Ugaritic ritual texts. There one will find much helpful material for understanding this genre of biblical law.

PSALMODY

The biblical psalms have very important parallels in the hymns and prayers preserved in the surrounding Near Eastern cultures. Egypt and Mesopotamia provide both the greatest number of these texts and the most important ones as well. Given the striking number of parallels between Israelite religious poetry and Ugaritic poetry, one would expect that Canaanite hymns and prayers would be even closer to the biblical texts. Israel's hymnic tradition probably developed largely under the influence of Canaanite poetic canons. It has been seriously argued that Psalm 29, for instance, is just a superficially edited Canaanite hymn originally addressed to Baal. Unfortunately, the many texts uncovered at Ugarit included only one Ugaritic text that could legitimately be considered a hymn, and there were no examples of prayers. Canaan proper has yielded even less, not much more than a few phrases gleaned from the Amarna letters. Some of the West Semitic inscriptions have properly been compared to the individual prayers of thanksgiving, but the corpus of the relevant inscriptions is quite small and therefore less helpful than could be wished. There are a significant number of Hittite prayers that should be considered and apparently some Hurrian prayers, though the present stage of our knowledge of Hurrian provides no adequate base for the use of these texts in comparative study.

Mesopotamian

There is still much work to be done in the study of Mesopotamian hymns and prayers, but the large corpus of Mesopotamian texts contains clear counterparts to Israelite hymns and individual laments. Both the resemblances and the differences should be noted.

Apart from stylistic differences in the poetic canons that govern Sumerian, Akkadian, and Hebrew poetry, the major discontinuities between Mesopotamian and Israelite psalmody can be attributed to the fundamental distinction between monotheistic and polytheistic religion. Mesopotamian texts make far greater use of divine epithets in the praise of their deities, and the invocation of the deity in Mesopotamian individual laments is normally extended with a long introductory section of praise built up of such epithets. This is in sharp contrast to the Israelite laments, which typically begin the lament proper with a very simple and short invocation of Yahweh. The difference probably arises from the need of the polytheist to clearly specify which god is being invoked, but this difference does not justify denigrating the intro-

ductory praise in the Mesopotamian texts as mere calculated flattery. The motif in Mesopotamian prayers of calling upon one god to intercede with another god is obviously rooted in polytheism, and the pervasiveness of the set formulas that occur in many Mesopotamian prayers expressing fear over bad omens or blaming one's suffering on the work of sorcerers owes a great deal to the multiplicity of independent powers in a polytheistic universe.

Despite these obvious differences, Mesopotamian hymns and prayers share much in common with their Israelite counterparts. Many of the same motifs and metaphors are found in the prayers of both cultures. The psychological approach to the deity is hardly distinguishable. Mesopotamian hymns tend to focus on what Claus Westermann, in studying the biblical hymns, has called "descriptive praise," the praise of the deity for what the deity customarily does or is, rather than focusing on what Westermann calls "narrative praise," praising the deity by narrating a particular action of the deity. There are exceptions, however, such as the hymn to Marduk celebrating his victory over Elam at the time of Nebuchadnezzar I.

Some differences are actually more apparent than real. Akkadian *shu-illa* prayers are typically accompanied by ritual directions following a ruled line at the end of the prayer. These normally indicate that the prayer was to be recited several times as accompaniment to a sacrificial offering. Biblical psalms lack such ritual directions, but it is clear from references in the Psalms and the historical books that the biblical laments and thanksgiving songs were also accompanied by sacrifice. In fact, the same Hebrew term, *todah*, designates both the thanksgiving song and the thanksgiving sacrifice. It is important to remember that, both when studying the Psalms and when studying the rules for sacrifice in Leviticus. The relative separation of word and ritual act in the biblical sources is a literary phenomenon that does not reflect what actually went on in worship. In addition to the brief ritual directions that accompany Mesopotamian prayers, Mesopotamia also provides us with more extended rituals for particular cultic celebrations, and these enable us to get a glimpse of how hymns and prayers of different genres could actually form a part of the same cultic celebration—a key point in Sigmund Mowinckel's cult-centered approach to the Psalms. Finally, one should note the occurrence in Mesopotamian prayers of the formula identifying the speaker in the form "I so-and-so, the son of so-and-so. . . ." These prayers were obviously intended for repeated use by different individuals; the supplicant needed only to insert his or her own name at the appropriate place. Such a formula is not found in the biblical psalms, but their stereotypical nature points to the same intention for their repeated use by different individuals in roughly analogous situations. In neither case, however, does such public use imply any lack of sincerity in the spirituality expressed in the text of the Mesopotamian or Israelite prayer. The works of professional composers of psalms were presumably preserved in both cultures precisely because they articulated for the masses their inchoate religious sensibilities. One must take the words of these prayers seriously.

Egyptian

Egyptian hymns and prayers also provide important parallels for the study of the biblical material. Psalm 104 is widely regarded as modeled on Amenophis IV's famous hymn to the sun god, and Egyptian enthronement hymns are helpful in the comparative study of the Israelite enthronement ritual and in the exegesis of such texts as Psalms 2, 110, and Isa. 9:1–6. Given the large number of Egyptian hymns and prayers belonging to carefully differentiated genres now available for study, the next few years should see significant progress in the comparative study of these texts.

Hittite

There are also a number of Hittite prayers that may be profitably studied for comparative purposes—one thinks especially of the plague prayers of the Hittite king Mursilis. Mursilis' religious interpretation of the plague as a judgment on his Hittite people because of their breach of a treaty with Egypt under an earlier Hittite king provides an interesting commentary on David's religious interpretation of the drought in his days as a judgment on Israel because of Saul's breach of the ancient treaty with the Gibeonites (2 Sam. 21:1–14). Moreover, Mursilis' pathetic appeal to the gods at least to tell him, through one or another of the various means of revelation, why they were angry, provides a striking parallel to the biblical statement that when Saul inquired of Yahweh, "Yahweh did not answer him, either by dreams, or by Urim, or by prophets" (1 Sam. 28:6).

Sumerian

Finally, one should mention the Sumerian laments over the destruction of important cult centers. These laments, such as the famous lament over the destruction of Ur, provide interesting parallels to the biblical book of Lamentations and to the Israelite public laments found scattered in the Psalms and else-where in the Bible. Motifs from pre-Israelite traditions of public lament very similar to those found in the Sumerian laments are adapted by such prophets as Jeremiah to give profound pathos to his description of Yahweh's anguish over the sin of his people.

WISDOM LITERATURE

Wisdom literature tends to be international in character, so it is not surprising to find striking Egyptian and Mesopotamian parallels to the biblical books of Proverbs, Job, and, to a lesser extent, Ecclesiastes. Mesopotamia provides several collections of moral admonitions similar to parts of Proverbs and Ecclesiastes, and there is a large collection of Sumerian and bilingual proverbs, though proverbs do not seem to have represented an important genre of Akkadian Babylonian literature. The numerous Egyptian works giving the "instructions" of a famous vizier, king, or wise man of the past are even more impressive as parallels to Proverbs. One of them, "The Instruction of Amen-em-Opet," appears to have been the literary model for structuring Prov. 22:17–24:22, though the passage in Proverbs can hardly be considered a direct paraphrase of the Egyptian text, much less a straight translation. Recent comparative study has shown the influence of Mesopotamian texts as well as a number of other Egyptian texts on Prov. 22:17–24:22. Its author was apparently well versed in a variety of international wisdom traditions and simply used Amen-em-Opet to provide a model structure in which to incorporate insights drawn from various sources. One should also mention the Aramaic proverbs preserved in the story of the Assyrian Sage Ahiqar.

The Mesopotamian texts dealing with the problem of the righteous sufferer give one a glimpse of the intellectual tradition within which the book of Job fits. It is a long tradition that includes an early Sumerian composition and an Old Babylonian Akkadian text. Its most elaborate literary expressions, however, are found in the long poem "I Will Praise the Lord of Wisdom" (Ludlul bel nemeqi) and "The Babylonian Theodicy," a text constructed in the form of a cycle of dialogues between the righteous sufferer and a friend. Other texts resembling Ludlul, though considerably shorter, have been found among the Akkadian documents from Ugarit. Ludlul and the texts similar to it have many points of contact with individual prayers of lament. In fact, Ludlul could be analyzed as the literary expansion of an individual thanksgiving song that incorporates major elements of the lament in its description of the evil from which the deity has delivered the worshiper. Such an analysis is very suggestive in explaining the development of the wisdom psalm from the individual thanksgiving song. In contrast to *Ludlul*, "The Babylonian Theodicy" owes more to the tradition of scribal-school debates with their convention of insulting or ironic address to one's opponent in the debate. The book of Job seems to have been influenced by both strands in the tradition. It has incorporated the psalmic lament motifs found in the *Ludlul* strand, but it has structured them in an expanded symposium inspired by the "Theodicy" strand.

OTHER GENRES IN GENESIS–NUMBERS

Outside of law, psalmody, and wisdom literature, one would be hard pressed to find Near Eastern parallels to the larger Israelite compositions. There is really nothing comparable in the preserved writings of the surrounding cultures to Genesis–Numbers or the Deuteronomistic History (Deuteronomy–2 Kings). For that matter, even individual books within these compilations have no real ancient Near Eastern counterparts. Nor do the books of the writing prophets or the book of Chronicles. What one can speak of are parallels to smaller genres used in the composition of these larger works.

Mythological Texts

The primeval history in the early chapters of Genesis contains a number of shorter stories with clear parallels in the surrounding cultures. The two creation stories (Gen. 1:1–2:4; 2:4–3:24) share certain features with some of the large number of creation stories known from Mesopotamia and Egypt. Given the structural similarities, the differences in detail between these accounts and the biblical stories are helpful in specifying the issue addressed in the Genesis accounts. The comparison of Gen. 1:1–2:4a with the Babylonian creation poem the *Enuma elish*, for instance, suggests a conscious polemic on the part of the biblical writer against the polytheistic theology reflected in this Babylonian myth. This account has been stripped of almost all the traces of the cosmogonic battle found in the Babylonian story, despite the fact that a similar form of this cosmogonic myth of the origin of world order was well known in Israel (Ps. 74:12–17; Isa. 27:1–2; 51:9–10; Job 9:13; 26:12–13). The closest parallels to the Israelite cosmogonic myth come from the Baal Epic at Ugarit—though the preserved Ugaritic texts do not explicitly tie Baal's

defeat of the sea dragon to creation—but there are also Egyptian and Hittite texts of a similar character (→ Baal).

The Fall story in Genesis 2–3 has no clear analogues, and the story of the first murder (Gen. 4) is only loosely paralleled by a Mesopotamian account of a debate between the shepherd and the farmer as to which of the two professions was superior. This debate between professions is a genre known in both Mesopotamia and Egypt, but the typical texts end on a far friendlier note than the Cain and Abel story. It is not until one reaches the Flood story that the external parallels are again compelling. The Genesis Flood story (chaps. 6–9) appears to be derived from Mesopotamian tradition, where the Flood story is known in a Sumerian version, in the Akkadian version found in the Atrahasis Epic, and in the well-known version of the Gilgamesh Epic. The Atrahasis Epic is particularly important because it shows that Genesis' linking of the creation of humankind and the Flood story in a history that leads to the present structures of society was not a unique achievement of Israelite theology. This move finds a remarkable, if partial, parallel in the Babylonian Epic. The Atrahasis Epic fills out the history between the creation of humankind and the Flood differently than the Genesis account does, and the Atrahasis Epic does not continue with an account of the origin of the various languages. But its linking of creation and the Flood account, with strong etiological elements similar to those found in the biblical Fall story, provides a theological interpretation of humankind's place in this world analogous to one level of the biblical text. The motif of the confusion of the languages does seem to be mentioned in a Sumerian myth, and the somewhat mysterious figure of Nimrod, mentioned without elaboration in Genesis, may have its background in very popular Akkadian heroic legends about Sargon the Great or Naram-sin. Moreover, the Akkadian genealogies of the Hammurabi dynasty and of the ancestors of the Assyrian kings have proven very helpful in the study of the background and function of the biblical genealogies in Genesis.

Patriarchal Stories

One can find parallels to motifs in the patriarchal stories in Genesis 12–50, but the parallels do not extend much beyond that level. The concern for a male heir integral to the patriarchal narratives is also reflected in the Keret and Daniel epics from Ugarit. The Egyptian story of Sinuhe has certain points of similarity to the story of Jacob's flight from Canaan to escape Esau's anger. Both Sinuhe and Jacob flee to another country where they stay for an extended period, marry into the family of the wealthy patron who receives them, and prosper in their new surroundings before returning to the land from which they had fled. The story of Moses' flight to Midian in the book of Exodus also follows this line with some variation. The Moses story does not emphasize the refugee's financial success in his new country, but it is closer to the Sinuhe narrative in the political motivation for the flight. In this connection one should also mention Idrimi's autobiographical account of his flight from and eventual return to his ancestral Aleppo.

The revelatory importance of dreams in these stories and elsewhere in the OT has many parallels in the ancient Near Eastern literature, and such texts as the Assyrian Dream Book show a very similar pattern of interpretation to that reflected in the Bible. One should also mention the Egyptian tale of the two brothers that provides an oft-cited but rather remote parallel to the incident with Potiphar's wife in the Joseph story. On the whole, however, the narrative art reflected in the patriarchal stories has no real counterpart in the preserved literature of the surrounding cultures.

Moses' Birth

There are more points of contact with elements in the other pentateuchal books. The parallel between the Akkadian birth story of Sargon the Great and the Exodus account of Moses' birth is particularly striking. In both stories a baby boy who cannot be kept by the real parents is placed in a reed basket and left in the water at the edge of a river. Eventually the child is discovered by someone else who adopts the child and raises it as his or her own.

Construction of a Sanctuary

The Near Eastern parallels to the legal and ritual material have already been noted, but there are also Near Eastern texts that provide parallels to the Exodus account of the building of the tabernacle, to the accounts in Kings and Chronicles of the building of Solomon's Tomple, and to Ezekiel's description of the future Temple. One thinks especially of the Sumerian text of Gudea in which King Gudea of Lagash relates how he was given the command in a dream to (re)build the temple of the city god Ningirsu. Gudea asks for further instruction, which the god provides, and after very careful preparation the temple is constructed, Ningirsu and his fellow deities are brought into the temple, and the gods bless the king. The text and the statues of Gudea showing him holding the divine blueprint given him by the gods reveal the very ancient background to the biblical references that speak of God's blueprint for the

tabernacle (Exod. 25:9, 40) or for the Temple (1 Chron. 28:11–19).

The concern for building or rebuilding the temple precisely according to the pattern originally given by the deity is reflected in "The Curse of Agade," an early Sumerian text that attributes the fall of the Akkad dynasty to Naram-sin's offense against Enlil's temple in Nippur. Naram-sin did major repair work on Enlil's temple, but according to this text he did it without sufficient regard to Enlil's wishes. The temple was a microcosm of the world, and Naram-sin's abuse of various parts of the temple resulted in dislocations in their macrocosmic counterparts in the external world. Thus when grain was cut in the gate where grain is not to be cut, grain was cut off from the land, etc. The same concern is still reflected in the late Neo-Babylonian building inscriptions that stress how the king rebuilt the temple precisely upon the original foundation trenches. If one missed the original line by so much as a finger's breadth, the results could be disastrous, resulting in the early collapse of the restored building. This understanding of the importance of following the divine pattern in temple construction is part of the background to the famous passage about God's foundation stone in Zion (Isa. 28:16–17). With regard to the detailed descriptions of the tabernacle and Temple and their contents, one should note that the building inscriptions of the Assyrian and Babylonian kings sometimes contain rather detailed descriptions of the architectural features of the temples they built.

The biblical story about the Mesopotamian prophet Balaam whom the Moabite king Balak hired to curse Israel (Num. 22–24) has been placed in a new light by the Aramaic wall inscriptions from Deir Alla that also mention this prophet. These texts are in a poor state of preservation and their precise data (ca. seventh century B.C.) is still disputed, but they indicate that a non-Israelite tradition about the seer Balaam was known in the Transjordan area among a presumably non-Israelite population group well before the period of the exile.

OTHER GENRES IN THE DEUTERONOMISTIC HISTORY

The Mesopotamians, Hittites, and Egyptians all composed annals and chronicles, but none of these texts that have been preserved compare in scope or in complexity with the account of Israel's history that scholars have designated the Deuteronomistic History and that includes the books of Deuteronomy, Joshua, Judges, 1 and 2 Samuel, and 1 and 2 Kings. That difference remains even though some of these Near Eastern historiographical texts resemble the

Deuteronomistic History in important features. The Assyrian Synchronistic History, for example, narrates the history of Assyro-Babylonian relations from ca. 1500 to 783 B.C., discussing each Assyrian king treated—only those who had relations with Babylon are included— along with his Babylonian contemporary or contemporaries. This synchronistic treatment is similar, though not identical, to the Deuteronomistic historian's synchronistic handling of the Israelite and Judean kings from ca. 922 to 722 B.C. Moreover, the Deuteronomistic historian's penchant for judging a king's reign and explaining his successes or failures on the very narrow ground of his religious performance is paralleled by a similar pattern in the Babylonian Weidner Chronicle. This text judges individual kings and explains their fate on the basis of their treatment of Marduk's temple Esagila in Babylon.

Despite such similarities, the biblical text appears far more complex. The Deuteronomistic historian's preservation and incorporation of major preformed blocks of earlier narratives with quite different agendas have given the biblical text an ambiguity that suggests a far more profound appreciation of the complexities of historical phenomena. One need only consider the account of the rise of kingship in 1 Samuel, with its disconcerting juxtaposition of pro- and antimonarchical sources, or the account of Solomon's reign in 1 Kings 1–11, with its peculiar mixture of lavish praise and harsh condemnation, in some cases with regard to the same actions, to illustrate the point. Just as in the case of Genesis–Numbers, the Near Eastern parallels tend to be parallels to some of these earlier narratives preserved in the Deuteronomistic History or to much smaller units or motifs.

The story of the Philistine capture and return of the Ark of the covenant has been compared to Babylonian accounts of the return of the cult statue of Marduk to Babylon after a period of foreign exile. The account of David's rise to power in 1 Samuel and the account of Solomon's succession to David's throne in 2 Samuel 9–20 and 1 Kings 1–2 have been explained as originally apologetic writings commissioned by these kings to justify their irregular accession to the throne on the analogy of such Near Eastern texts as the Hittite "Apology of Hattusilis III." One could even compare the Telepinus edict and Esarhaddon's account of his accession to the throne of Assyria after the assassination of his father, Sennacherib. Still at the level of genre, some scholars would see the Egyptian *Königsnovelle*, a narrative recounting a Pharaoh's accession to the throne, as a major influence on the narrative about Solomon's dream at Gibeon, but this is denied by other scholars.

At the level of the much smaller units of narrative, and especially at the level of the individual motif, the amount of comparative material is overwhelming. To take only one example, the narratives about military campaigns, which abound in the Bible and in Near Eastern literature, share many of the same ideas and motifs. It is clear from the Moabite stele of King Mesha and from numerous Mesopotamian texts, for instance, that the practices generally associated with "holy war" in Israel were not unique to Israel. The understanding of the outcome of battle as reflecting a judicial decision of the gods was also widespread, and stories about a city being taken by a stratagem are common.

Finally, one should note how the Deuteronomistic historian and many other biblical writers cite written correspondence of various sorts. The large collections of official and private letters from Mesopotamia, Egypt, Ugarit, and Palestine—including the Hebrew inscriptions from Arad and Lachish—have given a clear picture of the conventions governing actual letter writing, thus enabling scholars to better evaluate such literary citations.

PROPHECY

The phenomenon of prophecy was widespread in the ancient Near East. Prophets or prophetlike figures are attested among the Canaanites, the Arameans, the Hittites, in Mesopotamia, and in Egypt, but nowhere else did they leave a literary deposit comparable in any way to the books of the classical Israelite prophets. The Egyptian "Admonitions of Ipu-wer" and "The Prophecy of Neferti" are probably the two longest non-Israelite documents claimed by scholars as prophetic works, but their identification as prophetic is disputed. The latter is often regarded as political propaganda disguised as prophecy but actually composed after the events prophesied, and the former could be treated as political advice from a royal counselor. Caution is also in order in comparing the so-called "Prophecy of Marduk" from Mesopotamia to the biblical material. This text, in which Marduk explains away the ancient capture of his statue by the Hittites and the Assyrians as a business trip and a vacation that he decided to take but then treats the more recent capture of his statue by the Elamites as his judgment on sinful Babylon with which he has become angry, has points of contact with Israelite prophetic theology, especially in its theological interpretation of past history and in its insistence that the deity is in full control of that history. Marduk's promise for the restoration of Babylon even appears to be predictive, if scholars are correct in dating the text prior to Nebuchadnezzar I's conquest of Elam. On the other hand, the text does not mention any human intermediary through whom this revelation of Marduk was given, and its treatment of history might suggest a closer parallel to apocalyptic works such as Daniel in which the major part of "prophecy" is actually prophecy after the event. The Assyrian prophecy texts translated by Pfeiffer and Biggs in Pritchard's *Ancient Near Eastern Texts* may also be regarded as apocalyptic texts, if they are not simply omen apodoses.

In contrast, the collection of oracles concerning Esarhaddon attributed to various prophetic figures, but apparently all speaking in the name of the goddess Ishtar of Arbela, do appear to be genuine prophetic oracles, and the manner of their collection is suggestive for the study of the preservation and collection of the prophetic material in Israel. The Assyrian collection reflects no clear organizing principle, though it appears to be a collection made for some official purpose, and the concern to identify the speaker of the individual oracles may signal a legal responsibility that the prophet bore for his words. This would correspond to the earlier practice at Mari of taking legal symbols from the prophet, thus holding the prophet responsible for the reliability of his or her prophetic message. The Assyrian collection is rather short, however, and, unlike the majority of the prophetic books in the Bible, it does not even purport to be the collection of the oracles of a single prophet.

If the literary parallels to the prophetic books of the Bible are less than impressive, the same cannot be said for prophetic phenomena in general, nor for the content of particular oracles. Many of the motifs found in Israelite oracles are also attested in the oracles from the surrounding cultures. One thinks, for instance, of the common admonition "Fear not!" followed by a promise of divine assistance. It is found in the response of the Aramaic prophets to King Zakir of Hamath and Lu'ath, and it is very common in the Assyrian oracles.

The some twenty-eight prophetic texts in the Mari correspondence from the first half of the second millennium B.C. are particularly significant, both in the range of their parallels to the later biblical material and in their occurrence in an area and among a population group that might suggest some cultural link between the Mari phenomenon and the later Israelite development. In contrast to the traditional Mesopotamian preference for the technical, institutionalized practice of divination as the chosen means of obtaining communications from the divine world, Mari prophecy depends on inspiration and the initiative of a deity. The Mari prophets see themselves as the messengers or mouthpieces of the deity, speaking for the deity in the first person. Moreover, the reception of the prophetic message takes place in what may be defined broadly as an ecstatic state—a state characterized by somewhat abnormal behavior, if one may judge by the use of the same root to refer to the behavior both of the prophet and of the insane. In all these respects, prophecy at Mari resembles prophecy as it is known in the biblical texts.

Even at Mari, however, technical divination remains the favorite means of obtaining communications from the divine world. The authenticity of prophetic messages was tested by having the divination priests take the omens in the normal way and then comparing their results with the prophetic message. This preference for technical divination of various sorts as the primary means of revelation may account for the relative sparsity of literary collections of prophetic oracles. Mesopotamia's cultural equivalent to the biblical prophet as the central mediator between the divine and human worlds was the divination priest, and the cultural equivalent to the biblical prophetic book is perhaps the Mesopotamian omen collection, of which there are many very extensive examples. Such collections, if they ever existed in Israel, were not preserved in the canonical Israelite literature. The omen collections and the collections of incantations represent the two genres of literature that are very important in Mesopotamia, but are conspicuous by their absence from the Bible.

OTHER WRITINGS

Of the biblical writings not yet discussed, the one with the closest Near Eastern parallels is the Song of Songs. Both secular Egyptian love poetry and more religious love poetry from Mesopotamia have been compared to it. The memoirs of Nehemiah have been compared to votive inscriptions of Mesopotamian kings and officials who wanted their deeds on behalf of the god to be remembered and rewarded. Books like Ruth and Esther, on the other hand, present literary genres with no clear counterparts in the early ancient Near Eastern literature. Finally, the anti-Babylonian stories in the book of Daniel may reflect a late development of the Persian-sponsored anti-Nabonidus propaganda of the Marduk priests of Babylon. The particular development of these stories in Daniel, however, reflects a changed literary world. A literature of the powerless or stateless has taken the place of the older literature rooted in the national state. There is an analogy for this in the Aramaic story of Ahiqar, but this major shift in the kind of Israelite literature produced in the late postexilic period (second century B.C.) marks the end of the biblical period.

Bibliography

Hoftijzer, J., and G. Van der Kooij. *Aramaic Texts from Deir 'Alla.* Leiden: Brill, 1976.

Lambert, W. G., and A. R. Millard. *Atra-Hasis: The Babylonian Story of the Flood.* Oxford: Clarendon, 1969.

Mowinckel, S. *The Psalms in Israel's Worship.* Nashville, TN: Abingdon, 1967.

Pritchard, J. B. *Ancient Near Eastern Texts Relating to the Old Testament.* 3d ed. Princeton, NJ: Princeton University Press, 1969.

Roberts, J. J. M. "The Ancient Near Eastern Environment." In *The Hebrew Bible and Its Modern Interpreters.* Edited by D. A. Knight and G. M. Tucker. Chico, CA: Scholars Press, 1985. Pp. 75–121.

Westermann, C. *Praise and Lament in the Psalms.* Atlanta, GA: John Knox, 1981.

THE BIBLE AND THE LITERATURE OF ANTIQUITY: THE GRECO-ROMAN PERIOD

DAVID E. AUNE

HELLENISTIC LITERARY CULTURE

Early Judaism and early Christianity existed in a world in which the prevailing culture was Hellenistic. This culture, a legacy of Alexander the Great, was modeled on the thought, customs, and life-style of ancient Greece. The Roman Empire, which provided political and economic unity and stability to the entire ancient Mediterranean world after 41 B.C., included scores of native cultures, many of which were vitally concerned with the preservation of their own identities and traditions. Judaism, in both its Palestinian and Diaspora forms, constituted one such ethnic entity. Hellenistic Jewish literature, written primarily in Greek using Hellenistic literary forms and traditions, is the best preserved nativistic literature from the Greco-Roman period. That is not due to the survival of Judaism, for Christians rather than Jews preserved (and modified) the bulk of early Jewish literature written between 200 B.C. and A.D. 100. The history of this literature exhibits the increasing domination of Hellenistic literary culture.

Hellenism and Judaism were traditional societies that anchored the cultural and religious values of the present in the paradigmatic past as preserved by "approved" collections of literature. For Hellenism, that literature included Homer (appropriately labeled "the Bible of the Greeks") and the more than eighty other "classical" authors that constituted the so-called Alexandrian canon (including five epic poets, ten orators, nine lyric poets, five tragic poets, etc.). Approved authors were copied and recopied, studied in the schools, and used as literary and rhetorical models. Other authors were neglected and have largely perished. By the first century A.D. there was a widespread nostalgia for the past among both Greeks and Romans. Hellenistic authors became enamored with the literary style of the Attic prose writers of the classical period (450–330 B.C.) and tried to emulate their archaic style.

Opposite: A Roman wagon, perhaps meant to depict the holy Ark, can still be discerned among lintel decorations from the synagogue at Capernaum, late second–early third century A.D. The lintel decorations hint at the Greco-Roman influence felt in the region.

EARLY JEWISH LITERATURE

Early Judaism produced a large and varied body of literature from ca. 250 B.C. to the codification of the Mishnah, ca. A.D. 200. Much of early Jewish literature (excluding, however, several important groupings of literature, including Philo, Josephus, the Dead Sea Scrolls, the Targums, and rabbinic literature) has come to be associated with two collections, the Apocrypha and the Pseudepigrapha. "Apocrypha" (from a Greek word meaning "hidden") is a term referring to a collection of thirteen books (or additions to books) of Jewish origin but preserved (with the exception of 2 Esdras) as part of the Septuagint (LXX), i.e., the Christian OT in Greek, and not in the Hebrew OT. Though some of these documents were originally written in Hebrew or Aramaic (e.g., 1 Maccabees, Sirach, Tobit, Judith), they have survived only in translation. Since Greek versions of these writings were regularly included in copies of the LXX, they were widely regarded by some Diaspora Jews and later by Christians as sacred. Twelve of these books were included by Jerome in the Latin Vulgate and are part of the Roman Catholic OT. The literary genres represented by the Apocrypha include historiography (1 Esdras; 1 and 2 Maccabees), imaginative fiction or novels (Tobit, Judith, The Additions to Esther, and The Additions to Daniel), letters or homilies (Letter of Jeremiah), apocalypses (2 Esdras), and prayers (Prayer of Manasseh, Prayer of Azariah in Song of the Three Youths).

The word "Pseudepigrapha" means "forgeries" and is a generic term for those very diverse early Jewish compositions (fifty-two separate works are collected in Charlesworth, *The Old Testament Pseudepigrapha*) that unknown authors tried to pass off as works of famous ancient Israelites. The Pseudepigrapha includes many apocalypses (e.g., the *Apocalypses of Abraham, Adam, 1 Enoch, 2 Enoch, 2 Baruch, 3 Baruch*) and testaments (e.g., *Testaments of the Twelve Patriarchs, Testament of Moses*, and the so-called *Prayer of Joseph*). Several other genres are also represented including prayers (*Prayer of Jacob*), hymns (*Psalms of Solomon, Odes of Solomon*), novels (*Joseph and Aseneth, 3 Maccabees*), wisdom and instructional literature (e.g., *Pseudo-Phocylides*), expansions of OT texts (*Jubilees*, Pseudo-Philo's *Biblical Antiquities*), revelatory literature (*Sibylline Oracles*), and exhortation (4 *Maccabees*).

EARLY CHRISTIANITY AND HELLENISM

Early Christianity emerged from a Judaism already profoundly influenced by Hellenism. Thus the history of early Christian literature reflects a movement from Hellenistic Jewish cultural traditions toward an increasingly Hellenistic orientation. From a historical perspective, then, early Christianity was a Hellenistic religion. By the middle of the first century there were increasing tensions between pagan converts to Christianity and Jewish Christians. These tensions increased until Christianity gradually became separated from Judaism and came to be regarded as a religion in its own right.

At first glance, there appear to be five major literary genres in the New Testament: biography (the four Gospels), history (Acts), letter (the Pauline and general Letters), sermon (1 John and perhaps Hebrews), and apocalypse (the Revelation to John). While biographies and letters are more characteristic of Greco-Roman literary culture, history has possible models in both Greco-Roman and Israelite historiography, sermons have roots in both the Jewish synagogue and in the moral exhortation of popular Hellenistic philosophy, and the apocalyptic genre appears more exclusively linked with early Jewish literary traditions. Each of these literary forms must be examined more closely to determine precisely where they fit in the complex interrelationship that existed in the Hellenistic and Roman period between the Greco-Roman and the Israelite-Jewish literary cultures.

HISTORICAL LITERATURE

In the ancient world, comparable forms of historical writing arose only in Judaism and in the Greek world. These developments occurred independently of each other; they occurred at about the same time (sixth and fifth centuries B.C.); and they occurred in a similar historical and political climate (conflict with the mighty Persian Empire, 539–332 B.C.).

Greco-Roman Historiography

The English word "history" is derived from the Greek term *historia* meaning "investigation, inquiry" and was eventually used in the limited sense of the investigation of the past. Greco-Roman historians often consciously reflected about the problems, tasks, methods, and purpose of historiography and included discussions of such problems in prefaces and digressions. Historians in the Israelite-Jewish tradition, by contrast, rarely revealed what they thought of such matters. Greco-Roman historians also emphasized the accuracy of their narratives by claiming to have "seen" and/or "heard" the evidence recorded in their narratives and therefore tended to limit themselves to narrating contemporary or near-contemporary events. Historians were not specifically trained for their task. They simply applied general rhetorical training (the tertiary stage of Greco-Roman education permitting specialization in either rhetoric or philosophy) to the demands of writing history. One result was that the goals and forms of rhetoric were extremely influential in historiography. This typically included the tendency to "improve" sources by thoroughly rewriting them, the insertion of fabricated speeches as oratorical models, the use of dramatic episodes to involve readers emotionally, and the concern to change the attitude and behavior of readers by depicting individuals as paragons of virtue or vice.

There were several minor types of Greco-Roman historical writing (e.g., genealogy, ethnography, local history, chronography). The three important major forms were the historical (war) monograph, general or universal history, and antiquarian history. The *war monograph* narrated a contemporary war of great importance based on the assumption that political and military crises constituted the most important types of change in human history. The war monographs of Herodotus and especially Thucydides (fifth century B.C.) were models for this genre throughout antiquity. *General* or *universal history*, begun in the fourth century B.C. by Ephorus, treated either Greek or Roman history from the earliest reliable date down to the time of the author. Polybius (ca. 200–118 B.C.) is the earliest universal historian extant. *Antiquarian history* (the ancient counterpart of social history) combined various forms of systematic research into the past (ethnology, geography, genealogy, local history) with a chronological arrangement of individual states with particular emphasis on internal (political) and external (military) affairs. The *Roman Antiquities* of Dionysius of Halicarnassus (late first century B.C.) exemplifies this genre.

The three major forms of Greco-Roman history were all-inclusive literary forms that tended to embrace a variety of shorter forms, a feature particularly true of general and antiquarian history. Some of the major literary forms used in historical compositions include historical prefaces, dramatic episodes, speeches in both indirect and direct discourse (often constituting from 20 to 30 percent of the narrative), and digressions. The ideal purpose for which historians wrote was to be truthful, useful, and entertaining. Of these three, it was obviously easier to be useful and entertaining than to be truthful, since historical truth necessitated careful investigation. Many Hellenistic historians (Polybius was a striking exception) were armchair scholars who relied on rhetorical talents more than firsthand research.

Early Jewish Historiography

Narrative, whether historical or fictional, is one of the more characteristic styles of OT literature, where the Pentateuch (Genesis through Deuteronomy) is linked to the Former Prophets (Joshua through 2 Kings) to form a continuous narrative of Israelite history from creation to the aftermath of the fall of Jerusalem in 586 B.C. The increasingly sacrosanct status of this literature from the third century B.C. on meant that it automatically served as a literary paradigm and a source of themes for religious fiction and nonfiction alike. While the Greek historians distinguished between the mythological period (for which sources were unreliable) and the historical period, Israelite historians neither made nor appear to have been aware of any such distinction.

Several historical compositions have been associated with the Apocrypha, each of them very different from the others: 1 Maccabees, 2 Maccabees, and 1 Esdras. The only "historical" works included in the Pseudepigrapha are those that involve the interpretive and paraphrastic rewriting or expansions of the text of the OT historical books (e.g., Jubilees, Pseudo-Philo's Biblical Antiquities).

Under Ptolemy I of Egypt (died ca. 282 B.C.), Hecataeus of Abdera was commissioned to write Aigyptiaka ("On the Egyptians"), a flattering and propagandistic historical work that widely influenced Hellenistic historiography. The Hellenistic Jewish historians Artapanus, Eupolemus, and Pseudo-Eupolemus (all mid-second century B.C. and all surviving only in fragments quoted by later authors) used Hecataeus' history as a model for their own tolerant but propagandistic reinterpretations of biblical history. Their purpose was to demonstrate the antiquity and superiority of Jewish culture and civilization within a universalistic framework. While these authors all have basically historical intentions they, like many contemporary Hellenistic historians, manipulated "historical" data in the service of nationalistic interests.

1 Maccabees (ca. 100 B.C.) is an anonymous work originally composed in Hebrew or Aramaic. Written in a deliberately archaic style, this work was very probably intended by the author to be a continuation of the work of the Chronicler (1 and 2 Chronicles, Ezra, and Nehemiah). The work focuses on the causes and progress of the Maccabean revolt from ca. 175 B.C. with the accession of the Syrian king Antiochus IV and the eventual revolt of Mattathias and his sons until the death of the last surviving son, Simon, in 134 B.C. The work reflects a rapprochement between biblical and Hellenistic historiography. 2 Maccabees presents itself as an anonymous abridgement of a five-volume work of Jason of Cyrene. The work narrates Palestinian Jewish history from 180 to 161 B.C., overlapping 1 Maccabees. In its present form, the book is a typical example of tragic historiography, though in content it is thoroughly Jewish. 1 Esdras is a problematic work that closely parallels and appears dependent upon a portion of 2 Chronicles (35:1–36:23), all of Ezra, and a section of Nehemiah (7:38–8:12). Josephus (ca. A.D. 37–100) was a Jewish historian who wrote two extensive historical works in Greek closely following the conventions of Hellenistic historiography. The shorter of the two works is Wars of the Jews, which in form is a Thucydidean war monograph focusing on the first Jewish revolt of A.D. 66–73. The longer work (in twenty books), Antiquities of the Jews, used the Roman Antiquities of Dionysius of Halicarnassus as a model. Josephus follows the conventions typical of the tragic historiography of his day.

Luke-Acts as Hellenistic History

Originally, Luke-Acts was composed as a two-volume work with each "book" (cf. Acts 1:1) roughly equal in size (the ancient Gk. and Lat. terms for "book," logos and volumen, referred to the contents of one papyrus roll). In spite of the fact that Luke was separated from Acts to form part of the fourfold Gospel, Luke-Acts must be regarded as a single literary work. While it is legitimate to compare the other Gospels with Greco-Roman biography, the subordination of Luke's first book to a larger literary structure means that it cannot be considered biography. Until quite recently, scholars were generally united in regarding the author of Luke-Acts as a historian. Occasionally, connections between Acts and the Greek novel (i.e., narrative fiction) have been explored. More recently, the theological concerns of the author have been emphasized by several scholars. Yet these three views are not really mutually incompatible. First of all, most Greco-Roman historians of the late Hellenistic period were really "tragic historians." Influenced by rhetoric, they wrote to entertain, an intention to which the discovery and presentation of historical truth were usually subordinated. Second, virtually all ancient historians wrote either for the purpose of moral edification or gave expression to one or another ideology or wrote with (sometimes blatant) propagandistic purposes.

Luke is capable of writing elegant Greek, as the two periodic sentences in Luke 1:1–4 and Acts 15:24–26 indicate. Luke used many literary forms within the framework of Luke-Acts, including historical prefaces (Luke 1:1–4; Acts 1:1–5), a genealogy in typically Hellenistic ascending order (latest descendant to earliest ancestor, Luke 3:23–38), symposia (Luke 7:36–50; 11:37–54; 14:1–24), travel narratives, "we" passages, speeches (Acts contains thirty-two speeches constituting 25 percent of the narrative), quoted documents, dramatic episodes (e.g., Luke 4:16–30; 24:13–25; Acts 25:13–26:32), digressions (e.g., Luke 3:23–38; Acts 17:21; 18:24–25), and summaries (e.g., Acts 2:46–47). Paralleling the contemporary preference for archaism, he wrote extensive passages in Septuagintal Greek (e.g., Luke 1:5–2:52). Luke made innovative use of ancient historiographical traditions by treating early Christianity on analogy to an ethnic group. Like Israelite and early Jewish historians, he focused on Palestine and particularly Jerusalem, yet, like the general or universal histories of Greco-Roman historiographical tradition, he selectively treated the history of early Christianity throughout the various lands of the ancient Mediterranean world.

APOCALYPTIC LITERATURE

The term "apocalypse," from a Greek word meaning "revelation," is widely used as the name for a literary genre that primarily consists of a report of supernatural visionary experiences. The apocalypse is just one of many types of ancient revelatory literature. Judaism had canonical prophetic books (the end product of collections of edited oracles), testaments, revelatory dialogues, revelatory discourses, and revelatory revisions of Scripture as well as apocalypses. In the Greco-Roman world there were oracles, oracle collections, oracular dialogues, reports of dreams or visions, and procedures for magical revelation. While most surviving apocalypses originated in early Judaism from ca. 200 B.C. to A.D. 100, related forms of revelatory literature were also produced in Persia, Egypt, and in the Hellenistic world. Iranian and Hellenistic apocalypses tend to be included in larger, more encompassing literary forms, in contrast to Jewish and Greco-Egyptian apocalypses, which form independent literary compositions. Some apocalypses may reflect actual visionary experiences, while yet others appear to consist of fabricated vision reports using literary conventions characteristic of apocalyptic literature. Some works (like the Jewish 4 Ezra [another name for 2 Esdras 3–14] and the Christian Revelation and Shepherd of Hermas) seem to be combinations of visionary experience and literary artifice.

Early Jewish Apocalypses

Daniel is the only apocalypse in the OT, though sections of such prophetic books as Isaiah, Ezekiel, and Zechariah reflect the transition from prophecy to apocalyptic. Jewish apocalypses consist primarily of "autobiographical" vision reports mediated by an otherworldly revealer. Though usually related in the first person, all Jewish apocalypses are pseudonymous, that is, written in the name of famous ancient Israelites and set in periods centuries earlier than the actual date of composition. The substance of apocalyptic visions is highly symbolic, requiring question-and-answer dialogues between the visionary and an angelic interpreter. The visions, which reveal the events surrounding the end of the world and the secrets of the universe, are usually seen during the course of a guided tour through the heavens in which the ultimate goal is often the vision of God himself (e.g., 1 Enoch 1–13; 2 Enoch). In other apocalypses the visions are experienced in an earthly setting (e.g., Dan. 7–12; 4 Ezra; 2 Baruch). Jewish and other Near Eastern apocalypses usually function as protest literature, that is religious responses to social disorientation as well as political and economic oppression resulting from foreign occupation. Kingship in the ancient Near East was typically regarded as a divine institution upon which temporal prosperity depended. When native kings were overthrown, first by the Greeks and then by the Romans, the oppression and hardships that followed foreign domination were attributed to the interruption of the divine order. These wrongs were made right in eschatological fantasies in which a divinely appointed ruler or messiah was expected to appear, vanquish the foreign oppressors, and introduce an era of peace and prosperity.

Early Christian Apocalypses

In early Christianity, as in ancient Judaism, there was a tendency to create narrative accounts of eschatological events (e.g., Mark 13 and parallels; 2 Thess. 2:1–12; Did. 16). The Revelation to John, the only NT apocalypse, is the longest such narrative presented in the form of a single vision report extending from 4:9 to 22:11. The author has imposed a unifying literary structure on a variety of Jewish, Christian, and Greco-Roman sources and traditions. Unlike Jewish apocalypses, Revelation is not pseudonymous. For that reason the author does not conceal the true circumstances of composition but rather makes a special effort to relate his conception of the eschaton to the concrete situation of the seven churches to which he writes (Rev. 2–3). The three earliest Christian apocalypses reveal an increasing tendency to adopt the conventions of Hellenistic revelatory literature. The Jewish orientation of the Revelation to John is readily apparent. The *Shepherd of Hermas* (first half of the second century A.D.) combines Jewish with Hellenistic revelatory traditions, while the *Apocalypse of Peter* (ca. A.D. 135) is primarily dependent on Hellenistic revelatory conventions.

THE GOSPELS AND BIOGRAPHY

Since the earlier part of this century, the prevailing view among NT scholars has been that the Gospels represent a unique literary form created by early Christians to give expression to their faith with no real connections with ancient biographical literature. According to this view the oral kerygma (Gk., "proclamation") about Jesus (found in some evangelistic sermons in Acts, e.g., 10:34–43) was expanded by the addition of various kinds of discourse and narrative material to form the Gospel of Mark. More recently it has become apparent that the Gospels are much closer in *form* and *function* to Greco-Roman biographical literature than earlier scholars had recognized. Each of the four Gospels constitutes a Christian adaptation of the genre of Greco-Roman biography with distinctively Christian features.

Characteristics of Ancient Biography

The literary culture of ancient Israel never developed biography as an independent literary form, though OT narratives often focus on the lives and achievements of important political and religious personalities. The biographical literary forms that occur in early Judaism were largely borrowed and developed under Hellenistic influence (e.g., Philo's lives of Abraham, Joseph, and Moses). Even the twenty-two thumbnail sketches of various Israelite prophets presented in the anonymous first-century A.D. composition *The Lives of the Prophets* were probably composed in Greek (probably in Palestine) in a form analogous to the lives of the Greek poets (both are largely based on inferences from their works). Ancient character depiction, both east and west, had several common features: first, the focus is on a person's *public* rather than private life; second, people are depicted in conformity to *types* (i.e., as models of

community values) rather than as *individuals*; and third, human personality was regarded as *static* and not subject to development. These three factors drive a wedge between ancient and modern biography.

Greek biography has its roots in the fifth century B.C. and continued to evolve through to the end of antiquity. The function of biography was the stereotypical presentation of a person whose life exhibited Hellenistic social and cultural values and hence was worthy of imitation. Ancient critics carefully distinguished between history and biography, but in the Greco-Roman period, when the role of individuals in history was emphasized, the conventional distinction between history and biography became increasingly blurred. The nineteenth-century German classical scholar Friedrich Leo proposed a twofold typology of ancient biography that, though oversimplified, has proven influential: first, *Peripatetic biography* (e.g., Plutarch's *Lives*) was a chronological presentation suitable for depicting the careers of generals and politicians. The words and deeds of the subjects form the basis for praising them and presenting them as examples for imitation. Second, *Alexandrian biography* (e.g., Suetonius' *Lives of the Caesars*) tended to favor a systematic or topical presentation of a person's career, a form particularly appropriate for writers and artists. This approach emphasized particular Hellenistic virtues (e.g., courage, justice) as exemplified by deeds.

Greco-Roman biographical literature was an inclusive genre that framed other shorter literary forms. One of the major features of ancient biography was the use of various types of anecdotes under the conviction that a person's words and deeds revealed his or her character. The very general term "anecdote" (which in Gk. literally means "not published," i.e., transmitted orally) includes such specific forms as *chreiai*, "anecdotes," *gnomai*, "maxims," and *apomnemoneumata*, "reminiscences." Many collections of anecdotes circulated under the names of various famous people, and they were used (sometimes simply by attributing them to the requisite individual) as raw material for writing biographies.

Biographical Features of the Gospels

The Gospel of Mark, the first written Gospel (ca. A.D. 70), has more generic similarities to Greco-Roman biography than to any literary form within Judaism. Recent research into the language of Mark suggests that it was written in a popular *literary* style, neither the language of everyday speech as reflected in the papyri nor the elevated Greek of the wealthy and educated. Matthew and Luke show clear signs of a tendency to make Mark more literary by improving his style and by adding material to the beginning and end of Mark's narrative, stories of Jesus' origin and of his resurrection appearances and (in the case of Luke) his ascension. In *form*, Mark and the other Gospels are Greco-Roman biographies, while in *content* they preserve distinctively Judeo-Christian conceptions. The distinctive literary features of the Gospels, then, are the result of the combination of Hellenistic biographical conventions with the unique Christian perspective on the significance of Jesus.

The synoptic Gospels (Matthew, Mark, and Luke), like other Hellenistic biographies, incorporate a variety of constituent literary forms into their narratives. These include miracle stories, anecdotes (or *chreiai* and *apomnemoneumata*), sayings or aphorisms (*gnomai*), parables, and stories about Jesus. The content of the Gospels focuses on the ultimate religious claims made for Jesus on behalf of Christians, similar to the claims made for philosophers by Hellenistic biographers. The Jesus presented in the Gospels has a paradigmatic function since he both personifies and legitimates distinctively Christian beliefs and values, a function similar to that of the subjects of Greco-Roman biographies.

EPISTOLARY AND HOMILETIC LITERATURE

The letter was one of the more flexible of ancient literary forms. Almost any kind of written text could be framed by formal epistolary features and regarded as a letter.

Early Jewish Letters

The letter never quite achieved the status of an independent literary form in Israelite or Jewish literary culture. The only independent "letter" in the Apocrypha is the *Letter of Jeremiah*, which does not exhibit epistolary but rather sermonic form. Similarly, the pseudonymous *Epistle of Aristeas* is not actually a letter but an apologetic narrative about the origin of the Greek translation of the Hebrew Scriptures. The letter is used, however, as a constituent literary form and is frequently embedded in both historical and fictional narrative literature. Compared with the many studies devoted to Greek and Latin letters of antiquity (primarily documentary papyrus letters), Aramaic and Hebrew letters have been relatively neglected until recently, a fact primarily attributable to the paucity of surviving examples. The total number of Aramaic letters extant is about 120, primarily from the fifth and fourth centuries B.C.; six are embedded in the Aramaic portions of the

OT; eight of the fifteen extant letters associated with Bar Kochba, the Jewish revolutionary leader, are in Aramaic, ca. A.D. 132–35. Nearly fifty Hebrew letters are extant, mostly from 630 to 586 B.C.; eleven are embedded in OT documents; five of the fifteen Bar Kochba letters are in Hebrew.

Greco-Roman Letters

The Greco-Roman letters that survive from antiquity fall roughly into three classes: first, *documentary* letters, actual common letters recovered, usually from ancient garbage dumps in Greco-Roman Egypt; second, *literary* letters, letters written by educated people of antiquity and preserved in repeatedly recopied collections and regarded as models of epistolary composition and artistic literary expression; and third, *official* letters, letters drafted in royal or imperial chanceries dealing with diplomatic, administrative, and other governmental concerns and that have survived through being inscribed on stone or by being quoted in historical works.

Early Christian Letters and Homilies

Twenty-one of the twenty-seven documents in the NT are letters; twelve of the fifteen writings by other early Christian leaders not in the NT but collectively designated the "apostolic fathers" are also letters. The letter was obviously the most popular literary form in early Christianity. The flexibility of the letter form in the Greco-Roman world was carried over into Christianity. Opening and closing epistolary formulas were used to frame a variety of literary forms. The Revelation to John, though framed as a letter (cf. 1:4–5; 22:21), is really an apocalypse. The first extant martyr act, the *Martyrdom of Polycarp*, is similarly framed as a circular letter. Two NT documents commonly regarded as letters appear to be written homilies or sermons. 1 John has no formal epistolary features, and Hebrews has only an epistolary postscript. Most ancient letters, like modern ones, were written substitutes for oral communication necessitated by the physical separation of the writer from the reader(s).

The formal features of early Christian letters, while primarily reflecting Hellenistic epistolography, also exhibit some Semitic influences. Paul's characteristic salutation, for example, "grace and peace," combines an apparent wordplay on the typical Greek epistolary salutation *chairein*, "greetings," with the Aramaic/Hebrew epistolary salutation *shalom*, "peace." Further, Judaism had developed religious circular letters or encyclicals, which served both administrative and liturgical purposes (e.g., Esther 9:20–32; 2 Macc. 1:1–10; 1:11–2:18). After the process of reconstructing had begun after the debacle of A.D. 70, rabbinic authorities such as Gamaliel II directed encyclicals to various groups of Diaspora Jews (e.g., *b. Sanh.* 18d; cf. *2 Bar.* 77:19–26; 78:1–86:3); these have formal parallels with James, 1 and 2 Peter, and Jude, which are pseudonymous Christian encyclicals.

Early Christian letters tend to be more complex than most documentary, literary, or official Greco-Roman letters. They, like biography and the major types of historical writing, constitute an inclusive literary genre used to frame a variety of shorter literary forms. NT Letters contain a variety of constitutive literary forms, some of which must have been transmitted orally before they were preserved by being inserted into a letter. These include liturgical forms (grace benedictions, blessings, doxologies, hymns, confessions, eucharistic and baptismal sequences), kerygmatic formulas, and instructional forms (virtue and vice lists, codes of household ethics).

Some NT Letters are pseudepigraphical, i.e., written under the name of such famous Christian leaders as Paul, James, Peter, and Jude to gain a wider acceptance. Pseudonymity was an ancient literary phenomenon that originated primarily in Greco-Roman literary culture. While Israelite literary convention included *anonymity*, it was not until the Hellenistic period that pseudonymity came into vogue, primarily in connection with the writing of apocalypses in the names of ancient Israelite worthies. Pseudepigraphical compositions in early Christianity, as in the Greco-Roman world, were presented as written by someone other than the putative author. The widespread use of this phenomenon in antiquity generally, and in early Christianity in particular, suggests that many authors regarded pseudonymity as a justifiable expedient if the purpose for which they wrote was sufficiently important. There is widespread agreement among scholars that among the Pauline Letters, Ephesians and the pastoral Letters (1 and 2 Timothy and Titus) are certainly pseudonymous, while Colossians and 2 Thessalonians may be. Similarly, four of the seven general Letters are widely thought to be pseudonymous: James, 1 and 2 Peter, and Jude. Pseudonymity, which characterizes as many as ten of the twenty-seven documents in the NT, was a transitional way of dealing with the crisis in authority occasioned by the passing of the apostolic generation.

The relationship of the composition and structure of NT Letters to Greco-Roman rhetorical conventions is a subject that has only recently become the focus of scholarly research. Hellenistic rhetoricians described three types of rhetoric: *judicial* (the attempt to convince a court about past events), *deliberative* (the attempt to persuade an assembly about what to do in the future), and *epideictic* (entertaining oratory that celebrates common values). Ancient letter writers with some education automatically applied their rhetorical training in the composition of letters. Several handbooks on epistolary theory have survived that reflect the influence of rhetoric and provide model letters (e.g., Ps.-Demetrius *On Style* 4.223–35, and Ps.-Libanius *Epistolary Styles*).

Most early Christian letters have a basically deliberative character, though often they combine several epistolary functions. NT Letters with a primary function include Philemon and 3 John, both of which are basically letters of recommendation. 1 Thessalonians is primarily instructional but includes a focus on consolation (4:13–18). Galatians has been regarded by some as an apologetic letter (i.e., an aspect of juridical rhetoric), by others as a letter of advice (i.e., following the rules of deliberative rhetoric), and by still others as a combination of the two types. Romans is also problematic, for some scholars have proposed that it is an epideictic letter, while others have suggested that it is either apologetic or hortatory or even a combination of all three types. It is to be hoped that further research will clarify these questions.

Bibliography

Aune, D. E. *The New Testament in Its Literary Environment.* Philadelphia: Westminster, 1987.

Charlesworth, J. H., ed. *The Old Testament Pseudepigrapha.* 2 vols. Garden City, NY: Doubleday, 1983, 1985.

Collins, J. J. *Between Athens and Jerusalem: Jewish Identity in the Hellenistic Diaspora.* New York: Crossroad, 1983.

Grant, F. C. *Roman Hellenism and the New Testament.* New York: Scribner, 1962.

Hengel, M. *Judaism and Hellenism: Studies in Their Encounter in Palestine During the Early Hellenistic Period.* 2 vols. Philadelphia: Fortress, 1974.

Lesky, A. *A History of Greek Literature.* Translated by J. Willis and C. de Heer. New York: Crowell, 1966.

Schürer, E. *The History of the Jewish People in the Age of Jesus Christ.* Vol. 3, part 1. New English version. Revised and edited by G. Vermes, F. Millar, and M. Goodman. Edinburgh: Clark, 1986.

Stone, M. E., ed. *Jewish Writings of the Second Temple Period.* Vol. 2, section 2 of *Compendia Rerum Iudaicarum ad Novum Testamentum.* Philadelphia: Fortress, 1984.

THE BIBLE AND ITS INTERPRETERS: JEWISH BIBLICAL INTERPRETATION

MICHAEL FISHBANE

INTRODUCTION

Judaism is an exegetical religious culture *par excellence*, and the Hebrew Bible constitutes its foundation document and principal text. For over two millennia it has been reinterpreted for simple meaning, for spiritual-moral guidance, for theoretical insight, and for legal applicability. Whether one turns to the classical halakic (legal) or haggadic (theological-moral) texts of late antiquity (→ Haggadah; Halakah), to the homilies or synagogue poetry of medieval times, or to philosophical theologies and mystical theosophies of all periods, the matter is the same. Biblical exegesis either serves as the explicit structural feature of the composition at hand or as its implicit religious foundation. It has therefore been rightly observed that the majority of postbiblical literature is, in some way, an interpretation of the Hebrew Bible.

The reason for this is both simple and far-reaching. As with other book religions (like Christianity and Islam, and in certain respects even Hinduism), Judaism places a sacred Scripture at the very center of its religious life. Indeed, for Judaism, the Hebrew Bible is the sacred textual source of religious authority. This authority, in turn, derives from the belief that this Scripture is rooted in a divine source. It was presumed and believed from early rabbinic times in the first century A.D. that Scripture was an inexhaustible source of truth and meaning—only awaiting the creative human labor of exegesis for its full explication and adaptation.

INNER-BIBLICAL EXEGESIS

The contents of the Hebrew Bible have come to constitute (through exegesis) the prescriptive norms for behavior and the basis for all theological attitudes in Judaism. To be sure, such a notion of a comprehensive Sinaitic revelation did not develop with one masterstroke. A close examination of the Hebrew Bible discloses, in fact, that this document bears witness to a concern for the reinterpretation of its legal and nonlegal content already in ancient Israel itself. Materials perceived to be inexplicit, incomplete, or otherwise inadequate for ongoing religious life were variously explicated or revised. Significantly, these innovations and amendments were not represented as an independent exegetical tradition—complementary or supplementary to revelatory authority. They were, rather, incorporated within Scripture itself. But with the closure of the canon in early rabbinic times, this practice necessarily changed: exegesis then became part of nonbiblical literature.

The range of inner-biblical exegesis is surprisingly diverse. It includes such broad types as scribal, legal, theological, and prophetic exegesis. Within the first type, for example, there is evidence for an ongoing concern to explain or clarify the meaning of older words and the identity of ancient place-names. Thus the clarification of the general term *kilayim* (Heb., "mixtures") in Lev. 19:19 by the more specific term *sha'tnez* shows an early attempt to specify the types of textile mixtures proscribed. The later explication of *sha'tnez* as "wool and flax" in Deut. 22:11 shows that, in time, this word had also become obscure and was in need of comment.

Such supplementations into the received tradition illustrate one of the main purposes of inner-biblical exegesis: to clarify or adapt the received tradition while also preserving the authority of its instruction and formulation. This feature is found in many examples of legal exegesis. According to one type, where the law was unknown or inadequate, a new divine revelation was sought, received, and *added* to the divine corpus (cf. Lev. 24:10–23; Num. 9:14). In other cases, divine authority was safeguarded by the inclusion of supplementary addenda into the original law (cf. Exod. 23:9–11; Lev. 25:1–7). Even where these expansions are signaled by explicit formulas, the new element is presented as part of the revealed law, not as a human exegetical stratum. Similar considerations pertain to the book of Deuteronomy.

The overall tendency to preserve the integrity of the Sinaitic revelation continues into the latest biblical strata. For example, blatant contradictions with respect to the paschal offering in our pentateuchal sources are harmonized and re-presented as Mosaic law (2 Chron.

35:11–13). But a new feature is also at work. 2 Chron. 30:2–3 is clearly an attempt to reinterpret and apply an earlier revealed addendum to defer the Passover ceremony (Num. 9:10–14) based solely on human authority. No recourse is made to divine authority *even though* the new situation is decidedly not identical with the older one.

In addition to scribal and legal exegesis, there are also many examples of theological interpretation in the Hebrew Bible, as well as the reinterpretation and reapplication of old prophecies. In the first case, laws (like the law dealing with remarriage in Deut. 24:1–4) are often spiritualized or adapted for new homiletical purposes (cf. Jer. 3:1–5), and in the second case, oracles that had not been fulfilled were often reapplied to later times. The successive application of Jeremiah's seventy-year prophecy (Jer. 25:9–11) in postexilic literature, especially Daniel 9, is a case in point.

In sum, this early reflex of "biblical exegesis" anticipates several rabbinic concerns of later times: the protection of the divine authority of the laws, the tendency to obscure human innovations, the reapplication of old laws and prophecies, and, especially, the gradual emergence of an explicit exegetical culture. This latter feature is particularly evident in postexilic times; for not only were Ezra and his levitical aides involved in the explication of legal obscurities (Neh. 8), they were also engaged in polemical exegesis. Indeed, their attempts to sanction the exclusion of certain groups from intermarriage with the "community of the Exile" (the returnees) strike a new chord: group maintenance and integrity were now argued and assured via scriptural exegesis (cf. Ezra 9).

FROM ANTIQUITY TO THE REDACTION OF THE TALMUD (ca. 200 B.C.–A.D. 500)

By the postexilic period, then, most of the procedures and tendencies of later Jewish exegesis were well under way. The older sacerdotal structures of the pre-exilic period gave way in the Exile, so that new emphasis was placed —by the priests and increasingly the laity— on public teaching and interpretation of the Torah. In addition, the national decentralization brought on by the Exile sponsored diverse postexilic communities. Each of these groups laid claim to the same scriptural authority but differed radically as to its proper meaning and application. Clearly the Torah required interpretation for the sake of its ongoing vitality and authority. But how was it to be supplemented,

and what was to constitute the proper reading tradition?

The deep crisis of religious continuity that underlies such questions was ominous—both for the immediate sectarian developments and for the history of Judaism generally, for at root was the fundamental claim of the diverse postexilic communities to be the true heir of biblical Israel. In this context, the interpretation of Scripture took a new and fateful turn. It became the cutting edge of group boundaries, even as it provided the content of new religious behaviors, ideas, and hopes.

The Dead Sea Scrolls found at Qumran give paradigmatic expression to these issues. An initiate into the Qumran community was progressively introduced to its unique methods of exegesis, so that to grow in knowledge and authority in this group was inextricably bound up with accepting its claim to the true meanings of Scripture (CD 15:10–13). It is reported that the founder-teacher was granted divine guidance in the exposition of the laws of Moses. As a result, two Torahs were distinguished: the exoteric Torah, revealed to all Israel at Sinai, and an esoteric one known only to the covenanters and the basis of their legal behavior (1QS 5:7–12; 8:15–16; CD 3:12–16). The secret meanings and applications of the ancient prophecies were also revealed to the founder-teacher—as the remarkable *pesher* literature (commentaries explaining the hidden meaning of OT texts) of this group attests. It was the covenanters' conviction that their legal-ritual life and future expectations would be vindicated in the imminent final days.

The crucial relationship between right interpretation and right observance cannot be underestimated. At stake was the "true meaning" of the divine word. It is recorded, for example, that one early (proto?) Pharisaic group refused to share food with other pious Jews who did not conform to their ultrameticulous food regulations. Along different lines, the Sadducees mocked the Pharisees who "afflict themselves" (with the oral law). The derogation and refutation of the religious claims of rival groups through a condemnation of their modes of exegesis is a recurrent feature in NT sources as well (Matt. 15:1–3; Mark 7:1–3; Col. 2:8; 1 Tim. 6:3–4).

In time, one of these groups, the Pharisees, put forward a remarkable claim—one that was to be of inestimable significance for the history of rabbinic Judaism. Their claim was that their particular exegetical tradition had Sinaitic origins, that it was divinely given at Sinai to Moses, side by side with the written Torah, and that it had been preserved through an unbroken chain of transmission. This opinion was nothing short of revolutionary. The mythicization and retrojection of Pharisaic exegetical claims back to Sinai gave normative sanction to *two Torahs* —one and inseparable: an oral Torah and a written Torah. Indeed, if Judaism can be said to endorse a notion of progressive revelation, one would at least have to find it here. Whatever a scholar would claim via exegetical diligence, it was said, was *already* given at Sinai. When God spoke "*all* these words" (Exod. 20:1) at Sinai, said Rabbi Elazar ben Azariah, he spoke the exoteric Torah *and* the various—even contradictory!—words of human exegesis (b. Ḥag. 3a–b). Oral Torah is thus a progressive unfolding of the mysterious plenitude of the original divine revelation. "Turn it [i.e., Scripture], and turn it again," says an early source, "for all is contained therein" (m. 'Abot 5:22). The notion of a continuous revelation even found this remarkable formulation in later times: "The Holy One, Blessed is He, speaks Torah out of the mouths of all rabbis" (b. Ḥag. 15b).

Throughout the Tannaitic period—that is, from Hasmonean times up to the codification of law in the Mishnah (ca. 200 B.C.–ca. A.D. 200)—the Hebrew Bible was the central preoccupation of Jewish exegesis. At the beginning, some of the most basic exegetical tasks were performed by the Sopherim, or scribes. These scholars were concerned with such matters as establishing the fixed wording of Scripture and the punctuation and phrasing of words and sentences. Many of their textual and contextual observations were continued by the explications and semantic observations of the ancient rabbis.

The earliest legal exegesis (the halakic midrashim) in, for example, the *Sipra* and *Sipre* (classical rabbinic commentaries on Leviticus and Numbers respectively) reflect other procedures that had been developed to derive new applications from the old law, as well as new understanding of the plain sense of the text. The most notable difference between these new modes and the early "Sopheric" style of exegesis lies in their expanded notion of scriptural context. From a concern only with individual words or phrases, the sages turned to the entirety of Scripture as the context for their exegetical observations and correlations. This led to new types of exegetical logic and method. For example, although Exod. 13:16 states that divine teachings should be a sign "upon your hand," it is not stated whether the right hand or the left is meant. As this prescription was the textual basis of the ritual of donning phylacteries (small boxes containing scriptural phrases), this was no theoretical matter. The matter was resolved through a comparison of other scriptural passages where frequently "right" is in parallelism with "arm." The neutral word "arm" was thus deduced to refer to the left arm also here (cf. *Sipre Deut.*, 67). But despite this, it must also be noted that not all the legal rulings legitimated by scriptural reference are really exegetically derived. In some cases, it appears that these references merely serve as mnemonic guides for the legal scholars.

Diverse schools of Bible exegesis developed, and hermeneutical techniques became standardized. Among the most prominent exegetes of the first centuries were Rabbi Ishmael, who emphasized that the exegesis of Scripture must follow common usage and meaning, and Rabbi R. Akiba, who utilized every jot and tittle of the biblical text for exegetical derivations. The latter technique is traditionally traced to Nahum Gimzo. In the chain of exegetical method leading from Nahum Gimzo to Akiba, a momentous development occurred: Hillel (first century A.D.) formulated a list of hermeneutical *middot* (Heb., exegetical techniques; lit., "measures"). Rabbi Ishmael extended this classification to thirteen (*Sipra*, 3a). The categories are formal in nature and use analogical, elucidative, and syllogistic forms of argumentation. Among the types of procedures used, one may mention *klal u-phrat* ("general and specific," i.e., when a general formulation is followed by a specific one) or *gezerah shavah* ("grammatical similarity," when diverse passages are correlated on the basis of morphological similarities in the language used). These and other types use forms of deductive and inductive reasoning.

A strong formal resemblance has been observed between these old rabbinic hermeneutical rules and contemporary Greco-Roman techniques of rhetoric. In addition, the impact of the methods and terminology of the Alexandrine scribes cannot be disregarded. Quite certainly, the rationalization of methods of Jewish biblical exegesis at this time was part of a larger cultural enterprise that embraced the entire region. Classical antiquity was at an end, and its traditions were being reevaluated and reinterpreted. Homer and Bible gave way to Stoic philosophy and rabbinic exegesis.

The intense preoccupation with Scripture was not limited to legal matters. In addition to these, a broad species of haggadic *midrashim* (moral and homiletical interpretations of the Hebrew Bible) is preserved in the relatively early and great collections known as *Genesis Rabbah* and *Leviticus Rabbah* (compiled during the fourth and fifth centuries A.D.). This literature is replete with evidence of an at once playful and highly serious hermeneutical imagination. Philological and syntactical matters are repeatedly taken up; so too are matters of custom, moral behavior, and theology. As with legal midrash, so with the haggadic—there is the strong presupposition that Scripture is a seamless web. The exegete is permitted and encouraged to move back and forth across its surface, connecting texts and reconnecting them, harmonizing the contradictory and bringing the seemingly discordant into patterns of new and surprising concordance.

Through the vast exegetical enterprise, it is clear that the interpretation of Scripture is a cultural product. Many rabbis commented on diverse verses, and sometimes on a large sequence of them, but no extensive running commentary was produced by any one individual. To the extent that continuous commentaries do exist in this formative phase of classical Judaism, they do so as a cultural product, as anthologies organized around the structure of Scripture—comprising the opinions, observations, and sermonic précis of many scholars. This is a matter of immense significance. Scripture was the organizing prism of the people: it gave focus, structure, and of course authority to the theological speculations, the moral values, and the folk customs of the nation of Israel.

One counterdevelopment deserves comment. Though the Hebrew Bible remained authoritative for ancient halakic and haggadic exegesis, the legal corpus known as the Mishnah (redacted ca. A.D. 200) is a major classical text without an explicit scriptural and exegetical foundation. The formal and abstract style of the document may have derived from the influence of Roman legal style. In any case, because of the prestige of the Mishnah among the sages who continued the legal tradition, all parts of this legal document were quickly subjected to acute analysis. A dominant feature of subsequent Talmudic discussions, in fact, is the attempt to provide or establish the implicit biblical justification of the Mishnaic rulings. Proceeding along a different course, the exegetical discussions in such early collections as Sipra and Sipre started from the scriptural passages themselves and demonstrate how many of the rabbinic rules are derived from them. Both trends reflect a return to, and reemphasis on, biblical legal exegesis.

Concern with the *peshat*, the literal or plain sense of Scripture, and the *derash*, the halakic and haggadic modes of exegesis, did not exhaust the modalities of Jewish Bible exegesis in antiquity. Two other types are found: the allegorical and the mystical.

Like the *peshat* and *derash*, allegory arises as a result of a crisis in reading—where the text appears opaque or insufficient—for the allegorical impetus does not so much arise from problematics perceived when a text is viewed in its own right as from the encounter between an authoritative text and an attractive and religiously approachable body of religious or philosophical thought. The most notable example of this in Jewish antiquity is reflected in the works of Philo (ca. 20 B.C.–A.D. 50). Like his fellow intellectuals in Alexandria, Philo was confronted with the philosophic sublimity of Stoic-Middle Platonic thought and its apparently fundamental difference from the teachings of the Hebrew Bible. Faced with this clash of values, Philo (like other biblical allegorists before and since) engaged in a remarkable exegetical strategy: he read one thought-world (the Stoic-philosophical) in terms of another (the biblical-traditional). The result is a mode of syncretistic exegesis that harmonized these competing thought claims and established them as diverse levels of meaning. There is thus both the surface sense to Scripture and its *hyponoia*, a Greek term meaning its deeper and more spiritual sense. Significantly, this recognition (or assertion) of different levels of scriptural sense did not serve to eclipse the authority of the biblical text. It actually strengthened that claim, for the Stoic and other philosophical truths were not simply harmonized with or exegetically attributed to Torah; they were now dialectically discovered to be inherent in its very nature. Scripture is thus the best of books, for it is a book of many senses, including the philosophical. Correspondingly, philosophy is no alien product or challenge to biblical tradition but part of its comprehensive truth.

Philo's exegesis is profound and subtle. Human personages like Abraham and Sarah become figures of ethical-spiritual virtues; sacrificial rituals or images, like the cherubim, are read as guides to inner piety; legal texts, like the prescription to flee to the city of refuge, are construed in terms of the spiritual quest for God; and narratives, like the garden of Eden and the sin of Adam, are transformed into spiritual patterns that the discerning mind might use to perceive its proper place in Universal Mind, the true City of Man. Correctly read, then, the biblical text was nothing short of a spiritual-philosophical document, an expression of divine wisdom given to humanity to guide its perfectibility.

The capacity of the biblical text to sponsor new and unexpected levels of meaning is nowhere more evident than in mystical exegesis, whose main lines are observable from Tannaitic times. Typical are the ancient mystical interpretations of the Song of Songs. These love lyrics were read in a mystical sense, disclosing theosophical truths and providing descriptions of the Godhead. Thus, to enter the chambers of the beloved is to ascend into the recesses of the Divine Being; the physical description of the groom in the Song (5:10–16) was understood to veil the actual structure of the divine anthropos! In this way, mystical Bible exegesis served to reveal the illimitable depths of God himself. For it, the face of Scripture is nothing less than the surface play of divine mysteries, the outer map, as it were, of mystical visions and journeys. All this the mystic knows from experience; his exegesis merely confirms it.

THE MEDIEVAL PHASE TO THE ONSET OF MODERN TIMES
(A.D. 800–1700)

The four levels of scriptural meaning that developed in the early classical period anticipate their more sophisticated permutations in the Middle Ages. Indeed, the very concept of a multiple, fourfold meaning of Scripture is only first referred to in Jewish mystical texts from the thirteenth century, quite likely because of contemporary trends in Christian exegesis. From the fourteenth century these four senses were referred to by the acronym *PaRDeS* ("paradisal garden"), which stands for the *Peshat* (plain sense), the *Remez* (implied or allegorical sense), the *Derash* (halakic and haggadic exegesis), and the *Sod* (mystical sense) of Scripture. The widespread use of the term *PaRDeS* in Jewish sources does not, of course, mean that each level was equally valorized by all groups in all periods. But the acronym does signal a view of Torah and exegesis as the very source and method of all realizable Jewish truth.

The work of Rabbi Abraham Ibn Ezra (A.D. 1089–1164) is particularly characteristic of a Spanish trend toward rational, lexicographical exegesis and the attempt to write a systematic commentary. In the introduction to his Bible commentary, Ibn Ezra discusses the allegorical, midrashic, and Karaite approaches that preceded him and witheringly attacks their styles and conclusions. As for his own method, he says, "I shall be unbiased concerning the Torah and shall [first] investigate the grammatical form of each word with my full ability and then explain its meaning to what extent I am able." Since there are seventy "faces" to Torah, he goes on, the literal approach does not displace the midrashic interpretation, but when "it comes to the laws, rules, and regulations," the opinion "which is in accord with the bearer of Tradition [namely, the rabbis]" must be relied upon. "For God forbid that we get involved with the Sadducean [namely, Karaite!] contention which claims that [rabbinic] Tradition contradicts Scripture and grammar." Ibn Ezra was also greatly exercised by scriptural contradictions and blatant anachronisms in the text (see his comments on Gen. 12:6).

But for all his exegetical zeal for the *peshat* as the most valid method for recovering the ancient philological and historical sense of Scripture, Ibn Ezra was also a traditional Jew—and thus also recognized that his exegetical enterprise was ultimately subservient to the halakic basis of the community. He therefore remarked that, as a matter of principle, he would accept the legal *derash* of a passage in those cases where his method (of *peshat*) would contradict the meaning of a law as interpreted and practiced by the religious community. In this he was not alone. Similar considerations are referred to by Ibn Ezra's great Franco-German contemporary, Rabbi Samuel ben Meir (A.D. 1080–1160, known as Rashbam). He too was a devoted advocate of the *peshat* sense and advocated it above all others. "I have not come to interpret the halakic rules, even though they are of the essence . . . but I have rather come to interpret the *peshat* of Scripture, and [thus] I shall interpret laws and halakic rules by rational sense" (see his introduction to the laws of Exod. 21–23).

In this celebration of the *peshat*, Rashbam took a more determined and methodological position than his celebrated grandfather, Rashi (Rabbi Solomon ben Isaac, A.D. 1040–1105), who had been the first in northern France to advocate the *peshat* sense over the *derash* (cf. Rashi on Gen. 3:18; 33:20; although in actual practice the two methods are not fully distinguishable in all cases). This determination and methodological rigor even led Rashbam to provide the *peshat* of a passage *even where* it appears to diverge from the halakic *derash* (cf., e.g., his comments on Exod. 22:6). As is now clear, this strong emphasis on the literal, plain sense of the text was part of a larger historical development at this time—particularly noticeable in Christianity. Increasingly, reliance upon the traditional readings of Scripture was deemphasized in certain circles, and the achievements of human reason were privileged.

Medieval Spain was also the scene of another development: philosophical exegesis. If, as stated earlier, allegory is an exegesis born of a conflict between competing thought-worlds, the renewed recourse to *remez* by Jews who felt the keen challenge of Neoplatonic and Aristotelian philosophy is more than understandable. Since the works of Philo had long been lost to Jewish thought, the new conceptions that developed seemed little short of revolutionary. The Bible was now perceived as a book capable of bringing the adept to ultimate spiritual felicity, for it could guide the adept toward a rational, contemplative love of the God of the philosophers.

The work of Maimonides (A.D. 1135–1204) is a paradigmatic expression of this overall trend. He not only begins his magisterial *Guide for the Perplexed* with lexicographical considerations but actually devotes forty-seven chapters to a reexamination of the language of Scripture in an effort to reconcile it with philosophical truth. Though drawing upon older considerations regarding the appropriate use of metaphorical interpretation (*ta'wil*), Maimonides, who was much influenced by Islamic philosophy, put more emphasis on the distinction between the "inner" (*batin*) and "apparent" (*zahir*) levels of textual meaning than was common in contemporary Islamic philosophical circles. This distinction (based on an inner-Islamic development of *ta'wil* to include doctrinal matters) helped him resolve several issues at once. Not only was Maimonides well aware that the written Torah often presents God in highly anthropomorphic and anthropopathic images, which ostensibly violate and preclude a proper philosophical understanding, he was also highly conscious that even philosophical discourse, due to the inherent limitations of language, is often in need of literary figures and tropes (e.g., parables or similes). This Gordian knot was thus deftly cut by the realization that though the masses require figures and tend to read the surface images of Scripture literally, they would not thereby be led astray from the truth. As a divinely revealed teaching, the exterior level of Scripture is sufficient to guide the faithful to spiritual and moral excellence. Nevertheless, this level merely conceals the deeper and philosophically superior one, which establishes "the truth in all its reality."

Maimonides' method produced violent controversy in France and Germany. Though he himself did not disclaim the plain sense of Scripture and wrote a code of halakic observance, it was feared that focus on the inner, spiritual level of Scripture would subtly undermine the public spirituality of Judaism, based as it is on the performance of the divine commandments.

Nahmanides (1194–1274) was asked to mediate this acrimonious dispute, and his great prestige did in fact prove conciliatory. He was a man of vast erudition and interests—a fact reflected in the new style of synthetic commentary that he produced. Nahmanides' exegetical work entered into fruitful—if prolix—debate with the received opinions of his predecessors, from the ancient sages to Rashi and Ibn Ezra. Typically, his argumentation turns on the context and sequence of biblical language. But he did not stop there. Beyond "the way of *peshat*" and rabbinic legal exegesis, Nahmanides again and again drops hints about "the way of Truth"—the mystical sense (*sod*) of Scripture.

The *Book of Splendor* or the *Zohar* (thirteenth century) is the classical source of medieval Spanish Kabbala (mysticism). Though giving evidence of literal and figurative exegesis, its biblical expositions focus particularly on the luminous truths of *sod*. The early Kabbalists saw this as the fourth level of *PaRDeS*—hidden within the shell of outer meanings like the core of a nut, like the seeds of a pomegranate. In another image, *sod* is personified as the *Shekina*—or indwelling feminine aspect of God—who is veiled in the exterior garments of exoteric textual sense. This divine Bride beckons *even through* the plain sense of *peshat*. For those who can respond, the textual tokens of her bidding lend exegesis a deep erotic drive and

yearning—one that is no less than the love of God—to unveil Scripture and robe the Bride in the garments of mystical splendor (see *Zohar* 2:99 a–b).

Insofar as the mundane Torah is, in truth, a condensation of God in his infinite mystery, the Torah pulses with rhythms of the divine potencies that structure the cosmos. Exegesis thus begets entry into the mysteries and guides a spiritual journey into the emanationist structure of the Godhead. It is a subtle decoding of Torah or, better, a recoding of it into the theosophical truth that the mystic has been privileged to see. Accordingly, every person and every event described in Scripture—even the most apparently meaningless, like the genealogies of Genesis 36—veils the vitality of the divine. And insofar as the structure of the cosmos is perceived as a divine *Anthropos* whose earthly reflex is Man, mystical ascent into the recesses of God is also descent into the corresponding depths of the self.

POSTMEDIEVAL AND CONTEMPORARY TRENDS
(A.D. 1700–THE PRESENT)

Among the many striking patterns in the history of Judaism is the conjunction of its transformative moments with renewed vigor in biblical exegesis. New spiritual developments or crises continuously sponsored new views of Torah, revelation, and exegesis. This holds, as well, for the modern world—and all the complex spiritual transformations that have unfolded. Let us begin with Hassidism, the popular and late heir of Kabbala. Beginning in the mid-eighteenth century, this pietist movement has produced astonishingly subtle rereadings of Scripture and has guided Jews in exploring new levels of psychospiritual inwardness. For example, where the psalmist once cried, "Do not abandon me in old age," the Baal Shem Tov, the founder of the movement, is reported to have found here a watchword against spiritual aging. Now the text is an agonized plea for divine aid against the decrepitudes of ennui and routine in divine service.

In the more rationalist circles of the Enlightenment and post-Enlightenment period, the works produced reflect different exegetical trends. Moses Mendelssohn (1729–86) and his colleagues produced a commentary (called *Bi'ur*) that mixed philological economy and traditional perspectives. It focused on the *peshat* and gave considerable attention to aesthetic matters, as was fashionable at the time, though it clearly did not give expression to the new critical-historical temper of biblical studies then developing in Germany. These matters only begin to appear in Jewish commentaries with S. D. Luzzatto (1800–1865), of Italy. Hereby Jews were exposed to the liberal text-critical and historical assumptions of modern Bible scholarship—though hardly in the strident and radical forms then emerging in Europe. But as the Documentary Hypothesis took on its classical shape, and the religious-historical implications of this method of treating Scripture as any ancient document penetrated the traditional community, rebuttals were soon formulated. Perhaps the most thoughtful and penetrating was that of the important rabbinic scholar D. Z. Hoffmann (1843–1921), who also produced a significant series of commentaries on the books of Leviticus and Deuteronomy that combined in a distinctive manner traditional rabbinic perspectives and literary-critical observations.

Among liberal and secular Jews, the methods and achievements of biblical scholarship have been taken up without apology, though with varying nuances and emphasis. Inquiries into the biblical text have encouraged Jews to see their religious and national past in a new light. This has often meant an emphasis on certain aspects of biblical thought—like ethical monotheism and prophetic polemic against injustice—that serve nontraditional ideology. Thus, matters of ritual or national parochialism have been disregarded in favor of nonritual and universal values.

The relationship between Bible study and ideology has also had its reflexes in the secular and national realm. Thus, the massive reevaluation of the Documentary Hypothesis from a liberal-critical perspective, also influenced by national values, marks the voluminous achievement of Yehezkel Kaufmann (1889–1963). His refocus on the antiquity of monotheism and of many literary strands generally thought to be late gave new emphasis to the independence and integrity of Israel's ancient achievement.

An attempt to recapture the religious power of the Bible without abandoning critical sensitivities has been the achievement of Martin Buber (1878–1965) and Franz Rosenzweig (1886–1929). Both in their common Bible translation and in various books and essays, a close attention to the power of biblical language was felt to be a first step to transcending the crisis of a religious reading of the Bible for modern, nontraditional Jews. Such attention would lead, they felt, beyond the cant of "critical orthodoxies" to more penetrating literary and religious levels, even to an encounter with the divine presence. In this way, the Bible would open modern Jews to a new encounter with Israel's ancient God of history and holiness—though, to be sure, the sensibilities thus acquired would be related to the demands of the contemporary historical hour.

Bibliography

Fishbane, M. *Biblical Interpretation in Ancient Israel.* Oxford: Clarendon, 1985.

Idel, M. "Infinities of Torah in Kabbalah." In *Midrash and Literature.* Edited by G. Hartman and S. Budick. New Haven, CT: Yale University Press, 1986.

Rosenthal, E. I. J. "The Study of the Bible in Medieval Judaism." In *The Cambridge History of the Bible.* 3 vols. Cambridge: Cambridge University Press, 1963–70. Vol. 2, pp. 252–79.

Sarna, N. "Hebrew and Bible Studies in Medieval Spain." In *The Sephardi Heritage.* Edited by R. Barnett. London: Vellentine-Mitchell, 1971. Pp. 323–66.

Vermes, G. "Bible and Midrash." In *The Cambridge History of the Bible.* 3 vols. Cambridge: Cambridge University Press, 1963–70. Vol. 1, pp. 199–231.

THE BIBLE AND ITS INTERPRETERS: CHRISTIAN BIBLICAL INTERPRETATION

ROBERT L. WILKEN

THE EARLY CHRISTIAN AND PATRISTIC PERIOD (FIRST TO NINTH CENTURIES A.D.)

The Bible, like other classics of religion and literature, does not disclose its meaning without interpretation. The interpreter must know the language in which the text is written (or possess a reliable translation), identify names and places, understand stylistic conventions (metaphors and similes), and have some familiarity with the historical circumstances surrounding the text. For Christians, however, the Bible is also sacred Scripture. It is a holy book whose history narrates the story of salvation and whose teachings impart divine wisdom. As one medieval commentator put it: "The subject matter of all the Divine Scriptures is the work of restoration." It is the only book that is read regularly by Christians in public worship. It is at once a historical document and a book of faith handed on in the churches, and its interpretation has been shaped by the worship, practice, and teachings of the Christian communities. Even the texts that seem to yield their meaning readily depend on a tradition of understanding.

The earliest Christians were Jews for whom the Scriptures (i.e., the Jewish Bible, which was to become the Christian OT) was a living book. It was read in the synagogues, used as a guide for communal and personal life, and cited as an authority in debates. The necessity of interpreting these Scriptures had spawned a rich literature in the centuries prior to the beginning of Christianity, and it was these exegetical traditions that set the tone and spirit of early Christian interpretation.

Through the medium of Jewish exegetical traditions, the Jewish Bible and its history and prophecies provided a framework in which to view Jesus' death and resurrection, and in time belief in Christ began to transform the interpretation of these same Scriptures. Events (e.g., the Exodus), persons (e.g., Abraham), places (e.g., Sinai), and things (e.g., manna) now came to have a new dimension. The rock from which the Israelites drank in the desert (Num. 20) was now thought to represent Christ, and the deliverance through the Sea of Reeds (Red Sea) was now seen to foreshadow Christian baptism (1 Cor. 10:1–5).

Much of the study of the history of biblical interpretation has concentrated on the "method" employed by different interpreters. But already in the NT there is no consistent exegetical method even for a specific writer. More often than not, use rather than method shaped interpretation. Matthew quotes Jer. 31:15, for example, "A voice was heard in Ramah, wailing and loud lamentation," a lament over the exiles in Babylon, to mourn the murder of the male children in Bethlehem after Jesus' birth ("the holy innocents") by Herod (Matt. 3:16). Paul cites a law from Deuteronomy (25:4), "You shall not muzzle an ox when it is treading out the grain," to affirm his rights as an apostle (1 Cor. 9:8–12). In Galatians he allegorizes Abraham's two wives, Sarah and Hagar, to signify the two covenants, the one of freedom and the other of bondage. Other writers employ typology, e.g., the lifting up of the brazen serpent (Num. 21:4–9), to relate Christ's death on the cross to a scriptural event (John 3:14; cf. *Barn.* 12). Method is subservient to use.

The most perplexing and persistent problem for early Christian interpreters arose out of the relation of Christianity to the Jewish Scriptures. The first Christians were Jews who observed the Jewish law, but at an early stage Gentiles began to join the new communities, and in a very short time it became clear that one could not impose the Law on new converts who were not Jewish. Giving up observance of the Law was to create a particularly vexing problem for Christian exegesis. Moses had written: "You shall not add to the word which I command you, nor take from it; that you may keep the commandments of the Lord your God which I command you" (Deut. 4:2). Furthermore, Jesus had observed the Law and had said, "I say to you, till heaven and earth pass away, not an iota, not a dot, will pass from the Law until all is accomplished" (Matt. 5:18). Some Christians continued to observe the Jewish law, but most did not. How, then, asked the early interpreters, does one interpret those texts, especially in the Pentateuch, that enjoin observance of the Law?

In the writings of the NT (esp. Galatians, 2

Corinthians, Matthew, Hebrews) Christians had already addressed this question, and in the second century it emerged as a central theme in *The Letter of Barnabas* and in Justin Martyr's *Dialogue with Trypho*. These works offered the first detailed Christian interpretation of texts from the Jewish Bible. Justin's work centers on questions raised by a Jew named Trypho concerning the relationship of Judaism to Christianity. Why, Trypho asked Justin, do you Christians, who claim to be like us, not celebrate the Jewish festivals, or keep the Sabbath, or circumcise? Justin answers that the law of the Jews was only given for a fixed time and only intended for Jews. This law has now been abrogated by the new way in Christ (*Dialogue* 11), as had been announced by the prophet Jeremiah when he spoke of a new covenant (Jer. 31).

Some Christians in the second century (Marcion and his followers) proposed that the church give up entirely the Jewish Scripture. It seemed to them to be an alien document that spoke only about the Jewish people and about a lesser God. But the majority of Christians rejected these views, and Christian interpreters had to find a way to give the ancient laws and practices meaning for Christian faith and life. This was done by extending the meaning of these laws and practices to comprehend Christ and the Christian life. For example, circumcision was viewed as a type of baptism and the pascal lamb a type of Christ; the offering of fine flour referred to the Eucharist; and the twelve bells on the priest's robe signified the twelve apostles.

Another major exegetical development in the early period centered on Christian theological and exegetical issues. The key figure in this regard was Irenaeus, bishop of Lyon in the late second century, an opponent of the Gnostics. Irenaeus lived at the time when the establishment of the canon—the authoritative collection of Christian writings—was an issue of lively debate. Christians were using as Scripture the Greek translation of the Jewish Bible called the Septuagint (LXX). This translation included additional books (now called the Apocrypha by Protestants or the Deuterocanonicals by Catholics) and followed an order different from the Hebrew Scripture. It was, however, still a Jewish book. Pagan authors knew it and cited it as a Jewish work. It was the principal Scripture of the early Christian church, though many uniquely Christian works had begun to appear.

At first there was no collection of distinctively Christian books. But in time, partly in reaction to Marcion (who had developed a canon that included some Pauline Letters and excluded all Gospels except an edited version of Luke that fitted his own views), the authority of the four Gospels came to be recognized along with the Letters of Paul. Irenaeus is one of the first witnesses to this development. In time these books were supplemented by other early Christian writings. This collection came to be called the NT, and in turn the LXX received its Christian title, the OT. The Christian Bible, then, included two parts, one deriving from Judaism, the other from Christianity, but in the minds of Christian thinkers such as Irenaeus, the two parts constituted one book. The understanding that Christian interpreters had before them a single book became the basis for all later Christian interpretation.

Irenaeus was the first to interpret the Christian Scriptures as a unified document. His interest lay chiefly in the Gospels and the writings of Paul, but the overall framework of his interpretation was provided by the history of salvation beginning in ancient Israel and culminating in Christ, who sums up all things that began in Adam. According to Irenaeus, the Gnostics had misused and perverted the Scriptures to support false and idiosyncratic ideas contrary to the church's tradition. The aim of his work was to show the agreement of the Scriptures with the church's tradition, thereby retaining the Scriptures for the church. To do this he set forth for the first time the idea that the Scriptures have one central meaning, one scope. This unifying sense was found in the rule of faith (Lat. *regula fidei*), a simple creed used for catechetical instruction and at baptism by Christian congregations in all parts of the Roman world.

The faith expressed in this creed, summarized in the phrase "one God, Father and creator, one Christ, Son of God who became incarnate for our salvation, and Holy Spirit," became the key to interpreting the Scriptures. Irenaeus' approach to interpretation was to have enormous impact on later Christian interpretation. He repudiated piecemeal exegesis, that is, picking and choosing individual texts to defend arcane or idiosyncratic views, and insisted that the Bible was the church's book and had to be interpreted in light of central Christian beliefs. Tertullian, Athanasius, Augustine, and many others followed his lead in their exegesis of the Bible in theological disputes.

Works of interpretation in the late second and early third centuries took the form of treatises on disputed issues, as in Irenaeus' *Against Heresies* or Justin Martyr's *Dialogue with Trypho*; in apologies, e.g., Theophilus of Antioch's interpretation of Gen. 1–3; in homilies, e.g., Melito of Sardis on Exodus 14 and the Christian Passover; or in moral essays, e.g., Tertullian *On Patience*. But in the third century the commentary, a line-by-line exposition of the text, appears as a new literary form of interpreting the text of the Scriptures.

The earliest extant commentary of this type was written on the book of Daniel by Hippolytus of Rome (early third century). Though it is a verse-by-verse exposition of the text, it is not scholarly commentary but an occasional writing prompted by a fervent apocalyptic belief in Hippolytus' day that the end of the world was imminent. Hippolytus uses Daniel to assure the faithful that the end will not soon come and that they must learn patience and endurance. Already in the second century the Gnostic Heracleon may have written a commentary on John, but only fragments are extant (in Origen's commentary on John), and it is difficult to determine Heracleon's intention.

Origen

The commentary as a literary form established itself firmly within the Christian church with the writings of Origen of Alexandria (d. 254), the most significant early Christian biblical interpreter. Origen not only wrote several different types of commentaries, scholia (short comments on particular problems), series of homilies on individual books (e.g., Leviticus or Joshua or Matthew), and massive multivolumed learned commentaries, but he also prepared the Hexapla, an elaborate edition of the OT with several versions in separate columns, and wrote the first theoretical treatise on interpretation (Book 4 of his *De Principiis*). He realized the importance of Jewish exegesis, and though he frequently opposed Jewish views, he was often indebted to Jewish scholars, as, for example, in his interpretation of the Song of Songs. He was the first to recognize that interpretation was a scholarly as well as a spiritual and theological task.

Origen viewed the Bible as a book of divine oracles that spoke of God's relation to humanity. The Scriptures were written "not to narrate ancient history but for our instruction and use." For this reason he resorted to allegory, typology, and other forms of spiritual and moral interpretation. Like his predecessor Clement of Alexandria, Origen was influenced both by Philo the Jewish philosopher and by the Greek tradition of allegorizing classical texts. Allegory is a technique by which persons and things in a text are understood to signify something other than what they seem to refer to. It was first devised by interpreters of the ancient Greek poets (e.g., Homer), to bridge the gap between the text and contemporary philosophical and moral views. In time it was used to give a text a loftier meaning. The cave of the nymphs in the *Odyssey* (13:102–12), for example, was thought to signify not simply a cave but "images of higher things." In the first century Philo had employed allegory to deal with passages from the Jewish Scriptures that were offensive to current moral sensibilities, e.g., polygamy, or to make outmoded laws or practices spiritually edifying.

Allegory was particularly suitable to deal with passages from the OT the spiritual significance of which was not apparent to Christians. Commenting on Leviticus, Origen writes: "If I follow the 'simple sense' as some among us wish, without any recourse to the text's artifices and the obscurity of the allegory, I, a man of the church living with faith in Christ and placed in the midst of the church, would be compelled by the authority of the divine precept to sacrifice calves and lambs and to offer wheat cakes with incense and oil" (*Homilies on Leviticus* 1.1).

Unlike earlier interpreters, Origen set for himself the task of expounding every book of the Bible. He preached his way through entire books of the OT—Genesis, Leviticus, Numbers, Joshua, Jeremiah—and knew that his hearers were often genuinely perplexed and offended by it. The adoption of the commentary form made his task particularly arduous, because it required (even in a sermon) that "nothing be left unexplained." Origen's exegetical labors, his analysis of the text, his study of key biblical terms (e.g., the titles of Jesus in his *Commentary on John* or "justification" in his *Commentary on Romans*), his use of parallel passages to interpret puzzling concepts, his theological acuity and spiritual depth, his insight into human feelings (in his homily on the sacrifice of Isaac), all had one goal—to make the Scriptures intelligible and enlightening to Christians. His influence on later Christian interpreters is a monument to his success.

More than any other commentator in the patristic period Origen understood the central problems facing Christian interpreters of the Bible. In a sermon on the book of Joshua's account of the battle for the city of Ai, Origen observed that when the text is read in church his hearers ask, What does this history have to do with us? This question confronted Christian interpreters in every age, and the several exegetical techniques, allegory, typology, moral interpretation, all have one aim: to discover the current spiritual significance of the words and events recorded in the Bible. For Christians the Bible is a book about the living God, and its meaning is not exhausted by recounting past history. Whatever the text may have once meant, it must always have meaning for the present.

Although the patristic commentators were aware of their historical distance from biblical times, they recognized no discontinuity between the church and the Scriptures. The same God who inspired the Scriptures enlightened the interpreter. The Bible was a "carried book," interpreted within the context of a living tradition that could be traced back to the Bible itself.

The Bible in the Life of the Church

In the long history of interpretation, the Christian liturgy has been a key factor in giving coherence to biblical interpretation. Here the text did not serve simply to retell past history, but to re-present, along with the sacraments, salvific events in the midst of the Christian assembly. With the development of lectionaries, fixed cycles of readings, the day of the year on which the text was read and the readings that accompanied it came to be as salient a factor in determining its interpretation as the original setting in the book from which it was taken.

Much exegesis continued to focus on theological problems concerning Christian teaching, ecclesiastical problems, and catechesis. For example, "The Lord created me the beginning of his works" (Prov. 8:22) figured large in Athanasius' polemical work against the Arians because "me" in the text referred to "wisdom" and wisdom was identified with Christ. Some texts required extensive comment because they appeared to contradict fundamental tenets of the faith. Romans 9:16, for example, "it depends not upon man's will or exertion, but upon God's mercy" seemed to undermine responsibility for human actions. Others were interpreted in events and movements. "Go sell all and give to the poor" was the charter text for the monastic movement. Phil. 3:12, "I press on towards the goal," appears often in devotional works describing spiritual progress. In the first five centuries of Christian history the Scriptures were the textbook for theology, ethics, and spirituality.

As the commentary form (whose techniques had been learned from commentators on classical texts, e.g., the poems of Homer) became more familiar, interpreters began to address new kinds of questions to the text: authorship of individual books, author's intent, literary style and linguistic usage, historical setting, translations, and the reliability of the text itself. After Origen, the most outstanding representatives of the commentary tradition in the East were the Antiochene exegetes Diodorus of Tarsus, Theodore of Mopsuestia, and Theodoret of Cyrrhus (late fourth and fifth centuries). In their works, particularly those on the OT, they insisted that the prophets had first to be set within their own historical situation and could not be read solely as referring to Christ. It was illegitimate, Theodore argued, to apply one part of a verse to ancient Israel and the other to Christ. The interpreter had to determine in whose person the text was spoken. Some psalms referred only to David's lifetime; others were spoken in Christ's person, e.g., Psalms 2, 8, and 45. The Antiochenes sought to give a philological and historical basis to the task of exegesis without giving up the distinctively Christian interpreta-

tion. The prophets, wrote Theodoret of Cyrrhus, not only prophesied, but also used their words "for exhorting and legislating . . . [and] in teaching morals and doctrine" (*Patrologia Graeca* 80.861).

Jerome and Augustine

Among all the ancient commentators the Latin writer Jerome (d. 420) was the most learned. He alone mastered Hebrew and based his exposition of the OT on the Hebrew text, rendering it into Latin against strong opposition from Christian leaders and people. Augustine opposed the translation because he believed the LXX was the authoritative version in the church. Jerome's commentaries are filled with philological discussions, analyses of various translations, opinions of earlier commentators, and historical information. Jerome, like the Antiochenes, had contact with Jewish interpreters, and his commentaries on Isaiah, the Minor Prophets, Ezekiel, and others carry on a running debate with Jewish interpretation of prophecies. Although he recognizes that the prophecies (in Ezekiel, e.g.) were spoken to give hope to the exiles in Babylon, Jerome insists that they also refer to the coming of Christ and the new spiritual reality of the church.

In antiquity Christians wrote commentaries on all the books of the Bible, but all books did not have the same interest or appeal. In contrast to the classical Jewish commentaries—*Mekilta, Sipra,* and *Sipre* on Exodus, Leviticus, and Numbers (the legal sections of the Pentateuch)—Christian commentators were drawn to Genesis (esp. the first three chaps.), Isaiah, Ezekiel, the Minor Prophets, the Psalms. In the NT they favored Romans and the Gospels of Matthew and John. The wisdom books, however, were popular because they gave commentators greater freedom to develop distinctive spiritual or moral teachings, e.g., Gregory of Nyssa on the Song of Songs, or Gregory the Great on Job.

For Augustine (A.D. 354–430), however, the commentary was not the primary vehicle for his interpretation of the Scriptures. He did write commentaries—several (uncompleted) on Romans, a large work on the Psalms, a commentary on John, several on Genesis—but his major works are polemical, theological, spiritual, or educational tracts. In his early writings he seldom cites the Scriptures. But after his ordination he requested from his bishop time for detailed study of the Scriptures. After this period one can see how key biblical concepts enter into his thinking, e.g., the city of God (Ps. 87) in his work of that title, grace from Romans, love from the Gospel of John, and creation as a good gift of God (against the Manichees) from his study of Genesis. Although Augustine's initial reading of the Scriptures was aided by the allegorical exegesis he heard in the sermons of Ambrose, bishop of Milan, as he matured allegory gave way to a theological interpretation of history based on the biblical story that begins with creation and fall and ends with the beatific vision. This scheme, elaborated with unparalleled detail in the *City of God*, was to provide an overarching framework for later biblical interpretation.

Augustine also wrote a book on biblical hermeneutics, *On Christian Doctrine*, a work that drew on the first handbook of interpretation, Tyconius' *Book of Rules* (fourth century), which was a set of principles designed to guide interpreters into the distinctive features of biblical language and thinking. Like Tyconius, Augustine was concerned less with method than with content. Interpretation became more than a literary task; it was an aptitude or an ability. There could be no proper understanding of the Scripture that does not speak of the double love of God and of the neighbor. Augustine also developed here his notion of "signs," of the usefulness of obscurities in the Scripture, and of the importance of training in the liberal arts for interpretation.

In the East the great age of commentaries came to an end in the sixth century. With some notable exceptions, the commentary gave way to a new literary form, the *catena* (Lat., "chain"), a collection of citations from earlier commentators arranged according to the text of the Bible. Some *catenas* contained passages from a single author, but more often they included citations from several authors. The first great catenist was Procopius of Gaza (478–528), whose *catenas* on the first eight books of the OT, Isaiah, Romans, Matthew, and Job preserve passages from older exegetical works.

The Scriptures, however, continued to play a major role in Christian life through their use in theological discussions, in the liturgy, where they were read and expounded, and in spiritual and monastic writings. In the debate over iconoclasm (eighth and ninth centuries), Exod. 20:4, concerning the prohibition of graven images, and John 4:24 ("God is spirit, and those who worship him must worship in spirit and in truth") received extensive commentary. In the seventh-century Monothelite controversy, over whether Christ had one or two wills, Luke 22:42, "not my will but thine be done" (along with John 6:38), set the terms of the debate. One new form of interpretation, the sung metrical sermon (Gk. *kontakion*), usually associated with the name of Romanos Melodos (d. 556), became very popular in the East. It allowed the hymnist freedom to present biblical stories in dramatic form, to create dialogues, to develop the character of biblical figures (e.g., Adam and Eve, Abraham, Elijah), and to narrate the events of Jesus' life with uncommon liveliness.

The *kontakion* probably had its origin in Ephraem Syrus (306–73), the Syriac Christian poet and commentator. Ephraem wrote commentaries on Genesis, Exodus, Acts, and the Pauline Letters, but his liturgical poems are equally significant in the history of biblical interpretation. He believed that the language of the Scriptures was essentially poetic, and his writings employ the images of the Scriptures (e.g., bride, rock, vineyard, tree of life, mother, temple, nation) as the vehicles to interpret communal and personal Christian experience.

THE BIBLE IN THE MIDDLE AGES (TENTH TO SIXTEENTH CENTURIES)

In the West in the early Middle Ages the Bible became the basis for monastic prayer and meditation. The monks believed the interpreter should linger over the text and taste and savor its language and images, which spoke not only to the ears but also to the eyes (the vision at the beginning of Ezekiel, e.g.). They drew on Scripture to nurture spiritual growth and the pursuit of holiness and became skilled at extracting from the text what was important for Christian life. Interpretation was a spiritual discipline, and the exposition of the text a liturgical act.

With the discovery of the logical works of Aristotle in the eleventh century a new form of interpretation was born. This was the *quaestio* (Lat.), the practice of addressing logical and analytical questions to the text: why is this word used rather than some other? Does the author's statement follow from what was said previously in the book? Can one draw a deduction from the statement? What objections can be raised to the argument? This method, which allowed for a theological or philosophical analysis of the text, was particularly helpful in understanding Paul and other NT Letters, but it was less successful on narrative sections of the Bible or on devotional texts such as the Psalms. In time the *quaestiones* supplanted exposition of the text, and they were issued separately. These works, when they were arranged according to doctrinal subjects, came to be called Sentences, theological summaries that laid the foundations for medieval Scholasticism.

A new interest in exegesis as such, as distinct from the theological use of the text, emerged in the twelfth century in Paris at the Abbey of Saint Victor. Hugh of Saint Victor, who came to Paris in 1118, was the first to chart the new course. He objected to allegorical interpretations that ignored the meaning of the "letter." If one despises the "literal sense," said Hugh, one despises the Scriptures. The literal sense did not mean the historical sense, as understood today, but it referred to the meaning that the words have in the context of the text, the construction and syntax, and the metaphors and images. For example, in interpreting Isa. 4:1, "Seven women shall take hold of one man," the interpreter must recognize that the biblical writer is referring to war and depopulation and that in that setting sterility was a woman's worst reproach. Only when this is established can the interpreter move on to a spiritual application.

Hugh's disciples Richard and Andrew continued his work but in different ways. Richard employed the literal sense to construct a grand spiritual edifice, and Andrew turned to contemporary Jewish scholars to aid his understanding of the literal sense. The presence of Jewish exegetes has been a significant factor in shaping Christian interpretation of the Jewish Scriptures (OT). Often Jewish exegesis enters the picture because Jews offered a contrary view, but in other cases Jewish scholars gave access to the Hebrew version of a passage or to additional information about the text. This kind of exchange is evident in the early church in the writings of Origen, Jerome, or Theodoret of Cyrrhus, but it is also evident in the eleventh and twelfth centuries in writers such as Andrew, Rupert of Deutz (1070–1129), and others. Andrew's commentaries, almost unknown until recently, are particularly noteworthy because he was the first to have access to the interpretations of Rashi, the great medieval Jewish commentator. In some cases Andrew was so impressed by Jewish commentators that he was willing to adopt Jewish views even when they undermined traditional Christian teaching (e.g., the interpretation of "young woman" or "virgin" in Isa. 7:14–16). His fellow monk Richard criticized him because he sometimes cited Jewish interpretations without "answering" them with the Christian view.

The work of the Victorines was continued by men such as Herbert of Bosham, Peter Comestor, Stephen Langton, and later Nicholas of Lyra (d. 1349), the most influential medieval commentators. Lyra knew Hebrew but no Greek, and he was familiar with earlier Christian commentaries and with Rashi. For Lyra the literal sense was twofold—at once historical and theological. He recognized the historical character of the biblical text but insisted, for example, that the literal sense of the Psalms referred to Christ. Lyra's *Postillae perpetuae in universam Sanctam Scripturam*, a massive commentary on the entire Bible, became, along with the *Glossa Ordinaria*, the standard commentary in the later Middle Ages. It was the first biblical commentary to be printed after the invention of printing.

THE REFORMATION

It has been customary to set the sixteenth century Reformers off from the medieval exegetes, as though the Reformers were forerunners of the modern historical-critical method. Their exegesis of the Bible, however, moves within more traditional Christian attitudes toward the Scriptures. For them the OT was a Christian book, and the Scriptures as a whole are interpreted in relation to Christian doctrine. Martin Luther, for example, interpreted the plural name of God in Hebrew (*Elohim*) and the phrase "Let us make" in Genesis 1 as patristic and medieval commentators had, to signify the Trinity.

The Reformers, however, did introduce a new range of theological themes, and these profoundly altered the interpretation of the Scriptures. Many were trained as humanists, and this gave them an unusual appreciation for the importance of the biblical languages in exegesis. This was not, of course, unique to them, but it is a noteworthy feature of their work. One of Luther's most lasting accomplishments was the translation of the entire Bible into German from Hebrew and Greek. The great insight that informs the Reformers' exegesis is that the Scriptures speak about faith, hence of repentance and grace and of promise and hope. In Luther's commentaries on both the OT and the NT, these themes spring directly out of the biblical text, without being filtered through the medieval School traditions. Luther's exegesis focused always on the concrete life of the believer, of the church, on the people of God in the course of their pilgrimage in history. For this reason allegory appeared contrived and abstract in contrast to the concrete narrative of biblical history and the deeds of biblical heroes.

Luther's commentaries read like sermons. John Calvin's works, though no less theological, were more pedagogical. He was more attentive to detail, less repetitive, less given to imaginative soarings, and more systematic in developing the theological sense of the text. His humanistic learning was more apparent in the discussion of philological questions. He was unwilling to interpret the plural name of God as evidence of the Trinity. He was bolder than Luther in breaking with the traditional Christological interpretation of the OT. Calvin was always the teacher, explaining difficulties to his readers, noting apparent contradictions in the Scriptures, identifying false ascriptions of citations from the OT, and explaining the use of figures and metaphors.

Scriptural interpretation during the Reformation period profited from the humanistic learning that had swept across Europe. Besides promoting study of the languages of the Bible, Greek and Hebrew, the humanists also were interested in textual criticism, and they made available for the first time texts of classical Christian commentaries. Erasmus of Rotterdam, drawing on the work of the Italian humanist Lorenzo Valla (1406–57), who had compared the Vulgate and the Greek NT, edited the Greek NT (1516) with a new Latin translation. This edition was to have enormous influence in the sixteenth century. It also included extensive notes based on his study of early Christian commentators such as Chrysostom, Origen, Jerome, and Augustine. Another notable figure was Cardinal Cajetan (1469–1534), an opponent of the Reformation and a Thomist (a follower of Thomas Aquinas), whose studies led him to the conclusion that the Vulgate was no substitute for the Hebrew and Greek texts of the Scripture. His views, however, were repudiated at the Council of Trent (A.D. 1545–63), where the Vulgate was recognized as the approved version in the Roman Catholic church.

The centrality of exegesis during the Reformation gave way in the seventeenth century to a renewed interest in dogmatics. A number of commentators, however, who were not closely identified with the confessional traditions (e.g., Hugo Grotius or Jean Le Clerc), adopted a philological approach to the text. Grotius drew an analogy between the use of precedent to interpret the law and the role of tradition to interpret the Scriptures.

By the beginning of the eighteenth century other humanistic disciplines besides philology and grammar began to influence the interpretation of the Bible (e.g., ancient Near Eastern history, geography, archaeology). These new interests are apparent in the writings of scholars such as Richard Simon (1638–1712), Jean Le Clerc (1657–1736), and J. Ernesti (1707–81), to name only a few of the more noteworthy figures. Another important figure from this period was Johannes Bengel (1687–1752), a Pietist whose work in text criticism set a new standard. The Reformers had sought to disengage the Bible from traditional authorities. As philological and historical study gained momentum in the succeeding centuries, this legacy of the Reformation was to have unintended consequences. In their appeal to Scripture over and against tradition, the Reformers had not, of course, dispensed with tradition. The very claim, however, that only Scripture was authoritative (Lat. *sola scriptura*) fostered the idea that the Bible could be interpreted solely in relation to itself—"Scripture interprets Scripture." In time the Bible lost its context within Christian tradition and came to be viewed, paradoxically, as alien to the very tradition that had cherished it.

THE MODERN PERIOD

With the emergence of new historical disciplines in the eighteenth century and the application of these disciplines to the Scriptures, scholars began, unwittingly at first, to construct a new context to take the place of ecclesiastical tradition. The aim was to break free from the patterns that had shaped Christian interpretation for centuries. The Bible came to be seen more and more as belonging to the past. Its context was the ancient world; hence its interpretation was primarily a historical enterprise.

These two factors, the disengagement of the Bible from tradition in the name of an appeal to *sola scriptura* and the rise of historical study, changed the relation of interpreters to the Bible. The more the text was studied historically and philologically, the more the Bible appeared foreign to Christian faith and teaching. As the text was analyzed, compared with other ancient texts, dissected into sources, the more apparent it became that the Scriptures could not be read as an account of God's dealing with humanity in historical events, as had been assumed for centuries. The reliability of the biblical narrative came under question, and its unity as redemptive history began to unravel. The literal sense came to be identified with a historical sense that was distinct from its religious or theological sense.

By the beginning of the nineteenth century historical interpretation came to dominate biblical study, at least among academic interpreters. Interpretation now centered on questions of sources, on authorship, on the relation of the Scripture to other Semitic writings. For Gottfried Eichhorn (1752–1827) the Bible was an oriental book. J. Semler (1725–91) criticized the idea of canon. Canon appeared as a dogmatic and ecclesiastical category that stood in the way of a historical understanding of the NT. The divorce between theology and history reached its culmination in the work of David Friedrich Strauss. His *Life of Jesus*, one of the most celebrated religious works of the nineteenth century, argued that the historical tradition of the Gospels is too fragile to support faith. We must, he wrote, "reestablish dogmatically what has been destroyed critically."

Since the early nineteenth century most biblical scholars have assumed that the only legitimate approach to the Scriptures was historical. Some, however, have insisted (e.g., C. F. Staeudlin early in the nineteenth century) that the Scriptures are not explicable solely on the basis of grammar and history. Theological, moral, and philosophical considerations are appropriate—indeed, necessary.

The questions of modern scholarship, posed

with unprecedented power and clarity during the Enlightenment, are as urgent today as they were two hundred years ago. However necessary a historical interpretation of the Scriptures may be, the Bible is not simply a book from the past. The calm indifference of most Christians, i.e., those who read the Bible for edification and instruction, to a solely historical interpretation bears a message for biblical scholars. As Augustine wrote long ago, "Surely it is only a twisted mind that would maintain that books which have been so scrupulously preserved for thousands of years, which have been safeguarded by such a concern for a well-ordered transmission, that such books were written without serious purpose, or that we should consult them simply for historical facts" (*City of God* 15.20).

Bibliography

Barr, J. *Old and New in Interpretation.* New York: Harper & Row, 1966.

The Cambridge History of the Bible. 3 vols. Cambridge: Cambridge University Press, 1963–70.

Frei, H. *The Eclipse of Biblical Narrative.* New Haven, CT: Yale University Press, 1974.

Grant, R. M., and D. Tracy. *A Short History of the Interpretation of the Bible.* 2d ed. Philadelphia: Fortress, 1984.

Smalley, B. *The Study of the Bible in the Middle Ages.* Notre Dame, IN: University of Notre Dame Press, 1964.

THE BIBLE AND ITS COMMUNITIES

JAMES BARR

We tend to think of the Bible as a known and defined quantity with an unchanging and undifferentiated quality of authority and normativeness. Historically, however, this is not so. The Bible has not always existed, and it was in the communities of ancient Israel and of the early church that it came into existence. The terms that designate it are terms of these communities, and its role as norm and authority has varied in relation to the structures and patterns of religion in these communities.

The books of the OT as we have them today came into being over a very long period, at least a thousand years. Moreover, most books did not come into existence suddenly and completely as they do today when one author writes a book and "publishes" it. Rather, they came into existence gradually—older sources were incorporated, materials were edited, and further additions were made, whether in oral tradition that formed the basis for the text or after the writing down of a text. Thus during what we call "the biblical period" there was as yet no complete "Bible" in existence. Of what we now have, part was not yet in existence and part was in the process of development; and in all probability there were authoritative traditions, oral or written, that were later eliminated, altered, or simply lost, so that we no longer have them.

The NT came into existence during a much shorter time span, hardly over a hundred years, and a larger proportion of the books may be identified as the written product of one author at one point in time. Even then, however, books often refer to earlier traditions; the different Gospels are clearly literarily interdependent; some books and traditions have disappeared; and some works are clearly much later in origin than others. Thus the NT came into its complete form more quickly, but in essence the same relations apply. Any individual Christian community of, say, A.D. 70, or even of A.D. 100, can have had within its purview only a limited part of the written NT as we have it today. Here, once again, the people of the Bible did not possess our Bible.

TERMS DESIGNATING THE BIBLE

Correspondingly, there was in ancient times no one univocal term with exactly the same range of meaning as our word "Bible." The English word "Bible" is emphatically singular: there is only one Bible. But it is derived from the Greek *ta biblia*, "the books," for it was and is a collection of books. There was no such thing as a Bible in the physical form to which we are now accustomed, a single volume with all the books bound together. Not until the invention (in the Christian era) of the codex did such a form become possible, and it was the invention of printing that made a bound volume popular and familiar.

In ancient times the *biblia* were a collection of individual scrolls. This meant that there might be no fixed order to the books except where the contents (as in the Pentateuch or the historical books) made a certain sequence natural. It also made it less easy to define and separate authoritative scrolls from other religious writings, since both kinds might be kept in the same cupboard or storeroom. Jesus in the Nazareth synagogue was given the scroll of Isaiah to read, not a complete Hebrew Bible (Luke 4:17); the Ethiopian of Acts 8:28 was doubtless reading the same. The Qumran people had a sort of religious library, which contained scrolls that are part of our Bible and others that were their own books, unknown to us until recent discovery. A scroll was not necessarily identical with one "book" of our modern Bible; several short books, such as the twelve "Minor" Prophets, might be written on one scroll.

It is not surprising therefore that the term "the Bible" is not strictly a biblical term; the books do not use any such designation of themselves. Neither within the OT nor within the NT do the books make frequent explicit mention of other books of our Bible. There is of course much common matter between one book and another and there may be good reason to detect that one book is interpreting something said in another; but actual explicit mention of other books is rare and in each testament seems to be characteristic of the later portions. Thus Daniel learned "in the books" (Dan. 9:2) the number of years mentioned by Jeremiah. 2 Pet. 3:16 refers to Paul's letters and the difficulty of understanding them. But this kind of express cross-reference is infrequent. In spite of the close relationship between the Gospels, none of them refers to any other by name; Luke (1:1–4) refers to "many" other attempts at such narratives but leaves it vague whether others of our Gospels, or of their sources, are intended.

In fact, surprisingly, where there *is* mention of other books, this is more commonly of books that are *not* within our Bible than of books that are. Thus Kings often refers its readers for further information to "the book of the chronicles of the kings of Judah" (1 Kings 14:29) and the like, which books no longer exist. Paul asks the Colossians to take into account the Laodicean letter, which also is lost (Col. 4:16).

Our term "scripture" comes close to "Bible" when it is commonly understood as a collectivity, i.e., when "Scripture" means the same thing as "the Bible." There is no such expression in the OT, but it is frequent (*graphē*) in the Greek of the NT (and often plural). This word, however, was not then always identical in scope with our "Bible." In itself it meant "something written" and could apply to any piece of writing such as an inscription or a letter (numerous cases in the OT in Gk.); thus *graphē* was not then specialized in the sense of canonical sacred writings as "Scripture" now is in English. For religious purposes, of course, the sacred authoritative written texts were immensely the most important "written things," and these were often cited with the formula "as it is written." The term was not then a definition: it did not specify exactly which texts were included, nor did the use of it prove that the boundaries of what was "Scripture" were exactly defined. Moreover, the word might be used for "a scripture," i.e., an individual sentence or phrase, rather than the total body of holy writings, so that 2 Tim. 3:16 might read "all scripture [the totality] is inspired," but it might also read "every [passage of] scripture is inspired." Conversely, it would be possible for a religious writing to be called *graphē* without according to it the status of being part of the Bible in our sense. Within the Christian Bible the dominant use of "scripture" and of "it is written" is in reference to the OT.

In Jewish usage the main corresponding term in Hebrew is rather *miqra'*—that which is ritually recited; the expression focuses attention on the liturgical recitation of the text rather than on its being written. Another expression is *kitbe ha-qodesh*, "the holy writings." The expression Tenach or Tanach, now commonly used, does not go back to ancient times. It is an acronym formed from the first letters, T-N-K, of the names of the three sections of the Hebrew Bible: Torah (Law), *Nebi'im* (Prophets), and *Ketubim* (Writings). The Jewish Bible, needless to say, does not include the Christian NT. The term "Old Testament" is traditional in Christianity but is now sometimes felt to be tendentious in its implied judgment of Judaism, so that other expressions such as "Hebrew Scriptures" have come to be used.

PRESCRIPTURAL RELIGION

We have seen that in actual biblical times, or the earlier portion of them, religion was not yet governed by a defined Scripture. Faced with a religious problem, people did not turn to a written text, for their religion was not yet organized in that way. Quite possibly some traditions such as some legal ordinances had early been committed to written form, but many other religious traditions were transmitted orally. Neither the prophets nor the earlier kings appealed to any existing "Scripture"; prophetic words were mostly spoken, not written, in the first instance. People were related to God through holy persons and institutions, or they spoke with him verbally and directly; holy books were not considered an authoritative norm.

It was probably the Deuteronomic movement, around the eighth and seventh centuries B.C., that first made something like a "Scripture" central to Israel's religious life. Although various particular "books" (in fact, documents) are mentioned in other sources, Deuteronomy is the first major source for a solid and frequent mention of a basic authoritative "book of the law" in which the main divine commands are concentrated and set down. Especially at the end of the book there is a distinct emphasis on "all the words of this Torah which are written in this book" (Deut. 28:58; cf. 30:10; 31:24, 26). Similarly, it was in 622 B.C. that Josiah heard of the discovery of a "book of the Law" in the Temple, a discovery that greatly alarmed the king and caused him to take drastic steps in the reformation of religion (2 Kings 22–23). In 605 B.C. Jeremiah took a scroll and wrote on it all his past prophecies (Jer. 36); the king cut it up and burned it, but the prophet then rewrote the scroll and added more material for good measure. Deuteronomy states the future role of the law, which is to be preserved in written form and read by the kings so that they may learn obedience to God (Deut. 17:19), and it is also to be read publicly before "all Israel" on solemn occasions (Deut. 31:11). Such solemn public reading is particularly attested in the time of Ezra (Neh. 8); after the Exile (598–538 B.C.) the written Torah becomes paramount in the religious life of the nation, or at least of central currents within it. Thus in its later development Judaism became much more a scriptural religion and in this respect had undergone a substantial change as compared with its earlier pattern.

Christianity went through a similar process. It began without having or seeking to produce Scriptures of its own. Jesus wrote nothing and did not tell his disciples to write anything or even to memorize his words for future commitment to writing. Early Christian faith was spread by oral speech and tradition; there was not even a written account of Jesus' life. Neither Jesus himself nor the earliest Christians after him showed any sign of an intention that their faith should become a scripturally controlled religion as Judaism was by that time. It may have been felt that writing was not appropriate for the profoundest truth: the letter "kills" (2 Cor. 3:6). The living voice of persons who had been with Jesus was thought to be better than any book: this was felt by Papias as late as about A.D. 130. The first written texts were letters, which by their nature had to be written; it is only in 2 Peter, one of the later NT writings, that Christian documents (Pauline Letters) are mentioned in the same category as "Scriptures" (2 Pet. 3:16). In 1 *Clement* (late first century) there are copious citations from both the OT and NT but the terms "scripture" and "it is written" are used only for the former. The "holy writings" that Timothy had known from childhood were perhaps also the OT (2 Tim. 3:15).

THE OLD TESTAMENT IN EARLY CHRISTIANITY

The NT did indeed acknowledge previous Jewish Scripture as the Word of God and authoritative, and in this sense its religion is "scriptural" from the beginning. This makes more complex, but does not essentially alter, what has been said above. The meaning of the NT depends at a host of places upon the assumption that a verbally articulated Word of God was already known and acknowledged. This does not mean, however, that nothing could be said without citing previous written authority. On the contrary, the main starting point lay in the new Christian substance, in Jesus himself and in the events surrounding him, his acts and his teaching. To these events and teachings confirmation or exemplification from past Scripture was often given. But it was by no means necessary that this be done. Jesus' own characteristic teaching was through *parables*, newly created and fictional stories based on experience and imagination, just the opposite of an approach through a scriptural text. Jesus differed from the scribes because he spoke and acted on his own authority and not on the basis of a preexisting authority. Thus the undoubted authority of the OT as Word of God did not alter the fact that for the NT it was no longer the final criterion or the unique starting point; it was not an absolute, but its authority was relative to the supreme position of Jesus. Even where Scripture is taken as "inspired by God" (2 Tim. 3:16), it is said only to be "useful" or "profitable" for moral training and not the final arbiter of faith. Thus within early Christianity, in spite of the recognition of older Scripture as Word of God and fully authoritative, the total structure of authority was different, and Scripture fitted within a new pattern of relations.

COMMUNITY AND LITERARY PRODUCTION

Many biblical books must be regarded as a community product; they emerged from a process of tradition within the community. The community guarded this tradition, respected it, but also remolded it; it might allow it to be amalgamated with other traditions, to be modernized to fit newer conditions, or to be amplified with additional comments or rewritten in a newer form. But the community did not regard the works as simply the expression of its own sense of itself; it cherished them as works of leadership and authority that directed the community in a certain direction. This position of authority can be seen in different features such as the extreme importance of events narrated (creation, Exodus, resurrection), the presence of what was understood to be direct divine speech, the distinction of persons associated with books (Moses, Solomon, the early disciples), the normative force of their legal portions, their use as liturgical material, their role as historical memoirs, their ethical edificatory function, and their general educational use. Many books directed themselves in a critical (warning or reforming) manner to the community. In some books much importance attaches to a final editor or creative writer who brought various traditions together into a total work with its own viewpoint (Gen., Matt.). There is thus an interaction between community and literary production in which traditions are molded to guide the community in a certain way, although they may conflict with other traditions (cf. Jeremiah and Ezekiel; Paul and James; Matthew and Luke) and the community may receive these traditions with respect but with varying degrees of submission, acceptance, evasion, revision, and modification (e.g., the degree of implementation of Deuteronomy; the reaction in 2 Peter to delay of the end of the world).

CONTINUATION AND FINALIZATION

The transmission of sacred texts underwent two contrary impulses. One of these led toward the continuation of the process of composition: a good work could be continued, amplified, modernized. Explanatory glosses might be added. In major cases, a thorough rewriting might be undertaken. On the other side there was a force that favored finalization. A work had reached a stage at which no further change was desirable; it should henceforth be preserved as it was.

In the late stages of the development of Scripture, both these impulses can be seen at work. Books could be largely rewritten; their very excellence might encourage this. There is evidence that Jeremiah came out in two editions. On a larger scale, Chronicles was mainly a rewrite of Samuel/Kings, and *Jubilees* of Genesis. New works like Judith and Tobit carried forward the style of tales like Esther, and the Testament literature (best seen in the *Testaments of the Twelve Patriarchs*) expanded and recombined various biblical genres. Later Gospels (Matthew and Luke) carried forward the lines of earlier ones. The disciples of prophets amplified and altered the balance of the sayings of their masters; fragments of an apostolic letter might be similarly amplified and recombined. The impulse to continuation promoted the survival and the continued productivity of the biblical genres.

Finalization worked the other way. The text should be left alone. Existing words should be left as they are; new productions along the same lines should be discouraged. The very words of the text had come from God or from some source of unimpeachable antiquity and should on no account be modified. What was obscure should be elucidated by interpretation rather than improved by rewriting.

These forces were decisive in the formation of what was later to be known as the canon, understood as a collection of authoritative writings, and in the fixation of the text. Continuation meant that new books would be produced; finalization meant that they would not be encouraged and if produced would not be accepted. The same principles could apply to the actual text. Change a few words, add a word here and there, and it becomes a different book—so it could be argued—and all the more so where it was felt that religious and ethical decisions depended on the precise wording of the text. Deut. 4:2, which specifies that nothing is to be added to God's command or taken away from it, doubtless in the first instance meant that no substantial matter should be added to the ethical norms or subtracted from them; but the same principle could easily be extended to mean that the book that contained this command was the final version of it and, beyond that, that the actual wording of its text must be preserved.

These contrasting tendencies were expressed also on the level of interpretation. To rewrite a book entirely, adding new matter or altering its focus, can be called a kind of interpretation, but it is more like a restatement of the substance along literary lines similar to the original. The fixation of book and text encourages a different mode of interpretation: the exact form and wording of a text become data against which interpretation is set. Interpretation may then begin to look less at the general literary structure and more at each individual segment, which may thus be decontextualized; any portion of text, however tiny, may become decisive for the proof of law or doctrine. This tendency is supported by the idea that God is author not only of the books taken as wholes but of every small detail within them; since there is no redundancy, every detail is authoritative.

THE PRIMACY OF THE TORAH

Care should be used in talking about a Jewish "canon," since the concept is a Christian one and there seems to be no Jewish term for it. The central step was the elevation of the Torah, by now a virtually complete block of five books understood to be the Torah of Moses, to a position of religious primacy, a move traditionally associated with Ezra and belonging to the early postexilic community (sixth to fourth centuries B.C.). Other materials, later to form part of Hebrew Scripture, certainly already existed: much of the historical books from Joshua to Kings, the earlier portions of the Prophets, most of the Psalms, and doubtless much of Proverbs. This other body of material had long been recognized but did not yet have the same unity and finality as the Torah had: materials were still being added to the prophetic books until much later. Eventually the historical books and the books named after prophets came to be classified together and known as "the Prophets" (the division into "Former" and "Latter" Prophets is medieval). This classification, which eventually became neat and exact, may at first have been imprecise and fluid. The case of the Torah is clear, because it clearly formed a single block and had supreme religious authority. But some literature that later was classified as within the "Writings" could earlier have belonged to the same grouping as our "Prophets." This would fit the situation in early Christianity, where there is no clear sign of knowledge of the tripartite canon of Judaism and where the common term for older Scriptures is "the Law and the Prophets" (once, Luke 24:44, "the law of Moses and the prophets and Psalms"). Not all groups of Jews need have followed or accepted the same priorities, but the primacy of the Torah marked the dominant trend. It is possible that some laid just as heavy an emphasis on the prophetic books.

The Samaritans, like the Jews, had a Hebrew Bible, but it included only the Torah; their traditions showed influences from the historical books, but only the Torah had status as Scripture. This may be because the elevation of the Torah to primacy was extended by them to the point where no other Scripture existed at all. The Sadducees are said not to have accepted as binding any doctrines that could not be proved from the Torah alone. The Qumran community revered the biblical books (though no portions of Esther as yet have been found), but alongside them they had many other works, including the sacred rule of their own society; it is hard to think that such a document did not have authoritative status among them. Perhaps their writing of commentaries on biblical books is a sign that these were in a special category. Commentaries on the prophetic books such as Habakkuk and Nahum are prominent: in these books they found predictions about their own sect and its experience.

PALESTINIAN CANON GROUPINGS

The tripartite listing that finally emerged as "standard" for the Hebrew Bible contained the Torah as first part, the historical books from Joshua through Kings along with the four main prophetic "books" (Isaiah, Jeremiah, Ezekiel, and the twelve "Minor" Prophets) as the second part ("the Prophets"), while the third part, the "Writings," contained Psalms, Job, Proverbs, the five smaller Scrolls or Megilloth (Ruth, Song of Songs, Ecclesiastes, Lamentations, Esther), Daniel, Ezra, Nehemiah, and Chronicles. There are variations in order within the third group but the division between the three major groups has always been the same.

The completion and fixation of this canon is often ascribed to the "Synod of Jamnia," a series of rabbinic discussions held late in the first century A.D., in which it was sometimes discussed whether certain books like Ecclesiastes had full scriptural status. It is now considered doubtful whether these discussions dealt with the fixing of a canon at all, and some think that the canon now standard was achieved back in Maccabean times (second or first century B.C.). But even if the standard canon existed as a list, that does not mean that everyone knew of it or took it as binding. Josephus (first century A.D.) lists twenty-two books: five by Moses, then thirteen from Moses to Artaxerxes written by the prophets, and four containing hymns and ethical precepts. The number twenty-two is significant as being the number of letters in the Hebrew alphabet. Josephus' list may well correspond with the to-

tal contents of the standard canon (if we take Ruth with Judges, Lamentations with Jeremiah, etc.) but clearly cuts across the tripartite division of it. 4 Ezra 14:37–48 tells how ninety-four books were written, twenty-four for the general public to read and the other seventy only for the special class of the wise; these seventy would represent the apocalyptic books. As between these various views we have no real knowledge of controversies or of means by which they were settled or of mechanisms through which decisions about a canon could be reached or enforced. This fits with the absence of a term for "canon" that would have been used in such discussions. It is probable that the fading away of certain communities and the destructive effects of war eliminated alternatives and left one strongly represented opinion in control.

THE SEPTUAGINT

Greek-speaking Jews, especially in Egypt, had a translation, made from the third century B.C. onwards; it was called Septuagint (LXX) from the tale that seventy translators were engaged in the work. The books in Greek eventually included not only all that is now in the Hebrew Bible but a number of other books and longer texts of some (e.g., the Additions to Daniel, etc.). Some of these were translated from Hebrew or Aramaic and others were original writings in Greek but in biblical style. It is disputed whether all these materials counted as the Bible of Alexandrian Judaism; perhaps, as elsewhere, the question is a meaningless one. The Alexandrian interpreter Philo commented on the Pentateuch in detail but quoted other books little. The mere act of translation into another language meant that the exact verbal form of the original could not be preserved; but the legend of the (almost miraculously assisted) translation seemed to argue that the translation was as divinely inspired as the original had been and therefore fully authoritative. This was significant for Christianity, where the exact verbal form of the LXX was at times used for proof of doctrine even when it differed from the Hebrew. The LXX often differed in sense from the Hebrew (Masoretic) text, because it was made from a different text or an earlier edition, or misread the Hebrew, or through its translation technique. Both before and after the origin of Christianity steps were taken to revise the Greek and bring it closer to the Hebrew as it was now accepted; finally Jewish preference passed to these newer versions and back to the use of the Hebrew itself. The LXX was thus transmitted to us through Christian channels as the OT of the Greek church, and its books were those that were canonical in that church. Thus most, though not necessarily all, of Hebrew Scripture was already in Greek translation when Christianity began, and so were some books later considered apocryphal. The NT commonly cites the wording of the LXX but sometimes follows other versions.

THE HEBREW TEXT

During the first three or four centuries A.D. the Hebrew Bible was transmitted in a very narrow tradition of text. It was later provided with points, or vowel signs, and accents by Jewish scholars known as Masoretes (from the Hebrew word for tradition) and is therefore known as the Masoretic Text (MT). Within it variants of substance are very few. But much evidence suggests that in earlier times considerable variation in the Hebrew text existed. Numerous LXX renderings, at least in some books, came from a different Hebrew original, and are often supported by Qumran fragments or by the Samaritan Hebrew. One major Isaiah scroll from Qumran shows wide divergence in writing and spelling style from the Masoretic, while another approximates it more closely. And differences are not only in scribal minutiae. For instance, the chronological data of Genesis and Exodus differ substantially in the LXX, the Samaritan Pentateuch, and the MT, which suggests that these figures were being adjusted to different chronological systems up to a quite late date. Much of the variety within the Jewish transmission was probably obliterated in the wars with Rome. The ancestor of the MT was most likely not chosen through deliberate textual evaluation but through the choice of this or that manuscript as authoritative. Only gradually did the principle come to prevail that texts must be copied with the fullest precision in every detail, and absolute precision was never in fact attained. But the existence of a highly uniform text, variant-free in substance, favored the development of a very precise verbally related interpretation, in which every detail had potential religious import.

TARGUMS

For many Jews Aramaic rather than Hebrew was the major vernacular, and translations of biblical books into Aramaic, known as Targums, were important. Just when the main existing Targums originated is uncertain, but rules for the reading of them are already present in the Mishnah (a collection of legal material from the first two centuries A.D.). In general, the Targums are less important than the LXX as evidence for the biblical text, more

important as evidence for religious interpretation and supplementation with additional matter. In the end they functioned mainly not independently but as a supplementary text to the Hebrew.

THE LATIN BIBLE AND THE APOCRYPHA

Though chronologically later, this topic can be conveniently mentioned here. The older Latin Bible of the Western church was in its OT translated from the Greek and not directly from the Hebrew. Jerome's new version (around A.D. 400) went back to the Hebrew, and his thinking insisted on the "Hebrew truth" as basis for Christian use of the Bible. But this in turn involved the observation that a number of books already within the church's Bible were not within the Hebrew Bible. Jerome argued that only the books of the latter should be accepted; the rest should count as "apocrypha." Thus the "Apocrypha," as the term is generally used, are those books and portions of books that were within the older Christian OT but not within the Hebrew Bible, at least as the latter now, by the "standard" canon, was. Jerome's opinions on this matter were received with doubt, the books in question remained authoritative, and it was during the Reformation that his views bore fruit and Protestant Bibles mostly followed the Hebrew in the extent of their OT canon.

INTERPRETATIVE PATTERNS

The modes in which Scripture was interpreted, and the other authorities existing alongside of Scripture, influenced the conception that was held of scripture itself. In Judaism varying traditions prevailed. In Egypt Philo accepted Greek philosophy as the basic interpretative pattern: the texts were allegorically understood; textual details pointed to eternal verities. A sectarian community like Qumran took as key the principle that everything in Scripture concerned that same community; close verse-by-verse commentaries were written. The main current in Judaism emphasized the tradition handed down by the rabbis; this led to a two-source structure, with written Torah and oral law complementing one another. The oral law, originally passed on in unwritten tradition, was later gathered in written form in the Mishnah and further elaborated in the Talmud. Running interpretation of Scripture took the form of midrash, in which words, verses, and details were interrelated with similar features from elsewhere and embellished with story material; some of this overlapped with the Targums. In worship the entire Torah is read in sequence, selections only from the Prophets; the five Megilloth and some Psalms are also important. The oral law, when it quotes Scripture, quotes overwhelmingly the Torah; midrash is directed especially to the Torah and the Megilloth. Thus the tripartite canon has partial, but only partial, correspondence with degrees of importance in ritual use. The question of supremacy as between the Torah and the oral law is not a real one: the Torah is true, the rabbinic tradition is also true, and the question of canonical gradation between them does not arise.

NEW TESTAMENT USE OF ANCIENT SCRIPTURE

We have seen that Christianity from the beginning accepted Jewish Scriptures as the Word of God and authoritative; it is inexact however to say that they thus accepted "the Old Testament," first, because that expression was not yet so used (the Gk. word *diathēkē* means either a will or the covenant linking God and people; possible exception only at 2 Cor. 3:14, and if so an innovation there) and, second, because we cannot be sure that the books recognized were identical with any one "Old Testament" of today. Some books like Ecclesiastes, Esther, and Song of Songs are scarcely cited or used; some others like Wisdom are clearly influential (e.g., on ideas about Adam, creation, and sin); yet others like *Enoch* are actually quoted as authoritative prophetic works (Jude 14–15). To stress the precise boundaries of the canon is thus to force upon the NT an emphasis that it simply did not have. Nowhere does it show any interest in discussing or disputing the limits of anyone's canon, even where this could have been relevant (e.g., disputes with the Samaritans or the Sadducees).

The approach to past Scripture is not at all systematic; passages are used where they serve a purpose, many others are left unmentioned. There are few sequential commentaries or verse-by-verse expositions. Some have thought that books of scriptural "testimonies" existed and guided the choice of passages to be cited. Certainly Scripture is used very selectively, with a great preference for certain traditions such as those of Abraham and David and for the prophetic books, especially Isaiah and Daniel; a very large proportion of all express citations come from Isaiah and the Psalms taken together. The emphasis is "Christological," in that passages were seen as converging on the fulfillment of promise through Jesus and the church. As at Qumran, the present situation of the community was a key to the sense of Scripture: it was written "for us" (cf. 1 Pet. 1:12; 1 Cor. 9:10). The emphasis lies more on the realization of messianic prophecy than on the law. The importance of apocalyptic makes it all the more natural that *Enoch* was accepted as divinely given prophecy.

Although the Mosaic Law remained sacred, a change of emphasis took place. Jesus emphasized the "weightier matters of the law" as against minutiae of observance (Matt. 23:23). Reinterpretation of the law within the new Christian context encouraged allegorical understandings (e.g., Gal. 4:24; 1 Cor. 9:9–10), which were linked with typology (Adam and Christ, Elijah and John the Baptist) and became much more widespread as OT passages were more systematically explored. On the other side Jesus emphasizes Scripture itself as against the tradition of interpretation which contradicted it. Scripture was thus reaffirmed but the balance of its parts and the mode of interpretation were shifted to a different plane.

Another factor was the conception that the Holy Spirit had once again been shed forth. It was a common Jewish concept that the Spirit had departed from Israel after exilic times, when prophecy ceased. Now in the church the Spirit had again been shed forth. This could favor the discernment of "spiritual" meanings; it could act against bondage to a written text; and it could lead to productivity in "prophetic" utterances, some of which eventually appeared as books (Rev.).

NEW TESTAMENT BOOKS AND CANONS

Various factors favored the crystallization of the Christian traditions in a final written form. The practice of reading in church the letters of an apostle; the analogy of the OT read as Scripture; the special importance for Christian faith of the *original witnesses* of events and the danger that tradition might become distorted and facts forgotten; the rapid expansion into the gentile world, which made oral tradition, rooted in Jewish Palestine, more difficult to maintain—all these may have contributed. The sayings of Jesus himself were particularly cherished. Once the Gospels came into existence they quickly became central in church life and were liturgically emphasized. Their existence and their centrality in turn probably meant that most oral tradition about Jesus died away fairly soon.

Each Gospel may at first have had an attachment to a particular community; but the grouping of the four is explicit and is regarded as necessary in the writing of the early church leader Irenaeus (about A.D. 180). There are signs that, of the four, John suffered most questioning; it is little quoted in early sources and may have been regarded as favoring Gnosticism; when it was later seen that it could be used against that movement, it achieved acceptance. Mark, though doubtless the earliest, tended to drop into the background in comparison with the "fuller" three. The idea of combining the four into one narrative was tried out in Tatian's *Diatessaron* (also later second century), which was widely popular, especially in Syria, but the four-Gospel canon remained official in the main churches.

The Pauline letters seem to have been collected and some letters amplified or rewritten by Pauline disciples. They circulated in a collection of ten, later perhaps supplemented by the three "pastoral" Letters to Timothy and Titus. Hebrews was disputed until a late time, and of the catholic or general letters 1 Peter and 1 John had widest acceptance, James was more marginal, and the others were never widely used and were long omitted in certain areas. Revelation, if early popular, was also long opposed, its authorship disputed, and its standing damaged by reaction against millenarian movements in early Christianity. Conversely, various early Christian writings that in the end were not canonical were in the early years treated by some as on the same level with books now canonical, e.g., *1 Clement* or the *Shepherd of Hermas*, and some famous Bible manuscripts contain one or the other of these.

Thus the *core* of the NT canon was agreed upon quite early, but complete agreement in all aspects was only slowly reached, and indeed was never completely reached in all sections of the church. The arguments by which canonicity was determined are somewhat better known than in the case of the OT. Basically it came down to the authority of the opinion of respected senior persons in the churches. Authorship was naturally a consideration, but the question of who was the actual author was itself a matter of opinion; several rejected books bore the name of Peter. Theological content was also a consideration, but again the question whether a book accorded with the church's faith was a matter for the estimation of authoritative persons.

Two conflicts with heresy probably stimulated the creation of a fixed canon. Marcion separated Christianity sharply from its Hebraic past and formed a strictly limited canon of Pauline Letters plus the Gospel of Luke, all modified to remove Jewish elements. The Gnostics, conversely, produced numerous Gospels, apocalypses, and other works expounding their doctrines, often under the names of apostles like Peter or Thomas. Books of this sort are sometimes classified together as "New Testament Apocrypha," but they are unlike the standard OT Apocrypha in that they never formed part of the canon of the great churches.

With the completion and fixation of NT Scripture Christianity had come closer to joining Judaism in the category of scriptural religions. The "Old" and "New" Testaments had a definite shape. Yet it would be wrong to suppose that these written documents were paramount over all other instances of authority, for alongside them there stood the authority of the rule of faith and that of the bishops. The rule of faith crystallized in the creeds and, though the existing creeds may be later than the formation of the New Testament, in principle creed precedes Scripture, for it expresses the central affirmations of faith out of which Scripture arose and that therefore rightly interpret it. Thus early Christianity was never really a fully scriptural religion. It had a Scripture, the Word of God, but that stood in a complex relationship with other authorities. The idea that Scripture was entirely paramount over all other authorities comes more from the Reformation than from the NT. → Biblical Criticism.

Bibliography

Anderson, B. W. "Tradition and Scripture in the Community of Faith." *Journal of Biblical Literature* 100 (1981): 5–21.

Barr, J. *Explorations in Theology 7*. London: SCM, 1980.

_____. *Holy Scripture: Canon, Authority, Criticism*. Philadelphia: Westminster, 1983.

Sanders, J. A. *Torah and Canon*. Philadelphia: Fortress, 1972.

Von Campenhausen, H. *The Formation of the Christian Bible*. Philadelphia: Fortress, 1972.

PART ONE

THE BIBLICAL STORY: GENESIS–ESTHER

INTRODUCTION TO THE BIBLICAL STORY: GENESIS–ESTHER

DAVID J. A. CLINES

Traditionally, the Hebrew Bible has been divided into three sections: the Law (Torah), the Prophets, and the Writings. From a logical point of view, however, this division leaves something to be desired; for example, placing the collection of historical books (Joshua to 2 Kings) together with the prophetic books proper (Isaiah to Malachi) under the one heading, Prophets, is hard to justify. And there is not a lot of sense in placing Ruth among the Writings when its setting in time makes it an obvious appendage to the book of Judges or in including Daniel among the Writings rather than among the Prophets.

For the purposes of this volume, the OT has been divided into three somewhat different groupings of books: the Biblical Story (Genesis to Esther), Psalms and Wisdom (Job to Song of Songs), and the Prophetic Books (Isaiah to Malachi). This is the order to be found in most Christian editions of the Bible (though in Roman Catholic Bibles, Esther does not follow Nehemiah directly).

THE STORY IN ITS PRESENT FORM

The books Genesis to Esther are the narrative books of the OT. Together they contain two distinct story sequences, which are alike in many ways but which also show surprising and important differences. The first narrative sequence, which may be called the Primary History, runs from Genesis to 2 Kings, and the second, the Secondary History, from 1 Chronicles to Esther. Each sequence begins with the creation and recounts some of the history of the Hebrew people. But they conclude at very different points in the history: the Primary History concludes with the end of the Judean kingdom at the fall of Jerusalem in 587 B.C., and the Secondary History finishes in the fifth century B.C. with the installation of a Jewish prime minister, Mordecai, in the Persian government with consequent favorable treatment of the Jews throughout the Persian Empire.

The different points of conclusion are not the only sign that the two histories have fundamentally different outlooks on the past. For whereas the Primary History consistently stresses elements of decline, disaster, and failure in the national history, the Secondary History emphasizes positive aspects. The two histories thus represent alterna-

Previous page: Head of Moses; detail of a mosaic of Moses receiving the tablets of the law; from the Monastery of St. Catherine, Sinai, sixth century A.D.

tive ways of recounting the past, and in being juxtaposed within the Hebrew Scriptures—without any explanation of why both histories exist—they invite readers of the biblical text to make their own assessment of their significance. In this way readers are compelled to reexamine their own notions of what constitutes success or failure, blessing or curse, promise and fulfillment—which is to say, to reflect theologically in a creative way.

The Primary History (Genesis–2 Kings)

The Primary History contains the following twelve books: Genesis, Exodus, Leviticus, Numbers, Deuteronomy, Joshua, Judges, Ruth, 1 Samuel, 2 Samuel, 1 Kings, and 2 Kings.

Within the Primary History there are some obvious major divisions corresponding to significant phases in the national life. The death of Moses, who has been the key human figure in the narrative from Exodus to Deuteronomy, is clearly a crucial event, occurring as it does on the eve of the Israelite entry into the Promised Land. The opening of the book of Joshua, "After the death of Moses ... ," signals that transition and provides a model for other major transitions in the history. Thus Judges begins "After the death of Joshua," 2 Samuel "After the death of Saul," 2 Kings "After the death of Ahab" (though in this case the transition seems much less significant); 1 Kings begins just before the death of David. The Primary History is thus arranged around the lifetimes of important individuals: the patriarchs (Genesis), Moses (Exodus to Deuteronomy), Joshua (Joshua), the judges (Judges), Samuel and Saul (1 Samuel), David (2 Samuel), Solomon, Elijah, Ahab (1 Kings), and the other kings (2 Kings).

The narrative of the Primary History may be described as one of fair beginnings and foul endings. The first of those beginnings is the promise in Genesis 12 to Abraham that his descendants—the Israelite people—will be vastly numerous, that they will inhabit a land of their own, that they will be the object of divine blessing, and that they will be a blessing to other nations. But by the end of 2 Kings these promises are shown not to have been ultimately attained, even though there have been signals of their potential success along the way. By the end of the narrative sequence, ten of the twelve tribes of Israel have long ago been lost to view in Assyrian captivity, and the remainder have just now been submerged in Babylonian exile, Judah has been "taken into exile out of its land" (2 Kings 25:21), it has "come to the point" that Yahweh has "cast them [Jerusalem and Judah] out of his presence" (24:20), and the nations have experienced from Israel no blessing but either military domination (when Israel ruled an empire) or else insubordination (when Israel formed part of the Assyrian or Babylonian empires).

Fair beginnings are also announced by the various styles of leadership Israel experiences in the Primary History. Every type of leader—warrior, judge, king, and prophet—though represented as Yahweh's gift to the nation, proves disastrous or at least ineffectual. Moses the warrior-leader of the people can guide them to the Promised Land but not into it because of a personal failing; he can bring them divine law, but he cannot prevent the curses of Deuteronomy 28 falling upon them if they fail to be obedient. Joshua the warrior, whom no one is supposed to be able to withstand in his fight for territory for his people (Josh. 1:5) and whose function is to gain the land of Canaan as a possession for the Hebrews (1:6, 15), is at the end of his days still stiffening the resolve of his countrymen against "the nations that remain" (23:4) and urging them to remain loyal to the worship of Yahweh rather than "the gods of the Amorites *in whose land* you dwell" (24:15). The land is still the Amorites'!

The history of the judges, who are "raised up" by God (Judg. 2:16), is likewise a story of decline, from the first and unexceptionable judge Othniel, upon whom the spirit of Yahweh comes and who thereupon can overcome an oppressive "king of Mesopotamia" (3:10), to Samson. Samson, whom also the spirit of Yahweh "stirs" (13:25), but who—unlike other judges—cannot bring "rest" to his nation, cannot control the Philistine threat any more than he can control his own appetites, and he must suffer the indignity of having his era denoted "the days of the Philistines" (15:20). And if it is Samuel rather than Samson who is to be regarded as the last of the judges, even he fails conspicuously to fulfill his boyhood promise as purveyor of the word of Yahweh (1 Sam. 3), appointing his unscrupulous sons as his successors to the judgeship (8:1–3) and resisting the evident intention of Yahweh to institute a monarchy (e.g., 8:22).

The monarchy as an institution holds out great promise, but it too very soon proves its potential for disaster. The first king, Saul, chosen by divinely directed lot (1 Sam. 10:20–24), is very soon "rejected . . . from being king over Israel" (15:26), Yahweh having "repented" that he has made Saul king (15:11). The most esteemed of Israel's kings, David, is condemned out of his own mouth, sinning against Yahweh in the matter of Bathsheba and Uriah (2 Sam. 12:13) and in the numbering of the people (24:10). Though he is promised that his line will rule over Israel "for ever" (7:13, 16), he is also threatened with a prophecy that his dynasty will "never" be free from feuds and attacks (12:10). His son Solomon, who begins his reign by "loving" Yahweh (1 Kings 3:3) and building him a temple (1 Kings 6–7), in the end proves to be "not wholly true to the LORD his God" (11:4) and is told that Yahweh will "surely tear the kingdom from [him]" (11:11). In consequence, Solomon's son Rehoboam loses the allegiance of all the tribes except Judah (12:19–20), and Jeroboam, his northern rival, institutes unlicensed sanctuaries, which become "a sin to the house of Jeroboam, so as to cut it off and to destroy it from the face of the earth" (13:34). In the Northern Kingdom, the kings regularly follow the example of Jeroboam and lead their people into sin; Omri, for example, "walked in all the way of Jeroboam the son of Nebat, and in the sins which he made Israel to sin, provoking the LORD, the God of Israel, to anger" (16:26). In the Southern Kingdom, two kings are wholeheartedly approved of by Yahweh: Hezekiah (2 Kings 18:6), who nevertheless is the first to hear of the forthcoming exile to Babylon (20:16–19), and Josiah (22:2; 23:25), who nevertheless is killed in battle (23:29–30) despite a prophecy that he will be "gathered to [his] grave in peace" (22:20). Several others receive qualified praise, but of six of the last seven kings of Judah it is uniformly reported that they "did what was evil in the sight of the LORD" (e.g., 21:2).

The other institution of leadership in Israel is that of the prophets. They appear at various times in the course of the narrative from Moses (Deut. 34:10), who functions both as Yahweh's mouthpiece and as an intercessor for the people, through anonymous prophets in the period of the judges (Judg. 6:8–10; cf. 2:1–3; 10:11–14), bands of prophets in the time of Samuel (1 Sam. 10:5), and schools of "the sons of the prophets" in the time of Elisha, to the famous individual prophets Samuel, Nathan, Elijah, and Elisha. As a channel of communication between the divine and the human, the prophets hold greater promise than any of the other leaders, but nonetheless they are remarkably ineffectual: quite apart from the more trivial tasks of divination prophets were called upon to perform (like finding lost animals, 1 Sam. 9), their success in influencing national history is minimal. Disobedience to Yahweh's word as delivered by a prophet is very early on recognized as a fatal crime for a king: Saul is "rejected" from being king because he has rejected the "word" of Yahweh through Samuel (1 Sam. 15:23). Elsewhere, on the whole, the prophetic word does no more than announce a doom-laden future that is not open to adjustment (e.g., Ahijah's prophecy in 1 Kings 14:7–11) but that merely wakens echoes of the original prophecy as it comes to pass (cf. 15:29; also 2 Kings 9:25–26, 36; 10:10, 17). In the large stretch of the narrative given over to the activity of the prophets Elijah and Elisha (1 Kings 17–2 Kings 10) there is indeed an outstandingly successful confrontation between the prophet of Yahweh and those prophets of Baal that are supported by the royal court (1 Kings 18); nevertheless, it is not the prophet Elijah but the king Jehu who most decisively defends the worship of Yahweh when he "wipe[s] out Baal from Israel" (10:28), which is to say, from the nation as a whole. Prophets are indeed found designating future kings by anointing (1 Sam. 10:1; 2 Kings 9:1–10), but prophets do not make kings; it needs popular acclamation (1 Sam. 10:24–11:15) or a coup d'état (2 Kings 9:11–37) to achieve real political ends.

The direction of the Primary History, towards national decline and the negation of national hopes entertained at the beginning of the story, was, now that we come to recognize it, already foreshadowed by the opening chapters of Genesis. In Genesis 1–11, the primeval history, fair beginnings for the human race—before ever the scope of the narrative is narrowed down to the Abrahamic family—are very soon tarnished by human perversity. The primal couple is expelled from the Garden in no time at all (3:23), the first brother becomes the first murderer (4:8), the multiplication of humankind is accompanied by a corresponding increase in human wickedness (6:1, 5), and at Babel the first cooperative endeavor in human history leads immediately to a permanent "scattering" of the race across the face of the earth (11:9). Against that background it is perhaps not surprising that the focus on the Abrahamic family from Genesis 12 onward should reveal not some undoing of the primeval tragedy, but a long drawn out replay of it. There is not a lot of difference between Genesis 6:5–7 and 2 Kings 17:18–23: when God sees that humankind's thoughts are "only evil continually," he is sorry that he created them and determines to "blot" them out from the face of the ground by a great flood. Things are not very different when the Israelite people over many generations do "wicked things, provoking the LORD to anger" (2 Kings 17:11), and he "removes" or "casts" them "out of his sight" (17:18, 20, 23). The greatest difference between the primeval history and the rest of the Primary History is that in Genesis 1–11 every episode of human sin followed by divine punishment contains a further element of mitigation of the punishment; Adam and Eve, for example, though expelled from the Garden, do not actually die in the day they eat of the fruit, and Cain, though driven out from the tillable earth to be a fugitive, carries a divine mark of protection against any who might seek to slay him. In the remainder of the history as a whole, however, there is no mitigation, either realized or envisaged, of the fate of the Israelite people.

Or is there? Some have thought that the concluding paragraph of 2 Kings (25:27–30), recounting the release from prison in Babylon of the ex-king Jehoiachin of Judah, injects a note of hope on the very last page of the history, hinting perhaps that Jehoiachin's good fortune may one day be that of the people as a whole. It is true that Jehoiachin is given a royal pension and dines at the Babylonian king's table, at "a seat above the seats of the kings who were with him in Babylon" (25:28). But it is also true that Jehoiachin has spent thirty-seven years in prison in Babylon (twice the time he had lived in Judah; cf. 24:8), that he is still effectively a prisoner in the Babylonian court, that his pension is humiliatingly paid to him on a daily basis, and that at the time of writing Jehoiachin is already dead (25:30: "a regular allowance was given him by the king . . . as long as he lived"). None of this augurs well for the Jewish people, nor can this admittedly undisastrous conclusion reverse the downhill direction in which the whole of the Primary History has been moving.

The Secondary History (1 Chronicles–Esther)

The Secondary History begins with the creation, as does the Primary History, but it carries the story of the Israelite people much further, beyond the Exile to the Persian period of the fifth century B.C. This Secondary History consists of 1 Chronicles, 2 Chronicles, Ezra, Nehemiah, and Esther.

By comparison with the Primary History, the Secondary History is remarkable for its omission of any narrative for the period from the creation down to the death of Saul (1 Chron. 10)—genealogies fill the narrative gap—and for its exclusion of the history of the Northern Kingdom. Clearly the first crucial event in this history is not the Exodus or conquest of Canaan, but the reign of David and the establishment of his dynasty. In this history, David does not first rule over Judah and then extend his power over the northern tribes (cf. 2 Sam. 5:5); he is made king by "all Israel" from the beginning (1 Chron. 11:1).

The importance of David in the Secondary History is that he is represented as the institutor of the Israelite system of worship, especially of the Temple, which is his idea and which he instructs his son Solomon to build (1 Chron. 17; 22). The Levites also, who actually perform the worship of the Temple, are appointed by David (1 Chron. 23–26). Nothing is said of David's misdemeanors, and even the narrative of his exploits as a warrior seems to be included only by way of introduction to the story of his bringing the Ark as the focus of the worship of Yahweh to Jerusalem (1 Chron. 13).

The section of the history devoted to Solomon likewise has as its theme Solomon as the builder of the Temple (2 Chron. 1–9). Here too any negative aspects of the king's personality are passed over (cf. 1 Kings 2:1–3:1). Indeed, later kings of Judah are not depicted as uniformly righteous, but special emphasis is given to those who effect religious reforms or repair the Temple: Asa (2 Chron. 15), Jehoshaphat (19:4–11), Joash (24:4–14), Hezekiah (29:3–31:23), and Josiah (34:1–35:19). The history of the monarchy thus seems to be primarily a history of the establishment and maintenance of the worship of God; the function of kings is primarily to promote correct and lavish worship, and the function of the people is to provide the necessary funds and personnel for the Temple services.

In the postexilic section of the Secondary History in Ezra and Nehemiah the same interest is very evident. The return from exile in Babylonia is authorized by the Persian king Cyrus specifically to rebuild the Jerusalem Temple (Ezra 1:2), and the first action of the returned exiles is to rebuild the Temple altar "in its place" (3:3) and to reinstitute sacrifices there, even before the Temple itself has been rebuilt. The first major climax of these books is the completion of the Temple building "by command of the God of Israel and by decree of Cyrus and Darius and Artaxerxes king of Persia" (6:14) and the celebration of the traditional festivals (6:19–22). Other important moments in the narrative are the elimination of foreigners from the worshiping community (Ezra 10), the securing of the city and its people by the enclosure of a wall (Neh. 3–4; 12:27–43), instruction in the law of Yahweh (chap. 8), and cultic reforms (chap. 13). Nehemiah's closing words are in the closest harmony with the history's primary interest: "I established the duties of the priests and Levites, each in his work; and I provided for the wood offering, at appointed times, and for the first fruits" (13:30–31). And Nehemiah is not even a professional religious man, but a Jewish official in the Persian civil service.

The final book of the Secondary History, Esther, is set in Persia and so cannot directly concern itself with the worship of the Jerusalem Temple. But its theme, the preservation of the Jewish people from the threat of genocide against them, makes it a fitting conclusion to the Secondary History: in its present context, it affirms that the continuance of the worship of God by the people of God is guaranteed. The gravest threat to national existence has been faced and overcome, and the Jewish people, though "scattered" and "dispersed" (Esther 3:8) throughout the provinces of the Persian Empire, have their interests safeguarded by the presence at the Persian court of

Mordecai the Jew. He is not only "next in rank to King Ahasuerus" but also "great among the Jews" because he habitually "sought the welfare of his people and spoke peace to all his people" (10:3).

So the entire Secondary History concludes on an upbeat note. It harmonizes well with the outlook of the narrative as a whole, that the purpose for which history has existed is the worship of God. And the people of Israel, aided by the right-living kings of Judah, have, in fact, throughout the only history worth writing about, been carrying out that worship faithfully and joyfully. This quite different perspective on national history from that of the Primary History is particularly well illustrated by the way the two histories handle the question of the meaning of the Exile. For 2 Kings, the Exile is a punishment for national iniquity, an unredeemed disaster, and the end point of the whole narrative. But for 2 Chronicles, the Exile is punishment for pollution of the Temple (36:14), it is destined to come to an end at a time predicted by the prophet Jeremiah (36:21; cf. Jer. 25:11; 29:10), and it is no kind of end, for the book concludes not with the Exile but with an announcement of the plans of Cyrus to rebuild the Temple (36:22–23).

Conclusion

The OT presents us with, then, with two alternative tellings of the history of the Israelite people. Their difference in outlook does not necessarily make either of them unreliable; it only reinforces the fact that the telling of any story or any history must be selective and must reflect the intentions of some person or group.

The fact that the two histories are found within the same sacred Scriptures has a further meaning than that, however. Any community or individual with a commitment to those Scriptures does not have the freedom to pick or choose between the tellings of the story. They must come to terms with the coexistence of the conflicting narratives.

A very similar conflict of outlook exists between Psalms 105 and 106. These are both "historical" psalms in that they recount selected incidents from national history. But Psalm 105 is positive where Psalm 106 is negative. For Psalm 105, what happened to Israel in Egypt is that there God made his people fruitful and stronger than their enemies (105:24); for Psalm 106, it was a time when Israel ignored God's power and rebelled against him (106:7). Here too the reader, especially if he or she is a member of a religious group that uses these psalms, is not free simply to ignore the contrast.

THE BIBLICAL STORY AS IT HAS BEEN UNDERSTOOD

This understanding of the biblical story as essentially two competing historical narratives is not the way in which the books have been usually understood by the communities that have preserved them. This is because it has not been customary to look at ancient sacred books as literary works that generate meaning through their overall shape, their structure, and their dominant tendencies, that is, through their identity *as wholes*. These books, like the other biblical books, have tended rather to be valued piecemeal for their diverse *contents*.

Thus, the Primary History has been understood both in the Jewish and the Christian communities as containing *law* and *history*. It does, of course. In Exodus to Deuteronomy there is the legal foundation of the Israelite people, which remains essential for the moral and legal beliefs and practices of Jews today. Christians have generally tried to discriminate between the moral laws of these books, which they consider as having some kind of divine authorization, and the more strictly ritual laws, which they have regarded as applicable only to the Jewish people. These interpretations, which may or may not be valid, ignore the fact that the laws of the Primary History are *narrated*, i.e., set in a narrative context. It would be more appropriate to understand them— even the Ten Commandments—not as laws claiming universal truth but as texts that will yield meanings only as they are understood within the narrative framework that surrounds them.

The Primary History also contains a valuable collection of historical materials. In fact, for most of the period it covers, it is the only source we have for knowing anything at all about what actually happened. But it is plain from the structure of the history that its concern is not primarily historiographical in the sense of recording the events of the past. The narrative has an argument or a thesis it wishes to establish. And since that thesis concerns the religious meaning of the total historical period that it describes, our primary understanding of the narrative should be a theological one.

The Secondary History has been even less highly esteemed for its significance as a whole. Ever since the Septuagint Greek translation in the second century B.C. of 1 and 2 Chronicles under the heading *Paraleipomena*, "the omitted things," Chronicles has been regarded as no more than a supplement to Samuel and Kings rather than as presenting a distinctive view of the past and indeed of the purpose of creation. Ezra and Nehemiah, for their part, have been treated more as a continuation of the history of Genesis to 2 Kings carried forward into postexilic times than as further evidence for the argument of Chronicles.

A further effect of regarding the narratives as essentially history is the following. Both Jewish and Christian readers have always known that the history of Israel did not really come to an end with the Exile or with the postexilic age. So the particular point at which the two biblical histories conclude has seemed arbitrary to them and therefore meaningless. By contrast, to recognize the existence of the two sequences of narratives as literary works in their own right leads to an enlargement of meaningfulness.

So long as the narratives have been thought to contribute to a program other than their own—such as laying down the laws by which to live or providing information about the events of the past—their truly challenging and unsettling nature has lain unremarked. This is not surprising, for the communities that have preserved them have always been in the business of conservation, of themselves as much as of their sacred books. Once we acknowledge that the Bible contains in these two historical sequences two divergent ways of remembering the past we become obliged to make decisions for ourselves, not so much about the relative historical worth of each of the histories, but about whether it is possible to give allegiance to Scriptures that contain so much tension within themselves. There is no obviously or objectively correct decision; readers have to become personally involved. The history of the Bible's reception, even by groups that have esteemed it highly, is, in some important respects, a chronicle of misapprehensions of the Bible.

THE ORIGINS OF THE BIBLICAL STORY

What have been spoken of in this chapter as the two biblical histories did not originate as unified literary works and, indeed, never existed as such in biblical times. The histories as we have them now have an inner logic and coherence that do not depend on their authors. In fact, we may suppose that several different authors composed different parts of the histories at different times, in some cases deliberately intending their works to be read as sequels to narratives already written (e.g., Ruth as an appendix to Judges), at other times writing quite independently of the context in which their work is now to be found (e.g., Esther).

The Primary History

The twelve books of the Primary History are, with one small exception, the first books of the Hebrew Bible. Only Ruth, which belongs chronologically with Judges, is located elsewhere in the Hebrew canon, namely, in its third division, the Writings—for reasons no longer known. The Hebrew Bible, however, does not really regard Genesis to 2 Kings as a unified work because it breaks it apart with one of the major divisions of the canon: thus Genesis to Deuteronomy forms the Pentateuch (the Torah), and Joshua to 2 Kings the Former Prophets.

In modern critical scholarship it is customary to think of Genesis to 2 Kings not as a "Primary History" but as two large independent works composed at different times with differing purposes. These two works are regarded as either the Pentateuch and a Deuteronomistic History (Joshua to 2 Kings) or a Tetrateuch (Genesis to Numbers) and a Deuteronomistic History opening with the book of Deuteronomy.

The Pentateuch has for a century of scholarship been supposed to have been finally edited from various sources or documents in the fifth century B.C. In some versions of this Documentary Hypothesis, it grew by a process of accretion; the earliest narrative source, "J," of the tenth century B.C., was combined with a ninth-century narrative, "E," in the eighth century. In the seventh century, the laws of the book of Deuteronomy, "D," were attached to this narrative. Lastly, an exilic (sixth-century) Priestly work, containing both narrative and laws, was used as a framework for the older material; JEDP thus became, in the fifth century, the Pentateuch.

Though still defended by many scholars, this reconstruction has been challenged recently at every point. The dates and sequence of each of the sources have been questioned, J sometimes being thought postexilic, P pre-exilic. The existence of an E source has been doubted by many. Others have found the arguments for analyzing the sources behind the literature defective, and increasingly it is being felt that the growth of this diverse literary work is likely to have been very much more complex than the Documentary Hypothesis envisaged. No one doubts, however, that the materials from which the Pentateuch (or Tetrateuch) was written come from widely different periods. The material of Genesis and Exodus in particular must have existed for some centuries in oral form, and principles of selection and arrangement that we can no longer identify have shaped a good deal of the material. Surprisingly, few scholars have studied the question of what thesis the Pentateuch in its final form is attempting to sustain. But it may be suggested that its theme is the threefold promise to the Abrahamic family of land, posterity, and divine blessing. Since this promise was only partially fulfilled by the end of the Pentateuch, a more complete fulfillment lay in the future.

The Deuteronomistic History obviously comes in its final form from the sixth century, since the last narrated item refers to 561 B.C. The major critical issue is whether an earlier, pre-exilic edition of the book may be detected. If the first edition of this history was written during the lifetime of Josiah and under the influence of the religious reformation attributed to him, then the whole thrust of the work may perhaps have been very much more positive. The history could then be seen as a record of the graciousness of Yahweh toward the Davidic dynasty, in accordance with the prophetic promises of 2 Samuel 7 (cf. 1 Kings 11:12; 15:4; 2 Kings 8:19; 19:34). Most agree, though, that even if such were the theme of the first edition, the exilic edition, which not only recounts the untimely death of this much-praised king but also concludes with the exile of the people, effected an enormous alteration in its theme from a possibly positive to an almost certainly negative outlook. Some, indeed, have found a note of hope in its last paragraph reporting the release of Jehoiachin from prison (2 Kings 25:27–30), but that hardly prevents the impact of the total work being predominantly negative.

The Secondary History

The Secondary History has been subjected to a curious deformation by the canon of the Hebrew Bible. Not only is it removed as far as possible from the Primary History to the very end of the Hebrew Bible, but it is split in two and the order of its parts reversed. Ezra and Nehemiah, which of course relate the history of the centuries after Chronicles, are confusingly placed before Chronicles. The book of Esther, which belongs chronologically speaking with Ezra (to be precise, it forms an addendum to Ezra 4:6), is—like Chronicles, Ezra, and Nehemiah—one of the Writings but preceding Ezra and separated from it by Daniel (which rightly does precede Ezra).

It was long agreed by critical scholars that Chronicles, Ezra, and Nehemiah did actually once form a unified work, attributed to a Levite

83

or priest of the late fifth century B.C. called by scholars today the "Chronicler." While some now think that Ezra and Nehemiah are not the work of the Chronicler, there can be no doubt that all these books come from the same literary and religious circle. At some time in their early history, these books must have been regarded as part of the same work, because the first two and a half verses of Ezra have been copied to the end of 2 Chronicles (36:22–23), with the result that the forward-looking conclusion that 2 Chronicles already had has been much strengthened.

Chronicles evidently uses Samuel and Kings as its principal source; it is a matter of debate to what extent, if at all, the Chronicler had access to other old sources or whether he composed freely all the material not paralleled in Samuel and Kings. For Ezra and Nehemiah, the editor used a variety of historical documents including Persian administrative texts in Aramaic (e.g., Ezra 5:7–6:12; 7:12–26), records from Jerusalem archives such as the list of inhabitants of Judah in Ezra 2 and the people's pledge of loyalty to the law in Nehemiah 10, and above all the "memoirs" of Ezra (Ezra 7–10; Neh. 8–9) and Nehemiah (Neh. 1:1–7:73; 11:1–2; 12:31–43; 13:4–31).

The Chronicler's work has sometimes been thought to be politically motivated as a defense of the legitimacy of his Judean community against their northern neighbors, the Samaritans. Others have thought it an implicit expression of hope for the restoration of the Davidic monarchy. It seems more probable, however, that its audience is primarily the author's own community and its purpose was to assure them of the value of their life, even under foreign rule: they as a community are sustaining the worship of God, which is the primary function of Israel, indeed, the chief purpose of the world's creation.

Bibliography

Bailey, L. R. *The Pentateuch.* Interpreting Biblical Texts. Nashville, TN: Abingdon, 1981.

Clines, D. J. A. *The Theme of the Pentateuch.* Journal for the Study of the Old Testament Supplement Series, no. 10. Sheffield: JSOT Press, 1978.

Cross, F. M. *Canaanite Myth and Hebrew Epic: Essays in the History of the Religion of Israel.* Cambridge, MA: Harvard University Press, 1973. Pp. 217–90.

Fretheim, T. E. *Deuteronomic History.* Interpreting Biblical Texts. Nashville, TN: Abingdon, 1983.

Noth, M. *The Deuteronomistic History.* Journal for the Study of the Old Testament Supplement Series, no. 15. Sheffield: JSOT Press, 1981.

————. *The Chronicler's History.* Journal for the Study of the Old Testament Supplement Series, no. 50. Sheffield: JSOT Press, 1987.

Polzin, R. *Moses and the Deuteronomist: A Literary Study of the Deuteronomic History.* Vol. 1, *Deuteronomy, Joshua, Judges.* New York: Seabury, 1980.

Whybray, R. N. *The Making of the Pentateuch: A Methodological Study.* Journal for the Study of the Old Testament Supplement Series, no. 53. Sheffield: JSOT Press, 1987.

GENESIS

J O H N   S .   K S E L M A N

INTRODUCTION

Genesis and the Pentateuch

The book of Genesis comprises a narrative extending from creation to the death of Joseph. It can be divided into four large sections: Genesis 1–11, the beginnings; 12–25, the Abraham cycle; 25–36, the Jacob cycle; and 37–50, the Joseph story. Genesis is part of a larger literary complex of narrative and law commonly designated the "Torah" or the "Pentateuch." The three sources (J, also called the Yahwist; E, the Elohist; and P, the Priestly writer) that appear in Genesis continue through Exodus, Leviticus, and Numbers, with their characteristic language, concerns, and themes.

Cast as Moses' testament to Israel before his death and Israel's subsequent entrance into the promised land, Deuteronomy reveals a literary source different from J, E, and P; and the presence of the language and themes of this "D source" in Joshua, Judges, 1 and 2 Samuel, and 1 and 2 Kings has led to the conviction that these works form a great historical corpus (called the "Deuteronomistic History"), prefaced by an address of Moses to Israel in Deuteronomy and ending with the destruction of the kingdom of Judah (→ Elohist; Deuteronomy; Deuteronomistic Historian; Priestly Writer(s); Sources of the Pentateuch; Yahwist). The formation of a five-book Pentateuch from the Tetrateuch (Genesis–Numbers) was effected by the attachment of Deuteronomy to the preceding four books, an attachment governed in part by what might be termed "biographical" interests: Deuteronomy is Moses' farewell, his last words of instruction and warning to Israel; it ends with the death of this heroic figure whose birth and rise to leadership are recorded in Exodus. Thus understood, the Pentateuch relates the story of God's creation of the world and humanity; his choice of the ancestors and of Moses, God's chosen instrument in the liberation of slaves from Egypt and the creation of a people; the covenant and the proclamation of the law as a guide for the redeemed community; and God's care for Israel expressed in his provision for all their needs and his guidance of them through the wilderness to the border of the land of promise, where Moses preaches his final sermon to Israel before his death. It is also possible to speak of a six-book Hexateuch extending from Genesis through Joshua and carrying the story to the conquest of the land of Canaan under the leadership of Moses' chosen successor Joshua (→ Hexateuch).

Methods in the Study of Genesis

Modern study of the book of Genesis had its beginnings in the seventeenth and eighteenth centuries in the researches of R. Simon and J. Astruc. From those beginnings, the study of Genesis has moved in several directions. For some scholars, the history and society behind the text have been major concerns. The aim has been the reconstruction of Israel's history in its ancient Near Eastern context, especially through archaeology and the attempt to correlate its findings with the biblical literary record. The name of William F. Albright and those of his students are associated with this approach (→ Archaeology, History, and the Bible).

Other scholars have focused rather on the history and development of the book. The methods employed include source criticism, the recognition and isolation of the component narrative strands (for Genesis: J, E, and P) through the perspective of the Documentary Hypothesis given classic statement by Julius Wellhausen in his *Prolegomena to the History of Israel* (1883), and form criticism, the study of the origin and development, both oral and written, of the smaller constituent parts of these larger complexes and sources and the institutional setting of these identified units (→ Oral Materials, Sources, and Traditions). This method was employed with great success by Hermann Gunkel in his commentary on Genesis in 1901.

The attention of a number of scholars has shifted recently from the diachronic study of the parts of a composite like Genesis to the synchronic study of the finished product at the end of its development. The final form of the text can be approached as literature and studied with the appropriate tools of literary criticism (as in the work of Robert Alter) or as Scripture, as the sacred collection of writings normative for two communities of faith, Jewish and Christian. This method has been termed canonical criticism and is associated with the names of Brevard S. Childs and James Sanders (→ Biblical Criticism). These moves toward synthesis do not make irrelevant the gains of the traditional methods of source and form criticism; but they do bring into focus a reality sometimes not given sufficient attention by the more analytical methods, the final form of the text and the totality in which the constituent parts find their meaning and speak today.

Other contemporary approaches include feminist interpretation, which in Genesis would involve the examination of the role and status of women in the creation accounts of chaps. 1–3 and in the ancestor stories of chaps. 12–50. Sociology and anthropology have recently had considerable impact on OT studies; in Genesis, methods drawn from the social sciences have illuminated such issues as genealogies and kinship structures (→ Sociology of the Old Testament).

Major Themes of Genesis

Some prominent themes that occur throughout Genesis include the following: the theme of the promise, of blessing in place of curse, of election, and of familial strife.

The theme of God's promise (Gen. 12:1–3, 7) and its partial or incomplete fulfillment touches both the promise of descendants and of land. The promise of descendants is organized around a series of questions: how will Abram (Abraham) be the father of numerous descendants when he has not even one son? Which of his sons (Ishmael or Isaac) will be the bearer of the promise? Will the chosen son survive to carry on the line (chaps. 22, 27)? The partial fulfillment of the promise of descendants is recorded in the genealogy in Gen. 46:8–27. The promise of land is also delayed in fulfillment. The ancestors to whom Canaan is promised spend more time outside the promised land than in it: Abraham and Sarah in Egypt (chap. 12) and Gerar (chap. 20); Isaac and Rebekah in Gerar (chap. 26); Jacob in Haran (chaps. 29–31); Joseph in Egypt (chaps. 39–50); and Jacob, Joseph's brothers, and their families also in Egypt (chaps. 46–50).

Both of the promises are faced with obstacles that seem to make the promises humanly impossible to accomplish, obstacles that are overcome by divine intervention. To the promise of descendants, the obstacle is the barrenness of the matriarchs Sarah (Gen. 16), Rebekah (25:21), and Rachel (30:1). At the outset, Sarah's old age (17:17; 18:12) is a further obstacle. To the promise of land, the obstacles are its occupation by the indigenous population (12:6; 13:7) and the famines that provoke the ancestors' departure (12:10; 26:1; 41:54).

The second important theme is the blessing that is also promised by God to the ancestors, their descendants, and ultimately all humanity. There are two models of the activity or involvement of the Deity with humankind, and both models find a place in Genesis: salvation and blessing. By salvation is meant the deliverance of the community or of individuals from various crises and dangers by divine intervention. While the prime example of God's saving activity is certainly the Exodus, saving divine interventions occur as well in Genesis: the salvation of Abram and Sarai (Sarah) in Egypt (chap. 12) and Gerar (chap. 20); of Hagar and Ishmael in the wilderness (chaps. 16, 21); of Lot and his daughters in Sodom (chap. 19); and of Isaac from death (chap. 22).

Blessing, God's provision of human need, is an even more important theme in Genesis. The narrative begins with the blessing of humanity in 1:28 with progeny ("Increase and multiply!") and land ("Fill the earth and subdue it!"). The blessing is continued in the garden of Eden in Genesis 2, but blessing soon gives way to curse (chap. 3) and expulsion from the garden where the human needs for food and companionship were met. Humanity under the curse progresses to the fratricide of Cain and the universal violence and corruption that brought about the divine judgment of the Flood (chaps. 6–9). The blessing of humanity is renewed after the Flood, but the hubris of the tower builders of Babel threatens to start the whole cycle of sin and destruction over again. The dispersal of those who would challenge the sovereignty of God, however, leads into a new history of blessing inaugurated by God in the stories of the ancestors (→ Curse and Blessing; Salvation).

In Genesis, the theme of election appears pointedly in the mystery of God passing over the firstborn to choose the younger son. This theme is first announced in the story of Cain and Abel, where God looks with favor on the gift of the younger son. As the narrative continues, the divine choice falls not on Ishmael but on Isaac (Gen. 17, 21); not on Esau but on Jacob (chaps. 25, 27); not on Reuben but on Joseph (chap. 37); not on Zerah but on Perez (38:27–30; cf. Ruth 4:18–22); not on Manasseh but on Ephraim (Gen. 48:8–19); and not on Reuben, Simeon, or Levi but on Judah (49:8–12). If the major narrative strand in which these stories appear (J) was written in the Davidic-Solomonic era, this theme would have relevance for the accession to power of David and of Solomon, neither of whom was the oldest son (1 Sam. 16; 1 Kings 1).

The theme of rivalry, discord, and strife in the family has not until recently received the attention it deserves. Throughout Genesis, every familial relationship is riven by strife. There is discord between husband and wife (Gen. 3:12; 16:5; 27:1–13; 30:1–2), between wives (16:4–6; 29:21–30:24), between parent and child (27:11–12; 37:10), between brothers (chaps. 4, 27, and 37), and between other relatives (chaps. 13, 30). Like the theme of the choice of the younger son, this theme may be an indirect comment on the royal court of David. It may also reflect the strife and the hope for reconciliation between the two kingdoms.

COMMENTARY

1:1–11:32

The Beginnings

The narrative of Genesis 1–11 begins with the creation of the good world and of humanity as its blessed resident and regent. The divine intention was frustrated by human evil, however, in a story of progressive deterioration and alienation: from the primal act of disobedience (chap. 3) to another act of hubris (chap. 11) in which the boundaries that separate the divine and human worlds are challenged. Since Genesis 1 showed creation to be a process of separation and distinction, the ignoring or blurring of these distinctions reverses the very process of creation and brings about the return to chaos in the Flood.

The growth and spread of sin from disobedience (chap. 3) to murder (chap. 4) to total corruption (chap. 6) to universal destruction (chaps. 7–8) show humanity under the curse as the consequence of sin. But there is a parallel history of divine blessing and grace as well, a history that begins with the creation of a blessed humanity, wherein God continues to show his care for his sinful creatures and in which is renewed the blessing of all humanity (in chap. 9) and of a particular family (in chap. 12), which will become a source of blessing for all.

1:1–2:24

The Two Creation Accounts

1:1–2, In the Beginning. As most modern translations recognize, the P creation account (1:1–2:4a) begins with a temporal clause ("When, in the beginning, God created"); such a translation puts Gen. 1:1 in agreement with the opening of the J account (2:4b) and with other ancient, Near Eastern creation myths. The Hebrew verb *bara'*, "create," is used exclusively of divine activity; "heavens and earth" are a merism (an expression of totality by the use of two polar expressions) meaning "everything" (→ Creation).

The description of the precreation state in v. 2 probably is meant to suggest a storm-tossed sea: darkness, a great wind, the watery abyss. God's superiority over the sea here and in vv.

9–10 may be a reminiscence of the ancient Near Eastern mythic portrait of creation as the victory of order over hostile, chaotic forces like the divinized sea (→ Polytheism; Sea). The tripartite form and downward movement from "heaven" to "earth" to "sea" is frequent elsewhere in the OT (e.g., Pss. 135:6; 146:6; Amos 9:6).

1:3–31, The Six Days of Creation. The six days of P's creation week are described in solemn, repetitive language and are arranged in two sets of three, in which days 1 and 4 correspond, as do days 2 and 5, and 3 and 6. The first three days describe the divine work of separation (light from darkness, water above from water below, sea from land) that prepares a habitable world, while the last three days describe the inhabitants. Day 1 describes the creation of light, and day 4 the sources of light (sun, moon, stars); in day 2 the creation of the dome of the sky ("firmament" in the older translations) provides an air space and waters for the creatures of day 5, fish and birds; in day 3, dry land and plants are provided for the land animals and human beings of day 6 (→ Firmament).

The climax of the six days of creation is the creation of humankind on day 6, which differs from the other days in God's prior consultation of the heavenly court, Israel's demythologized version of the ancient Near Eastern pantheon (v. 26: "Let us make humanity"; cf. Isa. 6:8) and in the designation of humanity as the image of God (→ Image of God). The context suggests that humanity is the image of God in the dominion it exercises over the rest of creation; ancient Near Eastern parallels suggest that "image of God" is a royal designation, emphasizing the godlike nature of the ruling monarch. In the imageless religious tradition of Israel, the only acceptable image of God is the human being.

The divine command to humanity in v. 28 to reproduce prepares for the Genesis genealogies, the continuation of God's initial act of creation, and reaches its climax in the fruitfulness of Israel in Egypt (Exod. 1:7, 12).

2:1–4a, The Divine Sabbath. The P week of creation closes with God's resting on the seventh day and his blessing that day, which will be the Israelite Sabbath (Exod. 20:8–11). The language here is remarkably similar to that found at the end of the account of the construction of the desert tabernacle in Exod. 39:32, 42–43; 40:33 (→ Tabernacle). The creation stories of the ancient Near East often conclude with the construction of a dwelling for the victorious deity. In the Israelite use of this motif, human beings participate in the divine work of creation by extending and completing it. While most scholars consider 2:4a to be the end of the P creation account, echoing 1:1, some understand

87

it rather as the heading of the second creation account.

2:4b–24, The Second Creation Account.
Like P, the J creation account begins with a temporal clause, this time one that describes the precreation state as a waterless, lifeless desert. There may be echoes here of the Canaanite myth of Baal's struggle with a demonic adversary Mot (Death), as there are similar reminiscences of the combat myth of the creator-god Baal versus the Sea in 1:1–2 (→ Baal). The Israelite adaptation and reuse of the Canaanite myths of Baal versus the Sea in Genesis 1 and of Baal versus Death in his desert domain in Genesis 2 recall Yahweh's victory over the sea (Exod. 14–15) and the desert (Exod. 16–17) in the creation of Israel.

The water from the earth transforms the desert into a garden filled with the bounty of the earth; in the center of the garden stand the tree of life, a common ancient Near Eastern motif, and the tree of knowledge (→ Tree of Life, The).

Yahweh's first act of creation in J is the creation of a man from the clay produced by the mixture of the water and dry earth of Gen. 2:6, enlivened by the divine breath (→ Adam; Adamah; Flesh and Spirit). The man's responsibility in Eden, whose abundance comes from Yahweh and not from any of the fertility gods of polytheism, is to cultivate the garden and to obey the divine prohibition of eating from the tree of knowledge (→ Eden). The naming of the animals by the human being (vv. 19–20) is J's way of indicating human dominion over the created world (as in 1:28–30); it recalls the divine name giving in Genesis 1.

The J creation account reaches its climax in the creation of woman as a helping counterpart to the man; the creation of woman from man does not imply subordination, any more than the creation of the man from the earth implies subordination. The subordination of woman to man is effected by the frustration of the divine intention of equality.

2:25–3:24
Crime and Punishment

2:25–3:7, The Sin.
The reference to the nakedness of the man and woman is the beginning of the sin account, as the Hebrew pun of 'arummim, "naked," in 2:25 and 3:7 and 'arum, "crafty," in 3:1 suggests. Nakedness in the OT suggests weakness, neediness, and the like (Deut. 28:48; Job 1:21; Isa. 58:7). The unawareness of their nakedness on the part of the man and the woman suggests their unawareness of their dependence on God who provides in the garden for all their needs. "Good and evil" is another instance of merism; the "knowledge of good and evil" is thus the unlimited knowledge appropriate to divinity, as the serpent suggests in v. 5 ("You shall be like gods"). In v. 6 the woman "saw how good the tree was for food"; the language recalls God's delight in his creation (in the repeated "God saw how good it was" of Gen. 1), which culminated in blessing; here the woman's seeing will lead rather to curse (→ Fall, The; Serpent).

Ironically, what the man and woman discover is not that they are gods but that they are naked—weak, vulnerable, and helpless, having rejected their dependence upon God.

3:8–24, The Divine Judgment.
The J author continues the ironical tone of the narrative in the description of the human efforts to remedy the situation by attempting to cover their nakedness and hide from Yahweh. Unconscious irony marks the man's answer to the divine interrogation ("I heard your voice in the garden"), since the Hebrew idiom "to hear the voice of" means to obey—precisely what the man did not do.

In vv. 14–19, the divine judgment having been imposed on the participants, the order of their appearance in Genesis 2–3 (man, woman, serpent) is inverted; this literary reversal may imply the reversal of Yahweh's original intentions because of human sin. The divine judgment speech begins with a curse on the serpent (based on an etiology of the serpent's manner of locomotion) and a prediction of the enmity between the human and subhuman worlds. The curse of the woman involves the pain of childbearing, as the concomitant of the replacement of immortality (by eating of the tree of life) by progeny, and subordination to the man. Significantly, this cultural given of female subordination to the male is understood in the J narrative as the result of human sin rather than the divine intention. The curse on the man involves disharmony with the earth from which he was made and to which he will return in death, after a life of hard labor for food. The naming of the woman by the man in v. 20 (Eve; Heb. chawwah, "life") underlines the new situation of dominion by the man over the woman.

The J creation account ends on a note of grace, thus establishing a precedent that will operate in the other J sin stories to come. In place of their inadequate garments, Yahweh provides more durable clothing before expelling the man and woman from the garden; banished from the garden and kept from the tree of life, they are yet not separated from God's care.

Brokenness, disharmony, the sundering of relationships between God and humanity, between man and woman, and between the human and the nonhuman world (hostile serpent and cursed earth) are the result of sin and will continue to appear in Genesis 4–11.

4:1–5:32
Sin and Curse and the Blessing of Progeny

4:1–16, Cain and Abel. The sundering of the familial bond between husband and wife is now paralleled and intensified by another act of violence in the family, fratricide. While the conflict between Cain and Abel may indicate the enmity and rivalry between two ways of life, the pastoral nomad and the sedentary peasant farmer, their brotherhood may reflect the interaction and symbiosis of farmer and shepherd in the ancient Near East. Cain's act of violence is an attack on the integrity of the family, an offense against the divinely intended order of creation expressed in the command to reproduce. But Cain's sin is more than a rejection of the divinely established order; in arrogating to himself the divine sovereignty over life in ending a life, Cain has repeated the sin of his parents by making himself "like God."

There are several other important links between the Cain and Abel story and Genesis 3. The similarity of Yahweh's address to Cain in v. 7 and to the woman in 3:16 underscores the relationship between the two primal sins. Further, like his father, Cain the farmer will be cursed with unproductive land, which he has polluted with his brother's blood (vv. 11–12), and will be banished as a wanderer east of Eden (3:24; 4:16). Characteristically, the story ends not with judgment alone but with mitigating grace; the fugitive's life is protected by the tattoo that Yahweh places on Cain.

Several themes that will recur throughout Genesis make their first appearance here: the strife between brothers (Jacob and Esau, Joseph and the other sons of Jacob) and the rejection of primogeniture for the mysterious divine choice of the younger son.

4:17–25, The Descendants of Cain and the Birth of Seth. The ambiguity of human progress is highlighted by J's paralleling of advances in civilization and technology with the increase of violence. To Cain is attributed the building of the first city, an advance that will culminate in Genesis 11 in the building of a city that will challenge the supremacy of Yahweh. Among Cain's descendants are Jabal the ancestor of pastoral nomads, Jubal the ancestor of musicians, and Tubal-cain, the originator of metallurgy. Over against these descendants of Cain is set Lamech, who boasts of his vengeful reign of terror. This dark story of violence ends with a genealogy that moves from murderer to murderer; the framing of a genealogy by two acts that bring death stands in contradiction to the genealogical record of the continued life of a family. In sharp contrast to the surrounding darkness is the light that dawns in the an-nouncement of the birth of Seth, who fathers Enosh and a family of those who call upon Yahweh's name (v. 26), a family that will include Abram, who will call upon that same God (12:8).

5:1–32, The Descendants of Adam and Seth. Genesis 5 begins by recalling the P account of the creation of humanity in the divine image (Gen. 1:26–27) and of the divine command to reproduce (1:28). Obedience to this divine command is demonstrated in the following genealogy of 'adam. In Gen. 1:26 and in 5:1b–2, the Hebrew word 'adam has the generic and inclusive meaning "human being." In Gen. 4:25 ("'adam had relations with his wife"), 5:1a ("This is the record of the descendants of 'adam"), and 5:3 ("'adam was 130 years of age"), the generic noun has been transformed into a proper name. This transformation of "humanity" into "Adam" depends on the intervening J narratives in Genesis 2–4 that use ha-'adam ("the man") from Gen. 2:8 to 4:1.

In 5:3, Adam's begetting a son "in his image and likeness" understands human reproduction as the continuation of the creative act of God. There is a sharp contrast between the genealogy of Adam through Seth to Noah, in which the divine image and blessing are transmitted, and the curse-laden line of Cain in Genesis 4. The recurring pattern of the standard genealogical notice is: "A had lived X years when he fathered B [the firstborn male]; after B's birth A lived for Y more years and had other children. The whole lifetime of A was (X + Y) years; then he died." This pattern is altered twice. In v. 24, readers are told that Enoch, who "walked with God" (an expression of continuing service and constant performance of duty; Gen. 6:9; 24:40; 1 Kings 3:6; 2 Kings 20:3), "was no more"; and although this expression can mean death (Gen. 42:13, 32; Jer. 31:15), readers learn that "God took" Enoch (as he did Elijah in 2 Kings 2:9–10; cf. Ps. 49:15). In Gen. 5:29, Noah's genealogical notice is expanded by his naming (paralleling the naming of Seth at the beginning of the genealogy in v. 3) and by an etiology for the name. Noah's genealogical notice is further distinctive in that it begins in 5:32 and is concluded in 9:28–29, so that it serves as a frame to the Flood story and the post-Deluge renewal of creation (→ Noah).

Genealogies

The biblical genealogies have been the subject of several important studies in recent years. Two factors have provoked renewed interest in this generally neglected material. First, a larger context for the understanding of the genealogies has been provided by anthropological study of the form and function of genealogies in societies where they are still alive. Second, greater interest in the final form of the text has meant that the biblical genealogies can be studied as parts of a literary and theological totality.

Several significant features of genealogies ought to be mentioned. First, they can be *linear*, focusing on one individual in each generation, or *segmented*, in which more than one line of descent from a single ancestor is considered. The genealogies of Cain in Genesis 4 and of Adam through Seth in Genesis 5 both begin as linear genealogies and conclude as segmented ones. Second, the most important names in a genealogy are those that occur at its beginning and end (Adam and Noah in Gen. 5). The intervening names can show a high degree of variation and fluidity, with addition and subtraction of names depending on the purpose of the genealogy. To a person reciting or preserving a genealogy, such alterations reflect present social and political relationships rather than past biological history. Thus, it is possible to have differing linear genealogies from the same ancestor on the basis of changed relationships and different functions.

J and P, the two predominant pentateuchal sources in Genesis 1–11, both place a genealogy early in their material: J's genealogy of Cain in Genesis 4 and P's genealogy of Adam through Seth in Genesis 5. Both genealogies are linear (from father to firstborn son), with a segmented conclusion (Lamech's three sons and a daughter in Gen. 4:20–22; Noah's three sons in 5:32). Other genealogies in Genesis include the so-called Table of Nations in Genesis 10 (the descendants of Noah's three sons); 11:10–26 (the extension of the line of Shem to Abram); 25:1–26 (the descendants of Abraham); chap. 36 (the descendants of Esau); and 46:8–25 (the descendants of Jacob).

In regard to the Genesis genealogies in particular, some observations are in order. Theologically, the genealogies in Genesis 1–11 show a double movement of expansion (increase in the world's population in obedience to the divine command to reproduce) and of restriction (the singling out of one line of descent into which Abram will be born). The Genesis narratives share this focus on one family. Literarily, the Genesis genealogies function to create and underline the tension between the orderliness and fixity of the fundamental moments in human life (birth, death, continuation of family line) recorded in the genealogies and the disorderly, contingent openness of the related narratives. For instance, the story of the Flood and the preservation of Noah and the seed of human life in Genesis 6–9 is a narrative marked by contingency and questions about God's intentions and human fate: what does God mean to do with those

in the ark? Have the Flood waters abated? Will the dove return to the ark? But the bracketing of the Flood story by the genealogies in Genesis 5 and 10 demonstrates, beneath the flux and uncertainty of events, the unchanged intention of God, neither frustrated nor revoked by human or cosmic evil. On the other hand, if the genealogies tend towards a deterministic view of history, the narratives in which they are embedded present a history shaped by the indeterminacy of events and the freedom of the human participants in the story. Seen together, then, the genealogies and narratives of Genesis show, from different perspectives, God's sovereign control of history.

6:1–9:17
The Flood

6:1–4, Prologue to the Flood. As an introduction to the Flood story, J has used 6:1–4, a fragment of old mythic material with reminiscences of the ancient Near Eastern motif of "rebellion of the gods" in which a younger generation of gods challenges the authority of their divine elders and progenitors. Whatever the origin and history of this fragment, J has included it because it fits so well the narrative of the growth of sin and evil begun in Genesis 3–4. Gen. 6:1–4 is a story of the blurring of the distinction between the human and divine worlds, already heard in the challenges to the divine sovereignty in Genesis 3–4 and to be heard again in the story of the ill-fated tower in Genesis 11. The improper mating of heavenly beings and earthly women is an attack on the boundaries that are meant to separate the heavenly and earthly realms. It thus threatens the integrity of creation as God intended it (cf. Lev. 11:44–47; 20:24–26).

6:5–13, The Causes of the Flood. Following the mythic prologue, the narrative moves to the reasons for the Flood. The two sources (J and P) agree that the Flood was provoked by human evil. In J (vv. 5–8) there is an effective contrast between the evil inclination of the human heart and the pained heart of God. P specifies the evil as violence (vv. 11–12), graphically illustrated in the murderous behavior of Cain and Lamech in Genesis 4. The disordered violence that characterizes interhuman relationships parallels the disordered heavenly-earthly relationships portrayed in 6:1–4.

Set between these two pictures of unceasing human wickedness (J) and of violence and universal corruption (P) is Noah, who "found favor in the eyes of Yahweh" (J) and who "walked with God as a righteous and blameless man (P). The similar language in 1 Kings 9:4 ("If you walk before me . . . with a blameless heart") and in Ps.

101:2 and 6 points up the royal features of Noah. The description of Job as "righteous and blameless" (Job 12:4) recalls the linking in Ezek. 14:14 and 20 of Noah, Daniel, and Job as men saved by their own righteousness.

There are several interesting links between Gen. 6:1–13 and the creation stories in Genesis 1–3. In Gen. 6:2, the "sons of God" saw how beautiful ("how good") were the human women, a seeing that leads to a limited life span and eventual death (cf. Ps. 82:6–7). In Gen. 3:6 the woman "saw how good was the fruit of the tree of knowledge," a seeing that led to mortality. Similarly, when in Gen. 6:5 Yahweh saw how great was the evil of humanity, what he perceives is the reversal of Genesis 1, where "God saw how good" were the works of his creation, with its climax in the creation of humanity. Finally, Gen. 6:12 ("God saw the earth, and behold, it was corrupt") is a dark reminder of the conclusion of the six days of creation in Gen. 1:31 ("God saw all that he had made, and behold, it was very good"). The purpose of such echoes is to emphasize the meaning of the Flood as the reversal of the process of creation.

6:14–7:24, The Flood. The Flood story has traditionally been a parade example of the Documentary Hypothesis, by which the J and P versions of the Flood story can be identified and separated. The presence of more than one source can be seen in the doublets and in the irregularities and inconsistencies in the narrative. Such inconsistencies include, for instance, the distinction of the divine names "Yahweh" in J and "Elohim" in P (→Names of God in the Old Testament); the pair of each species brought into the ark in P (6:19–20) against the seven pairs of clean and the single pair of unclean creatures in J (7:2–3); and the forty days and nights of rainfall in J (7:4, 12) over against the Flood's cresting after 150 days in P (7:24).

Further, there are duplicate accounts of the divine command to Noah to enter the ark in 6:18–20 (P) and 7:1–3 (J), of the entrance into the ark by Noah and his family in 7:7 (J) and 7:13 (P), and the promise never again to destroy the earth in 8:21 (J) and 9:11 (P). More examples can be found in any standard commentary. Suggestions vary on how such originally disparate material was brought together; a recent proposal conceives of a Flood story from Priestly circles into which traditional epic material from J has been incorporated. Whatever the solution, the final product is not an unimaginative collection of material drawn from distinct sources, but an artful, unified composition arranged chiastically around the central affirmation in 8:1 that "God remembered Noah." A presentation of the chiastic structure of chaps. 7–8 will make this clear: A command to

enter the ark, 7:1–3; B two mentions of seven days' wait for the Flood, 7:4–10; C entry into the ark, 7:11–15; D Yahweh shuts Noah in, 7:16; E the Flood waters rise, covering the mountains, 7:17–24; F God remembered Noah, 8:1a; E' the Flood waters begin to recede and the tops of the mountains appear, 8:1b–6a; D' Noah opens a window in the ark, 8:6b; C' the raven and dove leave the ark, 8:7–9; B' two periods of seven days each waiting for the waters to recede and the earth to dry, 8:10–14; A' command to leave ark, 8:15–17. The first half of the chiasmus narrates the descent and return of the world to precreation chaos (cf. 7:17–24 to the first creation account in Gen. 1), while the second half moves toward the new creation, explicitly affirmed in Gen. 9:1–7.

Also noteworthy is the dependence of the biblical Flood story on such Babylonian sources as the Gilgamesh Epic and the Atrahasis myth. This ancient Near Eastern material was consciously reshaped and altered in accord with Israelite theological perspectives: e.g., Noah, the survivor of the Flood, is not immortal; the cause of the Flood is ethical (human sin) and not overpopulation, as in some ancient Near Eastern parallels—indeed the Flood is followed by the divine command to Noah to repopulate the earth.

Over against the forty-day downpour of rain in J (7:4, 12), P describes the Flood in more cosmic and mythological terms, with the reduction of the world to precreation chaos effected by the opening of windows in the firmament, the barrier holding back the waters above, and the upsurge of the subterranean waters (Gen. 1:6–8). Only a small bubble of order remains, in which is the vessel carrying the possibility of new life. In 7:21–23, the annihilation of all life is the divine punishment brought on by human evil and sin. While the primary focus of the Flood narrative is on the Flood as divine punishment, as the destruction of a thoroughly evil world, there is present as well a subtheme of the Flood as the divine means of purification, the cleansing of pollution from the earth (→Flood, The).

8:1–22, The End of the Flood. As was mentioned above, the dramatic climax and turning point of the narrative comes in 8:1, when "God remembered Noah." In v. 4, the ark comes to rest (a wordplay on the meaning of the name of Noah in Heb., "rest"). The gradual ebbing of the water and the drying of the earth (vv. 3–14) introduce the theme of the renewal of creation by recalling the gathering of the waters and the appearance of dry land in Gen. 1:9–12.

Our passage also foreshadows another kind of creation, God's creation of his people Israel, who pass through the sea on dry land in Exod. 14:16, 22, 29. Another shared motif linking the creation in Genesis 1, the Flood, and the passage of Israel through the sea is the mention of the wind in each of the narratives (Gen. 1:2; 8:1; Exod. 14:21). The parallelism of the conclusion of the Flood story with creation continues when Noah, at God's command, "brings forth" all the living creatures from the ark (v. 17), just as the earth "brings forth" plants and animals at God's command (Gen. 1:12, 24). The Flood story comes to an end as it began, with mention of the continuing evil designs of the human heart (6:5; 8:21) and the construction of an altar by Noah for the initiation of the postdiluvian system of divine service (cf. Gen. 12:8; 13:18; 22:9; 35:7).

9:1–17, Creation Restored. P continues the dominant theme of the renewal of creation with the repetition to Noah and his family of the command to primordial humanity to reproduce (Gen. 1:28; 9:1) and the divine blessing. The genealogy in Genesis 10 will demonstrate the obedience of Noah's family to this divine command. Unlike Adam, Noah was obedient and righteous; like him, Noah will be the progenitor of a reconstituted humanity. The prohibition of murder in vv. 5–6 is followed by the repeated divine injunction to increase and multiply; this repeats the pattern of murder followed by reproduction in Genesis 4–5. The narrative concludes with the establishment by God of a covenant with Noah and his descendants. The covenant with Noah initiated by God is unilateral, like the covenants with the patriarchs that follow; God binds himself by a promise, without imposing any obligation on Noah. Not surprisingly, this P covenant is similar to the P covenant with Abraham in Genesis 17. The idiom for "establishing a covenant" is employed in both accounts (9:9, 11, 17; 17:7, 19, 21). Other elements shared by Genesis 9 and 17 include the "eternal covenant" (9:16; 17:13, 19); the phrase occurs as well in Lev. 24:8; Num. 18:19; and Ezek. 16:60; 37:26 (all material related to P) and in the royal poem of 2 Sam. 23:5, as well as in Isa. 24:5; 55:3; 61:8; Jer. 32:40; and 50:5. In both Genesis 9 and 17 there is a sign of the covenant (the rainbow in 9:12, 13, 17; circumcision in 17:11). A final connection may be the expressions "remember the covenant" in 9:15–16 and "keep the covenant" in 17:9–10, given the equivalence of the verbs in the two versions of the command to sanctify the Sabbath (Exod. 20:8: "Remember the sabbath day"; Deut. 5:12: "Keep the sabbath day").

9:18–10:32

Noah and His Sons

9:18–29, Noah's Drunkenness and the Cursing of Canaan. Like Cain, Noah is identified as a farmer, a man of the soil (Gen. 4:2). As the first to practice viticulture and winemaking, Noah fits the pattern of those descendants of Cain who invented musical instruments and metallurgy (4:21–22). Noah's winemaking fulfills the prediction of his father Lamech that Noah would provide relief from the cursed ground and human toil (Gen. 5:29; cf. 3:17; 4:11–12).

This etiology is followed by the story of the sin of Ham and the cursing of his son Canaan. The story is obscure and seems to involve some breach of sexual propriety; "uncovering the nakedness of one's father" is prohibited in Lev. 18:7–8 (where, however, it refers to sexual relations with one's mother). The story is similar to Gen. 19:30–38, in which Lot's drunkenness is associated with sexual union with his daughters.

Whether sexual misconduct or simply lack of filial piety, Ham's act results in the cursing of his son Canaan, who is to be slave to his blessed brothers Shem and Japheth. The blessing of Shem is another step in the narrowing focus that culminates in Abraham, descendant of Shem (→ Canaan, Canaanites; Shem).

10:1–32, The Table of Nations. The prehistory of Genesis 10 is complex and obscure. It is a composite of J and P genealogical material with later interpolations. Its tripartite scheme of Noah's sons recalls the three sons of Adam (Gen. 4:1–2, 25), of Lamech (Gen. 4:19–22), and of Terah (Gen. 11:26).

As an ethnological statement, Genesis 10 has grouped and related peoples in perplexing ways that have been the subject of considerable examination. One recent study has suggested that the distinguishing features of the three lines of descent are sociocultural, based on distinct ways of life, group characteristics, and professions: Shem's descendants comprise the nonsedentary, migratory segment of the population, the nomadic tribes; the descendants of Ham, the sedentary agrarian population of village and town; and the descendants of Japheth, the maritime nations, the seafaring inhabitants of islands and coastal areas.

Whatever its original intent, in its present context Genesis 10 continues the segmented genealogy of Noah (Gen. 5:32; 9:28–29). Untypically, it moves from Japheth, the youngest of Noah's sons (vv. 1–5), through Ham (vv. 6–20), to Shem (vv. 21–31), the oldest son. The movement from the youngest son with his descendants to the oldest focuses attention on the genealogical line of descent in which the narrator is interested.

The spreading abroad (vv. 5, 32) and the dispersal (v. 18) of the peoples with their distinct languages receive a positive evaluation in Genesis 10 as a movement and distinction intended by God. A negative evaluation of the same phenomena is presented in the following episode in Gen. 11:1–9.

11:1–32
The End of the Beginnings

11:1–9, The Tower of Babel. This concluding narrative of the prehistory parallels Genesis 3 as a story of human rebellion against the limits and distinctions of the divine and human worlds. The individual rebellion of the first man and woman has become universal and characteristic of humankind. The cycle of creation (chaps. 1–2), sin and its progress (chaps. 3–4), and divine punishment (chaps. 6–8) begins again, with a statement of the unchanged evil of the human heart (8:21) followed by the renewal of creation (chap. 9) and a story of the worldwide extent of sin (chap. 11).

The hubris of humanity, the attempt to overcome the boundaries ordained by God, consists in the construction of a city with a temple-tower reaching to the heavens, challenging the supremacy of Yahweh. Thus the city builders will make a name for themselves. Since Hebrew *shem*, "name," includes the nuance both of fame or renown and of progeny, the city builders are engaged in an attempt to overcome the human fate of mortality as well (Gen. 3:4–5).

In an ironical comment of J, the Deity has to descend from his heavenly dwelling even to catch a glimpse of this product of human arrogance. The divine monologue in vv. 6–7 is similar to that in Gen. 3:22; this time the divine response is the confusion of language and the dispersal of the builders. While the universal extent of sin seems to call for a judgment as inclusive in its extent, Yahweh is faithful to his promise (8:21–22); the tower of Babel episode is followed not by a cataclysmic devastation but by the call of Abram, whose migration from Mesopotamia to Canaan is part of the great dispersal that follows Babel.

Gen. 11:1–9 shows some ambivalence about the works and achievements of civilization, a motif already evident in Gen. 4:17, where Cain is identified as the first city builder. The "achievement" of the city builders of Genesis 11 is alienation, inability to communicate, and dispersal. Given the context of J, perhaps we can see here an ambivalence toward Solomon's construction of the Temple, an ambivalence evident in the prophetic critique of Temple and Temple service. Such a reading of Genesis 11 would balance the critique of the royal theology of the divine king that some have seen at the beginning of the J material in chaps. 2–3.

11:10–32, From Shem to Abraham. The prehistory concludes with a ten-generation genealogy (like that in Gen. 5:1–32, which it continues) that traces the line of descent from Shem to Abram and his two brothers, Nahor and Haran. Nahor's twelve sons are listed in Gen. 22:20–24. Haran's son Lot will figure in several episodes in the Abraham cycle. The fact that several of the personal names in the Shem genealogy, including Nahor and Haran, are also place names of cities in Mesopotamia has been understood to support the Mesopotamian origins of the patriarchs (→ Haran; Nahor).

Myth

The relationship and dependence of the early chapters of Genesis on ancient Near Eastern myth raise the question of whether these chapters can themselves be designated as myths. The problem is compounded by the controversial issue of the definition of myth. While myth is notoriously difficult to define, at least the following characteristics are involved in its description. First, the language of myth is narrative and dramatic, and myths may have been related to ritual and cult; on occasion they served as the libretto, the interpretive text for the ritual. Second, the actors and participants in myth are supernatural agents (gods, angels, demons). Third, the action of myth is characterized by remoteness in time and space (in the beginning, at the end time, in the divine world). Fourth, myths are related to communities, for which they order human experience by providing a vision of the underlying structure of reality; myth informs the community about its origins, its identity, and its destiny. Fifth, the goal of myth is "salvation," broadly understood as whatever contributes to human well being.

If these characteristics are an adequate description of myth, there need be little difficulty in describing the material in Genesis 1–11 as myth, especially when so much of it is the Israelite version of ancient Near Eastern myth. Given the lack of consensus even on the proper definition of myth, however, perhaps it would be better to think of the stories of Genesis 1–11 as "parables," theological narratives whose intention is to present the Israelite view of the meaning of such fundamental realities as God transcendent and immanent, the creation, blessed humankind, the frustration of God's design by human sin, and the restoration and renewal of humanity by divine grace.

12:1–25:18

The Abraham Cycle

The Abraham stories are linked to Genesis 1–11 by the genealogy in chap. 11 that traces the line of descent from Shem to Abraham. The genealogies in Genesis 5, 10, and 11 have progressively narrowed the focus from Adam to Noah to Shem and finally to Abraham. The Genesis narratives continue this genealogical interest in the passages that deal with Abraham and his descendants Isaac, Jacob, and Jacob's sons, the progenitors of the people of Israel. In these narratives there is further narrowing and divine election (not Ishmael but Isaac; not Esau but Jacob).

Genesis 2–11 vividly portrayed humanity under the curse (Gen. 3:14, 17; 4:11; 5:29). Genesis 12 begins the narrative of humanity blessed, in the family of Abraham. If the blessing of Abraham is a centripetal force, promising the patriarch a son and descendants who will be the source of blessing for all humanity, there is also a centrifugal force at work: strife and deception in the family of Abraham. Deception on the part of Abraham endangers the matriarch and therefore the divine promise; family conflict breaks out between Abraham's wives, Sarah and Hagar, and their respective sons. Stories of strife and deception continue in the Jacob-Esau and Jacob-Laban stories, finally escalating to the disintegration of a family in the Joseph narrative. Yet through all this divine grace is at work, tending toward the reconciliation with which Genesis ends.

12:1–20

The Call of Abraham and His Response

12:1–3, The Call of the Patriarch. With the call of Abram there begins a new history of blessing, which is passed on in each instance to the chosen successor (Gen. 18:18; 22:15–18; 26:2–4; 28:14). The call of Abram is linked to the last narrative of the prehistory by catchwords: the settlers in the valley of Shinar propose to build a city, to make a name for themselves, and to avoid being dispersed. The human effort to secure community and renown is judged by God as human hubris. But the pattern of God's judgment mitigated by his grace in the J narratives of Genesis 2–11 continues, reaching a climax in the call of Abram, who is promised a great nation and a great name as the source of blessing for all humanity. What human beings failed to achieve by their own efforts comes to the family of Abram and through that family to all humanity as divine gift.

Not only do the promised blessings conferred on Abram recall the Tower of Babel narra-

tive. Yahweh's promised gifts of land, progeny, and earthly prosperity in 12:1–3 are a reversal of the curses in Eden (3:16–19) of a hostile earth, pain in human generativity, and endless human toil (→ Patriarch).

The opening of the Abraham cycle (vv. 1–3) is programmatic for the whole J narrative: association with the ancestors will bring blessing to humanity (30:27; 39:5; 50:20); separation from the blessed family results in curse (13:1–13; 19; 21). The Deuteronomist understands the promises to Abraham to be fulfilled in the success of David, to whom Yahweh gives a great name, a land, and an heir (2 Sam. 7:9–12).

12:4–9, The Patriarch's Response. Abram is directed by Yahweh to leave the security of his past ("your land, your kin, and the house of your father") to become a great nation. Obvious obstacles standing in the way of the promise are the barrenness of Sarai (11:30), complicated by the advanced age of the husband and wife (12:4), and the fact that the promised land is already occupied and inhabited (12:6; 13:7). Abram responds to the divine command by migrating to Canaan, which is identified as the land of promise (12:7) in a theophany (a visible manifestation of God) and a reaffirmation of the promise of land. Closing the section is Abram's construction of an altar on a site made holy by a theophany and his invocation of the name of Yahweh (13:4, 18; 22:9).

12:10–20, The Promise Endangered. In this episode, Abram's conduct threatens the promises of land and descendants. Directed by Yahweh to the land of Canaan, which is confirmed as the promised land in 12:7, Abram nevertheless leaves Canaan because of famine and travels to Egypt. Having put into question his relationship to the promised land, Abram adds the further complication of a deception that threatens to undo the promise of a child born of Sarai. Fearing that Sarai's beauty will lead to her husband's murder by those who would possess her, Abram directs Sarai to claim that she is his sister rather than his wife. This is the first of three versions of the endangering of the ancestress (Gen. 20; 26:1–11). It can also profitably be compared to the story of David's adultery with Bathsheba in 2 Samuel 11–12 and the story of Ahab's seizure of Naboth's vineyard in 1 Kings 21. All these narratives deal with royal desire (for Sarai, for Bathsheba, for a vineyard) and its fulfillment by violence (Abram in 12:12 is afraid that he will be murdered; Uriah and Naboth are actually murdered).

The story contains several ironic notes. Abram, who is to be the source of blessing, becomes rather the occasion of danger and curse to Sarai and to the Pharaoh; also ironic is the list of the wealth Abram acquires in Egypt, since it does not include his wife, described by

J as an essential element of a man's life (Gen. 2:23–24).

Two final observations on 12:1–20 are in order. First, in this narrative Abram experiences in advance what his descendants would later undergo: descent into Egypt because of famine, involvement with the Pharaoh, enrichment in Egypt, plagues, and release. Both stories involve a deception as well, the identification of Sarai as Abram's sister, and the request to celebrate a feast in the desert (Exod. 5:1–3). This same motif of the anticipation of the Exodus occurs in the Hagar stories in Genesis 16 and 21. Second, a noteworthy subtheme in the narrative is the contrast of Abram's plan with Yahweh's plan, a motif found prominently in the Joseph story (45:5–8; 50:20) and in wisdom literature (Prov. 16:9; 19:21).

13:1–14:24
Abraham the Shepherd and Sheik

13:1–18, Abram and Lot. Genesis 13 is the first of several narratives involving Abraham's nephew Lot. His birth was reported in 11:27, and his association with Abram is noted in 11:31 and 12:4–5. Genesis 13 describes the prosperity of Lot resulting from this association with the blessed family of Abram (13:1, 5). The family, however, is divided by conflict, and the strife leads to separation (v. 11). For Lot, separation from Abram means separation from the blessing. Abram ends the strife by inviting Lot to take what land he wishes. Lot chooses the well-watered Jordan plain, but his choice is not without a dark side. The narrator describes Lot's chosen territory as "like Yahweh's garden" (the site of the primal sin and the divine curse) and "like Egypt" (the place of oppression, as Gen. 15:13 indicates), and as including the doomed cities Sodom and Gomorrah (vv. 10–13).

The contrast the story builds between Abram and Lot is striking. To Abram Yahweh gives the land "forever" (v. 15), while Lot (v. 11) takes for himself land that is soon to be destroyed (chap. 19). Abram responds to the divine gift by building an altar at Hebron (v. 18), while Lot settles near Sodom (v. 12). Abram the tent dweller invokes Yahweh by name, while Lot the city dweller associates with the inhabitants of Sodom who are "evil and very sinful against Yahweh" (v. 13). The separation of Lot from Abram involves separation from the source of blessing to a place under the curse. The stories about Lot will continue in chaps. 14 and 19.

14:1–24, Abram's Rescue of Lot and His Tithe to Melchizedek. Genesis 14 cannot be aligned with any of the traditional pentateuchal sources. It is composed of annalistic material (battle reports) and a hero story cele-brating the military exploits of Abram. Its closest parallel is 1 Samuel 30, David's campaign against the Amalekites. The description of Abram as a "Hebrew" (v. 13) is unparalleled, as is his presentation as a sheik who can call up a large contingent of 318 servants and retainers.

The story begins with an account of a rebellion by vassals of Chedorlaomer, king of Elam; among the rebellious vassals are the kings of Sodom and Gomorrah. The victory of Chedorlaomer and his allies over a pentapolis including Sodom involves Abram because his kinsman Lot has been taken with all his possessions as spoils of the victor. (The reference to Lot may be secondary; at any rate it was the occasion for the placing of this story in its present context, after Gen. 13.)

On his return after his rescue of Lot, Abram is met by Melchizedek, king of Salem (Jerusalem, Ps. 76:2) and priest of God Most High (Heb. 'El 'Elyon; for the identification of this god with Yahweh cf. Pss. 47:2; 57:2; 78:35, 56). In his ceremonious greeting of a hero returning from his victory (cf. 1 Sam. 18:6), Melchizedek (who appears only here, in Ps. 110:4, and in the NT in Heb. 5–7) blesses Abram, who responds to the blessing with a tithe. The point of the story may be the legitimation of the sacral status of Jerusalem as far back as the ancestor Abram (cf. a similar concern in 2 Chron. 3:1). As adopted by J, the story has become part of the narratives dealing with Abram and Lot. The effect of Lot's separation from Abram in Genesis 13 is seen in Lot's loss of his freedom and his wealth (gained through his association with Abram) as spoils to the victorious kings (14:11–12). Lot recovers his freedom and his goods when, in vv. 13–16, he is reconnected with Abram (→ El; Hebrews).

15:1–17:27
The Covenant with Abraham and the Birth of Ishmael

15:1–21, The Covenant with Abram. The major concern of the divine speech in Genesis 15 is the promise to Abram of progeny and land. The assignment of this chapter to one of the pentateuchal sources (either J or E) is debated, and no attempt to divide the material into sources has been entirely convincing.

The chapter falls naturally into two parts (vv. 1–6 and 7–21), each with the same basic structure: an initial self-identification by the Deity (vv. 1 and 7); Abram's response, a complaint (v. 3) or a question (v. 8); Yahweh's reiteration of the promise of an heir and of numerous descendants (vv. 4–5) or of land (vv. 7, 18–21). In the first part, the expression "The word of Yahweh came to Abram," which occurs twice (vv. 1, 4), is a stereotypical prophetic formula (Jer. 1:2; Hos. 1:1; Mic. 1:1). This formula and the communication to Abram in a vision (Gen. 15:1) or a dream (v. 12) have suggested to some that we meet in Genesis 15 the first appearance of E material in the Pentateuch.

The second divine speech can be further subdivided into three sections: vv. 7–12, 13–16, and 17–21. The middle section, in which Yahweh speaks of the coming Egyptian oppression and the Exodus, interrupts the preparation for the ritual act in vv. 9–12 and its execution in v. 17. The passage of the symbols of the Deity between the parts of the sacrifice is an enacted ritual of self-cursing in which the one passing through the pieces of the slaughtered animals calls upon himself the same fate for not adhering to the pledge. Other instances of such self-imprecation are Jer. 34:18–19 and an Aramaic inscription of the eighth century B.C. (the Sefire treaty).

This ritual, described as a covenant (v. 18), is of the "royal grant" type, in which a king rewards a servant or vassal for past loyalty and faithful service and in which the obligations of the covenant do not fall upon the inferior party, but are self-imposed by the king. Since such royal grants often involved grants of land, boundaries had to be precisely and exactly drawn, as in v. 18 (→Covenant). The boundaries of v. 18 are the ideal limits of the Davidic-Solomonic state in the tenth century B.C.

The similarity of the patriarchal covenant to the royal covenant (2 Sam. 7:11–16; Ps. 89:19–37) has often been noted. To explain the similarity, it has been suggested that the old tradition of a covenant with Abraham was reshaped by contact with the royal theology and ideology of the ancient Near East, in its Israelite version. Such a covenant with Abraham, with royal features highlighted and perhaps retrojected (read back into the distant past), would supply a welcome and needed precedent for the innovation of royal ideology in Israel.

16:1–16, The Birth of Ishmael. The divine promise of progeny to Abram in Genesis 15 is followed by the birth in chap. 16 of his son Ishmael, as the result of Sarai's initiative and impatience. Verse 1 introduces the two principals in the story, the barren Sarai and Hagar her slave, who is given to Abram as a secondary wife and whose child will be considered legally the offspring of Sarai (vv. 2–3). Such substitute childbearing, reflected also in Gen. 30:1–13, was apparently an accepted social institution in the ancient Near East. Verses 4–5 introduce the motif of familial discord between the childless Sarai and the pregnant Hagar (cf. 1 Sam. 1:4–6) and between Sarai and Abraham. This theme of familial strife occurs throughout Genesis, between spouses (Gen. 3:12; 30:1–2), between brothers (Gen. 4:1–16, 27; 37), and between kin

(Genesis 29–31). Sarai's abuse of Hagar (v. 6) provokes the slave's flight, until she is commanded to return by a theophany in which the angel of Yahweh directs her to submit to her mistress's abuse (v. 9), with the assurance that "Yahweh has heard your [complaint of] abuse" (v. 11).

This discord between Sarai and Hagar takes up the language of the promise to Abram that "those who curse you [Heb. qillel] I will curse" (12:3). Because in 16:4–5 Sarai was treated with disdain by the pregnant Hagar (lit., Sarai was "cursed" [qillel] in Hagar's eyes), Hagar and her family will be separated like Lot (chap. 13) from Abram and the blessing (Gen. 16:6–8; 21:14–21).

The angelic annunciation of the birth of a son to Hagar in vv. 7–13 follows a standard biblical pattern that usually includes the following: first, the appearance of an angel of the Lord (Gen. 16:7; 18:2; Judg. 13:3; Matt. 1:20; Luke 1:11, 26) or of Yahweh himself (Gen. 16:13; 17:1); second, fear or prostration of the visionary (Gen. 17:3; Judg. 13:22; Luke 1:12, 29); third, the angelic promise to the visionary of the birth of a son (Gen. 16:11; 17:19; 18:10; Judg. 13:3–5; Matt. 1:20–21; Luke 1:13, 31); fourth, the name of the child, sometimes with an etymology (Gen. 16:11; 17:17–19; Matt. 1:21; Luke 1:31); fifth, the future achievements of the child (Gen. 16:12; 17:16, 19; Judg. 13:5; Matt. 1:21; Luke 1:15–17, 32–33, 35); and sixth, objection or question of the visionary (Gen. 17:17; 18:12; Judg. 13:8, 17; Luke 1:18, 34). Often the objection or question will be concerned with the obstacles (barrenness, advanced age, virginity) seemingly in the way of the accomplishment of the divine purpose.

Another noteworthy element in the annunciation of the birth of Ishmael is the striking similarity of Gen. 16:11 to Deut. 26:6–7 ("Since the Egyptians mistreated and abused us, we cried out to Yahweh, the God of our ancestors; Yahweh heard our voice, and he saw our abuse"). The "abuse" that is mentioned twice in the Deuteronomy passage and three times in Genesis 16 (vv. 6, 9, 11) occurs as well in Gen. 15:13, in the prediction of Israel's oppression by Egypt. In an ironic twist, it is Hagar the Egyptian who, in Genesis 16, endures slavery and abuse by Sarai. This link with the Exodus story is further underlined by Hagar's flight to the wilderness (Gen. 16:6–7; Exod. 14:3, 5) and her encounter there with an angel of the Lord (Gen. 16:7; Exod. 2:15–3:2; 14:19). In both cases (Sarai's mistreatment of the Egyptian slave Hagar and the oppression of the descendants of Sarai by Hagar's compatriots), a cry for help is answered by a compassionate God (Exod. 3:7–8).

17:1–27, The Covenant with Abraham. Genesis 17 is the P version of God's covenant with the patriarch, involving promises of a son and of the eternal possession of the land of Canaan. Like its parallel in chap. 15, it begins with a theophany; the Deity's self-identification here is El Shaddai (traditionally rendered "God the Almighty"); its probable original meaning is "God, the One of the mountain," an epithet that recalls the standard association of gods with their mountain abodes, like Baal's Mount Zaphon and Yahweh's Sinai and Zion (→ Mount, Mountain). This pre-Mosaic designation of God in P (Exod. 6:2–3) is followed by a divine command ("Walk before me and be perfect"; cf. Gen. 24:40; 48:15) that is similar to the command given to Solomon (1 Kings 3:6; 9:4) and to the appeal of Hezekiah (2 Kings 20:3). Such royal language is appropriate for the patriarch who will be the father of kings (vv. 6, 16).

The name changes of the ancestors to Abraham and Sarah (vv. 5, 15) imply both the authority of the giver of the new name (cf. Gen. 3:20) and the new destiny or mission indicated by the new name (cf. Gen. 32:29; Mark 3:16).

P's designation of the covenant with Abraham as "eternal" recalls P's "eternal covenant" with Noah in Gen. 9:1–17 and asserts the covenant's unconditional character and permanent validity. Similarly, the ritual institution of circumcision as a sign of the covenant recalls the divine institution of the Sabbath at the creation (Gen. 2:3) and the Noachian prohibition upon eating meat with the blood still in it (Gen. 9:4). Note, too, that circumcision as the eternal *sign* of the covenant recalls the role of the rainbow in the story of Noah (Gen. 9:12–16) and of the Sabbath in the revelation to Moses (Exod. 31:12–17).

While Ishmael will be the progenitor of a great people (Gen. 16:10; 17:20), God declares that the child of the promise will be born of the matriarch Sarah. Abraham's laughter (Heb. *yitzchaq* in v. 17), provoked by this divine declaration, provides an etymology for the name Isaac (v. 21).

18:1–19:38
The Fate of Sodom and Gomorrah

18:1–15, Abraham's Hospitality. Abraham is again repeatedly characterized (vv. 2, 6, 9, 10) as a nomadic tent-dweller, in tacit contrast to the urbanite Lot of Genesis 19. When three unexpected travelers arrive at his tent at midday, Abraham's hospitable invitation and solicitude are described in some detail (cf. 1 Sam. 28:24–25). He runs to greet his unexpected guests, then hurries off to instruct Sarah to prepare bread for a meal, runs again to choose an animal for the feast, and serves them (v. 8, lit., "stands before them") himself (→ Hospitality).

The accompaniment of a major deity by two attendants, a common feature in Canaanite polytheism, is reflected here in Yahweh and his two companions and, in demythologized form, in Pss. 23:6 (Yahweh's "goodness and kindness"); 43:3 (his "light and truth"); and 97:2 (his "justice and judgment").

The point of this first scene in the chapter is the announcement by Yahweh of the birth of a son to Abraham and Sarah, despite her barrenness and their advanced age. Sarah's incredulous laughter at this announcement (Heb. *titzchaq*) parallels Abraham's laughter in 17:17; however, Sarah's laughter, unlike that of Abraham, is judged negatively by Yahweh as revealing a lack of trust in the divine word.

18:16–33, Abraham's Intercession and Yahweh's Justice. With the typical politeness of a good host, Abraham intends to accompany his guests for part of their journey, as they continue on toward Sodom. In an interior monologue (vv. 17–19), Yahweh considers revealing his intentions to Abraham (cf. Amos 3:7). In the present Hebrew text, Abraham's dialogue with Yahweh begins with the statement that he is in attendance upon (v. 22, lit., "standing before" as in v. 8) Yahweh. This is one of the rare scribal adjustments of the text, which originally pictured Yahweh as "standing before" Abraham; it is not the anthropomorphism of the text that provoked the change, but the description (inappropriate to the scribes) of Yahweh standing in attendance before the patriarch. The description of Abraham in attendance upon Yahweh in 18:8 may have suggested the change of the text here.

While the two attendants make their way to the doomed city, Abraham intercedes for Sodom, raising the possibility of the influence of a righteous few on an evil majority. The same question is raised in Jer. 5:1, where the presence of only one righteous person could save Jerusalem, and in Ezek. 14:12–20, where the righteous will save only themselves. Also indicating the likely late origin of this passage are the echoes of Job in Abraham's intercession: mere dust and ashes (Gen. 18:27; Job 30:19; 42:6), Abraham presumes to question the Deity (Gen. 18:24–25; Job 9:12) about divine justice (Gen. 18:25; Job 9:22). The connections of Jeremiah, Ezekiel, and Job with Abraham's intercession have suggested to some commentators that Gen. 18:22–33 is a late addition to the text provoked by the religious crisis of the Exile of the sixth century B.C. and the questions about God's justice it raised. The prophetic denunciations of Jerusalem as Sodom (Isa. 3:9; Jer. 23:14; Ezek. 16:46–56) may give some credence to this view.

In his intercession for Sodom, Abraham assumes the function of a prophet (1 Sam. 7:5; 12:19, 23; Jer. 7:16; 11:14; 37:3; 42:2, 4, 20). And Abraham will be explicitly identified as a prophet in Gen. 20:7, where he is also involved in intercession. Of all the instances of prophetic intercession, however, the one most closely related to Gen. 18:22–33 is Amos 7:1–6. Not only does this intercession take the form of a dialogue between Yahweh and the prophet; but one of the punishments averted by Amos is a rain of fire (cf. Gen. 19:24).

19:1–29, The Rescue of Lot from Sodom. Genesis 19 takes up the story of Lot, who last appeared in chaps. 13–14. The account of Lot's hospitality to the two angels who traveled on to Sodom (19:1–3) is an abbreviated parallel to Gen. 18:1–8, but with several revealing differences. Abraham the tent dweller provides refreshment characteristic of a pastoral nomad: cream and curds (Gen. 18:8; cf. Isa. 7:21–22) and a choice steer. Lot is a city dweller who lives in a house in Sodom and meets the two strangers who arrive in the evening at the city gate. Abraham runs to greet the travelers and serves them himself; Lot stands and bows in greeting. In place of bread made from about a bushel of the finest flour (Gen. 18:6), Lot offers unleavened bread to his guests. Such differences may serve to contrast Lot's entertainment of the guests with the greater generosity of Abraham.

The meal is soon interrupted by the inhabitants of Sodom, who surround Lot's house and demand that he bring out his guests for gang rape. Lot's responsibility as host leads him to offer his two daughters to the mob, until he is rescued from their violence by the angelic visitors. There is an effective contrast between the hospitality of Lot, who "pressed" (v. 3—Heb. *yiptzar*) the visitors to stay with him, and the inhospitality of the townspeople who "pressed" (v. 9—Heb. *yiptzeru*) against Lot in their attempt to break into his house.

The violent, unnatural lust of humans for heavenly beings (vv. 4–11) is the reverse of the situation in Gen. 6:1–4 where, as a prelude to the Flood, divine beings mate with human women. Like Noah, Lot too will be saved from the cataclysmic disaster that will befall Sodom.

There is a close parallel account to Gen. 19:1–11 in Judg. 19:10–30. In both stories, there is a strong contrast between hospitality and the brutality of a violent sexual attack. In Judges 19, the men of Gibeah demand that the guest be brought out for sexual abuse. The host offers rather his daughter, or the concubine of his guest, who is put out and abused throughout the night and is found dead at the door the next morning. Homosexual acts, which threaten proper family relationships and boundaries (Lev. 18:22; 20:13; 1 Cor. 6:9–10; Rom. 1:26–27), run counter to the divine command to procreate (Gen. 1:28; 9:1, 7), a command that is part of the order of creation (→Homosexuality).

The danger to Lot's guests is averted when they afflict the inhabitants of Sodom with temporary blindness (cf. 2 Kings 6:18). After the angels order Lot to leave Sodom, he informs his sons-in-law, who treat his warning like a joke; their laughter (v. 14) reminds readers of Sarah's laughter at the promise of one of the angelic visitors that she would bear a child (18:12–15; this catchword also looks forward to Gen. 21:6). A second time the angels order departure and Lot again hesitates, irresolute, until the angels take Lot, his wife, and his daughters by the hand and lead them like children out of the city.

Outside the doomed city, when the angels direct Lot to flee with his family to the hill country, he asks rather to go to Zoar instead (19:20–23). In v. 30, he will change his mind and go to the hill country, one more indication of his confusion. When Lot's wife mirrors his irresolution and violates the prohibition of looking back (v. 17), she is turned into a pillar of salt (v. 26). One is reminded of the laughter of Abraham and Sarah in Genesis 17–18. Abraham's laughter at the promise of a child in 17:17 is passed over without comment; Sarah's similarly provoked laughter (18:12) is judged to be an indication of a lack of faith. The summarizing conclusion of the story in 19:29 is from P; it notes that "God remembered Abraham" and thus saved Lot, in a reminiscence of the high point of the Flood story in Gen. 8:1 ("God remembered Noah").

19:30–38, Lot's Daughters. Lot's passivity is underscored by the concluding episode in chap. 19. Since their husbands perished in the destruction of Sodom, the daughters of Lot realize their desire for offspring by incest with their father, another offense against the proper use of sexuality. Lot, who volunteered his daughters for sexual abuse by the men of Sodom, is plied with wine and becomes himself a passive object in the incestuous relations with his daughters, who give birth to Moab and Ammon. There are two more indications of Lot's passivity in the story. First, the Hebrew verb used in the episode for sexual relations (*shakab*, "lie [with]") generally has a masculine subject and a feminine object (as in Gen. 26:10; 30:15, 16; 34:2, 7; 35:22; 39:7, 12, 14). In the story of Lot and his daughters, the sexual stereotype of a patriarchal culture is reversed when the five uses of *shakab* have Lot's daughters as subject and their inebriated father as object. Second, it is noteworthy that the sons are named not by Lot but by his daughters (cf. Gen. 21:3).

Mention was made above of the connection of Gen. 6:1–4, the initial scene of the Flood story, to Gen. 19:4–11 and of the P conclusion to the destruction of Sodom in Gen. 19:29 to the climax of the Flood story in Gen. 8:1. The episode in 19:30–38 is similarly related to the closing scene of the Flood story in Gen. 9:18–

24, which also involves the violation of some sexual taboo by one of Noah's sons when Noah was overcome with wine. Given these links, it is not surprising that the two NT references to Lot connect him with Noah (Luke 17:26–29; 2 Pet. 2:5–7).

20:1–22:24
Stories from the Elohist

In this cycle of stories from the E source, each of the three stories displays the same structure: God instructs Abraham to initiate a course of action that will involve mortal danger to another family member (Gen. 20:13; 21:12; 22:2); the patriarch obeys (20:1–2; 21:14; 22:3); the threatening situation is about to be realized (20:2, 18; 21:16; 22:9–10); and God intervenes to prevent the expected outcome (20:6–7, 17; 21:19–20; 22:11–13).

20:1–18, Abraham and Sarah in Gerar.
The first of these stories is the E version of the wife-sister deception story that first appeared in Gen. 12:10–20. In E, Abraham and Sarah journey to the Negeb and settle in Gerar. The sexual relations between the Pharaoh and Sarah implied in chap. 12 are prevented here by a divine warning to Abimelech in a dream. Characteristics of the E source besides the divine name 'Elohim (Heb.) include the motif of the fear of God (20:8, 11), Abraham's prophetic intercession for the monarch (vv. 7, 17), and the justification of the patriarch's claim that Sarah is his sister (v. 12). While divine communication by a dream is sometimes seen as also characteristic of E, such dreams are ubiquitous in the ancient Near East and in the OT. The story ends with the enriching of Abraham (20:14; cf. 12:16) and the restoration of health and fertility to Abimelech's house, as a prelude to the pregnancy of Sarah (21:1–2). (For wealth and progeny as a sign of divine favor, see also Gen. 24:35–36.)

As the J version of the story in Genesis 12 included Abraham's proleptic experience of the Torah story of Egyptian oppression and liberation, so the E version focuses its attention on Abraham as a prophetic figure (cf. "the law and the prophets" in Mal. 4:4–5 and, in the NT, in Matt. 22:40 and Luke 24:27).

The story reveals an openness to non-Israelites. It is Abimelech the righteous Gentile who displays proper fear of God and receives a divine communication, while Abraham underestimates the extent of God's influence and power.

21:1–34, The Birth of Isaac and the Expulsion of Hagar.
In the present form of the tradition, Isaac serves chiefly as a link between the larger Abraham and Jacob cycles; the Isaac material is limited to the account of his birth

(chap. 21), his sacrifice (chap. 22), his marriage (chap. 24), his trip to Gerar (chap. 26), and his blessing of Jacob (chap. 27).

The E story of the birth of Isaac (21:1–8) repeats the motif of Sarah's laughter (v. 6) from 18:12; here it is an expression of joy at the birth of her son, not an indication of a lack of faith. Gen. 21:9 reintroduces Hagar the Egyptian and her son Ishmael (chap. 16) and the recurring theme of family discord. In 21:3, Abraham names his son by Sarah Isaac (Heb. *yitzchaq*). What Ishmael is doing in the Hebrew text of v. 9 is described as *metzacheq*, a verbal form derived from the same root as the name Isaac. Modern translations favor the interpretation "playing" for the verb, with the addition of "with her son Isaac" (which is not in the Hebrew) from the Septuagint (LXX). Perhaps the most economical and reasonable solution is to understand the LXX addition as interpretive and to translate the Hebrew in v. 9 thus: "Sarah saw Hagar the Egyptian's son, whom she had borne to Abraham, 'Isaacing' [i.e., taking the place of Sarah's son Isaac]." An angry Sarah orders Abraham to expel Hagar and the pretender to Isaac's rights. Sarah's demand is confirmed by a divine oracle (vv. 12–13), and so Abraham proceeds. His feelings are delicately hinted at in his solicitude for Hagar and Ishmael (v. 14). The imminent death of the child Ishmael in the wilderness to which Hagar has gone is averted by the angel of God (as will be the imminent death of Isaac in the next chapter). The angel repeats the divine declaration (21:13) that Ishmael will be the progenitor of a great nation (16:10). There is a subtle contrast between 21:12, where God instructs Abraham to "hear the voice" of ("obey") Sarah in her lack of compassion, and v. 17, where God twice "heard the voice of the youth" because of his compassion. This play reminds readers of the etymology of the name Ishmael ("May God hear") in Gen. 16:11.

As in Genesis 20, we meet the theme of the righteous Gentile in Hagar, who like Abimelech the God-fearer is given a message from God and whose child was saved by divine intervention.

Like Genesis 16, this chapter contains echoes of the Exodus story. When Sarah demands that Abraham "drive out" (v. 10) Hagar and her son, he "sends them away" (v. 14) to wander in the wilderness. Similarly, Moses asks Pharaoh to "send my people away" (Exod. 5:1) and so the people are "driven out" of Egypt (Exod. 6:1; 11:1).

The chapter is concluded with a pact between Abimelech and Abraham (21:22–34) to settle a dispute over water rights (cf. Gen. 13:6–7; 26:15–22).

22:1–24, Abraham's Sacrifice of Isaac.
In Gen. 12:1–3, Abraham was called by God to relinquish his past for the promise that he

would be the father of a great nation. In the divine command to sacrifice Isaac in chap. 22, Abraham is directed to give up the future and the promise as well. Since the style of this magnificently told story is spare and compressed, any apparent prolixity is meant to catch readers' attention. For instance, v. 2 emphasizes the enormity of what Abraham is asked by the piling up of synonyms: "Take your son, your only one, the one you love, Isaac." In wordless obedience Abraham journeys with his son and two attendants to Moriah. In v. 5, when he tells the attendants that "I and the boy ... will return," he unconsciously prepares for the unexpected conclusion of this dark story. In vv. 7–8, the poignancy of the story is highlighted by the dialogue between Abraham and Isaac, in which "father" and "son" are each used twice. The movement slows in vv. 9–10, as each act in preparation for the sacrifice is carefully described. The tension is finally resolved by a divine intervention in vv. 11–12, and Abraham's obedient loyalty is rewarded with a repetition of the promise (vv. 17–18).

Appended to the story of the binding of Isaac is Gen. 22:20–24, a list of the twelve sons of Abraham's brother Nahor. One of these sons is Bethuel, the father of Rebekah, who will become Isaac's wife in chap. 24.

Examined form-critically, this E narrative of Abraham's fidelity shows evidence of earlier stages and concerns. Verses 1–14 probably explain the origin of the form of worship of a particular sanctuary; they legitimate the substitution of an animal for child sacrifice. For the practice of child sacrifice, cf. 2 Kings 3:27; Jer. 7:31; Ezek. 16:20; for its prohibition, Exod. 13:15; Deut. 12:29–31; 18:9–12.

Genesis 21 and 22 are linked both by theme and by key word repetition. In chap. 21, Ishmael's expulsion, demanded by Sarah and approved by God, is carried out by Abraham, although it means the death of the child who was legally Sarah's. In chap. 22, Isaac, born to Sarah after long infertility, now is taken from her by Abraham's obedience to his apparent death. Both Ishmael and Isaac are exposed to death by the patriarch's obedience to God. A key word link can be seen in 21:14, where Abraham places (Heb. sam) bread and water on Hagar's back, and in 22:6, where Abraham places (Heb. yasem) the wood for the holocaust upon Isaac.

23:1–25:18
From the Death of Sarah to Abraham's Death

23:1–20, Abraham's Purchase of Land in Canaan. The purchase of a family burial plot occasioned by the death of Sarah is the subject of this P story. The transaction between Abraham and Ephron the Hittite seems to involve both Oriental politeness and ancient Near Eastern property law. Ephron's insistence that he sell to Abraham both the cave of Machpelah and the field where it is located reflects the attachment of certain feudal duties to the field, which Ephron would be glad to pass on to Abraham. In the present context, it foreshadows the eventual possession of the land of Canaan by Abraham's descendants, as does Jacob's purchase of land in 33:19. Abraham's death and burial here is recorded in 25:8–10. The burial of Isaac, Rebekah, Jacob, and Leah there is noted in Gen. 49:29–31 (→ Hittites; Machpelah).

24:1–67, The Wooing of Rebekah. The story of the mission of Abraham's steward to seek a wife for Isaac among Abraham's kindred in Mesopotamia is told twice, first in Abraham's instructions to his servant, followed by the narration in vv. 1–27 of the servant's arrival and then in the servant's retelling of the story to Rebekah and her family in vv. 34–49. The meeting at a well in vv. 11–27 that leads to a marriage is a stock scene that appears also in Genesis 29, Exodus 2, and John 4.

J has fashioned the account of the wooing of Rebekah upon the model of the call of Abraham. In 24:1, 35–36 we learn that, in accord with his promise in Gen. 12:2, Yahweh has blessed Abraham with long years, great wealth, and a son. The verb "bless" is a key word in this chapter, occurring in vv. 1, 27, 31, 35, 48, and 60. God's command "Go!" to the patriarch in 12:1 is complemented by Rebekah's "I will go" in 24:58 (and her family's "she will go" in v. 55). In 12:1, Yahweh commands Abraham to leave "your land and your kinsfolk and the house of your father." In chap. 24, the same expression occurs in whole or in part in vv. 4, 7, 38, and 40. Yahweh's promise to Abraham in 12:2 ("I will make your name great") is repeated in his servant's words in v. 35 ("Yahweh has blessed my master exceedingly and he has become great").

The echoes of Genesis 12 in this chapter make the point that Rebekah is an essential link in the transmission of the divine promise and is thus called by Yahweh, as Abraham was, to her matriarchal role. The climax of the account is Rebekah's one-word answer in v. 58, 'elek (Heb., "I will go"). The parallelism of 12:1, where Abram goes from his land, his family, and his father's house, with 24:4 and 38, where he sends his steward back to his land, kin, and father's house, forms a frame around most of the Abraham cycle of narratives.

The final element worthy of note is the comparison of Hagar in chap. 21, who, in departing from Abraham, moves away from the source of blessing and Rebekah in chap. 24, who, in agreeing to the marriage with Isaac, moves toward the blessing and becomes an honored member of the blessed family.

25:1–18, The Death of Abraham. Gen. 25:1 –18 recounts Abraham's marriage to Keturah after Sarah's death and a genealogy of their progeny. This is followed by a report of the patriarch's death and burial in the cave of Machpelah. The special status of Isaac is underlined in several ways in this material. Before his death, "Abraham gave everything that belonged to him to Isaac" while he gave "gifts" to the children of Keturah (vv. 5–6). As in the case of Hagar (21:14), Abraham sends these children away from Isaac (and thus from the blessing that he is to carry). After Abraham's death he is buried by his sons Isaac and Ishmael, a report followed by the statement that "God blessed [Abraham's] son Isaac" (25:11). The section concludes with a genealogy of the twelve sons of Ishmael and their father's death report. Thus, this chapter is structured with Isaac, his father's heir and blessed by God, in the middle with other children of Abraham ranged on either side (the sons of Keturah before and the sons of Ishmael after). The literary shape reflects the theological point that Isaac and his descendants bear a special status and a special destiny.

25:19–36:43

The Jacob Cycle

The chief themes of the Jacob material are announced in the account of the birth and youth of Jacob and Esau (25:19–34). As in the narratives about Abraham and his family, competition and family strife are the hallmarks of these stories: discord between the brothers Jacob and Esau that begins even before their birth and parental discord revealed in the love of Isaac for the elder Esau and of Rebekah for Jacob (25:28). After Jacob's departure from his murderously angry brother and his arrival in Mesopotamia, strife soon arises between Jacob and his kinsman Laban and between the wives of Jacob, the unloved Leah and the barren Rachel. Of climactic importance is Jacob's struggle with God on his return to Canaan. Fraternal and familial strife will be central to the ensuing Joseph story as well.

Another important theme of both the Abraham cycle and the Jacob material is deception: the deception of Isaac by Rebekah and Jacob, of Jacob by Laban, and finally of Laban by Jacob and Rachel. The theme of deception will continue powerfully and dramatically in the Joseph narrative as well. Its appearance throughout Genesis, from the deception of the woman in chap. 3 to the final deception of Joseph by his brothers in 50:15–17, shows it to be a major theme in the book.

The Jacob material can be approached in several ways. A traditional method has been source criticism, whereby the discrete elements of the composite narrative are distinguished and studied separately. J, E, and P are all present in the Jacob cycle of stories. For J, Jacob is a picaresque figure, a calculating deceiver and yet by divine choice the bearer of the blessing for his family and for those who come into connection with him. The character of Jacob undergoes a decisive and fundamental change in his contest with the Deity at Jabbok (32:23–32). In E, according to traditional source criticism, Jacob gains his brother's birthright not by deception but by Esau's exchange of it for food; Esau thus proves himself unworthy of the birthright that passes to Jacob. In the Elohist's view, Jacob's decisive encounter with God takes place at Bethel (chap. 28, of which vv. 11b–12, 17–18, 20–21a, and 22 are commonly assigned to E). In P, the encounter of Jacob at Bethel is recounted in 35:9–13.

Although source criticism has been one of the major advances in the study of a book like Genesis, there are problems associated with it. First of all, such neat and clear division of the material into its sources is not always possible. More recent study has understood the material not as the editorial compilation of sources, but as a corpus of material whose growth and development are more appropriately studied by tradition history. Further, it is debatable whether the fragmentary E material and the minimal P contribution offer any clear picture of Jacob independent of the Yahwist's presentation. Finally, such source criticism does not always pay enough attention to the unity into which the disparate material has been welded. For instance, is it really possible to assign the birthright incident in chap. 25 to E and the gaining of the parental blessing by deception in chap. 27 to J? Significantly, Esau in 27:36 combines both events with a wordplay on "birthright" (Heb. *bekorah*) and "blessing" (Heb. *beracah*) in a fragment of poetry in a chapter in which the direct discourse of Isaac is also cast in poetry (vv. 28–29; 39–40). In such an instance, the division of v. 36 into two sources would be illegitimate. The study of Genesis as literature by contemporary literary critics and as Scripture by canonical critics has brought back into focus the importance of the finished product now in our hands. While such perspectives do not cancel out the established gains of such historical-critical methods as source criticism, they do provide a salutary reminder that the final form of the text is the primary object of study and interpretation.

25:19–28:22

Jacob and Esau

25:19–34, The Birth and the Birthright. The story of the birth of Esau and Jacob begins with the motif of the matriarch's sterility (v. 21 —cf. Gen. 11:30; 30:1), a motif that highlights

Yahweh's accomplishment of his intent of numerous progeny from Abraham over apparently insuperable odds. The struggle of the twins even in Rebekah's womb provokes her to consult Yahweh, who announces the ultimate superiority of the younger brother (cf. Gen. 4:1–5; 37:5–11). The description in 25:25 of the firstborn Esau as "red" (Heb. *'admoni*) and "hairy" (Heb. *se'ar*) involve folk etymologies that indicate Esau's relationship to Edom (v. 30) and to Seir, a relationship spelled out in the genealogy of Esau in chap. 36 (→Edom; Edomites). This punning is continued in Esau's description in v. 30 of the requested food as "red" (*'adom*).

The conflict motif, first evident in the womb of Rebekah, continues through the delivery of the twins, as the second child to be born is already attempting to gain an advantage over his brother, by grasping his heel (v. 26). Conflict is also shown in the respective professions of the brothers (v. 27: Esau the hunter living in the wild, Jacob the tent-dwelling farmer) and in the opposing preferences of their parents (v. 28: Isaac's love for the firstborn Esau, Rebekah's love for Jacob).

The beginning of the fulfillment of the divine oracle proclaiming the divine choice of Jacob is recorded in the story of Esau's sale of his birthright to Jacob (vv. 27–34). The characters of the two brothers are well portrayed here—the impulsive Esau, thoughtless about the future in the face of present need, who sells his birthright to "stuff himself" (v. 30: the verb Esau uses means to stuff an animal with food), and the shrewd, calculating Jacob, leaving nothing to chance ("First sell . . . first swear" in vv. 31, 33). The concluding line in the birthright episode emphasizes Esau's carelessness in the assertion that "Esau despised [i.e., treated as worthless, contemptible] his birthright" (v. 34). In two other instances of the use of this verb, "despising Yahweh" (1 Sam. 2:30; 2 Sam. 12:9) brings upon the person guilty of this sin the divine curse. If that nuance is present here, there is a sharp contrast between Esau cursed and Jacob blessed.

26:1–11, Isaac, Rebekah, and Abimelech.
This is the third version of the wife-sister story that has already appeared in chaps. 12 and 20. The inclusion of this version here refocuses attention on Isaac and Rebekah, the dominant actors in the following story of Isaac's blessing. The mention of a famine in 26:1 recalls the J version in chap. 12; Abimelech, king of the Philistines in Gerar, recalls the E version in chap. 20. As in both previous tellings, a deception is involved in Isaac's statement that his wife Rebekah is his sister. The J account in 26:1–11, however, departs from the two previous versions in that the patriarch's wife is not taken into the harem of the foreign king.

Abimelech accidentally discovers the deception by his own powers of observation (v. 8). When the three versions of this story are compared synchronically, one can see that Gen. 12:10–20 is a proleptic summary of the Torah story in which Abram departs from Canaan because of famine and goes to Egypt where his family is oppressed by the Pharaoh and liberated by a series of plagues. The second story in chap. 20 designates Abraham a prophet in his intercession for Abimelech; also characteristic of prophetic material is the divine communication to Abimelech (20:3). Finally, Gen. 26:1–11 has a wisdom cast in that the means by which Abimelech uncovered the deception was not divine revelation (as in chaps. 12 and 20) but the use of his human powers of observation (→ Wisdom). Seen synchronically, then, the three accounts recall the division of the Jewish Scriptures into Torah, Prophets, and Writings (wherein is found the wisdom literature with its emphasis on human understanding and insight).

The presence of wisdom elements in the two J versions of this episode (the proverbial contrast between Abram's plan and Yahweh's plan in chap. 12; the nonrevelatory discovery of the truth in chap. 26) is not surprising. The composition of J as a national epic is effected in the tenth-century court of David and Solomon, a milieu where the wisdom influence would have been inescapable (see 2 Sam. 16:15–17:14; 1 Kings 10:1–9).

The theophany in Gen. 26:2–5 relates the transmission of the promise to Abraham of blessing, land, and numerous descendants (Gen. 12:1–3; 15; 17; 22:17–18) to his son Isaac. The divine blessing of Isaac is mentioned as well in 26:12, 24, and 29. The theophany introduces an important theme in Genesis: the divine presence abides with this patriarch (vv. 3, 24, 28) as it did with Abraham (Gen. 21:22) and will with Jacob (Gen. 28:15), Joseph (39:2, 21, 23), and Moses (Exod. 3:12). That elusive presence attains permanence in Israel when, under Moses' guidance at Sinai, Israel fulfills the divine command to "make me a sanctuary that I may dwell among them" (Exod. 25:8).

26:12–35, A Dispute over Water Rights.
This story begins by noting Isaac's success and increasing wealth because of the divine blessing. The enriching of the patriarch in a foreign land was present in Gen. 12:16 and 20:14–16; one is reminded of the tradition of the "despoiling of the Egyptians" in Exod. 3:21; 11:2; 12:35–36; and Ps. 105:37. The related motif of the success of an Israelite in a foreign court is a major factor in the Joseph story and in two late OT works, Esther and Daniel.

This J version of a dispute over water rights and its settlement by a pact between Isaac and

Abimelech is a doublet of the E account in 21:22–34, and it has connections with Gen. 13:5–7 as well; the departure of Isaac from Abimelech means the departure of the source of divine blessing for the Gentiles, which is association with a blessed descendant of Abraham (as in the Abram-Lot story in chap. 13). The covenant is concluded by a meal, as in Gen. 31:43–54 and Exod. 24:9–11 (→ Meals). Between the dispute and the pact is a second theophany to Isaac (Gen. 26:24). It begins with "Fear not!" a stereotypical introduction to an appearance of the Deity (cf. Gen. 15:1; 46:3), and repeats the assurance of divine presence, blessing, and numerous descendants. Like Abram in 12:8, Isaac responds by building an altar and calling upon the name of Yahweh. Gen. 26:34–35, a P addition about the marriage of Esau to a Hittite woman, forms a frame with 27:46 (also P) around the story of Esau's loss of his father's blessing.

27:1–46, The Deception of Isaac. In the J account of Isaac's deception, the patriarch, characteristically passive (as he was in the accounts of his sacrifice in chap. 22 and of his marriage in chap. 24), is managed by his determined wife. When Rebekah overhears that Isaac intends to give his blessing to Esau (as Sarah overheard the heavenly visitor's promise of a child in 18:10), she quickly works out a plan to assure that her beloved Jacob gains his father's blessing. The element of calculation in Jacob's character surfaces in his objection that, should the deception be discovered, he would receive not a blessing but a curse from his father (27:11–12). Rebekah's response ("On me be the curse, my son!") clears the way for Jacob to play his role in the deception, a passive role like his father's in the same story.

The disguise of Jacob involves his wearing his brother Esau's clothing; as will be seen, deception involving clothing is an important motif in the narrative about Jacob's beloved son Joseph (Gen. 37:31–33). Twice Isaac asks whether it is truly his son Esau, when Jacob presents himself dressed as his brother and with the food prepared for Isaac by Rebekah (27:18, 24), and twice Jacob answers affirmatively. When Isaac has conferred the blessing on Jacob, Esau appears; and Isaac's dialogue with his elder son (vv. 31–32) is an almost exact repetition of Isaac's dialogue with Jacob in vv. 18–19. There is one striking difference, however, between the two conversations of Jacob and of Esau with their father. In speaking to Jacob, Isaac calls him "my son" seven times (vv. 18, 20, 21 [twice], 24, 26, 27; also "his son" in v. 20) while only once (v. 37) does Isaac use "my son" to Esau, who speaks twice of himself as "your son" in vv. 31–32.

Isaac's blessing of Jacob involves fertility (vv. 27–28) and dominion (v. 29). The gift of "dew of heaven" (rain) and "oil of earth" echoes a Ugaritic expression used of the Canaanite goddess Anat, who is associated with fertility. The blessing of rain produces the abundance of grain and wine, two of the principal foodstuffs of the ancient Near East. The third of these basic foodstuffs, oil, may be suggested in the ambiguous "oil of the earth" that precedes the reference to grain and wine. The sequence of the fall rains followed by the grain harvest of the spring and the grape harvest of late summer (and the olive harvest of the fall) depicts a full agricultural year (cf. Deut. 11:14; 33:28; Joel 2:23–24; Ps. 104:13–15).

Isaac's blessing of Jacob includes dominion as well as fertility. In its emphasis on the superiority of the blessed son (Gen. 27:29, 40), the blessing echoes the oracle Rebekah received from Yahweh before the birth of the twins (25:23). The reference to the prenatal oracle declaring Jacob's preeminence over Esau reminds readers that it is Yahweh who is in control of the action in chap. 27.

This story of an energetic and resourceful woman who acts on behalf of her son and thus serves the hidden purposes of God reminds careful readers of the similar story of the mother of Moses in Exod. 2:1–10. Also worthy of note is the story of the wise woman of Tekoa who uses deception to assure the continued life of a son (2 Sam. 14:1–20).

The encounter of Esau with Isaac (Gen. 27:30–40) contains several interesting features. First, as Westermann has pointed out, the cry of Esau in v. 34 (at his discovery that Jacob has gained the blessing by deception) is a cry of lament ("he cried out a great and bitter cry") leading directly to petition ("bless me!"). The same verb for "cry out" is used in such laments as Pss. 77:1; 88:1; and 107:6, 28; its parallelism with "weep" in Isa. 33:7 and Jer. 48:5 prepares for Esau's weeping in Gen. 27:38. Isaac's reply to Esau repeats the two elements of the blessing (fertility and dominion) but in reverse order (v. 37: "I have made him your master . . . I have enriched him with grain and wine"). Chiasmus is also present in the reversal of v. 28 in v. 39 ("from the oil of the earth . . . from the dew of the heavens"). These reversals in form are probably meant to underline the reversal of expectations experienced by Esau. In being denied the blessing, Esau will reexperience the curses imposed upon the primal pair: dominion by a family member and separation from the productive earth (Gen. 3:16–19). As at the beginning of the story, Rebekah is once again the active party; when she learns of Esau's intention to kill his brother (cf. Gen. 4:8) after his father's death, she sends him to her relatives in Haran (Gen. 27:43). The chapter thus ends on the note of family strife leading to separation.

28:1–9, Jacob's Departure. In these verses Jacob's departure is described by P, as indicated by such characteristics as the divine name El Shaddai (Gen. 17:1; 35:11) and the divine command to increase and multiply (Gen. 1:28; 9:1, 7). In this account, Jacob gains his father's blessing on his father's initiative and without deception (v. 6). He goes to his mother's family not to escape Esau's murderous wrath but to seek a wife from Rebekah's family and to prevent a marriage with an inhabitant of Canaan (a "Hittite"), like Esau's (26:34; 27:46). To traditional source criticism, these differences with chap. 27 have led to the conclusion that P must have known of a different story of the blessing of Jacob by Isaac. To be noted, however, is the different point of the P blessing in 28:3–4—not rainfall sufficient for agriculture and fertility, and dominion over his brother but numerous descendants and land (cf. Gen. 17:5–8; 35:11–12). This difference made possible the meaningful integration of this P material into the larger account.

A focus on the fundamental human realities of birth, death, and marriage underlies all three blocks of P material in the patriarchal narratives (chaps. 17 and 23 and the passage under discussion). In chap. 17, God announces that Abraham and Sarah will be the parents of a child and through that birth the progenitors of a great people. Chap. 23 recounts the death of Sarah and her burial in a grave purchased from an inhabitant of Canaan (Ephron "the Hittite"). And Gen. 28:1–9 involves Jacob's journey to Mesopotamia to avoid intermarriage.

28:10–22, Jacob's Dream at Bethel. Jacob's night at Bethel on his flight to Haran serves as a point of transition from his home and family to an uncertain future in Haran. On his return to Canaan, there will be another night encounter with the Deity before his reentry into the land (32:22–32). After his return and reconciliation with Esau, he will again go to Bethel (35:1–15); in both accounts Jacob experiences a theophany (28:13, 35:9; cf. 48:3).

While source criticism has attempted to divide the account of Jacob's dream into its constituent J and E material (J: 28:10 11a, 13 16, 19a; E: 28:11b–12, 17–18, 20–21a, 22), tradition-historical analysis may point in a better direction by seeing the basic narrative in vv. 10–12 and 16–19, with expansions of this core in vv. 13–15 and 20–22. In the dream at a site sacred since the time of Abraham (Gen. 12:8), Jacob sees "messengers of God," members of the heavenly assembly in service of the Deity, ascending and descending a staircase between heaven and earth (for earthly tasks performed by such divine messengers cf. Gen. 19; 1 Kings 22:22).

Not only does Jacob see the divine messengers, he sees Yahweh as well, who reiterates the promises of possession of the land of Canaan, numerous descendants, and divine presence (Gen. 28:13–15). The conclusion of the promise is the blessing that will come upon the nations of the earth through contact with Jacob and his descendants; the accomplishment of this divine promise will be seen in the story of the prosperity of Laban through association with Jacob (30:27–30). Upon awaking, Jacob expresses his awe by word (28:17: "This is none other than the house of God; this is the gate of heaven!") and action (his consecration and renaming of the sacred site as Bethel [Heb., "house of God"; → Bethel]).

The original function of this story was probably to explain the founding of the sanctuary at Bethel. Bethel was an important site of worship after the secession of the northern tribes from the tribal union achieved by David and preserved by Solomon and their establishment of a kingdom that bore the name of the patriarch Israel. In designating Bethel as the site for one of the northern temples, the new kingdom reached back beyond the "innovation" of Solomon's Temple in Jerusalem to a site sacred to the ancestors (Gen. 12:8; 1 Kings 12:26–33; Amos 7:1–13). Genesis 14, with its account of Abraham at Jerusalem (vv. 18–20), may be a southern answer by Judah to the claim of ancestral antiquity for the northern temple at Bethel.

29:1–31:54

Jacob in Haran and the Return to Canaan

The story of Jacob's years in Mesopotamia with his uncle Laban is one of the narrative gems of the OT. Although there is evidence of more than one source, the narrative has been fashioned into a unity that makes source criticism difficult for this material. Form-critically, the narrative has been described as a novella, like that other masterpiece of Hebrew literary art, the Joseph story.

The family unity that welcomed Jacob to his mother's relatives is soon broken by Laban's duplicity in the arrangements made for Jacob's service to Laban and his marriages to Leah and Rachel. Laban's continuing sharp practice in the determination of Jacob's wages in livestock is overcome by Jacob's superior cleverness (30:35–43); a story that began with a reference to Laban's prosperity (30:27) ends with a reference to Jacob's wealth (30:43). Jacob's departure from Laban concludes with the making of a mutual nonaggression pact (31:44–54).

There are a number of obscurities in chaps. 30–31 (e.g., 30:27, 37–43; 31:29), some of which are probably due to the presence of technical lore about shepherding. That such lore was common to the pastoralists of the ancient Near East is demonstrated by the number of opaque and unusual expressions in the narrative that can be illuminated by parallel Akkadian material, as several scholars have shown.

It has been claimed that the material is arranged in a chiastic pattern, whose center is the birth of Jacob's children: A Jacob's arrival in Haran, 29:1–4; B contract with Laban, 29:15–20; C Laban's deception of Jacob, 29:21–30; D the birth of Jacob's children, 29:31–30:24; C' Jacob's trickery of Laban, 30:25–43; B' dispute with Laban, 31:17–42; A' departure from Laban, 30:43–54. This reversal in form mirrors the reversal of situation for Laban and Jacob. And note how the story is framed by Laban's kiss of welcome to Jacob (29:13) and Laban's parting kiss to his daughters and grandchildren in 31:55 (pointedly omitting a parting kiss for Jacob).

29:1–14, Jacob's Arrival in Haran. Arriving in his uncle's territory, Jacob makes inquiries about Laban of shepherds gathered at a well, waiting for the arrival of others to remove the stone from the mouth of the well, since its size and weight needed the concerted efforts of all. In v. 6 Jacob inquires about the well-being of his uncle (lit., "Is there peace to him?") and the shepherds answer affirmatively ("There is peace"). This *shalom* is soon to be lost in the contest in which Laban and Jacob are pitted against one another. When Jacob sees Rachel, he performs a heroic, superhuman feat of strength by moving the stone from the well alone and watering Laban's flocks. One is reminded of the earlier meeting of Abraham's steward and Jacob's mother Rebekah at a well (24:11–27). When Laban learns from his daughter of Jacob's presence, he goes quickly to meet him with an embrace and a kiss (29:13; 33:4; 45:14–15). The family bonds that are the basis of Laban's welcome of Jacob are expressed idiomatically in Laban's words (29:14), "You are my bone and my flesh" (cf. Gen. 2:23; Judg. 9:2; 2 Sam. 5:1 [= 1 Chron. 11:1]; 2 Sam. 19:13).

29:15–30, Laban's Deception and Jacob's Marriages. After a month's stay, the question of Jacob's working for Laban is brought up. The discussion about wages for such service begins in amicable fashion. Because of his love for Laban's younger daughter Rachel, Jacob proposes to work for Laban for seven years to earn the right to marry her; at the end of the years of service, he claims his right, and Laban celebrates the wedding with a feast (significantly, *mishteh*, the Heb. word for feast, means "drinking party"). At nightfall Laban brings his older daughter Leah to Jacob, who, after long feasting, unknowingly consummates his marriage with her.

There is a strong sense of irony in Jacob's indignant accusation of duplicity on the part of Laban. When he asks rhetorically "What is this that you have done to me?" his words recall the same question addressed to his forebears Abraham (Gen. 20:9) and Isaac (26:10) when their deceptions involving their wives are uncovered. After agreeing to another seven-year period of work for Laban, Jacob finishes the bridal week (cf. Judg. 14:8–18) with Leah and then immediately marries his beloved Rachel.

While the principal ironic reversal in the story is how Jacob the deceiver, in gaining his brother Esau's blessing, becomes Jacob the deceived, there are other ironic echoes of the Jacob-Esau story in the account of Jacob's marriages and the ensuing rivalry of his wives. The reference to Leah's "weak" eyes (v. 17) reminds us of Isaac's failing eyesight, which made Jacob's deception possible. While the differing parental preferences of Isaac and Rebekah were the source of family discord and separation, so Jacob's preference for Rachel over Leah brings about continuing family strife. As Jacob the younger son was helped by his mother, Leah the older daughter was helped by her father Laban. And in 30:16, Rachel will sell her marriage right to her older sister, as Esau sold his birthright to his younger brother. All these notes of irony are summed up in Laban's words to Jacob, "It is not done in our area to give in marriage the younger woman before the firstborn" (v. 26), words that must have recalled to Jacob his deceptive acquisition of the blessing of the firstborn.

29:31–30:24, Jacob's Children. The strife between the wives of Jacob is introduced in 29:30 with the observation that "Jacob loved Rachel more than Leah." It is continued in v. 31, where the fact that Leah was unloved (more vividly in Heb., "hated") leads to divine compassion and Leah's fertility, as she bears Jacob four sons (Reuben, Levi, Simeon, and Judah). In naming her firstborn Reuben, Leah says "Yahweh has looked on my misery" (v. 32), words that recall Hagar's naming of Ishmael (16:11: "Yahweh has listened to your [cry of] misery") and anticipate Jacob's statement that "God saw my misery" (31:42).

Gen. 30:1–2 introduces another recurrent theme, the matriarch's barrenness. There is an effective contrast between 29:31, where "Yahweh *saw* that Leah was hated and so opened her womb," and 30:1, where "Rachel *saw* that she had not borne sons to Jacob." Like Sarai in chap. 16, Rachel gives her maid Bilhah to Jacob; the children born of this union (Dan and Naphtali) are considered Rachel's. Rachel's words in 30:3 recall those of Sarai in 16:2 ("Perhaps I shall be given sons through her"). Leah also engages in this substitute childbearing by giving Jacob her maid Zilpah, who bears Gad and Asher (30:9–13).

105

In 30:14–16, Leah gives the fertility-inducing mandrakes (cf. Song of Sg. 7:13), found by her son Reuben, to Rachel for marriage rights with Jacob, after which Leah bears Issachar and Zebulun and a daughter Dinah (30:17–21). Just as God had seen Leah's misery and opened her womb (29:31) and heard her (in 29:33), so (in 30:22) "God remembered Rachel and listened to her and opened her womb." God's remembrance of Rachel parallels his remembering Noah (Gen. 8:1) and Abraham (19:29). As a consequence, she bears Joseph (vv. 23–24).

One concluding observation can be made on the echoes of Genesis 3 in 29:15–30:24. First, in his answer to the divine charge that they had sinned by attempting to be "like God" (Gen. 3:5), the man blames his wife (3:12: "She gave me some of the fruit, and I ate"). In 30:1–2 Rachel blames her husband for her childlessness ("Give me sons or I'll die!"), to which Jacob retorts angrily, "Am I in the place of God?" Second, the sequence of Jacob's years of hard labor for Laban and the birth of his children to his wives brings to mind the curses imposed on the first humans in Gen. 3:16–19, woman's pain in childbearing and man's hard labor in food production.

30:25–43, Jacob's Trickery of Laban. As Jacob begins to plan his return to Canaan, he engages in a lengthy proceeding with Laban, since he is a dependent in Laban's household. Laban admits that his wealth is the result of divine blessing because of his association with Jacob (30:27, 30). Laban's wish is that Jacob should remain in his service as a generously paid employee, while Jacob responds that he wants to work for his family. The meaning of the negotiations between Jacob and Laban is not completely clear, but apparently Jacob's inferior position as a dependent in Laban's employ does not allow him to return to his own land without Laban's agreement. At least Laban seems to have the right to retain Jacob's family and property should Jacob depart without his permission (31:43). In the end, Jacob accedes to Laban's wishes and proposes a way to be remunerated by taking for himself only the dark sheep and spotted and speckled goats. Laban's duplicity is seen in 30:35–36; after agreeing to Jacob's wages, he proceeds to take for himself all the unusually marked animals and to remove them several days' journey from Jacob. Since Jacob knows how to influence the breeding habits of the sheep and goats in his care so that they produce a large number of unusually colored offspring, he is able to outwit Laban. The means by which Jacob influences the fertility of the flocks are switches he takes from poplar trees; one is reminded of the fertility-inducing plants in 30:14. The story ends with a description of Jacob's great wealth (v. 43; cf. Gen. 12:16; 20:14; 26:12–13).

31:1–54, Jacob's Flight. The growing hostility of Laban and his sons toward Jacob, because of his increasing wealth, continues the theme of family strife that began in the account of Jacob's marriages (29:21–27). The charge of Laban's sons that Jacob "has taken all that belonged to our father" (31:1) echoes Esau's complaint in 27:36. The divine command to leave is communicated to Jacob in parallel accounts (by Yahweh in 31:3; by "the messenger of Elohim" in a dream in vv. 10–13); in source-critical terms, the first of these accounts is J, the second E.

When Jacob informs Rachel and Leah of his decision to depart, they overcome their mutual animosity to support this plan (a detail that may forecast the movement toward family reconciliation that Jacob will initiate in Gen. 33). Leaving with his family and goods in haste and stealth, Jacob is pursued by Laban, who is warned in a dream to do no harm to Jacob (31:24, 29). Laban is particularly angered by the theft of idols of his family deities that Rachel had taken without Jacob's knowledge (v. 19), perhaps as partial compensation for her father's dissipation of her bride price (→ Teraphim). In the search that Laban makes for these idols, there is an effective echo of the Jacob-Esau story. When Jacob gives Laban permission to search his party, Laban "feels through" what was in Rachel's tent. The Hebrew verb "feel through" (mashash) in vv. 34 and 37 is the same verb employed in 27:22 to describe Isaac's "feeling" of Jacob. As in chap. 27, a younger child (Rachel) deceives her father to gain what belonged to the father. Rachel's hiding of the idols in the camel cushion on which she sat and her excuse to her father for not rising from it (menstruation) may involve some broad humor at the powerlessness of Laban's sought-for gods. The episode ends with Jacob's upbraiding Laban and reminding him of his long and faithful service. Twice in this section (31:42, 53) Jacob's deity is identified as "the fear of Isaac" (i.e., "the Awesome One of Isaac," as the NAB renders it).

The chapter ends with the making of a covenant, a mutual nonaggression pact between Jacob and Laban (vv. 44–54). The different objects that serve as witnesses to this covenant (a stele in v. 45, a cairn of stones in v. 46), the different names given to the objects (Jegar-sahadutha and Galeed in v. 47, Mizpah in v. 49), and the two references to the covenant meal (vv. 46, 54) probably indicate the use of different versions of the treaty in the composition of this episode. While there is evidence of J and E material in this chapter, more recent traditio-historical criticism has tended to see in vv. 44–54 a basic J narrative with expansions and additions, rather than an interweaving of two distinct sources.

31:55–36:43
The End of the Jacob-Esau Cycle

31:55–32:23, Jacob's Embassy to Esau. In sharp contrast to Laban's greeting of Jacob (29:13), Laban kisses his daughters and grandchildren goodbye, but pointedly no kiss is given to Jacob (31:55). There follows a theophany (vv. 1–2), somewhat like the Bethel vision (28:12–17), in which Jacob encounters "messengers of God" (28:12; 31:11) and names the site Mahanaim ("two camps") after exclaiming "This is God's encampment!" (cf. "This is the house of God . . . the gate of heaven" in 28:17). The sequence in Gen. 28:1–22 of vision, naming, and erection of a monument is recalled in the vision and naming in 32:1–2, preceded by the setting up of a stele in 31:45, 51–53.

Jacob sends word of his return ahead to Esau, hoping to placate his brother. When he learns that Esau is coming with a large force, Jacob prays for divine aid (vv. 9–12). Several features of this petitionary prayer ought to be noted. Its essential features are the address to the Deity (v. 9), the petition (v. 11), and the motivation, reasons brought forward to persuade God to grant the petition (v. 12). The petition itself has parallels in Pss. 31:15 and 144:11. And the divine *chesed* (Heb., "steadfast love") and *'emet* ("fidelity") of which Jacob declares himself unworthy are associated with Abraham in 24:27. With characteristic practicality, Jacob follows the prayer with the division of his goods into two parts, in the hope of saving at least one if he is attacked by Esau. His dispatch of gifts to Esau (32:13–21) serves both to appease him and to act as a buffer between them.

Noteworthy in this section is the repeated reference to "face": in v. 16 ("Pass before my face"), v. 17 ("To whom belong these before your face?"), four times in v. 20 ("I may appease his face with the gift going before his face; afterwards I will see his face and perhaps he will lift up my face" [i.e., be gracious to me; cf. the same idiom in 19:21]), and in v. 21 ("The gift passed before his face"). These seven uses of "face" are clearly meant to bind this story with Jacob's following encounter with the Deity, in which he sees God face to face (32:30; cf. 33:10).

32:24–32, Jacob and His Mysterious Adversary. This story has provoked extended commentary (the earliest being Hos. 12:3–4 and Wisd. of Sol. 10:10–12). It is rich with motifs from myth and folklore—e.g., the trial of heroes, the loss by nocturnal demons of supernatural power at sunrise (vampires), the prohibition against fording a river by its protective deity, and the power gained by the knowledge of the adversary's mysterious and hidden name (cf. Rumpelstiltskin). While the story is complex, no attempt to divide it into J and E elements has won assent; as in other cases, expansions and development of a core in the tradition history of the story may be closer to the mark.

The chief difficulty with the story is the identification of Jacob's adversary with God. The standard pattern for the kind of tale found in 32:24–32, as analyzed by structuralism, is a hero (Jacob) on a quest (return to Canaan and reconciliation with Esau); the originator of the quest is God (31:3, 13), and the adversary with whom Jacob struggles is the opponent, whose task is to prevent Jacob from bringing the mission to a successful conclusion. At some earlier level of the story, the opponent may have been some Canaanite god attempting to keep Jacob from entering the land. But the point that makes the story so enigmatic in its final crystallization is the identification of both originator and opponent as God. This break with the conventional folktale pattern is the effect of Israelite monotheism, which cannot tolerate the possible dualism that might be implied by a powerful supernatural adversary to Yahweh.

Two etiologies, or accounts of origins, conclude the story. The first of these, involving the naming of the site, connects the story with Gen. 28:10–19 and 32:1–2 and suggests that at one point in its history the account may have been a story about the founding of a shrine at this place (→ Penuel). Any such etiology has, however, become almost invisible, as the story has been used to serve other functions. The second etiology here concerns a dietary taboo unwitnessed elsewhere in the OT.

In its present context, Gen. 32:24–32 is chiefly concerned with the blessing that Jacob receives (v. 26) and the change of his name to Israel (cf. Gen. 17:5, 15; 35:10), signaling a change of personality and destiny. The etymology offered for "Israel" in 34:28 involves contention; while it is not a philologically defensible etymology, it does fit in well with the theme of strife that runs through much of Genesis.

33:1–20, Jacob's Meeting with Esau. The confrontation of Jacob and his family with Esau and his four hundred retainers begins in tension, with Jacob dividing his family into three groups. In the ordering of these divisions (the slave women and their children first, Leah and her children second, and finally Rachel and Joseph), Jacob continues to demonstrate his affection for Rachel, which was one of the causes of discord in the family. The tension is resolved when Esau generously takes the initiative and runs to meet Jacob, humbly bowing, with embraces and kisses (v. 4; cf. 45:14–15). Esau's movement toward reconciliation is underlined by his address to Jacob in 33:9 as "my brother." Jacob responds by asking Esau, "Take, please, my blessing," thus restoring to his brother the blessing he had gained and reversing Esau's words in 27:36 ("Now he has taken my blessing").

Jacob's words to Esau in 33:10 ("Seeing your face is like seeing the face of God") link this scene to that preceding mysterious confrontation with the "face of God" in 32:30.

Up to this point in the chapter, both brothers have made gestures that signal the beginning of reconciliation: Esau's affectionate greeting of Jacob and his address to him as "my brother" and Jacob's restoration to Esau of the blessing. Gen. 33:12–17, however, show that reconciliation is only partial and incomplete. Despite Esau's efforts, the cautious Jacob finds excuses for parting with his brother, eventually settling not with Esau in Seir but in Succoth, in the environs of Shechem (→ Shechem). Shechem was visited by Abram after his arrival in Canaan (12:6); like his ancestor (chap. 23), Jacob purchases a piece of land from the local residents.

34:1–31, The Rape of Dinah. The story of the rape of Dinah is connected with its context by its concern with a child of Jacob, his only daughter; the twelve sons of Jacob, listed in 35:23–25, will be the chief concern in the Joseph story in chaps. 37–50. The introduction of Hamor and Shechem in 34:18–19 connects Genesis 34 to its setting by catchwords. The brief and laconic account of the rape is amplified by an exposition of the feelings of Shechem (v. 3: "He was deeply attracted to Jacob's daughter Dinah, and was in love with her, and spoke to her heart"). While the elders Jacob and Hamor try to negotiate a peaceful solution to the difficulty, Jacob's sons answer violence with violence, avenging the wrong done their sister by deceptively agreeing to intermarriage only after the circumcision of the Shechemite males (v. 15). The deception is completed when two of Dinah's full brothers, Simeon and Levi (29:33–34; 30:21), gain their revenge by the slaughter of the incapacitated males. This violent behavior of Simeon and Levi is an ominous prelude to the brothers' act of violence against Joseph (Gen. 37:20–27) and is recalled in Jacob's farewell discourse (Gen. 49:5–7) to his sons.

The story of the rape of Dinah has a number of connections with the similar story of Amnon's rape of Tamar (2 Sam. 13). These connections include the formulaic language in which the rape is described (Gen. 34:2: "He saw her . . . he took her . . . he lay with her and violated her"; 2 Sam. 13:6, 8: "in my sight"; 13:14: "he violated her and lay with her"). Also formulaically expressed is the reaction of Dinah's brothers (Gen. 34:7: "[Shechem] performed an act of folly in Israel; such a thing was not done") and Tamar's protest to her implacable half-brother (2 Sam. 13:12: "Such a thing is not done in Israel; do not perform this act of folly"). Murderous revenge by full brothers concludes both stories (Gen. 34:25; 2 Sam. 13:28–29).

35:1–29, Jacob's Return to Bethel. This chapter contains quite diverse material drawn from J and P. If the core of Jacob's Bethel experience in Gen. 28:10–22 is E, then 35:1–7 may be the J version of the Bethel sanctuary founding, including the rite of purification from foreign gods (cf. Josh. 24:14, 23; Judg. 10:16) and Jacob's instructions about a pilgrimage to Bethel (Gen. 35:1) in language reminiscent of Ps. 122:1 and Isa. 2:3, 5.

Gen. 35:8 is the first of three death reports in the chapter: the deaths of Rebekah's nurse Deborah, of Rachel in childbirth (vv. 16–20), and of Isaac in peaceful old age (vv. 28–29). The theophany and oracle in vv. 9–12 come from P, as indicated by the divine name El Shaddai (Gen. 17:1), the command to increase and multiply (1:28, 9:1), and the promise of royal descendants (17:6). Gen. 35:10 is the P account of the name change of Jacob to Israel; in the larger context of Genesis, it is a confirmation of the name change announced in 32:28.

There is some dispute about the source of 35:13–15. If they are from P, then vv. 9–15 may be the P version of the founding of the Bethel sanctuary. The genealogy in vv. 23–29 is also from P. It is prefaced by the curious story of Reuben's violation of his father's concubine Bilhah (v. 22). Such an act by an eldest son is not only a sexual offense; it is a challenge to the authority of the head of the family. Such a flouting of legitimate authority occurred twice in the early history of the Israelite monarchy, in uncertain situations where there was some doubt about who was the legitimate ruler (2 Sam. 3:7) or where rebellion was in progress (2 Sam. 16:21). In Jacob's farewell testament, this act of Reuben provides the reason for his loss of the authority normally held by the firstborn (Gen. 49:3–4). Finally, not only does Reuben's act recall the violation of Dinah (34:2, 5), it is another instance of strife in the family, especially of the discord between father and son(s) that is a dominant theme in the Jacob-Esau cycle, appearing most recently at the end of the story of the rape of Dinah (34:30–31), and that will appear again in the Joseph story.

36:1–43, The Genealogy of Esau. This chapter is a loose collection of material relevant to Esau, chiefly lists and genealogies of his descendants, placed here to complement the list of Jacob's sons in 35:23–26. Another possible connection between chaps. 35 and 36 is the descent of kings from both Jacob (35:11) and Esau (36:31–39).

The separation of Jacob and Esau in vv. 6–8 recalls the parting of Abram and Lot in chap. 13 and the unwillingness of Jacob to move too closely to Esau in 33:12–17. This division also prepares for the strife and separation of brothers in the Joseph novella.

Jacob and Esau, Israel and Edom

The lives and careers of the great figures of the OT, such as the liberator Moses or the ancestors from whom tribes or nations took their names, are not simply stories of individuals; rather such figures are sometimes portrayed as living out proleptically the later historical experiences of the people whose progenitors and saviors they are.

It has already been pointed out that the ancestor Abram anticipated in his life later experiences of his descendants: descent into Egypt because of famine, oppression by the Pharaoh (when Sarai is brought into the monarch's harem), the enriching of the ancestor in Egypt, divine intervention (described as "plagues"), and release. Similarly Moses underwent in his early life a kind of proleptic exodus: endangered by the Pharaoh, he was saved by a passage through water (Exod. 1:22; 2:1–10) and encountered God at Horeb after guiding his flock through the desert (Exod. 3:1–3).

What is true for Abraham and Moses is equally so for Jacob and his descendants (Israel) and Esau and his descendants (Edom). The brotherhood and strife between Jacob and Esau that mark the Genesis narratives are both reflected elsewhere in the OT. The relationship between the Jacob-Esau narratives in Genesis 25–36 and the texts dealing with the political interaction of Israel and Edom is complex; while the Jacob-Esau stories in Genesis include material drawn from ancient sources, at the same time they reflect later national-ethnic issues between the kingdoms of Israel (and later Judah) and Edom in the tenth century B.C. The influence can move in the opposite direction as well: i.e., it is likely that the Jacob-Esau cycle in Genesis had some influence on the literary shaping of OT texts dealing with the relationship of Israel and Edom in world affairs.

In the analysis of texts in which the eponymous ancestor's fate anticipates the historical fortunes of the people, a good starting point would be the annunciation of the birth of Esau and Jacob. In the oracle of Gen. 25:23 Rebekah is told that, of the twins to be born of her, "the older will serve the younger." The origin of this statement of Jacob's superiority over Esau

is probably the subjugation of Edom by Israel in the reign of David (2 Sam. 8:14; 1 Kings 11:15–16). Similarly, when Isaac promises Esau that he will "throw off his [Jacob's] yoke from your neck" (Gen. 27:40), the reference is probably to Edom's several attempts at independence from Israel (1 Kings 11:14–22, 25; 2 Kings 8:20–22; 14:7, 22).

The "brotherhood" of Israel and Edom is referred to in a number of OT texts. Such language reflects not only ethnic relationship but political alliance. In Deut. 23:7, the Israelites are instructed, "Do not abhor the Edomite, for he is your brother." The language of fraternity also appears in Num. 20:14. In Deut. 2:4, Moses is commanded by God to announce to the Israelites, "You are about to cross into the territory of your brothers the sons of Esau, dwelling in Seir." Brotherhood language appears as well in Amos 1:11 and Obad. 10, 12; in these texts, the theme of strife is heard in the description of Israel and Edom as warring, hostile brothers. In Amos 1:11, Edom is castigated for "pursuing his brother with a sword and destroying his treaty-partner." While the particular moment and events are not immediately clear, the "brother" referred to here is obviously Israel. In Obadiah 10, Edom's "violence to his brother Jacob" is specified as their standing by when Jerusalem was under attack.

Israel's hostility toward Edom reached a high point in the exilic period; Obadiah is certainly exilic, and many commentators consider Amos 1:11–12 to be an exilic addition to the book. The reason for this hostility and hatred is probably to be found in 1 Esd. 4:45, where Edom is said to have burned the Jerusalem Temple during the Babylonian attack in 587 B.C.; the same charge is probably the point of Lam. 4:21–22 and Ps. 137:7. Other anti-Edomite material from the exilic period includes Jer. 49:7–22 (a text with significant similarities to Obadiah); Isa. 34:5–6 (in which the destruction of Edom is described in almost apocalyptic terms); Isa. 63:1–6; Ezek. 25:12–14; 35; Joel 3:19; Mal. 1:2–5; and Lam. 1:2–5.

37:1–50:26

The Joseph Narrative

The Joseph narrative is one of the masterpieces of Hebrew narrative art, indeed one of the acknowledged masterpieces of world literature. It is a product of what Gerhard von Rad has called the Solomonic enlightenment, like another superb OT narrative, the court history of David (2 Sam. 9–20; 1 Kings 1–2). Beside being products of the court of Solomon (tenth century B.C.), both narratives share significant theological perspectives. For instance, both have been described as influenced to some extent by wisdom thought and literature. In a famous study, von Rad describes the Joseph narrative as a didactic wisdom story, and R. N. Whybray and others have made similar claims for the court history. Both narratives share a view of the Deity acting providentially rather than by direct intervention or theophany. Both show remarkable human characters surviving and prospering by their own wits, controlling their destiny by their natural gifts and superior ability.

Several questions are involved in discussing the relationship of the Joseph narrative to the rest of Genesis and to the Pentateuch. First, it is clear that the Joseph story is a bridge between Genesis and Exodus; the Joseph story begins with Jacob in Canaan (37:1) and ends with Israel in Egypt (47:27). The settlement of Jacob and his family in Egypt at the invitation of a Pharaoh well disposed toward them sets the stage for the appearance in Exodus of a Pharaoh "who knew not Joseph" and his oppression of Israel (Exod. 1:8–10). Second, the relationship of the Joseph narrative to what precedes it in Genesis, and particularly to the Jacob cycle, will be discussed below, but at least several obvious links may be mentioned here: both stories begin with a deception of a father by his offspring through an article of clothing; this deception leads to a separation of the brothers for twenty years; and the climax of both stories is the reconciliation of the estranged brothers and the abatement of family strife.

A more complex question is the relationship of the Joseph narrative to the pentateuchal sources: is it, like the preceding ancestral narratives, made up of individual narratives taken from different sources and then editorially woven together? Traditional critical scholarship answered this question positively, arguing that the sources identified in the prior material (J, E, P) are visible and can be isolated in the Joseph narrative as well. Evidence for this view included such doublets as the different patriarchal names: Jacob in 37:1 (identified as P) and 34 (identified as E); Israel in 37:3, 13 (both J); the attempts to save Joseph's life by Reuben (attributed to E) or by Judah (J); and the two versions of Joseph's fate, his sale to an Ishmaelite caravan (ascribed to J) and his kidnap by Midianite traders (in E). Such source analysis seemed to lead to the conclusion that the author/editor responsible for the final form of the Joseph narrative had at his disposal sources with variant tellings of the Joseph story. On the basis of such source-critical assumptions, some scholars felt confident in assigning Gen. 37:1–2 to P, 3a to J, and 3b to E.

More recent scholarship has been impressed rather by the unity of the Joseph story. From such a unitarian perspective, the Joseph narrative is described as a short story or a novella; those scholars who have argued for a wisdom cast to the Joseph narrative describe it more specifically as a "historicized wisdom tale" or a "didactic wisdom story" (other examples of which will be mentioned below). The coherence of the Joseph narrative seems to point not to a joining or interweaving of originally disparate variants, but rather to composition by a literary artist of exceptional skill. From this perspective, the use of different patriarchal names, Jacob and Israel, does not indicate several sources but rather different emphases in a single literary work, for whom the patriarch is both an individual and, as progenitor of the nation, a kind of "corporate personality." Nor is there a real contradiction in two brothers working in different ways to prevent the murder of Joseph. Reuben's words in Gen. 37:30 seem to indicate that he knew nothing of Judah's plan (worked out in Reuben's absence?) and the brothers' agreement to it. The Ishmaelite/Midianite accounts of Joseph's passage to Egypt are more of a problem; but, in the absence of clear evidence for sources elsewhere in the Joseph narrative, it can be resolved by understanding the Midianite account as a gloss, an expansion of a single source rather than a doublet from another source.

While Genesis 37–50 has been labeled for convenience as the Joseph narrative, a more precise description and delimitation of the extent of the Joseph novella would be Genesis 37 and 39–45. Chaps. 37 and 42–45 are a family story concerned with Joseph's rise to a position of prominence and superiority over his brothers. Chaps. 39–41 are a story within a story, a political tale of Joseph's career, with chaps. 40–41 stressing his divine gift of administrative and other wisdom.

Genesis 38 is a digression from the Joseph narrative; its position, as will be seen, is the result of the similarity of themes and motifs between it and the Joseph narrative. Chaps. 46–50 belong more properly to the Jacob cycle of stories. In Genesis 46 we find a theophany to Jacob, followed by an itinerary and a genealogy (the same sequence as in chap. 35); in chap. 47, Jacob's presentation to the Pharaoh; in chap. 48, his blessing of Joseph's sons Ephraim and Manasseh; in chap. 49, his farewell to his sons and his death; and in chap. 50, his funeral and burial.

The Egyptian locale of chaps. 39–50 of the Joseph story has led to attempts to relate the story of Joseph to what is known of Egyptian history. For a time, the intermittent presence of Asiatic slaves in Egypt and particularly the dominance of Egypt in the mid-second millennium B.C. by Asiatic Semites seemed to provide appropriate and reasonable historical background to the Joseph narrative (→Hyksos). Support for this hypothesis was drawn from instances of Egyptian "local color" (Egyptian names in 37:36; 39:1; and 41:45; Egyptian customs in 50:2–3, 26; and the like). More recent scholarship has tended to question this view; it finds a more likely background in the Solomonic era for the knowledge of Egypt displayed in the Joseph narrative. Solomon's marriage to a daughter of the Pharaoh (1 Kings 9:16; 11:1) points to an era of amicable political and commercial relations between Egypt and Israel and would explain the positive and benign attitude of the Joseph narrative to Egypt, its ruler, and its people.

We can conclude this introduction to the Joseph narrative by listing the themes that appear in it and that will be discussed in greater detail in the commentary: divine providence, i.e., the divine governance of the world and the divine conduct of human affairs by a hidden providence rather than by revelation or extraordinary divine intervention ("Yahweh was with Joseph"); the success of the unpromising ("rags to riches") and the related theme of Yahweh's mysterious choice of the younger son; strife and discord in the family; Joseph's wisdom and the associated theme of the tolerance and openness of wisdom to the non-Israelite world; the blessing of the Gentiles through contact with the descendants of Abraham (39:5, 21; 41:44–57); Yahweh's hidden plan prevailing over human plans ("Man proposes, but God disposes"; cf. Prov. 16:9). The appearance of a number of these themes in prior material in Genesis, particularly in J, raises the question of the relationship of the Joseph narrative to the Yahwist. From the perspective of source criticism, the presence of such themes in both Joseph and J indicated that here as elsewhere, the basic narrative strand in the Joseph narrative was J, with supplements from E and P. The view taken here is that the Joseph narrative is not part of the Yahwist's work but an independent and distinct literary work. The shared themes may point to some connection between J and the Joseph story: for instance, are both writers members of a group of like-minded religious thinkers, a "Yahwist school"? The common view that the composition of both J and the Joseph narrative was associated with the court of Solomon may be explanation enough for the coincidence of themes that they reveal.

Several recurrent motifs in the Joseph narrative deserve mention as well. Dreams and famine each appear several times in the preceding ancestral narratives (dreams in 20:3; 28:12; and 31:10–11, 24; famine in 12:10 and 26:1). Further, the motif of clothing, which appears in Gen. 27:15–16, plays a major role in the Joseph narrative as a symbol of the changing situations of Joseph and the other participants in the story.

Let us bring the introduction to the Joseph narrative to an end with a word on method. It is, of course, a truism that the object of study (in this case the Joseph story) determines to a considerable extent appropriate methods of interpretation. This seems to be clearly the case here in dealing with a literary work of a kind different from the patriarchal narratives of chaps. 12–36. Most of those texts were composite, often artfully achieved; and while the focus of study there was on the final form of the text, historical and genetic examinations of the development of the text contributed to our understanding of the text. As the work of an individual artistic imagination, the Joseph narrative is different, as several scholars have demonstrated. And so the method best suited to the Joseph narrative would seem to be the exercise of "close reading" in which particular attention is paid to the subtleties and delicacies of the text under examination and to the recurrent themes and motifs as they are played out in different circumstances and contexts. Dialogue plays an important role in the Joseph story as a revealer of character and of the never static relationships between protagonists. Therefore the speeches and dialogue of the characters should be carefully heard, with particular attention to the changes that mark even repeated speeches (42:9–20, 30–34). In the close reading of the Joseph novella, an extended analysis of chap. 37 will be undertaken, since this chapter introduces themes and literary motifs that will reappear at important points throughout the story.

37:1–36
Joseph's Descent from Canaan to Egypt

37:1–4, Joseph with His Father and Brothers. The twelve sons of Jacob, whose birth notices were recorded in Gen. 29:31–30:24 and 35:16–18, were brought together in the list of Gen. 35:23–26. They include Leah's six sons, the four of the slaves Bilhah and Zilpah, and the two sons of Jacob's beloved Rachel, Joseph and Benjamin. Gen. 37:1–2 introduce by way of exposition the principal characters of the Joseph story, in the following order of appearance: first, Jacob (vv. 1–2: "Jacob dwelt . . . these are the generations of Jacob"); then, Joseph (v. 2: "Joseph was seventeen years old"); and, finally, the other sons of Jacob (v. 2: "He was a shepherd with his brothers"). The rise of a shepherd to be a "shepherd of his people," their ruler and provisioner, is a motif that will reappear in the call of Moses (Exod. 3:1–10) and in the divine choice of David (1 Sam. 16:11–12; Ps. 78:71–72). In Gen. 37:3, we encounter the same order of precedence as in vv. 1–2 ("Israel . . . Joseph . . . all his sons").

111

The introduction twice of Joseph before his older brothers forecasts the impending crisis that will soon engage this family. Already subordinate to Joseph in their father's affection, Joseph's brothers are grammatically subordinate as well by their placement in prepositional phrases (v. 3: "with his brothers . . . with the sons of his father's wives . . . more than all his other sons"). Jacob's preferential treatment of Joseph and the discord and ill will that this favoritism engenders in the family are thus visible in incipient form in the first verses of the story.

The narrative goes on to note that Joseph brought his father bad reports about the four sons of Bilhah and Zilpah; in this detail Joseph is portrayed as an agent of familial discord, and we are reminded of the strife between the wives of Jacob (partly fought out through their slaves), strife now mirrored in the growing estrangement of the sons.

Only in v. 4 do the brothers appear as the subject of a sentence, when they see their father's greater love for Joseph, symbolized by the special garment that Jacob presents to Joseph. Jacob's love for his son Joseph is mentioned twice in vv. 3–4: "Israel *loved* Joseph more than all his sons . . . their father *loved* him more than all his brothers." While such doubling has sometimes been taken as evidence of two sources, we are dealing rather with a skillful escalation and intensification intentionally effected by this repetition; whether designated as sons of the patriarch or as brothers of Joseph, they still take second place in the affection of their father. Realizing this, "they hated him," and their hatred led to an inability to communicate ("They couldn't even greet him [by saying 'Shalom!' to him]").

Several concluding observations can be made about these opening verses of the Joseph story. First, the bitter hatred of the brothers of Joseph is played out against a background of relational and familial language: "son(s)" occurs five times, "father" four times, and "brothers" three times. The notable abundance of these terms highlights the poignancy of the estrangement and disintegration of this family. Second, the psychological acuteness of the author is evident in the manner in which these opening verses deal with the question of responsibility for the crisis in the family. All are implicated in this family drama: Jacob, because of his publicly displayed preference for Joseph; Joseph, because of the discord he stirs up by his bad reports about his brothers to his father; and the brothers, because of their hatred. All are implicated in this tragedy; no one is declared innocent. Finally, visible perception is a noteworthy feature of chap. 37 that is first alluded to in v. 4 ("The brothers *saw* that their father loved him more than all his sons").

Three times more in this chapter will the brothers' "seeing" be mentioned: in v. 18 they see Joseph at a distance; in v. 20 they conclude their plotting with the bitter words "Let's see then what becomes of his dreams!"; and in v. 25 the brothers see a caravan of Ishmaelites that they make part of their plot. This emphasis on visual perception stands in counterpoint to and powerfully reinforces the severing of fraternal bonds signaled by the inability of the brothers to speak to Joseph because of their intense hatred, further provoked by Joseph's talk about his dreams (vv. 5, 8). The accent on seeing is taken up in Joseph's mission to his brothers (v. 13): Jacob's command to Joseph in v. 14 ("See to the welfare of your brothers") will be fulfilled when Joseph becomes the provider for his family in Egypt (45:5–8; 50:20–21). The last instance of visual perception in chap. 37 is Jacob's recognition of his son's bloody tunic (v. 33). As will be shown below, in the brothers' next encounter with Joseph (chap. 42), "seeing" will give way to speaking and hearing.

37:5–11, Joseph's Dreams. The dreams of Joseph and the growing hatred of his brothers are coordinated in v. 5. His are the first of a series of dreams by the major characters in the Joseph narrative. Joseph is quick to relate to his brothers the dream of the sheaves in which Joseph's sheaf is surrounded by those of his brothers, which pay homage to him by bowing. It is noteworthy that the sheaves are of grain; this symbolism of sheaves of grain for Joseph and his brothers neatly points forward both to Joseph's management of Egypt's grain supplies (chap. 41) and to the grain-buying expeditions of his brothers (chaps. 42–43). In these expeditions the brothers will assume the posture of obeisance predicted in the dream (42:6; 43:26, 28). Now, however, the fulfillment of the dream is uncertain, for Joseph and his dream (in which he is surrounded by his brothers) are now "surrounded" by the hatred of his brothers: the hatred of Joseph's brothers mentioned in vv. 5 and 8 forms a frame around Joseph's recounting of the dream in vv. 6 and 7. The author closes the story of the first dream with the observation that the brothers hated Joseph as much for his talk about the dreams as for the dreams themselves.

Joseph relates more briefly the second dream of the sun, moon, and eleven stars bowing before him. Significantly, no retort from his angry brothers is recorded; this absence of response is an ominous sign of the breakdown in communication between Joseph and his brothers introduced in v. 4. Joseph does earn a rebuke from his father because of his second dream, which included prostration by parents as well as by siblings. By this rebuke, Jacob allies himself with his other sons ("I and your mother and your brothers") for the first time.

112

This alliance is underlined in v. 11, which concludes the scene with two sentences: in the first, the subject is "his brothers" (with Joseph unnamed in a prepositional phrase, "against him"—a grammatical reversal of the situation in vv. 1–3); in the second, we are told that "his father pondered the matter." Where Joseph had stood between his father and his brothers twice in vv. 1–3 (as implied in the order of their appearance in those verses), now in v. 11 "his brothers" and "his father" are placed in direct contact; the word order of the Hebrew is "Envious of him were *his brothers, and his father* pondered the matter."

37:12–20, Joseph Between His Father and Brothers.
In this scene, the brothers have departed to tend Jacob's flocks, and the patriarch decides to send Joseph to them. Israel's instructions to Joseph in v. 14 ("See to the welfare [*shalom*, lit., 'peace'] of your brothers") recall the inability of Jacob's other sons to greet their brother with "*Shalom!*" (v. 4).

In vv. 14–17 is recounted the curious scene of Joseph's wandering about during his journey to his brothers. The function of this scene is probably twofold: to build tension by delaying the eventual encounter of Joseph and his brothers and, more importantly, to show Joseph suspended between two worlds. Behind him is his reproachful father, before him his envious and hate-filled brothers. Joseph, his father's favorite and the "master of dreams" (v. 19), is here shown to be lost and dangerously vulnerable. In v. 18 the brothers spot Joseph at a distance (because of his distinctive garment?), and their smoldering anger finally boils over into violence. In plotting murder, the brothers of Joseph speak with unconscious accuracy when they say, "Let's see what will become of his dreams," a comment that will be ironically realized when they meet him again in Egypt.

37:21–36, Joseph Apart from His Father and Brothers.
We now come to the final act of separation and estrangement that has been building throughout this chapter. In this final scene, Joseph is a powerless and passive victim; this is shown particularly by the fact that Joseph is the object of thirteen of the verbs from vv. 23–35, most of which describe acts of violence. The active parties are Joseph's oldest brother Reuben, who tries to save Joseph by dissuading his brothers from their thoughts of murder, and Judah, who proposes an alternative to killing out of enlightened self-interest (selling him as a slave). Reuben and Judah will again appear as spokesmen for their brothers (42:37; 44:16–34).

In 37:23, their first act is to strip Joseph of his garment, that hated symbol and constant reminder of Jacob's special affection for Joseph. After throwing him into a cistern, they callously sit down to their meal. There will be another

meal later in the story at which the roles of powerful and powerless will be reversed (43:31–34).

Several motifs are employed in 37:23–25 that will recur elsewhere in the Joseph narrative. Already mentioned is the motif of the meal. More significant is the garment motif (v. 23), which appears at crucial points in the story (39:12–19; 41:14, 42; 45:22). Also prominent is the motif of Joseph's descent into the cistern (37:24); into Egypt (v. 25; 39:1); and into prison (39:20). The reference to the Egyptian prison in 40:15 and 41:14 with the same word used of the cistern in 37:22, 24, 28, and 29 ("pit") connects these three events as moments in the one downward movement of Joseph. Reuben's discovery that his plan to rescue Joseph has failed leads him to tear his garments (v. 29), a traditional gesture of grief that will be repeated by the other innocent party, Jacob (v. 34). Along with Jacob's donning of sackcloth, the gestures of Reuben and Jacob are an effective reprise of the garment motif.

As suggested above, the two variant explanations of Joseph's departure for Egypt (sold to Ishmaelites; kidnapped by Midianites) are evidence not of sources but of expansion. And taken together, these two variant explanations of Joseph's journey to Egypt preview subtly the whole Joseph story. In the first account, Joseph is sold by his brothers to Ishmaelite caravaneers who will bring Joseph down to Egypt along with their other goods (vv. 25–27). In the second account, passing Midianites bring Joseph up from the pit (v. 28). Thus at the moment of greatest danger and least hope for Joseph, the narrative in its final form alludes to the movement of Joseph both down to Egypt (39:1) and up from the pit (41:14).

To avoid an outright lie, the brothers stain Joseph's garment with the blood of a slaughtered goat and have the bloody garment brought to their father with the words, "We found this; see [lit., 'recognize'] whether it is the garment of your son [significantly, not 'our brother'] or not" (v. 32). When Jacob recognizes the garment, he assumes, as the brothers had intended, that Joseph has been killed by wild beasts. Jacob, who deceived his father, Isaac, with his brother's garments (27:15), is himself deceived by his sons with Joseph's bloodied garment. This example of punishment fitting the crime is further underlined by the slaughtered goat used in both acts of deception (27:9, 16; 37:31). The verb "recognize" that occurs twice in vv. 32–33 has a Janus-like function: it both looks back to 27:23 where Isaac "did not recognize" his disguised son Jacob, and it looks ahead to the tense and dramatic moment of the brothers' first meeting with Joseph, who recognizes them (42:7–8).

Jacob's lament for Joseph (37:35) is another instance of a character unconsciously speaking more truly than he knows (as in v. 20). At the end of the story, Jacob will *go down* (the descent motif) to his son, not to Sheol, the world of the dead, but to Egypt (46:3–4). Reuben's exclamation of dismay (37:30: "The boy is no more!") and Jacob's expression of grief (v. 35: "He refused to be consoled . . . thus did his father weep") remind one of the similar language in Rachel's mourning in Jer. 31:15 ("Rachel, weeping for her sons, refuses to be consoled . . . because they are no more"). The expression will be used again of Joseph by the brothers, in Egypt (42:13) and in their rehearsal to their father of the events of the trip (42:32). Jacob also uses it twice, in his responding lament (42:36: "Joseph is no more, and Simeon is no more!").

In his refusal to be consoled by "all his sons and daughters" Jacob rejects intimacy with his living children, preferring communion with his son Joseph, presumed dead. The chapter thus ends as it began, with Joseph, even absent, still a barrier preventing communication between family members. A family hostile and divided has become a family shattered by envy and hatred, treachery and deception, all culminating in a cruel act of violence.

38:1–30
Judah and Tamar

Gen. 37:36 brings the story of the breakdown of Jacob's family to an end, with Joseph in Egypt, sold (by Midianites) as a slave to a high official in Pharaoh's court. The story is continued in 39:1 in which Joseph is brought down to Egypt and is purchased (from Ishmaelites) by Potiphar. This narrative is interrupted by the self-contained story of Judah and Tamar. While its interposition between 37:36 and 39:1 of the Joseph narrative has long been a puzzle, the suggestion that it has been placed here because of the themes and motifs it shares with the Joseph narrative merits consideration.

38:1–11, Judah's Sons and Tamar's Marriages. The interpolated story begins with Judah's marriage and the birth of his three sons (vv. 1–5). Judah arranges a marriage for his oldest son, Er, with Tamar. Er's early death, the result of some unspecified offense against Yahweh, leads Judah to invoke the levirate custom in which the second son marries his dead brother's widow to provide offspring that will legally be recognized as his brother's, not his own (Deut. 25:5–10; Ruth 4:10; → Marriage). Onan's resistance to this customary law is expressed in his practice of coitus interruptus with Tamar, and for this offense his life is taken as well.

Judah has now only one son left. Fearful of endangering his third son's life and thus denying himself descendants, Judah temporizes, asking his daughter-in-law to return to her father's house (cf. Lev. 22:13) until his youngest son has reached adulthood. Tamar is thus confronted with the possibility of living as a childless widow, an extremely precarious situation for a woman in the ancient Near East.

38:12–30, Tamar's Plan and Its Discovery. The second part of the story begins with two acts of perception: Tamar *sees* that although Judah's third son Shelah has grown to adulthood, no marriage has been arranged (v. 14). Tamar takes the initiative by disguising herself as a prostitute and positioning herself where she will encounter her father-in-law. When Judah *sees* her (v. 15), he proposes intercourse, promising payment of a kid; at her request he leaves his seal and staff as a pledge of payment (→Seal).

After the intercourse but before Judah can send the agreed payment, Tamar, whose identity is still unknown to Judah, departs with his pledge. When she is discovered to be pregnant three months later, it is reported to her father-in-law, who calls for her death (cf. Deut. 22:22–24). But when Tamar triumphantly presents Judah's identifiable seal and staff, he admits his offense in not providing for her a husband who would give her a child. The story ends with the birth to Tamar of the twins Zerah (the first born) and Perez. As Num. 26:19–22 and 1 Chron. 2:3–4 indicate, Judah's three surviving sons (Shelah, Zerah, and Perez) become the progenitors of the most important clans of the tribe of Judah.

The descent of David from Tamar's younger son Perez is recorded in the genealogy in Ruth 4:18–22. In the NT, Perez makes an appearance in both genealogies of Jesus (Matt. 1:3; Luke 3:33). More surprising is the appearance of Tamar in the Matthean genealogy, along with three other OT women: Rahab, Ruth, and "Uriah's wife" (Matt. 1:3–6). Not only is the presence of women in a genealogical list unexpected; in each case there is something unusual or irregular in their marital unions. In Matthew's view, each of these women becomes a part of the divine plan in continuing the line in which the Messiah will be born of Mary, whose pregnancy could be viewed as irregular or scandalous because she had not yet come to live with her husband (Matt. 1:18). Tamar is one of the many women in the OT who show initiative within a patriarchal world.

The connections of the Judah-Tamar story with its context are multiple. First, there are several noteworthy contacts with the Jacob cycle: the birth of twins who struggle during delivery for the status of being the first born (Gen. 25:19–26); the choice of the younger twin to play an important part in the divine plan; a deception by disguise that involves a kid (27:9–16); Isaac's nonrecognition of Jacob, using the same verb in 27:23 that occurs in 37:32–33 and 38:25–26.

With the Joseph narrative, the Judah-Tamar

story shares such elements as the failure to recognize a family member (38:15; 42:8); a deception involving a kid and a means of identification (37:31; 38:17–18); the words of Jacob's sons ("recognize this garment") in 37:32 paralleled by Tamar's ("recognize to whom these belong") in 38:25. And Judah's recognition of his seal and staff (v. 26) recalls Jacob's recognition of Joseph's garment (37:33). In view of such links, one can conclude that while chap. 38 does interrupt the Joseph narrative, its multiple contextual connections nicely explain its placement.

39:1–41:57
Joseph in Egypt

This story-within-a-story deals with Joseph's career in Egypt from his descent as a slave in the power of others to his rise to a position of authority and power second only to Pharaoh's. The narrative that begins with Joseph being brought down to Egypt (39:1) will end with the whole world going down to Egypt (41:57), a movement that will include Joseph's brothers as well (42:2–3).

39:1–23, Joseph and Potiphar's Wife. The narrative skill that was evident in chap. 37 continues in the superbly told story of Joseph in Potiphar's house. The beginning of the story in v. 1 recalls 37:28, 36. The descent motif is mentioned twice in 39:1 ("Joseph was brought down to Egypt . . . the Ishmaelites who brought him down there"). Verses 2–3 introduce two of the major themes of the Joseph narrative: divine providence ("Yahweh was with Joseph"—vv. 2, 3, 21, 23) and the success of the unpromising (vv. 2–3, 23). The divine presence and Joseph's success in vv. 2–3 and 21–23 form an envelope around the chapter. But in both instances these assertions stand in contrast to Joseph's actual situation: he is a slave in Potiphar's house and a prisoner in Pharaoh's jail. Another important theme of both J and the Joseph story is the blessing that comes upon Gentiles through association with a descendant of Abraham (cf. 30:27–30), a theme that will be heard again in chap. 41 when Joseph's administration of Egypt's grain supplies brings prosperity and abundance.

Attention should be paid to a motif that will be employed throughout chap. 39. It occurs first in v. 1, where we learn that "Potiphar . . . bought [Joseph] from the *hand* of the Ishmaelites." From this neutral beginning, the motif of the hand is developed both positively (as a benefit to Joseph) and negatively (as a danger to him). In its positive development, when Joseph's master saw that whatever Joseph did prospered "in his *hand*" (v. 3), he put all his possessions "in his/Joseph's *hand*" (vv. 4, 6). The motif takes a negative turn in the story of the attempted seduction of Joseph, the handsome young slave, by Potiphar's wife (vv. 7–20). Her invitation is peremptory and blunt: "Lie with me!" (vv. 7, 12). In his refusal, Joseph speaks of the trust of his master who put everything "in my hand" (v. 8) and steadfastly refuses to commit this sin. In the present form of the text, which includes chap. 38, there is an effective contrast between Judah's questionable liaison with Tamar and Joseph's refusal of such with Potiphar's wife. There is also a contrast between the woman whose boldness preserves family continuity (Tamar) and the woman whose boldness betrays her marriage (Potiphar's wife).

When Joseph continues to rebuff her advances, Potiphar's wife abruptly replaces words with action, taking hold of Joseph by grabbing his cloak, which he leaves behind as he flees. Having failed to seduce him, she vindictively charges Joseph with attempted rape. Evidence of the crime will be the garment of Joseph, which she has "in her *hand*" (vv. 12, 13). In her accusation made first to the servants (vv. 14–15), the spurned seductress is careful to place the blame for the trouble on her husband ("*He* brought to us a Hebrew slave"). The reference to Joseph as a Hebrew may be a clever attempt to stir up xenophobic animosity on the part of the other servants toward the foreigner to whom the master had entrusted the management of his house. In repeating the charge to her husband (vv. 17–18), she places the blame squarely on Joseph ("The Hebrew slave whom *you* brought here broke in"). In both versions of the charge, there is a subtle but telling change. As she tells her story to servants and husband, she does not speak of Joseph's garment as "in her hand" but as "beside her" (vv. 15, 16, 18). In this way she directs suspicion away from herself by suggesting that Joseph disrobed, in preparation for rape. The story ends as it began. After being imprisoned by the deceived and angry Potiphar, Joseph is still blessed with the divine presence and with success. He finds favor in the eyes of the chief jailer (v. 21), who puts all the prisoners and all the activity of the prison "in the hand of Joseph" (v. 22).

In the introductory remarks to the Joseph narrative, we considered the suggestion by several scholars that wisdom thought had considerable impact on the narrative about and the characterization of Joseph. Such influence is not unlikely, given the setting in which wisdom flourished and in which the Joseph novella may have been composed—Solomon's court, in the tenth century. Indeed the parallels between Joseph and Solomon, the patron of wisdom, are several: both were sons of a best-loved wife who was not the father's first; both had older brothers; for both, dreams were important; and both married wives given them by Pharaoh. While wisdom influence is strongest in Genesis 40–41, Joseph's refusal to cuckold Potiphar by dalliance with his wife is in keeping with the warnings against adultery in such wisdom literature as Proverbs 5–7, ascribed to Solomon.

Attentive readers of Genesis 39 may have heard in it echoes of chap. 37. Both involve preferential treatment of a youth by a superior that leads to trouble; in both, an act of deception is accomplished by means of a garment. As in chap. 37, the language of visual perception is frequent in chap. 39. In v. 3, Joseph's master saw that Yahweh was with him, and in v. 4 Joseph finds favor in his master's eyes. Verse 6 describes Joseph as good looking; and in v. 7, Potiphar's wife raises her eyes to Joseph. In v. 13 she sees that Joseph has left behind his garment in her hand, and in v. 14 her first word to the other servants is "See!" Finally, Joseph's management of affairs in the prison meant that the jailer did not have to attend to ("see") whatever was in his charge.

Genesis 39 points not only back to chap. 37, but forward to chap. 42. Like Genesis 39, chap. 42 involves a deception (42:7), vilification, and a false charge by someone in a position of power (42:9–17) that lead to imprisonment (42:16, 29). This last connection is reinforced by the verbal link of "prisoners" (lit., "the ones who are bound") in 39:20, 22, and the verbal forms of the same root in 42:16 ("You will be imprisoned") and 42:24 ("He bound Simeon before their eyes").

Women in Genesis

Since Genesis 39 contains the last extended narrative about a woman in Genesis, this is an appropriate place to survey the treatment of women in the book. Interest in the women of the Bible and in their roles and status has been advanced by the recent advent of feminist biblical interpretation.

Women and Men. The starting point for any survey of women in Genesis is the recognition that the OT does not think primarily in terms of atomized individuals, but in terms of families, tribes, and clans. Lifelong celibacy seems to have been unknown, childlessness was, for men as for women, a grievous burden, and among the chief glories of God was his provision of family structures for those lacking these (e.g., Pss. 68:6; 113:9). As wife and mother, a woman played an important economic role and could earn great honor (see Prov. 31:10–31). A man, on the other hand, could play a role in the important public realm, in the public worship, for example, or the army or the government, and it was through the father that the key tribal and familial identities were transmitted.

A woman in biblical society passed from the authority of her father to that of her husband; women were thus dependent on their fathers before marriage and on their husbands after. A married woman's sexuality was the exclusive property of her husband, and therefore adultery by the wife was considered in the OT a crime of the greatest magnitude, an offense against the husband, and a challenge to the authority he exercised over his property. The double standard is evident in the fact that polygamy and concubinage were permissible, allowing the male more than one sexual partner.

Women and Children. As mother, the woman was to be chiefly involved in childbearing and childrearing. The greatest threat to the security of a woman was sterility, her inability to fulfill her conjugal obligation of providing her husband with children, especially with sons. A childless woman was cut off, as well, from the only position of honor and status generally available to women and the only legitimate authority that could be exercised by a woman over another person (her child). Divorce was the prerogative of the husband; barrenness as well as adultery were probably both considered sufficient reasons for divorce. The situation of a woman divorced by her husband for childlessness was desperate in the extreme, since no source of security from husband or male offspring was available to her. Against this background one can begin to understand the anguish and urgency of the barren women in Genesis (Sarah, Rebekah, and Rachel). In this context, the action of God in removing barrenness and giving sons to a woman can be seen as preserving not only the family line but the life and security of the woman.

While the OT literature, including Genesis, may today suggest the secondary and inferior status of women, there is another avenue that can lead to greater understanding of the elusive female roles and experience in Israel. Sophisticated archaeological research and the interpretation of the new data derived from archaeology by analytical tools from the social sciences provide this new avenue behind and through the literature to the society that produced it.

In premonarchical Israel of the settlement period, as in all human society, there was a basic division of labor between the specifically male role of protection (defense and warfare) and the female role of procreation (childbearing and childrearing). The third essential task of production (such subsistence activities as land clearing, home building, the production of food and clothing) was a role that could be shared by men and women. In pioneer or frontier societies, the greater the contribution of women to subsistence and production activities, the higher her status. An approximately equal share by women in such tasks gives them a position approaching equality.

While in normal circumstances an increase in the participation of women in production was accompanied by a decrease in reproduction, such was not possible in early Israel given the demographic crisis of underpopulation in Syro-Palestine at the end of the Late Bronze Age (1500 –1200 B.C.); hence, the emphasis on reproduction, confirmed in the divine command in Genesis to "increase and multiply" (1:28; 9:1). The threats to this imperative were several: a high rate of infant mortality; a mortality rate for childbearing females higher than that for males of similar age (Gen. 35:16–19); losses by death and captivity in warfare; and epidemic disease, which took its greatest toll in the preadult population and in the oldest adults.

According to one interpreter, the role of women in both childbearing and in subsistence tasks is reflected in Gen. 3:16, properly understood. Modern translations typically obscure this (e.g., RSV: "I shall multiply your pain in childbearing; in pain you shall bring forth children"). The word translated "pain" means in every other occurrence "toil, hard work, physical labor"; nowhere does it refer to the "labor" of childbirth. Accordingly, a more accurate translation would be: "I will greatly increase your toil [i.e., the participation of women in production and subsistence tasks] and your pregnancies [reproduction]. Along with your toil you shall bring forth children." In this view, Gen. 3:16 reflects an era and a society in which women had a high degree of participation in subsistence activities (particularly hoe agriculture), with no diminution of their reproductive roles (Gen. 1:28), because of the need for large families to repopulate and thus claim an area and to produce more workers for the tasks of food production and the like. If this analysis is correct, Gen. 3:16 may have its point of origin in the settlement period of the end of the Late Bronze Age and the beginning of the Early Iron Age.

The Primal Woman. Having provided this background on the roles and status of women in the OT, we can turn now to a discussion of the women who appear in Genesis. The first to be encountered is the woman created in the P account in Genesis 1. While Gen. 1:27–28 has been understood by some as a basis for the equality of the sexes, a more recent analysis has questioned this as inappropriate for P, which elsewhere presumes the patriarchal structures that 1:27–28 has been taken to question (e.g., the P genealogies that trace the descent through the male, circumcision as the sign of the divine covenant with humanity, etc.). Rather, Gen. 1:27–28 speaks of sexual differentiation as part of the created order in which God has placed the power of fertility, of replenishment and con-

tinuation. It is true that the task of the human species is dominion over the rest of the creation; but the representative of the species is the male, typically described in terms of such male concerns as dominion and rule. The second creation account (J) speaks of the creation of woman as one party in a partnership of equals, an equality suggested by the description of the man's need for a "helping counterpart" (2:20) and by the assertion that the woman is of the same stuff as the man (2:21–23). The creation of the man at the beginning of the J creation story and of the woman at its end is an example of the literary device of inclusion and not a basis for the subordination of woman. It is only after the sin of Genesis 3 that the divinely intended relationship of a partnership of equals is disrupted.

The roles that the primal woman experiences are typically wife (2:23–24) and mother (4:1–2, 25). Some have understood her as seductress as well, in her giving her husband the forbidden fruit (3:6); it is more likely that this gesture is not seduction but the woman's role of meal preparation in which the man accepts the food presented to him by his wife.

The Family Stories. Stories in which women play an important part occur with some frequency in the family stories that make up the bulk of Genesis 12–50. The first of these stories (12:10–20, with its parallels in chaps. 20 and 26) is a good illustration of the OT view of the woman as subject to her husband. Only divine intervention protects the ancestress and with her the promise of offspring, a promise endangered by the patriarch. The situation is reversed in chap. 16, where it is Sarai who manages the situation by proposing a plan for offspring, while Abram is the passive figure. This is the first of a number of stories in Genesis (and elsewhere in the OT) that deal with resourceful women. Even in this story the androcentric bias prevails; the emphasis on male issue is an indication of the power of androcentrism even in stories in which women are the main actors.

We meet another impressive woman, Hagar, the Egyptian maid of Sarah, in chaps. 16 and 21, stories of family discord. Perceived as a threat to Sarah's status as primary wife, Hagar is abused by her mistress and flees. Hagar is the first person in the Bible to be confronted by "the messenger of Yahweh" (16:7) and the only woman to whom the Deity promises numerous progeny (16:10). She is driven out in chap. 21 when her son Ishmael is perceived as a threat to Sarah's son Isaac; again she is addressed by "the messenger of Elohim" (21:17). The strife between wives will recur in chap. 30 and as part of the larger theme of strife within the family. Sarah and Hagar are both victims of a patriarchal system that gives a woman honor and status only if she can give her husband male offspring.

117

The stories interposed between chaps. 16 and 21 relate the promise of a son to Sarah (chaps. 17–18) and Lot's hospitality to his angelic visitors (chap. 19). A father's authority over his children is the unstated assumption of Lot's exposure of his daughters to danger. But the tables are turned when the inebriated Lot is himself made a sexual object by his daughters, two more of the resourceful women in Genesis. Twice in these stories of Abraham and Sarah and of Lot and his family, there are revealing details that speak indirectly of the inferior status of women. First of all, note the different divine reactions to the laughter of the ancestors: in 17:17 Abraham's laughter, provoked by the promise of a child to an old couple, is passed over in silence, while in 18:12–15 Sarah's laughter at the same divine promise earns her a sharp rebuke from the Deity. Second, Lot's indecision about leaving the doomed Sodom provokes the compassion of Yahweh (19:16), while his wife's similar indecision brings upon her divine judgment (19:26).

In the stories that feature Rebekah (chaps. 24–27), the ancestress will replicate the journey of Abraham to Canaan; she too will leave her kin and her father's house (24:39–40) to become the mother of Jacob. Significantly, her call comes not from God (12:1) but from Abraham. Genesis 26 and 27 neatly balance one another; in chap. 26 Isaac is the deceiver in a deception involving his wife, while in chap. 27 Isaac is deceived by a plan devised by his resourceful wife.

Like Genesis 16 and 21, chaps. 29–33 are stories of strife in the family, the discord between Jacob's wives, the unloved and fertile Leah and the beloved and barren Rachel. As in the Sarah-Hagar stories, both Rachel and Leah give their maids to Jacob for substitute childbearing (note the parallelism of 16:2 and 30:3). Rachel and Leah are important in these stories not as individuals but as maternal links in the patriarchal chain, intent on providing sons for their husband and survival for the clan.

In the story of the rape of Dinah (chap. 34), the narrative focuses on the negotiations between Abraham and the rapist's father, Hamor, and the vengeance of Dinah's brothers on Shechem and Hamor. Dinah's voice is never heard amid all these male activities. In chap. 38, Tamar the childless widow acts with initiative and resourcefulness to assure children for herself and, once more, continuation for the family. Hers is a story about the precarious situation of a woman with neither husband nor sons and about the double standard that allows a man more than one sexual partner without negative judgment. The final story in which a woman figures as a principal character is chap. 39, the attempted seduction of Joseph by Potiphar's wife. These final three stories about women in Genesis act as a counterpoint to the stories of the patriarchs' mothers and wives; they are stories of sexuality (rape, assumed prostitution, seduction) not in the service of procreation in obedience to the divine command to "increase and multiply" in Gen. 1:28 (→ Women).

40:1–23, Joseph the Interpreter of Dreams. In chaps. 40–41, our attention is directed to Joseph's divinely given knowledge of the future, as he decodes the dreams of his fellow captives. In chaps. 42–43, when the sons of Jacob are before their unrecognized brother Joseph, the focus is shifted to Joseph's experiential knowledge of the past. The two dreams of Pharaoh's officials remind readers of the dreams of Joseph in chap. 37 that brought about his move to Egypt; they also prepare for the two dreams of Pharaoh in Genesis 41. In chaps. 40–41 it is not Joseph the dreamer but Joseph the interpreter of dreams who is the narrator's concern.

Gen. 40:1–4 introduces the characters involved in the story: the royal cupbearer and chief baker, imprisoned for some unspecified offense; Pharaoh; and Joseph. In v. 3 Joseph is described as "imprisoned" (lit., "the one who is bound"); the same word is used to describe the situation of the two royal officials and to link chap. 40 to chap. 39, where "bound" appears in vv. 20 and 22. In 40:7 Joseph asks his fellow prisoners, "Why are your faces gloomy?" (the same question occurs in Neh. 2:2, a passage that also deals with a royal cupbearer). When he learns of their dreams and of their inability to understand, he announces that "interpretation belongs to God" (Gen. 40:8), an assertion that he will repeat to the Pharaoh in 41:16.

Because of their obscurity, the dreams of the two officials differ from those of Joseph with their more transparent symbolism. After the recounting of the dreams, Joseph tells the royal officials what they mean: in both cases they predict that "Pharaoh will lift up your head" (vv. 13, 19). In the case of the cupbearer, the expression means that Pharaoh will pardon him. The more normal expression for such an act of mercy is to "lift up the face" (of one prostrate before the king), which occurs, for instance, in 19:21 and 32:20. The variant and unusual expression "lift up the head" is used to produce the parallelism of the interpretation. In the case of the baker too, Pharaoh will lift up his head in an act not of pardon, but of decapitation.

In v. 14, Joseph appeals to the soon-to-be-released cupbearer that he remember Joseph and try to gain his release; but at the end of chap. 40, Joseph is still imprisoned, forgotten by the court official whose release he had predicted. At this low point in the story, Joseph's ability to interpret dreams reminds the reader that Yahweh is still with Joseph. And hope begins to dawn in the realization that dreams can become reality and that the Egyptian monarch can act mercifully toward Joseph as he did toward his cupbearer.

The motifs that occur in the Joseph story (descent, being forgotten, and the hope for ultimate restoration) appear in several of the lament and thanksgiving psalms. Psalm 30 is particularly interesting for the number of thematic and verbal associations it has with the Joseph story. Compare Ps. 30:8 ("to you, Yahweh, I cry out; you, O Lord, I beg for mercy") and Gen. 42:21 ("when he [Joseph] begged for mercy"); Ps. 30:9 ("What profit is there in my blood, in my going down into the pit?") and Gen. 37:26 ("What profit is there in killing our brother and concealing his blood?"). Ps. 30:3 ("O Yahweh, you brought my soul up from the nether world; you preserved my life from among those going down into the pit") could stand as a summary of the descent-ascent movement of the whole Joseph story. Such parallels remind readers that Joseph's descent into Egypt is like a descent into Sheol; and similarly, Israel's departure from Egypt in Exodus is its emergence from the world of the dead.

41:1–57, Joseph and Pharaoh's Dreams. Chap. 40 ended with Joseph still in prison. Despite his success in interpreting the cupbearer's dream and his appeal ("remember me . . . and mention me to Pharaoh"), the chapter ends with the note that the cupbearer "did not remember Joseph but forgot him" (v. 23). Joseph's situation will begin to change when Pharaoh's dreams cause the released courtier to remember him. Genesis 37–40 traced the descent of Joseph into cistern, Egypt, and finally prison. That these are three stages of a single downward movement is implied not only by the use of the same word (Heb. bor, "pit") for cistern (Gen. 37:20, 22, 28, 29) and dungeon (40:15; 41:14) but also by the use of the same verb to describe the brothers "throwing" Joseph into the cistern (37:20, 22, 24) and Potiphar "throwing" Joseph into prison (39:20). Chap. 41 begins the account of his ascent to a position of power and preeminence in Egypt. The event that brings about this reversal is Pharaoh's two troubling dreams, in which seven healthy cows are devoured by seven others, scrawny and ugly in appearance, and in which seven healthy ears of grain are swallowed up by seven others, thin and blasted by the east wind (vv. 1–7).

Pharaoh's dreams recall Joseph's in chap. 37 in several ways. First of all, the Pharaoh has two dreams that, like Joseph's, make the same point. Further, the underlying meaning of the dreams of Joseph and of the Pharaoh is the same: the weaker and inferior (Joseph, the gaunt cattle, and thin ears of grain) will dominate the stronger (Joseph's brothers, healthy cattle, and the good ears of grain). When Pharaoh's magicians and sages are unable to interpret the dreams, the royal cupbearer remembers Joseph and his skill in dream interpretation and speaks of him to Pharaoh (41:8–13). The failure of the king's counselors to interpret the dreams may involve an implicit critique of the gods of Egypt; neither they nor their devotees can interpret dreams that predict the future (cf. Isa. 41:22–23). This critique will become explicit in Exodus 7–8: in 7:11 the Pharaoh summons his "sages and sorcerers . . . magicians of Egypt," and, while in 7:12, 22, and 8:7 they can replicate the signs that Moses and Aaron perform, they are defeated in 8:18.

The summoning of Joseph to Pharaoh in Gen. 41:14 is the first step of the change of his status and fortunes, symbolized by the change of his prison clothing (cf. 2 Kings 25:29). As in 40:8, Joseph attributes his success in dream interpretation to God (41:16). The double recounting of the dreams in third-person narrative in vv. 1–7 and again in first person in vv. 17–24 is typical of Hebrew narrative art (Gen. 42:9–20, 30–34). Joseph not only interprets the dreams as predictions of seven years of abundance followed by seven years of famine (41:28–32); he also suggests a policy to deal with the future (vv. 33–36). Impressed by his sagacity, Pharaoh appoints him prime minister (vv. 39–40), and Joseph's wisdom is shown in his effective management of Egypt's food supplies (vv. 46–50).

Just as Joseph was stripped of his distinctive garment at the beginning of his descent (37:23), so his elevation is symbolized by an investiture with a fine linen garment (41:42). This is the fourth reference to the unifying theme of Joseph's garments, two of which are connected to his descent (37:23–33; 39:13–18) and two with his elevation (41:14, 42).

Joseph, like Solomon, marries a wife given him by Pharaoh (41:45). The birth and naming of his two sons are reported in vv. 51–53. These names summarize the whole Joseph story: the name Manasseh (understood by a folk etymology to be connected to Heb. nashah, "forget"), points back to the beginning of the Joseph story ("God has made me forget my trouble and the house of my father"); and the name Ephraim (linked to Heb. parah, "be fruitful") points forward to the end of the Joseph story ("God has made me fruitful in the land of my oppression"). In Exod. 1:7, 11–12, it is Israel's prolific fruitfulness that brings upon them oppression by the Pharaoh "who knew not Joseph."

There are several noteworthy features shared by Genesis 40–41 and Daniel. In Gen. 40:12, 18, Joseph begins his explanation of the two dreams of his fellow prisoners with the words "This is its interpretation," a statement echoed in Dan. 2:36; 4:2. The God-given ability to interpret dreams that Joseph demonstrates (40:8; 41:16) is characteristic as well of Daniel, who is also portrayed as an Israelite serving in a foreign court (Dan. 1:3–6; 2:23, 28, 47; 4:8–9, 18; 5:13–14). The inability of the monarch's magicians to explain the dream (Gen. 41:8) appears as well in Dan. 2:7–13; 4:6–7; 5:8. The reference in Gen. 41:8 to Pharaoh's agitation and troubled mind uses a rare Hebrew verb (only five occurrences in the OT) that appears twice in a similar context, the disturbance of Nebuchadnezzar because of a dream (Dan. 2:1, 3). Finally, in both the Joseph story and Daniel, the dream interpreter is honored by the king, who recognizes the God of the interpreter (Gen. 41:38–39; Dan. 2:46–49). That the book of Daniel drew on the Joseph story for the portrayal of its hero is significant, given the identification of Daniel as a wisdom figure in Ezek. 28:3. Apparently even in antiquity the wisdom character of the Joseph novella was recognized by the authors of Daniel; modern scholarship has only rediscovered it.

Dreams in Genesis

The dreams in Genesis, and in the OT generally, are understood as modes of divine communication to humans and are of two types: message dreams, in which the divine communication is auditory and understood with no need for an interpreter (as in chap. 20), and symbolic dreams, in which the divine communication is visual in symbols not immediately clear in meaning and which therefore need interpretation by the dreamer, the Deity, or by a "specialist" (as in chaps. 40–41).

The dreams in Genesis are sent to the patriarchs (including Joseph) and to several other characters in the narrative. Although there is no specific reference to a dream, chap. 15 has been understood by some interpreters as a report of a dream. The designation of the experience as a "vision" (15:1) taking place at night and involving sleep (15:5, 12) may point in that direction. If this understanding is correct, then Genesis 15 would be a symbolic dream, the interpretation of which is given by the Deity. Gen. 26:24 may also be an abbreviated report of a message dream of Isaac, involving, as it does, a theophany at night.

The first explicit reference to a patriarchal dream in Genesis is that of Jacob in 28:1–15. It is clearly a symbolic dream that is, again, interpreted by the Deity. Some interpreters have understood this episode to concern an incubation rite in which one sleeps in a shrine in the hope of receiving a divine communication in a dream (Gen. 28:16–19; 1 Kings 3:5–15). In the Jacob-Laban novella, the patriarch relates to his

wives a symbolic dream he received (Gen. 31:10–13). And the final divine communication to Jacob in 46:2–4 may also be a dream, given the reference to a vision at night. The two dreams of Joseph (37:5–11) are visual, but their point is so clear that no interpreter is needed.

Besides these patriarchal dreams, four other instances should be considered in which divine communications by dreams come to non-Hebrews: Abimelech, king of Gerar (Gen. 20:3–7), and Laban, Jacob's Aramean relative (31:24), both receive message dreams in which they are instructed not to harm the patriarch or his family. The other two pairs of dreams to non-Hebrew characters are those of the imprisoned cupbearer and baker (40:5–19) and those of the Pharaoh (41:1–7, 15–24). These are all symbolic dreams for whom Joseph serves as the interpreting specialist.

In classical source criticism, dreams were considered to be a characteristic of the Elohist source (E). According to this hypothesis, this northern source from the ninth century B.C. focused on the transcendence of the Deity and thus viewed dreams as the appropriate means of divine communication to humans in contrast to the anthropomorphic divine messages in J. The frequency and ubiquity of dreams in the OT and in the ancient Near East, however, have cast some doubt on whether this traditional association of dreams with E can be sustained (→ Magic and Divination).

42:1–45:28
From Enmity to Reconciliation

The angry question of Joseph's brothers in 37:8 ("Will you be king over us and rule us?") begins to be answered in chap. 41 with the elevation of Joseph to the position of vizier. First introduced in the narrative as a shepherd (37:2), Joseph has been raised to a position second only to that of Pharaoh. The dreams that become reality in chaps. 40–41 prepare readers for the realization of Joseph's dreams in regard to his brothers. Their arrival in Egypt is forecast in 41:57 ("All the world came to Egypt, to Joseph, to purchase grain, so severe was the famine in the whole world").

42:1–38, Joseph's First Meeting with His Brothers. Genesis 42 is the dramatic highpoint of the Joseph story in its portrayal of the initial meeting of Joseph and his brothers after their long separation. In this account, the brothers remain unaware that the Egyptian official is Joseph, the brother they presume to be dead, just as they are unaware of the deeper meaning of some of the statements they make. As mentioned above, 41:57 sets the scene by noting that famine had brought "the whole world" to Egypt, and among those who journey there to procure food is the family of Jacob. For the first time since 37:1–4 we meet in 42:1–5 all the principals, described in both filial and fraternal terms. In 42:1–3 the order of appearance is "Jacob . . . his sons . . . the brothers of Joseph"; in vv. 4–5, the sequence (in the Heb. text) is "Benjamin the brother of Joseph . . . Jacob . . . his brothers . . . sons of Israel." Several observations can be made about this sequence. First of all, vv. 1–3 reverse the order of appearance of the characters in 37:1–2 ("Jacob . . . Joseph . . . his brothers") and 37:3 ("Israel . . . Joseph . . . his sons"). Gen. 42:4–5, on the other hand, begins with "Benjamin the brother of Joseph," so that even the word order focuses attention on the special relationship between the favored youngest son and Jacob his father. Finally, we are reminded of the first of Joseph's dreams, in which his brothers' sheaves surround his; in 42:1–5 the order of appearance of the characters is "Benjamin the brother of Joseph" (v. 4) in the center of a frame formed by "his [Jacob's] sons" and "the brothers of Joseph" in vv. 1–3 and by "his brothers" and "the sons of Israel" in vv. 4–5. This "surrounding" of the full brother of Joseph may allude to the fulfillment of the first dream, a fulfillment made explicit in v. 6, when "the brothers of Jacob came and prostrated before him" (as predicted in 37:7).

In noting that Jacob did not send his youngest son, Benjamin, on the dangerous journey to Egypt, 42:4 portrays Jacob as repeating with Benjamin the same mistake that led to the division of his family. In vv. 6–17, when Joseph recognizes his brothers as they prostrate before him (as they will again in 43:26, 28; 44:14; 50:18), the narrator tells readers in an aside that "Joseph remembered the dreams" (v. 9). Joseph's concealment of his identity and the nonrecognition of him by his brothers vividly suggest the gulf separating them, a distance reinforced by Joseph's harsh questions and accusations. The brothers who hated Joseph "because of his dreams and his words" (37:8) now have reason to fear the realized dreams and the threatening words of their angry, unrecognized brother. In the discussion of chap. 39, it was pointed out that Joseph's experience of being falsely accused and imprisoned is now to be his brothers'; with roles reversed, they too will come to know what it means to be helpless and threatened with death by someone hostile and more powerful.

The brothers' response to this unexpected turn of events is appropriately couched in the language of court style and diplomacy ("my lord" in 42:10, "your servants" in vv. 10, 11, 13). On a deeper level, in their use of the diplomatic master-servant language, Joseph's brothers are brought unconsciously to an admission of the truth of Joseph's dreams of superiority. One part of the response of the brothers to the charge of spying seems at first to be irrelevant (v. 13: "We are twelve brothers, sons of the same man"). While their answer may suggest their bewilderment and confusion at the unexpected charge, it has as well an ironic function, in that their words to Joseph ("we . . . all of us") unwittingly include him among the sons of Jacob; this reference to "twelve brothers" raises the possibility of a restoration of fraternal bonds.

The brothers' first reference to Joseph is the neutral "and one is no more" (v. 13), echoing Reuben's cry of dismay in 37:30 and pointing ahead to Jacob's words in 42:36. At their mention of the youngest son still at home, Joseph demands that he be brought to Egypt by one of the brothers while the rest remain incarcerated. Joseph's demand for Benjamin may be his attempt to discover whether his murderous brothers have again acted against a favored son. In vv. 18–26, Joseph reverses his original threat by imprisoning Simeon and releasing the others to return home with food and to return with Benjamin. Simeon is chosen as a hostage because he is Leah's second son (29:33), who will be imprisoned until the arrival of Rachel's second son (35:18). The brothers do not realize that Joseph can understand them since Joseph had been using an interpreter; along with the harsh questions and accusations, this detail effectively reminds readers of the earlier breakdown in communication between Joseph and his brothers (37:4).

In the incarceration of Simeon, Joseph reconstructs the circumstances of the crime of the brothers against him. The question posed by this first test is: will the brothers abandon Simeon as they did Joseph? Joseph's request that the brothers bring Benjamin to him is the second test; how will the brothers react to the suggestion that Rachel's remaining son follow his older brother into Egypt? As Joseph listens, the brothers relate their fate to their old crime (v. 21: "We are being punished on account of our brother"). And as if by the law of talion ("an eye for an eye"), the remembered anguish of Joseph as he pleaded for mercy brings anguish upon them (→ Retribution). After weeping (as he will in 43:30 when he sees Benjamin and in 45:2 at the reconciliation), Joseph addresses his final words in this chapter to his brothers (42:34: "I will give back your brother to you"). This statement is intentionally ambiguous; while the brothers with their limited awareness understand it to be about Simeon, the brother restored is also Joseph himself.

The return of the brothers to their father, without Simeon but with the money they had brought to pay for grain, recalls Joseph's imprisonment in the cistern and the money paid for him by the Ishmaelites (37:28). The double discovery by the brothers of the money that Joseph has secretly placed in the grain sacks is one of the standard pieces of evidence for sources in the Joseph story. And it is not the only doublet in chap. 42. Others include Jacob's two addresses to his sons in vv. 1–2 ("he said" occurs twice, followed in the first instance by Jacob's question to his sons and in the second by his relating of information: "I have heard"). In vv. 3–5 the arrival of the brothers in Egypt is recounted twice ("They went down . . . they came"). Twice Joseph is said to recognize his brothers (vv. 7–8), and twice he accuses them of spying (vv. 9, 14). Most strikingly, in the instance under discussion, one brother discovers the money in his grain sack on the return journey (vv. 27–28), and all the brothers make the same discovery after they return home (v. 35). All but this last instance can be explained without recourse to sources as repetitions for emphasis; and, if this is so, then the remaining instance of the double discovery of the money is probably to be explained as an expansion (similar to the Midianite expansion in 37:28, 36).

The two adjacent scenes of the brothers before Joseph (vv. 6–20) and before Jacob (vv. 29–38) are similarly structured: the brothers appear before a relative (Joseph; Jacob) with an expected brother (Benjamin; Simeon) missing. Jacob responds to the news of this second missing son with a lament similar to that over Joseph in 37:33–35. Jacob's words form an inclusion with the beginning of the chapter: the descent of the brothers to Egypt (42:2–3) will bring about the descent of Jacob to the nether world (v. 38); and as Jacob refused to send Benjamin to Egypt (v. 4), so now he vehemently repeats that refusal (v. 38), giving the remarkably insensitive reason that, since Joseph is gone, Benjamin alone is left, as if the sons of Leah simply didn't matter! Reuben's words in v. 37 ("Put him [Benjamin] in my hands, and I will bring him back") recall 37:22, where Reuben intended to save Joseph "from their hands and bring him to his father."

Like Genesis 37, chap. 42 uses with frequency the language of seeing. In v. 1, Jacob sees his sons, who look at one another; in v. 7, Joseph sees his brothers and charges them, in vv. 9 and 12, with coming to see the land. In v. 21, the brothers remember how they saw the anguish of Joseph; in v. 24, Simeon is bound "before their eyes." And in vv. 27 and 35, they see the money in their sacks.

43:1–34, The Second Trip to Egypt. The pattern of pairs in the Joseph story (the dreams of Joseph, his fellow prisoners, and Pharaoh; Joseph's being thrown into cistern and dungeon [both Heb. *bor*]) is complemented by a pair of journeys by the brothers to Egypt. In Genesis 43–44, Judah replaces Reuben as spokesman to Jacob and to the Pharaoh for his brothers—not a surprising change after the foolish speech of Reuben in 42:37 in which he says that Jacob can

kill Reuben's two sons if Benjamin does not return safely! In 43:3, Judah reminds his father of the necessity of bringing Benjamin if they are to return to Egypt for more food. In answering Jacob's question about why they told the Egyptian about Benjamin (v. 6), Judah's version of the interrogation is somewhat different from the dialogue in chap. 42 in which they volunteered the information about a brother still at home. Judah's claim (43:7) that the Egyptian official asked them about Benjamin is another instance of the deception of Jacob by his sons (37:31–32).

The instructions of Jacob in vv. 11–12 are meant to remind readers of the description of the Ishmaelite caravan to whom Joseph was sold (37:25–28). Joseph's brothers are themselves to repeat that caravan journey, bringing with them the same gifts (gum, balm, resin) and Benjamin, the other son of Rachel. In chap. 37, a brother (Joseph) leaves home to join his brothers and ends up in a caravan to Egypt; in chap. 43, the brothers leave home in a caravan to rescue a brother (Simeon) in Egypt and find Joseph as well when he reveals himself to them (45:3–4).

Upon their arrival in Egypt, the brothers are brought to Joseph's house, fearful that they will be taken as slaves (as Joseph was) because of the money they discovered in their sacks. Joseph's steward stills their apprehension and releases Simeon to them. In their meeting with Joseph, they repeat the prostration (vv. 26, 28). Joseph "inquired after their peace" (v. 27), just as Jacob had instructed Joseph to do in 37:14. As Joseph wept at the first meeting with his brothers (42:24), he does so again upon seeing Benjamin (43:30). At the meal that follows, the apprehensive brothers are surprised at Joseph's knowledge of their ages, in his seating arrangements for the feast. The meal effectively recalls the meal at which the brothers callously discussed Joseph's fate (37:25); the meal served separately to Joseph (43:32) is not only an Egyptian custom, but a reminder that reconciliation has not yet been effected. The reference to the brothers seated "before Joseph's face" (v. 33) and his sending of portions of food to them "from his face" (v. 34) forms an inclusion with the references to Joseph's face in vv. 3 and 5 ("You shall not see my face unless your brother is with you").

44:1–34, The Final Test and Judah's Speech. Two scenes make up chap. 44. The first (vv. 1–13) comprises the brothers' departure with Joseph's goblet, their pursuit and accusation by Joseph's steward, and their discovery of the goblet. The second scene includes their return to Joseph's house and Judah's great speech.

As in Genesis 42, Joseph instructs his majordomo to hide the brothers' money in their sacks, adding to Benjamin's sack Joseph's divining cup. This silver vessel, used in fore-telling the future, recalls Joseph's predictive dreams about the future, dreams that provoked his brothers into selling him for silver. Also re-called is the theft and concealment by Rachel of Laban's household gods without Jacob's knowledge (31:19–35); now it is her son Benja-min who is similarly accused of stealing and concealing a sacred object. The brothers re-spond to this new and unsettling development with protestations of their innocence (44:6–8) and an oath that condemns to death anyone guilty of this theft (v. 9). Their aggrieved re-sponse to the steward is similar to Jacob's oath to Laban that if anyone in his party has Laban's gods "that one shall not live" (31:32; cf. 35:17–19). At the discovery of the cup in Benjamin's sack, the brothers express their anguish by tear-ing their garments (as the innocent Reuben and Jacob did in 37:29, 34). Benjamin, singled out for special honor in 43:34, is now singled out for death. Judah's words to Joseph in v. 16 ("God has discovered the guilt of your ser-vant") is not only a confession of their crime against Joseph, but also a reminiscence of simi-lar statements by the brothers in 42:28 and by the steward in 43:23. The truth of these three statements, which confess the mysterious in-volvement of God in the affairs of the brothers, is confirmed by Joseph in 45:5–8.

Joseph insists that only the guilty Benjamin will be punished by enslavement (44:17) while the others are free to "return in peace to your father" (an ironic reminder of the dispatch of Joseph by his father to "see to the peace of your brothers" in 37:14).

This decision provokes the great speech of Judah (44:18–34), a person changed from the one who suggests making a profit from the sale of an envied brother to one who can without rancor or resentment rehearse the sad history of his unhappy and divided family. Several features of this remarkable speech deserve special attention. First of all, it is filled with master-servant language: four times Judah refers to himself as "your servant" (vv. 18 [twice], 32, 33), three times to his brothers as "your servants" (vv. 21, 23, 31), and once to all of them as "his servants" (v. 19). With such language Judah unconsciously testifies to the truth and actualization of Joseph's two dreams. The second dream (37:9–10), in which the par-ents of Joseph join his brothers in doing him homage, is specifically referred to when Judah speaks of Jacob as "your servant my father" (44:27, 30). Second, Judah replaces jealousy with compassion as he speaks of his father's preferential love first for Joseph, whom he be-lieves to be dead (v. 20), and then for Benja-min. Judah's claim in v. 22 ("If he leaves his father, he will die") may involve an intentional ambiguity, since the subject of "he will die"

could refer to the death either of Jacob or of Benjamin because of their separation. Judah even recalls in vv. 27–29 Jacob's painful use of paternal and filial language only of Rachel's sons (42:36, 38). The change of Judah's char-acter is most dramatically illustrated in 44:32: the brother who initiated the sale into slavery of the first favorite now will himself endure slavery to secure the freedom of the second favorite. Judah's transformation is complete, from hatred, violence, and deception to a noble gesture of self-sacrifice for one more loved by Jacob than himself. Judah's offer prepares for the reconciliation, which he unknowingly fore-casts when in v. 31 he speaks to Joseph of Jacob as "your servant our father," a designation that suggests the possibility of the restoration of pa-ternal and filial bonds.

Like Genesis 43, the second scene in chap. 44 employs the frequently appearing motif of "face": in v. 14 the brothers fall before Joseph's face; in vv. 23 and 26 Judah mentions the im-possibility of seeing Joseph's face without Benjamin; and in v. 29 Judah recalls Jacob's warning of his death "if you take this one from before my face." The motif of "seeing" in vv. 23 and 26 (Joseph's face) is taken up negatively by Jacob in v. 28 ("I have not seen him [Joseph] since then") and by Judah in vv. 30–31 ("when he sees that the boy [Benjamin] is no more"). The expression "he is no more" in v. 30 was previously met in 37:30 and 42:13, 32, 36.

45:1–28, Recognition and Reconciliation. The transformation of Judah is matched by a transformation of Joseph, who answers the im-passioned plea of Judah with a long speech of his own. For the third time in the story Joseph weeps, as he did without the brothers' knowl-edge in 42:24 and 43:30. His first instance of unconcealed weeping in 45:2 prepares for the revelation of his concealed identity. In v. 3, the unexpected revelation ("I am Joseph; is my fa-ther still alive?") terrifies the brothers, given Jo-seph's previous harsh treatment of them. And their fears are not allayed when Joseph has them draw nearer, repeats "I am Joseph" and reminds them of their crime by adding "your brother whom you sold into Egypt" (v. 4).

Joseph continues his address to his brothers with words that form the theological center and focal point of the Joseph story (45:5–8): "It was for saving life that God sent me ahead of you" (v. 5). This assertion of the providential guidance and governance of Joseph and his family by God is repeated (as was Joseph's self-revelation) and expanded in v. 7: "God sent me ahead of you to ensure for you a remnant in the land and to preserve you alive as a great band of survivors." The association here of "rem-nant" and "survivors" occurs as well in 32:8 where Jacob divides his property so that, if

Esau attacks, "the camp remaining may survive." In 45:8 Joseph insists for the third time that "it was not you who sent me here, but God"; and, in describing himself as "*ruler* of all the land of Egypt," Joseph uses a word from his brothers' angry question in 37:8 ("Will you really *rule* over us?"). The brothers will use the word again in their report to their father ("Joseph is alive, and he is *ruler* over all the land of Egypt!"). Joseph concludes by sending his brothers to invite Jacob and all his family to settle in Egypt and share its bounty (45:9–11). The weeping of Joseph and Benjamin in v. 14 and Joseph's weeping over his brothers in v. 15 form an inclusion with v. 2, and echo their father Jacob's earlier reconciliation with his brother Esau (Gen. 33:4). Joseph signals the reconciliation and the restoration of fraternal bonds by embracing and kissing his brothers; and the brothers, for their part, end the estrangement that made even communication with Joseph impossible (37:4) by speaking with him (45:15).

Twice in the preceding material from chap. 45 the narrator uses effectively a technique of reversal of meaning of the same words uttered by different characters at different points in the story. Jacob's lamenting response in 42:38 to the news about the imprisoned Simeon ("Only one remains" [Heb. *nish'ar*]) is recalled when Joseph speaks of the survival of a "remnant" (Heb. *she-'erit*) in 45:7. By using these two related words, both derived from the same root, the narrator shows God's providence active in transforming lament into joy. Similarly Joseph's invitation to Jacob ("Come down to me," v. 9; cf. v. 13) recalls Jacob's lament in 37:35 ("I will go down to my son"). Since Jacob's descent will be not to his dead son in the nether world but to Joseph alive in Egypt, his lament has now been transformed into Joseph's joyful invitation to share in the bounty of Egypt.

In 45:16–20, the Pharaoh confirms Joseph's invitation and supplies his brothers with wagons in which they can bring their father and families back to Egypt. Before their departure, Joseph gives to each of his ten older brothers a gift of new clothing and to Benjamin, his full brother, three hundred silver shekels and five sets of new festal garments. In this last appearance of the garment motif, a symbol of favoritism and discord (37:3, 23) becomes a symbol of renewed relationship with the brothers and of Benjamin's special place (43:34). Joseph sends them off with gifts for his father and a warning against any further discord (45:23–24).

When the brothers return to Canaan and report to their father all that had happened and the invitation of Joseph and the Pharaoh to settle in Egypt, Jacob, who had grieved that he would be with Joseph only in the nether world, rejoices that he will see him alive (45:28).

46:1–47:27
Israel in Egypt

The climax of the Joseph story was reached in chap. 45, followed by its denouement and conclusion. The story that began with Jacob in the land of Canaan (37:1) ends with the patriarch settled in Egypt (47:27).

46:1–7, Jacob's Itinerary and Vision. The focus of chap. 46 moves from Joseph to Jacob. The itinerary of the patriarch's move from Canaan to Egypt that begins in v. 1 and continues in v. 5 brackets the theophany (in a dream?) experienced by Jacob. After arriving at Beersheba and sacrificing to "the God of his father Isaac," Jacob receives a divine oracle that begins with a self-identification formula ("I am God, the God of your father") and an admonition ("Fear not!"). It continues with God's confirmation of the invitation of Joseph and the Pharaoh to Egypt and concludes with the promises of numerous progeny (v. 3) and divine presence (v. 4; cf. Gen. 28:12–15). There is a sharp contrast between God's guidance of the patriarch Jacob by oracle and appearance and of Joseph by hidden divine providence (39:2, 3, 21; 40:8; 41:16; 45:5–8; 50:20).

Gen. 46:1–4 is closer in style and content to the ancestral narratives in chaps. 12–36 than it is to its immediate context in the Joseph story. The itinerary formula is similar to Gen. 13:1, 3; 20:1; and 28:10 and the double divine call of Jacob and his one-word answer in 46:2 are exactly parallel to Gen. 22:11. The reference in the oracle to the God of the fathers (cf. 26:24; 28:13) and the patriarchal promise of a "great nation" (cf. 12:2) also bring us back to the world of divine visitations to the ancestors (12:7; 15:1; 18:9–15; 26:2–5) at sacred sites (28:10–15; 32:23–32).

46:8–30, The Descendants of Jacob and the Reunion with Joseph. The name list of Jacob's descendants begins with a stereotyped formula ("These are the names of the sons of Israel who came to Egypt") that is repeated exactly in Exod. 1:1. This repetition links the Joseph narrative with its theme of Israel blessed,

---

Opposite: A group of western Asiatics (*third row from bottom*) seeks permission from an Egyptian dignitary to enter Egypt; copy of a wall painting from a tomb at Beni-Hasan, Egypt, nineteenth century B.C. In the book of Genesis, Abraham and Sarai (chap. 12) and later Jacob and his large family (chaps. 45–47) move to Egypt in time of famine.

prolific, and prosperous in Egypt (Gen. 47:27; Exod. 1:6–7) to the story of Israel redeemed in the book of Exodus. Gen. 46:8 also forms an inclusion with the end of the Joseph story in 47:27. If the name list is traditional and preexisted the Joseph narrative into which it has been inserted, it has been adapted to its new context by the reference in 46:12 to Genesis 38. The list begins with the children of the sons of Leah (vv. 8–15) and continues with the children of Leah's maid Zilpah (vv. 16–18). A striking departure from the formulaic monotony of the list is the heading of the list of the offspring of Joseph and Benjamin (vv. 19–22): "The sons of Jacob's wife Rachel" (set against the normal pattern established in v. 9 of listing the sons of the eponymous ancestors of the twelve tribes). After listing the sons of Dan and Naphtali, Bilhah's children (vv. 23–25), the list concludes with a notice that the family of Jacob who entered Egypt numbered sixty-six (v. 26), a number brought to seventy with the addition of Jacob himself, Joseph, and Joseph's two sons Manasseh and Ephraim (v. 27).

Joseph's reunion with his father Jacob (vv. 28–30) closes this section with Jacob's family fully reconciled. The reunion is described in the same way as Joseph's reconciliation with his brothers in 45:14–15; it ends (46:30) with Jacob repeating his words in 45:28.

46:31–47:12, Audiences with Pharaoh. After Joseph's reunion with his father, he goes to notify the Pharaoh of the arrival of his family and to obtain the monarch's permission to settle in Goshen. In preparing his brothers for their audience with the Pharaoh, Joseph instructs them to mention their desire to continue in their profession of pastoralism; perhaps the purpose of these instructions is to make clear that Joseph's family has no ambition to advance to positions of prominence in Egypt because of his power. The "abhorrence" of Egyptians for shepherds mentioned in 46:34 may refer to the Egyptian view of non-Egyptian Asiatic nomads (43:32).

Pharaoh's generous offer in 47:6 ("The land of Egypt is before you") recalls Abram's generosity in 13:9 ("Is not the whole land before you?") to Lot, who chooses territory that is "like the land of Egypt" (13:10) and Abimelech's similar offer to Abraham (20:15).

After the meeting of the Pharaoh with five of Joseph's brothers (47:1–6), Joseph brings his father to Pharaoh (vv. 7–10). At both the beginning and end of this section readers are informed that "Jacob blessed Pharaoh." The point made of Jacob's age (vv. 8–9) probably reflects the belief that an old man near the end of his life is in the most advantageous position to give a blessing (cf. chaps. 27, 48). Jacob's blessing of the Pharaoh is another instance of

the realization of the promise that Abraham's descendants would be a source of blessing for the Gentiles (30:27–30)—a theme announced by J (12:3; 22:18; 26:4; 28:14) and employed by the composer of the Joseph narrative (39:5). The concluding verses, 47:11–12, relate Joseph's keeping of the promise to care for his family that he made in 45:1–11.

47:13–26, Joseph's Administration. This section, only loosely related to its context, is the conclusion of the description of Joseph the wise and successful administrator of 41:46–57. These two passages bracket the story of Joseph and his family in 42:1–47:12. The story provides some Egyptian "local color" by attributing to Joseph's administrative skill the royal ownership of all Egyptian land and the Egyptian tax system. The phrase "to this day" in v. 26 indicates that this passage served to explain the origins of a practice current in the author's time.

While some commentators have suggested that 47:13–26 originally followed immediately after 41:57, one factor that might explain its present position is its function as an example of Joseph's claim that "God sent me ahead of you to save lives" (45:5). Joseph's saving of the lives of the Egyptian populace is mentioned twice, in 47:19 and 25; and note that Joseph's saving of the lives of Gentiles follows immediately a passage (47:7–12) that recalls the blessing that comes to Gentiles by association with the blessed descendants of Abraham.

47:27, The End of the Joseph Story. The Joseph story began with Jacob and his family in Canaan; it ends with Israel in Egypt (46:8–27). The increasing frequency of "Israel" as the patriarch's name indicates not multiple sources but the development of the patriarch from Jacob as an individual character to Israel the eponymous progenitor of the twelve tribes. The movement of the story from Canaan to Egypt is enclosed by the two similarly constructed sentences that begin and end the Joseph story: "Jacob dwelt in the land of his father's sojournings, in the land of Canaan" (37:1); "Israel dwelt in the land of Egypt, in the land of Goshen" (47:27). But Gen. 47:27 is Janus-like. If its first half points back to the beginning of the Joseph story, its second half ("There they acquired property, were fruitful and multiplied greatly") points forward to the book of Exodus, where "the descendants of Israel" will be described as "fruitful and prolific" (Exod. 1:7).

47:28–50:26
Supplementary Material to the Joseph Story

If 47:27 marks the literarily effective end of the Joseph story, the added material is concerned chiefly with Jacob and recounts his blessing of Joseph's sons, his farewell testament, his death and burial in Canaan (47:28–50:14). Only in the final verses of the book of Genesis (50:15–26) does the focus return to Jacob's sons, moving from fear on the part of Joseph's brothers of revenge by Joseph after their father's death to Joseph's reassurance and his own death.

47:28–31, Jacob's Preparations for Death.
This section begins with a summary reference to the span of Jacob's life (similar to the genealogical notices in Genesis 5), 130 years in Canaan (47:9) and 17 more in Egypt. As the time of his death approaches, he asks Joseph to swear that he will bury his father in Canaan. The oath and the accompanying gesture is the same as in 24:2, also part of the patriarch Abraham's preparations for death. The concluding words of this section, in which his father does obeisance to Joseph ("Israel bowed") may indicate the fulfillment of Joseph's second dream (37:9–10) where the obeisance of his parents is described with the same verb as in 47:31 (and cf. 42:6; 43:26).

48:1–22, Jacob's Blessing of Joseph's Sons.
Jacob's second act of preparation for death is the blessing of Manasseh and Ephraim (cf. chap. 27). Jacob begins by recalling the divine promise at Luz (Bethel; 28:14, 19; 35:7) of numerous descendants and of the land of Canaan as a permanent possession. The divine name that Jacob uses in 48:3 is "El Shaddai," a name that occurs in Gen. 17:1; 35:11; Exod. 6:3 (as a divine self-designation); Gen. 28:3 (Isaac's blessing of Jacob); and 43:14 (Jacob's blessing of his sons). With the exception of this last occurrence from the Joseph story, all the occurrences are P (→ El Shaddai).

Jacob's blessing of Joseph's sons in 48:5–6 involves an adoption that elevates them to a status equal to that of Jacob's first sons Reuben and Simeon (cf. 1 Chron. 5:1); this adoption is another instance of Jacob's special predilection for Rachel (Gen. 48:7) and those born of her. Joseph brings his two sons before the dying patriarch, who rejoices that God has allowed him to see not only Joseph's face again, but his sons as well (v. 11). The motif of Jacob seeing someone's face has appeared before (32:30; 33:10), as has the theme of God's providential direction of the affairs of Jacob and his family. When Israel places his right hand on the head of the younger Ephraim and his left on the firstborn Manasseh, Joseph assumes a mistake because of Jacob's poor vision (48:13–17); but Jacob insists (vv. 19–20) that it is no accident but rather God's intention that "his younger brother [Ephraim] shall be greater than he [Manasseh]." The reference to Jacob's failing eyesight and the divine election of the younger son

are clearly meant to recall the beginning of the Jacob story (cf. 25:19–23 and chap. 27). As Jacob blessed Joseph's sons with the promise of many descendants (vv. 16, 19), so in vv. 21–22 he reiterates to Joseph the divine promise of occupation of "the land of your fathers."

49:1–27, Jacob's Testament.
Jacob's last words to his sons are cast in the form of a farewell discourse, a fairly common biblical genre in which a dying elder gives instructions, exhortations, predictions, or blessings to his children or followers. The closest parallel to 49:2–27 is Deut. 33:6–25, Moses' blessings on the tribes of Israel before his death; the poem in Deuteronomy 33 forms the conclusion of the book of Deuteronomy, the whole of which is the Mosaic final discourse (→ Testament).

While the poetry of Gen. 49:2–27 contains many obscurities and unsolved puzzles, at least a few general observations are in order. First, the sayings to the tribal ancestors often involve wordplays that are impossible to render in translation. For instance, "Dan shall judge" in v. 16 is in Hebrew *dan yadin*; in v. 19, the Hebrew translated "As for Gad, raiders will raid him" is *gad gedud yegudennu*. The poem begins with the six sons of Leah (vv. 2–15), who are followed by the sons of the two maidservants in an order different from that of 30:5–13. In 49:16–21 the order is Dan (Bilhah's first son), Gad and Asher (Zilpah's sons), and Naphtali (Bilhah's second son). Rachel's sons, Joseph and Benjamin, end the list.

In the discourse, Reuben the firstborn is passed over as leader of his brothers because of his intercourse with Bilhah (Gen. 35:22), and the words addressed to Simeon and Levi recall their revenge for the rape of Dinah (chap. 34). The long section devoted to Judah (49:8–12) notes his preeminence among his brothers (a point made in the Joseph story by his replacement of Reuben as spokesman for the brothers); for the metaphor of the lion, cf. Num. 23:24; 24:9. Gen. 49:10–12, one of the most obscure passages in the poem, is a promise to Judah of dominion and royal sovereignty among the tribes because of Judah's military prowess.

The Joseph saying (vv. 22–26) is amplified with a blessing that promises fertility (cf. the similar blessing of Joseph in Deut. 33:13–16). The promised fertility includes agricultural bounty because of abundant rains, along with human and animal fertility ("the blessings of breasts and womb"). It may be no coincidence that agricultural plenty and human fertility are connected in Genesis 41, which recounts both Joseph's management of Egypt's grain production and the birth of his two sons. The number of divine names in 49:24–25 (Bull of Jacob, Shepherd, Rock of Israel, God of your father, El Shaddai) is striking.

Like the sayings about Judah, Issachar, Dan, and Naphtali (and perhaps Joseph, although the text is unclear), the Benjamin saying is based on an animal metaphor. Finally, the poem has incorporated a gloss in v. 18 (cf. Ps. 119:166).

49:28–33, Jacob's Death and Burial. Gen. 49:28 is a prose conclusion to the poem, in which the sayings are interpreted as blessings ("He blessed each of them; with a blessing appropriate to each he blessed them"). In vv. 29–32 are Jacob's instructions regarding his burial in the family burial plot in Canaan (cf. chap. 23) where are already buried the ancestors Abraham and Sarah, Isaac and Rebekah, and Leah (for Rachel's burial in Bethlehem, cf. Gen. 35:19–20). This section closes with the narration of Jacob's death in 49:33. The idiom used twice in this death report ("he was gathered to his kinsfolk") has appeared before, of Abraham (25:8) and Isaac (35:29). While the idiom may simply refer to interment in the family grave, it has also been suggested that the expression refers to the practice of secondary burial, the gathering and reburial of the bones of the deceased after decomposition of the body (→ Burial).

50:1–14, Jacob's Funeral. Joseph weeps as he mourns his father's death, in language reminiscent of Esau's reconciliation with Jacob in Gen. 33:4 and of Joseph with his brothers in 45:14–15. The embalming of Jacob (and of Joseph in 50:26) in preparation for the funeral procession to Canaan is another instance of Egyptian "local color" in material connected with Joseph. The reference to "the Canaanites who were dwelling in the land" in 50:11 recalls the same observation in Gen. 12:6 and 13:7. We are reminded that while the promise of numerous descendants is on the way toward fulfillment, the promise of the land is still unrealized (except for the burial ground purchased by Abraham in chap. 23, where Jacob is to be buried; and cf. 33:19). Gen. 12:6 and 50:11 form an inclusion around the ancestral narratives from the call of Abram to the death of Jacob.

50:15–26, Joseph's Final Reconciliation with His Brothers. After Jacob's death, former patterns of behavior reassert themselves. Fearful that Joseph might now revenge himself after their father's death (as Esau intended in 27:41), the brothers engage in a final act of deception when they bring to Joseph the fictitious dying request of Jacob that Joseph forgive his brothers. Once more, Joseph weeps, and his brothers prostrate before him with the words "Let us be slaves to you!" (as in 44:16, 33). In his reassurance to his brothers Joseph sums up again the meaning of the whole narrative: "You planned evil for me, but God meant it for good

. . . to preserve the life of many people" (50:20; cf. 45:5–8).

Joseph's adoption of the children of Manasseh's son Machir, expressed idiomatically (v. 23: "born on Joseph's knees," as in Gen. 30:3), recalls Jacob's adoption of his grandchildren (48:5, 13–20). Both adoptions reflect tribal history in which Ephraim, Manasseh, and Machir are counted among the tribes of Israel (Judg. 5:14). For another instance of longevity expressed by recording several generations of descendants born in one's lifetime, cf. Job 42:16. In his dying words (Gen. 50:24–25) Joseph repeats the promise of the land, the realization of which will be described in the narrative that extends from Exodus to Joshua.

God's intention to preserve life (45:5; 50:20) is not only meant to refer to the preservation of Jacob's family alone during the famine but has a wider scope. Because of Joseph's wise administration, all Egypt and indeed the whole world (Gen. 41:57) is blessed with abundant food. Seen in the context of the book of Genesis, the Joseph story, played out not in the land of promise but in the wider world, is linked to chaps. 2–4, a story of alienation and division of husband and wife that led to the expulsion from Eden and the tree of life, unremitting hard work to produce food, and murderous violence between brothers. In the Joseph story that concludes Genesis, these ancient curses are reversed and cancelled as Joseph lives with his reconciled family in a land of abundant food. The words of the wise serpent in Gen. 3:4–5 ("You shall not die! You shall be like gods, knowing good and evil") are transformed by the wise Joseph in his final theological summation in 50:19–20: "Am I in the place of God? Though you planned evil against me, God meant it for good, to keep alive a numerous people."

Bibliography

Brueggemann, W. Genesis. Interpretation: The Bible Commentary for Preaching and Teaching. Atlanta, GA: Knox, 1982.

Coats, G. W. Genesis; with an Introduction to Narrative Literature. The Forms of the Old Testament Literature, 1. Grand Rapids, MI: Eerdmans, 1983.

Gunkel, H. The Legends of Genesis. New York: Schocken, 1964.

Sarna, N. M. Understanding Genesis. New York: Schocken, 1970.

Speiser, E. A. Genesis. Anchor Bible, 1. Garden City, NY: Doubleday, 1977.

Vawter, B. On Genesis: A New Reading. Garden City, NY: Doubleday, 1977.

von Rad, G. Genesis. Old Testament Library. Philadelphia: Westminster, 1972.

Westermann, C. Genesis: A Commentary. Minneapolis, MN: Augsburg, 1984–86.

EXODUS

P. KYLE McCARTER, JR.

INTRODUCTION

The book of Exodus has two contrasting geographical settings. The first is pharaonic Egypt. The events described in chaps. 1–12 take place in royal building projects, along the banks of the Nile, or within the palace itself. The second setting is Mount Sinai. The background of chaps. 19–40 is a desert encampment at the foot of the sacred mountain. The change of locale from Egypt to Sinai is achieved by a trek through the wilderness (12:37–19:2).

The two principal topics of the book correspond to these two geographical settings. The first is Yahweh's deliverance of Israel from slavery in Egypt. The second is the institution of a system of worshipping Yahweh at Sinai. The two are linked by Yahweh's miraculous guidance of the people Israel on the march through the desert.

The account of the captivity in Egypt is a continuation of the story of the family of Jacob begun in Genesis. The immediate background is the family's departure from Canaan during a famine and settlement in Egypt on land granted to them by the king (Gen. 46–47). The canonical division between Genesis and Exodus corresponds to a major transition in the story. Jacob and his sons have died, and their descendants, the Israelites, have been enslaved by the Egyptians. The Exodus narrative tells how Yahweh keeps faith with his promises to the patriarchs and rescues their descendants from slavery.

The account of the institution of the system of worship is the first part of the long Sinai section (or, "pericope") which begins in Exod. 19:2, where the people encamp at Sinai, and extends to Num. 10:10, after which they set out on the march again. This pericope is the principal biblical repository of the regulations of the forms of service of Yahweh. The materials in Exodus describe the erection of the tabernacle or wilderness sanctuary and the inauguration of the system of worship. The materials in Leviticus prescribe the rules for the ongoing operation of this system, together with the requirements of ritual purity. The materials in Numbers include the regulations for the camp in the wilderness.

The account of the wilderness trek continues with the departure from Sinai in Num. 10:11 and the journey to the border of the promised land. Thus it provides a narrative connection between the exodus from Egypt and the conquest of Canaan. The principal themes of the wilderness story are Yahweh's miraculous sustenance of the people under inhospitable conditions and the people's anxious ingratitude.

Literary History

The literary character of the book of Exodus corresponds to its twofold division of setting and topic. The story of the captivity and escape from Egypt is told almost entirely in prose narrative. The account of the institution of the divinely ordained system of worship at Sinai is also presented as part of a narrative. Though it does include a few passages of true narrative, it is predominantly a mixture of nonnarrative materials—including laws, ritual regulations, and prescriptions for proper worship—presented in several long passages of divine discourse.

The narrative portions of the book are composed of the pentateuchal source documents conventionally called J, E, D, and P (→ Sources of the Pentateuch).

The Yahwistic Account (J). The basic thread to which the rest has been attached is the J account. The original form of this old story remains generally visible despite its reworking by subsequent editors. It presents the departure from Egypt as a continuation of the theme of the double promise made by Yahweh to the patriarchs. Israel is to become a great nation living in a productive land. The first part of this promise, the growth into a great nation, seems already very near fulfillment at the beginning of the Exodus story. The Israelites have become a strong and numerous people, a sign of the power of the blessing that accompanied the promise (Gen. 12:2–3). But the captivity in Egypt is a hindrance to the realization of the second part of the promise, the occupation of the land, and the king of Egypt, in his determination to reduce the numbers of the Israelites, poses a direct threat to the first part. Thus in the J narrative it is to safeguard his promise to the patriarchs that Yahweh commissions Moses to lead the people to freedom. Knowing that this can be achieved only by force (3:19–20), Yahweh strikes Egypt with repeated plagues until Pharaoh agrees to let the people go. In the end, the king who tried to

129

thwart the blessing of Israel asks Israel for a blessing for himself (12:32). Note that for J the goal of the Exodus is clearly the promised land (3:8, 17). Sinai is only a stop—albeit the most important stop—along the way. J's version of the proclamation of the covenant, which is preserved in chap. 34, links the covenant very closely to the conquest of the land (cf. 34:11). The covenant stipulations are largely concerned with agricultural festivals; thus the mandated mode of worship is also linked to the land (34:18–26).

The Elohistic Account (E).

The J account seems to be supplemented at many points by materials drawn from E, but it is often very difficult to distinguish E from J in Exodus. The criterion of divine names, according to which J is characterized by the use of "Yahweh" ("the LORD") and E by the use of "God," ceases to be reliable after the E account of the disclosure of the name "Yahweh" in chap. 3. The E narrative begins to refer to the deity as "Yahweh" as well as "God," so that the use of "Yahweh" is no longer a reliable indicator of J. E can still be recognized, however, by its formal, otherworldly tone. Yahweh does not act through natural agents in E as he does in J. Thus, for example, the agency of the east wind in J's account of the plague of locusts is lacking in E's account of the same plague (cf. 10:12–20). Similarly, in J's account of the apparition at Sinai Yahweh descends upon the mountain (19:18) and addresses the people, whereas in E's account he speaks from the sky (19:19; cf. 20:21). If Israel is to be joined to Yahweh in a covenant relationship, it will have to be "a people dwelling alone, not reckoned among the nations" (Num. 23:9). For E, then, the goal of the Exodus is Sinai itself (Exod. 3:12), and the meaning of the covenant is that Israel becomes "a realm of priests and a holy nation" (19:6).

Priestly Materials (P).

The basic JE narrative was substantially reworked to reflect the point of view of the Jerusalem priesthood, according to which the later Temple cult, with its various rituals and regulations, originated in the time of Moses and derived its authority from the Sinai revelation. In particular, the old JE account of the Passover (12:21–23, 27b, 29–39) was enlarged and revised to reflect the fully developed Passover celebration of later times (12:1–20, 28, 40–50). Other distinctive contributions from P include the enhancement of the role of Aaron, from whom the Jerusalem priesthood traced its descent, the furnishing of genealogical information, and the annotation of individual episodes to conform to P's chronological system and wilderness itinerary. In all, a significant amount of material was introduced from the P source, and the Sinai pericope was greatly expanded to ac-

commodate cultic and legal documents preserved in Priestly tradition.

The Priestly History.

In its present form, therefore, our book of Exodus is a part of the Priestly history that extends from Genesis to Numbers. According to this history, the world was created by Yahweh as a perfect and sacred system in which men and women had an important and well-defined role. It proved impossible for them to live safely in the divinely created world, however, so that Yahweh was obliged to make special provisions for their safety and welfare. The first such provisions were included in the covenant made with Noah and his descendants in Genesis 9. Then, when Yahweh chose to enter into a closer relationship with one human family, the covenant with Abraham was concluded (Gen. 17). The events narrated in Exodus provide the context for the next and most important stage of this covenantal history. This stage is marked by two special divine acts of disclosure. The first, described in 6:2–4, is the revelation of the name "Yahweh," which, as in the E account, was unknown to the patriarchs. For P, the events surrounding the Exodus derive their meaning from this revelation. The purpose of the rescue from Egypt is to demonstrate to the Israelites the awesome power associated with the name Yahweh ("and you will know that it is I, Yahweh your god, who brought you out," 6:7). The purpose of the "signs and wonders" is to demonstrate the same thing to the Egyptians (7:5). The second act of disclosure is the promulgation of the Sinaitic legislation, the rules by which human beings can live safely in a divinely ordered world. This revelation accompanies the covenant Yahweh makes with Israel, the third covenant in the Priestly scheme.

Deuteronomic Influence.

The Exodus narrative has been expanded or rearranged at several points to represent ideas scholars call "Deuteronomic" because they are based on the teachings of the book of Deuteronomy. This aspect of the text of Exodus is part of a larger phenomenon. Much of Exodus, Leviticus, and Numbers is paralleled in Deuteronomy, and there was a tendency during the last phase of the composition of these books to expand or revise the text to reflect Deuteronomic materials and ideas.

The Exodus Tradition

Underlying our present book of Exodus are early traditions, probably first transmitted in oral form, about the Exodus, the wilderness sojourn, and the revelation at Sinai. These are part of a larger complex of traditions that also includes the patriarchal sojourn in Canaan and the conquest. This complex was the basic myth, or sacred story, through which the ancient Israelite community expressed its identity. Modern scholarship has tended to separate these traditions and seek diverse origins for them, stressing in particular the original isolation of the tradition of the law-giving at Sinai from the others (→ Hexateuch). The meaning of the story does not derive from its individual components, however, but from their relationship to each other. Thus, though many of the details may have changed during its transmission, we must assume that the tradition had its present, complex form from the beginning, that is, from the time the Israelite community began its definitive period of formation in twelfth-century B.C. Canaan.

The meaning of the story has to do with the possession of the land. It involves three periods of preparation: a period of temporary residence in the land (the patriarchal sojourn), a period of exclusion from the land (the residence and captivity in Egypt), and a period of sanctification for return to the land (the wilderness). This preparation is followed by a triumphal reentry into the land and its conquest and settlement. The events described in Exodus belong to the end of the period of exclusion and the beginning of the period of sanctification. They should be understood in terms of the larger theme of the possession of the land. The hard labor at the end of the exclusion period is the opposite of the life that lies ahead in Canaan. The service of Pharaoh, who exploits the people's labor for himself, is the opposite of the service of Yahweh, who ensures that the people's labor in the land will produce crops that sustain them. The importance of the deliverance from Egypt is that it puts an end to the period of exclusion and looks ahead to the occupation of the land. The importance of the covenant made at Sinai is that it joins the people to the proprietor of the land and provides the rules by which they can prosper within the seasonal cycle of the land. As noted above, the Exodus and covenant retain approximately this significance in the earliest written version of the story (J). The wilderness sojourn, of which the revelation at Sinai is a part, corresponds to the period of sanctification in the larger story. It is the time of final preparation, when the people Israel learn to live in complete dependence upon Yahweh and receive the divine instructions by which they can live in the land.

Significance for the Ancient Community

As noted above, the events described in the book of Exodus were part of the basic story through which the ancient community expressed its identity. The God who rescued them from slavery in Egypt and brought them to himself in the wilderness was the God they now served (cf. Hos. 13:4–5). The "signs and wonders" in Egypt and the miracles in the wilderness, especially the deliverance at the sea, were paradigmatic illustrations of both the power of the God of Israel and the favor in which he held his people. These events were recited in worship both to praise Yahweh for his goodness in the past and to appeal for his help in present troubles. Examples of such liturgical materials have survived. Note, for example, the large role played by the plagues and the desert miracles in the so-called historical psalms (Pss. 78:12–16, 44–51; 105:23–43; 106:7–33; 135:8–9; 136:10–16). According to Deuteronomic law, and probably earlier, the story of the Exodus was to be recited during the celebration of the Passover (cf. Exod. 12:26–27), the Feast of Unleavened Bread (13:8), and the consecration of firstborn (13:14–15), thus preserving an understanding of the historical meaning of those ceremonies.

The Pre-exilic Community. For those who lived in pre-exilic Judah and knew the story as it was told in the J narrative, the Exodus was clear evidence of Yahweh's faithfulness to his double promise of land and progeny. As such, the story of the escape provided assurance not only of security but also of prosperity. The goal of the Exodus was the promised land, where the people now lived as heirs to the blessing that had permitted them to thrive even under the hardships imposed by Pharaoh. At the same time, the covenant bond established at Sinai formalized and clarified the people's relationship to their God, who guaranteed them possession of their land and who required them to make contributions from their flocks and fields and to assemble for worship at the major festivals of the agricultural year.

The Postexilic Community. For the community living in the time of the Second Temple (after 515 B.C.), the Exodus story was a part of the Priestly history. The plagues and the parting of the sea demonstrated the universal sovereignty of the God of Israel. The institution of the Passover service in Egypt and the tabernacle cult at Sinai demonstrated the continuity of the religion practiced by the postexilic community with the Mosaic period, from which the various institutions of worship derived their authority. For P, the revelation at Sinai was the fountainhead of the rules and practices that governed the life of the community. Laws, customs, and institutions that were accorded authoritative status, therefore, tended to be traced to this event. As noted above, the literary consequence of this tendency was the inclusion of a large body of diverse materials within the larger Sinai pericope (Exod. 19:1–Num. 10:10) of the Priestly history. Ultimately, this tendency accounts for the belief of the Talmudic rabbis that rabbinic law derives from the same great revelation to Moses on Mount Sinai (→ Halakah).

Historical Context

The general background of the story of Israel's enslavement by Pharaoh is the historical phenomenon of Asiatic laborers in Egypt. Slaves with Semitic names are known to have been working in Egypt at least as early as the eighteenth century B.C. and for about fifteen hundred years thereafter. The use of Asiatic slave labor was especially common during the New Kingdom (ca. 1550–1070 B.C.), and there are many references in the records of that time to the participation of foreign laborers, including Syrians and Canaanites, in building projects. The memory of a period of this kind of slavery in Egypt was an early component of Israelite tradition. It must have been based on the historical experience of some group of the ancestors of the later community. In the long process of the development of the tradition, however, the details needed for modern historians to date and explain this experience were lost. "The land of Rameses," in which the family of Jacob settled (Gen. 47:11), was in northeastern Egypt, where a royal residence was maintained from about 1300 B.C. onward. The region took its name from Ramesses II (ca. 1279–1212 B.C.), who sponsored building projects at several sites in the region, including Per-Ramessu and Per-Atum, the "Pithom and Rameses" of Exod. 1:11 (→ Pithom; Raamses, Rameses). For these reasons most modern historians have assigned the events of Exodus 1–15 to the New Kingdom, often specifically to the reign of Ramesses II. Thus Sety I (ca. 1291–1279 B.C.) would be the new king of 1:8 and Ramesses himself the Pharaoh of the Exodus. There is reason for great caution on this point, however. Despite the antiquity of the sites, the names Pithom and Rameses were not widely used as designations of cities before the seventh century, and the term "store cities" does not occur elsewhere in early biblical materials. Thus the second half of 1:11, the only specific link to extrabiblical evidence offered in the story, may be a late interpolation based on uncertain authority and, in any case, provides no basis for dating the Exodus to the Ramessid period. Thus many modern historians prefer to say nothing about the date of the events related in Exodus, except that, as basic components of the story that defined Israel, they must have taken place before the final formation of the Israelite community in twelfth-century Canaan.

COMMENTARY

1:1–7:7
Israel in Egypt

The first section of Exodus describes the enslavement of the Israelites in Egypt and Yahweh's preparations for their escape. Thus it sets the stage for the story of the plagues and the flight into the wilderness that follow. Yahweh's decision to act, however, is based not only on compassion but also on his past relationship with Israel's ancestors (2:23–25; 3:7–10), so that it is clear from the beginning that what he has in mind is not only a rescue but the reestablishment of his relationship with Israel on a new basis. When the people escape, they will "serve God" at his mountain sanctuary (3:12 [E]). Yahweh will renew his covenant with them (cf. 6:7 [P]) and lead them into the promised land (3:8, 17 [J]; 6:8 [P]). Thus the preparations made here are not only for the Exodus itself, but also for the revelations to be made at Sinai and the wilderness journey to Canaan. The most important part of these preparations is the commissioning of an individual who will serve as an intermediary between the people and their God throughout this long process. Thus by virtue of his commission here in chaps. 3–4 and 6, Moses will serve as the agent of Yahweh's punishment of the Egyptians and the leader of the march from the border of Egypt to the border of Canaan. This means that he is the dominant human figure not only of Exodus but of Leviticus, Numbers, and Deuteronomy as well.

1:1–22
The Oppression in Egypt

The opening of Exodus provides a transition from the stories about the patriarchs to the stories about the captivity in Egypt. At the end of Genesis, the sons of Jacob and their families were living as honored guests in the best land of Egypt (Gen. 45:17–20), which Pharaoh had granted them in gratitude for Joseph's service at the Egyptian court. Now, however, Joseph and his brothers have died. The land is filled with their descendants, but the Israelites of this new generation are no longer welcome in Egypt. The new Pharaoh recognizes no obligation to them. Their number and strength alarm him, and he begins to devise ways to control them. He presses them into the service of the state, and when this hard labor fails to check their vigor, he contrives the death of their male children.

There is an emphasis throughout this opening section on the increase in the number of Israelites. This is, in the first place, a part of an ancient and widespread literary pattern that is most easily seen in the well-known Mesopotamian story of Atrahasis. That story, like this one, begins with hard labor. At first the laborers are the younger gods, but they are replaced early in the story by a human labor force. The people work hard for centuries excavating canals. At the same time they multiply, until the land is crowded and noisy, and the gods become alarmed. In particular, the great god Enlil is disturbed by the clamor and cannot sleep. He orders that supplies be withheld from the people and that the land be afflicted with a drought. The people are decimated, but Atrahasis, the human hero of the story, eventually manages to end the drought with the help of Enki, a favorably inclined god. The people again multiply, and the land again becomes crowded. Enlil afflicts the people a second time, but Atrahasis and Enki fend off this disaster too. Finally Enlil instigates a great flood. All human life is in danger of being destroyed. Acting on Enki's instructions, however, Atrahasis constructs a large boat and saves his family, thus preserving human life. This story is often compared (and rightly so) with the biblical story of Noah and the Flood. Its literary pattern, however, is closer to the story of the affliction of the Israelites in Egypt. The people are working very hard, but they are nonetheless multiplying and filling the land. Pharaoh is alarmed, and, like Enlil, attempts to reduce their number by a series of afflictions, first imposing hard labor on them, then directing the midwives to kill their sons, and finally ordering their sons to be cast into the Nile. One of these sons, Moses, is saved by being placed in the Nile in an "ark" (the term is the same as that used for Noah's boat). The arks of Atrahasis and Noah preserve human life, while the ark of Moses preserves the life of the man who will eventually liberate his people from bondage.

Though the increase in the number of the people is part of an ancient literary pattern, however, it is also a thematic component of both the P and J narrative sources. The language used in 1:7 to describe the increase connects this story with a series of other passages in which a motif of divine blessing is expressed in terms of human fertility. The development of this motif began with the blessing of creation in Gen. 1:28, according to which the newly created men and women were to "be fruitful, multiply, and fill the earth." This blessing was articulated again after the Flood (Gen. 9:7) and then narrowed and conferred especially upon the family of Abraham (Gen. 12:3). The subsequent stories about the patriarchs show that the divine blessing continued to be effective for Abraham's descendants, and the references to the large number of Israelites in our passage represent a continuation of the motif, which will receive its climactic expression in the oracles of Balaam in Numbers 23 and 24. In its clearest form, this motif is a thematic component of the latest or Priestly redaction (edition) of the larger story, to which Gen. 1:28 and 9:7 as well as Exod. 1:1–7 and 13–14 are usually assigned. Thus the language of the blessing of creation is echoed precisely in v. 7, where we are told that the Israelites in Egypt "were fruitful ... multiplied ... and the land was filled with them." Note, moreover, that the theme of the blessing of Israel was already present in the older J narrative. The language used to describe Israel's increase in v. 12, for example, recalls Gen. 30:30, which characterizes the prosperity of Laban's household during Jacob's residence there. Both of these passages derive from the J narrative, in which the blessing of Israel was a major theme.

1:1–7, The New Generation of Israelites. The opening passage describes the transition of Israel's ancestors from a single family to a multitude of families. Thus the twelve sons of Jacob are listed in vv. 2–4 both to review the names of the individual members of the family that came to Egypt and to identify the ancestors of the tribes.

1:8–14, Hard Labor. As the story begins, Pharaoh declares his fear of the people of Israel. They are, he says, dangerously numerous. His solution is to put them to work building the store cities of Pithom and Rameses. Many commentators have questioned the suitability of this solution. Would it have been an effective way to reduce the population? Would the king have willingly diminished his own labor force? Some critics doubt that the themes of population increase and hard labor, though joined in the earliest written sources, were originally related. Note further that the story of Israel's hard labor finds its natural intensification not in the episode of the Hebrew midwives that follows immediately in vv. 15–22 but in the story of the deprivation of straw for brick making in 5:6–18. Thus this episode stands rather isolated in its present context.

1:15–22, The Hebrew Midwives. Pharaoh commands two midwives to kill all male children born to the Israelites, but the midwives will not cooperate and, in desperation, Pharaoh orders his soldiers to cast the male children of the Israelites into the Nile. The midwives refuse because they "fear God," that is, because they are women of moral scruples. The use of this general expression, rather than "fear Yahweh" (→ Fear of the Lord), raises the possibility that the women are not Israelites, but their names, Shiphrah and Puah, are Semitic, not Egyptian.

According to the present form of the story, the atrocities described here are to be understood as intensification of the hard labor just described. As noted above, however, the midwives episode is not a natural continuation of the hard labor episode. Instead, it represents an introduction to the story of Moses, the central figure of the story, who appears first as an infant endangered by Pharaoh's decree.

2:1–4:31
The Story of Moses

Only three human figures have prominent roles in the story of Israel's escape from slavery in Egypt. Of these, Aaron is little more than an extension of Moses himself, and Pharaoh is his antagonist. Moses is overwhelmingly the dominant figure. The keen interest the tradition took in him has influenced the growth of the narrative, which now contains considerable material about his early career. As just noted, the expected continuation of the story of Israel's hard labor in 1:8–14 is the story of the deprivation of straw for brick making in chap. 5. But the natural flow of the narrative is diverted at this point to make room for an account of Moses' childhood and sojourn in Midian. Though the story of Moses' infancy seems to have been known only to E, the tradition of the flight to Midian and sojourn there is represented in both of the early narrative sources (J and E), so that it must have entered the tradition at an early date.

2:1–10, Moses' Birth and Childhood. Moses is introduced as an infant hidden by his mother in the reeds of the Nile to protect him from Pharaoh's decree. Pharaoh's own daughter finds him, takes pity on him, and adopts him. With the help of his sister, who was secretly watching over him, the Egyptian princess arranges for the infant to be suckled by a Hebrew wet nurse, who is none other than the baby's mother. Thus the child Moses is rescued from death, nursed by his own mother, and raised in the Egyptian palace.

The infant who escapes mortal peril to grow up and become the leader of his people is a common motif in world folklore. In one group of such stories, the child's fate is foretold by an oracle, so that the king he is destined to replace exposes him at birth. Accordingly, some scholars have speculated that in an earlier version of our story Moses' role as liberator of the Israelites was foretold and Pharaoh's true purpose in drowning the sons of the Israelites was to eliminate the promised child. But no trace of such an oracle is preserved in our sources. Note, moreover, that the infant Moses is not exposed or cast into the water; he is placed among the reeds for protection. A closer parallel, therefore, is the so-called Legend of Sargon,

an Akkadian text describing the birth and rise to power of the third-millennium B.C. Mesopotamian ruler Sargon the Great. In this document, Sargon says that shortly after his birth his mother, a high priestess, put him in a basket of rushes caulked with bitumen and set him adrift in the river, where he was found and raised by an irrigation worker.

The Legend of Sargon is pseudepigraphal, having been composed long after the reign of Sargon the Great. Similarly, the story of Moses' birth, which seems to have been lacking in the J source, is legendary rather than historical in character (→ Moses). No individual but Moses himself is identified by name, not even his parents (cf. 6:20). Moses' own name (*moshe*) is explained in v. 10 as if it were derived from Hebrew *masha*, "draw out"; but in fact it was a common element in Egyptian names, often used by itself with the meaning "child" (cf. King "Thutmose"). Thus Moses was one of several Egyptian names in the early levitical genealogy, including Hophni, Phinehas, and Merari. This does not mean that Moses or any of the others was an Egyptian, but it does suggest that a portion of the tribe of Levi may have lived in Egypt at some time.

2:11–25, Moses' Flight from Egypt. Moses' Egyptian upbringing does not extinguish his identification with his people, and when he sees an Egyptian beating a Hebrew, he slays the assailant. Now sought by Pharaoh as a criminal, he flees eastward into the desert and comes to the land of Midian, east of the Gulf of Aqabah or Elath in northwestern Arabia.

The region south and east of Israel, which included Paran, Teman, and southern Edom or Seir, was regarded as sacred by the Israelites throughout the early biblical period. Horeb, the mountain of God, was here (3:1), and from here the God of Israel was said to march on behalf of his people (cf. Deut. 33:2; Judg. 5:4; Hab. 3:3, 7). Many scholars believe that the origins of Yahwism are to be sought in the vicinity of Midian, and it may be noteworthy in this regard that Moses' father-in-law is a "priest of Midian" (v. 16; cf. 3:1; 18:1) who in chap. 18 invokes, praises, and sacrifices to Yahweh. A distinctive culture, which archaeologists have tentatively designated Midianite, flourished in this region at the end of the second millennium B.C. Elsewhere in the Bible, the Midianites, though said in Gen. 25:2 to be descended from Abraham, are depicted as foreigners, sometimes regarded with hostility by the Israelites (e.g., Num. 31). In the Gideon story (Judg. 6–8) they are presented as camel-riding nomads, but the "Midianite" culture known from the archaeological record was largely sedentary.

Having rescued seven sisters from a group of hostile shepherds, Moses is befriended by their father, who takes him into his home and gives him Zipporah, one of his daughters, as a wife. She bears Moses a son, Gershom, whose name provides an occasion for wordplay involving the Hebrew term ger, "sojourner."

In this passage Moses' father-in-law is called Reuel. In Exod. 4:18, however, his name is Jethro (cf. chap. 18). The situation is further complicated by Judg. 4:11, where Moses' father-in-law is called Hobab and is said to have been a Kenite rather than a Midianite. Finally, Num. 10:29 speaks of "Hobab the son of Reuel, the father-in-law of Moses." Apparently there were at least two variants in this part of the tradition about Moses. According to the first, which was probably older, Moses' father-in-law was the Midianite Jethro. According to the second, which may have developed later in Judah, his father-in-law was Hobab the Kenite. Unless the name Reuel represents yet a third traditional variant, it must have arisen as an error based, perhaps, on the name of the father of Hobab or Jethro.

This account is followed by an editorial passage (Exod. 2:23–25) in which we are informed of two important events that have taken place offstage. The king of Egypt has died, so that it is now possible for Moses to return to Egypt (cf. 4:19). Yahweh, in the meantime, has taken note of the suffering of his people. The reference to the covenant with the patriarchs in v. 24 has the effect of incorporating the present events into the larger covenantal scheme of the Priestly history.

3:1–6, The Burning Bush. Moses leads his father-in-law's sheep to Mount Horeb, where he is astonished to see a bush that is burning but not consumed. He does not realize that what he has encountered is a messenger or angel of Yahweh in the form of a flame until, approaching the bush, he hears a divine voice speaking in the fire. Knowing that it is fatal for a human being to see a god (cf. 33:20), he covers his face and listens.

Horeb is another name for Sinai, the mountain at which the Israelites will assemble after their departure from Egypt (cf. v. 12). The name Sinai is probably hinted at by the designation of the burning bush in Hebrew as sene, as if Sinai meant "the mountain of the sene-bush" (cf. the designation of Yahweh as "the one who dwells in the sene-bush" in Deut. 33:16). The names Horeb and Sinai may derive from originally distinct traditions about the mountain of Yahweh, but in the present form of the story they are identical. The exact location of Mount Horeb is unknown; indeed, it had probably been forgotten by the time of the composition of most of the biblical literature. The present episode argues strongly for locating it in northwestern Arabia. The alternatives are discussed below in

connection with the wilderness itinerary (see 15:22–18:27, "The Journey to Sinai").

3:7–4:17, The Commissioning of Moses. Next is the Bible's most detailed account of the reception of a divine commission. It seems also to have been the paradigmatic account, having influenced the stories of the commissioning of Gideon (Judg. 6:11–24), Samuel (1 Sam. 3:2–14), and others. It is, moreover, a composite account, produced by the combination of two versions of the events. Thus Moses' charge is reported twice, in a short version that derives from E (Exod. 3:9–10) and in a much longer version taken from J (3:7–8, 16–22). The P version of Moses' commissioning is preserved in 6:5–13. In both of the present versions the message Moses receives includes an announcement and a commission. Yahweh has taken notice of the affliction of the Israelites in Egypt, and he is sending Moses to bring them out of the land. In the J version, he is told to lead them into a new land, which, according to v. 8, will be "good" and, in contrast to the confinement the Israelites have experienced in Egypt, "broad," i.e., open and free. It is described as "a land flowing with milk and honey," a stereotyped phrase referring to the raising of livestock and beekeeping, staple economies of the central Israelite hills. The land is identified by its present inhabitants, listed in the usual formulaic way. At the conclusion of the J version, Moses is told to instruct the people to despoil the Egyptians when they leave (cf. 11:2–3; 12:35–36).

In each version the commission is followed by two questions raised by Moses in objection to Yahweh's plan. His first question in the E version (3:11–12) regards his own ability to accomplish the task. God assures him that "I will be with you," but the "sign" offered—that Moses will lead the people to this very mountain, where they will "serve God"—is puzzling. We expect some kind of reassurance before the fact (cf. Judg. 6:15–21). Moses' second objection in the E version (3:13–15) is that the Israelites will demand to know the name of the God who has commissioned him. According to Elohistic tradition, then, the Israelites had forgotten or did not yet know Yahweh's name. It is now revealed in a mysterious way. God identifies himself as "I am who I am" (v. 14). The Hebrew word 'ehye, "I am," is thus associated with the name Yahweh, and Moses is to tell the people that "I am" sent him. "I am who I am" belongs to a category of expressions designated idem per idem, used in biblical Hebrew and related languages to refer to gods. In one way or another, they stress divine freedom, majesty, and mystery. Compare "I show favor to whom I show favor, and I show compassion to whom I show compassion" in 33:19, and "I say what I say" in Ezek. 12:25.

Moses' first objection in the J version (4:1–9) is that, despite Yahweh's statement to the contrary (3:18), the people will not believe him. Yahweh responds by giving him three magical transformations to perform to authenticate himself (cf. Deut. 13:1–2): he will be able to turn his rod into a snake and back into a rod again, to make the skin of his hand diseased and healthy again, and to turn the water of the Nile into blood. All three of these tricks suggest the deadly character of the power Moses will wield, and the last adumbrates the first plague (7:14–24). Moses' second objection in the J version (4:10–16) is that he is inarticulate and "heavy of mouth and tongue," an expression that may mean he has a speech impediment. Yahweh's solution is to assign Moses' brother Aaron to be his spokesman. In depicting the leadership of Moses and Aaron in this way, the J narrative prefigures the rule of the Davidic king and Aaronidic high priest in its own day. Note that at this point Aaron is called "the Levite" (v. 14), a title that could equally well be applied to Moses (cf. 2:1) but that here looks ahead to Aaron's role as ancestor of the levitical priests who presided in Jerusalem. Just as it was their responsibility to transmit the Mosaic law (cf. Lev. 10:11), so it was the responsibility of their ancestor to transmit the words of Moses himself.

At the end of the passage (v. 17) Moses is reminded to take along his rod, "with which you will perform the signs." The rod, then, is to be used not just for the serpent miracle (vv. 2–5) but to execute all the signs. This interpretation of the rod is characteristic of the E source, from which this notice derives.

4:18–31, Moses' Return to Egypt. The next passage combines a variety of narrative fragments under the general heading of Moses' return from Midian. It presents a number of interpretive difficulties. Without revealing his divine commission, Moses obtains permission from Jethro to return to Egypt. We are told that he prepares his wife and *sons* for the journey (v. 20), but we know only of Gershom (2:22), and 18:4 suggests that Eliezer was born after the Israelites left Egypt. Yahweh's orders in vv. 19 and 21–23 seem superfluous after the elaborate instructions Moses has already been given. Note, however, that vv. 22–23 introduce a new element, anticipating the final plague and giving it a clear rationale, which is lacking in chap. 11. Israel is Yahweh's firstborn (cf. Hos. 11:1; Jer. 31:9), and if Pharaoh refuses to release him, Pharaoh's firstborn will die.

The most difficult part of this passage is the enigmatic incident recorded in vv. 24–26. No motive is given for the attack. Presumably the attacker is some minor divinity, like the "man" who wrestled with Jacob at the ford of the Jabbok (Gen. 32:24–30). Thus the episode shows that the blood of circumcision, like pascal blood (12:13), was thought of as having the power to fend off demonic assaults. If this is the case, however, it is surprising that the attacker is called "Yahweh" (the Septuagint understandably modifies this to "an angel of Yahweh"). Nor are we told who is attacked or to whose "feet" (probably meaning genitals) Zipporah touches her son's prepuce, but the majority of commentators assume that Moses is intended in both cases. The simplest interpretation is probably that Moses became gravely ill on the journey and, thanks to the quick thinking of his wife, was restored to health by a healing ritual. As it stands, the story has become a vehicle for explaining the expression "bridegroom of blood" or "son-in-law of blood," which was current in the time of the writer but is obscure to us.

In any case, Moses arrives safely at Mount Horeb, where Yahweh has instructed Aaron to meet him. As they make their way back to Egypt Moses reports to his brother all that has happened, and when they arrive, they inform the people of Yahweh's plans.

5:1–6:1
The First Audience with Pharaoh

The confrontation between Moses and the Egyptian king in this passage establishes the pattern for the contest with Pharaoh in 7:8–15:21. Moses and Aaron ask permission for the people to go into the wilderness and celebrate a feast to their God. Modern scholars cite this as evidence that the Passover or some antecedent festival was celebrated by the Israelites before the official institution of the Passover described in chap. 12. Moses and Aaron make their request first as a demand in Yahweh's name, but Pharaoh retorts that he does not acknowledge Yahweh's authority. They then attempt to reason with the king, arguing that Yahweh might become angry at their failure to celebrate the feast and punish them. The language used at this point is that of the theophany at the burning bush (5:3; cf. 3:18), and, as predicted at that time (3:19), Pharaoh refuses, making it necessary for Yahweh to strike Egypt with plagues (6:1; cf. 3:20).

Pharaoh concludes from the request that the Israelites are idle, i.e., in need of harder work. He therefore commands that the straw needed for brick making be withheld from them. Clay without straw produces very brittle bricks, so that the Israelites are obliged to forage for stubble, and the result is much more work. When the Israelite foremen complain to Pharaoh, they learn the cause of the new policy. They go out to Moses and Aaron and chide them for their loss of favor with Pharaoh. When Moses in turn complains to Yahweh, however, he is assured

136

that everything is proceeding according to plan.

As we have seen, the episode of the bricks without straw continues the theme of hard labor introduced in 1:8–14. In discussing that passage, we noted an incompatibility between it and the stories leading up to Moses' birth. In light of that incompatibility the absence of Moses from 5:6–18 is striking. It is also noteworthy that, unlike other elements of the larger passage, the intensification of the labor of the Israelites is not anticipated in the theophany at the bush. Such considerations have led at least one modern commentator to the conclusion that there was an early tradition about the Exodus in which Moses played no part. A more moderate conclusion holds that both episodes (1:8–14 and 5:6–18) derive ultimately from an account of Israel's enslavement in Egypt that was related apart from or prior to Moses' appearance in the story. The first episode remains in such a position; the second has been incorporated into the larger narrative in the present position to link Pharaoh's intensification of the labor to the first request of Moses and Aaron.

6:2–7:7
The Mission of Moses and Aaron

The language of this passage connects it securely with the Priestly editorial remarks in 2:23–25. Yahweh has "heard the groaning" of the people and "remembered his covenant" (6:2; cf. 2:24), and he instructs Moses to announce his intention to deliver them from "their bondage" (v. 6; cf. 2:23). This, then, is the Priestly version of materials that have already been presented in their older (JE) form. The divine self-disclosure in 6:2–4 corresponds to the E account of the revelation of the divine name in 3:13–15. The commissioning of Moses and Aaron has its JE counterpart in chaps. 3 and 4. Within the context of the story as it is currently constituted, therefore, this passage must be understood as reiteration or confirmation of things already accomplished. Viewed as an independent unit, however, it is a new account of the same events. Its purpose is to incorporate the revelation to Moses and the work of Moses and Aaron into the larger Priestly history. The events now taking place in Egypt are interpreted as developments in the larger covenantal history that began with Noah and Abraham.

6:2–4, The Divine Self-Assertion. Yahweh speaks to Moses and identifies himself with the God who entered into a covenant with the patriarchs. He was known to them, he says, as El Shaddai (often rendered "God Almighty"). This epithet calls our attention to a series of thematic passages in the Priestly history having to do with Yahweh's beneficence toward Abraham,

Isaac, and Jacob and the covenant he made with them. In the most important of these, he appears to Abraham (Gen. 17:1) and Jacob (Gen. 35:11–12; cf. 48:3–4) and introduces himself with the words "I am El Shaddai." Now he begins his speech with the words "I am Yahweh." We know from the study of other ancient Near Eastern religious texts that the purpose of this kind of divine self-asseveration is not simply identification; it also asserts the authority and power of the god who speaks. The primary purpose of the divine speech in our passage, then, is a reassertion of Yahweh's ancient authority, linking present deeds to past promises and stressing the identity of the God who will perform the wondrous deeds that are about to begin.

In the process of this reassertion, however, certain especially interesting details are mentioned. The patriarchs, we are told, did not know the God of the fathers by his name, Yahweh. They knew him instead as El Shaddai. Though contradicted by the Yahwistic tradition (e.g., Gen. 13:4), this position is consistently maintained in Priestly materials. Knowledge of the divine name was reserved for those who would enter into the Sinaitic covenant and follow the rules of the sacred life. The disclosure of the name at this point, then, shows that the time has come for this holy relationship to be solemnized.

The meaning of "El Shaddai" is obscure. The prevailing scholarly opinion is that it is an archaic divine epithet, which may originally have meant "El (God), the One of the Mountain." In an eighth-century B.C. text from Deir Alla, Jordan, the Shaddayim (plural of Shaddai) are gods who meet in council to make decisions regarding the governance of the world. Thus Shaddayim may mean "mountain gods," i.e., those who meet on the mountain of the divine assembly (cf. the Olympians). If this is correct, the singular designation Shaddai or El Shaddai may have originally referred to a member of this group or, perhaps, to the presiding god of the assembly (cf. Zeus Olympios). The biblical evidence shows that this particular term was regarded as an ancient designation of Yahweh, known to those to whom his name had not been revealed, and this explains its thematic use in the Priestly history. The patriarchs were not beneficiaries of the final revelation, which begins only at this point.

6:5–13, The Commissioning of Moses. The P account of Moses' commissioning corresponds fairly closely to the composite JE account in 3:7–4:17. It includes the same two parts, an announcement and a commission. In keeping with the covenantal theology of the Priestly history, the announcement that Yahweh has taken notice of the affliction of the Israelites in Egypt is expanded to indicate that he has remembered his covenant with the patriarchs (v. 5). The commission has two parts: Yahweh sends Moses to the Israelites (vv. 6–8) and to Pharaoh (v. 10). Note again the emphasis placed on the identity of the God who is about to rescue Israel from bondage. The formula "I am Yahweh," used first in v. 2 and discussed above, is repeated three times in the announcement of deliverance that Moses is to repeat to the people (vv. 6–8). The people are to be told that after their rescue they will know "that I am Yahweh." In the Priestly history (as in the book of Ezekiel) a primary reason for Yahweh's redemptive acts is that his name will be known and his power recognized. Thus it is important that he should accomplish the rescue not secretively or quietly but "with an outstretched arm and with great deeds" (v. 6). The objection Moses raises in v. 12 corresponds to his two objections in the Yahwistic version in chap. 4. He is a man of "uncircumcised lips" (cf. 4:10; →Circumcision). His own people have refused to listen to him (cf. 4:1). How then can Pharaoh be expected to listen? Yahweh's response will be to commission Aaron to serve as Moses' spokesman (cf. 4:14–16), but this next commissioning is delayed until chap. 7. The narrative is interrupted now for the insertion of a levitical genealogy to which the editorial summary in v. 13 provides a transition.

6:14–27, The Aaronid Genealogy. The purpose of this genealogy is to legitimate the authority of the Aaronidic line of Levites through whom the Jerusalem priesthood traced its ancestry. Thus it is finally a genealogy of Aaron and Moses (note the order). Though it begins like a standard tribal roster, it changes after Levi and his two older brothers have been listed and Levi's position among the sons of Jacob has been established. Only Levi's family is traced beyond the second generation. The primary interest is in the line from which Aaron and Moses descended: Levi, Kohath, and Amram. Life spans are given only for these three, a detail that has the effect of linking Aaron and Moses with the early fathers in the Priestly scheme of history. The keenest genealogical interest centers on Aaron himself, so that the names of his wife and those of his father and one of his sons, Eleazar, are given. This reflects a special interest in Eleazar's son Phinehas, the only grandson of Aaron who is named. Phinehas is granted a "perpetual covenant" of priesthood in Num. 25:10–13, and the later high priests of Jerusalem traced their ancestry through him (cf. 1 Chron. 6:1–15). Note, finally, that in addition to Aaron and Moses there is a secondary interest here in Korah, the Levite who leads a rebellion against the authority of Moses and Aaron in Numbers 16. The details in Exod. 6:21 and 24 show the genealogical subordination of Korah (the eldest son of Kohath's second son) to Aaron (the eldest son of Kohath's firstborn).

6:28–7:7, The Commissioning of Aaron. The next passage is a continuation of the account of Moses' commissioning in 6:5–13. The two opening verses (6:28–29) provide an editorial recapitulation of the earlier passage, thus returning the narrative to the point at which it was interrupted for the insertion of the Aaronidic genealogy. Moses is then told that Aaron will be his spokesman. The image used is that of a god and his prophet: Moses' words will have the equivalent of divine authority for Pharaoh, and Aaron will serve as the messenger who transmits them. The theology of the earlier passage is also resumed here. The rescue from Egypt will not be achieved in secret but by "signs and wonders" (7:3) and "great deeds" (v. 4). "I shall lay my hand upon Egypt," says Yahweh (v. 4), an allusion to the plagues. All this will be done so that "the Egyptians will know that I am Yahweh" (v. 5). Again, the rescue must be performed in a spectacular and public fashion, because its purpose is not only to gain freedom for the people of Israel but also to demonstrate the power of the God of Israel. This point of view also explains the otherwise troubling phenomenon of the hardening of Pharaoh's heart, already alluded to once before (4:21). Even as he is demanding that Pharaoh release his Hebrew slaves, Yahweh is also causing him to be obstinate and refuse. Later on, we shall come to instances in which Pharaoh agrees to the departure of the Israelites, only to change his mind when Yahweh intervenes and hardens his heart (9:12; 10:20, 27). If the only objective in Yahweh's dealings with Pharaoh were to obtain the release of the Israelites, this hardening of the heart would seem capricious or self-defeating. Its necessity only becomes clear when we take account of the second objective, namely, the public demonstration of Yahweh's power.

7:8–13:16

The Plague Narrative

Yahweh, through the agency of Moses and Aaron, strikes Egypt with a series of afflictions of increasing severity, until Pharaoh finally agrees to release the Israelites. The report of the final plague, the slaying of the firstborn, is accompanied by an elaborate account of the Passover celebration. One widely accepted theory holds that the plague narrative originated as a "cult legend," that is, a story composed to explain a ceremony, in this case the celebration of the Passover, and to give the ceremony a historical basis. According to this theory, the original story said that the Israelites escaped from Egypt secretly at night, only to be overtaken by the Egyptian army at the Red Sea. An alternative view holds that a casual or coincidental reference to the Passover blood rite in the original account attracted the ritual materials into the story. In fact, most of the ritual elaborations in chaps. 12–13 derive from the latest of the pentateuchal sources (D and P). In the earliest of the pentateuchal sources (J), the people perform the Passover blood rite for protection against Yahweh's "destroyer" (12:21–23) and carry unleavened bread with them as they go (12:34, 39), but there are no further ritual details.

7:8–10:29
The First Nine Plagues

Plague is a weapon the God of Israel wields against the unjust and the enemies of his people. When the divine warrior marches, plague and pestilence go at his heels (Hab. 3:5). When the Philistines rout the Israelites and take home the holy Ark as plunder, a plague of mice and tumors breaks out in their cities (1 Sam. 4–6). When David angers Yahweh by taking a census of Israel, a plague decimates the country (2 Sam. 24). And in this account, whenever Pharaoh refuses to release the Israelites, a scourge of some kind strikes his land.

The plagues that afflict Egypt include diseases, infestations, and disasters of all kinds. Most of them correspond in some near or remote way to natural phenomena that were known in ancient Egypt. Noting this fact, many commentators have concluded that the memory of some historical natural disaster or series of such disasters was the basis for the story. Some have even attempted to reconstruct the event by combining the details of the biblical account with information derived from studies of the natural history of the Nile basin. The difficulty with such studies is that they do not take into account the complexity of the biblical plague tradition or its history. Although it is very likely, perhaps certain, that a knowledge of natural phenomena in Egypt lies behind many of the individual plague episodes, it is very unlikely that a single, historical chain of events gave rise to the complex of tradition as a whole.

The tradition of the plagues against Egypt is mentioned elsewhere in the Bible, notably in Pss. 78:44–51 and 105:28–36. Both of these psalms were probably composed in pre-exilic times (i.e., before the sixth century B.C.), thus earlier than the present form of the Exodus story. In both, the number of plagues is seven, not ten as in our account. Moreover, the psalms differ in the order of the plagues, both from each other and from our account, as the accompanying table shows.

The Plagues Against Egypt: Their Number and Order in Exodus and Two Psalms

EXODUS	PSALM 78	PSALM 105
1. blood	1. blood	1. darkness
2. frogs	2. flies	2. blood
3. gnats	3. frogs	3. frogs
4. flies	4. caterpillars/locusts	4. flies/gnats
5. cattle	5. hail/frost	5. hail
6. boils	6. cattle	6. locusts
7. hail	7. firstborn	7. firstborn
8. locusts		
9. darkness		
10. firstborn		

Our Exodus plague narrative is composite, a combination of a Priestly (P) account with an older Yahwistic (J) account. The latter can be reconstructed with some confidence. It almost certainly had not ten but seven plagues. The third (gnats), sixth (boils), and ninth (darkness) plagues were not included. The following list illustrates the form of this original Yahwistic plague narrative.

1. blood (7:14–15a, 16–18, 21a, 23–24)
2. frogs (7:25–8:15)
3. flies (8:20–32)
4. cattle (9:1–7)
5. hail (9:13–18, 23b–24, 25b–34)
6. locusts (10:1a, 3–11, 13b, 14b–20, 24–26, 28–29)
7. firstborn (11:4–8)

There is also Elohistic (E) material here, but its extent is difficult to determine. Many scholars doubt that there was an independent E account of the plagues and regard the scant E material they find in these chapters as a series of glosses on J. Others believe there was a complete E account but that much of it has been lost. Too little survives, in any case, to permit us to reconstruct its original form. Moses' rod, which is considered indicative of E (see the commentary above on 4:17), figures prominently in most of the materials assigned to E in the plague narrative. These include the following: the references to Moses' rod in vv. 15, 17, and 20 of the account of the first plague (7:14–24); accounts of the plagues of hail (9:22–23a, 25a, 35a) and locusts (10:12–13a, 14a) inserted into the J accounts of the same plagues; and the full account of the plague of darkness (10:21–23), which lacks any reference to Moses' rod and is sometimes assigned to P. As for the Priestly materials, there is general agreement among scholars about those portions of the narrative that describe the first six plagues (7:14–9:12). P accounts of the first two plagues, blood (7:19–20a, 21b–22) and frogs (8:5–7, 15b), have been incorporated into the J(E) account. The reports of the plagues of gnats (8:16–19) and boils

(9:8–12) derive exclusively from P. Aaron figures prominently in all of these episodes. In the reports of the later plagues (9:13–11:10), however, he recedes into the background, and it becomes much more difficult to detect P material. Only the addition of the Priestly formula of affirmation ("as Yahweh had spoken through Moses") in 9:35b and the final summary in 11:9–10 can be identified with certainty.

The underlying Yahwistic narrative was carefully organized, and its structure, though partly obscured by the editorial combination with the Priestly account, is still visible in the story. In the seven-stage J version the plagues escalated from three that were nuisances (blood, frogs, and flies) to three that destroyed property (cattle, hail, and locusts) to one that took human life (firstborn). Thus we can still observe a general intensification of the plagues from lesser annoyances to more serious afflictions. In the J version the scene of the confrontation between Moses and Pharaoh alternated strictly between an early morning outdoor setting (J's first, third, and fifth plagues) and a setting within the palace (J's second, fourth, and sixth plagues). In the present form of the story the outdoor setting introduces the first, fourth, and seventh plagues, while the palace is the setting for the second, fifth, and eighth. The third, sixth, and ninth plagues, which derive from other versions, mention no audience with Pharaoh. In the J version, Yahweh acted directly to execute the plagues, without first instructing Aaron to wield his rod or Moses to raise his hand. In the P version, however, some such agent seems always to have been used. In the present, composite narrative, the first three plagues are initiated by Aaron's rod and the last four by Moses' hand or rod; the fourth and fifth are executed directly by Yahweh himself.

7:8–13, Aaron's Rod. At the beginning of the episode of Aaron's rod (vv. 8–9) instructions for its use are given to Moses and Aaron. This is the P equivalent of 4:1–5, a J passage in which such a rod was given to Moses alone. When the divine instructions are carried out and the miracle is performed (v. 10), it is Aaron who wields the rod. The term for the creature into which the rod turns is not the same here as in 4:3. It may mean "snake," like the earlier word, but it is also possible that it means "crocodile." The Egyptian magicians turn their rods into crocodiles too, but Aaron's crocodile devours theirs. This contest sets the pattern for the first three plagues, which will be initiated by agency of Aaron's rod. The point is simply that, though the power of the Egyptian magicians is great, it is far surpassed by that of the servants of Yahweh.

7:14–24, The Plague of Blood. A well-known Egyptian text contains a complaint that the Nile has turned to blood and those who drink from it thirst for water. The natural phenomenon to which both this Egyptian text and the biblical story of the plague of blood point is probably the presence of red particles in the water of the Nile at the time of the annual inundation, which carried silt from the tropical red earth of the basin of the Blue Nile in Ethiopia and the Sudan. The presence of red microorganisms may sometimes have intensified the effect. According to our text, however, the water is turned to blood, not to the color of blood. It is thus undrinkable, and the Egyptians are obliged to dig wells (v. 24). Note also the additional details in the P portions of this composite account (vv. 19–20a, 21b–22). It is not only the Nile that is affected, but all natural bodies of water and even water stored in artificial containers. This effect is achieved through the agency of Aaron's rod, but the Egyptian magicians are able to duplicate it, and Pharaoh is unmoved.

7:25–8:15, The Plague of Frogs. The next is also a composite account. In the J version the frogs were brought up directly by Yahweh himself. The P materials in 8:5–7 introduce Aaron's rod as the agent. Again, the Egyptian magicians are equal to the task and produce their own frogs.

8:16–19, The Plague of Gnats. Other translations that have been proposed for the plague of gnats are "lice" and "mosquitoes." This plague has no equivalent in the lists in Psalms 78 and 105. Nor did it appear in the original Yahwistic narrative. This account derives strictly from Priestly tradition. Moreover, since there is no P account of the plague of flies that follows, it is safe to conclude that the plague of gnats arose as a variant of the plague of flies. Like the two previous plagues, this one is initiated by Aaron's rod. In this case, however, the Egyptian magicians are unable to duplicate the feat. Still, Pharaoh remains adamant.

8:20–32, The Plague of Flies. Some kind of biting flies is intended in the account of plague of flies, such as gadflies or stable flies. Yahweh brings them up himself in this strictly Yahwistic account. There is no Priestly material here, and nothing is said of Aaron's rod or the Egyptian magicians. A new motif is introduced, however. This plague discriminates between the Egyptians and the Israelites. There are no flies in Goshen, where the Israelites dwell. There is also a change in Pharaoh's attitude at this point. He seeks a compromise with Moses, granting the Israelites permission to sacrifice to their God within the land. This, however, is not in keeping with Moses' charge, and he declines, offering the excuse that Israelite offerings might be religious abominations to the Egyptians. Pharaoh then agrees to let the Israelites journey a short distance into the wilderness, but when the flies are gone, he hardens his heart again.

9:1–7, The Plague on the Cattle. This next passage is another strictly Yahwistic account. Aaron and the Egyptian magicians are not mentioned, and the livestock disease, which may be anthrax, is inflicted directly by Yahweh. Again a distinction is made between the Egyptians and the Israelites, whose cattle are not affected. Pharaoh is again unmoved.

9:8–12, The Plague of Boils. The sixth plague, like the third (gnats), has no equivalent in the lists in Psalms 78 and 105, and it was not included in the original Yahwistic plague narrative. This account derives entirely from Priestly tradition. It probably arose as a variant of the cattle plague, the boils "on man and beast" (9:9) referring to the carbuncles that appear on the skin at the onset of anthrax, a disease that afflicts humans as well as animals. Unlike the other plagues, which are initiated either directly by Yahweh or by agency of the hand or rod of one of his servants, this one begins in a unique way: Moses hurls ashes into the air. Aaron has returned, however, and so have the Egyptian magicians, though only as victims of the boils. Note that here for the first time Yahweh hardens Pharaoh's heart (see the commentary above on 7:8–10:29, "The First Nine Plagues").

9:13–35, The Plague of Hail. The destruction of the Egyptian crops by a hailstorm is described in a long, composite narrative. An Elohistic account (22–23a, 25a, 35) has been combined with the older Yahwistic version. There is no discernible Priestly narrative here, but note the standard Priestly formula of affirmation at the end of v. 35 (cf. 7:22; 8:15, 19; 9:12). The information given in vv. 19–21 and 31–32 is generally regarded as deriving from late, interpretive expansions, not one of the pentateuchal sources. The storm begins when Moses waves his rod toward the sky, though in the original J account Yahweh hurled down the hailstones himself (v. 23b). Again, the destruction does not extend to Goshen. As in the fourth plague (flies), Pharaoh agrees to release the Israelites, this time even admitting the justice of Yahweh's cause, but when the storm is over he reneges.

10:1–20, The Plague of Locusts. The next is another extended account, combining a short E version (12–13a, 14a) with the much longer J narrative. There is also a late expansion in vv. 1b–2, but no P material can be detected. In the J version the locusts were brought by the east wind, which was summoned by Yahweh himself (v. 13b; cf. 19). In the combined form of the story, however, the locusts come when Moses waves his rod over the land. As was the case after the preceding plague, Pharaoh admits his guilt and begs Moses to entreat Yahweh. When the locusts are gone, however, Yahweh hardens Pharaoh's heart (cf. 9:12).

10:21–29, The Plague of Thick Darkness. The ninth plague is a palpable darkness (cf. v. 21), associated by some commentators with a hot, dust-laden wind that blows into Egypt from the Sahara. Pharaoh is again inclined to negotiate. He offers to let the Israelites depart without their livestock, but Moses explains that all the animals must go, since it will be impossible to tell which will be needed for sacrifice before arriving in the wilderness. Yahweh again hardens Pharaoh's heart, and the king sends Moses away, threatening him with death if he returns. Negotiations have broken down. Note that the darkness is summoned by a wave of Moses' hand, like the seventh and eighth plagues in their E versions (9:22; 10:12). Like the third and sixth plagues, which are known only from a P account, it lacks any opening audience with Pharaoh. Thus it is sometimes assigned to E, sometimes to P. The account of the negotiations with Pharaoh in vv. 24–29 probably followed v. 20 directly in the original J narrative, but there was no plague of thick darkness in that narrative, and although darkness does appear in the list in Psalm 105 (as the first plague!), it is absent from Psalm 78. It is possible, therefore, that it arose as a variant of the plague of locusts, which "covered the eye of the land, so that the land became dark" (10:15).

11:1–13:16
The Final Plague

The next section describes the final plague and consequent departure of the Israelites from Egypt. Despite the drama and excitement inherent in this story, the narrative that contains it is very slow-moving. The reason for the slow pace is the presence in the account of substantial ritual material. The events related here were of such religious importance to the ancient community that they were celebrated regularly in the cult, and the form the celebration took has in turn influenced the description of the events. The departure from Egypt was memorialized by the rites of the Passover, and a full account of these rites as stipulated in Priestly tradition has been incorporated into our story. Accounts of the Feast of Unleavened Bread and the consecration of the firstborn are also included here. Though they seem to be diverse in origin, these observances are implicitly associated with the Passover by their inclusion here, and they are described in language that explicitly identifies them with the tenth plague and the events of the departure from Egypt.

141

11:1–10, The Announcement of the Tenth Plague. Chap. 11 looks back at the plague story and ahead toward the account of the Passover. In the original Yahwistic narrative the slaying of the firstborn was the climactic seventh plague. As a result of the compilation of this composite narrative, the death of the Egyptian firstborn, now the tenth plague, has become a part of (and indeed the introduction to) the story of the institution of the Passover. The opening section of this passage (vv. 1–3), however, is concerned with neither the firstborn plague nor the Passover. It looks ahead to the account of the spoliation of the Egyptians in 12:35–36. It is the E equivalent of the J passage in 3:21–22, and its editorial insertion at this point has created a serious narrative difficulty. When he begins to prophesy in v. 4, Moses seems to be speaking to Yahweh! But this makes no sense, and the end of the speech shows that he is addressing Pharaoh. Verses 4–8, then, were originally attached directly to the end of chap. 10. They represent a continuation of Moses' angry speech in 10:29.

The announcement of the death of the Egyptian firstborn is presented in a matter-of-fact way. No rationale of the kind we noted in 4:22–23 is offered. The purpose seems to be to afflict Egypt so dreadfully that, despite Pharaoh's obstinacy, his people will come humbly to Moses and ask him to leave (v. 8). The theme of discrimination that we have seen before is here too: the Israelite firstborn are to be spared (v. 7). We know from the law in chap. 13, however, that when the Israelites are living in the promised land, Yahweh will also claim their firstborn. As explained in the discussion of 13:1–16, the point of the rule requiring the consecration of the firstborn is that, as guarantor of the increase of family, flock, and field, Yahweh is entitled to the first fruits of each. The firstborn offering, in other words, is made in recognition of Yahweh's sovereignty over all life in the promised land. Thus the plague tradition, in stating that Yahweh finally took the firstborn of the Egyptians, implies that he has sovereignty over life in Egypt too and by implication life everywhere.

12:1–28, The Institution of the Passover. Chap. 12 opens with a long speech of Yahweh instituting the Passover celebration (vv. 1–20), followed by a speech of Moses to the elders of Israel describing the blood rite of Passover (vv. 21–27a). Much of Moses' speech (vv. 21–23) derives from J's account of the institution of Passover and thus represents a Yahwistic parallel to the Priestly account in vv. 1–20. According to the present form of the text, however, Moses' speech is to be read as an abbreviated report to the people of the instructions given by Yahweh. The instructions for the Passover ritual begin with the inauguration of a new calendar (vv. 1–2). "This month," which we know from 13:4 to be Abib (March–April), is now to be the beginning of the year, an arrangement that reflects the perspective of the Priestly author of this part of the passage. During the time of the Israelite monarchy, the end of the year (and thus the beginning too) came at time of harvest in the fall (cf. 23:16; 34:22). Beginning in the sixth century B.C., however, the Babylonian calendar was adopted, so that the month in the Jewish calendar corresponding to Abib has the Babylonian name of Nisan and is regarded as the first month of the year (→ New Year Festival).

The J account of the blood rite in vv. 21–23 makes no reference to the Passover meal described in the preceding P account. The blood rite is apotropaic, i.e., designed to avert evil, in this case a demon called "the destroyer" (v. 23) who has been sent by Yahweh to slay the firstborn of Egypt. Studies of similar festivals known to have been celebrated in pre-Islamic Arabia suggest that the purpose of such a rite was to ensure the safety of the flock by the sacrifice of one of the newborns at the time of lambing in the spring. In all probability, then, the Passover blood rite was already being celebrated annually by the Israelites prior to its association with the particular event of the slaying of the firstborn in Egypt. This, indeed, may be the sacrifice repeatedly referred to by Moses in his petitions to Pharaoh (e.g., 3:18). In our earliest source (J), however, the rite has already become associated with the tenth plague. The blood of the victim is understood as a sign to Yahweh (v. 23), and "the destroyer" is the agent of his wrath against the Egyptians. Verses 24–27a, in which the connection between the Passover sacrifice and the tenth plague is made even more explicit, are discussed below in connection with 13:1–16.

The details of the Passover meal described in the P material in vv. 1–20 show that it is a feast for beginning a new year and leaving the old one behind and, similarly, for setting out on the journey into the wilderness and leaving the life in Egypt behind. Symbolically, then, the clothes worn are the clothes of travelers (v. 11). The common factor in the stipulated foods is that none makes use of any product of the culture—or the year—being left behind. The lamb must be roasted, i.e., cooked directly in the fire without the use of any cooking pot or even water—thus it cannot be boiled (v. 9). The bread must be baked without leaven, a product of the previous year's harvest. We cannot identify the other food, "bitter herbs," with certainty, but it was probably some kind of uncultivated vegetable. Note too that because these foods have not been transformed by human culture (as by boiling or fermenting with leaven), they are suitable for sacrificial use. The pascal lamb is to be an unblemished male (v. 5), roasted whole (v. 9) like the burnt offering of Leviticus 1, and the bread is to be free of leaven, which, along with honey (another agent of fermentation), is excluded from all cereal offerings (Lev. 2:11). Thus the meal has the effect of purifying the Israelites for the life to come under Yahweh's guidance in the wilderness (or in the new year).

A well-known theory contends that the Passover meal, like the Passover blood rite, originated as part of an annual ritual that was secondarily combined with the tradition of the tenth plague. In particular, the meal is said to have originated as a nomadic ritual. Thus it requires no temple or sanctuary of any kind. The pascal lamb is taken from the flock and eaten along with unleavened bread (the usual bread of nomads). The participants wear nomadic dress (Exod. 12:11). In the biblical Passover tradition, according to this theory, this annual festival has been reinterpreted as a commemoration of the departure from Egypt and the escape from the plague on the firstborn. The Passover feast is now understood as a memorial meal. The bread is eaten unleavened because the people are in a hurry (cf. vv. 34, 39). The pastoral clothes are the clothes of travelers about to set out. The name of the ritual in Hebrew, *pesach*, whatever it originally meant, is now understood in reference to the sparing of the Israelite firstborn (v. 27): it is called "Passover" because Yahweh "passed over" (Heb. *pasach*) the houses of the Israelites (the meaning of the verb has also been explained in other ways, including "have compassion on," "leave out," and "protect").

In vv. 15–20 the Feast of Unleavened Bread is ordained (cf. 13:3–10). This arrangement has the effect of combining this feast with the unleavened bread rite in the Passover celebration (cf. Ezek. 45:21–24). Lev. 23:5–6, however, shows that the two were originally separate: Passover was a one-day feast celebrated on the fourteenth of the month, and Unleavened Bread was a seven-day feast that began on the fifteenth. Unleavened Bread was originally a festival celebrating the spring harvest, but, like Passover, it was partly reinterpreted as a commemoration of the departure from Egypt in both Priestly and Deuteronomic tradition (cf. Deut. 16:1–8).

12:29–36, The Death of the Firstborn. The next part of the narrative describes the events elaborately prepared for in the preceding passages. The threat in 11:4–8 is now carried out. Despite his own warning in 10:28, Pharaoh summons Moses and Aaron and addresses them in terms of complete capitulation. He no longer seeks a compromise or attempts to negotiate, so that, in contrast to his most recent

offer (10:24), he willingly releases the livestock. The Egyptian people are even more urgent, actually driving the Israelites away and willingly granting the gifts anticipated in 3:21–22 and 11:2. The verb used here in v. 36b, as well as 3:22, is a verb of plunder (cf. 2 Chron. 20:25), indicating that these valuables are to be understood as spoils of war. The Israelites leave Egypt not as escaped slaves but as conquerors.

12:37–42, The Departure from Egypt. The first stage of Israel's journey is from Rameses to Succoth, probably another name for Pithom (1:11). The "mixed multitude" that join the march are non-Israelites (the same term is used in Neh. 13:3); the early exegetical tradition associated them with "the rabble who were among" the Israelites in Num. 11:4. Even without this group, however, the total number who participated is said to have been six hundred thousand men in addition to women, children, and livestock (cf. Num. 11:21). The total, which derives from Num. 1:46, is impossibly large in terms of ancient demographics, and, even if we adopt the common expedient of understanding six hundred "thousands" as six hundred (military) contingents, it remains implausible. The other number given in this passage is also problematic. In a Priestly epilogue to the Egyptian period in Israel's history (vv. 40–42), we are told that the Israelites had been in Egypt for 430 years, a period forecast as 400 years in Gen. 15:13. In Gen. 15:16, however, it was stated that the Israelites would return in the fourth generation (cf. the four generations from Jacob to Aaron in Exod. 6:14–27 above). Numbers of this kind cannot be used as historical resources. They originated in the ancient interpretive tradition, having been calculated from information not available to us and on the basis of criteria that would not be acceptable to most modern historians.

12:43–51, The Ordinance of the Passover. The purpose of the next short Priestly passage is to stipulate who may participate in the celebration of Passover. In particular, the issue of non-Israelite participation is addressed, and it may be that the reference to the presence of "a mixed multitude" among the Israelites in v. 38 prompted an editor to place this passage at this point. Foreigners are excluded from the ritual meal, as are hired resident servants (the term is obscure). On the other hand, "sojourners," that is, legally resident foreigners, may participate if the males are circumcised, and this rule applies also to slaves. Since circumcision is also required of the Israelite males themselves, there is one law for both the native-born (the term anticipates the Israelites' residency in Canaan) and the resident foreigner.

143

13:1–16, The Consecration of the First-born. Early Israelite tradition held that Yahweh, as proprietor of the land and guarantor of life and fertility, was entitled to the first fruits of the harvest and the firstborn of both animals and humans (cf. 22:29–30). Every firstborn male, therefore, was subject to sacrifice to Yahweh. The rules stated here in vv. 12–13 require that such a sacrifice be carried out for all clean livestock. But for the firstborn of the ass, which is unclean, and for human firstborn, the substitution of a lamb is to be made.

Apart, perhaps, from vv. 1–2 this passage does not seem to have been a part of the Priestly history. It is a Deuteronomic addition intended to connect both the Feast of Unleavened Bread (vv. 3–10) and the rule of the firstborn (vv. 11–16) to events during the departure from Egypt. Exod. 12:24–27a above, another Deuteronomistic expansion, does the same for the Passover. As noted in the discussion of 12:15–20, the Feast of Unleavened Bread was originally an independent festival, but here, as in chap. 12, it is related to the Exodus (cf. Deut. 16:1–4). Similarly, the consecration of the firstborn was an ancient practice deriving from pre-Israelite times and originally having nothing to do with the Exodus. Here, however, it is related to Yahweh's slaughter of the Egyptian firstborn. Note the clear structural parallels between these two units (vv. 3–10, 11–16). Both look ahead to the time when the Israelites are living in Canaan (vv. 5, 11; cf. 12:25); both prescribe answers to questions sons will ask their fathers (vv. 8 and 14–15; cf. 12:26–27a); and both require that the words be worn as signs on the hand and frontlets between the eyes (vv. 9, 16). The original meaning of the last requirement, which gave rise to the wearing of tefillin (phylacteries) in postbiblical Judaism, is uncertain (→ Phylacteries).

13:17–18:27

The Sojourn in the Wilderness

The period spent in the wilderness was remembered as a distinct and important time in Israelite tradition. It was a time of transition between Egypt and Canaan, slavery and freedom. It was also a time of isolation, helplessness, and total dependence on divine sustenance. The biblical account of the period is found in two widely separated sections, the first describing the events that took place on the way from Egypt to Sinai (Exod. 13:17–18:27) and the second tracing the journey from Sinai to the plains of Moab on the border of the promised land (Num. 10:11–36:13). The separation was caused by the insertion of the legal materials now included in the Sinai pericope (Exod. 19:1–Num. 10:10). One of the results of the separation was the creation of duplicate accounts of certain episodes, such as the manna and quails (Exod. 16, Num. 11) and the water from the rock (Exod. 17, Num. 20). Both parts of the account are characterized by two dominant motifs, one positive and one negative. The positive motif is that of the miraculous provisions by which Yahweh ensures Israel's welfare. These include the water from the rock, the manna, and the quails; but the first and greatest is the miracle at the sea. The negative motif is that of the "murmuring" of the people. Oblivious to the miraculous things being done for them in the desert and heedless of the promises of the prosperity that lies ahead in the land, the people become anxious, complaining against Moses and longing to return to Egypt. Thus the wilderness period was remembered as a time of divine solicitude and miraculous protection but also of human ingratitude, discontent, and even rebellion.

13:17–15:21

The Crossing of the Red Sea

The familiar story of the crossing of the Red Sea is the result of a long and complex literary history, much of which can be reconstructed from a close examination of Exodus 14 and 15. Scholars agree that the old poem in 15:1–19 is the earliest account of the event at the sea. The prose account in 14:5–31 is composite, having been compiled from at least two different versions of the event, those of J and P, with occasional additions from E. A comparison of the descriptions of the events in these three sources reveals the development of the story in Israelite tradition.

According to the Song of the Sea, Yahweh hurled Pharaoh and his army into the waters and they sank (15:4–5). Yahweh's agent was evidently a raging ocean, whipped up by a violent windstorm, which the poet identifies as the divine breath ("the blast of your nostrils," v. 8). Pharaoh's army pursued the Israelites relentlessly (v. 9), but the divine wind continued to blow, and the Egyptians sank "like lead" (v. 10). Since they were hurled into the waters, we must assume that the Egyptians were traveling in boats or, less likely, along a cliff overlooking the sea. We are not told where the Israelites were or what they were doing while these events took place.

In the earlier of the two prose accounts in chap. 14 (J), the event is described as follows: Pharaoh pursued the Israelites and overtook them encamped by the sea (14:9a). The pillar of cloud moved between the two armies and kept them apart for the night (vv. 19b–20). Yahweh drove back the sea all night long with a strong east wind (cf. 10:13), so that the floor of the sea became dry (v. 21a). In the morning the pillar of cloud panicked the Egyptians (v. 24), locking up the wheels of their chariots (v. 25a, sometimes assigned to E), and they fled in terror (v. 25b). The sea returned to its normal flow just as the Egyptians were rushing toward it (v. 27a). Yahweh "shook off" the Egyptians in the sea (v. 27b)—meaning, perhaps, that he scattered and drowned them—and the awestruck Israelites watched the bodies of their enemies wash up on the shore (v. 30). The differences between this account and that in chap. 15 are subtle but clear. The wind is Yahweh's weapon in both. In the old poem the wind causes the sea to rage and casts the Egyptians into the waters. In the J account the wind causes the waters to back up, and the Egyptians, fleeing across the dried ocean floor, are drowned when the wind stops and the waters return. This version may have arisen in part from an interpretation of parts of the Song of the Sea, where we are told first that the wind caused the waters to stand up "like a heap" (v. 8) and then that the wind caused the waters to cover the Egyptians (v. 10). Though their original meaning was that the Egyptians were cast into a violent, wind-tossed sea, these verses were understood to mean that the wind blew the waters away from the seabed and then back again, trapping the Egyptians. Another factor that may have favored this change was the influence of a ritual in which the escape at the sea was memorialized and linked with the crossing of the Jordan into the promised land. This possibility is suggested by the ritual character of the account in Joshua 3, where we are told that the waters of the Jordan were stopped and stood up in "a single heap" (Josh. 3:16; cf. Exod. 15:8) while the people crossed over on dry land.

The later account in chap. 14 (P) tells the story very differently. Pharaoh pursued the Israelites with his entire army and overtook them at Pi-hahiroth (vv. 8, 9b). Yahweh told Moses to stretch out his hand over the sea (vv. 15-18), and when he did so, the waters divided. The Israelites crossed through the sea on dry land with walls of water on both sides (vv. 21-22, 29). When the Egyptians followed (v. 23), Moses was told to stretch out his hand again (vv. 26-27a), and the waters returned, covering the chariots, the horsemen, and the entire Egyptian army (v. 28). The most striking change that took place in the story between the composition of the J and P accounts was the addition of the motif of the parting of the sea. In the earlier version, the waters were not parted but driven back by the wind. It has been suggested that this change was influenced by the mythological tradition of the slaying and splitting of the sea dragon, to which we have allusions in several biblical passages (Ps. 74:13-14; cf. Isa. 27:1; Job 9:8; 26:12; Ps.

89:9-10). We know that by the sixth century B.C., the date to which P is usually assigned, the traditions of the slaying of the dragon and the escape at the sea had become associated, as Isa. 51:9-11 shows.

13:17–14:4, The Journey to the Sea. The Israelites set out from Succoth (12:37) and journey to Etham, "on the edge of the wilderness" (13:20; cf. Num. 33:6), the Wilderness of Etham being another name for the Wilderness of Shur (15:22). They are then told to turn back and encamp "in front of Pi-hahiroth, between Migdol and the sea, in front of Baal-zephon" (14:2; cf. Num. 33:7). Though these places must all lie somewhere in the eastern delta of the Nile, their exact location is uncertain (→ Pi-hahiroth; Migdol; Baal-zephon). What is clear is that the exodus will not follow the Way of the Sea ("the Way of the Philistines," 13:17), the direct route from Goshen to Canaan through the northern part of the Sinai peninsula (→ Trade and Transportation). Two reasons for this, deriving from two literary sources, are given. First, the Israelites would too quickly encounter armed resistance that way (13:17 [E]), a judgment affirmed by modern historians, who point to Egyptian military control of the Via Maris. Second, if the Israelites enter the wilderness, Pharaoh will assume they are trapped there and be lured into pursuing them, thus offering Yahweh an opportunity to "gain glory from Pharaoh and all his forces" (14:1–4 [P]). So the journey begins in a southerly direction, toward the desert and the Gulf of Suez (cf. 13:18). According to the J portion of this episode (13:21–22) the march is led by Yahweh himself manifested as a pillar of cloud by day and a pillar of fire by night, a mode of theophany that anticipates the storm cloud imagery of chap. 19. The Israelites make camp "at the sea" (14:2), evidently the Red Sea (cf. 13:18; 15:4). Hebrew *yam suph* seems to mean "Sea of Reeds," however, and it has become a commonplace of modern scholarship to point out that the ancient interpretive tradition associating this body of water with the Red Sea is incorrect. Recent research has argued that *yam suph* probably means "Sea of the End." It was used to designate any remote ocean or sea, but especially the Red Sea, including the gulfs of Suez and Aqabah or Elath (1 Kings 9:26; Jer. 49:21). Thus the sea involved in the episode that follows is probably the Red Sea after all.

14:5–31, The Escape at the Sea. Though the crossing of the Red Sea is often thought of in connection with the departure from Egypt, it is more correctly associated with the sojourn in the wilderness. The account of the wilderness period began in 13:17–18, where we were told that Israel entered the wilderness. The pillar of cloud and fire, the mode of theophany that characterizes the wilderness stories, appeared first in 13:21–22. The murmuring motif begins here in 14:10–14, and the salvation at the sea is the first and greatest of the miraculous provisions.

As explained above, the narrative in chap. 14 was produced by combining parallel accounts from J and P. A few details, such as the designation of the pillar of cloud as an "angel of God" in v. 19a, also derive from E. In the J narrative, Pharaoh changes his mind again, regrets the loss of his labor force (v. 5), and pursues the Israelites. Thus the events at the sea, which we have already described above, represent God's definitive solution to the threat of the vacillating Egyptian king. In the P account, however, these events are carefully orchestrated by Yahweh from the beginning (cf. v. 4). Pharaoh pursues the Israelites because Yahweh hardens his heart (v. 8), and the Egyptian soldiers follow them into the sea because he hardens their hearts (v. 17). Note, finally, the new motif introduced in vv. 10–14. When the Israelites see the Egyptian army following them, they become fearful, regret their decision to leave Egypt, and complain to Moses. This is the beginning of the "murmuring" theme, which will develop further in the account of the sojourn in the wilderness below.

15:1–19, The Song of the Sea. Many scholars think that the Song of the Sea is one of the oldest surviving specimens of Hebrew poetry. The language and poetic style are consistently archaic. Many also regard the poem as an eyewitness account that was accorded a position of special honor when the escape at the sea came to be memorialized in the liturgy of early Israel. Often called a victory song or hymn of thanksgiving, it has features characteristic of many literary types, but, taken as a whole, it cannot be identified with any one of the fixed genres of biblical or extrabiblical poetry. Though it may not have been included in any of the continuous narrative sources, it antedates all of them and was cited by incipit (opening lines) in at least one of them (v. 21, probably J). It has a two-part thematic structure. The first part (vv. 1b–12) is an account of the Red Sea event with parenthetical perorations on the propriety of praising Yahweh (v. 2) and his incomparability (v. 11). As explained above, this account describes the event at the sea as a terrific windstorm during which the Egyptians were hurled into the waters. The second part (vv. 13–18) describes the conduct of the Israelites to Yahweh's "mountain of heritage" (v. 17), that is, to Canaan. Yahweh guides the people first to his "holy encampment" (v. 13), causing grave concern to the peoples living in or near the promised land (the Philistines, Canaanites, Edomites, and Moabites). This encampment might be Sinai, Kadesh, or Shittim (→ Kadesh; Shittim).

15:20–21, The Song of Miriam. Before the insertion of the entire Song of the Sea into the narrative, it was cited by its incipit in one of the prose sources (probably J), where it is ascribed to Miriam, the sister of Aaron and Moses. The attribution to Moses himself in v. 1a, therefore, is secondary.

15:22–18:27
The Journey to Sinai

The names of the "stages" along the way from Rameses to the Wilderness of Sinai are systematically reported in the biblical narrative, and the list is recorded in even greater detail in Numbers 33. Such thoroughness is extraordinary in a story from which a detail as important as the name of the pharaoh was omitted. It is difficult to account for the precision with which the names of these places were preserved, unless we assume that the route continued to be known and followed in later times, perhaps by Israelite and Judean pilgrims to Sinai. Unfortunately, few of the stages can be identified today, and the location of Mount Horeb or Sinai has itself been forgotten, so that the itinerary of Israel's journey there can be traced only tentatively (→ Exodus). If the well-known tradition that identifies Mount Sinai with Jebel Musa in the southern part of the Sinai Peninsula is correct, then the route described here must proceed south along the eastern shore of the Gulf of Suez. The location of "Horeb, the mountain of God" near Midian in chap. 3, however, favors a route through central Sinai. The most direct road to Midian, north and east of the Gulf of Aqabah, is the Darb el-Hajj, or "Pilgrim's Road," which is still followed to Mecca, and it would not be surprising to find continuity between ancient and modern pilgrim roads.

15:22–27, The Waters of Marah. Yahweh sweetens the waters of "Bitterness" (Heb. mara), showing himself to be Israel's "healer" and promising to afflict Israel with none of the plagues of Egypt. He turned the waters of the Nile to blood, but he makes the waters of Marah sweet. He destroyed the grain crops of Egypt with hail, but he will rain bread on the Israelites (16:4). He sent a wind filled with locusts into Egypt, but his wind will bring quail in Num. 11:31. The awkwardness of Exod. 15:25–26 is a result of the insertion of Deuteronomic clichés about obedience. The reference to testing or proving in v. 25b reflects the Deuteronomic conception of the wilderness period as a time of teaching and testing (Deut. 8:3, 16).

16:1–36, Manna. Their thirst quenched, the people next complain of hunger, and Yahweh obliges them with a miraculous rain of bread from the sky (v. 4). The people marvel at the frostlike wafers, asking each other "What (Heb. *man*) is this?" Thus they name the bread *man*, "manna." This tradition stems from a natural phenomenon of the desert. The tamarisk bush, which grows in parts of the Sinai Peninsula, is infested with scale insects that suck its sap, some of which is excreted in the form of globules that crystallize in the sun and fall to the ground. This sticky substance is rich in carbohydrates and sugars and can support the life of a starving wanderer (→ Manna). It is still called *man* by the modern inhabitants of the Sinai, who regard it as a gift from God.

The sequence of events in vv. 1–12 is confusing because of the combination of narrative sources. In the P version (vv. 1–3, 6–13a, 22–26, parts of which may, alternatively, derive from E) the story is designed as another instance of Israel's "murmuring" (v. 2) and Yahweh's indulgence. The murmuring motif seems to have been lacking in the J version (vv. 4–5, 13b–15, 27–30), however, and the initiative for the gift of the manna comes from Yahweh. (Note, however, that, according to a Deuteronomic addition to v. 4b, Yahweh's purpose from the beginning is to test the people and teach them obedience [cf. 15:26] with regard to the special Sabbath provisions.) The P version also mentions a gift of quail (vv. 8, 12–13a), but in J the quail will come much later, when the people tire of the manna and crave meat (Num. 11).

17:1–7, The Water from the Rock. The site at which the miracle of the water from the rock takes place has two names, Massah and Meribah, understood in the story to mean "Testing" and "Contention." Meribah appears alone in Num. 20:13 (cf. Deut. 32:51; Pss. 81:7; 106:32), and it is possible that Massah was added secondarily. An association between the two is already present, however, in early poetry (Deut. 33:8), and it has been suggested they were the names of two different springs at the same oasis (Kadesh, according to Num. 20). A duplicate or parallel account appearing in Num. 20:1–13 explains why Moses and Aaron did not enter the promised land (cf. v. 12).

17:8–16, The Battle with the Amalekites. The Amalekites, nomads inhabiting the desert south of Judah, most often appear in the Bible as brigands (→ Amalekites). Their attack on the Israelites in this passage is thwarted by Joshua when Moses stands atop a nearby hill and, with the help of Aaron and Hur (→ Hur), raises his hands aloft. Divine images served as battle standards for other ancient Near Eastern peoples, and it may be that Moses is acting in lieu of such a standard, representing Yahweh "with outstretched arm" (6:6)—hence the altar name

"Yahweh is my standard" in v. 15. Verse 14 is probably a Deuteronomic addition, conforming our passage to the reference to these events in Deut. 25:17–19 (cf. 1 Sam. 15:2), which implies that the attack had a less favorable outcome for Israel.

18:1–27, Jethro's Visit. Moses is reunited with his wife and sons and confers with his father-in-law. Jethro advises Moses to share the burden of his counseling responsibilities. Note that the office of Moses under discussion is that of mediating between the people and Yahweh. Thus it is a prophetic office. Numbers 11 treats the same theme in terms of the distribution of Moses' "spirit" to seventy elders. It is surprising, then, to find a Midianite giving advice on religious matters to Moses, even if it is fatherly advice. It is true that Jethro praises Yahweh as the greatest of the gods (v. 11) and offers a sacrifice to him. Still, Jethro is a foreigner and not, we assume, a Yahwist, so that his praise of Yahweh must be like that of Balaam. As noted earlier in our discussion of 2:11–25, however, the religious affinity between Israel and Midian was very ancient, so that the advice recorded here may have a strong base in the tradition.

19:1–24:11

The Sinaitic Covenant

The next five chapters constitute the covenant pericope in Exodus. Chap. 19 is an introductory narrative describing the preparation of the people to receive Yahweh's proclamation of the covenant. Chap. 24 is a concluding narrative describing the ceremony of covenant ratification. The covenant proper, including the Decalogue and the laws of the so-called Covenant Code, is found in chaps. 20–23. The form of the covenant is especially significant. Yahweh speaks in the first person, identifying himself as the God who rescued Israel from slavery, enjoining upon the people a large body of law, and promising them a life of prosperity in the land in return for their strict loyalty to him. Scholars have detected in this covenant formulary an ancient Near Eastern literary pattern used in diplomatic documents known as suzerainty treaties. The purpose of such a document was to establish a relationship between a suzerain (that is, a king or lord) and a vassal. Speaking in the first person, the suzerain would identify himself, review his beneficent treatment of the vassal in the past, and call upon the vassal to obey a series of stipulations, promising to reward obedience and punish disloyalty. It seems clear that this pattern has influenced the formulation of the Sinaitic covenant. Yahweh is presented as a

147

suzerain who is owed allegiance because of what he has done and will do for his vassal Israel.

19:1–23:33
The Encampment at Sinai

Scholars do not agree about the literary history of 19:1–20:21. As in the preceding sections, the narrative in chap. 19 includes materials from J, E, and P. The dominance of the covenant-making theme seems to reflect the influence of the E version. The form of the Decalogue included here (20:1–17) is probably that of E. The motif of the people's fear and Moses' intermediary role (20:18–19) is in keeping with E's view of the role of the prophet, as is the statement that Yahweh spoke "from the sky" (20:22). On the other hand, the people's request in 20:19 seems to imply that God has not yet spoken. This suggests the possibility that the Decalogue is secondary or that it has been transposed with vv. 18–21. The present arrangement, according to which Yahweh proclaims the Decalogue directly to the people but mediates the other law through Moses, reflects the pattern stressed in Deut. 4:13–14. Some Deuteronomic influence may be suspected here, therefore, and the suspicion is strengthened by the presence of the Deuteronomic testing motif in 20:20 (cf. 15:25; 16:4). This does not mean that the Decalogue was originally absent from the story before it was inserted by a Deuteronomistic editor, though some scholars believe this to be the case. It seems more likely that an editor transposed the E version of the Decalogue with vv. 18–21 to reflect the Deuteronomic arrangement.

19:1–25, The Sinai Theophany. Yahweh appears to the people as a prelude to the proclamation of his covenant with them. The theophany experienced by Moses alone in chap. 3 is now shared by the entire community. In place of the fire in the bush, however, is a much greater fire enshrouded in dark clouds, so that the entire mountain seems to be burning. The imagery is that of a thunderstorm (vv. 16, 19 [E]), though some commentators detect volcanic language in v. 18 (J). Carefully drawn boundaries protect the sacredness of the precinct where the deity manifests himself (vv. 12–13; cf. 21–25), and the people are in a state of cultic purity, having washed their clothes and abstained from sexual activity (v. 15). The theophany itself is described somewhat differently in J (9–15, 18) and E (16–17, 19). In J, Yahweh descends onto the mountain in a smoking envelope of fire, out of which he addresses Moses. In E, however, his voice is in the thunder; that is, he speaks from the sky (cf. 20:22). The covenant is mentioned only in v. 5 in a passage that has the structure of the covenant formulary described above. This "covenant in miniature" (vv. 3–8a) is quasi-poetical in character and, though it has some affinities with Deuteronomistic thought, it probably derives from an independent source incorporated into the E narrative. In it Israel is called a "realm of priests," that is, a nation uniquely close to Yahweh and, therefore, holy (vv. 5–6).

20:1–17, The Decalogue. The rules of conduct grouped together here are called the Ten Commandments (lit. "ten utterances") on the basis of 34:28 (cf. Deut. 4:13; 10:4). The ten have been reckoned in different ways (→ Ten Commandments, The). The traditional Jewish division views the divine self-proclamation in Exod. 20:2 as the first "utterance" and the prohibitions of other gods and graven images (vv. 2–3) as the second. Most other traditions understand v. 2 as a preamble. Thus the prohibition of other gods is the first commandment and the prohibition of images the second in the most common Christian enumeration. The third commandment prohibits false swearing (v. 7). The fourth requires observance of the Sabbath (vv. 8–11), and the fifth calls for respect for parents (v. 12). The final five prohibit murder (v. 13), adultery (v. 14), theft (v. 15), false witness (v. 16), and coveting things belonging to another member of the community (v. 17). Most of these laws are prohibitions. All are apodictic, i.e., absolute and applicable in any situation. The first four pertain to the Israelites' relationship with Yahweh, the final six to their relationships with each other. Together they constitute the basic requirements of the covenant being established between Yahweh and Israel. The violation of any one of them would represent a breach of the covenant relationship, thus threatening the integrity of the community that is based on the covenant.

The narrative source drawn on here is probably E, but many scholars believe the Decalogue existed as an independent document before its incorporation into the E account. Deuteronomy 5 contains an almost identical version, which has been slightly reworked to reflect Deuteronomic ideas, just as the present account has been expanded to reflect the Priestly understanding of the Sabbath (v. 11). The form shared by Elohistic, Deuteronomic, and Priestly tradition seems to have been known to Hosea (Hos. 4:2; 12:9; 13:4). It is sometimes called the "Ethical Decalogue" to distinguish it from the so-called "Ritual Decalogue" preserved in Yahwistic tradition (34:11–26). According to the present arrangement of the narrative, the latter was given at the time of the renewal of the covenant, but it probably corresponds closely to J's version of the original covenant stipulations, which have not otherwise survived.

20:18–21, Moses the Mediator. The people are afraid of listening directly to the voice of God, and they ask Moses to mediate the commandments to them. As our text now stands, then, the Decalogue is the only part of the Sinaitic legislation communicated directly by Yahweh. The rest will be mediated through Moses. The literary-historical problem of this passage is noted in the introduction to this section (19:1–24:11).

20:22–23:33, The Covenant Code. According to 24:3, the covenant was concluded on the basis of both "the words" and "the ordinances." The former refers to the Ten Commandments, and the latter to the Covenant Code or, as it is often called on the basis of the reference in 24:7, "the Book of the Covenant." Formal considerations show that this collection is a combination of two bodies of law. The first begins in 20:22–26 and continues in 22:18–23:19. It consists of instructions for both cultic and social behavior expressed largely in the apodictic form we noted in the Decalogue. As we have noted, such rules are intended to define and sanction the sacred community. The second body of law was inserted into the middle of the first, so that it is now found in 21:2–22:17. It consists of rules or ordinances (21:1) of civil law expressed in casuistic, or case law, form ("if . . . then . . ."). Its purpose is to regulate the life of the community living in the promised land.

20:22–26, The Altar Law. Verses 22–23 are usually taken together to mean that images are prohibited because Yahweh is a heavenly, incorporeal god (cf. Deut. 4:15–40, which is a long interpretive reflection on these two verses). The altar law proper (Exod. 20:24–26) permits sacrifice at any sacred place (cf. Deut. 12:13) and thus antedates the reforms of the late Judean monarchs who destroyed the local altars ("high places") and restricted sacrifice to the Solomonic Temple (→ Josiah). An altar must be constructed of earth or unhewn stones without steps. As we noted in connection with the Passover ritual (12:1–28), natural materials not modified by implements of human culture are regarded as most suitable for sacred uses.

21:1–22:17, The Book of Ordinances. The beginning of this inserted document is clearly marked by 21:1. Case law of this kind is the predominant form in the great law codes of the ancient Near East (→ Law). The codes were not normative tabulations of currently practiced laws. They were royal proclamations expressing the king's responsibility for justice in his land and his commitment to the improvement of social conditions. The ordinances in Exodus 21–22 constitute a code that should be understood in the same way. It represents a series of improvements in the governance of the community

proclaimed by Israel's new divine sovereign. Thus many of the laws listed are specifically designed to make the enforcement of justice more equitable by limiting penalties or protecting the rights of powerless members of the community. For example, the purpose of the so-called *lex talionis*, or law of retaliation (vv. 23–25) is not to require vengeance but to restrict it. The laws are grouped roughly as follows: (1) laws pertaining to slavery, requiring a seventh-year manumission of Hebrew slaves and restricting the sale of daughters (21:2–11); (2) laws of capital crimes (21:12–17), exempting unintentional homicide but including murder (21:12–14), kidnapping (21:16), and crimes against parents (21:15, 17); (3) laws pertaining to personal injuries, including injuries to slaves, inflicted by other human beings (21:18–27) and by livestock (21:28–32); (4) laws pertaining to damages to property (21:33–22:16), including livestock (21:33–36, 22:3) and real estate (22:5–6); (5) laws involving contracts (22:7–15); and (6) laws regarding the payment of the bride-price (22:16–17; → Marriage).

22:18–23:19, Rules of Conduct. The next material concludes the document begun in 20:22–26. It is a diverse list of rules of conduct for the covenant community, expressed predominantly in the apodictic, second-person form. It has much in common with the "Ritual Decalogue" in 34:11–26. In contrast to the preceding book of ordinances, the arrangement of these rules seems to be random. There are some general groupings by subject matter, such as the rules pertaining to the administration of justice in 23:1–3, 6–9, and the rules for the liturgical calendar in 23:10–19, but even these are intertwined with unrelated rules (23:4–5, 13, 19b). Nevertheless, certain general themes seem to be present throughout. A conspicuous humanitarian concern is expressed in rules pertaining to the treatment of sojourners (resident aliens; → Stranger), widows and orphans, debtors, and the poor, and the rules of the fallow year (→ Sabbatical Year) and the Sabbath and other holidays are given a humanitarian interpretation (23:11–12). Most of the subjects touched on are religious. There are also a few general religious rules, including prohibitions of sacrificing or swearing to other gods (22:20; 23:13) and cursing God (22:28), and a few purity laws, including prohibitions upon bestiality (22:19), carrion eating (22:31), and boiling a kid in its mother's milk (23:19b), thus employing a nourishing agent of life to cause death. The dedication of a portion of the harvest, the firstborn of the herds and flocks, and the firstborn son are insisted upon (22:29–30; cf. 13:11–13). The concluding liturgical calendar stipulates three principal festivals (23:14–17): Unleavened Bread in the spring (cf. 12:15–20; 13:3–10), Harvest or Firstfruits at the time of the wheat harvest (later

Weeks), and Ingathering (later Succoth or Booths) in the fall (→ Feasts, Festivals, and Fasts).

23:20–33, Epilogue. Yahweh will send his messenger or angel to lead Israel safely to the promised land. He enjoins the people to serve no other gods in the land, and promises them in return prosperity together with victory over their enemies. Though this section now stands as an epilogue to the Book of the Covenant, its connection with the preceding material is tenuous. It is very different in style and subject matter, and it makes no reference to the ordinances just proclaimed. Though it seems to be based on an old narrative source, probably E (vv. 20–22, 25b–31a), it has been strongly colored by Deuteronomic ideas (cf. Deut. 7). It may have been an independent Deuteronomistic sermon on the conquest of Canaan, which was inserted at this point because of the prominence of the promised land and its produce in the cultic calendar at the end of the Book of the Covenant (23:10–19).

24:1–11
The Covenant Ceremony

The subject of the next section is covenant ratification. This is accomplished by two ceremonies, described in parallel accounts from two sources. In one of these accounts (vv. 1a, 9–11), which may derive from J or an independent early source, the central event is a covenantal meal. Moses is summoned to the mountain, along with Aaron and his two oldest sons, Nadab and Abihu (6:23; cf. Lev. 10:1–3), and seventy elders. They eat and drink, gazing upon the God of Israel. The vision is described in language similar to that of Ezekiel 1. It is unparalleled in its directness (cf. Exod. 33:18–23). This, then, is a unique moment, signaling a unique bond between Yahweh and Israel. Israel's leader, its priests, and representatives of its people are permitted to see its God. Ordinarily it would be fatal for a human being to look at a divine being (cf. Exod. 3:6), but the narrator explains that on this occasion Yahweh "did not raise his hand against the chief officers of the Israelites" (v. 11). In the other account (vv. 3–8), which derives from E, the central event is a rite involving "the blood of the covenant." Moses reads the law, the people assent to it, and the blood rite is performed. Many scholars think this pattern was influenced by a regularly celebrated ceremony of covenant renewal.

24:12–31:18
The Authorization for Divine Worship

Now that the covenantal relationship has been established, it is necessary that an apparatus be set up by which the Israelites can interrelate with their God. This will require the manufacture of certain special objects (the Ark, the altar, etc.) that will make human-divine contact possible and the designation of a special group of people (the Aaronidic priests) who will be able to manipulate the objects. Above all, a shrine or sanctuary must be erected (the tabernacle), where Yahweh will be present among his people. It is stressed that all these things are to be constructed exactly "according to the pattern of the tabernacle and according to the pattern of its furnishings" that Moses sees on the mountain (25:9, 40; cf. 26:30). This may indicate that Moses has a vision of the celestial sanctuary of which the earthly tabernacle is to be a replica (cf. Ezek. 40:1–2). Yahweh himself authorizes the preparation of each item and gives its specifications in Exod. 25–31. The carrying out of his instructions—the actual inauguration of the system of divine service—is described in chaps. 35–40 and Leviticus 8–9. Thus a pattern of command and execution determines the shape of the rest of the book, as the accompanying table shows. (On the sevenfold structure of 24:12–31:18, see commentary below on 31:12–18, "The Institution of the Sabbath.")

The Tabernacle and Its Furnishings

	COMMAND	EXECUTION
the contribution	25:1–9	35:4–29
the Ark	25:10–22	37:1–9
the table	25:23–30	37:10–16
the lampstand	25:31–40	37:17–24
the tabernacle	26:1–37	36:8–38
the sacrificial altar	27:1–8	38:1–7
the tabernacle court	27:9–19	38:9–20
the lamp	27:20–21	Num. 8:1–4
the priestly garments	28:1–43	39:1–31
the ordination ritual	29:1–46	Lev. 8:1–9:24
the incense altar	30:1–10	37:25–28
the bronze laver	30:17–21	38:8
the anointing oil	30:22–33	37:29
the incense	30:34–38	37:29
the craftsmen	31:1–11	35:30–36:7
the Sabbath	31:12–17	35:1–3

24:12–18, Introduction. Yahweh summons Moses to the mountain to receive the tablets of the covenant (24:12), and, as Moses ascends, the theophanic cloud enshrouds the mountain, with Yahweh's "glory," that is, the refulgent envelope that surrounds the divine person, in its midst. Thus the objects and institutions about to be established will provide a suitable repository for the safekeeping of the covenant documents (25:16, 21) and a shrine in which Yahweh's glory can "tent" within the Israelite camp (25:8) and accompany them on their journey. The basis of this introduction is a continuation of E's Sinai narrative (vv. 12–15a, 18b), into which has been inserted a Priestly notice about the descent of the glory (vv. 15b–18a).

25:1–27:21, The Instructions for the Tabernacle.

The tabernacle is the sacred dwelling where Yahweh's glory manifests itself among the people in the wilderness. In the older narrative sources it is presented as the tent of meeting, a simple tent-shrine, where the glory was intermittently present and oracles were received (Exod. 33:7–11; cf. Num. 11:16–30; 12:4–10). The prototype of this Israelite tent-shrine seems to have been a religious object of a type used by nomads over a very long period of time in the Near East. The *qubba* of pre-Islamic Arabian tribes was a small, dome-shaped tent constructed of reddened leather stretched over a frame of desert acacia. It was a portable sanctuary, often transported on camelback, that accompanied the community both on its seasonal journeys and on marches into battle. The tribal idols were kept within it. Other portable tent-shrines, antecedents of the *qubba*, are known from the ancient Near East. There are clear parallels between the *qubba* and the Israelite tabernacle, which, as it is described in Exodus 26, has a covering of reddened leather (26:14) and a frame of desert acacia (26:15). In the present shape of the biblical tradition, which is dominated by P's perspective, however, the character and significance of the tabernacle are somewhat more complex. The tabernacle is the site of Yahweh's abiding (not transitory) presence among the people. Thus the glory will take possession of the tabernacle in 40:34 and subsequently lead the community on its journeys, effectively subsuming the role played by the pillar of cloud and fire in the older sources. In the present section, moreover, and generally in materials deriving from Priestly circles, the term "tabernacle" refers to the entire elaborate shrine described in chaps. 25–27. The tabernacle proper is only a part of this larger structure (cf. 26:1) and is itself covered by a tent (26:7). In addition to the design of the earlier tent-shrine, the architecture of Solomon's Temple seems to have influenced the description of the tabernacle. The division into a "holy place" and a "Holy of Holies" (26:33), the outer and inner sanctuaries, is characteristic of Phoenician temple architecture, as are the sacred enclosure or court (27:9) in which the sacrificial altar stood (cf. 40:6–8) and the general use of curtain-draped frames and pillars to effect divisions (→ Temple, The).

25:1–9, The Contribution. The raw materials for the tabernacle come from gifts freely given by the people. The "contribution" or "offering" (RSV) referred to here is a rite that serves to set apart personal property for sacred use (→ Heave Offering).

25:10–22, The Ark. The Ark is a wooden box or chest in which "the testimony," i.e., the two tablets of the law, are deposited (v. 16). This "Ark of the testimony" will be stationed within the Holy of Holies of the tabernacle (26:34). It is covered with a golden "mercy seat" (RSV; → Ark), above which Yahweh speaks with the people, flanked by a golden pair of protective genii called cherubim (→ Cherub) and fitted with golden rings and acacia poles for conveyance like a royal palanquin. The details show that two conceptualizations have been combined in the Priestly understanding of the Ark. On the one hand, it is a covenant repository, and it will be routinely called "the Ark of the covenant" in Deuteronomistic literature. On the other hand, it is a cherub throne, the locus of Yahweh's invisible presence in the midst of Israel and an essential component of both the tabernacle and the battle camp.

25:23–30, The Table. The table held the "Bread of the Presence" (cf. Lev. 24:5–9; → Showbread). It was stationed in the holy place of the tabernacle, separated from the Holy of Holies by a curtain.

25:31–40, The Lampstand. The menorah also stood in the holy place. The botanical terms used to describe it suggest that its branched form originated in a concept of a sacred tree (→ Lampstand).

26:1–37, The Tabernacle Proper. The tabernacle proper is the structure that contains the holy place and the Holy of Holies. It consists of a wooden frame about 30 feet long, 30 feet high, and 15 feet wide, constructed of acacia planks (vv. 15–30) and draped with decorated curtains (vv. 1–6). This structure is covered with a goats' hair tent (vv. 7–14), which is covered in turn with tanned or reddened rams' skin and the skin of another animal, perhaps the dugong. The Holy of Holies is separated from the holy place by a veil or curtain suspended on four acacia posts (vv. 31–35), and the holy place is separated from the court by a screen supported by five acacia posts (vv. 36–37). The Ark is placed behind the veil in the Holy of Holies (v. 33), and the table and the lampstand are placed in the holy place, between the screen and the veil (v. 35). The incense altar, which was also located in the holy place, is described in 30:1–10.

27:1–8, The Altar. The sacrificial altar is a 7½-foot square, about 4½ feet high. The "horns" are protrusions from the corners, also known from archaeological discoveries. The excavated examples, however, are stone, whereas this one is wooden. It is difficult to understand how an acacia altar, even when laminated with bronze (v. 2), could withstand the sacrificial fires.

27:9–19, The Court. The altar of sacrifice stood outside the tabernacle proper in the court of the tabernacle, a rectangular enclosure measuring about 150 by 75 feet. It also contained the laver, which is described in 30:17–21.

27:20–21, The Lamp. Verses 20–21 seem to authorize the making of another cultic object. Lev.

151

24:2–4 shows, however, that the lamp mentioned here is the same as the lampstand of 25:31–40. Also note Num. 8:1–4, which is the passage corresponding to this one in the command and execution pattern. Thus the point of the present directive is not the authorization of a new lamp but the provision for the regular (not "perpetual") kindling of the lampstand.

28:1–43, The Instructions for the Priestly Vestments. Because Aaron and his sons are to be set apart as priests, they must wear garments designed "for dignity and splendor" (vv. 2, 40), appropriate to their office. All are provided with tunics, turbans, and sashes (vv. 39–43), as well as loincloths that permit them to enter the sacred precincts (cf. 20:26). The more specific instructions pertain almost entirely to the clothing of Aaron, i.e., the high priest. His principal garment, the ephod, is a belted loincloth with two shoulder straps (vv. 6–14). In contrast to the simple linen breechcloth called by the same name elsewhere in the Bible (1 Sam. 2:18; 2 Sam. 6:14), Aaron's ephod has ornate decorations, including a pair of lapis stones attached to the shoulder straps and engraved with the names of the twelve sons of Israel. Also attached to the straps is a pouched breastpiece (Exod. 28:15–30), covered with precious stones and containing the divining instruments called Urim and Thummim and thus designated "the breastpiece of decision" or "judgment" (→ Urim and Thummim). The ephod is worn over a blue robe hemmed with bells (vv. 31–35). The noise of the bells identifies the high priest as he crosses the boundaries between the zones of sacredness in the tabernacle, so that he will not be mistaken for an unconsecrated person and die (v. 35). A gold headpiece attached to the turban (vv. 36–38) is engraved "Holy to Yahweh," thus permitting the high priest to sanctify offerings brought by the people.

29:1–46, Instructions for the Consecration of the Priests. The consecration sets Aaron and his sons apart from the rest of the community as a sanctified group eligible to serve in the sacred precincts of the sanctuary and to provide a liaison between Yahweh and the people. In the preparatory first part of the ritual (vv. 1–9a), the initiates are bathed and dressed in the garments described in the preceding chapter. The sacrifice of ordination (vv. 9b–37) has three parts. The first animal is a young bull, which is offered as a "sin offering" (v. 14, RSV), or better, a purgation offering (see the commentary on Lev. 4). The sacrifice is not performed for the initiates, but on their behalf for the sanctuary, which it purges of ritual pollution. Some of the blood is smeared on the horns of the altar, drawing off the impurity and thus preparing the altar to receive the next sacrifice

(cf. 30:10). The second animal is a ram, which is immolated as a whole burnt offering (v. 18). Its purpose is expiatory. It atones for the sins of the initiates, thus making them eligible for the sanctification of the third sacrifice. The third animal is another ram, "the ram of ordination." Just as the blood of the bull was smeared on the horns of the altar, the blood of the second ram is daubed on the right earlobe, the right thumb, and the right big toe of the initiates. The blood again draws off the impurities, and the new priests are sanctified. Blood is also spattered on the priestly vestments, so that they, along with the men who wear them, become holy (v. 21). In vv. 22–28, provision is made for the future setting apart of the breast and the right thigh of sacrificial animals as reserved portions for the priests. When brought to the sanctuary, these will be presented to Yahweh (the "wave offering," → Worship), then given to the priests. The account concludes with the prescription of the regular sacrifices to be performed at the altar (vv. 38–42). This is evidently a charter for the daily Temple service of later times.

30:1–38, Further Instructions. Additional directives pertain to things that are needed by the priests for the safe and proper operation of ritual service to God. Thus, as we shall see, the incense safeguards the high priest against the danger of the holiness of the divine presence; the census payment forfends plague; the laver permits the removal of personal impurities; and the anointing oil sanctifies both the priests and the holy objects.
30:1–10, The Altar of Incense. Burning incense has both olfactory and visual properties (→ Incense). The function of the incense altar of the tabernacle is probably to be explained in terms of the latter. It is stationed directly in front of the veil at the entrance to the Holy of Holies (v. 6). It is lighted in the morning and evening when the high priest enters the holy place to tend the lampstand. The smoke covers the mercy seat, thus creating a boundary between the priest and the divine presence and protecting the priest's life (Lev. 16:13).
30:11–16, The Census Payment. Though later interpreted as a tax to support the operation of the Temple (→ Tribute, Tax, Toll), the stated purpose of the half-shekel payment is to prevent plague. Thus it is a ransom (RSV: "atonement money") paid as a precaution in case of ritual impurity. The reason this was required when a census was taken may have been that the chief purpose of a census was to determine manpower and enroll men for military duty, an activity to which much stricter purity rules applied. Note that the plague of 2 Samuel 24 broke out after David conducted a census that determined the number of "men who drew the sword" (v. 9).
30:17–21, The Bronze Laver. To perform cer-

tain ritual tasks in a state of uncleanness would be fatal (v. 20), so that it is necessary for the priests to wash before approaching the sacrificial altar or entering the tabernacle proper. Thus a bronze washbasin or laver is stationed between the two.

30:22–33, The Anointing Oil. Everything being set apart as holy, from the tabernacle to the priests, is to be anointed (→ Anoint). Moreover, the anointing oil itself is holy. It is to be compounded according to a precise recipe, a variety of spices and resins suspended in an olive oil base, which is not to be altered, and it is not to be applied to any profane person or object.

30:34–38, The Incense. The rules for the incense to be burned on the altar are similar to those for the anointing oil. The special blend is holy and must not be put to profane use.

31:1–11, The Appointment of Craftsmen. The artisans who are to manufacture the stipulated items have been divinely chosen and inspired (vv. 2–3). The chief craftsman is Bezalel son of Uri, the grandson of Hur (cf. 17:10; 24:14). He is a member of the tribe of Judah and, according to 1 Chron. 2:18–20, a Calebite (→Caleb). His first assistant is an otherwise unknown Danite by the name of Oholiab son of Ahisamach.

31:12–18, The Institution of the Sabbath. The day of solemn rest foreshadowed in the account of the manna in the wilderness (16:22–26) and stipulated by the fourth commandment (20:8–11) is formally instituted in vv. 12–18. The opening words of the speech addressed to the Israelites can be understood to imply a connection to the preceding account of the appointment of the craftsman, as if, "(You shall do all this work.) Nonetheless, you must keep my Sabbaths!" But the meaning is probably ceremonial and emphatic: "Above all, you must keep my Sabbaths!" There is, however, another kind of connection with the preceding passage and, indeed, with the entire account of the authorization of the system of divine service (24:12–31:18). Editorially, the long passage that extends from 25:1 to 30:10 is presented as a single speech. It is introduced with the simple formula, "And Yahweh spoke to Moses" (25:1). The same formula, or another almost identical to it, occurs six other times in the larger passage (30:11, 17, 22, 34; 31:1, 12). The effect is to divide Yahweh's instructions into seven utterances, of which the institution of the Sabbath is the climactic seventh. Note, finally, the designation in vv. 13 and 17 of the Sabbath as a "sign" between Yahweh and Israel. In Priestly theology each of the historical covenants was ratified by a visible token or sign. The rainbow was the sign of the universal covenant made with Noah (Gen. 9:12–13), and circumcision was the sign of the patriarchal covenant made

with Abraham (Gen. 17:11). The Sabbath is now proclaimed as the sign of the Sinaitic covenant. The cosmic significance of this sign—and thus of the covenant as a whole—is disclosed by a link to the Priestly account of creation (v. 17).

32:1–34:35

The Breaking and Renewal of the Covenant

The next three chapters stand between the two parts of the account of the wilderness sanctuary. The instructions for the erection of the tabernacle were given in the preceding seven chapters (25–31), and their implementation will be described in the succeeding six chapters (35–40). In between is a story of covenant breaking and renewal drawn primarily from the early narrative sources (JE). The story line broken off at the end of the covenant pericope in chaps. 19–24 is now resumed, and the covenantal relationship established in those chapters is completely and abruptly dissolved, then restored. The pattern is that of the "murmuring" motif, which was introduced as soon as the Israelites entered the wilderness (14:10–18). Oblivious to the divine provisions made for their welfare, the people become anxious and abandon their trust in Yahweh and Moses. As in the previous instances, the rift that is created is eventually healed through the mediation of Moses. At first, however, he is absent, and the mischief done is serious. The editorial links between this section and the tabernacle account are established by reference to the two tablets of the covenant. Yahweh summoned Moses to receive them in 24:12, and he gave them to him at the conclusion of his long speech about the tabernacle (31:18). In the course of this section Moses descends with the tablets (32:15–16) and breaks them in anger (32:19). He then cuts new tablets (34:1), and when the covenant has been renewed, Yahweh writes the words on them again (34:28). This brings the story back to the point when things went wrong: Moses again descends the mountain with the two tablets (34:29).

32:1–35

The Incident of the Golden Calf

The people's demand is for "gods who will go before us"; that is, they want palpable assurance of the divine presence among them on their march. This, however, is precisely what the tabernacle will provide. Thus the irony in the situation is that the thing the people are demanding is exactly what is being prepared for them on the mountain. Seen in this light, the manufacture of the golden calf is a travesty of the construction of the tabernacle just authorized. The image is fabricated from materials contributed by the people (vv. 2–4), just as the tabernacle is supposed to be (25:1–9). An altar is placed in front of it (v. 5), just as an altar is supposed to be placed in front of the tabernacle (cf. 40:29). The conflict, then, is one of modes and symbols of worship. The action taken by the people is not intended as a rejection of Yahweh. On the contrary, Aaron proclaims "a feast to Yahweh" as soon as the altar is in place (v. 5). The locus of Yahweh's presence, however, is not a tent-shrine but a calf, or rather a young bull. The biblical writers depict the worship of Yahweh with bull iconography as the standard error of the form of worship of the Northern Kingdom during the monarchical period. Jeroboam, the first northern king, introduced golden bulls into the sanctuaries of Dan and Bethel (1 Kings 12:26–28), and "the young bull of Samaria" (Hos. 8:5–6) seems to have been the chief icon in the sanctuary of the subsequent northern capital. Thus, like a very large number of ancient Near Eastern gods, Yahweh was worshiped in the form of a strong and virile young bull. Scholars disagree whether the bull was understood as an image of Yahweh himself or as a pedestal upon which he was believed to be invisibly present. In either case, however, the bull iconography was repudiated by one stream of Israelite tradition in favor of the iconography of the tabernacle and the Ark. It is this stream of tradition that is represented in the story of the golden calf, as in the Bible generally. Note that the people's utterance, "These are your gods, O Israel, who brought you up from the land of Egypt!" (Exod. 32:4, 8), seems inappropriate, since there is only one bull (cf. the correction in Neh. 9:18). The narrator is alluding to the two bulls at Dan and Bethel, which Jeroboam dedicated using identical words (1 Kings 12:28).

The unfavorable depiction of Aaron in this chapter contrasts sharply with his portrayal elsewhere in Exodus. The instructions in chap. 29 stipulated that only he and his sons would be ordained, a reflection of the actual situation in the highest rank of the Jerusalem priesthood, from which all Levites were excluded except one family of Aaronids (→Priests). Here in vv. 26–29, however, the Levites are said to have ordained themselves by their staunch behavior. We are not told which Levites these are, but they are certainly not Aaron's group. In earlier chapters Moses' inability to perform his duties without Aaron's help was emphasized, again a reflection of the views of the later Jerusalem priesthood. Here, however, Aaron's weaknesses are accentuated by comparison with Moses, who is exonerated from blame by his absence. These things suggest that the story originated in circles hostile to the

Aaronids at a time when there was a serious rift in the tribe of Levi.

Mesopotamian parallels to the smashing of legal tablets show that Moses' action is not just an expression of anger but a formal repudiation of the covenant. Moses' destruction of the bull, however, is not so easy to understand. It may be that burning it, grinding it up, dissolving its dust in water, and requiring the people to drink it is a way of obliterating it. The final stage is appropriate, because it was out of the mouths of the people that it came in the first place (v. 1). Some scholars draw a connection to the plague in v. 35, interpreting the drinking as an ordeal that identifies the guilty by making them sick (cf. Num. 5:16–28).

33:1–23
Yahweh's Presence Among the People

When the Israelites depart from Mount Horeb, will Yahweh go with them? Even though he led the march from Egypt personally in the pillar of cloud and fire (13:21), the incident of the golden calf has created doubts. A holy presence in the midst of such "a stiff-necked people" would endanger their lives (v. 5). As usual, the problem is solved by Moses' intercession. The scrap of early narrative in vv. 7–11 serves to highlight the intimacy of his relationship with Yahweh. In these verses the tent of meeting does not have the elaborated form of P's tabernacle. It is a simple shrine located outside the camp and attended by Joshua, who is identified as though for the first time (v. 11), even though he has appeared before without introduction (17:9; 24:13; 32:17). Verses 7–11, then, seem to be out of place here. Nevertheless, they are included to stress that "Yahweh would speak to Moses face to face, as one man speaks to another" (v. 11). It is on the basis of this special relationship that Moses makes his appeal for Yahweh to accompany the march, and Yahweh agrees (vv. 12–16). In a curious sequel, Moses makes another request. He asks to see Yahweh's "glory," but he seems to want to look directly upon the divine person. Yahweh's reply is, "You cannot see my face" (v. 20), and an arrangement is made whereby Moses is permitted a glimpse of Yahweh's back.

34:1–35
The Renewal of the Covenant

The issues raised by the golden calf incident have now been resolved, if not forgotten, and the broken covenant relationship can be formally restored. When this has been achieved, it will be possible to implement the instructions for the tabernacle.

34:1–28, The Proclamation of the Covenant. Having instructed Moses to prepare two new tablets, Yahweh again descends upon Sinai (v. 5; cf. 19:20) and proclaims his covenant with Israel. The relationship is renewed with reference to the future conquest of Canaan rather than the past escape from Egypt. Moreover, the covenant stipulations are not the same as those in chaps. 20–23. This is surprising, because it is the clear implication of v. 1 that the new tablets are to have the same thing on them that the broken tablets had, and v. 28 states flatly that Moses writes "the ten utterances" on the tablets. In the text of the chapter, however, there is a different list of apodictic laws (vv. 17–24) in place of the Decalogue. These difficulties have led scholars to the conclusion that chap. 34 preserves a part of the account of the making of the first covenant in the original J narrative, a parallel to the E and P account in chap. 20, even though it now stands as an account of the making of a second covenant, or rather a renewal of the first. The commandments in vv. 17–24 are sometimes called the "Ritual Decalogue" to distinguish them from the "Ethical Decalogue" that occupies the same position in the account of the broken covenant (20:3–17). But there is no Decalogue in vv. 17–24, a passage that stands much closer in tone and content to the apodictic rules of conduct in portions of the Book of the Covenant (20:22–26, 22:18–23:19).

34:29–35, The Shining of Moses' Face. In consequence of Moses' face-to-face dialogues with Yahweh, "the skin of his face radiated" with light. The Hebrew verb also permits the erroneous translation "was horned," giving rise to the curious notion, eternalized in Michelangelo's statue, that Moses had horns. In fact, however, Moses has been touched with the refulgent "glory" that, according to a belief widespread in antiquity, envelops the person of a deity. Compare the shining of Jesus' face in Matthew's account of the transfiguration (Matt. 17:2). The veil Moses uses in subsequent dealings with the Israelites is designated by a noun that occurs nowhere else in the Bible. Some scholars have supposed this tradition to have arisen from the use of a ritual mask, but it is precisely when he is involved in ritual activities that Moses' "mask" is set aside (v. 34).

35:1–40:38

The Inauguration of the Cult

The various tasks authorized in 24:12–31:18 are now carried out, and the divine service in the tabernacle is inaugurated. The account of the implementation follows that of the instructions

very closely. The only significant difference is the order of events. It was necessary for reasons explained below to implement the Sabbath law, collect the contribution, and appoint the craftsmen at the beginning of the work. This accounts for the only major variation in order, although there are certain minor variations having to do with the sequence in which various articles are made. Note, however, that there are several differences in arrangement between the received Hebrew text and the Greek text of chaps. 36–39. The most substantial of these differences are noted below. It is difficult to determine which arrangement is original.

35:1–3, The Rule of the Sabbath. The Sabbath law, which was given after the rest of the instructions (31:12–17), is put into effect before the actual construction begins, so that it can restrict the work.

35:4–29, The Contribution. The contribution is also shifted to the beginning. Though authorized at the end of the instructions, it must be collected before the work can begin.

35:30–36:7, The Appointment of Craftsmen. The appointment of Bezalel and the other craftsmen, though authorized at the end of the instructions, must be made in advance of the actual work.

36:8–38:20, The Construction of the Tabernacle. The order in which the tabernacle and its furnishings are made is not exactly the same as the order in which they were authorized. The tabernacle proper was authorized in chap. 26, after the articles to be stationed in it (25:10–40). It is built in 36:8–38, however, before the Ark, table, and lampstand (37:1–24). On the other hand, the sacrificial altar is built before the tabernacle court (38:1–20), just as in the instructions (27:1–19). (In the Gk. text of chaps. 36–38, the entire sanctuary, including both the tabernacle proper and the court, is constructed before any of the furnishings are made.) The incense altar, the anointing oil, the incense, and the bronze laver were authorized together in a collection of additional instructions (30:1–38). In the Hebrew text of chaps. 37–38, however, their manufacture is described in the natural positions—the incense altar, anointing oil, and incense in 37:25–29, in connection with the other furnishings of the tabernacle proper (37:1–24), and the laver in 38:8, in connection with the court (38:9–20). To the account of the making of the laver is appended the curious anecdote that the bronze with which it is made is taken "from the mirrors of the women who served at the entrance of the tent of meeting." The only other biblical reference to these women (1 Sam. 2:22) sheds no light on their identity or function.

38:21–31, The Record of Contributions. This tally of the gold, silver, and bronze contributed for the tabernacle contains at least two striking anachronisms. First, the supervisory role of Aaron's son Ithamar (v. 21) assumes that the disqualification of Nadab and Abihu described in Leviticus 10 has already taken place (Num. 3:4; cf. Num. 4:33). Second, the census reported in Numbers 1 seems to be one of the bases on which the contributions have been made.

39:1–31, The Preparation of the Priestly Garments. According to the arrangement of the received Hebrew text, the priestly vestments are the last things made. In the Greek text, however, they are the first.

39:32–43, Completion of the Work. The completed work is inspected by Moses, who finds it to be perfect and blesses the people. This passage stands as an epilogue to the account of the manufacture of the tabernacle in chaps. 35–39. It gives final reinforcement to the command and execution scheme, repeating three times that "according to all that Yahweh had commanded Moses, thus they had done" (vv. 32, 42, 43).

40:1–38, The Erection of the Tabernacle. The account of the actual erection of the tabernacle follows the command and execution pattern of chaps. 25–31 and 35–39. The instructions are given in vv. 1–15 and carried out in vv. 16–33. The final passage (vv. 34–38) records the divine response. The theophanic cloud covers the tabernacle, and Yahweh, clothed in his blazing "glory" enters the tabernacle proper. Thus the two theophanic traditions of Exodus, that of the pillar of cloud and fire and that of the tabernacle, are fused at the end. The tabernacle now assumes the bellwether role played by the pillar on the march to Sinai.

Bibliography
Childs, B. S. *The Book of Exodus: A Critical, Theological Commentary.* Old Testament Library. Philadelphia: Westminster, 1974.

Clements, R. E. *Exodus.* Cambridge Bible Commentary on the New English Bible. Cambridge: Cambridge University Press, 1972.

Greenberg, M. *Understanding Exodus.* Melton Research Center Series. New York: Behrman House, 1969.

Plaut, W. G. *The Torah: A Modern Commentary.* New York: Union of American Hebrew Congregations, 1981.

Sarna, N. M. *Exploring Exodus.* New York: Schocken, 1986.

LEVITICUS

JOHN H. HAYES

INTRODUCTION

Leviticus, the third book of the Torah (or Pentateuch), derives its English title from the Latin Vulgate, which in turn is dependent on the name assigned the book in ancient Greek translations. In Hebrew, the work is generally referred to by its opening word, *wayyiqra'*, "And He called." In early Judaism, the rabbis sometimes designated the book *Torat Kohanim* ("the Torah of the Priests"), a title very similar to the term "Leviticus."

The expression "Leviticus" implies that the work is concerned with priestly or levitical matters, although only 6:9–7:19; 8:1–10:19; 16:1–28; and 21:1–22:16 are matters strictly concerned with priests, and the Levites are mentioned only in 25:32–34. The book is actually a collection of matters on diverse subjects including laws and regulations concerning sacrifice, priestly ordination, dietary matters, purity and impurity, sexual relations, festivals, ethical concerns, the Sabbatical and Jubilee years, and a host of other issues.

Leviticus forms an integral part of the Pentateuch or Torah and, in fact, is the heart of the first five books of the Bible. In the book of Exodus, God reveals Torah (law) to Moses at Mount Sinai (Exod. 20–40). Included in these laws are directions for constructing the tabernacle (Exod. 25–31), which are carried out under Moses' direction (Exod. 35–39). In Exodus 40, Moses erects the tabernacle, making possible Israelite life and worship according to the commands of God. Leviticus picks up at this point.

The tabernacle was the place where God was present with his people (Exod. 25:8) and where he met and communicated with the community through Moses (Exod. 25:22; 29:43–46). The book of Leviticus details the manner of life and worship required of the community by God for the divine presence symbolized in the tabernacle to continue abiding in its midst (→ Tabernacle; Temple, the).

Leviticus interweaves narrative and legislation. The three narratives in Leviticus (8:1–10:20; 16:1–34; 24:10–23) continue the story line of Exodus. A similar pattern of interweaving narratives and blocks of legal materials follows in the book of Numbers. This suggests that the material throughout Exodus, Leviticus, and Numbers was put together by the same editor or editors.

The book of Leviticus itself now contains twelve major sections with each section marked off by a summarizing statement. These major summary statements appear in 7:37–38; 10:20; 11:46–47; 12:7b–8; 14:54–57; 15:32–33; 16:34b; 21:24; 23:44; 24:23b; 26:46; and 27:34. (Some sections also have minor internal summaries; see 13:59; 14:32). This division into twelve sections no doubt reflects the use of twelve as a symbolic number both indicating completeness and pointing to the twelve tribes of Israel. Before this material was edited into its final form, some of the twelve sections may have existed as separate and independent collections. For example, chaps. 1–7 or a shorter version of this material could have constituted a document serving as a small handbook on sacrifice.

In addition to the division into twelve sections, the book has been edited so that it contains thirty-six (3 × 12) divine speeches. Again there is the use of special numbers, three and twelve. Of these thirty-six speeches, introduced by "The Lord said," thirty-one are addressed to Moses, four to Moses and Aaron (his brother and high priest), and one to Aaron. These speeches primarily contain information in the form of laws and ordinances to the people at large, although a few are special and specific communications or directives.

COMMENTARY

1:1–7:38

Laws of Sacrifice

The sacrifices discussed in this section were unscheduled sacrifices offered to meet the religious and emotional needs of people and to fulfill the ordinances of God as circumstances demanded or opportunities presented themselves. The voluntary and unscheduled sacrifices discussed in chaps. 1–7 were in nature similar to those offered on a regular basis; only the particular occasions and motivations varied.

The material in these opening chapters of Leviticus falls into four natural divisions following the introduction in 1:1–2 and excluding the summary in 7:37–38. The first section, 1:3–3:17, discusses spontaneously motivated sacrifices and describes these with the donor's point of view in mind. The second section, 4:1 –6:7, discusses mandatory sacrifices required after the infraction of divinely ordained norms. Again these are described from the viewpoint of the donor. Both of these sections are presented as divine speeches addressed to Moses that he is then to communicate to the people of Israel as a whole since the information in these speeches concerns the community at large. In the third section, 6:8–7:21, the sacrifices previously described in 1:3–6:7 are regrouped and discussed primarily from the viewpoint of the priests who officiated at the sacrificial services of worship. Thus 6:8–7:21 contains divine speeches to Moses to be communicated to the priests (Aaron and his sons). Since the material in 7:22–36, the fourth section, concerns regulations relating to laypersons, the speeches here are to be communicated to the people of Israel, the community as a whole.

The Bible provides no theoretical discussion of the nature and function of sacrifice (→ Worship). Throughout the ancient world, sacrifice was a common phenomenon probably having its origin in the perceived need to provide food for the gods, a view still reflected (21:8, 22) but sometimes repudiated in the Bible (see Ps. 50:7–15).

In ancient Israel, sacrifice was understood as one of the means of sustaining and restoring the divinely created order. It was part of the ongoing process of human life and a means of contact and relationship with the divine. When normal personal and social life, the ordained orders of existence, or divine-human relationships were seriously disturbed, sacrifice functioned as part of the divinely ordained means to return life to normal.

Sin, or the disruption of divinely ordained order, was considered to have numerous consequences. First of all, it provoked the wrath of God (Lev. 10:6), even though he was slow to anger (Exod. 34:6–8), because it was contrary to divine will. Second, it polluted and defiled the sanctuary (Lev. 15:31) and the land (18:25). Third, it could pollute and defile the sinner, the agent of sin (Lev. 11:44). Fourth, sin disrupted and threatened the orders of society and creation (Lev. 26:14–39). The sacrificial system was a means of averting the consequences of sin and restoring harmonious relations.

Two other factors should be noted about sacrifice in ancient Israel. First of all, the ancients did not speak about "sacrifice" in general but about specific types of sacrifice. Second, the laws of sacrifice in Leviticus merely outline the technical aspects of rituals. The various sacrifices always belonged to larger contexts of worship in which prayer, hymns, and other forms of liturgy were integral parts. The various types of

divine service were not thought to be mutually exclusive.

1:1–2
Introduction

The opening of Leviticus indicates the association of this book with the book of Exodus. In Exodus 40, Moses had erected the tabernacle on the first day of the first month of the second year after the Exodus. Lev. 1:1 now continues the narrative and reports on divine communications made to Moses to be addressed to the people. The location of the revelation was the tabernacle (or tent of meeting) from which God had promised he would speak to Moses (Exod. 25:22; Num. 7:89). The tent of meeting was still situated at Mount Sinai.

The Israelite theologians and editors of the biblical texts made three assumptions about the people's laws and customs, and all are reflected in Lev. 1:1 and its context. First, all laws and customs regulating the people's life and order were divinely given and not the product of human promulgation. Second, Moses served as the mediator of these laws. Third, the laws and ordinances by which Israel was to live in the land of promise were given outside the land, and thus were not the product of normal social and political life in the land. Thus the laws presuppose a unique origin (God), a unique mediator (Moses), and a unique context (outside the land).

Although the stipulations regarding sacrifice are to be addressed to the Israelites (v. 2), the use of the word 'adam (Heb., "person") in the verse was understood to include non-Israelite sojourners and even foreigners (see 17:8). The formulation—"when any one of you brings an offering"—indicates the voluntary nature of some sacrifices and the importance of the worshiper's volition.

1:3–3:17
Voluntary Sacrifices

1:3–17, The Burnt Offering/The 'Olah. The 'olah (Heb.), "that which goes up [in smoke]," was completely burned on the altar except for the animal's hide, which would have presented problems in burning and was given to the officiating priest (7:8). Sheep, goats, cattle, and birds could be offered as whole burnt offerings. Animals were to be males without blemish, that is, normal healthy animals (see Mal. 1:8). The sacrificial system was not a place for one's discards, since the place of worship and the animals offered were related to divine perfection.

The slaughter and burning on the altar involved a number of steps. (Although the details are not spelled out identically in vv. 3–9 and

10–13, this is probably coincidental and the same procedures were used with goats and sheep as with cattle.) (1) The worshiper willingly brought the animal to the door of the tent of meeting (the entry to the sanctuary courtyard), probably to be approved by the priest as acceptable as a proper sacrificial specimen (v. 3b; see 22:18–19). (2) The worshiper laid a hand on the head of the animal, probably to attest ownership and to designate the animal as that particular worshiper's sacrifice (v. 4). (3) The animal was slaughtered on the north side of the altar (v. 11). Who killed the animal is not stated, although one would assume this and the further preparations were performed by the worshiper. (Only the priests, however, could perform the blood ritual and approach the altar that was off limits to laypersons.) (4) The blood of the animal was caught and thrown against the altar (v. 5). Blood from all animal sacrifices was brought into contact with the altar, thus returning "the life" to God so as to avert the wrath of God for having killed. (5) The animal was flayed, cut into pieces, and its entrails and legs washed to remove any blood and fecal material. (6) The cut-up animal was then placed on the altar by the priests and burned (vv. 6–9, 12–13).

Birds (pigeons and turtledoves), because of their size, were killed by the priest, who pinched off the head, drained the blood against the side of the altar, and burned the bird unplucked on the altar (vv. 14–17). The crop of the bird (with its feathers or contents, perhaps entrails) was removed before burning and cast aside. The removal of the crop with its food contents may have been comparable to washing an animal's entrails. Allowing birds to be sacrificed made it possible for even the poor to offer a burnt offering to God.

The function of the burnt offering is not spelled out in the text. At the end of vv. 9, 13, and 17, the burning on the altar is described as a "gift [not "an offering by fire" as in most translations], a pleasing odor to the Lord." Both "gift" and "pleasing odor" suggest that the burnt offering could be understood as a present offered to the Deity and thus should be considered as a thanksgiving sacrifice. The last phrase of v. 4, "to expiate on one's behalf" (rather than "to make atonement for him"), implies that this sacrifice was employed to make amends in some fashion. Lev. 1:4 and 16:24 are the only texts in the Bible, however, that explicitly relate the burnt offering to expiation (but see Job 1:5; 42:8). The burnt offering in general, and in the daily ritual especially (Num. 28:3–8), was probably presented to God to avert his wrath or to thank him for withholding wrath.

In other texts, the burnt offering is mentioned in connection with making petitions (1 Sam. 13:12), fulfilling a vow, or offering thanksgiving (Lev. 22:17–19). Probably, the unscheduled burnt offering was a general sacrifice used either to implore or to thank in circumstances where the worshiper wished to express extravagance, since the entire offering (minus the hide) was burned on the altar and no human party received benefit from the animal's flesh.

2:1–16, The Cereal Offering/The Min-chah. Grain products from cultivated crops could be presented to God as an offering. They could be presented uncooked as flour (v. 1); or cooked in an oven, on a griddle, or in a pan (vv. 4–5, 7); or roasted (v. 14). Flour and roasted grain were presented with frankincense (vv. 1, 15), an aromatic gum derived from the Boswellia trees of Arabia. Oil was either used in the preparation of the offering or poured upon it (vv. 1, 4–6, 15).

Only a part, "the memorial portion" of the cereal offering, was burned on the altar (vv. 2, 9, 16). This portion served to bring the giver to the attention of God. The remainder of the offering went to the priests. In presenting the offering to God, the giver transferred the cereal offering to the realm of the holy, that is, from human to divine ownership. It then fell into the category of the "most holy" (vv. 3, 10), which meant that only the priests, being holy, could eat it and then only in the Temple precincts, near the altar.

Two stipulations regarding the cereal offering are given in vv. 11–14. First, no leavening agent (generally sour dough) was to be used in preparing the cereal offering or mixed with it. Fermentation was considered a form of putrefaction and thus associated with decomposition and death. Second, salt, as a curing and preserving agent and thus a sign of permanence, was to be part of every cereal offering. Grain harvested early in the season and not yet fully dried and cured could be dried by heat or roasted and offered to the Deity (vv. 14–16).

The cereal offering when offered alone was understood as a freewill, voluntary gift on behalf of the worshiper. Along with wine it was offered to the Deity as part of the daily offering accompanying the meat sacrifice (Num. 28:3–8; see Num. 15:1–10), since the altar was to God as the table was to humans.

3:1–17, The Sacrifice of Well-Being/The Zebach Shelamim. Unlike the burnt offering and the cereal offering, the third type of voluntary sacrifice, the zebach shelamim, was eaten primarily by the donor in a festive meal.

The name for this sacrifice is variously rendered in modern translations "peace offering," "communion sacrifice," "shared offering," and so on. More important than the name in understanding the sacrifice are its nature and function. It could be offered in thanksgiving, to fulfill a vow, or as a freewill offering for no specific purpose (7:11–18). It was offered when life was proceeding normally and the worshiper was in a state of normal well-being or when some special occasion called for celebration. At one time all slaughter of animals in Israel may have been considered sacrifice and thus may have had to be performed at a sanctuary (see Lev. 17:1–7; Deut. 12:10–15). If this was the case, then all slaughter for food in those days would have fallen into the category of sacrifice of well-being.

Cattle, sheep, and goats could be sacrificed in this category without regard for the age or sex of the animals. The procedure for slaughter of the animal was similar to that for burnt offerings (Lev. 1), except in this case the animal could be slaughtered anywhere in the courtyard. Only certain parts of the animal were burned on the altar as a gift and pleasing odor to God: the suet and fat on the entrails and inside the body cavity, the two kidneys with their fat, and the appendage of the liver (1:3–4, 9–10, 14–15). The meaning of "the appendage to the liver" is uncertain; it may have been the diaphragm, the gall bladder, or merely the protruding lobe of the liver. In the case of sheep, the fat tail was also burned (v. 9a). According to one ancient source, the tail of the fat-tail sheep sometimes grew so heavy it had to be supported by a little cart pulled around by the animal.

This section concludes with a specific ruling at the end of v. 16 that declares that all the animal's fat (the suet, not normal body fat) belonged to the Lord, that is, was to be burned on the altar. A more general ruling occurs in v. 17 prohibiting the eating of suet and blood (see below 17:10–14).

4:1–6:7
Mandatory Sacrifices

That a new section begins and a change in subject occurs at 4:1 is indicated by the formula "And the Lord said to Moses." Even though this formula appears also in 5:14 and 6:1, these latter two occurrences mark off subunits within the larger section, since the addressee is the same as in the preceding material. All of 4:2 to 6:7 was to be circulated as public information as "Say to the people of Israel" (4:2a) indicates. Special concerns to be addressed to the priests begin a new section at 6:8.

Two types of mandatory sacrifices are discussed in 4:1–6:7. These are the "purgation offering" (generally rendered "sin offering") in 4:1–5:13 and the "reparation offering" (generally translated the "guilt offering") in 5:14–6:7. Both were related to wrongdoing committed unintentionally or inadvertently ("unwittingly") rather than brazen wrongs committed defi-

antly with no sense of contrition or confessional sorrow (see Num. 15:30).

According to Priestly theology, of which Leviticus is an expression, God had established the order and structures of life beginning with creation (Gen. 1:1–2:3). These orders included not only human-human and human-divine relationships but also human relationships with the world of nature. Appropriate actions and associations in all spheres of life constituted proper order. Within the human and natural orders, boundaries were set that structured life in terms of polar opposites. Such divisions included the following pairs: divine-human, holy-profane, life-death, human-animal, male-female, pure-impure, clean-unclean, kinship group–outsiders, and proper-improper ethical behavior. Actions that seriously transgressed these boundaries constituted wrongdoing or sin whether the action concerned ethical relations between humans or human relationships with the natural world. Thus an action that transgressed the division between clean and unclean was a refraction of order just as much as improper behavior toward another human being. Both constituted "sin," but, of course, some were obviously more serious than others. Some infractions, for example, threatened neither the health or well-being of society nor the divine-human relationship and thus only temporarily rendered unclean the person(s) involved.

4:1–5:13, The Purgation Sacrifice/The Chattat. Serious transgressions of the divine orders—the breaking of prohibitive commandments—were believed not only to offend God but also to produce an invisible contaminant that was attracted to and adhered to parts of the sanctuary. The contaminants thus polluted and defiled the sanctuary and threatened the Lord's presence there (15:31). At the same time, the Deity, like a human parent, was subjected to the consequences of his children's actions: he had to live with the pollution produced by their behavior. Elements in the sacrificial system functioned to hold the people accountable for their actions—thus taking sin and wrongdoing seriously—but also made possible the cleansing and purgation of the sanctuary and the placation of God—thus stressing divine forbearance and forgiveness. Blood placed on the altar purged the contaminants and the burning of part of the sacrifice as a gift, a pleasant odor, served to appease God.

First we read of the purgation sacrifice of the high priest (4:3–12). Since he was the supreme religious representative of the people, his inadvertencies brought liability on the whole congregation (4:3). High priestly inadvertent sins created a high level of impurity that penetrated into the holy place of the sanctuary. Thus the blood ritual that purged the impurity was performed inside the sanctuary proper (but not in the Holy of Holies, which was contaminated only by sins committed flagrantly or by wrongdoings not explicitly acknowledged). Blood was sprinkled seven times before the veil to the Holy of Holies (4:5–6) and then smeared on the horns of the altar of incense that stood in front of the veil (4:7a). The blood absorbed and cleansed away the impurity that had defiled the altar in the inner shrine. As in all purgation sacrifice rituals, the remainder of the blood was poured out at the base of the altar of burnt offering in the courtyard of the sanctuary (4:7b), reconsecrating the altar (see 8:15b).

Because of the prominence of the high priest and the fact that the purgation sacrifices were scaled according to the social standing of the wrongdoer, he was required to present a significant animal, a young bull without blemish (4:3). Only specific portions of the animal were burned on the altar (4:8–10; see 3:3–4). The remainder of the animal was taken to an uninhabited area ("outside the camp"), to the place where ashes from the altar were poured out, and there burned on a wood fire (4:11–12). Since the sin of the high priest representatively involved the entire community, including not only laypersons but also the priests, this purgation sacrifice could not be eaten by the priests. To have done so would have allowed them to benefit from an offering presented for their own guilt.

The requirements of the congregational purgation sacrifice (4:13–21) paralleled those for the high priest, since both involved the whole of the people. The conditions making the sacrifice both mandatory and possible were that the community committed some unintentional wrong and then, when the wrong was made known, became repentant (4:13–14a). Since the sin involved the whole community, the elders of the congregation laid their hands on the head of the bull (4:15). The function of the sacrifice and the blood ritual is stated in 4:20b: "the priest shall expiate on their behalf and it [the wrongdoing] shall be excused them."

In line with the socioeconomical scaling of the sacrifices, the purgation sacrifice of a rule (4:22–26) was a he-goat. Since the impurity and contamination caused by an individual's inadvertent wrong (even that of a leader) did not penetrate the inner shrine but only contaminated the outer altar, the blood was smeared only on the horns of the altar of burnt offering in the courtyard (4:25). The flesh of an individual's purgation sacrifice became the revenue of the priest who officiated at the altar when it was offered (see below 7:24–30).

Last, we read of the purgation sacrifice of an ordinary layperson (4:27–35). This could be either a goat or a sheep, in both cases a female without blemish (4:28, 32). The same features of the ritual applied in this case as in that for the ruler. A slightly fuller statement is made in 4:35b concerning the function of the ritual: "The priest shall expiate on the person's behalf with regard to the sin one sinned and the sin will be excused one." Repentant worshipers could leave the service of the purgation sacrifice knowing that their sins had been taken seriously, dealt with thoroughly, and purged conclusively.

There follows a section that presents four examples that necessitated the offering of a purgation sacrifice (5:1–6). It is uncertain whether these cases are presented as illustration or whether they were questionable and marginal cases about which there was uncertainty. The purgation sacrifice was required only in cases in which a negative or prohibitive commandment was broken. Thus acts of commission were always involved, not the failure to observe a positive or performative command.

The first case concerns one who failed to testify and to provide evidence in a case (5:1). Perhaps the public adjuration or curse was stipulated negatively—"Do not withhold evidence" (see 19:16b). Withholding evidence, even unintentionally, was a serious offense, since failure to testify could jeopardize justice and endanger proper social order.

The second and third cases (5:2–3) involve personal contamination through contact with uncleanness. Here the wrong seems to have been that the person forgot the uncleanness and did nothing to correct matters, thus prolonging purification beyond a week's time. Only impurities lasting at least seven days were considered serious enough to defile the sanctuary (see Num. 19:11–13, 20; Lev. 17:16).

The fourth case involves a rash oath (probably not to do some particular thing), which through forgetfulness the person broke (5:4).

Three stages are recognized in the process for offering a purgation sacrifice and thus being released from the responsibility of having polluted the sanctuary and affronted God. First, the person had to accept responsibility and show remorse. Second, the penitent had to confess the wrong (5:5). To whom confession was made is not stated, but it would certainly have involved a priest, since officiants at the sanctuary had to understand the circumstances before determining the nature of and participating in the ritual. The priests thus performed pastoral roles and looked after the care of souls in such situations, dimensions of their work frequently ignored. Third, the person's penalty in the form of a purgation sacrifice was offered at the sanctuary (5:6).

This section ends with special considerations given the poor with regard to sacrifices (5:7–13). In fact, the priestly material shows

161

more sympathy and consideration for the poor than any other body of literature in the Hebrew Scriptures. Persons who could not afford a goat or a sheep were allowed to offer less expensive animals, birds, as a sacrifice (5:7), and those who could not afford two birds were allowed to bring a cereal offering in the form of uncooked flour (5:11). Thus, in the case of the purgation offering, persons were allowed access to the cult regardless of their socioeconomical status. ("Cult" here means the system of worship of the religious community).

Two further aspects about these offerings of the poor are worthy of note. The person making an offering of fowl rather than of animals was required to bring two birds, one as a purgation sacrifice and another as a burnt offering (5:7). The reason is that a bird did not provide fat and internal matter to be burned on the altar. Thus an entire bird was icinerated on the altar serving as the gift, a pleasing odor for God to placate divine anger (5:10). The other bird, after some of its blood was put on the altar (5:8–9), became the property of the officiating priest, as was the case with all purgation offerings. In the case of the grain offering, no oil or frankincense was used, as was normally done (2:1). The oil and frankincense were associated with festivity, which was not a characteristic of the sacrificial ritual of purgation.

5:14–6:7, The Reparation Sacrifice/The 'Asham.

Sacrifices in this category were penalties or indemnities imposed for trespassing on the holy things of God (5:14–16). Items, both animate and inanimate, that had been consecrated by being presented or vowed to God—such as sacrifices, tithes, gifts, utensils of the sanctuary, and so on—could be contaminated or desacralized. For example, a layperson might accidentally consume the flesh of a sacrificial animal that had been presented to God as a reparation or purgation offering and had thus become holy and the perquisite of priests alone. When such holy items were wrongly used or desecrated, the trespasser was required to make restitution by paying the value of the desecrated thing plus 20 percent (but see 22:14). In addition, a fine in the form of a ram with a value relative to the desecrated thing was required. The priest calculated the value according to the weight of the shekel employed by the sanctuary, which might have differed from that used in ordinary business (5:15). (See chap. 27 for the legitimate desanctification of holy things.)

According to 5:17–19, persons who believed themselves to have trespassed on a holy thing were to be treated as if liable, although no actual wrongdoing was discoverable. Only the 'asham penalty was required in this case, since the real or imagined desecrated thing remained un-

known and restitution incalculable. This provision was obviously intended to meet the psychological needs of a person who understood life's treatment as indicating divine displeasure for trespass on a holy thing. Pastoral discussion and counseling by a priest would be assumed to reach such an opinion. Lev. 5:19b states the general principle involved: "[The one feeling liable] is [and is to be treated as] liable to the Lord."

In addition to direct trespass on a known holy thing (5:14–16) and suspected trespass (5:17–19), false oaths in the name of God also required a reparation sacrifice (6:1–7). The cases in 6:1–7 all involve acquisition through deceit followed by an oath in the name of Yahweh asserting innocence. In v. 2, the act of acquisition was deliberate and the deceit preceded the act. In v. 3a, the deceit followed the acquisition. One found something and lied about having found it (see Exod. 23:4; Deut. 22:1–4). One suspected of such illegal acquisition could be made to swear innocence by oath before God (see Exod. 22:7–13). A guilty party swearing innocence in the name of God made God an accessory to the crime and thus trespassed on his holy name.

When persons became remorseful and repentant about such wrongdoings and illegal acquisitions before apprehension, they could voluntarily take action to make amends. The process involved confession of the crime (noted in Num. 5:5–10, which closely parallels Lev. 6:1–7), restoration of the illegal acquisition plus a 20 percent penalty paid to the victim, and the presentation of a ram to God as a reparation sacrifice. In cases such as those in 6:1–7, no doubt a purgation sacrifice was also required in addition to the reparation sacrifice.

General principles in Israel's law are evident in these texts. First, in criminal justice, the focus of concern was the victim, not the perpetrator of the wrongdoing. Second, restitution rather than retribution and revenge predominates. Third, voluntary confession of a wrongdoing before apprehension and repentance over the sin reduced deliberate and premeditated wrongs to inadvertencies eligible for expiation. In addition, through confession malefactors righted matters with themselves by accepting the identity involved in the confession, through restitution they restored proper social relations, and through the 'asham payment they repaired their relationship with God.

6:8–7:21
Special Sacrificial Instructions to the Priests

A new subunit begins in 6:8–9 with the command to Moses to address the following stipulations to Aaron and his sons, the priests. The sacrifices previously described in 1:3–6:7, plus the priestly cereal offering (6:19–23), are discussed again with particular features highlighted.

6:8–13, The Burnt Offering/The 'Olah.

The regulations here are primarily concerned with the fire on the altar and the disposal of the ashes. Fire was to be kept burning on the altar continuously and burnt offerings left thereon all night. The priest responsible for cleaning away the ashes in the morning wore priestly dress (Exod. 28:42–43) while removing the ashes but changed clothes before carrying the ashes outside the sanctuary area. Working inside the sanctuary area, the priest was in the realm of the holy; moving outside, he crossed the boundary of the holy into the realm of the normal.

6:14–18, The Cereal Offering/The Minchah.

The supplementary material on the cereal offering has to do with the preparation and consumption of the flour minchah. It was to be prepared without leaven and eaten in the sanctuary precincts since it belonged to the category of the "most holy." The offering was divided among the priests and any priest could eat of it, since priests belonged to the category of the holy. Anything that touched the flour became holy and thus the property of the sanctuary.

6:19–23, The Priestly Cereal Offering.

The daily cereal offering presented along with the daily burnt offerings (Num. 28:2–8) was offered by the anointed priests, that is, the high priests, Aaron and his successors. This cereal offering was distinctive because, presented by the high priest, it was to be totally burned on the altar. The summary statement in Lev. 7:37–38 designates this cereal offering "an ordination offering," thus suggesting that it was to be the first offering by priests undergoing ordination. A general rule is stated in 6:23: every cereal offering presented by a priest must be totally incinerated on the altar.

6:24–30, The Purgation Offering/The Chattat.

The purgation offering, because it absorbed the pollution of the wrong committed, was surrounded by special precautions spelled out in this section. First, the location of its slaughter is identified as north of the altar (see 1:11), where the burnt offering was killed; this was thus a space carefully guarded by the priests against contamination (v. 25b). Second, the priest who officiated received the flesh of the offering as revenue and had to eat a portion of it (v. 26a), since the consumption by the officiating priest was part of the purgation process. The officiating priest was able to observe the purgation offering carefully throughout its handling lest it become mixed with other offerings. Third, since the purgation offering was most holy (v. 25b) and prone to contaminate anything it touched, it was eaten in a special place in the sanctuary courtyard (v. 26b). Fourth, whatever it touched became holy and any spattered blood had to be washed away within the sanctuary precincts before the garment was taken from the sanctuary (v. 27). Pottery vessels in which it was cooked had to be broken, since their porosity meant they absorbed contaminants, and metal cookers had to be thoroughly scoured (v. 28). Verse 30 reminds the priest that any offering whose blood was taken into the shrine, as was the case with the high priestly and communal purgation sacrifices, could not be eaten by the priests, since such offerings were made on behalf of the whole community (1:3–7; see 10:16–18) including all the priests (see 10:17–18). A priest could not eat the purgation offering made on his behalf.

7:1–10, The Reparation Offering/The 'Asham.

Little was said earlier about the sacrificial procedure and the disposition of the reparation sacrifice (5:14–6:7). That is rectified in this section. The laying of a hand on the reparation offering by the donor was not required, since the procedure involved in presenting a reparation offering left no doubt about the animal's ownership. The donor may not even have had to be present when the ram was sacrificed. No smearing of the blood was involved in the reparation sacrifice (v. 2) as with a purgation sacrifice (4:4–7), probably because a purgation sacrifice was generally also required. The wrong requiring a reparation sacrifice as penalty was directed immediately against God himself. The usual parts were burned on the altar (vv. 3–5) and the officiating priest became the owner of the flesh (v. 7) but could share portions with his fellow priests or sell them to them (v. 6a). The flesh had to be eaten in a holy place, i.e., in the sanctuary precincts (v. 6b).

The writer takes the occasion at this point to clarify matters not mentioned earlier but unrelated to the reparation sacrifice. Noted are the fact that the officiating priest received the hide of the burnt offering (v. 8), all cooked cereal offerings became the property of the officiating priest (v. 9), but uncooked cereal offerings presented as flour were shared by the priests in general without specific property rights (v. 10).

7:11–21, The Sacrifice of Well-Being/The Zebach Shelamim.

The motivation and occasion for sacrifices of well-being are described as threefold: thanksgiving, fulfillment of a vow, and spontaneous impulse. The thanksgiving offering included various forms of bread, both leavened and unleavened, with a sample of

163

each going to the priest but not burned on the altar (vv. 12–14). The flesh of the thanksgiving offering had to be consumed during the night after the animal's slaughter (v. 15). This encouraged conspicuous consumption in keeping with the festival atmosphere of the occasion. The time was for celebration with family and friends and for rejoicing before the Lord (Deut. 27:7). Offerings in fulfillment of a vow and spontaneous offerings could be eaten over two days, but what remained on the third day rendered the offering null and void (v. 18).

Even sacrifices of well-being had to be preserved from contact with uncleanness—both unclean objects and material and unclean humans (Lev. 7:19–21). One who ate while in a state of known uncleanness either from some personal source or from contact with an unclean substance committed sacrilege and was threatened with being "cut off from one's people." (Uncleanness, like holiness [6:18], was transmitted by physical contact.) Since this penalty was for transgression of a religious law, the punishment was to be meted out by God. Neither excommunication nor execution is meant! The threat appears to be the opposite of the ideal condition after death, namely, "to be gathered to one's people" (Gen. 25:8). To be cut off from one's people was to not be buried in the family tomb and thus to not join one's ancestors in the world of the dead.

7:22–36
Special Sacrificial Instructions to the People

Two small collections conclude the sacrificial regulations, both to be addressed by Moses to the people. The first (vv. 22–27) has to do with the prohibition against eating suet and blood. No animal suet was to be consumed; normal animal fat and the fat of fowl and game were not prohibited. The suet of an animal that died on its own or was killed by beasts could be utilized, probably in making soap or lubricating compounds, but not eaten (v. 24). All suet of a sacrificial animal was burned on the altar (3:16b). No blood of any animal was permitted as food (vv. 26–27).

The second collection (vv. 28–36) concerns the priests' share of the sacrifice of well-being. The worshiper personally brought to the priest the suet and the breast of the animal as a gift to the Lord. In presenting these to the priest, one elevated them in handing them over, thus transferring them from the realm of the normal and the ownership of the donor to the realm of the holy and the ownership of God. The fat was burned and the breast became the general possession of the priests (v. 31). The right thigh (the right foreleg) was ritually presented to the officiating priest as a perquisite (vv. 32–33).

Verses 34–36 affirm that this was to be a binding regulation for all times (see Num. 18:18; cf. Deut. 18:3).

8:1–10:20
The Ordination of Aaron and His Sons and the Consecration of the Sanctuary

In Exodus 25–31, God revealed to Moses directions for constructing the tabernacle sanctuary and its associated materials, for preparing priestly clothing for Aaron and his sons, for ordaining Aaron and his sons, and for consecrating the sanctuary. The directions for the first two are carried out in Exod. 35–40. The execution of the last two, namely, the ordination of Aaron and his sons (Exod. 29) and the consecration of the sanctuary (Exod. 30:26–30; 40:9–15), is the topic of Leviticus 8. A special convocation on the eighth day that provided the occasion for the initial service of Aaron and his sons is the subject of 9:1–24 and 10:12–20. The narrative about Aaron's sons Nadab and Abihu in 10:1–11 provides the setting for additional regulations on the priesthood (→ Priests).

8:1–36
The Ordination and Consecration Ritual

This chapter describes a ritual of initiation. With the completion and erection of the sanctuary (Exod. 35–40) and the revelation of the laws of sacrifice (Lev. 1–7), the scene was set for inaugurating the ritual of the sanctuary. A priesthood had to be set aside and ordained and the sanctuary consecrated. These two events were conducted as parts of a complex ritual process.

Just as Moses functioned as the mediator through whom divine revelation was made known, so did he function as the inaugurator of the cult. In such a role, Moses stood outside and above any normal office. He was the divine representative whom God assigned the task of establishing on earth the divinely ordained cultic institutions.

As v. 2 makes clear, only Aaron and his descendants were to be consecrated for service at the altar. At this point in the biblical narrative, Aaron's descendants were his four sons, Nadab, Abihu, Eleazar, and Ithamar (Exod. 6:23). Their ordination constituted a rite of passage through which they moved from the status of ordinary human beings to that of holy priests of the Lord.

Along with Aaron and his sons, Moses assembled the congregation to the front of the tent of meeting (Lev. 8:3–4) and explained to the people that the rituals they would witness were performed in fulfillment of God's earlier commands (v. 5). Thus the people participated, as witnesses, in the ritual.

Beside the general preparations (vv. 2–5), ten steps can be seen in the ordination ritual.

(1) The Presentation (v. 6a). Aaron and his sons were brought near, thus separating them from the general population and placing them in the area near the altar where their service would be performed.

(2) The Washing of the Candidates (v. 6b). Moses' washing of Aaron and his sons clearly identified them as the persons chosen and began the process of initiating them into "perpetual priesthood" (Exod. 40:15).

(3) The Investiture of Aaron (vv. 7–9). The garments symbolic of the high priestly office were placed on Aaron.

(4) The Anointment of the Tabernacle and Aaron (vv. 10–12). The anointment with oil set apart ("consecrated, made holy") the sanctuary, its furnishings, and the high priest, transferring them to the realm of the holy.

(5) The Investiture of Aaron's Sons (v. 13). The sons were dressed in the garb of their office.

(6) The Sacrifice of the Bull (vv. 14–17). The purgation offering of Aaron and his sons was treated in the same manner as the purgation sacrifice of a common person (4:27–35), with the blood placed on the altar of burnt offering and not carried into the shrine itself. Aaron and his sons were not yet fully priests (contrast 4:5–7), but since the sacrifice was of would-be priests, the flesh and hide of the animal were burned outside the camp. Ordination took place in the liminal margin between two states, partaking of both. The smearing of the blood on the altar cleansed it and the pouring of blood at the base of the altar served to reconsecrate it.

(7) The Sacrifice of the Ram Burnt Offering (vv. 18–21).

(8) The Sacrifice of the Ram of Ordination (vv. 22–29). This offering was treated as a sacrifice of well-being (see above on chap. 3). Moses as officiant received the breast (v. 29; cf. 7:31–32); although he was not a priest, as a relative of one he could eat of the sacrifice of well-being (see 10:14). The application of the blood of the ram to the right ears, the right thumbs, and the right big toes of Aaron and his sons (vv. 23–24) is to be understood as follows. These body extremities represented the whole person and the blood symbolized life (see 17:14). The smearing with blood indicated that Aaron and his sons had now passed safely across the boundary between the common and the holy. They now possessed new life, but life as members of the holy priesthood, having died as commoners (see below on 14:14–19).

(9) The Sprinkling with Blood and Oil (v. 30). This act represented the final phase of the transference of Aaron and his sons to the realm of the holy; the use of oil and blood from the altar bound the priests to the place of their fundamental service, the service of the sanctuary and the altar.

(10) The Ordination Meal (vv. 31–36). The sacrifice of well-being of the ram of ordination was offered, cooked, and eaten inside the sacred precincts.

Seven days were required before the ordination was complete and the priests could begin their duties. The text leaves unclear whether the same rituals were repeated daily over this period of a week during which the priests were to remain inside the sanctuary guarding the consecrated holy place. This seems highly unlikely. Seven days was the period of time required for persons to move in passage from one state of being to another (see 12:2; 14:8)—in this case from the realm of the common to the realm of the holy.

9:1–24; 10:12–18
The Convocation on the Eighth Day

On the eighth day, with Aaron and his sons fully ordained, the cult became operational. The cult, like creation, began normal operation on the eighth day. The convocation included the full participation of the community, and a series of sacrifices were offered. Two differences between the regulations of Leviticus 1–7 and the practices depicted here are noticeable. First, the blood of the priestly and communal purgation sacrifices was not taken into the inner shrine (see 4:5–7, 16–18). Second, the communal purgation sacrifice was a goat (9:15), whereas 4:14 requires a young bull (but see 16:5). No explanation is offered for these deviations. A possible explanation for the differences in the animal is that the book of Leviticus is composite, made up from sources of different dates. The practices in chap. 9 may be older than the regulations of chaps. 1–7.

After burning the sacrifices, Aaron, while still standing upon the elevated altar, blessed the people (9:22; see Num. 6:22–27). Aaron and Moses together then entered the tent of meeting, thus authenticating the right of Aaron to do so. They then exited and blessed the people (Lev. 9:23). Divine authentication of the service of the altar and of the priesthood of Aaron was given when divine fire instantly consumed the offerings on the altar, climaxing the service and indicating the presence and blessing of the Lord and his acceptance and approval of the sacrifices (9:24).

The instruction of the priests by Moses in 10:12–18 now appears to summarize 6:16, 26, and 7:28–34. If chaps. 1–7 did not exist, this teaching would have constituted the primary rules on priestly consumption of their perquisites from the sacrifices. In agreement with 6:14–18 and 7:28–34, the cereal offering is declared "most holy" and thus to be eaten by males of priestly descent and only in the sanctuary precincts beside the altar (10:12–13). The officiating priest's share of the sacrifice of wellbeing (here said to be both the breast and right thigh; cf. 7:31–32, where the breast goes to the priests collectively) was "holy," not "most holy," and could be eaten by the priests and their entire families, even away from the sanctuary but in a clean place (10:14–15).

The enigmatic events and the statements of Moses in 10:16–18, which have been integrated with the story of Nadab and Abihu (vv. 1–11) in v. 19, provide a setting for the general ruling in v. 18. The purgation sacrifice of a communal goat goes unmentioned after 9:15, but suddenly in 10:16 it is said to have been burned (not on the altar [v. 17] but outside the camp [see 4:21]). Moses castigates the sons of Aaron (and presumably Aaron himself) for not having eaten the purgation sacrifice on the principle that a purgation sacrifice whose blood is not taken inside the shrine must be eaten by the priests (v. 18). As noted earlier, the blood of a communal purgation sacrifice should have been utilized ritually inside the tent of meeting, according to 4:16–18. Apparently in older practice, represented in chaps. 9–10, whether the blood of the communal purgation sacrifice was taken into the shrine probably depended on the circumstances of its offering. Lev. 4:13–21 made it mandatory.

10:1–11, 19
The Nadab-Abihu Incident

Like the story of the golden calf constructed under Aaron's supervision (Exod. 32), the account of Nadab and Abihu is used as a negative example to highlight the importance of the preceding material and to stress the necessity of vigilant observance. In Exodus, as soon as the plans for constructing the tabernacle were revealed to Moses (Exod. 25–31), the people constructed the golden calf, thus endangering the life of the community. In Leviticus 8–9, the proper sanctuary had just been consecrated when two sons of Aaron took actions that threatened the sanctity of the Temple.

The sons' sin was using fire that should not have been in the Temple precincts. The word used to describe this fire (v. 1) is a Hebrew term that refers to something or somebody that is where it should not be (see Exod. 29:33; 30:33; Isa. 1:7). For their wrong, the sons are struck dead by fire from the Lord (v. 2). The point and moral of the story is summarized in v. 3: God declares, "By the ones approaching

me [the priests], I must be shown holy; and in the presence of the people, I must be glorified." The cult and its personnel must manifest the nature of God.

After the removal of the bodies of Nadab and Abihu by their kinsmen, the narrative occasion is used for five special instructions to the priests. Moses transmits two prohibitions (vv. 6–7) and God directly reveals one prohibitive and two performative commands to Aaron (vv. 9–11). First, priests are not to display signs of mourning—disheveled hair and torn clothes—while on duty; such mourning can be done by the people. For officiating priests to mourn risked the outbreak of God's wrath (v. 6). Mourning would not only preoccupy the priests' attention but also would be the introduction of the abnormal into the cultic ritual oriented to perfection. Second, once on duty and functioning in the Temple, the priests are not to leave their duty under any conditions (v. 7). (In later times, when an invading army stormed the Temple, priests were killed while faithfully continuing the performance of their duties.) Third, priests on duty are not to drink any intoxicant (wine or strong drink) that would interfere with their thinking and acting (v. 9). Fourth, distinguishing (separating) between the clean and unclean, that is, serving as the authorities in matters regarding purity and impurity, the holy and the common, is delegated to the priests (v. 10). Fifth, the priests are assigned the task of teaching the people all the statutes of God revealed through Moses. The priests are thus the custodians and transmitters of the Torah.

Probably some connection exists between this story of a Nadab and Abihu whose father, Aaron, built a golden calf (Exod. 32:35) and who were later slaughtered by God, and the accounts about King Jeroboam I (king in the north after the death of Solomon), who built golden calves (1 Kings 12:28–32) and whose sons Nadab and Abijah (= Abihu) were killed or died according to God's command (1 Kings 14:1–18; 15:25–30). Circles opposed to the Aaronite priesthood and to the employment of a golden calf in worship were probably responsible for the shape and content of some of the stories about Aaron and Jeroboam I.

11:1–47
Dietary Regulations and Defilement

Certain forms of food are permanently forbidden in the Hebrew Scriptures: suet and blood at all times and leavened bread during the Passover festival (3:17; Exod. 12:14–15). Certain animals and fowl were permitted and others prohibited as food. No vegetables or plants are described as taboo.

166

Leviticus 11 contains regulations on permitted and prohibited foods. (Deut. 14:3–20 contains very similar statements on the subject.) Lev. 11:2–8 describes the permitted and prohibited land animals (quadrupeds). The general principle in this area is stated in v. 3. Permitted animals must have cloven hoofs and ruminate (chew the cud). Eating anything prohibited defiled a person, rendering a person unclean. Mere contact with animals falling into the prohibited category did not defile a person as long as they were alive; thus horses, donkeys, and camels were usable as work animals. Only their carcasses defiled (v. 8). Nothing is said about the degree of defilement resulting from eating prohibited animals. One would assume therefore that uncleanness resulting from eating was covered by the regulations about carcass contact (see vv. 24, 28, 31, 40 and 17:15).

Verses 9–12 describe permitted and prohibited water creatures. In the permitted class were those with both fins and scales (v. 9). All others, such as shellfish and eels, were prohibited (vv. 10–12).

Because fowl did not lend themselves to such schematic classification, the writer provided a list of prohibited birds (vv. 13–19).

Winged insects (vv. 20–23) were forbidden except for certain types of hoppers (locusts, bald locusts, crickets, and grasshoppers).

Prohibited animals, water creatures, and insects were considered defiling agents when dead (vv. 24–28). Contact with their carcasses rendered a person unclean until the evening and their contact with one's clothing rendered the person unclean and required laundering of the garments. With the mere passage of time till the evening, a person's uncleanness dissipated.

All scurrying animals (vermin) and crawling insects and all reptiles were unclean and their carcasses defiled (vv. 29–31, 41–44). Items on which their carcasses fell had to be dipped in water and were unclean until the evening (v. 32). Their carcasses in a pottery item, vessels, small stoves and ovens, rendered unclean both the food within and the container itself, which had to be broken (vv. 33–35; see 6:28). Porous pottery absorbed, thus making thorough cleansing by scouring impossible. Water sources and seed for sowing were not rendered unclean by the carcasses (vv. 36–37).

The carcasses of edible animals that died on their own rather than being slaughtered also were contaminated (v. 39). Eating the flesh of such an animal rendered one and one's clothes unclean until the evening and required that the clothes be laundered (v. 40; see 22:8).

Verses 44–45 offer an appeal and rationale for avoiding the realm of the unclean. Avoiding contamination was to sanctify oneself and to strive after holiness. Since God was holy, striving for holiness was to imitate God. Since God had brought the people Israel up out of the land of Egypt, they were his in a special way and thus obligated to his demands. Verse 45b does not declare the people to be holy, as does Deuteronomy (see Deut. 14:2); it holds up holiness (the complete avoidance of the unclean) as an ideal goal.

Various attempts have been made over the centuries to explain the reasoning behind the material on the prohibited and permitted and the consequent defilement. This has especially been the case with the distinction between the clean and unclean foods, which has been explained as a means to disciplined obedience, an aid to good health, or as an avoidance of pagan practices. The clues to understanding the thinking behind the regulations actually lie in the worldview of the ancient Israelites, especially the priestly system.

The world was constituted into three realms and consequent states of being. These were the holy (Heb. *qodesh*), the common or normal (Heb. *tahor*), and the unclean or abnormal (Heb. *tame'*). Varying degrees existed in the realms of the holy and the unclean. The realm of the holy was that most closely related to the Deity and reached its strongest intensity in the innermost shrine of the sanctuary where God was uniquely present. Here also was concentrated the highest order and perfection. Persons and things could be transferred to the realm of the holy through ordination, consecration, gift, or vow. The realm of the unclean was the arena farthest from God and perfection. It was the realm of death, chaos, and the irregular. Geographically, it was associated with the wilderness, the uninhabited and the uninhabitable. The realm of the normal was the area of ordinary, everyday life.

Persons could move back and forth across the boundaries between the realms. The carcasses of animals, uncleanness, swarming and crawling things, and unclean animals with confused traits and uncharacteristic features belonged to the world of *tame* with its uncleanness, unorthodoxy, and impurity. Contact with the world of the unclean moved one across the boundary out of the world of the normal, and time and sometimes rituals were required to move one back from the world of the abnormal. The degree of the uncleanness determined the nature of the transition back to *tahor*.

The normal person could make contact with but not fully enter the realm of the holy—the realm of God, the priesthood, and the sanctuary. Rituals of preparation like bathing, abstinence from sex, and laundering of clothes were required before approaching the holy (see Exod. 19:10–11). Contact with the world of the holy was mediated to the ordinary person by the sanctuary, its ritual, and its priesthood. Property such as sacrifices and tithes could be and were transferred to the divine arena in

Temple ritual or personal vow. Some things so transferred (such as sacrifices) could be desanctified only through error and with penalty (the reparation sacrifice).

Just as the realm of the unclean could invade normal life, so could also the holy. As touching the unclean contaminated with uncleanness, so contact with the holy communicated holiness. Contact between the holy and the unclean was to be avoided at all cost and its consequences were considered enormous, as the case of Nadab and Abihu illustrated.

Dietary laws and defilement regulations were instituted and functioned to preserve the boundaries of the divinely created order. What God had put asunder, no one should join together.

12:1–8
Childbirth and Defilement

The subject of defilement, begun in the last section, continues in this new unit marked off with an introduction (v. 1) and a conclusion (vv. 7b–8).

Childbirth was a transitional period for mothers marked by a time of withdrawal from normal life and a three-staged readmission process. If the offspring was a male, the mother went through a seven-day period of uncleanness (v. 2a), probably characterized by isolation from the home and family. (Note that the father was apparently not present at the birth but had to be given the news; Jer. 20:14–15.) On the eighth day, perhaps following a ritual bath, she (along with the baby) would have resumed normal family life, except with regard to religious rituals. Thirty-three additional days had to pass before the mother could offer the sacrifices reintegrating her fully into the community and making normal participation in religious rituals possible (v. 4). The woman's uncleanness was associated with her bleeding at and following childbirth as v. 2b makes clear in its comparison with menstrual uncleanness (see 15:19–23). The time of uncleanness was double, fourteen and sixty-six days, if the child was female (v. 5), probably because in giving birth to a female the mother had a child who would also someday pollute with her blood flow.

Sacrifices required of the new mother, not for giving birth but for blood pollution, were a lamb as a burnt offering and a pigeon or dove as a purgation offering (v. 6). The latter was probably offered first to placate the Deity and purge the sanctuary (see 5:8). The burnt offering was probably understood as a thanksgiving presentation. The priest is described as handling all acts in the process, since the woman, still unclean, would not have access to the place of animal slaughter. The poor could substitute a second bird for the lamb (v. 2).

Only incidental reference is made in the text to the circumcision of the male child (v. 3), since this topic had already been covered in Genesis 17. Circumcision on the eighth day marked the transition of the male infant from being merely a human being to being a member of the chosen people.

13:1–14:57
Tsaraʿat Defilement and Cleansing

These chapters deal with what came to be called leprosy in the Middle Ages. The Hebrew expression applied to the ailments throughout the section is tsaraʿat. That the ailment does not refer to leprosy proper (Hansen's disease, known in antiquity as "elephantiasis") is indicated by a number of factors. First, the afflicted was expected to heal, even quickly, which is not the case with Hansen's disease. Second, houses and fabrics could be afflicted. Third, skeletal remains from biblical times in Palestine do not show evidence of Hansen's disease.

13:2–44
Diagnosis of the Ailment

This section discusses various characteristics of skin and head diseases, all suspected of fitting into the category of tsaraʿat. From the symptoms noted, it is impossible to determine the diseases involved and to label the troubles with modern names.

Persons suspected of or suspecting themselves to have "leprosy" were brought to a priest for examination (v. 2). An individual priest was "off duty" most of the time and thus among and available to the people.

If the person examined was clearly clean or unclean, the priest could rule on the case immediately. In other cases, various periods of confinement or quarantine were used: examination, seven-day quarantine, second examination, second seven-day quarantine, third examination, and bathing if the person had been declared unclean (vv. 3–6). Scalp and facial diseases could require shaving (vv. 33).

13:45–46
The Status of One Afflicted with Tsaraʿat

A person declared unclean was excluded from religious rituals and normal social relations. The person was deinstitutionalized both religiously and socially. Such a one moved completely into the realm of unclean. Clothing (torn), physical appearance (hair disheveled), mannerisms (covered lip and warning cry), and living space (alone outside the camp) all testify to the ostracism. The afflicted had to warn passersby of the danger of contacting defilement.

The diseased person was treated in this manner not only because of the real or assumed fear of contagion but also because of a theological motive, to protect the wholeness and well-being of society and to demonstrate the true status of the afflicted. Being without known cause, tsara'at was considered a punishment from God. As such, the person's presence in society was a threat to the community. Throughout the material describing the disease, it is called a "touch" or "stroke" implying an affliction from God. The disease was connected with death, since it gave the skin the appearance of a deceased person. The "leprosy" placed on Pharaoh (Exod. 4:6) and Miriam (Num. 12:10) is described as "flaky [not "white"] like snow." In the case of Miriam, the disease is described in terms of a stillborn child, "the flesh is half consumed when it comes out of the mother's womb" (Num. 12:12; see below on 14:14).

13:47–59
Garments with Tsara'at

Fabrics could have the affliction, in this case no doubt some fungus or mildew growth. If after two examinations and the passage of seven days, the disease had spread, the fabric was burned (vv. 47–52). If the disease had not spread after seven days, it was washed and if the color did not fade, it was burned (vv. 53–55). If the spot had not spread and had lightened in color, it alone was cut out and the fabric washed again (vv. 56, 58). Reappearance of the discoloration required burning of the entire cloth (v. 57).

14:1–32
Rituals of Cleansing and Reintegration of the Afflicted

When the afflicted was healed of the disease, a complex ritual process was employed, first, to effect the cleansing of the one afflicted and, second, to reintegrate the person into full standing in the normal life of the people. The transition involved both spatial and temporal dimensions.

14:1–7, The Cleansing Outside the Camp. The ritual of the day of cleansing took place "outside the camp" in the world of the unclean. The ritual involved the use of two living, small birds without defects, cedarwood, scarlet string, hyssop (an herb), and an earthen vessel (vv. 4–5). One bird was killed in the earthen vessel over running water and the blood was caught in the vessel. (Running water symbolized the intent of

the ritual, the removal of the contamination of the disease.)

At this point, the priest became the primary actor in the ritual. Using the bunch of hyssop and cedarwood (bound with the string along with the live bird) as a sprinkler, the priest sprinkled the afflicted person seven times with the slaughtered bird's blood. The diseased person was then pronounced clean and the live bird bearing blood was released into an open field (vv. 6–7). The blood sprinkled on the afflicted served as a ritual detergent to absorb and purge the person's contamination. The release of the live bird bearing blood was probably the means of offering back to God the life of the slaughtered bird in a ritual conducted away from the sanctuary proper. There is no indication in the text that the person's impurities had been transferred to the live bird.

14:8–32, The Ritual of Social and Religious Reintegration of the Afflicted. Although the afflicted was now pronounced clean and thus freed from the realm of the unclean, the person was not yet returned fully to the clean and the possibility of contact with the realm of the holy. This was effected through an eight-day process in three stages. First, the clothes of the afflicted were laundered, the person shaved of all body hair (becoming like a hairless infant), and bathed (v. 8a). These features of the ritual, like the washing of the priests in the ordination ritual (8:6), marked the transition of the afflicted into the marginal area between the boundaries of unclean and clean. Second, reentering the camp, the person spent seven days in the camp living outside the family abode (v. 8b). Seven days were thus spent in marginal life between the boundaries of the unclean and the clean just as the priests lived seven days on the boundary between the clean and the holy (8:33). On the seventh day, the body was again shaved and bathed and clothes laundered (v. 9), to prepare for the transition back into normal life. Third, on the eighth day, the afflicted offered the sacrificial requirements at the sanctuary, completing the transition to social and religious normality. The person's offerings and ritual material included a male lamb as a reparation sacrifice, a ewe lamb as a purgative sacrifice, and a second male lamb as a burnt offering, a cereal offering of flour and oil, and a separate measurement of oil (vv. 10, 12, 19, 20). Some of the sacrificial blood was placed on the person's right ear, thumb, and big toe (v. 14). Some of the oil, poured into the hand of the priest, was sprinkled seven times before the Lord to consecrate the remainder (vv. 15–16). Part of the oil was then placed on the right ear, thumb, and big toe and the remainder rubbed on the person's head (vv. 17–18). The application of the blood to the afflicted who had already been declared clean (see v. 6) symbolized the movement back to life from the realm of the dead and the application of oil confirmed that new status.

With the person now fully integrated back into the world of the living, the realm of the clean, the remainder of the sacrificial service was performed to purge the person's pollution from the sanctuary and to placate and thank God (vv. 19–20). The afflicted then could return home in full social and religious standing.

For the person too poor to provide the full retinue of animals, less expensive sacrifices could be substituted for the animals except for the reparation sacrifice, which was always a male sheep (vv. 21–32).

14:33–53
The Defilement and Cleansing of a House

Like humans and fabrics, houses could also be infected with tsara'at. This section outlines the procedures of diagnosis (vv. 35–38), remedial actions (vv. 39–42), and the determination of whether the case was irreversible (vv. 43–47) or reversible (vv. 48–55).

A house with suspicious growth on the walls was examined by a priest; the priest ordered removal of the household goods before inspection because, if a house were declared unclean, so were all its contents (vv. 35–36). If a preliminary examination confirmed the suspicion, the house was declared "off limits" for seven days (vv. 37–38). Both entering and living in the house during the period defiled one (vv. 46–47).

Upon second examination, if the growth had spread, the affected stones were replaced and the house's inside plaster scraped off and replaced. The contaminated stones and plaster were disposed of in a known place of uncleanness (vv. 39–42). If contamination reappeared, the entire house was pulled down and properly discarded (vv. 43–45).

If the house infection cleared after remedial actions, then the house was cleansed along the same lines as those used to cleanse the infected individual in 14:2–7 (vv. 48–53). Verses 54–57 summarize the chapter.

15:1–33
Genital Discharges and Defilement

A new unit begins with the speech formula of v. 1 and concludes with the summary statement in vv. 32–33. This section concerns the defilement produced by pathological male genital discharges probably resulting from gonorrhea (vv. 2–15), by normal ejaculation of semen (vv. 16–

18), by normal menstruation (vv. 19–24), and by pathological female discharges (vv. 25–30). All four cases are concerned with body fluids out of place, that is, with unusual discharges that moved beyond the normal body confines and thus transgressed boundaries.

The person with gonorrhea contaminated both directly, through contact and spittle (vv. 7–8, 11), and indirectly, through secondary contact with items on which the person lay or sat. Contact with the afflicted's bed or chair required laundering of clothes, bathing, and passage of a day to effect cleanness. Defiled inanimate objects had to be washed and pottery containers broken. After healing, the afflicted had to wait seven days (to confirm a cure), launder his clothes, bathe in running water, and offer two birds as a purgation sacrifice and a burnt offering (vv. 13–15). Although contaminated, the person with gonorrhea was never assigned the full status of total uncleanness like one suffering from "leprosy."

Semen contaminated both the person, and in intercourse both male and female, and any cloth or leather on which it fell (vv. 16–17). Bathing and washing were required. Couples after intercourse were required to bathe and were unclean until the evening because of semen. They were thus incapable of participation in religious rituals or attendance at the sanctuary (v. 18; see Exod. 19:15).

During the seven days of her menstrual period, a woman rendered unclean through direct contact or through secondary contact with that on which she lay or sat. Direct contact rendered one unclean until the evening (v. 19) and contact with her bed or chair required laundering, bathing, and passage of the day (vv. 20–23). Sexual relations with a menstruating female rendered the male unclean for seven days, and he became a contaminant (v. 20).

Females with pathological discharges were treated the same as menstruants (vv. 25–27) except that, like the person with gonorrhea, extension of the impurity beyond seven days required sacrificial expiation (vv. 28–30).

Verse 31 summarizes much of the system of thought lying behind the laws on defilement. Regulations and ordinances were revealed and taught so that the Israelites would be on guard against uncleanness that polluted the sanctuary (God's residence in their midst) and thereby avoid incurring the lethal anger of God.

16:1–34
The Ritual of Yom Kippur: The Day of Atonement

The stipulations regarding Yom Kippur have been given a narrative context so that 16:1 picks up where 10:20 broke off. This narrative context thus presents the ritual as the response to the episode of Nadab and Abihu, who had polluted the sanctuary with their sins and their corpses. The concluding paragraph (vv. 29–34a) makes clear, however, that what is being described had become and was limited to an annual event. The goals of the ritual were twofold; first, to cleanse the entire sanctuary of the defiling pollution produced by the priests' and people's wrongdoings (v. 33) and, second, to cleanse the people from their sins (v. 30).

16:1–10, The Sacrifices. The animals used in the ritual included the following: for the priests, a bull for a purgation sacrifice and a ram for a burnt offering, and for the people, two goats for a purgation sacrifice and a ram for a burnt offering (vv. 3, 5). Only one of the community's goats was slain, the other was "for Azazel" with the selection between the two being made by lot (vv. 7–10).

16:11–19, The Cleansing of the Sanctuary. Before conducting the ritual, Aaron, the high priest, bathed and donned simple linen garments (v. 5). The main portion of the ritual was thus performed without his wearing the elaborate regalia of the high priestly office (see 8:7–9). The bathing marked the high priest's temporary surrender of the exaltation of his office and the linen garments signified his identity with the people and their sin.

The priests' purgation offering was slaughtered and its blood caught (v. 11). Aaron then took a fire pan with coals from the altar and incense and, alone (v. 17), entered the tent of meeting penetrating into the Holy of Holies behind the veil. He placed the incense on the coals to make a cloud to cover the mercy seat atop the Ark, thus shrouding his direct confrontation with the Deity and his view of the mercy seat (vv. 12–13; → Ark). He then took blood from the slain bull (apparently exiting and reentering the Holy of Holies but leaving the burning incense before the mercy seat) and with his finger sprinkled blood once on the front of the mercy seat and then seven times on the ground before the mercy seat (v. 14), both cleansing and reconsecrating the Holy of Holies.

Then acting as a member of the community, he killed the goat for the people's purgation offering and repeated the ritual in the Holy of Holies (v. 15). Similar blood rituals were performed in the remainder of the tent of meeting (v. 16b) and on the altar of burnt offering in the courtyard (vv. 18–19). These blood rituals purged the Holy of Holies of defilement produced by the people's deliberate or inadvertent transgressions and purified and reconsecrated the altar.

16:20–22, The Cleansing of the People. The cleansing of the people was performed through the use of the live goat designated by lot "for Azazel" (v. 10). The high priest placed both his hands upon the head of the goat and confessed over it the iniquities, transgressions, and sins of the people, probably in generalized confessional formulas (v. 21b). Placing both hands on the sacrificial animal symbolized transference; the use of only one hand was to express ownership. The wrongs of the people were thus transferred to the goat and with the goat were sent into the wilderness, a place cut off from habitation (vv. 21b–22). The goat went "to Azazel" (vv. 10, 26). Whether Azazel was a place, a demon, or the personification of the "unclean" wilderness cannot be determined.

16:23–28, The Remainder of the Ritual. In the remainder of the ritual, the high priest reverted to his role as supreme representative of God, signified by a second bathing and the donning of the full high priestly regalia (vv. 23–24). Both the one who led the goat to the wilderness and the one who burned the remains of the sin offerings had to bathe to remove the defilement contracted in deposing of these sin-laden objects (vv. 26–28).

16:29–34a, Regulations on Yom Kippur. The concluding remarks specify details about Yom Kippur. Observed on the tenth day of the seventh month, the day was to be marked by abstinence from work (for both the native and the sojourner) and humiliation indicating penitence. The role of repentance in the observance is succinctly affirmed in the Mishnah: "If one said, 'I will sin and Yom Kippur will effect expiation,' then Yom Kippur effects no expiation. For transgressions between humans and God, Yom Kippur effects expiation, but for transgressions that are between persons, Yom Kippur effects expiation only if a person has settled affairs with one's fellow human being" (M. Yoma 8:9).

17:1–21:24

The Holiness of Life

This block of material is introduced by the speech formula in 17:1 (following the summary statement in 16:34b) and concluded by the summary statement in 21:24. Its central topic is the life of holiness lived in imitation of God. The material is structured into six speeches of the Lord to Moses (see 17:1; 18:1; 19:1; 20:1; 21:1; 21:16). Like the six days in which God established the orders of creation, so these six speeches outline the orders for the people's life of holiness. This block of material may once have existed as a separate collection as a booklet or code on holiness.

17:1–16
Sacrifice and Blood

The theme running through this entire chapter is the association of blood with life and of life with God. The first section (vv. 1–9) argues that all sacrifices, since they involve the taking of life and the shedding of blood, must be brought to the sanctuary where the blood can be properly disposed of. The second section (vv. 10–16) prohibits the eating of blood.

17:1–9, Sacrifices and the Sanctuary. This section mandates that all sacrifices must be made at the sanctuary, and since all slaughter of domestic animals is here considered sacrifice, then all animals must be slaughtered at the sanctuary.

The standard Hebrew text of v. 4 has suffered the loss of several words in scribal copying but these have been preserved in the ancient Greek and Samaritan versions. Verse 4 should read: "And does not bring it to the door of the tent of meeting so as to make it a burnt offering or a sacrifice of well-being to the Lord for its acceptance and for a pleasing odor, but slaughters it outside and does not bring it to the door of the tent of meeting to present it as a presentation to the Lord before the sanctuary of the Lord; blood-guilt shall be reckoned to that one; the person has shed blood and that person shall be cut off from the midst of his people." The requirement that all sacrifices and thus all slaughter of animals had to be done at the sanctuary was an effort to eliminate secular slaughter of animals for food. Secular slaughter of animals had been sanctioned by Deuteronomy (12:15–18); apparently Lev. 17:1–9 was an attempt to counter this and its attendant practice of pouring out the blood "upon the earth like water" (Deut. 12:16). Such practices were for the Priestly author the equivalent of sacrificing to some "demons" of the field (Lev. 17:7). Verses 8–9 extend the regulation to include non-native sojourners.

According to v. 4, to slaughter an animal without giving the blood (= life) back to God through the means of priestly disposal against the altar (v. 6a; see 3:2, 8) was to be guilty of murder.

17:10–16, Prohibition Against Eating Blood. Throughout the Priestly texts of the Bible, the eating of blood is prohibited and, in fact, is treated as the primeval prohibition given Noah when humans, after the Flood, were allowed to give up a purely vegetarian diet and slaughter animals for food (see Gen. 9:3–4; Lev. 3:17; 7:26). The one eating blood in the land—native or sojourner—is threatened with being "cut off from one's people" (v. 10).

A twofold rationale is given for not eating blood in v. 11. First, "the life of the flesh is in the blood," and the "life" (or "soul," Heb. *ne-*

phesh) that animals, like humans, possess is given by and belongs to God (see v. 14). Second, God declares, "I have given it to you for the altar to expiate on behalf of your lives because it is the blood with the life that expiates." The disposal and application of the blood at the altar is the divinely given means for humans to make amends for having taken life. To refuse to return the blood (life) to God made one a murderer (see v. 4).

The blood of game and fowl, which were killed in hunting for food and thus could not be presented at the sanctuary, was to be poured out and covered with dust (v. 13). With a kill, the hunter must momentarily pause and function like a "priest." Animals that had died on their own or been killed by beasts and thus not properly bled nor their blood treated ritually were unclean and eating their flesh rendered one unclean until evening and required personal bathing and the laundering of one's clothing (v. 15; see 11:39–40). Not to undergo this ritual cleansing rendered one to blame for possibly more serious offenses (v. 16), namely, prolonged uncleanness (see 5:2) or exclusion from ritual occasions and the sanctuary.

18:1–30
Prohibited Sexual Relations

18:1–5, Introduction. The life of holiness prohibited sexual relationships and therefore marriage between certain persons (vv. 6–18) and forbade certain other sexual practices and relationships (vv. 19–23). The regulations on these matters were prefaced with an introduction that designated such relationships as the practice of the inhabitants of the lands of Egypt and Canaan and therefore to be shunned (vv. 3–5). The expulsion of the pre-Israelite occupants of the land of Canaan is attributed to their having defiled the land through such practices, and the Israelites are warned that they too can be vomited out by the land if they follow such abominable customs (vv. 24–30).

18:6–18, Forbidden Marriage and Sexual Relationships. Sexual relationship ("to uncover the nakedness of") and therefore marriage between men and certain women were considered abnormal and prohibited. The two near female relatives that occur to us in this connection but are not mentioned in the list as prohibited sexual partners are a man's own daughter, who was surely prohibited (see Exod. 21:9), and nieces, who appear not to have been prohibited.

Most of the prohibited parties were near blood relatives, but not those in vv. 17–18 who were relatives through marriage. Marriage to any in the group would have produced confusion in human relations and thus introduced disorder. (Note that some of the patriarchs of the nation would have been guilty of unholiness according to these standards [see Gen. 20:12; 29:21–30; Exod. 6:20] and that Israel poked fun at its near neighbors for incestuous origins [Gen. 19:30–38]).

18:19–23, Other Prohibited Sexual Relations. Five other forms of sexual activity are prohibited in these verses: first, sex with a woman during her menstrual period (v. 19; see 15:24; since menstrual blood was unclean and represented death, such sexual relations involved mixing life [semen] with death); second, sex with another man's wife (v. 20); third, devoting one's offspring, the product of sex, to Molech (v. 21; see below on 20:1–5); fourth, homosexual sex, with another male (v. 22; the Hebrew Scriptures do not comment on lesbianism); and fifth, sex with animals (v. 23). All of these acts were considered abnormal, crossing the boundaries ordained by God.

18:24–30, Concluding Exhortation. The series of prohibitions concludes with a warning that pre-Israelite occupants of the land of Canaan were expelled because they defiled the land with their sexual practices, and the Israelites too can be "vomited" out by the land if they follow such abominable customs.

19:1–37
The Life of Holiness

19:1–2, 37, Holiness in Imitation of God. This chapter, in spite of its apparently disorganized and eclectic quality, may be viewed as the Priestly parallel to the Ten Commandments. In fact, the basic content of all the Ten Commandments appears here. The expression, "I am the Lord (your God)," occurs fifteen times in the text serving both to stress the origins of the ordinances and to divide the material into subunits. The initial call to the people is to be or become holy as God is holy (v. 2). Holiness is affirmed as a quality inherent in the Deity but also as a goal for the people to strive for. The life of holiness is then illustrated by diverse examples, some based on legal and cultic stipulations and others not. Verses 3–8 concern the life of holiness in relationship to God and vv. 9–37 concern the life of holiness as it is lived out in personal and human relationships. Verse 37 is a summarizing statement repeating the intent of v. 2.

19:3–8, Holiness Toward God. Four examples are used to speak of holiness toward God: first, to fear (or revere) one's mother and father (v. 3a); second, to observe the Sabbath days (v. 3b; the seventh day but also the "Sabbaths" of the festivals; see 16:31); third, neither to turn idols nor to manufacture molten images (perhaps of the Lord, v. 4); and fourth, to observe cultic regulations, for example, in the eating of the sacrifice of well-being offered to fulfill a vow to God (vv. 5–8). Interestingly, respect for parents is parallel to respect for God. This text resembles the Ten Commandments in that honor of parents is placed among the duties to God, i.e., in the first half of the commandments.

19:9–36, Holiness in Human Affairs. The description of human affairs begins with groups most distant from the center of the social order: the poor and resident aliens. For their benefit, some areas in field and vineyard were to be left unharvested and ungathered for their gleaning (vv. 9–10).

Verses 11–12 deal with relationships between business associates and prohibit stealing through stealth, deception, lying, and swearing falsely over such matters in the name of God (see 6:1–7).

Relations with those more available to the person are noted in vv. 13–15. Neighbors should not be oppressed (or deprived) or stolen from. Hired servants must be paid on the day of their labor and the blind and deaf must not be taken advantage of. Adherence to such principles is to fear (revere) God.

In legal matters, justice was to be disinterestedly administered (generally done by a group of the person's peers). Partiality should not be shown to the poor and weak nor deference to the rich and powerful (v. 14). One is admonished to be neither a troublemaking gossip and accuser nor a silent nonparticipant when possessing evidence that could affect a neighbor's capital case (v. 16; see 5:1).

One is admonished not to harbor a grudge and repress feelings of hostility against another. Instead, one is advised to confront directly (reproach and reason) the other (see Isa. 1:18) and have it out. Repression of feelings instead of open interchange and externalization of the hurt are seen as eventually leading to sinful action and certainly to slander and deceit (v. 17; see Prov. 25:9–10; 26:24–26). Harboring hatred in the heart is seen as possibly leading to vengeance (in court or out) and grudge bearing. Over against the latter two sentiments and dispositions, the writer proposed the alternative: "Love your neighbor as (or as one like) yourself" (v. 18). In vv. 17–18, the love commandment (in v. 18) parallels "reproach your neighbor" in v. 17, which would suggest a meaning like "treat others as you would (or should) like to be treated," but without implying any sentimental affection.

With v. 19, the material seems to begin anew. The first portion of v. 19a parallels v. 2 and precedes a sequence beginning with the second portion of v. 19a, which parallels v. 3 and what follows it.

Verse 19, like Deut. 22:9–11, prohibits mixing of species across boundaries. Breeding, planting, and weaving must be done to preserve the independence of plant and animal species "according to their kind" (see Gen. 1:12, 24), thus respecting the divinely established natural boundaries and reflecting wholeness.

Verses 20–22 parallel vv. 5–8 and require, in addition to an indemnity, a reparation sacrifice by a man who has voluntary sex with an unfree woman who is betrothed to another man. Such relations with a free woman would have involved a capital offense (v. 20b). The reason for the payment of a reparation sacrifice in the case of a betrothed slave girl and her lover is that the man was an intrusive figure in a divinely sanctioned arrangement and therefore guilty of trespass against a holy thing (see commentary above on 6:1–7).

Fruit trees were to be considered "uncircumcised" for three years and their produce forbidden; in the fourth year all fruit was holy; only in the fifth year was the owner to eat the produce (vv. 23–25). Such a practice represented a gradual transition process, with the first fruit of trees like those of humans, animals, and grains being dedicated to God. Such gifts of the "first" embodied Israel's sense of being a tenant in God's land. As is clear from this example, the laws beginning in vv. 19 are concerned with the observances and holiness of personal practices rather than interpersonal practices (unlike vv. 9–18). They concern matters relating to life in the land.

Practices prohibited in vv. 26–29—eating blood, practicing sorcery or necromancy with its "contact" with the dead, and disfiguring the hair or the body—either defiled and defaced the person and/or threatened one's relationship with the family after death.

Making one's daughter a prostitute (for the sake of income) profaned the female and threatened the land with defilement (v. 29; see 18:24–30). Sabbath and sanctuary may appear to be oddly associated in v. 30 but reference to them peculiarly placed in this context. Neither is the case. Sabbath and sanctuary go together throughout the Priestly material (note the Sabbath text amidst directions on tabernacle construction [Exod. 35:1–3]). As the Sabbath is the culmination of creation, so the building of the sanctuary is the culmination of the stay in the wilderness. God is described speaking six times in giving directions about building the sanctuary paralleling the six days of creation (Exod. 25:1; 30:11, 17, 22, 34; 31:1). Sabbath and creation are related (see Exod. 20:8–11) and failure to observe the Sabbaths (see Lev. 26:34–35, 43), like defiling the Temple, threat-

ens life in the land. So does prostitution, the topic of v. 29.

One should not be defiled by mediums and wizards who practice necromancy since their contact with the dead brings defilement, which threatens life in the land (v. 31).

Honoring the older generation is to revere God (v. 32) and to claim the promise of long life in the land (see Exod. 20:12).

Sojourners or resident aliens should not be wronged; they should be shown the same love as natives (Lev. 19:18). Their presence among the people is a constant reminder of Israel's time in Egypt—a time without land (vv. 33–34).

The final challenge is a call to personal integrity reflected in honesty and justice in business (vv. 35–36). The Lord can make his demands for holiness not only because he is holy but also because he brought the people out of Egypt and therefore they belong to him in a unique way (v. 36b).

20:1–27
Penalties for Various Infractions

This chapter specifies punishment for some of the wrongs described in the preceding chapters but especially those in chap. 18. Other than the speech formula (v. 1), the unit contains no special introduction. A lengthy admonitory conclusion (vv. 22–26) offers a rationale for obeying the divine ordinances and striving for holiness.

20:2–21, 27, The Penalties. The description of penalties opens with a lengthy statement (vv. 2–5) condemning anyone, native or resident alien, who gives a child to Molech, a matter already mentioned in 18:21. The nature of this wrong has been widely discussed since antiquity without consensus.

Two factors are fundamental in understanding what was involved in this matter. First, the name usually rendered "Molech" (actually *hammolek*, Heb., "the Molech") is probably a distortion of the title *hammelek* (Heb.), which means "the king" and would have been a designation for God (→ Molech). Second, the ritual involved was clearly a part of the Judean cult and was carried out in the name of the national god, the God of Israel. That this was the case is demonstrated by the fact that giving one's offspring to Molech defiled the sanctuary and profaned God's holy name. This act was possible only if something was done in the name of God. Thus the Lord, the God of Israel, was "the king" (*hammelek*; the full title occurs in Isa. 6:5 *hammelek yahweh seba'ot*) to whom the child was given. Therefore 20:2–5 legislated against an element in the national cult. To understand the Priestly prohibition we must examine the history of the practice.

In early Israel, people were required to consecrate to the Lord ("declare holy") everything that opened the womb among humans and animals (Exod. 13:1–2). The firstborn became the property of the Temple, although it was assumed that firstborn children would generally be redeemed (Exod. 13:13b) according to desanctification rules (see below on Lev. 27). Income from the redemption of firstborns and the sale of the unredeemed was a major source of Temple funds (see 2 Kings 12:4). The verb "pass over" (Heb. *'abar*; Exod. 13:12) and this early dedicatory practice may have been the origin of the term "Hebrew" (*'ibri*; → Hebrews). The "Hebrew slave" in Exod. 21:2–6 and Deut. 15:12–18 would then have been one of the unredeemed that could be purchased from the Temple (note the role of the Temple in Exod. 21:5–6) at good prices (Deut. 15:18).

In the eighth century B.C., apparently during the reign of Ahaz, the ritual of "passing over" the child to God came to be understood in sacrificial terms, and children were actually burned as sacrifices to "(the Lord) the king" (see 2 Kings 16:3; 23:10; Jer. 7:31; 32:35; Mic. 6:6–8), as was the case in contiguous cultures, especially Phoenicia.

Deuteronomy later (probably in the latter part of Hezekiah's reign) prohibited the actual sacrifice and burning of children (Deut. 18:10; see also 12:31). Jeremiah later denied that God had commanded the practice of child sacrifice (Jer. 32:35). Ezekiel held that God had once established the ordinance requiring child sacrifice but now finds it odious (Ezek. 20:25).

The Priestly legislation in Lev. 20:2–5 attempted to eliminate entirely the practice of devoting children to the Lord (*hammelek*) and, thus, the potential for child sacrifice. In Numbers, the Levites are interpreted as the substitute for the firstborns thereby rendering unnecessary any transference to the holy of the firstborn (Num. 8:16–18). The penalty for devoting a child to *hammelek* was severe according to Lev. 20:2–5—stoning inflicted by the people of the land and failure to be gathered to one's people after death inflicted by God.

Consultation of wizards and mediums and thus the world of the dead, still apparently accepted as legal even if not reliable in the time of Isaiah (Isa. 8:19–20), was placed under the penalty of God (Lev. 20:6) and treated as a sign of unholiness (v. 7). Verse 8 described the Lord as the one sanctifying the people, that is, giving ordinances by which the people can live holy lives. Cursing father and mother (see Exod. 21:17), an act against divinely established social orders, was placed in the category of a capital crime (Lev. 20:9).

The death penalty is prescribed (or "permitted," depending on whether the verbs are translated "shall be [or may be] put to death") for both parties in seven types of sexual relations: a man and his neighbor's wife (v. 10), a man and his father's wife (v. 11), a man and his daughter-in-law (v. 12), a male with another male (v. 13), a man with a woman and her mother (v.14), a man with an animal (v. 15), and a female with an animal (v. 16).

Other sexual "misconduct," probably assumed to be protracted, is to receive lesser penalties. Sexual relations, perhaps marriage, between stepchildren results in God's placing them under the threat of an early death (v. 17). Sex with a menstruating female (v. 18; see 15:24), and marriage with an aunt (v. 19) or aunt-in-law (v. 20), or sex with a living brother's (presumably ex-) wife (v. 21) are all condemned, but execution of any penalty is left in the hands of God.

The regulation on mediums and wizards (v. 27) appears to be a misplaced law that perhaps once appeared earlier in the chapter (see v. 6). It prescribes stoning for necromancy. This form of divination involved contact with the dead, a practice considered defiling by Priestly theology for its failure to respect the boundary between life and death.

20:22–26, The Rationale. The reasons offered for obedience to the divine statutes in the conclusion are twofold. Obedience protects against the defilement of the land, which could result in expulsion of the people (vv. 22–24a; see 18:2–5, 24–30). Just as God had separated out and chosen his people from among the nations, so must they separate and choose between the permitted and prohibited, the clean and unclean, and thus imitate the divine.

21:1–24
Regulations for the Priests

This section, to be addressed to the priests, contains regulations regarding priestly holiness in terms of their contact with the dead (vv. 1b–6, 10–12) and whom they may marry (vv. 7–9, 13–15) as well as statements on the status of blemished priests (vv. 17–23).

21:1b–9, Regular Priests. Regular priests were forbidden contact with and being in the presence of a human corpse except for the closest of kin—parents, children, brother, and unmarried sister (vv. 2–3). Being a leader (Heb. *ba'al*) among his people, the priest (*kohen*) should not defile himself (v. 4). Signs of mourning—special cutting of the hair, shaping of the beard, and cutting of the body were prohibited (v. 5). Contact with the dead defiled (see Num. 19) and changing the body's appearance was an affront to God's holiness (→ Priests).

Priests were forbidden to marry certain women who had been profaned by other sexual partners (Lev. 21:7). For a priest's daughter to become a prostitute (or engage in sexual infidelity to her husband) reflected on the holiness of the father, since it threatened the purity of the priestly line. She was to be executed through burning (v. 9).

21:10–15, The High Priest. Restrictions were even more rigorous for the high priest; he was forbidden any signs of mourning (see 10:6–7) and prohibited from being in the presence of any corpse even those of his own parents (vv. 10–11). He could not leave the sanctuary during emergencies caused by death of a near relative but had to continue his ritual duties (v. 12).

A high priest was required to marry a native prepubescent female, that is, a girl without experience of sexual intercourse (vv. 13–14). His "seed" or family line must not be profaned (v. 15). Such precautions may have sought to assure that any child born to his wife was his.

21:17–23, Blemished Priests. In the priestly system, any male descendant of the house of Aaron inherited the right to the priesthood, but one with a physical abnormality (vv. 17–21) was prohibited from functioning in the Temple ritual, though he could share in priestly perquisites ("the bread of his God"), both the "most holy" (consumed in the sanctuary) and the "holy" (consumable by priests and their families in any clean place; v. 22). A blemished priest could not approach the altar or enter the sanctuary shrine, for to do so would have profaned the holy things (altar and shrine) of God (v. 23). Abnormality had no place in the ritual service of God.

22:1–23:44

Holy Things and Holy Times

The ninth section of the book, which follows the summary statement in 21:24, contains two divine speeches to Moses: the first, in chap. 22, to be addressed to the priests and the second, in chap. 23, to be addressed to the general population.

22:1–33
The Holy Things and Priestly Responsibility

This entire chapter is devoted to instructions to the priests regarding their custody and care of the "holy things"—gifts and sacrifices—contributed by the people. The priests are warned that they must be scrupulous about such sacred things (v.2). The remainder of the chapter spells out how this is to be done.

The temporarily unclean priest was warned not to approach a holy thing (vv. 6–7). The placement of the regulation about not eating the flesh of animals that died or were killed in v. 8 could suggest that originally this regulation applied only to priests and was subsequently extended to the general population (see 17:15; and Ezek. 44:31). Priests are warned to be vigilant lest they incur guilt and be struck dead for their profanation (Lev. 22:9; see 10:1–2).

Verses 10–16 spell out who could eat the sacrifices presented to God. Only the priest's share of the sacrifice of well-being is discussed. A priest's entire household, including permanent slaves either purchased or born in his house, could eat of it. Excluded from consuming the sacrificial flesh were all native laypersons, temporary settlers attached to his household, hired servants, and any daughter married to a nonpriest (unless she was a childless divorcee or widow who had fully returned to the household of the father; vv. 10–14.) If an unqualified person accidentally ate of the sacrificial flesh, the uneaten portion had to be returned and a 20 percent penalty on the value of the sacrifice had to be paid (v. 14). Priests are reminded of their duty to avoid situations in which their irresponsibility could bring guilt on others (v. 15).

Verses 17–30 outline some of the criteria by which the priests evaluated the acceptability of sacrifices offered to fulfill vows or as freewill offerings. Burnt offerings so offered had to be males and had to be unblemished (vv. 19–23). Concession is made in the case of freewill offerings; they could have minor defects (v. 23). Genitally injured or castrated animals, even acquired from foreigners, could not be offered as sacrifice (vv. 24–25).

Firstborn animals (see Exod. 22:30) had to remain with their mother for at least seven days before being given to the Temple (Lev. 22:27). A mother and its offspring were not to be sacrificed on the same day (v. 28). This regulation, like Exod. 23:19b; 34:26b; and Deut. 14:21b, which prohibit cooking the young in its mother's milk, expresses horror at the unnecessary abnormality of such a practice (see also Deut. 22:6–7). The priests were held responsible for seeing that the people properly offered and properly consumed their thanksgiving sacrifices, the ones least under the supervision of the priesthood (Lev. 22:29–30).

The conclusion to chap. 22 admonishes the priests to remember that a goal of the cult was to manifest the holiness of God in the midst of the people (vv. 31–32a; see 10:3). As so frequently in this material, the redemption and election of the people of Israel are given as the motivating and obligating factors in obedience to the law (vv. 32b–33).

23:1–44
Holy Times and Sacred Seasons

Israel conceived of not only things (gifts, sacrifices, and "devoted" objects), persons (the priesthood and given and "devoted" individuals), and places (the sanctuary and its precincts), but also times as especially holy, dedicated to God, and belonging to the realm of the holy. These times are discussed in chap. 23 (see also Exod. 23:14–17; 34:18–24; Num. 28–29; Deut. 16:1–17).

23:3–4, The Sabbath. This seventh-day observance is discussed elsewhere in this volume (see Genesis, "Commentary," 2:3; Exodus, "Commentary," 16:22–30; 20:8–11; 23:12; 31:12–17; 35:1–3; Numbers, "Commentary," 15:32–36; Deuteronomy, "Commentary," 5:12–15). The nature of the Sabbath observance became the pattern for the especially sacred days in the calendar, namely, the first and seventh day of Unleavened Bread (Lev. 23:7–8), the Feast Day of Weeks (v. 21), and the first, tenth, fifteenth, and twenty-second of the seventh month (vv. 24, 27, 34–36).

23:4–8, Passover/*Pesach* and Unleavened Bread/*Matsot*. These celebrations are discussed elsewhere in this volume (see Exodus, "Commentary," 12:1–28; Deuteronomy, "Commentary," 16:1–8). Lev. 23:4–8 decrees that both the first (the fifteenth of the first month) and seventh days (the twenty-first of the first month) would be special days with Sabbath regulations applicable (cf. Deut. 16:8; → Passover, The).

23:9–14, First Sheaf/*'Omer Reshit*. Priestly legislation required that a sheaf of newly harvested grain (along with a special burnt offering) be presented to God before any of the new crop was eaten by the people. This sheaf was to be presented on "the day after the sabbath" (v. 11). The context would imply that the sheaf was presented on the sixteenth day of the first month, following the "Sabbath" day of no occupational work ("laborious work") on the fifteenth. This meant new grain could be eaten after the presentation.

23:15–21, Feast of Weeks/*Shavuot*. The day following seven weeks after "the day after the sabbath," or fifty days later, was the Feast of Weeks or Pentecost (cf. Deut. 16:9; → Pentecost).

23:22, Regard for the Poor at Harvest. Reference to reaping gave the Priestly writer occasion to comment on care for the poor (see 19:9–10).

23:23–25, The Day of Trumpet Blasts. The first day of the seventh month, later referred to as New Year's Day (Rosh Hashanah) was a "Sabbath" day. Since several days in the seventh month were sacred, the day the month was begun had to be clearly noted (→ New Year Festival).

23:26–32, Yom Kippur. (See commentary above on chap. 16.) The only new element noted here is the admonition to begin fasting on the ninth day in the evening.

23:33–36, Feast of Booths/*Sukkot*. This fall festival was the most important of the sacred occasions in early Israel. It concluded the old harvest year, looked forward to the new agricultural season, and marked the turn of the year, the transition from the old to the new. In early Israel, the festival was probably a three-day affair (see Hos. 6:1–3; Amos 4:4) that combined the features of Rosh Hashanah, Yom Kippur, and Booths (→ Tabernacles, Festival of).

23:37–38, Summary Statement. This section was apparently the original summary to the festival calendar of 23:4–36. Verses 1–3 and 39–43 appear to be insertions. The reference to the sacrifices of these holy times are spelled out in detail in Numbers 28–29.

23:39–43, Features of *Sukkot*. This appendix to the directions for *Sukkot* concerns the gathering of the *hadar* fruit (traditionally understood as the citron) and, according to tradition, the making of the *lulab*, a festive spray (v. 40). Both were used during the festival. A straightforward reading of the text suggests that the branches were collected for building booths (sukkot), impermanent shelters used in the fields at harvest time and then abandoned. Here the booths have been secondarily associated with life in the desert following the Exodus (vv. 42–43).

24:1–23
Oil, Bread, and Blasphemy

Part of this chapter reiterates and expands on material already presented in Exodus; it also contains the third narrative in Leviticus. The rationale for the ordering of the contents of chapter is not clear.

24:2–4, Oil for the Menorah. A similar passage (Exod. 27:20–21) occurs in the divine directions to Moses for building the Tabernacle and its furniture (→ Lampstand).

24:4–9, Bread for the Table. This unit expands on Exod. 25:23–30 and stipulates the conditions relating to the "showbread" placed on the table in the inner shrine: the number twelve and the size of the loaves, their arrangement on the table, the use of frankincense, the fact that they are gifts to God, the placement of new loaves by the high priest on the Sabbath, and the restriction of the consumption of the old loaves to the priests (→ Showbread).

24:10–23a, Blasphemy in the Camp. Three texts in the Torah in addition to this one report a condition in which Moses is uncertain of what action should be taken and must await divine direction (Num. 9:6–14; 15:32–36; and 27:1–11). All four cases involve the following features: first, an issue arises or an offense is committed; second, Moses is consulted but has no immediate verdict; third, after a time, God reveals to Moses what should be done; and fourth, the divine verdict is carried out or formulated as a binding legislative statement.

In Lev. 24:10–23, a male of mixed parentage (which seems to play no major role in the story) engaged in a fight committed blasphemy. The description of his act in v. 11 should be translated: "He pronounced the name cursing (Yahweh)." His crime thus consisted not just in using the personal name of the nation's God (Yahweh) but in cursing God with the use of this special name. The verdict decreed was death by public stoning after the witnesses had laid their hands on him, transferring to the culprit the consequence of having heard the curse (see commentary above on 16:21).

The formulation of the ruling in vv. 15b–16 includes the resident alien among those covered by the law against blasphemy (perhaps the reason the culprit is described as of mixed parentage).

In the final editing of this material, vv. 17–22 were incorporated although they are not intrinsically relevant to the case. Verses 17–18 and 21 affirm the death penalty for murder and equal compensation in the case of an animal's death. The latter ruling limits settlement in property damage totally to compensation.

25:1–26:46

The Land's Sabbath and the Jubilee—Blessings and Curses

These two chapters focus on the theme of the land, a central concern of the material in chaps. 18–26 (see 18:3–5, 24–30; 19:33–34; 20:22–26).

25:2–7, The Land's Sabbath. The interests of this text differ remarkably from other statements about the Sabbatical Year (see Exod. 21:1–11; 23:10–11; Deut. 15:1–18). Other texts are concerned primarily with the relationship of sabbatical regulations to the social order (→ Sabbatical Year). Lev. 25:2–7 is primarily concerned not with social ramifications but with the land itself. The land is to have a Sabbath, a period of freedom from human exploitation; it must experience complete rest, a "sabbath of the Lord" (v. 4). Normal agricultural pursuits were to be suspended and what grew of itself was not to be gathered in and treated under normal property regulations (vv. 4–6). Everyone, including slaves, resident aliens, and even beasts of the field, was to have access to what the land produced of its own (vv. 6–7).

25:8–17, The Jubilee. The function of the Jubilee was to redistribute the land to its original owners, so as to prevent the amassing of large estates and to retain the people's direct association with the land and their ownership of it (→ Jubilee).

The Jubilee was to be proclaimed on Yom Kippur after the passage of forty-nine years (vv. 8–9). Thus the "fiftieth" year was to begin on the tenth day of the seventh month of the forty-ninth year and probably included the remainder of that year. In that case, it was not in reality a fiftieth year. A general release was to be proclaimed in which one's holding was returned and all slaves and indentured servants were freed (v. 10). Since the period overlapped a Sabbatical Year, the same rules applied about people "eating" the land's yield directly from the field (vv. 11–12). Since property in such a system could not be sold, but in fact only leased and only for the time until the next Jubilee, transactions were stipulated to be based on this consideration (vv. 13–17).

25:18–24, Theological Underpinning. The theological rationale for these idealistic institutions (which, so far as is known, were never implemented) was that the land belonged to God; the Israelites were only his tenants. The landowner set the terms of tenancy: "the land shall not be sold in perpetuity" (v. 23).

25:25–28, The Poor and Their Property. A person forced to sell one's landholding had redemption (repurchase) rights if funds became available through a next of kin (a redeemer relative) or through one's own efforts.

25:29–34, Urban Property. Since the concern of the Jubilee was with farmland as a means of livelihood, only farm and village land was covered by the release (v. 31). Redemption rights on urban property were for only one year; thereafter the dwelling was considered sold in perpetuity (vv. 29–30). The exception to the urban property rule was the levitical cities (see Num. 35:1–8) where any Levite always possessed the right to redeem dwellings and where houses were to be returned in the Jubilee (vv. 32–33). Levites were not to trade the common land that went with their cities (v. 34).

25:35–55, Provisions for the Poor. Persons who became stricken with poverty were to be maintained by the community, although without property they would be like temporary settlers (attached to a native's household) or resident aliens, that is, without full rights (v. 35). Neither advanced nor accrued "shares" were to be taken of goods and materials supplied the poor, money was not to be lent at interest (see Ps. 15:5; Ezek. 18:8; Deut. 23:19–20), and food was not to be sold at a profit (Lev. 25:36–37; →Loan).

The poor who had to sell themselves into slavery to a native to pay debts were not to be treated as slaves, but as hired laborers or temporary residents. At the Jubilee, they and their children (one could not sell a wife) were to be released (vv. 39–40). Israelites were not to be sold as slaves on the open market, since they were all God's servants and ultimately divine property (v. 42). Israelites were allowed to buy non-natives as slaves, from both foreign nations and from non-natives living in their midst (vv. 44–45). These could be bequeathed in perpetuity to one's descendants (v. 46). Israelites who sold themselves to non-natives living in the land were to be sold with rights of full redemption and Jubilee release (vv. 47–55).

26:1–2, Reverence for God. Before the pronouncements of blessings and curses, the writer reports God as summarizing what reverence for him embodies. First, nothing should be constructed and venerated that replaces the Deity or stands between the divine and the people since only he is their God (v. 1). In all the Priestly legislation, only the sanctuary and the priesthood stand between the people and God. Second, the sacred seasons (the Sabbaths) set apart as holy must be observed. The ebb and flow of human time and the temporality of human existence must be intersected by sacred pauses that bear witness to the divine ordering of time and that manifest human submission to that ordering. Third, human life must be lived so as to avoid the impure, the unclean, and the sinful and their resulting contaminating pollutions and thus to show reverence for the divine sanctuary, the sacred space of God's presence (v. 2).

26:3–33, Blessings and Curses. Most treaties and law codes establishing patterns of relationships between parties in the ancient world concluded with the pronouncement of blessings as the reward for obedience and curses as the consequence of disobedience (see Exod. 23:20–33; Deut. 27–29). The blessings and curses in Lev. 26:3–38 once either concluded a covenant document or law code (chaps. 25–26; cf. 25:1; 26:46) or else were conceived along the lines of such a document (→ Covenant; Curse and blessing).

26:3–13, The Blessings. It is significant that the blessings occur as a list of ten: (1) "I will grant your rains on schedule" (v. 4); (2) "I will establish peace [Heb. *shalom*] in the land" (v. 6a); (3) "I will drive away the vicious beasts" (v. 6b); (4) "I will look favorably upon you" (v. 9a); (5) "I will make you fertile" (v. 9a); (6) "I will multiply you" (v. 9a); (7) "I will establish my covenant with [or keep my obligation to] you" (v. 9b); (8) "I will establish my dwelling place in your midst" (v. 11); (9) "I will travel along in your midst" (v. 12a); and (10) "I will be your God" (12a).

The consequences of the blessings are fertility, tranquility, safety, success in battle (even with *shalom* one still had enemies!), and the abiding, beneficent presence of the God who in bringing the people out of Egypt broke their burdensome yokes of servitude and allowed the people to stand upright and free (vv. 11–13).

26:14–33, The Curses. God's promised hostile action to be taken against his people for disobedience is correlated with the people's unwillingness either to obey the divine commands or to accept the curses as disciplinary and reformative. Both lack of obedience (vv. 14, 18) and deliberate opposition to God (vv. 21, 23, 27) are noted as the bases for divine oppression.

Again, it is significant that the number of first-person references is twenty-four ($= 2 \times 12$). This underscores the severity of the divine response to the people's continuing disobedience and obstinancy. The twenty-four divine actions are: (1) "I will wreak misery upon you" (v. 16a); (2) "I will look with disfavor on you" (v. 17a); (3) "I will chastise you" (v. 18); (4) "I will break your proud glory" (v. 19a); (5) "I will make the skies like iron and the earth like copper" (v. 19b); (6) "I will chastise you sevenfold" (v. 21); (7) "I will let loose wild animals against you" (v. 22); (8) "I will walk contrary to you" (v. 24a); (9) "I will smite you sevenfold" (v.24b); (10) "I will bring a sword against you" (v. 25a); (11) "I will send pestilence" (v. 25b); (12) "I will shatter your supply of bread" (v. 26); (13) "I will walk in hostility contrary to you" (v. 28a); (14) "I will personally chastise you sevenfold" (v. 28b); (15) "I will destroy your cult places" (v. 30a); (16) "I will cut down your incense stands" (v. 30a); (17) "I will heap up your carcasses on your broken fetishes" (v. 30a); (18) "my soul will abhor you" (v. 30b); (19) "I will lay your cities in ruin" (v. 31a); (20) "I will make your sanctuaries desolate" (v. 31a); (21) "I will not savor your pleasing [sacrificial] odors" (v. 31b); (22) "I will devastate the land" (v. 32); (23) "I will scatter you among the nations" (v. 33a); and (24) "I will unsheath the sword against you" (v. 33a).

26:34–38, The Land and People After Judgment. The sabbatical rest (see 25:2–7) that would be denied the land if the divine ordinances were not kept would be made up when

179

the people were exiled from the land so that it was left to lie desolate and untilled (vv. 34–35; see 2 Chron. 36:20–21).

26:39–45, Human Contrition and Divine Remembrance. In spite of the horrible curses, with their vision of devastated land and an exiled people, the material holds out hope for the future, a hope built on human contrition and repentance and on divine fidelity to the covenant.

The pattern of contrition on the part of those that survive the catastrophes is developed in the following stages. First, they shall feel heartbroken over their iniquities and the iniquities of their fathers (v. 39). Second, they shall confess these iniquities committed in their transgressions against God in walking contrary to divine will (v. 40). Third, they shall acknowledge that God walked contrary to them and brought them into exile in the land of their enemies (v. 41a). Fourth, when they have done these things, then they shall humble their stubborn hearts and, fifth, make up for their iniquities, atoning for their sins through living and suffering in the exile (vv. 41b, 43).

God promises that he shall then remember especially his covenant with Jacob but also the covenant with Isaac and Abraham and the land (v. 42). While the land makes up its Sabbaths and the people languish in exile atoning for their sins, God promises that he will neither completely destroy them nor finally annul his covenantal promise to award the land to their ancestors (vv. 43–45).

27:1–34
Evaluation and Desanctification of Holy Things

This chapter is only loosely integrated into the book of Leviticus and thus gives the appearance of an appendix. The incorporation of chap. 27, however, was used to bring the units in Leviticus to the number twelve and the number of divine speeches to thirty-six. This obvious editorial activity indicates that the separate books of the Torah were edited individually at their final stage.

This chapter concerns the evaluation and desanctification of persons and things given to God in various ways. Since they became "holy" as divine and sanctuary property, a person had to make special arrangements and payment to have the desanctifiable thing or person transferred out of the realm of the holy and back to the realm of the normal or clean.

Many things belonged to God according to divine ordinance; tithes, various sacrifices, the firstborn, and so on. These were given or passed over to God. Other things could be especially given to God through vows, dedications, and "devotion." Some of these items could be desanctified legitimately and others not (see commentary above on 5:14–19). The income from desanctification was apparently a significant source of funds for the sanctuary and its priesthood (see 2 Kings 12:5).

27:2–13, Holy Things from Vows. Vows were promises made contingent upon divine aid (see Gen. 28:20–22; 2 Sam. 15:7–12; Ps. 66:13–15) and could include the promise to give humans to God (Judg. 11:29–40). One who was ill, for example, might pledge the monetary worth of a person of a certain age if recovery occurred. When divine aid was received, for example, in a recovery from illness, then the promised vow was presented to God (→ Vow). This text does not discuss the actual giving of persons to God, but only the monetary equivalent.

Lev. 27:2–8 set the evaluations for humans along age and gender lines without regard for health or earning capabilites. Females were assessed at one-half, three-fifths, or two-thirds that of males (vv. 5, 3–4, 6, 7). Children under one month of age could not be vowed, probably due to their uncertain viability. For a poor person, the equivalency was set not according to the established scale of vv. 3–7, but by the priest according to the person's ability to pay (v. 8).

Vowed animals that were eligible to be sacrificed could not be redeemed, exchanged, or substituted; otherwise both the vowed and secondary animal became Temple property (vv. 9–10). Vowed animals unclean by nature or from condition that the Temple could not later use for sacrifice could be redeemed at the appraised value plus 20 percent (vv. 11–13).

27:14–25, Holy Things from Dedication. A person might dedicate ("set apart, make holy") real estate to God, either house (vv. 14–15) or land from inherited property (vv. 16–25). The priest made an assessment of the property's value. The value of land was calculated either according to the amount of seed required to plant it or according to its yield (v. 16; the meaning is unclear) and according to the date in relation to the Jubilee (vv. 17–18). Both house and land could be redeemed, if the donor had second thoughts, by paying the assessment plus 20 percent (vv. 15, 19). If one dedicated a portion of inherited land and did not redeem it, then the land became God's possession after the (unspecified) time of redemption passed. If one dedicated property that had already been sold, it passed into God's possession at the Jubilee. Either way the land was henceforth to be treated as "devoted" and thus nonredeemable (vv. 20–

180

21). One could dedicate a purchased field for the number of years remaining until the Jubilee and thereby dedicate the value of the harvests for that period (vv. 22–23a). Verse 23b may mean that the one dedicating a purchased field had to pay the total amount on the day of the appraisal, or that the priest set the annual evaluation once and for all on the day of dedication and that evaluation was paid during each of the years until the Jubilee. Dedicated purchased land was to revert to the original inheritor at the Jubilee (v. 24). (For v. 25, see commentary above on 6:6.)

27:26–27, Holy Things from Firstling. Since the firstborn belonged to God, these could not be dedicated (v. 26). A firstborn that was unclean could be redeemed since it was not eligible to be sacrificed to God (v. 27).

27:28–29, Holy Things from Devotion. Items vowed to God could be redeemed from or sold by the sanctuary unless they were animals that could be sacrificed. Devoted items, in contrast, were pledged and given to God without the possibility of redemption for sale (→Ban). In the Scriptures, things most often devoted (declared *cherem*) are materials and personnel captured in war (Num. 21:1–3; Deut.13:13–18; 1 Sam. 15:3). Devoted objects became Temple and priestly property ("most holy") or else were destroyed (Num. 18:14; 21:2–3). Lev. 27:28 describes the "devotion" of property under nonmilitary conditions and classifies it as nonredeemable and nonsalable. Since it was most holy, anyone appropriating the "devoted" thing also became "devoted" and was to be put to death (v. 29; Deut. 7:25–26: Josh. 7:10–26).

27:30–33, Holy Things from Tithes. Tithes belonged to God, but grain and fruit tithes could be redeemed at their appraised value plus 20 percent. Verse 32 contains one of the few biblical references to tithes from the herds and flocks (see 2 Chron. 31:6), presumably required in addition to the firstlings (see Deut. 14:22–28). The choice of the animal tithe is depicted as occurring arbitrarily—every tenth animal passing under the shepherd's staff.

Bibliography

Bailey, L. R. *Leviticus*. Knox Preaching Guides. Atlanta, GA: John Knox, 1987.

Bamburger, B. J. "Leviticus." In *The Torah: A Modern Commentary*. Edited by W. G. Plaut. New York: Union of American Hebrew Congregations, 1981.

Levine, B. *In the Presence of the Lord: A Study of Cult and Some Cultic Terms in Ancient Israel*. Studies in Judaism in Late Antiquity, 5. Leiden: Brill, 1974.

Milgrom, J. *Studies in Cultic Theology and Terminology*. Studies in Judaism in Late Antiquity, 36. Leiden: Brill, 1976.

Wenham, G. T. *The Book of Leviticus*. New International Commentary on the Old Testament. Grand Rapids, MI: Eerdmans, 1979.

NUMBERS

D E N N I S T. O L S O N

INTRODUCTION

The Book of Numbers is the fourth book of the OT. Numbers derives its name from the census lists of the number of people in each of the twelve tribes of Israel in Numbers 1 and 26. The Hebrew title for the book, "In the Wilderness," comes out of the first verse of the book and accurately describes its setting. Numbers is the story of the people of Israel in the wilderness as they travel toward the promised land of Canaan.

Issues in Critical Study

The most distinctive feature of the book of Numbers is its great variety of literary forms and topics. The book includes stories and laws, travel itineraries and census lists, lists of personal names and lists of instructions for worship, reports of military battles and accounts of legal disputes. This variety has led scholars to study the book from a number of different perspectives.

Critical study of Numbers has uncovered the existence of separate literary sources or layers that have been woven together. These sources or traditions are usually termed J for the Yahwist, E for the Elohist, and P for the Priestly traditions (→ Sources of the Pentateuch). In general, it is agreed that the J and E sources tend to be earlier layers and are concentrated in Numbers 11–25. There is some disagreement on the extent to which the earlier J and E traditions can be isolated from one another. The later Priestly material, while scattered throughout the book, is most in evidence in chaps. 1–10 and chaps. 26–36. It is generally agreed that supplementary material was added to the book sometime after the inclusion of the Priestly tradition.

Study of the book of Numbers has also involved attempts to reconstruct the original oral forms and traditions that preceded the writing of the literary sources. Attention has been focused on the twelve-tribe system; the ordering of the camp of Israel in Numbers 2; the traditions about the Levites in chaps. 3–4; the wilderness murmuring traditions in chaps. 11, 12, 13, 14, 16, 17, 21, and 25; the Balaam cycle in Numbers 22–24; and the allocation of the land in chaps. 26 and 34. Those interested in historical issues in ancient Israel have focused their attention on such problems as the early conquest traditions in Numbers 13, 14, 21, and 32; the levitical cities in chap. 35; the development of the Israelite priesthood in Numbers 16–17; and the census lists in chaps. 1 and 26. Numbers has also provided an important source for the understanding of OT law, particularly in regard to ritual, festival, and purity laws (Num. 5–9, 15, 19, 27, and 36).

It is clear that the relative age and subject matter of the materials that make up the present book of Numbers are enormously varied. Some of the traditions have their roots in the actual tribal community of ancient Israel. For example, it is probable that the lists of the twelve tribes of Israel in the census lists in chaps. 1 and 26 derived in part from tribal genealogies in ancient Israel. Before the rise of the monarchy in the tenth century B.C., these genealogies played a sociopolitical role in unifying the diverse tribes that made up Israel. These tribal lists or genealogies have now been significantly reshaped for theological purposes into census lists in the present form of the book. The Balaam oracles in Numbers 22–24 provide an example of ancient Hebrew poetry from the earliest times in Israel's history. Yet the oracles also show evidence of having been reshaped and edited over a long period of time. The original age of much of the remaining material in Numbers is difficult to determine because it has been taken out of its original social or historical setting and placed within the present unified theological portrayal of the wilderness wandering of the Israelites from the area surrounding Mount Sinai to the eastern edge of the promised land. It is clear, however, that the material in Numbers has originated and been shaped in many different periods, ranging from the earliest to the latest times in Israel's history.

It is probable that the definitive shaping of the book of Numbers in roughly its present form occurred sometime during the Babylonian exile (587–538 B.C.). The Jewish community in exile struggled to understand its relationship to God and the promised land in light of the crisis of being driven out of the land. But the definitive structure of the book of Numbers seeks also to address every new succeeding generation of God's people as a generation standing in hope on the edge of the promised land. The new wilderness generation that is poised on the threshold of entering the land of Canaan functions as a paradigm for every new generation of God's people.

Overarching Framework

The central problem in the interpretation of the book of Numbers has been the failure to detect a convincing and meaningful structure for the book as a whole. Numerous interpreters lament the difficulty of determining any coherent structure or outline for the book of Numbers. This perception of haphazard arrangement and incoherence has caused Numbers to be one of the least studied and appreciated books of the Bible. In contrast to Numbers, the structure and story line of Genesis, Exodus, and Leviticus is fairly clear. The book of Genesis moves from "the generations of the heavens and the earth" (Gen. 2:4) at creation through the generations of the ancestors of Israel. Exodus and Leviticus tell the story of the generation that experienced the Exodus out of Egypt and the events and laws associated with Mount Sinai. If we jump over Numbers for a moment to the book of Deuteronomy which follows, we see that Deuteronomy is composed of Moses' last words to another new generation of Israelites who had not experienced the Exodus or Sinai events. But how did that new generation appear? How and where was that transition made from the old generation of the Exodus and Sinai to the new generation of God's people on the edge of the promised land in the book of Deuteronomy?

That important transition is made precisely in the book of Numbers. In fact, the transition from the old generation of the wilderness to the new generation of hope and promise on the edge of the promised land forms the primary structure and theme for the book of Numbers as a whole. This structure is marked by the two census lists of the twelve tribes of Israel in Numbers 1 and 26. The census lists divide the book into two halves.

The first census list in Numbers 1 introduces the first half of the book, which includes chaps. 1–25. This first half of Numbers recounts the eventual death of the old generation of God's people out of Egypt as they march in the wilderness toward the promised land. The death of this old generation who had experienced the Exodus and Sinai events is precipitated by the people's continued rebellion against God, coming to a climax in the spy story in chaps. 13–14.

The second census list in Numbers 26 introduces the second half of the book, which includes chaps. 26–36. This second half of the book recounts the emergence of a new generation of God's people as they prepare to enter the promised land. The theme of this part of Numbers is not rebellion and death, but new life and hope. This overarching structure of the death of the old generation and the birth of a new generation of hope provides the interpretive framework for the other varied contents of the book of Numbers.

Importance

The later traditions of both the Jewish and the Christian communities have underscored the continuing importance and relevance of the book of Numbers. The apostle Paul in the NT Letter of 1 Corinthians recounts the story of the wilderness generation in Numbers as an example that ought to apply to his readers: "Now these things happened to them as a warning, but they were written down for our instruction" (1 Cor. 10:11, RSV). The Jewish community continued its interpretation of the book through the *Midrash Sipre* on Numbers and the Talmud, which focused in large part on the legal material within the book. The Aaronidic benediction or blessing that is an integral part of both Jewish and Christian worship services comes from Num. 6:22–27. The key importance of the book, however, remains the inclusion of Numbers as part of Scripture for both Jews and Christians. The book wrestles with the transition from the old generation to the new generation. How is faith transferred from one generation to another? How does the story of a generation of the past become the story of a present generation? These are some of the central questions Numbers addresses.

COMMENTARY

1:1–25:18

The Death of the Old Generation

The first half of Numbers recounts the fate of the old generation of Israelites who had been eyewitnesses to the Exodus out of Egypt and the revelation of God on Mount Sinai. The beginning of this first generation was marked by a census list in Exodus 1 with seventy people counted among the twelve tribes of Israel (Exod. 1:5). The new census list of the twelve tribes of Israel that appears in Numbers 1 marks a major transition in the people's wandering. They have been liberated from the bondage of Egypt. They have received God's commandments and entered into a covenant with God at Sinai. Now with Numbers 1, this generation that is the first to have come out of Egypt is ready to organize and begin its march in earnest toward the promised land of Canaan.

Initially, the members of this old wilderness generation appear obedient as God organizes them into a holy military camp. This obedience and positive tone, is, however, marred by a number of rebellions against God by the Israelites. These rebellions constitute a resumption of the series of rebellions that take place already in Exodus 16, 17, and 32. The most serious rebellion is portrayed in the spy story in Numbers 13–14 in which the people refuse to trust God to lead them into the land of Canaan. This rebellion of the people provides the basis for God's judgment of death on the old generation and his promise of hope to the new generation to follow.

1:1–10:36
The Preparation and Inauguration of the March of the Holy People of Israel

This section of Numbers is dominated by a positive tone. The people of Israel obediently follow God's instructions to prepare for the march from Sinai to the promised land. The people of the twelve tribes of Israel are counted in a census and then organized into a four-sided military camp with three tribes on each side. Laws are given that preserve the holiness of the camp. The people obediently prepare for a holy war against the native inhabitants of the promised land. These preparations for the journey through the wilderness make up Num. 1:1–10:10.

This section prepares for the march of the people through the wilderness. Then Num. 10:11–10:36 recounts the actual inauguration of the march and the events of the first three days. The holy camp sets out for the first time from the Wilderness of Sinai to the Wilderness of Paran. The first three days of the journey occur without incident. All seems to be proceeding smoothly.

1:1–54, The Census of the Twelve Tribes. The book of Numbers begins with the people situated in the Wilderness of Sinai fourteen months after the Exodus out of Egypt. God commands Moses to take a census of the twelve tribes of Israel. The census is not to be of all the people but only of the males who are over twenty years of age who are able to go to war (1:2–3). One person from each tribe is chosen to supervise the census (1:4–16). The results of the census for the twelve tribes are given in 1:20–46, with a grand total of 603,550 males over twenty years of age. The emphasis of this first census in Numbers is on the number of fighting men who are available for combat. In light of the goal of the promised land, this census is a preparation for the entry and conquest of Canaan.

The census in Numbers 1 is the first census of the people since leaving Egypt. The only previous full-scale census of the twelve tribes of Jacob occurred at the end of Genesis 46 and

lists the sons of Jacob and their offspring as numbering seventy people. The book of Exodus begins by repeating this list of the sons of Jacob or Israel and the number of their families as seventy persons. Exod. 1:6–7 then reports the death of Joseph and "all his brothers and all that generation" as well as the emergence of a new and greatly expanded generation. This census at the beginning of Exodus marks an entirely new generation as well as a major transition from a state of blessing and prosperity to slavery and oppression (Exod. 1:11).

The Census Lists in Numbers 1 and 26

Two separate critical issues are involved in the study of the census lists in Numbers 1 and 26: the lists of the names of the twelve tribes of Israel and the high numbers reported in the census lists.

The earliest version of the names of the twelve tribes of Israel is given in 1:5–15, in which the tribal leaders are chosen to carry out the census. The names of the tribes occur in the following order: Reuben (the oldest son and thus the first tribe listed), Simeon, Judah, Issachar, Zebulun, Ephraim, Manasseh, Benjamin, Dan, Asher, Gad, and Naphtali. Other lists of the twelve tribes occur in 1:20–43; 2:3–31; 7:12–83; 10:14–28; 13:4–15; and 26:5–51.

It is probable that these tribal lists in Numbers are dependent upon even earlier versions of the twelve-tribe list in the book of Genesis, most notably the narrative of the twelve sons of Jacob in Gen. 29:31–30:24. This genealogical story about the birth of the twelve tribal ancestors is rooted in a time in Israel's history when the tribal genealogy functioned to unify the society, since there was no king or other centralized government. With the rise of kings in Israel, the genealogical lists of the twelve tribes lost this sociopolitical function. The genealogies were then taken into the religious sphere and used in the emerging literary tradition to express the ideal Israel.

A second issue connected with the census lists in Num. 1:20–43 and 26:5–51 is the high numbers of people counted in the census for the twelve tribes. Num. 1:46 gives a total of 603,550 Israelite males over twenty years of age in the first generation in Numbers. Num. 26:51 states a total of 601,730 for the second generation. The enormous size of the numbers has often struck commentators as amazing or impossible. How could the tiny clan that began in Exodus 1 with the census list of seventy persons swell to over 600,000 fighting men plus women and children and the elderly in the course of a few hundred years?

Many solutions have been offered. Some have suggested a possible alternate meaning for the Hebrew word for "thousand" as a "tent-group." For example, the tribe of Reuben is counted in Num. 1:20–21 as forty-six "thousand," five hundred. The number could, however, be translated as forty-six "tent-groups" with a total of five hundred people. This would significantly reduce the numbers in each of the tribes. While this and other proposed solutions may be possible, it is clear that the present form of the text intends these figures to be taken as they stand as "thousands" and not "tent-groups."

In any case, the high numbers in the census lists are difficult to reconcile historically. Their present role in the book of Numbers, however, seems in part to serve a broader theological purpose. The numbers appear to express the extent to which God has graciously blessed Israel in multiplying their descendants to such large numbers. God's promises to Abraham of innumerable descendants (Gen. 15:5; 17:4–8) are certainly in view. The emergence of the new generation in Egypt that "increased greatly" and "grew exceedingly strong" (Exod. 1:5–7) is part of this same theological concern to underscore God's faithfulness to his promises. The large number of fighting men counted in Numbers 1 also ought to be grounds for great confidence as the Israelites near the border of the promised land. The spy story in chaps. 13–14 will show, however, that the people will fail to have confidence and will not trust God to bring them into the land. In short, the problem of the historicity of the numbers is important, but it should not cause us to lose sight of the theological message that the census numbers convey within the present form of Numbers and the Pentateuch.

2:1–34, The Holy Camp Prepared for the March to the Promised Land.

Numbers 1 relates the number of people in the tribes of Israel. Chap. 2 specifies the arrangement of the camp by which this large community of tribes is to travel through the wilderness. The camp is arranged in concentric circles of holiness, for it is a holy war in the promised land of Canaan for which God is preparing his people. Verse 2 indicates that the tent of meeting where God meets Moses and speaks to him stands at the center of the camp (→ Tabernacle). The Levites, who are a tribe especially set aside to serve in important priestly functions, are also situated in the center of the camp around the tent of meeting (v. 17; →Levites). The holiness of the Levites is protected by the provision for a special and separate census in chaps. 3–4.

Numbers 2 continues by describing the arrangement of the other twelve tribes around the center of the camp occupied by the tent of meeting and the Levites. The three tribes headed by the tribe of Judah (Judah, Issachar, Zebulun) are placed on the east side of the camp and thus lead the march (vv. 3–9). The group led by Reuben (Reuben, Simeon, Gad) forms the south flank of the camp and sets out in second place (vv. 10–16). The tent of meeting and the Levites at the center of the camp are designated as the next group to set out (v. 17). The west side of the camp includes the three tribes led by Ephraim (Ephraim, Manasseh, Benjamin) that are next in line (vv. 18–24). The fourth group of three tribes led by Dan (Dan, Asher, Naphtali) sets out last (vv. 25–31).

This almost monotonous recitation of the tribal groups in the camp serves to create an atmosphere of careful and meticulous obedience to God's commands. The final verse in chap. 2 hammers the point home: every member of every family of the people of Israel did as God commanded (v. 34). The impression is given of an eager and obedient people encamped and ready for God's holy war in the promised land. The sense of readiness and expectation begins to rise.

3:1–4:49, The Special Census of the Levites.

Numbers 3 opens with an important generational formula: "These are the generations of Aaron and Moses." The book of Genesis contains eleven of these generational formulas, beginning with Gen. 2:4a ("These are the generations of the heavens and the earth") and extending through Gen. 37:2 ("These are the generations of Jacob"). These generational formulas function as the primary overarching structure of the book of Genesis in its present form. A later editor has probably added the generational formula in Num. 3:1 after those in Genesis were already in place. Num. 3:1, however, now extends the overarching generational framework from Genesis into the present form of the book of Numbers. The formula also serves to reinforce the linkage of Numbers with the generations of Genesis that was already evident in the connection of the census lists in Numbers with the tribal genealogies in Genesis.

Apart from their function as the primary framework or structure for the book of Genesis, the generational formulas also function in two other ways. On one hand, some of the genealogies recount several generations, mentioning only one ancestor in each generation (e.g., Gen. 5:1–32, from Adam to Noah). These vertical or linear genealogies serve to narrow the focus of the line of promise down to a smaller and more exclusive group. The progression begins with "the generations of the heavens and the earth" (Gen. 2:4a) and with "the generations of Adam" (Gen. 5:1) but then quickly narrows its focus down to "the generations of Jacob" (Gen. 37:2). Placing the generational formula "These are the generations of Aaron and Moses" at the end of this progression in Num. 3:1 serves to narrow the focus of the narrative even further to one group within the tribes of Jacob or Israel: the priests and the Levites who are the generations of Aaron and Moses. The line of the promise is concentrated on an ever smaller group of people. The arrangement of the camp in Numbers 2 further underscores the narrowing of the focus as the priests and Levites occupy the center of the camp.

On the other hand, the generational formulas in Genesis sometimes also introduce horizontal or segmented genealogies, which usually have a depth of only two or three generations with several members of each generation mentioned (e.g., the children of the three sons of Noah in Gen. 10:1–31). These segmented genealogies in Genesis keep the broader arena of the cosmos and the other peoples of the world in view. Israel exists within a wider world and in the context of many peoples. The people of God are not alone but live within the framework and for the sake of the larger human community (Gen. 12:1–3). This inclusive motif is continued in the book of Numbers as well. The census list of the twelve tribes as well as the numerous other lists of the twelve tribes of Israel remind readers that the priests and Levites, "the generations of Aaron and Moses," do not exist in isolation. Rather, the priests and Levites live and work within the context of the larger community of God's people.

Thus, the dual perspective of a narrowing focus within the broader context of humanity that is evident in the generational formulas and genealogies in Genesis has been extended by a later editor into the book of Numbers. The more narrow focus on the priests and Levites (3:1) is counterbalanced by a concern to include all Israel within the purview of God's concern. The census list of all twelve tribes in chap. 1 maintains the inclusive dimension. It continues the story of "the generations of Jacob" (Gen. 37:2). The census list of the Levites in Numbers 3–4 carries the narrowing of the focus begun in Genesis one more step to "the generations of Aaron and Moses" that includes the representatives of priestly, levitical, and Mosaic offices in Israel (Num. 3:1).

These two concurrent emphases of exclusion and inclusion, of narrowing and broadening, are also evident in the account of the census of the Levites. Two different numberings of the Levites are actually prescribed in Numbers 3–4. The census in chap. 3 is to include every male Levite over the age of one month (3:15). The context that surrounds this census of the Levites in chap. 3 emphasizes the Levites' role as a substitute for all the firstborn

of the Israelites who rightfully belong to God. Thus, the purpose of the census in chap. 3 is to check whether the number of Levites corresponds with the number of firstborn children in the other tribes. The results show that the number of Levites falls short of the total number of firstborn Israelites. These extra Israelites are then to be redeemed by another method: the payment of money (3:44–51). The Levites serve on behalf of and for the sake of the larger community of all the twelve tribes of Israel. This stresses the broader or inclusive character of the mission of the Levites.

The second levitical census in Numbers 4 includes only those male Levites between the ages of thirty and fifty years old (4:2–3). The context of this census deals with the Levites' role in the service and maintenance of the tent of meeting. The Levites are to serve the sons of Aaron who are the high priests in the worship life of the tabernacle (3:5–10). Therefore, the Levites serve both the larger community of Israel and also the more exclusive group of Aaron and his sons. The duties of each of the families of Levites are delineated in chap. 4. Again, the impression is left of an obedient people and priesthood preparing for the march through the wilderness (4:49).

5:1–6:21, Laws for Preserving the Holiness of the Camp—Ritual Impurity, Suspected Adultery, and Nazirite Vows. The preparations for the inauguration of the march continue with provisions for dealing with those within the camp who are considered impure or unclean. The requirement of purity or cleanness is an important concept in the OT. Purity meant being free from any physical, moral, or ritual contamination. Contamination resulted from such things as the contact with a corpse, the involuntary flow of fluids from the sexual organs, a skin disease usually translated incorrectly in English versions as "leprosy," or the eating of prohibited foods (→ Purity).

The existence of unclean or impure individuals within the holy camp with God and the priests at the center constituted an affront to God and a threat to the well-being of the community. Numbers 5–6 provides instructions for dealing with the danger of impurity. These chapters are a composite of various laws and supplements that were added at a later stage in the composition of the book. Num. 5:3 instructs the people to put those who are unclean outside the camp since God is in the midst of the camp. Num. 5:4 records the people's obedient response to God's command.

Chap. 5 continues by turning from a concern to preserve the community's relationship with God to a concern to maintain harmonious relationships among the people within the community. Verses 5–10 mandate that a person who sins against a neighbor must confess the wrongdoing and make full restitution plus 20 percent of the total loss. This corresponds to the law in Lev. 6:5. Numbers goes on, however, to consider a case not addressed in Leviticus, namely, when the person wronged is dead and has no relatives. In such a case, the priest is to receive the restitution.

Num. 5:11–31 continues the concern to maintain harmony within the community and to uncover any acts that endanger the purity of the community. A trial by ordeal is prescribed for a woman suspected of adultery. The concern is both to unmask a hidden sin and to vindicate one who is unjustly accused. The woman is to come to the priest at the sanctuary, drink a mixture of water and dust (v. 17), and take an oath (vv. 19:22). The result of the ritual will determine whether she is innocent or guilty of the breach of the marriage relationship. Such trials by ordeal were used in the ancient Near East in legal cases in which direct evidence and eyewitness accounts were lacking. The whole community was in danger as long as a judgment about the alleged wrongdoing was not made.

Num. 6:1–21 further elaborates the concern for maintaining the holiness of the camp. These verses address the Nazirites, those laypeople within the community who have been set aside as expecially holy to God through commitments to abstinence from alcohol, uncut hair, and avoidance of contact with the dead (→ Nazirites). Num. 6:1–8 clarifies the nature of the Nazirite vows. Verses 9–12 make provisions for remedying the accidental violation of Nazirite vows through contact with the dead. The ordinary layperson could be cleansed from such contamination by washing in a special mixture prescribed in chap. 19. The special instructions for cleansing that are prescribed for the Nazirites in Numbers 6 underscore their exceptional holiness. Verses 13–21 detail a ritual for terminating the Nazirite vow; this implies that the vows were to be of limited duration. Any commitment to the holy God of Israel, whether by a priest or a Nazirite, was to be taken with the utmost seriousness and discipline for it impinged on the holiness of the whole community.

6:22–27, The Priestly Blessing of the Community.

These verses are perhaps the best known of the whole book of Numbers. They record the words of God's blessing that the priests are to pronounce over the congregation. This blessing continues to be used as part of the worship services of many different Christian and Jewish traditions.

The blessing is couched in poetic Hebrew style and is probably one of the oldest portions of Scripture. The elevated style is suggested by the parallelism and expansion of thought and words. In Hebrew, the first line of the blessing in v. 24 consists of three words, the second line of five words, and the third line of seven words. Each line in turn consists of two clauses. The Lord (Yahweh) is explicitly named as subject in the first clause of each of the three lines. That the Lord is the source of blessing is emphasized again in the closing statement in v. 27 in which God says, "I will bless them." The "I" is emphatic in the Hebrew.

The first line of the blessing in v. 24 speaks of God's blessing and keeping. Blessing refers to God's gifts of posterity, land, health, the presence of God, and all other things that make life possible and full (Deut. 28:2–14). God's keeping of his people involves guarding and protecting from evil (Ps. 121:7–8). The second line of the blessing in Num. 6:25 uses the metaphor of light to refer to God's face as it shines benevolently upon God's people. This shining of God's face results in his being gracious and delivering the people in times of trouble (Ps. 67:1).

The third line of the blessing in Num. 6:26 brings the blessing to a crescendo. The Aaronidic blessing moves from the general blessing of the first line to the shining of God's face in the second line to the active movement of God to lift up his face and send blessing and grace specifically toward the people. The goal of God's blessing is summed up by the final word of the benediction, Hebrew *shalom* or "peace." *Shalom* refers to more than simply the absence of conflict. It encompasses all of God's good gifts of health, prosperity, well-being, and salvation.

This richly worded blessing comes at the end of the section in chaps. 5–6 that is concerned about the holiness and well-being of the entire community. It highlights God's ultimate will for all the people as one of blessing and peace. The Aaronidic benediction stands as an affirming centerpiece in this opening section of Numbers, which is overwhelmingly positive in its tone. God is blessing the community, and the people are obediently and eagerly following his commands.

7:1–89, The Offerings of the Twelve Tribes for the Altar.

The portrait of an obedient people continues in Numbers 7. In thankful response to God's establishment of the priesthood and promise of blessing (6:22–27), the people bring offerings for the dedication of the altar. Num. 7:1–9 recounts the offering of oxen and wagons that will enable the Levites to transport the altar and tent of meeting on the march toward the promised land. Verses 10–88 are a repetitive account of the offerings for the altar brought by each of the twelve tribes of Israel on each of twelve consecutive days. The amount and type of offering are exactly the same for each tribe. The careful repetition underscores the unanimous and strong support for the tabernacle and its priesthood. Every tribe has an equal and strong commitment to the worship of God.

Num. 7:89 is probably a later insertion. In its present context, the verse affirms the sanctuary as the true locus of God's presence and revelation. The community's commitment to the support of God's sanctuary and priesthood and his revelation at the tent of meeting in the preceding verses is part of the ongoing dialogue between God and the people. God is shown to be faithful to his promise to be present in the midst of his people, and the people are shown to be obedient in their response. This image of God's speaking to Moses in the tent of meeting that is now located at the center of the camp (chap. 2) is in contrast with the scene in Exod. 33:7–11. There the grave sin of the golden calf necessitated locating the tent of meeting not in the middle but on the outside of the camp. Here in Numbers the tent of meeting has been restored to the center, and the holiness of God's people has been reestablished.

8:1–26, The Obedient Response of Aaron and the Levites. The meticulous obedience of the people in Numbers 7 is followed by evidence of the obedience of Aaron and the Levites. In 8:1–4, God commands Aaron to light the seven lamps in the sanctuary and to ensure that the light beamed forward in front of the lampstand. Verse 3 states that Aaron did exactly as God commanded; v. 4 again underscores Aaron's obedience in constructing the lampstand. The details for the lampstand's design are given in Exod. 25:31–40. The lampstand or menorah is shaped into a flowering tree with seven branches and symbolizes the life-giving power and light of God's presence (→ Lampstand).

The next section (Num. 8:5–26) tells of the dedication ceremony for the Levites as the substitutes for the firstborn of Israel. Numbers 3, 4, and 7 described the census of the Levites, their duties in caring for the sanctuary and its furnishings, and the gift of oxen and wagons for transporting the sanctuary. All that is now required is the official dedication of the Levites to their tasks. The ceremony is a sign that the actual inauguration of the march of the holy camp of Israel is soon about to take place.

The Levites' dual roles as servants of Aaron and his sons (v. 19) and as substitutes for firstborn of Israel (v. 16) are again stated. Verse 17 traces the consecration of the firstborn back to God's slaying of all the firstborn of Egypt (Exod. 13:2, 15). This reference to the Exodus out of Egypt opens up the way to Numbers 9 and its reference to the celebration of the Passover.

Again, however, the stress in Numbers 8 is placed on the obedience of Moses and Aaron and the people in dedicating the Levites to God's service (v. 20). Emphasis is also placed on the obedient service of the Levites in doing what God commanded through Moses (v. 22). The chapter closes with the age requirements for the Levites' service in the tent of meeting. They are to begin at twenty-five and retire at fifty years of age. Num. 4:47 presents a different age range for the Levites—from thirty to fifty years of age. There is no obvious reason for the discrepancy, apart from a difference of tradition.

9:1–14, The Celebration of the Second Passover. We move from the obedience of the priests and Levites in chap. 8 to the obedience of all the people in chap. 9. That obedience is expressed in the celebration of the most important festival in Israel, the Passover (→ Passover, The). The first Passover in Exodus 12 had been the prelude to a new beginning in the Exodus out of Egypt. This second Passover signals the reconstitution of Israel after the golden calf debacle had endangered their status as God's holy people. This second Passover in Numbers marks as radical a new beginning as the first Passover in Exodus. Verses 4–5 pick up the characteristic theme of the opening chapters of Numbers: the people obediently follow the words that God speaks to them through Moses.

The subject of the Passover provides an occasion for a legal decision regarding cases in which a person is unable to observe the festival at the appointed time. Two possible situations are raised. What if someone comes in contact with the dead and is thereby rendered unclean? Is the Passover of such importance that the unclean person should still observe the festival on the appointed day—the fourteenth day of the first month (vv. 6–7)? And what if someone is on a journey during the appointed time of the celebration of Passover (v. 10)? God decrees that a special supplemental Passover on the fourteenth day of the *second* month should be observed by those unable to observe the festival on the fourteenth day of the *first* month (9–11). This concession should not, however, be construed as a license for laxity in keeping the Passover (v. 13). As a matter of fact, the festival is so important that it should be observed even by the foreigners who live among the Israelites.

It has been argued that the two dates for the Passover, with one in the first month of the year and the other in the second, represent two different traditions, one from northern Israel and the other from the south. The story of Hezekiah's Passover in 2 Chron. 30:1–3 may be a hint of such divergent traditions. In any case, the traditions have now been reshaped to emphasize the importance of the festival and the people's careful observance in obedience to God's command.

9:15–23, God's Guidance Through the Cloud and the People's Obedient Following.

This section carries forward the theme of Israel's obedient following and is a sign of the imminent beginning of the march from Sinai to Canaan. The image of God's presence in the cloud and its association with the tent of meeting here in Numbers appears to be a reshaping of the traditions found in Exodus. In Exod. 13:21–22, the cloud is shaped as a pillar that goes in front of the people and guides them in the Exodus out of Egypt after the celebration of the first Passover. Just as the cloud marked a new chapter in Israel's life in the Exodus, so too the appearance of the cloud motif after the second Passover in Numbers 9 signals a major new transition in the life of the people. The march toward the promised land after the reorganization of the holy camp is about to commence.

The cloud in Num. 9:15–23, however, does not go in front of the people as it did in Exod. 13:21–22. Rather, in accord with the tradition in Exod. 33:7–11, the cloud is closely tied with the tent of meeting or tabernacle, which in Numbers 9 stands in the middle of the camp. In Exodus 33, the tent of meeting was located outside of the camp because the sin of the golden calf had rendered the community unclean. In Numbers 9, however, the tent of meeting has been restored to the camp's center and with it the cloud as a sign of God's presence and guidance.

The central theme of this section and of all the opening chapters of Numbers is sounded in a refrain repeated three times (vv. 18, 20, and 21): "At the word of the LORD the people of Israel set out, and at the word of the LORD they made camp." These and other verses in this section contain a chorus of affirmations of Israel's diligent obedience in following God's instructions.

10:1–10, The Signal of the March Soon to Begin—The Silver Trumpets.

The role of the cloud and God's leading of the people in Numbers 9 is complemented by the leadership and guidance provided by the sons of Aaron through the blowing of the silver trumpets. Verse 2 suggests two functions for the trumpets. One is to summon the congregation to a gathering. When both trumpets are blown, the whole congregation is to assemble at the tent of meeting (v. 3). When only one trumpet is blown, only the leaders are to gather at the tent (v. 4). A provision that may have been added secondarily establishes the procedure for calling the people together when they come to the promised land. A special alarm signal would gather the people at times of war. The trumpets would also summon the people at times of religious festivals as a remembrance of God's faithfulness (vv. 9–10). This first function lifts readers' attention for a moment to the future goal of the march—life in the promised land.

The second function for the trumpets turns readers' attention back to the immediate context. The trumpets are a signal of the time for breaking camp and the inauguration of the march. The sound of the trumpets gives notice to the twelve tribes to move out according to the order assigned in the arrangement of the camp in chap. 2 (10:5–6). This latter function points to the beginning of the march that is to begin immediately in 10:11.

10:11–36, The Actual Inauguration of the March of the Holy Camp of Israel.

At long last, the camp of the twelve tribes of Israel begins its climactic march from the Wilderness of Sinai toward the promised land. The preparations for the march that were designed to maintain the purity and holiness of the camp have been elaborate and meticulous. The plodding and repetitive style of the narrative in Numbers thus far creates in readers a sense of impatience and anticipation of this moment when the camp finally picks up and moves. "They set out for the first time at the word of the LORD through Moses" (v. 13).

According to v. 11, the tribes set out nineteen days after the day that the census was taken (Num. 1:1) and eleven months after arriving at Mount Sinai (Exod. 19:1). Num. 10:14–28 indicates that the tribes begin the march precisely in the order prescribed in chap. 2. The Levites obediently carry out their tasks of taking down the tabernacle and transporting it in accordance with the instructions in chap. 3.

Num. 10:29–32 is typically thought to be from a much older narrative tradition than any of the previous material in Numbers. The mention of Hobab as the father-in-law of Moses in v. 29 raises problems, since the name of Moses' father-in-law in Exod. 3:1 is Jethro. Hobab may simply be an alternate name for Jethro from a different tradition, or the Hebrew term for "father-in-law" may have here the wider meaning of "a relative by marriage." Moses asks Hobab to be a guide for Israel, since he is of the desert tribe of the Midianites and thus well acquainted with the wilderness. Initially, Hobab refuses, but Moses insists and promises that God will be as gracious to him, a foreigner, as he will be to Israel (vv. 30–32). Hobab's response was presumably positive (see Judg. 1:16; 4:11).

The mention of a human guide in Hobab is balanced in the verses that follow by a reaffirmation of the role of the Ark (Num. 10:33) and the cloud (v. 34) as instruments of God's guidance on the journey. Just as the cloud and the trumpets were paired as complementary divine and human instruments of leadership (9:17; 10:2), so too the human guide who is a foreigner and the divine presence in the cloud and Ark are paired as complementary means of leadership for the people. A subtle interaction is suggested here between the divine and the human as well as an openness to guidance and wisdom from those who come from outside Israel.

The words of Moses in vv. 35–36, which announce the breaking and making of the camp, are seen as ancient tradition and have an almost liturgical flavor. They reinforce the impression of the inauguration of the march as a liturgical procession with the holy God at the center leading the faithful people through the wilderness. This impression of a totally obedient and holy people is, however, about to be shattered.

11:1–20:29
Repeated Incidents of Rebellion and Atonement: The Death of the First Wilderness Generation Begins

The transition from the portrait of the people's complete faithfulness in Numbers 1–10 to the portrait of their repeated rebellions beginning in chap. 11 represents a totally unexpected turnabout in the flow of the story. In 11:1 we encounter the first instance of a complaint and rebellion by the people in the book of Numbers. It is a rebellion for which readers are totally unprepared. The abrupt and shattering break of the narrative flow between 10:36 and 11:1 reflects the shattering break in the relationship between God and his holy people. Throughout chaps. 11–20, Israel continually rebels, and God punishes Israel with plagues and military defeats. God offers signs of atonement and forgiveness, but the people still keep slipping back into rebellion. A general rebellion of the people in Numbers 11 is followed by the first rebellion in the wilderness by two leaders of the people, Aaron and Miriam, in chap. 12. The most serious rebellion occurs in the story of the spy mission into the promised land in chaps. 13–14. This story provides the definitive basis for understanding the whole book of Numbers in terms of the death of the old generation and the birth of the new generation of hope on the edge of the promised land. After a word of hope is offered in Numbers 15, the people and even the Levites resume their rebellious ways. Chap. 20 recounts an act of rebellion even by Moses and Aaron against God. Aaron's death and the succession of his son Eleazar as priest in 20:22–29 is a sign of the coming end of the first generation of Israelites out of Egypt and the beginning of a new generation.

11:1–3, The First Rebellion by the People Against God. Numbers 11 marks a dramatic shift from the positive tone in chap. 10, in which people looked forward to the promised land and

were sure of God's care and protection (10:29). Num. 11:1–3 involves the first example of the people's murmuring against God in the book of Numbers. The motif of the people's murmuring in the wilderness occurred previously in the book of Exodus, where the complaints were typically understood as legitimate. In response to the intercession of Moses, God met the people's needs in a positive way (e.g., Exod. 15:22–25; 17:1–7). In the book of Numbers, however, the people's complaints are understood as acts of faithlessness. The complaints rouse God's anger and punishment, which is mitigated only by Moses' intercession. Num. 11:1–3 provides a clear and concise example of this second form of the murmuring story and establishes the theme for the entire section that it introduces (chaps. 11–20).

The people's complaining arouses the fire of God's anger, which burns the fringe areas of the camp (11:1). Before the divine fire continues any further toward the center of the camp, Moses prays on behalf of the people and the fire is removed (v. 2). The name of the place is then called Taberah (Heb., "burning"). The location of Taberah is unknown.

11:4–35, The Craving of Meat at Kibroth-hattavah: Another Rebellion. This rebellion story probably evolved from an original story only about the provision of quail in response to the people's request for meat. The story of the provision of additional leaders to support Moses was then added as the story developed in the course of transmission (vv. 16–17, 24–30).

A rabble stirs up the people's desire for meat and for the variety of food they had in Egypt. This craving for meat is a rejection of the gracious gift of manna that God had provided so faithfully as food for the people throughout their journey through the wilderness (vv. 4–9). Everyone joins in the complaint that angers both God and Moses (v. 10).

The next section is a dialogue between these two. Moses laments the burden of leadership that God has placed on his shoulders (vv. 11–15). He, in turn, commands Moses to select seventy elders from the twelve tribes to share the burden of leading the people. He also commands Moses to have the people prepare to eat meat for an entire month, until it becomes loathsome to them (vv. 16–20). The people's desire for meat and their yearning for Egypt are signs of faithlessness and a rejection of God's gift of manna. Moses himself expresses doubt that God will be able to make good on his promise to provide a whole month's supply of meat for 600,000 people, but God tells him simply to wait and see (vv. 21–23).

God stops talking and begins acting through his spirit or wind. The fact that the Hebrew word for "spirit" is the same as "wind" helps to tie together the two actions of God in vv. 24–35. In the first action (vv. 24–30), God takes some of the spirit from Moses and places it upon the seventy elders who stand at the tent of meeting in the holy center of the camp so that they may share the leadership of the tribes. The episode involving the two people prophesying in the camp illustrates the need to allow for the possibility that persons outside the institutional leadership of God's people may have genuine words and insights from him (vv. 26–30).

In the second action (vv. 31–35), God sends forth a "wind" that brings flocks of quail from the sea so that they fall far outside the camp. The quail lure the people to leave the security of the holy camp. As they eat the quail that lies at a day's journey outside the camp. God is angered and sends a plague upon the people. The story provides an explanation for the name of the place, Kibbroth-hattavah, which in Hebrew means "graves of craving" (v. 34). The precise location of Kibbroth-hattavah is unknown.

12:1–16, The Rebellion by the Leaders, Miriam and Aaron.

Thus far, only the people and not the leaders have joined in the rebellions. Numbers 12, however, introduces the complaint of Miriam and Aaron against Moses. The preceding episode in 11:26–30 opens the door to the possibility of legitimate prophets and revelation outside the official or institutional leadership of the tribes. Chap. 12 wrestles with the limits of such revelation. Miriam is described in Exod. 15:20 as a prophetess and as a sister of Aaron and of Moses. The implicit question in this story is this: can prophetic or any other revelation override Mosaic revelation? In other words, is prophecy subordinate to the authority of Moses and the Mosaic tradition? It has been suggested that behind this story lies a conflict between specific priestly or prophetic groups in Israel's history. The evidence for such a conflict is far from clear, and, in any case, the story in its present form has in mind the broader issue of the relationship of Mosaic tradition to prophecy in general.

The scene opens with Miriam and Aaron speaking against Moses because he had married a woman from Cush. The Bible often identifies Cush with Ethiopia (e.g., Isa. 20:3,5). The unnamed wife is, in any case, a foreigner. This initial objection is only a smoke screen, however, for the real cause for the rebellion by Miriam and Aaron. In two rhetorical questions, these two challenge Moses' unique role as the supreme channel of the words of God. After a note about Moses' humility (Num. 12:3), God appears and emphasizes the role of Moses as the unique and supreme vehicle of divine revelation (vv. 6–8).

God punishes Miriam and Aaron by making Miriam leprous, which renders her unclean so that she must remain outside the camp for seven days until she is again allowed inside the camp. Moses demonstrates his integrity by interceding on behalf of Miriam, who had been the one who had opposed him (v. 13). A question that naturally arises is why God punished Miriam with leprosy and not Aaron. It may be that the story was originally only about Miriam and Aaron was added secondarily. Another explanation may be that the writer simply could not tolerate having Aaron the high priest rendered unclean by leprosy. The requirements of purity or cleanness for the priests were very strict (see Lev. 21).

13:1–14:45, The Spy Mission into the Promised Land: The Decisive Rebellion.

More than any other story in Numbers, the narrative of the spy mission in chaps. 13–14 provides the foundation for the unifying theme of the book, which is the death of the old generation in the wilderness and the birth of a new generation standing expectantly on the threshold of the promised land. The purpose of the census at the beginning of the book was to count all who were "able to go forth to war" (1:3). The twelve tribes were then organized into a holy camp as an army marching toward Canaan (chap. 2). The spy story in chaps. 13–14 records the first military action of the twelve tribes of Israel, who have been prepared in this way for a holy war.

Scholars are generally agreed that the story in Numbers 13–14 consists of at least two interwoven layers or literary sources, one older and one later. For example, one layer or tradition seems to assume that the area that the spies covered was confined only to southern Canaan around Hebron (13:22–24). A later layer extended the territory of the reconnaissance to include the entire land of Canaan from the Wilderness of Zin on the southern edge to Rehob on the northern (13:21). Another tension in the text that is a sign of multiple layers is the designation of the faithful spies among the twelve. In an earlier tradition, Caleb was apparently the only spy among them who was faithful to God (13:30). In the later tradition, Joshua was also included as a faithful spy (14:6).

Numerous suggestions have been made for the origin of the spy story. Some have proposed that the original story was about a successful conquest of a part of Canaan from the south by a tribe claiming Caleb as an ancestor. The story was then reshaped into a failed conquest story that provided a rationale for the entrance into the promised land from the eastern border of Canaan rather than the southern. Others have proposed that the story originated as a polemic by Judah in the south, represented by Caleb, against the northern tribes. In any case, the story

191

in its present form has been significantly re-shaped for theological purposes and has lost any major thrust that it may have once had as one tribe's polemic against another.

The spy story in Numbers 13–14 begins with the Israelites in the Wilderness of Paran poised on the southern edge of the promised land of Canaan (12:16; 13:3). At last the Israelites have reached the doorstep of their destination. God commands Moses to send twelve men, one from each tribe, to spy out the land (13:2–24). After forty days, the spies return and report what they have seen. Initially, the spies give a favorable report about the fruitfulness of the land, but they warn against the inhabitants who are strong and who live in large fortified cities (13:25–29, 31–33). Caleb and later Joshua, two of the spies, counter the unfavorable report of the others by urging the Israelites to trust in God and to proceed to conquer the land (13:30; 14:6–9). The people respond faithlessly by refusing to go into the promised land and by desiring to choose their own leader and return to Egypt (14:1–4).

God then appears and tells Moses that he will disinherit the people and instead make of Moses a new and even greater nation than the Israelites (14:10–12). The anger of God is so severe because the nature of the people's rebellion is unprecedented. The people's wish to choose their own leader and go back to Egypt is, in effect, a total rejection of God whose essence and name was "Yahweh your God who brought you *out of* the land of Egypt, *out of* the house of bondage" (Exod. 20:2). This rebellion goes beyond the sin of the golden calf at Mount Sinai, which was not so much a rejection of God as an attempt to shape God into their own image (Exod. 32:4–5).

Numbers 13–14 is a story of high hopes and bitter disappointment. All the promises to the ancestors of Israel in Genesis, which extend through Exodus and Leviticus, have looked forward to this time when the people finally are on the verge of entering the promised land. Coupled with this high sense of anticipation, the census in Numbers 1, which counted an enormous total army of over 600,000 people, and the elaboration of the carefully ordered military camp with God visibly in its midst should have provided grounds for complete faith and confidence. The tone of events in chaps. 1–10 is entirely positive. The initial spying out of the land reveals a beautiful and fruitful land, one that "flows with milk and honey" (13:27). The prospect is bright indeed.

But then comes the fateful rebellion. The people refuse to enter the land, afraid of the death that may await them and afraid to trust God to make good on his promise. As a result, God announces the punishment of death on this old, sinful generation.

Moses intercedes and asks God to forgive the people just as he had done after the sin of the golden calf in Exod. 32:11–13 (Num. 14:13–19). While God had allowed the people to live and be reconstituted as his holy people after the golden calf incident in Exodus 32, the rebellion in Numbers 13–14 is a more serious matter. God agrees to forgive the people by allowing the next generation of Israelites to enter the promised land. The old wilderness generation, however, is condemned to die in the wilderness over the course of the next forty years (14:20–35). At this point, the story is explicitly linked to the census list in chap. 1, which contains the recurring formula "all your number, numbered from twenty years old and upward," now also used by God to designate who will die in the wilderness (14:29). Only two members of the old generation will enter the promised land: Caleb and Joshua, the two spies who trusted that God would be faithful to the promise to bring the people into the promised land (14:30).

But out of the darkest moment of the entire Pentateuch comes the birth and the promise of a new generation of God's people. The children of the old generation whom the rebels used as an excuse for not entering the land (14:3) will become the new vehicles of God's promise (14:31). The new census list in chap. 26 will be a concrete sign of the birth of this new generation of hope even as it signals the final demise of the old wilderness generation.

Numbers 14 concludes with two brief episodes. In vv. 36–38, the ten rebellious spies who refused to trust God to bring the people into the land die in a plague. Their deaths are a sign of the coming punishment that will eventually fall upon all members of the older generation. As if to confirm the people's failure to comprehend their own sin, they change their minds and resolve to go and fight the Canaanites. But Moses warns them that God will not be with them. They go anyway and are soundly defeated in battle (vv. 39–45). The death of the old rebellious generation has begun.

15:1–41, A Sign of Hope: Regulations for Life in the Promised Land.

Numbers 15 is a collection of legal material that has been inserted at a relatively late stage of composition between two narratives, the spy story in chaps. 13–14 and the story of the rebellion of Korah, Dathan, and Abiram in chap. 16. Numbers 15 contains a number of laws concerning sacrifices and offerings that the people are to present to God when they live in the promised land (vv. 1–21). The next section includes regulations for sacrifices that atone for unintentional sins by the community (vv. 22–26) or by an individual (vv. 27–31). These laws concerning intentional and unintentional sins are followed by the legal case of a man gathering wood on the Sabbath day (vv. 32–36). Because the degree of guilt and punishment of the man is unclear, the case is referred to God's judgment. Originally the case may have had something to do with the law against kindling a fire on the Sabbath (Exod. 35:3) or with kindling a fire for a sacrifice to foreign gods. In the present context, however, the case provides a concrete example of the law that immediately precedes it concerning sinning flagrantly or "with a high hand" (Num. 15:30). Such deliberate and defiant sin must be punished severely. Thus, this legal case and the laws that precede it share a common theme: the role of intentionality in determining the degree of guilt and punishment. Sins done unwittingly bear less guilt and can be atoned through sacrifice (v. 28), while a blatant and intentional act of disobedience (v. 30) involves great guilt and severe punishment.

Num. 15:37–41 continues with instructions to the people to wear tassels on their garments as reminders of God's commandments (→Fringes). This section was included as part of the Jewish liturgy of the postexilic period as part of the prayer known as the "Shema" (→ Shema). The last verse of the chapter, v. 41, strongly reaffirms God's relationship to the people after the trauma of the rebellion in chaps. 13–14. In fact, the whole chapter functions in this way to provide reassurance to the new generation that God will indeed bring them into the land. The laws presuppose that the new generation will indeed live in the promised land (15:2, 18). They look forward to new generations in that they are to apply "throughout your generations" (vv. 14, 15, 21, 23, 38). The tassels on the garments serve as a reminder of God's covenant to future generations (v. 38) and of Israel's perpetual duty to observe God's commandments and to safeguard their own sanctity (v. 40).

In relation to chaps. 13–14, the laws of Numbers 15 function as profound promise for the future. In relation to the rebellion of Korah, Dathan, and Abiram in chap. 16, these same laws function as threat and burden. The laws in Numbers 15 are mediated exclusively through Moses, a fact repeatedly stressed (vv. 1, 17, 22, 23, 35, 36, 37). In the present shape of these chapters, Moses' unique role as God's mediator in chap. 15 apparently provides the reason for the otherwise unprovoked rebellion by Korah in chap. 16. Moreover, Korah's blatant and defiant revolt provides an example of sinning "with a high hand" (15:30), which requires the penalty of death, as we shall see.

16:1–35, The Rebellion of Korah, Dathan, Abiram, and 250 Leaders.

A number of older and later traditions have been combined in this account of a rebellion against Moses and Aaron. The revolt is led by a subordinate levitical priest named Korah and by Dathan, Abiram, and 250 other lay members of the community. One is also mentioned as a rebel in v. 1, but he does not appear again. The earliest form of the story may have focused only on a rebellion by Dathan and Abiram, members of the tribe of Reuben (vv. 12–15). The story was then expanded to include 250 laymen who claimed the right to offer incense but were refuted in a test (vv. 2b, 4–7, 18, 35). A further elaboration introduced Korah, a Levite, as one of the rebels (vv. 1a, 8–11, 16–17). These separate traditions have been expanded and tied together by one or more editors. The judgment on Korah stresses the subordinate role of the Levites in relation to the sons of Aaron in priestly duties. The issue of whether this conflict between Levites and sons of Aaron reflects an actual historical struggle within the priesthood in either the pre-exilic or postexilic period in Israel is a matter of some debate.

In its present context, the rebellion in Numbers 16 simply confirms the faithlessness of the old wilderness generation that was already demonstrated in the debacle of the spy story in the preceding chapters. In a sense, the story in Numbers 13–14 and the story in chap. 16 signal the unraveling of the careful organization and preparation of the people at the beginning of the book (chaps. 1–4). The census and the holy camp in chaps. 1–2 prepared for the first military engagement, which should have occurred in the spying out of the land in chaps. 13–14. The spy story, however, ends in total failure. Moreover, the census and the preparation of the Levites for their important task of caring for the Ark and serving the sons of Aaron in Numbers 3–4 should have brought satisfaction and fulfillment to the Levites. Instead, Korah, the Levite, leads a rebellion against Moses and Aaron and challenges their legitimacy as leaders here in chap. 16.

The cause of the complaint against Moses in v. 3, "You have gone too far," is not clear in the immediate context. In the larger context and in the present shape of the text, however, Moses' exclusive role as mediator of the laws in Numbers 15 seems to provide the necessary background to the revolt. As we saw in our analysis, the laws in chap. 15 also function to dramatize the grave nature of the revolt in chap. 16. The revolt is an example of sinning openly and defiantly with "a high hand," which demands a judgment of being cut off from among the people (15:30). The judgment on Korah and his cohorts also serves to clarify the nature of the call in 15:40 for all God's people to be holy. The rebels incorrectly use their status as a holy people to seek their own advantage rather than obeying God's appointment of Moses and Aaron as their rightful leaders.

193

The story begins with the complaint of Korah and the Levites against the supremacy of Aaron and his sons in the practice of the priesthood (16:3–11). The rebels say Moses and Aaron have "gone too far" (v. 3), but Moses replies that the Levites have "gone too far" (v. 7) in their rebellion. A test is established whereby Korah and his company are to bring censers with fire in them on the following day in order that God may choose who is to serve as priests.

The story then proceeds to the challenge voiced by Dathan and Abiram, two laypersons from the tribe of Reuben. They yearn to return to Egypt, which they ironically remember as "a land flowing with milk and honey" (v. 13), the stereotypical designation for the promised land of Canaan. They also throw Moses' own words in his face. Moses attempted to comfort Korah and the Levites concerning their subordinate but privileged role by saying (v. 9), "Is it such a small thing that the God of Israel has separated you?" Dathan and Abiram turn the words back on Moses with a sarcastic twist (v. 13): "Is it such a small thing that you have taken us up out of a land flowing with milk and honey?" Their words belie a lack of faith in God's promise to bring the people into the promised land. They blatantly reject the authority of God's appointed leader, refusing to heed Moses' call to come and stand before him: "We will not come up" (v. 14).

The rebels are then judged by God in a manner that corresponds with their complaints. Korah and the Levites claim to be full priests. As a test of whether God will accept them as priests, the rebels light censers to offer incense as only priests are to do. Rejecting this democratizing of the priesthood, God commands Moses and Aaron to separate themselves from the people so that God's wrath may consume the entire congregation (v. 21). Although Moses is very angry with the people (v. 15), he and Aaron reveal the quality of their character and leadership by pleading with God to judge only the guilty ones and to spare the rest of the people (v. 22). God complies, and Moses then asks the people to stay away from the dwellings of Korah, Dathan, and Abiram to see whether God will judge them (v. 26).

God then begins the judgment as the earth opens up and swallows the rebels. In accord with their complaints (v. 13), they do indeed die in the wilderness (vv. 31–34). And in accord with their complaints, these rebellious Levites offered incense to the Lord but were burned and killed as they did it (v. 35). Thus, God vindicates the rightful authority of Moses and Aaron.

16:36–50, Another Rebellion by All the People. God commands Moses to have Aaron's son, Eleazar, gather the bronze censers that the Levites had held as they were consumed in the fire of judgment. The bronze is to be hammered into a cover for the altar. This may have been intended as a supplemental covering or simply another tradition about an altar covering, since a similar bronze overlay is mentioned in Exod. 38:2. In Numbers, the covering serves as a sign to remind the people that only priests of the family of Aaron are to burn incense at the altar (Num. 16:36–40).

But the people soon slip back into their rebellious ways. They begin to accuse Moses and Aaron of killing the people of God, which includes Korah, Dathan, Abiram, and 250 others. God comes down and threatens again to destroy all the people of Israel since "all the congregation" is rebelling (vv. 41, 45). Whereas the question earlier had concerned God's justice in destroying the whole people when only a few were guilty (16:22), now God could destroy all the people since all were involved in rebellion.

Moses and Aaron exemplify the quality of leadership as they again seek the good of the people rather than their own good or glory. They fall on their faces in an act of intercession on behalf of the people. Moses then instructs Aaron to take a censer throughout the camp and offer incense to make atonement for the people. The plague that is God's judgment kills 14,700 people before Aaron is able to step in to stop the spread of the plague through his intercession (vv. 45–50). Aaron's exclusive role as priest (Heb. *kohen*) is again vindicated, this time in a positive way. God had rejected and killed the Levites when they attempted to offer incense. In contrast, Aaron's offer of incense is accepted by God, and it effectively stops the spread of the plague. Leadership, priestly or otherwise, is to be exercised for the sake of the community, not for self-glorification.

17:1–13, Aaron's Almond Rod. The previous two incidents of rebellion against Aaron's exclusive role as priest in chap. 16 demonstrate the unwillingness of the people to accept the need for a priesthood. This section in Numbers 17, however, confirms once and for all God's sole appointment of Aaron and his sons to the priesthood. At the end, the people finally acknowledge their need for a priesthood to represent them at the altar (vv. 12–13). The aim of the original form of this story of the almond rods may have been to legitimate the Levites as priests. In the present shape of the story, however, the focus has been shifted from the Levites as a group to Aaron as an individual by having his name written on the rod representing the tribe of Levi (v. 3).

The story begins with God proposing a test to determine which tribe is to assume the privileges and responsibilities of the priesthood. God instructs Moses to collect twelve almond rods or branches and to write the names of the twelve tribes upon them. Aaron's name is to be written on the rod representing the tribe of Levi. Moses deposits the rods in the tent of meeting overnight. God suggests that the tribe whose rod sprouts on the following day will be considered the chosen tribe for the priesthood. God intends that the test will put an end to any further complaints from the people concerning the priesthood (vv. 5, 10). The rebellions that preceded clearly provide the reason for this test.

On the next day, the rod of Aaron is the only one of the twelve rods that sprouts buds, blossoms, and ripe almonds. God tells Moses to display Aaron's almond rod in the sanctuary as a visible sign of Aaron's rightful claim to the priesthood. The people come to recognize the necessity for a special priestly group to represent them at the tabernacle (vv. 8–13). The test and the previous rebellion stories in Numbers 16 clearly affirm God's choice of Aaron as priest of the people of Israel. We lack exact evidence of any historical conflicts over the priesthood in the history of Israel that may have formed the original background to this sequence of narratives. As the narratives stand, they simply reaffirm the uniqueness of the Aaronidic priesthood among all the other tribes or groups (→ Aaron; Priests).

18:1–32, The Rights and Responsibilities of the Priesthood of Aaron and the Service of the Levites.

The preceding narratives finally convince the people of the necessity of the priesthood. They now can recognize the importance of providing the tithe offerings and sacrifices necessary to sustain the priesthood. The nature of these offerings as well as the role of the Aaronidic and levitical priesthood are spelled out in Numbers 18.

The chapter begins by stressing the responsibility of the priesthood to bear the sin of the community and to protect the community from drawing near to the holy vessels of the inner sanctuary. The Levites are to form a second circle of protection around the tent of meeting. The priests and Levites protect the people from compromising the holiness of God's presence in the sanctuary, thus guarding against the wrath of God and the death that it brings (vv. 1–5). The service of the priests and Levites is a gift from God to the community for their own good. Support of the priesthood ought then to be done out of a spirit of thankfulness and not only one of obligation (vv. 6–7).

In vv. 8–20, God speaks directly to Aaron rather than through the mediation of Moses. This is unusual and serves again to underscore Aaron's special role as priest. These verses summarize the sacrifices, the first-fruit offerings of the harvest, the firstborn animals, and the de-

voted items from holy war that are the priest's due. Many of these same laws are found elsewhere (e.g., Lev. 6–7, 27). The rationale for offering to the priest is stated in Num. 18:20. The priests will not inherit any of the property in the land of Canaan. Their only source of sustenance will come from the offerings given to God.

The Levites are specifically addressed in vv. 21–29. Although they had been involved in the preceding rebellions (16:1, 7), God reaffirms the role of the Levites' service to the sons of Aaron and their right to the tithe offering of the people. The provision for the support of the Levites in these verses leaves no doubt that their role remains crucial to the plan of God for the people. Like the Aaronidic priesthood, the Levites have no inheritance in the land and must be supported through the people's offerings (v. 24).

The Levites are to receive the tithe or one-tenth offering in return for their service in the tent of meeting. In turn, the Levites are to give a tithe of their tithe to the priests, or sons of Aaron. Moreover, the tithe is to be the best part of the offering. This ordinance emphasizes the important but subordinate role of the Levites in relation to Aaron. The rest of the offering, however, belongs to the Levites (vv. 25–31). The note in v. 32 reminds the Levites that any further rebellions like Korah's will lead only to death.

19:1–22, The Ritual of the Red Heifer and the Purification of the Unclean.

The first half of the book of Numbers recounts the death of the members of the old wilderness generation in successive stages, leading up to the census and organization of the new generation in chap. 26. The presence of death and its threat to the community permeates these chapters. Several rebellions have already resulted in the deaths of thousands. Death occurs in the plague in 11:33; the punishment of the ten unfaithful spies in 14:37; the military defeat in 14:45; the punishment of Korah, Dathan, and Abiram and the other rebels in 16:33–35; and the plague that killed 14,700 people in 16:49.

After the rebellion of Numbers 16, the position of the priestly house of Aaron, which stands at the center of the wilderness camp, is reaffirmed in chap. 17. Chap. 18 follows by reconstituting the legitimate but subordinate role of the Levites in the next circle of holiness in the midst of the camp. Chap. 19 moves on to consider the major threat to the holiness of the laypeople in the rest of the camp by contamination through contact with the dead. Num. 5:2–3 has already stressed the seriousness of the threat to the holiness of the camp through touching a corpse. Given the several incidents of death among the people thus far and the theme of the death of the old generation in the first half of the book (chaps. 1–25), the concern

195

of Numbers 19 for cleansing those contaminated by contact with the dead seems entirely appropriate.

The ritual of burning a red heifer or cow and using the ashes for a water of purification for the unclean probably reflects an ancient ritual. The details are contained in vv. 1–10. The redness of the heifer, the unusual burning of the blood of the animal (v. 5), and the scarlet stuff (v. 6) all seem to signify blood and its potent ability to cleanse that which is polluted. Cedarwood and hyssop (or marjoram) are other cleansing agents thrown into the fire as ingredients of the purificatory ashes (v. 6; see Lev. 14:4 and Ps. 51:7). The ashes are to be gathered up and kept for mixing with water to cleanse the people from sin and impurity (Num. 19:9). There is no mention in vv. 1–10 of its specific use for purifying those who have touched a corpse.

This link of the ritual of the red heifer with cleansing those who have come in contact with the dead was established with the addition of the ritual laws of vv. 14–19. These verses deal in detail with the issue of uncleanness through contact with the dead and may reflect an originally independent tradition. Verses 11–13 serve as a literary bridge that now binds the red heifer ritual with the concern for uncleanness from the dead. Thus, the ashes of the red heifer in v. 9 are identified in the present shape of the text with the ashes in v. 17. The notes in vv. 13 and 20 emphasize the importance of the cleansing ritual and focus the concern on preserving the holiness of the sanctuary of God at the center of the wilderness camp. The presence of God and the mechanisms for worship and life among the people can be maintained in spite of the continuing deaths of the people of the older wilderness generation.

20:1–29, The Ultimate Rebellion by Moses and Aaron Against God.

The rebellion of the central leaders of Israel, Moses and Aaron, signals the pervasiveness of the sin of the old generation. Numbers 20 opens with a note about the death of one of the leaders, Miriam, who had rebelled along with Aaron in chap. 12. Her death and burial in the wilderness is a sign of what lies ahead for Aaron (v. 28) and for Moses (v. 12; cf. Deut. 34:5). None of the leaders of the old wilderness generation will lead Israel into the promised land.

The story of Num. 20:1–13 appears to be a reworking of a similar story about the people's complaint of a lack of water in the wilderness in Exod. 17:1–7. Both stories include the complaint about a lack of water, the rod used by Moses, and the name Meribah for the place. The primary aim of the story has been changed, however. The story in Exod. 17:1–7 illustrates God's care for the people, whereas the focus of the narrative in Num. 20:1–13 is on the extension of the rebellion even into the leadership of Moses and Aaron. The story shows that the sin of Moses and Aaron leads to God's prohibition upon their entering the land of promise in Canaan. It should be noted that the book of Deuteronomy gives an alternative explanation for Moses' not being allowed to enter the promised land. Deut. 3:26 and 4:21 suggest that the prohibition was part of Moses' vicarious suffering on behalf of the people for their sin. In either case, it is understood that the effect of the sin of the people has somehow extended even to God's closest servant, Moses.

The precise nature of the disobedience by Moses and Aaron has been much debated. It is not immediately clear how their actions constituted an act of faithlessness against God. The most probable explanation may be found in God's command in Num. 20:8 to take the rod and to *tell* the rock to produce water. Instead of just telling the rock to yield water, however, Moses strikes it two times (v. 11). The striking of the rock was not part of God's original instructions. Moses' failure to comply exactly with God's instructions is in contrast to the early chapters of Numbers in which God's commands are obeyed with an almost monotonous and repetitive correspondence (1:54; 2:34; 7:1–89; 9:15–23). Readers sense in chap. 20 a breakdown in the relationship between the leaders and God.

This breakdown in leadership is heightened by the question that Moses and Aaron pose to the rebels (v. 10, italics mine): "Shall *we* produce water for you out of this rock?" The question assumes that it is Moses and Aaron who have the power to produce the water, not God. This arrogance, particularly on the part of Moses, is in marked contrast to the portrait of a humble Moses in 12:3. Moreover, the primary sin in the spy story in chaps. 13–14 was the people's desire to trust in themselves rather than in God's power (14:11, 39–45). Now this sin of pride that forgets the divine source of all power and blessing has even reached into the leadership of Moses and Aaron. They too show themselves to be part of the old rebellious generation who are condemned to die outside the promised land.

The circles of holiness within the camp that were so carefully organized in Numbers 1–10 have slowly been undone. The people of the twelve tribes in the outer circle of the camp rebelled in chaps. 13–14. The Levites who surround the tent of meeting in the midst of the camp rebelled in chaps. 16–17. Now even the leaders closest to God, at the center of the camp, the priest Aaron and the leader Moses, rebel in Numbers 20. The fate of the whole generation of Israelites who first came out of Egypt is now sealed. Except for Joshua and Caleb (14:30), none of them, not even Moses, will set foot in Canaan. The holy camp of Israel will have to be reorganized with a new generation of Israelites (chap. 26).

Num. 20:14–21 recount Edom's refusal to allow the Israelites to pass through its territory on the way to the promised land. Edom was descended from Esau, the twin brother of Israel's ancestor Jacob (v. 14; cf. Gen. 25:26; 36:1; Amos 1:11). In spite of this kinship, Edom refuses the Israelites passage so that they are forced to take a detour around Edom (Num. 20:21). This lengthening of the journey provides the occasion for another murmuring incident in Num. 21:4. The incident with Edom also provides another example of Israel's leadership going its own way without consulting God. There is no command of God to Moses to approach Edom. Moses seems to be acting on his own (v. 14). Not even a promise of reimbursement will work (v. 19). The failure of Moses' mission may be related to his failure to involve God in carrying it out.

Verses 21–29 narrate the death of Israel's first high priest, Aaron. Aaron's death is described with little fanfare, a somber reflection on his rebellion at Meribah in vv. 1–13. Aaron's priestly garments are stripped and placed on his son Eleazar, who takes over the role of high priest for Israel. The death of Aaron and the succession of Eleazar to the priesthood are a sign of the coming end of the first generation and the beginning of a new generation of hope and promise. The continuance of the priesthood in Eleazar, however, indicates God's ongoing commitment to Israel and the institutions through which God works his will for the sake of the people.

21:1–25:18
The End of the First Generation: Signs of Hope Coupled with Ultimate Failure

A major break in the narrative occurs with Numbers 21. For the first time in this predominantly negative section of Numbers, a positive tone is struck with the story of Israel's military victory over the Canaanite king of Arad. Ever since chap. 11, Israel has continually rebelled and God has punished the people with military defeats and plagues. This negative portrait is abruptly altered by the positive conquest story in 21:1–3, which is followed by another rebellion (21:4–9) and then another positive conquest story with victories over two kings, Sihon and Og (21:10–35). A lengthy section involving King Balak and the prophet Balaam follows (22:1–24:25). The Balaam cycle concludes with a series of climactic promise oracles to Israel. A final rebellion story in 25:1–18 narrates the death

of the remaining members of the old and unfaithful generation of the wilderness who continue to rebel in spite of God's promises and faithfulness. This section concludes the first half of Numbers (chaps. 1–25) by weaving together accounts of ultimate failure by a generation past and notes of profound promise for a generation of the future.

21:1–3, God Gives Victory over Arad to Israel. One of the purposes of the original form of this story was to explain the name of a place called "Hormah," which in Hebrew means "destruction" (v. 3). A conflict at Hormah had also been mentioned at the end of the spy story in 14:39–45. The story in 21:1–3 seems to be an alternate tradition about this same conflict at Hormah. In the context of the present narrative, this successful conquest of Arad at Hormah signals God's continuing faithfulness and intention to bring Israel into the promised land. When Israel trusts in God alone, then God will give victory to Israel. The Hormah story in 14:39–45 makes the same theological point in negative terms: when the people disobey and do not trust in God but only in their own strength and resources, they will suffer defeat.

21:4–9, Another Rebellion by the People. In spite of God's gracious act of faithfulness in 21:1–3, the members of the old wilderness generation immediately return to their grumbling ways. The long detour in their journey was necessitated by Edom's refusal to let the people travel through its territory (20:21). The detour causes the people to grow impatient. They complain to Moses and God about the lack of food and water and about the manna, which they detest. The people had complained about the manna before, in 11:6, and their complaint stirred up God's anger in the form of a plague (11:33). In 21:4–9, God's anger manifests itself in the form of poisonous serpents whose bite is deadly (v. 6). The people confess their sin to Moses, and Moses intercedes for them. God instructs Moses to set up a bronze serpent on a pole. Anyone who is bitten by a serpent and looks at the bronze serpent will live (vv. 8–9).

This story provides some background to 2 Kings 18:4, which mentions the bronze serpent made by Moses. People had been burning incense to the bronze serpent as part of their worship. King Hezekiah destroyed the bronze serpent because it apparently had too many associations with the pagan worship of the Canaanites who lived in the land before Israel and for whom the serpent was an important symbol in worship. Thus, Hezekiah banned the symbol to avoid any associations with idol worship. In Num. 21:4–9, however, the bronze serpent is a positive symbol of God's healing power.

197

21:10–35, Israel Marches On with Victories over Sihon and Og. In spite of the preceding rebellion, God continues to lead the people on their march toward the promised land. The first section (vv. 10–20) describes the itinerary of the Israelites as they camp and then move on from place to place toward their goal. Most of the place names mentioned are unknown. Two poetic passages or songs are included in these verses. The first song (vv. 14–15) is drawn from the "Book of the Wars of Yahweh." This book was apparently a collection of ancient songs or accounts, similar to the "Book of Jashar" mentioned in Josh. 10:13. The brief song in Num. 21:14–15 is not straightforward in its meaning, although the general sense seems to be an account of the victories or travels of Israel in the areas named. The second song (vv. 17–18) is inserted after the note about God's gift of water to the people at a place called Beer, which in Hebrew means "well." God continues to provide for his people as he leads them through the wilderness.

The next section (vv. 21–35) recounts two decisive military victories by Israel over Sihon, king of the Amorites, and Og, king of Bashan. The form of the account of the conflict with Sihon is similar to that of the story of the Edomites in 20:14–20. The Israelites request permission from Sihon to pass through his kingdom. They pledge not to take anything from the fields or wells as they pass. Sihon denies their request. In 20:14–20, when Edom refused passage to the Israelites, they avoided a conflict by taking a detour around Edom. In 21:21–26, however, Sihon attacks Israel and is soundly defeated. God gives Israel a foretaste of the conquest of the promised land. For the first time, Israel successfully captures cities and land, although they are still on the east side of the Jordan River just across from the promised land of Canaan (v. 25). An ancient song that may have formed the basis for the narrative of the victory over Sihon in vv. 21–26 follows in vv. 27–30. Jer. 48:45–46 contains a slightly different form of the same song. The note about Israel's settlement in the land of the Amorites in Num. 21:31–32 provides the background for the controversy about the settlement of Reuben and Gad in the Transjordan area in chap. 32.

A second military encounter occurs in 21:33–35. Israel defeats Og, who is king of Bashan. Israel obediently carries out the requirements of holy war and leaves no survivors (v. 35). As a result, God assures them of victory, and Israel is given the land of Bashan to possess. Once again when the Israelites are faithful and obedient, God shows his faithfulness by giving them victory over their enemies (→ Ban). Deut. 2:26–37 and 3:1–7 contain parallel accounts of Israel's victories over Sihon and Og. Whether one of the two parallel accounts in

Numbers 21 and Deuteronomy 2–3 is dependent on the other is a matter of debate. The two may also be independent but parallel forms of a common tradition. In any case, the function of Num. 21:21–35 in its present context is to show God's faithfulness in giving victory to Israel as Israel moves toward the promised land. For the first time since the spy story in Numbers 13–14, the travels and victories of the Israelites in chap. 21 have moved Israel once again to the edge of the promised land "in the plains of Moab" (22:1). This hopeful setting provides the stage for the climactic promise oracles that Balaam speaks over God's people in the ensuing three chapters.

22:1–24:25, A Crescendo of Hope: Balak and Balaam and the Blessing of Israel. Two main characters stand out in this enigmatic story. The first character is Balaam, a professional prophet or seer who travels about and curses military enemies for money (→ Balaam). He is, in a sense, a hired gun, and his only weapons are words that have the power to curse. The second figure is Balak. He is the king of Moab, a country that borders the promised land of Canaan on the east side, just across the Jordan River. Balak fears that the large number of Israelites moving through his nation will attack and devastate his kingdom. He has no faith in his own army and so decides to turn elsewhere for help.

The story tells how King Balak decides to send his messengers to hire the professional curser, Balaam, to curse the millions of Israelites who are camped on the plains of Moab. Throughout the story, the Israelites remain oblivious to the drama taking place outside their camp. They rest in peace, totally unaware of the curse that threatens them and of God's persistent efforts to block the curse and, instead, to bless Israel.

When Balaam is asked by Balak's messengers to curse Israel, God first tells Balaam not to go. Balaam complies with God's command and refuses to go with the messengers to Balak. Finally, however, Balaam does go with his ass. They find some roadblocks along the way but eventually reach King Balak. Balak carefully makes the necessary preparations for Balaam to curse Israel. In three successive attempts, however, Balaam can only speak words of blessing and not of curse upon Israel. Balaam's last blessing upon Israel is the most extravagant of all, as he promises a glorious future for Israel.

The Balaam story has been a source of intense fascination and great diversity in the history of biblical interpretation. Some commentators have viewed Balaam as a true and faithful prophet of God, and others have seen him as an evil and false prophet. This variation in interpretation is due in part to the complexity of the biblical tradition itself concerning Balaam. Numbers 22–24 is an essentially positive portrait of Balaam. He ends up faithfully speaking God's words. But Deut. 23:3–6 conveys a very different opinion of Balaam and uses his association with the Moabites as a reason that Moabites and Ammonites are prohibited from ever entering the assembly of God's people (see also Num. 31:8). This tension in evaluating the figure of Balaam probably extends all the way back into the oral tradition when stories about the legendary professional curser named Balaam circulated among Israel and its neighbors. Archaeologists have discovered writings on plaster panels in a temple at Deir 'Allah near the Jordan River that refer to a famous professional prophet named Balaam. These inscriptions are evidence that different traditions and stories about Balaam were well known and circulated widely. This variety of traditions has been incorporated into the biblical record.

The Balaam cycle falls into three parts. The first episode in Num. 22:1–14 relates the mission of Balak's messengers as they try to convince Balaam to come with them. In Balaam's first encounter with God, God tells him not to go to Balak and he obeys (22:7–14).

The second episode is a folkloric tale about Balaam and his ass. In Balaam's second encounter with God in 22:15–20, God reverses the earlier decision and this time commands Balaam to comply with the messengers' request and go to Balak (v. 20). Balaam saddles his ass and begins the journey. In what now amounts to Balaam's third encounter with God, however, God seems again to reverse the decision to allow Balaam to go. An angel of God stands in the road and blocks the way. Only the ass sees the angel. Balaam is blind to his messenger from God and so angrily beats his ass who has turned off the road to avoid the angel (22:22–23). The ass sees the angel again on the road in a narrow place, but again Balaam fails to see the angel (22:24–25).

As they continue on the journey, the ass sees the angel a third time and simply lies down in the road since there is no way to go around the angel. Balaam angrily begins to beat the ass, and the ass opens its mouth and asks why Balaam is beating his faithful animal (22:21–30). Then God opens Balaam's eyes, and Balaam sees the angel of God. The angel chastises Balaam for treating his ass so harshly, since it was the ass who saved him from being killed. Balaam begs for forgiveness, and the angel instructs Balaam to go ahead with his mission to Balak. Balaam is to speak, however, only what God commands him to speak (22:31–35).

The third major episode in the Balaam cycle (22:36–24:25) reports the repeated attempts of Balak to have Balaam curse Israel. Each attempt is thwarted, however. Balaam ends up blessing rather than cursing Israel on three

different occasions (22:41–23:12; 23:13–26; 23:27–24:25). Ironically, Moab, not Israel, becomes the one cursed by Balaam (24:17).

The experience of Balaam and his ass (22:21–35) is parallel to the experience of Balaam and King Balak (22:36–24:25). The ass was caught three times between the angel's sword and Balaam's stick. Balaam is likewise caught three times between Balak's demands to curse Israel and God's prohibitions. Moreover, in each of the three incidents with the ass and the angel, the intensity rises at each stage toward a climax. Balaam becomes increasingly frustrated. In the same way, the anger of King Balak grows with each of the three oracles of blessing that Balaam pronounces upon Israel. As in the incident with Balaam and the ass, God's apparent arbitrariness is simply evidence of his control of Balaam and Balak and his resolve to bless Israel in face of all outside pressures to the contrary.

In general, Balaam's oracles of blessing all reaffirm the promises made to the ancestors in the book of Genesis. God's initial promise made to Abraham in Gen. 12:1–3 provided for land, descendants, and blessing. Balaam's first oracle in Num. 23:7–10 mentions Israel's positive relationship with God and Israel's great population (23:8, 10). The second oracle concentrates on God's faithfulness to the promises that he had made and on the irreversibility of his blessing of Israel (23:19–20). The third vision describes how Israel will shortly be given victory over its enemies and enjoy peace and prosperity in the promised land (24:3–9).

This last blessing moves somewhat beyond the promises to the ancestors in Genesis and looks forward to a distant time when a king or messiah would arise in Israel (24:14–19). Balaam describes what God would do to Israel "in the latter days" (24:14) as he points to a coming king in 24:17: "I see him, but not now; I behold him, but not nigh: a star shall come forth out of Jacob, and a scepter shall rise out of Israel" (RSV). The image of a star could be used as a metaphor for a royal figure (Isa. 14:12), while the scepter or royal staff symbolized the authority of a king. The original fulfillment of this oracle was probably understood as coming with the reign of King David in Israel, but the promise of a king or messiah was then extended beyond David to a future hope for a messiah who would usher in God's kingdom in the end days.

Scholars are generally agreed that the oracles of Balaam are good examples of Hebrew poetry that may be dated early in Israel's history (→ Poetry). Evidence also suggests, however, that the Balaam oracles have been edited and reshaped in the course of transmission at various points in Israel's history.

The Balaam cycle in Numbers 22–24 plays an important role in the overall theme of Numbers: the death of the old sinful generation and the birth of a new generation of hope on the edge of the promised land. The story of Balaam has been placed in a strategic position in the book of Numbers at the end of the first generation (chap. 25) and the beginning of a new generation (chap. 26). The oracles of blessing that Balaam speaks sound a crescendo of hope and promise at the conclusion of the first generation. Even so, the first generation returns immediately to the way of rebellion and disobedience. The sin that follows in chap. 25 is the final rebellion of the old generation. The ensuing plague kills the last members of the generation counted in chap. 1.

In the midst of the dismal end of the old generation of the wilderness, a new generation of hope arises and is affirmed by the powerful oracles of Balaam. The oracles point beyond themselves to a time to come. It will be a time of prosperity, strength, victory, and hope. Through Balaam, God blesses Israel with accolades and promises unsurpassed in the entire Pentateuch. Thus, Balaam stands at the end of one generation and points ahead to the coming of a new generation of God's people.

25:1–18, The Final Rebellion: The Death of the Remainder of the Old Wilderness Generation.

This last episode in the first half of Numbers brings the story of the generation who experienced the Exodus and Sinai to an end. The story of Balaam in chaps. 22–24 had demonstrated God's faithfulness to the promises that he had made to the people of Israel. In contrast, the story in Numbers 25 shows the fickle and shallow nature of the faith of God's people.

Israel here has every reason to be hopeful and faithful. The Balaam oracles describe the glorious future that is theirs as they stand again on the threshold of the promised land. The setting is a replay of the spy story in chaps. 13–14, in which the people likewise had every reason to have hope and trust in God. And yet the Israelites in Numbers 25 quickly and easily turn from their God to worship a false god and commit sin. The Balaam story described how even an ass can recognize an angel of God. Even a pagan prophet like Balaam can see God and do his will. Numbers 25 reveals that the same cannot be said of this old generation of God's own people. Balaam in chaps. 22–24 sees glorious visions of a great future. The Israelites in chap. 25 see only their own people playing the harlot, prostituting themselves with the foreign women of Moab and Midian. The story of the Israelite apostasy draws a sharp contrast between the faithfulness of God and the faithlessness of the old wilderness generation.

It is generally agreed that 25:1–5 represents an earlier version of the story that focuses on the women of Moab, the punishment of the chiefs of the people, and the role of the judges in carrying out the sentence. This earlier story was then expanded in vv. 6–18 by including the women of Midian, the punishment of all the people (v. 9), the role of Phinehas in carrying out a specific act of punishment, and God's consequent promise of a perpetual priesthood to him. Some of these elements are found in a version of the story in Ps. 106:28–31, which may have provided source material to the writer of Numbers.

The inclusion of the women of Midian in seducing the Israelites into the worship of other gods provides the justification for the later attack against Midian in Numbers 31. The punishment of all the people by a plague as a sign of God's wrath repeats a motif found in some of the other rebellion stories in Numbers (11:33; 14:37; 16:46). The role of Phinehas in killing Zimri the Israelite and Cozbi the Midianite woman was a meritorious act that legitimized Phinehas and his descendants as priests forever. Some commentators have seen this as an attempt to vindicate the priesthood of Phinehas and his line during a time in Israel's history when the legitimacy of that priesthood was in doubt. The notes in Ezra 8:2 and 1 Chron. 9:20 concerning Phinehas have been suggested as reflexes of this concern to validate Phinehas' priesthood in the postexilic period.

The great sin of Numbers 25 is the worship of other gods, in this case the god named Baal of Peor. The phrase in v. 1 describes the sin as playing the harlot with the women of Moab. This has a double sense. It refers to actual sexual intercourse with foreign women (see Exod. 34:12–16; Deut. 7:3–4). But it also refers to participating in the common ancient Near Eastern practice of cult prostitution that was a form of worship of certain fertility gods. The Israelites succumbed to pagan seduction both in a physical and a religious sense. Moab (Num. 25:1) and Midian (v. 6) are close neighbors; their identification in this story is not surprising.

The specific sinful act that enraged Phinehas was the intermarriage of the Israelite Zimri and the Midianite Cozbi. Phinehas killed them with a spear, presumably in the act of sexual intercourse. God interprets the killing as a sacrifice for the atonement of the people (v. 13). Priests usually sacrificed animals, but in this extreme case the two people directly involved in the sin were killed. Phinehas acts in concert with the jealous anger of God and is rewarded with the promise of the priesthood for him and his family.

The narrative of Israel's apostasy in Numbers 25 brings to a close the life of the first generation of Israelites out of Egypt. The twenty-four thousand people who die in v. 9 are presumably the last contingent of the old generation. They have been taken off the stage to make room for the coming of a new generation of Israelites who again stand on the edge of the promised land.

200

The advent of this new generation of hope and promise is signaled by the second census list of the twelve tribes of Israel in Numbers 26.

26:1–36:13

The Birth of the New Generation on the Edge of the Promised Land

The second half of the book of Numbers begins with the second of two census lists that appear in the book. The first census list (chap. 1) signaled the preparation of the first generation of Israelites out of Egypt for the march through the wilderness toward the promised land. The second census list (chap. 26) signals the preparation of an entirely new generation on the edge of the promised land. Numerous parallels between chaps. 1–25 and chaps. 26–36 enhance the sense of symmetry between the first and second halves of Numbers. This symmetrical construction conveys the impression that the new generation is given similar opportunities and guidance with the hope that it will fare better than the old generation that had died in the wilderness.

For example, the census list in chap. 26 uses the same formula for God's command to count the people (v. 2) as in 1:2–3. The lists of the twelve tribes in Numbers 1 and 26 have exactly the same order, except for a minor reversal of Manasseh and Ephraim. A census of the Levites follows the twelve-tribe census in both cases (chap. 3–4 and chap. 26). A legal discourse involving women in Numbers 5 parallels the legal discourse involving women (the daughters of Zelophehad) in Numbers 27. Laws concerning vows in chap. 6 find an echo in the laws concerning vows in chap. 30. Provisions for the Levites in Num. 18:21–32 are paralleled by the provisions for the levitical cities in Numbers 35. The list of offerings given by each tribe for the dedication of the altar in chap. 7 and the laws concerning offerings in chap. 15 find a parallel in the list of offerings to be given at the appointed feasts and holy days in chaps. 28 and 29. The celebration of the Passover in chap. 9 is mirrored in 28:16–25, where instructions for the future celebration of the Passover are given to all succeeding generations.

The list of spies in Numbers 13 is also echoed in the list of tribal leaders chosen to divide the land of Canaan in Numbers 34. The itinerary of Israel's wilderness journey in Numbers 1–25 is summarized in chap. 33. The story of the spies and the rebellion of Israel in chaps. 13–14 is taken up and used as a lesson for the new generation in 32:6–15. Moreover, the victory of the first generation of Israelites over Sihon and Og in the Transjordan prepares the way for the new generation of the tribes of Reuben, Gad, and the half-tribe of Manasseh to settle there in Numbers

32 (32:33). One final echo involves the last act of the first generation, which was apostasy in connection with the Midianites in 25:16–18. This act of seduction of the first generation of Israelites by the Midianites is avenged by the second generation in a holy war in chap. 31.

These parallels between chaps. 1–25 and chaps. 26–36, however, should not obscure the real differences in the characterization of the old generation and the new one. The old generation began with its census in the wilderness, a place of hardship and despair (1:1). The second generation begins its journey poised in expectation and hope on the edge of the promised land in the plains of Moab (26:3).

The first generation had been at the edge of the promised land twice before. When spies surveyed the land of Canaan and reported back, the people rebelled and were condemned to return to wander in the wilderness for forty years (chaps. 13–14). The members of the first generation were given the opportunity to come again to the threshold of the land of Canaan, but again they rebelled and so suffered their final death (chap. 25). In contrast, the new generation begins its life on the edge of the promised land (26:3) and remains there until the end of the book (36:13). Moses reminds the new generation of the wanderings of the preceding generation (33:1–47) and of the place where the new generation now stands (33:48–49). The new generation is also reminded of the goal: the new land to which they are going (33:51).

The fate of the first generation, as it attempted to live as God's holy people, led to ultimate death and failure (11:1–25:18). But the fate of the second generation is left open. Signs of hope appear along the way as disputes move toward peaceful resolution rather than open rebellion (27:1–11; 32:1–42; 36:1–13). Laws are given to the second generation that can apply only when they actually settle in the promised land (chaps. 27, 34–36). Such laws are a subtle promise that there is hope for this new generation to enter the land of promise. In contrast to the death of a whole generation in a series of rebellions and judgments in the first half, the second half of Numbers does not record the death of any Israelite. The Israelites are victorious in their first military engagement against the Midianites (chap. 31).

The second generation in Numbers 26–36 represents an entirely new beginning. Its destiny lies before it as it stands on the doorstep of the land of Canaan. Thus, the second half of the story of the second generation remains undecided and untold. The outcome is a question mark. Will the members of this new generation be faithful and enter the promised land? Or will they rebel and fail as the first generation had done? It is with this undecided future that the book of Numbers comes to an end.

26:1–65
The Second Census of the Twelve Tribes and the Levites: A New Generation

This second census of the twelve tribes of Israel and of the Levites is very similar in form to the census taken in Numbers 1–4. The same formulas are used in the command to take the census. The sequence in the list of tribes is virtually identical. The symmetrical construction of the two census lists suggests that they are intended to function together as the pillars of the structure of Numbers.

One significant difference between the two lists in chaps. 1 and 26 is that the second census list adds an enumeration of the various subclans within each tribe. An example is the tribe of Gad. Num. 1:24–25 simply lists the tribe of Gad and his family. Num. 26:15–18 enumerates the various subclans within the tribe of Gad (e.g., a son Zephon and the Zephonites). Many of the names for the subclans appear related to the list of the children of the twelve sons of Jacob in Gen. 46:8–27. This elaboration of the family groups within the tribes in Numbers 26 functions to express the development of the tribes into a new generation that now has branched out into various subclans. The newness of this generation is underscored by the fact that the names of the leaders of the tribes or clans in chap. 26 do not appear in the earlier census list in chap. 1 nor in any of the other previous lists of clan leaders in Numbers. The second census list represents a totally new generation.

Two important passages in Numbers 26 help to guide our interpretation of this second census list. First of all, vv. 52–56 suggest that the purpose of this second census list is primarily to determine the size of the territory that will be assigned to each of the twelve tribes when they enter the promised land. The focus has been shifted from the census as military preparation for war in Numbers 1. The formula that is repeated fourteen times in chap. 1, "all those who were able to go forth to war," is dropped entirely from the narrative of the census in chap. 26,

---

Opposite: Four of the twelve tribes of Israel (*clockwise from top:* Judah, Reuben, Ephraim, and Dan, each represented by a standard-bearing medieval knight) on the way to the promised land; frontispiece to the book of Numbers from the *Duke of Sussex Pentateuch,* ca. A.D. 1300. Numbers 2 specifies that the tribe of Judah was to camp with tribes to the east and lead the march. The tribes of Reuben, Ephraim, and Dan were to camp to the south, west, and north, respectively, and to lead those contingents.

with one exception (v. 2). The emphasis has shifted from the people's military preparation as the means of gaining the land to their receiving the land from God as a gift. The focus is not so much on conquest as on receiving the land as a gift from God and dividing it fairly among the tribes.

The second important passage in Numbers 26 is vv. 63–65. These verses explicitly pick up the theme of the whole book—the death of the old generation and the birth of the new generation of God's people. The spy narrative in chaps. 13–14 was the first to establish this overarching theme explicitly. The note in 26:63–65 takes it up and applies it to the second census. An entirely new generation has now arisen to take the place of the old. This text represents a programmatic summary of the structure of the book of Numbers. The second census is a sign that God's judgment upon the first generation has been completed. But the census is also a sign that God's promise of a new generation of hope has also been fulfilled.

27:1–11
The Daughters of Zelophehad and the Inheritance of Land: A Legal Dispute Resolved

The preceding chapter of Numbers had already established the principle of keeping the promised land equally and fairly divided among the tribes and families of Israel (26:52–56). To ensure that the land remained with the tribe to which it was first apportioned, the land was passed from eldest son to eldest son within the same family. A problem arises, however, as is intimated already in the census list in 26:33–34. Zelophehad had five daughters but no sons. After his death, his daughters urge Moses to allow them to inherit their father's land. In this way the land will remain in the same family, even though there are no sons. But this would contradict the custom that only males can inherit property.

Faced with this dilemma, Moses consults God for instruction on this unprecedented case. Is it more important that only males inherit property or that the land remain in the same family? God agrees with the daughters that the land must remain in their family's possession, even if it means violating the other custom that only males receive inherited land (27:5–11). The further issue of what should happen to the land when the daughters marry is not addressed here. That issue will be taken up in the conclusion of the book of Numbers when the daughters of Zelophehad will again appear (36:1–12). God affirms a high priority to the equal distribution of the economic base for each family. Other rules may be bent in order to ensure the well-being of each of the tribes and families of God's people. This legal dispute involving the daughters of Zelophehad provides an interesting look at the way in which new case law may have been developed in the absence of precedents. The successful resolution of the case and its relation to the promised land provide a positive and hopeful tone as the first incident recorded in the life of the new generation.

27:12–23
The Succession of Leadership from Moses to Joshua

God reminds Moses that he may only see Canaan and not actually enter it. Like his brother Aaron, Moses will die outside the promised land. The reason given is the sin of Moses and Aaron at the waters of Meribah of Kadesh when they rebelled against God's word (v. 14). The story is recounted in 20:1–13. As our commentary noted there, the precise nature of the sin or rebellion by Moses and Aaron is unclear. Nevertheless, the sin becomes the warrant for the prohibition of these two leaders to enter the promised land. The book of Deuteronomy provides an alternate tradition. In Deut. 3:26, Moses must die outside the land not because of his sin but because of that of the people.

The reminder of Moses' impending death causes him to plead to God for a new leader for the new generation of God's people. They already have a new priest in Eleazar. The succession of Aaron's priestly office to Eleazar and the death of Aaron were narrated together in Num. 20:22–29. Num. 27:12–23 narrates only the succession of the Mosaic office and not the actual death of Moses, which comes much later in Deuteronomy 34. Instead, we here read of the succession to the Mosaic office of Joshua, who was one of the faithful spies who God promised would enter the promised land (14:30). Joshua has frequently appeared as a close assistant to Moses (11:28; Exod. 17:8–13).

Joshua, however, is not to function simply as another Moses. Moses is to give only some or a portion of his authority to Joshua (Num. 27:20). While Moses spoke to God face to face in a most intimate and direct way (12:6–8), Joshua will have to rely on indirect divine guidance provided by the priest and his casting of lots with the Urim and Thummim (cf. Exod. 28:30; 1 Sam. 28:6). The era and revelation associated with the figure of Moses remain in some way unique and unrepeated in the history of Israel. Moses and Joshua will lead the people together in a coregency during the time of transition that will end with the death of Moses in Deuteronomy 34. Then Joshua will assume sole leadership of the people, but his leadership will be guided by the book of the Torah of Moses (Josh. 1:7–8).

Although the roles of Joshua and Moses are different, an essential continuity between the two leaders also exists. The laying of hands on Joshua by Moses underscores this continuity (Num. 27:18, 23). The imposition of hands transferred the power of authority, blessing, or sin from one to another. In any case, the one becomes a representative of or substitute for the other. Jacob blessed his grandsons by laying on his hands (Gen. 48:14). People could transfer their guilt or sin to another person or a sacrificial animal by placing their hands on the head of the person or animal (Lev. 1:4; 24:14). The Levites' function as substitute for all firstborn children was symbolized by the laying on of hands by the people of Israel (Num. 8:10–12). In chap. 27, authority is passed from Moses to Joshua by the imposition of hands. In this way, new leadership was publicly transferred from one generation to the next.

28:1–30:16
Further Ritual and Legal Regulations for the New Generation's Life in the Promised Land

This section includes a systematized program of sacrifices that Israel is to offer once in the land of Canaan and laws that remove any ambiguities about women and the legitimacy of their vows. Most commentators are agreed that this section of laws is among the latest parts of the book of Numbers and of the whole Pentateuch. Much of it may have been added to Numbers during the postexilic period in Israel's history. The primary function of these laws in the present structure of Numbers is to offer guidance and indirect assurance of the new generation's life in the promised land of Canaan.

28:1–29:40, A Systematized Program for Sacrifices in the Promised Land. Chaps. 28–29 provide a systematic list of the dates and quantities for the sacrifices that Israel is to offer God. The dates mentioned include the daily sacrifice in the morning and in the evening (28:3–8), the Sabbath sacrifice (28:9–10), the sacrifice on the first day of the month (28:11–15), and the sacrifices for the festivals. These include the Feast of Unleavened Bread (28:17–25), the Feast of First Fruits (28:26–31), the first day of the seventh month or Trumpets (29:1–6), the tenth day of the seventh month or the Day of Atonement (29:7–11) and Tabernacles (29:12–34) together with its eighth day of assembly, attested in Lev. 23:36 but no other Pentateuchal calendar (29:35–38). The various kinds of offerings or sacrifices include the whole offerings (the burnt flesh of animals), cereal offerings (grain and oil), drink offerings (wine), and purification offerings (the goat) (→ Worship).

This summary of the sacrifices appears to be based on much similar material scattered in Exodus 29, Leviticus 23, and Ezekiel 45–46. The sacrifices listed here are in addition to other votive and freewill offerings given by the people (Num. 29:39). The purpose of these offerings is to purify and dedicate the people of the new generation as they look forward to living in the land of Canaan. The enormous quantities of animals and grain and wine presuppose a settled agricultural life in the promised land. Therefore, these laws function as a hopeful sign that the new generation will soon enter Canaan. The laws in Numbers 15 had a similar role in their placement after the debacle of chaps. 13–14.

30:1–16, Women and Vows. Vows in the Bible typically took one of two forms. They could be made to give something to God, usually a sacrifice of some kind. Or a vow could involve abstaining from something as a sign of thankfulness or dedication. Examples include Jacob's vow of a tenth of his possessions to God (Gen. 28:20–22), Israel's vow to destroy the Canaanite cities in return for victory (Num. 21:2), Hannah's dedication of her son Samuel (1 Sam. 1:11), and the Nazirite vows of abstention (Num. 6:1–8). The vow may be seen as a type of freewill offering or sacrifice; this would explain its position following the laws concerning sacrifices in chaps. 28–29 (29:39).

The issue in Numbers 30 concerns situations in which a woman's vow may or may not be made void by the objection of a father or husband. The general principle is established at the outset: vows made to God by men are not to be broken (v. 2). In regard to vows made by women, the general principle followed is that the immediate objection of a father or husband to a woman's vow nullifies it without penalty (vv. 5, 8, 12). If a woman's husband does not protest the vow at first and only later objects, however, then he is responsible for fulfilling the vow and any penalty involved (v. 15).

In the patriarchal society of ancient Israel, women were often economically dependent on men. In certain circumstances, the ultimate responsibility for fulfilling vows made by a woman could rest upon her father or her husband. The laws in Numbers 30 thus protect the husband or father from the requirement to honor a woman's vow in special cases. But the laws also protect women and the integrity of their vows by requiring a clear and immediate response by a father or husband if the vow is to be nullified. Otherwise, the vow stands and the man bears the responsibility and any guilt incurred in not fulfilling the vow. The overriding concern is that the holiness of the people in the land be preserved and that all obligations to God be clearly fulfilled in a proper manner.

31:1–54
Revenge on the Midianites:
A Foretaste of the Conquest to Come

This section recounts a war of revenge on the Midianites led by Moses in his last act of military leadership. The narrative may be based in part upon the account of the conquest of the five Midianite kings in Josh. 13:21. The battle against the Midianites in Numbers 31 is the first military venture undertaken by the new generation of Israelites, and the success of their mission is overwhelming. This battle functions as a dress rehearsal and builds confidence and hope for the actual conquest of the promised land of Canaan that lay ahead.

The Israelites send out one thousand soldiers from each of the twelve tribes to fight the five Midianite kings (vv. 5–8). They kill every Midianite male and the prophet Balaam in revenge for the Midianite seduction of the Israelites into apostasy in Numbers 25. The guilty Israelites in chap. 25 were immediately punished by a plague (25:9). God commanded Moses at that time also to punish the guilty Midianites for having lured the Israelites into the false worship of a pagan god (25:16–18). Moses obeys this command in chap. 31 by a holy war of revenge upon the Midianites. The prophet Balaam, who is depicted as a faithful spokesperson for God in chaps. 22–24, is accused in 31:15–16 of having counseled the Midianite women into leading the Israelites astray in the false worship of Baal Peor. Thus, Balaam is included among those who are killed (v. 8).

Although every male among the Midianites is killed, Moses is angry because the Midianite women who played an important role in seducing the Israelites in Numbers 25 were not killed. He instructs the Israelite warriors to kill all the Midianite women who have been sexually active, but all virgins may be kept alive (31:17–18). Moreover, the purity of the camp and the Israelites is also to be protected through strict adherence to the purity laws in connection with touching the dead in battle (vv. 19–20) and in purifying all booty through fire and water (21–24).

The bulk of the rest of the chapter deals with the distribution of the spoils of the war, which includes both captives and animals. The booty is divided equally between soldiers and the people (v. 27; cf. 1 Sam. 30:21–25). A proportion of the booty is given to provide support for the priests and Levites (Num. 31:28–31). The list of the enormous quantities of booty that follows underscores God's faithfulness in leading the people in military success (vv. 32–47). It is discovered that not one Israelite died in the battle. In a response of thankfulness to God for protection in battle, a special offering is given in support of the sanctuary (vv. 48–54).

The narrative of the Midianite war plays an important role in portraying the obedience of the new generation of Israelites that leads to God's blessing. The battle and the division of booty illustrate how the new generation puts into practice the laws given to the old generation earlier in Numbers. The trumpets are sounded in accordance with the instructions in 10:1–10 (31:6). Numbers 19 outlined procedures for purification after contact with the dead; these procedures are followed in 31:19–20. Guidelines were given in Numbers 18 to ensure adequate support of the priests and the Levites. These guidelines provide the basis for the division of the booty in 31:25–47. In Numbers 7, each tribe of the old generation had demonstrated its devotion to God by giving offerings to the support of the sanctuary. This devotion is echoed in the new generation's generous offerings to the sanctuary (31:48–54). Numbers 31 is an example of laws obediently followed and put into action.

The new generation's victory in the Midianite war functions as an undoing or reversal of two incidents in the experience of the old generation. The first is the spy mission into Canaan in Numbers 13–14. Standing there on the edge of the promised land, the people had failed to trust God to lead them in victory. The result was death in the wilderness. In the first military expedition of the new generation in Numbers 31, however, the people trust God and obey his command to avenge the Midianites. The new generation experiences a resounding victory, and not one Israelite is killed in the process (v. 49). This first military victory of the new generation serves to undo the first military defeat of the old generation in Numbers 13–14.

The second incident in the life of the old generation here reversed is the apostasy in Numbers 25. The Midianites had led the people to worship a pagan god. The Israelites had been conquered not by military strength but by religious seduction. In Numbers 31, the roles are reversed, as the Midianites are conquered and the Israelites are victorious. The victory over the Midianites signals a new and fresh start for the new generation of Israelites. The victory strengthens the hope and trust of the people as they look forward to entering the long awaited land of promise.

32:1–33:56
Words of Warning and Encouragement: Reminders from a Generation Past

Chap. 32 inserts a note of warning and one of hope into the story of the new generation of God's people. A potential crisis erupts that may upset the whole plan of entering the promised land. Two of the Israelite tribes desire to settle outside the land of Canaan on the east side of the Jordan River. Moses is angered by their request and warns the people that they may become like the old generation who died in the wilderness. A compromise is achieved, however, and the crisis averted.

Chap. 33 is a summary of the itinerary traveled by the old generation of Israelites from Egypt through the wilderness to the edge of the promised land. It contains a list of places where the people camped along with notes that provide both words of warning and words of encouragement to the new generation camped at the threshold of the promised land.

32:1–42, A Crisis Averted: The Request of Reuben and Gad to Settle Outside the Land of Canaan. This section is typically understood by commentators to be a composite of two or more layers of material that have been combined to form the present narrative. The earliest parts of the story may be found in vv. 16–27 and 34–38. In its present form, the story recounts the request by Reuben and Gad to settle on the east side of the Jordan River. It was this territory that the Israelites captured from Sihon and Og in 21:21–35 (32:33). Since the Jordan River forms the eastern boundary of the land of Canaan, their request seems to suggest a desire not to enter the promised land of Canaan. Moses fears that the other tribes will be discouraged and lose heart if Gad and Reuben stay and do not cross the Jordan River into Canaan with the other tribes.

Moses draws a parallel with the experience of the old generation in the spy story in Numbers 13–14 and the request of Gad and Reuben. Like the spies' negative report of the land, Gad and Reuben's request may dishearten the people and cause them not to trust God to lead them into the land. If that happens, the fate of the old generation, which was death in the wilderness, may become the fate of the new generation as well (32:6–15). The lesson of the past becomes a paradigm that interprets the potential rebellion of the new generation again on the edge of the promised land. The outcome of the second generation remains an open question. If they rebel, God may again punish them.

The people continue to live under the threat of God's judgment.

The last word in this episode, however, is one of promise and encouragement. Reuben and Gad propose a compromise whereby they will join the other Israelites in conquering the land of Canaan. Only after the conquest is complete will they return to the territory on the east side of the Jordan to settle there. Moses accepts the compromise as a reasonable one, and the crisis is averted (vv. 16–27). He instructs Joshua and Eleazar to enforce the compromise agreement, and Reuben and Gad pledge their commitment to the plan (vv. 28–32). Moses then grants the territory and its cities to these two tribes and also to half of the tribe of Manasseh as their possession (33–42).

This story plays an important role in the larger structure of Numbers, as it explicitly applies the central theme of the spy story in chaps. 13–14 to the new generation of God's people. Both the promises and the warnings from the old generation are focused on this new one. The final fate of this second generation is unknown at this point, but the successful resolution of the potential crisis brings the episode to a close on a note of hope and promise.

33:1–56, The Travel Itinerary of the Old Generation: Warning and Encouragement for the New Generation. Chap. 33 consists of a list of campsites of the Israelites as they traveled from Egypt to the boundary of the promised land. Many of the names of the campsites are found only in this list (vv. 13, 19–29). Most of the actual locations of the campsites in the wilderness are today unknown. The list of places may reflect a combination of one or more actual itineraries used by travelers or pilgrims in ancient times, but the precise background of the itinerary is very difficult to reconstruct.

Several of the names of the campsites do occur, however, elsewhere in the Pentateuch, and some have specific incidents connected with them. These incidents are recalled to engender hope in the new generation. For example, the recollection of God's victory over the Egyptians (v. 3) and over the Canaanite king of Arad (v. 40) would serve to encourage the new generation about to engage the Canaanites as they enter the land. Other incidents are recalled as warnings to the new generation: the judgment on the worship of false gods (v. 4) and the death of Aaron for his sin (vv. 38–39) are mentioned. The list of campsites is followed by a general word of assurance from God to the people about their imminent entry into the land of Canaan (vv. 50–54). The chapter concludes with a word of warning if the people do not carry out the conquest of Canaan faithfully

and obediently (vv. 55–56). The overall effect of the lengthy and detailed list of encampments is to underscore God's faithfulness in bringing Israel through the long and arduous wilderness journey. Such faithfulness ought to inspire confidence and trust in God as the people enter the promised land.

34:1–36:13
Law as Promise: Divine Commands Concerning the Anticipated Residence of the People in the Promised Land

The book of Numbers concludes with a series of laws and instructions that assume that the conquest of Canaan is near at hand. These final chapters of the book strike a uniformly positive note as the new generation looks forward to its life in the land that had been promised to its ancestors for generations.

34:1–29, Boundaries and Divisions of the Land. The chapter outlines the procedures for the future division of the land of Canaan. It opens with precise instructions from God for drawing the boundary lines of the Promised Land. The boundaries in chap. 34 exceed those of Israel at any point in its history. The portrait of the land here is thus an idealized one; the promise in a sense always outdistanced its fulfillment in a particular historical time. And yet the land is a very tangible and carefully delineated promise from God; it is not simply an otherworldly or nebulous hope.

The description of the land in chap. 34 corresponds very closely to the description of the area covered by the spies in chaps. 13–14. The southern boundary is in the Wilderness of Zin (34:3), and the northern boundary extends to the entrance of Hamath (v. 8; cf. 13:21). The eastern boundary is the Jordan River (34:12), and the western boundary is the "Great Sea" (v. 6; cf. 13:29). These precise correspondences between the spy story and the boundaries of the land delineated in Numbers 34 suggest that the original promise of the land to the old generation has now been extended in its entirety to the new generation.

35:1–34, Establishment of Levitical Cities and Cities of Refuge: Maintaining the Purity of the Promised Land. Provisions having been made in chap. 34 for the division of the land among the people, chap. 35 makes provisions for cities for the Levites to occupy and for pasturelands on which to graze their livestock (vv. 1–8). This material may in part be dependent on the list of levitical cities in Joshua 21. Numbers 18 provided for the support of the

Levites from the offerings of the people because the Levites "will have no inheritance among the people of Israel" (18:24). The levitical cities are thus not the permanent possession or inheritance of the Levites but rather a place for them to live and pasture their flocks.

Forty-eight cities were to be designated as levitical by the twelve tribes of Israel with the larger tribes contributing more cities than the smaller (35:7–8). In this way, the Levites, who guarded the holiness of God and the sanctuary, would be distributed throughout the land of Israel.

Six of the levitical cities were also designated as cities of refuge to which a person who had killed another person could flee (34:6). Detailed instructions for the cities of refuge and for determining guilt and intention in the matter of murder or manslaughter are given in 35:9–34 (→ Murder). The holiness of God's promised land could be threatened through the shedding of human blood, one of the most serious defilements. Murder and its defilement of the land could be expiated only through the blood of the murderer (vv. 33–34). The cities of refuge, however, provided a place of sanctuary for a person who had killed another citizen unintentionally. Such a person would be admitted only after determination by the elders of the city that the killing was in fact unintentional. Guidelines for such a determination are given in vv. 16–25. The person was then to remain in the city of refuge until the death of the high priest; the violation of this provision would make the person vulnerable to blood revenge by a relative of the victim (vv. 26–28). Related matters concerning the number of witnesses required for a murder conviction and the prohibition of paying ransom to expiate a murder are also given (vv. 30–32). The overall intent of these laws is to ensure the purity of God's holy land, which the new generation is about to receive.

36:1–13, The Daughters of Zelophehad Revisited: Maintaining the Equal Distribution of Land Among the Tribes. Chap.
36 resumes the case of the daughters of Zelophehad and the inheritance of their father's land in the absence of any male heirs, which first appeared in Numbers 27. There it was decided that the daughters could inherit their father's land in order to keep the land within the family. Here another question arises. May the daughters of Zelophehad marry outside their own tribe, or must they marry only men in their own tribal group in order to prevent the alienation of the land (vv. 1–4)? God is consulted and proclaims that the daughters may marry any man as long as he is a member of their own tribe, Manasseh (vv. 5–9). The overriding concern is that the ancestral land remain within the tribe that originally inherited it (v. 9). The daughters of Zelophehad comply with the directive from God, and this brings the commandments of God concerning the land in the last part of the book of Numbers to a positive and hopeful conclusion (vv. 10–13).

The stories of Zelophehad's daughters in Numbers 27 and 36 form a frame that brackets all the material related to the new generation counted and organized in the second census list in chap. 26. Most of the material contained within this frame relates to life in the promised land. Thus, the two narratives of the five daughters of Zelophehad function as a positive confirmation of God's promise that the land will indeed one day be given to the new generation of God's people. Moreover, the case of the daughters and the land affirms the flexibility of the tradition and its need for new interpretation with the experience of each new generation. This adaptability provides a warrant for a new interpretation from another tradition that readers will encounter in the book of Deuteronomy, which follows Numbers as the fifth book of the Pentateuch.

Bibliography

Budd, P. J. Numbers. Word Biblical Commentary. Waco, TX: Word, 1984.

Gray, G. B. A Critical and Exegetical Commentary on Numbers. International Critical Commentary. Edinburgh: Clark, 1903.

Noth, M. Numbers, A Commentary. Philadelphia: Westminster, 1968.

Olson, D. T. The Death of the Old and the Birth of the New: The Framework of the Book of Numbers and the Pentateuch. Chico, CA: Scholars Press, 1985.

Plaut, W. G. The Torah: A Modern Commentary. New York: Union of American Hebrew Congregations, 1981.

DEUTERONOMY

RICHARD D. NELSON

INTRODUCTION

Deuteronomy presents itself as a series of addresses offered by Moses to Israel just before its entry into the land of promise. Law giving, wilderness, and the conquest of the east bank of the Jordan are behind Israel. Canaan with its blessings and dangers lies before the people. A large number of introductory formulas and summaries are scattered through the book (1:1–5; 4:44, 45–49; 5:1; 12:1; 26:16; 29:1; 31:1), making a description of its literary shape and its history of composition difficult.

Deuteronomy has two introductions in the form of speeches given by Moses. In the first (1:1–4:43), Moses reviews history from Mount Horeb (Deuteronomy's name for Sinai) to the point of transition into Canaan and exhorts Israel to loyalty. In the second introduction (4:44–11:32), he exhorts and motivates Israel to obey the Torah (God's instruction to Israel), again reviewing history at several points. The central core of Deuteronomy consists of chaps. 12–26. Here Moses promulgates a law designed to shape Israel's life in the land as God's faithful people. The last part of the book, chaps. 27–34, directs this law at Israel's future life in Canaan.

The parts and sections of the book may be outlined in this way:

1:1–4:43, Part One: Moses reviews history
  1:1–3:29, The road from Horeb
  4:1–43, Transition to the law
4:44–11:32, Part Two: Moses preaches about the law
  4:44–6:9, First principles
  6:10–11:32, A motivational introduction
12:1–26:19, Part Three: Moses proclaims the law
  12:1–14:21, Purity in worship
  14:22–16:17, Life in the new land
  16:18–20:20, The structures of society
  21:1–26:19, Interpreting traditional laws
27:1–34:12, Part Four: The story continues
  27:1–30:20, Covenant making
  31:1–34:12, Transition to Canaan

The original book of Deuteronomy seems to have consisted of the reform-oriented law code proper (chaps. 12–26), framed by an introductory exhortation (chaps. 5–11) and some concluding chapters that directed the law at the readers of the book (chaps. 27–30). There is no agreement whether an even earlier and shorter form of the book once existed. A puzzling feature of Deuteronomy is its alternation between second-person singular and plural address. The plural portions often seem to be somewhat later than the singular portions, but there is no completely satisfactory explanation for this phenomenon.

In its original form, Deuteronomy was addressed to Israel in the period of the monarchy (about the eighth century B.C.) by a group or an individual writing in the name of Moses. Just as Moses was the mediator for God's law, Deuteronomy sought to mediate God's will for the people in a new period of crisis and transition. The precise nature of the intended audience remains uncertain, but there are indications that the Northern Kingdom of Israel provided the original context, rather than Judah. There are close affinities to the northern prophet Hosea, especially in the use of the concept of covenant. The absence of any reference to the Davidic dynasty or Jerusalem and the demand for a radical reform of the kingship point to the Northern Kingdom, as does Deuteronomy's focus on Shechem (11:29–30; 27:1–26).

Although its date cannot be fixed precisely, Deuteronomy provides us with clues to the crisis that caused it to be written. This crisis was partly religious. Loyalty to the God of Israel had been undermined by the worship of Canaanite gods. One source of this syncretism was the cities (13:12–18), which had retained much of their Canaanite heritage in spite of their inclusion in the Israelite state. Another source was the local sanctuaries or "high places" scattered throughout the country (12:2–3). There the gods of Canaan and the God of Israel were worshiped side by side, sometimes with fertility rites alien to Israel's traditions. Certain prophets were compounding the problem by authorizing syncretism and the worship of other gods (13:1–5). One practical result of Israel's lapse in religious loyalty was the precarious economic position of the levitical priests, whose cause Deuteronomy champions.

Another facet of the crisis was social. Deuteronomy reflects a breakdown in family solidarity caused by social change (21:18–21; 25:5–10). The shift from a purely agricultural barter economy to a money economy in which wealth could be accumulated and lent at interest had caused a critical social problem. Farmers who had worked their ancestral lands for generations were losing them to those classes who were in a position to lend them money. Sometimes the inability to satisfy a debt led to the enslavement of the farmer and his family (15:12–18). The gap between the rich and poor was widening and the traditional institutions to protect the poor needed to be revitalized (→ Economics in Old Testament Times).

A third aspect of the crisis was political. The judicial system was corrupted by bribery and had become unfair to those most in need of justice (16:18–20). The authors of Deuteronomy clearly believed that the power and wealth of the monarchy needed to be sharply curtailed. They saw the king's professional army and the royal penchant for international adventurism as problems (17:16–17). Perhaps the danger of Assyrian control or even conquest was already ominously apparent.

To meet this crisis, Deuteronomy offered itself to Israel as a reform law. It imagined and described a new society, one based on renewed dedication to God and God's law. Deuteronomy's vision was fully utopian in the positive sense of the word, calling Israel to restructure itself in the spirit of Mount Horeb.

There would be a seven-year cycle of tithes offered to God and the poor, culminating in a release of all debts and a national rededication to the law. There would be zeal for religious purity at all levels of society. God's law would penetrate all areas of life. The king would become an ordinary citizen whose primary task would be to study the law. Ancestral lands would be protected. Fair justice for all would be the rule, and the economic system would protect the poor from the greed of the rich. The ancient traditions of holy war would be revitalized. Most importantly, the tempting danger presented by the local high places would be eliminated by centralizing all sacrificial worship at a single national sanctuary.

This reform of Israel's life before God was directed at the original readers of Deuteronomy by means of the theological concept of the covenant. Deuteronomy explicitly identifies itself as the content of a covenant made in the land of Moab, itself a renewal of the covenant made at Mount Horeb. This covenant is summarized in 26:16–19 and 27:9–10: Israel is to be God's people and the Lord will be Israel's God. The theme of covenant is further supported by the presence of extensive blessings and curses of the sort used to guarantee ancient treaty documents.

It is often thought that the entire book of Deuteronomy may reflect the shape of ancient Near Eastern treaties and follow the format of some regular ceremony of covenant renewal. It may be more reasonable to look to the prophet Hosea as the source of this covenant concept. In any case, God's covenant with Israel does not only concern the past but transcends generations to confront any audience of Deuteronomy directly with its challenge.

Great rhetorical skill was used to convince readers to adopt the far-reaching reforms proposed by the book. Such skill points to some group that knew Israel's historical and legal traditions well and were practiced in presenting it to lay audiences. Scholars have suggested the prophets, the sages, and the Levites as possibilities. Like Moses, the authors of Deuteronomy were mediators of God's law who did not just promulgate it but explained it (5:22–31). Readers were encouraged and motivated to obey through repetitious, sermonic language, through repeated calls to remember the past, and through explanations that tried to rationalize the laws and uncover their meaning.

Deuteronomy did not seek to reform external behavior only but inner attitudes toward God and neighbor as well. It endeavored with great urgency to engage and change readers before it was too late, and that urgency is visible throughout the book. Deuteronomy confronts each reader personally and demands a personal response, best summarized by 6:4–9 and 10:12–13.

Characteristic theological themes permeate Deuteronomy. God is the central focus. This is the God of the Exodus (5:6), the God of history who has given victory in war and the promised gift of land (7:17–24; 9:1–6). This is also the Creator (10:14), the God of nature who blesses Israel with rain and fertility (11:10–17).

Israel is the people chosen by God (7:6; 10:15; 14:2). God loves Israel (7:8), and love becomes the basic principle of the relationship between him and Israel (6:5). This love is known to Israel through its memory of God's redemption in the Exodus (7:8; 9:26; 15:15) and nurture in the wilderness (8:2–4; 29:4–5). God's supreme gift to Israel is the good land, the land promised long ago to the patriarchs. The goodness, richness, and fertility of this land is constantly emphasized (8:7–10; 11:10–12), but this land also contains within it the temptation to forgetfulness and apostasy (7:1–6; 8:11–20).

Forgetful, apostate Israel is a people in critical danger. Discipline is part of God's parental love (8:5). The Lord is a jealous God who will not countenance the worship of other deities (5:9; 7:9–10). Israel must be a holy people, loyal only to the God who has liberated it (26:18–19). Israel is to worship the Lord alone, and to do so only in the place which he has chosen. Loyalty to God means following his will not only in matters of religion, but in political affairs and daily life. Yet Israel's record so far has been dismal. Israel is a stubborn and rebellious people (9:7–14) and punishment in the form of national destruction is imminent (29:18–28).

Two ways are set before Israel: the way of obedience and life and the way of continued disobedience and death (30:15–20). The future

210

remains open, but Israel must choose and do so immediately. The terrible curses of chap. 28 hang over the future. Yet the proper choice is so easy and obvious that it is really no choice at all. The law of God is near and easy to obey (30:11–14). Remember what God has done for you (7:18; 8:2; 16:3) and do not forget (6:12; 8:14–18). Circumcise your heart (10:16). Choose life (30:19)!

Deuteronomy underwent a second major stage in its compositional history after its adoption by King Josiah as the reform law of the kingdom of Judah (2 Kings 22–23; → Josiah). Somehow, a century after the collapse of the Northern Kingdom to which it had probably been directed, Deuteronomy appeared in Jerusalem, where it initiated a spectacular but short-lived reform (622 B.C.). Naturally, the Jerusalem Temple was assumed to be the central sanctuary the book called for. Josiah abolished the local high places in Judah and extended the reform into the territory of the former Northern Kingdom as well. He also centralized the Passover in Jerusalem (16:1–8).

During the reign of Josiah (or perhaps somewhat later, early in the Exile), Deuteronomy was utilized as the first part of a long historical work we today call the Deuteronomistic History. This work tells the story of Israel in the land and stretches through the books of Joshua, Judges, 1 and 2 Samuel, and 1 and 2 Kings. Deuteronomy was integrated into this history by the addition of the first introductory speech (chaps. 1–3 and parts of chap. 4). This historical review by Moses became the first in a series of summary reviews that punctuate the Deuteronomistic History at critical points of transition: Joshua 1 and 23, 1 Samuel 12, 2 Samuel 7, 1 Kings 8, and 2 Kings 17. In this way, Deuteronomy was directed at a new audience and became the interpretive key for understanding the later history of the people. Israel prospered or suffered as a direct result of its obedience or disobedience of this law. Chap. 31 and portions of chap. 34 were also added by this Deuteronomistic historian to link Deuteronomy to the conquest under Joshua and Israel's life under the law (→ Deuteronomistic Historian).

The final stages in the history of Deuteronomy's composition took place in the Exile. Two related short additions (4:29–31; 30:1–10) call on the people to return to God and promise a return from exile. The addition of the Song of Moses (chap. 32) pointed beyond exile and punishment to God's vindication of the people in the face of their enemies. The Blessing of Moses (chap. 33) speaks of God's gracious will for the people and dreams of a better future. At the very latest stage, Deuteronomy became the fifth of the books of the Torah, or Pentateuch (Genesis through Deuteronomy). Portions from the Priestly writer were added to effect this merger: 1:3; 4:41–43; 32:48–52; 34:1a, 7–9 (→ Sources of the Pentateuch).

Deuteronomy plays a central role in the Hebrew Bible. As the authority and norm of the reformation sponsored by King Josiah, it may legitimately be considered the first book of the Bible to be treated as Scripture and in that sense canonized, that is, admitted to the Bible. Indeed the book seems to claim canonical status for itself (4:2; 12:32; 31:24–26). Ideas and language from Deuteronomy helped shape the final form of the Pentateuch and the books of Jeremiah and Amos. Deuteronomistic theology undergirds the entire presentation of history in the Former Prophets (Joshua, Judges, 1 and 2 Samuel, 1 and 2 Kings).

As the last book of the Torah and the first part of the Deuteronomistic History, Deuteronomy may have served as a catalyst for linking these two complexes in the canonization process. In its present place in the canon, it links the narrative of desert wandering to the conquest of Canaan.

The reforming law became an important part of emerging Judaism in the Second Temple period. That the Jerusalem Temple was the only legitimate sanctuary was taken for granted. Passover was celebrated according to the dictates of Deuteronomy as a Jerusalem festival. The Shema and the verses following it (6:4–9) became a focus for the practice of piety. The influence of Deuteronomy may be traced in passages such as Ezra 9:12; Neh. 1:8–9; 13:1–3; and Tob. 1:6–8, as well as in the teaching of Jesus (Matt. 18:16; Mark 7:10; 12:29–30).

The humane spirit of Deuteronomy, its concern for justice, and its call to love God above all else have challenged both Judaism and Christianity to ongoing reform through the centuries.

COMMENTARY

1:1–4:43

Moses Reviews History

The law of Deuteronomy (chaps. 12–26) is introduced by two successive speeches of Moses. The second one (4:44–11:32) is primarily exhortation. This first speech emphasizes history. Moses surveys the story of Israel from Mount Horeb (1:6) to Beth-peor (3:29) in a connected way and applies the lessons of this history to his audience (1:16–17, 29–30), especially in chap. 4.

Thus the basis for the law Moses is about to deliver is a review of Israel's experience with

God. Ancient Near Eastern treaty documents began with similar reviews of history as prologues to the practical commands and prohibitions of the treaties themselves. It is very uncertain, however, whether such treaties actually influenced the shape of Deuteronomy. Scholars have also speculated that covenant renewal ceremonies in Israel may have followed a similar pattern, with historical review preceding a reading of God's law, but again certainty eludes us. It would be natural, however, for any agreement between two parties to reflect on their past relationship as a basis for their shared future. Certainly this is the pattern of Deuteronomy. Reference to the past (9:7–10:11; 11:2–7; 29:2–9) provides the basis for God's gift of the law and a motive for Israel to keep it.

Chaps. 1–4 were prefaced to the book to integrate the book into the larger whole of the Deuteronomistic History. They find their counterpart in chap. 31, where the transition from Moses to Joshua is completed and the story moves on to that told in Joshua through 2 Kings. By adding these chapters, the Deuteronomistic historian addressed the book of the law to an audience somewhat later than the original readers of Deuteronomy, to Judah in the late monarchy or early Exile. The law of Deuteronomy is introduced as the evaluative principle according to which the following story of Israel in the land is to be understood. The themes of victorious conquest (2:24–3:11), allotment of the land (3:12–20), and the leadership of Joshua (3:28) prepare for the following book of Joshua. The theological principle that obedience leads to success and disobedience results in destruction (1:41–44; 4:3–4) is the key to understanding the history of Judges and 1 and 2 Kings. In the present shape of the Hebrew Bible, this introduction also links Deuteronomy to the other books of the Pentateuch, covering many of the same traditions reported in Numbers.

Themes important to Deuteronomy as a whole are introduced: love and election (7:6–8; 10:15; 14:2), the dangers of apostasy (13:1–18), a concern for justice (16:18–20; 17:8–13). The focus of this introduction is God, who has guided Israel (1:31–33; 2:7) and given them victory in war (2:24–3:11). God also chose Israel in love (4:31, 37) and remains with them because of loyalty to past promises (1:8, 11). God has given the gift of the law. Now it is time for Moses to explain this law (1:5) and for Israel to adopt it as the basis for their new life in the land (4:1, 5, 14).

The original readers of Deuteronomy were meant to apply to themselves this situation of transition from old to new. The literary technique of distinguishing and merging three generations helped them do so. These chapters speak of the former evil generation whose fate is to be taken as a warning (1:35; 2:14–16), of the present generation that is Moses' audience and that must be attentive and faithful in the face of the crisis of transition to new leaders and a new land (1:39; 3:28), and of a future generation that will experience the punishment and mercy of God (4:25–31). Yet all three generations merge into one in those to whom the book is addressed (1:26; 4:11, 40). Israel in the monarchical period had suffered destruction, yet looked forward to God's mercy. They too faced the challenge of applying old traditions to a new situation.

1:1–3:29
The Road from Horeb

Moses begins his speech with a review of history that leads up to the place and time at which, according to the literary premise of Deuteronomy, he is addressing a new generation of Israel (1:5; 3:29). Retelling older traditions about the wilderness and conquest, these chapters cover about the same ground as the narrative portions of Numbers 11–31, but rely on traditions somewhat different from those preserved there. These stories are kept clearly in the past from the standpoint of Moses and his audience by the repeated phrase "at that time" (e.g., 1:9, 16, 18; 2:34). They have been joined together into a larger story tracing Israel's progress from Mount Horeb (Deuteronomy's name for Mount Sinai) to the stopping point opposite Beth-peor. Linking passages describe the people's movements in the first person plural: 1:19; 2:1, 8, 13; 3:1. A different sort of progress is the transition from the previous disobedient generation to the present one (1:35; 2:14–15) and a consequent shift from failure to success (cf. 1:42; 2:33; 3:3).

1:1–8, Introduction. As an introduction to Deuteronomy as a whole and to its opening review of history (1:9–4:43) in particular, these initial verses answer the questions "Who?" "Where?" "When?" "What?" and "To whom?" Moses is the "who," the speaker of the words that follow. God is the actual source of Moses' words, however, for they are spoken at God's command (1:3). Moreover, Moses quotes God directly (vv. 6–8), as he will continue to do throughout Deuteronomy.

The people are at the end of an arduous journey. Pinpointing the "where" is made impossible by the piling up of contradictory geographical expressions, but the general locale, "across the Jordan" in "the land of Moab," is clear enough. The people are near the crossing point, about to invade Canaan. They will still be there when Deuteronomy draws to a close (29:1; 32:49). The "when" is the eleventh month of the fortieth and last year of wilderness wandering. Mount Horeb is in the past.

The conquest of the land east of the Jordan is complete. Now is the moment of transition into the land of promise.

The "what" about to be spoken by Moses is law (Heb. *torah*), but more particularly law that will be explained, expounded on, and clarified (1:5). *Torah* proves to be the opposite of cold legalism in every way. Deuteronomy is a book of "preached law," applied with careful concern to life lived in the new land. This land is described expansively and, in words reminiscent of a legal formula, placed by God at Israel's disposal (vv. 7–8). It is promised land, sworn to the patriarchs and their children.

These children are those "to whom" this law for a new life in the land is expounded. The former faithless generation has died (1:35). A new generation now awaits the move across the Jordan into nationhood. Yet those who hear the speech of Moses are also "all Israel" (v. 1), a universal address used more than a dozen times in Deuteronomy. This preached law addresses an audience that transcends generations, one that includes the original readers of Deuteronomy in the period of the monarchy. They are carried back in time to stand before Moses and to hear him explain the law that must shape their new life as the Israel they ought to become.

This introduction calls readers to give careful attention to what is to follow. Deuteronomy is to be taken with utmost seriousness. It is a law commanded by God and mediated by Moses. It is a law founded on the authority of God, who chose the patriarchs, promised the good land, and fulfilled that promise through victorious conquest. All Israel, as the beneficiary of God's gracious acts, is now to listen.

1:9–18, Judicial Organization. Even before Israel left Mount Horeb, it was structured into a society shaped by God's justice. These verses utilize an old tradition, similar to the traditions preserved in Exodus 18 and Numbers 11, to implant in readers a concern for justice and to argue that a fair judicial system is expected of God's people. Here are revealed the first sketchy outlines of Deuteronomy's visionary portrayal of what life in the land ought to be like. There must be fearlessly impartial justice for both fellow Israelite and resident foreigner, for the powerful and the powerless alike. That is God's way (vv. 16–17).

The problem faced by Moses is, paradoxically, caused by God's blessing, the population explosion promised to the patriarchs (Gen. 15:5). It is a problem that will only get worse (Deut. 1:11). The people agree to a structure for handling legal disputes. This system would rely on well-qualified personnel and would penetrate every level of society from the tribes down to small groups of ten families.

This first story in the historical review establishes basic themes in Deuteronomy: concern for resident foreigners (10:19) and an interest in justice and juridical structures (16:18–20; 17:8–13). Deut. 1:18 presents this story as just one example of how Moses prepared Israel for life in the land. In actual fact, of course, Israel was not always a just society (Amos 5:7, 10–12; 1 Kings 21). Deuteronomy remembers, however, that Israel had once been in harmony with God's justice and dreams that this might be so again.

1:19–46, A Failed Invasion. Moses tells his audience (and Deuteronomy its readers) an illustrative story based on traditions similar to those preserved in Numbers 13–14. This is a cautionary tale, a negative example of what must never happen again. It calls forth fidelity by portraying rebellion. It evokes courage by describing both cowardice and bravado.

Israel's disobedience is put in the worst possible light. It follows a wholly positive scouting report (Deut. 1:25; the bad news about Canaan is saved until v. 28). Israel mutters treason secretly in its tents. The people accuse God of hating them and impugn his motives. Reversing the standard formula of holy war, they insist that they will be delivered into the hand of the Amorites, a grim self-fulfilling prophecy.

The fear and infidelity of Israel's insurrection are undercut for readers in two ways: positively by Moses' two speeches of encouragement (vv. 20–21, 29–33) and negatively by the outcome of the story. Moses stresses that parental concern is obvious from what God has already done for Israel. Israel cannot question the Lord's motives, for he fought for Israel in Egypt (cf. vv. 30, 27). God does not hate Israel but carries Israel like a beloved child (cf. vv. 31, 27). Israel's querulous question of v. 28, "wherever are we going?" receives its answer in God's providential wilderness leadership (v. 33).

The narrative illustrates that rebellion against God leads to disaster. The land the Lord swore to give, he now swears to withhold (vv. 34–35). Even Moses suffers from God's anger (v. 37). Pointed back in the ominous direction of the Red Sea, the people instead compound their rebellion against the command of God (cf. vv. 26, 43) out of a false confidence in the ease of a campaign they had earlier dreaded. The results are defeat and God's refusal to listen to their tears. The people remain frozen at Kadesh (v. 46), no longer on the road to their destiny.

Themes are introduced that recur later in Deuteronomy: God's anger with Moses (3:26; 4:21; 34:4), faith and courage in war (7:17–21; chap. 20), and Israel's unworthiness (8:11–18; 9:1–9). Later readers were meant to apply the lesson of their forebears' folly to their own situation. Like Caleb, Joshua, and Israel's little ones (1:36, 38–39), these readers faced challenges of fidelity that had overwhelmed their ancestors. They were the survivors of defeats believed to have resulted from God's punishing anger. Now they needed courage to face the future and faith to bring into being the sort of community envisioned by Deuteronomy. God's past acts as parent, leader, and warrior could evoke such faith and courage.

2:1–25, Through Neighboring Territories. Historical recitation continues, based on traditions similar to Num. 20:14–21. Because Israel's goal is the conquest of the Amorites (Canaanites), non-Amorite nations are to be left alone (Edom, Deut. 2:4–7; Moab, v. 9; Ammon, vv. 18–19). Just as God is giving Israel a homeland, so has he already given these nations lands previously promised to their ancestors Esau (v. 5) and Lot (vv. 9, 19). Edom is given the fullest treatment. Israel is cautioned lest Edom's fears lead to war. Purchasing food and water would defuse tensions. Israel is reminded that Edomites are a related people and that experience has demonstrated that God would provide.

These warnings, along with the parenthetical comments of vv. 10–12, 20–23, breathe a cosmopolitan, universalistic spirit. Israel's God is also the God of these nations and has dispossessed other peoples to give them promised lands. This broad vision implies disapproval of those acts of aggrandizement against these nations that preoccupied much of the foreign policy of the Israelite and Judean monarchies. An imperialistic state is not what Deuteronomy is proposing (17:16).

The Zered marks the boundary of Moab here, but it is also a watershed of another sort (2:14). The former generation has died not just from natural causes but through God's direct action (v. 15). Now the new generation to whom Moses is speaking is ready for the conquest. Israel's fearsome reputation has preceded them (v. 25; cf. v. 4). Classic holy war language announces that Sihon will be at Israel's mercy, and warlike imperatives mark the transition from peace to war (v. 24).

2:26–3:11, Sihon and Og. Moses continues his review of recent history with the conquest of the east bank of the Jordan. The defeat of Sihon and Og was a standard item in Israel's national memory (29:7–8; Num. 21:21–35; Ps. 136:17–22). The accent falls on Sihon; the story of Og reiterates and seconds the point. In Deuteronomy's version, God is the prime mover behind the conflict and its outcome. The battle results from Sihon's intransigence, insists the narrative. Israel is not the aggressor. Moses peacefully proposes to keep to the roads lest crops be trampled and people harassed, to buy food and water, and in general to act as circumspectly as Israel al-

ready has done in Edom and Moab. Israel's true objective, claims Moses, lies across the Jordan. Yet God is really behind the whole event, strengthening Sihon's resolve to resist, encouraging Israel with promises of success, and handing them a pair of victories.

These victories are wonderfully complete, involving the whole east bank from Moab's border in the south to Mount Hermon in the north. The numerous defeated cities are put under the ban (→ Ban) according to the standards of Deut. 20:10–18, leaving Israel with rich booty. The note in 3:11 about Og as the last of the ancient powerful ones and his huge "iron bed" (perhaps a basalt rock formation) underscores the wonder of Israel's victory.

As an object lesson in courage and obedience, this success story is the reverse of the defeat of 1:19–46. Here the emphasis is on scrupulous obedience (2:37). The high fortifications of Canaan engendered fear in 1:28; here no city is too high or too strong for Israel to conquer (2:36; 3:5). Deuteronomy's original readers could face the uncertain future with courage. God is in ultimate control of events and gives victory to the faithful and obedient.

3:12–29, Foretastes of the Future. These last items in the historical review point forward to events that will take place after the speech of Moses is finished. They prepare his audience for the coming conquest and the first readers of Deuteronomy for whatever challenging transitions lie before them. Four topics are covered in four distinct sections, each marked by a first-person statement of Moses and the expression "at that time": vv. 12–17, 18–20, 21–22, and 23–29.

First (vv. 12–17) Moses recalls the allocation of the land east of the Jordan and the call for those tribes to aid in the rest of the conquest. The geographical description serves to solidify Israel's ill-defined eastern frontier. The exhortation of vv. 18–20 focuses on national solidarity. The very fact that God has already given these tribes their rich grazing land means they are now obligated to help secure this same gift for their fellow Israelites. In the spirit of Deuteronomy, the "haves" join the "have-nots" for the common good. In a preview of 31:3–8, Moses then charges Joshua to have confidence in the future based on God's past victories (vv. 21–22).

The topic of conquest leads naturally to Moses' submissive request and God's angry response to it, which itself leads back to the issue of Joshua's succession. Moses somehow bears the sin of the generation that died in the desert (1:37; 4:21–22). He cannot enter the future, but he is at least permitted to view it from afar, as he will eventually do in chap. 34. This dialogue underscores the richness and goodness of the promised land. It also suggests that the effects of disobedience cannot be facilely undone, a grim fact that Deuteronomy's original readers needed to face.

The movement toward Canaan stops with 3:29 and will not begin again until chap. 31. Now both Israel and the readers of Deuteronomy, primed for the challenges of the future, wait opposite Beth-peor for Moses to speak.

4:1–43
Transition to the Law

Chap. 4 is a bridge between the review of history in chaps. 1–3 and Moses' extended exhortation about the law, which begins with 4:44–5:1. In this chapter Moses takes up God's revelation of law from several different perspectives (4:1–40). Then Moses enacts one specific command of the law (vv. 41–43).

This material has a complex history of development. The basic exhortation consisted of vv. 1–14 and 21–22, encouraging readers to obey the whole law of Deuteronomy in the land and to teach it to their children. This would have been the link between chaps. 1–3 and the rest of Deuteronomy provided by the Deuteronomistic historian. At a somewhat later period, vv. 15–18 and 23–28 were added to highlight the specific temptation of image worship and warn that such worship would inevitably lead to destruction and exile. These verses have an outlook similar to 29:22–28. This warning was later broadened by 4:19–20 to include the worship of heavenly bodies. These additions taken together represent the viewpoint of the early Exile. At a still later and more optimistic period, another writer contributed vv. 29–40, material similar in purpose and outlook to 30:1–10. These verses urge those who have suffered defeat and exile to repent and return to God. The report of the three cities of refuge (4:41–43) represents the final stage in this process of successive addition.

In spite of its complicated background, chap. 4 gives an impression of overall unity as an exhortation to keep the law of Deuteronomy, offering several different perspectives on a single central principle: obedience to the law leads to life and prosperity, but disobedience means death (cf. 30:15–20).

4:1–40, Exhortation to Obedience. Moses moves from history to exhortation, urging Israel to perform the law he is about to promulgate and explain. The balance shifts from memory of the past to encouragement for the future. Those who read these words were motivated to keep the reforming law of Deuteronomy in their life in the land (vv. 5, 14). They were to pass on this

law unchanged (v. 2) to future generations (vv. 9–10; cf. 6:7, 20; 11:19; 31:13; 32:46). The law is described with a variety of terms—statutes, ordinances, commandments—but most strikingly as God's covenant (4:13; cf. v. 31; →Covenant).

Repetition urges careful attention to prevent forgetfulness (vv. 9, 15, 23). Lest readers imagine that this law was for past generations only, Moses emphasizes the ever-present "today" of its challenge (vv. 8, 26, 38, 40), while also evoking a "far-off" future that actually corresponds to the original readers' present (v. 25). Dramatic quotation (v. 6), the call for a universal quest for precedents (vv. 32–34), and the invocation of heaven and earth as witnesses (v. 26; cf. 30:19; 31:28; 32:1) all add to the rhetorical impact.

A wide variety of motives for obedience are offered. Some are rational. Because you know that the Lord is the only God, you must keep this law (4:39–40). Because you saw no form on Mount Horeb, you must never make idols (vv. 15–18). Some motives are negative: the Baal of Peor incident (v. 3; cf. Num. 25:1–5) or God's anger with Moses (4:21–22). Apostasy will eventually lead to national destruction and exile to an idolatrous land (vv. 26–28). The awesome fire of theophany, God's visual manifestation (vv. 11, 15, 33), is sharpened into the fire of a jealous God (v. 24; cf. 5:9; 6:15).

Yet positive motives for obedience predominate: long life, the land, prosperity (4:1, 4, 40). The law is Israel's prized possession, surpassing the allotment God has given other peoples (vv. 6, 8, 19). The primary motive for obedience is, however, the character of a God who is near and easily found (vv. 7, 29). God is compassionate, never forgetting the covenant (v. 31). He has given the land as a gift for all time, exile notwithstanding (v. 40). Two mighty deeds demonstrate God's regard for Israel. The Exodus was an unprecedented act of election (vv. 20, 34) that, along with the gift of the land, showed God's love (v. 37) and uniqueness (vv. 35, 39; cf. 6:5). The second great act was the revelation on Mount Horeb, manifesting his tolerance (4:33) and discipline (v. 36; cf. 8:5).

This exhortation reveals the fundamental patterns of Deuteronomic thought. The Baal of Peor incident (4:3–4) is paradigmatic. If you obey, you will live; if you commit apostasy, you will be destroyed. The assertion that there is an inevitable correlation between one's behavior and one's fate is basic to Deuteronomy's worldview. The future is always seen in terms of reward or punishment. This concept lies behind the use of blessings and curses in chaps. 27–28 to motivate obedience and can be traced throughout Deuteronomy's language of warning and exhortation (11:26–27; 30:15–20).

Deut. 4:24–31, however, reveals that there is more to the theology of Deuteronomy than this stark formula of retribution. Idolatry and disobedience will indeed result in destruction and exile from the land, punishments from a jealous God. Yet heartfelt return and renewed obedience will lead to a restoration of Israel's relationship with this merciful God (cf. vv. 31, 24). In contrast to all those things a false god cannot do (v. 28), Israel's God will neither fail nor utterly destroy Israel, nor forget the covenant (v. 31). And this, God's graciousness, is the most fundamental theological theme of Deuteronomy.

4:41–43, Cities of Refuge. The literary convention of the direct discourse of Moses is dropped for a moment to report the establishment of three cities of refuge in territory east of the Jordan. This note assures readers that Moses obeyed the law of 19:1–13 at the opportune time, perhaps as a way of motivating readers to strict obedience as well.

4:44–11:32

Moses Preaches About the Law

A second introduction (4:44–49) initiates a second speech of Moses, which prepares for his promulgation of reforming law in chaps. 12–16. Although historical recital continues to be part of his presentation (Exodus, manna, golden calf) as in the first speech, here the emphasis shifts to exhortation. The Ten Commandments are placed first and the role of Moses as mediator (5:23–31) is emphasized. In this way, the whole of Deuteronomy is viewed as an outgrowth of the Decalogue, as God's will communicated by Moses to Israel.

The theological themes of Deuteronomy are developed in this second address to motivate obedience to the law and to encourage reform. This is done through a variety of rhetorical formats: sermonic exhortations centered on the basic principle set forth in 6:4–9 (5:23–6:9; 10:12–11:32), shorter individual sermons (6:10–9:6), and a first-person reminiscence (9:7–10:11). Moses' address focuses on God's grace, protection, and election. It explores the dangers of life in the land, particularly apostasy and the temptation to forget the past. The importance of strict obedience to the law and the education of future generations is emphasized, along with the rewards of obedience. This second introduction ends with the contrast between the blessing that results from obedience to this law and the curse that follows on disobedience (11:26–32).

4:44–6:9

First Principles

The Ten Commandments are presented as the foundation for the rest of the law of Deuteronomy. They have been inserted in their present place in the book, interrupting Moses' recollection of the fearful fire of Horeb that breaks off at 5:5 and picks up again at 5:23. They have special authority, literally graven in stone, complete in themselves (5:22). By their placement here, they authorize and legitimate the rest of the book. Deuteronomy thus claims to be a continuation of God's revelation from Horeb (5:31), mediated by Moses in the same way as the Ten Commandments (5:5, 27).

The setting for Moses' re-presentation of the Decalogue is provided generally by 4:44–49 and then more pointedly by 5:1–5. Following the commandments themselves, Moses drives home their implications for his listeners (5:23–6:9). He continues the mode of historical recollection with 5:23–31, which returns to the topic of mediation begun in 5:4–5. Then he shifts back to the direct imperative address of 5:1, concluding with the extended imperative of 6:4–9.

4:44–5:22, The Ten Commandments. Cf. Exod. 20:2–17. An introduction (4:44–49) sets forth the basic dramatic premise of Deuteronomy: that Moses is addressing the law to Israel after the events recalled in chaps. 1–3. Then Moses summons Israel to hear the covenant made at Mount Horeb forty years ago (5:2, 4–5). This covenant and its law are now directed at a new generation (5:3; cf. 29:10–15). These Ten Words are addressed to a community that transcends time, for whom it is always "today." God's challenge was not just for the ancestors. It was directed at the original readers as well. They too had been slaves in Egypt (5:15) and had been liberated to stand at Horeb (5:4–6).

The Ten Commandments may be viewed as a concentrated version of the entire law of Deuteronomy. They provide a brief description of the love for God called for by 6:4–5. They serve as prologue to the whole law and provide, with the curse list in chap. 27, a frame for it. Like Deuteronomy as a whole, they represent preached law, law set forth with rhetorical flourish, law set in the historical context of God's acts (5:6, 15). Deuteronomy's interest in servants (12:18; 16:11), sojourners (10:19; 24:14, 17, 19–21), and even animals (22:1, 4; 25:4) is echoed in the Sabbath commandment. Deuteronomy's concern to motivate the law to evoke willing obedience is present as well (5:9–10, 11, 15, 16).

The self-identification of the God who speaks, the God of the Exodus (5:6), is the most important word. God's act of redemption is both the claim he has on those who hear and their motivation to rise to the challenge of these commandments.

These commandments describe how liberated Israel should live out their relationship to the God who freed them. Such a relationship demands fidelity. There could be no other gods, no empty use of the Lord's name, no violation of the rest implicit in the Exodus. Such a relationship affects the entire society, cutting across generation and class. Because fidelity to God means limits must be set on behavior, these commands are mostly negative, marking off margins and boundaries. They are concerned not with "religious" life or the life of priests, but with the day-to-day existence of the ordinary Israelite before God and in relation to neighbor. The "neighbor" of 5:20–21 is a central focus of Deuteronomy's social ethic (19:4, 11, 14; 22:24; 23:25; 24:10). These commands protect a fellow Israelite's right to life, to a secure marriage and respect as a parent, to fair legal process, and to property.

Deuteronomy's call to a reformed Israel is founded on God's oneness (6:4) and the constant danger of apostasy and idolatry. Here the commandments begin as well (5:7–9). This is no philosophical monotheism, but the personal claim of the God of the Exodus (→ Monotheism). God's claim on Israel means there can be no other gods and no images of these gods or of the One God. Imageless worship is rationalized in 4:15–18, but here the motive for obedience is provided by God's "jealousy" (4:24; 6:14–15), a powerful emotion springing from the depth of his personhood. There are both threat and promise implicit in this jealousy, according to the old confessional formula employed here (Exod. 34:7; Num. 14:18; cf. Deut. 7:9–10). The implication of 5:9 is either that all three or four generations alive at that one time would be included or that children who followed in their forebears' sins would share in their punishment. In overwhelming contrast to the numbers three or four, thousands of those who love God (5:10) will be the objects of God's covenant loyalty.

God's personal name Yahweh (→ Names of God in the Old Testament) must not be lifted up for any idle, unnecessary, or frivolous purpose, especially in the taking of empty or false oaths (5:11). It is not to be employed to do magical harm, as though to coerce God into action. False prophets must not use it to speak empty words (18:20–22).

Although the Sabbath (5:12–15) is not mentioned in the rest of Deuteronomy, its motivation in the Exodus from Egypt and Israel's servitude there certainly is (15:15; 24:18, 22). Here Sabbath represents a day of liberation, founded on Israel's own journey from bondage to "rest" in the good land (cf. 12:10; 25:19). It is a part of ordinary life (in contrast to the great festivals of chap. 16) set aside as holy, given back, as it were, to God, and so ordered that all levels of society may participate in God's gift of rest.

The command to honor parents (5:16) is addressed not just to children but adults, who in the extended family system of ancient Israel would have continued to live under the authority of their parents for many years. This situation would naturally lead to conflict, especially over matters of land inheritance. In critical economic circumstances there might also have been strong motives to deprive aged parents. Deut. 21:18–21 offers a specific legal process for a related situation. This is one place in OT law where a woman as mother has equal rights with a man. The motivational promise involving the inheritance of land and long life are especially appropriate for this command, both being special interests of Deuteronomy (8:1; 16:20). Deuteronomy adds further motivation to the parallel in Exod. 20:12 by underlining that this is God's command and promising that things will "go well."

The command of Deut. 5:17 did not concern all killing (for capital punishment, see 17:2–7 or 19:12; for warfare, see chaps. 20–21), but rather outright murder and careless accidental killing. Probably the issue of legally inappropriate vengeance (19:4–10) also comes into play here.

In the OT, adultery (5:18) did not correspond to our notions of the act; it was a much more limited issue focused on the rights of the wronged husband. Other sorts of sexual partnerships and marital issues are regulated by chaps. 22–25.

Scholars often assert that 5:19 originally referred to kidnapping a free Israelite and point to Deut. 24:7 as an example. Probably by the time these commandments were included in Deuteronomy, theft in general was meant.

The false, empty, and purposeless witness forbidden by 5:20 refers to testimony in court against an accused person. Deut. 19:15–21 also shows concern for possible abuses of the criminal justice system, which relied on the testimony of witnesses.

Coveting (5:21) moves into the sphere of the psychological and attitudinal. The first Hebrew verb used implies strong desire leading to an actual move to possess, but the second verb in the Deuteronomic version (Exod. 20:17 is different) refers to a completely internal feeling. Deuteronomy is concerned not only with deeds, but also with motives (15:10).

Those who first were confronted by these words were intended to hear, learn, and do what was commanded (5:1). By describing the life

Israel ought to live as a nation freed from Egyptian bondage, these commandments sought to convert readers to become what God's act of liberation had already made them, his covenant people.

5:23–6:9, The Essence of the Law. Moses explores the meaning of God's law, especially as concentrated in the Ten Commandments. The impact of God's commandments is to be total and uncompromising, involving heart, soul, and strength, molding both individual and public behavior. The original readers of Deuteronomy were to appropriate this reforming law personally and live their lives in the good land of promise by its standard.

Deuteronomy was a reforming law, a new look at God's will for the new situation of Israel in the monarchy. It was law heard, as it were, a second time (5:25), an addition to what had already been encountered (5:31). For this reason it was important to authorize or legitimate the Deuteronomic reinterpretation of the law for its audience. To do this, the mediatory role of Moses is stressed (5:23–27, 31; 6:1). Moses reminds his listeners of how mere flesh, mortal and weak, seemed too vulnerable to hear the terrifying voice of God a second time. Encounter with the living God threatened death. The people's request for an insulating medium for revelation was approved. Thus Deuteronomy claims for itself divine authorization and authority and presents itself to readers as God's own words mediated by Moses.

Deuteronomy urgently seeks to motivate its readers to observe its precepts. The deadly power of theophany (5:23–27) is emphasized, along with God's almost wistful wish for Israel's fidelity (5:29). The potential rewards of prosperity and long life in the rich, good land are reemphasized (5:29, 33; 6:2–3). God's own nature motivates obedience as well. The Lord is God alone, unique in power with a sole claim on Israel's loyalty. Unlike Baal, who was manifested at scores of local high places around the country, the one true God had one true place of worship (chap. 12). The Lord is one, and therefore has no doubleness of purpose or intention. Such a God, and only such a God, is worthy of total obedience.

This law is to be appropriated personally, internalized by those whose lives it claims (30:14). They are to pay close attention to it and observe it scrupulously, as the language of 5:32; 6:6, 8–9 insists (→Phylacteries; Mezuzah). They are to teach it to future generations, literally "sharpening" it for their instruction (6:7). This law must permeate every sphere of life, be bound on each Israelite, and displayed publicly for all to see (6:7–9). It is law lived not only externally, but also with heart and soul, an expression of love for God and humanity.

6:10–11:32
A Motivational Introduction

This transition to the promulgation of law that begins in chap. 12 makes every effort to connect the law to the lives of the original readers to motivate their adoption of Deuteronomy and obedience to it. A number of different formats are used to change attitudes, create repentance, and evoke obedience. Eight short sermons (6:10–9:6) are followed by a first-person historical narrative (9:7–10:11) and a long exhortation (10:12–11:32). The overall purpose is to prepare readers for what is to follow, to cultivate an attitudinal seedbed in which the law of Deuteronomy could take root and flourish.

The sermons (6:10–9:6) require special comment. They are literary creations imitating Israel's tradition of exhortative oratory. They resemble sermons of a military, liturgical, or prophetic nature found elsewhere in the OT. Each of these sermons starts with a citation of some characteristic situation in which the audience might find itself, or perhaps of a tradition from Israel's past. From there the sermon draws conclusions and makes applications to the readers' own lives.

Shared themes hold these sermons together. The first (6:10–15) begins an exploration of what the situation will be when the land has been occupied. It also introduces a call to remember that permeates the other seven, either explicitly or implicitly. Thus 6:16–19 is itself an example of remembering a story from Israel's tradition, as is 8:1–6. The issue of remembering in order to educate the next generation is presented in 6:20–25. The call to remember and never to forget is explicit in 7:17–26; 8:1–6; and 8:7–20. Two of these units seem to be literary imitations of war sermons of the sort delivered to the troops on the eve of battle (7:17–26; 9:1–6).

6:10–15, Do Not Forget. The situation presupposed in this sermon is that the land has been given as promised. Its agricultural richness is described in an attractive way, perhaps following the fashion of ancient vassal treaties. The central theme is that God alone has given these good things. Israel has contributed nothing. The homiletical application is the sharp imperative of v. 12. Never forget the God who is identified by the act of exodus liberation. In contrast to your former servitude, serve God. Swear only by his name and by no other, as might be required in making treaties with other, more powerful nations. This challenge is motivated by reference to God's character as revealed by the Ten Commandments (5:9). The grim result of forgetting this jealous God could be total destruction, complete removal from the rich land he gave.

This sermon convinces readers to obey the law of Deuteronomy in order to remain loyal to

God. Any complacency they might have felt about their security in the land is shattered. Any pride they might have had in the military accomplishments of their kings or in the prosperity that characterized some periods of the monarchy is here undermined. Reading between the lines a bit, this sermon may also counter the temptation to enter into a vassal treaty with some foreign power.

6:16-19, Do Not Test God. This sermon recalls a tradition of wilderness testing, preserved for us in Exod. 17:1-7. A simple reference is enough, for readers know it well. The tradition is applied to readers in the fashion of a canonical text. Do not push God too far through disobedience. This unit seeks to motivate obedience by means of a negative historical lesson and a positive reference to the divine victories that gave Israel their good land.

6:20-25, A Child's Question. The situation from which this sermon begins is the rhetorical device of a question put into the mouth of a child. Deuteronomy is concerned with the issue of transmitting the tradition to coming generations. The answer to this question provides the sermonic application in the form of a confession of Israel's classic historical faith. Each succeeding generation of Israel is included by the repeated use of "us" as the object of God's liberation, gift, and command (vv. 21-24). The meaning of the law of Deuteronomy is found in the past acts of God and in the present and future blessings to which obedience leads. True "righteousness," that is, existence in accord with a right relationship to God, is found in keeping this law.

These verses seek to inculcate respect for the law through a recital of God's gracious history with Israel and by pointing to the rewards of obedience. Because a healthy relationship with the God of the Exodus is only possible through this law, it must be taught to each succeeding generation, just as Deuteronomy itself is teaching it to its original readers, who represent a new generation in the land.

7:1-16, A People Set Apart. The situation envisioned in this sermon is again the completion of the conquest. What is called for is the single-minded application of the ban, the wholesale destruction of Canaanite culture and religion (vv. 2, 16). Israel must make no treaties with these seven nations nor ever intermarry with them (though 21:10-14 permits marriages to foreigner captives, probably from nations other than these seven).

The motive advanced for such vigilance focuses on Israel's special relationship with God (7:6-10). Israel is holy, set apart for his purposes (v. 6). Israel was chosen specially by

God not out of any merit on their own part, but because he has a personal attachment to them based on love and the promise to their forebears. The fidelity of God to the covenant over uncountable generations has been revealed in the Exodus and Ten Commandments, along with the pattern of individual retribution for the apostate. A further motive for wiping out Canaanite religion is offered by the promise of fertility for family, field, and flock (vv. 13-14), an especially appropriate counter to Baal's claim to be the one who bestows fertility. Obedience also leads to good health. The plagues of the Exodus tradition will be reserved for enemies (v. 15).

The original readers of Deuteronomy could certainly see themselves included in God's graciousness to the thousandth generation. On the other hand, they had experienced the grim effects of Israel's involvement with international alliances and the dangers created by at least one foreign queen, Jezebel. Certainly these readers still lived in an environment of uneradicated Canaanite religion and were all too likely to credit Baal for the blessings of fertility. These verses urge them to see themselves as a people set apart, a people defined, on the one hand, by the gracious blessing of the God of the Exodus and, on the other, by their own obedience to the reforming law of Deuteronomy, particularly those portions that forbid Canaanite religious practices (12:29-13:18).

7:17-26, Memory Cures Fear. This is a literary imitation of a war sermon of the sort delivered before battle in the tradition of Israel's holy wars (cf. 20:2-4). The postulated situation is fear and despondency over the numerical superiority of the enemy. The admonition is classic to the ideology of holy war: do not be afraid (1:29; 20:1; 31:6). The key to this confidence is the memory of the past victories of God, the Divine Warrior. The hornets of v. 20 seem to be a metaphor for the divinely induced panic by means of which God wins holy war victories (2:25; cf. Exod. 14:24-25; Judg. 7:19-22).

This sermon seeks to bring its original readers back to traditional, premonarchical values and institutions, to the ban and the ideology of holy war. These traditions had been replaced by the institutions of the royal state, a state with a standing army and a tolerant attitude toward the Canaanite enclaves and urban centers still to be found in Israel. In the militaristic spirit that pervades the book of Deuteronomy, this sermon insists that these Canaanites represent an unfinished task for Israel. Their continued presence is given a rationalistic explanation (Deut. 7:22), but it cannot be tolerated (vv. 23-24). The royal policy of accommodation is to be rejected. Canaanite culture is to be eradicated without any concern for the intrinsic value of what must be destroyed (vv. 25–26).

8:1–6, The Staff of Life. This unit begins and ends with its central point, a call to obey the law (vv. 1, 6). This point is hammered home through theological reflection on Israel's tradition of wilderness wandering. The wilderness is seen as paradigmatic for Israel's entire experience with God (29:5–6). Those forty years were a training ground, an experience of parental discipline designed to test and temper the character of Israel. The key lesson was that of the manna, which taught that the importance of the "necessities of life" is only relative. The real staff of life is not bread, but that which comes out of God's mouth, every word that he decrees. God's law as set forth in Deuteronomy is Israel's true source of life in the land.

8:7–20, Remember and Obey. The sermonic situation is Israel's future presence in the land. A poetic description of the good land (vv. 7–10) leads to a portrayal of the twin dangers of pride and forgetfulness in vv. 11–13 and 17–20. Sandwiched between are vv. 14–16, a hymnlike recital of God's saving deeds and wilderness lessons, which undermine smug pride and must themselves never be forgotten. This sermon is constructed around the opposition between remembering, which leads to obedience, and forgetting, which results in apostasy. A second contrast is created by the land with its dangers of forgetting and the wilderness with its remembered lessons. Both land and desert are colorfully portrayed (vv. 7–9 and 15). The good land presents Israel with a test as dangerous as any offered by the wilderness. The wilderness lesson of humility counters the pride engendered by the land.

The point is sharpened by vv. 19–20, which threatens punishment and destruction. This reflects an outlook similar to 4:25–26 and 6:14–15 and is often thought to come from a somewhat later writer. In any case, this threat harmonizes with the rhetorical power of the rest of the sermon in its impact on the original readers, who are living out the situation described. Their life in the good land has led them to forget, to become prideful and self-congratulatory, to worship other gods. National destruction looms on their horizon. From such readers, these verses urge a renewal of memory, seeking to counter pride with humility and calling for a new commitment to the God who brought Israel out of Egypt.

9:1–6, Dangerous Complacency. After a renewed bid for attention through solemn rhetorical address (5:1; 6:4), the dramatic premise of the book of Deuteronomy is restated by 9:1. Moses is addressing the law to Israel after the events recalled in chaps. 1–3. In format, this unit is a literary imitation of a war sermon, words addressed to Israel before battle. As such its purpose would be to build confidence in the military support of God, the Divine Warrior (vv. 1–3). Yet the actual homiletical situation is the same as the previous unit: the danger of self-righteousness and complacency on the part of Israel already settled in the land (v. 4). This sermon intends to counter such complacency by asserting God's true reasons for the conquest, reasons that have nothing at all to do with any alleged virtue or sincerity on the part of headstrong and stubborn Israel. Instead, the conquest is described as punishment for the wicked Canaanites (18:12) and as a result of God's promise to the patriarchs. Here we see Deuteronomy's concern that readers should obey the law with a proper attitude, not out of self-righteousness but out of gratitude for God's gracious, unmerited gift of the land.

9:7–10:11, Rebellion and Forgiveness. Moses now returns to the mode of historical reminiscence to explore the topic of Israel's rebellion and God's forgiveness. The story of Israel's rebellion is told from Moses' own point of view (9:7–24). Then as a flashback, parts of it are retold with an emphasis on intercession and forgiveness (9:25–10:11).

The first telling, enclosed in the repetition found in 9:7 and 24, dwells on Israel's disobedience and underscores its enormity. Israel was chronically rebellious, as the examples of 9:22–23 demonstrate. Even at Horeb, the high point of God's revelation, they "quickly" (9:12, 16) turned to make a molten idol, a sin so grave that Moses performed the symbolic act of shattering the tablets of the law, indicating that the covenant with God had been smashed as well. This was so terrible an apostasy that Moses lay fasting forty days and nights before God. This loathsome idol had to be burned, broken, ground up, and washed away. God's reaction matched Israel's catastrophic sin; he threatened in fury (9:19–20) to destroy them and start the process of election over from the beginning (9:14). The fire of revelation (9:10) became the fire of terror (9:15). God's words to Moses (9:12) carried a terrible message of rejection. They are your people, Moses, not mine.

The second telling, enclosed in the repetition of forty days and nights in 9:25 and 10:10, emphasizes Moses' intercession and God's forgiveness, exploring the implications of 9:18. Moses used telling arguments to turn God around. This is your people, your inheritance. Remember the patriarchs. Guard your own reputation, lest it be said you were powerless to give us a land or lest your motives for the Exodus be questioned. Here Moses practiced the other side of the office of mediator, interceding for the people, as did the prophets. God responded with commands that indicated that Israel's life with God would go on. The reinscribed Ten Commandments were to be put into an Ark that in itself promised Israel future journeys and conquests. In 10:4, Israel found itself back where it had been in 9:10, as the repeated language indicates. In 10:10 the story returns once more to the intercession, this time to announce climactically that God had decided not to destroy them. Israel could go on because the covenant had not been irrevocably shattered.

A side issue is introduced by 10:6–9. The tasks of the tribe of Levi will be to carry the Ark, minister before God in worship, and bless in his name (→ Levites). While these verses reflect Deuteronomy's concern for the status of the Levites, they also serve to contemporize this historical narrative for the original readers (10:8). This story of rebellion and forgiveness would have struck home. Their own history had been poisoned by recidivist tendencies toward idolatry, not the least in the form of Jeroboam's golden calves (→ Jeroboam I). God's wrath and destruction loomed on the horizon. They needed to hear that repentance and forgiveness were still possible and that the institutions of national faith could still continue after disobedience and punishment.

10:12–11:32, Incentives for Obedience. The exhortations of 6:5–9, 13 are taken up again and directed at readers through the imperatives of 10:12–13, 19–20 and 11:1, 8, 18–21. Fear, love, and serve God, and keep the law. The metaphorical imperatives of 11:18–21 call for an ongoing internal appropriation of Deuteronomy in all areas of Israel's life. A rich variety of motivations for obedience are offered. Some motivational material is attached to the imperatives directly: God's intent for good (10:13), the ability to conquer (11:8), long life in the land (11:21).

Longer motivational sections are interspersed between the imperative sentences. God's own character as reflected in the election of Israel provides the focus for 10:14–18, 21–22. Because God elected this tiny, enslaved people, they should now keep his law. Election requires internal circumcision along with the external ritual (10:16). God's greatness is reflected in concern for the marginal people in society (10:18), a concern characteristic of the law that will follow (e.g., 24:17–22). The motivational impact of God's discipline in history is the topic of 11:2–7, where the traditions of the past are recounted in hymnic praise. The fertility of the well-watered land is portrayed in 11:9–17 as further incentive. The rains of April and October are sent by God, but this direct divine provision also means that drought threatens if apostasy occurs. A complete, nearly effortless conquest is promised, again to motivate obedience (11:22–25).

Reflecting the blessings and curses that conclude Deuteronomy (11:29; chaps. 27–28), this exhortation sets forth a simple choice of weal or woe (11:26–28; cf. 30:15–20). The law that is to follow is not a set of cold legal precepts, but a "way" that leads to blessing (11:26). As the transition to law giving is completed, there is once more a reminder of Deuteronomy's dramatic premise (11:30–31) and a direct appeal for the original readers to obey what is to be set before them "today" (11:32).

12:1–26:19

Moses Proclaims the Law

As a renewal of Israel's traditional law in order to renew Israel as God's people, these chapters form the heart of Deuteronomy. This reformed law is built upon older legal traditions, particularly those found in Exod. 20:22–23:19, the "Book of the Covenant." Moses' promulgation of new law for life in the land of promise provides the analogy for Deuteronomy's reform of law offered to its own readers.

Israelite law has two basic forms. Apodictic laws simply command or forbid behavior (e.g., 14:3; 15:1; 17:1). Casuistic laws set forth a situation and follow it with its appropriate result or penalty (e.g., 17:2–5; 21:1–8). Both apodictic and casuistic laws stand behind Deuteronomy's reformed legal presentation. Motivational and explanatory expansions have often been added to the basic laws to induce obedience (15:2–6, 15; 21:9).

The Deuteronomic restatement of the laws in the Book of the Covenant represents a utopian reform of older laws to meet the challenges of a new day. Deuteronomy's call to centralize all sacrifice leads to numerous changes (cf. Deut. 15:19–23; Exod. 22:29–30; Deut. 16:1–17; Exod. 23:14–17; Deut. 19:1–13; Exod. 21:12–14). Other modifications reflect Israel's shift to a money economy in monarchical times. This shift caused a social crisis that widened the gap between rich and poor and led to the enslavement of many free farmers to satisfy debts (Deut. 15:1–11; Exod. 23:10–11; Deut. 15:12–18; Exod. 21:1–11). Some changes seek to undo the social damage caused by changing times, reflecting Deuteronomy's concern for fairness and human dignity (Deut. 24:10–13; Exod. 22:26–27).

In the context of royal infringements on the traditional rights of free Israelites, Deuteronomy revitalizes old institutions that had become obsolete under the monarchy (holy war in Deut. 20; levirate marriage in 25:5–10). To meet the challenge of syncretism and the temptation offered by Baal worship, these laws call for fidelity in religious practices (14:1–21; 16:21–22).

221

12:1–14:21
Purity in Worship

Deuteronomy's reform law begins with worship as the center of Israel's life before God. In contrast to past practice, all sacrifice is to be centralized in one place to safeguard the purity and unity of God's covenant people in the face of tempting Canaanite religious practices. The revolutionary renewal of society described by the rest of the law begins with an equally revolutionary reform of Israel's religious life.

12:1–28, Centralization. Although Israel may have earlier had some sort of national worship centered around the Ark, ordinary religious life was focused on the local sanctuaries scattered around the country. It was to these high places within easy walking distance that the Israelites took sacrifices and tithes and to which they repaired for the major festivals. It was to this local altar that fugitives ran for asylum and to the local priest that ordinary folk went for guidance in religious matters (→ High Place).

In a revolutionary attempt to preserve traditional values, Deuteronomy calls for the consolidation of all sacrifice at a single central sanctuary. As Amos and Hosea testify, monarchical Israel's worship at local holy places had often resulted in apostasy to Canaanite practices, the express context for this centralization law (vv. 2–3, 29–31). Deuteronomy seeks to avoid such contamination through a radical, perhaps utopian demand for centralization. This move reflects the theology of God's oneness (6:4). Another theological underpinning is Deuteronomy's "name theology," which protects God's transcendence by asserting that, although God is not actually present at the central sanctuary, his name is at home there (vv. 5, 11). At the same time, the "name" of Canaan's gods is to be wiped out (v. 3).

This radical challenge addresses lay people, not religious specialists. It does not concern itself with technical detail, but with a comprehensive call to centralize, the motivation of which is renewed obedience. Its utopian flavor is balanced by the pragmatic considerations of ordinary life. Repetition is used to fix this call in the mind of readers and to cover every eventuality.

The effects of this primary law of centralization on Israel's religious and juridical life will focus many of the laws to follow (14:22–29; 15:19–23; 16:1–17; 17:8–13; 18:1–8; 19:1–13). The call of Deuteronomy for reform was also concerned with things other than centralization, but this was its most important and most revolutionary facet. The book itself gives no clue as to the identity of the place chosen by God, although Shechem is hinted at, but eventually this radical principle would find its realization in the kingdom of Judah under King Josiah, who took it for granted that Jerusalem was meant (2 Kings 22–23).

The basic content is repeated five times. Because God has chosen this place, bring all your sacrifices to offer and eat them there (Deut. 12:5–6, 11, 14, 18, 26). Repetitious enumeration covers every type of sacrifice (→ Worship). The special focus of vv. 13–14 is whole burnt offering, while that of vv. 17–19 is the eating of tithes and firstlings. The mood of these offerings is one of joy (vv. 7, 12, 18). Typically, their social effects are not ignored (vv. 12, 18–19) and motivations are set forth: God's blessings, the security of the land, and general well-being (vv. 7, 9–10, 25, 28). The point is sharpened through repeated contrast. What Israel is to do is not like the former practices (v. 8), not done in every place (v. 13), not performed locally (v. 17), and not like secular slaughter (v. 26).

The practical problem of secular butchering is taken up by vv. 15–16 and 20–25. In the ancient world, all slaughter was viewed as a sacramental act, but in Deuteronomy's schema such noncentral, nonsacrificial killings had to be thoroughly secularized. Blood, as the essence of life, was still not to be eaten, however, but poured out in a completely secular manner, "like water."

12:29–13:18, Other Gods. The topic of this unit is how life in the land could lead to apostasy. These verses urge readers to fidelity and drastic action in the face of syncretism. Three times in these verses the tempting refrain "let us follow other gods" (13:2, 6, 13) recurs.

The possibilities suggested were all part of the actual experience of the original readers. General curiosity (12:29–31) is followed by three more specific scenarios. That a prophet should entice Israel to false worship (13:1–5) would have been a possible reaction to disasters from which God seemed impotent to protect Israel (cf. the thinking of Jer. 44:16–18). The prophet described would have been particularly tempting because he performs the sign thought to authorize a word truly sent by God (Deut. 18:22). In fact, this is actually the case in a sense, for his message is a test from God. The secret enticement of relatives and friends (13:6–11) would be especially tempting, resulting in the agonizing choice reflected by 13:9. Again this represents a real temptation resulting from intermarriage, one that Israel's royal families, at least, certainly experienced. The Canaanite cities that had been assimilated into the nation were also a dangerous source of temptation (13:12–18).

The original readers, living in an environment of apostasy, are challenged to take drastic action. God hates these detestable Canaanite practices (12:31). Such situations are tests

(13:3). God rescued Israel from Egypt, but these Canaanite gods played no role in Israel's history. Israel's zeal can deflect God's anger and lead to blessing (13:17). Undergirding this challenge is the canonical authority claimed by Deuteronomy itself (12:32).

Apostasy was an objective reality that had to be excised from national life (13:5). There is an uncompromising call for loyalty to God in the demand that one cast the first stone at one's apostate kinfolk (13:8–9). An idolatrous city must become the target of an internal holy war and ruthlessly applied destruction. From such zeal, Israel is to learn a salutary lesson (13:11).

14:1–21, Clean and Unclean. Quoting several traditional apodictic commands (vv. 1, 3, 21), Deuteronomy insists that both Israel's mourning customs and diet must correspond to the people's status as children of God, as a nation set off as holy. Election affects even the most personal and ordinary aspects of life. The customs forbidden by v. 1 seem to have been part of Baal worship, and the unclean animals forbidden as food may have been associated with Canaanite rituals. Boiling a kid in its mother's milk may also have been a non-Israelite religious practice. An animal that had died naturally would contain blood, forbidden for eating. Unclean animals are "abominations" (v. 3), things that defile and endanger one's relationship to God (7:25; 12:31). Incentive to knowledgeable obedience is provided both by rules of thumb (14:6–10, 19–20) and traditional lists (14:4–5, 11–18; cf. Lev. 11).

14:22–16:17
Life in the New Land

The life Deuteronomy envisions for Israel in the land implies a radical reform of both religious and social practices. These are not seen as separate issues. Rather religion and social concern interpenetrate. Deuteronomy's proposed seven-year cycle of tithes and Sabbatical Years has revolutionary social effects (14:28–29; 15:4). On the other hand, the secular practices of money-lending and slave release receive clear religious motivations (15:9, 15). This reform even modifies Israel's three traditional religious festivals, restructuring them according to Deuteronomy's concerns for centralization, social justice, and the memory of God's saving acts.

14:22–29, Annual and Third-Year Tithes. Using a traditional apodictic law (v. 22), Deuteronomy explores the implications of the centralization law and a money economy for the practice of tithing agricultural produce, a concern picked up from 12:17–19. These tithes are to be eaten as a joyful meal of communion fellowship at the central sanctuary. Geographic distance need be no barrier to obedience, for money can be used to eliminate any need to transport the food itself to the central sanctuary. The plight of the Levites, who would feel the economic impact of centralization, is a concern as Deuteronomy seeks to cushion the revolutionary effects of its proposed reform. The tithes of years three and six of the seven-year cycle (15:1–18) are to be used instead for social welfare and distributed to society's marginal members, again including the Levites.

The reforming intent of these verses is to restructure Israel's use of tithes along the lines of centralized sacrifice and social concern. The monarchy's stratified society and monetary economy are clearly in view. Typically, motives are provided to urge obedience: a lesson in reverence for God and the prospect of further blessing (14:23, 29).

15:1–11, The Seventh-Year Release. Israel's traditional practice of letting the land rest fallow every seventh year is restructured by Deuteronomy into a revolutionary solution to Israel's social inequities. The introduction of a money economy and the resulting alienation of ancestral lands had created a society with wide economic disparities. Israel's peasant farmers were under severe economic pressure, in constant danger of losing land and freedom to rich creditors.

The traditional law of release is cited in v. 1 and then reinterpreted in v. 2. A permanent and total remission of debt every seven years is intended, as implied by v. 9. Issues of motivation and attitude are explored in vv. 3–11. Those in a position to lend are to do so without a grudging eye to the calendar. The motive for lending is the plight of one's fellow Israelite, not economic advantage. The institution of a seven-year debt release converts the oppressive practice of lending into a mechanism for social benevolence.

The intended utopian ideal is presented in vv. 4–5. Perfect obedience would lead to a society without poverty. The reality of poverty presented in v. 11 is seen as an opportunity for generosity. The vision of Israel as a major creditor nation motivates obedience (→ Ownership).

15:12–18, Hebrew Slaves. Building on traditional law preserved in Exod. 21:2–6, Deuteronomy extends the principle of release to those victims of economic pressure who have been sold into slavery for debt. In this case, the seven years are the years of a slave's service, a different matter from the calendar cycle of Deut. 15:1–11. Reflecting its revolutionary social spirit, Deuteronomy goes beyond Exod. 21:2 by insisting on a generous provision for released slaves so that they can retain their independence. If a strong sense of affection should mean that a slave wishes to stay, he or she may be converted to the status of a permanent slave. The ceremony is a desacralized version of Exod. 21:5–6, made necessary by the institution of a central sanctuary. Here again Deuteronomy is concerned with proper attitude and motivation (Deut. 15:10), the most telling motivation being the memory of Egyptian slavery.

15:19–23, Firstborn Males. Deuteronomy sets forth a reformed presentation of the traditional principle that any firstborn male animal must be set aside for God (Exod. 22:29–30). The basic apodictic law is cited in Deut. 15:19a, then explored within the limitations of the centralized system of animal sacrifice. The basic idea is that this animal belongs to God. Therefore no economic benefit can be derived from it. It must be eaten as a communion sacrifice at the central sanctuary. Any animal unfit for sacrifice is to be eaten at home as a completely secular meal (12:15–16, 20–25), shared by clean and unclean participants together.

16:1–17, Festival Calendar. Deuteronomy restates Israel's traditional religious calendar to convert these formerly local celebrations into pilgrimage festivals at the central sanctuary, as summarized in vv. 16–17. The emphasis is on the place chosen by God (vv. 2, 11, 15). Interested in probing meaning rather than giving details, Deuteronomy has stripped the Feast of Weeks and the Feast of Booths of much of their distinctive character, along with many traditional practices appropriate only to their observance at local shrines. We no longer read of bringing loaves of bread before God or of dwelling in booths (Lev. 23:15–21, 39–43; → Pentecost; Tabernacles, Festival of). Although the dates of these latter two festivals remain tied to the harvest schedule (Deut. 16:9, 13), the offerings are no longer closely specified and vary with the situation of the worshiper (vv. 10, 17). The character of the celebrations has been flattened out into joy over God's blessings in general (vv. 11, 14–15), rather than over any specific feature of the harvest. The shared celebration of the marginal classes of society is heavily emphasized, motivated by the memory of shared slavery (vv. 11–12, 14).

The celebration of Passover also had to be brought in line with the principle of centralization. What had traditionally been a domestic festival is converted to a public one. What had been a rite of protection for the home and flock is transformed into a sacrifice performed at the central sanctuary. Because the Passover animal is now seen as a sacrifice, the field of choice is widened to include cattle and not just a lamb or kid (v. 2; cf. Exod. 12:5), and the animal is boiled according to early sanctuary custom (Deut. 16:7; cf. 1 Sam. 2:12–14; Exod. 12:9). The practice of eating unleavened bread seems to be both local and centralized in Deuteronomy's restructured festival. Leaven is removed from the whole of Israel's territory, but unleavened bread is specifically eaten at the central sanctuary by the pilgrims in their temporary lodgings (Deut. 16:3–4, 8).

These verses urge a revolutionary change in worship practice, yet they demonstrate a concern to preserve tradition. The actual date of Passover does not have to be given, for this is less a promulgation of new law than an attempt to reform well-established practice. Deuteronomy is concerned with attitude and with memory. What is important is that Israel remember that Passover happens in the same month, on the same day, and at the very same time as the Exodus (vv. 1, 3, 6). Israel eats unleavened bread because as the bread of affliction and haste it helps them remember that important night (v. 3). Had this reform proposal been adopted by Deuteronomy's original readers (as it eventually was in Judah, 2 Kings 23:21–23), it would have meant far-reaching changes in the religious life of every Israelite. For Deuteronomy, this dislocation would have been justified by the elimination of dangerous local sanctuaries and a renewed appreciation of the Exodus and the blessings of God (→ Feasts, Festivals, and Fasts; Passover, The).

16:18–20:20
The Structures of Society

Deuteronomy goes on to describe the judicial, political, and social structures of Israel's reformed life. Chaps. 17 and 18 deal with legal procedures and public persons (king, priest, prophet). Chaps. 19 and 20 concentrate on issues involving the community as a whole (asylum, warfare). These laws do not offer a complete constitution for renewed Israel but instead concentrate on those areas of life in which Deuteronomy sees the greatest need for reform. Concerns for fairness, fidelity to God, priestly rights, and centralization dominate this material. There is a distinct flavor of nostalgia and a desire to return to premonarchical values, particularly in the portrayal of the central tribunal of justice, the royal office, and the practice of war.

16:18–17:13, The Justice System. These verses demand a reform and restructuring of court process, first on a local level (16:18–20) and then on a centralized national level (17:8–13). Sandwiched between these concerns is material dealing with religious apostasy. Various older apodictic and casuistic laws provided the skeleton for the presentation of these matters in Deuteronomy.

The discussion of local justice springs from three apodictic laws about impartial justice in 16:19, expanded by a proverb about bribes and some typical Deuteronomic motivation in 16:20. Here the judicial task traditionally performed by the elders falls under some sort of centralized appointment procedure.

The centralized tribunal is presented in casuistic form ("if," 17:8). This is not a court of appeal for the accused, but a resource for local judges who would formerly have turned to the priests of local sanctuaries in cases made difficult by the absence of clear-cut testimony or those involving fine questions of law. Legal distinctions involving intentional or accidental death, contradictory pleas, and various types of assault often fell into this category (17:8). Such cases would have been handled by imposing oaths or ordeals on the parties involved (Exod. 22:8, 11; Num. 5:11–31). Both civil and religious judges staff this central tribunal (Deut. 17:9, 12). To undermine its authority is presented as a very serious capital crime, an evil to be purged from Israel.

Deuteronomy urged these reforms on its original readers in the knowledge that improved judicial structures were needed to bring unbiased justice to all classes of society (16:19; 17:6–7; cf. 24:17). It is difficult to decide how much of this law reflected actual practice and how much was utopian proposal. In any case, Deuteronomy's general intentions are clear. The justice dispensed by local elders was to be brought under some kind of central control. The role of the local sanctuaries in deciding puzzling cases was to be superseded by courts attached to the central sanctuary. Priestly and civil justice were to work in harmony.

Strikingly, the king's role in preserving justice is completely bypassed in this reform. It was traditionally to the king that parties would appeal the decisions of the local elders. Reading between the lines, we may assume that Deuteronomy had a low opinion of the royal capacity for unbiased judgment. At the same time, Deuteronomy seems to be convinced that its own reformed court system would have no need for an appeal process.

A concern for purity in worship is sandwiched between this proposal to restructure courts. Three apodictic laws (16:21, 22; 17:1) forbid a sacred pole (→ Asherah) beside the central altar, any stone pillar, and all defective sacrifices (cf. 15:21). Such abuses had motivated the demand for the centralization of worship in the first place. A situation similar to those discussed in 13:1–18 is presented in a casuistic format ("if," 17:2). The general crime is described as transgressing God's covenant and is illustrated by representative specific examples. The appropriate punishment is stoning. This coordination of religious purity with judicial fairness is hardly a surprise. Both had to be achieved if Israel was to become the people God wished it to be.

17:14–20, Kings. Deuteronomy reflects a low opinion of kingship. Doubtless, this was a result of the grim experience Israel had had with its kings. Instead of protecting the worship of God, the monarchy had introduced foreign forms of worship. Instead of providing justice for all classes of society, the kings had piled up riches. Instead of bringing peace and prosperity to the land, they had embroiled Israel in repeated wars and brought the danger of Assyrian conquest ever closer.

Deuteronomy nevertheless acknowledges that kings would still be part of Israel's reformed life in the land, but seeks to bring the monarchy under the control of God's law. The intent is not really to promulgate a reformed political constitution, but to describe in a utopian way what the attitudes and behaviors of Israel's king ought to be. This is less a description of what to do than what to avoid. The result is an insubstantial figure who is more like a student of Torah than a traditional king. He is a "citizen king," one whose status does not separate him from the rest of the people.

In accordance with the ideal in both Judah and the Northern Kingdom, he must be God's choice. His reward is long life for himself and his dynasty, again a wish appropriate to either of the two kingdoms. One wonders what unfortunate historical memories lurk behind the requirements that he be an Israelite, that he eschew a large harem or an impressive chariot force, and that he avoid hoarding wealth. Certainly Solomon comes most directly to mind, but Israel's whole grim experience with kingship is in view. The puzzling v. 16 may refer to trading mercenaries for horses.

The tool for reforming the kingship is to be the book of Deuteronomy itself. The king is to transcribe a personal copy of this law, preserved under the guardianship of the levitical priests. Constant study will lead him to fear God and scrupulously obey the law. It will also prevent royal haughtiness and unconcern for his fellow Israelites. This is a clear instance of Deuteronomy's own view of itself as a reforming law that can convert all Israel to what the nation ought to become. To do this the law must be written on doorposts and gates, on stones and altars, and in books (6:9; 27:2–8; 31:24–27).

18:1–8, Levitical Priests. These verses seek to reform Israel's treatment of the Levites, whose distressed condition is reflected elsewhere in the book. It is uncertain whether the terms "priest" and "Levite" are supposed to be synonymous here or whether two separate groups are intended. If the latter is the case, vv. 6–8 demonstrate that priests and Levites are thought to have equal status, in contrast to later developments. The intention is to induce lay Israelites to support priests and Levites with their rightful shares of the sacrificial offerings. This is rationalized by pointing out that Levites have no inherited rights to the land. Their heritage is God. The levitical share of the promised land must come to them indirectly from those with a direct inheritance. The last three verses of this unit seek to cushion the economic effects of centralization on those Levites who would live at a distance from the central sanctuary.

18:9–22, Prophets. This unit seeks to reform Israel's attempts to learn about divine will, the future, or other hidden mysteries. Its purpose is to encourage its readers to listen to those prophets who follow in the tradition of Moses. As a first step, all divination and magical techniques of inquiry must be eliminated (vv. 9–14), in accordance with Israel's traditional law (Lev. 19:31; 20:6, 27; cf. 1 Sam. 28:3). The fate of their Canaanite practitioners is a warning, as is the assertion that these are "abominations" that destroy the integrity of Israel's relationship with God.

The only proper medium of revelation for Israel is the prophet (Deut. 18:15–18). Here Deuteronomy gives an etiology or rationale for the institution of prophecy as it was known in monarchical Israel. Not just one, but a long series of prophets is in view (cf. 17:14 where more than a single king is obviously intended). The suitability of prophetic mediation is illustrated by Israel's experience on Mount Horeb. It is precisely prophets like Moses that Deuteronomy envisions. Such prophets indeed mediate the divine word, but also serve as intercessors for the people (9:7–10:11) and teachers of Torah.

The ways in which prophecy itself might become a problem are covered by vv. 19–22. Both unheeding audiences and presumptuous prophets are warned. Some advice is given to help with the recognition of prophetic words that are to be ignored. Prophecy in the names of other gods is easily rejected, but false prophecy in God's name is a more serious matter. This dilemma requires the application of a pragmatic criterion that, although clearly useless for judgments on individual oracles, is certainly a way to evaluate a prophet's overall performance (→ Magic and Divination; Prophet).

19:1–21, Asylum and Other Matters of Justice. Deuteronomy continues its reform of Israel's system of justice (16:18–20; 17:8–13), concentrating here on vengeance and asylum (vv. 1–13) and the unsupported malicious witness (vv. 15–21).

Israel's legal institution for dealing with murder was blood vengeance. A member of the victim's family, the "avenger of blood," would hunt down and kill the murderer. In tension

with this custom was the principle of asylum, which permitted anyone who had unintentionally caused death to seek shelter at the altar of the local sanctuary (Exod. 21:12–14). Deuteronomy's revolutionary call for a central altar required that the institution of asylum be modified so that the basic fairness of the whole process could be preserved. Otherwise, the great distance to the central sanctuary would lead to frequent miscarriages of justice. Such cities of refuge are also mentioned in Num. 35:6, 13–14 and Josh. 20:7–8, both texts dependent on Deuteronomy. There is no evidence that these utopian provisions were ever actually carried out.

The basic reform law creates cities of refuge (Deut. 19:1–3). Distances are to be surveyed (or perhaps roads prepared) to ensure that every accidental killer would have a fair chance of reaching them. A representative case of manslaughter is offered in vv. 4–7 to demonstrate how distinctions between murder and accidental death can be made by analyzing the circumstances. If national expansion should make distances too great (cf. 12:20), three more cities must be designated (vv. 8–10; cf. 4:41–43). Finally, the problem of illegitimate claims of asylum by intentional murderers is illustrated by a contrasting representative case (vv. 11–13). The rational for this reform is that any miscarriage of justice involving human death would endanger the whole nation and subvert God's gift of the land (vv. 10, 13).

Between these two sections, v. 14 pursues another matter of justice, the displacement of ancient boundary markers, probably as a result of economic pressure by the rich against the poor. Deuteronomy seeks to halt this practice of alienating ancestral lands by insisting that it too undermines the structure of God's good gift.

Israel's court system depended almost entirely on the testimony of witnesses. The traditional principle that two such witnesses are always required is quoted in v. 15 (cf. 17:6) to introduce the special case of a single, unsubstantiated witness to a charge of apostasy. This is an example of a matter that must be taken to the central tribunal described in 17:8–13. Again fairness is the issue. The lying witness must receive the exact punishment that would have fallen on the innocent victim as a salutary lesson for the rest of the nation. The lex talionis ("an eye for an eye"; 19:21) is quoted to forestall any temptation to leniency. The principle of just and appropriate retribution must be upheld.

20:1–20, War. Although war in Israel had become the province of the king, Deuteronomy seeks to reform warfare according to the older, premonarchical theology of holy war. These verses envision citizen soldiers rather than professionals employed by the king. This is war as it ought to be, war fought by God on Israel's behalf. God as the Divine Warrior fights with a heavenly army against Israel's foes with weapons such as lightning, storm (Judg. 5:20–21), and earthquake (Josh. 6:20). At the critical moment, usually at the break of dawn, a divinely induced panic falls on the enemy and routs them (Deut. 2:25; Judg. 7:22). Because such war was a sacred enterprise, the war camp had to be kept ritually clean (Deut. 23:12–13). Success was followed by the imposition of the ban, by means of which the fruits of victory were dedicated to the true victor, God.

In the theology of holy war, the faith of Israel is decisive, not the respective size of the armies or the presence of chariots. In a dramatic portrayal of events before battle, a priestly war sermon (20:2–4; cf. 7:1–6; 9:1–6) repeats the message of 20:1. The memory of the Exodus is Israel's basis for confidence. Then the military officers address the troops proclaiming exemptions for all whose presence might dilute the army's fearless faith (v. 8). The issue of fairness and of honoring God's gifts is important here as well. Those who have not yet tasted the fruit of what is theirs by right must not be denied (cf. 24:5).

The discussion of siege warfare also presupposes monarchical Israel, involving distant offensive campaigns. Again the tone is utopian and idealistic. Cities not in the promised land (20:10–15) are to be offered terms resulting in forced labor. Only a limited ban is imposed when they are conquered. Foreign cities in Israel's territory receive no terms and are to be totally destroyed (vv. 16–18). At the same time there is a humane concern to ameliorate the destructive effects of siege warfare (vv. 19–20). The half-humorous motivation offered by v. 19 seems to suggest that even the trees deserve fairness.

Deuteronomy's reform stands opposed to those royal military practices known to its original readers, insisting on a return to older ideals of warfare in harmony with God's will for Israel. Royal compulsion is set aside (vv. 5–8). The practice of war must not subvert Israel's joy over God's gift of the land. In place of professional troops, there is to be a militia whose ad hoc nature is clear from v. 9. The barbaric prosecution of total war (cf. 2 Kings 3:25) is limited. The ancient ban, which undermines the purposes of royal warfare (cf. 1 Kings 20:26–43), is restored. The conquest of Canaanite cities, the source of the apostasy infecting the nation (Deut. 20:18), must be taken up again. This is a revolutionary challenge to return to a utopian past, directed at readers who have suffered from the adventurism of their kings and who have a well-founded fear of invading armies numerically and technically superior to themselves. This unit seeks to rebuild their confidence in God's protection and urges

that they restructure the practice of warfare along traditional models.

21:1–26:19
Interpreting Traditional Laws

As a reform document, Deuteronomy takes up laws from Israel's traditions and recasts them for a new age. Many of these laws can be found in a somewhat different form elsewhere in the Pentateuch. The result is not a complete legal code, but a selection of those laws most in need of revision or reemphasis.

By modern standards, the organization of the laws is problematic, but such disorder is typical of ancient law codes. A wide range of topics is covered by chaps. 21–25: unsolved murder, family life and sexuality, religious purity, economic exploitation. Deuteronomy's special concern for social justice for the powerless surfaces in many laws. In chap. 26 a description of the ceremony for offering tithes at the central sanctuary provides an opportunity to review God's saving acts once more. A concluding transitional exhortation leads into the last major section of the book.

21:1–9, Unsolved Murder. Israel believed that the objective guilt of a homicide could endanger the rest of society. Guilt was viewed as an objective reality totally apart from any issue of morality or punishment. Ideally, the murderer's execution should remove this danger, but in an unsolved death other steps had to be taken. This procedure is not a sacrifice (which involves a relationship to God), but an act of expiation. Therefore the animal, killed away from the central sanctuary, has its neck broken as a sign of its nonsacrificial function (Exod. 13:13). The guilt that threatened the community is transferred to the animal. Speaking for their city, the elders wash their hands as a symbol of their innocence and as a way of transferring the guilt by means of the flowing water. Both the animal and the place are special in the sense that no human benefit has been derived from them. They are empty vessels for the guilt.

The characteristic reforming concerns of Deuteronomy are visible here. It is the land given by God that is contaminated by blood guilt (Deut. 21:1). The priests must be included in the process (v. 5). The quasi-magical ceremony of expiation must be supplemented by prayer, for in the end it is God who must cover the guilt and who does so out of concern for the people he redeemed (v. 8; → Atonement; Expiation).

21:10–21, Aspects of Family Life. The reform urged on Israel is applied to three facets of family life. First, Deuteronomy advocates the just treatment of female captives (vv. 10–14), women without male protectors in society. They are given legal status and some protection from unrestrained greed. The female prisoner of war makes a new start with new clothing, putting her old life behind her. She is fairly treated by being given a month to mourn those who have been killed or left behind. In the case of a subsequent divorce, she is no slave to be sold off but may leave freely, for her husband has received his benefit from the relationship.

Again, fairness must be maintained in the situation described in vv. 15–17. When the father assigns his sons their shares of the inheritance before his death, the rights of the less-favored wife must be preserved. Here Deuteronomy asserts the principle of fairness over against what may have been a traditional custom of free choice on the father's part, reflected in Gen. 48:13–20. As a widow, the mother would be supported by her son, who is to receive his proper double share as firstborn. This narrow special case seems to be used to advocate justice in general for women in polygamous marriages.

In 21:18–21, Deuteronomy seeks to reform the breakdown in family life that it senses as characteristic of its own era (cf. 5:16; 27:16). Clearly the absolute power parents once had over children has disappeared, and the village elders must become involved. The seriousness of the son's offense is shown by his drastic punishment, which purges the evil from the nation and serves as a salutary lesson.

21:22–22:12, Laws Enhancing Solidarity.

If anything serves as a common theme for this diverse grouping of laws, it may be the concept of solidarity. Israel's solidarity with God is protected when the purity of the land is guarded from the ritual pollution of a hanged body, something offensive to God (21:22–23). The transvestism forbidden by 22:5 may have been a pagan religious practice or viewed as deviant sexual behavior, but in either case it is labeled an "abomination" that subverts Israel's relationship to God. In a similar vein, various mixtures seen as contrary to nature are forbidden (vv. 9–11). The impropriety of these practices must have been clear enough to the original readers as to require no explanation.

The solidarity of the social order is enhanced by 22:1–4. This basic law (v. 1) with its several variations (vv. 2–4) goes beyond the older formulation of Exod. 23:4–5 to a wider definition of national fellowship, even with unknown and far-distant Israelites. The law of the parapet (Deut. 22:8) eliminates a physical risk and, more importantly, guards against blood guilt, a danger to the whole community. National solidarity in dress would be enhanced by wearing tassels (v. 12), a practice for which Deuteronomy provides no rationale (→ Fringes).

The law about birds (22:6–7) has overtones of conservation and humane treatment for animals. There seem to be echoes of the thinking that lies behind laws forbidding boiling a kid in its own mother's milk or destroying fruit trees (14:21; 20:19; see also Lev. 22:27–28). In any case, the welfare and life of the whole community is seen as affected and that may explain the inclusion of this law here.

22:13–30, Sexual Behavior.

Sex was not considered to be a matter of private moral decision in Israel; it was something of community concern. These laws regulate sexual behavior out of concern for fairness to the parties involved and a recognition that the whole community has a stake in these matters. Although these laws are one-sided and operate from an exclusively male viewpoint, they did offer women some limited protection from the worst excesses of male domination.

The concern for fairness is clearest in vv. 13–21. The husband's charge may be a vicious pretext for divorce, but the parents may be able to clear their daughter's name by showing the "token" of her virginity, a cloth stained with the blood of her wedding night. Both mother and father share this parental role (cf. 21:18–21). The husband is punished severely because he has defamed her and the nation as well. She is justly protected from further attempts at divorce. If her parents cannot prove her previous virginity, however, she is assumed to have committed a "folly in Israel" (22:21) and is stoned beside her father's house as a sign of the shame she has brought to her family. Whether she turns out to be guilty or innocent, this is no private matter of her personal morality, for the reputation of the nation is at stake (vv. 19, 21).

Five laws guarding sexual purity follow. Adultery and rape are seen as offenses against the husband or father of the woman involved. There seems to be no concern for rape as a crime of violence against the woman herself in these laws. If both parties are caught in adultery, that is, if the woman is married to someone else, both must die, for this is an evil to be purged from Israel (v. 22). The case is similar if she is betrothed, since that was the legal equivalent of marriage (vv. 23–24).

Deuteronomy's concern for fairness is evident if the couple is discovered in the country, for then this must be considered a case of rape by force in virtue of the circumstances (vv. 25–27). If the raped woman is not married or betrothed (vv. 28–29), the matter is less serious, a clear indication that rape was viewed as a crime against the victim's husband. In this case it is a crime against her father, and he is compensated for the loss of her bride price (cf. Exod. 22:16–17). She is, however, protected by the law from a life of shame and the destruction of her prospects for marriage (cf. 2 Sam. 13:13, 16, 19) by marriage to her attacker without any future threat of divorce.

The series concludes with an apodictic prohibition designed to protect the integrity of the extended family in a polygamous context (Deut. 22:30; cf. 27:20). Sexual relations with a stepmother did not occur only as a mere clandestine affair (as Gen. 35:22); it could also result from a son's inheriting his father's wives and concubines (1 Kings 2:22).

23:1–14, The Purity of Israel. Deuteronomy seeks an idealistic return to traditional concepts of purity in the worship assembly and the war camp, settings in which the people were a sacral gathering, united for the purpose of worshiping God and fighting under God's guidance. The motive for revitalizing these laws was not hatred of foreigners or hygiene, but a desire to strengthen Israel's relationship with a loving, protective God (vv. 5, 14).

A five-part apodictic list restricts participation in the worship assembly (vv. 1–8). Castration may have been an aspect of Canaanite worship, although v. 1 more likely reflects the idea that it was simply offensive for someone less than whole to participate in sacred activities (cf. Lev. 21:17–23). The precise nature of those barred by Deut. 23:2, offspring of an irregular union of some kind, is unclear, but Moabites and Ammonites seem to fall under this rubric, given their traditional origin (Gen. 19:30 38). Two items from the wilderness tradition support their exclusion, and the technical language of Deut. 23:6 implies that no political treaties may be made with them. In contrast, resident Edomite and Egyptian families might eventually gain admittance based on Edom's kinship and Egypt's hospitality to Israel's ancestors.

The sacrality of the war camp was part of the holy war tradition that Deuteronomy seeks to revive. Concepts of ritual pollution (cf. Lev. 15:16–17) and aesthetics are combined here. God's protective presence in the camp is both the rationale and the motivation for these practices.

23:15–25:19, A Renewed Society. These diverse laws protect the harmony of relationships, both with God and with other human beings. Deuteronomy seeks to reform Israel into a society of wholeness and social concord. The motivations offered for obedience describe the nature of this society. "Abominations" and evils that subvert the nation's relationship to God would be prevented (23:18; 24:4, 7). Instead there would be blessing in the land of promise (23:20; 24:19) and approval from God (24:13). Israel would remember the lessons of the past (24:9, 18, 22; 25:19) and behave accordingly. There would be joy, life, dignity, and social harmony (24:5, 6, 13, 15; 25:3).

Such a society requires, first of all, a healthy relationship with God. Therefore sacral prostitutes of either sex are forbidden and money earned by such persons is banned from the sanctuary (23:17–18). Vows to God must be kept (23:21–23). Even labor disputes (24:15) and commercial fraud (25:13–16) undermine Israel's harmony with God and must be avoided.

The divorce law (24:1–4), written from an exclusively male perspective, does not give guidance for divorce procedures in general. These are reviewed only to set up the specific prohibition of remarriage to a previous husband by a divorced woman. Divorce is taken for granted as a simple dismissal of the wife by her husband (and not vice versa). The stated grounds could be minor: some undefined impropriety (v. 1) or simple dislike (v. 3). Clearly divorce was an institution by means of which injustices against women were perpetrated, but Deuteronomy is concerned here only with a danger to Israel's relationship with God. Divorce is reformed so that it is permanent rather than temporary, lest God be offended.

Renewed Israel would be a society in which marriage is affirmed (24:5), kidnapping is prevented (24:7), and "leprosy" (which included a wide variety of skin diseases) is regulated by the priests (24:8–9). The innocent are protected from unfair applications of the principle of communal guilt (24:16). Modesty is preserved between women and men and the danger of injury or infertility forestalled in cases like the one described by 25:11–12.

The society envisioned here would take special care of its poor and marginal members. Escaped slaves are not to be returned or reduced again to slavery (23:15–16). This is remarkable, for escaped slaves were a dangerous class and the obligation to return them was a common provision of ancient treaties. A divorced woman is to receive a document that clarifies her status in the community (24:1). Hired servants, who live from hand to mouth, are to be paid promptly (24:14–15), protecting workers from oppression and employers from sin. Powerless people such as sojourners, orphans, and widows are guaranteed justice and economic protection (24:17). Even criminals deserve dignity and consideration. Verdicts must be clear and punishments humane, carried out in the presence of the judge responsible (25:1–3). Even domestic animals have certain rights (25:4).

Lending is envisioned as a way the rich extend social benefits to the poor, not as a way of acquiring interest (23:19–20). The economically marginal could thus be helped over times of crisis. This conception of credit is even more remarkable when one remembers that all debts were to be canceled every seventh year (15:1–6). Moreover, the practice of taking pledges or collateral is strictly regulated to protect the domestic life and dignity of the debtor and to prevent undue hardship (24:6, 10–13). Because such pledges were taken not for their intrinsic value, but to pressure the debtor into payment, Deuteronomy is depriving the practice of much of its oppressive power. Such regulations show that Deuteronomy is thinking of the economic structure of a small town in which the borrower and the lender interact on a daily basis.

The poor are protected from hunger through the social support institution described in 24:19–22, while property owners are themselves protected from abuses of a similar custom in 23:24–25. These practices eliminate the need for direct handouts or begging, thus protecting the dignity of the poor, who must work for what they receive.

The institution of the levirate marriage (25:5–10) offers protection for a man who dies without a son to inherit his property and carry on his name and, less directly, for his widow who needs support and a niche in society. The brother (or other close relative) of the deceased was obligated to marry his widow in order to produce a son, who was then considered to be the son of the dead brother. This ancient practice of surrogate fatherhood rests on the institution of the extended family, in which brothers live together (v. 5). The possibility of refusal, which does not seem to exist in the levirate law presupposed in Genesis 38, is now offered the recalcitrant brother (see Ruth 4:1–8). Now compliance depends only upon social pressure (Deut. 25:9–10).

26:1–15, First Fruits and Tithes. The presentation of the law ends, as it began in chap. 12, with worship. By describing what an individual was to do when the land was first settled, Deuteronomy seeks to establish two continuing liturgical events, providing appropriate liturgical recitations for each.

The offering of first fruits ties together the themes of deliverance, God's gift of the fertile land, the central sanctuary, the gifts due the priests (18:4), and concern for society's marginal people. In the context of Deuteronomy, these first fruits must be taken to be the same as the annual tithe (12:17–18; 14:22–27) brought to the central sanctuary and enjoyed by all. There are two declarations (26:3 and 5–10), each followed by a presentation, first by the priest (v. 4) and then by the farmer (v. 10). The creedal prayer of thanksgiving reviews Israel's experience of salvation. It moves from the national story to the worshiper's personal story, tying God's present gift of agricultural fertility to his past acts of deliverance. The contrast between past and present is sharp. Jacob's wandering (or perishing) as a landless alien and slavery in Egypt are set over against rest and freedom in the rich land of promise.

The tithe of the third year (vv. 12–15) adds the theme of obedience and reiterates the issues of social concern and the land's richness. Third-year tithes were to be distributed to the economically distressed at home, not taken to the central sanctuary (14:28–29). The worshiper's profession of obedience and prayer for blessing are thus addressed to God in heaven (26:15).

26:16–19, Concluding Summary. These verses conclude the legal portion of Deuteronomy begun with chap. 12 (cf. v. 16 with 12:1). The literary premise of the book is restated by the "today" of 26:17. The theological concept of covenant is introduced to lead into chaps. 27–30. The audience is with Moses in Moab, about to conclude a covenant agreement with God. Each party has made a solemn declaration of the covenant relationship. God has taken Israel as a treasured, holy people and promised them a high position among the nations. Israel has declared this God to be their God. Israel's obedience to his commandments is a factor in both declarations, and obedience with total heart and soul is urged upon them.

27:1–34:12

The Story Continues

Materials from a variety of sources work together to focus the reform law of Deuteronomy for readers and to challenge them to accept its authority over their lives. Chap. 27, speaking of Moses in the third person, describes a permanent display of this law before the people and a future ceremony by which they put themselves under its authority. Chap. 28 represents a further speech by Moses in which he sets forth the blessings and curses that give this law power over Israel's future. This is followed by a motivational address set into the context of a covenant made in the land of Moab (chaps. 29–30). Portions of this speech were added during the exilic period and help focus the meaning of the law for those who had already disobeyed it and been punished (30:1–10).

The transition from the age of Moses to the readers' present is carried forward by the Deuteronomistic historian's concluding narrative, which sets out the law of Deuteronomy as the standard by which Israel's continuing story is to be understood (chap. 31). The Song of Moses (chap. 32) and the Blessing of Moses (chap. 33) each had a separate history of transmission before its inclusion in Deuteronomy. In their present context, they focus the law of Deuteronomy on Israel's future life in the land, an existence marred by disobedience yet empowered by God's vindication and blessing. The last chapter concludes both Deuteronomy and the entire Pentateuch with the death of Moses.

27:1–30:20
Covenant Making

Chaps. 27–30 direct the law of Deuteronomy at its readers by using the concept of covenant to challenge readers to live according to its precepts. In chap. 27 Moses sets forth a covenant ritual of curses by which Israel will accept its responsibility to live under the law. Blessings and curses (chap. 28) motivate obedience and cast the entire book into the shape of a covenant document.

Covenant was a vital theological concept for Israel, used to describe the nature of God's relationship to the patriarchs and to the nation. Although some scholars trace the covenant concept back into Israel's earliest days, it may be that the prophets and Deuteronomy are the sources for this idea in Israel. The covenant was described as based on God's own past saving acts, shaped by precepts or laws, instituted by a covenant ceremony, and empowered by curses and blessings. This covenant format follows the analogy of human legal agreements and, more specifically, ancient Near Eastern international treaty practice. In its final form, Deuteronomy follows this covenant format closely.

The covenant theme is carried forward by chaps. 29–30, in which the book of Deuteronomy becomes the content of a second covenant, one made between God and Israel in the land of Moab. The Ten Commandments are described as the covenant document given at Mount Horeb (4:13; 5:2–3; 9:9, 11, 15). In a similar way, the entire written law of Deuteronomy is converted into the expression of God's covenant will for Israel delivered in Moab (29:1, 9, 14–15, 21).

27:1–26, The Shechem Ceremony. Moses no longer speaks alone, but with elders (vv. 1–8) and priests (vv. 9–10), for the focus now turns to the future, when Moses will no longer be with Israel. Instructions for what is to be done on Ebal and Gerizim (11:26–32; 27:2–26) bracket his promulgation of law (chaps. 12–26), for Deuteronomy wants to direct this law at its original readers, who live in the land of promise. It is to them that it will be displayed on plastered stones (27:2–4, 8). Whatever relationship the altar on Ebal (vv. 5–7) might bear to the central altar of the rest of the book, it certainly signals the beginning of Israel's life as a worshiping community in the land, those to whom this book is really addressed.

Moses gives instructions for a covenant ceremony of blessing and curse, but provides here only the curses in an ancient series of twelve laws concerning deeds done in secret. Secret behavior could not be controlled by social pressure or legal process, but it could be regulated by curse, the threatening power of which was taken for granted. The people here

agree to each curse with an "amen" and thus mark themselves off from any who would do such things. Many of these curses deal with concerns found elsewhere in Deuteronomy. Idolatry, honor for parents, and murder are topics of the Ten Commandments (vv. 15–16, 24). Displacement of a boundary marker (v. 17) was dealt with in 19:14 and intercourse with one's father's wife (27:20) in 22:30. Deut. 27:20, along with v. 22, was intended to protect the integrity of the extended family. The rights of strangers, orphans, and widows (v. 19) are basic themes of Deuteronomy. Bribes (v. 25) are the topic of 16:19.

The summary curse of 27:26 impels obedience to the whole law of Deuteronomy. Like the Ten Commandments, these curses concentrate the law into an intense, memorable list with a powerful impact. The Shechem ceremony aims Deuteronomy's reforming law directly and forcefully at its original readers. They are the people of the future addressed by Moses, for whom the law is written publicly and plainly (v. 8). As the people of God they are to obey (vv. 9–10) and respond to this law with their own "amen."

28:1–68, Blessings and Curses. Ancient treaties were often guaranteed by a concluding list of blessings and curses that gave the agreement power to regulate behavior. Deuteronomy uses curses and blessings for the same purpose, to motivate obedience to the covenant said to have been concluded between God and Israel on the plains of Moab. The basic structure of this covenant is set forth by vv. 1 and 9, which go over the ground of 26:16–19 and 27:9–10. The blessings will follow obedience (28:2); the curses will overtake Israel if they disobey (v. 15). There is some balance between blessing and curse (vv. 3–6 and 16–19; 7 and 25; 12–13 and 43–44), but the curses are much more extensive and colorful. Their intended purpose is to motivate obedience to the law of Deuteronomy (v. 58) before it becomes too late. The preponderance of curses over blessings underscores the urgency of Israel's need to reform.

These motivating blessings and curses are appropriate for their intended audience in monarchical Israel. They reflect a rural, agricultural life on the one hand and a deep concern over international affairs on the other. The curses are very similar to those found in certain Assyrian treaties, and it seems likely that Deuteronomy made use of Assyrian curse language in formulating these frightful imprecations. Since Assyria was notorious for its wartime atrocities, this borrowing deepens the impact of this unit.

Taken together, these curses and blessings impact on a wide area of life. Fertility (vv. 3–5, 8, 11, 16–19, 38–40, 42) and rain (vv. 12, 23–24) were gifts that Israel was often tempted to associate with the gods of Canaan. Their inclusion here makes a statement about God's demand for exclusive worship. Other curses deal with sickness (vv. 21–22, 27–28, 35, 59–60). Israel looked to its God for military protection (v. 7), but these curses threaten defeat (v. 25), conquest by cruel foreigners (vv. 33, 49–57), and heartbreaking exile (vv. 36–37, 63–68). The blessings and curses are generalized to sweep all readers into their net (vv. 3, 13, 29, 43–44). The curses are also personalized (vv. 30–32) and made as frightful as possible (vv. 26, 34, 53–57) so that no reader might escape their power.

As the curses unroll, transitions are visible. A conclusion of sorts seems to be reached in vv. 45–46, but then a new section of curses begins, vv. 47–57. Here Israel's failure to obey seems no longer just a possibility, but a certainty. The curses focus on invasion by a ruthless enemy and the horrors of siege warfare. Then another new introduction begins vv. 58–68. This section portrays Israel's future as a reversal of saving history, an exile back to Egypt, to a hopeless existence far from rest in the promised land. The most terrible thought of all may be v. 63, which describes God as taking grim pleasure in Israel's destruction (→ Curse and Blessing).

29:1–30:20, A Covenant in Moab. A renewal of the covenant in Moab (29:1, 12) provides the occasion for an oration by Moses. Israel is urged to adopt the reforming law that Deuteronomy presents in written form (29:20–21, 27; 30:10). The entreaty becomes insistent and impassioned. A sense of crisis looms. Today is the moment of decision (29:4). Choose life and not death (30:19).

A review of saving history (29:2–8) reminds Israel that past crises were times of providence and education. The meaning of those events was hidden then but now has been revealed. Deuteronomy urges the adoption of its own particular interpretation of past traditions. Israel is to seize the present moment of crisis as an opportunity for decision and obedience. A renewed dedication to the covenant is required of all, from the greatest to the least (29:10–11). The nature of this covenant relationship is epitomized by v. 13, repeating 26:17–19. The original readers are directly included in the moment of decision by vv. 14–15.

This covenant is guaranteed by curses (chap. 28) that will fall on any man or woman or group who worships a strange god, the rest of the nation being endangered by the guilty one marked off for catastrophe (29:18–21). An effective literary device (vv. 22–28) carries the audience forward into a grim potential future. A vivid dialogue set into a blasted landscape portrays the destruction and exile that will result if this covenant is violated.

Israel is to concentrate on faithful obedi-

ence to what is openly revealed in Deuteronomy. The mystery of God's ways remains an impenetrable secret best left to God (v. 29), but this law is not difficult to keep; it is clear and understandable (30:11–14). God's will for Israel is within easy reach; it need not be sought out in some epic quest. Israel is faced with the simplest of choices: life or death (vv. 15–20). Moses, backed up by the witness of heaven and earth, sets before Israel two clear ways. Apostasy means adversity and eventual exile. Obedience means prosperity and long life in the land of promise.

Although a somewhat different and later situation seems to be addressed by 30:1–10, there too Israel is called upon to repent and reform. These verses, resembling 4:29–31 in outlook, speak to an audience that has already experienced national destruction and exile. The path of return is set out step-by-step. Take these blessings and curses to heart in the land of exile and return to God through renewed obedience (30:1–2). Then God will gather and restore you to the prosperous land once more (vv. 3–5), circumcising your hearts so that love for God and obedience will become second nature to you (vv. 6, 8). The curses will be transferred to your enemies, while the blessings will shower on you (vv. 7, 9; cf. 28:4). All this will happen if you obey and wholeheartedly return to God (v. 10).

31:1–34:12
Transition to Canaan

This concluding section provides readers with bridges that connect the reform law of Deuteronomy to their own lives. Moses initiates a regular routine of reading Deuteronomy before the assembled community and gives final instructions that carry forward into the book of Joshua (chap. 31). The Song of Moses and the Blessing of Moses (chaps. 32–33) represent his last testament to Israel. These point forward into a future that is the readers' own present. The Song is a witness to the apostasy in which they have participated, as is the written law of Deuteronomy itself (31:19, 21, 26–27). Yet along with the Blessing of Moses, the Song also points beyond disobedience and punishment to God's gracious will for Israel. The future is ultimately determined not by Israel's infidelity, but by God's fidelity. Chap. 34 continues the transition to the story of Israel under Joshua and summarizes the career of Moses.

31:1–29, Preparing for the Future. A major turning point is reached with this unit. Moses' long speeches are over. There is a return to the narrative, which is picked up from where it left off in 3:23–29. Attention shifts to preparation for Israel's future in the land. This future (which is the original readers' present) will be grim. Following an ingrained predisposition to rebellion already evident to Moses, Israel will violate the covenant by worshiping foreign gods and idols and be punished by God's wrath (31:16–18, 20–21, 27–29).

Since Moses will not cross the Jordan because of age and God's command, Joshua is prepared for his role as military leader. In turn, Moses encourages both the people and Joshua to bravery (vv. 2–8). The transition from Moses to Joshua is made in a different way by vv. 14–15, 23, probably a fragment of tradition from some other source. Here the tent of meeting, the point of rendezvous between Moses and God, is the locale of God's direct authorization of Joshua (→ Tabernacle).

The law is the focus of other preparations for the future. The written law, which is Deuteronomy, is entrusted to the priests and elders. It is to be read at the Feast of Booths every seventh year, the year of debt remission (vv. 9–13; cf. 15:1–11). This is to be an educational and motivational opportunity for coming generations. The book of the law is given to the Levites to be set beside the Ark as a witness against Israel's future disobedience (31:24–27). Another witness against Israel will be provided by a song that Moses writes down and teaches Israel (vv. 19–22; the Song of Moses, chap. 32).

This chapter was intended to connect the book of Deuteronomy to those to whom it was first addressed. They were living in the grim future for which Moses has prepared. The law had been passed on to them. Deuteronomy witnessed against their present apostasy, but at the same time it offered them a chance for renewal and obedience (31:10–13).

31:30–32:52, The Song of Moses. Moses, about to die, offers some last words to Israel in the form of a song. This is spoken rather than sung, indicating its didactic nature. Moses is represented as one with prophetic vision, uncovering the meaning of the past while providing a vision of future and a challenge for the present. He tells the story of Israel from election through apostasy and punishment to God's gracious vindication. Like the law (31:26), this song is to be a witness against Israel (31:19, 21), describing the consequences of the apostasy against which Deuteronomy warns. It is directed at the Israel in Moses' future (31:29), those who have experienced punishment in the shape of enemy conquest.

The poem (32:1–43) uses the traditional format of a lawsuit in which God brings Israel to trial for its infidelity. God calls witnesses to observe the proceedings (vv. 1–3) and then summarizes the prosecution's case (vv. 4–6). The details of the case then follow: God's past graciousness (vv. 7–14), the indictment (vv. 15–18), the guilty verdict, and the sentence of total destruction (vv. 19–25). At this point, the poem abandons the lawsuit format and moves on to assert God's continued vindication of Israel for the purpose of preserving his own honor.

The introduction (vv. 1–3) addresses the heavens and earth, invoked as witnesses against Israel throughout Deuteronomy (4:26; 30:19; 31:28). Water metaphors underscore the beneficial and refreshing intent of Moses' teaching. The song's theme is present in 32:4–6a: God has proven faithful; the people have been faithless and perverse. The poem's central metaphor is God as a rock, the symbol of solidity and stability (vv. 4, 15, 18, 30, 31; cf. 37).

Israel's story begins with the nation's election at the time of the origin of all peoples (vv. 8–9). When parceling out the peoples of the earth to their gods, God kept Israel as a personal inheritance. He found this people in the wilderness and adopted them (a tradition of election found also in Hos. 9:10). God gave Israel the land of promise (Deut. 32:13–14), nurturing them richly, sometimes from the most unpromising places. Complacency in prosperity, however, led to the worship of other gods (vv. 15–17; cf. 6:10–12; 8:7–20). Israel forgot the Rock who had given birth to them (32:18). Israel's idolatry roused God to jealous anger, and punishment followed in the form of invasion and defeat by a cruel people (vv. 19–25). The curses of chap. 28 had struck home.

Disaster does not have the last word, however. Punishment is not carried to its ultimate conclusion but is moderated (32:26). God's inner thoughts reveal that this is not because of Israel's own merit, however, but grows out of his own concern for self. The enemy people whom God had employed against Israel would misinterpret complete destruction and take the credit for themselves (v. 27). These enemies are not wise enough to see the divine pattern behind their victories (vv. 28–30). They are corrupt in origin and poisonous, and the vengeance of God is stored up against them (vv. 31–35).

Israel's vindication begins when their power has reached low ebb (v. 36). Israel's false gods have been unable to help them (vv. 37–38). In contrast, the only one worthy of the designation "God," the one who kills and gives life, takes an impressive martial oath to be vindicated against all enemies (vv. 39–42). The hymnic conclusion (v. 43) applies God's vindication to Israel's own vindication.

This poem confronted its readers, those who had themselves experienced this history of apostasy, punishment, and vindication, with the law of Deuteronomy. They were not to imagine that national catastrophe meant that their God was powerless. Based on the confession that Israel's Lord alone was God (v. 39) and a conviction that he would turn back to rebellious Israel once punishment has run its course (cf. 30:1–10), readers were urged to recognize God's rock-solid faithfulness and to respond with loyalty and obedience.

233

In the prose section that follows, the center of interest moves back to the law, its transmission to future generations, and its vital importance to Israel's life in the land (vv. 45–47). Moses' impending death is referred to again in vv. 48–52, reflecting traditions like those found in Num. 20:10–13 and 27:12–14.

33:1–29, The Blessing of Moses. Blessings spoken by a leader near death were thought to be exceptionally powerful in shaping the future. This material had a history of its own before being used in Deuteronomy to point to Israel's coming life in the land. A diverse collection of tribal sayings is framed by vv. 2–5 and 26–29 to create a unified poem. The introduction describes God's coming in awesome theophany from Sinai as king over Jeshurun (a poetic name for Israel). Verse 4 connects this poem to its context, the giving of the law by Moses. God's power and love are emphasized, along with Israel's unity. The conclusion speaks of the conquest and the gift of the land. It stresses the protection and providence of God, who rides the clouds (cf. Pss. 68:4; 104:3) to give Israel victory.

The sayings themselves reflect a time of peace and prosperity for the Joseph tribes (Ephraim and Manasseh) and Benjamin, the heartland of the Northern Kingdom. Reuben is small and struggling. Dan has moved to its second home in the north. It is indicative of a northern perspective that Judah is separated from the other tribes and Simeon receives no mention at all.

Some of these sayings are less blessings than statements or aphorisms that characterize a given tribe's life in some way. Benjamin dwells safely, protected between God's shoulders (or the slopes of their hills; v. 12). Dan is aggressive (v. 22). Naphtali is sated with favor (v. 23). Zebulun and Issachar are addressed directly with a command to rejoice, followed by a description of their sanctuary at Mount Tabor and the riches that come from their access to the sea (vv. 18–19).

Closer to the idea of a blessing are sayings that are wishes and prayers. Moses wishes Reuben continued existence and Asher prosperity and security (vv. 6, 24–25). There is a prayer for Judah's reunification with the other tribes (v. 7) and a more extensive one for Levi (vv. 8–11). Levi has proved its fidelity to God (cf. Exod. 17:1–7; 32:26–29; Num. 20:1–13 for similar traditions). Levi's role seems to be insecure in some way. The prayer is that God defend them and prosper their undertakings. To them belong the sacred lots (→Urim and Thummim), the task of teaching law to Israel, and sacrifice. The Joseph tribes receive a fertility blessing along with a description of their military prowess (vv. 13–17). A tradition similar to Exod. 3:1–3 is referred to in the mention of the bush in v. 16.

The Blessing of Moses is tied to the Song of Moses through the use of the ancient name "Jeshurun" for Israel (32:15; 33:5). The Blessing portrays the results of God's vindication of Israel that was promised by the Song. These blessings are also integrated with the entire book of Deuteronomy as a description of life in the land, offering a positive balance to the curses of chap. 28. The warlike ones connect to the coming conquest.

On the other hand, this chapter moves beyond Deuteronomy's penchant for exhortations and warnings, concluding the book with a picture of Israel's future that seems to transcend the categories of obedience and disobedience to the law. Yet, like Deuteronomy as a whole, it offers a utopian vision of what Israel ought to be like when its life is lived out under God.

34:1–12, Moses Dies. Moses' final words are finished. The narrative returns to where it left off in 32:48–52. This chapter looks back, providing the conclusion for Deuteronomy and the entire Pentateuch as well. Moses' career is reviewed as that of a prophet with the closest possible communion with God, as one through whom God worked wonders (34:10–12). His extraordinary age and vigor testify to his virtue, and the thirty-day period of mourning to his popularity (vv. 7–8).

This is also a transition to the rest of Israel's story, reported in the books that follow. Moses' mountaintop view points forward to the conquest and life in the land promised to the patriarchs. In ancient legal practice, a survey was one way of transferring land ownership. The past is decisively over: Moses is dead and his grave cannot be found. Joshua is empowered to carry the story forward, and the people accept his leadership.

Thus the challenge of the future was set before the original readers of Deuteronomy. For them, this challenge came in the form of the law written in this book. Continued life in the land of promise would depend on their obedience to that law.

Bibliography

Achtemeier, E. *Deuteronomy, Jeremiah.* Proclamation Commentaries. Philadelphia: Fortress, 1978.

Clements, R. E. *God's Chosen People: A Theological Interpretation of the Book of Deuteronomy.* London: SCM, 1968.

Levenson, J. D. *Sinai and Zion: An Entry into the Jewish Bible.* San Francisco: Harper & Row, 1987.

Nicholson, E. W. *Deuteronomy and Tradition.* Philadelphia: Fortress, 1967.

von Rad, G. *Deuteronomy.* Old Testament Library. Philadelphia: Westminster, 1966.

JOSHUA

WALTER E. RAST

INTRODUCTION

The Book of Joshua poses a problem for the reader of the Bible. Approximately one-half of it is a book of wars, in which God is a divine warrior who fights at the head of his people. This forthright militaristic portrayal may block the way to a fruitful engagement with the book. Yet it seems that the Jewish and Christian communities decided wisely in including the book of Joshua in the scriptural canon. Despite any negative reaction readers may have, this book provokes us to reflect on some of the issues of war, territorial claims, and nationalism. At the same time it encourages thought about the problems of the justice and mercy of God, of holding one's commitments in a pluralistic world, and of achieving an understanding of life based in covenant. This commentary, devoted to the study of the growth and structure of the book, its social and religious questions, and its theological perspective, is intended as an aid to such reflection.

Literary History

New ground was broken in the literary study of Joshua when the German scholar Martin Noth proposed that the book of Joshua was part of a large historical work from Deuteronomy through 2 Kings. Noth termed this work the "Deuteronomistic History," since he held that its point of view was often identical with that of the book of Deuteronomy. According to a widely accepted interpretation, Deuteronomy was the product of a movement in the latter third of the seventh century B.C. (→ Deuteronomy). Influenced as this so-called Deuteronomic movement was by the prophets of Israel, the purpose of the great historical work that sprang from it was to trace the downfall of the northern and southern kingdoms of Israel to the people's growing unfaithfulness to the covenant, which finally called forth the divine judgment upon both kingdoms. The Deuteronomistic History was thus very different in style and theology from the J (Jahwist), E (Elohist), and P (Priestly) accounts, which make up the bulk of the Pentateuch. According to most scholars, the Deuteronomistic History was produced by several historians either around the time of Josiah's reform in Judah in the late seventh century B.C. (→ Josiah) or during the Exile, after 587 B.C.

Along with other scholars, Noth also stressed that the Deuteronomistic historians used earlier material but interpreted it according to this theology. This understanding of the literary character of the book of Joshua, which is followed in this commentary, makes it essential that we be aware of earlier and later levels of tradition in the texts. Almost every chapter contains earlier material that now stands in the new context of the Deuteronomistic historians' interpretive framework. This presentation makes an effort to point out both the earlier traditions and the historians' purposes in incorporating them.

Forms in the Book

Older materials in the book can often be identified by their form. One such example is the short piece of ancient verse found in Josh. 10:12b–13 (→ Jashar, the Book of), raised as a cry of victory in the Valley of Aijalon. Older sagalike stories also occur, such as much of the story of Rahab in chap. 2. The historians likewise made use of lists compiled considerably before their time. Such lists are the defeated kings in 12:9–24 and a registry of cities in 15:20–62 and 18:21–28. Some parts of the conquest traditions in chaps. 8–11 also suggest older material formalized long before the historian received it. Similarly, the distribution of the land in 13:1–15:19 and 17:1–18 and the "divisions by lot" in 18:11–20 and 19:1–51 are archaic, having originated probably somewhat before the tenth century B.C. No doubt the account of the "cities of refuge" in chap. 20 and the narrative of the disputed altar in 22:10–34 were also of earlier vintage.

The favorite literary form of the historians themselves was the declamatory speech. Such speeches appear at crucial turning points in the history of Israel. Examples can be found in 1:10–11; 1:13–15; 3:3–5; and 3:9–13 where they are given by the leaders, or in 1:16–18 where such a speech is made by the people, or in 2:8–13 by Rahab. God also addresses his people in this form in 1:2–9 and 3:7–8, as does Joshua in his final oration in chap. 23.

All speeches stress the covenant between Israel and God, and throughout the book the historians assess the history of Israel by means of the Israelites' faithfulness to the covenant or their rejection of it.

Purpose

A single conviction dominates the book of Joshua—that Israel was destined to become a covenant people in a special land prepared for them by Yahweh. Such a promise of land had been made to the ancestors (→Promise), yet the historians gave it a new dimension by making the inheritance of the land contingent on Israel's keeping the Torah given to Moses. It was Joshua who saw to it that the commands originally given to Moses were carried out. Thus the period of the original entry was a successful one. Israel followed Joshua as "the Lord's servant" just as they had Moses. The historians were firmly of the conviction that, if Israel had continued to follow the Torah, they would not have fallen on the evil days detailed in 2 Kings 17 and 24–25.

The Problem of Historicity

The Deuteronomistic History is more interested in interpreting the past than in giving a chronicle of events exactly as they happened. Some of the difficulties of historicity in the book of Joshua are: Joshua's eminent role in chaps. 1–11 and 22–24, but his virtual absence in 12–21, raising the problem of the specific place of this leader in Israel; the highly embellished story of the conquest of Jericho in chaps. 5–6; the frequent use of the formula "unto this day" in the book (4:9; 5:9; 6:25; 8:29), indicating a later explanation of older material; the mixture of different types of lists in chaps. 13–21; and the contrasting presentations of a swift conquest of the land by Israel in this book as against the more gradual settlement indicated by Judges 1.

The above points suggest that, whatever we may have in the way of historical memory in the book of Joshua, it has often been put through the sieve of later interpretation. Archaeology can sometimes help to clarify what lies behind the book, but archaeology also has increased the difficulty in some cases. There are also differences of opinion on how archaeological evidence is to be interpreted when applied to texts such as those of the conquest in Joshua 6–12. The lists in Joshua 13–21, too, can sometimes be illuminated by archaeological survey and excavation, but since these lists date to a time later than Israel's entry into the land, they often cannot provide us with information about the earlier period.

We are left, then, with records and interpretations that report or tabulate important developments in the history of early Israel in the land of Canaan, even though the specific details of that important period have often been obscured, and its actual history was undoubtedly much more complex. Despite this, it is fair to say that the book of Joshua does introduce us to the struggles that accompanied Israel's settlement in the land. More than that, it provides us with an indispensable description of the developments through which the independent tribes began to merge into the larger group called "the children of Israel."

COMMENTARY

1:1–2:24
Preparation for Entering the Land

These two chapters differ greatly in content. Joshua 1 contains a speech by God to Joshua and one by Joshua to the people. Joshua 2, on the other hand, consists of a narrative regarding the spies of Jericho. Both chapters build on the charge in 1:2: "Arise, cross over this Jordan."

1:1–9, God's Speech to Joshua. This section fulfills two purposes. First, it shows that Joshua is to carry through what Moses initiated but could not complete, bringing Israel to the land promised to the fathers. Second, it links Joshua to Moses by stressing Joshua's role as the one who, like Moses, is to see that all the law of the Lord is carefully observed, for only then could a successful entry into the land be made.

1:10–18, Joshua's Command to the People. For the first time in the book Joshua "commands" the people. This verb appears often in the Deuteronomistic historians' vocabulary. In their view nothing could occur unless divine action stood behind it. For that reason it is God above all who commands, because all authority derives from him. But in the Deuteronomic view it is "Yahweh's servants," such as Moses, who transmit the divine commands. This verb, therefore, stresses Joshua's authority to speak and act on behalf of the God of Israel, as Moses had done.

Joshua commands the officers to prepare the people to cross the Jordan. The term "officer" apparently refers to a group whose primary function was keeping records. If this is so, it could be evidence for the existence of writing already in early Israel. The title also denotes an overseeing function as in Exod. 5:14–15. It is not clear, however, whether mention of such functionaries gives us an insight into the social organization of early Israel or whether it is a feature retrojected from a later period. In any case, this group of specialists appears in several places in the book (e.g., 3:2).

The brief Deuteronomistic speech ascribed to Joshua in 1:13–15 reasserts what was earlier

236

attributed to Moses (Deut. 3:8–20), that the two and a half Transjordanian tribes should cross the Jordan to help their kinsmen conquer their land there. The people respond with a statement of loyalty, which again has a Deuteronomic tinge to it: "As we heeded Moses in everything, so we will listen to you" (1:17).

2:1–24, The Spies at Jericho. The historians proceed to tell the story of the spies. This is clearly a piece of older narrative that fits well at this point, not only in providing the first contact of the Israelites with the land but also in introducing tension into the story of the capture of Jericho. In the forefront are Rahab the harlot and the two Israelite spies, in the background the king's secret police trying to smoke out the potential menace of these outsiders. The tension in the story is in the relation of the spies to Rahab, which is characterized by the mutual suspicion of two inimical parties. Tension is also found in the flight of the spies to the hill country and their pursuit by the king's men.

The story of the spies at Jericho is one of a group of biblical spy accounts (e.g., Josh. 7:2–5; Num. 13; Judg. 18:2–10). No doubt such stories had a firm basis in reality, reflecting familiar military practices. Yet the various references to Rahab in the book do not suggest a unified account so much as a remembered tradition that has been incorporated at several points. When we examine the story of Rahab's family as this is taken up subsequently in 6:22–25, it becomes evident that this part was joined secondarily to the account of Jericho's conquest, since the walls of Jericho had already fallen when Rahab and her family are said to have been delivered. Most likely, therefore, the tradition of the spies and Rahab was joined to the narrative about Jericho by the Deuteronomistic historians themselves.

Some features of the story of Rahab in Jericho are graphically illustrated by archaeology. The city described in the story fits well with what we know of Canaanite cities about the time Israelites were establishing themselves in the land. That the gate of Jericho was closed up at night recalls excavated examples of gates of Bronze Age Canaanite cities that were constructed for such protective purposes. The statement is also made that Rahab's house was "in the city wall" (2:15), a phrase that suggests a unique type of "casemate wall" excavated at several sites by archaeologists. This kind of fortification, known already in the Late Bronze Age, consisted of two parallel walls around the circumference of a city; crosswalls separated off rooms within them. Perhaps it was in such a group of rooms that Rahab lived, although the wall of Jericho may also have been simply a single one with houses built up against it.

The account of the spies, then, is not merely an interlude. In returning they report that Yahweh was about to give the land into Israel's hands, and the Canaanite inhabitants would be unable to resist Israel's advance (2:24). The notion that the Canaanites became faint of heart derives from the idea of holy war, as held by the Deuteronomistic historians (→ War). According to this belief, every conflict was a contest between Israel's God and its opponents. Israel was to have courage, since it was Yahweh who would fight its battles. The "enemies" would be struck down in utter panic (cf. 10:10) before the intervention of God as the divine warrior.

3:1–5:15
Crossing the Jordan

Entry to the promised land could not be made without crossing the Jordan River, the natural barrier between Transjordan to the east and Canaan to the west. Thus it is understandable that the conquest should place the river crossing as the first event and describe it with a greater amount of imagination than in the case of subsequent events. In fact, the crossing became a matter of festive memory. It is essential to bear in mind that chaps. 3–5 contain various elements that accrued in the course of liturgical celebration of these events. Three such items in particular can be singled out: the role of the Ark, the traditions of stones being set up in the Jordan and at Gilgal, and the site of Gilgal, where the festival of entry into the land seems to have been celebrated.

3:1–17, The Ark and People Cross the Jordan. The Ark appears for the first time in Joshua in 3:3. This object, described in Exod. 25:10–22, seems to have originated during the early tribal period, at which time it had a prominent role as the place where Yahweh met his people and communicated his word to them. Later it was deposited in the Jerusalem Temple, from which it was borne into the streets during festivals celebrating the God of Israel as "king of glory" (Ps. 24:7–10).

The Ark very early had a place in the wars of Israel, where it served as a symbol of divine presence and protection (1 Sam. 4–6). That it is the priests and Levites who are said to transport it probably has resulted from the liturgical influences in this account. It was characteristic of the Deuteronomistic school to make little or no distinction between these two groups of liturgical officiants.

Thus the role of the Ark in the story of Israel's crossing makes it possible for us to discern influences from later liturgical reenactment of the conquest tradition. A group of ritualistic formulae are introduced into the tradition of the crossing of the Jordan. The Israelites lodge on the edge of the Jordan for three days (3:1–2) before passing over the river. The crossing itself is described less as a military maneuver than as a liturgical procession, with a space of two thousand cubits between the people and the leaders carrying the Ark (3:4). The people "consecrate" themselves (3:5), and just as the feet of the priests are "immersed" in the water (3:15), the miraculous event occurs. The waters open up and the people cross, as they had done in leaving Egypt (cf. 3:16 with Exod. 14:22). After all had crossed and the priests came out of the water, the waters returned to their place. The present shape of the text is thus a fusion of historical memory and an ongoing liturgical representation of this evocative series of experiences. The authors perceive the events through the lens of theological commitments and their own life of worship.

Many scholars have connected this liturgical form of the crossing account with a shrine established at Gilgal. Gilgal indeed is mentioned as the key location to which the people came after crossing (4:19–20; 5:9–10), and commemorative stones erected there became a lasting testimony to its importance as a center of worship.

In this same narrative the motif of holy war continues to be accented by the Deuteronomistic historians (3:10). Yahweh fights for his people as they place full confidence in him. He drives out the peoples before them, so that they may enter the land under his protection. The Ark carried before them is the visible sign of this presence.

4:1–5:1, The Twelve Stones as Memorial of the Crossing. The liturgical descriptions of the passage through the river continue in this section, the events again being connected with Gilgal (4:19–20), a site still unidentified by archaeologists. The name Gilgal, meaning "circle," no doubt recalls the circular position of the twelve stones set up at this site (cf. also 5:9). Actually two accounts are given of where the stones were placed. In one (4:9), they were set up in the river bed where the priests had stood with the Ark. In the other (4:4–8), twelve men were appointed by Joshua to carry twelve stones from the Jordan, apparently to Gilgal. Both accounts, of course, agree that the stones were a memorial to the divine guidance in crossing the river.

Such descriptions provide us with valuable insights into Israelite worship. The worship of early Israel was rooted in the celebration of God's dynamic action in continuously meaningful events. The twelve stones, which also point to connections with the twelve tribes, were not cultic stones like the Canaanite "pillars" (see Deut. 12:3; → Pillars), but commemorated a specific saving event.

5:2–12, Circumcision and Passover at Gilgal. Two additional ritual events are narrated before Israel's departure from Gilgal takes place. First, since the Israelite males who had been in the wilderness for forty years had not been circumcised, a ceremony of mass circumcision at Gilgal was carried out. Verse 8 states that in this representative act "the entire nation" was circumcised. Not only does this indicate the importance that circumcision as a rite attained, it also points to the way later memory reflected on this important act. In this manner the entire people were prepared to enter the new land and to take part in the wars of conquest.

The second rite, a celebration of Passover, is briefly decribed in vv. 10–12. The date given for the observance ("fourteenth day of the month in the evening") is the prescribed day for Passover of the later Priestly tradition (Exod. 12:6; Lev. 23:5). As to why the Passover was being observed at this time and place, vv. 11–12 offer an answer: the manna with which the people had been supplied ceased. Thus the Passover here initiates a new time in which the Israelites begin to eat food from the land they are about to occupy.

There may be yet another meaning, however. Since the crossing of the Jordan paralleled the crossing of the sea in the Exodus, and since the Passover was so central to that great episode (Exod. 12:1–27), so here the same feast had to be celebrated because another momentous act of God's deliverance was about to occur.

5:13–15, A Meeting with the Lord's Military Commander. This eerie description seems to be a fragment of early tradition. Its inclusion here is especially powerful because Jericho was the first of the cities to be confronted in the conquest. Just as the attacks against the cities of Canaan are about to begin, Joshua beholds the mysterious commander of the Lord's army with an unsheathed sword ready for the fight.

Several other traditions tell of such a figure sent by Yahweh with a sword in hand (Num. 22:23; 1 Chron. 21:16). In 5:14 not only a commander but also Yahweh's army is mentioned, and this adds even greater emphasis to the encounter. Israel is about to enter hostile territory. Yet Israel's strong and courageous leader can have confidence that the heavenly army will be on his side. Like Moses (Exod. 3:5), Joshua removes his shoes in the presence of this awesome personage.

6:1–12:24

The Conquest of Canaanite Cities

6:1–27, The Destruction of Jericho. It has already been noted that the story of Jericho is not a simple historical description, but a recollection carried on in ritual celebration. The description of priests bearing the Ark, the blowing of the *shophar* (ram's horn), the prescribed order and times for encircling the city, and the observance of days are all from the rubrics of ritual celebration. The additions from a later age are also evident in v. 25, where it is noted that Rahab's family continued to a later time in Israel.

Whether the conquest of this city is to be taken largely as a later liturgical creation or whether this town actually fell to Israel will remain a debated problem for a long time to come. Here is a case where archaeology cannot seem to resolve the problem. The excavator of Jericho, Kathleen Kenyon, held that the archaeological evidence is unclear about whether a city existed on the site at the time of Joshua's conquest.

A more serious problem in the narrative, however, is the motif of the commanded destruction of everything in Jericho except those items earmarked for the Lord's treasury (vv. 18–19). This notion, called the "ban," is found often in the conquest narrative and is an element in the institution of holy war. The idea was important to the Deuteronomistic historians because they were convinced that Israel's failure had come from intermingling with the religious culture of the Canaanites. According to them, therefore, everything belonging to a captured Canaanite city such as Jericho was to have been offered to God through destruction. Had Israel carried this out throughout its history, as Joshua led them to do earlier, it would have removed this danger and even warded off the eventual destruction of both kingdoms (see Deut. 20).

As unsettling as the ban is to the modern Western ear, it, like holy war, fostered an absolute confidence that God was indeed directing all that was occurring. In the account of Jericho each step was prescribed and the outcome was preordained; all that Israel needed to do was to follow. Because Joshua had such undaunted faith in this divine guidance in the war, he was not only successful, but his reputation became great throughout the land (v. 27).

7:1–26, Achan's Sin and the Defeat at Ai.
The story of Achan is the most elaborate account in the Bible of a failure to carry out the ban and its consequences (cf. 1 Sam. 15:1–33). Achan's taking of forbidden things from Jericho resulted in a curse upon the Israelites, so that their superior force of several thousand men was thrown back in defeat at Ai. The divine anger could only be turned away if the forbidden things held by Achan were removed (v. 13).

In addition to informing us about the ban, this story illustrates how the Israelites saw evil and its effects spreading beyond a single person to a larger group. Since all of Achan's family, and even his cattle and possessions, had become infected with Achan's misdeed, they too were put to death or destroyed. A stone heap in the Valley of Achor south of Jerusalem on the way to Jericho became a reminder of this distressing event (v. 26).

Although in these ideas of the ban and punishment we are dealing with conceptions bound to an earlier time, the story of Achan can make us aware of the continuing importance of corporate responsibility. To be sure, we are well rid of the tribalism that extracted punishment for guilt from innocent members of a group. At the same time, the privatism and apathy that dominate so much of modern life are also failings, and a prophetically informed conscience, such as that of the Deuteronomistic historians, will not allow these to go unchallenged either.

8:1–29, The Destruction of Ai.
The capture of Ai takes place by means of a brilliant strategy. The occupants of Ai are lured from their city at the same time that a small group of Israelite ambushers attack the city from the opposite side and burn it. The army of Ai is thrown into pandemonium and the Israelites rout them thoroughly.

Ai, identified with et-Tell, nine miles northeast of Jerusalem, is the site of imposing ruins dating to the Early Bronze Age, a thousand years before the Israelite entry into the land. At the time the latter was happening, only a small village stood on the site, and it may have been with this village that the events recorded here were concerned. Problems exist, however, since excavation has produced no evidence of a destruction of this village dating to the time of Israel's entry into the land. Therefore the narrative may also be simply a story based on the earlier ruins, although that interpretation also cannot be taken as assured. In any case, the story of Ai alerts us to the danger of reading Joshua as simple historical description.

8:30–35, An Altar on Mount Ebal.
This section gives the impression of being out of place. The account may, however, make sense if it is recalled that in Deut. 27:1–8 Moses commanded Israel, once they entered the land, to build an altar on Mount Ebal and to set up stones with the Torah written on them. Apparently it was thought that this would be an appropriate place for the tradition that Joshua fulfilled this dictate, despite the fact that the rest of the chapter has nothing to do with either Shechem or Mount Ebal.

9:1–27, The Treaty with the Gibeonites.
The land that Israel entered was inhabited not only by Canaanites but also by a number of differing ethnic groups (v. 1). One of these was the Hivites, better known today as Hurrians.

Although their main city was Gibeon, several other cities were also included in their territory (v. 17). Archaeological exploration has made a strong case that Gibeon is el-Jib, about five and a half miles northwest of Jerusalem.

The Gibeonites are here described as concocting a scheme to enter into a covenant with the Israelites, so that they might not be destroyed by them. The story shows how strong was the notion of covenant (treaty) in the world in which the Israelites lived. Covenants were serious relationships. They were religiously sanctioned and enforced by the threat of curse and death (vv. 19–20). Thus, even though the Israelites were stunned to find they had been deceived by the Gibeonites, they could not cancel the covenant obligations.

This chapter is a little window into what must have been the complex history of the entry of the Israelites into the land. It ends with a note about later times when the Gibeonites served at the altar in Jerusalem as "hewers of wood and drawers of water" (v. 27).

10:1–27, The Battle with the Five Kings. Because of Gibeon's treaty with the Israelites, and because Gibeon was located so close to Jerusalem, Adonizedek, king of Jerusalem, enlisted a coalition of kings to move against the inhabitants of this city. As these five kings gathered for war at Gibeon, Israel answered the latter's appeal for help. Thoroughly routing the enemy, the Israelites pursued the fleeing armies into the Valley of Aijalon where, in the heat of battle, Joshua uttered an old piece of verse calling upon the sun and moon to stay in their place (vv. 12b–13a). That an astronomical event such as an eclipse may have occurred is possible, but it seems more likely that, since the quotation is from the book of Jashar, the occurrence was metaphorical in the original poetry, although the prose explanation in v. 13b interpreted it literally. The focus in the account is on God's mighty deliverance of Israel in the battle (v. 12a).

10:28–43, The Capture of the South. Archaeologists have debated whether all of the conquests recorded in this section took place as described or whether these texts have greatly telescoped the events. We know from other biblical texts and sometimes from archaeology that most of the cities named eventually became Israelite. But in the case of some of them, this did not occur until the monarchy was well established. Gezer (v. 33), for example, did not become an Israelite city until the time of Solomon (1 Kings 9:16–17). And despite the defeat of the king of Jerusalem recorded in v. 23, in reality this city was first taken only by David (2 Sam. 5:6–10). It makes no great difference theologically, however, whether some parts of the

land were occupied early or late. For the historians all of it was a divine bestowal upon a nation that, despite some lapses, was faithful in following Joshua.

11:1–15, The Battle of Upper Galilee. In this final part of the conquest story, the scene shifts to the north and to territory later allocated to the tribes of Naphtali and Zebulun. The two foci are the battle at the "waters of Merom" and the destruction of the great city of Hazor.

As in the case of the southern battle in chap. 10, the king of Hazor called for a coalition of northern cities (Achshaph, Shimron, and Madon) to come out against Israel. The large site of Tel Hazor has been excavated recently, and the director of the work, Yigael Yadin, attributed the destruction of the Canaanite city (→ Hazor) to the incoming Israelites, with the latter's own smaller settlement being built over the earlier ruins.

11:16–23, The Grand Finale of the Conquest. This section is a summation of the Deuteronomistic historians' interpretation of the period of conquest. Here it is stated that the entire land from the Negev to Mount Hermon was taken, and that God's hand was in all events, including the resistance offered by the inhabitants. Thus God was able to establish his people in their own territories (v. 23). Only the Gibeonites (v. 19) and the Anakim in Gaza, Gath, and Ashdod (v. 22) were untouched by the conquest.

12:1–24, A List of Kings Defeated by Israel. This chapter contains a summary list of the "kings of the land" (vv. 1, 7) defeated by Joshua. Most of these "kings" were local rulers over city-states. Some, like the Transjordanian kings Sihon of Heshbon and Og of Bashan, controlled larger territories.

The list must have had a teaching purpose and thus was probably formulated much later than the time of Israelite penetration into the land. Its intent was to show how Moses and Joshua had led Israel to victory first in Transjordan and then west of the Jordan River. Evidently the list is a telescoped summation rather than a description of events at the time of the Israelite entry, since it required a longer time for Israel to become dominant in the land than the list implies. Comparison must be made with Judges 1, which describes a more gradual settlement in different areas of the country.

13:1–21:45

Traditions of Land Assignments

These chapters become more meaningful if readers study them alongside the geography of the land of Israel, since frequent reference is made to locations of territories and towns. It is possible to discuss here only the most important locations and proposals for their identifications (see Color Map 3; → most individual place names).

13:1-33, Allotments in Transjordan

13:1-14, The Unpossessed Land. In comparison with 10:40-43, this description presents a very different picture of the conquest. Large parts of the land, especially along the Philistine coast and in Lebanon to the north, remained untaken. These verses fit well with what is presently known from archaeology, and they are also closer to the descriptions in Judges 1. In neither Philistia nor Lebanon did Israel gain a foothold until the time of David nearly two centuries after Joshua.

The nine and a half tribes mentioned in v. 7 were settled west of the Jordan River. The distribution of land to the two and a half tribes east of the Jordan (cf. Num. 32:33-42) is introduced in vv. 8-13. Verse 14, on the other hand, notes the landless status of the Levites, who were set aside for special religious purposes.

13:15-23, The Territory of Reuben. Reuben's area lay directly east of the upper half of the Dead Sea. Its southern border was the Arnon River, the spectacular gorge known today as Wadi Mujib in modern Jordan. The tradition of the slaying of Balaam (v. 22) does not appear in the account of Balaam in Numbers 22-24, and it is bewildering why Israel is said to have killed this foreign seer who placed an unusual blessing on the people.

13:24-28, The Territory of Gad. The territory of Gad was east of the Jordan River, extending from near the north end of the Dead Sea to the Jabbok River (modern Wadi ez-Zerqa). The description has the border going as far as the southern edge of the Sea of Galilee or Chinnereth, but this area was controlled by Manasseh, as the following shows.

13:29-31, The Territory of Manasseh. This tribe, which had more extensive holdings west of the Jordan, occupied territory stretching east and southeast from the Sea of Galilee. The Transjordan allotments are concluded with a summation statement in vv. 32-33.

14:1-19:51, Allotments West of the Jordan

14:1-5, Introduction. The focus of the description is on territories west of the Jordan River. Those in charge of the distribution here were Joshua, Eleazar the priest, and "the heads of the families of the tribes of Israel" (JB). It was they who apportioned the territories by lot according to the divine command given earlier to Moses (Num. 26:55). Lots are referred to throughout this account of the inheritance of the land. Although having some features of

magic, the use of lots is better understood as an element in the divine gift of the land, which Yahweh alone could distribute.

14:6-15, The Allotment of Hebron to Caleb. Caleb's claim rested on an earlier pledge made by Moses (Num. 14:24-25). Caleb's request included the area around Hebron (formerly Kiriath-arba), one of the prominent towns of the southern Judean hills. As in the case of the earlier account, he again demonstrates courage in vowing, even at his advanced age, to take Hebron from the Anakim.

15:1-12, The Boundaries of Judah. Judah's boundary on the south (v. 2) cut across the Negev from the south end of the Dead Sea to the Mediterranean Sea. The northern boundary (v. 5) began at the northern tip of the Dead Sea and continued across the hill country to the Mediterranean. Because the northern boundary skirted Jerusalem on the south (v. 8), it placed this city in the territory of Benjamin. Later, after the division of the kingdom, the city that David had made the capital of all Israel became the capital of the Southern Kingdom alone.

15:13-19, The Family of Caleb in Hebron. A further piece about Caleb is introduced at this point, probably because this clan's activities were centered around a major city in Judah, namely, Hebron.

15:20-62, A City List from Judah. This section contains an independent list of the cities of Judah. Scholars have debated its date, but a widely held view is that it was put into final form at the time of King Josiah (640-609 B.C.). On the other hand, there may be earlier parts reflecting an official tally of cities during the early monarchy.

The list has an interest in the four regions of Judah: the Negeb ("extreme south," v. 21), the Shephelah ("lowland," v. 33), the "hill country" (v. 48), and the "wilderness" (v. 61). In addition, it is arranged according to a series of twelve provinces, each with a capital city, suggesting the conditions of the monarchy.

15:63, Jebusite Jerusalem. This brief notation fits well with the account incorporated by the Deuteronomistic historians in 2 Sam. 5:6-10. There the city of Jerusalem was in the hands of the Jebusites until David's army conquered it.

16:1-17:18, Allotments to the Joseph Tribes

16:1-4, General Introduction. Although not mentioned until v. 4, "the sons of Joseph" refers to Ephraim and Manasseh, the two large tribes of northern Israel. Here their southern boundary is very generally traced from the Rift Valley below Jericho to the Mediterranean Sea.

16:5-10, The Territory of Ephraim. The tribe of Ephraim was allotted its land in the central hill country. With a line beginning near Jericho, its southern boundary followed the Brook

241

Kanah to the Mediterranean Sea. At this western end the area became lowland and coastal plain. The great city of Gezer, located within this territory, remained non-Israelite until Solomon's time (v. 10; 1 Kings 9:16).

17:1–13, The Territory of Manasseh. The account begins with an apportionment of land to a family within the tribe of Manasseh, the Machirites. This family traced its ancestry to Machir, Manasseh's first son (Gen. 50:23). Seeking a special allotment, the Machirites were assigned several territories in Gilead in Transjordan. Thus, as is mentioned elsewhere (Num. 32:33–42), Manasseh possessed land on both sides of the Jordan River.

The boundary descriptions for Manassite territory west of the Jordan (vv. 7–13) situated this tribe north of Ephraim, and in fact the southern boundary edged up on territories and towns properly in Ephraim (vv. 8–10).

17:14–18, Joseph's Colonization of the Hill Country. Archaeological survey has shown an upward swing in the intensity of settlements in the hill country during the time the Israelites were settling in Canaan. It is possible that terracing was introduced during this period, making a new type of farming in the hilly areas possible. In any case, Ephraim and Manasseh's large territories included newly cleared forest areas (v. 18).

18:1–19:51, Allotments to the Seven Remaining Tribes

18:1–10, Joshua at Shiloh. Joshua 18–19 report the distribution of land to the seven smaller tribes north of Ephraim. Whereas Joshua earlier (14:6) was said to have apportioned the land while at Gilgal, here he is at Shiloh in the land of Ephraim.

18:11–28, The Territory of Benjamin. The description shows the inheritance of Benjamin wedged between the larger areas of Judah on the south and Ephraim on the north. The northern border passed north of Jericho to Bethel, bending back to the south on the south side of Jerusalem and from there once more to the Rift Valley.

19:1–9, The Territory of Simeon. At some point Simeon's territory was absorbed into Judah, and thus its original boundaries are indefinite in the descriptions. Its most famous city was Beer-sheba (v. 2).

19:10–16, The Territory of Zebulun. The land alloted to Zebulun lay between Asher along the coast to the west and Issachar in the southern Galilee to the east. The Bethlehem mentioned in v. 15 is, of course, not the famous one in the land of Judah.

19:17–23, The Territory of Issachar. Issachar's inheritance included the fertile hilly land surrounding Mount Tabor as a western boundary, with its territory extending eastward to the Jordan River below the Sea of Galilee.

19:24–31, The Territory of Asher. Located along the coast north and south of modern Haifa, Asher included such prominent cities as Achzib (v. 29).

19:32–39, The Territory of Naphtali. Naphtali's inheritance stretched along the western side of the Sea of Galilee and included the territory north and west of the same sea.

19:40–48, The Territory of Dan. In its earliest history in the land of Canaan, Dan had settled southwest of Jerusalem in territory made famous by the stories of Samson (Judg. 13:2). As v. 47 shows, Dan lost this territory under pressure from the Amorites (Judg. 1:34) and probably the Philistines (Judg. 13:1–2). Thus this tribe migrated to upper Galilee north of Naphtali. Its boundaries there, however, are only imprecisely described.

19:49–51, Joshua's City and Summation. To Joshua finally was presented his own city by the people of Israel (v. 49).

In summary, it can be seen that Joshua 19 is based in part, at least, on a list of cities similar to the one noted in 15:20–62. It is also apparent from Judg. 1:27–36 that the northern tribes, including Manasseh, did not win swift victories over the Canaanites, as the book of Joshua would have it. They only gradually attained dominance over these areas.

20:1–21:45, Cities of Refuge and Cities for Levites

20:1–9, Cities of Refuge. The establishment of sanctuary cities gives us a glimpse into the way ancient Israel handled the social implications of homicide (cf. Num. 35:9–34; Deut. 19:1–13). Since in Israelite belief the blood carried the life of a person, the shedding of blood not only deprived an individual of life but was also a blow against the corporate group from which the victim came. The "redeemer" (v. 5) was a member of the tribe obligated to see that justice was done by taking the life of the slayer.

Three cities on each side of the Jordan were appointed to protect a person who had killed unintentionally. Fleeing to the gate of any of these cities, an "unwitting" slayer could receive asylum with the town's elders as long as the current high priest lived. Upon the latter's death, the slayer could return home.

21:1–42, Cities for the Levites. The Levites, as has been stressed (14:3; 18:7), received no allotment of land but lived among the other tribes. The history of the Levites shows how they developed from being like the other tribes to a group devoted to special ritual activities. Some have held that the Deuteronomistic historians' interest in the levitical priests indicates that they themselves were from this circle, although the point is disputed. Joshua 21 records forty-eight cities scattered among the twelve territories as special cities for the Levites. Included with these cities were also surrounding lands for livestock and presumably also for cultivation. **21:43–45, The Conquest of the Land Concluded.** This summary is from the Deuteronomistic historians. It closes off the materials dealing with conquest and settlement, and also capsulizes the historians' theological perspective, especially their belief that the land was the most tangible sign of God's deliverance of Israel. As the historians view it, toward the end of Joshua's life the land was broadly occupied by Israel, and each part was happily settled.

22:1–24:33
Three Concluding Chapters

22:1–34, The Transjordanian Tribes Return Home. Earlier the two and a half tribes east of the Jordan River had been commissioned to assist the tribes west of the river to settle their lands (1:14–15). Upon their return when all of this was concluded, they built an altar near the Jordan River. This action clearly violated the key Deuteronomic precept (Deut. 12:13–14) that sacrifices and offerings were to be offered only at the central sanctuary of Israel. Shiloh was such a central sanctuary earlier, and later Jerusalem became for the Deuteronomic movement the only legitimate place of worship.

So serious is this violation seen to be that the western tribes prepare for battle against their Transjordanian kinsmen. But the mediation of Phinehas and "the leaders of the community" (NEB) reduces the tension. The eastern tribes present an apology that they meant their altar to serve only as a "witness" of their continuing allegiance to Yahweh. Indeed, their confession in v. 34 is that "Yahweh is God."

Through this episode the Deuteronomistic historians again assert that faithfulness to Yahweh and the covenant must never be compromised. And this included purity of worship in a centralized liturgical system in Jerusalem.

23:1–16, Joshua's Final Speech. The final chapters of this book are something like the closing movement of a symphony. A brief conclusion in 21:43–45 gives way to a new section in chap. 22. Joshua 23 then presents the last oration of the great leader, which is followed by the important Shechem assembly in 24:1–28. Only in 24:29–33 is the final note struck. Unlike a symphony, however, this undulating movement is no doubt the result of several stages in the book's composition.

Joshua's speech is one of the key addresses in the Deuteronomistic History, and again it is mainly the work of the historians. At the heart of the speech is the notion that Yahweh had set Israel aside on a land given by promise, making a covenant with this people that was grounded "in the book of the Law of Moses" (v. 6). Faithfulness to the covenant meant the rejection of Canaanite forms of worship, and above all, intermarriage. Since vv. 14–16 suggest that the people have already gone into exile, or are just about to be deported, the thoughts of Joshua's speech date not far away from the Babylonian exile that began in 587 B.C.

24:1–28, The Gathering at Shechem. It is generally agreed that Joshua 24 contains old traditions about a covenant ceremony at Shechem to which a good deal of Deuteronomic expression has been added (for instance, the listing of the peoples west of the Jordan in v. 11).

A key question for this chapter is whether this ceremony was one in which the various tribes of Israel for the first time gathered together to pledge their loyalty to Yahweh or whether it represented an ongoing, perhaps annual, ceremony of covenant reaffirmation. Scholarship has tended toward the first of these views, taking chap. 24 as an indispensable source of information about the way the tribes came together into a unity in early Israel. Most importantly, however, this great assembly at Shechem sums up the historians' perspective, which can be seen throughout the book. Like Joshua, Israel was called to be Yahweh's servant. Nothing more important could be said by all of Israel than the response given in v. 21: "It is Yahweh we wish to serve" (JB).

24:29–33, A Trilogy of Burial Traditions. The conquest and settlement history of the book of Joshua closes with brief accounts of the burials of its most important actors: Joshua, Joseph, and the high priest Eleazar. With these prosaic reports the book concludes. Yet taken as a whole the book of Joshua is far from prosaic. It abounds with a sense of urgency. Promise and responsibility are in tension throughout. According to the Deuteronomistic historians who have passed on this rich material, nothing is more wondrous than the covenanting God who gives his people a place and a future. The proper response to him is the committed covenant life that his promise evokes—a life of faithfulness and obedience.

Bibliography

Auld, G. A. "Cities of Refuge in Israelite Tradition." *Journal for the Study of the Old Testament* 10 (1978):26–40.

Boling, R. G. *Joshua.* Anchor Bible, 6. Garden City, NY: Doubleday, 1982.

———. "Jericho Off Limits." *Biblical Archaeologist* 46 (1983):115–16.

Gottwald, N. K. *The Tribes of Yahweh: A Sociology of the Religion of Liberated Israel, 1250–1050 B.C.E.* Maryknoll, NY: Orbis, 1979.

Kenyon, K. M. *The Bible and Recent Archaeology.* Atlanta, GA: Knox, 1978.

Lapp, P. "The Conquest of Palestine in the Light of Archaeology." *Concordia Theological Monthly* 38 (1967):283–300.

Mendenhall, G. E. "The Hebrew Conquest of Palestine." *Biblical Archaeologist* 25 (1962): 66–87.

Miller, J. M. "Archaeology and the Israelite Conquest of Canaan: Some Methodological Observations." *Palestine Exploration Quarterly* 109 (1977):87–93.

Miller, J. M., and Tucker, G. M. *The Book of Joshua*. Cambridge Bible Commentary. Cambridge: Cambridge University Press, 1974.

Noth, M. *The Deuteronomistic History*. Journal for the Study of the Old Testament Supplement Series, no. 15. Sheffield: University of Sheffield, 1981.

Weippert, M. *The Settlement of the Israelite Tribes in Palestine*. Studies in Biblical Theology, Second Series, 21. Naperville, IL: Allenson, 1971.

Wenham, G. J. "The Deuteronomic Theology of the Book of Joshua." *Journal of Biblical Literature* 90 (1971):140–48.

Wright, G. E. "Conquest." Chap. 5 in G. E. Wright, *Biblical Archaeology*. Rev. ed. Philadelphia: Westminster, 1962.

Yadin, Y. "Is the Biblical Account of the Israelite Conquest of Canaan Historically Reliable?" *Biblical Archaeology Review* 8 (1982): 16–23.

JUDGES

J. CHERYL EXUM

INTRODUCTION

Title and Scope

The English title of the Book of Judges derives from the Latin, *Liber Judicum* (Heb. *shophetim*; Gk. *kritai*) and refers to the leaders of Israel in the critical period between the occupation of the land of Canaan under Joshua (→Joshua) and the establishment of the monarchy under the leadership of Samuel (→Samuel; Saul). The death of Joshua, reported in chap. 1, marks the end of an old era, the period of conquest, and begins a new era, the period of the judges. The period of the judges extends beyond the book of Judges into 1 Samuel, where Samuel, in addition to being a prophet, is also a judge (1 Sam. 7:15–17; cf. 1 Sam. 4:18, for Eli). Whereas the book of Joshua dealt with the occupation of the land of Canaan and its allotment among the Israelite tribes, Judges deals with Israel's inability to drive out all the inhabitants of the land and the reasons for Israel's failure to do so. It thus presents a different picture from Joshua, where the conquest is sudden and complete (though a careful reading of Joshua reveals inconsistencies in its version of the conquest). In Judges, Israel is still engaged in a struggle to wrest the land from the Canaanites and must repeatedly respond to attacks from hostile neighbors.

The book may be divided into three parts: a double introduction, which deals with Israel's failure to conquer Canaan completely, first from a military and then from a religious perspective (1:1–3:6); the main body of the book, consisting largely of the adventures of the individual judges (3:7–16:31); and a double conclusion (chaps. 17–21), which sets the stage for the transition to the monarchy by painting a picture of moral decline and political dissolution in a time when "there was no king in Israel and every man did as he pleased" (21:25). The stories of the judges are thus framed by an introduction that looks back to the book of Joshua and a conclusion that looks forward to the books of Samuel and Kings.

Who Were the Judges?

The main body of the book presents twelve figures as leaders of Israel: Othniel, Ehud, Shamgar, Deborah, Gideon, Tola, Jair, Jephthah, Ibzan, Elon, Abdon, and Samson. The number corresponds to the twelve tribes of Israel, but not every tribe is represented by a judge; most of the judges are from the central hill country. The exact duties of these figures are not at all clear. None is actually called a "judge" (apart from the introduction in 2:16–19, that title appears only once, in reference to God, 11:27). Only nine are said to have judged Israel (Othniel, Deborah, Tola, Jair, Jephthah, Ibzan, Elon, Abdon, and Samson), whereas some appear on the scene to "deliver" Israel from its enemies (Othniel, Ehud, Shamgar, Gideon, Tola, and Samson).

It has become customary to distinguish between "major judges"—the military leaders about whose exploits we have stories—and "minor judges"—the relatively obscure figures who appear in a list (10:1–5; 12:[7]8–15) and about whom we know almost nothing apart from the fact that they "judged Israel." Since Jephthah appears both in a story and in the list of minor judges, he is usually assigned to both categories.

The Hebrew word *shaphat* ("to judge") has a wider semantic range than the English, meaning not only to judge in the forensic sense but also "to govern" or "to rule" (cf. 2 Kings 15:5; Pss. 2:10; 148:11). When applied to the minor judges, for whom no military functions are reported, the title suggests they may have been local rulers responsible for civil administration and jurisdiction (note that while they are said to "judge Israel," their sphere of influence is local). The major judges, except Deborah, are not judges at all in the judicial sense. The term "charismatic" is often used to describe their leadership; for the most part they are divinely inspired by the "spirit of the Lord" to lead individual Israelite tribes against their enemies and their leadership is limited to a particular crisis. Jephthah is appointed commander and head (Heb. *ro'sh*) by the elders of Gilead on condition that his military campaign against the Ammonites prove successful (11:9–11), but his duties, apart from military leadership, are not described. In contrast, Deborah appears to have rendered legal decisions to Israelites who came to her in the hill country of Ephraim (4:5); and from his home in Ramah, Samuel went on a circuit to Bethel, Gilgal, and Mizpah, apparently giving case decisions in all of these places (1 Sam. 7:16). The paucity of our knowledge about the political organization of Israel in this time makes it impossible to be precise about the actual functions of its leaders. We seem to be dealing with two forms of leadership, represented by "judges" and "deliverers," which have been combined by the editors of the book under the concept of judges of Israel.

The Composition of the Book

Judges is the second book in the traditional division of the Bible known as the Former Prophets (Joshua, Judges, Samuel, Kings) and the third book of an account of Israel's history that many scholars believe begins with the book of Deuteronomy and continues through Kings (excluding Ruth, which in the Hebrew Bible belongs to the Writings). This composition, called the Deuteronomistic History because of its noticeable affinities with the style and theological outlook of Deuteronomy, presents a comprehensive religious history of Israel from the Exodus to the Exile (→ Deuteronomist; Deuteronomistic Historian). Whereas scholars disagree regarding the date and number of editions of the Deuteronomistic History, most believe it underwent at least two major editions, one in the seventh century B.C., during the reign of the Judean king Josiah (see 2 Kings 22–23), and the other, exilic (sixth century B.C.). In composing their religious history, the Deuteronomistic compilers used earlier sources, but their selection and presentation of the ancient material also reflect the particular religious and political issues of their own time. From Israel's historical vicissitudes the Deuteronomistic historians draw a lesson about God's discipline and mercy (see 1 Samuel, "Commentary"; 2 Samuel, "Commentary"; 1 Kings, "Commentary"; 2 Kings, "Commentary").

The kinds of sources available to the compilers for different periods of Israelite history and the way they dealt with these sources differ for each of the books of Joshua, Judges, Samuel, and Kings. Judges itself has a long and complex editorial history. The Deuteronomistic historians probably drew much of their material from local or tribal traditions, which one can imagine arising orally and later fixed into written form. The folkloristic character of the Samson stories, for example, is readily evident. Some scholars think that the editors had a book of "savior" or "deliverer" stories at their disposal. If the minor judges represent some kind of official list, this would mean the editors had access to an annalistic source. They have also included an inspiring victory song (Judg. 5), which is one of the oldest literary compositions in the Bible.

The present form of the book gives the impression that the judges exercised authority over a unified Israel and that they followed one another in an unbroken succession. Closer examination, however, reveals the artificiality of this picture. Chap. 1 details the struggle of individual Israelite tribes to establish themselves in their own particular territory. Moreover, in the individual stories of the judges, the tribes act independently or, at most, two or three tribes band together against a common threat. The exception is Judges 5, where Deborah and Barak lead a coalition of tribes against the Canaanites. The overall picture, then, does not support a view of Israel as a militarily and religiously unified tribal organization but rather suggests that the settlement process was largely a local affair and the influence of the judges too was essentially local. That this picture is not immediately apparent results from the way Judges has been organized: tribal traditions have been nationalized and placed within a chronological framework so that local heroes, some of whom originally may have been contemporaries exercising authority in different geographic areas, have now become a series of deliverers of "all Israel."

In their organization of the book, the editors of Judges are primarily interested in presenting a religious interpretation of Israel's history during the period of the judges. They view this history as repetitive, illustrating again and again the consequences of unfaithfulness. The stories of the major judges appear within the framework of a cyclical pattern that illustrates this theological perspective. The main elements of the pattern are: the Israelites do what is evil in the eyes of the Lord by turning to other gods; as a result the Lord gives them into the hands of oppressors for a stated period of time; the people cry out in their distress; and the Lord raises up judges who deliver them. After the story of deliverance, the land is said to "have rest" for periods of forty or eighty years.

A few things should be noted about this editorial framework. It is frequently described by scholars as a pattern of apostasy/punishment/repentance/deliverance, but in fact, the Israelites repent only once (10:10–16), and other elements of the pattern also vary somewhat. God does not, therefore, act strictly in accordance with retributive theology; instead, a tension emerges between divine mercy, which is moved to intervention by Israel's plight, and divine justice, which demands that as a consequence of disobedience, the Israelites shall not prosper in the land that the Lord promised to their ancestors (2:1–3; 20–23; cf. Deut. 11:13–17; Josh. 23:12–13).

Although its basic orientation is cyclical rather than linear, Judges does move forward. The pattern itself exhibits variation; for example, the rest formula appears for the last time after the story of Gideon, and few elements of the pattern occur in the story of Samson. Thus by the end of the main body of the book, the cyclical pattern of history has exhausted itself. A deterioration in the character of the judges themselves can also be observed. By the end of

Judges, the pressing question becomes how Israel can break out of the repetitive pattern that has characterized its life in Canaan since the death of Joshua (2:11–23). Samson, unlike the judges before him, does not succeed in delivering Israel from its oppressor—in this case, the Philistines. Where is the leader who can do so? (Ancient listeners knew, of course, as we do, that David is that leader.) The concluding stories of Judges (chaps. 17–21) even more explicitly acknowledge the crisis of leadership. They look toward the institution of kingship as providing a possible answer to Israel's moral and political problems.

Life in the Time of the Judges

The editors of Judges were concerned not with history per se but with its religious interpretation. As a result, it is impossible for us to get behind their highly stylized, artificial presentation of events to establish a chronology for the period or to discover very much about Israel's political or religious organization during this time. Nevertheless, scholars have sought to reconstruct as much as possible about the actual historical situation. If the chronology of the book itself is followed, the figures for the number of years of oppression, the judges' tenure of office, and the periods of rest add up to 410 years (not including the time of Eli and Samuel). The significance of the figures is lost to us (recall the frequent appearance of the round numbers 20, 40, and 80), and 410 years is much longer than the generally accepted dating of the period of the judges between the initial occupation under Joshua, roughly 1200 B.C., and the accession of Saul, around 1020.

Many of the places mentioned in Judges have been excavated, and archaeology has added considerably to our knowledge of life during the period (→ Archaeology, methods of). Sociological and anthropological methods have also recently been applied to the biblical evidence with important results. Using archaeological and extrabiblical evidence such as the Ugaritic texts, the Alalakh tablets, and the Amarna letters, scholars have been able to shed light on life in Syro-Palestine prior to the emergence of Israel as a political entity. The conflict between "Canaanite" and "Israelite" society is essentially one between a city-state society and a rural, tribal social system. Canaanite social structure was hierarchical, maintaining a clear distinction between the privileged ruling class and its subject population. In Israel, considerable power resided at the ground level, with the extended family serving as the primary social and economic unit, and, beyond it, the clan and the tribe. Israel's economy was based primarily upon pastoralism and agriculture and its early social organization shows little evidence of the division of labor and professional classes of the city-state.

The religious conflict is related to the societal one. Canaanite polytheism and religious practices stand in tension with the Lord's demands for Israel's absolute loyalty and with the largely egalitarian nature of Israelite faith—particularly for men, but perhaps also offering greater equality to women during this period than later. In periods of social disturbance, such as represented by the numerous military crises in Judges, and also in societies where power is centered in the domestic, rather than the larger political, sphere, women traditionally exercise more power (see, e.g., the story of Deborah, chaps. 4–5). The stories in Judges reflect Israel's rural and tribal base. They also illustrate Israel's antipathy toward the Canaanites and their way of life, as well as the attraction of Canaanite worship for Israel (e.g., the story of Gideon's ephod, chap. 8) and the appeal of Canaanite power structures (Gideon's son's city-state kingship, chap. 9).

Evidence of a centralized administration is lacking. The theory, once widely accepted by biblical scholars, that premonarchical Israel was a six- or twelve-tribe amphictyony, or tribal league, organized around a central sanctuary has now been generally discredited. Although Judges 20–21, which depicts a united Israel with the Ark of the Lord at Bethel, fits this picture, its historical value is questionable. But the individual stories of Judges do bear witness to occasional instances of tribal cooperation under "charismatic" leaders against common enemies. This apparently segmentary tribal organization served Israel until external pressures, such as the threat posed by Philistine expansion, combined with David's political shrewdness to produce a new form of political organization. (Saul's monarchy is best viewed as transitional between this older tribal, rural order and the new order represented by the Davidic monarchy, with its central administration, hierarchy, and dynastic succession.)

COMMENTARY

1:1–3:6

Double Introduction

1:1–36

Introduction, Part One: The Military Problem

Judges begins with the words, "After the death of Joshua," a beginning comparable to that of Joshua, "After the death of Moses." The Israelites seek a divine oracle (through what means is not specified) to determine which tribe should lead the attack against the Canaanites. Their question indicates that Israel's conquest of the promised land is far from complete. The Canaanites are the indigenous population Israel was supposed to drive out (Deut. 7:1–5; 20:16–18; Josh. 23:6–13); other terms used for the inhabitants of the land are Perizzites (Judg. 1:4–5) and Amorites (v. 34). Judges 1 appears to be based on ancient sources clearly at odds with Joshua's picture of a sudden and complete conquest. It functions to enhance the role of Judah, the tribe from which the Davidic kings will come, and to play down the accomplishments of the other tribes. Some consider it a more realistic account of Israelite settlement, as opposed to Joshua's idealized version. The tribes fight more or less on their own, and though some successes are reported, the account quickly becomes a list of failures to conquer the Canaanites. The Israelites were unable to overthrow the city-states in the fertile plains, occupying instead the mountainous regions and steppes. This was essentially the situation until the time of David.

The geographical movement in the chapter is from south to north; a similar movement may be observed in the book as a whole, which begins with Othniel as the judge from the south (3:7–11, also mentioned here in v. 13) and ends with Dan in the north (chaps. 13–18). For groups about whom success is reported (Judah, Caleb, and Joseph), lively anecdotes appear to break up the otherwise matter-of-fact account (1:5–7, 11–15, 22–26).

1:1–21, Victories in the South. First to be reported are the victories in the southern hill country on the part of Judah and groups associated with it: the tribe of Simeon, the Calebites, and the Kenites. Judah has a central role here and also in chap. 20. The location of Bezek, the site of their first victory, is uncertain. They capture Adonibezek (= the prince of Bezek), cut off his thumbs and big toes, and bring him to Jerusalem, where he dies (vv. 5–7). Only in the next verse, however, is Judah said to have captured Jerusalem, and that statement is contradicted by v. 21, which relates that the Benjaminites did not drive out the Jebusites from Jerusalem. Josh. 15:63 makes the same statement about Judah. In Josh. 18:28, Jerusalem belongs to the territory assigned to Benjamin. That Jerusalem was on the border between the two tribes may explain the discrepancy. In any event, it is David who actually conquers Jerusalem (2 Sam. 5:6–10).

According to Judg. 1:10, Judah attacked Hebron and defeated Sheshai, Ahiman, and Talmai; whereas v. 20 assigns Hebron to Caleb, and both it and Josh. 15:14 credit Caleb with victory over the three sons of Anak—Sheshai, Ahiman, and Talmai (the Anakim are elsewhere identified as giants, Deut. 2:10–12, 20–21). Caleb was early assimilated to the tribe of Judah. The Calebite Othniel conquered Debir, winning Caleb's daughter Achsah as a wife in the bargain (cf. David's bride price of Michal for two hundred Philistine foreskins, 1 Sam. 18:25–27). Since Othniel is assigned the Negeb (the desert area in the south), Achsah shrewdly asks her father for springs of water (Judg. 1:14–15). The story appears also in Josh. 15:13–19. Josh. 10:36–39, on the other hand, attributes the conquest of both Hebron and Debir to Joshua. The Kenites, related to Moses through marriage (→ Kenites), are mentioned as accompanying the tribe of Judah (Judg. 1:16). Judah and Simeon totally destroy Zephath; the verb used refers to the sacrificial ban or *cherem* (Heb.; → Ban), which is frequently invoked in Joshua, but only twice in Judges (see also 21:11). The name Hormah is a wordplay on *cherem*. The statement in 1:18 that Judah took Gaza, Ashkelon, and Ekron is anachronistic. These cities were members of the Philistine pentapolis and did not come under Israelite control until much later. Perhaps we should read the word "not" in v. 18, with the Septuagint (LXX). Verse 19 offers a more sober assessment of the situation, showing Judah in possession of the hill country, while attributing their inability to conquer the cities of the plain to the Canaanites' military superiority.

1:22–36, Setbacks in the North. Of the central and northern tribes, victory is reported only for the tribe of Joseph. Their capture of Bethel is based on deception. Deception, it turns out, figures importantly throughout Judges, from Ehud's deception of Eglon (chap. 3) to Delilah's deception of Samson (chap. 16). Manasseh and Ephraim, the two tribes into which the tribe of Joseph was divided, were unsuccessful against the city-states of Beth-shean, Taanach, Dor, Ibleam, Megiddo, Gezer, and their dependencies (RSV: "villages"). Failure is also reported for the northern tribes of Zebulun, Asher, and Naphtali. That in later times Israel was able to subjugate these Canaanite enclaves is noted in vv. 28, 30, and 33, which inform us that the Canaanites were subjected either to forced labor or to taxation as a form of vassalage, depending on how one understands the Hebrew term. Probably the latter is meant. According to v. 34, the Danites were unable to get a foothold in the plains. Chap. 18 will return to their plight, describing their migration from the central hill country around Zorah and Eshtaol to the north, where they take over an unsuspecting city in a surprise attack.

2:1–3:6
Introduction, Part Two: The Religious Problem

The second part of the introduction to Judges seeks to explain the military setbacks detailed in the first part. Why, in light of God's promises to give Israel the land, has Israel not been successful? How does one account for the continued presence of Canaanites in the land? This introductory section begins by interpreting the continuing presence of the native population as punishment for Israel's unfaithfulness (2:1–5) and ends by describing the nations as a means to test Israel (2:20–23) and to teach war to the generations of Israelites who had not experienced it (3:1–6). These three different but interrelated explanations frame the programmatic description of life under the judges that provides the theme of the main body of the book (2:6–19).

2:1–5, The Lord's Angel. A divine messenger, or "angel," appears to announce that Israel's disobedience is the reason for its failure completely to conquer the Canaanites. Israel broke God's command not to form alliances with the inhabitants of the land (cf. Exod. 34:12–16; Deut. 7:2–5). As a consequence, God refuses to drive out the Canaanites; they will remain a troublesome presence in the land and their gods will lead Israel astray (a pointed example of Canaanite worship becoming a "snare" to Israel is Gideon's ephod, 8:27). Gilgal was Israel's base in the conquest narratives of Joshua. The etiological story of Bochim (of uncertain location) rests upon a wordplay; the place is called Bochim (Heb., "Weepers") because the people wept (2:4–5).

2:6–19, The Cyclical Pattern of Apostasy, Oppression, Deliverance. Verses 6–9 (= Josh. 24:28–31) offer a flashback to the time of Joshua. They function to contrast the faithfulness of Joshua's generation with the unfaithfulness of the present generation (v. 10). Verses 11–19 present an elaborate statement of the schema of apostasy, oppression, and deliverance, which serves as the framing device for the stories of the major judges. The Israelites forsake the Lord and worship the gods of the local population. The god Baal and the goddess Astarte are well known to us from the Ugaritic literature. The Bible uses these names, in the singular or plural, as general designations for the Canaanite deities (similarly the name of the goddess Asherah [plural, Asheroth], 3:7). The Israelites' apostasy provokes the Lord's anger, and he gives them over to their enemies (here again the nations are a means of punishment, 2:14–15). Although the Lord raised up judges to save them (v. 16; according to v. 18 the Lord acted out of pity for their plight), they did not listen to their judges (v. 17), and when the judge died, they behaved even worse than before (v. 19). Israel's faithlessness and stubbornness are thus underscored, and it becomes obvious that the Israelites are doomed continually to repeat this pattern. Whatever successes they have in the land are due to divine mercy, and not any merit on Israel's part. No lasting relief from this cycle is envisioned, so that the implicit question becomes, how can the pattern be broken?

2:20–3:6, The Nations That Remain. Verses 21 and 23 contradict the claim in Joshua that God gave all the land into Joshua's power (see esp. Josh. 10–12). The nations said to remain comprise a standard list of indigenous people—Canaanites, Hittites, Amorites, Perizzites, Hivites, and Jebusites (v. 5; cf. Deut. 7:1 for the "seven nations")—as well as the Philistines, who occupied the coastal plain to the south, and the Sidonians (Phoenicians) on the northern coast (Judg. 3:3). The Jebusites were the native population of Jerusalem. The Israelites intermarry with these peoples and, as a natural outcome, serve their gods (v. 6), both in explicit violation of God's commands.

3:7–11

Othniel

The account of the first judge consists almost entirely of framework formulae: apostasy (v. 7); oppression (v. 8); cry for help (v. 9); deliverance (vv. 9–10); rest (v. 11). For this reason, some interpreters have suggested that Othniel was supplied by the editors of Judges in order to have a judge from Judah (recall the prominence given to Judah in chap. 1). The foe ("Cushan of the Double Evil," king of Aram Naharaim [RSV, Mesopotamia]) also appears contrived, since it is unlikely Mesopotamia would have threatened southern Israel. Some (JB, e.g.) emend "Aram" to "Edom," thereby obtaining a southern adversary. According to 1:13–15, Othniel was the conqueror of Debir. The spirit of the Lord that comes upon him (v. 10) is a divine force that animates various leaders, often causing them to perform extraordinary deeds (Gideon, Jephthah, Samson, and later Saul and David are all inspired by the spirit at some point in their lives).

3:12–30

Ehud

The story of the next deliverer, Ehud, is set within the familiar editorial framework (vv. 12–15, 30). The oppressor is Moab, Israel's neighbor east of the Dead Sea, which, according to v. 13, enlists the help of the Ammonites, to the north of Moab in Transjordan, and the Amalekites, Israel's traditional enemies from the desert

249

(Exod. 17:8–16). They capture the "city of palms," a common designation for Jericho; it is not, however, altogether clear whether the main action of the story takes place west of the Jordan near Jericho or in Transjordan. The Israelite territory primarily affected is Benjamin, and from this tribe the Lord raises up the deliverer Ehud. Ehud is "restricted in his right hand"; the Hebrew expression refers either to a physical handicap or, more likely, as in 20:16, to left-handedness (LXX and the Vulgate [Vg.] read "ambidextrous"; cf. 1 Chron. 12:2). Ehud achieves deliverance by assassinating Eglon and leading his compatriots from the hill country of Ephraim (Benjamin and neighboring Ephraim) to victory over the Moabites.

As tribute bearer, Ehud has access to the Moabite king, and as a left-handed man he is able to conceal a sword on his right thigh. The assassination account is punctuated by grim and scatological humor. Having dismissed his followers and returned alone from Gilgal, Ehud secures a private interview in the king's cool roof-chamber by proffering Eglon a "secret message" (v. 19). To Eglon's surprise, the "message from God" (v. 20) turns out to be death. King Eglon is grossly fat—so obese, in fact, that the fat closes over the blade and the hilt of Ehud's sword. His name, which suggests a pun on the word for "calf," makes his assassination appear as a grotesquely humorous sacrifice of a fatted calf. The details are related with relish: Ehud's deed is not immediately discovered because Eglon's servants think their master is leisurely relieving himself. Thus they wait before entering the roof-chamber, giving Ehud ample time to escape and muster his troops. The Moabites, presumably thrown into confusion by the loss of their king, are defeated by Ehud and his followers at the fords of the Jordan.

3:31
Shamgar

No editorial framework accompanies the brief note about Shamgar. Shamgar seems to interrupt the cyclical pattern, since 4:1, which introduces the judgeship of Deborah, begins the cycle anew with "after Ehud died." Apparently Shamgar was well known, since his name appears in 5:6 for dating purposes. The mention of the name in Judges 5 may be the reason for the insertion of the reference to Shamgar here. Some LXX manuscripts place the Shamgar notice after the conclusion of the Samson story in 16:31. Like Samson, Shamgar fights the Philistines, and his mighty exploit of killing six hundred Philistines with an oxgoad is reminiscent of Samson's slaughter of one thousand Philistines with the jawbone of an ass. The name Shamgar may be Hurrian. The matronymic "son of Anat [RSV: Anath]" is suspicious; Anat was the Canaanite goddess of war. It has been proposed that "son of Anat" is a military title and that Shamgar was a mercenary.

4:1–5:31
Deborah

The story of Deborah's victory over the militarily superior Canaanites in the north is told in two versions, one prose (chap. 4), the other poetry (chap. 5). The accounts differ in details, but it would be a mistake to try to harmonize them or to prefer one over the other as the more "correct" or "likely" version. Each should be considered on its own merits. The poem, which is older, offers a more dramatic, but also more elliptic, presentation.

4:1–24
The Prose Account

4:1–5, Introduction to Deborah. The editorial framework (vv. 1–3) introduces Deborah's judgeship; the concluding formula of the framework, "and the land had rest for forty years," occurs at the end of chap. 5. Israel suffers twenty years of oppression at the hands of Jabin, king of Canaan, and his general, Sisera, whose chariots outfitted with iron gave them a military advantage over the Israelites. The reference to Jabin who reigned in Hazor is problematic, since Josh. 11:1–11 reports Israel's defeat of a Canaanite coalition under Jabin, king of Hazor, in the time of Joshua. Jabin is not mentioned in the account of chap. 5, and the real antagonist there and in chap. 4 is Sisera, whose name is not Semitic and who may have belonged to the Sea Peoples (→ Sea Peoples). In contrast to Othniel and Ehud, of whom we are told, "the Lord raised up a deliverer" (3:9, 15), Deborah is already judging Israel when the crisis occurs. The judge Deborah is also identified, v. 4, as a prophet and by a Hebrew phrase usually translated "wife of Lappidoth," but perhaps meaning "fiery woman" (cf. the NEB footnote, "spirited woman"). Her sphere of influence is the hill country of Ephraim.

4:6–10, Deborah Commissions Barak. In her role as prophet and judge, Deborah summons Barak from the tribe of Naphtali and commissions him to lead the Galilean tribes of Naphtali and Zebulun against Jabin's army under Sisera. Her role can be compared to that of another prophet and judge, Samuel, who commissions Saul to fight the Amalekites (1 Sam. 15). Barak, however, is unwilling, unless Deborah accompanies him. She agrees, but prophesies that God will give victory over Sisera to a woman. The surprise for Barak—and for anyone hearing the story for the first time—is that the victor is not Deborah, which might be expected, but another woman, Jael.

4:11, The Kenites. This verse prepares for Jael's assassination of Sisera by explaining the presence of a group of Kenites, considered by some scholars to have been itinerant smiths, in the north near the site of the battle. Hebrew *cheber* is usually taken as a proper name, Heber; however, it has been argued that the word, whose basic meaning is "group," refers to an ethnic unit. If this is the case, v. 11 refers to a Kenite group that had separated from the main tribe whose home was in the south (cf. 1:16). The Kenites had ethnic ties with Israel through Moses' Midianite father-in-law, Hobab.

4:12–16, The Lord's Victory over Sisera's Forces. Topographical details of the battle are not entirely clear. Barak's forces advance from Mount Tabor, north of the plain of Esdraelon, while Sisera's army and chariots proceed from Harosheth-of-the-Gentiles to the river Kishon. The battle takes place in the Plain of Esdraelon near the river Kishon, and victory gave Israel control over this strategic area (→ Esdraelon). Victory is attributed to God's intervention (v. 15); the entire army was slain except Sisera (v. 16).

4:17–22, Jael's Victory. Sisera, the general who had "nine hundred chariots of iron" (4:3, 13), is reduced to flight on foot. He is met by Jael, a woman of the Kenite group, who offers him refuge in her tent. The condition of peace (i.e., an alliance) between Jabin and these Kenites explains Sisera's willingness to seek protection there. Over against this alliance, however, must be weighed the ethnic bond between the Kenites and Israel, perhaps the deciding factor for Jael. Jael's actions give every appearance of generosity: when Sisera asks for water to drink, she gives him milk, and Sisera trusts her to stand guard at the entrance of the tent. Jael, however, takes a tent peg and a hammer—tools that she most likely wielded skillfully, since pitching the tent was probably women's work, as it is among the bedouin today—and kills Sisera, apparently while he is sleeping. Barak, in pursuit of Sisera, is met by Jael, who invites him into her tent to view the enemy's body. Just as he was overshadowed in the battle scenes by Deborah, so Barak is overshadowed in the murder scene by Jael. The glory has been snatched from Barak's hands, and Deborah's prophecy, "The Lord will sell Sisera into the hand of a woman," finds its fulfillment.

4:23–24, The Conclusion: Victory Is the Lord's. The prose account of chap. 4 concludes by ascribing victory to God (cf. v. 15).

These verses thus form an appropriate transition to the song in chap. 5, which praises God for granting victory to his people.

5:1–31
The Song of Deborah

The poetic account, traditionally known as the Song of Deborah, is both about Deborah and Barak and, according to v. 1, sung by Deborah and Barak. The verb in v. 1, however, is feminine singular, which may indicate that Deborah was regarded as the singer, with Barak added later; in v. 12 Deborah is the one called on to sing. The poem extols God and his people, who bravely joined the Lord's battle (vv. 2, 9, 11, 13). The ancient poem, dating from about 1125 B.C., exhibits a repetitive style similar to the older, Canaanite poetry from Ugarit (→ Ras-Shamra). Its vivid descriptions, striking imagery, effective repetitions, and skillful use of various poetic techniques have rightly earned it the designation as a literary masterpiece. Unfortunately, the text and its meaning are often obscure. If the traditional dating is correct, the poem comes from a period not far removed from the events themselves.

5:1–12, Praise of God and Human Heroes. The poem begins with a call to "bless the Lord" (v. 2), and continues with an evocation of the Lord, the God of Sinai, marching forth from the region of Edom (vv. 4–5). The Hebrew text of vv. 6–12 is uncertain, and many quite varying interpretations have been offered. The verses appear to contrast the precarious social and economic conditions before Israel's victory with the situation after. In v. 7 Deborah is called a "mother in Israel"—a title indicating her authority and prophetic leadership (cf. the use of "father" for male prophets; 2 Kings 2:12; 13:14); elsewhere the title appears only in reference to a city (2 Sam. 20:19, referring to its status in Israel). The reference to Deborah as a mother at the beginning of the poem is balanced by the mention of Sisera's mother at the end.

5:13–23, The Battle. These verses are extremely important for the light they shed on premonarchical Israel's political organization. In contrast to the prose version, which mentions only the tribes of Naphtali and Zebulun, the poem praises Ephraim, Benjamin, Machir, Zebulun, Issachar, and Naphtali for their heroic participation in the battle, while censuring Reuben, Gilead, Dan, Asher, and Meroz for not responding to the muster. The list differs from the traditional twelve-tribe reckoning, which is later (see Gen. 29:31–30:24; 35:16–26; Gen. 49; Num. 26; Deut. 33). Meroz, which appears in an obscure context (v. 23), is otherwise unattested. Machir and Gilead appear instead of Manasseh and Gad, to which they are respectively related. Noteworthy is the absence of the tribes of Levi, Simeon, and Judah, particularly the last which apparently was not reckoned as part of "Israel" at this time, and which historically always had a tenuous relationship with the northern tribes (→ Judah).

In contrast to the battles led by the other major judges, in which Israel defends its territory against the encroachments of hostile neighbors, Israel here fights a Canaanite coalition in the plain, where the Canaanites had a clear military advantage. Victory meant the breakdown of the Canaanite city-state system and gave Israel control over central and northern Palestine. The setting at Taanach by the waters of Megiddo places the battle in the Esdraelon somewhat south of the battle site in chap. 4. According to vv. 19-22, the forces of nature intervened on Israel's behalf. Apparently the Canaanite chariots became bogged down in the marshy terrain created by the flooding of the Kishon.

5:24-31, Defeat of Sisera. The poem ends with the juxtaposition of two "domestic" scenes. The first heaps extravagant praise upon Jael for killing Sisera (vv. 24-27). Her violation of the laws of hospitality and deception of Sisera are viewed with hearty approval, as was Ehud's use of a ruse to assassinate Eglon earlier (3:12-30). Here, apparently in contrast to chap. 4, Sisera is struck down while standing. The second scene (vv. 28-30) ironically shifts perspective to that of Sisera's mother, anxiously awaiting the return of her son from battle and attempting to assure herself that his delay is caused by the amassing of booty.

Verse 31 concludes the story of Deborah's judgeship. The period of rest is twice as long as the period of oppression (4:3) but only half that of the period of rest after Ehud (3:30).

6:1–8:32

Gideon

6:1-10, Introduction. The editorial framework of apostasy/oppression/cry-for-help appears in vv. 1-6. The seven-year oppression takes the form of raids from Transjordan on the part of the Midianites, the Amalekites, and the people of the East (→ Midianites; Amalekites). Their forays across the Jordan, particularly into the territory of the tribe of Manasseh, severely threaten the local population's means of livelihood (vv. 2-6, 11). In response to Israel's cry, God sends a prophet (v. 8). Unlike the previous account, where the prophet Deborah was also the judge and deliverer, this anonymous prophet recites God's saving deeds (vv. 8-9), accuses Israel of disobedience in serving the gods of the Amorites (= Canaanites, v. 10), and

then disappears from the scene. The accusation recalls that of 2:1-3, except that the consequences of disobedience are not spelled out (cf. also 10:11-14). In 2:3 God warns Israel that foreign gods will be a "snare" for them; this is precisely what happens at the end of Gideon's judgeship, when "all Israel prostituted themselves after [Gideon's ephod] . . . and it became a snare to Gideon and to his house" (8:27). Verses 7-10 are lacking in 4QJudg. (→ Scrolls, The Dead Sea).

6:11-18, Gideon's Commission. In contrast to Othniel and Ehud, whom God "raised up" to deliver Israel, and to Deborah, who was already judging Israel when the crisis occurred, Gideon, from the Manassite clan of Abiezer, is commissioned by a divine messenger (RSV, JB: "angel") to deliver Israel. Like Barak before him, Gideon is hesitant, and his reply, v. 13, expresses his doubt (cf. the hesitancy of Moses [Exod. 3:10-12] and Jeremiah [Jer. 1:5-8] to accept God's call). God's response, "I will be with you," Judg. 6:16 (cf. v. 12; Exod. 3:12), turns attention away from Gideon's merits to the God who will be the source of his victory. Gideon, whose doubtful and hesitant nature will become clearer as the story continues, requests a sign (Judg. 6:17).

6:19-24, Gideon Experiences a Vision of God and Builds an Altar. The messenger reveals his divine identity and Gideon, in a response typical of such visionary experiences, fears death because he has seen God (see Gen. 16:13; 32:30; Exod. 3:6; 33:20; Judg. 13:22). On the basis of God's words of assurance to him (Judg. 6:23), Gideon builds an altar and names it "The Lord Is Peace" (v. 24). The account displays a number of similarities to the apparition to Samson's parents in Judges 13.

6:25-32, Gideon Destroys Baal's Altar and Builds an Altar for the Lord. These verses relate how a Canaanite sanctuary became an Israelite one. The Asherah Gideon was commanded to cut down was probably a wooden pole that served as a fertility symbol associated with the Canaanite mother goddess Asherah. It is further desecrated when Gideon uses it as firewood for a sacrifice to the Lord. Because Gideon is afraid, he carries out the deed by night; his character begins to emerge as not only hesitant (6:15, 17) but also timorous. Gideon's destruction and desecration of the Canaanite religious site and erection of an altar to the Lord in its place is used to explain the name Jerubbaal. One would not expect a follower of the Lord to bear a Baal-name; thus the story presents the name as meaning "Let Baal contend" and as bearing witness to Baal's impotence to defend his sanctuary. Some take the identification of Gideon with Jerubbaal as a sign of the fusion of two different, though related, traditions.

6:33-40, Preparations for Battle; Gideon's Tests. The Midianites and their allies encamp in the valley of Jezreel, at the eastern end of the Plain of Esdraelon, the site of the previous battle under Deborah and Barak. In addition to his own clan (Abiezer) and tribe (Manasseh), Gideon summons the neighboring tribes of Asher, Zebulun, and Naphtali (all but Zebulun are mentioned in 7:23 as pursuing Midian). Next to the coalition under Deborah (chap. 5), this is the largest muster of tribes mentioned in the battles of the judges (see commentary below on chap. 21). What was perhaps originally a victory of the clan of Abiezer over the Midianites may have been expanded to include other tribes in the area that would have been affected by Midianite incursions (note the tension between Gideon's three hundred troops and the muster of the tribes in 7:23, and the comparison of Abiezer's accomplishment with Ephraim's, without mention of the other tribes, in 8:2). In spite of his animation by the spirit of the Lord (6:34), Gideon, still hesitant, tests God two times (6:36-40).

7:1-8, Preparations for Battle; the Lord's Tests. Gideon's forces camp on a hill near the spring of Harod (probably in the vicinity of mount Gilboa); the Midianites are to their north in the plain below (vv. 1, 8). Now God makes use of two tests, designed to reduce drastically the number of Gideon's troops and thereby ensure that the Israelites will acknowledge God rather than their own might as the source of their deliverance. The first test is straightforward: the fearful are sent home (v. 3; cf. Deut. 20:8). The second test has to do with the warriors' manner of drinking water (Judg. 7:4-7). The text is problematic and the reason for preferring those who lapped with their tongues over those who knelt down to drink is not clear. Perhaps the point is that God chooses the least likely (least cautious) warriors to demonstrate that victory is due solely to God's intervention (v. 7; cf. 7:2). Victory is the result of God's action, not human endeavors.

7:9-15, Gideon Reassured. Again, Gideon's fearfulness and hesitancy are brought out. God reassures him by sending him down to the Midianite camp to overhear the recounting of a dream and its interpretation. Since dreams were regarded as divinely inspired, the enemy's dream of Gideon's victory offers Gideon confirmation of God's providence.

7:16-23, The Battle. Gideon's three hundred troops, divided into three companies and supplied with horns (Heb. shophar) and jars with torches in them, advance against the Midianites at the beginning of the middle watch (the night was divided into three watches), before the relief sentries would have become familiar with the appearance of the landscape by night. That Gideon's men could have blown horns and broken jars while holding torches in their left hands and horns in their right and also sounding the battle cry, "For the Lord and for Gideon" (vv. 18, 20), contributes to the spectacular nature of the account. The Midianites, thrown into a panic, flee, attacking their own companions (vv. 21-22). Victory is attributed solely to God (v. 22), and the account, with its sounding of the horn and absence of human involvement in battle, is reminiscent of the highly ritualized capture of Jericho in Joshua 6. Verse 23 reintroduces the warriors of Naphtali, Asher, and Manasseh, who rally to the aid of Gideon's three-hundred-strong force.

7:24-8:3, Ephraim's Involvement. The tribe of Ephraim plays a central role in Israel's history (→Ephraim). Here they capture and execute the Midianite princes Oreb ("Raven") and Zeeb ("Wolf"). They are angry with Gideon for not calling them to join in the battle against Midian, apparently a reference to the earlier muster in 6:35 and 7:23 and not to Gideon's summons in 7:24. Gideon diffuses their anger with a sagacious response (8:2). A similar situation occurs under Jephthah, but with quite different results (see commentary below on 12:1-6).

8:4-21, Gideon's Pursuit. Like the preceding section, these verses tell of the capture and execution of two Midianite leaders, here called "kings" and given the names Zebah and Zalmunna (meaning in Heb. "Sacrifice" and "Protection-Withheld"). Gideon and his three hundred followers cross the Jordan River into Transjordan. Their requests for provisions, first from the citizens of Succoth ("booths") and then Penuel ("face of God"; see Gen. 32:30), meet with refusal on the grounds that Gideon is not yet clearly the victor. Gideon threatens cruel reprisals (Judg. 8:7, 9). Gideon's forces catch the remainder of the Midianite army off guard in their camp at Karkor (location uncertain) and capture Zebah and Zalmunna. A victorious Gideon returns with his captives and fulfills his threats against Succoth and Penuel (vv. 13-17). Verses 18-21 introduce a new motive, blood revenge. To avenge the slaughter of his brothers at Mount Tabor (cf. 4:6), Gideon orders his son Jether to slay Zebah and Zalmunna. But the young man, like his father earlier, is afraid. Gideon, who by now has ceased to show fear and has begun taking action on his own initiative (8:1-17), kills them himself.

8:22-23, Gideon Is Offered the Kingship. Although the text repeatedly stresses God's role as the true deliverer of Israel (7:2, 7, 9, 22), the Israelites credit Gideon with the deliverance (8:22) and offer him a hereditary monarchy. They use the term "rule" (Heb. mashal) rather than the usual verb "to be king" (*malak*). Gideon's refusal is praiseworthy (some, however, have argued that v. 23 represents a positive, rather than a negative, answer). The antimonarchical sentiment that God alone is the proper ruler for Israel appears elsewhere (see esp. 1 Sam. 8:7) and plays a significant role in Israel's self-understanding. Nonetheless, there are hints that something is amiss here: one of Gideon's sons bears the suspicious name Abimelech ("My Father Is King") and according to 9:2, Gideon's sons rule over at least an area of Israel. Thus even if Gideon himself refuses the kingship, his decision will shortly be overturned by his son (see commentary below on chap. 9).

8:24–28, Gideon's Ephod. Although he refuses the kingship, Gideon allows himself some of its trappings: he requests a large share of the spoil, the golden earrings of the enemy, here identified as Ishmaelites. The Ishmaelites were related to Israel through Abraham's son by Hagar (Gen. 16), the Midianites through Abraham's second wife, Keturah (Gen. 25:1–4); for similar alternation of terms, see Gen. 37:25–28. From the spoil, Gideon makes an ephod, which becomes the source of idolatrous worship for Israel (Judg. 8:27; cf. 2:3). The ephod was either a priestly vestment or ritual object, perhaps an image (cf. 17:4–5). It was used in divination (see 1 Sam. 23:9–12; 30:7–8). Gideon, who began his career by tearing down the Baal altar (Judg. 6:25–32), finishes by leading Israel into apostasy. In contrast to the other stories of the judges, Israel's apostasy begins while the judge is still alive and the judge contributes to it. The rest formula, which belongs to the editorial framework, appears for the last time in the book in 8:28.

8:29–32, Transition. Judg. 8:29–32 forms the transition to the account of Abimelech's abortive attempt at monarchy. As with the minor judges (see commentary below on 10:1–5), we have a report of the number of sons Gideon had, his death, and his burial. Abimelech is here introduced as one of Gideon's sons, by a legitimate wife of secondary rank ("concubine" in most English translations) whose home is Shechem.

8:33–9:57

Abimelech

8:33–35, Introduction. The story of Abimelech begins in a way similar to the accounts of the major judges, with Israel's apostasy. This time the specific god Israel worshiped is named, Baal-berith, "Lord of the Covenant." Abimelech, however, does not illustrate the cycle of apostasy/punishment/cry-for-help/deliverance, but rather interrupts the cycle. He is an oppressor, not a judge or deliverer. Moreover, this is not a story of oppression of "all Israel" or even of one or two tribes; only the city-state of Shechem and its territory are affected.

9:1–6, Abimelech Is Made King. Abimelech's power base is Shechem, a Canaanite city-state with a long history (→ Shechem), now somehow incorporated into Israelite territory and administered ("ruled") by Gideon's sons. Through his mother's influential kinspeople, Abimelech convinces the Shechemite leaders that the rule of one who is their blood relative is preferable to the rule of the seventy sons of Jerubbaal (Gideon). Seventy is a conventional number of largeness or totality (cf. 2 Kings 10:1; Judg. 1:7; 12:14); the citizens of Shechem give Abimelech seventy pieces of silver, with which he hires "worthless fellows" or "ruffians" to provide his personal entourage (9:4). These followers sound very much like the *'apiru* (Heb.) known to us from other sources (→ Khapiru; cf. also 11:3; 1 Sam. 22:2). Abimelech kills his half-brothers, except Jotham the youngest, and is made king (Heb. *melek*) of the city-state Shechem.

9:7–21, Jotham's Speech. Jotham stands on Mount Gerizim, one of the two mountains overlooking Shechem (the other is Mount Ebal, which some identify with Mount Zalmon, 9:48), and excoriates the Shechemite leadership with a fable (vv. 8–15) and a curse (vv. 16–20). The fable, one of two examples of that genre in the Bible (see also 2 Kings 14:9; 2 Chron. 25:18), is strongly antimonarchical. It illustrates both the folly of kingship (only the worst and least qualified aspire to it) and its dangers (it destroys those who place their reliance on it). The bramble offers scant shade but is a prime cause of fire (v. 15). A monarchy founded on murder can come to no good and inevitably will destroy those who support it. Jotham's call for the mutual destruction of Abimelech and the Shechemite leaders (v. 20) anticipates their fate.

9:22–33, Conflict Between Abimelech and the Shechemites. Abimelech is said to have ruled over Israel for three years (the verb is *sarar*, not *malak*); however, there is no evidence to suggest that his influence extended beyond Shechem and its territory. According to 9:41, Abimelech lived at Arumah, southeast of Shechem, with Zebul acting as his deputy in Shechem. Verses 23–24 show the principle of retribution at work: God, by means of an evil spirit, brings about conflict between Abimelech and the Shechemites to punish Abimelech's mass murder and the Shechemites' support of him. The retributive theme is repeated in 9:56–57. Gaal the son of Ebed ("son of a servant") incites insurrection against Abimelech with a highly nationalistic speech during the harvest festival, when spirits were high and tensions easily excitable. Abimelech's deputy Zebul ("Prince") alerts Abimelech and counsels him to quell the rebellion in a surprise attack upon Shechem.

9:34–45, Abimelech Puts Down the Revolt. These verses report two successive and related campaigns, the surprise attack upon Gaal (vv. 34–41) and an ambush against the city using a stratagem similar to that employed in the capture of Ai (Josh. 8) and Benjamin (Judg. 20:29–48). Abimelech destroys the city and its inhabitants. The custom of sowing the city with salt (9:45), otherwise unattested in the Bible, has analogues in other ancient cultures and apparently symbolizes the finality and irreversibility of the destruction.

9:46–57, Campaigns Against Shechem's Tower and Thebez. When the people of Shechem's Tower hear of Abimelech's victory and violence, they take refuge in the temple of El-berith ("God of the Covenant"; cf. Baal-berith, 8:33). Shechem's Tower is either a quarter of the city or an outpost of it, but at any rate a separate place from the scene of the battle in 9:42–45. Abimelech burns down the stronghold, killing all the people (vv. 46–49). When he tries the same siege tactic against Thebez—perhaps in an attempt to extend his influence and support now that his base in Shechem has been destroyed—a woman throws a millstone on his head that crushes his skull. His death illustrates the imprudence of drawing too close to a defended city wall. By having his armor bearer run him through, Abimelech hopes to avoid the stigma of an ignominious death, for to be killed by a woman was a disgrace for a warrior. Ironically, this is precisely what is remembered about him (2 Sam. 11:21). Judg. 9:56–57 attributes these events to God's retributive action in fulfilling the curse of Jotham. It is worth noting that Abimelech is not punished for establishing a monarchy but for killing his brothers. As in the earlier stories (e.g., 4:15, 23; 7:2, 22), so here also God is in complete control of events. Charismatic leadership is preferable to a monarchy founded on violence, but charismatic leadership is not without its problems, as we saw with Gideon and as we will see even more clearly with Jephthah and Samson.

10:1–5
The Minor Judges

No editorial framework introduces the minor judges. Judg. 10:1–5 together with 12:(7)8–15 have the appearance of an annalistic list, which,

along with the judges' names, gives information about their tribal or city affiliation, the length of their judgeship, and their death and burial. The minor judges are presented in succession (note the repetition of "after him"). For three of them —Jair (10:3–5), Ibzan (12:8–10), and Abdon (12:13–15)—we are given interesting family details, which testify to their substance and prestige. All are said to have "judged Israel," but whatever functions they exercised are not reported, and in spite of the pan-Israel perspective suggested by the phrase "judged Israel," nothing in the descriptions of these figures indicates a sphere of activity beyond a particular city or tribe.

Many suggestions have been put forward about the office held by the minor judges, but the fact is that the information in the list is too meager to permit any meaningful conclusions. The editors of the book of Judges apparently intend us to see these figures as exercising the same office as the other (major) judges, even though they report no stories about their delivering Israel from oppression (but note that Tola [10:1] is said to "deliver Israel" "after Abimelech"). Perhaps they governed local areas in times of peace.

Judg. 12:7 sounds as if it too belongs to the list. If so, the editors presumably interrupted the list because at this particular point they had substantial material to include about one of the judges' activities.

10:6–12:7
Jephthah

10:6–16, Theological Introduction. The Jephthah story interrupts the list of minor judges, 10:1–5; 12:8–15. The framework formula (10:6–10) is here elaborated into a full-scale indictment of Israel's apostasy. Similar theological elaborations occur in chap. 2 and in 6:7–10. For the first time, Israel actually repents (10:10, 15–16), but God does not, as at other times, raise up a deliverer in response to Israel's cry for help. The Gileadite elders appoint Jephthah their leader (11:4–11) and only later does God confirm their choice (11:29). In contrast to the following account, where the conflict is limited to Ammon and Gilead, 10:9 introduces a wider Israelite perspective (note that Jephthah is appointed leader only over Gilead, not over "all Israel").

10:17–11:11, Jephthah's Appointment as Leader. In response to pressure from the Ammonites (from central Transjordan), the elders of Gilead (in northern Transjordan) seek out Jephthah to be their leader. The elders represent a form of local leadership evidenced throughout

255

the biblical period. Jephthah had earlier been driven away from his Gileadite homeland by his half-brothers, jealous of their inheritance rights (11:2); 11:7 suggests that this may have been a political action involving the elders. The elders choose Jephthah because of his military skills (11:1), a consideration that outweighs his objectionable origins and current status as leader of a band of outlaws (for the same expression, see 9:4; see also 1 Sam. 22:2). Jephthah negotiates with the elders to have himself made not only their leader against the Ammonites (Judg. 11:6, 11) but also their head (vv. 8, 9, 11). "Leader" (Heb. qatsin) may represent a temporary military leadership, and "head" (Heb. ro'sh), a permanent civil one. Thus Jephthah is appointed for the present crisis and for the future, if he succeeds in ridding Israel of the Ammonite threat (v. 9). The agreement is ratified at Mizpah (cf. 1 Sam. 11:14–15; 2 Sam. 5:3; on Mizpah, see commentary below on 20:1–17).

11:12–28, Jephthah Negotiates with the Ammonites. Jephthah tries to settle Israel's differences with Ammon through diplomacy. The Ammonite king contends that Israel took part of their land in central Transjordan between the Arnon and Jabbok rivers. Jephthah's laborious counterargument has two main points. First, he rehearses Israel's encounters with Edom, Moab, and Sihon, king of the Amorites, in the process of entering the promised land (see Num. 20–24), arguing that Israel conquered and took possession of the land of the Amorites because it was God's will to give Israel the land, and a nation has a right to whatever its god gives it through conquest (Judg. 11:15–25). It is often claimed that the description fits Moab better than Ammon, but the fact that Ammon had conquered part of Moabite territory may help explain the confusion. The territory in dispute, the land east of the Jordan River between the Arnon and the Jabbok (v. 13), was taken in battle from Sihon, king of the Amorites (v. 22). Chemosh, according to the Bible and the Mesha Stele, was the national god of Moab, but may also have been worshiped by the Ammonites (→ Mesha). Jephthah's second point is that since Ammon laid no claims to the land during the three hundred years Israel occupied it, they have no right to dispute it now (v. 26). Jephthah's lengthy attempt at negotiation proves unsuccessful.

11:29–40, Jephthah's Vow and Its Tragic Consequences. Like Othniel and Gideon before him, Jephthah is animated by the spirit of the Lord (v. 29), but in Jephthah's case this takes place after he had assumed leadership. In return for victory over Ammon, Jephthah vows to sacrifice as a burnt offering to God the one who meets him upon his return from battle. Some commentators have argued that he may have had in mind

an animal, but both the language and the nature of a vow (namely, an extreme measure that would ordinarily entail the offer of something quite precious) suggest that a person was meant.

The Hebrew Bible generally condemns human sacrifice (Lev. 18:21; 20:1–5; Deut. 12:31; 18:10; but see also Gen. 22; Exod. 22:29–30; and Mic. 6:7–8), and the actual biblical examples of the practice, which are few, view it with horror (see 2 Kings 3:27; 16:3; 21:6). God gives Jephthah a great victory (Judg. 11:32–33) and thus Jephthah must fulfill his part. A vow, once uttered, was irrevocable (v. 35; Num. 30:2). Jephthah's reaction (Judg. 11:35) makes clear that he had not expected the one to meet him to be his daughter. His daughter courageously accepts her fate, requesting only a two-month delay to lament her virginity, since to die childless was a great misfortune. Jephthah too will die childless, since his daughter is his only child. The sacrifice itself is treated in less than one brief verse (v. 39); the details are too terrible to receive elaboration. The young woman's tragedy is tempered by the company of women who grieve with her (vv. 37–38) and who, after her death, remember her in a yearly ritual (v. 40). RSV and JB, following LXX and Vg., read "to lament," but the Hebrew verb has the sense of "recount" or "commemorate" (cf. its only other occurrence in 5:11). The most startling feature of the narrative is the absence of any condemnation of Jephthah's sacrifice of his daughter to God.

12:1–7, Civil War Between Gilead and Ephraim. Some commentators understand the conflict as originating in Ephraim's reaction to the threat to its influence in Transjordan posed by the assertion of Gileadite authority. Unlike Gideon before him (8:1–3) and in marked contrast to his own lengthy attempt at negotiations with the Ammonite king, Jephthah does not seriously pursue diplomacy as a means of placating Ephraim's anger at not having been called up to join the battle against Ammon. Moreover, Jephthah and the Ephraimites have different versions of the events (12:1–3), and the text gives us no clue which to believe. Fighting breaks out and the Gileadites gain the upper hand. They seize the fords of the Jordan and slay any Ephraimite trying to escape to his own territory. Anyone trying to cross over into the area west of the Jordan had to say the word "shibboleth" (meaning "ear of grain" or "torrent of water"). The Ephraimites, who spoke a different dialect of Hebrew, pronounced it differently from the Gileadites, and thus betrayed their true identities. The information about Jephthah's term of office, death, and burial (v. 7) links Jephthah with the list of minor judges, where the same type of information is summarily presented.

12:8–15

The Minor Judges

See commentary above on 10:1–5.

13:1–16:31

Samson

It is frequently observed that Samson does not behave like a judge. He does not lead any Israelite troops into battle but rather engages in personal vendettas against the Philistines. When one considers his wild escapades and sexual liaisons, his character leaves much to be desired. Unlike the major judges before him, he does not achieve Israel's deliverance from its oppressor. Nonetheless, for the editors of the book, Samson was a judge (15:20; 16:31), and what were probably originally folktales—rowdy adventure stories told by an oppressed group as an outlet for their frustration at their inability to gain the upper hand over their more powerful oppressors—have been given a theological interpretation. The stories in their present form repeatedly remind us that Samson is the instrument of God (13:25; 14:4, 6, 19; 15:14, 18–19; 16:28–30). Even if he is ultimately unsuccessful in ridding Israel of the Philistine menace, his final act brings glory to God (16:28–30).

The setting is the Shephelah in the vicinity of Zorah and Eshtaol (13:25; 16:31), with specific events related to the surrounding area: Timnah, Etam, Ramath-lehi, Hebron, the valley of Sorek. In the period of Israelite settlement, this area came increasingly under the Philistine sphere of influence. Ashkelon and Gaza, members of the Philistine pentapolis, are visited by Samson, and Gaza is the scene of his death. The Philistines, Sea Peoples who came from the Aegean and settled along the southern coast of Canaan in the twelfth century B.C., sometime after Israel, posed a serious threat to Israelite existence during the time of the judges and in the early days of the monarchy (see above commentary on 1:1–21; 4:1–5; → Philistines). Philistine pressure forced the Danites to migrate from their assigned territory in southwest Palestine to the far north of the country (see Josh. 19:40–48; Judg. 17–18). Samson's failure completely to defeat the Philistines, in spite of his victories, may reflect Dan's inability to get a stronghold in the plain.

13:1–25, Samson's Birth. Only two elements of the editorial framework appear in the story, apostasy and oppression. There is no cry for help, and deliverance from the oppressor is not achieved. Unlike the deliverers before him, Samson is chosen by God before birth. He is set apart as a Nazirite "to begin" or "to be the first" to deliver Israel from the Philistines (v. 5), but it will remain for David to complete the task.

Judges 13 has features in common with other birth accounts (see 1 Sam. 1; Gen. 18; 16:7–16). There are also strong similarities to Gideon's visionary experience in Judg. 6:11–24. The account enhances Samson's mother's role and portrays her as more perceptive than her husband. The divine messenger's appearance and announcement are to her alone (13:3–7). When Manoah manages to get an audience with the messenger and seeks to obtain more information, the messenger tells him even less than he told the woman (vv. 8–14). Whereas Manoah is unaware of the messenger's divine identity (v. 16), his wife senses it from the outset (v. 6). Manoah's fear of death upon witnessing the revelation of the messenger's identity is an appropriate response (vv. 15–22; see commentary above on 6:19–24); but his wife displays greater theological acumen, recognizing the divine intention behind the events (13:23).

Samson's Nazirite status (vv. 4–5, 7) has perplexed commentators. The Nazirite regulations of Numbers 6 do not fit the picture in Judges 13–16, where Samson is a lifelong Nazirite consecrated before birth, who may never cut his hair. The injunctions against wine and beer and against unclean food are placed on the mother in Judg. 13:4, 7, and 14; presumably they apply to the child. Samson does not behave like a Nazirite and, moreover, chaps. 14–15—where Samson touches a carcass (14:8–9) and presumably drinks at the feast (14:10)—make no mention of Nazirite status. Nazirite status appears to be a later development in the tradition to provide a theological rationale for the strong man's strength that resides in his hair (16:17), a common folklore motif.

14:1–15:20, Samson's Marriage to a Philistine Woman and Its Consequences. Israelites and Philistines live side by side and even intermarry (though for faithful Israelites this is not desirable, 14:1–3; recall Deut. 7:3–4), but relations between the two peoples are strained. Samson's marriage may be of the *tzadiqa* type, in which the wife continues to dwell in the house of her father (see 15:1). The account of Samson and the Timnite is modeled on the story of Samson and Delilah in Judg. 16:4–22. In both cases Samson is persuaded by a woman to reveal a secret: in 14:15–18, the answer to his riddle; in 16:4–22, the explanation of his great strength. The Philistines are behind each woman's attempt to learn Samson's secret, and each time the woman breaks down Samson's resistance by casting doubt on his love (14:16; 16:15). The woman betrays Samson's secret to the Philistines, and this leads—directly in 16:21 and indirectly, through a series of reprisals, in

14:19–15:13—to the handing over of Samson to the Philistines. Samson's riddle (14:14), based on his private experience (14:5–9), would have been insoluble had the Philistines not gotten the answer from Samson's wife by threatening to burn her and her father's house (14:15). Ironically, the fate she sought to avoid befalls her (15:6). Her betrayal of Samson's riddle to the Philistines occasions a series of reprisals between Samson and the Philistines (14:19–15:8) that finally leads to the Philistine attack on Judah and the Judahites subsequently handing over Samson to their oppressors (15:9–13). The Judahites are thus portrayed in a negative light; like Delilah, they deliver Samson into Philistine hands.

The spirit of the Lord inspires Samson's unusual feats of prowess (13:25; 14:6, 19; 15:14; see commentary above on 3:10). The spirit enables Samson to kill one thousand Philistines with the jawbone of an ass, providing the name of the place, Ramath-lehi, which means "hill of the jawbone" (15:14–17). Immediately thereafter, however, Samson falls victim to thirst and appeals to God (15:18). His response not only reveals his dependence on God; it also makes a crucial theological point: the strong man cannot save himself. God provides Samson with water, and another place receives its name, En-hak-kore, "the spring of the caller" (15:18–19).

16:1–3, Samson and the Harlot of Gaza. This brief anecdote offers another illustration of Samson's enormous strength and equally large libido. The Philistines fail in their only attempt to trap Samson without a woman's help.

16:4–22, Samson and Delilah. On the similarity with the story of Samson and the Timnite, see the commentary above on Judg. 14:1–15:20. That Delilah was Philistine is not stated in the text, but in view of Samson's other liaisons, it is quite likely. Her first two unsuccessful attempts to discover the source of Samson's great strength involve binding Samson (vv. 6–9, 10–12). The third attempt comes perilously close to the secret, since it has to do with Samson's hair (vv. 13–14). Her fourth attempt succeeds, and Samson is captured, blinded, and imprisoned by the Philistines (vv. 15–21). Verse 22 offers a sign of hope and a hint of victory to come.

16:23–31, Victory at Gaza. What appears initially as a victory for Dagon, the Canaanite grain god worshiped by the Philistines, becomes the victory of God. While the Philistines praise their god (vv. 23, 24), Samson calls on his (vv. 28, 30). He acts as the agent of God's punishment, in particular for the ignominy he has suffered at the hands of the Philistines (v. 28). Samson's death is not, strictly speaking, a sui-

cide, since God grants his prayer for death, accepting him as an instrument through which to carry out the divine plan (v. 30). His death is viewed as achieving an important result, killing more Philistines than he had killed in his lifetime. The story closes with the statement that Samson judged Israel twenty years. No rest formula occurs, the cyclical pattern of Judges is at an end, and we move into the final chapters of the book on a somber note.

17:1–21:25

Double Conclusion

The concluding chapters of Judges sound a recurrent theme, "In those days there was no king in Israel" (17:6; 18:1; 19:1; 21:25). The first and last times this phrase occurs, the implications are spelled out: "every man did what was right in his own eyes." Neither judges nor deliverers appear in the concluding stories, and significantly, the threat to Israel is no longer external but internal. Even when no foreign oppressor appears on the horizon, conditions do not improve, for Israel left to its sinful ways pursues a course that threatens its political and religious survival. From the evidence of the major judges, it would seem that charismatic deliverers who arise in time of need have not provided the kind of stable leadership Israel requires. Moreover, beginning with Gideon, whose ephod led to apostasy, followed by Jephthah, who makes a human sacrifice, and Samson, who failed to live up to his calling, the judges themselves have displayed disturbing weaknesses. A serious crisis of leadership emerges. By illustrating the depravity and anarchy of the times when Israel had no king, Judges 17–21 looks forward to the monarchy as a possible solution. The degree to which kingship provides a solution to Israel's problems receives attention in the following books of Samuel and Kings.

17:1–18:31

Conclusion, Part One: The Origin of the Sanctuary at Dan

Although they contain no explicit censure, these chapters offer a subtle and ironic polemic against the sanctuary at Dan, which, along with Bethel, was a national sanctuary of the Northern Kingdom (see 1 Kings 12:26–33). The Danite sanctuary is founded on theft (Judg. 18:14–26) and violence (18:27); its main ritual objects are stolen images made by human hands (17:4; 18:24, 27, 31) from stolen silver (17:1–4). Judges 17–18 also portrays the levitical priesthood in a negative light, as do the following chapters.

258

17:1–6, Micah's Image and Other Ritual Objects. The strange account begins abruptly with a theft, a curse, and the making of a molten image. From the outset Micah is presented negatively. He steals a large sum of silver from his own mother (eleven hundred pieces of silver is the amount each Philistine lord promised Delilah, 16:5) and engages in apparent syncretistic religious practices that belie his name (the full form, which appears in vv. 1–4, is Micah-yahu, meaning "Who is like Yhwh [the LORD]?"). Molten images are forbidden in Exod. 20:4–6; Deut. 5:8–10; Exod. 34:17; and Deut. 27:15; and warnings about the dangers of syncretism appear in Judg. 2:1–5; 6:7–10; and 10:10–15. Whereas Gideon made an ephod that led to apostasy (8:27), Micah has a shrine (lit., "house of god[s]") with a graven image, a molten image, an ephod, and teraphim. The terms "graven image" and "molten image" (RSV) may indicate a single carved statue covered with silver, but elsewhere in the account they seem to indicate two different images (18:17, 18). On the ephod, see above commentary on 8:24–28; teraphim were statues used in worship (→ Teraphim). Whereas the exact nature and function of all this ritual paraphernalia are obscure, there can be little doubt that the piling up of these terms is meant as ironic disapproval. The image, after all, is made from stolen silver; and though Micah's mother consecrates all of it to the Lord, she obviously keeps the larger portion.

17:7–13, Micah Employs an Itinerant Levite as His Priest. Micah installs a Levite from the tribe of Judah as his family priest. Whereas 17:5 indicates that a priest did not have to be a member of the tribe of Levi (cf. 2 Sam. 8:18), these verses show that a Levite was especially desirable. Micah believes that having a Levite as his priest will bring him God's favor (v. 13), but the following events will prove him wrong.

18:1–6, The Danite Spies Consult God Through Micah's Levite. The Danites' appearance on the scene, seeking an inheritance, looks back to the beginning of the book (1:34). From their base in the area of Zorah and Eshtaol (see commentary above on chaps. 13–16), they send out spies who, coming upon Micah's house, recognize the Levite's voice (18:3). Either they knew him or, more likely, they recognized his dialect as Judahite or perceived him to be a priest on the basis of what they overheard him saying. He "inquires of God" on their behalf—probably a reference to divination by means of the ephod and teraphim—and gives them a highly ambiguous answer. "Your way is before the Lord" (v. 6) is not a clear promise of divine blessing, and its obscurity perhaps functions to dissociate God from the questionable conduct of the Danites.

18:7–26, The Danites Steal Micah's Priest and Ritual Paraphernalia. Laish in the far north was desirable because of both its fertile land and its military vulnerability, there being no allies to come to its defense (vv. 7–10). Upon hearing the spies' report, the tribe of Dan journeys to Laish (vv. 11–13). On the way, they steal Micah's images and ritual objects (vv. 14–26). The Levite reveals himself as an opportunist happy to accompany the Danites as their priest (v. 20), and the Danites are bullies who intimidate Micah, threatening bloodshed, when he protests their plunder (vv. 23–26).

18:27–31, The Sanctuary at Dan. In an attack that resembles holy war, with its total slaughter and destruction by fire, the Danites capture Laish. They rebuild the city, naming it "Dan" after their eponymous ancestor, and establish their shrine with Micah's stolen image and priest. Only the graven image is mentioned; the other ritual objects have dropped out of the picture. But the syncretistic nature of this form of worship is nevertheless intimated by the phrase "Micah's image which he made" (v. 31). Only now do we learn the priest's name, Jonathan the son of Gershom, son of Moses (i.e., Moses' grandson or simply a member of the Gershomite branch of Levites). The copyists, reluctant to associate the name of Moses with a questionable type of religious service, changed the name (*mosheh*) to Manasseh (*menasheh*) by inserting a suspended "n" in the Hebrew text. The captivity of the land (v. 30) may refer to the deportation that took place under the Assyrian ruler Tiglath-pileser III in 734–732 B.C. (see 2 Kings 15:29). The reference to the house of God at Shiloh seeks to make the two religious centers contemporary (→ Shiloh).

19:1–21:25

Conclusion, Part Two: Violence at Gibeah and War Against Benjamin

The pan-Israel perspective of these chapters reveals the hand of a later editor, since the kind of tribal organization envisioned can hardly have preceded the consolidation under the monarchy (see "Introduction" above). The events recounted show how utterly low Israel has sunk without a leader (19:1; 21:25). The threat of dissolution through internecine warfare was avoided under Gideon (8:1–3), but fighting between tribes did take place, albeit on a smaller scale, under Jephthah (12:1–6). In Judges 19–21, one Israelite tribe is nearly wiped out by a confederation of the others. Near anarchy and moral depravity characterize the times. The crimes of rape and murder are punished by the Israelite assembly with violence that does not stop short of mass rape and murder.

19:1–9, A Levite Fetches His Wife from Her Father's House. These chapters exhibit a stronger antilevitical sentiment than Judges 17–18. The Levite here is not simply worse than the Levite of chaps. 17–18 but is possibly the most disreputable character in the book. None of the characters in this grisly story are named. The Levite is from the central hill country of Ephraim; his wife of secondary rank (see commentary above on 8:29–32) is from Bethlehem in Judah, south of Jerusalem. Her reason for returning to her father's house is not clear. A reference to harlotry, following the Hebrew, does not make a great deal of sense in this context. It has been suggested that the Hebrew means she divorced him. Many modern translations follow the versions in reading, "she was angry with him" (so RSV, JB).

The Levite's weakness of character is hinted at when he allows his father-in-law repeatedly to persuade him to remain in Bethlehem. First he is too irresolute to leave on his journey at a reasonable hour, and then too stubborn to remain yet another night. Had he left early in the morning as intended, the outrage at Gibeah might have been avoided. The woman does not participate in either the decision making or the merriment (vv. 4–9). In what follows, she is clearly treated as an object.

19:10–21, The Decision to Spend the Night in Gibeah. The Levite rejects his servant's suggestion to spend the night in Jebus (Jerusalem) because he could expect no hospitality from foreigners. Jerusalem was a Jebusite city (see commentary above on 1:21); Gibeah, north of Jerusalem, was Israelite, belonging to the tribe of Benjamin. They receive no hospitality in Gibeah (vv. 15, 18), however, until an old man from Ephraim, a resident alien in Gibeah, takes them in for the night. Gibeah was King Saul's hometown, and an anti-Saul polemic is noticeably at work in Judges 19–21.

19:22–30, The Rape of the Levite's Wife. In the night their merriment is interrupted by Benjaminite ruffians who demand that the man be brought outside so that they might sexually assault him. The account has striking similarities to Gen. 19:4–11, except that here an assault is carried out, making this story perhaps the most gruesome in the Bible. The host offers his virgin daughter and the Levite's wife as substitutes. In Genesis 19, Lot's offer of his two virgin daughters is viewed by many scholars as demanded by the conventions of hospitality, which require that the guest be protected at all costs. In Judges 19, in contrast, the host offers one of his guests, and, in fact, only the Levite's wife is thrown out to the mob. It is not certain whether the host or her husband throws her out.

The men of Gibeah rape and abuse the help-

less woman all night. When the Levite opens the door in the morning "to go his way"—not to see what has happened to his wife—and finds her lying on the threshold, his crass response underscores his depravity, "Get up, so we can go" (v. 28). He puts her on his ass, travels home, and chops her body into twelve pieces, which he sends through the territory of Israel. It is not at all clear that the woman was dead when he dismembered her—a point that clearly concerned the translators of the LXX and Vg., who added "for she was dead" in v. 28. (Is this a morbid parody of Saul's mustering of Israel, 1 Sam 11?) The abuse of the woman by her husband, her host, and the mob reflects Israel's moral and spiritual deterioration.

20:1–17, The Tribes Assemble Against Benjamin. All Israel responds to the crime by assembling at Mizpah "as one man." "Dan to Beersheba" is a conventional designation for the northern and southern extent of Israel; Gilead refers to northern Transjordan. Mizpah was a sanctuary on the border between Ephraim and Benjamin. For the first time in Judges, we have something that looks like a tribal confederation taking united action in response to the crime of one of its members. The historical value of the account is questionable, however; it has been suggested that an original story about warfare resulting from rivalry between Ephraim and Benjamin has been expanded to include all Israel. The figures given for the number of warriors involved are greatly exaggerated.

The Levite's testimony (vv. 4–6) confirms his baseness. He magnifies the threat to himself ("me they sought to kill," v. 5) and neglects to mention that he remained in the safety of the house while "my wife they ravished." His final statement, "and she is dead," preserves the ambiguity whether the woman was alive or dead when he dismembered her. The tribes march against Benjamin and demand that the criminals be given to them to execute the death penalty. The Benjaminites refuse, thereby assuming solidarity with the guilty, and the battle lines are drawn. The heavy odds against Benjamin are somewhat compensated for by the elite corps of left-handed or ambidextrous men skilled with the sling (v. 16; see also 3:15; 1 Chron. 12:2).

20:18–28, Benjamin Twice Defeats Israel. The Israelites go to Bethel to inquire of God by means of the oracle. Bethel and Dan (see commentary above on 18:27–31) were the two principal sanctuaries of the Northern Kingdom; in 20:27 we learn that the Ark was at Bethel. The question as to which tribe should lead the advance (v. 18) is the same question asked in Judg. 1:1, with regard to the Canaanites. The answer is also the same, indicating the primacy of Judah in these two narratives. Unlike Judg. 1:2, God does not promise victory and, indeed, Benjamin defeats Israel. As in Judg. 2:4, the Israelites weep before God in a ritual lament and inquire again, this time asking not who should attack first but whether they should do battle at all (v. 23). It is a question they should have asked earlier. Again they fight Benjamin, are defeated, and lament before God at Bethel, fasting and offering sacrifices (vv. 24–26). Again they inquire of the oracle, and this time God promises them victory (vv. 27–28).

20:29–48, The Defeat of Benjamin. Two accounts of the same event may have been combined in these verses. On the third day, Israel defeats Benjamin by an ambush similar to the attack on Ai under Joshua (Josh. 8; see also Judg. 9:34–45). Judg. 20:35 attributes victory over Benjamin to God. Only six hundred Benjaminites escape, while Israel destroys the rest of the tribe in what sounds like an implementation of the ban (v. 48), but in this case is war against their own kinspeople!

21:1–25, Wives for Benjamin Obtained Through Violence. Israel again weeps before God at Bethel, ironically this time, not because they could not defeat Benjamin, but precisely because they have (v. 3). They are distressed that one tribe faces extermination, and they question how to find wives for the few Benjaminites who remain (20:47) since they themselves have slain the Benjaminite women (20:48). The solution is to carry out the ban against Jabesh-gilead, which had not joined the war against Benjamin, sparing only four hundred virgins. As these were not enough, and everyone else was under oath not to give their daughters as wives to Benjamin, the Benjaminite men are told to kidnap wives from the dancers in the annual vintage festival at Shi-

loh. Since the women would have been stolen rather than given in marriage, their families would not be guilty of breaking the oath. Thus the book of Judges comes to a close with the outrage at Gibeah repeated on a mass scale by the whole assembly of Israel. To punish the violence done to one woman (and the threatened crime against the Levite), the Israelites kill many innocent women, women from Benjamin and women from Jabesh-gilead who are not virgins. They take by force four hundred virgins from Jabesh-gilead and capture others from Shiloh. At the end of Judges, Israel lacks direction; all behave as they please. This is the editor's final word on Israel's plight without a king.

Bibliography

Bal, M. *Death and Dissymmetry: The Politics of Coherence in the Book of Judges.* Chicago: University of Chicago, 1988.

Boling, R. G. *Judges.* Anchor Bible, 6A. Garden City, NY: Doubleday, 1975.

Gottwald, N. K. *The Hebrew Bible: A Socio-Literary Introduction.* Philadelphia: Fortress, 1985.

———. *The Tribes of Yahweh.* Maryknoll, NY: Orbis, 1979.

Gray, J. *Joshua, Judges, Ruth.* New Century Bible Commentary. Grand Rapids, MI: Eerdmans, 1986.

Malamat, A. "The Period of the Judges." In Vol. 3, *Judges,* of *The World History of the Jewish People.* Edited by B. Mazar. Tel Aviv: Massada, 1971. Pp. 129–63.

Mayes, A. D. H. *Judges.* Old Testament Guides. Sheffield: JSOT Press, 1985.

Polzin, R. *Moses and the Deuteronomist: A Literary Study of the Deuteronomic History.* New York: Seabury, 1980.

Soggin, J. A. *Judges.* Old Testament Library. Translated by J. Bowden. Philadelphia: Westminster, 1981.

RUTH

ADELE BERLIN

INTRODUCTION

The Book of Ruth is a short narrative independent of the long narrative running from Genesis through 2 Kings but similar to it in style and outlook. There are two main traditions regarding the placement of Ruth in the canon (→ Canon). In Christian Bibles, which derive their order from the Septuagint and Vulgate, Ruth is found after Judges, for this is the period in which the story is set. Jewish Bibles follow the tradition of placing Ruth in the Writings, as the Masoretes did. Although there is some variation in the Masoretic ordering of the books in this section, in modern printed Hebrew Bibles Ruth is the second of the Five Scrolls, because it is read publicly on the festival of Shavuot (Weeks, Pentecost), the second festival in the year commencing with Passover.

According to rabbinic tradition, the main theme of Ruth is *chesed*, loyalty or faithfulness born of a sense of caring and commitment. *Chesed* is a Hebrew term used to describe God's relationship to Israel as well as the relationship among members of a family or a community. All of the main characters in the book, Naomi, Ruth, and Boaz, act with *chesed*. Naomi, although she technically had no responsibility for her widowed daughters-in-law, was concerned that they find new husbands; she went out of her way to see that Ruth did. Ruth, on her part, had no obligation to Naomi, but she remained steadfastly with her, even giving up her native land and religion; all of her actions were directed toward finding support and protection for Naomi. Boaz too took upon himself a commitment beyond what was required; not only was he willing to redeem the family's land, but he was eager to marry Ruth and enable the family name to be perpetuated. God also manifested his *chesed*, by virtue of which the individuals are repaid for their loyalty by finding security and fulfillment, and the family that came close to destruction finds new life and continuity.

Closely related to the theme of *chesed* is the theme of family continuity. The male members of Naomi's family who might normally be expected to perpetuate the family are quickly removed from the story, and it is through the women, an elderly widow and a non-Israelite, that family continuity is achieved. Nor is this the only time in the Bible that such is the case. The book of Ruth calls attention to its similarity to the story of Judah and Tamar (in Gen. 38; cf.

Ruth 4:12) and to the matriarchs Rachel and Leah, "who built the house of Israel" (4:11). The first two chapters of Exodus also recount how, through the fertility and quick action of the women, Israel survived and grew to nationhood.

Another important element in the book, related to the national interest, is David and his ancestry. The book culminates with the Davidic genealogy and the last word in the book is "David." In addition, the Judean and Bethlehemite interests are strongly felt at several points in the story. The book may be read as a glorification of David through the glorification of his ancestors. What fine stock the ideal king of Israel is descended from! And how fitting for his ancestors that they were to produce a figure like David.

A secondary motif that runs through the story is emptiness/fullness. This applies to the land—famine/harvest—and to the main characters, Ruth and Naomi, who first suffer death and then celebrate birth. Naomi gives expression to this thought in 1:21: "I went away full and the Lord has brought me back empty." On both a human and a national level, in small and large ways, emptiness is replaced by fullness and completion.

The book of Ruth is a masterpiece of literary artistry. This short narrative, often called a short story or novella, seems disarmingly simple on the surface, but, like most biblical narrative, it is complex and sophisticated. The plot contains numerous symmetries and operates on various levels: the romantic, the quasi-legal, the familial-national, and the moral-religious. The characters are developed through their speech and actions; little of their inner life or the narrator's evaluation is expressed. Like most of the Bible, Ruth is written with great economy. Words are chosen carefully and their recurrence often signals significant connections or developments. Frequently occurring terms, like *chesed* and *go'el* (Heb., "redeemer"), point to the main concepts of the story. Although Ruth is not poetry, its language is elevated and elegant. The book leaves readers, as it leaves its characters, with a sense of fulfillment.

It is difficult to establish the date of composition accurately. Certainly in its final form, Ruth cannot predate David, although the story is set in an earlier period. Because of its affinity in language and content to some of the early parts of the Bible such as Genesis, Judges, Samuel, and the prose sections of Job, it is often dated between 950 and 700 B.C. If we interpret it as a glorification of David, then its date might be closer to the time of David, around 950–900 B.C. The period of David and Solomon saw a great flourishing of Israelite culture and the formation of some of the earliest parts of the Bible. It seems appropriate that Ruth might have been a product of this literary effort.

On the other hand, certain late linguistic features, especially Aramaisms, have prompted some scholars to date the book to the exilic or postexilic period (the sixth century B.C. and later). This view is reinforced by those who interpret the book as a polemic against the decree of Ezra that the returning exiles should divorce their foreign wives (Ezra 9–10; Neh. 13:23–29). This interpretation seems forced, but the exilic and postexilic periods were times during which many national traditions were preserved and became a source of comfort and encouragement. Many people looked forward to the reestablishment of the Davidic dynasty, and they would no doubt have derived hope from the book of Ruth.

It is, of course, entirely possible that the book was composed in an early period and was subsequently edited, thereby acquiring late characteristics as well. The uncertainty regarding its date of origin, however, does not diminish the book's significance or the pleasure that we derive from reading it, for these are timeless.

COMMENTARY

1:1–5, Setting the Scene. The story is set in the days of the judges, before the monarchy, but its pastoral tone is in marked contrast to the wars and violence of the book of Judges. A famine provides the impetus for the migration of a Bethlehemite family to Moab (cf. Gen. 12:10 and 42:1–2 for other famines that lead to sojourns in foreign lands).

After having been introduced by their positions in the family—husband, wife, sons—the characters are introduced by names whose meanings appear to be symbolic: Elimelech, "My God is king," this being the period before human kings ruled Israel; Naomi, "Pleasantness," a woman whose lot in life turns bitter (cf. 1:20) and then fortunate; then Mahlon, "Weakness, Sickness," and Chilion, "Annihilation, Consumption," sons who die young and leave no offspring. Although Elimelech is named first, Naomi quickly becomes the focus of attention and other characters are named in reference to her: "Naomi's husband," "her two sons," "her daughters-in-law."

Since there was no ban on marriages between Israelites and foreigners in the early biblical period (cf. Joseph, Moses, David, and Solomon), it is quite natural that Naomi's sons should marry local Moabite girls. From the point of view of the dynamics of the story, however, this fact is crucial, for Ruth's loyalty to Naomi's family is extraordinary precisely because Ruth is not an Israelite. The name "Ruth" probably derives from the word for "friend, companion"; Orpah means "back of the neck" (as seen when one turns away). The character of Orpah, who is not bad but represents the norm or the expected, serves as a contrast to Ruth, who goes far beyond the norm in maintaining her loyalty.

1:6–15, Plans to Return to Bethlehem. The action of the story commences with Naomi's intention to return to Bethlehem now that the famine is over. Since she cannot provide for her widowed daughters-in-law, she begs them to return to their own mothers' homes where they may find security in the form of remarriage. Both daughters-in-law initially refuse to leave, and this elicits a moving plea from Naomi (1:12–13) in which she calls Ruth and Orpah "daughters" (as she does Ruth throughout) and stresses that if she could have more sons for them to marry, she would gladly marry and bear children. But, alas, she is too old; and even if she were not, Ruth and Orpah would have to remain husbandless until these children were grown. This may seem to refer to the levirate marriage (see Deut. 25:5–10), but, since these new sons would not be paternal brothers of the deceased, as the levirate law of Deuteronomy requires, it is more likely that these words are exaggerated rhetoric, whereby Naomi attempts to convince her daughters-in-law how hopeless it is for them to look to her for support. There is also a note of bitter frustration on Naomi's part that she could not provide for Ruth and Orpah. Orpah is persuaded to depart at this point, but Ruth remains steadfastly with Naomi. Naomi urges Ruth to follow Orpah's example, but to no avail.

1:16–18, Whither Thou Goest. In moving rhetoric Ruth pledges her loyalty to Naomi. She will remain with Naomi always: while going and while lodging, in life and in death. In what amounts to a change of identity, from Moabite to Israelite (for there was as yet no formal procedure or even the theoretical possibility for religious conversion), Ruth adopts the people and God of Naomi. Religion was bound up with ethnicity in biblical times; each people had its land and its gods (cf. Mic. 4:5), so that to change religion meant to change nationality. Boaz recognizes the enormity of this in 2:11. Ruth is apparently totally accepted when she comes to Bethlehem, but the narrative continues to refer to her as "the Moabitess."

1:19–22, Arrival at Bethlehem. Naomi's return after her long absence creates a stir. She contrasts her name, "Pleasantness," with her present condition, deeming it inappropriate. The motif of emptiness/fullness finds expression in v. 21. Indeed, Naomi is now empty but will be fulfilled at the end of the story. The land, however, which had been emptied by famine, is now enjoying the barley harvest. The harvest sets the scene for the action in the next chapter.

2:1–23, Ruth Gleans in the Field of Boaz

2:1, Boaz. A new character is introduced. As in the case of the other characters, first his status and family connection are given, finally his name. The meaning of "Boaz" is obscure, although it has been explained as "In him there is strength." More important is the fact that he is a man of substance from Elimelech's family.

This chapter and the following one are each composed of three scenes: Ruth and Naomi at home, Ruth with Boaz, and Ruth returns home to Naomi.

2:2, Ruth and Naomi at Home. Ruth tells Naomi that she is willing to go out to glean in the fields. Gleaning is a form of charity in which the poor are permitted to gather the grain left by the harvesters (cf. Lev. 19:9; 23:22; Deut. 24:19). This underscores the poverty of Naomi and Ruth's willingness to support her.

2:3–17, Ruth with Boaz. Ruth happens on the field of Boaz (but readers sense that this is more than coincidence). At this time she does not yet know of Boaz or his relationship to the family. She appears throughout this section as hardworking, humble, and grateful for her good fortune.

Her fortune is indeed good, for Boaz accords her a number of special privileges in an incremental progression. She is invited to glean in his field for the entire harvest instead of moving from estate to estate; the male workers are warned not to bother her; and she is permitted to drink from the workers' water. Later she is invited to share a meal with the harvesters; they are ordered to let her glean among the sheaves, are cautioned not to shame her, and are even told to pull out stalks for her from the bound sheaves.

Most significant is the way in which the relationship between Ruth and Boaz develops. Boaz first refers to Ruth as "a young woman" and then addresses her as "my daughter," the same term used by Naomi, suggesting that Boaz feels a paternal protection toward Ruth. Ruth is at first surprised to have been singled out, since she is

Opposite: Scenes from the story of Ruth; Ruth gleaning after reapers in the field during the barley harvest (*bottom*) and Ruth with Boaz (*top*); illustration from the *Admont Bible*, ca. A.D. 1130–1150.

a "foreigner"; a wordplay is involved in v. 10: the words "take cognizance of" and "foreigner" are from the same root, nkr. Then, in v. 13, Ruth addresses Boaz as "my lord" and refers to herself as "your maidservant, even though I am not [worthy of being] one of your maidservants." Ruth and Boaz both change their terms of reference, raising Ruth's status vis-à-vis Boaz, but on different planes. Ruth takes herself from foreigner (to whom Boaz has no obligation) to maidservant (to whom Boaz has some obligation); Boaz's terms for Ruth move from "young woman" (neutral) to "daughter" (family). This process will culminate in chap. 3.

2:18–23, Ruth Returns Home to Naomi. The first turning point of the story is reached as Naomi learns that Ruth has gleaned in Boaz's field and Ruth learns of Boaz's family connection. Even before learning Boaz's name, Naomi blesses the one who has taken cognizance of Ruth (using the same term that appeared in 2:10). When she hears that it is Boaz, Naomi blesses God, "who has not abandoned his *chesed*," and she tells Ruth that Boaz is a relative, in fact, a go'el, a redeemer or family protector. Naomi encourages Ruth to accept the invitation to remain in Boaz's field throughout the harvest.

The go'el, usually translated "redeemer" or "next of kin," is one legally responsible for protecting the interests of the family. His main obligation is to buy land that must be sold or buy back land that has already been sold, so as not to let property be alienated from its original line of ownership (cf. Lev. 25:25; Jer. 32:7–10).

3:1–18, At the Threshing Floor.

As in the previous chapter, there are three scenes, the second being the longest and most important. The tension escalates as the relationship between Ruth and Boaz develops.

3:1–5, Ruth and Naomi at Home. This section parallels 2:2, but here it is Naomi who takes the initiative. She seeks "security" for Ruth, meaning a husband, as she did in 1:9. "Boaz our kinsman with whose girls you were" is immediately juxtaposed, forcing Ruth and the reader to view Boaz not as a father/master, but as a potential husband. Naomi does not call Boaz "our relative" or a go'el, as in chap. 2, but "our kinsman," as the narrator did in 2:1 when introducing Boaz. Naomi continues by outlining a plan whereby Ruth will approach Boaz at night at the threshing floor. The nature of this meeting is left ambiguous; there are undercurrents of a sexual encounter mixed with matters of family business and propriety.

3:6–15, Ruth with Boaz. During the harvest season the grain was threshed in the evening wind at an appropriate spot in the field and then guarded to prevent damage or theft. For this reason, Boaz was lying at night at the threshing

265

floor. Ruth, doing as Naomi told her, approached him and "uncovered the place of his feet" (this may be a euphemism). It was perhaps Naomi's intention that Ruth should make her presence known to Boaz after he had eaten his dinner and lain down, but before he had fallen asleep. Boaz, however, does not become aware of Ruth until about midnight, when he is startled to find a woman "at the place of his feet." He asks, "Who are you?" a direct request for personal identification, in contrast to "Whose young woman is this?" in 2:5, which seeks to put Ruth in her family context. Naomi uses the same phrase, "Who are you?" in a different sense in 3:16. Ruth's response to Boaz is significant but difficult to interpret: "I am Ruth your handmaid; spread your skirt/wing over your handmaid for you are a go'el." Ruth has raised herself from "maidservant" (2:13) to "handmaid" and has come to seek Boaz's protection in his role as go'el. "Spreading the skirt/wing" means taking one under protection, into the family; it recalls the same phrase used by Boaz in 2:12 in reference to God's protection. It is not clear whether Ruth is specifically proposing marriage here or not.

Boaz responds to this potentially embarrassing situation by making it seem that Ruth is doing him a favor rather than the reverse. He declares Ruth blessed (as Naomi did Boaz in 2:20) and views her coming to him as another, even greater, act of chesed. Indeed it is, for it shows that Ruth's actions were not motivated by selfishness, but out of family solidarity. Boaz adds that Ruth is a "worthy woman" (Heb. 'eshet chayil), and by using this term he equates Ruth's status with his own; the narrator had used a counterpart term meaning "man of substance" (Heb. 'ish gibbor chayil) to describe Boaz in 2:1. Ruth is no longer a servant or a daughter, but a woman fit to marry Boaz. The major turning point of the story has been reached.

But just when we think a happy ending is in sight, we are told that there is another go'el, a closer kinsman who has a prior claim. Boaz bids Ruth "lodge [here] tonight"—this is the first time that Ruth has not "lodged" with Naomi, as in her declaration of 1:16—and promises to clear up the matter of who will act as go'el. He sends Ruth home early in the morning, thus protecting her reputation, and again provides her with food.

3:16–18, Ruth Returns Home to Naomi. Naomi greets Ruth with the words "Who are you?" meaning "What has happened? Has your status changed?" As before, Ruth tells Naomi what has transpired, emphasizing that the grain was sent especially for Naomi, for Boaz had said, "Do not return empty-handed to your mother-in-law." There is no record of his having said these words; Ruth wants to reinforce Naomi's positive image of Boaz as caring for the family. Naomi expresses her confidence that Boaz will expedite the matter of the redemption.

4:1–17, Go'el, Marriage, Progeny. The other go'el, left nameless in the story, is located by Boaz at the city gate, the commercial center of the town, and apprised in the presence of witnesses of the legal situation. The legal situation is complicated and puzzling. First of all, we are informed for the first time that Naomi has put up for sale or has already sold land that belonged to Elimelech. The go'el would have the first option, indeed the obligation, to buy it. The nameless go'el is willing to do his duty in the matter of the land but is put off by a further complication. According to Boaz, the go'el who acquires the land also acquires the obligation to perpetuate the name of the deceased on his inheritance. Now this sounds like the law of the levirate, in which the widow of a man who died childless marries the brother of the deceased so that their firstborn may perpetuate the deceased's name (Deut. 25:5–10). If the transaction narrated in 4:1–12 is a form of the levirate, however, it is a form at variance with Deut. 25:5–10, which pertains only to the brother of the deceased. Neither Boaz nor the nameless go'el is the brother of Mahlon (nor apparently of Elimelech, despite Boaz's use of the phrase "our brother, Elimelech"), and therefore neither would be obligated to marry Ruth. Whatever the precise legal background may be, Boaz's obscure warning in 4:5 has the happy effect of dissuading the primary go'el from acquiring the land, so that when Boaz marries Ruth, as seems to have been his intention since 3:11, he, Ruth, and their children retain possession of the family inheritance. Unless one accepts an emendation in the text of 4:5, there is no mention in this verse of marriage. When Boaz makes his legal declaration in 4:9–10, however, he acquires both the land and Ruth as a wife. He has thus extended his role as go'el beyond the norm and thereby matches with his chesed the family loyalty already manifested by Ruth.

An ancient legal practice validating the transfer of real estate is noted in 4:7–8. Apparently it was no longer practiced by the time the book was written or edited. The removal and transfer of the shoe is an added confusion with the loosening of the shoe in the ceremony of rejection of the levirate (Deut. 25:9–10).

Wishes for progeny and communal status are given; they express the continuity with the patriarchs, hopes for many children, and continued prominence in Bethlehem. A more specific connection is made with Tamar and Judah because Boaz (and David) is a descendant of Judah; and through Ruth, as through Tamar, the family lineage is rescued and perpetuated.

A son is born to Boaz and Ruth. He is Naomi's comfort and fulfillment and the family's continuity and protector. Naomi takes him to her bosom and the women of the town proclaim "A son is born to Naomi." This helps to keep Naomi a central character; this is the culmination of Naomi's story no less than Ruth's.

4:18–22, The Davidic Genealogy. A brief genealogy listing three generations from Obed to David concludes the action of the story (v. 17). This is followed by a longer, more formal genealogy beginning with Perez, the son of Judah, and ending ten names later with David. Boaz occupies the significant seventh position. There is no mention of Mahlon, "the name of the deceased." There is no consensus on whether this genealogy was part of the original story or a later addition. In either case, it serves to focus on David, either to explain and legitimize David's ancestry or to legitimize a wonderful story about otherwise obscure people by linking them to the great national hero.

Bibliography

Beattie, D. R. G. *Jewish Exegesis of the Book of Ruth*. Sheffield: JSOT Press, 1977.

Berlin, A. *Poetics and Interpretation of Biblical Narrative*. Sheffield: Almond, 1983.

Campbell, E. F. *Ruth*. Anchor Bible, 7. Garden City: Doubleday, 1975.

Gordis, R. "Love, Marriage, and Business in the Book of Ruth." *A Light Unto My Path: Old Testament Studies in Honor of Jacob M. Myers*. Philadelphia: Temple University Press, 1974. Pp. 241–64.

Rauber, D. F. "Literary Values in the Bible: The Book of Ruth." *Journal of Biblical Literature* 89 (1970): 27–37.

Sasson, J. M. *Ruth, A New Translation with a Philological Commentary and a Formalist-Folklorist Interpretation*. Baltimore, MD: Johns Hopkins University Press, 1979.

1 SAMUEL

ROBERT L. COHN

INTRODUCTION

Literary Analysis

The identification of the First Book of Samuel as a separate book derives from the Septuagint (LXX), in which Samuel and Kings are each divided into two parts and together constitute the four "Books of Kingdoms." Hebrew tradition, on the other hand, did not recognize 1 Samuel as an individual book until the printed edition of the Bomberg Bible of 1517. Thus the literary analysis of 1 Samuel apart from 2 Samuel is necessarily truncated, for the two books were transmitted and canonized together. But, by the same token, analysis of 1–2 Samuel apart from 1–2 Kings is incomplete, because 1–2 Kings completes Samuel's story. In short, every literary unit in the Bible grows in meaning from the ever larger literary contexts in which one considers it.

Although the division of Samuel into two books may seem artificial, 1 Samuel does possess its own literary logic, which begins with the birth of Samuel and ends with the death of Saul. In fact, the book falls clearly into two parts centering upon these two figures: chaps. 1–12 chart Samuel's career from his birth to his farewell address; and chaps. 13–31 start with the notice of Saul's reign and conclude with the account of his death. But this division is not rigid: Saul is introduced as early as chap. 9 and Samuel continues to function after chap. 12. Yet these appearances are subordinated to the stories of Samuel and Saul, respectively. Similarly, the second account of Saul's death in 2 Samuel 1 properly forms part not of Saul's story, but of David's. Unlike the first account of Saul's death in 1 Samuel 31, the second account is presented not as an objective narration but as a post factum, tendentious report by a messenger to David. Only in 2 Samuel 1, after Saul's death, does David function independently—in 1 Samuel he is regarded always as the servant of Saul and his story is always subordinated to Saul's.

At the same time, we must not overemphasize the break between the two parts of 1 Samuel. The narrative strategy of the book depends upon the weaving of stories of successors into the lives of their predecessors: Samuel's into Eli's, Saul's into Samuel's, and David's into Saul's. In each case the narrative aims to reflect God's readiness to provide new leadership for his people as old institutions and individuals fail. With a sense of historical evolution as well as ideological revolution, the narrative of 1 Samuel moves us in stages toward the Davidic dynasty.

Composition

The classic theory of composition of 1 Samuel, fully articulated by Julius Wellhausen, perhaps the greatest critical scholar of the Bible in the nineteenth century, divides the book into an early promonarchical source and a late antimonarchical source. The opposition of these two sources is most visible in the account of Saul's accession to kingship (chaps. 8–12), in which Samuel's strenuous opposition to the people's request for a king is interwoven with his enthusiastic support for Saul. Later theories insist that the source division is far more complex, that more than two sources are represented, and that compilation and redaction took place in several stages.

The final stage is the most evident. Most scholars agree that the last hands to work on 1 Samuel belonged to Deuteronomists, those anonymous writers and compilers of the books beginning with Joshua and ending with Kings that tell the story of Israel's life as a nation in its land. Unlike other parts of this Deuteronomistic History, however, 1–2 Samuel seems not to have been much edited or expanded in this last stage. The strict structure and formulaic introductions and conclusions so apparent in Judges and Kings are lacking here. Yet certain characteristic Deuteronomistic features surface: for example, the rehearsal of Israel's history of disobedience culminating in the need of a decision for or against God (1 Sam. 12:6–25) and the oracle against a "house" by a "man of God" (1 Sam. 2:27–36). If the Deuteronomists made only minor repairs to the materials of 1 Samuel, it was because those materials already fit their agenda well. True to the Deuteronomic understanding of the covenant, these pre-Deuteronomistic traditions showed how Saul's disobedience to God's command eventually led to his destruction, while David's faithfulness was rewarded by God. Furthermore, these materials subordinated the "secular" leaders to the word of God as mediated by the prophet Samuel.

Most scholars also agree that the materials in 1 Samuel came from originally independent narratives such as the tales of the Ark, the Saul cycle, and the rise of David. The Ark narrative appears to have been an Israelite version of a common ancient Near Eastern type of tale about captured deities wreaking havoc upon the enemy captors. The Saul cycle likely arose among partisans of Saul eager to champion his political cause and his military prowess. Only as a result of this cycle's combination with the David materials did Saul become a pitiful psychotic with no chance of success. The romanticized story of David's rise from a shepherd of sheep to a shepherd of God's people may have been composed during his reign to legitimate him against strong opposition or may be part of a much later attempt to underscore his exemplary qualities.

Between these earliest materials and the Deuteronomistic redaction, there must have been other contributions to what became 1 Samuel, but here there is less agreement among biblical scholars. One popular view posits a prophetic history in which the earliest materials were arranged in three sections: the story of Samuel (chaps. 1–7), in which the prophet Samuel replaces the priest Eli as the leader of all Israel; the story of Saul (chaps. 8–15), in which the prophet Samuel acts as both king maker and king breaker; and the story of David's rise (chaps. 16–31), in which God chooses his own king whom the prophet Samuel anoints privately (chap. 16) and, finally, confirms to Saul (chap. 28). In this history the prophet functions as sole intercessor even after the kingship is established with God's blessing. This focus on the prophet's role may reflect a northern Israelite perspective rather than the perspective of Jerusalem where dynastic succession was well established. According to this view, the prophetic history nicely served the purposes of the Deuteronomists.

Importance

1 Samuel documents momentous changes in the character of the Israelite polity that took place roughly between 1050 and 1000 B.C. The book traces the beginnings of monarchy, the central institution of Judah and the cause of and the evidence for God's blessings upon Israel. It shows how this institution, which many from the very outset must have perceived as alien to Israelite identity and to the covenant tradition of early Israel, came to be not only accepted by Israel but embraced by God. The book depicts the difficult transition from rule by charisma to rule by dynastic kingship by showing the inadequacy of judge, priest, and prophet to provide the stability necessary for national development. The book also explains the difficult problem of why, despite God's approval in principle of monarchy and his selection of the first king, that king failed and a new

start had to be made under David. Saul is shown as a foil to David, who can do no wrong for he alone is the man after God's own heart.

The treatments of the central personalities of the book constitute paradigmatic studies in the highly nuanced biblical vision of the relationship between divine control and human initiative. Thus Samuel, Saul, and David are all "chosen," but they exercise their freedom under God very differently. Samuel protests the people's rejection of him to God but carries out God's order to anoint Saul king. Saul sees himself caught between the demands of the God who chose him and those of the people he rules and shows what happens to a leader who gets his priorities reversed. David's success depends on both God's favor and his own acumen; the complex interrelationship between these forms much of the dynamic of the engaging David cycle. So leadership under God has many human faces. 1 Samuel reads as a work deeply sensitive to the uses and abuses of human power and to the abiding ineluctability of divine election.

COMMENTARY

1:1–12:25

The Life of Samuel

The first part of 1 Samuel focuses on the life of the prophet Samuel, taking us from his birth (chap. 1) to his farewell speech (chap. 12). After chap. 12 the spotlight shifts to the first king, Saul, although Samuel plays a supporting role until his death in chap. 25. Samuel functions as priest, judge, and prophet—a kind of composite of premonarchical leadership roles. Like Moses, in whose image he is in many ways drawn, he intercedes with God on behalf of Israel. Although he surrenders his governing role to the king, his intercessory role remains crucial. Indeed, the books of Samuel are written not from a royal but from a prophetic perspective that accepts the institution of monarchy but is critical of individual kings. Although the torch is passed to Saul and then to David, the book is rightly named after Samuel.

1:1–4:1a

The Coming of Age of Samuel

Unlike the accounts of many biblical figures who claim our attention only after they assume leadership, the story of Samuel, like those of Moses and Samson, begins before his birth. In this section the young and maturing Samuel is contrasted with the old and decaying Eli to underscore the dramatic new leadership Samuel will bring to Israel. The narrative heightens the contrast by opposing the piety of Samuel's parents to the corruption of Eli's sons. The climax of the section is reached in the first and only encounter of Samuel and Eli—when they come to terms with the invasive divine word that officially launches Samuel's career.

1:1–2:11, Samuel and His Parents. The story of Samuel's birth establishes both the piety of the family from which he hails and the reason that he, like Moses, comes to grow up in the house of the one he will displace. The tale begins with an unhurried narration aiming to root Samuel firmly in Israelite tradition both genealogically (1:1) and gynecologically (1:2), for like Isaac, Jacob, and Samson he is born of a long-childless mother. Next, Elkanah's piety is indicated by the description of his annual pilgrimage to Shiloh and by the special sacrificial portion that he reserved for his beloved but barren wife Hannah. The verb forms in 1:7b signal the end of the parenthetical background (1:4b–7a) about Elkanah's yearly ritual and the beginning of the story's action. Thus, the tale starts: "One day when Elkanah sacrificed . . . [Hannah] wept and did not eat" (1:4a, 7b). Despite Elkanah's compassionate response to her (1:8), Hannah now turns to God to pray for a son. Eli sees her, and the narrator, by contrasting our privileged view of Hannah's behavior with Eli's external observations, makes Eli look obtuse. Yet the priest reacts generously to Hannah's explanation, though she reveals nothing of the content of her prayer and vow. Ironically, the petition that he blesses will directly impinge upon him and his house. Eli is thus introduced as decent but lacking in-sight, a characterization that subsequent events will confirm.

Having devoted considerable attention to the tradition of the plight of the barren but beloved co-wife, the narrator swiftly telegraphs the conception and birth of the long-desired son (1:19b–20). No ordinary conception this but a joint venture, for after "Elkanah knew Hannah his wife, the LORD remembered her." His "remembering her" here means more than mere memory; it suggests the common northwest Semitic notion of a god's kindly treatment of a suppliant. Note that there is no "annunciation"; God enters the story not through speech but conception. Hannah alone knows what she had prayed for, and she alone sees the child as an answer to that prayer. The focus thus falls on Hannah's faith expressed both in the meaning of "Samuel," the name she gave the child ("because from the LORD I have asked him," 1:20), and in her fulfillment of her vow (1:21–28).

The emphasis on Hannah's piety continues in the narrative of the presentation of Samuel to Eli (1:21–28) and in the prayer following (2:1–10). The narrative is told from Hannah's perspective—Elkanah is identified as "her husband" (1:22, 23) and Samuel as "her son" (1:23). Refusing to accompany "the man Elkanah and all his household" to Shiloh, she stays behind until she weans Samuel and is ready to deliver him to the priest. Then alone she treks to Shiloh and confronts Eli again. Elkanah is noticeably absent as Hannah returns to God at Shiloh what she received from God at Shiloh. Only at the very end of the scene do we hear that Elkanah was there too (2:11), a silent partner as his wife fulfills her vow and puts her son in the service of God.

The psalm that Hannah prays (2:1–10), usually regarded by critics as a late insertion, serves well to conclude Hannah's story and to preface the books of Samuel, for it celebrates the divine justice that reverses human expectations. It looks back to the barren woman (2:5) who has given birth, and it looks ahead to the king (i.e., David) whom God will empower (2:10). The movement of 1–2 Samuel is nicely encapsulated in the inclusio formed by the word "horn" in the first and last verses of the psalm: the poet begins with Hannah's good fortune ("my horn is raised up in the LORD," 2:1) and ends with the success of the king ("and he will raise up the horn of his anointed one," 2:10). As an expression of Hannah's thanksgiving, the psalm thus also sets the theme of the entire book.

2:12–36, Eli and His Sons. We turn from a tale of a mother's triumph to one of a father's tragedy; Eli's woe follows hard upon Hannah's joy. The narrator identifies the sons of Eli (whose names were mentioned earlier [1:3]) as "sons of Belial" (2:12), a derogatory epithet meaning "perverse" that Hannah earlier disclaimed in responding to Eli's charge (1:16). Next their habitual sin is detailed: they flout the "law of the priests" (2:13; stated here in legal rhetorical form) by greedily demanding the sacrificial meat and denying God his due.

By means of juxtaposition the narrator contrasts these "young men" (Heb. na'arim), sinful in "the LORD's sight" (pene Yhwh, 2:17), with the "boy" (na'ar) Samuel, who ministers "before the LORD" (pene Yhwh, 2:18). Indeed the reports about little Samuel's physical and spiritual growth (2:11, 18, 21, 26; 3:1) punctuate this tale of the corruption of Eli's sons. As Eli's natural sons degenerate in our eyes, his "adoptive" son blossoms. Meanwhile Samuel's natural parents have not abandoned him. The narrative stresses Hannah's ongoing maternal concern by mentioning her annual visits and gifts to her son (2:19). Hannah exits from the narrative with a notice of her remarkable fertility (2:21) preceding the report of Eli's sons' fornication (2:22).

Eli finally learns of his sons' perversity not from his none too keen observation but from the people. In both the narration (2:22) and in Eli's own words (2:23–24), the text stresses that Eli does not *see* himself but *hears* from others about his sons. Clearly he is not in control of his own family, let alone of his people. And his protests to his sons fall on deaf ears (2:25), deaf because God has his own plans for them. Eli asks his sons, "But if it is against the LORD that a person sins, who will pray for him?" (2:25). Though Eli asks the question rhetorically to condemn his sons, the answer ironically is hinted at in the next verse. There we are reminded that "the young man Samuel grew and prospered, with the LORD and with people" (2:26) at the same time that Eli's sons are sinning against people and God. Though there is no help for Eli's sons, Samuel will act precisely as intercessor later in the narrative by praying for the people. That Eli cannot even imagine such intercession is a sure indication that new leadership is needed.

The end of this unit (2:27–36) is an oracle against the house of Eli by an unnamed man of God. Its length and style identify it as a contribution of the Deuteronomistic writer eager to show God's tight control over events (cf. 1 Kings 13). This oracle appears to look ahead to Saul's massacre of the Elide priests of Nob (1 Sam. 2:31; cf. 22:6–23), the escape of Abiathar alone (2:33; cf. 22:20–23), and Solomon's banishing of Abiathar from Jerusalem (cf. 1 Kings 2:26–27). Here Eli is held directly responsible for his sons' behavior (1 Sam. 2:29), so that God appears justified in decimating and demoting Eli's house. To confirm the accuracy of these long-range predictions, a short-range sign is offered: the death of Eli's two sons on the same day (2:34; cf. 1 Kings 13:3). So when these two degenerates next appear (1 Sam. 4:4), we know that their days are numbered. Hannah's song echoes in this oracle: one house will be cut down and a faithful priest raised up (2:35). But though we expect Samuel to be this new priest —indeed, the narrator reiterates his priestly behavior immediately following the oracle (3:1)— events belie our expectation. The oracle rather looks ahead to the installation of Zadok and his house to replace the deposed Abiathar (cf. 1 Kings 2:35).

3:1–4:1a, Eli and Samuel. With Samuel's parents blessed and Eli's sons cursed, the text now turns to the encounter between the two principals. The pregnant stillness of the first verse hints that that encounter will be climactic: neither divine word nor prophetic vision breaks through these days. Eli, already shown as blind to his sons' deeds, is now physically blind as well. But it is not quite dark for Samuel—or for

Israel—because the lamp still burns. The old man lies sleeping while the young lad is awake to the word of God. There is a comic touch to this scene: God speaks while his appointed priest sleeps and the young man Samuel races between them trying to figure things out. Just as Eli misread the meaning of Hannah's moving lips, so too does he misunderstand the source of the persistent voice Samuel is hearing. But similarly, just as he accepts Hannah's explanation, so now he accepts God's judgment against his house (3:18). God's oracle here is like a précis of the one in chap. 2, and again Eli is held responsible for his sons' misdeeds.

The chapter ends with the solution to the problem stated in 3:1. There "the word of the LORD was precious" and Israel lived with divine silence. But now Samuel becomes a channel for the word of the LORD and his reputation spreads throughout the land. So although Eli and his sons still live, they are no longer in control. The center of gravity has shifted to Samuel.

4:1b–7:17

The Philistine Interlude

But Samuel does not take over directly. In this section Samuel is depicted as a "judge" (7:15) who, following the pattern in the book of Judges, saves Israel from its enemies. Thus the Philistine defeat of Israel (4:10) precedes Samuel's assumption of leadership of an Israel leaderless for a formulaic twenty years (7:2). This section begins with Israel's loss to the Philistines and old Eli's death (4:10–18) and ends with Israel's triumph over the Philistines under Samuel's leadership (7:3–14). Between defeat and victory the scene shifts to Philistine territory for the tale of the adventures of the captured Ark of the covenant. This originally independent narrative, in which neither Shiloh nor Samuel figures, is fit into the space between the end of Eli's priesthood and the beginning of Samuel's judgeship. With clear allusions to the story of the plagues in Egypt, this narrative humorously shows God's power within the enemy camp in preparation for the Ark's "exodus" and Israel's victory under Samuel.

4:1b–22, The Defeat of Israel. Two tragedies are interwoven here: the national and the personal. Israel goes down to the Philistines (4:1–11), and Eli and his daughter-in-law die, though for different reasons, as a result (4:12–22). Linking the two tragedies is the Ark of the covenant. The report of its capture by the Philistines occurs midway through this unit and both caps the defeat of Israel and precipitates the death of Eli (→ Philistines). The chapter begins with the unexpected slaughter of Israelites by the Philistines (4:2) and the elders' call for the Ark (4:3), which was believed to ensure Yhwh's presence in the battle. Lest there be any doubt about this motivation, the narrator calls the Ark by its full name: "the ark of the covenant of the LORD of hosts who is enthroned upon the cherubim" (4:4). Ominously, though, the already cursed (2:34) sons of Eli accompany the Ark to battle.

In 4:6 the scene shifts to the Philistine camp where we see the Philistine reaction to the Ark. In their benighted pagan way they assume that Israel is polytheistic, but they do correctly identify the Ark with incomparable divine power. The identification of these "gods" with those that plagued the Egyptians (4:8) foreshadows the plagues that will soon strike the Philistines themselves. By stressing the Philistines' great fear of God, expressed in their emphatic direct address (4:7–9), the author allows them to defeat the Israelites but does not compromise God's power.

Meanwhile back at Shiloh Eli awaits word of the battle (4:13), "watching," though, we soon discover, he cannot see (4:15). In a scene calculated to draw out the tragic effect of the new bad news, the messenger first informs the city and only then approaches Eli (4:14). Then he repeats his credentials twice as if trying to avoid what he is about to say (4:16). At last he gives his report (4:17), but he reverses the chronological order of the last two disasters as given by the narrator (4:11). Though his intent may be to soften the blow, the climactic news that the Ark has been captured topples Eli and kills him. Not his sons' death but the Ark's capture pushes him over the edge; our last view of him is again as a pious though powerless priest. And the narrator concludes his life with the formulaic conclusion of a judge's reign (4:18), for, from the Deuteronomistic perspective, every major figure between Joshua and Saul was a judge.

In a kind of human interest footnote to the death of Eli, the author recounts the impact of the events on Eli's daughter-in-law. Only after Hophni and Phinehas are dead are they differentiated by the information that Phinehas is survived by a pregnant widow. The narrator reverses the order of disasters yet again, putting the death of her husband last (4:19). And though we might think that it is this personal tragedy that sends her into premature labor and sudden death, her own last words suggest otherwise. She names her son Ichabod in memory of the lost Ark (4:21) and mourns its capture as she expires (4:22). This sad little incident hammers home the overriding tragedy we have just witnessed.

Finally, it should be noted that Yhwh is completely silent in this chapter. The loss of the battle and the Ark are not attributed to him, nor is his purpose clear in permitting his Ark to be captured. Israel could have suffered for the sins of the house of Eli in some other way. So though the scene ends in death and desperation, we anticipate some explanation for this strange turn of events.

5:1–12, The Hand of God upon the Philistines. That explanation is not long in coming, for our attention is now directed to Philistine country and the manifestation of God's power against the Philistine god Dagon (5:1–5) and against the Philistine people themselves (5:6–12). The first evidence that the capture of the Ark did not signify the humbling of Yhwh comes in a mock battle with Dagon. The Ashdodites, who are shown to understand the Ark as Yhwh's physical representation, set it up beside Dagon in his temple to symbolize Yhwh's honoring of Dagon's might (5:2). But, comically, Dagon is twice found toppled, the second time with hands and head cut off (5:4), a mutilation motif known from Canaanite mythology. Only the results of the battle are reported, not the battle itself, because for a biblical author Yhwh's battle with an idol could only be a mock battle. Yet it is clear both to the Philistines and to us that Yhwh had defeated Dagon just as he defeated Pharaoh, the symbol of the gods of Egypt. And lest there be any doubt, the doubling of Dagon's downfall (5:3, 4), just like the doubling of Joseph's dreams, guarantees that the occurrence was no accident (cf. Gen. 41:32).

Having punished the god, Yhwh turns to punish the people by striking the Ashdodites with plague. A phrase commonly used to refer to plague, "the hand of the LORD was heavy," encloses the action (1 Sam. 5:6, 12; cf. Exod. 9:3; Hab. 3), but here control by the LORD's hand underscores his cutting off of Dagon's hand. The nature of the plague is not altogether clear. The Masoretic scribal tradition read "hemorrhoids" for the written "swellings" (5:6). But the LXX includes a verse here that tells of mice swarming upon the land from the Philistine ships. The combination of mice and swellings has suggested to commentators bubonic plague carried by rats and often spread among seacoast cities. In any case, the later fashioning of both golden tumors and golden mice (6:4, 5) would seem to presuppose a plague involving both.

The Ark is rapidly passed from Ashdod to Gath to Ekron, and by implication, to the other Philistine cities—Ashkelon and Gaza—as well (see 6:17), bringing tumors and death wherever it goes. Prominent are the cries of fear and desperation of the Philistines (5:7, 8, 10–11) who, like the Egyptians before them (cf. Exod. 12:30–33), want to rid their land of the source of the plague.

6:1–7:1, The Return of the Ark. Just as the biblical storyteller delighted in elaborating the ironic predicament of the Philistines smitten by their prize trophy, so too he relishes detailing the careful plan that the Philistines prepare for returning it. Bypassing the fallen and powerless Dagon, they ask their priests for aid (6:2). The priests respond with an extraordinarily lengthy plan (6:4–9) for sending back the Ark, but also with a test to determine if the source of the plague is really the god of Israel. They propose a "reparation offering" (6:3) to accompany the Ark back to Israelite territory. The five golden tumors and mice serve, on the one hand, as a sacrifice that decontaminates Philistine territory (hence, the need for a new cart and unyoked cows) and, on the other hand, as a payment of tribute symbolically representing the five Philistine lords and their cities. The priests further determine that if the young postpartum cows can, unnaturally, ignore the cries of their newborn calves and proceed without guidance to Beth-shemesh, then it must be Yhwh's power in the Ark that leads them now and that caused the plague in the first place (6:7–9).

Prominent throughout this choral instruction is the parallel to the Exodus story. Thus, just as the Egyptians "sent forth" the Israelites with "golden vessels" (Heb. *kele zahab*; Exod. 12:35), so too the Ark is to be "sent off" with the "figures of gold" (*kele hazzahab*; 1 Sam. 6:8). Consciously too the priests recall the Egyptians as a negative example for their countrymen: they are warned not to harden their hearts and be made sport of, as the Egyptians were (6:6; cf. Exod. 10:2).

In 1 Sam. 6:10–16 we see the journey of the Ark and its reception in Beth-shemesh from the Philistine perspective. From their purchase on the border, the Philistines hear nothing; no Israelite dialogue is recorded. Instead, with the Philistines, we watch as the men of Beth-shemesh rejoice (6:13) and sacrifice (6:15). When the Philistines finish their observation and return home (6:16), we too can see nothing further and the scene ends. The appearance of levitical priests, anachronistically here, is probably a late interpolation suggested because Beth-shemesh was a levitical city (→ Levites; Priests).

After a formulaic conclusion and etiology (6:17–18), the story takes a surprising turn. In an epilogue (6:19–7:1), some number of Israelites are slain for looking into the Ark. The tale then ends with a question that points to the theme of the whole: the Ark and its god are not to be taken for granted, owned as a prize possession. The naked power of Yhwh will strike out at Israelite and Philistine alike. So the Ark is sent off to Kiriath-jearim, a town on the border of Judah, Dan, and Benjamin, and put in the charge of someone especially consecrated to care for it. That way, presumably, it will pose no danger. But then, Yhwh would also seem to be set at a distance. To solve this new problem, Samuel reemerges.

7:2–17, Samuel's Intercession. Balancing Israel's defeat at the hands of the Philistines in chap. 4 is Israel's victory over the Philistines here. While the house of Eli fell then, now the star of Samuel rises. And, not coincidentally, Samuel names the place of victory Ebenezer (Heb., "stone of help"; 7:12), the name of the site of the earlier slaughter (4:2, 10).

This unit begins with the predicament of the Ark apparently out of commission and Israel mourning God's absence. Into this scene comes Samuel who initiates a ceremony with Deuteronomistic trappings of a covenant renewal: the disposal of Canaanite icons, a water-pouring rite, the people's admission of guilt, a sacrifice, and prophetic intercession. Samuel's order to put away the foreign gods recalls Joshua's covenant renewal at Shechem (Josh. 24:14), while his care in offering the sacrifice contrasts sharply with the practice of the sinful sons of Eli. Samuel's intercessory role is spotlighted here. "I will intercede on your behalf," he announces (1 Sam. 7:5). He becomes the answer to the question that for Eli was unanswerable (2:25): "Who will intercede for the sinner?" The scene seems to continue the pattern of the book of Judges—apostasy, punishment through the agency of an enemy, cry to the LORD, and deliverance by a judge—though here apostasy follows, not precedes, divine abandonment. By successfully enlisting God's aid, Samuel accomplishes what neither Eli's priesthood nor the Ark could: the elimination of the Philistine threat.

The concluding narration (7:12–17) stresses Samuel's continued intercession: "and so the hand of the LORD was against the Philistines all of Samuel's life" (7:13). Thanks to Samuel, the equilibrium lost when the house of Eli fell apart is restored. Finally, the summary of Samuel's functions and regular circuit (7:15–17) telescopes the rest of his life in preparation for our next view of him as an old man. But also the report of his successful "judging" of Israel sets a backdrop against which the people's demand for a king to "judge" them and fight for them (8:20) appears unwarranted.

8:1–12:25
Samuel Prepares for His Successor

The lion's share of narrative space devoted to Samuel concerns his relationship with his successor, Saul, just as most of Saul's story is enmeshed with David's. The problematic of the book of Samuel is the quest for godly and durable leadership in Israel, so that the transitions between leaders prove to be the flash points of

273

narrative interest. In this section the issues surrounding the introduction of kingship to Israel are brought together. While some circles in Israel regarded this institution as necessary and desirable, others saw it as a threat to inherited tribal traditions. Both perspectives are represented in this section. Sources favorable to Saul are sandwiched in a narrative quite hostile to monarchy. Together they form a five-unit bloc, alternating between anti-king and pro-Saul views. As a result monarchy emerges as an institution fraught with ambiguity. Born out of human rebellion, it is nonetheless supported by God; kingship may bring disaster but also salvation. Samuel appears in this seesaw story as both bitter lame-duck leader and joyful patron of his successor.

8:1–22, The People Request a King. Wayward sons in the Bible frequently bring ruin upon their fathers' houses (e.g., Ham, Abimelech, Absalom), but here the repetition of the motif first with Eli's sons and now with Samuel's points to a larger literary scheme. Just as Eli's two sons abused the priesthood and led to Samuel's judgeship, now Samuel's two sons pervert justice and provoke the people's request for a king. A new order—the monarchy—is about to emerge.

The unit centers on Samuel's lengthy harangue on the evils of kingship (8:10–18). It is bracketed on either side by dialogues in which Samuel intercedes between the elders' demands and God's responses (8:4–9, 19–22). The elders speak as representatives of the people as a whole who will later appear en masse to reap the fruits of the negotiations (10:17–27). Although judicial corruption provides a reasonable motive for the elders' request for new leadership, their blunt style and revolutionary demand conspire to make Samuel the more sympathetic figure. The narrator's neutral comment about Samuel's age (8:1) becomes in their mouths crude and cruel ingratitude when addressed to the man whose intercession had kept the Philistines at bay for a generation (8:5). Moreover, when they request a king "to judge us like all the nations," they show themselves eager to cast off their unique role as God's special people (cf. Deut. 17:14–15). Samuel's reaction reveals for the first time in his story a fragile ego stung by rejection. What reportedly irks Samuel is not the threat to the covenant, the desire to mimic the nations, but only the threat to himself, expressed in the words: "Give us a king to judge us" (1 Sam. 8:6). God rejoins gently that it is not Samuel but he whom the people have rejected. The allusion to the Exodus (8:8) aligns the people's request with an unbroken series of apostasies reaching back to the beginning of Israel.

Samuel's recitation of the excesses of royal rule (8:11–18) begins and ends with ironic jabs at his audience. At the outset he calls his speech "the justice of the king" (8:11) yet details only injustice. And he concludes with the reminder that all this tyranny will be brought to you by "your king whom you have chosen for yourselves" (8:18). Many scholars have argued that this litany of deprivations and persecutions actually reflects the hardships suffered under Solomon and that the passage is a late Deuteronomistic composition. Yet opposition to monarchy as such never again surfaces in Deuteronomistic writings. Moreover, the royal corruption depicted here matches that of Canaanite kings from as early as the Late Bronze Age (ca. 1500–1200 B.C.). So it is more likely that this picture represents the view of those circles who, from the beginning, opposed monarchy, even if our text bears later Deuteronomistic markings.

The unit concludes with the elders' reiteration of their demand and God's reiteration of his order to Samuel to do what they say. God appears reluctant but resigned to the change in leadership, but Samuel, by again seeking God's reassurance, reveals his abiding resentment.

9:1–10:16, Samuel Privately Anoints Saul. Juxtaposed to the account of God's concession to popular outcry stands a folktale about God's gracious provision of a king for his people. With the elders' carping plaint still reverberating, the narrative cuts away to a quiet pastoral scene and the charming story of a man who, in search of his father's lost asses, finds a kingdom instead. This story comes at kingship from a different angle: Samuel is depicted not as national judge but as local seer, not threatened by kingship but embracing God's chosen. Kingship here is all God's idea, not the people's. Unlike chap. 8, in which we saw events through Samuel's eyes, this story proceeds from Saul's point of view. The difference in perspectives is the key to resolving the apparent conflict between the two tales. Saul lacks the readers' privileged access to the elders' request or knowledge of Samuel's pique. Saul experiences only Samuel's solicitude and God's onrushing spirit.

The tale begins with Saul's pedigree (9:1), syntactically identical to the one given Samuel (1.1), but continues not with a birth story but with the mature Saul. This initial parallel marks Saul as, in some sense, Samuel's equal and prepares us for the role about to be thrust upon him. And Saul's distinctive good looks give him a further credential for leadership. The action proper is narrated through Saul's perceptions: we hear his father sending him out (9:3), follow his journeys (9:4), share his anxieties (9:5, 7), and search for an unnamed seer (9:11–13). Only when Saul and his servant actually arrive does the narrator intrude with Samuel's name (9:14) and reveal that Saul's quest for the seer is reciprocated by Samuel's search for him.

Throughout, Saul appears quite childlike, following the lead of others. Initially his servant, presumably his inferior, soothes his anxiety, leads him to the seer, and supplies the gift for him. Then he submits without a word to the instructions of Samuel (9:22–10:8), who dominates the rest of the unit. Although in the tradition of Moses (Exod. 3:11) and Gideon (Judg. 6:15), he questions Samuel's acclamation of him (1 Sam. 9:21), he silently follows Samuel to dinner, to sleep, and to his anointing. The elevation of this simple man is yet another enactment of the lyric of Hannah's song.

If Saul's star is rising, Samuel's is falling. Because he is seen from Saul's perspective, Samuel here lacks the judicial, executive, or military functions he wielded earlier. Samuel only anoints and predicts signs to confirm the legitimacy of the anointment. In fact, before he even appears in this chapter, he is demoted by the very terms used to refer to him. First, the servant tells of a "man of God in this city" (9:6), that is, a local clairvoyant. Then the narrator, in an explanatory gloss (9:9), tells us that the figure formerly called "seer" (Heb. ro'eh) is in his day called "prophet" (nabi'). Both terms get deflated in the story. Saul's concern that "we bring" (nabi') a gift to the man of God (9:7) defines the term (by the play on the unrelated homonyms) as one who receives gifts for his services. And though the maidens drawing water call Samuel a "seer," he does not "see" very well. Pointedly, the narrator tells us, "The LORD had opened the ear of Samuel" (9:15), not the eye, to tell him of Saul's arrival. And even when Samuel sees Saul (9:17), he does not recognize him until God expressly identifies him. Samuel then looks rather ludicrous as he proclaims, "I am the seer" (9:19). The seer of this story sees only what God tells him to see; Samuel here functions purely as an instrument for God's elevation of Saul to "king designate" (nagid).

From the perspective of this unit, monarchy derives exclusively from God's compassion. God's first words to Samuel (9:16) echo that earlier summons to Moses before the Exodus. There too he "saw" his people and "heard their cry come up to me" (Exod. 3:9). Now the Philistines are the new Egyptians, oppressing God's people and calling forth God's salvation. Saul is a new Moses. Monarchy here presents no challenge to the ancient traditions; it simply fulfills God's promise to his people to be with them. The "king designate" takes his place in a long line of divinely chosen saviors, not, as in the previous chapter, as the symbol of the people's latest rebellion against God. The hand of God lurks here in subtle ways too: a coin is found to give to the prophet (9:8) and maidens appear to point the way to the seer (9:11–13). But these are no chance occurrences. The onrush of God's breath upon Saul confirms to him

all that Samuel has told him. Indeed, to all present he becomes another person (10:11–12), no longer recognizable as the "son of Kish" but as an ecstatic to be identified in terms of his prophetic "father" (the leader of a group of prophets).

As positive as the story is toward Saul, it leaves us wondering just a bit about what the future holds. Saul has been anointed privately as nagid (Heb., "king designate") but the public "election" as melek ("king") still lies ahead. And Samuel's warning that Saul must wait at Gilgal for seven days for Samuel to come to offer sacrifice raises the specter of trouble ahead in light of Saul's already demonstrated childlike behavior. The unit is rounded off by a return to the problem that launched it, the lost asses of Kish, and Saul's assurance to his uncle that they had been found. With the note on Saul's silence about his anointment, the narrator prepares us for the public selection in the next unit.

10:17–27, Samuel Orchestrates the Public Selection of Saul as King. Verses 17–27 may originally have followed upon 8:22. There the elders have been dispersed to their cities to convey Samuel's response to their demand for a king, while here Samuel assembles "all Israel" at Mizpah to execute that demand. The negative view of the king resumes here: again God interprets the people's request for a king as their rejection of him (10:19). At the same time, the intervening positive view of Saul comes into play. Again Saul is described, this time from the point of view of the people rather than the narrator, as the tallest among them (10:23), and Samuel acclaims his uniqueness (10:24). Moreover, those who accompany Saul, enspirited by God, are called "sons of valor," while those who denigrate him are termed by contrast "sons of Belial [wickedness]" (10:26–27).

Yet the interweaving of positive and negative perspectives lends an ironic tone to the whole. Though the selection of Saul by lot indicates God's direct hand in the matter, in other stories the casting of lots determines not a hidden hero but a hidden sinner whose sin has brought divine wrath upon the whole people (e.g., Josh. 7; 1 Sam. 14:24–45). Then too at the crucial moment our champion, Saul, is nowhere to be found: is his hiding a sign of the modesty or of the childish fear that we saw earlier? And does Samuel's acclamation of Saul's greatness after the people drag Saul into the open (1 Sam. 10:24) carry a sincere or a sarcastic tone? These ambiguities are the inevitable result of the dovetailing of pro-Saul and anti-king traditions.

The unit ends with two final ambiguities that point ahead to a rocky future for kingship. The narrator alludes to Samuel's dire warnings of "the justice of the king" (8:11) when he tells of Samuel's writings of "the ways of the kingship"

(10:25) in a book. Second, the wicked fellows' question, "How will this one save us?" raises questions about Saul's abilities before they are even tested. That question casts a giant shadow over the subsequent story of Saul's reign.

11:1–15, Saul Demonstrates His Leadership. Having been demanded by the elders at Ramah, privately anointed by Samuel in his city, and publicly selected by lot at Mizpah, Saul is now popularly acclaimed as king at Gilgal. Like colonial American cities each claiming that "George Washington slept here," important Israelite shrines preserved traditions connecting them with Israel's first king. One only wonders why no tale naming Bethel, Samuel's other haunt (7:16), is extant. But these tales have been transformed into a single linear narrative subordinating Saul to Samuel. In this unit that aim is most blatant, for Saul hears of the plight of Jabesh-gilead and responds to it quite without Samuel's intervention. Yet Samuel's name is included with Saul's in the rally cry to battle (11:7), and it is Samuel who leads the people to Gilgal to proclaim Saul's kingship. At every stage of this extended accession of the first king, the prophet Samuel remains in control; indeed, in the next unit (chap. 12), he has the last, and a foreboding, word.

Because the Philistines would seem to be the major threat to Israel (9:16), this tale of Saul's initial victory over the Ammonites comes as a surprise, and for that reason it probably has a historical basis (cf. Judg. 11; 1 Sam. 12:12; 31:11–13). The purpose of the tale is not to chronicle a battle but to demonstrate Saul's leadership. The tale fits the pattern of those of the "judges" and incorporates elements of holy war ideology. The enemy threat calls forth a hero empowered by God's spirit to muster the tribes and lead them to total victory. The pattern is broken, however, by the unlikely weeklong reprieve given Jabesh by the Ammonites (11:3), a respite that gives the author time to dramatize the transformation of Saul from farmer to general. The conclusion to the war also breaks the pattern, this time definitively, for now the judge becomes king. In triumph Saul appears magnanimous, demanding amnesty for those who doubted him (11:13) and thus winning total support.

12:1–25, Samuel's Farewell Address. The last unit in this section ends the extended narrative about the beginning of monarchy on a sober note and concludes as well the era of the "judges," for Samuel, the last judge, takes leave of his people. This lengthy sermon and valedictory address marks Samuel's last public appearance, and he takes the occasion both to review Israel's history and to lay out the options that lie ahead. In terms of the larger Deuteronomistic

History, this speech thus constitutes a major structural pivot between two different periods.

The first verse resumes the language of 8:7: Samuel reminds the people that kingship was all their idea, not his. He proceeds to extract from them a confession that he was an honest and honorable leader undeserving of their rejection. Against the backdrop of Samuel's justice, the people's demand for a king again appears ungracious. Having established his own unblemished leadership, Samuel recalls all of the "righteous acts" of God. Specifically, he alludes to those of God's salvific acts that featured heroes whom he deems his predecessors: Moses and Aaron, Jerubbaal, Bedan (perhaps another name for Jephthah), and Jephthah. The series ends with Samuel naming himself in the third person (12:11) as the final deliverer before kingship begins. This slip into the third person points to the author's intention: to punctuate his history with the career of Samuel, the last of the old order.

With the "and now" of 12:13, the speech shifts into the present and the choices that will determine the future. In Deuteronomistic language Samuel sets forth the people's choice: obedience to "the commandment of the LORD" or disaster (12:14–15; cf. Deut. 30:15–20). To prove his contention that the people have sinned in requesting a king, Samuel calls for divine confirmation in the form of an out-of-season thunderstorm. Struck by this miracle the people for the first time admit their sin (1 Sam. 12:19). Yet precisely at this point Samuel turns the tables and offers comfort and hope. Despite their sin, he promises, God will not forsake them, and he, Samuel, will continue to pray for them. So this speech envisions an important ongoing function for Samuel and his prophetic successors during the monarchy: as intercessor and instructor (12:23) he is not replaced by the king but remains superior to him.

Samuel's swan song, though antimonarchical in its general thrust, nonetheless looks ahead to kingship with hope in God's continued faithfulness toward Israel and the prophet's continued intercession on Israel's behalf. Samuel's last word on kingship is thus more moderate and positive than his first. The intervening narrative, which looks at kingship from several different points of view, issues in this cautious look ahead.

In summary, the combination of "pro" and "anti" perspectives on kingship in 1 Samuel 8–12 created a wholly new examination of the beginnings of monarchy. Although the positive view of Saul in 9:1–10:16 and 11:1–15 would seem to contrast sharply with the negative view of kingship we saw in 8:1–22; 10:17–27; and 12:1–25, in these "anti" units not the person of Saul but the institution of kingship is attacked. Only the wicked "sons of Belial" challenge Saul himself (10:27). Conversely, in the "pro" passages, where Saul is viewed as a savior, the institution of kingship as such is never discussed in general terms. It presents no threat because it is taken for granted, not viewed as a novelty. The effect of this combination is to place the hero Saul in an ambiguous position, the first incumbent of an institution hedged about with question marks. Ironically, it will be the institution and not the hero who survives.

13:1–31:13
The Reign of Saul

The second part of 1 Samuel spans the career of Saul as king but is principally concerned with his relationship to David. Although Saul does not die until the last chapter, God's rejection of him at the outset casts a pall over his reign. The subsequent anointment of David sets the two on a collision course that runs through nearly every chapter. One finds only sparingly in this narrative the political, military, social, and demographic details that would be necessary to reconstruct a rudimentary picture of the early monarchy. Instead, one finds a story of two giant personalities caught up in a struggle of love and power that sends Saul spiraling downward and leaves David positioned to assume control.

13:1–15:35
The Beginning of the Fall of Saul

The reign of Saul begins with three successive tales in which disobedience to an order exposes his foolishness and leads God to reject him. While in the previous section not Saul but the institution of monarchy was attacked, here Saul proves a failure while monarchy persists. Saul's ritual infractions may seem on a first reading minor, hardly weighty enough to justify his punishment; God may appear to be looking for a pretext to depose Saul. Yet the sequence of errors suggests habitual behavior unbefitting God's chosen. Still, with the deck seemingly stacked against him from the start, he remains a sympathetic character.

13:1–22, Samuel Condemns Saul. The historian's difficulty in chronicling Saul's reign is pointed up in the formulaic verse with which the story of the first king opens, for the crucial age and regnal years have been dropped in transmission. This inauspicious opener is followed by the troubling report of a victory against the Philistines by Jonathan, as yet unidentified, for which Saul apparently takes the credit (13:3–4).

Next, sandwiched between accounts of Philistine might comes the first of the three episodes depicting Saul in a compromised position (13:8–15). The extended description of Israelite fear in the face of overwhelming Philistine power (13:5–7) gives teeth to the explanation that Saul gives Samuel for his failure to wait for the prophet's arrival (13:11–12). Moreover, the narrator is careful to point out that Saul did wait the seven days as Samuel had commanded and that Samuel appeared only afterward, just in time to condemn the king: "And so as he was finishing the offering of the burnt offering, here comes Samuel!" (13:10). Saul eagerly greets Samuel and responds to his question unaware, it seems, of any guilt; his response to Samuel's harsh words of judgment can only be shocked silence.

On the one hand, it is almost as if the old Samuel is eager to abort the term of a successor he never wanted. Saul's sin hardly seems grievous enough to warrant God's rejection. On the other hand, because Saul did not keep the "appointment," or commandment (Heb. *mitzwah*) of God, God is justified in "appointing" (*wayetzawwehu*) a successor to him (13:13–14); the word play clinches the connection between the two acts and thus the justice of Samuel's charge. At this point, however, we sympathize with Saul, who seems to have followed the commandment and broken it at the same time.

The rest of the unit returns to narration about the Philistine might. We see Saul and Israel staying put while the Philistines send troops in several directions at once. Then the narrator flashes back to explain that the Philistine monopoly on iron prevented the Israelites from fashioning swords and spears. In light of Saul's inaction and Israel's weakness, the courage of Jonathan in the next chapter stands out even more sharply.

13:23–14:46, Jonathan's Valor and Saul's Folly. In this second episode of Saul's kingship, Saul looks bad again, this time in contrast to his son Jonathan. While Saul sits encamped under a pomegranate tree, Jonathan wreaks havoc behind the Philistine lines. When Saul at last goes to battle, he precipitously utters an oath of vengeance that nearly destroys the heroic Jonathan.

The focus on Jonathan in this chapter shows us the man who could succeed Saul were his kingdom to continue. But since we already know that Saul's kingdom will not survive (13:14), Jonathan, whose bravery and popularity clearly exceed his father's, becomes a poignant figure. The episode begins with the first identification of Jonathan as Saul's son (14:1) and thus as a logical candidate for succession. Already a victor in war with only half as many troops as Saul (13:2–3), Jonathan now sets off on a solo expedition to break the deadlock with the Philistines. While Jonathan is accompanied in this daring act over rough terrain (14:4–5) by only his armor bearer, Saul, with six hundred troops, sits motionless. Saul, it is noted, has with him a priest from the rejected house of Eli (14:3), not an associate to inspire our confidence. As he sets out, Jonathan shows himself appropriately pious, again in contrast to Saul. While Saul countermanded Samuel's order for fear of desertion by his troops, Jonathan righteously affirms that God can save with many or few. Moreover, he waits for a sign from God before proceeding (14:8–12). Saul, on the other hand, having called for the Ark (or the ephod, according to the LXX) before battle, dismisses the priest and marches out without knowledge of God's will (14:18–19).

Although Saul's rashness does not lose the battle for him this time, his next impetuous act nearly costs him his son: he lays a curse on anyone who eats before he defeats the Philistines (14:24). Jonathan, who speaks rather pompously and disparagingly of his father after unwittingly disobeying his father's order (14:29–30), places the onus of guilt squarely upon Saul. And the altar that Saul builds, pointedly the very first (14:35), does little to assuage our growing sense that Saul cannot redeem himself.

Flushed with victory, Saul decides, again rashly, to pursue the Philistines to the last man (though, ironically, in the very next chapter he will fail to follow God's order to do precisely this to the Amalekites). This time he does inquire of God, but God does not respond because of the curse brought down by Jonathan's sweet tooth. After the casting of lots points to Jonathan as the culprit, the confrontation between father and son exposes sharply their contrasting personalities. Without apologies or excuses, the righteous Jonathan tells what he did, albeit in a manner that makes ludicrous both Saul's order and his own willingness to die: "I surely did taste with the tip of my staff in my hand a bit of honey; here I am ready to die" (14:43). But Saul, missing the irony, is adamant that he shall die. Saul is determined to follow strictly his own rashly taken oath, yet he has interpreted God's commandments freely and will do so again. Finally, the soldiers intervene on Jonathan's behalf, acclaiming his victory and charging Saul with stupidity. Saul departs without a word, though clearly humiliated, having surrendered to the people's will as he will again in the next episode—with grievous consequences for himself.

14:47–52, Summary of Saul's Reign. Abutting this unflattering view of Saul are two positive reports about Saul's military achievements (14:47–48, 52) bracketing a short family tree. Again we are reminded that in the eyes of some, Saul did valiantly despite the general negative

impression we get from the episodes. The final author has positioned this regnal summary, however, not at the end of the Saul narrative but close to the beginning, between two tales of Saul's recklessness. In so doing he suggests that the reign of Saul is, for practical purposes, over. The narration also serves the purpose of introducing members of Saul's family soon to come into play. Finally, the mention of Saul's victory over the Amalekites (14:48) connects this summary to the subsequent story, which views that battle differently.

15:1–35, God Rejects Saul. In this unit Saul's poor judgment, which we have seen twice already, seals his doom. By failing to execute the *cherem* (Heb.; → Ban) against the Amalekites, Saul directly contravenes God's command and merits God's rejection. Yet the matter is not quite so simple: Saul is no villain and Samuel, who pronounces his fate, is not just a mouthpiece for God. In the complex dialogue between the two principals, we see the anguish of two men caught between the divine will and their own freedom.

The episode begins with God's uncompromising demand for extermination of the Amalekites, a sacred duty that rightly falls upon the first king who has defeated his enemies round about (14:47; cf. Deut. 25:17–19). With the imperatives of 1 Sam. 15:3 stated in the singular, there can be no ground for misunderstanding—or the excuses that Saul will later give. Dutifully, Saul sets out for battle, but mercifully he pauses to send the Kenites away (15:6). Although this thoughtfulness would seem to be unimpeachable, it is just that kind of independent judgment that, we next discover, has led Saul to "have mercy upon" (*wayyachmol*) not the women and children as we might expect, but the king and the best of the livestock and "upon all the good things" (15:9). Saul has utterly subverted God's commandment of *cherem* by taking the good things instead of devoting them to God.

God reacts by repenting of his choice of Saul as king, but Samuel, crying all night, apparently takes Saul's side. While Saul builds a self-congratulatory monument (15:12), Samuel approaches to deliver a devastating critique. In his subsequent dialogue with Saul, Samuel repeatedly offers him a chance to confess his sin, but obdurate Saul fails the test.

Saul treats Samuel's initial question (15:14) as a request for information rather than for confession. And in his answer he shifts the blame for capturing sheep and oxen to the people and takes personal credit for executing the *cherem*—this in pointed contrast to the narrator's objective report that Saul and the people together did the sparing (15:9). Saul altogether fails to mention Agag and invents out of whole cloth a supposed sacrifice to the LORD for which the livestock have been reserved. To Samuel's second set of questions (15:19), Saul responds in a similar way, this time claiming total personal obedience and heaping all the blame on the people. Given every chance to confess, Saul, unlike Jonathan in the previous episode, mounts a cover-up.

With keen psychological insight Samuel diagnoses Saul's problem: he is "little in [his] own eyes" (15:17), the victim, we might say, of an inferiority complex. When Saul finally does confess, he confirms this judgment in admitting that "I feared the people and obeyed their voice" (15:24). For the third time in three chapters we see Saul giving in to the people's wishes, following them rather than leading them, putting his public image before his responsibility to God, who alone is to be feared and obeyed. Saul's confession comes too late, however—only after Samuel, in formally metered couplets, has announced his verdict (15:22–23). In fact, though, Saul has condemned himself: since he was willing to kill Jonathan for unwittingly breaking his own oath, how much more so does he deserve punishment for knowingly defying God's order?

Saul, realizing that all that is left to him is the appearance of royalty, asks for Samuel to accompany him, but Samuel initially refuses. As God's spokesman he reiterates mechanically his reasons: you have rejected God, so he has rejected you (15:26); just as you have torn my robe, so has God torn the kingdom from you (15:28). His revenge upon Agag he explains with similar bloodless logic: as you have made women childless, so shall your mother now be (15:33). Yet, in the end, Samuel's sympathy for his favorite wins out and he consents to honor him (15:31). The last verse of the chapter confirms that Samuel's prophetic duties have not diminished his abiding love for Saul.

16:1–18:30
David in the House of Saul

Having rejected Saul, God wastes no time in finding a successor to him. This time, though, the king is unambiguously God's man; the people have no voice in his selection (16:1). David's resounding successes make us wonder whether Saul's failure was God's way of rejecting the people's choice. In this section David is twice introduced to Saul, who twice takes him into his house. As musician David appears sensitive and intellectual, while as warrior he shows bravery and faith in God. These qualities endear him to Saul's son Jonathan and daughter Michal. By the end of the section, David has established formal bonds with both, but he has also earned the undying jealousy of Saul.

16:1–13, Samuel Anoints David. Despite his reluctance, Samuel sets out at God's command to find a replacement for Saul. Whereas

Saul came to Samuel as if by accident, Samuel sets out purposefully to find David, thus underscoring God's greater initiative this time. Yet the anointing scene seems calculated to stress the similarities between Saul and David to show that David is indeed the proper successor. Both anointings are secret: in the case of David, even he is not told why he is anointed and his kingship remains hidden until Saul is dead. Both Saul and David are of similar social station before they are chosen. Saul claims to be of the least important tribe and clan (9:21) and is found while searching for his father's asses. David is the youngest of Jesse's sons and tends his father's sheep. The motif of the youngest or least likely who becomes the greatest clearly replays Hannah's song. Like Saul, David must be brought in from the wings to be anointed; neither seeks the position suddenly thrust upon him.

In this tale the power of Samuel continues its eclipse. Just as his ability as a "seer" was mocked in the story of Saul's anointment, here he wrongly assumes that the first son of Jesse upon whom he lays eyes must be God's choice, apparently because of his physical resemblance to Saul (16:6–7). God chastises Samuel for relying solely on outward appearance, yet when David is chosen, it is precisely his good looks that the narrator describes (16:12). Whether David, unlike Saul, has inner as well as outer substance only time will tell.

16:14–23, David Comforts Saul. Immediately following the rush of God's spirit onto David (16:13) comes its departure from Saul (16:14), as if it fled directly from one to the other. Ironically, the inheritor of the divine spirit is brought in to soothe a Saul possessed by an evil spirit also "from the LORD." More ironic still, he succeeds and wins Saul's gratitude and love. While David is described so promisingly as a sensitive artist and military warrior (16:18), Saul is pictured as pathetically unstable. As he was once led by his servant to the prophet Samuel, who held the key to his future, now he is directed by another young man to David, who has inherited that future.

17:1–54, David Defeats Goliath. Just as 1 Samuel provides multiple perspectives on Saul's initiation into kingship, so too it offers several introductions of David. First he is anointed by Samuel, then brought to the moody Saul, and now celebrated as the victor over Goliath and introduced again to Saul. Twice as long as most other chapters, this one tells its story at a leisurely pace developing folktale motifs and including traditions missing in many Greek manuscripts (17:21–31; 17:55–18:5).

17:1–10 presents the Philistine enemy personified in the ten-foot-tall Goliath, whose fearsome appearance and military equipment are described in more detail than those of any other biblical combatant. His fierce challenge panics the Israelites (17:8–10) but, remembering Hannah's proclamation that God punishes the arrogant (2:3–4), readers already anticipate Goliath's downfall.

Next the text backtracks to introduce David, the challenger-to-be. Emphasized here are David's youth, his simple shepherd life, and his obedience to his father. Striking also is the echo of the Joseph story (Gen. 37:12–14), for there too the father sends the youngest son off to the older brothers and asks for word from them. Just as Joseph provokes resentment, so does David, and just as Joseph eventually triumphs, so, biblical logic predicts, will David.

In his first speech in the Bible, David reveals the two sides of his character, which the rest of 1 and 2 Samuel will develop. As he becomes acquainted with the dire straits of Israel, he displays his bravery and devotion to God, but not before he twice inquires about what is in it for himself (17:26, 30). In resolving, then, to challenge Goliath, David has determined to win the battle for God but also for the hand of the princess. He accomplishes both aims. David's practical and devotional dimensions are also revealed in his encounter with Saul. To convince Saul of his ability to defeat Goliath, the untrained David naively relates to the king his practical experiences protecting his father's flocks from lions and bears. But it is only when David invokes God's protection (17:37) that Saul responds. Unable to wear Saul's armor, David symbolically refuses to play Saul; he is his own man and this is his battle.

In this battle the verbal duel is more important than the military maneuvers. To Goliath's taunts about David's primitive weapons, David responds with a resounding proclamation of God's ability to save without any human weapons at all. Like the plagues on Egypt, this victory has an ulterior motive, "that all the earth may know" (17:46) God's power (cf. Exod. 9:14). Having declared his faith, David—and the narrator—make short work of Goliath.

17:55–18:30, Saul's Recognition and Jealousy of David. In this unit various traditions have been structured into a thrice repeated pattern of two parallel episodes and a narrated summary about David's successes and popularity. The first sequence features the separate introductions of David to Saul and to Jonathan. Although Saul's ignorance of David's identity would seem to contradict 16:14–23, in which Saul already knows David intimately, the interest here is to legitimate David as a victorious warrior acclaimed by the king. Together that episode and this one show David fighting Saul's inner and outer battles. For his part, the brave Jonathan finds in David a kindred spirit. The language of love used to describe their relationship is found frequently in ancient Near Eastern texts to describe the loyalty of king and subjects, so here there are likely both personal and political connotations. Importantly, Jonathan gives David his clothes and armor, and David wears them, symbolically assuming the role of crown prince.

After a summary about David's success (18:5), the second pair of episodes sketches Saul's abrupt change of attitude toward David. In the first, Saul reacts jealously to the adulation of David the warrior by the young women of Judah. His inner thoughts are given voice (18:8) to show us that he already intuits what the future holds: "only the kingdom is not yet his!" In the second episode this quite rational fear takes the form of irrational "prophesying," the raving of a man possessed (18:10), and he lashes out, ironically, at the man whose music formerly soothed his spirit. The second summary statement is more pointed than the first. Now we are told specifically that the Lord was with David (18:14) and that the people "loved" him (gave him their allegiance), while Saul stood in awe of David's success.

The third repetition of the pattern features two stories of Saul's efforts to do away with David without bloodying his own hands. Saul promises each of his daughters to David in return for David's victories against the Philistines, though he really intends for David to die at the Philistines' hands (18:17b, 21a, 25b). Though at an earlier stage of tradition the story likely told how David, through marriage to the king's daughter, established a rightful claim to inherit the loyalty of the northern tribes, in its present form it aims to develop the theme of Saul's jealousy and his unsuccessful effort to destroy David. By the end, David has won from Saul his own son and daughter leaving the king isolated. The final summary raises the tension to the breaking point. Now the desperate Saul "saw and knew that the LORD was with David" (18:28), and he is even more afraid than he was before. The three summaries thus map the rising tide of Saul's realization and concomitant fear of the enemy in his own court and of his recognition of God's hand in it all.

19:1–23:28
Saul in Pursuit of David

In this section Saul takes his vendetta against David into the open. But David has important allies—Saul's own son and daughter, the prophet Samuel, and the priest Abiathar—whose defection contributes to Saul's feeling of isolation. The pursuit is narratively orchestrated as a cat-and-mouse chase; we are led back and forth from Saul to David, from pursuer to escaper, but Saul never catches David. Instead we witness Saul's rising desperation until, in the next section, he becomes the one who is caught.

19:1–24, Jonathan, Michal, and Samuel Shield David from Saul.

Saul's public pursuit of David begins with four short episodes in which those people closest to Saul prevent him from killing David. First, Jonathan warns David of Saul's intention and then convinces Saul that to kill David would be to shed "innocent blood" (19:5). Importantly, Jonathan dissuades Saul from killing David by appealing to his sense of justice and by depicting David as God's agent against the Philistines. The next scene (19:9–10) virtually repeats 18:10–11 and is placed here to illustrate the wild and repeated fluctuations of Saul's mood. Saul, just reconciled with David through Jonathan's intervention, now erupts violently against him, not coincidentally just as David wins another victory against the Philistines. It was the popular adulation following David's earlier victories that initially set Saul against David. In the third episode Michal follows her brother's lead and intercedes to protect her husband from her father. Sending David out the window and, apparently, over the city wall, she improvises a dummy in David's bed out of the teraphim (household idols) and some goat hair. When her masquerade is discovered, she disclaims responsibility and places the blame on David. Michal here shows the independence that will later (2 Sam. 6) be turned against David himself.

The last scene picks up the story of the fleeing David who until now has not been credited with a single word; his friend and his wife have done his talking for him. But now David pours forth words to the prophet who had anointed him. In a popular folktale form (cf. 2 Kings 1), the text relates how Saul's attempt to seize David is frustrated as his messengers are repeatedly rendered useless by the contagion of ecstatic prophecy. Finally, Saul himself appears, but he too is possessed and unable to take David, who again escapes. This is the second time that the origin of the saying, "Is Saul also among the prophets?" is given an explanation. While the first story of ecstatic possession signaled God's choosing of Saul (10:6), this one, symmetrically, underscores God's rejection of him. Thus Jonathan by persuasion, Michal by deception, and Samuel by prophecy have deflected Saul's wrath. But from here on David is on his own.

20:1–42, David and Jonathan Part.

Escaping from the raving Saul, David returns to Gibeah for what turns out to be his parting rendezvous with his beloved Jonathan. Jonathan, whom we last saw successfully pacifying his father, appears stunned at David's new charge against Saul. While this seeming contradiction may be the result of the juxtaposition of different sources, it serves in the text as we have it to emphasize Saul's erratic behavior. In a lengthy conversation (20:3–23) David devises a scheme to test Saul's intentions and Jonathan decides how to inform David of them. At the literary center of this dialogue Jonathan sounds the theme that carries forward the rest of the book: the inevitability of David's kingship. Before agreeing to David's plan, Jonathan invokes the "chesed Yhwh," the mutual loyalty of those bound together in sacred covenant (20:14), to elicit an oath from David. Jonathan, not overcome by the emotions of the moment, makes David swear to protect his house after David has established himself. Again, after describing the secret message relayed with the arrows, Jonathan reminds David that the LORD stands "between" them, guaranteeing their fidelity (20:23).

David's absence from the new moon feast arouses, as he predicted, Saul's suspicions, and Jonathan's excuse for him provokes Saul to attack Jonathan himself with his ever-ready spear. But in the midst of his fury, Saul backhandedly affirms his son's affirmation of David's kingship, for he correctly sees that David's life is the price that must be paid if Jonathan is to assume the throne (20:31).

According to plan, the grieving Jonathan the next morning shoots the arrows beyond his servant to signal to David Saul's murderous intentions. But then, seemingly rendering the signal superfluous, he sends the servant home and embraces David directly. Again a splicing of sources is indicated, yet by having the bad news transmitted through a sign, the text allows the final scene between the two comrades to be a poignant leave-taking. Jonathan repeats his prayer that the Lord will stand between himself and David but extends their mutual loyalty to their progeny (20:42; cf. 20:23). Though they now part, God will continue to join them. On this pregnant note they go their separate ways, David to return only after Jonathan is dead.

21:1–22:5, David Flees from Saul.

From here on out David's path goes in two directions. At the same time that the narrative shows him fleeing from Saul, it has him edging closer to his own kingdom. As he escapes from the present crises, he prepares for the future. The featured story in the account of David's flight from Saul centers on David's use and Saul's abuse of Ahimelech, the priest of Nob and great-grandson of Eli. Arriving alone, hungry, and defenseless at Nob, David requests from the priest the two prerequisites of the successful fugitive: food and a weapon. But he does so with the aid of a verbal ruse to calm the nervous priest.

Ahimelech, believing him to be on a mission from Saul, gives him not just any bread and sword but, the story emphasizes, the holy bread and the sword of Goliath, symbolizing perhaps David's authority over the priesthood and the military. Placed strategically between David's two requests is the seemingly irrelevant but actually ominous note about the presence of Saul's mercenary, Doeg the Edomite, at Nob while David masquerades as Saul's trusted servant (21:7).

Filling in the time interval until Doeg reports to Saul about David's appearance at Nob, the text includes three more stations on David's path of escape. At the first, the Philistine city of Gath, David improvises his second masquerade (21:10–15). Preceded in Gath by his reputation as "king of the land," an ironic foreshadowing of his future position, David feigns madness to avoid capture. His behavior recalls the recent "prophecy" of Saul with the important difference that, whereas Saul was actually possessed, David is in full possession of himself. From Gath David goes to Adullam in southern Judah where he attracts a following of Apiru types (→ Khapiru) who will serve him as a personal army (22:1–2). Here clearly the text shows David with his eye on his destiny. Similarly, at his next stop in Moab he alludes to his future when he deposits his parents there in the care of the king "until I know what God will do with me" (22:3). As in the book of Ruth, here Moab serves as refuge for displaced Bethlehemites. The unit ends (22:5) with a prophetic word noteworthy both because it establishes David as the recipient of prophecy and because it directs David back to Judah and, ultimately, a confrontation with the king from whom he has until now fled.

22:6–23, Saul Slaughters the Priests of Nob. The scene now shifts to Saul, who eliminates his priestly support at the same time that David obtains his very own priest. In contrast to the ever-moving David, Saul now sits in state at Gibeah (→ Gibeah). Ranting on to the silent tribesmen surrounding him about their ingratitude and their conspiracies against him, he reveals his sense of utter isolation. Referring to David only as "son of Jesse" (22:7–8), Saul makes him into a distant, nameless enemy. Only Doeg the Edomite breaks the silence with his eyewitness account of the visit of "the son of Jesse" to Nob. But Doeg, while reporting nothing of David's ruse, adds the information that "Ahimelech, the son of Ahitub" inquired of God for David (22:10). The text seems to present Doeg with his own motivation for not telling the whole story, on the one hand, and adding an important fact, on the other. If Doeg had been forcibly detained at Nob (21:7), he may have had his own gripe against Ahimelech. By making it seem that Ahimelech knowingly conspired with

David against Saul and by stressing divine inquiry, Doeg baits Saul against the priest and his house. Indeed, in his report about Ahimelech, Doeg places divine inquiry in first position, because Saul is most threatened by David's having the access to God, which he now lacks. And Doeg, in contrast to Saul's again silent servants, readily slaughters the priests at Saul's command and executes, perhaps at the same time, his own revenge (22:18b–19).

The text describes the total destruction of Nob in precisely the same language as that of God's command to Saul to destroy Amalek (15:3). But while Saul failed to fulfill God's command to destroy the foreigners, he ruthlessly, through the foreigner Doeg the Edomite, fulfills his own order to slaughter Israelite priests. Saul's disobedience then and lack of humanity now come into sharper relief when seen in light of each other.

But if Saul is credited with destroying the priests, thereby fulfilling the prophecy of the man of God to Eli (2:27–36), David, with guilt on his conscience (22:22), promises to protect the one son of Ahimelech who escapes. Saul, rejected by the prophet Samuel, now has cut off his priestly link to God as well, while David has inherited both.

23:1–28, Saul Chases David. In this chapter Saul's actual pursuit of David is telescoped in two tales. While the king devotes all his energies to capturing David, David exercises the duty of a king by defeating the national enemy in battle. This is the point of the first episode in which David, not Saul, does battle on his own initiative against the Philistines and, like the judges of old, "saves" (23:2, 5) the Judahite town of Keilah. In this battle David apparently exploits the services of Abiathar (not, however, mentioned until 23:6), for he twice inquires of God before going into battle. In two further inquiries, he discovers the intentions of both Saul and the men of Keilah (23:11–12). The doubled questions and answers underscore David's reliance on God and God's support of David.

Saul meanwhile, bereft of priests and access to certain knowledge, gropes in the dark. First he plans to besiege Keilah, but David escapes. Then, responding to the Ziphites' voluntary offer to turn David over, Saul demands from them better reconnaissance, but David eludes him again. Saul's fruitless insistence on sure information (23:22–23) highlights the contrast with David who has such knowledge for the asking. Finally, a Philistine attack calls Saul away from his pursuit of David leaving the fugitive providentially reprieved (23:26b–28).

Between the two tales of David's escapes is placed the short episode of Jonathan's visit (23:14–18). Jonathan's encouragement thus occupies the literary center of the narrative of

Saul's manhunt. More explicitly than ever he predicts David's future as king and his intention to be second in command (Heb. *mishneh*, 23:17; cf. Esther 10:3). He also provides objective confirmation of Saul's increasing desperation, for he adds, "Saul my father also knows this." The cutting of a "covenant" concludes this last rendezvous of the intimate friends, just as it marked their first meeting (1 Sam. 18:3). In this chapter, then, God's assistance is mediated through oracles, through Jonathan, and ironically at the end, through the Philistines.

23:29–26:25
David Confronts His Enemy

After successfully eluding Saul, David turns the tables and twice confronts Saul and mercifully spares his life. Between these two scenes comes the episode of David and Abigail, which forms a narrative analogy to them. Again David refrains from taking vengeance and leaves his destiny in God's hand. Indeed, the lesson he learns from Abigail in chap. 25 prevents him from killing Saul in chap. 26, as Abishai urges him to do. In sequence the three tales show David's growing mastery of his emotions and willingness to put his fate in God's hands.

23:29–24:22, David Spares Saul's Life.
The first scene depicts an accidental encounter between pursuer and pursued in which David skillfully gains the upper hand. Discovering Saul preoccupied in relieving himself in the front of the cave where he and his men had been hiding, David cuts off Saul's skirt, symbolically emasculating him. Suddenly realizing that the man his men called "your enemy" (24:4) is, in fact, "the LORD's anointed" (24:6), David is stricken with remorse and prevents his men from killing Saul.

In the lengthy speech that follows David confronts Saul with the physical evidence of his mercy and innocence. Dramatically producing Saul's skirt, David challenges Saul to "see" (a verb repeated four times in 24:10–11) David's sinlessness and not to listen to hearsay reports about him. Forswearing vengeance, David declares his reliance on God's justice (24:12, 15). Saul's response is moving, for he humbles himself and declares David's righteousness. More importantly, he adds his voice to the growing chorus of those who acclaim David's future kingship (24:20).

25:1–43, David Saved from Bloodguilt.
Although the story of David and Abigail initially appears to be unrelated to the episodes of David's encounters with Saul, this story too shows David forbearing from murder and consequently acclaimed as future king. Perhaps the isolated notice of Samuel's death at the outset (25:1) is meant to account for the new dimension of David we see here. His link to kingship now deceased, David strikes out on his own, ready to take vengeance against those like Nabal who stand in his way.

Nabal, a rich but stingy rancher, refuses David's request for food in return for what David claims has been his protection of Nabal's flocks. Nabal appears as a one-dimensional character whose name, as in a morality play, describes him: *nabal* means fool or churl in Hebrew (cf. Isa. 32:5–8). Wholly a skinflint, he responds to David's politely worded plea (1 Sam. 25:6–8) with sarcasm. He stigmatizes David as a servant disloyal to his master (25:10–11), a charge that, ironically, will soon be applicable to one of his own servants, who takes up David's cause before Abigail.

Abigail is Nabal's opposite in every way. Introduced by the narrator as intelligent and beautiful at the beginning of the story (25:3), she remains in the wings until warned by Nabal's servant that David plans to attack her husband and his men. Then she emerges to use both her intelligence and her beauty to prevent David's revenge on her husband and win his heart for herself. Her lengthy, carefully crafted speech (25:24–31) to David is the centerpiece of the entire chapter. Sending tribute to David on ahead with her servants, she arrives alone ready to deal woman to man. Quickly she deflects attention from her husband, whom she dismisses as a crank, to herself, for she accepts the blame for Nabal's behavior (25:24–25). As a supplicant she then presents her gift and prophetically proclaims David's impending kingship. Because David fights "the battles of the LORD" (25:28), she says, his vendetta against Nabal is senseless; bloodguilt would destroy his stainless record (25:26, 31). Finally, having persuaded David of the folly of vengeance, she gives him a way to save face by making herself, not Nabal, the beneficiary of his change of heart (25:31). David responds exactly as Abigail must have hoped, for he blesses God and her as well and accepts her gifts in lieu of murdering Nabal's men, the "pissers on the wall" (25:34), as David none too delicately calls them.

The scene shifts abruptly to Nabal seen through Abigail's eyes. She returns home after her rendezvous with the future king to find her husband, whose life she has just saved, having a feast without her, ironically "like the feast of a king" (25:36). She saves her news until he is sober enough to appreciate it, the next morning when the fool who feasts like a king is just another "pisser" (25:37). His two-stage death allows for both natural and supernatural causation. David's reaction to the news of Nabal's death is no surprise, and Abigail, without a tear, responds to David's summons with the same alacrity she had shown twice earlier (25:18, 23, 42).

The tale aims not only to depict David's learning that revenge does not befit the LORD's anointed. As the final verses remind us, behind the story is the historical reality of David's cementing by marriage alliances with clans that will support him in his drive for power: Abigail, the widow of the Calebite chieftain, and Ahinoam, who may well have been none other than the wife of the reigning king, Saul (25:42–43; 14:50).

26:1–25, David Challenges Saul. The second account of David's sparing of Saul's life is usually identified by critics as another version of the one in chap. 24, but in its present context it plays a rather different role. It depicts a David more calculating and more in control than does the earlier story and a Saul stripped of all power and hope for the future. In this, their last meeting, David is cold and distant, challenging Saul to justify his conduct toward him but finally looking toward God, not the impotent king, for his reward.

The first verse replicates 23:19, but while in that episode it was Saul who sought reconnaissance to entrap David, here David sends out spies to pinpoint Saul's position. Earlier Saul chanced into the cave where David and his men were hiding (24:3), but here David plans his entrance into Saul's camp (26:6–7). Whereas in the first encounter David's remorse over cutting off Saul's skirt makes him prevent his men from killing Saul, here David coolly calculates that to slay God's anointed would be counterproductive. Here David seems more intent to demonstrate his own righteousness than to show mercy for the king. In detached third-person formality, David asks as he stands over the sleeping Saul, "For who can raise his hand against the anointed of the LORD and be guiltless?" (26:9). Alluding to the recent death of Nabal, David rather smugly declares that Saul too shall die in due course. While in 24:6 an impassioned David fumbles for the right words to prevent his men from attacking Saul, in 26:11 the same sentiment has become a cold formula.

David's control of the situation is underscored by the thrice repeated mention of Saul's slumber. First, from afar David sees Saul sleeping with his army surrounding him (26:5). Next, with Abishai, David enters the camp and approaches the sleeping Saul who lies unprotected, for his army too sleeps (26:7). Finally, as David and Abishai steal out of the camp, the narrator explains that this deep sleep was divinely sent (26:12), and we again see God's hand behind David's fortune.

When David does awaken Saul, he is far away atop a mountain. The physical distance between them now symbolizes their irreparable rupture. David taunts Abner and protests to the suddenly awakened Saul. Though Saul, as earlier, familiarly calls David "my son," David replies correctly, "my lord king" (26:13–17). David is finished reasoning with Saul: he declares and Saul must listen. David claims that Saul's pursuit has forced him into apostasy (26:19); he wants only to return to his own land and his God. Saul's confession and apology do not move David. David challenges Saul to reclaim his captured spear, but there is no indication that Saul retrieves it. As he captured Goliath's sword, so now he possesses Saul's spear; Saul is left defenseless. In David's final words he talks past Saul to God (26:22–24). In return for sparing Saul's life, David seeks protection not from Saul but from God. In his last words Saul blesses David, but David does not respond; it is too late to make amends (26:25).

27:1–31:13
Saul and David Part Ways

In this final section of 1 Samuel, Saul and David never meet. David escapes to Philistine territory and raids the enemies of his own tribe, Judah, all the while pretending to fight the battles of his overlord, the Philistine Achish. He thus establishes a power base in Judah for his rapid rise to kingship after Saul's demise. Meanwhile, Saul has abandoned his pursuit of David to fight the Philistines. But the ghost of Samuel warns him that the battle is lost, and the last chapter relates the predicted death of Saul. By alternating stories of David and Saul, the narrative communicates the simultaneity of the destinies of the once and future kings but also the contrast between those same destinies.

27:1–28:2, David Among the Philistines. Despite Saul's apology to David and blessing upon him, David does what he claims Saul has forced him to do (26:19) and seeks refuge among the Philistines. In this second flight to Achish he faces him not alone (cf. 21:10–15), but with his whole retinue; he need not fear and feign madness now. Instead, he feigns loyalty. Granted his own property by Achish, as favored servants often were in ancient Near Eastern city-states, David professes to return the favor by fighting Achish's battles. In fact, David raids the enemies of Judah including the Amalekites (27:8), the enemy against whom Saul failed to complete the *cherem* (15:9). This narration plays upon that memory, for David, under no command to execute the *cherem*, leaves no one alive anyway and brings back booty in addition. While Saul is condemned, David is implicitly praised, for he outsmarts the hated Philistines and Achish trusts him completely.

284

The narrative transforms what must have been an embarrassing historical memory—the defection of the future king to the enemy camp—into a piece of dramatic irony. David, who came to Saul's attention by battling the Philistine giant, now flees that attention as a soldier for the Philistines just at the time that Saul will meet his death at their hands. Yet David, it is claimed here, only *feigned* service to the Philistines. He thus escapes Saul and, as we shall see, any involvement in the battle that brought on Saul's death.

28:3–25, Saul Learns His Fate. Breaking into the account of David's success comes the story of Saul's nadir. Not coincidentally Samuel's death is again reported (28:3), for with David in the wings, the Philistines encamped against him, and God silent, the entrapped Saul has only Samuel to turn to. The text plays upon Saul's name, *wayyish'al sha'ul* ("and Saul asked," 28:6), to point up the irony that the one whose name means "ask" gets no answers from God. So powerless that he must break his own edict rather than revoke it, Saul disguises himself and goes to a necromancer still in the land and persuades her to practice despite her fear of the king.

The woman's success gives us a unique picture of an Israelite view of the dead and gives Saul confirmation of his worst fears. Samuel, enraged at Saul's summons, which the dead apparently cannot resist, responds by hinging two new predictions upon one old fact. He predicates disaster upon Saul's disobedience in the battle against Amalek. Now, finally, Saul hears explicitly what he has always known in his heart about David. Now too he knows that tomorrow is doomsday for him, his sons, and Israel (26:16–19).

The audition over, Saul falls prostrate "from the words of Samuel" (28:20). The woman had seen Samuel but not heard his words; Saul had heard the words but not seen the apparition (28:13–14). Starved physically, Saul is now crushed spiritually as well. Again the seeing of the woman is stressed, for it is Saul's appearance that prompts her to insist that he eat to revive himself. Like a condemned prisoner on death row dining on steak and champagne the night before his execution, Saul eats the fatted calf. The secret nocturnal visit over, Saul returns to his troops, and the narrator returns to the interrupted story of David among the Philistines (28:21–25).

29:1–30:31, David Victorious. Having prepared us—and Saul—for Saul's imminent demise, the narrator turns back to the story of David and Achish to explain how, despite his alliance with Achish, David had nothing to do with the Philistine defeat of Israel and the death of Saul. By repeating the phrase "And the Philistines gathered all their troops" (29:1), which preceded the episode of Saul's consultation with the necromancer at Endor (28:1), the text indicates the simultaneity of Saul's unsuccessful masquerade before the necromancer and David's successful bamboozling of Achish. As Saul is discovering that he cannot escape an ignoble end, David escapes from an uncomfortable vassalage to Achish and prepares for his new beginning.

Despite his own trust in David, Achish is forced by his allies to send David away from the battle and back to his fief at Ziklag (29:4; cf. 27:6). The irony of Achish's defense of David before the justly suspicious Philistines is highlighted by the innocent honesty of his words, "And I have not found in him a fault" (29:3). More ironic still are the gentle words with which Achish breaks the news to David. He amplifies his praise of David and downplays the Philistines' objections so as not to hurt him: "but in the eyes of the princes you are not so good" (29:6). And in response to David's feigned pique, in which David with intentional ambiguity expresses his desire to "battle against the enemies of my lord the king" (29:8), Achish compares the scheming David to "a messenger of God" (29:9). David submits without another word, rescued from having either to fight against Saul, God's anointed, or betray his new lord Achish. Instead he soon finds himself in a position to continue building his own power base by distributing gifts to his Judean countrymen (30:26–31).

Upon his immediate return to Ziklag, however, he confronts apparent catastrophe. Although we are told that it was the Amalekites who burned the city and took the women and children captive, David and his men see the result but must discover the source. Trusting in God (30:6) and summoning the priest Abiathar with the ephod, David begins that process of discovery. To David and, we remember, not to Saul the oracle speaks, and David sets out to pursue the as yet unidentified raiders. Further information is provided by the abandoned Egyptian slave who just happens to cross David's path. Whereas all avenues to knowledge are closed to Saul, David's way is strewn with clues. Whereas the battle against the Amalekites proved to be Saul's undoing, David's battle against the same people paves the road to his success. Far from being condemned for capturing the Amalekite flocks and herds, David is lionized and distributes the spoil both to his own men who stayed behind and to his countrymen whose support he will later need. The juxtaposition of Saul's pathetic, lonely last supper at Endor and David's triumphant, providential massacre of the Amalekites sets the stage for the final chapter in Saul's life.

31:1–13, Saul Defeated. With but a single line of direct discourse—Saul's request to his armor bearer to slay him—the author hurriedly sets the inevitable concluding scene. Whether the author understood Saul's suicide as a final show of force or a failure of nerve, Saul's end is a tragic one, made more so by the unadorned reportage of the narrator. Saul's sons are killed before him, and the armor bearer follows Saul's example. The death of the leader routs the Israelites, and the Philistines easily advance (31:1–7).

The epilogue (31:8–13) adds a last ironic note. Saul, who had grown increasingly isolated and "little in his own eyes" (15:17), was not to be left abandoned in death. The men of Jabesh-gilead, whom Saul had bravely saved in the first battle of his career (11:1–11), now rescue the bodies of Saul and his sons from Philistine disgrace and give their bones proper burial. In this touching tribute to their fallen leader, Saul's followers demonstrate their abiding loyalty.

Bibliography

Birch, B. C. *The Rise of the Israelite Monarchy: The Growth and Development of 1 Samuel 7–15.* Society of Biblical Literature Dissertation Series, 27. Missoula, MT: Scholars Press, 1976.

Garsiel, M. *The First Book of Samuel: A Literary Study of Comparative Structures, Analogies and Parallels.* Ramat Gan, Israel: Revivim, 1983, 1985.

Gunn, D. *The Fate of King Saul: An Interpretation of a Biblical Story.* Journal for the Study of the Old Testament Supplement Series, no. 14. Sheffield: JSOT Press, 1980, 1984.

Halpern, B. *The Constitution of the Monarchy in Israel.* Harvard Semitic Monographs 25. Chico, CA: Scholars Press, 1981.

Hertzberg, H. W. *I and II Samuel, A Commentary.* Old Testament Library. Philadelphia: Westminster, 1965.

McCarter, P. K., Jr. *I Samuel.* Anchor Bible, 8. Garden City, NY: Doubleday, 1980.

Miller, P. D., Jr., and J. J. M. Roberts. *The Hand of the Lord: A Reassessment of the "Ark Narrative" of I Samuel.* Baltimore, MD: Johns Hopkins University Press, 1977.

Miscall, P. *I Samuel, A Literary Reading.* Bloomington, IN: Indiana University Press, 1986.

Sternberg, M. *The Poetics of Biblical Narrative.* Bloomington, IN: Indiana University Press, 1985.

2 SAMUEL

DAVID M. GUNN

INTRODUCTION

Content and Context

Reading the Second Book of Samuel as a separate book is rather like reading a single chapter in an episodic novel. The story makes sense but keeps directing us beyond itself to its larger context. In the case of 2 Samuel, that context is the great story of God and Israel—its origins, nationhood, and eventual removal from the land—told in Genesis–2 Kings.

2 Samuel belongs to the part of the story that recounts Israel's nationhood in the promised land and its attempt to adapt religious and political institutions to changing circumstances. Running through both books of Samuel is a major interest in leaders and the nature of leadership. 1 Samuel tells of the transition from the period of judges to a monarchy under Saul (see 1 Samuel "Introduction"). The priest Eli, the prophet-judge Samuel, and Saul himself each hold center stage for a time.

The story is not just Israel's story, however; it is also God's. Above all, it is about Yhwh's attempt to maintain or recreate a relationship of loyalty between God and people. (The Hebrew text has preserved only the consonants of the divine name, Yhwh, perhaps originally Yahweh; English version: "the LORD.") Yhwh takes the people's desire for a human king as a rejection of divine sovereignty. Thus Saul, designated by God at the people's insistence, must be rejected in favor of one who is freely chosen by God (a man "after [God's] own heart," 1 Sam. 13:14). That man is David.

The story of David's rise, woven into the story of Saul, finds fulfillment in the story of his kingship in 2 Samuel. In turn, just as the account of Saul's end dovetails into 2 Samuel, so the account of David's death dovetails into the beginning of 1 Kings, which continues the story of monarchical Israel.

It may be helpful to regard the book as having three main parts. First is the story that lies between the death of Saul and the consolidation of the kingdom under David (chaps. 1–8). In the center is a story of the king's private life and its repercussions upon the kingdom; it becomes an account of his loss and regaining of the throne (chaps. 9–20). Finally some narrative and poetic units form a coda or epilogue connected to what has gone before not by plot but by theme and allusion (chaps. 21–24).

Composition

Attempts to reconstruct the history of the composition of the book have depended largely on observations about writing style, plot (where a plot line seems to begin and end), and literary genre (for we find various kinds of material such as prose anecdotes, archival lists, annalistic reports, a psalm, short stories, etc.). The results remain speculative. Suggested dates for individual units often differ widely, in some cases ranging from near the time of the events depicted (tenth century B.C.) to the period of the Exile (sixth century B.C.). This uncertainty over dating, together with a dearth of external evidence relating directly to the events of the book, also make it difficult to determine the historical accuracy of the material.

Most commonly accepted of the ideas about sources is the view that chaps. 9–20 together with 1 Kings 1–2 was originally a separate document. This "story of King David" is often referred to as the "court history" or "succession narrative," since some have seen the struggle between David's sons to succeed him on the throne as its primary theme. A case has been made for including most of chaps. 2–4 (the war between David and Saul's son Ishbosheth) with this material and possibly parts of chaps. 6 (David and Michal) and 7 (the promise of a Davidic dynasty). But where this postulated document originally began is uncertain.

Many critics believe that another account, a "story of David's rise" can be traced in 1 Samuel and 2 Samuel, finishing in chap. 5 with David's coronation over all Israel (though some include chap. 8, David's victories over the neighboring states). Likewise, the story of the Ark's coming to Jerusalem (chap. 6) is often seen as the original conclusion to an "Ark narrative," which began in 1 Samuel 4–6. Other parts of the book appear to have had origins in a variety of sources—popular, prophetic, liturgical, and bureaucratic.

Isolating the original components of 2 Samuel has always been a tentative matter. It is now doubly so, as recent studies in the "poetics" or "art" of Hebrew narrative cast doubt on much of the evidence appealed to by source critics. The further problems involved in determining the editorial stages through which the material might have passed are, in the view of increasing numbers of scholars, insuperable.

Hypotheses, however, abound. Most commonly accepted is the hypothesis that the last stage was the incorporation of the material into a "Deuteronomistic History"—Deuteronomy through 2 Kings—composed during the Exile in the sixth century B.C. (→ Deuteronomist; Deuteronomistic historian; Deuteronomy). (Some think that an earlier edition was written near the end of the seventh century.) While the exilic dating of the final form of Deuteronomy–2 Kings still looks relatively secure, however, the idea that these books were composed as an independent work, separate from Genesis–Numbers, faces serious criticism.

Perhaps more helpful to modern readers than hypotheses about editorial history is some understanding of how the kind of Hebrew narrative we find in the books of Samuel works to unfold meaning. We need to be aware, for example, that the narrator is fond of using repetition, and variation on the basis of it, in a way that much modern Western writing tends to avoid. We also observe that the narrator is generally reticent about telling readers what to think. Thus, for example, readers are often left to judge characters for themselves on the basis of their speech and actions. And speech can rarely be taken as the plain, unvarnished "truth." Characters in Hebrew narrative, like people in real life, present their own point of view or attempt to manipulate someone else's point of view. Constantly we find ourselves invited to fill gaps of information or meaning. Why has this character done this? Has something happened about which we have not been told? Why does this character's report of an event not match the narrator's account?

Meaning emerges little by little as we try out one way of reading against another. But because the text is so open to interpretation, the process of discovering meaning is never complete. Reading 2 Samuel, which contains some of the finest prose in the Hebrew Bible, is always a rich experience of discovery.

Meaning

The David of 2 Samuel starts life in 1 Samuel, in Hannah's hymn (1 Sam. 2:1–10). A mother gives thanks for the gift of a child (Samuel) and speaks, prophetically, of the king, the "anointed one" to whom Yhwh will give power. As the child is a special gift to the barren woman, so the kingdom is a special gift to David. Both gifts are freely given by God.

Giving and grasping are at the center of the story. It is when David allows choice to lie in the hands of others, especially Yhwh, that he most seems to flourish. Then he provokes readers to contemplate forbearance, to recognize providence as reality (e.g., 1 Sam. 24; 26; 2 Sam. 15–16). It is when he cannot rest content with the risk entailed or accept injured esteem issuing from rejection that he falters (e.g., 1 Sam. 25; 2

Sam. 11–12). Then we are confronted with a reality we know only too well, the reality of deceit, greed, and violence that makes us judge the David story so "realistic," so "plausible."

Yhwh gives David the kingdom, the house of Israel and of Judah (cf. 2 Sam. 12:8). But David's life consists not only of the public world. What happens privately in his own house (palace and family) will have an impact on the nation. As his mighty men are fighting the Ammonites (chap. 10), David seizes Bathsheba (chap. 11). As the one house (the house of Israel) is secured, another (the house of David) begins to crumble. In the story of Amnon and Absalom that follows, both family and nation will be torn apart (chaps. 12–20).

The kingship arose out of the people's search for security. But David's story in 2 Samuel embodies an old truth: human security all too readily generates corruption. Kingship, God-given or not, turns out to be no talisman (cf. 1 Sam. 8; Deut. 17:14–20). Our story retells a story told and retold in Genesis–2 Kings: Yhwh alone is sovereign, Yhwh alone offers security, and even then the people of Yhwh cannot acquire that security and fashion it their own way.

Thus David here embodies the nation that is given the land but falters in the receiving of it (in Joshua and Judges). His son Solomon falters in turn. Too soon the glory of Yhwh's house that Solomon has built (→ Temple, The) gives way to the expanding glory of his own house, from the security of which he serves other gods! So is torn from his house the house of Israel (the Northern Kingdom).

The house of Yhwh is no talisman. The larger story ends with it ruined, the people dispersed. So too with the house (dynasty) of David. 2 Kings concludes with a brief note about the exiled Davidic king, powerless in the house of his Babylonian conqueror.

The promise of an enduring house for David seems in 2 Samuel 7 to be unconditional but turns out to have limits. God, we may hear the story saying, offers a gift that is lasting—a gift to Abraham, to Moses, to David. But God cannot be taken for granted. That comment catches the story of the nation from entry into the land to exit. The promise of a "house" offers a gift that establishes order. But in itself no institution can secure order, no institution is secure. The promise cannot be presumed upon. It is not a crutch but an invitation to share in God's gift for the future.

David is not an ideal character. Rather the story that he inhabits points to various ways, negative as well as positive, in which a relationship between Yhwh and humankind might work. The original readers of the story perhaps sat in exile and wondered whether they might hope to rebuild a broken house. Why, they asked, had the old one been destroyed? But it is not just their story. As Deuteronomy helps us to see (cf. Deut. 4–6), the readers of Genesis–Kings are those who "today" stand beyond a river and yearn to cross and to build or rebuild a house. This is a story for them, wherever their "today" might be.

COMMENTARY

1:1–8:18

David's Kingdom Established

The first major movement of the book begins where the story of 1 Samuel has come to rest, with the death of Saul (→ Saul). It ends with David on the throne, king of both Judah in the south and Israel in the north (2 Sam. 5:1–5). Jerusalem, lying strategically between the two regions, has become David's capital (5:6–9).

By the end of the section important questions raised early in 1 Samuel have been resolved. The failure of the families of Eli and Samuel, priest and prophet, had led to a crisis of leadership (1 Sam. 1–8). The problem has been met by the institution of kingship in the person of David, chosen by God and promised by God a stable and enduring dynasty or "house" (2 Sam. 7). The symbol of the system of divine service, the Ark, has apparently found rest after much wandering and prominence at the center of the new kingdom (chap. 6; → Ark). The long-standing threat of national neighbors (cf. Judg.; 1 Sam.) appears to have been finally overcome. By the close of chap. 8 David appears to be established in power, in control of cult and state, and blessed by God.

1:1–27

The News of Saul's Death

1:1, Connections. The opening of the story resonates with earlier beginnings: "After the death of Saul" revives memories of Judges ("After the death of Joshua," 1:1) and Joshua ("After the death of Moses," 1:1), and beyond that the opening of Exodus ("Then Joseph died . . . and there arose a new king over Egypt, who did not know Joseph," 1:6, 8). Readers are at a pivotal moment.

Other stories, from 1 Samuel, also come to mind, creating some fine ironies. The narrator introduces David to us at his city of Ziklag, gift of the Philistines (1 Sam. 27:6) against whom Saul has just died fighting (1 Sam. 31). David has returned from slaughtering the Amalekites (→Amalekites). That information reminds us of Saul's ill-fated campaign that led to his rejection as king for having spared some of the booty (1

Sam. 15). In striking contrast stands David's amazing good fortune in not only recovering his own family and property but also seizing much booty (1 Sam. 30).

Thus to speak of David in the context of Ziklag and the Amalekites is to say something about the way that providence has moved, at times strangely, with David against Saul. To cap the irony, it is an Amalekite, of all people, who brings David word of Saul's death.

1:2–16, Message and Mourning. The narrator describes the messenger scene in terms that allude to Eli's hearing of Israel's defeat, the capture of the Ark, and the deaths of his two sons (1 Sam. 4). That story grew out of the failure of the priestly government (1 Sam. 2:22–36), which also led to God's choice of Samuel as the new leader. Now we are at another pivotal moment when the leadership is about to change. David will succeed Saul, by Yhwh's choice.

Yet the story of the message is not quite what it seems, for what the messenger says does not fit well with the narrator's account in 1 Samuel 31. Did Saul die by his own hand or by that of the Amalekite? Is the Amalekite lying, hoping to gain a reward? If so, he is mistaken, for his deed is rewarded by execution.

David takes the lie to be truth (or so it appears) and condemns him for having slain "Yhwh's anointed." Earlier, in Exodus and Leviticus, anointing has been associated with the Aaronidic priests; in 1 Samuel, however, it comes to refer to the king chosen by God (→Messiah). Occurring in this sense first in Hannah's song (1 Sam. 2:10), it is used frequently of Saul by various characters and of David by Jonathan.

With Saul at his mercy (cf. 1 Sam. 24; 26), David explains his restraint in terms of not putting forth his hand against Yhwh's anointed. Whether that restraint is an exercise in piety or in political shrewdness is not told to readers directly. Perhaps it contains a measure of both. Although Samuel never tells him so, David seems aware that Saul has been rejected as king by God (1 Sam. 15) and that his own anointing (1 Sam. 16) has been an anointing for kingship. Yet he does not presume to seize immediately what may still lie in God's gift for the future. Rather he bides his time, building his power base (his small army and his circle of well-treated "friends" [1 Sam. 30:26]) and waiting for others to see to Saul's demise. Dramatically now (2 Sam. 1:14–16) he proclaims his innocence of Saul's blood by publicly mourning for him, by naming him once more (for the last time) as "Yhwh's anointed" and by having the Amalekite put to death.

1:17–27, A Song of Lament. David rounds off his public disclaimer with a lament for Saul and Jonathan ("to teach the people of Judah";

289

→ Poetry). It crowns their death in glory and proclaims his own deep bond with Jonathan. Yet the song may also leave us uneasy. Were father and son truly "in life . . . not divided" (see 1 Sam. 19–20)? "How are the mighty fallen!" runs the refrain. Is that praise or a judgment? For so it might have been said of Goliath (1 Sam. 17)! Divided from Saul in life, David claims him in death. That makes good politics, but it may leave his true feelings masked behind the words.

2:1–5:5
The Gift of the Kingdom

2:1–7; 5:1–5, King of Judah and Israel.
The way to the throne is now clear. As in times past, David consults the oracle to determine his next move (2:1; cf. 1 Sam. 23:1–14; 30:6–9). Sure enough, the ascent to Hebron in Judah turns out to be the right one. At Hebron the leaders come of their own accord to anoint him king over the southern nation ("the house of Judah"; → Hebron). Not that he was a person they could easily ignore, for he had not come alone but had brought with him a powerful military presence (v. 3).

Part of greater Israel is now David's. The remainder, the northern nation ("the house of Israel"), will not become his without opposition. The story of enthronement culminates in 5:1–5 with the northern tribes claiming kinship with him ("we are your bone and flesh," 5:1) and professing to know that even when Saul had been alive it had been David who had fought at their head, David whom God had designated to lead them. So David makes a treaty ("covenant") with them and they anoint him king over the Northern Kingdom. That makes him at last king of all Israel.

2:8–3:5; 3:17–30, War Between Brothers.
The opening and closing scenes (2:1–7; 5:1–5) frame the story of the ongoing conflict between the ailing house of Saul and the ascendent house of David. And at the heart of the story lie two power brokers, the generals Abner (for Saul's son Ishbosheth) and Joab (for David; → Abner; Joab).

Ishbosheth, the narrator infers, is largely a pawn in Abner's hands: "And Abner son of Ner, commander of Saul's army, took Ishbosheth son of Saul, and caused him to cross over to Mahanaim [a town east of the Jordan]; and he made him king over Gilead [a region east of the Jordan] and the Geshurites [in the far northeast] and Jezreel [in the north, between the Galilean and Samarian hills] and Ephraim [the main northern territory] and Benjamin [central territory and Saul's homeland] and all Israel [the entire land, probably including Judah]" (2:8–9). As the list expands, the claim to kingship looks increasingly hollow. Ishbosheth sits across the Jordan, virtually in exile, his power fragile and growing weaker (3:1).

Initially the issue is put to a kind of trial by combat. "Let the young men [or soldiers] arise and make sport before us," says Abner to Joab (2:14), clothing in jest the deadly seriousness of the occasion. But the contest solves nothing, since all twenty-four combatants fall dead, and war ensues.

The battle goes against Abner and the northerners but the narrator rapidly passes over the details (2:17) in favor of two scenes from the aftermath. In the first (2:18–23), Abner reluctantly slays Asahel, the son of Zeruiah, who was also Joab's brother (and David's nephew—Zeruiah was David's sister, according to 1 Chron. 2:16). In the second (2 Sam. 2:24–28), Joab agrees to call off the pursuit, faced with a united band of Benjaminites under Abner who are determined to fight to the death (vv. 25–26).

In both cases the personal tensions peculiar to opponents in a civil war are focused sharply. Abner pleads with Asahel to give up his pursuit, lest by slaying Asahel Abner start a blood feud with Joab (v. 22; cf. 3:27). Likewise, Abner challenges Joab to bid his troops stop pursuing "their brothers," lest "the sword devour for ever" (v. 26; note the repetition of "brothers" in Joab's reply).

There is a disheartening familiarity in this struggle between "brothers" right at the outset of David's reign; the story of the book of Judges is pockmarked with such strife, culminating in the virtual annihilation of Benjamin, the very tribe fighting so desperately here (Judg. 8:13–17; 9:1–57; 12:1–6; 20:1–21:25; cf. 5:14–18, 23). In turn, struggle between brothers will darken much of what remains of David's story in 2 Samuel and in 1 Kings 1–2. And within little more than a generation the kingdom will be split once more, brother against brother (1 Kings 12).

Within this struggle too readers see the close intertwining of personal and public concerns. The fact that Abner had killed his brother, Asahel, will perhaps tip the scales for Joab when deciding how to respond to Abner's secret visit to David (3:23–25). Abner has come as a spy, asserts Joab (3:25)—and given the extent of the enmity between them, private as well as public, why should Joab see it differently? While David was dealing "in peace" with the enemy general, Joab was out winning David's battles (3:22).

3:6–16, Rizpah and Michal.
Abner's decision to desert Ishbosheth is crucial to the plot, for it leads to his death and thereby to the death of Ishbosheth (chap. 4). And crucial to the decision is a quarrel over a woman, Rizpah, one of Saul's concubines (3:6–11). The brief episode lies between a list of sons born to David's wives

in Hebron (3:2–5; listed in order of birth)—a list that readers will want to remember from chap. 13 onward—and the account of David's recovery of his first wife, Michal, the daughter of Saul (3:12–16; cf. 1 Sam. 18:20–27; 19:11–17).

Neither Rizpah nor Michal has a voice in the narrative; they are disposed of like property. Whether David, who already has at least six wives, wants Michal for herself is not indicated—has, indeed, never been indicated (cf. 1 Sam. 18:20–27). As a symbol of his alliance with the house of Saul, however, her presence with him is politically invaluable. Yet she has her own presence, powerfully suggested by the grief of Paltiel, her second husband, at her departure (2 Sam. 3:16). Of Rizpah, on the other hand, we can glimpse nothing. Both characters remind us that however much the Abners, Joabs, and Davids protest their loyalty, good faith, or piety, it is a soldier's world in which they seek to wield power. The two women will return to confront both David and readers again (chaps. 6, 21).

3:31–39, More Mourning. With the death of Abner, David cannot lose. He can, however, capitalize on the deed, and he does so at Joab's expense. His mourning for the enemy general is extravagant; and, caught up in the fever, the people weep and lament also. David's language is extravagant: "as one falls before the wicked you have fallen," he exclaims (3:34), conveniently forgetting for a public moment that the "wicked" Joab is his right arm. But his extravagance makes its point; it was not David who killed Saul's general.

4:1–12, The End of Ishbosheth and His Assassins. When two of Ishbosheth's unit commanders treacherously assassinate their master in his bed in the noontime heat, David is presented with yet another opportunity to write his own version of history and demonstrate his loyalty to Saul and his restraint in the taking of the kingdom. Alluding directly to the execution of the Amalekite in chap. 1 (vv. 10–11), he has the brothers Rechab and Baanah similarly dispatched (v. 12). Then he is ready to receive the gift of the house of Israel, the completion of his kingdom. And this duly takes place (5:1–5; see 2:1–7).

5:6–8:18
Consolidation

The story of the kingdom is now one of consolidation and centralization.

5:6–16, Jerusalem. David moves to counter the separatist politics of north and south by seeking a new, centrally located capital in the Jebusite (Canaanite) city of Jerusalem near the borders between Judah and Benjamin. (The reference to the "blind and lame" in vv. 6–8 is best understood as sarcasm, by the Jebusites toward David and vice versa; → David, City of.)

The narrator then pauses to add a word about the new king's growing power, "for Yhwh, the God of hosts [armies], was with him" (v. 10). Furthermore, David knew his success to be the doing of Yhwh "for the sake of his people Israel" (v. 12). David's relationship to Yhwh appears to be as firmly established as his kingdom.

Yet a jarring note follows (vv. 13–16). "And David took more concubines and wives from Jerusalem"—an unusual and interesting order of priority for Yhwh's chosen king! Moreover, to elaborate the king's establishment by first speaking of him "taking" from the city is to remind readers of Samuel's impassioned warning to the people about the ways of kings in 1 Sam. 8:10–20. The king, says Samuel, will take and take from you. It recalls too the law of kingship in Deut. 17:14–20. "He is not to multiply wives for himself," runs the law of Moses, "or his heart will turn away [from God]" (v. 17). These passages haunt the whole story of kingship in Samuel and Kings.

Later, when we read the story of David's taking of Bathsheba (chaps. 11–12), the phrase "he took wives from Jerusalem" will be seen to have strikingly foreshadowed the taking of Uriah's wife.

Verses 13–14 continue, "and more sons and daughters were born to David. And these are the names . . ." Yet only the names of sons follow. David perceives Yhwh's action toward him to have been "for the sake of Israel" (v. 12). Does that include daughters? Or are daughters of no account in David's Israel? These verses, then, bring back into focus those voiceless women, Rizpah, Saul's concubine, and Michal, Saul's daughter, taken for David from the weeping Paltiel.

5:17–25, Philistines. The focus switches from internal consolidation (both public and domestic) to the issue of external security and the defeat of the new nation's most pressing enemy, the Philistines (→Philistines). With success on the front, the king is ready to continue centralizing power by establishing his capital as a center of worship (chap. 6).

6:1–23, The Ark. With its relocation from Baalah (i.e., Kiriath-jearim; cf. 1 Chron. 13:6; 1 Sam. 7:1–2; the Hebrew text may be garbled here) to Jerusalem, the wanderings of the Ark seem to be over. Great rejoicing marks the account. Two incidents, however, disturb the triumphal tone.

First is Yhwh's anger when Uzzah touches the Ark, which in turn prompts David's anger and fear of Yhwh (2 Sam. 6:6–10). The Ark, the narrator reminds us, is a sacred object and represents the awesome and sometimes unpredictable power of the sacred (→ Ark; Holiness). Yhwh does not need Uzzah to prop up the Ark of God. Set against such mystery, Uzzah's very human reaction is made to appear of secondary importance. But if this is what can happen to Uzzah, what response might a deliberate sin of some magnitude bring forth?

The incident reminds both David and readers that David's relationship with Yhwh does not guarantee divine blessing on all he does. Is it even Yhwh's will that the Ark be brought to Jerusalem? In contrast to the preceding accounts of the Philistine battles, David has made no inquiry of Yhwh before acting. Now, fearful because of the setback, he waits for a divine sign (cf. v. 12).

The second incident is the quarrel between David and Michal over his dancing in public. The precise nature of his action in Michal's view is unclear (v. 20: "uncovering himself" [RSV] or "exposing himself" [NAB] may equally be "flaunting himself" or "showing off," i.e., without implying nakedness). Plainly, however, she thinks that it is debasing for a king; hence the heavy sarcasm of "How the king of Israel has distinguished himself today!" (NIV).

The narrator introduces her as "Michal the daughter of Saul" (v. 16 and again in v. 20), not "Michal the wife of David," thereby distancing her from David and reminding readers of her royal lineage. Here is a daughter who does count in David's kingdom, at least to the extent that she is useful to the new king. She can buttress his claim to the throne and no doubt produce a son who will then conveniently inherit both royal houses.

But this daughter is not prepared to be so used. She pits her sense of royal dignity against his public posturing. Like her father, she cannot win the contest, for Yhwh is on David's side, has chosen him above Saul, as David himself is only too ready to tell her. "And Michal the daughter of Saul had no child to the day of her death" (v. 23)—the due reward, readers might suppose, for opposing Yhwh's chosen. Yet in another sense David's is a pyrrhic victory, for not through her will David's line be able to legitimize succession to the throne of Saul. And without her son, the obvious heir, the way is open for the bitter struggle between brothers that will plague the latter part of David's story.

7:1–29, A House. Chap. 7 develops two elements of chap. 6—divine service and dynastic succession. Tying them together is a play on the word "house." David, dwelling comfortably in his house (palace) of cedar, decides that the Ark too should have a house (temple) (v. 2; cf. vv. 5–7). Nathan the prophet, here introduced for the first time, makes an instant response: "Go ahead, do whatever you have in mind; for Yhwh is with you."

Alas, his advice proves less than sound. As we have already seen, the fact that Yhwh is with David does not give him *carte blanche* to do as he chooses. And Yhwh hastens to tell the prophet that very night to sort out his theology. On the contrary, Yhwh suggests with some sarcasm, a house is the least of the Deity's concerns.

Yhwh turns the conversation around instead. Rather than you build me a house, the Deity says, I will build you one (vv. 11–16). The "house" in mind is, of course, a royal house or dynasty. The Deity offers the prospect of a peaceful transfer of power with a successor from among David's sons taking the throne with Yhwh's blessing. Let that heir, then, build a "house for my name" (though whether this refers to building, literally, a temple or rather to building, metaphorically, a royal house or, perhaps, nation—the "house of Israel"—which is dedicated to Yhwh, is far from clear).

Yhwh is making here a major concession, for the history of Israel's leadership to this point has been one dissociated from dynasty. Again and again sons have proven unworthy successors and leadership has had to devolve elsewhere (e.g., Samuel and his sons, 1 Sam. 8:1–3; Eli and his sons, 1 Sam. 2:22–36; Gideon and his son, Abimelech, Judg. 8:22–9:57).

The prophecy hugely reinforces David's sense of being favored. He responds enthusiastically in a long prayer, acknowledging Yhwh's gift to Israel and to him (2 Sam. 7:18–24). Yet he hovers curiously between the security of knowing great blessing and the insecurity of needing to have it confirmed for the future. With elaborate rhetoric the king urges Yhwh to "confirm for ever the word which you have spoken" (vv. 25–29).

8:1–14, Further Conquest. Having drawn us into the world of cult and prophecy the narrator now pulls us back to where these themes entered, the Philistine war (8:1; cf. 5:17–25). Now all the nation's borders are secured. The list takes readers on a grand tour of Israel's boundaries.

Skirting the edge of the Deuteronomic law ("nor is he to multiply greatly for himself silver and gold," Deut. 17:17), the king dedicates gifts and booty of silver and gold to Yhwh (2 Sam. 18:11). So "Yhwh gave David victory everywhere he went" (v. 14).

8:15–18, The Bureaucracy. This first movement of David's story comes to rest with a bland summary: "So David reigned over all Israel; and he did what was just and right for his whole people" (v. 15). A brief list of officials follows. It begins with Joab, the army commander, and includes the "recorder," the priests, the secretary, the commander of the Cherethites and Pelethites (the professional guard)—and some more priests! "And David's sons were priests" (v. 18).

Again, therefore, we find equilibrium disturbed (as earlier in 5:13–16). For David's sons to be priests is to flout the Mosaic law that draws the priesthood exclusively from the tribe of Levi (→ Levites; Priests). (Many versions, like many commentators, have attempted to smooth the text by rewriting it—cf. 1 Chron. 18:17.) Just as we sense completion at hand, the narrator unsettles us. David, chosen and supported by Yhwh, is no simple model of piety.

9:1–20:26
Kingdom and Family

The story moves into a new phase. Consolidation gives way to a new struggle for power within the kingdom. The story of the Ammonite war (chap. 10) has tempted readers to consider the greatest threats to David to lie beyond Israel's borders in the realm of international politics. Subdue those outside, it suggests, and all will be well. The story of David's taking of Bathsheba and murder of Uriah (chaps. 11–12) and the subsequent story of rape, murder, and rebellion (chaps. 13–20) tell otherwise. It is a threat from within, a corruption that grows from within himself and his own family, that most menaces David's exercise of power. From this point on, despite enlivening moments, David's story becomes increasingly bleak.

Nathan's prophecy (chap. 12) presses us to see that David's crime and the events of chaps. 13–20 are part of a chain that is anchored in David's sin. Ironically, one of the seeds of disruption lies in the very thing that David so earnestly desired—the divine promise of a "house" (chap. 7). While that promise offers the king security and stability by sanctioning the transfer of kingship to one of David's offspring (7:12), it opens up the question "Which one?" The appetite for power by and on behalf of various sons permeates the remainder of David's story, both in chaps. 13–20 and, equally bloodily, in the closing chapters of his life (1 Kings 1–2).

Though David is eventually restored to his throne, his power is in reality held by others, men of violence, most notably Joab. Moreover, the signs of division in the kingdom have already reappeared with the quarrel between north and south (2 Sam. 19:41–43) and the withdrawal of support by some northerners under Sheba ben Bichri, of Saul's tribe of Benjamin (chap. 20).

9:1–13
Mephibosheth, Son of Jonathan

The story of Mephibosheth's coming to court, in chap. 9, is transitional. On the one hand, it looks back to David's time at Saul's court, when Jonathan loved him (1 Sam. 18:1; 19:1; 20:17), dealt loyally with him (1 Sam. 19–20), and had him swear never to "cut off [his] loyalty [kindness]" from Jonathan's house (1 Sam. 20:14–17; cf. 20:42). And in raising the question of David's relation to Saul's family, the story brings to mind again the division between David and Michal, Saul's daughter (2 Sam. 6:20–23). On the other hand, the chapter looks forward to the forthcoming story of the rebellion of Absalom, David's son (chaps. 15–20), of which it forms part of a subplot.

David's action in summoning the lame Mephibosheth (9:3, 13; cf. 4:4) is clothed in the language of loyal dealing (vv. 1, 7). Yet once more we find ambiguity as Mephibosheth grovels fearfully before the king (v. 8).

David's generosity means restoring to Mephibosheth land that is in any case Mephibosheth's by right of inheritance. The produce, from the labor of Ziba's considerable household (v. 10), is to be brought to the king's table—far beyond Mephibosheth's needs and leaving, no doubt, a handsome surplus for the court. And for the heir of a defeated royal house to eat at the conqueror's table is itself an ambiguous honor. That way David has this heir of Saul under his scrutiny. Mephibosheth is effectively a prisoner.

We shall again glimpse this picture of Mephibosheth, "who used to eat always at the king's table" (v. 13; cf. vv. 7, 10), at the very end of the larger story (Genesis–2 Kings). Jehoiachin, defeated king of Judah and heir of David, is released from prison in Babylon by Evil-merodach—"and he used to eat food always before [the king] all the days of his life." His prison has but changed its appearance (as he changes his clothes, 2 Kings 25:29). Ironically, the fate of Saul's house and of David's will turn out to be the same.

10:1–12:31
War, Adultery, and Murder

The account of the Ammonite war in chap. 10 becomes, in 11:1, both starting point and background for the crucial story of David, Bathsheba, and Uriah. The war report is then resumed in 12:26–31, which details the taking of the Ammonite capital, Rabbah. Thus the domestic story of David's adultery and murder is framed by the public story of war and conquest. The taking of the city of Rabbah parallels the taking of Bathsheba and the life of Uriah.

10:1–19, The Ammonite War. From seeking to "deal loyally with [Mephibosheth] for Jonathan's sake" (9:1, 7)—and for the sake of internal security?—David now turns his attention beyond Israel's borders and seeks to "deal loyally with Hanun the son of Nahash [king of the Ammonites], as his father dealt loyally with me" (10:1). He sends envoys, says the narrator, "to console [Hanun] over [the death of] his father" (v. 2; → Ammonites).

But if we have been suspicious of David's motives in treating Mephibosheth "loyally," we might also wonder a little here. Is the narrator expressing only the publicly stated intent of the mission? Concern for the security of his borders and the maintenance of a treaty of nonaggression must be at least David's objective (as many historians have observed). But Hanun's advisors appear doubly suspicious. They persuade the new king that the mission is in fact espionage preparatory to an Israelite assault on the capital. Or is it that they too have a hidden agenda and wish to provoke a war to destroy the growing power of Israel under David while there is still time? The episode conjures a memory of Abner's visit to David (chap. 3) and Joab's accusation that the enemy general had come to spy (3:25).

Talk of "treating loyally" and "consoling" can all too easily conceal ulterior motives. What "seems to be" and what "is" in David's story—as in Genesis–2 Kings as a whole—turn out, so often, to be rather different things. As much as human beings struggle to communicate what "is" through what they say, they have an even greater propensity for using words to fabricate appearances. And between speaker and listener, moreover, there is always a void in which lurks the possibility of misunderstanding. So here we are not surprised to see the language of loyalty turned into the language of enmity; and as readers we are left struggling to know what lies behind what seems.

The account of the war that inevitably follows the humiliation of David's envoys also unsettles our sense of knowing exactly the time frame of the events. When we read that the Ammonites hired the Syrians of Zobah and Rehob (10:6) in the first phase of the war (vv. 6–14) and note the Syrian king Hadadezer in the second phase (vv. 15–19), we begin to wonder whether this episode is not a flashback to the campaigns recounted in chap. 8 (cf. 8:3–12).

If, on the one hand, we think of the Ammonite war as subsequent in time to the events of chap. 8, we are struck by the rapidity with which what appeared secure has again become a threat. If, on the other hand, we read the war account as a flashback, we may be struck by the irony of the context in which David's adultery and murder have been set. It is at the very peak of his power, when Yhwh is giving him victory wherever he goes (8:14), that the king most conspicuously fails. Security breeds insecurity; success incubates failure. It is as the gift of the kingdom is being made complete that Yhwh's chosen one chooses to grasp most rapaciously what is not his to grasp. In short, it is at its most secure that David turns out to be most open to failure.

11:1–27, David, Bathsheba, and Uriah. The story is full of irony, starting with the narrator's dry comment that "At the turn of the year [i.e., the spring], at the time when kings march out [to battle], David sent Joab, and his servants with him, and all Israel . . . and David stayed in Jerusalem" (v. 1). So while the army besieges Rabbah, David takes an afternoon nap and then besieges Bathsheba.

The narrator gives us few explicit clues to the inner feelings or thoughts of the characters. Bathsheba's point of view, particularly, is concealed. Rather, events unfold through David's eyes. The nature of the king's interest in Bathsheba is thus implicitly revealed. The word "bed" sets the tone, and we see that what he sees is "a woman" and "a very attractive woman" (v. 2). In due course we hear, with David, only the stark content of her message: "I am pregnant" (v. 5).

In the word choice, readers may also find a clue to another dimension of the story. David, we are told, was walking on the roof of "the king's house" (rather than "his house"). This is about a woman and a *king*, and that means a story about a disparity of power, not only that existing between a woman and a man, but between a woman and the most powerful man in the land. Bathsheba (and later Uriah) is the object of a king's transactions. The text is full of the word "send" (twelve times in chap. 11).

The narrator provides another piece of important information. Bathsheba was "purifying herself from her uncleanness" (v. 4), that is, from her menstrual period (→ Purity). David's paternity of the child she conceives will be beyond dispute.

The interchange between David and Uriah follows directly (vv. 6–13). Readers know David's words cloak deceit from beginning to end. His asking after the welfare of Joab and the army is a sham, merely the pretext to get Uriah home. "Go down to your house," he says to the soldier (v. 8), adding lightly, as man to man, "and wash your feet"—a euphemism for sexual intercourse. The suggestion is designed to sound like indulgent generosity, especially since to follow it would be to break the rules of purity (v. 11; Exod. 19:14–15; Deut. 23:9–14; cf. 1 Sam. 21:5; Ps. 132:1–5). But, of course, to both David and readers the suggestion really means much more than "sleep with your wife." Rather, it means David's opportunity to pass off paternity to Uriah, the deceived husband.

With David's failure to subvert Uriah, the scene shifts again (2 Sam. 11:14–25). David does not hesitate. "In the morning" he sets murder in motion. Ironically, the faithful Uriah carries his own letter of doom.

But does Uriah really not know what is happening? Can the affair, the subject of so much message sending, have remained hidden from the man who slept with "all the servants of his lord"? If David can speak in code, why not Uriah? Understood thus, Uriah's refusal to go down to his house is in fact his refusal to compromise his own house, to condone David's crime and so to embed further the corruption in the king's house. Does he therefore go to his death knowingly, still the king's loyal servant, but with his own integrity intact? In that case the irony of his death is turned against David. It is Uriah who is in charge of it, not David. It is Uriah the Hittite (whose name in Hebrew means "Yhwh is my light") who rules in Jerusalem.

The narrator switches back for a brief moment to Bathsheba. Our focus is brought to bear on the marital relationship that has been destroyed: "And the *wife of Uriah* heard that Uriah *her husband* was dead, and she lamented over *her lord*" (v. 26, emphasis added). The proper social customs are observed: Bathsheba enters a period of mourning, feeling what we know not. Then David who began the episode ends it by once again sending to have her brought to his house, this time as his wife. She bears his son.

"Let not this thing be evil in your sight," David says to Joab concerning Uriah's death (v. 25). "But the thing that David had done was evil in the sight of Yhwh" (v. 27), concludes the narrator. Thus the first part of the story of adultery and murder closes with our glimpsing Yhwh's perspective. And that will preface Yhwh's action.

12:1–25, Judgment. The act of "sending"— people, words—has characterized David's manipulation of his power in chap. 11. Now it is Yhwh's turn. "And Yhwh sent Nathan to David" (12:1). What the prophet will wield against David are simply words, but they will be powerful words that will shape David's future. Then Yhwh will wield death against David's house as David has against Uriah's.

In the parable of the poor man's ewe lamb, Nathan deploys words that are slippery, an apt weapon against the David of slippery words. He teases readers with the parable's alternative referents: the lamb is pictured as a child but also as one who "ate his morsel and drank his cup"—language often used in sexual imagery—

and "slept at his breast"; she became to him like a "daughter" (Heb. *bath*, as in *Bathsheba*!). The parable sucks the king in and extracts from him self-judgment.

Suddenly we are confronted with what was so palpably absent in chap. 11. As David sits in judgment upon others his feelings are opened up to our view. He responds to the account with passion and invokes Yhwh's name in righteous anger. We recognize once more the David who could so tellingly lend his emotions to a public occasion (e.g., at the deaths of Saul, Abner, and Ishbosheth, chaps. 1–4). And if his outburst in 12:5 means "the man who has done this deserves to die" (RSV; but it may mean something like " . . . is a hellish fiend"), it doubly exposes his own hypocrisy. He, after all, approved taking and slaughtering not a lamb but a woman and a man.

He speaks of restitution. If "fourfold" is read (12:6, Masoretic Text [MT]; the Septuagint [LXX] has "sevenfold") there may be here a foreshadowing of the premature deaths of four of David's children: Bathsheba's first child, Amnon, Absalom, and Adonijah. "Let not this thing be evil in your sight, for sometimes the sword devours one, sometimes another," David had said to Joab (11:25). "So now," says Nathan (for Yhwh), "a sword will not turn aside from your house, a lasting sword. . . . Thus says Yhwh: Behold, I am raising up evil against you from your house" (12:10–11).

"I gave you," says Yhwh, "your master's house . . . I gave you the house of Israel and Judah (v. 8). "House" is ambiguous. It is kingdom, dynasty, extended family. One meaning slides into another. Just so, the king's private and political lives merge, often mirror each other. What he does in the one has a way of impinging on what he does in the other.

Yhwh's gift has been met by David's grasping. He has taken what is not his to take—Bathsheba and the life of Uriah. Therefore, says the prophet in Yhwh's name, "I will take your wives in your sight, and give them to your neighbor [cf. Samuel's words to Saul, 1 Sam. 15:28], and he shall sleep with your wives in the sight of this sun [i.e., with everyone's knowledge]" (v. 11). The words foreshadow Absalom's treatment of David's concubines (16:20–22).

David's response is powerful. In recognizing his sin against Yhwh he recognizes his ultimate antagonist in the matter. Somehow Uriah and Bathsheba become secondary. Readers too may sense that the stakes are higher than the individuals concerned, for at issue is Yhwh's choice and support of David. Can the Deity countenance the rejection of the chosen one? On the other hand, at what cost can the Deity afford to continue supporting him? Nathan's response points to ongoing support but at a price, paid first by the child conceived in adultery. We shall see it paid in turn by a succession of others in David's house—family and kingdom—in the episodes to come.

Powerful too is David's response to the child's death. Against what his servants expect he shrugs aside his loss, symbolizing his commitment to living by asking for food and eating (compare Saul's equally symbolic reluctance to eat in 1 Sam. 28:20, prior to his death). At the heart of David's action seems to be his recognition of Yhwh's power to give and take life (cf. v. 23).

The king's speech to his servants (vv. 22–23) may evoke different responses in different readers—as resignation, indifference, or even callousness. But there is a softening in the picture at the close. As we read of David renewing his relationship with Bathsheba, we note, at last, an affective verb: "And David comforted Bathsheba, his wife, and went in to her, and slept with her" (v. 24). A son is born and Yhwh's response, as if mirroring David's, is also affective: "And Yhwh loved him."

12:26–31, The Taking of Rabbah. Abruptly we are thrown back into the political world, where fighting and taking/capturing dominate the scene. It is too a world of appearances, for although Rabbah has effectively fallen to Joab, the king must be seen to be its captor. Torture (perhaps—so, e.g., Josephus and KJV, but few modern English versions) and forced labor are the lot of its people (v. 31). The momentary note of contrition and comfort is lost in the glorification of war.

13:1–14:33
Rape, Murder, and Exile

13:1–39, Tamar and Her Brothers. We meet three characters. Two are sons of David—Absalom and Amnon, whom we have met before as third-born and firstborn, respectively, in the list of sons born to David at Hebron (3:2–5). Introduced between them is a daughter, Tamar, sister of Absalom, half-sister of Amnon.

From the beginning the familial relationships are sharply focused by constant definition and redefinition of characters (as the point of view changes) in terms of "son," "sister," "brother," and "father." This is a story of sickness within a family, where the very ties that betoken solidarity and protection are perverted into the means to commit crime.

That Tamar, the sister, is described at the outset as "beautiful" is perhaps ominous, given the way the David and Bathsheba story had started (11:2; Bathsheba is "very attractive"). And, indeed, so it proves: Amnon loved her and wanted to sleep with her (13:1–2).

But already our understanding has come under strain. We are first struck by the verb "love," which was, together with other affective language, so obviously missing from David's story. Yet the word is immediately defined in terms of "doing something to her" (v. 2). "Love" looks more like "desire" and will soon most resemble "lust." (In the same way we will come to put quotation marks around the word "wise" used of Jonadab, "a very wise man," in v. 3.) Unlike David with Bathsheba, however, Amnon is unable simply to send for and take Tamar, because as a young marriageable woman (most English versions read: "a virgin") she is subject to strict oversight. Hence he must use subterfuge to take her (cf. David with Uriah).

Thus the son's story both imitates that of the father and differs from it. And at the heart of the difference is perhaps the outcome for the woman. Bathsheba, whose taking is described in such dispassionate terms, is finally offered comfort by David. Tamar, excessively "loved" at the beginning (vv. 1–4), is at the end excessively hated by her rapist (vv. 11, 14–17; he "seizes," "overpowers," and "rapes" her). The violent fluctuation is conveyed also in the dialogue: "Come, lie with me, my sister" (v. 11) gives place to "Get this [woman] out of my presence" (v. 17).

By contrast too, Shechem, who raped Dinah, Leah's daughter, ends by loving her, speaking tenderly to her, and asking his father to get her to be his wife (Gen. 34:1–4). But there the contrast stops, for her brothers will not consider a marriage, since her honor (by which they really mean their own) has been slighted. Shechem is slaughtered and Dinah disappears from view, locked up in perpetual dependency upon her do-nothing father and dominating brothers. A similar fate awaits the now unmarriageable Tamar, shut up, desolate, in the house of her brother Absalom (2 Sam. 13:20) while her angry father, like Jacob (Gen. 34:30–31), does nothing.

"And King David heard all these things and was very angry" (v. 21). Some ancient versions add here: "but he did nothing to vex his son Amnon because he loved him, for he was his firstborn." Again the woman is pushed to the margin. Abused by her brother, she is ignored by her father in the interests of the firstborn son. David, the lastborn (1 Sam. 16:11), has forgotten his own beginnings. The king, the assiduous taker of women, will not take up his daughter's cause.

Mention of favoritism toward the firstborn also prods us to reflect on Absalom's response to his sister's plight. Is the rape the beginning of his hate toward Amnon or but another episode in it? With Chileab, the second-born son (2 Sam. 3:3), unmentioned, does that make Absalom and Amnon rivals for the succession?

David's cynical disposal of Uriah was left to a chance enemy arrow. Absalom, however, leaves nothing to chance—"When I say to you, 'Strike Amnon,' then kill him" (13:28). Here is a character who knows how both to bide his time and to act. He also knows how far to push David. So he flees to Talmai, king of Geshur, his maternal grandfather (v. 37; cf. 3:3).

The narrator's closing remarks typically provoke questions. For which son did David mourn (13:37)? And if David "was comforted" (or "consoled"; cf. 12:24, David "comforted" Bathsheba) over the death of Amnon, did he welcome it all along or at least see in it someone else's solution to his dilemma? Did he really suspect nothing, as Absalom pressed him to let Amnon go to the sheepshearing (13:24–27, especially v. 26)? Or was David, after all, acting once more through abstaining?

His attitude toward both Amnon and Absalom may thus be complex. A hidden factor becomes evident only when we remember the larger setting of the story. David's hands are tied by his own evil (chap. 11), for the sons have merely mimicked the king, their father. To function as judge would thus be to expose himself fatally to a charge of hypocrisy. He would then be like his ancestor Judah, condemning the other Tamar to death (Gen. 38).

14:1–33, Absalom's Return. Again the plot turns on coded words—a parable intended to provoke the hearer to self-judgment (vv. 4–21; cf. 12:1–7; 1 Kings 20:35–42). Again a woman is at the center of the episode, apparently not this time as a victim of a man's grasping, but as a mediator and reconciler.

It is Joab, however, who initiates the attempt to bring Absalom back to court. And notice how David perceives that Joab is behind the action (2 Sam. 14:19). That happens after the woman has made her judgment against the king (v. 13), as she seeks desperately to mitigate her dangerous effrontery. Her speech subtly transforms the story of threat to the widow and son in the parable into an account of the threat that has forced her to risk confronting the king in this way.

She has been threatened, she says, by "the people" (the word could also mean "army") and, in particular, by "the hand of a man who would destroy me and my son" (v. 16). She is speaking to the king now in her own voice, not the voice of the widow in the parable, but she allows the two voices to flow together, for she cannot openly accuse the king's general (perhaps standing nearby—cf. v. 21) of intimidating her. But she has no need to do so. In the language of violence David unerringly recognizes "the hand of Joab" (v. 19).

Whether or not it is wisdom to grant Joab's request remains to be seen. (And what is Joab's motive in making it?) Nor can we be sure that the wise woman thinks it to be wise, since the narrator never tells us what she thinks. The parable and judgment are put in her mouth by Joab (v. 3)—put there, moreover, to the accompaniment of other words of coercion (according to her) that the narrator mischievously neglected to mention (vv. 2–3). Thus her role as reconciler must be reconsidered. The nature of her wisdom remains elusive, to be sought perhaps in her skill as playactor and wordsmith. Perhaps she is simply trying to stay alive in a world where men wield power ruthlessly and capriciously.

Absalom's return is thus woven from words of deception and violence. That is both ominous and appropriate—for certainly violence is a language both he and Joab understand well, as the field burning exemplifies (vv. 28–33). Throughout the whole episode reconciliation is constantly compromised—by fear and coercion (the wise woman's speech), by the aggression of Absalom's message to Joab (vv. 28–33), by the king's refusal to let his son come into his presence (v. 24; so Absalom, like Tamar, dwelt apart in his house), and finally by the wordless reunion that conceals as much as it reveals (v. 33).

Absalom's story began in 13:1: "And Absalom, David's son, had a beautiful sister, whose name was Tamar." With Amnon dead and Absalom back in Jerusalem, the narrator pauses to fill in some details (14:25–27). They are details full of irony. We read of Absalom's unsurpassable beauty (a fateful thing in King David's family), of the absence of blemish in him (like a sacrificial animal), of the cutting of his extraordinary hair (like a Nazirite; cf. Num. 6:1–21; Judg. 13:3–5; 16:17), and of his three sons and one daughter. For once, the sons are unnamed, the daughter named: she was called Tamar, and, adds the narrator, "she was a beautiful woman to look at" (2 Sam. 14:27; cf. 11:2; 13:1). Readers might well tremble for this Tamar too.

15:1–16:14
Rebellion and Exile

Now comes the story of Absalom's rebellion. In effect, it puts David back to the beginning of the book, with the kingdom in the grip of civil war. This reverse, however, has a curiously positive effect. As the king journeys across the Jordan into the wilderness (cf. 17:29), he rediscovers for a moment some of his sources of strength.

There is symmetry in the way the narrative of exile and return unfolds. It draws our attention to similarities and differences between particular scenes, especially in the journeys to and from the Jordan (15:13–16:14; 19:15–20:3). Framed by these journeys are the central scenes of debate (between Hushai and Ahithophel, 17:1–14) and battle (between the armies of David and Absalom, 18:1–17). Each culminates in a messenger scene (17:15–21; 18:19–32) and an account of the king's response (17:22; 18:33–19:8).

15:1–12, Absalom Steals Hearts. The story gathers speed. From the picture of Absalom's ostentation (v. 1), and his cultivation in Jerusalem of support for himself and disaffection for the king (vv. 2–6), the narrator moves to Hebron, where David had been made king (vv. 7–12; cf. 2:4, 5:3). Four years (LXX; the MT has "forty") are traversed in a few sentences, compounding our sense of the rapid growth in Absalom's popular backing. That, of course, raises questions. What was David doing all this time? Is it possible that Absalom's claims about his father's failure to provide justice are well founded?

The son cloaks his visit to Hebron in piety, claiming that he must fulfill a vow to Yhwh, as though it were the Deity who had brought him back to Jerusalem (15:7–8). Two verses later and rebellion declared, that implication might seem a striking blasphemy on Absalom's part. Yet Nathan's prophecy should nag our memory —"Behold," says Yhwh, "I will raise up evil against you out of your own house" (12:10–11; cf. 15:14). Perhaps, ironically, there may be truth in Absalom's deceptive words after all. There is irony too in the picture of the man "without a blemish" offering sacrifices to Yhwh while he summons Ahithophel, David's counselor, to betray his own father, Yhwh's chosen king.

The return of Absalom, begun with Joab's observation that "the heart of the king was [set] on Absalom" (14:1), culminates in "the hearts of the men of Israel [going] after Absalom" (15:13), for Absalom "stole the hearts of the men of Israel" (v. 6). With their hearts in the grasp of Absalom, the men of Israel who had given David the kingdom now revoke their gift. The roles of father and son are reversed. It is now David's turn to go into exile.

15:13–16:14, From Jerusalem to the Jordan. The speed with which David abandons his capital more than matches the rapidity with which rebellion overtakes him. Indeed, there is a touch of pathos, if not farce, in the response to Absalom by the conqueror of Rabbah. Barely has the flight begun before we find him in conversation with a powerful mercenary captain, referring to Absalom as "the king," and, of all things, urging this vital ally to desert him (15:18–22).

Read from another perspective, however, things may look different. David's flight is in the interests of preserving the city from the ravages of war and his response to Ittai illustrates his understanding of freedom.

Ittai is made no unwilling captive to a contract. Instead, he matches David's gift of liberty with his own commitment. In Ittai's view, de-

spite all appearances to the contrary, David is still his lord "the king" (v. 21). And in his commitment lie the seeds of David's restoration. Ittai will play an important role in making David's kingship real again (18:2).

It is similar with the Ark (15:24–29). Instead of grasping at it as a guarantor of success (like the Israelites in 1 Sam. 4), David returns it to the royal city. "If I find favor in Yhwh's sight," he remarks, "he will bring me back . . . but if he says, 'I have no pleasure in you,' behold, here I am, let him do to me what is good in his sight" (2 Sam. 15:25–26).

Shimei of Saul's house expresses vehemently the view that Yhwh has indeed no delight in David (16:5–12): the rebellion is divine vengeance "for the blood of the house of Saul, whose place as king you took. . . . See, your own evil is upon you, for you are a man of blood" (v. 8). Abishai's violent response (he is Joab's brother)—"Let me go over and take off his head" (v. 9)—is what we might expect of the participants in this world. David's restraint—"Leave him alone and let him curse" (v. 11)—is by contrast extraordinary. And again it is expressed in terms of Yhwh's doing.

Shimei we know to be wrong. It was, of course, Yhwh who gave David Saul's throne. The story was remarkable for David's restraint toward Saul, above all at the cave at En-gedi and in Saul's camp at Hachilah (1 Sam. 24; 26). But perhaps Shimei is also, unconsciously, right. As already observed (on 15:7–8, 14), given Nathan's perspective (12:10–11), it may well be David's own evil that is now upon him.

As for blood, we may recall an earlier flight from court—Saul's court—when David had recklessly taken supplies from Ahimelech the priest at Nob, knowing a spy to be there, and costing the blood of eighty-five priests and more, "men and women, children and sucklings" (1 Sam. 21–22; cf. 1 Sam. 15:3). We see too the blood of the civil war (2 Sam. 2–4), of the wars to secure borders—Moabites measured out for death (8:2), twenty-two thousand Syrians slain (8:5), eighteen thousand Edomites (8:13), and much more—and, of course, the blood of Uriah (11:14–25; 12:9–10). Has David no hand in any of this?

Yet that view of David as a man of blood need not dominate here. If we so choose, we may rather enjoy the king who lets power pass into the hands of others whom he trusts.

The account of David's progress out of the city has almost a ritual quality to it. It is full of participles indicating continuing action; the verb "pass over" ("pass on," "cross over") is repeated sixteen times (similarly in Josh. 3–4, the account of crossing the Jordan); and it is narrated at a measured pace, scene by scene.

In the procession comes the Ark (2 Sam. 15:24–29), though that is turned back. But then David and the people with him, in the attitude of mourning, ascend the Mount of Olives (v. 30). Here word comes of Ahithophel's treachery, to which David responds with a prayer: "Yhwh, please turn the counsel of Ahithophel into folly" (v. 31). "And it came to pass," continues the narrator, "that when David came to the summit, where God was worshiped, behold, Hushai came to meet him" (v. 32). As the story unfolds it will become clear that Hushai is the answer to David's prayer. The king's friend (v. 37; 16:16) will persuade Absalom to reject Ahithophel's advice and so allow David to escape safely across the Jordan (17:1–22). The narrator makes explicit the connections in 17:14: "For Yhwh had ordained to frustrate the good counsel of Ahithophel, in order that Yhwh might bring evil upon Absalom."

Ahithophel, summoned to treachery as Absalom offered sacrifices at Hebron, finds his best counsel rejected. Hushai, called to loyalty as David prays "where God is worshiped," finds his deceptive counsel accepted. Irony is a hallmark of Yhwh's workings in this story.

16:15–17:23
Debate, Message, and Escape

With David at the Jordan, the narrator switches scene to Jerusalem. Ahithophel and Hushai are introduced side by side (16:15–16), and their battle of words will dominate the section.

First (A) Ahithophel advises the new king to take possession publicly of his father's concubines. So Absalom goes in to them on the roof of the king's palace, "in the sight of all Israel" (16:22)—a roof last mentioned as the place from which David saw Bathsheba bathing (11:2). Now Nathan's judgment is fulfilled: "I will take your women in your sight [says Yhwh], and I will give them to your neighbor, and he shall lie with your women in the sight of this sun . . . before all Israel" (12:11–12).

The narrator then (B) interposes a comment on Ahithophel's counsel: it was considered by all alike to be equivalent to the divine oracle (16:23). Implicitly Ahithophel is pitted against God.

The central scene of debate follows (C). It hinges on whether pursuit should be immediate (Ahithophel) or cautiously prepared (Hushai, playing for time; 17:1–14).

Ahithophel's advice is expressed in terms of an apt and ironic metaphor. By killing the king alone, he says, he will "bring all the army [or people] back to you as a bride comes back to her man" (v. 3, following the LXX; so RSV, NAB). The army is depicted as a woman desired by Absalom. Kill but one man, David (the old husband), and she can come to him as a bride. We recognize the scenario. It is David, Bathsheba, and Uriah again, but with David this time playing Uriah's role! The advice ("word"),

says the narrator, was "right in Absalom's sight" (v. 4). Just so had David assured Joab, "Let not this matter [word] be evil in your sight" (11:25)—to which the narrator had responded, "But [it] was evil in the sight of Yhwh" (11:27).

Absalom's decision to prefer the counsel of Hushai draws from the narrator a comment (B') that puts firmly in divine perspective the previous evaluation of Ahithophel's wisdom. It may undoubtedly be good, but it cannot stand against the power of Yhwh (v. 14).

Finally (A'), it is Hushai's turn to offer advice to the old king, David, via the priests who had returned with the Ark, Zadok and Abiathar (17:15–22). And in the adventure of the messengers (vv. 17–21), we recognize a striking allusion to the story of the spies at Jericho in the house of Rahab (Josh. 2). It is as though we are witnessing the conquest of the land in reverse.

Realizing that David has gained the time needed to escape safely, Ahithophel tidies his affairs and hangs himself (2 Sam. 17:23); for, like the divine oracle (cf. 16:23), he can see the outcome. Now readers know that both Yhwh and Ahithophel have foreseen Absalom's doom. That fate is no longer open to doubt. Interest now lies in the manner of the son's destruction and in David's response.

17:24–19:8
Battle, Message, and Mourning

The story of the ensuing battle and the death of Absalom centers around David's struggle to come to terms with his conflicting roles as king and as father.

17:24–29, Prelude. The stage is set. Absalom too crosses the Jordan, "with all the men of Israel" (v. 24).

Some brief items then bear witness to the strange twists and turns of loyalties in David's world. Mahanaim, where David finds refuge (vv. 24, 27–29), is the place from which Ishbosheth, son of Saul, had waged war against him (chaps. 2–4). Amasa, whom Absalom—now also across the Jordan—sets over the army in Joab's place, is David's nephew, Joab's cousin (though his genealogy poses some difficulties).

Shobi, a son of Nahash, is from conquered Rabbah of the Ammonites (chaps. 10–12). Machir, the son of Ammiel, was the guardian of Saul's grandson, Jonathan's son, Mephibosheth (9:4). They, together with Barzillai the Gileadite (see also 19:31–39), offer king and people manna in the wilderness (cf. v. 29).

18:1–18, Battle. The army is put under the command of Joab, his brother Abishai, and Ittai from Gath, the mercenary captain. Thus, when

David adds that he too will go out with the army, his offer sounds a little lame; he already appears superfluous. Perhaps he has been remaining in Jerusalem too long (cf. 11:1) and is not the soldier he once was. Whatever their underlying reasons, the soldiers put a flattering construction on their insistence that he stay behind. To this he responds meekly, "Whatever is good in your sight, I will do" (vv. 1–4).

Yet he must still interfere: "Deal gently with [or perhaps protect] the young man Absalom" (v. 5), he commands the generals, unwilling to let them do what is good in their sight in the matter of his rebel son. The narrator adds that all the people heard this order, but leaves us to guess at their reaction—enthusiasm, indifference, dismay?

Two things rapidly become clear. First, Joab is determined to be rid of Absalom. Second, David's command, expressing his commitment to his son, has great potential for straining his men's loyalty and destroying morale. The man who reports Absalom's whereabouts is unwilling to kill him not simply because of his sense of loyalty and obedience to the king. He knows only too well how quickly he would find himself alone, a convenient scapegoat (like the Amalekite who claimed to have killed Saul [chap. 1] and the captains who killed Ishbosheth [chap. 4]). Thus soldier and general are set at odds.

18:19–19:8, Message and Mourning. The point is brought home in chap. 19 as the army slinks into the city as though loser rather than victor, "for the army heard that day, 'The king is grieving for his son' " (vv. 2–3). General is set at odds with king: "you have made it clear today," says Joab to David, "that commanders and servants are nothing to you. . . . So now, get up, go out and placate your servants!" (vv. 6–7). We come full circle—as at the outset, the king does what he is told.

At the center of the story of Absalom's death is David's reception of the news. The account is teased out by an elaborate messenger scene, neatly linking battlefield and waiting king through a switch in point of view at 18:24. Like a thread through the account is the question, how will the king take the news of Absalom's fate? Who will tell him and how? Will the messenger become the object of violent displeasure?

In the event, both young Ahimaaz, whom Joab tries to protect, and the Cushite, an African no doubt backed by long experience, prove able to deflect the king from anger. The Cushite's indirect language on top of Ahimaaz's hedging is brilliantly framed. It conveys the message without the brutality of the fact and in terms that force the king to see the news as his people must see it: "May the enemies of my lord the king be like the young man, and all who rise up against you for evil" (v. 32).

David's moving outburst (v. 33) ends the scene. That may be read as a poignant expression of a father's grief that invites us to identify with David's ordinary humanity. Or it may be read critically, through Joab's eyes (19:5–7), revealing the king's absurd self-indulgence. It invites at least those responses along, perhaps, with others more nuanced.

At the close of the episode we glimpse the king, sitting mute at the gate, reviewing his triumphant army and nursing his parental anguish. We have an even more vivid image of the son, suspended between heaven and earth (18:9) —most appropriately for one who so aspired to raise himself up. For the man with the splendid hair this too is a fitting end—ensnared by his handsome head. (Josephus makes it his hair and so it is often portrayed in Western art.) And for the man without a blemish who is paying the price of his father's sin as well as his own there is also apt irony: for he is a ram caught in a thicket (cf. Gen. 22:13).

19:9–20:3
David's Return

Joab ejects David from his private chamber of grief into the world of public appearances. In doing so he makes apparent to readers the fragility of David's power. Perhaps too he makes that apparent to David. Whatever the talk of providence and the hands of God (chaps. 16–17), it is, in this view, victory in battle and control of the army that counts.

19:9–14, David Sways Hearts. The fact that David has been deposed cannot be glossed over. The prelude to restoration is thus a passage that exudes compromise and irresolution (vv. 9–10). David must sway some hearts and minds. He makes his play hard for the support of Judah, his power base from the beginning. He calculates that by appointing his kinsman Amasa as army commander he can win over the remaining rebel forces and risk alienating the loyal Joab (vv. 11–14). The strategy works (v. 14), but it also proves divisive (19:41–20:3).

19:15–20:3, From the Jordan to Jerusalem. The road to exile saw a gradual decline in the quality of the relationships between David and the people he meets on the way. The loyalty of Ittai the foreigner and mercenary was striking. Hushai, the king's friend, risked his life to do what David asked, though that is perhaps what we should have expected from a friend. Ziba *appeared* to be a loyal subject, although his story of Mephibosheth's expectations (that he gain the crown) sounded suspiciously strained. Shimei was openly hostile.

The return has some interesting and ironical variations. Shimei is now making a passionate (and desperate!) declaration of loyalty.

Mephibosheth's story—which, when heard in light of his lameness, carries a ring of probability—compromises Ziba and makes David's earlier judgment look more than a trifle hasty. Moreover, it leaves David in doubt about Mephibosheth and occasions an even more dubious judgment, that they are both equally in the right or the wrong! Whereas Hushai had wished to go on with the king but had gone back at his insistence, Barzillai resists the king's wish to go on and goes back at his own insistence, making it clear that he values a way of life independent of king and court. In stark contrast to the quiet loyalty of Ittai, the foreigner, the men of Israel who hotly claim kinship with the king are only too quick to refuse to have anything more to do with him.

Return, therefore, also reveals an undercurrent of decline. Both the inverted order of the scenes in the journeys to and from the Jordan (i.e., A B C B' A') and the ostensible occasion, a victorious restoration, lead us to expect the return to be narrated as a movement from a low point back to a high one. Instead, the movement to restoration is counterpointed by a falling tone. David's return is far from triumphal.

The return has some important links to the story ahead. The meeting with Shimei (19:16–23) resonates with the earlier encounter (16:5–13). Again an apparently magnanimous David refuses to acquiesce to Abishai's hardheaded ethic of power and offers mercy: "And the king said to Shimei, 'You shall not die'; and the king gave him his oath" (19:23). Yet when it is David's time to die, he will charge Solomon, "do not leave [Shimei] unpunished," but "send his grey head down with blood to Sheol" (1 Kings 2:9). Solomon will oblige, like David with Uriah, at arm's length (1 Kings 2:36–46). It is a jarring scene with which to bring David's story to a close, especially since it is clothed in a heavy layer of pious rhetoric.

The quarrel between the men of Israel and men of Judah takes us back to the civil war with which the book began, but also beyond that to Judges (e.g., the quarrel between the men of Gilead and the men of Ephraim in Judg. 12), to Joseph and his brothers, or to Jacob and Esau. For the nation-family to be riven by jealousy and status seeking is not new.

Moving ahead, we hear Sheba's words echoed in the northern secessionist cry against Rehoboam, Solomon's son (1 Kings 12:16). The nation's unity is fragile at best. With Rehoboam the split will become permanent.

The return ends where the journey into exile began, with the concubines whom the king left behind "to keep [watch over, guard] the house" (2 Sam. 15:16, 20:3; cf. 16:21–22). Unable to keep in order his own house (family), unprepared to guard his own house (city and nation), he leaves ("forsakes," 15:16) the women whom he has taken for his pleasure. They are expected to do what he will not do—with a rapacious Absalom descending upon the palace! But now deeming them tainted by Absalom's intercourse, he will do what patriarchal honor and political wisdom dictate. He "takes" them and "gives" them . . . a prison cell, "the house of keeping"! "So they were confined until the day of their death, widowed by the living" (20:3).

Thus these women are condemned by a man's sin to be shut out of society. Their fate at the hands of Absalom and David compounds that of Tamar (13:20) at the hands of Amnon and David (who offers her no help or consolation). They are both members and victims of David's house. Unlike the king's mercenary captain (Ittai; 15:19–20) or his cursing enemy from the house of Saul (Shimei; 16:11–12; 19:21–23), his women will receive from David no gift of freedom.

20:4–26
The Aftermath of Restoration

20:4–22, War Between Brothers. Given back the kingdom, David now takes action against those who choose to have no part in the giving. Amasa is commissioned to eliminate Sheba. Why he delays beyond the appointed time is unclear, though what little we know of Amasa already suggests either incompetence or treachery as possibilities. His death comes by deception, like the death of Abner in chap. 3. Joab is once more firmly in control.

A wise woman's speech marked the beginning of Absalom's return to Jerusalem (chap. 14). Another wise woman's speech marks the close of David's return (20:14–22). Her wisdom is her way with words—her ability to seize Joab's attention, to recognize the force of his demand, and to sell it to the besieged inhabitants. Joab, like his brother Abishai (16:9; 19:21), wastes no time with political opponents but deals effectively in death. The woman bows to that reality, but in doing so prevents more destruction in the family of Israel—the swallowing up of the city Abel Beth Maacah, a mother in Israel. (Verse 19; the city's name in Hebrew, ironically, means something like "mourning the house of Maacah"; Maacah was the name of Absalom's mother; 3:3.)

20:23–26, The Bureaucracy. The plot of the central section of the book (chaps. 9–20), the story of sin, exile, and restoration, now seems to be exhausted (though it will briefly resume in 1 Kings 1–2, in the story of Solomon's accession to the throne). Marking its end, as its beginning, is a list of David's officials (2 Sam. 20:23–26; cf. 8:15–18). A few changes stand out: there is no mention of David administering justice and equity to all his people; there is now an officer in charge of forced labor (20:24), foreshadowing the issue that will divide the kingdom (Adoram appears again in 1 Kings 12:18); and while David's sons are no longer listed as priests, another non-Levite appears in their place.

21:1–24:25
Last Words

The book draws to a close with chaps. 21–24. Like much of chaps. 1–8, it is fashioned, anthology style, from apparently disparate narrative accounts, lists, and poetry. Though no longer continuing the plot of the central section, it draws some of its characters from previous parts of 2 Samuel, and in this and other ways is closely linked to the body of the book. It soon becomes clear, however, that the events recounted need not all be considered as occurring in time after the events of chap. 20. The section encompasses the whole of David's life.

The material is clearly structured in a chiastic pattern, $A B C C' B' A'$. It starts and ends with narratives of famine, plague, and death, where the action stems from a divine oracle and ends with God "heeding supplications for the land" (21:1–14; 24:1–25). Between these lie anecdotes and lists suggesting David's military power. At the center are two poems of David—a hymn of thanksgiving (chap. 22) and his own "oracle," his "last words" (23:1–7).

21:1–14, Rizpah and the Sons of Saul. In response to a long famine David consults the divine oracle ("sought the face of Yhwh") and receives what is to readers a puzzling response: there is "bloodguilt" on the house of Saul "because he put to death the Gibeonites" (v. 1). We know nothing of such an event. The narrator hastens to explain, reminding us of the story of the Amorite (Canaanite) Gibeonites' covenant with the Israelites (Josh. 9) and informing us that Saul had indeed attempted, "in his zeal for the people of Israel and Judah" (2 Sam. 21:2), to wipe out the Gibeonites—plainly without success. Ironically, in seeking to implement what the Israelites had originally been commanded, Saul now stands condemned for violating their subsequent oath, made through deception.

A moment's reflection reveals the issues of "guilt" and justice here to be highly complex. When does one covenant (or promise or commandment) override another? For how long must "bloodguilt" haunt a house? If Saul's house has blood on its hands, what of David's?

David's response is to allow the Gibeonites to name their compensation. Their request, obliquely, is for blood. The king takes them up with alacrity: "What are you saying [exactly]? I will do it" (v. 4). So seven sons of Saul are given into the hands of the Gibeonites for execu-tion. Once again, conveniently for David, the house of Saul is reduced, and the blame laid at another's door.

The story is troubling. Does the oracle require the deaths of the sons or does David only get from it the answer that he wants in the first place? (We see something similar, perhaps, in Judg. 20:18–28.) It is the Gibeonites who determine that only blood will compensate for blood, and David who encourages them in their demand.

Against Gibeonites and David—and Yhwh? —is set Rizpah. Against bloodguilt that traverses generations and swallows up the innocent is set a mother's care. Rizpah's loyalty traverses death as she fends off from her dead kin the ravening wildlife, the counterpart of the human world that consigned the sons to death. The Hebrew meaning of her name captures, with some irony, something of her spirit: she is "glowing coal," daughter of "falcon."

At the beginning of the book Rizpah was the voiceless pawn in a man's quarrel (3:6–16). At the end she is still voiceless and still a pawn, as she watches her sons destroyed in another quarrel between other men. Yet she succeeds in exercising power through the only action open to her—her mourning and her defiance of the gratuitous humiliation by exposure that was part of the execution (cf. Sophocles *Antigone*). Her action shames David into bringing the bones of Saul and his sons home, into their family tomb, in their own land.

21:15–22, Philistines Again. The narrative breaks off into some anecdotes of the Philistine wars—anecdotes of fights against descendants of giants. First we read of a tiring David rescued by his nephew Abishai—of whom we have earlier heard him exclaim in exasperation, "What is there between you and me, you sons of Zeruiah?" (16:10; 19:22; cf. 3:39). Among the items that follow, one is startling: Elhanan of Bethlehem slew Goliath of Gath, "the shaft of whose spear was like a weaver's beam" (21:19). That is exactly how the Goliath whom David slew is described in 1 Sam. 17:7. So who did slay Goliath?

The narrative of 2 Samuel invites readers to question characters' actions, to probe behind their speech, and to find so often that appearance is not reality. Now it seems that even the narrator may not have all the "facts" reliably arrayed. Perhaps the "truth" of the narrative lies beyond the mere ordering of "facts." Meaning is found when what is important to readers and what seems important in the text interact. The narrator reminds us here that this is not a "story brought live," but a story of life woven out of many strands of information and many perceptions of value. There will be many times when we cannot make it all "fit."

302

22:1–51, The Righteous Psalmist. The song in chap. 22 is found also in Psalms as Psalm 18 with small variations. Its position here at the end of the books of Samuel links it to the song of Hannah at the beginning (1 Sam. 2:1–10). That also is in psalm form. It not only reflects Hannah's own situation but foreshadows the concern with kingship of the two books; it ends with the expectation that Yhwh "will give strength to his king, and raise the horn [exalt the power] of his anointed" (1 Sam. 2:10). David's song is related to a specific occasion ("on the day when . . .") that turns out, however, to be occasions of deliverance throughout his life, including escape from Saul. It too reaches its climax with "Yhwh's anointed," now specified as David himself (2 Sam. 22:51).

The opening imagery of Yhwh as rock (vv. 2–3; cf. vv. 32, 47) is apt for one who found refuge at the Rock of Escape (1 Sam. 23:24–29). The psalmist then recalls his cry in his distress, his enemies like waves sweeping over him, and the coming of Yhwh in lightning, thunder, and clouds of a storm (2 Sam. 22:4–20). In the central section (vv. 21–28) the psalmist reflects on his own righteousness, the reason, as he sees it, for his reward. The focus then shifts back to God but in order to speak of what the psalmist can do through God's support (vv. 29–51). As noted, it comes to rest on David and his descendants (v. 51).

Distress, theophany, and rescue are described in graphic terms. Participants, emotions, situations, actions—all are heightened into extremes. So too are the protestations of righteousness and achievement. In Psalms, in the context of much similar poetry, this characteristic might slip by the reader unnoticed. In the present prose context it stops readers short: "I was blameless before [Yhwh]," proclaims David, "and I kept myself from guilt" (v. 24). One effect of this lengthy self-adulation, therefore, is to proclaim not righteousness but self-righteousness, not piety but hypocrisy. That is a reading hard to resist.

23:1–39, Last Words and Mighty Men. So it is too with the "last words of David" (23:1–7). As David's (non-Levite) sons had become priests, so now the king transforms himself into the divine oracle: "The spirit of Yhwh speaks by me" (v. 2). David speaks of ruling justly and being rewarded for it. "For a lasting covenant [Yhwh] has made with me, ordered in all and secure" (v. 5). These are confident words, yet hedged about with questions: "For is it not thus, my house, with Yhwh? . . . Will he not cause [all my deliverance and desire] to spring forth?" These are rhetorical questions, of course, but they invite scrutiny.

The poem shifts focus to the field (v. 4), to threatening thorns and the "weapons" of those who root out the forces of chaos (vv. 6–7). The vision is like that of David's psalm (chap. 22). Good arms itself for battle with evil, a David against a Goliath. (But, we might wonder, was it not Goliath who armed himself with iron and the shaft of a spear?) So the poem dissolves into a listing and telling of this weaponry—of the anointed's mighty men and their deeds (vv. 8–39).

In the center of the chapter is one of those great stories of David (vv. 13–17). In an unguarded moment he buys water at the price of other men's blood. We see the man who commands intense loyalty and who is alert to providence as he refuses to drink the water, pouring it out to Yhwh, blood upon the ground. That reminds us of the David who would not reach out against Saul, Yhwh's anointed (1 Sam. 24, 26), or who turned Abishai's sword back to its sheath when Shimei cursed him and called him a "man of blood" (16:5–13; cf. 19:21–23).

In turn, however, to think of David as a "man of blood" raises disturbing recollections of other occasions, as we have noted before (in 16:5–12)—recollections of the slaughter of the priests of Nob (1 Sam. 22:11–23, esp. v. 22), or the murder of Uriah (2 Sam. 11), or the execution of the seven sons of Saul (chap. 21).

In fact, the tale of the water of Bethlehem is surrounded by recollections, for the chapter is full of names. As we recognize them we bring the whole story into review. David's psalm speaks only of himself, of his God, and of his righteousness. The lists of mighty men tell a different story. They tell of a house secured by many, with blood and pain and not always with righteousness.

The narrator reminds us of Abishai (23:18) who, we recall, saved David from the giant (21:15–17). Within a verse or two (23:24) another name, Elhanan from David's hometown, has resurrected that unsettling anecdote of Elhanan and Goliath (21:19). Asahel takes us back to the civil war and Joab's killing of Abner (2 Sam. 2–3); Benaiah takes us forward to Solomon's ruthless disposal of Shimei at David's behest (1 Kings 2:36–46)—Shimei of whom the king said, "You shall not die," and gave him his oath (2 Sam. 19:23).

The list in 23:24–39 is particularly rich in allusion to the Bathsheba story. Names jump out: Eliam (Bathsheba's father? cf. 11:3), Nathan, Zobah, and the Ammonites (chap. 10), Joab (chaps. 10–12). Finally (23:39) it comes to rest upon none other than Uriah the Hittite! We might hear other oracular words: "Why have you despised the word of Yhwh, doing what is evil in his sight? Uriah the Hittite . . . you have slain with the sword of the Ammonites; so now a lasting sword will not turn aside from your house" (Nathan in 12:9–10). Is the psalmist blameless before Yhwh? Is his house secure?

David's story has a way of shifting out from under us. It is a story that refuses to be tamed, secured, or neatly ordered.

24:1–25, King and People. Why Yhwh's anger is kindled against Israel we are not told. The divine anger is worked out, however, through David who, as in chap. 21, appears a ready champion of this particular word (again, perhaps, an oracle or a decision by lot, with the questions put by the inquirer). To number the people is to number the army (the same word in Hebrew). A census is a tool for centralizing power; its purpose is usually to raise taxes and an army. The great irony of this story is that it is Joab, the power broker at the center of this centralized government, who protests against the action (24:3–4).

What exactly is wrong with the census is also unexpressed, though in the eyes of Yhwh (and the prophet Gad) it is perhaps its potential for military aggrandizement at the expense of trust in the power of Yhwh. That would take us right back to Samuel's speech about the grasping ways of kings, when the people first ask for a king (1 Sam. 8:10–12).

Yet once more it is difficult not to be impressed by David. He is boldly penitent (2 Sam. 24:10, 17). He invites action against himself and his own house rather than the ordinary people: "these sheep, what have they done?" (v. 17). He is unwilling to make an offering to Yhwh that has cost him nothing (v. 24).

His choice of the plague is couched in piety: "let us fall into the hands of Yhwh, for his mercy is great; but let me not fall into human hands" (v. 14). He thus eliminates the crucial second option, that he flee three months before his foes—the only option in which he is the focus and the spread of death might be contained. So once more a question hangs over our reading. Is the king who promoted the census unwilling still to relinquish power in the interests of his people? Is he unwilling to return to his roots, houseless, living by his wits, pursued by Saul in the wilderness? Instead, he bequeaths on Israel the deaths of seventy thousand people.

"And Yhwh heard supplications for the land, and the plague was averted from Israel" (v. 25). But Yhwh had halted the plague before David had prayed for the people or offered his sacrifice (v. 16). Why, we are not told. And all along, while David thinks that he is the cause of the plague and that the expiation of his sin is the key to everything, we know that it is Israel that is the object of God's anger. David has been merely God's unwitting tool in the expression of that anger.

Saul seems to haunt this last episode of the book, like the first. David, so different from Saul, is yet so alike. David, induced by Yhwh to offend, reminds us of Saul, driven by the spirit to fits of jealous rage. Though both stand at the focal points of their stories, Yhwh's action pushes us to see that they are not the ultimate focus of Yhwh's concern. Rather they facilitate Yhwh's dealings with the covenant community. At heart the story is about God and the people.

Bibliography

Ackroyd, P. R. *The Second Book of Samuel.* Cambridge Bible Commentary on the New English Bible. Cambridge: Cambridge University Press, 1977.

Berlin, A. *Poetics and Interpretation of Biblical Narrative.* Sheffield: Almond Press, 1983.

Brueggemann, W. *David's Truth in Israel's Imagination and Memory.* Philadelphia: Fortress, 1985.

Interpretation, vol. 35, no. 4 (October, 1981); vol. 40, no. 2 (April, 1986).

McCarter, P. K. *II Samuel.* Anchor Bible, 9. Garden City, NY: Doubleday, 1984.

Newsome, J. D., Jr. *1 Samuel. 2 Samuel.* Atlanta, GA: Knox, 1982.

Sternberg, M. *The Poetics of Biblical Narrative.* Bloomington, IN: Indiana University Press, 1985.

Trible, P. *Texts of Terror.* Philadelphia: Fortress, 1984.

1 KINGS

P. KYLE McCARTER, JR.

INTRODUCTION

The First Book of the Kings is the tenth book of the Hebrew Bible, the eleventh according to the arrangement of the Septuagint, in which Ruth stands between Judges and 1 Samuel. Kings is referred to as a single book in the Talmud; it was not divided into two in the Hebrew tradition until the late Middle Ages. But the division came much earlier in the Greek tradition, which treats 1 and 2 Kings with 1 and 2 Samuel as a canonical unit called 1–4 Kingdoms. The divisions between books correspond to the deaths of major figures: Saul at the break between 1 Samuel and 2 Samuel, David at the break between 2 Samuel and 1 Kings, and Ahab at the break between 1 Kings and 2 Kings. The four books of Samuel and Kings together with Joshua and Judges form the traditional canonical division called the Former Prophets. Modern scholarship recognizes this division, with Deuteronomy as an introduction, as an editorial unit, the Deuteronomistic History (see "Literary History" below).

1 Kings relates the history of Israel from the death of David and accession of Solomon to the death of Ahab and accession of Ahaziah. The book divides roughly into four parts. The first part describes the transfer of power from David to Solomon (1:1–2:46). The second part is an account of the reign of Solomon (3:1–11:43), which gives special attention to his erection of the Temple. The third part recounts the early history of the divided monarchy (12:1–16:28), describing the secession of the northern tribes after Solomon's death and the reigns of the first rulers of the independent kingdoms of Israel and Judah. The fourth part is an account of the reign of Ahab (16:29–22:53), in which the prophet Elijah plays a major role.

and in the inscription of King Mesha of Moab (cf. 2 Kings 3:4–8). Ahab is named in the inscriptions of the Assyrian emperor Shalmaneser III, who also mentions the Damascene kings Hadadezer, who may have been the Ben-hadad contemporary with Ahab (20:1), and Hazael (19:15). There is no other direct evidence in contemporary sources, but much can be learned indirectly and inferentially from contemporary records of events that took place outside of Israel and Judah. Archaeological study of Israelite sites also provides primary information. Later histories of Israel, such as that of the first-century historian Josephus, are based largely on the biblical text and have limited independent value. The materials Josephus quotes from the "Annals of Tyre" and other Phoenician sources, however, provide a valuable supplement to the biblical account of the relations of Solomon and Ahab with their Phoenician allies.

In the final analysis, however, the basic source for the history of this period is the biblical record itself. Because of its long and complex literary history, it must be used very cautiously for historical reconstruction, but when critically interpreted, it provides a fairly clear picture of the sequence of events. Solomon's economic successes were not sufficient to eliminate the regional factionalism that had troubled David's reign (cf. 2 Sam. 20:1–22). When Solomon died in about 930 B.C., the northern tribes refused to accept the rule of his son, Rehoboam, and made Jeroboam, an Ephraimite officer in Solomon's labor force, their king (1 Kings 12). The now independent kingdoms of Israel and Judah endured a period of weakness and intermittent civil war that lasted until the reign of Omri (ca. 876–869 B.C.), who seems to have stabilized Israel and established a rapprochement with Judah.

Historical Background

Only very limited historical information can be derived from extrabiblical written materials from the time described in 1 Kings (→ Chronology, Old Testament). Neither David nor Solomon is mentioned in contemporary extrabiblical sources. The scope of Shishak's incursion in the time of Rehoboam (14:25–28) is better understood because of a list of conquered cities he had carved on the wall of the temple of Amun-Re at Karnak. But no king of Israel or Judah is named in contemporary records before Omri, who is mentioned in Assyrian records

Literary History

Scholars regard 1 Kings as part of an editorial unit that extends from Deuteronomy through 2 Kings. This unit is an account of the Israelites' experiences from the time they first approached the promised land under the leadership of Moses until the time of their exclusion from the land at the beginning of the Babylonian exile. The purpose of the account is to evaluate the people's experiences on the basis of the rules of conduct set forth in the Deuteronomic law code (Deut. 12–26). Thus the work as a whole is called the Deuteronomistic

History (→Deuteronomist; Deuteronomistic Historian).

The Deuteronomistic History was composed by one or more writers utilizing a variety of materials drawn from both archival and narrative sources. Some of these materials were annalistic, having been preserved, we assume, in the palace or Temple archives in Jerusalem. The present text of 1 Kings contains citations of three lost works of this kind: "the book of the acts of Solomon" (11:41), "the Book of the Chronicles of the Kings of Israel" (e.g., 14:19), and "the Book of the Chronicles of the Kings of Judah" (e.g., 14:29). Other sources of the Deuteronomistic History seem to have been transmitted in prophetic circles. Various stories about holy men, prophets, and kings—some legendary in origin, others historiographical—have been incorporated into the larger history. Groups of such stories were probably already combined into larger narratives before their incorporation into the Deuteronomistic History. The most important of these is the Elijah-Elisha narrative complex now underlying 1 Kings 17–2 Kings 10.

The Deuteronomistic History is a product of the Babylonian exile, having reached its final form after the last event reported in 2 Kings, the release of Jehoiachin from prison in 560 B.C. (2 Kings 25:27–30). Nevertheless, many scholars believe that much of the history was completed earlier, during the reign of Josiah (639–609 B.C.) and in the midst of the reforms instituted by Josiah, which seem also to have been based on principles expressed in the Deuteronomic law code (cf. 2 Kings 23). Of these principles, the most important for an understanding of the books of Kings are, first, the insistence on the sacrificial worship of Yahweh, God of Israel, at a single, divinely chosen sanctuary and, second, the absolute prohibition of the worship of foreign gods.

The Central Sanctuary. Deuteronomy 12 requires that offerings be brought to Yahweh only in the place he chooses, a single, central sanctuary. Israel's prosperity in the land is closely tied to the establishment of this sanctuary and its preservation as the exclusive place of sacrifice. Because Jerusalem was understood in Deuteronomistic theology to be the chosen place, the erection of the Temple of Yahweh by Solomon is presented as a landmark event in the Deuteronomistic History (see commentary below on 5:1–9:25). Later, when the kingship of Israel is taken away from Solomon's heir, the rule of Judah is said to have been left to him for the sake of David and Jerusalem, the chosen city (11:32; see commentary below on 11:26–40). On the negative side, Jeroboam's establishment of rival sanctuaries at Dan and Bethel is presented as a uniquely heinous crime (see commentary below on 12:25–33). Together with other crimes, "the sin of Jeroboam," as the perpetuation of these sanctuaries by his successors is called, is shown to have led finally to the destruction of the Northern Kingdom (2 Kings 17:21–23). The Southern Kingdom too was endangered by violations of the law of the central sanctuary. All of the kings of Judah before Hezekiah are said to have permitted local places of worship, conventionally referred to as "high places," to remain in use. Thus, Rehoboam and his successors are condemned for tolerating shrines "on every high hill and under every green tree" (14:23; cf. Deut. 12:2 and commentary below on 14:21–24).

Foreign Gods. Deuteronomy 13 requires that anyone—whether a prophet, a family member, a wife, or a friend—who induces an Israelite to worship a foreign god should be put to death. The tolerance of such subversive individuals by the kings of Israel is an important theme of 1 Kings, where the particular problem is that of foreign wives who entice their husbands to worship foreign gods. According to the understanding of the Deuteronomistic editors, this was the crime for which Solomon was afflicted with adversaries and his heir deprived of the rule of the Northern Kingdom (see commentary below on 11:1–13). The quintessential foreign wife, however, was Jezebel, who actively promoted worship of Baal in Israel (16:29–33).

The Deuteronomistic editors provided synopses at the beginning and end of the account of the reign of each king (→ Deuteronomistic Framework). Generally speaking, the purposes of these synopses were to coordinate the chronologies of the northern and southern kings, to provide statistical information drawn from archival sources, and to offer editorial evaluation based on Deuteronomistic principles. The religious policies of seven of the kings of Judah are evaluated positively (Jehoshaphat, Jehoash, Amaziah, Azariah, Jotham, Hezekiah, and Josiah), although the favorable evaluation of the first five of these is qualified by their failure to remove the high places. The northern kings are condemned without exception, usually for perpetuating "the sin of Jeroboam."

Significance for the Ancient Community

The age of Solomon was remembered by the later community as a golden age. The king's dominion was broad (4:21), his wisdom was internationally acclaimed (4:34), and his wealth was fabulous (10:14). The people were prosperous and happy (4:20). Nevertheless, the biblical account of the reign of Solomon has a dark side and concludes with a stern divine judgement. The purpose of the account was not to invite the ancient community to reminisce on glories of the past or to stimulate national pride. As a

306

part of the Deuteronomistic History, it offered the people of Judah sober reflections on what its authors regarded as centuries of national wrongdoing.

The original edition of the Deuteronomistic History was addressed to the people of Judah living in the latter part of the seventh century B.C. For them, the story of the reigns of Solomon and the kings of the Divided Monarchy illustrated the need for the measures instituted by Josiah's reform. Solomon's erection of the Temple was the culmination of a long process by which the divinely chosen place of sacrifice had been established. Most of Solomon's kingdom was taken away, however, because he condoned the worship of foreign gods in Jerusalem. Later, the Northern Kingdom was destroyed because Jeroboam and his successors abandoned Jerusalem, and many kings of Judah incurred Yahweh's anger by permitting sacrifice at local shrines. In the time of Josiah, however, the worship of foreign gods was prohibited and the high places were being dismantled. The lesson of history was clear: if the people of Judah supported their king's policies, they could avoid the fate of their northern kin. Because of Yahweh's special regard for David and Jerusalem, moreover, they could expect to find security in the chosen city under the rule of the Davidic king (11:13; 15:4–5).

For the audience of the final edition of the Deuteronomistic History, the people of Judah living in exile in Babylon, the stories of the kings afforded evidence of the recurrent wrongdoing that justified Yahweh's punishment of his people. The crimes of Manasseh, Josiah's predecessor, had been so heinous that Josiah's reforms could save Judah only temporarily (2 Kings 21:10–16; 23:26–27). Jerusalem had been tested with "the line of Samaria, and the level of the house of Ahab" (2 Kings 21:13) and found wanting. In keeping with Yahweh's warning to Solomon (1 Kings 9:6–9), the people had been excluded from the land, and the Temple itself had been laid in ruins. Nevertheless, as Solomon himself had foreseen (1 Kings 8:46–53), there was hope even in captivity for those who would confess their crimes, look toward the site of the Temple, and return to the faithful service of Yahweh.

COMMENTARY

1:1–2:46

The Accession of Solomon

The opening chapters of the book describe Solomon's assumption of David's throne. The cir-

cumstances are suspicious: Solomon is not David's eldest living son, and those who oppose his accession are slain as soon as he becomes king. The document upon which chaps. 1–2 are based seems to have been addressed to an audience that was aware of these circumstances. It was probably composed early in Solomon's reign to explain the events leading up to the succession and demonstrate the legitimacy of the new king.

All of these materials now belong to the larger Deuteronomistic History, however, and the principal significance of the accession of Solomon for the Deuteronomistic historian is the fulfillment of the divine promise made in Nathan's oracle that David would have a son who would build a temple to Yahweh and for whom Yahweh would establish an enduring dynasty (2 Sam. 7:11b–16, esp. v. 13; cf. 1 Kings 2:12, 24, 33b, 45; 8:20).

1:1–53, The Accession of Solomon. At the beginning of the story, David is still alive, but old and debilitated. He cannot live long, and the question of the succession is the central theme of the narrative. Of David's many sons, only two are still alive. Adonijah is the older of the two (v. 6; cf. 2:22) and, thus, the heir presumptive. He has the support of Joab, David's chief general, and Abiathar, one of David's two high priests (v. 7). His rival is his younger brother, Solomon, who has the support of Benaiah, another ranking military figure, Zadok, the other high priest (v. 8), and Solomon's mother, Bathsheba. As explained above, the narrator's purpose is to defend the legitimacy of the accession of Solomon. To achieve this, he first shows that David exercised his right to set aside primogeniture (the law of the firstborn) and designate his successor. In vv. 32–35, therefore, the old king names Solomon his heir, fulfilling a promise made long before (vv. 17, 30). At the same time, the narrator presents Adonijah as an unworthy candidate for the throne by pointedly associating him with his elder brother Absalom, a rebel (v. 6). In vv. 5–6, therefore, Adonijah appears as a very handsome man who procures a chariot with horses and fifty runners and declares himself king—in short, as another Absalom (cf. 2 Sam. 14:25; 15:1, 10).

2:1–12, The Death of David. The narrator shows that two of the executions ordered by Solomon at the time of his accession were carried out in compliance with the deathbed instructions of his father. David condemns Joab for the murders of Abner (2 Sam. 3:27; →Abner) and Amasa (2 Sam. 20:10; → Amasa), crimes for which bloodguilt was attached to David (reading the superior Gk. text of 1 Kings 2:5). He also condemns the Benjaminite agitator Shimei for abusing him and imposing a curse on him (v. 8;

307

2 Sam. 16:5–14). By contrast, David stipulates that Barzillai, the Gileadite who provided for David's troops during Absalom's revolt (2 Sam. 17:27–29; 19:31–39), should be given favored treatment at Solomon's court. A Deuteronomistic expansion of David's words (1 Kings 2:3–4) links the duration of the dynasty to the new king's obedience to Mosaic law, and the biblical story of David's life concludes with a Deuteronomistic succession summary (vv. 11–12), including a calculation of the length of his reign (v. 11; cf. 2 Sam. 5:4–5).

2:13–46, The Death of Solomon's Enemies. Solomon is now king, and those who opposed him are executed one after another. The narrator's purpose is to justify these executions. Adonijah, though given an opportunity to live under the protection of the court (1:52), asks to marry Abishag the Shunammite, the young woman who nursed David during his last illness (1:3–4). Because claiming the harem of the previous king is a standard way of claiming the kingdom itself (cf. 2 Sam. 16:21–22), Solomon interprets Adonijah's request as an attempt to reestablish his claim to the throne, an open act of treason, and orders his execution. Joab is executed not for his opposition to Solomon—though that is the reason for his flight to the asylum of the altar (1 Kings 2:28; cf. Exod. 21:14) —but in compliance with David's deathbed orders (1 Kings 2:5–6; see above). Shimei, who was also condemned by David (2:8–9), is given an opportunity to live under house arrest in Jerusalem, but he violates the terms set by Solomon and forfeits his life. Another opponent of Solomon, the priest Abiathar, is exiled, but his life is spared because of his early assistance to David (cf. 1 Sam. 22:20–23; 23:6; 30:7–8) and his service as high priest (2 Sam. 8:17; 20:25). A comment by a Deuteronomistic editor (1 Kings 2:27) connects the banishment of Abiathar with the prophecy in 1 Sam. 2:33.

3:1–11:43

The Kingship of Solomon

The biblical account of the reign of Solomon is a loose collection of miscellaneous materials, much of which seems to be drawn from archival sources. The arrangement, which is topical rather than chronological, has a two-part structure presenting the positive and negative sides of Solomon's kingship. The first part (3:1–10:29) depicts the grandeur of his reign and reports his great achievements. It begins with a vision in which he receives divine favor and is granted great wisdom (3:4–15), and it continues with

events and catalogues of information that illustrate both the wisdom of Solomon and its consequences in effective administration and the accumulation of wealth. The second part (11:1–43) describes the religious misconduct into which Solomon's foreign wives led him and identifies the external and internal adversaries who caused conflict throughout his reign. The first, positive part of the account of Solomon's kingship is dominated by the story of the erection of the Temple, which has been elaborated with editorial remarks stressing its supreme importance in the Deuteronomistic understanding of the reign. The long tirade on Solomon's foreign wives that introduces the second, negative part of the account (11:1–13) is almost entirely Deuteronomistic in composition. These things suggest that the larger two-part structure is itself a result of Deuteronomistic editorial activity. A similar, two-part topical arrangement into positive and negative aspects is also visible to some extent in the final, Deuteronomistic arrangement of the accounts of the reigns of both Saul and David.

3:1–28

The Divine Gift of Wisdom

Biblical tradition associates wisdom in general with Solomon. What he requests at the beginning of his reign, however, is a specific and pragmatic kind of wisdom, the ability to govern his people well. The attribution of this type of wisdom to a good king was commonplace in ancient Near Eastern tradition, and it is found in the Bible in the cases of David (2 Sam. 14:17, 19, 20) and other good kings. Such wisdom was regarded as the basis of an enduring kingship and a successful reign (cf. Ps. 72).

3:1, Solomon's Marriage to Pharaoh's Daughter. The general circumstances of Solomon's alliance with Egypt can be reconstructed from the scattered references preserved in 1 Kings. Early in Solomon's reign an Egyptian army captured the Canaanite-Philistine city of Gezer on the border of Israel. At the same time Solomon married an Egyptian princess, and the pharaoh gave his daughter the city as a dowry (9:16–17). Solomon brought the pharaoh's daughter into the City of David (3:1), where she lived until a house was built for her nearby (9:24). The unidentified Egyptian king is thought to have been one of the pharaohs of the weak twenty-first dynasty (ca. 1070–945).

3:2–3, Sacrifice at "High Places." These two verses are editorial (Deuteronomistic), having been inserted ahead of the account of Solomon's visit to the high place at Gibeon. The later Davidic kings will be censured for their failure to remove the high places (14:23; 15:14; 22:43), but Solomon's action in this chapter is mitigated by the fact that the Temple has not yet been built.

3:4–15, The Dream at Gibeon. Solomon's revelatory dream belongs to the widespread ancient Near Eastern practice of incubation dreaming, by which an individual slept in a sanctuary in the hope of receiving a divine message. Partial biblical parallels include Jacob's dream at Bethel (Gen. 28:11–19) and Samuel's call at Shiloh (1 Sam. 3:2–18). Gibeon, which lay northwest of Jerusalem, seems to have been a prominent city in the time of David and Solomon (→ Gibeon). Although the statement in 1 Kings 3:4 that Solomon made regular sacrifices there of a thousand whole burnt offerings must be an exaggeration, the Gibeonite high place and altar clearly constituted an important cultic center before the erection of the Temple in Jerusalem.

As explained above, the gift Solomon requests is the wisdom to govern well. Yahweh is so pleased that he gives Solomon more than he has asked for: he will receive *unparalleled* wisdom (v. 12) and, with it, wealth and fame (v. 13).

Note, finally, that the story of Solomon's dream has been expanded editorially by the insertion of certain materials lacking in the parallel version of the event in 2 Chron. 1:3–13, which seems to have escaped Deuteronomistic editing. Thus, 1 Kings 3:6 has been elaborated to connect Solomon's succession to David's throne with the dynastic promise in 2 Samuel 7; 1 Kings 3:14 has been added to qualify Yahweh's promise; and v. 15 has been altered to shift the place of sacrifice from Gibeon to Jerusalem.

3:16–28, The Judgment of Solomon. The account of the divine gift of wisdom is followed by an example of its practical application. The sagacity with which Solomon arbitrates between two prostitutes convinces the Israelites that "the wisdom of God was within him" (v. 28).

The story of the wise judge who identifies the true mother of a disputed child by ordering that the child be cut in half is very widespread in world folklore. Of some twenty-two examples that have been collected, the closest to the biblical story is a Jain tale of two women, widows of the same man, who claim to be the mother of his child and, therefore, the rightful head of his household and heir to his estate. When the magistrate rules that the estate should be divided and the child sawn in half, the true mother earnestly relinquishes all claims, pleading that the child should not be harmed. The magistrate awards her both the estate and the child.

4:1–34
Solomon's Administration

The organization of Solomon's government is described here in materials drawn largely from archival sources. The arrangement of the larger narrative, in which this section follows immediately after the section concerned with Solomon's wisdom, suggest that the governmental structures described here are reflections of the king's divinely given aptitude for wise rule. Under these policies, we are told, the people thrived (v. 20). As noted below, however, many modern historians question both the wisdom and effectiveness of the fiscal policies involved in the division of the kingdom into administrative districts (vv. 7–28).

4:1–6, Solomon's Cabinet. A comparison of this list with the two lists of David's high officials in 2 Sam. 8:16–18 and 20:23–26 shows substantial continuity between the two administrations. Jehoshaphat (1 Kings 4:3) and Adoniram/Adoram (v. 6) were already in office under David (2 Sam. 8:16; 20:24). Benaiah, who is now in charge of the army (cf. 1 Kings 2:35), served as commander of David's personal bodyguard (2 Sam. 8:18; 20:23). The other officers named here are sons of men who served under David. (The reference in 1 Kings 4:4 to Zadok and Abiathar as priests is out of place here, where Zadok's son is already in office [v. 2] and Abiathar has been banished [2:26–27].)

4:7–28, The Twelve District Officers. Solomon's kingdom is organized into twelve administrative districts presided over by officers whose chief responsibility is the collection of revenues for the maintenance of the royal household. Each district officer has the responsibility for providing for Solomon's court during one month out of the year (vv. 7, 27), and it is this arrangement, rather than the traditional tribal division, that dictates the number twelve. While some of the districts correspond closely to tribal boundaries, others do not. The place of Judah in the list is not clear. "The land" of v. 19b is evidently Judah, as many ancient versions make explicit. Unlike the other district officers, the officer in charge of Judah is not named. Moreover, there seem to be twelve districts *apart from* Judah, and it has been suggested that Judah was exempt from the taxation imposed upon the other parts of the country.

Noting the departure of the list from the traditional tribal allotments, many historians believe that Solomon deliberately tried to weaken tribal loyalties to strengthen the central government. Another purpose for this new arrangement may have been to incorporate newly conquered territories into the kingdom. If so, it seems likely that the reorganization was begun under David, who was responsible for the conquests, and it has been conjectured that David's census (2 Sam. 24) was the beginning of the process.

The conclusion to the list of officers in 1 Kings 4:7–19 is found in vv. 27–28, a miscellany of materials about Solomon's reign having been inserted in between (vv. 20–26). We are told in v. 21 that his dominion extended from the Euphrates ("the River") to the border of Egypt, probably the Brook of Egypt (cf. 8:65), the traditional southern border of Canaan (→ Egypt, Brook of). This statement is usually explained as the nostalgic hyperbole of a writer living long after the time of Solomon, and it is true that the language of the insertion in 4:20–26 is that of the postexilic period. It is quite possible, however, that territories as far away as Tiphsah on the shore of the Euphrates (v. 24) acknowledged at least a nominal fealty to Solomon at the beginning of his reign. David defeated an Aramean coalition that included armies from the western bank of the Euphrates as well as southern Syria (2 Sam. 8:3–13), and the victory brought tributaries to David from as far north as Hamath on the middle Orontes (cf. 2 Sam. 8:9–12).

4:29–34, Solomon's Wisdom. A collection of loosely related remarks has been gathered here to form a paean on Solomon's legendary wisdom. As in the case of vv. 20–26 above, the language suggests that this passage is a late insertion, anticipating the eventual attribution to Solomon of all kinds of anonymous sayings and songs (Prov. 1:1; 10:1; Eccles. 1:1; Song of Sg. 1:1; Pss. 72:1; 127:1), though this does not preclude the possibility that the assertions made in the present section are based on old tradition. Solomon's wisdom is compared favorably with that of the Egyptians and the people of the East, presumably the Mesopotamians, unless the term means "ancient times" rather than "the East." He is said to have been wiser than certain great sages of the past whose names are obscure to us. The statement in 1 Kings 4:33 that Solomon spoke about trees and animals brings to mind not only such proverbs as that about the industry of the ant in Prov. 6:6 (attributed to Solomon in Prov. 1:1) but also Jotham's fable about the trees in Judg. 9:7–21 and Samson's riddle about the lion and honey in Judg. 14:14. A similar use of natural history is found in wisdom materials from Aramean, Mesopotamian, and Egyptian sources.

5:1–9:25

The Temple of Solomon

As explained in the introduction, Solomon's erection of the Temple was understood by the Deuteronomistic historian as the most important event of his reign and a crucial juncture in the larger story of Israel's experience in the land. In Deuteronomy 12, Moses promised the people that, when they entered and conquered the promised land, Yahweh would give them "rest" from their enemies (Deut. 12:9, 10). The promise of rest was linked to the establishment of a single, central sanctuary, "the place that Yahweh will choose" (Deut. 12:5, 11, 14), to which the worship of Yahweh would be confined. Though the time of "rest" seemed at hand after the conquest led by Joshua (Josh. 21:43–45; 22:4; 23:1), the promise could not be fulfilled until the land was fully pacified and the central sanctuary established. These things were left for David and Solomon. David fought the wars that finally pacified the land (2 Sam. 8) and conquered Jerusalem and brought Yahweh's Ark there (2 Sam. 5–6). Now Solomon builds the Temple.

5:1–12, Negotiations with Hiram of Tyre. Extrabiblical sources indicate that Hiram, king of the Phoenician city of Tyre, was an energetic and successful ruler, especially remembered for his building projects (→Hiram). He was an ally of David (cf. v. 1), whose palace he helped build (2 Sam. 5:11). Now he sends a delegation to renew the diplomatic relationship with David's son, and Solomon asks him for help in the construction of a temple for Yahweh. The contract calls for timber, including the fabled cedar of Lebanon, to be shipped to Jerusalem in exchange for large quantities of wheat and olive oil.

Though probably based on earlier materials, this passage is cast in the distinctive rhetoric and style of the Deuteronomistic historian. The language of Solomon's proposal to build the Temple (1 Kings 5:5) recalls the promise made to David in Nathan's oracle (2 Sam. 7:4–17), a key Deuteronomistic passage. Indeed, David wanted to build the Temple himself (2 Sam. 7:2), but, according to the understanding of the author of the present passage (1 Kings 5:3), this was impossible because of the constant warfare during David's reign.

5:13–18, The Organization of the Corvée. The source of manpower for Solomon's Temple project is "a levy of forced labor" (RSV), or corvée. This was an old institution, known from fourteenth-century Canaanite texts, which Solomon and perhaps David (cf. 2 Sam. 20:24) revived in Israel. Apparently it was not the same as the "forced levy of slaves" (RSV) imposed on foreigners, from which Israelites were exempt (1 Kings 9:20–22). The present passage refers to the conscription of "all Israel" for several months out of each year (5:13–14). Work details go to Lebanon to assist in the harvest of timber and to the Israelite hills to quarry and transport. The use of corvée labor in Solomon's various

310

building projects is thought by historians to have been a major source of popular resentment during his reign and a contributing factor in the secession of the northern tribes after his death (cf. 12:4).

6:1-38, The Building of the Temple. Solomon's Temple stands 30 cubits high (about 45 feet). Its floor plan is a rectangle 60 cubits long by 20 cubits wide (about 90 by 30 feet). Entrance is from a forecourt (the "vestibule," "porch," or "portico") into the nave or holy place and, beyond the nave, the inner sanctuary or most holy place. If the cedar altar mentioned in v. 20 is the same as "the bronze altar in front of Yahweh" in 8:64, it is located in front of the Temple next to the molten sea described in 7:23-26 (cf. 2 Chron. 4:1 and esp. 2 Kings 16:14). The interior walls are completely linked with carved cedar, and the floor is covered with cypress planks. The doors are made of carved cypress and olivewood, and a pair of olivewood cherubim is placed in the inner sanctuary. There is very generous use of gold overlay throughout the structure (→ Temple, The).

7:1-12, The Palace Complex. The secular part of Solomon's construction in Jerusalem includes the administrative halls and residential chambers that, collectively, make up the king's own "house" (v. 1). Presumably the House of the Forest of Lebanon is so named because of its extensive cedar paneling. References to it elsewhere suggest that it may function as a treasury (cf. 10:17) and an armory (cf. Isa. 22:8b), among other things. The Hall of the Throne or Hall of Judgment (1 Kings 7:7) must be the place where the king dispenses justice. Like the Hall of Pillars (v. 6) and the private residential chambers of Solomon and the pharaoh's daughter (v. 8), the Hall of the Throne may be a compartment of the House of the Forest or an independent structure.

7:13-51, The Temple Furnishings. The elaborate bronze work of the Temple is crafted by a Phoenician named Hiram, who is not to be confused with the king of the same name. According to v. 14, he is the son of a man from Tyre and an Israelite widow from the tribe of Naphtali (Dan in 2 Chron. 2:14), whose tribal allotment lay in the far north near Phoenician territory. The description of his skill is reminiscent of that of Bezalel, the chief craftsman of the tabernacle, in Exod. 31:3 and 35:31. According to 1 Kings 7:46, his foundry is in the rich clay beds of the Kikkar or Ghor, the plain of the lower Jordan and Dead Sea, between the towns of Succoth and Zarethan.

Hiram's task is to produce the bronze furnishings that will be displayed outside the Temple. Two freestanding pillars with pome-granate capitals will stand on the forecourt flanking the door to the nave (vv. 15-22). The significance of their names, Jachin and Boaz, is not known, but they may be the incipits, or opening words, of Temple inscriptions (Heb. *yakin*, "May he establish" . . . ; *bo'az*, "With him strength . . ."). The molten sea (vv. 23-26) is an enormous bronze cauldron resting on the backs of twelve bronze oxen, three of which faced each of the four cardinal directions. In 2 Chron. 4:6, the molten sea is described as a laver for priestly oblations (cf. Exod. 30:17-21), but its rim is at least 10 feet above the ground, and Hiram makes ten other lavers, positioning them atop ten bronze stands (1 Kings 7:27-39). The molten sea may be a symbolic object, emblematic of Yahweh's founding of the earth upon the seas (e.g., Ps. 24:2).

1 Kings 7:48-50 is concerned with a second group of furnishings. These are made of gold rather than bronze, they belong inside the Temple rather than outside, and they are not made by Hiram. The somewhat unclear text of v. 48 indicates that Solomon makes them himself or, perhaps, that he simply puts them in place. In the latter case, we are probably to assume that they are gold furnishings made for the tabernacle in the wilderness by Bezalel and other craftsmen in the time of Moses (Exod. 25-31; 35-40). Many scholars believe that 1 Kings 7:48-50 is a late expansion, based on the tabernacle account in Exodus.

8:1-66, The Dedication of the Temple. The ceremonial conveyance of Yahweh's Ark into the Temple corresponds to the rites of neighboring peoples by which the image or statue of a god was brought into a newly constructed shrine. The basis of this passage, therefore, is an old account of the dedication of Solomon's Temple. The ceremony takes place in the month of Ethanim, later Tishri (September-October), which was probably reckoned as the beginning of the year in the time of Solomon (→ New Year Festival). The community assembles before the king, who supervises the ritual. The Ark is taken up by the priests, carried into the Temple, and placed in the inner sanctuary. As the procession moves into the Temple, lavish sacrifices are offered (v. 5), the primary purpose of these being the sanctification of the new sacred precinct. The effectiveness of the ceremony is shown by the appearance of a theophanous cloud in the Temple as the priests withdraw from the inner sanctuary (cf. Exod. 40:34-35). The ceremony concludes with further sacrifices (1 Kings 8:63-64), the so-called peace offerings (RSV), which were characteristically made at times of rejoicing and which were eaten by the people after the removal of the blood, fat, and kidneys (Lev. 3). The seven-day feast mentioned in v. 65 is presumably the Feast of Tabernacles or Succoth, which was celebrated at this time of year (cf. Lev. 23:39).

In the course of its transmission, the original account of the ceremony of dedication was gradually elaborated to conform to details of the knowledge of the Ark and the Temple in later times (cf. "to this day," v. 8). Verses 7–9 probably derive entirely from this later development, which led eventually to the extensively expanded version in 2 Chron. 5:2–6:2.

In his dedicatory oration (1 Kings 8:14–61), Solomon praises Yahweh for his loyalty to Israel and petitions him to accept the Temple and interact with his people there. He describes the new shrine as a place from which divine justice can be dispensed (vv. 31–32) and supplications can be heard in time of war, drought, and famine (vv. 33–40). This long speech, which is replete with Deuteronomistic language, is recognized as one of the programmatic passages in the Deuteronomistic History. From the viewpoint of this history, with its emphasis on the importance of the central sanctuary, the erection of the Temple was a major landmark in the history of Israel. It represents the culmination of two of the primary themes of the Deuteronomistic History. The first of these is the promise made to David in 2 Samuel 7 that his son would succeed him as king and build the Temple. Solomon proclaims this promise, paraphrased here in 1 Kings 8:16–19, to have been fulfilled (v. 20), and then, on the basis of the same promise (v. 25), he asks Yahweh to permit David's dynasty to endure. The second theme is the divine promise of a time of "rest" for Israel after the conquest of the promised land and the establishment of a central sanctuary at "the place that Yahweh will choose." Thus, near the end of his long speech (v. 56) Solomon blesses Yahweh for granting this rest to his people. Note, finally, that the speech was further expanded in vv. 41–53 by an exilic writer, whose contribution shows a special concern for the people taken away as captives of war (vv. 46–51; see Introduction, "Significance for the Ancient Community").

9:1–9, A Vision of Destruction. Yahweh appears to Solomon again, as in his dream at Gibeon (chap. 3). This time the message is in response to Solomon's long prayer in the preceding section and, specifically, to his petition for the endurance of the Davidic dynasty (8:25). Yahweh promises to grant the petition, but only on the condition of Solomon's strict loyalty and obedience to Yahweh's laws. This passage was added by a Deuteronomistic editor after the destruction of the Temple, explicitly referred to in 9:8, to qualify the promises cited in chap. 8 in the spirit of the similar qualification in 3:4–15. The warning about the worship of other gods (9:6) looks ahead to the condemnation of Solomon in 11:1–13.

9:10–14, The Land of Cabul. This episode concerns a district of twenty towns on the border of Israel and Phoenicia in the Galilee. A village called Cabul lying southeast of Acco on the border of the tribal territory of Asher (Josh. 19:27) preserved the name in later times. The author seems to relate the name of the district to Hiram's dissatisfaction with the towns, and it has been suggested that Cabul is being interpreted as ka-bul, Heb. for "as nothing," that is, "good for nothing." But the point of the wordplay is elusive. Cabul may mean "[property] encumbered by debt," that is, "mortgaged property."

9:15–23, The Corvée. The projects said to have been built with corvée labor include not only the Temple and palace complex (chaps. 7–8) but also the Millo (which, unless 2 Sam. 5:9 is an anachronism, Solomon rebuilt; → Millo) and the wall of Jerusalem (on the levy of forced labor or corvée, see 5:13–18). Although the Solomonic city wall has not been exposed by excavation, its parameters are fairly well known. The pre-Israelite and Davidic wall surrounded only the southeastern hill or City of David. Solomon's expansion of the city to the north and building of the Temple necessitated the construction of new fortifications. Excavations immediately to the west of the Temple Mount have shown that the Solomonic wall did not extend beyond the summit of the northeastern hill. Outside of Jerusalem, Solomon is said to have "built" (that is, refortified) a number of Israelite cities. It has been suggested that this building activity was a response to the threat represented by the rise of Shishak to power in Egypt (cf. 14:25–26). Archaeologists have discovered a network of fortresses in the Negeb that seem to have been built by the Israelites at about the same time. Excavations at Hazor, Megiddo, and Gezer (9:15) have revealed similar gates, which must be assigned to a national building program in the tenth century and thus very probably to the time of Solomon. The insertion of the parenthesis in vv. 16–17a was occasioned by reference to Gezer at the end of v. 15. (For the events alluded to here, see commentary above on 3:1.)

9:24, Pharaoh's Daughter. This is a miscellaneous detail. (See commentary on 3:1 and 9:15.)

9:25, Solomon's Offerings. The purpose of the regular offerings is to maintain the sacral integrity of the Temple. Thus the meaning of the last sentence is not "So he finished the house" (RSV), which is grammatically difficult and inconsistent with the fact that the Temple has already been finished and dedicated, but rather "Thus he would restore the house." The three occasions probably correspond to the three feasts of Unleavened Bread, Harvest or Weeks, and Ingathering or Tabernacles (cf. Exod. 23:14–17), as explicitly stated in 2 Chron. 8:13.

9:26–10:29
Solomon's Wealth

After the long section on the Temple (5:1–9:25), the subject of the various enterprises and accomplishments of Solomon's reign resumes. The particular themes now are his wealth and fame, both of which are understood as consequences of his wisdom.

9:26–28, The Red Sea Fleet. The exact site of Ezion-geber, Solomon's Red Sea shipping port, is unknown (→ Ezion-geber). It lay at or near Elath (here Eloth; cf. Deut. 2:8; 2 Chron. 8:17) on the Gulf of Aqabah. The Israelite ships are steered by the much more experienced sailors of Phoenicia. The location of Ophir is unknown (→ Ophir), but it was probably in the southern part of the Arabian peninsula (cf. Gen. 10:26–30). The gold of Ophir was highly prized (Isa. 13:12; Job 28:16; Ps. 45:9; 1 Chron. 29:4).

10:1–13, The Queen of Sheba. Sheba, Seba, or Saba was a land in the part of the Arabian peninsula corresponding to modern Yemen (→ Seba, Sabeans). When they clashed with the Assyrian kings in the eighth century, the Sabeans were still ruled by queens. The tradition of a visit by an earlier queen of Sheba to the court of Solomon suggests that the Sabeans were already actively involved in trade along the caravan routes of the Arabian subcontinent in the tenth century. Solomon's maritime activities in the south brought him to the attention of the those who had their own trading interests in the region.

This episode has been included to enhance the theme of the legendary wisdom of Solomon. The queen comes to Jerusalem to test Solomon with riddles (v. 1). She leaves praising his sagacity and the good fortune of his subjects, and her acknowledgement of the good fortune of the Israelites is all the more significant because —like that of Jethro, Balaam, Rahab, and others —it comes from a foreigner.

10:14–29, Solomon's Wealth. Solomon's reputation for wisdom drew people from all over the earth to Jerusalem, bringing valuable gifts with them. Gold was so abundant during Solomon's reign, we are told (v. 21), that people were contemptuous of silver (cf. v. 27). Thus, when Solomon's gold shields (vv. 16–17) are taken away by Shishak and replaced with bronze shields by Rehoboam (14:26–28), the change may be understood symbolically as a descent from a golden age to a bronze age. It is impossible to say how much historically reliable information is preserved in these notices about Solomon's fabulous wealth and wisdom. The references to the two types of shield in vv. 16–17 and the ornate throne in vv. 19–20 are likely to have been based on recollections of actual treasures preserved in the House of the Forest of Lebanon (cf. 7:2) and used by later kings for ceremonial occasions (cf. 14:27–28). The ships mentioned in 10:22 are probably the Red Sea fleet (9:26–28), as their cargo of "gold, silver, ivory, apes, and baboons" (not "peacocks") indicates. Their designation as "ships of Tarshish" does not indicate that they sailed to the Mediterranean ports called Tarshish in Spain or Cyprus, but rather that they were large ships capable of transporting metal ores long distances from such ports. It has long been recognized that the two places with which Solomon is said to have traded for horses are Kue, that is, Cilicia in southern Anatolia, and Musri, a land located in the Taurus mountains between Cilicia and Arpad in northern Syria. Instead of *musri*, "Musri," our received Hebrew text has *misrayim*, "Egypt," a confusion that gave rise to the prohibition of trading with Egypt for horses (Deut. 17:16), but the references to the kings of the Hittites and the Arameans in 1 Kings 10:29 shows that it was in the north that Solomon's horse trading was conducted.

11:1–43
The Condemnation of Solomon

As explained in the introduction to the larger account of the reign of Solomon (3:1–11:43), the Deuteronomistic editors responsible for the arrangement of the account believed that Solomon's reign ended in failure because he erected places of worship for other gods. In their understanding, this was a consequence of his marriages to foreign women (11:1–13), and it was the cause of the troubles he had with various adversaries (vv. 14–40).

11:1–13, Solomon's Wives. Solomon's reputation as a great lover, the husband of a thousand wives (v. 3a), was legendary. He became the idealized bridegroom of the Song of Songs (cf. Song of Sg. 3:6–11), which was eventually ascribed to his authorship (Song of Sg. 1:1). The popularity and persistence of this part of the Solomon tradition can be accounted for by the tendency of a people to take delight in the sexual prowess of their monarch, whose virility represents the welfare and productivity of the community as a whole. Nevertheless, there was probably a substantial historical basis for Solomon's reputation, though his polygynous behavior seems less likely to have been motivated by an amorous disposition than by diplomatic perspicacity. We have already noted the circumstances of his marriage to the pharaoh's daughter (see 3:1), and there were probably other diplomatically motivated marriages to women from neighboring countries.

This passage in its present form, however, is a Deuteronomistic composition that presents Solomon's marriages to foreign women in a wholly negative light. The basis for this judgment is the prohibition of foreign wives in Deut. 7:3–4 (clearly evoked here in 1 Kings 11:2), because of the danger that they might induce their husbands to worship foreign gods (cf. Deut. 13:6–11; 17:17a). Josiah will dismantle three shrines to foreign gods that Solomon is said to have built on the outskirts of Jerusalem (2 Kings 23:13).

Solomon, then, has forsaken the God "who appeared to him twice" (1 Kings 11:9), and we recall in this connection the interpolated Deuteronomistic qualifications of the promises made on the occasion of both appearances (3:14; 9:1–9). In particular, the perpetuation of David's dynasty was linked to Solomon's obedience to divine law in 9:4–5. Because of his failure to keep Yahweh's commandments, therefore, Solomon's kingdom is going to be taken away and given to one of his servants, whose identity will be revealed shortly (11:26). Solomon's son will inherit the rule of the tribe of Judah, a dispensation made "for the sake of David and for the sake of Jerusalem, which I have chosen" (v. 13) in keeping with the Deuteronomistic view of Jerusalem as the chosen place of worship (cf. the discussion at 8:1–66). As for the rest of the tribes, Yahweh is going to "tear" them away—the verb anticipates the symbol of the torn garment in 11:30–31.

11:14–22, Hadad the Edomite. The events described here seem to have occurred early in Solomon's reign (cf. vv. 21–22, 25), but if so, Hadad's hostility did not prevent Solomon from maintaining a trading port at Ezion-geber (9:26). This episode shows that the Edomite royal family, like the Israelite, was linked to the Egyptian court by a diplomatic marriage. It may be that the kings of the weak twenty-first dynasty attempted to maintain a balance of power in Palestine in this way.

11:23–25, Rezon Son of Eliada. David's war against Hadadezer, king of the Aramean state of Zobah, and his allies is described in 2 Sam. 10:1–19 and 8:3–8. Rezon, a refugee from this war, seems to have had a career that paralleled that of David in some respects. He gathered a personal fighting force and eventually established a kingdom in Damascus, henceforward the most powerful state in southern Syria. Note that David administered Damascus through an Israelite prefect after the defeat of Hadadezer (2 Sam. 8:6). It has been plausibly suggested that David sponsored Rezon, who "fled from Hadadezer . . . his master" (1 Kings 11:23), and that

Rezon rebelled at the time of David's death. This may be the import of the obscure statement "and he abhorred Israel" (RSV) in v. 25.

11:26–40, Jeroboam Son of Nebat. This is an account of the prophetic proclamation of kingship to Jeroboam, the "servant" of Solomon to whom the bulk of the kingdom was promised in 11:11. Jeroboam's encounter with the prophet Ahijah (vv. 29–39) is set in the context of a brief sketch of the circumstances of his first, abortive attempt at a coup. More complete information is preserved in the Greek text of 11:43 and 12:24. Jeroboam seems to have come to the king's attention while still living in the Ephraimite hills. He was put in charge of the local detachment of the corvée (cf. 5:13–18; 9:15–23) and given the task of fortifying his hometown of Zeredah. From there, he was brought to Jerusalem to work on the bulwarks of the City of David. He became very powerful—the Greek text mentions a personal force of horse-drawn chariots—and eventually aspired to the kingship itself. But when he attempted to seize power ("lifted up his hand against the king," 11:26–27 [RSV]), the coup was not successful, and he was obliged to flee to Egypt, where he found refuge with Shishak (ca. 945–924 B.C.), the founder of the twenty-second dynasty.

In many respects Ahijah's role parallels that of another Ephraimite prophet, Samuel. Here he designates Jeroboam king, and in chap. 14 he will reject him, just as Samuel designated and rejected Saul (1 Sam. 10:1; 13:13–14). The symbolic act involving the tearing of the cloak into twelve pieces is reminiscent of a similar gesture involving Samuel and Saul (1 Sam. 15:27–28). Ahijah's Shilonite background may also be significant in view of Samuel's connections with Shiloh (1 Sam. 1–3) and, more especially, of Solomon's banishment of the scion of the Shilonite priesthood from Jerusalem (1 Kings 2:26–27; cf. 1 Sam. 14:3; 22:20).

In its present, expanded form, Ahijah's oracle expresses the rejection of Solomon's dynasty in favor of Jeroboam in the Deuteronomistic language of 1 Kings 11:11–13. Solomon's son will be permitted to retain one tribe, so that David will always have a parcel of land (not "lamp" [RSV]) "in Jerusalem, the city I chose for myself to place my name there" (v. 36, cf. 8:29, 44; 9:3; Deut. 12:5). Note that Jeroboam's designation as king includes a conditional promise of a "sure house" or enduring dynasty (1 Kings 11:38) expressed in language reminiscent of that used of the Davidic dynasty (cf. 1 Sam. 25:28; 2 Sam. 7:16).

11:41–43, The Death of Solomon. The account of Solomon's reign concludes with a typical Deuteronomistic synopsis. Though it is likely that his reign was a long one, "forty years" (v. 42) is probably an estimate.

314

12:1–16:28
The Early Kings of the Divided Monarchy

These chapters are concerned with the secession of the northern tribes under the leadership of Jeroboam and the reigns of the kings of the now independent realms of Israel and Judah before the accession of Ahab.

12:1–24
The Secession of the Northern Tribes

The people of Israel, the Northern Kingdom ruled by Saul, actively sought David's rule (2 Sam. 5:1–3) and willingly accepted Solomon. But when Solomon's heir deals highhandedly with them, they refuse to accept him as king. Instead, they follow a fellow Israelite, Solomon's adversary Jeroboam (cf. 1 Kings 11:26–40).

12:1–20, The Assembly at Shechem. At Solomon's death, his son Rehoboam becomes king of Judah. His succession to the kingship of the northern tribes, however, seems to require a separate investiture, a renewal of the agreement made between David and the "elders of Israel" at Hebron (2 Sam. 5:3). This time the negotiations take place at Shechem, where Rehoboam meets with representatives of the northern tribes. The issue is royal leniency. The Israelites agree to follow Rehoboam if he will lighten the burden of labor imposed by Solomon. This request is not remarkable in itself: some such gesture promising improved conditions was expected at the beginning of a king's reign. Rehoboam's response, then, shows him to be particularly callous and inept. Rejecting the advice of the elders who had counseled his father, he is persuaded by his own privy council, a group contemptuously referred to as "the children who had grown up with him" (1 Kings 12:8, 10), to promise no more than to replace his father's whips with "scorpions," probably a more painful kind of scourge. The Israelites walk out, taking up the old slogan of Sheba, a Benjaminite who tried to foment a rebellion of the northern tribes against David (2 Sam. 20:1–2). When Rehoboam sends Adoram, the boss of the corvée (called Adoniram in 1 Kings 4:6; 5:14), to compel the Israelites to cooperate, they stone him to death. Rehoboam flees Shechem, and the northern tribes are in open rebellion.

Jeroboam, in the meantime, has heard of the death of Solomon and returned from Egypt (12:2–3). He is presented in this account as the chief spokesman for the northern tribes (vv. 3, 12), but v. 20 suggests that he is not summoned until the negotiations break down. In any case,

we should probably assume that he continues to be supported by Shishak, who wants to neutralize the power of Jerusalem in southern Canaan.

12:21–24, The Oracle of Shemaiah. Rehoboam's plans for a war to force the submission of the northern tribes are cancelled by an oracle proclaiming the division of the country to be the divine will. Shemaiah is mentioned nowhere else in Kings, but see 2 Chron. 12:5–8, 15.

12:25–14:20
The Condemnation of Jeroboam

The dynastic promise made to Jeroboam in 11:37–38 is quickly revoked. As we shall see, the condemnation of Jeroboam and his house will become a paradigm for the condemnation of all the northern kings, not only because the fall of the houses of Baasha and Omri will recapitulate the fall of the house of Jeroboam, but also because the particular crime of which Jeroboam is accused by the Deuteronomistic editors, the erection of places of worship to rival Jerusalem, will be perpetuated by all the northern kings.

12:25–33, The Golden Calves of Dan and Bethel. Evidence of Jeroboam's rebuilding of Shechem has been found at the site (→ Shechem). It will serve as the royal residence in the north until displaced by Tirzah after Baasha's coup (15:33). The reference to Penuel shows that Jeroboam also has power in northern Transjordan. The author of the present passage, however, suggests that Jeroboam feels insecure in spite of these refortified strongholds. He fears that the regular pilgrimages his people made to Jerusalem will incline them to return their allegiance to Rehoboam. This anxiety leads him to establish his own sanctuaries in the north. From the Deuteronomistic point of view, this was done in cold disregard for Yahweh's choice of Jerusalem. It was "devised from his own heart" (12:33), that is, not commanded by Yahweh through Moses, and the illegitimacy of the scheme was exacerbated by the consecration of nonlevitical priests, the construction of high places, and the institution of a festival beginning the fifteenth day of the eighth month to rival the Feast of Tabernacles celebrated one month earlier in Jerusalem (Lev. 23:34). Modern analysis of Jeroboam's religious policies, on the other hand, suggests that he was appealing to old Yahwistic traditions in the north, not innovating arbitrarily. Bethel was an ancient sanctuary with strong patriarchal associations (Gen. 12:8; 28:10–22). The bull was probably also a very old and authentically Yahwistic symbol. The animal represented the Deity, who may have been thought of as invisibly present on its back. It has been plausibly suggested that Jeroboam chose the bull iconography in an attempt to compete with the Ark iconography of Jerusalem. In any case, though the present narrative depicts the bulls not as pedestals but as idols (cf. 1 Kings 14:9) to which sacrifices were offered (12:32), there is no suggestion that Jeroboam introduced any kind of non-Yahwistic cult. From the Deuteronomistic perspective of the present account, however, the installation of the bulls was a heinous crime ("the thing became a sin," v. 30), for which Jeroboam's kingship would be rejected and his family condemned (14:9–11). Moreover, "the sin of Jeroboam," which his successors perpetuated (e.g., 15:26, 34), would prove to be the fatal mistake of the Northern Kingdom, leading finally to the exile of its people (2 Kings 17:21–23).

13:1–34, The Man of God at Bethel. The basis of this narrative is a story about prophetic authenticity. A man of God comes to Bethel from Judah and delivers an oracle predicting the desecration of the altar by the burning of human bones. A prophet from Bethel intercepts him on his way home and tricks him into violating the strict terms of his mission. For this violation, the man of God is condemned in an oracle uttered by the prophet from Bethel, and when he returns to the road, he is slain by a lion. Ironically, the oracle authenticates the man of God's mission at the same time that it condemns him. Realizing this, the prophet retrieves the body of the man of God and buries it in his own tomb, instructing his sons to bury him alongside the man of God.

The Deuteronomistic historian used this story as a vehicle for his condemnation of Jeroboam's cult at Bethel. He understood the altar oracle to refer to Josiah's desecration of the high places of Samaria (cf. v. 32), as described in 2 Kings 23:15–16. Despite a few small discrepancies, the words of the oracle are tightly linked to the report of its fulfillment, and Josiah is even mentioned by name in 1 Kings 13:2. When the oracle is fulfilled, moreover, the mission of the man of God is remembered, and his bones, together with those of the prophet, are spared (2 Kings 23:16–18).

14:1–20, Ahijah's Oracle. Ahijah of Shiloh, the prophet who proclaimed the conditional promise of a dynasty to Jeroboam (v. 2; cf. 11:29–31), now announces the condemnation of his house. The occasion is a visit to Shiloh made by Jeroboam's wife to consult Ahijah about the illness of her son Abijah. Though she disguises herself, the deception is both unnecessary, since the old prophet is blind, and futile, since Yahweh has warned him of her coming. Ahijah announces that not only Abijah but every male in Jeroboam's house will perish (14:10). The new king alluded to in v. 14 is Baasha, who will be the assassin of Jeroboam's son and heir, Nadab (15:25–29). Just as the dynastic promise made to Jeroboam implied a promise of male progeny, so the condemnation of the dynasty involves the elimination of his sons. The grisly language of the oracle (14:10–11) will be echoed in the condemnations of the houses of Baasha (16:1–4) and Ahab (21:21–24). The pattern thus established presents the denunciation of one royal family after another throughout the early history of the Northern Kingdom. The Deuteronomistic editors saw this as a consequence of the perpetuation of "the sins of Jeroboam" (14:16) and, making explicit reference to the Assyrian deportations of Israelites to places "beyond the Euphrates," they expanded the condemnation of the house of Jeroboam into a condemnation of the Northern Kingdom as a whole (vv. 15–16). The passage ends with the standard synopsis for the end of a king's reign (vv. 19–20).

14:21–15:24
The Early History of Judah

The reigns of the kings of Israel and Judah are presented together in strictly chronological order. Rehoboam, Abijam, and Asa—three kings of Judah—are described in succession because they all came to throne before a change of ruler in the north, that is, they were all contemporaries of Jeroboam.

14:21–24, Synopsis of Rehoboam's Reign. These verses contain the introductory Deuteronomistic synopsis of the reign of Rehoboam. His capital, Jerusalem, is described here in the usual Deuteronomistic way as the divinely chosen city. During Rehoboam's reign, however, the people of Judah disregarded the rule of the chosen sanctuary and celebrated their religious rites "on every high hill and under every green tree," a Deuteronomistic cliché that evokes the description of the pre-Israelite shrines in Deut. 12:2 and anticipates the final condemnation of the Northern Kingdom in 2 Kings 17:10. The list of abominations that Rehoboam is accused of tolerating is also Deuteronomistic and formulaic (→ Asherah; High Place; Pillars [3]). The role of the religious functionaries called "male cult prostitutes" in 1 Kings 14:24 is unclear; but they are prohibited by Deuteronomic law (Deut. 23:18), and Asa and Jehoshaphat are said to have eradicated them from Judah (1 Kings 15:12; 22:46).

14:25–28, Shishak's Invasion. Shoshenq I (ca. 945–924 B.C.), the biblical Shishak, was a man of Libyan ancestry who founded the twenty-second dynasty and ruled Egypt from a city called Bubastis in the eastern Delta. As we have seen, he gave Jeroboam asylum after his first, abortive revolt against Solomon (11:40), evidently as part of a policy of neutralizing the power of Jerusalem in Palestine. It is tempting, therefore, to interpret his invasion as continuing support for Jeroboam in his struggle against Judah. The biblical accounts give the impression that the raid was directed only at Jerusalem (v. 25) or the fortified cities of Judah and Jerusalem (2 Chron. 12:4), and Rehoboam seems to have had to strip both the Temple and the palace for tribute to save the city (1 Kings 14:26; for Solomon's gold shields, see commentary above on 10:14–29). The editorial insertion of the present account immediately following a denunciation of Rehoboam's religious policies (14:22–24) implies that the attack was divine punishment for the religious inconstancy of Rehoboam, and the leaders of Judah, and this is made explicit in the parallel account in 2 Chron. 12:5. But the city list Shishak left at Karnak names cities captured as far east as Penuel in Transjordan, which had been fortified by Jeroboam (cf. 1 Kings 12:25), and as far north as Megiddo, where a fragment of a Shishak stele has been found. Thus we must conclude that Jeroboam, once his own kingship was established, lost favor with Shishak and that the invasion was an attempt to reassert Egypt's ancient control over Palestine as a whole.

14:29–31, The Death of Rehoboam. This is the concluding Deuteronomistic synopsis of the reign of Rehoboam, with which has been included a notice about the constant warfare between Rehoboam and Jeroboam (v. 30; cf. 15:7b).

15:1–8, The Reign of Abijam. The rule of Abijam, who is called Abijah in Chronicles (e.g., 2 Chron. 13:1), is described here entirely in formulaic Deuteronomistic notices, which condemn him for continuing Rehoboam's religious policies (1 Kings 15:3). The reference in v. 7 to warfare between Abijam and Jeroboam is supplemented in 2 Chron. 13:3–20 by an account of a major battle fought on the southern boundary of Ephraim in which Judah is said to have been victorious.

15:9–24, The Reign of Asa. Asa is the first of several kings of Judah whose reigns are evaluated positively by the Deuteronomistic editors because of their religious policies. He is said to have banned both "male cult prostitutes" (cf. 14:24) and idols from Judah. He removed Maacah, his mother or grandmother (cf. 15:2; 10), from the office of queen mother because she had honored the goddess Asherah with "an abominable image" (RSV), which Asa cut down and burned. He is also credited with having enriched the Temple with gold and silver votives (v. 15). Except for his failure to eliminate the high places (v. 14), his success is qualified only

by the statement that "in his old age he was diseased in his feet" (v. 23), probably a euphemism indicating venereal disease. This detail is presented in a way that suggests the illness was a divine punishment for some kind of sin.

The war against the Northern Kingdom continued during Asa's reign. Baasha of Israel (see 15:33–16:7) sets up an embargo against Judah by fortifying the city of Ramah, a few miles north of Jerusalem. By stripping the Temple and the palace again (cf. 14:26), Asa is able to induce Ben-hadad, the Aramean king of Damascus, to invade Naphtali. The account speaks of an existing alliance between Ben-hadad and Baasha and alludes to an earlier alliance between Damascus and Judah (v. 19), but we know nothing else of either of these arrangements. In any case, the presence of an Aramean army in the northern Galilee forces Baasha to withdraw from Ramah, which Asa dismantles, using the building materials to fortify the border cities of Geba and Mizpah.

15:25–16:28
The Early History of Israel

The reigns of six northern kings (Nadab, Baasha, Elah, Zimri, Omri, and Ahab) are described in succession, because they all came to the throne before a change of ruler in the south, that is, they all were contemporaries of Asa.

15:25–32, The Assassination of Nadab. Nadab succeeds his father, Jeroboam, and reigns two years before being slain in a coup led by a member of the tribe of Issachar named Baasha. The assassination takes place while the Israelites are besieging the city of Gibbethon, which at this time is in Philistine hands. Baasha secures his position by exterminating all the descendants of Jeroboam (v. 29). These events are presented as the fulfillment of Ahijah's oracle (14:10).

15:33–16:7, The Reign of Baasha. Baasha's twenty-four-year reign is reported with the usual editorial formulas. As a usurper (15:27–28), he inaugurates a new dynasty, and his son Elah will succeed him as king. There is also a new seat of government, Tirzah, which lies north of Shechem in the direction of Baasha's tribal homeland of Issachar (cf. 15:27). Because Baasha's religious policies are the same as those of Jeroboam, however, his dynasty is condemned in an oracle that echoes that of Ahijah the Shilonite (cf. 14:7–11).

16:8–22, The Rise and Fall of Zimri. Two military coups, spaced only seven days apart, are recorded here. Zimri, a chariotry officer, kills Baasha's heir Elah, then takes his own life a week later when Elah's chief military officer,

Omri, arrives with the army. The assassination of Elah takes place in Tirzah, the seat of the Baasha dynasty, in the home of Arza, the officer "over the house," that is, the supervisor of the royal estates (cf. 4:6). Elah's death and Zimri's subsequent massacre of the family of Baasha are presented as the fulfillment of the oracle of Jehu son of Hanani (16:1–4). Zimri's own reign lasts only as long as it takes the army to receive the news at Gibbethon, where a siege is again under way (cf. 15:27), and march to Tirzah. Nothing else is known of Tibni son of Ginath, who competes briefly with Omri for supremacy.

16:23–28, The Reign of Omri. A new dynasty needs a new capital, and Omri finds an excellent prospect on a previously unfortified summit in the hills of Manasseh. The site affords a clear view of the surrounding valleys, and the Hebrew name *shomron*, "Samaria," probably means "place of watching," that is, "Lookout Mountain." Thus, the notice tracing the name to a certain Shemer, the original owner of the hill, is not likely to be historical. Nevertheless, the tradition of the purchase of the site, formally transferring its ownership to Omri, is important: Compare David's purchase of the threshing floor of Araunah (2 Sam. 24:24–25), the site of the Temple of Solomon (1 Chron. 21:28–22:1).

Apart from the notice about Samaria, however, the reign of the founder of the first stable dynasty in the Northern Kingdom is described in a surprisingly brief account. Omri's seizure of power at Tirzah was described in 1 Kings 16:15b–22, but apart from the usual introductory and concluding synopses, no further details of the political or religious history of his reign are provided. We know, nevertheless, that Omri was a powerful and important king who brought stability to Israel, based in part on the establishment of cordial relations with both Phoenicia and Judah (→ Omri). Archaeological evidence shows that he inaugurated a vigorous period of building and fortification, of which the limestone city he and Ahab erected at Samaria is the best example. An inscription of Mesha, the Moabite king contemporary with Ahab (cf. 2 Kings 3:4–27), credits Omri with having seized control of the Madeba plateau in central Transjordan.

16:29–22:53

The Reign of Ahab

The accounts of the reigns of Ahab and his two sons, Ahaziah and Jehoram, have been greatly expanded by the inclusion of stories about Elijah and Elisha, which occupy most of the narrative from 1 Kings 17 to 2 Kings 10. Ahab's own reign, moreover, is given an especially full treatment because of the interest taken in it by the Deuteronomistic editors, who regarded the crimes of Ahab and Jezebel as exemplary of the kind of behavior that led finally to the destruction of the Northern Kingdom.

16:29–34

The Accession of Ahab

The synopsis that introduces the account of Ahab's reign is followed by a notice about a contemporary event, the rebuilding of Jericho, included by the editors as a part of the prophecy and fulfillment scheme of the larger Deuteronomistic History.

16:29–33, Summary of Ahab's Reign. The indictment included in this synopsis is the most severe imposed on any Israelite king. Ahab, we are told, was guilty not only of Jeroboam's sin, the perpetuation of rival sanctuaries outside of Jerusalem, but also of Solomon's. Jezebel is presented as another instance, perhaps the paradigmatic instance, of a foreign queen who induces an Israelite king to worship a foreign god (cf. 11:1–13). Her father was the Tyrian king Ittobaal (biblical Ethbaal). The marriage between Ahab and Jezebel was probably arranged by their fathers as part of an alliance made necessary by the burgeoning power of the Aramean state of Damascus under the successors of Ben-hadad, son of Tabrimmon (cf. 15:18–19). From the Deuteronomistic point of view, the marriage was a terrible mistake, because it introduced the worship of "Baal," as Jezebel's god is called, into Israel. Here, as often elsewhere in the Bible, Baal is used as a generic term for any foreign god. In this case, Baal should be Melcarth, the god of Jezebel's homeland of Tyre (→Phoenicia). We know that the cult of Melcarth enjoyed international popularity at this time, as shown by the dedication to him of a stele erected near Aleppo by Ben-hadad of Damascus, possibly the son of the Ben-hadad who aided Asa in his struggle against Baasha (15:18). On the other hand, the fully developed biblical tradition clearly understands the Baal of the Elijah cycle to be the widely worshiped Syrian and Canaanite god Baal Haddu or Hadad. This Baal was above all else a rain-giver, and it is over the issue of giving and withholding of rain that Yahweh's prophet Elijah will challenge the authority of Baal in the narrative that follows.

16:34, The Rebuilding of Jericho. The fortification of Jericho under Ahab was probably undertaken because of the threat posed by the Moabites, upon whom Omri and Ahab imposed tribute but who rebelled against Israel after Ahab's death (2 Kings 3:4–27). The death of the eldest and youngest sons of Hiel, the builder of Jericho, is presented here as the realization of the curse uttered by Joshua in Josh. 6:26.

318

17:1–18:46
Elijah and the Drought

The stories about Elijah and Elisha in 1 and 2 Kings probably derive from an old northern complex of prophetic legends and miracle stories. They are composed of a number of discrete episodes, most of which seem to have been independent in origin, though they may have already been combined into a single narrative unit before their incorporation into the Deuteronomistic History. The first group of stories, found in chaps. 17 and 18, are unified around the theme of Elijah's role in the drought that occurred during Ahab's reign.

17:1, The Announcement of the Drought. Elijah the Tishbite makes his first appearance in the narrative suddenly and without preparation. "Tishbite" has been explained as meaning "from Tishbi in Gilead" or "one of the settlers in Gilead," but no other introduction of the man of God is provided, and many scholars believe that the beginning of the Elijah story has been lost. Nevertheless, the point of Elijah's proclamation to Ahab is clear: the life-giving rains that water the land are under the control of Yahweh and not, by implication, of Baal. Thus the contest that will take place on Mount Carmel in chap. 18 is already in view, and the intervening drought will demonstrate the futility of Ahab's support for the worship of Baal. The effect of a drought lasting for even a part of three seasons (17:1; 18:1) would have been devastating. Josephus quotes a Tyrian source recording a year-long drought in Phoenicia during the reign of Ittobaal (Ethbaal), Ahab's father-in-law and contemporary.

17:2–7, The Ravens of the Wadi Cherith. Elijah's first place of refuge in this flight from Ahab was in Transjordan, but the exact location is uncertain. The motif of the hero fed by wild animals is very widespread in world folklore.

17:8–16, The Phoenician Widow. Elijah's second place of refuge is the Phoenician city of Zarephath or Sarepta (→ Zarephath), where he finds shelter with a widow. In place of the miracle of the ravens is the miracle of the unfailing jar of meal and cruse of oil, another common folklore motif. The closest biblical parallel is found in 2 Kings 4:1–7 in the Elisha cycle, where the widow of one of the sons of the prophets is sustained by a bountiful jar of oil (cf. 2 Kings 4:42–44 and, more remotely, Matt. 14:13–21; 15:32–38; Mark 6:30–44; Luke 9:10–17; John 6:1–14).

17:17–24, The Revival of the Widow's Son. This miracle also has a close parallel in the Elisha cycle (cf. 2 Kings 4:18–37). In the present story, the widow's reactions have thematic importance. When her child is on the verge of death, she angrily blames the catastrophe on Elijah. Various forms of guilt or impurity that might otherwise be inconsequential become dangerous in the presence of the holy man (1 Kings 17:18). When her son is revived, however, she is moved to acclaim the special powers of Elijah, which the transmission of vitality from his body to that of the child has demonstrated (v. 21), and to acknowledge the veracity of the word of Yahweh (v. 24).

18:1–46, The Contest on Mount Carmel. The Carmel promontory, which rises precipitously out of the sea at modern Haifa and dominates the surrounding lowlands, seems to have been thought of as a sacred place throughout antiquity. It is against the power of the greatly venerated Baal who was lord of Carmel that Elijah pits the power of Yahweh in a contest of sacrificial altars. The people can no longer go on "hobbling on two crutches" (v. 21); they must choose. The authentic god will be the one who answers "by fire" (v. 24). Despite the prayers and self-lacerations of his prophets, the Carmelite Baal does not respond. But when Elijah prays, a lightning bolt ("the fire of Yahweh") falls from a clear sky and ignites the altar (v. 38).

The story of the contest between Elijah and the prophets of Baal seems to have been an originally independent narrative. Yahweh is vindicated when the lightning falls, and the adversary is the local Baal of Carmel. In the larger account of the drought, this Carmelite Baal is understood to be the great rain-giving Baal Hadad, and Yahweh is vindicated when Elijah returns and the rain begins at his word (cf. 17:1). The clouds gather after the combustion of Yahweh's altar and the slaughter of the prophets of Baal, as Elijah performs a rite of some kind on the summit of the Carmel headland overlooking the sea (vv. 42–44).

The contest between the gods follows a meeting of the two human antagonists. Ahab greets Elijah as the "troubler of Israel," an expression suggesting the ritual pollution of a community and, therefore, the inducement of communal hardship by the violation of an oath or sacred rule (Josh. 6:18; 7:25; 1 Sam. 14:29). Ahab's point is that Elijah is responsible for the drought, but Elijah replies that it is Ahab who has "troubled Israel" by violating Yahweh's commandments.

19:1–21
Elijah at Mount Horeb

Elijah's journey through the wilderness to Mount Horeb is the most important of a series of episodes that present him as the new Moses. The altar he built on Mount Carmel using twelve stones, "according to the number of the tribes of the sons of Jacob" (18:31–32), is reminiscent of Moses' altar and twelve standing stones "according to the twelve tribes of Israel" set up on

Mount Sinai (Exod. 24:4; cf. Josh. 4:8). Now he makes a journey of "forty days and forty nights" to Horeb (1 Kings 19:8; cf. Exod. 24:18b) and enters "the cave" (1 Kings 19:9), which might be the same "cleft of the rock" from which Moses saw Yahweh's back (Exod. 33:22). Like Moses, Elijah watches as Yahweh passes by (1 Kings 19:11; cf. Exod. 33:19-23). Note, finally, that Elijah will part the Jordan and cross on dry ground (2 Kings 2:8), just as Moses did at the Red Sea (Exod. 14:21), and he will ascend into the sky in Transjordan opposite Jericho, where Moses died (2 Kings 2:6-11; Deut. 34:1, 6). At that time Elisha will take Joshua's role of understudy (1 Kings 19:21; cf. Exod. 24:13) and successor, recrossing the Jordan on dry ground (2 Kings 2:14; cf. Joshua 3).

19:1-8, The Journey to Horeb. Many scholars think pious Yahwists made pilgrimages to Sinai during the time of the Israelite and Judean monarchies. The notices of the stages in the wilderness in Exodus and Numbers, summarized in Numbers 33, seem to preserve precise records of one or more routes through the desert. Thus Elijah is often seen as a pilgrim in the present passage. His expressed motivation, however, is not pilgrimage but refuge. Alarmed by Jezebel's threat, he flees first to Beer-sheba, the southern limit of Judah, then one day's journey farther into the desert, where he sits and despairs of his life. The "pilgrimage" itself is a miraculous journey of forty days and nights without food or water, for which he is prepared by an angel who requires him to consume a double portion of both before the trek begins.

19:9-18, The "Still Small Voice." Like Moses before him (Exod. 33:12-23), Elijah watches from a cave as Yahweh passes by at Sinai. The wind, earthquake, and fire of Exodus 19 appear again, but this time Yahweh is not present in them. Instead, the word of Yahweh comes to Elijah in a "slight whispering sound" or "still small voice" (RSV). Many scholars interpret this account as a deliberate rejection of the storm theophany in Yahwism because of its special associations with the Canaanite rain god Baal. The rejection comes at a time when Israel is divided between the worship of Baal and Yahweh, and the danger of syncretism is great. It is clear, in any case, that according to the prophetic point of view from which the Elijah story is told, this incident represents a transition from the spectacular theophanies witnessed by early Israel to the quiet transmission of the divine word to the prophets.

The divine whisper instructs Elijah to appoint three men to office. The third of these appointments will be made immediately, when Elisha is called to become Elijah's apprentice (1 Kings 11:19-21) and, eventually, his successor (2 Kings 2). The first and second appointments will be made by Elisha, not Elijah, when the former reveals to Hazael that he is going to become king of Syria (2 Kings 8:7-15) and then, with the help of an anonymous young prophet, anoints Jehu, the bane of the house of Omri, as king of Israel (2 Kings 9:1-10).

19:19-21, The Call of Elisha. Though Elisha will not appear again until the story of the ascension of Elijah in 2 Kings 2, a thoroughly enigmatic account of his call has been inserted here in consequence of 1 Kings 19:16 above. The picture of twelve teams of oxen working a field at the same time is not impossibly unrealistic, providing that we do not suppose that Elisha is driving them all. Nevertheless, it is tempting to suspect that the number twelve originally had some symbolic significance, now obscured by the abbreviation of a long narrative. The cloak used in Elisha's investiture is evidently the one that will be passed on to him and used in the miraculous splitting of the Jordan in 2 Kings 2:8, 13-14. The impromptu and unexplained sacrifice of the oxen may also be a part of Elisha's investiture, comparable to the bull and two rams sacrificed during the ordination of the high priest (cf. Exod. 29).

20:1-43
The War with Ben-hadad of Damascus

Chaps. 20 and 22 form a continuous narrative interrupted by the story of Naboth's vineyard. These two chapters are markedly different from those that immediately precede and follow them and from chap. 21. Elijah, who has dominated the story up to this point, is absent, though he will return in chap. 21 and 2 Kings 1. In fact, he seems to be completely unknown. Ahab is still here, but he is presented in a less harsh light. Jezebel is not mentioned. It is clear, then, that chaps. 20 and 22 derive from a source that was originally unrelated to the Elijah-Elisha narrative from which most of the surrounding material was drawn.

Note further that the name of Ahab appears only three times in chap. 20 (vv. 2, 13, and 14) and once in the main narrative of chap. 22 (v. 20) before the Deuteronomistic synopsis in 20:39-40. Most often he is called simply "the king of Israel." There is material similar to this elsewhere, much of it embedded within the Elisha stories and especially in 2 Kings 6:24-7:20, in which the conflict between Ben-hadad of Damascus and an anonymous "king of Israel" is described. This raises the possibility that the events described in chaps. 20 and 22 did not occur in the reign of Ahab, whose name has been added secondarily in its few occurrences. This possibility is enhanced by the historical problems raised by these chapters. We know from Assyrian records that Ahab was an ally of Damascus in 853 B.C., when a coalition of Syrian and Palestinian states engaged Shalmaneser III in a major battle at Qarqar on the Orontes. It also seems clear that this anti-Assyrian coalition stayed together until at least 845, several years after Ahab's death in about 850. Only Damascus and Hamath are named as confederates after 853, however, and it is possible, though unlikely, that Israel withdrew. If this is what happened, then we can conclude that chaps. 20 and 22 refer to events that took place between 853 and 850. "Ben-hadad," then, must be the throne name of Hadadezer, who, as we know from the inscriptions of Shalmaneser III, was the king of Damascus contemporary with Ahab. If chaps. 20 and 22 have been wrongly assigned to the reign of Ahab, however, "the king of Israel" portrayed here is probably Jehoash, the grandson of Jehu. Many of the details given in the account of his reign correspond to events described here. Though he inherited an army reduced to almost nothing (2 Kings 13:7; cf. 1 Kings 20:27), he was able to rally and recover cities lost by his father to the Arameans (2 Kings 13:25; cf. 1 Kings 20:34). He also won a major victory at Aphek (2 Kings 13:17; cf. 1 Kings 20:26–30). If this solution is correct, the Ben-hadad who appears here in chaps. 20 and 22 was Ben-hadad son of Hazael (2 Kings 13:24).

20:1–12, Ben-hadad's Provocation of Ahab. The armies of the Aramean kingdom of Damascus besiege Samaria. Ben-hadad, the enemy king, makes certain demands on the city, but because of textual uncertainties, it is difficult to tell exactly what these are. The king of Israel seems at first to agree to give Ben-hadad whatever he wants, but when Ben-hadad insists on having his servants enter the city to choose what they want, the Israelite king becomes suspicious and refuses to comply. There follows a boastful Aramean threat (v. 10) countered by a proverbial Israelite retort (v. 11). The time of battle is at hand.

20:13–21, The First Engagement. An Israelite victory against overwhelming odds is achieved with Yahweh's help. An anonymous prophet conveys the divine promise of success, which also includes tactical instructions. Ahab is told to strike first (v. 14), thus taking the overconfident Arameans by surprise. The first to march out to battle are "the young men of the provincial governors," an otherwise unknown group, followed by the regular militia ("all the people of Israel," v. 15). Ben-hadad, who has been drinking with his field officers, is unable to stop the Israelite advance, and the Arameans are routed.

20:22–34, Ahab's Victory over Ben-hadad. The next engagement takes place at Aphek, east of the Sea of Galilee. The Arameans have chosen this region, an open plateau, because they believe they were defeated at Samaria by the Israelites because "their gods are gods of the hills" (v. 23). This provides the occasion for another divine promise of success to Israel: Yahweh will prove that he is a God of flatlands as well as hills (v. 28). When the battle is over, Ben-hadad asks for clemency, and his life is spared on the condition that he return cities taken from Israel by his father.

20:35–43, The Condemnation of Ahab. For the first time in this independent source (chaps. 20 and 22) the prophetic message is unfavorable to the king of Israel. He is censured by another anonymous prophet for releasing Ben-hadad, when Yahweh requires that he be put to death (v. 42; cf. 1 Sam. 15:9). The condemnation of Ahab in 1 Kings 20:42 looks ahead to his death in chap. 22.

21:1–29
Naboth's Vineyard

This story is not a part of the story of the conflict between Ben-hadad and the king of Israel in chaps. 20 and 22. Elijah, who played no part in chap. 20, returns to utter a final condemnation of Ahab and his dynasty. Thus the larger Elijah-Elisha narrative resumes from chap. 19. It is noteworthy that in the arrangement of the Greek text, the story of Naboth's vineyard follows chap. 19 immediately. The arrangement of the received Hebrew text is the result of an editor's wish to place the episode after the condemnation of Ahab in 20:35–42. The crime of Ahab is that he has "killed, and also taken possession" (21:19 [RSV]). The latter means that he has deprived an innocent citizen of something that rightfully belongs to him. From the prophetic perspective according to which this story is told, this is the quintessential royal crime. As the prophet Samuel warned before the first king was crowned, it is the way of kings to treat people this way (1 Sam. 8:11–17). Ahab's personal denunciation is expanded in 1 Kings 21:21–22 to a condemnation of his dynasty that associates it with the condemned houses of Jeroboam (14:10–11) and Baasha (16:3–4).

Jezebel plays her most prominent role in this episode. Her contrivance of Naboth's unjust execution suggests that the Phoenician queen has acquired an extraordinary knowledge of Israelite law, with its requirement of two witnesses (Deut. 17:6; 19:15) and death by stoning (Deut. 17:5).

Ahab's unexpected reprieve (1 Kings 21:27–29) explains why the full sentence is not imposed until the end of the reign of his son Joram (Jehoram in 22:50), when the extermination of the family will occur (2 Kings 10:10–11). Ahab's blood will indeed be licked by dogs, but in Samaria (1 Kings 22:38), not Jezreel (21:19; but see 2 Kings 9:25–26).

22:1-40
The Death of Ahab

This section is a continuation of the narrative begun in chap. 20. The old prophetic account of the death of the king of Israel at Ramoth-gilead in vv. 1-28 has been filled out with an editorial synopsis concluding the account of the reign of Ahab (vv. 39-40).

22:1-28, The Prophecy of Micaiah Son of Imlah. Ramoth-gilead, an important Transjordanian outpost located on one of the main roads to Damascus, was the headquarters of one of Solomon's district officers (4:13), but now it is in Aramean hands. Ahab decides to join forces with Jehoshaphat, his contemporary in Judah (22:41), to restore the city to Israel. As we know from 2 Kings 8:18, 26, this alliance was sealed by the marriage of Ahab's daughter Athaliah to Jehoshaphat's son Jehoram. The primary interest of the story, however, is not the alliance of Israel and Judah or even the preparations for war. It is the problem of authentic and inauthentic prophecy. Ahab's prophets predict battlefield success for Israel. A prophet called Zedekiah son of Chenaanah dramatizes this outcome with a symbolic act using iron horns, perhaps in evocation of the oracle on the tribe of Joseph in Deut. 33:17. But there is one dissenting voice. Micaiah son of Imlah reports a vision of Israel scattered like sheep without a shepherd —that is, he foresees that Ahab will die in the battle.

It is Micaiah's vision that is authentic. In Jeremiah's indictment of false prophets who give favorable oracles (Jer. 23:16-22), the true prophet is the one who has stood in the divine courtroom and received Yahweh's commission (Jer. 23:18). Thus, Micaiah authenticates himself by his report of a vision of the divine courtroom (1 Kings 22:19-23). He says that he saw Yahweh seated on his throne (cf. Isa. 6:1), flanked by the celestial armies, and heard Yahweh asking for volunteers (cf. Isa. 6:8). Micaiah watched as "a spirit" was commissioned to be "a lying spirit in the mouth of all of [Ahab's] prophets" (1 Kings 22:22). Thus the favorable oracle reported by the other prophets is a hoax, sent by Yahweh to entice Ahab to his death.

The conflict between Micaiah and Zedekiah is often compared to that of Jeremiah and Hananiah (Jer. 28). In the end, Zedekiah's viewpoint prevails, and Micaiah's counsel is rejected. He is arrested and, like Jeremiah, placed in the custody of a "son of the king" (1 Kings 22:26; cf. Jer. 36:26; 38:6).

22:29-38, The Battle. Ahab's strategy to protect himself has been obscured by confusion in our received Hebrew text. Fortunately, the versions preserve the original reading. "I will go into battle disguised," he says (v. 30), "but you," he tells Jehoshaphat, "wear my robes!"

The Aramean king has commanded his charioteers to look for the king of Israel, so that Jehoshaphat, dressed as Ahab, is immediately hard pressed, while the real Ahab successfully avoids attention. Soon, however, Ahab is felled by a randomly shot arrow. Both the happenstance of the shot and the arrow's fortuitous penetration of a seam in Ahab's armor (v. 34) are ironic signs of the futility of the elaborate precautions. Micaiah's oracle has been proved authentic, and Ahab will not return to Samaria "in peace" (cf. vv. 27-28).

22:39-40, Summary of Ahab's Reign. This concluding synopsis is from the hand of a Deuteronomistic editor. The reference to Ahab's "ivory house" (v. 39) has been illustrated by the discovery of numerous fragments of carved ivory inlay, once attached to paneling and furniture, in the ruins of Ahab's palace at Samaria (→ Ivory; Samaria, City of).

22:41-53
The Successors of Asa and Ahab

22:41-50, Jehoshaphat of Judah. Jehoshaphat's kingship, like that of his father, Asa (cf. 15:9-15), is evaluated positively by the Deuteronomistic editors. He is said to have finished the job begun by Asa (15:12) of eliminating "male cult prostitutes" (22:46). His only shortcoming was his failure to dismantle the high places. The intent of the cryptic notice in v. 47 may be that Edom was ruled by Judah through a prefect during Jehoshaphat's reign. Evidently it was Jehoshaphat's ambition to revive the Red Sea trade of Solomon's reign, but his fleet seems to have been wrecked while still in port at Ezion-geber. We are also told that he refused an offer from Ahaziah to undertake a joint shipping venture.

22:51-53, Ahaziah of Israel. After this introductory synopsis, with its wholly negative evaluation, the account of Ahaziah's reign continues in 2 Kings 1.

Bibliography

Devries, S. J. I Kings. Word Biblical Commentary, 12. Waco, TX: Word, 1985.

Gray, J. I & II Kings: A Commentary. 2d ed. Old Testament Library. Philadelphia: Westminster, 1970.

Long, B. O. I Kings. Forms of the Old Testament Literature, 9. Grand Rapids, MI: Eerdmans, 1984.

Montgomery, J. A. Kings. International Critical Commentary. New York: Scribner's, 1951.

Nelson, R. First and Second Kings. Interpretation. Atlanta, GA: Knox, 1987.

Robinson, J. The First Book of Kings. Cambridge Bible Commentary on the New English Bible. Cambridge: Cambridge University Press, 1972.

2 KINGS

B U R K E   O .   L O N G

INTRODUCTION

The Second Book of the Kings is part of an editorial unit that begins with the book of Deuteronomy, includes Joshua, Judges, and 1 and 2 Samuel, and concludes with the books of Kings (→ Deuteronomist; Deuteronomistic Historian). In this final book, the ancient Deuteronomistic historian continues to evaluate his people's experience with the northern and southern monarchies after the death of Ahab (ca. 851 B.C.). The story moves through the destruction of the Northern Kingdom (ca. 722; 2 Kings 17) and comes to rest in the aftermath of Judah's and Jerusalem's demise in 587 (2 Kings 25).

Although the subject of the book is royal history, its theme is the moral and religious failure that led to the loss of national identity and autonomy. In the turmoil that followed Jerusalem's destruction, the Deuteronomistic historian drew a warning from this catastrophe and hinted that hope might be extracted from the favorable treatment accorded Jehoiachin, the last Judahite king, who lived on as a captive in Babylon (2 Kings 25:27–30). (For further information related to 1 and 2 Kings, its sources, literary history, and major themes, see 1 Kings, "Introduction.")

Modern readers confront 2 Kings as an ancient version of history and so must infer the one or more writers' intentions and the ancient readers' reception of the book from the text itself. Historians ask questions about this or that factual event mentioned in the story and collate the biblical versions with scattered extrabiblical evidence. In the last analysis, however, one is left not with history pure and simple, but with *historiography*, a story told by an author who claims to be bound by the facts rather than free to pick and choose among them, like writers of fiction.

Accordingly, a primary aim of the following commentary is to discern in this story the main transactions between writer and readers, that is, between the Deuteronomistic historian and what scholars assume to have been his ancient audience. Due allowance for modern readers is made as well. The unifying motifs and perspectives of the work, its ruling concepts, its rhetoric of persuasion, all add up to the writer's presentation of a distinctive interpretation of Israel's history. At various points, historical and linguistic information aid in understanding the book's claims. Historical information alone, however, is insufficient to grasp the sense of the literary whole presented to both ancient and modern readers. One needs also to be sensitive to literary matters: compositional techniques, cues, motifs, and allusions that guide readers along certain paths of perception and suggest coherent intentionality in the work. The comments that follow focus on this ancient literary rendering of history that modern men and women in church and synagogue continue to read for self-understanding and inspiration.

COMMENTARY

1:1–10:36

The Divided Kingdom to Jehu's Revolt

The division of Kings into two parts (1 and 2 Kings), with the dividing point in the midst of the reign of Ahaziah, is the work of later editors. In 2 Kings, the Deuteronomistic historian simply continues the synchronistic account of the Divided Kingdom begun at 1 Kings 12.

1:1–18

Ahaziah (ca. 851–849 B.C.)

The reign of Ahaziah was introduced at 1 Kings 22:51–53. Here, the writer records a first event during the reign of Ahaziah (v. 1) and then recounts in 2 Kings 1:2–17 a tradition about Elijah, already known from 1 Kings 17–19; 21 (→Elijah). Typical concluding formulas (2 Kings 1:17b–18) close out Ahaziah's rule.

The Deuteronomistic historian draws a lesson from the king's death. Misguidedly, Ahaziah solicits an oracle from a Philistine god, Baal-zebub (the name means "lord of the flies," perhaps a conscious parody on a Caananite epithet, *ba'al zebul*, "Prince Baal"). What the king received was a death word spoken by Elijah, prophet of Yahweh (→Baal-zebub; Prophet).

The narrator weaves the action into a fabric of moral combat. An ailing king reaches out first, sending messengers to solicit an oracle from the god of Ekron, one of five Philistine cities, but the God of Israel intervenes and commissions Elijah to intercept the royal emissaries with a prophecy of punishment. Angered, the king then pursues Elijah and, having forgotten his original concern, repeatedly sends royal militiamen to fetch the prophet. His initiative fails disastrously (vv. 9–12), and a Yahweh counterthrust takes over in v. 13. In the end, Elijah repeats his prophecy, and the narrator notes its fulfillment (vv. 16–17; cf. 1 Kings 16:34; 17:16). The king died, just as foretold.

On the one hand, the question, "Is there no God in Israel that you go to inquire of Baal-zebub . . . ?" (JPS; 2 Kings 1:3, 6; cf. v. 16), finds its answer in Elijah's assault-by-oracle upon a king who has sought other powers. On the other hand, Ahaziah's question about Yahweh's prophet, "What kind of man was he who came to you?" (RSV, v. 7), receives its reply in Elijah's conjury of consuming fire. Like the great contest in 1 Kings 18:20–40, the struggle is between Yahweh and the gods of Canaan and between their respective earthly stand-ins. Ahaziah lost, and the Deuteronomistic historian adds this accounting to the string of apostasies in the Northern Kingdom.

2:1–25
Elisha Succeeds Elijah

Seen in relation to the whole of 1 and 2 Kings, this unit occupies a pausal moment between two regnal periods. Elijah, the champion of Yahwism (i.e., traditional Israelite monotheism) against the Baalists of the Northern Kingdom, departs earth and story, leaving behind a successor to carry on the austere voice of prophetic witness. The Deuteronomistic historian arranged originally independent narratives (now reflected in vv. 1–15, 16–18, 19–22, and 23–24) like itinerary points on a map. Elijah and Elisha move from Gilgal to Bethel (vv. 1–2, 3–4) to Jericho (vv. 5–6) to the Jordan River (vv. 7–8a) and cross into the Transjordan (vv. 8b–14). At v. 14b, the direction reverses. Elisha, who is now alone, fords the river back to Jericho (vv. 14b–17, 18–22), whence he moves on to Bethel and beyond (vv. 23–25).

The effect of this ordering of events is to build a certain suspense toward that climactic moment beyond the river when the crack between temporality and eternity opens to Elisha's sight. At the outset, everybody is aware that Elijah is to be taken away: the readers (v. 1), Elisha, and those members of a prophetic association, the "sons of prophets" (vv. 3, 5; see 2 Kings 6:1). No one, however, knows the time or place. The characters repeatedly suppress conversation about the event while steadily moving toward it. Finally, repeated words and phrases (2 Kings 2:7–8, 14) define a private space beyond the Jor-

dan where one learns for the first time that the departure of Elijah has to do with empowering a successor (vv. 9–10). Suddenly Elijah ascends into the heavens in a visionary whirlwind (v. 11; cf. the similar language of vision reports in Judg. 13:19–21; 2 Kings 6:17). In this visionary space beyond the Jordan and away from bystanders, the prophets confront the power of God, as though containment of the Holy were necessary to bring the power of divinity into the ordinary human realm (cf. the miracles of healing in 1 Kings 17:17–24; 2 Kings 4:33–35; the temptations of Jesus in Luke 4:1–13).

Elisha brings back to the human community Elijah's power to perform wondrous deeds (2 Kings 2:14–15). The members of the prophetic band seek some assurance, however, that Elisha is really alone and that Elijah will not pop up somewhere to demand his accustomed honor. Their futile search (for a corpse? for Elijah himself?) shows that the succession has taken place and that homage to a new leader is justified. The narrator assures readers of the same point in vv. 19–24. Elisha quickly demonstrates the terrifying power he holds from Elijah and God—for repair of misfortune and for curse.

Elijah's departure is filled with memory and echo. Like Moses (Deut. 34:6), Elijah leaves the earth without a trace except in the legacy of succession (cf. Deut. 31:7–8, 23; Josh. 1:1–9). The transition from Moses to Joshua marked continuity in Yahweh's giving of *torah* (divine teaching) and constancy in covenanted partnership with God. In this later day, the transition from Elijah to Elisha suggests a true and steady voice for allegiance to God in a Northern Kingdom that lives in the shadow of Jeroboam. At the same time, this pausal moment between the reigns and between the two great prophets is a station on the way from that first hint of Yahweh's victory (1 Kings 19:15–18) to its consummation in a military slaughter inspired by Elisha (2 Kings 9–10).

3:1–10:36
From Jehoram to Jehu

The circumstance that determined the literary organization of this large complex of tradition is that Jehu, a military commander in Israel's army, murdered both Jehoram and the Judean king Ahaziah, thus bringing to an end two regnal periods and launching his own brief rule. The literary problem for the Deuteronomistic historian was to take account of this fateful meeting of three kings and still follow his preferred technique of presenting each regnal period as an enclosed block of tradition, with introductory and concluding summaries. The solution was to begin conventionally with an introduction to Jehoram of Israel (3:1–3), recount events during his time (3:4–8:15), and, without concluding Jehoram's rule, resume the sequence of Judean kings (8:16–24), getting quickly to Ahaziah (8:25–27). Jehu murdered this Judahite while simultaneously revolting against Jehoram of Israel (8:28–9:29). In this way, the historian presents the end of both Jehoram and Ahaziah and the rise of Jehu as an occurrence within the regnal period of Ahaziah. From these circumstances, the writer goes on to recount incidents during Jehu's reign (9:30–10:33) and concludes with the usual summary (10:34–36).

Elisha is placed at or near the center of all these events. Most of what the historian considered relevant to Jehoram's reign is drawn from freely circulating stories or collections of tales about Elisha (3:4–8:15). Even the destructive energies of Jehu are presented as having been commissioned and legitimated by Elisha (9:1–10).

3:1–3, The Regnal Summary for Jehoram.
This summary is typical of most others in the books of Kings (cf. 1 Kings 14:21–24; 2 Kings 13:1–2; the synchronistic date in v. 1 contradicts 1:17—such inconsistencies appear fairly frequently in 1 and 2 Kings and remain an unresolved problem for historians). While condemning the religious loyalties of Jehoram (all northern kings are thus summarily treated), the Deuteronomistic historian nonetheless softens his judgment. Unlike his father and mother, Ahab and Jezebel (cf. 1 Kings 17–21), the king put away the phallic religious object, the stone "pillar of Baal." The word "baal" means "lord" or "master-owner," but as a proper name it can refer to various local deities (cf. 1:2) and to a widely revered Canaanite god associated with storms and fertility (→ Baal; Pillars).

3:4–27, The Campaign against Moab.
Although this unit may have undergone extensive development prior to its being included in the books of Kings (cf. 1 Kings 22:1–37), it is now unified around three dialogues (vv. 7–8, 10–12a, 14–15a), a prophetic address (vv. 16–19), and two action sequences (vv. 4–6 and 20–27), which lead into and away from the moments of direct speech. Mesha, king of Moab, rebelled against his overlord, Jehoram of Israel. With his allies, the kings of Edom and Judah, Jehoram wages war against the rebel, but, as v. 27b shows, with less than a clear victory (→ Edom; Moab). Between this main crisis and its qualified resolution, the narrator develops a secondary problem, the lack of drinking water for troops and animals (vv. 9–10). To overcome this threat, Jehoram presses for the aid of a reluctant Elisha, whose double promise of water and military victory leads to a miracle of double duty: water comes to slake the thirst of Israel's forces and to confuse the enemy (vv. 11–20, 22–23).

The narrator builds an invidious contrast between Jehoram and the Judean Jehoshaphat. A man of uncertain devotion, Jehoram put together the expedition against Moab, but when his success was threatened, he decried his fate as though he were a victim of Yahweh, not his chosen hero: "Alas! The LORD has called these three kings [us] to give them [us] into the hand of Moab" (v. 10). Later, Elisha imputes to the king some vestige of his infamous father and mother (v. 13), Ahab and Jezebel, those exemplars of apostasy (see 1 Kings 18–19; 21). In contrast, it is Jehoshaphat who suggests guidance through a Yahwistic prophet (2 Kings 3:11), and it is his merit alone that justifies Elisha's (and Yahweh's) attention. It is a point of Deuteronomistic theology to prefer kings in the Davidic line (cf. 1 Kings 11:36–39; 2 Sam. 7:11–16).

Elisha is portrayed as a defender of true Yahwistic religion after the manner of Elijah, his master. He is the one who "poured water on the hands of Elijah" (2 Kings 3:11) and of whom Jehoshaphat says, "The word of the LORD is with him" (v. 12; cf. 1 Kings 17:24). The narrator notes that "the hand of Yahweh [the rush of divine power] came upon him" (v. 15; cf. 1 Kings 18:46) and depicts events as flowing from prophecy to fulfillment (vv. 16–17, 20–24). This successor to Elijah reproves Jehoram and approves Jehoshaphat. Like his predecessor, he denies to the Northern Kingdom any sort of religious legitimacy.

Yet when the Israelite armies abruptly withdraw from their assault on Kirhareseth (2 Kings 3:27), victory is less than clear cut. Following a human "burnt offering" to the Moabite god Chemosh, "great wrath came upon [against] Israel," and Jehoram's armies withdrew (→ Chemosh). Such sacrifices to appease the anger of the national god horrified the historian (2 Kings 16:3), and he may have understood that the Israelites were gripped with dread at this sight of Moabite devotion—yet another sign of uncertain devotion to Yahweh—and so lost their victory (so several ancient versions, followed by NEB: "The Israelites were filled with such consternation at this sight that they struck camp and returned home"). On the other hand, the tradition upon which the Deuteronomistic historian drew may have implied that the Moabite god accepted the sacrifice and then defended the city, letting loose great terror against Israel. The idea that military success comes from the deity's guiding and protective strength is not only found in the Bible (e.g., Josh. 10:7–11) but is also enunciated by Moabite scribes themselves (→ Moabite Stone, The).

The biblical story speaks, then, with a double voice. Ultimate triumph eludes the Israelites, but Moab is spared final defeat. Yahweh brings about partial victory, but Chemosh too wields power in the world. Nonetheless, for the narrator any contest between Yahweh and the gods is really no contest at all (cf. 1 Kings 18:20–40; 20:26–30). Through Yahweh and Yahweh's prophet, Jehoram achieved some success but without changing God's judgment of the apostate Northern Kingdom.

4:1–44, Miracles of Elisha. Although presented as part of Jehoram's reign, these originally independent traditions (vv. 1–7, 8–37, 38–44) make no mention of the king. Instead, they emphasize Elisha's larger-than-life dealings with ordinary folk and portray him as carrying on Elijah's penchant for rescuing the destitute and the dead (cf. 4:1–7 with 1 Kings 17:8–16; 2 Kings 4:8–37 with 1 Kings 17:17–24). Elisha cares for the hungry just as he did when freshly enlivened with his mentor's spirit (cf. 2 Kings 4:38–44 with 2:19–22). The narratives express adulation for Elisha. In keeping the king apart from these signs of Yahweh's power, the Deuteronomistic writer suggests indirectly that Jehoram is blind to these matters of faith (cf. 6:24–33).

The story of Elisha and the Shunammite (4:8–37) is a centerpiece to the collection of stories in chap. 4. Against a background of the Shunammite's admiration for Elisha (vv. 8–10), the drama encompasses three movements: first, in fulfillment of prophecy, a son is born to this woman who was without child and married to an old man (vv. 12–17); second, the son sickens and dies, creating a crisis for both mother and prophet (vv. 18–25a); third, responding to urgent demands, Elisha intervenes and restores the dead son to life (vv. 25b–35). Dramatic intensity finally drains away in a meeting between the prophet and the woman (vv. 36–37).

In the end, the narrator completes a thematic and structural symmetry. The Shunammite first appeared in deferential respect toward Elisha; she questioned and pleaded, even rebuked him, while demanding his help (vv. 16, 27–28); and now at the end, she falls at his feet in a posture of near worship (v. 37; cf. Gen. 18:2; 19:1; 2 Kings 2:15). In this closing moment, Elisha declares her son restored (2 Kings 4:36b), as earlier he had announced his imminent birth (v. 16). Occurring only as part of the annunciation (vv. 14–17, 28) and restoration (v. 36), this "son" motif spans the narrative's main action. A son is given in promise, lost in sickness, and restored by the mother's pursuit of a holy man's power.

Yet, Elisha's unrivaled claim to center stage is subverted during those moments of pursuit. When the child dies, disturbing the assurances of promise and fulfillment, the woman suddenly emerges as a clearheaded, forceful mother urgently concentrated on rescue. She pushes past every obstacle, including those formalities that kept her standing in the doorway while the men discussed how they might reward her kindness to them (vv. 12–15). Now, on her approach to Mount Carmel, she brushes aside the standard greetings (v. 26), "grabs hold of Elisha's feet," and turns even that gesture of submission (cf. v. 37; 1 Sam. 25:23) into one of assertiveness (2 Kings 4:27). Neither Elisha nor his protocol-conscious servant know what lies behind the woman's headlong intrusion onto Mount Carmel. Elisha is singularly blind: "The LORD has hidden it from me and has not told me" (v. 27).

The Shunammite unwittingly presses an advantage against a prophet whose status has been diminished by ignorance. She calls due a moral chit. Her rebuke (v. 28) and insistence (v. 30a) demand that Elisha accept the moral consequences of his miracle and address the situation personally. Elisha seems to understand, although—still clinging to formality—he speaks nothing directly to the woman. The narrator notes simply that "he arose and followed her" (v. 30b). Readers, however, have been shown a clearheaded mother challenging convention and those who cling to it and extracting from Elisha a direct response he seems not to have entirely wanted.

Events finally vindicate the Shunammite's insistence and restore Elisha to his pedestal (vv. 31–37). By announcing the miraculous birth, Elisha played the part of the wonder worker who dispenses largesse among his patrons. In restoring the son, he merely worked his magic again. Within these conventions, the Shunammite challenges prophetic privilege and wins. She is a victress, even if Elisha does not quite admit her moral claim. Her bowing to the ground in reverence (v. 37) returns to him the status of beloved miracle worker.

Perhaps one should temper admiration for Elisha with the experience of a mother's grief and the knowledge of Elisha's blindness. God did not tell all to his prophet, as readers are made keenly aware. Elisha knows less than he needs to know and does less than he is able to do and surely less than one might expect of a hero. Homage is due this prophet, but not without reservation, for his power and position seem in need of moral restraint.

Verses 38–44 show Elisha fully restored to his accustomed role of miracle worker and beloved master of a prophetic guild. In vv. 38–41, we see him wondrously detoxifying a meal for his disciples in a time of famine (cf. Exod. 15:22–25). In 2 Kings 4:42–44, we see him miraculously feeding one hundred men from what had been only a small amount of food (cf. 1 Kings 17:8–16).

5:1–27, Elisha, Naaman, and Gehazi. In this narrative, Elisha again helps a person in distress, this time a non-Israelite and, ironically, a commander of those armies that so often threatened the Israelite kingdom (see 6:8, 24; 10:32–33; 13:22). Naaman the leprous commander is healed and recognizes Yahweh as the source of his cure (5:15). Gehazi's crass failure to honor this moment draws Naaman's disease onto himself (vv. 20–27). God extends his concern to all the earth (v. 15) and to all human beings who are made in God's image (Gen. 1:26–27). Yet the power of God in the world is not just restorative. It also demands righteousness and is a punishment to those who trifle with it. Perhaps the narrator saw in this story a metaphor for the history of Israel's kingdoms.

The unity of the narrative is best imagined as a series of waves rolling along a line, each bearing energy for the next. One wave carries Naaman from leprosy to cure (2 Kings 5:1–14). A problem emerges as part of the background summary (v. 1) and is resolved by a miracle, as the flesh of this "great man" becomes like that of a "little child" (v. 14).

Borne within this wave is the energy for another. The readers' knowledge that the God of Israel had really given Naaman his success and public reputation (v. 1) stands in ironic contrast to Naaman's intransigently arrogant attitude toward Elisha and the land of Israel (vv. 11–12). Naaman's spirit needs reform as much as his flesh requires healing.

From this point, the writer turns to spiritual transformation (vv. 15–19a). Having been healed (the Hebrew at v. 14 reads literally "his flesh turned back"), Naaman "turns back" to Elisha (v. 15a) and speaks as a convert to Israel's religion (v. 15b). He even wants to reward Elisha for his services. When refused, he insists on a pardon in advance for unavoidable semblances of his old self (bowing, in military duty, to the Syrian god Rimmon) when his heart is truly wed to Yahweh (vv. 17–18; →Rimmon). At the same time, a narrative loop on the level of narrator and reader is closed. Naaman's awareness of the Lord finally converges with that of writer and readers, who already at the outset knew of Yahweh's hand in the Syrian's successes.

A last pulse of energy arises when Gehazi witnesses Naaman's transformation (vv. 19b–27). His latent opportunism drawing encouragement from misapprehension (v. 20), Gehazi sullies this high moment by turning it to self-serving advantage (vv. 21–24). Therefore he stands accused, convicted, and punished for grasping at the very same material outpouring of gratitude that his master refused (vv. 25–27a).

The narrator's final clipped remark draws this tale of reversals and contrasts into a single ironic circle. One recalls Naaman, who was leprous (v. 1), and now reads that Gehazi, who was whole, "went out from his presence, leprous as snow" (v. 27b). Naaman, a foreigner, was healed in body and spirit; Gehazi, an insider, inherits the leper's excludedness (see Lev. 13:45–46).

While Elisha presides in authority and power, a foreign convert affirms the singularity of God (cf. Exod. 18:10–11; Josh. 2:9–11). Next to Elisha, Israel's king seems ineffectual and, next to Naaman, simply uninterested in piety. In this way, the story may indirectly assess Jehoram's reign.

6:1–7, An Axehead Recovered. The tradition in 6:1–7, which follows a common narrative pattern (cf. Exod. 15:22–27; 17:1–7), is one of several brief stories about Elisha that stress in uncomplicated ways his marvelous powers in the service of others (cf. 2 Kings 2:19–22; 4:1–7, 38–44; 13:20–21). The prophet is cast here with "sons of prophets," i.e., members of an established occupational group who "sit before" him (RSV: "dwell under your charge") and who look to him for direction (cf. 4:1; 4:42–44). The narrative seems intended to glorify Elisha, and—like all pious legends—to inculcate attitudes of reverence toward him.

6:8–23, Elisha and the Syrian Threat. In contrast to 5:1–27, this narrative depicts Elisha as an adversary to the Syrians. The enemy king's military campaigns having been continually frustrated (the recurrent sense is strong in 6:8–10), and having at last laid the blame on Elisha, he orders his troops to seize the prophet at Dothan (a strategic point controlling access to the hill country north of Samaria; vv. 11–14). Because Elisha has extraordinary powers and is wrapped in supernatural protection, however, the prophet disarms the personal threat (vv. 18–19) and has the king of Israel send the enemy home with great feasting (vv. 20–23a). With this turn, action that began in Syria returns to its source. A closing comment (v. 23b) notes that the continuing hostilities (vv. 8a; 5:2) had been wondrously dissipated by Elisha's power.

Ironic play on two motifs turns this story toward playful admiration of Elisha. First, there is a double sense of "seeing" in the story. The prophet is a man of preternatural sight. He continually frustrated Syria's bellicose intentions (vv. 8–10), and now the Syrian king—who is limited to natural sight—embarks on a comic quest. He wants to be told the facts plainly: "Will you not show me who of us is for the king of Israel?" (v. 11). The same verb brings a report to the king, "it was told [shown] him . . ." (v. 13). The king's messengers even describe Elisha's early warnings to the Israelites on exactly that level of ordinary military intelligence and with the identical word ("the prophet . . . tells [shows] the king of Israel," v. 12). Later, a similar ironic contrast depicts supernatural against natural perception. Elisha prays that his servant will "see" the unseen heavenly forces that guard him (v. 17), and the menacing Syrian soldiers are struck blind, captured, and made to see again (vv. 18–20). In all this, the narrator takes us through a see-scape: from contrasting Elisha's "seeing" with the Syrian's being shown, to blindness supernaturally sent by forces "seen" only by the prophets, to natural sight supernaturally restored. It is no contest. Elisha divulges the secrets and manipulates the players out of his private reservoir of supernatural powers.

The second ironic motif is a contrast between military forces. Syria sends "horses and chariots and a great army" to seize Elisha (vv. 14, 15), but this overwhelming horde faces the visionary "horses and chariots of fire" deployed around the prophet (v. 17). The scene dramatizes panic through the servant's ordinary sighting of the enemy and then quickly diffuses it in a vision induced by prayer. One sees the protective shield of Elisha and recognizes that the force of Yahweh is concentrated in and about Elisha.

Even the king of Israel must finally submit to this extraordinary power when deciding what to do with the duped prisoners (vv. 21–23). Elisha's words in v. 22 are difficult. He seems to suggest that when capture has come as a gift of the prophet's miracle working, the victims are owed their life, perhaps just as obviously as they had been deprived of sight or shown to be without second sight. Such is the power of this prophet in Israel, whom the Syrian army foolishly sought to restrain. Perhaps the narrator is showing his own answer to that question raised by Elijah in 1:3. There is a God in Israel, and Elisha is his prophet.

6:24–7:20, Famine Relieved, Oracle Fulfilled. This is another of the stories that depict Elisha in relation to a continuing Syrian military threat (see 6:8–23; 8:7–15; cf. 5:1). One must assume that the narrator took Jehoram to be the unnamed "king of Israel" in the narrative (6:26). Several known kings of Syria had the name Benhadad, and we do not know that the writer had one specific ruler in mind. In any event, the point seems not to record history so much as to draw moral and religious lessons from historically colored stories.

In the preceding narrative (6:8–23), Elisha is presumed to be on good terms with the Israelite king. Now, having lost all hope during the siege of Samaria, Jehoram blames Elisha for his trouble and despairs of any help from the Lord. In the meantime, unbeknownst to Jehoram, deliverance is wrought by God—just as Elisha prophesied. Thus, two converging sequences of events (breaking the siege and actualizing Elisha's prophecies) vindicate the prophet's unwavering confidence in God and dramatize Elisha's prescience and power.

The trajectory from city under siege to city rescued grows less distinct as the path from prophecy to fulfillment emerges more sharply (7:1–2, 16–17, 18–20 [the last verses may be editorial elaboration]). Yet, the move from word to event is not narrated directly. One wanders through a landscape of four lepers' comic self-absorption (7:3–10), and the miracle that befuddles leper and king alike and is the cause of Samaria's relief is revealed to the readers alone —and then only as a secondary comment in retrospect, not as an event witnessed firsthand (7:6–7).

Through this indirect means, the writer portrays, not a miracle, but how various people deal with its aftereffects. The characters themselves remain unenlightened; they bump into cryptic prophecies (the king and his aide, 7:1–2), discover strange happenings (the lepers and the king's men, 7:8, 15) and offer ill-informed explanations for what they see (the king, 7:12; the Syrian troops, 7:6b). Readers must finally complete the narrative sequence begun in 6:24–25 by inferring that the siege was broken. The narrator notes only that Elisha's prophecy, which did not look directly to the end of the military campaign, found its fulfillment.

In sum, the narrator and the readers taken into his confidence (7:6–7) see one sequence of events from a point outside narrative time (how the siege of Samaria was broken by a noise sent by Yahweh and how, coincidentally, Elisha foresaw the outcome). Constrained by their finitude, the people embedded in the narrative see another sequence (how a siege camp was abandoned, leaving provisions for the taking, fulfilling Elisha's word).

Elisha dominates one's perspective on events. He is calmly prescient (he knows the king pursues him, 6:32; and he knows the famine will end, 7:1–2). It is this power rooted in foreknowledge and insight into God's ways that the narrator seeks to generate in the readers' experience (7:6–7, 16–20). From this point of sighting, one admires Elisha and appreciates the humor with which the story has been told.

8:1–6, The Power of Elisha's Fame. Although v. 1 appears to link this narrative to the Shunammite's story in 4:8–37, the two traditions may have been originally independent of one another. The Deuteronomistic historian need not have presupposed the death of Elisha, as may seem to be the case, but only the fame of the "great things" attributed to him (v. 4b); in fact, the prophet's death is reported in 13:20–21, during the reign of Jehoahaz.

The writer implies that even in his absence, when merely talked about by others (vv. 4–6), Elisha helps those in need. He had spun a strand of Elisha's exploits in chaps. 3–7, and here, within one tiny episode, Gehazi does the same. There is a momentary congruence between the narrators (the Deuteronomistic historian and a narrator-character Gehazi) and their subjects (the king within the story and the readers without). Narrative recollection refracts completely the power of Elisha, as though the mere glow from a flame transmits warmth. The woman receives its benefits (the king restores her property), and even Jehoram—in contrast to some of his other appearances—seems on the side of God's benevolent aid eased into the world.

8:7–15, Elisha, Ben-hadad, and Hazael.
This narrative takes readers back to the larger canvas of political history, against which were set most of the preceding stories about Elisha. The narrator opens a period of severe troubles for Israel at the hand of Hazael and attaches this new beginning to the mysterious inner movements of Elisha's spirit (vv. 10–13). The incident also marks the beginning of fulfillment, for Elisha's predecessor Elijah, speaking for the historian, had already seen the shape of Hazael bulking in the distance and read its meaning as chastisement for an apostate people (1 Kings 19:17).

The narrator builds on a conventional literary pattern: in a situation of distress, a person seeks an oracle from a prophet ("inquire of the LORD"), receives God's answer, and then witnesses its realization (cf. 1 Kings 14; 22; 2 Kings 3). Here, the pattern is modified by dialogue and multiple prophecies (2 Kings 8:11–13) that seem to elaborate and explain an original cryptic oracle (v. 10). Elisha's word to Hazael is ambiguous. One message seems intended for the king: "You [Ben-hadad] shall surely recover." Another is meant for Hazael as information or perhaps wily suggestion: "but the LORD has shown me that he [Ben-hadad] shall surely die." As though foreshadowing biblical interpreters who have struggled with such incoherence or with the moral implications of a prophet who may be suggesting that Hazael deliberately lie, Elisha probes in some trancelike state the ambiguity of his own speech. "He fixed his face, and set [it] until he was ashamed. And the man of God wept" (v. 11).

From this opaqueness springs another modification to the literary pattern—a second dialogue that is, by comparison to vv. 10–11, limpid. Hazael's question about weeping (v. 12a) blends into the specter of gruesome oppression of Israel. In self-abasement, he refuses such worldly glory, and this quickly elicits Elisha's unambiguous announcement ". . . you are to be king over Syria" (v. 13).

When the narrator tells of events that fulfill that prophecy (vv. 14–15), he seems to suggest that Hazael by violence gave history a little self-serving push. Perhaps he even acted at Elisha's suggestion. In any case, one comes to Hazael's accession forewarned, acquainted with his route to power and Elisha's mysterious hand in it. Integrated into the Deuteronomistic history, Hazael will become an external villain, the counterpart to the Baalizing kings and queens who threaten Israel from within. The books of Kings suggest that somehow both are within God's grasp (cf. Isa. 10:5; Jer. 25:9; Gen. 50:20).

8:16–27, Two Kings of Judah.
Turning from Elisha to narratives having to do more directly with the kings, the Deuteronomistic historian summarizes the reign of Joram of Judah (8:16–24) and then opens the reign of his successor, Ahaziah (8:25–27). The stage is now set for a major event: Jehu, a rebel from among the Israelite military commanders, comes to power.

8:28–9:29, The Rebellion of Jehu.
The process by which underlying sources have been forged into the present narrative is obscure. In its final form, however, readers gradually learn that while Joram lay wounded in Jezreel (8:29), Jehu was chosen to make good Yahweh's prophesied retribution on the house of Ahab (9:1–16). He begins to avenge the transgressions of Ahab and Jezebel by assassinating Ahab's descendant, King Joram of Israel (vv. 17–28). The murder of Ahaziah (vv. 27–28) seems a byproduct of this plot, and, unlike the death of Joram, it is not explicitly interpreted as fulfillment of prophecy.

The Deuteronomistic historian regards these events as a turning point in the history of the monarchy. In Elijah's time, the struggle to preserve an exclusive devotion to Yahweh had been idealized in the confrontation between Elijah and the Baalists—Ahab, Jezebel, and the prophets of Baal (1 Kings 18). In that confrontation, a foreshadowing glimpse of the eventual resolution to the conflict was linked to Jehu (1 Kings 19:17–19). Now, as the dynasty of Omri comes to an end, the writer alludes to those older confrontations through repetition of prophecy (cf. 2 Kings 9:7–10 with 1 Kings 21:21–24; 2 Kings 9:25–26 with 1 Kings 21:20–24). Jehu's stirrings in Jezreel begin Yahweh's long foretold judgment on the Omrides.

The twist of narrative plot is set in 9:16 as the paths of Joram, Ahaziah, and Jehu come together at Jezreel. The town was in the north in a valley that separated the central hill country from Galilee, on the road to the east Transjordanian territory. The kings of Israel may have had a palace there (cf. 1 Kings 21:1).

Joram and Ahaziah had fought together at Ramoth-gilead (precise location unknown). Joram had been wounded, and both kings withdrew to the royal lands in Jezreel (2 Kings 8:28–

29). Meanwhile, in Ramoth-gilead (9:1–13), a prophet sent out from Elisha had designated Jehu to be king in Israel and charged him with exacting Yahweh's punishment on the house of Ahab (9:1–10). The selection by a prophet is an old custom (cf. 1 Sam. 10:1; 16:13; 1 Kings 11:29–39). Jehu's fellow commanders offered him open acclamation (2 Kings 9:11–13), and, emboldened by their support, Jehu took up the charge (he coyly downplayed its significance at first) and began to claim his future in conspiracy (vv. 14–16).

Background complete, the writer sets the narrative clock running forward (vv. 17–28). Tension builds around the question of when and how Jehu's murderous design will become known to Joram and Ahaziah and, for readers, what the outcome of Jehu's conspiracy will be. A series of reconaissance missions (vv. 17–20; note the repeated "Is it peace?") leads into, and defines, the climactic moment when Joram discovers the truth and is murdered (vv. 23–24). Doing the bidding of prophecy and its fulfillment, Jehu disposes of the body (v. 26).

Like an inexorable corollary, Ahaziah's death follows. The narrator closes out the regnal period of Ahaziah in v. 28. (Verse 29 is possibly a scribal correction; apparently understanding that Jehoram of Israel reigned twelve years [3:1] and that Ahaziah ruled for one year [8:26], a scribe has corrected 8:25 "twelfth year of Joram" by writing in 9:29 "eleventh year" so as to allow Ahaziah a full year of rule.) Now that both sitting monarchs are dead, subsequent events will be treated as occurrences fully within the regnal period of Jehu (9:30–10:36).

9:30–37, The End of Jezebel. This narrative tells how Jehu eliminates Jezebel, who is assumed to be both his political and religious opponent. Earlier, Jezebel had been cast as a malignant figure, the powerful queen mother in Israel who is also a Phoenician princess, supporter of Baal worship, and enemy of Elijah (1 Kings 16:31; 18:19; 19:1–2; 21:1–16). Here, she faces Jehu as a queen (the painted eyes suggest royal affluence, not—as in our culture—lurid sexual attraction). Her death, however, is prophecy vindicated (cf. 2 Kings 9:36 with 1 Kings 21:23); it marks Jehu's first step toward the righteous triumph of Yahweh religion over those in Israel who worshiped the Baal of Canaan.

Yet, the queen mother's words flung at Jehu, "Is it peace, you Zimri, murderer of your master?" offer intriguing resonance to the incident. Like Zimri, Jehu was a military commander who "conspired against" and assassinated his king (1 Kings 16:9–10); like Zimri, Jehu moves to eliminate all opposition, and in fulfillment of prophecy (1 Kings 16:11–13). Despite this prophetic justification, Zimri came to his end after only

seven days on the throne and failed to win the historian's approval (1 Kings 16:15–19). Jehu will not escape condemnation either, despite the view that his military coup serves God's ends (10:29–31). Thus in recalling Zimri, Jezebel implicitly comments on Jehu. To this extent she not only epitomizes evil for the historian but—like an unwitting prophetess—she presages the mixed moral evaluation of Jehu himself.

10:1–27, Purge of the Baalists. This narrative presents Jehu's action in two phases: first, the murder of Ahab's and Ahaziah's family and supporters—a political act seen as fulfilling a religious aim already prophesied by Elijah (vv. 1–11, esp. vv. 10–11); and second, religious reform in Samaria (vv. 18–27). The incidents in vv. 12–14 and 15–17 are transitions between the two phases.

While these self-contained episodes reflect their original independence, they have been arranged according to a geographic and thematic unity. Jehu moves from Jezreel (vv. 1–11) to Samaria (vv. 18–27), the capital of the Northern Kingdom (cf. 1 Kings 16:24). At the same time, he eliminates political rivals to himself and competition to Yahweh. The move from one place to the other is bridged by two incidents situated "on the way" to Samaria (2 Kings 10:12–14, 15–17).

These transitional reports relate ancillary steps that Jehu took in realizing his transformation from prophet-charged rebel to zealously Yahwistic monarch. Verses 15–17 introduce Jehonadab as witness to Jehu's reforming "zeal for the Lord" (v. 16), and thus announce Jehu's Elijah-like defense of true religion. Just as Jehonadab was bidden to watch, so readers too are asked to take Jehu's ruthless actions as singleminded religious devotion and fulfillment of prophecy (vv. 10, 17).

From Jezreel Jehu first deals with Ahab's "seventy sons" (the number traditionally means the whole family, all the descendants, as in Exod. 1:5; Judg. 8:30). A cleverly worded challenge causes Samaria's leaders to switch their loyalty to Jehu (2 Kings 10:2–5). In response, he asks them to demonstrate their good faith by delivering up the heads of Jehu's rivals. Their compliance and stylized declarations show that this grim exchange represents the substance of negotiated agreement, or covenant, between two parties (cf. Josh. 9:8; 2 Kings 16:7; 1 Kings 20:31–34; Neh. 5:12; Exod. 19:8; 24:3, 7; → Covenant).

Turning to Ahab's supporters in Jezreel (2 Kings 10:8–11), Jehu makes an object lesson of those public reminders of death—which are also the private tokens of newly won political support. The point of the somewhat obscure exchange in v. 9 seems to be, yes, Jehu killed his *master*, but, inferring from the heap of heads, God alone delivered the *kingdom* into Jehu's hands. All is made legitimate by citing Elijah's prophecy (v. 10; cf. 1 Kings 21:21–22). Thus justified, Jehu immediately slays those Jezreelean supporters of Ahab (2 Kings 10:11).

The next two scenes (vv. 12–14, 15–17) portray Jehu moving with determination toward Samaria, the control of which will proclaim both physically and symbolically that he is master in the kingdom. Seemingly by chance, Jehu slays "kinsmen" of the Judean Ahaziah ("forty-two" may be a traditional number; cf. 2:24). As Jehu had struck at the Judean kingdom after murdering the Israelite monarch (9:27), so he attacks Judean loyalists after killing those attached to the house of Ahab. In so recording matters, the writer twice raises a disturbing question: will the Davidic line survive this threat posed by Jehu? (See 11:1–20.)

2 Kings 10:15–17 describes a second compact of solidarity with Jehu (v. 15b; cf. vv. 5–6; on "give the hand" as a gesture of fealty, see 1 Chron. 29:24; and, in the context of international treaties, Ezek. 17:18). Jehu invites a newly loyal subject, Jehonadab son of Rechab, to witness Jehu's "zeal for the LORD" (2 Kings 10:16). The expression recalls Elijah's singleminded defense of Yahweh worship (1 Kings 19:10, 14). Whatever Jehonadab's political importance to Jehu (the Rechabites have been connected with riding and chariotry, on the basis of the Heb. root of their name) or whatever his religious allegiances (some think the Rechabites were staunch devotees of an austere Yahwism; cf. Jer. 35:1–19), Jehonadab is made a harbinger of harsh religious reform (→Rechab). As the image of Jehu had been earlier elided with Elijah (2 Kings 9:22–23), so now with Jehonadab as witness, Jehu will show Elijah's characteristic zealotry for a kingdom exclusively devoted to Yahweh.

The final section of the narrative itemizes Jehu's purge of the Baal cult from Samaria (vv. 18–27). Feigning devotion, he calls together the worshipers of Baal, and, in a stageplay calculated to appeal to their expectations that the king supports the national god of Samaria (vv. 18, 23), Jehu orders the people slain. Concluding notes briefly report the destruction of the temple and its sacred objects (vv. 26–27; the "pillar" that was burned may have been the "Asherah," a wooden symbol of Baal's consort [1 Kings 16:33; cf. Deut. 16:21; 12:3]; →Asherah).

Living up to his advanced billing (1 Kings 19:17), fulfilling those execrations that Elijah hurled at the house of Ahab (1 Kings 21:21–29), and undoing precisely what Ahab had put in place (cf. 2 Kings 10:26–27 and 1 Kings 16:32–33), Jehu concludes Elijah's struggle. He embodies the prophetic impulse that shapes events into meaningful history.

10:28–36, Conclusion to Jehu's Reign. The Deuteronomistic historian closes out the time of Jehu with three items: first, theological appraisal, vv. 28–31 (normally these statements are part of a king's opening summary); second, a notice that Jehu gave up territory to Hazael of Damascus (vv. 32–33), implying the fulfillment of Elisha's premonition (8:12; the "Black Obelisk" monument from Nimrud extolls the Assyrian Shalmanezer III, who defeated Hazael in 841 B.C. and collected tribute from Jehu); third, the usual concluding formulas (10:34–36).

The Deuteronomistic historian is of two minds about Jehu. The loss of territory was a consequence of Jehu's religious shortcomings (vv. 31–32), and he persisted in following Jeroboam's ways (v. 29). But his heroic place in the narrative derived from carrying out God's wishes (v. 30). This limited approval, while reported as God's speech, is taken as a prophecy. When it is expressly fulfilled (15:12), it will link subsequent events to God's unseen hand.

11:1–17:41

The Divided Kingdom to Israel's Demise

In this section, the narrator continues the story of both kingdoms during a period of mutual weakness. Steady encroachment on Israelite and Judahite territory eventually led to Assyrian domination of Israel and Judah. The account spans the years from ca. 843 B.C. (Jehu rules in Israel and queen mother Athaliah usurps the throne in Judah) to 722 B.C. (Hoshea of Israel is carried into exile, ending the Northern Kingdom, while Ahaz reigns in Judah, beholden to the Assyrian Tiglath-pileser).

The writer emphasizes Judahite affairs. This comes as an abrupt change, since after the division of Solomon's kingdom in 1 Kings 12, the narrator stressed the northern realm and its waywardness. Here, one lingers over Athaliah (11:1–20), Jehoash (11:21–12:21), Amaziah (14:1–22), and Ahaz (16:1–20). The treatment of Athaliah extends the theme of purging Baalistic and Omride influence to the Southern Kingdom and highlights a concern for theocracy and Jerusalemite Temple protocol (11:4–18). These same issues, which were already evident in 1 Kings 6–9, are also prominent in the presentation of Jehoash (2 Kings 12:4–16, 17–18), Amaziah (14:14), and Ahaz (16:10–18). The rest of the kings appear summarily. Often their reigns are reduced to little more than opening and concluding formulas (13:10–13; 14:23–29; 15:1–38).

331

11:1–20, Athaliah of Judah (843–837 B.C.).
This account continues the theme of ridding the kingdom of the influences of Ahab and Jezebel. Athaliah was their daughter (8:26); her death is portrayed as necessary to reform in Judah. As Jehu eliminated a Baalist king and exterminated non-Yahweh worship in Israel (chaps. 9–10), so a Judahite Yahwist priest, Jehoiada, executes a Baalist queen mother and—perhaps anticipating the reform of Josiah (23:4–20)—presides over the destruction of Baalism in Judah. At the same time, continuity of David's dynasty, which had been pronounced inviolate by God (2 Sam. 7), was assured.

Despite frequent attempts to postulate that divergent sources have been merged into one account, the narrative is continuous. A brief sketch introduces the villainy of Athaliah (of Ahab's house) and the heroism of Jehosheba (of David's house through Joram). Then the writer describes, first, the crowning of Joash, the single prince remaining after Athaliah's murderous sweep among the royal sons (2 Kings 11:4–12); second, the nearly concurrent execution of Athaliah, who had been attracted by the clamor of coronation (vv. 13–16); third, the religious purge carried out after her death (vv. 17–19). The narrator concludes with a summary, the very last phrase of which circles back with emphasis to a central event: "for [it was] Athaliah [whom] they slew with a sword [at the] king's palace" (v. 20b; cf. v. 16).

In the first sequence, Jehoiada assembles a military force (the identity of the Carites of v. 4 is uncertain) and makes of it a rank of loyalist guards, bound by covenant oath to protect the young heir apparent. Their orders (vv. 5–8) are not easy to understand. Apparently, both the royal palace and the Temple are to be guarded, but a special contingent is to protect Joash (cf. v. 11). The instructions having been carried out (vv. 9–11), Jehoiada then conducts the coronation ceremony and Joash receives the signs of office (v. 12). The meaning of "testimony" (JPS: "insignia") is not entirely certain. Many take it to refer to a written, divinely sanctioned warrant for kingship. Customary acclamation follows (cf. 1 Kings 1:39).

These same events are depicted through Athaliah's eyes. Hearing the clamor and seeing the royal celebration, she concludes that her rule has been violated and overthrown. Her cry of protest recalls the shriek of recognition on the lips of her brother Joram as he was about to be slain by Jehu (2 Kings 11:14; cf. 9:23).

Athaliah's death—outside the Temple, thus preserving its sanctity—completes the parallel with events in the Northern Kingdom. As Joram's murder cleared the way for religious reform, so too Athaliah's will lead to pitiless destruction of Baalist elements in Judah.

The basis for reform is a covenant of loyalty, not between soldiers and Jehoiada and sanctioned by God, but between king, people, and the Lord in which the earthly kingdom itself is constituted as the "LORD's people" (vv. 17–20). This Deuteronomistic belief was woven into the fabric of David's dynasty (cf. Deut. 7:6–11; Exod. 19:5; 1 Kings 2:1–4). Here, it authorizes sweeping reform to insure that this "people of the LORD" will be devoted exclusively to Yahweh. Athaliah's religious influence is wiped out with the same zeal as had been attributed to Jehu and Elijah (cf. 1 Kings 18; 2 Kings 9–10). Joash triumphantly processes to his palace seat, to reign over a cleansed nation.

Carrying little more than a patronym, Athaliah is remembered for her Pharaoh-like violence against the young men of Judah. Her reign ended as it began, irregularly, and the narrator recognizes her without the usual opening and concluding formulas that bestow legitimacy upon a monarch. The blood of Israelite apostasy, however, has flowed into Judah—through Ahaziah and his mother Athaliah (8:26–27) and, before that, through Joram his father, who was husband to a daughter in the house of Ahab (8:18). The Deuteronomistic historian views this poison and its purgative seriously, for not since Solomon's lapse (1 Kings 11) had there been such evil to counteract in Judah. Jehoiada's antidote begins a pattern of restoration and renewal that will find its analogies in Hezekiah and Josiah (2 Kings 18–20; 22–23), and its final undoing in Manasseh (2 Kings 21).

11:21–12:21, Jehoash (ca. 837–800 B.C.).
The rule of Jehoash begins and ends with the usual introductory and concluding summaries (12:1–3, 19–21). The narrator reduces a forty-year reign to accounts concerning Temple repairs (12:4–16) and turning aside Hazael's threat against Jerusalem (vv. 17–18). Jehoash is evaluated both positively (v. 2) and negatively (v. 3; cf. the different view in 2 Chron. 24). Repairs to the Temple illustrate his "doing what was right in the eyes of the LORD," while robbing the Temple treasury merited a punishment of conspiracy against him (2 Kings 12:17–18, 20–21; cf. 1 Kings 15:27–30; 16:9–13; 2 Kings 15:10, 14, 25, 30).

The first report (12:4–16) suggests that the priests ignored the king's orders to make repairs to the Temple with revenues received from their "benefactors" (JPS, vv. 5, 7; RSV: "acquaintances"; the exact meaning is uncertain).

Jehoash then put his own "secretary" in charge of a new system for collecting the funds and carrying out the work (vv. 9–12). The same procedure was used by Josiah, with similar praise noted for the honest workers who managed the funds (22:3–7; cf. 12:15 with 22:7). No new ritual objects were made—all the precious metals went for repairs (12:13–14)—and the priests continued to earn their livelihood from dedicated offerings (v. 16; cf. Lev. 5:15–19). These various details (cf. 1 Kings 7:45–50) suggest what was important about Jehoash: he enforced shared oversight of Temple affairs, diverted substantial sums to the piety of Temple repair, and depended not so much upon the priests as upon the honesty of the workers.

Consequently, it is shocking to read that when Jerusalem was threatened by Hazael ("at that time" [2 Kings 12:17] allows no precise temporal link to the preceding material), Jehoash strips the Temple of its valuables, apparently signifying vassalage to Syria. While saving Jerusalem, this action (cf. v. 18 with 16:7–9) subtracted economic support from Yahwistic religion. The narrator probably understood this tribute as a punishable transgression (v. 20; cf. 20:12–19 with 2 Chron. 28:16–21; Ezek. 23:1–49; Jer. 2:18–19).

13:1–25, Jehoahaz and Jehoash (ca. 816–785 B.C.). In this section, the focus is shifted to Israel and a miscellany of items related to the dynasty of Jehu is presented. The material derives from various sources and seems confusing because both northern and southern kings have identical names, J(eh)oash (vv. 10–13). The first section (vv. 1–13) summarizes the reigns of Jehoahaz and Jehoash with typical introductory and concluding formulas (vv. 1–2, 8–9, 10–13). Remarks in vv. 3–5 follow a schematic pattern of transgression, punishment, plea for help, and divine rescue (cf. Judg. 2:11–16; 3:7–11, 12–30; Deut. 26:7–9; 2 Kings 14:26–27). A second section provides supplementary information in three parts: first, Elisha's symbolic action, which "prophesies" the terms of Jehoash's military successes (13:14–19; cf. 1 Kings 11:30–33; Jer. 13:1–11; 19:1–13); second, Elisha's death (vv. 20–21), which marks his exit from the Deuteronomistic History; third, continual hostilities between Israel and Syria; these statements correlate limited victory with Elisha's prophecy (vv. 19, 22–23, 24–25).

The purpose of this compilation may be inferred from the writer's explicit comments in vv. 3–6 and 22–23. Since Jehu had been promised a dynasty to the fourth generation (10:30), the chaos during the regnal years of his sons is presented as a near disaster. Only God's promise (cf. 15:12), compassion for the people (v. 4b), and, moreover, fidelity to his covenant with the forefathers (v. 23) stood in the way of total collapse. Such generalized reflections make it impossible to identify with assurance any particularities of historical events, such as the identity of the "deliverer" in v. 5 (RSV: "savior"; see 14:26–27). In any case, these commitments were enough to override the sons' addiction to Jeroboam's ways (13:2–3, 11) and grant reprieve to the dynasty. Perhaps the revival of a corpse by Elisha's bones (vv. 20–21) makes a symbolic point about national life that can persist in decay. But God's patience is not infinite. Israel's final punishment is only delayed, not avoided, as chap. 17 will make clear.

14:1–22, Amaziah (ca. 800–783 B.C.). The narrator interrupts the summary of Israel's kings with a more elaborate account of the Judean Amaziah. The usual introductory and concluding formulas (vv. 1–4, 18–22) enclose reports of various incidents during the reign (vv. 5–6, 7, 8–14). Because vv. 8–14 deal largely with Jehoash, a later editor may have added a summary of this Israelite's reign as well (vv. 15–16; cf. 13:12–13).

Amaziah is remembered for his revenge against those who murdered his father (14:5; cf. 12:20), his assault against Edom in the Valley of Salt, probably at the southern end of the Dead Sea (v. 7), and his disastrous attempt at warring with Jehoash of Israel (vv. 8–14).

The writer claims that Amaziah was good (v. 3), but not good enough. The king perpetuated the "high places," those ancient countryside shrines scorned by the Deuteronomistic writer (v. 4; → High Place). Even though scrupulous about some commandments in the teaching of Moses (v. 6; cf. Deut. 24:16), Amaziah nearly destroyed Judah by his foolish actions (2 Kings 14:8–14). For that, he suffered his father's fate, a murderous conspiracy (v. 19).

Verses 8–14 suggest, however, that Amaziah's poor showing redounds to the glory of Jehoash and the continued success of Jehu's dynasty. The writer gives no motivation for Amaziah's challenge to Jehoash, "Come, let us look each other in the face" (v. 8; the idiom means to "confront one another in battle"; cf. v. 11). Instead, one is induced to accept Jehoash's fable with its application to Amaziah as correct (vv. 9–10; cf. Judg. 9:7–15). Owing to his defeat of the Edomites, Amaziah is swollen with self-intoxicating ambition, and he risks the kingdom for his own glory (v. 10; cf. the nonmoralistic motivation attributed to Amaziah in 2 Chron. 25:6, 10, 13). Not only is he unlike David (2 Kings 14:3), but Amaziah foolishly challenges a royal house that is sustained by God to its fourth generation and protected by the age-old promise to the patriarchs (10:30; 13:23). Naturally, disaster follows. Amaziah loses decisively to Jehoash, and the Temple treasury is again depleted (v. 14). In this matter, besides suffering death by conspirators, Amaziah "did in all things as Joash his father had done" (v. 3; cf. 12:17–18).

14:23–15:38, The Kingdoms from Jeroboam II to Ahaz.

In this section, the narrator compresses some fifty years into a rapid summary of eight overlapping regnal periods, two from Judah and six from Israel. Brief notes, heavily interpreted with theological commentary, suffice to represent the accomplishments of various monarchs (e.g., 14:25; 15:5; 15:10). As usual, formulaic opening and concluding summaries delineate discrete periods of time: Jeroboam II, ca. 785–745 B.C. (14:23–29); Azariah (Uzziah) of Judah, ca. 783–742 (15:1–7); Zechariah and Shallum, ca. 746–745 (15:8–16); Menahem, ca. 745–736 (15:17–22); Pekahiah, ca. 736–735 (15:23–26); Pekah, ca. 735–732 (15:27–31); and Jotham of Judah, ca. 742–735 (15:32–38).

The writer presents the final years of Israel, with a sidelong glance at Judah, as a period of chaos, assassinations, and foreign intervention. Through it all runs a current of divine energy that is visible in moral judgment and prophecy fulfilled (cf. a similar summary at 1 Kings 15:1–16:28). Jeroboam II expanded the borders of Israel "according to the word of the LORD" (2 Kings 14:25 27); Azariah of Judah (called Uzziah in 15:13, 32) was struck with leprosy from the Lord, presumably a punishment for not removing the "high places" (15:4–5); so too Zechariah lost the kingship to Shallum—thus ending the prophesied four generations of Jehu's house (15:9–12). Not all the kings' fortunes are thus glossed, but the overall impression is unmistakable. Both Israel and Judah are at risk in this perpetual chaos—Israel because its kings persisted in the ways of Jeroboam I; and Judah, because its kings kept those country shrines even while maintaining political stability and otherwise "doing what was right in the eyes of the LORD." In this, the writer looks to the eventual demise of both kingdoms. On the nearer horizon, the writer anticipates the influence of Tiglath-pileser (15:29) and the troubles from a military assault on Judah (15:37).

16:1–20, Ahaz of Judah (ca. 742–727 B.C.).

The regnal period of Ahaz is introduced and concluded with standard formulas (vv. 1–4, 19–20). Within this framework, the narrator represents the king's rule with two incidents: first, a threat on Jerusalem that Ahaz turned away by concluding an alliance with Assyria (vv. 5–9) and, second, extensive alterations to the Jerusalem Temple according to Ahaz's command and Assyrian custom (vv. 8–18). Tucked away inside the first account is a brief mention of Edomite incursions on Judah's southern territories (v. 6).

Apparently, the narrator meant one to judge Ahaz's actions negatively. Noteworthy is the allusion to moral infection from the northern kings and the nations round about (vv. 3–4). Ahaz "walked in the way of the kings of Israel" (RSV), and (the language becomes emphatic) he "even consigned his son to the fire, in the abhorrent fashion of the nations that the LORD had dispossessed before the Israelites" (JPS). Only Jehoram and his son Ahaziah among Judah's kings were similarly aligned with northern monarchs (8:18, 27). And only Manasseh, who will be blamed for Judah's eventual downfall (21:10–15), is similarly condemned for following the customs of those dispossessed Canaanites (21:2–9; cf. 17:29–33). The narrator measures Ahaz by the scale of the Israelite kings, who could do no right, and of Manasseh, whose wrongdoing brought an end to the Davidic house.

Ahaz's action in vv. 5–9 recalls Menahem of Israel (15:17–20; cf. 1 Kings 15:15–20). Jerusalem is threatened by a coalition of Israelite and Syrian forces. (Isa. 7 8 reflects the same circumstances, and 2 Chron. 28:5–21 offers a very different version of events.) Like Menahem, who bargained with Assyria to stave off his own destruction (2 Kings 15:19–20), Ahaz calls upon Assyria to help him maintain a hold on Judah. The narrator clearly envisions a treaty in vv. 7–9, and Ahaz seals the pact with riches drawn from the Temple treasury. The alliance saved Jerusalem but at the cost of lessening the monarch's independence and the wealth of the kingdom and of the Temple. The price would have been too high for the narrator, who likened Ahaz to the hated northern kings.

Moreover, Ahaz does not dislodge the Assyrian influence from the heart of his kingdom. The king orders alterations to the Temple in Jerusalem (vv. 10–18) and thus foreshadows those innovations in worship in Manasseh's time that the Deuteronomistic historian will condemn without compromise (21:2–9). Ahaz oversees the religious establishment (vv. 11, 16) and, like Solomon, builds and furnishes a Yahwistic shrine (cf. 1 Kings 7–9; cf. the "bronze altar" of vv. 14–15 with 1 Kings 8:64). But he uses Assyrian blueprints.

The historian viewed these events in a negative light. Ahaz called for aid from the very power that had already ravaged the Northern Kingdom. He corrupted Temple worship in Jerusalem with an altar of Assyrian design and introduced changes in the Temple furnishings "because of the king of Assyria" (v. 18). In short, Ahaz lived by the standards of others and placed Judah on a surface slipping toward destruction.

17:1–41, Hoshea of Israel (ca. 732–723 B.C.).

This section recounts the destruction of

the Northern Kingdom—an event that has been anticipated repeatedly by the writer—and explains the religious failures that led to catastrophe. The chapter is a good example of how the writer construed historical events with theological and didactic purposes foremost in mind (cf. Josh. 23–24; 1 Sam. 8; 2 Sam. 7; 1 Kings 12:25–33; see "Introduction").

Though scholars disagree on the details, it seems likely that the traditions have undergone editing and supplementation. The resultant text, however, is coherent in its larger outline. Hoshea's rule opens with the usual formulaic summary (2 Kings 17:1–2; the evaluation of the king is severely abbreviated) and moves to a report concerning the demise of the Northern Kingdom (vv. 3–6). This is followed by an extensive explanation of the reasons for its fall (vv. 7–23a). Narrative flow resumes at v. 24 with an account of resettlement in Samaria (vv. 24–32; v. 33 is a summarizing conclusion expressing continuous action, "the LORD they [repeatedly] worshiped, and their gods they [continuously] served after the fashion of the peoples . . ."). A final section stops temporal sequence again and offers commentary on the situation in Samaria (vv. 34–41). Hoshea receives no concluding summary.

As in other spaces between regnal periods when he interrupts the flow of time, the writer fills this pausal moment with material of great thematic consequence (cf. 1 Kings 2:12b–46; 12:1–20; 2 Kings 2:1–25). Here, one reads a doubly phased theological commentary on the fate of the two kingdoms.

First, the transgressions of Jeroboam are like a systemic poison that runs through Israel's lifeblood, ending in death (17:7–18, 21–22; cf. 1 Kings 12:26–32; 13:33–34; 14:1–18; 15:29; 16:7; 2 Kings 9:6b–10). The people worshiped other gods (RSV: "fear" [v. 7] does not mean psychological terror but attitudes of reverence bound to actions of obedience; see Deut. 4:10; 5:29; 6:24); they "sinned against the LORD their God" (2 Kings 17:7, RSV); that is, they "transgressed" against the teaching, the *torah*, of God by carrying out prohibited religious practices (vv. 9–11) despite warnings by the prophets (vv. 7, 13; cf. Jer. 3:12–14; 7:3). Israel indeed "rejected his [God's] statutes and his covenant which he made with their fathers" (a reference probably to the Sinai covenant, which bound God and Israel into a partnership of command and obedience [Exod. 19:4–6]); they chased after "useless things" or "delusion," perhaps meaning the religious habits of nations round about (2 Kings 17:15; "false idols" in RSV is misleading; JPS: "delusion" or KJV: "vanity" are better choices); they made molten calves (the archetypal image of apostasy, recalling Exod. 32 and 1 Kings 12). In short, led astray by King Jeroboam, the people did all manner of things

that implied a diluted loyalty and weakened attachment to Yahweh (2 Kings 17:16b–17, 21–22; cf. Deut. 18:10). Thus, retributive destruction came upon a misguided kingdom.

The writer also mentions the Southern Kingdom and suggests that Judah—like its most recently cited king, Ahaz (2 Kings 16:3)—will go the way of Israel (17:13, 19–20). In fact, many of the faults attributed to the Northern Kingdom are elsewhere associated explicitly with the Judahite monarchs, e.g., burning incense, divination, sacrifice by fire, worshiping the "hosts of heaven" (vv. 16–17).

A second phase of comment reveals the persistence of just those "sins" cut off by the Assyrian invasion (vv. 24–33) and radically extends the duration of this condition into the writer's own day (vv. 34–41). Resettlement of the devastated kingdom brings with it comic malfeasance. Brought from cities in Babylonia and Syria whose locations are not altogether certain, strangers to the land bring god-strangers from foreign lands (only Nergal, god of the underworld [v. 30] can with certainty be identified). Ironically, the settlers (who probably bear no relation to the "Samaritans" of the Second-Temple period) must be taught true religion by a Yahwistic priest brought out of exile. But the instruction fails, and confusion persists. The people simply add the worship ("fear") of Yahweh to that of their own gods. In short—and here the writer's irony is evident—they replicate the transgressions of the Israelites before them and especially Jeroboam, who, like them, was accused of appointing "all sorts of people as priests" (2 Kings 17:32; cf. 1 Kings 12:31). Further commentary (2 Kings 17:34–40) reiterates that the broken "covenant" persists even to the writer's own times (v. 41b).

Israel lost its soul and after that its land and after that its identity. A similarly lost and confused offspring peopled Samaria in the aftermath. With the destruction of Israel went the loss of that Deuteronomistic ideal of one people, one God, and one covenant. From the vantage point of the Deuteronomistic historian who wrote after Judah's own collapse in 587 B.C. (chaps. 24–25), this event in Hoshea's rule is both explanation and warning for those Judeans who must endure their own exile, learn from their mistakes, and accept the claim that their kinsfolk's misdeeds have been their own. Deliverance follows upon true religion or "fear of Yahweh" (v. 39).

Later in the story, Hezekiah will be presented as a king who takes this lesson to heart (chaps. 18–19). He wholly trusts Yahweh, and for this singular steadfastness he and Jerusalem will be delivered from the grasp of the same Assyrian foes who conquered Hoshea and the Northern Kingdom (the verb translated "deliver" in v. 39 is the same as in 18:30–35).

18:1–25:30

The Last Days of Judah

The narrator now turns to the Southern Kingdom with a fixed gaze on its coming destruction in 587 B.C. The writer had already discretely anticipated this eventuality in 1 Kings 8:23–53; 9:3–9; and 2 Kings 17:19–20. Now the matter presses with overt references (20:16–19; 21:10–15; 22:15–19; and 23:26–27). A series of eight monarchs, each set within his regnal period and framed with the usual introductory and concluding summaries, spans some 140 years from Hezekiah (ca. 727–698) to the last Judahite king, Zedekiah (ca. 597–587). The writer wrestles with the reality of failure and explains in theological terms this catastrophic end to the covenanted nation, the throne of David, and the Temple of God. Despite the faithfulness of Hezekiah and Josiah (18:3; 22:2), the transgressions of Manasseh and the peoples whom he led astray (21:1–9) could not be overcome save by purging the body politic "as one wipes a dish, wiping it and turning it upside down" (21:13; cf. 23:26–27).

The books of Kings close with devastating frankness. Even those left in Judah under a Babylonian-appointed Judahite governor do not escape continued turmoil (25:22–26). Oddly, it is a Babylonian who provides an image of healing in this landscape of despair. Evil-merodach "raised the head of Jehoiachin, king of Judah, from prison," and granted him special privileges among the vanquished kings in Babylon (25:27–30).

One should not claim too much for this note of grace. Perhaps the narrator wrote his account because he envisioned some future for a people in exile or a remnant in Judah. In that case, his voice may be heard in Gedaliah's: ". . . dwell in the land, and serve the king of Babylon, and it shall be well with you" (25:24; cf. Jer. 29:1–7).

18:1–20:21

Hezekiah (ca. 727–698 B.C.)

Framed within typical introductory and concluding formulas (18:1–8; 20:20–21), the writer represents the reign of Hezekiah with at least four originally independent accounts: first, exile of the Northern Kingdom (18:9–12), which essentially recapitulates 17:3–6; second, Sennacherib's invasion of Judah and the survival of Jerusalem (18:13–16; 18:17–19:37; many scholars think that these two units were originally separate and may even have referred to different occasions); third, Hezekiah's illness, with an oracle of recovery (20:1–11); fourth, Hezekiah's involvement with Babylonia and Isaiah's announcement of troubles (20:12–19).

The literary history of these materials and their relation to historical events has been much debated, and there remains no consensus. Chaps. 18–19 seem most difficult. Scholars have seen multiple versions of one invasion or two invasions refracted in several traditions. It is also difficult to match the information contained in chaps. 18–19 with that in the parallel tradition of Isaiah 36–37 and with an Assyrian inscription that mentions Sennacherib's invasion of Judah (→ Sennacherib).

However one decides these matters, it is clear that the writer produced an idealized portrait of Hezekiah. (The idealization is carried much further in 2 Chron. 29–32.) What mattered most about the Assyrian invasion was that Jerusalem was not taken and that the eventual demise of Judah had been forestalled. For this, Hezekiah's piety gets the credit (2 Kings 18:5–6; 19:1–20) and Sennacherib's prideful blasphemy, the blame (19:4, 16, 21–28). Even the full twenty-nine years accorded to Hezekiah (18:2) results from the king's faithfulness, for in his fourteenth year God grants him fifteen more years to rule (20:6). In the end, however, Hezekiah's open trafficking with a Babylonian king, Merodach-baladan, elicits an oracle of doom—as though a transgression against God was in need of requital (20:12–19). However admirable a priest-king, Hezekiah's deeds were not sufficient to remove entirely the threat of losing everything to the Babylonians (20:17).

18:1–12, Hezekiah. In this section, we are first given the standard data about the king—the date of his accession relative to the reign of his counterpart in the Northern Kingdom and his age upon assuming the throne (vv. 1–2). Verses 3–9, however, give an unusually positive evaluation of his reign: Hezekiah's reforms made him one of the Deuteronomistic historian's few heroes. This faithful and devoted monarch even destroyed the bronze snake that, though cast by Moses (see Num. 21:4–9), had become an occasion for idolatry (v. 4; →Nehushtan). The result, as Deuteronomistic theology would lead one to expect, was national independence and military success for Judah under this obedient king (vv. 7–8). This stands in marked contrast to the fate of the perfidious schismatics of the Northern Kingdom, exiled for their willful violation of the covenant and commandments of Moses (vv. 9–12).

18:13–19:37, The Siege of Jerusalem. Many scholars believe that 18:13–16 originally had nothing to do with 18:17–19:37 and that, moreover, the latter consists of two different versions of the same incident, 18:17–19:8 and 19:9–37. Nevertheless, the text coheres around a single thematic opposition: the confidence of the Assyrians (focused in the Rabshakeh, an Assyrian officer speaking for Sennacherib) contrasted with the narrator's view that the Assyrians blaspheme and mock Yahweh (focused in the words of Hezekiah, 19:4, 16, and the prophet Isaiah, 19:21–28, esp. vv. 22–23). If the Rabshakeh's words mark him as a blasphemer (18:33; 19:12; in v. 25, he even claims to have been sent by Yahweh himself), then Hezekiah's words imply a deep faith in God (18:3–4, 15–19; cf. 20:3). In short, Hezekiah exemplifies exactly the quality of spirit that the writer mentioned in his introductory summary (18:5–6). Through this theological lens, the siege of Jerusalem sharpens into an archetypal struggle between the powers of unfaith and faith, personalized in Sennacherib and Hezekiah, respectively.

A conventional scene sets the stage in 18:13–16 (cf. 12:17–18; 14:14; 16:8–9; 1 Kings 14:25–26). Presumably in response to Hezekiah's rebellious acts toward Sennacherib (2 Kings 18:7), the Assyrian armies invade Judah, and Hezekiah sues for peace (v. 14). The massive tribute that, incidentally, marked Hezekiah as a temple robber like some of his predecessors, does not appease the invaders. Sennacherib moves to destroy Hezekiah's independence altogether.

The Rabshakeh's first mission comes in two phases (18:19–25, 28–35). Its central theme is the trust that has been placed in Egypt and Yahweh, neither of whom—the Assyrian claims—can bring about deliverance. A key word, "rely" or "trust" and its associated noun, "confidence," link the entire rhetorical play to the writer's image of Hezekiah, who utterly "relied upon" God (18:5; cf. vv. 19, 20, 21, 22, 30). Rabshakeh hopes to induce Hezekiah, or if not him, the people, to switch allegiances and put their "trust" in the Assyrians (vv. 31–35).

The second diplomatic mission (19:9b–13), this time presented as an exchange of letters, draws down this subject matter to the ideas most evident in 18:29–32 (cf. "deliverance" in 19:10–11 with 18:29–30, 33–35; cf. "gods of the nations" in 19:12 with 18:33–35). This cross-reference of motifs amounts to a new emphasis. Readers hear the Rabshakeh's second burst of bravado with Hezekiah's characterization of it in mind. It is "mockery" of the living God (19:4, 16 bracket Rabshakeh's words in vv. 10–13). Thus, the good and pious king exposes a fundamental theological issue implied in human action and words. God is defamed, and his reputation must be defended or avenged. That is precisely what Hezekiah asks for (19:19) and what the outcome of events will demonstrate (19:29–37).

The narrator develops images of an ideal prophetocracy, a people governed by God through a faithful king guided by a prophet whose words from God do not fail (cf. prophecy fulfilled, 19:7, 35–37). Nothing less than the voice of God confirms this perspective

(19:20–34). The poem in 19:21–28 (which may have been drawn from another source) now functions as prophetic oracle and, by implication, ridicules Sennacherib for denigrating the Holy One of Israel. In an ironic turnabout, Sennacherib is put on trial for exaggerating his own *self*-reliance in contrast to Hezekiah who relies on God (in 19:22–23 the verbs "mock" and "revile" are those that Hezekiah used in vv. 4–5 and 16).

These heroes and anti-heroes play out a cosmic struggle between the gods. Not surprisingly, Hezekiah's petition (19:15–19) conforms to the stylized epic form associated with the great prophet Elijah, who similarly defended Yahweh and asked that God himself appear among all the peoples (cf. 19:19 with 1 Kings 18:37; see also 1 Kings 20:28; 2 Kings 5:15).

20:1–11, Hezekiah's Illness. This tradition may have originally been independent of its present context, since v. 6 implies that Jerusalem has not yet seen its victory. Relative to chaps. 18–19, however, the incident amounts to a flashback in which the narrator fills an ellipsis in the earlier sequence of events (the phrase "in those days" in v. 1 makes only the vaguest temporal association with the preceding passage).

The narrator remains fixed on Hezekiah's piety, but by including divine recognition and personal reward, he "canonizes the saint" while rehearsing his deeds. Facing an oracle that he would not recover from illness, the king weeps bitterly and recalls his faithfulness to God's ways (v. 3; his words are similar to those of the Deuteronomistic writer who routinely evaluates all kings in the introductory summaries). Seized by a new oracle, Isaiah delivers a promise of deliverance (vv. 5–6).

The oracular language invokes Davidic ideals (see 2 Sam. 5:2; 6:21; 7:8; 1 Kings 1:35; 8:16–21). Moreover, God declares that Hezekiah's and Jerusalem's deliverance (the verb "deliver" recalls 2 Kings 18:33–35; 17:39) will be "for my own sake and for the sake of my servant David" (20:6b). Forthwith, healing begins, and Isaiah, as though cut from the miracle-worker mold of Elijah and Elisha, orders curative action (v. 7). The theological issue of defending God and the kingdom that had been promised to David for all time (2 Sam. 7), however, overwhelms simple medical arts. Hezekiah's goodness is singled out for reward, but the importance of that linkage is quickly subsumed under grander principles—the reputation of God and the sanctity of David's (God's) kingdom (20:6). The viewpoint fits perfectly with 19:34.

Given these associations, a miraculous "sign" that the prophecy may be relied upon seems anticlimactic (vv. 8–11). Yet, human understandings and kings are weak. Perhaps the writer is ambivalent in his approval of Hezekiah, who proved unable to save Judah from its ultimate fate after all.

20:12–21, Envoys from Babylon. Before Sennacherib's assault on Jerusalem, Merodach-baladan ruled in Babylon (→ Merodach-baladan). This fact and the imprecise temporal connective, "at that time," shows again how little the writer cared for strict chronology. By including this tradition at the end of Hezekiah's rule, he seems to suggest another "sign" wherein a prophet reads some incident as a cipher of God's intentions (cf. 2 Kings 13:18–19; visions too are taken similarly, e.g., Jer. 1:11–14; 24:1–9).

The details are somewhat obscure. Receiving the Babylonian envoys with open arms, Hezekiah "shows" them the privy treasures of Judah. The language is emphatic, as though the tour alone were tantamount to concluding a treaty with a foreign power (cf. 1 Kings 20:1–6). Isaiah disapproves and announces God's punishment (2 Kings 20:16–18). Resigned to judgment, Hezekiah suggests that such an ignoble end is the price to be paid for short-term "peace and security" (probably through an alliance with Babylon).

In the end, Hezekiah's heroic size is trimmed a bit. Trust in God, which put him on rank with David, will be insufficient to counteract the flagrant evils of others in the Davidic line. Cast as a prophecy of punishment for Hezekiah, Isaiah's words (vv. 17–18) allude to Judah's tragic end as well (cf. 2 Kings 17:18–19).

The section concludes with a summary (2 Kings 20:20–21) of Hezekiah's reign.

21:1–26
Manasseh and Amon (ca. 697–640 B.C.)

In this section, the writer rapidly summarizes the reigns of two Judean kings, Manasseh (ca. 697–642) and his son Amon (ca. 642–640). Only one "event" is mentioned, a conspiracy against Amon reported in stereotypical form (vv. 23–24; cf. 15:10, 14, 25, 30). The rest of the chapter consists of introductory and concluding formulas for each king (21:1–2, 17–18, 19–22, 25–26) and a lengthy theological review of Manasseh's religious failings (vv. 3–16). This parade of sins greatly expands the evaluative element that is normally included in a king's introductory summary (cf. for Amon, vv. 20–22). Unmoored from its usual berth, the review is comparable in importance to the homily on Israel's demise (17:7–23), the enumeration of Solomon's many women and many gods (1 Kings 11:1–13), and the appraisal of Jehu (2 Kings 10:28–31; cf. similar summaries in Judg. 2:11–15; 3:7–8).

The writer catalogs Manasseh's actions—they correspond to all the condemned deeds attributed elsewhere to Judean kings—and likens him to the northern apostate, Ahab (v. 3; cf. 8:18, 27). The writer also anticipates in virtually every detail those things that Josiah will do to counteract Manasseh's influence (21:3a = 23:8b; 21:3b = 23:4; 21:4–5 = 23:12; 21:6a = 23:10; 21:6b = 23:24; 21:7 = 23:6). Manasseh's deeds, moreover, will be cited as a kind of benchmark for disasters in times to come (23:26–27; 24:3–4).

Obviously, Manasseh is a key figure in the larger Deuteronomistic story. Whatever else might have been reported about his reign (its fifty-five years surpassed those of any other Judean, and one has a less hostile impression of him from 2 Chron. 33 and Assyrian inscriptions), Manasseh is memorialized as the cause of Judah's failure. He is even more wicked than the Amorites (v. 11), whom tradition remembered as having been driven from the land covenanted to Israel (Josh. 24:15; Judg. 6:10). Thus the announcement of judgment, imitating prophetic speech, is irrevocable (2 Kings 21:10–15). Even Hezekiah and Josiah, antecedent and succedent foils to Manasseh, cannot undo the effects of his transgressions (23:26–27; 24:3–4).

Unmistakably, Judah is on a course of self-destruction. One should expect no change in God's purpose, if prophecy is to have its fulfillment. And in the books of Kings prophecy is always fulfilled.

22:1–23:30
Josiah (ca. 639–609 B.C.)

Within the typical introductory and concluding summaries (22:1–2; 23:28–30) the writer epitomizes the rule of Josiah by recounting pious action during the king's eighteenth year (22:3–4; 23:23). The writer assembled materials from various sources and, with generous use of stereotyped vocabulary, shaped them into a coherent account of religious reform: first, Josiah repaired the Jerusalem Temple, following the procedures established by Jehoash (22:4–7 [cf. 12:9–16]); second, a "book [scroll] of *torah*" is found in the Temple, which stimulates renewed commitment to God and his teachings (22:8–23:3); third, on this basis, Josiah commands and personally carries out reforms in the south (23:4–14), north (23:15–20a), and in Jerusalem, with its renewed Passover festival (23:21–23). More general statements and commendations conclude the account in 23:24.

This text has been crucial to a number of debates among historians. Taking the "book of *torah*" as essentially equivalent to Deuteronomy 12–26 and 28, literary historians date Deuteronomy close to the reign of Josiah and, from this conclusion, go on to assign relative dates

339

to other documents that make up the first books of the Bible (→ Deuteronomy; Sources of the Pentateuch). Historians of politics and religion look upon Josiah's actions as important but cannot easily establish the sequence of historical events and correlate the version in 2 Kings with 2 Chronicles 34–35.

These matters aside, it is clear that as presently arranged, the rule of Josiah draws into itself thematic strands from the larger Deuteronomistic History. The account has its formal antecedents in Hezekiah, Jehoash, and Jehu (2 Kings 18; 12; 9–10). Its details refer to other reports of the reform of worship: the "high places" of Solomon and Jeroboam (23:13; cf. 1 Kings 11:5, 7; 23:15; cf. 1 Kings 12:32); the altar of Manasseh (2 Kings 23:12; cf. 21:5); actions of former but unnamed kings (23:4, 5, 10–12, 19). Also, some narrative elements were anticipated in earlier material: Josiah's Temple renovation (22:4–7; cf. 12:9–16); the oracle guaranteeing Josiah a fitting burial (22:20; cf. 1 Kings 14:13); the renewed commitment to torah and covenant (2 Kings 23:1–3; 11:17); centralization of worship in Jerusalem (23:8; cf. 18:4); setting aside the wrongs of Jeroboam, formulated as prophecy-fulfilled (23:15–20; cf. 1 Kings 13:1–3).

This Deuteronomistic system of cross-referencing interprets Josiah's reign as a time of convergence and culmination. The transgressions of those who went before, especially Jeroboam and his corrupting effects upon Judeans, are put right (23:4–12). Even the wrongs of Solomon, whose allegiance tilted toward the gods of his foreign wives (cf. 1 Kings 11:1, 5), are corrected (2 Kings 23:13). Josiah reaffirms the book of torah (22:8, 11) as the heart of the body politic, as David himself had exhorted it must be (1 Kings 2:3), only to have his hopes undone by Solomon (1 Kings 11:11). Josiah commands the people to "keep Passover as written in this book of the covenant" (2 Kings 23:21). This memorial to the Exodus from Egypt (Deut. 16:1–8) had never been properly observed, that is, celebrated in Jerusalem (2 Kings 23:9), by any of Josiah's predecessors (but cf. 2 Chron. 30:13–27).

A concluding remark in 2 Kings 23:25 praises Josiah for turning back to God (cf. the language of Deut. 6:5). Josiah perfectly fits the writer's image of an upright king. He reacts to hearing the book of torah in repentance and mourning ("rent his clothes," 2 Kings 22:11; cf. 19:1). In a highly stylized Deuteronomistic oracle (22:16–20) the prophetess Huldah announces a personal reprieve because of his penitence (cf. 20:5–6; 1 Kings 21:28–29). Like no king before or after, he acts "according to the torah of Moses" (2 Kings 23:25), identified here with the "book of the covenant" found by Shaphan (22:8; 23:2). The claim of Josiah's sin-

gularity need not be taken literally (cf. 2 Kings 18:5; Deut. 34:10). The writer suggests that Josiah lives up to the standard set by King David, who similarly was said to have lived by the "torah of Moses" (1 Kings 2:3; cf. 9:4).

Yet, for all his exemplary qualities, Josiah cannot overcome the fateful repercussions of Manasseh's transgressions (2 Kings 23:26–27; 21:10–16). All reformers, though floodlit for a time in praise, move offstage in more subdued light: Jehu (10:28–33), Jehoash (12:17–18), Hezekiah (20:12–19). Not even this last and most celebrated reformer can reverse God's judgment (23:26–27). In a system of moral tit-for-tat, Yahweh himself seems bound by the rules—unless, of course, the kindness that will be shown to Judah's last Davidic king (25:27–30) hints at God's freedom to initiate action also, for his own sake.

23:31–25:30
The Last Kings of Judah

In this section, the Deuteronomistic historian recounts the collapse of Judah's political and religious vitality, which, for him, was necessarily centered on the royal Temple in Jerusalem. With customary formulas, readers move through the reigns of four kings: Jehoahaz (ca. 609 B.C.; 23:31–35); Jehoiakim (ca. 608–598; 23:36–24:7); Jehoiachin (ca. 598–597; 24:8–17); Zedekiah (ca. 597–586; 24:18–25:7). It was during Zedekiah's rule that the Babylonians destroyed Jerusalem and its Temple and exiled its leaders (25:8–21). The writer's last word is a sort of postscript in which he contrasts the continuing turmoil among those who remained in Judah (25:22–26) with the relative calm in Babylon, where Judah's last king survives unexpectedly as a privileged prisoner (25:27–30).

Modern historians view the decline of Judah after 605 B.C. as part of a larger struggle between Egypt and Babylon to control vast territories in the ancient Near East. Judahite kings ruled a portion of the land bridge between these great powers and, thus, were drawn into their conflicts. Tribute and forcible change of name, which are prominent here (23:33, 34; 24:17), were gestures and signs of vassalage. A Babylonian document records provisions delivered to Jehoiachin in exile (→ Jehoiachin).

For the Deuteronomistic historian, Judah's problems were not due to geopolitical forces but to a failure of religious nerve. While denouncing the four Judean kings for their evil deeds (23:32, 37; 24:9, 19), the writer ultimately faults Manasseh, whose transgressions move God to destroy Judah and Jerusalem (24:20). The prophecy of that angry judgment (21:11–15) must find its fulfillment in tragic events guided by God (20:17; 24:2–3; 24:13).

The writer fixes on the loss of Jerusalem but

emphasizes the destruction of its Temple, God's dwelling place (25:9, 13–17, drawing selectively from elements in 1 Kings 7:15–50). The covenant people are at an end, their center broken, their people dispersed to Babylon. The few symbols of sacred order that remain, that is, the Temple implements and a last Davidic king, are in Babylon too and offer only tenuous continuity with God's favor. Continued turmoil among the ruins of Jerusalem forces a surviving remnant to flee to Egypt (2 Kings 25:22–26).

If conditions are bleak in Jerusalem, there is perhaps hope among the Babylonians. That was, after all, the counsel of Gedaliah (cf. the parallel account in Jer. 40:7–41:8). And the Babylonian king does offer some favor to Judah's last king (2 Kings 25:27–30). At the least, the Davidic house survives but without regnal authority.

Scholars dispute whether the closing tone of the Deuteronomistic work is one of hope or despair. It is neither, exactly. The tale is a cautionary one, told to explain the catastrophe that befell Israel and Judah. The narrator, who wrote among the exiles in Babylonia (note the change to reckoning by Babylonian regnal dates, 25:8, 27), seems to offer an exhortation as well: life can go on with the Babylonians (25:24) and in Babylon (25:27–30; cf. Jer. 29:1–7) so "it shall be well with you" (25:24). The thought may be troubling to modern people of faith. The writer suggests that life with the God of covenant is demanding, even perilous, but that the survivors—scarred and chastised—are exhorted, perhaps commanded, to carry on nonetheless with this same God, whose promises to the people Israel even this catastrophe has not terminated.

Bibliography

Gray, J. I and II Kings. 2d rev. ed. Philadelphia: Westminster, 1970.

Halpern, B. The First Historians. San Francisco: Harper & Row, 1988.

Hobbs, T. R. 2 Kings. Waco, TX: Word, 1985.

Miller, J. M. and J. H. Hayes. A History of Ancient Israel and Judah. Philadelphia: Westminster, 1986.

Nelson, R. First and Second Kings. Interpretation. Atlanta, GA: Knox, 1987.

Robinson, J. The Second Book of Kings. Cambridge Bible Commentary on the New English Bible. Cambridge: Cambridge University Press, 1976.

1 CHRONICLES

RODDY L. BRAUN

INTRODUCTION

Unity and Place in the Canon

The First and Second Books of the Chronicles form a single unit, and this introduction serves as an introduction to both 1 and 2 Chronicles. In the Greek Bible, and hence in Latin and English Bibles as well, they are placed with the so-called historical books, whereas in the Hebrew Bible they are usually found at the very end of the last group of books, "the Writings" (→ Canon). The quotation ascribed to Jesus in Matt. 23:35 = Luke 11:51 indicates that, by the time of early Christianity, Chronicles already held the latter position (see commentary below on 2 Chron. 24:21).

In the biblical tradition, Chronicles is closely associated with the books of Ezra and Nehemiah; 2 Chron. 36:22–23 is repeated in essence in Ezra 1:1–3a. This same association is seen in the apocryphal book of 1 Esdras, which presents a continuous story running from 2 Chronicles 35 through Nehemiah 8 (see 1 Esdras). Because of this and the correspondences in vocabulary, style, and interests, it has become scholarly orthodoxy to attribute Chronicles and Ezra-Nehemiah to a single author, often referred to as the "Chronicler."

Nevertheless, remnants of another tradition may also be seen. Although other explanations are possible (Ezra-Nehemiah could have been accepted into the canon prior to Chronicles to supplement the books of Samuel and Kings), Chronicles follows rather than precedes Ezra-Nehemiah in the Hebrew canon. Moreover, the inclusion of the same verses at the end of Chronicles and the beginning of Ezra-Nehemiah (where they are usually considered original) could equally well be a device used to join works originally independent so as to indicate an original unity. It is an undisputed fact that Ezra-Nehemiah makes use of materials from various other sources in its presentation, and recent studies have pointed to significant differences in vocabulary, style, and thought (e.g., the attitude toward the north and ideas on messianism and repentance) that make it difficult to assume that the same author is responsible for both Chronicles and Ezra-Nehemiah in their present form.

The books of Chronicles embrace the period from creation to the dawn of the Persian Empire in the second half of the sixth century B.C. The period from Adam to Israel's first king, Saul, however, is covered only in the form of lengthy genealogies (1 Chron. 1–9), much of which, like 1 Chronicles 23–27, is often considered secondary, that is, composed or inserted later. Most of the remainder of 1 Chronicles 10–2 Chronicles 36 is probably due to the work of a single author. (The exceptions lie principally in the form of expansions of earlier lists, as in 1 Chronicles 12 and 15, and elaboration of the duties of the Levites. See the commentary below.) This author used as his major source the traditions in 1 Samuel 31–2 Kings 25, which he probably had available to him in a slightly different text from the one we now have (→ Texts, Versions, Manuscripts, Editions). By omission, addition, and alteration of that text, he wrote a new or radically revised picture of Israel's history, which must have been meant to portray more adequately his understanding of Israel's past and of its future hope.

Of the additional material supplied, some may have been based upon other sources available to the writer, but much is quite clearly his own composition. No satisfactory name has yet been found to describe the resulting literature. The most appropriate analogy is perhaps to be found in the biblical commentary itself. Another comparison frequently drawn looks upon Chronicles as a forerunner of later Jewish literature called *midrash*, in which a biblical text is elaborated upon, often fancifully, for purposes that may be devotional, educational, or merely entertaining (→ Midrash; Haggadah).

The Author's Audience and Age

In view of the uncertainty concerning the ending of Chronicles, it is impossible to say with precision when the author lived. The present ending of the book would place the beginning of the Persian era, i.e., the mid-to-late sixth century B.C., as the earliest date for his work. If, however, an earlier ending of the book has been supplanted by the present form of the books of Ezra-Nehemiah, that date would have to be moved later. Recent scholarship, accepting the unity of Chronicles and Ezra-Nehemiah as a given, has considered the age of Ezra and Nehemiah (late fifth century B.C.) as the *terminus a quo* of the book, and a few scholars have dated it as late as the second century B.C. A date sometime during the fourth century B.C. (late

Persian, early Greek period) is the date most in favor with biblical scholars.

More recent studies have tended at least to permit, if not to favor, an earlier rather than a later date, although it cannot be said that any consensus has developed. If Chronicles is removed from Ezra-Nehemiah and certain portions of Chronicles are recognized as later additions to the book, there is nothing to require a date later than the return from exile as the earliest possible date for the work. Supposed anti-Samaritan polemic is not present in Chronicles itself (→ Samaritans), and study of military organization and equipment has so far been unconvincing. The matter of the author's age must, however, be left an open question.

The Author's Message

While it may not be possible to place the author in a specific historical context, his message to his readers does much to bring to life his audience and the problems that they faced. At the center of his concern is surely the Temple and its worship, and to that end the entire history of the nation is directed (→ Temple, The). The whole work of David and Solomon, with which no less than twenty-six of the sixty-five chapters of the books are concerned, is directed toward the construction of the Temple. That interest in the Temple itself is maintained throughout the remainder of the book, whether its original conclusion be met in the account of the removal of the Temple vessels (2 Chron. 36:18) or Cyrus's edict to rebuild the Temple (2 Chron. 36:22–23) or the rebuilding of the Temple itself (Ezra 1–6).

Together with this interest in the Temple, its vessels, and its personnel, two other interests are apparent. First, the author regularly emphasizes the involvement, participation, and support of *all Israel* in those activities associated with the Temple. All Israel recognizes the kingship of David and Solomon (1 Chron. 11:1; 12:38–40; 29:22–25) and consents to and participates in the activities leading to the building and dedication of the Temple (1 Chron. 13:1–5; 2 Chron. 7:8–10). After the division of the kingdom into the Northern Kingdom, Israel, and the Southern Kingdom, Judah, the history of the northern tribes is, in a sense, regularly omitted. The activity of various kings of Judah in and toward the north, however, is regularly noted, as is, frequently, the positive response of representatives of the north (e.g., 2 Chron. 11:13–17; 19:4; 28:8–15; and esp. 2 Chron. 29–31).

Second, the author's interest in the *Davidic dynasty,* although problematic, cannot be ignored. That this interest is prominent and extends beyond the dedication of Solomon's Temple is most apparent in the speech placed in

the mouth of Abijah in 2 Chronicles 13 (see esp. vv. 5 and 8). Nevertheless, this emphasis is rare throughout the remainder of the book, and one senses that the monarchy exists primarily, if not solely, for the sake of the Temple. At the end of Chronicles no special attention is directed to the Davidic line (cf. 2 Kings 25:27–29), and it is, in fact, the Persian king Cyrus who becomes Yahweh's instrument to restore the Temple. In the account of the rebuilding of the Temple in Ezra also, there is at best little emphasis upon the Davidic line (cf. 3:2), and in later chapters of the book no mention at all. Perhaps events of the postexilic period presented the author, or a later one, with a difficulty he was incapable of fully resolving. Even in the absence of the Davidic kings who were originally responsible for the Temple, life goes on around the Temple, and more and more on the basis of a legal code closely associated with the Temple. The messianic hope, to the degree that it survived, was increasingly transferred to a future age.

The Message of the Book

The author pictures the people of God worshiping at the Jerusalem Temple planned and built by two kings, David and Solomon, whose kingship and work were given unanimous and enthusiastic support by all true Israelites of both north and south. There is here, and in the activities attributed to other kings throughout the history of the chosen people, a breadth of concern that indicates the author was open to the acceptance of those whose earlier associations had been with Israel rather than Judah. The sole criterion was their allegiance to the Lord as seen in acknowledgement of the unique status of the Jerusalem Temple and, to a lesser degree, the Davidic dynasty. The author must therefore have stood firmly opposed to others who would have severed all ties with the north (cf. Ezra 4). At the same time his understanding of God's ways would hardly be compatible with a more apocalyptic tendency developing in other circles (→ Apocalyptic Literature).

This understanding of God's ways is most commonly summarized under the name "retribution." Obedience to God is rewarded, and disobedience punished. We will have opportunity to note frequently that the Chronicler's portrayal especially of the post-Solomonic kings of Judah is governed completely by this theology (see, e.g., commentary on 2 Chron. 33). Portions of his sources that do not correspond to that understanding are altered accordingly.

Special attention should be given to those expressions used in conveying this theology. Faithful kings are those who *seek* God (2 Chron. 31:21). They engage in reforming activi-

343

ties, which include also the involvement of the northern tribes (2 Chron. 30). As a result, God causes them to *prosper*, that is, they have sizable families, engage in building operations, are victorious over their enemies, receive tribute, and enjoy God's *rest* (2 Chron. 14:6). To be unfaithful means to *forsake* the Lord or his Torah, often with no additional description added (2 Chron. 12:1). The accompanying statement of God's punishment is often equally vague (cf. "wrath has gone out," 2 Chron. 19:2; 32:25), but most commonly it includes defeat in warfare and exile. Sometimes it is as explicit and concrete as leprosy (2 Chron. 26:19), afflictions of the bowels (2 Chron. 21:19), and foot disease (2 Chron. 16:12).

Finally, however, Chronicles knows of another avenue to God's mercy and blessing, and that is *repentance* (2 Chron. 12:6, 12; 33:12). God speaks regularly to his people through the prophets, and it is ultimately the refusal to hearken to this prophetic voice (2 Chron. 24:17–22) that brings judgment. This opinion is expressed most fully immediately preceding Judah's final exile (2 Chron. 36:15–16) and should be understood as the final reason for its destruction. At the same time, this means that repentance and new obedience still lie open as the effective avenue to God, in whatever age and circumstances the readers may find themselves.

COMMENTARY

1:1–9:44
The Genealogical Prologue

1:1–54
From Adam to Israel (Jacob)

By genealogy, the writer moves rapidly from creation to Israel/Jacob, where his consuming interest lies. The tracing of Israel's ancestors back to Adam, and hence to God, demonstrates the divine plan in history and Israel's special role in that plan.

1:1–4, From Adam to Noah. The names of the ten "antediluvian" fathers, including the listing of all three of Noah's sons, are identical to those in Genesis 5.

1:5–27, From Noah to Abram. The writer identifies Abram with Abraham in the first editorial comment in the book. This genealogy, like Genesis 10 from which it is taken, lists ten postdiluvian fathers and apparently means to list

seventy descendants of Shem, Ham, and Japheth, symbolic of the theoretical seventy nations of the world. The characteristic structure of the unit, in which Noah's sons are dealt with in reverse order of their significance, is also taken from Genesis 10 and becomes characteristic of Chronicles.

1:28–54, From Abraham to Israel (= Jacob). These names too are taken with little alteration from Genesis (cf. Gen. 11, 25, and 36). The lists of the sons of Seir and the rulers of Edom (1 Chron. 1:38–54) seem unnecessary, and their presence is probably due to the desire for completeness and the practice of relating geographically close peoples by genealogy.

2:1–8:40
The Sons of Israel

As indicated by the sheer volume of the material, the author here arrives at the focal point of his interest. "All Israel" includes *all* the tribes, both northern and southern, descended from the patriarch Israel/Jacob.

2:1–2, The Sons of Israel (Jacob). This listing of Israel's sons is the most extensive in the OT, including Levi, Joseph, and Benjamin as separate tribes. It is most closely related to Genesis 46, although it is not identical with it.

2:3–4:23, The Sons of Judah. The structure of this unit is complex and debated. The argument that its arrangement is chiastic (that is, in the pattern of *A B C C' B' A'*, or the like) centering on David in the unit (Ram-Caleb-Jerahmeel, Jerahmeel-Caleb-Ram) may be accepted as reflecting the structure of the unit without implying unitary authorship.

Subordinate lines have to this point been dealt with first, but this procedure is reversed in the current unit. Here the descendants of Judah (2:3–4:23) are listed prior to those of his brothers. The sons of Perez (v. 5) are given prior to those of Zerah (vv. 6–8), and Ram assumes pride of place among Hezron's sons (vv. 9–17). Therefore, by structure and content, the writer points both to the importance of the inclusion of all of the tribes of Israel within his "all Israel" and to the special position occupied by Judah, from whose line David is to come.

The listing of Judah's five sons (vv. 3–4) is derived from Genesis 38; Perez's sons Hezron and Hamul (1 Chron. 2:5) are named in Gen. 46:12, and Zerah's line through Zimri, Carmi, and Achar (1 Chron. 2:6–8) is treated in Josh. 7:1, 18. The author, however, has made at least two significant alterations. First, while Joshua 7 reads Zabdi, Chronicles has, probably in view of divergent textual evidence, chosen Zimri, possibly because of its association with Temple music (Heb. zamar, "to make music"). While no other OT tradition links Ethan, Heman, Calcol, and Darda to the Judahite Zerah, 1 Kings 4:31 applies the gentilic "the Ezrahite" to Darda and further attaches to Heman, Calcol, and Darda the qualifying "sons of Mahol," a term perhaps related to religious dance (Heb. machol, a dance; cf. Ps. 149:3; Exod. 15:20). It seems the author, aware of the tradition linking Heman and Ethan with the Temple and its music (cf. the superscriptions to Ps. 88 and 89) and noting the fortuitous similarity of the name Zerah with Ezrahite, has on that basis and in view of his love for sacred music incorporated Ethan and his associates into the line of Zerah and hence Judah. Thus Chronicles may well preserve here the tradition that certain Temple guilds were not "levitical" in the strict sense of the term but may have traced their origins to pre-Israelite inhabitants of the land and made their entrance into various Israelite genealogies from outside. Second, the writer has also altered the name Achan (Josh. 7:1, 18) to Achar (Heb. 'akar, "to trouble"), an association made previously in the name of the valley called Achor (cf. Josh. 7:23–24).

1 Chron. 2:9–17 cover the age from Hezron to David. Verse 9 has no parallel elsewhere in the OT and has probably been constructed by the author to form the framework of the remainder of chap. 2, joining three groups of peoples, including the line of David, to Judah through Perez's son Hezron.

Jerahmeel (→ Jerahmeel) and Chelubai (who it appears certain should be identified with the Caleb of vv. 18, 42, and the wilderness tradition) are regularly associated with the southern territory of Judah, but the Jerahmeelites are regularly viewed as non-Israelites (1 Sam. 27:10; 30:29), and Caleb is named the son of Jephunneh who is further defined as a Kenizzite (Num. 13:6; 32:12). Their inclusion in Judah's genealogy here, as is already the case with Caleb in Num. 13:6; 34:19, probably reflects a recurring pattern by which non-Israelites were incorporated into Israel (→ Caleb).

The author is at particular pains to present the genealogical connection between Judah and David as an unbroken line. He accomplishes this by connecting Amminadab to Hezron through the otherwise unknown Ram, and Boaz to Nahshon through the similarly unknown Salma. The similar genealogy in Ruth 4:18–22 is probably dependent upon Chronicles. That David's genealogy nevertheless remains incomplete is apparent in that only nine generations are named, far too few to span the period of more than nine hundred years from the settlement in Egypt to Solomon's Temple that the biblical chronology requires.

The numbering of David here as the seventh son of Jesse (1 Chron. 2:15) is perhaps symbolic, standing in contrast to 1 Sam. 16:10 and 17:12–14, where he is the eighth. 1 Chron. 2:16–17 make it clear that David invested leadership of his troops in his own relatives and that Absalom's choice of Amasa to replace Joab (2 Sam. 17:25) was similarly conditioned.

1 Chron. 2:18–55 and 4:1–7 are lists of descendants of Caleb (Chelubai) and Jerahmeel. In the chiastic structure of the unit, the two genealogies of Jerahmeel are found in 2:25–33 and 34–41; they are well preserved. Calebite material occurs in vv. 18–24 and 42–55, as well as in 4:1–7, and its precanonical history is more complex. (For details, see the larger commentaries listed in the Bibliography, especially those by Williamson and Braun.)

The material gathered here is without real parallel elsewhere, and the individuals named are largely unknown. Since only David's line is derived from Ram (2:9–17), all remaining genealogical data related to Judah have been gathered under Hezron's remaining sons, Caleb and Jerahmeel. The materials are fragmentary, related to various localities and, we must assume, ages. Some of the names given are not those of individuals but of cities and occupational groups (cf. vv. 51–55). The fact that descendants of Caleb, traditionally associated with the southern extremes of Judah, are in vv. 42–55 and 4:1–7 located nearer the center of the tribe's territory suggests that the misfortune of the Exile has led to a resettlement of the people.

The author's aim here is to document the relationship of various families, groups, and cities to Judah. We can assume that some honor, if not political, economic, and social advantage, accrued to being a member of the sole tribe to survive the exile. Study of the genealogies at hand suggests that many whose fortunes came to be associated with Judah had assumed that status by a long process of absorption. These genealogies serve to legitimate that process.

1 Chron 3:1–9 includes a listing of David's immediate family. This list of nineteen sons and one daughter of David consists of two parts: first, vv. 1–4, names of six sons born to six different wives while David was king in Hebron, based on 2 Sam. 3:2–5; second, vv. 5–9, sons born to David in Jerusalem, four by Bathshua (in 2 Sam. 11–12, Bathsheba) and nine others. For similar lists see 1 Chron. 14:3–7 and 2 Sam. 5:14–16. 1 Chron. 3:9 adds mention of David's daughter Tamar. (On David's rule at Hebron, see commentary on 1 Chron. 11 and 29:27.) The different form of Bathsheba's name may be intended to veil David's adultery, which is also absent from 1 Chronicles 17.

1 Chron. 3:10–16 spans the years from Solomon to the Exile. These verses name all the ruling line of Judah from Rehoboam through

345

Josiah with the exception of the wicked queen Athaliah (2 Kings 11), who was the daughter of Jezebel and Ahab of Israel and not of Solomon's line.

Four sons of Josiah are named. The first of these, Johanan, is otherwise unknown, and the fourth, Shallum, is in Jer. 22:11 identified with Jehoahaz. Their rather unusual order of rule appears to have been Shallum, Jehoiakim, Jehoiakim's son Jehoiachin, and Zedekiah (2 Kings 23–25; 2 Chron. 36). It has been conjectured that Shallum rather than Jehoiakim may have been chosen to rule after Josiah's death because of the pro-Egyptian posture of the latter, who was duly placed upon the throne by the Egyptians after the brief reign of his younger brother. There is confusion in the texts over whether the Zedekiah who was Judah's last king was the son of Josiah, as in the Hebrew of 2 Kings 24:17 and the Greek of 2 Chron. 36:10, or a son of Jehoiakim or Jehoiachin, as in other texts.

1 Chron. 3:17–24 covers descendants of Jeconiah. This list of exilic and postexilic descendants of David stretches eight generations beyond the Exile, or to about 400 B.C. Jeconiah's son Shenazzar (v. 18) has been commonly identified with the Sheshbazzar (→ Sheshbazzar) of the return (Ezra 1:8, 11; 5:14–17), and the Zerubbabel who is in 1 Chron. 3:19 the son of Jeconiah's third son, Pedaiah, is elsewhere the son of his eldest, Shealtiel (cf. Hag. 1:12, 14; Ezra 3:2; Neh. 12:1). Neither Zerubbabel's brother Shimei nor any descendant of David named in the generations following him is mentioned in the remainder of the OT or in the NT genealogies of Jesus. A Shelomith, however, is named on one recently discovered seal as the wife of one Elnathan, who is on yet another seal named governor of Judah, and impressions on storage jars from Ramat Rahel may mention his second son Hananiah as well. Similarly, the Anani of v. 24 could be the individual named in an Aramaic letter dated to 407 B.C. (see James B. Pritchard's Ancient Near Eastern Texts, p. 492). At a minimum, the inclusion of such a lengthy list of Davidides suggests the Davidic nobility occupied a significant role in the history and theology of the postexilic period, although no messianic significance appears to be attached to them.

For 4:1–7, see 2:18–55 above. Verses 8–23 appear to be constructed of isolated and fragmentary bits, perhaps to provide the final part of the chiastic structure of 2:1–4:23. (See commentary above on 2:3.)

4:24–43, Sons of Simeon. Simeon (→ Simeon) is regularly listed second in tribal enumerations in the OT. The relatively scant treatment accorded him here, in contrast to Judah, is again indicative of the author's interest.

This unit has three basic parts, typical of a number of those of less significant tribes (see chap. 5): first, descendants of Simeon, 4:24–27; second, their settlements, vv. 28–33; third, other data, vv. 34–43. Each unit seems to be composite.

For other lists of Simeon's descendants see especially Gen. 46:10; Exod. 6:15; and Num. 26:12–13. In Chronicles the third son is Jarib, while all other lists have Jachin. The list of Simeonite cities is drawn from Josh. 19:2–8. The relationship of 1 Chron. 4:34–37 to both the preceding and the following verses is obscure, and we know nothing of the names given there. The historical notes appended in vv. 38–43 cannot be attached to other known events, but it seems likely the author found them in conjunction with other material related to Simeon.

5:1–26, Reuben, Gad, and East Manasseh. The presentation of these three tribal groups is a unity, as is clear from the terminology in vv. 11, 18, and 26. The result is that all of the tribes located in Transjordan are placed together. Signs of unevenness, such as the multiple conclusions in vv. 18–21 and 25–26, do exist, suggesting multiple authorship.

Most of the individuals named here are otherwise unknown. The exception is Reuben's four sons (v. 3), whose names are found also in Gen. 46:9; Exod. 6:14; and Num. 26:5–6. Joel (1 Chron. 5:4) and those listed after him, however, are not linked into this genealogical structure. The sons of Gad and Manasseh listed in Gen. 46:16; Num. 32:34, 38; and Josh. 17:2 are not included here nor are any of the descendants listed here named elsewhere in the OT.

The author's "all Israel" theme is most clear in his presentation of Reuben (1 Chron. 5:1–10), here placed immediately north of Moab. Like his brother Simeon, Reuben disappeared early as an independent tribe. (The ninth-century Moabite stone names Gad as Israel's southernmost tribe in Transjordan; → Moabite Stone, The.) Here, however, Reuben's territory is dutifully noted as stretching from Aroer on the Arnon in the south to Nebo and Baal-meon, opposite Jericho, in the north, as in Num. 32:34, 38 and Josh. 13:8–13.

Recent studies have also indicated that, although it has often been assumed on the basis of Genesis 48 that Reuben's birthright was transferred to Joseph's sons, Ephraim and Manasseh, 1 Chron. 5:1–2 is the only OT tradition that states this directly. While equally explicit that leadership was to be vested in Judah, the blessings associated with the birthright are reserved for two significant northern tribes, Ephraim and Manasseh.

To the account of the territory of Gad (vv. 11–17) and Manasseh (vv. 18–22) in Gilead (→Gilead) and Bashan (→Bashan), both of which

346

have narrower and wider meanings, are joined two reports of military encounters characteristic of the retributive theology of Chronicles. In a period of religious faithfulness, the Transjordanian tribes are victorious in warfare against their Arabian neighbors (vv. 18–22). In a period of unfaithfulness characterized as religious harlotry after its model in 2 Kings 17, however, God gives those same tribes into the hands of Tiglath-pileser of Assyria for exile (ca. 733 B.C.). Both the military and the theological terminology is similar to that found frequently in Chronicles (cf. 1 Chron. 4 and 12; 2 Chron. 13 and 14).

6:1–81, Descendants of Levi. The length of this section, second only to the attention devoted to Judah (2:3–4:23), reflects the writer's obvious interest in the priestly family (→ Levites; Priests). Much is considered secondary by many scholars. The chapter is composed of four units.

1 Chron. 6:1–15 lists the sons of Levi and Aaron. This is the most extensive listing of the priestly line in the OT, extending from Levi to the Exile. Our list appears dependent upon Ezra 7:1–5, which in turn relies upon the traditions found in Neh. 11:10–11 and 1 Chron. 9:11.

Earlier lists seemed intent on placing the otherwise unknown Zadok within the levitical line of Ahitub. Ezra 7:1–5 makes Zadok the twelfth priest after Aaron and apparently sees Ezra himself as the priest of the return. Our list secures the twelfth position for one of Zadok's sons, Ahimaaz of Azariah (1 Chron. 6:9), who served as Solomon's priest (1 Kings 4:2), and counts the priest of the Exile, Jehozadak, as the twenty-third priest in that line. It might then be assumed that the next priest, whether it be the Ezra of Ezra 7:1, Jehozadak's son Joshua of Hag. 1:1 and Zech. 6:11, or another unknown priest, would be the priest who would participate in the worship of the Second Temple.

1 Chron. 6:16–30 names three groups of Levites tracing their lineage back to Levi's three sons, Gershom, Kohath, and Merari. Verses 1–4 are identical in substance with Exod. 6:17–19 and Num. 3:17–20. 1 Chron. 6:20–30 adds additional names. The relevance of this information is seen in vv. 31–47, which make it clear that, of the three levitical groups associated with Temple music, Asaph is attached to Gershom (vv. 39–43), Heman to Kohath (vv. 33–38), and Ethan to Merari (vv. 44–47). The purpose of vv. 25–28, which appear as something of an insertion in the line of Kohath, is to make a Levite of Samuel, who exercised priestly functions (1 Sam. 2:11, 18) although named as an Ephraimite (1 Sam. 1:1).

1 Chron. 6:31–53 adds other Levites and priests (see commentary above on vv. 16–30). The lists differ to a greater or lesser degree from those given earlier. Each levitical line is here extended by one or more generations and made to terminate with the patriarch of a group of Temple musicians duly appointed by David for the music of the Temple. At the same time, the levitical musicians are differentiated in rank both from other Levites (v. 48) and from the Aaronidic priests (vv. 49–53). Among the musicians, pride of place belongs to the family of Heman, who is named first and whose genealogy reaches back to Levi and Israel (vv. 33–38). The priestly line reaches to Ahimaaz, priest at the time of David (cf. 2 Sam. 15:27), as do apparently the other lists as well.

1 Chron. 6:54–81 lists the levitical cities (cf. Josh. 21:1–42, upon which our passage seems to be based, although rearranged). Scholarly consensus tends to date the original list of levitical cities in the reign of David or Solomon, since cities such as Gezer (1 Chron. 6:67) were not in Israel's hands until that time, while Gezer, Golan, and Ashtoreth were lost early in the ninth century. It has been persuasively argued that the levitical cities were provincial administrative centers, located principally in occupied territory for supervision of the royal estates (and cf. 1 Chron. 26:30–32). While textual obscurities abound, it is difficult to avoid the conclusion that originally forty-eight cities were named, with each of the twelve tribes contributing four. The nine cities of 6:55–59 should be viewed as the combined contribution of Judah and Simeon, although this is not stated explicitly, and it is surprising that nothing is made of the fact that the priestly cities stem from Judah and Benjamin, the heart of postexilic Judah (v. 60; cf. v. 65).

Verses 66–81 give the allotments to the remaining Kohathites (vv. 66–70), to the Gershomites (vv. 71–76), and to the Merarites (vv. 77–81). Aijalon and Gath-rimmon (v. 69) are, in Josh. 21:24, from the tribe of Dan, and it seems likely that the omission of Dan here, as in 1 Chron. 7:12, is intentional on the part of a later writer.

7:1–5, Descendants of Issachar. The enumeration of Israel's northern tribes begins with Issachar, as would be expected from 2:1. Only four generations are listed, insufficient to fill the interval from Egypt to David. The information available to the writer appears skimpy and has perhaps been supplemented from a military census list.

7:6–19, Descendants of Benjamin, Dan, Naphtali, and Manasseh. One would expect the genealogy of Issachar to be followed by that of Zebulun (cf. 2:1; 12:32–33; 27:18), mysteriously absent from 1 Chronicles 2–9. The list of Benjamin's descendants in 7:6–12 begins abruptly (the RSV's "the sons of . . ." is not found in the Hebrew), has little in common with other OT lists (cf. Gen. 46:21; Num. 26:38; 1 Chron. 8:1–2), and quite possibly reflects a postexilic tradition in which Benjamin occupied a more significant position. Benjaminite warriors total 61,434, in contrast with smaller numbers in 1 Chron. 12:29 and Num. 1:37 and 26:41.

Comparison with Gen. 46:21–25 indicates the text of 1 Chron. 7:12 is fragmentary and corrupt. While Shuppim, Huppim, and probably Aher are to be identified as sons of Benjamin (see Gen. 46:21; Num. 26:38), Hushim is, in Gen. 46:23, the sole son of Dan, followed by the sons of Naphtali, as in 1 Chron. 7:13. The final phrase of v. 13, "the offspring of Bilhah," is meaningless here unless preserving a part of Gen. 46:25, where it points to Dan and Naphtali as Israel's sons through Rachel's handmaiden Bilhah. It thus seems likely that here, as in 1 Chron. 6:61, 69, mention of the tribe of Dan has been purposely omitted and that here, in tandem with the replacement of an original Benjaminite list dependent upon Genesis 46 by a postexilic one, Zebulun has also been omitted and the end of the Benjaminite list obscured.

The list of the descendants of Manasseh (1 Chron. 7:14–19) is to be compared with Num. 26:29–34. Gen. 46:20 provides no parallel to these names.

7:20–29, Descendants of Ephraim.
Cf. Num. 26:35–36, the only other Ephraimite genealogy available to us. Both similarities and differences are apparent, and direct dependence is unlikely. The list's seventeen generations that lead to the well-known hero of the conquest, Joshua, are too numerous to be included in the period between Israel's stay in Egypt and the birth of Joshua and, together with the occurrence of several sets of similar names (cf. Tahath, twice in v. 20, and Tahan in v. 25), suggest that our genealogy may be a conflation of two parallel but divergent ones. Verse 28 appears to give settlements of Ephraim and v. 29 of Manasseh (cf. Josh. 16–18), uniting rather unexpectedly the genealogies of Joseph's two sons. (Note also the occurrence of "Joseph" to include Ephraim and Manasseh in 1 Chron. 2:2.) Together Ephraim and Manasseh formed the nucleus of the Northern Kingdom, and they remained central to the Chronicler's concern (cf. 2 Chron. 31:1).

7:30–40, Descendants of Asher.
Asher is here, as in 1 Chronicles 12, placed last in the tribal listing (see also 2 Chron. 30:11; for 1 Chron. 7:30–31 see Gen. 46:17, upon which this passage is dependent, and Num. 26:44, more divergent). There are no known parallels to 1 Chron. 7:32–38, which appear to trace the remainder of Asher's family through Heber's

children named in v. 32. Verse 40 recalls the terminology of the military census seen also in vv. 1–5, 6–12. Shemer/Shomer (vv. 32, 34) is suggestive of the owner of the hill upon which the northern capital, Samaria, was built (1 Kings 16:24).

8:1–40, Descendants of Benjamin.
See also 7:6–13 and the references given there. The extensive references to Benjamin here and in chaps. 7 and 9 are evidence of the intense interest in Benjamin in the postexilic period.

Chap. 8 consists of four units based on Benjaminites living in four areas: vv. 1–7, sons of Benjamin and Ehud at Geba; vv. 8–12, sons of Shaharaim in Moab, Ono, and Lod; vv. 13–28, Benjaminites at Aijalon, Gath, and Jerusalem; and Benjaminites in Gibeon and the genealogy of Saul. A later hand, in harmony with the position of chap. 9, has added the notation that "these dwelt in Jerusalem" (v. 28, cf. 9:3, 34).

The sons of Benjamin listed in vv. 1–2 cannot be harmonized with other OT lists, including 7:6, with which it has only Bela in common (although Becher [Heb. beker] probably lies concealed in "his firstborn" [Heb. bekoro] of 8:1, which is consonantally identical). This first unit seems to have as its goal the descendants of Ehud (→ Ehud) in vv. 6–7, although we know nothing of the names given or the "move" to Manahath mentioned there.

The same is true of the persons and events of vv. 8–28. Verses 29–38 are essentially identical with 9:35–44, where they are more likely to have been original. Perhaps 9:1 is meant to stand as the conclusion to chaps. 2–8 rather than the introduction to chap. 9.

9:1–44
Israel After the Exile

This chapter is closely related to Nehemiah 11, a composite list of those dwelling in and around Jerusalem at the time the city's walls were rebuilt by Nehemiah. The writer of Chronicles, however, apparently also had other material at his disposal. Because of limitations of space, we shall confine ourselves to the more significant variations between these chapters.

Verse 1 joins chaps. 2–8, which are pre-exilic in orientation, with chap. 9, which is postexilic. Verse 1 should probably read "they are written in the book of the kings of Israel and Judah," by far the most common title of the source referred to frequently in 2 Chronicles, and possibly "and Israel and Judah were exiled" as well, since northern tribes are named in v. 3.

Verses 2–3 introduce the chapter. Verse 2 differs significantly from Neh. 9:2 in understanding the following lists to refer more exclusively to those dwelling in Jerusalem (cf. 1 Chron. 9:34). Verse 3, in a strong statement of the "all Israel" theme, includes descendants of Ephraim and Manasseh in Jerusalem, who are to be understood as representatives of all of the northern tribes (cf. Ps. 78:9, 67–68). Both texts show their composite nature in that the groups named in the introductory verses do not correspond to those mentioned in the remainder of the chapter.

Verses 4–6 list the Judahites in Jerusalem. Neh. 11:6 names 468 descendants of Judah through his son Perez. Chronicles also includes descendants through Judah's sons Shelah and Zerah and counts a total of 690.

1 Chron. 9:7–9 lists the Benjaminites. After "Sallu, the son of Meshullam," the two lists are entirely different.

Verses 10–13 list six priestly families. The relationship to Nehemiah is quite close, although the Azariah of v. 11 is, in Neh. 11:11, Seraiah (see commentary on 1 Chron. 6:11–14), and three generations have dropped from the genealogy of Adaiah (9:12). Maasai (v. 12) is to be identified with Amashsai (Neh. 11:13), since their genealogies, though more divergent, are consistently similar. The number of priests here is 1760; in Nehemiah, 1192.

1 Chron. 9:14–16 names three levitical families that Chronicles traces to the three chief levitical groups: Merari, Asaph, and Jeduthun. (Merari is not named in Nehemiah.)

Verses 17–32 list the gatekeepers. Chronicles is vastly expanded by the addition of one Shallum, to whom primary attention is directed (v. 17), and by the extensive listing of duties in vv. 24–32. The gatekeepers actually belong to the same line as the high priests and, despite the reference to Phinehas centuries earlier, their installation is attributed to David and Samuel (v. 22), as if to span all ages.

Verse 33 lists the singers. Though of considerable importance elsewhere in Chronicles (cf. chaps. 16, 25), they are not mentioned elsewhere in this chapter or in Nehemiah 11.

1 Chron. 9:34, like v. 3, places all of those previously named in Jerusalem.

Verses 35–42 are lacking in Nehemiah, which, however, does conclude with a reference to Benjamin. The reference to Kish in v. 36 (cf. 8:30) has led to the inclusion of Saul's genealogy, the most extensive in the OT and apparently extending to exilic or postexilic times. Ner, whose name is inserted here in v. 36 as brother of Kish (cf. 8:30), is in v. 39 Kish's father, contrary to 1 Sam. 14:51. The genealogy stands in contrast to 1 Chron. 10:6, which states that all of Saul's house died in his war with the Philistines. The verses apparently formed the original bridge between chaps. 1–9 and Saul's battle in chap. 10.

David and Solomon

Current study indicates that the work of David and Solomon forms a single unit centered in the construction of the Temple. Within that framework, chap. 10, recounting Saul's death, serves as an introduction to David (chaps. 11–21), while chaps. 22–29, concerning themselves equally with David and Solomon, are a transitional unit leading to Solomon (2 Chron. 1–9).

Since within these chapters the relationship between Chronicles and the books of Samuel and Kings is very close, even verbatim at times, and the dependency of Chronicles upon Kings is well established, we shall in such cases concentrate upon the divergences to illuminate the special message of Chronicles.

10:1–21:30
The David History

The significance of David for Chronicles has long been recognized. The result has been a one-sided view in which David is elevated to messianic or near messianic proportions and the work of others, such as Solomon, denigrated. That this view has now been modified helps us grasp more clearly the central role that the Temple and its worship played for the writer.

10:1–14, The Death of Saul. Compare 1 Samuel 31, from which Chronicles is taken. The action begins abruptly with the Philistine war, since the writer was interested only in Saul's death. Although there are minor variations throughout the chapter, two of these are clearly important for the writer. First, v. 6 reads "So Saul died, and his three sons, and all his house —they all died together." Instead of "all his house," 1 Sam. 31:6 reads "all his men." Chronicles wants to impress upon the reader that Saul's dynasty has been completely destroyed (note the absence from Chronicles of any parallel to 2 Sam. 2–4, which depicts the continuing struggle with Saul's house) and that no opposition to David's reign is possible from that quarter. That this view is not sustained in 1 Chron. 8:29–40 and 9:35–44 suggests a different author is responsible for those units. Second, vv. 13–14, an addition by our author, state unequivocally that Saul's defeat and death were due to his unfaithfulness (a nonspecific term met repeatedly in Chronicles) in that he did not keep the Lord's word or "seek" him. While it is possible to relate this judgment to specific acts in Saul's life, such as his improper offering of a burnt offering (1 Sam. 13), his sparing the king and the animals of the Amalekites (1 Sam. 15), and his inquiring of the medium at Endor (1 Sam. 28; reflected also in what is probably an explanatory gloss in 1 Chron. 10:13b, "and also consulted a medium, seeking guidance" [RSV]), it is more likely that the author wished simply to paint Saul's entire life as one of faithlessness. Therefore "God killed him, and turned the kingdom over to David, the son of Jesse." Divine vengeance has its way with Saul, but divine grace raises up a David to do God's will.

11:1–12:40, The Rise of David. In narrating David's rise, the author is at pains to demonstrate the complete and unanimous consent given his kingship by all Israel.

1 Chron. 11:1–9 is a brief statement of the beginnings. In agreement with the alteration of the text in 10:6 (see above), Chronicles bypasses the material found in 2 Samuel 1–4, which includes the anointing of David as king over Judah (only) at Hebron (2 Sam. 2:1–11) and David's continuing struggle with Saul's family, and proceeds immediately to David's anointing over all Israel (1 Chron. 11:1–3; cf. 2 Sam. 5:1–3), adding only that this was "according to the word of the Lord through Samuel" (1 Chron. 11:3). Note also the omission of 2 Sam. 5:4–5 (= 1 Chron. 3:4), which mentions that partial rule. The "all Israel" theme is sounded strongly in 1 Chron. 11:4, which now reads "David and all Israel" instead of the simple "the king and his men" of 2 Sam. 5:6.

David proceeds immediately to the capture of Jerusalem (2 Sam. 5:6–10). Textual problems make conclusions difficult here, but it is clear that David's general Joab plays a significant role not mentioned in Samuel. The laudatory words of 1 Chron. 11:9, with which the Chronicler was doubtless in agreement, belong already to his source in 2 Sam. 5:10.

1 Chron. 11:10–47 is a list of David's mighty men, moved here from the appendix to 2 Samuel in chap. 23. The reason for this is made clear in the introduction provided by the writer in 1 Chron. 11:10: it is to serve as additional example of those who supported David's kingship, again in harmony with God's word (cf. v. 3). The text reflects pervasive confusion between the "three" and the "thirty," both of which would have varied in composition and probably size from time to time. The list of David's mighty men is extended by some seventeen names in vv. 41–47 (beyond Uriah). Their origin is unknown, and they differ also in form from the first part of the list.

1 Chron. 12:1–23 depicts events at Ziklag and the stronghold. This unit, also unique to Chronicles, continues to depict the widespread support extended to David and is well summarized by v. 22: "So day by day they kept streaming in to David to help him, until there was a great army, like the army of God." To that end, groups are listed: Benjaminites who came to David at Ziklag (vv. 1–7); Gadites who

came to David "at the stronghold in the wilderness" (vv. 8–15); Benjaminites and Judahites who came to David "at the stronghold" (vv. 16–18); and Manassites who came to David at Ziklag (vv. 19–21).

None of those named in the chapter is otherwise known. Emphasis seems to be directed to the fact that early in his career, while Saul was still alive, David was supported by Saul's kinsmen of Benjamin and that leaders from two more remote northern tribes, Gad and Manasseh, also supported David. Amasai's speech (v. 18) is clothed in the ancient language of prophetic inspiration, which is used by Chronicles also of the levitical choir (2 Chron. 20:14), the priests (2 Chron. 24:20), and even the Persian Cyrus (2 Chron. 36:22). This again reflects the writer's own judgment: God is with David and with those who help David.

1 Chron. 12:23–40 concludes the story of David's rise. This unit devoted to David's supporters concludes with a numbering of warriors from north and south who came to Hebron for David's anointing (vv. 23–37) and with a description of the festival attending that anointing (vv. 38–40). The number of tribes included is the largest in the OT, including both Levi and Ephraim/Manasseh. The massive number of warriors (about 340,000) is indicative of the writer's enthusiasm for his subject.

Some measure of unevenness in composition is present. The numbers attributed to the southern tribes, which are listed first, are uniformly smaller than those of the northern tribes. The inclusion of Levi and the priest of Solomon's day, Zadok, described with typical military terminology, have suggested to some that that material is secondary.

The entire unit is concluded with vv. 38–40, an exuberant description of the festivities celebrated by those gathered for the coronation. The themes of "all Israel," "with a perfect heart," and "of one mind" are profuse here (see "Introduction" above). The three-day feast itself is described so extravagantly that some have considered it an indication of the writer's messianic viewpoint. While such a view would appear unwarranted, the "great joy" that results (v. 40) is normally reserved by the Chronicler for occasions dearest to his heart, such as the appointment of the levitical singers (15:16), Solomon's coronation (1 Chron. 29:9, 17, 22), and Hezekiah's reformation (e.g., 2 Chron. 29:30).

13:1–14:17, David, the Ark, and the Levites. With David securely in office, the author moves directly to his primary concern, Israel's worship, bypassing 2 Sam. 5:11–25, to which he will return in 1 Chronicles 14. After the second (successful) attempt to move the Ark and the completion of levitical arrangements (chaps.

15–16), the dynastic oracle of chap. 17 places all in readiness for one of David's sons, Solomon, to build the Temple.

1 Chron. 13:1–14 rehearses the first attempt to transfer the Ark, in vv. 1–4. The writer again provides his own introduction in which the "all Israel" theme predominates. David makes the decision to move the Ark in consultation with all the leaders of Israel (v. 1), who agree to invite their brethren from throughout the land to join them. Inclusion of priests and Levites is explicit.

Verses 5–14 are dependent upon 2 Sam. 6:1–11, although with greater variation, especially in vv. 5–9. The narrative begins with the Ark at Kiriath-jearim, presupposing its earlier history (cf. 1 Sam. 4–7). Instead of "the chosen men of Israel, thirty thousand" (2 Sam. 6:1, RSV), however, Chronicles has David assemble "all Israel, from the Shihor of Egypt to the entrance of Hamath" for an undertaking so significant. It has been observed that this is in fact the most extensive delimitation of the extent of the Holy Land in the Bible (see also 2 Chron. 7:8; 30:5, where limits are similarly set in conjunction with festivities surrounding Solomon and Hezekiah).

Of other variations from Samuel, some are probably stylistic, others an attempt to make sense of a difficult text (e.g., "Chidon" in 1 Chron. 13:9), and still others substitute more conventional religious terminology. So David "assembled" Israel (v. 5), from the same Hebrew root (qhl) found in "assembly, congregation" in vv. 2 and 4 and throughout the Priestly writings, instead of merely "gathering" them (2 Sam. 5:1), and the divine name Yahweh is commonly altered to the less personal "God." 1 Chron. 13:14 has been altered to avoid the impression that the Ark of God did not occupy a special tent or house of its own.

The reason for the failure of the first mission is, if somewhat obscure, still that of 2 Samuel 5. For a second explanation see 1 Chron. 15:13. 1 Chron. 14:1–17 points to David's prosperity. This section, found in 2 Sam. 5:11–25 and bypassed earlier in favor of the Ark narrative, is now included. Its inclusion here may be insignificant, or it may serve as an example of the prosperity God extends to those who serve him faithfully.

For 1 Chron. 14:1–2, cf. 2 Sam. 5:11–12. That Chronicles did not find David's relationship with Hiram of Tyre offensive is perhaps surprising (cf. 2 Chron. 2).

1 Chron. 14:3–7 lists David's children. The wording presupposes the earlier list in 2 Sam. 3:2–5, although omitted by Chronicles at that point in the story. The list is sometimes in agreement with Samuel, sometimes with 1 Chron. 3:5–8, and sometimes with neither.

1 Chron. 14:8–16 includes the Philistine wars. The "all Israel" theme is emphasized

again by the addition of "all" before Israel in v. 8. David's obedience here is exemplary, and the result is victory (v. 16). Some alterations of text, especially in vv. 8 and 16, may be to bring the text more into harmony with Isa. 28:21 (reading "Gibeon" instead of the "Geba" of 2 Sam. 5:25). That David had the Philistine idols "burned" rather than picked up (1 Chron. 14:12; cf. 2 Sam. 5:21) is surely meant to his credit.

1 Chron. 14:17 is a summarizing conclusion added by Chronicles after the style of 2 Sam. 5:10 = 1 Chron. 11:9. Such statements as this are incorporated and added frequently by the writer at significant places throughout his work (cf. 29:25; 2 Chron. 11:13–17).

15:1–16:43, The Ark Is Brought to Jerusalem. The writer returns to his primary concern, the Ark of the covenant and the levitical priests. His canonical source is 2 Sam. 5:12b–20a, which is embedded in 1 Chron. 15:25–29 and 16:1–3, 43 and has been supplemented with appropriate psalms and by other materials of unknown origin.

It appears clear from the repetition of similar lists (cf. 15:4–10 with 15:11; 15:17–18 with 15:19–24 and 16:5–6) that also differ from each other (note the position of Obed-edom in 15:18, 21, 24; 16:5) that this section is composite. While certainty is impossible, it seems likely that at least 15:4–10, 16–24 and portions of 16:38–42 are later additions. We shall leave open the question of 16:8–36.

1 Chron. 15:1–3 is introductory, and, like vv. 4–24, without parallel in Samuel. These brief verses are replete with the emphases of Chronicles: the Ark, the Levites (who are termed "chosen of the Lord"), "all Israel," and of course David himself, whose preparations for the Ark are now described.

1 Chron. 15:4–10 names six levitical families and their chiefs. This section, which is commonly considered late, includes the familiar Kohath, Merari, and Gershom, and three lesser known families, all of whom are derived through Kohath (cf. Exod. 6:18; 1 Chron. 6:2, 18). Perhaps mention of the Aaronidic priests in 1 Chron. 15:4 (and in vv. 11, 14) is the work of a later editor.

1 Chron. 15:11–15 names the same six levitical chiefs, as in vv. 4–10, with the addition of the priests Zadok and Abiathar. Although v. 13 is textually difficult, it seems clear that the previous failure to bring the Ark to Jerusalem is ascribed to the fact that the Levites did not participate or did not participate properly, a deficiency stated as remedied in v. 15.

1 Chron. 15:16–24 is a list of levitical and priestly musicians. Three leaders are named in vv. 17–18 (Heman, Asaph, and Ethan) followed by eleven assistants and two gatekeepers (Obed-edom and Jeiel). These are repeated in

essence in vv. 19–24 (cf. also 16:5–6), where the cymbals are apportioned to the leaders and the remaining musicians (including Obed-edom and Jehiel; but cf. 15:23b) are to play harps and lyres. This second list appears to be an even later updating in that it adds a musical director, two other gatekeepers, and seven priestly trumpeters (vv. 22–24). According to current studies, the occurrence of Ethan instead of Jeduthun as the third levitical family dates both lists as relatively late.

1 Chron. 15:25–16:3 is taken from 2 Sam. 6:12–19, with characteristic emphases of Chronicles added: first, more emphasis upon the participation of all Israel (cf. 1 Chron. 15:25), although the "all Israel" theme, like that of joy, was already present in 2 Sam. 6:15–19; second, participation of Levites (not priests) in the sacrifices (1 Chron. 15:26–27) and in the music is expanded and made more explicit; third, the priestly acts of David are curtailed, e.g., the sacrificial acts are described more carefully and the priestly "linen ephod" of 2 Sam. 6:14 is exchanged for a byssus tunic (1 Chron. 15:27, where mention of the linen ephod is late); fourth, the mention of the negative reaction of Saul's daughter Michal is omitted, perhaps merely to avoid ending the account on a negative note.

1 Chron. 16:4–7 names Levites (and priests) before the Ark in Jerusalem (cf. 15:4–26). According to Chronicles, Asaphites were to minister before the Ark in Jerusalem, while the families of Heman and Jeduthun were to serve at the tabernacle, which Chronicles (alone) places at Gibeon (cf. 16:37–42).

As a part of the festivities surrounding the placement of the Ark, the Chronicler (or a later writer) includes portions of three psalms. Verses 8–22 are taken from Ps. 105:1–15, part of a psalm of thanksgiving. By omitting the remainder of that psalm the writer has permitted vv. 12–15 of that psalm to stand as a kind of timeless principle of God's protection of Israel.

1 Chron. 16:23–33 is identical with Psalm 96, a psalm of praise to Yahweh the king, with minor changes for which no reason is apparent. For vv. 34–36, cf. Ps. 106:1, 34–36, which includes the familiar "Give thanks to the Lord, for he is good, because his steadfast love endures forever" (also in Ps. 107:1), a prayer that God would gather Israel from the nations, and the doxology to Book 4 of Psalms. Perhaps these verses were meant to remind Israel also of the remainder of Psalm 106, most fitting for a nation in exile.

At least in the final form of this passage (1 Chron. 16:37–43), David leaves Asaph and his family to minister before the Ark in Jerusalem, while the priest Zadok and the families of Heman and Jeduthun are to do the same at Gibeon, where Chronicles locates the tent of the Lord. Presumably the priest Abiathar also remains at Jerusalem (cf. 15:11). Perhaps an earlier form of the chapters left Asaph and the Levites in Jerusalem and placed the priests at Gibeon, where, the Chronicler may have reasoned, the tent of the Lord must have been (see commentary above on 2 Chron. 1:2–6).

17:1–27, The Promise to David. This chapter is based on 2 Samuel 7, surely one of the most significant passages of Scripture. Two chief points are made by means of a play on the word "house": a member of David's house, one of his descendants, will build a house (i.e., a temple) for Yahweh, v. 12; and the kingdom of David's house will be established forever, vv. 12–14. Thus OT (and NT) messianism will be forever after linked with David.

While divergences between the texts of Samuel and Chronicles have perhaps been overinterpreted in the past, significant differences do occur. First, Chronicles omits the phrase "and Yahweh had given him [David] rest" from 2 Sam. 7:1, since the verbal root embodied in that form is significant for him in explaining why Solomon rather than David built the Temple (see commentary below on 1 Chron. 22:6–10). In 1 Chron. 17:10, another form of the same root is altered to "I will subdue" for the same reason. Second, 2 Sam. 7:14 had alluded to at least the possibility that the chosen seed of David would commit transgression. Since Chronicles presents Solomon's conduct as blameless, the omission of these words from 1 Chron. 17:13 is suggestive, although not essentially altering the meaning of the original. Third, David's prayer places greater emphasis upon the fact that Yahweh has already begun to bless David's house, v. 27 (cf. 2 Sam. 7:29).

18:1–20:8, David's Wars. Chronicles probably includes these accounts largely because they were in its source (cf. 2 Sam. 8–21, with many omissions). Perhaps at the same time, though generally positive toward David (cf. 1 Chron. 18:6; 19:13; 20:3–4) and pointing to God's blessing upon him, they point to his age as a period of warfare in which construction of the Temple was not permitted, in contrast with the age of Solomon, marked by peace and the building of the Temple (see 1 Chron. 22). That spoil from his wars was used for construction of the Temple appears more of an afterthought (18:8, 11) than the purpose for their inclusion.

For 18:1–17, see 2 Samuel 8, with which this chapter is largely identical. Apart from minor differences of text and style, we may see the mind of the writer at work in 1 Chron. 18:2, which appears to absolve David from atrocities in war (cf. 2 Sam. 8:2), and in 1 Chron. 18:8, which adds that Solomon used the bronze taken from Hadadezer for the Temple. (Verse 11 is found already in 2 Sam. 8:11–12.) The larger numbers in 1 Chron. 18:4 (a thousand chariots and seven thousand horsemen compared to seventeen hundred horsemen alone in 2 Sam. 8:4) may be due to the exaggeration for which the writer is often cited, but may also stem from a different text (the number of foot soldiers [20,000] remains the same in both texts). Noteworthy in the light of the idealization of David often posited of Chronicles is his omission of 2 Sam. 8:13a, "David made a name for himself," and the transference of some of his victories to Abishai (1 Chron. 18:12; cf. 2 Sam. 8:13).

1 Chron. 19:1–19 relates David's war with the Ammonites and Aram (see 2 Sam. 10). The writer omits 2 Samuel 9, recounting David's kindness to Saul's son Mephibosheth, since he has stated that all of Saul's house was slain in his final battle with the Philistines (see commentary on 1 Chron. 10:6). Apart from minor differences due to textual error, style, and updating, there is little indication of the writer's hand apart from several cases of hyperbole that appear to glorify David (cf. vv. 6–7 with 2 Sam. 10:6–7; v. 18 with 2 Sam. 10:18).

1 Chron. 20:1–8 tells of additional warfare. Chronicles includes in vv. 1–3 only the beginning and end of the lengthy account of the Ammonite war found in 2 Samuel 11–12, omitting David's adultery with Bathsheba and the subsequent murder of her husband Uriah, as well as David's condemnation by the prophet Nathan. Also omitted is 2 Sam. 13:1–21:17, partially from a desire for brevity, but also because it describes in vivid detail the "evil from his own house" (2 Sam. 12:11) that would befall David by way of punishment and thus contradicts a basic premise of the writer, that David faced no opposition in his kingship. He has, in 1 Chron. 20:4–8, picked up the narrative from 2 Sam. 21:18–22, which leads immediately to the account of David's census, in which he is more interested because of its relationship to the Temple.

In 1 Chron. 20:4, the writer has perhaps omitted "Gob" (2 Sam. 21:18) as unknown, replacing it with the better known Gezer. The addition of "they were subdued" (1 Chron. 20:4) suggests a fulfillment of 1 Chron. 17:10 is here being expressed. In 20:5, Chronicles so rearranges the text that Elhanan kills Lahmi, the brother of Goliath, rather than Goliath himself (cf. 2 Sam. 21:19), erasing the tension with David's slaying of Goliath in 1 Samuel 17. Thus a general picture of David's faithfulness is presented, and Yahweh rewards that faithfulness with victory in war.

21:1–30, David's Census. The writer omits the other materials of 2 Samuel 22–23 (he has used the list of David's mighty men in 1 Chron. 11:11–41a) and proceeds to David's abortive census (2 Sam. 24), which in its concluding verse spoke of an altar built by David with divine approval (1 Chron. 21:6) and hence provided a convenient connection to the Temple narrative.

Textual variations from its Samuel source are numerous in this chapter, and since they represent no clear theological direction, it has been felt the author was here using a different text type. Manuscripts from Qumran do show some cases in which texts of Samuel agree with readings in Chronicles.

Several variations are worthy of note. First, in 1 Chron. 21:1 it is Satan (→ Satan) rather than God (2 Sam. 24:1) who incites David's census, reflecting a developing and popular piety that preferred not to predicate evil directly of God. Second, David's guilt in conducting the census is actually heightened. His general, Joab, takes issue with him concerning the matter and is himself responsible for the decision not to count Levi and Benjamin. Third, the value of the future site of the Temple is elevated in that David pays Ornan not the fifty shekels of silver named in 2 Sam. 24:24, but six hundred shekels of gold (1 Chron. 21:25). The number of potential warriors in Israel and Judah might represent a similar hyperbole, but the numbers (1,570,000 in Chronicles, 1,300,000 in Samuel) do not differ substantially enough to present a strong case for that. Finally, David's decree is altered to refer to altar and Temple (21:26; 22:1), and the divine approval of the entire operation is made explicit by fire from heaven (21:26).

With the Levites set aside for their work (chap. 15), the Ark in Jerusalem (chap. 16), and the site for the Temple chosen and approved (chap. 21), all is in readiness for the erection of the Temple, which is the central concern in chaps. 22–29 (and 2 Chron. 1–8).

22:1–29:30
Transitional Unit

Chaps. 22–29 are normally considered a part of the David history; they deal equally with Solomon, however. Since they have no parallel in Samuel, we may see in them again the intention of the writer(s) most clearly. Leaving aside chaps. 23–27 for the moment, which are probably later additions (see commentary on chap. 23), chaps. 22, 28, and 29 serve to bind the work of David and Solomon into one; they are composed principally of three speeches and a prayer of David spoken to or in direct reference to Solomon: 22:6–16, David's first speech; 28:2–21, David's second speech; 29:1–5, David's third speech; and 29:10–19, David's prayer. He, in turn, is set forth in them as the divinely chosen builder of the Temple.

22:2–5, David Gathers Workers and Material for the Temple. There seems to be no prior tradition to this effect (but cf. 1 Kings 7:51 = 2 Chron. 5:1). Many of the details are derived from the Solomonic portions of Kings. The reason given here for David's preparations is Solomon's youth and immaturity (cf. 1 Chron. 29:1).

22:6–19, David's First Speech. Solomon is designated to build the Temple. This is indicated in three ways. First, the entire unit is modeled upon the account of Joshua's installation in Joshua 1. Second, the "rest" theology of Chronicles referred to previously in 1 Chronicles 17 is given its rationale in 22:6–10. David has been forbidden to build the Temple because he had "shed very much blood, and waged great wars" (cf. 1 Kings 5:3–5, significantly omitted by Chronicles). His seed, however, who will be a man of rest, will build the Temple, and that "man of rest" is identified by name as Solomon, whose name means "peace." Third, three elements of a literary form for the induction of an individual into an office have been isolated: the formula of encouragement, such as "Be strong and be courageous; do not be afraid and do not be terrified" (1 Chron. 22:13); the description of the task for which the individual is inducted; and the formula of accompaniment, "The Lord is with you." Each of these items is found in Joshua 1 and David's speech as well (vv. 11, 13). Most significantly, however, the task to which Solomon is inducted is that of building the Temple.

In vv. 11–13, Yahweh's presence is directly related to obedience to the Torah and prosperity (cf. again Josh. 1:6–8), laying the basis for the doctrine of retribution, which will find fuller expression in 1 Chron. 28:9. 1 Chron. 22:14–16 and 17–19 are probably to be considered a later addition from the hand of a more priestly disciple.

23:1–27:34, Levitical Organization. These chapters are highly composite and represent, in part if not in totality, a later addition to the book. All levitical organization is here linked with David, just as is all law with Moses and all wisdom with Solomon. Divisions of the Levites are covered in chap. 23, priests in chap. 24, singers in chap. 25, gatekeepers in chap. 26, and other appointees in chap. 27.

1 Chron. 23:1–32 lists divisions of the Levites. This chapter is probably late or composite, since v. 2 is a duplicate of 28:1 and internal duplicates and discrepancies abound (e.g., the levitical age in 23:3 and 24; the sons of Shimei in vv. 9 and 10). This chapter is composed of three units.

Verses 1–6 list levitical duties. David's death and Solomon's coronation will not be described

until 29:22–30. Thirty-eight thousand Levites are numbered at age thirty or above, a high number in comparison with other OT figures (cf. Num. 3:39; 1 Chron. 12:27; Num. 8:23–26; 2 Chron. 31:17). The fourfold division of the thirty-eight thousand is also unusual in that twenty-four thousand (similar to the number of divisions of priests [1 Chron. 24:18], musicians [25:31], and probably gatekeepers [26:12, 17–18]) are set aside to "direct the work of Yahweh's house" (see also 27:1–15). Striking is the designation of six thousand as "officers and judges" (23:4; cf. 2 Chron. 19:4–11 and Deut. 17:8–13).

1 Chron. 23:7–23 includes sons of Gershom (vv. 7–11), Kohath (vv. 12–20), and Merari (vv. 21–23). On this conventional threefold division of the Levites and for alternative genealogies, see chap. 6. Moses' association here with the Levites rather than the Aaronidic priests is strongly affirmed (1 Chron. 23:13–14). The same nine family heads of Kohath are also named in 24:20–25. Since these "genealogies" extend at most three generations beyond the patronymic heads, it is apparent that they, in fact, establish rather than demonstrate levitical ties.

1 Chron. 23:24–32 adds more levitical duties. With the granting of rest to Israel, the task of the Levites is changed by David's decree from carrying the tabernacle to regular assistance in the Temple (v. 26). These verses, like vv. 13–14, emphasize the subordinate role of the Levites and probably reflect a later addition. Levites are here counted above the age of twenty (v. 27).

1 Chron. 24:1–31 gives divisions of the priests (and further levitical arrangements). Twenty-four priestly groups are named (vv. 7–19), preceded by a lengthy introduction. All are derived from Aaron's sons Eleazar and Ithamar, since Nadab and Abihu suffered untimely deaths (v. 2; for the priestly genealogy, see commentary above on 6:1–15). Zadok is here firmly implanted in Eleazar's line, opposite Abiathar, who is from Ithamar's line. Abiathar was removed from office by Solomon (1 Kings 2:27). 1 Chron. 24:19 affirms that priestly duties were established not by David, but by Yahweh himself.

For vv. 20–30, see commentary above on 23:7–23. Five of the families named are here extended by a single name, and an otherwise unknown branch of Merari's family, Jaaziah, is added.

In 25:1–31 the musicians, like the priests and Levites in chaps. 23 and 24, are enumerated and then divided into twenty-four courses. The chapter contains two units, which are themselves composite.

In vv. 1–7, David and the levitical heads set aside three families of levitical musicians (Asaph, Heman, and Jeduthun [v. 1], who are named again in vv. 2–5 and 6 in the order Asaph, Jeduthun, Heman; for the singers, see also 1 Chron. 6; 15:16–24; 16:4–7, 41–42). A total of 288 (24 × 12) singers is counted (1 Chron. 25:7), presupposing both the twenty-four sons named in vv. 2–4 and the twelve members of each course in vv. 9–31. While Asaph is regularly listed first and would appear to be formally recognized as preeminent, only four families trace their lineage to him, and it is, above all, Heman, with no less than fourteen sons/families, who is in the ascendancy.

The prophetic nature of the work of the singers is here emphasized repeatedly (vv. 1, 2, 3, 5), as in 2 Chron. 20:14; 29:25; and 35:15. We may sense in such terminology the desire to elevate the work of the singers beyond that of more menial Temple servants.

It has been noted that of Heman's sons named in 1 Chron. 25:4, the last nine (from Hananiah on) differ in form from the first five and are identical or similar in form to regular Hebrew verb forms. Some have understood these words to stem from a psalm verse or the beginnings of various psalms.

Verses 8–31 describe the casting of lots. The order in which the lots fall here seems to presuppose the order of the sons in vv. 2–4, also in that all of Heman's remaining sons are grouped together in vv. 23–31.

1 Chron. 26:1–32 lists gatekeepers and other Levites. For the gatekeepers (vv. 1–19) see 9:17–32. Three groups are mentioned, stemming from Korah (26:1–3, 9) and Merari (vv. 10–11), whose levitical genealogies are given, and Obed-edom (vv. 4–8), for whom none is given. Apparently both Obed-edom and Korah had difficulty establishing levitical credibility. Verses 12–19 again detail the casting of lots. The predominance of Shelemiah, whose name is variously spelled throughout this section, is apparent both in that he is assigned to the most important, or east, gate and that his son Zechariah is chosen to fill the vacancy at the fourth gate.

Verses 20–32 add "other Levites." As in 9:22–32, where the functions of the gatekeepers are similarly expanded, Levites are placed in charge of the Temple precincts and treasuries. This section abounds in textual and other difficulties. 1 Chron. 26:26–28 make the point that the dedicated gifts of all Israel's leaders, from the time of Samuel down to David, were brought to the Levites for use in the Temple service. Two additional families of Kohathites, those of Izhar and Hebron, are named to "outside duties" west and east of the Jordan respectively, apparently pointing once again to broader responsibilities of the Levites.

1 Chron. 27:1–34 is a listing of other Davidic officials. While we know little about administrative arrangements in David's age, it seems quite certain that sweeping administrative changes did take place. This chapter is composed of four independent, probably unrelated units.

Verses 1–15 list commanders of the monthly courses. Twelve divisions of twenty-four thousand each are listed, reminiscent of the twenty-four courses of priests, musicians, and gatekeepers. Each of the twelve heads is included in the first sixteen names of the list of David's heroes in 11:10–47.

1 Chron. 27:16–24 is a listing of tribal heads. The order of the tribes is closest to that of 1 Chronicles 2, but other details are reminiscent of the census of Numbers 1. Unlike 1 Chronicles 21, fault for the census here appears to fall largely on Joab rather than David.

The king's officials are, in 27:25–31, divided into three groups, those responsible for the king's storehouses or treasuries (v. 25), agriculture (vv. 26–28), and livestock (vv. 29–31). Probably none of the individuals named here is otherwise known in the OT, although an Azmaveth is listed among David's heroes in 11:33.

1 Chron. 27:32–34 names other Davidic advisers. Perhaps these enjoyed a close personal relationship with David, in contrast to the more formal list of 1 Chron. 18:14–17 (= 2 Sam. 8:15–18; 20:23–26). The Jonathan named is not Saul's son, whose death is recorded in 1 Chron. 10:2, but an otherwise unknown "uncle" or friend of David.

With the listing of David's officials, the writer concludes his list of those placed in office by David, giving expression by so doing that priestly, levitical, and secular organizations alike were to be attributed to David.

28:1–21, David's Second Speech.

Chap. 28 resumes the thought of chap. 22, interrupted by chaps. 23–27. Having earlier informed Solomon of his task as Temple builder, David assembles Israel's leaders and gives them the same information.

The list of officials in 28:1–2a has probably been revised in view of the insertion of chaps. 23–27 (for David's speech [28:2b–10] cf. 22:6–13). David repeats that his own plans to build the Temple, termed a "house of rest" for the Ark in a further development of that term (v. 2; see commentary above on 22:9), have been rejected by God because he was a warrior and had shed blood (28:3). God has instead chosen Solomon for that task (v. 6), and that choice is this time expressed in terms of divine election (Heb. bachar). Verses 4–5 are perhaps secondary, referring that election also to Judah. In vocabulary often borrowed from his sources but especially dear to Chronicles (cf. "all Israel," "a perfect heart and a willing spirit"), vv. 8–10 exhort Solomon to obedience to God's commands, which will result in prosperity, while failure to do so will result in rejection. The statement of

v. 9, "If you seek him, he will be found by you; but if you forsake him, he will reject you forever," is the first explicit statement of the dogma of retribution that dominates 2 Chronicles.

Verses 11, 12a, and 19 tell of the transfer of the Temple plans received by David "from the hands of Yahweh" to Solomon. Verses 12b–18 are a later elaboration of that theme.

Verses 20–21 place for the first time all of the people at Solomon's disposal and repeat the ingredients of the formula of installation (see chap. 22). In addition, the doctrine of retribution is reformulated positively: God will not forsake Solomon until his work is finished.

29:1–9, David's Third Speech. As Moses appealed to Israel for freewill offerings for the construction of the Temple and Israel responded generously to that appeal (Exod. 35:5–29), so David appeals to the princes of Israel and receives their gifts. In the materials named, as well as in the pervasive note of generosity (1 Chron. 29:5, 9), the influence of the tabernacle narrative is clear.

29:10–19, David's Blessing. This splendid prayer, which probably reflects the thought and liturgical style of the exilic or postexilic period, blends three major psalm types (hymn, thanksgiving, and petition) and is replete with the terminology of Psalms. David praises God (vv. 10–12, in notes later echoed in the doxology of the Christian "Lord's Prayer"), thanks God for the offerings received (vv. 13–16), and asks God's continued presence with his people and especially Solomon in the construction of the Temple (vv. 17–19). In describing Israel as sojourners, pilgrims, and without hope (v. 15), the author appears to move from Temple festivity to the more troubling days of the Exile (cf. Neh. 9).

Nevertheless, the notes of generosity, joy, and the perfect heart continue to dominate (1 Chron. 29:17–19).

29:20–25, Solomon's Enthronement. Solomon is enthroned in a two-day ceremony marked by the blessings of the people, sacrifices of at least three thousand animals, an eating and drinking before God, the formal anointing as Yahweh's prince, and a pledge of loyalty on the part of Israel's chiefs and warriors (see 1 Chron. 12:38–39). The anointing of Zadok at the same time may be out of place but is not impossible. The note of joy is again present (29:22), and the epitome of the "all Israel" theme appears to be reached (cf. vv. 21, 23, 25) when it is noted in v. 24 that, in spite of the evidence to the contrary in 1 Kings 1–2 and elsewhere, "all the sons of King David" vowed their allegiance to Solomon. Even as with David, recognition of Solomon is complete and unanimous, and no opposition is voiced to his reign. 1 Chron. 29:25 is indicative of the author's appraisal of his reign.

29:26–30, The Death of David. The mention of David's seven-year reign at Hebron is surprising, but even here there is no indication that his rule there was over only a part of Israel (see 1 Chron. 11:3). The usual evaluation of David's reign is lacking in both Kings and Chronicles, but 29:28 is surely commendatory. Interested readers are referred to the words of Samuel, Nathan, and Gad. The idea for such concluding summaries is probably borrowed from Kings and completed utilizing the names of prophets known to be active in the reign of the king referred to.

Bibliography
See 2 Chronicles, "Bibliography."

2 CHRONICLES

RODDY L. BRAUN

INTRODUCTION

INTRODUCTION

See 1 Chronicles, "Introduction."

COMMENTARY

1 CHRON. 10:1–2 CHRON. 9:31

David and Solomon (continued)

1:1–9:31
The Solomon History

These chapters are devoted almost exclusively to the king's role in the construction of the Temple; only chap. 1 and 8:16–9:31 are more general in nature. Even more than in the case of David, it will be seen, the author depicts Solomon as the king divinely chosen to erect the Temple, the king whose kingship was accepted by all Israel unanimously and enthusiastically, and the king whose personal life was without fault.

1:1–17, The Beginning of the Reign of Solomon. Verse 1, which would have immediately followed the story of David's death in 1 Chronicles 29 before Chronicles was separated into two books, begins the Solomon narrative by restating 1 Chron. 29:20. The similar note in 1 Kings 2:12 occurs only after Solomon has ruthlessly eliminated all opposition to his rule.

For 2 Chron. 1:2–6, see 1 Kings 3:3–4, generally favorable toward Solomon but critical of his activity on the high places, as with all kings except the reformers Hezekiah and Josiah. But in Chronicles, the high place at Gibeon, termed "the great high place," has been legitimized in that the tent of meeting (not to be identified with David's tent in Jerusalem, 2 Chron 1:4, but with the tabernacle, v. 5) and the bronze altar for sacrifice were located there (cf. 1 Chron. 16:39; 21:28–30). Solomon thus begins his reign not with a sacrifice at a proscribed high place, but as a pious king at the head of a procession of "all Israel" (cf. 1 Chron. 13:1) seeking the Lord (cf. Saul in 1 Chron. 10:13–14). Whether there is any historical accuracy to this position or, as seems more likely,

it is a construct of the Chronicler to preserve Solomon's integrity, cannot be determined with certainty.

2 Chron. 1:7–13 demonstrates Solomon's wisdom (see 1 Kings 3:5–15; 4:1). The wisdom, knowledge, riches, and honor promised Solomon were doubtless in keeping with the author's view of Solomon's greatness. Note the omission of much of 1 Kings 3:6, highly laudatory of David; of 3:14, which would have left room for Solomon's apostasy; and of 3:15, which notes that Solomon returned to Jerusalem and sacrificed.

Chronicles inserts (in 2 Chron. 1:14–17) the demonstration of Solomon's prosperity from 1 Kings 10:26–29, which is surprising in view of its omission of 1 Kings 3:16–28 and 4:2–33 and its use of portions of 10:26–29 in 2 Chron. 9:27. Perhaps especially 1 Kings 4:20–34 is one of those sections (see 1 Chronicles, "Introduction") of such importance for the writer that he has omitted its rote repetition in order to include it in his work in a more important and programmatic way.

2:1–8:16, The Building of the Temple. With these chapters the author comes to the high point of his work, already of supreme importance also in 1 Kings 5–8.

2 Chron. 2:1–18 describes the relations between Solomon and Huram (see 1 Kings 5, rewritten here with considerable skill), though here the name of this well-known Tyrian king appears as Hiram. Solomon assigns 153,600 aliens to the work (2 Chron. 2:2, 17–18; 1 Kings 5:13–18 mentions an additional levy of 30,000 Israelites conscripted to work by rotation in the forests of Lebanon) and requests Huram to provide timber for the Temple and a chief craftsman. Huram responds by sending one Huramabi, whose mother was a Danite and whose father was from Tyre (2 Chron. 2:13–14). This Huramabi is perhaps to be identified with (a second) Hiram (1 Kings 7:13–14), whose mother is, however, from Naphtali. King Hiram also agrees upon a price for the timber.

The tendentious character of the narrative is apparent in that, first, Solomon's letter to Huram provides opportunity to propound the significance of the Temple (2 Chron. 2:4–6). While agreeing with the Deuteronomistic historian that the Temple is not God's dwelling (1 Kings 5:3) but the place where his name dwells, emphasis falls primarily upon the Temple as a place of worship and sacrifice (the Hebrew *qatar*, conventionally translated "to burn incense," probably has this broader meaning in 2 Chron. 2:6). Second, the terminology associated with the building of the Temple and with Huramabi is heavily dependent upon the tabernacle narrative (cf., e.g., vv. 7–8, 14 with Exod. 28 and 35, and the designation of Huramabi as a "skilled" worker in vv. 7, 13 with the description of Bezalel in Exod. 31:1–5). Huramabi is, as one writer has called him, practically a second Bezalel, and his unusual name has been considered a conflation of Hiram/Huram and Bezalel's assistant Oholiab, also a Danite (Exod. 31:6). Third, the figure of Solomon presented is more proficient, more pious in Chronicles than in Kings. He leads his people to Gibeon to sacrifice, takes the initiative with Huram, sets the price for the timber, and expounds the meaning of the Temple. All is then in readiness for the work to begin.

2 Chron. 3:1–5:1 describes the construction of the Temple, an abbreviation of 1 Kings 6–7. Chronicles replaces the opening reference dating the building of the Temple in the four hundred and eightieth year since the Exodus with one identifying the site of the Temple with Ornan's threshing floor (1 Chron. 21:18; 22:1) and Mount Moriah (Gen. 22:2), the first known mention of the Jewish and Islamic tradition identifying the Temple site with Isaac's trial. The Chronicler omits the details concerning the construction of the Temple (1 Kings 6:4–20) as well as all mention of the building of Solomon's palace, which required no less than thirteen years (1 Kings 7:1–12), most of the details concerning the two pillars Jachin and Boaz (1 Kings 7:15–22), and all mention of ten bronze stands (1 Kings 7:27–37). His only significant addition appears to be 2 Chron. 5:6b–9, which may have been omitted from Kings by error. Other minor differences may be due to the author's knowledge of the Temple in his own day.

2 Chron. 5:1–14 depicts the placement of the Ark in the sanctuary and is largely identical with 1 Kings 7:51–8:11, except for vv. 11b–13, found in Chronicles only. The following variations appear to reflect the writer's interests: first, the Levites rather than the priests are named as bearing the Ark (2 Chron. 5:4; cf. 1 Kings 8:3). Second, 2 Chron. 5:5 mentions the tent of meeting, which is for Chronicles the tabernacle at Gibeon (1:2–6) and not the tent that David made for the Ark in Zion. The point of vv. 4–5 is that the Ark was brought up from Zion and the tent/tabernacle from Gibeon. The mention of the "levitical priests" (normally a Deuteronomic expression) in v. 5b may already be secondary and is then borrowed by Kings from Chronicles. (1 Kings 8:4b is lacking in the Greek, though present in the Hebrew.) Third, between the two

halves of 1 Kings 8:10, Chronicles contains a major insertion (vv. 11b–13), sometimes judged late, calling attention to both the sanctity of the priests (v. 11b) and to the presence of the Levites and singers, Heman, Asaph, and Jeduthun, clothed in garments of fine linen (cf. 1 Chron. 15:27) and with their musical instruments. Fourth, the presence of the glory of the Lord in 2 Chron. 7:1–3, where it is absent from the parallel in 1 Kings 8:54–62, has suggested to some that 2 Chron. 5:11a, 13b–14 are secondary here.

2 Chron. 6:1–42 contains Solomon's blessing and prayer, and is largely identical with 1 Kings 8:12–53. Verses 1–2, like 1 Kings 8:12–13, stand contrary to the basic emphasis of the Deuteronomistic History upon the Temple as the place where God's name dwells and perhaps stems from an earlier day when such precision was felt unnecessary (2 Chron. 6:18–20; 1 Kings 8:27–29). 1 Kings 8:16 seems to say God had chosen no city but had chosen David —Chronicles rephrases this to parallel the choice of Jerusalem and David (2 Chron. 6:5–6). Verse 13 may well have dropped out of the Kings text, since 1 Kings 8:54 mentions Solomon's rising from the kneeling reported only in that verse.

At the end of Solomon's prayer, Chronicles attaches Ps. 132:8–9 (2 Chron. 6:41–42). These verses join Yahweh's choice of Zion as his resting place (Ps. 132:8, 13–14; cf. 1 Chron. 17:1, 10; 22:8–10; 28:2) with his choice of David (2 Chron. 6:4, 10, 11, 17) and so were admirably suited to his own interests. Too much, probably, should not be made of the omission of 1 Kings 8:53, touching upon the Exodus, although the Exodus certainly does not occupy for Chronicles the dominant place it does elsewhere in the OT. The theme of rest expressed here through the quote from Psalm 132 was probably suggested by its mention in a third speech of Solomon reported in 1 Kings 8:56–61 but omitted by Chronicles. Like 1 Kings 5:3–6, this third speech centered on the rest denied David but granted Solomon.

2 Chron. 7:1–22 concludes the dedication (cf. 1 Kings 8:54–9:9). Chronicles presents in this section an account (clearly of paramount importance for the writer) that is both highly dependent upon his source and unusually independent as well.

First, on 7:1b–2, cf. 1 Kings 8:10–11 and 2 Chron. 5:11a, 13b–14, where it is perhaps secondary, Chronicles perhaps thinking this a more appropriate place for the appearance of the divine glory (Heb. *kabod*). Chronicles adds only the consuming fire of 7:1b, indicating the divine approval and recalling 1 Chron. 21:26; Exod. 24:17; 40:34; and Lev. 9:23–24. To this account of the divine epiphany Chronicles adds the worship of the people (7:3), whose praise is again summarized with the characteristic words "his steadfast love endures forever" (cf. v. 6 and 5:13).

Second, special attention is due at this point to the omission of 1 Kings 8:54–61, Solomon's concluding prayer pointing to this occasion as marking the rest that God has promised his people and as the culmination of his promises to Moses and David (1 Kings 8:56). These verses (1 Kings 8:54–61) also state clearly both poles of that divine retribution seen in 1 Chron. 28:9 that will dominate the writer's presentations in 2 Chronicles 10–36. Recall also the omission of other significant sections, such as 1 Kings 5:3–6.

The report in 1 Kings 8:62–66 already contained themes common to Chronicles, such as the note of "all Israel" (vv. 62, 65), numerous sacrifices (vv. 63–64), feasting (v. 65), and joy (v. 66). Chronicles has nevertheless again indicated the participation of priests and levitical musicians (2 Chron. 7:6) and lengthened the dedicatory feast by seven days, perhaps believing that the dedication of the altar and Tabernacles (the feast of the seventh month) ought not overlap. Most significantly, God's goodness to "David his servant and Israel his people" has been altered to include mention of King Solomon.

On vv. 11–22, cf. 1 Kings 8:62–66. Yahweh's speech at his second appearance to Solomon is altered to include the designation of the Temple as a "house of sacrifice" (2 Chron. 7:12). It has been observed that, especially in the words of v. 14, four avenues of repentance are uncovered (to humble oneself, pray, seek, turn) that will lead to God's hearing, forgiving, and healing of people and land and that such a theology is meant to proclaim to the exiles that no circumstances are too formidable to prevent God from fulfilling his promise. These terms are indeed the heart of the writer's theology from this point on and point to the dedication of the Temple as the beginning of a new era in Israel's history. Notice too that in these verses the conditional nature of the covenant with Solomon is retained (vv. 17–18; cf. 1 Kings 9:4–8), as is the mention of the Exodus (v. 22; cf. 1 Kings 9:9).

For 2 Chron. 8:1–18, cf. 1 Kings 9:10–28, which presents something of a miscellany of remarks here before concluding its account of Solomon's reign. While textual corruption appears likely in places (cf. the mention of 250 officers in v. 10 with 1 Kings 9:23), the writer of Chronicles has found several statements unacceptable and rewritten them to reflect more favorably upon Solomon.

First, 1 Kings 9:10–13 spoke of cities that Solomon had sold to Huram, obviously to finance his building operations. The Chronicler, thinking such an action unworthy of Solomon, has simply reversed the direction of the transaction.

Second, 1 Kings 9:15–19 had spoken briefly of building operations of Solomon, including a house for the pharaoh's daughter. While textual corruption seems probable here, Chronicles has Solomon active in the otherwise unknown Hamath-zobah, probably to be identified with Hamath, the ideal northern boundary of Israel (cf. 2 Chron. 7:8), and Tadmor, the significant Syrian city of Palmyra, and explains the move of the pharaoh's daughter from the city of David (1 Kings 9:24) as due to Solomon's concern for the sanctity of the Ark (2 Chron. 8:11).

Third, the brief note of 1 Kings 9:25 concerning Solomon's thrice-yearly sacrifices is taken as the opportunity to present what must be understood as the conclusion to the Temple narrative, 2 Chron. 8:13–15. Solomon's offerings are multiplied to include also the daily, weekly, and monthly offerings, and the appointment of the priests, Levites, and gatekeepers according to David's command is mentioned. In conclusion, the simple statement of Kings, "So he finished the house," is elaborated: "Thus was accomplished all the work of Solomon from the day the foundation of the house of the LORD was laid until it was finished. So the house of the LORD was completed" (v. 16, RSV).

8:17–9:31, Solomon's Riches and Wisdom. 2 Chron. 8:17–18, together with 9:1–24, which repeats almost verbatim 1 Kings 10:1–25, provide a fitting description of Solomon's prosperity. The same is true of 9:25, which, however, varies more from 1 Kings 9:26.

From that point on, Chronicles proceeds more selectively. 2 Chron. 9:26, "And he [Solomon] ruled over all the kings from the Euphrates to the land of the Philistines, and to the border of Egypt" (RSV), is inserted at this point from 1 Kings 4:21 before repeating vv. 27–28 from 1 Kings 10:27–28. But most significantly, the entire content of 1 Kings 11:1–40 is omitted, and the Solomon history is concluded by appending in vv. 29–31 a form of 1 Kings 11:41–43 amended only by the replacement of "the book of the acts of Solomon" with mention of prophets known to be active in Solomon's day: Nathan, Ahijah, and Iddo (cf. 1 Chron. 29:29).

The result is that Solomon ends his reign as he has begun it—as a perfectly faithful king. Gone is all reference to foreign women, who turned away his heart to follow foreign gods. Absent is all negative evaluation, such as that of 1 Kings 11:6, "So Solomon did that which was evil in the sight of the LORD, and did not wholly follow the LORD, as David his father had done" (RSV). Omitted also are the references to Yahweh's anger (1 Kings 11:9) and the resulting decision to tear the kingdom from Solomon (although not during his life) but to retain a single tribe for the sake of David (1 Kings 11:9–13).

Likewise omitted is the opposition that God raised up against Solomon from Hadad the Edomite, Rezon of Syria, and Jeroboam (1 Kings 11:14–40). Solomon thus dies, in the presentation of Chronicles, as the king who has not only built the Temple but who remained faithful throughout his life and whose life has accordingly witnessed that God-given prosperity that regularly attends such faithfulness: building operations (2 Chron. 8:3–6), riches and wisdom (9:22, 27–28), and receipt of tribute from foreign kings (9:24). At the end of Solomon's life there is faithful obedience to God; hence there is peace, unity, and prosperity, with the Temple and its services standing firmly at the center of the nation's existence.

10:1–36:23
Post-Solomonic Kings of Judah

With the death of Solomon the writer adopts a different manner of dealing with his subjects. After giving his account of the division of the kingdom (2 Chron. 10), he normally omits those portions of Kings dealing with the Northern Kingdom (cf. 1 Kings 12:25–14:20). Concerning the Southern Kingdom, evaluations of the various rulers are generally accepted at face value; these are, however, understood rigidly in terms of the dogma of retribution. Obedience results in prosperity, expressed in terms of wealth, wisdom, "rest," building operations, a large family, victory in warfare, and tribute from foreign nations. Disobedience results in punishment, most commonly in the form of defeat in warfare. Prophets appear upon the scene frequently, interpreting events in that light, and while repentance is always a possibility, rejection of the prophetic message leads to individual, and ultimately national, disaster.

10:1–12:16
The Reign of Rehoboam
(ca. 922–915 B.C.)

The Chronicler devotes considerable space to Rehoboam, including not only all of the material of Kings except that related exclusively to Jeroboam but also considerable material of his own (cf. 11:5–23; 12:1, 3–8, 12). In so doing he expresses his own theology.

10:1–11:4, The Division of the Kingdom. Cf. 1 Kings 12:1–24, repeated here almost verbatim. But Chronicles omits most of 1 Kings 11, which describes both Solomon's faithlessness and Jeroboam's place in the divine plan.

Recent textual studies indicate that some ancient versions of Kings gave Jeroboam little part in the schism between north and south (cf. the current confusion in the text of the RSV between 1 Kings 12:2, 12, and 20). On the basis of various Greek manuscripts, it appears likely that Chronicles was the first to judge Jeroboam a chief cause of that schism, a viewpoint later inserted into Kings from Chronicles. Earlier versions of Kings had Jeroboam returning from Egypt only in 12:20.

Note should be made that in 1 Kings 11 the term "Israel" is used for the northern tribes, whence it is borrowed by Chronicles and used in the same sense. In 1 Kings 12:19, for example, "Israel" is used in contrast with the house of David. At other times, however, a theological distinction is made. Thus Kings speaks of the words of the prophet Shemaiah to "all the house of Judah and Benjamin, and to the remainder of the people" (12:23), which Chronicles rephrases as "all Israel in Judah and Benjamin" (2 Chron. 11:3). Precise meaning of the term must also be derived from the context.

11:5–23, Rehoboam's Faithfulness. The passage is without parallel in Kings and apparently placed here to establish a principle. 1 Kings will report (14:25) that Shishak of Egypt successfully invaded Jerusalem in the fifth year of Rehoboam, a judgment accepted by 2 Chronicles (12:2). Since retribution is not only certain but swift, the author has apparently concluded that Judah was faithful for three years (defined as walking "in the way of David and Solomon," 2 Chron. 11:17) and apparently became disobedient in the fourth year (12:1–9).

This three-year period of faithfulness results in God-given prosperity, expressed concretely in terms that will be met repeatedly. First, Rehoboam engages in building operations in Judah and Benjamin, especially fortified cities (2 Chron. 11:5–12; cf. v. 23). While most of the cities named are reasonably well known, it is disputed whether the list actually comes from the time of Rehoboam or from a later date. Second, "All Israel," represented by the priests and Levites who had been driven out of the north by Jeroboam's religious innovations (cf. 1 Kings 12:25–33) and others "who had set their hearts to seek the Lord" (2 Chron. 11:16), immediately recognized the legitimacy of the Jerusalem Temple. Third, Rehoboam fathers no less than twenty-eight sons and sixty daughters of his eighteen wives and sixty concubines. Fourth, despite Rehoboam's apparent foolishness, as reported in chap. 10, leading to the division of the kingdom, Chronicles nevertheless remarks upon his wisdom (2 Chron. 11:23). Such prosperity, the writer wants to say, is the reward of the faithful!

12:1–16, Rehoboam's Apostasy. Kings had reported (1 Kings 14:25–28) the invasion of Shishak, which is outlined also in that king's own annals. In line with his theology of retribution, the Chronicler adds his own comments in 2 Chron. 12:1 and in the words of Shemaiah in v. 7, making that disaster due to the fact that Rehoboam and "all Israel with him" *forsook* the law and so abandoned the Lord (cf. 1 Chron. 28:9). His words in 2 Chron. 12:6–8 are more nuanced, and perhaps specifics are out of place. The writer clearly wants to affirm both that Shishak executed punishment in some form upon Judah/Jerusalem because of Rehoboam's unfaithfulness and that because Rehoboam and Israel's leaders *repented* ("humbled themselves," vv. 6, 7 [twice], 12), they were spared complete destruction (vv. 7, 12). God will grant them "some deliverance" (v. 7), although they will be servants of Shishak. It may well be that the writer has tried to include here a description of the circumstances of his own age, which were themselves more complicated than simple formulas could describe.

The phrases evaluating conditions show something of that same ambivalence. Kings contains no evaluation of Rehoboam but does contain a more extended statement on the evils of Judah, including Judah's erection of idolatrous high places (1 Kings 14:22–24). Chronicles states that Rehoboam did evil and adds its own characteristic vocabulary, "for he did not set his heart to *seek* the LORD" (emphasis mine; cf. 1 Chron. 10:14). The statement that "conditions were good in Judah" (2 Chron. 12:12, RSV) is certainly unusual.

For vv. 15–16, see 1 Kings 14:29–31. The reference to the "Book of the Chronicles of the Kings of Judah" has again been replaced with two prophetic sources: Shemaiah (cf. 2 Chron. 12:5) and Iddo, previously named in 9:29.

13:1–22
The Reign of Abijah (ca. 915-913 B.C.)

The brief story of Abijam in 1 Kings 15 includes only the customary introduction (1 Kings 15:1–2; repeated here in vv. 1–2); a somewhat expanded statement of his evil ("he walked in all the sins which his father [i.e., Rehoboam] did before him," 1 Kings 15:3) contrasting him with David (vv. 4–6); the mention of his continual warfare with Jeroboam (v. 6); and a closing notice (vv. 7–8). Chronicles features, instead, a single battle between Abijah (perhaps a more "Yahwistic" form of the name Abijam) and Jeroboam, which serves as the stage for a lengthy speech of Abijah, surely reflecting the thought of Chronicles itself.

First, the "kingdom of the Lord" (2 Chron. 13:5, 8) has been given to David and his descendants for ever. Second, Jeroboam and his followers have *forsaken* God, rebelling against his chosen king Rehoboam when he was young

and immature (v. 6; cf. 1 Chron. 29:1) and replacing the legitimate ministry of priests and Levites with illegitimate priests serving "nothing gods" (2 Chron. 13:9), i.e., the golden calves who are pictured as being present with Jeroboam (v. 8). Third, the Lord is with Abijah and his people, however, who have not forsaken the Lord but have Aaronidic priests and Levites performing the services of God.

In such circumstances, of course, the course of the battle is never in doubt. Those who fight against the Lord cannot succeed (v. 12). The battle itself is related in terms reminiscent of holy war. Although Abijah's army numbers "only" 400,000 men versus Jeroboam's 800,000 —both unrealistically large numbers—the men of Judah, with priestly trumpeters at their head, cried to the Lord (v. 14) and shouted (v. 15), and "God defeated Jeroboam and all Israel before Abijah and Judah" (v. 15, RSV). With no fewer than 500,000 Israelites slain, the message of the battle is made explicit: "Thus the men of Israel were subdued at that time, and the men of Judah prevailed, because they relied upon the LORD" (v. 18, RSV). So, the writer surely wishes to state, those who are faithful to God will regularly triumph over their enemies!

Following the battle, additional evidence is given for the principle of retribution: Abijah captures cities in Israel, including Bethel, and takes them from Jeroboam (v. 19), "grows mighty" (v. 21), and has a large family of fourteen wives, twenty-two sons, and sixteen daughters (cf. 11:18–22); while, Jeroboam, on the other hand, never recovers his power, is smitten by the Lord, and dies (13:20).

The unknown prophet Iddo is again cited as the source for further information (v. 22; cf. 12:15), and Abijah is buried peacefully.

It is difficult to determine the reason the writer has used the reign of Abijah (whose evaluation as an evil king it was necessary to reverse) to introduce such a programmatic statement of faithfulness and illustrate it so elaborately. Perhaps, with Rehoboam's defeat before Shishak an established fact, Abijah's reign simply presented the first convenient opportunity to do so. At any rate, the picture of the "ideal Israel," with Davidic king and legitimate priesthood at its head, is here painted clearly.

14:1–16:14
Asa (ca. 913–873 B.C.)

Kings evaluates Asa very highly (cf. 1 Kings 15:9–24). Three items, however, would have been adverse to the theology of Chronicles: first, it is noted he had war with Baasha (1 Kings 15:16); second, he made a treaty with Ben-hadad of Damascus; third, in his old age he had diseased feet (1 Kings 15:23). With those problems in mind, Chronicles has expanded the sixteen verses of Kings into some forty-seven and divided Asa's reign, like that of Rehoboam, into two distinct periods.

14:1–15:19, Asa's Faithfulness. Asa is one of the kings most highly regarded by the Deuteronomistic historian, who concludes that his heart was "wholly true to the Lord all his days" (1 Kings 15:14). Asa even engaged in reforms of the system of worship and contributed to the Temple treasury (1 Kings 15:12–15). His only shortcoming was that the high places were not abolished (1 Kings 15:14), a criticism made of every king of Judah except Josiah.

In view of Asa's faithfulness, Chronicles expands this first and positive portion of Asa's reign. After rephrasing his cultic reforms (2 Chron. 14:3), Chronicles adds other signs of Asa's prosperity. Three times it is stated that the land had *rest* under him (vv. 1, 6, 7), marking a further development of the rest theology expressed most fully in 1 Chron. 22:8–10. Asa also engaged in building operations (the fact that they are listed as fortified cities is insignificant). In addition to the explicit statement that he *prospered* (cf. 1 Chron. 28:8), we are told he fielded an army of 580,000 from Judah and Benjamin. This happened because, in response to Asa's plea, the people had *sought* the Lord (2 Chron. 14:7).

As a further mark of Asa's prosperity, a battle with one Zerah the Ethiopian is recounted (vv. 9–15). Although Zerah had an army of a million men (!), Asa's cry to God indicates his trust in him (v. 11), so that Zerah and his army were totally decimated before "the Lord and his army" (v. 12). Notes of the "fear of the Lord" (v. 14) and the plunder of the enemy (vv. 13–15) add to the note of holy war and parallel the thought in 13:13–19. While it may be disputed whether a historical kernel underlies this account, in its present position it serves as an example of military victory following upon faithfulness.

2 Chron. 15:1–7 contains the words of Azariah, designated a prophet by the fact that the spirit of the Lord came upon him (v. 1), and is again full of the thought and vocabulary of Chronicles. This is true above all of vv. 2 and 4, where the doctrine of retribution is stated in classic form (*turned, sought, was found*). The specific time referred to in vv. 3–6 when Israel was without the true God, a teaching priest, or Torah is unclear, but the age of the judges is the most likely. More important are the marks of unfaithfulness cited and the resulting warfare and distress. In view of that negative example, Asa is exhorted to courage and action (v. 7).

2 Chron. 15:8–19 contains additional reforms. Azariah's exhortation leads Asa to renewed reforms, including, significantly, removal of (all?) idols from Judah, Benjamin, and "the cities which he had taken in the hill country of Ephraim" (v. 8, RSV). Thus Asa, like Rehoboam (11:16), welcomes converts from the north and, like Abijah (13:19), makes military incursions into the north. These reforms and his covenant with those from Judah and Benjamin as well as from Israel (Ephraim, Manasseh, and Simeon; 15:9) appear to presage those of Hezekiah and Josiah, which are similarly marked. The ceremonies attending this covenant, which is probably associated with the Feast of Pentecost in the third month, are described in terms similar to other festive events —trumpets, rejoicing, "all their heart," "whole desire," "was found by them"—such as David's coronation at Hebron (1 Chron. 12), Solomon's accession (1 Chron. 29), and the dedication of the Temple (2 Chron. 7). In conclusion, it is stated yet again that "the LORD gave them *rest* round about" (emphasis mine; 15:15).

2 Chron. 15:6–19 largely repeats 1 Kings 15:13–15, the removal of Asa's grandmother Maacah for her idolatry. But Chronicles has reconciled the statement of 1 Kings 15:14 that the high places were not taken away with its own position that Asa removed some high places (14:3) by adding "from Israel" (i.e., the north).

16:1–14, Asa's Faithlessness. Verses 1–6 describe Asa's war with Baasha of Israel and his alliance with Ben-hadad of Syria (cf. 1 Kings 15:16–22). The warfare that Kings notes as lasting throughout Asa's reign is here dated to his thirty-sixth year (v. 1; cf. 15:19). Baasha's embargo of Judah results in an alliance by Asa with Ben-hadad. In the holy war context, such an alliance is always a sign of lack of faith and calls for retribution (cf. Isa. 8:1–15; → Ban).

In 2 Chron. 16:7–10, the words of Hanani express Chronicles' theology. The prophet condemns Asa's lack of faith, recalls his victories over the Ethiopians and Libyans when he trusted in the Lord, and indicates that from now on he will have war. Asa not only rejects the words of the prophet but adds to his evil by having him imprisoned and inflicting other undefined cruelties upon the people.

Verses 11–14 recount Asa's last days. Asa's diseased feet, placed only in "old age" by 1 Kings 15:23, are dated by Chronicles in the thirty-ninth of his forty-one-year reign. Chronicles adds that even this final indignity did not lead Asa to trust, but that he turned to doctors instead. The burial notice is an expanded form of that found in Kings.

We could conclude that Asa is marked at his death as an unrepentant and faithless king. That would be to ignore the generally positive evaluation of him taken over from Kings, however, together with the extensive reforms and prosperity attributed to him earlier. It should be noted that the Chronicler's theology devotes no less than thirty-five of his years to peace and prosperity, with only the final five to warfare and bodily affliction. The total picture, therefore, is overwhelmingly positive and highly suggestive of the two kings evaluated most strongly by Kings and Chronicles, Hezekiah and Josiah.

17:1–20:37
Jehoshaphat (ca. 873–849 B.C.)

Chronicles contains some hundred verses devoted to King Jehoshaphat, of which some sixty-three (including most of chaps. 17, 19, and 20) have no parallel in the fifty verses of Kings. On the other hand, 2 Chronicles 20 is a nearly verbatim copy of 1 Kings 22.

Jehoshaphat was highly regarded by the Deuteronomistic historian, who concluded, as with his father Asa, that he did that which was right except that the high places were not removed (1 Kings 22:43). The Chronicler accordingly uses Jehoshaphat's reign to restate a number of his previous emphases and to add new dimensions to the work of the pious king, apparently finding only two matters in the account of Kings to which he felt it necessary to take exception.

2 Chron. 17:1–6 points to Jehoshaphat's prosperity. The story of Jehoshaphat begins by stating his faithfulness and presenting examples of the resulting prosperity. His building operations included garrisons not only in Judah, but also "in the cities of Ephraim which Asa his father had taken" (v. 2). Because he sought the Lord, God was with him and established his kingdom (v. 3). Jehoshaphat received tribute from Judah (sic) and had great riches and honor. Verse 6 even states, contrary to 20:33 (cf. 14:3), that he removed the high places from Judah. These are the regular marks of a pious king in Chronicles.

2 Chron. 17:7–9 describes Jehoshaphat's faithfulness further in that, in his third year, i.e., early in his reign, he sends a group of five princes, nine (or ten) Levites, and two priests throughout Judah teaching the book of the Torah (see also 19:4–11).

2 Chron. 17:10–19 describes Jehoshaphat's military might. The marks of God's blessing are again stereotypical. Jehoshaphat is feared by the surrounding nations, two of whom, the Philistines and Arabs, bring tribute. He builds fortresses and store cities and has an army of no fewer than 1,160,000 men, not counting those in the fortified cities throughout the land!

In 18:1–34, Jehoshaphat joins Ahab of Israel to fight against the king of Aram at Ramoth-gilead. Apart from vv. 1–2, which restate Jeho-

shaphat's honor and riches (cf. 1 Kings 22:1–2, where the position of Jehoshaphat is more honorific and Ahab more treacherous), these verses are almost a carbon copy of 1 Kings 22:3–35a.

The reason for the inclusion of the chapter is difficult to determine, since Chronicles will voice somewhat gentle exception to it (see 2 Chron. 19:1–3). Perhaps the writer, who is intensely interested in prophecy, was struck by the presentation of that phenomenon here. The only obvious tendentious alteration is in 18:31, where Jehoshaphat's outcry to God results in his being helped (cf. 1 Kings 22:32–33).

The writer somewhat surprisingly omits the rather gruesome details surrounding Ahab's death, even though it was in accord with the prophetic word (2 Chron. 19:1–3; cf. 1 Kings 22:35b–38). He is more interested in the safe return of Jehoshaphat to Jerusalem (2 Chron. 19:1) and in his meeting with the prophet Jehu, the son of the prophet Hanani who had prophesied to his father Asa (16:7). Jehu condemns Jehoshaphat for his association with the wicked Ahab, although the punishment is very general ("wrath has gone out against you from the Lord") and is immediately blunted by noting that "some good things" were found in him, including his destruction of the Asherahs and establishing his heart to seek the Lord.

2 Chron. 19:4–11 demonstrates Jehoshaphat's zeal for the Lord in that he personally undertakes "missionary work" to "bring back" the people "from Beersheba to the hill country of Ephraim" (v. 4; i.e., in both Judah and Israel) to God. Jehoshaphat appoints lay judges throughout the land, exhorting them to judge justly and impartially, and does the same with Levites, priests, and family heads in Jerusalem. This "supreme court" in Jerusalem had a priest in charge of religious matters and a representative of the king in secular matters, assisted by Levites. Jehoshaphat's final words to them (v. 11) are closely akin to the installation genre utilized by David in 1 Chronicles 22.

Since these verses are without parallel, it is disputed whether they have a historical basis or whether they might be a product of the writer's understanding of the name Jehoshaphat, which means "Yahweh judges." That priests and Levites at one time exercised a teaching and judicial function in Israel is clear (cf. Deut. 17:8–13); whether a specific example of that is given here is impossible to say with certainty.

2 Chron. 20:1–30 describes Jehoshaphat's battle of faith. In the face of attack by Moabites, Ammonites, and Meunites (see RSV footnote), Jehoshaphat responds as a faithful king should. He proclaims a fast throughout the land and assembles Judah to seek the Lord (vv. 3–4).

2 Chron. 20:5–12 contains Jehoshaphat's prayer. This prayer before the Temple in Jerusa-

lem, like David's earlier, points to the omnipotence of God and the impotence of the people without him (v. 6; cf. 1 Chron. 29:10–19). Drawing upon traditions as diverse as Abraham, the gift of the land, and the Temple (2 Chron. 20:7–9), Jehoshaphat casts himself and his people upon God's mercy. It is quite probable that the exilic or postexilic situation of the Jews is prominent here in the writer's mind (cf. the prayer in Neh. 9, which voices many similar themes).

The prophetic response to Jehoshaphat's prayer comes through Jahaziel, a member of the levitical choir (2 Chron. 20:14). Enveloped by the "fear nots" of the priestly oracle in vv. 15–17 is the reminder that the battle belongs to God, who will deliver his people without any need on their part to fight. In response, Jehoshaphat, Judah, the Jerusalemites, and the remaining Levites worshiped and praised God.

The battle, which might better be termed a liturgy, takes place in the wilderness of Tekoa. Jehoshaphat urges faith in God and his prophets (cf. Exod. 14:31) in order that they might succeed (cf. 1 Chron. 29:23). The appointed singers, obviously to be considered Levites, break forth with their favorite chorus, "Give thanks to the Lord, for his steadfast love lasts forever" (cf., e.g., 1 Chron. 16:41; 2 Chron. 5:13), and with the outbreak of their singing God's ambush of the enemy is sprung (20:21–23). In typical holy war language, the scene is described as one of panic in which Israel's enemies destroy themselves. When the people of Judah arrive, they find nothing but dead bodies, and nothing remains but to pick up the spoil, which requires no less than three days (v. 25).

The journey to the Jerusalem Temple is more like a choir procession, and the language that speaks of musical instruments (esp. trumpets), joy, and rejoicing is reminiscent of other occasions of great festivity (cf. 1 Chron. 15:25–28; 2 Chron. 7:1–10). Fear once again descends on the surrounding countries (20:29; cf. 17:10), and God gives Jehoshaphat rest, even as he has Solomon and Asa (1 Chron. 22:8–10; 2 Chron. 14:1, 6).

2 Chron. 20:31–34 reproduces 1 Kings 22:41–46 without significant alteration. The repetition of the statement that the high places were not taken away, which stands in conflict with 2 Chron. 17:6, is probably due to careless editing exhibited rather commonly by the writer, who appears unconcerned about this type of inconsistency. Finally, the Kings account refers us to the "Book of the Kings of Judah" for more information, while Chronicles refers to the words of Jehu in the "Book of the Kings of Israel."

1 Kings 22:47–50 is rewritten significantly in 2 Chron. 20:35–37. Trading alliances, like military alliances (16:7–9; 19:1–3), are obviously anathema to the writer. Eliezer prophesies destruction of a fleet built to go to Tarshish, and the result is as predicted.

21:1–20
Jehoram (ca. 849–842 B.C.)

Jehoram is the first king the Chronicler portrays as completely evil. In doing so, he again adopts the evaluation of Kings (2 Kings 8:18) and, in view of the material presented there (vv. 16–24), has no need to condition that judgment.

Of Jehoram, Kings had reported only his evil, together with the usual closing formulas. Kings appears to attribute Jehoram's evil to the fact that the daughter (or sister) of Ahab (i.e., the wicked Athaliah) was his wife; that, because of his promise to David, God refused to destroy Judah; and that Edom and Libnah revolted during his days.

The Chronicler includes almost all of this material, since it conforms perfectly to his scheme of retribution. He has however expanded his account significantly.

Verses 1–4 are a list of Jehoram's brothers. Although without parallel elsewhere, at least the names may well be based on a historical source. The statement of v. 3 that Jehoram was made king because he was the eldest at least suggests that he was otherwise unfit, and the notice that he murdered his brothers (v. 4) adds to that possibility.

Verses 5–10 are taken from 1 Kings 8:16–24, with only minor variations. Although the wording of the dynastic promise in 2 Chron. 21:7 appears to be sharpened, one somehow feels it has been done dispassionately, and it is not Judah, as in 1 Kings 8:19, but the house of David itself that is the benefactor of the promise. The portrayal of the Edomite revolt here (2 Chron. 21:8–10a), as in Kings, is unclear, but the outcome is surely meant to be negative for Jehoram and Judah. The final phrase of v. 10, "because he had *forsaken* the Lord" (emphasis mine), is the Chronicler's typical addition.

Verses 12–15 speak of a letter from the prophet Elijah, who may well have been dead by this time (cf. 2 Kings 2), condemning Jehoram for his unfaithfulness (2 Chron. 21:13; cf. v. 11) and promising a plague upon the nation and Jehoram's family in general and sickness for Jehoram in particular. The vocabulary and generalized nature both of Jehoram's "unfaithfulness" and of the resulting punishment strongly suggest this letter is a free composition of the Chronicler, who may well have felt that Elijah's activity, while centered in the north around Ahab, should include the similar activity of Athaliah in the south as well.

Verses 16–20 reflect the outcome of that prophecy. Philistines and Arabs revolt and despoil the king's house, his wives, and sons so that only Jehoahaz (who is the Ahaziah of 22:1) remains. Jehoram himself is smitten with an affliction of the bowels (21:18–19) and dies in pain and, quite obviously, in humiliation and disgrace. His burial notice (no fires [v. 19], "with no one's regret," "not in the tombs of the kings" [v. 20]) indicates the disdain of the public (and the writer) for him, as does perhaps the omission of the closing reference to other sources of material on his life (though present in Kings). Nobody, the writer seems to be saying, really cared.

22:1–9
Ahaziah (ca. 843–842 B.C.)

Verses 1–6 are taken from 2 Kings 8:25–29 with little variation. Ahaziah's mother, Athaliah, is cited as the cause for her son's evil (2 Chron. 22:2–3), as she had been for her husband earlier (21:6). Ahaziah's action in joining with Joram of Israel in war against Syria is also related more directly to evil counsel received from the house of Ahab (22:5; cf. 2 Kings 8:27).

Verses 7–9 represent a summary rewriting of 2 Kings 9:14–28, told here with the entire emphasis upon Ahaziah and provided with interpretative comments. Above all, it is stated that Ahaziah's death in visiting Joram was ordained by God (2 Chron. 22:7). There are other minor differences between the two accounts, such as the circumstances surrounding Ahaziah's death, and Chronicles adds the explanation that Ahaziah was buried because he was the grandson of Jehoshaphat, who sought the Lord with all his heart (v. 9).

22:10–23:21
Athaliah (ca. 842–837 B.C.)

For vv. 10–12, cf. 2 Kings 11:1–3. Athaliah takes advantage of the death of her son Ahaziah to kill the remainder of the royal family of Judah. Ahaziah's sister, Jehoshabeath (Kings: "Jehosheba"), however, hides her nephew Joash with her six years in the house of the Lord while Athaliah serves as the only queen ever to reign over Judah (or Israel). Chronicles makes explicit that this Jehoshabeath was the wife of Jehoiada the priest (v. 11), who appears unannounced in 2 Kings 11:4.

2 Chron. 23:1–15 recounts Jehoiada's revolution (cf. 2 Kings 11:4–16, with which our text is often in verbatim agreement). The Chronicler, however, includes the following in his account of placing Joash on the throne.

First, while Kings speaks of the captains of the Carites and of the guards (v. 4), i.e., various Temple officials, Chronicles pictures a much broader conspiracy involving five captains of hundreds (23:1) who gather the Levites from Judah and the heads of father's houses from Is-

rael to place Joash on the throne. Indeed, apart from Jehoiada, there is no explicit participation of priests and Levites in the Kings account.

For Chronicles, the priests and Levites alone enter the Temple (v. 6) and take up guard around Joash (v. 7). And while the participation of the people of the land is duly noted, the mention of Judah's obedience and the participation of the singers with their musical instruments is added (vv. 8, 13; cf. 2 Kings 11:9, 14).

Second, when Jehoiada presents Joash before the initial assembly, Kings states only that he showed them the king's son. Chronicles states dramatically: "Behold, the king's son. Let him reign, as the Lord spoke concerning the sons of David" (2 Chron. 23:3; cf. 2 Kings 11:4).

2 Chron. 23:16–21 contains Jehoiada's covenant. In 2 Kings 11:17–21 there is reference to two covenants, one religious and one civil. Chronicles speaks only of the religious covenant in which all agree that they should be the Lord's people. The scope of the reforms that follow, including destruction of the house of Baal, is the same in both texts, but the "watchmen" whom Jehoida installs for the Temple in Kings (11:18) are placed under proper levitical supervision, and opportunity is taken to add additional reference to their position with reference to Moses and David (vv. 18b–19). The notes of joy and peace and quietness voiced in 2 Chron. 23:21, however, are already found in the Deuteronomistic source (2 Kings 11:20; see 1 Chronicles, "Introduction"), another example of a note first sounded there but intensified in Chronicles.

24:1–27
Joash (ca. 837–800 B.C.)

On Joash, see 2 Kings 12, which affirmed that "Je[ho]ash did what was right . . . all his days, because Jehoida the priest instructed him" (v. 2, RSV), although the high places were not taken away. Kings, however, also contains two items incongruous with that position as understood by Chronicles: tribute paid to Hazael of Syria (vv. 17–18) and Joash's death in a conspiracy (vv. 19–21). Accordingly, Chronicles has characteristically retained the general evaluation of Joash as good but divided his reign into two distinct periods.

24:1–14, Joash's Faithfulness. 2 Kings 12:2 is rewritten so that Joash did good only so long as Jehoida the priest lived (2 Chron. 24:2). Verse 3, which speaks, though very briefly, of Joash's family, is probably to be considered a part of the indication of Joash's blessing (cf. 2 Chron. 13:18–21), as is the account of the reforms undertaken in vv. 4–14, a more drastic rewriting of 2 Kings 12:4–16.

While detailed comparison is impossible

here, Chronicles' rewriting characteristically gives more importance to the work of the Levites (vv. 5, 11), although, if the present text is a unit, vv. 5b–6 would mark a rare case in which the writer is critical of the Levites. Other changes, such as placing the offering chest "outside the gate of the house of the Lord" (v. 8) rather than "beside the altar" (2 Kings 12:9), reflect the writer's view of what was permitted in his own day. Once again, some of the problem is laid at the feet of Athaliah (v. 7). The writer also apparently considered it unlikely that sufficient money was not raised to pay both for Temple repair and for the precious vessels (v. 14; cf. 2 Kings 12:13–14).

24:15–16, Jehoiada's Death. The praise of the priest Jehoiada is indicated in that he lived no less than one hundred and thirty years and was buried among the kings.

24:17–27, Joash Under Judgment. This is 2 Kings 12:17–21 rewritten and expanded. The words are fully characteristic of Chronicles. Judah forsakes the house of the Lord, and "wrath came upon Judah and Jerusalem" (2 Chron. 24:18; cf. 19:2). The significance of the prophetic warning is both reminiscent of 12:12 and anticipatory of the final judgment upon Judah's fall in 36:12–16.

The prophetic message is delivered this time by a priest, Jehoiada's son Zechariah. Judah has *forsaken* the Lord and so has *been forsaken* by him (24:20; cf. 1 Chron. 28:9) and cannot prosper (cf. 1 Chron. 29:23). Zechariah's murder indicates a final refusal to respond to divine correction, and its mention in Luke 11:51 (as well as Matt. 23:35, where he is improperly called the son of Barachiah, confusing him with the literary prophet of the same name, Zech. 1:1) indicates that already at that time Chronicles stood near the end of the Hebrew canon.

Retribution is once again swift. The Syrian invasion (2 Chron. 24:23–24; cf. 2 Kings 12:17–21) is described both as a result of Judah's having forsaken the Lord and as an execution of judgment upon Joash. Missing, however, is any indication that Joash used the contents of the Temple treasuries to buy off Hazael (cf. 2 Kings 12:18).

For the closing notice, 2 Chron. 24:25–27, cf. 2 Kings 12:20–21. The conspiracy mentioned in Kings is here explicitly related to the murder of Jehoiada's son, and the two conspirators are designated as a Moabite and an Ammonite through their mothers, probably a further dishonor. Finally, Chronicles does not permit Joash to be buried among the kings (cf. 2 Kings 12:21). The work to which readers are referred for further information is here the "Midrash of the Book of Kings," a name found otherwise in the OT only in 13:22 and later used as the generic name for the imaginative explanation of a biblical text (of

which one might consider Chronicles one of the earlier examples). It is unlikely that the reference to this source or others in such notices was to any existing document.

25:1–28
Amaziah (ca. 800–783 B.C.)

For Amaziah's reign cf. 2 Kings 14:1–14, 17–22. Kings concludes that Amaziah did "what was right in the eyes of the Lord, yet not like David his father; he did in all things as Joash his father had done" (v. 3), although noting that the high places were not removed (v. 4). Chronicles states, instead, "he did what was right ... yet not with a blameless heart." After a brief and nonjudgmental note that Amaziah killed ten thousand Edomites and took Sela (v. 7), however, 2 Kings 14:8–14 reports that Amaziah was defeated in a war he had provoked with Jehoash of Israel and killed by his own people in a conspiracy (vv. 17–20).

Chronicles accepts Kings' basic evaluation with some difference in phraseology (v. 2) and omits reference to the high places. But vv. 5–13, without parallel in Kings, describe an action in which Amaziah, who has conscripted 300,000 from Judah and Benjamin and hired 100,000 from Israel, is confronted by a nameless prophet who tells him that "God is not with Israel, with all these Ephraimites" (v. 7) and that if he proceeds in this way, God will defeat him (v. 8). Amaziah somewhat reluctantly discharges the men from Ephraim and is victorious against the Edomites (v. 11, the only connection with 2 Kings 14:7). The men of Judah kill another 10,000, but those discharged by Amaziah fell upon cities of Judah "from Samaria to Beth-horon" (v. 13) and killed 3,000 people.

Verses 14–16 describe as a further consequence of the Edomite war that Amaziah set up Edomite gods, worshiped them, and rejected the advice of yet another prophet who condemned that action. Verses 17–24 repeat in essence Amaziah's defeat before Israel from 2 Kings 14:8–14, adding only a phrase indicating that this was God's decree, since they had sought the gods of Edom (2 Chron. 25:20). A similar addition in v. 27 indicates that the conspiracy against his life also began from the time when he turned away from the Lord. Unlike Joash, however (24:25), he is nevertheless buried "with his fathers" (v. 28).

26:1–23
Uzziah (ca. 783–742 B.C.)

Chronicles' method of portraying Uzziah is by now familiar. Kings had reported briefly concerning Uzziah, whom it usually names Azariah, that he did that which was right, that he reigned no less than fifty-two-years, and that he died a leper (2 Kings 14:21–22; 15:1–7). To illustrate and harmonize that data, Chronicles adds as examples of his prosperity, and perhaps in virtue of his unexcelled fifty-two-year reign, that he built Eloth and restored it to Judah (2 Chron. 26:2) and that his *prosperity* was due to his *seeking* God in the days of a certain Zechariah, whose identity is uncertain but who is surely to be considered a priest and who instructed him in the fear of God (v. 5; cf. 24:2).

Most extensively, however, Chronicles' additions in 26:6–15 depict those building operations, victory in warfare, large army (307,500), fame, and strength that were his so long as God helped him.

In contrast, vv. 16–20, likewise without parallel in Kings, explains Uzziah's leprosy. He was *unfaithful* to the Lord (vv. 16, 18; *see* 1 Chronicles, "Introduction") and became angry with Azariah and his eighty fellow priests when they warned him not to enter the Temple to burn incense, and so he broke out with leprosy.

The concluding notice is again altered to refer us to the annals of a prophet, Isaiah in this instance (v. 22), and Uzziah's burial place, while royal in some sense, is due to his leprosy and clearly not meant to be identical to that of the other kings (cf. v. 23 with 2 Kings 15:7).

27:1–9
Jotham (ca. 742–735 B.C.)

The brief account of Jotham in 2 Kings 15:32–38 notes, in addition to the expected formulas, only that Jotham did what was right "according to all that his father Uzziah had done" (v. 34), although the high places were not removed; that he built the upper (i.e., northern) gate of the Temple (v. 35); that in his days Judah began to be threatened by Syria and Israel (v. 37); and that he was buried with his fathers (v. 38).

One would assume, particularly with the mention of the impending warfare with Syria and Israel, that Jotham's reign would be divided into a good and bad portion as have those of other kings. Instead, Chronicles, accepting as usual the Deuteronomistic evaluation of Jotham as good, adds only that he did not enter the Temple as Uzziah had done (27:2), lists additional building activities on Ophel and in Judah (vv. 3–4), and has Jotham war successfully against the Ammonites, who pay him tribute for at least three years. The mention of the threat from Syria and Israel is omitted, and it is stated instead that Jotham "became mighty, because he ordered his ways before the LORD" (v. 6, RSV). His burial notice also is unchanged.

The reason for permitting Jotham such a perfect reign is difficult to determine and suggests either that the Chronicler simply had little information or interest in Jotham and was hurrying on to Ahaz and Hezekiah or that he was introducing here the pattern that he would use with Ahaz (all evil) and Hezekiah (essentially good).

28:1–27
Ahaz (ca. 735–715 B.C.)

Chronicles, like 2 Kings 16 (cf. esp. 2 Kings 16:1–4), views Ahaz as entirely evil. Verses 1–4 make his idolatry and apostasy more explicit.

Verses 5–8 tell of the Syro-Ephraimite war (cf. 2 Kings 16:5–6, rewritten and expanded here, and Isa. 7). The incursions of Syria, Israel, and Edom (2 Chron. 28:17) are here separated, Judah apparently suffering defeat before each in turn (vv. 5, 6, 17) "because they had *forsaken* the Lord" (emphasis mine; v. 6).

When the Israelites are returning 200,000 Judeans and much spoil to Samaria, they are, as is typical in Chronicles, met by "a prophet of the Lord," an otherwise unknown Oded, who expresses the Chronicler's thoughts: Judah has been given into their hand because of her unfaithfulness, but the anger of Samaria, who has "sins of her own" (v. 10), has exceeded the divine plan (v. 9). He urges them to return their kinsmen with the further warning that the wrath of God is upon them (v. 11).

Unlike many of the southern kings, the people of Samaria react positively to the prophet's warning. Under the leadership of certain men of Ephraim, named in v. 12, who confess that their guilt and God's anger upon them is great (v. 13), the captives are clothed, fed, and returned to Jericho.

In vv. 16–25, it is the threat of the Edomites (cf. 2 Kings 16:6) and Philistines that leads Ahaz to appeal to Assyria for help. Ahaz's faithlessness is repeatedly emphasized (2 Chron. 28:19, 21, 22–24), concluding with idolatry (which the writer defines as the "ruin of him and all Israel"! v. 23), the dismantling of the Temple vessels, and the closing of the doors of the Temple itself (v. 24)! As might be expected, Chronicles denies Ahaz a burial place with the kings (v. 27).

Thus, in immediate conjunction with the fall of the north to Assyria (30:6, 7), the south under Ahaz reverts to a position analogous to that of the north. A faithless king rules, idolatry is rampant throughout the country, and the Temple doors are shut. Indeed, the situation in the north is in some ways preferable to that in the south, for in the north there is found a prophet of the Lord, and those who listen to his voice, recognize their guilt and respond, if not in repentance, at least in obedience. The way is thus prepared for the work of Hezekiah, who will be, in the Chronicler's eyes, Judah's best king.

367

29:1–32:33
Hezekiah (ca. 715–687 B.C.)

Hezekiah is shown to be the king most favored by Chronicles by both content and by the sheer volume of space devoted to him. Of chaps. 29–31, only 29:1–2 have a parallel in Kings; chap. 32 is more closely related to 2 Kings 18–19.

29:1–36, The Rededication of the Temple.

On vv. 1–2, see 2 Kings 18:1–3. Chronicles accepts the high evaluation of Kings but omits at this point specific reference to Hezekiah's removal of the high places (cf. 31:1; 2 Kings 18:4), as well as the laudatory evaluation of 2 Kings 18:5–8, which states that there was none like him before or after him, that he trusted in the Lord (v. 5), that the Lord was with him, and he prospered (v. 7).

Hezekiah's charge to the Levites is contained in 2 Chron. 29:3–11. As it has done with David and Solomon, Chronicles moves immediately to Hezekiah's concern for the Temple. In the first month of his first year (cf. Ezek. 45:18–20), he opens the doors of the Temple, with the Levites even beginning work the first day (2 Chron. 29:17), thus reversing the work of Ahaz (cf. 28:24). Hezekiah's speech recalls that of David in 1 Chron. 28:2–10 and calls on the Levites to sanctify the Temple in view of the fact that the fathers have been *unfaithful, forsaken* the Lord (v. 6), and in effect closed the Temple (v. 8), thus incurring God's *wrath* and causing the captivity of their families (v. 9; cf. 28:23). The vocabulary of v. 10 recalls David's in 1 Chron. 28:2, and the closing charge to the Levites recalls David's to Solomon in 1 Chron. 28:9 –10.

The Levites, with fourteen representatives of all the significant groups named, begin their work on the first day and complete it on the sixteenth day of the first month, i.e., two days after Passover (2 Chron. 29:12–19).

Verses 20–24 contain the purgation offering. The "all Israel" nature of the offering is emphasized repeatedly in v. 24.

The Levites are installed in vv. 25–30 (on David's commandment, only here conveyed through the prophets Nathan and Gad; see esp. 1 Chron. 15–16; 2 Chron. 8:12–15). Primary attention falls on the musicians and singers and the joy with which they worshiped (29:30).

Verses 31–36 complete the dedication. The emphasis upon the willing heart recalls 1 Chron. 29:17–18. Sacrifices are so numerous that the Levites, described as more conscientious than the priests (2 Chron. 29:34), had to assist the priests. Verses 35–36 are parallel to 8:16, marking the conclusion of Solomon's work.

30:1–27, Hezekiah's Passover.

Hezekiah moves rapidly to celebrate the Passover on the fourteenth day of the second month, prescribed in Num. 9:3 as the date for those unable to do so in the first month.

2 Chron. 30:1–12 contains Hezekiah's invitation to "all Israel and Judah . . . Ephraim and Manasseh" (v. 1) and from Beersheba to Dan, the ideal limits of the land (v. 5). The couriers point to the faithlessness of the northerners and their plight in captivity to Assyria (vv. 6–8), inviting them to the Temple in Jerusalem, "which he has sanctified forever," and urging them to repent so that their brothers and sons might return to the land (v. 9).

The courier's message is met with mocking by many in the north, but some men (to be preferred to the "only a few" or "however, a few" of the RSV) *repent* and come to Jerusalem. In Judah too God gave the people *one heart* to do what the king and princes commanded "by the word of the Lord" (v. 12).

Verses 13–27 describe the Passover. The priests and Levites are shamed by the zeal of the laity, who cleanse Jerusalem of illegitimate altars (vv. 14–15). In view of the ritual uncleanness of many from the north (Issachar is here added to the tribes named in v. 11), Hezekiah offers a particularly gracious prayer for the people (v. 19), so that God hears and forgives them (v. 20). The festival is celebrated with great joy for fourteen days, as was Solomon's feast of dedication (2 Chron. 7:8–10). The final acknowledgement of prayer heard recalls Solomon's prayer in 7:12–15.

31:1–21, Other Religious Reforms.

The chapter is without parallel in Kings. 2 Kings 18:1–8 had spoken of reforming actions of Hezekiah, including removal of the high places in Judah. Chronicles, however, envisions "all Israel" engaged in a massive reform that resulted in the removal of the high places not only in Judah and Benjamin but in Ephraim and Manasseh as well (31:1).

Verse 2 details the appointment of the priests and Levites (cf. esp. 8:12–15, 16, where Solomon's similar act marks the conclusion of the Temple narrative).

Hezekiah's offerings (31:3–10) recall Solomon's in 2 Chron. 7:5; the generosity of the people recalls that of David and the people in 1 Chron. 29:1–9 and the tabernacle narrative upon which that was dependent. Notice especially the blessings (v. 8; cf. 1 Chron. 29:10, 20; 1 Kings 8:55) and the overabundance of offerings (v. 10).

Storerooms are prepared for "the contributions, the tithes, and the dedicated things" (vv. 11–12, RSV), and placed in charge of the appropriate Levites. Allotments are also made to the priests living throughout the land, although the details of vv. 16–19 are far from clear.

Verses 20–21 summarize Hezekiah's reign. Notice the characteristic words of Chronicles:

seeking, the *whole heart,* and prosperity (*see* 1 Chronicles, "Introduction").

32:1-33, Hezekiah and Assyria; Hezekiah's Last Days. For the Assyrian crisis (vv. 1-23), see 2 Kings 18-20; Isaiah 36-39. The Chronicler's introduction (v. 1) suggests a change in Hezekiah's fortunes at this point, but as vv. 20-23 make clear, that is not the case.

The Chronicler's rewriting of his sources here evidences considerable skill. The account of Hezekiah's capitulation to Sennacherib in 2 Kings 18:14-16 is omitted, probably as inappropriate to Hezekiah's faithfulness, although the text of Kings is confused here (*see* 2 Kings, "Commentary"). 2 Chron. 32:2-8 reflects preparations taken by Hezekiah for warfare, which are themselves signs of the blessings of God that he enjoyed as a result of his faithfulness: building operations and military provisions (vv. 3-6). Hezekiah's brief exhortation (vv. 7-8) echoes themes heard throughout the work: be strong; don't be afraid; God is with us (cf., e.g., 1 Chron. 22:13; 2 Chron. 19:5-7; 20:15-17, 20).

2 Chron. 32:9-19 (esp. vv. 9-15) is more closely related to 2 Kings 18:19-35. God responds to the prayer of Hezekiah and Isaiah (2 Chron. 32:20), and the result in the somewhat disparate material of 2 Kings 19:7, 35-37 is reshaped and summarized nicely in v. 21. Verses 22-23 apply God's deliverance not only to Hezekiah's victory over Sennacherib but to all his enemies. Hezekiah, like Solomon and Asa before him (1 Chron. 22:8-10; 2 Chron. 14:5), enjoys *rest,* gifts are brought to the Temple and to Hezekiah, and he is honored before all nations.

2 Chron. 32:24-33 tells of Hezekiah's last days (on v. 24, cf. 2 Kings 20:1). Hezekiah's sickness, which would appear unjustified in view of the writer's theology, serves here only as a prelude to his failure to respond appropriately to the healing granted him (2 Chron. 32:25, 31). His pride resulted instead in *wrath* upon him, Jerusalem, and Judah (v. 25). On account of his *repentance,* however, that wrath, which in 2 Kings 20 related to exile to Babylon, was not to come during the days of Hezekiah.

2 Chron. 32:27-33 gives more examples of Hezekiah's prosperity—riches, building operations, and prosperity (cf. 31:21; 32:22-23). His closing notice is altered to refer us to the prophet Isaiah, and the note is added that he was buried with the sons of David and that all Jerusalem and Judah did him honor.

In summary, despite difficulties presented in the source, including foreign invasion and sickness, Hezekiah is considered more favorably than any king after Solomon. Indeed, in many ways his reign marks a reversal of that of Ahaz and is pictured as parallel to that of Solomon. Solomon ruled over a united Israel, completed the construction of the Temple, and set in motion the personnel and service of the Temple; Hezekiah rededicates the Temple, reestablishes those same services, restores the ideal of the single central sanctuary, and, perhaps most significantly, brings north and south together in a common worship. That picture is surely the one that the Chronicler wishes to set before his readers as ideal and divinely approved.

33:1-20
Manasseh (ca. 687-642 B.C.)

Cf. 2 Kings 21:1-18, which is wholly negative about Manasseh.

33:1-9, Manasseh's Wickedness. Verses 1-9 are essentially identical with 2 Kings 21:1-9, depicting Manasseh's fifty-five-year reign and wickedness. Notice the parallel of David and Solomon already in v. 7 of Kings.

33:10-13, Manasseh's Captivity and Repentance. Verses 10-13 are without parallel in Kings and commonly considered unhistorical. Assyrian records list Manasseh as a vassal, but there is no suggestion that he rebelled. While it is quite likely that he may have had to appear before the Assyrians at some such place as Damascus, as did Ahaz (2 Kings 16:10), his deportation here to Babylon (v. 11) is striking and may indicate, as has been suggested, that Manasseh, in both his exile and repentance, is being considered a type of the Exile. The tradition of Manasseh's prayer of repentance is continued in the Prayer of Manasseh recorded in the Apocrypha (→ Prayer of Manasseh, The).

33:14-17, Manasseh's Prosperity and Reforms. The prophetic summary of 2 Kings 21:10-15 pictures Manasseh as Israel's archvillain, as a result of whose sins Jerusalem and Judah will be destroyed without remnant. (This prophetic censure may be that referred to in 2 Chron. 33:10, the ignoring of which led to Manasseh's captivity.) In *repentance,* however, Manasseh is restored, and these verses, again without parallel, picture Manasseh as the typical pious king, engaged in building operations and even in the reform of worship. The sole negative note remaining is the continued existence of the high places.

33:18-20, Closing Notice. In addition to the usual inclusion of a prophetic reference (here, anomalously, the "Chronicles of the Seers"), this notice too includes repeated reference to Manasseh's repentance and God's acceptance of that prayer, obviously matters of great importance for the writer. Chronicles has retained the burial notice of Kings, which has Manasseh buried on his own property rather than with the other kings (cf. 2 Kings 21:17-18).

33:21–25
Amon (ca. 642–640 B.C.)

Kings pictured Amon as evil like his father Manasseh (cf. 2 Kings 21:19–26); since the Chronicler viewed Manasseh as repentant, he has had to modify his report accordingly, adding that Amon "incurred guilt more and more" (v. 23, RSV). The conspiracy that led to his death is also reported in Kings. Chronicles omits his burial place, in the gardens of Manasseh.

34:1–35:27
Josiah (ca. 640–609 B.C.)

For 2 Kings 22–23, Josiah was the king without equal, who, on the basis of the book of the law found in the Temple in the eighteenth year of his reign (i.e., 622 B.C.), undertook extensive religious reforms, including removal of the high places in both south and north. Nevertheless, because of the wickedness of Manasseh, the Lord remains firm in his resolve to destroy Jerusalem.

34:1–7, Josiah's Reforms. On vv. 1–2, cf. 2 Kings 22:1–2, repeated here almost verbatim. Verses 3–7, however, are without parallel and place the beginnings of the reform in Josiah's eighth and twelfth years. While described much more briefly here than in 2 Kings 23 (since much of the work has been assigned to other kings, especially Hezekiah), that reforming work does include the removal of the high places both in Judah and Jerusalem and in Manasseh, Ephraim, Simeon, and as far as Naphtali (vv. 3, 6).

34:8–28, The Book of the Torah. Verses 8–28 are very similar to 2 Kings 22:3–20, with typical alterations. Josiah's officials are specifically sent to repair the house of Lord (2 Chron. 34:8) and deliver money that the Levites had collected from north and south (cf. 24:4–14, where they are restricted to the south only, v. 9). It is added that the work was under the direction of the Levites, who are nonetheless skillful musicians (34:12–13). Verse 21 adds "those left in Israel" to Judah as the object of Josiah's inquiry.

Verses 22–28 are reproduced closely from 1 Kings 22:14–20, which exhibits a number of facets of the Deuteronomistic theology that has also broadened in Chronicles. This is true in particular of Judah's *forsaking* the Lord, occasioning the outpouring of God's *wrath* (2 Kings 22:17). Josiah was also "penitent" (RSV; perhaps better translated "immature"; cf. 1 Chron. 29:1 and 2 Chron. 12:7) and *humbled himself* (2 Kings 22:19), repeated and reemphasized in 2 Chron. 34:27. As in Kings, Josiah's repentance spares him the sight of the impending destruction.

34:29–33, Josiah's Covenant. Cf. 2 Kings 23:1–3. Notice again a familiar theme of Kings adopted by Chronicles, "with all his heart and all his soul" (v. 31; cf. 2 Kings 23:3). Josiah's role in pursuing the covenant is more pronounced, and "all the people" who joined in the covenant are identified as those present in Jerusalem and Benjamin (2 Chron. 34:32). The two uses of Israel in v. 33, however, may apply just as well to the north or to *both* north and south.

35:1–19, Josiah's Passover. At this point Kings includes the details of Josiah's reform (2 Kings 23:1–23), which conclude with a brief mention of the Passover (vv. 21–23). Chronicles has inserted these at the beginning of Josiah's reign and now elaborates extensively the Passover proceedings, as if to climax Josiah's reign.

Emphasis here falls, as might be expected, on the proper appointments and ceremony, perhaps reflecting these as they were in the author's own day. The work of David and Solomon is considered primary, both in the construction of the Temple (2 Chron. 35:3) and in the levitical arrangements (v. 4). The reason for the apparent change in levitical function given in v. 3 is not apparent, but the change is probably meant to be significant. The generosity of Josiah (v. 7) and his officers (v. 8) provides yet another bridge with similar ceremonies in the book, as does the participation of the Levites, singers, and gatekeepers, who are apparently here (v. 15) not considered Levites.

Verse 16 recalls the completion of Solomon's work in 8:16 and Hezekiah's in 29:35. The reference to Samuel in v. 18 is problematic. 2 Kings 23:22 speaks of the age of the judges, and it is possible that the author here simply wants to list a prophet from the end of that era, one who also marks the beginning of the monarchy (cf. also the reference to Solomon at Hezekiah's Passover in 2 Chron. 30:26). Josiah's Passover would thus seem to be given wider significance, encompassing "all Judah and Israel who were present" (35:18), though this is perhaps due only to the Kings source the author had before him.

35:20–27, Josiah's Death. Cf. 2 Kings 23:28–30. Chronicles omits 2 Kings 23:24–25, including the highly laudatory words of v. 25. Josiah's death in battle at the hands of Pharaoh Neco has obviously presented some problems for the writer's understanding of God's ways in history, and he has accordingly included a command from Neco as inspired prophecy, disobedience to which occasioned Josiah's death. Other minor alterations in the narrative are probably due to the attempt to make Josiah's fate more compatible with the earlier words of Huldah's prophecy (2 Chron. 34:27–28). Jeremiah's lament in his honor is not preserved, and the reference is not to our book of of Lamentations. The omission of the customary burial notice and other variations in this final section have suggested to some the use of another source than Kings.

36:1–23
The Last Kings of Judah

The writer moves rapidly, almost prosaically, over the details of 2 Kings 23:31–25:30, omitting much but also adding considerable comment of his own. It is obvious that the final fate of the nation has already been determined.

36:1–4, Jehoahaz (609 B.C.). Cf. 2 Kings 23:30–34. Omitted is the name of his mother, the evaluation of him as evil (cf. Jer. 22:10–12), his bondage in Riblah, and the reference to his death, which is replaced with mention of his deportation to Egypt.

36:5–8, Jehoiakim/Eliakim (ca. 609–598 B.C.). Cf. 2 Kings 23:34–24:6. Striking is Chronicles' brevity, omitting Jehoiakim's taxation (2 Kings 23:35), his rebellion against Nebuchadnezzar (24:1), and the important rationale for Judah's destruction (24:2–4), including mention of the Chaldeans, Syrians, Moabites, and Ammonites (and, according to the Septuagint, the Samaritans) as God's instruments to destroy. Instead, Chronicles adds mention of a captivity of Jehoiakim in Babylon (36:6) and of a deportation of some of the Temple vessels to Babylon (v. 7).

36:9–10, Jehoiachin (ca. 598/597 B.C.). Cf. 2 Kings 24:8–17, drastically abbreviated. Verses 10b–16a are omitted, which recount the exile of the king, his family, at least a sizable portion of the population of Jerusalem, and all the treasures of the Temple and the palace, with specific mention that the golden vessels Solomon had made were cut in pieces. Chronicles mentions only the exile of Jehoiachin and the "precious vessels" of the Temple.

36:11–16, Zedekiah (ca. 597–587 B.C.). Cf. 2 Kings 24:18–25:17. In vv. 12b–14, without parallel in Kings, the writer gives the reason for Judah's destruction. Zedekiah did not *humble himself* before Jeremiah, who spoke from the mouth of the Lord. He also rebelled against Nebuchadnezzar after swearing an oath to him by God (cf. 2 Chron. 35:21–22 and Ezek. 17, esp. v. 16). The priests and people are also characterized as unfaithful and as having polluted God's holy house (2 Chron. 36:14).

Nevertheless, as we have seen repeatedly, their ultimate sin was their failure to respond to the prophetic voice in repentance. Because of God's mercy he sent prophet after prophet, but they were scorned and mocked until finally there was no more forgiveness (vv. 15–16; cf. 7:14; see 1 Chronicles, "Introduction").

36:17–21, The End of Judah. Verses 17–21 are comparable to 2 Kings 25:1–21, but different in important ways. Kings had emphasized the destruction of the remainder of the city, the poorest of the people, less valuable items from the Temple, and the leaders of Zedekiah's government. Chronicles concentrates instead upon the Temple and its vessels, which are pictured as both carried to Babylon (v. 18) and destroyed (v. 19), and indicates that the entire population was killed or deported (vv. 17, 20). The land thus lies empty and fallow, enjoying a "sabbath rest" for seventy years until the rise of Persia (i.e., about 539 B.C.), in fulfillment of the prophecy of Jeremiah and as a supposed punishment for the failure to observe that rest throughout at least a significant period of its history (v. 21, cf. Jer. 25:11–13; 29:10–14; Lev. 26:34–39).

36:22–23, Cyrus's Edict. Verses 22–23, essentially identical with Ezra 1:1–3a, raise the vexing problem of the original conclusion and the purpose of the Chronicler's work (see 1 Chronicles, "Introduction"). The rise of Cyrus the Persian is here associated with the fulfillment of the prophecy of Jeremiah. Yahweh has "stirred up" Cyrus to make his proclamation that Yahweh has both given him all the kingdoms of the earth and commanded him (Cyrus!) to build him a Temple in Jerusalem. The stage is thus set for Israel's return from the Exile and for the rebuilding of the Temple.

Bibliography

Ackroyd, P. R. *I & II Chronicles, Ezra, Nehemiah.* Torch Bible Commentary. London: SCM, 1973.

Braun, R. L. *1 Chronicles.* Word Biblical Commentary, 14. Waco, TX: Word, 1986.

Coggins, R. J. *The First and Second Books of Chronicles.* Cambridge Bible Commentary on the New English Bible. Cambridge: Cambridge University Press, 1976.

Myers, J. M. *1 Chronicles.* Anchor Bible, 12. Garden City, NY: Doubleday, 1965.

———. *2 Chronicles.* Anchor Bible, 13. Garden City, NY: Doubleday, 1965.

Williamson, H. G. M. *1 and 2 Chronicles.* New Century Bible Commentary. London: Marshall, Morgan, & Scott, 1982.

———. *Israel in the Books of Chronicles.* Cambridge: Cambridge University Press, 1977.

Wilson, R. R. *Genealogy and History in the Biblical World.* New Haven, CT: Yale University Press, 1977.

EZRA

RALPH W. KLEIN

INTRODUCTION

The Book of Ezra contains a theological history of the postexilic community, from the first return in 538 B.C. to the end of the first year of Ezra in 457 B.C. Ezra 1–6 describes the return from the Babylonian exile and the rebuilding of the Temple; Ezra 7–10 describes the first year of the work of Ezra.

While the majority of the book is written in the standard Hebrew of the postexilic period, Ezra 4:8–6:18 and 7:12–26 are written in imperial Aramaic. The first of these sections contains letters sent to the Persian kings Artaxerxes or Darius and their replies (4:8–16; 4:17–22; 5:6–17; 6:3–12), but it also contains Jewish narrative that connects these letters to one another. The narrative was one of several sources available to the author of the book of Ezra. The second section, 7:12–26, is the Persian king's commission to Ezra.

The account of the work of Ezra, conventionally called his memoir, consists of paragraphs written in the first person (7:27–9:15), as well as in the third person (7:1–26; 10:1–44; Neh. 8, and part of Neh. 9:1–5). All of the Ezra memoir may once have been written in the first person and may come from Ezra himself. It is probable that Nehemiah 8 originally stood between Ezra 7–8 and 9–10 and that Neh. 9:1–5 stood between Ezra 10:15 and 10:16.

Williamson proposes that the Ezra memoir and Nehemiah memoir (see Nehemiah, "Commentary") were combined about the year 400 B.C. into a work that juxtaposed the lives of the two great leaders of the restoration and brought their careers to a climax in Nehemiah 8–10. This document, basically Ezra 7:1–Neh. 13:31, lay before the editor who composed Ezra 1–6. By adding the latter chapters in about the year 300 B.C., he wanted to show that the Jerusalem Temple of his day and its form of divine service were the legitimate successors of pre-exilic Israel. Other scholars believe that Ezra and Nehemiah are part of the Chronicler's history, which consists of 1 and 2 Chronicles, in addition to Ezra and Nehemiah (see 1 Chronicles, "Introduction").

According to Ezra 1–6, the LORD brought about the return of the exiles and the rebuilding of the Temple through the favorable actions of the Persian kings. The book seems to foster a collaborative attitude toward the Persians. This may explain the absence of any reference to the Davidic ancestry of Sheshbazzar and Zerubbabel.

The book of Ezra is concerned about the purity of the community in Jerusalem and gives the impression that this community was made up primarily of those who returned from exile. Continuity with pre-exilic Israel is based on the return of the Temple vessels through Sheshbazzar and on the restoration of both the altar and the Temple on their former sites. The delay in the building of the Temple is not blamed on the people's concern for their own comforts (as in Hag. 1:4) but on the actions of the enemies of Judah and Benjamin, who persistently opposed the work in Jerusalem and disheartened the people. The celebration of the Feast of Tabernacles after the completion of the altar (Ezra 3:4–5) anticipates the joyful dedication of the Temple (6:16–18) and the equally joyful observance of the Passover a few months thereafter (6:19–22). The Temple was completed by Zerubbabel, the governor, and Jeshua, the high priest, with the hearty endorsement of the prophets Haggai and Zechariah.

Ezra, who was linked to Aaron by his genealogy and to Moses by his attitude toward the law, was sent by the Persian king in 458 B.C. to make inquiries about conformity to the law in Judah and Jerusalem and to appoint officials to teach the law. When a problem arose about intermarriage with peoples of the land, Ezra appointed a commission to remove the foreign wives and children and so to create a purified community. For Ezra's additional actions on behalf of the law—reading and teaching it publicly—and the people's subsequent covenant to keep the law's prescriptions, see Nehemiah, "Commentary," chaps. 8–10.

COMMENTARY

1:1–6:22

Return from Exile and Rebuilding of the Temple

1:1–4:7

A Narrative in Hebrew

1:1–11, The Return Under Sheshbazzar.
Cyrus the Persian began his rule in Babylon in

October 539 B.C. His permission for the Jews to return home is seen in Ezra as the fulfillment of a prophecy made through Jeremiah (Jer. 29:10) that the LORD would bring the exiled Judeans home after a seventy-year captivity. The author expresses in these opening verses a positive, collaborative attitude toward the Persian authorities of his day (cf. Isa. 44:24–45:6). The generosity of Cyrus to the Jews was part of a wider policy toward all the peoples held captive in Babylon (→ Cyrus II; Persia). The Hebrew decree issued by Cyrus (Ezra 1:2–4) is paralleled by a similar Aramaic record in 6:3–5. The Hebrew copy of the decree provides for the repatriation of the Jews in addition to the rebuilding of the Temple. It is unclear whether these verses are an authentic document available to the author (perhaps the text of a herald's proclamation) or whether the author created this decree on the basis of 6:3–5.

Those Jews who elected not to return to Jerusalem were urged to offer financial support to those who planned to return (v. 4). Only members of the tribes of Judah and Benjamin were present in Babylon and available for the return. The clergy consisted of priests (descendants of Aaron) and Levites (non-Aaronidic descendants of Levi, who were assigned the less important tasks in the system of worship). That the return pleased God is shown by the reference to all who returned as "those whose spirits God had stirred up." Material assistance from gentile neighbors makes the return resemble the Exodus from Egypt (cf. Exod. 3:21–22; 11:2–3; 12:35–36).

The Jewish leader of the return was Sheshbazzar, the prince (Ezra 1:8) or governor (5:14) of Judah. Appointed by Cyrus and entrusted with the Temple vessels (1:7–11), he laid the foundation of the Temple (5:14–16; but see 3:10–12). Sheshbazzar is a Babylonian name ("May the sun god Shamash protect the father"), although he is clearly Jewish. Recent studies have undermined the proposed identification of him with Shenazzar (1 Chron. 3:18). The length of his tenure at the head of the restoration community is unknown but was probably fairly brief.

The Temple vessels themselves establish a continuity between the Solomonic Temple and the postexilic Temple, lending an aura of authenticity to the latter. An exilic prophet had also announced that the returning exiles would bring the vessels of the LORD home (Isa. 52:11–12).

2:1–70, The List of Those Who Returned.

This list presupposes that Zerubbabel has replaced Sheshbazzar (v. 2). Zerubbabel is called the son of Shealtiel in 3:2, 8; 5:2 (cf. Neh. 12:1) and in the book of Haggai (where he is also given the title of "governor," Hag. 1:1; 2:2), but a genealogy in 1 Chron. 3:17–24 makes him the son of Shealtiel's younger brother, Pedaiah. It is possible that Pedaiah was his physical father, while Shealtiel was his father according to the rule of levirate marriage (Deut. 25:5–10). In any case, the genealogy in 1 Chronicles identifies him as a descendant of David. The silence about this in Ezra may result from the author's acceptance of Persian domination and the absence of any hope for deliverance through the Davidic house. The list may be a composite summary of a number of returns to Palestine made during the reigns of Cyrus and his successor, Cambyses. Some have taken it as a census of Judah from about the time of Nehemiah (cf. Ezra 2:2). A copy of this list, with many variations in the numbers and in spelling of names, appears in Neh. 7:6–73, which is probably its original location.

The list of leaders in Ezra 2:2 should include a twelfth, Nahamani (cf. Neh. 7:7). Jeshua was the grandson of Seraiah, the last chief priest before the destruction of Jerusalem (2 Kings 25:18). Laity are listed in Ezra 2:3–35 (identified by family in vv. 2–20 and by place of residence in vv. 21–35); priests (about one-tenth of the total population), a few Levites (cf. Ezra 8:15), and other Temple personnel (Temple servants and Solomon's servants [cf. 1 Kings 9:20–21]), in Ezra 2:36–58; and those who could not prove their ancestry, in vv. 59–63. The latter were excluded temporarily from the priesthood until a high priest could be installed who could consult Urim and Thummim, the dicelike objects that had been used in earlier days to determine God's will in matters that were beyond human wisdom (→ Urim and Thummim). The "governor" mentioned in v. 63 is designated by a Persian term (*tirshata'*). It is not clear whether the author intended to refer to Sheshbazzar, Zerubbabel, Nehemiah, or some other official. Since the vast majority of people could prove their ancestry, the continuity between the restored community and the community before the Exile is affirmed (cf. the twelve leaders mentioned in v. 2).

The whole assembly numbered 42,360, plus some 7,337 male and female servants and 200 singers (vv. 64–65). The totals cannot be harmonized with the numbers assigned to the individual families in the list (did copyists make errors, or do the larger totals include women?). The high number of servants may indicate that the postexilic community was not so impoverished as many assume. The gifts for the Temple (2:68–69) are discussed in Neh. 7:70–72, where the text is more nearly complete. The priests, Levites, and some of the people settled in Jerusalem, but all the rest of the people returned to their own towns (v. 70). The list presupposes that the community in Palestine was composed almost exclusively of Jews who had been in exile (cf. Jer. 24:4–10). Though this does not conform to historical fact, it does reflect the exalted station of the eastern Diaspora in the author's theology.

3:1–6, The Reestablishment of the Altar. Jeshua (identical with Joshua of Hag. 1:1) and Zerubbabel, the joint leaders of the restoration community, reestablished the sacrificial altar on its old site—thus stressing continuity with preexilic Israel. The LORD himself had indicated where the altar of burnt offering for the first Temple should be by answering David's petition at the threshing floor of Ornan (1 Chron. 22:1). The restored altar was presumably made of unworked stones, as prescribed in the Mosaic law (Exod. 20:25). While occasional sacrifices had taken place in Jerusalem during the Exile (Jer. 41:5), the returning leaders may have considered the existing altar unclean.

Fear of hostile neighbors led to scrupulous observance of the law in hopes of ensuring God's protection (Ezra 3:3), but it also kept the community from engaging in other building projects at this time (cf. 4:4–5). The text implies that the altar was set up in September 538, but the major period of activity for Jeshua and Zerubbabel was in 520 and later. The author may have mistakenly identified Zerubbabel with Sheshbazzar. In any case, he emphasized that regular worship was initiated without delay.

The people celebrated the Feast of Booths or Tabernacles (Heb. *Sukkot*), which began on the fifteenth day of the seventh month, and offered up daily sacrifices required for this feast (cf. Lev. 23:33–36 and the detailed laws of Num. 29:12–38). Thereafter, all appointed feasts were kept (Ezra 3:5), surely including Passover/Unleavened Bread, the Feast of Weeks (Pentecost; *Shavuot* in Heb.), and Booths again (Lev. 23).

3:7–13, The Foundation of the Temple Laid. Though sacrifices began on the first day of the seventh month (September 17, 538), the foundations of the Temple were not yet laid (3:6) or, perhaps, "the Temple was not yet repaired." It is possible that the activities described in these verses were actually undertaken during the reign of Darius, while the altar itself was restored during the reign of Cyrus. The second year mentioned in v. 8 is the second year of the exiles' work on the house of God, not the second year after their return from exile. With the permission of Cyrus, they arranged for cedar logs to be imported from the Phoenician cities of Sidon and Tyre. Logs had also been imported for the Temple in Solomon's time (2 Chron. 2:16). Joppa was located just north of the modern city of Tel Aviv. The masons and carpenters who were hired for the reconstruction (Ezra 3:7) recall similar workers who were used in building Solomon's Temple (1 Chron. 22:2, 15).

Levites twenty years of age or older were appointed to supervise the work, although Mosaic law set the minimum age limit at thirty (Num. 4:23, 30) or at twenty-five (Num. 8:24).

Perhaps it was necessary to lower the age limit because of the few Levites who were part of the community (Ezra 2:40–42).

The ceremony at the beginning of the repairs echoes the dedication of Solomon's Temple (1 Kings 8; 2 Chron. 5–7) and of David's bringing the Ark to Jerusalem (1 Chron. 15–16). The cymbals were played by the levitical sons of Asaph (Ezra 3:10), who are identified in 2:41 as singers. Their song (v. 11) appears to be a citation of Ps. 106:1 and the refrain in Psalm 136, praising the LORD in advance for the completion of the Temple. The Levites, who once had been assigned to carry the Ark, were given new duties by David after the Ark was placed permanently in the Temple (cf. 1 Chron. 15–16; 23–26; 2 Chron. 7:6; 29:25–26).

While most of the people shouted when the repairs were begun, many of the older priests, Levites, and other leaders, who had seen the Solomonic Temple years earlier, cried. Did some fear they would not live long enough to see the completion of the Temple? Or did the plans for the restored Temple seem pale by comparison with the original (cf. Hag. 2:3; Zech. 4:10)? The din from the combined shouting and weeping aroused the attention of hostile neighbors (4:1), with nearly disastrous consequences.

Throughout this chapter the theme of continuity plays an important role. The altar was placed on its old site and erected according to the law of Moses. The Feast of Booths was kept "as it is written," and there are many parallels between the repairs of the Temple and the construction and dedication of the first, Solomonic Temple. Even the singers praised the LORD according to the directions of David. The author of chap. 3 is building an argument against those who might question the validity of the postexilic Temple and its worship.

4:1–3, Offer of Assistance Refused. The noise created by the rites of 3:10–13 attracted the attention of hostile neighbors, who offered to assist with the building of the Temple and who claimed to have worshiped the God of Israel since they had been brought to Palestine by the Assyrian emperor Esarhaddon (681–669 B.C.), presumably to fill a gap left after the Assyrian deportation of the population in 721. Their offer was categorically rejected. Why?

A passage from 2 Kings 17:41 suggests that the new residents in Samaria were syncretistic, worshiping the LORD but also their native deities. The Jewish community in Ezra argued that they alone had been commissioned for this work by Cyrus.

4:4–5, Opponents Stop the Building of the Temple. Once their offer to help had been rejected, the people of the land employed various strategies to frustrate work on the Temple. Work on the Temple had begun under Cyrus (559–530), and it was only resumed under Darius I (522–486).

4:6–7, Summary of Letters. These verses describe negative reports about the Jews that were sent to the Persian authorities long after the completion of the Temple, first in the reign of Ahasuerus (Xerxes), 486–465, and then in the reign of Artaxerxes I, 465–424.

4:8–6:18
A Narrative in Aramaic

Aramaic was the official diplomatic language of the Persian Empire. The document incorporated into the text contains a number of official records and a Jewish narrative. It is currently debated by scholars whether only the letters themselves (4:8–16; 4:17–22; 5:6–17; 6:3–12) were available as sources to the author of Ezra or whether the correspondence had been woven together into an Aramaic chronicle prior to its editing by the bibical writer.

4:8–16, A Letter from Rehum to Artaxerxes. Rehum and other Samarian leaders wrote to the Persian king that Jews who had returned from exile had attempted to rebuild the walls of Jerusalem and that this effort constituted rebellion and could lead to a decrease in revenue for the king. The Samarians claimed to have been settled in Palestine by Osnappar, that is, Ashurbanipal (669–627 B.C.). "Beyond the River" (Trans-Euphrates) is an administrative title for the area from the river Euphrates to the Mediterranean. The words of v. 14 suggest that the Samarian officials and the Persian authorities were treaty partners (cf. the "salt of the covenant" in Lev. 2:13; Num. 18:19; 2 Chron. 13:5) who required mutual support of one another. They informed the king that the state records of his predecessors, including those of the Babylonian kings, would show that Jerusalem had always been rebellious and that was the reason that it was destroyed in 587 B.C.

4:17–23, The Reply of Artaxerxes and Its Consequences. The Persian king replied to the Samarians that a search through the state records had confirmed their accusations: Jerusalem had constantly been rebellious. Since some of his predecessors had ruled over "Beyond the River" and been successful in collecting taxes (v. 20), Artaxerxes made a decree that the work on the walls of Jerusalem should be brought to an immediate end. Perhaps this failed attempt to rebuild the walls of Jerusalem lies behind the report of Jerusalem's broken walls and destroyed gates at the beginning of Nehemiah

(Neh. 1:2–3). After receiving the king's reply, the Samarian officials immediately went to Jerusalem and brought the work of the Jews to a halt through the use of force.

4:24, Work on the Temple Stopped. This verse treats vv. 6–23 as a digression and continues the story of v. 5, where the people of the land had stopped work on the Temple from the time of Cyrus to that of Darius. The digression justifies the Jewish rejection of help from their neighbors, since subsequent history proved that the Samarians had no positive interest in the restoration of Jerusalem.

5:1–5, Opposition to Renewed Temple Building. Haggai and Zechariah, whose words are preserved in the canonical books named after them, gave prophetic support to the efforts of Zerubbabel and Jeshua to rebuild the Temple (cf. 3:8). Tattenai, the governor of "Beyond the River," asked the Jews if they had proper authorization for rebuilding the Temple, but he did not stop their construction projects while he sought a ruling from higher Persian officials. His leniency is interpreted as God's providence: "The eye of their God was on the elders of the Jews" (v. 5).

5:6–17, A Letter from Tattenai to Darius. This letter repeats and expands upon information provided in vv. 1–5. The technique of building with courses of stone interspersed with wood is known from other places in the ancient Near East (cf. 1 Kings 6:36; 7:12; Ezra 6:4). In vv. 11–17 is the Jews' defense of their building activities. They claimed that the God of heaven and earth was the deity whose Temple they were rebuilding—such a God would require a magnificent building. Because of the sins of their ancestors, God had delivered them to the Babylonian king, Nebuchadnezzar (606–562), who destroyed the first Temple and exiled the population (2 Kings 25). Cyrus, here identified as king of Babylon, granted permission for the Jews to rebuild the Temple on its former site in the first year of his reign (cf. 1:3), and he restored to them the ceremonial vessels that had been removed from the first Temple. Sheshbazzar, to whose care the vessels were entrusted and who had also been named governor (cf. 1:8) by Cyrus, repaired the foundations and began the rebuilding of the Temple immediately after his return. In chap. 3, the laying of the foundations is credited to Zerubbabel and Jeshua during the reign of Darius. The ascription of this work to Sheshbazzar and the claim of uninterrupted work on the Temple (which contradict 4:4–5, 24; Hag. 1:2, 4, 9) seem to be attempts by the restoration community to impress the Persian authorities that the edict of Cyrus had not been ignored. Tattenai and his associates ask that the Jewish

375

claims be checked against the official records in the city of Babylon. As it turned out, the records actually were found in Ecbatana, the summer residence of the Persian kings (6:2).

6:1–12, Darius Replies. The king began his reply to Tattenai and his associates with a quotation of the original decree of Cyrus (vv. 3–5). This decree authorized the building of the Temple, with support from the royal treasury, and it provided for the restoration of the Temple vessels to the Jewish community. If this Persian financial support had actually been provided, it is hard to imagine why the Temple was delayed as long as it was. Strangely, the decree mentions only the height and breadth of the building. If the length is restored from the account of Solomon's Temple (1 Kings 6:17, 20), the Temple would be a cube, 60 cubits on each side. But since this would make it much bigger than Solomon's Temple (60 cubits long, 20 cubits broad, and 30 cubits high), this reconstruction is unlikely. Perhaps the text should be restored to make the new Temple have the same dimensions as Solomon's.

Darius endorsed the earlier provisions and ordered the group associated with Tattenai not to interfere with the Jews. He also mandated financial support for the building project and for the daily sacrifices. In exchange for this support, he asked that prayers be offered for the life of the king and his sons. Cyrus made a similar request in a famous inscription: "May all the gods whom I have settled in their sacred cities ask daily Bel and Nebo for a long life for me" (see James B. Pritchard *Ancient Near Eastern Texts,* p. 316). Jeremiah too had urged the exiles to seek the welfare of the city where they had been taken as captives and to pray on its behalf (Jer. 29:7). If people dared to change the decree of Cyrus or disobey it, they would be impaled and their houses destroyed (Ezra 6:11).

The governor referred to in 6:7 is probably Zerubbabel, although the immediate context of this verse might suggest Sheshbazzar (cf. 5:14). In v. 12 the decree refers to the God who has caused his name to dwell in Jerusalem, which is so similar to a characteristic phrase of Deuteronomy (e.g., Deut. 12:11) that one suspects that a Jewish scribe helped give expression to the royal decree.

6:13–15, Completion of the Temple. Tattenai and his associates complied with the king's decree, and the building of the Temple went forward with the support of the prophets Haggai and Zechariah. Neither Zerubbabel nor Jeshua is mentioned in these verses. It is often proposed that Zerubbabel's term of office ended before the Temple was finished. God's command and the Persian decree enabled the elders (cf. 5:5, 9) to finish the task. The mention of Artaxerxes is out of place in v. 14, since he ruled long after the dedication of the Temple. Perhaps his provisions for the Temple at the time of Ezra (7:12–27) led to the addition of his name here. The Temple was finished on March 12, 515 (or on April 1, 515, if the word "third" in v. 15 is emended to "twenty-third" to avoid making the work end on a Sabbath day).

6:16–18, Dedication of the Temple. More than seven hundred animals were sacrificed at the dedicatory rites, although Solomon had offered up almost sixty times as many (1 Kings 8:63)! The priests and Levites were installed according to their divisions and courses. While 1 Chronicles 23–26 ascribed these divisions to David, the author here traces them back to the time of Moses (cf. Exod. 29; Lev. 8; and Num. 3, 4, and 8).

6:19–22
The Celebration of the Passover

The language is Hebrew once more. Passover was celebrated by those who had returned from exile and by those who had separated themselves from the surrounding pollutions. The joy at Passover and the subsequent seven-day celebration of the Feast of Unleavened Bread expressed the people's thanksgiving for the assistance of Darius, who is here given the unusual title of "the king of Assyria."

7:1–10:44
The Initial Work of Ezra

7:1–26
A Third-Person Narrative About Ezra

7:1–10, Ezra's Return. Ezra is provided with a genealogy that traces his ancestry back to Aaron, the chief priest. Seraiah, identified in the genealogy as Ezra's father, preceded him by about 150 years, since he was a pre-exilic high priest (1 Chron. 6:14). Perhaps Ezra's father was in fact a different Seraiah, and the names between his father and the pre-exilic priest of the same name were lost accidentally. Ezra is also called a scribe skilled in the law of Moses. He may have been secretary of state for Jewish affairs in the Persian bureaucracy. The law that he desired to teach is the Pentateuch, although it is impossible to tell whether it was identical with the present text of that document. The seventh year of Artaxerxes I was 458 B.C. (Many scholars in the past have put Ezra in the time of the second Artaxerxes, that is, at 398.) The period intervening between his reign and the last date of the previous chapter, 515, is passed over in silence. Ezra was accompanied by laypeople (the people of Israel) and clergy (priests, Levites, singers, gatekeepers, and Temple servants; cf. 8:1–14). His nine-hundred-mile trip lasted about fourteen weeks, from the twelfth day of the first month (April 8) to the first day of the fifth month (August 4).

7:11–26, The Letter Commissioning Ezra.

Verse 11 provides a Hebrew introduction to the letter that, like other governmental documents, is written in Aramaic. The letter commanded Ezra to lead Jews to Jerusalem (v. 13); deliver gifts to the Temple from the Persian authorities, the people of Babylonia, and Babylonian Jews (vv. 15–18); make inquiry about compliance with the law in Judah and Jerusalem (v. 14: 10:16–17); and appoint magistrates and judges to teach the law (7:25).

The law of Moses was very likely already known in Judea (cf. 7:25), and those who did not yet observe it were to be instructed to do so. Artaxerxes required the treasurers to support the Jewish community with grants and to exempt the clergy from various kinds of taxation (7:21–24). The grants were enormous. One hundred talents of silver, for example, was the amount of tribute paid by all Judah to Pharaoh Neco (2 Kings 23:33). Ezra 7:23 suggests that Israel's God would be angry with the king and his sons if the grants were not paid. God's law is equated with the king's law in v. 26; failure to obey it could be punished with execution, banishment, confiscation of goods, or imprisonment.

7:27–9:15

A First-Person Narrative About Ezra

7:27–28, Doxology.

This first person account, written in Hebrew, thanks God for giving Artaxerxes the idea of beautifying the Temple (by improving its worship practices) and for giving Ezra favor before the Persian authorities.

8:1–14, The List of Those Who Returned with Ezra.

After naming the priests from the lines of Phinehas and Ithamar first (unlike Ezra 2), the list identifies some fifteen hundred laymen from twelve families, suggesting that the total number of persons with Ezra was about five thousand. Hattush (v. 2), a descendant of David (cf. 1 Chron. 3:22), heads the list of laypeople.

8:15–36, Ezra's Trip to Jerusalem.

Ezra discovered that no Levites had decided to make the trip with him. Perhaps they had heard of the inferior status that would be afforded them in the land of Israel. Ezra's urgent request of Iddo for additional returnees led to 38 Levites joining his entourage, plus 220 Temple servants to assist the Levites. As in chap. 2, the Temple servants, whom David is credited with establishing, outnumbered the Levites. The names of the river Ahava and of the place Casiphia are otherwise unknown.

Ezra proclaimed a fast before he set out on the trip home to secure God's protection on the way. While Nehemiah was provided with a military escort (Neh. 2:9), Ezra refused to ask for similar help. He had assured the king that his God would protect all who seek him, and to request an escort from the Persian king might seem to express doubt about God's ability to care for his own.

Ezra entrusted the gifts he was bringing along to twelve priests, who were responsible for them until they could be turned over to the authorities in Jerusalem. Six hundred and fifty talents of silver would amount to nineteen tons; a hundred talents of gold would be three tons. Clines estimates that Ezra's entire treasure would be equal to the annual income of one hundred thousand to five hundred thousand people. These inflated totals may be an attempt to give glory to the Temple, or they may result from a misunderstanding of the original figures in the list.

The delay caused by the need to recruit Levites led to a departure of Ezra's entourage from Babylon on the twelfth day of the first month (8:31; cf. 7:9). They arrived in Jerusalem safe and sound—delivered from the hand of the enemy and from ambushes—and rested three days before turning over the gifts to two priests and two Levites (8:33).

Ezra and the other exiles offered a series of sacrifices in thanksgiving for their safe arrival. All the numbers given are multiples of twelve, which may imply that the restoration community was the legitimate continuation of the twelve tribes of pre-exilic Israel. The king's officials in "Beyond the River" offered financial assistance for the returnees in their conduct of the Temple worship. The final two verses of the chapter describe the returnees and their actions in the third person and so are not an original part of the first-person narrative.

9:1–5, Crisis over Mixed Marriages.

Pentateuchal law ruled out marriage with the inhabitants of Canaan (Exod. 34:11–16; Deut. 7:1–6) for fear that "their daughters would play the harlot after their gods and make your sons play the harlot after their gods" (Exod. 34:16). In Ezra's time there was intermarriage with the non-Jewish peoples of the lands, who are denoted in Ezra 9:1 by a stereotyped list of the pre-Israelite inhabitants of the land. The marriages were between Jewish men and non-Jewish women; the officials of the community led in this offense. Ezra dramatically expressed his shock and fasted, while he was surrounded by faithful Jews who trembled at the contrast between the law of God and the behavior of their fellow Jews.

9:6–15, Ezra's Prayer. Ezra confessed the sins of Israel throughout its history but also noted the gracious actions of God that had restored the Jewish community within the Persian Empire and had allowed them to repair the Temple. The recent sin of intermarriage violated commandments given by the prophets, prohibiting the marriage of Jewish men or women with outsiders. The law as stated occurs in none of the extant books of the Prophets, though its essential content is recorded in the pentateuchal laws cited in the previous paragraph. Since Ezra no doubt regarded Moses as a prophet (Deut. 18:15; 34:10; Hos. 12:13), such laws could be considered prophetic. Ezra claimed that the calamities Israel had experienced were less than the nation deserved (cf. Isa. 40:2), and he proposed that the sin of intermarriage raised the possibility that God would wipe out the community completely. While individuals had intermarried, the whole community bore the responsibility and faced the consequences of this guilt.

10:1–44
A Third-Person Narrative About Ezra

10:1–17, Decision to Expel Gentile Wives and Children. The people echoed Ezra's confession of sin and entered into a covenant to expel the foreign wives and their children from Ezra's religious community. Ezra spent a night fasting and mourning in the chamber of Jehohanan the son of Eliashib (v. 6). Those who date Ezra to 398 have seen this meeting with Jehohanan as crucial since Eliashib was the high priest in Nehemiah's time (Neh. 3:1). Jehohanan, then, would have been high priest at the end of the fifth century and the beginning of the fourth century (cf. Neh. 12:22–23). Cross, however, suggests that the names of another Eliashib and J(eh)ohanan have fallen out of the list of high

priests before the Eliashib of Nehemiah's time, and this reconstruction allows the dating of Ezra to 458. Others suggest that Jehohanan was not a member of the high-priestly family at all.

When the community assembled during inclement weather to express its contrition, it requested the creation of a special commission to carry out the removal of the gentile wives and their children. Only four men expressed opposition. Did they want more severe actions? The assembly met on the twentieth of the ninth month (December), Ezra appointed the commission on the first of the tenth month, and the work was completed on the first day of the first month. Within a year of Ezra's departure from Babylon (cf. Ezra 7:9), a purified community had been created in Jerusalem.

10:18–44, The List of Those Involved in Mixed Marriages. There were twenty-seven clergy (members of the high priest's family, other priests, Levites, singers, and gatekeepers) and eighty-four to eighty-six laity (in twelve family divisions) who had intermarried—out of a community of some thirty thousand. The problem was largely confined to the upper strata of the society (cf. 9:2).

Bibliography
Clines, D. J. *Ezra, Nehemiah, Esther.* New Century Bible Commentary. Grand Rapids, MI: Eerdmans, 1984.
Cross, F. M. "A Reconstruction of the Judean Restoration." *Journal of Biblical Literature* 94 (1975):4–18.
Holmgren, F. *Ezra and Nehemiah: Israel Alive Again.* International Theological Commentary. Grand Rapids, MI: Eerdmans, 1987.
Myers, J. M. *Ezra-Nehemiah.* Anchor Bible, 14. Garden City, NY: Doubleday, 1965.
Williamson, H. G. M. *Ezra, Nehemiah.* Word Biblical Commentary, 16. Waco, TX: Word, 1985.

NEHEMIAH

RALPH W. KLEIN

INTRODUCTION

The Book of Nehemiah contains an account of the career of Nehemiah, the story of Ezra's public reading of the Torah (instruction), and a number of lists from the postexilic period. Nehemiah 1–7 describes Nehemiah's return to Palestine and his rebuilding of the wall of Jerusalem; Nehemiah 8–10 depicts Ezra's reading of the law and the responses to it; Nehemiah 11–13 reports further acts of Nehemiah.

The history of Nehemiah is based primarily on the Nehemiah memoir, an autobiographical narrative in which the author frequently appeals to God to remember him and hear his prayer (1:1–7:73a; 12:31–43 [partly]; 13:4–31). A first edition of this memoir (chaps. 1–7) may have been composed a year or two after Nehemiah's arrival in Jerusalem in 445 B.C. A second edition, contained in the present book of Nehemiah, gives Nehemiah credit for a number of later reforms in the community (see esp. chap. 13).

The materials dealing with Ezra are drawn primarily from the Ezra memoir (see Ezra). Nehemiah 8, the present text of which makes Ezra and Nehemiah contemporaries, is thought to have dealt originally only with Ezra and to have had a location within the Ezra memoir between Ezra 8 and 9. An earlier version of Neh. 9:1–5 may have been located between Ezra 10:15 and 10:16 or at the end of Ezra 10.

About the year 400 B.C., an editor combined the Ezra memoir with the Nehemiah memoir, thus juxtaposing the lives of the two great leaders of the restoration and bringing their careers to a joint climax in Nehemiah 8–10. He added, from the Temple archives and other sources, the prayer in Neh. 9:6–37, the pledge to keep the law in Nehemiah 10, the report of the repopulation of Jerusalem in Neh. 11:1–2 (plus vv. 3–20), and an expanded description of the dedication of the walls in Neh. 12:27–43. A later hand provided the lists in 11:21–12:26. Toward the end of the fourth century, an editor added Ezra 1–6 to the Ezra-Nehemiah narrative and produced the present books of Ezra and Nehemiah.

The book of Nehemiah can be summarized as follows: Nehemiah, authorized by the Persian authorities, led a group of Jewish exiles home and rebuilt the walls of Jerusalem despite the persistent opposition of Sanballat of Samaria and his allies. Nehemiah corrected abuses dealing with loans and the charging of interest and generously provided for others at his table, with no help from the taxes enjoyed by former governors (chap. 5). He also resolved to relocate to Jerusalem people whose genealogy could be correlated with the list of those who returned with Zerubbabel (chap. 7).

Before the actual repopulation of Jerusalem had taken place, the people requested Ezra to read them the law (8:1). This reading was explained by the Levites and heard by the people with a mixture of joy and weeping. On the basis of their study of the law, the people revived the correct celebration of the Feast of Tabernacles (8:17). Thereupon, the people separated themselves from foreigners and confessed their sins (9:1–3). After a speech rehearsing the history of Israel's sinning and the LORD's repeated benefactions (9:6–31), the community entered into a covenant to walk in God's law and to do all his commandments (10:28).

This purified community relocated one of every ten persons from local towns to Jerusalem (11:1–2) and then dedicated the walls (12:27–43). Lists identify those who lived in Jerusalem (11:3–24) and in the villages (11:25–36) and those who served as priests, Levites, and high priests at various times in the restoration period (12:1–26). The final paragraphs of the book report reforms effected by Nehemiah (12:44–13:31).

COMMENTARY

1:1–7:73a

The Return of Nehemiah and the Rebuilding of the Walls of Jerusalem

1:1–11, Nehemiah's Response to the Destruction of Jerusalem's Walls. In November/December (the Jewish month Chislev) of 445 B.C. (the twentieth year of Artaxerxes I), Nehemiah, who lived in Susa, one of the three capitals of the Persian Empire, received a discouraging report about the physical condition of Jerusalem (→ Shushan; Persia). Hanani, who delivered the report, was a brother of Nehemiah.

Nehemiah engaged in various acts of sorrow (weeping, mourning, and fasting), during which he confessed his own sin and that of the people. According to the kind of retributive theology characteristic of Deuteronomistic thought, sin was the moral cause of the Exile and of the dismal state of affairs in Jerusalem. The formulaic list in v. 7 does not allow us to identify the specific sins he may have had in mind. Verses 8–9 are a loose paraphrase of Deut. 30:1–5. Nehemiah identified the people in Jerusalem as heirs of the original group that experienced God's redemption in the military acts of the Exodus (Neh. 1:10; cf. Deut. 9:29). He prayed that God would remember the promise revealed to Moses and bring about the restoration that was supposed to follow acts of repentance.

In addition, Nehemiah appealed to the LORD to pay attention to the prayer of himself and the people—whose obedience and dedication to God are indicated by the term "servants" (Neh. 1:6, 10)—and to give him a favorable response from "this man" (i.e., Artaxerxes I).

A cupbearer tasted the king's wine to thwart assassination attempts and also guarded the royal living quarters. Some Septuagint manuscripts identify Nehemiah as a eunuch instead of a butler, but this is probably only a confusion in the Greek text and not a reflection of the Hebrew. Nehemiah's opponents would have used his condition as a eunuch to disqualify him for leadership in the community (cf. Deut. 23:1) if he had in fact been castrated.

2:1–10, Artaxerxes Authorizes Nehemiah to Return and Rebuild the Wall.

Four months later, Nehemiah found an opportunity to present his case before the king. The king's solicitous question about his depression led to great anxiety in Nehemiah. A royal official should not bother the king with his own personal problems! But Nehemiah revealed his concerns, after praying to the God of heaven (cf. 1:4–5), wishing the king a long life and referring to the spoiled condition of his home city, where his ancestors had been buried. His silence about the name Jerusalem may mean that he knew of the city's rebellious reputation among Persian officials (cf. Ezra 4:9–16).

The king's favorable attitude toward Nehemiah may have been enhanced by the queen's presence, before whom the king may have wanted to appear generous. Her name was Damaspia, as we are told in the classical writer Ctesias. Perhaps the king was also generous because of the start of a new year (the incident is dated to Nisan, the first month of the Jewish year). Nehemiah named a time span for his absence, which surely was not as great as the twelve years that his first term in Jerusalem actually lasted (Neh. 5:14). In addition, he requested safe passage and a supply of lumber from the royal forest to use in repairing the gates and walls and in building (or repairing) a house for himself. Nehemiah attributed the king's generosity to the intervention of God's good hand (cf. Ezra 7:9; 8:18).

Accompanied by a military guard (cf. Ezra, who refused such a guard, Ezra 8:22), Nehemiah presented his credentials to the governors of the various provinces through which he passed. Two officials, however, were displeased by his coming, and Nehemiah interpreted their opposition to him as hostility toward the Israelites as a whole. Sanballat, whose name is of Babylonian derivation ("May the moon god Sin give life"), was governor of Samaria, though Nehemiah never uses this title in connection with him. Instead, he calls him the Horonite, which may be a term of derision. Sanballat continued as governor of Samaria until at least 407 B.C.; the names of his two sons, Delaiah and Shelemaiah, known from the Elephantine papyri, show that he was a worshiper of Yahweh (the ending "iah" is a shortened form of the name Yahweh). Tobiah, the other opponent, who also has a Yahwistic name, is called an Ammonite. According to the Pentateuch, Ammonites were to be excluded from the worship assembly of Israel (Deut. 23:3), but Tobiah had ingratiated himself with some of the rulers in Jerusalem (Neh. 6:17–18; 13:4–5), and this was no doubt an irritant to Nehemiah. Tobiah was probably an assistant to Sanballat rather than the governor of Ammon (→ Sanballat; Tobiah).

2:11–15, Inspection of the Walls.

Nehemiah inspected the walls and gates by night before he informed the Jewish officials what his plans were. The city at the time of Nehemiah included the Temple area and the spur to its south, called Ophel (→ Color maps 15 and 16). He left the city by the Valley Gate, which exited into the Tyropoeon (or Central) Valley, and proceeded around the city in a counterclockwise direction. The Dung Gate (through which rubbish was removed from the city) and the Fountain Gate were on the southern end of Ophel. His difficulty in traversing the east side of the city may have been caused by the collapse of a series of terraces built there in monarchical times.

2:16–20, Opposition to Nehemiah's Plans.

When Nehemiah reported on his inspection tour to the Jewish officials, he made mention of his divine and political authorization (v. 18). A ruined Jerusalem brought its people and its God into disrepute (v. 17; cf. 1:3). The people immediately accepted Nehemiah's proposal to rebuild the walls and gates, but strong opposition was raised by Sanballat, Tobiah, and a previously unnamed Geshem, who controlled vast areas south and east of Jerusalem. The opponents ridiculed the project and suggested that Nehemiah was engaged in rebellion against the Persian Empire. Nehemiah, in reply, called on the God of heaven (cf. 1:5; 2:4) and denied his opponents civic, legal, and liturgical rights in Jerusalem.

3:1–32, A List of Those Who Worked on the Wall.

Despite the fact that this list is at times obscure and incomplete, it is of great value to geographers of Jerusalem and Judah in the postexilic period. Five administrative centers are mentioned (Jerusalem, v. 9; Beth-haccherem, v. 14; Mizpah, vv. 15, 19; Beth-zur, v. 16; and Keilah, vv. 17–18). The area included in Judah was perhaps less than half of the preexilic kingdom of Judah (cf. the area of pre-exilic Judah [see Color map 7] with that of later Judea [see Color map 11]). On the north and west, the workers were able to repair the older walls and gates (vv. 1–15), but on the eastern side a whole new wall had to be constructed closer to the crest of Ophel (vv. 16–32). Archaeologists have found remnants of this wall that are 2.75 meters thick.

Eliashib (v. 1) was high priest during the time of Nehemiah (cf. Ezra 10:6). The Sheep Gate (Neh. 3:1, 32) was probably on the eastern end of the northern wall; the Fish Gate (v. 3) was on the northwest corner, facing the Mediterranean Sea; the Water Gate (v. 26) was on the east, near the spring of Gihon (since Nehemiah's wall was built to the west of the pre-exilic city wall, the old Water Gate was outside the new wall); the Horse Gate (v. 28; cf. Jer. 31:40) was also on the east, near the Temple area (note that priests did the work on this area of the wall).

4:1–5, Ridicule by Opponents.

Sanballat and Tobiah made fun of Nehemiah's efforts and scoffed at his ability to build a formidable defensive wall. Nehemiah's prayer is much like the imprecatory psalms (e.g., Ps. 109), which wish harm to one's enemies. The Hebrew text of Neh. 4:4 has a play on words between the words "despised" and "plundered." The acts of the opponents deserved a punishment to fit their crime. Nehemiah identified the hostility toward the Jews as a sin that would provoke God's own anger. Since God clearly intended that Jerusalem should be reestablished, any opposition to the building plans was opposition to God himself.

4:6–23, Wall Building and Guard Duty.

As building on the wall progressed, so did the opposition—Sanballat and Tobiah on the north, the Ammonites on the east, the Arabs on the south, and the Ashdodites on the west. While the enemies planned to disrupt the project by guerrilla raids (v. 11), the Judeans themselves were losing their morale. Verse 10 seems to be a lament song, bemoaning their loss of strength and the abundance of the debris.

The Jews who lived away from Jerusalem appealed to those working in Jerusalem to escape danger by returning home (v. 12). Nehemiah, however, rallied his workers by assembling them and reminding them of the capabilities of the LORD as a great warrior (vv. 14, 20; cf. Exod. 15:3). He urged the people to fight for their families and their homes. This assembly was held in an exposed place so that it might impress the opponents with the military capabilities of the Jews.

Nehemiah divided his workers into three groups. One contingent served as soldiers, armed with various kinds of weapons (Neh. 4:16). Another group, the porters, reserved one hand for their labors and the other for a weapon (v. 17). The builders themselves, who needed both hands for their task, had a short sword girded on their side (v. 18).

Since the circumference of the city was about 1.5 miles, Nehemiah appointed a trumpeter to rally the forces in case of crisis. He also lengthened the work day from the usual sunset (Deut. 24:15) to the time when the stars appeared. He increased both security and efficiency by eliminating the daily commuting to the workers' hometowns. All spent the night in Jerusalem, fully dressed, and ready for any emergency. Nehemiah not only claimed credit for all of these innovations, but he also set an example of readiness himself.

5:1–13, Socioeconomic Problems.

A severe famine and the need to pay royal taxes forced a number of Judeans into an economic crisis. In order to get food, people offered their sons and daughters as pledges for loans (v. 5). Others mortgaged their fields, vineyards, or homes. A third group went into debt to pay their taxes.

A cry of moral outrage (v. 1) arose because children, especially daughters, were being sold into debt slavery to their fellow Judeans (cf. Exod. 21:7–11). Since all the crop money went to creditors, there was nothing left over that they could use to redeem their children (Neh. 5:5). Nehemiah was enraged, and he contended with the moneylenders who were mistreating their own flesh and blood. The point at issue seems to involve the practice of demanding pledges from debtors, rather than with the taking of interest (despite the translation in RSV; → Loan).

Previously, Jews had been buying back their sisters or brothers who had been forced to sell themselves into debt slavery to gentile masters. But now people were selling themselves into slavery to fellow Jews, with the result that the community had to use its precious money to pay off Jewish creditors. Nehemiah urged his colleagues to stop such outrageous loan practices. Anything taken in pledge—fields, vineyards, olive orchards, and houses—should be returned to its rightful owner.

The creditors agreed to follow Nehemiah's reforms, and he sealed their commitment with an oath administered by the priests. In a symbolic curse, he asked that anyone who did not follow through on these reforms be shaken out, like pockets. By their "amen," the creditors agreed to be bound by the stipulations of the oath.

5:14–19, Nehemiah's Generosity. Nehemiah's first term as governor lasted from 445 to 433/432 B.C. In distinction from his predecessors, he refused the governor's food allowance, which amounted to about 40 shekels of silver a day (roughly one pound). His piety and his sympathy for the people's heavy tax burdens (vv. 15, 18) were behind this generous policy. Nehemiah persisted in his work on the wall at considerable expense and assigned his servants to fill in wherever they were needed. Daily he fed some 150 officials in addition to numerous foreign guests. One modern commentator has estimated that the oxen and six sheep he butchered every day would provide enough meat to serve some 600 to 800 people. His prayer for God to remember his generosity to the people (v. 19) is repeated in 13:14, 22, and 31. It expresses a strong belief in the doctrine of retribution (cf. 6:14). Of course, Nehemiah also recognized that forgiveness was ultimately possible only because of God's great mercy (13:22).

6:1–14, Escapes from Enemy Plots. Two of his opponents, Sanballat and Geshem, invited Nehemiah to a meeting in the plain of Ono, some twenty-five miles northwest of Jerusalem. Their intentions were to do him bodily harm and to stop his work on the walls. Nehemiah declined their invitation with an ironic excuse: he was too busy working on the walls to meet with them! After receiving four negative replies to his invitation, Sanballat sent a fifth invitation in an open letter delivered by a courier. Sanballat charged that the wall building was part of a rebellion designed to make Nehemiah king. He also alleged that prophets were hailing Nehemiah as king, and he threatened to send word of these activities to the Persian king if Nehemiah failed to meet privately with him. Nehemiah categorically branded the charges as futile attempts to frighten the Judean community and make them weak. In his prayer he asked God, therefore, to strengthen his hands so that the work might be completed.

A second effort to discredit Nehemiah came in an invitation from the prophet Shemaiah, urging him to seek asylum in the Temple. While laypeople could seek asylum by grasp-

ing the horns of the altar in the Temple courtyard (1 Kings 1:50–53; 2:28–34), it was not permitted for them to enter the Temple itself. If Nehemiah had followed Shemaiah's invitation, he would have violated an important law. Nehemiah angrily rejected this invitation and accused Shemaiah of being paid off by Tobiah and Sanballat. Perhaps Shemaiah's suggestion that he enter the Temple in defiance of the law helped Nehemiah to see through his pretensions. Nehemiah prayed for God to punish Tobiah and Sanballat appropriately. He also mentioned a prophetess Noadiah and a group of other prophets who wanted to make him afraid, though the details of these incidents are not preserved.

6:15–19, Completion of the Wall. The repairs of the wall were completed on October 2, fifty-two days after they had been begun on August 11. This speedy completion may have resulted from the high dedication of Nehemiah. It needs to be remembered that he did not restore the severely damaged eastern wall, but relocated it further up on the ridge. Archaeologists have not been impressed with the workmanship on the "wall of Nehemiah" that they have unearthed.

The speed shown in this task convinced Nehemiah's enemies that the wall had been completed solely with the help of God (v. 16). Consequently, their own self-confidence and self-esteem suffered.

All during this period ("in those days," v. 17), a lively correspondence was carried on between the nobles of Judah and Tobiah the Ammonite. Tobiah and his son Jehohanan had both married women from Jerusalem, perhaps women of some importance (cf. 3:4, 30, in which Meshullam seems to possess a high rank). The nobles tried to mediate between Nehemiah and Tobiah, but Nehemiah observes that Tobiah himself tried to intimidate him (6:19).

7:1–73a, The List of Those Who Returned. Only the first five verses of this chapter are new; the rest of the chapter is duplicated by Ezra (see Ezra, "Commentary," 2:1–70). Nehemiah, who was governor of Judah, appointed his own brother as governor of Jerusalem. This man's name was Hanani or Hananiah (alternate spellings of the same name); several English versions give the impression that Nehemiah appointed two people with nearly identical names. Hanani feared God, and he also was faithful to both Nehemiah and to the Persian authorities. Verse 3 deals with details of the security system for Jerusalem. Apparently, the gates of the city were to be closed during the midday hours, when the guards might be drowsy. Lay inhabitants of Jerusalem were also appointed for security purposes at positions near their own homes and wherever else they were needed.

Jerusalem at the time of Nehemiah may have comprised thirty or forty acres, but the population seemed sparse to the governor, and this increased the security risks about which he was worried. Nehemiah decided to remedy this situation by bringing 10 percent of the province's purely Jewish population to Jerusalem (cf. 11:1). To determine genealogically who was eligible to be transferred to Jerusalem, he referred to the extant list of those who had returned from the Exile, which was probably a composite summary of a number of returns to Palestine during the reigns of Cyrus and Cambyses.

In Neh. 7:70–72, the list notes the donations given to the Temple. The unnamed governor in v. 70 was especially generous, and Nehemiah may have believed that his own gifts made him that governor's legitimate and worthy successor. According to a plausible reconstruction of v. 73a, the priests, the Levites, and some of the people lived in their country towns, but the leaders lived in Jerusalem.

7:73b–10:39
The Climax of the Work of Ezra

7:73b–8:12, Ezra Reads the Law. This unit originally was part of the Ezra memoir and probably did not refer to Nehemiah (the reference to him in 8:9 is lacking in the Greek translation known as 1 Esdras). Chap. 8 belongs chronologically after Ezra 8. Thus the public assembly here described took place on the first of the seventh month (8:2), whereas the assembly called to deal with the problem of mixed marriages (Ezra 10:9) came together on the twentieth of the ninth month. In later times, the first day of the seventh month was celebrated as New Year's Day (Lev. 23:24–25; Num. 29:1–6).

The book from which Ezra read for five to six hours (Neh. 8:3) was very likely some form of the Pentateuch (note "the Torah of Moses" in 8:1; 13:1). Since the books of Ezra and Nehemiah are not explicit about the extent of this torah-book, one's view of its identity may be colored by one's view of the composition history of the Pentateuch. Some would restrict this torah to the book of Deuteronomy or the so-called Priestly portions of the Pentateuch.

Ezra had six (lay?) officials on his right and seven on his left (unless Meshullam, the seventh person on his left, is the result of a textual error; see 1 Esd. 9:44). Ezra stood on a platform, much like the one Solomon used at the dedication of the first Temple (2 Chron. 6:13), and opened the

scroll containing the Torah. The people assented to the reading by calling out "amen, amen" and by prostrating themselves to the ground. Thirteen Levites helped the people understand the Torah, perhaps by translating it on the spot into Aramaic or by moving among the people and explaining it after every paragraph had been read.

The people heard the Torah with a mixture of joy and weeping (Neh. 8:9 and 12). Weeping expresses the sorrow people felt for failing to observe its demands. Ezra reassured them that the joy of the LORD offers protection against the judgments that the Torah proclaimed against transgressors (v. 9). Since the day of the law reading was holy to the LORD (vv. 9, 10, 11), Ezra commanded the people not to mourn or weep and to celebrate the occasion in a festival meal. All were urged to share their food with those unprepared for this meal, though we are not told why some were unprepared.

8:13–18, Celebration of the Feast of Booths. The people resolved to study the Torah just as Ezra had done (v. 13; cf. Ezra 7:10). On the basis of this study, they held a unique celebration of the Feast of Tabernacles (Booths), unparalleled since the days of Joshua (here called Jeshua the son of Nun, Neh. 8:17). This festival was normally held on the fifteenth to the twenty-second days of the seventh month (Lev. 23:33–36, 39–43). Perhaps Ezra's celebration marked the first time that the Feast of Booths had been held at the central sanctuary since Israel was gathered at Gilgal during the time of the conquest or the first time in centuries that the booths represented Israel's wilderness wanderings and not just the way people lived at harvest time.

Each day of the festival Ezra read from the book of the Torah. According to Deut. 31:10–13, the Torah was to be read every seventh year. The solemn assembly or holiday on the eighth day is in accord with the ordinances of Lev. 23:36 and 39 and Num. 29:35–38 (cf. Deut. 16:13–15).

9:1–5a, National Day of Mourning. This national day of mourning fits best between Ezra 10:15 and 10:16 or at the end of that chapter. The position after Ezra 10:15 would place this incident on the twenty-fourth of the ninth month of Ezra's first year; the position at the end of Ezra 10 would place it on the twentieth of the first month of his second year. In either case, it seems to be related to the incident in which Ezra forced the people to divorce their foreign wives, and it is not a direct sequel to Nehemiah 8.

This section reports that the people resolved to separate themselves from all foreigners and spent half the day in reading the Torah and in making confession of their sin. In its present context, this act of separation shows the purity of all those who entered into covenant (9:38). The worship was led by Levites, who are listed in vv. 4–5; they also are the ones who recited the following prayer.

9:5b–37, Confessional Prayer.

The prayer begins with words of blessing and praise for the LORD, whose righteousness in judging Israel is acknowledged toward the end (v. 33).

First among God's praiseworthy acts is his creation and preservation of the entire world (v. 6). God's uniqueness is reflected in his worship by the whole host of heaven (the stars or heavenly beings).

This mighty God is the one who chose Abram, took him from southern Mesopotamia to the promised land, and entered into a covenant with him to give him the land. God's fidelity to this relationship (his righteousness) brought about the fulfillment of these promises (vv. 7–8).

God also heard the cries of distress in Egypt and led Israel to freedom in the Exodus (vv. 9–11). During the wilderness wanderings, he guided Israel in a pillar of cloud and fire and gave them the Sabbath, commandments, and laws at Sinai. He also fed them with manna and provided water from the rock; he told them to proceed with the conquest of the land, in fulfillment of his promises (vv. 12–15).

Despite numerous rebellions and the apostasy in the incident of the golden calf (cf. Exod. 32), God showed his readiness to forgive and be merciful. While he led them by the pillars of cloud and fire more than once and gave them food, water, and clothing over a forty-year period, he gave the Torah only once. Finally, at the end of the wilderness period, he gave them victories over the kingdoms of Sihon and Og in Transjordan. Increase in population among the descendants of the exodus generation served as a fulfillment of God's earlier promises, and he subdued before them the various peoples and kings of the Canaanites. The richness of the God-given land is described in terms of its many crops. The notice in v. 25 that they "became fat" may have a double meaning: it can be a sign of blessing and prosperity or it can be a prelude to stubbornness, haughtiness, and rebellion (cf. Deut. 32:15).

The behavior recounted in these verses follows the pattern of the Deuteronomistic History (→Deuteronomistic historian). God's goodness is followed by Israel's rebellion—Israel rejected the law and killed the prophets! Evidence for killing prophets in OT times is very slim, and the charge, so frequent in the NT, is first raised in the Bible here. It dramatically illustrates how Israel rejected the prophetic word. As in the book of Judges, sin was followed by deliverance into the hand of enemies, a cry to God for deliverance, and his raising of saviors to deliver them (Neh. 9:27). After a period of rest, the whole cycle would begin again. God delivered them "many times" (v. 28) and patiently warned them over "many years" (v. 30). The spirit, which had instructed them in the wilderness period, spoke through the prophets, but the people refused to hear. The history of Israel in the land, as in Ezek. 20:28–29, is very brief, and the moral is clear: because of its disobedience in the face of repeated warnings and divine acts of mercy, Israel was turned over into the hands of great nations like Assyria and Babylonia.

Neh. 9:32–37 resembles the communal laments in the book of Psalms. The poets affirm God's covenant loyalty and ask him not to overlook the hardships they have experienced since the invasion of Assyria. The history reported in this chapter demonstrates that the LORD has dealt faithfully and Israel has acted wickedly (v. 33). Since the ancestors refused to "serve," those who pray these words "serve" or become slaves in the rich land that had once been given to the ancestors. Here the Persian rule is not viewed from a collaborationist perspective. The people complained that the produce of the land went to the victorious kings, who forced them to work on state labor projects and who requisitioned livestock whenever they wanted to. The last words of the prayer are poignant: we are in great distress.

9:38–10:39, A Pledge to Keep God's Law.

The community entered into a covenant to walk in God's law and to do all his commandments. A number of the areas identified as in need of correction required Nehemiah's direct actions later in the book: mixed marriages, the Sabbath, the wood offering, first fruits, levitical tithes, and proper care of the Temple. It seems that after Nehemiah's efforts at reform, the community as a whole resolved to put these abuses to an end permanently. From a historical perspective, therefore, chap. 13, which mentions Nehemiah's efforts on these problems, preceded chap. 10. For the editor of the books of Ezra and Nehemiah, however, this making of a covenant served as the climactic work of Ezra and Nehemiah.

The list of signatories includes Nehemiah, Zedekiah (perhaps Nehemiah's chief official), twenty-one priests, seventeen Levites, and forty-four heads of the people. The vast majority of names can be found in other lists in Ezra and Nehemiah. Their inclusion here shows that the entire community agreed with what had been covenanted. In 10:28, the groups within the community are called people (laity), priests, Levites, gatekeepers, singers, and Temple servants.

The decision not to enter into mixed marriages (v. 30; cf. 13:23–30) is based on Exod. 34:11–16 and Deut. 7:1–4, where marriages with the pre-Israelite inhabitants of the land are prohibited. No provision is made here about mixed marriages that already existed (cf. Ezra 10).

The people also resolved not to purchase goods on the Sabbath or other holy days (Neh. 10:31; cf. 13:15–22) and to observe the Sabbatical Year by letting the land lie fallow (cf. Exod. 23:10–11; Lev. 25:2–7, 20–21) and by canceling all debts (cf. Deut. 15:1–8). Thus, by this unique combination, both farmers and merchants/employers alike would share equally in the observance of this year (cf. Neh. 5:1–13; → Sabbatical Year).

An annual Temple tax was designated to provide sacrifices and to make repairs on the Temple (10:32–33). The community decided by lot when the various families would bring an annual wood offering to keep the fire on the altar burning perpetually (v. 34; cf. 13:31; Lev. 6:8–13). Gifts in kind are specified in Neh. 10:35–36: first fruits of crops and livestock (cf. 13:31) and firstborn sons. Firstborn sons and the firstborn of unclean animals would be redeemed. Tithes from the crops were perquisites for the Levites (Num. 18:26–32; cf. Neh. 13:10–14). A final pledge not to neglect the Temple (10:39) seems to respond to the complaint of Nehemiah in 13:11.

11:1–13:31

Further Acts of Nehemiah

11:1–2, Action to Increase Population. By casting lots, the community decided to bring one of every ten people in Judea to live in Jerusalem. Neh. 7:1–5a had also been concerned with the low population of the holy city.

11:3–24, A List of Family Heads in Jerusalem. This list shows the success of the repopulation effort by identifying those who lived in Jerusalem: people of Judah (vv. 4b–6); people of Benjamin (vv. 7–8); leaders (v. 9); priests (vv. 10–14); Levites (vv. 15–18); gatekeepers (v. 19); Temple servants (Nethinim; v. 21); and singers (v. 23). Pethahiah (v. 24) was an official in charge of Jewish affairs connected with the Persian monarch. How his office was related to that of Ezra or Nehemiah cannot be determined. Verses 1–19 are roughly paralleled by 1 Chron. 9:2–17.

11:25–36, A List of the Settlements in Judah and Benjamin Outside of Jerusalem. The editor of Ezra-Nehemiah thought it appropriate to specify the population in the rest of Judah (cf. vv. 1–3, 20). (For identifications of the various place names, see the book-length commentaries listed in the "Bibliography.")

12:1–9, A List of Priests and Levites from the Time of Zerubbabel and Jeshua. The authenticity of this list is widely questioned. It may have been artificially reconstructed from 12:12–25 to provide a list of clergy from the first period of the restoration community.

12:10–11, A List of High Priests from Jeshua to Jaddua. Jeshua, the first in the list, was high priest in 520 B.C., and Jaddua, the last, was a contemporary of Alexander the Great, who died in 323 B.C. Since there are only six names in the list, this creates an average tenure of more than thirty years. Cross argues that papponomy (the naming of a baby after his grandfather) was used within the high-priestly line. He conjectures that an additional Eliashib and Johanan should be inserted before the Eliashib of v. 10 and an additional Johanan and Jaddua before Jaddua. His reconstructed list of high priests is as follows (additions marked with brackets): Jeshua, Joiakim, [Eliashib I], [Johanan I], Eliashib II, Joiada I, Johanan II (an emendation for "Jonathan"; cf. vv. 22–23); Jaddua II; [Johanan III]; and [Jaddua III]. Cross locates Ezra in the time of Johanan I and Nehemiah in the time of Eliashib II. Critics of his solution have pointed out that there is no necessary reason to conclude that papponomy was practiced at this time in the high-priestly line, that the relationship between Joiakim and Eliashib I that Cross proposes (brothers) is contradicted in 12:10–11 (Eliashib is the son of Joiakim), and that the chronological difficulties are not so severe as Cross implies.

12:12–26, A List of Priests and Levites from the Time of Joiakim. The dating of this list to Joiakim is found in vv. 12 and 26. The latter reference puts both Nehemiah and Ezra during the high-priesthood of Joiakim. While this is not accurate historically (Nehemiah's high priest was Eliashib; 3:1), the editor of this list was intent on showing the unified character of their work, a concern that is also behind the present arrangement of chaps. 8–10. Neh. 12:23–25 puts the list of Levites in the time of Johanan (= Jonathan of v. 11). While Johanan is called the son of Eliashib in v. 23, the Jonathan of v. 11 is Eliashib's grandson. Some, therefore (e.g., NEB), translate the Hebrew word *ben* (usually, "son") in v. 23 as "grandson."

12:27–43, Dedication of the Wall. This dedication, which one might expect to have taken place shortly after the completion of the building, is reported now after a series of intervening events and lists (8:1–12:26). A double procession emphasizes the joint contributions of Ezra and Nehemiah to the founding of the postexilic community. Ezra led a procession that proceeded around Jerusalem in a counterclockwise fashion; Nehemiah led another group clockwise around the city. Both groups came together in the Temple square. Apparently the two processions walked along the top of the wall. The sacrifices at the dedication were "great," that is, many; the joy was also great. The verb "rejoice" is used three times in v. 43; the noun "joy" is used two times. The joy on this occasion did not cause the political troubles it did at the beginning of the restoration of the Temple (Ezra 3:13).

12:44–47, Contribution Supervisors Appointed. This paragraph associates the appointment of contribution supervisors with the completion of work on the city. The community's happiness with the clergy continued from the time of Zerubbabel to the time of Nehemiah (v. 47). Authority for the various distinctions within the clergy is traced back to the efforts of David and Solomon (→ Levites; Priests).

13:1–3, Separation from Foreigners. The action described in these verses prepares readers for Nehemiah's treatment of Tobiah in the next paragraph. The ban on Ammonites and Moabites is recorded in Deut. 23:3–6. Balak, king of Moab, had hired Balaam to curse Israel during their trip through the wilderness (Num. 22–24).

13:4–9, Misuse of Temple Chambers. While Nehemiah had returned to Mesopotamia after completing his first term as governor, Eliashib (not the high priest of 3:1, etc.) had allowed Nehemiah's enemy Tobiah to take over one of the rooms in the Temple. When Nehemiah returned to Jerusalem for his second term, he immediately banished the Ammonite Tobiah from these quarters and threw out all his furniture. Perhaps Eliashib and Tobiah had concluded that Nehemiah would never return. From the Temple area Tobiah would have been in a good position to develop his local contacts (cf. 6:17–19).

13:10–14, Provisions for the Levites. Because the people had provided no income for the Levites, they had fled to the countryside, leaving the Temple understaffed. Nehemiah brought the Levites back to the city and saw to it that tithes were once again paid and that treasurers were appointed to collect and distribute the contributions. Three times in this chapter he asks God to remember his good deeds and reward him for them (vv. 14, 22, 31; cf. v. 29).

13:15–22, Reform of the Sabbath Day. Ezra's work was thirty years old at the time of Nehemiah's second term, and people had begun to violate the Sabbath commandment, which his torah demands be enforced. Nehemiah warned that the present offenses might lead to the same dire consequences as the offenses of the ancestors—destruction of the city and exile. By closing the gates of the city during the Sabbath, he tried to ensure that no burdens would be carried into the city and no commerce would take place. He warned those merchants who set up their shops just outside the city on the Sabbath and appointed the Levites to guard the gates in order to keep the Sabbath holy.

13:23–29, A Crisis of Intermarriage. Nehemiah noted that many Jews had married women from Ashdod, Ammon, and Moab and that the children of these unions often could not speak Hebrew. We are not told that he dissolved existing marriages, but he did rebuke those who had intermarried, both verbally and physically. He forced the community to swear not to intermarry with foreigners in the future, that is, to keep the law recorded in Deut. 7:3. The criticism of Solomon's marriages with foreign women in Neh. 13:26 is an important argument against the notion that one person wrote both 1–2 Chronicles and Ezra-Nehemiah, since Solomon's foreign marriages are not reported in Chronicles, but only in 1 Kings 11.

Nehemiah acted decisively against one of the grandsons of Eliashib, the high priest during his first term, who had married the daughter of his archenemy, Sanballat. Nehemiah expelled them from the community and asked God to "remember" them because they had violated the requirement that a high priest should never marry a Gentile (Lev. 21:13–15; in Ezek. 44:22, the prohibition against having a gentile wife applies to all priests; on the levitical covenant, see Mal. 2:4–8).

13:30–31, Summary of Reforms. These verses rehearse Nehemiah's efforts to cleanse the community from foreign influence and to regulate the duties of the priests and Levites and the offerings of the people. The final prayer for God to remember him makes no additional requests for rewards.

Bibliography

Clines, D. J. *Ezra, Nehemiah, Esther.* New Century Bible Commentary. Grand Rapids, MI: Eerdmans, 1984.

Cross, F. M. "A Reconstruction of the Judean Restoration." *Journal of Biblical Literature* 94 (1975):4–18.

Holmgren, F. *Ezra and Nehemiah: Israel Alive Again.* International Theological Commentary. Grand Rapids, MI: Eerdmans, 1987.

Myers, J. M. *Ezra-Nehemiah.* Anchor Bible, 14. Garden City, NY: Doubleday, 1965.

Williamson, H. G. M. *Ezra, Nehemiah.* Word Biblical Commentary, 16. Waco, TX: Word, 1985.

ESTHER

DAVID J. A. CLINES

INTRODUCTION

The Book of Esther is the story of the greatest threat to the survival of the Jewish people. It recounts how a series of happy coincidences, allied with the courage and wisdom of the Jewish woman Esther, so successfully averted the threat that not a single Jewish life was lost.

The story of Esther exists in two principal versions. The first is the ten-chapter form we find in the Hebrew Bible and in Protestant translations of the OT. The second is the sixteen-chapter form appearing in the Septuagint (Greek) version of the Bible and in Roman Catholic translations. The material that appears in the Roman Catholic but not the Protestant Book of Esther is put by Protestants in the Apocrypha, where it is known as The Additions to Esther. (See The Additions to Esther, "Introduction" and "Commentary.") The Additions do not appear in Jewish Bibles.

History

Given the serious threat to the Jewish people narrated by this book, readers are naturally eager to know whether the events it depicts actually occurred or whether the book is fiction. Most scholars agree that the book is essentially a fictional account in which a good deal of historical detail is incorporated.

There is no doubt that the Persian king Ahasuerus of the book of Esther is the historical Xerxes (486–465 B.C.) known to us from the Greek historian Herodotus' *History of the Persian Wars*, especially Books 7–9 (→ Ahasuerus). The events narrated in the book of Esther as occurring in his third year (1:3) would fit into the period before his departure for his ill-fated expedition against the Greeks (483–479); the four years between his deposition of his queen Vashti and the installation of her successor Esther in his seventh year (2:1) coincide with those four years of his absence from Persia. The book of Esther also contains many details of Persian life that we find confirmed from extrabiblical sources, such as the extent of the empire from India to Ethiopia (1:1), the impressive postal system (3:13; 8:10), the keeping of official diaries including records of the king's benefactors (2:23; 6:1–2), and the use of impalement as a form of punishment (2:23; 5:14; 7:10).

But the plausibility of the chronological framework and the accuracy of the local color do not amount to a demonstration of the book's historicity. It is more significant that the essential plot of the book hangs upon a considerable number of improbable coincidences—for example, that there should be a Jewish queen on the Persian throne at the very time when genocide of the Jews is being plotted; that Mordecai's service to the king (2:21–23) is not rewarded at the appropriate time but brought to the king's attention merely hours before Haman, the prime minister, arrives to ask for Mordecai's life (6:1–3); or that Haman, in begging for his life at Esther's feet, should be thought by the king to be attempting to rape the queen and for that reason be executed (7:8–10). The combination of coincidences, none perhaps entirely improbable in itself, brings the historical credibility of the work into question.

Function

If the book is not a historical narrative, what is its function? Clearly it addresses itself to the Jewish community as an affirmation that God is just as concerned with the survival of the Jewish people as they themselves are and that no danger to them can arise that will not issue in "relief and deliverance" (4:14). Within that affirmation stands the assertion that Jewish and gentile interests are not necessarily contradictory (despite Haman in 3:8) and that Jews should expect to enjoy security through peaceful cooperation with their gentile masters. The more ostensible function of the book is to recount the origin of the Jewish festival of Purim (9:20–32)—a goal it manifestly does not accomplish if the book is not historical. But what it does do is to insist that this festival celebrating Jewish survival should not be an acclamation of Jewish military might or Jewish diplomatic cunning but serve as reminder of an occasion when simply "rest" or "relief" came the Jews' way (9:16, 18); at Purim the order of the day should be domestic merrymaking and the exchanging of gifts rather than solemn or militaristic ceremony (→ Purim, The Feast of; Lot, Lots).

Structure and Plot

The book has a clearly demarcated beginning, middle, and end; chaps. 1–2 form the exposition, chaps. 3–9 the complication, and chaps. 9–10 the resolution. The exposition contains seven distinct scenes, and the complication nine scenes.

The plot proper begins with the refusal of the Jew Mordecai to do obeisance to his superior Haman, on the religious ground that Haman the Agagite comes from a race once hostile to the Jewish people. From Haman's angry response there develop two arcs of tension, the one the question of what will happen to Mordecai, the other the question of what will happen to the Jews, since Haman has determined that the whole of Mordecai's race should suffer for Mordecai's intransigence. Mordecai's fate is first determined when the king, discovering that he has failed to reward him for an earlier favor, elevates him to a position of honor. The fate of the Jews still hangs in the balance, however, so long as the unalterable Persian decree Haman has issued against them remains in force. Only when Mordecai dispatches a second decree that, while not literally canceling the first, effectively annuls it, are the Jews safe. The fateful day on which a mass assault, a veritable pogrom, against them was planned becomes a day on which—on the contrary—they manage to kill their enemies throughout the empire without loss of a single Jewish life.

COMMENTARY

1:1–2:23

Exposition

1:1–4, The Royal Banquet for the Officials. The story begins at some distance from the main action of the plot, with the depiction of a sumptuous 180-day banquet for officials from all over the Persian Empire. The function of this scene is principally to portray the magnificence and luxury of the Persian court as a backdrop to the decidedly shabby treatment that will be meted out to one of the subject races of that empire, the Jews.

1:5–9, The Royal Banquets for the Citizens of Susa. The narrative focus sharpens on a briefer, but equally pretentious pair of banquets given immediately thereafter by the king and the queen for the citizens of the Persian capital Susa. The king's banquet for the males is, according to the Persian custom, primarily an extended drinking bout, the only rule for its conduct being that "the drinking is to be unstinted" (1:8). The ostentation of the men's banquet and the elaborate description of the decor of the palace pavilion where it is held contrast with the perfunctory notice given to Queen Vashti's banquet for the women (1:9). But at least the queen,

who will prove a mainspring of action in this chapter, has been introduced, even though her strict subordination to the king is emphasized with the notation that her own quarters, where she gives her banquet, are "the palace that belonged to King Ahasuerus" (1:9).

1:10–22, Vashti's Refusal to Obey the King's Command. On the seventh and closing day of the festivities and thus presumably as the climax to his self-advertisement, the king sends for Vashti to appear before him at the men's banquet "to show off her beauty" (1:11)—to his advantage rather than hers. Contrary to custom and expectation, she refuses. It is all the more alarming that she gives no reason for her refusal, not even the fact that the king is tipsy. A feminist reading of the narrative is today inescapable, but the author more probably intends a satire against Persian men as incapable of commanding their wives' obedience. It is hardly to the credit of this absolute monarch, fabulously wealthy and masterfully supreme in every sphere, that on the domestic front he can be so decisively worsted. He, rather than Vashti, has become the spectacle.

Vashti's unelaborated refusal forms an amusing contrast to the histrionic reaction of the king and his counselors. While the outcome is (perhaps) tragic for Vashti—though we observe that her punishment, never to come again before the king (1:19), is conceivably her dearest wish—it is in other respects pure farce. It involves the whole elaborate machinery of Persian law and administration—to say nothing of the postal service—in asserting the right of every man in the empire to be master in his own house. And it is implied that the story of Vashti's independence will spread like wildfire throughout Persian lands, every wife in the empire waiting only for this sign from the empress to break out in long-stifled rebellion against her husband.

2:1–4, The King's Decision to Seek a New Queen. We move closer to the main action of the story in this chapter as we discover how the Jewish girl Esther, who will be indispensable for the salvation of her people, comes to be queen on the Persian throne. Certainly her ancestry will be no recommendation for the post of successor to Vashti; only a nationwide beauty contest, open to virgins everywhere regardless of ethnic background or social status, will succeed in replacing a Persian queen with a Jewish one. It is an extra piece of satire against the king, and so against Persians, that he cannot think how Vashti may be replaced without the advice of his counselors.

2:5–11, Esther's Admission to the Court. Esther is an improbable candidate for the throne of Persia, being not only Jewish but also the descendant of captives (2:6) and lacking both father and mother to promote her cause. She is, however, beautiful. It is only later that we learn of her other qualities. For the moment it is her beauty alone that gains her entrance to the harem and, once there, to the favored position in the eyes of the harem-master.

2:12–18, Esther's Accession to the Throne.
The depiction of the twelve-month course of beautifying treatments for potential bedfellows of the king is hard to take seriously; it highlights the extravagance and artificiality of the court. A hint is dropped of Esther's character when we learn that she takes no advantage of the custom of taking possession of the most expensive jewelry and clothes for her night with the king. But we cannot be sure that it signifies her modesty or unwillingness to enrich herself at the king's expense; could it be her innate cunning (which we will have clearer tokens of in later scenes) to distinguish herself from her competitors by dressing "down" for the occasion, or is she making a silent protest at Persian ostentation?

The king, in choosing Esther for nothing other than her good looks, no doubt thinks that he has now got himself a "little woman" who will be receptive and obedient. The banquet he gives for her (2:18) contrasts with the banquet given by the more self-confident Vashti.

2:19–23, Mordecai's Discovery of the Plot Against the King.
This episode serves a foreshadowing purpose; it will become truly functional only for the events of chap. 6, when Mordecai's good deed is rewarded. Mordecai appears to be a palace official, with his seat "at the king's gate," though perhaps the story gains in punch if we see him as simply one of the crowd of loungers who gather outside the palace gate. We do know that he walks in front of the harem to pick up gossip on how Esther is faring (2:11). In either case, his position enables him to overhear a plot to assassinate the king, and because he still has contact with Esther he can pass the news on to her. She, because she stands so high in the king's favor, has ready access to him and can inform him of the plot "in the name of Mordecai" (2:22).

Up to this point everything has been setting the scene. The real action of the story will begin only in chap. 3.

3:1–8:17

Complication

In the ten scenes that form the complication, or main action of the plot, we are confronted with a constantly changing grouping of the four main characters of the plot—Esther, Mordecai, Ahasuerus, and Haman.

3:1–6, Haman's Promotion and Mordecai's Refusal to Honor Him.
The focus shifts from the figures of Esther and Mordecai to the axis of Mordecai the Jew and Haman the prime minister. Haman is not himself a Persian, but an "Agagite." We never hear in nonbiblical literature of such a racial designation in the Persian Empire, but Jews know that Agag was not only the foe of Saul who indirectly cost him his kingship (1 Sam. 15:8–33), but also the king of Amalek, the tribe that was the archetypical enemy of Israel (Exod. 17:14–16; Deut. 25:17–19; → Amalekites). Jewish readers immediately understand that Haman will play the role in this story of the "enemy of the Jews" (Esther 8:1). In this connection, note that just as Haman's descent recalls Agag, so does Mordecai's recall Saul (2:5; 1 Sam. 9:1). But whereas Agag is Saul's downfall, Mordecai will be Haman's.

Why Mordecai refuses the customary obeisance to Haman remains unclear. The narrative makes no judgment on Mordecai's behavior or its motive; it is simply the datum of the text from which the narrative will take its rise. If there is a recklessness or an excessiveness about Mordecai's behavior, there is an irrationality about Haman's, who promptly decides that to humiliate Mordecai would be beneath his dignity and that the only adequate retribution would be to wipe out the whole people of Mordecai. This is the first notice we have of the nervousness and overreaction characteristic of Haman, the outsider and parvenu.

3:7–15, Haman's Plot Against the Jews Gains the King's Consent.
Haman first chooses by lot the most suitable day for carrying out his design; the casting of lots by an astrologer among the Persians is attested by the Greek historian Herodotus. The impression is given that Haman remained firm to his evil design throughout the whole of the twelfth year of Ahasuerus, from the first to the twelfth month (though 3:7 may mean that the lot casting determined on one day in the first month which would be the fateful day for the Jews). The day fixed upon is the thirteenth day of the twelfth month; thirteen is an unlucky number among Babylonians and Persians. Could this be a hint that the day will turn out worse for Persians than for Jews?

Haman's speech, like the courtier Memucan's in 1:16–20, states first the precise offense, then a proposed solution, and then the advantages to be gained. In both cases the disproportion between the actual events and the proposed punishment is striking. Haman cunningly mixes truth, half-truth, and innuendo: the Jews are indeed scattered throughout the empire (though Haman manages to make that

389

sound like a conspiracy); they do indeed have their own customs, but it is a misrepresentation to suggest that means that they therefore do not obey the king's law. (Haman is playing upon the fact that the same word means "custom" and "law.")

His offer of an enormous bribe, equivalent to two-thirds of the annual budget of the Persian central government, does not alert the king to the likelihood that Haman cannot be acting disinterestedly out of pure concern for the king's welfare.

4:1–3, Mordecai Hears the News. Mordecai's reaction to the threat of genocide against the Jews is not dismay at what damage his principles have done to his people, but a public protest ("at the king's gate") at the injustice that now has royal assent. Mirroring Mordecai's public response is the more private and religious response of the less powerful Jews throughout the empire; though God is not mentioned in the book, their fasting is a sign of their religious commitment (→ Fasting; Sackcloth).

4:4–17, Mordecai Impresses on Esther the Need for Action. In this brilliant narrative, communication between Mordecai and Esther passes through three stages. In the first (4:4), no words are spoken, and the gift of clothes that Esther sends to Mordecai is rejected. In the second (4:5–9), a message, both oral and written, is sent from Mordecai to Esther, but the words are not reported. In the third (4:10–17), words from Esther, from Mordecai, and from Esther again are narrated. The whole narrative represents a movement from ignorance to understanding to decision. Esther is the one who initiates each of the communications, but Mordecai's part is equally crucial: it is he who gives news of the king's decision, challenges Esther to approach the king, and convinces her against her inclination to act courageously.

In this scene Esther comes of age; by the end of it she is no longer acting as merely the adoptive daughter of Mordecai who obeys him in everything (cf. 2:10, 20), but as the one who takes charge, Mordecai going away and doing "everything that Esther had commanded *him*" (4:17; my emphasis). The change has come about through Mordecai's argument that staying out of the king's presence is no less dangerous than entering it: "do not think that in the king's

palace you have more chance of escape than do the other Jews. ... If you keep silence, you and your family [including Mordecai!] will die" (4:13–14). But Esther does not need only to be convinced intellectually of the right action; she needs also the support of her compatriots, expressed in an exceptionally rigorous period of fasting that is in keeping with the enormity of her undertaking.

5:1–8, Esther's First Audience with the King and Its Outcome. The difficulty in approaching the Persian king lies in not being summoned (4:11), and now that the king has apparently tired of her and she has not been called to his presence in the last month, there is little reason to think that she will again be summoned. There is no extrabiblical evidence for this rule of the Persian court, but it is in harmony with the picture the book has drawn of the exceptional severity of the Persian autocracy.

Since the king offers Esther anything she wants, up to half his kingdom, it seems strange that she does not ask there and then for the deliverance of her people. From a narrative point of view, her invitation of the king and Haman to a banquet retards the resolution of the plot for another three chapters and keeps the tension alive. But from the point of view of the characters, we are perhaps meant to know that it is impolite (and risky) to take monarchs' extravagant promises at face value and that some more delicate bargaining needs to be done before the safety of her people is secured. And who is to say what will count as half the kingdom, especially if the head of the prime minister is at risk? In this narrative we have simply the first exchange in a play of oriental courtesies.

Even more surprising is her refusal, at the first banquet (5:6–8), to say what her request actually is. But what she commits the king to, in extending the invitation to the second banquet, is the granting of her petition sight unseen, without any quantifying of fractions of the kingdom. Unlike the first banquet, which she said she had already prepared when she invited the king, the second will be prepared only when the king has agreed, by accepting her invitation, to give her exactly whatever she will demand. So ingenious is her logic that by the end of her speech she is able to represent what *she* wants as "what the king has said" (5:8); it has all been a subtle play of bargaining.

5:9–14, Haman Grows More Incensed Against Mordecai. The domestic setting of this scene makes Haman's malice all the more sinister. There is a parallel with Ahasuerus in the setting of his palace in chap. 1: Haman at home, worsted by his inferior, Mordecai, and in desperate need of counsel about his next move, mirrors Ahasuerus in the palace, worsted by his inferior Vashti. Like Ahasuerus who must put every woman in the kingdom in her place in order to assert his own dignity, Haman must butcher the whole race of the Jews to conquer his own sense of inferiority and alienness. All his honors do him no good, he pathetically admits (5:13), so long as one Jew does not offer him the customary respect. Haman's friends rightly understand that Haman has been so publicly dishonored that something more than Mordecai's death is required: it must be public humiliation. The pole 50 cubits (80 feet) high, on which Mordecai's body is to be impaled, will stand in Haman's courtyard but be visible throughout Susa. And Mordecai's death must not be an act of private vengeance, but authorized by the king.

6:1–14, Mordecai Is Rewarded by the King. With a flurry of coincidences the narrative now suddenly begins to move toward a resolution favorable to the Jews. The king is by chance that night sleepless. By chance the passage in the royal chronicles recording Mordecai's benefaction to the king is read aloud before him. By chance Mordecai has not already been rewarded. Haman is by chance the first afoot in the palace in the morning ready to give the king advice—advice without which Haman cannot act against Mordecai, the very man the king delights to honor. All these key events are such pure chance that readers are compelled to wonder whether they are chance at all and not the workings of a hidden providence (cf. 4:14).

Any courtier would have served the king's purpose, but for the sake of the irony it is Haman who must give advice on how Mordecai should be honored and who alone is in the position to propose honors for Mordecai because he has come to seek authorization for Mordecai's execution. There is irony too in the way the king unintentionally destroys Haman by keeping from him the name of the man he wishes to honor, just as Haman had intentionally kept from the king the name of the people he wished to destroy (3:8). Haman's dearest desire for himself is intimacy with Persian royalty; hence the thrill when he is invited to private dinner parties with the king and queen (5:9, 12) and his ambition to wear clothes the king has already worn and ride on the horse the king has himself sat on. This is the psychology of the outsider who can never believe he has truly become an insider. As the roles of the honored and the endangered are reversed, Haman adopts Mordecai's garb while Mordecai is clothed in the garment Haman had coveted for himself.

7:1–10, The Fall of Haman. Here the narrative reaches its first major climax. The fate of the Jewish people remains undecided and will not in fact be settled until chap. 9. But here the fall

of their archenemy is a clear enough sign that they will escape his design upon them. In the three scenes depicting Haman at the court of Ahasuerus his fate has been disclosed: in the first (3:8–15), Haman has initiated the conversation and has achieved his purpose; in the second (6:4–11), the king has initiated the conversation and has diverted Haman from his purpose; and now in the third (7:1–10), Haman is excluded from the conversation and has his own purpose turned against him.

In this scene Esther reappears; she is now in firm control. With her characteristic subtlety, she reponds to the king's repeated offer of the half of his kingdom with the apparently minor request for her own life—and for that of her people; surely this request has no financial implications on the scale of half a kingdom! Since the king has to this moment known neither that Esther is Jewish nor that the race whose death warrant he has signed is that of the Jews, it only gradually dawns on him what the significance of her request is. Paradoxically, in the moment when she pleads for her own safety she puts herself in her greatest danger by revealing her Jewishness, for the unalterable law of the Persians and Medes (cf. 1:19) still stands written against them. And in the moment when she is most obedient to Mordecai's exhortations to her, she first disobeys his one command—not to make known who her people are (2:20).

Everything is happening too fast for the king, and for the first time in the story he is without counselors to turn to. When he has to make a decision for himself, his first instinct is to run away—out into the garden, for more than the wine (7:2) has made him dizzy this evening. Whether he realizes it or not, Esther has pointed the finger of accusation against him as well as Haman; for who has "sold" the Jews to death (7:4) and who has "bought" them except Ahasuerus for the one part and Haman for the other? The culprit, and the "foe and enemy" (7:6), is perhaps not only Haman in his genocidal design, but also the king who, in his fecklessness, agrees to mass murder without even inquiring who its victims are to be.

When the king returns from the garden, he has evidently not yet decided between his queen and his prime minister, for it is the sight that meets his eyes that determines his move. He sees Haman on his knees beside Esther, begging for his life; whether he really believes Haman is trying to assault or rape Esther or whether he simply finds it convenient to put that construction on Haman's posture, the king knows how to behave once his "property" is threatened. To his decidedly theatrical cry of outrage, "Will he even assault the queen in *my* presence, in *my own* house?" (7:8; my emphasis), Esther raises no objection; but this is hardly callousness, for is it not true that Haman by his plot has already "assaulted" the queen, even in the palace? Haman's end, quickly narrated, is a nice piece of dramatic irony: he is impaled on the stake he himself has prepared (cf. Prov. 11:27; 26:27). The story folds back on itself, reminding us that the previous impalement was that of the conspirators against the king (Esther 2:23), while this impalement is of the man who has plotted against both the queen and the man who saved the king from the first conspiracy.

8:1–17, Haman Is Replaced and His Plot Overturned. A major narrative problem still remains to be solved. Even after the death of Haman, the edict against the Jews still stands, and, being written in the king's name and sealed with his ring (3:12), it is irreversible. How can unalterable law be altered?

It is not enough that Mordecai is elevated to the position of prime minister. Nor will it be of any help for Esther to beg the king tearfully to "avert the evil design of Haman the Agagite" (8:3). The king is not unsympathetic (8:7), but he refuses to regard it as his problem. Esther and Mordecai have his permission to take any action they care to about the decree and "write whatever [they] like about the Jews" (8:8). Mordecai now has the king's signet ring, and any edict he seals with it cannot be revoked. But there is a sting in the tail, for the edict of Haman has also been sealed with the selfsame ring! Write what you like, says the king, so long as it does not alter, contradict, or revoke what has already been written!

The plot has encountered a conundrum. Before we are told the terms in which it will be solved, we are tantalizingly treated to an elaborate description of how the letters conveying its solution are dispatched (8:9–10). Then at last we learn of Mordecai's ingenious ploy: a second decree, not contradicting the first verbally, but effectively annulling it by giving authorization to the Jews to defend themselves against anyone who tries to carry out the first decree. If attack and defense are both recommended by the Persian government, what is the honest citizen to do on the thirteenth of Adar?

Not very surprisingly, both the Jews and the inhabitants of Susa regard the issuance of the decree as a bloodless victory for the Jewish cause, and throughout the empire it is so clearly felt that the Jews now have the upper hand that many Gentiles convert spontaneously to Judaism (8:17).

9:1–10:3

Resolution

9:1–19, What Actually Happened on Adar 13? Though the intellectual problem is solved, readers are still curious to know what, if

anything, actually happened on the day assigned for the massacre of the Jews. The Jews, in fact, do not wait for anyone to attack them but take the initiative in slaying 75,800 of their enemies (somewhat surprisingly, since hitherto Haman has been the only enemy of the Jews we have heard of). They themselves apparently do not suffer a single casualty.

The narrative does not linger too long over the unsavory details but tends to concentrate on the pacific results of the killing. Adar 13 is noted not as a day of triumphant bloodletting, but as a time when a reversal of expected fortunes occurs, as a day of gaining mastery, as an occasion of self-defense, and above all as a gaining of relief from hostile neighbors (9:1, 16). What is celebrated thereafter is not the victory itself, but the day(s) of rejoicing after the victory (9:17–19). A distinct program of demilitarization of the memory has been going on.

9:20–32, The Institution of the Festival of Purim. So signal an event in Jewish history is bound to be commemorated. It is the community in the first place that decides to celebrate the events (9:19, 23). But this being the Persian Empire, and Mordecai and Esther now being officeholders in that empire, we are hardly surprised that they should take it in hand to give the celebration the full Persian bureaucratic treatment. So Mordecai harnesses the resources of the chancellery and the imperial postal system, and Esther duplicates the whole undertaking rather unnecessarily (9:29–32), both of them dispatching letters throughout the empire in order to ensure that annual celebrations be carried out by Jews everywhere. In the fashion of a prudent bureaucrat, Mordecai even prevents potential conflict among the Jews over which day to celebrate by authorizing commemorations on both of the days suggested.

The name by which this festival of rejoicing for deliverance (not of gloating over slain enemies) is to be known is Purim, "lots." The name probably originally referred to a Persian spring festival at which lots were cast to determine destinies and fortunes for the coming year. But in this narrative the word "pur" has been linked with the "lot" cast by Haman to determine the most propitious day for the extermination of the Jews (3:7). This is not a major element in the plot, but it serves to give a specifically Jewish dimension to a festival much older than the Jews' first celebration of it. Today Purim remains a major festival of the Jewish year, an occasion of feasting, gift giving, and charity. Its principal religious ceremony is the public reading, once in the evening and once in the morning, of the book of Esther from a special scroll (Heb. *megillah*).

10:1–3, Mordecai as a Symbol of Jewish Success. This closing note, perhaps later appended, of the high office and esteem of Mordecai is probably not intended to detract from the significance of Esther, but to round off the story with a cameo portrait of the possibility and desirability of Jewish-gentile cooperation. A Jew who is highly esteemed by his compatriots (10:3) may still be a Persian official of the highest rank, to the advantage of Jews and Gentiles alike.

Bibliography

Anderson, B. W. "The Place of the Book of Esther in the Christian Bible." *Journal of Religion* 30 (1950):32–43.

Berg, S. B. *The Book of Esther: Motifs, Themes and Structure*. Society of Biblical Literature Dissertation Series, 44. Missoula, MT: Scholars Press, 1979.

Clines, D. J. A. *The Esther Scroll: The Story of the Story*. Journal for the Study of the Old Testament Supplement Series, no. 30. Sheffield: JSOT Press, 1984.

————. *Ezra, Nehemiah, Esther*. New Century Bible Commentary. Grand Rapids, MI: Eerdmans; London: Marshall, Morgan and Scott, 1984.

Moore, C. A. *Esther*. Anchor Bible, 7B. Garden City, NY: Doubleday, 1971.

————. *Studies in the Book of Esther*. New York: Ktav, 1982.

PART TWO

PSALMS AND WISDOM

INTRODUCTION TO
PSALMS AND WISDOM

J A M E S L. K U G E L

Beside historical writings, bodies of legal material, prophetic collections, and the like, the Hebrew Bible contains numerous songs, prayers, compilations of wise sayings, and similar compositions. These are sometimes found in the midst of narratives (as the "Song at the Red Sea," Exod. 15, is found in the midst of the Exodus narrative), but they exist as well in independent collections such as those of the books of Psalms, Proverbs, Job, Ecclesiastes, and the Song of Songs. Indeed, these works are sometimes spoken of as the "poetic and didactic" books of the Bible, and the name, though inexact, represents well the view that such books stand apart from the rest of the Bible by virtue of their special "literary" or "poetic" character. Indeed, it was apparently such a judgment that led to the arrangement of books that is now found in many modern Christian Bibles (and whose roots ultimately go back to the Old Greek Bible of the Jews, the Septuagint), an arrangement that groups the material according to the categories (Law and) History, Psalms and Wisdom, and Prophecy. In introducing this middle group, Psalms and Wisdom, we shall thus be dealing with a collection of different writings that struck early readers of Scripture as fundamentally similar because of their literary artistry and poetic character—but that nonetheless appear to modern scholars as quite diverse in their origins, literary types, life setting, and structure. Although there is some overlap between the two broad categories "Psalms" and "Wisdom"—some psalms, as we shall see, are redolent of the wisdom worldview—it will be best to deal with each of these separately.

PSALMS

The book of Psalms (or "Psalter") is a collection of one hundred and fifty brief compositions that might generally be described as praises and prayers addressed to God. As such, these compositions are hardly unique in the Bible; as noted, narratives also contain songs of praise like the Song at the Red Sea, as well as personal prayers, and prophetic collections contain compositional units similar to those found in the Psalter. Indeed, some psalms themselves occur both within the Psalter and outside of it (e.g., Ps. 18 = 2 Sam. 22). Thus our book of Psalms is in some sense an arbitrary collection of diverse materials—in

Previous page: Head of David; one of several medallion mosaics in the apse of the Church of St. Catherine, Sinai, sixth century A.D.

fact, as scholars have come to see, a collection of smaller collections reflecting quite different origins and original purposes.

How did our Psalms come to be written in the first place? Much recent research has suggested that, like other divine praises known from elsewhere in the ancient Near East, the Psalms—or at least many of them—were connected with the formal worship conducted at specific sacred sites, sites like the great Jerusalem Temple, where animals and other sacrifices were offered up to honor Israel's God. The precise role of the Psalms in sacrificial worship is, however, far from clear. Remarkably, there is no mention of psalmody in prescriptions in the Pentateuch for sanctuary worship, but it seems likely that psalms and sacrifices were somehow coordinate forms of worship, the sacrifices constituting a standardized and quite tangible medium of human-to-divine communication, and songs and prayers constituting a more diverse, and wholly verbal, medium. The latter might have had, thereby, a somewhat more specific, even personalized, character: after all, there is not merely one "formula of thanks," "prayer for aid," and so forth in the Psalter, but dozens, and this diversity may bespeak an effort to create in the Psalms a verbal expression that, while perhaps accompanying standard sacrifices, would serve to connect the offering with the particular circumstances and motivation of the offerer(s).

This hypothesis is supported by the very words of some of the psalms found in our Psalter. There are, of course, numerous psalms that are expressions of community celebration, and these doubtless served as liturgies for such occasions as the various festivals and holy days described in the Pentateuch. But there are others of a more individual character, psalms that evoke states of distress such as illness or personal intrigue, or that offer thanks for God's having "heard my cry" in time of need. Yet these evocations—curiously!—lack detail: the identity of the psalmist's "enemies" or the precise nature of the dire straits involved is glossed over. They are alluded to starkly as "the Underworld," "the Pit," or represented metaphorically by wild beasts or similar perils. Apparently this lack of specifics was intentional, a way of tailoring the individual's plea or praise to his or her circumstances, but in such a way as to permit the reuse of a particular text again and again by different worshipers.

Thus, a great many, indeed, most of our psalms were likely connected to the formal worship of God through sacrifices at sacred sites, and their form and very words reflect this original life setting. Indeed, much of recent Psalms scholarship has been devoted to exploring that life setting in detail, and to classifying psalms into different putative genres or literary types, depending on whether the psalm was apparently intended for the individual or the community, and whether its intent was principally praise or petition (→ Psalms, The). Such classification notwithstanding, it would be a gross distortion to reduce our Psalter to a collection of verbal accompaniments to sacrificial worship which, in the absence of such a form of worship, now lack a significant context. Quite the contrary. Indeed there is clear evidence that well within the

397

biblical period, psalmody itself had developed something of an independent existence: the singing or speaking of the words of existing psalms (as well as the creation of new ones inspired by extant models) became a form of individual or group devotion outside of the sacrificial setting, and under such new circumstances, the very words of the Psalms themselves sometimes took on new meanings. Since late antiquity, the book of Psalms has been the focus of Jewish and Christian spirituality, providing much of the actual liturgy for synagogues and churches (as well, again, as a model for new liturgical compositions), and the recitation of psalms as a form of individual devotion has similarly flourished since ancient times. Thus, however diverse the origins and purposes of its various components, the Psalter has in effect taken on a unified identity and use all its own, as a manual of prayer and praise through the ages.

THE WAY OF WISDOM

"Wisdom literature" is a modern critical term used to describe a kind of writing that flourished not only in ancient Israel but throughout the ancient Near East. Its hallmark in the Bible is the *mashal* (Heb., "proverb"), that pithy, two-part sentence that embodied some fundamental truth about life. The *mashal* is the basic building block of the books of Job, Proverbs, and Ecclesiastes, and is well known in other parts of the canon also, especially in the book of Psalms and prophetic oracles. (It is also characteristic of some books in the Apocrypha, such as Sirach and Wisdom of Solomon.) But to understand the *mashal* and the books that are collections of *meshalim* (Heb., "proverbs"), it is necessary first to understand something about "wisdom" itself.

Wisdom was not only a class of writings in ancient Israel; it was first and foremost a way of life and of understanding the world. The wise man or sage was one who sought to look deeply into the meaning of things, and as such he was a valued member of society. He was associated with various (related) professions: royal counselor and court adviser, judge, teacher, scribe. The sage in the ancient Near East was one who knew how to interpret dreams—the portrayal of both Joseph and Daniel in the Bible is redolent in many particulars of the world of wisdom—and to interpret other mysteries as well, the movement of the stars and planets, omens of animals and birds, indeed, of the natural world in its fullness. Although some of these pursuits have little to do with the biblical books in question, they belong to the same organic unity and bespeak, to a great extent, the same mentality.

What is that mentality, the "world of wisdom"? Among its fundamental tenets is the belief that the world makes sense, that underlying all the apparent confusion and injustice and disorder of daily existence is a basic pattern, an ordering by which all such phenomena can ultimately be understood. This pattern itself is sometimes referred to as *hokmah* (Heb., "wisdom") as in Prov. 3:19:

> By wisdom the Lord founded the earth;
> by understanding he established the heavens.

398

One who can perceive the pattern, or at least part of it, is said to have "found" or "acquired" wisdom—but such is no easy undertaking according to Ps. 92:5:

> How great are your creations, Lord,
> and most profound your plans;
> a simple man does not know,
> nor a fool understand this.

How then could one go about glimpsing this underlying pattern? "Whence then comes wisdom, and where is the place of understanding?" (Job 28:20).

An outsider to the world of wisdom might say that acquiring wisdom was first and foremost an act of faith, a willingness to believe, despite at times considerable evidence to the contrary, that all is happening according to plan and that the old verities about divine justice, the triumph of righteousness, and the necessity for fair and pious conduct were still the best guide in leading one's life. But biblical wisdom texts themselves present another answer: evidence of the workings of this pattern and order does indeed present itself, if only one is sufficiently discerning and takes the "long view." As Ecclesiastes observes, "Better is the end of a thing than its beginning" (7:8). How so? Beginnings, however auspicious, can go awry, and that which started off so well can come to naught. The thing completed, on the other hand, is unarguable: how it *may* turn out was beforehand a matter of opinion, but once it *has* turned out it is simply a fact. And what is life but a series of processes that are ever moving toward their conclusion, often ending up in configurations that would surprise their beginnings? So, of course, "Better is the end of a thing than its beginning" because it is only the "end of a thing" that counts.

So it is that we can discern one of the cardinal virtues in the world of wisdom: patience. Indeed, the proverb from Ecclesiastes just cited is, in its entirety, "Better is the end of a thing than its beginning, and the patient one better than the haughty." For only with patience can one hold back from snap judgments and escape the prison of the moment. In fact, the English word "patience" corresponds well to the whole spirit of Israelite wisdom, for it suggests not only an ability to wait things out, but also an ability to accept discomfort and suffering (the Latin root of "patience" means suffering and is present in, for example, the English use of "patient" for someone suffering from a disease and under a doctor's care). So too the sage is one who has patience and knows that, however much at any given moment the world seems to be in imbalance and he himself or others are forced to suffer in a manner that appears unjust, sooner or later the underlying order will appear; things will be set aright again, or a previously unknown explanation will become apparent. So it is, for example, that Joseph, whom we have already seen as having many of the characteristics of the sage, is swept up by events beyond his control, sold as a slave to Egypt, then falsely accused and thrown into prison. A "fool" —that is, the opposite of a "sage" and the constant foil of sages in books like Proverbs and Ecclesiastes—would certainly despair under such circumstances or undertake desperate action, but Joseph, sage that he is, patiently greets each new turn, and ultimately assumes his place as ruler over Egypt. When, at last, he reveals his true identity to his brothers, he urges them not to blame themselves for having dealt ill with him, for their actions were only part of the divine plan (Gen. 45:5–8); later he says, "As for you, you meant evil against me, but God meant it for good, to bring it about that many people should be alive, as they are today" (Gen. 50:20).

Proverbs

This virtue of patience is very much in evidence in our biblical book of Proverbs, a collection of wise sayings and exhortations from different periods and geographic centers. One who first looks into Proverbs will immediately be struck by the "old-time" morality found in this book. Here are no surprises: honesty, diligence, self-restraint, and humility—"the wise man's path" (Prov. 15:24)—are endlessly praised, while their opposites are unceasingly condemned. Read in sequence, its chapters take on the quality of a litany of virtues, a kind of propaganda tract for the way of wisdom. Through this array of praiseworthy traits, it is perhaps patience (in the sense in which we have described it) that dominates the picture, though the concept itself is scarcely invoked. For though the "fool" or the "wicked" (the two are synonymous in Proverbs) may gain immediate satisfaction, it is the "sage" or the "righteous" who wins out in the end, as in Prov. 10:17–18:

> The fear of the Lord lengthens life,
> but the years of the wicked will be short.
> The hope of the righteous ends in gladness,
> but the expectation of the wicked perishes.

Patience is not only the proper attitude of the sage in the face of the wicked man's immediate gratification or of his own suffering or frustration; it is also that by which the ultimate justice of the world, the great pattern underlying human existence, will ultimately become apparent. Thus, Prov. 13:18, 21:

> Poverty and disgrace come to him who ignores instruction,
> but he who heeds reproof is honored.
> Misfortune pursues sinners,
> but prosperity rewards the righteous.

Indeed, what are continence, abstemiousness, respect for parents and teachers, humility, and the other virtues of Proverbs but a reflex of that general attitude of patient moderation that is the hallmark of the righteous sage?

It is virtually a logical consequence of this mentality that wisdom itself is properly associated only with old age. A young person may strive to master the sages' teachings (the "son" spoken of, or to, in so many proverbs is, apparently, a young initiate setting out on the path of wisdom), but only with age can one overcome youth's impetuousness, and only with age can one see the truth of wisdom's dictates confirmed in the end. So is it that the word "old man" is virtually synonymous with "sage": "Wisdom is with the aged, and understanding in length of days" (Job 12:12). For the same reason Elihu is reluctant to speak out in the book of Job (32:6–7):

> I am young in years, and you are aged;
> therefore I was timid and afraid to declare my opinion to you.
> I said: "Let days speak, and many years
> teach wisdom."

The old man knows the lessons of the past (Deut. 32:7) and the lessons of his own life; but more than that he is one who has endured, and this in itself bespeaks his mastery of the path of wisdom—thus Prov. 16:31:

> A hoary head is a crown of glory;
> it is gained in a righteous life.

We have seen how the notions of "patience" and "suffering" are intertwined, and it is perhaps not surprising that suffering too is addressed in Israelite wisdom literature. But is suffering, as "orthodox" wisdom would have it, always the reward of wickedness?

Job and Ecclesiastes: Two Challenges

This is the question of Job, the sage whose wisdom is challenged by personal catastrophe and physical suffering in order that his ability to endure patiently and reverently be put to the test. Most of our biblical book of Job is taken up with "dialogues" between Job and his comforters, sages come from the proverbial centers of wisdom and who therefore represent the wisdom worldview in its purest form. They attempt a particular form of "comforting" known to us from elsewhere in the Near East—an attempt to bring the sufferer to accept his suffering as part of the divine plan, and therefore as just, no matter how great his pain. That this is what comforting is all about or that wisdom's whole world of patience and plan underlies their remarks is nowhere stated; it did not have to be. It is evident in their very identity as sages. But the person of Job here is set in contrast to those of his fellow sages: he is, in Eliphaz's first words, "impatient" (Job 4:5) because he dares to challenge the canons of wisdom and refuses to accept their comfort. The book as we have it is therefore not so much an exposition of wisdom teachings (wisdom's basic teachings are assumed by the very form of the book, though eloquently reiterated in the comforters' words) as it is a serious challenge to it: these are the meditations of an author disturbed by wisdom's pat verities in the face of human suffering—though he is willing, in the end, to give God the last word.

Ecclesiastes is another book that presumes the world of wisdom as we have described it and that also seeks to question its dictates, albeit in a somewhat different fashion. Its author knows the version of the world espoused by sages but sets out (Eccles. 2) to put everything to the test: is hokmah, the path of wisdom and restraint enjoined by the sages, the best in life, or is its opposite, siklut (Heb., often translated as "folly," the word in Ecclesiastes means self-indulgence and hedonism) the way to choose? Although the answer is quick in coming (Eccles. 2:13), the book's search is far from over; indeed, it implies that learning the truth of wisdom's way is a lifelong task. For the book of Ecclesiastes is framed by its author's life: the young hedonist of chap. 2 ages as his book progresses, and at each turn he propounds new insights in his clipped *meshalim*. But he does not hesitate to confess his frustration: however much the ancient verities seem validated here and there, he is nonetheless baffled at the world's unfairness. How, for example, can one continue to maintain that the righteous are rewarded in old age and the wicked are cut off, when our very experience tells us differently? "Surely it happens that a righteous man may perish in his righteousness, and that a wicked man may live long life in his wickedness" (Eccles. 7:15). It is all *hebel* (Heb.), not so much "vanity" (as this word is often translated) as something insubstantial, ungraspable, futile. In this very judgment is a summons to go on, and as our author continues his quest he sometimes contradicts what he has said before; at the end of his book he is apparently an old man (Eccles. 12 presents a moving description of the progress of old age); indeed, at the very end he is spoken of in the third person, already dead (Eccles. 12:9–10). Considered as a whole, Ecclesiastes is a remarkable book, a collection of wise sayings that is at the same time a quarrel with wisdom teachings, a sort of brief intellectual autobiography of one who was not content merely to transmit the accepted maxims.

Song of Songs

Having made mention of the major works of wisdom literature in the Hebrew Bible, we ought as well to say a word about the Song of Songs, since it too is connected to wisdom's world. Anyone who reads the Song will recognize in it a series of love lyrics between a shepherd girl and her rustic lover. Yet the very presence of this book within Israel's sacred Scriptures, indeed its collocation with other books of wisdom, suggests that this external form was understood as just that, an outer covering that, like proverbs generally, required deep inspection for its full significance to emerge. Read in such a manner, the Song yielded a meaning fully consonant with the teachings of wisdom: for what was the significance of the on-again, off-again encounters between lover and beloved, the alternating evocations of nearness and frustrating distance, but that God's ways with his people are similarly trying, alternatingly blissful and unfulfilled? Patience, the sagely virtue, is a human being's sole recourse; this is the hidden sense of the Song's refrain, "Do not stir up, oh do not arouse Love before its time." And yet, in this context, there is something wonderful about the lovers' urgent desire for one another, a suggestion that the sage's life was not merely the colorless, rather passive, submission to divine will that we have described, but something vibrant as well, a passionate and vital devotion.

POETIC FORM

It remains only to say a few words about the form of the *mashal*, and more generally about the form in which not only much of Israel's wisdom literature but the Psalms and a great deal more in the Hebrew Bible are written. For the basic unit that makes up almost all of the Bible's songs, psalms, proverbs (*meshalim*), oracles, sayings and the like is a clipped, two-part sentence that might be represented schematically like this:

$$\underline{\hspace{3cm}} / \qquad \underline{\hspace{3cm}} //$$
$$\qquad A \qquad\qquad\qquad\qquad B$$

The notations / and // represent two different sorts of pauses, partial and full, and might be said to correspond to the comma and semicolon or period in our system of punctuation. The first part of the sentence (A) ends in a slight pause, the second in a longer one; these pauses in turn are expressive of the relationship between the two parts. For B, although separated from A by a slight pause, is nonetheless a continuation of it and its completion; whereas the break between B and the next line is more substantial—B is "end-stopped" and does not flow into the next line. A brief example (Ps. 111:1–3) will make the structure clear:

> I will praise the Lord with all my heart / in the company of the upright and the assembly //

> Great are the works of the Lord / studied by all who have pleasure in them //

> Splendor and majesty are his work / and his righteousness endures forever //

Each of the above lines is just the sort of two-part sentence described, in which the B part is both separated from A by a brief pause (the above translation, taken from the RSV, does in fact divide each A clause from B with a comma), yet grammatically and semantically connected to it. The end of each line is, by contrast, more final (RSV punctuates with periods). How are these two grades of separation achieved? In the examples cited, one might note that the first two A parts are complete statements in and of themselves, grammatically independent, while their following Bs cannot stand alone; this is one very common way of articulating B's separate-yet-connected status. The third line contains two potentially independent clauses, but B's "and" here serves to emphasize the connection.

This "adding on" or "seconding" style of writing, in which each A was followed up, carried further, or otherwise completed by its corresponding B (and, on occasion, by a third clause, C) was very versatile, both easily accomplished and yet elegant in its regularity; it created an oscillating pattern of partial and full disjunction, of brief lines with a short break in the middle and a longer break at the end. This is what constitutes the "poetry" of the Bible, though it is a form of poetry that involves neither rhyme nor regular meter, but only the approximate regularity imposed by the brevity of A and B (each usually consists of only two to four words in Hebrew) (→Poetry). It also is a form that frequently has an emphatic character: B is sometimes made to restate A or intensify its meaning as in Ps. 92:12:

> The righteous man will flourish like a palm tree / [indeed] like a cedar in Lebanon he will grow great //

Now when one turns to the wisdom proverb, this same emphatic sort of sentence recurs (its prominence has in fact led this particular style to be labeled, somewhat misleadingly, *parallelism*, because B often *parallels* A in grammar or meaning). An example is Prov. 10:1:

> A wise son makes a father glad / but a foolish son is his mother's sorrow //

But one also finds a more subtle use of the bipartite form, in which, for example, there is an implicit comparison between A and B, as in Prov. 11:22:

> A golden ring in a pig's snout / a beautiful woman poorly behaved //

Here mere physical beauty is compared to the dazzle of gold: it is doubtless of value, but, shackled to an uncouth spirit that leads it about, it loses all its charm. This is the meaning of the proverb, but we have hardly exhausted the evocativeness of its image in which our perception of physical beauty is made to precede the nonphysical qualities as the golden ring precedes the pig in its peregrinations. Another comparison (which is also informative about how the makers of proverbs saw their own handiwork) is Prov. 26:9:

> A thistle alights in a drunkard's hand / and a proverb in the mouth of a fool //

The thistle comes into the drunkard's possession not by design but rather by mishap: groping around on the ground, the victim of his own inebriation, he accidentally gets jabbed. So is it with fools who pretend to be sages and even recite proverbs: they have not taken possession of the proverb *intentionally*—that is, through the systematic pursuit of and devotion to the way of wisdom—but casually, accidentally, and without real understanding. Far from being truly the fool's possession, his proverb is his adversary, it pricks him and does him no good.

Merely knowing the words, then, did not necessarily imply understanding: indeed, establishing the precise relationship between A and B was sometimes the whole point of the proverb. Often that relationship was not so much "Just as A ... / so B ... //" (as we have seen it to be in the previous examples), but more "Since A ... / therefore B ... //" or "You know A ... / now understand B ... //." This is really how the previously cited proverb, Eccles. 7:8, is to be understood:

> Better is the end of a thing than its beginning / and the patient one better than the haughty //

Everyone knows—for the reason explained above—that the project completed is infinitely more valuable than the project just undertaken; *since that is so*, our proverb argues, so one who is patient and is able to follow things through their course is better than one who is "haughty." Now haughtiness is no more the precise opposite of patience in Hebrew than in English, but in formulating this proverb as he has, our author is in fact relating the two. When one considers the haughty person, with his take-charge, "What's-going-on-here?" attitude, and compares his stance to the taciturnity and apparent passivity of the patient one, the former's course may indeed be appealing. But beware, says our proverb: just as you know that the end of a thing is better than its beginning, so understand patience ultimately wins out over haughtiness. We see a similar example in Prov. 27:6:

A friend's criticism is trustworthy / false are an enemy's kisses //

The first part of the proverb (a more literal translation would be: "The wounds of a friend are trustworthy") is one whose truth has been experienced by all: who has not been stung by a friend's criticism, a criticism whose reliability is vouchsafed by its very source? A friend does not criticize to hurt, but to correct and set aright (cf. Prov. 15:12; 19:25; 27:5 [the verse just preceding ours]; and esp. 28:23). However clear that lesson may be, its opposite may prove nonetheless elusive: flattery has its appeal, and we may welcome praise ("kisses") even when of notorious provenance. Hence our proverb's true import: you already know that the barbs of a friend are sincere; now understand, therefore, that an enemy's kisses are by the same logic not to be trusted. Their source utterly undermines their substance. One final example is Prov. 10:18:

One who conceals hatred has lying lips / one who spreads slander is a fool //

No doubt the truth of A and B is clear enough, but what is the relationship of the two to each other? To repeat, A and B are not to be understood merely as juxtaposed assertions, but as *significantly* juxtaposed, and the unfolding of that significance is what is meant by understanding a proverb. So here we begin by noticing that the two actions described in A and B are in fact opposites. The first involves not telling when telling is warranted, for if, instead of making a clean breast of one's hatred and its cause (allowing, thereby, the hated person to seek to make amends), one instead covers over that hatred, the result is hypocrisy, "lying lips" in the words of our proverb. Part B, on the other hand, involves a form of telling that is not warranted, that is, the telling to others about a person behind the person's back that is called in the Bible *dibbah* (Heb., "slander"; as in Gen. 37:2; Prov. 25:10). But these two actions are not unrelated, for the *not telling* involved in dissembling hatred often leads to the *telling* of *dibbah*, and one who hypocritically hides feelings in front of an enemy will often slander that enemy when he or she is not around. So it is that the two are juxtaposed here, just as in biblical law (see Lev. 19:16–17); indeed, the import of this juxtaposition is quite similar to that of Prov. 25:9–10, whereby failure to confront a disputant openly leads to "disclosing a secret" to others, which in turn may backfire and turn oneself into the ultimate subject of others' *dibbah*.

Such are the ways of wisdom—and more than wisdom! For such pithy, dense, two-part sayings are found not only within the corpus of "wisdom literature," but here and there in narrative and in biblical law as well. (Indeed, the connection of the world of wisdom to such legal compilations as are found in Deuteronomy or in Leviticus, has

405

become increasingly apparent in recent years.) The two-part sentence upon which the *mashal* is built is, as explained, the basic building block of what is called biblical poetry, and its self-enclosed, couplet-like quality apparently had wide appeal. This sentence form, with its infinite potential for subtle juxtaposition, intensification, and refinement, might truly be said to be the vehicle of choice for biblical Israel's literary creativity, one most fully evidenced in the Bible's Psalms and wisdom literature.

Bibliography

On the Psalms:

Kugel, J. L. "Topics in the History of the Spirituality of the Psalms." In *Jewish Spirituality: From the 16th Century Renewal to the Present.* Vol. 1. Edited by A. Green. New York: Crossroad, 1987. Pp. 113–144.

Miller, P. D. *Interpreting the Psalms.* Philadelphia: Fortress, 1986.

Westermann, C. *Praise and Lament in the Psalms.* Translated by K. R. Crim and R. N. Soulen. Atlanta, GA: Knox, 1981.

On Wisdom:

Crenshaw, J. L. *Old Testament Wisdom: An Introduction.* Altanta, GA: Knox, 1981.

Kugel, J. L. *The Idea of Biblical Poetry: Parallelism and Its History.* New Haven, CT: Yale University Press, 1981. Pp. 1–58.

von Rad, G. *Wisdom in Israel.* Translated by J. D. Martin. Nashville, TN: Abingdon Press, 1972.

JOB

EDWIN M. GOOD

INTRODUCTION

Overview

The praise the Book of Job has received may put some readers off. After all, who feels equal to comprehending "one of the grandest things ever written" (Carlyle)? But Job is too well worth the effort of understanding for readers to pass it by in favor of the mediocre. And, unlike the mediocre, the excellent requires effort of its readers, a willingness to work mentally, to read a passage again when comprehension does not come immediately, to think hard about what one has read.

It is most useful for modern readers to approach Job as fiction. Job refers only to itself; it does not factually portray anything outside itself. To view the book as fiction may help to keep distractions about it at bay. One does well to think of Job, Eliphaz, and the others as characters in a story, not as actors in history.

Outline. The book consists of five parts:

Part One (1:1–2:13): The opening tale
Part Two (3:1–31:40): Dialogue with the friends
Part Three (32:1–37:24): Speeches of Elihu
Part Four (38:1–42:6): Dialogue with Yahweh
Part Five (42:7–17): The closing tale

Summary. In the opening tale, the great man Job loses his wealth and children and is subjected to a painful disease after discussions between God and a character I will call the Prosecutor. Expected to curse God because of this experience, Job refuses to do so. Three friends come to comfort him and sit with him in silence for seven days.

Job opens the dialogue by cursing his birthday (chap. 3), and the friends then reply, urging Job to admit his fault and return to good terms with God. Job insists that he has done nothing to deserve the punishment he is receiving. Neither side persuades the other of anything, and Job closes with a long speech (chaps. 29–31) describing his pleasant past life and lamenting its loss. With a series of curses on himself, he calls on God to answer him. Elihu, a previously unmentioned friend, suggests that both Job and the friends were wrong about the suffering (chaps. 32–37).

Now the deity speaks to Job "out of the whirlwind," asking hard questions about the universe and the habits of various powerful animals, challenging Job to reply (38:1–40:2). Job is noncommittal (40:3–5), at which the deity insists that he answer and invites him to control human evil, a monstrous creature named Behemoth and another named Leviathan (40:6–41:34). Then Job speaks in a conciliatory way, saying that he now has firsthand knowledge (42:1–6).

At the end (42:7–17), God criticizes the friends and reinstates them in his favor. Job is comforted for his troubles, receives twice his former wealth and a new family of children, and comes to a satisfactory death.

The opening and closing tale are prose narrative, and the middle three sections, all speeches, are in poetry (save for one-line introductions to the speeches and a brief introduction of Elihu in 32:1–5). The dialogue between Job and the friends falls into a consistent pattern. Job speaks (chap. 3), and Eliphaz replies (chaps. 4–5). A second speech of Job (chaps. 6–7) is followed by a speech of Bildad (chap. 8), and after Job's third speech (chaps. 9–10) comes one by Zophar (chap. 11). The same pattern occurs in chaps. 12–20, with Job speaking between each of the friends. The third cycle begins like the others, with a speech of Job (chap. 21) and one of Eliphaz (chap. 22), then Job again (chaps. 23–24) followed by a short speech of Bildad (chap. 25). Job then speaks without interruption (chaps. 26–31), and there is no speech by Zophar in this cycle. Thus the speeches create three cycles, the third slightly skewed in structure; Job has both the first word (chap. 3) and the last (the summation speech, chaps. 29–31).

Elihu's speech is divided into four parts by opening formulas; the dialogue between Job and Yahweh (38:1–42:6) also falls into four parts, two long speeches of Yahweh and two short ones of Job.

Origins of the Book

Language. Job is written in an extremely sophisticated, "learned" Hebrew, with a higher proportion of words unique to itself than any other book of the Hebrew Bible. The issue of language is raised otherwise only by some theories that the book was originally composed in Aramaic or in Arabic. Such proposals cannot be demonstrated. That a work so subtle and complex in style is a translation seems unlikely, and theories that it was not originally Hebrew have found very few supporters.

Authorship. One Jewish tradition names Moses as the author of Job, but otherwise there was little speculation about it. Reticence about attempting to identify the author is well advised. Some scholars believe there was more than one author, others that one or several editors gave the book its final form. Surely it is the work of more than one mind, if only in the sense that it underwent changes in the process of copying and, perhaps, of editing. But authors or editors left no discernible traces of identity.

Location of Writing. Because chaps. 40–41 describe animals that some scholars identify as a hippopotamus and a crocodile, they have argued a location in Egypt, where these animals are native. The commentary will show that I do not think Behemoth and Leviathan are those animals. That the language is Hebrew indicates that the book was written in Israel. No regional dialect is identifiable, and no specific part of the territory can be determined. The book is not, however, set in Israel. Its characters come from places in Edom, southeast of Israel (→ Edom). Yet that setting is no more reason for thinking Job was composed in Edom than the setting of *Hamlet* in Elsinore is reason to think that Shakespeare wrote the play in Denmark. Some passages betray knowledge of desert travel and of various wild and domestic animals, but geographical location plays no part in the book's meaning.

Date. If we cannot say where Job originated, it is equally difficult to say when. Ezekiel referred to Job as an important person alongside Noah and Daniel (Ezek. 14:14–20). Moreover, tradition put him in the patriarchal period and made the book one of the oldest in the Bible. Modern scholars are skeptical of this claim to antiquity, but dates proposed range from the tenth to the third century B.C. The book itself is completely silent about its time, with no allusions to historical events or topical subjects (some take 12:17–19 as a depiction of the Exile). If we could be certain of the history of the Hebrew language or of the relations between one text and another, we could more confidently assign a date. Some affinities of Job 3 with Jer. 20:7–18, for example, do not allow certainty of which passage came first. Stylistic similarities between Job and Isaiah 40–55 have also been alleged. Those connections suggest a time either before the early sixth century B.C. (if Job is prior) or in the late sixth or early fifth century B.C. (if Job is later). Job 7:17–18 is almost surely a parody of Psalm 8, but no one can be sure when Psalm 8 was written. Job 3:4 is a parodistic allusion to Gen. 1:3, a creation account usually dated after the Exile in the sixth century B.C. Such evidence suggests but does not prove that Job was composed and completed after the Babylonian exile.

Composition. Here we ask about the process through which the book achieved its final form. One supposes either that an author "composed" the book over a long or short period or that it is "composite," brought together from diverse sources. But our modern assumptions about books are inappropriate for ancient ones. The process of copying by hand, the only way ancient books could be circulated, means that we cannot be sure we are reading what an "original" author wrote. The structure of the book outlined above may provide some bases for guesses. Chaps. 1, 2, and 42 are written in a relatively simple prose style that some scholars have compared to folktale. The poetry in the middle of the book is very complex and difficult, full of unusual words and unusual thoughts. Supposing that a single mind tends not to produce such different kinds of writing, scholars propose that one or more poets took an existing folktale (to which Ezekiel referred?) and inserted the poetic dialogues into it. On the other hand, Elihu turns up in chap. 32 without prior mention and disappears at the end of chap. 37 without later mention. Most scholars think that the Elihu speeches were interpolated into the book by another poet; they note the Hebrew style in these speeches differs from that of the rest of the book. Some scholars have argued that the speeches of Yahweh (chaps. 38–41) were added or modified later.

More complications: chap. 28 breaks suddenly into the debate with a puzzling discussion of mining, metallurgy, and wisdom. Arguing that it was inserted later, scholars seldom explain why. In the third cycle of speeches, Bildad's (chap. 25) is unusually short, and Zophar has no speech at all. Some scholars, noticing what seems self-contradiction in Job's speeches around Bildad's, wish to add 26:5–14 to Bildad's speech and put together a speech for Zophar from such passages, now in Job's mouth, as 24:18–20, 22–25 and 27:8–23. Such observations lead scholars to postulate several stages in the book's composition. All such conclusions can be no more than guesses, as we have no copies of Job representing these stages. In my opinion, a poet probably used the existing prose tale as an occasion for the debate, Elihu's entrance was staged by a later editor, and perhaps chap. 28 was added by someone with great sensitivity to the argument around it. I doubt that the third cycle is garbled, and I think the Yahweh speeches belong. In any case, the book as it now stands is the one we have to read, and omitting later additions gives us no demonstrable access to the minds of earlier authors.

Relations to Other Works

The Relation of Job to Other Literature.
No book is an island, unrelated to any other.
Some literary theorists think that every book
is but a comment on other books. Job has
forerunners in Mesopotamia, Canaan, Egypt,
and perhaps even Greece in the use of dialogue
form, and some of those dialogues deal with the
meaning of suffering. But Job seems unique in
the ancient world, with no clear indications that
its dialogue was influenced in style or form by
these other works. The problem of undeserved
suffering is a staple of ancient literature from
early in the second millennium B.C. on, and the
problem was solved in varied ways. But I find no
ancient Near Eastern work that has influenced
the ways in which Job handles the problem.

The book is often classed among other Near
Eastern and biblical works as "wisdom literature" on the basis of a high value placed on
wisdom in those works. The term is modern,
not ancient, referring in the Hebrew Bible to
Job, Ecclesiastes, and Proverbs, along with a
few psalms. Job is the only one of those books
with the dialogue structure and a short but not
fragmentary narrative; its point of view is diametrically opposite, for example, to most of the
proverbs, in which wise people are righteous
and good and fools are wicked and unsuccessful. Job's friends display the attitudes of the
wise in Proverbs but show them false and unproductive. Perhaps Job belongs in the wisdom
literature as the exception to its rigidities.

Job in the Biblical Canon. In the Hebrew
Bible, Job appears either before or after Proverbs
among the Writings (Heb. *Kethubim*), the third
division of the canon. Such different place-
ments have yet to be explained. In the Christian
OT, Job appears most often as the first of the
Writings, preceding Psalms (where it is in Christian Bibles today), sometimes at the end of the
Writings before the Prophets, sometimes after
the Prophets. We do not know how Job was used
in the Jewish community, whether it had a place
in synagogue reading or in what contexts it was
studied. Early Christian sermons indicate that
Job provided texts for preaching, and some
church fathers, e.g., Clement of Alexandria, Origen, and Chrysostom, wrote commentaries and
treatises on Job. The book was translated into
Greek in the Septuagint, but modern scholarship has shown how thoroughly this version
eviscerated the hard edge of the Joban arguments. Since most Christian interpreters dealt
with the book in Greek, they had a rather pale
text to read.

Job and Modern Culture. In modern times,
when people are willing to ponder a Bible not
blandly consonant with the central strands of
their religious traditions, Job has come into its
own. Since William Blake's rather wild engrav-
ings, and Kierkegaard's independent interpretation of Job in *Repetition*, many modern writers
have used the book to comment on human problems, e.g., Archibald MacLeish (*J.B.*), Robert
Frost (*A Mask of Reason*), Joseph Roth (*Job*, a
novel), the Yiddish author I. L. Perets (*Bontsye
Schwaig*), and Robert Heinlein (*Job, A Comedy
of Justice*). Some critics interpret Franz Kafka's
The Trial as a transposition of Job. The modern
Italian composer Luigi Dallapiccola has set parts
of Job to music, and the English composer Ralph
Vaughan Williams wrote *Job, A Mask for Dancing*. Like much of the Bible, the book has become
an important artifact of culture and no longer
the exclusive property of religious communities.

COMMENTARY

1:1–2:13

The Opening Tale

Ezekiel mentions Job, with Noah and Daniel, as
one of the most righteous ancient worthies
(Ezek. 14:14, 20). The righteous Noah we know
from Genesis 6–9; the Daniel referred to by
Ezekiel we know not from the Bible but from a
Canaanite epic about a good king named Dan'el;
Job we know only here. All three figures, Noah,
Dan'el, and Job, were able to save others by their
righteousness. Ezekiel's reference suggests that,
like Noah and Dan'el, Job was a folk hero, the
epitome of "righteousness," whom our story
calls "scrupulously moral" (Job 1:1, 8; 2:3).

The story in Job 1–2 and 42:7–17 resembles
a folktale in some respects; it has the "once
upon a time" beginning (1:1–5), formulaic
structural markers ("It was the day," 1:6, 13;
2:1), the messengers' refrains ("And I escaped
all alone to tell you," 1:15, 16, 17, 19), the
formal greetings between Yahweh and the
Prosecutor (1:7; 2:2), and the repeated formula
describing Job (1:1, 8; 2:3). Yet this narrative is
not naive—it is pure in its simplicity and density. If calling Job 1–2 and 42:7–17 a folktale
leads readers to expect something rough, we
should not call it that. It seems unnecessary to
designate the genre more closely than as story
or narration.

The story structures itself in six parts, the
first general and introductory, the others successive episodes:

Episode A (1:1–5): Job's character and circumstances

409

Episode B (1:6–12): First scene in Yahweh's court
Episode C (1:13–22): Job's first calamity
Episode D (2:1–7a): Second scene in Yahweh's court
Episode E (2:7b–10): Job's second calamity
Episode F (2:11–13): The arrival of the friends

The outer episodes frame the story, the first describing Job, the last showing a ritual action, seven silent days (2:13), which make us expect that something is about to happen.

The middle four episodes alternate between Yahweh's court and Job's troubles in the land of Uz, a balanced regularity that is underscored by the formal similarity between episodes B and D. Yet balance is also upset by the change from episode C, told from Job's point of view as the messengers come one by one, to episode E, which narrates the calamity objectively and comments on it in the dialogue between Job and his wife. Moreover, episodes B–D all begin with the same phrase, "It was the day when," and end with similar conventional formality, but episode E plunges abruptly into action with no structural prelude.

The tale drives from a beginning in permanence and certainty to a transitional conclusion, though it presents a mixture of symmetry and difference. The similar remarks made about Job in 1:22 and 2:10 suggest that he has successfully met the Prosecutor's challenges to his moral integrity, though neither he nor his possessions remain intact. The issue has apparently been resolved. On the other hand, at the beginning and in both scenes in Yahweh's court, Job is described as "one who avoids evil" (1:1, 8; 2:3), but the friends come because of "all the evil that had come upon him" (2:11). The "feast days" of Job's sons in episode A (1:4, 5) turn to a death day in episode C (1:13); the meeting "days" of Elohim's sons in B and D (1:6; 2:1) issue in Job's suffering; and all give way in episode F to seven "days" of silence (2:13). By this point, it seems that the tale's problem has been intensified: evil formerly avoided is now present; days formerly joyful are now tragic and painful.

With the transition implied in the seven days of silence, we must wonder: what is the problem of this story, and is it resolved or intensified? To the latter we must say, "Both." For the former we must look again at the transactions between the Prosecutor and Yahweh.

To Yahweh's incautious boast about Job (1:8), the Prosecutor's response is heated: "Is Job religious [fears God] for nothing?" (v. 9). The rhetorical question calls for a negative answer, and the heat of the Prosecutor's reply overrides logic: Yahweh has "hedged around" Job and his goods with "blessing," but those goods have "burst out over the earth." If Yah-

weh ensures so responsive a piety as Job's, he ought not to boast about the man as if he were responsible for it.

The Prosecutor's challenge is extremely powerful. He proposes that Yahweh "touch" Job's possessions and goes on: "If he doesn't curse you to your face . . ." (1:11). The statement is a self-curse that omits the result clause. The curse formula is, "If A happens (or does not happen), may B happen." Usually the "B" clause is omitted (Job 31 presents a series of such curses, and in some, e.g., vv. 7–8, 9–10, the "B" clause is present). According to Job 1:11, the Prosecutor is willing to call down a calamity upon himself. He proposes neither a test ("Let's see if he flunks") nor a wager. The Prosecutor puts his own welfare on the line: the present clause implies the continuation, "May something awful happen to me!"

The word "bless" (Heb. brk), occurring several times in these chapters, sometimes seems to mean "to bless" (e.g., 1:10, 21), its usual meaning (→ Curse and Blessing), but sometimes appears to mean the opposite (1:5, 11; 2:5, 9). In the latter sense, have we a euphemism, a word substituted to avoid saying the unacceptable (e.g., that a person might, heaven forbid! curse the deity)? Or does the text present a deliberate ambiguity?

The Prosecutor proposes to call down a presumably nontrivial calamity upon himself if Job fails to "curse" (brk) Yahweh. That seems only fair, if Job's calamity is to be serious. The fact that in chap. 2 the Prosecutor is as healthy as before suggests that the curse has not been fulfilled. Indeed, Job did brk Yahweh, in the hymn in 1:21: "May Yahweh's name be blest." But in 2:5, when the Prosecutor repeats his self-curse, Job's wife urges him to do what the Prosecutor was sure he would do: "Curse (brk) Elohim and die!" (v. 9). Job accuses her of talking foolishness (v. 10) and does not do it, arguing that only good comes from God (if 2:10 is an assertion; if it is a question, he expects to receive both good and evil from God).

The Prosecutor never reappears. The reason is quite clear: Job did not brk Yahweh the second time, and the Prosecutor's prediction was fulfilled. This eventuality indicates that the ambiguous "bless/curse" is a structural element in the story.

Who is this "Prosecutor"? Most translations refer either to "Satan" or to "the Adversary." The Hebrew reads "the satan," the definite article showing that the word is a title, not a proper name. The term occurs several times in the Hebrew Bible meaning a legal opponent. He is certainly not the devil, who in Judaism had various names, "Satan" among them, while Christianity preferred Satan to others (→ Satan). In Job 1–2 and in Zechariah 3, "the satan" is a member of the divine court whose job is to maintain law and order, a kind of district attorney who brings malefactors to justice. The term "Prosecutor" shows that the word is a legal title, while "the Adversary" still suggests the later idea of a principle of evil. Understanding "the satan" as Yahweh's opponent has raised unnecessary questions about divine morality in the treatment of Job. By ancient lights, there is no such problem. A curse operated objectively, automatically, and without moral entailments.

Job has done nothing to put him in trouble with Yahweh, and yet at the end of chap. 2, his trouble is deepened, not resolved. His possessions are gone, his children are dead, his suffering is unremitting, his wife's support is ambiguous, and the friends who arrive to "console and comfort him" (2:11) perform funeral rites as if he were already dead (vv. 12–13). The debate in Yahweh's court is apparently settled, but the debate in the land of Uz has only begun.

3:1–31:40
The Dialogue

3:1–11:20
The First Cycle of Speeches

3:1–26, Job. Job had refused, even on serious provocation, to curse God. Now, after a week's silence, he curses (3:1) not the deity but "his day," i.e., (v. 3) his birthday.

His curse (vv. 4–5) alludes to creation: "That day, let there be darkness" (v. 4a) parodies Gen 1:3: "Let there be light." By images of God's and light's absence, of darkness dominating, avenging, and terrifying day, Job curses his birthday as a reversal of the first process of creation. In vv. 6–7, his curse on the night of his conception cancels time, which creation set in train (v. 6), and human procreation, which imitates divine creation (v. 7). Calling for those who by magic can control the Sea (a mythic enemy of the deity in Job) and Leviathan (see 40:15–41:34) for the reversal of night and dawn (v. 9), Job further invites the undoing of the creation. Light (v. 9) has become "toil" (v. 10). Job comes very close to cursing the deity without actually saying the words. Cursing the creation and all of its cosmic and human effects covers everything the deity has done.

The rest of the speech focuses on himself in two stanzas each beginning with "Why?" (vv. 11–19, 20–26). In the first, Job wishes he were dead, stillborn (vv. 11–12, 16), asleep (v. 13). Death is the leveler, sleep in company with kings, counselors, and princes (vv. 14–15), the absence of oppression and power (vv. 17–19). Death wishes are unusual in Israelite culture

(see Elijah, 1 Kings 19:4; Jonah, Jon. 4:3, 8). Still, because Israelites thought the deity did not visit the realm of the dead (Ps. 139:8 and Amos 9:2 are startling exceptions), Job's perception of death as freedom must include the notion of liberation from God.

Even though extending the idea to toilers and the world's weary (Job 3:20–26), Job is thinking primarily of himself. The Prosecutor's description of Yahweh's protecting him by "hedging" around him (1:10) feels to Job like constriction (3:23). He is reduced to animal conditions (v. 24), but, most surprisingly, "I was terrified of something, and it arrived, / what I feared comes to me" (v. 25). A most intriguing statement! Has his remarkable piety been motivated all along by the fear of suffering?

The last couplet (v. 26) drains away emotion. Life's positives, "tranquil," "quiet," "rest" (cf. vv. 13, 17), have given way to the negative, "turmoil" (cf. v. 17). Job's questions here flow from his curse on the creation and his birth: "Why am I alive? Why is anyone who prefers to be dead alive?" He does not ask, "Why did this happen to me?"

4:1–5:27, Eliphaz. This is the longest and most elaborate of the friends' speeches. Praising Job for strengthening others in trouble (4:2–5), he is sure that, because Job is religious, he will never experience the troubles of the wicked (vv. 6–11). But his frightening vision (vv. 12–21) has taught him that every human is liable to error (5:7a). Describing the fool's brief career (vv. 2–5), he counsels Job to turn to God, who puts down the strong and raises the weak (vv. 8–16). Finally he assures Job that the "discipline" of suffering (v. 17b) will bring him to a satisfying end (vv. 17–26).

But the speech is not as generously positive as that summary suggests. In 4:6, for example, Eliphaz says, "Is not your religion your confidence, / your hope, and the integrity of your ways?" The question is very ambiguous. "Religion" (lit., "fear") and "integrity" (Heb. tom) characterized Job in chaps. 1–2 (see, e.g., 1:1; 2:3), and here they are sources of his "confidence" (kislah). But in Job (8:14; 31:24) and elsewhere (Ps. 85:9), that word and its cognate kesel appear to denote misplaced confidence, and they are related to the noun kesil, "fool, stupid." Again in 4:8, Eliphaz says, "As I have seen, those who plow iniquity / and sow toil, harvest it too." The parallelism indicates a similarity between "iniquity" and "toil." Job has said that he received "toil" (3:26); Eliphaz must think that he has also "plowed iniquity." Thinking that "the race is born to toil" (5:7) does not remove the difficulty, for Eliphaz says in the same breath (v. 6) that humans are responsible for it.

411

Eliphaz is at least unkind to describe the plowers of iniquity as "finished by [God's] nostril's wind" (4:9) after the "great wind" that killed Job's children (1:19). He tactlessly refers to the sons of the fool who "are crushed in the gate, no rescuer near" (5:4). Job suffers very much as Eliphaz describes the fool's suffering (vv. 4–5). The generous advice, couched as "If it were I, I would . . ." (vv. 8–24), sounds rather hollow in the light of these implicit similarities between Job and the fool and the wicked. Eliphaz is good at promises: "In six troubles he will rescue you, / in seven, evil will not touch you" (5:19). But evil *has* "touched" Job. The Prosecutor urged Yahweh to "touch" his goods and himself (1:11; 2:5), and Eliphaz himself said that it "touched" him (4:5). He is clearly not on Job's side emotionally or rationally.

Eliphaz has introduced a new term into the discussion. Job did not ask about justice, but Eliphaz brings it up very quickly: "Think, who that was innocent has perished, / where have moral people been destroyed?" (4:7). Those rhetorical questions expect negative answers, and they are modified, if at all, only by his idea that all human beings sin by virtue of being human (4:17–21). Eliphaz's question contains the idea, common in the Hebrew Bible, of divine retributive justice. The deity governs justly, rewarding righteous people with health and prosperity and punishing wicked ones with calamity and suffering. The suffering of the innocent or the happiness of the wicked are contradictions in terms. If suffering is punishment for wickedness, a sign of the deity's just handling of human affairs, there can be no undeserved suffering.

Job did not raise this issue. He skirted it in 1:21 with the idea that Yahweh both gives and takes, and in 2:10 he avoided it either by ascribing both good and evil to the deity (if 2:10 is a question) or by asserting that anything the deity does must be good (if it is a statement). In chap. 3, he damned the whole creation, wishing he were dead; but he did not wonder why he, being good, suffered. Eliphaz has brought up the question, and by his apparent identification of Job with fool and wicked has proposed that Job deserves what has happened to him. From now on the question of deserved suffering becomes a central issue.

6:1–7:21, Job. "Passion," said Eliphaz (5:2), "murders the fool." Job clearly takes it personally: "Would that my passion could be weighed" (6:2). Eliphaz said that the deity "wounds" in order to heal (5:18). Job hopes God will "crush me, free his hand and cut me down" (6:8–9). So Job defines "hope" as "crushing," a word Eliphaz used to describe general human ephemerality (4:19) and the particular fate of the fool's

sons (5:4). Job's second speech is a wild, stream-of-consciousness spray of confusing, contradictory images, as if it depicted a man trying to think in the throes of pain.

In chap. 3 he wished that his life could be cancelled; now he both complains that the deity attacks him (6:4) and desires that he would attack him and put him out of his misery (vv. 8–9). Job lacks the strength to continue and wishes for help to die (vv. 11–13). Yet the metaphor (vv. 15–20) of wadis in the desert that store water in winter ice but suddenly go dry in the summer, causing death to caravans, shifts toward a wish *not* to die, as the caravans are first "eager" (v. 19) and then "ashamed because they trusted" (v. 20). The friends are like them: "You stare at ruin, and you're scared" (v. 21—the pun is in Hebrew too).

They fear that his "ruin" may put them in a dangerous legal, moral, or physical situation (vv. 22–23). Or do the healthy, being sure they know what suffering means, worry that it might happen to them? Is it the fright Job admitted in 3:25: "what I feared came to me"? It is important that just here Job begins to use legal terms. The friends are planning an "indictment" of him, they accuse him of having "erred" (6:24–27). He asks them (v. 24) to "instruct" him about his guilt. For the first time Job has become conscious of the issue of guilt, and his "innocence" is at stake (v. 29). Why is he being dealt with as if he were guilty? "Does not my palate understand a disaster?" (v. 30). He now thinks in terms of Eliphaz's understanding of the relation between suffering and wrongdoing.

Perhaps that is why Job turns at 7:1 to address the deity, who could solve the problem if he so wished (6:8–10). All through the dialogue, Job addresses the friends in the plural and the deity in the singular (some apparent exceptions are troubling). Verse 7 includes a singular imperative in Hebrew ("Consider that my life's a wind"), and in v. 8 a singular second-person pronoun ("Your eyes will be on me").

Describing his pain and desolation (vv. 1–6), Job emphasizes his evanescence in vv. 7–10. He is a "wind," invisible, disappearing. "Your eyes will be on me, but I'll not be there"; the last clause reappears as the last word of the speech, v. 21, with a similar idea: "You'll search for me, but I won't be there." God must act soon, before it is too late.

When complaining bitterly, Job likens himself to the Sea or a sea monster, opponents of the deity in combat myths (v. 12), imagery ironically opposite to his actual insubstantiality. Like Eliphaz, Job has dreams in which the deity terrifies him (v. 14). He cannot understand why he is worth all this attention, expressing his amazement (vv. 17–19) in a splendid parody of Psalm 8:

What's a man, that you magnify him so,
set your mind on him,
visit him every morning,
test him every moment?
How long will you not turn your gaze
away,
let me be till I swallow my spit?

He is not perfect ("I sin," he says in v. 20), but he cannot see that it is that big a thing. "Why not lift my guilt, carry away my iniquity?" (v. 21). There is the guilt again. His perception of his situation has changed from seeing it positively as God's doing in chaps. 1–2; now he is guilty. Surely God has but to see how ridiculous it is for him so to treat Job. But it will soon be too late (v. 21).

8:1–22, Bildad. Bildad's bluntness would be refreshing if he had any ordinary kindness. After one sarcastic couplet comparing Job's words to "a gusty wind" (v. 2), he jumps into his ideas, that God is unbendingly just and always responds favorably to the right human approach. Job has but to "search" for him and "ask mercy" (v. 5) to be repaid with a greatly improved future (v. 7).

Bildad shows, in a metaphor of a plant, that wicked folks receive what they deserve (vv. 11–12), admitting that bad people, like plants, may look prosperous for a time (vv. 16–17). But their hope "perishes" (v. 13), and they are "swallowed up" from their places (v. 18). He even brutally assures Job that "if your sons have sinned against him, [God] has sent them off in custody of their guilt" (v. 4).

He is sure, however, that good people are in no ultimate danger. Job will live happily later (vv. 7, 21). But the theory fails to solve an inconsistency: Job is good now, and by the theory, his goodness ought to be recognized now. Bildad implicitly acknowledges that God is treating him as if he were not what he is: "If you are pure and moral, though now he rouses up against you, he will repay your innocent dwelling" (v. 6). Just that "later" upsets Job, for little time is left.

Bildad's closing comment (8:22) alludes rhetorically to the end of Job's previous speech: "You'll search for me, but I won't be there" (7:21). Bildad uses the same final word: "The tent of the wicked will not be there." However, it is not exactly comforting. "The tent of the wicked" becomes the analogue of the sufferer.

9:1–10:22, Job. Job begins with a near quotation from Eliphaz (4:17): "How can a man be innocent with El?" (9:2). Eliphaz was talking morality, but Job is talking law: "If one wished to enter a case against him, he couldn't answer him once in a thousand" (v. 3). Although using the same word ("innocent"), they do not mean the same thing by it. Participants in this dialogue often talk past each other.

Job's speech intertwines a number of images around the central theme of law. God is both powerful and in charge of justice. The power is unreasonably directed against Job, and he sees no justice at work. Borrowing the language of hymnic praise of a God who does wonders in nature (as in Ps. 136 or Isa. 40:12), Job reverses its implications: "He who removes mountains, and they don't know / whom he's overturning in his anger; / who shakes earth from its place, / and its pillars shudder; / who speaks to the sun and it does not rise, / and puts a seal on the stars" (Job 9:5–7). This is chaotic power that does not maintain order but undoes it, that prevents human comprehension of the divine: "Ah, he passes me by, and I don't see him, sweeps on, and I don't discern him" (v. 11). Reverting in v. 14 to the language of trial, Job emphasizes his inequality with an opponent whom he "though innocent, couldn't answer" (v. 15a) and from whom he must "beg mercy" (v. 15b). The judge is also the prosecutor who "enlarges my wounds" (v. 17) and brutally "gorges me with bitter things" (v. 18).

Innocence is of no use, and Job's emotion rises to hysterical pitch as he describes himself as "perfect" (Heb. *tam*, v. 21; cf. 1:1, 8; 2:3). The deity is indifferent to moral stature: "He finishes off both perfect and wicked" (v. 22). Job moves very quickly from seeing God as amoral to accusing him of immorality: "Earth is given over to a wicked hand; / he covers its judges' faces— / if not, then who is it?" (v. 24). Only God can be the subject of that astounding statement. He is not merely amoral but so "wicked" that he does away with his own kind (v. 22).

In v. 27, Job speaks directly to God, as he did in chap. 7. His pain is evidence that God thinks him guilty (v. 28), and he has no hope of a fair outcome to the trial: "I'll be condemned" (v. 29). He is already condemned, and the muck of guilt will cling to him (vv. 30–31). Turning away from address to God (9:32–10:1), Job resumes it only at 10:2.

Meanwhile, he reflects on the difference between human and divine: "For he's not a man like me whom I could answer" (9:32). That is not just theology but represents the problem of the trial. Because God is both wicked and not human, no fair trial is possible. Job introduces and at the same time rejects the idea of a third-party advocate: "There's no arbiter between us / to lay his hand on us both" (v. 33). We will meet this "arbiter" and others like him in chaps. 16, 19, and 40.

Address to God resumes at 10:2 as a report of what he intends to say. In v. 3 it is sarcastic: "Is it good to you that you oppress, / despise your hands' toil, / and beam upon the counsel of the guilty?" Is God actually "not a man"

(9:32)? "Have you fleshly eyes; do you see as a man sees?" (10:4). If God is the creator (vv. 8–11), it seems either that he is no greater than a human being, thus not deserving so much power, or that he is undermining creation: "Recall that you made me like clay, / yet you're turning me back to dust?" (v. 9). Job is put under guard (v. 14), hunted down (v. 16), attacked as if by troops (v. 17). He has proclaimed his "perfection" (9:21) and the deity's "wickedness" (9:24), but he cannot know whether he is guilty or innocent (10:15).

Discouraged, worn down by pain and by the assaults of friends and deity alike, he closes his part of this cycle of speeches (v. 18) by returning to the theme of his beginning: "Why did you bring me out of the womb?" In chap. 3 he thought it would be better to be dead, and in 7:16 and 19 he proposed to be left alone. He ends with a figure of the darkness to which he will go, "deep shadow, all disordered, which shines like dusk" (10:22). It is the mirror image of his beginning at 3:4: "That day, let there be darkness."

But Job has come to a different point. Then being alive was too terrible; now he wants to be dead because his structure of assumptions has fallen apart. Divine power is not correlated with divine justice, and, though he deserves the latter, he is subjected to the assaults of the former.

11:1–20, Zophar. Job was worried in chap. 9 about answers. Zophar is sure that if Job received an answer directly from God (11:5) he would understand that he is getting off easily: God "lets some of your guilt be forgotten" (v. 6—or "exacts from you less than your guilt deserves"). But Zophar is more concerned with Job's understanding of the matter than with objective facts. Job does not comprehend (vv. 7–9) that the deity is so transcendent as to be unknowable. There is no hindering him (v. 10), no contradicting him (v. 11), because humans are invincibly stupid. That appears to be what Zophar's proverb means (v. 12): "A hollow-headed man will be intelligent / when a wild ass colt is born human."

"Be intelligent" is a verb cognate to the noun "heart," the organ in which Israelites conceived thinking and planning to take place. Yet if the race's problem is a flaw of the heart, how can Zophar so lightly propose (vv. 13–14) that Job just "prepare [his] heart" and "if guilt is in your hands, send it away"? If only all human flaws could be so readily mended.

Zophar is sure that nothing more is wanted than what Job has known to make the vision of a better life reality: "Your life will rise above noon [like the sun?] / gloom will become like morning [past?—a strange image]" (v. 17). Yet he must have his last twist of the knife: "The eyes of knaves will be exhausted, / refuge per-

ished from them, / their only hope to breathe their last" (v. 20). Job said in 6:8–9 that his "hope" was to be crushed and cut down by the deity. Zophar implicitly identifies Job with the knaves of this world.

12:1–20:29
The Second Cycle of Speeches

12:1–14:22, Job. In the first cycle, the friends argued for God's moral governance of the world, and Bildad and Zophar explained Job's punishment by his guilt. At first Job wished he could get out of his life of suffering and appealed to the created order, but shortly he began to think more about the question of justice and a trial that would establish his innocence. Yet Job thinks that justice has gone wrong, as his situation reverses the structure that everyone assumes. If there is to be a trial, is Job already presumed guilty?

In this opening speech, Job spends about half his time addressing the friends (12:2–13:19a) and about half addressing God (13:19b–14:22). He flings the friends a textbook example of sarcasm: "In truth, you are the people, / and with you dies wisdom" (12:2). If Zophar knows the divine secrets (11:6–7), Job can claim at least as much intelligence as they (12:3). They, on the other hand, are contemptuous in principle of any sufferer (v. 5) because they have the security available to "violent" people (v. 6).

He appeals to the creation, to "Behemoth" (cf. 40:15–24) and to birds, plants, and fish (12:7–8), all of whom know God's control (vv. 9–10). But the friends mistakenly persist in thinking that such control is fair and just, and Job piles up evidence that it is no such thing (vv. 13–25). God's "wisdom" is the arbitrary, unprincipled power to change nature (vv. 13, 15, 22) and to overturn human order (vv. 14, 16–21, 23–25). It might remind us of prophetic descriptions of the reversals of human power, except that Job describes divine retribution on human power with the insidious language of subversion (v. 19), deprivation of discretion (v. 20) or of "mind" (v. 24), contempt (v. 21), consignment of people to precreation "chaos" (v. 24; cf. Gen. 1:2) and to "lightless dark" (Job 12:25). As in chap. 9, this control, far from sustaining the created order, disintegrates it.

But Job persists in wanting the trial (13:1–2): "I want to speak to Shaddai, / desire to argue the case to El" (v. 3). Is that not strange? If God is so cynically careless of order and principle, why does Job want a trial over which he is judge? He continues to hold inconsistently both that the deity's justice is untrustworthy and that a trial is the solution to his own problem.

Meanwhile, he is fed up with arguing with the friends. Silence would be their wisdom (v. 5), as they speak "perversely" (v. 7) and try to "trick" God (v. 9). They argue with "dusty proverbs" and hold up "shields of clay" (v. 12). Job wants to speak with God, "whatever happens" (v. 13). Verse 15 is a famous passage:

> He's going to slay me; I cannot wait,
> but I must argue my ways to his face.

The first line has been discussed a great deal, especially because the KJV translators rendered it wrongly: "Behold, though he slay me, yet will I trust in him." It is a splendid religious concept, but it does linguistic damage to the line. The verb "he will slay me" is not a subordinate clause, and the verb KJV renders "trust" means rather "to wait, tarry" (RSV says "hope," which is also not quite correct). The words "in him," moreover, reflect a traditional interpretation of the Hebrew lo', "not." The interpretation, pronouncing the word in the same way, leaves out of account the letter aleph (') and reads a preposition with an object, "to him or it" (Heb. lo). It is too bad to lose from Job so valuable a religious concept as that of trusting in the deity no matter what the deity does, but other passages propose the same idea (see, e.g., Hab. 3:17–18). Here the notion is a sudden, radical contradiction of what Job says otherwise in this and other speeches, and he never returns to it. I do not reject the translation for that reason; I reject it because the text does not say it.

This is a moment of the most powerful intensity. Job must gather all of his courage (13:14) to declare that he has "marshalled a case" and to insist that he knows he is "innocent" (v. 18). But he looks forward to no positive outcome, and as he begins his address to the deity (v. 19b), he must request that God "remove your hand from me, / and don't fall on me with terror of you" (v. 21). We have seen something of that terror in Job's descriptions of God's awful, chaotic power.

Now he calls for an accounting: "Let me know my guilt and sin" (v. 23). Punning on his name (Heb. 'iyyob), he wonders (v. 24) why God counts him as his "enemy" (Heb. 'oyeb). He assumes that he is being punished for guilt. But he, the human, is too worn out and ephemeral to justify all of this divine attention (13:24–14:6). He compares himself to a "drifting leaf" and "dry straw" (v. 25) and wonders in passing if such weakness may be the very reason that God watches and tries him (14:3). The trial and the creation come together in v. 5: "You've set him limits he cannot exceed" may mean both limits of nature, as in the images of ephemerality (13:28–14:2), and legal regulations that humans may not transgress. It is as if God forces the human to be guilty simply by being created. "Gaze away from him [the human], and he'll

cease" (14:6). Only if God leaves us alone can we even die in peace.

The implication of v. 6 leads to the remarkable analogy between a felled tree and human evanescence (vv. 7–12). The tree has hope, does not "cease" (v. 7), can sprout again with the right water. "A man lies down and doesn't get up" (v. 12). The Hebrew Bible has no expectation of a pleasant afterlife, and the analogy to the tree has a rueful tone. Job goes on to wish (vv. 13–15) that, as a special case, he might have an afterlife, that God might conceal him among the dead ("in Sheol," v. 13; →Sheol) until he is ready to deal with him. He would wait eagerly for a positive outcome (v. 15). But it is for nothing. The idea is raised only to be dropped. The physical world wears away, "and you destroy a man's hope" (vv. 18–19). Nothing is there for Job except "his flesh's pain" and a lamenting soul (v. 22).

Job had said in 12:10 that "every living soul" is in God's hand. Now he sees that to be in that hand is only pain, to be not merely in contrast but in opposition to God. Job (Heb. 'iyyob) has definitely become enemy ('oyeb).

15:1–35, Eliphaz. Speakers in this debate typically begin with sarcastic remarks about the others' arguments (Bildad, 8:2; Zophar, 11:2–3; Job, 12:2–6). Eliphaz too shrugs his shoulders at the notion of answering "windy knowledge" (15:2) and arguing against "useless talk" (v. 3). Job threatens "religion" (lit., "fear" [of God]) and constrains "complaint" (v. 4). Ancient Israelite piety saw no contradiction between fear of a powerful God and willingness to complain about what that God did to them. Both were central elements of the concourse between humans and deity. Eliphaz seems to worry that, because Job is unacceptably guilty, he may undermine his religious freedom to complain. Job is becoming the prosecution's star witness in this trial. Every word he speaks ensures a guilty verdict. "Your mouth condemns you, not I, / your lips testify against you" (v. 6).

Job is claiming too much. "Were you born the first human?" (v. 7). Eliphaz pours scorn on the grandiose idea that Job thinks he is Adam's equal. He is only asking questions, to be sure, but they imply that Job thinks of affirmative answers to them. And Eliphaz is sure that he and the others know as much and understand as well as Job does (vv. 9–10).

It is not at all clear that he is right to think that. His next question is incredible: "Are El's consolations too slight for you, / the gentle word against you?" (v. 11). If that is irony, it is stupidly insensitive. "Consolation" is the wrong term for what both he and Job assume the deity has done to Job, and if the situation proposes a "word" to Job, it is hardly "gentle" (but Zophar said in 11:6 that it is gentler than Job deserves).

Eliphaz goes on to criticize Job for losing his mind and talking wildly (vv. 12–13). He can hardly be both ironic and critical. If, on the other hand, he is serious, he has abandoned rationality. To think that God *is* both consoling and gentle with Job is to refuse to experience the real world.

But perhaps he is doing that. In v. 14, Eliphaz repeats the theological doctrine he had proposed in chap. 4, that the human race is condemned before it starts; and he echoes Job's parody in 7:17 of Psalm 8 and the nature of divine attention: "What is a man, that he can be pure, / innocent, one born of woman?" Did Job misconstrue God's heed to humans as serious, though vindictive? Eliphaz insists (vv. 15–16) that the deity finds everyone less than himself, and, especially a human like Job, contemptible: "He doesn't trust his holy ones, / and the sky is not pure in his eyes. / What then of one horrible and corrupt, / a man who drinks wrongdoing like water?" The "holy ones" are probably members of the divine court, such as the "sons of Elohim" in chaps. 1–2, and the drinker of wrongdoing is surely Job.

The image leads Eliphaz to a detailed, conventional description of the fate of wicked people (vv. 20–24), "terrible sounds" and destruction in a time of well-being (v. 21), darkness (vv. 22–23), starvation (v. 23), "strain and stress" and attack (v. 24). Verses 25–27 portray the aggressive rebellion and active, if temporary, prosperity of the wicked. Verse 29, at least, proposes that it will be temporary; but Eliphaz confuses himself in v. 30 by saying both "He won't escape from darkness" and "He'll escape with the wind in his mouth."

Eliphaz is sure that what looks like a good life for the wicked is at best fleeting, cut off before its prime (v. 32), dropping blossoms and fruit before ripeness (v. 33). An image of sterility in v. 34 gives way to an oddly mixed metaphor of fruitfulness and uselessness: "conceiving toil and bearing guilt, / their womb fosters deceit" (v. 35).

The entire speech contains not one word of encouragement. In his first speech, Eliphaz ambiguously assured Job that the matter was not hopeless. Here Job is the outstanding case of corruption in an already corrupt universe (v. 16). Eliphaz seems to have given up on Job's rehabilitation.

16:1–17:16, Job. In the first cycle, speakers alluded to one another a good deal, sometimes in indirect rather than direct reference. In the second cycle, we find less such interaction, though it is not absent. In 16:2, for example, Job turns Eliphaz's closing shot at the wicked as "conceiving trouble" (15:35) back on him, calling the friends "troublesome comforters." He

wishes that "windy words have an end" (v. 3), echoing Eliphaz's condemnation of his "windy" wisdom (15:2). Eliphaz had criticized him in 15:6 as testifying against himself, but Job replies, "my emaciation . . . testifies against me" (16:8). Later, describing God, who "runs against me like a warrior" (16:14), Job ironically reverses Eliphaz's image of the human rebel, "playing the hero," who "runs toward" God in attack (15:26). These responses are almost explicit answers. It is simply that there were more and subtler responses in the first cycle; as the dialogue proceeds, one discerns more talking past one another than before.

Except for chap. 3, Job turned, in earlier speeches, to speak directly to God, complaining of mistreatment or requesting special attention. Here he addresses God only twice, very briefly, with a couplet at 16:7b–8a and a quatrain at 17:3–4, both with second-person pronouns. After these speeches, he immediately discusses God in the third person. Later speeches contain very little address to God. It is important to our perception of Job's character and feelings that he drastically reduces his direct speech to the deity in the latter parts of the dialogue. Job's isolation increases as the book goes along.

Yet the dialogue *is* painful. The friends do not diminish Job's pain by "piling up words" against him (v. 4), and his own talk does not stop it (v. 6). After complaining that God causes his alienation and forces him to be a witness (vv. 7b–8a) so that his very condition is legal testimony ("my emaciation . . . testifies against me"), he describes how God increases his pain with a metaphor of attack by a beast that "tears" its prey (v. 9; cf. Gen. 37:33). God uses human mobs against him (v. 10), "abandons me to the vicious, / flings me to the hands of knaves" (v. 11). Job suffers military assault: he is used for target practice (v. 12c), troops surround him (v. 13), besieging forces break through a wall (v. 14). He emphasizes the deity's immediate, physical force: "He shook me up, grabbed my neck and broke me apart" (v. 12a–b). The troops stand aside while God (the verbs are masculine singular) "splits open my guts without pity" (v. 13) and "runs against me like a warrior" (v. 14). It is a most unpleasant image of a violent God, and the irony is deepened by Job's certainty that his despair has no effect on this viciously tyrannical deity (vv. 15–16) and that his purity ought to justify the opposite treatment.

Even that graphic image of Job's feelings does not prepare us for the outburst in vv. 18–21. Job expects to be murdered and calls on the earth itself not to conceal the evidence: "Earth, do not cover my blood, / do not provide a place for my outcry!" (v. 18). Since God knew that Cain had murdered Abel because "the voice of your brother's blood is crying out to me from

the ground" (Gen. 4:10), Job wishes no concealment of the traces of his murder by God.

Earth is not the only witness. "Even now,
Ah! my witness is in heaven, / my supporter is
on high" (Job 16:19). This passage moves
beyond 9:33, where another third party, an "arbiter," was denied. Here Job asserts the "witness's" presence and his power to "interpret"
Job to God (v. 21a) and to make a decision in the
case (v. 21): "And he will decide for a hero
against God, / between Adam and his friend."
The translation is controversial; JPS prefers "let
him arbitrate between a man and God," and RSV
has "that he would maintain the right of a man
with God." But the verb means to decide in a
case, and I believe that it is a decision "for" Job
(the "hero") and "against" God.

It is fascinating that Job refers to a third
party with power to carry out a legal decision
against the deity. It causes some difficulty, no
doubt, with the idea of the Hebrew Bible's
unequivocal monotheism, though one might
argue (somewhat lamely, I think) that bitterness leads Job theologically astray. The provocation to be bitter is very great.

From this emotional highpoint, Job slides
quickly down into deep discouragement. Time
is running out, and "I own the grave" (16:22–
17:1). Even the somewhat feisty-sounding demand addressed to God (17:3–4) has a certain
formulaic tone to it. His heart is not in it. People
spit on him (v. 6), and he is reduced to a shadow
(v. 7). The temperature rises a bit in vv. 8–10.
Job's suffering moves "good" people not only to
shock but to opposition: "The guiltless rouses
up against the impious" (v. 8). People who conceive themselves as good oppress those who,
they think, deserve punishment. Job's suffering
hardens the dogmatism of those who think
themselves pure. It is the same contempt for the
sufferer that Job noted in 12:5, and it rests in the
same fear he saw in his friends' eyes (6:21). More
helpful would be a wise person, but Job knows
better than to expect to find one (17:10).

So he falls back to lethargy and the wish for
death: "My days are past, / my purposes shattered" (v. 11). He has no hope except death (cf.
the ends of chaps. 7 and 10), no companions
except "muck" and "maggot" (v. 14). Death
would be better.

18:1–21, Bildad. Job himself predicted that
his outburst would anger the friends (17:8–9).
However, he seems to have confused them,
since Bildad begins almost unintelligibly.
Verses 2–3 are addressed to someone plural
(plural verbs and pronouns), criticizing them for
delaying the friends' speaking ("we," v. 2b) and
for considering them as stupid animals (v. 3).
Such charges would be perfectly comprehensi-
ble if addressed to Job in the singular. Is Bildad
so upset that he has forgotten his grammar? Or

is he speaking to Eliphaz and Zophar? If the
latter, his criticism of their failed arguments and
of a supercilious attitude toward him (editorial
or royal "we"?) introduces a serious disharmony among the friends.

In v. 4, he speaks directly to Job in the second line: "Will earth be abandoned on your account?" But no more; from then on, Job is
included only by the implication of context.
These disputants are talking past each other!
Like Eliphaz, Bildad proffers no word of assurance or positive expectation, but his series of
images is interesting. He goes from the metaphor
of cattle in v. 3 to the image of a beast of prey
who tears only itself ("preys angrily on his
soul," v. 4). "Will earth be abandoned on your
account?" The rhetorical question expects a
negative answer, and a quotation from Job ("A
rock disintegrates from its place," 14:18) ridicules Job's pretensions to greatness and influence. The extinguished lights in 18:5–6 continue the ridicule (Bildad is still having difficulty with singular and plural; v. 5 refers to
"knaves," v. 6 to a singular "he"), and vv. 7–10
play out an elaborate image of trapping, which
harks back to the beast of prey. He then moves
into an image of sickness and death, which begins with "shiver" (v. 11) and moves to famine,
disaster, and the minions of personified Death
snatching a sick person from a tent (vv. 12–14).

Reference to the tent leads to the poignant
picture of a tent occupied by someone else and
the dwelling sprinkled with sulphur (v. 15) to
disinfect it and then shifts to the metaphor of a
tree that dries away from root to twig (v. 16). The
dying tree merges in vv. 17–19 with the picture
of the dying or dead person whose very "memory" and name die (v. 17). He is chased "out of
the world" (v. 18) and deprived of survivors (v.
19). The ancient world, expecting no future life,
laid its hopes on the memory of the descendants, which Bildad summarily rips away from
Job. The images of disintegration from v. 5 on
illustrate Bildad's quotation from Job in v. 4 ("A
rock disintegrates from its place"), which
seemed scornful there.

But Bildad closes with another self-contradiction: "They shudder over his day in the
west, / in the east the hair stands on end" (v.
20). Having depicted the wicked person as lost
from the world and memory, he now describes
the catastrophe as notoriously worldwide. The
dwelling, dissolved in vv. 15–16, returns as
"the evil dwellings" in v. 21. Bildad seems
confused from beginning to end of the speech.
Its multiple images would be interesting if they
did not result in a contradiction.

19:1–29, Job. Job begins by repeating Bildad's
opening words, "How long?" (cf. 18:2). We can
imagine this indignant quatrain spoken in a
parodying tone of voice: "How long will you

pain my soul, / pulverize me with talk?" (v. 2). It is also exaggerated: "These ten times you've insulted me" (v. 3). It has been only five times, but ten is a good round number, even if an exaggeration.

Much of the rest of this relatively short speech revolves around images of distance and closeness, of travel and staying at home. Job asks, "Have I truly strayed?" but insists that "my straying stays at home with me" (v. 4). In 6:24, he asked about error with the same verb, and perhaps here he suggests that his "error" is like a house guest who goes nowhere and bothers no one. Echoing Bildad's metaphors of trapping, he describes how God "circled his net" over him (19:6). Justice is undiscoverable (v. 7).

The next stanza (vv. 8–12) piles up travel images: blocked roads and darkened paths (v. 8), devastation around the walker (v. 10), God's "gangs" who build a highway and camp around his tent (v. 12), the latter an image of home set against words of journey. These images are combined with military ones. Job experiences again God's attacks (v. 11) and the gangs (the word often refers to raiding parties) building a highway for an army to pass on the way to siege. The object of all of these military attentions, Job notes, is merely his "tent" (v. 12). Proportion has been abandoned.

Images of distance become psychological rather than physical in vv. 13–19. Job begins with the verb "to distance" and lists those who were once close and are now, by God's agency, far: brothers, acquaintances, visitors (vv. 13–14), strangers given hospitality (v. 15), slaves (vv. 15–16), his immediate family (v. 17), social inferiors (v. 18), and social equals (v. 19). The reversals are ironic. "Those who know me are alien (Heb. zaru) from me" (v. 13), and his maids think of him as "alien" (zar) and foreign (v. 15). A slave refuses his commands, and the young "heckle" rather than respect him (v. 18). His wife recoils from his "stinking" breath (v. 17, zur, a pun on zar, vv. 13, 15). Most surprising, "I am loathsome to my own children" (v. 17). Has Job forgotten that they are dead?

Suddenly, images of distance give way to those of unbearable closeness: "My bones cling to my skin and flesh" (v. 20); God's "hand has touched me" (v. 21)—the same verb as in 1:11 and 2:5, used also of the wind that "touched" the house and killed his children in 1:19; both friends and God "pursue" him (v. 22). Yet in the midst of these metaphors comes a poignant plea for a positive closeness: "Pity, O pity me, you my friends" (v. 21). It is a very brief change from the sarcastic invective that Job and the friends usually use on each other.

These images of motion taken and blocked (vv. 4–12), of psychological distance (vv. 13–19), and of painful closeness (vv. 20–22) suggest change itself as the essence of Job's suffering. In vv. 23–24 he shifts radically to permanence:

"Would that my words were written, / would that they were engraved in an inscription / with an iron stylus and lead / forever in rock they were incised." As in 16:18, where he called on earth to testify to the martyr's blood, Job is anxious that his complaint not be lost. He wants the testimony not of mute fact but of "words," the unmistakable meaning of his story, to be permanently "incised" in a public monument.

If only what he says next could be deciphered! Ironically, it was written not in rock "with an iron stylus and lead" but on papyrus or parchment. I can read the first line of v. 25, but the six lines following (vv. 25b–27) are unintelligible to me. Each word is readable, but the words do not join in sentences that make sense. Nearly every interpretation of these lines rests on a scholar's proposal to rewrite some part of them. Since I reject doing that, I can give readers no help with them.

The first line of v. 25 is clear: "As for me, I know that my avenger lives." The line is familiar to music lovers from Handel's Messiah: "I know that my Redeemer liveth." But the word is not "redeemer," much less "Redeemer." Job is not referring to a divine savior or to Jesus. The Hebrew go'el alludes to a custom known from passages such as Num. 35:19 and Deut. 19:6, 12, that refer to "the avenger of blood." When someone was killed by a member of another tribe or clan, the injured clan appointed one of its number to take vengeance on the murderer on behalf of the deceased. The person so appointed was the go'el, the "avenger," not a "redeemer," because Job's go'el furthers the opposition between God and himself. God is attacking Job, not enhancing friendship, as we have seen in chap. 16 and earlier in this chapter. The figure of the "avenger" is born of Job's desperate awareness that God "considers me like his foes" (v. 11). It reminds us of the earlier third parties, the "arbiter," whose existence Job denied in 9:33 but who could hypothetically intervene between two parties in a dispute, and the "witness" of 16:19–21, whose presence with God Job affirmed with great certainty and who has, he thought, the power to decide the controversy. Job makes a more serious move with the avenger. This is the kin who takes vengeance on the guilty enemy for damage done to the sufferer.

The exploration of divine justice has come to this pass. Because that justice, so confidently proclaimed by the friends, turns out on examination to be injustice, its solution cannot be acquiescence, the mediation of the "arbiter," or the controversy of the "witness." Only revenge is left. The avenger, moreover, "lives." A commission of vengeance is given only on the death of someone. For Job to be avenged, he must, it seems, be dead, but by the same token the avenger must be alive. Significantly, Job does not address God in chap. 19. For the first time since chap. 3, his speech is entirely with-

418

in himself or to the friends. Conceivably, part of the garbled passage in vv. 25–27 could have been addressed to the deity, but there is now no way to know.

When the text returns to intelligibility in vv. 28–29, Job is warning the friends of danger to themselves from a "sword" as "fury on wrongdoing" (v. 29). Whose sword is it? Does he threaten them with the avenger's attentions or with God's sword, which has so far pursued no one but Job? Like him, the friends will soon learn about judgment. The sword will make them "know that there is a trial" (v. 29). Something legal is still in Job's mouth as he ends his part of the second cycle.

20:1–29, Zophar. Zophar can hardly wait to leap into the discussion. He begins with "therefore," which we would expect in the middle of a sentence, and his first quatrain, vv. 2–3, seems breathless. He is taking it personally: "I hear indication of an insult to me" (v. 3), of which Job also complained (19:3).

Like the other friends in this cycle, Zophar has no word of reassurance or support. He emphasizes images of sudden, radical reversal. Bad people's "triumphal shout" and "joy" are short (20:5), and they themselves disappear like dreams (v. 8). They "ascend to the sky" and "reach into the clouds" (v. 6; an allusion to the Tower of Babel, Gen. 11:4?), then perish like dung (Job 20:7). The seen becomes unseen (vv. 7b, 9). Their lusty bones will "bed" in the dust (v. 11), a painfully ironic consummation of lust in the bed of dust, echoing Job's expectation of going down to Sheol's dust with his hope (17:16).

The images of 20:12–23 center on eating and oppose sweet to bitter (vv. 12, 14), good taste (vv. 12–13) to vomit (v. 15), and gall and poison (vv. 14, 16) to honey and butter (v. 17). The knave cannot see the latter (v. 18), because moral retribution is at work. The wicked person, oppressing the oppressed, taking what is not one's own, having ulcers (vv. 19–20), gives the signs and causes of wrong. Zophar proclaims the justice that meets injustice: "There's nothing left for him to eat, / therefore his property cannot increase" (v. 21). He is not the model of consistency here. Verse 21 pictures the person with nothing to eat, v. 22 with plenty to eat, v. 23 with something to eat. Eliphaz too exaggerated the case and contradicted himself (15:20–21). Perhaps Zophar is discussing different situations at different times. Yet the friends claim the certainty of correlation between sin and suffering, between goodness and prosperity. That they contradict themselves as they describe it suggests that the principle is itself self-contradictory.

Zophar's images of battle and storm (20:24–28) are also not utterly meticulous. "He flees an iron weapon, / a bronze bow cuts him down" (v. 24). The crescendo from iron to bronze would be effective if a "bronze bow" were good for anything or even if a bow could "cut down" someone. Perhaps one expects too much: Zophar called attention to his own agitated state at the beginning. Yet the rest of the speech has some relatively consistent pictures of reversal and opposition and a nicely developed bit on the shift from sweet to bitter. Here his reversal of situation pretends precision but fails to deliver it. The battle moves to the cosmos itself. Supernatural fire (v. 26), sky and earth (v. 27), storm and flood (v. 28) fight to bring the sinner down. Zophar sounds very like a hellfire preacher, with his reference to "the wrathful day" (v. 28).

His conclusion reverses two positive terms: "This is the lot of evil humankind from God, / the heritage that God bespeaks him" (v. 29). One may receive a "lot" (or "portion") in a special banquet (see, e.g., 1 Sam. 1:4–5), and "heritage" is usually a bequest. The images of food in Job 20:12–23 and those of property in vv. 19–21 come to climax with this ironic promise. The knave—Job's category—has no positive gift from God to anticipate.

The negativity of the friends in this cycle is thorough and consistent. It is hard to suppose that they could go further in the third, but they do.

21:1–28:28
The Third Cycle of Speeches

21:1–34, Job. The second cycle (chaps. 12–20) was an unfriendly one. The friends turned unfriendly to Job, concentrating on lurid visions of how the wicked are punished, with the implication that Job is undergoing some version of these punishments. Job turned unfriendly to God, progressively diminishing direct speech to him from the long passage in 13:19b–14:22 through the brief remarks in 16:7b–8; 17:3–4, to the absence of address to God in chap. 19. Twice he asserted a new assurance for the presence of third parties to his dispute: a "witness," whose power to decide he affirmed in 16:19–21, and an "avenger," whom he "knows" to be alive in 19:25. These figures of Job's imagination are, as it were, "anti-Prosecutors," who advance beyond the "arbiter" whose existence Job denied in 9:33. Job has implicitly agreed with the friends that he is being punished and has continued to desire a trial to clear him, though his references to the helpers may indicate doubt about it. But the vivid, horrific terms in which he has described God's attacks on him match the friends' visions of divine punishment on sinners.

The third cycle takes the argument into interesting, unexpected turns. Eliphaz wondered (15:11) whether Job found God's "consolations too slight." Job suggests sarcastically that, if the friends listen carefully, they may receive "some consolation" (21:2). Their increased certainty that he is hopelessly guilty may console them. But v. 3b presents a strange singular: "And after I've spoken, you [masculine singular] can scoff away." Is he addressing Zophar, as most scholars think, or Eliphaz, who, in the established pattern, will speak next? Or, as the singular has been before, is it addressed to God, a passing, truculent shot—"You up there!"? The latter may be implied by his next questions (v. 4): "Now for me, is my complaint with humans? / Why shouldn't my breath be short?" The answer to the first must be negative: "No, the complaint is with someone other than humans." The second, like Job's exhortation to the friends, suggests the magnitude of the complaint: "Face me and be appalled, / lay your hands on your mouths. / If I recall it, I'm frightened, / and my flesh grasps a shudder" (vv. 5–6). The friends refuse to realize that the problem originates not with the sufferer but with the punishing deity.

That is what is so appalling. Job's condition requires the thought that *God has done this without any good reason.* If God punishes by suffering—and Job and the friends think he does—the effect ought to result from a discernible cause. The friends have not found one, and Job can find none in himself that is proportional to the suffering. Not only has he not done enough to justify the divine reaction; he has done nothing whatever to justify it. An inexplicable blow from the back of God's hand has thrust rudely away Job's entire system of laws, assumptions, assurances, and truths on which his daily living rested comfortably. "My flesh grasps a shudder" —a strange expression. Perhaps he can find nothing more solid to grasp.

In the rest of the speech, Job proposes an understanding of life and the world exactly the opposite of the one that has just dissipated. Job and the friends have supposed that God rewards with prosperity those humans who please him and punishes with suffering those who displease him. They have assumed that prosperity rewards virtue, suffering punishes vice. Turn it upside down, Job proposes, and one has just as accurate a view of the world. "Why do the wicked live, / mature, and increase strength . . . ?" (v. 7). He does not ask *whether* the wicked live this way; he asks *why,* assuming that they do. Verses 8–12 provide a series of pictures of healthy fertility in family and flocks (vv. 8–11), happy children and music (vv. 11–12), exactly the opposite of what Job experiences. His herds are destroyed, his children neither dance nor sing. But he is the model of virtue, and those who prosper are "the wicked."

They manage, moreover, to keep God at arm's length, tell him to his face that "knowing your ways does not please us" (v. 14), that service to him is unprofitable (v. 15). Yet something less attractive lurks in their thoughts (v. 13): "They wear out their days with good"—an odd but somewhat attractive way to picture decline to death, but not so odd as the next line— "are terrified at the moment of Sheol." Such terror of death might motivate the distance from God articulated in vv. 14–15. An alternative reading of v. 13b is: "They go down to Sheol in peace." I see no basis except personal preference to choose one reading over the other. The duality persists in v. 16. "Their good is not in their hand" might mean that it is in the deity's hand, whether the wicked like it or not, or, if the line is a question, as RSV has it ("Is not their good in their hand?"), that prosperity or happiness is actually in these people's own power. Job wishes (vv. 19–20) that those people would receive a deserved punishment, but he does not see that they do (v. 17). The person who dies "all secure and at ease" comes to the same dusty end as the bitter one who has never had it good (vv. 23–26). But the thought is different from the one in chap. 3. There the sameness of destiny was pleasant. Here it is unfair that the unhappy righteous have no better prospect than the prosperous wicked.

The friends apparently try to appeal to contrary evidence (v. 28), but Job proposes unaccustomed sources of wisdom (v. 29). Wayfarers, gypsy nomads, traveling caravaneers—not the polite society Job and his friends know—have a different sense of the world: "On a calamitous day a wretch is spared" (v. 30). People do not receive what they deserve (v. 31): "When he has done something, who pays him back?"

The wicked wealthy person has a funeral attended by crowds, and the "clods of the wadi" where he is buried "taste sweet to him" (vv. 32–33). As the images of death throughout this chapter put the cap on the images of life, so Job turns upside down the friends' reflection on life. Certainly God rewards those who please him and punishes those who displease him. But they are completely mistaken about who pleases God: *he rewards the wicked.* Job cannot imagine their being more wrong: "How you console me with empty air, / and your replies leave only fraud behind!" (v. 34). He began the speech by saying that they might receive some "consolation." He closes it with the irony that they "console" him only with puffs of wind.

22:1–30; 25:1–6, The Friends. I will look at the speeches of the friends in the third cycle together. There are only two; Zophar has no third speech. Bildad's speech is unusually short, and he says nothing new.

Eliphaz's opening statement, echoing his first stanza in chap. 15, comes very quickly to a climax: "Are you not in fact greatly wicked, / with no end to your misdeeds?" (22:5). He has not said that quite so bluntly before, and his process of getting there is interesting. Asking if a human "benefits" God, he answers that one "benefits only himself" (v. 2). Verse 3 repeats what he said before, that God is indifferent to Job's "innocence." Appearing to grant that "innocence," the next rhetorical question, "Does he charge you out of your religiousness?" (v. 4), calls for a negative answer. Seeming to say that God does not accuse Job for being good, he really says that Job must be guilty if God charges him. He makes a similar point in v. 5, still retaining the form of the rhetorical question—but "Are you not?" demands the affirmative answer "Yes, I am." It is a sneaky switch in a series of rhetorical questions that call for negative answers.

Eliphaz now leaps at Job with a series of specific accusations. In vv. 6–11 he specifies Job's moral crimes, and in vv. 12–20 he describes theological faults. In his conclusion, vv. 21–30, Eliphaz proposes a solution to Job's dilemma. He delivers the accusations with utter certainty, and we must imagine Job's jaw dropping in astonishment. The whole is a tissue of invention. Job has done none of what he is accused of in vv. 6–9. Eliphaz's assurance that wicked people suffer means that people who suffer are wicked. Thus, if Job has not crushed the arms of orphans (v. 9), he must have done something just like it. His accusation is structured exactly like certain oracles of the prophets. The opening "because" governs the accusations in vv. 6–9 and introduces the resulting punishment by "therefore" (cf., e.g., Hos. 2:7–8; Isa. 8:6–7, and many other passages). But "because" is followed by sheer fiction, made the more ironic by contrast to the praise of Job's compassionate care for those in trouble, an allusion with which Eliphaz began his first speech (4:3–4).

He now moves to the theological sins (vv. 12–20). Assuming that Job must grant God's transcendence (v. 12), he purports to quote Job about the limits of divine knowledge: "And you say, 'What does God know? / Does he give order through the thick cloud? / Clouds conceal him, and he does not see, / and he walks around on the circle of the sky'" (vv. 13–14). Job has said nothing of the sort but has consistently complained that God "sees" too much (e.g., 7:19–20; 13:27; 14:3, 6; 16:9). To accusations of deeds Job has not done, Eliphaz adds criticisms of thoughts he has not expressed. He nearly gives his game away when he blurts out about those who remain distant from God (v. 17) that God "filled their houses with good" (v. 18)—which was precisely Job's claim in chap. 21, namely, that God showers good on the wicked. And v. 19, "the righteous see and rejoice, / the innocent

mocks it," remarkably echoes Job's sarcasm in 17:8–9 about how his plight hardens the attitudes of "good" folks.

As suddenly as he began his frontal attack, Eliphaz leaves it to propound a solution (vv. 21–25) and to predict a happy future (vv. 26–30). However, his head is not yet quite together. "Then benefit him [God]," he says, forgetting that in v. 2 he denied that a human *could* benefit God. The advice is conventional: take instruction (Heb. *torah*, with a hint of submitting to rules), turn to the deity, put wrongdoing at a distance (vv. 22–23). He should give up crass materialism in favor of the divine treasure (vv. 24–25), a metaphor wearied by vast overuse. The result will be a future filled with success: pleasure in God (v. 26), prayer answered and vows paid (v. 27), decision definitively made (v. 28), rescue of lowly sinners from the depths (vv. 29–30). It sounds so easy, but it ignores the depth of evil Eliphaz ascribed to Job earlier in the speech. Is this the work of a rational mind?

If Eliphaz's last contribution combines unjust accusations with ostensibly warm hopes for Job's future, Bildad's hardly has time for more than a "good-bye." His style is the tersest of the three, but this speech is short even for him, only ten lines. He makes but two points. In 25:2–3, he affirms the utter power of God, and in vv. 4–6 he argues that nothing in the creation can measure up to divine standards. Neither point is remotely new, and the second, interestingly, circles back to where the discussion began. Bildad echoes Eliphaz's point (4:17–18): "How is any man righteous with God, / how is one born of woman pure?" (25:4) and adds another (cf. 15:15), even the moon and stars are not pure (25:5). So we return to the beginning, and it seems that the friends have learned nothing. Eliphaz lambasts Job but, strangely, promises him a future; Bildad closes with Eliphaz's cynical view of the human race; and Zophar—well, Zophar is reduced to silence.

23:1–24:25, Job. In chap. 21, Job argued that the converse of the conventional notion of retribution is correct: the wicked are rewarded and the good punished. In this speech he focuses on the divine absence. "Oh that I knew, and could find him, / could enter his throne room" (23:3). I have wondered before, why, given Job's strictures against God, does he insist on a trial with God as judge? If, as he argued in chap. 21, God rewards evil, what is the trial's attraction? He even talks about it in positive terms, anticipates that God will say something that he will understand (v. 5), expects personal attention (v. 6), and thinks that he may win a case rationally handled (v. 7). In chaps. 9 and 13, the trial seemed already decided—and lost.

Discouragement resumes in force, as Job boxes the compass in unsuccessful search for God (vv. 8–9). He is "not there" in the east, cannot be discerned in the west or perceived in the north, and when Job reaches the south (v. 9b), he understands: "He hides in the south." God deliberately avoids him, and Job thinks he understands that too: "Because he knows the way I'm on; / he'll test me, I shall emerge as gold" (v. 10). God avoids the sufferer precisely because the trial will turn out in Job's favor or because God will be publicly shown unjust. Job, after all, has been flawless in his conduct (vv. 11–12). But God is arbitrary: "His soul wishes something, and he does it" (v. 13). There is no time between desire and deed, and the thinking comes later: "He will come to terms with my sentence" (v. 14). That is enough to raise Job's abject fright (vv. 15–16). Yet that terrorism does not "silence" Job with the prospect of darkness (v. 17).

God is still irresponsibly absent. "Why are not proper times treasured by Shaddai, / and those who know him don't see his days?" (24:1). The proper times are probably times for trial, which God simply ignores. The divine absence, however, becomes for Job an explanation of errant behavior by humans, as he accuses God, in chap. 24, of responsibility for human wrong. The accusation is implicit, since Job does not address God directly.

Chap. 24 is very difficult, complex in images and ambiguous in language, full of verbs with unspecified subjects and pronouns with unclear antecedents. Translators have an inordinately hard time with it, changing singulars to plurals and finding conjecture necessary. It is no wonder that modern scholars have tried to recover from chap. 24 traces of "lost" parts of Bildad's speech (chap. 25) and of Zophar's nonexistent one. Any interpreter must confess uncertainty about this passage.

God's absence explains why humans go bad, oppressing the weak, stealing their goods, and behaving arrogantly with them (vv. 2–4). Job compares them with the wild asses (vv. 5–8), who live by the wits they can muster. Humans live in the same way, whether they are the oppressors (v. 9) or the oppressed (vv. 10–11). But the comparison to wild asses suggests that Job is not criticizing these people morally. It is the fault of God: "From the city the dying cry out, / the throats of the wounded call, / but God thinks nothing amiss" (v. 12). If God fails to give people guidance because he is absent, and if he ignores trouble about which he ought to care, can one expect anything but beastly behavior? Job makes an interesting advance on his revised theory of divine retribution. In chap. 21 he argued that God rewards misbehavior. Here he implicitly argues that God *causes* it.

In the two following stanzas, Job draws an opposition between humans and God, vv. 13–17 specifying the evil humans do, vv. 18–24 the deeds of God. The controlling image of vv. 13–17 is the opposition of light and darkness. Human wickedness depends very much on darkness, from the murderer who can kill in broad daylight but expands his activities at night (v. 14) to the adulterer's use of twilight (v. 15) and the thief's dependence on darkness (v. 16). But all of these wrongdoers are "rebellers against light" (v. 13) and "familiar with darkness's terrors" (v. 17).

The subject of v. 18 must be God. Verse 13 began with the emphatic Hebrew pronoun "they." Likewise, v. 18 begins with a pronoun "he." As the implicit cause of the human sins in the earlier verses, God is the obvious referent of this emphatic singular. Verses 18–24 are, if anything, more difficult than vv. 13–17. Divine curses cause barrenness in soil and humans (vv. 18, 20–21), dryness overcomes melting snow (v. 19). In one line, "Wickedness is bought like wood" (v. 20c), Job explicitly blames God for social disorder. God seems to raise up strong people in order to cast them down (vv. 22–24). Some of these images modify the earlier emphasis on God's absence, but Job reaffirms it: "They are exalted a little, and he is not there" (v. 24). This claim is the divine counterpart to Job's threat (7:21) that he would not be there. God departs "swiftly" (24:18) from the scene and leaves behind disaster and chaos. All of this reflects the absence of which Job complained when he looked for the trial among all points of the compass (23:8–9).

And again we must wonder why Job wants a trial with this God. Not only is he absent; he is corrupt and a corrupter. Delving deep into the ground of human evil, Job finds there the work of God. Will such a deity acquit an uncorrupted human being? The statement about God in this chapter is devastating, and Job challenges the friends at the end: "If it is not so, who will prove me a liar / and bring my words to nought?" (24:25). The friends are not equal to the challenge. Bildad returns, in the next chapter, to a conceded point, that God is mighty and transcendent, and Zophar falls back on silence. Elihu (chaps. 32–37) tries to meet the demand of 24:25 but surely fails, and Yahweh (chaps. 38–41) makes no effort to do so. Job has already won the argument. But he still has a good deal left to say.

26:1–27:23, Job. The opening reply to Bildad is sharply sarcastic, emphasizing Job's weakness and the poor argument directed against him. "By whose help have you declared these words? / Whose breath is it that comes out from you?" (v. 4). It sounds like a nearly sinister accusation of guilt by association. It is even more devastating that vv. 2–4 are cast entirely in the second-person *singular*, which Job has used otherwise only to address God. Is he speaking to

422

God or to Bildad? One may try taking it both ways. To Bildad, he tramples on whatever remains of kindliness and scorns their wisdom and help. To God, he criticizes help, "deliverance to the arm without strength," advice, knowledge—none of which God has conveyed to him. The divine absence, indeed, is his subject. Verse 4 even suggests that God must have help from someone else to speak.

Verses 5–14 characterize the creation in terms of power. This identification might appear to agree with the friends' assessment of God's transcendence (and therefore some scholars assign these verses to Bildad). Yet the tone, tinged with the foregoing sarcasm, is not normal theology. The cosmos is under the thumb of a cruel, harsh tyrant, who causes the dead to "writhe in agony" (v. 5), strips the place of the dead naked (v. 6). The universe lies passive under his rule (vv. 7–10), or "the sky's pillars tremble, / stunned by his rebuke" (v. 11). The usual divine enemies, Sea, Rahab (Isa. 30:7; 51:9–10), the "fleeing Dragon" (Isa. 27:1), who are respectively "stilled," "smashed," and "pierced," are joined in Job 26:12–13 by a surprising one, "Sky," who has also been somehow undone (the crucial verb is obscure). The presence of Sky is surprising because sky deities are never displaced in ancient mythologies. It is as if Job is making up mythic themes and dubious theologies. And he responds to the friends, implicitly, that they have trivialized God's doings: "Oh, these are but the edges of his ways. / What whispered word do we hear of him, / and the thunder of his might who understands?" (v. 14). Only a tiny corner of God's power reaches human knowledge, and therefore Bildad's and Eliphaz's certainties are misplaced (Zophar's confidence seems to have left him). Bildad's limping reference to moon and stars is blown apart by Job's account of the cosmic powers.

Yet we do not know how Job has received his knowledge. Why should we believe his account more than theirs? It is never clear that we should. The first surprise in chap. 27 occurs when Job takes an oath on God's own life. From what he said in chap. 24, an oath on the life of a radically unjust God would seem a strange thing. The oath is, as so often in Job, a self-curse, calling down an unspoken disaster if he speaks "viciousness" or "deceit" (v. 4). And its basis is Job's staunch statement of utter certainty about his own "integrity" and "righteousness" (or, as I have sometimes translated the word earlier, "innocence"): "I'm damned if I'll say you [plural: the friends] are right; / until I perish, I'll not turn away my integrity. / To my righteousness I hold fast, will not weaken it; / my heart finds nothing from my days to taunt" (vv. 5–6). In effect, Job claims here that he is the exception to chap. 24, that the God who has corrupted the whole world has failed to corrupt him.

He now proceeds to redefine God—the second surprise. In 13:24 Job wondered why God thought of him as "enemy," and in 19:11 he decided that God "considers me like his foes." Moreover, in 16:9 he referred to the deity as "my foe" (same word as in 19:11), and in 9:24 declared that in God's hand, the world is in a "wicked hand." At last, in 27:7 he combines two ideas, that God is his enemy and that God is "wicked" and "vicious," unlike himself (see v. 4): "Let my enemy be considered wicked, / the one who rises against me, vicious." The thought is out: Job has but one "enemy." Not only is he alienated from this God, but he condemns him, claiming implicitly that he is the moral superior of God. Job is the righteous (v. 6), God the wicked (v. 7).

The third surprise: Job has redefined God, and now he redefines himself: "For what hope has the godless when he is snipped off, / when God carries off his life?" (v. 8). "Godless" is not quite right for the Hebrew word, which has to do rather with ritual pollution. The important thing is that, having condemned God, Job uses the term to describe himself, defines himself as not only distanced from God but repugnant to God. To maintain the integrity of his own moral stance, which he has solemnly sworn, Job redefines God as wicked enemy and himself as polluted, alienated, godless. The meanings of these words are radically turned on their heads. Job has no more "hope" of a better fate (vv. 9–10) now than he did back in 6:8–9, when he wished God would "crush" him and finish the matter.

He cannot imagine, though, how the friends can miss the truth of what he says. Offering to help them understand (27:11), he reminds them of what they have seen and of their incomprehension: "You, of course, have all seen it, / and why, then, are you so utterly vapid?" (v. 12, more literally, "why do you puff a gust of wind?"). To underscore his point, he slightly skews a quotation from the end of Zophar's last speech (20:29), which described the desperate fate of the wicked as their rightful "lot" and "heritage" from God. "They receive this lot of evil humankind with God, / this heritage of oppressors from Shaddai" (27:13). Zophar spoke of the "lot" from God, Job with (the connivance of?) God. And Job refers in the plural to those who "receive" the heritage from Shaddai. He divides, then, the plural "evil humankind" who are on God's side from himself, the singular "godless" (v. 8). And he proceeds, in vv. 14–23, to use that singular term to describe the sufferings of the hopeless opponent of a powerful deity. It is a scathing parody on the friends' conventionalized visions of the sufferings of the wicked—so effective that many modern scholars propose to assign these verses to Zophar's missing speech. He even proposes (v. 17) that the "righteous" and the "pure" will profit from looting the wealth of the "godless." But one

423

must remember that Job has inverted the terms, and the "righteous" and "pure" are on the side of God, who is the "wicked enemy." And, as we might expect, the very forces of nature, which are under the complete control of God (26:5–14), participate in the destruction of God's hapless enemy (27:20–23). Job closes with an ambiguous description of mockery, ambiguous because it is not clear whether it is the "east wind" (v. 21) or God himself who "claps his [or its] hands over him, / whistles derisively at him from his [or its] own place" (v. 23).

28:1–28, Job. The consensus of scholars is that this chapter, usually referred to as the "Hymn to Wisdom," was a late addition to the book. Still, here it is, a beautiful poem that makes very good sense in its context. But it is surprising. Immersed as readers have been in issues of righteousness and virtue, it is unexpected to find a description of mining and metal-working technologies. But these topics bring readers to the center of "wisdom," for the ancient world understood wisdom, it seems, principally as skill.

The first part, vv. 1–11, runs a kind of circle from the knowledge implied in mining (vv. 1–2) through distance (vv. 3–4) and discovery (vv. 5–6), around ignorance (vv. 7–8), and back to the hard work of knowledge (vv. 9–11). At this point, one encounters the first question about wisdom and where she is to be found (vv. 12–14; the Heb. noun "wisdom" is feminine, but we have the example of Prov. 1–9 for thinking it may be personified). Neither humans (Job 28:13) nor the cosmic powers of Abyss and Sea know where she is. The knowledge in the first part gives way to ignorance about wisdom. The middle section (vv. 15–19) is a somewhat repetitious catalogue of gems and other objects of great value, none of them in any way commensurable with the value of wisdom. Question and answer, very like vv. 12–14, again ask whence wisdom comes (vv. 20–22) and then respond with another answer of ignorance. Neither earthly life (v. 21) nor cosmic powers (v. 22; → Abaddon; Death) know more than "rumor." But in the last section (vv. 23–28) God's understanding and knowledge come into play. He is the origin of wisdom and even "dug her out" (v. 27; the same verb as "digs" in v. 3). And he has informed humans about wisdom: "Now, the fear of the Lord, that is wisdom, / and avoiding evil is understanding" (v. 28). The contrast with the standard understanding of wisdom in vv. 1–11 is complete. Wisdom has nothing to do with knowledge, and the ancient Israelites would have found our research universities, laboratories, and government grants unthinkable. Wisdom for them arises from religion ("fear of the Lord" = religion) and from morality. To be wise is to be religious and to avoid evil. Where have

we seen that remark before? We were told that Job "feared God [or was religious] and avoided evil" back in 1:1. More than that, God himself described Job in the same terms (1:8; 2:3). Job possesses what the poem presents as the divine definition of wisdom. This chapter adds to Job's powerful assertion of his moral righteousness (27:4–6) the claim to divinely certified wisdom. Yet one has the hunch that, just as Job redefined righteousness and wickedness as they applied to God and humans in chap. 27, perhaps this very claim to wisdom also has its ironic twist. Perhaps insofar as wisdom involves "avoiding evil," as v. 28 has it, it constitutes avoiding God. Job surely has no illusions left but has, in Nietzsche's famous phrase, "transvalued his values."

29:1–31:40
Job's Summation

The summation divides itself into three parts, corresponding to these three chapters. Chap. 29 describes the "good old days" when Job was happy. Chap. 30 sketches the miserable present. Chap. 31 prepares for the trial, as Job pronounces a series of curses to clear himself from the cloud of accusations over him. The speech, then, is a final preparation for the trial, about which we have heard so much. With the self-curses in chap. 31, moreover, Job circles back to the curses on his birthday, with which he began the dialogue in chap. 3.

29:1–25, Job's Past. Job describes his past situation in a symmetrical structure (which coheres with that shown by Habel, The Book of Job):

Part One (29:2–6): Past blessing
Part Two (29:7–10): Past honor and admiration
Part Three (29:11–17): Administration of justice
Part Four (29:18–20): Expected blessing
Part Five (29:21–25): Past honor and admiration

The thematic connections of parts four and five with parts one and two are evident, and the content seems simple enough. Beloved by God (vv. 2–6), respected by the people (vv. 7–10), helper of the weak and scourge of the wicked (vv. 11–17), flourishing in prosperity (vv. 18–20), influential as if he were a king (vv. 21–25), one might almost think Job has forgotten his pain. However, he has not, and what he says is not as simple as it seems.

"Would that I were as past months, / the days when God watched over me" (v. 2). When Job discussed God's "watching" him before, it has included sometimes "guarding" (10:12), sometimes "stationing a guard" (7:12; 10:14), "watching" his paths in connection with putting his feet in stocks (13:27). God "watches" him too much, more like a hostile prison guard than like a benevolent hospital nurse.

Though 29:4–5 is generally positive ("my autumn days," v. 4a, refers to his youth, as autumn in Palestine is the beginning of the year, not the end), an odd duality appears in v. 6. "My steps were washed with milk" seems a pleasantly positive image of luxury. But one is able to translate with the word "milk" only by correcting the word in the Hebrew text on the plausible supposition that it is misspelled. What is there in Hebrew is a word that means "rage" ("footsteps washed with rage" is quite a different metaphor) or, even more interestingly, "poison." Multiple meanings may be confusing, but they can also be interesting. In this instance, it sounds as if the great man is in danger of assault or assassination.

Job's description of the people's respect for him (vv. 7–10) is equally interesting. We might have thought from chaps. 1–2 that Job was a nomadic herdsman, but he speaks here of "going out to the gate of the city / to take my seat in the square" (v. 7). The city gate was where legal business was done in Israel. There was no professional judiciary, it seems, and wise, elderly men were expected to sit in the gate to act as intermediaries in disputes and to hear legal cases. Job speaks of his "seat" as if he always occupied the same one. But most interesting is his description of people's attitudes toward him: "Young people saw me and hid, / old ones rose and stood, / princes restrained words / and laid their hands on their mouths, / the voices of leaders were hidden, / and their tongues stuck to their palates" (vv. 8–10). Respect is there but also terror. The young hide, not only in admiration; princes are quiet by self-restraint, leaders silenced by voices that refuse in fright to work. These lines point to respect, but they also bear a negative connotation. Job's self-satisfaction at well-deserved success conceals underneath an arrogant man's testimony to the success of his arrogance.

As Job describes his administration of justice, one discovers that he is an activist jurist, personally leading and assisting the handicapped and punishing the hurtful (vv. 12, 15, 17). Besides acting justly, that quality describes his very character, the "robe and turban" that he wears (v. 14). In contrast to the silence of his social inferiors in vv. 8–10, this justice is accompanied by sound, the "cry" that calls attention to the need for justice (v. 12) and the joyful "song" of the widow (v. 13). But Job is also violent, breaking the wrongdoers' jaws (v. 17) recalls the princes' "hands on their mouths," v. 9).

Job's expectation of future blessing (vv. 18–20) has interesting and mixed images. Just what "I'll die with my nest" means ("with" is

odd in Heb. too) is not clear, but it seems a bit contradictory to "multiply days like sand" (both v. 18). Then one finds a pleasant image of a plant with well-watered roots and misted twigs (v. 19). Yet the second line, "Dew lodging on my twigs," is ambiguous. Dew notoriously disappears at first sun, and "lodging" explicitly means a temporary stay. The line at least exhibits a somewhat strange choice of words. There is even a hint of double meaning in v. 20, where "my bow successful in my hand" points at first to military prowess. But the word "successful" might also mean something like "changed" or "exchanged" in a less than positive sense.

The last stanza, vv. 21–25, repeating the silence idea but less harshly than in vv. 9–10, points to motifs of kingship, i.e., "they waited for me as for rain, / opened their mouths as for showers" (v. 23; see Ps. 72:6), and "I chose their way, sat at the head, / lived like a king among the troops" (v. 25). The phrase "the light of my face" (v. 24) is also a royal reference (see, e.g., Prov. 16:15) as well as a divine one (see Num. 6:25; Ps. 4:6). Is Job claiming divinity? After chap. 27, anything seems possible. The old duality appears here too. "If I smiled at them, they did not believe it," he says (29:24). Why not? Was it so rare that people were pleased? Or so unusual that they are surprised and incredulous?

What is clear throughout the speech is Job's satisfaction with his past honor. What is not nearly so clear is whether, even as he himself describes it, others were so satisfied.

30:1–31, Job's Current Plight. In 29:24, Job remarked on others' reactions to his smile (the verb could also be translated "laugh"). As chap. 30 opens, the reversal has taken place: "And now they laugh at me" (v. 1). In derision. They "shout" (v. 5) and "bray" (v. 7). He is "their [mocking] song" and "word" (v. 9). And as he closes the chapter, Job refers to his sounds: weeping (vv. 25, 31), crying out (vv. 20, 28), disgusting noises in his bowels (v. 27). In chap. 29 the oppositions of sound and silence showed Job's power and others' weakness. In chap. 30 sound and silence show Job as weak, his opponents strong. The movement is visible even in the structure of the chapter. Three times (vv. 1, 9, 16) he begins a new thought with "And now." In vv. 1–8, he expresses contempt for his tormenters' worthlessness. In vv. 9–15, he describes the terrifying brutality of their tormenting. And in vv. 16–19, he ascribes this torment directly to God. He goes on to complain to God about the mistreatment and his expectation of death. In vv. 24–31, he returns to his feelings of pain and hopelessness. From being the king "who consoles mourners" (29:25), Job has become the mourner: "My lyre has become mourning, my flute a weeping voice" (30:31).

425

Job's contempt for his tormenters comes to the surface in a vivid figure: "And now they laugh at me, / those much younger than I, / whose fathers I disdained / to station among my sheepdogs" (v. 1). He is still thinking of inferiors and superiors. The rest of the section (vv. 1–8) is a confusing mixture of prepositions with singular and plural verb forms. For example, "What is their hands' strength to me?" (v. 2a) surely refers to the tormenters of v. 1. But the next line includes a singular preposition (lit., "upon him [or it] perishes vigor"), which might refer to "strength," giving something like "the vigor of which is gone," or might be an unusual third-person reference to Job himself, giving "whose vigor is gone." Depending on how one reads that preposition, vv. 3–4 either continue Job's description of his tormenters or describe his own bad state. Complication arises again in v. 5: "From the community they cast out, / shout over him as over a thief." Who are they, and who is he? The singular, we would think, ought to refer to Job, and "over him" repeats "upon him" in v. 2a. Then one would want "vigor" in v. 2 to be Job's and vv. 3–4 to describe him. But the plural verb, "they cast out," works best if it continues the "they" that began at v. 1, with vv. 2–4, referring to the laughers. To make sense of both vv. 2 and 5, it seems that one needs vv. 2–4 to refer at the same time to both Job and his persecutors.

These details are indicative of the trouble the book of Job can present readers. Such trouble is compounded in vv. 5–8, where the tormenting pursuers ("they cast out") in v. 5 seem suddenly and fantastically to merge with the pursued, described like wild donkeys ("bray," v. 7; cf. 24:5–8) and social outcasts.

The next stanza (vv. 9–15) has some images familiar from chaps. 16 and 19. Job has become the (mocking) "song" of his pursuers (v. 9; cf. Ps. 69:12; Lam. 3:14). They "detest" him, "spit" at him (v. 10), because God hates him. The disdainful God "has loosened his bowstring," casting aside the weapon to show the victim's complete helplessness, "and humiliated me" (v. 11). Motivated by God's contempt, Job's tormenters "put off the bridle," which might mean casting off restraint or becoming wild beasts (cf. the donkey's bray, v. 7). From v. 12 on, one returns to a siege metaphor, as in chap. 19, with "building up roads" (v. 12), coming against Job like a "breach" (in the wall, v. 14). In v. 15, he becomes both the dumping ground ("Terrors are dumped over me") and airy, evanescent vapor ("my standing is driven off like the wind, / my safety sweeps away like a cloud"). The controlling image seems to be military attack by God and his agents, an attack motivated by hatred and contempt.

God is responsible. He "bores out my bones" (v. 17; cf. 16:12–13), an image of surgery that

gives ceaseless pain: "my gnawing pain never lies down." After the unintelligible 30:18, he refers again to God's contempt, "He has flung me to the muck" (v. 19; cf. 9:31), as if the useless corpse were dropped in the sewer. Job presents a verbal conclusion to his being "song" and "word" to his tormenters (30:9): "I'm a cliché, like dust and ashes" (v. 19). The first phrase stems from the activity of making proverbs, and it suggests the proverbs and metaphors bandied about by "miserable comforters." He is indeed a cliché to an entire culture. Mention Job, and someone will invariably speak of patience. So does the misreading of Job in James 5:11 control our implicit reading.

Now Job addresses God (30:20–23), almost exactly in the middle of the summation. Since the long speech in 13:19b–14:22, Job has spoken to God only briefly, in 16:7b–8; 17:3–4; 21:3 (one line); 26:2–4. He will do so only twice more (40:4–5; 42:1–6). But he says nothing new here. God responds to him inappropriately, no matter what he does: "I cry out to you, and you don't answer me, / I stand [silent], and you examine me" (30:20). To complain that God has "been changed to cruelty toward me" (v. 21) may seem odd, since Job has complained about cruelty for some time. But his main complaint is the unpredictable, inconsistent character of tyranny: "You lift me to the wind, make me ride, / you dissolve me, level me" (v. 22). The first line reminds us of God riding the clouds (Ps. 68:4) or the wings of the wind (Ps. 18:10), but the second returns to the ground with a thump. Job can be sure of nothing but death (Job 30:23). And he has been sure of that for a long time.

In the difficult last stanza (vv. 24–31), Job curiously changes his tune. Verse 24 is nearly unintelligible, but in v. 25 Job claims constant concern for other sufferers, using the same kind of curse formula the Prosecutor used in chaps. 1–2: "If I did not weep for a difficult day, / or my soul grieve for the poor ..." He ought to be rewarded for that. "I hoped for good, and evil came, / waited for light, and darkness came" (v. 26). His body is ravaged by suffering (vv. 27, 30), his colleagues are indifferent (v. 28), his only company is the animals of the uninhabitable desert (jackals and ostriches, v. 29), and his musical instruments, usually employed for happy song and dance (as in chap. 21), now become mourning and weeping. And he has apparently reverted to the friends' position. He has been good, and he deserves reward. Has Job reversed himself so suddenly?

31:1–40, Job's Oaths. Job has received good press for this part of his speech: "The Code of a Man of Honor" is Robert Gordis's title (see Gordis, p. 339). The ethical system involves not only external action but also inner attitudes and principles of ethical thinking. The chapter is a series of oaths, some in the form we have seen without a result clause, some in the more complete form with result clause. These oaths are often interpreted as Job's final preparation for the trial, whose ups and downs in his mind we have followed since the idea first came up in chap. 9. Yet the redefinitions in chap. 27 seemed to render the notion of a trial impossible. If God has become Job's vicious enemy, and if Job is as righteous as he has claimed, the trial will be unjust by definition, and he can hope only for death (30:23).

It is a very complex, powerful series of oaths and other kinds of statements. An outline may help to see it clearly:

Questions: retribution (31:1-4)
Oaths and statements (31:5-12)
  Oath without result: fraud (31:5)
  Statement: integrity (31:6)
  Oath with result: impurity (31:7-8)
  Oath with result: adultery (31:9-10)
  Statement with "for": crimes (31:11-12)
Oaths, questions, and statement (31:13-18)
  Oath without result: justice (31:13)
  Questions: God and common origin
    (31:14-15)
  Oath without result: aloofness (31:16-17)
  Statement with "for": care for poor (31:18)
Oaths and statement (31:19-23)
  Oath without result: clothing for poor
    (31:19-20)
  Oath with result: fairness (31:21-22)
  Statement with "for": fear of disaster (31:23)
Oaths and statement (31:24-28)
  Oath without result: wealth (31:24)
  Oath without result: power (31:25)
  Oath without result: idolatry (31:26-27)
  Statement with "for": crimes (31:28)
Oaths and statements (31:29-34)
  Oath without result: arrogance (31:29)
  Statement: curse (31:30)
  Oath without result: food (31:31)
  Statement: hospitality (31:32)
  Oath without result: hypocrisy (with "for")
    (31:33-34)
Statement and oaths (31:35-40)
  Statement (exclamation): challenge to trial
    (31:35)
  Oath without result: pride (31:36-37)
  Oath with result: soil (31:38-40)

Such a design enables readers to visualize what Job is saying. At first glance, the speech looks rather disjointed. From the covenant of v. 1 (where Job is denying not lustful thoughts about young women, but connection with a goddess) to the covenant with his soil in vv. 38-40, he ranges over sins he has not committed and attitudes he has not had. Some are like those of which Eliphaz gratuitously accused

him in chap. 22. The subjects, as indicated in the outline, comprise an impressive claim to moral honor, interspersed with statements of assurance that God knows his integrity (31:6), that some crimes are notoriously actionable (vv. 11, 28), that he has not cursed loosely (v. 30) and has hospitably opened his doors (v. 32). He denies improper attitudes such as despising justice due to the slave (v. 13), being pleased at others' misfortune (v. 29), concealment of something out of fear of displeasure (vv. 33-34). These are sins we take seriously, attitudes we are taught to avoid. We respond positively to this epitome of the ethical person. Such a response lends credence to the first characterization of Job we saw as "scrupulously moral" (1:1, 8; 2:3).

We must remember, however, that these are actually curses that Job calls down on himself. The curse in the ancient world was no casual expression but was the most powerful way one had to set in motion forces of action and reaction. The curse worked itself out, objectively and irresistibly, and even God could not hinder it. Our culture has nothing that corresponds to it, and we tend not to understand why other cultures have taken curses so seriously. As the Prosecutor did in chaps. 1-2, Job lays his own future and welfare on the line. If he is mistaken about anything in his claims to moral integrity, the unspoken catastrophe will strike him still further down.

But not only himself. Unusually, four of these curses do contain the statement of the catastrophe (what I have called the "result"). In 31:21-22, the result matches the evil denied: "If I have shaken my fist at the orphan / because I saw my helpers in the gate, / may my arm fall from my shoulder, / my forearm be broken at the elbow." In vv. 38-40, the evil of exploiting the soil is matched by the soil's growing inedible produce. In vv. 7-8, the penalty for having "strayed from the way" and having an impure stain on his hands falls partly on Job ("may I sow and another eat") and partly on others ("and my descendants be uprooted"). It is surprising, as in 21:19-20, that Job opposed the idea that one's descendants might be punished for another's sin, though the law allows it (Exod. 20:5). But worse comes in Job 31:9-10: "If my heart has been fooled over a woman, / and at my neighbor's door I have lain in wait, / may my woman grind for another, / others kneel over her." Job calls for the effects of his sexual misdeeds to fall not upon himself or upon his partner in adultery but upon his innocent wife!

With this series of curses on himself, Job demands divine attention as the Prosecutor did at the beginning. He calls for the trial again: "Oh that I had someone to hear me— / here is my mark; let Shaddai answer me—/ and the inscription my accuser has written!" (v. 35). He even reverts to royal language about himself: "Like a prince [I will] approach him" (v. 37), having tied the "inscription" (presumably the written indictment) on himself "like a wreath" (v. 36). Yet that picture of the emaciated victim getting up from the ashes to march around with a "paper crown" (a phrase from Habel, p. 439) provides a comic parody of Job's arrogant parading to his seat of justice in 29:7–10. Does the comic occur to Job?

The most interesting aspect of this speech is 31:2–3: "What is God's portion from above, / Shaddai's inheritance from on high? / Is it not disaster for the vicious, / calamity for evildoers?" We have seen several of those words in chap. 27. "Portion" and "inheritance" were God's reward to the "evil" and "oppressors" in 27:13 and are now punishment to the "evildoers." "Vicious" characterized God in 27:7. Job has reverted to retributionism. The curses exhibit him as the model of the ethical person, the follower of the rules and the attitudes inculcated by the ancient Hebrew superego. He has climbed from despair about a fair trial (chap. 23) and the savage redefinition of terms that portrayed him as the deity's moral superior (chap. 27), and he trots out the weary old rewards and punishments to which he so furiously objected before. He *deserves* acquittal because he is free of the improprieties he describes. How has Job made so stark a shift of position? Was he so enraptured by his memory of past power and influence as to wish to recapture them? Does he suppose that, getting them before by obedience to the rules, he might regain them by the same route?

And what now? Surely the next activity must be God's direct entry on the scene. At the very least, he must respond.

32:1–37:24

The Speeches of Elihu

Thinking we would hear the voice of God, we get instead Elihu, who is angry at the elderly incompetents who cannot show Job how he is wrong. Elihu is young and brash, given to long prefaces and pretentious language, not a very attractive character. Most scholars think his speeches were inserted into the book. They speculate variously about the interpolation, e.g., that Elihu gives a different answer to the problem of suffering from the others or that he gives the right answer to the problem, thus relieving God of answering it (a popular Jewish understanding of Elihu in the Middle Ages and later). Perhaps Elihu is here *because* we expect God, and his often boring speech maintains tension

by delaying the entrance of the divine voice. That seems indeed a better reason than the other two. His idea of suffering is only marginally different from the others, and it is evidently not the "right" one.

The speech is boring, and we need not devote a great deal of space to it. After the introduction, the speech falls into four basic sections: 32:6–33:33; 34:2–37; 35:2–16; and 36:2–37:24.

32:1–5, Introduction. In the narrative introduction, Elihu gives his genealogy and notes his anger.

32:6–33:33, Elihu I. Most of the speech (32:6–33:7) is preface, grumbling about the others' inability to deal with Job. They are old but not wise; he is young but "full of words" (32:18), which are about to burst him "like unopened wine, / like new wineskins" (v. 19). He reassures Job with a straight face that there is nothing to fear from him (33:6–7).

At 33:8 begins the one-sided debate, to which Job never replies. Quoting Job's claim to moral perfection in skewed form ("I am pure, without transgression, / I am clean, have no iniquity," v. 9), he argues, like Eliphaz, that no human can claim purity, and one must admit imperfections and sins (v. 27). To Job's claim that God has made him his enemy (vv. 10–11), Elihu opposes a divine revelation that shows humans where they are wrong. As Eliphaz said (chap. 4), messages come through dreams (33:15–18), and Elihu interprets suffering as God's education that transforms the sinner into a righteous person (vv. 25–26). He even alludes to Job's witness-interpreter (16:19–20), postulating an "angel over him, / one interpreter out of a thousand" (v. 23). Suffering, like dreams and angels, is a medium for the divine message to restore the sinner. God "does all these things / twice, thrice with a man, / to turn his soul back from the Pit" (33:29–30). If Job does not want to debate, Elihu will proceed: "Be silent," he says pretentiously, "and I'll familiarize you with wisdom" (v. 33).

34:1–37, Elihu II. The second speech is addressed to the friends—or the world: "Hear my words, you wise people" (v. 2) and "Therefore, intelligent men, listen to me" (v. 10). It is strange that Elihu would compliment the friends, when he so disdained them in chap. 32.

Elihu says, as did Bildad (8:3), that God "does not bend justice" (34:12). But he and the others know what justice is: "Justice we will decide for ourselves; / we know among us what is good" (v. 4). Job does not qualify, for he "wanders in company with evildoers, / walks with wicked men" (v. 8). Elihu's vision of the divine control over humans (vv. 19–30) is perhaps more detailed than that of the friends, at least as vivid in its depiction of punishment,

428

and more aware of divine compassion than either Job's or the others'. Job is wrong about God: "He hears the outcry of the oppressed. / He gives content—and who finds that bad?" (vv. 28–29).

At the end, Elihu addresses Job briefly and a bit cryptically (v. 33): "Does he repay you out of what is yours because you despise?" But he turns back to the "intelligent men" (v. 34) and quotes them: "Job does not speak with knowledge" (v. 35) and "adds to his sin, / in transgression jeers among us" (v. 37).

Elihu may be a bore. But one thing can be said for him: only he among the friends both refers to and addresses Job by name.

35:1–16, Elihu III. Sometimes one feels an unreality in Elihu, as if he were not quite in touch with this world. He quotes Job: "Is this what you consider justice, / that you say, 'I am more righteous than God'?" (v. 2). Job said the opposite of that in 9:2. Elihu goes on, "For you say, 'How is he of use to you? / How do I profit from my sin?' " (35:3), putting into Job's mouth a word ("to be of use") that only Eliphaz has used (22:2, 21). Of course, Job implied in 27:6–7 that he is God's moral superior, and perhaps one should credit Elihu with shrewd insight. His promise that he will "refute your words" (35:4) after quoting words that Job has not used is nevertheless pretentious.

In vv. 5–8, Elihu repeats Eliphaz's idea that a human's action has no effect on God (22:2–3). Sin does not diminish God, nor does excellence add to him. Job had agreed with the former in 7:20, as he had agreed with Elihu's next contention (35:11), that humans should accept instruction from animals (12:7–8). And he has staunchly agreed with Elihu's remark (it sounds inadvertent, as if Elihu were not perceiving reality again), "There they [the beasts, perhaps] cry out, and he [God?] does not answer, / before the pride of the evil ones" (35:12). Elihu can only assure Job that he is wrong to think that God pays no attention to him (vv. 13–14; Job has complained that he does).

36:1–37:24, Elihu IV. The last speech verges on an exalted vision of a world filled with God's glory. But Elihu nearly throws it away by bragging: "Certainly my words are not lies, / faultless knowledge is in your presence" (v. 4).

In vv. 5–25, he amplifies his point made first in chap. 33, that God instructs humans through suffering. "If they are bound in fetters, / trapped in cords of misery, / he is telling them their deed / and their transgressions" (36:8–9). If they pay attention, they will have pleasure (v. 11), and if they do not, "They will cross the channel, / die without knowing" (v. 12; "channel" implies the myth of a river before the place of the dead). Suffering itself is the oppor-

tunity to learn: "He rescues the miserable in their misery, / opens their ears in their torment" (v. 15). Job must avoid wickedness and despair (vv. 17, 20) and join in praising God's power and instruction (vv. 22–25).

In the rest of the speech (36:26–37:24), Elihu expands on God's power in nature without abandoning his theme of divine instruction. The wonders of rain (36:27–30) are a means for informing humans about "judgment" (v. 31) and for telling people about "wickedness" (v. 33). A remarkable picture of a storm, complete with sound and light effects (37:2–4), underscores the divine control. Elihu's account demonstrates how important water was in that culture, where rain, frost, snow, clouds, moisture, and storm were central. Both humans and animals depend on it (vv. 7–8), and God controls to his ends not only storms (vv. 9–11) but also events involving dryness, "the things that whirl" (v. 12; e.g., "dust devils, cyclones"). He makes everything "find its goal" (v. 13). Elihu insists that Job is far inferior to this powerful God. Moreover, vv. 14–20 anticipate Yahweh's following speech. Elihu asks questions in some of the same ways as will Yahweh: "Do you know about the cloud-rolls, / the marvels of perfect knowledge, / you whose clothes are hot / when the land lies still from the south wind? / Can you hammer out the clouds with him, / strong as a cast-metal mirror?" (vv. 16–18). In these verses, Elihu points to oppressive qualities of God's control. In the final stanza (vv. 21–24), he emphasizes both positive power ("From the north gold comes forth," v. 22) and negative ("Shaddai—we cannot find him," v. 23). Yet just his righteous power, which "does not oppress" (v. 23), arouses fear: "Therefore men are afraid of him, / he does not see any who are wise of heart" (v. 24). Elihu does not recollect his earlier claim for exalted wisdom.

The effect of Elihu's intervention is an odd one. He proposes a new meaning for human suffering, as a teaching device from God, and he shows a high appreciation for God's natural power, for both support of life and its destruction. But he surrounds the nuggets of semiprecious metal with so many clods of ordinary dirt as to weary the miner beyond reason. The style is wordy, convoluted, often hardly intelligible. Translating excellent poetry is hard but exhilarating; translating Elihu is just hard.

38:1–42:6

Dialogue with Yahweh

Each character has two speeches. Yahweh speaks "from the whirlwind" in 38:2–40:2, and Job responds in 40:4–5. Yahweh resumes at length, 40:6–41:34, and Job answers in 42:1–6. Never has Job been so terse.

38:1–40:2, Yahweh. Yahweh is not terse. Having been silent for so long, it is as if he bursts into speech as the sea bursts out of the womb (38:8). Why he comes from a "whirlwind" (v. 1) is not entirely clear. Storms were portents of divine presence in Israel (e.g., Ps. 18:7–16; 77:17–19), though whirlwinds were not especially prominent in this regard. The whirlwind is devastatingly powerful, and it certainly lends an awesome atmosphere of darkness and noise to accompany God's cosmic outpouring.

Does he refer to Job at all? "Who is this who darkens counsel / with ignorant words?" (v. 2) could as well mean Elihu, whom we might picture scuttling away in terror. God has heard enough questions; he will now ask them and expect answers (v. 3). The questions are hard, with more than a tinge of sarcasm in them. "Where were you when I laid earth's foundations? / Tell me, if you know so much. / Who set its measurements—surely you know!— / or who stretched the line out on it?" (vv. 4–5). Verses 4–38 pass across the regions of the universe: earth, whose foundations rest on pedestals, the laying of which elicited the song of the morning stars (vv. 4–7); Sea, limited by "bar and doors" and clothed in cloud (vv. 8–11); morning, which shakes the wicked out of "the skirts of earth" (vv. 12–15); the watery Deep (v. 16) and the realm of Death (v. 17); the roads of light and darkness (vv. 19–21); the realms of weather, snow and hail (vv. 22–23), winds (v. 24), storm (vv. 25–27, with the lovely picture of rain falling in a kind of divine exuberance on uninhabited barren ground); the origins of nature's water (vv. 28–30); the stars and constellations (vv. 31–33); and back to the rainstorm (vv. 34–38, with a side glance at the Egyptian gods Thoth and Sekwi, v. 36). He draws an astounding portrait of a world full of complicated, powerful forces and uses it to ask whether Job can control it. "Have you commanded morning?" (v. 12). "Have you entered Sea's springs?" (v. 16). "Can you raise your voice to the cloud?" (v. 34). Yahweh promised questions, and we have questions. What is the purpose of this series of questions, the answers to which must be, "No, I haven't" or "No, I can't" or "I don't know"?

The same may be said for the rest of the speech (38:39–39:30) about the animals and their qualities: the lioness and her prey (38:39–40); ravens and their food (v. 41); the birth season of rock goats and fallow deer (39:1–4); the freedom of the wild ass (vv. 5–8); the untamable wild ox (vv. 9–12); the ostrich's stupidity and speed (vv. 13–18); the war horse and its courage (v. 19–25—the only domesticated animal in the group); the hawk and eagle (or vulture; the Hebrew word means both) and their affinity for height (vv. 26–30). Does Job control the animal or give it its quality? "Can you hunt prey for the lioness?" (38:39). "Who sets the wild ass free?" (39:5). "Do you give the horse his strength?" (v. 19). They are again questions the answers to which are "No, I can't" or "No, I don't" or "I don't know."

After asking these questions, Yahweh speaks directly to Job: "Will an accuser of Shaddai yield, / God's arbiter answer it?" (40:2). It is a fascinating echo of Job's agents. He had denied the existence of the "arbiter" in 9:33. By implication, Yahweh wonders whether any of the helpers (the "witness" of 16:19 or the "avenger" of 19:25) can be of assistance to Job with this deity, whose universe has just been described so vividly.

Does this mean, as is often said, "What makes you think you have anything to say? Shut up and do as I tell you"? Is it an answer to any of Job's questions? Yahweh makes no reference to suffering or to justice. Is the cosmological outburst simply irrelevant to the book? Are Job's suffering and his questions about it beneath the notice of the God who at least allowed it?

40:3–5, Job. Job seems to feel so, in his noncommittal reply: "Oh, I am small, what could I reply to you? / I put my hand on my mouth. / I spoke once, and I will not answer, / twice, and I will add nothing" (vv. 4–5). Is that "All right, I will shut up," or is it "If you're going to be like that, I have nothing more to say"? The former is acquiescence to being trampled down, the latter is resignation to the inevitable but not acceptance of it, Job the "refusenik." In either case, Yahweh looks and sounds like an overwhelming tyrant. But we cannot be sure of the outcome, as each has one speech yet to give.

40:6–41:34, Yahweh. Yahweh begins the second speech like the first (v. 7), and we think more strongly than ever of the tyrant. He refuses to accept Job's prior response and requires a better one. If Job's answer was acquiescent, Yahweh wants either a more heartfelt agreement or something else. If the answer was refusal, perhaps he wants agreement.

He asks a new question (v. 8), aimed at Job and his questions: "Would you even annul my order, / treat me as guilty so you may be innocent?" To make the issue one of guilt and innocence, of wickedness and morality, a duality whereby, if Job is right, then God is wrong and vice versa, is to "annul my order." "Order" can also be translated "justice," and it has to do with both moral justice and cosmic structure. Yahweh means it in both senses. The world does not spin on the axes of guilt and innocence, and ever since Eliphaz raised the question of justice back in 4:7, the conversation was deflected, at least in Yahweh's judgment, from its proper aim. Suffering is not a sign of guilt, and the dialogue between Job and the friends went off on a wrong tangent.

If Job still thinks guilt and innocence is the issue, Yahweh has some friends he wants to lend him. If God is guilty, then let Job deal with the problems of justice and immorality in the human world (40:9–14). Let him be the king he said he was in chap. 29 and exert his power against the wicked: "Strew about the furies of your anger, / see everyone high, bring them low, / see everyone high, humiliate them, / and trample wicked people where they stand" (vv. 11–12). Once he has won Yahweh's own acclaim for that "victory" ("I will praise you," he says, v. 14), he can go on to Behemoth (vv. 15–24) and Leviathan (41:1–34).

Scholars once interpreted those two astonishing creatures as a hippopotamus and a crocodile, respectively. More recent awareness of various mythological beings in the Bible and the discovery of Leviathan in Canaanite mythology have led scholars to view Behemoth and Leviathan as imaginary monsters, creatures of myth and fantasy. Behemoth belongs to the same act of creation as does the human ("whom I made with you," v. 15) but primal in that creation ("the first of God's ways," v. 19) and extremely powerful (v. 16). "His bones [are] tubes of bronze, / his limbs like iron rods" (v. 18). He can even withstand the power of the river (vv. 23–24), which may be oceanic water rather than a freshwater river. Yahweh describes him as living where "all the wild animals play" (v. 20), suggesting an aspect of pleasure. Behemoth may be a lovable monster.

Leviathan is emphatically not, for he is beyond any sort of human control (41:1–8). One does not fish for him (41:1–2), make him a pet (v. 5—a ludicrous image: "Can you play with him like a bird, / put him on a leash for your little girls?"), market him (v. 6), hunt him (v. 7). "Put your hand upon him— / think of the fight; don't do it again" (v. 8). He is a frightful monster, frightening even to God (41:9) and the gods (v. 25). The description of him emphasizes his unbreachable armor (vv. 13–17), his fiery breath (vv. 18–21—even his sneeze is a flash), his immovable bulk (vv. 23–24). No weapon is of any use against him (vv. 26–29), and he churns up the surface wherever he goes, whether on land (v. 30) or in the sea (vv. 31–32). No one surpasses him for power or terror. "He looks on everything lofty, / he, king over all proud beasts" (v. 34).

Yahweh does not taunt Job with these animals. He simply describes them in all of their unconquerable might. His invitation to Job to rule presents a progression: first the realm of humans (40:9–14), then the realm of natural power beyond human force (Behemoth, vv. 15–24), and finally the realm of supernatural, mythic power above creation (Leviathan, 41:1–34). The implication is clear: if Job wants to control the deity by the power of his moral innocence, he must contend with forces that, though less than the deity, are more than Job can handle. But Yahweh has already suggested (40:8) that guilt and innocence are not the issue.

42:1–6, Job. Job begins by acknowledging God's overwhelming power: "I know that you can do everything, / no plan is inaccessible to you" (v. 2). Job alludes to omnipotence in the first line, omniscience in the second. Now, thinking about what Yahweh said to him, he quotes 38:2 (inexactly): " 'Who is this who obscures counsel ignorantly?' Therefore I told, and didn't understand, / wonders beyond me, and I didn't know" (42:3). It is an odd sentence, in which the first phrase of the second line completes the first phrase of the first, and the second parts of the two lines are parallel. Job admits having spoken beyond his competence. He quotes again, more exactly, from 38:3 and 40:7: "Hear, and I will speak, / I will ask you questions and you instruct me" (42:4). Yes, Job has heard, and he says so in v. 5: "With ears' hearing I hear you, / and now my eye sees you." Some scholars think "hear" ought to be translated in the past tense, and some think it ought to read "I heard of you." Either reading conveys the idea that secondhand knowledge is replaced by firsthand knowledge, the immediate sight of God that Israelite tradition firmly refused (e.g., Exod. 33:20; though there is the counterinstance in Exod. 24:9–11 where seventy-four people "saw" God and—amazingly—"he did not lay his hand on" them). But "now" does not necessarily stand in contrast with the first line. Both lines claim firsthand knowledge as opposed to the lack of knowledge attested in Job 42:3. The knowledge has a most surprising result, a "therefore": "Therefore I despise and repent / of dust and ashes" (v. 6). An astounding shift! Job takes a religious action to forswear religion. "Dust and ashes" stands for the ritual surrounding repentance, the machinery and concept of guilt and innocence as the central issue of human life, and Job rejects all of it. Accepting what Yahweh said in 40:8, he takes it a step further. It is another indication that Eliphaz moved the debate off center when he introduced the notion of retribution, categorizing the world by guilt and innocence. Job was so sure of his own moral purity that the slur seemingly cast on it by the friends' retributionism seduced him into seeking a way out. The friends urged him to repent. And so he does, but not as they thought. He repents of repentance.

42:7–17

The Closing Tale

To many readers, the closing tale is an anticlimax. The fireworks are over, the point has been reached, and people are bothered that, after all the talk about rewards and punishments, Job gets back his fortune twice over. We have been led to think that "Hollywood endings" are sentimental and tacky. But here it is, and we need to examine it.

42:7–9, The Friends. Yahweh comes immediately to the friends with an angry criticism: "You have not spoken truth of me, as has my servant Job" (v. 7). He requires of them a sacrifice, in Job's presence and with Job's intercession (v. 8). On performance of that requirement, everything will be all right. It is interesting that the friends, whose theology is most impeccably Deuteronomic and prophetic, are so thoroughly condemned. That suggests, as other parts of the book do, that Job is not as close to the center of the biblical tradition as is sometimes thought—or at least the text itself, apart from its interpreters, is more radical.

42:10–12, Job's New Wealth. Job is restored to his friends and relatives (v. 11), who reverse the alienation of which he complained in 19:13–19 and succeed in "consoling and comforting" him. The three friends came originally to do that (2:11), and Job complained bitterly in the dialogue that they failed miserably. The consolation and comfort are for "all the evil that Yahweh had brought upon him" (v. 11). The tale assumes, on the one hand, that it *was* evil, not in a moral sense, but in the sense of something unpleasant to endure, and, on the other hand, that Yahweh did it. Not only did the Prosecutor disappear from the story, but the story seems to have forgotten him entirely. In any case, his action did not preclude the principle that God is in charge. The relatives also give Job rich gifts, "each one *qesitah* and one gold ring." A *qesitah* is a large unit of exchange; Jacob bought land at Shechem for one hundred *qesitahs* (Gen. 33:19). This is not coinage but probably a weight of precious metal, and, with a gold ring, it adds up to a large sum. Yahweh has "blessed" him more now than before. He acquires twice the number of animals he had before (Job 42:12), but we see no mention of slaves. Does this "blessing" reverse the rejection of the retributive theology in the dialogue with Yahweh? One could argue that, just as Job knew better than to take literally the intercession to restore the friends (v. 9), he knows better than to take the flocks and herds as a sign of his virtue. They are just flocks and herds.

42:13–17, Job's New Family. The fantasy world of the tale is evident here. No new wife is mentioned, and the one we met in chap. 2 was the mother of ten grown children. Suddenly, with no reference to the passage of time, she is the mother of ten more, and in a trice, they are grown. Job's wife deserves better than she receives in this book. Not only does she seem mainly a machine for producing babies, but one of Job's curses on himself turned her in prospect into the slave and sexual toy of other men (31:9–10). All the sharper is the contrast with the daughters, more beautiful than anyone and, unusually, sharing the inherited wealth with their brothers (42:15). They are carefully named: Jemimah, "Dove" (or perhaps an epithet for a Canaanite goddess, which might mean "progenitress"); Keziah, "Cassia," used anciently for perfume and incense (or perhaps "bow"); and Keren-happuch, "Horn of Antimony," used anciently as mascara is used now. It is interesting that the text deals so carefully with the daughters, seeming to tell us so much while actually telling us very little. But Job himself remains the focus, a grand old man whose 140 years after the catastrophe are twice the normal life span (Ps. 90:10) and more than Moses' 120 years (Deut. 34:7). "Then Job died, old and sated with days" (Job 42:17).

Any summary of this huge, sprawling, complex book would gravely insult its integrity and its depth. The only thing to do is to read it again.

Bibliography

Dhorme, É. *A Commentary on the Book of Job.* Translated by H. Knight. London: Nelson, 1967.

Glatzer, N. M., ed. *The Dimensions of Job: A Study and Selected Readings.* New York: Schocken, 1969.

Good, E. M. *In Turns of Tempest: A Reading of Job.* Stanford, CA: Stanford University Press. Forthcoming.

Gordis, R. *The Book of Job: Commentary, New Translation, and Special Studies.* New York: Jewish Theological Seminary of America, 1978.

Habel, N. C. *The Book of Job: A Commentary.* Old Testament Library. Philadelphia: Westminster, 1985.

Janzen, J. G. *Job.* Interpretation: A Bible Commentary for Teaching and Preaching. Atlanta, GA: Knox, 1985.

Pope, M. H. *Job: Introduction, Translation, and Notes.* Anchor Bible, 15. 3d ed. Garden City, NJ: Doubleday, 1973.

Terrien, S. L. "The Book of Job: Introduction and Exegesis." *The Interpreter's Bible.* Edited by G. A. Buttrick et al. Nashville, TN: Abingdon, 1954. Vol. 3, pp. 877–1198.

PSALMS

C A R R O L L   S T U H L M U E L L E R

INTRODUCTION

External Format

Unique among biblical books, the book of the Psalms is not subdivided into chapters but into five books of uneven length (Pss. 1–41; 42–72; 73–89; 90–106; 107–150). Each psalm, moreover, typically begins with a title or descriptive label, except for 34 "orphan" psalms. In the Greek version (the Septuagint [LXX]), which tends to add new titles, 18 of these "orphan" psalms are given supplementary information. The enumeration of the 150 Hebrew psalms (in the Masoretic Text [MT]) also is different in the Greek version (the LXX has 151):

HEBREW (MT)	GREEK (LXX)
Pss. 1–8	Pss. 1–8
9–10	9
11–113	10–112
114–115	113
116	114–115
117–146	116–145
147	146–147
148–150	148–150
————	151

Both divisions are ancient and neither one is objectively preferable: i.e., Psalms 9–10 in the Hebrew were originally a single psalm, favoring the Greek division; Psalms 114–115 are two psalms, favoring the Hebrew; both traditions divide a single psalm into Psalms 42 and 43. The liturgical books of the Greek and Latin churches have followed the Greek enumeration. *This commentary adopts the Hebrew enumeration of the individual psalms*, as do most English versions of the Bible.

The Hebrew text generally considers the title a separate verse. Because Christian liturgical tradition included the title neither in song or recitation nor in theological discussions, the titles were not included in the versification. The Hebrew form is followed by the NAB, JB (French ed.), and JPS but not by the RSV, KJV, NIV, TEV, or the JB (English ed.). *This commentary considers titles as separate verses.* Citations of verses in the Psalms in this commentary will therefore differ from the verse numbers in the RSV and many other English versions. Titles receive considerable attention in rabbinical commentaries. They offer important information, even if obscure for us today, about the attitude for praying the psalms, as well as their liturgical usage and accompaniment by musical instruments. As an integral part of the psalms, the titles declare that the spirit and style of worship in any age belong to the inspired tradition of the Bible.

Date of Composing and Editing the Psalms

The division into five books offers some clues to the date during which Israel's sacred songs were collected in postexilic Israel and to the religious spirit of those times. (See the introduction to each of the five books in the commentary.)

Book One (Pss. 1–41) consists almost exclusively of "Psalms of David" (except Pss. 1–2, 10, and 33) and is dominated by laments. Book One reflects the decadent or, at best, the despondent state of religion after the return from exile, as seen in Haggai and Isa. 56:9–57:13; 63:7–64:11. The fact that the royal Davidic psalms are scattered and that the titles refer to David's shared humanity, not to his royal status, reflects the demise of the dynasty.

Book Two (Pss. 42–72) gives new attention to Jerusalem's Temple liturgy in the psalms of Korah (Pss. 42–49) and Asaph (Ps. 50). These may date from the time of the religious reform of Ezra in the latter part of the fifth century B.C. (Ezra 7–10; Neh. 8–9) and the composition of the two books of Chronicles.

Book Three (Pss. 73–89) belongs almost exclusively to Asaph and Korah, while the psalms in *Book Four* (Pss. 90–106) are almost completely untitled. Psalms 96–99 enhance the Temple liturgy as prefiguring the final or eschatological age. These books were added as the momentum of Ezra's reform continued.

Book Five (Pss. 107–150) is the most liturgical of all, with attention to Jews in the Diaspora on pilgrimage to Jerusalem, a situation possibly reflecting international stability and communication effected by the conquests of Alexander the Great. Psalms 120–134 constitute a booklet for pilgrims; Psalms 113–118, for the three major pilgrimage festivals. In Books Four and Five, composition of psalms has definitely passed from the control of the guilds under the names of David, Korah, and Asaph, to a wider group of worship leaders.

The collecting and arranging of psalms did not stop at that time. The Greek version added Psalm 151. At Qumran, the manuscripts disclose a tendency to stabilize the order of psalms according to that of our Bible by the middle of the first century A.D. The Psalm Scroll (11QPs^a), with a different sequence especially for Books Four and Five and with new psalms, including Psalm 151 of the Greek, represents either an earlier stage or a freer approach for worship.

The Literary Form

The psalms collected in the five books can be classified as hymns of praise; prayers of supplication, of thanksgiving, of confidence, and of wisdom; as compositions for the royal family of David; and as processional and entrance liturgies.

Hymns begin and frequently end with a community call to joyful worship; the body of the psalm consists of a motivation to praise Yahweh based upon his great deeds in creation and history as remembered and reenacted liturgically. These psalms center upon life and joy.

Laments or supplications exhibit a strong prophetic influence, especially from Jeremiah, in which Israel came to realize that suffering, even that provoked by sin, individual or national, has a positive role in returning the people to Yahweh and in appreciating the personal compassion of Yahweh. These psalms are grammatically divided into the singular and the plural. Yet even the voice of a single suffering person voiced the faith and prayer of the community.

Confidence and thanksgiving become central to a smaller series of psalms. Thanksgiving psalms are the most difficult to identify. Even the Hebrew word for thanks basically means praise and only derivatively does it express gratitude. In giving thanks, Israel is only responding with praise to what Yahweh does.

Wisdom psalms, like Proverbs or Ecclesiastes, represent a nonliturgical origin, mirror a piety of sophisticated scribes, and concern themselves with retribution for virtue and sin. Because earthly results do not provide for adequate reward and punishment, these psalms begin to infer belief in life after death (Pss. 1; 49).

The table "The Psalms: Classified According to Their Form" lists some psalms more than once since the determination of literary form is uncertain. Psalms, as well as literary and liturgical forms, evolved over the centuries. Psalm 14 is repeated as Psalm 53; Psalm 40:14–18 exists separately as Psalm 70; Psalm 108 is composed of Pss. 57:8–12 and 60:7–14 (→ Biblical Criticism; Poetry).

COMMENTARY

PSALMS 1–41

Book One

The first two psalms are united by the exclamation "How happy" (Heb. *'ashrey*; Pss. 1:1; 2:12). In fact, the same phrase bonds together the first book of Psalms (Pss. 1:1; 41:1), forms a link with the second and third books (Pss. 89:16; 106:3), and is a frequent refrain in the fifth book (Pss. 112:1; 119:1–2; 128:1; 137:9; 146:5). This word, more secular than *baruk* (Heb., "Blessed"), reaches out into daily life. The psalms were intended as everyone's book, even though in the postexilic age the collection became more formally liturgical. Psalm 2 was originally composed for the coronation of a Davidic king and keeps alive the memory of David and his dynasty.

Psalm 1. The opening psalm manifests its close contacts with the wisdom tradition (→ Wisdom). The opening phrase, "Happy that one," occurs frequently in Proverbs within the context of reward and punishment (e.g., Prov. 28:14); other statements about meditating upon the law day and night are found in Josh. 1:8; and the sequence of "walk, stand and sit (or abide)" in Ps. 1:1 recalls the exhortation in Deut. 6:4–9. A comparison may be made with Jer. 15:5–8. Yet Psalm 1 is less tragic in tone than Jeremiah, less legal and ritual than Deuteronomy, and closest of all to wisdom literature. Psalm 1 presumes a body of instruction upon which to meditate. It reflects a person of experience, totally dedicated to the traditions of Israel. The psalm can be divided into vv. 1–3, the way of the righteous; vv. 4–5, the way of the rebellious; and v. 6, conclusion.

Verses 1–3 move from the past tense, where one has taken a clear position with Yahweh (v. 1), to a present tense of satisfaction (v. 2), to a hope for a happy future (v. 3). The Hebrew term *derek*, "way," indicates the conduct of individuals (Ps. 37:5–7) or of all Israel (Isa. 40:3), a way mysteriously directed by God, yet clear in its moral expectations.

Some interpreters discern anticipation of reward and punishment beyond the grave here: v. 3 may refer to the tree as "transplanted" beyond the present conditions of earth; v. 5 employs a definite article with judgment, possibly foreseeing a final reckoning. Early Christian writers interpreted the tree as the cross and the life-giving water as baptism.

Psalm 2. Composed very probably for a royal coronation at Jerusalem, perhaps for one of the last kings such as Josiah (640–609 B.C.), who

The Psalms
Classified According to Their Form

Hymns of praise

Motivation from nature: 8; 19:1–7; 29; 33; 89:1–19; 93; 96; 104; 148; 150

Motivation from history or Torah: 19:8–14; 24; 33; 46; 47; 48; 68; 76; 78; 81; 100; 105; 107; 113; 114; 117; 134; 135; 136; 145; 146; 147; 149; 150

Canticles of Zion: 46; 48; 76; 84; 87; 122

Entrance or processional hymns: 15; 24; 68; 95:1–7a; 100; 132

Yahweh-King: 24; 29; 47; 93; 95:1–7a; 96; 97; 98; 99; 149

Royal Davidic psalms

Coronation or anniversaries: 2; 72; 89:2–38; 101; 110; 132

Supplication: 20; 21; 61; 89; 144:1–11

Thanksgiving: 18

Marriage: 45

Prophetic psalms: 50; 81; 82; 95:7b–11

Prayers of supplication

For the assembly: 12; 36; 44; 58; 60; 74; 77; 79; 80; 83; 85; 90; 94; 106; 108:7–14; 137; 144:1–11

For the individual: 3; 4; 5; 6; 7; 9–10; 13; 14; 17; 22; 25; 26; 27; 28; 35; 38; 39; 40:14–18; 41; 42–43; 51; 53; 54; 55; 56; 57; 59; 61; 63; 64; 69; 70; 71; 86; 88; 102; 108:2–6; 109; 120; 123; 130; 139; 140; 141; 142; 143

For the sick: 6; 16; 30; 31; 38; 39; 41; 61; 69; 88; 91; 103

Seven penitential psalms: 6; 32; 38; 51; 102; 130; 143

Curses: 10:15; 31:18–19; 40:15–16; 55:16; 58:7–12; 59:11–14; 68:22–24; 69:23–29; 83:10–19; 109:6–20; 137:9; 139:19–22; 140:9–11

Thanksgiving psalms

For the assembly: 22:23–32; 34; 65; 66; 67; 68; 75; 76; 92; 107; 118; 122; 124; 135; 136

For the individual: 18; 23; 30; 31; 40:2–12; 63; 66; 103; 116; 118:5–21; 138; 144:1–11

Prayers of confidence: 11; 16; 20; 23; 27; 41; 52; 62; 63; 84; 91; 115; 121; 125; 126; 129; 131; 133

Wisdom psalms: 1; 25; 32; 34; 36; 37; 49; 62; 73; 75; 78; 111; 112; 119; 127; 128

Acrostic psalms: 9–10; 25; 34; 37; 111; 112; 119; 146

Some psalms are listed more than once since they can be classified in more than one of these categories.

pledged himself, as Psalm 1 would enjoin, to obey the ancient laws and traditions (2 Kings 22–23), Psalm 2 moves with skillful balance: vv. 1–3, earthly kings, who speak in their own voice, in revolt, (v. 3); vv. 4–6, a heavenly setting of peace for ratifying the choice of a new Davidic king, concluding with an oracle from Yahweh; vv. 7–9, the words of consecration (2 Sam. 7:14; Isa. 9:6–7; Pss. 89:27–28; 110:3) and other ritual actions; 2:10–12, advice to princes and, indirectly, to the new king.

In v. 2, the term "anointed" indicated a special relationship with Yahweh, as it does elsewhere for altars (Exod. 29:36), priests (Exod. 28:41), prophets (1 Kings 19:16; Isa. 61:1), and especially kings (1 Sam. 10:1; 16:3). Ps. 2:4, "The Lord laughs" denotes his supreme control (Ps. 37:13), not necessarily a laugh of ridicule or disdain (Ps. 59:9). God paralyzes the efforts of all opponents (2:5) and with a decree fixes the limits of chaos (v. 7). Israel's land is created anew in peace (Jer. 5:22; Job 28:26). Beginning with v. 9, the text does not appear to be in its original form, perhaps by disuse after the end of the dynasty. As a result, one may say that the text here is disturbed or "corrupt." "Shatter the clay vessels," like the symbolic actions of the prophets (Jer. 19:10–11; 28:10), announced the end of all opposition. The action has some overtones of ancient magical practices (Num. 5:11–31), yet here Yahweh clearly determines the outcome by obedience to the divine will. Despite a tone of fierceness within the psalm and its exclusive concern for the king, Psalm 2 modulates into a statement of calm protection for all who take refuge in the Lord.

Through this psalm, especially v. 7, the early church proclaimed its faith in Jesus' messiahship and divine enthronement at his resurrection from the dead (Acts 4:25–26; 13:33; Heb. 1:5; 5:5).

Psalm 3. The first major collection of psalms, attributed to the guild "of David," begins with Psalm 3 and extends to the end of Book One. This guild under the patronage of David (1 Sam. 16:18; Amos 6:5) had, at first, exclusive rights to psalm writing. Psalms 3–4 have traditionally been considered prayers for morning (Ps. 4:5, 9) and evening (Ps. 3:6). A sequence of words identical in the Hebrew further bonds these psalms together: foes or distress (3:2; 4:2); many say (3:3; 4:7); my glory or honor (3:4; 4:3); I call and the Lord hears (3:5; 4:2, 4); and I lie down and sleep (3:6; 4:9).

Although the title refers to David's flight from his son Absalom (2 Sam. 15–18), the reference to "my holy mountain" (Ps. 3:5) presumes a date after Solomon had constructed the Temple (2:6). The title declares that no darkness is bleaker than betrayal within one's family.

This individual lament begins with a cry for

help to Yahweh (3:2–4), continues with a meditation about Yahweh, one's true confidence (vv. 5–7), and concludes with a stirring supplication for help (v. 8) and a final ritual blessing (v. 9). Two key words set up a strong tension between the foes who are many (vv. 2 twice, 3, 7) and Yahweh the source of salvation (vv. 3, 8, 9). Many of the lines begin dramatically: "Yahweh, how many!" (v. 2); "Many say" (v. 3); "But you, Yahweh" (v. 4); "My cry to Yahweh" (v. 5); "I" (v. 6); "Rise, Yahweh" (v. 8); and "With Yahweh is salvation" (v. 9). Verse 8 resonates with the traditional summons (Num. 10:35; Pss. 7:7; 44:27; 68:2) and links the rise of a new day to Israel's march into the mystery of its divinely directed future.

Psalm 4. More serene than Psalm 3 but with a more disturbed text, the prayer of supplication in Psalm 4 sustains confidence within a setting, or at least a remembrance, of Temple sacrifice (v. 6). Possibly composed by a priest betrayed by colleagues (v. 3), the psalm concludes with renewed assurances for the person faithful to Yahweh (Lev. 26:3–45). The final reference to sleep intimates the practice of prayer at night (Ps. 119:62) in the Temple and the reception of favorable dreams from the Lord (Gen. 15:12–21; 37:5, 9).

An opening cry for help (Ps. 4:2) is followed by reflections addressed either to persecutors or fellow worshipers (vv. 3–6); the psalm then modulates from ridicule to gratitude (vv. 7–9).

Verse 2 appeals to a just God fulfilling covenant promises to Israel and asks that "in distress you open wide" my horizons and remove oppressive borders. The same Hebrew word, here translated "open wide," occurs in Gen. 26:22 for the name of a well within a spacious area for living. Ps. 4:3–6 blends the thinking of wisdom literature (the good are blessed, the evil punished, Ps. 1) with references to the covenant and Temple ritual. The difficult v. 5 is translated in the Greek, "Be angry and sin not," which is quoted in Eph. 4:26. The Hebrew infers anxiety within extended periods of prayer.

Ps. 4:7b, spoken by the "many" in Psalms 3–4, declares sarcastically that the light of Yahweh's face has vanished. Verse 8 announces that a person receives greater joy from one's interior peace than from abundant material resources (Pss. 17:15; 84:11).

Psalm 5. A morning prayer for accompanying Temple sacrifice (Pss. 3; 4) or possibly a ritual at the Temple gate (Pss. 15; 24), Psalm 5, a supplication, repeats in its second half the sequence in the first. The introduction (vv. 2–4), like the entire psalm, is addressed to Yahweh, worshiped as holy (vv. 5–7) and good (vv. 8–9); the wicked fall (vv. 5–7, 10–11) but the upright are joyful (vv. 8–9, 12–13).

Verses 2–4 begin as though God, alive within the Temple, may be deaf and silent (Ps. 22:2–3). Salvation is given to the righteous, who in faith wait upon the Lord (Isa. 7:4; 30:15–18) and follow the way of the Lord (Ps. 5:8). Verse 3, "my King and my God," recalls Isaiah's vision in the Temple (Isa. 6). Dawn was the time of sacrifice (2 Kings 3:20; Amos 4:4) and salvation (Ps. 46:6; Isa. 33:2; 37:36).

Ps. 5:5 can be translated: "A no-god takes pleasure in evil; but you, no evil one is ever your guest." This rendition leads to an entrance liturgy, proclaiming the purity of the true worshiper (Pss. 15; 24). The psalmist in entering the Temple submits to God's mysterious ways (Ps. 5:8; Ps. 1; Isa. 40:3–5; 43:16–20).

Ps. 5:10–11 points to deceit as the most serious sin, for it reaches deeply into communication between friends (12:3–5). "Let them bear their guilt"; possibly such openness will bring a conversion (34:22). "All who take refuge in you" repeats the antiphonal response in Psalm 2.

Psalm 5 states that righteousness, not birth as an Israelite, brings one into God's presence; it hints, if only vaguely, to opening that presence to righteous Gentiles.

Psalm 6. The first of the seven penitential psalms (Pss. 6; 32; 38; 51; 102; 130; 143) is a filigree of stereotypic phrases found throughout psalms of supplication, with repetition of words (hear and shamed, twice; terrified, three times; Yahweh, seven times). Yet it remains a poem with high emotional intensity established by the I-Thou relation, the life-death polarity, and the effective use of questions and commands.

Verses 2–4 involve supplication and petition, beginning with imperatives and ending with a question; vv. 5–6, emotional fear of death, again with imperative and question; vv. 7–8, acute physical suffering; vv. 9–10, confidence, beginning with imperative and concluding with a clear statement.

The psalm labors under the relation of suffering and sin, whether this be the sin of an individual or of the group. God as healer never addresses simply physical or emotional ailments but the whole person as bonded within Israel. Healing includes conversion. This psalm became very popular within Israel, at first as morning prayer, except on Sabbaths and festivals. Because of the reference to "the eighth" in the title, it was sung at circumcisions; for Christians, it announced the resurrection on the day after the Sabbath.

"How long?" (v. 4) occurs approximately thirty times in the Hebrew Scriptures. The question is left unanswered.

"In Sheol, who offers you praise?" (v. 6). Sheol is the grave, a place of murky silence and of no return, with little or no contact with Yahweh (Pss. 94:17; 143:3; Job 7:9). Only very late in the postexilic age was the notion of God's presence with the dead in Sheol accepted (Ps. 139:8). Belief in life after death is found earlier only within popular religious beliefs (1 Sam. 28:8–25; 2 Kings 2:11; → Hades; Sheol).

Psalm 7. A person betrayed and persecuted seldom follows clean lines of response and closure but reacts with melancholic, abrupt transitions, with anger and imperfect grammar. Such is the case in Psalm 7. The editor, however, has imposed a reasonable development; vv. 2–3, summary introduction; vv. 4–6, confession of innocence; vv. 7–9a, trial beginning; vv. 9b–10, prosecution of the wicked; vv. 11–12, hymnic interlude; vv. 13–17, verdict and punishment; v. 18, thanksgiving. This lament wrestles with the biblical problem of reward and punishment, particularly when the question touches personal relationships. God is present as one seeks to sort out the parts from a web of emotions and confusion. The title, as interpreted in the Aramaic Targum, asks readers to reread David's persecution by the Benjaminite Saul in order to respond to betrayal by leaving the outcome in God's hands (1 Sam. 18–31).

The introduction is relatively calm, repeating the stereotypic phrase "I take refuge in you, Yahweh, my God" (Pss. 11; 16; 31). In view of 7:8, the reference may be to Yahweh's presence in the sanctuary where disputes were sometimes settled (Exod. 22:6–8; Num. 5:6–10). Lions (Ps. 7:3) were to be found in Israel up to the time of the Crusaders. In pleading innocence and taking no initiative to punish evildoers, the psalmist will risk death if there is any dishonesty (vv. 4–6). "Guilt on my hands" refers to a deliberate breach of personal trust.

The trial gets under way, presided over by the Lord in an assembly of peoples or, as some scholars read the text, of lesser gods (Ps. 82:1). The style is suddenly majestic and definitive, as befits action in God's throne room. Ps. 7:9b–10 modulates into a calmer, legal action of indicting the wicked party. Verse 10b reads literally, "Searcher of heart and kidneys," a reference to the seat of reason and emotions.

Verses 13–17 appear excessively stark in their realism. Yet not even God can forgive, much less reward the unrepentant sinner. Such people do not need divine punishment, for they destroy themselves (Prov. 26:27). Ps. 7:18, a liturgical conclusion, reminds us that God takes seriously each betrayal of trust.

Psalm 8. Psalm 8, a hymn of praise, resolves into peaceful joy the somber and at times agonizing outcries of Psalms 3–7, yet in v. 4 it is linked with them as a prayer at night. Verses 2 and 10, calling for praise of Yahweh, form an envelope, technically an inclusio, around the body of the psalm that provides the motive for singing to the Lord's name. The language reaches high poetical flights, yet the thought is simple enough: humanity, which feels overwhelmed by the universe, if redeemed by the Lord, has this world at its feet.

This psalm's history of composition and use is long and complex. Originally it was composed in honor of a Davidic king; the phrase "our Lord" was a title for kings (1 Kings 1:11, 43, 47); only in the postexilic age was it directed to Yahweh (Neh. 10:29; Ps. 135:5). The king empowered by Yahweh was considered the source of harmony. Like Genesis 1–3, Psalm 8 delicately blends human excellence and human lowliness. In the postexilic age the psalm became a popular night prayer and still later was sung in the New Year's festival celebrating creation. Job 7:17–21 reversed the sense of v. 5, while the LXX made "the son of man" (possibly to be translated more inclusively as "the child of earth") "for a little while less than the angels" refer to the small stretch of time till the Messiah comes. The NT calls upon the psalm to announce the messianic presence in Jesus (Heb. 2:6–10; 1 Cor. 15:20–28). Matt. 21:15–16 recalls the early link with the Davidic dynasty. Not suprisingly, Christian liturgies reserve the psalm for Sundays and major Christological feasts.

The motivation for praise is sung by special choirs, narrating, questioning, and answering (Ps. 8:3–9). Verse 3 announces definitive victory with only a hint of the violent struggle over chaos in creating the good order of the universe (Pss. 29; 89:6–13; Isa. 51:9–10). New creation delights in the sound of new life in "babes and sucklings." Ps. 8:6, "little less than gods," like Ps. 7:8; 1 Kings 22:19; Job 1:6; and Isa. 6:1–7, refers to the divine assembly; later these figures are renamed angels. Humankind, redeemed and lifted up from its lowly state by the Lord, shares in the divine governance of the world. The harmony of nature depends upon the harmony of men and women among themselves and with their God. Ecology belongs to the theology of redemption.

Psalms 9–10. While the question is not completely settled, many solid reasons support the unity of Psalms 9–10. First, ancient manuscripts, especially the LXX and the Vulgate (Vg.), unite them. For this reason, after Psalms 9–10, the liturgical tradition of the Greek and Latin churches generally numbers its psalms one behind the Hebrew (see Introduction above). Second, very unusual for psalms in the first book, Psalm 10 has no title. Third, similar words, especially for the poor and the wicked, some even rare in biblical Hebrew, occur in both psalms. Third, some scholars discern an acrostic pattern uniting both psalms, an arrangement by which new lines begin with successive letters of

the alphabet. Yet in Psalm 10 considerable ingenuity is needed to locate the proper letter. The acrostic form is frequently associated with the wisdom movement (or "tradition"). Yet Psalms 9–10 do not share the tranquil spirit of wisdom nor its distance from the Jerusalem liturgy.

While the literary form varies between hymn, supplication, reflection, thanksgiving, and confidence, the atmosphere is generally somber, at times anguishing, and therefore one understands Psalms 9–10 best as a lament from the individual. The clue to the form of Psalms 9–10 is to be sought in liturgical ceremony at the Jerusalem Temple where the Lord is enthroned (Pss. 9:5, 8, 12; 47:6). Part One of the service includes 9:2–13, praise and thanksgiving, with an introduction (vv. 2–3), motivation for praise in God's protection of the individual and the nation (vv. 4–11), and a hymnic interlude (vv. 12–13). Part Two includes 9:14–21, an appeal for justice, with prayer (vv. 14–15, 20–21) and reflection (vv. 16–19). Part Three includes 10:1–18, a cry of distress over the prosperity of the wicked (vv. 1–11), followed by prayer (vv. 12–15). Part Four includes 10:16–18, hymnic conclusion of confidence.

The opening hymn (9:2–13) begins with "I praise the Lord with all my heart; I announce all your wonders!" (For translating the first word as "praise" instead of "thanksgiving," see Gen. 29:35; 49:8.) The word "wonders" occurs forty-five times in the OT, twenty-seven in the Psalms, and refers to the Lord's great acts of creation and redemption as they reach the ordinary Israelite (Ps. 71:17) and all the nation (Ps. 75:1), both in Israel's history (Ps. 44:2) and in cosmic creation (Ps. 136:4). Problems arise later in Psalms 9–10 from this broad perspective concerning earth and history. Praise involves faith in the Lord's justice (9:5) to fulfill every promise and hope of the righteous person (Exod. 34:6–7). The psalmist does not flinch from stating clearly at the outset that the Lord is always dependable and just (Ps. 44). Beneath 9:11 lies the rich theology of knowing or cherishing the name of the Lord and all that the Lord personally stands for in relation to Israel. "Those seeking you" is another phrase so frequent (about 165 times in the OT) that we cannot adequately unpack its richness. In v. 13 it is translated "avenger of blood," referring to the obligations of a kinsperson to "seek" the integrity of the family by executing anyone who murders a family member (Lev. 25:23–55; Num. 35:16–29).

Ps. 9:14–21 comprises an appeal for and reflection on justice. The gates of death are contrasted with the gates of daughter Zion in vv. 14–15, so that justice is the door to life, injustice to death. Because the gates of death were firmly closed forever, does the psalmist also imply eternity for life with God? Not clearly, but these intuitions prepare for such a theological development. The end of v. 17 includes two Hebrew words difficult to translate, *higgayon selah*. The first implies meditation (1:2), the accompanying sound of the harp (92:4), and the movement of the heart (19:15). The second word probably indicates a pause. The liturgy calls for silent reflection, to be terminated abruptly: "Rise, Lord!" (9:20).

In 10:1–15 the acrostic arrangement is no longer clearly visible; the tone is somber, even desperate. The psalmist confronts the just Lord with the proud and prosperous wicked: "Why, Lord?" in startling contrast to the confident "Rise, Lord" (9:20). A personal bonding in faith enables the psalmist to be this forceful without being arrogant or skeptical. The statement about the Lord's forgetfulness surges with agony (v. 11; Pss. 13:2; 44:25; 77:10). Here the conclusion is carefully arrived at "in the heart," or seat of reason. It will be repeated more vigorously in the final appeal.

Even though the external situation has not improved in 10:16–18, the faith of the psalmist has been strengthened by describing it as it is; and the conviction emerges that "you hear, Lord," a phrase that is the turning point. The final Hebrew words are somewhat uncertain, yet even so they reflect the simplest and deepest human desire for peace and shelter.

Psalm 11. A psalm of confidence, Psalm 11 witnesses to the faith of a devout Israelite, weathering the collapse of the nation's leaders and the betrayal of personal friends. The psalm begins and ends with strong trust in the Lord (vv. 1a; 7); in between we encounter the advice of false friends (vv. 1b–3) and the motivation for loyal confidence in the Lord (vv. 4–6).

In v. 1a, rather than "flee like a bird to your mountain" (Gen. 19:17; Judg. 6:2; 1 Sam. 14), the psalmist declares, "I take refuge in the Lord" (Pss. 2:12; 7:2; 16:1). Some understand this to be a statement about the right of asylum in the Jerusalem Temple (Exod. 21:12–14; 1 Kings 1:50–53). Yet in Ps. 11:1b–3, all the underpinnings of life are obliterated, be they laws or leadership or buildings.

Nothing but Yahweh is left for one's confidence. Verse 4 follows the tradition that the Lord's normal throne is above the heavens (Pss. 18:7; 20:7; 29:10; 1 Kings 8:27); the Jerusalem Temple is an earthly mirror of the heavenly house of the Lord, yet only on condition that Israel remains faithful (Ezek. 10). Ps. 11:4b denotes a God who sees hidden reality and explores unknown places. Verse 6 bursts with the Lord's fierce anger against the wicked, recalling the destruction of Sodom and Gomorrah (Gen. 19:23–24).

Psalm 12. A communal lament, Psalm 12 involves people suffering from deceit, particularly at the hands of their own religious leadership. In fact, the key words all center around speaking. The structure follows a chiastic arrangement, forming a letter X (Gk. *chi*), so that the second upward stroke follows the steps in reverse of the downward stroke. After the call for help (v. 2a), we find A lament, vv. 2a–3; B prayer, v. 4; C words of the wicked, v. 5; D Yahweh's own words, v. 6; C' choral response of the devout, v. 7; B' prayer, v. 8; A' lament, v. 9.

As the psalm advances to its center moment in v. 6, symbols and other people drop away and God speaks directly in an oracle of salvation. God saves, not by changing the human situation, for in the final verse nothing changes. That verse even repeats a phrase from v. 2, "sons of men" or "children of earth." Yet if people "wait upon me," as the Lord here advises, salvation has already begun.

Verse 7 poses a serious question: how can God's pure words be purified seven times over? This notion seems to result from the suffering of faithful ones who thereby attach themselves ever more personally to the Lord.

Psalm 13. A personal lament, Psalm 13 describes a desperately sick person (v. 3), abandoned by friends who gloat over this miserable end of virtuous living. The psalm consists of lament (vv. 2–3), petition (vv. 4–5), and statement of confidence (v. 6).

"How long?" (vv. 2–3), a biblical formula for fright and exasperation, demands an explanation from the provident God who has let things get completely out of control. God even "forgets" (Pss. 9:19; 10:12; 42:10). Verse 3a can be translated, "How long do I lay up counsel in my heart," as though to say, "must I keep on learning forever from my pain?"

"Look! Answer me!" These strong words (vv. 4–5) challenge God to scrutinize me through and through. The phrase ends with the affectionate, "My God! Illumine [or open] my eyes," which long for life and not death, for God and not oblivion.

"I indeed will scrutinize your steadfast love and rejoice in your salvation . . . you care for me tenderly" (v. 6; cf. 2 Cor. 12:9–10).

Psalm 14. Psalm 14 is textually disturbed (yet repeated again in Ps. 53 in much better condition) and mixes features of prophetic diatribes against evil (Jer. 5) with a discussion of foolishness that recalls wisdom literature. The overall attitude seems to reflect a personal lament, possibly composed during the decadent reign of Manasseh (2 Kings 21:1–18; 698–642 B.C.). After the introduction (Ps. 14:1), the universal collapse of morals is described (vv. 2–3), a verdict against the wicked awaits fulfillment (vv. 4–6), and a prayer begs for the Lord's return to Jerusalem (v. 7).

"There is no God," displays a practical atheism (v. 1). God is useless and ineffective, so why bother? Verse 3 is quoted in Rom. 3:10–18 along with six other OT passages, all of which found their way into some Greek manuscripts of Psalm 14 and even into a Hebrew manuscript.

Psalm 15. Composed for a service at one of the Temple gates (Ps. 118:19), Psalm 15 along with Psalm 24 enabled a person once guilty or at least under suspicion to be declared worthy of acceptance. The liturgy did not remove the requirement of confessing one's fault and making full restitution (Num. 5:5–10) but recognized the need for a final arbiter to ensure that all prerequisites were properly fulfilled.

The psalm combines the question-answer method and the concern for morality as in prophecy (Isa. 33:14–16) or in wisdom literature (Prov. 30:2–6). After the initial question, probably spoken by a representative of the congregation (Ps. 15:1), the officiating priest or Levite responds (vv. 2–5a) and officially welcomes the party (v. 5b).

In v. 1 the words for sojourn, dwell, and tent recall early, nomadic days and remind the worshiper that even at Jerusalem there is no unconditional assurance of eternal presence (Ps. 11:4).

In vv. 2–5a the list does not include ritual requirements (Lev. 15) or serious sins like apostasy but those faults that disrupt family and neighborhood. The prohibition of lending at interest reflects the ancient practice of the extended family and its obligations to help. Currency did not yet exist and precious items were given as pledge. In the ancient Near East, interest rates were exorbitantly high (e.g., 33 1/3 percent in Babylon; 50 percent at Nuzi).

Psalm 16. A prayer of confidence, especially for Levites, Psalm 16 addresses a time of severe sickness and disqualification from the sanctuary (Lev. 21), a time as well of moral collapse among fellow Levites. The parallels with Isa. 56:9–57:13 place the composition in the early postexilic age around 500 B.C. After a call for help (Ps. 16:1a), the confusing religious scene is put before us (vv. 1b–4), followed by an expression of confidence (vv. 5–8) and rewards (vv. 9–11).

Significantly, the psalmist does not take refuge in anything sacred, not even in the sacred word but states that his good comes only "in

you, Lord." Verses 1–3 are disturbed in the Hebrew, mirroring confusion and degeneracy in levitical ranks.

"The Lord, my portion and cup" (v. 5) identifies Levites who, though they possessed no property (Josh. 13:14; Deut. 10:9), were a symbol of an attitude proper for all Israel (Pss. 73:26; 142:6). Verse 7 refers to prayer at night (Pss. 4:9; 91:5–6; 119:62).

The rewards of confidence included a return to health (16:9–11). Yahweh will not allow this devout worshiper to be consigned to the grave. In the Hebrew text, v. 11 repeats six key words or ideas from the psalm and is clearly the finale. The Greek translation, reflecting a later clear belief in resurrection and personal immortality, read v. 8, "I see Yahweh before me always [in paradise]" and shifted the conclusion to v. 10 where the psalmist is "not consigned to corruption." The LXX reading was accepted at Qumran (1QS 4:11–14) and in Acts 2:23–28.

Psalm 17. Word parallels and the act of praying at night (vv. 3, 15) connect Psalms 16 and 17. Sorrow and outrage, which Psalm 16 pushes to the background, Psalm 17 brings forward prominently. Psalm 17 may also expand upon the conditions, listed in Psalm 15, for entering the sanctuary. While the Hebrew text is seriously damaged, the sense and structure seem clear: first, an appeal to Yahweh (v. 1) with a protest of innocence (vv. 2–5); second, a request for an oracle (v. 6) with prayer (vv. 7–9b) and lament (vv. 9c–12); third, an appeal to Yahweh (vv. 13–14a) with lament (v. 14bc); and fourth, the conclusion (v. 15).

The opening appeal may be translated either "Hear, just Lord" or, with justifiable emendation, "Hear, Lord, my plea for justice." Verses 1 and 15 reason from the psalmist's righteousness, not God's. Again one encounters deceit among religious people (Ps. 12).

In vv. 2–5 the psalmist protests his innocence, derived from the pure light of the Lord's presence (v. 2), which searches the mysterious darkness of each person's heart (Jer. 12:3) during prayer at night (Ps. 17:3). The image extends from heart (reasoning) to mouth (speaking) to feet (acting).

After the initial request for an oracle from the Lord (v. 6), lovely images of divine care are introduced: "at your right hand" (Ps. 16:8); "apple of your eye," literally, "the little image in the pupil of your eye" (Deut. 32:10; Prov. 7:2); "shadow of your wings" (Deut. 32:11; Isa. 51:16; Lam. 4:20), possibly an allusion to residing in the shadow of the wings of the cherubim, which were located on either side of the Ark (Exod. 25:20; Isa. 6:1–2; Ps. 36:8). In 17:9c–12 the psalmist speaks with the agonizing accents of suffering and betrayal (Jer. 12:3).

Ps. 17:13–14 is textually corrupt. The message seems to be all earthly gifts are from God, but only for the righteous do these gifts lead to peace. The difference comes from bonding with the Lord.

Liturgy seems to reach beyond orthodox limits (v. 15). "I will see the vision of your face," yet no one can see God and live (Exod. 33:20; Isa. 6:5). "Upon awakening I rejoice before your presence" (Num. 12:8), yet belief in the resurrection will not be clarified till Dan. 12:1–3, around 165 B.C. Or is the text referring simply to awakening after a night vigil in the sanctuary? In a context of visions at night, intuitions of resurrection ought not to be dismissed.

Psalm 18. A biblical masterpiece and a majestic ode of thanksgiving, Psalm 18 summons a universe of cosmic images to announce Yahweh's giant steps through the life of faithful Israelites. Rather than be terrified at the roaring darkness and the grinding of people into dust, one is instead caught up in ecstatic wonder at Yahweh's immediate presence in Israel's history and in the marvelous protection of the chosen people. Thanksgiving, however, centers less in Yahweh than in the work that Yahweh is accomplishing among the Israelites. Images describing manifestations of God, exalted vocabulary, and stately Temple ceremonies, enable one to envision the awesome world of the spirit where each person battles for salvation (cf. Eph. 6:10–17).

Although this psalm seems to be repeated in 2 Samuel 22, only vv. 9, 10, 17, 22 are identical. Stylistically, Psalm 18 reflects many features of Israel's earliest poetry (Deut. 32–33; Exod. 15; Hab. 3). Rather than an eschatological poem dealing with the final age of complete divine renewal, Psalm 18 reflects Canaanite literature about the yearly struggle of the gods' creating the world anew in harmony and fertility (Pss. 29; 89:10–14; 93). The psalm is composed in an early age, with additions in v. 51 about the Davidic royalty and, in v. 2, the title "my strength," a word very similar to the Hebrew name of King Hezekiah (727–698 B.C.), who saw Jerusalem survive the massive army of Assyria (2 Kings 18–20).

The psalm proceeds: introduction (vv. 2–7); theophanic presentation, with Yahweh's departure from heaven (vv. 8–13), upheavals on earth (vv. 14–16), and deliverance (vv. 17–20); historical presentation, with the righteous rewarded (vv. 21–31) and military victory (vv. 32–46); and epilogue, with thanksgiving (vv. 47–50) for the Davidic royalty (v. 51).

Most probably, the opening line of the psalm belongs to the title and could be translated, "I Yahweh have pity on you, Hezekiah." This line is missing in 2 Samuel 22; the verb "pity," sometimes translated "love," never has

God as its object. In Ps. 18:3, "my rock" is a title given to Yahweh only in Jerusalem psalms (Ps. 95:1).

Ps. 18:5–6 voices a litany of death! "Breakers of death" refers to the angry sea, which swallowed its victims, never to release them. Israelites were not seafarers and dreaded the open waters. God answers "from his [heavenly] temple" (Ps. 11:4). In 18:7–8 the clash of symbols is typical of Semitic poetry: raging waters, smoke from Yahweh's nostrils, and fire from the Lord's mouth. Symbols such as these communicated a mysterious divine presence that could not be rationalized as in the stately symbolic world of Greece and Rome. The psalmist is delivered against all odds, "because the Lord delights in me" (v. 20b).

The psalm leaves aside theophanic symbolism and enters the world of conscience (vv. 21–31). Verses 21–25 recall the entrance liturgies of Psalms 15; 24. This fact raises the question whether or not the preceding verses were also part of Temple ritual, inaugurating a solemn service. Ps. 18:26–27 stuns readers with its lapidary style after the extravaganza of the preceding section. At times, one needs the sober truth. God does not tolerate being mocked or the covenant being ridiculed. The measure for divine righteousness is gauged from caring for the lowly. In vv. 32–46, the language reflects "holy war," a phrase found in Mic. 3:5 and Joel 4(3):9. It refers to warfare in the book of Joshua as well as in the very late apocalyptic literature (Zech. 14; Dan. 7–12). As Israelites kept the ancient law (Josh. 1; Dan. 1), the mighty power of Yahweh was on their side to fight their battles. "Holy wars" seemed to be more religious instruction and Temple liturgy than actual military venture. Yet if conflict occurred, Israel would be mightily empowered. Vengeance must be left to Yahweh, who sets the record straight (Ps. 18:48). Paul, in declaring that vengeance belongs to God alone, substantiates his words by appealing to the OT (Lev. 19:18).

Psalm 19. Resting between the royal Davidic Psalms 18 and 20, Psalm 19 may have found its place in the Psalter because of the relation of vv. 5b–7 to Isa. 41:1–5, which refers to royalty. Ps. 19:5b–7, which acclaims the resplendent way of the sun, acts as a bridge from the first part, praising the glorious Creator in vv. 2–5a, to the praise of Israel's glorious law in vv. 8–11. According to Babylonian mythology, as exemplified in the prologue to Hammurabi's law code, the sun god Shamash grants the code of laws to the king. Verse 12, in turn, provides a transition from the glory of the law in vv. 8–11 to the darkness of disobedience in vv. 13–14. The psalm concludes with v. 15.

The entire psalm holds together primarily through the image of splendid light across the universe and within the law, which in turn casts its shadow should there be any opposing disobedience, and secondarily through the rubric of God's mysterious word, manifest through the good order of the universe (vv. 2–5a) and in Israel's law (vv. 8–15). Each section expresses the sense of mystery, the first concerning all the world by using the common name for God (Heb. 'el), the second specifically for Israel by using the proper name Yahweh. The first section comes from an early period, possibly that of David around 1000 B.C., and the second section from the days of Ezra around 428 B.C.

The luminous yet mysterious wonder of the world proclaims not only God's glorious presence (vv. 2–5a), but its orderliness and balance set the stage for appreciating the law in vv. 8–11. The structure of v. 2 is chiastic: A B C C' B' A': "The heavens proclaim the glory of God; the work of God's hands is revealed in the heavenly vault." The imagery in v. 3 is exquisite: water gurgling from rocks in the daytime, wind breathing through the space of the night (cf. John 3:8). Ps. 19:2 can be compared to the sacred place, v. 3 to the liturgical action within it. While v. 4 denies that any voice is heard, v. 5 announces its message throughout the universe (Rom. 10:18).

Ps. 19:5b–7 unabashedly incorporates the mythology of Babylon and Egypt about the sun god, so that the sense of mystery is not lost. The natural law of the universe that lies behind the laws and traditions of Israel reaches beyond rational understanding.

Law in vv. 8–11 embodies early clan traditions, enactments in the Torah, and later practices—all that governs the good order of Israel. Most of all, law expresses the qualities of Yahweh—perfect, loyal, luminous, pure, sweet, and just. So described, law almost becomes the immediate presence of Yahweh with Israel.

The transitional v. 12 speaks of "your servant" (so v. 14) and of law's abundant reward (so vv. 8–10). In vv. 13–14, sins of inadvertence or ignorance are mentioned first, the stage after willful sins have been confessed and restitution made (Num. 5:5–10) and before the ceremony at the temple gate (Ps. 15). Then more serious, presumptuous transgressions are cited (Gen. 20:6; Exod. 32:21, 30–31).

Ps. 19:15 concludes: "How pleasant is God's word and the rhythm of one's heart in meditation before you, Yahweh, my rock, my redeemer." Redeemer carries the early meaning of the Hebrew word go'el, one's kinsperson with the obligations of blood relationship (Lev. 25:23–55).

Psalm 20. The sequence of verses in Psalm 20 follows that of a service before battle: v. 2, introduction as the king arrives at the Jerusalem Temple; vv. 3–6, ritual sacrifices and intercessory prayer; vv. 7–9, priestly assurance of vic-

tory; v. 10, concluding prayer (1 Sam. 7:9; 13:9–12; 2 Chron. 20:1–19). Because the Ark is not said to be carried into battle (1 Sam. 4:1–11; Psalm 68), one may presume a date of composition in the late pre-exilic period.

"A time of crisis" (Ps. 20:2) grips the nation (Gen. 35:3; Ps. 50:15). "The name of the God of Jacob" extends God's pledge of fidelity and compassion (Exod. 34:6–7) to "Jacob," possibly all Israel (Isa. 2:5–6) or else to the southern tribe of Judah (Jer. 5:20), God's chosen people (Exod. 19:3; Isa. 41:17).

Ps. 20:3–6 summarizes Temple services. "Offerings" of grain or animals were partially burned on the altar with the rest used for sacred meals (Lev. 2–3); "holocausts" were completely consumed on the altar in total adoration of the God of life (Lev. 1). The practice of raising banners has biblical precedence (Num. 10:13–28). "Victory" is the same Hebrew word generally translated "salvation," one instance among many of deriving sacred vocabulary from nonreligious words.

An oracle may have been given by the priests (Ps. 12:6) before the response in 20:7–9. The phrase "holy heavens" shows that the earthly tabernacle was a symbolic replica of God's dwelling in the heavens (11:4). While Israel prepares for war, the people confess that victory does not result from instruments of war (Isa. 30:15–17). "Lord, grant victory to the king" or "Save the king" in Ps. 20:10 inspired the joyful shout honoring royalty in England.

Psalm 21. The royal psalm Psalm 21 has a less defined setting within the Temple ritual than does Psalm 20. After the introduction in 21:2, Yahweh is addressed in the name of the king (vv. 3–7); the transitional v. 8 leads to an address to the king in the name of Yahweh (vv. 9–13). Verse 14 functions as a conclusion to the ceremony and repeats a key phrase of v. 2, "in your strength."

"Victory" (v. 2) is understood according to its use in Ps. 20:6. "Heart's desire" is a request granted to those possessed of God's spirit (1 Sam. 10:7; 13:14). God never jealously hoards divine gifts but gives them freely. "Path of days for ever and ever" implies not only a mystery reserved to Yahweh (Ps. 8:9) but also a fulfillment through offspring (2 Sam. 7:16; Ps. 89:30).

The blessings for the Israelite king are reversed for the enemy in 21:9–13. Although the language is figurative (Isa. 13:7–8; Lam. 5:10), one must never underestimate the inhuman fury of warfare (→ War). It took OT religion many centuries to extricate itself from linking military means with establishing God's kingdom.

Psalm 22. Consecrated by the dying breath of Jesus on the cross and frequently chosen by NT writers to communicate better the mystery of the cross (thirteen times, nine in the account of the

Passion), Psalm 22 has equally deep roots in OT religious life. The motif of being called from the mother's womb (vv. 10–11) links Psalm 22 with Jeremiah (Jer. 1:5; 20:14–18), the songs of the suffering servant (Isa. 49:1; Gal. 1:15) and Job (3:3–12).

The role of Psalm 22 as a carrier of Israel's faith in times of distress appears in its stages of composition. First, after a long ordeal of sickness and imprisonment (vv. 2–22), an individual sufferer realizes that God is truly listening (v. 22) and so anticipates a liturgy of thanksgiving in the Temple, including a sacred meal (vv. 23–27). Then by its exquisite beauty, the psalm found its way into Temple liturgy and became the property of all Israel. Within this communal setting, the psalm absorbed later developments about outreach to the nations (Isa. 56:1–8; Jonah) and life after death (Dan. 12:1–3). At this point vv. 28–32 were added. Then from the cross, Jesus again individualized the psalm. Jesus cried out according to the vernacular form of the Aramaic language, not the classical rendition of the Hebrew. In death, human cords and childhood memories hold firmly. Finally, the Evangelists in their preaching and writing gave the psalm a new communal setting, weaving its phrases into their story of the Passion.

The long opening section is divided into seven units: vv. 2–3, introductory cry of agony; vv. 4–6, confession of faith; vv. 7–9, lament; vv. 10–11, prayer of confidence; v. 12, prayer; vv. 13–19, lament; and vv. 20–22, prayer.

Verses 2–3 and 20–22 form an inclusio by repeating three key words: distant, save or salvation, and hear. Translations sometimes appeal to the LXX for modifying the starkness of the Hebrew thought. Verse 2, "Distant from my salvation," and v. 22, "You hear me," are made to read "Distant from my outcry" and "my wretched self." The Greek version is less threatening to the theology that God always hears prayers. Keeping the Hebrew intact, one not only preserves the inclusio, an important Hebrew rhetorical device, but one also realizes that the transition to a prayer of thanksgiving (vv. 23–27) came from a silent perception of faith, "God hears!"

Three times repeating in vv. 4–6 "our ancestors trusted in you," the psalmist will not abandon faith, even though seemingly abandoned by God. Yet is the psalmist protesting too much and about to give up? It is difficult to distinguish the mystic darkness of faith (Ps. 139:11–12) from the black void of unbelief (1 Sam. 28:8–25; John 13:30).

Ridicule and shame besmear the psalmist in 22:7–9. He is like a worm (cf. Job 25:6). Though the ancestors were not shamed (Ps. 22:6), the psalmist definitely is and so is experiencing the reverse of what faith teaches. When v. 9 is paraphrased by the leaders against Jesus on the cross (Matt. 27:41–43), the Evangelist was associating Jesus with the devastated psalmist.

A series of metaphors in vv. 11–19 articulate physical and psychological pain. Therefore, it is better not to take literally "they pierce my hands and my feet" (v. 17b). In fact, the Hebrew does not support this reading but declares, "Like a lion [they maul] my hands and my feet." This phrase is never quoted in the passion narrative.

It is not at all surprising, as in vv. 23–27, for a psalmist who has endured extreme physical suffering and severe psychological onslaught on faith to align himself with the isolated outcasts of society. He invites the poor and lowly to a thanksgiving banquet. In vv. 28–32, the group is swelled by other outcasts: foreigners (v. 28), the sick, the dying and possibly the dead (v. 30), all excluded from public worship (Lev. 21; Deut. 23:2–9). If the dead are included in the invitation (the Hebrew text is uncertain), then these lines would not have been added until around 165 B.C. (cf. Dan. 12:1–3). Yet, if Psalm 22 circulated principally within popular religious circles, where belief in the afterlife was accepted more readily, then this final section could have originated much earlier.

Psalm 23. The early church sang Psalm 23 as the baptized person emerged from the font and proceeded into the newly illumined church for Eucharist. Contemporary churches turn to this psalm for Holy Communion and funerals, depending whether one stresses the early walk through darkness or the later banquet.

The psalm shows an overlay of covenant traditions about journeying through the wilderness and renewing the covenant; the release of an individual from trial (Ps. 121); the return from exile (Isa. 40:1–11; 41:10; Jer. 31:10); a liturgical ceremony of thanksgiving and sacred meal (Pss. 111; 118). If we keep the Hebrew reading of 23:6b, "I will return," the psalm is one of confidence; or if we follow the Greek and read "I will dwell," as in Ps. 27:4, the psalm turns into a thanksgiving.

In 23:1b–4, the language is metaphorical about the "Lord, my shepherd" (Gen. 49:24; Isa. 40:11; Ezek. 34:11–31; → Shepherd). Yet metaphors gradually give way to realistic expressions: "path of righteousness" or "straight path," depending whether one understands the phrase as symbolic or realistic; "valley of darkness" is still metaphorical in the first word, realistic in the second; "at my side" describes concretely Yahweh's continual presence. Ps. 23:5–6 describes a thanksgiving sacrifice and a sacred meal before returning home. Yahweh is no longer the shepherd but the host at home. The final phrase, "the path of one's days," recalls the way of obedience that leads to the promised land (Deut. 6) and interior rest (Ps. 95:11).

Psalm 24. One encounters in Psalm 24 an entrance liturgy far more elaborate than Psalm 15. Ps. 24:1–2 was sung during a solemn procession with the Ark through the city or countryside (Pss. 68; 132). Upon arrival at the "gates of justice" (Ps. 118:19), questions are asked to receive a repentant person and all Israel into full communion (Ps. 24:3; Num. 5:5–10). Finally, the Levites return the Ark to the Holy of Holies (Ps. 24:7–10). Questions and answers as well as solemn acclamations were sung by separate choirs.

Verses 1–2 recall the ancient cosmogony about the earth's foundations upon underground "seas and ... ocean currents" (Gen. 7:11; Exod. 20:4; Ps. 136:6; → Water).

In 24:3–6 the stable order of creation was not preserved by ritual but by a moral life. Prophetic influence may be detected here (Amos 4:4–5; 8:4–8; Hos. 4:1–3). "Who shall go up?" is a phrase that refers to Israel's Exodus out of Egypt and to its pilgrimage to Jerusalem (Amos 3:1; Jer. 31:12; Ps. 122:4), which later rabbis ascribed to Moses' ascent of Mount Sinai to receive the law (Exod. 19:3). With "clean hands and pure heart" one truly seeks the Lord, not some false god (Ps. 31:7). The Hebrew word "to seek" means to visit a sanctuary (Amos 5:5) and worship God (Amos 5:6) as well as to inquire into God's ways (Ps. 9:11) and to repent (Ps. 78:34).

In 24:7–10 the language is militaristic, but in the sense of the "holy war" (Ps. 18:32–46) in which God alone wages war for Israel (Exod. 15:1–18), surrounded by the heavenly hosts (1 Sam. 4:4; Ps. 29:1).

Psalm 25. The alphabetical or acrostic arrangement of Psalm 25 is almost perfect. Each new line begins with the succeeding letter of the Hebrew alphabet, except that two letters are missing and two are doubled! Such an arrangement along with other didactic aspects suggests that this is a wisdom psalm. Yet, similar to Psalms 9–10, the overriding tone includes reference to sin and troubles, characteristic of the lament, thereby hinting that we have a blend of literary forms. Key words support this mixture: "Yahweh" is used ten times, to sustain the religious spirit; "shamed," four times, for supplication; while the wisdom aspect is supported by the use of "way," ten times, "to learn," three times, and "the poor," twice.

A clear development of thought is not evident, the absence of which is typical of a reflective piece where the purpose is wisdom, not logical achievement. An overarching chiastic form (Ps. 19:2) is evident: 25:1, 22, calling upon Yahweh; vv. 2–3, 19–21, saved from the foes and not shamed; vv. 4–5, 16–18, following the path of Yahweh and the relief of heart's tensions; vv. 6–7, 11–15, covenantal love; and at the center the covenantal love of Yahweh that leads in the right way, vv. 8–10.

The first major section (vv. 1–7) stresses the need to "wait" (Isa. 30:15–18); otherwise one will be shamed by sad results (Pss. 22:7–9; 44:10) and be in danger of breaking faith (Hab. 2:1–6). The directions for "the way" must be learned from God; they cannot be self-taught. People sinful from youth (Gen. 8:21; Job 13:26) make no claim except that based on God's compassion (Jer. 31:1–6).

Ps. 25:8–10 is central because it repeats the key covenant formula of Yahweh's "loving kindness and fidelity" (Exod. 34:6–7). The stereotypic phrase, Ps. 25:20, "I take refuge in you," occurs frequently (Pss. 2:12; 7:2; 11:1). When in great anxiety, one can often do nothing more than repeat memorized formulas.

The conclusion (25:22) resides outside the alphabetical sequence, perhaps because it was to be sung antiphonally after each line.

Psalm 26. With continuous allusions to Temple ritual, Psalm 26 appears to be part of a ceremony for acceptance into the worshiping assembly (Pss. 15; 24). On the basis of 26:6–8, the author appears as a Levite, for a while under suspicion and banned from the altar (Pss. 42–43; 84).

Structurally, the psalm is carefully knit together: an inclusio and repetition of key words unites the entire psalm (26:1 and 11) and the lines of the introduction (vv. 1 and 3); the Hebrew text shows repeated chiasms (Ps. 19:2) especially in vv. 4–5; contrasts between the assembly of the righteous and of the wicked, between the person of the psalmist (first-person singular, twenty-nine times) and Yahweh; frequent verbs of walking and standing; the covenant virtues of love and fidelity (Exod. 34:6–7). After the introduction (Ps. 26:1–3), two stanzas juxtapose the assembly of the wicked with that of the just (vv. 4–7, 9–12).

"I walk in integrity" (v. 1) implies completion, sincerity, trustworthiness, all that is expected for calm and capable interaction within community and family (Pss. 18:26; 19:8a). Ps. 26:2 is close to Jeremiah's protestation in the first of his confessions (Jer. 12:3) where the Lord responds (Jer. 12:5) with the expectation of still stronger trust. Like Psalm 16, the Lord is the only refuge for the psalmist. Ps 26:3 repeats the covenantal virtues of "kindness and fidelity" (Exod. 34:6–7).

Ps. 26:4–5, 9–10 repeats the prophets' demand for moral and social integrity if ritual is to be acceptable (Isa. 1; Mic. 3; cf. Matt. 12:6–13). Ps. 26:6–7 brings us fully into the Temple: ritual washing of hands (and feet) to symbolize cleanliness and trustworthiness (Exod. 30:17–21); processions around the altar (Pss. 68:25–

445

28; 118:27); and a thanksgiving sacrifice (Amos 4:5; Jon. 2:10).

Psalm 27. Two poems of confidence (vv. 1–6) and supplication (vv. 7–14) are so closely interwoven that it is difficult to know if they ever existed independently. Psalm 27 oscillates between longing for the Lord, awareness of a powerful enemy, and reaffirmation of one's trust in the Lord. While vv. 1–6 sound more strident in expressing confidence and in using military language, vv. 7–14 proceed more cautiously within community situations.

Each section moves toward and away from a center. Part One is as follows: v. 1, confession of trust in question form; vv. 2–3, answer; v. 4, the center of longing; v. 5, a new affirmation of trust; v. 6, reward for trust and Temple sacrifice. Part Two is as follows: v. 7, address to Yahweh; vv. 8–9, petition and longing; v. 10, the center of confessional trust; v. 11, petition for guidance; vv. 13–14, reward for trust and challenge to persevere.

In vv. 1–6 the presence of the Lord in Jerusalem's Temple does not depend upon the faith of the psalmist; rather, this faith depends upon the Lord's presence, initially understood as present in God's great deeds in Israel's history and then, symbolically, as these are celebrated anew in the Temple and in people's lives. "The Lord is my light" (v. 1). The phrase occurs only here in the OT (cf. John 8:12). Light has important roles: ceremonially (Exod. 25:31–40; 34:29–35; 40:34–38); prophetically (Isa. 10:17); and eschatologically (Zech. 14:7). Here it seems closer to the prophetic way of distinguishing integrity from deceit (on "evil people . . . devour my flesh," cf. Mic. 3:2–3). Language such as "dwell in the house of Yahweh each day of my life" and "to gaze," or, literally, "to behold a vision" through faith, indicates that with this faith the psalmist returns joyfully to the ritual of sacrifice and song (Ps. 27:6).

To seek the face of God (v. 8) was a stereotypic phrase that referred to visiting a sanctuary (Deut. 31:11; Ps. 42:3). The Canaanites thought it possible to behold the faces of the gods by looking at external images, but the Israelites did not. The psalmist was seeking, through faith, the interior and personal presence of the Lord (Pss. 24:6; 123:2). Forsaken by family (27:10; Jer. 12:6) and community (Ps. 27:12; Deut. 19:15–21), the psalmist prays in 27:12: "Do not give me over to the throat of my foes," that is, to the greed which dominates the life of the foes (Mic. 3:2–3). "Be strong-willed" repeats the encouragement of Josh. 1:6–18 for entering the promised land (cf. Hag. 2:4).

Psalm 28. An individual supplication, Psalm 28 is addressed to the "deaf God" (v. 1; Ps. 22:2–

3) and was composed at least partially during a serious illness, which barred one from the sanctuary (Ps.16; Lev.21); it consists of lament (28:1–5) and thanksgiving for a cure (vv. 6–7). Verses 7–8, focusing upon the anointed king, may have been added after the cure of King Hezekiah (Isa. 38). The sequence from lament to thanksgiving or statement of confidence is normal.

In Ps. 28:1–5 God seems mute and deaf like the idols ridiculed in Ps. 115:5–6. The word "pit" or "grave" originally meant a quarry (Isa. 51:1), well, or cistern (Gen. 21:25, 30), which when empty became a place for detaining people (Jer. 38:6). The term also came to signify the abode of the dead, because of the dank, dark, and unhealthy conditions of these cisterns (Pss. 30:4; 88:7; Isa. 38:18). By contrast, "prayers . . . [like] hands are lifted up towards the Holy of Holies." "Prayers," the same word as in Ps. 22:2, conveys the shrill sound of urgency. Evil or rebellious people speak of peace mockingly (cf. Isa. 57:19b–21). Ps. 28:4–5 skillfully contrasts the deeds of the wicked and the kindly ones of the Lord; each has its own inevitable result of sorrow or blessing.

In vv. 6–7 it is not clear if the phrase "I give God thanks" refers to a thanksgiving sacrifice (Ps. 26:7) or to a song of praise. The former seems likely in view of the overall ritual setting. The Greek version of 28:7 enhances the notion of healing from sickness.

Psalm 29. Probably one of the earliest psalms, Psalm 29 appears as a significant link between several competing and at times hostile perceptions of God. Various similarities relate Psalm 29 with the Song of Moses (Exod. 15), the theophany of Mount Sinai (Exod. 19), and the enthronement of Yahweh in Psalms 46–48, 93, 96–99. In this psalm, Israel's theology seeks to surround Yahweh, the warrior God and Savior of the desert, with the glorious accoutrements of the creator God, who overcomes the chaotic forces of nature, prominent in Canaanite city temples. Exodus 15 and Psalm 29 do not have the theological and liturgical finesse of Psalms 46–48 or 96–99. Psalm 29 extends a bridge into the Canaanite world of Baal worship through several significant word parallels. Yet Psalm 29 actually parodies Baal worship since power and enthronement are granted exclusively to Yahweh (→ Baal).

A psalm of such majesty was headed for frequent use and adaptation. The LXX places it on the last day of the Feast of Tabernacles (Lev. 23:33–43) and relates it to the prayer for rain (Zech. 14:16–19). The Talmud linked it with the Feast of Weeks (Pentecost), which commemorated the giving of the law to Moses on Mount Sinai (Exod. 19). Psalm 29 may have made its own contribution to the story of Pentecost in Acts 2; it was sung by the early church for the ancient feasts of Pentecost, Epiphany, and Transfiguration.

Psalm 29 begins with a call to adore Yahweh (vv. 1–2); moves to the motivation for praise in a fearsome thunderstorm (vv. 3–4, 5–6, 8–9b; v. 7 is a later addition); and concludes with the enthronement of Yahweh (vv. 9c–11).

In vv. 1–2 "children of the gods," a phrase drawn from Canaanite religion (Heb. *bene 'elim*), constitute the heavenly council of Yahweh (Gen. 6:2, 4; Job 1:6; Pss. 82:1; 89:6; 1 Kings 22:19), lesser gods subservient to Yahweh, an embarrassment when this line is quoted in Ps. 96:7 (where they become the "families of nations"). They are to ascribe "Glory!" to Yahweh, a word announcing the manifestation of Yahweh's loving power in redeeming Israel, recognizable only through faith (Exod. 16:7; Ps. 81:17; → Glory).

One hears (29:3–9) the seven mighty claps of thunder (which the Hebrew word *qol* or "voice" can mean), splintering the cedars of Lebanon, sweeping the desert and its wadis or valleys into writhing swells of sand and roaring cataracts. The phrase in v. 8, *midbar kadesh*, occurs in Canaanite literature meaning "the awesome desert." In Psalm 29, Israel changed *kadesh* from the adjective "awesome" to a proper name, designating the oasis of Kadesh-barnea far to its south, where the people encamped during the period of wandering the desert (→ Kadesh). The storm has thus been rerouted south, making a half circle around the promised land, where the Israelites are at peace.

In vv. 9c–11 the Lord is enthroned "above the flood waters," a word used elsewhere only in the Flood story (Gen. 6–9; Sir. 44:17) but here referring to the massive waters thought to reside above the earth (Ps. 148:4). From this heavenly temple, Yahweh imparts strength (an inclusio with v. 1) and *shalom* (Heb.), the wholeness of a happy, harmonious life. With the untamed storm, a glorious symphony fills the universe and echoes in the Jerusalem Temple.

Psalm 30. Once seriously sick, the psalmist offers thanksgiving for a return to health. At a much later period the title was expanded (something unusual in these early psalms) to refer to the dedication of the Second Temple in 515 B.C. Because the word "dedication" reads *chanukkah* in Hebrew, some associate the title with 1 Macc. 4:52–59 and the rededication in 164 B.C., on a feast called Hanukkah. In both cases national mourning, like a serious sickness, ended. After thanksgiving by a solo voice (Ps. 30:2–4) and then the congregation (vv. 5–6), one hears in vv. 7–11 of sickness and prayer and in vv. 12–13 the conclusion.

Verses 2–6 show that this psalm followed the official theology that death was like slipping into silent oblivion (Pss. 6:6; 16:10), not the position of popular religion, which accepted some kind of personal existence after death (1 Sam. 28:8–25; 2 Kings 2:11). The Bible always associates healing with a message about Yahweh as savior, and therefore conversion from sin was a prerequisite, offered by a compassionate, faithful God (Hos. 7:1; 14:4–5). The Bible also looks upon sickness as a communal disease in which the sins of all the people affect one another (Hos. 6:1–3). Physical helps for healing were used (2 Kings 20:1–11). Ps. 30:5 may refer to a grateful memorial sacrifice.

In vv. 7–11 the first two verses seem textually corrupt, yet the general thought is that success is always a temptation to indifference toward God, especially for religious people. Arguing with God (v. 10) recalls the confessions of Jeremiah (Jer. 12:1–5). The Hebrew verbs in Ps. 30:12 permit a present-tense translation, so that sickness is completely out of the system: "you turn my lament into dancing" (Jer. 31:13).

Psalm 31. Psalm 31 is a complex psalm borrowing heavily from Jeremiah and other psalms; it shows that God does not always require artistic creativity as much as sincere fidelity, in this case of serious sickness and desertion by friends. The memory of sacred texts sustained this sick person: vv. 2–4a, identical with Ps. 71:1–3; v. 8b is similar to Ps. 10:14; v. 10a to Psalms 35; 38; 39; 71; v. 11b to Ps. 38:11; v. 13 to Jer. 22:8; v. 14 to Jer. 20:10; v. 18 to Jer. 17:18. This psalm is the first example of an anthological style with similarity to modern hymn writing.

The structure is unusual in that psalms generally begin with supplication and move into thanksgiving (Ps. 22). This one begins with confidence (vv. 2–9), drops into supplication, where the language is more graphic but also more derivative (vv. 10–19), follows with thanksgiving (vv. 20–23), and ends with a liturgical addition (vv. 24–25).

With extraordinary daring, possible only with the humble, the psalmist (vv. 9–11) challenges God to be faithful to the divine promises, which v. 4 identifies with the name or specific vocation of God towards Israel. The title, "my rock," locates the psalmist at Jerusalem (Pss. 18:3; 95:1). Ps. 31:6 became Jesus' final word from the cross (Luke 23:46), repeated again in the death scene of Stephen (Acts 7:59). Jesus too in severe agony could not be creative but found peace in sacred Scripture and the company of this psalmist. Ps. 31:8 completes the covenant formula about Yahweh, faithfulness (v. 2) and bonding love (Exod. 34:6–7). Though deserted by foes, neighbors, and friends, the psalmist thinks as a member of Israel.

As the psalm turns into supplication (vv. 10–19), the language shows more signs of bor-

447

rowing. It begins with the classic call of lament (Ps. 51:3), "Have mercy on me," a word that recognizes distance and undeserved recognition; the appeal here is to God's concern for suffering people. Ps. 31:11b reads, "My strength drains away because of my sinfulness," which the Greek, Syriac, and most versions change to "because of my misery" by a slight variation of Hebrew letters. One should retain the Hebrew reading, not only because the more difficult reading is preferred as less likely to have been a correction, but also because of the connection of sickness with sin in the Bible (Ps. 30). Ps. 31:14 recalls the whispering crowd that threw back into Jeremiah's face as a nickname the threat that he had been calling down upon the nation: "Terror on every side" (Jer. 6:25; 20:3–4, 10).

The thanksgiving in Ps. 31:20–23 may have been a public sacrifice in the Temple, "the shelter of your presence." The psalmist hoped others would find their faith strengthened by his example. Verses 24–25 were added later from the repertoire of Temple thanksgiving services.

Psalm 32. The second of the seven penitential psalms (Ps. 6 was the first), recited by Ashkenazi Jews as night prayer on each Monday and by priests in the Greek church for personal purification before conferring baptism, Psalm 32 shows some of the repetitive qualities of Psalm 31; its didactic style removes some of the latter's intensity. Yet it rings with sincerity.

The psalm may have been an instruction at the Temple, composed by an individual whose spiritual and physical life changed as a result of a confession of sin. The development is as follows: vv. 1–2, introduction by Temple priest; vv. 3–7, edifying autobiography about the power of grace; vv. 8–10, instruction; and v. 11, liturgical addition.

The title announces this psalm as a "*maskil*," from a Hebrew word meaning "to be wise or skillful," a clue to the wisdom instruction to follow. "Happy is that one" recalls Psalm 1 and its wisdom characteristics. The vocabulary for sin and forgiveness in vv. 2–3 reminds one of Psalm 51. Divine forgiveness always presumes not only admission of faults, at times publicly if the offense was public, but also restitution (Num. 5:5–10). Paul quotes Ps. 32:1–2 about the futility of human works if one does not look to God for the grace to confess sin (Rom. 4:6–8).

From the autobiographical account in Ps. 32:3–7, one learns that the psalmist was physically ill (cf. Ps. 30 for the connection of sickness with sin). Once the psalmist stopped dissimulating and covering up, God extended a cover of forgiveness over the sins. Ps. 32:6–7 addresses a prayer of gratitude to God, equally a lesson for others. The final instruction in vv. 8–10 is spoken by the priest. On "senseless like the horse and mule," see Prov. 26:3; Sir. 30:8.

The final line of Ps. 32:9 is an awkward intrusion. Verse 10 expresses the orthodox position, especially prominent in the wisdom literature, that the wicked are punished and the virtuous are blessed. This statement does not harmonize well with Psalm 31.

Psalm 33. Because Psalms 1–2 were added later as a general introduction to the Psalter and Psalm 10 originally was a continuation of Psalm 9, Psalm 33, therefore, is the only orphan psalm without a title in the first book (Pss. 1–41). A late composition, it was attached here by a repetition of a key word, "exult," at the end of Psalm 32 and at the beginning of this psalm. Reasons for arguing postexilic authorship include "Sing a new song" in v. 3 (Isa. 42:10; Pss. 96:1; 98:1); a wisdom style, prominent in the postexilic age; and stereotypic phrases common with other late psalms (v. 1 and Ps. 97:12; v. 2b and Pss. 98:5; 147:7). Yet there are also touches of originality, which flow mostly from its oral composition: repetitions (33:1, 7, 9, 11) and the continual use of word pairs such as "spoke/commanded," "plan/design," and "nation/people." Most of all this psalm presents a theology of the divine word.

After the call to praise (vv. 1–3), an initial motivation is given from Yahweh's fidelity (vv. 4–5) and omnipotent word (vv. 6–7). This motivation extends to Yahweh's providential control: across the earth (vv. 8–12) and through human plans (vv. 13–19). The conclusion comes in vv. 20–22. The divine name Yahweh (thirteen times) and the covenant formula of mercy and fidelity keep the focus upon Israel, God's chosen people (v. 12).

The first stanza (vv. 1–7) opens with musical instruments echoing the symphony of heaven and earth (→Music). With this "new song," Yahweh is creating anew at the moment of worship; the final age is at hand. This psalm is not like most of wisdom literature, generally aloof toward Temple ceremony (Ps. 1; Prov. 10–31). Ps. 33:4–7 places the universe within the covenantal kindness and fidelity of the Lord (Exod. 34:6–7).

In Ps. 33:8–12 one observes an earth teeming with people, all within the embrace of Yahweh's loving concern and strong control. The people Israel (vv. 11–12) are chosen forever because they have a role in the eternal plan of Yahweh (cf. Rom. 9:1–5; 11:25–36). Implications for world salvation are not developed as they are in Isaiah 40–66 and Jonah.

Heaven is not a silent retreat where the deity resides at a remove from humanity; Yahweh is continually looking down (Ps. 33:13) on everyone (v. 14), even into each human heart (v. 15). Not even kings are exempt (v. 16). Like most OT literature, the psalm does not extend God's plans beyond any person's lifetime (v. 19; Pss. 6:6; 30).

The psalm closes in 33:20–22 with the classic vocabulary of confidence. It does not center upon musical instruments as in the introduction, or upon plans and interaction as in the body of the psalm, but upon the person of Lord. Verse 22 contributed the final words to the ancient classic Christian hymn, *Te Deum*.

Psalm 34. Psalm 34 is another acrostic poem like Psalms 9–10 and 25, but in it the alphabetic sequence is almost perfect, except that the letter *waw* is missing and 34:23 was added both to complete the number of letters in the Hebrew alphabet and to ensure a happy ending. After a hymnic introduction (vv. 2–4), the first major section gratefully narrates the Lord's intervention to save (vv. 5–11) and the second provides typical wisdom instruction (vv. 12–23).

The title (v. 1), one of few lengthy ones in the first book of the Psalter, is curious with historical inaccuracy. The Philistine king's name was not Abimelech but Achish, an error due to the similarity of *b* and *ch* in Hebrew writing. Therefore, the title evolved during the written, not the oral stage. According to 1 Sam. 21:11–16, David pretended to be insane (lit., acted in bad taste) and showed himself a madman (enthusiastically beyond control). The first of these verbs shows up in Ps. 34:9 in the positive sense, "taste and see . . ."; the second verb in v. 4, again positively as "glorify the Lord." Because of these words the editors found a way to put a very late psalm under the patronage of David.

The opening phrase in vv. 2–11, "I will bless," recognizes God's gracious, strong presence in life, generally expressed liturgically, for instance, in a sacred meal (Exod. 18:10–12). Ps. 34:3 begins a series of references to a person oppressed, afflicted, and troubled but now thanking God for deliverance. The phrase "angel of the Lord" (v. 8) is generally a circumlocution for simply saying "the Lord" (so Gen. 31:11–13; Exod. 3). Angels appear in the Bible to unite earth with activity in the heavenly court (Zech. 3:1–10) and to surround God's servants with care (Josh. 5:14; 2 Kings 6:17). This reference to supernatural protection is unusual for wisdom literature and more in accord with Israel's popular piety, which believed the world was inhabited by good and evil spirits (Ps. 91; → Angel; Angel of the Lord).

The characteristics of wisdom literature come to the fore in 34:12–23, with an address to children or pupils common in all ancient wisdom literature (Prov. 1:8; 2:1). Ps. 34:12–16 constitutes one of the longer quotations of the OT in the NT in a context calling for a patient response to insult (1 Pet. 3:10–12). The necessity of patiently persevering through trials (Ps. 34:16–20) will be stressed ever more in the NT (Heb. 12:6, 12). "Not a bone shall be broken" in Ps. 34:21 may be the text cited in John's passion narrative (John 19:36).

Psalm 35. A long, somewhat monotonous and repetitive psalm, Psalm 35 stems from an individual who oscillates between sorrow, anger, curse, and thanksgiving, between narrative and intercession. Some of the lines are rapid and direct (vv. 21–24) with vigorous images (vv. 5–8) and strong emotions (vv. 13–16). The Hebrew text is not well preserved, overloaded perhaps with glosses and corrections, so that translations differ in their reconstruction. If God can speak through an ungifted though religiously inspired person (cf. Ps. 31), likewise God's normative word can come through canonical texts damaged in transmission. In either case one may be uncertain about the precise meaning and yet be spiritually moved by the overall attitude and general message. The simplest, unadorned answer, in broken accents, becomes heroic in the actual setting of life's tragedies.

Because of the circuitous, emotional response, some think of Jeremiah as a source for the psalmist (Jer. 18:18–23; 20:10–13). The psalmist enters no proof of innocence; it is enough that God knows. Unlike Psalms 6 and 31, there is no mention of sickness.

The psalm is divided according to the enemy and the type of image: 35:1–10, images of warfare and the hunt, against impostors; vv. 11–18, images of mourning, against ingrates; and vv. 19–28, images of legal procedure, against perfidious people.

In v. 1, the demand, "Take up my [legal] case, Lord," exhibits a person confident of innocence before human and divine tribunals. "I myself [no other] am your salvation" (v. 3) emphasizes the personal response of Yahweh. The word "salvation" ought to be taken in its original meaning, to liberate by removing barriers and providing space for the psalmist simply to live again. In vv. 7–8 the example of the *lex talionis* (Lat., "law of retribution"), "an eye for an eye . . ." (Exod. 21:23–25; Ps. 7:16), does not vindicate vendettas and revenge but states a law of reality: we become in our heart and facial features as well as in the events of life what we think and do. Violence breeds violence. Liars are caught in the web of their own lies.

The types of mourning cited in 35:11–18 were not sanctioned officially in Israel's manuals for ritual (Exod. 25–31; Lev. 1–9; 16; 23–24), until after the Exile. God was the God of the living, not of the dead. Sackcloth was donned for public mourning apart from worship at the Temple (Gen. 37:34; 2 Sam. 3:31). Fasting is not even explicitly mentioned for Yom Kippur in Leviticus 16, but fasting with sackcloth was undertaken privately by David at the death of his son (2 Sam. 12:16). When Moses fasted, it was rather in awesome trembling before the wonder of the divine presence (Exod. 34:27–28), not out of a sense of sinfulness. During and after the Exile, fasting was prescribed for all Israel on fixed days commemorating national calamities (Joel 1–2; Zech. 7:1–14; → Fasting). This psalm then, through prophetic influence, is to be associated with the people's popular religion rather than with official Judaism. "I prayed with bowed head" accurately communicates for us what the Hebrew declares more poignantly: "My prayer returns to my bosom or heart." Ps. 35:15–16 is severely damaged textually.

In vv. 17–26 the psalmist entreats God to move from inertia to activity, from silence to a verdict against the oppressors (Ps. 44:24–27). Too long have they been ridiculing God's justice by abusing the psalmist. Ps. 35:27–28 provides thanksgiving after a proper verdict from the Lord.

Psalm 36. Yahweh's mercy and fidelity, the core covenant intuitions (Exod. 34:6–7), are viewed either as repudiated by the wicked (Ps. 36:2–5 and 11–13) or as celebrated by the faithful (vv. 6–10). Yahweh as Lord of the covenant is the sole remedy to universal injustice.

In vv. 2–5 the opening phrase is most unusual: "The oracle of the wicked" (cf. the beginning of Ps. 110, where the phrase "oracle of Yahweh" occurs). The sinner, by opposing God, thinks to be godlike. Ps. 36:2b is quoted by Paul in a chain of OT passages (Rom. 3:10–18). Ps. 36:5 reminds one of Mic. 2:1–2, where wicked people, complacently lying on their couches at night, plot ways to satisfy their greed; then with the break of day they seize whatever they want. Words like "understand" (Ps. 36:4) and "way" (v. 5) are telltale signs of wisdom influence (cf. Ps. 1; Prov. 1:10–18; 10:5).

Ps. 36:6–10 offers a celebration of Yahweh's covenant presence. The Lord's kindness and fidelity (Exod. 34:6–7) reach into the heavens; the Lord knows no limits in arranging everything for the sake of the chosen people Israel. This idea returns almost verbatim in Ps. 57:11 and echoes in the preaching of Second Isaiah, Isaiah 40–55 (Isa. 40:12–14), and in Ps. 139:7–10. In all these cases, the writer appears to be in severe crisis. These are the occasion either for destroying faith or for extending it beyond the limits of previous theological statements. Ps. 36:8–10 is recited by Ashkenazi Jews as they put on the tallith or prayer shawl. For "shadow of your wings" in v. 8, see Ps. 17:8. "River of your delights" (v. 9) was later taken as a reference to paradise; the word for "delights" stems from the same root as does the word "Eden." The image of light is often linked with water as here, "In your light we see light." These images occur in Jeremiah (2:13; 17:13), where Yahweh is the "fountain of living water," and in the Gospel of John: "fountain . . . leaping up to provide eternal life" (4:14) and "I am the light of the world"

(9:5). Understandably, Ps. 36:9–10 came to be used for the blessing of a baptismal font.

Verses 11–14 are a fitting conclusion that alludes again to the covenantal qualities of kindness and fidelity and to the arrogance of the wicked and their downfall.

Psalm 37. This acrostic Psalm 37, like Psalms 9–10, 25, and 34, perfectly executes its sequence of letters. It shares many key themes with Deuteronomy, like the possession of the land (Ps. 37:3, 9, 11) as well as blessings and curses for the obedient and disobedient (vv. 22, 37–38), only here the focus has passed from the nation Israel to the individual Israelite. This fact favors a date in the postexilic period when the interests and possibilities of Israel shrank considerably from where they were in the pre-exilic days of royalty. This transfer of the question of retribution to the individual turned out to be a conspicuous aspect in wisdom literature. If one compares Psalm 37 with other wisdom pieces, one finds that unlike Proverbs it does not seek to form disciples and unlike Job it does not seek to solve problems. Rather it provides points for meditation and for preaching within the postexilic assembly. The author was an elder sage (v. 25).

On the question of retribution the author displays the good sense to avoid stereotyped simplicity. Despite a hewing of the traditional position (vv. 1–2, 25), other verses recognize that neither are the virtuous immediately blessed nor are the wicked quickly reduced to disgrace (vv. 7–9, 12, 35). Neither does the psalmist take the next step and seek a final solution after death (Pss. 1, 49, 139).

The development within the psalm is not clear. One may detect an introduction (vv. 1–9) and a conclusion (vv. 34–40) by the frequent use of the imperative mood. In the central part, one observes the ruin of the impious (vv. 10–15), prosperity as the gift of Yahweh (vv. 16–26), and a return to fidelity (vv. 27–33). Logically, one can begin almost anywhere and proceed in any direction. This poem is not so much instruction or proof as quiet meditation. Nor is it mysticism for saints—it centers on earthly problems, temptations, and occasional lapses.

"Do not fret," or stir with anger and frustration (v. 1)—such is not proper for the calm attitude expected of a sage! "Let your confidence be in the Lord and do what is good" (v. 3) gives a fine balance between interior trust and external action. "Delight in the Lord" (v. 4) puts a proper stress upon delicate sensitivity (Isa. 58:14). In Ps. 37:13, "the Lord laughs," as in Ps. 2:4, but nonetheless this is a rare attitude of God in the Bible. The foolish, egotistic pretentions of the wicked are too amusing to be taken seriously. This smile is like that of the elderly grandparent at the feverish activities of youth. (For the *lex talionis* in v. 15, see the commentary above on Ps. 35:8.) Jeremiah develops a similar theme. Sin always brings suffering; suffering can be disciplinary and redemptive, depending on one's attitude (Jer. 2:19; 5:25; 30:11; 31:18). Laws regulating debtors (Ps. 37:21) are frequently enough discussed in the OT: 2 Kings 4:1; Amos 2:6; and 8:6. Interest rates were staggering (see commentary above on Ps. 15:4–5). The phrase in 37:27, "to dwell forever," applies to one's offspring. In fact, the Hebrew word "to dwell" denotes a tent, not a permanent type of home (Ps. 15:1; 2 Sam. 7:5–7). In Ps. 37:28, "his faithful ones" derives from the covenant word in Hebrew for loving mercy, chesed. Wisdom literature, however, as in Proverbs, Job, and Ecclesiastes generally, refers neither directly to the covenant nor to other aspects of Israel's history and worship. The ending (v. 40) is similar to other psalms in the first book (Pss. 2:12; 7:1; 11:1), perhaps a deliberate way of incorporating this poem into the collection.

Psalm 38. The third of the seven penitential psalms, recited as evening prayer on the third day of the week by the Ashkenazi Jews, is not exceptional in style; it is repetitive and stereotyped. Yet it looms powerfully before us because of its intense recital of physical pain and emotional isolation and because of its honest acceptance of responsibility (vv. 5, 19). Unlike Job, the psalmist does not argue his innocence but simply pleads for human recognition and compassion.

All indications point to leprosy, which breaks out with oozing sores (vv. 4, 6, 8), blinds the eyes (v. 11), and distorts the limbs (vv. 4, 7). Lepers were quarantined and prohibited from mingling in ancient society (v. 12; Lev. 13). They were "no-persons," no longer a spouse, parent, or child, with no national or religious identity (cf. Luke 17:11–19). Like the dead, they were isolated even from God (Ps. 6:6).

The author must have ruminated upon ancient prayers in leprous solitude: parts of 38:5, 6, 12, and all of 19–20 reflect Psalm 35; v. 2 from Ps. 6:2; vv. 21–22 from Ps. 22:2, 12, 20. From these biblical prayers the leper was encouraged to present a new plea before the Lord and before the society of Israel. The psalmist was convinced that God was concerned about a person's physical ugliness and moral guilt as well as about society's taboos and banishment.

This prayer of supplication can be divided as follows: 38:2–3, call for help; vv. 4–11, serious sickness; vv. 12–21, isolation and even persecution; and vv. 22–23, repeated call for help.

The title in v. 1, "for remembrance," indicates that this psalm was received into Temple liturgy, possibly for the readmission of cured lepers (Lev. 14). The phrase refers to a liturgical practice of remembering the name of the Lord at sacrifices (Ps. 70). The Aramaic Targum specifies a daily offering (Lev. 2:2), the Greek an offering for the Sabbath (Lev. 24:7).

The request in v. 2, "chastise me not angrily," implies suffering that disciplines and purifies (Jer. 2:19; Isa. 53:5). The psalmist begs that it be done with minimum wrath. "Arrows" indicate the piercing sharpness of the pain; they may also be associated with the sense of being under a curse from evil spirits (Ps. 91:5; or 1 Sam. 18:10, where the text speaks of a "divine evil spirit").

In Ps. 38:4–11 the sickness seems to correspond to leprosy. The severity is intensified by the pounding of the heart (vv. 9, 11) and a consuming fever (v. 8). Yet the psalmist is able to direct "all my desire" toward the Lord. In v. 6 the sufferer does not argue against personal guilt and foolishness (Ps. 107:17; Prov. 24:9). The word for "sores" is from a root that means to unite, here with hostile forces that strike blows and cast spells. The verb in v. 9, "I roar from anguished heart," is generally used of lions (Ps. 22:14).

Even "those [once] loving me ... stand at a distance" (38:12) with devices to keep the psalmist far away (v. 13), so that the leper neither hears nor is able to converse (vv. 14–15). Verses 16–21 pursue the reasons why Yahweh should cross the barrier into unclean territory and intervene.

The conclusion (vv. 22–23) calls upon a key word of Psalm 22, "Be not distant" (vv. 2, 12, 20), and begs God not irreverently, only with urgency, to "hurry" (Ps. 22:20).

Psalm 39. The piety of Psalm 39 seems highly individual, even if the title, in attributing it to "Jeduthun," links it with one of the guilds of psalm writers for worship (2 Chron. 5:12; 35:15–19). To Jeduthun are attributed two other exquisite compositions (Pss. 62:1; 77:1). These, with Psalm 39, may have offered a more quiet or reflective type of worship.

Psalms speak often enough of the brevity of life, but only here do they ask God for peaceful insight into its meaning. Psalm 39 is not blindly accepting whatever happens; it struggles, even with the danger of rash questioning, though it prays to be spared such a fault. As with Psalm 16 and frequently with the confessions of Jeremiah (12:1–5; 15:10–21; 20:7–18) and dramatically with the songs of the suffering servant (Isa. 49:4), security is not obtained by answers from God, certainly not by gifts from God, but only in personal bonding with the Lord.

After an introductory apology for speaking (Ps. 39:2–4), the psalmist reflects on the inconstancy of life (vv. 5–7) and poignantly petitions God for assistance (vv. 8–12). The psalm concludes with supplication (vv. 13–14).

If the psalmist intends (vv. 2–4) to trust

God, then silence is appropriate. Verse 3b is variously translated; it probably had to be heard in its abruptness to be understood: "I kept silent without any good." The insolence of the wicked had blown the flames of dissatisfaction red-hot in the heart, and one hears the desperate cry to God: "To my weeping do not be deaf" (v. 13; Ps. 22:2–3).

After an initial prayer for insight (39:5), there follows, it seems, an acceptance of life's transitoriness (v. 6a). Yet the Hebrew now begins three lines with the very abrupt word '*ak*, as though the previous statement is inadequate even if found frequently in the OT (Pss. 62:10; 90:3–6; Job 7:6–10; Eccles. 5:9–16). The psalmist follows the traditional position that after death no personal existence is assured (Ps. 6:6).

The psalmist (39:8–12) begs God for deliverance, simply by being with him. Strong, dissenting forces merge: peace from waiting upon the Lord, a sense of sin and of deserving the punishment, panicking at being dissolved into nothing, and confessing that punishment chastens and purifies.

Verses 13–14 allude to earlier lines in the psalm (vv. 5–8). The conclusion gets nowhere. The psalmist makes contradictory requests: "hear my prayer" and "turn away!" Yet such contradiction may be sustained in God's presence.

Psalm 40. In Psalm 40, an editor in the postexilic age stitches together two earlier psalms (the second of these occurs identically in Psalm 70), drawing upon the experience of the Exile to state that the Temple and its sacrifices are not absolutely necessary, only very helpful, as Israel seeks to rebuild the Temple and reconstitute worship. In uniting a psalm of thanksgiving (40:2–12) with one of supplication (vv. 14–18)—actually an unusual sequence—and adding a transitional v. 13, the inspired editor has produced a new work, stressing dependency upon God for authentic Temple worship.

The opening song of thanksgiving in vv. 2–12 reads better stylistically if vv. 7–9 are deleted, yet their presence strengthens the need of interior attitudes for proper worship. Waiting upon the Lord (v. 2) implies that a dark period continues, as one waits patiently and expectantly (Isa. 25:9; 40:31). Second Isaiah (Isa. 42:10) and the time of the Exile (Ps. 33:3) provide the context for the "pit of destruction" and the time for a "new song." National resurgence corresponds with the individual's moment of being rescued, possibly from serious sickness (Ps. 30:3–4). Ps. 40:4 announces a community festival at which Psalm 40 is to be sung. Verse 5 warns against false worship, certainly a danger in postexilic Israel (Isa. 56:9–57:13; Ps. 16), a danger wherever ritual and ceremony have high priorities. The formula "happy that one" shows the touch of wisdom literature (Ps. 1:1; 32:1), which continues in v. 6, recognizing a divine mystery even in the most meticulous ordering of life (Prov. 8:22–31; Sir. 43:28–33). This verse may also allude to the "wondrous deeds" of Israel's history, reenacted in sanctuary worship (Deut. 5:1–5; 26:1–11).

Ps. 40:7–9 interrupts the sanctuary hymn of thanksgiving to introduce a strong prophetic warning against excessive ritual and formal religion (1 Sam. 15:22–23; Isa. 1:10–16; Mic. 6:6–8; Jer. 7). The major types of sacrifice are enumerated: "sacrifice," an all-purpose word; "oblation," generally of grain (Lev. 6:7–16); "holocaust," an act of adoration in which the entire offering is consumed by fire (Lev. 1); "sin offering," a ritual after the offense has been confessed and restitution has been made (Num. 5:5–10; → Worship).

The phrase "ears you have dug [or pierced or opened] for me" refers to a procedure by which a slave's ears were pierced at a sanctuary as a sign of perpetual servitude to the master (Exod. 21:5–6; Deut. 15:12–18) and that was understood metaphorically as obedience to the Lord (Prov. 28:9; Isa. 50:4–5). The passage was translated very differently in the Greek, "a body you have given to me," to be picked up in Heb. 10:5–7 for Christ's obedient offering of himself on the cross, which removed the necessity of all other sacrifices. In Ps. 40:9 the law within the heart alludes to a long sequence of texts, all insisting upon the interior attitude necessary for covenant and worship (Deut. 6:4–9; Jer. 31:31–34; Ezek. 36:26–27; Ps. 37:31).

Ps. 40:10–11 returns to the community assembly in the Temple commemorating its covenant with the Lord. Verse 12 ends the hymn of thanksgiving, referring to the covenant of "love and fidelity" (Exod. 34:6–7), whereas Ps. 40:13 functions as a transition to the prayer of supplication that follows.

Verses 14–18 (identical with Ps. 70) express the powerlessness of people left to themselves. Those who seek the Lord in community worship (40:17; 27:8) ought not to be shamed by the ridicule and success of wicked people. It is sufficient to be held within the strong gaze of the Lord.

Psalm 41. The prayer of a sick person, Psalm 41 is a psalm of supplication transformed into one of confidence by a new introduction and conclusion. The complicated structure exhibits a long history before its final editing. We are dealing as much with an inspired tradition as with a single inspired author. The psalm follows a chiastic structure (see commentary above on Ps. 19:2): *A didactic introduction and prayer of* confidence, 41:2–4; B prayer of the psalmist, v. 5; C words of the enemy, vv. 6–8; C' words of the enemy, vv. 9–10; B' prayer of the psalmist, v. 11; A' didactic conclusion with Temple worship, vv. 12–13. Verse 14 functions as a conclusion to the first book of the Psalter (see Pss. 72:18–19; 89:53; 106:48; 150).

In Ps. 41:2 the exclamation "Happy that one," occurs for the first time since the opening psalm. This person "is solicitous for the poor," a word conspicuous in wisdom literature for careful regard and resultant insight. "Not hand him over to the life [or greed or curse] of his enemy": the word for life (nepesh) can mean throat and hence greed, but because of vv. 7 and 8, it may carry a curse from the enemy. Biblical people lived dynamically in the world of spirits and demons; blessings and curses were taken seriously (→ Demon; Devil).

The prayer (v. 5) combines a sense of sin with sickness (Ps. 30). Ps. 41:6–8, 9–10 permits the enemies to speak for themselves; the sins that inflict sickness are those of the larger world. The biblical concept of sickness linked it at once with community responsibility and community offenses. In vv. 8–9, "whisper" can refer to casting a spell (Ps. 58:6), and "a deadly thing" reads, literally, "a word of Beliyyaal," possibly hinting at a demonic curse. Sickness involved the evil world not only of people but also of devils (→ Magic and Divination). The betrayal of close associates (41:10) reminds one of Jer. 12:6; the line is quoted in the passion narrative in reference to Judas Iscariot (John 13:18).

After a prayer, wisdom style picks up again in Ps. 41:11–13 with its theory of retribution: the evil are punished and the good are rewarded by God. "Stand before you" refers to Temple worship. The psalm may have been an offering at the sanctuary from a sick person now restored to health who is now repaying a vow (Neh. 10:35–36; 13:31).

PSALMS 42–72

Book Two

In Books Two and Three we meet two new guilds of composers: Korah (Pss. 42–49; 84–85; 87–88) and Asaph (Pss. 50; 73–83). Both groups functioned prominently at the postexilic Temple (1 Chron. 16:5, 37; 2 Chron. 5:12; 20:19), although Asaph sustained a prominent position while Korah seems to have been demoted to gatekeeper (1 Chron. 26:1, 19) and baker of sacred bread (1 Chron. 9:31–32). This loss may be reflected in the melancholic tone of the first psalm in the two collections of Korah. Korah psalms at times reflect a more pensive or sensitive author, nonreligious wisdom (Pss. 45; 49), as well as the exalted praise of Zion (Pss. 46–48). Asaph psalms appear more vigorous, self-confident, and historical (Pss. 50; 78).

The "Elohist Psalter" begins here with the psalms of Korah and extends to the end of the Asaph psalms (Ps. 83). The name for God is generally Elohim instead of Yahweh, which otherwise dominates the psalms.

Psalms 42–43. Two psalms in enumeration but one in structure, Psalms 42–43 share a refrain at the end of each of three stanzas. The pen of a master poet is exhibited here: in the intricate structure, the correspondence of imagery and mood, the play on words and sounds, and the momentum forward. Ps. 42:2–6 places us, timid and afraid, in desert terrain, thirsty, saddened in personal exile by the memories of Temple worship. Ps. 42:7–11 transports us, scorned by enemies, absorbed in suffering, strong and affirmed, to mountains that roar with mighty, even destructive waterfalls. Ps. 43:1–5 directs our gaze to future hopes, into a sanctuary flooded with light, pure and clean after the rains.

The language and images in the elegy (42:2–6) evoke memories of Temple worship. The psalmist is "athirst" not just for the Lord but also for the Temple, where the Lord's bountiful presence was symbolized by water (Ps. 46:5; Ezek. 47). Ps. 42:3b originally read, "When will I go and see the face of God," an expression for visiting a sanctuary (Deut. 31:11; Ps. 27:4) derived from the Canaanites who had material figures of their deities. Later a scribe corrected the reading, "When will I go and be seen before God," for no one can see God and live (Exod. 33:20). Sacred meals are recalled, now only a memory of tears. "I pour out my soul" expresses sorrow drawn from the ritual of pouring water (1 Sam. 7:6; Isa. 57:6). The refrain (Ps. 42:6, 12; 43:5) shifts the meaning of Hebrew words: "the multitude" in 42:5 now describes "the tumultuous" soul; the word for worship modulates into being "downcast."

In 42:6–12 the geography is that of upper Galilee at the base of Mount Hermon, snow-capped year round, with waterfalls and gushing springs. Water is now destructive, and the psalmist uses a Hebrew word, tehom, which summons images of the sea monster Tiamat and the angry depths of the sea (cf. Ps. 89:10–11). Yet Mount Hermon turns up small in comparison to the (religiously) exalted heights of Mount Zion (Ps. 68:16–17). The melodies of the Temple begin to return (42:9).

In 43:1–5, the psalmist experiences a public vindication from the Lord, who allows this member of the Korah guild to return to Jerusa-

lem, "your holy hill" (Pss. 2:6; 3:5), to participate in the worship and to bask in the light of
God's face (Pss. 31:17; 44:4). Light indeed
bursts out as the dominant motif in this third
stanza. "God, my God" originally read "Yahweh, my God" before the phrase was changed
for the Elohist Psalter.

Psalm 44. A communal lament composed after a serious military defeat, Psalm 44 could fit
into various occasions: when King Jehoshaphat
(873–848 B.C.) was faced with an Edomite invasion from the south and ordered fasting and
public prayer (2 Chron. 20); when the Assyrians
finally left Judah with Jerusalem alone intact
and the rest of the country in ruins during the
reign of Hezekiah (727–698 B.C.; 2 Kings 18:13–
19:37); or at the tragic death of King Josiah in 609
B.C. (2 Chron. 35:20–25). The psalm begins in
hymnic style with a creed confessing God's great
redemptive acts for Israel (Ps. 44: 2–9); a community lament challenges the faith (vv. 10–17);
a reflective meditation follows (vv. 18–23); and
finally there is a prayer for help (vv. 24–27).

Verses 2–9 provide a chant for a large choir,
except for vv. 5 and 7 in the singular for solo
voices and v. 9 a refrain to be sung repeatedly
by the congregation. Other stylistic flourishes
add strength, such as the repetition of the emphatic Hebrew word ki, "indeed," three times
in v. 4. The language reflects the "holy war"
fought on. Israel's behalf by the Lord (cf. Ps.
18:32–46).

In 44:10–17 the creed is reversed; even the
vocabulary used in v. 8 is introduced into v. 11
in reverse meaning. Evidently creeds and theology have their limits! Not that they are
wrong, but the mystery of God extends beyond
the bounds of human speech (cf. Rom. 11:33–
36). "Sheep for the slaughter" is a very common phrase: Jer. 11:19; 12:3; Zech. 11:4, 7. In
Ps. 44:16 a solo voice rings out over the words
of the large choir.

Verses 19–23 are like Job in miniature, reflecting upon useless and undeserved suffering.
The psalmist will speak to God (vv. 18–20, 23)
and in between insert words about God (vv. 21–
22). Verse 23 is cited by Paul, who then declares
that one can overcome even death "because of
him who loved" (Rom. 8:35–36). A similar answer occurs at the end of the psalm.

In Ps. 44:24–27 the psalmist dares to challenge God to "Arise! Why are you asleep!" For
God to sleep, especially in times of Israel's serious need, contradicts Ps. 121:4 and 1 Kings
18:27. God hides (Pss. 10:11; 13:2) and forgets
(Ps. 10:12)—a deaf and dumb deity (Ps. 22:2–
3). The psalmist's final appeal is to God's loving and faithful kindness, the technical phrase
for the covenant (Exod. 34:6–7). The solution
lies not in victory but in a strong, even mystical
union between God and Israel.

Psalm 45. As a nonreligious marriage song,
Psalm 45 is the only such example in the Psalter
and, as such, is capable of comparison with the
Song of Songs. Composed for a royal marriage,
the psalm leaves one undecided about time and
locale. Some favor the Northern Kingdom with
its ivory elegance at Samaria (v. 9; 1 Kings 22:39;
Amos 3:15; 6:4) and its contact with Tyre and
Sidon (Ps. 45:13; 1 Kings 16:31).

Ancient rabbinical and early church writers
consistently recognized here an announcement
of the messianic king. The Aramaic Targum addresses this ode to the "Messiah King." The
psalm draws many of its images and words
from Isaiah's remarks about the promised king
and the future kingdom of God: beauty (Isa.
33:17); warrior (9:5); justice (11:5); humble
(11:4); and oil of gladness (61:3). The symbolic
interpretation, moreover, of perceiving the relation between God and Israel like that of
spouses in marriage derives from the prophet
Hosea and continues throughout the OT and NT
(Hos. 2:21–22; Isa. 54; Matt. 9:15; John 3:29;
Eph. 5:22–33; Rev. 21:1–2). The human situation, here of marriage, is not only found worthy
of modeling the divine, but the human institution is also challenged anew to live up to a divine ideal.

Psalm 45 includes a rather elegant introduction (v. 2) and conclusion (vv. 17–18) and centers upon the bridegroom (vv. 3–10) and the
bride (vv. 11–16). According to the title, the
psalm is to be sung according to the melody of
the song "Lilies." The introduction in v. 2 is
every bit as solemn as that for Psalms 49 and 78.
The poet sings excitedly, majestically.

The bridegroom in 45:3–10 is acclaimed
principally as king. Surrounded with power
and dignity, he is to protect the poor and secure justice against any opposing or deviant
forces whether at home or abroad. "Your
throne, O God" in v. 7 could be equally well
translated "your most honorable throne"; the
Hebrew word 'elohim can be considered an adjective of majestic grandeur or awesome power:
Gen. 1:2, where the "spirit of God" is sometimes
translated "a mighty wind," or 1 Sam. 18:10,
which reads, literally, "a divine evil spirit,"
namely, "an overwhelming, preternatural evil
force." Ivory luxury (Ps. 45:9) reminds us of the
northern capital of Samaria (Amos 3:15; 6:4),
though Solomon's throne was inlaid with ivory
(1 Kings 10:18) and Tyre was known for trafficking in ivory (Ezek. 27:15). The queen mother (Ps.
45:10) stood at the king's right hand. While
wives remained hidden in the royal harem, the
queen mother enjoyed rather free access to the
king (1 Kings 1:11–14). Ophir was a region in
southern Arabia and a supplier of fine gold (1
Kings 9:28; 10:11).

Ps. 45:11–16 provides another impressive
introduction. "Forget your people" inculcates

more than loyalty to the husband; the foreign princess is not to import foreign religious beliefs and practices (1 Kings 11:1–10). Ps. 45:12 implies honor as given to divinity (see v. 7 above); kings represented all Israel in their role as children or firstborn of God (Pss. 2:7; 110:3; Isa. 9:5).

The concluding praise in Ps. 45:17–18 is reserved for the king and bridegroom. The last line imparts a religious blessing.

Psalm 46. Psalm 46 is the first in a trilogy praising God for Jerusalem and its Temple and also served as the inspiration for Martin Luther's hymn, "A Mighty Fortress Is Our God." The composition of the psalm may have sprung from the seemingly miraculous deliverance of Jerusalem from the cruel Assyrian army (701 B.C.; 2 Kings 18:13–19:36). This psalm, like Psalm 48, contains many mythological, Canaanite references honoring the creator, who struggled against chaotic forces to bring and keep peace (Isa. 51:9–10; Ps. 89:10–11). Mythology and history merge here. As historical details of Judah and Assyria drop away, the focus is on Yahweh's supreme, creative presence with Israel.

Psalm 46 divides neatly into vv. 2–4, praise of Yahweh-Creator in mythological language; vv. 5–8, praise of Jerusalem in historical terms; and vv. 9–12, praise of God with almost mystical awe. The Hebrew places the refrain only after the last two sections, allowing it to focus explicitly on Israel's religion.

Verses 2–4 reflect the land of Canaan as always open to invaders from desert and sea (cf. Ps. 29). Mythology, wrong in its false identification of deity, nonetheless rightly enabled Israel to appreciate the mysterious power of Yahweh's protection.

In 46:5–8 the monstrous force of water is tamed to become a stream, joyfully flowing with life from the Lord's presence in the Temple (Isa. 66:12; Ezek. 47; Zech. 14:8–9). The language is religious metaphor, for no springs actually flowed from the altar. This motif probably derives from a ritual of pouring water at the Temple (Ps. 42:5). The metaphor was expanded to visualize the garden of paradise at the Temple (Gen. 2:10; Isa. 33:17–24; Sir. 24). The reference to the break of morning (Ps. 46:6) may allude to the departure of the Assyrian army (2 Kings 19:35) and, symbolically, to the end of night's dangers (Ps. 91:5). The refrain (46:8) links the psalm with Isaiah through the titles "God of Jacob" (more than fifty times in Isaiah) and "God with us" (Heb. 'immanu'el; Isa. 7:14).

Ps. 46:9–12 perceives the Temple ritual as a vision, ceremonially reenacting and spiritually reliving Yahweh's great deeds for Israel (Ps. 44:2–9). The God of peace silences the strident sounds of war (→ Jerusalem; Temple, The).

Psalm 47. In Psalm 47, a battle hymn, Israel attributes its successes to Yahweh. Composed after a military victory, it sustained Israel's hope for the world domain of Yahweh (Isa. 44:6–8; Zech. 2:14–17). Only after Israel's ambitions for empire had collapsed did the psalm assume its final meaning for worshiping Yahweh.

There are two calls for praise (Ps. 47:2, 7), with the motivation after the first more patriotic (vv. 3–5) and after the second more religious (vv. 9–10a). Each stanza ends with a reference to the ritual enthronement of Yahweh (vv. 6, 10b). Various Temple ceremonies are reflected here (cf. Pss. 24; 68). The first part was sung during a procession with the Ark through the city (47:2–5) and its return to the Holy of Holies (v. 6), the second part during the obeisance of vassal nations before the princes of Israel. Jews recite this psalm seven times before sounding the trumpet to begin the new year. Christians associate the psalm with the Feast of the Ascension.

Clapping of hands and shouting (vv. 2–5) were ceremonial actions originally associated with military or political action (Josh. 6:16, 20; 1 Sam. 10:24; 1 Kings 1:39–40). The epithet "Lord, Most High" goes back to an early period (Gen. 14:18–20), and that of "Great King" was used of Assyrian and Babylonian monarchs (Isa. 36:4, 13; 2 Kings 18:19, 28). Ceremonial trumpets were prominent in political celebrations (Josh. 6:20; 2 Sam. 15:10; 1 Kings 1:39; Ps. 81:4).

In 47:8, the injuction to "sing skillfully" refers to an artistic quality in the service. Later Christian writers interpreted it to mean singing wisely, that is, with faith. Verse 10 provides one of the very few references in the Psalms to Abraham (cf. Isa. 51:2, where Sarah also is included), the source of blessing for all nations (Gen. 12:1–3).

Psalm 48. In the opening stanza of Psalm 48 one meets a litany honoring Yahweh and Jerusalem, with titles drawn from Canaanite mythology (vv. 2–4). This use of Canaanite language in Israel's religion is not suprising at Jerusalem, a cosmopolitan capital where cultures merged, including especially those of the sophisticated Canaanites. Yet the psalm remembers a startling victory for Israel. The mythological references are historicized within Israel's experience before becoming the language of faith (vv. 5–9; Chap. 46). Similar to Psalms 46–47, the third section focuses upon liturgical functions, here a procession through the city (48:10–15).

The occasion is difficult to pinpoint since details have been erased in the interest of allowing a symbolic expression of Yahweh's intervention in any age for people of strong faith. From a theological perspective, Jerusalem becomes the center or navel of the earth (Ezek.

5:5; 38:12) with directions explicitly to the north (Ps. 48:3) and the east (v. 8), implicitly to the south (v. 11, "right hand," directions were given facing east) and the west (v. 14, the word for "future" also serves for "west").

The psalm commences with reference to God's home. "Recesses of the north" (v. 3) in Canaanite literature referred to Mount Cassius, the major point of assembly for the gods (so Isa. 14:13). Yet Jerusalem is not the bulwark of Israel's faith, only God provides that support (Ps. 48:4).

Verses 5–9 attest to the memory of a near defeat and wondrous deliverance, perhaps like the invasion of Sennacherib in 701 B.C., is relived through Temple ceremonies; the faith of the people is intensified (vv. 5–9). "Ships of Tarshish" recall a battery of texts about fear and havoc: 1 Kings 22:49, a wreck of Israelite ships heading south in the Gulf of Elath; Jon. 1:3, a place in Spain, again with shipwreck in the story; Ezekiel 27, the collapse of Tyre under the image of shipwreck.

During the procession (vv. 10–15), the covenantal graces of Yahweh's loving-kindness and strong fidelity are celebrated. The final words in the Hebrew, 'al mut, "beyond death," not only enunciated the permanence of the holy city of Jerusalem, but they form a wordplay and inclusio with the title of Psalm 46, 'al 'alamot, "For the maidens." The latter word may refer to the 'almah, or "maiden," in Isa. 7:14 (note the other parallels with Isaiah in Ps. 46). This association may indicate that the 'almah to give birth to the messianic king (Isa. 7:14) is none other than Jerusalem.

Psalm 49. A difficult psalm, disturbed in the Hebrew text, especially v. 15, advances two positions about death, one that ultimately seems to make life and perhaps God meaningless and another that dares to reach beyond death. Developing within the wisdom tradition, always several steps distant from the Temple rituals and its priests, this psalm reached independently for a new solution (cf. Pss. 1; 16). The text represents a dialogue between a rigidly conservative position as found in the Torah (Lev. 21) and in Ecclesiastes and Job (life is not to be explained beyond human experience) and the views of popular religion (life with God extended beyond one's limited time on earth).

After the imposing introduction in Ps. 49:1–5, a chiastic structure appears (see commentary above on Ps. 19:2), so that the conservative position at the center is surrounded with the more advanced one: A self-confidence, 49:6–7; B earthly possessions, vv. 8–9; C overcoming death, v. 10; D the center piece, repeating the conservative position, vv. 11–15; C' overcoming death, v. 16; B' earthly possessions, vv. 17–18; A' self-confidence, vv. 19–20. The refrain (v. 21) repeats the older position.

The first of the Korah psalms (Pss. 42–43) began in a melancholy way but ended with Temple worship flooded with light; this last one in the Korah collection also begins pessimistically with the theologically conservative position but comes around to life beyond the limits of earth.

The solemn introduction in 49:2–5, similar to that of Pss. 45:2 and 78:1–11 and accompanied by the "music of the harp" (Ps. 33:2), ends quietly and quickly so as to allow time for a new view of life and death. The touch of wisdom literature is very evident. Rich and poor, people of lowly or noble birth, are all invited; distinctions disappear in the face of death.

According to 49:6–10, wealth can never provide enough resources to ransom someone from the grip of death and prevent the person from descending into the silent abode of the pit (Ps. 6:6). Ps. 49:10 denies what it is hoping against hope to be true, yet in this hope it is intuiting what is theologically unacceptable in public worship. The hope must be contemplated along with the melody of the harp.

Verses 11–15 are the centerpiece of the psalm and the heart of the problem. Orthodox theology refused to look beyond life on earth for fear of contamination with sorcery and mediums (Deut. 18:9–14). In its fear it showed its limits in dealing with the pastoral question of dying and death (Ps. 44). Ps. 49:13, repeated again in v. 21, was an enigmatic proverb intended to stir discussion as much as to settle it.

Even though vv. 16–21 go the same route as vv. 6–10, they are nonetheless dominated by the statement in v. 16, "God will ransom my life from the pit. Indeed, God takes me." After this verse we find the Hebrew particle selah, requesting a pause for meditation. The Hebrew verb "to take" is a strong word, used of people like Enoch and Elijah taken alive from earth by divine intervention (Gen. 5:24; 2 Kings 2:11). The verse is not necessarily speaking of being saved from premature death. The psalmist separates out the wealthy but unjust person who will never see light but will vanish in oblivion. The enigmatic refrain, repeated again at the end, is all the more mysterious and open to question in view of Ps. 49:16.

Psalm 50. The first of the psalms of Asaph, the only one in Book Two of the Psalter, is a harbinger of those to follow in Book Three (Pss. 73–83). The author shows up as energetic and confident, from the sanctuary itself, tackling serious prophetic threats to sanctuary worship. If we are in the pre-exilic age, the time of splendid Temple worship, the strident voice of the prophets was still ringing in his ear (Amos 5:21–25; Isa. 1:11–20; Jer. 26). Asaph directly faces the challenge.

After a solemn prelude similar to the preceding psalm yet this time like a theophany

(Ps. 50:1–6), the author critiques worship (vv. 7–15) as unacceptable to God because of social injustices (vv. 16–21). The conclusion sounds one final warning (vv. 22–23).

Verses 1–6 recall the spectacular theophany of Sinai and the high liturgical pieces of Exodus 19; Habakkuk 3; and Psalm 68. Yet this introduction also blends in prophetic material, summoning the heavens and the earth for a public legal hearing (Mic. 1:2–4; Isa. 1:2–3). If prophetic preaching was fiercely honest, God appears just as formidable "in a consuming fire and roaring storm." The covenant material enables the author to take a firm position within Temple and tradition (Exod. 19; → Theophany).

A dead conscience lies behind the feverish ritual in Ps. 50:7–15, reeking with sacrificial smoke on one side and, on the other side, ignoring public morality (cf. Hos. 7:8). People think that ritual wraps its sacred mantle round them to hide the rotten morality of their lives. Ritual, however, is no alibi for sinning. "If I were hungry . . ." (v. 12) recalls other episodes of idolatry (Deut. 32:38; Bel and the Dragon). Ps. 50:14–15 uses ritual language ambiguously; we are not sure if the overtones are positive or negative. After all, the author comes from Temple personnel. (For the various types of sacrifice, see commentary above on Ps. 40:7.)

Ps. 50:16–21 does not suggest that the listeners recite the Torah and then commit robbery, adultery, lying, and slander against one's family. Rather, and particularly if priests and Levites are being addressed, leaders are afraid to condemn what the people are doing lest they lose their stipends (Deut. 18:8). They even encourage sin to receive greater sin offerings and so "they feed off the sins of my people" (Hos. 4:8). Tolerating such deviousness, they give the impression that God also is deaf and blind to the situation (cf. 50:3).

In concluding the entire psalm, 50:22–23 echoes phrases from the minor conclusion (vv. 14–15) and realistically warns once more against the sin of religious externalism. The guild of Asaph remains faithful to covenant and Temple, recognizing a proper place for sacrifice.

Psalm 51. In writing this fourth of the seven penitential psalms (Ps. 6), a classic prayer for Lent and the forgiveness of sin, the writer meditated long upon prophetic literature, especially Jeremiah, Third Isaiah (Isa. 56–66), and Ezekiel, so that even if the psalm is composed in the first-person singular, it reflects social sins and their effect upon the community: for v. 3, see Isa. 63:7; for vv. 5–6, see Isa. 59:12–13; for v. 7, see Ezek. 16:2–4; Jer. 3:25; for v. 8, see Ezek. 36:25.

The style shows expert balancing and development. Guilt and sin dominate in Ps. 51:4, 11; heart and spirit in vv. 12, 19. Sin and sinner occur six times and God one time in vv.

3–11; sin and sinner only one time and God six times in vv. 12–19. The sequence of the verbs, wipe out, wash, and cleanse, in vv. 3b–4 is repeated in reverse order in vv. 9, 11b. Structuring like this is intended for effective communication in public assembly and worship, not for private prayer. While the psalm stresses the need for personal spirituality, this quality is achieved through the community, all Israel at the Temple.

Despite its intensity, the psalm flows easily: vv. 3–4, introduction; vv. 5–8, confession of sin; vv. 9–11, prayer for forgiveness; vv. 12–14, prayer for moral renewal; vv. 15–19, promise or vow of thanksgiving; and vv. 20–21, liturgical addition.

In vv. 1–2, David's sin with Bathsheba is a reminder that serious sin is comparable to adultery because it violates God's love. The dependence upon late prophecy rules out Davidic authorship.

Verses 3–4 are a storehouse of Hebrew vocabulary for sin and forgiveness: *chanan*, "graciousness shown to nonrelatives and outsiders"; *chesed*, "loving bonds within family and tribe"; *rachamim*, "compassion," from the Hebrew for "womb"; *machah*, "wipe or blot out"; *pesha'*, "rebelliousness"; *kibbes*, "thoroughly wash [i.e., in cold water, beating the clothes against rocks and bleaching them in the sun]"; *'awon*, "twisted out of shape"; *chatta'*, "like arrows missing the mark"; and *taher*, "clean as not to contaminate others." With the clash of images behind these words, the text points out the disruption wrought by sin upon human nature as created by God and bonded in covenant with God and community. Only God can restore the lost harmony between the individual and society (→ Sin).

The confession of sinfulness (vv. 5–8) begins with a conscience sensitive to wrongdoing (v. 5), an admission of guilt (v. 6) and of powerlessness to remedy the situation (vv. 7–8). Verse 5, very similar to Isa. 59:12, stresses the first-person "I" with a verb that reaches beyond theoretical knowledge to an inner experience. Ps. 51:6a turns the focus just as pointedly upon God: "Against you, against you alone . . . and that which is evil in your eyes I did." Whatever harm sin inflicted upon people touched not just the holiness but the kindliness of God (cf. Luke 9:48; 15:18). Ps. 51:6b is perplexing at first, for if it is linked with v. 6a, it may imply that our confession of sin justifies God's punishment. More correctly, if it is associated with God's kindliness in vv. 3–4, God is seen to be just by living up to the covenantal promises of forgiveness (Exod. 34:6–7). In this case fidelity is a better word than justice.

Ps. 51:7–8 reflects the two sides of sexuality: v. 7, the association of shame and even uncleanness with sexual activity and with the sexual organs, and v. 8, the sacredness of sexuality and of the transmission of life. While shame bestows a healthy safeguard around an area easily abused, it also manifests strange habits and practices in every culture, even in ancient Israel (Lev. 15). In Ps. 51:7 the wrongness does not consist in conception and birth but in the way that sexuality can become a selfish, even harmful activity. One can just as easily say, "In sin I eat or work," for one may easily overeat or become a workaholic. Verse 8, translated specifically in a context of v. 7 and sexuality, reads, "You [God] are pleased with fidelity amid [conjugal] intimacy; in such secret moments you impart the experience of true wisdom."

The prayer for forgiveness in vv. 9–11 draws upon the memory of Temple worship: happy songs of praise; hyssop, a small bushy plant used for sprinkling to signify cleanliness (Lev. 14; Num. 19) and divine protection (Exod. 12:22). One of the Hebrew words for sin (*chatta'*) is used as a verb here to mean "cleanse," as though if one thoroughly realizes the ugliness of sin, one will purge and purify oneself completely.

In the prayer for moral renewal (Ps. 51:12–14), the psalmist admits that only God creates; the Hebrew word *bara'* has only God as its subject. The new creation will be total and integrated, as the phrase "sturdy spirit" implies.

In vv. 15–19 conversion fires one with zeal. From guilt (as blood signifies, Isa. 1:15; Hos. 4:2) to innocence, from death to life, the psalmist breaks into songs of praise and is restored to the Temple assembly (Pss. 15; 24). Yet Temple sacrifice did not achieve this transformation, only God did. Lest the previous verses be misinterpreted with anti-Temple bias, 51:20–21 were added.

Psalm 52. The title, "maskil of David," introduces four of the least prominent psalms (Pss. 52–55) and, in this case, one of the more damaged textually. "Maskil" is a favorite wisdom word (Ps. 47:8). A wisdom psalm similar to Psalms 1 and 37, Psalm 52 discusses the lot of the liar (vv. 3–7) and the honest person (vv. 8–11), specifically contrasting worthy and unworthy priests (Ps. 16).

The mention of Doeg in the title (vv. 1–2) alludes to his part in the massacre of the priests at Nob (1 Sam. 21:8; 22:11–19). In the psalm some priests are "killing" others by lies and intrigue.

The style of addressing the wicked in person (Ps. 52:3–7) is unusual in the Psalter, but normal with prophecy (Amos 4:6–11). With a slight change, Ps. 52:3b reads, "the devout one of God," possibly said in sarcasm to the wicked priests. The ancient versions have different renditions. God "will snatch and tear you away from the tent," i.e., from the Temple (v. 7; Ps. 15:1).

During the rapid demise of the wicked priests (52:8–11), the others will stand in silence, smiling in disbelief. "Green olive trees" is another reference to priesthood "in the house of the Lord" (cf. Zech. 4:1–3, 11–14). Ps. 52:11 sees the persecuted, righteous priests reinstated in the Temple assembly of "your devoted ones."

Psalm 53. This Psalm is identical with Psalm 14 but for three exceptions. The divine name Yahweh drops out, as is customary in the Elohist Psalter (Pss. 42–83; see commentary above introducing Book Two), in favor of the generic form for God, "Elohim." The title adds, "According to Mahalath. A maskil." (For the relation of the latter word to wisdom literature, see the commentary above on Ps. 52.) *Machalat* derives from a Hebrew root signifying sickness or sorrow. It may be the name of a song for the sick, according to whose melody this psalm was to be sung, or it may join this psalm to such a group of prayers. Ps. 53:6 rings with a more strident tone than Ps. 14:5–6.

Psalm 54. All the customary sections, even the standard vocabulary of supplication, occur in this short poem, Psalm 54: vv. 3–4, call for help; v. 5, motivation; vv. 6–7, prayer of confidence; and v. 8, thanksgiving.

The title in vv. 1–2, like others for a "Psalm of David" in Book Two, is more extensive and more liturgical than those in Book One, as here with the reference to "stringed instruments." For the Ziphites' betrayal of David, see 1 Sam. 23:19 and 26:1.

Expressions in Ps. 54:3–5 are repeated in other psalms, a fact that indicates a repertoire of stock phrases for supplication: "save me" in Pss. 3:8; 6:5; 7:2; "hear my prayer" in Pss. 4:2; 17:1; "give ear" in Ps. 5:2; and "your name" in Pss. 20:2; 52:11. Ps. 54:5 is identical with Ps. 86:14. Blessing by the name flows over into the NT (so Acts 3:6; 4:12). The freewill offerings (vv. 8–9) are sacrifices not under obligation by ritual or personal vow.

Psalm 55. Psalm 55, poorly preserved, contains obscurities due as well to occasional Aramaic forms, a sign of late editing. As with Psalm 52, the author seems to have been a priest, disturbed by the decadent state of Temple worship in the postexilic period (cf. Ps. 16; Isa. 56:9–57:13). Jerusalem may be occupied by foreigners (Ps. 55:10–12).

The following outline directs us through the complicated form: vv. 2–3b, introduction with stereotyped phrases (Ps. 54:3–5); vv. 3c–16, lament; vv. 17–18, prayer for help; vv. 19–20, confidence; vv. 21–22, lament; and vv. 23–24, confidence. Sickness (vv. 5–6) and betrayal (vv. 14–15) leave little energy for good order and self-control. While the introduction is somewhat flat, the rest of the psalm evinces vigor and passion.

Verses 3c–16 range over many human reactions to distress. Emotional distress and probably physical sickness are detected in vv. 5–6: heart tremor, terrors of death, fear, and shaking. Verses 7–9 evince gentle sensitivity (Song of Sg. 2:14), susceptible to disappointments at times tragic (Ps. 74:19). Jeremiah's longing to flee to a desert inn is recalled (Jer. 9:1). In Ps. 55:13–15 the psalmist faces treachery among closest friends, again with parallels in Jer. 12:6; 20:10; Job 19:19; and Psalm 16. The Aramaic Targum supplies the name of David's betrayer, Ahithophel, who later committed suicide (2 Sam. 16:15–17:23). Ps. 55:15 points to a priest as author. The language in v. 16 is reminiscent of the opening of the earth to swallow the jealous Levites of the Korah clan (Num. 16:31–34). (For the netherworld or Sheol, see the commentary above on Ps. 6:6.)

Ps. 55:17–18 reflects continuous prayer. Verse 18 influenced the practice among the rabbis of praying: in morning, honoring Abraham (Gen. 19:27); at midday, honoring Isaac (Gen. 24:63); and at evening, honoring Jacob (Gen. 28:11). The early church adapted these three hours to Christ's resurrection in the morning, ascension at noon, and rest in the tomb at night.

The psalm ends with a statement of confidence (Ps. 55:23–24). Many phrases become familiar in the NT: Matt. 6:25–34; 10:19; and Luke 12:22–31. The ultimate basis for trust is the person of "you," where the Greek adds Lord or Yahweh, the sacred name avoided in the Elohist Psalter (Pss. 42–83).

Psalm 56. A supplication (Psalm 56), possibly from a priest (v. 14), begins a series of *miktam* psalms (Pss. 56–60; 16). This word from the psalm's title possibly designates atonement. The texts of these psalms are poorly preserved. The sequence is somewhat complex because we do not know the accompanying Temple service. Part One includes 56:2a, call for help; vv. 2b–4, lament and confidence; and v. 5, refrain. Part Two includes vv. 6–10, lament, curse upon the enemy, and further lament; and vv. 11–12, refrain. Part Three includes vv. 13–14, thanksgiving offering in the Temple.

A phrase in the title, translated literally, reads, "dove of silent distant places." The Greek reads this phrase as "the people removed from the sanctuary" and the Aramaic Targum as "the community of Israel, composed of a silent dove in the time of the distant deportation from their cities." Dove, therefore, appears as a symbol of Israel (Ps. 68:14; Mark 1:10).

The first section (Ps. 56:2–5), like the closing one, imparts a typical liturgical cast to the psalm: "Have mercy, God" (Ps. 51:3) and "process before God in the light of the living" (Ps. 43:3–4). Confidence is restored not simply by Temple services but by encounter with the person of God. Life is not a divine plan with troubles and joys but an ever-intense search for God within the mystery of one's life. The Hebrew text of 56:5 moves with a solemn cadence; it contrasts God with "flesh," humanity in its weakness.

In vv. 6–12 jealous adversaries from the ranks of the priesthood employ intrigue and spying (Jer. 12:6) to draw religious people into open antagonism and displays of passion, reactions destructive to an image of piety. "My tears ... in your flask" blend memories of sorrow with the custom of carrying water in a goatskin container for treks in the dry wilderness (Gen. 21:15). Suffering and tears strengthen the psalmist in resolve to seek the Lord (Ps. 42:4). The Hebrew word for "counting" or "determining my wandering" is from the same root as "book" at the end of 56:9, supporting the previous impression that divine providence principally involved confronting the mystery of God's personal presence. There is a long tradition for writing names in a book to ensure a permanent relationship with God (Pss. 69:29; 139:16; Exod. 32:32; Job 19:23; Mal. 3:16).

In Ps. 56:13–14 a vow is fulfilled through thanksgiving sacrifice (→Vow). The reference to light reflects the dazzling sunlight over the land of Israel and the important role of lamps in Temple services and, generally, in Israelite life (Ps. 43:3–4; cf. John 1:4; 8:12; →Lamp; Lampstand).

Psalm 57. Another song from the individual laments false accusations and harassment, probably from fellow priests as in Psalm 56. Verses 2–6 petition God for help, ending with a refrain. After a transitional v. 7, one hears a quiet, somewhat plaintive song of thanksgiving, again with refrain, in vv. 8–12. Verses 2 and 9 refer to night vigils in the Temple.

The phrase in the title, "Do not destroy," indicates a song according to whose melody this psalm is sung (Pss. 59; 75). The mention of David's flight from Saul into a cave (1 Sam. 22:1–2; 24:1–23) extends God's protection from a ritual in the Temple to everyday details of life.

In vv. 2–6 "wings" refer to the cherubim on either side of the Ark, where God was said to be invisibly enthroned (Pss. 17:8; 36:8; Exod. 25:17–22; Isa. 6:1–2); the psalmist takes refuge in this intimacy with God (Pss. 2:12; 7:2; 11:1; 16:1). "Love and fidelity" describe the principal attributes of the covenant God (Exod. 34:6–7). Ps. 57:4–5 and the transitional v. 7 repeat the *lex talionis* (Pss. 7:16; 35:8) whereby God does not stand idly by when innocent people are persecuted. Unjust suffering can purify a person and unite one more fully with God. (For the presence of lions, see commentary above on Ps. 7:3; Amos 3:4.) The refrain (Ps. 57:6) rhetorically extends the domain of God, who is worshiped in the Temple across the cosmos. The language about heaven and earth, as in Isaiah 40–55, is highly poetical.

Ps. 57:8–12, repeated in Ps. 108:2–6, celebrates the conclusion of a night vigil in the Temple, symbolizing the end of dark oppression. Dawn represents God's dramatic end of oppression (Ps. 46:6; Isa. 37:36) and the extension of God's warm care in the light of a new day (Ps. 139:9). "Lyre and harp" spread the soft music of peace (Ps. 33:2). Ps. 57:11 has been drawn almost verbatim from Ps. 36:6. The liturgical refrain closes the psalm.

Psalm 58. Psalm 58 is a communal lament, with a Hebrew text poorly preserved and in which v. 10 almost defies translation. Some of the most violent images in the Psalter occur here, moving in a world of magic and a dreadful miscarriage of justice, yet all the while pulsing with extraordinary vigor. The time of composition reaches from pre-exilic days (cf. Deut. 18:9–14) into the early postexilic period (cf. Isa. 56:9–57:13). Ps. 58:2–3 introduces the conniving judges; vv. 4–6 their embodiment of evil; vv. 7–10, their punishment; and vv. 11–12, the vindication of the righteous.

Curiously, the title (v. 1) stipulates that a psalm of brute force follow the melody of a song entitled "Do not destroy" (Pss. 57; 75). Is this a way of controlling anger?

The opening phrase in 58:2–3 is generally amended to address the immoral judges as "gods," similar to the use of Hebrew 'elim or 'elohim for princes in Ps. 45:7 and for judges in Ps. 82:1, 6. Pompous, self-confident judges are sarcastically compared to lesser gods (Ps. 29:1; Deut. 4:19).

In Ps. 58:4–6 the phrase about being wicked "from the womb" does not refer to the Christian doctrine of original sin, unknown in these ancient times, but to a sense of total depravity. For their sly manipulation of justice, magistrates are compared not only to snake charmers, who procured oracles from the "whispering" of snakes, but also to the snakes themselves (Pss. 41:8; 140:4; Gen. 3:1).

The seven curses in Ps. 58:7–10 intensify their fury with each new statement; seven signifies completion. Though vv. 11–12 repeat a hyperbole common in the ancient Near East (Ps. 68:24; Isa. 63:1–6), the image nonetheless remains revulsive. It affirms the theological fact that God communicates in the Bible through human style and passion.

Psalm 59. A lament for an individual at a time of serious crisis within Israel is adapted to communal supplication (vv. 6, 14). Not only the refrains but also other words like "arise," "awake," and "visit" (Ps. 44:24–27), or "deliver me," "protect me," "God my stronghold" (Pss. 7:2; 9:10) carry a strong sense of communal worship. The discouraging situation may have resulted from traitorous Israelites conniving with foreign conquerors. As with other psalms in this particular collection from the guild of David, the text is poorly preserved.

Parallel movement is perceptible in 59:2–10 and 11–18: lament and petition, vv. 2–6, 12–14; refrain about despicable dogs, vv. 7, 15; confidence of divine help, vv. 8–9, 16–17; and final refrain about "God, my stronghold," vv. 10, 18.

In vv. 2–10 the psalmist protests innocence from any serious offenses (for the vocabulary of sin, see commentary above on Ps. 51:3–4). The contempt shown here for dogs is typical of the Bible. They prowl through garbage heaps (1 Kings 14:11; Mark 7:27–28), savagely run in packs (Ps. 22:17), even provide a title for male prostitutes (Deut. 23:19). Ps. 59:9, "You, Lord, indeed laugh at them," signals a victory celebration over a rival (Pss. 2:4; 37:13; Isa. 37:22). For reading a refrain in Ps. 59:10, it is necessary to correct the poorly transmitted text in accord with v. 18.

Verses 11–18 identify the offense as lies and intrigue. The psalmist prays that such sinners be caught in the web of their own deceit (Pss. 35:8; 57:7). With their collapse the psalmist sings "at dawn," always a time of transition to a new day of divine favor (Pss. 46:6; 90:14) and therefore a moment for prayer (Pss. 5:4; 57:9; 92:3). The Hebrew word *chesed*, generally translated "steadfast kindness" within family or treaty relationships and used repeatedly in acclaiming the God of the covenant (Exod. 34:6–7), here stresses the strength of blood and covenant bonding (Ps. 59:10 and 18; Jonah 2:9; Pss. 44:27; 94:18).

Psalm 60. Because of its many historical and geographical references, Psalm 60 is difficult for modern readers. It is fired by faith in God's mysterious presence within Israel's history. That the land was truly theirs by promise (Gen. 12:1–2; Deut. 34:1–4) and by right of settlement (Josh. 1:1–9) is presumed in the ancient oracle (Ps. 60:8–10). Colossal military defeats shake this faith to its foundations (vv. 3–6) and lead to prayer (vv. 11–14). Verse 7 functions as a transition from the communal lament to an ancient oracle. Verses 7–14 occur almost identically in Ps. 108:7–14.

In Ps. 60:1–2 the long title adds a panoramic scope of history and geography. It is to be sung "according to the [melody of] lily of testimony," also used for Pss. 45:1; 69:1; and 80:1, psalms of high emotional intensity. "Testimony" recalls the tables of the law and the origins of Israel (Exod. 31:18), a historical moment thrown into doubt by later military defeat. Aram-naharaim is an ancient name for Mesopotamia, the birthplace of Abraham and Sarah as well as the wives of Isaac and Jacob (Gen. 11:27–28; 24; 29–30). Aram-zobah, north of Damascus, and Edom, south of the Dead Sea, were conquered by David (2 Sam. 8:3–14).

The lament in Ps. 60:3–6 brings memories of Psalms 44 and 74, though more positively. The metaphor of earthquake (60:4) evokes the language of Amos (1:1; 4:11; 6:11; 8:8; 9:1). In Ps. 60:6 "banner" and "flee" are spelled almost alike in Hebrew. With painful irony the banner leading forward to victory becomes the instrument for fleeing backward. Verse 7 is a transitional verse. "Loved one," the name for the vineyard in Isa. 5:1 and for Solomon in 2 Sam. 12:25, appeals to God's tenderness (Hos. 11).

Ps. 60:8–10 speaks of the ancient promise to the patriarchs and its initial fulfillment under Joshua and David. Shechem, about forty miles north of Jerusalem, quickly made an alliance with the newly settled Israelites. Succoth was east of the river Jordan where Jacob thanked God for his safe return to the promised land (Gen. 33:17–18). Gilead is a large area also east of the Jordan; Manasseh and Ephraim represent the principal northern tribes. "Ephraim my helmet" alludes to the major military force, and "Judah my scepter" the place of royalty.

Ps. 60:11–14 ends with the faith that only God restores Israel's hopes. The military might of David or of the northern tribes was no more lasting than human flesh. A reassuring though grim response is given in Isa. 63:1–6.

Psalm 61. Psalm 61 is a lament from a Levite as in Psalms 42–43, a sick person, an Israelite in exile, or a king in some distress—the subject is not clear. Typically, Israel's prayers become ever more inclusive. Psalm 61 opens with calling upon God (vv. 2–3a), prays for relief (vv. 3b–5), and concludes with thanksgiving (vv. 6, 9). Verses 7–8 were added, in a different meter, as intercession for the king. Many phrases are reproduced elsewhere in the Psalter.

The "shrill cry" at the beginning imparts a note of urgency (Ps. 17:1). Ps. 61:3 remains ambiguous. "Earth's end" may refer to exile (Isa. 41:5; 42:10) or possibly to the edge of the grave (Jon. 2:7–8). Ps. 61:5 provides prayer for a return to the Temple (Pss. 17:8; 27:5). Ps. 61:6 and 9 manifest a certitude of being heard, the appropriateness of a vow (Ps. 50:14), and thanksgiving sacrifice (Ps. 4:4–6). Thanksgiving gives to God only the joyful acknowledgement of God's care. The prayer for the king (Ps. 61:7–8) links the covenantal qualities of Yahweh as merciful and faithful with the eternal promises granted to David (2 Sam. 7:22–29; Ps. 89:2–5).

Psalm 62. A scribe uses the setting of a psalm of confidence (vv. 2–8) to communicate a message from the wisdom tradition (vv. 9–13). Throughout, one perceives the composure of a book like Proverbs. Yet it is the God of wisdom, not wisdom itself, who brings rest and strength. The major theme, "only in God," is stylistically evident in the Hebrew text, which begins six lines with the emphatic particle 'ak, "only," and the final two lines with another such particle, ki, "indeed." To have refrains at the beginning rather than at the end of strophes is unusual and attracts attention to the lovely way of singing one's soul to rest "only in God." The sequence flows easily: vv. 2–5, refrain and external threats; vv. 6–9, refrain and internal peace; and vv. 10–13, meditation upon social morality within the peace of God's presence. "Jeduthun" (v. 1) belonged to one of the guilds of singers at the postexilic Temple (1 Chron. 16:41; Pss. 39; 77).

In Ps. 62:2–5 silence is more than a quality; literally, "only in God silence is my soul." Customary titles for God provide a litany of praise: "my rock," Ps. 18:3; "my salvation," Ps. 27:1; and "my fortress," Ps. 46:8, 12. Not to be disturbed means to share in the stability of Jerusalem (Ps. 46:6). While prosecuted, the psalmist calmly sees through the lies of hypocrites (Isa. 30:12–13; Ezek. 12:24).

The psalmist's interior peace (Ps. 62:6–9) contrasts with the deceit of the persecutors (vv. 4–5). First a new litany in praise of God (v. 8), then wisdom addresses "my people." "Pouring out one's heart" reflects a Temple ritual for the pouring of water to express interior trust (Ps. 42:5).

Ps. 62:10–12 evinces the trademarks of prophetic discourses for social justice, only here less stridently (Amos 8:4–8; Mic. 2:1–2). Another litany in praise of God is embedded within the final advice, typical of wisdom literature with its numerical form (Prov. 6:16–17) and its insistence upon human cooperation. While admitting human weakness (Ps. 62:10), with God providing strength and bonding in love, the respondents are expected to give a proper accounting of their lives (Ezek. 18).

Psalm 63. Though a lament, Psalm 63 breathes such tranquility it almost modulates into a prayer of confidence. As it reaches out to speak in the name of the king, the individual merges into the community. The words are reminiscent of Psalms 27, 42–43, 84, and 91 and their desire for dwelling peacefully with God, yet here the tone never reaches the thirst and darkness of Psalms 42–43, nor the distance of Psalm 84, nor the demonic dangers of Psalm 91. Such peace befits a morning prayer, as Psalm 63 became for the early church. The

Armenian church prays Psalm 63 at the Eucharist.

After the introductory lament (v. 2), the language moves in the direction of a narrative of thanksgiving with most of the verbs calling for continuous action (vv. 3–7). In vv. 8–9 the verbs imply completion and confidence in God. The final section focuses on the king (vv. 10–12).

The title associates this psalm with David's experience when he wandered in a wilderness (1 Sam. 24). Ps. 63:2 includes a cry from the depths, "God, my God!" and adds emphatically, "you!" as though God were already present. "I seek you" represents the word from Israel's wisdom literature for discovering God in everyday affairs. The same word stands for "dawn" and explains the use of this psalm for morning prayer. In vv. 3–7 "I looked" has the sense of seeking a vision of the mysterious God in sanctuary worship. "Strength and glory" are associated with the Lord of the sanctuary (Pss. 24:8; 29:1–2). "Better than life" implies a sense of life beyond earth (cf. Phil. 1:21; 3:11). "I bless you in my living" so that life itself, received totally from God, becomes the psalmist's return to God. The strophe ends with a night vigil in the Temple and a sacred meal, gratefully celebrating God's gift of life (cf. Exod. 18:9–12; 24:11).

Ps. 63:8–9 blends the thought into an expression of confidence, again within the sanctuary and beneath the wings of the Lord (Ps. 57:2) where "my soul clings toward you," Hebrew language for intimacy and longing. Ps. 63:10–12 concludes with a final prayer for the king.

Psalm 64. Psalm 64 comprises an individual's lament over intrigue. Because of ties with wisdom literature (v. 10) as well as the subject matter itself, the psalm reaches beyond the limits of Israel's land and history. The psalm imparts a personal touch to a common, disquieting problem. Hounded by deceit, the psalmist is not discouraged. The poor transmission of the text, especially the almost untranslatable v. 7, has not deprived the style of its vigor. After the call for help (vv. 2–3) because of evil schemes (vv. 4–7), God intervenes to restore trust (vv. 8–10), a cause for rejoicing (v. 11).

Opponents who scheme secretly are to be feared more than an enemy in open warfare, not only because it is difficult to second-guess them, but also because their religious appearance makes one doubt one's own faith (vv. 2–3). Although the images in vv. 4–7 are drawn from the hunting and stalking of animals, the secret manipulation of details hints as well at sorcery (Pss. 58; 91), always possible when religious people are laying the snares.

Ps. 64:8–10 presents God's response with words from the preceding section, like shooting arrows. God meets the schemers on their own

ground (Ps. 18:26–27) and shatters their sham of religious righteousness. The lex talionis shows up again (Ps. 35:8); the results of sin turn out to punish the sinner. "All humanity," Israelite or not, understands this kind of language and peers to the depths of what is really happening. The psalm ends (Ps. 64:11) with the motif of seeking refuge in the Lord (Pss. 2:12; 7:2).

Psalm 65. Psalm 65 is a national hymn of thanksgiving to celebrate the end of a drought. It was possibly used for the Feast of Tabernacles, when prayers were offered for rainfall (Lev. 23:33–43; Zech. 14:16–21). In the spirit of pilgrimage, the Greek version extends the application to "exiled people as they begin their return."

A rather long introduction locates the psalmist within the sanctuary thanking God and offering appropriate sacrifice (Ps. 65:2–5). The next two stanzas allude to the struggle of God the creator with angry oceans (vv. 6–9) and the quiet presence of God the re-creator in rainfall (vv. 10–14).

In vv. 2–5 the opening line is generally translated according to the ancient versions, yet the Hebrew text may be correct: "for you, God, silence is praise," a possible reference to congregational reverence (Hab. 2:20) as the thanksgiving sacrifice was placed on the altar for burning. The service included burning a small part of the animal in adoration, followed by a sacred meal (Deut. 16:1–15; Exod. 18:9–12; Ps. 22:23–27). Ps. 65:5 refers to this sacred meal. The opening verse inspired the dialogue in the "preface" to eucharistic prayers: "Let us give thanks to the Lord our God; it is right and just." (For vows, see Pss. 22:26; 50:14; for a description of the ceremony, Ps. 118:19–20, 26–28.)

In Ps. 65:6–9 the psalmist's words sweep back to God's struggle in creation (Ps. 89:10–11; Isa. 51:9–10), which was also a battle for justice (Pss. 24; 97). The Temple was the place where God maintained harmonious order in creation and in history. The world's inhabitants marvel at such signs (1 Sam. 10:7; Isa. 7:10–14) and wonders (Isa. 40:5).

Ps. 65:10–14 rejoices in a bountiful rainfall, not just the heavy precipitation in late November through February, but also the special gift of the early rains in October and early November as well as the late rains in March and early April (Deut. 11:10–17; Joel 2:23). The literal translation of Ps. 65:12b, "The tracks of your chariot overflow with fat," blends ancient images: God rides upon a chariot through the sky (Pss. 18:11; 104:3); "fat" signifies abundance of life or its best part, reserved for the altar (Ps. 20:4), a sign of rejoicing (Ps. 23:5) and prosperity (Prov. 11:25); "tracks . . . overflow" recalls the overladen cart dropping some of its produce along the way.

1 Illustration in a bound tenth century Latin manuscript (the *Gerona Beatus*) showing Noah receiving a green branch from the dove that he had released from the ark (Gen. 8). The ark, with Noah's family and tiers of animals, floats atop flood waters filled with drowned bodies. The return of the dove signals the end of the Flood.   **2** Two of six panels that depict the story of creation; from a seventeenth-century Armenian Bible preserved in the Armenian Patriarchate, Jerusalem. The first panel (*top*) shows God creating heavens and earth from dark, watery chaos (Gen. 1:1–2). The second panel (*bottom*) apparently shows the creation of light (vv. 3–5) and the dome of the sky (vv. 6–8).   **3** The beginning of the book of Genesis, with illuminated initial word panel; from the Hebrew *Duke of Sussex Italian Bible*, copied by Moses Akrish, Italy, 1448.

1 The sacrifice of a ram; shown on a frieze inlaid with mother-of-pearl, ivory, red limestone, and schist; from a temple at Mari, mid-third millennium B.C. In Genesis, God asks Abraham to sacrifice his son Isaac, but a ram is sacrificed instead after divine intervention (chap. 22).   2 Two embracing warriors and a deity with a horned tiara depicted on a ritual basin from a temple at Ebla; Middle Bronze Age, early second millennium B.C.   3 An Egyptian harvest scene showing oxen trampling grain; mural from the Tomb of Mennah, scribe of Thutmose IV (fourteenth century B.C.); Thebes, Egypt. Israelite law regulated many aspects of farming, including the separation of harvested sheaves using animals (see Deut. 25:4).   4 Rebekah offers water to Abraham's servant Eliezer (see Gen. 24:10–27); detail from one of forty-eight surviving miniatures from a sixth century manuscript now called the *Vienna Genesis*.

1 The crossing of the Red Sea (see Exod. 14:21–15:21) as depicted in the *Rylands Haggadah*; Spain, ca. 1325–1350. The crossing of the Red Sea is the culminating event in God's rescue of the Israelites from oppression in Egypt.
2 Brickmakers at work; detail of an Egyptian wall painting in the Tomb of Rekhmere, Thebes, Egypt, fifteenth century B.C. The Israelites were forced to make bricks during their oppression in Egypt (see Exod. 1:13–14; 5:6–9).
3 Egyptian officials dragging captive western Asiatics after them; bas-relief from the tomb of Haremhab, viceroy under Amenophis IV and his successors, fourteenth century B.C. **4** Sec-tion of a wall painting that apparently depicts Moses giving water to the twelve tribes of Israel from a well in the wilderness; from the synagogue at Dura-Europos, third century. The biblical narrative mentions several instances where the twelve tribes are given water in the wilderness (cf. Exod. 15: 2–25, 27; 17:1–7; Num. 20:1–13).

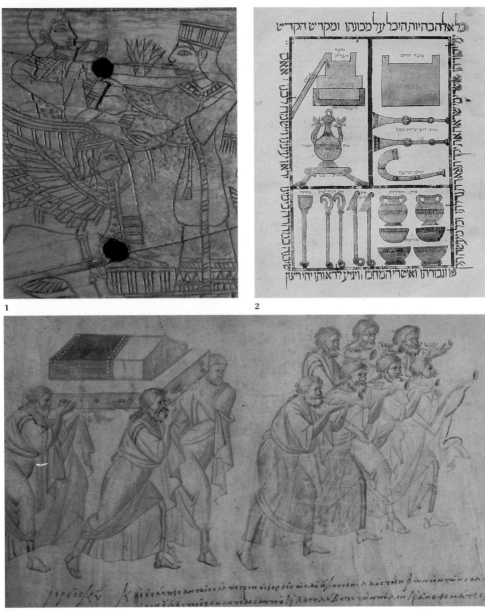

1 Detail of an ivory plaque from Megiddo showing the king and his attendants, thirteenth–twelfth century B.C. The king of Megiddo is listed among those kings defeated by Joshua and the people of Israel (see Josh. 12). 2 Israelite sanctuary vessels, as depicted on one of two facing pages in a Hebrew Bible copied and illuminated in Spain in the late thirteenth century. In Exod. 24:12–31:18, the Israelites are given instructions for building a tabernacle and consecrating a priesthood for divine worship. Among other furnishings, the tabernacle was to have an incense altar (depicted top right), a sacrificial altar and laver (both top left), and various altar utensils (bottom). 3 The march around Jericho led by seven Israelite priests blowing seven rams' horns before the holy Ark (see Josh. 6); detail from *The Joshua Roll*, tenth century.

1 David—poet and musician as well as commander and king—is depicted with mantle, military footgear, crown, and harp; frontispiece to Psalms from the *Vivien Bible*; Tours, 845–846. Musicians and guards are pictured around David.   2 Solomon, David's successor as king of Israel, judges between two women who both claim to be mother of the same child (see 1 Kings 3:16–18); illustration in a Hebrew manuscript from France, ca. 1280. In the biblical narrative, Solomon threatens to cut the child in two, then grants it to the woman who protests.   3 Assyrians transporting cedar wood by sea; bas-relief from the palace of Khorsabad, eighth century B.C. According to 1 Kings 5, Solomon used cedar transported by sea from Lebanon in building the Temple.

A5

1 Two Assyrian officials in profile; fresco from Til Barsib, mid-eighth century B.C. From the mid-eighth to the mid-seventh centuries B.C., the Assyrian Empire under Tiglath-pileser III, Sennacherib, and other rulers attained its greatest extent, with the drastic consequences for Israel and Judah recounted in 2 Kings. 2 Assyrian war chariot with armed charioteers; bas-relief from the palace of Ashurbanipal in Nineveh, seventh century B.C. 3a, 3b Ezekiel's vision of dry bones brought to life when he prophesied as the LORD commanded (Ezek. 37:1–14); panels of a wall painting from the synagogue at Dura-Europos, third century. God is symbolized here by a hand reaching down from the sky. The left panel apparently depicts God transporting Ezekiel to the valley of dry bones, where Ezekiel is told to command the bones to reassemble and array themselves with flesh. The bones here seem to have flesh already. At right, the winged figures per-

1

2

3b

haps represent the Spirit entering the bodies at Ezekiel's command, and the people at far right are perhaps the bodies fully restored.

1 A medieval artist's rendering of the bountiful tree that King Nebuchadnezzar of Babylon saw in a dream reported in Daniel 4; illumination from the *Leon Bible* of 960. Nebuchadnezzar (605–562 B.C.) appears in 2 Kings 24–25 and 2 Chronicles 36; Nebuchadnezzar's army conquered and burned Jerusalem, exiling many of its inhabitants to Babylon.   **2** Two life-size archers; enameled tiles from the palace of Persian king Darius I in Susa, ca. 515 B.C. Under the Per-sian king Cyrus II, who ruled Babylonia from 539 to 530 B.C., Judean exiles were allowed to return to Jerusalem and begin rebuilding the Temple. It was during the reign of Darius (530–522 B.C.) that the rebuilding actually occurred (see Ezra 4–6, Haggai, and Zech. 1–8).

1 Scenes from the sacking of Jerusalem by Antiochus IV Epiphanes and the beginning of the Maccabean revolt (see 1 Macc. 1–2); panels of the frontispiece to Maccabees in the *Bible of San Paolo Fuori Le Mura*, ca. 870. At top, Antiochus is seated at center receiving sanctuary vessels plundered from the Temple. At bottom, Mattathias is seated at center, surrounded by his sons. **2** A depiction of personified wisdom; detail of the beginning of Ecclesiasticus (Sirach) in the *Martial of Limoges Bible*, late eleventh century. **3** Judith carrying the head of Holofernes after decapitating him with his own sword (see Jth. 13:1-10); from an illuminated Hebrew manuscript, the *Rothschild Miscellany*, Italy, ca. 1470. **4** Bronze coins from the last two Hasmonean rulers. At left, the coin of Antigonus II, who ruled in Jerusalem as high priest from 63 to 40 B.C. At right, the coin of John Hyrcanus II, who ruled briefly from 40 to 37 B.C.

Psalm 66. Although structurally a complex psalm, the themes of deliverance from trials and of thanksgiving at a sanctuary appear clearly and repeatedly in Psalm 66. A close reading perceives that the three major sections are carefully integrated. Each includes special lines for praise and then for thanksgiving: vv. 1–4, 5–7, for past deliverance; vv. 8–9, 10–12, for a recent deliverance of Israel; and vv. 13–15, 16–19, for the deliverance of the psalmist.

The psalm is animated by an artistic melange of individual and community, of formal and spontaneous prayer, of past and present deliverance. While Psalm 66 transports one back into the past with Moses in the Exodus and with Second Isaiah (Isa. 40–55) in the return from Exile, it challenges readers to relive these experiences of salvation in their own lives (cf. Deut. 5:1–5; 6:20–25). In Ps. 66:1a some Christian manuscripts, including the Vg., add, "A psalm of the resurrection," in accord with the psalm's spirit of new life after harsh trials.

Verses 1b–7 recall the Exodus out of Egypt and the return from the Babylonian exile. Points of contact show up with Psalms 96–100 and Isa. 40–55. The opening invitation is identical with those of Pss. 98:4a and 100:1. Although "the glory of his name" occurs in Ps. 29:2, here the psalmist does not invoke "the children of the gods." (For a similar theological refinement, see the commentary below on Ps. 96:7.) In summoning "all the earth," the psalmist confesses that what happens to Israel affects all other nations. "Come and see" (Ps. 66:5) refers to ceremonies symbolizing a great act of salvation, probably the Exodus through the Red Sea. Verse 6, "There let us rejoice" may indicate the sanctuary, some say at Gilgal near the river Jordan. Psalm 114, which combines crossing the Red Sea with the passage through the river Jordan, may also have originated at Gilgal. God "rules forever" by enabling Israel to relive the Exodus in other deliverances like the return from Exile.

Ps. 66:8–12 focuses upon a deliverance within the recent experience of the Israelite community. The references to being tested (Ps. 95:9; Jer. 12:3; Job 23:10), tried as silver (Ps. 12:7; Isa. 1:25), brought into a snare (Ps. 57:7; Ezek. 12:13), severely constrained (Deut. 28:53), and walked upon by others (Isa. 51:23) accumulate images for painful trials from throughout the OT, summarized in passing through fire and water (Isa. 43:2). God is mysteriously preparing a new Israel, as one sees has been the result in the biblical references just cited.

Ps. 66:13–20 first presents a liturgy of thanksgiving performed publicly by the psalmist and then refers to personal trials that the psalmist expressed by referring to biblical traditions about Israel's sufferings and deliverance by God. Holocausts were completely burned on the altar out of adoration and total self-giving to God; other offerings were partially burned on the altar, thus providing food for a sacred meal of thanksgiving (Exod. 18:9–12; Deut. 26:1–11; 1 Kings 8:62–64). Ps. 66:16–19 recalls personal confessions of deliverance as in Ps. 22:23–27.

Psalm 67. The interpretation of the short, intense Psalm 67 depends upon the translation of the verbs in vv. 7–8 and upon the sequence of its lines. If the verbs are read in the past tense, which most authors prefer, then the psalm thanks God for bountiful crops (cf. Lev. 23). If the verbs are rendered as a prayer or exhortation, grammatically possible ("May the earth give its fruit . . . and may God bless us"), then the psalm turns into a community lament after a poor harvest! Within the psalm the enigmatic *selah* calls for a pause after vv. 2 and 5; v. 5 thus becomes the centerpiece with its announcement of God's providential care over the nations of the world. Without the *selah*, the psalm divides into three sections with the emphasis upon the refrain after each (it is supplied after v. 8). In this case the nations stand in awe at what God is doing for Israel, as in Isa. 40:1–5. Each explanation is legitimate, depending upon the occasion for worship. The image of harvest announces the final salvation (Hos. 14:5–9; Isa. 45:8; 61:11).

The service opens with the priestly blessing from Num. 6:24–26. The "way" of God (Ps. 67:3) leads through the farmers' fields; "salvation" consists in rain and a good harvest. The refrain thanks God, the source of all good gifts.

Psalm 68. Like a centuries-old cathedral, Psalm 68 manifests exceptional antiquity, major historical and theological developments, confessions of faith at times of crises, ravages of war, and neglect and further use—artistic accretions not always in good taste or in the name of the best theology. Within Psalm 68 several significant movements are detected. One is historical: from the period of Moses (vv. 2–4, 7–9) to settlement in the land (vv. 5–6, 10–11), from the time of Deborah and the judges (vv. 12–15) to the capital and Temple at Jerusalem (vv. 16–19), military adventures (vv. 20–24), victory celebrations (vv. 25–28), political and military problems (vv. 29–32), and prophetic hopes (vv. 33–36). This sweep through history theologically accepts dramatic changes, like that from the wilderness austerity with Moses to the cosmopolitan grandeur of David and Solomon, or that from the sacred object of an Ark carried by the people in their journeys to the sacred place of the Temple where people came to pray before the Ark, or that from charismatic rule by judges and prophets to the autocratic institution of kings, or the change from great deeds of salvation in early history to their ceremonial symbolism in Temple ritual, or the geographical transfer of places of worship from the meeting tent in the wilderness to the sanctuary of Mount Tabor and finally to the Jerusalem Temple. Psalm 68 can be read and celebrated on many different levels. Though a unified composition, it has aged over centuries of inspired composition and use.

Verses 2–4 and 5–7 each form a minihymn with its own call to praise and its own motivation. Verses 2–4, set in the Sinai wilderness, repeat the summons to break camp under God's guidance (Num. 10–35). Here, however, the passage moves from the second-person summons ("Arise, Lord") to the third-person statement ("God arises"). The statement becomes more generic or symbolic; each day in the land is like breaking camp and moving onward. Because this psalm is in the midst of the "Elohist Psalter" (see commentary above introducing Book Two), the divine name changes from Yahweh to Elohim or God, the first of twenty-three times in the psalm, with Yahweh used only once in 68:18 and an abbreviated form, Yah, in v. 19. In vv. 5–7 God is acclaimed with Canaanite imagery as one "who rides upon the clouds" (Pss. 18:11; 104:3) but associated closely with the compassionate and faithful God of the covenant (Exod. 3:7–8; 34:6–7). This new cultural way of addressing God helped to win Canaanites to the worship of Yahweh. What they attributed falsely to their gods truly exists in Yahweh.

After the solemn introduction, Ps. 68:8–11 begins over again, echoing the theophany of Mount Sinai (Exod. 19) and the victory song of Deborah (Judg. 5). This latter may have been originally composed for a celebration at the sanctuary on Mount Tabor (Judg. 4:12–14). Already the biblical accounts do more than record events; they provide texts for sanctuary worship so that application can be made to the lives of later generations of Israelites. Ps. 68:12–15 continues to catch memories of the days of the judges, when women spread the news of victory and divided the spoils (Judg. 5:30). (For the comparison of Israel to a dove, see Hos. 7:11; 11:11.)

Ps. 68:16–19 records the installation of the Ark in the Jerusalem Temple, transferring to the Temple the theological significance of Sinai. God, accordingly, is no longer revealing the law but, through the Levites and priests, is interpreting and applying the law (Deut. 31:9–29). Ps. 68:19 reads, "You [God] have gone up the mountain ... received human beings as gifts ... the Lord God within the [holy] dwelling." At first this verse mirrored a ceremony in which the Ark was returned to the Holy of Holies after a triumphal procession through the city (Pss. 47; 132) and the booty of war, includ-

ing slaves, was offered to the Temple (Josh. 9:23; Neh. 7:72). Later Israelite armies no longer marched to war, so weak and minuscule had the country become. The scribes were scandalized that God should need gifts, particularly slaves. A new reading, therefore, was provided in what is called the style of midrash or rabbinic interpretation. Moses, not Yahweh, ascends the mountain of Sinai and receives gifts from Yahweh, namely the Torah. Eph. 4:7–13 relies upon the midrash and reinterprets the passage about Christ who ascends on high and, by sending the Spirit, confers the gifts of leadership in the church (→ Midrash).

Ps. 68:20–24 continues to celebrate the military victory, v. 24 with violent but stereotypic language (Ps. 58:11; Isa. 63:1–6). Many biblical allusions occur here: the defeat of King Ahab near Bashan (1 Kings 22:29–40) and the end of the wicked queen Jezebel (2 Kings 9:30–37), all with the lesson that evil is not tolerated by God, whether among foreigners or Israelite royalty. Ps. 68:25–27 continues the ceremony with a new procession. The presence of northern tribes at Jerusalem points to the reign of David or, better, of Solomon (1 Kings 12). The procession of both women and men into the inner courts of the sanctuary also points to a pre-exilic period before this area was reserved to Levites and priests. The psalm continues with prayer (vv. 29–32), inferring military humiliation, therefore an addition from a later inspired composer. Another minihymn, with God again enthroned in the heavenly heights (v. 5), reaches like the earlier parts of the psalm across the nations of the earth to conclude this extraordinary song of national thanksgiving.

Psalm 69. One of the longer laments of an individual sufferer, Psalm 69 is also one of the most quoted psalms in the NT, especially in the passion narrative. Moreover, it contains an extensive curse of the enemy (vv. 23–29), thus providing an opportunity to deal theologically with both the early Christian use of this psalm as well as with the curse tradition itself.

The psalmist is a disciple of the prophet Jeremiah and like this prophet was hounded unjustly (v. 5), even by close friends and family members (v. 9). The delicate sensitivity of this writer shows up not only in the personal agony of forced isolation (v. 21) but also in the resultant outburst of anger and cursing (vv. 23–29). It is not surprising that the writer becomes physically sick (vv. 4, 15–16, 19). There are a number of contacts between the book of Jeremiah and this psalm: vv. 2–5, in the deep mire, Jeremiah 38; v. 4, crying out, Jer. 45:3; v. 8a, shame before God, Jer. 15:15; v. 9, betrayed by family and friends, Jer. 12:6; and v. 21, God knows the brokenhearted and their shame, Jer. 15:18; 18:23; and 23:9.

The sections are clearly identifiable: v. 2a, call for help; vv. 2b–5, lament; v. 6, confession of sin; v. 7, prayer; vv. 8–13, lament; vv. 14–19, prayer; vv. 20–22, lament; vv. 23–29, curse of the enemy; v. 30, final prayer; vv. 31–34, thanksgiving; and vv. 35–37, later addition (Ps. 51:20–21). The gloom turns out to be heavier, the words of thanksgiving shorter, the anger against the enemy fiercer than in Psalm 22.

The title suggests that the psalm be sung according to the melody of a song named "Lilies," like Psalms 45; 60; and 80, all highly emotional compositions. In calling for fasting and sackcloth in 69:11–12, the psalmist is following popular religion, manifested in the prophetic books (Josh. 7:6; 1 Sam. 7:6; 1 Sam. 12:16; Isa. 58). These acts were not a part of official worship as defined in the Torah, where all symbols expressed life in honor of the God of life (Lev. 17:11; 21). Only during and after the Exile did these acts enter officially into Israel's religious customs (Joel 1:13–14; Zech. 7). Like Ps. 35:13, Psalm 69 may have been a bridge between the earlier, nonofficial and the later official practice.

The slanderers sat openly and shamelessly "at the [city] gate," where everyone came and went, the obvious place for news and gossip (1 Sam. 4:13), for business even as important as lawsuits (Deut. 17:5; 21:19). Evil closes in upon the psalmist from all sides, like angry flood waters (Ps. 46:3–4), swirling one into the netherworld (Pss. 6:6; 16:10; 49:15).

There are frequent citations of Psalm 69 in the NT: v. 5 in John 15:25; v. 10 in John 2:17; Rom. 15:3; and Heb. 11:26; v. 22 in Matt. 27:34; vv. 23–24 in Rom. 11:9–10; v. 25 in Rev. 16:3; v. 26 in Acts 1:20; and v. 29 in Rev. 3:5. As seen already with Ps. 68:19 and Eph. 4:8, NT writers carefully chose not only an OT text but also the most appropriate version of it. In the latter case, the midrash was preferred over the normative Hebrew text. NT writers, moreover, read OT passages within the context of their own times and experiences.

Ps. 69:10a, "zeal for your house eats me [alive]," when quoted in John 2:17 and further explained in John 2:21, undergoes substantial change in meaning. For the psalmist, zeal was directed principally toward the house of Israel, secondarily toward the Temple; he was the one being eaten alive by hostile reactions to his zeal. For John, Jesus' own zeal for the holiness of the Temple consumed him emotionally as he drove out the money-changers. Later the image changes so that his body becomes the Temple, to be consumed on the cross by the jealous rage of persecutors. Events in the life, death, and resurrection of Jesus influenced the way in which the OT passage was understood.

The other major theological matter raised by Psalm 69 revolves around the curse of the enemy. The explanation of such curses involves a number of issues. Semites were a particularly emotional and eloquent people; they blessed and cursed with intensity. Some of the rhetoric followed its own literary patterns, so that Ps. 137:9 does not mean to dash babes against the city walls but rather that the enemy city and its inhabitants be conquered at any cost.

The OT, like the sequence between the various books of the NT, exhibits stages in developing traditions, evident in comparing 2 Sam. 24:1 with the later explanation in 1 Chron. 21:1. A particularly gnawing problem was the relation of Israel to the foreign nations and to the enemies within its own ranks, never satisfactorily solved—but neither was the doctrine of life after death (Ps. 6:6). The pronouncement of a sacred curse upon the enemy as well as upon a person suspected of a crime was intended to go into effect only if the person or group was really guilty (Num. 5:18–28; Deut. 27:15–26). Israel did not have internal police forces or prisons; the judicial process was handled speedily. The curse was one way of hurrying the procedure and leaving the result completely in God's hands.

Biblical anthropology did not easily distinguish sin from sinner or the individual from the community. This outlook had its disadvantages, but it also kept people thinking in a communal and responsible way. Based upon the preaching of Jeremiah (2:5, 19; 31:18), as developed within the fourth song of the suffering servant in Isaiah (52:13–53:12), some Israelites believed that the sorrow inflicted upon the sinner or the servant could be turned into a purifying and transforming force for the larger community. One must be human to pray, and oppressors are known to dehumanize their victims. As a result, those who have not been dehumanized must pray in place of those who have been victimized, and on such rare occasions there is only one possible prayer, that God destroy the oppressor. The people who wrote the curse psalms had suffered radically for sin. Such suffering serves to explain the prominence of the curses as well as the bitter tone of these psalms.

Psalm 70. From the viewpoint of literary excellence and textual preservation, Psalm 70 is one of the finest. It is repeated in Ps. 40:14–18, though with some textual disturbance and with the reintroduction of the divine name Yahweh. Psalm 70 is within the "Elohist Psalter" (see commentary above introducing Book Two). The title to Psalm 70 adds that it is to be employed with memorial offerings (Exod. 30:11–16; Lev. 2:2). The opening verse of Psalm 70 became the traditional way for beginning the divine office of psalms and readings in Christian monastic communities.

Psalm 71. An elderly (vv. 9, 18), sick (v. 20) person evokes the memory of other psalms for strength to withstand persecution or rejection in Psalm 71. Verses 1–3 are identical with Ps. 31:2–4a; vv. 5–6 similar to Ps. 22:10–13; v. 7a to Ps. 31:12, 13; v. 12a to Pss. 22:12; 35:22; v. 12b to Pss. 38:23; 40:14; v. 13 to Ps. 35:4, 26; v. 18 to Ps. 22:31, 32; and v. 19 to Ps. 36:6. While a patchwork without title, nonetheless, Psalm 71 offers its own quiet insight into old age. Other biographical details show up: the author was faithful from youth and once an instructor in the community (71:5, 17), possibly consecrated like Samuel as a Nazirite before birth (v. 6; 1 Sam. 1:22 according to 4QSam[a]), or at least a Levite or priest.

The sections of the psalm are not clearly differentiated. After the introductory statement of confidence in "you, Lord" (Ps. 71:1–3; an unusual invocation of Yahweh in the Elohist Psalter), the psalm continues with petition and motivation for the lament (vv. 4–13), follows with hope (vv. 14–21), and concludes with anticipated thanksgiving (vv. 22–24).

Verse 6 associates the psalmist with a tradition, inaugurated by Jeremiah with calmness (Jer. 1:5) and later with agony (Jer. 20:16–17) and continued with outreach toward the community of Israel by the suffering servant of Isaiah (Isa. 49:1). Instinctively the psalmist realizes that suffering is not wasted if it unites one with righteous persons whose own failure and agony spoke to Israel. The psalmist appears as a sign or portent (Ps. 71:7), whose life of suffering becomes a more effective instrument of help to others than words had ever been. The psalmist is comforted by the prophetic ministry of signs and symbolic actions in Jeremiah and Ezekiel (Jer. 28; Ezek. 12:6, 11; 24:24, 26). There are moments of revolt and anger (Ps. 71:13) but this single verse of cursing is mild compared to the preceding Psalm 69.

Concern for the community shows up in a scribal correction with 71:20. While the "spoken" form, sustaining a mournful sound in its words, saw "me," namely, the psalmist, surrounded with hostile adversaries, the written text was changed to "us," the congregation, those who identify themselves and their faith with the psalmist.

Psalm 72. Book One of the Psalter began and now Book Two ends with attention to the royal family of David. Psalm 72, like others composed for royal festivals (Pss. 2, 45, 89, 110, 132) and similar to other biblical passages centering on the Davidic dynasty (2 Sam. 7; Isa. 7:14; 11; Jer. 23:1–6), exhibits signs of reinterpretation. Once David's family had suffered eclipse, it survived only as a hope for the future. New texts were composed, either like Isa. 55:3–5 in which the Davidic promises were restored to the people or

like Zech. 6:9–15 where they were confided to the high priest. These revisions were drastic in their theological implications.

Such is the case of Psalm 72, composed, as the title declares, "for Solomon," since it reflects hopes of justice for the needy and of fertility for the country, with promises of eternal dynasty, qualities associated with royalty in the ancient Near East. With serious military reversals, yet seemingly miraculous survival, in the reign of Hezekiah (727–698 B.C.; 2 Kings 18–20), the influence of contemporary texts like Isa. 9:5–6 and 11:1–9 is apparent in this psalm. Other additions came during the postexilic period, again from the Isaian tradition (Isa. 11:10). As in other cases, one encounters as much an inspired tradition as an inspired text. This tradition kept alive the expectations of social justice. The memory of a world kingdom from the days of David and Solomon ensured that the messianic hope would in some way involve the whole world. For everyone it means that initial hope must collapse for a fulfillment greater than the first dreams.

After the introduction (Ps. 72:1–4), four short stanzas acclaim the right exercise of justice and the prosperity of the country (vv. 5–7, 8–11, 12–14, 15–16). The psalm ends with v. 17. Verses 18–19 mark a formal conclusion to the second book of the Psalter, v. 20 to the major collections of psalms from the guild of David.

The opening words of vv. 1–4, "God, give your decrees to the king," probably accompanied a ritual act of handing to the king the scroll of the laws; or, since Israel was an oral culture in which important political events were enacted publicly, the decrees may have been given by proclamation. "He shall judge your people" significantly points out that the people are God's, not the king's. "To judge" is repeated twenty-five times in the psalm, an indication of the seriousness of proper public order. The judgment extends first of all to the poor, who will loom large on the messianic canvas (Zeph. 2:3; 3:12; Isa. 41:17). If a good order embraces the poor and defenseless, then it will certainly be universal, and the mountains will resound with *shalom* (Heb., "peace"), the integral, all-embracing fulfillment.

Ps. 72:5–7 paints a panorama of peace and justice. To the extent that this vision reflects God's hopes, it will be eternal. Rain is a major symbol of abundance (Hos. 6:3; Isa. 45:8; 55:10–11; Joel 2:23).

Ps. 72:8–11 revives the vast extent of the kingdom, reached only in the days of David (Gen. 15:18; Exod. 23:31; Josh. 1:4; Zech 9:10), not the more limited boundaries of post-Solomonic days (Deut. 34:1–2; Judg. 20:1; 1 Kings 5:5). The reference to Tarshish (in western Spain) and Arabia comes from the postexilic work of Isa. 60:6–10. Episodes from the time of Solomon (1 Kings 10) were given a new symbolical meaning, so that the center of the world was no longer associated with the Davidic dynasty but in the Jerusalem Temple. Ps. 72:12–14 may have been sung as a sacred meal was placed before the people (2 Sam. 6:17–19; 1 Kings 8:62–66). The ritual blessing at the end (Ps. 72:17) is formulated from the promises to Abraham (Gen.12:2–3; 22:17–18), bestowed also upon Isaac (Gen. 26:1–5).

Ps. 72:18–19 concludes the second book (Pss. 42–72) and ties in well with the blessing of the preceding verse. Ps. 72:20 states a determination to add no new collection of psalms from the guild of David, perhaps in order to close the Psalter.

PSALMS 73–89

Book Three

The "Psalms of David" have ended, except for the straggler Psalm 86, and the major collection of Asaph is given (Pss. 73–83) to complete the "Elohist Psalter" (see commentary above introducing Book Two). A second group of psalms from the guild of Korah appears next (Pss. 84–88, except 86). The final, Psalm 89, comes from the repertoire of psalms for Davidic kings, though possibly composed by a non-Israelite close to the royal family. With the third book the three principal guilds of psalm writers have completed their contribution to the songs and prayers of Israel.

Psalm 73. Psalm 73, an Asaph psalm, treats the topic of retribution for good and wicked people more vigorously than Psalms 1 or 37, more confidently than Psalm 49 or Job, with less cynicism than Ecclesiastes. The writer, like the author of Psalm 16, appears at home in the sanctuary, something to be expected in the Asaph collection (1 Chron. 16:7, 37). The style of questioning and challenging God about human affairs appeared occasionally in early literature (Exod. 3:11; 5:22; 32:11) but became solidly placed in biblical tradition with Habakkuk (Hab. 1:5, 13b) and especially with the confessions of Jeremiah (Jer. 12:1–5; 15:10–21). The single earlier work of Asaph (Ps. 50) showed the ability to absorb and control prophetic elements otherwise antagonistic to Temple worship. The Hebrew text is not the best; 73:10 and 20 make little sense.

The psalm divides into a series of dialogues about the good and wicked: first, vv. 1–12, the unhappiness of the just (vv. 1–3) and the prosperity of the unjust (vv. 4–12); second, vv. 13–20, confiding to God the lot of the just (vv. 12–

17) and the unjust (vv. 18–20); and third, vv. 21–27, the crisis and its quick solution for the just (vv. 21–26) and for the unjust (v. 27). Verse 28 concludes within the Temple.

Verses 1–12 begin with absolute faith in the goodness of God. Whatever the problem, the biblical writer never doubts God's goodness, only how to reconcile it with human events. The first confession of Jeremiah begins pointedly: "You are faithful, Lord, but I must still argue against you" (Jer. 12:1); God's reply in v. 5 never answers the question but rather insists upon stronger faith (Jer. 12:5). In the Hebrew text of Ps. 73:1, "How good toward Israel is God!" "Israel" is generally changed to read "the just," a variation quite simple in the Hebrew, so that the personal dialogue of the psalm explicitly embraces all the people. Verses 4–5 sweep rhetorically beyond the truth. If one were to inquire of wicked people, they would admit to their share of sickness and troubles. Yet prosperous people can hide their problems more easily than the poor. Privacy is seldom a poor person's luxury. What the wicked cannot mask are the effects of luxury on their puffy faces (v. 7); their dangling jewelry reinforces their cruel indifference toward others (v. 6).

Verses 13–20 begin as emphatically as v. 1, with an effective use of sound in the Hebrew text: "Indeed, a pure heart is empty and useless!" The image of washing hands comes from the Temple ritual (Ps. 26:6) and indicates ambiguous feelings toward the Temple that the psalmist will resolve in 73:28. Yet for the psalmist to walk in the attractive way of the wicked would end in treacherous action toward "the generation of your children," to the covenant faith of one's offspring, who are really God's children (v. 15; Gen. 17:7). Ps. 73:17 may refer to night vigils in the Temple (Ps. 42:4), where in silent darkness the psalmist finds the strengthening light of God's word (Ps. 139:11–12).

Ps. 73:21–27 begins in desperation, always the moment of surrendering, either to despair or, heroically, to God. God grants a passing intuition of eternity, the memory of which sustains a person for years afterward. Eternity, however, is not time but the endless embrace of Yahweh. The language of vv. 23–26 recalls Ps. 16:5 and is exquisite with strong repetitions of "you" and "I" (73:23) or with the contrast between a heart like flesh wasting away and a heart with the endurance of a rock because of its experience of the Lord's delight (v. 25). Within the Temple, the psalmist adds a new story of salvation to affirm for all the people the traditional salvation history of Israel (v. 28).

Psalm 74. Perhaps only a Temple guild as self-confident as Asaph could write so realistically concerning the tragedy of 587 B.C., the destruction of the Temple and the Exile of Israel, all the while sustaining faith in the covenant upon which Yahweh seems to have reneged (v. 20). For these various reasons Psalm 74, along with Psalm 79, enables Jewish people to commemorate national tragedies, so that the absent God can be tracked down by intuitions of faith. Such catastrophies as the breaching of the city walls by the Babylonians (2 Kings 25:3–4), the burning of the Temple (2 Kings 25:8–10), and the murder of Gedaliah by fellow Israelites (2 Kings 25:25) were commemorated by days of mourning and fasting during the Exile and afterward (Zech. 7; 8:19), eventually subsumed in the one day of Yom Kippur (Lev. 16). Very different from prophecy, this psalm never puts any blame on the people's sins; it is too close to the agony to speculate about the cause of such a tragedy.

The grammar of verbs within the psalm leads to its explanation and divisions: imperatives addressed to God that Yahweh live up to promises (Ps. 74:1–3, 18–23); perfect or completed tense of verbs representing the total victory of the enemy (vv. 4–9, 12–17); and imperfect or incompleted tense of verbs for Yahweh's impotent distance from Israel's tragedy (vv. 10–11). If one recognizes chiastic structure here, then God is at the center, dealing with divine anger by remaining indifferent and inactive. The psalm enables Israelites to bring the silence of broken hearts before the silent Yahweh. Implied in the presence of God is a faith, albeit plunged in dark agony, that God affirms what is happening and that this God remains faithful to the covenant.

Verses 1–3 begin with the challenging "Why?" frequent enough in Israel's laments (Pss. 10:1; 22:2; 44:24). Yahweh is not asked but told, with the imperative mood of the verb, to "remember" the Mosaic covenant (Exod. 34:6–7) and the promises to Jerusalem (Ps. 46). God is told to walk through the ruins of the desecrated holy place, as though God may have forgotten what has happened.

Ps. 74:4–9 allows one to walk through the stages of Jerusalem's destruction: v. 4, the enemy has broken through the walls and set up victory banners within the city; vv. 5–6, they plunder and destroy; and v. 7, the Temple is put to the torch. In Isa. 63:7–64:11 the agony of such moments turns into the question "Why do you remain silent, Lord?" the only kind of prayer possible. The denial of prophetic presence in Ps. 74:9 overlooks Jeremiah, who remained in Jerusalem throughout the final chaotic days. Evidently the author's problem is precisely with a Jeremiah who announced such an outcome as God's punishment against a sinful people (Jer. 26; 28). Religious people such as those in the guild of Asaph need time to suffer silently before discussing prophetic predic-

tions. The psalmist refuses to accept the ruins of Jerusalem and Temple as a "sign" that God spoke through the prophets. In exile, the author of Second Isaiah argued repeatedly on Jeremiah's side against the position of this psalm (Isa. 44:24–45:7). Other writers, earlier (1 Sam. 3:1; Lam. 2:9) as well as later (1 Macc. 4:46; 9:27), have recognized the silent void of prophecy.

Ps. 74:12–17, again with the perfect tense of completed action, compares the destruction of Jerusalem with the chaos before the earth was created. If the psalmist confesses that God created good order and fruitful life out of such uncontrollable darkness, then the implication is whispered: God can do it again. This description of creation is one of the closest in the Bible to Canaanite descriptions. In the silence of God, the psalmist felt obliged to reach beyond the nonexistent orthodoxy, for how can creeds exist in the absence of the God whom they confess? Verses 18–23 conclude this strange statement of faith ordering God to "remember" and to "rise" and "defend," again to "remember" and not to "forget."

Psalm 75. The question of retribution in Psalm 75 recalls wisdom literature (Pss. 1; 37), yet the focusing upon God as judge leads in the direction either of prophetic psalms (Ps. 50) or even of eschatological psalms (Pss. 96–99). Deliverance from injustice points to thanksgiving. A vigorous style (75:5–6) and strong imagery (vv. 4, 9) point one to the Temple. In fact, Temple liturgy may be the clue to appreciating this work: v. 2, a communal expression of thanksgiving; vv. 3–6, an oracle from the Lord, delivered by a priest or Temple prophet; vv. 7–9, the verdict upon the wicked, recited by a choral group; and vv. 10–11, a conclusion of praise sung by an individual cantor.

The call for thanksgiving in v. 2 associates God's imminent judgment against the wicked with God's "wondrous deeds" in Israel's history, as these are acclaimed and symbolically reenacted at the Temple. The litany of God's saving acts explains the divine name (Exod. 3:13–15).

The oracle in Ps. 75:3–6 is placed at a fixed time, possibly on one of Israel's three major feast days (Lev. 23). Ps. 75:4, typical of other Temple services, introduces Canaanite images of the world's collapse until God brings stability (Pss. 46:2–4; 74:12–17). "Horns," a symbol of strength from animal life (Ps. 22:22; Dan. 8), came to be associated with the corners of the altar and divine strength (Lev. 4:7; Ps. 118:27). The latter use may have prompted the psalmist to think of the animal-like force and fury that the wicked directed against the Lord as though they were divine.

Ps. 75:7–9, reaching to the four corners of

the universe, east, west, desert (to the south of Israel), and mountains (to the north), announces the presence of the judge, lifting up the lowly, humbling the proud (1 Sam. 2:3–8), pronouncing the sentence of punishment under the symbol of "cup," sometimes a good omen (Pss. 16:5; 23:5) but here one of pain, even agony (Ps. 11:6; Isa. 51:17–22).

Psalm 76. The concern for divine judgment against the opponents of Israel, whether internally within the ranks of the chosen people (Ps. 75) or externally from foreign invaders as in Psalm 76, continues to dominate the Asaph psalms. Psalm 76 may well be one of the earliest in the Psalter, for it refers to Jerusalem as the capital of Judah and Israel, therefore it can be no later than Solomon. Ps. 76:11 may allude to David's victory over the Edomites (2 Sam. 8:13–14) and over Hadadezer at the entry of Hamath in Lebanon (2 Sam. 8:3–12). Theologically, Psalm 76 lines up with Korah psalms (Pss. 46–48), though it is less doctrinal, more empirical, and consequently earlier.

Psalm 76 speaks about God gloriously enthroned at Jerusalem in vv. 2–4, addresses God about past victories in vv. 5–7 and about new victories in vv. 8–10, and again speaks mostly about God in vv. 11–13. Verses 2–4 provide an excellent setting by recalling the ancient and mysterious figure of "Melchizedek, priest and king of Salem," who acclaimed Abraham's victory over the four kings of the north by a ritual meal of bread and wine (Gen. 14:18–21). The Hebrew words for "peace," "his name," and "there" (i.e., at Jerusalem) sound much alike and tie these lines together. In Ps. 76:8–10 the battles are not fought by Israel but by the Lord, so that the heavenly and earthly temples merge together and an awesome silence stuns all human forces into immobility (Hab. 2:20). This is a theophany of justice, not of wonder, as God arises to save the poor and defenseless (Ps. 75:8). Ps. 76:11 may refer to Edom and Hamath, or these words can be translated for what they mean, "humanity" (the actual reading, "Edom," requires a slight modification) and "anger," so that the sense would be, "The anger of all humanity will be turned to your praise," certainly the sense of the entire psalm.

Psalm 77. Although composed in the singular, Psalm 77 does not reflect an isolated person in the guild of Asaph but speaks for all Israel at a time of sorrow. The tragedy is not named, but the association with the preceding psalm implies a military defeat or some public calamity. Despite the intensity lurking beneath silent darkness (vv. 3, 6), the psalmist remains detached from God's anger and Israel's sins. If we take seriously the presence of selah or "pause" after vv. 4, 10, and 16, the psalm divides as

follows: vv. 2–4, introductory call for help from God; vv. 5–10, lament; vv. 11–16, a confession of faith; vv. 17–20, an ancient hymn of praise; and v. 21, a conclusion of confidence. The reference to "Jeduthun" in the title, as in Pss. 39 and 62, brings together psalms of subtle gentleness.

In 77:2–4 the psalmist cries aloud to God, if only to break the pall of silence over the night vigil (Pss. 6:7; 22:3; 32:4). Ps. 77:4 recalls the refrain in Psalms 42–43.

The opportunity for meditating during the night leads, in 77:5–10, to inner perplexity. Beneath the silence there stirs serious anxiety, yet such human emotions lead to the remembrance of God's compassion. It is only a question, but for the person of faith, a question of critical consequence: has God forgotten pity and compassion? If so, then God has reneged on the covenantal promise and revelation in Exod. 34:6–7. The confession of faith in Ps. 77:11–16 begins in a surprising way: has God changed? The remembrance (one of the key words in this psalm along with meditation) of God's deeds in Israel's history revives faith. The reference to foreign peoples suggests that this psalm addresses military defeat.

Verses 17–21 represent an ancient hymn, inserted here as a conclusion to the Temple service. The armed forces of foreign countries, massed against Jerusalem, evoke the remembrance of the ancient creation stories where God overcomes chaos and brings order and prosperity. The Temple symbolized this victory and assured its repetition (Pss. 46; 74:12–17; 93). Typical of other texts (Exod. 15:1–18; Isa. 51:9–11), this hymn associates the renewal of creation with the Exodus out of Egypt.

Psalm 78. The opening lines of Psalm 78 (vv. 1–11) bear the marks of wisdom literature (Prov. 3:1; 4:2). Individual verses are chiseled finely as in Proverbs where each two or four lines serve as independent units. In Psalm 78, however, these verses are like gems in an elegant setting, as each blends into the continuous epic style. The psalm also diverges from wisdom literature, at least as known in Proverbs, Ecclesiastes, and Job, by its concern for Israel's history, its extended treatment of its subject (to become the second longest poem in the Psalter), and in its strong testimony for the Jerusalem Temple.

Psalm 78 shows its closest affinity to Deuteronomy 32 and appears, as a historical epic composed by Jerusalem priests to explain the destruction of Shiloh, where the Ark resided in the early days of Samuel (1 Sam. 1:1–7:2), and the orientation of all Israel around the new shrine at Jerusalem. Yet history is not recited simply to know the past but rather to be assured of God's direction in later ages. Most of all, the psalm insists that catastrophes, which seem to break continuity and invalidate divine

469

promises, fit into a larger pattern under God's direction. After God's mysterious control, the next most decisive factor in history is Israel's fidelity or infidelity.

The psalm presumes the Philistine destruction of Shiloh in 1050 B.C. (1 Sam. 4) and the transfer of the Ark to the Jerusalem Temple by Solomon (1 Kings 8). It also envisages a bonding of the northern and southern tribes in worship at Jerusalem, consequently suggesting a date of composition either during the reign of Solomon (970–924 B.C.) or, better, toward the end of the reign of King Hezekiah (727–698 B.C.). At this latter time, Jerusalem emerged from near destruction and extended its control again over the north (2 Chron. 30:1–22). Events of collapse and restoration had emphasized the mysterious ways of Israel's history under God's direction. Important for the theology of history in this psalm is God's plan, first, for a unified Israel and, second, its location in Judah and Jerusalem instead of in the northern tribes and Shiloh.

The psalm begins and ends in the land of Israel, its theological point of concern. It breaks chronological order, regarding the earlier events in Egypt, to indicate that history was not being recited for its own sake. After a lengthy, solemn introduction (Ps. 78:1–11; Deut. 32:1–6), the first recital extends from v. 1 to v. 41, the second from v. 42 to v. 72. Each of these, like Deuteronomy 32, is subdivided: first, God's gracious acts in vv. 12–16, 42–55, and Deut. 32:7–14; second, Israel's rebellion in vv. 17–20, 56–58, and Deut. 32:15–18; third, divine anger and punishment in vv. 21–32, 59–64, and Deut. 32:19–25; and fourth, judgment and new beginning in vv. 33–41, 65–72, and Deut. 32:26–43.

The introduction in Ps. 78:1–11 follows a well-known pattern (Deut. 32:1–6; Ps. 50:1–6). These opening verses combine, like the rest of the psalm, remembrance of God's mighty deeds for Israel with warning and rebuke, exhortation and promise. The speaker would be an authoritative person at Jerusalem with a thorough command of tradition, manifesting a profound faith in God's presence not only in glorious moments but also in disaster and punishment. That speaker affirms nothing breaks the continuity of Israel's history.

Ps. 78:2 refers to proverbs (comparisons) and obscure riddles (as in the Samson story, Judg. 14:12) or to words spoken by God to prophets (Num. 12:8; Ezek. 17:2). Such sayings require contemplation and a heart willing to be challenged by God. Matt. 13:35 states that Jesus too spoke in parables, so that as people pondered the comparison, unanticipated insights into the mystery of God came to light. Ps. 78:8–11 is addressed principally to the northern tribes, since eventually the psalmist appeals to them to seek unity with all Israel at the Jerusalem Temple. The ancestors (v. 8) are the patriarchs, parents of all twelve tribes.

The point of comparison in vv. 12–32 is always to be located in God's gracious deeds for Israel. These wondrous acts are principally those in the wilderness of Sinai, providing food, drink, and direction. Yet the Hebrew text in v. 12 centers not so much upon wonders as upon "you, that very God, working wonders." The participle keeps the action in the present tense, implying that now God is doing the same. Yet, in vv. 17–20 the people forget quickly and "test God," as in Exod. 16:3; 17:2, 7; and Ps. 95:9. In Num. 11:4–6 the problem was not food and drink, which they had, but rather the kind of food, "the cucumbers, melons, leeks, onion, and garlic," which they craved. Testing God turned into a demand for a different kind of God, one who catered to sensuality and selfishness.

God's anger flared against them in Ps. 78:21–32, verses that still concentrate upon God's goodness and strength in caring for Israel. Anger is the exasperation of goodness taken for granted and betrayed or, as in v. 21, goodness that is not accepted as a permanent quality in God but only as an occasional exercise that cannot be counted upon in the future. Faith here is not a body of doctrine but adherence to the person of God as gracious and faithful (cf. Exod. 34:6–7).

Despite the serious break in the continuity (the previous generation was not to enter the promised land, Num. 14:20–23), the next generation will participate in the same promises (Ps. 78:33–41). These verses repeat, only now more reflectively, what had already been said in the preceding section. Verse 38 is the pivotal verse for the entire Psalter, the halfway mark of its 5,896 verses; Ps. 80:14 contains the middle letter of the Psalter. Verse 38 emphasizes that at the center of biblical religion must be a confession of a merciful God who turns anger away from the people. This verse was recited with Ps. 78:38 and Deut. 28:58–59 and 29:8, when a person was scourged forty lashes less one (cf. 2 Cor. 11:24).

Within Ps. 78:42–72 the second major recital of Israel's history is given. It begins with the plagues in Egypt, chronologically out of place but theologically well placed. Because the preceding section ended with the new generation, which will enter the land and be brought into contact with the Canaanites, this new section emphasizes God's preferential care for Israel against the non-Israelites. In the plagues God was acting for his people against foreign oppression. The plagues are adapted to the produce of Israel, vines and sycamores instead of the flax and barley stricken in Egypt (Exod. 9:31). In Ps. 78:54 God not only brings the people into the Holy Land but also establishes a major sanctuary for the Ark of the covenant at

Shiloh. After the account of God's gracious deeds for Israel (vv. 42–55), the people rebel (vv. 56–58), and God allows the holy city of Shiloh to be leveled and the Ark to be captured by the Philistines (vv. 59–64). Again this serious break in continuity did not end God's fidelity to the covenant. A new generation and a new Temple at Jerusalem become the pledge of the future.

The psalm ends, affirming that this sacred history teaches that God's skillful hand and dedicated heart are always guiding the people. No break nor collapse snaps the bond of God's presence. God continues to lead the people into their destined future. The end of the Northern Kingdom did mean the end of the northern people's participation in the covenant. Many new breaks will occur, like the destruction of Jerusalem, yet Israel's history proceeds with God's direction. The citations of this psalm, or allusions to it, in the NT point out the strength of this promise for the future: v. 2 in Matt. 13:35; v. 3 in 1 John 1:1–4; v. 18 in 1 Cor. 10:9; v. 24 in John 6:31; v. 37 in Acts 8:21; and v. 44 in Rev. 16:4.

Psalm 79. Asaph, the author of this present collection of psalms, tackles hard theological and pastoral problems. With the backing of Deuteronomy, Psalm 78 discussed at length such abrupt changes as the destruction of the holy city of Shiloh and of the Northern Kingdom and concluded that these do not break the continuity of God's plans for the chosen people. Their life and worship will continue at Jerusalem. Psalm 79 faces up to the tragedy of Jerusalem's destruction. The guild of Asaph is courageously addressing Israel's national destiny: in Psalm 78, past history; in Psalm 79, the disaster of Jerusalem's reduction to ashes; in Psalm 80, the restoration of the nation; and in Psalm 81, the national return to liturgical worship.

The reflective style of Psalm 78 is impossible with the memory still tortured with agony and guilt. Psalm 79 becomes one of the most plaintive pieces in the Psalter. Many religious attitudes convulsively relate with one another: the sins of Israel and those of the nations; defilement of the Temple and God's glory; and God's compassion and the groans of prisoners. The psalmist supports his faith by delaying over lines from many other biblical laments: v. 1 from Jer. 26:18; v. 4 from Ps. 44:14; v. 5 from Ps. 89:47; vv. 6–7 from Jer. 10:25; v. 8 from Ps. 142:7; v. 9 from Pss. 23:3; 25:11; 31:4; v. 10 from Ps. 115:2; v. 11 from Ps. 102:21; v. 12 from Ps. 89:51–52; and v. 13 from Ps. 100:3.

Ps. 79:1–4 gives a description of ruin; vv. 5–7, a prayer against the enemy; vv. 8–9, a request for pardon; vv. 10–12, a call for revenge; and v. 13, a promise of thanksgiving. Today Psalm 79 is recited by Jews on Friday evening at

the western wall, the only section of the Second Temple in existence, and on the ninth day of Ab (the fifth month of the Jewish calendar), commemorating the various destructions of Jerusalem.

In vv. 1–4 the psalm opens onto a Temple defiled, a city strewn with corpses and bleeding with the blood of God's covenanted people. Neighboring nations are not horrified, not even moved to compassion; they scornfully joke about Jerusalem. The psalmist draws phrases from the prophets, especially from Jeremiah, who announced that if Jerusalem continued in sin, it was doomed (Jer. 7:30; 32:34). Once Jeremiah had been ridiculed (Jer. 28) and threatened with death (Jer. 26) for making this prediction.

Ps. 79:5–12 pours out reactions pell-mell, oblivious to some of the contradictions: revenge against the enemy and an appeal to God's compassion, the sacrilegious scene and the appeal to God's glory. It is more than an issue of Israel's distress, it involves God's honor. The psalmist will shame God into acting on Israel's behalf. In v. 12 the psalmist requests the sevenfold vengeance of Cain (Gen. 4:15). The final verse returns to the theology of Psalm 78. Future generations will look back upon this tragedy. It did not break the covenant or deny the fidelity of God. In God's subsequent compassion they will find a motive for their faith and thanksgiving.

Psalm 80. Typical of a psalm, as the title indicates, to be sung like Psalms 45, 60, and 69 "according to [the melody of] Lilies," Psalm 80 is characterized by great themes handled with restraint and nobility. A double national tragedy, the collapse of the Northern Kingdom and a severe setback for the Southern Kingdom, is being lamented. Yet the traumatic effects are moderated by epithets acclaiming God as savior, by confessions of faith and a refrain. The psalm combines hope with a memory of great sorrow, optimism about a restoration of northern tribes with realism about new blows against the Southern Kingdom. Psalm 80 reflects the preaching of Jeremiah in chaps. 30–31. A likely date for composition falls within the reign of Josiah (640–609 B.C.).

Though 80:15–18 is textually damaged, one may detect a sequence of prayer and ceremony: vv. 1–3, an opening confession of faith, almost in the style of a hymn, with a petition for help; vv. 5–7, a lament of quiet agony; vv. 8–12, a second confession of faith acknowledging the gift of the promised land; and vv. 13–20, another lament almost with a touch of panic and again a reflective petition for help.

In vv. 2–4 the opening title for God, "shepherd of Israel," shows the preference of the Asaph psalms for pastoral images (Pss. 74:2;

78:52; 79:13) and for the northern tribes of Ephraim and Manasseh. God as gloriously "enthroned [over the mercy seat above the Ark] between the Cherubim" (Exod. 25:17–22; Ezek. 1) contrasts with the hidden, even pitiable presence of God within Israel's recent history. Such is the type of understatement in many Asaph psalms. The refrain alludes to the priestly blessing in Num. 6:24–26 (Ps. 67:2) and adds: "bring us back," a request for national restoration and for inward turning to God.

Ps. 80:5–7 echoes lines from Psalm 42, in which the memory of Temple worship and its sacred meals becomes a sad way to describe the silencing of these rituals. Ps. 80:6 in the Hebrew ends with a vague allusion to "triple tears," which Rabbi David Kimchi (ca. A.D. 1160–1235) accommodated to the three exiles: all the people in Egypt; the northern tribes in Assyria; the southern tribes in Babylon.

Verses 9–12 recall, like Ps. 44:2–9, the early redemptive acts of God, especially the settlement in the promised land. The psalmist generously draws the boundaries according to the widest limits (2 Sam. 8:3; 1 Kings 5:1, 5; Ps. 72:8). Whatever be the surface details of life, the psalmist will not compromise the promises received from long tradition. Israel's understanding of these promises had to collapse completely before they could be revived in a new, more spiritual kingdom of God.

Many of Israel's earthly sanctuaries, once the places of worship for the patriarchs upon entering the land of Canaan (Gen. 12:6, 8; 28:10–22) and later important centers of instruction and worship, are now silenced in their charred ruins (Ps. 80:13–20). God nonetheless remains enthroned in a heavenly sanctuary (v. 15; Ps. 11:4), able to fulfill ancient promises. Ps. 80:19, which treats the gift of "new life," literally asks for revival of the nation. Out of such resurgence Israel will develop a belief in personal immortality (Dan. 12:1–3).

Just as Ps. 78:38 is the middle verse of the entire Psalter, Ps. 80:14 contains the middle letter 'ayin in the Hebrew word "forest." In Hebrew manuscripts it is always elevated above the line. The name of this letter means "eye," with the spiritual sense that the eye of a compassionate God is always upon Israel.

Psalm 81. Psalms 81 and 95 have much in common but also differ significantly: compare Ps. 95:9 with Ps. 81:8. Psalm 95 reflects Jerusalem theology and ritual; Psalm 81, with explicit reference to Joseph, the religious thought and ceremony of the northern sanctuaries. Yet Psalm 81 survived at the Jerusalem Temple. Its points of contact with Deuteronomy indicate a time for final editing during the reform of King Josiah (640–609 B.C.; 2 Kings 22:1–23:30). "The day of our feast" (Ps. 81:4) is likely the Feast of Tabernacles or Succoth, the final harvest festival, announced with trumpets (Lev. 23:33–43), at times simply called "the feast" (1 Kings 8:2; Neh. 8:14).

After the solemn introduction (Ps. 81:2–6b) and a prophetic call for silence (v. 6c), two alternate rituals are provided: one that speaks about Israel in the third person (vv. 7 and 12–17) and another addressed to Israel in the second person (vv. 8–11). Each concludes with a sacred meal.

Verses 2–6 summon a full orchestra for the opening hymn. "New moon" refers to the New Year's celebration announced by trumpet blasts (Lev. 23:23–25); the "full moon" came on the fifteenth day when the Feast of Tabernacles began (Neh. 8:1–18). Temple prophets gave their instruction at times in parables and riddles (Ps. 78:2; Num. 24:4, 16) and spoke about hidden knowledge received in visions (Mic. 3:6–7).

Ps. 81:7, 12–17, a prophetic warning against hardness and sin, may have been preceded by a proclamation of Scripture (Deut. 26:1–15). God delivers the people over to the consequences of their hard, stubborn hearts (Deut. 29:18; Jer. 3:17), yet suffering can purify and renew the people (Jer. 2:19, 30; 31:18). "The finest wheat" and "honey from the rock" combine a memory of God's care for Israel in the wilderness (Exod. 17:1–7) and the abundance of the promised land flowing with milk and honey (Exod. 3:8, 17; Ezek. 47:1–12).

Ps. 81:8–11 begins with a reference to God's thunderous descent upon Mount Sinai, a secret place of revelation. After condemning the worship of Canaanite gods, Yahweh declares, "It is I, Yahweh, your God, bringing you up from the land of Egypt." The participial form of the Hebrew combines praise with contemporaneity: Sinai and the Exodus are now.

Psalm 82. The prophetic speech in Psalm 82 summons wicked judges before the divine tribunal (v. 1), marshals the evidence against them (vv. 2–4), pronounces the verdict and sentence (vv. 5–7), and ends with an acclamation of God's universal power (v. 8). Judges are called "gods" (Heb. 'elohim) in that they stand in the place of God (Exod. 4:16; Ps. 45:7). If they do not act as Yahweh would, then they are relegated to the status of false Canaanite gods, to be condemned and swept away (Isa. 14:12–15).

The trial is placed in the heavenly assembly (Ps. 89:6–9; 1 Kings 22:19–23) and based on impartial care for the needy (Lev. 19:15). The final judgment as announced by Jesus is to depend on the same criteria (Matt. 25:31–46). Ps. 82:5, in announcing the chaotic dissolution of the earth with its evil, declares the strong bonds between the moral and physical order.

Psalm 83. The last of the Asaph psalms, typically composed with strength and broad perspective, is also the final psalm in the Elohist Psalter (see commentary above introducing Book Two). Psalm 83 may also be one of the earliest in the entire book of Psalms. Its geographical references reflect the hostile nations circling Israel in the period of the judges (1250–1050 B.C.; Judg. 4–5, 7–8), except that the reference to Assyria comes from the ninth century. It is possible, however, that a much later author drew these names from the ancient past to symbolize all angry forces through the ages (cf. Isa. 66:19). (To identify the nations listed in Ps. 83:7–12, → entries for the individual names.)

After the call for help (v. 2), a long lament voices the fear and anger of Israel as armies march against its land (vv. 3–9). Lines similar to the prophetic oracles against the nations follow, drawing down a divine curse upon them (vv. 10–19). These sections may have originated in sanctuary services before war (1 Sam. 4:4–9; 7:5–9), but the prophets turn them into a theological discussion of the role of the nations in the salvation of Israel (cf. Amos 1:3–2:16; Isa. 13–23). This final section transforms the military assualt into an attack upon Yahweh as supreme God. Such an early text is not announcing the worship of Yahweh by other nations, only that Yahweh controls world events for the sake of the chosen people, Israel, and that survivors from these nations will join Israel, a phenomenon happening continuously from the time of the Exodus out of Egypt (Exod. 12:38).

Psalm 84. The second group of psalms from the guild of Korah (Pss. 84–85, 87–88) begins with the same melancholic tone as the first (Pss. 42–49). Psalm 84, along with Psalms 63 and 120–134, may have been sung on pilgrimage to the sanctuary. In 84:7 the reference to rain may locate the psalm at the festival of Tabernacles (Lev. 23:23–43; Zech. 14:16–19). The psalm is structured as follows: vv. 2–4, a meditative introduction; vv. 5–8, on the journey; vv. 9–12a, prayers and reflection at the Temple; and vv. 12b–13, preparations for the return journey. The Hebrew text is frequently difficult and variously translated.

Verses 2–4 begin with peaceful sadness. The desire for God touches every side of the psalmist's person: soul, the center of breathing and responding to life; heart, the center of reflection and understanding; and flesh, the site of deeply felt weakness. The mention of a bird adds a touch of delicate sensitivity (Gen. 8:6–12; Jer. 4:25).

Ps. 84:5–6 begins as v. 13 ends, with a formula about the happiness of dwelling in the house of the Lord and trusting always in the Lord (Ps. 1:1). The two moments coalesce in "ever singing the Lord's praises." In 84:7a the rare and difficult Hebrew word *baka'* with a slight emendation can be read as "tears." The ancient church hymn to Mary, "Salve Regina," followed the Latin Vg. with a phrase common in ordinary speech: "in this [earthly] vale of tears." Tears offer a parallel to the early rain in the second part of this verse. Yet that passage too is not absolutely safe textually and can be translated, "The choir intones blessings [for God]."

After a ceremonial prayer for the king (vv. 9–10), the psalmist's personal reflection is recorded (vv. 11–12a) and, finally, the prayer for a safe journey home (vv. 12b–13).

Psalm 85. Psalm 85 is a national lament not nearly as intense as those of Asaph (Pss. 74; 80); it is moderated by ritual and the repetition of key words. Ritual, in fact, may explain the unusual structure. The ceremony begins with a hymn of confidence (85:2–4) and follows with lament and prayer (vv. 5–8). An oracle of peace from a Temple prophet marks the centerpiece of the service (vv. 9–10), and afterward there is a meditation upon the oracle (vv. 11–14). The Hebrew text exhibits an effective use of key words: *shub*, or "return," in vv. 2b, 4b, 5a, 7a, 9b; *'eretz*, or "land," in vv. 2a, 10b, 12a, 13b; *shalom*, or "peace," in vv. 9b, 11b, 14b; and *chesed*, or the Lord's "steadfast love," in vv. 8a, 10b, 11a. For these and other reasons, the psalm may be a prayer for a return from Exile and for a new era of peace in the promised land.

Verses 2–4 focus at once on land, always the recipient of God's blessings when the people are faithful (Amos 9:13–15), otherwise the victim of devastation (Jer. 14:1–22; Joel 1–2; Isa. 24). The new exodus cannot start without forgiveness of sin (Isa. 40:1–2; 43:25).

Ps. 85:5–8 borders on the outer edge of impatience. Must suffering for one's sins continue indefinitely (Pss. 74:1; 77:8–10; Isa. 63:7–64:11)? As at the end of Psalm 44, the final appeal is to *chesed*, the steadfast love uniting Yahweh and Israel in covenant. Ps. 85:9–10 responds with an oracle pronouncing peace, yet peace with its own expectations (Isa. 57:19–21; Jer. 14:13). Therefore the warning is given in Ps. 85:9b, "Let them not return to foolishness." In meditating upon the oracle in vv. 11–14, the psalmist links the gift of new peace with the covenantal promises of Yahweh (Exod. 34:6–7). This "truth" or "fidelity" springs from the earth in the righteous living of people.

Psalm 86. The sole psalm of David in Book Three and an individual's lament, Psalm 86 remains an anomaly in a section otherwise dealing with national sorrows. Its contacts are with other "Psalms of David" in Book One or in Book Five (Pss. 138–145). The psalm, moreover, is more a filigree of phrases from elsewhere in the Psalter than an independent creation (e.g., v. 1b from Ps. 40:18a; v. 2 from Ps. 25:20; v. 3 from Ps. 57:2–3). Verse 14 is lifted out of Ps. 54:5 and breaks the spirit of gratitude here. This anthological method becomes even more common in Book Five (so Pss. 135; 143).

A style such as this presumes time to moderate one's initial shock over tragedy and to meditate. More verses deal with confidence and thanksgiving in the center of the psalm than with lament at the beginning and end. The transitional v. 11, asking Yahweh to "teach me your way," begs for still more time to enable more profound appreciation.

After the initial call for help (vv. 1–7), a hymn of confidence is voiced (vv. 8–10) and then one of gratitude (vv. 11–15). The psalm ends with renewed lament and prayer (vv. 16–17). The covenant theology of Exodus 34 returns at important moments: in v. 5, to induce God to respond and in v. 15, to sustain thanksgiving. Yahweh shows up differently from all other gods (v. 8) precisely because of his loving-kindness and fidelity and therefore a penchant to forgive (which Voltaire called God's *metier* or normal life-style). These qualities that make Yahweh to be truly God define what the Bible means by divinity and show the complete deficiency of all other pretenders at divinity. This monotheism leads to a rare biblical statement on universal salvation (v. 9). The same sequence from Yahweh's extraordinary kindness and forgiveness, to the nothingness of other gods, to universal salvation marks the writing of Second Isaiah. It may have been this prophet's interpretation of the Mosaic covenant that led to Psalm 86.

Psalm 87. Textually one of the most difficult in the Psalter, Psalm 87 leaves us guessing about its meaning. The phrase three times repeated, "this one [or everyone, in v. 5] was born there," in a context speaking of major foreign countries, leaves the first impression of new life for all nations by their worship of Yahweh. Their names will be recorded in the book of the living (v. 6; Pss. 56:9; 69:29; 139:16). Perhaps like other isolated statements about the salvation of the nations (Amos 9:7; Isa. 49:6), this one was too important to suppress and yet too difficult to integrate with other biblical positions—so Psalm 87 was neglected. It adds a special contribution to other psalms from the Korah guild honoring Jerusalem (Pss. 46–48).

The psalm may possibly have a more restricted meaning, referring not to foreign nations but to individual converts from their midst (Isa. 44:5) or simply to Israelites living among them and always tempted to apostasy.

This sequence is suggested: Ps. 87:1–3, Yahweh's choice of Zion; vv. 4–6, Zion, mother of all; and v. 7, conclusion.

Psalm 88. Completely isolated and close to death from serious illness, without the luxury of community liturgies or traditional prayers as in Psalm 86, the psalmist is hardly a human being, only a cadaver ready for the grave in Psalm 88. This is not a theological commentary on death but a prayerful diary of personal depression. For this psalmist, all answers to the absurdity of death smack of pious simplicity; prayer is the only refuge. "Dialogue" may best direct us through the psalm: 88:2–3, calling to God for a hearing; vv. 4–6, a lament oblivious of God; vv. 7–9, dialogue with a hostile God; vv. 10–13, another appeal to God; vv. 14–17, again the silent God; and vv. 18–19, conclusion.

The title attributes the psalm to the family of "Heman" within the guild of Korah, a group well known for liturgical songs and leadership (1 Chron. 6:17–18; 16:41–42). The psalmist, however, in sickness experiences a silent isolation from worship. "Ezrahite" indicates a native-born person, possibly from early Canaanite stock (Lev. 19:33–34). "Mahalath," from the word for sickness, suggests a sad melody (Ps. 53).

In 88:2–3 the appeal to "God, my salvation" extends through day and night. After setting up this contrast, the psalmist, in vv. 4–6, suddenly turns completely away from God and peers into the dark, inactive, formless experience of Sheol (Ps. 6:6). In 88:7–9 the psalmist paradoxically turns to God from this pit where God is said to remember no one. The sickness, like leprosy (Lev. 13), puts friends, who have once experienced one's deepest thoughts, at a distance. Again in Ps. 88:10–13 the psalmist appeals to God from Sheol, introducing aspects of Israel's creed and worship into the unclean abode of the dead; these lines bristle with contradictions. Verse 13 had led to this psalm's use as a traditional morning prayer, the normal time for interceding with God (Ps. 5:4; 30:6). The psalm concludes in 88:18–19, very similar to the end of the first half (vv. 8–9).

Psalm 89. Psalm 89 provides a commentary on 2 Samuel 7 and the perpetual promises to the Davidic family. By a skillful transfer of titles from God to David, this psalm places in the king's hands the power of God to bring peace out of chaos, to induce life out of sterility. Psalm 89 belongs to the repertoire of royal psalms (Pss. 2; 45; 72; 110). Located at the end of Book Three, it links this book (with only one psalm of David, Ps. 86) with the Davidic sponsorship of psalm writing. The psalm ends with a long lament, as though God had reneged upon divine promises by permitting a major military defeat.

Psalm 89 is frequently quoted or alluded to in the NT: vv. 4–5 in Peter's Pentecost discourse (Acts 2:30); v. 21 in Paul's speech at Pisidian Antioch (Acts 13:22); v. 11 in Mary's canticle (Luke 1:51); and v. 53 in Zechariah's canticle (Luke 1:68).

The psalm divides into three major sections, stitched together by the key words of covenant, steadfast love, and fidelity (Exod. 34:6–7). Quite a few other parallels help achieve a compact unity within this long psalm. First is a hymn honoring Yahweh: vv. 2–3, invitation; vv. 4–5, oracle for the king; and vv. 6–19, Yahweh's supremacy over all gods (vv. 6–9), over the universe (vv. 10–15), and over the liturgy (vv. 16–19). Second is an oracle honoring the Davidic king: v. 20a, introduction; vv. 20b–28, the king as Yahweh's representative; and vv. 29–38, divine promises to the king. Third is a lament over the rejection of the king: vv. 39–53.

For a further explanation of the title's reference to an Ezrahite (v. 1), see the commentary above on Ps. 88:1. The opening lines (89:2–3), in announcing a hymn of praise for Yahweh, center upon the covenantal qualities of Yahweh as merciful and faithful (Exod. 34:6–7); these are linked with the stability of the heavens, for who can ever disturb the movement of the sun and stars (so Jer. 31:35–37). Ps. 89:4–5 transfers the same words and image to the dynasty of David. Royalty receives unconditional, divine promises, as in 2 Samuel 7, and so exhibits more stability than the Mosaic covenant, dependent upon the people's obedience. The king, as "my chosen one," represents all Israel, God's chosen people (Exod. 19:5–6; Deut. 7).

The cosmic hymn to Yahweh (Ps. 89:6–19) is sung in part by the heavenly hosts (vv. 6–9), another part by a combined choir of heaven and earth (vv. 10–15), and the final section by an earthly assembly (vv. 16–19). The hymn opens with Yahweh enthroned in the heavenly sanctuary (Ps. 11:4), surrounded by an assembly of holy ones, "children of the gods" (cf. Pss. 29:1; 82:6), the host of heaven (1 Kings 22:19)—various names drawn from Canaanite religion and represented by the statues of the cherubim on either side of the Ark (Exod. 25:17–22). Decisions about the Davidic dynasty are first ratified before the heavenly throne. In Ps. 89:10–15 the mythology about Baal's conquering the sea (Ps. 29) is transferred to the one supreme God, Yahweh, who overcomes the sea monsters of evil and chaos to create a new stable world, the home of the Lord's kindness and fidelity. The final lines of the hymn (89:16–19) bring us to the earthly sanctuary where the Davidic king is waiting.

Verses 20–38 present an oracle (cf. v. 20a

with Pss. 2:7; 110:1) along prophetic lines (Isa. 2:1), promising the king many of the powers reserved to Yahweh. The strong arm of the Lord crushing sea monsters (Ps. 89:11) now strengthens the king (v. 22). The Lord who rules the sea and the ocean currents (vv. 10–11) places the hand of the king over these forces. "Kindness and fidelity," God's special qualities (vv. 2–3), rest with the king.

The final section consists of a lament (vv. 39–46) and a prayer (vv. 47–52), stitched closely with the preceding two parts: kindness and fidelity (vv. 2–3, 15, 25, 29–30, 34, 50); "right hand" of Yahweh (v. 14), of the king (v. 26), and now of the enemy (v. 43); and ancient eternal promises to David (vv. 4–5, 37–38, and 50–51). Military disaster poses a serious threat to Yahweh and the religion of Israel. The strong, stereotyped phrase, "How Long!" bursts out (cf. Ps. 6:4). Ps. 89:53 concludes Book Three (cf. other such concluding verses, Pss. 41:14; 72:18–20; 106:48).

PSALMS 90–106
Book Four

The psalms here are almost completely unassigned. After the major collections of David, Korah, and Asaph in the first three books, this collection appears like an appendix. Psalms 101 and 103 come like stragglers from the David guild. The name of Moses bonds these psalms together: 90:1; 99:6; 103:7; 105:26; and 106:16, 23, 32.

Psalm 90. Psalm 90, a communal lament, stems perhaps from a sick person too young for death and humbly conscious of sin. Because life is short and irreversible, the psalmist begs God for immediate forgiveness. Perhaps this divine action will bring a return to good health (v. 13). Little is granted to conscious survival after death (Ps. 6:6), nor does the psalm allude to God's great historical deeds in Israel's favor. The absence of these ideas brings the psalm into the realm of wisdom literature. Major sections may be spotted by stylistic changes: 90:1–2, hymnic introduction; vv. 3–12, wisdom stanza about the shortness of life; and vv. 13–17, prayer for assistance. The Hebrew text is poorly preserved and variously translated.

"Man of God" in the title (v. 1a) surrounds Moses with the authority of a charismatic figure like Samuel (1 Sam. 9:6) and Elijah (1 Kings 17:18, 24). The opening hymn (Ps. 90:1b–2) praises Yahweh for giving birth to the cosmos just as Yahweh later begets Israel as a favorite people. Comparing the earth to Israel declares that each has an origin, a character, and a purpose uniquely bestowed by Yahweh. Suffering disrupts this divine order and, therefore, poses a fundamental problem.

Verses 3–12 begin with reflection common to the sages: life for everyone is very short, so quickly the sentence is delivered, "return to dust" (v. 3), possibly a reference to Gen. 3:19. Because life is transitory, "a thousand years are like yesterday." The psalmist refers to the suddenness of death and one's descent into the dark grave of Sheol; from this passage, 2 Pet. 3:8 concludes that the Messiah will appear unexpectedly. Even children are not always guaranteed survival, as Ps. 90:5–6 (textually very corrupt) says: "Their offspring change as grass changes; in the morning it sprouts and flourishes and in the evening it fades and withers." "Hidden sins" (v. 8) refers to violations of ceremonial taboos and other unknown infringements (Ps. 19:13; Lev. 5:14–19).

"Seventy" (Ps. 90:10) was not a normal life span, since the average life span of a person at this time was forty-four years. According to Jer. 25:11, "seventy" indicated the full number of years for the Exile. "Daybreak" (v. 14) refers to a revival of life, a special time for prayer (Pss. 30:6; 46:6; 143:8), to realize the wisdom of divine providence.

Psalm 91. This psalm of confidence, Psalm 91, was prepared for an entrance and departure liturgy at the Temple; other examples for solemn entry occur in Psalms 15 and 24, with a longer service in Psalm 95. At the beginning there is a blessing from a priest (Ps. 91:1–4) and a promise of protection from Yahweh (vv. 5–9); similarly at the end, a blessing for the return into daily life (vv. 10–13) and an oracle promising God's protection (vv. 14–16). Although there is some contact with wisdom literature (Prov. 3:13–16; Job 5:17–26), closer bonds tie Psalm 91 with the Blessing of Moses in Deuteronomy 32 (see the title for Ps. 90). Because of allusions to pestilence and sickness, the psalm is adapted to a prayer service for good health that included exorcism of demons.

Ps. 91:1–2 invites the worshiper into the protection of the Temple, possibly for a night vigil (Pss. 1:2; 42:4). The wings of the cherubim on either side of the Ark (Exod. 25:17–22) symbolize Yahweh's protective overshadowing (Pss. 17:8; 36:8). The darkness of the night contrasts with the blinding glory of the Lord's presence (1 Kings 8:10–13; Ps. 139:11–12), which does not reflect blind superstition but a personal bonding with "my God in whom I trust." Fearful demons (cf. Isa. 34:14; Tob. 3:8; 6:15; Eph. 2:2; 6:12) prowl the night, killing the firstborn of Egypt (Exod. 12:29) and the army of Sennacherib (Isa. 37:36). The exorcism of evil spirits leads to new promises from God (Ps.

91:5–8). The "noonday demon" (v. 5) may refer to sunstroke or else to voluptuous living with false security (→ Satan).

The second blessing from the priest before departure (vv. 10–13) asks the protection of the angels, so that each individual Israelite is led as all the people were conducted through the wilderness (Exod. 23:20; 32;34). God does not remove the dangers but provides strength for the struggle that purifies and strengthens. The promise of a long, peaceful life (Ps. 91:16) represents a supreme biblical gift (Ps. 23:6; 34:13; 54:9), a sign of the final age (Isa. 51:6; 65:20), possibly of eternal happiness (Ps. 1:3; 16:8).

Psalm 92. Psalm 92 is a hymn of thanksgiving with a strong wisdom influence, possibly by an elderly priest (v. 15) after some deliverance. The psalm bears the earmarks of worship. After opening with a fully orchestrated call to worship (vv. 2–4), vv. 5–6 offer motivation from Yahweh's mighty deeds for Israel (Ps. 136). Next, one meets wisdom's instruction about retribution (92:10–12) and a closing benediction upon righteous people (vv. 13–16).

The title (v. 1) assigns Psalm 92 to Sabbath services. The people are to rejoice (v. 3) as God did at the end of creation (Gen. 2:3). The psalm, like the Sabbath, combines joy over nature's beauty with care for moral harmony between people. The divine name Yahweh occurs seven times in the psalm, perfect for "Sabbath" which means "seventh."

In Ps. 92:2–6 music from many types of instruments becomes an intuitive, almost mystical way of providing dialogue with God and of reliving the Lord's wondrous deeds toward Israel. The Hebrew word for melody comes from a root that signifies quiet, repetitive prayer. Daily Temple sacrifices at dawn and in the evening may have been one of the early settings for this psalm (Exod. 29:38–42).

Ps. 92:7–12 gives an instruction prompted by wisdom literature and its concern about proper retribution for the wicked and the just. Wisdom, close to nature, also shows a penchant to think about creation (Prov. 8:22–31). Because of the Sabbath (Ps. 92:1), the praise of "your works, Lord" (v. 6) may direct attention to the works of God's hand across the heavens and the earth (Gen. 1:1–2:4; Ps. 8:4). The wicked will be buried in darkness. At this early age the text refers to oblivion, not to eternal damnation.

The comparison of the just to palm trees and the cedars of Lebanon (92:13) evokes memories of many biblical passages about strength and uprightness (Pss. 1:3; 29:5; 80:11), wealth and beauty (1 Kings 5:21–23), and future, messianic blessing (Hos. 14:5–6; Isa. 41:18–19). The everlasting Sabbath will have arrived.

Psalm 93. The Greek version as well as the Talmud assign Psalm 93 to the eve of the Sabbath (Ps. 92:1), when God had completed the created world for habitation. The thought and language echo the Canaanite myths of creation (Pss. 29; 89:10–14) and the divine enthronement (Pss. 96–99; Zech. 14:16–19). Each Sabbath marked a new victory of Yahweh as king, allowing the worshiper to begin life anew, in harmony with creation and covenant.

The style is rapid, condensed, and forceful, almost like thunder, effective with repetition, and controlled in its development. Ps. 93:1–2 lays out the setting; vv. 3–4 orchestrate the liturgical action; v. 5 concludes gloriously. Though in a different mood, Ps. 19:2–5 presents a similar scenario.

The opening words, "Yahweh rules as king," echo the shouts in 2 Sam. 15:10 and 1 Kings 1:11, except that here the name of the king is first, emphasizing the person of Yahweh rather than the moment of enthronement. Yahweh's normal throne is above the floodwaters in the heavens (Pss. 11:4; 29:3). In 93:5 the phrase "your precepts" may possibly read "your throne," so that the psalm ends as it begins, in the heavenly sanctuary.

Psalm 94. A national lament, Psalm 94 utilizes many literary forms such as narrative, interrogation, mourning, and instruction, with a clear, vigorous style and a sincere, forthright attitude. The structure, after the introduction (vv. 1–2), follows the format of chiasm (see commentary above on Ps. 19:2): A pretensions of the lawless (vv. 3–7); B questions (vv. 8–10); C the center with Yahweh's care for persecuted people (vv. 11–15); B' questions (vv. 16–20); and A' pretensions, with resolution in Yahweh (vv. 21–23). The Greek version and the rabbinical tradition add a title: "Of David, for the fourth day of the week."

In vv. 1–2 the language is less violent than it seems, if one recalls that it uses stereotypic formulas (Pss. 18:48; 58:11; Isa. 34:8; 35:4). Vengeance is often the response of someone who loves dearly and witnesses abuse heaped upon a loved one. More than once Israel shouted to God: "Rise up!" (Pss. 7:7; 44:24). The word for "pride" (94:2) is from a root, "to rise up" arrogantly. When vv. 3–7 record the insolence of the wicked, prophetic language merges with the psalm (cf. Amos 8:4–6; Mic. 2:1–3). The center of the psalm (94:11–15) records the Lord's reaction (Ps. 12:6). Ps. 94:11 and 15 contain a notion, frequent in Jeremiah, that punishment can be purifying and instructive (Jer. 2:19, 30; Prov. 3:12). Human plans are no more substantive than breath or *hebel*, a Hebrew word sometimes translated "vanity" (Eccles. 1:1–2). Such empty and dark silence was almost the lot of the psalmist (Ps. 94:17), a line

that is dramatically reversed in v. 19. The questions in vv. 16–20 reflect agony but not doubt, as they lead to the finale (vv. 21–23).

Psalm 95. The Greek version assigns Psalm 95, like Psalms 90, 92, 93, to the Sabbath or its eve. Later rabbinical tradition associates it with the New Year's festival, preparing for the Yahweh-as-king songs, Psalms 96–99. Significant similarities and differences show up in comparison with Psalm 81, with mention of Meribah and Massah, of the hardening of heart, of testing God in Psalm 95 or the people in Psalm 81. This present psalm belongs at Jerusalem, where Yahweh alone is invoked as "rock" (Ps. 18:3).

A procession makes its way toward the Jerusalem Temple, possibly beginning at the Gihon sanctuary (1 Kings 1:33), up the Kidron valley, and climbing to the Temple mount (Ps. 95:1–5). Before the Holy of Holies, there is a ceremony of adoration and prayer (vv. 6–7a) and then of biblical reading and sermon. The ceremony concludes with the prophetic oracle in vv. 7b–11. The hypothesis of biblical reading and sermon explains the abrupt transition in v. 7b. The literary style stands out clearly: vv. 1–7a, two hymns with a call to praise in vv. 1–2 and 6 to be sung by the entire congregation, and with motivation for praise in vv. 3–5 and 7a to be chanted by a special choir; and vv. 7b–11, an oracle by a Temple prophet (Ps. 50).

Ps. 95:1–2 encourages the people in their procession: "Come, let us draw near God's face" (cf. Ps. 42:3); v. 6 calls upon the people at the Temple to fall prostrate before the Lord. Yahweh, "a great king over all the gods" (v. 3), stands in contrast with the various gods worshiped by Solomon's wives on a neighboring hill. God, in searching out the peaks of the mountains and the depths of the valleys, appears as king over the universe as well as over the height and depths of the human heart (cf. Job 11:7). In creating sea and dry land, God is master of all creation, even in its hostile forms (Pss. 29; 89:10–11).

The transition to the prophetic oracle begins with "Today!" as in Deut. 4:40; 5:3; and 6:6. Meribah and Massah are the places where the people angered God and where Moses struck the rock for water (Exod. 17:1–7; Deut. 6:16; 8:15). If the present generation continues with the same stubbornness, then they will be exiled from the land of rest (cf. Deut. 12:8–12).

Psalm 96. Psalm 96 is the parent of hymnology, sacred compositions composed of phrases and lines from the Bible: compare v. 1a and Ps. 33:3a; Isa. 42:10a; v. 2b and Isa. 40:9; 52:7; v. 4b and Pss. 48:2; 95:3; vv. 7–9 and Ps. 29:1–2; v. 10b and Ps. 93:1c; v. 10c and Ps. 9:9b; v. 11a and Ps. 97:1; v. 11b and Ps. 98:7b; and v. 13 and Ps. 98:9. The psalm itself became part of a new hymn in

1 Chron. 16:8–36, which combines Pss. 105:1–15; 96; and 106:1, 47–48. Biblical writers continued to adapt older passages to new historical and religious settings.

Because Psalms 96–99 were intended for Temple worship (the Greek version indicates for the Feast of Tabernacles), these psalms are not so much addressing the final age of the world as its anticipation in liturgy (Zech. 14:16–19). The structure stands out clearly: two calls for praise, Ps. 96:1–3, 7–9; two motivations, vv. 4–6, 10–13 (→ Eschatology).

Verses 1–3 draw heavily from Isaiah 40–55 to relive within the liturgy the herald's announcement of a new song. For the sake of Israelites, not the nations, Ps. 96:3 proclaims, "the nations' gods [Heb. 'elohim] are worthless ['elilim]."

In citing Ps. 29:1–2, the psalmist makes two theological corrections in 96:7–9: "children of the gods" becomes "families of nations" and, instead of Canaanite phrases about thunder, ritual gifts are presented in the Temple. (For the acclamation "Yahweh reigns as King," see the commentary above on Ps. 93:1.) Yahweh's world kingship is exercised for the sake of divine justice, fulfilling the covenantal promises to Israel (Exod. 34:6–7).

Psalm 97. Like Psalm 50, Psalm 97 too draws upon prophetic preaching to insist that true worship includes social justice. Psalm 97 is heavily dependent upon Isaiah 40–55, the great prophetic book of consolation from the Exile and weaves the key word "righteousness" (Heb. *tsedeq*) in and out of the psalm. Yahweh will always be true to divine promises and so exemplify "justice" and "righteousness." Concerned this much about liturgy, the psalm is not announcing the end, technically called "eschaton," but a momentary fulfillment in Israel's liturgy, especially at the Feast of Tabernacles (Pss. 29; 93; 96; Zech. 14:16–19). Other major sources for the author are Pss. 18:8–16; 77:17–20; and Habakkuk 3.

Ps. 97:1–6 describes a theophany like the awesome manifestation of Yahweh on Mount Sinai (Exod. 19) and traditional hymns dependent on that episode (Judg. 5; Hab. 3; Ps. 68). Altogether these brilliant songs announce a continuously glorious presence of Yahweh in Israel's history. The liturgy reenacts what the eyes of faith recognize in hidden depths. Liturgy brings such reality to the surface at least for the day. Twice righteousness enters the theophany: at the base of Yahweh's throne (97:2b) and in heavenly proclamation (v. 6a).

In vv. 7–12, motifs and imagery from literature about "the day of the Lord" bring a fiery judgment upon all who set up rival deities and abuse the rights of people (Zeph. 1:14–18). Life-giving light will envelop Yahweh's faithful ones, those with the Lord's concern for the poor and the hopes of Israel (Isa. 2:2–5; 60:1–4; → Justice).

Psalm 98. The spirit, literary form, and themes of the two preceding psalms continue in Psalm 98 with the same heavy dependence upon Isaiah 40–55. In fact, the final verse repeats the end of Psalm 96. While Second Isaiah was singing of the glorious new exodus to the homeland, Psalm 98 repeats the melodies back in the land of Israel. Even if the fulfillment of Second Isaiah's expectations hardly lived up to the excitement and grandeur of the announcement, nonetheless by faith one can relive such hopes and so anticipate their final realization through Temple liturgy (vv. 4–6). Again salvation and justice are joined carefully together (Isa. 46:13; 51:5, 6, 8) so that Israel is advised that the glorious fulfillment of divine promises requires the pursuit of social justice with the compassion of the covenant God (Ps. 98:3). Yahweh's future is mysteriously linked with Israel's obedience.

Psalm 99. Yahweh's royalty is not a myth like that of Canaanite gods; it is closely associated with Israel's history and institutions as well as with justice for the people. References to king and priesthood allude to the pre-exilic age and, especially, the time of First Isaiah (Isa. 1–39). Psalm 99 is divided into three stanzas: vv. 1–3, enthronement of Yahweh; vv. 4–5, Yahweh's concern for justice in the rule of kings; and vv. 6–9, Yahweh's reception of prayers from three mediators. The doxology of Isa. 6:3, "Holy, holy, holy," becomes a refrain, expanded with each stanza. The refrains keep the focus entirely upon the Lord as enthroned above the Ark (Exod. 25:17–22). In Ps. 99:5, however, the Temple and Ark are rightly presented as "the footstool" for Yahweh; the normal presence of God is in heaven (Ps. 11:4).

The great priest-intercessors are named: Moses (Exod. 17:11–15; 32:11–14); Aaron (Exod. 28:29–30; Num. 17:11–15); and Samuel (1 Sam. 7:7–12; 12:19). Because of God's holiness, human mediators are needed, trained in the traditions and in dialogue with Yahweh. God, who once led by the pillar of cloud (Exod. 14:24; 33:9–10; Num. 10:34), in Ps. 99:7 just as truly directs the people through priests at sanctuaries.

Psalm 100. If Psalms 91–99 constitute a booklet for worship on Sabbaths and important feasts, Psalm 100 is their final doxology. It consists of two minihymns: vv. 1–3 for the procession and vv. 4–5 for the thanksgiving service within the Temple, leading to a sacred meal (Ps.

478

81:11, 17). The call to praise in each case breaks with excitement. Yahweh made Israel by bringing it out of Egypt to be a chosen people (100:3; Exod. 3:7–10; 19:3–6). "Steadfast love" and "fidelity" conclude the psalm with the major attributes of God as Lord of the covenant (Ps. 100:5; Exod. 34:6–7).

Psalm 101. A discourse from the throne, possibly on the day of coronation (Pss. 2; 110) or on some other royal festival (Pss. 18; 72), Psalm 101 begins with a call to praise (101:1) and a promise to live and judge morally (vv. 2–3a). Specific pledges are mentioned, some negative (vv. 3b–5) and some positive (vv. 6–7). In the conclusion, the psalmist affirms that justice shall prevail (v. 7). A strong influence from wisdom literature is recognizable (Prov. 4:14; 6:12–19; 8:15–16).

The opening words, "steadfast love and justice," accord to the Davidic royalty the major goals of the Mosaic covenant (Ps. 89:2–5; Exod. 34:6–7); they also bring the support of Moses to the throne. A series of "I" statements pledge the king's word to the cause of moral integrity (Ps. 18:21–25). The hope within the final verse in Psalm 78 will be pursued (cf. Gen. 20:5–6; 1 Kings 9:4). The negative side of what is unacceptable (Ps. 101:3b–5) as well as the positive requirements (vv. 6–7) recall the conditions for entering the sanctuary (Pss. 15; 24). The king was the guardian of the Temple and of the Torah (1 Kings 8). These lines stress the king's personal obligation by using the first person, "I hate . . . I do not know . . . I destroy." The break of morning (Ps. 101:8) was not only the time for judicial procedures (Jer. 21:12), but it was also the moment of salvation (Ps. 46:6; Isa. 37:36).

Psalm 102. In the fifth of the seven penitential psalms, the lament of a sick person merges with lamentation over devastated Jerusalem. Yahweh's everlasting presence provides the theological backdrop. Unlike Psalm 51, words for sin and guilt are conspicuously absent. As the prayer of an individual, the psalm is suffused with tender sensitivity; this attitude is directed in turn to the stones and dust of Jerusalem. National mourning over fallen Jerusalem keeps the individual's lament from excessive introspection and adds the element of faith in Yahweh's eternal presence and promises. Publicly expressed pain leads to personal strength and a vision beyond older limitations. The influence of prophecy and wisdom may have opened the door of the psalmist's vision for Jerusalem and the world. Ps. 102:2–12, 24–25 record the individual's lament, vv. 13–23, 26–29 a lament over Zion that leads to new confidence.

Jewish tradition in the Mishnah (m. Ta'an. 2.3) assigns this psalm to fasting days (Zech. 7:5;

8:19). The opening call for help (Ps. 102:2–3) speaks in the traditional language of prayer. There follow other accepted expressions for sorrow; "my bones burn with fire within" (v. 4) repeats the urgent pleading of Jer. 20:9. Groans from physical pain direct us to a very sick person, without appetite, sleepless, gaunt and emaciated, in danger of premature death, and, worst of all, quarantined and lonely. The sound of an unclean bird, the night owl (Ps. 102:7; Lev. 11:17), captures the whole scene.

Ps. 102:13–23 weaves in passages and themes from prophetic literature of the exilic and postexilic ages. The rebuilding of Zion will bring a new glorious presence of Yahweh to the wonderment of the nations (Isa. 40:5; 41:5; 59:19; 60:2). The psalmist is still speaking from loss (Ps. 42), for in quoting Lam. 5:19, Ps. 102:13 replaces the "throne" of Yahweh with "the memory of you." In v. 19 the psalmist requests a writing tablet to record these words. Future generations will be supported in their faith by Yahweh's restorative power and love (Ps. 22:31–32).

Ps. 102:24–29 returns first to personal lament and then, like the preceding section, to confidence. The Lord not only acts with loving concern but is forever present with the chosen people, as the promises to Zion and the stability of the earth testify. Heb. 1:10–12 calls upon these words so that Christians may find in Jesus an eternal sanctuary and stable earth.

Psalm 103. In many ways a transitional poem, in the first part Psalm 103 relates with Psalm 102, grateful for a return to health (103:1–18); in the second part, as a hymn of praise, it introduces Psalm 104. The psalmist expresses gratitude for both physical and spiritual healing. Sickness and sin (unlike Ps. 102 in this regard) are linked together (like Ps. 30); pardon is frequently begged of God because of its promise in the ancient covenant (103:7–8; Exod. 34:6–7). Like Psalm 102, personal questions are linked with communal problems and traditions and thereby receive a solid basis for an answer. The psalm comes from the postexilic age, quoting Isa. 57:16 in 103:9, Isa. 55:9 in v. 11; and Isa. 40:6–8 in vv. 15–16. It draws upon Israel's traumatic experience of sin and suffering. It is sung on the Day of Atonement by Jews (Lev. 16) and each morning by Greek Christians.

After the opening hymn (vv. 1–2), the psalmist asks for pardon and healing (vv. 3–5), relying upon the promises of the covenant (vv. 6–18); vv. 19–22 conclude with joyful songs of praise for Yahweh in the heavenly sanctuary.

Verses 1–5 identify the major ingredients of a blessing, that is, publicly proclaiming God's gifts through moral strength and physical health. "Soul," which derives from a Hebrew word for "throat," provides the way not only for manifesting life or death by breathing but also for interacting personally with one's environment. Healing, consequently, involves the entire community and its sensitivity to social justice and the earth's ecological balance. Health presumes the end of selfish abuse of others and of the world. In v. 5, "your life" is a different type of Hebrew word, meaning "adornment." If one follows the translation in ancient versions, "desires" (Gk.) or "body" (Syriac), the reference then is to sexual vitality and the ability to share life in family (so Gen. 18:11–14; cf. Rom. 4:19–20).

In Ps. 103:6–18 justice certainly embraces "the rights of the oppressed" and punishment upon wrongdoers, yet justice is most of all a divine attribute: Yahweh's way of living up to divine assurances of forgiveness, rooted in the covenant (Exod. 34:6–7). The history of Israel becomes a "way," revelatory of a merciful God. Isa. 55:6–11 revels in the mystery of God's ways as high above earth as the heavens are, yet soaking the earth like rain and returning to God through earthly produce and human lives. Therefore in Ps. 103:17 Yahweh's "steadfast love" and "justice" parallel each other and merge together. These verses are a commentary on the first and last sections of Second Isaiah (Isa. 40 and 55). Ps. 103:19–22 introduces Israel's praise into the heavenly sanctuary where God is enthroned (Pss. 11:4; 29).

Psalm 104. Gen. 1:1–2:4a is turned into magnificent poetry. Psalm 104 shows many parallels with an Egyptian hymn to the sun god Aten, composed during the reign of the monotheist Akhenaton (ca. 1380–1362 B.C.). Psalm 104 does not acclaim creation but Yahweh the creator; Yahweh appears not primarily as all-powerful but as all-merciful. Yahweh creates a happy world where even the lion's roar becomes a prayer (v. 21). The psalm does not reason from creation to the existence of God, but vice versa. It proceeds from faith in the covenant God of kindness and fidelity (Exod. 34:6–7) to a new appreciation of creation. God's people Israel are at the center. Ps. 104:30 accounts for the Christian use on the Feast of Pentecost.

Verses 1–9 acclaim the royal creator, who in vv. 10–18 is dispenser of nourishment; in vv. 19–23, master of the seasons; in vv. 24–26, Lord of earth and sea; and in vv. 27–30, controller of life and death. Verses 31–35 provide a glorious finale. The psalm also divides according to the days of creation in Genesis 1: first day, creation of light, vv. 1–2a; second day, creation of the firmament or sky, vv. 2b–4; third day, separation of heaven and earth, vv. 5–9, and the adornment of earth, vv. 10–18; fourth day, creation of heavenly bodies, vv. 19–

20; fifth day, creation of ocean creatures, vv. 25–26; and sixth day, creation of terrestrial creatures and humankind, vv. 21–23. Verse 24 is like the refrain in Genesis 1, "And God saw that it was good!"

Ps. 104:1–9 begins with, "Bless the Lord" (Ps. 103:1–2, 19–22), an important theological formula. Here the active form of the verb occurs, an indication of early origin. Later Hebrew tradition turned it into the passive, more dignified form, "Blessed be the Lord." The latter phrase is followed by an account of what God has done for the chosen people (Gen. 24:27; Exod. 18:10–12; 1 Kings 8:56–61). This account belongs to a liturgical reenactment of God's gracious deeds and to a hymn of praise. Praise, therefore, is much less Israel's gift to God than it is a recognition and ritual reliving of God's gifts to Israel.

The language of praise (Ps. 104:1–4) and of cosmogony (vv. 5–9) can be traced back into ancient mythology: the Lord's palace built above the heavenly waters (Pss. 11:4; 18:5–10; 29:10), surrounded by stars and moon and wind as attendants and servants (Pss. 29; 82; 103:20). Ps. 104:9, repeated almost verbatim in Jer. 5:22, refers to the taming of primeval chaos.

Ps. 104:10–18 reveals the abundant graciousness with which God creates. Very clearly God is at the source of whatever human beings need for physical nourishment and delight, even of "wine to make the heart joyful" (v. 15). Verses 19–23 show Yahweh to be master of the seasons of the year and of the passage from night to day. The heavenly bodies, which regulated the seasons, were worshiped as divine by many people (Deut. 4:19), but here (Ps. 104:1–4) they are God's heavenly retinue and servants. When vv. 24–26 extend God's control over the oceans, the imagery is unusually tranquil as compared with Ps. 89:10–11 and Isa. 51:9–10. The Lord even makes sport of the sea monster Leviathan, a feat declared impossible for human beings (Job 40:25–32).

In Ps. 104:27–30, Yahweh directs life and death through the gift or withdrawal of the spirit. The sequence life, death, new life through the spirit follows the common biblical pattern for Jerusalem or the people Israel. Those persons upon whom God bestows promises generally succeed at first, undergo serious difficulties to the seeming frustration of faith (Ps. 44), but rise to a fulfillment never anticipated earlier.

In the glorious finale (Ps. 104:31–35) Yahweh reaches down from the heavenly sanctuary touching the earth with smoke, a symbol of divine manifestations (Exod. 19; Judg. 5:4–5; Hab. 3:3–6). Such a world has no place for sinners. The psalm, therefore, sees a world of good people, innocent of any innate corruption, with God's gift of goodness.

Psalm 105. Writing at the time of the Exile, the author of Psalm 105 draws upon Israel's history as far back as the age of the patriarchs to establish the thesis that people frequently go through a cycle of promise, followed by setbacks, but climax in a new possession. No gift, especially the promised land, was Israel's by right, only by the grace of God. The poem communicates this major message by the repetition of three key words: "patriarch, servant, or chosen one" (vv. 6, 9–10, 17, 25, 26, 42–43); "land or territory" (vv. 7, 11, 16, 23, 27, 30, 31, 32, 33, 35, 36, 41); and "word or promise" (vv. 11, 14–15, 19, 27, 42). Land accordingly turns out to be God's most ancient and continuous promise, reaching back to the patriarchs. Israel had to go through many experiences of land possessed, lost, and regained, to realize that land is always and foremost a grace. The importance of Psalm 105 is affirmed in its choice to form, with Psalms 96 and 100, a trilogy for worship in 1 Chron. 16:7–36.

After an invitation to seek God's presence (Ps. 105:1–6), the basis of development (from loss to new possession) is provided in vv. 7–11 with the eternal promises to the patriarchs. Verses 12–45 dwell upon various ways God protected his people: vv. 12–15, the patriarchs amid hostile kings and vv. 16–22, imprisonment in Egypt, first of Joseph and then, in vv. 23–38, of all the people. Verses 39–41 recall the difficulties in the wilderness, whereupon vv. 42–45 close the psalm.

Verses 1–6 offer a new way for the exiles to view their situation. With liturgical language the psalmist calls upon the people to "inquire of the Lord . . . constantly seek God's face" (v. 4). This language implies turning to Yahweh in the Temple for an answer (1 Kings 14:5; 22:5) and, through the Temple services, to contemplate God's past redemptive actions. The psalm thus instills a longing for returning to the land and rebuilding the Temple. Like Abraham, Israel is about to receive a call to go forth to the promised land. The patriarchs are not prominently mentioned outside of Genesis, except in selections from the prophet of the Exile (Isa. 51: 2–3; 54:9). Ps. 105:7–11 reaches behind the Mosaic covenant to assure Israel that, despite its breaking of the covenant laws, the patriarchal promises remain intact. The land is affirmed as the allotted portion for all Israel in language reminiscent of Levites for whom the Lord was their allotted portion and cup (Ps. 16:5; Deut. 32:9). All Israel was a priestly people (Exod. 19:6) whose lives, especially in the promised land, were to make important contributions to worship (Deut. 26:1–11).

In Ps. 105:12–45 the plagues of Egypt are lined up differently than in Exod. 7:14–11:10 and Ps. 78:43–51. The purpose of the biblical accounts is a theological elaboration for the religious instruction and worship of later generations. Chronological accuracy was not to the point. Darkness is recorded first (105:28), though it was the ninth plague in Egypt (Exod. 10:21–23), to show that opposition to Yahweh wraps a person in obscurity and shame. By contrast (Ps. 105:39) Yahweh will provide light at once for Israel to depart and to be led through the wilderness. Verses 25–29 form a long, important chiasm (see commentary above on Ps. 19:2) in which the central line, v. 27, states that "words or signs" go together, so that the words of Moses and Aaron were seen in their inner strength by the wonders that accompanied them. Verses 42–45 bring together the three principal key words. The psalm ends with the people still in Exile, but ready to obey the Lord's precepts. Otherwise all is lost.

Psalm 106. A communal lament over the dismal conditions of the postexilic age (Ps. 16; Isa. 56:9–57:13; Zech. 7–8), Psalm 106 follows the pattern of Deuteronomy not only in the sequence of events in Egypt and during the wandering in the wilderness but also with prophetic warning, instruction, and comfort for contrite hearts. The psalm treats Israel's inexplicable guilt and God's inexhaustible mercy. A comparison with Psalm 105 exhibits surprising differences. While each psalm relives the Exodus and wilderness experiences, Psalm 105 molds it into a praise of God, Psalm 106 into a communal lament. Israel's religion is not subject to divine fate if such divergences occur from the same traditions and are due to Israel's reactions. The sins of early Israel are repeated again during and after the Exile.

The incorporation of Psalm 106 (along with Pss. 96, 105) into a Temple service (1 Chron. 16:7–36) testifies to the psalm's existence before 400 B.C. and its popularity for rebuilding hope. Lines or phrases are frequently woven into NT preaching: Ps. 106:10 in Luke 1:71; v. 20 in Rom. 1:23; v. 28 in 1 Cor. 12:2; v. 37 in 1 Cor. 10:20; v. 45 in Luke 1:72; and v. 48 in Luke 1:68; Rev. 19:4.

The preaching style of Deuteronomy, which dominates Psalm 106, makes it difficult to section it off into poetic stanzas, but the following outline may direct study and worship. After a short entry chant (vv. 1–3) and prayer (vv. 4–5), the psalm divides into two main parts: first, Israel's ingratitude in Egypt and in the wilderness (vv. 6–23) and Yahweh's just punishment (vv. 24–27); second, Israel's disobedience before and after entering the promised land (vv. 28–39) and the Lord's new punishment and grace (vv. 40–46). Verse 47 is a final prayer for the psalm and v. 48 a doxology for Book Four of the Psalter (Pss. 90–106).

481

Ps. 106:1–5 begins with the popular postexilic refrain, "Hallelujah," used twenty-three times as an introduction or conclusion to psalms within Psalms 104–150. The Greek and Latin translations generally transliterated the word (without the initial *h*, hence the "Alleluia" spelling within the Roman and Orthodox churches) rather than translating it as "Praise the Lord." Two other congregational responses occur, generally paired together: "Praise [or, Give thanks to] Yahweh, for God is good" and "God's kindness lasts forever" (Pss. 107:1; 118:1, 2, 3, 4, 29; 136). The confession of sin that is to follow becomes a way for the community to praise God's fidelity and goodness. In this setting of a family tradition of faith, the individual humbly and peacefully asks God, "Remember me."

Ps. 106:6–27 recalls, with sorrow and hope, the Lord's extraordinary interventions and Israel's rebellious or indifferent response in Egypt and in the wilderness. The opening verse repeats traditional words for sin and repentance (Ps. 51:3–4). Israel's faith rested squarely upon God's willingness to forgive repeatedly (Exod. 34:6–7). Such was the way that God was to be remembered and named (Ps. 106:8). Goodness was no easy gift from God; the language of v. 9 recalls God's battles against chaotic, evil forces, symbolized by water (Exod. 15; Pss. 29; 89:10–11; Isa. 51:9–10). In the wilderness, cowardice (Num. 14:1–4), sensuality (Exod. 32; Num. 11:4–6), and selfish ambition (Num. 12; 16) provoked Israel's sinful responses. Similar to Hosea's and Jeremiah's intuition, sin is described in a touching way as a forgetfulness of God (Hos. 2:13; Jer. 3:21). Moses appears as the great intercessor before God (Num. 14:13–19; Ps. 99:6). The Exile is traced to sin similar to that of the Israelites in the wilderness, who died in perpetual exile (Num. 14:20–38). Ezek. 20:23 quotes Ps. 106:27 to announce the Exile.

Verses 28–47 move the thought to a hopeful setting, advancing beyond the point of sentence and punishment where the preceding section ended. Like the people in the wilderness, those in Exile were severely tempted to worship the Babylonian gods who seemed to have defeated Yahweh. Yet Israel's defeat was planned by Yahweh to purify and strengthen morally the chosen people (Isa. 44:9–20; 44:25–26; 45:4–7). Even Moses, for some mysterious offense, must die with the people in the wilderness (Ps. 106:32; Num. 20:6–13; Deut. 1:37–40; 34). The story of sin continues, even with human sacrifice (Ps. 106:37; Gen. 22; 2 Kings 16:3; Jer. 7:31). Yahweh still remembers the covenant and its pledge of forgiveness (Exod. 34:6–7). Ps. 106:48 completes Book Four (Pss. 90–106) with a doxology similar to that at the end of Psalms 41, 72, 89.

PSALMS 107–150
Book Five

The final book reflects the full flowering of postexilic Temple liturgy and Ezra's religious reform in 428 B.C. (Ezra 10; Neh. 8–9). A first series of "Hallelujah Psalms" (Pss. 111–118) includes the "Egyptian Hallel" (Pss. 113–118), which was sung for the three great pilgrimage festivals of Passover, Weeks, and Tabernacles (Exod. 23:14–17). The "Psalms of Ascent" (Pss. 120–134) constitute a small booklet to accompany pilgrims to or from Jerusalem. Psalm 136 is the "Great Hallel" for Sabbath services. Psalms 146–150 conclude the Psalter with an exultant "Te Deum" or "Glory to God in the Highest" (→ Feasts, Festivals, and Fasts).

Psalms 107, 119 are, possibly, introductory psalms, Psalm 107 to the entire ensemble of Book Five and Psalm 119 to the "Psalms of Ascent." Psalm 137 is untitled, typical of unclassified songs always finding their way into a hymnal. A final group of "Psalms of David" show up, generally in a very poor textual condition, due to long neglect (Pss. 108–110; 138–145).

Psalm 107. An intricate, yet carefully structured and free-flowing hymn of praise, Psalm 107 draws motivation from Israel's history (vv. 1 and 4–32) and was later adapted to thanksgiving for the return from Exile (vv. 2–3) and augumented with another hymn colored by the concerns of the wisdom tradition (vv. 33–42). Each stanza within vv. 4–32 has four sections clearly marked off by refrains: first, a narrative about a distressing situation, traveling across land or desert (vv. 4–5), imprisonment (vv. 10–12), illness and sin (vv. 17–18), traveling by sea (vv. 23–27); second, a prayer refrain (vv. 6, 13, 19, 28); third, an account about deliverance (vv. 7, 14, 20, 29–30); and fourth, a thanksgiving refrain (vv. 8–9, 15–16, 21–22, 31–32). The theology of the psalm, God's loving and effective answer to dire human needs, is summarized by key words: in the first refrain, "distress" or "trouble"; in the second refrain, "God's wonderful works" and their recipients, "the children of men [or earth]" (Heb. *bene-'adam*).

The liturgical ceremony at the Temple can be reconstructed as follows: v. 1 at the gate of the Temple and vv. 4–32 comprising four sections, each of which consists of narratives recited by a special choral group and two refrains by the entire congregation. The second refrain, more confessional in style, may have been sung by the priests. Some verses or themes are reflected in the NT: v. 9 in Luke 1:53; v. 20 in Acts 10:36; 13:26; v. 26 in Rom. 10:1–7; and vv. 23–32 in Mark 4:25–31.

Ps. 107:1–3 begins with stereotypic expressions of praise (cf. Ps. 106:1). The phrase, "redeemed of the Lord," reflects the preaching, during the Exile, of Second Isaiah, who transformed a nonreligious word, "kinsperson," with its accompanying obligations (Lev. 25:23–55) into a technical, theological word, "redeemer" or "to redeem" (so Isa. 35:9; 51:10; 62:12). Ps. 107:3 deliberately adapts the psalm to Israelites scattered in foreign lands, a new phenomenon called the Diaspora, a Greek word for "scattered abroad."

Verses 4–9 lay out the consequences of being lost in a desert wilderness: hunger, thirst, and inevitable death. Yahweh responds according to the law of desert hospitality (Gen. 18:1–5). God cannot do otherwise, once having heard the cry of distress, for Yahweh is to be named by kindness and fidelity (Exod. 34:6–7). The deliverance of travelers, lost physically or morally, becomes part of Israel's repertoire of praise for Yahweh. Such language implies aimless wandering (Exod. 23:4; Isa. 53:6), a way that needs to become straight in its directions and just in its morals (Pss. 25:8; Isa. 40:3).

Ps. 107:10–16 blends words for imprisonment due either to physical coercion from others or to one's own moral condition. Rebellion against God's word leads to punishment (Josh. 1:18; Ps. 106:33). Israel spurned God's counsel (Num. 14:2; Isa. 5:24) and so was destined for execution. They were already as good as dead (Ezek. 37:1–14). God breaks the bars of oppression and reverses the death sentence (Isa. 45:2).

Ps. 107:17–22 considers simultaneously physical health, moral integrity, individual status, and community responsibility (Pss. 6; 30; 38; 69; 88). Just as the imprisonment in the preceding section links physical and moral chains in a condition near to death, likewise here the condition leads a person and (symbolically) a community close to the dark, silent grave (Pss. 6:6; 16:10). For these reasons, healing consisted of more than a physical cure. Only God, therefore, is the true, effective physician, converting the community in its attitudes, reaching tenderly to the sick person, securing moral transformation (Exod. 15:26; Hos. 5:13; 6:1; 11:3).

Ps. 107:23–32 corresponds with many other biblical passages. The sea was almost always portrayed as a hostile, dangerous place (Pss. 29; 46:2–4; 89:10–14; Mark 4:35–41). Only Yahweh can overcome this demonic force and deliver Israel (Exod. 15:1–18; Isa. 51:9–10).

Ps. 107:33–35 is drawn from Second Isaiah, prophet of the Exile (Isa. 42:15; 43:19) and leads into the final hymn with its strong wisdom coloration (Prov. 23:34; 30:18–19; 31:14; Job. 12:21, 24).

Psalm 108. A composite psalm, Psalm 108 is made up of vv. 2–6 from Ps. 57:8–12 and vv.

7–14 from Ps. 60:7–14. The change of the divine name from Yahweh to Elohim is preserved as in the Elohistic Psalter (Pss. 42–83, see commentary above introducing Book Two). Joined together, Psalm 57, an individual's lament, modifies the fierceness of Psalm 60; Psalm 60, a community lament, provides a larger setting for the isolation in Psalm 57. All three psalms locate the solution to suffering and oppression somewhere in between the exclusively military and exclusively religious response.

Psalm 109. Psalm 109 is a lament from an individual who is slandered (vv. 4, 20, 29), falsely judged (vv. 7, 31), weak and probably sick (vv. 23–24), isolated and rejected (v. 25). The psalm consists of an opening lament (vv. 1–5), an extended curse of the enemy (vv. 6–20), a prayer for help and further lament (vv. 21–29), and finally a vow to offer public thanksgiving when exonerated (vv. 30–31). The strong influence of Jer. 18:19–23 is recognized, and therefore the composition is generally placed during the Exile or later. Repetition of words argues for unity of authorship. There are a number of reasons for thinking that the long imprecation in vv. 6–20 is mainly a quotation from the enemy: first, while the psalmist speaks generally in the plural about others, these verses use the singular; second, the curses of the adversary are mentioned in vv. 20, 28; third, the psalmist relates a separate set of curses against the enemy in v. 29. (For a further explanation of biblical curses, see commentary above on Psalm 69.)

Ps. 109:1–5 reveals a God functionally dead or nonexistent (Pss. 14:1; 22:2; 28:1), no more effective than the statues ridiculed by the prophet of the Exile (Isa. 44:9–20; Ps. 115). Such a weak God is put to shame by the psalmist's foes, who are efficient in hatching plots. The psalmist, like Jeremiah, feels betrayed by close friends (Jer. 11:18–19; 12:6). In Ps. 109:6 the word for accuser (Heb. satan) generally indicates strong opposition (2 Sam. 19:23; 1 Kings 5:18) and, in the postexilic age, a superhuman adversary (Job 1:6; Zech. 3:1). The curse may include demonic opposition. (For the lex talionis in Ps. 109:17, see commentary above on Ps. 35:8.) Ps. 109:25 shows contact with a phrase in Ps. 22:8, but the two psalms remain widely apart in attitude.

Psalm 110. Psalm 110 rose and fell with the Davidic dynasty; the text became obscure as the ritual of the dynasty ceased with the end of the monarchy. Psalm 110 becomes more intelligent as we associate it with other biblical passages involving royalty (2 Sam. 7; Isa. 9:6–7; Pss. 2; 89:2–38). Each verse indicated a long ceremony in the multiday ritual of a royal coronation.

Ps. 110:1a begins with the announcement of the Temple prophet: "The oracle of Yahweh for my lord [the crown prince]." In the Jerusalem Temple, the crown prince is being introduced to the assembly. "Sit [as supreme judge] at my right," that is, directly south of the Temple where the royal administrative buildings were situated. (Directions were always taken facing east, so Ps. 48.) At this point the assembly processed solemnly to the reception hall in one of these buildings. Ps. 110:1b refers to the ritual of vassals, no longer enemies, making their obeisance to the new king (Ps. 2:1–3, 8). Ps. 110:2, "Your strong scepter the Lord extends to you," is the signal for investing the crown prince with the symbols of royalty (Ps. 2:9). The scepter extends "from Zion," the center of the universe (Ezek. 5:5; 38:12) around which world history revolves.

With Ps. 110:3 the assembly is back again in the Temple for the most solemn moment of all, the consecratory words by which the crown prince becomes king. The form accepted by the Jerusalem scribes reads, "Your people offer themselves willingly on this, your day of strength; in holy splendor from the womb of dawn yours is the dew of your youth." The Greek depends upon a slightly different set of vowels within the same consonants: "Yours is regal power on [this] day of your birth; in the splendor of the holy ones, from the womb before the daystar, I beget you" (cf. Ps. 2:7). Both versions acclaim the mysterious origin of the king's position and power. Dew appears "miraculously" without rain (Hos. 14:6; Ps. 133:3; Job 38:28).

In Ps. 110:4 the king is declared "priest forever according to the order of Melchizedek," one of the titles of the Jebusite kings who ruled Jerusalem before its capture by David (Gen. 14). This title became highly controversial. It was taken over by the Hasmonean kings against the Zadokite family who controlled the high-priesthood up till then (1 Macc. 10:21; 14:41). Still later the Samaritans legitimated their priesthood as that of Melchizedek against that at Jerusalem. Qumran saw in Melchizedek the messianic figure (11QMelch); the NT recognized here a prototype for the priesthood of Jesus that was thereby eternal (Heb. 7:24, 28) and superior to that of Aaron (Heb. 5:10; 6:20; 7:11).

Ps. 110:5 continues at the Temple. The new king is enthroned "at the pillar" reserved for royalty (2 Kings 11:14; 23:3), directly north of the holy place. Therefore "The Lord['s dwelling] is at your right hand." With rhetorical flourish, Ps. 110:5–6 announces the invincible power of the new king. Verse 7 locates the final ceremony in this week or more of pageantry at the spring of Gihon, the supplier of water for the city and also a sanctuary where Solomon was crowned (1 Kings 1:38–40). Here the king drinks from consecrated water, symbolic of receiving life from

God, and with uplifted head leaves the sanctuary to begin his reign.

Psalm 110 is one of the most cited OT passages in the NT, principally v. 1 in connection with Christ's resurrection (Matt. 22:44; 26:64; Acts 2:34–35; 1 Cor. 15:25; Heb. 1:13; 10:13). In the NT, royalty is not normally claimed for Jesus during his earthly life, only after his resurrection when he rules by sending the Spirit to his disciples.

Psalm 111. Psalm 111 is an alphabetical or acrostic psalm (like Pss. 9–10; 25; 34), with each half-verse beginning with the next letter of the alphabet. This and other didactic features (111:10) suggest a postexilic composition when the wisdom tradition was strong. Psalm 111 relates well with Psalm 112 in rhythm, ideas, and vocabulary: righteousness in 111:3; 112:2; steadiness in 111:8; 112:8; and remembrance in 111:4; 112:6. Together they lead to the "Egyptian Hallel" (see commentary above introducing Book Five). Psalm 111 celebrates a righteous God, Psalm 112 a righteous person.

Ps. 111:1–3 introduces a didactic hymn; vv. 4–6 root all blessings in the covenant because Yahweh is faithful (vv. 7–9). Verse 10 concludes on a strong wisdom note.

"The assembly of the righteous" (v. 1b) is gathered in a public edifice, possibly a school. Yahweh's works are "studied for their delights." The word "studied," from the Hebrew word *da-rash*, lies at the root of a special type of rabbinical interpretation called "midrash." The works pondered by the group center around the Exodus, the Lord's care in the wilderness with the food of manna (Exod. 16; Ps. 81:11, 17), and the gift of the land. Ps. 111:10 states that "the fear of the Lord is the beginning of wisdom," meaning that the basis and support of a wise person are found in reverence towards God and neighbor (cf. Prov. 1:7; Job 28:28).

Psalm 112. Linked carefully with the end of Psalm 111, Psalm 112, again of the wisdom school, follows the same alphabetical method. The traditional position that the just are rewarded and the wicked are left poor and barren (Pss. 1; 37) imparts a steady peace here. Benefits redound both to the just person (vv. 112:1–3) and to the neighbor (vv. 4–6), with protection against adversity (vv. 7–8) to the confusion of the wicked (vv. 9–10). This solution was not always obvious (Ps. 49; Job) but seemed more than sufficient for the majority of cases in times of peace. In Ps. 112:3 "wealth and riches" are identified with "righteousness," a word, however, that in postbiblical Judaism also signified "generosity" (NAB; Sir. 3:30; 7:10). Words like "light" (Ps. 27:1) and "compassionate and just" (Exod. 34:6–7), normally attributed to Yahweh, are here bestowed on the righteous person. The psalm does not end in revenge but in the satisfaction that wickedness does not succeed.

Psalm 113. Psalm 113 is a song related to some of the most frequently cited and ancient canticles (Exod. 15; Deut. 32; Judg. 5; 1 Sam. 2) and to the songs of the poor (Zeph. 2:3; 3:12; Isa. 41:17–20). Psalm 113 begins the "Egyptian Hallel," sung partly at the beginning (Pss. 113–114) and partly at the close (Pss. 115–118) in the context of the three pilgrimage festival dinners (Exod. 23:14–17). Psalm 113 indicates some kind of antiphonal singing: v. 1, a request to begin; vv. 2–4, choral response; v. 5, question by a solo voice; and vv. 7–9, choral response.

"Servants of the Lord" in v. 1 indicates anyone loyal to Yahweh, especially under trial (Deut. 34:5; Isa. 42:1; Ps. 79:2). The choral response in 113:2–4 reaches to people true to the covenant even at a distance from Jerusalem (Mal. 1:11; Ps. 107:3). Thrice "the name of the Lord," Yahweh, is acclaimed, affirming the special relation of the people with their God. In reply to the question (113:5), the choir responds that Israel's God is distinguished by "raising the poor" from disgrace. During the Exile, Israel realized its impotence, like many saintly persons (Gen. 16:2; 20:18; 1 Sam 1:5) who became typical of all Israel (Isa. 54:1–10; 66:7–16).

Psalm 114. The hymn in Psalm 114 possesses high literary and liturgical qualities involving parallelism, brevity, imagination, and surprise. All verses, except the final one, comprise a call to praise, so the Greek version united Psalm 115 with it. The psalm may have been composed for the sanctuary at Gilgal near the river Jordan (Josh. 5; 1 Sam. 10:8) and was later transferred to the Jerusalem Temple with its symbolism of water flowing from the rock of sacrifice (Ps. 46:5; Ezek. 47). One may suggest an early date since the two kingdoms, Israel and Judah, are united.

Ps. 114:1–7 quickly moves from the Red Sea to the river Jordan and overlooks the long, trying period of the wilderness (Ps. 95:7b–11). Israel celebrated and relived the crossing of the Red Sea at a more convenient geographical location, which, however, was unlike the Red Sea area and was surrounded with mountains. A similar ritual "actualization" occurs throughout Joshua 1–6. The final line, sung by a solo voice in contrast to the choral singing of Ps. 114:1–7, consists of participles, a verbal form that, in Hebrew, emphasizes the present. It is happening now as God supplies life in response to Israel's prayer (Deut. 5:1–5).

Psalm 115. Originating in a service like Josh. 7:19; Mic. 7:7–20; Isaiah 12; and Amos 4:6–13, with confession of faults, forgiveness, and

praise of Yahweh, Psalm 115 represents a religious service especially for Diaspora Jews living among foreigners and tempted to apostasy. The psalm was ideal for pilgrimage to Jerusalem (see commentary above introducing Book Five). The heart of the service was vv. 12–15, a priestly blessing (Num. 6:22–27), preceded by renewed consecration to the Lord of the covenant (vv. 1–2) and a prayer of confidence (vv. 3–11), followed by thanksgiving (vv. 16–18).

Verses 1–2 reflect the agonizing taunt of Ps. 79:10 and attribute strength and glory "not to us," or as the Aramaic Targum reads, "not because of our justice" (Ps. 138:2). All confidence rests with the Lord of the covenant (Exod. 34:6–7). Ps. 115:3–11 ridicules the helpless gods of conquered people, something commonly done (2 Kings 18:33–35; Isa. 44:9–20). For Israel, the religion of other nations appeared like fetish idolatry. Israel is divided between priests, laity, and "God-fearers," converts who were not completely following the full laws of circumcision and food (cf. Acts 10:2, 22). Ps. 115:17 reflects the ancient, traditional opinion about the afterlife (Pss. 6:6; 30:10).

Psalm 116. Intended for a Temple service of thanksgiving (vv. 9, 14, 18–19; Pss. 65:5; 100:4), Psalm 116 mirrors a person fulfilling vows if released from critical sickness (116:3, 8) or from bonds and execution (vv. 3, 16). The many Aramaic expressions represent a late composition from a Jew in the Diaspora. The psalm may be divided as follows: vv. 1–2, confession of faith in Yahweh's regard for the needy; vv. 3–4, expression of distress; vv. 5–11, chant of praise and thanksgiving; and vv. 12–19, sacrifice of thanksgiving in the Temple. The Greek version, which unites Psalms 113–114, separates 116:10–19 as a distinct psalm. Sung as the "Egyptian Hallel" (Pss. 113–118; see commentary above introducing Book Five), this psalm belonged to the second segment toward the end of the sacred meal (Matt. 26:30).

In Ps. 116:1–2 the psalmist is able to love because the Lord has been loving and caring all along; this psalm does not begin with a silent, deaf God as do Psalms 22:2 and 28:1. Yet the phrase "my voice, my supplication" implies a loud, persistent supplication (Ps. 28:2). In 116:3–4 the understanding of the afterlife is traditional (Pss. 6:6; 115:17); still God's presence with an unclean, sick person is not traditional, as the rules in Leviticus 21 point out. In Ps. 116:15 the psalmist slips into an attitude shared with Ps. 139:8, with its own Aramaic expressions.

Ps. 116:5–11 begins the chant of thanksgiving, based on the covenant's intuition of a kind and faithful God (Exod. 34:6–7; Pss. 111:4; 112:4; Isa. 49:10; 54:10). The "simple" or "little ones" (Ps. 116:6) are vulnerable people, at times naive, who seem to trust too easily (cf. Pss. 9:11; 19:8; 119:130; Prov. 1:22). According to Ps. 116:10, faith remains as a sturdy support even when a person's emotions are crying out against faith (Pss. 22; 44; Job 14:2).

Ps. 116:12–19 recognizes that God's goodness and gifts cannot be purchased. Temple sacrifice, therefore, gives nothing to God but recognizes ever more fully God's gifts by enabling one to surrender oneself symbolically with the holocaust of joyful adoration (Lev. 1). The "cup of salvation" is the wine shared at a sacred meal, a metaphor for the joy already received from the Lord and shared with others, intensified by the Lord's presence (Ps. 23:5). While, previously, death meant fearful silence, in 116:15 it becomes a precious moment of rest in the Lord. Liturgy has slipped beyond death to the ever-living God (Ps. 22:28–32; 49:16).

Psalm 117. The shortest of psalms, Psalm 117 is a hymn of praise. It raises the persistent question, are the nations being granted a place in the Mosaic covenant? Rom. 15:11 recognizes universal salvation here. Yet the motivation for praise (Ps. 117:2) reserves the gifts of "love and fidelity" (Exod. 34:6–7) "for us." Does that mean exclusively for Israel? There seems to be here, however, at least an indirect confession from the Gentiles of faith in God as revealed through the Mosaic covenant.

Psalm 118. The "Egyptian Hallel" (Pss. 113–118), sung for the three pilgrimage feasts, concludes in Psalm 118. It accompanied the fourth cup of wine at the Passover meal. It may also have been used for an entrance ritual (v. 19; Pss. 15; 24). Several details indicate that it was most of all at home with the Feast of Tabernacles, with reference to tents (118:15), day (v. 24; Ps. 81:4), light (118:27), plants used for the family tent (v. 27), and hosannah (v. 25). Long usage meant additions and shifts, so that the structure became complex. The psalm moves between community thanksgiving (vv. 1–4, 22–29) and individual thanksgiving (vv. 5–21). It allows for individual adaptation within its larger pattern. Some Hebrew manuscripts begin separate psalms at vv. 5 and 25.

Verses 1–4 begin with a traditional community expression of gratitude (Pss. 107:1; 136:1; Ezra 3:11) embracing all Israel, lay, priests, and God-fearing converts (Ps. 115:9–11).

Ps. 118:5–21 is adaptable to many forms of individual thanksgiving: people freed from severe restrictions (vv. 5–9), from harassment by outsiders (vv. 10–16), or from sickness (vv. 17–18). It probably permitted additions for other situations. Verses 5–9 refer to something like occupation by foreign troops (Lam. 1:3) or confinement in death (Ps. 116:3). Everyone, but especially people with nomadic background, possesses a basic necessity of being "set free"

from burdensome restrictions (Gen. 26:22; Ps. 31:9). "The Lord is with me. . . . What can any human being do to me?"—a common refrain (Ps. 56:5, 12) repeated in Rom. 8:31. Taking refuge in the Lord is another familiar response (Ps. 2:12; 7:1; 11:1). In 118:10–16 the language is so strong that one suspects a king is speaking about a national disaster or an individual is identifying personal tragedy with the nation's or someone in the Diaspora is persecuted for the faith by surrounding Gentiles. "Cut off" refers to circumcision and, in 1 Sam. 18:22–27, to a great massacre. The language of gratitude in Ps. 118:14 is taken from the nation's song of deliverance in Exod. 15:6, 12. In Ps. 118:17–18 sickness is now seen as a chastisement that disciplined and purified one (Deut. 4:36; Jer. 10:24; Isa. 54:8). The gates of justice may be named from the ceremony of receiving a person into full membership after sin or uncleanness (Pss. 15; 24).

Ps. 118:22–25 allows the congregation to absorb all individuals again in communal thanksgiving as at the beginning. "The stone rejected by the builders [now] the cornerstone" refers to the enigmatic text of Isa. 28:16, in which the prophet refers to the testing of one's faith and one's faithful reliance upon the Lord (Isa. 7:9b; 30:15–18). The phrase probably became a proverb suitable for many situations. In Matt. 21:42–43, Jesus refers to sincere Israelites whose lives show the fruits of the kingdom of God; Mark 12:10–12 relates the passage to the death of Jesus, Luke 20:16–18 to the necessity of making a clear decision for or against Jesus. Acts 4:11 speaks of the stone "spurned," weaving in a passage from Isa. 53:3.

It is evident that "this is the day the Lord takes action" (Ps. 118:24a); the present tense here reflects the liturgical custom of actualizing the past moment of a great redemptive act. The Hebrew form of v. 25a preserves the origin of the refrain, "Hosannah," originally a call for help (Pss. 12:2; 28:9) or mercy (2 Sam. 14:4) but later a stereotypic word for praise (so Matt. 21:9). This verse was repeated seven times on the last day of Tabernacles as the congregation processed up to and around the altar (Ps. 118:27).

Verses 26–27 offer a blessing upon "the one who comes in the name of the Lord." Here the phrase refers to any devout Israelite; eventually in Judaism it became a messianic title (Matt. 11:3). Ps. 118:27a, with its reference to light, may provide the occasion at the end of the service for imparting the priestly blessing from Num. 6:22–27.

Psalm 119. On first reading, Psalm 119 seems exceptional for nothing except its length. It is the longest of all psalms but does not display exceptional poetry, or vivid images, or original insights, or excitement about anything; it just exhibits a quiet, meditative tone about "law"

486

with no internal development. One can start at the end and read the verses backward, and it makes equally good sense. Yet Psalm 119 was not composed for the epic moments of life but for the 90 percent of time in which life is uneventful, even monotonous. Psalm 119 becomes the moment of prolonged contemplation in God's presence.

Each stanza of eight verses begins with the succeeding letter of the Hebrew alphabet, and all eight verses start with the same letter. Each verse has one of eight synonyms for law, except that v. 90 has a ninth synonym and v. 122 none at all. The author of Ps. 119 must have been a persistent type of person, yet did not want to be stereotyped as rigid.

The psalmist meditated intently, especially upon Deuteronomy but also upon Proverbs, Job, Jeremiah, and Ezekiel, and to a lesser extent upon Isaiah 40–66, writing in what is called an anthological style. Little derives from the historical or former prophetical books of Joshua through 2 Kings. Despite its legal appearance, there seems to be no contact with the priestly tradition of the Pentateuch. Some examples of borrowing are: v. 2 and Deut. 4:29; Jer. 29:13–14a; v. 25 and Job 40:13; vv. 33–40 and Prov. 4:13; v. 31 and Deut. 10:20; v. 70 and Isa. 6:10; v. 76 and Isa. 51:3; v. 85 and Jer. 18:20a; and v. 89 and Isa. 40:8. The sources lean toward a style of lament, with a strong secondary impulse of instruction and exhortation. Psalm 119, therefore, is difficult to categorize, yet its overall appearance tilts towards a wisdom psalm. It stems from a contemplative type of person within the Deuteronomic school. The author may have intended this work for new converts (vv. 19, 67, 176).

"Law," as inferred already, is not to be interpreted as a legal code, or as the Torah or five books of Moses, or as the tradition of the scribes. It is the Lord who teaches the law (vv. 12, 19, 26, 64, 68); and so in keeping the law, one seeks the Lord (vv. 2, 10, 19, 48). Law is not kept simply by human determination but through prayer and the Lord's assistance (vv. 10, 18, 25, 26, 36). Obedience to this law becomes a source of unfailing joy (vv. 24, 35, 77, 92). Law thus becomes an important part of conversion and reformation (vv. 19, 67, 176). Law is identified with the inner force of conscience in a person persistently in touch with the Scriptures and prayerfully in God's presence. Such a law is the most binding and most liberating of all, for it represents one's best self formed by God along the way of the Scriptures.

The psalmist seems to be peering into the mystery of a personal, loving, caring God. Prayer at night is taken for granted (vv. 55, 62, 147); prayer is requested seven times a day (v. 164), giving rise to the seven "hours" of the monastic office in Christianity.

The alphabetical style adds its own mystic tone. Each letter is seen as a gift from God, enabling a person to refine ever more carefully the least dictate of God's will. This style endows a person with inner strength and consistency.

Psalm 119 shows no interest in Israelite history and institutions. Temple and feast days seem far from the mind. This psalmist may have been among the first of the pietists, the forerunners of individualistic religion. Yet the anthological style meant that the author was not a stranger to sanctuary worship, only not the most active participant.

Some scholars look upon Psalm 119 and especially its later stanzas as an introduction to or a part of the "Psalms of Ascent" for pilgrimage (Pss. 120–134). Pilgrims often passed through hostile territory (119:81–88) and were grateful at the end (vv. 89–96), with prayers during the stay at Jerusalem (vv. 97–128) and before departure (vv. 129–136), with further reflections for the return journey (vv. 137–160) and upon arrival home (vv. 161–176).

Psalm 119 adapts itself to private retreat. One can substitute for "law" any aspect of life that is from God, important yet difficult to appreciate, understand, or even accept: for example, sickness or death in a family; crucial turns in life, church, or politics beyond one's control; or an inspiration to be of service to others.

The Psalms of Ascent

Psalms 120–134 are each entitled "A Song of Ascent" or, in some older Bibles, "A Gradual Psalm." Various reasons are offered: there is the steplike or progressive rhythm of repeating words from the previous verse (Pss. 121:3–5; 123:1–2; 127:1–2; 130:5–6); fifteen psalms were to be sung on the fifteen steps from the Court of the Women to the Court of Israel in the Temple (Ezek. 40:22, 37; m. Mid. 2.5 6); they allude to return from Babylonian exile (Ezra 2:1; 7:9); and, most probable of all reasons, they were chanted by pilgrims to and from Jerusalem, especially at the time of the harvest festivals, as the "Egyptian Hallel" (Pss. 113–118) was sung at Jerusalem during these feasts.

This sequence of psalms may reflect a pilgrimage to Jerusalem: the announcement (Ps. 120), beginning (Ps. 121), and joyful arrival at Jerusalem (Ps. 122) where prayers (Ps. 123) and thanksgiving (Ps. 124) are offered, and after a pause (Ps. 125), processions with sheaves (Ps. 126), invocation (Ps. 127), with blessing and curse (Pss. 128–129), expiatory sacrifice (Ps. 130), a renewal of covenant obligations (Ps. 131), and another procession honoring Jerusalem (Ps. 132), a communion sacrifice or sacred meal (Ps. 133), and a farewell to the Levites at the Temple (Ps. 134).

The psalms share many literary qualities: brevity, formal blessings, hymnic sentences, repetitions, allusions to Jerusalem, and Aramaic expressions. Their imagery generally reflects farm life and agricultural vistas, family and homelife. The tone is mild, well adapted to people tired from a tedious journey.

Psalm 120. Psalm 120 is a prayer for help combining sorrow and confidence. Verse 1 calls for help because of the distressful circumstances of the Diaspora and the difficulties of the journey to Jerusalem. Verses 2–4 respond in the only way possible in a culture without internal police forces, by a curse that places the evil situation squarely in God's hands (Ps. 69). In vv. 5–7 the foreign lands stretch as far north as Meshech near the Black Sea (Gen. 10:2) to Kedar in southern Arabia (Isa. 21:13–17). Despite its dangers the psalmist confesses the need (Ps. 120:7) to go on the pilgrimage to pray for peace.

Psalm 121. Psalm 121 is a quiet dialogue between parent and child or between priest and lay person. Verse 1 is the question, vv. 2–8 the reply. Or even more intricately, vv. 1 and 3 are by the lay person; vv. 2 and 4 by the priest, who pronounces the blessing in vv. 5–8.

Lifting one's eyes to the mountains implies a yearning look toward Jerusalem (Ps. 42:2) and a fearful glance at hostile mountains along the way. The blessing in 121:2 is founded on Isa. 41:10, 13–14; 42:5 and was repeated frequently (Pss. 115:15; 124:8; 134:3; 146:6), as it is in Christian prayers. That God does not slumber or sleep (121:4) reassures anyone doubtful, as in Pss. 7:7; 44:24. Ps. 121:5 reads in 11QPs[a], "By night the Lord is your keeper, by day your shade at your right hand," like a promise given to Abraham (Gen. 28:15). God will protect the pilgrim not only from sunstroke (2 Kings 4:18–20) and the evil influence of the moon but also from demonic attack (Ps. 91:5–13).

Psalm 122. Joyfully arriving at Jerusalem (vv. 1–2), the pilgrim praises the holy city (vv. 3–5) and prays for its peace (vv. 6–9). The walls of Jerusalem offer security after the dangerous journey for those obeying the law of pilgrimage (Deut. 16:16–17). The reference to "the house of David" reflects postexilic hopes for a Davidic Messiah (cf. Zech. 9:9). Christians think of Jesus' pilgrimages to Jerusalem (Luke 2:49; 9:51; 19:41) and their own invitation to an assembly of worship (Heb. 12:22–24).

Psalm 123. Although beginning almost the same way as Psalm 121, Psalm 123 has a tone of lament over the memory of personal and national sorrows. A quiet, wholesome trust sustains the pilgrim, despite an arrogant smirch from oppressors. The psalm was composed at a difficult time (cf. Neh. 2:19–20; Isa. 63:7–64:11; Zech. 1:15).

Psalm 124. Psalm 124, a hymn of community thanksgiving composed for an occasion such as the completion of the city walls after a period of internal indifference and outside harassment (Neh. 12:27–47), was easily adaptable for pilgrims. "Were it not for the Lord," the psalmist, like Israel, would never have survived (Ps. 94:17; Gen. 31:42). People are summoned to witness publicly to their faith in the holy city as well as their own deliverance by the Lord (Pss. 107; 118). A series of precise images sweeps us forward: fire, torrential rain, wild animals, a helpless bird; people were in danger of being swallowed up in death (cf. Num. 16:30). The psalm recalls the mythological accounts of chaotic waters associated with Jerusalem (Pss. 29; 46). Ps. 124:8 repeats a standard prayer of confidence (Ps. 121:2).

Psalm 125. This psalm of confidence, Psalm 125, was composed during foreign occupation or subversion from evil leadership within (Isa. 56:9–57:13; Ps. 16). It was ideal for pilgrims reflecting upon the perils of their own hostile environment at home and on the journey. In the opening expression of assurance (125:1–3), righteous Israelites merge into city, mountains, and Temple and these into God, a God who surrounds the chosen people with complete protection (Zech. 2:9[5]; 2 Kings 6:17). Ps. 125:4–5 asks a blessing upon the upright, those who are "straight and true with God," but upon the wicked, "those who bend and twist their ways," an expulsion from the community (Pss. 18:26–27; 35:8). The psalm ends with a liturgical blessing (Ps. 128:6).

Psalm 126. Psalm 126, another psalm of confidence, may have been composed for the festival of Tabernacles, when the people celebrated the autumn harvest and prayed for rain (Lev. 23:33–43; Zech. 14:16–19), but which was at times a feast of disappointment (Hag. 1:6; 2:16; Neh. 8:9–18). Ps. 126:1–3 dreams about a happy future under God's direction (Gen. 37:5–11; 20:3–7; 1 Kings 3:5–15). Ps. 126:4–5 prays for the speedy fulfillment of dreams, like sudden rainfall in the wilderness, or for a sure fulfillment, like sowing seed in the dark earth with hopes for a good harvest (cf. John 4:36–38; Gal. 6:9). The sequence of joy into sorrow with new hope may also be observed in Jeremiah 31.

Psalm 127. Psalm 127, a wisdom psalm, examines the special blessings of a large family for the virtuous person. It may have been composed to greet the birth of a child, yet it was ideal for pilgrimage since the child represented the continuity of Israel within the family home of the Temple. The association of wisdom, blessings, and Temple attracted the name of Solomon in the title (cf. Ps. 72). In 127:1–2, and throughout the Bible, to build a house meant to have a family (Deut. 25:9; Ruth 4:11). If the Lord does not give children, then every effort at building a physical home is useless. Ps. 127:3–5 witnesses to the blessing of children and the protection that they provide against false witnesses at the city gate (Deut. 25:7; Ruth 4:1–2, 11).

Psalm 128. The preceding psalm ends and Psalm 128 begins with the formula "Happy that one . . ." (cf. Ps. 1). Each, a wisdom psalm, emphasizes the happiness of children for the married couple, here compared to olive plants (Ps. 52:10; Hos. 14:7). At Jerusalem the pilgrim received this formal blessing upon the family. The wife is portrayed living within the private interior of the home with little visibility. The psalm retains the notion of earthly retribution for a virtuous or wicked life (Lev. 26).

Psalm 129. Psalm 129 blends lament, thanksgiving, and most of all, confidence so as to overcome deep disappointments. The tone and images are calm and peaceful, plowing fields and cleaning the housetop, yet the significance is traumatic in that the live flesh of the back is being turned over in the plowing (cf. Isa. 1:4–9) and the withered lives of people are being burnt up like grass. The psalm reflects the sad disillusionment upon returning from exile (Hag. 1:6; Ezra 3:12; Neh. 1). The psalm is a pilgrimage through Israelite history from oppression in Egypt (Ps. 129:1–2; Hos. 11) to the difficulties through the centuries from foreign invaders (Ps. 129:3–4; Jer. 31:15–20) and the destruction of Jerusalem (Ps. 129:5; Lamentations). A liturgical blessing, which may have become a popular greeting (Ruth 2:4), closes the psalm.

Psalm 130. More personal than Psalms 15 and 24, Psalm 130 also prepared a worshiper for full entry into the Temple through "the gate of justice" (Ps. 118:19). It includes a word or oracle from the priest (130:5) in preparation for sacrifice. The Aramaic Targum interpreted "sentinels" (vv. 6–7) as Levites who signal the morning sacrifice (Lev. 6:5–6). The strong attitude of compunction makes it one of the most popular of the seven penitential psalms.

After a plaintive cry for pardon (Ps. 130:1–2) and an admission of guilt (vv. 3–4), the tone moves to confidence (vv. 5–7a) and the assurance of forgiveness (vv. 7b–8). The sincerity of the psalmist shows in a skillful choice of words and style. "Depths" reveal an abyss of torment (Pss. 18:16; 69:3, 15) and opaque darkness (Ps. 18:29) beneath the psalm's calm rhythm. Ps.

130:5 positions one humbly before the Lord but three times declares, "I wait!"

Psalm 131. Forgiveness, with memories of failures and guilt, induces a humble attitude toward God (v. 1) and toward one's neighbor (v. 2), so that a community exhortation is appropriate (v. 3). Biblical humility is not so much a state of soul but a healthy, honest relationship with others. The psalmist does not venture recklessly into God's domain (cf. Gen. 3:1–7; Exod. 3:6; Isa. 40:12–14).

Psalm 132. While other "Psalms of Ascent" tend to be subdued and date to the postexilic era (see the Short Essay "The Psalms of Ascent"), Psalm 132 sings enthusiastically and reaches back into early history when David conquered Jerusalem and solemnly brought the Ark from Kiriath-jearim to the holy city (1 Sam. 7:1; 2 Sam. 6–7). 2 Chron. 6:41–42 associates Psalm 132 with Solomon's dedication of the Temple. The first half inaugurates a procession at Kiriath-jearim, repeating David's oath to bring the Ark to Jerusalem (vv. 1–5) and concluding at Jerusalem with the installation of the Ark in the Holy of Holies and prayer for the king (vv. 6–10). In the second half, God (through the priests) declares an oath in favor of David's dynasty (vv. 11–12), associating it with the divine presence at the Temple (vv. 13–16) and ending with a prayer for the king (vv. 17–18). With the disappearance of the dynasty after the destruction of Judah, the pilgrimage to Jerusalem reaffirmed Israel's hope in a Messiah to appear in the Temple. A psalm that originated with a strong political statement connecting the dynasty with the Mosaic covenant and the Ark at Jerusalem ends with nonpolitical aspirations.

A wordplay in vv. 1–5 associates "afflictions," "my eyes," and "sleep," so that David's total concern, indeed his willingness to suffer, is directed towards the Ark. Verses 6–10 locate the beginning of the procession at "Ephrathah," referring to David's clan within the tribe of Judah (Gen. 35:19; Ruth 4:11; Mic. 5:1[2]) and at the "fields of Jaar," "Kiriath-jearim," a village directly west of Jerusalem. "Arise" (Ps. 132:8) announces the beginning of the procession (cf. Num. 10:35; Ps. 68:2). Yahweh's "resting place" is a name for the Temple (Isa. 66:1; 1 Chron. 28:2) with important religious consequences (Ps. 95:11). The clothing (132:9) would be priestly and royal vestments (cf. Zech. 3:3–5). In Ps. 132:17–18 "horn" symbolizes strength (Ps. 18:3; Ezek. 29:21); "lamp," one's presence before God (Exod. 27:20–21; 1 Kings 11:36).

Psalm 133. Psalm 133 is ideally suited to express the joyful companionship of pilgrims at Jerusalem. Closely associated with wisdom (Prov. 15:23; 16:16), it declares that harmony anoints a family and neighborhood as though they were a high priest directing worship at the Temple. Scented oil symbolized peace, health, and joy (Pss. 23:5; 45:8; Exod. 30:22–33). Mount Hermon, reaching over nine thousand feet into the sky and continually capped with snow, became a source of abundant water and dew. Dew is symbolic of blessings (Hos. 14:5; Ps. 110:3), especially "life forever" in family descendants.

Psalm 134. The last of the "Psalms of Ascent," Psalm 134 presents a final evening service at the Temple (Ps. 8:4; Josh. 1:8; 1 Chron. 9:33) with a blessing upon the Levites (Ps. 134:1–2) and a priestly blessing upon the people (v. 3; Num. 6:22–27; Pss. 121:2; 124:8). Psalm 134 may provide the rubrics for a much longer farewell service.

Psalm 135. Like Psalms 96–97 and 119, Psalm 135 presents a mosaic of biblical passages: compare v. 1 and Ps. 113:1; vv. 1–2 and Ps. 134:1; v. 3a and Ps. 136:3a; v. 4 and Exod. 18:11; 19:5; and vv. 15–20 and Ps. 115:4–11. In the postexilic age, a repertoire of sacred literature and formulas was available. The difficulty of detecting a poetical sequence may be due to the psalm's purpose of indicating various liturgical actions. Three minihymns are present: 135:1–4, 13–14, 19–21. Verses 4–21 were sometimes joined with Psalm 136 as part of the "Great Hallel," so that Psalm 135 was sung every Sabbath except the one before New Years; on the eighth day of Passover, it was attached to the "Egyptian Hallel" (Pss. 113–118).

For the call to praise in 135:1–4, cf. Pss. 8:2; 134:1; Exod. 19:5; and Mal. 3:17. All depends upon God's initial election of Israel as a special possession. Ps. 135:5–18 provides motivation for the hymn, first from creation (vv. 5–7), beginning with "I know," a solo voice from the choir. The sea was always a mysterious, fearful place (Pss. 42:7–12; 107:23–32). The scanning of Israel's history (135:8–12) covers the plagues in Egypt and the early settlement in the land. The first Canaanite kings defeated by Israel were Sihon and Og (Num. 21:21–24, 31–34). Ps. 135:13–14 recapitulates creation and history in the remembrance of the divine name Yahweh; all flows from the self-revelation of God's person within the Mosaic covenant, a remembrance acted out liturgically in Temple ceremonies and prayers. (For vv. 15–21, cf. Ps. 115:4–11.)

Psalm 136. To be chanted antiphonally between a solo voice or special choir and the entire assembly, Psalm 136, a most solemn hymn, is fittingly called the "Great Hallel" or "Great Praise" (see commentaries above introducing Book Five and on Ps. 135). After the introduction (135:1–3), Yahweh is acclaimed for great deeds: in creating the universe (vv. 4–9), in redeeming Israel from Egypt (vv. 10–16), and in conquering the promised land (vv. 17–22; Deut. 34:1–4). Ps. 136:23–26 either summarizes everything as Yahweh's love or else extends that love to the return from Exile. In any case, each moment of God's intervention from the beginning of creation was directed towards Israel's joy and peace.

The opening exclamation can be translated either as "Give thanks!" or "Praise!" The latter meaning is even more germane to this Hebrew word: to lift or cast (Lam. 3:53), praise (Ps. 49:19), or confess sin (Ps. 32:5b)—the context determines the lifting of oneself to God. The refrain begins with the Hebrew particle ki, best translated in its original meaning, "Yes!" or "Indeed!" Nature and history do not give the reason for praise as they direct one's joyful faith already stimulated by what Yahweh has been doing. The word for "loving-kindness" or "mercy" is also pregnant with many connotations: at times "strength" (Isa. 40:26; Ps. 59:10) or "pledge" (Gen. 20:13; Isa. 55:3). Therefore, it connotes love that is enduring and dependable. The refrain became extremely popular in postexilic Israel (Pss. 106:1; 107:1; 118:1; Jer. 33:11; Ezra 3:11).

"God of gods" (Ps. 136:2) originally referred to elevating Yahweh above all other gods (Deut. 10:17), but here it means "God is certainly God." "Lord of lords," similarly. Creation according to the designs of wisdom (Ps. 136:5) directs God's activity across heaven and earth for the sake of Israel (Prov. 8:22–36; Sir. 24). Ps. 136:13 reflects Yahweh's struggle against monstrous, even superhuman hostile forces to free Israel from oppression (Exod. 15:3–8; Isa. 51:9–10). (On Ps. 136:17–20, see Ps. 135:10–11.)

Psalm 137. Psalm 137, a communal lament, closest of all to a funeral dirge, may be divided between vv. 1–4, lamenting the impossibility of chanting songs honoring Jerusalem in enemy lands and vv. 5–9, first lamenting the holy city destroyed before one's eyes and then cursing the two great enemies, Babylon, which burned Jerusalem to the ground (2 Kings 25) and Edom, which looted the countryside afterward (Obad. 8–15; Isa. 63:1–6). The psalm was written with the same agony as present in Isa. 63:7–64:11, between 537 and 520 B.C., perhaps by a repatriated singer from the guild of Asaph (Ezra 2:41; Ps. 79).

Ps. 137:1–4 begins with a contrast of "rivers of Babylon" and the stream of one's tears (Ps. 42:4), between remembering and forgetting (137:1, 5, 6, 7). The tormentors who ask, "Where is your God?" (Pss. 79:10; 115:2) hardly want a song to this God. "Songs of Zion" may dictate the placement of this psalm here, after the Zion songs in Psalms 120–134, 135–136. (For curse psalms, see the commentary above on Ps. 69; and for atrocities of war, expressed in the metaphor of dashing children against city walls, Hos. 14:1; Nah. 3:10.) The metaphor expressed the capture of an enemy city, at which time defenders, born within the city, were frequently overwhelmed and killed by the assaulting troops.

Psalm 138. The last series of "Psalms of David" commences with Psalm 138, generally in poor textual condition (Ps. 141:5–7). The author, writing from a foreign land, is quite conscious of the community and its covenant (138:2b, 8; Exod. 34:6–7). Two hymns of thanksgiving (Ps. 137:1–3, 4–6) are completed by a song of confidence (vv. 7–8).

Verses 1–3 begin in a fashion similar to the canticles of the redeemed in Isa. 12:1; 25:1. The phrase, "in the presence of the gods [Heb. *'elohim*]," became embarrassing to the scribes. The Greek and Latin versions read "angels" (NAB); the Syriac, "kings"; the Aramaic Targum, "judges." Originally *'elohim* could have a generic meaning of exalted authority (Ps. 45:7) or Yahweh's heavenly court (Pss. 29:1, 9; 89:6–9) or discredited foreign gods (Ps. 82; Deut. 4:19).

In Ps. 138:4–6 the recognition of Yahweh's gracious deeds by the nations depends upon Israel's faith and its manifestation to outsiders (Isa. 40:9). Ps. 138:8 confesses that the Lord of the covenant outlasts every difficulty.

Psalm 139. Topically one of the most beautiful of psalms, textually Psalm 139 is one of the most difficult. Once the unity is established by an inclusio, bonding vv. 1–3 and 23–24, then the lament in vv. 19–22 controls the meaning of vv. 4–18. Darkness comes from the encirclement of disloyal, hostile people, possibly apostate Jews in foreign lands. As at night, this darkness enables the psalmist to peer deeply into the heavens and into the depths of human existence, perceiving the presence of Yahweh, otherwise hidden by the glare of daylight. With no mention of Israel's history or Temple, the psalmist is related to wisdom literature like Job, yet even stronger ties show up with prophecy (Jer. 11:20–21; 12:3; 17:10; Isa. 40; 49).

Persecution (Ps. 139:19–22) plunges the psalmist into a dark mystery where God is pursued in the paths of knowledge (vv. 4–6), into the farthest reaches of the universe (vv. 7–12), into the silent moments of conception and birth (vv. 13–18). The introductory hymn (vv. 1–3) is paralleled by a confession of innocence (vv. 23–24). The psalmist is not so much seeking wisdom as reaching for peace with God.

When the verb "know" in v. 1 is left without an object, the implication is that Yahweh knows everything. The juxtaposition of sitting and standing (cf. Deut. 6:7; Ps. 127:2), journeying and resting in Ps. 139:2–3 intends to include every moment in between.

Verses 4–6 leave the psalmist in fear and awe at the mystery of God within oneself. To be hemmed in is expressed using language of siege and adversity (Judg. 2:15; Jer. 10:18). The psalm, therefore, is not written from a peaceful setting. When Ps. 139:7–12 reaches to the limits of sky and earth, the psalmist is defiantly saying to persecutors, you cannot hound me away from God. In fact, to locate God in the highest heavens or in Sheol speaks defiantly to the narrow limits of Israel's theology. Deut. 30:12 forbad seeking God in the skies; Pss. 6:6; 88:10–13 denied God's presence in Sheol. This search for God through impenetrable, even forbidden darkness is not to be dismissed as black magic (139:11–12).

Verses 13–18 move from the dangerous darkness of public life to the warm, life-sustaining darkness of the mother's womb. The psalmist senses the kindly protection and wise planning of Yahweh. "My inward being," (lit., "my kidneys,") refers to the seat of conscience (Ps. 16:7) and personal integrity (Jer. 12:2), where one learns true wisdom (Ps. 51:8). This and other classic texts on pregnancy confess God's presence already forming the entire future of the person (Pss. 22:10–11; 71:5–6; Jer. 1:5; Isa. 49:1; Job 10:8–12). God sees "my embryo," an Aramaic expression for something unfinished, and inscribes the entire future "in your book." From Ps. 69:29; Exod. 32:32–33; Dan. 7:10; 12:1, and many other texts, this expression assures a person of faith that a happy, peaceful outcome will ensue. Ps. 139:18b, "when I awake, behold you are still with me," may originally have indicated light at the end of an earthly trial, but the Aramaic Targum saw here an allusion to the resurrection.

Verses 19–22 pray for the destruction of the wicked, a prayer that would have eliminated the need of a psalm like this. Verses 23–24 end with a door opening into the unknown future, later understood as "the way of eternity."

Psalm 140. Laborious with words rare or unusual, Psalm 140 represents the prayer of an Israelite innocently accused, possibly the victim of a curse. The opening section contains a double prayer for deliverance (vv. 2 and 5), each time followed by lamentation (vv. 3–4 and 6); there follows an expression of faith in Yahweh (vv. 7–9), a curse upon the slanderers (vv. 10–13), and a final prayer of confidence (vv. 14–15). The dismal, deceitful situation reflects the early postexilic age as described in Isa. 56:9–57:13 and 59:1–15.

The opening appeal is against people with venomous tongues who may have put a curse upon the psalmist (Ps. 140:4; Pss. 41:8; 58:6); the image of a snare trapping the unsuspecting victim is equally frequent (Pss. 140:6; 91:3; 124:7). Ps. 140:3b is included in a series of passages quoted in Rom. 3:10–18 (see the commentary above on Ps. 14:3). The confession of faith (140:7–9) uses familiar expressions from the repertoire of Israel's prayer (Pss. 16:2; 22:11b; 31:15; 35:3; 60:9). The curse against the enemy (140:10–13; see the commentary above on Ps. 69) incorporates the *lex talionis* (Ps. 35:8). Reminiscences of the fiery destruction of Sodom and Gomorrah (Gen. 19; Ps. 11:6) and the opening of the earth to swallow Dathan and Abiram (Num. 16:32–33) explode upon readers. The concluding prayer of confidence presumes eventual vindication.

Psalm 141. Psalm 141 is even more textually disturbed than Psalm 140. In fact, vv. 5–7 are unintelligible in the Hebrew with a wide variety of restructuring in modern translations. Yet Psalms 117, 138, 141, and 142 were chanted each evening for the lighting of lamps within the Temple evening service; today Psalm 141 is frequently sung with the burning of incense at Christian vesper services. The psalm opens with an appeal to God for assistance (vv. 1–2) against temptation (vv. 3–4). After the perplexing vv. 5–7, another prayer for help is directed against deceitful adversaries (vv. 8–10).

Verse 1 voices a classic appeal to Yahweh (Pss. 17:6; 22:20; 38:23). The evening sacrifice consisted of prayers, incense consumed in adoration, cereal and lamb offerings partly burned and partly given to the priests for livelihood (Exod. 30:8; Lev. 2:1; 6:1; Num. 28:3–8). This custom was faithfully followed in the postexilic age (Ezra 9:5; Dan. 9:21; Jth. 9:1). Through prayer one seeks wisdom and circumspection (Ps. 141:3; Prov. 13:3; Eccles. 5:1, 4–6). God "inclines the heart to evil" (Ps. 141:4) in that only God's grace, freely offered and freely received, opens the heart to goodness. When rejected, God leaves a person.

Psalm 142. Psalm 142, a lament, stems from an individual falsely accused and under dark confinement; prisons as known today did not exist (Lev. 24:12; Num. 15:34; Jer. 38:6). The composer borrowed freely from other laments (Pss. 16; 22; 27; 30). The structure is typical: a call for God's attention (142:2–3a), a lament (vv. 3b–5), and a prayer for help (vv. 6–8). The title associates the psalm with David's hiding from Saul in a cave (1 Sam. 22:1), certainly an encouragement for anyone under persecution who, like David, is assured Yahweh's special care.

For Ps. 142:2, see Pss. 30:9 and 77:2. Consolation is found in memorized prayers. Ps. 142:3 literally speaks of pouring out "my meditations," my continuous mumbling of prayers. The psalmist in v. 5 challenges the Lord: "Look carefully to the right [where a friend ought to be] and see; there is no one willing to acknowl-

edge me." Verse 6 accumulates familiar phrases, especially drawn from the Levites (Ps. 16:5; Num. 18:20), but here applied to all Israel, which recognizes a personal consecration to the Lord (Ps. 73:26).

Psalm 143. The last of the seven penitential psalms, Psalm 143 confesses that only through Yahweh can anyone arrive at goodness and persevere in it. The popularity of this psalm is exemplified by the Greek church's recitation of it every morning. One meets an initial appeal to Yahweh (vv. 1–2), a lament (vv. 3–6), a new call for God's attention (v. 7), and petitions (vv. 8–12). The psalm is a potpourri of prayers across the Psalter; almost every line can be documented elsewhere. Verse 2 acknowledges the powerlessness of anyone to be a righteous person left to themselves (Job 15:14; 25:4) and is quoted by Paul (Rom. 3:9, 20; Gal. 2:16). Ps. 143:5 indicates the value of memorized prayers (Pss. 77:4; 119:52). Ps. 143:7 follows the traditional position of no remembrance of Yahweh in Sheol, the place of the dead (Ps. 6:6). The psalm ends in the company of the suffering, obedient servant (Deut. 34:1–5; Isa. 42:1; 50:4–9a; 52:13–53:12).

Psalm 144. Just as Psalm 18 was considered a most typical psalm of David and inserted as chap. 22 in the appendix to the Davidic narrative (2 Sam. 21–24), Psalm 144, almost at the end of the "Psalms of David" in the Psalter, draws upon Psalm 18 to thank God for the glorious Davidic tradition and to beg God for its renewal in dreary postexilic Israel (Isa. 56:9–57:13; Ps. 16). In fact, this redaction in the postexilic age may have dictated the predominance of laments in the "Psalms of David" and the reduction of David's image in the titles to small, even sinful human proportions. Part One (vv. 1–11) represents the royal Davidic tradition, drawing upon Ps. 18:3, 5, 10, 15, 17; Part Two (144:12–15), a fragment of a psalm, adapts wisdom traditions to the later age. The text has been damaged by neglect or scribal incompetence.

After the opening hymn (vv. 1–2), an admission of human frailty (vv. 3–4) leads to a theophany and a prayerful refrain requesting God's intervention (vv. 5–8), to an expression of gratitude with a repetition of the refrain. Verses 12–15 ask for peaceful prosperity in the family (v. 12), farmlands (vv. 13–14a), and cities (v. 14bc). The psalm concludes joyfully (v. 15).

After a hymnic introduction from Psalm 18, human weakness is confessed with the images and expressions of Pss. 8:5; 39:6–7, 12; Job 7:17–18; 14:2; Eccles. 6:12 and leads to a cry of desperation that God break through the postexilic desolation with a marvelous theophany. This is not a prayer for the messianic age but for urgent help now. The language is drawn from Pss. 18:10, 15; 104:32; Isa. 64:1–4. The reference to foreigners who swear falsely (Ps. 144:7–8) may point to apostate Jews or to those who intermarried in postexilic Israel (Isa. 56:6–57:13; Neh. 9:2). The new song (Ps. 144:9; Isa. 42:10; Pss. 33:3; 96:1) prepares for the addition of a new prayer in 144:12–15.

Psalm 145. An alphabetic psalm (Pss. 9–10) with the line beginning with the Hebrew letter *nun* supplied at 145:13b in the Greek, Syriac, and 11QPs[a], Psalm 145 is typically restrained in its creativity. An anthological method appears throughout: compare v. 1 and Ps. 30:2; v. 2b and Ps. 34:3; v. 3a and Ps. 48:2. Structure is often obscured by the alphabetic approach, but it may be helpful to recognize: the call to praise in vv. 1–2, 4–7, 10–12; motivation in vv. 3, 8–9, 13–20; and conclusion in v. 21.

With this poem, the "Psalms of David" are concluded, even though the major collections ended at Ps. 72:20. Rabbi Eleazar ben Abina (fourth century A.D.) assured anyone who recited Psalm 145 three times daily a place in the world to come (b. Ber. 4b). It is recited daily in the synagogue for morning, noonday, and evening prayer. Verse 2 was incorporated into the traditional Christian hymn of praise, "Te Deum," and vv. 10, 15–16 into grace before meals. Yahweh's domain according to this psalm will be universal (vv. 15, 16, 21), but especially over Israel (vv. 10b, 18–20), and eternal (vv. 1, 2, 13, 21). These qualities are reinforced by the inclusive and enduring nature of an alphabetic psalm.

Verses 4–9 draw praise from the roots of the covenant (Exod. 34) and may refer to the remembrance (Ps. 145:7) of Yahweh's great deeds for Israel as reenacted in liturgy (Pss. 102:13–18; 111; 135:13). Ps. 145:15–16 is drawn from Ps. 104:27–28. Because the Lord is close, manifest, and just "to all who call with sincerity" (145:17–18), the only requirement is a turning to God with faith in God's graciousness and fidelity, excluding whatever smacks of deceit, frivolousness, or superstition. The final phrase, "for ever and ever," is placed after each "letter" or verse in 11QPs[a] and may represent a community refrain.

Psalm 146. The last five psalms may constitute the final doxology of praise (Pss. 41:14; 72:18–19; 89:53; 106:48). Psalm 146 exhibits a strong anthological style and draws especially from Psalms 103–104. After the call to praise (146:1–2) and an exhortation from the priests (vv. 3–4), the motivation comes principally from Yahweh's care for the defenseless (vv. 5–9), Yahweh's role as king (v. 10).

Verses 1–2 transform one's entire life into praise through the reception of Yahweh's gift of life. The second half of v. 2 hints at a translation such as, "let my entire life be music to my God." Verses 3–4 contrast the eternal God with every

human resource that ends in death (Gen. 3:19; Ps. 104:29–30). The text may connote, at least vaguely, the psalmist's aspiration for eternal life (Ps. 49:16–20).

Ps. 146:5–9 begins in the style of wisdom (Ps. 1:1) but proceeds with participles in hymnic style: making heaven and earth ... guarding fidelity, securing justice ... giving food ... opening [the eyes of] the blind. Worship acknowledges creation as happening now and links it closely with social justice (Pss. 96–98). Ps. 146:6 is recited in a prayer of thanksgiving in Acts 4:24. The anthological style is enhanced in 11QPs[a] with the insertion after Ps. 146:9 of Pss. 33:8 and 145:10–12.

Psalm 147. Like Psalm 146 in its strongly anthological style, Psalm 147 also draws from Psalms 33 and 104 as well as from Isaiah 40; 55; 56; and 61. Three hymns, with frequent use of participles, are stitched together: Ps. 146:1–6, Yahweh, Lord of history; vv. 7–11, Lord of nature; and vv. 12–20, God of Zion, where the creative word is announced. The Greek and Latin versions separate vv. 12–20 as a separate psalm, enabling them to catch up numerically with the Hebrew text. The references to Jerusalem in the first and third stanzas create literary unity. Because of the mention of the city walls in v. 2 and of rain in the second and third stanzas, the psalm may have close links with the dedication of the walls (Neh. 12:27–43) and with the Feast of Tabernacles (Zech. 14:16–19).

Ps. 147:1–6 joins creation with Yahweh's care for the poor and outcasts. The creator God who reaches into the stars (Isa. 40:26) appears as a healer for personal sorrows (Hos. 11:3; Jer. 30:17); both acts proclaim a message of salvation about a compassionate God. The second hymn (Ps. 147:7–11) contrasts the strength of a merciful God with the weakness of the instruments of war. The fear of the Lord is identified with hope in the Lord's steadfast love, bonding everyone with the God of the covenant.

Verses 12–20 begin within the Temple at Jerusalem, and from the word of proclamation and prayer there goes forth a creative word (Ps. 33:6; Isa. 55:10–11) to bring important snow in winter, especially on the mountains north of Galilee. The melting of this snow and the later rains assure abundant crops in the new agricultural year (Deut. 11:10–17). This stanza of the hymn leads up to Israel's faith as a chosen people (Deut. 7:5–15; Isa. 44:1–5). In Ps. 147:19–20 the creative word, giving ever-new life, is identified with the Torah (Deut. 4:7–8; Sir. 24).

Psalm 148. Psalm 148 is a hymn of praise that allows many comparisons: with scribal lists from ancient Egypt; with Psalms 33; 103–104; Genesis 1; Job 38; Song of Three Youths 28–68; and with St. Francis's "Canticle to the Sun." Psalm 148 consists of an invitation to the heavens and their inhabitants (vv. 1–6) and to the earth and its inhabitants (vv. 7–13a) to praise Yahweh. Each section consists of imperatives completed by the exhortative clause, "Let them praise the name of the Lord" (vv. 5, 13a), each with its own finale (vv. 6, 13b). Verse 14 centers this universal phrase in Israel. While the first stanza descends from the angels, to sun, moon, and stars, down to the body of rain clouds above the earth, the second stanza ascends from sea monsters, to earth's surface, to animals and humankind. A lovely symmetry directs the liturgical action.

Verses 1–6 place the liturgical action in the universe beginning before God's throne in the heavens (1 Kings 8:27; Pss. 11:4; 18:5–20), surrounded by the heavenly court (1 Kings 22:19–23; Job 38:7; Pss. 29; 82). Later tradition speaks of a series of heavenly spheres (2 Cor. 12:2; T. Levi. 3:1–8), drawing one ever more closely to the divine presence. All of these heavenly creatures are completely subject to Yahweh's will.

Ps. 148:7–13 brings together sometimes hostile sea monsters (Ps. 89:11; Isa. 51:9–10) and wild beasts (Isa. 11:6–8), mountains that quake and spit fire (Ps. 46:2–4), kings at times belligerent (Isa. 10:5–6; Jer. 6), together with young men and maidens, old and young (Ps. 68:25–28; Jer. 31:4, 13) into the liturgical choir. In Ps. 148:14 the "horn" or strength (Ps. 18:3) of Israel appears supreme in this sacred assembly. Israel is God's chosen and beloved, joined to them by steadfast love (Exod. 34:6–7).

Psalm 149. Psalm 149 struggles to sustain the universal praise of Psalm 148 in the postexilic age, possibly when Nehemiah overcame opposition to rebuilding the city walls (Neh. 2:17–20; 12:27–43). The opening words, "sing a new song," allude to the final or eschatological achievement (Isa. 42:10; Pss. 96:1; 144:9) with the extravagant language of Israel's "holy war" tradition (Ps. 18:32–46).

The opening stanza calls for praise (149:1–3) based on the motive of Yahweh's care of the poor (v. 4); the second stanza is a call to battle (vv. 5–6) to achieve victory and peace (vv. 7–9a); and v. 9b, like the close of Psalm 147, centers the action in Israel.

Ps. 149:1–4 blends the titles "chosen people" (Exod. 6:6–7; Deut. 7:6–7; Ps. 95:7), "Maker" (Isa. 44:2; Ps. 100:3), and "King" (Isa. 44:6; Pss. 96–100). In Psalms 148–149 Yahweh creates and rules the universe for the sake of chosen Israel, even for their lowly ones (cf. Isa. 60:14).

Ps. 149:5–9a, with slight emendation, calls upon all "the clans" (instead of "couches" in v. 5). The "two-edged sword," literally "sword of double mouths" (v. 6; Isa. 41:15), devours with double fury, a phrase for the clear, swift justice of God's word (cf. Heb. 4:12; Rev. 1:16; 2:12). So certain is the victory that it is already written in the heavenly records (Pss. 69:29; 139:16).

Psalm 150. If Psalms 146–150 are not the final doxology (cf. Ps. 146), certainly the last psalm fills that position magnificently. While the Psalter opens with a series of "Psalms of David," characterized mostly by lament, it concludes with exuberant praise.

Psalm 150 rings with either hallelujahs or *halleluhu* (Heb., "Praise him") or *hallelu-'el* ("Praise God"), ten within the body of the psalm, vv. 1b–5, or thirteen if one counts the conclusion in v. 6 along with the opening and closing hallelujah, typical of Psalms 146–150. The rabbis recognized the symbolism of ten in the ten words of the commandments (Exod. 34:28) or thirteen in the thirteen times that God the Creator speaks in Genesis 1 or in the thirteen divine attributes in Exod. 34:6–7.

Yahweh is praised in the heavenly sanctuary (Ps. 11:4), in the firmament that upholds the heavenly waters, and for mighty deeds in Israel's history (Deut. 3:24), ceremonially reenacted (Ps. 106:2). The musical instruments include even the pipe, only here in a formal liturgy (Gen. 4:21; Job 21:12). Music catches the pulse and breath of the universe, the inutterable longings of the spirit (cf. Rom 8:22–23; 2 Cor. 5:2).

The Hebrew text adds, "The book is complete; there are 2,527 verses." The Greek, Latin, and Syriac versions as well as llQPs[a] have a Psalm 151 (see Psalm 151).

Bibliography

Allen, L. C. *Psalms 101–150*. Waco, TX: Word, 1983.

Anderson, A. A. *The Book of Psalms*. 2 vols. Grand Rapids, MI: Eerdmans, 1981.

Craigie, P. C. *Psalms 1–50*. Waco, TX: Word, 1983.

Dahood, M. *Psalms*. Anchor Bible, 16, 17, 17a. Garden City, NJ: Doubleday, 1966, 1968, 1970.

Kraus, H. *Theology of the Psalms*. Minneapolis, MN: Augsburg, 1986.

Mowinckel, S. *The Psalms in Israel's Worship*. Nashville, TN: Abingdon, 1962.

Murphy, R. E. *Wisdom Literature and Psalms*. Nashville, TN: Abingdon, 1983.

Rogerson, J. W. and J. W. McKay. *Psalms*. 3 vols. Cambridge Bible Commentary on the New English Bible. Cambridge: Cambridge University Press, 1977.

Stuhlmueller, C. *Psalms*. Old Testament Message Series, 21, 22. Wilmington, DE: Glazier, 1983.

Weiser, A. *The Psalms*. Philadelphia: Westminster, 1951.

Westermann, C. *Praise and Lament in the Psalms*. Atlanta, GA: Knox, 1981.

PROVERBS

CAROLE R. FONTAINE

INTRODUCTION

Date and Background

The Proverbs, the oldest of the "wisdom" books of the Hebrew Bible, has a complex history and literary form. The book bears the title "The Proverbs of Solomon, Son of David, King of Israel" and hence follows the traditional ascription of authorship of this work, as well as Ecclesiastes and Song of Songs, to Solomon. This would suggest a date in the tenth century B.C., but, in fact, the book is not a unified composition. Rather, it comprises collections dating from various periods in the history of ancient Israel. The book of Proverbs probably received its final editing in early postexilic times (latter part of the sixth century B.C.) and hence reflects the needs of the later community as well as the "practical ethics" of the earlier monarchical period.

More than other biblical traditions, "wisdom literature" exudes something of a cosmopolitan air, which reflects its origin in a wisdom tradition common to the ancient Near East. The literary genres found in Proverbs, Job, and Ecclesiastes and the content they convey have parallels in Mesopotamian and Egyptian literature. Moreover, it is clear that, in a number of instances, such extrabiblical literature has had a direct impact on the Israelite traditions. For example, Prov. 22:17–24:22 reflects a classic Egyptian wisdom text, *The Instruction of Amenemope* and the "problem literature" of Mesopotamia bears a striking resemblance to the tone and form of Job. Nevertheless, the Israelite sages subsumed the teachings of their neighbors into a fully Israelite perspective, one integrated with the teachings of the Torah and Prophets. Although wisdom literature speaks of God more as "Creator" than as "Redeemer" or "Covenant Lord" and understands persons as individuals rather than as members of the covenant community of Israel, in the final analysis the same worldview undergirds both the teachings of Proverbs and the teachings of the rest of the Hebrew canon. (For example, compare wisdom's concept of retribution to the laws of Deuteronomy or the oracles in Amos 3:3–8.)

In biblical wisdom literature, this common Yahwistic perspective (a perspective based on the unique characteristics of Israel's God) is expressed as "Fear of the LORD." This catch-phrase refers to the religion of ancient Israel in its entirety and involves both the beginning of wisdom and knowledge (Prov. 1:7; 9:10) and the implicit end of wisdom's search (Job 28:28). Without a right relationship to the Holy One of Israel, no intellectual efforts can hope to succeed nor can life be preserved (Prov. 3:5–8). "Foolishness," then, as the antithesis of wisdom, must be understood not so much as ignorance or inability of intellect but as a moral position that denies the necessity of this prior orientation of heart and mind toward the Deity.

Literary Description

Major Sections. Proverbs may be divided into a series of major collections, many of which bear superscriptions and may be distinguished by use of like form or content. These are the following:

1:1–9:18, wisdom poems and instructions
10:1–22:16, "The Proverbs of Solomon"
22:17–24:22, "The Words of the Wise" (superscription restored from 22:17a, see below)
24:23–34, further "Words of the Wise" (lit., "also these [belong] to the wise ones")
25:1–29:27, "Further 'Proverbs of Solomon,' Copied by the Men of Hezekiah, King of Judah"
30:1–14, "The Words of Agur, Son of Jakeh"
30:15–33, mostly numerical sayings (no superscription)
31:1–9, "The Words of Lemuel, King of Massa, Which His Mother Taught Him"
31:10–31, acrostic poem on the woman of worth (no superscription)

Many of these collections may be subdivided further, based on criteria of form and content. For example, the first Solomonic saying collection, 10:1–22:16, easily divides into two sections, 10:1–15:33 and 16:1–22:16, based on the preference in the first for antithetic parallelism and in the second for synonymous parallelism (→ Parallelism; Poetry). It should also be noted that the Greek text (Septuagint, LXX) of Proverbs differs considerably from the Hebrew text (Masoretic Text, MT) in both content and arrangement.

Literary Forms: The Proverb. The basic generic unit of the book is the *mashal*, or "saying"/"proverb" (→ Proverb). This Hebrew word has two basic meanings: "to be similar to" and "to rule over," and we find both of these aspects embodied in the biblical saying and proverb. First, these forms encapsulate or make visible the relationships inherent in the events they have observed. In Prov. 16:18, we read:

Before destruction, pride;
and before a fall, haughtiness of spirit.

This proverb expresses a connection between a psychological attitude and the subsequent effects of that orientation. Once this "similitude" is understood, the proverb then allows people to "rule over" such situations wherever they are encountered, fulfilling the second meaning of *mashal*. Quoting this proverb to someone possessed of a prideful and haughty disposition acts as a warning against the "comeuppance" so often observed to be the outcome of such attitudes. Proverbs are not simply "observational" but, rather, persuasive sayings that exert social control. The citation of a proverb or saying to analyze a situation (whether social or literary) may be termed a "proverb performance" (see Fontaine).

Although the term *mashal* may refer to other "sentence" forms such as the taunt (Jer. 24:9) or parable (Ezek. 17:2), in wisdom literature it is most often used to refer to a two-lined proverb that exhibits parallelism between its members. The second line in some way restates the thought of the first, either through agreement (synonymous parallelism), disagreement (antithetic parallelism), or expansion of the basic idea (formal or synthetic parallelism). The simplest way to establish parallel structure is through the use of a standard "word pair," namely, two words traditionally used in conjunction to convey a contrasting or coordinate meaning. "Father/mother," "righteous/wicked," "wise/foolish" are typical examples of wisdom word pairs.

Ancient Israel also knew of one-lined "traditional" sayings that circulated among the people (see, e.g., Judg. 8:2, 21; 1 Sam. 24:13; 1 Kings 20:11). However, the presence of the second line, which produces parallelism, indicates an artistic attempt at literary shaping and, hence, usually signals the saying's origin among the educated class of "sages" rather than the "folk." For purposes of definition, the term "saying" is here used to refer to the single-line form, while "proverb" designates its artistic cousin, which displays parallelism. (Other scholars have distinguished the saying from the proverb on the basis of content; the former is merely an observational statement drawn from experience while the latter incorporates a value judgment on the experience.) Despite the differences between the style and origin of the literary proverb and those of the traditional or "folk" saying, the experiential content, outlook expressed, and use of the two forms are strikingly similar.

The short or "pithy" nature of the proverb and saying helps characterize the style of these forms. The *mashal*, whether folk or literary, incorporates observations of the world in a witty, imaginative, and striking way that enhances memorization. These observations work as "portable" categories that, when applied to new and ambiguous events, help people organize their experiences in familiar and socially approved ways. An African proverb of the Yoruba tribe expresses this function of proverbs quite nicely: "A proverb is like a horse: when the truth is missing, we use a proverb to find it." By mounting a horse (as opposed to a pig or hedgehog), one obtains an "overview" of what is happening on the ground and hence is no longer bound by a limited perspective. In the same way, applying a known and accepted proverb to an immediate context allows a group to integrate the new events into its earlier experience, thereby gaining greater perspective. The use of a proverb, then, suggests the existence of a situation that necessitates comment to restore the group's social stability. Although proverbs are typically used in ways that support a group's worldview, they may also be used to challenge such perspectives. Indeed, this is precisely the way great religious figures such as Ezekiel, Qohelet (Ecclesiastes), and Jesus often use proverbs.

Specialized proverbs include the "better than" form and its negative counterpart, the "not good" proverb. In both, a value judgment is typically being made, as the proverb moves from a simple comparison to an explicit statement that "x is better than y" or "x is not good." Examples of the former occur in Prov. 3:14; 12:9; 15:16–17; 16:8, 19; 17:1; 19:1; and 27:5, 10b. "Not good" proverbs are found in 17:26a; 18:5a; 20:23b; 24:23b; 25:27a; 28:21a; a variation on the form is found in 17:7; 19:10; and 26:1 (see Murphy, pp. 66–67).

Another variation on the simple proverb/saying form is the riddle (Heb. *chidah*). Here the language conceals the relationship between the topic of the sentence and the comment concerning it. Such concealment stands in direct opposition to the way a proverb or saying works to explicate the connection between topic and related comment. Although the riddle in its pure form is found only in Judg. 14:10–18, the term occurs in parallelism with *mashal* in Prov. 1:6. This text indicates that the sages considered mastery of the riddle to be within their purview. Disintegrated riddle forms underlie Prov. 5:1–6, 15–23; 6:16–19, 23–24; 16:15; 20:27; 23:27, 29–35; 25:2–3; 27:20; and 30:15–33 (see Crenshaw, p. 242).

Numerical Saying. Closely related in form to the proverb and riddle is the numerical saying, which provides a list of items with an explanatory "title line" that indicates common features of the list. Title lines may occur at the beginning ("Four things on earth are small, but they are wisely expert," Prov. 30:24) or at the end of the list (Exod. 21:10–11). The number of items in such lists follows numerical conventions: two, three, and seven are the favorite numbers. In "graded" numerical sayings, the title line gives two numbers, x and x + 1, which are then explicated in the following list ("Under three things the earth trembles; under four it is not able to bear up," Prov. 30:21). Like other wisdom forms, this graded pattern has been observed in the literary traditions of Israel's neighbors. The numerical saying may be related both to the riddle and the list, the latter of which orders items by categories in ways allowing for easy memorization.

Commands: Admonitions and Prohibitions. Unlike the proverb, which is generally expressed as a third-person observation, admonitions and prohibitions are expressed as commands using second-person ("you") or third-person ("he/she") language. The admonition is the positive and the prohibition is the negative realization of the command. Although the proverb seeks to persuade by couching its insight as "impersonal" truth to which one ought to assent on grounds of reason, the command makes its appeal to hearers far more directly, as if hoping to order compliance. "Motivational clauses" are often appended to the command, usually beginning with "for," "because," or "lest" (e.g., Prov. 4:21–22; 5:7–10), suggesting that the sages still hoped to convince students rather than to rely on simple coercion. Commands are found mainly in Proverbs 1–9 and in the longer, unified compositions in the later collections influenced by the "instruction" form (e.g., 22:17–24:22).

The Instruction. From the Egyptian court, the (Egyptian) sebayit, or "instruction" genre, which is longer than the proverb or command, finds its way into Prov. 1:1–9:18; 22:17–24:22; and elsewhere. Usually beginning with the phrase "the instruction that X made for Y," Pharaoh or one of his court officials or sages writes a testament filled with good advice for his successor. The instruction usually addresses the hearer as "my son," builds up its arguments by making use of proverbs, admonitions, and prohibitions, and includes a liberal sprinkling of motive clauses. The instruction covers a wide range of topics necessary for a young man's success in diplomatic circles: how to handle arguments, proper table manners and conduct before a monarch, guides to handling the various threats posed by familiarity with women, and so on. The instructions in Proverbs have many of the same features as their Egyptian cousins, but they tend to have a more "theological tone," perhaps a reflection that they are less closely associated with the royal household and more related to the didactic goals of sages teaching in Jerusalem. If these compositions in Proverbs 1–9 do come from the postexilic period, a time when the monarchy no longer existed, then this move beyond royal circles is quite understandable as a response to the wisdom community's changing needs. Instructions are found in Prov. 1:1–19; 2:1–22; 3:1–12; 3:21–35; 4:1–9; 4:10–19; 4:20–27; 5:1–23; 6:20–35; 7:1–27; 22:17–24:22; and 31:1–9.

Wisdom Poems. Like the instruction, the wisdom poem is a long, unified composition. It may include proverbial sayings, admonitions, prohibitions, rhetorical questions, and hymnic elements as well as other forms. Found in Prov. 1:20–33; 8:1–36; 9:1–6, these poems are marked by a most unusual feature, the personification of wisdom as a woman. Speaking directly to prospective students, Woman Wisdom sounds like prophet, lover, counselor, and goddess as she expounds the goals of the sages and entices her hearers with the promise of rich reward—life itself. Such an exalted female figure, speaking with divinely sanctioned authority, must be considered rare in Israel's patriarchal monotheism. Consequently, some scholars have seen in these compositions a borrowing of goddess traditions from Israel's neighbors. Others view wisdom poems as a culmination of Israel's own traditions about the constitutive role of real women in society, developing at a time when a new authority figure was needed to replace the king as mediator between human and divine spheres of life (see Camp). Prov. 3:13–18, 19–20 may also be considered wisdom poems, although Woman Wisdom is there spoken of in the third person, rather than speaking directly.

Acrostic and Alphabetizing Poems. These forms take their organizing principles from the twenty-two letters of the Hebrew alphabet and, hence, consist of twenty-two or twenty-three lines. In Prov. 31:10–31, we find a complete acrostic poem, one in which each line begins with successive letters of the alphabet. In 2:1–22, aleph and lamed, the letters that begin the first and second halves of the alphabet, respectively, play a significant role in the structure of this instruction, hence, allow one to speak of an alphabetizing poem. Attempts to locate other alphabetizing poems of twenty-two lines each in Proverbs 2–7 are less convincing since

the present text must be rearranged to yield the hypothetical structure.

The Role of Proverbs in Ancient Israel and the Canon

Questions concerning the place of the book of Proverbs in Israel's life are closely related to concerns over its origin and date of composition. There is firm evidence for the existence of court and temple schools in Mesopotamia and Egypt. Such schools preserved vigorous literary traditions, including wisdom literature with all its characteristic forms and typical themes. Since Israel consistently links kings and court counselors with the wisdom tradition (so the ascription of proverbs to Solomon in 1 Kings 4:32, to Hezekiah's men in Prov. 25:1, to Lemuel in Prov. 31:1–9, and to Ahithophel in 2 Sam. 15–16), it is reasonable to posit similar schools in Israel, which trained court officials and scribes in the pre-exilic era and potential leaders as well as scribes in the postexilic period. Direct evidence for such institutions is, admittedly, slim.

However, the court does not provide the only possible setting for the origin and use of the book of Proverbs. Scholars have demonstrated that wisdom literature functioned in tribal settings to settle disputes, a goal not unrelated to the courtly, diplomatic use of wisdom. Some biblical sayings and proverbs may have had such "folk" origins. Similarly, the emphasis on the "torah of your mother" (Prov. 1:8b), the role of Lemuel's mother in the transmission of his royal instruction (31:1), as well as the figure of Woman Wisdom herself remind us that education of children in the ancient world began in the home. Hence, the family must also be considered a probable setting for the origin and use of some of the materials found in Proverbs.

Within the context of the Hebrew Bible, the book of Proverbs is often considered by scholars to represent the tradition of "old wisdom" against which the later wisdom books of Job and Qohelet (Ecclesiastes) revolt. The measured confidence in human reason and the ability to respond appropriately to the world, the trust in Israel's god, Yahweh, and the notion that Woman Wisdom is accessible to humanity are transmuted in subsequent wisdom literature.

Opposite: The opening of the book of Proverbs from the second volume of a two-volume Hebrew Bible; Italy, ca. A.D. 1300. The border, with its delicately painted animals and foliage, exhibits a Renaissance influence common to illuminated Hebrew manuscripts from Italy.

These later authors respond to an increasingly ambivalent world, one affected by the continuing social and political trauma of the changes wrought by the Exile and the new philosophical claims of Hellenism. "Following the rules" laid down by "old wisdom" no longer provides a guarantee of success. Wisdom is hidden with God (Job), and in the face of the great leveler—death—sage and fool come to the same unsatisfactory end (Qohelet).

Despite such seeming disenchantment with the "rules" for the good life laid down in the "old wisdom" of Proverbs, the wisdom tradition embodied there enters the intertestamental and Christian eras with renewed vigor. The Jewish communities of the Diaspora produced the apocryphal books the Wisdom of Jesus the Son of Sirach (Ecclesiasticus, written around 180 B.C.) and the Wisdom of Solomon (first century B.C. to first century A.D.) as well as the Mishnaic tractate 'Abot ("Fathers"). These "proverbial" works attest to the use of wisdom by their communities to meet the ethical and philosophical challenges of Greco-Roman culture (→ Ecclesiasticus; Wisdom of Solomon, The; Mishnah; Diaspora).

For early Christians, the methods of wisdom argument and the figure of Woman Wisdom become especially important for explicating the meaning of the person and ministry of Jesus of Nazareth. Not only does Jesus teach using the *mashal* forms of the sages (→ Parables), thereby challenging the religious and ethical assumptions of his time, but the theology embodied in Woman Wisdom undergirds the application of *logos* theology, theology of the "Word" to Jesus in John 1. In 1 Cor. 1:24, Paul explicitly identifies Jesus as the "wisdom [Gk. *sophia*] of God." Despite the change of gender, literary threads bind the two human-divine mediators together into a single figure who can not only promise life, but deliver it as well. Moreover, the figure of Sophia, the Greek version of Woman Wisdom, takes on a life of her own in the Gnostic tractates from Nag Hammadi. Indeed, the female "self-revealer," who speaks so paradoxically in the Nag Hammadi *Thunder, Perfect Mind,* sounds like nothing so much as Woman Wisdom in her speeches in Proverbs 1–9. For Gnostic Christians, with their fondness for gospel in proverb rather than narrative form (*The Gospel of Thomas*), the metaphors of Woman Wisdom and the literary forms exemplified in the book of Proverbs lent vitality and a Hebraic accent to their understanding of Jesus Christ. The rediscovery of these Gnostic materials in modern times has enhanced our appreciation of the role of wisdom and the book of Proverbs in the religious and literary heritage of Christians and Jews (→ Logos; Wisdom; Nag Hammadi; Gospel of Thomas).

COMMENTARY

1:1–9:18
Theological Introduction: Wisdom Poems and Instructions

1:1–7
Superscription and Introduction

1:1, Superscription. The superscription, which introduces the book, labels its contents as *meshalim*, or proverbs, even though much of the ensuing literature consists of longer poetic compositions that depart from the strict two-line proverb form. Ascription of authorship to Solomon is based on tradition, namely, the wisdom vignettes found in the first book of Kings as well as the statement in 1 Kings 4:32 that Solomon authored three thousand proverbs, probably of the "nature wisdom" type (cf. 1 Kings 4:33). Yahweh's gift of wisdom to Solomon (1 Kings 3:3–15) and this king's subsequent display of that royal and judicial wisdom in 1 Kings 3:16–28 (judgment of the two prostitutes) and 1 Kings 10:1–10 (riddle contests; the "hard questions" of v. 1; with the Queen of Sheba) all work to create a picture of an astute, judicious, and creative monarch—a fitting figure to preside over teachings of the "good life." Attribution of important literary traditions to famous kings was common practice in the ancient Near East.

1:2–6, The Sage's Program. Similar to a teacher passing out a syllabus on the first day of class in modern educational settings, the sage makes clear the purpose of the material that follows. The piling up of infinitives in vv. 2–4 (it is worth noting that the translations of the NEB and RSV insert the word "men"), along with the multiple use of specialized wisdom vocabulary, suggest that the acquisition of wisdom is an all-encompassing process that must be approached with the same care with which it is described in these verses. However arduous the enterprise might be, the ignorant and the young will be richly rewarded for their work, and even the wise will acquire greater expertise by reflecting on the matters that follow, many of which are explicitly related to the ability to understand and use wisdom's literary forms. The mention of righteousness, justice, and fair dealing in v. 3b, classic virtues extolled by the Torah and the Prophets, adds a special Israelite flavor to this wisdom curriculum. On the whole, the opening is reminiscent of that of the Egyptian *Instruction of Amenemope* (see Simpson, p. 242):

> The beginning of the instruction about life,
> The guide for well-being,
> All the principles of official procedure,

The duties of the courtiers;
To know how to refute the accusation of one who made it,
And to send back a reply to the one who wrote,
To set one straight on the paths of life,
And make him prosper on earth;
To let his heart settle down in its chapel,
As one who steers him clear of evil;
To save him from the talk of others,
As one who is respected in the speech of men.

The nautical metaphors in *Amenemope* are hinted at in v. 5b, "and the discerning may acquire the art of steering" (RSV, NEB: "acquire skill"; JB: "the art of guidance"). The Hebrew term *tachbulot* is related both to the word for a woman writhing back and forth with labor pains and the twisting of ropes to change the course of a sailing craft. In both cases, extreme physical effort produces the desired end, a successful birth or change of course. The knowledge of when to push or pull, expending just the right amount of effort at just the right moment, is the type of practical mastery that is one of the goals of wisdom instruction.

1:7. The introductory section ends with a contrastive proverb about "fear of Yahweh," the Hebrew Bible's terminology for its religion. This phrase should be understood not as simple fright but as involving awe, reverence, and obedience to the Lord. Without this proper prior commitment (which the foolish implicitly spurn by rejecting wisdom and discipline), no intellectual enterprise is sound. Hence, the acquisition of wisdom is not simply an "academic" pursuit but, fundamentally, a theological and spiritual activity.

1:8–19
The Sage's First Introduction

1:8–9. Most appropriately, this instruction opens with the imperative "Listen, my child" (literally "my son," but this term is often translated inclusively elsewhere, as in "children of Israel" for the literal "sons of Israel"). Egyptian wisdom stresses the importance of listening carefully to one's elders, and a similar notion is found here as the parental authority of mother and father is stressed. The prohibition in v. 8b ("do not forget") balances the admonition "listen . . . ," thus emphasizing harmony within the teachings of both parents. Similarly, v. 8 suggests that true understanding consists of taking in information and remembering it. A motivation in v. 9 tempts the young listener with a metaphor that suggests Egyptian body ornaments often worn by successful officials. Here such ornaments allude to the beauty of wisdom teachings. The garlanded head and shoulders of the wise youth stand in implicit contrast with the feet of wicked companions that "run to evil" (v. 16, perhaps a gloss from Isa. 59:7).

1:10–16. This section, which pictures the sinners taking counsel to tempt the unsuspecting youth, twice (vv. 10, 15) repeats the sage's "my son/child" of v. 8. Such repetition emphasizes the instruction as heartfelt advice "for one's own good," rather than as an expression of casual disapproval of certain companions. The sinners of v. 10 lie in wait for the innocent "without cause." (Note the importance of this term in the prologue to the book of Job: the Adversary wonders if Job worships God "without cause" [Job 1:9b]; in Job 2:3b, God is incited to afflict Job "without cause.") The description of the intended victims as harmless has the effect of defusing the very real danger of such behavior: reprisal will not come from the victims, but from the ultimate outcome of a life of criminal acts (see commentary below on 1:17–19). As the description continues, we discover that the sinners are motivated by greed (vv. 13–14) and share a surprising degree of cooperation and camaraderie ("one purse for us all!" 14b), which might be expected to deceive the unwary into a desire to be part of this closely knit group. The sage meets this threat directly with a forceful one-two punch, another balanced set of negative ("My child, don't go! . . .") and positive ("withhold your foot! . . .") commands (v. 15). The teacher understands well youth's desire to "fit in."

1:17–19. An example of "proverb performance" occurs in v. 17 with the citation of an out-of-context proverb (the sage was not discussing birds previously, but warning against the temptations of wicked companions) to categorize a social situation and suggest its proper resolution. Here, our informed youth, like the wary and observant bird, will not be tempted to join in, for he sees the net spread before him, a tactic "without cause" or "in vain" since he is forewarned. Verses 18–19 conclude the instruction with a typical appeal to wisdom's understanding of retribution: those who seek to dig pits for others fall into the very same pit themselves (Prov. 26:27). Even when that pit is "Sheol," the underground cavern in which Israelites believed the dead led a shadowy, unconscious existence, the result is the same (→ Retribution).

The Personification of Wisdom

The figure of personified wisdom is something of an anomaly in Israelite theology. What are the origins of this figure, and what role does it play in the literary and theological structure of the book of Proverbs? Scholars have recently offered a series of reflections on this female personification ranging from simple acknowledgement that abstract nouns in Hebrew are feminine in gender (e.g., "Torah," "Understanding") to complex formulations that provide Woman Wisdom with a divine genealogy. Given the literary function of female imagery as a "frame" (Woman Wisdom and Woman Stranger in Prov. 1–9; Lemuel's mother and the Woman of Worth in Prov. 31) for some collections of proverbs as well as the importance of this figure for later Christian reflections on Jesus and Jewish reflections on the *Shekinah* (Heb., "the female indwelling presence of God"), Woman Wisdom and her more clearly human sisters, the "strange," "foreign," and upright women, deserve full consideration. Attempts to understand this personification have proceeded in several directions: consideration of the figure as hypostasis, as a goddess, as a human female, or the trivialization of the significance of the female personification. We will consider each option in turn.

Woman Wisdom as Hypostasis. This view sees Woman Wisdom as an extension of the attribute(s) of the "High God," Yahweh, in this case the wisdom of God, which takes on a differentiated life of its own. Wisdom, which is essentially an aspect of God's omniscience and capacity to act effectively, becomes Woman Wisdom. Although she appears as an independent actor on the stage of creation, nuances concerning her origin in and dependency on Yahweh convince those who endorse this interpretation that she is an authentically Israelite, Yahwistic figure. Nonetheless, the relationship between Yahweh and Woman Wisdom may be more easily accounted for by attention to the literary roles played by these two figures in wisdom texts rather than by the appeal to hypostasization (see "Woman Wisdom as an Israelite Woman" below; see also Prov. 8:1–36).

Woman Wisdom as Goddess. In acknowledging the international, especially Egyptian, influence on the first nine chapters of Proverbs, this view sees Woman Wisdom as an adaptation of the goddess traditions of Israel's neighbors. In Egypt, the goddess Maat stood for justice, probity, and social and cosmic order; she was literally the undergirding of the throne of the pharaoh and provided the measure according to which the hearts of the dead were judged in the underworld. She is the first creation of the creator god in one Egyptian myth, and in various texts she is conceived as both his daughter and the master plan by which he creates. Though never appearing as either a "personal" goddess or a particularly active character in the texts that survive from ancient Egypt, she is, nonetheless, an important figure in Egyptian wisdom instructions. Her protective amulets were worn by sages as well as placed around the necks of the dead in hope of a good judgment. She is often depicted holding an ankh, the symbol of life, in one hand and a scepter, a symbol of power, in the other. Such symbols remind one of the image of Woman Wisdom in 3:16, with long life in her right hand and honor and wealth in her left. Of the more active, personal Egyptian goddesses, Hathor, "Lady of the Tree," and Isis, the salvific mother-goddess, are also regarded as part of the iconographic heritage of Israel's Woman Wisdom. Scholars subscribing to this hypothesis often date Proverbs 1–9 to the Solomonic period, a judgment based on connections between Solomon's court and related Egyptian practices.

Nor is the pantheon of goddesses in Woman Wisdom's family tree exhausted by reference to Egyptian parallels. Scholars also appeal to connections between Woman Wisdom and Canaanite and Mesopotamian goddesses. Noting the striking similarities in the way Woman Wisdom and Woman Stranger/Foreign Woman are described by the sages, some have considered the Babylonian Ishtar and her fertility cult to be the figure behind Woman Wisdom's "evil twin," Woman Stranger. Likewise, a Canaanite vine-goddess or (still yet to be discovered) goddess of wisdom have also been postulated as figures from whom the sages adapted Israel's version of the divine "totemic female" who confers the abundance of life's blessings on her followers.

Based on our increasing knowledge of Sumerian texts, we might also note the special relationship between the Sumerian goddess of love and war, Inanna (later fused with the Semitic Ishtar), and Enki, the god of wisdom and sweet waters. As a result of her crafty behavior, Inanna receives the me, divine ordinances by which human society is organized, from the drunken Enki and successfully bears them away to her city, thereby assuring its place among the competing city-states of Sumer. Inanna's dangerous journey to the "Great Below," the underworld of the Sumerians, seems related to the Woman Stranger, whose house leads down to death (Prov. 2:18). Upon her return, she consigns Dumuzi, the royal mate whose rule is legitimated by his alliance with the goddess, to the demons of the Great Below in her place. This punishment occurs because of his refusal to mourn properly the loss of the divine wife. This motif reminds us of Woman Wisdom in Proverbs 1, scoffing at those who ignored her and who are now beset by calamity. Dumuzi's life is eventually restored for six months of every year when his sister Geshtinanna, the vine-goddess (and perhaps another fructifying aspect of Inanna), offers to take his place in the underworld, thus presenting us with another divine female figure who, like Woman Wisdom, brings life.

The unanswered question of this scholarly reconstruction is the manner in which Israelite sages would have borrowed material from traditions so roundly condemned elsewhere in the canon, even though such borrowing and free adaptation is in keeping with wisdom's international spirit and origins. Still, it may be that by "co-option" of surrounding goddesses to create the Yahwistically subordinated figure of Woman Wisdom, Israel met its own psychological need for female imagery of the divine without serious compromise of patriarchal monotheism.

Woman Wisdom as an Israelite Woman. Camp's recent seminal work, *Wisdom and the Feminine in the Book of Proverbs*, which questions the potentially mysogynist argument for a divine precursor of Woman Wisdom and ignores the real, human role models that might have given rise to personified wisdom in Israel, provides a much needed balance to the "goddess" hypothesis. After examining the literary roles played by women in the Hebrew Bible and relating them to the social roles of real women, Camp was able to isolate a number of features present in Woman Wisdom and Woman Stranger that result from literary traditions about women in society. These include: wife and mother; lover; harlot and adulteress; the wise woman; female user of indirect means; and female authenticator of written traditions. Camp suggests that the social crises of the postexilic period provided the impetus for drawing on family-centered imagery to authenticate the wisdom tradition embodied in Proverbs. She further argues that Woman Wisdom replaces the king as mediator for those who seek to understand God's new ways of interacting with the human community (see Camp, pp. 79–149). Moreover, since the feminine is always viewed as ancillary and contingent with androcentric thought, it serves logically as a natural mediator between a male god and the male students who are the sages' audience.

In examining further the literary roles played by Israelite women as these affect the interpretation of Woman Wisdom, we might note that many of these characterizations fall within the sphere of "the sought-for person" ("princess/bride") so often found in folk literature. The bride who is also a counselor and helper to her prospective mate, the wife who confers material blessings on the hero through their marriage, and the (royal) father who bestows the sought-for person on the hero after his completion of a long search or set of arduous tasks seem to be represented in the relationship between Yahweh, Woman Wisdom, and the person (usually male) who is enjoined to seek her. Yahweh bestows wisdom upon Solomon in 1 Kings 3, thus legitimating the reign of one who was not first in line for the throne. Similarly, in Prov. 4:8, students are told to "embrace" Woman Wisdom and to

502

"grasp" her and her instructions (Prov. 3:18 and 4:13). Using this reconstruction, we can readily understand the figure of Woman Stranger as folk literature's "false bride," whose claims sound so much like her legitimate rival's (cf. Prov. 9). The language of love and desire applied to the sought-for one, Woman Wisdom, continues into the Greco-Roman period (so Wisd. of Sol. 6:12-16; 8:2, 16; Sir. 14; 15; 51). It is likely that the fullest understanding of the origin and function of the figure of Woman Wisdom will combine aspects of these first three hypotheses.

Trivialization of Woman Wisdom. By ignoring the human and divine antecedents of Woman Wisdom and Woman Stranger, some commentators on the text have preferred to deal minimally with the significance of this female imagery. In such treatments, Woman Wisdom and Woman Stranger become "mere" literary devices whose symbolic meaning becomes relatively insignificant, despite its anomalous appearance in androcentric literature. Woman Wisdom is seen as the embodiment of the sages' teachings (but why as *woman*?) or the voice of the world-order addressing men or as a sort of Teacher Temptress, urging male students to greater learning by use of sexually nuanced speech. Some note the way Woman Wisdom often incorporates prophetic modes of speech into her poems and, as a result, view her as prophet and preacher. However, it is unlikely that any ancient Israelite would have viewed a female figure lifting her voice in the streets in quite such positive terms.

Given the importance of the ring or "envelope" structure in the canonical wisdom books (i.e., the blasphemous poetic speeches of Job are framed or ringed by the highly moral prose folktale; the scathing questions of Qohelet are sandwiched inside royal ascriptions and comments of a pious editor), one cannot ignore the canonical function of Woman Wisdom and the Woman of Worth in Proverbs 31 as an important guide to the interpretation of the book. For this reason, failure to explore seriously the significance of Woman Wisdom imagery is no longer an option.

1:20-33
Direct Address Wisdom Poem

1:20-21. The introduction of Woman Wisdom's speech places her clearly in the public eye, like a prophet, prostitute, or a woman coming to the city gates for judgment (Gen. 38:14; Ruth 3:11; cf. Camp, p. 129). Her appeal is made in the most open way (no esoteric, hidden wisdom here!), on many levels.

1:22-28. Opening with the poignant phrase "How long? . . ." (cf. Jer. 4:14, 21; 12:4), this

rhetorical question prepares the audience for the ensuing series of reproaches, threats, and announcement of doom. The text's form and content evoke a notion of someone judging on behalf of God, even though reference to the Deity does not occur until v. 29b, and there obliquely as "fear of Yahweh." This notion strengthens Woman Wisdom's claim to be heard and, by extension, the sage's authority as one who discloses wisdom to his students.

The speech stresses Woman Wisdom's availability to the simple (those untutored, but capable of learning). Are these the same persons addressed in 1:4? Use of the word "knowledge," also found in 1:4, seems to confirm this identity. Similarly, there is an implicit link between Prov. 1:22-23 and the opening commands in the sage's first instruction (1:8). Verses 10-19 gave an example of "your father's instruction"; now the female figure of wisdom explicates "the Torah of your mother." The inclusion of Woman Wisdom, thus, provides for total instruction.

Despite Woman Wisdom's willingness to pour out her spirit and make known her thoughts, her offer will not remain valid in perpetuity for those who persist in rejecting her (vv. 24-28). Moreover, her reproaches echo the pathos of Yahweh's questions to the people in Micah 6:3.

1:29-33. The calamity that overtakes the mockers and fools is once again viewed as their "just deserts" in the reproach of vv. 29-30 and the announcement of doom in vv. 31-32. In ancient Israel, no act could be separated from the consequences it produced; rather the effects were implicit within the deed just as a seed contains the future plant. The positive side of this "act-consequence" relationship is rehearsed in a proverb (v. 33) that offers security to those who follow Woman Wisdom's counsel.

2:1-22
The Second Instruction

2:1-11. Making use of a twenty-two-line alphabetizing structure (see Murphy, p. 56, for discussion) and numerous repetitions of vocabulary items from chap. 1, this instruction builds up its argument through a series of "if/then" sequences ("if": vv. 1, 2, 4; "then": vv. 5, 9). Motivations ("for," "because") in vv. 9, 10, 18, 21 intensify the argument. In v. 3, the student is to echo back the cry of Woman Wisdom heard in 1:20-21 and search for her, the "sought-for one," more diligently than for treasure (v. 4). In v. 6, we see once more that it is Yahweh who bestows wisdom on those who search. Moreover, the impact of this statement is amplified by the recognition, in v. 5, that the search for wisdom is equivalent to the search for God. There are many paths to spiritual growth, but only one destination.

2:12–22. The topic again is the excellence of wisdom teaching as a guard against evil companions, here represented as both male (as in the first instruction) and female. Who is the "Woman Stranger" and "Foreign Woman" of v. 16, against whom the youth must be on guard? Some have postulated the fertility goddess Ishtar (Canaanite Astarte) as the one who tempts young men into apostasy; v. 17 suggests an Israelite adulteress may also function as the Woman Stranger. The goddess Inanna/Ishtar (see the Short Essay "The Personification of Wisdom") descended to the "Great Below" or underworld "Land of No Return" in a famous ancient myth; this may be alluded to in v. 18. However, Lev. 20:10 mandates the death sentence for simple adultery, thus supplying another possible meaning for this warning. Similar warnings against relationships with women are found in the Egyptian *Instruction of Ani* and the *Instruction of Ptahhotep*. Contrasting proverbs on the fates of the upright and the wicked in vv. 21 and 22 confirm and round out the argument of the instruction (→ Foreigner; Asherah).

3:1–12
The Third Instruction

3:1–4. A series of positive and negative commands with motivations organized into six couplets (vv. 1–2, 3–4, 5–6, 7–8, 9–10, 11–12) moves from general advice in vv. 1–4 to specific commands in vv. 5–12. Similar thoughts are found in sections three and four of the *Instruction of Amenemope*. Just as the sins of the wicked bring death, so adherence to wisdom's teaching lengthens life and brings healing and prosperity (vv. 2, 8, 10). Like the commandments of the Torah in Deut. 6:8, wisdom teaching is to be bound to one's body (Prov. 3:3) where it acts as a constant reminder of right conduct.

3:5–12. Excellent as wisdom may be, no one who possesses it can hope to be truly wise when compared to Yahweh. The limitations of human wisdom are clearly stated (vv. 5, 7). Verses 11–12 anticipate some of the reflections of the book of Job on the relationship between wisdom, adversity, and the God-fearing person.

3:13–20
Two Descriptive Wisdom Poems

3:13–18. Strong Egyptian influence marks this section, which deviates from the normal instruction form in that it consists of two hymns

to wisdom or wisdom poems (vv. 13–18, 19–20). Making use of the "blessing" formula ("How happy/blessed is the person who finds wisdom!") in v. 13, this section concludes with a wordplay on the same Hebrew root in v. 18b ("those who take hold of her are blessed"). Is the wisdom alluded to here personified Woman Wisdom? Imagery in v. 16 describing wisdom in terms associated with the Egyptian goddess Maat suggests an affirmative answer. The "tree of life" motif in v. 18, perhaps to be associated with Hathor as goddess of the sycamore tree, is also popular in the *Instruction of Amenemope* (→ Tree of Life, The).

3:19–20. A hymnic interlude on the relationship between Yahweh, Woman Wisdom, and creation also draws heavily on Egyptian themes, where Maat constitutes the plan by which the creator god creates the world. Association of wisdom with water ("deeps," "dew") virtually equates wisdom with life in the minds of those who exist in arid climates (v. 20).

3:21–35
The Fourth Instruction

3:21–26. The typical instruction style resumes as the sage draws conclusions from the previous sections. As in the first instruction (1:8–19), we find the teachings of wisdom gracing the neck and safeguarding the ways of the feet. From top to toe, wisdom bestows protection and the untroubled sleep of a clear conscience on those who adhere to the ways of discernment and sound judgment. The confidence that wisdom brings is once again closely related to the protection God bestows: both function to guard the steps and paths of their followers (vv. 25–26).

3:27–35. A series of prohibitions on various matters demonstrates that failure to do good, when it is in one's power to do so (vv. 27–28), is strongly condemned as wrongdoing (vv. 29–30). The temptation to envy (and hence emulate) the seeming security of the wicked is first discouraged by a prohibition in v. 31 and then countered with four proverbs assuring the hearer that, while the wicked are detestable to Yahweh (cf., e.g., Deut. 7:25; 12:31; 18:12) and the mockers soon to be mocked, the righteous, wise, and humble find favor in God's sight (Prov. 3:32–35).

4:1–9
The Fifth Instruction

4:1–4a. Family tradition, a motif familiar from Egypt, is evoked here to authorize the sage's advice, which follows in vv. 4b–9. Despite the prominence of this literary tradition of instructions, oral teachings are also important in vv. 3–4a. (A number of textual irregularities in the Hebrew text are customarily solved by reference to the LXX [see esp. the NEB].)

4:4b–9. After the introduction invoking traditional authority in the previous section, we find the father's advice couched in language appropriate to admonitions concerning the choice of a mate. As in Dumuzi's union with Inanna, Woman Wisdom will exalt those who embrace her (v. 8), crowning the searcher who is rewarded after finding this sought-for female (v. 9; cf. 1:9; 3:22), protecting the faithful and watching over them (v. 6). The use of positive and negative imperatives throughout this section, along with key words such as "commands," "live!" "grace" (though this term is not used in the NT sense of the word), and "honor," forms a summons that is not easily ignored. Verse 7a may legitimately be translated in a variety of ways. However, on the basis of previous discussion of the divine female, the translation "wisdom is first" is preferred. Woman Wisdom will bring all good things in her train once acquired as a mate. Hence, she is the first thing that must be sought by inquisitive students.

4:10–27
The Sixth Instruction

4:10–23. The catchword "life" begins and ends this section of traditional teachings with an insightful, if perhaps overdrawn, description of "the wicked" sandwiched between in vv. 14–17. The now familiar theme of the "path," with its associated terms ("step," "run," "stumble") is developed further and provides a link, along with the verbal root "life/live" (4:4b), to the previous instruction that ended with Woman Wisdom placing a garland of grace on her lover's neck. These motifs occur clustered together earlier in Proverbs 3. In Prov. 3:2, the sage's teaching prolonged life; in v. 3 those same wisdom teachings bound around the neck led to straight paths in v. 6 and health to the body in v. 8. In 3:22, discernment and sound judgment lengthened life and provided grace for the neck, leading to feet that do not stumble (v. 23) and sweet sleep (v. 24). Now, all these aspects of the right path appear conjoined once more, but the sleep described is that of the wicked, who cannot retire fulfilled unless evil has been done (4:16).

4:23–27. The instruction ends with more imperatives concerning control of the body. In ancient Hebrew thought, the heart (v. 23) was comparable to the modern term "mind" as the locus of thought, will, emotion, and memory (→ Heart), making it the focus of the strongest warnings. As in other instructions, the potential perversity of language is a special subject for wisdom admonitions (v. 24; cf., e.g., 6:2, 12; 8:13; 10:6, 11), even as the special and positive attributes of "mouth," "word," "command," "speech," and "lips" are celebrated elsewhere (cf. 2:6; 4:5; 5:7; 8:8; 10:11). One might expect both such concerns to be shared by those whose main work is literary. These authors are shrewd observers of the inevitable deception and trickery present in human communication, problems that may be attributed as much to the inherently ambiguous nature of language as to the dastardly intent of some language users.

5:1–23
The Seventh Instruction

5:1–6. This instruction begins with language nearly identical to that found in 4:20, with "my wisdom/my insight" in v. 1 substituted for the word pair "my words/my advice" found earlier. That these "loaded" terms may be freely interpreted in light of each other should occasion no surprise, given the sages' view of the preeminence of language as a tool for complex communication. The Woman Stranger, who is the subject of these admonitions, is dangerous precisely because she too knows the use of smooth speech (v. 4). The use of "honey" imagery carries erotic overtones familiar from the Song of Songs and the lovesongs of Inanna for her mate, whom she names "the honey-man" (see Pritchard, p. 645). Possible allusions to Inanna's descent or Israelite punishment for adultery are again developed as in 2:18. The sweet/bitter contrast found in vv. 3–4 is present in the Aramaic wisdom text "The Words of Ahiqar" ("Be not [too] sweet, lest they [swallow] thee: be not [too] bitter [lest they spit thee out]"; see Pritchard, p. 429). It probably represents a standard proverbial contrast. Her death-dealing "way of life" (Heb. 'orach-chayyim, v. 6 [cf. 2:19]) presents a wordplay on the "length of days" ('orek-yamim) in Woman Wisdom's right hand (3:16).

5:7–14. After a reprise consisting of the standard introductory formula, this section of positive and negative commands further develops the sage's warnings against Woman Stranger. The "door of her house" (v. 8) carries both sexual allusions and, perhaps, oblique reference to the gateposts of Inanna, which served as a divine emblem of her religion. The remainder of this passage reminds one of the fate of Samson in the hands of Women Strangers in Judges 14–16.

5:15–20. The language of love and fertility abounds in this section, which recommends the joys of marital love as an antidote to the slippery allure of the Woman Stranger. Thus, it is clear

505

that the sages do not condemn sexuality per se—far from it!—but rather forbid sexual behavior that they consider inappropriate. In their judgment, part of the excellence of a loving wife is her exclusive availability to her husband. That the prostitute or Woman Stranger, on the other hand, owes her loyalty to no one because she is available to many is precisely one of the reasons why she is to be avoided. This theme is also clearly developed in Akkadian wisdom counsels (see Pritchard, p. 427), texts that report that "reverence and submissiveness are not with her."

5:21–23. Three instances of proverb performance round out the sage's discourse on sexuality. Though the topic of much of the seventh instruction has been the evil, life-killing behavior of the Woman Stranger in contrast to the safety of the beloved wife, these proverbs (vv. 21–23) are addressed to men, presumably those who have disregarded such teachings. Although, once again, the intended audience of the instructions is male, such difficulties in "matching" the referents of proverbs to the context situations are typical of proverb performance (cf. Eccles. 4:9–12 where the imagery of a "threefold cord" is applied to the situation of two partners).

6:1–19
Miscellaneous Counsels

A number of short units appear together here: advice on standing surety on loans that may be defaulted (vv. 1–5), an expanded *mashal* on the diligence of the ant (vv. 6–11), a section describing the ways of the troublemaker (vv. 12–15), and a numerical saying on things hateful to God (vv. 16–19). Though the content of these passages is unrelated, they are linked together by bodily imagery.

6:1–5. Only the first section, which finds a parallel in the *Words of Ahiqar,* uses the typical instruction form as it advises the person standing pledge for a loan to rectify this situation while there is still time. The motif of word and mouth as a potential snare, which is repeated elsewhere in the instructions, appears again in v. 2. The "palm of the hand" is struck in v. 1, symbolizing the making of a bargain, and occurs again in v. 3 as the hand of the neighbor. The more common term for hand (Heb. *yad*) appears in the proverbial images of the bird and gazelle escaping from hunters' hands (v. 5).

6:6–11. The *mashal* of the ant represents typical "nature wisdom" and develops the theme of detrimental sleep, an activity of the body, in vv. 9–10. Folded hands, familiar as an image of sloth in Eccles. 4:5, appear in Prov. 6:10b.

6:12–15. The behavior of the villainous, worthless man is painted in terms of body language (cf. 10:10; 16:30) that expresses his evil intent (by magic or by colleagues lying in wait for his signal?). Typically, he is fully and suddenly repaid according to the laws of the act-consequence relationship (cf. 24:22; 29:1).

6:16–19. Telling body language is again the topic of the customary "x, x + 1" numerical saying. Verses 16–17 follow the descriptive pattern familiar from the lament Psalms and Song of Songs, moving from the top of the body to the bottom (eye, tongue, heart, feet). Study of traditional societies has shown that "troublemaking" activities such as gossip and slander are strategies typically used by those of lower status to cope with social problems. Hence, this text may provide an index of problems in postexilic Israel (disputes over inheritance and land claims?) rather than simply representing the behavior of a few "bad apples."

6:20–35
The Eighth Instruction

6:20–26. The instruction style resumes in vv. 20–21 with imagery familiar from 1:8 and 3:3. The author supplies motivations evoking the clarity and protective qualities of parents' teachings in vv. 22–23 (some scholars place v. 22 after 5:19, a judgment based on the presence of the feminine gender in both verses). Bodily imagery (tongue [v. 24], beauty and eyes [v. 25]) link this instruction to other units in chap. 6. Concrete reference to prostitution occurs for the first time in Proverbs in v. 26. Previously, there had been reference to foreign or strange women. Verse 26 suggests that the prostitute, like the thief (v. 30), is also hungry.

6:27–35. Two rhetorical questions, which may be interpreted as proverb performance, open this section that compares adultery to theft and, in so doing, reminds readers that adultery with married women was condemned as much for its violation of men's property rights as for its inherent dishonesty or immorality (cf. Exod. 20:14–15 and Deut. 5:18–19 where the two are clustered together). While thieves are allowed to make sevenfold restitution (contrary to Exod. 22:1–9), no amount will compensate the jealous husband (cf. 5:9–11).

7:1–27
The Ninth Instruction

A story exemplifying the temptations of the Woman Stranger (vv. 6–23) stands between a standard introduction (vv. 1–5) and typical admonitory conclusion (vv. 24–27). Egyptian and Mesopotamian influence may be discerned in

vv. 6, 16, 19, 26–27. Moreover, imagery familiar from previous instructions is used freely (cf., e.g., 1:20; 3:3; 6:21). To call Woman Wisdom "sister," that is, "bride," is to gain salvation from the perils of Woman Stranger (v. 4), even though the recommended figure could hardly be described as "stay-at-home" (cf. 7:11b; 1:20).

8:1–36
Wisdom's Second Speech

The pinnacle of wisdom thought appears here in the self-proclamation of Woman Wisdom, a form of literature familiar from texts listing the miraculous deeds of Isis, an Egyptian goddess, and dating to the Hellenistic period. This "wisdom speech" presents a view of Woman Wisdom as more than a teacher, desirable human mate, or attribute of Yahweh. The translation and interpretation of no passage in Proverbs is more hotly contested than this one, no doubt because Woman Wisdom's claims are so difficult to assimilate within later Judaism and Christianity. Significant parallels to this passage are found in the "Hymn to Wisdom" of Job 28, some of the material in the "Yahweh speeches" of Job 38–42, Sir. 1:1–10; 4:11–19; 14:20–15:10; 24:1–19; and Wisd. of Sol. 7:22–8:1. The view of wisdom found here becomes important for the *logos* theology in the prologue of the Gospel of John and elsewhere in the NT (Matt. 11:19; Luke 11:49; Matt. 23:34–36; 1 Cor. 10:4; Col. 1:15–16).

8:1–3. Once again, Woman Wisdom stands in this introduction in full view of the people, in the places where power is exercised and choices are made (vv. 2–3; cf. 1:20–21).

8:4–11. Woman Wisdom's speech is deliberately described here in terms that refute and undercut the seductive language of Woman Stranger in Proverbs 7, as though the sage has become aware that his fascination with Woman Wisdom's "evil twin" might prove dangerous. Motifs familiar from 3:14–15, where Egyptian influence was noted, occur here, and the "simple ones" or untutored (1:4, 22) are again addressed.

8:12–21. Despite problems in the Hebrew text, the meaning of this section of Woman Wisdom's self-praise is reasonably clear. Woman Wisdom's relation to kingship is explicated in vv. 15–16 and allows at least three possible interpretations: first, the goddess Maat's special function of undergirding the throne (and hence, justifying the reign) of pharaoh; second, the Mesopotamian fertility goddesses' (Inanna/Ishtar) role in certifying human males as fit for kingship through the sacramental sacred marriage rite; and third, the special link between rulers and wisdom in Israel and the ancient

Near East (cf. 1 Kings 3; 2 Sam. 14:17; Isa. 11:2). The last option rests on a pragmatic observation: kings who routinely display poor judgment in governing their subjects have trouble in maintaining their grasp on power. The pattern of "x loves those who love x" in v. 17a is familiar from Egyptian theological language. Moreover, 17b finds echoes in Wisd. of Sol. 1:1 and 6:12.

8:22–31. This most disputed section of Woman Wisdom's speech involves her exact relationship to Yahweh and to creation. Verse 22 is the crux. Should the Hebrew verb and its object *qanani* (v. 22a) be translated as "begot me," following the Targum, Greek, and Syriac versions? Those who adopt this option usually render the phrase "created me" to avoid sexual connotations (cf. Eve's statement in Gen. 4:1 and the epithet of the Canaanite mother-goddess [see Pritchard, pp. 131–32]). Or, should one read "acquired/possessed me" with the more literalistic ancient authorities: Aquila, Symmachus, Theodotion, and Jerome? Modern commentators are divided on the issue (cf. Vawter, pp. 207–14).

The translator's view of Woman Wisdom's nature helps determine the selection of an appropriate translation. Since we have earlier noted Woman Wisdom's literary appearance as the "sought-for person" who bestows needed abilities and goods upon her human seekers (1:9; 3:22; see commentary above on 4:4b–9), it is not unreasonable to find this motif applied to Woman Wisdom's relationship to the Creator. Though the translation "Yahweh possessed me, at the beginning of his acts" is preferred here, Camp's translation of vv. 22–25 (see Camp, p. 84) deserves a hearing, since it seeks to incorporate the "fleshly" overtones of verbs in the text:

> Yahweh conceived me at the beginning of his way,
> the first of his acts of old.
> Ages ago I was woven in the womb,
> at the first, before the beginning of the earth.
> When there were no depths, I was brought forth,
> when there were no springs abounding with water.
> Before the mountains had been shaped,
> before the hills, I was brought forth.

It should be noted that the Hebrew verb *cholaleti*, here translated "brought forth" (vv. 24–25), derives from the root *chyl*, which is generally associated with the physical activity of the *female* in giving birth. Hence, one must ask if Yahweh, in the manner of a female, gives birth (metaphorically?) to Woman Wisdom? Though Woman Wisdom appears to exist prior

507

to the rest of creation, is used as a model or principle in Yahweh's subsequent creative activity, and does not serve as an attribute of Yahweh (so with Vawter and others), nevertheless, she must have come from somewhere.

Disputes over vv. 22–31 continue in v. 30 since the translation of 'amon remains problematic. Does it mean "master craftswoman," an analogy with the "artisans" of Jer. 52:15 (so, apparently, with the LXX), or "nursling, darling child," an analogy with Lam. 4:5 and Esther 2:7, or was it revised to yield a different form altogether? Egyptian parallels may be adduced to support either reading, for Maat is both playful child and master plan for creation. But on the whole, the purport of the passage, with its allusions to delight and play, suggests that "darling child" is preferable.

8:32–36. Woman Wisdom's remarkable speech concludes with a surprising invitation: those who find her find life itself (v. 35). This is the kind of language that is normally used only of Yahweh, but here Woman Wisdom is fully endowed with divine attributes since she appears as guarantor of earthly salvation. Students who reject her invite death (v. 36).

9:1–18
The Tenth Instruction

Reference to two banquets (9:1–6; 13–18), the first given by Woman Wisdom and the second by another manifestation of her "evil twin," Woman Foolishness, is divided by assorted counsels (vv. 7–12) in the final instruction, which serves as a literary, theological introduction to the proverb collections.

9:1–6. Woman Wisdom's house is described as a mansion. Some scholars have found deeper significance in the phrase "seven pillars" (v. 1). The term may allude to wisdom's architectural role in creation (cf. 8:30), since the ancients believed the world to be supported by seven great pillars, or it may refer to the literary structure of Proverbs 2–7 (see Murphy, p. 52; → Pillars). Woman Wisdom is connected with women other than the "mother" of the sages' traditional word pair ("father/mother" in 1:8; 6:20; 10:1; and elsewhere), since she is served by maids who do her bidding (v. 3), in much the same way that devotees of a fertility goddess solicit worshipers for their deity. Woman Wisdom's banquet (vv. 5–6) is one of the few in the Hebrew Bible that does not lead to disastrous consequences for those who attend.

9:7–12. Counsel on the correct handling of the scoffer or mocker (vv. 7–8, 12) forms a ring around the centerpiece of wisdom teaching in v. 10: "fear of Yahweh" is the beginning of wisdom

(cf. 1:7); knowledge of the Holy One, understanding. While a sage or righteous person profits from correction (vv. 8b, 9), the scoffer turns on the one who attempts a reproof (vv. 7–8a). As with all acts, the consequences will be borne by the actor (vv. 11–12). Verse 11 suggests this section is to be interpreted as Woman Wisdom's "table talk" at her banquet.

9:13–18. Oddly, the last portion of the instructional introduction to Proverbs is not a speech by Woman Wisdom, but another brush with her opposite counterpart. Sitting like a prostitute where she may oversee potential customers (v. 14), her call to passersby (v. 16) is a parody of Woman Wisdom's summons (v. 4), complete with an example of proverb performance (v. 17) to spice her proposition, even as Woman Wisdom spiced her wine (vv. 2, 5). Her connection with the underworld, familiar from 5:23 and 7:26–27, ends the section, replacing the sweet taste of stolen water and secret food with the odor of death.

10:1–22:16
"The Proverbs of Solomon"

Beginning with 10:1, one moves from lengthy, unified compositions of wisdom poems and instructions to the collections of proverbs. The first collection, associated with Solomon explicitly through its superscription in 10:1a, contains 375 proverbs. This is the same numerical value given to the name "Solomon" in Hebrew, which appears in the superscription. The compiler of this section seems to be working at joining together two collections of approximately the same size, that is, chaps. 10–15 and 16–22, since a number of peculiarities (repetitions of sayings, vocabulary peculiar to one section and not the other, patterns linking a series of proverbs, preferred type of parallelism) occur at the "seam" in 14–16 (see Murphy, p. 64). In addition, a cluster of "Yahweh sayings" (15:33–16:9) located near the center of the book (16:17) seems to provide a theological core for the collection.

Commentators customarily consider morally neutral or observational proverbs as belonging to an earlier "old wisdom" stage of the collection, with any theological proverbs representing a later, pietistic attempt to incorporate these insights into a Yahwistic framework. However, such a thesis need not be necessary, especially if Proverbs 1–9 dates to the Solomonic period. Rather, it would not be surprising to find "theological knowledge" present at all stages of Israelite wisdom reflection, since wisdom in the ancient Near East was habitually viewed as a gift from the gods. In general, content alone is not an infallible guide to the date of a text's composition. Rather, content ought to be considered along with structural features in the literature before any final determination is made.

Attempts to provide a social or even a literary context for this collection of proverbs have proved highly speculative, since "sentence literature" resists the type of analysis that has proved so fruitful in determining contexts for longer compositions. Proverbs such as one finds here might have originated and been employed in a variety of contexts: family or tribal settings, court or scribal schools, or simply in society at large (see "Introduction" above). Search for a literary structure in these proverb collections has proved as elusive as the quest for social context. However, it is generally recognized that proverbs were grouped together by a variety of methods: content ("royal" proverbs in 16:10–15); wordplay and "catchwords" ("hear" in 15:29–32); preferred form of parallelism (antithetic parallelism in chaps. 10–15); or other mnemonic devices.

10:1–15:33
The Antithetic Collection

10:1–32. After the superscription (10:1a), the first proverb ties what follows to the preceding instructions in an explicit way. The use of "son" as the topic of 10:1, along with the "father/mother" word pair (cf. 1:8; 6:20) suggests that what follows provides "midrash" or commentary on the earlier teachings. That such is indeed the case is confirmed by the way the proverbs of chap. 10 restate the vocabulary and themes present in 1–9: righteous/wicked contrasts (vv. 2–3, 24–25, 27–32), the theme of language (vv. 18–21, 31–32), and the catchwords "life" (vv. 16–17) and "wisdom" and "wise men" (vv. 13–14). Crop gathering in the summer (v. 5) recalls the wise ant of 6:8; the winking troublemaker (v. 10) reminds one of the same gesture made by a plotter (6:13). The stirring up of dissensions (10:12a) suggests that the gossip (6:19b) who is hated by Yahweh; the positive path to life (v. 17a) stands in contrast with the paths to life not attained by those who consort with Woman Stranger (2:19b). The fool, who takes pleasure in doing evil (v. 23), alludes to the imagery of 2:14 and 4:16. Only one clearly observational, neutral saying is found: the poor are ruined by lack of goods, but wealth is the fortified city of the rich (10:15). However, this comment is immediately contextualized by v. 16 and later by v. 22. The sages would prefer to believe that wealth is a gift of Yahweh that confirms its possessor's righteousness. Otherwise, the standard act-consequence relationship is displayed throughout the chapter.

11:1–31. Various catchwords link the proverbs of this chapter together: "righteousness" (vv. 4–6), "upright" (vv. 5–6), "justice" (vv. 18–19), and "blessing" (25–26). "Delight" or "fitting" ties 11:1 to 10:32 (see Murphy, pp. 68–69), and that which is detestable to Yahweh (11:1, 20) recalls the numerical saying of 6:16. The theme of the requisites for survival is developed in vv. 3–11, where the sages recommend, not unexpectedly, righteousness, knowledge, and integrity rather than confidence in wealth. The proverb warning against standing surety for a pledge (v. 15) distills the instruction of 6:1–5. The mysteries of generosity are attested (vv. 25–26); moreover, tree of life imagery appears in vv. 28 and 30. Women appear as topics in both positive and negative form (vv. 16, 22). The proper use of language, a favorite subject, recurs (vv. 9, 12–14).

12:1–28. The contrast between wicked/evil and righteous/upright is developed in vv. 3, 5–7, 10, 12–13, 17, 20–21, 26, 28, with the wise/foolish motif a second major interest (vv. 15–16, 23, 27). The benefits and pitfalls of language are treated (vv. 6, 8, 13–14a, 17–19, 22, 25) with a keen observation on the stressful effects of anxiety (v. 25a). A "better than" saying on the follies of pretense and a synonymous proverb on righteousness as the way to life break the regular antithetic pattern in the rest of the proverbs. Verse 22 includes a parallel with chapter ten of the *Instruction of Amenemope*. Catchwords include "wickedness" (vv. 1–3), "righteous/wicked" (vv. 5–7), "righteous" (vv. 10, 12–13), "fool" (vv. 15–16), "tongue" (vv. 18–19), "evil/trouble" (vv. 20–21), and, in vv. 26 and 28, both "way" and "righteous/ness" are used.

13:1–25. Antithetic relationships between the behavior of the wise/diligent and the proud with sluggards/mockers, as a variant for the former comparison (vv. 1, 4, 10, 13, 15–16, 18, 19b–20), continue as the main topics. The righteous and wicked are compared (vv. 5, 6, 9, 17, 21–22, 25) and the wealthy/poor contrast appears in v. 8 (also implicitly in vv. 11, 23). The effects of hope and longing on the human spirit are observed in vv. 12, 19a, and a cynical proverb on the deceptive appearances of wealth occurs in v. 7. Synthetic parallelism marks the praise of wisdom teaching in v. 14, a proverb perhaps evoked by the tree of life imagery in v. 12 and the term "command" in v. 13. Catchwords continue to bind short units together: "desire/soul/life" (vv. 2–4); "righteous/wicked" (vv. 5–6); "righteous" (vv. 21–22); and "poor/rich" (vv. 7–8). In addition, wordplays occur in vv. 15–19, 20.

14:1–35. A midrash on the two banquets described in 9:1–6, 13–18 opens this chapter, which continues the juxtaposition of wise and foolish behavior (vv. 1, 3, 6, 8, 15–16, 18, 24, 29, 33). Wicked/foolish images stand in contrast with those involving the righteous/upright (vv. 9, 11, 22, 32, 34), whereas the poor/rich form another pair of contrasts (vv. 20–21, 31). Psychological insights undergird vv. 10, 12–13, 30, and two royal sayings arise for the first time (vv. 28, 35). "Fear of Yahweh" proverbs appear three times (vv. 2, 26–27), with the latter two occurrences breaking the antithetic pattern in favor of synonymous parallelism. Various verbal roots act as catchwords, along with other typical vocabulary: "to know" (vv. 6–8); "fool" (vv. 7–8); "to be great" (vv. 28–29).

15:1–33. The same antithetic pairs apparent in chaps. 10–14 round out this collection: wise/prudent versus fool/mocker (vv. 5, 12, 14, 18, 20 [cf. 10:1], 21, 24, 31–32); righteous/wicked (vv. 6–9, 19, 26, 28–29). Language provides an important topic (vv. 1–2, 4, 7, 23, 28), and "popular psychology" appears in vv. 1, 4, 13, 14, 30. Two "better than" sayings (vv. 16–17) point out that abundance is not everything, if accompanied with strife (cf. *Amenemope* VI, 9:5–8 in Pritchard, p. 422, as noted by Murphy, p. 70). Imagery of death and the underworld marks vv. 10–11, 24, 27. Verbal roots for "to be good" in vv. 2–3, and "to be glad" in vv. 20–21, 23 act as catchwords, along with other typical language: "heart/mind" (vv. 13–15), "righteous" (vv. 28–29), "hear" (vv. 29, 31–32), etc.

"Yahweh proverbs" abound in this transitional chapter (vv. 3, 11, 16, 25, 29, 33), with "detested by Yahweh" forms occurring in vv. 8–9, 26. The awesome sovereignty of God is conveyed not simply by content—the good and the wicked, even the underworld lie open to Yahweh's sight—but also by repetition of this theme. The collection ends appropriately with the equation of "fear of Yahweh" to the teachings of wisdom (15:33).

16:1–22:16
The "Royal" Collection

Breaking away from the pattern of antithetic parallelism, this collection displays more varied forms, more attempts at thematic arrangement, and high valuation of the monarchy and, perhaps, reflects a city rather than rural background.

16:1–33. A cluster of "Yahweh proverbs" (vv. 1–7) begins this chapter, with these forms continuing to punctuate the rest of the proverbs in vv. 9, 11, 20, and 33. People may fret, plan, and wonder, but in the end it is Yahweh who prevails. Verse 2 recalls the Egyptian scribal god Thoth who weighs the heart of the dead against the measure of Maat. The diverse ways of the

king are discussed in vv. 10, 12 (cf. 8:15), 13–15, where the monarch is seen as the upholder of Yahweh's just order, an idea created as much by the placement of these verses after the Yahweh proverbs as by their actual content. The topic of language occurs in vv. 21, 23–24, 27–28. "Better than" sayings appear in vv. 8, 16, 19, 32, and psychological observations in vv. 25–26. An admonition to acquire wisdom, a precious commodity in v. 16, recalls 4:5 and 3:14. Variants for some of these proverbs exist: cf. v. 2 with 21:2, v. 5b with 11:21, and v. 25 with 14:12. Catchwords continue to unite short groups of proverbs (vv. 10–11, 12–13, 18–19, 21–24, 27–29), but thematic development is the more important organizing technique in this chapter.

17:1–28. A great variety of topics is treated here, with unusual stylistic features and few catchwords ("companion" in vv. 17–18, "joy/cheerful" in vv. 21–22). References to the caprice of human language occur in vv. 4, 7, 20, 27–28, and reflections on proper conflict resolution are discussed in vv. 9, 13–14, 26. The wise are the subjects of vv. 2, 10, 24, with fools appearing in vv. 12, 16, 21, 25. The image of Yahweh testing the heart (v. 3) reflects the Egyptian influence already noted in 16:2. Other subjects appear briefly: bribes in vv. 8, 23; friendship in v. 17; parent-child relationships in v. 6; standing pledge in v. 18; treatment of the poor in v. 5; and role reversal in v. 2. The sage continues to record insights on psychological stress: a "better than" saying in v. 1 celebrates peace and quiet, with a cheerful disposition found to be the best medicine in v. 22.

18:1–24. The main topic is the power of speech, developed in vv. 4, 6–8, 13, 20–21, though the benefits of wealth receive some attention (vv. 11, 16, 23), along with conflict resolution and justice in court (vv. 17–19). The negative and positive side of friendship frame the chapter in v. 1 and v. 24, respectively. Yahweh appears as a strong tower to the righteous in v. 10 and the "Donor" of wives in v. 22, much as God was seen to be the provider of Woman Wisdom in the instructions of chaps. 1–9. A person's spirit can sustain or be crushed, according to the "psychology" of v. 14. Perhaps the strongest programmatic statement occurs in v. 21: death and life are both in the "power of the tongue," that is, language. Catchwords are used in vv. 10–11, 18–19, 20–21. Verse 12b shows how a phrase may be reused in a new context; it appeared earlier in 15:33.

19:1–29. Emphasis on family relationships (vv. 13–14, 18, 26), wisdom (vv. 11, 16, 20, 25, 27), and folly in its various modes (vv. 1, 10, 22b, "mockers" in vv. 25, 28–29, sluggards in vv. 15,

24) accompany the resurgence of the instruction style in vv. 18, 20, 23, 27, as the sage urges the "son" to take instruction. Insights on the life of the poor and their relationship to Yahweh occur in vv. 7–8 (note the shift from sentence style), 10, 17. Discussion of the false witness (vv. 5, 9, 28) involves the reuse of phrases; vv. 5a and 9a are identical. Various catchwords, associated with the topics above, appear in vv. 1–2, 6–7, 13–15, 18–19, 20–21, 26–27, 28–29. As in 18:22, Yahweh is the provider of a good wife in v. 14, even as parents provide an inheritance.

20:1–30. A wide range of topics and styles (cf. vv. 6–7, 18) characterize this chapter, which opens with "mocker" in v. 1, a reference that provides a tie to 19:28–29. Royal sayings appear in vv. 2 (cf. 19:12a), 8, 26, 28, with reuse of the image of "winnowing" evil in vv. 8, 26. An allusion to Yahweh's maintenance of just weights, a motif familiar from 11:1 and 16:11, occurs in vv. 10, 23, with other Yahweh proverbs occurring in vv. 12, 22, 24, 27. The proverb on gossips (v. 19) provides a variation on 11:13, and the typical advice against standing surety on a pledge (v. 16) is repeated exactly in 27:13. The gray hair of the old (v. 29), a white badge of wisdom, recalls 16:31. Violence is recommended as an efficacious corrective in v. 30 (for similar statements, see 13:24; 19:18, 25). Numerous catchwords are used throughout this chapter.

21:1–31. These verses provide readers with the sages' cast of typical characters: the wicked (vv. 4, 7, 10, 12, 18, 27, 29); the mocker (vv. 11, 24); the craving sluggard with idle hands (vv. 25–26, cf. 19:24; 20:4); the false witness (v. 28, cf. 14:5; 19:5, 9, 28); and the quarrelsome wife (vv. 9 [= 25:24], 19). On the positive side, Yahweh appears in vv. 1, 2 (cf. v. 2a with 16:25a, v. 2b with 17:3), 3, 30–31; the wise in vv. 11, 20, 22; the righteous and diligent in vv. 5, 21; and the king in v. 1. Beyond the familiar themes and catchwords with which these characters are associated, the idea of "plan" and "way" unites thoughts present in vv. 2, 5, 8, 16, 29. Additionally, remarks regarding proper attitude toward sacrifice occur toward the beginning and end of the chapter: in v. 3, Yahweh prefers justice and righteousness to sacrifice; in v. 27, the sacrifice of the wicked, brought with evil intent, is "detestable." Both proverbs echo the programmatic statements of Psalm 50. Yahweh figures as absolute sovereign over human events in Prov. 21:30–31: no counsel prevails against God, no human plan can, by itself, bring salvation.

22:1–16. As this large collection ends, treatment is given to the themes of generosity to the poor (vv. 9, 16); the training of children (vv. 6, 15); the value of a good name (v. 1); and, of course, the wicked (vv. 5, 8); the mocker (v. 10);

the sluggard, now feigning fright of lions to avoid work (v. 13); the prudent (v. 3); and the king (v. 11). Even as Yahweh was the source of a good wife (18:22; 19:14), those feeling God's wrath will fall into the "Pit"-like mouth of Women Strangers (22:14). Thus, the major Solomonic collection of 10:1–22:14 ends as did the instructions in 9:13–18, with the image of woman as the way to death.

22:17–24:22

"The Words of the Wise"

This section of Proverbs, a free adaptation of the highly moral Egyptian *Instruction of Amenemope*, returns to the longer, more developed instructional style. However, instead of the unified poems of Proverbs 1–9, we find here a series of positive and negative commands, expanded by the addition of motivation clauses and sayings to enhance their authority. The antithetic parallelism of the previous Solomonic collection is found only in 24:16 (Murphy, 74).

Only a third of the material in these chapters is actually based on the Egyptian text. It appears in 22:17–23:11 and in different order than it does in *Amenemope*. Parallels to the Aramaic *Words of Ahiqar* are also evident in 23:13–14 (see Whybray, pp. 132, 136). Direct address, to "my son," appears in 23:15, 19, 26; 24:13, 21. The topics treated range from table manners among the powerful (23:1–3, 6–8) to the dangers of alcoholism (23:20–21, 29–35), suggesting that this instruction may date from the monarchical period as training material for those entering court service (cf. 22:21 and commentary above on 1:2–7). Other typical wisdom themes also appear: treatment of the poor, the oppressed and their relationship to Yahweh (22:22–23; 24:11–12); the excellence of wisdom (23:23; 24:3–7, 13–14); family relationships and discipline of the young (23:13–16, 24–25); envy of sinners (23:17–18; 24:1–2, 15–20); the dangers of harlots (23:27–28); and advice against guaranteeing debts (22:26–27). The rest of wisdom literature's cast of characters are also to be found in this instruction: the fool (23:9; 24:7, 9); the angry man (22:24–25); the king (22:29; 24:21); and Yahweh (22:19, 23; 23:17; 24:18, 21–22; implicitly in 23:11 [cf. Num. 35:19] and 24:12).

22:17–23:11

The Egyptian Prologue

22:17–21. The title of this instruction has been mistakenly embedded within the first sentence in Hebrew in v. 17. The Hebrew text may

511

be translated, following the LXX, "The Words of the Wise. / Give ear and hear my words, / and apply your mind to my teaching." In addition, the Hebrew *shlshwm* of v. 20 must be understood to mean "thirty" in view of the Egyptian *Amenemope*, which is divided into "thirty houses" (that is, chapters). Efforts of commentators to divide this instruction into thirty distinct units have not been particularly successful, however. Verse 21 reflects the typical concern of officials in traditional societies to entrust messages only to those capable of delivering them accurately.

22:22–23:11. Reference to boundary markers (22:28; 23:10–11) also occurs in *Amenemope*, as well as in Prov. 25:25 and elsewhere in the Hebrew Bible (Deut. 19:14; 27:17; Isa. 5:8–10). A common method of oppressing the poor, especially widows vulnerable by having no male protector but the Lord, is dispossessing them of their land. Since a boundary marker sets the limits of a field and provides "legal" evidence of ownership, their movement or removal is forbidden and will be avenged by Yahweh (Prov. 23:11).

23:12–24:22
The Sage's Instruction

Issues such as the exemplary benefits of wisdom, the plight of the drunkard, the temptation to envy the wicked or fall prey to the harlot are developed in this section. As in previous verses, the sage invokes Yahweh to lend authority to his teachings. Prov. 23:29–30, which focuses on the drunkard, may be a remnant of an earlier "riddle" (see "Introduction" above). Prov. 24:5–7 has implicit parallels in Prov. 11:14; 20:18. Elsewhere in the Hebrew Bible, too many counselors lead to the downfall of Absalom in 2 Samuel 17. (On the significance of the "weighing the heart" motif in 24:12, see 16:2 [cf. 21:2].) The Greek text for this instruction has five additional verses occurring after 24:22.

24:23–34
Further "Words of the Wise"

This short collection is usually understood to be an appendix of the previous instruction.

24:23a. The first half of v. 23 may be interpreted as a heading for this collection. It might, however, have a more specialized function, namely, a title linking 24:23–34 to 22:17–22, since this half-verse could also be rendered

"These also belong to the [collection of 'Sayings of] wise men'" (Skehan, quoted in Murphy, p. 76).

24:23b–25. Concern about impartiality in judgment is common in the Hebrew Bible (cf., e.g., Prov. 18:5; 28:21; 31:5; Lev. 19:15; Deut. 1:17; 16:19; Amos 2:6; 5:7–10; Isa. 10:2, 11:3–5; Mic. 3:9, 11).

24:26–29. This miscellany of saying, admonition, and prohibitions begins (v. 26) and ends (vv. 28–29) with a focus on proper speech. Verse 28 reflects the experience of the law court. The admonition (v. 27) comments on the prudential road to success. The final prohibition (v. 29), one directed against revenge however well-justified, finds a striking parallel in Matt. 6:12, 14–15.

24:30–34. This "example story" concerning the self-generated plight of the sluggard provides insight into what the sages mean by the word "instruction" (v. 32), used so often in Proverbs 1–9. Reflection on life's events or on humanity's foibles may engender a paradigmatic insight, which can be used to help someone avert disaster or achieve success. Verses 33–34 are identical to Prov. 6:10–11. For other comments on the sluggard, cf. Prov. 6:6; 26:13–16.

25:1–29:27
"Further 'Proverbs of Solomon,' Copied by the Men of Hezekiah, King of Judah"

Another collection of proverbs is here attributed to Solomon. Although this attribution is probably another example of traditional ascription of, rather than actual, authorship, the information, "copied by the men of Hezekiah" (25:1), is generally considered historically accurate and gives an insight into wisdom activity at the royal court. The number of proverbs in this section (approximately 130) is equivalent to the numerical value of the Hebrew name Hezekiah as it was traditionally calculated. Like the previous Solomonic collection, this one may also be divided into two minor groupings, Proverbs 25–27 and 28–29, each internally structured by the typical devices observed earlier (i.e., catchwords, wordplay, onomatopoeia, topic). Proverbs 25–27 prefers comparisons, prohibitions, the topics of natural world and trade, and uses antithetic parallelism far less than is usual. Proverbs 28–29 returns to antithetic parallelism as it treats the themes of the poor, the king, and justice.

25:1–27:27

The Comparison Collection

25:1–28. The topics of the king (vv. 2–7, 15), language (vv. 11, 15, 23), treatment of one's neighbor (vv. 8–9, 17–18), and psychological insights (vv. 20, 25) highlight this chapter of extended comparisons (more than one verse) and commands. Other typical wisdom motifs are also present: false witness (v. 18); behavior at court (vv. 8–10); the boaster (v. 14); the quarrelsome wife (v. 24 = Prov. 21:9); the righteous (v. 26); and the wise (v. 12). Missing are the typical antithetic contrasts between wicked and righteous, wise and fool. Particularly noticeable are comparisons using lush, evocative imagery drawn from nature. Golden apples (v. 11), the refreshing coolness of snow or cold water (vv. 13, 25), wind and rain (vv. 14, 23), all work to cast their content into especially memorable form with the crafted beauty of their similes and metaphors. The gentle tongue, which patiently breaks the bones of the powerful (v. 15), must be a special insight of the sages who habitually counsel against hot-tempered, ill-mannered, and loud-mouthed assaults on convention. Here it is clear they do not think their students should simply endorse the status quo but should rather choose available and effective means to change it. Such recommendations also highlight the sages' lack of ultimate power in Israelite social structure: where kings are concerned, they may counsel, but they cannot command.

26:1–28. The fool (vv. 1 [cf. 19:10a], 3–12 [cf. 10:13b; 19:29b for v. 3b]), the sluggard (vv. 13–16), and the malicious users of language for quarrels, gossip, and deceit (vv. 20–26, 28; v. 22 = 18:8) are the main topics of this chapter. Imagery drawn from the natural world again serves as a vehicle for the sages' observations in vv. 1–5, 9, 11, 13, 17, 20–21, 27. Weapons technology gone out of control due to "human error" forms an appropriate counterpoint in vv. 8, 10, 18–19. Unlike fools of earlier chapters, whose behavior carried moral overtones, those pictured here are simply foolish, thoughtless persons whom those in authority would do well to recognize and avoid entrusting with serious matters (vv. 1, 6, 8, 10). Verses 4–5 present a striking contrast in counsel on how to handle reprimanding a fool. These two verses demonstrate that the insights couched in proverbial form are not eternal "truth" carved in stone but, rather, depend on context for their application. (This is no doubt why the fool will never understand how to use a proverb correctly [vv. 7, 9; cf. Sir. 20:20].) The character portrait of the sluggard is painted with wicked clarity: idlers use any excuse, however ludicrous, to avoid work (v. 13; cf. 22:13; 24:30) and are too lazy even to feed themselves (26:15 = 19:24). Both sides of the act-consequence relationship are affirmed here: no curse "without cause" will find an innocent victim (26:2) and those who dig pits for others will not escape falling in themselves (v. 27; cf. 28:10; Ps. 7:15; Eccles. 10:8; Sir. 27:25–27).

27:1–27. Explorations of the relations between friends and neighbors (vv. 9–11, 14, 17, 19); strange paradoxes (vv. 5–7); uncertainty (v. 1); and human psychology (vv. 4, 17, 19, 20 [cf. 30:15–16]) are nestled among typical wisdom concerns: the fool (vv. 3, 22); prudent behavior (v. 12; cf. 22:3); pledges for loans (27:13 = 20:16); language and boasting (vv. 2, 21); nagging wives (vv. 15–16); and success in one's work (vv. 18, 23–27). Imagery from nature is important in vv. 3, 7–8, 15–16, 18–19, and in vv. 23–27, which provide a small "instruction" on farming (cf. Isa. 28:23–29). Again, context is everything: honey is sweet, but not to the satisfied; to the hungry person, even something bitter is counted as sweet (Prov. 27:7). A friend may be better than kin under the right circumstances (v. 10, cf. 18:24; Sir. 37:6); a rousing blessing given too early becomes a curse (Prov. 27:14); and too much affection can mask more sinister motives (v. 6).

28:1–29:27

The Ruler's Collection

Returning to the antithetic parallelism that characterized the earlier Solomonic collections, this section favors the two-lined proverb rather than commands and extended comparisons. The topics are those important to rulers: justice, treatment of the poor, the nature of power, along with typical wisdom concerns (righteous/wicked, wise/fool, father/mother).

28:1–28. Explicit and implicit contrasts between the righteous and wicked (vv. 1, 4, 10, 12, 13, 16, 18, 28), the rich and poor (vv. 3, 6, 8, 11, 19 [cf. 12:11], 20, 22, 25, 27), and the nature of rulership (vv. 2, 3, 15–16, 28) provide the main topics in this chapter. Yahweh appears as protector and instructor of those who are "godfearing" (vv. 5, 25) and is the implicit referent of the verb "fear" in v. 14 (cf. Sir. 37:12). "Torah" is mentioned specifically in Prov. 28:4, 7, 9. Although "Torah" has been used in the general sense of "teaching" throughout Proverbs, the highly juridical, moral tone of this chapter suggests that the Torah, Israel's legal tradition, is also implied here. Family relationships are the subject of vv. 7, 24, and wisdom themes of flattery/rebuke (v. 23), wise/fool (v. 26), guilt (v. 17), and justice (vv. 5, 8, 21 [cf. 24:23]) round out the selection of proverbs. The Hebrew text of vv.

2–3 is difficult and usually restored from the LXX, a situation that gives rise to varying modern translations.

29:1–27. In the same way that Proverbs 10, the first chapter of the proverb collections, was composed of proverbs that took up themes developed in Proverbs 1–9, so the last chapter of the proverb collections is marked by its use of items that had previously appeared in slightly different form (29:1b = 6:15b; cf., e.g., 29:2 with 11:10; 28:12, 28; 29:5 with 11:9; 29:11 with 12:16; 29:13 with 22:2; 29:20b = 26:12b). The main topics are again the contrast between wicked and righteous (29:2, 6–7, 10, 16, 27), and proverbs about rulers (vv. 2, 4, 12, 14, 26). The contrast between the man who loves (Woman?) Wisdom and the one who goes to prostitutes (v. 3) builds on the imagery present in Proverbs 1–9, while mockers and fools are contrasted with the wise in 29:8–9, 11. Once more, the sages who generally condemn violence in others recommend it (vv. 15, 17, 19, 21; cf. 13:24; 19:18) to control their own families and domestic slaves. Apparently the patient, gentle tongue of 25:15 is to be used only when the one being corrected is of higher status and capable of self-defense.

30:1–14
"The Words of Agur, Son of Jakeh"

Commentators disagree on the precise length of this section, with vv. 4, 6, or 14 serving as possible ending points for the passage. Topical groupings seem to organize these verses (see Murphy, p. 80).

30:1–4
Agur's Oracle

30:1. Although the heading of this collection is understandable, the rest of the Hebrew verse makes little sense. The names Agur and Jakeh do not occur in the rest of the Hebrew Bible and should perhaps be translated literally (Agur = "I am a sojourner"; Jakeh = an abbreviation of "Yahweh, blessed is he") as a symbolic answer to the riddle in v. 4. Agur, then, would stand for Israel, the perpetual sojourner people (cf. Gen. 47:9), and for the "son" of Yahweh, who is the referent of the questions of Prov. 30:4 (see Murphy, p. 80). The word "Massa" (v. 1a) is usually interpreted as a name (so too in 31:1) of a tribe or of an area in north Arabia associated with one of Ishmael's sons in Gen. 25:14 and 1 Chron. 1:30 (see Whybray, p. 172). Such a reference here is not out of the question, since the Hebrew Bible contains many traditions about the fabled wisdom of "the sons of the East" (1 Kings 5:10;

Jer. 49:7). However, "Massa" may also be translated "oracle," even though the following verses are not oracular in form. Prov. 30:1b ("Ithiel," "Ucal") is corrupt and usually emended to read "there is no god"; "I am not god"; "I am weary, O God, I am weary, I am worn out."

30:2–4. Agur's opinion of his own intelligence when compared to the wisdom of the Holy Ones (cf. 9:10) is in keeping with the concept of wisdom's limits as developed in Proverbs 1–9 and throughout the proverb collections. The cosmological questions in Prov. 30:4 draw on the same tradition of God's actions found in Job 38, Isa. 40:12, and Sir. 1:2–3.

30:5–14
Answers, Admonitions, and Observations

The remainder of the passage may be divided into four units: vv. 5–6, an instruction on God's word; vv. 7–9, a prayer framed in numerical saying style; v. 10, a prohibition against defaming slaves; and vv. 11–14, four proverbs on the "breed" or "generation" of the wicked. The instruction in vv. 5–6 seems related to Ps. 18:30 (= Prov. 30:5), Deut. 4:2 (cf. Prov. 30:6a), and Job 13:10; 24:25b (cf. Prov. 30:6b). Whybray finds the notion of "not adding to the word" characteristic of late wisdom's insistence on the reliability of sacred Scriptures, a judgment that provides a postexilic date for this unit as well as the entire Agur passage (see Whybray, p. 173). The prayer of vv. 7–9 steers the traditional middle way of "nothing too much" recommended throughout the book of Proverbs. The typical "father/mother" word pair occurs in the extended description of the wicked (vv. 11–14), where each line begins with the word "generation."

30:15–33
Mostly Numerical Sayings

Some commentators take the conclusion of chap. 30 to be an extension of the discourse of Agur, in which case these numerical sayings may have been taken over from Israel's neighbors to the south (where the names Agur and Jakeh have been attested in south Arabian inscriptions) and east. The collection consists of five numerical sayings (vv. 15b–16, 18–19, 21–23, 24–28, 29–31), of which all but vv. 24–28 are sayings built on the same pattern, referring first to three things, then to four things. Interspersed with these are sayings (vv. 15a, 17), interpretations (v. 20), and commands (vv. 32–33).

30:15–16. The saying about the leech and her daughters (a reference to a leech's two suckers?

514

see Whybray, p. 176) is difficult to understand. Are the words "Give! Give!" to be understood as the names of the leech's children, the cry of the leech and her daughters, or are they in some way related to 15b, whose referents (Sheol and the barren womb) could also be understood as uttering the same exclamation? Some commentators have suggested that the word for leech refers to a bloodsucking demon (cf. the [Akkadian] *lilitu* [= Lilith] nightdemon of Babylon and Israel). The saying may have been placed here because of its symbolic connection to the four insatiable items in 15b–16: the underworld that is greedy for lives; the barren womb desperate for children; parched land; and fire that exists only so long as it has fuel to consume.

30:17–20. The ravens and vultures who pluck out the mocking eye connect the saying in v. 17, reminiscent of 30:11–14, to the numerical saying in vv. 18–19, whose catchword is "way." Punishment for reviling one's parents is death in Exod. 21:17, a judgment echoed here by reference to the ancient horror of lack of proper burial. The saying about the mysterious "ways" (Prov. 30:18–19) may refer to lack of visible means of propulsion or movement that leaves no trace, with "the way of a man with a fertile woman" as a reference to either procreation or sexual attraction generally. The saying about the adulteress (v. 20) makes use of the euphemism of eating for illicit sexual behavior (cf. 9:13–18) and probably appears here because of its topical relationship to v. 19b, as well as the occurrence of the catchword "way."

30:21–33. Inappropriate or undesirable human behavior (vv. 21–23, 32–33) provides a frame for the noble, amazing, and stately aspects of the natural world, a favorite source of knowledge for traditional wisdom teaching. The unbearable human types of vv. 21–23 seem to display a progression of sorts: the slave-turned-king in v. 22a could easily be the gorged fool of v. 22b; the unloved (and for that reason perhaps barren) wife of v. 23a might easily be displaced by a slave girl providing sexual services for her master in v. 23b (cf. Hagar and Sarah in Gen. 16:1–6). Ants (Prov. 6:6–8), rock-badgers, locusts, and lizards are all praised (30:24–28) for their cooperative efforts or abilities to prevail in seemingly impossible situations, thereby demonstrating that wisdom is not to be measured by size. The stately stride and bearing of certain animals (vv. 29–31) is probably to be associated with power. (Two of the terms of this 3/4 saying must be restored from ancient versions: the Greek reads "the cock that proudly struts among the hens" for the Hebrew "one girded about the loins"; various translations are advanced for the "king with his [Heb.] *'alqum* with him" in v. 31b, where the meaning of

'alqum is not known. It may be that the text is corrupt here, and some other stately animal was the original referent.) The effects of pressure are the topic of vv. 32–33, although the relationship between the two verses is obscure, since v. 32 uses the instructional style while v. 33 appears to return to the itemization of examples seen in the numerical saying. Since the words "nose/blood" in v. 33a can also mean "anger/bloodshed" in Hebrew, v. 33b may in fact be a variant of the preceding line (see Whybray, p. 179), though another translation for v. 33b, such as "so the stirring up of dissension produces lawsuits," could also provide a suitable climax for the saying while leaving the text intact.

31:1–9

"The Words of Lemuel, King of Massa, Which His Mother Taught Him"

Instructions in the ancient Near East were often made for kings and princes of Egypt and Babylon, but this is the only surviving example of an instruction made by a woman, though royal wives could, in certain circumstances, wield considerable power (1 Kings 1:11–13; 15:13; 2 Kings 9:22; 11:1). Here we are provided with a concrete instance of the "torah of your mother" mentioned previously by the sages (Prov. 1:8b, 6:20).

31:1–3. The Greek text does not read "Lemuel" as a proper name but translates v. 1 with "my words have been spoken by God—the oracular answer of a king, whom his mother instructed." (On the meaning of "Massa," see commentary above on 30:1.) Foreign influence appears in 31:2–3, as is evident in the use of the Aramaic words for "son" and "kings." Verse 2 reads, literally, "What, my son?! . . with a threefold repetition of the interrogative "what," which functions either as an interjection to highlight the intensity of the mother's comments or to refer to that which follows. The ascription to mothers of advice against involvement with women is common in traditional literature. Verse 2a may reflect a folk belief that sexual excesses quite literally shorten a man's life. Verse 2b is usually interpreted with reference to the LXX or other versions; the Hebrew text reads "your ways" for the conjectured "your loins."

31:4–9. The mother's instruction continues with advice on the appropriate and inappropriate uses of intoxicants (vv. 4–7) and duties of the king (vv. 5b, 8–9). The sentiment in vv. 4–5, that drunkenness may impair judgment and the

515

righteous exercise of power, echoes earlier concerns about partiality in judgment (24:24) and abuse of strong drinks (20:1). On the other hand, when all hope is gone, strong drink may act as a palliative (31:6–7). The Talmud records that compassionate women in Jerusalem used to offer drugged wine to condemned prisoners to minimize their sufferings (so the note to Luke 23:27 in JB). The wine that Jesus refuses in Matt. 27:34 (cf. Luke 23:27; Mark 15:23; John 19:28–30) was probably meant for this purpose. Prov. 30:8–9 explicate the legal role of the king: the ruler is the upholder of the rights of the oppressed, a human mediator who acts on God's behalf to enact justice (cf. the portrait of the ideal king found in Isa. 11:1–5).

31:10–31
Acrostic Poem on the Woman of Worth

The "woman of worth" (others translate: "a capable wife" or "a perfect wife"), who balances and explicates the imagery of Woman Wisdom found in Proverbs 1–9, provides a fitting ending to the book of Proverbs. This wisdom poem is an acrostic (see "Introduction" above), that is, each line begins with a succeeding letter of the Hebrew alphabet (cf. Pss. 9–10; 25; 119; Lam. 1–4). This stylistic device changes the typical word order in Hebrew sentences and causes some problems in the creation of a logical development of thought. Placed after the teaching of Lemuel's mother, this passage could easily be taken as a further development of her instruction, but its internal structure makes clear that it was originally an independent composition.

Though the family pictured here is prosperous and of high status, the wife who maintains it is praised by the sages for symbolic reasons. The poem about her expresses the great value placed on the family as *the* important social and religious unit within Israelite society, both in the premonarchical period and in postexilic Judaism from which this composition probably comes. It is not surprising to see her depicted as wholly "male-identified," that is, from the perspective of her fulfillment of roles that enable the lives of the men who depend on her. Nevertheless, the picture presented here acts as a corrective to the view that women are dangerous beings who sap away men's lives and fortunes. Though a human female, the imagery used paints a portrait of the benefits of Woman Wisdom *inside* the household rather than *outside* in the streets and markets, as in Proverbs 1–9.

31:10–12. The opening question suggests how unlikely sages consider the prospect of finding a woman of worth, which is not surprising given their general view of women (cf. 11:22; 21:9, 19; 22:14). Said to be more precious than jewels in 31:10 (NEB: "coral"; JB: "pearls"), this language directly recalls Woman Wisdom in 3:15 and 8:11. The one who succeeds in finding her (31:10) does not lack material goods (v. 11), reminding us of those who find Woman Wisdom and are materially rewarded by their association with this sought-for person in 3:13–14 and 8:17, 21 (see Camp, p. 188). Her gift of "good" to her husband (31:12) recalls the proverb of 18:22 where "he who finds a wife finds good, and he receives favor from Yahweh."

31:13–19. No sluggard, the woman of worth works diligently even though her household is equipped with servants (vv. 14–15, 17–18). She engages in the typical tasks of spinning, weaving, and sewing, "woman's work" of paramount importance in the ancient world (vv. 13, 19). Verse 16 seems to indicate that she engages in at least some activities that are usually reserved for men, such as the purchase of real estate. Historical evidence suggests, however, that women of extremely high (and extremely low) status have always had more freedom than "average" status women to move about in the public domain, so that the range of activities attributed here to the wealthy wife need not surprise us.

31:20–27. The "provider" motif (vv. 21–22, 24–25) continues, interspersed with description of her wise, righteous, and compassionate actions (vv. 20, 26). Her generosity to the poor, along with her wise speech, loyal instructions (Heb. *torat-chesed* or "teaching of steadfast/covenant love"; →Loving-kindness) give a living example of the "mother's torah" (1:8; 6:20; and 31:1). All these attributes contribute to her husband's good name (31:23) and allow him to earn the respect of his peers when he appears in places of power, especially the legal assembly.

31:28–31. Her single-minded devotion to the needs of others earns her, in vv. 28–30, the praise of those for whom she lives. Verse 29 reads, literally, "many daughters" rather than the "many women" usually rendered. The selection of this language is in keeping with the "male-identified" tone of the poem, although it is also possible that this term, rather than "women," was selected because it provides a superior rhyme in Hebrew. "A woman who fears Yahweh" (v. 30) may originally have read "a woman of understanding," as it appears in the LXX. The change may have been made by the final redactor of Proverbs to distinguish the woman of worth from Woman Wisdom, who appears as Understanding in 8:14 (see Camp, pp. 96–97). Within the context of this poem, the effect of such a statement is to suggest that women in the community for whom this text is "Scripture" most properly worship God through fulfillment of their domestic roles, rather than through forms of observance (such as public religious leadership) that men assign to themselves. The command to provide for the woman of worth suggests that, although she is the source of all good things, she may not automatically have shared in the profits of her own labor (31:31a). Verse 31b concludes the poem and the book with a return to the imagery of Woman Wisdom: the works of the woman of worth will praise her in the same city gates where Woman Wisdom issued her call (1:21; 8:3).

Bibliography

Camp, C. V. Wisdom and the Feminine in the Book of Proverbs. Bible and Literature, 11. Sheffield: Almond, 1985.

Crenshaw, J. "Wisdom." In Old Testament Form Criticism. Edited by J. H. Hayes. San Antonio, TX: Trinity University Press, 1974. Pp. 225–64.

Fontaine, C. R. Traditional Sayings in the Old Testament: A Contextual Study. Bible and Literature, 5. Sheffield: Almond, 1982.

Murphy, R. E. Wisdom Literature: Job, Proverbs, Ruth, Canticles, Ecclesiastes, Esther. Forms of the Old Testament Literature, 13. Grand Rapids, MI: Eerdmans, 1981.

Pritchard, J., ed. Ancient Near Eastern Texts Relating to the Old Testament. 3d ed. with supplement. Princeton, NJ: Princeton University Press, 1969.

Simpson, W. K., ed. The Literature of Ancient Egypt: An Anthology of Stories, Instructions and Poetry. New ed. New Haven, CT: Yale University Press, 1973.

Vawter, B. "Prov. 8:22: Wisdom and Creation." Journal of Biblical Literature 99 (1980):205–16.

Whybray, R. N. The Book of Proverbs. New English Bible Commentaries, Old Testament. Cambridge: Cambridge University Press, 1972.

ECCLESIASTES

JAMES L. CRENSHAW

INTRODUCTION

Mystery of the Name

The author of Ecclesiastes gives his name as Qohelet, which occurs seven times (1:1, 2, 12; 7:27; 12:8, 9, 10). In two instances in the Hebrew text (7:27; 12:8), the name has a definite article ("the Qohelet"). Although feminine in form, Qohelet is construed as masculine since it occurs with verbs of the latter gender. The Hebrew verb *qahal*, from which the name Qohelet is derived, means "to gather, to assemble," always with reference to people. So, in 1 Kings 8–12, an author uses this verb to refer to Solomon's assembling of the people to dedicate the Temple. The book of Ecclesiastes connects its author with King Solomon (Eccles. 1:1, 12; indirectly in 1:12–2:26), but this royal fiction vanishes at 2:26, perhaps reappearing in the epilogue (12:11, "one shepherd").

What does the word Qohelet connote? Scholars understand it in various ways: as a personal name, pen name, acronym, or function. Its use as a reference to Solomon is unlikely, since the article, which may preface the word Qohelet, and the identification of the author as a professional wise man (12:9) point to a functionary other than a king. To be sure, Egyptian precedent for royal authorship of wisdom literature exists, but the author's perspective outside Eccles. 1:12–2:26 is that of a subject. One interpreter has proposed that the word Qohelet conceals the author's name, just as Yaqeh (RSV: Jakeh), Agur's father in Prov. 30:1–2, is said to be an abbreviation for "Yahweh is the Holy One." However, no one has discovered a suitable explanation for the putative acronym Qohelet.

The usual explanation is based on Ezra 2:55, 57 and Neh. 7:59, where the offices of scribe and binder of gazelles, untranslated in RSV as "Hassophereth" and "Pochereth-hazzebaim," are designated by words formed as feminine participles. Understood on the basis of this analogy, the word Qohelet describes an office that relates in some way to assembling people (or proverbs?). The Septuagint Greek translation renders the word in this way, associating the noun for assembly with the word for a public gathering (Gk. *ecclesia*). Jerome followed this lead in the Latin Version, the Vulgate, but emphasized the role of speaking before an assembly. Protestant Reformers adopted Jerome's notion of a preacher, and modern translations have generally followed suit, despite its inappropriateness. Awareness of this difficulty has led one scholar to understand the verb *qahal* in the sense of harangue (cf. Neh. 5:7) and to think of Qohelet as an "arguer," as in a diatribe. Still another interpreter suggests that the term refers to a living assembly of wise sayings in the same way that wisdom may be personified as a woman.

One problem with assuming that Qohelet assembled students in a school is that he sets his view over against traditional wisdom. Indeed, his teachings undercut the established wisdom of the time, rejecting its fundamental premise and major conclusions. Moreover, he seems to have democratized education, offering his insights to the populace at large, if the first epilogist has preserved authentic memory (Eccles. 12:9). Perhaps this disciple has also remembered correctly that Qohelet's primary function as teacher was to assemble proverbs (12:9–11). There may be a subtle hint in 7:27 that the name Qohelet refers to this process of assembling proverbial data in the search for comprehensive wisdom. Such a departure from the typical use of *qahal* as referring to people would not be the only instance in which Qohelet forged a distinctive language. After all, in his view people were no better off than animals.

Unity of the Book

The first-person pronoun punctuates the book of Ecclesiastes, leaving the impression that a single author is responsible for its content. However, the book concludes with a section that refers to the author in the third person (12:9–14). These comments resemble an epitaph (12:9–11) and a polemical corrective (12:12–14). Furthermore, since 1:12 seems to be the author's introduction to the book, 1:1 may be viewed as a secondary superscription based on 1:12. In addition, a thematic statement, which may derive from Qohelet, forms an envelope around the book (1:2; 12:8). In any event, there is sufficient evidence to question the literary integrity of Ecclesiastes. This suspicion is heightened by the presence of contradictions, particularly with regard to the ultimate fate of the wicked. Does Qohelet think God will judge them or not? Because the book answers this question both positively and negatively, critics usually attribute these opposing views to different authors.

Scholars have developed four theories to account for the book's formation: first, the author wrote most of the book, but editorial comments were added at a later time; second, the author quotes traditional wisdom and contradicts it; third, the author enters into dialogue with an interlocutor, real or imagined; and fourth, the book reflects a single author's changing views over the years, as it also realistically describes life's ambiguities.

Beyond the superscription and epilogues, additions to the book seem to occur in contexts dealing with reward and retribution (2:26a; 3:17a; 8:12–13; 11:9b; perhaps 5:18 and 7:26b). These additions may derive from the same hand that was responsible for 12:12–24, which reaffirms traditional views and brings Qohelet's teachings in line with Torah piety. Earlier theories about multiple editors (a Sadducean, a sage, a pious one, and another editor) have lost their attraction, but few contemporary interpreters are willing to abandon the theory of an editor altogether. After all, such editorial activity altered many biblical books, and Qohelet's radical views would have invited editorial revision. In at least one instance, material was very poorly integrated into the book (10:1–4, 8–20).

Contrasting opinions appear throughout the book. Qohelet openly opposes any teacher who claims to possess absolute truth (8:17). Indeed, an adversarial stance pervades the material, leading some scholars to suggest that Qohelet quotes his opponents without the usual indications for a change in speaker. One scholar has isolated the citations 2:14a; 4:5; 4:6; 7:5–6a; 9:17; 10:2; 10:12, and several interpreters assume that Qohelet used an approach that is best described as "Yes, but . . ." Although conceding the general reliability of a particular view, Qohelet proceeds by appealing to a fact of life that contradicts and, thereby, refutes it.

Early Christian interpreters recognized such competing views, attributed them to different speakers, and thus pointed to the dialogical character of the book. As a result Qohelet's unorthodox sentiments were neutralized. Thesis stood over against antithesis in such a way that all teachings were relativized. Modern interpreters have continued this line of reasoning by isolating a "good" and a "bad" in Qohelet's views on a given subject or by emphasizing polarities within the book. In one instance, the juxtaposition of opposites is undeniable (3:1–8).

If Qohelet assembled his reflections about life over a long period of time, it may be amiss to expect logical consistency. Furthermore, life's ambiguities themselves may have struck Qohelet as noteworthy. Indeed, the very confrontation between Hebraism and Hellenism produced compromises, and Hebraism alone included its share of contradictions.

Structure

Qohelet's reflections begin with a thematic statement (1:2) and a poem (1:4–11); they conclude with a poem and the same thematic statement (11:7–12:7; 12:8). Together with the superscription (1:1), and an elaboration of the thematic statement (1:3), the epilogues (12:9–14) enclose the book in a kind of envelope. The rest of the book includes a few easily recognizable units, for example, the royal experiment in 1:12–2:26 or the praise of companionship in 4:9–12. Nevertheless, the precise structure of the book defies description.

Several interpreters have sought the clue to the book's structure in refrains that seem to introduce or conclude various segments. However, the sevenfold exhortation to eat, drink, and enjoy life (2:24–26; 3:12–13; 3:22; 5:17–19; 8:15; 9:7–10; 11:7–10) illustrates the difficulty of this approach; the first text concludes a unit and the last one introduces a new unit.

Others have sought to discern the structure of the book in polar opposites and Greek rhetoric, according to which there is a complete balancing of the material in the two halves of the book. But none of these theories is adequate, for some collections of sentences have not been fully integrated into the book. In the book's unity of tone, theme, and topic, one receives the impression that a single teacher has observed life's ambiguities and reflected on their meaning, using favorite words: do, work, good, wise, time, know, toil, see, under the sun, fool, profit, portion.

Historical Setting

The effort to establish the historical setting of the book has also been unsuccessful. The hypothesis that the original language was Aramaic has virtually disappeared because of the discovery at Qumran of Hebrew fragments of the book. Nevertheless, the language is an Aramaizing Hebrew, closest to other late canonical texts. Two Persian loan words occur (pardes, "park"; medinah, "province"). Phoenician and Egyptian origins have been posited, but the evidence, although inconclusive, favors Palestine (references to reservoirs, leaky roofs, wells, farmers' attention to the wind, and the Temple). The so-called historical allusions do not enable a precise dating (4:13–16; 8:2–4; 9:13–15; 10:16–17). The meager political data point to a period before the Maccabean revolt in 167 B.C., and the attitude toward foreign rulers fits best in the Ptolemaic period (→ Ptolemy). The Zenon business archives from about 250 B.C. reflect a political situation of economic prosperity in the upper echelons of Jewish society. Qohelet may have belonged to the privileged class shortly after this time.

Literary Expression

The fundamental genre of the book is reflection arising from personal observation. Qohelet's language calls attention to both aspects, the observing and the subsequent reflection ("I said in my heart, I saw, I know, there is"). The issue of literary genre is not entirely clear, however, and other critics propose that the book be understood as royal testament, diatribe, or *mashal* (Heb., a "comparison"). Nonetheless, the Egyptian royal testament is limited to 1:12–2:26, and monologue may be more apt than diatribe, for Qohelet emphasizes the debate in his own mind. The term *mashal* is too broad to be useful.

Of course, the book includes many other literary types such as autobiographical narrative, example story, anecdote, parable (often called an allegorical poem), antithesis, and proverb. The proverb itself occurs in many forms: truth statements, better sayings, numerical sayings, instructions, traditional sayings, maledictions, and benedictions. Qohelet was fond of better sayings (4:3, 6, 9, 13; 5:5; 6:3, 9; 7:1, 2, 3, 5, 8; 9:4, 16, 18) and the emphatic "nothing is better than" (2:24; 3:12, 22).

What was the essence of Qohelet's reflection about life? His primary word denies earlier optimistic claims about wisdom's power to secure one's existence. Moreover, he observes no discernible principle of order governing the universe, rewarding virtue and punishing evil. The creator is distant and uninvolved, except perhaps in cases of flagrant affront like reneging on religious vows. Death cancels all imagined gains, rendering life on earth absurd. Therefore the best advice is to enjoy one's wife, together with good food and drink, during youth, for old age and death will soon put an end to this relative good. In short, Qohelet examined all of life and discovered no absolute good that would survive death. Profit is thus the measure of life for him. He then proceeded to report this discovery —that there was no profit—and to counsel young men in the light of this stark reality. In sum, Qohelet bears witness to an intellectual crisis in ancient Israel, at least in the circles he taught in.

The Larger Environment

An intellectual crisis struck other cultures as well, though not all at the same time. One expects, therefore, to find some common themes throughout the ancient Near East. This universality of ideas has led to claims of Hellenistic influence on Qohelet, specifically the concepts of chance, vanity, profit, portion, and the phrase "under the sun." Similar arguments about Egyptian influence have been advanced, especially the royal testament, the phrase "eternal home," the idiom of casting bread upon waters, and the idea of *carpe diem* (Lat., "enjoy the day"). Papyrus Insinger, and the "Instruction of 'Onkysheshonky," roughly contemporary with Qohelet, are especially significant in this regard. Moreover, scholars have pointed to parallels between Mesopotamian literature and Qohelet. Siduri's advice to Gilgamesh is strikingly similar to Qohelet's advice to young men. The Gilgamesh Epic also probes the themes of death and the ephemerality of life. Other texts such as "I Will Praise the Lord of Wisdom" stress the hiddenness of God; "The Babylonian Theodicy" espouses pessimism at its very core, blaming the gods for evil, a view from which Qohelet shrinks (7:29); and "The Dialogue Between a Master and His Slave" mentions a threat posed by women and sets up polarities in a way that commends neither alternative. Such parallels do not necessarily require the notion of literary dependence, and Qohelet forges his distinctive worldview out of personal experience. His eyes and ears were open to insights regardless of their origin, and those themes that are not the result of polygenesis were probably "in the air."

Canonization and Text

Qohelet's radical views have branded his teachings an alien body within the Hebrew Bible. How, then, was the book accepted into the canon? The usual answer is that the attribution to Solomon paved the way for its approval as Scripture, although that alone did not work in the case of Wisdom of Solomon and the *Odes of Solomon*. A better answer is that the book's epilogue removed the sting from Qohelet's skepticism and advocated traditional views concerning observance of Torah.

The Hebrew text of Ecclesiastes is in good condition. Fragments dating from the middle of the second century B.C. include part of 5:13–17, substantial portions of 6:3–8, and five words from 7:7–9.

COMMENTARY

1:1, The Superscription. Verse 1 resembles the introduction not only to the sayings of Agur (Prov. 30:1a) and Lemuel's mother (Prov. 31:1a), but also to some prophetic collections (Amos 1:1a; Jer. 1:1a). The allusion to Solomonic authorship is more specific than that in Eccles. 1:12, which could refer to *any* Davidic ruler in Jerusalem.

1:2–3, A Thematic Statement and Its Elaboration. The repetition of the word for brevity and futility provides an idiom for the ultimate absurdity. Qohelet assesses everything as ephemeral and devoid of substance. Hence, human toil under the sun yields no lasting profit. This brief unit sets the tone of the entire book.

1:4–11, An Absence of Novelty. An eternal sameness characterizes movements in nature and society. The impressive poem in 1:4–11 describes the endless rounds of an exhausted sun, the circling of the wind, and the never-ending flow of streams to a sea that is not filled by all the water that enters it. The poet moves on to describe the tedious monotony in society: the wearisome words that no one can ever fully declare, the acquisitive eye, the eager ear, and the frustrated search for something new. The illusion of novelty derives from human forgetfulness, which he declares to be universal and permanent. The poet allows the ambiguous word "generations" to describe heavenly bodies and human beings, uses the euphemism "goes" for death, achieves emphasis by withholding the subject "wind" until the latest possible moment, gives the impression of monotony by repeating several words, and signifies comprehensiveness by alluding to the four points of the compass.

1:12–2:26, A Royal Experiment. In 1:12–2:26 Qohelet states his findings and reinforces them with two proverbs (1:12–18), describes the examination of pleasure (2:1–11) and of wisdom and folly (2:12–23), and draws a conclusion that the best thing to do is to enjoy life (2:24–26). Qohelet introduces himself in 1:12 and reports on his resolve to search for and spy on everything that happens, which he takes to be God's gift, an unpleasant, sorry business. Everything is futile, herding of the wind (chasing it? feeding it?). The proverb (1:15) about the impossibility of straightening the crooked (back?) or counting what is lacking points to human impotence in the face of divine determinism. Solomon's reputation for exceptional wisdom prompts Qohelet's boast to have surpassed all others in this regard, but this notable achievement brought only more sorrow. In short, the noble aim of the sages is here dismissed as chasing the wind.

When Qohelet describes his experiment, he turns to the exploration of what pleasure has to offer. This too is futile, he asserts. His acquisitions are typical of ancient kings: houses, vineyards, gardens, reservoirs, servants, riches, and concubines. His indulgence knew no limit, for he had the means to satisfy every desire, and, as king, he could do so without fear of being challenged. But the flirtation with sensual gratification issued in a feeling of utter futility

(2:11, which combines the three negative assessments thus far: futility, chasing the wind, and devoid of profit).

Qohelet turns to assess the life of the intellect, examining wisdom and its opposite. He grants the essential correctness of the proverbial saying that the wise person can see but fools walk in darkness. Therefore, wisdom is relatively superior to folly. However, in the long run, there is no advantage to the wise, who suffer the same fate that fools experience. Because both wise and fool die and remembrance is quickly erased, Qohelet draws a shocking conclusion: "So I hated life," 2:17. Inheritance exacerbates the feeling of repugnance, for some people toil endlessly and achieve wealth only to leave it to someone who may lack intelligence.

This test of sensual pleasure and wisdom convinces Qohelet that everything is absurd and empty. Therefore, he observes that the best course is to enjoy life, if God makes such possible. The words "good in God's presence" and "sinner" are entirely amoral; they refer to people who are fortunate and unfortunate respectively. Even one's capacity to enjoy life lies in divine hands, and the individual can do nothing about this reality.

3:1–15, Reflections on Time. The remarkable poem in vv. 1–9 takes the form of fourteen opposites, each introduced by the word "time." Qohelet then draws some conclusions about the relationship between deity and time (vv. 10–15). The poem on time begins with personal events, birth and death, and concludes with public events, war and peace. The chiastic form permits the poem to end on a favorable note (vv. 1, 8: birth, death, war, peace; v. 8: love, hate, war, peace). (In a chiasm the elements occur in an inverted order, e.g., good bad, bad good.) In many cases the first and third are closely related, as are the second and fourth (for example, weeping and laughing, mourning and being happy). If this tendency is consistent, the reference to throwing and gathering stones may be erotic, as rabbinic interpreters insisted, for the parallel verbs connote passion and its absence. The images in v. 5 may, however, derive from commerce, agriculture, or mythology. Although everything has its proper time, human beings (even astrologers?) cannot discover that moment. Qohelet declares that God created everything beautiful in its time and planted mystery (hiddenness? a sense of eternity?) in the human mind; however, that dubious gift opened doors for no one. This situation, which is judged to be permanent, results from God's desire to instill fear in humans. Meanwhile, the Deity is busily engaged in chasing after the past.

3:16–4:3, The Tears of the Oppressed. Because God fails to keep times of judgment, the oppressed shed bitter tears. Moreover, despite Qohelet's conviction that God has set a time for judgment, the facts speak for themselves: virtuous people are crushed by vicious and powerful persons. The cherished belief in reward and retribution does not accord with experience. Qohelet attributes a strange motive to God for delaying proper reward and punishment: God is testing human beings to demonstrate that they have no advantage over animals. Both people and beasts share a common fate, and no one knows whether human breath ascends or animal breath descends at death. After all, every creature came from dust and will return to it (cf. the divine curse in Gen. 3:19 and Job 10:9, 34:15). The sorry human lot, which evokes a pathetic refrain in Qohelet ("and there was no comforter for them," 4:1), goads him into praising those who have never been born over those for whom light has exposed human misery.

4:4–6, Proverbial Wisdom. Insights from the past are valuable, but how does one know which road to follow when there is a choice? Qohelet attributes human toil to envy, and he sees advantages both in work and in its opposite. To be sure, fools sit idly and live off their fat (or the aphorism may mean that God rewards laziness with plenty of meat to eat), but a morsel is better than working for more food without success.

4:7–12, The Advantages of Companionship. A traditional saying, which is also attested in Mesopotamia: "A threefold cord is not quickly broken," acknowledges the need for companions. Qohelet comes close to questioning the sage's egocentricity in this section, but he never really gives it up. It is good to have a friend to lift one out of a pit into which one has fallen, to provide warmth on a cold night, and to fight against a robber. In each instance, the argument rests on the advantages that accrue to one who has a companion. The ego is still paramount here as in the royal experiment, where the phrase "for myself" occurs often. Qohelet thinks it strange that a person who has no relative or friend works without pausing to ask why he is depriving himself of the good life.

4:13–16, The Fickle Crowd. There is no lasting allegiance, for the people quickly forget a ruler whose achievements were truly amazing. Qohelet observes that a poor but intelligent ruler is superior to an old foolish king who does not fully appreciate the insights of people in the royal court. This is true, Qohelet insists, even if the young person emerged from prison—or even from birth in poverty—to the throne. But this anecdote, which echoes the story about Joseph, becomes somewhat confusing with the introduction of a second youth. Either this is an example of imprecise syntax or it illustrates the fickleness of subjects who always welcome a new ruler as one who will deliver them from an unpleasant situation.

5:1–9, On Religious Obligations. Because of the great distance separating human beings from God, they should speak sparingly, in Qohelet's view. Furthermore, their words must be truthful, for it does not pay to call attention to one's lack of integrity. Here Qohelet's language echoes Deut. 23:21, fulfilling a vow when one has made it, but he stresses the advisability of avoiding oaths in the first place. The word for a "mistake" is a technical term for unwitting offenses listed in Hebrew Bible laws. The messenger is an angel (of death, as in Egyptian literature?) or a priestly emissary. Qohelet thinks that verbosity opens the door to affront, just as dreams generate anxiety and emptiness. The primary obligation is to fear God, and that includes an acknowledgment that the Deity has no special fondness for fools. Qohelet even advises against the prophetic voice of protest over oppression, noting that a hierarchy of responsibility rises to the supreme earthly ruler, or perhaps one step higher to God.

5:10–6:9, Disappointments in Owning Wealth. Various factors over which one has no control lead to disenchantment with wealth: bad investments, sickness, increasing overhead costs, worry, and the inability to "take wealth with one." Qohelet exposes human jealousy, the grasping to have more than a neighbor possesses and the desire to satisfy an insatiable lust for possessions, to public scrutiny. The person who loves money will merely see it slip through the fingers like quicksilver. Whereas a laborer sleeps soundly from exhaustion, a rich person lies awake from overeating and from anxiety. Qohelet thinks of a particular example, a person who acquired a fortune and lost it, although he had a son who would have inherited the largess. Reference to emerging from and returning to the womb naked echoes a similar remark in Job 1:21. Perhaps Qohelet here implies a miserly existence, one in which a person is too stingy to light a lamp during the evening meal. It grieves Qohelet that some people have wealth but lack the capacity to enjoy it, since God's gift should enable such enjoyment. The meaning of God's keeping someone occupied with (or afflicting?) the joys of the heart is unclear (5:20). Is the sentiment comforting or distressing? In any event, Qohelet does not consider longevity the answer, for a long life is hollow unless it is marked by pleasure and a proper burial. That is why an abortive birth is better; the dead infant never experienced the full range of human suffering.

6:10–12, A Transitional Unit. Qohelet returns to the idea that there is nothing new, ironically alluding to the name of the first earth creature (Heb. *'adam*), who cannot compete with God (perhaps an allusion also to Job). Reference to the multiplication of words reinforces the suspicion that Job is the target of this comment. The fundamental orientation of ancient wisdom—the ascertainment of what is good for human beings—is here dismissed as beyond discovery.

7:1–14, A Collection of Proverbs. This unit calls attention to the relative worth of many things. The key word is "better," sometimes used in the sense of good. The author uses alliteration, especially in the play on similarities between the Hebrew words for oil and name, as well as brambles, pot, and laughter. Qohelet insists that God's works are inalterable, whether good or evil, and advises persons to visit the house of mourning rather than a place of festivity, for the end is preferable to the beginning.

7:15–22, On Moderation. Qohelet warns against extreme virtue or vice because qualities call special attention to oneself. It has been argued that Qohelet warns against self-righteousness rather than excessive goodness.

7:23–29, Seeking and Finding. The mysteries of wisdom and woman occupy Qohelet's attention, prompting him to acknowledge that wisdom is too deep, hence impenetrable, and that the seductress is more bitter than death. In his view, the fortunate individual escapes her trap.

8:1–9, Rulers and Subjects. Qohelet warns against tarrying when a king becomes angry, for no one can call him to account. But the king is unable to master "the day of death."

8:10–17, The Mystery of Divine Activity. The delay in punishing the wicked encourages villainy. An editorial gloss reaffirms divine justice in the face of such brutal facts (8:11–13). However, Qohelet reiterates the injustice of society, the reversal of reward and punishment, and repeats his advice to enjoy oneself.

9:1–10, The Shadow of Death. Death's lengthening shadow extends throughout the book; it is particularly dark in this unit. Qohelet thinks that God's disposition toward humans is unfathomable, resulting in a common fate for everyone regardless of their religious activities. Qohelet uses irony in conceding that the living have an advantage, since the traditional saying about a living dog and a dead lion is negated by what follows.

9:11–12, Time and Chance. According to Qohelet, chance governs human lives. As a result, it does no good to strive for excellence in the belief that such effort will produce pleasant results. There is no way to plan for the unexpected or to compensate for randomness.

9:13–18, On Wasted Wisdom. Qohelet offers an example, perhaps hypothetical, of skill that did not bring the expected success. A poor but wise man could have saved a village when a great king attacked, but everybody forgot him (or he did save it and everyone promptly forgot him). Qohelet praises wisdom more than weapons, but admits that the former can easily be overlooked and thwarted.

10:1–20, A Collection of Proverbs on Wisdom and Folly. This section is not fully integrated into the book. Connections with other material are not obvious, but word associations with other sections do occur. The fool proclaims his own stupidity, or thinks all others are stupid. Qohelet complains about reversals in society (fools riding horses), warns about dangers lurking in domestic chores, expresses dismay over rulers who drink too much, mentions the function of bribes, and alludes to a proverbial saying about a bird carrying slander to its object.

11:1–6, The Element of Risk. Some risk always resides in commercial enterprises and agriculture, but intelligent persons venture nonetheless. The image of casting bread on waters is also found in the Egyptian "Instruction of 'Onkysheshonky." The mystery of pregnancy does not preclude union between lovers, and ignorance of the wind ought not prevent the sowing of seed.

11:7–12:7, Youth, Old Age, and Death. An exquisite poem depicts a collapsing house and wasting human body and achieves thematic unity by the use of verbs ("remember," "rejoice") and nouns ("darkness," "light"). In addition, a repeated formula ("before . . .") occurs three times. The images for death are complex: the breaking of a cord that held a lamp and the shattering of a pitcher as a result of a faulty pulley at the well. The ensuing puff of dust and release of God's breath signal the end, thus evoking Qohelet's solemn refrain about emptiness and futility. In this poem the reference to a creator seems out of place; the word may allude to one's wife (well) and/or grave (pit).

12:8, A Thematic Statement. Verse 12:8 forms an envelope structure with 1:8, and in so doing emphasizes Qohelet's view that life is futile.

12:9–14, Two Epilogues. Two editors praise Qohelet for his integrity, reliability, and elegance, although conceding that his sayings provide painful education, and warning against any additional works such as this. One epilogist states what he thinks Qohelet should have but did not say: fear God, keep his commandments, for God will judge every secret deed.

Bibliography
Crenshaw, J. L. *Old Testament Wisdom.* Atlanta, GA: Knox, 1981.

————."Qoheleth in Current Research." *Hebrew Annual Review* 7 (1983):41–56.

Gordis, R. *Koheleth: The Man and His World.* 1951. Reprint. New York: Schocken, 1968.

Murphy, R. E. "Qoheleth's 'Quarrel' with the Fathers." In *From Faith to Faith.* Edited by G. Y. Hadidian. Pittsburgh, PA: Pickwick Press, 235–45.

Sheppard, G. F. "The Epilogue to Qoheleth as Theological Commentary." *Catholic Biblical Quarterly* 39 (1977): 182–89.

von Rad, G. *Wisdom in Israel.* Nashville, TN: Abingdon, 1972.

SONG OF SONGS

MARCIA FALK

INTRODUCTION

One of the most celebrated collections of ancient love poetry, the Song of Songs—also known in English as the Song of Solomon—is the only book of love poems in the Bible, and as such it has been the subject of much speculation and controversy. For centuries, both Jewish and Christian traditions justified the place of the Song of Songs in the canon by viewing it as a spiritual allegory that recounts the love of God and the people of Israel (the Jewish interpretation), or of Christ and the church or the individual soul (the Christian reading). But these modes of interpretation, imaginative and moving as they may be, do not explicate the primary level of the text, which is explicitly about human love and nowhere mentions God.

Another centuries-old interpretation presents the Song of Songs as a drama with fixed characters, such as King Solomon and his country bride, or two country lovers (shepherd and shepherdess) and the king. But it is difficult to find evidence of dramatic structure in the Song: acts, scenarios, and dramatis personae are not indicated, and there is hardly a trace of coherent plot. Rather, the Song has a variety of contexts that shift frequently in no apparent dramatic sequence and within which many different voices seem to speak. There is no reason to assume only a few fixed speakers in the Song and even less justification for viewing King Solomon as a central character. Although Solomon's name is mentioned in the Hebrew title, this title was bestowed not by the Song's original author or authors but by later compilers, who may also have been responsible for giving the Song its semblance of structural unity.

About the Song's authorship and origins very little is known. Tradition ascribes the work to King Solomon, but this view is discounted by modern scholars, who generally agree that the Song's authorship cannot be specified. Nor is its date of composition determined: scholarly speculation ranges from 950 to 200 B.C. In the past two centuries, scholars have hypothesized about the original context and function of the Song, proposing, for example, that it was a cycle of wedding songs or the liturgy of an ancient fertility cult. These theories, however, are not only unprovable but unconvincing, because they attempt to force the varied material of the text into confining molds. It is finally simpler and more illuminating to view the Song as a collection of different types of love poems that did not necessarily all derive from the same author or serve the same function in their original society. The stylistic similarities and repetitions among the poems may best be explained as literary conventions of ancient Hebrew verse, particularly if one accepts the view that the Song was, in its earliest stages, popular oral literature.

Well beyond the time of its original composition, the Song continued to be orally transmitted. Through the present day, Ashkenazic Jews ritually chant it on the Sabbath of the Passover holiday, and in many Sephardic Jewish communities it is chanted on the eve of every Sabbath. With good justification is it called the Song of Songs, meaning the most supreme song: its many musical phrases have inspired hundreds of melodies, of many genres and styles, in both the religious and nonreligious Jewish communities. It has also been a popular source of imagery for Hebrew poets over the ages.

COMMENTARY

Though theories concerning the origin of this text can never be proved, it seems likely that the Song was orally composed and transmitted over an extended period of time before being transcribed, compiled, and finally canonized. Many scholars conclude that the Song was, in its earliest form, several distinct shorter poems, although there is disagreement about the number of poems comprising the whole. One postulation is to divide the Song into thirty-one poems, corresponding to the biblical chapters and verses, after 1:1 (title), as follows: 1:2–4; 1:5–6; 1:7–8; 1:9–11; 1:12–14; 1:15–17; 2:1–3; 2:4–7; 2:8–13; 2:14; 2:15; 2:16–17; 3:1–5; 3:6–11; 4:1–7; 4:8; 4:9–11; 4:12–5:1; 5:2–6:3; 6:4–10; 6:11 (6:12 is an indecipherable fragment); 6:13–7:5; 7:6–9; 7:10–13; 8:1–4; 8:5a; 8:5b; 8:6–7; 8:8–10; 8:11–12; and 8:13–14.

Because it is my view that the Song is an anthology of lyric poems rather than a structural unity implying sequence, this commentary is organized in a different way from others in the volume. Rather than proceeding sequentially by chapter and verse, it offers an overview of the different types of poems in the Song and of the poetic material that recurs among the poems, including specific kinds of metaphoric passages and the most frequently appearing contexts, themes, and motifs.

Types of Lyric Poems in the Song. The thirty-one poems that comprise the Song may be categorized into several types, all of which may properly be considered "lyrics" in several senses of the term; that is, they are all brief, sensual, musical poems in which intensely subjective experience is recorded.

Over half the poems in the Song may be categorized as "love monologues"—poems in which a single speaker, female or male, speaks to or about a beloved with words of praise, invitations to lovemaking, or descriptions of fantasies. Examples of this type of poem are 1:2–4; 1:9–11; 1:12–14; 2:4–7; 2:14; 2:16–17; 3:1–5; 4:1–7; 4:8; 4:9–11; 6:4–10; 7:6–9; 7:10–13; 8:1–4; 8:5b; and 8:6–7. Another six of the thirty-one poems might be termed "love dialogues," or conversations—again, entailing praises and invitations, and sometimes employing coyness or games of hide-and-seek—between two lovers; these are 1:7–8; 1:15–17; 2:1–3; 2:8–13; 4:12–5:1; and 8:13–14.

Other types of poems in the Song are less obviously "love poems" and sometimes less apparently lyrics; they may not be to or even directly about a beloved, and some of them are spoken by plural voices or unidentifiable speakers. There are five monologue poems that fall into these types—1:5–6; 2:15; 3:6–11; 8:5a; and 8:11–12—and two dialogues—6:13–7:5 and 8:8–10. In addition, there is one poem that is somewhat longer than the others and that takes a composite form—5:2–6:3. Set in a variety of contexts and spoken by several speakers, this poem seems least to resemble the lyric archetype. However, it is framed in its entirety as the monologue of a woman who declares herself to be in a state of dreaming ("I sleep and my heart is awake"). Everything that happens in the poem may thus be viewed as taking place in her dream or in the recounting of it. In this sense the poem is really the speech of a single speaker, about—if not directly to—her beloved, and it may be regarded as a complex lyric form. It should also be noted that all the poems in the Song, even those having unidentifiable speakers or enigmatic subject matter, have some erotic reference, albeit at times indirect. In several poems, erotic experience is suggested by means of symbols (such as the vineyard, representing female sexuality), which establish their meaning by their recurrent appearances in the Song. Thus, when

viewed as part of the larger collection, the individual poems of the Song all finally emerge as types of love lyrics.

The Wasf. The *wasf*, a specific kind of passage describing the human body, appears several times in the Song within different types of lyrics. Although not found anywhere in the Bible outside the Song, the *wasf* is common in Arabic literature and takes its name from an Arabic word meaning "description." *Wasfs*, or fragments of *wasfs*, appear in the following places in the Song: 4:1–7; 5:9–16; 6:4–7; and 6:13–7:5. Fairly rigid in form, the *wasf* is essentially a catalogue that proceeds in sequence—from top to bottom or bottom to top—to depict parts of the male or female physique in metaphors drawn from the realms of nature and artifice. While these metaphors are often based on visual perceptions, they sometimes appeal to other senses, as in the tactile "breasts like fawns" (4:5; 7:3) or the fragrant and sweet-tasting "lips like lilies" (5:13b).

Often surprising on first encounter, the metaphors of the *wasfs* have been both the bane and delight of scholars and readers, who have been variously baffled, bemused, and entertained by them. The repeated comparisons of a woman's hair to a flock of goats (4:1b; 6:5b), for example, or of her forehead to a slice of pomegranate (4:3b; 6:7) have caused some biblical scholars alarm. In truth, however, these images need be no more puzzling than those of European and English Renaissance verse, which sometimes derive from them. The trick to appreciating them is proper visualizing—seeing them in their full context—and then taking the metaphoric leap. Often the text itself provides the clues to its own mysteries, if we only read it carefully; sometimes we may need to fill in a bit of geographical or cultural background to appreciate an image fully.

For example, in 4:1b and 6:5b, the woman's hair is compared to a flock of goats *that winds down Mount Gilead*. The text directs us to view the image from afar, picturing a flock of goats wending its way on the mountainside. If we are familiar with Israel's landscape, we will visualize black goats against a paler background. Thus, viewed from a distance, the graceful pattern of the goats of Gilead may suggest dark waves of hair falling down a woman's back.

So too we are told in 4:3b and 6:7 that the woman's forehead *seen through her veil* is like a slice of pomegranate. When a pomegranate is sliced open, one sees a gleam of red seeds through a white membrane—may this not call to mind the appearance of rosy skin when glimpsed through the mesh of a white veil?

If some of these images seem a bit far-fetched, we should at least appreciate their inventiveness. And although to us they may seem unusual, we should keep in mind that, in their own time, they may have been quite conventional—the standard literary stock of the oral poet.

Just as *wasfs* occur more than once in the Song, so other kinds of material also recur from poem to poem. Three layers of such material that we may isolate and analyze are those of context, theme, and motif.

Contexts. Physical context, or a sense of place, is not equally crucial to all the poems in the Song. While the mood or argument of some poems depends greatly on physical setting, other poems seem not to "take place" anywhere in particular but to focus more on interior (emotional) space. Nonetheless, each poem has an ambiance created or suggested by either an explicit or an implied setting. Context shifts frequently in the Song, from poem to poem and sometimes within poems, and this kaleidoscopic movement creates an exciting richness of texture. Four identifiable contexts, either separately or in combination, provide backdrops for the various different poems. These are: the cultivated or habitable countryside; the wild or remote natural landscape and its elements; interior environments such as homes, halls, and bedrooms; and city streets.

All the love dialogues and many of the love monologues in the Song take place, at least in part, in the habitable countryside. Pastures, groves, hills, ravines, gardens, and blossoming spring landscapes—so numerous it seems pointless to cite examples—all provide tempting and conducive sites for lovemaking and for invitations to love. Either of the lovers may take the initiative in these lush, idyllic settings, which, for the most part, set the stage for young, romantic love: the pleasure of anticipation finds more expression here than the satisfaction of consummation. Although the lovers are often separated in the countryside (he tending flocks while she looks for him; she hidden in the rocks like a dove while he seeks to see her and hear her voice), reunions are invited and expected. Thus the poems set in these habitats are often playful in tone and suffused with feelings of happy arousal.

While the natural world is essentially benign, in several poems nature appears as an awesome presence. The miragelike wilderness (3:6; 8:5), the mountain lairs of wild animals (4:8), powerful seas, torrents, and rivers (8:7), and the staring eye of the sun (1:6, 6:10) can provoke anxiety, suggest mystery, or set a bold dramatic backdrop. In poems having these contexts, the intimacy of the lovers may be threatened and the mood may be reverent, even awestruck.

Interior environments such as the winehall, the bedroom, the king's chambers, and the mother's home, on the other hand, are all very supportive of intimacy, even more so than the habitable countryside. It is in these places that fantasy is given its freest reign; the female speaker wishes she could bring her lover here (3:4; 8:2); in the seclusion provided by four walls, she imagines and anticipates his embrace (2:4–6; 8:2–3). The interior environment is by far the most private place in the Song, and thus it is most protective of the microcosmic world-of-two.

In sharp contrast stands the public urban realm, where the lovers are most vulnerable to attack. The watchmen who roam the city streets are of no use to the woman in her frantic search for her lover (3:1–4); on another of these searches they find and beat her (5:7). The daughters of Jerusalem—city women—are less aggressive than the watchmen, but they are hardly sympathetic. In 1:5–6, they are seen by the country woman to scorn her dark beauty; in 5:8–9, they seem unconcerned to help the distressed speaker in search of her lover until they have been tempted—and thus engaged, more out of self-interest than altruism—by a description of his beauty and charm. In 8:1, the speaker exclaims that if only her lover were her brother, she would not be afraid to kiss him "outside," implying that because he is *not* her relative, she does not dare kiss him in the streets, lest she become the object of scorn.

Themes and Motifs. Implied in our analysis of contexts in the Song are some of the themes that intertwine in the poems. For example, because the private world-of-two is often pitted against the public domain, we may expect to find secret romances; and, indeed, banishment of the beloved during the daytime—when, presumably, the lovers cannot be safely alone—is a recurring theme (2:17; 4:6; 8:14). Related to it are other themes having to do with separation, such as search for the lost beloved (1:7–8; 3:1–5; 5:2–6:3) and beckoning the beloved closer (2:10–13; 2:14; 4:8; 7:11–12; 8:13). In addition, several poems address what seem to be negative relationships between individuals and others in the outside world, another expression of tension between microcosm and macrocosm (the country woman and the daughters of Jerusalem in 1:5–6; the little sister and her siblings in 8:8–10; the male speaker and King Solomon in 8:11–12). Finally, underlying many of the poems and explicit in a few (see esp. 8:6–7 and the opening verse of 7:6–9) is the theme of the power and beauty of love itself.

Interwoven among these dominant themes are lighter strands of meaning that may be regarded as motifs. For example, as mentioned above, the use of vineyards as a symbol for female sexuality is a motif that appears in several different poems in the Song. Other motifs are: the garden as both place and metaphor; regality and wealth as metaphors, figures, and foils; flora and fauna, and artifice, as complementary sources of imagery; and eating and drinking as erotic metaphors. Reading the Song with these motifs in mind, one notices oft-recurring links among the individual poems. After several readings—as contexts, themes, and motifs reveal themselves more clearly— the individual poems accrue resonance, and the collection as a whole gains in richness and depth.

Mutuality and Interrelationship. Finally viewed in its totality, as a richly variegated collection of distinct but interrelated poems, the Song of Songs emerges as a stirringly sensual text, appealing at various moments to each of the senses and not infrequently to several at once. Beyond this, the Song is especially striking for its expression of mutuality in relationships between women and men, and between human beings and the natural world. Indeed, in this regard the Song is special not only as a book of the Bible but as a classic of Western civilization. In the Song of Songs, women speak as assertively as men, initiating action at least as often; men are free to be as gentle, as vulnerable, even as coy as women. Men and women similarly praise each other for their sensuality and beauty, and identical phrases are sometimes used to describe lovers of both genders. Domination and subordination between the sexes, or, for that matter, sexual stereotyping of any kind, have no place in the Song. Remarkably, the Song seems to describe a nonsexist world, and thus it can act for us as an antidote to some of the themes of biblical patriarchy.

Consonant with this mutuality between the sexes, in the world of the Song no domination exists between human beings and the rest of nature; rather, interrelationship prevails. The presentation of natural phenomena as both contexts and metaphors in the Song reveals a nonalienated and nonnaive stance. Nature is neither idealized as good nor subjugated because wild; it is, simply, a part of the world in which we live—and in which, the Song emphasizes, we love. Thus although it is primarily a book about romantic love, the Song of Songs says a great deal, by implication, about a wide range of human relationships and about how to live in the world.

Bibliography

Exum, J. C. "A Literary and Structural Analysis of the Song of Songs." *Zeitschrift für die alttestamentliche Wissenschaft* 85 (1973): 47–79.

Falk, M. *Love Lyrics from the Bible: A Translation and Literary Study of the Song of Songs.* Sheffield: Almond, 1982.

Murphy, R. E. *Wisdom Literature: Job, Proverbs, Ruth, Canticles, Ecclesiastes, and Esther.* The Forms of the Old Testament Literature, 13. Grand Rapids, MI: Eerdmans, 1981. Pp. 97–124.

Pope, M. *The Song of Songs.* Anchor Bible, 7c. Garden City, NY: Doubleday, 1976.

Trible, P. *God and the Rhetoric of Sexuality.* Philadelphia: Fortress, 1978. Chap. 5.

PART THREE

THE
PROPHETIC
BOOKS

INTRODUCTION TO THE PROPHETIC BOOKS

JOSEPH BLENKINSOPP

THE LATTER PROPHETS

Together with the historical books (Joshua through Kings, known in the Hebrew Bible as the "Former Prophets"), the fifteen prophetic books form the central section of the Hebrew Bible. In the Septuagint (the Greek version of the Hebrew Scriptures, designated with the Roman numeral LXX) the order is different, with the prophetic books coming at the end. The indications are that this collection of prophetic material was in place, more or less as we have it today, by the beginning of the second century B.C. Writing about 180 B.C., Jesus ben Sirach lists Isaiah (Sir. 48:22–25), Jeremiah (49:6–7), Ezekiel (49:8–9) and the twelve Minor Prophets (49:10) in that order. Later in the same century we begin to hear allusions to "the law and the prophets" (Prol. to Sir.; 2 Macc. 15:9), a phrase familiar from the NT. The complete scroll of Isaiah from Qumran (1QIsaᵃ), dated on epigraphical grounds (that is, on a study of the script) to the second century B.C., suggests further that by then the text of prophetic books was well on the way to being firmly established. From the Qumran community we also have the earliest commentaries on prophetic books (Isaiah, Hosea, Micah, Nahum, Habakkuk) known in Hebrew as *pesharim*; these too point in the same direction, since the capacity to generate commentary is one of the clearer indications of canonical status.

The inclusion of the histories within the category of prophecy, explained in Jewish tradition by prophetic authorship (Josephus *Against Apion* 1:37–41; *b. B. Bat.* 14b–15a), points to a broad expansion of the semantic range covered by the term "prophecy" in the later period. We can detect this tendency as early as Chronicles (probably about the middle of the fourth century B.C.), the author of which lists several prophets and seers among his sources and also speaks of the composition and rendition of liturgical music as a form of prophecy (1 Chron. 25). The writers of apocalypses also thought of themselves, and were thought of by others, as fulfilling a prophetic role (2 Esd. 15:1; Rev. 1:3).

All of this, however, leaves open the question what meanings should be assigned to the term when used of those to whom canonical books are attributed. It would be well to bear in mind that those

---

Previous page: Head of Jeremiah; one of several medallion mosaics in the apse of the Church of St. Catherine, Sinai, sixth century A.D.

whom we think of as *the* prophets formed only a small and in some respects anomalous minority among Israelite prophets at any given time. It may also be disconcerting to discover that when they themselves speak of contemporary prophecy, they more often than not condemn it as inauthentic (e.g., Jer. 23; Ezek. 13). It therefore remains to be determined in what relation they stand to the phenomenon of prophecy in general and in what sense the term may be appropriately used of them (→ Prophet).

WHAT IS A PROPHETIC BOOK?

To speak of these fifteen units of varying size—from Obadiah with 21 verses to Jeremiah with 1,364—as "books" may be somewhat misleading for modern readers. A book is generally understood to be a self-contained production of one author, less commonly several, published on a specific date and protected by copyright law from the intrusion, well meaning or otherwise, of later hands. In all of these respects prophetic books are quite different. Critical study has established that the sayings of the original "author" have in many cases been edited and amplified over a period of several centuries. Isaiah, for example, was active during the second half of the eighth century B.C., but it is acknowledged that the second and third parts of the book (Isa. 40–55 and 56–66) cannot be earlier than the sixth century B.C., and even in the first part (Isa. 1–39) there are sayings and entire sections (e.g., much of Isa. 13–27) that are post-Isaian. In some instances we can see this process of adaptation and expansion at work. Isa. 15:1–16:11 contains a long oracle in verse directed against Moab. (There is another version in Jer. 48 that complicates the issue of authorship.) It is followed by what is clearly the comment of a later seer: "This is the word which Yahweh spoke concerning Moab in the past; but now Yahweh says . . ."—and a new oracle follows (Isa. 16:13–14). We conclude, then, that in most cases prophetic books reached their present form as the result of a cumulative process of editing, adapting, and expanding. This redactional history continued until the individual books and the collection as a whole achieved such an authoritative status that no further adaptation or commentary was deemed permissible.

THE FORMATION OF PROPHETIC BOOKS

Attempts to reconstruct the formation of prophetic books have to be based almost entirely on internal evidence. That the prophets delivered their messages orally is amply attested. Since they functioned for the most part in the public and political domain, it is not surprising that their sayings were often widely disseminated. Amaziah, priest-in-charge at Bethel, could quote verbatim a particularly ominous oracle of Amos (Amos 7:11). At his trial for sedition in 609 B.C. Jeremiah was saved from death by the timely quoting of a saying of

The Location of the Prophetic Books in the Hebrew Scriptures and in the Old Testament

THE HEBREW SCRIPTURES

The Law	The Prophets	The Writings
Genesis	*Former Prophets*	Psalms
Exodus	Joshua	Job
Leviticus	Judges	Proverbs
Numbers	Samuel	Ruth
Deuteronomy	Kings	Song of Songs
		Ecclesiastes
	Latter Prophets	Lamentations
	Isaiah	Esther
	Jeremiah	Daniel
	Ezekiel	Ezra-Nehemiah
	The Twelve:	Chronicles
	Hosea	
	Joel	
	Amos	
	Obadiah	
	Jonah	
	Micah	
	Nahum	
	Habakkuk	
	Zephaniah	
	Haggai	
	Zechariah	
	Malachi	

THE OLD TESTAMENT

Genesis	2 Chronicles	Daniel
Exodus	Ezra	Hosea
Leviticus	Nehemiah	Joel
Numbers	Esther	Amos
Deuteronomy	Job	Obadiah
Joshua	Psalms	Jonah
Judges	Proverbs	Micah
Ruth	Ecclesiastes	Nahum
1 Samuel	Song of Songs	Habakkuk
2 Samuel	Isaiah	Zephaniah
1 Kings	Jeremiah	Haggai
2 Kings	Lamentations	Zechariah
1 Chronicles	Ezekiel	Malachi

In the OT the prophetic books appear at the end and include among them Lamentations and Daniel.

Micah from more than a century earlier (Jer. 26:17–19; Mic. 3:12). In many cases individual sayings and collections of sayings would have been written down shortly after they were delivered, a practice for which we have Assyrian parallels from the seventh century B.C. In 605 B.C. Jeremiah dictated from memory sayings delivered by him over a period of more than two decades. When this collection was read to King Jehoiakim by Jehudi his secretary, he tore it up and threw it on the fire, after which Jeremiah produced a second and amplified edition now part of the biblical book (Jer. 36). In some cases writing may have been an emergency measure, undertaken when the prophet was unable to deliver the message orally. Amos may have had recourse to writing after being expelled from the kingdom of Samaria (Amos 7:12) and we recall that Jeremiah, in the case just cited, was debarred from speaking in the Temple precincts (Jer. 36:4–6). Writing could also have had the purpose of authenticating predictive prophecy (e.g., Isa. 30:8; Jer. 30:1–3). The need to preserve prophecies when political or military disaster threatened must also have been a factor and may help to explain why written prophecy dates from the Assyrian crisis in the eighth century B.C.

While we have little information on prophetic disciples during the high period of Israelite prophecy, it is difficult to see how the sayings of prophets outside of the royal establishment and the temple could have been preserved and transmitted without some kind of support group. In several cases the first stage toward the formation of a prophetic book would have been the memorizing, collecting, and writing down of smaller collections of sayings. Some would have been held together by formal or stylistic features, e.g., a recurring refrain (Amos 4:6–12; Isa. 5:24–25; 9:8–10:4), or an initial formula (e.g., the woe sayings in Amos 5:18–20 and Isa. 5:8–23). Others had in common a particular theme (e.g., Jer. 23:9–40) or bore on a particular historical occurrence (e.g., Isa. 7:1–8:15). In the course of time these collections would have been put together, usually in some meaningful arrangement, and amplified with a biographical or autobiographical memoir where available. It is also possible that some sayings of unknown origin were simply attached to one, or in some cases more than one, named collection (e.g., Isa. 2:1–5 = Mic. 4:1–5).

In Israel as elsewhere prophetic activity tended to intensify during periods of political, military, or cultural crisis. The Mari oracles come from the last decades of that kingdom's existence before its conquest by Hammurabi (ca. 1765 B.C.); in Israel the most intense period of prophetic activity occurred more than a millennium later during the final decades of Judah's existence (640–586 B.C.) before its conquest by another Babylonian king. It is reasonable to conclude that the collecting and editing of the sayings of Amos and Hosea were one aspect of the Judean response to the fall of Samaria in 722 B.C. After the fall of Jerusalem one hundred and thirty-five years later a major effort was made, for the same reasons, to collect prophetic texts, adapting them to the needs of communities in the Diaspora and the homeland. While prophetic activity continued during the postexilic period, the dominant tendency was retrospective (e.g., the allusion to "former prophets" in Zech. 1:4; 7:7), moving in the direction of the interpretation of earlier prophecy as the basis for claims in the religious sphere (e.g., Dan. 9:1–2).

In its present form, therefore, the Latter Prophets is the end product of a cumulative process extending over several centuries. Those involved in this process did not share our critical perspective on prophecy and were less interested in historical authenticity than in serving the needs of the communities to which they belonged. Hence the pattern of judgment followed by salvation (often expressed in terms of final fulfillment) that is a prominent structural feature of many of the books. The finale of Amos, for example, imposes a new interpretation on the book by making it into a prophecy of salvation *through* judgment (Amos 9:11–15). This too is part of the total meaning for modern readers.

THE LITERARY CHARACTER OF PROPHETIC WRITINGS

Since the only way to understand the prophetic authors is through the texts, we must, so to speak, make our way upstream from the book in its present form to the smaller collections and eventually to the individual sayings. These sayings can often be identified by formal characteristics and a more or less regular internal structure. This is, of course, true of all forms of oral or written communication that purport to be understood by a specific audience in a given culture. The determination of form or genre is therefore not just an exercise in literary criticism but an essential precondition for grasping intention and meaning. Since the culture of modern readers is different from that of the biblical author, this task will not always be easy. The difficulties are not, however, insuperable.

The basic prophetic unit is, undoubtedly, *the proclamation of judgment or salvation*, the former much more in evidence than the latter in the pre-exilic prophets. Since it is presented as a verbatim communication from the Deity who has commissioned the prophet as his spokesman, it is couched in the divine first person and is generally introduced by such formulaic expressions as "thus says Yahweh," "the word of Yahweh came to me," and the like. The judgment saying is often preceded or followed by an *indictment* that explains the verdict in the words of the prophet. Understandably, the form and wording of this indictment-verdict unit often reflect the sphere of law (e.g., Isa. 3:13–15), which has influenced other forms of prophetic discourse, e.g., the trial speech (Isa. 1:2–6; 41:1–4) and the case history (e.g., Ezek. 18:5–18).

Though especially prominent, the forensic sphere is only one aspect of social life on which prophetic speech draws for its characteristic forms. From the sphere of worship and the ritual of daily life are drawn hymns (Isa. 42:10–13; Jer. 33:11), laments (Jer. 14:17–18), funeral dirges (Amos 5:2; Isa. 14:12–20), the description of the righteous based on qualifications for worship (Isa. 33:14–16; cf. Pss. 15 and 24). More familiar to modern readers would be songs (Isa. 5:1–2), parables (Isa. 28:23–29), allegories (Ezek. 16), reproaches (Amos 4:6–11), and woe sayings (Mic. 2:1–2; 7:1–7; Hab. 2:6–17; these examples can be verified and supplemented by consulting the individual commentaries in this volume).

But it is not enough to identify these units: they must be understood in the context in which they occur, which is not necessarily or even generally identical with the social context to which they refer. Amos, for example, uses ironically and subversively forms of speech otherwise familiar to his audience. The book opens with oracles against foreign nations—one of the oldest and best attested of prophetic genres —but by including Israel in the list, the normal expectations aroused by the genre are subverted and the entire book is given the character of indictment (Amos 1–2). In like manner he makes use of the familiar call to worship only to condemn the worship of his contemporaries (Amos 4:4–5) and of the funeral dirge as an advance announcement of death and disaster (Amos 5:1–2).

With the passing of time we note the gradual breakdown of these relatively simple forms and the prevalence of longer discourses. Something of this is already apparent in Hosea, but it emerges most clearly in Jeremiah, Ezekiel, and Second Isaiah (Isa. 40–55). This transformation at the literary level may signify a shift in the understanding of the prophetic role and in the social context in which the role was played out. Jeremiah's Temple sermon (Jer. 7:1–8:3) illustrates the prophetic function of preaching, which was not then, as it is now, the responsibility of priests. After the destruction of the Temple, the exilic communities may have evolved something akin to the synagogue in which the longer discourses of Second Isaiah and the sermons attributed to Moses in Deuteronomy were first heard. At the same time, we note that prophecy is becoming more of a literary activity. One of the clearer indications is the figurative and allegorical narratives of which Ezekiel makes generous use (e.g., Ezek. 12–24) and that earned him a reputation among his contemporaries as a skillful user of words (Ezek. 20:49; 33:30–33). There is also an increasing tendency, noted earlier, to comment on earlier prophecy. Ezekiel 7 appears to be a prophetic sermon based on the fourth vision of Amos (Amos 8:1–3), and a good part of Third Isaiah (Isa. 56–66) relates to Second Isaiah as commentary on prophetic text.

BIOGRAPHICAL AND AUTOBIOGRAPHICAL NARRATIVE

In addition to collections of sayings, fragments of prophetic biographical and autobiographical narrative have also come down to us. The author of the so-called Deuteronomistic History (Joshua through Kings) has woven into the fabric of his story popular "legends" about seers and ecstatics, especially in recounting the history of the Northern Kingdom. The most extensive of these deal with Elijah (1 Kings 17–19; 21; 2 Kings 1–2) and his disciple Elisha (2 Kings 2–9; 13:14–21), and it is clear that they have been excerpted from a much larger cycle of hagiographical narrative.

Beginning in the eighth century B.C., and no doubt because of the mortal danger posed by the Assyrians, there is a notable shift in emphasis from the person to the message of the prophet and, correspondingly, from stories about prophets that quote their sayings to collections of oracles in which the biographical element, when present, is minor and incidental. Amos contains only one short biographical passage recounting his confrontation with the priest of the state sanctuary at Bethel (Amos 7:10–17). Here, too, we have the impression of an excerpt from a longer narrative, perhaps from an alternative version of the reign of Jeroboam II, one less sympathetic to that king than the version incorporated into the history (2 Kings 14:23–29, with perhaps a covert allusion to Amos in v. 27). A similar situation confronts us with the third-person account of Isaiah's intervention in the crisis of 734 B.C. when Syria and Israel attempted to force Judah into an anti-Assyrian alliance (Isa. 7:1–17; cf. 2 Kings 16:5). The Isaiah sayings collection has also been supplemented by a much more extensive narrative cycle taken, with modifications and additions, from the history (Isa. 36–39; cf. 2 Kings 18–20). Here we encounter a rather different figure from the Isaiah of the sayings: a miracle worker and holy man not unlike Elisha and one who plays a supportive rather than critical and disruptive role in affairs of state. In other instances narrative serves to introduce and contextualize specific sayings (e.g., Hos. 1:2–9; cf. 3:1–3 in the first person).

Beginning in the last decades of the independent existence of Judah, there seems to be a renewed interest in the personal history of the prophet. Unlike Amos and Hosea, Jeremiah was clearly the object of considerable biographical interest. Starting with the superscription to the book (Jer. 1:1–3), a greater effort is made to place sayings and discourses in a chronological and topographical framework (e.g., Jer. 3:6; 21:1; 22:11; 24:1; 34:1, 8–11). What, however, sets the book apart from its predecessors is the inclusion of longer biographical passages (Jer. 26–29; 32), especially the sustained account of his role in events immediately preceding and following the fall of Jerusalem (Jer. 37–44). Whoever authored this long biographical memoir—perhaps his faithful attendant Baruch—it is agreed that the book as a whole, including these continuous narrative sections, has been edited and expanded by a Deuteronomistic hand during the exilic period. A careful study of the editorial procedures involved in this rewriting reveals an intent to present Jeremiah as a prophet after the manner of Moses (Deut. 18:15–19) and as the last in a prophetic series beginning with Moses. This intent is already apparent in the call narrative (Jer. 1:4–10; cf. Exod. 3:1–4:17), less obviously in assigning to Jeremiah a forty-year ministry (Jer. 1:2–3, corresponding to the years 627–587 B.C.). It is to the Deuteronomistic school that we owe the portrait of Moses as prophetic figure whose mission meets with opposition but is ultimately vindicated by God. Not surprisingly, therefore, the book is rounded off with the last chapter of the Deuteronomic History that begins with Moses and ends with the Exile (Jer. 52 = 2 Kings 24:18–25:30).

The same profile of the prophet destined to a mission from the earliest years, or even from conception, who is opposed and persecuted but ultimately vindicated by God appears in the passages in Second Isaiah known rather inappropriately as the "servant songs"

(Isa. 42:1–4; 49:1–6; 50:4–11; 52:13–53:12). While not all of these passages may refer to the same individual, we hear of an intermediary who is set aside for a special mission from conception (Isa. 49:1), who experiences failure, rejection, and persecution (Isa. 49:4; 50:6–9; 52:13–53:9), and who is finally vindicated, perhaps posthumously (Isa. 53:10–12). That this anonymous figure is designated "servant of Yahweh" may also suggest a connection with Deuteronomistic usage following which the designation "servant" is used of prophetic intermediaries in general (e.g., 2 Kings 9:7; 17:13, 23; 21:10) and preeminently of Moses himself (e.g., Num. 12:7–8; Deut. 34:5).

The greater attention given to biographical narrative, detectable in Jeremiah, the Deuteronomistic portrait of Moses, and the Isaian Servant, corresponds to a development in understanding the prophetic function. Prophecy could still consist in a simple mandate to speak on behalf of the Deity, but there is now in addition the idea that the call can involve the entire life of the individual. This pattern of prophetic biography was further developed in the Greco-Roman period (e.g., *The Martyrdom and Ascension of Isaiah*, Bel and the Dragon, *The Lives of the Prophets*) and left its mark on early Christian presentations of Jesus, especially in Luke.

CALL NARRATIVES AND VISION NARRATIVES

In the prophetic books themselves, biographical interest has concentrated primarily, and in some cases exclusively, on the critical moment of the commissioning of the prophetic intermediary. In both the ancient and modern worlds extraordinary circumstances accompany this event, whether a dream (often repeated on successive nights), a vision, or significant psychic and behavioral changes. Since the intermediary always acts on behalf of a particular constituency, the commission must always be validated in some way by the society or a particular group within it. One way in which this could happen is illustrated by the call of Samuel at the ancient tribal sanctuary of Shiloh (1 Sam. 3). In the course of an incubation ritual (sleeping in the sanctuary to receive a revelation from the Deity worshiped there), Samuel heard a voice calling him that was deemed to be an authentic revelation after the third occurrence. After receiving a message that he was to transmit to those concerned, his prophetic role was publicly acknowledged (1 Sam. 3:20). It may also be noted that though his experience was auditory, it is called a vision (1 Sam. 3:15, 21).

The call of Elisha (1 Kings 19:19–21) illustrates a rather different kind of commissioning, since what is involved here is prophetic succession and endowment with authority vis-à-vis the guilds of dervishlike ecstatics known as "sons of the prophets." Elijah performed the symbolic act of placing his mantle, the distinguishing mark of the master prophet, over the disciple-elect. At a later point (2 Kings 2:9–12), the transmission of the spirit had to be validated by acts of spiritual power including extrasensory perception (cf. 2 Kings 6:17), precognition (2 Kings 8:7–15), and various miracles, the first of which involved the prophetic mantle of the master (2 Kings 2:13–14). Here too the acknowledgment of the commissioning is explicitly noted (2 Kings 2:15).

Both of these accounts have been incorporated into the Deuteronomistic History, no doubt undergoing some editing in the process. In the prophetic books themselves, most of the call narratives are written in the first person and are, with the possible and problematic exception of Hosea (3:1–5), accompanied by visions. Isaiah's vision of the heavenly court (Isa. 6:1–13), closely paralleled by that of Micaiah (1 Kings 22:19–22), may represent a special Judean variant since it appears to have taken place in the Temple and represents the prophetic intermediary as royal messenger or herald. After a purification ritual, Yahweh as king calls for a volunteer, the prophet offers his services, and the commissioning follows. The same scenario has been assumed for the exilic Isaiah (40:1–11) though in this instance the situation is less clear and the command in vv. 1–5 is addressed to a plurality. That Judean prophetic books are either introduced under the title "vision" (Isaiah, Obadiah, Nahum) or as words received in vision (Amos, Micah, Habakkuk) may indicate a special regional characteristic, though one that was not, of course, unique.

Habakkuk, the only pre-exilic prophet to be named such (Heb. *nabi'*) in the title, provides a brief glimpse of the preparation for receiving a visionary revelation, probably in the Temple (Hab. 2:1–2), and an equally brief description of the behavioral changes that tended to occur during this period of waiting (Hab. 3:16); cf. the similar situation of an anonymous exilic seer announcing the fall of Babylon (Isa. 21:6–10).

Amos describes his commissioning only indirectly, in the course of defending himself before the priest Amaziah. While the interpretation of this passage (Amos 7:14–15) has long been in dispute, Amos appears to be saying that his commission came to him directly in a private capacity, not after apprenticeship in a prophetic guild. Various attempts have been made to establish a connection between the vision series (Amos 7:1–9; 8:1–3; 9:1–4) and the prophetic commissioning. In the first two visions, which threaten locusts and drought respectively, Amos successfully discharges the prophetic task of intercession. The third vision, presaging earthquake and military disaster, might be thought to mark the point at which Amos received his charge to preach against the kingdom of Samaria and its ruler, especially since it is followed immediately by the defense of his prophetic calling. This, however, is only one of several possibilities.

The description of Jeremiah's call to be prophet to the nations is also accompanied by visions of the same type as the third and fourth of Amos (Jer. 1:11–19; cf. Amos 7:7–9; 8:1–3). They are in the first person, the prophet is shown an object, the significance of the exhibit is explained, and the explanation depends on either a symbolic explanation of the object or an ambiguity of pronunciation. The actual commissioning that precedes (Jer. 1:4–10) follows a different and distinctive pattern found also in the earlier of the two versions of the call of Moses (Exod. 3:1–4:17): divine address, expostulation of the intermediary-designate, confirmation and encouragement designed to overcome his hesitation, the giving of a sign (absent in Jeremiah), an act of installation accompanied by a form of words ("behold, I have put my words in your mouth"), and finally the specifics of the mission. While the similarities may be explained in part by the Deuteronomistic intent to portray Jeremiah as a "Mosaic" prophet, the pattern itself is older than either of these examples, as may be seen in the nonprophetic commissioning of Gideon in what is certainly a pre-Deuteronomistic narrative (Judg. 6:11–18).

The account of Ezekiel's call also conflates two quite different narratives: the vision of the chariot-throne (Ezek. 1:4–28) and the commission to speak unwelcome words, signified by having the prophet-elect eat a papyrus scroll containing lamentations (Ezek. 2:1–3:3). The latter is the original commissioning (with later expansions in Ezek. 3:4–9; 3:10–15) to which the "school" of Ezekiel has prefaced the chariot-throne vision, so that the call emanates from the one enthroned thereon (Ezek. 1:28). This detailed description of the *merkabah* (Heb., "chariot"), which was to become a major source of Jewish mystical speculation, marks a transition from the earlier, relatively simple prophetic vision narrative to the complex scenarios produced by the writers of apocalyptic tracts (e.g., Daniel and the Enoch cycle).

The visions of Zechariah, dated to 519 B.C., are also of a different kind and symptomatic of the changing perception of the prophetic function in the early postexilic period (Zech. 1:7–6:8). One of the most interesting innovations is the presence of a supernatural agent, the angelic interpreter, in the vision. His function is to explain what is going on, and in many cases he does this with reference to motifs in earlier prophetic books: the seventy years of exile (Jer. 25:11; 29:10), the smiths (Isa. 54:16–17), the measuring line (Ezek. 42:20), the north country (Jer. 1:13–16), the wall of fire around Jerusalem (Isa. 4:5), and others. Here too we see the shift from the classical prophetic mode of direct communication to the indirect mode of interpretation, including the interpretation of prophetic texts.

THE PLACE OF PROPHECY IN THE BIBLE AS A WHOLE

One way of viewing the Latter Prophets in the context of the Hebrew Bible canon is as a supplement to the history (Former Prophets). Chronologically, the correspondence is not exact, since we know that five of the Latter Prophets (Joel, Jonah, Haggai, Zechariah, Malachi) are postexilic, and of these the last three were always known to be postexilic. The three longer books (Isaiah, Jeremiah, Ezekiel) were apparently grouped together in chronological order for practical reasons as early as the second century B.C., and the twelve Minor Prophets also appear to have been arranged in what was thought to be chronological order (in LXX the series also begins with Hosea but the next five are arranged somewhat differently).

A strong argument can be made in favor of the supplement theory in that the Deuteronomistic historian does not so much as mention any of the Latter Prophets with the exception of Jonah (2 Kings 14:25), not originally part of the collection, and Isaiah (2 Kings 19:1–7, 20–37; 20:1–19), but a very different Isaiah from the author of the sayings. The role of the prophets who are mentioned in the history also corresponds closely enough to that of Latter Prophets to justify this conclusion. One of the chief aims of the exilic historian was to explain the massive disasters that had occurred within living memory. Many of his contemporaries were raising serious questions about the justice and ethical character of the God of traditional religion who, it seemed, had abandoned them to their fate. The historian's reply is that, throughout the history beginning with Moses himself, Yahweh had sent "his servants the prophets" to warn the people of the consequences of their infidelity. The reading of the prophecies, therefore, served as a reminder of the justice of God's ways and as a guide to the moral requirements flowing from the covenant relationship (see, e.g., Zech. 1:1–6). At the same time, these texts were edited and expanded to testify to the assurance of salvation beyond judgment (e.g., Isa. 40–55; Amos 9:11–15; Mic. 4:1–5; Zeph. 3:14–20), an assurance that could also be extended to the gentile world (e.g., Isa. 45:22–23; 66:18–21; 19:24–25; Zeph. 3:9–10; Jon.).

The relation of prophecy to law is one of the most important and difficult issues in biblical theology. It can be shown that much of the ethical teaching of the pre-exilic prophets was based on stipulations of law the antiquity of which cannot be doubted (e.g., Amos 2:8; cf. Exod. 22:26–27). At the same time, this teaching also contributed to the mature formulation of Israel's legal traditions. The Deuteronomic law (Deut. 12–26) betrays the pervasive influence of prophetic preaching that may also have contributed to the final form of the Decalogue (see esp. Hos. 4:2; Jer. 7:9–10). The tendency to subordinate prophecy to law and to the figure of Moses, the fountainhead of both, is already apparent in Deuteronomy which carefully circumscribes the scope of prophetic activity (Deut. 13:1–5; 18:15–22) and insists that prophecy represents a lower order of mediation than that of Moses (34:10). The Deuteronomistic history also assigns to prophets the task of preaching the law and warning against the consequences of nonobservance (e.g., 2 Kings 17:13–20). We may find here the source of the view, which was to become normative in Judaism, that the primary role of the prophet was to serve as a vital link in the transmission of the law from Moses down to the present (m. 'Abot 1:1).

A quite different line of development was followed by those who read prophetic texts as predicting the future and heralding the consummation of history. As suggested earlier, the first stage of this eschatological reinterpretation of prophecy has to be recovered from the texts themselves. The sects that begin to emerge clearly in the latter part of the Second Temple period (the second century B.C.) found this mode of interpretation especially congenial. The author of the visions in Daniel, for example, thought of the prophetic books as containing a coded message about the future, with special reference to the destiny of the group to which he belonged (e.g., Dan. 9:1–2). In the biblical commentaries of the Qumran sect we even find the idea that the prophetic author did not himself know the meaning of his prophecy that was only now revealed to the initiates within the sect (1QpHab 7:1–2). Something of the same approach is apparent in early Christian interpretations of prophecy with reference to the events of the life of Jesus (e.g., Matt. 1–3) and the founding and development of the Christian movement (e.g., Acts 2:24–32; 15:15–18). In spite of challenges from different quarters, this interpretive scheme of prophecy and fulfillment has remained to the present an essential aspect of the Christian appropriation and use of the Hebrew Scriptures.

These views of prophecy traditional in Judaism and Christianity have to be balanced against the results of the historical-critical investigation of the texts that began in earnest about the middle of the nineteenth century and is still in progress. The principal aim of historical–critical analysis was to arrive at the authentic sayings through a critical reading of the texts and thus be in a position to determine the identity and agenda of the prophetic author. Stated in general terms, the conclusion was that the biblical prophets were concerned primarily with contemporary social and political realities rather than with prediction. In mediating the tradition through an intense personal experience of the divine, they brought about a new religious consciousness, at once ethical and spiritual, over against the popular religion of the day centered on the sacrificial cult. With the benefit of hindsight, we can now see the extent to which this critical work was colored by the cultural prejudices of the nineteenth and early twentieth century—for example, dogmatic evolutionary ideas of religious development and a devaluation of ritual. The critical rediscovery of prophecy has, nevertheless, been enormously influential, bearing, for example, on the religious interpretation of history and the social responsibilities of synagogue and church. It has also enabled us to get into clearer focus one of the most fundamental contributions of prophetic religion, namely, the idea of people called to be instruments of service.

Bibliography

Blenkinsopp, J. *A History of Prophecy in Israel.* Philadelphia: Westminster, 1983.

Clements, R. E. *One Hundred Years of Old Testament Interpretation.* Philadelphia: Westminster, 1976. Pp. 51–75.

Tucker, G. M. "Prophetic Speech," *Interpretation* 32 (1978):31–45.

von Rad, G. *Old Testament Theology.* Vol. 2. New York: Harper & Row, 1965.

Westermann, C. *Basic Forms of Prophetic Speech.* Philadelphia: Westminster, 1967.

Wilson, R. R. *Prophecy and Society in Ancient Israel.* Philadelphia: Fortress, 1980.

ISAIAH 1–39

GERALD T. SHEPPARD

INTRODUCTION

Few books of the OT have supplied more fuel to the fire of Jewish and Christian interpretation than the book of Isaiah. Ben Sira's eulogy in the early second century B.C. illustrates the positive perception of the prophet (Sir. 48:22b–25):

> . . . a great man trustworthy in his vision.
> In his days the sun went backward;
>   he lengthened the life of the king.
> By the power of the spirit he saw the last things.
> he comforted the mourners in Zion,
> he revealed what was to occur to the end of time,
> and hidden things long before they happened.

The Dead Sea Scrolls and the NT show equal enthusiasm for Isaiah's "vision" (Isa. 1:1) of the future, while later rabbinic Judaism viewed Isaiah as a superlative expositor of the Torah. The book offered an unparalleled chiaroscuro of God's judgment and comfort to Israel. For Jews the words of comfort spoke accurately of Israel's restoration after the judgment of exile. For Christians these same prophetic words of promise found such perfect fulfillment in the birth, death, and resurrection of Jesus Christ that the book was occasionally called "the Gospel within the Old Testament."

Up to the modern period, interpreters viewed the book of Isaiah as a unified literary composition. The book as a whole expressed the words of the eighth-century Isaiah. Historical criticism in the modern period threatened this view by demonstrating that the prophet could not have written many parts of the book. This evidence has often led commentators in the modern period to focus only on certain prescriptural traditions that underlie the formation of the later biblical book: either on the reconstructed "genuine" oracles of Isaiah or on major editorial levels in the history of the book's composition. Conversely, some recent literary approaches have tried to defend the unity of parts or of the whole book based on evidence of aesthetic or structural features analogous to those found in other literary classics. The effect of these two approaches has been either to atomize the book into fragments that might yield access to the "intent" of some historical author/redactor or to defend the coherence of the book in a literary-aesthetic manner at the expense of its historical claims as a book of Scripture.

This commentary on Isaiah 1–39 seeks to benefit from the insights gained from both of these approaches but will concentrate specifically on the question of how older prophetic traditions were put together as elements in the later composition of a book of Scripture. The designation Scripture carries the assumption that the book of Isaiah belongs to a larger context of scriptural books and that its primary import depends on this function within the religions of Judaism and Christianity. From the perspective of the history of the composition of this book, Isaiah 1–39 cannot be treated as an isolated literary unit. It derives in its present form from editors, who are responsible for the book of Isaiah as a whole, and belongs, as well, to two quite different Jewish and Christian scriptures.

The Relation of 1–39 to 40–66

The book of Isaiah easily divides, as Martin Luther observed, into "two books." The first, Isaiah 1–39, is organized around a complex scenario of narratives—roughly in chronological order according to the presumed activity of the prophet Isaiah—together with collections of the prophet's oracles of judgment and promise. The second part, Isaiah 40–66, consists entirely of prophetic poetry, without any historical narratives, and predominately explicates God's comfort and promise to Israel.

Premodern interpreters had long observed the absence of any direct reference to the name of the prophet in Isaiah 40–66. Obvious differences in literary style, vocabulary, and content between Isaiah 1–39 and Isaiah 40–66 had already been noticed, though the clear resonances throughout the entire book seemed to assuage any anxiety over historical dissimilarities between the two parts of the book. Even the recognition, made occasionally by the sixteenth-century Protestant reformer John Calvin and his predecessors, that the audience of Isaiah 40–66 was a group of Babylonian exiles in the sixth century B.C. instead of Judeans under Assyrian threat in the eighth century B.C. could be explained by appeal to the extraordinary character of prophecy. Only in the modern period did acceptance of different historical origins for parts of the book challenge the traditional Christian assumption that "the literal" sense of the entire book of Isaiah could be identical with the original "intent" of the eighth-century prophet.

To bring historical and literary evidence against the traditional assumption that Isaiah wrote the entire book was not, intentionally, an impious attack on Scripture. It reflected, instead, a modern interest in grasping a more accurate sense of "history," which was encouraged by archaeological discoveries and a new facility in ancient languages. Often the goal was to honor the traditional priority given to a biblical author's intention by finding precisely what the "genuine" words of that historical figure were. For the book of Isaiah, these investigations proved, first, that Isaiah 40–66 must have derived from a much later period than did most of 1–39 and, second, that many traditions, even in Isaiah 1–39, were written by someone after the time of Isaiah. These two historical conclusions deserve careful consideration before any contemporary interpretation of the book of Isaiah can be set forward critically and clearly.

Scholars have, for many years, observed that the latter half of the book addresses the conditions of people in the Babylonian exile; in the time of Isaiah, Assyria alone was a threat and Babylon was viewed as a friendly, historically minor nation (see Isa. 39). Furthermore, on its own terms, the prophet's message in Isaiah 40–55 describes social circumstances in which the audience is positioned in a time after "former things" have been fulfilled. This fulfillment could have occurred only during the time of the Babylonian exile (see Isa. 40:21; 41:4, 27; 42:9), a fulfillment that provides the basis for the prophet's argument that trustworthy "new things" can be announced. Among these "new things," the prophet states that Cyrus will expedite the restoration of the nation of Israel and its return to the promised land. The logic of the prophet's argument turns on a recognition that the historical setting is the Babylonian exile and that previous oracles have been fulfilled in that time. For that reason, the prophet can mock other prophets who pretend to promise things without similar proof, namely, that they actually have come to pass (see Isa. 41:21–24). This prophet to the Babylonian exiles could not be identified with the historical Isaiah without either violating the logic of the argument or introducing a strange understanding of prophecy, one at odds with even a traditional view of how prophets performed and what they foresaw. Still, a modern admission of underlying similarities in theme and subject matter between the two parts of the books inspired critics to call this later unknown prophet Second Isaiah. One could speculate, without explicit biblical support, that this later prophet must have been a gifted disciple of the eighth-century "First Isaiah."

A second set of critical observations concentrated on Isaiah 1–39 and built upon the foundation of the preceding observations. For example, Isaiah 1 appears to be composed of fragments of older oracles, but certainly the last verses of the chapter echo the language of Isaiah 40–66. When this chapter came to serve as an introduction to the larger book of Isaiah, the editors of Isaiah 40–66 apparently added a note at the end of it. The fact that Isaiah 36–39 has been taken, with few changes, from 2 Kings 18:13–20:19 provides another sign that some editor of Isaiah 1–39 borrowed non-Isaian material from other biblical books. Also, recognition of the Babylonian provenance of much of Isaiah 40–66 led naturally to suspicion regarding the eighth-century origins of prophecies against Babylon in Isa. 13:1–14:23 and in 21:1–10. The content and style of these chapters clearly reflect the same milieu as the oracles in the latter half of the book.

More recently, these historical-critical, scholarly views that, at the outset, threatened the literary unity of the book of Isaiah have provided the means for showing just how integrally related the two parts of the book are to each other. The composition of Isaiah 1–39 reflects a systematic editorial accommodation of the older traditions retained in Isaiah 1–39 to those of Isaiah 40–66. So, for instance, the oracles against Babylon in Isaiah 13 and 21 anticipate the judgment against Babylon in the latter half of the book. Concomitantly, especially in Isaiah 56–66, the prophetic traditions often quote and interpret oracles found in the first half of the book. In other words, both parts of Isaiah have been edited to resonate each with the other. Isaiah 1–39 is already an admixture of traditions, including some contemporary with those of Isaiah 40–66. An independent collection of Second Isaiah prophecies probably never existed. The designations "First" and "Second" Isaiah for Isaiah 1–39 and 40–66, if they are intended to refer to independent literary compositions, prove to be glittering generalities that fail to reflect the complexity of the history of traditions in the book. The newly recognized evidence of subtle and pervasive redactional contributions throughout Isaiah 1–39 makes its interpretation as a whole impossible without reference both to Isaiah 40–66 and to the place of the book of Isaiah within a larger collection of scriptural books. At a minimum, Isaiah 1–39 never existed as an isolated unit of literature, either separate from the present book of Isaiah or independent from its scriptural context.

The nature of the composition of Isaiah 1–39 discloses another factor typical in the formation of biblical books. The editors of biblical books generally show no interest in disclosing their participation. Except for brief mention of Isaiah's writing oracles down in the form of "a book" (in 8:16 and 30:8), Isaiah 1–39 retains no indications of either the social phenomenon of prophecy itself or the identity of, or historical forces influencing, editors responsible for the later stages in the formation of the biblical text. The form and function of this biblical text resist any attempt to make these matters the key to its meaning, though they may certainly prove essential to illumine the text from a modern perspective. A historical reconstruction of even a historically "genuine" prophetic oracle may recover traditions that existed prior to their incorporation into a Scripture. Such an exercise in reconstruction should provide information helpful in reading the later context of Scripture, analogous to the way the study of the etymology of a word aids an understanding of its subsequent usage in the context of a particular sentence. However, conclusions reached from investigations in tradition history should never be confused uncritically with the meaning of the biblical text.

When read as part of Scripture, the text of Isaiah 1–39 belongs fully to the warp and woof of history. In this context, Isaiah 1–39 overtly represents prophetic traditions against the background of the major events of the eighth century B.C. Yet, these chapters are contextually tied to another historical episode of prophecy, that in Isaiah 40–66, which pertains to the Babylonian exile of the sixth century. This ordering of traditions in the book follows a logic and purpose at odds with that of historical writing, both ancient and modern. The very survival of the book over so many centuries implies that there was some other, very strong assumption regarding the value of this literature. Its value was determined less by the text's perfection, measured according to most historical standards, than by how well it could meet some specific religious expectations of future readers, who continually endeavored to preserve and understand it. It remains, as do most edited literary constructions that survive for centuries, the object of compromise and an approximation—from a historical perspective, "a reed shaken in the wind."

The preservation of the book of Isaiah with all of its modern historical duplicities finds justification precisely because this text is not just any text, but one with a specific historical pedigree. In Judaism it is a manifestation of the revealed Torah, wisdom, promise, and judgment of God. Christianity adds the assumption that the subject matter of the book of Isaiah is the gospel of Jesus Christ. Through its claim to additional revelation, made manifest by the addition of a "New Testament," Christianity altered the context of the book of Isaiah and changed its semantic import by making it part of an "Old Testament" of Christian Scriptures. This modification of the Hebrew Scripture to "Old Testament" within Christian Scripture itself grew out of historical responses to events in the life of the early church. Commentary on Isaiah 1–39 must necessarily be conscious of this complicated relation of text to history and to its religious subject matter whenever one speaks about the "meaning" of these texts, at least as we have received them as treasures from the past.

The aim of this commentary will be to describe, in historical and literary terms, the form and function of a scriptural text rather than to offer a pious or impious reading of a reconstructed history. In this regard, awareness of the history of religions and of religious comparativist insight into the nature of religions generally may prove as illuminating as detailed knowledge of the social history of ancient Israel. So too the internal register of wisdom and spiritual knowledge found in a Jewish or Christian believer may resonate more appropriately with certain key motifs and traces in this text than any purely "literary-aesthetic" approach.

The Composition of 1–39

The older prophetic traditions preserved in Isaiah 1–39, as well as in the book as a whole, are not organized simply around events in the life of Isaiah. Instead, Isaiah 1 and the recapitulation of the same themes in the last chapter, Isaiah 66, place emphasis topically on the word of God to God's chosen people and city, Jerusalem/Zion. These two chapters form the introduction and a retrospective conclusion to the book. In these chapters, one learns that the people of God have fallen into iniquity and have abused sanctuary worship. Zion abounds with injustice like Sodom and Gomorrah and almost experiences their fate. The rebellious inhabitants of Jerusalem will be purged with the fire of exile, so that a "few survivors" remain the only hope for restoration. The city will be destroyed, but it will be restored later as a citadel of justice and righteousness. Both chapters end with the same bleak image of the purge in which a fire will burn such that "none can quench" (1:31; 66:24). By this means the activity of Isaiah the prophet has been made secondary to his message, namely, the enduring word of God and its implications for the past, present, and future of both the people and the city of God.

Attentive to this larger pattern, Isa. 40:1–2 provides the major transition between the two parts of the book and maintains the same topical orientation as that found in the introduction and conclusion (see 66:13). "Comfort" is declared both to "my people" and "to Jerusalem" at a time when the "iniquity is pardoned." This emphasis on the people and the city, found as well in the introduction and conclusion, is again picked up by the title of the book in Isa. 1:1 (also 2:1) in its explicit reference to both "Judah and Jerusalem." The announcement of comfort in 40:1–2 assumes the aftermath of the Babylonian exile and clearly provides an introduction to the second half of the book in the light of the whole. Thus, the introduction and conclusion reinforce the basic pattern of the book of Isaiah, one that divides the oracles into a period of God's wrath (2–39) followed by a later time of comfort (40–65).

Isaiah 12 occupies a similar pivotal position. It occurs after a long section associated with the Syro-Ephraimite war (5:8–11:16) and before the edited collection of oracles against the nations in Isaiah 13–23. Once more there is an explicit reference to the same basic themes of God's present anger and future comfort, with an assurance that plays on the name of Isaiah: "God is my salvation" (12:2). Even the name of the prophet is not strictly historical datum but provides a typical expression of the prophet's message. In Isaiah's name we hear an adumbration of the central theme of Isaiah 40–66. In this way, "Isaiah" is personally linked to his message throughout the prophetic book of Scripture associated with him.

An attentive reading of Isaiah 2–39 will discover subsections comprising oracles of the same or a similar type. A basic distinction is made between judgment oracles and promise or salvation oracles. The promise oracles of 2:2–4 and 4:2–6 provide a framework around a long section of judgment oracles. As in the introductory chapter, each of these promise oracles contains prophecy of a future restoration of Jerusalem. Isa. 2:2–4 adds an explicit reference to the revealed Torah (Heb., "law/teaching") of God that will be taught from Zion. The oracles between these promises similarly concern Judah and Jerusalem. This entire first section of the book of Isaiah is followed by the parable-like summary of this same message in the song of the vineyard (Isa. 5). Starting with Isa. 5:8 is a collection of oracles oriented around the events of the Syro-Ephraimite war (7:1–9). Using an editorial device, the composers have broken apart two original collections of prophetic oracles—a group of seven woe oracles against leaders in Judah and a cluster of judgment oracles directed against Ephraim (the Northern Kingdom, Israel)—to form a double *inclusio* or framework of oracles around the so-called testimony of Isaiah in 6:1–9:7. The last of these woe oracles concludes with a repeated refrain borrowed from the judgment oracles against Ephraim (see 10:4b).

Next, a series of promise oracles to Judah and judgments against Assyria follow in Isaiah 10:5–11:16. Isaiah 12, then, is another "song" that serves as a transition, similar to that of Isa. 5:1–7, between the preceding section and a collection of oracles against the nations in Isaiah 13–23. In the song of Isaiah 12, the preceding theme of God's anger is taken up and reversed, and a specific assurance of "comfort" is added that did not occur before and is found again only in Isaiah 40–66. After the oracles against the nations, a group of promissory eschatological oracles occurs in Isaiah 24–27; they take up a number of themes and motifs from the first part of the book and project them into a vision of future restoration. One, then, finds in Isaiah 28–32 a return to judgment oracles against Judah and Jerusalem, followed, once more, by promise in Isaiah 33–35. Isaiah 34 and 35, in this last section, comprise virtually a mosaic of themes found only in Isaiah 40–66 and, therefore, they clearly anticipate the latter half of the book, which then becomes integral to the interpretation of Isaiah 1–39. Finally, there is a cluster of narratives in Isaiah 36–39 that pertain to a later Assyrian threat, after the end of the Syro-Ephraimite war.

This brief sketch demonstrates that a variety of criteria have governed the composition of Isaiah 1–39. Collections of judgment oracles are regularly followed by collections of promise oracles. A formal introduction begins the book, while "songs" in Isaiah 5 and 12 mark off whole sections and provide summarizing commentary on them. These songs also provide a transition between collections of different types. Moreover, in Isaiah 1–39, diverse traditions are often found clustered together in association with historical events of national significance (e.g., the Syro-Ephraimite war). In this manner, editors ordered the traditions on the basis of unrelated criteria, e.g., the literary type of the traditions, sequence of historical events, features in the biographical presentation of the prophet, and topical concerns.

The context of Isaiah 1–39 allows both for the time-bound quality of the prophet's activity and for the timeless claim of the text on future readers. This complexity suggests a high degree of adaptation of traditions over a long period of time. In the present biblical context, one may detect principles of ordering retained from earlier periods of composition alongside different principles that pertain to a later reworking of the same traditions. The persistent anonymity of the editors, as well as their concern with preservation and the subtlety of their technique, suggests a certain anxiety of influence. The editors are not in any modern sense "authors." Instead, they stand behind the text and push it forward in the name of Isaiah and with an import that may include but, at the same time, exceed their own views.

In support of this general pattern of organization in Isaiah 1–39, there are a number of repeated key motifs or refrains in these chapters that provide nuance and continuity throughout the differing subcollections. For example, in the judgment oracles of Isa. 2:6–22 there is a repeated poetic refrain that the high or proud will be brought low (2:11, 17). This same refrain, perhaps derived from an older form in 2:6–22, recurs after the song of the vineyard in 5:15. Such repetition throughout various subcollections of prophetic traditions establishes topical resonance between different sections of the book. For example, the aforementioned refrain, the high brought low, introduces the same theme in the judgment against Assyria in 10:33–34 and, again, in the promise oracles to Judah in 25:11–12 and 26:5. In a very similar way, an expression perhaps once belonging to the song of the vineyard in Isaiah 5 appears in 3:13–15 and elevates "the vineyard" into a key metaphor throughout Isaiah 2–39. Later plays upon the rare expression "briars and thorns" that overtake the vineyard recall the same set of motifs and are variously applied throughout Isaiah 6–39 (see 7:23–25; 9:18; 10:17; 27:4; 32:13).

As a last example, one finds around the testimony of Isaiah a repeated refrain: "On account of all this, his anger is not turned away; [in fact,] his hand is stretched out still" (5:25; 9:12, 17, 21; 10:4). In the transitional song of Isaiah 12, this same expression appears as a thematic summary of the first part of the book of Isaiah. Only there do we find that God's "anger is turned back" and that "comfort" will follow (v. 1), as in Isaiah 40–66. Once again the refrain has become an idiom for integrating and interpreting diverse traditions. The same expression of God's wrath is later applied to the "rod" of God's anger, Assyria (14:24–27). Certain motifs and refrains become idioms that express a continuity in the message of Isaiah 1–39, and many of them are not carried over into Isaiah 40–66. They help to knit the diverse traditions of Isaiah 2–39 into a distinctive religious statement, separate from the continuation of prophecy in Isaiah 40–66.

However, a variety of features link the two parts of the book together editorially, including the presence of traditions from the second part within the first (e.g., Isa. 34–35) and citations from Isaiah 2–39 in so-called "Third Isaiah" (Isa. 55–66). Various promise oracles and "messianic" interpretations in the first part anticipate the traditions in Isaiah 40–66. (For discussion of these chapters as involving a "Second" and a "Third" Isaiah, see Isaiah 40–66, "Introduction.") In the discussion of the "former" and "latter" things in Isaiah 40–55, the first part of the book is associated with the "former" things, and the last part is described as the "latter" or "new" things declared by the prophet. The claim in 44:24–45:7 that the appearance of Cyrus fulfills the "former" prophecy of Isaiah likewise holds the two parts together. The pattern of promise and fulfillment is analogous to that asserted for Jeremiah in Ezra 1:1.

The transition between 1–39 and 40–66 is achieved structurally by continuing the voice of the prophet in the first part into the second. The opening words of Isa. 40:1–2 reflect the voice of God (see Isa. 51:12) and are reminiscent of what belongs to a prophetic call. In 40:6, the response is the "I" of the prophet, who, in this context, can be associated only with Isaiah. Although the familiar voice of the human prophet occurs in the two parts of the book, the word of God is not made independent of human prophetic expression—the biographical identity of the prophet becomes vague and belongs only in the distant background of the text. Priority is given to the word of God itself; the prophet's personality "withers" and "fades" biographically from our view like the "grass" and "flower" of Isa. 40:8. Other topics, themes, and key words form a bridge between the parts of the book as a whole. We find the anger of God in the first part turns to "comfort" in the second (12:1; 40:1; 49:13; 51:3, 12; 52:9; 66:13–14). The "guilt/iniquity" (1:4) spelled out in the first part is "pardoned" in the second (40:2). The "servant" in Isaiah 40–55 bears the guilt of Israel representatively; a lengthy confession follows in 64:4–8. We have already seen how Jerusalem/Zion is a key object of address throughout the book (e.g., Isa. 1; 40:2; 66). Also, the divine name "The Holy One of Israel" becomes a distinctive expression for God in all the major sections of Isaiah. The third part of the book (Isa. 55–66) takes up these key themes and, with citations from Isaiah 2–39, provides a unified topical statement reflecting the content of the book as a whole.

In sum, certain repetitions establish moments of contextual and topical resonance between subcollections of Isaiah 1–39 and become crucial idioms by which different prebiblical traditions can be read together biblically, that is to say, as part of the same book in the context of other scriptural books. We have already seen how idioms such as God's "anger" and "comfort" go beyond either purely literary or historical analysis of biblical traditions. They prove essential to the formation of Isaiah 1–39 as a book of Scripture precisely because they assert how the older traditions relate to the subject matter of Scripture itself. Through resonance with each other, these inner-biblical plays in Isaiah 1–39 are constitutive of the biblical context and cause a single cumulative and memorable word to emerge from the context of the subcollections of these originally independent historical traditions.

The Historical Isaiah and the Book of Isaiah

The entire book is associated with "Isaiah" by the title in 1:1. The form of the title resembles that attached to other prophetic books. This editorial feature confirms that Isaiah belongs among other prophetic books, in the shadow of the Torah and separate from other writings such as Solomonic wisdom books. The title emphasizes that the message of God was delivered through the prophet Isaiah, a message bearing its own marks of continuity that are indicative of Isaiah's own personal stamp and provide a unifying strand within the book. By viewing the prophetic traditions that make up this book as part of a Scripture, the interpreter can settle for neither a purely historical reconstruction of prophetic traditions in the book nor an ahistorical literary assessment of the text. Though these and other investigations are integral to the larger task of biblical interpretation, the weight of interpretation must be, finally, on the form and function of the text that has been preserved as Scripture in the religions of Judaism and Christianity. At the same time, it is not the intention of this approach to reduce commentary on this text to subjective theological impressions, but to offer descriptions of how the book continues to make claims upon its readers. Such an approach assumes that the traditional definition of the "literal sense" sought to preserve a semantic level of significance to religious interpretation that cannot be sustained by a modern identification of that sense strictly with a historical author's intent.

The association of the prophet Isaiah with the entire book implies some unity to the message within the book and invites one to ask special historical and biographical questions. At the outset, these questions are similar to those any interpreter faces in considering the books of Moses, the psalms of David, the Solomonic books, or even the Letters of Paul in the NT. For example, Moses is associated with Genesis through Deuteronomy in the biblical tradition. However, there are changes in voice—from first-person reports to third-person descriptions of him. Even historical conservatives have recognized problems in attributing to Moses the account of his own death. Likewise, the book of Psalms, though associated with David, contains hymns assigned to figures either before his time (Ps. 90, Moses) or after (Ps. 72, Solomon). Again, within the Proverbs of Solomon, some collec-

tions are assigned to non-Solomonic authors (see Prov. 30:1; 31:1). The ending of Ecclesiastes is clearly the product of a later editor, as is the beginning. In none of these instances do we find evidence of a modern concern with historical authorship.

Rather than subjecting the biblical texts to questions arising from modern notions of authorship, one can begin with another inquiry. How is the message of Isaiah related to presentation of the prophet's life in this book? Implicit in this question is a recognition that the message of the prophet has a double voice, the human voice of a prophet and, behind it, the voice of God. A reading of Isaiah as Scripture entails an effort to hear the word of God as it is mediated through the human testimony of the words and deeds of the prophet. The biographical presentation of Isaiah provides a crucial element in the tapestry of these ancient human words by which the word of God is made available to later religious interpreters.

A primary concern, therefore, is to describe how the details of the prophet's life are presented in the book of Isaiah and to define the implications for interpretation of the book. First, by speaking of biographical "presentation" instead of modern historical biography, a distinction is made between the "historical" Isaiah as modern historians might try to reconstruct the "life" of an ancient person and the depiction of the biblical Isaiah as he appears in the book of Isaiah. Both a biblical and a historical portrayal of Isaiah, if they are sufficiently realistic, clothed in idiosyncratic dress, and existing to some degree in a memorable world of accidental events, are equally "flesh and blood" renderings of the prophet. What incites modern speculation about the historical Isaiah is a recognition that the biblical Isaiah appears as a believable, vital "life" caught up in the exigencies of historical experience. Without examining here the relationship between the historical and the biblical Isaiah, the concern of this commentary acknowledges and seeks to sustain the biblical presentation as constitutive of the book of Isaiah and integral to the syntax of the entire book. One should not confuse the recovery of a more "reliable" historical portrait of the eighth-century B.C. prophet with the discovery of a more reliable "Scripture," since ancient traditions do not become Scripture through their fidelity to principles of modern historiography. The transformation of ephemeral prophetic and nonprophetic traditions into a biblical book of prophecy belongs to another set of political and religious factors, with an entirely different purpose in mind.

Second, in Isaiah 2–39 the book's editors have made some effort to present the traditions in chronological order, according to the major historical events that punctuated the ministry of the prophet. The opening chapters of Isa. 2:5–5:7 represent Isaiah's earliest period of prophecy, when he pronounced judgment against the wrongdoing of complacent national leaders in Jerusalem. The narratives in Isa. 6:1–9:7 pertain to the later events of the Syro-Ephraimite war (735–733 B.C.) during the time of Ahaz. The note in Isa. 20:1–6 recounts the still later Philistine revolt against Assyria (713–711), and the reports in Isaiah 36–38 take up the subsequent interactions of Isaiah with Hezekiah when Jerusalem came under siege by the Assyrian king Sennacherib in 701 B.C. Isaiah 39 technically belongs before these events, since Merodach-baladan ruled Babylon in 721–710 B.C. Recalling a minor incident in the life of the prophet, this chapter makes clear that Jerusalem would not be rescued from the Babylonians in the way it had been spared from the Assyrians (Isa. 36–37). Therefore, Isaiah 39 now offers an impressive transition from the period of Assyrian hostility represented by Isaiah 2–39 and that of Babylonian captivity presumed by the chapters that follow. This biographical drive is so integral to the organization of materials in the first part of the book that many premodern interpreters speculated that the latter half of the book derived from the last phase of Isaiah's life during the time of Manasseh. This estimate held sway despite the lack of any mention of Manasseh in the title of the book.

Finally, the highly stylized depiction of the prophet in Isaiah 36–39 is complemented by some vivid images of the prophet's life in Isa. 6:1–9:7. The autobiographical sections in chaps. 7 and 8 provide an introduction to the prophet as a well-known public figure, with a family and children. He appears as one profoundly well versed in religious traditions and worship, one who has compassion—"How long, O Lord?" (6:11)—for those whom God has destined for destruction. Like any other human being, he depends on God's warning and encouragement regarding his actions during a time of crisis (8:11–15). A consistent element in his message appears to be that righteousness and trust in God, rather than international alliances, will provide Judah's only security. In spite of his despair and the resistance to his message, Isaiah finds the courage to "hope in" God and, at God's request, to record his teaching as a source of hope for later generations. The prophet's consistency, eloquence, and fearless confrontation of kings has given later interpreters good reason to speculate that he was probably a highly educated, stately, or even royal-like figure. The content of Isaiah's oracles suggests someone with detached compassion, without the type of passionate identification characteristic of Hosea. He appears well versed in wisdom traditions, but without Amos's zeal for biting satire. As a result, biblical readers easily sense that Isaiah has a personality distinct among biblical prophets. This dimension contributes to the impression that he is subject to familiar human frailties and that the word of God can be perceived only through the necessary limitations of its human mediators.

Isaiah and Christian Scripture

Because Isaiah 1–39 never existed as an independent unit of literature, an awareness of its wider context in Scripture should inform any commentary upon it. First, the aforementioned relationship of Isaiah 1–39 to 40–66 affects the manner in which the former has meaning as part of the book of the Isaiah. Second, the fact that Isaiah 36–39 derives essentially from 2 Kings 18:13–20:19 shows that the book of Isaiah belongs to a larger collection of scriptural books in the Hebrew Bible. Similarly, for example, "the Lord God is my strength and salvation" in Isa. 12:2 cites Exod. 15:2. Third, a Christian re-visioning of Isaiah occurs in light of the earliest kerygma (proclamation of the "good news"; → Kerygma) regarding the nature and significance of Jesus Christ and, later, through understanding Isaiah as part of an "Old Testament" alongside the "New." Such change in context introduces a change in the semantic import of the literature, and a biblical commentator must be conscious of this diversity. The first of these factors has already been considered, but the last two need further comment.

Some explicit verbal allusions to Isaiah do appear elsewhere within the Hebrew Bible (e.g., Ps. 119), though the book retains a high degree of independence in the collection of biblical books. One of the most significant connections between the book of Isaiah and other books of Scripture derives from the assumption that they share the same subject matter. The central subject matter of the Hebrew Bible is clearly the Torah, manifest most explicitly in Genesis through Deuteronomy—"the book of the law" (see Josh. 1:8). In the traditions of Isaiah 1–39 we find references to "torah" in the sense of the prophet's teaching (see Isa. 8:16, 20; 30:9). However, at a later editorial level another view of the Torah of God, reminiscent of the Mosaic law, has been introduced (see 2:3; 5:24; 42:4, 21, 24; 51:4, 7). Analogous to the relation between the prophetic word and God's word, the torah of the prophet now is identified with the divine Torah, known most clearly in the book of Moses. If "torah" in Isa. 1:10 once meant simply the teaching of the prophet, in the editorial formation of the book it gained new meaning, one that assumes the complementarity of the revealed Torah given to Moses. On the one hand, one can readily understand how Isaiah 1–39 and the book of Isaiah came to be read as commentary on the Mosaic Torah within Judaism. On the other hand, the lack of any explicit harmonization of the Isaian traditions with the Mosaic Torah intensified the demand for interpretation of the book as a part of Scripture.

Besides an understanding of the book of Isaiah as the Torah of God, Jewish interpretation also found in it a source of prophetic promise and judgment in the past, present, and future for contemporary interpreters, as well as a basis for attaining biblical "wisdom" rivaling that of the Solomonic books. In other words, the subject matter of the book of Isaiah is expressed through different biblical idioms of law, prophecy, and wisdom as major rubrics under which it could be studied as a guide to believers. In rabbinic Judaism, the presence of oral Torah in the form of the Mishnah and the Talmuds encouraged a dialectical or midrashic assessment of Isaiah. This way of interpretation sought to disclose the law of God as a guide to the obedient life.

The earliest followers of Jesus shared the interpretations of Scripture of their Jewish relatives and neighbors, except that the teachings of Jesus altered their perception of the overarching subject matter of the Bible. For the first Christians, the essential message of the Bible became the gospel of Jesus Christ, which arguably could still be complementary to the older rubrics of Jewish law, prophecy, and wisdom. The legal exposition of Isaiah ceased being a primary means of biblical interpretation (though it remained such in later rabbinic Judaism). At least, what survives in the NT is an orientation to Isaiah as wisdom (see James 1:10–11) consonant with the gospel and, above all, as prophetic promise that finds fulfillment in the kerygma of Jesus Christ.

Two sets of texts from Isaiah 1–39 were cited by more than one NT writer and can be considered representative moments of consensus in the Christian appropriation of Isaiah. First, Isa. 6:9–10, with its statement that God will prevent an understanding of the revealed word, provided Christians with an explanation for why Jesus spoke in parables (Matt. 13:14–15; Mark 4:12; Luke 8:10). Only the insiders could understand. In John 12:40 the disbelief of Jesus' own disciples, despite the many signs shown them, could be explained by citing Isa. 53:1 followed by Isa. 6:10. The refusal of Jews in Rome to accept Paul's testimony is explained by the same prophecy (Acts 28:25–27). Finally, in Rom. 11:7–8 the same words of Isaiah account for why Jews generally rejected the gospel and why the gospel is now offered to the Gentiles. Numerous allusions in the NT

play upon this popular interpretation. The disappointment among the first Christians that most Jews rejected the new revelation of Jesus made sense when it was viewed as a fulfillment of the Isaian prophecy.

Second, Isa. 28:16, "I lay a foundation stone in Zion," and 8:14, "a stone of stumbling and a rock of offense," were commonly used to explain both the offense and the hidden significance of Jesus. In 1 Peter 2:6, 8, these verses are cited along with Ps. 118:22, "the stone which the builders rejected." Commonly in the Psalms and in other OT books God is referred to as a "rock" or as "my rock." In a related metaphor, the term "stone" could be considered to belong to this same vocabulary. Jesus represents the rejected stone that now has become the foundation or cornerstone for the house of the elect. It was customary for Christian interpretation of OT symbols for God to include reference to Jesus Christ. Hence, Jesus is the spiritual "rock" (1 Cor. 10:4). As an explanation of how the gospel came to be announced to Gentiles rather than only to Jews, Paul (Rom. 9:33) depends on both Isa. 1:9 and 8:14. The depiction of conditions after the Exile—"a few survivors" (1:9)—could be explained in Christian terms as a consequence of Israel's trying to obey the law through works rather than by faith. Isa. 8:14, then, proves to be a prediction of the later Jewish rejection of Jesus. In this way, an argument regarding how Jews should have obeyed the Torah is followed by a prophetic witness to the Jewish rejection of Jesus, who is "a stone of stumbling and a rock of offense."

At a minimum, these examples illustrate that the subject matter of the book of Isaiah in the Christian Bible was ultimately the gospel of Jesus Christ. The differing contexts of this book in two different Scriptures elicited very different ways of making sense of the book for the sake of faith. Isaiah became one of the most widely cited OT books in Christian preaching regarding the prophetic interpretation of the significance of Jesus' words and deeds, as well as a common authoritative resource in disputes over Christian doctrine.

The Text

Unlike some of the other prophetic books, Isaiah shows a remarkable consistency in preservation from the earliest available manuscripts to the received Hebrew Masoretic texts of the tenth century A.D. The discovery of copies of Isaiah from about 100 B.C. among the Dead Sea Scrolls (esp. 1QIsa), confirmed the pre-Christian antiquity of the book of Isaiah as it currently exists. The Greek translation, the Septuagint (LXX), and other versions contain only minor differences from the Hebrew text.

COMMENTARY

1:1-31

The Prologue

The opening section of Isaiah contains a title and an introduction to the book. The introduction (vv. 2-31) consists of a series of independent prophetic traditions (vv. 2-3, 4-9, 10-17, 18-20, 21-26, 27-31) that are loosely linked to each other through key words or themes. Most of this chapter, with the exception of 1:27-31, once provided an introduction to a smaller collection of prophetic oracles, perhaps 2:1-10:6 or 21:1-32:20. Certainly the last unit, 1:27-31, appears to be a later, postexilic addition that presupposes themes in Isaiah 40-66 and anticipates the final chapter, Isaiah 66. The concluding verse, 1:31, now plays upon—a fire "not quenched"—the last verse of the book, 66:24. Isaiah 66 is similarly concerned with the redemption of Jerusalem as "Zion" (v. 8), along with a variety of related motifs and themes already found in this chapter. Therefore, in its present form, this chapter provides a prologue including in its scope both Isaiah 2-39 and the entire book of Isaiah.

1:1, The Title of the Book. Modeled after the same style as the titles in Amos. 1:1 and Hosea 1:1, a very brief ascription of the book to Isaiah the prophet prefaces the book. The content of the entire book is described in technical prophetic terminology as a "vision" (cf. 2 Chron. 32:32) "which he saw concerning Judah and Jerusalem." The expression "Judah and Jerusalem" occurs only here and in the subsequent title of Isa. 2:1, otherwise the order of these terms is reversed (3:1, 8; 5:3; 22:21). This sequence in the title corresponds to the order in which the nation and city are treated in the introduction that follows (1:2-31): first, judgment against the rebellious people of God; and second, implications of that rebellion for the city of Jerusalem (Zion) and its inhabitants. The preoccupation with Judah, the Southern Kingdom, and its capital city probably accounts for the listing only of the kings of Judah during the time of Isaiah, with no mention of their counterparts in the Northern Kingdom, Israel.

1:2-31, A Topical Introduction. Chap. 1 summarizes and prefigures the content of the book of Isaiah through a scenario of God's purging and redeeming the nation of Judah. The people of Judah, brought up as God's offspring, have forgotten their divinely appointed heritage and grown ignorant of their relationship to God. Their disobedience consists of open rebellion (vv. 2, 28) and sinful acts (vv. 4, 28). Verse 3 epitomizes the prophet's indictment against

them: "An ox recognizes its owner; even an ass [knows] its master's crib. [But] Israel does not recognize [anything]; My own people do not understand at all." There is redemption for only a "few survivors" (v. 9), those who "return to her [Zion] by righteousness" (v. 27; 35:10). In this scenario, Jerusalem as "Zion" appears as a central motif. Due to the corruption of its inhabitants, the city is called "Sodom" and "Gomorrah" (v. 10) and "a harlot" (v. 21). However, someday it will again be called "the city of righteousness, the faithful city" (v. 26).

The concept of the redemption and preservation of Zion plays a highly significant role in the composition of Isaiah, especially in chaps. 2-39. Repeatedly the prophet assures the leaders and the people that they must not be afraid. "Zion" is God's special habitation, his "holy mountain," that will not ultimately fall to the enemy. Belief in the "inviolability of Zion" may derive from the eighth-century prophet himself or from a later period, perhaps the reign of Josiah in the seventh century, after the Northern Kingdom had been taken into exile by the Assyrians. Regardless, it now accurately highlights an important, recurring note throughout the presentation of the prophet's message in Isaiah 1-39.

The title and the introduction form the prologue to the book and provide a specific context for an interpretation of the prophetic traditions within the book of Isaiah. On the one hand, the whole book is associated with the eighth-century B.C. prophet Isaiah and his message. Just as the book of Psalms came to be associated with David, despite the presence of later psalms (Ps. 72, "of Solomon"), and just as Proverbs is linked with Solomon, despite later editing (Prov. 25:1), so the unity of the book of Isaiah is asserted by its relationship to the prophet and his message. Anticipating a later distinction between parts of the book in terms of the "former" and "latter things" (chaps. 41-48), 1:27 distinguishes between prophetic claims upon Zion "before" the Exile and those "afterward." On the other hand, the introduction places an emphasis on the topical import of the prophet's word as a source of the word and law of God. Though the Assyrian siege of Jerusalem in 701 B.C. still shimmers here and there behind some of the traditions in Isaiah 1, the present context employs them to make a historical generalization regarding God's judgment and redemption of Judah. Biographical dimensions of the prophet himself find no place in this introduction, just as they remain absent in Isaiah 40-66. In the book of Isaiah generally, the message of the prophet takes precedence over interest in the exigencies of the prophet's "life." The introduction itself aims at the enduring implications of that message for future generations by emphasizing a pattern of divine response to the chosen people: God's wrath is a means of purging; it is accompanied by a demand for repentance and right action and is followed by a vision of the full restoration of both the people and the city.

2:1–4:6
Promises and Judgments of Zion

In the initial section of prophecies, two promise oracles serve as brackets around a collection of judgment oracles. The topical concern in the introduction, God's word to both Judah and Jerusalem, is amply illustrated throughout these prophecies. Their setting suggests a period of relative calm before the storm, of complacency and injustice that the prophet eloquently condemns.

2:1–5
Zion, City of God's Law and Word

2:1, A Second Title. The title in 2:1 is remarkably similar to that in 1:1, though shorter in form. It repeats the inverted order of "Judah and Jerusalem" in contrast to the usual expression in the oracles themselves. This title helps to distinguish the introduction from the oracles that follow. The title appropriately corresponds to the section 2:2–4:6, with its threats and promises directed solely to the southern nation and its capital.

2:2–5, Zion, the City of God's Law and Word. The stress on the law or Torah and God's word (v. 3) from Zion, together with the ideal of a permanent end to war (v. 4), suggests that the tradition derives from some time after the destruction of Jerusalem. As in later, apocalyptic literature, the description of the city's restoration is here accompanied by cosmic changes "in the latter days" (v. 2). Most of this oracle (vv. 2–4) is identical with Mic. 4:1–3, and the title in 2:1 may also be intended to argue for its original association with the prophet Isaiah, rather than Micah.

In most collections of prophetic oracles, judgment oracles precede oracles of promise, instead of the order here. One explanation for this variation may be that the ordering does, in fact, place a promise oracle (2:2–5) immediately after the negative conclusion of the introduction. In addition, 2:2–5 makes an excellent transition by picking up themes from Isaiah 1, and yet, because of the title in 2:1, one is not permitted to confuse it with the introduction itself. It predicts the restoration of Zion and foresees a time when the word and the Torah ("teaching" or "law") of God will be taught to the entire world from Jerusalem.

The term "torah" in 1:27 probably means simply "the teaching" of the prophet Isaiah (cf.

8:16). However, Isa. 2:3 appears to interpret this same word contextually in terms of the larger revealed Torah, which came to be associated with the "Book of the Law" (Gen.–Deut.; see Josh. 1:8). In the formation of Jewish Scripture, the book of Isaiah was edited to reflect its role in a larger collection of books, with the Torah as its central subject matter. As a result, one may appreciate why later Jewish interpretation viewed Isaiah primarily as prophetic commentary on the revealed Torah. Isa. 2:2–5 points to this larger context for the book of Isaiah but does not take the next step of demonstrating practically how parts of Scripture will be read in the light of each other.

2:6–22
The Proud Made Low

In a peroration of judgment against arrogant and idolatrous leaders, the prophet's message is made memorable by a refrain that describes the humiliation of the proud. By contrast, "God alone will be exalted in that day" (vv. 11, 17). Some of the argument against dependence on soothsayers, diviners, and graven images seems more pertinent to later conditions of apostasy during the Exile and afterward. Nevertheless, the composition follows logically after the preceding unit because of its assurance that God will be exalted, which is similar to the preceding claim that the mountain of God "shall be established as the highest of the mountains" (2:2).

3:1–4:1
Judgment on Judah's Leaders and Zion's Daughters

Continuing the theme of God's wrath against wicked leaders and the immorality of rich landowners, the message points again to a coming social upheaval that will expose their false security.

3:1–12, Misguided Leaders. The prophets describe an impending famine and political anarchy. Children and random survivors suddenly become national leaders. Merely having a mantle becomes grounds for holding a position of authority, but such candidates will resist the opportunity because there is no food at home. Again, this portrayal recalls the preceding unit, reflecting a catalogue of consequences for those who, in a time of relative prosperity, arrogantly hold high offices and lead the people astray. In the last verses, the righteous have hope of receiving help according to their own deeds, while the wicked will reap what they have sown.

3:13–15, Against the Vineyard's Destroyers. This unit interrupts the consistent theme and style of the tradition in which it now stands. Its reference to God's judgment of "the people" offers a loose contextual bridge to the preceding verse, with its mention of "my people." The sudden mention of "the vineyard," with no explicit explanation of what it symbolizes, presumes some prior knowledge of its usage in Isaiah's oracles. The term occurs rarely in this way, once with an explanation in the "song of the vineyard" (Isa. 5:1–7) and again, in 27:1–7, in a promise of restoration that depends upon elements in 5:1–7. Verses 13–15 may have belonged originally with 5:1–7, perhaps between 5:3 and 5:4, in which case they once would have formed part of a juridical parable. In a juridical parable, the king or audience is asked to judge a case. After the case is decided, the one presenting it as a parable implicates the judge. The ones judging unknowingly judge themselves. Other examples of this type of parable in the Bible include David's confrontation with Nathan in 2 Sam. 12:1–13, as well as his being tricked by the wise woman of Tekoa (2 Sam. 14:4–17). In the context of Isaiah, these verses provide a graphic, summarizing indictment ("It is you!") directed against the leaders in Judah, one that resonates with the more detailed explication of the metaphor in 5:1–7. This vineyard imagery becomes a major way of explaining the rationale and the nature of God's judgment in Isaiah 1–39.

3:16–4:1, Complacent Daughters of Zion.
The city's wealthy women are mocked for their self-preoccupation, which is illustrated by an obsession with hairstyles, lavish clothing, and jewelry. Judgment will fall upon them no less than upon the corrupt men who have been the city's leaders.

4:2–6
The Glory of Survivors in Zion
The oracle at 4:2–6 maintains continuity with the oracles immediately preceding it through the theme "the daughters of Zion." Here they emerge "in that day" washed clean of past "bloodstains." Similar to that of Isa. 2:2–4, the promise of God involves an end to the judgment of Zion. In this section, only 2:2–4 and 4:5 speak of Zion as a "mountain," though the related depiction of the proud brought down and God being exalted is a recurring feature throughout. The oracle secures, from a perspective after the Exile, confidence that Zion will be restored and will surpass its former glory. An implicit assumption is that God will carry his chosen people through the worst purging judgment, without ever abandoning the goal of blessing them when they are transformed into an obedient and righteous nation.

5:1–7
The Song of the Vineyard

Verses 1–7 introduce "a song of my beloved," the owner of a cherished vineyard (vv. 1–2). Despite thoughtful planting, loving care, and diligent protection of the fertile field, the vineyard yields worthless, sour grapes. This poetic complaint is suddenly ("and now ..." v. 3) transformed into a demand for legal adjudication by the listeners, the inhabitants of Jerusalem and Judah (vv. 3–4). The guilty party, still cast in metaphorical terms, is sentenced by the prophet (vv. 5–6). Then the author deciphers the parable explicitly and provides a summarizing indictment of the people of Jerusalem and Judah (v. 7). The tradition may derive originally from a longer juridical parable (see Isa. 3:13–15) and certainly retains the force of an invitation to judge unknowingly one's self. As poetry it depends on an analogous observation about what is natural and unnatural, in a manner typical of wisdom literature (see Prov. 25:19; 26:11; Sir. 27:6). Prophets frequently use the logic of wisdom literature to make their arguments incisive and unavoidable (see, e.g., Amos 3:3–8). In its present context, this song represents one of several key "songs" (see Isa. 12; 26) in Isaiah 1–39 that mark transitions between prophetic subcollections and summarize the import of prophetic traditions, either immediately preceding or following them. As "songs," these traditions contribute to our conception of the message of the book by looking forward to a time when Israel "will have a song in the night" (30:29), and especially, "a new song" (42:10).

Finally, some distinctive elements that occur in the song of the vineyard have been picked up and used again in other parts of Isaiah 2–39. For example, the expression "briars and thorns" occurs nowhere else in the Hebrew Bible and is applied repeatedly to describe the effect of God's judgment on Judah and other nations, especially Assyria (7:23–25; 9:18; 10:17; 32:13). This unit is significant because, as with the first chapter, a general pattern of God's response to believers is established that can apply to later generations, long after the specific historical events that the prophet himself addresses.

5:8–30
One Side of a Framework of Judgment Against Ephraim and Judah

Around the testimony of Isaiah, 6:1–9:7, two sets of judgment oracles have been placed to form a double *inclusio* or bracketing frame. The outer framework contains seven woe oracles: six on one side, and one on the other. Within this framework is another *inclusio* composed of judgment oracles punctuated by a refrain, "for all this his anger is not turned away; his hand is stretched out still" (5:25; 9:12, 17, 21). To distinguish the entire framework from the traditions that follow, the same refrain has been added as a conclusion to the seventh woe oracle (10:4). This editorial arrangement contributes significantly to the way in which these oracles are read together in the book of Isaiah. Addressing similar parties, as did the oracles in Isa. 2:6–22 and 3:1–12, the woe oracles on both sides (5:8–23 and 10:1–4) criticize rulers and leaders in Jerusalem. Thus they have the effect of maintaining continuity with the earlier oracles in chaps. 2–3, while placing further emphasis on the responsibility of leaders who, during the events lying behind 6:1–9:7, bring about the destruction of northern Israel. The core traditions of the testimony complement the poetry of the framework through narrative descriptions of the prophet Isaiah's encounter with the Judean king Ahaz and other national leaders.

Alongside the woe oracles in this section, the other judgment oracles in the framework are directed against both Judah and Israel. They foresee the defeat of northern Israel by the Assyrians (5:26–30). The intrigue attested within the testimony itself centers on this very issue, whether or not Judah should join a coalition with Israel and Syria against the Assyrians around 735 B.C. These events immediately precede northern Israel's defeat and exile in 722. The refrain associated with these judgment oracles that surround the testimony is employed editorially as a major motif elsewhere in Isaiah 1–39, even finally applied in judgment to the victorious Assyrians (Isa. 14:24–27).

5:8–24
Six of Seven Woe Oracles

The woe oracles condemn various groups of people in Jerusalem and Judah, including wealthy land holders, drunkards, arrogant sages, and corrupt judges. The seventh woe oracle (10:1–4a) probably once stood at the beginning of this collection. In their correct order, the first two oracles make the most substantial case against Jerusalem's leaders and now provide an initial heightening of certain concerns illustrated by the core traditions in the narrative testimony of Isaiah (6:1–7:9). These words of judgment in the woe oracles complement the scenario presented in the preceding song of the vineyard. In both, a promising situation is undone by a variety of self-indulgent actions on the part of those most responsible for the preservation of the southern city and country.

5:8–14, The First Two Woe Oracles. The first oracle describes the accumulation of property by a few, as well as the undermining of the relationship between families and their land in a farm economy. The victims become sojourners in their own country and have no means to survive. The second of these oracles contrasts the thirst for excessive drink and entertainment with the starvation of persons who should be held in high esteem. The threat in v. 14 recalls the judgment of exile and designates those addressed as Jerusalem's "nobility."

5:15–17, The Proud Made Low. The nobility and throngs of people who will "go down" (v. 14) are linked now to the familiar refrain of 2:6–22 in which the proud are "brought low" and "humbled." This echo of an opening section of the book of Isaiah establishes a consistent idiomatic rendering of the divine word of judgment across these prophetic traditions, one applicable to Judah as well as to Assyria (10:33–34).

5:18–24, The Fourth, Fifth, and Sixth Woe Oracles. The prophetically misguided, the morally inverted, those wise in their own eyes, drunkards, and bribe takers are the objects of indictment in the fourth, fifth, and sixth oracles. A threat follows, introduced by a typical "therefore" as in the previous woe oracles (v. 13). In these threats the theme is that of famine and drought in the land. In v. 24 a number of expressions occur that are similar to the language in the judgment on the vineyard in 5:5–6. There is, however, a new theme struck in the second half of v. 24. The prophetic judgment is identified with the demands of the law, like that found in Deuteronomy (see Amos 2:4). Here, the interpretation of the book of Isaiah is held together within a larger context of Scripture, including the Torah revealed through Moses. Although the prophetic oracles themselves do not directly cite the book of the Torah, this note assures readers that these books belong together and make sense as Hebrew Scripture.

5:25–30
Judgment Oracles, "His Anger Is Not Turned Back"

The judgment oracle in 5:25 is directed against the Northern Kingdom, in contrast to the preceding woe oracles. It is followed by a graphic description of how God will use Assyria as an agent of his wrath.

5:25, A Sentence of Judgment. As part of a framework around the testimony in 6:1–9:7, this oracle helps to explain the reason for God's eventual destruction of both northern Israel and southern Judah. By contrast, the historical events within the testimony depict only the intrigue between prophet and the Judean king just prior to the exile of the Northern Kingdom, more than a century before Judah would suffer a similar fate.

Verse 25 begins abruptly with a hinge word, "therefore," like that introducing the threat following a woe oracle in the immediately preceding verse. One would normally expect an indictment to precede this threat as part of a single prophetic speech. However, the effect of this unusual use of older traditions heightens the force of the threat and allows the indictment of the preceding woe oracles to justify this threat as well. The threat in v. 25 clearly belongs to a group of invective-threat oracles, distinct from the woe oracles and ending with a familiar refrain: "On account of all this, his anger is not turned away; his hand is stretched out still." These same two lines are repeated verbatim at the end of oracles of the same type (see 9:12, 17, 21) and after the last woe oracle (10:4) on the other side of the testimony. Again this refrain, like "the proud made low" (5:15–17), becomes a major way of expressing the enduring nature of God's word, eventually applied even against Assyria (14:24–27).

5:26–30, Assyria as the Agent of God's Wrath.
God "whistles" for Assyria, who responds obediently as a trained animal obeys its master. Assyria's attack is compared to that of a lion seizing its prey. The land of Israel is left devastated, appearing as a place of "darkness, distress, light darkened by its cloud." This description is the same as that found in the testimony (8:22), followed by a promise that, after the Exile, those who walked in darkness will "have seen a great light."

6:1–9:7

The Testimony of Isaiah

The collection in the next passages includes prophetic autobiographical reports and narratives about the prophet's interaction with King Ahaz and concludes with promises of God's restoration. The primary historical event behind these various materials is that of the Syro-Ephraimite war (roughly 735 B.C.), which developed in response to the growing military power of Assyria (→ Assyria, Empire of).

In 738, the Assyrian king Tiglath-pileser initiated a campaign from the north into Syria and Palestine. In the reign of Judah's king Ahaz (735–715 B.C.), northern Israel formed a coalition with Syria against Assyria. Judah, having the benefit of some distance from the direct challenge of Assyria, refused to join that coalition. In an effort to force collaboration, the kings of Syria (Rezin) and Israel (Pekah) sought to replace by force the Judean king in the city of Jerusalem. Ahaz had many advisers during this precarious situation, including the prophet Isaiah (→ Ahaz).

The Syro-Ephraimite war inspired Judah to form an alliance with Assyria that led to the defeat of Syria and the Northern Kingdom, Israel. The Assyrians exiled all able-bodied Israelites in 722 B.C., the last record of the northern tribes in human history (→ Exile). More than a century later, Judah faced a similar exile under the Babylonian usurpers of the Assyrian legacy (→ Babylon).

When Isaiah's word was finally rejected by King Ahaz, God instructed the prophet to "bind up the testimony" concerning these events (8:16) as a future "teaching" and a later proof of the prophet's veracity. Much within the traditions of 6:1–8:18 may derive from this specific occasion, though the older material has been expanded to address a future audience. Accordingly, the composition of 6:1–9:7 underscores the abiding significance of Isaiah's prophecies associated with a historical turning point in the life of ancient Israel.

6:1–13

Isaiah's Vocational Justification

Sometimes described as "the call of Isaiah," the autobiographical statement by the prophet in 6:1–13 is properly a report of his commissioning to deliver a particular message of judgment to the people of God. It is dated to the same year as the death of King Uzziah (736/35 B.C.). The king's son, Jotham, died either before his father (perhaps having served as co-regent) or shortly after. Ahaz, Jotham's son, was king of Judah when Isaiah sought to carry his divinely appointed commission as a prophet to the Southern Kingdom. The narratives that follow (Isa. 7–8) illustrate the prophet's confrontation with Ahaz during the intrigue of the Syro-Ephraimite war.

The account opens with Isaiah's vision of God in his temple. Immediately the prophet recognizes that he is a human observer of Yahweh's heavenly council. He properly fears for his life, since the realm of the holy can be dangerous to the profane world (→ Holiness). After a purification ritual, Isaiah hears God's request that someone be found to represent the heavenly ones on earth by announcing their decision. A similar scene is described by the prophet Micaiah, son of Imlah, in 1 Kings 22:19–23. In that case, a spirit volunteers to incite the royal prophets to lie to King Zedekiah, leading him to doom. In Isaiah 6, the prophet himself volunteers to be the messenger. However, the message he hears is harsh. Moreover, it is coupled with a command to dull the people's senses so that they are not able, through the hearing of it, to change their actions and be healed or redeemed.

In his prophetic role as intercessor for God's chosen people, Isaiah pleads with God, "Lord, how long?" (cf. Amos 7:2, 5). The answer offers no reassurance: every house will be empty, and the land will be, like the vineyard in 5:1–7, utterly desolate. Only the final line offers the slightest hope—a "holy seed" will survive in the stump of the tree that has been cut down and burned. This possibility hints at a concept, developed less ambiguously later in the book, of a surviving remnant of Judah through which God would restore the nation of Israel.

This commissioning report implies the same fate for Judah as for Israel. The woe oracles against Judean leaders and the judgment oracles against the Northern Kingdom surrounding the testimony underscore this assumption. The fragile optimism at the end appears as an afterthought, without in any way ameliorating the coming disaster. Only in time, well after a full contemplation of the torturous events of national devastation for both nations, can one detect a faint glimmer of hope in the stump that is left, a glimmer that will someday adumbrate a great light to those who walk in the darkness of exile (9:2).

7:1–8:15
The Prophet, King Ahaz, and the Syro-Ephraimite War

In a series of events associated with the names or naming of three children, Isaiah is depicted in the turmoil of social unrest in Judah (735–733 B.C.). The fulfillment of his commission in chap. 6 moves from direct conversation with Ahaz in chap. 7 to indirect communication with the leaders and the people regarding the word of God. The king's and the people's lack of response to the prophet's message has already been anticipated by the commissioning in chap. 6.

Occasionally, ordinary public activities of prophets could carry extraordinary significance. Beside professing oracles, prophets could dress or behave in ways that symbolized their message. Just as Hosea's marriage constituted a symbolic act of prophecy, so Isaiah's children, by their very names, carried a message throughout their lives. The Emmanuel child in 7:14 seems to belong to some unnamed woman, whereas Isaiah's son Maher-shalal-hash-baz is born of "the prophetess," who is surely his wife. Unfortunately, nothing more is said about her, and nothing is known about her contribution, if any, to the message of Isaiah. In the formation of prophetic books, such historical detail becomes increasingly secondary to the message of the prophet. In this respect, a theocentric set of concerns takes the place of an anthropological interest in the phenomenon of prophecy. This tendency in the formation of biblical books coincides with the demise of classical prophecy and the formation of a Scripture in the postexilic period.

7:1–9, Ahaz and Isaiah on the Highway to Fuller's Field. In the period prior to the siege of Jerusalem, God instructs Isaiah to meet King Ahaz at a particular place with a message of hope. The account in vv. 2–9 now has a historical introduction taken from 2 Kings 16:5, reminding us that the larger context of Isaiah includes a collection of other scriptural books. Verse 2 confirms Ahaz's fear about the coalition of Syria and the Northern Kingdom. Isaiah meets the king soon after, accompanied by the prophet's son, Shearjashub (meaning, "a remnant shall return"). Isaiah's message is one of comfort and assurance that God will destroy Ephraim and Syria, but with the provision that the king "not fear": the king should not seek alliances with foreign nations instead of trusting in God alone to defend the nation. The ultimatum at the end of v. 9 falls, as the context later confirms, on deaf ears.

7:10–17, Emmanuel as an Unwanted Sign. In an effort to convince the frightened king, Isaiah offers to provide any confirming sign Ahaz might be able to imagine. Attempting to conceal his unwillingness to obey the prophetic word, in a gesture of false piety, Ahaz refuses to "test God" (see Deut. 6:16). The prophet retorts with a judgment oracle that repeats not only the claim that Syria and the Northern Kingdom will cease to exist on their land, but that a similar disaster will befall Judah. The time of the destruction of the two northern nations is tied to the birth and early childhood of a boy named "Emmanuel" (lit., "God with us"). The name symbolized that the presence of God can be a source of the greatest comfort to the righteous (Ps. 139) or, as in this historical moment, an assurance of certain judgment to those subject to God's wrath (Amos 9:2–4).

"A Young Woman/Virgin Shall Conceive and Bear a Son and Shall Call His Name Emmanuel"

Differences in the English translations confirm that a range of problems are raised by Isa. 7:14 for Jewish and Christian interpreters. The Hebrew noun for "young woman" neither requires that she be a virgin nor precludes that possibility. The LXX rendered this noun as "virgin," which was taken in Matt. 1:22–23 to be a promise fulfilled in the birth of Jesus Christ. However, many other Greek translations rendered the same noun as simply "young woman." Of course, this issue is not a minor one in the history of interpretation. Martin Luther allegedly offered a hundred gulden to anyone who could show a reference in the OT to a married woman designated by this term. One might argue that the "young woman" in Prov. 30:19 is by implication not a virgin. In addition to this matter of controversy, the Hebrew in Isa. 7:14 does not specify the tense of the relevant verb. The most recent translation of the Hebrew Scripture by the Jewish Publication Society reads, "a young woman has conceived"; the choice of the future tense, "will conceive," reflects a decision that more aptly favors the NT interpretations of this verse but is not dictated conclusively by grammar alone.

A distinction needs to be made between a narrowly focused historical interpretation of Isa. 7:1–17 and the way in which the prophetic context of Isa. 7:18–9:7 has played upon the original ambiguities of 7:14 and rendered its semantic implications, so that the older oracle now applies to other periods long after the time of the prophet. Within Isa. 7:1–17, the historical setting seems explicit enough. Because Ahaz refuses to ask for a sign to confirm divine deliverance from the Syro-Ephraimite threat to the north, the prophet rebukes the king and offers the sign anyway. Before a child named "Emmanuel" will reach an age sufficient to eat solid food, the northern threat will be removed, but Judah will then face an even greater threat than the current one. In this original historical setting, "the woman" appears to be a person known to the king and to Isaiah, and the child's life should be contemporaneous with events of the next few years. One may certainly speculate on the earliest historical identity of the woman. She may have been Ahaz's spouse, Isaiah's wife ("the prophetess," see 8:3), or some other woman.

Within 7:1–9:7, the original historical situation has been interpreted within a larger context of future prophecies. Consequently, the import of the child has gained a profundity far exceeding whatever were the original political circumstances of Isa. 7:1–17. The reference to the child's eating "curds and honey" has been applied to a future Assyrian attack on Ahaz (7:20–21) and applied, by a later editor, to the miraculous sustaining of those who are left in the land of Judah after its defeat (7:21–22). The unusual name "Emmanuel" (Heb., "God with us") now harbors in it prophetic implications for the destruction of Judah as well as Syria and Ephraim (8:6–8) and, finally, for the nations in the future that will so threaten Judah (8:9–10). The "child sign" seems to continue in 9:1–7, where the birth of a child (9:6) portends a comparable claim of God's presence with Israel (9:4) in the period after the Exile, when "the people walked in darkness" (9:2). Even if the original tradition of 9:1–7 was once an independent, nonmessianic "royal psalm," its present context in the book invites a messianic interpretation. So too Isa. 7:14 has similarly engendered messianic expectations regarding the Emmanuel child among both Jews and Christians, expectations based on the warrants of the text's "scriptural" context in 7:1–9:7.

7:18–24, Future Implications. As a series of interpretations based on the Emmanuel prophecy, a set of four "in that day" prophecies follows. The first two concern God's use of Assyria in a manner typical of the prophecy of the eighth-century B.C. prophet. The last two "in that day" oracles (vv. 21–22 and 23–25) are more complicated. The first seems to combine an initially negative picture—farms reduced to a few surviving livestock—with the impression that each cow will produce an "abundance of milk." Instead of continuing the immediately preceding references to milk curds and wild honey as a sign of desperate people living off a barren land, one can imagine a land miraculously flowing with milk and honey. The second of these oracles returns to a description of destitution like that in the commission (6:11–12), repeatedly employing the unusual pair of words "briars and thorns" indicative, again, of conditions depicted earlier in the song of the vineyard in 5:1–7.

8:1–4, A Third Child and a Bleak Future. As a further sign of the impending collapse of Syria and Ephraim, the prophet secured officials to witness a large tablet he had prepared on behalf of his future son, Maher-shalal-hash-baz. Though what was legally accomplished remains unclear—perhaps it was a dedication to his son —the tablet undoubtedly became a matter of public record. By this means, Isaiah confronted everyone with the terrifying name, meaning "spoil speeds, booty hastes." As with Emmanuel, a certain moment in the child's development would not be reached before the announced judgment would fall upon the north.

8:5–10, Further Import of Emmanuel. In the present context, the prophecy in vv. 5–8 takes up once more threats associated with the Emmanuel child (7:17). The metaphors contrast the meager water supply of Shiloah with the abundance of the Tigris in the Mesopotamian valley, home of Assyria. The floodwaters of that great river will rise up to the necks of those who dwell in Judah. However, the next prophecy (vv. 9–10) moves in a very different direction. As in

Ps. 2:2, the nations, undoubtedly including Assyria and later Babylon, plot against the people of God. They will be "broken," and the concluding explanation, "for God is with us," plays once more upon the name Emmanuel. Here the Emmanuel child represents a sign for future hope after the judgment upon Israel.

8:11–15, Fear God, Not the Nations. The same message Isaiah has given to Ahaz is summarized in a general way. The lesson missed by Ahaz has likewise been forfeited by the people. The entire nation has failed to trust Yahweh for their security, in spite of God's threat that by such disobedience "both houses of Israel" (v. 15) will stumble, become ensnared, and be "broken."

8:16–22
A Written Testimony for the Future

In the present context, this binding and sealing of a "testimony" and "teaching" (lit., "*torah*") pertains to a moment in the life of the prophet when he first began to collect his oracles in written form. The "disciples" are probably students of the prophet or, at least, members of a group aligned with Isaiah the prophet. Some scholars speculate that these disciples could be simply Isaiah's children.

The written collection of oracles is clearly intended to represent the enduring message of the prophet up to the time of the collapse of Samaria in 722/721. Furthermore, vv. 19–22 anticipate its continuing value to still later students of the traditions of Isaiah during the period of the Babylonian exile. Though they will be tempted to consult various alien mediums, they are to remain faithful to the prophetic teaching of Isaiah. The final note about exile echoes the same condition of darkness, distress, and gloom that was forecast by the oracle (5:30) just before the testimony.

9:1–7
A Child of Messianic Hope

The foreboding implications of Isaiah's message during the time of Ahaz are contrasted with promises that indicate a reversal in the historical predicament of Israel. Besides the obvious transition in 9:1, from the "darkness" of 8:22 to the "light" of 9:2–7, the reference to a child being born recalls the earlier use of children as prophetic signs in the book of Isaiah.

If 9:2–7 were treated as an independent unit of tradition, it could be considered an ancient "royal psalm," possibly used in festival celebrations concerned with the enthronement of a king in Judah, perhaps with either Josiah or Hezekiah. Similar remarkable epithets ("Wonderful, Counselor, . . ." v. 6) are found in Egyp-

tian hymnology in praise of the pharaoh and are typical of exaggerated language employed in ancient Near Eastern royal eulogies. Nevertheless, just as other royal psalms have been transformed into messianic psalms in the formation of the book of Psalms (e.g., Ps. 2), this hymn in its present context no longer points back eulogistically to a familiar royal figure. Instead, it looks forward eschatologically to a restoration of the promise to David of a kingdom with "no end" (v. 7). In the context of this book, this hymn offers, at a minimum, messianic hope for the period after the Exile (8:21–22). Cyrus came to be viewed in these terms (so Isa. 44–45), though not in a manner that would end interpretation of these messianic texts. Later generations of Jews and Christians would look for yet another future person who could more completely fulfill what is here promised.

9:8–10:4
The Other Side of a Framework of Judgment Against Judah and Ephraim

9:8–20, Judgment Oracles, "His Anger Is Not Turned Back." Three judgment oracles with identical concluding refrains indict the Northern Kingdom for wrongdoing, arrogance, and refusal to trust in Yahweh. Before the last of these oracles, their original audience is made clear by the claim, "Together they are against Judah" (v. 21). Undoubtedly, "they" denote northern Israel and Syria, as mentioned in the testimony (e.g., 7:1–2).

10:1–4, The Seventh Woe Oracle. The woe oracle in 10:1–4 is the last of an original collection of seven. The rest are clustered together in Isa. 5:8–24 as part of the framework around the testimony of Isaiah. This one offers a lengthy attack on corrupt Judean judges who leave the people without any recourse to justice. An editor has added the refrain, familiar in the preceding oracles of judgment, to the end of this woe oracle. This final repetition concludes the subsection (5:8–10:4) by highlighting a recurring theme, the way in which God's "anger" and "hand" address both Israel and Judah.

10:5–11:16
Woe to Assyria and Promise to Judah

Though the opening sections of the book of Isaiah have given most weight to woe, in these traditions in 10:5–11:16 a more positive note is struck. This collection is composed of prophetic judgments against Assyria and future promises to Judah. In their present context, they often pick up elements from judgment oracles in the previous sections and interpret them in terms of a divine promise that the enemy will be defeated and Judah will be restored.

A key motif that weaves throughout this section and connects it contextually to the previous section is a play upon the term "rod." It first occurs in the testimony (9:4) in a series of metaphorical synonyms, including "yoke" and "staff." Here, the judgment against Assyria begins with its identification as the "rod" and "staff" of God's anger (10:5). However, Assyria arrogantly assumed its victory really was achieved by means of its own "hand" (10:10, 13, 14), in contrast to the above-mentioned refrain, "his [God's] hand is stretched out still" (5:25; 9:12, 17, 21; 10:4). God mocks Assyria's folly by asking if an "ax," "rod," or "staff" really has any power over the one who wields it (10:15). Israel, then, is encouraged not to fear Assyria, which is merely a "rod" and "staff" in God's hand (10:24), and is promised that the "yoke" of Assyria will someday be removed from around Israel's neck (10:27). Finally, a messianic king is to arise as a "shoot of the stump of Jesse" (see Isa. 6:13) who will chastise the wicked with the "rod" of his mouth (11:4).

10:5–15, Assyria, the Arrogant Rod of God. This account of God's anger with Assyria turns on a theological principle found elsewhere in the OT. Though God does not have the same relationship with other nations as with Israel, these other nations are instruments of divine activity in the world. Hence, God is concerned about how they will assess the historical experience of Israel. In a similar way, Deut. 32:27 explains that God will turn away from punishing Israel if the other nations begin to say, "Our hand is triumphant; Yahweh did not perform all this."

10:16–19, Assyria, Like a Condemned Vineyard. As Yahweh threatened to burn and devour even the "briars and thorns" of the vineyard (5:1–7), so Assyria confronts divine punishment.

10:20–23, A Remnant Shall Return. The interpretation introduced by the stereotypic phrase "in that day" stands in contrast to the last two lines of the preceding oracle against Assyria. There the "remnant" or "remainder" of trees, which symbolize Assyria, will be so few a child could write on all of them. Here, the few Judahites who survive the Exile will be a symbol of hope (→ Remnant).

10:24–27a, God's Anger Turns Toward Assyria. Encouraging those in Zion not to be afraid, the prophet foresees a time when the anger against Judah will be directed against their present enemy, Assyria (see 14:24–27).

10:27b–32, The Advancing Enemy. An enemy, probably Assyria, traverses the map in its march toward an attack upon Jerusalem.

10:33–34, The Proud Assyrians Made Low. Echoing phrases from 2:6–22 and 5:15–17, what the Assyrians were instrumental in doing to arrogant leaders of Jerusalem and Judah will now be done to them.

11:1–9, A Shoot from the Stump of Jesse. Picking up on the brief note in 6:13b, the next verses continue the messianic promises of 9:1–7 in terms that require a fundamental change in the natural order of animal and human relations (vv. 6–9). The text envisions a time of "shalom" when everyone in the world will have full knowledge of Yahweh.

11:10–16, A Second Exodus for the Remnant Among the Nations. In a further interpretation of Ephraim and Judah as "the seed" in the stump of Jesse (11:1), a promise oracle identifies Judeans scattered among the nations as a special "ensign." A second time (v. 11), the Diaspora will be drawn together from the nations to form the nation of Israel (→ Diaspora).

12:1–6

Anticipatory Praise

The song of chap. 12 expresses confidence in God and praise for God's promised blessings. It stands between the first major collection of Isaiah's oracles and the oracles against the nations (chaps. 13–23). Its most important role in the book is to foreshadow the contribution of Isaiah 40–66. The crucial lines occur in the first verse: "Your anger turned away; you comforted me." This is the only occasion, outside the refrain in the framework around the testimony, that this same noun and verb ("anger," "turned") are found together in the book of Isaiah. Moreover, the second line is the only place in Isaiah 1–39 where an overt statement is made regarding God's "comforting" Judah, the basic theme of the second half of the book. Isa. 40:1 opens accordingly: "Comfort, comfort my people, says your God." The second verse in chap. 12 picks up again the basic message of the prophet to Ahaz (Isa. 7; 8:11–15). The assertion that God's name will be "exalted" echoes the refrain in 2:11, 17 and 5:16.

The purpose of the song is to cast the traditions of 1–39 within the perspective of the book as a whole. The two basic parts of the book of Isaiah are presented as belonging to two different periods: a time of God's anger against Judah and Jerusalem (Isa. 1–39) and a time of comfort (Isa. 40–66). Already Isa. 1:24–26, in the introduction to the book, hinted at this same temporal distinction between a period of prophetic condemnation followed "afterward" by restoration. In Isaiah 40–55, this same distinction is made between the revelation of "former things," which by implication are found in Isaiah 1–39, and "new" or "latter things" in Isaiah 40–66. Historical events of the eighth century B.C. clearly do surface at many places in Isaiah 1–39, though the wider context of the book transforms the older prophecies generally into a message addressed to later generations. In Isaiah 12 "the word of God" appears as part of a transhistorical description of the nature of God's activity in the world.

In sum, Isaiah 12 illustrates once more that the book of Isaiah is not primarily an antiquarian record of prophetic activity but is intended to provide a depiction of the nature of God's relationship to a chosen people, and to humanity in general. This organization of ancient traditions in Scripture presumes their value to later generations and, like the psalm in Isaiah 12, addresses future readers in a "present tense." However, this specific orientation to ancient prophetic traditions does not deny that they finally remain a tapestry of human words, deriving from different times and places. Editorially, these traditions cohere under the impress of the presentation of the prophet Isaiah, dependent upon, but not determined by, ordinary concerns of history.

13:1–23:18
Oracles Against the Nations

Commonly within the biblical books of prophecy, oracles against various nations are found clustered together. Similar collections occur in Amos 1:3–2:6, Jeremiah 46–51, and Ezekiel 25–32. The earliest comparable example of oracles against a foreign nation occurs as part of the activity of the Moabite seer Balaam (Num. 22–24). As in that instance, the use of prophecy against other nations is often associated with holy war, and the first verses of the oracle directed to Babylon in Isaiah 13 suggest just such an application. However, the scope of God's confrontation with the nations in Isaiah 13–23 far exceeds that of a particular moment of prophetic activity. It extends to the entire world (13:11), involves cosmic changes (13:13), and entails a final reordering of relationships among all the nations. In the most radical terms, God will "in

that day" be able to call Egypt "my people" and Assyria "the work of my hands" (19:24–25). A comparison of Isa. 13:1–16 with the opening verses of the prophetic promises in Isaiah 24–27 shows that these oracles against the nations are linked closely to an equally radical vision of the restoration of Israel. Just as Judah and Israel experience the wrath of God in response to their disobedience and yet look forward to a promise of divine restoration, so, too, judgment of nations according to the "purpose" or "plan" of God (see Isa. 14:24–27; 19:12, 17; 23:8–9) has beyond it a promise of future world peace.

Other elements within Isaiah 13–23 show how the place of these oracles within the larger composition affects their interpretation. Some repeated expressions within the judgment prophecies against Judah in Isaiah 1–12 recur in these threats against the nations. The imagery of the proud made low (13:11; 14:8–15; 16:6; 17:4) resonates with the refrain in 2:6–22. In 14:24–27 a direct play is made upon the refrain "his hand is stretched out still" in the judgment oracles of 5:25 and 9:8–20. At several places one hears again about the "rod," "staff," or "yoke" of nations that will be broken (14:5, 25, 29) in a manner that clearly recalls the same motifs in the promises present in 9:4 and throughout 10:1–11:16. This set of repeated words and phrases, which deepens in its religious significance, serves to provide continuity throughout the book.

The depiction of how God uses and relates to other nations precedes a similar concern with God's relation to the Persians in Isaiah 40–66. The appearance of Cyrus is introduced in 41:25 by the expression "I stirred up one from the north," using the same verb as 13:17, "I am stirring up the Medes against them." As with the nations, Cyrus's actions conform to God's "purpose" or "plan" (44:28; cf. 14:26), though he does not realize it (45:5; cf. 5:5–15; 14:5). Likewise, the threat against Babylon (13:17–22) closely parallels similar prophecies in 46:1–4 and 47:1–15. Once again, Isaiah 13–23 is significant because it marks out a specific religious vocabulary, providing transhistorical terms by which a believer can describe the world and the role of nations within it.

13:1–22, Against Babylon. The title (v. 1) sets the segment of traditions in chap. 13 apart from the preceding ones and associates it with the prophet Isaiah in the same style of 2:1. This and many of the prophecies that follow are designated by a technical term that can be translated either "oracle," "load," or "burden" (e.g., 13:1; 14:28; 15:1; 17:1).
13:1–16, A Holy War. The oracle encompasses the principal elements of a holy war, including inducement for national leaders to summon a public lamentation (cf. Joel 1:13–14; 2:15–17).

The nature of this battle leads to consideration of "the Day of the Lord" and a final cosmic punishment of evil throughout the whole world. Though the title has assigned this threat to Babylon, the elusive nature of the opening lines allows these words against Babylon to be viewed as a typological account of the final victory of God over all the world's unrighteous "in that day."

13:17–22, The Downfall of Babylon. Only here does the imagery identify explicit historical parties. The Medes, long-time allies of the Babylonians, will turn against them. Certainly, in the present context this threat anticipates the rise of the Persians and the defeat of the Babylonians, who were victorious over Judah about a century after the time of Isaiah's prophetic activity. Clearly, this portion of the book presumes the historical context of Isaiah 40–66.

14:1–27, Judah in Contrast to Babylon and Assyria

14:1–2, The Captors Are Captives. Judah and Israel are promised that those who took them into exile will one day become slaves themselves (see 61:5–7).

14:3–23, Taunt Against Babylon. The proud boasts of Judah's antagonist are portrayed as so pretentious as to be an assault on heaven itself (vv. 13–14). Hence, Babylon faces complete humiliation. In mockery of Babylon's sense of superiority, the dead in that once great nation will be left unburied in the streets.

14:24–27, Israel's Judgment Applied to Assyria. It is promised to Judah that Assyria will reap the same consequences as did the Northern Kingdom, Israel. The refrain in 5:25; 9:12, 17, 21; and 10:4, found within the framework around the testimony of Isaiah, is taken up and applied to Assyria (14:26–27). Likewise, the author proclaims a fulfillment of the promise in 9:4 regarding God's breaking of the "yoke" and "burden" that troubles Judah.

14:28–32, Against Philistia. Its title indicates that the date of the oracle in 14:28–32 coincides with the death of Ahaz, even as the commission report in Isaiah 6 is dated to the year Uzziah died. The death of a king represented a momentous and potentially dangerous period in which some word from God might seem timely. As in Isa. 10:5, a Mesopotamian power is called a "rod" of God. Philistia will suffer the effects of famine and destruction.

15:1–16:14, Against Moab. Two prophecies of threat occur in 15:1–9 and 16:1–5, followed by a lamentation with an additional prophecy in 16:12–13. Isaiah 16:4b–5 provides a messianic promise of the restoration of David's throne about to be fulfilled after the destruction of Moab.

17:1–11, Against Damascus and Israel. The core of the prophecy in 17:1–6 probably derives from the period of the Syro-Ephraimite war (735–733 B.C.). Damascus and Israel, the northern opponents to Judah at that time, provoke God's anger. In expressions familiar already (2:6–22), "the glory of Jacob [Israel] will be brought low" (v. 4). Within this judgment is a promise (vv. 7–8) that "in that day" people will recognize "their Maker" and no longer worship objects of their own making. This concern with idolatry seems typical of conditions in the exilic period. By wedding traditions from different periods, the prophecy gains a topical quality and is no longer interpreted solely in connection with a singular historical event.

17:12–14, Against Assyria. The judgment directed to Damascus and Israel is followed by an oracle against their enemy, Assyria. Though these verbs do not explicitly name the one to be defeated, the expressions chosen hark back to descriptions of Assyria. The "roar of many waters" recalls the imagery in 8:5–8. The "roaring" noise is reminiscent of the description of the Assyrian onslaught in 5:26–30. The sudden terror "at evening time" in v. 14 undoubtedly brings to mind the events of 701 B.C., when Jerusalem was under siege and wondrously rescued by divine intervention (see Isa. 37:33–38). The last verse offers a summary and an appraisal of how these events fit into the plan of God, similar to the summary in 14:26–27. In the description of those who "spoil," "rob," or "plunder" echoes the name of Isaiah's child Maher-shalal-hash-baz ("spoil speeds, booty hastes"; see Isa. 8:1–4). By not explicitly naming the enemy, the text asserts a pattern of how God can respond to any who might be temporarily victorious against God's own people.

18:1–7, Against Ethiopia. The mention (v. 1) of ambassadors who arrive on papyrus ships to visit Judah may harbor references to the Ashdod rebellion of 713–711 B.C. or, earlier, to the organization of an anti-Assyrian rebellion by Egypt between 705–701 B.C. In both cases Hezekiah seems to have joined the coalition. All attempts to find security through alien alliances, rather than by reliance on God alone, are doomed. The last verse, like that of 19:24–25, gives a note of promise, pointing to a time when even the Ethiopians will come to worship at Mount Zion, and it anticipates the same hope as found in Isa. 45:14.

19:1–15, Against Egypt. Under Hezekiah, Judah often looked to Egypt as an ally in the hope of fending off northern enemies. This oracle offers a general threat against Egypt, prophesying anarchy among those who desperately consult mediums for advice (cf. Isa. 8:18–19), drying up of the Nile, and a confusion of the wisdom for which the princes of Zoan (a city in the northeastern delta region of Egypt) had been famous. The last verse contains a direct play on the language of the threat against Israel in 9:14, confirming again the topical character and vitality of these expressions describing divine wrath.

19:16–24, Israel, Egypt, Assyria: "In That Day." A series of five "in that day" oracles provides brief promissory comments that look boldly into the future. The hope expressed is remarkable in its universal breadth, envisioning the complete realization of the promise to Abraham, that through Israel all the nations of the world will someday be "blessed."

20:1–6, Assyria Against Egypt and Ethiopia. A further comment conveys another divine response to Egypt, and now Ethiopia. The reference in the title to Ashdod suggests the time of the Philistines' revolt of 713–711 B.C., when they were defeated by the Assyrians. Isaiah is presented as performing the symbolic act of walking naked and barefoot for three years as "a sign and a portent" (v. 3). This act signifies that Egypt, and Ethiopia to the south, will both suffer the same fate, as a result of their coalition with Judah in revolt against Assyria in 705–701.

21:1–10, Against Babylon. Similar to 13:17–22, the prophecy in 21:1–10 looks to the future of Judah's later antagonist. Babylon will fall to the Elamites and Medes and will be replaced as a major power by the Persians. The lamentation here is comparable to that of Isaiah 47. Again the fortunes of Assyria are made parallel to the later spoiler of Judah, Babylon.

21:11–17, Against Arabia. Dumah (v. 11), Tema (v. 14), and Kedar (v. 16) are probably all provinces of Arabia (Gen. 25:13–15). The underlying events remain obscure, despite a specific time of fulfillment mentioned in v. 16. The later Greek translation of the Hebrew Bible emended "Dumah" to read "Idumea" (Edom), which might be suggested by the reference in v. 11 to Seir, a region of Edom. However, the sequence does not require that Seir and Dumah be synonymous, for the second merely describes in poetic terms the location and activity of the prophet. From whatever period these oracles may derive, they proclaim further the universal nature of God's judgment on the nations.

22:1–14, Against the "Valley of Vision." The present context makes clear that Jerusalem (see vv. 8, 10) is the object of the prophecy against the "valley of vision." The Old Greek translation unnecessarily emended the word for "vision" to "Zion" to remove any ambiguity in the title. The title is taken from v. 5 and conforms in style to other titles in the oracles against the nations. Moreover, "vision" is a term summarizing the preaching of Isaiah, with its focus on the destiny of Judah and Jerusalem (Isa. 1:1; cf. 21:2). The oracle contrasts the unabandoned celebration of a temporary victory (vv. 1–2) with the impending destruction of the city. One can readily imagine such a response when Judeans claimed dramatic relief from the siege of Jerusalem in 701 B.C. (Isa. 37:36–38), in contrast to their despair when the Babylonians sacked the city many decades later, in 586 B.C.

This tradition, similar to Isaiah 39, overtly anticipates the conditions of Babylonian exile to which Isaiah 40–66 offers hope. The account is not simply a historical recollection of past events but is presented as a lesson to be learned regarding what God expects of those who seek salvation in the light of past divine judgment and continuing promises.

22:15–25, Against Hezekiah's Royal Officials Shebna and Eliakim. The officials mentioned in 22:15–25 are also cited in the narratives of Isaiah 36–37 (= 2 Kings 18–19). The reference to Shebna appears to be an editorial addition based on Isa. 36:3 and 37:2. The text announces judgment against two leading officials associated with Hezekiah, just as the king himself looks to the future judgment in Isaiah 39. In contrast to the king, whose prayers gain him personal redemption, the other leaders under Hezekiah meet their own fates according to their belief or lack of it. Shebna is portrayed as presumptuous and subject to divine wrath (vv. 15–19), whereas Eliakim, who bears the weight of the hope symbolized by the house of David, meets defeat in the end.

These elusive accounts about individuals known elsewhere in Scripture solely by their names illustrate God's continuing attention to the obedience and disobedience of specific individuals during a time of national judgment. The last verse warns that the actions of none of these leaders was exemplary enough or sufficiently effective to avert Babylonian exile.

23:1–18, Against Phoenicia. Any collection of prophetic oracles aimed at the nations of "the whole earth" (see 13:5; 23:17) would seem incomplete without including the mighty sea traders on the northern coasts of Palestine. As in many of the other oracles, the tone is more one of lamentation than of prophecy, but with a clear note of judgment and, finally, promise at the end. Actual historical circumstances are ambiguous, though the destruction of Phoenicia is explicit. Their destiny belongs to the "purpose" of God (vv. 8–9) and, as before, results from God's hand stretched out in anger (v. 11). The once great sea trader is reduced to playing the harlot "among all the kingdoms of the world upon the face of the earth" (v. 17). This note of universality recalls the same tone present at the beginning of the oracles against the nations in 13:5, 13. The final words are a promise to Israel that all the trading goods will "be dedicated to the Lord" and will supply needs for those who remain loyal to God.

24:1–27:13
Promises and Visions of the Future

Regarded by most scholars as one of the latest sections to be included in the book of Isaiah, chaps. 24–27 combine a great variety of traditions, including lament (26:7–19), thanksgiving (24:14–16a), judgment oracles (24:1–13), and promises cast as songs (26:1–6; 27:2–5) or as standard prophetic oracles (27:6–11). Interspersed throughout this collection are citations from different parts of Isaiah, including a full revision of the song of the vineyard according to a new vision of the future (27:2–5; cf. Isa. 5:1–7).

What is contextually significant about this loose collection of traditions is their aim to interpret the earlier oracles against the nations (13–23) explicitly in terms of God's future restoration of the world. Just as Babylon appears in 13:1–16 first as an unnamed representative nation, so here in chap. 24 and in 25:1–4, a representative city is the object of divine wrath. This city is described in various ways throughout these chapters: "the city of chaos" (24:10), "the palace of aliens" (25:2), "the lofty city" (26:5), "the fortified city" (27:10). Scholars have speculated without consensus regarding its original historical identity. It seems clear the biblical writers intended that the identification of this city should remain elusive, foreshadowing Israel's antagonists, as yet unnamed, in the final confrontation of God with the world's evil powers. The destruction of this enemy city stands in sharp contrast to the restoration of the city of Jerusalem, "Mount Zion" (25:6–8, 9–12). The respective fates of these two great cities, facing a reversal of their fortunes in the course of God's plan or purpose in history, constitutes a major theme within these chapters. Threats from the enemy city and its arrogant assertions of control in human affairs are interpreted from God's point of view, which looks for "that day." When "that day" comes, the world will be purged through the fire of divine wrath so that all people may live, at last, in peace, justice, and obedience to the laws of God.

Scholars debate how these traditions form a coherent composition. Chaps. 24–26 seem to interweave (in a liturgical manner similar to Isa. 33) prophetic threats against the enemy with various prayers, including songs of lament, praise, and thanksgiving from the righteous survivors in Judah. The last chapter contains a series of short, additional eschatological judgments, each introduced with the formula "in that day" (27:1, 2, 6, 12).

24:1–26:21
The Purging Judgment of an Evil World and Israel's Praise to God

Chaps. 24–26 alternate prophetic words of judgment against unnamed enemy nations with the prayers of the redeemed in Jerusalem: 24:1–13, prophetic judgment; 24:14–16, description of praise; 24:17–23, judgment; 25:1–5, praise; 25:6–12, promise, praise, judgment; 26:1–6, praise; and 26:7–21, lament and a reassuring divine response. The collection contemplates "that day" and the final defeat of an unnamed enemy city that is a rival to Jerusalem.

24:1–13, Both the Earth and the City of Chaos Will Mourn. The surface of the earth will be catastrophically "twisted" and its inhabitants "scattered" (v. 1). This ultimate judgment of the world occurs because the people have broken the laws of "the everlasting covenant" (24:5). This same expression is used elsewhere in Hebrew Scripture to designate the special covenant God made with Noah and the world surviving the flood in Gen. 9:16. An allusion is probably being made, as well, to legal ordinance regarding land polluted with blood (Num. 35:33). This combination of allusions links the text of Isaiah to the written Torah of Moses (Gen.–Deut.) with its account of covenants of revealed "laws" and "statutes" that postexilic Israel is to obey.

The last verses (7–13) describe various scenes of devastation among the people of the nations. Their joy, their singing, and their drinking of wine in celebration all come to an end. Only "a few" people survive (v. 6), and the streets of the "city of chaos" (vv. 10–13) are deserted and its gates in ruin.

The "Torah" in Isaiah 1–39

Because the "Torah" may be viewed as the central subject matter of the Hebrew Bible, the significance of this term in Isaiah 1–39 becomes important both for understanding later Jewish interpretation of these traditions within Hebrew Scripture and for appreciating Christian options for interpreting Isaiah in the context of Christian Scripture.

The term *torah* has a range of meaning that includes "teaching, instruction, and law." This noun gained popularity as an expression of the content of the message of priests, prophets, and sages. The wide occurrence of the term to embrace the full range of biblical traditions made it an ideal concept to express the locus of biblical revelation. With the promulgation of the five-book Mosaic Torah under Ezra in the fifth century B.C., a literary standard or "canon" was established that highlighted the Torah as revealed law, with accompanying interpretation through biblical narratives and prose (see Deut. 1:5). Later, other books of Hebrew formed a "fence" or "halo" around this conception of the Torah and were viewed as commentary upon it. This scriptural ordering of traditions is similar to that of the Christian Gospels in the NT, followed by the Pauline Letters and other writings, as various witnesses to the one gospel of Jesus Christ.

The term *torah* occurs seven times in Isaiah 1–39 and twelve times in the entire book. Four of the seven instances in the first part of the book seem to equate *torah* simply with the oracles and interpretive traditions of the prophet. In 8:16 and 30:9, Isaiah's prophecies are written down and designated as "torah and testimony" and "the torah of the Lord." Also, in 1:10 and 5:24, God's torah is associated with the word of God delivered by the prophet Isaiah. However, the reference in 24:5 concerns "the statutes" and "an everlasting covenant," distinct from the teaching of Isaiah. Both of the remaining references (2:3 and 8:20) probably belong to the exilic and postexilic periods, when the Torah was specifically identified with the law revealed to Moses. Torah in Isaiah 40–66 consistently presumes a revealed Mosaic legislation as the norm against which to judge Israel's failure and the guide to future obedience and divine reward (see Isa. 42:4, 21, 24; 51:4, 7).

In sum, the book of Isaiah has identified the prophetic "word" and *"torah"* ("teaching") of Isaiah with the one Torah revealed in Hebrew Scripture. With these warrants, Jewish interpretation properly viewed Isaiah as commentary on the Mosaic Torah and assumed this same Torah to be a primary subject matter of the book of Isaiah. Though these literary connections are visible enough within Hebrew Scripture, the book of Isaiah still retains remarkable independence from specific interpretations of the Mosaic Torah. The possibility of reading the book as a source of divine promise or wisdom was, therefore, not negated by any harmonizing program in the late stages in the formation of the book. Christians, with differing views concerning the legal Torah, sought to minimize this connection in order to concentrate on promissory and sapiential (wisdom) interpretations of Isaiah, which find fulfillment or full disclosure in the gospel of Jesus Christ.

24:14–16, Songs of Praise, with a Note of Lamentation. Across the promised land, people rejoice and glorify God for what has happened throughout the world. It is logical to assume this voice, though unnamed, rises from those in Judah who have seen their vindication "on that day." The final verse expresses what

may be a cryptic word of warning from the prophet to those who too readily rejoice in the defeat of their enemies. The last expression, dependent on 21:2, produces a mysterious effect, though it may be a text error and is omitted from the Old Greek translation.

24:17–23, Enemies Thrown into the Pit. Besides describing God's continuing confrontation with the surface of the planet ("the earth staggers," v. 20), this text reports that those who try to flee from the cities, as well as the disobedient "hosts of heaven," will be as prisoners in the pit. The pit is here a symbol of the dark recesses in which the shades of the dead roam with no escape. The "hosts of heaven" is a parallel expression to "the kings of the earth" and may indicate the stars that were thought to regulate human fate. More likely (and certainly a common assumption within the history of interpretation), these divine beings are to be identified as rebellious angels (Gen. 6:1–4). In the end, a restored Jerusalem, from which God will reign, will arise (v. 23).

25:1–5, Praise to God for the Destruction of "the Palace of Aliens." A prayer glorifies God for doing "wonderful things," including the destruction of the "the city" of the enemy, which will never be rebuilt. God himself is Israel's "shelter" in the storm that destroys the alien aggressors.

25:6–12, Promise, Praise, and Judgment Against Moab. Various traditions support the pattern of these verses. God will provide a banquet for the elect, and death will be "swallow[ed] up forever." Verse 8 provides a hint of the words of comfort, which occur in the latter half of the book, that God will himself wipe away the tears of those who once suffered. Praise by the people follows in v. 9, language reminiscent of Isaiah 12. The last verses add a searing judgment against Moab, whose pride will be laid low (2:9, 11, 17).

26:1–6, A Song of Zion, a "Strong City." Picking up the central message of Isaiah, the author portrays Jerusalem as a city of "salvation," "perfect peace," and refuge for those who continue to maintain "trust" in God. Conversely, "the lofty city," which offered false security through moral compromise and international alliances, will be "made low, . . . cast . . . down to the dust" (v. 5), recalling again the imagery from Isa. 2:6–22.

26:7–21, A Hymn of Lament and an Assuring Divine Response. An extensive song of lamentation is followed by an assurance to the effect that in "a little while" (v. 20) the time of God's judgment of the nations will be complete and the answer to the prayers of Israel's past will be answered. It expresses hope, once

563

more, for a time of peace (v. 12) and a restoration of the nation (v. 15). Within this portrayal is a remarkable affirmation that "your dead will rise" and that divine light will fall on the darkness of the realm of the shades in Sheol (v. 19). Probably, as in Ezek. 37:1–14, the language is a hyperbolic expression of confidence that God will restore the nation of Israel, but without an explicit or developed conception of the resurrection of individuals. This ambiguity leaves open other possibilities for later readers who contemplate a more explicit conception of the restoration of the dead within the religious beliefs of Judaism and Christianity.

27:1–13
"In That Day" and "Those to Come"

In a series of four additional notes, the future is explored as a series of wondrous reversals of the earlier devastations of Judah and Israel.

27:1, Slaying of the Serpent Leviathan.
Employing the common ancient Near Eastern symbolism of Leviathan, the monster of chaos, the prophet confirms God's cosmic victory over the forces of evil in the world.

27:2–5, A New Song of the Vineyard, "In That Day." These verses provide the best example in the book of Isaiah of a full recasting of an earlier oracle of judgment (5:1–7) according to a message of promise that allows a reverse interpretation of its imagery. This recasting is significant since the theme of "the vineyard" and motifs within the "song" of Isaiah 5 became constitutive throughout Isaiah 1–39.

Yahweh is presented immediately as the owner of the vineyard and as the one who waters and guards it. The key motif of "briars and thorns," applied repeatedly in Isaiah 1–39 to symbolize the implication of God's wrath (5:6; 7:23–25; 10:17; 32:13), can never invade this vineyard. On the basis of this promise, Israel is twice encouraged to make peace with God.

27:6, "Jacob Shall Take Root." As in the preceding new song of the vineyard, this promise takes up a memorable theme and asserts it in unequivocably positive tones. What was a mere seed in the stump in the commission of Isaiah (6:13b) becomes subject to a promise of new growth (so Isa. 4:2; 11:1, 10). The emphasis here is on restored Israel "filling the whole world with fruit," consonant with a theme in this section and in the oracles against the nations regarding God's judgment and renovation of the entire earth.

27:7–11, The Fortified City Lies Desolate.
As in the beginning of this section, an unnamed city is deserted, its population decimated. Connected to this bleak picture is the assurance that,

through the experience of exile, "the guilt of Jacob" has been removed. In relation to the unnamed city itself, the prophet condemns a group of people who remain "without discernment." Perhaps the city of Samaria and the people later described as "Samaritans," who came to be regarded by many postexilic Jews as a misguided people (→ Samaritans), provide the historical background. Regardless, in the context of Isaiah 25–27, a city is portrayed as representative of false centers of power and pretension that can be contrasted with God's chosen people and city of Zion.

27:12–13, The Exiled Return. The section concludes with the remnant of exiled Israel returned to their land and to "the holy mountain" of Jerusalem.

28:1–33:24
Judgments and Promises to Judah

The pattern of judgment followed by promise oracles is basic to the book of Isaiah. Consistent with this pattern, Isaiah 28–35 offers a collection of, essentially, judgment oracles against Judah in chaps. 28–32, followed by a liturgical condemnation of Assyria in Isaiah 33, and then oracles of promise in chaps. 34 and 35. A closer examination suggests further resemblances between these chapters and other sections of the book. Within Isaiah 1–12, there were seven "woe oracles" against Judah (5:8–24 and 10:1–4) around the testimony (6:1–9:7), followed by judgments against Assyria, which were introduced with a woe oracle in 10:5–11. The same pattern may be observed in the organization of Isaiah 28–32. The collection of judgments is introduced and segmented with woe oracles (see Isa. 28:1; 29:1, 15; 30:1; 31:1), followed by a liturgical condemnation of Assyria that begins with a woe oracle as well (see 33:1).

In very general terms, the prophecies in Isaiah 2–9 concentrated on Judah's response during the time of the Syro-Ephraimite war; those in Isaiah 28–32 are mostly related to later events associated with Hezekiah's rebellion against Sennacherib (705–701 B.C.), as are the subsequent narratives in Isaiah 36–37. Despite this evidence of different historical periods underlying these prophetic oracles, these historical backgrounds play a persistent but limited role in the present context. The editors have presented the prophecies in continuity with the pattern present in earlier portions of the book. The chapter reinforces the now familiar scenario of God's judgment, followed by the assurance of divine promises, national restoration, and world peace. Throughout the various subcollections, editors have ensured that the language reverberates with certain recurring idioms indicative of the message and distinctive style of Isaiah.

28:1–29
Woe to Ephraim and to the Rulers in Judah

28:1–6, Proud Ephraim Is Brought Down. The woe oracles in the first section of the book concerned Judah (5:8–24; 10:1–4) and were preoccupied with excessive drinking on the part of leaders as a sign of the fading glory (v. 4) of the nation. Now, with the addressee as Ephraim, the author picks up again the familiar motif of the proud being cast down to the earth (v. 2). The punishment, which seems to assume the exile of the Northern Kingdom, introduces the rest of the judgment oracles in Isaiah 28–32 as focusing on Judah, which remains in the land.

28:7–13, Misguided Priests and Prophets. An indictment is made of those who, like the Ephraimites, remain drunken and resistant to the consistent message of Isaiah not to resist the Assyrian threat (v. 7). The meaning of the repeated lines (vv. 10, 13) continues to be debated, and they vary greatly from translation to translation. The Old Greek version took the words to mean "affliction upon affliction, hope upon hope." These repetitious monosyllables may be part of a chant used by children in learning the alphabet. Whether the line is a childish ditty or drunken nonsense, it indicates how they misunderstood the word of God and serves as a sign associated with their punishment.

28:14–22, Rulers of Jerusalem Rebuked. The nation's political leaders are portrayed as "scoffers" (vv. 14, 22), who have made a "covenant with death." Foreign alliances again fly in the face of the prophet's message to believe and have no fear; God has made a promise to Zion.

28:23–29, God's Actions Are Like Those of a Wise Farmer. Drawing on common knowledge about the different times and the various planting and harvesting techniques that ensure a successful farm, a parable is provided that explains the diverse ways in which God responds to his people. The wisdom of such a farmer is comparable to the wisdom of God. This analogy perhaps answers those who question the counsel of the prophet during the Assyrian crisis.

29:1–24
Woe Ariel, City of David

29:1–8, The City Under Siege. Jerusalem (Ariel) is under siege as a judgment of the Lord, but the siege is suddenly averted by a "visitation" of the Lord (vv. 5–6). The occasion for this saying was probably the wondrous abandonment of the siege by Sennacherib in 701, as described in Isa. 37:33–38.

29:9–12, A Spirit of Deep Sleep. Consistent with God's statement in the commissioning of Isaiah in 6:9–10, the people will be blind to the truth of the prophet's word, though their eyes are wide open. Although the prophet's message is clearly present before them, it is like a sealed book, they cannot appropriate it.

29:13–14, Lip Service in Worship. The same theme of a lack of understanding, despite a verbalization of beliefs, leads God to increase the confusion of the wise in Judah.

29:15–24
Woe to Ones Hiding from God's Counsel

29:15–16, Those Who Turn Things Upside Down. Many of the prophet's earlier oracles mocked the Assyrians for thinking they were more than a mere "rod" of God's wrath (10:15). The unresponsive in Judah are here portrayed as equally foolish, thinking they are the potter when they are only the clay. They falsely assume they can do things in secret that will never be exposed.

29:17–24, A Vision of Promise. This note offers assurance that the deaf will someday hear and those blind to the message in Judah will understand it. These words clearly set the preceding judgments of Isaiah 28–29 within the context of a divine plan in which the destruction is intended to purge the nation of disobedience and lead to a time of discernment and restoration.

30:1–33
Woe to the Rebellious Children

30:1–5, "A Plan, but Not Mine." Warning is given to those who, as did Hezekiah, seek alliances with Egypt as a way to hold off the enemy. All these efforts lack God's counsel and will end in public shame.

30:6–7, Egypt's Worthless Help. These obscure words seem to describe the dangerous route of emissaries from Judah who seek Egypt's help. The reference to Rahab, a mythical monster of chaos, makes mockery of the great images of gods in Egypt, which are intimidating in appearance but powerless to move.

30:8–17, A Book of Divine Instruction Despised. As in the testimony (6:1–9:7), the prophet is once more presented as making a public record of his message, which the officials have refused to hear or acknowledge. As in the commissioning of Isaiah (6:9–10), the leaders of Judah actively seek to be ignorant of the prophet's message, even encouraging prophets to lie so that the oracles may be heard as they wish them to be. An indictment and threat follows (vv. 12–14) that finds vivid analogy to Judah's ruin with a break in a wall and a shattered vessel. Finally, the oracle repeats what has been heard before, namely, that Judah has rejected the central message of Isaiah (v. 15) and will, therefore, fall victim to its enemies.

30:18–26, A Wondrous Restoration. As in 29:17–24, promise is juxtaposed with the announcement of divine wrath to clarify the purpose and goal of the chastisement of God's chosen people. In terms like that of Isaiah 24–27, the graciousness of God will conclude the period of punishment by establishing a whole new situation for Zion. The blindness and dumbness that have plagued Judah will disappear. Idolatry will be abandoned; the natural order will be transformed so that rain will be unusually abundant; and the moon will be as bright as the sun. God will completely heal "the wounds inflicted by his blow."

30:27–33, The Fall of the Assyrians. Consistent with the preceding assurance is a statement that anticipates the sacking of Nineveh, the capital city of Assyria, in 612 B.C. After abandoning the siege of Jerusalem in the time of Hezekiah, the Assyrian king confronts the full retribution of God, and Judah exults in the triumph of God over the long-familiar adversary.

31:1–32:20
Woe to Those Who Go Down To Egypt

The prophet explores a theme familiar within this section of the book by continuing to denounce those who seek security in an alliance with Egypt.

31:1–3, Egypt Instead of the Holy One of Israel. In a poignant reminder that horses and chariots are not comparable to the power of God, Judah is warned, once more, against making foreign alliances. Judah's dependence on such alliances entails a political compromise that explicitly rejects the counsel of Yahweh.

31:4–9, Yahweh as a Lion. The description of God as a wild beast in pursuit of prey recalls the imagery of Assyria's attack upon Judah (Isa. 5:29–30). God, like a hovering bird, will protect Jerusalem.

32:1–8, Eyes Shall See, Ears Shall Hear. As with other prophecies of promise, a common feature in Isaiah is the appearance of an ideal king who will "rule in justice." Accompanying this event will be a reversal of the responses by the people listed in the commission of the prophet (6:9–10). They will, at last, "see" and "hear"; their minds will become rational; and they will be able to speak clearly (v. 4). Verses 6–8 probably derive from later, postexilic interpretation cast in language typical of wisdom literature. A series of proverbial sayings contrast the actions of "the fool" and "the scoundrel." The writer seems to assume that when the people can hear and see normally again, then the logic of wisdom will be applicable in a standard fashion. This passage illustrates well both the independence and complementarity of wisdom and prophecy.

32:9–14, Women Who Are at Ease. In a threat against wealthy women, similar to that of 3:16–17, the prophet summons them to mourn (vv. 9–12) over the destruction to come "in little more than a year." The description of the destruction of the city plays directly upon the language of the song of the vineyard in Isa. 5:1–7. In place of a fruitful economy, there will be "thorns and briars"; the once "joyful city" will be deserted, and its "watchtower" will be inhabited by wild animals.

32:15–20, Justice as a Future Promise. A fitting positive conclusion to all that has preceded in Isaiah 2–32 looks toward the time when all the promises given will be fulfilled. The final wisdom saying, "Happy are those ..." (v. 20) provides comfort for those who will live in the time of "peace." Such will be the reward for those who obey the prophetic instruction to seek "righteousness, quietness, and trust forever" (v. 17). By so referring to the essence of the prophet's message to troubled eighth-century B.C. Judah, the earlier sections in the book are brought to a crescendo and made to apply to later readers. These verses may once have belonged to the conclusion of an edition of Isaiah's oracles completed during the reign of Josiah, an edition that included much of Isa. 2:5–32:14.

33:1–24
Woe to the Destroyer

A summary of the prophet's message is accompanied by an appropriate response by the people. Chap. 33 is a composite of once independent units or fragments of tradition, suggesting a special function prior to its placement here. It may once have been a prophetic liturgy that expressed, in a later period, the people's recognition of Isaiah's prophecies and their desire for God's salvation. Performed with antiphonal responses, this impressive oral tradition contains the laments of the people and a challenge to them to be righteous, as well as a vivid denunciation of their enemy. The different traditions have not been harmonized and are, therefore, readily discernible: vv. 1–6, a prophetic threat against "the destroyer"; vv. 7–9, a lamentation of the people; vv. 10–13, another threat against the enemy; vv. 14–16, a Torah interrogation like that found in Pss. 15 and 24:3–6; vv. 17–19, a promise oracle; vv. 20–22, a hymn of confidence like that of Psalm 23; v. 23, another threat; and v. 24, a prophetic promise to Judah. Whether or not the unnamed enemy was Babylon, as seems plausible, the context of this chapter makes it representative and applicable to future times when foes rise up against those who look to the words of Isaiah and hope for a messianic age of peace.

34:1–35:10
The Future of Zion

Much like those in the preceding chapter, the traditions in chaps. 34–35 are editorial compositions that recall the earlier traditions in Isaiah 2–32 and anticipate those found in Isaiah 40–66. Whoever composed them had traditions from both these parts of the book of Isaiah at hand. Chaps. 34–35, a learned transition between these differing sets of traditions, weaves them together thematically. The subtle relationships between these two chapters suggest that they were originally composed together. They build on a familiar pattern of judgment against the nations (34:1–17) and promises of deliverance to Judah (35:1–10).

34:1–17
Judgment Against the Nations

Continuing important themes found in the oracles against the nations (Isa. 13–23), chap. 34 addresses a prophetic judgment to all the people of the earth, expressing the rage of God "against all the nations" (v. 2). In a melange of poetic descriptions, the prophet paints a picture of bloody consequences, deserted strongholds, and the ruins of once famous cities overtaken by nature. The perspective is cosmic—"the skies will roll up like a scroll" (v. 4)—and depicts a final confrontation between God and all the nations of the earth. A prime example is made of Edom, whose name will be changed to "No Kingdom." An unusual note is the command that one should "seek and read from the book of the Lord" (v. 16). This admonition presumes the existence of some authoritative "book" of prophecy. In theory, this phrase once could have referred to some unknown collection of oracles, perhaps either an earlier collection

of Isaiah's prophecies or oracles against the nations. Nonetheless, in its present context, this authoritative book seems to refer to the book of Isaiah as a whole. This tradition belongs to the latest stages in the formation of the book, and presents an admonition to its future readers. Cast in the voice of the prophet Isaiah, this reference is comparable to that of Moses in Deut. 31:26–29.

35:1–10
A Summary of God's Promises

Resembling 32:15–20, chap. 35 brings the oracular prophecies in the first part of the book to a rapturous crescendo. The wilderness left in the wake of Judah's destruction will blossom; the weak will be made strong; waters will flow in the desert; and wild animals will no longer roam the ruins of the city. This great reversal of earlier misfortunes will be greeted by the people as they march to Zion with joyful songs. Note how songs punctuate the book of Isaiah (5:1–7, 12) and offer guides to interpretation of the prophecies within it.

Many of the expressions in 35:1–10 are direct citations of or allusions to the oracles in Isaiah 40–55. At the same time, the passage contains numerous references to the preceding traditions. In v. 4, Isaiah's central message, "Be strong, fear not," is reaffirmed. In vv. 5–6, the blindness and deafness of those who have heard the word of God through the prophet recall the report of the commission of the prophet in Isa. 6:9–10. The depiction of a "highway" echoes similar accounts in 19:19–25 and 27:12–14. The effect, within this context, gives readers an epitome of the promises of God throughout the book of Isaiah. The portrayal of restoration far exceeds the historical experience of Judah both after the return from the Babylonian exile and after the return from the Diaspora to the land of Israel. Its horizon lies in the ultimate renovation of the entire world and, consequently, in the hope of future readers of this prophetic book.

36:1–39:8
Jerusalem and Further Intrigue with the Assyrians and the Babylonians

With the exception of the long prayer of Hezekiah in 38:9–20, chaps. 36–39 are taken verbatim from 2 Kings 18:3–20:19. The first two chapters concern the siege of Jerusalem in 705–701 B.C. by the Assyrian king Sennacherib and God's wondrous deliverance. The last chapter finds, in the visit of a Babylonian king, a prediction of Judah's later devastation and exile under the Babylonians in 586 B.C.

567

The change in the context of these traditions, from their former place within the books of 1 and 2 Kings to their use in the book of Isaiah, entails a natural shift in their interpretation. Concern with the city of Jerusalem remains prominent in these chapters. The prayer of Hezekiah paradigmatically shows how one should respond to Isaiah's message and, by analogy, summons a similar response from postexilic Jewish believers. Hezekiah's illness, like Judah's exile, is perhaps something God "has done" (38:15); the king's prayer to be restored to health and to be allowed to live (v. 16) corresponds to the national hope of Judah. There is a resonance between personal and communal experience in this text. Such resonance is reinforced by God's response to Hezekiah, which includes a defense of Jerusalem from further attacks by the Assyrian king (38:6).

Finally, Isaiah 39 serves to shift readers' attention away from the events around the Assyrian threat in the eighth century B.C. to later Babylonian destructions in the sixth. Topically, it prepares readers for the "comfort" given to those in Babylonian exile (Isa. 40–66). In 40:2 this very focus on the fate of Jerusalem is expressed again, as it is throughout the book of Isaiah generally (see Isa. 1).

36:1–37:38
God's Deliverance of Jerusalem from Sennacherib

The siege of Jerusalem in 701 B.C. and the claim of the city's sudden deliverance occasioned a wide variety of responses, both as a subject in the oracles of the prophet and in these narrative accounts. Elsewhere in Scripture additional narrative reports are provided in 2 Kings 18:13–16 and in 2 Chron. 32:1–23. There is even an account in the annals of Sennacherib that makes reference to Hezekiah and to the siege of Jerusalem, though without mention of a sudden departure by the Assyrians. The relation between historical events and these differing traditions remains a perennial topic of scholarly debate. The biblical traditions obviously are written with a purpose in mind other than chronological reporting of historical events. The overall structure and selectivity of these reports reflect the same perspective. A scenario of similar events is repeated in both 36:1–37:9a and 37:9b–39. Each narrative includes an Assyrian threat to Heze-

Opposite: Assyrian battering ram and archers (top) and Judahite exiles carrying provisions (bottom); scenes from the Assyrian conquest of the Judahite city of Lachish in 701 B.C., as shown on reliefs from the palace of Sennacherib, Nineveh. The Assyrians also threatened Jerusalem and King Hezekiah (Isa. 36:1–37:38; 2 Kings 18:13–19:37).

kiah, Hezekiah's response, Isaiah's prophetic word of assurance, and deliverance as fulfillment of the word of the prophet. In both accounts, there is an escalation of the threat and of the tension felt by the king. In the first, the king assumes mourning dress and goes to the Temple to pray (37:1); in the second, his lengthy prayer forms part of the report (37:16–20). In the first, Isaiah sends a brief message of promise to the king (37:6–7); in the second, the prophet's oracle starts a long denunciation of the enemy (37:22–29). In the first, the Assyrian king is diverted by a false rumor (37:8–9a); in the second, an army of the heavenly hosts directly intervenes and slays 185,000 Assyrian soldiers while they sleep (38:36). These accounts appear remarkably suitable to the larger purpose of the book of Isaiah, with its concern for the restoration of Jerusalem. They explore the way in which human responses move God to leave a blessing when one might expect only a curse.

36:1–37:9a, Rescued by a False Rumor. The first scenario of events gives greatest weight to the intimidation by and verbal abuse of the Rabshakeh to the inhabitants of Jerusalem. "The Rabshakeh" is a title, perhaps meaning "chief cupbearer." The position of this person may have been similar to that of Eliakim, the steward of Hezekiah's palace. Addressing Hezekiah by name, the Rabshakeh publicly denounces the confidence of Hezekiah and the people that God will save them from the Assyrian king. The effect of this caustic speech is heightened by the Jerusalem officials' interruption of it and their request that the emissary speak in Aramaic rather than in Hebrew, which the city's inhabitants could understand. Refusing this request, the Rabshakeh intensifies his denunciation and in a lengthy argument encourages the people of Jerusalem to defect before it is too late (36:13–20). The author creates suspense through the details describing the officials rending their garments while bearing the news to the king of Jerusalem. The king rushes to the Temple to pray and sends for Isaiah, who can give a fresh word from God. According to the word of God, the Assyrians take seriously a false rumor and abandon the siege. A common human experience, falling prey to a false rumor, is here seen specifically as an act of divine intervention.

37:9b–38, A Wondrous Deliverance. The opening connection with the preceding account is vague. In any case, a further confrontation takes place between the king of Assyria and Hezekiah. This time the Assyrian message is brief and focused on discrediting Yahweh as powerless against the Assyrian deities. Hezekiah takes the letter to the Temple and offers an extensive prayer that expresses his confidence in God and the need to show the world of nations that "you alone are the Lord" (v. 20). The word of God through Isaiah recalls common themes in chaps. 2–35; for example, the lofty will fall (v. 29); God will bring things to pass according to a divine plan (v. 26); and God has intimate knowledge of the nations regardless of their acknowledging God (v. 28). This word is accompanied by a divine promise regarding the remnant of Judah that will take root and grow from "out of Jerusalem." The assurance by God, that "I will defend this city" for the sake of David (v. 35), points again to a view of Zion's inviolability, which is affirmed throughout Isaiah 1–39. The deliverance is tersely described and expanded by an account of the death of the Assyrian king in a coup carried out by his sons while he was worshiping his gods. Yahweh's willingness to save Jerusalem has been illustrated graphically here and prepares the reader of this book for the hope expressed in Isaiah 40–66, namely, that through mighty acts of God the city will be rebuilt out of the rubble of Babylonian destruction.

38:1–22
Hezekiah's Recovery from Illness

Within the context of internationally significant events attested in Isaiah 36–37 and 39, the story of Hezekiah's recovery may seem incidental and very personal. Hezekiah has been ill and is near death. Isaiah brings word to the king that he will soon die. Rather than acquiescing to this oracle, King Hezekiah asks God to remember that he has done consistently as king that which God has demanded. A new word comes through Isaiah that includes an assurance that fifteen more years will be added to the king's life, that Assyria will not conquer Jerusalem in this time, and that the sundial will reverse itself as a sign (vv. 5–8, cf. 7:11) of God's will to do these things. A lengthy prayer of Hezekiah has been inserted subsequently (vv. 9–20). The story concludes with a note regarding the way in which Hezekiah was healed.

This story is significant since it presents Hezekiah as an exemplary believer and illustrates how prayers of the righteous can change God's response. The last two verses are out of place because the question in v. 22 has already been answered by vv. 7–8, as in an earlier version of the same story (2 Kings 20:8–11). The sequence of elements in the original story has been disturbed by the addition of the prayer (vv. 9–20) so that Hezekiah now appears to offer two prayers. The former may be considered a summary of its later written counterpart. The first, as found also in 2 Kings 20, simply asserts his innocence; the second account (Isa. 38:9–20) consists of a complaint, reminiscent of laments in the Psalms, that ends with communal praise: "We will sing . . . at the house of the

Lord" (v. 20). The similarity to the psalms of David is conspicuous. This presentation has the effect of illustrating how the Psalms offer models of prayers to be offered by individuals in times of stress and calamity.

39:1–8
Jerusalem and the Future Babylonian Threat

The account in chap. 39 corrects any impression gained from the preceding account that might seem to preclude the possibility of the capture of Jerusalem at a later time. The king of Babylon, a minor kingdom during the time of the mighty Assyrians, pays a visit to Jerusalem and to King Hezekiah. Hezekiah proudly displays all the national treasures. After the visit, Isaiah asks the king of Judah what he showed to the Babylonian king. When the prophet hears that it was everything of value, he delivers an oracle of judgment. The Babylonians will someday return with a great army to rob Judah of all that Hezekiah has proudly shown. The only compensation to Hezekiah, presumably because of his obedience to God (38:3), is that the calamity will not occur in his generation. Hezekiah responds with thankfulness that, at least in his days, there will be "peace and truth." Ironically, the same king who saw the most dramatic deliverance of Jerusalem is the first to hear of a distant threat against the city from the Babylonians.

The placement of this story after the preceding chapters appears intentional, since the historical events are prior to those referred to in Isaiah 36–37. Within the book of Isaiah, this tradition brings a fitting conclusion to Isaiah 1–39, for it predicts the Babylonian exile, which the oracles in Isaiah 40–66 turn to address. The opening words of Isaiah 40 replace words of judgment with comfort, both to the people in Babylonian exile and to the city of Jerusalem. The unjust city that now lies in ruins will be fully restored to become the righteous city that God had purposed it to be from its beginning (Isa. 1 and 66).

Bibliography

Ackroyd, P. "Isaiah I–XII, Presentation of a Prophet." *Vetus Testamentum, Supplements* 29 (1978): 16–48.

Childs, B. *Isaiah and the Assyrian Crisis.* Studies in Biblical Theology, 2nd ser., 3. London: SCM, 1967.

Clements, R. *Isaiah 1–39.* New Century Bible Commentary. Grand Rapids, MI: Eerdmans, 1980.

Holladay, W. *Isaiah: Scroll of a Prophetic Book.* Grand Rapids, MI: Eerdmans, 1978.

Kaiser, O. *Isaiah 1–12.* Old Testament Library. Philadelphia: Westminster, 1983.

———. *Isaiah 13–39.* Old Testament Library. Philadelphia: Westminster, 1974.

ISAIAH 40-66

RICHARD J. CLIFFORD

INTRODUCTION

Isaiah 40–55 and 56–66 are collections of prophetic speeches dating to the second half of the sixth century B.C. and appended to chaps. 1–39, the bulk of which records the eighth-century ministry of Isaiah of Jerusalem. The separation and delineation of chaps. 40–66 is the achievement of critical scholarship in the last two centuries; even the names "Second" and "Third" Isaiah are modern designations for these two anonymous collections. Prior to the Enlightenment, it was assumed that Isaiah wrote chaps. 1–66 of the Book of Isaiah in the eighth century B.C.

Chaps. 40–55 are easily dated. The author assumes throughout that his hearers in Babylon are aware that Cyrus II, king of Persia, will conquer the Neo-Babylonian Empire. Such an assumption was possible only after Cyrus deposed his sovereign Astyages of Media in 550 B.C. and conquered Croesus of Lydia in 547. Second Isaiah must have preached, therefore, in the 540s, probably until the entry of Cyrus's army into Babylon in 539. The author of chaps. 56–66, probably a disciple, preached in Jerusalem to a mixed community of residents and those who had returned from exile in Babylon. Most, if not all, of these chapters come from the period between Cyrus's edict in 538 and the rebuilding of the Temple in 515.

The Prophetic Tradition

Both prophets spoke from a centuries-old prophetic tradition. The pre-exilic institutions (esp. monarchy) that defined the prophet's social role had been destroyed by the deportations of the early sixth century B.C., but the prophetic literary tradition survived. That tradition divided God's relations with Israel after the conquest into three successive stages, sin, punishment, and restoration; each involved a prophetic task. The first was the period of Israel's sin, during which prophets prepared the people to submit to impending divine punishment at the hands of the Assyrians (Amos, Hosea, Isaiah) and the Babylonians (Jeremiah, Ezekiel). The second stage was the punishment itself, exile; the prophets preached submission and hope of restoration (Jeremiah and Ezekiel). Second Isaiah belongs wholly to the third stage; he preached restoration. Like other prophets who anticipated in their own lives the divine plan for Israel, the prophet-servant exemplifies acceptance of the exilic punishment and obedient return. His task was to deepen the spirit of acceptance and to lead the return. The author of Third Isaiah defined what restoration meant. To be present physically in Zion is not enough; the people must await a winnowing judgment that will make them true Israel.

Isaiah's own version of the tradition influenced Second and Third Isaiah. Zion is the dwelling of the all-holy God, where Israel comes to life. Isaiah preached the decree of judgment he heard in the divine assembly (chap. 6); the author of Second Isaiah preached the decree of restoration he heard (40:1–11). The Assyrian king had been the instrument of punishment for Zion (10:5–19); the Persian king was the instrument of the restoration for Zion (44:24–45:13). Second Isaiah also exploits several times the darkness-light sequence of 8:16–9:7 for exile-restoration. He utilizes, of course, other traditions, e.g., the new exodus-conquest tradition from Hosea 2 and Ezekiel 20.

Third Isaiah is eclectic, borrowing Second Isaiah's servant language to describe the righteous poor who will inherit the land and occasionally turning its predecessor's new exodus-conquest notion into the righteous path that leads to life, a theme of wisdom literature. From Isaiah comes the idea of a winnowing judgment in Zion separating out true Israel (1:21–28; chaps. 28–33). Pre-exilic denunciations of false leaders and false worship are used to resolve community conflicts. New is his judgment oracle; instead of indicting all Israel, it distinguishes between the wicked and the righteous, assigning a different lot to each. New also is a lack of specificity about the human agency that will accomplish the divine plans, a harbinger of later apocalyptic literature.

Appropriate Method of Study

A major problem affecting interpretation of both prophets is how to determine the length of the units that make up their collections. The dominant approach today, heir to both the source criticism of B. Duhm's influential commentary of 1892 and the form criticism of H. Gressmann, J. Begrich, and C. Westermann, is especially sensitive to "logical inconsistencies" and to what is typical and recurrent in the chapters. The method is quick to find sources and insertions, e.g., the idol passages (e.g., Isa. 41:21–24) and the four "servant songs" (Isa. 42:1–4; 49:1–6; 50:4–11; 52:13–53:12), and to define the unit based upon a judgment about its genre. Not surprisingly, such an approach concludes there are between forty-five and seventy separate and relatively brief units in chaps. 40–55. J. Muilenburg's pioneering 1956 commentary, unusually appreciative of poetic originality and rhetoric, argued for nineteen lengthy compositions. In this commentary I follow Muilenburg, though with emphasis upon the prophet's program of action. I propose that there are seventeen substantial speeches, which advance their ideas with remarkable subtlety and compactness. The boundaries proposed for some speeches are tentative.

Message of Second Isaiah

The prophet's persistent use of five paired concepts provides a convenient entry into the style and thought of the chapters (and a further argument that the speeches are long and closely argued). By the interplay of these concepts, he interprets the national tradition to the exiles and exhorts them to act. The first two pairs are "first" and "last," and Babylon and Zion. "New things" sometimes means the new exodus-conquest, which is contrasted with the "first things," the old exodus-conquest; Israel must leave Babylon (Egypt) and journey to Zion (Canaan). The new act is validated by its resemblance to the ancient one. Babylon, like Egypt of old, is the land of oppression and false gods (chaps. 46, 47), to be stripped by Yahweh of her "lords" (the gods Bel and Nebo) and her children (inhabitants). Zion, on the other hand, is to be glorified by the return in the exodus-conquest of her Lord and children (49:14–26; 50:1–52:8; chap. 54). The next two contrasts are also linked: Yahweh and the gods, Israel and the nations. In the polytheistic ancient Near East, a god was acclaimed supreme by powerful action. The most powerful action was creation, which in the ancient East was creation not just of the physical world but of a fully articulated society. In Second Isaiah, creation occurs through the defeat of the enemies that keep Israel from coming into being in Zion; the enemies are both historical (Babylon) and suprahistorical (the sterile and impassable desert that bars the people's return to Zion). Only Yahweh predicted Cyrus's victory over Babylon and the journey through the desert (esp. in the great trial scenes, 41:1–42:9; 43:9–44:5; 44:6–23; 45:14–25; and in chaps. 48 and 49), proving he creates Israel by mere word. The fourth polarity, Israel and the nations, is closely related to the third, because each nation reflects on earth the power of its patron god. The nations' mute and immobile statues reflect only the nothingness of their heavenly patrons. Israel, however, when it acts by taking part in the exodus-conquest through the sterile desert, witnesses to the supremacy of Yahweh (43:9–10; 44:6–7; and 55:4–5). The fifth and last polarity is the servant and Israel. The servant, honored and obedient friend of Yahweh, represents what all the people are called to be; hence there is a polar relationship between servant and people. Like the servant, Israel is called to accept the Exile as just punishment from Yahweh (50:4–11) and to march in the exodus-conquest (42:1–9; 49:1–13; 52:13–53:12).

The servant in Second Isaiah has fascinated readers from earliest times. The loyalists of the book of Daniel understood themselves as the servants, "the wise" (playing on a meaning of 52:13; RSV: "he shall prosper") whose death aids the many to understand (Dan. 11:32–35). The righteous sufferer in the Wisdom of Solomon draws on the same speech, as do NT passages like Mark 10:45 and Acts 8:28–35. Modern controversy about the servant stems largely from B. Duhm's *Die Theologie der Propheten* in 1875, which isolated "the servant songs" (42:1–4; 49:1–6; 50:4–11; 52:13–53:12) as the work of an author other than Second Isaiah. Scholars have attempted to identify the servant with many different historical figures, but without reaching a consensus. In recent years interest has turned to the servant's function rather than his identity. Most still hold, however, that the servant songs are additions to the text.

This commentary proposes the songs are integral to their contexts. Duhm, influenced by source criticism from pentateuchal research, failed to recognize the servant–people dialectic. "Servant" in Second Isaiah has a politico-religious meaning: an official whose relationship to his god or king is one of loyalty and love, in keeping with the personalized politics of the culture. His task was to see that the people did the will of his sovereign; he stood over against them on the side of his god or king and also represented them to the sovereign. The servant's dialectical role is especially clear when he anticipates in his own person the divine plan for all the people. Moses fled Egypt and met God at Sinai (Exod. 1–4) before the people did in Exodus 19–24. Jeremiah underwent in his famous confessions the people's anguish of exile. (Both Moses and Jeremiah, significantly, serve as models for the portrait of the servant in chap. 49). The servant has submitted to the Exile and is preparing to return to Zion in a new exodus-conquest. The people are called to be like the servant or, more accurately, to be the servant, accepting exile and returning to Zion.

572

The structure of chaps. 40–55 shows no overall design. Isa. 40:1–9 and chap. 55 are obviously opening commission and final exhortation. Cyrus appears from chap. 41 to 48, and Zion, as a developed theme, from 44:24 to the end.

The complex speeches have a single aim: to persuade the exiled people to join the servant in that act through which they will become Israel once more, the exodus-conquest.

Was Second Isaiah's basic prediction largely mistaken? Despite the conquest of Babylon and the resumption of national life in Zion, many scholars suggest that his predictions of unalloyed happiness and political power remained entirely unfulfilled (see Whybray). One must respect, however, his either/or preaching of creation: *either* the triumph of Babylon and the desert *or* the creation of Israel in Zion by their defeat. The problem of "unalloyed happiness and political power" becomes the stuff of Third Isaiah's preaching.

The divine word, however, did exceed its late sixth-century B.C. realization. The message lived on to animate "the wise" of Dan. 11:32–35, the righteous of Wisdom of Solomon, and early Christians, all of whom looked for the regeneration of Israel through the vicarious action of the servant.

Message of Third Isaiah

Though scholars are not all agreed that chaps. 56–66 are from a single author, a minority postulating the chapters to be an anthology from different times, there is a consistent message. To the returnees, uncertain about their claim on the land and what it means to be Israel in a still devastated Zion, the prophet preaches that Yahweh in a future act of judgment will rebuild the community in Zion so that the divine glory will be revealed. To be Israel means adhering to the commandments and awaiting that creative visitation. The divine act will separate true Israel from the wicked, who oppress their neighbors and close themselves to the coming renewal.

The coming judgment of upholding the poor and putting down the wicked seems, to some scholars, to reflect class conflict between the Zadokite party, who wanted to rebuild the Temple according to Ezekiel 40–48, and the visionaries of Third Isaiah, who expected God to create directly a new, egalitarian community. There is undoubtedly class conflict behind the chapters, but to be specific regarding the groups is difficult. Hebrew rhetoric customarily dramatizes moral choice as a conflict between wicked and good groups; hence, sociological conclusions must remain tentative.

Chaps. 56–66 are structured around a centerpiece, chaps. 60–62, the glorification of Zion; five speeches precede it, and five follow. Chaps. 60–62 are framed by a lament ending with the coming of Yahweh to Zion (Isa. 59:20–21) and by a poem that reports the coming of Yahweh to Zion (63:1–6). The latter poem is followed by a lament (63:7–64:12). The first section, 56:1–8, declares righteousness to be the only criterion for entry into the new Jerusalem, even for foreigners. The last section, 66:18b–24, depicts a great procession to Zion, with foreigners bringing their gifts.

COMMENTARY

40:1–55:13
Second Isaiah

40:1–11
God Decrees Salvation for Exiled Israel

The scene, like chap. 6 of Isaiah, is the divine assembly in heaven, presided over by Yahweh, the God of Israel. In comparable scenes outside the Bible, the gods, after discussion, decree what will happen on earth. In such scenes within the Bible, Yahweh's decree is supreme; discussion is only about which of the thoroughly subordinate heavenly beings will carry it out (1 Kings 22:19–23; Job 1:6–12; 2:1–6). This scene alludes to and reverses Isaiah 6, in which Israel's punishment was decreed and the prophet sent to announce it. The voices in 40:1–5 are those of the heavenly courtiers implementing the decree. In vv. 6–8, one of them speaks to the prophet, who, like his master, Isaiah of Jerusalem, is told to announce what he has seen and heard to the people of God. Jerusalem, personified as a mother and queen, is told to go up to a high mountain and announce the coming of Yahweh to the cities of Judah.

40:1–2, Convey the News of Release! A heavenly official conveys the divine command to the court in v. 1. The period of punishment is over. Ancients often imagined divine visitations lasting for a set term; Jeremiah, for instance, saw the Exile as lasting seventy years (Jer. 25:11; 29:10).

40:3–5, Build a Highway for Our God. An official commands the assembly to build a road through the desert separating Babylon from Palestine, impassable because of its lack of water and precipitous slopes (like the deserts of

Sinai and the Negeb rather than the sandy Sahara). "Highway" alludes to the exodus-conquest from Egypt to Canaan through the Wilderness of Sinai as well as to the triumphant procession of God's people to his shrine after his creation victory (cf. Exod. 15:13–18); it may also refer to the processional ways of Babylonian feasts. Israel's return home will manifest Yahweh's glory because the nations will see that Yahweh is able to snatch his client people from Babylon and revive them in his own land.

40:6–8, The Prophet's Commission. A courtier tells the prophet to publicize on earth what he has seen and heard, just as his prophetic predecessor had been told to do in 6:9. Attending the divine assembly is a mark of the authentic prophet: "For who [among the false prophets] has stood in the council of Yahweh, and seen and heard his word?" (Jer. 23:18). The prophet as representative of the people must (Isa. 40:6) express the community's exhaustion, and does so in traditional lament language; they are "like grass killed by the withering wind" (cf. Pss. 90:5–6; 103:15–16). Isa. 40:8 provides the courtier's response, "Yes, the people are broken but God's word is able to revive them."

40:9–11, Jerusalem Announces the Coming of the Lord. The news is conveyed first to Zion, who is to go up to a mountain and announce to the cities of Judah that their God comes, as a shepherd (a traditional designation for king) leading the flock in a new exodus-conquest (cf. Exod. 15:13–18; Ps. 78:52–55).

40:12–31
Strength for an Exhausted People

In the opening scene, the heavenly messenger states that the word of Yahweh will overcome the weakness of the people (40:7–8). The prophet must, therefore, encourage the people exiled in Babylon, and this he does in a series of three rhetorical questions, showing their fears to be groundless: fear of the nations seemingly greater than they (vv. 12–17), fear of the religion (cultic images) and kings of their oppressors (vv. 18–23), and fear of the other gods (vv. 25–26). Yahweh will provide strength for the journey to Zion (vv. 27–31). A series of questions designed to destroy preconceptions about how God acts in history is found also in Job 38–41, where they bring Job to a new openness to God's ways.

40:12–17, The Nations Are Nothing Before Yahweh. Verse 12 asks who gathered the raw material of the universe, and vv. 13–14 who planned its arrangement into a beautiful world. For Second Isaiah, the answer is "Yahweh alone." Verses 15–17 state that the nations,

whom Israel fears, are merely part of the raw material effortlessly weighed out by Yahweh (v. 12). Note the correspondence between the weighing of the material of the universe in v. 12 and the weighing of the nations in vv. 15–16. Verse 15 should be translated: "See, the nations are a drop in the pan [of the scales], like clouds on the scale are they reckoned. See, the coastlands lift it [the pan] like dust."

Symmetry in Isaiah 40:12–17

VERSE 12	VERSES 15–16
waters	drop of water
heavens	clouds of heaven
earth	dust of earth
mountain	Mount Lebanon
hills	

40:18–24, Neither Statue nor King Represents the True God. In the ancient Near East the deity became present to the earthly worshiper by cult statues and/or by the king as son of god. The earthly form resembled, however crudely, the heavenly being, and hence represented the god on earth. In vv. 18–19, the prophet radically criticizes cult images: they represent mere human activity. He points rather to the Maker of the world, who is above such representation (vv. 21–22). The other representatives of the gods, kings ("shoots," "plantings," and "roots," in the palace language in the culture), rule by Yahweh's sufferance, liable to be blown away by his storm wind (vv. 23–24).

40:25–31, No Heavenly Being but Yahweh Can Impart Strength. Having shown the earthly images of the gods to be powerless, the prophet turns to the gods themselves, who were sometimes believed to be visible in the stars; these "gods" serve Yahweh in the heavenly army and march at his command (vv. 25–26). Since there exists no other divine power save Yahweh's, how can Israel say its God pays no heed (v. 27)? Yahweh's strength is available to those who wait for him, enabling them to make the journey toward Zion.

41:1–42:9
The Verdict in Favor of Israel

The relentless questioning of the previous section, 40:12–31, was addressed to Israel so as to convince it that only Yahweh was powerful. The questions in this section are addressed to the nations and their patron gods to the same end and, further, to demonstrate that Israel has a mission to the nations. It is a great trial, in which the entire world is summoned before the divine creator and judge. There are two parallel sections; ancient hearers were able to grasp the out-

	I. 41:1–20	II. 41:21–42:9
Summons to trial	41:1, 5–7	41:21–22b
Interrogation and		
verdict on		
nations/ gods	41:2–4	41:22c–29
Commission of		
Israel	41:8–20	42:1–9

line and interplay of the two versions of the one trial. In each section, the nations are summoned to bring their "gods" (their statues) before the divine judge and to prove their gods predicted the great events that were reshaping the world, the victories of Cyrus the Persian. A god's prediction of Cyrus's victories would prove the word of that god controlled human history; that god would be the supreme god. But the gods provide no predictions; they are shown by their silence to be nongods, nonexistent. Yahweh then declares that he has predicted Cyrus's victories and Israel's rebirth, that his word brought it about. Yahweh's people are therefore vindicated, and the gods' peoples are censured.

41:1–20, The First Trial Scene. The nations are summoned and asked to prove their gods are behind Cyrus by bringing forth oracles predicting his successes (vv. 1–4). Verses 2–3 show that Cyrus embodies the storm wind of Yahweh, already seen to be controlling history in 40:7 and 24, enabling him to uproot kings; like the wind he is not bound by roads. Verses 5–7 describe the fearful nations coming with their statues to the trial. Repetition of several words and phrases in vv. 5–7 and 8–13—"fear," "ends of the earth," "help," "say," "encourage"—show the contrast between the nations and Israel. In vv. 5–7, the gods are silent while the fearful people who made them chatter away aimlessly; in vv. 8–13, Israel is silent while Yahweh commissions it. Israel is given a mission in vv. 14–20. In vv. 14–16 the mountains and hills, which make the desert impassable, are to be leveled to make the highway announced in the heavenly assembly (40:3–4). Israel threshes the mountains, and the divine storm wind carries the refuse away. The other danger of the desert, its life-threatening sterility, is so tamed that rivers, ponds, and trees abound (vv. 11–19). When people see the desert mastered, they will acknowledge that Yahweh is unique (v. 20). Second Isaiah sees the return to Zion as the defeat of the desert, just as the old tradition saw the first exodus-conquest as the defeat of the sea; each form of chaos kept the people from its land.

41:21–42:9, The Second Trial Scene. The second scene repeats the outline of summons (41:21–22b), legal questioning (41:22c–29), and commission (42:1–9) but varies the emphases.

In the second scene, the questioning of nations and the commission to Israel is more specific. **41:21–29, Summons, Interrogation, and Verdict.** After the summons, the divine judge asks what gods have predicted Cyrus's conquests, meaning what gods by mere word have brought them about. The statues' silence shows the gods had done nothing. The judge-questioner finds the gods null and void, like precreation chaos before divine shaping (vv. 24, 29). Yahweh is the one who predicted and is now bringing about what is happening. Second Isaiah does not identify the predictions about Cyrus; probably they are Isaian texts about Yahweh's control of the Assyrian king (e.g., 10:5–19) and about the restoration of Zion.

42:1–9, The Commission of the Servant. After exposing the gods by debunking their images, Yahweh turns affectionately to Israel and says it can communicate his gracious power by its activity (vv. 2–4). Verse 4 probably refers to the justice introduced into the land at the accession of ancient kings, like David, who "became king over all Israel and . . . administered justice and righteousness to all his people" (2 Sam. 8:15). Former royal functions are now exercised by all the people, as elsewhere in Second Isaiah. Verses 5–8 summarize and develop the preceding point. Yahweh creates a peopled universe; Israel has a special call to make Yahweh known to the rest of the peoples (vv. 6–7). By accepting its commission to take part in the exodus-conquest and victory over the desert, Israel will image forth Yahweh's lordship. Yahweh will not be represented to the world by statues (v. 8). Verse 9 is the last word of the judge, summarizing his verdict on world history and pointing to the future.

42:10–43:8
Israel Called to Hear and See God Who Acts

Psalms 96 and 98, which both begin with "Sing to Yahweh a new song" and with other language nearly identical to v. 10, provide important clues to the genre of the passage: a hymn of victory. The whole world, animate and inanimate, is called to praise Yahweh, who has created the world by defeating forces hostile to human life. Israel, however, has a special role: "Tell among the nations, 'Yahweh reigns!' " (Ps. 96:10; cf. Pss. 96:3; 97:8–12; 99:1–9).

42:10–12, Hymnic Introduction. As in Psalms 96 and 98, the whole world is to praise Yahweh for creating.

42:13–17, Yahweh Defeats Threatening Sea. Yahweh is portrayed as a sleeping warrior aroused at last to defend his people (v. 13); such warriors worked themselves into a frenzy before marching to the battlefield (v. 14). Verses 15–16 show the warrior pushing back Sea to its proper sphere so that life-supporting dry land can appear, as in Ps. 104:5–9: "I will dry up mountains and hills, all their vegetation I will dry. I will make rivers into coastlands [meaning, the formless waters are now bound by coasts], pools I will dry up." Chaotic waters and primordial night are placed in their proper spheres so that human life is possible. Yahweh, who alone made the world, is alone worthy to be praised (Isa. 42:17).

42:18–25, Israel's Distress Is Punishment for Its Sin. Israel is to recognize the truth of the teaching (v. 21b) about light following exilic darkness (8:16–9:7). That teaching is proven true in its present distress (42:22); divine glory will shine forth through human weakness. Its suffering was not from chance or its enemies' power (vv. 23–25) but from the just will of Yahweh (v. 21).

43:1–8, Yahweh Calls His People to Journey. The people are not to remain ignorant of their new situation. The time of punishment is over; they are called to pass through fire and water to join others in the march homeward. Verse 8 undoes the grim decree of Isaiah in 6:9–10, "Go on hearing but do not understand; go on seeing but do not perceive," which introduced the period of punishment.

43:9–44:5
Israel a Witness to Yahweh

Like 41:1–42:9, Isa. 43:9–44:5 is a trial scene, contrasting the nations and their gods with Israel and its God, Yahweh. The emphasis is almost entirely upon Israel and the way it witnesses in both past and present. Israel is called a witness here, in 44:8–9, and in 55:4; in each case the people witness to the nations that Yahweh is the sole powerful deity. By its prosperity Israel had always been a sign of its patron's fidelity and power: "May God be gracious to us and bless us. May he make his face shine on us, that your way be known on earth, your saving power over all the nations" (Ps. 67:1–2). The king, however, had a special witnessing role, providing the visible sign of Yahweh's creation victory: "I will place [the king's] hand on the Sea, on the Rivers his right hand. . . . Yes, I will make him my firstborn, the highest of the kings of the earth" (Ps. 89:27; see also Ps. 18:43–44). But before it can witness to Yahweh's supremacy, Israel must acknowledge its sinful refusal to worship, and experience divine forgiveness (43:22–28).

43:9–15, Israel Is to Witness Yahweh as Sole Deity. As in 41:1–42:9, the nations are summoned by the divine judge: can their gods prove their unhindered word caused Cyrus's success? Before they even reply, Yahweh appoints Israel as witness to his supremacy. A subtle chiastic, or envelope, structure underscores Israel's witnessing.

A *Appointment of Israel as witness:* "you are my witnesses," v. 10a, elaborated in v. 10bcd.
  Its witnessing: no God except Yahweh exists, v. 10ef; no God except Yahweh acts ("saves"), v. 11ab.

B *Proof:* I am the only God who acts effortlessly according to his word, v. 12ab.

A' *Appointment of Israel as witness:* "you are my witnesses," v. 12c.
  Its witnessing: no God except Yahweh exists, vv. 12d–13a; no God except Yahweh acts [no other god can stop his work], v. 13bc.

Part B is central. Verses 14–15 answer the obvious objection: if Yahweh is supreme, why is Israel still captive to Babylon? The answer: Yahweh has already knocked down Babylon's gates.

43:16–21, The New National Story. Yahweh provides a new script for the nation. They are no longer to recite as their national story (v. 18) the crossing of the sea and the defeat of Egypt (vv. 16–17) but instead the crossing of the desert, now made so fertile and friendly that even its wild animals honor Yahweh. The people are created anew and show it by praising God.

43:22–28, Israel Must Be Forgiven. The probability of Israel recognizing and witnessing Yahweh's new deed is slight, since it has failed to recognize Yahweh's hand in the punishment of the Exile: "But you did not call me, you did not weary yourself [in prayer, cf. Pss. 6:6 and 69:3] on my account, O Israel" (Isa. 43:22). Divine forgiveness is needed for Israel to witness (v. 25), since the people cannot act by themselves (vv. 26–28).

44:1–5, Israel, Like the Desert, Will Be Healed. The passionate commission in vv. 1–2 shows the depth of divine love. As the desert was healed of its aridity and enmity with God (43:19–20), so will the people be healed (44:3–5). The wind of God, which had devastated the people (40:7), here heals them. The people will bear the names that will mark them as Yahweh's people.

44:6–23
Witnesses to Their Maker

Most commentators regard vv. 9–20 as an addition by someone other than Second Isaiah, and

576

many translations print the verses as prose. The verses, however, continue the topic of witnessing begun in vv. 6–8, and their arrangement as prose is simply an editor's decision; they can just as easily be arranged in poetic lines, despite some lines overloaded due to textual corruption. The scene is a cosmic trial, by now familiar from 41:1–42:9 and 43:9–44:5. Familiar too is the logic: the nations witness to their gods (in the form of statues), whereas Israel witnesses to Yahweh. The question: what god predicted contemporary events so as to prove his or her unimpeded word shaped historical events? The poem consists of five stanzas of eleven to thirteen lines each, except for the fourth, which has thirty-two lines.

44:6–8, Israel's God Shapes History. Israel has heard his prediction of contemporary events and must therefore confess that only he is supreme among the gods. It has experienced the God who acts and is therefore a true witness to Yahweh's supreme control of history.

44:9–11, The Nations' Gods Shape Nothing. Ironically, the prophet calls the nations "creators" and the statues they create "their witnesses." Since the nations' metal and wooden witnesses can do nothing, their creators are shamed when summoned to stand and answer the divine judge (v. 11).

44:12–13, Creators of Metal and Wooden Gods. Ancient statues were made either of metal or of wood overlaid with precious metal. In the first of the two parallel tableaux, the metalworkers' labor leaves them exhausted, drained of strength (v. 12). In the second tableau, woodworkers produce a statue in human form to dwell in a house of god (v. 13)!

44:14–20, The Raw Material of the Statues. Ritual texts from Babylonia give elaborate directions for planting and nurturing sacred trees from which statues were made. In v. 14, the artisan goes out to the nursery and selects the right tree. The emphasis throughout is on the wood before the artisan "creates." In its raw state, the wood is useful for warming oneself and baking bread. After its shaping it will be useless and a cause of shame (vv. 9–11). The artisans do not realize their folly.

44:21–23, Israel, and All the World, Is Called to Show Forth Yahweh's Glory. Yahweh declares Israel to be the servant, the favored one, whom he has created and to whom he remains loyal (v. 21). Israel has failed to recognize its call to show forth its patron's supremacy and hence needs forgiveness to do so (v. 22). The people are to join all parts of God's world in giving praise, including the trees of the forest!

44:24–45:13
Cyrus Is the Instrument of Yahweh

In the eighth century B.C., Yahweh chose the Assyrian king to be his human instrument, "the rod of my anger" (10:5). To Second Isaiah in the sixth century, Cyrus the Persian king becomes the instrument of divine mercy by allowing exiled populations to return to their homelands and by helping to rebuild native temples. As Israel resisted seeing the Assyrian king as Yahweh's instrument so they resist seeing Cyrus in that role. The purpose of the speech, therefore, is to convince them of Cyrus's role in the divine plan (45:1).

In all three sections of the speech (consisting of twenty, thirty-three, and twenty lines, respectively), Second Isaiah alludes to the great poem of chap. 10. "My shepherd, he will do my pleasure," in 44:28, reverses "the rod of my anger," in 10:5; "I will give you treasures of darkness," in 45:3, alludes to "to take spoil and seize plunder," in 10:6; and clearest of all, "Does the clay say to the potter?" in 45:9, rewords "Shall the axe vaunt itself over the one who hews with it?" in 10:15.

44:24–28, Yahweh Decrees the Rebuilding of Zion by Cyrus. Verse 24 powerfully states for Israel the sole divinity of Yahweh; the proof is that he alone made heaven and earth. Those who worship other gods, therefore, do not speak the truth (v. 25); only Israel's prophets speak the truth on behalf of the one God (v. 26ab). And the prophets have revealed God's decree, expressed in the threefold "who says" of vv. 26c, 27a, and 28a: the rebuilding of Jerusalem and its daughter cities, the victory over cosmic waters, and the commission of Cyrus to rebuild the Temple. The three commands are aspects of one act. Chaotic forces hostile to the existence of the people are to be curbed; city and temple, essential for peoplehood in the ancient Near East, are to be rebuilt. Cyrus, destroyer of the Babylonian Empire, will do the building by his royal decrees.

45:1–8, All Will Acknowledge Yahweh's Choosing of Cyrus. Yahweh commissions Cyrus in the elaborate palace language of the day; he will march before his armies and give him plunder (vv. 1–3b). Cyrus will at length acknowledge that it is the God of Israel who is giving him success (v. 3cd). Three times in this section the successful mission of Cyrus leads to acknowledgment that the God of Israel is the only God, vv. 1–3, 4–5b, and 5c–7. The third acknowledgment is climactic; not only is Israel's God solely responsible for Cyrus's victories, but he alone is responsible for creating all that exists (vv. 6–7). Verse 8 invites that world to display the victory: the heavens are to rain down the waters, now tamed, that give life; the earth, made fertile, is to bloom.

45:9–13, Israel Must Accept God's Plan. All creation is called to celebrate, but God's own people balk. Like the foolish Assyrian king (10:15), they do not see Yahweh controlling events. Fools in the biblical sense, they deserve the harsh questions of v. 11. The discourse ends appropriately with vv. 12–13. Yahweh is the complete master, creating and directing the earth with human beings and the heavens with angelic beings (v. 12).

45:14–25
Zion Is the Site of Victory

The previous speech clarifies, for the first time, Cyrus's role in restoring the people. This speech makes clear, for the first time, the full significance of Zion, the goal of the journey the people are to undertake. Temples and holy cities in the ancient East were often celebrated as the place where creation took place, as the polar opposite, therefore, of primordial chaos. Even the nations acknowledge this function of Zion.

The passage's unity is shown by the approximately equal four stanzas (seventeen, fourteen, fifteen, fourteen lines, respectively) and the recurring Hebrew words, "pray, address fervently," "be hidden, secret," "save, be victorious," "be righteous, reliable," "be ashamed." Other passages with similar themes, Isa. 2:1–4, on the one hand, and Psalms 2 and 72, on the other, show Isa. 45:14–25 to be a single scene. Isa. 2:1–4 foresees the day when the nations hear the voice of Yahweh and stream toward his mountain, and the psalms show the defeated enemy kings bringing tribute.

45:14–17, The Tribute of Kings. Yahweh announces that foreigners will bring tribute to Zion and confess that "only in your midst is God, there is no other God." That it is Zion who is addressed by the nations is clear from the Hebrew; the reiterated second-person feminine pronoun (customarily used of Zion) and the confession that Yahweh is in her midst is frequent in Zion songs (in Pss. 46, 48, and 76). The nations speak from the end of Isa. 45:14 to v. 17; change of person within a speech is not unusual in Hebrew style. Their confession that Yahweh is a hidden God (v. 15) refers to his apparent withdrawal when his people were exiled.

45:18–19, Yahweh Founds the Earth and Sanctuary. Yahweh vigorously restates the nations' confession, proclaiming himself the only creator. The phrase "he found it" describes both the founding of the earth and the founding of Jerusalem (Pss. 48:8; 87:5) and of his sanctuary (Exod. 15:7). The world is no longer chaos,

where God's word does not sound, but habitable land (Isa. 45:18f–19b), where Yahweh can speak and be sought in his shrine (v. 19cdef).

45:20–21, God Summons the Nations. From the secure site of cosmic victory and just governance of the universe, Yahweh summons the nations to a trial. As in other trial scenes, 41:1–42:9 and 43:9–44:5, he asks the nations which of the gods they carry with them spoke the word that foretold and effected Cyrus's victories. Only Yahweh spoke the word.

45:22–25, Only in Yahweh Is Prosperity to Be Found. Since Yahweh is the only God, all nations must journey to his shrine to find blessing (v. 21). To the one God is due their homage (vv. 23–24a). The nations will be ashamed because their patron gods are nothing (v. 24bc). Yahweh is the reason for Israel's triumph (v. 25).

46:1–13
Yahweh Carries His People to Zion

Ancient poetry spoke of Yahweh carrying Israel: "You have seen what I did to Egypt. I carried you on eagle's wings and brought you to myself" (Exod. 19:4); "He spread his wings, he lifted [Israel] up, he carried him on his pinions" (Deut. 32:11). Second Isaiah draws on that tradition in 40:11: "He will carry them in his bosom." The word "carry," connoting the great act by which Israel moved from being a slave in Egypt to being Yahweh's servant in Canaan, succinctly expresses the contrast between the Babylonians, who carry their gods as they flee their city, and Israel, who is carried to the city of its God (vv. 1–7). A second characteristic of Israel's God is his word, which effects what he predicts (vv. 8–10). Israel is to allow itself to be carried to Zion by its God, who acts through Cyrus (vv. 12–13).

46:1–4, Yahweh Carries Israel. Verses 1–2 picture the Babylonians carrying statues of their gods Bel and Nebo, fleeing the city before the invasion of Cyrus. The statues bob up and down with the motion of the pack animals. How different are the survivors of Israel, who have been carried and can count on being carried in the future because of the fidelity and unmatched power of Israel's God (vv. 3–4)!

46:5–7, There Is No Other God. The assertion in v. 4 that Yahweh will carry Israel is proven here as in 40:18–20. Human beings made the other gods. The motionless and dumb statues prove the deities cannot carry their clients.

46:8–13, Come to Zion. Second Isaiah rebukes the rebellious of Israel who do not trust the God who has carried them from of old (v. 8). Their God has spoken the word that is moving Cyrus to bring them home (vv. 9–11). The exiles are literally far from the place where justice is placed (cf. 45:14–25); they must allow themselves to be carried to Zion.

47:1–15
Lady Babylon Is Dethroned

Fair maiden Babylon (not "daughter of Babylon") is to descend from her throne (v. 1) and be silent (v. 5), in contrast to Dame Zion, who goes up to a high mountain and loudly proclaims the coming of her Lord (40:9). Babylon's "lords," Bel and Nebo, have departed (chap. 46). Her children, those who worship in her midst, are lost (47:8–9). Zion, on the other hand, is about to have the "divorce" from her Lord reversed (50:1) and see the return of her children (49:14–26). She will be told, "Arise, shake off the dust, sit [on your throne], O Jerusalem" (52:2).

The genre is a taunt song, like those against Tyre (Ezek. 27:1–36), the prince of Tyre (Ezek. 28:1–10, 11–19), and the king of Babylon (Isa. 14:3–21). It asks contemptuously: where now is the strength you used to dominate others? Since it is Yahweh the judge who speaks, the taunt song is a judgment finding Babylon guilty of opposing the divine plan that had made it Yahweh's instrument (vv. 6–7). It did not recognize Yahweh's lordship but claimed ultimate power for itself (vv. 8d, 10f).

47:1–5, Queen Babylon Becomes a Slave. Yahweh commands the queen to leave her throne and city stripped as a prisoner and to assume a slave's duties.

47:6–7, Babylon Exceeded Her Mandate. As in Isa. 10:5–14, in which the Assyrian king exceeded Yahweh's mandate by redrawing God-given boundaries and boasting, "By the strength of my hand I have done it" (10:13), so Babylon was unnecessarily cruel (47:6) and thought herself to be immortal, a divine claim (v. 7).

47:8–9, The Sentence. She loses her claims to glory—her marriage to the city gods and her throng of citizen-worshipers—at a single stroke. The very suddenness suggests divine intervention.

47:10–11, Babylon's Delusion. The queen is now taunted for her renowned lore, which allowed her to predict the future and to assure success. In v. 10, Babylon utters a threefold boast, and in v. 11, disaster is said three times to come upon her. As each wave hits, the great merchant city is unable to use its wealth to avert it.

47:12–13, Her Seers Cannot Save Her. Babylon is allowed "benefit of counsel" in her trial, but her famous diviners offer no useful advice. How could they know the future, which is in the hands of Yahweh?

47:14–15, Her Resources Offer No Help. Her seers and her vast network of traders cannot save her. With the queen herself, they leave the once-great city.

48:1–22
Openness to the Interpreting Word

Chap. 48, a carefully constructed poem, affirms that every act of Yahweh is accompanied by an interpretive word, which invites the people to respond appropriately. Such a word accompanied the first great deed that created Israel, the creation/exodus-conquest, so that rebellious Israel would not credit its idols with the deed (vv. 3–6b). In this time of a new creation/exodus-conquest, signaled by Cyrus, Yahweh gives such a word (vv. 6c–8), transmitted through the prophet (v. 16d), a word that invites both belief (vv. 17–19) and action (vv. 20–21). The theme of the word of the Lord gives the whole chapter a coherence.

There are other arguments for the chapter's coherence, apart from the poem's logic. The same verb, "call oneself, be known," with humans as subject, occurs three times in the first section (vv. 1–11) and, in the second section (vv. 12–21), three times conveying the meaning of "call, summon," with Yahweh as the subject. The second section, vv. 12–21 (thirty-seven lines), repeats the first section, vv. 1–11 (thirty-eight lines), the same way 41:21–42:9 repeats 41:1–20. The first part bids Jacob to hear (48:1–2) because, in view of Israel's rebelliousness, a divine word always accompanies the divine deed, whether in the past or the present (vv. 3–8). The second part bids Jacob hear (vv. 12ab), reiterates the link between word and deed (vv. 12c–13), and declares that the new deed is Cyrus's defeat of Babylon, accompanied by a prophetic word (vv. 14–16). Verses 17–19, like vv. 9–11, restate the divine purpose, intent on good even in the face of Israelite obstinacy.

48:1–2, Israel Names Itself Invalidly. At the beginning of the first part, Israel, addressed with its titles expanded severalfold, is declared to be worshiping invalidly. The invalidity is explained in v. 2. Verse 2a, lit., "but from the holy city are they called," means that the people are known from their city of origin, the city of God. If the people do not worship in their God's city, they do not worship validly. During the Exile, it was of course impossible for Israel to worship in Zion; Ezekiel and Jeremiah acknowledge the fact (Jer. 29; Ezek. 11:16). But for Second Isaiah, the exilic period is over, and Zion again exercises its claim as the exclusive place for Israelite worship.

48:3–8, Word Precedes Deed. Yahweh predicted the first creation/exodus-conquest so that Israel would know who was the true author of the deed and not credit it to an idol (vv. 3–6b). The prediction probably consisted of the pentateuchal promises of progeny and land to the patriarchs and the promise of Canaan to Moses. Today (vv. 6c–8), Yahweh predicts a new creation/exodus-conquest so that Israel will know its true author. The prophet is aware of Israel's tendency to say, "I knew it already"; hence to deny as Yahweh's all acts contrary to its own expectations and biases.

48:9–11, The Divine Purpose Shall Stand. Though negative upon first reading, vv. 9–11 are positive, stating Yahweh's work will proceed irrespective of popular response. The work is founded on Yahweh's zeal for his name (v. 11). Verse 10 declares that Israel's present distress is not an argument against God's sovereignty; its distress was due to deliberate testing.

48:12–16, Yahweh Predicts Cyrus. In vv. 12–13, beginning the second part, Israel hears the familiar recital concerning the creation of heaven and earth and of all who dwell therein (vv. 12–13). When Yahweh summons those whom he has created, all of them utterly dependent upon him, can any one of them claim to predict and interpret what the creator is about to do (v. 14ab)? The new deed is Yahweh's choosing Cyrus (vv. 14c–15). Just as Yahweh was not silent about the old deeds but predicted and interpreted them (vv. 16a–c), so he is not silent about today's act, "Now the Lord Yahweh has sent me [Second Isaiah], endowed with his spirit" (v. 16d).

48:17–19, The Divine Purpose Stands, Whether Israel Obeys or Not. Israel has heard the word interpreting the significance of Cyrus. If they would only heed the new promise, their prosperity would be like Israel when it obeyed the ancient word. In words reminiscent of the promise to Abraham and Sarah (cf. Gen. 22:17–19), they would live and not be cut off (Isa. 48:18–19).

48:20–21, Leave Babylon! The proper response to Yahweh's word delivered through the prophet is an act: they are to become part of the new exodus procession. On the way their conversation is to express their redemption. They will experience the prosperity promised in v. 18bc, even in the infertile desert. Verse 22 appears to be an addition denying to the

wicked a share in the prosperity enjoyed by the obedient.

49:1–26
The Servant Is Commissioned to Lead the People

The nations see a double restoration: the servant Israel, who has lost all the insignia of peoplehood in the Exile, embarks on a new creation/ exodus-conquest (vv. 1–13, fifty-five lines); Dame Zion, who has lost her children and buildings, is rebuilt (vv. 14–26, fifty-three lines). The commission of the servant is modeled on the commission to Moses and to Jeremiah. There are two types of commission in the Bible: the type represented in 1 Kings 22:19–22, Isaiah 6, and Isa. 40:1–9, in which the prophet in the divine assembly willingly assumes responsibility for communicating heavenly decisions to those on earth, and the type represented in Exod. 3:1– 4:17 (Moses), Judg. 6:11–24 (Gideon), and Jer. 1:4–10 (Jeremiah). In the latter type, the person resists the call, and his resistance must be overcome by signs and dialogue. Moses cites the people's lack of confidence in him (Exod. 4:1) and his lack of eloquence (Exod. 4:10). Jeremiah (whose commission is modeled on Moses') points to his youth and lack of eloquence (Jer. 1:6). The dialogue in Isa. 49:3–5, "he said," "but I said," "and now Yahweh says," is reminiscent especially of Jer. 1:4–10, "but I said," "Yahweh said," "and Yahweh said to me." The servant, who is to lead the new exodus-conquest, is clearly modeled on Moses and Jeremiah.

Further evidence for the unity of the passage is the Second-Isaian device of creating two sections of approximately equal length that each make the same point (cf. 41:1–20 and 41:21–42:9; 48:1–11 and 48:12–21). In 49:1–13, the servant's resistance is overcome; in vv. 14– 26, the disbelief of Dame Zion. Verses 8–12 are a natural continuation of the commission in vv. 1–7; the call to the new Moses is fulfilled in the exodus-conquest of vv. 8–12. Verse 14, which begins the second section, would be impossibly abrupt without the preceding lines.

49:1–13, The Commission of the Servant. The nations are invited to look on, as in 52:13– 15, while the servant narrates his commission to them. They will be astonished when they see a people they thought had been annihilated restored, with a divinely chosen leader (vv. 1–6), land (vv. 8–12), and a holy city with temple and citizens (vv. 14–26).

In the dialogue between God and the prophet, modeled on those between God and Moses (and Jeremiah), the prophet's plea of exhaustion (v. 4) is ruled out as an impediment to the task. The task is specified in v. 5abc: to bring

Israel back to Yahweh in Zion. The task of the universal God's servant cannot be limited to Israel (v. 6). The nations will be enlightened when they see the servant, humbled in the defeat of exile and rescued by the God who chose him (v. 7).

Before going on to vv. 8–13, a word needs to be said about how the servant, called "Israel" in v. 3, can have a mission to Israel. As pointed out in the introduction, many commentators distinguish an individual servant of the four "servant songs" (42:1–4; 49:1–6; 50:4–11; 52:13–53:12) from servant Israel elsewhere in Second Isaiah. They therefore excise "Israel" in v. 3. This excision is unwarranted and unnecessary if one understands that servants of gods or kings were understood dialectically, in relation to their master and to their people. All Israel is called to be like the servant.

Isa. 49:8–13 specify the task. Just as Moses led the people to Canaan and apportioned the land (v. 8), so the servant will bring forth the people from bondage and will lead them through the desert, now tamed by Yahweh, to Zion (vv. 9–11). The people will proceed to Zion (v. 12) not only from Babylon, but from all places of exile (including Syene in Egypt). All nature is to praise Yahweh, for he has comforted his people (cf. 40:1).

49:14–26, Dame Zion Is Consoled. The gathering of the exiles is only half the story. As in Jer. 31:15–22, one of the sources for this section, the bereft mother must be consoled. As divine-human dialogue persuaded the servant in Isa. 49:1–6, so dialogue with Yahweh gradually turns the mother's discouragement and exhaustion to amazed joy. The mother's fatalism, expressed in her proverbs (vv. 14, 24), is fully addressed by Yahweh's repeating and reversing them (vv. 15, 25). In v. 16, Yahweh adapts the well-known metaphor of constant remembrance in Deut. 6:8, "You shall bind them [the words of the Law] as a sign on your hand, and they shall be a symbol on your forehead." The glory of a city is its walls, buildings, and thronging crowds. Mother Zion will joyfully contemplate her complete restoration (Isa. 49:17–21), in contrast to Dame Babylon, who suffered the loss of her "lords" and of her children in chap. 47. Just as the nations see the people's rise in 49:7, so they do here; kings are summoned by a flag (cf. 11:10–11) to bring the prisoners home and bow down before the people of the only God (49:22–23). Because it is Yahweh who contends, no tyrant can gainsay his intent to gather all his people (vv. 24–25). In the defeat of the enemies, who are forced to eat their own flesh and blood (an allusion to cannibalism in siege-induced famine, as in the curses of Lev. 26:29 and Deut. 28:53–57), all flesh will acknowledge Yahweh as Israel's God.

50:1–51:8
The Disciple Reveals the Divine Plan

Isaiah, frustrated by his eighth-century audience's refusal to prepare for the judgment, commanded his disciples to write down his message (8:16–18; 30:8–14) so that when judgment finally came, the people would see that their defeat resulted from Yahweh's plan. In this speech, the prophet declares that he is one of those disciples of Isaiah (50:4–9); his faithful bearing of punishment and his rescue enable him to teach his fellows where salvation is now to be found (50:10–51:18).

Since most scholars deny that 50:4–11 has anything to do with 51:1–8, it is necessary to demonstrate the passage is a unit. Some phrases are repeated in both sections with only slight variation, suggesting a deliberate reprise: "near is the one who declares me innocent," in 50:8a and 51:5a; and the repetition of the metaphor "to be worn out like a garment" in 50:9cd and 51:6cde and 51:8ab. Moreover, the pattern of the thanksgiving psalm has shaped the whole. The thanksgiving psalm is essentially the report of a rescue; the singer tells how he or she was rescued by God from an affliction—illness, false accusations, inability to visit the Temple, or the psalmist's own folly. Having been rescued, the psalmist can now declare before the assembly the wonderful rescue of God, and thus invite the whole community to give praise. Sometimes the psalmist becomes a teacher, teaching trust in God on the basis of the experience of rescue. Ps. 34:1–13 is a good example: "I sought Yahweh and he answered me. . . . Come, O children, listen to me and I will teach you the fear of Yahweh. What person is there who desires life, and covets many days, that he may enjoy good things? Keep your tongue from evil, and lips from speaking deceit." The prophet describes his suffering and rescue in 50:4–9 and teaches the people on the basis of that experience (50:10–11; 51:1–3, 4–5, 6, 7–8). The suffering in 50:4–9 is specific: it is the second stage in the prophetic scenario, the time of punishment that preceded the present time of salvation.

50:1–3, Because of Your Sins Yahweh Left His Wife and Children. Isa. 49:14–26 spoke of Dame Zion's loss of husband and children. Isa. 50:1–2b declares this double loss did not occur because of Yahweh's weakness but because of the people's sins; no one heeded Yahweh's words (v. 2ab). Verses 2c–3 show that this double dismissal cannot have come from anyone wresting them away from Yahweh, since he alone is powerful. Yahweh alone made the world by pushing back to their boundaries the waters that once engulfed earth (v. 2efg; cf. commentary above on 42:13–17); he also created the exilic night, covering the heavenly luminaries so that darkness enveloped the earth (3ab).

The last phrase requires comment. In the first of the two Isaiah passages concerning disciples mentioned above, 8:16–9:7, the eighth-century prophet spoke of the impending judgment as darkness and distress: "In the former time he humbled the land of Zebulun and the land of Naphtali, but in latter time he will glorify the way of the sea, the land beyond the Jordan, Galilee of the nations. The people who walked in darkness have seen a great light." Second Isaiah seems to have taken the sequence of darkness-light from this text as descriptive of his prophetic scenario of punishment and restoration. Hence 50:3 declares that Yahweh deliberately created the period of exilic darkness, when wife and children were sent away.

50:4–11, The Disciple Teaches the People. Second Isaiah is one of the Isaian disciples who knows the divine plan of darkness-light, punishment-restoration, so that he can teach the exhausted people. Daily the disciple receives instruction (v. 4). In the period of darkness, he submitted to the punishment sent by God, unlike the rebellious ones spoken of in 30:8–14. (There are remarkable verbal echoes of 30:9, 12 in 50:4, 10). Like the faithful lamenter in Lam. 3:30, he gave his cheek to the smiter and was filled with insults (Isa. 50:5–6). Like the sufferer in the thanksgiving psalms, he did not give up, for Yahweh was there (vv. 7–9). Now the disciple can teach those among the people who "fear Yahweh" (v. 10a) yet "lie in a bed of pain" (v. 11f) to "walk in the light of your fire." The last phrase is obscure, but may allude to Isa. 2:5, "O house of Jacob, come let us walk in the light of Yahweh," i.e., now that the light of restoration has come, let it light your path to Zion.

51:1–8, Yahweh's Consoling Presence Is Now Found in the Holy City. The four stanzas (vv. 1–3, 4–5, 6, 7–8) all develop in different ways the teaching of the disciple of 50:10–11: the presence of Yahweh that was with me in the period of dark exile is now, in the period of light, to be found in Zion. All four stanzas begin with a masculine plural imperative, the usual form for addressing all Israel. In 51:1–4, Yahweh blessed Abraham and Sarah by giving them progeny. Yahweh will "comfort" Zion and give her progeny as David "comforted" Bathsheba in 2 Sam. 12:24. Isa. 51:4–5 refer to Isa. 2:1–4, where Yahweh's teaching and word go forth from Zion to the nations. Isa. 51:6 alludes to songs of Zion like Psalms 46 and 48, which declare Zion to be the firm point in a tottering universe. Isa. 51:7–8 focus on those prepared to come to Zion, assuring them that mere human

beings cannot harm them, for Yahweh's victory is forever.

Because of the fidelity of the disciple who knew that Yahweh was with him in the period of darkness, the people learn that in the period of light Yahweh will be with them in Zion.

51:9–52:12
Prayer to Yahweh the Warrior

The stanzas in 51:9–52:12 appear at first glance to be unrelated, and few commentators see them as a single speech. Many regard the placement of the three similar imperatives in 51:9, 51:17, and 52:1 as later editing. They admit Isa. 51:9–16 is a lament with response, but view 51:17–23; 52:1–2; 52:3–6; 52:7–11; and 52:11–12 as separate sections or fragments. This commentary proposes that the section is modeled on the communal lament, examples of which include Psalms 44 and 74, and Isa. 63:7–64:12. Communal laments contain a recital of the events that brought Israel into being (51:9–11) so as to pose the question, Will Yahweh allow that act to be undone by the present enemy? Communal laments also contain vivid descriptions of the present crisis (51:17–23) and urgent pleas for help (51:9ab). Divine responses recur throughout this speech, 51:12–16, 21–23; 52:1–2, 7–10. Another argument for the unity of the section is that the opening recital of the creation of Israel in 51:9–11, describing the return of the redeemed to Zion in v. 11, receives a response only in 52:11–12. Also, Dame Zion's loss of her children (51:20) is not redressed until 52:7–12.

51:9–11, Appeal to the Warrior. Hebrew style sometimes uses the concrete noun for the abstract quality, "arm" for "power," and "feet" for "messenger," e.g., 52:7. As in 42:13–14 and Ps. 78:65, the divine warrior is asleep and needs to be aroused by his needy clients. Appeal is made to the act of creation that brought the people into existence—the defeat of Sea, when the waters that covered the entire earth were forced back to their proper boundaries, the upper and lower oceans (cf. Ps. 104:5–9; Isa. 43:12–16; Gen. 1). Second Isaiah identifies creation and exodus-conquest, for the defeat of Sea allows the entry of the people into Canaan. The question is posed acutely: will you let Babylon annul your creation?

51:12–16, Yahweh's Response to the Appeal. Yahweh proclaims himself their consoler (v. 12a). His question, "Who are you to fear a mere mortal?" seems to rebuke the people's question, "Was it not you . . ." in vv. 9e and 10a. Can the people have so forgotten their creator as to fear mere humans (v. 13)? The oppressed shall be saved (v. 14), for "I am Yahweh your

God," who defeated Sea and said, "You are my people" (vv. 15–16). Verse 16ab seems awkward and interrupts the connection between v. 15 and v. 16cd. It may be parenthetical, an assurance given to the servant that Israel is already protected.

51:17–20, The Suffering of Jerusalem. Jerusalem is to rouse itself rather than Yahweh, who, as the preceding section shows, has always been alert (v. 17ab). Nonetheless, there is compassion despite this rebuke. Jer. 25:15–29 equates the effect of suffering Yahweh's punishment with drunkenness in a way not dissimilar from Isa. 51:17. Dame Zion is disgraced in having no children to lead her home (vv. 18, 20). A Ugaritic text describes the ideal son: he "takes [his father] by the hand when he is drunk, carries him home when he is sated with wine" (see Pritchard, *Ancient Near Eastern Texts*, p. 150). Reversal of Zion's fortunes consists not only of vengeance on her enemies (vv. 22–23) but also of restoration for her children.

51:21–23, Jerusalem's Enemies Drink Her Cup. From Jerusalem reeling from the blows of Babylon (v. 21), Yahweh takes her cup and forces her enemies to drink from it.

52:1–2, Jerusalem Is Awakened and Adorned. With the same imperatives in which she earlier had addressed Yahweh (51:17), she is told to rise and array herself in queenly garments (contrast Babylon in 47:1–3), for the enemies that stripped her are gone.

52:3–6, I Will Not Permit My Name to Be Profaned. The verses are later glosses. Israel will be redeemed without money (v. 3), meaning that no conventional army will redeem it. Israel was attacked for no reason by the Egyptians and by the Assyrians (the enemy in Isaiah's time). Yahweh will act, and in that act people will recognize him as God (vv. 4–6).

52:7–10, Yahweh Is Spied Approaching Zion. Yahweh's approach is described through the eyes of the sentries on the walls. 2 Sam. 18:19–33 similarly builds suspense through the device of sentries' conversation. The lament of Jerusalem is answered; Yahweh has come as redeemer.

52:11–12, Leave Babylon for Zion! In the new exodus-conquest the people are to bring back the vessels taken by Nebuchadnezzar when he destroyed the Temple (2 Kings 25:14–15). They shall not go out in haste as in the first exodus (Exod. 12:11; Deut. 16:3), for the Babylonians are defeated. Yahweh leads a peaceful procession, protecting the people, like the pillar of cloud in the first exodus. The arm of Yahweh has acted (Isa. 51:9).

52:13–53:12
The Servant Justifies the Many

There is widespread agreement on the dimensions and genre of the speech in 52:13–53:12 but not on its meaning. Divine speech in the first person (52:13–15; 53:11b–12) frames a speech by a different speaker in the third person. The genre utilized in 53:1–11a is the individual thanksgiving psalm, but it is radically transformed. The thanksgiving is essentially the psalmist's report to fellow Israelites (often called "the many") of his rescue by God from an affliction that separated him from God and community. "The many" are invited to give thanks with the psalmist: "With my mouth I will give great thanks to Yahweh; I will praise him in the midst of the many" (Ps. 109:30). Second Isaiah, however, alters the genre; the rescued person is silent, and the many tell of his rescue of them.

The material is traditional, but its arrangement is startlingly new and has given rise to many questions. Who are the speakers in 53:1–11a, the nations or Israel? Who is the servant? Does the servant die and undergo resurrection? How does the servant "bear the sins" of the many?

52:13–15, Kings Are Amazed at the Transformation of the Servant. In 49:7 the nations were startled to see the once-exhausted servant leading the people to Zion. Here Yahweh gives a judicial verdict in favor of the servant and against those who interpreted his condition as divine rejection.

53:1–11a, The Many Acknowledge the Servant Has Borne Their Sin. In thanksgiving psalms, the person rescued speaks of his vindication to the many, but here the many speak while the servant is silent, thus illustrating v. 7 (cf. Ps. 39:2, 9). They can hardly believe their rescue came from one so lowly (Isa. 53:1–3). Servants in the Bible were often of lowly origin: Moses, Gideon, and Jeremiah all reminded God of their lack of talent; even David in the estimate of his family was totally unsuitable as a candidate for kingship (1 Sam. 16:1–13).

In Isa. 53:4–6, the speakers declare the servant has borne their sins. Here we must attempt to answer two difficult questions: who are the speakers, and how does the servant bear others' sins? The speaker seems to be exiled Israel, not the nations. In Second Isaiah the nations are spectators at the reemergence of Israel. They are part of important scenes as chorus, not protagonist. Israel, therefore, is "the many" whose sin the servant bears.

How does the servant bear the sins of Israel? One must avoid reading NT ideas into the Isaian text (Mark 10:45; 14:24; and parallels use similar language to interpret the death of Jesus) or denying vicarious suffering in the OT simply because it is not found anywhere else. A good starting point is the observation that most Hebrew words for sin can mean both the act and the state resulting from the act. "To bear the sin" therefore means to bear the consequences of sin. The people of the Exile, for example, had to bear the consequences of the sins of their pre-exilic ancestors, "Our fathers sinned and are no more [they are not living so as to suffer the consequences of their act], and we bear their sins" (Lam. 5:7).

How could the servant bear the sin of his contemporaries, "the many"? A partial answer is given by 50:4–11, in which the disciple accepted the sufferings of the Exile as sent by God; he offered his back to the smiters, his cheek to those who plucked his beard. Most of the exiles did not regard the Exile the way the servant did, to judge from the preaching of Jeremiah and Ezekiel. They fled from it, either attempting to return prematurely or giving up all hope of return and settling in. They did not bear the consequences of their sin. True expiation could come about only through obedient submission in the period of punishment and obedient return in the period of restoration. But so long as Israel, in the person of the servant, acted obediently, the nation continued to exist. In 53:4–6, the many finally come to this awareness.

Verses 7–9 speak of an unjust trial ending in a disgraceful death. Actual death seems unlikely; the servant's rehabilitation in vv. 11b–12 would have to be a heavenly judgment scene. Rather, a "death experience" is described, like the psalmic "going down to the pit" (e.g., Pss. 28:1; 30:3; 88:4; 143:7). The servant's entire life, from birth (Isa. 53:2) to death, was one of suffering and rejection.

In the last stanza of the speakers' statement, 53:10–11a (unfortunately the text is damaged), the many see that the servant's suffering was part of God's plan. There is a hint in v. 10d, explicit in vv. 11b–12, that his reward is to possess the land; in Deuteronomy "to lengthen the days" is a phrase describing life in the promised land.

53:11b–12, The Servant's Reward. The servant's self-conscious acceptance of the pain of exile as the deserved punishment from God, his "bearing of the sin" of Israel and his leading it in the exodus-conquest, wins him the great prize—possession of the land. To be in God's land, Zion, makes one righteous, pleasing to God. Isa. 8:16–9:7, which speaks of possessing the land after the darkness of defeat, provides important clues to the meaning of the verses. Verse 11a should read, with LXX, "he shall see the light," a reference to the dawning light in

9:2. Isa. 9:3 likens the joy of possessing the land to the joy of warriors dividing spoil (v. 12ab).

Due to the servant's exemplary bearing of the guilt of all Israel, the whole people is now free to enjoy the great gift—the land. The servant's suffering is accepted as valid, while the many—and the nations—look on in amazement.

54:1–17
Yahweh Returns as Husband to Zion

Zion, the wife of her Lord and the mother of her inhabitants, has been at the center of Second Isaiah's preaching since 44:24–45:13, a text that provides Cyrus's commission to rebuild her. Whether indirectly, through mention of her counterimage Babylon (chaps. 46; 47), or directly (45:14–25; 49; 50:1–51:8; 51:9–52:12), interest in Zion has been constant. The prophet had to contend with the exiles' reluctance to leave the splendid city of Babylon for unwalled and ruined Jerusalem. He therefore emphasizes Yahweh's guarantee to make Zion the most beautiful and secure city in the world.

The unity of the chapter is suggested by the sections of approximately equal length: 54:1–5, twenty-one lines; vv. 6–10, twenty lines; and vv. 11–17, twenty-two lines. This device has been seen before in 48:1–11 and 12–22 and in 49:1–13 and 14–26. There is a clear logic to the drama: Yahweh exhorts Zion to rejoice at her husband's return (vv. 1–5), assures her that his return will be permanent (vv. 6–10), and then specifies how his protecting presence will be mediated (vv. 11–17). The fact that a tent is mentioned in vv. 1–5 and a temple-city in vv. 11–17 is no argument against unity. Old Canaanite tradition, preserved in the Ugaritic texts, portrays the gods as living either in a majestic tent or in a palace of wood and stone. Psalm 84 speaks of Yahweh living in a tent (vv. 1–2) and in a house (v. 4).

54:1–5, Zion Is to Sing at Her Husband's Return. Like the once barren Hannah, who sang, "The barren woman has borne seven, but she who has many children is forlorn" (1 Sam. 2:5), Zion is told to sing of her miraculous birth. Isaiah had praised Zion as a "quiet habitation, an immovable tent, whose stakes will never be plucked up, nor will any of its cords be broken" (Isa. 33:20, RSV). Elsewhere in the Bible (Ps. 48; Rev. 21:9–27) the sacrality of the divine dwelling is extended to the entire city. Here the old dimensions of the tent city are too narrow for the hordes of Zion's children and must be extended (Isa. 54:2–3). The shame attached, in ancient Israel, to a woman without husband, children, or property will be removed by her husband, the creator of the world (vv. 4–5).

584

54:6–10, Yahweh's Love Is Everlasting. Yahweh's return is rooted in his loving commitment; in vv. 6–10 "Yahweh says," or a variant, is repeated five times. The contrast in v. 7 is clear in the Hebrew, lit., "small moment" and "large mercy." Love's oath this time is permanent, the same oath through which Noah was promised that there would never again be a flood (Gen. 9:11). Even storms paradoxically show the new security of Zion (Isa. 54:10), where Yahweh's eternal love is available to all his people.

54:11–17, Rebuilding the City. Verse 11 alludes to the storm and loneliness that have shaken Zion, and promises rebuilding with precious stones befitting God's dwelling (vv. 12–13). Isa. 2:1–4 predicted the exaltation of the mountain of the house of Yahweh, whence Yahweh's teaching would go forth. Zion's inhabitants are appropriately called disciples ("taught by Yahweh"), who prosper because of their observance of the teaching. Songs of Zion, especially Psalms 46, 48, and 76, sang of Zion as the one firm point in the universe where God's enemies are defeated, and Isa. 54:14 echoes those promises of safety. Verses 15–16 explain why Zion is secure: Yahweh, as creator of all, controls even the enemies and the makers of their weapons. The last couplet, v. 17cd, interprets renewed Zion as the "patrimony" of Israel, given in the new exodus-conquest. Those who live in it are righteous.

55:1–13
Come to the Life Offered in Zion

Contrary to most commentators, I take chap. 55 as a single speech: vv. 1–5, eighteen lines; vv. 6–11, twenty-one lines; and vv. 12–13, nine lines. Stanzas 1 and 2 are parallel, each inviting the people to Zion, where life is offered. Stanza 3, half the length of the first stanza, concludes the invitation by an announcement of the procession to the shrine. Correspondence in length between lines of a single section has occurred before, e.g., in 40:12–31, with stanzas of eighteen, twenty-two, and twenty-six lines respectively. The best proof of unity, however, is the parallelism and interplay of vv. 1–5 and 6–11, as well as their natural connection to vv. 12–13.

55:1–5, Come to the Banquet in Zion. This section makes use of the genre of the gods' or goddesses' invitation to a banquet, attested from the late second (in the Ugaritic texts) to the late first millennium (Prov. 9; Sir. 24). In this genre, the deity invites humans to a banquet, first offering food, and then life, fellowship with the deity. Proverbs 9 is a good example: "Whoever is inexperienced, let him turn in here, whoever lacks understanding, I say 'Come eat of my food,

and drink of the wine I have mixed. Leave aside folly and live, walk in the path of insight. For with me your days will be multiplied, and the years of your life increased' " (Prov. 9:4–6). To enter the banquet hall of Dame Wisdom, one must "leave aside folly," an injunction implicit in Isa. 55:2 and explicit in 55:7–8, "Let the wicked person leave his way."

What is the meaning of "to live" in v. 3b? In Proverbs 9 it is the intentional search for wisdom, which brings one close to God. In Isa. 55:3, the bond with God exists through the covenant, in pre-exilic days made with the Davidic king but now with those who come to Zion. The Davidic king witnessed the power of Yahweh to the world (cf. Pss. 18:43–45; 89:20–27; see commentary above on Isa. 43:9); the witnessing is now to be performed by the people who return to Zion, an instance of the transferral to the whole people of tasks once performed by kings and prophets.

In the ancient Near East, king and temple were closely associated. The building, or rebuilding, of a temple, signifying the renewal of creation, was celebrated with a great feast. The previous speech, 54:11–17, narrated the building of the Temple. Celebration of divine and human kingship (in the democratized sense) is therefore appropriate.

55:6–11, Come to Where Yahweh's Word Bears Fruit. The thought advances as it did in the first section: the summons to the sanctuary (v. 6 is to be translated, "Seek Yahweh where he may be encountered, call upon him where he is present"), the insistence upon conduct appropriate to the divine presence (vv. 7–8), the movement from food ("providing seed to the sower, bread to the eater") to life with Yahweh through commission ("accomplishing what I desire, succeeding in what I command").

Jer. 29:10–14 provides an impressive parallel to the passage, declaring that God's *plans* are to bring Israel back to where they will *call upon me, seek me,* and *I will be found by you* (vocabulary similarities to Isa. 55 are in italics). According to Jeremiah, when seventy years (the period of punishment in his reckoning) were up, Israel was to come back and find God once again in the Temple. Second Isaiah held the same basic belief but expressed it in different language.

Verses 8–11 develop the idea that human plans (not RSV: "thoughts"), like human life, depend utterly upon the heavens. Only those will live who obey the divine word, which accomplishes all its purposes.

55:12–13, The Procession Along the Sacred Way. Verses 12–13 conclude the chapter and the prophecy. The prophet urges the exiles to join him in a new creation/exodus-conquest, before which all nature is in awe (v. 12). The

585

plants of the desert are replaced by evergreens, which shall stand by the highway, a memorial to the new exodus, just as the twelve stones of Joshua were to the old (Josh. 4:6–7).

56:1–66:24
Third Isaiah

56:1–8
Yahweh Will Gather Yet More Worshipers

A divine speech invites two hitherto excluded categories, eunuchs and foreigners, to become members of the holy people. In the coming judgment only those who observe the commandments will be among God's people. They will be brought to "my holy mountain" (v. 7). "Salvation" and "deliverance" refer to a future divine visitation, like that foretold in Isa. 1:21–28. The prophet's words function like the entrance rites, Psalms 15 and 24; Isa. 33:13–16 and 55:6–7, that admitted one to the Temple. The alternation between first and third person is not a sign of later editing; such alternation, even within a single verse as in v. 6, is common, especially in divine speech.

In v. 1, the imperatives, "Keep justice and do righteousness," define membership in Yahweh's people: righteous conduct in God's presence (v. 2cd; → Righteousness). The Bible sometimes defines roles by citing the divine command to the person in the role, e.g., man and woman, in Gen. 1:28, "Be fruitful and multiply"; Israel, in Lev. 19:2, "You shall be holy, for I Yahweh your God am holy"; judges, in Deut. 17:18–18:1. The word "righteousness" (RSV: "salvation") characterizes both divine and human activity in Isa. 56:1bc; the righteous God comes to a righteous people. In v. 2, only those who obey the commandments are admitted into the divine presence. "This" in v. 2a refers primarily to the righteous acts that follow; these acts are examples of the general imperatives of v. 1b. Sabbath observance is paired with a general avoidance of evil (v. 2cd); juxtaposition of general and concrete precept is characteristic of prophetic preaching, e.g., Isa. 1:16–17; Jer. 22:3, and Ezek. 45:9. Sabbath observance was emphasized in the Exile and thereafter because it defined the people, who had lost other insignia; it is not an externalizing and trivializing of religion. In the face of the divine declaration of what makes a people holy, human words of exclusion have no weight (Isa. 56:3). Foreigners "who have attached themselves to Yahweh" and who carry out the tasks of the law of Moses are admitted here and in 66:20; elsewhere foreigners per se are excluded and even reckoned as enemies (60:10; 61:5; 62:8). Eunuchs were

excluded from "entering the assembly of Yahweh" in Deut. 23:1; male worshipers were to be physically integral. The two groups are addressed in inverted order (vv. 4–7). In vv. 4–5, eunuchs who observe the Israelite religion will have "a hand and name" in the Temple and in Jerusalem. "Hand" here, as in 1 Sam. 15:12 and in 2 Sam. 18:18, means "monument"; "hand and name" is a hendiadys (two words coordinated by "and" that refer to one thought) for a monument causing one's name to be remembered. The eunuch who has no son to carry on his name, "a dry tree," has a future within the future of the people. In Isa. 56:6, no less than seven clauses—all expressing fundamental loyalty to God—impress upon the foreigner-converts how deep their conversion has to be. "Covenant" (v. 6) means the totality of commandments. "To bring to my holy mountain" (v. 7) alludes to venerable poetry such as Exod. 15:17, Deut. 32:13, and Ps. 78:54, in which Yahweh leads his people through the wilderness from Egypt to worship at his holy mountain in the land of Canaan. "Rejoice," in the parallel verse, refers to joyous and vocal participation in worship (Isa. 56:7cdef). The last phrase of v. 7, "my house shall be called a house of prayer for all the peoples" (cited in Mark 11:17 and parallels), invites those who had been excluded to the sole place of encounter between Yahweh and the community. Verse 8, the climax, declares that the welcome to the two categories of outcasts provides only one part of a yet more ambitious divine plan: to invite yet more people to the flock. Righteous conduct, not simply physical membership, makes a member of the community.

56:9–57:13
Punishment for the Idolatrous Oppressors of the Faithful

Whether the passage 56:9–57:13 is a unity is debated; the relevance of 57:1–2 to the rest is unclear to many commentators, as is the connection of 56:9–12, a denunciation of careless leaders, to 57:3–13, a denunciation of idolaters. But the passage is a unity; denunciation of leaders prior to condemnation of the people is attested elsewhere (e.g., Hos. 4:1–10; Amos 6:4–7). Moreover, typical Third-Isaian vocabulary unifies the whole section: "come" in Isa. 56:9, 12; "understand" in 56:11; 57:1; "beds" in 57:2, 7, 8; "to place in the heart" in 57:1, 11; and the Heb. root nchl, "valley" in 57:5, 6, and "inherit" in 57:13.

56:9–57:2, Divine Punishment Against the Careless Leaders. Divine punishment is announced to the leaders first and then to the people. God's summoning of the wild beasts to attack the unprotected flock or vineyard (both traditional images of the people) occurs in Jer.

12:9–13; Ezek. 14:15; and 34:5. "His/its watchmen" (Isa. 56:10) has no clear antecedent; it probably refers to Yahweh by anticipation, the speaker of the opening summons to the beasts. "Watchmen" is a term for prophets (Hos. 9:8; Jer. 6:17; Ezek. 3:17; 33:7), who are usually imagined to be on the walls of a city, but here they may be shepherds in the field because the dogs are probably shepherd dogs (cf. Job 30:1). At any rate, the leaders are blind, deaf, sleepy, wine-sodden, intent only on their appetites, neglectful of the people. Such, alas, are the shepherds, declares Isa. 56:11c; they are without understanding, thinking the future to be a mere repetition of the present (v. 12). Refusal to see a novel, divinely fashioned future was also condemned by Isaiah in chaps. 28–32. Isa. 57:1–2 provides a conventional description of the injustice brought about by the irresponsible, selfish shepherds. Psalms 12, 37, 49, and 73 all describe an unjust world in which the righteous person suffers at the hands of the wicked. Ps. 12:1 is the prayer of one trapped in such a world, "Come to rescue, Yahweh, for the godfearer has disappeared, for the faithful have vanished from the children of men." Though the syntax of the obscure Isa. 57:2 suggests that the oppressed person of v. 1 is expressing the hope of one day being rescued, the laments just cited suggest another, more plausible, interpretation: the verse continues the complaint of the just person that the unjust are flourishing (cf. Pss. 10:3–11; 73:4–9).

57:3–13, Divine Judgment in Favor of the Righteous. The divine judge summons the guilty people, "the children of diviners" and adulterers (v. 3), because of their false worship and infidelity. The rites described in vv. 5–9 are not prescribed by Yahweh; those who engage in them condemn the one God (v. 4; cf. 37:23). The rites of 57:5–9 aim to protect and enhance the fertility of humans, animals, and the soil, a deep concern of farmers in arid Palestine. Sacrifice of the firstborn child, forbidden in Israel (Exod. 13:1–2, 11–16; → Firstborn, First Fruits, Firstling), placated the god, who would then not claim subsequent children. The sexual rites were apparently carried out with cultic prostitutes representing gods or goddesses to promote fertility. The shrines are conventionally described by earlier prophets as being "under the terebinths" (Hos. 4:13) and "under every green tree" (Jer. 2:20; 3:6, 13). Such activity constitutes a covenant with the gods (Isa. 57:8c). Verse 6 plays on v. 13; a remote and arid valley (Heb. nachal) symbolizes your inheritance (nchl), whereas the righteous will inherit (Heb. nachal) the fertile land; "portion" and "lot" are also terms for the land allotted by God to Israel. Verse 9 is obscure; oil and perfume are given to a god whose epithet is "the king," and envoys are sent far and wide. The actions may honor El, the king

of the Canaanite pantheon, to whom children are offered and for whose blessing sexual rites are carried out. Israel does not grow weary of this fruitless cultic activity (v. 10), does not revere God as ultimate (RSV: "fear"), does not invoke (RSV: "remember") Yahweh; Israel mistakes Yahweh's silence for impotence (v. 11). In vv. 12–13, Yahweh, as sole God, announces his judgment: "I hereby pronounce judgment upon your deeds" (lit., "your judgment and your deeds," a hendiadys). By this decree, Yahweh decides in favor of the aggrieved righteous of 57:1–2 and against the unrighteous of vv. 3–11. The righteous, those who hope in Yahweh alone, will inherit the land. The author has drawn on Psalm 37, with its reversal of the fortunes of the good and the wicked, especially vv. 9, 11, 18, 22, 29, 40, and also upon Isa. 65:13–14.

57:14–21
God Will Lead the Humble Faithful

This speech, alluding to earlier prophetic texts that declare God's wrath or absence, refers to specific sins of Israel. God's wrath will not be permanent; it will be turned into loving care by free divine decision. Second Isaiah's call for a new exodus from Babylon becomes a metaphor for "the way" of the wisdom literature, on which the righteous consciously place themselves.

57:14–17, The All-Holy Dwells with the Lowly. "Build up a highway" alludes to 40:3 except that "way" and "stumbling block" become metaphors, as in Psalm 1 and Proverbs 1–9. Isa 57:15 impressively declares the Most High to be on the side of the lowly, bringing them to life. Verses 16–17, like 54:7–8, attribute God's wrath to Israel's sin and not to divine impotence. "A contrite or broken spirit" is the way to assure his return (→ Wrath). The words recall Ps. 51:17, "My sacrifice, O God, is a spirit broken; a heart broken and crushed, O God, you will not reject." As in 1 Kings 8:27–30, 33–34, a stark contrast is drawn between God's lofty dwelling and his gracious presence to those who repent. Isa. 54:7–8 is incorporated in v. 16 but changed considerably. Modern translations generally interpret v. 16cd after the Septuagint (LXX) paraphrase: "For spirit will come forth from me and I have made all breath," but the literal Hebrew text is to be preferred: "Yes, because of me spirits flag, [for] it is I who made the breath of life"; all is attributed to God. This stage of the speech, the self-willed wandering of the people, ends in v. 17c.

57:18–21, Yahweh Turns and Leads the Lowly. God then "sees" their confusion caused by his absence in v. 18, just as he saw the people's plight in Exod. 2:25 and Isa. 58:3a.

587

Spontaneously he resolves to heal them; he will lead them along the right path to where their ritual mourning, "the fruit of their lips," will find acceptance. In 57:19–21, God unambiguously declares his will to save the repentant in Zion and in far-off lands and to punish the wicked. As in Psalm 1, where the wind blows the wicked like chaff, the wicked here are uprooted, ceaselessly churned by the sea. Israel far and near is to turn to God who dwells with the lowly.

58:1–14
The Fast That Yahweh Wants

Though some scholars believe that chap. 58 is a composite (vv. 1–3a plus 5–9 making up the original kernel), the passage develops a single idea coherently: liturgical fasts win Yahweh's favor only when people act justly by caring for the poor. Verses 13–14 include sabbath observances among the required acts of justice, as does 56:1–8; Israel did not reduce obedience to social justice alone.

58:1–3b, The Prophet Is Instructed. Verse 1 instructs the prophet to speak like a trumpet (cf. Hos. 8:1) and gives a reason for the ensuing judgment: the people seek oracles from priests and prophets but do not "do righteousness" (the same phrase expressing total fidelity, as in 56:1). Popular frustration at God's silence is felt particularly at the fasts (Isa. 58:3a), which had been observed on the fourth, fifth, seventh, and tenth months since the destruction of Jerusalem in 587 B.C. (Zech. 7:1–7; 8:19).

58:3c–5, The Prophet Denounces the Fasts. Though the people approach God as if they were a righteous nation (v. 2cd), they oppress their neighbor. Their self-abasing gestures are not accepted (v. 5).

58:6–14, Proper Repentance and Its Fruits. In v. 6 begins the first of three long conditional sentences; the others begin at vv. 9c and 13. What Yahweh requires in the first sentence is that they liberate and care for the poor, the needy who are victimized by the wicked (→ Poor). For their fasting to be accepted, they must reverse the behavior described in vv. 3b–4. Verses 8–9b depict what the divine response will be to such conversion: their light and healing will shine forth; God will lead them and will answer their prayer.

In the second conditional sentence, if you free the poor (vv. 9b–10) then your light will shine, and Yahweh will lead you (vv. 10b–11 = v. 8). Verses 11d–12 show the happy effects of God's favor: the people will have water in abundance, and their city will be rebuilt, the goal of the fasts.

In the third and climactic "if . . . then" series, righteousness is interpreted as keeping Yahweh's Sabbath, a day for joy and for casting off willful conduct (v. 13). As in 56:7–8 and 57:13, Yahweh's protection is described in terms of exodus-conquest. Isa. 58:14 cites the great poem of Israel's origins: "He will put them on the high places of the earth, he will let them eat the produce of the field" (Deut. 32:13). There is a progression in the fruits of repentance in the three sections, culminating in the third: secure possession of the land.

59:1–21
Those Who Repent in Zion Will Be Saved

Most scholars believe that chap. 59 is a redactional unit, i.e., its unity is the work of an editor rather than the prophet. The prophet rebukes a complaint, typical of community laments, that Yahweh is silent (v. 1ab), vigorously showing that the people, not Yahweh, are responsible for their plight (vv. 2–8). A traditional lament follows in vv. 9–15b. Verses 15c–20 are the divine response to the lament: judgment in favor of the righteous. Verse 21 is generally seen as an addition.

59:1–8, Prophetic Rebuke of a Lament Complaint. In communal laments such as Pss. 44:9–25 (esp. vv. 23–24); 74; 77 (esp. vv. 7–10); 89:38–51; and Lamentations, the people complain of God's indifference at his people's suffering in order to rouse him to action, e.g., "Why do you hold back your hand?" (Ps. 74:11a). Isa. 59:1 alludes to such a complaint about Yahweh's power. Such near blasphemy deserves the prophetic rebuke of vv. 1–8. The first part of the rebuke, vv. 2–4, vigorously directs the blame away from Yahweh and onto the people, declaring that "your" sins are the reason for God's absence; the Hebrew suffix "your" is repeated nine times in eight verses. The description of "your" sins (vv. 1–4) resembles other cultic rebukes (e.g., Ps. 50:16–21; Isa. 1:14–15). Isa. 59:4 mentions legal abuses (Job 5:1; 9:16; 13:22) show the legal context). The word "no one" in Isa. 59:4a, like "no one" in Pss. 12:1–2; 14:1, 3 (= Ps. 53), provides part of a conventional description of corrupt society. Isa. 59:5–8 includes traditional language for deep-rooted perversity (cf. Ps. 58:3–5): evil conduct ends in frustration (the vain weaving in Isa. 59:6) and death (the poison of v. 5). Human life is a path (a metaphor repeated six times). As is common in Third Isaiah, words from the one section recur, often without development, in another: "hand," "blood," "no one," "justice," which appear in vv. 1–4, reappear in vv. 5–8.

59:9–15b, The Lament. The people now lament God's absence from their suffering for the reasons shown them by the prophet: they themselves have made a corrupt, self-enclosed society that cannot save itself. "Therefore" (v. 9) they lament, i.e., lift up to Yahweh their dashed hopes for "redress" and "vindication" (better than RSV: "justice" and "righteousness" in vv. 9ab, 11cd, 14). The "path" metaphor of the rebuke in vv. 7–8 is continued in the lament of vv. 9b–15: "righteousness has not caught up with us," "we walk in gloom," to grope along a wall, to stumble, to enter. The lament lays out before God the community's disappointment and sadness (vv. 9–11), its living with the consequences of sin (vv. 12–13), and its corrupt institutions (vv. 14–15b). The climactic example of social corruption, oppression of the righteous ("the one who turns from evil is despoiled," v. 15b), is important; it will be picked up by v. 20b, only "those who turn from sin in Jacob" will be redeemed in Yahweh's judgment.

59:15c–20, Yahweh Sees and Comes as Redeemer to Zion. The total corruption of the people is abhorrent to Yahweh (v. 15cd). Because there is not one just person to intervene for the people, someone like Moses in Exodus or the servant in Isa. 53:12, Yahweh alone must right things (Isa. 59:16). As a warrior he arms himself (vv. 17–18; cf. 42:13–17; 51:9–11) and goes out against his enemies. The whole world will fear the name of the Lord when they see this redeemer, like a pent-up stream and a roaring wind, coming to vindicate repentant Zion (59:19–20; cf. 1:27–28). Verse 20b follows up on v. 15b; the innocent victims of social injustice will be rescued.

59:21, The Spirit and the Covenant. The next verse seems a comment on rather than an integral part of the preceding passage. The wind, or spirit, of Yahweh as he comes to the city (v. 20) is declared to be a permanent feature available to the inhabitants of the renewed city, enabling them to be faithful and to give praise to Yahweh. In Num. 11:23–30, the spirit is given to all the people in response to the question, "Is the hand of Yahweh shortened?" just as in Isa. 59:1.

60:1–22
Zion's Glory

Chap. 60 is the first of three sections, the others being chaps. 61 and 62, that speak of God's grand design for Zion and for its inhabitants; the chapters constitute a striking change from the judgment of the preceding and following chapters. The prophet, in chaps. 60–62, draws on a variety of traditions: Zion songs (such as Pss. 46, 48, and 76) in which enemy kings are defeated

at the foot of the holy mountain; royal songs (such as Pss. 18:43–45; 22:27–28; 72:8–11, 15) in which the king is saved from his enemies who recognize the grandeur of Jerusalem; Isaian texts (such as 2:1–5; 8:22–9:7) in which Israel is bathed in divine light; and Second-Isaian texts (such as 49:14–26; 54) in which God promises Dame Zion that the nations will bring back her dispersed children and rebuild her walls. Using these traditions Third Isaiah composed chap. 60, a unified poem asserting the brilliance and vitality of God's city. This transformation of the present devastated Jerusalem has no timetable: "I Yahweh will hasten it in its time" (v. 22). The poem consists of a preamble, vv. 1–3, and three sections of approximately equal length, vv. 4–9, 10–16, and 17–22.

60:1–3, Preamble. Verse 1 summons the city to rise up from its lowliness and shine with the brilliance of Yahweh. "Light," "Yahweh," "glory [of Yahweh]," occur in parallelism, showing that God's presence in the temple-city (the two are not really separate here) is symbolized by light. Divine light overcame primordial night at creation (Gen. 1:1–5; cf. John 1:5) and overcame the night of foreign domination (Isa. 8:22–9:2). In Isaiah the light embodies itself in the teaching given on Mount Zion (2:5), to which the nations make pilgrimage. These verses make that contrast even more stark; outside the circle of God's presence all is primordial night.

60:4–9, Worship in Zion with the Wealth of the Nations. The section 60:4–9 is unified by the summons to Dame Zion (v. 4) and by her surprised and delighted question (v. 8; cf. the similar sequence of summons and question in 49:18, 21). Unlike chaps. 49 and 54, however, the section does not primarily announce restoration of children to barren Zion but the arrival of worshipers at the one place where true worship can be offered. Jews in exile, "your sons . . . your daughters," must therefore come to Zion (60:4). Zion's joy (v. 5) comes from participating in celebration and from seeing the nations acknowledge the sole divinity of Yahweh. The nations' tribute—gold, frankincense, flocks, and rams—is exclusively for the worship of Yahweh, not the enrichment of the people. The caravans (v. 6) are an allusion to Ps. 72:10–11. The answer to Zion's astonished question (Isa. 60:8) about the sailing ships states the purpose of all the activity: the honoring of Yahweh in Zion.

60:10–16, Foreigners Will Rebuild Jerusalem. The nations supplied materials for worship in the previous section; here they rebuild the city and Temple. There seems to be no sharp distinction between city ("walls" in v. 10a) and Temple ("sanctuary" in v. 13c); the entire city is hallowed. To the city once abandoned and rejected, with no trade routes ("no one passing through" in v. 15), there comes building material (vv. 11–13) with which the foreign kings can build (v. 10). Kings present their tribute with Eastern gestures of submission (so Ps. 72:8–11) as they acknowledge the city of Yahweh (Isa. 60:14).

Verse 12 is generally considered a later addition; it is metrically overlong, and its harsh threat seems out of keeping with the tone of the rest. Israel knows its Lord by his act—the pouring in of precious building material.

60:17–22, Replacement of the Old Order. Conventional building materials are inadequate for the new city; moreover, the city's rulers require renewal (v. 17). Third Isaiah here as elsewhere does not distinguish sharply between the physical city and its spirit, the inner and the outer. In addition, Hebrew royal poetry often pairs virtues, e.g., "righteousness and justice are the foundation of your throne, steadfast love and fidelity walk before you" (Ps. 89:14). Such paired virtues characterize ideal governance, e.g., Isa. 1:26; 9:7; 11:4–5. Isa. 60:17, lit., "I will make your governance Peace and your officials [not RSV: 'taskmasters'] Righteousness," promises that the rulers of the new city will govern according to the divine plan. As a result of that governance, the cry "Violence" and "Wrack and Ruin" will no longer be heard (v. 18ab). Walls and gates are also given names expressing their essence, customary in the ancient Near East (v. 18cd). Next, sun and moon are replaced by the light/glory of Yahweh (vv. 19–20; cf. vv. 1–3; Rev. 21:23). In the dramatic perspective of this poem, everything becomes insignificant except the brilliant presence of God in Zion. In Isa. 60:21–22 all of Dame Zion's children are declared righteous, the climax of the several renamings in the poem. "Righteous" means acceptable to God; they are therefore given the land, the reward of the righteous (Ps. 37:29). In Isa. 60:22, God's blessing enhances vitality; the least shall become a clan. The last verse, v. 22cd, entrusts the timetable of the transformation to God, "In its time I will hasten it."

61:1–11
The Prophet Is Sent to the Poor

Chap. 61 is a single poem with a single theme: Yahweh appoints the prophet to announce to the poor they are to be glorious among the nations. In vv. 10–11 he leads the revived community in a thanksgiving that anticipates the salvation he so decisively announced in vv. 1–3. The central section, vv. 4–9, develops the theme of deliverance for the poor. Underlying the poem is the biblical conviction that the 'anawim, the poor (victims of the wicked who wait for Yahweh), will see Yahweh reverse their

situation, since injustice insults Yahweh, the creator of a just world. (Jesus begins his public ministry in Luke 4:18–19 with Isa. 61:1–2.)

61:1–3, The Prophet Is Anointed to Preach Liberation to the Poor. Third Isaiah confidently proclaims that the spirit of Yahweh is upon him, enabling him to preach this message of liberation. Pre-exilic writing prophets, with the exception of Ezekiel, generally were endowed with the Deity's word rather than with the spirit of God, perhaps to differentiate them from popular ecstatics. The Second-Isaian servant, however, was granted the spirit (42:1; 48:16d), and the speaker continues that tradition here. Only priests and kings were regularly anointed in pre-exilic Israel, with the possible exception of Elijah in 1 Kings 19:16. "Anoint" here (as perhaps in the Elijah text) may be figurative for "appoint," parallel to "send" in the next verse. "To announce good news" is properly the work of sentries or messengers, who, in Second Isaiah and elsewhere (40:9; 52:7–8), announce a specific event in the immediate future. The good news here, however, is a reversal of fortune that lies in the unspecified future; lack of specificity is suggested by the parallelism of "year" and "day" in Isa. 61:2. The five terms for the afflicted in vv. 1–2 are synonyms. All the terms describe the righteous poor, unjustly kept from their reward. As in 42:7 and 49:9, those for whom salvation has not yet occurred are called prisoners. The year of release for the poor is at hand (Lev. 25:39–41; Ezek. 46:17). In Isa. 61:2, RSV's "day of vengeance" is better translated "day of vindication," a time when God rights wrongs. Verse 3 is confused, lit., "to place [?] for the mourners of Zion"; it is perhaps a corrupt repetition of v. 2c. It is certain, however, that "to give them a turban instead of ashes" (v. 3b) parallels "comfort all the mourners" (v. 2c). In v. 3bcd the mourners are clothed in priest's attire; "turban" and "a splendid garment" are preferable to RSV's "garland" and "mantle of praise." Oil, turban, and garments suggest the consecration of priests (Exod. 28–29; Lev. 8). The liberated, festally attired people are to be "righteous terebinths," long-lived trees with spreading branches, which constitute an apt symbol for the restored and vital people who will show forth God's power to bring victory.

61:4–9, Restoration and Glory. To this revived group is given the privilege of rebuilding the ruins of God's land (v. 4). Of vv. 5–7, Ibn Ezra, eleventh century A.D., wrote perceptively: "The other nations will resemble the Israelites, and the Israelites will be like the Aaronites; the Israelites will therefore receive the abundance of nations as their tithes." Priests in the ancient Near East lived off the revenues of temple lands and the offerings of the faithful; they were thus left free for divine service. The difficult Hebrew of v. 7ab, lit., "Instead of your shame, a double portion; and people cried out 'shame their lot,' " is probably to be read as follows (corrected words are in italics): "Because *their* shame was double, shame *and spitting* [cf. 50:6] their lot, therefore they shall inherit a double portion in their land, everlasting joy shall be upon their heads." Just as the Israelites saw priests as specially blessed by Yahweh, so the nations will see the renewed community as blessed.

61:10–11, Song of Thanksgiving. As in thanksgiving psalms, which are public celebrations of divine rescue of a person or community from near destruction, the speaker of v. 1 anticipates celebrating divine rescue. Lament psalms sometimes praise God proleptically, before the actual salvation (e.g., Pss. 22:22–28; 31:21–24). The priestly metaphor continues in the clothing with festal garments (v. 10; cf. Exod. 29:5–9); Isa. 61:10e reads, "like a bridegroom who 'priests it' with a turban," i.e., wears a splendid priestly turban. Like 55:3–5, which speaks of the royal people revealing God's glory to the nations, so these verses speak of a priestly people performing the same task.

62:1–12

Prayer for the City's Restoration

Commentators agree that chap. 62 comprises, at least, a redactional unity. The prophet announces the city's new name, indicating a change of mission (vv. 1–5). The sentries remind God of the promise; on its basis they urge the people to open the transformed city to those still exiled (vv. 6–12).

62:1–3, Prayer for a New Name. So great is the contrast between the ruined city and the traditional promises about it that the prophet must break forth into ardent prayer on behalf of Zion (v. 1). Some scholars suggest that the "I" of v. 1 stems from God, who is now breaking his silence. Yet the verse is a prayer like vv. 6–7, not an announcement of action, as in Pss. 78:65–66 and Isa. 42:13–17. The praying person will not cease *until* Zion's victory and triumph are so visible "that the nations will see your victory . . . and call [reading an infinitive] you by a new name, which the mouth of Yahweh will give." In the Bible, name reveals essence, and a change in name, a new direction, e.g., Abram and Sarai to Abraham and Sarah in Gen. 17:5–15, and Jacob to Israel in Gen. 32:28. The new name of Zion is only given in Isa. 62:4; it is Yahweh's to assign (vv. 2d, 4). Verse 3 views the vindication of Zion as the bestowal of a splendid crown and royal turban, the investiture signifying bestowal of office.

62:4–5, The New Name. As in Gen. 17:5, 15 and 32:28, the old name is nullified before the new one is assigned. "Abandoned" and "Desolate" yield to "Hepzibah" (a woman's name meaning in Heb. "my delight rests on her," said by the delighted parent) and Beulah ("married"). The verses allude to 54:1–8, and perhaps to Hosea 2, where Yahweh, the husband, supplies the grain and wine to the wife, as he does in vv. 8–9 of our passage. Most scholars read v. 5, by a slight change, "your builder [i.e., God]," instead of the senseless "your sons" of the Masoretic Text (MT). Verse 5a refers back chiastically to v. 4d to "marry," and v. 5b to "delight." It is always Yahweh who initiates marriage in the Bible.

62:6–7, The Sentries Are to Pray. Every walled city had its sentries to watch out for the welfare of the inhabitants. These are to join in the prophet's fervent prayer that Zion's victory and triumph (v. 1) arrive soon. Day and night they will lift up to Yahweh, "cause him to remember," the condition of the city; they are neither to rest themselves nor let Yahweh rest until Jerusalem is rebuilt in such a way that it wins praise over all the earth.

62:8–9, God's Oath, the Sure Foundation of the New Name. Yahweh swears that Israel will eat the grain and the wine it produces, and not be forced to use it for tribute to foreign kings.

62:10–12, Preparation to Welcome the Remaining Exiles. In chap. 49, after Zion was assured that her children would return, God promised to raise an ensign to guide the nations carrying the exiles home (49:22). Here the inhabitants of Zion themselves, certain of her vindication, are to go out, complete the highway into the city, raise the ensign among the peoples (v. 10), and repeat (vv. 10–11) the proclamation of Second Isaiah (40:3, 10). Isa. 62:12 reworks Isa. 11:10–12, though the purview of our prophet is limited to the exiles. "They" are the returning exiles, and "you" are Zion, the city that makes all who come into it holy.

63:1–6

Day of Punishment for the Nations

All commentators agree vv. 1–6 are a unit, many suggesting that this judgment followed by the lament of 63:7–64:12 and the lament with judgment in chap. 59 frame chaps. 60–62. Purification of Zion is but one task of the righteous and powerful God; the other is punishment of the nations who exceeded their mandate to be the instruments of God's wrath against Israel (63:1–6). As in Isa. 10:5–19 and 14:24–27, which together describe the divine punishment of the Assyrian king for excessive cruelty in carrying out his role as the "rod of my anger" (10:5), the nations are punished for their excessive cruelty to Israel before and during the Exile. The wrath of God constitutes anger directed at injustice done by the wicked against God's people.

In 63:1, a speaker, presumably in Zion, asks the approaching bloodstained warrior who he is. The speaker is perhaps a sentry on the city wall but more likely is a speaker in a ritual, as in Ps. 24:7–10, "Who is this king of glory?" (cf. Ps. 118:20). The ritual questions are asked to allow the warrior to recount his exploits. Edom had become the enemy because of its incursions into ill-defended Judah during the Exile (Ps. 137:7; Lam. 4:21–22; Ezek. 25:12; 35:1–15; Obad. 13–14). Along with its capital Bozrah, Edom provides, therefore, the appropriate site for the punishment inflicted upon all sinful nations. To the first question, "Who are you?" the answer is, "I [Yahweh], acting in justice." To the second, "Why are your garments red?" the answer is that they are bespattered from Yahweh's battle in Edom (cf. Isa. 34). The warrior acted alone, possibly because there is no Cyrus here to do his will, but more probably because only Yahweh can redress such massive injustice. Yahweh acted alone against Egypt in Exodus 1–15 and against the Assyrian king in Isa. 10:5–19; 14:24–27.

Isa. 59:15–20, the other side of the frame enclosing chaps. 60–62, announces that Yahweh, after repaying his enemies, "will come to Zion as Redeemer" (59:20). In this scene the warrior arrives at the gates, seeking admission to his city. Are the people ready to welcome the God who demands righteous conduct?

63:7–14
A Communal Lament: The National Story

Nearly all scholars agree that 63:7–64:12 forms a single impressive communal lament. All the conventions of the form appear: the recital of the deeds that brought Israel into existence (63:7–14) with mingled complaint against God, prayer for rescue, and acknowledgment of sin in 63:15–64:12. Other biblical laments, such as Psalms 44, 74, 77, 80, 83, and 89, similarly retell the creation of Israel as Yahweh's people in his land and complain that Yahweh no longer protects their secure dwelling in his land or sanctuary. They ask: will Yahweh allow his act to be nullified by mere human enemies? The lament is to be dated sometime before the rebuilding of the Temple in 515 B.C.

In 63:7–14, the speaker recites before Yahweh the story of Israel's origins in order to persuade him to be faithful to that original loving act. Verses 8–14 tell a single story: God freely chose his people and became their savior in

Egypt, his presence leading them through the wilderness (vv. 8–9). Their rebellion and consequent punishment (v. 10) did not nullify God's work because Moses succeeded in persuading God to appear among them again and lead them to his holy land (vv. 11–14). Verse 8ab presents a divine declaration making them his people, like divine declarations in Exod. 6:6–8; 19:5–6; 20:2–3, and Lev. 26:11–12, where the divine word creates a people. Egypt, to be sure, is not mentioned, but v. 9b alludes to the Exodus, "No angel, no messenger (but) his presence saved them" (cf. Exod. 32:34; 33:2–3, 14–16). Yahweh's lifting and carrying Israel (Isa. 63:9) utilizes the venerable tradition of God's carrying the people to Canaan (cf. Exod. 19:4; Deut. 32:11; Isa. 40:11; and chap. 46). With Isa. 63:10 the history departs from other communal laments (except Ps. 106) by including among the "days of old" the rebellion and punishment of the people, their repentance under Moses, and Yahweh's return to them as guide to the land. Isa. 63:10 is central because of its position (eight bicola, or poetic lines, preceding and following), by its picking up earlier phrases (e.g., emphatic "they" in v. 8; "to become their enemy" echoing "to become their savior" in v. 8c; "he fought against them" echoing "he redeemed them" in v. 9c) and by its shifting of the traditional "his presence" of v. 9c to "his holy spirit" (a shift of terminology that will be extended in later verses to "his holy spirit" [v. 11], "his glorious arm" [v. 12], and "spirit of Yahweh" [v. 14]). Moses is the subject of "he remembered" (v. 11), in spite of scholarly opinion proposing God or the people as subject. The people are the subject of a plural verb in the immediately preceding verse, whereas the verb in v. 11 is singular; God could not be the subject, since the complaint of vv. 11c–14a is governed by "remembered." Verse 11 should be translated: "then remembered the days of old Moses his servant." The exceptional Hebrew word order, verb-object-subject, of v. 11 frames (with v. 9d) v. 10 by the phrase "days of old." In vv. 11c–12b, Moses first complains that Yahweh neglects him, Yahweh's servant, exactly as he does in his pentateuchal complaints (Exod. 32:30–34; 33:13–16; 34:9; Num. 11:10–15). He uses the polite third person, appropriate to a servant addressing his master (cf. 1 Sam. 26:19–20; 2 Sam. 7:18–29). Yahweh's drawing him out of the water could refer either to Exodus 2 or, metaphorically, to drawing him out of danger (cf. Pss. 18:16; 30:3; 40:2). Only afterward, in Isa. 63:12c–14a, does Moses plead for the people, using the traditional argument that Yahweh's honor ("to make for himself a glorious name" in v. 12d) demands that he remain faithful to the Exodus. Verses 13–14a, which have frequently been emended, make perfect sense if they are divided properly:

"[Where is] the one who caused them to walk through the deep like a horse in the steppe? They did not stumble, like a beast in the plain." (For the parallelism of "cause to walk" and "they did not stumble," cf. Jer. 31:9.) Isa. 63:14b is the divine response to Moses' complaint: "The spirit came down and rested upon him"; i.e., Moses is the mediator of the spirit to the people. This particular version of the national story, in which the people's rebellion did not definitively end Yahweh's presence, is designed to encourage the people to pray, using the language in 63:15–64:12, that Yahweh come down to meet them despite their sin.

63:15–64:12
The Lament Prayer

As comparable communal laments make clear, the historical recital is exactly tailored to the aim of the lament. Psalm 44, for example, recalls Yahweh's conquest of Canaan before it complains that the enemy overruns the land. Psalm 89 tells the story of the powerful installation of the Davidic king as highest of the kings of the earth (Ps. 89:27) before complaining that the king is suffering defeats. Our text tells how, despite the people's sin that made God their enemy, Moses' intercession occasioned the return of the spirit that led them to the shrine. In the prayer, the people complain that the shrine is in ruins (Isa. 63:18; 64:10–11) and that Yahweh has become their enemy (63:17, 19; 64:5, 7), just as he had been in the days before Moses' intercession (63:10). Moses' success in persuading Yahweh to return to his people emboldens the people to pray for a new divine-human encounter (64:1–5b). Communal lamentation typically mingles direct prayer in the imperative mood, motives for divine action, questions such as "How long?" or "Where are you?" and descriptive complaint.

63:15–19, Look Down, Our Father, and Turn to Your Servants! The prayer builds on the recital. Verse 15 asks God to look down from his holy and glorious abode upon the plight of the people, using the very adjectives for his dwelling that described his presence in days of old ("*holy* spirit" and "*glorious* arm"). As in 63:11–14, it asks where now are the power and compassion evident in earlier days. With its reference to "our Father" and "our Redeemer," v. 16 harks back to God calling Israel "my children" and becoming their redeemer in 63:8–9. The vigorous complaint of vv. 17–19 reproaches God—to whom it attributes for the moment all initiative—for allowing Israel to appear as if it had no protecting God. The speaker hints that God's honor is at stake. We are your special property (lit., "heritage"); it is your sanctuary

that is destroyed (v. 18); no one would ever judge that we are your people from the condition we are in (v. 19). This reproach resembles Moses' complaint in 63:12c–14a, which reminded Yahweh his honor was in question ("to make for himself an everlasting name," v. 12d).

64:1–7, O That You Would Come Down to Rescue Us! The prayer asks (v. 1) that Yahweh not only look down (63:15) but come down from the heavens, just as the spirit of Yahweh came down upon Moses and the people in 63:14b. The same Hebrew word for "come down" is used in both verses. In Israel's venerable poetry, Yahweh appeared in storm to rescue his people in time of need (Exod. 15:4–10; Judg. 5:4–5; Deut. 33:2–5; and esp. Ps. 18:6–19 = 2 Sam. 22). Isa. 64:1–5 make up an extended wish, dependent upon the syntax of v. 1a, that Yahweh come down now as he came down in days of old (63:14b). The second half of 64:3 should be excised as a doublet of v. 1b. Verse 4 continues the wish of v. 1 and should be translated, "as when you do wonders we do not expect, what was not heard of, not perceived, what eye had not seen, O God, except you, who act for those who wait for you." The verse perhaps alludes to Isa. 48:6–8, which predicts salvation in such terms and prays for the fullness of the Second-Isaian promise. Though some scholars interpret "meet" in v. 5 in its frequently attested hostile sense, so that Yahweh attacks the righteous person (so JPS), the verb "to meet" (like other Hebrew verbs of solemn encounter) can be used in a friendly sense as well (e.g., Gen. 32:2). Here the verse is to be read, "Oh, that you would meet [favorably] the one who rejoices in doing justice," thus aptly concluding the prayer for Yahweh's coming down to the sanctuary.

Isa. 64:5c–7 continue the prayer that Yahweh come down by their stark portrayal of God as absolute master—even to the extent of attributing the people's sin to his absence, his "hiding his face"—and the people as mired in sin.

64:8–12, Our Father, Look Down! The thought returns to the recital of 63:8–9, God as Father, Israel as his children. As the Father who created us, pity the work of your hands! The people appeal to Yahweh's care for his creation, not to their virtue. The recital of 63:7–14 ended in v. 14bcd with Israel led to Yahweh's holy territory or shrine. Their ruined shrine suggests to the nations that Yahweh is not able to sustain into the present his past saving action. The psalm ends with a question: will you keep silent? The people have faith enough to hold Yahweh to the promise contained in the act that brought them to existence.

593

65:1–25
The Righteous Shall Inhabit the Land

Scholars generally agree that chap. 65 is a unified whole, though, as is often the case with Third Isaiah, there is disagreement whether the entire chapter was composed as a single unit, or whether segments were gradually added to a core, vv. 1–16a. Those who hold the latter opinion point to the exclusive concern with the wicked-righteous contrast in vv. 1–16a and with the righteous alone in vv. 16b–23, and suggest that v. 24, with its obvious reference back to v. 1, artificially links the two originally separate sections. The date of composition too is debated, though recent scholarship rightly rejects a Hellenistic date for the rites of vv. 3–5 in favor of the late sixth century. This commentary proposes an originally single composition chiefly because dual judgment upon the wicked and righteous in Jerusalem was frequent in some Psalms (e.g., 50; 76) and elsewhere in Third Isaiah (56:9–57:13; 58; 59). The emphasis throughout chap. 65 is on the city, or land (sometimes called "mountain," singular or plural) purified of sinners.

65:1–7, Sentence upon a Faithless People. Some prophetic judgments portray Yahweh wronged by the people and hence justified in condemning them. In Isa. 1:2–3, Yahweh is the loving father of ungrateful children, and in Amos 2:9–12, the gracious giver of leaders who are not heeded. Yahweh here is eager to be worshiped and inquired of at the Temple, the meaning of "seek," "ask," "find," but the people seek other gods (Isa. 65:1d–5). They do not use Yahweh's name (v. 1d). They anger him (vv. 3ab, 5cd) by worshiping in unauthorized places (v. 3cd), by seeking oracles from the dead through the practice of incubation (sleeping in a tomb to receive communication in dreams, v. 4ab), by not observing the dietary laws (v. 4cd), by assuming they have become holy, set apart, and warning off the profane lest their holiness be contaminated (v. 5ab). Such willful behavior offends the one who has always been accessible to those who approach in the right spirit (v. 5cd). The just God, who punished false worship in the past, announces punishment for it now (vv. 6–7). "It is written" (v. 6a) may cite an actual text regarding divine justice or it may state an axiom: sin is always punished. The verses declare the present sins to be equivalent to pre-exilic sins "upon the mountains, upon the hills" (e.g., Deut. 12:2; 2 Kings 16:4; Hos. 4:13; Ezek. 6:13).

65:8–10, My Chosen Ones Will Inherit the Land. These verses are crucial to the speech. The destruction threatened in vv. 1–7 is not directed at all Israel (v. 8). Yahweh is about to do a new thing and will bring forth a group from the people who will inherit the land. Just as farmers do not destroy a cluster of grapes since it contains the juice that will become wine, so Yahweh will not destroy all Israel since among them are "my servants." They will inherit the delightful pasture stretching from west (Sharon) to east (Valley of Achor that terminates near Jericho). Third Isaiah alludes to the servant of chaps. 40–55; through the servant(s), Israel will continue to exist.

65:11–12, The Sword for Those Who Forsake Yahweh. The same judicial act that gives a future to "my servants" (v. 8) punishes the idolaters. They preferred the gods Gad ("Fortune") and Mani ("Destiny") to Yahweh, who invites obedience and righteous behavior (v. 12c; cf. vv. 1–2, 24). Biblical judgment is not a decree but an act upholding the righteous and putting down the wicked so as to make known the righteous God.

65:13–16, The Judgment Itself. These verses describe the judicial act: the righteous and the wicked are publicly assigned their places. The verses have in view the new creation (vv. 17–25); they announce who will inhabit the new land. The wicked are addressed directly in the second person; the righteous, in the third person. God's new city/land/mountain(s) are only for the holy. Like the old entrance liturgies, e.g., Psalms 15; 24; and Isa. 33:13–16, which admitted only the obedient to the sacred precincts, these verses admit the obedient to the new Jerusalem described in Isa. 65:17–25. "My servants shall eat . . . shall drink" in v. 13 points ahead to vv. 21–22. "My servants shall sing . . ." in v. 14 points ahead to vv. 18–19. In v. 15, the chosen will use the name of the rejected sinners as a curse; i.e., they will say of their enemies, "May you meet the fate of the sinners who were excluded from the new creation!" Verse 15b, "May Yahweh slay you," seems to be a later attempt to supply the words of a curse. Whoever bless themselves (in the new creation) can be sure that God is there to effect the blessing (v. 16), another pointer to vv. 17–25. In v. 16ef, "the former troubles," i.e., the iniquitous present age when the wicked reign unchecked, are to end with the new creation. The whole section echoes Psalm 37, where "the meek" and "the lowly" inherit the land, and it anticipates the Beatitudes in Matt. 5:2–12 and Luke 6:20–26. In the light of the Isaian context, the Beatitudes are judgments regarding who may enter the kingdom of God.

65:17–25, New Heavens and New Earth. These verses echo and expand chaps. 60–62. Where Yahweh lives there can only be victory and life; evil and premature death have no place. Verse 20 is widely regarded as a later addition; in any case the verse is somewhat confused. No invaders will take the homes and farms of the righteous; they will enjoy the land throughout their long lives and will be seen by all as blessed by Yahweh (vv. 21–22). God's readiness to hear prayer in the shrine will be respected by the people (v. 24), not abused as in 65:1–2 and 65:11–12. The paradisal scene, which recalls Genesis 2, Isa. 2:1–4, and Isa. 11:6–9, represents the world Yahweh intended. Biblical creation is not the formation of the physical universe alone, but of a people.

66:1–16
Judgment in Jerusalem in Favor of the Righteous

Verses 1–16 provide a judgment oracle: the ritual acts of one group of Israelites are condemned, and another group's acts are accepted. Some scholars find several discrete units here, but the condemnation of one group of Israelites and the upholding of another is common in Third Isaiah (e.g., 56:9–57:13; 58; 59; 65). The group relying on ritual alone without regard for obedience (vv. 3–4) and denying the imminent coming of Yahweh (v. 5) will not enter the New Jerusalem. The new city is created by an act of divine judgment (vv. 5–16).

66:1–2, Where Does Yahweh Dwell? Solomon prayed at the dedication of the Temple: "Will God dwell on earth? See, heaven and the highest heaven cannot contain you, how much less this house that I have built! . . . Yet hear the prayer of your servant and your people Israel when they pray toward this place" (1 Kings 8:27, 30). The Temple is the place where God graciously meets the penitent people. The prophets from the beginning protested empty ritual; even the Psalms rebuke it, e.g., Psalm 50. Third Isaiah reiterates this criticism; he is not rejecting worship as such, since pure and obedient worship characterizes life in the New Jerusalem. He dwells with the obedient and with those who hope for his coming.

66:3–4, False and Disobedient Worship. The worship of those who do not respond when Yahweh calls, i.e., who are disobedient (v. 4c), is equated with murder and false worship (v. 3): "the one who slaughters oxen (in sacrifice) is a slayer of humans." These shocking equations are the strongest of the three passages in Third Isaiah that equate disobedient worship with pagan worship; the others are 57:5–10 and 65:2–5. Entry into temples was carefully regulated in antiquity; humans had to negotiate that holy realm according to divinely given rubrics so as not to offend the gods. The worshipers in our text have not followed the divine commands; their refusal to obey incurs divine wrath (66:4).

66:5–6, Yahweh's Theophany Rejects the Scoffers. Against those who scoff at his coming, Yahweh cites their ridicule of his true servants: "Let Yahweh show his presence that we may see your joy!" Those doubting the freedom of God to act will be disgraced when the storm god is manifested in thunder from the Temple.

66:7–9, Mother Zion Gives Sudden Birth to Children. Yahweh comes as warrior at the birth of the city. In Second Isaiah, Zion was portrayed as a mother whose barrenness was healed by the children surrounding her (48:17–21; 54:1–8). Here the talk is not of returning exiles but of birth pangs and instantaneous birth. Later apocalyptic literature makes frequent use of the metaphor of birth pangs for the conflicts preceding the end time. These verses are but one of several descriptions of the creation of the new city; others are chap. 60 and 65:17–25. In all of them, the emphasis is on a purified people rather than on buildings. The marvelous birth also alludes to the once barren ancestral wives, to Sarah, to Leah, and to Rachel, who became fruitful as a result of a divine visitation.

66:10–14, Rejoice and Be Comforted in Jerusalem! The figure of childbirth continues. The newborn children rejoice with their mother and drink from her breasts (vv. 10–11). A divine word accompanies the new creation. The unfulfilled promise of 48:18–19, "If only you would heed my commands, your peace would be like a river," is at last fulfilled in 66:12. The maternal metaphor continues with Yahweh becoming the mother, a remarkable portrayal of God as feminine. So close is Yahweh to Zion that her nurture is credited to him. The mother comforts Israel the son; his body thrills with joyous satisfaction. The public transformation of Israel is itself the judgment (v. 14cd).

66:15–16, Judgment in Storm. These verses pick up 66:6, in which Yahweh from his Temple roared in thunder against his enemies. Verses 5–16 are a single judgment scene; Yahweh upholds his faithful ones and condemns their enemies. Verses 7–14 are the judgment in favor of the faithful ones, predicted in vv. 2 and 5. Verses 15–16 are the other side of the same coin, the punishing of those who violated the canons of true worship (vv. 3–4) and scoffed at the coming of Yahweh (v. 5). Verse 14d immediately prepares for vv. 15–16. The imagery is drawn from the picture of the storm god vanquishing his enemies with wind, lightning ("fire"), and sword. The Bible frequently depicts the triumph of the righteous by showing the defeat of their wicked oppressors; it does not portray good and evil abstractly but good and evil people in conflict.

66:17–24
Judgment in Jerusalem

Much of Third Isaiah has been concerned with the appearance of Judge Yahweh in Jerusalem, to uphold the righteous and to put down their oppressors, acknowledged by all as just and holy. The Isaian tradition affirms that judgment takes place in Jerusalem, which is thereby transformed into a righteous city (e.g., 1:21–28; 4:2–6). Songs of Zion celebrate the defeat of Yahweh's enemies at the foot of the holy mountain (e.g., Pss. 46:6; 48:3–8; 76:1–2).

66:17–18a, Addendum to the Judgment Scene of vv. 15–16. In the ancient world, people prepared themselves for encounter with the gods by rituals that separated them from the profane world; often they bathed, donned special clothing, and abstained from sexual activity. Those preparing themselves for false worship will be attacked by Yahweh in the judgment described in vv. 15–16. Verse 17 extends into v. 18a: "They shall one and all come to an end—oracle of Yahweh—for I know [following the LXX and the Syriac version] their deeds and their plans."

66:18b–24, The Final Judgment in Jerusalem. These verses have in mind the indefinite future. The subject in v. 18b is uncertain ("I [Yahweh] am coming," or "the time is coming"), as is the mood (perfect or participle) of the first "come" in v. 18. Presumably the time is subsequent to the purification of Zion described in the previous chapters. Judged and restored Zion is now a place where "my glory" of vv. 18b and 19 is visible. Yahweh gathers those who will see his glory. He will give them a sign, a convincing display of divine power, which "the survivors" will use in preaching the divine glory in far distant lands. "Survivors" suggests that the preachers are those who have survived the judgment of Zion. It is not clear if the survivor-emissaries are Israelites or Gentiles from the first gathering in v. 18b. In any event non-Israelites bring the scattered children of Zion to the holy mountain in a procession like Israel's to Zion. Some of the exiles will become priests and Levites; living in foreign lands has not disqualified them from this office. Verses 22–23, like 65:17–25 and 66:7–14, affirm that the New Jerusalem is not a matter of buildings but of obedient people living long and worshiping Yahweh. Isa. 66:24 continues the same scene; the establishment of peace is the defeat of the rebellious, whose bodies lie at the foot of the holy mountain as a testimony to the divine victory. The prophet may be alluding to an actual site to the south of Jerusalem, the Valley of Hinnom (Heb. *gehinnom*, whence the English "Gehenna"), the site of a city dump, which was full of fire and worms. The harshness of the final verse was recognized by the Masoretes (rabbinic scribes), who directed that, when it was read in the synagogue, v. 23 was to be read again so that the book would end on a hopeful and merciful note.

Bibliography

Clifford, R. J. *Fair Spoken and Persuading: An Interpretation of Second Isaiah.* Theological Inquiries. New York: Paulist, 1984.

Hanson, P. D. *The Dawn of Apocalyptic.* Philadelphia: Fortress, 1975.

Muilenburg, J. "Chapters 40–66." The *Interpreter's Bible.* Edited by G. A. Buttrick et al. Nashville: Abingdon, 1956. Vol. 5, pp. 381–773.

Westermann, C. *Isaiah 40–66.* Old Testament Library. Philadelphia: Westminster, 1969.

Whybray, R. N. *Isaiah 40–66.* New Century Bible. Grand Rapids, MI: Eerdmans, 1975.

JEREMIAH

THOMAS W. OVERHOLT

INTRODUCTION

The first two sentences of the Book of Jeremiah summarize the book's contents—the "words of Jeremiah"—and assign it a date—the reigns of the last four kings of Judah (1:1–3). One soon discovers, however, that the book is neither a straightforward chronicle of that historical period nor simply a verbatim collection of the prophet's utterances.

Even casual readers of the book of Jeremiah will observe three things, the first of which is that its content is diverse and loosely organized. There is no narrative or plot line or any other principle of organization (e.g., chronological order or arrangement by topic) that encompasses the book as a whole. Instead, one finds a variety of literary forms in both poetry (e.g., oracles of judgment and of salvation, individual laments) and prose (e.g., biographical narratives, sermons, a letter). Sometimes these forms occur in homogeneous units (2:1–3:5, oracles of judgment; chaps. 37–44, biographical prose); sometimes they are widely dispersed (the individual laments are scattered through chaps. 11–20). A number of different audiences (kings, nobles, priests, other prophets, the general populace, foreign nations) and problems (the threat of war, drought, contemptible behavior) are addressed, and a variety of metaphors employed (see, e.g., 2:1–4:4; 12:7–13). Whole verses, or passages, may even be repeated (6:12–15 and 8:10–12; 10:12–16 and 51:15–19).

A second observation is that some sections of the book seem to have a special biographical interest. Though the oracles of judgment reveal little about the prophet himself, the opposite is the case for the narratives of chaps. 26–29 and 36–44, which report his activity in the framework of datable historical circumstances. Third, one observes that Jeremiah seems to have been embroiled in controversy with officials of the state (chaps. 26; 36–37), priests (20:1–6), and other prophets (chaps. 28–29).

These observations give rise to a like number of questions to which we must turn before beginning the commentary: what types of literary material are found in Jeremiah, and how are we to understand the way these were combined to form the present book? To what extent does the book provide us with biographical information about the prophet? What was the importance of the prophet and the traditions about him in the context of the social, political, and religious settings of the period during which the book of Jeremiah came into existence?

Literary Form and Composition

The book of Jeremiah contains both poetry and prose. Materials of these two types tend to be gathered into different sections of the book, although intermixing of types is frequent (→ Poetry).

The poetry consists of prophetic utterances of several types, concentrated in chaps. 1–25 and 46–51. The most common form is the "oracle." The use of direct address couched in the first person (the "I" is God, not the prophet; see 2:1–3) shows that these were thought of as God's words delivered through the prophet to a specific audience. They tend to be brief and composed in one basic pattern (e.g., 5:10–14). This pattern contains an introduction (v. 10), an accusation (vv. 11–13), a formula signifying that the message is from God (v. 14a), and an announcement of God's judgment against the people (v. 14b). These elements and this order are not, however, invariable. Thus, in the complaint (or "lawsuit") form of the oracles, the prophet states on God's behalf a grievance against the people (e.g., 2:5–9), but there is no announcement of judgment.

Oracles like these are common to prophets both in the Old Testament and elsewhere (→ Prophet). Beside the specific content of what he says, Jeremiah's uniqueness is sometimes evident in stylistic variations on the form. One of these is his use of rhetorical questions, which often set the stage for an accusation directed against his audience (e.g., 2:11–12, 32; 3:1–5). It would seem that, like any effective speaker, Jeremiah made use of forms he and his audience were familiar with, but modified them to suit his own purposes.

Another type of poetry important in the book of Jeremiah and occurring in no other prophetic book is the personal complaint, or lament (see 11:18–12:6; 15:10–21; 17:14–18; 18:18–23; 20:7–18). These complaints share certain formal characteristics with the individual lamentations in the Psalms. Since the latter are usually understood to have been used in a ritual context and by a variety of different persons, the question of the extent to which these complaints give us useful information about Jeremiah himself has been hotly debated (see the Short Essay "Jeremiah's Complaints").

The major prose passages in Jeremiah may be classified into two types, biography and prose sermons. The former are narratives that speak about Jeremiah in the third person, reporting things that he did and said and placing these within an identifiable social and historical context (see 19:1–20:6; 26; 28–29; 36; 37–45; 51:59–64). The prose sermons, in which Jeremiah sometimes refers to himself in the first person (e.g., 11:6, 9; 16:1), are reports of speeches the prophet is said to have delivered (see 7:1–8:3; 11:1–14; 16:1–13; 17:19–27; 18:1–12; 21:1–10; 25:1–14; 35:1–19). Occasionally, the same incident will be reported in both types of prose (e.g., cf. 7:1–15 with chap. 26; 25:1–11 with chap. 36).

Authorship of the "biographical" passages has often been attributed to Baruch, a scribe associated with Jeremiah, who on two occasions wrote down a collection of the prophet's utterances (36:4, 32). However, such attribution of authorship cannot be verified (→ Baruch). Though these passages are somewhat scattered, their arrangement is roughly chronological. They do not, however, constitute a connected biography in the modern sense of the term.

Besides being couched in the first person, the "prose sermons" have two other formal characteristics: most begin with a special heading ("the word that came to Jeremiah from the Lord"), and several display a three-part structure that includes a summons to repentance (e.g., 7:3–7; 11:3–7; 17:21–22), a description of the people's lack of repentance (7:8–11; 11:8–10; 17:23), and an announcement of the punishment that will inevitably come to them (7:12–15; 11:11–17; 17:27). The sermons also contain a large number of stock words and phrases (e.g., "rising up early and sending/speaking" [RSV: sending/speaking "persistently"] in 7:13, 25; 11:7; 25:3–4; 35:14–15; "turn every man from his evil way" in 18:11; 25:5; 35:15; "other gods" in 7:6, 9, 18; 11:10; 16:11, 13; 35:15). Examples of this stereotypic language can be found in other portions of the book, both poetry (cf. 23:22) and prose (cf. 26:3; 36:3, 7), as well as in Deuteronomistic writings (cf. Deut. 6:14; 2 Kings 22:17). The latter fact has led to the view that these "sermons" are a Deuteronomistic reworking of the prophet's message (→ Deuteronomist).

The case for a Deuteronomistic revision of the prose sermons is not conclusive, however. Some of the stereotypic language found in them (e.g., the first of the examples cited in the preceding paragraph) is unique to Jeremiah, and this may suggest that both Jeremiah and the Deuteronomists were influenced by a style of expression used in Judah (or among a specific group of Judeans) during the late seventh century B.C. There are similarities between the point of view of the prose sermons and that of the Deuteronomistic writings—for example,

the idea that Judah's downfall could be attributed to its having rejected the word of God sent via the prophets (cf. Jer. 7:25–34; 25:4–11; 26:4–6; 29:17–19; 35:15–17; 36:1–31; and 44:4–6 with 2 Kings 17:13–18; the Deuteronomists' belief in the authority of the prophetic word is stated in Deut. 18:15–19). Often, however, these ideas can be found in the pre-exilic edition of the Deuteronomistic History, so there is no need to explain their presence in Jeremiah as the result of an exilic revision of his words.

It is also important to note that Jeremiah's religious viewpoint was not in complete harmony with the Deuteronomists'. For example, whereas they take a positive interest in the Jerusalem Temple and make it the central institution in Judah's religious life, Jer. 7:1–15 (cf. chap. 26) condemns the people's excessive trust in the Temple and its rituals. Therefore, though they are in important respects similar, it seems best not to think of the Jeremian traditions as having undergone a systematic Deuteronomistic revision. We will return to this point below.

Composition. We have seen that the book of Jeremiah contains material of several distinct literary forms and that these are sometimes found in relatively homogeneous blocks, but we should not infer from this that there were corresponding written sources from which an editor or editors constructed the book in its present form. The relationships among the types of material are more complicated than that. We have already noted, for example, that the larger sections of the book contain a mixture of literary forms (e.g., chaps. 1–25 are composed largely of poetic oracles but also contain examples of both biographical prose and sermons). In addition, language characteristic of the prose is also found in the poetic oracles (e.g., the phrase mentioned above, "turn every man from his evil way," appears in 23:14, 22).

Despite the intermixing of literary forms, several major blocks of material can be identified within the book of Jeremiah. Chaps. 1–25 seem to constitute a unit composed largely of poetic oracles and prose sermons. This block begins with an account of how Jeremiah was commissioned to be a prophet (1:4–19) and ends with a reference to a "book" in which the prophet's utterances were recorded (25:13). Much of the material in chaps. 26–45 is more "biographical" in nature, and what is not, chaps. 30–31, makes up a block the content of which shows a preoccupation with prophecies of hope for the people's future. Chaps. 46–51 are a collection of oracles directed against Judah's traditional enemies among the surrounding nations.

Within these larger blocks one can find smaller groupings united by such things as a common theme (e.g., 2:1–3:5, Judah's unfaithfulness to its God; 21:11–23:8, criticism of Judean kings; 23:9–40, Jeremiah's prophetic opponents) or by their relationship to a specific historical situation (e.g., chaps. 27–29 reflect disputes over foreign policy during the reign of Zedekiah). That chaps. 27–29 have to be seen as a separate block of tradition is evident not only from their content but also from several stylistic features of the Hebrew text that set them off from other material in the book: the name of the Babylonian king appears there as "Nebuchadnezzar," whereas elsewhere the spelling is "Nebuchadrezzar"; proper names compounded with God's name, Yahweh, tend to appear in their shortened form (Heb. *Yirmeyah*, "Jeremiah") rather than their full form (*Yirmeyahu*); and Jeremiah (as well as his opponent, Hananiah) is referred to by the title "the prophet."

A basic datum about the book, then, is that it contains chunks of material that from the standpoints of literary form, style, and content are to some extent different from each other. The question is, How are we to interpret this fact? Are these implications for the history of the book's composition? For example, some have held that, in its original form, prophetic speech was poetic and that, therefore, only the poetic oracles found in the book could be considered the original and authentic words of Jeremiah. But it would seem that there is no way to be certain either that the prophet spoke (or wrote) only poetry or that all the book's poetry stems originally from him. In fact there is general agreement between the message contained in the "prose sermons" and that in the oracles, and some have held the view that both derive ultimately from the prophet.

So, we are faced with something of a paradox: the present form of the book of Jeremiah is both difficult and easy to understand. The difficulties stem largely from the variety of literary forms it contains and the fact that there appears to be no completely satisfactory way to explain their distribution. In addition, the specific historical setting of many individual passages is unclear. The identity of the "enemy from the north" mentioned in chaps. 4–6 has been debated for years, but no consensus has emerged. Even where seemingly firm dates are given (e.g., 1:2, 626 B.C.), reasons have been found to doubt their accuracy.

On the other hand, it is easy enough to grasp the book's broad thematic unity, namely, a concern to interpret Judah's present historical circumstances in terms of the people's past behavior and to make projections about its future. This is a concern that the prophet would have shared with many others, and one that could have motivated both the preservation of and reflection on his words.

What seems clear is that the prophet himself began the process by which his utterances were,

from time to time, reinterpreted in the light of current events and written down. The incident reported in chap. 36 provides an illustration. According to the narrative, in the year 605 B.C. Yahweh instructed Jeremiah to make a written collection of oracles, which he had uttered over a period of two decades (assuming the traditional date for the beginning of his activity [1:2]). Verse 29 indicates that a dominant theme of this collection was the threat that Judah would be conquered by "the king of Babylon."

Now, a number of oracles in chaps. 4–6 and 8–10 speak of an attack by an unspecified enemy from "the north," though in the early days of his activity the Babylonians were not yet a power to be reckoned with. By 605 B.C., however, they were the dominant nation in the region, and it seems plausible to assume that, when he gathered together his oracles of judgment against the people of Judah, he specifically designated Babylon as the agent through whom God would punish them. Behind this reinterpretation of his earlier oracles lies the assumption that they were as relevant in 605 as they were when they were uttered—indeed, that their predictions were just then on the verge of being fulfilled.

Seven years later, in 597, the Babylonians did overrun Judah and Jerusalem and carry the king and some of Jeremiah's countrymen into exile (2 Kings 24:8–17). Since Nebuchadnezzar installed a new king on the throne and Judah retained its identity as a nation, the question would have arisen whether these events could be considered the complete fulfillment of the prophet's predictions. Chapters 27–28 show that Jeremiah faced this issue by incorporating Nebuchadnezzar's activity into his conception of God's plan for the nation and by opposing those who believed that Judah had been sufficiently punished and that soon its fortunes would be restored.

Nor was it the prophet alone who engaged in the reinterpretation of earlier predictions of national disaster (see commentary below on 4:5–6:30). Not even the poetic oracles were immune to alteration in response to the catastrophe of the nation's collapse. Thus, in 15:2, the triad of terms, "sword, famine, and pestilence," which occurs frequently in Jeremiah (seventeen times, with occasional variations in order; see, e.g., 14:12; 21:9; 24:10; 27:8, 13), is altered to include a fourth, "captivity." The latter term refers obviously to the Exile.

But chap. 36 also illustrates the difficulty that attends any attempt to construct a series of steps in the composition of the book of Jeremiah as we have it. The narrative itself is clear enough: during the years 605–604 B.C. the prophet is said to have twice dictated to Baruch a collection of his utterances spanning the whole period of his activity. The second scroll

599

was dictated after the king destroyed the first. It contained "all the words" of the first scroll, as well as "many words like them" (36:32). If we assume that the second edition of the scroll formed the nucleus for the subsequent collection of materials associated with Jeremiah, then we should be able to find that scroll in the present book, as well as evidence of the contents of its predecessor. But we cannot, at least not with any certainty. Over the years a variety of hypotheses about the contents of the scroll have been offered, some of them quite complicated. Even a brief sampling of opinion—it has been claimed that the scroll is to be found in chaps. 1–6, or in 1:4–9 plus chaps. 46–47 plus 4:5–6:26 plus 14:1–15:3, or in chaps. 1–11, or in the "prose sermons"—indicates both the variety of hypotheses that have been proposed and the lack of consensus on the matter.

Behind the discussion of the book's composition lies the problem of how one is to judge the authenticity of the various materials that form its content, the criterion of "authenticity" being that the words can be understood to have come from the prophet himself. Among those who sought to identify the prophet's "original" words, there was for many years a bias in favor of the poetic oracles, but this view has increasingly been challenged. Some have argued that certain prose passages (e.g., chap. 27) should be understood as containing "genuine" words of the prophet. Others contend that at the very least the prose, especially the sermons, preserves the gist of what Jeremiah said. But we may note again that there is no consensus on an inventory of authentic Jeremiah utterances, and it may well be that this search is flawed by an overemphasis on tying the contents of the book exclusively to the prophet's life and activity.

This judgment is not to deny that the prophet's life is important for understanding the present shape of his book. Other things, however, are also important. Above all, we need to ask *who* was responsible for collecting and preserving his words and *why* they felt it important to do so. As we shall see, the community must have played an important role in Jeremiah's actual prophetic activity. The community or groups within it also had a stake in preserving traditions about Jeremiah's activity.

It is possible, for example, that in its present form the prose of the book has been shaped by the need of Judeans living in exile in Babylon to provide themselves with a reasonable interpretation of the events of their recent past. The fall of Jerusalem (597 B.C.), and ultimately of the nation (587), were social and political disasters that precipitated a crisis in Judean religion. People now asked whether God had abandoned his people and whether the promise that a member of David's house would always sit on the throne in Jerusalem (see 2 Sam. 7; Ps. 132) was defunct. In an attempt to answer such questions, the Judeans in exile (re)interpreted traditions about the prophet. But in doing this they were only continuing a process begun by Jeremiah, who, as we have already seen, on at least one occasion set a collection of his older oracles in the context of an emerging national crisis. In the final analysis, we should take a rather broad view of the "authenticity" of materials in the book. Both prophet and those who preserved the traditions of what he did and said felt free, as occasion demanded, to reapply words they understood to be those from God to situations different from those in which they were first uttered.

We have several times mentioned the lack of any apparent principle of organization in the book of Jeremiah. This trait, shared with other prophetic books, has sometimes been attributed to the theory that, in their present written form, they represent loose assemblages of sayings and stories that at first circulated orally. In the case of Jeremiah, this explanation is not sufficient, since we know that the process of committing his prophecies to writing began with the prophet himself (chap. 36). Still, studies of oral performance and transmission in modern cultures suggest a way of understanding how the reinterpretation of the prophetic traditions may have proceeded. What such studies reveal above all is the influence of the audience upon narrators, who shape their material in response to the audience's makeup and concerns.

It was Judeans in and after the Exile who were the primary audience for the emerging written compilation of Jeremiah materials. It is safe to assume that those who had not given up their religious beliefs would have been intensely interested in discovering both a reason for their fate and some prospects for their future compatible with traditional notions about the relationship between God and his people. This quest for understanding, at the hands of exilic editors of the Jeremian materials, would account both for their being preserved and for the form in which they have come down to us.

This understanding of how the tradition developed raises another question about the book's composition: was the Jeremiah tradition reworked into a "Deuteronomistic edition" sometime during or after the Exile? The presence of prose sermons that in content closely agree with the Deuteronomistic interpretation of the nation's history has led some to suggest that it was. But the evidence is ambiguous. Note, for example, that both Jeremiah and Deuteronomy stress the necessity for the people to be obedient to the stipulations of God's law (e.g., Jer. 6:16–21; 7:1–15; 11:1–13; 22:9; 34:8–22; Deut. 5; 7:12–16). Both aim to guide the people's actions so as to safeguard their possession of the land (e.g., Jer. 7:3, 7; 25:5; 35:15; Deut. 11:8–22; 12:1; 16:20; 19:8–9; 23:20; 25:15), and in both the message is couched in essentially conditional terms (e.g., Jer. 4:1–4; 5:7–17; 26:1–6; Deut. 11).

Such similarities, which are not confined to the prose sermons, may represent basic agreement between Jeremiah and the Deuteronomists (the first edition of whose history dates from the time of Josiah, the late seventh century B.C.) on the interpretation of current events. Furthermore, it is difficult to see how conscious editing of Jeremiah could have resulted in such compositional disarray.

Alternatively, we can envision a communal attempt to find relevance in the traditions about what the prophet did and said that proceeded in a much more varied, piecemeal, and gradual way (see, e.g., commentary below on 2:1–4:4 and 8:4–10:25). The quest for understanding, not compositional coherence, guided the formation of the book. In fact, much of the sense of coherence one feels when reading the book of Jeremiah derives from a consistent interpretation of the nation's fate: disasters came because of the people's unfaithfulness to Yahweh. This viewpoint is evident not only in the prose "Temple sermon" (7:1–15) and the "Deuteronomistic" reflections on the covenant (11:1–14), but in shorter prose insertions like 3:24–25 and in 17:19–27, both of which share the point of view of the prose sermons.

If this is the way the tradition grew, perhaps all we can say about the final form of the book is that it represents a loosely structured compilation of the Jeremiah materials available at the time when the text as we have it was written.

Text. The original language of the book of Jeremiah is Hebrew, but there is an important Greek version dating from about the third century B.C., the Septuagint (LXX; → Septuagint). A special problem arises for interpreters of Jeremiah because of two significant differences between the LXX and the Hebrew Masoretic Text (MT), upon which English translations are based (→ Masorah): the LXX of Jeremiah is approximately one-eighth shorter than the MT, and in it the "oracles against the nations" appear following 25:13 (in the MT they form chaps. 46–51).

Studies of manuscripts from the Essene library at Qumran (→ Scrolls, The Dead Sea) have revealed that by the first century B.C. two different Hebrew traditions of the book of Jeremiah existed, one apparently identical to the MT, and the other closely resembling the LXX. Since the longer version frequently repeats verses and adds details to the narrative but seldom offers any change in basic content, the most likely explanation is that the MT represents an expansion of an earlier Hebrew text corresponding to the LXX.

The text of Jeremiah 27–29 can serve as a case in point. The MT contains a number of verbal embellishments: it is fond of titles (e.g., "the prophet"; cf. 28:5; 29:29), and it continually identifies the king of Babylon as Nebuchadnezzar (27:8, 20; 28:3, 11, 14; 29:1–3). The LXX identifies Nebuchadnezzar the first time he is mentioned, 27:6, but omits his title thereafter. Moreover, the LXX expands the so-called messenger formula ("Thus says the Lord") by adding "of hosts, the God of Israel" (27:21; 28:2, 14; 29:8, 25). In addition to these differences, there are a number of shorter expansions in the MT, like the phrases "the people, and the cattle which are on the face of the earth" (27:5) and "and I will scatter you, and you will perish" (27:10).

There are, finally, a number of expansions in the MT a verse or more in length, e.g., 27:7, 12b–14a, 17, 21; and 29:14. One of these, 29:16–19, clearly disrupts the context in which it occurs. But despite these considerable differences between the two versions of the text, the important observation is that the narrative is, in all its essentials, the same. The expansions in the MT are, for the most part, simply expansions of ideas or actions already present in the shorter text.

The Prophet in His Book

Like other prophetic books, Jeremiah begins with a superscription (1:1–3) that locates the prophet in a specific historical setting. Here we learn that he was born to a priestly family of the village of Anathoth (approximately three miles northeast of Jerusalem) and that his prophetic activity began in the thirteenth year of King Josiah's reign (626 B.C.) and continued until the second conquest of Jerusalem in 587.

The book of Jeremiah is unique, however, in the amount of additional information it seems to supply us about its prophet. The prose sections sometimes give detailed descriptions of Jeremiah's interaction with his fellow Judeans (king, princes, priests, prophets, and the general populace; e.g., chaps. 26; 27–29) and, sometimes, even with foreign emissaries (27:1–11; 39:11–14). Chaps. 21–45 contain a great many specific dates (e.g., 25:1; 36:1; 39:1–2), as well as references to events that can be easily dated (e.g., 21:1–2; 24:1; 34:1, 6–7), and chaps. 37–44 focus on the prophet's activity at the time of Nebuchadnezzar's second conquest of Jerusalem.

We also appear to have information of a more personal nature about the prophet. Though the narratives tell us that audience reaction to his message was often hostile (e.g., 26:7–9; 43:1–4) and that he sometimes was abused as a result of what he said (e.g., 20:1–6; 37:15; 38:1–6), the laments seem to reveal Jeremiah's own feelings about the difficulty of his task and the hardships he was forced to endure in its performance (e.g., 11:18–20; 15:10, 15–18; 20:7–12, 14–18). We are even told he was forbidden to take a wife (16:1–4). On the other hand, we have no information about his age, personal appearance, means of support, and the like, and we do not know the date of his death, though he is often assumed to have died in Egypt (chap. 44).

For this sort of information we are dependent largely upon the "biographical" prose and the poetry of lamentation. However, there are critical problems associated with each of these bodies of material. It has sometimes been argued that the biographical prose was written by Baruch, a trained scribe who was closely associated with Jeremiah (32:12–16; 26:4–19, 27–32; 43:3). There is no firm evidence for this supposition, however, and since much of the material is scattered through chaps. 19–36 and has affinities with the Deuteronomistic understanding of the nation's fate, the assumption that we are dealing with a "biography" of the prophet is questionable. As regards the laments, the form and language are to some extent stereotypic, reflecting lamentations in the book of Psalms, which should make us wary of taking at face value all the apparent individual references in the Jeremian laments. Still, it is hard to deny the impression that these lamentations contain elements that are specific to Jeremiah's situation (see the Short Essay "Jeremiah's Complaints").

Date of Jeremiah's Call. The question of the accuracy of the traditional date for the beginning of Jeremiah's prophetic activity (the "thirteenth year of Josiah" is 626 B.C.; so 1:2; 25:3) may serve as an example of the difficulties that attend any attempt to construct an accurate "biography" of Jeremiah. Note first that, though there are references to later kings Jehoiakim and Zedekiah, there are no accounts of Jeremiah interacting with Josiah, and it is even difficult to locate any of the book's contents specifically in that king's reign (3:6–10, the only passage so dated, may be a later addition). Jer. 2:18 seems to assume that Assyria is still a viable power, thus presupposing a date prior to 614. Apart from these texts, the most one can do is argue that the religious situation in Judah in the period before Josiah's reform (621 B.C.; see 2 Kings 22:1–23:25) would have provided appropriate occasion for delivering the oracles of chaps. 2–3.

There is a second problem. Apparently, from the very beginning of his career Jeremiah expected that Judah would suffer military defeat at the hands of an unnamed enemy from "the north" (1:13–16). Oracles announcing this threat are found in chaps. 4–6 and 8–10 (see 4:6; 6:1, 22; 10:22). But in the years following

626 B.C. such an attack did not materialize, and it is not even clear whom the prophet identified as the foe. A common suggestion has been the Scythians, a nomadic people from the north whose unsuccessful attack on Egypt was described by the Greek historian Herodotus, but the lack of direct evidence makes this hypothesis unlikely (→ Scythians).

The problem is complicated by the fact that two passages dated to the period 605–604 B.C. specifically identify the Babylonian king, Nebuchadnezzar, as the agent of imminent destruction (25:1, 8–9; 36:9, 29). Are we to infer from this that the prophet was wrong in his first prediction, and that two decades later he suggested a new identity for the invaders? Some have been reluctant to accept this conclusion on the grounds that as a true prophet Jeremiah could never have been wrong or change his mind about such a serious matter. Such a view, however, fails to allow for an ongoing process of reinterpretation of earlier utterances by the prophet himself and his successors, and thus represents a too static notion about how prophecy operates.

A third problem involves the relationship of Jeremiah to Josiah's reform of the nation's religious establishment and to the document important for that reform (2 Kings 22:8–13), generally believed to be an early version of the book of Deuteronomy. Again, the evidence is ambiguous. Some have seen in the sermon on the covenant (Jer. 11:1–13) explicit reference to the reform (cf. 2 Kings 23:1–3) and an indication that Jeremiah supported it. However, the "Deuteronomistic" character of these verses makes confidence in such a view difficult (see commentary below). Jer. 6:19 is not so open to the latter criticism, but the exact referent of "my law" is uncertain. The Temple sermon, 7:1–15 and 26:1–24, might suggest that Jeremiah opposed the Jerusalem Temple establishment and must therefore have opposed a reform that had as its centerpiece a religion purified and centralized in that location. On the other hand, in 3:1 and 34:8–22 he seems to draw upon Deuteronomy's formulation of the law mandating centralization (cf. Deut. 24:1–4; 15:1, 12–18).

Perhaps, as some have suggested, Jeremiah ceased to act as a prophet for a time during the heyday of Josiah's reform. The oracles in chaps. 1–25 contain few indications of date, so this hypothesis cannot be proven, though there is precedent for such a period of withdrawal in Isa. 8:16–17.

One way to solve these problems is to argue that the traditional date for the call of Jeremiah is inaccurate. This can be done in several ways. One can emend the text of 1:2 and 25:3 on the grounds that they originally read "twenty-third year," i.e., 616 B.C. One can eliminate these chronological references altogether as later additions, or one can understand "thirteenth year" as the date of the prophet's birth rather than his call. But to do any of these involves one both in an argument from silence (assuming that since Jeremiah did not come right out and *say* things that allow us to link his utterances to the reign of Josiah, he was not active then) and a willingness to overlook or explain away the specific evidence of the text (the references to the "days of Josiah" in 3:6 and 36:2, to "Assyria" in 2:18, and to the beginning of his prophecy in the "thirteenth year of Josiah").

"Biography" in the Service of Community.

We have seen that there is little biographical information about the prophet to be found in the poetic oracles and that we must be careful about accepting at face value what we encounter in other materials. The search for the "historical Jeremiah" is an intriguing one, precisely because, by comparison with other prophetic books, in Jeremiah we seem to have so much information at our disposal. But we must also ask how much accurate data about the prophet's life we can expect to derive from material so preoccupied with interpreting the historical experiences of a nation.

The broader question is this: in what sense can the book of Jeremiah be considered the prophet's biography? And to the extent that it is, what is the relationship between "biography" and community? Egyptian tomb inscriptions written centuries before the emergence of the Israelite state in Canaan reveal the existence of a literary form that has been called "biography" or "autobiography." These inscriptions often contain a report of the person's installation in office by the pharaoh, a description of his assignment and his conduct in it, narratives about his birth and death, and the like. These are some of the very elements found in the book of Jeremiah. It is important to note, however, that these biographies present their subjects as the performers of a public function and give an account—to the gods and to the public—of the person's conduct in office. Contrary to modern expectations, these documents do not focus on the development of individual traits of character and personality. Where these appear at all, they are subservient to the person's performance of his public role.

One might well ask whether it is not a necessary feature of a biography that it be centrally interested in its subject. If the so-called biographical prose in Jeremiah (e.g., chap. 26) seems more concerned with depicting the people's rejection of God's message to them and the ultimate consequences of that than the life of the prophet, then perhaps we should not speak of "biography" at all. Still, it is obviously not the case that such passages as chap. 26 lack all interest in the prophet's personal history.

What we appear to have in Jeremiah is biography employed as a vehicle for addressing topics of larger than individual concern. The crucial question is not *whether* the narratives refer to historical traditions about the prophet. We assume that to some extent they do, since the descriptions are often extremely concrete (with dates, names, and events corresponding to those found in 2 Kings and in extrabiblical sources), and the laments contain convincingly personal references. Furthermore, prophecy is a social phenomenon. Intense emotional dialogue is basic to the functioning of an intermediary (see the Short Essays "The Interaction Between Prophet and God" and "The Social Dynamics of Prophetic Behavior"). Judging from comparative studies of prophets and similar intermediaries, the social dynamics of prophetic behavior depicted in these Jeremiah texts seem realistic. The question is, rather, *how* the overall purpose of the narrative affected the use of these historical traditions.

The Book in Its Contexts

The book of Jeremiah is not the product of a single person operating in a closely circumscribed time and place. To understand it, therefore, we must be aware not only of the contexts in which the prophet worked, but also those contexts in which traditions about his work were known, appreciated, and preserved, culminating in the book as it has come down to us. The time during which this development took place can be divided into two distinct periods, before the Exile and after.

Judah Before the Exile

Politics. According to the traditional date, Jeremiah's prophetic activity spanned the last four decades of Judah's existence as a nation (626–587 B.C.; 1:1–3). This period was a time of increasing internal factionalism and shifting foreign alliances.

The beginning seemed auspicious enough. Perhaps as early as 629, King Josiah (640–609) took advantage of Assyria's increasing weakness to reestablish Judah's independence and in the process brought under his control former Israelite lands to the north. As part of this effort, he undertook a major reform of the nation's religious establishment (2 Chron. 34:1–8; → Josiah).

For Judah, however, the growing weakness of Assyria was in the long run a mixed blessing, since it both permitted and was hastened by the rise of the Neo-Babylonian Empire. In the years 614–609 the Babylonians and their sometime allies, the Medes, inflicted a series of defeats upon the Assyrians, which brought that empire to an end. Egypt, looking out for its own interests, had by this time become an ally of Assyria, and in 609 Pharaoh Neco marched north through Palestine to join in the attempt to recapture the city of Haran. Josiah moved to intercept him but was killed by the Egyptians in battle at Megiddo.

The death of Josiah was an important turning point, and a profound embarrassment. In retrospect we can see that the notion that Judah could exist as an independent nation, controlling Palestine as it had in the days of David and Solomon, was an illusion. It is symbolic of Judah's fate that two of its last four kings were installed by foreign powers (2 Kings 23:34; 24:17).

Still, not all of Jeremiah's contemporaries had such insight into their situation, and continuing hopes for national independence remained a source of internal tension until the very end. Probably, they did not share the embarrassment of the later writer of 2 Kings, who was left virtually speechless: Josiah, to whose life so many words had been devoted (2 Kings 22:1–23:25), was in death accorded a single verse (23:29). Josiah's fate falsified the assumption of Deuteronomists and prophets alike that the righteous and God-fearing person and nation will prosper.

After Josiah's death, Neco continued toward Syria, and the Judean "people of the land" installed Josiah's second-oldest son, Jehoahaz, as the new king. This selection, which violated the normal order of succession, suggests that Jehoahaz, like Josiah, pursued an "anti-Egyptian" foreign policy. This would explain why, on his return from the north three months later, Neco deposed Jehoahaz and replaced him with his elder brother, Jehoiakim (2 Kings 23:30–35), who proved to be a friend of Egypt in its struggles against Babylonia.

During Jehoiakim's reign, Babylonian power continued to increase. In 605 Nebuchadnezzar decisively defeated the Egyptians at the northern Syrian city of Carchemish, and in 604 he captured the Philistine city of Ashkelon, a close neighbor of Judah. About the year 603 Jehoiakim formally became a vassal of the Babylonian king, but after three years he revolted (2 Kings 24:1). Nebuchadnezzar was occupied elsewhere for several years, but in the spring of 597 he mounted a siege against Jerusalem, which fell on March 16 of that year.

Three months before the city's fall, Jehoiakim died (it is possible he was assassinated by opponents) and was succeeded by his son, Jehoiachin. The latter survived the siege but was among those persons and objects of booty carried off by Nebuchadnezzar into exile in Babylon (2 Kings 24:8–20). He was replaced by Zedekiah, the third son of Josiah to become king in Jerusalem in a decade.

Zedekiah's situation was not an easy one. Although Judah had been decisively defeated

and was again a vassal of Babylon, the voices of nationalism were still heard. Even among those who understood the defeat as God's punishment were some who felt that their chastisement was now complete and that restoration would soon follow (see commentary below on chaps. 27–29). The fact that the previous king, Jehoiachin, continued to live in captivity in Babylon, where he was recognized as king by his captors and was able to exercise some measure of control over royal properties in Judah (2 Kings 25:27–30; → Jehoiachin), further complicated Zedekiah's situation. Early in his reign it appears that Judah and some of its neighbors began to plot a revolt against Babylon (see chap. 27), but nothing came of this. Later, Zedekiah did rebel. In January 588 Nebuchadnezzar began a siege of Jerusalem, which continued with one short respite until the walls were breached in July 587. Judeans were again carried into exile, but this time the city and its Temple were completely destroyed (2 Kings 25:1–21).

The Babylonians appointed a Judean nobleman, Gedaliah, to be governor over what remained of the former Judean state, but by 582 he was dead at the hands of a political rival. Fearing Babylonian reprisals, some of his followers fled to Egypt (2 Kings 25:22–26). Tradition has it that they carried the prophet Jeremiah with them against his will (Jer. 43–44).

Beginning in chap. 21, the book of Jeremiah contains many passages that either mention specific dates or refer to events that can be dated from other sources (e.g., 21:1–2; 25:1; 27:1; 34:1–2; 36:1; 37:1; 39:1–2). Since the prose narratives are concentrated in this part of the book, it is not surprising that many dates should appear here. What is particularly interesting is that the majority of these refer to two particular moments: 605 (the fourth year of Jehoiakim, and the year that Nebuchadnezzar defeated the Egyptians at Carchemish and became king of Babylon; e.g., 25:1; 26:1) and 597–587 (the reign of Zedekiah). The political fate of the nation dominates the book.

One of the notable features of Judean politics during the last decades before 587 was the division of the leaders into factions, or parties. The book gives these groups no names, but they can be identified by their views on foreign policy. One group, comprising kings Jehoiakim and Zedekiah and many of the nobles and religious leaders, was committed to Judean political autonomy. As a practical matter, this group generally favored alliance with Egypt and other steps designed to preserve, or (during most of the period) regain, independence from Babylon. The other, made up of a smaller group of nobles and their supporters among religious functionaries, believed that in the present circumstances it was necessary to submit to the suzerainty of Babylon. Both were able to rationalize their position on the basis of the religious tradition. Jeremiah sided with the latter group, and something of the bitterness of the dispute can be gathered from chaps. 27–29.

Among Jeremiah's consistent supporters in his confrontations with various kings were members of a particular noble family, the house of Shaphan. Shaphan himself had been Josiah's secretary and had had a prominent role in that king's religious reform (2 Kings 22:3–20). Shaphan had three sons: Ahikam, who was also involved in Josiah's reform and who later defended Jeremiah from an attempt to condemn him to death for treason (2 Kings 22:12–13; Jer. 26:24); Elasah, who once served as a messenger for both King Zedekiah and Jeremiah (Jer. 29:3); and Gemariah, who supported the prophet in the face of King Jehoiakim's hostility (Jer. 36:10, 12, 25). On the latter occasion Jeremiah's position was also supported by Gemariah's son, Micaiah (Jer. 36:11–13). One other member of the family is known: Gedaliah, son of Ahikam, whose politics can be inferred from the fact that Nebuchadnezzar appointed him governor after 587 and, according to tradition, put Jeremiah under his care (Jer. 39:14). This connection of the prophet with the house of Shaphan allows us to trace the pedigree of what some have called the "pro-Babylonian" party back to the time of Josiah's reform.

Religion. As in politics, the official religion of Judah during the decades before the Exile was dominated by the legacy of Josiah, who relatively early in his reign carried out a thoroughgoing institutional reform. 2 Kings 22 and 2 Chronicles 34 differ in their reports on the chronology of his activity, but the latter account, which sees it as extending over a period from approximately 628 to 621, is the more probable. The reform's main features, removal of foreign religious practices from both Jerusalem and its environs and from regions farther to the north (2 Kings 23:4–5, 15, 19–20) and centralization of worship in the Temple at Jerusalem (2 Kings 23:8–9; see Deut. 12:1–14), fit well with Josiah's political program of gaining independence from Assyria and reasserting Judean control over formerly Israelite territories to the north. A law book found in the Temple after the reform was already in progress (2 Kings 22:3–13; in all probability some portion of the present book of Deuteronomy) gave the activity additional impetus and occasioned a ceremony in which king and people formally renewed their covenant with God, pledging to keep his commandments (2 Kings 23:1–3).

From Jer. 44:15–19 we can infer that the reform was generally effective in bringing communal worship of other gods under control. But the enhanced position of the Jerusalem Temple and its priesthood also had the effect of providing a conceptual justification for foreign policy decisions that Jeremiah felt compelled to oppose (see 7:1–15; chaps. 27–28). The last decades before 587 were thus a period of intense politico-religious conflict between two groups of the nation's elite, each containing both prophets and members of the ruling aristocracy.

Reading through the book of Jeremiah gives one the impression that widespread apostasy among his countrymen was the feature of Judean society that disturbed the prophet most. Jer. 2:1–4:4, for example, is concerned entirely with that topic. The people are accused of forsaking their God, indeed, of trading him for other, less effective gods (2:9–13). In some of these oracles, apostasy appears to be both a religious and a political issue. In the prophet's view the adopting of new gods had diminished rather than enhanced the chances for national survival (2:14–19, 26–28, 36–37). It is not surprising that the nation's leaders (kings, princes, priests, and prophets, 2:8, 26–28) are singled out for special blame.

If Josiah's reforms were successful, how can we account for this emphasis? The oracles of chap. 2 have often been considered among the oldest in the book, and the situation mirrored in them might be the one that existed at the beginning of the reform. Moreover, although Josiah effected changes in public practices, private religious preferences of long standing may well have persisted. Another factor seems of greater importance. The Jeremiah traditions preserved for us in the book begin with the prophet but were brought to completion by a community that survived the nation's collapse and the prophet's death. The book both predicts and reflects upon Judah's end. And how could such a dire fate be explained? Already during Jeremiah's lifetime, one explanation, applied to the fall of the Northern Kingdom, Israel, was gaining acceptance, namely the Deuteronomistic notion that the nation fell because it had abandoned its God (2 Kings 17:7–18). It is, therefore, not so important to assess the actual level of apostasy during various stages of Jeremiah's career as to recognize that many of the passages of the book that take up this theme do so explicitly in the framework of reflection on the cause of the nation's demise (e.g., 7:16–20; 9:12–16; 11:9–13, 17; 13:1–11; 16:10–13; 22:8–9).

It is not always easy to discern precisely what Jeremiah intended in his accusations relating to the people's religious practices. The criticisms of his prophetic opponents, for example, can be quite general and vague (23:10–11, 14, 15b, 22b). Perhaps we can say that his central concern was with what he perceived to be the leaders' unwillingness to take God and his demands seriously (5:12–13, 20–25; 6:10; 7:21–26; 8:4–7; 15:5–9; 17:5; 22:21). But of course that is a judgment that can only be made on the basis of a particular point of view. It will become apparent that Jeremiah's opponents may reasonably have assessed their own religious position quite differently.

Society. Jeremiah seems little concerned with details of the nation's socioeconomic life. There are several references to oppression of the powerless by the powerful (2:34; 5:26–29), as well as a standard catalog of offenses reminiscent of the Decalogue: stealing, murder, adultery, and false swearing (7:9; cf. 5:2, 7b–8). The latter is part of a "prose sermon" that sets out the terms for the people's continued existence in the land and, in the process, elaborates a conceptual framework for understanding Judah's demise. One passage alludes to the potential for social chaos in a general pattern of deception and slander in personal relations (9:4–6, 8); another pictures the prophet as embroiled in an actual dispute concerning the manumission of slaves during the period of the final siege of Jerusalem in 587 (34:8–22). There are several references to breaking God's "law" (26:4; 44:10), as well as to the "covenant" (11:1–13; 22:9), all of which can be understood in the context of reflection on the nation's fall.

By contrasting to the much shorter book of Amos (see, e.g., Amos 2:4–8; 4:1–3; 6:4–7; 8:4–7), Jeremiah's lack of emphasis on socioeconomic conditions in Judah may seem surprising. Though it would be wrong to conclude that such matters were of little importance to Jeremiah and to those who transmitted the traditions about him, it does seem to indicate that in their day it was actions in the political arena that were perceived as most critical for determining the nation's future. What was at stake was national survival, and it was clear that the really important decisions affecting this lay in the realm of foreign policy.

In retrospect, Josiah's legacy proved to be uncertain. His reform of religious institutions, certainly a move that many considered exemplary, was part of a larger effort to make Judah independent from Assyria and establish it as a sovereign power governing an expanded territory. Whatever the fate of the reform, it is clear that in subsequent decades decisions to strive for such national autonomy led inexorably to the disasters that dashed all such hopes.

We can assume that both parties to the dispute anticipated Judah's survival. Kings Jehoiakim and Zedekiah, along with their supporters in the political and religious establishments, interpreted survival in terms of autonomy from the dominant regional power, Babylon. The group to which Jeremiah belonged hoped for a cultural and religious survival that did not depend upon political independence. Therefore, the insistence upon autonomy in the face of Babylon's overwhelming military power seemed to them suicidal. To make things more difficult, each side was convinced that its position corresponded to God's plan for his people.

Pre-exilic Judean society was the context for Jeremiah's prophetic activity not just in the sense that it gave him something to talk *about*; it was also the context *within* which he worked. It is obvious that the prophet's oracles imply an audience, but the dynamics of his relationship to it were more complicated than the simple utterances of a message.

The book of Jeremiah contains many instances of social interaction between the prophet and others. There are references to his acting as an intercessor with God on the people's behalf; 42:2–6 seems to represent an "ideal" instance of such activity (see also 15:11; the thrice-repeated prohibition of intercession—7:16; 11:14; 14:11—implies that such activity was common). The fact that even his opponents continued to consult him (21:2; 37:3, 16–17; 38:14; 42:1–3) indicates a public acknowledgment of this aspect of the prophetic role.

But we learn most about disputes between the prophet and members of his audience. Some of the references to opponents are general in nature (1:17–19; 15:19–20; 17:14–18; 18:20; 20:8, 18), but others are more specific. Jer. 20:1–6 describes a public dispute with a high-ranking priest of the Temple, and this is only one of the attempts made by persons in positions of power to control the prophet's activity (cf. 11:21; 26:7–9; 29:26–28; 32:2–5; 37:13–15, 20–21; 38:15–16, 24–28). In the first instance Jeremiah was publicly punished (20:2). Evidently, a prophet was to be both consulted and controlled.

Over time Jeremiah's activities aroused such feelings of hostility that opponents plotted actively against him (11:18–19; 18:18, 22–23; 20:10; see the general references to "persecution" in 15:15; 17:18). Still, there is evidence of a certain reluctance to deal too harshly with him (38:1–13).

Among the important opponents that Jeremiah had to face were other prophets, who appeared to him to be mere supporters of the social and political status quo (23:14, 16–17; 27–29). Jer. 26:7–19 indicates that it was not easy for Judeans to pass judgment on the validity of competing prophetic claims. Some made the acceptability of the message itself their criterion (v. 11b; see 37:13–15), but for others overt behavior was the critical concern (v. 16). In a culture that assumed the existence of prophets, one apparently had to give the benefit of the doubt to those who displayed recognizable prophetic behavior (cf. Jeremiah's reaction to the prophet Hananiah, 28:11b).

All this took place within the framework of partisan dispute that we have already identified. That Jeremiah had defenders in high places in the government seems to have been an important factor in his survival (26:24; cf. 39:11–14).

Communities After the Fall of Judah. The Exile began with a deportation of Judeans after the fall of Jerusalem in 597 B.C. For the next decade there were two communities and two living kings of Judah, and they faced a double task of accounting for the nation's fall and deciding on a course of action for the future. Their religious tradition made it easy enough to understand the disaster as God's punishment. The question now became whether the punishment could be considered complete and a restoration of fortunes expected. Some apparently held such a view (see chaps. 28–29). But Zedekiah's revolt against Nebuchadnezzar and the subsequent capture and destruction of Jerusalem made the question moot. Additional Judeans were deported to Babylon in 587, and again in about 582. Jer. 52:28–30 sets the total number of deportees at four thousand six hundred, though the discrepancy with 2 Kings 24:10–17 suggests that, if this number is accurate at all, it must refer only to adult males. We know that the exiles were the select of Judean society: royalty, nobility, soldiers, craftsmen, and religious leaders. According to 2 Kings 25:12, only the poorest remained in the land.

Not much is known about the life of the exiles in Babylon. There are indications that they built houses, raised families, and pursued livelihoods (Jer. 29:5–6; Isa. 55:1–2; → Exile). We are plagued with a similar lack of information about the other post-587 Jewish communities. Apparently, some who had fled the war and taken refuge in surrounding countries returned to the devastated homeland (40:11–12), but if Lam. 5:1–18 is any indication, life in Judah was difficult. When civil strife in the remnant community resulted in the death of the Babylonian-appointed governor, Gedaliah, some of those Judeans fled to Egypt (2 Kings 25:22–26; Jer. 41–43). Nothing is known about this group, though there is evidence of a continuing Jewish community at Elephantine on Egypt's southern border during the Persian period (→ Syene).

From the religious point of view, the main problem posed by the Exile was to understand why it had happened and what its implications were for the continued existence of God's people. The distinctive emphases in the book of Jeremiah as a whole seem to derive from such a need to understand. This concern would have been shared by both the prophet and those who transmitted and developed the traditions about him. The goal of the book they produced was not simply to preserve Jeremiah's words; it was to understand Judah's fall and the people's future.

It seems probable that this shaping of the tradition took place during the early decades of the Exile. Some passages show a certain bias in favor of the exilic community, identified as the "good figs" by comparison to the "rotten figs" who were left behind (chap. 24). Speculation about the length of the Exile was important to them (25:11; 29:1–14). We might even imagine the curiously anachronistic Sabbath regulation of 17:19–27 as deriving from attempts during the Exile to codify laws concerning religious practice.

The fact that there are many promises of eventual restoration of the people to their land is also in harmony with the hypothesis of an exilic setting (e.g., 3:14–18; 23:1–4, 7–8; 24:5–7; 27:22; 29:10–14, 32; 30:1–3; 46:27–28; 50:4–5, 19–20). Many of these passages occur in prose; many mention both Judah and northern Israel in a comprehensive promise of restoration. The "Deuteronomistic" explanation of the collapse of Israel and Judah as God's punishment for their wrongdoing allowed the people to believe that their defeat signaled neither that God was powerless to defend them nor that he had completely and finally abandoned them. There was hope for the future.

Point of View

The book of Jeremiah is a long and complex work. Though not, strictly speaking, a summary, the following sketch of the point of view toward it that has been developed in the preceding sections is offered for readers who wish to begin with an overview of the book's contexts and purpose.

Where did the material in the book of Jeremiah come from, and why was it preserved in its present form? There can be no single answer to this question. Rather, we must take into consideration the differing circumstances of the individuals and communities responsible for the preservation and development of Jeremiah traditions.

There are indications that the prophet himself made the first move to preserve formally his utterances in writing (see chap. 36). He did this after two decades of activity (1:1–3; 25:3; 36:2). It appears that the scroll he dictated was not simply a compilation of his earlier oracles but an interpretation of them in light of a new political situation (the unnamed enemy from the north of 1:13–16 and chaps. 4–6 was now specifically identified with the Babylonians; see 25:8–9; 36:29).

The purpose of dictating the scroll was not simply to preserve his writings, however. Under the circumstances (36:4–8), the scroll was a necessary alternative way of delivering his message to its intended audience, the Judean people and their rulers.

The scroll had another function as well. Jeremiah was not the only Judean prophet of his day; he was often in competition with others performing that role (see 6:13–15; 23:9–22;

chaps. 27–29). Since they were all Judean prophets, they shared common patterns of behavior. Both Jeremiah and Hananiah, for example, spoke in the name of Yahweh and performed symbolic actions to augment the force of their utterances (see chaps. 27–28). They contradicted each other in their views of the political future of Judah and called upon their contemporaries to make important decisions. Without the benefit of hindsight, as provided by a record of Jeremiah's words, it was not easy for those who heard them to distinguish "true" prophets from "false."

It is clear that the simple claim to be a prophet was not always sufficient to win acceptance. Throughout his career, Jeremiah (like the others) needed to establish his own credibility, to gain a following so that he could influence behavior. He attempted to do this by the claims he made (see 26:12–15; 1:4–10), the message he proclaimed, the actions he performed (see 19:1–20:6 and the Short Essay "Jeremiah's Symbolic Actions"), and by direct attacks on his opponents (e.g., 6:13–15; 37:19). Making a collection of his earlier oracles and claiming that they referred to the present, looming Babylonian threat would have been one way of arguing for his legitimacy, especially in view of the criticism that was leveled against him, that his prophecies had not been fulfilled (so 17:15; 20:7–8). At this stage preserving the words was but one of a repertoire of rhetorical strategies utilized in his performance of his prophetic role.

The situation of the exiles was different. They did not have to argue for the legitimacy of Jeremiah's message, since history had already vindicated it; they could simply assume that he had been a true prophet. Their main problem was to make sense out of their current situation. In this effort they found Jeremiah's interpretation of Judah's fate (see, e.g., 4:13–18; 26:1–6) made-to-order and used it. In the process they shaped many of the traditions that had come down to them in the light of their own concerns (note how the conditional message of 26:1–6 is altered in 7:8–15; see also 7:16–8:3; 11:1–17; 15:2). Some of these developments produced statements with which Jeremiah probably would not have agreed (see chap. 24).

It is difficult to be certain when this process of reinterpretation and growth came to an end. The circumstances reflected in 17:19–27 and 22:24–30 may indicate that it continued into the postexilic period. In addition, for many years the book seems to have circulated in two written forms, identifiable in the texts we now refer to as the MT and the LXX. Everything that came to be included in the book of Jeremiah shared the authority of the prophet. Neither Jeremiah nor those who followed him seem to have believed that the significance of Yahweh's words was ex-

hausted in the context during which they were first uttered.

Though it is beyond the scope of this commentary, it should at least be mentioned that the tradition lived on past the time when it was committed to writing and beyond the "Old Testament period" into the canons of the Jewish and Christian religious communities. The task of reinterpreting the words in new contexts—always full of hazards—has nonetheless continued.

The narrative of chap. 36 seems to promise that of all prophetic books Jeremiah will most easily yield to our view the authentic, original words of the prophet himself. We have already seen, however, that this promise remains unfulfilled, for the "original" scroll cannot be identified with confidence. The reason is by this time clear: the traditions in the book of Jeremiah were preserved as the result of separate actions over several generations, each of which was in response to a particular and immediate need. It is obvious that these needs shaped the collections. And it is understandable that, occupied with their own concerns, the exilic editors obscured the boundaries of the earlier collections. It is for this reason, therefore, that the following commentary does not make a systematic effort to isolate Jeremiah's "genuine" words.

COMMENTARY

1:1–25:38
Confronting the People with Words and Deeds

1:1–3
Superscription

The superscription is a statement in the third person giving information about the prophet Jeremiah and his activity. Such prefixes are a standard feature of most prophetic books in the OT.

The superscription contains four elements. It begins with a phrase that serves as the title of the collection ("The words of Jeremiah"). This is followed by biographical information ("the son of Hilkiah, of the priests who were in Anathoth in the land of Benjamin"), a statement about the basis of his prophetic authority ("to whom the word of the Lord came"), and a chronological reference fixing the dates of prophetic activity ("in the days of Josiah . . . [and] until the captivity of Jerusalem in the fifth month"). The first and third of these elements are always present in superscriptions to prophetic books, though frequently a single phrase serves for both (Hos. 1:1; Obad. 1:1). The second and fourth are sometimes absent. This suggests that the purpose of the superscription is to make two claims about the collection that follows: that it stems from a single, known individual and that, since this individual spoke at the command of Yahweh, the collection as a whole is to be viewed as containing Yahweh's words. The superscription asserts the authority of the prophet to legitimate the authority of the collection of traditions associated with him.

It seems unlikely that the author of the superscription believed that all the material in the collection represented Jeremiah's words (e.g., the extensive biographical narratives are obviously *about* his activity). What is evident in the superscription and in the collection, which it introduces, is the assumption that the activities of Jeremiah shed light on the relationship between Yahweh and his people.

The Jeremiah superscription has several peculiarities. For one thing, it has more biographical detail than most. This element is in character with the book as a whole and adds a poignant dimension to the prophet's complaint about persecution at the hands of the "men of Anathoth" (11:18–21). A second peculiarity is the precision in dating, specifying the exact beginning and end of Jeremiah's activity. However, the latter date (July 587 B.C.) contradicts reports in the collection of Jeremiah's activity subsequent to the fall of Jerusalem (40:1; 42:7; 43:8; 44:1, 24–25).

1:4–19
Jeremiah's Call

This passage contains an account of how Jeremiah came to be a prophet (1:4–10), plus a report of two visions. The first vision stresses Yahweh's determination to bring his words, uttered by the prophet, to fulfillment (1:11–12); the second sketches the content of those words: Judah will be destroyed by an enemy attacking from the north as punishment for its unfaithfulness to Yahweh (1:13–16). Verses 17–19 reiterate vv. 7–9. The passage thus makes the claim that Jeremiah was a designated prophet of Yahweh, ties the general content of his message to this commission, and addresses two problems that emerged during the course of his subsequent activity: the delay in the fulfillment of his prophecies, which tended to undermine his authority as a prophet (cf. 20:7–8), and the opposition that he encountered from people who rejected his message (cf. 11:18–12:6).

1:4–10, The Call. Jeremiah's call is described as a confrontation and dialogue with Yahweh that proceeds through four stages: commissioning, objection, reassurance, and sign. Since this

is the same general pattern one finds in reports of the commissioning of Moses (Exod. 3), Gideon (Judg. 6:11–24), and Isaiah (Isa. 6), the account forges a link between Jeremiah and these great figures from the people's past. The language itself is sometimes stereotypic (e.g., the "Ah, Yahweh God" of Jer. 1:6 reflects the vocabulary of lamentation; cf. 4:10; 14:13; 32:17; Josh. 7:7; Judg. 6:22). However, the whole is presented as something the prophet actually experienced.

Such a call report is appropriate for someone thought to stand in special relationship to a god. Not just in ancient Judah, but in many cultures, the deity is understood to take the initiative in appointing persons to function in the role of intermediary. Call narratives make a formal claim that dialogue with the deity has occurred. In doing so they refer to a part of the prophet's experience that, because of its private character, would otherwise be unavailable to others. But though there is every reason to believe that they are based upon real experiences, the purpose of call narratives is not primarily (auto)biographical. Rather, their main function is rhetorical—to assert a claim to authority that is prior to and legitimates the claim made every time the prophet addresses an audience with a specific message from the god.

Of course, the authority of an intermediary is not established by a call narrative alone. It is primarily the prophet's behavior—both words and actions—that, when deemed appropriate by some portion of the audience, leads to a public affirmation of the prophet's authority. The call narrative can thus be viewed as a theoretical explanation of the cause of that behavior, which shifts the responsibility for it to the deity.

It is probable that the narrative as it stands reveals traces of other uses to which the tradition about Jeremiah's call experience was put. For one thing, intermediaries typically stand between specific peoples and their deities. Jeremiah was no exception; with great consistency he conveyed the rebukes of Yahweh to his Judean compatriots. Yet the narrative refers to him as a "prophet to the nations." Though chap. 27 records an instance in which Jeremiah spoke to foreign emissaries who had assembled in Jerusalem, the focus of his activity was national, not international. The phrase therefore may represent an interpretation by the exilic preservers of the tradition: since Jeremiah's activity had placed him directly in the middle of an important foreign policy dispute (see commentary below on chaps. 27–28), his original call was presumed to have mentioned international responsibilities.

Similarly, the claim that part of Jeremiah's task was "to build and to plant" (v. 10) does not correspond well with what we know about his activity. The phraseology of v. 10 has parallels elsewhere in the book. Once it describes Yahweh's options in dealing with his people (18:7–10), and once his punishment of them (45:4). Otherwise, the reference is to the possibility of political restoration after the long period of Babylonian dominance (24:6; 31:27–28; 42:10; cf. 12:14–17). It seems likely that the reference to building and planting represents a drawing out of the implications of Jeremiah's words in the period after the judgment he proclaimed had become reality.

1:11–19, Two Visions. There are close parallels to these patterned vision reports in Jer. 24:1–3 and Amos 7:7–9; 8:1–3, but it is not necessary to conclude from this that they are merely literary constructions. Comparative studies show that highly stereotypic vision experiences are nonetheless real to those who have them. A vision report constitutes a claim to have received a revelation from the deity and legitimizes subsequent behavior (cf. 1 Kings 22:17–23; 3:5–15). Visions both convey a message and authorize its delivery. They are a vital component of the prophetic process.

It is another question, however, how much the present account was shaped by subsequent events. The reference to invasion by a northern enemy could encompass both the rather general pronouncements on that theme in chaps. 4–6 and the later references to the Babylonians in 25:8–9 and 36:29 (cf. 21:1–10), and v. 15 appears to mirror 39:3.

On what occasions would the prophet himself have related the account of his commissioning? Comparative studies show that intermediaries sometimes recite their visions as part of a specific public act, and such a possibility cannot be ruled out. In 26:12 we see, however, that during a conflict, when his authority was challenged, a much simpler statement could suffice. Amos 7:10–17 provides an example of a prophet's appeal to his commission in response to a challenge to his authority. The fact that this is a narrative in the third person shows that others could utilize this appeal for the same purpose, namely, to establish the authority of Amos's words. In any case it is clear that the position of the account of Jeremiah's call at the head of the entire collection provides the underpinning for all the material that follows.

In fact the need to assert the legitimacy of Jeremiah's activity would have recurred, both during the period of his activity and subsequently, when his words were appealed to as authoritative. Whether or not the call narrative in its present form stems from the prophet himself, the claim it makes is crucial to his acceptance by the people. Prophets cannot function unless their claims to authority are acknowledged by at least some members of their audience.

The Interaction Between Prophet and God

The call narrative provides us with an important clue to the nature of the relationship between prophet and deity: broadly speaking, we must think of revelation in terms of dialogue, not monologue. It is easy to overlook this fact because the utterances of Jeremiah are understood to be the words of Yahweh. The book is replete with formulaic expressions that underscore this assumption: "Thus says Yahweh" (e.g., 6:22), "the word of Yahweh came to me saying" (1:4; 2:1), "Yahweh said to me" (3:6, 11), and similar phrases. In addition Yahweh gives Jeremiah visions (1:11–19), instructions (6:27; 7:16), and information (11:18–19).

But in addition to the visions reported in chap. 1, there are other passages that portray the prophet in dialogue with Yahweh (5:1–6; 12:1–6; 14:11–18; 15:10–21). The prophet's vehement response to words from Yahweh is mirrored in the diatribes of 17:14–18 and 20:7–18. Moreover, speech addressed to Yahweh was an integral part of Jeremiah's intercessory function (7:16; 11:14; 14:11; 15:11; 27:18; 37:3). Jeremiah considered standing in Yahweh's "council" to be an important prophetic experience, one that involves dialogue (23:18, 22).

Since the effectiveness of a prophet depended upon acceptance by an audience, reports of such dialogue should be seen as part of the rhetoric by which Jeremiah and those who transmitted the traditions associated with him sought to legitimize his words.

2:1–4:4
Accusations and Exhortations

The tone of this section is accusatory. The crime is apostasy, the people's abandonment of their God. The language is hyperbolic. It seems unlikely that the Judeans had abandoned their traditional god, Yahweh, altogether (as 2:11 suggests). What Jeremiah represents and forcefully states is the point of view of those Judeans who condemned any deviation from the ideal of exclusive loyalty to Yahweh.

In chap. 3 the idea of the people's "return" to Yahweh emerges as a theme. We learn that there are prior conditions for such a return (3:1) and that the people have refused to turn back to God (3:7, 10). Nevertheless, they continue to be invited to do so (3:12, 14, 22; 4:1). is this content that sets the passage off from the preceding and following units (the call, and a series of oracles about an enemy from the north).

The chapters are rich in the use of figurative

language, especially metaphor. Such language is nonliteral. It proposes identifications we know are not exact, making comparisons on the basis of presumed common qualities.

By far the greatest number of metaphors and similes are drawn from the realm of love and sexuality: the happy marriage (2:2), adultery (3:8, 20), prostitution (2:20, 33; 3:1–3, 6, 8), and even animal sexuality (2:23–24). Figures of speech are also drawn from agriculture (2:3, 20, 21), physical geography (2:31), social and economic life (2:11, 13, 14, 26, 32), and religious law (4:4). In most cases they refer negatively to the people's behavior.

Metaphors are suggestive and open-ended. By using an analogy that invites reflection, the prophet adds force to his accusation. We can imagine members of his audience asking, "Have our actions toward Yahweh really been like those of an unfaithful spouse? Must we then take them as seriously as we would behavior that disrupts a marriage? If we ourselves would be angry and prone to strike back when confronted by such behavior, why should Yahweh act any differently?"

The passage focuses on the past, but the historical allusions are rather general and vague (e.g., 2:7b, 14–16, 20). In particular there is an ambiguity in the use of the term "Israel," which sometimes refers to the whole people in the period before the monarchy (2:3), sometimes to the Northern Kingdom (3:6, 8, 11, 18), and sometimes to Judah (2:26–28). This ambiguity, as well as the fact that we have here a mixture of poetry and prose (3:6–10, 15–18, 24–25), raises the question of why the separate units within this section occur in their present order. An obvious suggestion is that some units were originally composed as comments on others. In particular, the units woven together in 3:6–4:4 form a complex fabric of elaborations and clarifications. Since 2:1–3:5 plus 3:19–20 seem to be the verses that elicited the comments, they are probably the oldest. Still, it is difficult to be confident that even here everything originated with Jeremiah. It is possible, for example, that 2:20–28 owes its present shape to an attempt to explain why Judah fell to the Babylonians.

The whole section 2:1–4:4 provides a good example of the complex way in which the Jeremiah tradition grew. Far from being concerned to preserve only the actual words of the prophet, the transmitters, motivated by an overriding interest in understanding the implications of those words for their current situation, willingly incorporated commentary into the text.

2:1–3:5, Inexcusable Sin and Yahweh's Judgment. In 2:14–19 there is an allusion to a sequence of historical events. First "Israel" (the Northern Kingdom) was destroyed (by Assyria

in 722 B.C.). Then the Judeans (note the shift to the pronoun "you" in v. 16) suffered a blow at the hands of Egypt, presumably the death of Josiah in 609 B.C. (see 2 Kings 23:28–30). Verse 17 offers an interpretation applicable to both these disasters. Yet despite the warnings of history, Judean officials ("you," v. 18) continue to seek national security in the form of alliances with foreign governments. To the prophet these overtures are tantamount to forsaking God. Verses 29–30 make essentially the same point— that the people have failed to learn the lessons implicit in their past misfortunes—but without alluding to any specific event. Such statements clearly rest on the theological assumption that Yahweh is in control of historical occurrences, which he manipulates according to his own purposes, in this case punishment and instruction.

3:6–10, Israel and Judah's Harlotry. These verses can be thought of as an attempt to clarify the potentially ambiguous reference to "Israel" in 2:14–15. The distinction between the Northern Kingdom (Israel) and Judah is made explicit, and the latter is criticized for not having heeded the warning implicit in the destruction of the former.

3:11–14, Judah Worse Than Israel. There now comes an elaboration in which the unfortunate Northern Kingdom is viewed more favorably than Judah (v. 11). The grounds for this comparison are not stated explicitly, but can be inferred from v. 10: Judah failed to heed the warning implicit in Israel's defeat. The contrast between the two is heightened by the allusion to 3:5. The same presumed willingness of Yahweh not to be "angry for ever," which gave the Judeans a false sense of confidence in their own future security, is offered as the basis of Israel's hope of restoration. The conditions for this restoration are that they acknowledge the cause of the nation's downfall—as interpreted by the prophet—and make whatever changes in behavior are required for a "return" to Yahweh. Again, there is a contrast with the Judeans, whose statements of confidence had no effect upon their behavior (3:5b). There is, however, a significant Judean modification in this pro-Israelite statement: Israel's restoration will not be as an independent nation, but as part of a group based in Jerusalem (v. 14).

The contrast set up in these verses is reminiscent of chap. 24, where the Judean exiles are designated "good figs" and their compatriots who remained behind after the Babylonian victory in 597 B.C. are the "bad figs." Historical adversity is interpreted as punishment, and wrongdoers who have been punished are elevated in status over those who have not. Ezek. 16:51–52 may indicate that this theme was a topic of speculation during the Exile, which is probably when the reflections contained in Jer. 3:11–14 originated.

3:15–18, Return and Restoration. This unit clarifies the idea of a restoration to Zion introduced in v. 14. The point of view is clearly exilic: the Ark, and presumably the Temple in which it was housed, no longer exists, and the people of both Israel and Judah are assumed to live to the north of their original homeland. Jerusalem will become the focal point of a new order, which will incorporate other nations as well.

3:19–20, God's Children. These verses return to the theme of 2:1–3:5 and may originally have been contiguous with them.

3:21–25, Return and Healing. Appropriating from vv. 11–14 the theme of Israel's "return," vv. 21–23 add a positive response. The latter motif is further elaborated in the prose unit, vv. 24–25.

4:1–2, Return and Blessing. These verses set out the conditions for some future act of "return" to Yahweh, which will have benefits for other nations as well (cf. 3:17). The term "Israel" is ambiguous, but the allusion to 3:15–18 suggests a reference to the people assembled in the coming restoration.

4:3–4, Admonition and Threat. Prefaced by a new heading, addressed to the "men of Judah and inhabitants of Jerusalem," the subject (warning) and figure of speech (circumcision) change. At first glance, we seem to have a warning that suggests a way to avert a coming disaster, but its position at the end of the larger section suggests that it may have been placed here as a further interpretation of Judah's downfall.

4:5–6:30
An Enemy from the North

The focus of the unit 4:5–6:30 is on the threat of an invasion from the north (4:6; 6:1, 22), a theme introduced in 1:13–15. Though this threat is referred to in several other passages (10:22; 13:20; 15:12), the enemy is not identified until 25:9, where the Babylonian king, Nebuchadnezzar, is named. The unit combines descriptions of an enemy attack with more standard oracles of judgment, interspersing interpretations of the calamity's cause.

The "attacking enemy" passages (4:5–8, 13–17, 19–22, 23–28, 29–31; 6:1–5, 22–26) picture Judah, especially Jerusalem (4:6, 14, 16, 31; 6:2, 6, 23), invaded by a nation that, though anonymous, is clearly a great international power (4:7). Stereotypic language of attack is employed (cf. Isa. 5:26–30). In addition, the derogatory reference to Judah's dependence

upon foreign alliances (4:30) echoes 2:18. One has the impression that the attack is impending, if not already in progress (4:15–17, 19–21, 29; 6:24–25). There are calls to flee (4:5–6a; 6:1), references to destruction (4:6b–7, 20, 23–26, 29; 6:2–8), and lamentations (4:8, 13, 19, 31b; 6:24, 26).

The oracles of judgment (5:1–9, 10–17, 20–29, 30–31; 6:9–12, 13–15, 16–21) are somewhat loose in form; for example, one incorporates elements of dialogue (5:1–6), another rhetorical questions (5:22, 29). They are addressed to the Judeans (5:1, 11, 20), against whom they level, in rather general terms, a variety of accusations: they have violated Yahweh's law (5:1–2, 4–5, 25–26; 6:19), refused to take him seriously (5:11–13; 6:10, 17), and worshiped other gods (5:6–8, 23–24; cf. 2:11, 20); their officials are corrupt (5:30–31; 6:13–15a; cf. 2:8). As a consequence, Yahweh is about to intervene to destroy them (5:6, 14–17; 6:11–12, 15b, 21). One senses an echo of 2:30, namely, the idea that the people have refused to be instructed by their past misfortune (5:3).

The interpretations included in 4:5–6:30 make it clear that the disaster is not just a random event, but an act of judgment by Yahweh in response to the Judeans' own behavior (4:8, 12, 17–18, 22, 26b, 28; 5:19; 6:6–7, 27–30). The accusations contained in the judgment oracles underscore the same point. This explanation is timeless in the sense that it could be applied to any disaster that befell the nation (that is the implication of 2:30 and 5:3). Though the unit contains no unambiguous historical allusions that would allow us to date the attack or identify the enemy, it is clear that those who collected these traditions viewed them from the perspective of the Babylonian exile. The few prose sections that occur here point to the destruction of Jerusalem as Yahweh's act of judgment against Judean apostasy (4:11–12, 27; 5:18–19), but they contain an expression of hope as well: Yahweh will not "make a full end" of the people (4:27; 5:18). Those in exile were conscious of being that remnant (see commentary above on 3:11–14).

Jer. 5:18–19, a straightforward attempt to explain the Exile, has close parallels in Jer. 9:12–16; 16:10–13; 22:8–9; Deut. 29:22–28; and 1 Kings 9:8–9. These passages tend to follow a common outline: after a narrative introduction, the question of why Yahweh has destroyed his people is posed. The answer is invariably apostasy, and the punishment exile. If not the mark of a Deuteronomistic "edition" of the book of Jeremiah, these passages are at least in agreement with the viewpoint of the Deuteronomists.

Within the unit several different attitudes toward the prophets are displayed. Apparently, those who announced misfortune were ignored (5:13; cf. 2:30, which suggests persecution), whereas those who prophesied "peace" received a favorable response (5:31; 6:13–15). This implies the importance of the audience in prophetic activity (see the Short Essay "The Social Dynamics of Prophetic Behavior"). The comment in 4:10 that Yahweh had "deceived" his people points in another direction. The deception referred to seems to be the conviction—dashed by the Exile—that Yahweh would guarantee Judah's security, precisely the message of the prophets whom Jeremiah considered false (6:13–15). The writer held Yahweh responsible for this conviction, presumably because he sent the prophets who reinforced it. The uncritical attitude about prophecy reflected here (i.e., everyone who claims to be a prophet is one) differs from Jeremiah's willingness to make judgments between competing prophetic claims.

Among the prophets, Jeremiah was not alone in having to combat an assumption on the part of his audience that the nation was secure from the threat of military defeat (5:12; 12:4; 21:13; cf. Amos 9:10; Isa. 5:18–23; Mic. 2:6; 3:11). Mic. 3:11 specifically links this confidence to the presence of Yahweh in their midst, as does Jeremiah in his Temple sermon.

7:1–15
Jeremiah's Temple Sermon

Two passages, 7:1–15 and 26:1–24, refer to the same event, an occasion on which Jeremiah stood in the Temple and addressed those who entered with the message that unless they changed their behavior Yahweh would certainly destroy Jerusalem and its sanctuary. What differentiates them is their points of view on this event. Jer. 7:1–15 is a "prose sermon" and concentrates on the prophet's words; chap. 26 is "biography" and gives more details about the interaction between Jeremiah and his audience.

The confrontation occurred in 609 B.C., a time of political upheaval in Judah and the region. King Josiah had been killed in battle by the Egyptians, who later deposed his son Jehoahaz after only three months' reign and replaced him with a more trustworthy ally, Jehoiakim. A struggle between Egypt and Babylon for the control of Palestine was under way, and in Judah questions of national security and prosperity were paramount.

Jeremiah's message seems to have attracted considerable attention, since a group consisting of priests and prophets instituted a legal proceeding against him. They accused him of prophesying the destruction of Temple and city and sought to have him executed (26:8–9, 11).

Deuteronomy's legislation assumes that Israel had both an interest in and a right to exercise control over the activity of prophets, and it provides two instances in which a sentence of death might be handed down: if the prophet spoke in the name of some god other than Yahweh or if the message spoken was not commanded by Yahweh (Deut. 13:1–5; 18:20). Both the fact that Jeremiah spoke in Yahweh's name and the nature of his defense (26:12b, 15b) indicate that the latter was the substance of the charge against him.

As a guide to adjudicating such a case, Deut. 18:21–22 sets forth the criterion of fulfillment of prophecy—if the specific prophecies do not come to pass, then Yahweh has not sent the prophet. By this criterion, Judah's current political situation might seem to confirm the message of peace uttered by Jeremiah's prophetic opponents (cf. 6:13–15) and to discredit his message of doom (20:7–8 shows that the failure of prophesied events to occur was a major problem for Jeremiah). But such a criterion is difficult to apply satisfactorily (see the Short Essay "The Problem of 'False' Prophecy").

The princes, before whom the case was argued, acquitted Jeremiah, but not, as we might expect, by affirming their conviction that Yahweh had in fact sent him with a message of doom. To the contrary, it was sufficient that he had come forward and spoken in Yahweh's name. When the elders then cited the precedent of Micah (whose century-old prophecies of doom still awaited fulfillment, 26:17–19), they explicitly rejected content of a certain type—threats by Yahweh against his own people—as a criterion for acceptable prophecy. The implication of the whole proceeding is that persons who manifest a certain kind of behavior recognizable as "prophetic" are to be given the benefit of the doubt and considered prophets.

The Uriah episode (26:20–23) shows that other factors could enter into such decisions. Like Jeremiah, Uriah prophesied in the name of Yahweh that the nation would be destroyed. But in his case, the king and princes wished to put him to death and succeeded in doing so. Since such a message would seem to undermine national security, their action is not very surprising.

It would appear that the behavior of Jeremiah and Uriah was essentially the same. The crucial difference in their situations seems to have been that Jeremiah had strong supporters among the princes (26:24). It is difficult to know why he had such a following (religious-political affiliation? family ties?) while Uriah did not, but the narrative clearly illustrates the importance of a group of supporters for prophetic activity.

The Social Dynamics of Prophetic Behavior

Prophetic communication is dialogical at two levels. On the one hand, the prophet both hears and responds to the deity (see the Short Essay

"The Interaction Between Prophet and God"), and on the other, the prophet's audience does not receive the words passively; its reactions make a difference. Research in the social sciences has shown that "charisma" is, in some sense, always attributed. An audience will judge positively a prophet whose behavior fits certain stereotypes and whose message is acceptable from the standpoint of certain sociopolitical and religious convictions.

We may observe that prophecy can only occur in societies that harbor a belief in the existence of a god (or gods) able and willing to intervene in the events of the world, as well as the conviction that one legitimate mode of such intervention is the words and actions of human intermediaries. The Judah of Jeremiah's day was such a society. The Temple sermon, however, makes it clear that such beliefs do not preclude a critical evaluation of prophetic activity (cf. 5:12–13). Indeed, we see not only that evaluation occurred, but also that it was affected by differences of opinion. Sometimes, portions of the intended audience are unwilling to listen to the prophet at all (6:10).

The Temple sermon is not the only indication that a prophet's audience assumed the function of judging what was acceptable as prophecy (see 20:1–2; 26:7–9, 16–19; 29:24–28; 38:5). In reality the hearers decided *who* was to be considered a prophet, since without acceptance it is impossible to function in that role. The case of Uriah shows that rejection sometimes took extreme forms (26:20–23; cf. 2:30).

Unanimous support of a prophet is not the issue. But since communication between the divine and the human worlds stands at the heart of the process of intermediation, some level of human acceptance and support is necessary. The different fates of Jeremiah and Uriah show that the relative power of the group of supporters can also be of great importance. The struggle to gain support was a continuing one for Jeremiah (see commentary on chap. 28 and the Short Essay "Jeremiah's Symbolic Actions").

At the core of the dispute mirrored in the Temple sermon incident is a difference of judgment about the nation's fate. Jeremiah's accusations and threat of disaster were opposed, especially by members of the political and religious establishment, though they knew that his was not a new view about the people's fate (26:18). The basis of their confidence was not just wishful thinking, but a religious conviction mirrored in the words, "This is the temple of Yahweh. . . . We are delivered!" (7:4, 10). This conviction was anchored in the royal ideology: Yahweh had chosen Jerusalem to be his habitation, had

founded David's house as the royal line in it, and had established both forever (2 Sam. 7; Pss. 89; 132; Isa. 29:1–8). It was strengthened by historical experience: by Jeremiah's time both dynasty and Temple had endured for nearly four centuries.

Jeremiah's interpretation of Judah's fate, shared by the Deuteronomists and many in exile who wanted to understand the reasons for the nation's fall, was based on the conviction that the covenant between Yahweh and his people was conditional. He described the confidence of the Judeans in the worst possible light—it was based on a "falsehood" that had allowed them to think that they could break Yahweh's law with impunity—and countered their belief with a reference to the fate of Shiloh. The analogy between the two cities is close. In the days before the monarchy, Shiloh had been the resting place of Yahweh's Ark and the only known location apart from Jerusalem of a "temple" of Yahweh (1 Sam. 1:9; 3:3). Furthermore, one may observe a similar mechanical view of the security afforded by Yahweh's presence during times of crisis in the Israelites' manipulation of the Ark at the time of the Philistine wars (1 Sam. 4:3). Nonetheless, Shiloh had been destroyed, according to Jeremiah, because of the people's "wickedness." The same could happen to Jerusalem.

This was not simply a theological dispute. Ideology and foreign policy were intermeshed, and we know that Jeremiah did not hesitate to draw specifically political inferences from his convictions (see chaps. 27–29). The fact that the book contains two accounts of the Temple sermon suggests both that some such occurrence was an important skirmish in Jeremiah's ongoing confrontation with Judah's rulers and that it provided significant material for exilic collectors of the Jeremiah tradition.

There is, in fact, evidence that the account in 7:1–15 is a product of the community of exiles: though the tone of Jeremiah's message seems to be conditional—if you mend your ways you will be spared (vv. 3–7; cf. 26:2–6)—the treatment of the Shiloh analogy in vv. 8–15 implies that the nation's fate is already sealed. The tradition has been preserved for us in such a way as to acknowledge and explain the nation's fall.

Jeremiah's Struggle Against "Falsehood"

The Hebrew word *sheqer* (basically, "lie") occurs frequently in the book of Jeremiah. In the main it is used in three interrelated contexts: reference to a pervasive but false sense of national security (7:4, 8), to Jeremiah's opponents among the prophets (6:13; 27:14, 16; 28:15), and to loyalties to gods other than Yahweh (3:23; 10:14; 16:19).

Though the term can refer to everyday prevarication (37:14), such usage is rare. Rather, it labels—as the Temple sermon passages show—a certain attitude about the relationship between Yahweh and the nation, the social and political implications that were drawn from that attitude, and the utterances of those who espoused it. What the prophet struggled against was a pervasive falsehood that he understood to be present at the core of Judah's national existence and that he saw as a serious threat to that existence (see the Short Essay "The Problem of 'False' Prophecy").

The term *sheqer* is widely distributed in the book, occurring in all three major types of material—poetry, biographical prose, and prose sermons. Such occurrence may be taken as an indication both that we are dealing with a major theme of Jeremiah's message and that those who collected and preserved the traditions associated with him shared his concern to interpret the nation's fate, as well as his general point of view on that matter.

7:16–8:3
Supplements to the Temple Sermon

Jer. 7:16–8:3 is not part of the Temple sermon, but a separate unit made up of three sections that loosely approximate the oracle form (accusation, followed by an announcement of Yahweh's intervention). The accusations focus on religious practices, especially the worship of gods other than Yahweh and the offering of sacrifices. Because of these acts, Yahweh "has rejected and forsaken the generation of his wrath" (7:29) and will destroy their land.

The passage contains phrases characteristic of the prose sermons. Some of these it shares with the Deuteronomist (e.g., "provoke me to anger," 7:18 [cf. 1 Kings 14:9]; "obey the voice of Yahweh," 7:28); others are peculiar to the Jeremian prose (e.g., "cities of Judah and streets of Jerusalem," 7:17, 34; "I have persistently sent," 7:25).

The unit is not really a sermon, however, for it takes the form of Yahweh speaking to Jeremiah (7:16, 27–28) about Judah. Nor does it present an entirely accurate picture of the prophet's activity, since the prohibition recorded in v. 16 does not jibe with accounts of Jeremiah's intercessions, some coming from late in his career (18:20; 21:1–2; 37:1–10; 42:1–22; for a parallel to 7:17–20, see 44:15–19).

It is best to see the unit as an exilic comment on the cause of Judah's destruction, an event mirrored in 8:3. The prohibition against intercession serves to strengthen the judgment about the seriousness of the people's actions

and perhaps also to protect Jeremiah's reputation as a prophet by heading off the charge that his intercessions had been powerless to prevent the nation's fall. The same prohibition occurs in two other prose passages devoted to elucidating the cause of exile (11:14; 14:11). The unit is located where it is in the book probably because, like 7:1–15, it focuses on unacceptable religious practices and is concerned to reflect upon the causes of exile.

8:4–10:25
Coping with Catastrophe

Jer. 8:4–10:25 has ties to the "enemy from the north" oracles of 4:5–6:30, though in general its component sections differ from these in form. Oracles of judgment are infrequent (8:4–13; 9:2–9). Instead, one finds cries of lament and mourning (8:18–9:1; 9:10, 17–22; 10:19–21), a "dialogue" (8:18–9:1) in which the speakers change with confusing rapidity (Jeremiah, 8:18–19a; the people, 8:19b; Yahweh, 8:19c; the people, 8:20; Jeremiah, 8:21–9:1), and a polemic against idols that contains a hymn of praise to Yahweh (10:1–16).

Twice an attack from the north is mentioned (8:16–17; 10:22; cf. 4:13), drawing a specific connection to chaps. 4–6, though now the invasion is viewed as unstoppable (8:17). There are additional reflections of the immediately preceding chapters in 8:8–13 (against the Judean leaders; cf. 5:30–31 and 6:13–15, which is repeated almost verbatim), 8:18–19a and 8:21–9:1 (Jeremiah's personal reaction to the people's fate; cf. 4:19–21), 8:19b (on Zion's security; cf. 7:4, 10), 9:7 ("refine" and "test"; cf. 6:27), 9:9 (cf. 5:9, 29), and 8:19 and 10:1–16 (polemic against idols; cf. 7:17–18, 30).

The dominant theme of the unit is coping with disaster. No hope is expressed that, if the people repent, they can avoid catastrophe. Rather, the nation's downfall seems already to have occurred, though perhaps in the not too distant past. In all likelihood, the poetry of these chapters reflects the Exile but has not yet developed elaborate rationalizations of it, which is evident from the relatively large number of poetic passages in which either the people or the prophet are pictured as struggling with a disaster that seems at the very least to be virtually complete (8:14–15; 8:18–9:1; 9:10, 17–22; 10:19–21). The mood is typified by the wailing of the people: "How we are ruined! We are utterly shamed, because we have left the land, because they have cast down our dwellings" (RSV). By contrast, the prose of 9:12–16 is much more dispassionate in its attempt to explain the disaster (cf. 5:18–19).

This unit, then, does not simply mirror the warnings of chaps. 4–6. Though it takes up the same theme of attack from the north, it presupposes a later time. This recognition allows us to surmise why it came to be placed here. The Temple sermon (7:1–15) and its supplement (7:16–8:3) may be considered the pivot of a larger section of the book, chaps 4–10. Following the warnings of a possible invasion from the north (chaps. 4–6), the Temple sermon establishes that the punishment such a disaster would represent is irrevocable. Chaps. 8–10 indicate that this judgment has been executed. Since this organization would have been motivated by reflection on the events of 587 B.C., the overall organization of the passage mirrors the concerns of the exilic community. Along these lines we can note that in the Temple sermon there is a tension, if not a contradiction, between the open-ended warning that allows for the possibility of repentance and escape (7:5–7) and the announcement that punishment is inevitable (7:13–16). The parallel account of the sermon in 26:4–6 agrees with the former, not the latter, sentiment.

Repetition in the Book of Jeremiah

Even apart from the occurrence of various formulas like "Thus says Yahweh," the book of Jeremiah contains a great deal of repetition. Frequently, this is at the level of words and phrases (e.g., "to pluck up and break down . . . build and plant," 1:10; 12:14, 17; 18:7–10; 24:6; 31:28; 42:10; 45:4), but sometimes passages several verses in length are repeated (e.g., 6:13–15 and 8:10–12; 10:12–16 and 51:15–19). Occasionally, whole episodes are reported from different points of view (7:1–15 and 26:1–24; 21:1–12 and 37:3–10; in both these sets the first passage is a prose sermon, the second a biographical narrative).

There is no single explanation that will cover all such repetitions. Sometimes the influence of standard prose conventions of Jeremiah's day or of the Deuteronomists may account for the choice of specific vocabulary. At other times we may be confronted with favorite expressions of the prophet (or some transmitter of his traditions, e.g., 2:13 and 17:13; 5:9, 29 and 9:9; and 11:23b; 23:12b; 48:44b and 49:8b). Some doublets are likely the result of the oral transmission of the oracles (e.g., 6:13–15 and 8:10–12).

It is striking that many such repetitions occur in interpretive prose sections devoted to specifying the causes of the Exile and speculating on the shape of the people's future. That is true, for example, of four of the six passages linked to 1:10 (12:14, 17; 24:6; 31:28; 42:10), as well as of the prohibitions against intercession (7:16; 11:14; 14:11), 9:15b (mirroring 23:15), 15:13–14 (cf. 17:3–4), and 16:14–15 (cf. 23:7–8).

Jer. 22:3 repeats 21:12 in the course of elaborating the short oracle against the king in which the latter verse appears (21:11–14). The compilers of the tradition obviously found some verses to be relevant to more than one context. Thus, a combination of polemic against idols and hymn of praise came to function both as a part of a larger description of Judah's actions (10:12–16) and as an assurance of Yahweh's power to bring about the defeat of Babylon (51:15–19). A statement of assurance (30:10–11) became part of a collection of oracles concerned with the people's future restoration (chaps. 30–31), as well as of an oracle directed against a specific enemy, Egypt (46:27–28). The same words were used to describe Judah's northern attacker (6:22–24) and, later, Babylon's (50:41–43).

Taken as a whole, the repetitions in Jeremiah give us a hint of the long and lively process of collection and compilation that lies behind the present form of the book.

11:1–17
The Broken Covenant

Both the opening formula ("The word that came to Jeremiah from Yahweh") and its general contents identify Jer. 11:1–17 as a prose sermon. The parallel to 7:1–20 is especially close: both begin with a statement of what is required of the people (7:3–7; 11:2–5), followed by a declaration that they have actually been disobedient (7:8–11; 11:6–10), an announcement that Yahweh will intervene to punish them (7:12–15; 11:11–13), and a prohibition—because of their apostasy—against the prophet's interceding on their behalf (7:16–20; 11:14–17).

Because it is prose, this unit is better described as a "sermon" than an "oracle," though it contains the elements of a traditional oracle of judgment. Addressed to "the men of Judah and the inhabitants of Jerusalem," it accuses them of having failed to obey Yahweh's commands (11:8a, 9–10, 13) and announces the punishment that Yahweh will levy against them (v. 11). Verses 12–13 mirror the language of the oracles (cf. 2:26–28).

The striking feature of the unit is that its argument develops the theme of the covenant relationship between Yahweh and his people. The presence of this issue, plus the fact that the passage contains no date or datable allusion, has led to considerable debate over its setting and reference. There are three main options.

First, Jeremiah might be referring to the covenant made at the time of Josiah's reform (cf. 2 Kings 23:1–3; note that the same participants— men of Judah and inhabitants of Jerusalem— are mentioned in both). This reference is an appealing interpretation because it would provide us with at least one clear indication of the prophet's attitude toward the reform, but it cannot be proven.

Second, Jeremiah might be referring, in a general way, to the Sinai covenant (rather than to Josiah's specific renewal of it) to provide a context for his condemnation of the people's behavior. Though specific mention of this covenant is somewhat rare in the prophetic books, precedents are available (e.g., Hos. 8:1–3).

Third, many have seen this unit as an example of Deuteronomistic editorial activity. Especially in vv. 3–5, the language corresponds closely to Deuteronomy (cf. v. 3 with Deut. 27:14–26, v. 4 with Deut. 4:20, v. 5 with Deut. 8:18 and 31:20, and vv. 4–5 with Deut. 26:8–9), and, like the Deuteronomistic History, the passage displays a well-developed covenant theology. (On the matter of a "Deuteronomistic edition" of Jeremiah, see Introduction.)

The term "covenant" presents a problem. The occurrences are almost exclusively in prose sections, which are either exilic in date or do not refer to the relationship between Yahweh and his people. The topic in chap. 34 is an agreement on the part of the king and the people of Jerusalem to free their Hebrew slaves (34:8, 10, 13, 15, 18). The context of the occurrence in 22:9 is an exilic interpretation of the causes of the nation's collapse, and in 31:31–34 it is a description of a "new covenant." The remaining occurrences outside of chap. 11 are in passages that refer to the eventual restoration of the people to their land and seem to be products of exilic reflection and hope (3:16; 32:40; 33:20–21, 25; 50:5). The only occurrence in the poetry (14:21) is in a communal lamentation in which the people, anxious to influence Yahweh to act on their behalf, remind him of their long-standing relationship with him.

The fact that the exilic community elaborated the idea of covenant does not require one to view 11:1–13 as purely a product of the Exile. Jer. 7:1–15, and its parallel in chap. 26, show that the prose sermons may derive ultimately from Jeremiah's speeches. As we have seen, the theme in chap. 11 mirrors that of chap. 2, and if we understand v. 8b to refer to the collapse of Israel in 721 B.C. (see commentary above on 2:1–3:5), v. 11 can be taken to refer to the impending fate of Judah.

The sermon proper ends at v. 13. The following prohibition against intercession (vv. 14–17) no longer speaks of the covenant, and probably represents an editorial addition after the fashion of 7:16–8:3.

Though it is likely that the wording of this sermon on the covenant is exilic, it is possible that, in its essentials, it goes back to Jeremiah. One might object that even if it contains no explicit reflections on the catastrophe of 587 B.C., thematically it is quite similar to them. However, such an interpretation of the people's history was in the air during the decades before the Exile. We see it reflected in the pre-exilic Deuteronomists' view of the fall of Israel (2

Kings 17:1–18), as well as in Jeremiah's oracles (e.g., chap. 2; 4:16–18). When Judah and Jerusalem were finally destroyed by the Babylonians, the prophet's analysis was ready to hand as a tool for interpreting what was now past.

11:81–12:6
Jeremiah's First Complaints

In two pairs of speeches, words of Jeremiah are followed by words of Yahweh. The first pair (11:18–23) loosely resembles an oracle of judgment; the second (12:1–6) has the form of a dialogue.

Jeremiah's speech in 11:18–20 begins as a narrative describing how Yahweh revealed to him the plotting of his enemies and ends as a prayer for vengeance against them. This is followed by a speech of Yahweh addressed specifically to "the men of Anathoth," which includes both an accusation against them (11:21) and an announcement that Yahweh will send against them, as punishment for their deeds, an attacking army that none will escape (vv. 22–23). In contrast, 12:1–4 finds Jeremiah speaking directly to Yahweh, complaining about his opponents (even accusing Yahweh of having strengthened them, v. 2a), justifying himself (v. 3a), and requesting vengeance upon them (v. 3b). Yahweh's response is in two parts: a rebuke of the prophet (v. 5) and words of comfort for him in the face of his enemies' attack.

The accusation leveled against the opponents differs in the two sections. In the first there is specific mention of a plot to murder Jeremiah (11:19b), as well as reference to the attempt by the men of Anathoth to use death threats to control his activity as a prophet (v. 21b). In the second the primary reference is not to actions against Jeremiah, but to the people's false sense of security: they do as they please in the confidence that Yahweh will not "see" (which assumes he will not bring about) their "end" (v. 4).

Several difficulties arise if one tries to read these two pairs of speeches as a single unit. One is the difference in the accusations against the prophet's enemies. Another is the tone of warning in 12:6, which seems out of place after the earlier revelations to Jeremiah about his enemies' activity (11:18–19). It is therefore best to assume that they were originally two separate units. Each is a complete communication, with the enemies the focus of the first and the prophet himself the focus of the second.

There are strong echoes of the psalms of lamentation in these complaints. Compare, for example, 11:18–19 with Ps. 56:5; the cries for vengeance in 11:20a and 12:3a with Ps. 26:1–3; 12:1b with Ps. 10:1–4; and 12:4b with Ps. 10:13b. This does not mean that Jeremiah

617

could not have spoken these words, but it does suggest that we cannot assume uncritically that he did (see the Short Essay "Jeremiah's Complaints").

Furthermore, it is impossible to identify specific settings for these two units. The first alludes to an attempt (or series of attempts) by the men of Anathoth to control Jeremiah's activity as a prophet. The second reflects a negative response by his audience to his message that their overconfidence in Yahweh's protection has set them up for disaster.

Given this uncertainty about historical setting and the use within them of stereotypic language, what can one learn from these units about Jeremiah himself? In particular two things seem clear: that in the exercise of his prophetic function he encountered serious opposition and that as a result he sought help from Yahweh.

It is interesting that the source of opposition is specified as the "men of Anathoth" (11:21, 23) and kinsmen (12:6). There is a strong tradition that Anathoth, about three miles northeast of Jerusalem, was a residence of priests (Josh. 21:18; 1 Kings 2:26) and the home village of Jeremiah, himself a member of a priestly family (1:1; 29:27). Chap. 32 shows that not all the prophet's relationships with citizens of Anathoth were strained. What, then, can one make of this opposition? One obvious point is that priests, together with prophets, were prominent among Jeremiah's opponents (see 26:7–9, 11). The probable reason for their hostility was his condemnation of the doctrine of national security based on the royal ideology and his prediction of the destruction of Temple and city. He attacked their vested interests, and their negative response was predictable.

What is most clearly reflected in these units is the process of intermediation, seen from the prophet's point of view. Jeremiah felt himself a man caught in the middle, under attack from both sides. Compelled to function as a prophet, he understood himself to be criticized by Yahweh for lack of proper performance (12:5). Yet he could not perform his function effectively in the face of strong opposition to his legitimacy, for that is the thrust of his opponents' attack: their attempt to silence him with a threat (11:21b) presumes their judgment that he was not a valid prophet and that, as an impostor, he must die (see Deut. 18:20; Jer. 26, and the Short Essay "The Social Dynamics of Prophetic Behavior").

Jeremiah's Complaints

At five places in the book of Jeremiah, one encounters poetry that seems to voice the prophet's personal complaints against both his human enemies and God (11:18–12:6; 15:10–21; 17:14–18; 18:18–23; 20:7–18; there may be a total of seven individual poems here, assuming breaks after 11:18 and 20:13). These poems have been given various names, which in turn have implications for how we are to understand them. To refer to them as "complaints" or "confessions" emphasizes the personal dimension of their contents, suggesting that in them one sees the prophet bemoaning his fate and lashing out against his opponents. To refer to them as "laments," however, emphasizes the stereotypic nature of much in their language and calls to mind their close affinities with the generic prayers of lamentation, which had a place in Israelite ritual.

With respect to form, there are three elements that recur in these poems: descriptions of the adversaries' behavior (11:18–19, 21; 12:6; 15:10; 17:15; 18:18, 22b; 20:7b, 10), appeals to God to act against the adversaries (11:20; 12:1–4; 15:15a; 17:14, 17–18; 18:21–23; 20:11–12), and the prophet's attempts at self-justification (12:3a; 15:11, 15b–18; 17:16; 18:20b; 20:7–9—in the form of a rebuke of his opponents). In three places, God's responses to the complaint are given (11:22–23; 12:5; 15:19–21).

All these elements are characteristic of the individual psalms of lamentation, with which Jeremiah's complaints also share similarities in vocabulary and expression. The latter are too numerous to list, but the following may serve as illustrations: cf. Jer. 11:20a; 12:3a; 20:12 with Ps. 26:1–3; Jer. 15:15 with Ps. 69:7; Jer. 15:17 with Pss. 26:4–5; 88:8–12; Jer. 15:18 with Pss. 38:5–8; 42:10; Jer. 17:18 with Ps. 35:4–6; Jer. 18:18, 22b with Ps. 57:6; Jer. 18:21–22 with Ps. 109:6–15; Jer. 20:7–8 with Ps. 22:6–8; and Jer. 20:10 with Ps. 31:13.

It is probable that the individual laments of Psalms are standard prayers used during the performance of certain Temple rituals. Though no one would deny they were uttered by real persons with real problems, it is pointless to try to discern behind them specific individuals and situations. The Psalms, therefore, attest more to stereotypic patterns than to individual creativity, a conclusion strengthened by the virtual absence of historical allusions in them.

Given the similarity between Jeremiah's complaints and these psalms of lamentation, one must raise the question of the extent to which the form gives us any accurate biographical information about the prophet. There have been arguments at both extremes on this issue. Many have seen a personal crisis of vocation and faith reflected in these poems. A few have argued that such laments could never have broken loose from their liturgical setting and become purely "spiritual" utterances, but must always have remained tied to the liturgy. In this view the prophet of the laments is enacting his role as intercessor between God and the nation, and his distress expresses the people's fate.

Because it emphasizes individual emotions and experience to the exclusion of communal patterns of behavior, the former view seems too "modern." The latter, however, is based on the dubious assumption that forms of speech at home in public rituals could not, or would not, be dislodged and used on other occasions. The truth, no doubt, lies somewhere between these extremes.

Despite important similarities, certain features distinguish Jeremiah's complaints from the lament psalms and encourage the perception that his complaints contain references to the prophet's own experiences. For example, there is the matter of God's answer to the complaint. In the psalms of lamentation, one often finds a sudden shift in tone from distress to confidence: God has heard the prayer of the righteous sufferer and has (or will) come to the rescue (20:11; cf. Pss. 6:9–10; 22:22–31; 56:12–13; 109:30–31). Although one of the responses incorporated into Jeremiah's complaints has a similar tone (11:22–23), the other two are, above all, rebukes of the prophet for his weakness (12:5; 15:19–21). In addition, certain verses seem to have derived from specific experiences of the prophet. In 17:15 the speaker quotes his adversaries, who have taunted him because "the word of the Lord," which he has spoken, has not come to pass, a theme echoed in 20:7–8. The "I" of 18:20 must refer to a single individual who interceded with God on behalf of a larger group, with which he now finds himself in conflict. There is a reference to the adversaries as "men of Anathoth" (11:21–23) and kinsmen (12:6), and we know that Anathoth was Jeremiah's home village (1:1; 32:6–8). Furthermore, it is clear from references to the internalizing and speaking of God's "words" that the speaker was (or was pictured as being) a prophet (15:16, 19; 17:15–16; 20:7–10). On the other hand, the reference in 15:17 (cf. 16:5–9), which seems so personal, actually uses stereotypic language (cf. Pss. 26:4–5; 88:8–9). Hence, it is difficult to have confidence in 15:17 as a reflection of Jeremiah's actual experience.

It should be noted in passing that the social situation suggested by the complaints is entirely realistic. Anthropological field studies of contemporary cultures yield numerous examples of intermediaries contesting with their gods, encountering hostility in their audiences, and suffering in their private lives the pervasive (and often negative) effects of the demands of their role.

It is uncertain whether the present order of the complaints is chronological. What can be said is that the picture they present of the prophet's situation becomes increasingly dismal. The first three contain answers, albeit somewhat harsh, from God, but none thereafter do. The last has the tone of abject despair (20:14–18).

Other prophets faced opposition (e.g., Amos 7:10–17; Isa. 8:9–22), and one may assume they felt frustrated. But there are no complaints attributed to them. So, it is not entirely clear why these poems, attributed to Jeremiah, were even preserved. Their picture of a threatened and complaining prophet has been both puzzling and disconcerting and has frequently led to theological explanations: they illustrate the truth that God chooses and empowers just such persons to serve him; or they reveal the plight of one of the last of Israel's prophets, who had experienced through his own suffering and disappointment the hopelessness of actually carrying out the prophetic mission. Whatever the truth of such explanations, it will be more in harmony with the view of the book and its contexts sketched in the Introduction to ask what social factors might be involved in their creation and preservation.

One may start with the assumption that the picture the complaints present of a man who suffered both with and at the hands of his contemporaries has some basis in actual experience. That one who suffers might publicly complain is no more than one would expect. That in doing so he would utilize his culture's standard vocabulary of complaint is not surprising. Those complaints that were formalized as poems may originally have been part of the rhetorical arsenal used by Jeremiah in the conflict with his prophetic opponents: they would certainly (from his point of view) establish a stark contrast between his faithfulness to Yahweh's difficult commission and the easy task of prophets who spoke only what the people wanted to hear, a message of peace.

As the tradition developed, the complaints must have been preserved, at least in part, because they were attributed to Jeremiah. But it also seems clear that they fit well the contexts in which the book of Jeremiah came into being. The picture they give of suffering would have been useful to persons trying to make sense of the events of the times, whether in the prophet's day or during the Exile. The "lessons" to be learned from them (e.g., that in such times even a prophet must suffer and may become discouraged and angry, or that God's anger with the people had become so intense that it carried away innocent and guilty alike) no doubt differed from person to person. But to emphasize only the biographical dimension of these complaints is to miss their larger message and that of the book.

12:7-17
Yahweh's Response to Disaster

The unit 12:7-17 has two parts, vv. 7-13 and 14-17. The first may be considered a lament, not because of the language it uses (in contrast to Jeremiah's complaints), but on the basis of the underlying sympathy expressed in v. 7 and in the repeated phrase "my heritage" (vv. 7, 8, 9). We learn at the beginning of the lament both that Yahweh has abandoned his heritage (v. 7) and his reason for doing so, namely, the people have displayed hostility toward him analogous to that of a wild beast, v. 8. What follows is essentially an elaboration on the first issue, which uses a series of metaphors and describes the enemies as wild beasts (v. 9, accepting Holladay's translation of the first phrase: "Does the hyena look greedily on my possession for me?") and as shepherds (= kings; see 2:8; 23:1-4). These have brought destruction upon the land of Judah (vv. 10-11a, 12). The account seems to assume that this devastation has already occurred. In addition, reference to those who have not learned the proper lesson from the events (v. 11b) suggests that the catastrophe referred to may have been the military harassment of Judah that culminated in Nebuchadnezzar's first conquest of Jerusalem (597 B.C.; see 2 Kings 24:1-2, 10-16). Verse 13 may be a reference to drought.

In the second section, 12:14-17, there is a change from poetry to prose and from reflection on Judah's fall to an address directed at its neighbors. The theme is the restoration of Judah and, after suitable punishment ("plucked them up," vv. 14, 15), of its former enemies as well. The "plucking up" recalls 1:10, though as applied to Judah in v. 14, its meaning is reversed: that nation will be rescued from captivity. This restoration of Judah's enemies is conditional, depending upon their conversion to the religion of Yahweh (vv. 16-17). The latter is symbolized by the swearing of oaths in Yahweh's name. Such oaths seem to have been common (see 1 Kings 1:29; 2:24), and the assumption here is that the specific god mentioned in them could be taken as an indication of where one's religious loyalties lay. The passage is connected thematically with vv. 7-13 (note the word "inheritance" in vv. 14, 15), but the viewpoint is clearly exilic. Judah's punishment had been accomplished. Hope for restoration was the logical sequel to preceding laments.

13:1-11
A Vision of Destruction

Jeremiah is instructed by Yahweh to purchase and wear a linen undergarment and, subsequently, to make two trips, one for the purpose of burying it and the other for the purpose of retrieving it. The unit concludes with an interpretation of this series of actions (vv. 8-11). The description is highly pictorial and is often considered to be an account either of a symbolic action or of a vision.

The plausibility of the former view depends in part on the location of the place to which the prophet was sent. The text reads "Euphrates," but a round trip from Jerusalem to that river would involve a journey of approximately seven hundred miles. To circumvent this problem, it has been suggested by some scholars that the reference is to "Parah," a spring some six and a half miles to the northeast of Jerusalem, a manageable journey. But "Euphrates" may be the better reading, since there is another reason to believe that we should not consider this text to represent a symbolic action: the account has the form of a dialogue between Jeremiah and Yahweh; nowhere does it mention an audience before whom the actions were performed and to whom the accompanying words were addressed (see the Short Essay "Jeremiah's Symbolic Actions").

It is best to see this passage as a vision report. The dialogue form provides the key to this understanding (cf. 1:11-12, 13-16; Amos 7:1-9; 8:1-4). No audience is necessary. The vision communicates to the prophet Yahweh's attitude about the current situation, which can then be taken up into the proclamations he delivers to the people. The message is clear enough. The undergarment—purchased and worn, hidden away and spoiled—is a metaphor for the intimate relationship that existed between Yahweh and Judah, which the latter's rebellious actions have brought to ruin (v. 11). Indeed, there is a double sense in the picture of the garment's being "spoiled": the former intimacy is no longer possible, and the nation will be made to suffer as a result (v. 9). The mention of the Euphrates in this connection is entirely appropriate and calls to mind the earlier oracles concerning a foe from that northern region who would despoil (or had already) the Judean countryside. One may observe that the action depicted preserves the main parts of an oracle of judgment, an accusation and an announcement of punishment.

13:12-27
More About Judah's Fate

The unit 13:12-17 contains four short sections on the theme Judah's fate. The first, vv. 12-14, opens with the prophet quoting a proverb that seems to suggest that prosperity and good times are the norm. The anticipated response of the people suggests that this saying expresses their conviction. But Jeremiah reinterprets the proverb by transferring it to a different context—from social drinking, symbolizing the good life, to drunkenness, providing a metaphor for the disaster that will befall Judah (cf. 25:15–29, and also Ezek. 23:33, where an explicit reference is made to the fall of Samaria).

Jer. 13:15–17 contains a general call for the people to respond to Yahweh's words, followed by a threat about the dire consequences of not doing so. Failure to respond will cause the prophet to weep, since "Yahweh's flock is taken captive." The latter phrase suggests a date after 597 B.C.

There follows an address to the "queen mother" (vv. 18–19), who might be either the senior wife of a ruling king (beyond childbearing age and perhaps no longer an active conjugal partner; e.g., Bathsheba in her later years) or a widow and the mother of the ruling king. The queen mother, a person of importance in Judean society, seems to have functioned mainly as a counselor (see 1 Kings 1:11–40). The oracle assumes that a deportation has already occurred, perhaps that of 597 B.C. Note that 2 Kings 24:12 specifically mentions the queen mother among the exiles.

The longest section, vv. 20–27, returns to the theme of the enemy from the north. The dispersal of the "flock" (v. 20; two Hebrew words for "flock" are used) may contain a double entendre, suggesting the scattering both of the Judean army (contrast the reference to the strength of the attacking "shepherds" and "flocks" in 6:3) and of the population (see 23:1–3) as well as the loss of countryside and livestock (cf. 5:17). Use of birth pangs as a figure for acute distress suffered in the face of impending attack recalls 6:24. The question "Why?" (v. 22) sounds like an attempt to explain the Exile, but this interrogation could be a device for presenting an accusation against the people. Certainly the answer to this question, that they have "forgotten" Yahweh and "trusted in a lie" (25b), corresponds to a main theme of Jeremiah's proclamation (see the Short Essay "Jeremiah's Struggle Against 'Falsehood' "). It also provides a plausible conceptual framework for the attitude of the people mirrored in vv. 12–14. The accusation of "harlotry" recalls 3:2, 9.

It is difficult to discern a specific original setting for these sections. The last may come from the period before the first deportation of Judeans to Babylon, but it is improbable that the others do. Together they form part of a rather loose assemblage of oracles and interpretations that begins in 12:7.

14:1–15:9
Reflections on the People's Lamentations

The heading of this passage (14:1) announces that the topic is a drought. The first sections may

in fact reflect a real drought, but later in the unit the people's fate is described in terms of military defeat. However, both drought and warfare result in the destruction of the people, and both are susceptible to the same interpretation.

The unit begins with a description of the effects of a drought (14:2–6), which is followed by a confession and plea addressed to Yahweh by the people (vv. 7–9) and his response to them (v. 10). The focus then shifts to Jeremiah; vv. 11–16 record (in prose) a dialogue between him and Yahweh and vv. 17–18 his lamentation over what has happened to his people. Following another segment of communal lamentation (vv. 19–22), Yahweh comments to Jeremiah on the futility of interceding for such a people (15:1–4). The final section is reminiscent of an oracle of judgment (vv. 5–9). From 14:11 on, references to the nation's fate are dominated by images of war: the standard pair "sword/famine," or a variation on it, occurs six times (14:12, 15, 16, 18; 15:2; cf. 15:3, 9); 14:18a suggests a city under siege; 14:19b (= 8:15) and 15:6b–9 mirror a military attack. Only 14:22a mentions drought.

Though it can be segmented into smaller sections that differ in style and content, there are also indications that this passage should be treated as a single unit. First, Jerusalem is the focus of attention (14:2; 15:5; cf. 14:17). Second, the tone of lamentation is pervasive. Taken together, 14:2–6 and 7–9 display the standard form of a psalm of lamentation (description of distress, vv. 2–6; confession, v. 7; plea for help, vv. 8–9a; expression of confidence, v. 9b), and vv. 19–22 have the same elements in identical order. Verse 7, especially, mirrors the language of the Psalms (cf. Pss. 25:11; 32:5; 38:18; 79:9; 109:21; 143:11). Jer. 14:17–18 and 15:5 also echo the language of lamentation. Third, the problems of intercession on behalf of the people (14:11–12; 15:1) and false prophets are each dealt with twice. This observation may offer a clue as to why several of the smaller units were combined into the larger text.

The lamentations were occasioned by disasters—drought and war—that the text views as past occurrences. The responsibility for these events is placed directly on the people (14:10, 14–16, 18b; 15:4, 6), who themselves are pictured as acknowledging it (in the "confession" section of their laments, 14:7, 20). The fact that the people engage in pleas to Yahweh for assistance, however, indicates that they did not view the breach between themselves and Yahweh as pessimistically as the prophet did (cf. 14:11–12; 15:1).

One can only speculate about the precise setting of the original segments. The condemnation of Jeremiah's prophetic opponents (14:13–16) would fit the intensity of the prophetic struggle, which characterized the years 597–587 B.C. (see chaps. 27–29). Jer. 14:13 may even represent an attempt by Jeremiah to excuse the people's behavior by laying the blame for it at the feet of his prophetic opponents. On the other hand, there are some indications of the context of the unit in its present form. The expansion of the standard list, "sword, famine, and pestilence," to include "captivity" (15:2) and the reference to the sins of King Manasseh (15:4; a theme of the exilic Deuteronomists, see 2 Kings 23:26–27) suggest exilic reflections on the fall of Judah. If 14:18a refers to a siege of Jerusalem, that of 588–587 is the most likely candidate (it lasted about eighteen months, and during it there was famine in the city, 2 Kings 25:3). Such a reference would provide another indication of an exilic date for this text.

Taken as a whole, this unit should be viewed as a literary construction, a small, independent collection of Jeremiah traditions. That it is not a ritual text utilized on the occasion of a national fast for seeking aid in the face of drought or enemy attack is indicated by the form of the first lament (the description of distress in 14:2–6 is in the third person, not the first, as we would expect in a prayer), by the dialogue between the prophet and Yahweh that appears parenthetically in the middle of it, and by the exilic interpretations it contains. Its presence at this particular point in the book of Jeremiah is perhaps best explained by the proximity of other lamentations, the prophet's own complaints found in 11:18–12:6 and 15:10–21.

15:10–17:27
Complaints and Interpretations

At the beginning and near the end of the unit 15:10–17:27, one finds additional examples of Jeremiah's complaints to Yahweh (15:10–21; 17:14–18). Their theme is persecution, the result of the people's hostile reaction to his prophetic message (15:15b–17; 17:15–16; cf. 11:21). These complaints bracket a miscellaneous collection of materials that focus on that message, justifying it both theoretically and by reference to the actual destruction of the nation. At the end there is a section on the Sabbath, which may be understood as a priestly application of the lesson of the Exile to the postexilic situation (17:19–27).

15:10–21, Two Complaints. This unit consists of two complaints (vv. 10–14, 15–21) cast in the form of dialogues (see the Short Essay "Jeremiah's Complaints"). Verses 10–14 present some special difficulties. First, Jeremiah laments his birth because everyone makes light of (or, curses) him. Yet the reason given for this reaction, that he has been neither a lender nor a borrower, sounds curiously weak by compari-

son to the rationale for opposition supplied in vv. 15b–17; 17:15–16; and 20:7–10. Second, vv. 11–12 are difficult to translate. The Hebrew text makes it clear that the speaker is Yahweh (v. 11 begins, "Yahweh said"), and the gist of what follows is that he has (or will) protect Jeremiah in times of distress (cf. NEB; the RSV conveys an entirely different sense). Third, in vv. 13–14 the addressee shifts abruptly, as Yahweh utters a threat against the people. In the earlier complaints, there were responses both to the prophet (12:5–6) and to the people (11:21–23), but these were not directly connected. Since Yahweh's response to the prophet's complaint (vv. 11–12) completes the dialogue, it seems likely that the following threat, mirroring as it does the destruction of Jerusalem, conveys exilic interpretation, the purpose of which is to vindicate the prophet's earlier message.

In the speech that begins the second dialogue, Jeremiah laments the fact that he is persecuted and protests his own righteousness (vv. 15–17), claiming that his dedication to Yahweh's word has made him a social outcast. He ends with the accusation that (contrary to vv. 11–12) Yahweh has not protected him (v. 18). Yahweh's response combines insistence that Jeremiah "return" to his task (v. 19) with an assurance of protection (vv. 20–21) in language reminiscent of 1:18–19. This second complaint has close affinities with some of the Psalms. Like the earlier complaints, it seems to reveal a prophet caught, by the nature of his task, between an insistent God and a hostile audience.

16:1–13, Symbolic Actions. This section contains reports of three symbolic actions (see the Short Essay "Jeremiah's Symbolic Actions"), followed by an interpretation that places them in the context of the Exile. In the first (vv. 1–4), the prophet is instructed to remain unmarried and childless, since the coming warfare will be utterly destructive of families ("sword," "famine"). In the second (vv. 5–7), he is told not to participate in mourning rites. The rationale for this prohibition is that Yahweh intends to remove his "peace" from the land, with the result that death (in war) will become so widespread as to undermine normal mourning customs. The third (vv. 8–9) incorporates a prohibition against participation in festive social gatherings, since Yahweh is about to bring "mirth" and "gladness" in the land to an end (elsewhere in the book this language is associated with the fall of Judah to the Babylonians; cf. 7:34; 25:10).

What follows by way of interpretation of these actions (vv. 10–13) is a standard piece of exilic reflection on the causes of the nation's demise. These verses assume that that national catastrophe has already occurred. In addition, they provide an explanation for it that justifies the suffering Yahweh inflicted on his people. These verses may have been included at precisely this location in the book because of their thematic connection with the preceding complaint (15:17).

16:14–17:4, Hope and Doom. Parts of this section alternate between words of hope and of doom in a manner reminiscent of Isaiah 9–11. Jer. 16:14–15, a repetition of 23:7–8, voices the exiles' hope for restoration to the homeland. Verses 16–18 evoke an image of the completeness of the people's defeat and give the standard reason for it, apostasy. The chapter's only poetic verses, 19–20, take up a theme of thanksgiving (v. 19a; cf. 2 Sam. 22:3 and Ps. 18:2) and deal with rival gods in a fashion similar to 10:1–16 and 14:22. Jer. 16:21 and 17:1–4 are threats, the first quite general and the second mentioning apostasy (v. 2; cf. 2:20) and apparently assuming the Exile (v. 4; cf. 16:13). Thus, this section is dominated by two of the main concerns of the exilic community: to identify the cause of its present situation and to contemplate a more favorable future.

17:5–13, Wisdom Poetry. This section, a collection of wisdom psalms, comes as a surprise. There is a remarkable similarity between vv. 5–8 and Psalm 1, and vv. 9–10 have parallels in Ps. 26:1–3 and Jer. 11:20a and 12:3a. Verse 11 is a proverb on the theme of the impermanence of unjustly acquired wealth, and vv. 12–13 pair praise of Yahweh with the observation that all who forsake him, "the fountain of living water" (cf. 2:13), will perish. The underlying theme is that evil will inevitably be punished and good rewarded. We can thus think of these fragments as expressing an explanation of the nation's demise. This and the presence of the key word "heart" (vv. 1, 5, 9, 10) may account for the inclusion and the present location of this collection in the book.

17:14–18, Complaint. Like other complaints, this one contains an appeal to Yahweh for help (vv. 14, 17–18), a description of the adversaries' behavior (v. 15), and a self-justification (v. 16). This time, however, there is no response from Yahweh. The opponents' hostile derision centers on the fact that the words Jeremiah has uttered against the nation have not come to pass (Ezek. 12:21–28 echoes a similar problem), suggesting a date sometime before 597 B.C. At least some of Jeremiah's audience was no longer willing to take him seriously, to acknowledge his authority as a prophet of Yahweh, which would have made his social position precarious indeed (see the Short Essay "The Social Dynamics of Prophetic Behavior"), and it is easy to conceive of such a social setting giving rise to a complaint like this one. It is worth noting that by way of self-justification Jeremiah denies responsibility for the offensive content of his message (v. 16). He was, again, a man caught in the middle.

17:19–27, Sabbath Admonition. This extended reflection on keeping the Sabbath is an anomaly in the prophetic literature. It begins with an accusation that the people have failed to heed the warning to keep the Sabbath (vv. 20–23). A conditional statement then follows, to the effect that, if the people again observe the Sabbath, the Davidic dynasty will be perpetuated, Jerusalem will remain inhabited, and the broader Judean population will continue to worship in the Jerusalem temple. Infraction of the Sabbath ordinance, however, will lead to the destruction of Jerusalem. Some of the language is characteristic of the Jeremiah tradition (vv. 20, 25: "men of Judah, inhabitants of Jerusalem" occurs fourteen times in Jeremiah; see 11:2, 9), and some is reminiscent of Amos (v. 27: the kindling of a devouring fire; cf. Amos 1:4, 7, 10, 12, 14; 2:2).

The institution of the Sabbath seems to have existed in Israel from a comparatively early date (→ Sabbath). There are laws requiring its observance (e.g., Exod. 20:8–11; 23:12), and it is mentioned in historical narratives (2 Kings 4:23) and prophecy (Amos 8:5; Isa. 1:13). But this particular interpretation of the Sabbath's importance appears to be postexilic (cf. Neh. 13:15–18). The passage thus appears to be a rather late priestly attempt to defend current religious and political practice by linking failure to observe the Sabbath to the national catastrophe of 587 B.C. and by justifying the absence of a king in postexilic Israel.

This entire unit (15:10–17:27) is, then, a mixed collection of prophetic complaints and reflections on the prophet's and the nation's fate. The materials come from a variety of times and historical contexts, from before the Exile until after the restoration of the people to their land. What the various sections have in common is their struggle to understand events.

18:1–20:18
Narratives and Complaints

18:1–12, The Potter. The heading identifies this narrative, in which Jeremiah draws an analogy between a potter's activity and Yahweh's, as one of the prose sermons. The description of the potter at work (vv. 1–4) demonstrates that the artisan has total control over the clay with which he works, and that is the point of the analogy: Yahweh has the power to do as he wishes with his people (vv. 5–6). In vv. 7–10, however, the focus changes abruptly. Instead of

623

the "house of Israel," the subject is any "nation," and Yahweh's power to build is explicitly paired with his ability to destroy (see 1:10). Verse 11 returns to the original train of thought. Its threat of punishment directed against Judah can be viewed as an application of the general principle stated in v. 6, and this is followed by a call to repentance (cf. 7:5-7). The people's response (v. 12) occurs in the form of a quotation. The language is extremely self-incriminatory, suggesting an exilic interpretation, the intent of which is to blame the nation's collapse on the behavior of its citizens.

Thus, the narrative contains several layers of interpretation. There is the original prose sermon (vv. 1-6 plus 11), which seems to preserve the gist of one of Jeremiah's public addresses (see commentary above on 11:1-17). The "quotation" is probably exilic and has the effect of absolving both Yahweh and Jeremiah of responsibility for Judah's fall to the Babylonians. As for vv. 7-10, concern with the conversion of other nations seems more appropriate to the late exilic or the postexilic periods (cf. Isa. 42:6; Zech. 2:10-12); the verses are clearly not Deuteronomistic (cf. Deut. 4:19-20).

18:13-17, Israel's Apostasy. The condemnation of "the virgin Israel" expressed in these verses develops the rather vague self-incrimination of v. 12. The basic accusation is apostasy. Rhetorical questions, which expect the answer no, contrast the constancy of nature with the inconsistency of the people. Together with the reference to exchanging Yahweh for other gods (vv. 13-15a), they are reminiscent of oracles earlier in the book (cf. 2:9-13, 32; 3:21), as is v. 16a (cf. 4:7). However, though in 4:7 it is an attacking enemy that makes the land desolate, v. 16a holds the people responsible. This and the fact that v. 16b expresses the same sentiment as Lam. 2:15-16 (post-587 B.C.) and v. 17a mirrors the prose of 4:11 suggest that 18:13-17 may be a product of exilic interpretive activity.

18:18-23, Complaint. These verses make up another of Jeremiah's complaints. Verse 18, quoting an anonymous "they," describes the behavior of his adversaries that motivated the complaint: angered by his announcement that the activity of certain elite groups in Judean society (priests, wise men, prophets) would come to an end, they were plotting against him. Since the downfall of the nation is the most obvious context in which such an end could come about, we may infer that the message to which they were reacting spoke of Judah's destruction.

The other parts of a traditional lamentation follow in rapid succession. Verse 19a is an appeal for aid. Verses 19b-20a—"Hearken to the voice of my adversaries, 'Will evil be repaid for good?' For they dug a pit for my life"—describe the adversaries' behavior, and v. 20b is a self-justification. Verses 21-22a are another appeal for aid, this time in the form of a call for the destruction of his opponents' families. The siege imagery employed is a variation of a favorite triad, "sword, famine, and pestilence" (occurring in some combination twenty-nine times in Jeremiah). There are echoes here of an earlier accusation against the people that they had spoken falsely by claiming that Yahweh would "do nothing" and that, therefore, they would not "see sword or famine" (5:12), as well as echoes of Yahweh's answer to the first complaint: he will punish the prophet's enemies by giving their young men to the sword and their children to famine. Verse 22b repeats v. 20a, and the complaint ends with yet another appeal for aid: Yahweh knows of their plots against Jeremiah, and therefore should overthrow, not forgive, them.

Following an introduction in narrative prose (v. 18), the complaint focuses on the adversaries' behavior and the appeal for Yahweh's action against them. There is little by way of self-justification. The claim that Jeremiah's enemies are plotting to kill him (vv. 18a, 23a) picks up the theme of the first complaint (11:19, 21) and is in harmony with more general references to persecution in 15:15 and 17:18.

What was behind such extreme behavior? We can infer from the "quotation" (v. 20a) that Jeremiah's adversaries were convinced of the correctness of their own position and actions, which they believed were in the best interests of national security and destined for success (cf. 5:12). Jeremiah's attack, alluded to in v. 18, denied both contentions (see the Short Essay "Jeremiah's Struggle Against 'Falsehood' "). In their view, his attack was treasonous. They were angered by what he said (11:21) and were convinced it was false prophecy (17:15). This was not simply a religious dispute, but a political one as well. In the last decades before the catastrophe of 587 B.C., there were two identifiable political factions in Judah, and the prophet identified himself with one of them (see commentary below on chaps. 27-29). The plots against the prophet can be easily explained in the context of the ongoing dispute between these factions. Thus though the complaint is grounded in episodes of the prophet's life, it also offers more clues about prophecy as a social process than it does specific biographical information (see the Short Essay "The Social Dynamics of Prophetic Behavior").

19:1-20:6, Symbolic Action and Persecution. This biographical narrative describes one of the prophet's symbolic actions and an official response to it. Though it is presented in the form of instructions from Yahweh to Jeremiah, 19:14 implies that the action was carried out.

Jeremiah was told to buy a ceramic pot, assemble a group composed of elders of the people and senior priests, go with them to a valley south of Jerusalem (→ Hinnom, Valley of), and proclaim there a specific message addressed to the "kings of Judah and the inhabitants of Judah." The latter contains a general threat of impending disaster (v. 3), an accusation that the people have been guilty of apostasy and of offering child sacrifices (vv. 4–5; → Topheth), and a more specific threat that "this place" (the valley, but by extension the city as well) will be attacked and, after experiencing the horrors of a siege, defeated (vv. 6–9). The comment that this defeat will make void the plans of Judah and Jerusalem can be seen as a reference to the foreign policy of Jeremiah's opponents.

The symbolic action itself follows. Jeremiah breaks the pot and announces that "this people and this city" will be irreparably broken because of their apostasy. The idea that the city will be made "like Topheth" harks back to the destruction and burial mentioned earlier (vv. 7–9, 11) and also to the defiling of the religious site itself during Josiah's reform (2 Kings 23:10).

The reference to child sacrifice (vv. 4–5) is puzzling. It could indicate that such offerings, attested in the time of Manasseh (2 Kings 21:6), had resumed after the death of Josiah. This is uncertain, however. Jer. 44:16–18 suggests that Josiah's reforms of worship persisted after his death, and the force of vv. 12–13 seems to rely on Topheth's still being defiled. It is conceivable that vv. 2b–9 are an exilic interpretation elaborating on the accusation and threat from the vantage point of what had already happened. Support for this view is provided by the close correspondence between vv. 4–5 and 2 Kings 24:3–4—the exilic Deuteronomists' description of Manasseh's sins.

Following this incident, Jeremiah went to the court of the Temple and delivered a summary of his threat before a wider audience (vv. 14–15). This occasioned a response by Pashhur, a Temple priest and administrator, who beat Jeremiah, placed him in stocks, and put him on public display (20:1–2). The prophet's response was to rename the priest "Terror on every side" (v. 3; cf. 6:25, where this phrase describes the people's response to an invasion from the north, and 20:10, where it describes Jeremiah's response to his enemies' actions). The name symbolizes the fact that Pashhur will be a "terror" both to himself and to his friends: they and the whole land will suffer death, plundering, and exile at the hands of the Babylonians (vv. 4–6). The assertion that Pashhur has misled his friends (v. 6b) is the key to this condemnation. His reaction to Jeremiah's message was based on a partisan political position, supported, of course, by an appropriate religious ideology. From his own standpoint Jeremiah was convinced that this position would lead to disaster.

Jeremiah's Symbolic Actions

In addition to prophets' words, one sometimes encounters reports of prophetic deeds unusual enough to merit special attention. Within the OT, such "acts of power" can be separated into two categories. There are, first of all, acts that are within the capabilities of any individual to perform. These are often referred to as "symbolic actions." Jeremiah's breaking of a pot (19:1–15) and Isaiah's walking the streets naked and barefoot (Isa. 20) are examples of actions of this type. Second, there are actions, often referred to as "miracles," that appear to go beyond what we normally think it possible for human beings to do. Isaiah's causing the shadow on the sundial to move backward (Isa. 38:7–8 = 2 Kings 20:9–11) and the stories of Elijah and Elisha recalling the dead to life (1 Kings 17:17–24; 2 Kings 4:32–37) are examples. In the OT, most actions of this type are attributed to Elijah and Elisha. The attempt to understand these accounts does not depend upon belief that such things actually happened.

Although there are no "miracles" in Jeremiah, there are a number of "symbolic actions": his refraining from marriage, mourning rites, and feasting (16:1–9), his breaking of the ceramic pot (19:1–13), his wearing of yoke-bars (27:1–22), his buying a field in Anathoth and protecting the deed (32:6–15), his setting wine before the Rechabites (35:1–19), and his sending a book to Babylon with instructions that it be read aloud and then destroyed (51:59–64). Some might also wish to include the prophet's "eating" of Yahweh's "word" (15:16) and his carrying a "cup of wine" around for various persons to drink (25:15–29), though the second, especially, seems unlikely to refer to an actual occurrence. The account of how Jeremiah hid stones in the pavement at the entrance of the pharaoh's palace (43:8–13), though in character with the other symbolic actions, seems to come from an exilic editor who knew of Nebuchadnezzar's campaign into Egypt in 568 B.C. In addition, the book provides accounts of symbolic actions performed by three other persons, Hananiah (who broke the yoke-bars that Jeremiah had been wearing, 28:10–11), Pashhur (who beat Jeremiah and put him in the stocks, 20:1–2), and King Jehoiakim (who cut and burned the scroll containing Jeremiah's oracles as it was read to him, 36:23). Pashhur's action has the special feature that it apparently involved the exercise of legal authority.

Though there are no miracles reported in the book of Jeremiah, an examination of stories of that type can give us some insight into the symbolic actions. Frequently, the miracle stories in the Elijah and Elisha narratives speak of a response by those who witness the act. Whether these witnesses are inclined to be well disposed or ill disposed toward the prophet, the nature of the response is always essentially the same, namely, to acknowledge the prophet's power and, therefore, his authority (see 1 Kings 17:24; 18:39; 2 Kings 1:13–14; 2:15; 4:37).

It is worth noting that acts of this type are relatively common in shamanistic performances of certain native North American and Arctic peoples (e.g., Paiute, Kwakiutl, Tungus), as well as those of other types of intermediaries (e.g., shaking tent "conjurers" of the Ojibwa). In these contexts, one of the major functions of such acts is to engender belief in the power and authority of the practitioner. Even where these "miracles" are widely known by members of the audience to be sleight of hand and where some of the audience is skeptical of the ritual, the fluid performance of such acts enhances the chances of acceptance for the intermediary. This structural similarity suggests that the accounts of Elijah's and Elisha's "miracles," whatever the reality of the events that underlie them, may have played an important role in the process by which these prophets gained acceptance.

The accounts of symbolic acts in Jeremiah are simple and fairly regular in structure: the action is performed before an audience and is accompanied by words. The act is usually performed first, with the words following as an interpretation, but this is not always the case (see 19:1–13; 51:59–64). Sometimes a response is noted, and when this is the case it is always negative. The context suggests that the act and accompanying words are integral parts of a rhetorical situation. Their aim is forceful and convincing communication.

Symbolic actions have sometimes been understood as quasi-magical acts in which the prophet sought to set into motion that effect which his words anticipated. Others have seen them from a more theological perspective, namely, as symbolizing the guaranteed result of Yahweh's intended action, which had been revealed to the prophet. Observations about the miracle stories suggest a somewhat different way of understanding them. Prophets were dependent upon public support. They could not

function without some measure of it (see the Short Essay "The Social Dynamics of Prophetic Behavior"). Moreover, continuing support could not be taken for granted. In the prophets' constant struggle to be accepted by and make an impact upon their audience, fluid actions reinforcing and reinforced by words would force a reaction and might predispose some toward acceptance of prophet and message. Symbolic actions may be seen as part of the rhetorical repertoire by which the prophet sought to gain the assent and support of an audience.

20:7–18, Complaints. These verses contain the last two of Jeremiah's complaints. The first (vv. 7–13) begins with a self-justification (vv. 7–9), followed by a description of the adversaries' behavior (v. 10), an expression of confidence (v. 11) and appeal for aid (v. 12; 11:20 is a close parallel), and a closing expression of confidence (v. 13). The latter has seemed to some to be too optimistic to stem from the prophet himself, but, given v. 11, it makes more sense to attribute it to him than to an exilic editor. Such a person, after all, would have known that neither Jeremiah nor the nation had been delivered.

What may one know about the dynamics underlying and giving rise to this complaint? Jeremiah accuses Yahweh of forcing him into a position where he is a laughingstock and an object of mockery (v. 7); Yahweh is requiring him to deliver a message of doom (cf. 17:16) that events of history have so far failed to confirm. The reaction of his audience to that message is stated somewhat more generally than in other complaints, but it fits the picture gained from the earlier ones (see commentary above on 18:18–23): they wish to eliminate him and his rival message about the nation's future. Both Jeremiah (along with his allies, for we may view him as a spokesman for his party) and his opponents were confronting the question of how the nation's future might best be secured. The rival positions had political and military implications, and the intensity of the conflict mirrors the seriousness of the stakes.

The Pashhur event seems not to have occasioned this complaint. These two episodes may have been placed in close proximity because they share a key phrase, "terror on every side" (20:3, 10).

Self-curses like the one that follows (vv. 14–18) are not, strictly speaking, part of the lamentation form (see the Short Essay "Jeremiah's Complaints"), but they certainly represent a "complaint" in the broad sense. Its obvious difference from the preceding complaint is the tone of abject despair, and its inclusion here has the effect of turning confidence into gloom. The most obvious interpretation of the curse is psychological. In this case, v. 18 would refer back to vv. 7–13 (and even to 1:5): Jeremiah's despair was the result of his impossible task. At the same time, v. 16 may suggest rage over the fate of the nation and thus hint at a social element in the curse.

Those who collected and preserved the Jeremiah traditions knew, of course, of the nation's demise. They were in a position to understand the sufferings of the prophet in a broader historical context. That they set this gloomy outburst at the end of the entire series of his complaints can scarcely have been an accident.

21:1–23:8
The Fate of Kings and of the Monarchy

The unit 21:1–23:8 is held together by a common subject, the kings of Judah, and a common theme, the royal ideal of justice and righteousness (21:12; 22:3, 13–17; 23:5–6; cf. Ps. 72). At its core is an orderly sequence of oracles, which begins with a general condemnation addressed to the "house of David" (21:11–22:9), progresses through utterances directed at specific kings (the arrangement is chronological—22:10–12, Jehoahaz; 22:13–19, Jehoiakim; 22:24–30, Jehoiachin), and ends with a general cry of "woe" concerning the deeds of the "shepherds" (kings) that becomes a promise of restoration for the nation (23:1–8).

The narrative about Zedekiah with which the unit begins is out of chronological sequence, but given the point of view of the exilic collectors and arrangers of the Jeremiah tradition, its position is logical. For them, the downfall of the nation and its last king was the decisive event to be recalled and understood, and they gave it pride of place in this collection dealing with the fate of the monarchy. It is worth noting that the sequence of kings addressed begins with Jehoahaz (609 B.C.). Josiah (640–609) is referred to as an exemplar of the royal ideal (22:15–16) but not addressed.

21:1–10, Jeremiah Responds to Zedekiah. This prose sermon has striking similarities with the biographical narrative in chaps. 37–38. In both, Zedekiah sends emissaries to Jeremiah (one, a priest named Zephaniah, appears in both accounts) to ask him to intercede with Yahweh, and, in both, his reply makes it clear that Jerusalem is doomed (it will be "burned with fire," 21:10; 37:10). The counsel to citizens to flee the city (21:8–10) appears almost verbatim in 38:2–3. There are some differences in detail. Jer. 21:2, 4 presupposes that a Babylonian siege of the city is in progress, whereas 37:5, 11 speaks of the siege having been lifted. In addition, the specific attention given to

Zedekiah's fate (21:7) does not appear in chaps. 37–38. The setting of 21:1–10 must, therefore, be the period either just before or just after the temporary interruption in the Babylon siege of Jerusalem occasioned by Nebuchadnezzar's response to an Egyptian military challenge in the winter and spring of 587 B.C.

Jeremiah's reply to Zedekiah (vv. 3–7) was brutal: the city would be captured and he and the other survivors killed, for Yahweh himself was taking up arms against them. This prophecy seems not to have been literally fulfilled; Zedekiah was humiliated, blinded, and led away into captivity (cf. 2 Kings 25:4–7; Jer. 39:4–7). According to Jer. 52:11, he died there. This, plus the fact that the section is pure judgment with no accusation at all (as one might expect if the intent were to explain the nation's fall), suggests that the book here presents the essentials of a message addressed to Zedekiah, a logical extension of Jeremiah's straightforward statement on foreign policy reported in chap. 27.

The prophet's encouragement for the people to defect (vv. 8–10) recalls his own attempt to leave the city and undermines the credibility of his protestation to his captor that he was not deserting to the Babylonians (cf. 37:11–15).

21:11–22:9, Kingship. This general condemnation of Judean kings is composed of a matched pair of statements, the second of which (in prose) is longer and more elaborate than the first. Each begins with an address to the king (21:11; 22:1–2 adds his servants and subjects), followed by an exhortation for him to live up to the ideal of righteous rule familiar from Psalm 72 (21:12a; 22:3, developed after the pattern of 7:6). Both threaten destruction if the king fails to respond (21:12b, 14; 22:5–7).

Each has a unique feature. The first contains an explicit condemnation of those who hold to the belief that Yahweh will not allow his nation and city to fall (21:13; on this false sense of security, see 7:1–15 and the Short Essay "Jeremiah's Struggle Against 'Falsehood' "). The second ends with a Deuteronomistic interpretation of the nation's fate (cf. 5:18–19), which moves the focus of attention from the king to the people.

22:10–12, Jehoahaz. This brief call to mourning reflects the fate of Jehoahaz, who was deposed by Pharaoh Neco after a reign of only three months and carried away captive to Egypt, where tradition says he died (cf. 2 Kings 23:31–34).

22:13–19, Jehoiakim. Jehoiakim is condemned for his failure to live up to the kingship ideal (vv. 13–15a, 17; cf. 21:12; 22:3), and his actions are contrasted with those of his father, Josiah, who did (vv. 15b–16). The announcement of the fact and form of his death (vv. 18–19) is apparently not historically accurate (the account of Jehoiakim's death three months before the fall of Jerusalem contains no indications of violence and is silent on the matter of his burial; see 2 Kings 24:6), which seems to indicate that this oracle was delivered while he was still alive.

22:20–23, Concerning Lebanon. These verses interrupt the sequence of oracles against kings. The identities of both the addressee (presumably, an "inhabitant of Lebanon," v. 23) and the "enemies" (who have already been destroyed, but whose captivity lies in the future, vv. 20, 22) are unclear. Verse 21 is the kind of accusation that is elsewhere made against Judah (cf. 2:20–25), and v. 23b recalls 6:24. Their inclusion here may be due to the reference to the scattering of the "shepherds" (i.e., kings; cf. 23:1–4) in v. 22.

22:24–30, Jehoiachin. The poetic portion of the oracle against Jehoiachin (vv. 28–30) raises, but does not answer, the question of why he and his children were carried into exile. The focus is rather on the announcement that he will have no successor on the throne. In the first instance, this would refer to the transfer of the succession to Zedekiah's lineage, but from the point of view of the exiles, it could be understood to refer to the end of the Davidic dynasty. Immediately after the Exile, a grandson of Jehoiachin, Zerubbabel, was appointed by the Persians to be governor of Judah. Some seem to have hoped that he would reestablish the Davidic dynasty of kings (see Hag. 2:20–23; →Zerubbabel). Those who opposed such a move may have made use of—may even have created —these verses. The prose introduction, which specifically mentions Nebuchadnezzar and says that nothing can stand in the way of the permanent exiling of Jehoiachin and the queen mother (note that the children are not mentioned), is an exilic clarification (before 587 B.C. the hope remained alive that Jehoiachin would be returned to his throne; see 28:1–4), which may postdate the king's death in captivity sometime after 560 B.C. (2 Kings 25:27–30).

23:1–8, Restoration. This concluding section, which speaks of the return from exile and the restoration of the monarchy, is exilic in origin. The earlier kings are held responsible for the Exile (vv. 1–2), but the real interest is in the restoration of the exiles to their native land and in a reformed monarchy (vv. 3–4). The following verses elaborate these points, but in reverse order. The restored monarch will continue the Davidic line. He will conform to the kingship ideal (cf. 21:12; 22:3; 33:14–16), and under him both Judah and Israel will dwell securely (contrast 21:13). The ingathering of the exiles (cf. 3:18) will supplant the exodus from Egypt as the paradigm for God's deliverance of his people from captivity (vv. 7–8 = 16:14–15).

23:9–40
Against the Prophets

The heading "concerning the prophets" (v. 9a) sets off the unit 23:9–40 from the preceding one devoted to kingship. Two oracles of judgment follow.

23:9–15, Judgment on Prophets. In the first (vv. 9–12), the focus is not yet exclusively on the prophets. Jeremiah's reference to his own emotional state (v. 9) is, as in 4:19, ambiguous. It seems probable that these verses provide us with clues about the psychology of revelation, though it is possible that the outbursts reflect an emotional reaction to conditions that the prophet observed among the people (cf. 4:20; 23:10). The accusation (vv. 10–11), directed against "both prophet and priest" (cf. 5:30–31; 6:13–15; 14:18), employs the language of drought. Both it and the following threat (v. 12) are quite general.

The second oracle of judgment (vv. 13–15) compares the prophets of Israel with those of Judah. The point is not to weigh the offenses of each group, but to show that Judah is as guilty as Israel was and can, therefore, expect a comparable punishment (cf. the Jerusalem-Shiloh analogy of the Temple sermon, 7:12–15). The accusation against the Judean prophets (vv. 14, 15b) is, again, somewhat vague. One may infer from the reference to "falsehood" (v. 14) that they were "peace" prophets. The threat (v. 15a) is stated in general terms. In fact, there is nothing in these two oracles to suggest a date of composition after the fall of Jerusalem.

The following sections present variations on the theme "I did not speak to the prophets, yet they prophesied." The application of the term "prophet" to these (from Jeremiah's point of view) inauthentic speakers raises the issue of how one is to distinguish "true" from "false" prophets (see the Short Essay "The Problem of 'False' Prophecy").

23:16–17, Prophets of Peace. This prose section clearly identifies these prophets with the message of assured national security that Jeremiah strongly opposed (see 6:14 = 8:11 and 7:1–15). Their message is not from Yahweh but is "a vision of their own mind."

23:18–22, The Prophet in God's Council. Against such activity, this text proposes a norm for the reception of authentic messages, which seems to presuppose some type of visionary experience, namely, standing "in the council of Yahweh" (vv. 18, 22). It is clear what one will hear in such a council: unless the people repent (v. 22b), they will be punished (vv. 19–20 = 30:23–24). Since the prophets were not commissioned by Yahweh (v. 21), we may infer that they had not stood in his council and were guilty of uttering a message that contradicted what was spoken there. The irony of this oracle is that Jeremiah criticizes his opponents for a failure that, in retrospect, he apparently shared (v. 22; cf. 25:3–5).

23:23–32, Prophesying Lies. This prose passage continues the theme of prophetic conflict. The problem here is that the author seems to disparage dreams (vv. 28–29), though in Israel they were considered, at least by some, a legitimate source of revelation (cf. Gen. 20:6; 28:12; 31:10; Num. 12:6; Deut. 13:1–5). Furthermore, it is not common in Jeremiah to find opposition to prophets couched in terms of "dreams." In 27:9 the prophet enumerates various intermediaries, including dreamers, but reverts to referring only to prophets when he addresses Judeans (27:14–15, 16–18; 29:8–9 is very similar to 27:9–10). The focus of 23:23–32 is actually on the content of the prophets' message. They justify this message by claiming it to be revelation ("I have dreamed," v. 25; "says [Yahweh]," v. 31), but (according to the author) they have really received it from each other (vv. 27, 30). That their message is characterized as "falsehood" (vv. 25–26, 32) indicates that the topic is still the peace prophets.

The criterion by which these prophets were judged false probably differed within various contexts. For Jeremiah himself, it would have been a matter of his conviction about the validity of his own message. He would have considered those with whom he differed fundamentally to be wrong. But from the point of view of the exilic preservers of the tradition, Jeremiah's view had been vindicated by the events of history. In fact it seems best to consider vv. 16–17 and 23–32 to be exilic elaborations on vv. 18–22. The sheer quantity of this interpretation (twelve verses commenting on an original five) may be due to the fact that, for the exiles, the existence of contention among Yahweh prophets in the pre-exilic period was a well-known scandal. It is this retrospective stance that justifies the otherwise virtually incredible condemnation of Yahweh prophets for engaging in standard prophetic behavior (v. 31). One may also note that what appears to be the ultimate criterion for judging the prophets "false," that their message did not "profit" the people (v. 32b), could not have been effectively used by their contemporaries. Indeed, neither the prophets of "peace" nor those, like Jeremiah, of "doom" had been able to save Judah.

23:33–40, "The Burden." This passage abandons the theme of the preceding sections. It reflects antagonism between Jeremiah and his audience, though its sense is somewhat obscure. Verse 33 is a wordplay on the Hebrew homonyms of *massa'*, meaning "utterance" and "burden." The question, "What is the *massa'* [utterance] of Yahweh?" receives the reply (following the LXX), "You are the *massa'* [burden]." The question seems a sarcastic pun, implying that any "utterance" from Jeremiah, a well-known prophet of doom, will be a "burden" on the people. The reply reverses the judgment: it is the questioners who are the real "burden." Thus, this text seems to reflect the familiar sphere of conflict with the prophets of peace.

Verses 34–40 are probably an exilic elaboration of the prophetic conflict issue. They threaten punishment for individuals who take up such derision of Jeremiah's position (v. 34), continuing the wordplay of v. 33 (vv. 36–38). One may continue to inquire after Yahweh's word (vv. 35, 37), but now the criterion for judging authenticity is clear: Jeremiah's position has been vindicated by the events of history, and the Exile has become a perpetual source of shame for the people (vv. 39–40).

The Problem of "False" Prophecy

There is abundant evidence in the book of Jeremiah for conflict among prophets (cf. 5:30–31; 6:13–15 = 8:10–12; 14:13–16; 23:9–40; 27:1–29:32). The point of contention seems to be the content of the prophecies: some predict that the nation will dwell securely and at peace; others convey a message of doom. The narrative about Hananiah and Jeremiah (chap. 28) highlights this conflict in a striking way, since on the surface the two seem indistinguishable except for the content of their messages. Such conflicts were not unique to Jeremiah's time (see Mic. 3:5–12), though they may have intensified during the last decades of Judah's existence.

In Israel, as in other societies, periods of intense prophetic activity coincided with times of crisis. Thus, the decision about how to respond to a prophet was a matter of some urgency, and criteria for making a judgment became a necessity.

Among the exiles, there was apparently some ambivalence about the evaluation of earlier prophecy. This is strikingly illustrated by two passages that refer to the same message, "it shall be well with you" (4:10b; 23:17a) but understand its origin in opposite ways. In 23:16–17, the point is that the prophets have made up their message of peace; it was not from Yahweh (cf. Lam. 2:14). Jer. 4:10, however, suggests that it is Yahweh himself who is responsible for the deception of his people (cf. 1 Kings 22:19–23, and Jeremiah's complaints about Yahweh in 15:18 and 20:7. It seems that the conflict between apparently genuine prophets gave rise to a crisis in confidence about prophecy itself. The implication is that the prophets' audience possessed no sure criterion by which to judge between competing claims.

Though the conflict between prophets is a major theme in the book of Jeremiah, we can discern there no foolproof method for distinguishing among them. Jeremiah's charge that Yahweh had not commissioned his opponents (23:21) begs the question of how one might know this to be the case, and his own personal conviction on the matter would not be useful to other persons caught between competing claims. The attempt to distinguish between the forms in which the revelation came (cf. 23:27–28) is probably exilic, and in any case is not consistently applied (cf. chap. 28). In fact, with respect to the narratives dominated by prophetic conflict (chaps. 27–29) it is easier to list things that are not a factor in the prophet's evaluation of his opponents—association with cultic functionaries (27:9–10), personal immorality (not a factor in chap. 28 and only marginal in 29:23), and the fulfillment of prophecy (cf. Deut. 18:20–22 and commentary below on 28:9 and 37:16–21)—than to locate a specific criterion. People were apparently forced to respond to the prophets on the basis of an evaluation of their message.

Anthropological studies of contemporary societies may provide some perspective on the problem. It would appear that there are basically four criteria by which audiences evaluate prophetlike intermediaries: their behavior conforms to established patterns; their message conforms to traditional customs and beliefs and is adequate to the special circumstances in which it is uttered; they claim to have received a special commission from a deity; and they are successful (what they predict comes to pass, the specific problem is resolved, or the like). Evaluations of individual intermediaries do not necessarily involve all four of these criteria.

Both in Israel and elsewhere, the interpretation of crises, whether national, local, or personal in scope, took place within the range of possibilities offered by the particular culture within which the intermediary functioned. This means that inevitably both worldview and the more mundane facts of history, politics, and society were factors in the judgments made about them. In the Judah of Jeremiah's day, the crucial decisions seem to have been closely related to assumptions about the nation's destiny that mirrored religious convictions and had concrete implications for political action. The judgment that a particular prophecy was "true" was, as always, dependent upon the viewpoint and commitments of the person(s) making it (see

commentary below on 38:14–28). The confrontation of Jeremiah and Hananiah (chap. 28) is a case in point.

24:1–10
A Vision of Figs

The setting of the narrative in chap. 24 is the period following Nebuchadnezzar's first conquest of Jerusalem. The dialogue format of the vision report recalls 1:11–12, 13–16 and, even more precisely, Amos 7:7–9 and 8:1–3.

The interpretation of what was seen, two baskets of figs, suggests a straightforward comparison of the exiles of 597 B.C. (the good figs) with King Zedekiah and the others who remained behind in Jerusalem (the bad figs). The former may look forward to restoration in their homeland; Yahweh will "build them up" and "plant them" (v. 6; cf. 1:10) and will "give them a heart to know" him (v. 7; cf. 31:33). The latter will be destroyed. The inclusion among the "bad figs" of "those dwelling in the land of Egypt" (v. 8) may stem from an exilic editor, since the only flight of Judeans to Egypt we know about came after 587 B.C. (see chaps. 42–44).

The book of Jeremiah contains a number of prose narratives about the reign of Zedekiah. In general, these display one of two points of view. The majority are in agreement with the present chapter in looking favorably upon the exiles and opposing Zedekiah and those who remained in the land after 597 (cf. 21:1–10; 29:1–32; 37:1–38:13; 38:24–39:18). In others, however, Jeremiah acts to enlist Zedekiah's aid in forestalling complete disaster. To this end he advocates submission to Babylonian rule (cf. 27:1–28:17; 38:14–23).

As it happens, the last major unit of the book's first part (chaps. 1–25) contains two such narratives, 21:1–10 and 24:1–10. These narratives frame two smaller collections of material, one concerning Judean kings (21:11–23:8) and the other, prophets (23:9–40). The narratives do not fit smoothly into this context. Although 21:1–10 does deal with a king, it is out of harmony with the chronological sequence of the oracles against the kings that follow, and 24:1–10 introduces an altogether new topic, namely, an apology for the community of exiles. However, the two narratives complement each other rather well. Both have as their subject Zedekiah, Jerusalem, and the fate of the exiles (21:8–9 advocates surrender, a voluntary joining of those in exile whom 24:4–7 identifies as "good figs"). The focus of attention in the former is the fall of the nation and in the latter the restoration of the exiles (note the contrasting tone of 22:24–30). Between these narratives stand two small collections directed against the leaders responsible for the national catastrophe (see 21:12; 22:5; 23:1–2, 21–22).

It would, therefore, appear that the present arrangement of chaps. 21–24 is the result of an ongoing process of reflection by Judeans living in Babylon after 587 B.C. on the causes of the nation's collapse and on the position of their own community of survivors (in relation to those who remained in Palestine after 587? see 39:10; 40:7–12) in Yahweh's plan for the future.

25:1–14
Confronting the People: A Summary

The narrative in 25:1–14 is dated 605 B.C., and a cross-reference is made to Nebuchadnezzar, who that year emerged as a power in the Near East by defeating the Egyptian army (→Carchemish) and assuming the throne in Babylon. Chap. 36, an account of how Jeremiah dictated two versions of a scroll containing all the words he had spoken since the beginning of his prophetic career, carries the same date (see 25:1; 36:1). From 36:3, 29, one can infer that the content of those scrolls corresponds to the message given in summary form here (v. 3). Thus, as in the case of the Temple sermon, the book provides a prose sermon and a biographical narrative that grow out of the same event. We can also infer that what remains of these two scrolls may be found in chaps. 1–25, though there is no consensus on the identification of this material (see Introduction).

The structure characteristic of the prose sermons is evident here: a summons to repentance (vv. 3–6), followed by a description of the people's unrepentance (v. 7) and an announcement of punishment (vv. 8–11a). The stereotypic language of Jeremian prose predominates, e.g., "his servants the prophets" (v. 4; cf. 7:25; 26:5; 29:19; 35:15; 44:4), "other gods" (v. 6; over a dozen occurrences, including 7:6, 9, 18; 11:10), and "the voice of mirth" (v. 10; cf. 7:34; 16:9).

The passage has two distinctive features. First, it makes an explicit connection between the enemy from the north and Nebuchadnezzar (v. 9). It is not a matter of great importance that the tradition, as it has come down, makes it impossible to establish the identity of the enemy Jeremiah was referring to in the earlier oracles and visions (see 1:13–16; 4:5–6:30). By 605 the identification with the Babylonian king would have been obvious, and it is reasonable to assume that Jeremiah himself reapplied older oracles to the new situation.

Second, there is a section on the punishment of Babylon "after seventy years" (vv. 11b–14), a reference that is mirrored in 29:10. The sentiment echoed here is like that in Isa. 10:12–19, but the dates do not make sense: beginning with the conquest of Babylon by the Persians (538 B.C.) and adding seventy years yields 608 B.C., three years before the time of the narrative, whereas starting from the captivities of Judeans in 597 and 587 yields dates for the fall of Babylon at 527 or 517. Other computations (from the fall of Nineveh in 612 until that of Babylon, or from Nebuchadnezzar's accession in 605 until the fall of Babylon) are equally inexact. Whatever the arithmetic, it is clear that the people's crimes have been serious and the period of their punishment will be lengthy. Perhaps it is best, therefore, to see the number seventy as a way of indicating passage of two (or more?) generations. Whether the figure was originally suggested by Jeremiah is difficult to judge, though the reference to him by name in v. 13 suggests that the section as it now stands is an exilic reapplication of Jeremiah's own reapplication of his earlier oracles.

25:15–38
Yahweh's Wrath Against the Nations

The unit 25:15–38 contains two general oracles against Judah's traditional enemies. Unlike regular oracles of judgment, these make no accusations but contain only threats of punishment. Beginning at this point, there is a major difference between the order of the Hebrew and the Greek texts (see Introduction): the LXX omits v. 14 and inserts the oracles against the nations found in chaps. 46–51 (MT) between vv. 13 and 15, though in a slightly different sequence. This difference, plus the fact that a new topic (the cup of Yahweh's wrath against the nations) is introduced in v. 15, suggests that the inclusion of vv. 15–38 at this point is the work of exilic editors (see v. 18b, which refers back to the catastrophe of 587 B.C.). The list of kings to whom the cup is to be delivered (vv. 18–26) occurs in roughly the same order as the more extensive oracles against the nations (chaps. 46–51) but is more inclusive.

It is possible that the mention of "nations" in vv. 13–14 provided a convenient key for the attachment of these oracles. One may also note that v. 29 expresses a reaction that would be quite understandable on the part of the exiles (cf. Ps. 137), and, from their perspective, it is perfectly appropriate that the list of nations that Yahweh will punish (vv. 18–26) should begin with Judah and end with Babylon.

Verse 30 introduces a separate, though related, oracle, that elaborates the themes of Amos 1:2 (Yahweh "roars" like a lion, threatens the "shepherds," i.e., the leaders of the nations). In Amos, this verse serves as an introduction to a collection of oracles against the nations (Amos 1:3–2:16), but it might just as well be a conclusion. Considering its location in the LXX, that may have been its original function in the book of Jeremiah.

632

26:1–45:5

Narratives Concerning the Nation's Fate

26:1–24
Jeremiah's Temple Sermon

Chapter 26 contains the narrative account of what happened on an occasion when Jeremiah delivered a message in the Temple, precipitating an open controversy with and among members of his audience. (See commentary above on 7:1–15 for a discussion.)

27:1–29:32
Prophecy and Politics

These prose narratives deal with events that occurred during the year 594 B.C. Chaps. 27 and 29:1–23 have been considered prose sermons, chaps. 28 and 29:24–32 biographical prose. Such labeling shows just how problematic strict distinctions in the Jeremiah prose can be, since in structure and theme the passage forms a single unit.

These chapters are distinguished stylistically from the remainder of the book by the presence of both long and short spellings of Hebrew proper names like Jeremiah, Zedekiah, Jeconiah, and Hananiah (e.g., Yirmeyah, here 9 times, including 28:5–6, but absent elsewhere in the book; Yirmeyahu, here only in 29:27–30, but 110 times elsewhere). In other parts of the book, the longer spellings predominate. Furthermore, except in 29:21, "Nebuchadnezzar" is spelled with an n, rather than with the more usual r ("Nebuchadrezzar" occurs twenty-eight times elsewhere in Jeremiah), and there is a tendency to use formal titles like "the prophet" with prophets' names (see 28:5–6). On the differences between the MT and the LXX in these chapters, see Introduction.

The narrative flows continuously and proceeds chronologically. This is evident in the episodes described in chaps. 27–28 and is probable for chap. 29, which presupposes an interval after 597 during which the Babylonian exiles could begin to settle down and which, in the MT, is connected by a conjunction to the preceding narratives ("And these are the words of the letter . . .").

These narratives also have a thematic unity: they are preoccupied with the problem of the duration of Babylonian rule (27:6, 9–10, 14–15, 16–17; 28:2–4, 12–14; 29:4–9, 24–28). Here one sees Jeremiah dealing with the problem of the day: how to understand the significance of the capture of Jerusalem in 597 and the subsequent exiling of King Jehoiachin and others to Babylon (see 2 Kings 24:8–17). The fact that the city and nation were not completely destroyed

rendered the meaning of the events ambiguous, leaving open the question of how long the submission to Babylonian authority would continue.

There was a basic difference of opinion on this matter. The faction to which Jeremiah belonged believed that Yahweh had granted Nebuchadnezzar a lengthy hegemony in the region—the exact duration is somewhat vague, but approximates three generations (27:7; 29:6, 10; cf. 25:12). The inaccuracy of these dates is an indication that these formulations may indeed go back to the dispute of 594 B.C. An opposing faction was convinced that, after a short period (28:2–4 says two years), the power of the Babylonians would be broken.

The narratives stress a religious interpretation of the political events. Jeremiah believed that Yahweh had established Nebuchadnezzar's power in the region (chap. 27). His opponents, on the other hand, presumably accepted defeat and exile as Yahweh's doing but thought of them as sufficient punishment for the people's behavior. They believed that Yahweh would now restore the nation (so chap. 28), and they set themselves in opposition to Jeremiah's interpretation.

It is important to note that there is adequate theological justification in the Judean religious tradition for both these positions. Jeremiah's viewpoint mirrors the Sinai covenant, in which national security and prosperity are contingent upon obedience to Yahweh's commandments. His opponents' position reflects the ideology of the royal covenant, according to which the nation may be punished by Yahweh but will not be finally abandoned by him (→ Covenant).

But this was not simply a dispute over points of doctrine. It is a struggle between two political parties, each seeking support for its position on the prime foreign policy issue of the day: the relationship of Judah to the dominant power in the region, Babylon. One may infer from the narrative in chaps. 27–28 that the specific dispute involved a proposal being entertained by Judah and its allies to revolt against their Babylonian suzerain. Presumably, they had found encouragement in a rebellion in Babylon during the year 595–594 (according to 28:1, the consultation of envoys and anti-Babylonian agitation took place in 594–593).

The stakes were high. For Jeremiah and his group (they might be called the "pro-Babylonian" party) the survival of those Judeans who remained in the land after 597 depended upon continued submission to Babylonian rule. (Jer. 27:13 shows that Jeremiah still believed survival was possible; but 24:8–10, which is the product of reflection among the exiles in Babylon after 587, stands in contrast.) For their opponents (whose nationalism prompted them to resist Babylonian domination and to seek support from the greatest of Babylon's rivals, Egypt) the issue was the political independence of Judah.

From the narrative one infers that Jeremiah was a public spokesman for one of these parties and Hananiah for the other. That the public utterances of such prophets played an important part in the struggle between competing ideologies is indicated by Jeremiah's attacks on the prophets associated with the rival party (27:9–10, 14, 16; 28:1–17; 29:8–9, 15, 20–32). Apparently, Jeremiah feared the prophets for their ability to influence opinion and action in the direction of aggressive nationalism.

These chapters contain parallel accounts of how Jeremiah confronted the problem of false prophecy, first at home and then among the exiles. The outline of the accounts is the same: there is a message (submission to Babylonian rule, chap. 27; defining the length of the Exile, 29:4–9), a negative response to that message by a prophet or prophets (28:1–4, 10–11; 29:15, 21–23, 26–28), and a resolution (a curse against the opposing prophet, 28:15–17; 29:21–23, 30–32). In chap. 27, this message is addressed in sequence to three different audiences (foreign emissaries, the Judean king, and the priests and people of Judah), and the accounts of these occasions are parallel in structure and vocabulary. Jer. 27:19–22 appears to be an exilic interpretation reflecting the final catastrophe of 587.

The narratives make it clear that, in the decade following the national catastrophe of 597, the people were confronted with a choice between two diametrically opposed positions. Each had concrete policy implications, and each was supported by one or more persons who, through their behavior, claimed to be prophets of Yahweh (both Jeremiah and Hananiah performed symbolic actions and prefaced their utterances with the formula "Thus says Yahweh"). The choice the audiences of the day were confronted with was both practical (what course of action will be most likely to ensure the nation's survival?) and theoretical (how can "false" prophecy be distinguished from "true"?).

That there were no easy, foolproof criteria for making the latter judgment is demonstrated by Jeremiah's reaction to Hananiah (see the Short Essay "The Problem of 'False' Prophecy"). According to the narrative, he initially proposed the criterion of fulfillment as the critical test of validity (28:6–10; cf. Deut. 18:22), and Hananiah's prophecy would seem a perfect opportunity to use such a rule, since his prediction was specific enough to be tested by future events (28:3–4, 11). But Jeremiah apparently did not wait for two years to pass. When he later condemned Hananiah, he made no mention of the prophecy not being fulfilled, but instead reverted to the general charge that Yahweh had not commissioned him. In effect, Jeremiah could

only reassert his former claim that Yahweh had willed the present international situation and that, therefore, the only hope for national survival lay in submission to the Babylonian king (28:13–14; 27:11–12; cf. 21:8–10, where this message is applied to a later, more desperate situation).

The message to the exiles is the same: their future prosperity depends upon settling in and making the most of a long captivity (29:4–6). Here, too, there is an elaborate refutation of his prophetic opponents' assertions about the duration of exile. Though v. 23 seems to introduce personal immorality as a criterion for judgment in the case of Ahab and Zedekiah, the main issue is clearly political. Since Nebuchadnezzar executed these two prophets (vv. 21–22), it is reasonable to assume that he considered their activities a threat. It is likely that they expressed views on the length of his reign that were perceived as spreading unrest among the Judean captives.

Verses 24–28, which report a letter from one of these prophets to a priest in Jerusalem reprimanding him for not exercising his responsibility to control the prophet Jeremiah (see the Short Essay "The Social Dynamics of Prophetic Behavior"), are reminiscent of 20:1–6. Jer. 29:16–19, absent in the LXX, has nothing to do with the prophets. It is an exilic tirade after the fashion of chap. 24.

30:1–31:40
The Book of Consolation

Chaps. 30 and 31 form an independent unit preoccupied with the restoration of the people rather than the more usual condemnations of their behavior. Because of their content, they have come to be referred to as "the book of consolation."

The fact that 29:10–14 speaks of the future restoration of Judeans to their land (after "seventy years"; cf. 25:1–14) may have motivated the inclusion of these oracles at this point in the book. The theme of hope is continued in the narratives of chaps. 32–33, and it is also possible that the placing of such material at the beginning of the account of Judah's last days (chaps. 32–35; 37–44) was intended to make their proclamation about the people's future seem less an afterthought and more directly a part of Yahweh's plan. Thus, the position of the unit in the book itself might be viewed as part of an effort to console the exiles.

The core of the "book of consolation" is 30:5–31:22. Apart from some apparent supplements, it is a prophecy of the restoration of the old Northern Kingdom of Israel, overrun a century earlier by the Assyrians, who dispersed its population (721 B.C.; 2 Kings 17:1–6). The nouns of address (Jacob, 30:10, 18; 31:11; Israel,

30:10; 31:2, 4, 7, 21; Ephraim, 31:6, 9, 18, 20; Rachel, 31:15; note also the mention of Samaria in 31:5) clearly indicate this interest in northern Israel. Where the larger framework of the passage mentions Judah, it tends to do so in connection with Israel (30:3–4; 31:27, 31; the exception is 31:23–25).

This unit displays a logical sequence of thought. Though there is a note of hope in 30:7, 17, the focus is on the distress of the nation, whose ruin the prophet justifies as Yahweh's punishment of the people's sins. There follows in 30:18–22 and 31:2–6 an account of the restoration of northern Israel's land and cities, the multiplication of its population, and the return of prosperity and festivities, culminating in a pilgrimage to Zion (31:6). To this point no mention has been made of the Israelites deported by Assyria, and 31:15–20 begins with Rachel weeping for these, her lost children. In response, Yahweh promises to bring about their return, a change of heart made possible by their repentance (vv. 18–19). The unit concludes with a summons to the dispersed Israelites to return (31:21–22). The reversal of fortune is portrayed in a striking way: the "strong man" who a century earlier had quaked before the attackers like a woman in the pangs of labor (30:6) will now be sheltered (31:22).

Several verses in this unit should be considered later supplements. Jer. 30:8–9 is prose and takes up the image of the "yoke," which is central to chaps. 27–28, suggesting that it comes from the time of the Exile. Jer. 30:10–11 is a virtual doublet of 46:27–28, though the latter would seem to preserve a form closer to original (note the repetition of the phrase "fear not" at the beginning of the second verse). The idea that Yahweh will not make a "full end" of his people (see 4:27; 5:10, 18) is repeated, and is also transformed into a general threat against the people's enemies. Jer. 30:16–17 calls for vengeance against those who destroyed Jerusalem, and despite the conjunction, "therefore," does not follow logically from vv. 12–15 (how can "great" sin be the cause of vindication?). It is not clear to what 30:23–24 refers. These verses appear again in 23:19–20, and fit that context better. Finally, 31:7–14 contains striking parallels to the language of what biblical scholars call Second Isaiah, i.e., Isaiah 40–55 (cf. Isa. 40:3–5; 43:1–7; 48:20–21; 49:9–13; the idea that Yahweh has "redeemed" his people, v. 11, mirrors an important theme in Second Isaiah; cf. Isa. 41:14; 43:1, 14; 44:22–24). These verses seem to anticipate a restoration of the exiles to a Judean homeland (Zion, v. 12), something quite different from the pilgrimage from their own land to Zion envisioned in v. 6.

Is it possible that Jeremiah could actually have addressed the Northern Kingdom, Israel, over a century after its fall? The key to this ques-

tion is found in the fact that these words about restoration end with a summons (31:21–22). Beginning in the 620s, King Josiah of Judah apparently made attempts to extend the boundaries of his kingdom into the northern Israelite region, which for a century had been controlled by Assyria. 2 Kings 23:4, 15 reports that his religious reform extended to Bethel (see also 2 Chron. 34:6–7), and since he was killed in a battle against Pharaoh Neco near the city of Megiddo (2 Kings 23:29–30; cf. 2 Chron. 35:20–24), one may infer that he had extended his influence at least that far north. Though the exact extent of Josiah's expansion is unknown, there is also archaeological evidence to suggest that he fortified towns in Judah and controlled territory on the Philistine coast. All this activity was possible because of increasing Assyrian weakness after the death of Ashurbanipal in 627 B.C.

Viewed in this context, the poem can be interpreted as a propaganda piece for Josiah's political and religious program, and it may be among Jeremiah's earliest utterances. Northern Israel would again be incorporated into Yahweh's realm, and would again be ruled by its own king, Josiah (30:21). Zion would again be the religious center to which northerners made pilgrimages, a practice that had been stopped by the first Israelite king, Jeroboam (1 Kings 12:26–33), but had reappeared by Jeremiah's day (41:4–5).

However, Josiah's hope failed, and eventually Judah fell as well. During the Exile, one had to envision the restoration of both northern Israel and Judah. By means of supplements and an editorial framework, the exilic assemblers of this little "book" (30:2) offered "consolation" to both north and south.

Jer. 30:1–4 and 31:23–26 provide the framework for the core unit. It begins with the usual formula of the prose sermons and announces that Yahweh will "restore the fortunes" of his people, mentioning first Israel and Judah (30:3; necessary to make connection with the content of what follows) and then Judah alone (31:23–25; necessary for the exilic situation).

The "book" ends with a supplementary group of three prose oracles, each beginning with the same introduction: "Behold, the days are coming, says Yahweh" (31:27, 31, 38). The first two of these mention both Israel and Judah, the last Judah alone. Verses 27–30 focus on a "proverb" (cf. Ezek. 18:2) to explain the hardships encountered by the survivors of Judah's fall as a result of the previous generation's sins (cf. 32:18; Deut. 5:9–10; Lam. 5:7). It is possible that the term "fathers" is intended to refer to the pre-exilic Judean rulers. The hope is expressed in terms that mirror Jer. 1:10. The second oracle pursues a line of thought similar to that of the core unit (cf. 31:22) but does so in terms of a different category, the "new covenant." Since the old one had not worked (cf. 2:22, 13:23), a new basis for the relationship between Yahweh and the people was necessary. What is new is the God-given ability to obey, an echo of which can be heard in 24:7 (see the Short Essay "Expressions of Hope in the Book of Jeremiah"). The third oracle (vv. 38–40) announces the restoration—for all time—of Jerusalem. Verses 35–37 comprise a poetic oracle assuring that Yahweh's relationship with the "descendants of Israel" (the context makes it unlikely that northern Israel alone is meant) will be perpetual. The same imagery is used in 33:19–26 with reference to the Davidic dynasty and levitical priesthood.

Expressions of Hope in the Book of Jeremiah

One of the problems encountered by interpreters of Jeremiah is the necessity of accounting for the inclusion of passages containing an element of hope in a collection attributed to a prophet whose message seems to have been perceived as consistently negative (cf. 20:7–8; 36:28–29; 38:1–4). In addition to the "book of consolation," there are over two dozen briefer passages of this type.

One may begin with the observation that the element of "hope" is included within the prophet's original commission: he was "to pluck up and break down, to destroy and to overthrow, to build and to plant" (1:10). Echoes of this theme recur in oracles later in the book (12:14–17; 24:4–7; 31:28; 32:41).

The expressions of hope are sometimes addressed to individuals or small groups (35:18–19; 39:15–18; 45:2–5), but most often to a whole people or to a larger group representative of them. Frequently, these are Judeans (24:4–7; 27:22; 29:10–14, 32; 32:14–15, 36–41, 42–44; 33:10–11), but in a surprising number of instances the reference is to northern Israel, either mentioned alone (3:12–14; 30:5–31:22) or together with Judah (3:15–18; 5:10; 12:14–17; 23:5–6; 30:3–4; 31:27, 31; 33:4–9, 14–16, 23–26; 50:4–5, 17–20). The oracles against foreign nations also contain occasional promises of a brighter future (46:26b; 48:47; 49:6, 11, 39).

Several themes recur in these passages. One notices first the prominent associations of hope with Jerusalem (33:9, 10–11), its Temple (31:12), and its royal dynasty (33:17–18, 19–22). Both Zion (3:14, 15–18; 31:6; 50:4–5) and the restored Davidic dynasty (23:5–6 = 33:14–16; 33:23–26) are important in the future of northern Israel, as well as of Judah. A second and closely related theme is the restoration of Judah to its land (24:4–7; 27:22; 29:10–14, 32; 32:14–15, 36–44; 33:12–13).

A third theme—dramatic, though less frequent—is that in the future Yahweh will make a "new covenant" with his people. Its fullest statement may be found in 31:31–34, which contains the following elements: (a) both northern Israel and Judah are to be included; (b) the new covenant will not be like the old (broken) Sinai covenant, in that (c) obedience will now be possible, because the law will no longer need to be taught but will be written upon the people's hearts; (d) Yahweh will again be their God, and they his people; (e) he will forgive their past sins; and (f) by implication (v. 34b) this new covenant will endure forever. Clearly, this covenant is not completely "new." It is, rather, a revision of the Sinai covenant, which depended upon the people's obedience to Yahweh's law, the covenant's stipulations. Jeremiah favored this view of the people's relationship to Yahweh and struggled against the attitudes fostered by confidence in the unconditional covenant that was the foundation stone of the royal ideology (see 7:1–15).

There are other passages, similar to 31:31–34, that suggest how this theme developed. Though the narrative about the faithfulness of the Rechabites (see chap. 35) does not use the term "covenant," it does end with the promise that, because of their obedience to the commands of their founder, the Rechabites will endure forever. Since the point is to contrast the actions of the Rechabites with those of the disobedient populace of Judah, the oracle of hope directed to this group (35:18–19) affirms that obedience is the true basis for an everlasting covenant.

The problem is, of course, that in the Jeremiah tradition the people are viewed as having been persistently and irredeemably disobedient (e.g., 2:22; 13:23; condemnations approximating 35:14–15 occur six times). Jer. 24:4–7, which dates from the period after 597 B.C., takes this into account: when he restores the exiles to their land, Yahweh will "give them a heart to know" him and will be their God—"new covenant" elements (c) and (d). Jer. 31:31–34, which one may presume to be exilic, states the theme fully, and 32:36–41 repeats its key elements, (c), (d), and (f)— specifically, now, an "everlasting covenant." Jer. 50:4–5 and 50:17–20 refer to both northern Israel and Judah (a); the first speaks of an "everlasting covenant" (f), and the second seems to imply (c)—no sin is found in them.

One passage seems to contradict this theme: 33:19–26 reasserts the unconditional covenant with David (2 Sam. 7:11–16). It is possible that this sentiment reflects an enthusiastic response to Evil-merodach's release of the captive king, Jehoiachin, from captivity ca. 560 B.C. (2 Kings 25:27–29).

These hopeful statements did not all originate in the same historical setting. Some evidently derive from Jeremiah's earliest period of activity (30:5–31:22). Jer. 32:14–15 is apparently related to an episode that occurred toward the end of the prophet's career, and many other statements are clearly exilic. They share the characteristic of assuming a disastrous past and, on the basis of theological reflection about current circumstances (e.g., Josiah's expansion to the north, the deportations of 597 and 587, the release of Jehoiachin), of projecting a future restoration.

How "realistic" were such hopes? Those related to Josiah's political program must have had a high degree of plausibility, at least in the short run. The others were tied to the traditional Judean worldview, now reformed in light of the lessons of history (as interpreted by prophets and Deuteronomists). They affirmed the people's heritage, and one must assume that they too would have seemed highly plausible. It was a plausibility that even apparent disconfirmation could not destroy. When Josiah's attempt at expansion failed, the oracles first directed to northern Israel were altered to include Judah. The oracles of hope are one part of a living tradition associated with the prophet Jeremiah.

32:1–35:19
Tales of Life Under Siege

Chaps. 32–35 display a loose thematic unity: the events they narrate all took place in Jerusalem during periods of siege by the Babylonians. Chaps. 32–34, set in 588 B.C., form a subunit in which the introduction (32:1–5) provides an abbreviated account of the final narrative (34:1–22). These three chapters are similar in content to chaps. 21, 24 and 37–38, but unlike them say a great deal about hope for the future. Chap. 35, set in 597, which speaks of the reason for the coming destruction of the nation but has nothing to say of hope, is the link that joins these siege passages to chap. 36.

Jer. 32:1–5 serves as an introduction to this little collection of narratives. It is 588, Jerusalem is under siege, and Zedekiah (cf. 37:15; 38:1–6) has imprisoned Jeremiah for prophesying, first, that Yahweh will deliver Jerusalem to Nebuchadnezzar; second, that Zedekiah will not escape but will be given into the hand of the king of Babylon, brought before him, and taken to Babylon, where he will remain until Yahweh "visits" him; and third, that fighting against the Babylonians will not be successful.

The reference in v. 5 to Yahweh "visiting" the captive king in Babylon is ambiguous. The term usually connotes punishment, either of the nation (e.g., 5:9) or of an individual (e.g., 25:12; 29:32; 36:31). Jer. 27:22 and 29:10, however, report that Yahweh will "visit" his people in exile

for the purpose of restoring them to their land. Since the parallel passage (34:5) is unique in its prediction of relatively peaceful circumstances surrounding Zedekiah's death, and since being carried off into captivity would in itself constitute harsh punishment, one should probably see this reference to Yahweh's "visitation" as offering solace to the doomed king. Such optimism would be appropriate to these chapters.

Jer. 32:6–15 reports a symbolic action. The narrative begins with Yahweh announcing that Jeremiah's cousin Hanamel would soon arrive and offer the prophet an opportunity to redeem a field in Anathoth, which was part of the family land holdings (for the legal background, see Lev. 25:25). Hanamel arrived, the purchase was made (the act was deliberately public, v. 12), and Baruch was charged with preserving the deed. An interpretation of the act follows: a time is coming when real estate holdings will again be secure in Judah. There is hope for the land.

Symbolic actions such as this one served to enhance the power of a prophet's utterances (see the Short Essay "Jeremiah's Symbolic Actions"). It is also worth noting that when Hanamel arrived, Jeremiah invoked the criterion of fulfillment ("then I knew that this was the word of Yahweh," v. 8). During a siege, when his message of hope might not have seemed credible, he needed all the persuasive power he could muster.

The prayer (vv. 16–25) and Yahweh's answer (vv. 26–44), which follow the symbolic action, contain one of the largest concentrations of stereotypic language in the book—some of it shared with the Deuteronomists ("bring . . . out of the land of Egypt," "land flowing with milk and honey," "other gods," "provoke me to anger"). Both prayer and answer are heavily overlaid with interpretation. The basic prayer (vv. 16–17a, 24–25) highlights the siege and the symbolic action and takes the form of a lamentation (so the vocabulary: "Ah, Lord Yahweh," v. 17; cf. 1:6, 4:10; Josh. 7:7; Judg. 6:22; "Behold, thou seest," Jer. 32:24; cf. Lam. 3:59–60). Uttered in public and containing another evocation of the criterion of fulfillment, it adds rhetorical force to the prophet's speech. Verses 17b–23 contain a standard exilic period interpretation for the cause of exile.

The stereotypic language in Yahweh's answer occurs mainly in vv. 28–35, which repeat the idea that the city's fall in 597 was the result of the people's apostasy, committed despite persistent warnings by the prophets. Following the new heading in v. 36 one finds Yahweh's words of hope for a restoration from exile, addressed to the city of which Jeremiah had said "it is given" to the Babylonians. These words speak first of a renewal of the people's election (v. 38) and a new covenant relationship with Yahweh (vv. 39–41; cf. 31:31–34), and then return to the real estate theme of the symbolic action (vv. 42–44). The focus is on life in the Palestinian homeland.

Jer. 33:1 ties the next narrative unit to the date (588) already established in 32:2. The chapter contains a collection of prose oracles (note the new headings in vv. 4, 10, 12, 14, 19, and 23), and v. 3 provides the key to its intention: "Call on me and I will answer you and report to you great and inaccessible things you have not known." What are these things? Clearly, they are not explanations of the causes of the nation's collapse (vv. 4–5), since such were well known. The "great things," rendered conceptually inaccessible by the disaster of 587, are rather Yahweh's promise to cleanse his people of their past sins and to restore their fortunes (vv. 6–13). Because vv. 10 and 12 presuppose the destruction of Jerusalem and v. 3 echoes a way of thinking about the people's future found also in Second Isaiah (cf. Isa. 48:6), one may assume that the compiler lived during the Exile. The question of the people's future, still open, is here addressed in terms of restoration to the homeland.

Although 33:14–26 (absent in the LXX) continues to speak of restoration, the subject changes to the Davidic dynasty. Verses 14–16 parallel 23:5–6 but also mention Yahweh's promise to Israel and Judah (presumably, that recorded in 2 Sam. 7:11–16) and emphasize the security of Judah and Jerusalem in those coming days. Verses 17–18 promise that there will always be both a descendant of David to sit upon the "throne of the house of Israel" and levitical priests offering sacrifices in the Temple, and vv. 19–22 expand upon this theme by likening the permanence of the "covenant" with David to that of the regular alternation of day and night (cf. 31:35–37) and by promising to multiply greatly descendants of David and the levitical priests. Connected historically with David's priest, Abiathar, and Jeremiah's home village of Anathoth (see 1 Kings 2:26–27), the Levites were of special interest to the Deuteronomists, another indication of the exilic provenience of this section (→ Levites). A final elaboration in vv. 23–26 employs both the regularities of nature and the idea of Yahweh's election of his people to underscore the hope for future restoration.

At the beginning of chap. 34, Jerusalem is depicted as under siege and the surrounding Judean countryside as, for the most part, in the hands of the invading Babylonians, but Jeremiah is not yet in prison (vv. 1–2, 6–7). It is, therefore, chronologically prior to chaps. 32–33, though the oracle with which it begins (vv. 2–5) was adapted by the compiler as an introduction to these chapters (32:1–5). The version given in this chapter lacks the final note about the futility of fighting the Babylonians (32:5)

and adds a reference to Zedekiah's peaceful death in Babylon (cf. 52:11; 2 Kings 25:7 makes no mention of his death).

The bulk of the chapter (vv. 8–22) is devoted to a narrative about the treatment of Hebrew slaves, which is set during the temporary lifting of the Babylonian siege of Jerusalem (vv. 21–22; cf. 37:5). Verses 8–11 provide the background: after years of neglect (see v. 14b), owners had released their Hebrew slaves in accordance with the law (Deut. 15:1, 12–18). Their motives for doing so were perhaps a mixture of religious (repentance, v. 16; demonstrations of faithfulness to Yahweh's law in a time when it was necessary to call upon him for assistance against attack by aliens) and practical considerations (during a siege it might be difficult to feed slaves, and there would be no agricultural work for them to do; it might also be assumed that free persons would fight harder in defense of their city). In the prose oracle that follows, one learns from the accusation (vv. 12–16) that subsequently (perhaps after the siege was lifted) the owners reneged on their agreement and reclaimed their former slaves. Because of this action, Yahweh would deliver them into the hands of their enemies, causing the Babylonians to return and destroy the city and countryside (vv. 17–22; cf. 21:7; 32:4).

Jer. 35:1 gives only a general date for the final narrative in this section ("the days of Jehoiakim"), but v. 11 allows us to locate the event more specifically in 597, during the siege preceding the first conquest of Jerusalem.

The chapter describes a symbolic action that begins with an account of Yahweh's instructions to Jeremiah to take a group of Rechabites to the Temple and publicly offer them wine to drink and of the prophet's compliance to act in this way. The response of the Rechabites is of central importance: they refuse to drink wine on the grounds that, since the days of "Jonadab the son of Rechab our father" (ca. 842 B.C.), they have faithfully kept the latter's command that they not drink wine, build houses (they had to live in tents), or engage in farming.

Jeremiah's interpretation of this action takes the form of an oracle of judgment (vv. 12–17). The accusation compares the Rechabites, who had been faithful to the commands given them, with the people, who had not obeyed Yahweh but had ignored the prophets and continued in apostasy. The announcement of judgment is quite general: Yahweh will bring "evil" upon Judah and Jerusalem (v. 17a).

The narrative closes with an oracle of salvation directed to the Rechabites (vv. 18–19). Because they have kept their father's commands, their line will continue forever. The terminology ("never lack a man"; cf. 33:17–18) recalls the royal ideology, but in this context it is clear that permanence depends upon obedience. The passage thus agrees with and offers yet another statement of the prophetic and Deuteronomistic views of the people's history.

The identity of the Rechabites is unclear. Some have seen in them a guild of metalworkers and have interpreted the commands as guild restrictions and not indications of cultural conservatism (holding to a supposed "nomadic ideal"). In any case, Jeremiah points not to their social location, but to their faithfulness to religious tradition. The symbolic action in which they cooperated was a demonstration of the importance of faithfulness to commandments that were the basis of a group's existence.

36:1—32
The Beginnings of the Book of Jeremiah

Chap. 36 provides a narrative account of how, in 605 B.C. (v. 1), Jeremiah undertook to collect all the prophecies he had uttered from the beginning of his career and to bring them to the attention of his countrymen, especially their leaders. It seems likely that the prose sermon of 25:1—14 refers to the same events, focusing on the prophet's words. Both chapters make reference to a "scroll" (25:13; 36:2, 28), and there is general agreement by interpreters as to the content of the message (cf. 25:5—6, 8—11; 36:3, 29). The narrative is composed of three episodes with identical structure, but of differing length.

Verses 1—4 describe the way in which Jeremiah's prophecies were committed to writing. The prophet is instructed by Yahweh to write on a scroll all the words he has spoken to him about "Jerusalem [reading with the LXX] and Judah and all the nations" from the "days of Josiah" until the present. Jeremiah follows this instruction by dictating these words to his scribe, Baruch.

Verses 5—26 recount the public reading of these prophecies. Jeremiah instructed Baruch to go to the Temple on a fast day (vv. 5—6, 9; we are not told why the prophet could not go himself or what the specific occasion for fasting was) and there read the scroll aloud. The goal of this action was to stimulate a change in the people's behavior (v. 7). Verse 8 states in a general way that Baruch executed these instructions.

Verses 8—26 give a more detailed picture of what happened. Approximately one year after the scroll was dictated (vv. 9, 22), Baruch took it to the Temple, where it was read three times during the course of a day, twice by Baruch himself (to "all the people," v. 10, and "all the princes," v. 12) and once by Jehudi, a servant of the court (to King Jehoiakim and the assembled princes, v. 21). For each occasion the narrator records a response. The first reading caught the attention of the princes (vv. 11—12). The second aroused fear among the assembled princes (v. 16), who first established the authority of the scroll (by determining that it had in fact originated with Jeremiah, vv. 17—18) and then sent Baruch (and Jeremiah) into hiding (v. 19). The king's response was quite different (vv. 22—26): he showed no fear, but cut the scroll in strips, burned it in a warming fire, and ordered the arrest of Baruch and Jeremiah.

Finally, 36:27—32 tells that Jeremiah was instructed to write a second scroll, a command he again executed by dictating to Baruch. In addition to all the words that had been on the first one, the new scroll contained an oracle, which condemned Jehoiakim for burning the first scroll (vv. 29—31), and "many" additional prophecies (v. 32). The prediction of Jehoiakim's death (vv. 30—31) seems to agree roughly with 22:18—19 but not with 2 Kings 24:1—7.

There is a noticeable relationship between the account in 2 Kings of Josiah's response to the "scroll of the law" found in the Temple (2 Kings 22:3—23:24) and Jehoiakim's to the scroll containing Jeremiah's prophecies: Josiah tore his clothes, sought prophetic guidance (2 Kings 22:11—14), and burned the offending ritual objects; whereas Jehoiakim, showing no fear, tore and burned only the scroll (Jer. 36:22—26). And this was despite the fact that the menacing content of the two scrolls was essentially the same (2 Kings 22:14, 16; Jer. 36:3, 29). From the standpoint of Jeremiah and those in exile who agreed with him, this comparison is highly unfavorable to Jehoiakim. It is possible that the narrative of Jeremiah 36 is consciously patterned after the Deuteronomistic account of Josiah's reaction to the scroll.

Again, in this narrative, one finds the family of Shaphan singled out from among the princes as staunch supporters of Jeremiah. The first public reading of the scroll was at the chamber of Gemariah (v. 10), where Micaiah took an interest in it and reported what he heard to the princes (vv. 11—12). Gemariah was among those who urged King Jehoiakim to attend to the scroll's words (v. 25). Several years earlier, it was apparently the support and influence of another member of that family, Ahikam, which was crucial in saving the prophet's life (26:1, 24). The political dispute that divided the Judean leadership is clearly in evidence here (see Introduction).

37:1—44:30
The Fall of Judah and Its Aftermath in Palestine

The book of Jeremiah contains two accounts of the fall of Jerusalem. One (chap. 52) is virtually identical with 2 Kings 25 and does not mention the prophet at all. The other (chaps. 37—44) features Jeremiah as an important actor in these events and offers an explicit interpretation of their cause.

37:1–2, Zedekiah's Disobedience.

The first two verses in chap. 37 set the stage for the entire narrative by stressing two aspects of the situation: Judah's king, Zedekiah, was a vassal of the Babylonian king, Nebuchadnezzar; and Zedekiah and the majority of Judeans did not respond positively to the words of Jeremiah. The descriptions that follow, of conflicts between Jeremiah and various opponents, can best be seen in the context of the struggle between parties that characterized Judah's last decades.

37:3–38:28, Zedekiah Consults Jeremiah.

The events reported in these chapters occurred during the period 588–587 B.C. After a temporary lifting of the siege in either summer 588 or early winter 587 (vv. 5, 11), the Babylonian armies returned to Jerusalem, and the city fell in July 587. Three consultations between Zedekiah and Jeremiah provide the structure of the passage. These consultations are separated by accounts of confrontations between the prophet and the Judean princes.

In the first consultation (37:3–10), Zedekiah sent messengers to the prophet, requesting that he "pray for us." Presumably, the intention was to try to secure permanent deliverance for the city. Jeremiah's response was an oracle of doom against the city (vv. 7–8 explicitly contradicting the hope that must have arisen following the lifting of the siege). The episode is reminiscent of 21:1–7, which suggests another instance of the same occurrence being recorded in both prose sermon and biographical narrative forms (see chaps. 7 and 26; 25:1–14 and 36:1–32; 21:8–10 and 38:2–3). Verse 4 anticipates the reaction to this message: the imprisonment of the prophet.

Verses 11–15 reveal that during the interlude in hostilities Jeremiah tried to leave the city. The author does not report what motivated this action, though an errand in connection with a purchase of real estate (chap. 32) is a possibility. As he reached one of the city gates, he was arrested as a deserter. Though he protested to the contrary, the fact that he had given advice to others to desert (21:8–10; 38:2–3, 17–18) and that some Judeans had already done so (38:19) makes the charge seem reasonable. The princes punished him with a beating and imprisonment.

Verses 16–21 record the second consultation. This time Zedekiah himself sent for the prophet and, when he had been brought from prison, asked him, "Is there a word from Yahweh?" Jeremiah's response was a short oracle of doom against the king, followed by a protestation of his own innocence (v. 18 is reminiscent of 26:15) and a plea that he be transferred

out of the control of the princes and placed under the king's own guard.

It is worth noting that, according to the narrative, Jeremiah used the criterion of fulfillment of prophecy against his opponents (v. 19). Apparently, it was a handy argument, when the circumstances permitted its use (contrast chap. 28; see the Short Essay "The Problem of 'False' Prophecy"): Jerusalem had already fallen once (597) and had again come under serious attack, so who now could believe in prophecies of peace? This point raises an interesting question. Jeremiah had been persecuted both because his message was unpopular and because for so long the doom he predicted did not come to pass (e.g., 17:14–18; 20:7–12). Then came the national disaster of 597 and the siege of 587, seemingly obvious fulfillments of his prophecies. Yet the present narrative shows that his status among important segments of his audience changed, if at all, only for the worse. In addition the activity of Hananiah a decade earlier (chap. 28) demonstrates, and 37:19 implies, that the "peace" prophets continued to be influential. Matching predictions with occurrences seems not to have been a very powerful tool for judging among prophets.

In the second conflict episode (38:1–13), the princes accuse Jeremiah of treason, saying that he has urged people to desert to the Babylonians, thereby weakening the city's defense. They demand his death, but when Zedekiah hands him over to them, they arrange the execution in a strange and ineffectual manner (vv. 5–6). Soon, with the king's blessing, he is rescued.

The third consultation (38:14–28) involved some curious negotiations between Zedekiah and the prophet. The king wished to ask a question, but the prophet was afraid of two things: that he would be put to death, and that what he said would not be heeded (v. 15). After receiving Zedekiah's assurances, Jeremiah delivered the message that only surrender to the Babylonians could now avert complete disaster. The king suggested that, if he wished to live, he should not let the princes know the content of this message. So when they asked, he lied, and was returned to prison until the city's fall.

This, then, is what the final stages of the party conflict in pre-exilic Judah had come to: counsels of desertion and imprisonment for the prophet who uttered them. Especially in the face of Jeremiah's obvious lack of success in gaining support for his position (37:2; 38:15), desertion can be seen as the logical extension of the "pro-Babylonian" party's foreign policy. What he sought was a way to remain in the land (see chap. 27; this idea seems to underlie the oracle in 38:17–20, and is evident in chaps. 39–43), though events brought this hope to nothing. It is probable that the exilic shapers of these narratives, who knew of this dashed hope, are responsible for the harsher tone of the oracle in 37:6–10.

This was a time when prophets were consulted, but not universally honored. Politically, they had taken sides, and it appears that the supporters of each were mainly his fellow partisans. Even the failure of prophecies to be fulfilled, supposing that it was recognized, did not shake the partisans' faith in their prophets (see 37:19). Jeremiah was consulted, but his words went unheeded.

Jer. 38:4 gives a clear indication of what the powerful elements in Judean society expected of their prophets: they should be upholders of the status quo (see 26:7–9). Jeremiah's activity was perceived to be detrimental to the national welfare, and so he was imprisoned. In the end he could no longer proclaim his words publicly lest he be killed (38:24–28). He took himself out of action: a prophet who does not operate publicly is no threat because he is no prophet.

39:1–43:13, Defeat, Exile, and Prophetic Response. Though these chapters tell a tale of destruction and exile, they continue to reveal the prophet's positive attitude toward the land of Palestine. Thus, after the fall of Jerusalem, Jeremiah chose to remain in the land rather than join the large community of Judeans in Babylon (39:11–14; 40:1–6). For a brief time the remnant in Palestine prospered (40:10–12), and even after the assassination of Gedaliah, the prophet counseled his companions to stay rather than flee to Egypt (42:10–12). This was Jeremiah's bias: he chose to stay. The narratives of chaps. 39–43 allow one to sense an element of hope that was dashed by events. Such hope is not present in the other account of Jerusalem's fall (Jer. 52 and 2 Kings 25).

Jer. 39:1–10 is a summary of Babylon's actions against Jerusalem and its inhabitants after the fall of the city and is essentially the same as that found in 52:4–16 and 2 Kings 25:1–12.

Jer. 39:11–14 contains the suprising claim that Jeremiah counted among his defenders in high places Nebuchadnezzar himself. At first glance this seems implausible. Yet he had tried to leave the city during a temporary lull in the siege (37:11–13), and he had a history of preaching submission to Nebuchadnezzar (chaps. 27–29; 38:17–23) and even of suggesting defection (21:8–10; 38:2–3). Since there were Jewish deserters among the Babylonians (38:19), it is not unreasonable to assume that Nebuchadnezzar had been made aware of all this. Furthermore, we can infer that Nebuchadnezzar had knowledge of local events from the fact that Gedaliah, whom he appointed governor of Judah (40:5; 2 Kings 25:22) and to whom Jeremiah was entrusted, was of the house of Shaphan, one of the mainstays of the "pro-Babylonian" party.

Verses 15–18, an oracle to Jeremiah's rescuer, Ebed-melech, was uttered during the siege (v. 15) and is out of place here.

The point of view of the narrative is clear in 40:1–6, an expanded account of Jeremiah's release. Here the prophet is given a choice about where he will reside. Moreover, the Babylonian officer in charge gives an interpretation of the causes of the city's fall—essentially irrelevant to the narrative—that reflects the sentiments of the Judean community in exile.

The Judeans who remained in Palestine rallied around Gedaliah, who as governor stood for a policy of obedience to Babylon, and prospered (40:9–12). But their prospects were undermined by his assassination (40:13–41:18). Especially because Babylonian soldiers were among those slain, this act had the appearance of a rebellion. It caused consternation among the survivors because of the reaction they expected from the Babylonians (40:15; 41:2–3, 17–18; 43:3).

What motivated the assassination? The perpetrator, Ishmael, was a member of the Judean royal house (41:1) and during the war had been a freedom fighter (head of a military unit, 40:7–8; 2 Kings 25:23; on "captain of the forces," see 2 Sam. 24:2; 1 Kings 15:20). Thus, it is possible that this act was a last gasp of the old party struggle. Given the magnitude of Judah's defeat in 587, this was less likely an attempt to actually assume leadership than an act of revenge. From one point of view, Gedaliah, like Jeremiah, could be considered a traitor.

Chap. 42 presents a textbook case of intercession. Inclined to flee Egypt (41:17–18) but uncertain about what they ought to do, the people and their leaders went to Jeremiah (as in divination, the initiative lay with them, not the prophet) and requested that he consult Yahweh on their behalf, swearing to obey whatever he might command. After a ten-day wait, Jeremiah received a message from Yahweh and transmitted it to them: they were to remain in the land. Furthermore, they had no need to fear Nebuchadnezzar, since Yahweh would cause him to be favorably disposed toward them (vv. 10–13). They were forbidden to go to Egypt, though their motivation for doing so (v. 14) seems quite reasonable.

Jer. 42:18–22 begins with a new formula (see v. 9) and contains a brief recapitulation of Jeremiah's message and the request that occasioned it. However, there is a new element here, the prophet's reference to his own history of being rejected by the people to whom he spoke (v. 21). The gloomy pessimism that results would have been appropriate for Jeremiah, but would also fit the views of exilic interpreters who knew what had happened and who must have understood the flight to Egypt as yet another in a series of self-destructive acts by those who had been left behind after the first deportation to Babylon.

The message was in fact unacceptable, and was branded a "lie" (43:1–3), the very charge that Jeremiah had leveled against his prophetic opponents (see the Short Essay "Jeremiah's Struggle Against 'Falsehood' "). The people quit the land and went to Egypt (vv. 4–7), carrying Jeremiah with them. There the prophet is said to have performed a symbolic action, predicting a Babylonian invasion of the land in which they had taken refuge (vv. 8–13; see the Short Essay "Jeremiah's Symbolic Actions"). These latter verses are probably the work of an exilic interpreter who knew of Nebuchadnezzar's campaign against Egypt in 568 B.C.

44:1–30, Jeremiah and Other Judeans in Egypt.

Broadly speaking, the narrative of chap. 44 takes the form of a dialogue between Jeremiah and the Judeans who had come to Egypt. The prophet speaks twice, the people once. In each case the speech is prefaced by a historical review. The theme is the cause of the nation's misfortune and the lessons that are to be learned from it.

Jeremiah's first speech begins with a review of the 587 disaster, which he attributes to the people's failure, despite the warnings of the prophets, to cease worshiping other gods (44:2–6). This speech is followed by an oracle of judgment, which accuses his audience of having forgotten the lessons of their past wickedness (they have continued in Egypt to serve other gods and have not walked in Yahweh's "law" and "statutes," vv. 7–10) and threatens that Yahweh will, but for a few fugitives, utterly destroy them (vv. 11–14).

The people refuse to accept these words and respond with a historical retrospective of their own: in the past, when they freely worshiped the queen of heaven (the reference may be to the long and apparently prosperous reign of Manasseh; cf. 2 Kings 21:1–18), they prospered; only after stopping such worship (i.e., after the reform of Josiah in 621) did they fall on hard times (vv. 15–19). The description of idolatry focusing on the "queen of heaven" takes up a theme already encountered in 7:16–20, a passage that derives from the exilic community.

The content of Jeremiah's response to this argument essentially repeats his first review and oracle (vv. 20–30). In addition the criterion of fulfillment of prophecy is again mentioned (v. 28; cf. 37:19): the remnant that escapes Yahweh's destruction of the Judeans in Egypt will know that the prophet had been correct. And as a sign that this punishment is coming, Yahweh will give Pharaoh Hophra to his enemies as he had Zedekiah (vv. 29–30). One has the impression that the author of this passage knew of the death of Apries (Hophra) ca. 569 at the hands of

a usurper, as well as of whatever misfortune overtook the Judeans in Egypt.

The chapter, then, accounts (yet again) for the fall of Judah and Jerusalem in 587 and also for the disappearance from the historical scene of the Judeans who had remained behind in the land after the second deportation. What hope remained for the Judeans must now rest solely with the community in Babylonia (see chaps. 24; 29). This assessment, the interpretive capstone of chaps. 37–44, must reflect the thinking of some within the exilic community.

45:1–5
An Oracle to Baruch

The opening verse of chap. 45 dates the oracle to 605 B.C. and connects it specifically to the narrative of chap. 36. The oracle of judgment against the nation (v. 4) reflects 1:10 and 36:29. The oracle of deliverance addressed to Baruch (v. 5) echoes 39:18 and is "fulfilled" by the event reported in 43:6.

Why should this short oracle have been placed here, out of chronological sequence and separated from the narrative to which it belongs? The answer may well be that here it served the needs of the exilic interpreters, whose reflections on the people's destiny can be discerned both in additions made to the traditions and in the order in which these traditions are arranged. Chaps. 37–44 in fact narrate how the prophecies compiled by Jeremiah in 605 were fulfilled. As they are enclosed by two chapters that speak of the collection and utterance of these prophecies (36 and 44), the reader can hardly miss the point. Yahweh had indeed been behind these events. The results had been painful, but at least they were intelligible.

46:1–51:64
Oracles Against the Nations

Oracles against foreign nations are a distinct and relatively common genre of prophetic literature. Collections like the one in these chapters may be found in Amos 1–2, Isaiah 13–23, and Ezekiel 25–32 (cf. also Nahum, Obadiah, Zeph. 2). That chaps. 46–51 of Jeremiah were collected and at first transmitted separately is indicated by the fact that their position in the MT differs from that in the LXX, where they follow 25:13. The latter position is more like that of the collections in Amos, Isaiah, and Ezekiel, but the position in the MT does provide a more dramatic ending for the book: an announcement of the destruction of Babylon, the enemy that had destroyed Judah and carried its inhabitants into exile.

Though we do not know exactly how oracles of this type were used, the genre appears to be quite old. Prophets at Mari spoke against foreign kings, and Jer. 28:8 indicates that Israelite prophets had performed in a similar fashion "from ancient times." It is possible that such oracles were directed against specific enemies in times of war.

In contrast to the oracles of judgment against Judah and the reflections on the people's fate so common in the rest of the book, this collection displays a certain kinship to chaps. 30–33: by announcing the downfall of their enemies, it sets the stage for a restoration of the people's fortunes. The defeat of the foreign nations is generally seen as Yahweh's doing, and sometimes it is specifically said that his motivation is vengeance for what they have done against his people (e.g., 46:10; 50:15, 28). In fact, it is possible to see a contradiction between Jeremiah's insistence that Judeans must submit to Nebuchadnezzar's rule (chaps. 27–29) and the announcements of Babylon's pending destruction (chaps. 50–51), texts that the editors present as contemporaneous (cf. 27:1; 28:1; 51:59). In the first, the Babylonian king is represented as Yahweh's "servant" (27:6), in the second as "monster" (51:34).

46:1
Heading

The heading in 46:1 clearly announces this new major section of the book as oracles against the nations.

46:2–28
Against Egypt

The chapter contains two oracles, each with a prose heading giving its date. The first, vv. 2–12, is set in 605 B.C. (v. 2). It looks back on Egypt's defeat at Carchemish (vv. 6, 12), which it interprets as an act of Yahweh's "vengeance" (v. 10) —presumably, for the death of Josiah at the hands of the pharaoh in 609. The term "vengeance" appears more frequently in Jeremiah than in other prophetic books. Sometimes it refers to Yahweh's actions against his own people (5:9, 29; 9:9) or against Jeremiah's enemies (11:20; 15:15; 20:12), but most often to those against Egypt or Babylon (46:10; 50:15, 28; 51:6, 11, 36).

Verses 13–24 are set in the time of Nebuchadnezzar's campaign against Egypt ca. 568 B.C. (v. 13). The Babylonian attack is in progress (vv. 16, 20–21, 22–24), and victory is anticipated (vv. 14, 19). Egypt's downfall is interpreted as Yahweh's "punishment" (vv. 21, 25; for similar statements against other nations, cf. 48:44; 49:8; 50:18, 27, 31; 51:18, 44, 47, 52). Though these verses are addressed to lower Egypt (v. 14, Memphis), the prose supplement to the oracle is directed to upper Egypt (vv. 25–26, Thebes). The oracle ends with a word of assurance to Israel (vv. 27–28 = 30:10–11), although v. 28b harks back to its own punishment, showing the double need of those in exile to understand the reason for their captivity and to see hope for the future.

Several stages of growth can be discerned in this section about Egypt. The first of the oracles is appropriate to the situation after Egypt's defeat at Carchemish in 605 (vv. 3–12), and the second (vv. 14–24) to the period around 568. Behind the latter we can imagine members of the exilic community gloating that Egypt, the failed ally of the old nationalist party, was itself now succumbing to the Babylonians (cf. 37:3–10). Verses 27–28 express a hope for restoration to the land, along with yet another statement about the meaning of the Exile. The entire collection, held together by a prose framework (vv. 2, 13, 25–26), probably comes from the late exilic period.

47:1–7
Against the Philistines

Though the prose introduction to chap. 47 specifies a date for this oracle (v. 1), a specific historical allusion is uncertain. The contents are quite general, but it is clear that from the author's perspective the disaster coming to the Philistines is Yahweh's doing (vv. 4b, 6–7).

48:1–47
Against Moab

The little collection in chap. 48 begins with four general oracles concerning Moab's destruction (vv. 1–9, 11–12, 14–20, 28–33), each of which is followed by a prose supplement expanding on the main theme of the preceding oracle (v. 10, warfare; vv. 12–13, vessels; vv. 21–25 and 34–36, cities under attack). Two of the prose passages are themselves expanded with statements to the effect that Yahweh is responsible for Moab's demise (vv. 26–27, 38–39). Though Yahweh is twice mentioned as speaker in the oracles (vv. 15, 30), his role in Moab's troubles is not specified (v. 33b may be an allusion to it).

The statement that, because of the defeat, the Moabite god, priests, and princes will be carried into exile (v. 7; cf. 11) is echoed in the following oracle against Ammon (49:3) and in Amos's oracles against the nations (Amos 1:5, 6, 15).

Verses 40–46 explain Moab's destruction as punishment for having "made himself great" against Yahweh (vv. 42, 44; cf. 46:13–24). Moab and Judah were traditional enemies, and there are no allusions that allow us to locate this accusation in a specific historical setting. It is possible, however, that the author had in mind the role of the Moabites as Babylon's allies prior to

643

597 (cf. 2 Kings 24:2). Finally, v. 47 speaks of a future restoration of Moab's fortunes (cf. 46:26b; 49:6, 39).

49:1-39
Against Ammon, Edom, Damascus, Kedar, Hazor, and Elam

49:1-6, Ammon. The oracle against Ammon is quite general in content (on v. 3, see 48:7). Again, the destruction is interpreted as retaliation for oppression of Yahweh's people (vv. 1-2; for a possible historical setting, see 41:15 and commentary above on 48:40-46). It concludes with a promise of restoration (cf. 46:26b; 48:47; 49:39).

49:7-22, Edom. The poetic portions of the oracle (vv. 7-11, 14-16) interpret Edom's fate as Yahweh's punishment (v. 8), though the cause of his action is not specified. The prose of vv. 12-13 contains a confusing reference to drinking from a cup reminiscent of 25:15-29. Verses 17-22, also prose, are dominated by two images: Edom will become like Sodom and Gomorrah, and Yahweh will act like the devouring lion. The latter motif is repeated in the oracle against Babylon (50:44-46).

49:23-39, Damascus, Kedar, Hazor, and Elam. The last three oracles are quite general and do not speak of Yahweh's punishment or vengeance. The only link of the pronouncement against Damascus to Yahweh's action is the stereotypic formula in v. 27 (cf. Amos 1:4). The oracle concerning "Kedar and the kingdoms of Hazor" apparently refers to desert-dwellers in the region between Judah and Babylon. Nebuchadnezzar is identified as the destroyer in both the editorial introduction (v. 28a) and the body of the oracle (v. 30b, which may be a later addition). The introduction (v. 34) to the oracle against Elam, a kingdom to the east of Babylon, provides the date 597, and the two nations may have been in conflict about that time. Elam's destruction is attributed to Yahweh, but no motivation for it is mentioned. Again, there is a concluding promise of restoration (cf. 46:26b; 48:47; 49:6).

50:1-51:64
Against Babylon

The collection in chaps. 50 and 51 begins with a general oracle of destruction (50:2), followed by prose supplements that speak of an attack against Babylon by a nation from the north (vv. 3, 8-10; cf. 50:41-43), the restoration of Israel and Judah (vv. 4-5; see the Short Essay "Expressions of Hope in the Book of Jeremiah"), and yet another reflection on the cause of the Exile (vv. 6-7). Evidently, questions raised by the great

national disaster of 587 could not be laid to rest once and for all, and explanations of it bore repeating (cf. 46:27-28).

In 50:11-16, a general oracle of destruction that specifies Yahweh's motivation as vengeance is followed by a prose elaboration that interprets the event as his restoration of Israel and Judah to their land (vv. 17-20). In the remainder of the chapter, oracles and prose alternate. The former speak of Yahweh's motivation (v. 24b) and interpret Babylon's downfall as punishment (v. 31). The latter elaborate these themes: the vengeance occurs because of the destruction of the Temple (v. 28) and because Babylon has magnified itself against Yahweh (vv. 28-30); Babylon's desolation will be like that of Sodom and Gomorrah (vv. 39-40; cf. 49:18); Yahweh will attack Babylon like a savage lion (vv. 44-46, mirroring 49:19-21). In a language reminiscent of Second Isaiah, vv. 33-34 speak of Yahweh as the redeemer of Israel and Judah.

The oracle of 50:41-43 speaks in vague terms about an attack by an enemy from the north (cf. vv. 3, 8-10; 51:48). Later, the enemy is specifically identified with the Medes (51:27-28). Such use of enemy language parallels earlier portions of the book, where Judah's northern enemy is first unspecified and then identified with the Babylonians (see commentary above on 25:1-14).

The passage 51:1-33, 38-44, depicts an attack on Babylon in which the countryside has already been taken (vv. 30-33, 38-43) and its captives are about to be liberated (v. 44). In the midst of this description comes Jerusalem's curse against Babylon and Yahweh's response that he will take vengeance upon Babylon (vv. 34-37). Verses 45-58 are general oracles proclaiming Yahweh's punishment of Babylon. Indeed, the theme of 51:1-58, including its two short prose elaborations (vv. 11b, 24), is that Babylon's destruction should be seen as Yahweh's retribution (vv. 5, 6, 10, 11, 24, 34-37, 44, 47-53, 56).

Jer. 51:59-64a reports a symbolic action (see the Short Essay "Jeremiah's Symbolic Actions"). Jeremiah sends a "book" of oracles against Babylon to Babylon with Baruch's brother in about 594. These are to be read publicly and then tied to a stone and cast into the Euphrates, symbolizing Babylon's fate. Taken at face value, this judgment would contradict the favorable interpretation of Babylonian hegemony that Jeremiah espoused during the reign of Zedekiah (see chaps. 27-29). It has been suggested that the original intention of Jeremiah's action was to rebut the prophecies of Ahab and Zedekiah to the effect that the Exile would be short (see 29:4-9, 20-23). On this interpretation, reading and then destroying a set of anti-Babylonian prophecies would have the effect of stressing

Jeremiah's rejection of this optimistic view. The editors who placed this story at the end of the oracles against Babylon had a different purpose in mind, however. With it they claimed that Jeremiah had uttered these prophecies and even delivered them to Babylon long before the events to which they allude.

The short notice in v. 64b marks the end of the book of Jeremiah proper.

52:1–34
Historical Appendix

The narrative of chap. 52 is a close parallel to 2 Kings 24:18–25:30. The only major differences between the two are that this chapter omits the story of Gedaliah (2 Kings 25:22–26; but this story is told in detail in Jer. 40–41) and adds an accounting of the number of persons exiled on the three separate occasions when the Babylonians carried away Judean captives (vv. 28–30). The latter element is absent in the LXX of Jeremiah 52.

Bibliography

Bright, J. *Jeremiah: A New Translation with Introduction and Commentary*. Anchor Bible, 21. Garden City, NY: Doubleday, 1965.

Carroll, R. *From Chaos to Covenant: Prophecy in the Book of Jeremiah*. New York: Crossroad, 1981.

_____. *Jeremiah: A Commentary*. Old Testament Library. Philadelphia: Westminster, 1986.

Holladay, W. *Jeremiah 1*. Hermeneia. Philadelphia: Fortress, 1986.

Nicholson, E. *Preaching to the Exiles: A Study of the Prose Tradition in the Book of Jeremiah*. Oxford: Blackwell, 1970.

Overholt, T. "Prophecy: The Problem of Cross-Cultural Comparison." *Semeia* 21 (1981): 55–78.

_____. *Prophecy in Cross-Cultural Perspective: A Sourcebook for Biblical Researchers*. Atlanta, GA: Scholars Press, 1986.

Perdue, L., and B. Kovacs, eds. *A Prophet to the Nations: Essays in Jeremiah Studies*. Winona Lake, IN: Eisenbrauns, 1984.

LAMENTATIONS

NORMAN K. GOTTWALD

INTRODUCTION

Literary Analysis

Lamentations consists of five closely structured poetic compositions on the topic of the destruction of Jerusalem, poems that both evoke the scenes of catastrophe and articulate the psychic and religious trauma of the survivors. It shares a pervasive lament idiom with Psalms, Job, and the prophetic books of Jeremiah, Ezekiel, and Second Isaiah (Isaiah 40–55).

All of the laments use an acrostic contrivance that distributes the entire Hebrew alphabet of twenty-two letters in sequence throughout each of the first four chapters and then, in the final chapter, echoes this device through the use of exactly twenty-two short verses. In chaps. 1 and 2, each three-line strophe opens with a word starting with one of the letters in alphabetic sequence, yielding sixty-six lines in all. Chap. 3, also sixty-six lines long, achieves a denser acrostic form by beginning every line with an acrostic word. Chap. 4 reverts to a single use of each acrostic letter, but differs in having only two-line strophes, yielding forty-four lines. The combined line count of sixty-six in the last two laments equals the length of each of the first three laments.

The acrostic structure constrains vocabulary and word order and also breaks the flow of Lamentations 1; 2; 4; and 5 into twenty-two subunits. Hence, Lamentations presents discrete laments, brief cameos of description and terseness of speech. This conciseness is augmented by the decision to give each strophe only three (or two) lines (Ps. 119 devotes eight lines to each acrostic letter). Compactness of form channels and reinforces strongly expressed emotions while guarding against bombast and mawkishness.

Aptness of expression in the first four poems is enhanced by the disproportion in length between the two parts that form each line or sentence; the second part is generally shorter than the first. Such imbalance produces a falling rhythm that is said to "limp," "choke," or "sob" in sympathy with the mournful contents. The final lament, by contrast, maintains an even length between the two sentence elements.

The tendency for the acrostic artifice to break the compositions into fragments is countered by skillful shifts in speaker and point of view, creating continuities of description, feeling, and thought that span several acrostic strophes in pleasingly varied ways. The shifts in speaking voice correspond closely to the conventions of the funeral song, the individual lament, and the communal lament.

Influence of the funeral song (cf. 2 Sam. 1:17–27) shapes the speeches by the poet in 1:1–11, 17; 2:1–12; 3:48–51; and 4:1–6, in which he bewails the fall of Fair Zion (or Daughter of My People) as a personified city. No typical funeral is in view, however. Although likened to a widow and bereaved mother, Zion's "husband" is not dead (only remote and hostile), nor are all her "children" dead since some have survived to remember and ponder what has happened by composing and reciting these very laments. The speech of the poet takes on a dialogic character and addresses Fair Zion in chiding and consolatory manner, inciting her to cry out to Yahweh for deliverance (2:13–19). This same voice declaims a prophetic oracle announcing punishment on Edom and the end of guilt and exile for Judah (4:21–22).

Contours of the individual lament are adopted when personified Jerusalem speaks as a suffering woman (1:12–16, 18–22; 2:20–22). "Mother" Zion incorporates all the pain and anger of her Judahite "children," confessing their collective sins and calling upon God to mitigate or terminate the horrible and extreme suffering. We are made acutely aware that this woman is an imaginative figure who both embodies and stands off from particular Judahites whose condition she reports and bewails. This personification admirably succeeds in infusing mass suffering with the personal meaning that only a specific human sufferer can give it.

The individual laments of chap. 3 are not framed or marked as personifications; they derive their collective reference in part by association with surrounding chapters and more directly from their juxtaposition with an enclosed communal lament (vv. 40–47). Read by themselves, the cries of the unnamed "man" (vv. 1–24) and a subsequent "I" speaker without specified gender (vv. 52–66) are typical individual laments of anonymous sufferers so plentiful in the Psalms. In context, the elusive and ambiguous identity of the speakers in chap. 3 may be entirely purposeful.

Chap. 5 stands apart as a communal lament without the separate speaking voice of the poet or any personification of city or people. Judah speaks in a united voice that erases many earlier ambiguities and brings dramatic closure to the troubled book.

Composition

Lamentations was almost certainly written in the sixth century B.C. to commemorate the destruction of Jerusalem by the Neo-Babylonians in 587. The stock of lament language was, by this time, already richly developed in Israelite religion. Moreover, the genre of lament over a destroyed city probably owes much to ancient Mesopotamian tradition and practice that continued unabated until late biblical times.

The first four laments share vocabulary and stylistic devices, modulation of speaking voice, formal features, and the acrostic scheme. These similarities imply, if not a single author, at least a group or "school" of lament traditionists. On the other hand, each lament is self-contained, displaying marked individuality. Since there are no conspicuous signs that the laments were written "from scratch" as parts of a single work, one may argue for their independent composition, followed by later redaction (compilation). It is possible that the redactor was author of one or more of the laments (chap. 5?) and that minor modifications were made in the text during the course of the book's composition.

The separate laments were created for recitation at annual fast days observed at the site of the ruined Temple during the Exile (Zech. 7:1–7; 8:19). Apparently some form of ritual practice continued at the Temple site throughout the Exile (Jer. 41:5). Other communal laments suitable for these commemorative fasts are Psalms 44, 60, 74, 79, 83, 123, 137. By comparison with the latter, Lamentations displays a high level of artistic complexity, subtlety, and cohesion.

The aim of the acrostic-building poet(s) seems to have been to foster a comprehensive catharsis of grief and confession linked to an inculcation of faith and hope, to be accomplished literally by covering the subject "from A to Z." This explanation of the acrostic form is more satisfying than other theories about the magical power of letters, instructional techniques for scribes, or aids to memory. The impulse to explore the trauma until the topic is "exhausted" is both realized and held in check by the acrostic principle that imposes economy of expression on otherwise boundless grief and shock.

Collection of the individual laments may have been occasioned by a notable event such as the release from exile and anticipation of rebuilding the Temple. This notion has been questioned by some interpreters because there are no traces of release from exile or Temple rebuilding in Lamentations. Nevertheless, the Mesopotamian practice of using just such bleak laments on the occasion of cleansing and rebuilding a temple site suggests that the somberness and restrained hope of the exilic compositions might have been retained as a deliberate reminder of dark days, even after the redactor was aware that the situation had changed for the better.

Amid the rich details of the five laments in their final form, the strongest statement of faith and hope, underscored by the triple acrostic and even by repetitions of the same acrostic word (note the threefold "good" as the acrostic term in 3:25–27), is positioned at the center of the work. By contrast, some scholars have argued for the presence of chiastic structure, namely, for the correspondence of chaps. 1 and 5 (general "distanced" descriptions) and chaps. 2 and 4 (detailed "emotionally involved" descriptions). However, this pairing of the laments oversimplifies the evidence, since chaps. 1 and 2 form the closest pair in terms of the speaking voices and chaps. 4 and 5 are most similar in their inventories of population groups. While there is no unequivocal progression of thought in the compilation, readers may discern Judah's increasingly profound understanding of its traumatic situation.

Function as Scripture

It is likely that, by the time of Second Isaiah (Isaiah 40–55), the idioms and concepts of the Lamentations "school of thought" had reached Babylonian Jews (cf. Isa. 47; 51:17–23; 54:1–8). The notion of the "satisfaction" of Judah's sin and guilt through prolonged exile is shared by Lam. 4:22 and Isa. 40:2. Moreover, Second Isaiah's use of liturgical genres to communicate his message may owe something to the proven appeal and endurance of communal lament practice based in exilic Jerusalem and demonstrated in Lamentations. Familiarity with Lamentations is also evident in Third Isaiah (Isa. 56–66), 2 Chronicles, Sirach, and Baruch, the latter modeled in part on Lamentations itself.

Following the destruction of Jerusalem in 70 A.D. the reading of Lamentations on the ninth of the month of Ab became part of the festal calendar of postbiblical Judaism. Lamentations Rabbah, a Jewish midrash redacted at the end of the fifth century A.D., interprets the biblical text verse by verse and contains a large collection of sayings, stories, and homilies.

The tradition of Jeremiah authorship for the book, aided by an erroneous understanding of 2 Chron. 35:25, has contributed to a popular view of Jeremiah as the weeping or sorrowful prophet. Christian liturgies have included Lamentations in readings for Holy Week, thereby referring its descriptions to the sufferings of

Christ. Over the centuries, Lamentations often has been set to music, from Gregorian chants through the work of major composers beginning with the Renaissance. Its subject has frequently been applied to later national calamities (e.g., in Polish history and the Jewish Holocaust) and to the fall of other great cities (e.g., Constantinople).

In the Hebrew Bible, Lamentations is reckoned as one of the five Megilloth, or "Scrolls," read at major festivals (the others are Song of Songs, Ruth, Ecclesiastes, and Esther). English versions, following the Septuagint and the Vulgate, place Lamentations after Jeremiah.

In its original setting, Lamentations performed a basic task of historical "grief work." It bridged the gap between primal grief and outrage at the fall of Jerusalem and the ethics and theology by which Jews interpreted the events and oriented their lives. By linking the idioms and concepts of lament to a major historical crisis, Lamentations provided a paradigm according to which Jews and Christians might struggle with the meanings of calamity and work out strategies for living through world-shaking catastrophes, reaching to the wars and massacres of the twentieth century.

Authorship and Setting

To what traditions and to which spokespersons in Judah can we attribute Lamentations? In past interpretation, there has been an overly simple search for a single source. In place of the claim for Jeremian authorship, now almost universally dismissed, scholars have sought to identify sources for the book in the following streams of tradition: prophecy, Deuteronomistic thought, kingship (Davidic-Zion) traditions, priestly theology, or wisdom teaching. In truth, no one such tradition adequately accounts for the book, since, in the riptide of national collapse, the streams were mingling and forcing new channels of thought and action.

Lamentations shares with prophetic and Deuteronomistic thought the firm belief that Judah's "sins" precipitated the catastrophe. This belief is dressed out in the prophetic image of the people as a faithless defiled woman (1:8–9, 17–18, 20; 4:6). In accord with critical prophets, Lamentations condemns the superficial assurances of "false" patriotic prophets who also joined corrupt priests in murdering innocents (2:14; 4:13). The prophetic belief in judgment on the nations as well as on Judah is firmly attested in Lamentations (1:21–22; 4:21–22, cf. 3:58–66), as is the necessity of contrite confession and wholehearted conversion (1:18, 20; 3:39–42; 5:7, 16, 21).

Wisdom affinities with Lamentations show up prominently in 3:25–39, a text in which the transcendent mystery of God is declared, suffering is seen as disciplinary as well as retribu-tive, the long-range justice of God is affirmed, and patient waiting on and hope in God is inculcated.

Royal traditions, namely, those associated with the Davidic line and with Zion, are most evident in the astonished outcries of passersby who thought Jerusalem to be impregnable (2:15–16; 4:12) and in the communal lament of those who trusted totally in their king as "the anointed of Yahweh" (4:20). The poet joins the personified Zion in expressing shocked disbelief at the enemy's violation of the sacred Temple (1:10; 2:6–7, 20). These texts suggest that all the special privileges of David and Zion, which depended on the faithfulness of Judah, have now been justly canceled. It is true that Judah's political leaders are not unambiguously condemned. Nevertheless, the censure of priestly and prophetic complicity with civil rulers presupposes censure of the latter. Moreover, "our fathers sinned and are not" (5:7; cf. 2:9), may refer to the political leadership swept away by death and exile. The focus of Lamentations on faulty religious leadership may be due to the postdestruction reality in which the political leadership is no longer in power. In addition, "old-style" priests and prophets may still be vying for control of the reconstituted religious life in Jerusalem and, thus, threatening the status and credibility of the Lamentations traditionists.

In sum, anyone adhering rigidly to the conventions of a single theological tradition could hardly have woven the web of poetic argument in Lamentations. Strict prophetic and Deuteronomistic adherents viewed the covenant with God as irrevocably broken. Followers of traditional wisdom tenets had little precedent for grappling with the sociopolitical and religious ramifications of the city's fall. Ardent Davidic-Zion loyalists could not abide the breach of the unconditional promises to the holy city, its Temple, and king. Those who thought that Judah's regime and society were just (or at least) as good or better than those of other nations would not have understood or sympathized with the notion that "sins" explained Judah's sad end.

The ritual setting for Lamentations was the ruined Temple site at which place fasting, prayer, and sacrifice were carried on with the apparent permission of the Babylonian overlords. The poets of Lamentations were "priests" in the sense that they were religious personnel. Since, however, the priestly establishment had been shattered with the city's fall, these postdestruction religious leaders may have been former prophets, scribes, political or private laity, or even lower order or non-Jerusalemite priests; their positions were probably without stipend.

Lamentations, in its final form, exhibits a striking and innovative amalgam of prophetic, Deuteronomistic, and wisdom notions that subordinates and neutralizes Davidic-Zion traditions without rejecting them outright. This theology of active engagement with national crisis is the work of poets and pastoral leaders who communicated directly and concretely with the demoralized survivors of 586 B.C.

COMMENTARY

1:1–22, First Lament of Poet and Zion. The chapter is divided equally between a lament of the poet (vv. 1–11) and a lament of the personified city, Fair Zion, who, as the object of suffering, becomes through her speaking an independent character (vv. 12–22). The two laments are bound together in a pattern of anticipation and recall by introducing two short cries of Zion into the poet's speech (vv. 9c; 11c) and by inserting a comment by the poet within Zion's speech (v. 17). Verse 7 is overloaded with four lines (NEB gives a likely correction, as also in 2:19).

The note struck by the poet and confirmed by Zion is that the city is bereft of comfort from any source. Her plight is described in lurid fashion: subjection to conquerors and betrayal by former allies, contempt and gloating by her enemies, decimation of her populace by death and exile, profanation of the Temple by the enemy and cessation of festivals, and a dire shortage of food.

Zion takes up her lament by voicing the incomparability of her pain and picturing the angry assault of Yahweh in the metaphors of individual lament. An ironic disintegration of established religious language occurs when God's murder of his people is called "a festival" and a grape-treading harvest (v. 15). Although confessing fully her rebellion, Zion cites mitigating factors in her punishment that merit Yahweh's reconsideration, at least in providing for punishment of Zion's destroyers (vv. 21–22) as well. Uniquely in the OT, Lamentations identifies a past event with the Day of Yahweh as the time of his judgment (v. 12), and Zion pleads that this recently enacted Day of Yahweh be extended to fall upon the arrogant enemy (by inference Babylonia, whose ally Edom is named in 4:21–22).

2:1–22, Second Lament of Poet and Zion. When compared to chap. 1, the proportions and contents of the speeches by poet and Zion in chap. 2 undergo considerable change. While Zion has much less to say, the poet grows more articulate and reflective, directly addressing Zion and struggling with her to grasp the enor-

mity of the events she has experienced. Again, the Day of Yahweh as judgment is stressed, though this time as a demonic festival at the Temple site, a place at which praise of deity is reversed by God's terrible destruction of his own religious center (vv. 5–7, 22).

The poet moves into close emotional and ideological sympathy with Zion. In line with Zion's speech in chap. 1, he depicts Yahweh as the direct destroyer of the city's fortifications, palaces, and Temple by using a variety of descriptive statements and personifying metaphors. He is overcome by the sight of famished infants dying in their mothers' laps (vv. 11–12). Moreover, consistent with Zion's very first words (1:12), the poet's initial words to Zion bemoan the incomparability and boundlessness of her plight, "for great as the sea is your ruin" (2:13). He deplores the fact that Zion was misled by prophets who gave "slick" oracles of cheap optimism that were out of touch with reality (v. 14). To be sure, Yahweh's decree of judgment remains defensible; nonetheless, the means chosen to punish are bitter and hard for the poet to accept, especially the abrasive taunts of the enemy and the death of children by famine (vv. 17–19).

In her brief lament, Zion enlarges on the poet's disgust and outrage at the gross extremities of the punishment (vv. 20–22). Unlike her speech in chap. 1, she mentions neither her own sins nor the sins of the enemy deserving punishment. Her stress is on the utter unnaturalness of women cannibalizing their own children and of priests and prophets cut down in the sacred Temple precincts. Zion's outcries are grief-stricken and horror-driven reflexes: Look at what you have done, Yahweh! Look at those to whom you have done it, the dying children!

3:1–66, An Individual Laments. The central lament of the collection uses different literary conventions. However, the central theological problem is implicit in the raging grief, guilt, and horror of chaps. 1–2, namely, how are we to understand and live with a merited punishment that has produced such shocking and excessive results, one that creates new injustices?

The stark and solemn intonation of the initial verse, "I am the man who has seen affliction by the rod of his wrath," breaks sharply with the previous personification of Fair Zion. Nonetheless, this new language operates on a similar "wavelength" in expressing the enervating burden of suffering at God's hand.

The major difficulty in interpreting this chapter is the veiled identity of the speakers. This problem may not have existed when the lament was recited in worship, since intonations in delivery, explanatory rubrics, even different speaking voices, may have clarified the issue. The shift to a written text created a new

649

context of meaning, less immediate and more dependent on the eye and experience of the reader. The readactor may have left the speakers in anonymity as an artifice to deepen readers' involvement in the engagement with suffering: what do we learn about national suffering when we see it through the lens of individual sufferers who have attained hope and meaning amid all their adversities?

The precise identity of speakers may not be as crucial for understanding the argument as commentators have usually thought. Nevertheless, any careful reading of this chapter requires some tentative conclusions about who speaks to whom and with what import. Many options have been proposed, yielding a rich variety of nuances to the function of chap. 3 within the book.

Is the "man" of vv. 1–24 Jeremiah, the poet, an anonymous sufferer, or a masculine personification of the people? Second Isaiah uses both the feminine Zion and masculine Servant personifications for the people. Traces of the same practice occur in the Jacob references of Lam. 1:17; 2:2–3. And who declaims the lofty theological truths of 3:25–39? Is this still the voice of the "man" who has now found answer to his lament? Or is this the voice of the poet, expounding and enlarging on the more tentative "hope" of the "man" in vv. 21–24? Lastly, whose is the "I" voice (or voices) of vv. 48–66? Verses 48–51 read like an interjection of the agitated poet. However, is the speaker once again the "man," or is it Fair Zion (cf. v. 48), or yet another voice, or even, as some have thought, the solo voice of the liturgical leader in a communal lament?

In the midst of these speeches by individuals, an unmistakable communal lament, which seems at first wholly out of place (vv. 40–47), breaks forth. It lacks both the confident insight and faith that precedes it and the certainty of hearing and deliverance that follows. While this national lament is premised on complete sincerity ("Let us lift up our hearts, not our hands, to God in the heavens!" v. 41), it is otherwise "stuck" at a level of frustrated religious traditionalism in which faith and hope are not yet internalized and integrated with grief and contrition.

By enfolding the frustrated communal lament within faith-affirming and hope-engendering individual laments and meditations, the author (confirmed in his intent by the redactor) points toward a life-giving way that has been found by sufferers whose discoveries increasingly inform the outlook of the people on their road to new life.

4:1–22, Third Lament of Poet and City.
This lament, teeming with vivid scenes of hardship and disgrace among the survivors in Jerusalem, is divided, like chaps. 1 and 2, between two speakers. Striking, however, is the minimal presence of Fair Zion (only in vv. 3, 6, with a trace in v. 10), until she emerges in prophetic proclamation at the end (vv. 21–22). In place of the Fair Zion speeches in chaps. 1 and 2, the city expresses itself in a communal lament (vv. 17–20). The individualized presentation of Judah's suffering, characteristic of chaps. 1–3, gives way here and in chap. 5 to overt communal discourse by the collective body of sufferers.

The lament as a whole lays bare the physical, sociopolitical, and moral fragility of the upper classes. Political and religious leaders failed equally. Perfidious prophets and priests are rejected as though they are lepers (vv. 13–16). The lamenting people acknowledge their misplaced trust in allies and in their own king (vv. 17–19). The prophetic announcement of the end to Zion's punishment vindicates the hope expressed in chap. 3 and is to be read not as jingoism, but as Judah's renunciation of all false hopes.

5:1–22, The Community Laments.
In this communal lament, the author introduces perspectives of economic hardship, social disorder, and political restrictions among the inhabitants of the Babylonian subprovince of Judah. Such a description of Judah's reproachful situation is designed to elicit divine intervention.

Significantly, the lament holds to the paradox disclosed in chap. 3 and sustained by the poet in chap. 4, namely, that Judah has both sinned and been sinned against. This time, however, the insight is internalized and expressed by the whole community. Judah's ambivalence and schizophrenia about the tension between deserved and undeserved suffering is resolved. The people are now enabled to own up to their sins (vv. 7, 16) at the very same time they appeal for their disgrace and oppression to be relieved (vv. 1, 17–20). The lament focuses on this new maturity. In a closing appeal to Yahweh, the people seek a restored relationship with their God (v. 21).

There is a critical caveat, however, expressed in the final troubled question, "Or have you utterly rejected us? Are you angry with us beyond recall?" (v. 22). Has Judah learned her lesson too late? Does God still honor a covenant with the Judahites or has he broken off his relationship with them irrevocably? The unclouded confidence of 3:25–39, 52–66 is not yet firmly within the people's collective grasp. Even so, the overarching sense of the book is that the enduring trust situated at the center of the collection in chap. 3 will in time prevail among those who mourn Jerusalem by praying to Yahweh.

Bibliography

Albrektson, B. *Studies in the Text and Theology of the Book of Lamentations.* Lund: Gleerup, 1963.

Gottwald, N. K. *Studies in the Book of Lamentations.* 2d rev. ed. London: SCM, 1962.

Gwaltney, W. C., Jr. "The Biblical Book of Lamentations in the Context of Near Eastern Lament Literature." In *Scripture in Context II: More Essays in Comparative Method.* Edited by W. W. Hallo et al. Winona Lake, IN: Eisenbrauns, 1983. Pp. 191–211.

Hillers, D. R. *Lamentations.* Anchor Bible, 7A. Garden City, NY: Doubleday, 1972.

Lanahan, W. F. "The Speaking Voice in the Book of Lamentations." *Journal of Biblical Literature* 93 (1974): 41–49.

Miller, P. D., Jr. "Trouble and Woe: Interpreting the Biblical Laments." *Interpretation* 37 (1983): 32–45.

Mintz, A. "The Rhetoric of Lamentations and the Representation of Catastrophe." *Prooftexts* 2 (1982): 1–17.

Tigay, J. H. "Lamentations, Book of." *Encyclopaedia Judaica.* Vol. 10, cols. 1368–75.

EZEKIEL

ROBERT R. WILSON

INTRODUCTION

The Book of Ezekiel has always been difficult to understand. Since antiquity ordinary readers have found the book's language, images, and theology puzzling, while scholars have often been embarrassed both by the contents of the book and by their own inability to produce an adequate commentary on it. In the history of Christian biblical scholarship, the interpretive difficulties associated with the book were already apparent as early as Jerome (ca. A.D. 340–420), whose commentaries are filled with apologies for his inability to clarify obscure passages. Other early Church Fathers resorted to numerological interpretation to squeeze theological meaning from the text, and their more modern counterparts have sometimes employed textual emendation or radical surgery to solve the book's problems.

In Jewish tradition the interpretation of Ezekiel has been particularly difficult because some of the legal material contained in chaps. 40–48 contradicts the laws of the Torah. The Babylonian Talmud reports that this fact caused some rabbis to advocate withdrawing the book from circulation, a fate that was avoided only through the extraordinary efforts of Hananiah son of Hezekiah, who successfully reconciled the contradictions (b. Šabb. 13b; b. Ḥag. 13a; b. Menaḥ. 45a). Equally troublesome to the rabbis was the vision of God's glory described in Ezekiel 1, a passage that they feared might lead to dangerous mystical speculations or even destroy the interpreter who probed too deeply into its mysteries. According to the Talmud, Hananiah son of Hezekiah was again able to persuade his colleagues not to withdraw Ezekiel, although Jerome reports that some rabbis prohibited the reading of the beginning and end of the book by anyone under the age of thirty (b. Ḥag. 13a).

In spite of the interpretive problems associated with Ezekiel and the occasional efforts to withdraw it from circulation, there is no indication that early Jewish or Christian interpreters ever questioned the canonicity or divine inspiration of the book. In most biblical manuscripts it appears after the books of Isaiah and Jeremiah as the third of the major prophets, an order that more or less accurately reflects the historical sequence in which the books were composed. However, the Babylonian Talmud (b. B. Bat. 14b) also knows of a tradition that places Ezekiel after Jeremiah but before Isaiah. This arrangement is based on the contents of the books rather than on the chronology of their creation and is reflected in some biblical manuscripts.

Even a brief survey of the history of the study of the book of Ezekiel suggests that scholars are not ever likely to agree on a definitive interpretation of this complex and puzzling book. However, many of the difficulties associated with understanding the book can be minimized by bearing in mind the historical, sociological, and religious settings in which the book was produced and by cultivating a sensitivity to the book's structure and peculiar literary style.

The Prophet and His Times

Unlike many of the prophetic books, which are difficult to date precisely and which contain oracles that have been lifted from their original historical contexts, the book of Ezekiel often assigns very precise dates to the oracles and visions that it contains and to the events that it records (1:1–3; 3:16; 8:1; 20:1; 24:1; 26:1; 29:1, 17; 30:20; 31:1; 32:1, 17; 33:21; 40:1). These dates root the book in a specific historical context and suggest that an understanding of that context is necessary for a proper understanding of Ezekiel's prophecies.

The Exile and Its Theological Implications. The book's own chronology places Ezekiel's prophetic call in Babylon during the fifth year of the Exile of King Jehoiachin of Judah (1:2), and the latest dated oracle in the book is assigned to the twenty-seventh year of the Exile (29:17). The prophet was thus active at least between July 593 B.C. and April 571 B.C., although the bulk of his oracles are dated to the relatively brief period between his call and the arrival of the first Jewish exiles in Babylon (January 585 B.C.), not long after the Babylonians destroyed Jerusalem (33:21). Ezekiel's prophetic activities thus partially overlapped those of Jeremiah and must be seen against the chaotic background of the last years of the Judean state.

The Political Situation. The political crisis that led to the fall of Jerusalem had been developing for a number of years before Ezekiel began to prophesy. After the death of the Assyrian king Ashurbanipal (669 B.C.), the widespread empire that he had ruled began to break apart. With this political instability came a rebirth of nationalism on the periphery of the empire, especially in Babylon, Egypt, and Palestine. In Judah King Josiah was able to establish a kingdom that was relatively free from Assyrian control, and he moved to reclaim Assyrian territory that had historically been part of the Northern Kingdom, Israel. In connection with his political expansion, he also instituted a religious reform that restored the worship of Yahweh to the land (2 Kings 22–23; 2 Chron. 34–35). However, this period of Judean independence was relatively brief. Even as Josiah was rebuilding his state, Egypt and Babylon were beginning to struggle with each other for control of the old Assyrian Empire. During this struggle Josiah was killed when he tried to prevent Pharaoh Neco II from coming to the aid of the Assyrians in their fight with the Babylonians and the Medes (609 B.C.). At Josiah's death, his son Jehoahaz became king, but after only three months Pharaoh Neco returned to Judah, deposed Jehoahaz, and installed another son of Josiah, Jehoiakim, as king. Judah became an Egyptian vassal, and Jehoiakim levied heavy taxes on the people in order to pay the required tribute (2 Kings 23:31–35). This move caused great dissatisfaction in the land and encouraged some political groups to oppose the king's pro-Egyptian policy. During this period of unrest, the power of Babylon gradually grew, and by 603 B.C. Jehoiakim was forced to become subject to the Babylonians. This shift of allegiance gave rise to further political disputes in Judah, with some factions advocating a pro-Babylonian foreign policy, others counseling a return to reliance on Egypt, and still others arguing for the restoration of a politically independent Judean state.

Thinking that the power of the Babylonian king, Nebuchadnezzar II, was declining, Jehoiakim rebelled in 601 B.C. and again threw in his lot with Egypt. This was a serious miscalculation, which the Babylonian king eventually punished. Late in 598 B.C., the Babylonian army moved against Judah and laid siege to Jerusalem. Sometime during this period Jehoiakim died or was killed, and his son, Jehoiachin, was placed on the throne. In March 597 B.C., the new king surrendered Jerusalem to the Babylonians. Jehoiachin was deported to Babylon, along with a number of palace and Temple officials and craftsmen, including the prophet Ezekiel (2 Kings 24:14–16; Ezek. 1:1–3). The Temple and royal treasuries were drained, and some of the Temple vessels were either destroyed (2 Kings 24:13) or taken to Babylon (Jer. 27).

For Ezekiel and his fellow exiles, the events of 597 marked the beginning of the Exile. However, for those left in Jerusalem, life continued on its normal course. Nebuchadnezzar installed Jehoiachin's uncle, Zedekiah, on the throne but

continued to use the title "king" to refer to the exiled Jehoiachin. This move added to Judah's instability by encouraging disputes over the legitimacy of Zedekiah. Many people left in Judah apparently accepted his authority (2 Kings 24:18–20; Jer. 22:24–30), while at least some of the exiles continued to recognize Jehoiachin as king (Ezek. 1:2). Nevertheless, during the first years of his reign, Zedekiah managed to maintain a stable foreign policy and remained a faithful vassal of Babylon, in spite of the continued presence of groups advocating pro-Egyptian and nationalistic positions. However, in the end he was unable to resist his pro-Egyptian advisers, and he joined with other nearby rulers in an attempt to break away from Babylonian control (Jer. 27–28). This conspiracy, which was probably encouraged by Pharaoh Psammetichus II, was not successful, and Zedekiah was forced to reaffirm his loyalty to Nebuchadnezzar (Jer. 29:3; 51:59).

In spite of the inability of Zedekiah and his fellow rulers to remove the Babylonian yoke, popular pressure for revolt continued in Judah. Although Zedekiah apparently had some misgivings about further provoking Babylon (Jer. 21:1–7; 37:3–10, 17; 38:14–23), he eventually gave in to pressure from some of his own advisers and rebelled, probably with assurances of aid from Pharaoh Hophra, Psammetichus' successor. This time Nebuchadnezzar acted more quickly and decisively. In 588 B.C. he invaded Judah, destroying a number of cities, and laid siege to Jerusalem. The city finally fell in the summer of 586 B.C. (Some scholars date the fall to the summer of 587.) Zedekiah and some of the royal court attempted to flee the country but were captured by the Babylonians. The king's sons were killed, and he himself was blinded and taken captive to Babylon. Jerusalem was destroyed, most of its inhabitants were deported to Babylon, and the Temple was burned. Nebuchadnezzar attempted to restore some political stability by appointing a Judean noble, Gedaliah, to be governor over the "poor of the land" who still remained in Judah. However, Gedaliah was soon murdered, and the land again became politically unstable. The Babylonian response to these events probably included another deportation (582 B.C.) and the incorporation of Judah into the Babylonian province of Samaria, but the available historical sources provide no further information.

The Religious Situation. The political chaos that eventually led to the fall of Jerusalem triggered a number of theological problems, both for the exiles in Babylon and for the people who remained in Judah. These problems began with the first deportation (597 B.C.), when Israel's religious leadership was split between Jerusalem and Babylon. Both groups naturally attempted to provide theological interpretations of the events that had just occurred, but these interpretations did not always agree, and the result was a growing religious controversy that reached crisis proportions after the final destruction of the city and the Temple. Several important theological issues were involved. First, there were debates over the meaning of the first deportation. Some Israelite religious leaders, principally the authors of the books of Kings and the prophet Jeremiah, had for some time been warning the people that the sins of Judah and its kings would eventually be punished by God (2 Kings 21:8–9, 14–15; 23:26–27, 32, 37; 24:1–9; Jer. 14:1–15:4; 36). Therefore, when the first deportation occurred, there was general agreement, even among the exiles, that the prophecies of judgment had come true. However, there were disputes about the completeness of the judgment. Did God's exile of Jehoiachin and his officials represent a final word of divine judgment, or were the people who remained in Jerusalem still in danger of additional punishment if they did not change their ways?

Second, there were debates about the length of the Exile and the possibility of return to the land. These debates initially arose after the first deportation and intensified after the second one. Jeremiah and the writers of Kings sometimes speak as if the deportations represent God's complete and final rejection of Israel (2 Kings 21:10–15; 24:3; Jer. 14:1–15:14; 17:1–4). But Jeremiah's ultimate word on the subject was to prophesy a return after a long but limited exile. Other prophets, however, disagreed and soon after the first deportation began to speak of a rapid return of the exiles and a restoration of normal worship in the Temple (Jer. 27–32).

Third, there were debates about the status of the exiles in Babylon after the first deportation. Did the fact that they had been removed from God's chosen city mean that they had been rejected and were no longer part of the true Israel? This issue was obviously of great concern to the exiles, who were anxious to clarify their religious status (Ezek. 11:14–21). Furthermore, the theological status of those in exile had a direct bearing upon their religious life in Babylon. Did the fact that the exiles were separated from the land of Israel mean that they could no longer worship God? If they were free to worship, then what form should that worship take? These questions took on new urgency after the second deportation, when Israel was geographically scattered in Babylon, Israel, and Egypt. Disputes over the identity of the true Israel continued to be a feature of religious life until the issue was finally resolved in favor of the Babylonian exiles.

Fourth, between 597 B.C. and 586 B.C. there were increasingly heated debates among prophets reflecting differing points of view. These debates can be seen most clearly in the book of Jeremiah, where Jeremiah is often portrayed in conflict with his fellow prophets. While he warned of the imminent destruction of Jerusalem by the Babylonians, other prophets were confidently predicting that the city would be spared (Jer. 6:14–15; 14:13–14; 23:13–40). While Jeremiah was speaking of a long exile, the prophet Hananiah was telling Jerusalemites that the Exile was almost over (Jer. 27–28). While Jeremiah was advocating surrender to the Babylonians, exiled Judean prophets in Babylon were counseling revolt (Jer. 29:15–32). Although it is easy in retrospect to determine which prophets were speaking truly and which were not, the people who lived at the time had a great deal of difficulty adjudicating these conflicting prophetic claims. People finally came to be suspicious of all prophets, and even major prophets like Jeremiah and Ezekiel had to defend their prophetic authority at every turn. The words of Ezekiel were particularly open to question because he prophesied in Babylon, and many Israelites apparently doubted that true prophecy could exist outside the land of Israel.

Finally, the destruction of Jerusalem and the Temple in 586 B.C. provoked intense debate about the nature of God's relationship to the city. An important element of the royal theology of Jerusalem was the belief that God had elected David and his descendants to be the eternal rulers of Israel (2 Sam. 7). Furthermore, at the same time God had elected the city as the divine dwelling place forever. Once Solomon built the Temple, God took up residence there and was enthroned above the cherubim in the Holy of Holies. Because of God's eternal presence in the Temple, both the city and the Temple were inviolable. This belief in the eternal election and invulnerability of Jerusalem was celebrated in Israel's worship (Pss. 2, 42, 46, 78, 110, 132) and was accepted, at least in modified form, by some of Israel's prophets. Isaiah, for example, held that God might punish the city but would not finally destroy it. There would always be a remnant after the judgment, and a Davidic king would always remain on the throne (Isa. 7:10–25; 8:1–10; 28:1–22; 29:1–24; 30:15–28; 33:1–24). Even during the last days of the siege the prophetic opponents of Jeremiah continued to proclaim that the city was inviolable because of God's eternal dwelling in it.

However, when the city finally fell, serious questions had to be raised about this theology. Did the destruction of the city and the Temple mean that God had broken the divine promise and rejected Jerusalem and David's line? Or, even worse, had God lacked the power to defend the city against the Babylonians? These questions had a particular urgency for the Babylonian exiles, most of whom, like Ezekiel, were former officials in Jerusalem and participants in rituals that celebrated God's eternal presence. Clearly it was necessary for the exiles to find some satisfactory theological explanation for the situation in which they found themselves if they were to retain their ancestral faith.

The Person of the Prophet. Unlike Jeremiah, whose book contains a number of biographical narratives, Ezekiel is a dark and enigmatic figure in the history of prophecy. Very little is known of his personal life. He was the son of Buzi, who is otherwise unknown, and came from a priestly family. Presumably Ezekiel functioned as a priest himself until his deportation to Babylon in 597 B.C. (1:3). There he was settled near Nippur at Tel-abib (3:15), a site whose name suggests that it was an ancient ruin pressed into service as a settlement for the exiles. He was married, although his wife suddenly died just before the fall of Jerusalem (24:15–18). Nothing is known of his fate after his last dated oracle. Postbiblical sources do supply accounts of his death, but these are usually considered unreliable.

Even though the book of Ezekiel contains little biographical information, it does shed a great deal of light on the prophet's behavior, much of which appears bizarre to modern readers. As a prophet he was the recipient of elaborate visions (chaps. 1–3, 8–11, 40–48) in which he was sometimes transported from one place to another. He is said to have performed strange symbolic acts (chaps. 4–5), some of which appear to be physically impossible. In some of his oracles (e.g., chap. 7), his words appear irrational, and he seems to have lost all self-control. When God commands the prophet to act, he seems unable to do so until he has been energized by the spirit (2:2). Finally, from his call until the fall of Jerusalem he claims to have been bound, confined to his house, and struck dumb (3:22–27; 33:21–22).

To many modern commentators, Ezekiel's strange behavior appears pathological, and there have been a number of attempts to discover the specific psychological and physiological diseases from which he suffered. Such procedures are always risky when ancient texts are involved and, in addition, overlook the probability that the entire book is a literary creation. However, to say this is not to imply that the book is a work of fiction. It is likely that the behavior and experiences described had a basis in reality. But it is also likely that they have been elaborated in writing for the benefit of the exilic audience. If so, then the narratives might yield information about the prophet's actual behavior, but they are better interpreted literarily for the light that they might shed on his overall message, the communication of which was the prophet's goal from the beginning. The descriptions of bizarre behavior may well have been part of the message that Ezekiel wished to convey.

The Original Audience. The book provides overwhelming evidence that Ezekiel prophesied only in Babylon, where his audience would have consisted of his fellow exiles. He presumably also had a small band of disciples that accepted his prophetic authority, revered his message, and preserved his words for later generations. His primary audience would therefore have been the former elite of Jerusalem, including a number of government officials, scribes, and priests. This would have been a relatively well educated audience and one well versed in the religious traditions of Jerusalem.

The fact that Ezekiel sometimes directs his oracles to the people in Jerusalem rather than to the Babylonian exiles has led some scholars to argue that he, in fact, traveled back and forth between the two locations. To support this line of reasoning they point to the prophet's detailed knowledge of events in the Temple (chaps. 8–11) and to the resemblances between his oracles and those of his Jerusalemite contemporary, Jeremiah. However, prophets often address oracles to people who are not present, and there is no reason to suppose that Ezekiel felt constrained to be in the actual presence of the people to whom he was speaking. As for his knowledge of events in Jerusalem, including the oracles of Jeremiah, the book of Jeremiah itself indicates that there was a lively exchange of correspondence between the community in Jerusalem and the exiles. Jeremiah wrote letters to some of the exiles, and in turn exiled religious leaders wrote to Jerusalem to complain about Jeremiah's prophecies, of which they obviously knew (Jer. 29). There is therefore no reason to suppose that Ezekiel ever prophesied outside of Babylon. He returned to Jerusalem only in his visions, but he very likely kept in touch with events in Jerusalem, about which he and all the rest of the exiles would have been greatly concerned.

Ezekiel as a Literary Work

Many of the interpretive problems connected with the book of Ezekiel stem from its unusual character as a literary composition. On the one hand, the book gives an overall impression of structural unity. On the other hand, the individual oracles are quite unlike those in earlier prophetic books. Where the oracles of earlier prophets are usually relatively brief and coherent, those of Ezekiel are often long, highly ornamented, repetitious, convoluted, and sometimes obscure. An understanding of the book's message must be based on a thorough understanding of how the book came to be in its present literary form.

Structure and Contents. Three major structural devices are used to give coherent shape to the book of Ezekiel. First, the book makes extensive use of dates to mark important events and oracles, and these dates indicate that the book is organized chronologically. The book opens with the earliest event (ca. 593 B.C.), the prophet's call (1:1–3; 3:16). The next dated event (592 B.C.) is the great Temple vision, which definitively explains to the prophet the fate of Jerusalem (8:1). The prophet's important account of the history of Israel's sin (chap. 20) is dated to 591 B.C. The beginning of Jerusalem's siege (24:1) is dated in 588 B.C., while the various oracles against foreign nations (chaps. 25–32) bear dates between 587 and 585. News of Jerusalem's fall (33:21) is said to have reached Babylon in 585, and the eschatological vision of the restored Temple (chaps. 40–48) is assigned a date of 573. This neat chronological arrangement is disturbed only by the later revision of an oracle against Tyre (29:17), which bears the date of 571.

The chronological ordering of material in the book is reinforced by a second structuring device, the arrangement of oracles and visions according to content. Thus chaps. 1–24 contain primarily words of judgment against Judah and Jerusalem, while chaps. 34–48 record primarily words of promise to the exiles. This last section is immediately preceded by the pivotal chap. 33, which repeats the prophet's call and records the news of Jerusalem's fall. Between these two large units containing words of doom and salvation respectively, the prophet has inserted a collection of oracles against foreign nations (chaps. 25–32). These chapters serve as a transition between the oracles of judgment (chaps. 1–24) and the oracles of promise (chaps. 34–48) by sharing the character of both their neighbors. On the one hand, the oracles against foreign nations contain words of judgment directed at Israel's enemies just as the preceding chapters speak of judgment against Israel. On the other hand, the announcement of disaster to Israel's foes functions obliquely as a promise to Israel, just as the following chapters contain explicit promises to Israel.

This organization of the book according to content is not perfect. There are a few words of promise mixed in with the oracles of judgment in the first part of the book (11:14–21; 16:60–62; 17:22–24), and this section also contains calls for the people to repent (14:6; 18:30–32). Similarly, the words of promise in the latter part of the book are occasionally mixed with references to judgment (e.g., 34:1–10; 36:16–32). Nevertheless, readers are left with the overall impression

that, up to the time of the fall of Jerusalem, Ezekiel spoke mainly words of judgment and that after the fall he switched to words of promise. The organization of the book thus reinforces two of the most prominent themes found in the individual oracles. First, Jerusalem is destined to be destroyed for its sin, and nothing can be done to save it. There can be no talk of salvation until after the judgment has occurred. Second, after Israel has been punished, God will be faithful to the promises made to David and will restore Jerusalem's status as the eternal divine dwelling place. In spite of their severe punishment, both the people and the city remain God's elect.

Finally, a measure of literary structure is achieved in the book through the use of repetitive images and words. This device is used on many levels, but the most obvious example is the verbatim repetition of part of the prophet's call narrative (3:16–21; 33:1–9), the second occurrence of which marks a crucial shift in the prophet's message. Connected with this example are the narratives of the onset and removal of the prophet's dumbness (3:22–27; 33:21–22), which are also correlated with the two reports of the prophet's call and with the fall of Jerusalem. Equally important from a theological standpoint are the three long vision reports, which are closely linked linguistically and thematically. The first vision describes the appearance of God's glory in Babylon and provides the occasion for the prophet's call (chaps. 1–3). The second vision graphically portrays the judgment on Jerusalem and the Temple and the movement of the divine glory out of the sinful city (chaps. 8–11). This vision serves as the introduction to the longest and most complex of Ezekiel's oracles of judgment. Finally, the third vision (chaps. 40–48) summarizes the oracles of promise and describes the return of the divine glory to a rebuilt and reconsecrated Temple.

The various literary devices that have been used to structure the book reinforce each other, so that readers' overall impression is one of unity. The book has been carefully organized at some stage of its compositional history, and that organization itself conveys part of the prophet's message.

Process of Composition. Given the overall impression of unity that the book of Ezekiel makes on readers, it is not surprising that since antiquity interpreters have treated the book as the work of a single author. Even with the rise of modern critical scholarship in the middle of the nineteenth century, the book managed to escape scholarly dissection. When critics gradually came to believe that Israelite prophets originally gave their oracles orally and that oral prophecies were by necessity brief and compact, it was clear that Ezekiel did not fit this typical pattern. Scholars therefore concluded that Ezekiel must have composed his oracles originally in writing, intending them to be read and studied rather than heard. To be sure, some scholars believed that the present Masoretic Text (MT) of Ezekiel had been corrupted during the process of transmission, and they therefore sought to restore the original text, usually on the basis of the Septuagint (LXX). However, they did not challenge the basic consensus that Ezekiel was the product of a single authorial mind.

When the challenge finally came, it came not on literary grounds but on religious grounds. Some scholars began to believe that ecstasy was a basic part of the prophetic experience and that literature created while the prophet was in an ecstatic state must necessarily be poetic. This romantic notion led scholars to be suspicious of prosaic passages in prophetic books and encouraged the elimination of such passages as later additions. When these critics looked at Ezekiel in this light, they saw clear signs of ecstasy coupled with long, repetitious, and very unpoetic oracles. The conclusion to be drawn was clear. The prosaic passages in the book must be the work of the prophet's disciples or later editors, and an attempt must be made to remove these editorial layers to recapture Ezekiel's original words. With some variations, this approach to the book has dominated biblical scholarship in the twentieth century and is best represented in the mammoth commentary of Walther Zimmerli (see Bibliography below).

However, there are several problems with this sort of approach to the book. First, the various applications of this form of research have produced little agreement on what in the book is original to the prophet and what is the work of the disciples. While this fact in and of itself does not invalidate the method of research being used, it does prompt the interpreter to despair of ever achieving definitive results. Second, the theory that the book consists of a collection of original oracles augmented sporadically by later editors conflicts with the book's rather cohesive literary structure. On the whole, the book does not appear to be the product of random editing. Finally, there are no good reasons for thinking that the oracles in the book were originally in oral form and at least three good reasons for suspecting that Ezekiel was a written composition from the beginning.

The first reason for treating Ezekiel as an original written composition is that while the prophet is often told to deliver oracles to the people, he is rarely portrayed as doing so. Instead he is pictured sitting in his house and restricting his activities among the people. This point cannot be pressed too far, but the description of the prophet may be indicative of a shift away from earlier modes of prophetic activity. Second, the assumption that Ezekiel was written from the beginning can easily account for the complex oracles and symbolic acts that the book contains. While complex prophecies are difficult to deliver orally and hard for hearers to understand, written prophecies are easily elaborated and invite careful and repeated study. Finally, the physical limitations that the exile placed on prophets like Ezekiel and Second Isaiah (Isa. 40–55) would have encouraged the production of written prophecy. Before the Exile, prophets could go to the nation's capital or to a major shrine and deliver oral prophecies addressed to the whole nation. With the Exile, however, Israel was scattered throughout Israel, Egypt, and Babylon. Communication would have been impossible or at least severely hampered without writing. The geographic dispersion of Israel would probably have encouraged prophets to write down their oracles and distribute them to the widely separated Israelite communities rather than try to rely on traditional oral methods of delivery.

Considerations such as these have led some scholars in recent years to revive the older theory that Ezekiel was first composed by the prophet in writing during the period indicated by the dates in the book. This approach has been applied most successfully in the commentary of Moshe Greenberg (see Bibliography below) and will be adopted in the commentary that follows. It will be assumed that Ezekiel initially created his prophecies in written form, although he or his disciples may have subsequently revised them in the light of changing conditions or later revelations. For the most part such later editorial activity is difficult to detect, and no systematic attempt will be made to treat any but the most obvious cases. The period of composition is assumed to be that delineated by the book itself, although there are a few examples of much later material.

Literary Style: Prophecy in Search of Form. It is not clear precisely when the transition took place in Israel between prophecy that was originally oral and prophecy that was originally written. Early prophetic books, such as Amos, still show signs of oral composition, while the latest ones, such as Haggai, Zechariah, and Malachi, were clearly produced first in writing. Precisely where Ezekiel fits in this spectrum is uncertain, but it is likely that he was a major transitional figure. As the first exilic prophet, he had to come to grips with both the limitations and the possibilities that writing offers. On the negative side, writing makes prophecy less malleable and less able to respond quickly to new situations and new audiences. After a certain point, written prophecies tend not to be altered but rather to be interpreted. On the positive side, writing permits a more detailed elaboration of the material and opens up the possibility of creating new literary forms. The result is a powerful and effective means of communicating the prophet's message.

As one of the first to produce written prophecy, Ezekiel had few models to guide him in his search for forms appropriate to the new medium. To be sure, there were the traditional patterns that prophets had followed in creating spoken oracles, and he could and did develop those. But he also experimented with new forms, some of which influenced later prophetic writings and some of which left little trace in later literature.

Autobiographical Narrative.

Among the biblical prophets who left books, Amos was the first to try to communicate the divine word by recounting his own experiences with God. In the prophet's vision reports (Amos 7–9), he described to his hearers his encounters with God and embedded his oracles in this narrative context. Similarly, Hosea used an account of his marriage to portray to his audience the relationship between Israel and God (Hos. 3:1–5), and Jeremiah used autobiography to report his reactions to his prophetic task (e.g., Jer. 11:18–12:13). However, in all three of these cases biographical narratives are also employed, and in the case of Jeremiah they dominate a large portion of the book (Amos 7:10–15; Hos. 1:2–11; Jer. 20–52). However, Ezekiel develops the autobiographical approach in a massive way. With the exception of 1:2–3, the entire book takes the form of a first-person narrative. No one else talks about the prophet; rather, he tells his own story. Furthermore, in his extensive vision reports, he leads his readers through the vision as he himself experienced it. Even though he may understand in retrospect the significance of what he saw, he resists the temptation to summarize or interpret for members of his audience. Rather, he allows an awareness to dawn on them just as it had dawned on him. By using this method, the prophet is better able to convince his readers of the truth of his message.

In addition to using the autobiographical narrative literally, Ezekiel sometimes uses it symbolically. His life and behavior become signs that his readers must interpret just as they must interpret his words. This phenomenon is particularly noticeable in his prophetic actions (e.g., chaps. 4–5), where everything that the prophet does takes on a larger significance. These acts are sometimes highly developed literarily, with the result that Ezekiel describes his actions as if he were a character in a surrealistic drama. Even the prophet's "normal" behavior at times has a symbolic quality to it that invites study and analysis.

Older Prophetic Traditions.

Ezekiel was, of course, heir to Israel's prophetic traditions and drew from them literary and thematic material, which he then transformed. His prophetic roots are particularly clear at the literary level. Thus, for example, he introduces his oracles with a standard prophetic formula, modified slightly to fit his autobiographical format: "Thus said the Lord [to me]." He adopts from earlier prophecy the divine oath ("as I live said/says the Lord") and often uses it to reinforce the truth of a prophecy. Ezekiel takes over the vision report, which was employed sparingly in earlier prophetic traditions, and uses it to compose a major part of his book (chaps. 1–3; 8–11; 40–48). In chaps. 8–11 and 40–48 he also introduces the figure of a heavenly guide who leads the prophet through the vision and supplies necessary interpretation. Such guides eventually became a routine part of vision reports, appearing in Zechariah, Daniel, and a number of postbiblical apocalypses. Ezekiel makes considerable use of accounts of symbolic prophetic acts. Such acts had appeared occasionally in earlier prophecy, but Ezekiel's descriptions are much more highly elaborated than those of his predecessors (cf. chaps. 4–5). Finally, he continues to use the old prophetic literary pattern usually called "the announcement of judgment to the individual." Oracles of this sort usually begin with a description of the addressee's crime, often using verbs in participial form, and then move on to an announcement of the penalty, typically introduced by the messenger formula ("thus said/says the Lord"). Lying behind some of the prophet's most complex oracles is this simple pattern, which was a basic part of prophetic speech at least as early as Amos.

In addition to developing older prophetic speech patterns, Ezekiel also drew on the prophetic traditions themselves. One of the models that shaped his work was certainly the prophetic story, a number of which may be found in the books of Samuel and Kings. The fact that these stories were already in written form when Ezekiel used them made their appropriation relatively simple, and as a result there are numerous thematic and linguistic links between Ezekiel and the earlier prophetic narratives. Similarly Ezekiel seems to have known of the work of Hosea and Jeremiah, two prophets outside of Ezekiel's own theological tradition. From them, as well as from the books of Samuel and Kings, he drew their characteristic emphasis on the covenant, as well as the notion that God's promises to Jerusalem were contingent on the behavior of the people.

New Literary Forms.

In addition to elaborating older prophetic literary forms, Ezekiel also developed new ones. Earlier prophets had used a number of vivid literary images and figures of speech to help communicate their messages, but Ezekiel enormously extended the range and complexity of the images that he used. He created a highly metaphorical type of discourse that closely resembles what modern readers would recognize as allegory (e.g., chaps. 16–17). These "allegories" are so complex that they are sometimes difficult to interpret, and the situation is not helped by the prophet's tendency to lose control of his images by allowing the underlying historical reality or the prophet's own theological perspective to skew them beyond recognition. Yet even though the prophet seems not to have completely mastered this new form, his work influenced later biblical writings (e.g., Dan. 2, 7–12).

Ezekiel also seems to have been the originator of the "disputation oracle." Such oracles usually begin with the quotation of a saying current in the community that the prophet is addressing. The common wisdom expressed in the saying is then vigorously refuted, sometimes by the citation of cases expressed in legal form (e.g., Ezek. 12:21–28; 18:1–32; 33:10–20).

One of the most characteristic inventions of Ezekiel is the "proof-saying," the components of which he took from older traditions and applied to prophetic oracles. The proof-saying is marked by the use of the formula "and you will know that I am Yahweh," which is attached to God's first-person account of a divine action. It is employed frequently in judgment oracles, where God concludes the announcement of judgment by announcing that the promised disaster will reveal God to the people. The people are assured that they will encounter God in judgment, which cannot be interpreted as the result of impersonal natural forces.

Priestly Tradition. Because of his priestly background, Ezekiel was thoroughly familiar with ritual language and with priestly law, so it is not surprising that he used this language in formulating his oracles. In addition, many members of his original audience must have originally had connections with the Temple, so the prophet's use of priestly terminology would have been a particularly effective means of communication. Priestly vocabulary abounds in the book, and there are particularly close ties with the priestly law code known as the "Holiness Code" (Lev. 18–26). The links here are so strong that some scholars have suggested that Ezekiel was actually the author of the code. However, it is more likely that both the prophet and the code have been strongly influenced by ancient priestly legal traditions.

Literary Elaboration. Throughout this discussion of Ezekiel's literary style it has often been noted that he tended to elaborate any literary form that he used. This elaboration is so characteristic of the prophet that it deserves comment in its own right. Ezekiel's writing is baroque. It is thoroughly ornamented, filled with detail, convoluted, and often repetitious. His arguments, descriptions, and allegories are easily diverted from their course, with the result that they sometimes appear to ramble and to be logically inconsistent. These characteristics have often been traced to crude editorial work by Ezekiel's disciples or to textual corruptions introduced by later scribes. However, it is more likely that the text simply reflects the way that the prophet wrote. His peculiar, ornate style must always be kept in mind whenever an attempt is made to interpret his oracles.

The Text of the Book. The Hebrew text of Ezekiel is often thought to be poorly preserved, although this judgment is usually made without taking into account the prophet's peculiar literary style. The Greek translation (LXX) is often more compact than the MT and frequently omits duplicated material and ornamentation. In the LXX the prophet's arguments are often clearer, and apparent inconsistencies are removed. This fact has led many scholars to assume that the LXX is based on a Hebrew text that lacked the corruptions of the present MT, and they have therefore used the Greek to reconstruct the original Hebrew.

However, it is also possible that the translators of the LXX were simply doing the best that they could with a difficult Hebrew text. The differences between the two versions may simply reflect the efforts of later communities to present a coherent translation. In short, the LXX may represent an attempt at communication and interpretation rather than a more original text. It is not currently possible to decide between these two alternatives, and for this reason the commentary that follows uses the MT as its base. Only in a few cases will alternative readings be suggested on the basis of the ancient versions.

Ezekiel's Message and the Exilic Crisis

Despite the complexity of the book of Ezekiel, the prophet's message is relatively simple and can be easily summarized. The city of Jerusalem and the people of Judah would inevitably be punished because of their sins, which were both religious and social. Not only was the current generation sinful and deserving of punishment, but the entire history of Israel had been a history of disobedience and rebellion against God (chap. 20). Repentance might still save individuals who led a righteous life (chap. 18), but the righteous few, if they existed at all, could not save the rest of the nation. This message applied both to the deportees of 597 B.C. and to the people who remained in the land.

Yet, in spite of this unequivocal message of doom, Ezekiel also prophesied that after the city had been destroyed and the people punished, God would bring the exiles back to the land, and the Temple would be restored according to a divine plan (chaps. 40–48). However, the return will be a pure act of grace. God will bring the people back in order not to profane the divine name (36:16–32). In contrast to Jeremiah, who believed that the Exile would cause Israel to recognize its sins and repent and that because of this repentance God would restore the people to the land (Jer. 31:16–22), Ezekiel was pessimistic about the long-range religious effects of the Exile. Although there might be a few, including some in the prophet's own community, who might remain righteous, the bulk of the exiles did not pay attention to the prophet's message. Therefore, in Ezekiel's scenario for the return, God will first restore the people to the land to preserve the holiness of the divine name. The people will then realize what God has done. They will repent and live faithfully in the land, newly purified from their sin.

Ezekiel's general message also contains some explicit answers to the practical theological questions that were raised by the fall of Jerusalem and the Exile. First, the fall of the city did not mean that God was powerless to defend it. Rather, God had deliberately deserted the Temple so that it could be captured by the Babylonians (chaps. 8–11). Ultimately this disaster was the direct act of God and not simply the result of shifting political fortunes in the ancient Near East. At the same time, God's fidelity to Jerusalem had not been diminished. The departure of the divine glory from the city was only temporary, and God would in due time take up residence in a rebuilt and resanctified Temple.

Second, from Ezekiel's perspective the people in Babylonian exile are the true Israel, and they will be the ones to return to the land and rebuild the nation (11:14–21). Other Israelites in exile and those left in the land after the fall have been cut off from the community of faith and have no role to play in the future. This narrow view of the identity of the true Israel will be shared by many of the exiles who finally do return and will be one of the sources of the theological debates of the postexilic period.

Finally, in the face of conflicting prophetic words immediately before the fall of the city, Ezekiel lays claim to absolute prophetic authority. Throughout the book a number of literary devices are employed to support the notion that Ezekiel always speaks with divine authority. His word is in fact the direct word of God, which is delivered to his audience without human interference or interpretation. Ezekiel's prophecies are therefore a safe guide for surviving the Exile. When the exiles hear an oracle from Ezekiel, they truly know that a prophet has been among them (33:33).

COMMENTARY

1:1–3:27
Introduction to the Prophet and Prophecy

The introduction to the book of Ezekiel places the prophet in his historical context (1:1–3) and describes in extraordinary detail his initial call to prophesy (1:4–3:27). However, both the contents and literary structure of these verses also introduce some of the major themes of the prophet's message, so the call narrative can be seen as an introduction to the book as well as to the personal experiences of the prophet.

Because of the unusual length, complexity, and apparent repetitiousness of this introductory material, scholars have often seen the book's first three chapters as the work of several editors and have tried by various methods to reconstruct Ezekiel's original account of his experiences. In particular, the watchman's call (3:16–21) and the story of the prophet's dumbness (3:22–27) are usually thought to be editorial additions because material from these verses is repeated, sometimes verbatim, in chap. 33. However, there is no scholarly agreement on the original form of these chapters, and Ezekiel's normally complex and repetitious literary style should caution readers against performing radical surgery on the text. It is also likely that even clear editorial additions have a role to play in shaping the overall message of the text.

1:1–3
The Superscription

The book of Ezekiel begins with a brief autobiographical statement (v. 1) followed by an editorial comment (vv. 2–3). Together they describe the background of the prophet and the date and location of his activities. He dates his initial call to "the thirtieth year," although the precise meaning of this date is obscure. Some scholars have suggested that it refers to the age of the prophet when he received his call, although the Hebrew idiom used here is not the standard one for expressing age. Others have suggested that, like the other dates in the book, "the thirtieth year" refers to the year of King Jehoiachin's exile. If so, then it would contradict the explanation of the date given in v. 2. Furthermore, the date in v. 1 would represent the latest date in the book rather than the earliest and would place the prophet's call after his other dated oracles. This odd situation can be avoided by assuming that "the thirtieth year" refers to the date of the book's composition rather than to the prophet's call, but such an interpretation is not in harmony with the text, which clearly connects the date to the prophet's initial vision.

The Targum (a translation of the Hebrew text into Aramaic, often with accompanying interpretation) was the first to suggest that Ezekiel's call occurred thirty years after Josiah's religious reform (2 Kings 22:3). While this calculation is accurate if the explanation of v. 2 is accepted, there is no biblical evidence to suggest that Josiah's reform was used by other authors for dating important religious events. Whatever the meaning of "the thirtieth year," an editorial comment equates it with the fifth year of Jehoiachin's exile and thus places the prophet's call in July 593 B.C.

Ezekiel is identified as one of the officials exiled to Babylon during the first deportation (597 B.C.). He was a priest, presumably of Zadokite descent, and would probably have served in the Temple before his exile. His initial vision occurred beside the Chebar Canal, near the Babylonian city of Nippur, in the vicinity of which some of the exiles had been settled. The prophet further specifies the location as Tel-abib ("mound [deserted since the time] of the flood"), a site that also must have been in the neighborhood of Nippur (3:15). By the fifth century B.C. there was at Nippur a flourishing Jewish community that traced its origins to the exiles of Ezekiel's time.

The bank of a stream may have been a traditional place of worship and divine revelation during the latter part of the Exile (cf. Dan. 10:4; Ps. 137:1), but in Ezekiel's time some Israelites doubted that genuine prophecy could occur outside of Israel. Ezekiel is therefore careful to stress a theme that will recur throughout the book. His vision was clearly of divine origin and took place when God seized or possessed him. God's "hand" came upon the prophet and exercised divine control over him (cf. 1 Kings 18:46). Elsewhere in Ezekiel God's hand or Spirit will energize the prophet and leave no doubt that his words and deeds are not his own but come directly from God (Ezek. 3:22; 8:1; 37:1; 40:1). Ezekiel is a human agent, who is compelled to do God's will.

1:4–3:21
The Call of the Prophet

Israelite prophets did not always record their initial encounter with God, and when they did do so they tended to be relatively brief (cf. Amos 7:14–15; Isa. 6:1–13; Jer. 1:1–10). In contrast, Ezekiel devotes the better part of three chapters to describing his call. Although some of this extensive description may be the result of later reflection and elaboration on the meaning of his initial experience, challenges to the prophet's authority may also have prompted him to give an unusually detailed account. Ezekiel's words would have lacked credibility not only because he was prophesying on foreign soil, but also because his prophetic message challenged many of the fundamental beliefs of his audience.

Ezekiel's call seems to have taken place in two stages. During the first stage the prophet saw his initial vision (1:4–28), was commissioned to be a prophet to Israel, and was given an indication of the contents of his message (2:1–3:15). In the second stage, which followed the first by seven days, he was called to be a watchman for the house of Israel (3:16–21).

1:4–28, The Throne Vision. The MT of the prophet's initial vision is occasionally repetitious and contains what appear to be dislocated phrases. For this reason, most scholars assume that the account has been secondarily elaborated, either by Ezekiel himself or by later editors. However, there is no scholarly agreement about the nature or even the location of these elaborations, so it is best simply to follow the text as it now stands. In spite of occasional roughness in the MT, the general outline of the vision is clear, and there can be no doubt about what the prophet saw. In the vision he came face to face with God's glory, the overwhelming radiance that surrounds the Deity (→ Glory).

As he does in his other major visions (cf. 8:2–11:25; 40:1–48:35), Ezekiel here recreates the experience as it occurred rather than first summarizing or interpreting it. He thus forces the reader to repeat the prophetic experience and to share the prophet's growing comprehension of the vision's significance.

At first the prophet saw only a glowing storm cloud being blown by a strong north wind. As the cloud drew nearer, however, he realized that the glow was in fact a cloud of fire, in the midst of which he gradually perceived four strange creatures. Each of them had a vaguely human form, but they each also had four wings and four different faces. Their feet were bovine, and they had human hands under their wings. They were arranged in a square, with their wing tips touching, and as a result they could face all of the cardinal points at the same time and could move in any direction without turning. In the midst of the creatures was an awesome brightness that flashed like lightning. Beneath the creatures were sparkling wheels that touched the earth. Each wheel contained all-seeing eyes and was composed of a "wheel within a wheel," either two different-sized wheels in the same plane like the hub and rim of a wagon wheel or, more likely, two identical wheels at right-angles to each other to facilitate movement in all directions. As the creatures drew nearer, Ezekiel was able for the first time to hear the roar of their wings and to see above them a crystalline expanse on which rested the likeness of a throne (→ Firmament; Throne). On the throne was the glowing likeness of a human form, and the prophet then knew that he was seeing "the appearance of the likeness of the glory of God." When Ezekiel realized what he was seeing, he fell on his face to the ground.

Scholars have made a number of attempts to probe beyond the prophet's description to uncover its underlying reality. Some have claimed that he saw only an electrical storm and then elaborated what he saw with his own imaginative details. Other scholars have pointed to artistic representations of fantastic animals and chariots that bore the images of some ancient Near Eastern deities. More specifically, scholars have argued that Ezekiel had in mind the Temple cherubim, the winged creatures flanking the Ark above which God was enthroned (cf. 1 Sam. 4:4; 2 Sam. 6:2; 1 Kings 6:27; Pss. 80:1; 99:1) (→ Ark; Cherub).

To be sure, Ezekiel's vision was shaped by motifs from Israelite tradition and was deeply rooted in his own priestly background. Fire, storm, and wind are often said to accompany God's appearance (cf. Exod. 19; Deut. 33:2; Judg. 5:4–5; Pss. 18:7–15; 68:7–10), and the prophet's knowledge of the Temple cherubim helped him to recognize what he was seeing in his vision. However, the description in the vision cannot be taken too literally, for the prophet constantly reminds his readers that the images used to describe the vision only approximate what he actually saw. He often uses the terms "appearance" and "likeness" to remind his audience that his description is not exact, and he employs in his description a number of evocative but incorporeal words having to do with brightness and fire. Like his Jerusalemite predecessor Isaiah, who saw the Temple cherubim transformed into flaming seraphim (Isa. 6), Ezekiel sees natural objects that have taken on supernatural dimensions. The visionary combination of vague, evocative images with concrete but fantastic objects helps the prophet to describe the divine reality that he saw but that cannot ultimately be described.

The theological significance of the vision is not elaborated until Ezekiel's later vision of Jerusalem's destruction (Ezek. 8–11). However, Ezekiel's original readers could not have failed to recognize that he had seen God's divine throne, normally located in Jerusalem, come to rest on Babylonian soil. For a Zadokite priest, who believed in God's eternal presence in Jerusalem, this would have been a shocking idea and one that would require additional explanation. However, at this point in the book it is not clear whether God's appearance has positive or negative implications for the exiles. That question will ultimately be answered only as the book progresses, but a partial answer is given in the divine word that follows the initial vision.

2:1–3:15, The Prophet's Commission. After Ezekiel recognizes the significance of his vision, he hears God's voice for the first time (1:28–2:1). Having fallen to the earth at the conclusion of the vision, the prophet is now commanded to rise. He is addressed, as he is throughout the book, with a title often translated literally "son of man." In Ezekiel's time this title had none of the theological overtones it was later to acquire and simply means "one who is a member of the human species." The address thus emphasizes the contrast between the human prophet and the divine glory. However, in spite of the divine command to rise, Ezekiel is unable to do so until the Spirit sets him on his feet (2:2). The motif of the enabling Spirit is found throughout the book and gives rise to the curious picture of a prophet who seems incapable of carrying out his prophetic tasks without divine aid. He speaks only the divine word that is put in his mouth and does only what the Spirit enables him to do (cf. 3:27). By portraying Ezekiel in this way, the book underlines the point that he has no control over his prophetic activities. Everything that he does or says comes directly from God, and the prophet does not interfere with the divine message in any way. Unlike the illegitimate prophets of whom Jeremiah speaks (Jer. 23:30), Ezekiel cannot be accused of stealing other prophets' words or giving his own interpretation of what God said. Ezekiel's readers know from the beginning of the book that they are reading only the word of God.

The content of the divine message is clear as soon as the prophet receives his commission. After being told to prophesy to the rebellious house of Israel, both to the people in exile and to those who remain in the land, the prophet is commanded to eat a scroll, which is filled with words of mourning, lamentation, and woe. He does so and reports that the scroll tastes sweet, in spite of its devastating contents (2:10–3:3). This striking episode seems to be the literary reflection of a statement made by Jeremiah in one of his complaints: "Your words were found, and I ate them, and your words became to me a joy and the delight of my heart" (Jer. 15:16). While Jeremiah's original statement expressed his own prophetic experience and explained why he was willing to continue to act as God's prophet (Jer. 15:15, 17–18), Ezekiel's literary development of the statement has an entirely different function. By speaking of eating the scroll, Ezekiel again indicates that his announcements of coming disaster are not his own but are dictated by God, who has literally put the divine words into the prophet. Because the divine word is in written form, the image also implies that the entirety of the writing of Ezekiel, that is, the whole book, is of divine origin. Just as Jeremiah delivered a scroll of his oracles to the king of Judah to see whether God's word would be accepted or rejected (Jer. 36), so also Ezekiel delivers to the exiles and to other Israelite communities a prophetic book to which they must respond.

The remainder of the commissioning narrative in fact concentrates not on the dismal contents of the prophet's message but on the people's reaction to it. God's initial address to the prophet characterizes as rebels the people who will read or hear his words, and this description is repeated throughout the remainder of the narrative. The phrase "for they are a rebellious house" echoes like a refrain in these verses (Ezek. 2:5, 7; 3:9) and clearly implies that the success of Ezekiel's work is in doubt. God is giving the people one more chance to hear the announcement of certain destruction and to save themselves by repenting, but God also has little hope that the people will listen. Instead, it is likely that the people will actively oppose Ezekiel and will thereby seal their own fate, making divine judgment inevitable. For this reason God warns the prophet to resist popular opposition and promises to strengthen and protect him during the ordeal that lies ahead.

The reasons for opposition to Ezekiel's message of judgment are easily understood, for he addressed his words both to his fellow exiles in Babylon and to the people who remained in Jerusalem. The former group may well have felt that it had already experienced God's judgment and should now be forgiven and brought back to the land (cf. 18:1–32). The latter group agreed that the exiles had been punished but also felt that the people left in the land had been spared and could now claim special status as God's elect (cf. 11:15). In contrast to these two views, Ezekiel prophesied that both groups were still rebels, and both were required to repent to save themselves. The ultimate failure of the prophet's mission thus seems to have been assured from the start.

3:16–21, The Watchman's Call. Many scholars feel that the narrative of Ezekiel's second call is redundant after the initial call vision (1:4–3:15). In addition, these verses are repeated in a more elaborate and sometimes clearer form in 33:1–9, where they seem to mark a new phase in the prophet's career following the fall of Jerusalem. For this reason scholars tend to see the watchman's call as a secondary addition based on material found in chaps. 18 and 33. However, even if these verses are accepted as a later editorial expansion, it is still necessary to try to understand why they were inserted in their present location and how they modify the narrative that they follow.

According to the book's own chronology, Ezekiel was overwhelmed by his initial vision for a period of seven days (3:15). At the end of that time, God again spoke to the prophet and appointed him to be a watchman for the house of Israel. The image of the watchman is used elsewhere of the prophetic office (Jer. 6:16–21), and its meaning in such contexts is clear. Like a watchman on a city wall, the prophet is to warn the people of an approaching enemy (2 Sam. 18:24–27; 2 Kings 9:17–20). However, a curious feature of the use of the image in Ezekiel is that God is both the one who appoints the protective watchman and the one against whom the people must be protected.

This unusual situation immediately becomes apparent when God gives Ezekiel examples of a prophetic watchman at work. These examples are framed in legal language, presumably drawn from Ezekiel's priestly tradition, and describe the various situations that might occur when God pronounces a formal death sentence against an individual. Four cases are considered: first, the wicked person who does not repent because the prophet has not issued a warning; second, the wicked person who does not repent even though the prophet has issued a warning; third, the righteous person who turns away from righteousness and does not repent because the prophet has not issued a warning; and fourth, the righteous person who remains righteous because the prophet has issued a warning. The case of the wicked person who repents after hearing the watchman's warning is omitted, possibly an indication that Ezekiel did not really expect this case to occur.

These cases are unusual in that they do not emphasize the watchman's success or failure in bringing about repentance. Rather they are concerned with whether or not the watchman actually issues a prophetic warning. The prophet who issues such a warning saves his own life, while the prophet who does not issue a warning bears the responsibility for the death of the wicked. The call narrative thus sharply emphasizes the warnings against prophetic rebellion that were present in the initial call vision (2:8) and underlines the importance of the prophet's persistence in his task, even though he sees no apparent results. In this way the narrative further stresses the initial call vision's doubts about the effectiveness of the prophet's mission. As chap. 4 makes clear, God has issued a sentence of death against the city of Jerusalem, and Ezekiel must warn the people of the danger. However, there seems to be little hope of saving the city.

3:22–27
The Prophet's Dumbness

Of all of the difficult passages in Ezekiel, the narratives of the onset and removal of the prophet's dumbness have provoked the widest range of interpretations, none of which is totally satisfactory. The sources of the difficulty are readily apparent. According to Ezekiel's own account, immediately after his second call he was possessed by God and told to go to "the valley." There the divine glory appeared to the prophet, as it had in chap. 1, and he responded in his typical fashion by falling stunned to the ground. After being raised by the Spirit (cf. 1:28–2:2), Ezekiel was commanded to shut himself up in his house. He was then told that he would be bound so that he could not go out among the people and that he would be struck dumb so that he could not act as a "reprover" to them. However, God promised that Ezekiel's mouth would be opened when there was a divine word to be given to the people (3:22–27). According to the book's own chronology, this dumbness lasted until the fall of Jerusalem, a period of more than seven years. The removal of the dumbness is narrated in the context of a repetition of the prophet's call to be a watchman, so that both the call and the opening of the prophet's mouth are clearly correlated with the city's destruction (33:21–22; cf. 24:26–27).

The immediate literary context makes it difficult to understand the dumbness literally, for in chap. 4 the prophet begins a series of oracles against the people and against Jerusalem, reproving both for their sins. Later in the book he issues calls to repent (14:6; 18:21, 30–32; 33:11), a fact that indicates that his speech consisted of more than the delivery of announcements of doom. This has led many scholars to assume that the dumbness was somehow symbolic or that it lasted only a few hours or days, perhaps being brought on by the sudden death of the prophet's wife and the traumatic events surrounding Jerusalem's fall (24:15–27). Others have suggested that Ezekiel actually suffered from some physiological or psychological malady. However, none of these explanations helps to interpret the narrative in its present location in chap. 3.

Like other problematic passages in Ezekiel, this one is perhaps best interpreted as a literary expression of a prophetic experience that caused the prophet to have a new understanding of his call. The prophet's confinement to his house may reflect the fact that he did not deliver his oracles orally in public as did earlier prophets but produced them first in writing (cf. 8:1; 14:1; 20:1). The dumbness may indicate that from his call until the fall of Jerusalem Ezekiel spoke only words of judgment against the city and reserved his calls to repent for the exiles. This interpretation would generally be in keeping with the present literary organization of the book, which places most of the judgment oracles before the narrative of the fall of Jerusalem in chap. 33 and locates most of the oracles of promise after this point. In addition, the dumbness may indicate that, for this period of time, the prophet did not exercise one of his normal prophetic functions, perhaps that of interceding on behalf of the city and the people. Later in the book he is explicitly forbidden to intercede for the people (14:3–5; 20:3), and they are again allowed to approach God through the prophet only after the city falls (36:37).

4:1–24:27
Prophecies of Judgment Against Judah and Jerusalem

After the introduction of the prophet and his message, the next section of the book concentrates on announcements of the disasters that are about to happen to Jerusalem, to the rest of the people in Judah, and to the people already in exile. Although there are occasional promises in these chapters, there is a pervasive feeling of impending doom. From the beginning it is clear that the destruction of Jerusalem is inevitable, and nothing that the people can do will alter this situation.

4:1–5:17
Symbolic Acts of Judgment

The announcement of Jerusalem's fate is introduced by narratives of several symbolic actions that were performed by the prophet. However, unlike the symbolic acts of earlier prophets, which were brief, pointed, and designed to have an immediate impact on the audience (cf. Isa. 20:1–6; Jer. 13:1–11; 19:1–13; 27:1–11), Ezekiel's symbolic acts are literary representations of the originals. As literary representations, they tend to be highly complex and well developed. They are meant to be read and studied, and the point they make is not always immediately clear. Their complexity also invites later reinterpretation by the prophet, his disciples, and later generations of readers.

4:1–17, Symbols of Siege and Exile. The major theme, Ezekiel's announcement of judgment, is clearly stated by his first symbolic act, which portrays in miniature the coming siege against Jerusalem (4:1–3). From this point, he repeatedly assures his readers that the city and its inhabitants can in no way escape the wrath of the Babylonians. As a Babylonian architect or military commander might do, the prophet draws the city on a sun-dried brick and then sketches in mounds, ramps, and battering rams —the military installations and machines designed to seal off the city from outside relief and eventually to breach its walls (→ Battering ram; Siege). The symbolism of the act then shifts as the prophet is told to take a more personal role and to act out the enemy attack against the city. He is to place an iron plate between himself and the city and to press the siege against it. The plate is a symbol of separation and in this instance represents a barrier that exists between God and the people in Jerusalem. The inhabitants of the doomed city are to be cut off from God until the destruction is complete. The prophet's direct participation in the siege also implies that God is actively involved in the attack on the city.

In 4:4–8 Ezekiel is made to bear symbolically the punishment that is to be laid on the people. First he is commanded to lie on his left side for 390 days to represent the number of years that the house of Israel, namely, the Northern Kingdom, must be punished (vv. 4–5). The interpretation of these verses is problematic, and the number has puzzled interpreters since antiquity. The sudden use of the name "Israel" in its narrow sense as a reference to the Northern Kingdom, destroyed by the Assyrians in 722–721 B.C., is unexpected, since the remainder of the unit concentrates on the imminent siege and exile of the Southern Kingdom of Judah. The period of 390 years is not susceptible to any satisfactory interpretation. The LXX contains entirely different figures. Their significance is easier to understand, but they are suspect for that very reason, and it is likely that the numbers in the MT are original, whatever their meaning. If 390 years are calculated backwards from the prophet's own time, then the period of punishment would have begun about the time the Temple was built by Solomon. Thus the whole history of the north would have to be seen as a period of punishment, a proposition that makes no sense. If the 390 years are calculated from the fall of Samaria in 722/721 B.C., then the prophet would be indicating a period of punishment that would end much later than the one projected for Judah. However, he explicitly rejects this interpretation elsewhere and predicts that Ephraim and Judah will be restored to the land at the same time (cf. 37:15–23).

Easier to understand is the second part of the act, which involves the prophet's lying on his right side for forty days to portray forty years of punishment and exile for Judah (vv. 6–17). This figure differs from Jeremiah's prediction of a seventy-year exile (Jer. 25:11; 29:10) but at least gives the act a plausible interpretation. The prophet is to persist in his odd and lengthy action without deviation, just as he was bound at his call to speak only the word that God gave him (cf. Ezek. 3:25–26).

In 4:9–16 Ezekiel adds additional details to his portrayal of a people suffering a siege. During his symbolic act he is to eat bread composed of a mixture of grains, there being no single grain available in sufficient quantity to make up a loaf. The prophet may drink each day only a measured quantity of water, about two-thirds of a quart. While the scarcity of food and water refers particularly to conditions in Jerusalem during the expected siege, the symbolic action has been broadened to include references to the lives of the exiles, both those who will be driven from the city and those who are already in Babylon. They are to eat ritually unclean food outside of the land. The prophet's resistance to eating bread baked on human dung was apparently a futile effort, for he was still required to eat unclean food to demonstrate the conditions of exile, something that would have been a particular violation of priestly regulations.

5:1–17, Symbols of Jerusalem's Fate.
Ezekiel's symbolic description of the fate of Jerusalem continues in a complex action (5:1–4), which is then interpreted at length for readers (5:5–17). The prophet is to cut off his hair, an act that itself represents the loss of personal identity associated with exile (cf. Isa. 7:20), and then is to divide the hair into three portions. A third he is to burn in the midst of the city that he has portrayed on the brick (4:1–2), a third he is to strike with a sword, and a third he is to scatter to the wind. From the latter portion he is to take a few hairs—presumably representing an exiled remnant such as the members of the prophet's own community—and is to preserve them, although even some of these will be burned. The interpretation of the act is clear. The treatment of the hair represents the fate of the people in the besieged city (v. 5). Because the people have rebelled against God, there will be a divine judgment against them. The city will endure the horrors of a protracted siege (v. 10), and God will this time have no pity on the people (v. 11). A third of them will die by fire during the siege, and a third will be killed by the sword. The remainder will be scattered in exile. Even there they will have no rest, for God will make them desolate and a reproach among the nations. The destructive divine fire will reach even to the remnant, which will continue to be punished as God harries the exiles with famine, disease, and bloodshed. Of

the remnant of the city driven into exile, only a smaller remnant will survive (vv. 3, 13–17). However, there may be a slight hint in the passage that the fire that burns the remnant is redemptive for the rest of Israel (v. 4).

6:1–7:27
Oracles Against Land and People

From symbolic representations of Judah's coming destruction, Ezekiel turns to prophetic words directed against the land, the people, and the city. Like the earlier prophetic actions, these words help to actualize the events of which they speak.

6:1–14, Prophecy Against the Mountains. Up to this point, the prophet has concentrated on the fate of Jerusalem and the exiles already on foreign soil. Now he is commanded to set his face toward the mountains of Israel and thus to focus his attention on the entire country—the mountains, hills, ravines, and valleys. The message for the rest of the land is identical to that delivered to Jerusalem, and the people outside the city will not be able to escape from the coming judgment. Ezekiel is to prophesy that all of the land of Israel will be devastated, a prophecy that was in fact fulfilled as the Babylonian armies advanced on Jerusalem in 587–586 B.C.

It is noteworthy that the prophet does not elaborate on the destruction of the cities themselves but concentrates instead on the destruction of the illegitimate religious installations that are the symbols of Israel's sin. He particularly singles out the platforms or high places, which were often located on hills near towns and which perhaps were used for the worship of underworld deities and deified ancestors (→ High Place). The people who in life worshiped other gods at incense altars will now be slain before those same altars, and their bones will defile Israel's illegitimate places of worship. The people have not been willing to know God through appropriate worship in the Temple or through obedience in response to God's great acts of deliverance (cf. Exod. 7:5; 14:4, 18). Therefore the people are condemned to know God only through divine punishment and destruction. God is known through the revelation of the divine name, but that revelation now leads to judgment rather than salvation (Ezek. 6:1–7; cf. Exod. 3:13–22; 20:2) (→ Knowledge).

However, just as there will be refugees from Jerusalem, so there will also be a few who survive the devastation of the land. In exile they will understand what they have done and will witness to future generations that God does indeed punish rebellion (Ezek. 6:8–10). For their benefit Ezekiel is to portray God's delight in destroying sinful Israel and the abominable ritual practices that the people have instituted (6:11–14).

7:1–27, Prophecy of the End. Ezekiel's announcement of judgment to the mountains of Israel is followed by a horrifying oracle directed at all of the inhabitants of the land. The literary structure of the oracle vividly reproduces the words of a prophet so thoroughly possessed by the divine spirit that he no longer has any control over his words or actions. He is obsessed by the judgment that he must announce. The oracle regains a degree of rationality briefly in v. 23, when God gives the reason for the destruction of the people. However, the remainder of the oracle generates its impact through the seemingly endless repetition of key words and images. The piling up of phrases gives the oracle a breathless quality as it rushes toward its crushing climax. Over and over the prophet repeats his devastating message until his words pound the reader like a hammer. Disaster approaches. An end has come upon the land. Doom is near. God will not spare any of the people and will not pity them. The people are helpless against the approaching enemy. Prophets, priests, elders, and king are terrified and can do nothing. God will be known to Israel only in the irreversible judgment that will repay the people for their sins.

The passage has roots in a number of prophetic traditions, particularly those dealing with the "Day of the Lord," the time when God would appear to confront Israel for good or ill. This concept seems to have been well known as early as the eighth century B.C., but the prophet Amos first gave it the strongly negative overtones that it retains in most of the prophetic literature (Amos 5:18–20; 8:1–14). The disciples of Isaiah further developed the idea (Isa. 13), and the work of both prophets may have influenced Ezekiel's choice of words and images. For Ezekiel the Day of the Lord certainly refers to the imminent Babylonian attack on Jerusalem and not to some more distant eschatological appearance of God (→ Eschatology; Judgment, Day of).

8:1–11:25
Vision of Jerusalem

In September of 592 B.C. Ezekiel traveled through visionary transport to Jerusalem, where he witnessed activities in the Temple. More important, he also saw how God and the other inhabitants of the heavenly world were reacting to human events there. The vision thus becomes an ominous portent of the judgment that is to come on the city and the Temple and demonstrates that behind historical events is a spiritual reality that gives them theological significance. The prophet here dramatizes for his readers God's direct involvement in Jerusalem's destruction and forestalls any interpretation of this event that would simply ascribe it to the shifting winds of ancient Near Eastern politics.

The Temple vision is closely related to the prophet's initial call vision, both literarily and theologically. The Temple vision picks up and elaborates the description of the divine glory in chap. 1 and also provides a theological explanation for the glory's presence in Babylon. The general sequence of events in the Temple vision is relatively clear, although some of its elements seem obscure or out of place. This is particularly true for the progress of the cherubim and the glory out of the Temple, and it is possible that at some points the prophet or his disciples have added material or elaborated the original text in the light of later events and traditions. However, it is also important to remember that the Temple vision, like the call vision, has a dreamlike quality to it. Objects and events sometimes blur and do not always have the sharp outlines that would be expected in the ordinary world. Ezekiel preserves this dreamlike quality, leading his readers through the vision as he himself experienced it. He provides minimal interpretation of what he saw and expects his readers to understand the significance of what is being described.

8:1–18, The Abominations in the Temple.

The Temple vision begins with a description of Ezekiel sitting in his house in Babylon (cf. 3:24). The elders of Judah are sitting in front of him, although the purpose of their visit is not clear. Presumably these leaders of the exilic community have come to seek a prophetic oracle concerning Jerusalem's fate. They may also have hoped that the prophet would intercede with God on their behalf in order to prevent the city's destruction. If so, the prophet's response was quite different from what they expected. As in similar situations later in the book (14:1; 20:1), Ezekiel does not provide the oracle that the elders seek but instead describes a visionary trip to Jerusalem that underlines the hopelessness of the city's plight.

Ezekiel reports that, as the elders were waiting for a response, he was possessed by God. When the prophet went into trance, he saw a fiery humanoid figure resembling the one he had seen at the conclusion of his call vision (cf. 1:26–28). The figure is clearly intended to represent God's glory; and God, through the agency of the Spirit, lifts the prophet into the heavenly realm and transports him to Jerusalem, where he is placed at an entrance to the Temple (8:1–4; for a diagram of the Temple, →Temple, The). From this point on God continues to speak to Ezekiel and to guide him through the Temple, but God in the form of the divine glory is also a visible participant in the events that the prophet describes.

The visionary tour of the Temple begins at the northern entrance to the inner court, where the people had set up a statue, perhaps a representation of the Canaanite goddess Asherah but in any case an image that had no rightful place in orthodox Israelite worship (vv. 5–6). To continue the tour, the prophet burrowed through a wall to enter a secret inner room, the walls of which were decorated with carvings of fantastic animals that were probably connected with a non-Israelite cult. There he saw seventy representative elders of Israel conducting some sort of priestly rite. Among them was one Jaazaniah, who is otherwise unknown but who is, ironically, said to have been a son of Shaphan, the scribe who was intimately involved with Josiah's religious reform (2 Kings 22) and whose family protected Jeremiah during the final chaotic days of the siege (Jer. 26:1–24; 36:1–32). Clearly religious corruption had reached to the highest levels, and now representatives of the most important and faithful families in the land were secretly performing illegitimate rituals, thus destroying the sanctity of God's house (Ezek. 8:7–13).

This picture of aberrant worship is reinforced when the prophet is shown women participating in mourning rites for Tammuz, the ancient dying and rising fertility god of Mesopotamia, whose yearly trip to the underworld was the occasion for wailing among his devotees. Elsewhere Ezekiel is shown men symbolically turning their backs on the Temple so that they could face the east to worship the sun (vv. 14–16).

Up to this point in the vision, God has concentrated on showing Ezekiel aspects of Israel's religious sins, something that surely would have been a major concern for the prophet, who functioned as a priest before his deportation. However, the first part of the vision ends with God pointing out that the people have compounded their ritual sins by filling the land with violence. Violations of the social order are also an important part of Israel's sin, even though Ezekiel tends not to emphasize them as much as did his contemporary, Jeremiah. Both Israel's religious and social abuses are a direct insult to God and provide the motivation for the divine destruction of the people. In the very heart of the Temple, where God was supposed to be the most accessible, the prophet is told that God will not pity the people and will not hear them when they beg for mercy. The Temple has ceased to be a place where God and Israel can meet and communicate, and in this sense the Temple has lost its appropriate function (vv. 17–18).

Interpreters sometimes feel that Ezekiel's description of abominations in the Temple is exaggerated, given the fact that Josiah had recently purified Judah's religion and removed from the Temple a number of pagan ritual objects, including some belonging to religious activities described by Ezekiel (2 Kings 23:4–14). However, it is worth noting that Hezekiah had also reformed Temple worship, only to have the same aberrant practices reintroduced by his successor Manasseh (2 Kings 18:4–8; 21:1–16). It is probably safe to conclude that Israel's appetite for Canaanite and Mesopotamian rituals was stronger than its interest in sustaining religious reform and that Josiah's reforms were therefore short-lived.

9:1–11, The Slaughter of the Idolaters. After hearing God's final word of judgment against the city, the prophet is shown the beginning of the judgment itself. Although there is no doubt in Ezekiel's mind that the Temple will actually be destroyed by the Babylonian army, the vision makes clear that God is the real destroyer of the Temple and the people. Once God has acted, all hope for the city is gone.

The divine judgment begins when God summons six armed executioners of the city, who approach the Temple from the north, the traditional invasion route of enemy armies and the direction from which divine judgment was usually thought to come (Jer. 1:13–16; 4:5–31; 5:15–17; 6:1–5, 22–26). They are accompanied by a scribe clothed in linen, the traditional garb of priests (Exod. 28:29–42) and angels (Dan. 10:5; 12:6–13). The seven appear to be a contingent from an enemy army, but in fact are God's agents, members of the heavenly court (cf. 1 Kings 22:19–23). As they approach, the divine glory, since the time of Solomon enthroned above the cherubim-flanked Ark (1 Kings 8), begins its slow journey out of the Temple. God instructs the scribe to mark with the Hebrew letter *taw* the foreheads of those in the city who have grieved over the religious and social abominations committed in it and then commands the executioners to slay the rest, sparing no one and beginning with the elders before the Temple. As the slaughter is carried out, the prophet is shocked by its completeness. Apparently few, if any, were worthy of bearing the mark, a situation that goads the prophet into making an objection, one of the few personal responses that he makes in the book. The Temple, a traditional place of sanctuary, has not provided protection for people in the city. The prophet therefore wants to know if there is any salvation from the divine wrath (v. 8). God's response indicates that the sin of Jerusalem is so great that no escape is possible, but this statement does not comment on the fate of those already in exile.

10:1–22, The Departure of God's Glory. The religious abominations and social injustices described in chap. 8 have defiled the Temple and robbed it of its sanctity so that it could no longer serve as a place of sanctuary. As a result, the Temple could not protect the people from God's wrath, and in chap. 9 the prophet witnessed God's further desecration of the sanctuary through the slaughter of the elders. In chap. 10 Ezekiel describes the completion of a process already begun (9:3). Because the Temple has been desecrated, it is no longer a fit dwelling place for the Holy One of Israel, and the prophet traces the slow departure of the divine glory as it leaves the Temple and the city. As Ezekiel watches, the Ark and the Temple cherubim are transformed into the divine throne borne by the heavenly cherubim, and God's glory leaves the Holy of Holies, the inner sanctum of the Temple, and migrates to the threshold of the house (vv. 1, 3–5). God then commands the scribe to take coals from beneath the cherubim and to scatter them over the city to destroy it (v. 2). Before he can do so, however, one of the cherubim hands him the coals, and God thus directly provides the supernatural fire that will destroy the city (vv. 6–8).

It is at this point in the vision that the prophet recognizes the connection between what he is seeing and what he saw in Babylon during his call vision. He therefore describes the divine throne and the attendant cherubim in great detail, repeating much of what was said in chap. 1, but varying a few details. At the end of this description he describes the further movement of the glory to the east gate of the Temple (vv. 9–22).

11:1–25, Oracles of Judgment and Hope. As the prophet accompanies the divine glory out of the city, he sees twenty-five men at the east gate. These men are sometimes identified with the twenty-five sun worshipers of 8:16, although in that passage no specific names are mentioned. In any case, in chap. 11 they are indicted by God, and the prophet is told to deliver a judgment oracle against them. The precise nature of their crimes is unclear. They are accused of devising iniquity and giving wicked counsel to the city, a charge that may be related to the conflicting political advice being given to King Zedekiah by his advisers. They are then quoted as saying that there is no need to build houses, because "it [the city] is the pot and we are the flesh" (v. 3). The latter part of this statement is a reference to Jerusalem under siege, and Ezekiel develops the image in great detail in 24:1–14. The meaning of the first part of the statement is uncertain, but it may be that the accused were advising pouring all of the city's resources into defense rather than into building homes for those dispossessed by the previous Babylonian invasion. Ironically, the need for strengthening the city's defenses may be due to these same advisers' misguided foreign policy.

The judgment oracle that the prophet delivers to the men elaborates somewhat on their crimes and prescribes a very specific punishment (11:5–12). They are accused of increasing the number of those slain in the city, a possible reference to the results of the men's political advice or to the results of their defense-centered economic policies. They have acted out of fear of foreign attack, and their judgment will therefore take the form of making that fear into a reality. They will be taken out of the city and slain by foreigners at the border of Israel. This specific description of the judgment is sometimes thought to be a reference to the capture and killing of members of the royal court who fled from Jerusalem as the Babylonians captured it in 586 B.C. (2 Kings 25:4–7). Such an interpretation is possible but cannot be considered certain. A foretaste of the judgment occurs immediately when one of the men, Pelatiah, dies as Ezekiel is prophesying, thus provoking another of the prophet's anguished objections (Ezek. 9:8). Pelatiah's sudden death indicates the truth of the prophecy and suggests that the remainder of the men will be killed in due time (11:13).

Following the judgment oracle against the twenty-five men, God levels a charge against all of the inhabitants of Jerusalem (vv. 14–21). Those who were left in the city after the first deportation (597 B.C.) had apparently interpreted that event as divine judgment on the deportees and concluded that they had now been totally cut off from God and from the nation of Israel. Those who remained in the city therefore not only felt that they were the rightful heirs to the positions of leadership that had been vacated by the exiles but also claimed to be the heirs to the land of Israel and to the special divine promises that went with it. In short, those still in the land claimed to be the true Israel and sought to exclude the exiles from the religious community.

God's judgment oracle against the inhabitants of Jerusalem rejects this claim both obliquely and directly. In telling Ezekiel what the Jerusalemites are saying, God refers to the exiles as "your brothers . . . the whole house of Israel" (v. 15). By referring to the prophet's companions in this way God implies that the exiles are in fact the true Israel and not those left in Jerusalem. This notion is made explicit in the judgment oracle itself, in which God admits to having scattered the exiles but at the same time claims to have been a "small sanctuary" to them in the nations where they now live (v. 16). When this statement is set in the context of what Ezekiel has seen earlier in his vision, its meaning becomes clear. God has rejected Jerusalem and the Temple, thus dooming the people who still dwell there, and is even now in the process of leaving the city. At

the same time, the divine glory is present among the exiles in Babylon. Where God dwells, there is the true Israel, and the exiles have access to God, even though they live on foreign soil. This is the significance of Ezekiel's initial vision. God has temporarily taken up residence among the exiles and has rejected the Temple and the city.

At the same time, God's presence in Babylon is only a pale copy of the divine presence that formerly dwelled in Jerusalem, and that presence must be restored if the people are to live as the true Israel. The judgment oracle against the inhabitants of Jerusalem is therefore followed by a promise to the exiles (vv. 17–21), one of the few that Ezekiel will give before the fall of the city (chap. 33). God promises to return the exiles to the land of Israel and to give them that land as a possession. There the former exiles will remove the abominable religious objects that were left in Jerusalem when it was destroyed, and God will institute a new social and religious order to ensure that the sins of the past will not be repeated. The people will be given a new heart and spirit so that their loyalty will no longer be divided among various gods but will be single-mindedly devoted to God (cf. Jer. 32:39). The stony hearts that made the people insensitive to God's word will be removed and replaced with human hearts that will enable Israel to follow God's laws. Then the covenant relationship between God and the people will be restored to its original state.

Following the giving of this promise, Ezekiel reports that the divine glory with its attendant cherubim left Jerusalem, pausing briefly on the mountain east of the city. The Spirit then transported the prophet back to Babylon, where he reported his vision to the exiles (Ezek. 11:22–25).

Ezekiel's Temple vision would have had a major theological impact on his exilic audience, which was composed primarily of Jerusalemite officials, people who believed in the eternal election of Jerusalem and the Davidic house, the eternal presence of God in the Temple, and the inviolability of the city. To them the prophet's message would have come as a shock. God had in fact rejected the elect city and had migrated temporarily to Babylon. The removal of the divine presence allowed the city to be destroyed by the Babylonians, but God had already begun the process of destruction by pouring divine fire over the city and its inhabitants. However, God would ultimately return to Jerusalem to create a new Israel that would be totally responsive to the divine word. Ezekiel thus left most of the old Jerusalemite royal theology intact, but transformed it in a way that would have made it difficult for his readers to accept. God's eternal election of the city became in a sense contingent on the obedience of the people, a notion that cut at the very heart of the theology of Ezekiel's readers.

12:1-20
Symbols and Oracles of Exile

The first part of chap. 12 contains accounts of two symbolic actions by the prophet, together with their interpretations. Unlike the prophetic actions in chaps. 4–5, the ones here are relatively simple and easily interpreted.

In the first account (12:1–16), the prophet is told to prepare during the day an exile's pack, which probably would have consisted of essential clothing and household goods that could have been gathered quickly and carried easily. Then at night the prophet is to dig through the wall, as a would-be exile might do to escape from a besieged city. The departure would be under cover of darkness in order to mask the escapee's actions, and the unexpected exit through the wall could perhaps be interpreted as an attempt to avoid being seen by the enemy, who would have been watching the gates. The prophet is then to shoulder his pack and go into exile while covering his face so that he cannot see the land. The point of this last act is not clear, but it may be intended to dramatize the exile's grief at leaving the land.

Although the general symbolism of this act seems quite straightforward, God repeatedly warns the prophet that the people are rebellious and will deliberately refuse to understand the significance of what the prophet is doing (vv. 1–6). This warning about the rebelliousness of the people echoes the warning given at the prophet's call (2:1–3:15) and prepares him for the failure of his mission.

After Ezekiel performs his symbolic act (12:7), God tells the prophet that his audience has refused to understand what is happening and that an interpretation must be supplied. The obvious meaning of the act is that the people in the besieged city of Jerusalem will be forced to go into exile, a fate that Ezekiel's audience may have hoped could be avoided. However, when the interpretation is actually given (vv. 10–16), it is much more specific. The Exile is associated with the prince, Zedekiah, who together with his court will be forced to abandon Jerusalem by night. (Ezekiel uses the title "prince" to refer to Zedekiah and reserves the title "king" for the exiled Jehoiachin.) The prince will have to carry his own baggage and dig through the wall in an attempt to escape. However, God will trap the prince and his retinue and bring him to Babylon, but he will not see the land. His courtiers will be scattered, although a few will escape to testify to the abominations committed in Jerusalem.

The interpretation's description of the fate of the prince closely resembles the actual events

connected with Jerusalem's fall in 586 B.C. When the Babylonians breached the walls of the city, Zedekiah tried to escape with his court by leaving the city through a gate near the king's garden. The escape was not successful. The Babylonians captured Zedekiah on the plains of Jericho and brought him to Nebuchadnezzar at Riblah. There Zedekiah's sons were slain, and he himself was blinded before being taken to Babylon in chains (2 Kings 25:4–7; Jer. 52:4–11). The close correspondence of these events with Ezekiel's prediction concerning the fate of the prince has led many scholars to assume that the interpretation in 12:10–16 is in fact "prophecy after the fact." While this is certainly a possibility, it is worth noting that Ezekiel's prince and the historical Zedekiah escaped from the city in slightly different ways. Furthermore, Ezekiel's description contains a number of motifs commonly found in narratives dealing with exile. It is therefore likely that Ezekiel's original description of the fate of the prince was a bit more general than it is in the present text and that the actual historical events of the siege have influenced the shaping of the narrative after the fact. However, the extent of that shaping cannot be determined.

The second symbolic act (12:17–20) is much more direct than the first. Ezekiel is told to tremble while eating bread and drinking water. This display of fear is immediately interpreted as a reference to the inhabitants of Jerusalem, who continually live in fear, knowing that they are about to be punished for the violence that they have committed in the land. Destruction will soon come upon them and cannot be escaped.

12:21-14:11
Oracles on Prophets and Prophecy

The events leading up to the fall of Jerusalem were accompanied by a major crisis in the prophetic office. As frequently is the case in chaotic times, prophets responded to events by giving conflicting messages concerning the way people should react and by predicting different courses for future events (cf. Jer. 23; 27–29). In times of prophetic conflict, people are likely to question prophetic authority, and prophets often respond to this situation by undergirding their own authority in various ways and by undermining the authority of their prophetic rivals. An interest in strengthening Ezekiel's prophetic authority played a major role in shaping the accounts of his call, and in Ezek. 12:21–14:11 additional attention is given to problems connected with the prophet's own oracles and to the activities of other prophets.

12:21–28, The Fulfillment of Prophecy. The end of chap. 12 contains two oracles dealing with the same theme: the apparent nonfulfill-ment of prophecies of judgment. Both oracles have the same basic form. A saying of the people is quoted, and God then responds by showing the falsity of the people's words. In the first case (vv. 21–25), God complains that people are say-ing that prophecies concerning the land of Israel have been so long delayed that they have lost their validity. In this period such an attitude would cause people to ignore not only the judg-ment oracles of Ezekiel but also those of his contemporary Jeremiah, who was likewise pre-dicting Jerusalem's destruction. In response to this proverb God assures both Ezekiel and the exiles that the fulfillment of the judgment ora-cles is at hand. The prophets predicting salva-tion will no longer have any credibility, for God will bring about the predicted disaster during the lifetime of Ezekiel's audience (cf. Jer. 23:9–32).

In the second oracle (Ezek. 12:26–28), the people are apparently willing to believe that the prophetic announcement of disaster will become a reality, but they are saying that judg-ment will take place only in the distant future. Again God assures Ezekiel and the people that the judgment will no longer be delayed but will take place immediately.

13:1–23, Condemnation of False Prophets and Diviners.

Having dealt with the problems associated with judgment oracles, Ezekiel now records two oracles directed against prophets of salvation (13:1–16) and against diviners (13:17–23). Both of these oracles have roughly the same form, that of the classic prophetic announce-ment of disaster. They begin with an instruction to Ezekiel to prophesy (vv. 2, 17) and then move on to a woe oracle describing the crimes that the addressees have committed (vv. 3–7, 18–19). This description leads logically to an announce-ment of disaster, introduced with the formula "thus says the Lord" and sometimes containing additional references to the reasons for the judg-ment (vv. 8–16, 20–23).

The first judgment oracle is aimed at proph-ets in Jerusalem, who are predicting that the city will miraculously escape destruction, as it did in Hezekiah's time (2 Kings 19:35–37). Be-cause of this misleading advice, the people in the city do not realize that they are in danger and therefore do nothing to save themselves. The activities of these prophets are well known from the book of Jeremiah, where they are por-trayed as a persistent hindrance to Jeremiah's activities (Jer. 6:14; 8:11; 14:13–16). Although their point of view is deeply rooted in orthodox Jerusalemite theology, Jeremiah feels that their message during the final days of the siege is simply wrong, and he accuses them of lying and misrepresenting God's word (Jer. 23:9–32). This indictment of the peace prophets contains a number of phrases and motifs that are also present in Ezek. 13:1–16, and it is likely that the latter passage has been influenced by Jere-miah's at some stage in its formation. There is also some evidence of editing after the fall of Jerusalem, especially in 13:9, where the focus of the oracle suddenly shifts from Jerusalemite prophets to prophets in exile, who will not be allowed to reenter the land of Israel along with the rest of the returnees. This later editorial ac-tivity may also help to account for some of the repetitions in the passage, although it must al-ways be remembered that Ezekiel's literary style is normally convoluted and highly orna-mented.

The oracle against the peace prophets begins when God indicts them for inventing their pro-phetic message (13:1–7). They are accused of prophesying from their own minds (lit., "hearts") and then introducing these fabrica-tions with formulas identifying them as divine oracles. Like jackals they inhabit ruins and feed on the dying and the dead. Furthermore, they have not built a wall to protect the people against their enemies and have not climbed high on the wall to fill the breaches made by the enemy battering rams (v. 5). The building of the wall refers to the prophet's responsibility to warn the people of approaching danger so that they may repent and save their lives. Unlike Ezekiel, who was specifically commissioned as a prophetic watchman to warn Israel to repent (3:16–21), the peace prophets speak of no dan-ger, issue no warning, and thus leave the people unprotected. In addition, these prophets ne-glect a genuine prophet's second major duty, that of protecting the people by interceding with God on their behalf. This intercessory function of the prophet is elsewhere traced to Moses, who in the wilderness stood in the breach and protected Israel from God's wrath (Ps. 106:23).

Because of the damage that the peace prophets have done to Israel, God's hand will now be upon them, not as a sign that they are genuine prophets but as a sign of judgment (Ezek. 13:9). The prophets have misled the people and built for them a wall held together with whitewash rather than mortar, a wall that appears to be solid but that will crumble in the face of God's stormy judgment (vv. 10–11). The divine judgment will now destroy the wall, the people, and the prophets who mislead them by building the insubstantial wall based on false hopes of peace (vv. 12–16).

The oracle against the prophetesses (13:17–23) condemns them too for inventing prophetic words and attributing them to God, but it con-centrates on the prophetesses' work as diviners. The precise nature of their activities is unclear, but they apparently involved the making of arti-cles of clothing to serve as amulets or to aid in divination (→ Amulet; Magic and divination). The prophetesses may have also used barley as a means of divination, although the reference to grain and bread in v. 19 may be to the form of payment for their services rather than to the materials used in the process. Divinatory activities of this sort were condemned by Israelite law (Deut. 18:9–14), and God therefore accuses the diviners of profaning the divine name and destroying the people. Because of their crimes the diviners' paraphernalia will be destroyed and their perverted oracles will no longer be allowed to ensnare the innocent.

14:1–11, A Warning to God's Prophets. Although Ezekiel's primary concern in these chapters is with false prophets and false interpretation of prophecy, he is reminded sharply in 14:1–11 that even God's genuine prophets must constantly be on guard against violating the divine will. At his call Ezekiel was warned not to rebel against the divine word that he would be given (2:8), and he is now cautioned against being overly influenced by the people in his audience.

The warning is triggered by a visit from some of the exiled elders (14:1). The purpose of their visit is not made clear, however, until God reacts to their presence by denouncing their reason for coming (v. 3). They have come to inquire of God. Inquiries of this sort required the prophet to serve as an intermediary between the human and divine worlds. The people would come to the prophet and present questions and requests directed to the Deity. The prophet would mediate those requests to God and then would return to the people the divine response. Such a procedure was a normal part of religious life and was the preferred method of communicating with God. In Israel the prophet, rather than the diviner, was thought to be the proper method of determining God's will.

God's angry response therefore comes as a shock. These people have worshiped idols, and their sins now make God unwilling to listen to their requests (v. 4). Instead God will respond to them directly in judgment and destroy them from the midst of Israel (vv. 4–5, 7–8). The prophet is not to mediate their requests but is allowed only to urge them to repent and reject their idols (v. 6). Furthermore, any prophet who is deceived by the people and who, as a result, presents their requests to God will share the fate of the sinners. Both will be cut off from the land and destroyed. In this way God will purge the evil that exists in Israel (vv. 9–11). The right to approach God through the prophet is not absolute but depends on the obedience of the people. When they deliberately sin, access to God can be denied as part of the divine judgment.

14:12–23
Individual Salvation and God's Justice

Up to this point the book of Ezekiel has given the clear impression that no one in Jerusalem is without sin and that this fact will make the judgment on the city total and inevitable. Ezekiel has also spoken of the Israelites already in exile as rebels and prophesied that they too will be subject to further destruction. There have been a few references to a remnant that will return to the land (5:3–4; 11:14–21), but for the most part the fate of the exiles is bleak. However, even the brief references to a remnant would have raised a question in the minds of Ezekiel's audience about the mechanisms through which one might survive the Exile and become part of the restored community. A partial answer to this question can be deduced from 14:12–23, although the main point of the passage lies elsewhere.

Ezek. 14:12–23 consists of four hypothetical cases (vv. 12–20) and an application of these cases to the situation of Jerusalem (vv. 21–23). The four cases are given in typical legal form and deal with God's reaction to a hypothetical nation's sin, specifically the sin of trespass, an offense against something holy or the violation of a sacred oath (cf. Lev. 6:2–3). In each of the four cases, God sends a different punishment on the land: famine (Ezek. 14:13), devastation by wild beasts (v. 15), slaughter by the sword (v. 17), and pestilence (v. 19). The same point is then made in all four cases. God punishes everyone who is guilty. Even if three legendary examples of virtue, Noah, Daniel, and Job, lived in the land, their righteousness would save only their own lives and could not be transferred to their children in order to save them (vv. 14, 16, 18, 20).

The three examples mentioned are traditional, ancient Near Eastern wisdom figures who were renowned for their patience and goodness. Noah was, of course, the hero of the Flood story, who survived because in his generation he alone was righteous (Gen. 6:9). In this case he was even able to save his family. Job's patience and faithfulness were proverbial even in antiquity, and the old folktale of Job's trials became the starting point for the biblical book of Job (Job 1). Daniel cannot be the hero of the book of Daniel (the names are spelled differently in Hebrew) but is probably the legendary king Dan'el, the good and wise ruler who is the subject of the Ugaritic tale of Aqhat. The fact that Ezekiel uses three non-Israelite examples of righteousness to illustrate the principle that personal righteousness leads to individual salvation may hint that he considered this principle to be a universal one. He certainly develops it in great detail in chap. 18, where he applies it to the exilic community. However, the point of the examples in 14:12–20 is not to develop a doctrine of individual salvation but to illustrate God's absolute justice. Only the guilty are destroyed; only the righteous are saved.

That this is the proper interpretation of vv. 12–20 becomes clear when Ezekiel applies the examples to Jerusalem (vv. 21–23). In keeping with what has been said in the book up to this point, the sin of Jerusalem is assumed, and the city is visited with all four of the previously mentioned acts of judgment: sword, famine, evil beasts, and pestilence. Technically speaking, no one in the city is delivered, as the righteous were in the hypothetical examples. The word "deliver" is not used in the application. Nevertheless, some people in the city, perhaps including some of the children of Ezekiel's exilic audience, do escape. However, their survival is not intended to indicate that they are righteous. Rather they have been allowed to escape so that they can be living examples of the evil that provoked God to destroy the city. When Ezekiel's audience sees the evil in their own children, then the exiles will recognize that God acted justly in judging Jerusalem (vv. 22–23).

15:1–8
Meditation on the Vine

Ezekiel's oracle of the vine can be broken easily into two parts. The first part consists of a series of rhetorical questions concerning the vine (vv. 1–5), and the second part compares the vine to Israel (vv. 6–8). The meaning of the first question is uncertain but probably has to do with the ultimate uses of the vine when compared with the other trees of the forest. Assuming that, in a poor land like Israel, everything that is given living space must in some way be utilitarian, God asks whether anything useful can be made from the vine. The answer is obviously no, since the vine contains too little usable wood, and its fibers are so flexible that it cannot even be made into an efficient peg (v. 3). Therefore the vine can only be used as a fuel. After it has been charred and partially burned, it is even less useful than it was originally. It is now only fit for further use as fuel, and it will therefore be consigned to the flames again (vv. 4–5).

The comparison between the uses of the vine and the fate of Jerusalem is clear. Like the vine, Jerusalem is worthless for any purpose except burning. God will therefore give up the city to destruction. If some escape the burning, as did the people who were left in the city after the first deportation of 597 B.C., they will be burned again until the city is totally consumed (vv. 6–8).

16:1–63
Allegory of the Adulterous Wife

Ezekiel's long oracle comparing Israel to an adulterous wife is composed of three major parts: an extended metaphor of Jerusalem as an adulteress (vv. 1–43a), an uncomplimentary comparison between Judah and her sisters Samaria and Sodom (vv. 43b–58), and a promise of God's fidelity (vv. 59–63). The whole oracle is held together by the image of the adulterous wife, but there is no logical progression from one part to another.

16:1–43a, Jerusalem as Adulteress. The bulk of the oracle is devoted to developing an extended metaphor of Jerusalem as an adulterous wife. The idea of comparing Israel's relationship with God to the relationship between a faithless wife and her husband seems to have originated with Hosea, whose broken marriage became a symbol of the estrangement between God and Israel (Hos. 1–3). The image was further developed by Jeremiah, who compared the worship of other gods and the making of foreign alliances to adultery (Jer. 2–3). Ezekiel develops both of these themes but sets them in the context of Israel's earlier history by giving a biography of God's eventual bride.

Throughout the metaphor the language of sexuality is explicit, and at times it appears crude to modern readers. Even in antiquity, the images were shocking, intended to make an instant impression on the prophet's readers. The images were also dangerous, for they were closely related to the themes of the fertility cults and were easily open to misinterpretation by Ezekiel's audience. Although the image of the adulterous wife is highly developed, the underlying historical reality is never completely hidden and sometimes intrudes into the metaphor, warping it slightly.

The extended metaphor is set within the classic prophetic form of an announcement of judgment to an individual. The faithless wife is confronted with a detailed indictment describing her crimes (Ezek. 16:1–34), and then judgment upon her is announced (vv. 35–43). The indictment begins with a reminder of Jerusalem's origins: her father was an Amorite and her mother a Hittite (v. 3). This statement reflects the actual background of the city. Before David captured it and made it his capital, Jerusalem was a Jebusite city closely related to the Hittites, and before that it was in Amorite hands. However, in the metaphor the young woman who is Jerusalem represents not only the pagan city that became Israel's religious and political center, but she also represents the nation of Israel as a whole. When the prophet begins to describe the young woman's life, it is the history of Israel that

673

underlies the metaphor, not the actual history of the city. The actual history of the city does not concern Ezekiel again until vv. 40–42, when the reality of the impending siege of Jerusalem intrudes into the metaphor.

The young woman was rejected by her parents, and the proper birth rituals were not performed for her. Like many unwanted children in antiquity, she was left in an open field to die. However, God saw her in this pitiful condition and ordered her to live. When she grew to sexual maturity, God married her and made a covenant with her (v. 8), a reference to the covenant at Sinai where God and Israel entered into a special relationship (→ Covenant). As an attentive husband, God then gave to Israel all of the things that had been denied by her parents. She was bathed, anointed with oil, and clothed with fine garments, with the result that she became famous for her beauty (vv. 9–14). Lying behind this description may be a remembrance of the glorious days of the old Solomonic empire, but it is equally likely that Ezekiel here refers to no particular historical period.

Jerusalem was both the religious and the political capital of Israel, and Ezekiel therefore appropriately describes Israel's sins in both of these areas, tying the two together with images of prostitution and harlotry. The prophet apparently has no particular period of Israelite history in mind, for he elsewhere portrays Israel as sinful from the very beginning of its life as a nation (chap. 20).

Turning first to Israel's religious sins, God accuses the nation of committing adultery with other gods. The clothes that God had given her she used to make tent-shrines. Like the Israelites at Sinai, who melted down their jewelry to make an idolatrous golden calf (Exod. 32:1–10), so later Israel used God's gold and silver to make forbidden images in human form and then worshiped them with the clothing and food that God had provided (Ezek. 16:15–19). Included in the offerings were the children that Israel had born to God (vv. 20–21), a reference to a religious practice that existed in monarchical times outside of Jerusalem in the Valley of Hinnom, where children were sacrificed by fire to the underworld deity Molech (→ Molech).

However, Israel's sins were not only religious. She also committed adultery by making political covenants and treaties with other nations, thus violating her covenant with God and showing a lack of trust in God as Israel's sole protector and defender. These political arrangements were usually unfavorable to Israel, often resulting in the loss of Israelite territory (v. 27), but the nation continued to engage in them, even during the final years of its existence, when King Zedekiah vacillated between pro-Babylonian and pro-Egyptian foreign policies. Concluding treaties with foreign nations

inevitably involved Israel's paying heavy tribute in return for political stability, a practice that Ezekiel sarcastically likens to a prostitute paying her customers in her eagerness to commit adultery with them (vv. 23–34).

The judgment that God announces upon Israel is appropriate for the crime (vv. 35–43). In Israelite law adultery was punished by stoning the offenders (Lev. 20:10; Deut. 22:23–29), a punishment in which the whole community participated to restore wholeness to the society. In this case, the agents of divine punishment will be the other nations, the very lovers whom Israel had desired. Specifically, the Babylonians will destroy Jerusalem, tearing down its altars, burning its houses, and slaughtering its inhabitants.

16:43b–58, Jerusalem and Her Sisters. Returning to his original image of Jerusalem as the child of pagan parents (v. 3), Ezekiel compares the city's conduct to that of her mother (vv. 43b–45). Just as Jerusalem's mother had neglected and rejected her, so Jerusalem has rejected her children by offering them as sacrifices to other deities (vv. 20–22). Furthermore, when compared to her "sisters," Samaria, the capital of the Northern Kingdom, Israel, and Sodom, the notoriously sinful city of antiquity, Jerusalem's sin appears even more blatant. Samaria and Sodom had both neglected the poor and committed all sorts of religious abominations (Gen. 18–19; 2 Kings 17), and God had therefore destroyed them. But the terrible sins of Jerusalem make these two proverbial sinners appear righteous. The conclusion to be drawn from the comparison is obvious. God destroyed Samaria and Sodom because of their sins, and Jerusalem's even greater sins will surely provoke a similar punishment (Ezek. 16:46–52).

After announcing judgment on Jerusalem, God unexpectedly promises that the city will be restored (vv. 53–58). However, the reinstated capital will not enjoy a preeminent status among the other nations (cf. Isa. 2:2–4). Rather it will be restored only after Sodom and Samaria have been restored. Like her sisters, Jerusalem has become a proverbially wicked city, and she will continue to be compared with them even after the fortunes of all three have been changed. This comparison will shame Jerusalem, which will continue to be disgraced for what she has done.

16:59–63, God's Fidelity. The long and convoluted oracle of judgment ends with a surprising word of promise. Given the sharply negative tone of the first thirty-three chapters of Ezekiel, this promise seems out of place, and most scholars consider it a later addition. However, although the promise is at odds with the book's final literary shape, there is no reason to conclude that Ezekiel could not have delivered occasional promises before the fall of the city.

Even though Jerusalem/Israel has been unfaithful to the marriage agreement with God and has committed adultery, God remains faithful to the covenant with Israel. This covenant is eternal, in spite of historical evidence to the contrary. Reversing the situation described in vv. 53–58, God now promises to forgive Jerusalem and restore its former preeminent status. Israel will truly know God in this act of grace and will never again rebel.

17:1–24
Allegory of the Eagles

Ezekiel's tale of the two eagles is called both a riddle (*chidah*) and an allegory (*mashal*). The former term refers to an enigmatic saying that requires interpretation, while the latter refers to a comparison between two things. In the allegory, the kings of Judah are being compared to cedars and vines, and the kings of Babylon and Egypt are being compared to eagles. To understand the riddle, it is necessary to have some knowledge of political events in Jerusalem between the first deportation in 597 B.C. and the fall of the city in 586 B.C. (see "Introduction" above for historical details).

17:1–10, The Allegory. Although at first glance the tale of the eagles seems to resemble a fable in which animals or plants engage in actions appropriate to humans (cf. Judg. 9:7–15), the opening of the story indicates that it operates on a more symbolic level. A large eagle, traditionally considered a royal bird of great power, takes the top of a Lebanese cedar and plants it in a "land of trade." The cedars of Lebanon were famous in antiquity because of their size and strength, and, consequently, were used throughout the ancient Near East as a building material, particularly in monumental royal construction projects. When Solomon built his royal residence and the Temple in Jerusalem, he imported large quantities of Lebanese cedar, and indeed one of his buildings contained so much of this wood that it was called "The House of the Forest of Lebanon" (1 Kings 7:2). Jerusalem, which is located on a mountain, is therefore appropriately symbolized in the allegory by Lebanon and the Davidic king by the cedar. The identity of the "land of trade" and the "city of merchants" (Ezek. 17:4) is ambiguous at this point in the allegory. The reference becomes intelligible only against the historical background of the first deportation. After planting the cedar shoot in the foreign land, the eagle takes some of the "seed of the land," presumably the seed of "Lebanon," and plants it in fertile soil, where it flourishes. However, the cedar vine, for no apparent reason, reaches out toward another eagle,

which transplants it to equally fertile soil (vv. 3–8).

At the end of the tale, God addresses Ezekiel in a new oracle, asking whether or not the vine will survive (vv. 9–10). The answer to this question is not obvious unless the reader already understands the meaning of the allegory. Moreover, the divine replies that follow are equally puzzling. God supplies a negative answer to the initial question, suggesting that the first eagle will pull up the vine without much effort (v. 9). In addition, the cedar is not deeply rooted enough to withstand the east wind, a natural force elsewhere associated with God's powerful acts in the world (Exod. 10:13; 14:21).

17:11–21, The Interpretation. Although Ezekiel's original audience would have immediately understood the allegory, God nevertheless provides an oracular interpretation of it. The first eagle is Nebuchadnezzar, who deported the Israelite king Jehoiachin and Ezekiel's fellow exiles to Babylon in 597 B.C. Nebuchadnezzar then placed the Davidide Zedekiah on the throne in Jerusalem and made a treaty with him, thus providing all the conditions necessary for political stability in the land. However, Zedekiah rebelled and sought military support for his revolt against the Egyptian pharaoh Psammetichus II, the second eagle of the allegory. Ezekiel, like Jeremiah (Jer. 27:4–15), considered this move not only a political blunder but also a violation of God's will. Therefore the judgment will take place on two levels. On the human level, Nebuchadnezzar will besiege Jerusalem and deport Zedekiah to Babylon, where he will die. On the divine level, God will trap Zedekiah and judge him by taking him to Babylon, destroying his army in the process (Ezek. 11:11–21).

The interpretation of the allegory is straightforward and, for the most part, does not appear to have been crafted after the fall of Jerusalem. In fact Nebuchadnezzar was not able to capture Jerusalem easily (cf. v. 9), and the description of Zedekiah's fate (vv. 16, 17–21) does not seem to know of the actual events surrounding the fall of the city. Only in v. 17 has a later editor reinterpreted v. 9 as a reference to the fact that the Egyptian pharaoh did not come to the aid of the besieged Jerusalem.

17:22–24, An Oracle of Restoration. After the description of the certainty of judgment in the preceding verses, the announcement of restoration (vv. 22–24) comes as a surprise. God promises to select a Davidide from among the Babylonian exiles and restore him to the throne in Jerusalem. The monarchy will again flourish after the fall of the city. This oracle is not an interpretation of anything in the earlier allegory and is related to it only through the use of the same literary images. It is therefore likely that the promise was added to Ezekiel's original oracle after the fall of the city.

18:1–32
Questions About God's Justice

Like 12:21–28 and 33:10–20, 18:1–32 is essentially a disputation oracle that states a popular saying and then argues against it. The overall unit is composed of three parts: first, the statement of a proverb concerning intergenerational retribution and the arguments against it (vv. 1–20); second, the application of the principle lying behind the refutation to the stages of an individual's life (vv. 21–29); and third, a call to repent (vv. 30–32).

18:1–20, Intergenerational Sin and Punishment. The disputation oracle begins by quoting a proverb that was current in Jerusalem and probably also among the exiles: "Fathers have eaten unripe grapes, and the children's teeth are set on edge." The meaning of the proverb is clear. One generation is suffering the consequences of a prior generation's actions. In the context of Ezekiel's historical situation, just after the first deportation, the use of the proverb implies that the exiles are being punished for the sins of their ancestors. This point of view was widely accepted by people in the prophet's own time and is represented to some degree by the book of Kings, which attributes the Exile primarily to the evils committed during the reign of Manasseh rather than solely to the deeds of the people living at the time of the fall of Jerusalem (2 Kings 21). Jeremiah also accepted this explanation, at least in part, and prophesied that the proverb will cease to be true only after God has brought the exiles back from Babylon (Jer. 31:29). In Ezekiel's oracle, however, God orders the people to stop using the proverb immediately. As the one who controls the lives of all humans, God decrees that children shall not die for their parents' sin. Only the individual who sins shall die (Ezek. 18:4).

This principle by which God actually assigns punishment is then illustrated by three cases stated in legal form. In the first case (vv. 5–9), a righteous father lives because he has not committed iniquity, even though he may have a son who is not righteous. In the second case (vv. 10–13), the wicked son of a righteous father dies and bears the legal responsibility for his own death. The righteousness of the father cannot benefit the son. In the third case (vv. 14–18), the son of a wicked father sees the sins of his father and avoids them. The son lives and is not made to suffer for his father's sins.

In each of these three cases Ezekiel defines righteous or unrighteous conduct by citing specific examples of righteousness or wickedness.

As one might expect, Ezekiel's priestly background leads him to choose examples from the priestly laws, particularly from the Holiness Code (Lev. 17–26). Thus, the righteous person is one who does what is just and right, does not participate in ritual meals at mountain sanctuaries, does not worship idols (Lev. 19:4), does not commit adultery (Exod. 20:14), does not approach a menstruous woman (Lev. 18:19), does not violate the laws governing business practices (Exod. 22:25; Lev. 6:2, 4; 19:13; 25:14, 17, 36–37), feeds the hungry, clothes the naked, and judges justly (Lev. 19:35). Conversely, the unrighteous person violates these prescriptions.

After giving specific examples, God summarizes the basic principle again. When the people ask why the righteous son did not die for the sins of his father, God replies that the son did what was right, and because of this he lived. Only the person who sins shall die (Ezek. 18:19–20).

Ezekiel did not create the principle of retribution illustrated in these verses. Deut. 24:16 already enunciates it clearly. Parents are not to be put to death for the crimes of their children, nor are children to be punished for the crimes of their parents. This law was intended to counter the practice of punishing all of the members of a criminal's family, even if they had no part in the crime (cf. Exod. 20:5; Deut. 5:9; Josh. 7:24–25; 1 Sam. 22:19; 2 Kings 10:1–11; 25:7). However, Ezekiel stresses a direct correspondence between sin and punishment more strongly than did his predecessors, and he does so for a very specific reason. Ezekiel seeks to emphasize the notion that the exiles and those who remain in the land are suffering for their own sins and not for the sins of prior generations. The people using the proverb imply that they are being punished without cause and that their present state is due to someone else's actions. Therefore the proverb must be rejected, and the exiles must admit their guilt.

18:21–29, Individual Sin and Punishment. After arguing against the popular proverb on the grounds that only the individual that sins shall die, Ezekiel extends the principle to successive stages in the life of a single individual. In this case two examples cast in legal form are provided. In the first case, a wicked person repents and thereafter lives a righteous life. As a result, his past sins are not remembered, and he lives (vv. 21–23). In contrast, the righteous person who commits iniquity dies for his sins, and none of his previous righteous deeds have any bearing on his fate (v. 24).

In contrast to the wicked people who are questioning divine justice, God in fact distributes rewards and punishments according to a clear and just principle. Only the righteous are rewarded, and only the wicked are punished.

676

18:30–32, A Call to Repent. In spite of the gloom that pervades most of the book of Ezekiel, the prophet's oracles on individual reward and punishment imply that some of the exiles may in fact escape destruction and may even live to return to the land. However, this goal can only be achieved by individual repentance and persistence in the righteous life. The oracle therefore ends with a call for the people to repent. Even though God is determined to punish the guilty, there is no divine pleasure in the death of the wicked. God sincerely desires repentance, even though the possibility of its occurring is remote (vv. 30–32).

19:1–14
Laments over the Monarchy

Ezekiel's lament over the monarchy is divided into two parts. In the first part (vv. 1–9), he develops an allegory concerning a lioness and compares the fates of two of her cubs (vv. 1–4, 5–9). In the second part of the lament (vv. 10–14), the prophet shifts the images in the allegory and speaks of the fate of a maternal vine and her offshoots. Both parts make use of the poetic structure that is typical of Hebrew dirges. Each pair of lines in the dirge consists of a triply accented line followed by a shorter, doubly accented line. Dirges are normally addressed to the person or thing being lamented, and they usually emphasize the contrast between the addressee's present pitiful state and former glory.

19:1–9, Allegory of the Lioness. In the first allegory, a lioness raises a cub and teaches it to hunt, but when the young lion grows strong, it becomes a man-eater. The surrounding nations are alarmed and capture the young lion, taking it in shackles to Egypt (vv. 1–4). When the lioness sees that the cub will not return, she raises another cub. This one too becomes a man-eater, making cities desolate and terrifying their populations. Again the nations trap the young lion, and this time bring it in shackles and neckstock to Babylon so that it can never return to its land (vv. 5–9).

The historical reality lying behind the allegory is far from clear. Scholars agree that the first cub must refer to King Jehoahaz of Judah, who was the son of Josiah and Hamutal. After Josiah's sudden death, Jehoahaz reigned briefly until he was deposed by Pharaoh Neco and deported to Egypt, where he died (2 Kings 23:30–34). Even so, Jehoahaz was far from being the international threat pictured in the allegory, and it must be assumed that Ezekiel has inflated the power of the Judean monarchy for dramatic effect. The second cub could allude to either Jehoiachin, who had in fact already been deported to Babylon when Ezekiel wrote, or

Zedekiah, the reigning monarch. The latter interpretation is attractive because he too was a son of Josiah and Hamutal (2 Kings 24:18), a fact that would allow the dirge to be read narrowly as a comparison between the two sons of Hamutal who later became kings. Hamutal herself would then be the lioness of the allegory, and the dirge would have to be read as an anticipation of the deportation of Zedekiah to Babylon in 586 B.C. However, this narrow interpretation is undercut by the second allegory (Ezek. 19:10–14), where the mother seems to represent a corporate entity such as Jerusalem or the nation as a whole rather than a specific individual. It is therefore preferable to identify the lioness as Jerusalem, the royal house, the nation of Israel, or the tribe of Judah. Of these possibilities, the last has the advantage accounting for the major images used in the allegory. The tribe of Judah was traditionally symbolized by a lion (Gen. 49:9) and was the tribe from which the Davidic dynasty came.

19:10–14, Allegory of the Vine. In the second allegory the mother is compared to a vine that grew luxuriantly because of its favorable surroundings. Its strongest branches became scepters for rulers, and its height made it clearly visible from a distance. Then the vine was uprooted, and the east wind made it wither. The vine was burned and transplanted to a wilderness, where it will die in drought. Nothing will be left from which to make a ruler's staff.

The language of the allegory closely resembles that of chap. 17, and it is likely that the general subject matter is the same. However, the allegory is very general, and it is difficult to identify any of the symbols with certainty. The maternal vine is presumably Jerusalem, the royal house, or the tribe of Judah (as in vv. 1–9), and the strong branches represent the various great kings that arose during Israel's history, although no specific king can be readily identified. Rather the allegory concentrates on the vine as a whole and deals with the fate of the Davidic royal house. In the allegory the vine is destroyed many times over, and it is likely that here, as elsewhere, Ezekiel's description has been colored by the traumatic events surrounding the siege of Jerusalem. Nevertheless, the main point of the allegory is clear. The Davidic dynasty can no longer flourish and will be utterly destroyed. Verse 14 seems to imply that after its destruction, the Davidic line will not be restored, an idea that Ezekiel elsewhere rejects (37:24–28).

20:1–44
The History of Rebellious Israel

Ezekiel's judgmental account of Israel's history is highly complex and full of interpretive difficulties. The first part of the account follows a regular pattern (vv. 1–26), but later there are breaks in literary continuity that lead many scholars to suspect that Ezekiel or his disciples have elaborated the original text and introduced some confusion into the overall argument. At the same time, there is no scholarly agreement concerning the location of these editorial additions.

The whole chapter contains an uncharacteristically large amount of Deuteronomistic language and theology, a fact that seems to indicate that the prophet knew of and was influenced by the Deuteronomistic tradition. At the same time, the basic theology of the chapter is peculiar to Ezekiel. The same is true of some of the historical events that are mentioned. In such cases, it is necessary to conclude either that Ezekiel has remembered events that have left no other traces in the biblical record or that he is presenting a history that is already deeply colored by his own theological interpretation of Israel's past. Of these two possibilities, the latter is more likely.

20:1–4, Inquiring of God. The oracle is dated to August of 591 B.C. As in 8:1 and 14:1, the entire unit is presented as God's response to exilic elders who have approached Ezekiel to inquire of God. The subject of their inquiry is not specified, although it presumably had to do with the city of Jerusalem and its fate. However, as in 14:1, their attempts to communicate with God are cut short. Their sins have made such communication impossible, and God refuses to listen to their requests. Instead, Ezekiel is commanded to present an account of their past crimes, a task that he performs by giving his own version of Israel's early history.

20:5–26, From Egypt to Exile. Ezekiel's primary account of Israel's history consists of three episodes, all of which have the same basic structure. In each case God acts graciously toward Israel, but Israel responds by disobeying God's laws and by worshiping other gods. Because of the people's sins, God is determined to destroy them but does not do so in order to protect the sanctity of the divine name.

Following this pattern, Ezekiel begins his account with the Israelites in Egypt before the Exodus (vv. 5–9). In Egypt God revealed the divine name to Israel and swore to bring the people out of Egypt and to give them a glorious land (cf. Exod. 6:2–8). In return, God required that the people reject the idols that they had worshiped, a requirement that is not recorded in the Exodus narratives in their present form (but note Josh. 24:14). However, the people did not listen but continued to worship other gods. God therefore contemplated destroying them in

Egypt but finally did not do so in order not to profane the divine name. Such a decision is not recorded in the existing biblical accounts of the Exodus, but the stories of Israel in the wilderness do tell of two occasions when Moses saved the people by appealing to the necessity of preserving the sanctity of the divine name. After Israel created and worshiped the golden calf (Exod. 32:1–6) and after the people rejected the land that God had given them (Num. 14:13–19; Deut. 9:28), God threatened to destroy Israel but was prevented from doing so by Moses, who successfully argued that such an act would dishonor the divine name by making it appear to the nations that God was unable to fulfill the promise of deliverance that had been made to Israel in Egypt. Ezekiel has apparently taken this motif and applied it throughout Israel's early history.

After the Exodus, the same basic pattern is repeated during the time of the first wilderness generation (Ezek. 20:10–17). From Egypt God led the people to Sinai, where they were given life-giving laws, including the distinctive law of the Sabbath (Exod. 20–40). However, Israel again rebelled and refused to obey the laws, violating the Sabbath and worshiping other gods (cf. Exod. 16; 32). God again considered destroying the people in the wilderness, but did not do so in order to preserve the sanctity of the divine name. In this case too Ezekiel has generalized on isolated incidents that occurred during Israel's wilderness wanderings but has overlooked the main historical point. God did in fact condemn to death all of the wilderness generation because of their refusal to accept the land (Num. 14:13–19).

God then turned to the children of the wilderness generation (Ezek. 20:18–26) and warned them not to follow in the ways of their ancestors. The second wilderness generation, however, was just as wicked as the first. God therefore determined to destroy them in the wilderness but did not do so to protect the sanctity of the divine name. Instead God swore to scatter the people among the nations (v. 23). Thus, according to Ezekiel, the Exile was decreed as punishment for Israel's sins even before the people entered the land (cf. Ps. 106:26–27). However, at the same time the prophet indicates that the Exile is not to be equated with the destruction of Israel. This refusal to interpret the Exile as the equivalent of the destruction of the nation provides an oblique note of hope in an otherwise dismal oracle.

This third example of Israel's rebellion is noteworthy not only because it was the occasion on which God decided to exile the people, but also because after this event God made it virtually impossible for Israel to improve its conduct. As punishment for their sins, God gave the people bad laws that would lead them to defile themselves by offering their children as sacrifices (Ezek. 20:26). The reference here is to the law requiring the dedication of firstborn children to God (Exod. 22:29), a law whose ambiguity was later clarified by stipulations allowing firstborn children to be redeemed through animal sacrifice (Exod. 13:11-13; 34:20). It is likely that in Ezekiel's day people appealed to this law to justify their participation in the cult of Molech in the Valley of Hinnom outside of Jerusalem, where children were sacrificed to the deities of the underworld.

20:27-29, Israel in the Land. Ezekiel's treatment of Israel's life after it entered the land is strikingly brief and appears to be an intrusion into the flow of the argument. The prophet summarizes the people's behavior by saying that they worshiped other gods as their ancestors had done. This comment is anticlimactic after the preceding history leading from Egypt to the promise of exile.

20:30-44, Implications for the Future. At the end of his history of Israel's apostasy, Ezekiel is told to address the elders again concerning both the present and the future. Speaking to the present, God repeats the point of vv. 1-4. The elders have repeated the sins of their ancestors and therefore may not inquire of God through the prophet (vv. 30-31). At the same time, this refusal of the elders' inquiry does not mean that exilic Israel is doomed to a future without God. The people will not become like the rest of the nations, which worship idols (v. 32). Instead, God promises the people a new exodus, which will involve a purifying return to the wilderness (vv. 33-38). In the future the exiles will be gathered from the places where they have been scattered, and they will be led into a wilderness where God will impose divine kingship on them. Like a shepherd who counts sheep for sacrifice by making them pass under a rod, so God will examine the individual exiles and remove the rebels from them. The new wilderness will be a time of judgment, and the survivors will be obliged to obey the covenant (v. 37). Even though the exiles continue to rebel, they cannot cease to be God's people, and God will not finally reject them.

After this involuntary period of judgment and purification, God promises to bring the remnant back to the land and to reestablish worship. No longer will God refuse the people's request for an audience, but their offerings will again be accepted. The divine presence will return to the land, and the proper relationship between God and people will be restored. When the people witness these events, they will know God through acts of restoration rather than through acts of judgment, and then they will recognize their sins. In the end God will restore the people for the sake of the divine name and will not give them what they actually deserve (vv. 40-44).

20:45-21:32
Oracles of the Sword

In this section Ezekiel or his disciples have woven together several oracles that may have originally been written on different occasions. The collection opens with an allegory against the southern forests (20:45-49). This initial unit is then linked to an oracle concerning the divine sword; this second oracle is presented as the interpretation of the opening allegory (21:1-7). The reference to the sword is the occasion for including two additional oracles dealing with swords: the song of the sword (21:8-17), and a description of the sword of the king of Babylon (21:18-32). By use of these thematic links the entire section coheres.

20:45-49, Allegory of the Forest. In this oracle Ezekiel is told to prophesy against the southern forests, specifically the forest of the Negeb. The divine message is that all of the trees of the forest, the green ones as well as the dry ones, are to be burned. The total burning will be a sign to everyone that God is the agent of the destruction.

The symbolism of the allegory is unclear. Presumably the fire represents God's judgment, as it does elsewhere in Ezekiel, but the identity of the area to be burned is obscure. It is impossible to understand the oracle literally, since the Negeb was a dry, desolate area of southern Judah that contained little vegetation of any sort and certainly no forests (→ Negeb, The). It is likely, therefore, that the prophet here refers simply to Judah as a whole. The designation "southern" is appropriate if Judah is compared with the old Northern Kingdom, Israel. This old division of the land may lie behind the allegory.

The vagueness of the allegory also impressed the prophet, who apparently did not understand what was being communicated. He therefore complained that his audience was accusing him of speaking only in incomprehensible riddles and allegories. Apparently in response to this complaint, God then provided the interpretation contained in the following oracle.

21:1-7, Unsheathing God's Sword. The interpretation supplied for the preceding allegory clearly identifies the object of God's wrath as Jerusalem and its sanctuaries. However, in the interpretation the prophet changes the agent of destruction from fire to sword. The reason for this shift is not clear, since both images are appropriate in descriptions of the Babylonian conquest of the city. As is true throughout Ezekiel, it is clear here that God is the actual destroyer of Jerusalem. It is a divine sword that will rage through the city, destroying both the righteous and the wicked together (vv. 1–5).

To dramatize the devastation foretold in the oracle, Ezekiel is commanded again to become a sign for the exiles (cf. 12:1–7, 17–20). He is to wail and mourn to indicate the seriousness of the loss of the city and the destruction of its inhabitants. When people ask the reason for his behavior, he is to respond by describing the terror that will inevitably come on the Jerusalemites as they anticipate their destruction (21:6–7).

21:8–17, The Song of the Sword. In the poem describing God's sword, the prophet communicates his dreadful message by using repetition and by piling up evocative images (cf. chap. 7). The result is a passionate, urgent song that fully captures Ezekiel's horror as he watches the divine sword do its deadly work. The poem begins with an ominous description of the sword's construction. It is sharpened and polished so that it can be an efficient instrument of destruction (21:8–11). With the preparation of the sword completed, the prophet's attention is drawn to the sword's purpose: the slaughter of God's people. The prophet is told to cry and wail when he realizes that Jerusalem cannot escape destruction. God will no longer use the sword simply to test the city's willingness to obey but will use the blade only for slaughter (vv. 12–13).

After seeing the use to which the sword will be put, the prophet is himself drawn into the action. He is to clap his hands, and that act will make the sword fall on the people. God then joins the prophet's action whereupon it becomes clear that the real agent of Jerusalem's destruction is God acting through the prophet (vv. 14–17).

21:18–32, The Sword of the King of Babylon. From the divine agent of Israel's destruction Ezekiel turns to the human agent, the king of Babylon. Just as the prophet was earlier told to dramatize the siege by drawing Jerusalem surrounded by the enemy (4:1–3), so now he is commanded to sketch the invasion route by which Nebuchadnezzar will come to Jerusalem. Ezekiel dramatically draws a fork in the road leading from Babylon. One of the road's branches leads to Jerusalem, while the other leads to Rabbah, the capital of the Ammonites. The oracle then graphically describes the Babylonian king standing at the fork in the road and consulting various types of omens to determine which road to take. The omens point to the road

to Jerusalem, and the city's fate is sealed (21:18–23).

The significance of Ezekiel's oracle is immediately made clear. God has not forgotten Israel's sins. Therefore Jerusalem will be destroyed, and Zedekiah will be stripped of his royal robes and removed from the throne (vv. 24–27).

As an afterthought, Ezekiel or his disciples have added an oracle against the Ammonites (vv. 28–32). Although Ammon originally escaped when the Babylonian oracles directed the king toward Jerusalem, the Ammonites too will feel God's wrath. Against them will be turned the divine sword that had been prepared for use on Jerusalem.

22:1–31
Oracles Against the Uncleanness of Jerusalem

In this section Ezekiel or his disciples have assembled three oracles dealing with the impurity of Jerusalem and its inhabitants. The individual units may well have originated at different times, and the prophet has made no effort to weave them together into a larger literary unit.

22:1–16, A City of Blood. The first oracle in the section fits the standard prophetic pattern of an announcement of judgment. The unit begins with a general indictment of Jerusalem for its crimes. The offenses of the city are of two general sorts: bloodshed and idolatry, that is, crimes against people and crimes against God. Both types of crimes have made Jerusalem notorious among the nations and brought it to the brink of judgment (vv. 1–5).

The general indictment of the city and its inhabitants is then made specific by citing a representative list of sins (vv. 6–12). Some of these crimes are included in indictments elsewhere in Ezekiel (see esp. chap. 18). Many of the offenses are violations of priestly law as set out in the Holiness Code (Lev. 17–26). Included are mistreatment of parents (Exod. 21:17; Lev. 20:9); oppression of aliens, widows, and orphans (Exod. 22:21–22; Deut. 14:29); desecration of holy things and Sabbaths (Lev. 19:30); slander (Lev. 19:16); eating ritual meals at pagan shrines; a variety of sexual offenses (Lev. 18; 20); and improper business practices.

On the basis of this indictment, God announces a judgment (Ezek. 22:13–16). Israel will be scattered in exile among the nations, and everything in Jerusalem that is impure will be destroyed.

22:17–22, The Smelting of the City. The image of God refining Jerusalem to remove its impurities is already present in Isa. 1:22, 25. Ezekiel here may be giving his own interpreta-

680

tion of Isaiah's earlier oracle. Both prophets refer to the ancient process by which silver was extracted from the ore in which it was embedded. During the first stage of refining silver, minerals were added to the silver ore, and the whole mixture was heated in a smelting furnace. The intense heat melted the ore and caused the metals mixed with the silver to form sulfides. At this point the smelters removed the metal sulfides (dross or slag) and discarded them. Then the silver, still mixed with some lead, was further refined.

In Isaiah's original oracle, the smelting image was used to describe the process by which God would purify the city until all of the wicked (the dross) were collected and discarded and only the remnant (the silver) remained. As is frequently the case, however, Ezekiel changed Isaiah's image dramatically. In Ezekiel's oracle, God begins by announcing in advance the results of the smelting process. Before the work even begins, God tells the prophet that all of Israel has become dross, which is fit only to be discarded. The people have become the bronze, tin, iron, and lead that are removed as slag. There is no silver, no one worth saving, among them (Ezek. 22:17–18; cf. Jer. 6:27–30). Because God has reached this conclusion, the prophet is to announce the people's punishment, which will take the form of burning them in the smelting furnace of Jerusalem. However, because there is no silver in this ore, nothing good comes from the smelting process. The furnace of God's wrath only melts the dross, which is then discarded (Ezek. 22:19–22).

22:23–31, An Indictment of Jerusalem's Inhabitants. In the last oracle in this section, the prophet addresses Jerusalem and condemns various leaders who should have tried to prevent the city's destruction but did not. It is important to remember that Ezekiel's audience in Babylon also contained some of Jerusalem's leaders, so the oracle pertains to them as well. Because of the actions of the leaders, Jerusalem remains impure. The leaders have taken treasure and destroyed people in the city. The priests, who should have been concerned with the purity of the city, have violated God's law, desecrated holy objects, and failed to distinguish the holy and the unholy, the clean and the unclean. The princes, who should have guaranteed justice, have murdered for unjust gain. The prophets speaking in God's name have lied to the people. The landowners ("people of the land") have committed robbery and extortion against the poor. When God looked for a prophet to protect the people from the divine wrath, no one could be found (cf. chap. 13). Therefore God has already poured out judgment on the leaders. The way in which Ezekiel refers to the judg-

ment as already having taken place (22:31) suggests that he is referring here to the judgment that occurred in 597 B.C., when the leaders in Ezekiel's audience were deported to Babylon. In this case the message is intended for the exiles, even though the oracle itself is addressed to Jerusalem. Alternatively, it is possible to interpret the entire oracle as a retrospective statement of the reasons for Jerusalem's fall. In this case the oracle would have been written after 586 B.C. by Ezekiel or his disciples.

23:1–49
Allegory of the Two Sisters

Chap. 23 contains an expanded allegory dealing with two adulterous sisters, Jerusalem and Samaria. Ezekiel first used this literary image in 16:43–63, and it is likely that chaps. 23 and 16 have influenced each other at various points in their compositional history. In addition, chap. 23 has undergone several later expansions at the hands of Ezekiel or his disciples, with the result that there are breaks in the continuity of the argument during the latter part of the chapter (vv. 35–49).

As he did in chap. 16, Ezekiel bases the allegory in chap. 23 on Hosea's image of God and Israel related to each other as husband and wife (cf. Jer. 2–3). Again Ezekiel develops this image in great detail, using graphic, crude, and explicit sexual language to portray Israel's adulteries. As in chap. 16, the prophet's intent is to shock his readers into realizing how drastically they have violated their covenant relationship with God.

23:1–34, The Judgment of the Sisters. In chap. 16 Ezekiel compared Jerusalem with her "sisters," the proverbially wicked cities of Samaria and Sodom, to dramatize Jerusalem's depravity. In chap. 23 the prophet uses the image in a more strictly historical way. He first tells allegorically the story of Samaria, the capital of the Northern Kingdom (Israel) after the political division of Ephraim and Judah following the death of Solomon. Samaria's history, which culminated in the city's destruction at the hands of the Assyrians, should have been an object lesson for Jerusalem, the capital of the Southern Kingdom (Judah), but Jerusalem did not learn from her "older" sister (cf. Jer. 3:6–10). Therefore Jerusalem is condemned to share the same fate as Samaria.

In developing the allegory, Ezekiel sometimes distorts or emphasizes too strongly the actual events of Israel's history, but in general the course of the allegory can easily be followed. The tale begins with two sisters who were the daughters of the same mother, a reflection of the fact that, until Solomon's death, Judah and Israel were both part of the larger nation of Israel. Ezekiel assigns the names Oholah and Oholibah to Samaria and Jerusalem respectively, although the specific meaning of these names is not clear. Both are based on the Hebrew word meaning "tent," and the prophet may intend the names to evoke the preconquest period, when Israel lived in tents, or to refer to the tent of meeting, the portable shrine that housed God's presence until a permanent Temple was built by Solomon (→ Tabernacle). Some scholars have suggested more specific meanings for the names, although there is still much debate on this issue. It is possible that the prophet simply wanted to use two different names that resembled each other.

According to the allegory, the adulteries of the two sisters began in Egypt, though it is not clear in this case what the prophet means by "adultery." Knowing that they were adulteresses, God nevertheless married them and had children by them (vv. 1-4). This picture of Israel's early relations with God closely follows the symbolic actions in Hosea 1 and 3 and may reflect the fact that Israel rebelled against God even before the covenant ("marriage") was made at Sinai (Exod. 14:10-18; 15:19-26; 16:1-36; 17:1-16).

After this brief introduction to the history of the sisters while they were still together in Egypt, Ezekiel jumps to the time of the division of the Northern and Southern kingdoms and traces their separate stories. In both stories he uses the adultery image primarily to refer to the practice of making political alliances with other nations, a practice that he viewed as the equivalent of rejecting God's sovereignty (cf. 16:23-34; Hos. 8:9-10; Isa. 7:1-9). Thus Oholah played the harlot with the Assyrians, a reference to the Northern Kingdom's various treaties with Assyrian kings (2 Kings 15:19-22; 17:1-6). As a punishment for this crime, God gave Israel into the power of the Assyrians, her former lovers (Ezek. 23:5-10; cf. 16:35-42). Samaria was destroyed, and the Northern Kingdom ceased to exist (722/721 B.C.).

The story of Oholah/Samaria should have been a warning to Oholibah/Jerusalem and should have led her to change her ways, but this was not the case. She too committed adultery with the Assyrians and compounded that sin by inviting the Babylonians to commit adultery with her (23:11-21). Lying behind this indictment is Judah's long history of political alliances with Assyria (2 Kings 16:7-9; 18:1-36) and later with Babylon (2 Kings 20:12-21). This history continued up to Ezekiel's own time and culminated in Zedekiah's vacillating foreign policy that included leagues with both Babylon and Egypt (see "Introduction" above).

The description of Jerusalem's crimes leads directly to a graphic picture of her punishment (Ezek. 23:22-31). God will punish the adulteress

by leaving her to the mercy of her former lovers, the Babylonians and all of their allies (v. 23; cf. 16:35-42). Now rejected by God, the adulterous wife is no longer under the protection of God's law, which mandated death by stoning as the penalty for adultery (Lev. 20:10; Deut. 22:22-24). The laws of other nations were not so kind. The Babylonians will mutilate the adulteress, strip her, and leave her to the mercy of her enemies. Her children will be killed and burned. Jerusalem will be exposed to the horrors of siege, capture, and exile. She will drink from the same cup as her sister, Samaria, and will share the same fate.

The reference to the two sisters sharing the same cup (Ezek. 23:31) provides the occasion for the inclusion of a brief song that develops this image (vv. 32-34). The song, which may have been part of the original oracle or may have been added later, reinforces the point that Jerusalem will have to suffer all of the torments that Samaria suffered.

23:35-49, Supplementary Indictments.

The remainder of chap. 23 contains several new indictments and announcements of judgment against Jerusalem. Much of this material seems to have been influenced by the contents of chap. 16 and may have been added to chap. 23 after the initial allegory was composed. The additional charges amplify the earlier oracle but do so in a way that is anticlimactic after the allegory's horrifying description of judgment.

After a summary of the preceding oracle (v. 35), the prophet includes a new indictment of both sisters (vv. 36-42). Again the charge is adultery, but this time the adultery image clearly refers to the worship of other gods rather than to the making of foreign alliances (cf. 16:15-22). The people have profaned God's sanctuary and Sabbaths and have offered their children as sacrifices to the underworld deities (see commentary above on 16:15-22; 20:26). They have invited foreign lovers to the Temple, presumably a reference to the introduction of foreign practices into Israelite worship (cf. 8:5-18; 13:17-23).

The importation of other gods is the equivalent of adultery (23:43-44). Therefore the sisters will be judged by "righteous men," who will impose the penalty for adultery (v. 45). The identity of these righteous people is uncertain. If the reference is to the Babylonians as the agents of God's punishment, which is the case in the rest of the chapter, then the prophet is clearly being ironic or else implying that the Babylonians are righteous when contrasted with Jerusalem. On the other hand, the reference may be to those in exile who have been able to repent and keep themselves righteous (cf. 18:14-17). If so, then the prophet envisions a situation in which the righteous remnant of the exiles will participate in the judgment of the rest of Israel.

The penalty for adultery is referred to explicitly in 23:46–49, where God commands the prophet to call up the enemy army that will punish Israel. As is true elsewhere in Ezekiel's allegories, the literary image is invaded by the historical reality of the siege of Jerusalem. The adulterous Jerusalem will be stoned and killed by the sword. The survivors will be killed and the houses of the city torn down. The fate of Jerusalem will serve as a warning to the rest of the nations, and in the judgment Israel will come to know God.

24:1–14
Allegory of the Pot

Ezekiel's allegory of the pot takes the form of a brief song about preparing a pot and its contents for cooking (vv. 3–5). The allegory is then extended and obliquely interpreted (vv. 9–14), and this interpretation has in turn been expanded by a later addition (vv. 6–8). The result is an image that contains some inconsistencies, but the overall meaning of the allegory remains clear.

At the beginning of the allegory, God tells Ezekiel to record in writing the precise day on which the oracle is given. It is January 588, the beginning of the Babylonian siege of Jerusalem (vv. 1–2). The exiles, of course, will not receive word of the siege until later, and when they do they will then be able to recognize the truth of the prophet's earlier oracle.

Following the instructions concerning the date, God gives the allegory that the prophet is to utter. It is in the form of a song, instructing someone to fill a pot with water and fill it with pieces of prime meat and bones. The pot is then to be put on the fire and the meat cooked. Taken by itself, the song is innocuous, and if it were to be heard in isolation from its present context it might even be understood as a positive image of the preparation of a bountiful feast. However, the introductory note on the date of the allegory forces readers to give the image a more negative interpretation. It must now be connected with the Jerusalemites' earlier statement about Jerusalem: "This city is the caldron, and we are the flesh" (11:3).

The first of the two expansions and interpretations of the allegory immediately develops this negative note (vv. 6–8). However, instead of focusing on the contents of the pot, as one might expect, this interpretation focuses on the pot itself. The bloody city of Jerusalem is likened to a corroded kettle, which contaminates everything in it. The contamination of the city stems from innocent blood that has been spilled within its walls, a reference perhaps to the oppression of the poor or to the deaths caused by the kings' foreign policies. No attempt has been made to atone for the blood or cover it, so God

will now expose the blood and make atonement impossible. The pot will be emptied and purified (v. 6). If this reference is to be interpreted as part of the allegory, it may refer to the exiles of 597 B.C., who were removed from the city before its burning and purification in 587–586.

After this reflection on Jerusalem's sin, which appears to be a digression, there is a second interpretation that better fits the original allegory (vv. 9–14). The bloody city of Jerusalem and its inhabitants will be burned until people (the contents of the pot) are thoroughly cooked and charred. Then the city itself (the pot) will be burned until its impurities are removed. God will not spare the city again but will burn it until it is pure.

24:15–27
The Death of Ezekiel's Wife

In 24:15–27 the prophet is again told to act as a sign for the exiles to dramatize for them what their own future will be. As is often the case, Ezekiel reports the sign as he experienced it and does not supply an interpretation until the meaning of the sign is actually revealed to him.

The symbolic act begins when God tells the prophet that "the delight of [his] eyes" will be taken away from him with a single stroke. In response to this event the prophet is not to weep, sigh aloud, or wear the clothes of mourners. He is to do nothing to make his grief public. This prophecy is immediately reported to the exiles, but its meaning is not immediately clear. To what does the phrase "delight of your eyes" (v. 16) refer? Is it a human being? If so, who is it? In the context of the beginning of the siege of Jerusalem, does it perhaps refer to the city itself? The ambiguity is not resolved until Ezekiel's wife dies on the evening of the day that the prophecy was reported to the people. Then the prophet responds as he was directed (vv. 17–18).

When the exiles inquired about Ezekiel's peculiar response to his wife's death, he interprets the sign for them (vv. 19–24). In this interpretation, the phrase "delight of your eyes" is given a double meaning. It refers to the Temple, which symbolizes God's presence in Jerusalem, and it also refers to the children whom the exiles were forced to leave behind in the city when they were deported in 597. God will desecrate the Temple, and the sons and daughters of the exiles will be slaughtered (v. 21). In response to these two events, the exiles are not to mourn publically, presumably because the destruction was deserved in both cases.

At the end of the symbolic act Ezekiel receives an additional divine word concerning the fatal day of the Temple's destruction. When the judgment actually takes place, a fugitive from the city will report the news, and the prophet's dumbness will then be removed (vv. 25–27). This prophecy is finally fulfilled in 33:21–22.

25:1–32:32
Oracles Against Foreign Nations

After the last of the major judgment oracles against Jerusalem and Judah, Ezekiel has inserted a collection of judgment oracles against foreign nations. Similar collections appear in other prophetic books as well (Amos 1–2; Isa. 13–23; Jer. 46–51), and it may be that certain types of Israelite prophets were expected to deliver such prophecies as a form of protection or retaliation against the nation's enemies. For this reason judgment oracles against foreign nations are often considered the equivalent of promise oracles for Israel. By destroying Israel's enemies, God is in fact bringing salvation to Israel. While this view of the oracles may help to explain why Ezekiel placed them between oracles of judgment against Israel (chaps. 1–24) and oracles of promise (chaps. 34–48), it does not explain the purpose of the oracles. If the oracles were intended simply to predict divine vengeance against Israel's enemies and to reassure the besieged Jerusalemites, then one would certainly expect Ezekiel to have included oracles against Babylon in the collection. However, anti-Babylonian oracles do not appear. Rather all of the nations condemned in the oracles either played some role in the events surrounding the destruction of Jerusalem or were active in trying to prevent Babylonian rule from being established in Palestine. Throughout the book Ezekiel's theological view of Babylon is that God, who is the true ruler of all nations, has chosen Nebuchadnezzar as a divine instrument to punish Israel for its sins. Therefore anyone who interferes with Nebuchadnezzar's actions is opposing the will of God and deserves to be punished.

The oracles in the collection contain an unusually large number of specific dates, although the arrangement of the oracles is not strictly chronological. The dates serve two functions. First, they anchor most of the prophecies in the period between the beginning of the siege of Jerusalem and its completion. The siege was a time of intense political activity in Israel, and many of the nations condemned in the oracles were involved in this activity in various ways. Their interaction with Jerusalem probably prompted the oracles dealing with their fate. Second, the dates are designed to guarantee the truth of the oracles by showing that they were actually delivered before the events they describe.

Although oracles against foreign nations are sometimes thought to be the work of exilic or postexilic disciples of the prophets, there is no reason to doubt that Ezekiel composed the oracles contained in chaps. 25–32. However, some of the oracles appear to have been heavily edited, either by Ezekiel himself or by his disciples.

25:1–17
Oracles Against Israel's Neighbors

The collection of prophecies against foreign nations opens with a set of oracles against four of Israel's nearest neighbors: Ammon (vv. 1–7), Moab (vv. 8–11), Edom (vv. 12–14), and the Philistines (vv. 15–17). All of these nations had a long history of contentious relations with Judah, but most of the indictments are rather general in character. When specific charges are made against a particular nation, they usually reflect events occurring after the fall of Jerusalem in 586 B.C. Although the indictments are not dated, the references to Jerusalem's fall suggest that most, if not all, of the oracles were produced after the city was destroyed.

All of the oracles follow the same general literary pattern, that of the classic prophetic announcement of judgment. The indictment of the nation is introduced with the word "because," and the description of the crime is followed by an announcement of punishment, introduced by the word "therefore," often followed by the formula "thus says the Lord."

25:1–7, Against Ammon. Ezekiel records two oracles against Ammon. In the first (vv. 2–5), the Ammonites are condemned because they mocked Judah when the Temple was destroyed by the Babylonians. For this reason, Ammon is to be invaded by an unnamed people from the east, presumably the Babylonians or their successors. In the second oracle (vv. 6–7), Ammon is accused of rejoicing over Israel's destruction. As a punishment, Ammon will have to share Israel's fate.

25:8–11, Against Moab. Although there were longstanding political tensions between Judah and Moab, the Moabites are charged only with denying the special religious status of Judah and comparing the Judahites to the rest of the nations. Because Moab did not recognize Judah's privileged position as God's elect, Moabite cities will be invaded and given into the power of people from the east (cf. v. 4).

25:12–14, Against Edom. In contrast to the two preceding oracles, which treat theological themes, the oracle against Edom is purely political. Relations between Judah and Edom had been acrimonious for years before Jerusalem fell, but the Edomites earned the undying hatred of the late biblical writers by invading southern Judah after the Babylonians had destroyed Jerusalem (cf. Jer. 49:7–22; Obad. 1–14). It is not surprising that Ezekiel condemns the Edomites for this vengeful, opportunistic act. Because of their crime, God will completely destroy them and leave the country a wasteland.

25:15–17, Against the Philistines. The indictment against the Philistines is also politically oriented. Like the Edomites, they too are charged with taking vengeance on Judah, although the precise events to which the prophet refers are unknown. It is possible that Nebuchadnezzar gave Judahite territory to the Philistines. Because of their crimes the Philistines will be destroyed by God.

26:1–28:26
Oracles Against Phoenicia

Ezekiel's oracles against Phoenicia focus on the island city-state of Tyre, which, along with Egypt, Babylon, and Assyria, was one of the major political powers in the ancient world. The island location of the city provided good protection from outside attack and allowed Tyre to participate in Near Eastern political intrigues with relatively little risk. At various points in its history Tyre paid tribute to Assyria and Babylon, but the Tyrian homeland was not successfully invaded until the time of Alexander the Great. Tyre's economy was always oriented toward the sea, and the city became immensely wealthy through an extensive network of trading relationships. In Ezekiel's own time Tyre was one of the nations that joined with Judah in an attempt to stop the Babylonian advance to the west (Jer. 27).

Ezekiel's opposition to Tyre is presumably grounded in its anti-Babylonian policies. Because he saw Babylon as God's chosen agent for the punishment of Jerusalem, the prophet interpreted Tyre's anti-Babylonian activities as a violation of God's will. In addition, Ezekiel may have traced some of the abominable religious practices in the Temple to Tyrian influence.

26:1–21, The Destruction of Tyre. Ezekiel's first oracle against Tyre is dated in March/April of 587/586 B.C. The actual date is uncertain because of textual variants, but the oracle is probably to be related to Nebuchadnezzar's siege of Tyre, which began shortly after the fall of Jerusalem. The siege lasted thirteen years and finally ended with the negotiation of a treaty between the two parties.

The oracle as a whole consists of four sections. In the first section (vv. 1–6), God condemns the city for exulting over the additional trade that it will enjoy by virtue of Jerusalem's destruction. Because of Tyre's heartless reaction to Judah's suffering, the island kingdom will be engulfed by the surrounding nations, which will obliterate all signs of Tyrian occupation and reduce the island to bare rock.

In the second section of the oracle (vv. 7–14), the general threat of punishment by the nations (v. 3) is made much more specific by describing in graphic detail the successful siege, which Nebuchadnezzar will mount against Tyre. This amplification of the earlier judgment oracle (vv. 1–6) was probably inspired by the beginning of the actual Babylonian siege, although vv. 7–14 must have been added to the chapter before the end of the siege, since Ezekiel's prediction of the Babylonian destruction of the city was never realized.

In the third section of the oracle (vv. 15–18), Ezekiel anticipates the reaction of the surrounding nations to Tyre's dramatic fall. Addressing the city directly, the prophet describes the way in which its death cries will shake the entire Palestinian coast and terrify the kings who were once Tyre's trading partners. They will put on mourning garments and lament the vanquished city. As in all laments (cf. chap. 19), the dirge of Tyre's neighbors contrasts the city's former glory with its present miserable state. The powerful, renowned city that once terrorized the entire coast has now disappeared entirely (26:17–18).

The final section of the oracle (vv. 19–21) expresses the significance of Tyre's destruction in theological terms. Although Nebuchadnezzar may be the direct cause of the city's demise, God is actually the one who causes Tyre to be engulfed in the waters of the cosmic sea, the primeval deep that lies beneath the earth. God will then consign the city to the underworld, the realm of the dead, where all life ceases. Ezekiel uses the image of a descent into the underworld elsewhere in his oracles against foreign nations (cf. 28:8; 31:14–18), and it is extraordinarily well developed in his oracles against Egypt (32:17–32). The latter passage in particular has probably influenced his description of Tyre's fate.

27:1–36, A Lament for the Ship of Tyre. In this long and beautifully crafted oracle, Ezekiel laments the anticipated destruction of Tyre at the hands of the Babylonians. Like his other laments (cf. chap. 19), this one describes first the previous glorious state of Tyre (vv. 3b–25a) and then its present grievous condition (vv. 25b–36). However, rather than describing the city's downfall literally, the prophet does so allegorically. Quoting Tyre's boast of its perfect beauty, Ezekiel compares the proud island to a beautiful, stately ship.

The prophet first describes the beauty of the ship's construction (vv. 3b–7). The materials in the ship, like the wealth of Tyre itself, came from countries throughout the Mediterranean Basin and represented the finest quality that the

685

ancient world had to offer: fir from Senir, cedar from Lebanon, oaks from Bashan, pines from Cyprus, linen from Egypt, and purple goods from Cyprus (Elishah). The crew that operated the ship and made possible Tyre's extensive trading activities likewise came from a wide variety of locations (vv. 8–11).

After dealing with the ship and its crew, Ezekiel turns to the merchandise that the ship carried. Tyre derived its income from transporting cargo from one city to another along the Mediterranean coast, so the prophet provides a detailed account of the sorts of goods that would be loaded at each port (vv. 12–25a).

At the end of its rounds, the heavily loaded ship headed into deep water, where it met disaster. A strong east wind wrecked the ship, and all its crew and cargo sank into the sea (vv. 25b–27). The wind in this case probably represents the Babylonian army, which Ezekiel had already predicted would destroy Tyre (26:7–14).

All of Tyre's trading partners then mourn for the destroyed ship (27:28–31) and raise their own lament (v. 32). They describe Tyre's former trading activities that enriched both the city and the entire region (v. 33), and then they record their horror at Tyre's disappearance (vv. 34–36).

28:1–19, Oracles Against the Rulers of Tyre. In chap. 28 Ezekiel records two prophecies against the rulers of Tyre (vv. 1–10, 11–19). Both of these oracles share a similar theme, although they are quite different in form. In both cases the prophet condemns the ruler for his pride and speaks of his downfall in mythological terms. Because of this mythological dimension, many scholars see behind the oracles a Mesopotamian or Canaanite myth in which a primeval figure, who lived in a fruitful garden on a cosmic mountain, was deposed and sent into the underworld as punishment for a sin that he had committed. Traces of such a myth are alleged to exist in Genesis 2–3 and Isa. 14:12–20, but to date no myth resembling the scholarly reconstruction has been found in extrabiblical sources.

In the first prophecy (Ezek. 28:1–10), Ezekiel delivers a standard announcement of judgment against the prince of Tyre. In the initial indictment (vv. 2–5), the prophet amplifies a prominent theme of chap. 27, Tyre's pride in its immense wealth and power. Ezekiel accuses the prince of actually claiming to be God or at least of claiming divine wisdom. Like the legendary Dan'el (see commentary above on 14:12–23), the prince was indeed wise and used his wisdom to amass enormous wealth, but his wisdom also led him to claim equality with God. Because of the ruler's pride, he will be the target of divine judgment (vv. 6–10). God will bring strangers (presumably the Babylonians)

against him and will destroy his wealth and power. They will kill him, forcing him into the underworld, the realm of the dead. There the once proud prince will become vividly aware that he is only human.

In the second prophecy (vv. 11–19), Ezekiel raises a lament over the ruler of Tyre and describes his downfall in mythological terms. The prince was once perfect in wisdom and beauty and lived in Eden, the garden of God (cf. Gen. 2–3). In the garden the ruler was dressed in garments covered with precious stones and was accompanied by a guardian cherub. The ruler was in fact perfect, until he committed an unnamed sin. Because of this sin, God cast the ruler from his mountain abode, and the cherub drove him from the garden. The ruler will be exposed before the nations and consumed by divine fire because he defiled his sanctuaries (Ezek. 28:18); all people will be appalled because of his dreadful fate.

Although it is certainly possible to interpret the oracle as it stands as a description of the anticipated destruction of Tyre at the hands of the Babylonians, there are several features of the prophecy that suggest Ezekiel may be likening the fate of the prince to the fate of the Zadokite high priest in Jerusalem, who in Ezekiel's view, defiled the sanctuary there (cf. chap. 8). In 28:13, the list of precious stones that adorned the Tyrian prince is identical to the list of stones on the breastplate of the Israelite high priest (Exod. 28:17–20; 39:10–13). In Ezek. 28:14, the cherub is reminiscent of the cherubs that flanked the Ark in the Holy of Holies of the Jerusalem Temple, while the fire stones may recall the glowing coals on the Temple altar. The cherub's expulsion of the ruler resembles Ezekiel's description of the cherub that provides the fire to destroy Jerusalem (10:1–8). Finally, the description of the ruler's fate resembles the descriptions that Ezekiel provides throughout the book when he describes Israel in exile. If these references to Israel in 28:11–19 are intentional, then the oracle may have a dual function. In its present context it is certainly a condemnation of the pride and power of Tyre and expresses the prophet's hope for that city's destruction. But Ezekiel's readers could hardly have missed seeing in the oracle reminders of their own sin, which led to their expulsion from Jerusalem. In reading this oracle they were confronted again with the prophet's sharp message of judgment. They were in exile because of their own crimes and were no better in that respect than their pagan neighbor.

28:20–23, Oracle Against Sidon. To the collection of Tyrian oracles, Ezekiel has appended a short oracle against Sidon, another Phoenician coastal city that depended on trade for its livelihood. The judgment is described in very general terms, and no reason for God's anger is given. In Ezekiel's day Sidon had ceased to be a major political power and was probably already under Babylonian control. The city regained some of its former importance from about 586 to 573 B.C., and it is possible that the oracle is a late addition.

28:24-26, A Promise to Israel. At the end of this large collection of judgment oracles against Israel's neighbors, Ezekiel has added a promise oracle to Israel. At first this oracle appears to be out of place, but it must be remembered that prophecies of judgment against Israel's enemies can also be considered oracles of reassurance to Israel. This interpretation of the preceding collection has apparently prompted the prophet to make the implied reassurance explicit. The oracle proclaims that in the future Israel's neighbors will be able to do no harm to God's people. Israel will be gathered from exile and brought back to dwell securely in the land. God will be faithful to the divine promises to Jerusalem, and when the nations see this faithfulness, both Israel and the other nations will recognize God's power.

29:1-32:32
Oracles Against Egypt

Ezekiel's seven oracles against Egypt make up the book's largest collection of prophecies against foreign nations. The reason for the prophet's extraordinary concern with Egypt is clear. Egypt was normally viewed as Israel's traditional enemy, the nation that had originally enslaved the Israelites, thus prompting God's great act of deliverance in the Exodus (cf. 20:5-7). After the Exodus, the two nations continued to interact politically, and on a number of occasions Israel and Judah looked to Egypt for help in resisting the power of the Assyrians and the Babylonians. However, this sort of reliance on Egypt almost always turned out badly for Israel. In Ezekiel's own time Egypt's promise of aid had led Zedekiah to rebel against Nebuchadnezzar, an act that the prophet predicted would lead to Jerusalem's destruction (chap. 17). In fact Pharaoh Hophra did make an attempt to relieve the city during the Babylonian siege, but he was not successful. Thus in Ezekiel's eyes Egypt was not only a traditional enemy and an unreliable ally but was also the nation most fully devoted to opposing God's plan to use Nebuchadnezzar to punish Jerusalem. For all these reasons, the prophet's anti-Egyptian oracles are particularly harsh.

29:1-16, Oracle Against the Pharaoh. Ezekiel's first oracle against Egypt is dated January 587 B.C., and was probably prompted by Pharaoh Hophra's unsuccessful attempt to raise the Babylonian siege of Jerusalem. The oracle consists of three parts. In the first part (vv. 3-6a), the pharaoh is compared to a sea monster dwelling in the Nile. God, however, will subdue the monster, catching it with a hook as one catches a fish and throwing it into the desert as food for scavengers.

This initial image of judgment is expanded in the second part of the oracle (vv. 6b-9a), which also gives the reasons for the pharaoh's punishment. Egypt has been an unreliable ally, a weak reed that breaks and injures anyone who leans on it for support (cf. Isa. 36:6). For this reason God will completely destroy Egypt with the sword and will make the country a wasteland.

The final portion of the oracle (Ezek. 29:9b-16) amplifies the judgment still further and describes Egypt's fate in terms that closely resemble those that the prophet used earlier to describe the judgment on Judah (cf. 4:4-8; 20:32-38). God will desolate Egypt from one end to the other so that the land cannot be inhabited for forty years. The people will be scattered in exile among the nations, but at the end of forty years God will gather the Egyptians again and return them to their land. However, the restored Egypt will have only a shadow of its former power.

29:17-21, The Substitution of Egypt for Tyre. This oracle, the latest dated oracle in the book, is set in April of 571 B.C., shortly after the end of Nebuchadnezzar's unsuccessful siege of Tyre. The prophet or his disciples were apparently worried that the earlier prophecies against Tyre had not been fulfilled. To explain this situation, God tells Ezekiel that Egypt is to be given to Nebuchadnezzar as compensation for the effort he expended trying to capture Tyre. When Babylon finally plunders Egypt, Israel's own monarchy will be restored (v. 21). As later events developed, Ezekiel's substitute prophecy against Egypt was not fulfilled either. Nebuchadnezzar apparently did campaign in Egypt and may have even exacted tribute from the pharaoh, but the country was not destroyed in the way that the prophet predicted.

30:1-19, Prophecies Against Egypt. This collection of oracles contains three undated prophecies against Egypt. The first (vv. 2-9), predicts the coming of the day of God's judgment on Egypt. The precise nature of the judgment is unclear, but the evocative language used to describe it is reminiscent of that used in earlier prophecy to describe God's judgment of Israel (cf. Amos 5:18-20; Ezek. 7:10-13). The second oracle (vv. 10-12) makes the agent of judgment clear. Nebuchadnezzar will ravage Egypt just as he destroyed Israel. The Nile,

Egypt's reliable source of life-giving water, will dry up, and the land will become desolate. The third oracle (vv. 13–19), elaborates further on the extent of the destruction by mentioning specific cities (mostly in the delta) that are to be destroyed.

30:20–26, The Pharaoh's Broken Arm. In April of 587 B.C., shortly before Jerusalem's fall, Ezekiel received an oracle in which God claimed to have already broken the arm of the pharaoh so that he could no longer wield a sword. The oracle is repetitious, but its point is clear. God will strengthen the power of Nebuchadnezzar against Egypt, and the Egyptians will not be able to defend themselves. As a result they will be scattered in exile among the nations.

31:1–18, Allegory of the Cedar. This allegory comparing the pharaoh to a Lebanese cedar came to Ezekiel in June of 587 B.C. In it God likens the Egyptian to a great cedar, which in fact is the mythological world tree. Its top reaches the clouds and its roots grow down into the underworld, where the subterranean waters of the great deep nourish the tree so that it flourishes and provides shade and shelter for animals and nations. Even the trees in the garden of Eden are not its equal (vv. 1–9).

In the interpretation of the allegory (vv. 10–14), the great height of the tree, which seems to be a positive image in the allegory, is interpreted negatively as a symbol of the pharaoh's pride in his great power. Because of his pride, he will be cut down like a tree and be sent into the underworld. There the pharaoh, who, like all Egyptian rulers, claimed to be divine, will discover that he is mortal like all humans. When the pharaonic tree is felled and sent to Sheol, the realm of the dead, the other trees that depended on the great tree will also be cast down into the netherworld. Egypt's allies will share its fate when the nation falls (vv. 15–18).

32:1–16, Lament over the Pharaoh. In March of 585 B.C. (MT) or 586 (LXX), after the fall of Jerusalem, Ezekiel was commanded to deliver a lament over the pharaoh. However, the lament departs from the usual pattern in a significant way. While a lament normally contrasts the addressee's former glory and present ignominious condition (cf. chap. 19), here the description of the pharaoh's present condition is replaced by an announcement of coming judgment. The lament is anticipatory and looks forward to what can be said of the pharaoh when God finally punishes Egypt for its pride. The account of the coming judgment is given in very general terms, some of which recall earlier anti-Egyptian oracles. The pharaoh, who considers himself a proud and powerful lion, is in fact a sea monster

(cf. 29:3–5), which God will capture and expose as carrion in the open field. When Egypt is destroyed, the heavens themselves will grow dark, just as they did when God plagued Egypt before the Exodus (32:2–8; cf. Exod. 10:21–23).

The general images used in the lament are made specific when God reveals that the cause of the pharaoh's downfall will be the king of Babylon, through whom God will act to destroy Egypt (Ezek. 32:9–16). Other nations will be appalled at Egypt's degradation. All of its people will be slaughtered, and the land will be uninhabited.

32:17–32, Egypt in the Underworld. In April 586 B.C. or 585 B.C. Ezekiel was again told to utter a lament against all the people of Egypt. This time the dirge takes the unusual form of a trip through the underworld. The Egyptians, who once boasted of their power and beauty, are made to share the fate of those who are murdered and thus die unnaturally. They go down into Sheol, where they meet other murderers, who were themselves slain. Assyria, Elam, Meshech, Tubal, Edom, and Sidon all preceded Egypt into the underworld, but the anticipatory lament is also an assurance that Egypt will soon join them and share their common fate.

33:1–33

The Fall of Jerusalem

In chap. 33 the long anticipated report of the fall of Jerusalem marks the turning point of the book (vv. 21–22). After this climactic event, Ezekiel turns from announcing Israel's judgment to delivering oracles of salvation. Before making this shift, however, the prophet inserts several prophecies that seem simply to repeat earlier material in the book. It is important to recognize that these repetitions are not redundant but are an important part of Ezekiel's message at this crucial point in Israel's history.

33:1–9, The Watchman's Call. The account of the fall of Jerusalem is prefaced by a repetition of Ezekiel's call to be a prophetic watchman (vv. 1–9). The description of the watchman's task is first given in general terms (vv. 2–6) and then Ezekiel is again commissioned (vv. 7–9). The prophet's call repeats virtually verbatim much of the call narrative in 3:17–21, and the basic point of the address is the same (see commentary above on 3:17–21). God cautions the prophet that he must issue the prophetic warning to the people or forfeit his own life. Although the fall of Jerusalem is a turning point in the history of Israel, the prophet's task remains the same after the fall as it was before. The destruction of the city has done nothing to change the fact that the people are still sinful. They must therefore be given the prophetic warning if even greater judgment is to be prevented from occurring in the future.

33:10–20, Individual Punishment and Reward.
After recommissioning Ezekiel, God repeats the message of 18:21–32 as an indication of what the prophet must say to the people (see commentary above on 18:21–32). The people who survive the destruction of Jerusalem, whether they live in Judah or in Babylon, are not to interpret their survival as a sign of their righteousness. They are still rebels, and the basic principle of chap. 18 still applies to them. If they repent of their wicked ways and remain righteous, they will live. This is what God intends (v. 11). However, if they refuse to repent or if they turn away from righteousness, then they will die for their sins.

33:21–22, The Fall of Jerusalem.
Given the way in which Ezekiel has caused his readers to anticipate the fall of Jerusalem, the actual account of the event is surprisingly brief. Word of the city's defeat arrived in Babylon in January of 585 B.C., roughly six months after the actual event. At this moment the prophet's dumbness was removed, and he entered a new phase of his work (see commentary above on 3:22–27).

33:23–29, The Fate of the Survivors.
Immediately after the fall of Jerusalem, Ezekiel delivered an oracle to survivors of the siege who were still living in Judah. They had apparently interpreted their survival as an indication of God's favor and were now also claiming to be the true Israel (v. 24; cf. 11:14–21). In the oracle God emphatically rejects the refugees' claim, pointing out that they still worship idols and commit all sorts of social abuses. God indicates that they too will be destroyed, with the result that the land will be uninhabited. When this devastation occurs, the only hope for Israel's restoration will lie with the exiles in Babylon.

33:30–33, Israel in Babylon.
Although Israel's last hope consists of the exilic community in Babylon, the chapter closes on an ominous note. The Babylonian exiles can live and be restored to the land only if they admit their sins and heed the prophetic warning to repent (vv. 10–20). However, God reminds Ezekiel that the people do not understand what he is saying. They come for oracles, but to them his words are no more than songs that entertain rather than edify. If this situation continues, an additional judgment on the exiles cannot be avoided.

34:1–39:29
Oracles of Hope and Restoration

After the fall of Jerusalem, Ezekiel was again free to concentrate on delivering words of salvation to Israel, although these words are sometimes still associated with judgment. As a class, the prophecies of salvation do not have the consistency of theme that pervaded the judgment oracles in the first part of the book, and it is likely that the prophet's views on the future went through several stages of development in the early years of the Exile.

34:1–31
Israel and Its Leaders

In chap. 34 Ezekiel has collected several oracles dealing with Israel's leaders. He expresses their relationship to Israel by using the image of the shepherd, an old Near Eastern image that was usually used to describe the role of the king but that could be employed to characterize other leaders as well.

34:1–10, Against the Shepherds.
Like Jeremiah (Jer. 2:8; 10:21; 22:22; 23:1–8; 25:34–37; 50:6), Ezekiel believed that many of Israel's problems could be traced to the fact that the people had been misled by their leaders, particularly by their kings. In Ezek. 34:1–10 God presents an indictment against Israel's shepherds, who have destroyed sheep for their own gain and have not taken proper care of the weak and sick. As a result, the sheep have been scattered (vv. 2–6). This indictment seems to attribute the Exile to the failings of Israel's leaders, rather than to the sins of individual Israelites, and is thus a slightly different perspective on the Exile than the one that the prophet usually gives. Speaking not only to the past but also to the present leaders of the exilic community, God warns that the leaders will be held directly responsible for the people in their charge (vv. 7–10).

34:11–16, God as Israel's Shepherd.
In place of the corrupt shepherds, God promises to take personal responsibility for the exiles in the future. As the shepherd who will gather the sheep that have been scattered, God will reassemble the exiles and restore them to the land of Israel, where God will care for the sick and the weak.

34:17–24, Judgment of the Sheep.
From oracles against Israel's leaders, Ezekiel turns to the people themselves. Continuing to use the image of sheep and shepherd, God warns that there are sheep that are taking all of the good pasture and even fouling the drinking water so

that the rest of the sheep cannot drink (vv. 17–19). These fat sheep, which push the weaker sheep away from water and food, will be separated from the flock, although the precise nature of their fate is unclear. God will then give the remaining sheep a new shepherd, David, who will again rule over them.

The precise meaning of this allegory is not clear, although it certainly implies that some of the exiles are making it difficult for the rest to survive. Ezekiel may be identifying the leaders of the exilic community as the fat sheep, or he may be thinking of the wicked who have refused to heed the prophetic warning to repent. In any case, the oracle suggests that there were conflicts among groups of exiles and that only some of the exiles, perhaps the members of the prophet's own community, would be brought back to the land, where the Davidic monarchy would be restored.

34:25–31, The Covenant of Peace. When the weak sheep have been restored to the land and the Davidic dynasty reestablished, God promises to make a new covenant with Israel (cf. Jer. 31:31–34). This covenant will be a covenant of peace, which will restore proper and harmonious relationships of all sorts in the land. Israel will again know God not in acts of judgment but in an act of restoration. The people's shame will be removed, and they will be made to dwell securely in their own land. As a symbol of this renewed relationship with God, the land itself will no longer be an enemy of its inhabitants but will willingly yield its fruit to sustain them (cf. Gen. 3:17–19).

35:1–36:15
Edom and Israel

Returning to the theme of 25:12–14, Ezekiel delivers a sharp oracle of judgment against Mount Seir, the home of the Edomites (35:1–15). This oracle and the one that follows it (36:1–15) are somewhat convoluted and appear to have been subject to several editorial expansions, an indication of the hatred that later writers continued to have for Edom. Lying behind the oracles are the Edomite attempts to occupy Judahite territory after the fall of Jerusalem, and it is even possible that Edom aided the Babylonians in the final battle against the city.

In the indictment against Mount Seir, God recalls the long history of enmity between Edom and Israel and alludes to Edom's unreliability as an ally (35:5). Because of this, Mount Seir will be made a wasteland, and its inhabitants will be held responsible for the Israelite blood that they have shed (vv. 3–4, 6–9). Referring to Edom's boast that it could now take Judahite territory unhindered (vv. 10, 12), God swears to desolate Mount Seir and to destroy Edom for its anger and envy (vv. 14–15).

After delivering an announcement of judgment to Mount Seir, God turns to announce restoration to the mountains of Israel (36:1–15). Although in the past God had decreed judgment against these same mountains (chap. 6), they will now be reinhabited. Furthermore, God supplies a reason for giving this promise to Israel, something that is fairly unusual in biblical prophecy, which rarely mentions God's motives for bringing salvation. Because the Edomites have laid claim to God's land and have helped to destroy the mountains of Israel, which have become an object of reproach among the nations, God will make the mountains fruitful again and will repopulate them with the returned exiles. The mountains will now sustain the Israelites and will no longer be an object of reproach.

36:16–38
The Vindication of God's Holiness

After the prophecy of the restoration of the mountains of Israel, Ezekiel has inserted a remarkable oracle that signals a radical shift in his views on salvation. Up to this point the prophet has stressed the necessity for the exiles to repent and to remain righteous if they were to return to the land (chaps. 18, 33). However, in this oracle God reveals that the exiles will be brought back even though they are still wicked.

The oracle begins with a brief introduction (36:16–21), which rehearses Israel's history and the reasons for the Exile. When the people were still in the land, they defiled it by worshiping idols and committing crimes against each other. Therefore God sent Israel into exile (cf. chaps. 16, 20, 23). However, even in exile they profaned the divine name because their presence implied that God was not capable of maintaining them in the land as a holy people (see commentary above on chap. 20).

To protect the divine name, which in this oracle almost assumes the status of an independent entity (cf. Deut. 12), God promises to gather the Israelites from exile and bring them back to the land. There God will purify them and remove the idols that they continue to worship. God will give the people a new heart of flesh so that they will again be sensitive to the divine word (cf. Ezek. 11:19; Jer. 31:31–34). Filled with God's spirit, Israel will now be able to observe the laws that they could not obey previously. Because of God's gracious acts, the people will finally recognize their sinful past and will remain obedient with the help of the Spirit (Ezek. 36:22–32).

At the conclusion of the oracle, the general promises of vv. 22–32 are made specific. The deserted cities of Israel will be repopulated, and the land will again be tilled. When the land again becomes fruitful, the surrounding nations will recognize God's hand at work (vv. 33–36). The nation will prosper and increase, and God will again be responsive to Israel's requests. The divine-human relationship that had been broken before the Exile will finally be restored (vv. 37-38).

37:1–28
Israel's Restoration

Further details concerning Israel's restoration are presented in chap. 37, which consists of an allegorical vision (37:1–14) and an oracle on the nature of the restored community (37:15–28).

37:1–14, The Valley of Dry Bones. Ezekiel's dramatic vision of the valley filled with dry bones is undated, but it must have been received after the Exile had been under way long enough for the people to have lost their hope of ever returning to the land. Unlike the prophet's earlier visions (1:1–3:15; chaps. 8–11), this one is allegorical. However, the prophet still follows his usual practice of leading his readers through the vision as he experienced it (37:1–10). Only after the vision has been described in all of its complexity does he provide an interpretation (vv. 11–14).

The vision begins when God transports the prophet by means of the Spirit (cf. 3:12–15; 8:3) and brings him to a valley or plain, presumably the same plain where Ezekiel saw his initial vision of God's presence in Babylon (1:1–3:15). The valley is full of bones, which have lain on the ground long enough for them to have been stripped of their flesh and dried by the sun. God leads the prophet on a tour through the valley, and he is impressed by the number and dry condition of the bones. God then asks the prophet if the bones can be made to live again. The prophet seems genuinely surprised at the question, since the reanimation of such old bones seems out of the question, and he replies that only God can answer that question. By way of response to the prophet, God invites Ezekiel to participate directly in the vision rather than simply observing it. He is to prophesy to the bones and command them to reassemble themselves and clothe themselves with flesh. When the prophet does what God commands, the bones begin to arrange themselves in their proper order with a noise that shakes the valley, and then they array themselves with flesh. The prophet is then ordered to prophesy to the Spirit, which enters the bones and reanimates them (vv. 1–10; cf. Gen. 2:7). Just as in an earlier vision Ezekiel's prophetic word began the judgment and death of the people (Ezek. 11:13), so now his word helps to restore the nation. In the history of Israel, God speaking through the prophet is the one who kills and the one who gives life.

Scholars have sometimes assumed that Ezekiel's striking image of the dry bones was drawn from his actual observation of battle-fields, but the real source of the image is to be found in the interpretation of the allegory (37:11–14). The exiles, who feel that they have been cut off from God, have been lamenting that their bones have dried up and their hope for restoration destroyed (cf. Ps. 31:10; Prov. 17:22). Without God's presence they consider themselves virtually dead. However, God promises to open the graves of the exiles, to reanimate them with the divine Spirit, and to return them to their land.

Although the interpretation in Ezek. 37:11–14 seems to have originally understood the opening of Israel's graves as yet another literary image describing God's restoration of the exiles, later Jewish and Christian interpreters understood the image literally and saw in the passage a reference to the actual resurrection of the dead. The language of vv. 12–13 is vague enough to support both interpretations, and the more literal interpretation may even have been in the mind of Ezekiel and his disciples (see commentary below on 37:15–28).

37:15–28, Oracle of the Two Sticks. Immediately after Ezekiel's great vision of restoration, he is told to perform a symbolic action for the exiles. He is to take two pieces of wood, symbolic perhaps of royal scepters, and to inscribe on them the names "Joseph" and "Judah," the names given to the Northern and Southern kingdoms of Israel and Judah. The prophet is then to hold these two pieces of wood together in his hand (vv. 15–17). When the exiles ask the meaning of this act, Ezekiel is to deliver to them an oracle in which God promises to reunite the Northern and Southern kingdoms, which shall again become one nation (vv. 18–19). In additional elaborations of the sign, Ezekiel prophesies the gathering of the exiles and their purification in the land of Israel (vv. 20–23). Furthermore, God promises to restore the Davidic dynasty to rule the reunited Israel. God's covenant with Israel and the Davidic house is indeed eternal, and the people are not to conclude from the Exile that God has rejected them (cf. 16:60; Isa. 55:3; 61:8). God will again take up residence in Jerusalem and will dwell eternally in the Temple (Ezek. 37:24–28).

Ezekiel's prophecy of restoration for Ephraim and Judah involves considerably more than a return of the exiles currently living in Babylon. The Northern Kingdom, destroyed by the Assyrians in 722–721 B.C., had not existed for many years, and its restoration would require radical divine activity (cf. 4:4–8). Ezekiel's placement of this oracle between his vision of the dry bones and the account of the apocalyptic battle between God and Gog (chaps. 38–39) may indicate that the prophet himself expected a literal resurrection of dead Israelites (37:12–13) and that he looked for this salvation to be accomplished as a result of divine activity on a cosmic scale.

38:1–39:29
Oracles Against Gog

Ezekiel's oracles against Gog and his allies seem to have had a long and complex literary history. Many of the images and motifs in the prophecies are drawn from Jeremiah's ominous predictions of the coming of an unnamed foe from the north (Jer. 1:14; 4:6; 6:1, 22; 10:22; 13:20), while the notion of defeating God's enemies on the mountains of Israel appears to have been inspired by Isaiah's oracles against Assyria (Isa. 14:24–25; 17:12–14; 31:8–9). The name Gog itself may refer to Gyges, who ruled Lydia in the seventh century B.C., and the names associated with Gog (Magog, Meshech, Tubal, Gomer, Beth-togarmah [38:2, 6; 39:1]) appear in Gen. 10:2–5 as peoples and nations in Asia Minor. All of this suggests that Ezekiel's original oracle was directed against a foe from Anatolia to whom the prophet assigned the name Gog. After Israel's return to the land, Ezekiel apparently expected an attack by this northern enemy and his allies, but the prophet also believed that God would defeat the enemy and allow Israel to continue to dwell securely in its own land. However, not long after the original oracle was recorded, perhaps even during Ezekiel's own lifetime, Gog began to be interpreted as a symbol of all of Israel's enemies, and God's defeat of Gog was increasingly seen as a cosmic battle at the end of time. When these shifts in interpretation occurred, explanatory additions were made to the original oracle, thus making it convoluted and difficult to follow.

38:1–13, Prophecy Against Gog. The initial prophecy against Gog begins with an announcement of God's judgment. God will lead Gog and his allied hoards from the north and bring them against the mountains of Israel, where the returned exiles are dwelling securely (vv. 2–9). Gog will not be aware of this divine leadership and will assume that he is following his own desires to attack the defenseless Israelites and seize their possessions (vv. 10–13).

38:14–23, Elaboration of the Judgment. The first section of this second prophecy against Gog summarizes the beginning of the first prophecy (38:2–9). At some indefinite future time, after Israel has returned to its land, Gog will gather his allies and attack Israel (vv. 14–16). God then makes the real purpose of the attack clear. Gog is the enemy of whom the earlier prophets Jeremiah and Isaiah had spoken, and God will now destroy Gog in a cosmic battle that will shake the very foundations of the earth.

God has in fact led Gog to Israel for this very purpose. When the nations see God's victory, then they will recognize the divine power at work on Israel's behalf (vv. 17–29).

39:1–16, The Results of the Battle. Ezekiel's third oracle against Gog repeats again the basic scenario of God's victory. God will bring Gog from the north to attack Israel, but he and his allies will be defeated through God's direct intervention (vv. 1–6). This victory will demonstrate the holiness of the divine name to all the nations (vv. 7–8).

After describing God's victory, Ezekiel turns to the very practical matter of purifying the land after the battle. The purity of the land was an important issue for the Zadokite priesthood of which Ezekiel was a part, and he wanted to be sure that the dead bodies of Gog and his hoard would not contaminate Jerusalem and render it unfit for ritual purposes. The Israelites are to collect the enemy weapons and burn them, a process that will last for seven years. Then for seven months the people will bury the bodies in the Valley of Hinnom (the Valley of the "Travelers," [v. 11], the Valley of Those Who Have "Passed On"), and that famous place of pagan worship will be appropriately renamed "Valley of Gog's Hoard" (v. 15). At the conclusion of all of this work, the land will finally be purified (vv. 11–16).

39:17–29, The Eschatological Feast. If it is assumed that chap. 39 is arranged in some sort of historical sequence, then vv. 17–29 are clearly out of place, since Gog was killed and buried in the third oracle and cannot now appear as the main course in the eschatological banquet. It is therefore best to understand 39:17–29 as a prediction of events that were to occur as part of the judgment described earlier and not as a sequel to Gog's burial.

As part of the judgment against Gog, God will summon the birds and beasts of the land to feast on the sacrificial meal that God has prepared from the remains of Gog and his hoard (vv. 17–20). This dramatic end to Gog will demonstrate to the nations God's glory (vv. 21–22).

At the end of the prophecies against Gog, Ezekiel has inserted a summary of the divine plan for Israel's salvation (vv. 25–29). God will restore the people to preserve the sanctity of the divine name. When Israel has returned to its land, then the people will recognize their past sin and will repent, living a righteous life with the help of the Spirit.

The apocalyptic motifs that have entered chaps. 38–39 suggest that Israelites in exile began to fear that the promises in chaps. 34–37 were not going to be realized (→ Apocalyptic Literature). As Ezekiel and his disciples continued to read these prophecies, they increasingly began to see them being fulfilled only at the end of time as part of a great cosmic act of divine salvation. The present placement of chaps. 38–39 in the overall structure of the book encourages an apocalyptic reading of the promise oracles and also suggests that the following material, the great concluding Temple vision, is also to be read eschatologically, as an event that will occur only at the end of time.

40:1–48:35
Vision of the Restored Jerusalem

In April or October 573 B.C., Ezekiel received a vision of the restored Temple in Jerusalem. The vision contains explicit details of the Temple complex and the laws that are to govern it. As a result, it is likely that the prophet intended his words to be a blueprint to be followed by the returned exiles. Where his vision differs from analogous laws in the Pentateuch, it can probably be assumed that he wanted to reform existing priestly practice. The Temple plan was likely to have been the most important part of the book for the prophet and his community, for it dealt with the building and resanctification of the Temple that were necessary before God could return to the city and before sacrifices could again resume. Ezekiel's temple was not, however, the model actually used by the returning exiles, and this fact encouraged the prophet's disciples to interpret the vision eschatologically. This interpretive shift was encouraged by the present position of chaps. 38–39 and caused the temple plans finally to be interpreted as a temple that God would cause to be built at the end of time. It is likely that this shift in interpretation also encouraged additions to be made to Ezekiel's original work, although the prophet's normal lack of stylistic uniformity makes such additions difficult to detect.

40:1–43:12, Vision of the Restored Temple. Ezekiel's vision began when God transported him in visions to the Temple mount in Jerusalem, now exalted greatly as Isaiah had predicted (Isa. 2:2). A heavenly intermediary then guided Ezekiel through the Temple precincts, moving generally from the perimeter toward the interior and taking specific measurements as they went (Ezek. 40:1–4). After giving the details of the outside wall, they moved to the exterior gatehouse and rooms, the outer court, the gatehouses of the inner court, the porch, the sanctuary (nave), the Holy of Holies of the Temple proper, and the side chambers to be used by the priests (40:5–42:14). The prophet and his

companion then returned to the outer wall. The concern throughout the tour is to mark the boundaries that will separate the sacred from the profane and thus to protect God's holiness from contamination. Once this has been done, God can return to the Temple, and in fact in 43:1–12 Ezekiel describes the return of the divine glory, whose departure the prophet had witnessed in chaps. 8–11.

43:13–46:24, Regulations Governing Temple Activity. With the boundaries between the sacred and the profane established and the divine glory once again in the Holy of Holies, it is possible for Temple worship to begin again. Ezekiel therefore turns to a description of the altar of burnt offerings, which is to be properly purified by the Levites and Zadokite priests before it is used (43:13–27). After the altar is in place, the prophet deals with the laws governing access and worship. Non-Israelites are not to be permitted to enter, as they were previously, and the sanctity of the Temple is to be guarded by the Levites, who are to act as gatekeepers. However, because of the Levites' past sins, only the Zadokite priests are actually allowed to perform sacrifices. The Zadokites themselves are to be subject to stringent ritual laws (44:1–31). The sanctity of the city of Jerusalem is to be protected by surrounding it with land taken from the allotments of the various tribes, and the scope of the prince's participation in Temple worship is strictly defined (45:1–17).

The prophet then turns to the subject of worship and describes the religious calendar. First the provisions for the annual sacrifices are given (45:18–25), and these are followed by the regulations for repeated sacrifices (46:1–15). Additional restrictions on the prince are set in place, and additional provisions are made for isolating the offerings because of their holiness (46:16–24).

47:1–12, The Stream of Life-giving Water. After discussing religious regulations, the heavenly intermediary leads the prophet back to the door of the Temple, where the prophet observes water flowing from the sanctuary. The water becomes deeper as it moves away from its source and gives life to the plants near it, eventually sweetening the salty water of the Dead Sea. The water may possibly represent the cosmic river that flows from the Temple, here conceived as the center of the world. At the very least the river is a vivid symbol of the life-giving powers of the Temple.

47:13–48:35, The Allocation of the Land. Now that the Temple has been constructed and staffed and sacrifices have begun, the land may again be inhabited. Ezekiel therefore turns to an account of tribal boundaries. In general the borders follow those described in Num. 34:2–12, but all of the tribes are given equal allotments. As in Ezek. 37:15–28, Ezekiel assumes that all of the twelve original tribes will be reconstituted. In addition, land is set aside for God, and within this holy sector special allotments are given to the Zadokite priests, the Levites, and the Temple. What is left within the sacred portion of land is given to the prince (47:13–48:29). Finally, the prophet describes Jerusalem and its gates, one gate being assigned to each of the tribes (48:30–34). With all of the boundaries properly drawn and the country reinhabited, life will return to an ideal state. God's continuing faithfulness to Jerusalem will be symbolized by the new name that will be given to the city: Yahweh is there.

Bibliography

Carley, K. W. *The Book of the Prophet Ezekiel*. Cambridge Bible Commentary on the New English Bible. Cambridge: Cambridge University Press, 1974.

Cody, A. *Ezekiel*. Old Testament Message, 11. Wilmington, DE: Glazier, 1984.

Cooke, G. A. *A Critical and Exegetical Commentary on the Book of Ezekiel*. International Critical Commentary. Edinburgh: Clark, 1936.

Eichrodt, W. *Ezekiel*. Old Testament Library. London: SCM, 1970.

Greenberg, M. *Ezekiel, 1–20*. Anchor Bible, 22. Garden City, NY: Doubleday, 1983.

Wevers, J. W. *Ezekiel*. The New Century Bible Commentary. London: Nelson, 1969.

Zimmerli, W. *Ezekiel*. 2 vols. Hermeneia. Philadelphia: Fortress, 1979, 1983.

DANIEL

W. SIBLEY TOWNER

INTRODUCTION

Daniel was a figure well known in biblical and extrabiblical tradition long before the book of Daniel itself was composed. In the Canaanite texts of the fourteenth century B.C. found at the ancient Syrian coastal city of Ugarit (modern Ras-Shamra), mention is made of a righteous hero, Dnil, who was noted for his fairness as a judge. In Ezek. 14:14, 20, this Daniel is mentioned alongside two non-Jewish heroes of the OT, Noah and Job, as one of the most righteous men in memory. The Canaanite past of Daniel is reinforced by another reference (Ezek. 28:3) in which Daniel and the king of Tyre are compared at the point of wisdom. This prehistory devolves upon the book of Daniel to the extent that Daniel continues to be notably wise, notably righteous, and, because of these virtues, a man capable of receiving divine communication through the intermediation of angels regarding the future destiny of the world.

Structure and Content

The structure of the book of Daniel can be schematized as follows:

1:1–6:28, The public history: Tales about Daniel and his three friends
  1:1–21, Four Jewish heroes do well in Babylon
  2:1–49, Daniel, the dream interpreter
  3:1–30, The three young men in the fiery furnace
  4:1–37, Daniel, spiritual counselor to a mad king
  5:1–31, The handwriting on the wall
  6:1–28, Daniel's passion in the lions' den
7:1–12:13, The private history: Dreams and visions recounted by Daniel
  7:1–28, The vision of "one like a son of man"
  8:1–27, The vision of the ram and the he-goat
  9:1–27, The meaning of the seventy years
  10:1–12:13, The great apocalypse of Daniel

The dates given internally suggest that the two parts of the book overlap. The entire story is said to begin in 606 B.C., the third year of Jehoiakim, king of Judah (1:1), and to conclude seventy years later in 536, "in the third year of Cyrus, king of Persia" (10:1). Such a span of time would imply that Daniel, who was taken as a lad

to serve in the Babylonian court, completed his career at a ripe age of more than eighty years.

The Crucible of Composition

The first six chapters of Daniel surely have roots in the wisdom tradition of Israel. They present Daniel and his friends as wise men, dream interpreters, and ideal courtiers who, though observant Jews and unwilling to compromise with idolatry, were nonetheless able to win their way in the foreign courts of Babylon and Persia. The function of these stories is pedagogical. It is to provide role models for the people of the *chasidim* (Heb., "devout ones") who wrote the book of Daniel. The second half of Daniel, on the other hand, has as its basic function the foretelling of the future, a function that we often associate with OT prophecy. This section of the book deals with the crisis of history's culmination. Such concern descends from the earlier tradition of prophetic eschatology. Beginning with Amos, the prophets had spoken of the Day of Yahweh as a day of crisis initiating the onset of a new age. Their vision had remained this-worldly, however. Even as late as Isa. 65:17–25 (probably written in the early postexilic era), the renewed and perfected world beyond the day of crisis was still the familiar world of houses and vineyards, wolves and lambs. Apocalyptic eschatology, by contrast, comes to view the Day of the Lord as a great divide, a point of radical disjunction between this world and the fundamentally altered world of the new age. The scope is cosmic. Themes of creation myth—divine struggle against evil, world catastrophe, new Eden and new Adam—all appear in the apocalyptic vision of the new age. The new world that lies beyond history is a recapitulation of the Eden that lay before it. Although the apocalyptic scheme is not yet fully visible in Daniel, the book stands in a trajectory that links the realistic eschatology of the prophets with the mature, cosmic apocalyptic eschatology of *Enoch*, 2 Esdras, and the NT book of Revelation.

Students of Daniel inevitably question where author and audience would have been situated to draw upon such diverse strands of tradition and to weave together the complex book that stands before us. In *The Dawn of Apocalyptic*, Paul D. Hanson looks back early in the postexilic period to find conflict between the remnants of the prophetic movement and the triumphant priestly rulers. With Persian sponsorship of priestly restoration and the reconstruction of the Temple in 520–515 B.C., a stable order emerged that sought to guarantee a right relationship between God and God's people, Israel. Central to this right relationship was the Temple itself, with its order of sacrifices and its priestly staff. These priestly circles extended the divine covenant of order out into every aspect of Israelite life, including worship, relations with foreign peoples, ritual cleanliness, and even diet.

Arrayed against this stable and dominant group, in the opinion of Hanson, were visionaries who, because of the eschatological promises of the prophets (particularly Isaiah of the Exile, Isa. 40–55), had expected more from this age of restoration than they found to be possible under the aegis of the priests. In their disaffection with the unshakable status quo, they began to express their hope for a better order in increasingly radical, even sectarian terms. This dissident apocalyptic tradition never enjoyed public success through the centuries of the Persian Empire, but it achieved a kind of fruition under the impact of persecution by the Hellenistic tyrant Antiochus IV Epiphanes (175–163 B.C.). In that era, the devout and steadfast *chasidim*, or saints, who are both the authors and the audience, make public through the book of Daniel the visionary hope for the future cherished through the centuries by those who claimed the prophets as their ancestors. In it they also reveal their willingness to draw upon the legendary traditions of their people to set forth the heroes of the faith in all of their integrity.

Language

From Dan. 2:4b through the end of chap. 7, Daniel is written in Aramaic, found elsewhere in the OT, primarily in Ezra 4:8–6:18 and 7:2–26. Elsewhere the book is written in Hebrew. No one knows why this is the case. Were one of the two languages neatly confined to the narrative section of Daniel, chaps. 1–6, and the other to the apocalyptic vision, chaps. 7–12, one could simply postulate dual authorship. But as is obvious, the Aramaic portion of Daniel overlaps the narrative and the apocalyptic portions of the book. That its present bilingual character goes back to its beginnings is attested by the fact that in the fragments of the text of Daniel found at Qumran, written not much more than a century after the book itself, the same transition points between Hebrew and Aramaic occur. Perhaps the most widely accepted explanation for the bilingualism of the book is that Daniel was originally written in Aramaic and that the beginning and the end of the book were later translated into late biblical Hebrew (rife with Aramaisms) to make the book more acceptable to the devout and observant Jewish audience that treasured it. By the time Daniel was written, Aramaic might have been the more likely language of choice of the author, since Aramaic had long since become the lingua franca of the Middle East, and had largely displaced Hebrew as the language of Palestine. At the same time, the issue that confronted the authors of the book most dramatically was how to survive as Jews and how to maintain Jewish lore and tradition at the necessary high level of consciousness. To these ends, the use of at least some Hebrew might have been signally important.

Date

Daniel is one of the few OT books that can be given a fairly firm date. In the form in which we have it (perhaps without the additions of 12:11, 12), the book must have been given its final form some time in the years 167–164 B.C. This dating is based upon two assumptions: first, that the authors lived at the latter end of the historical surveys that characterize Daniel 7–12; and second, that prophecy is accurate only when it is given after the fact, whereas predictions about the future tend to run astray. Based upon these assumptions, the references to the desecration of the Temple and the "abomination that makes desolate" in 8:9–13; 9:27; and 11:31 must refer to events known to the author. The best candidates for the historical referents of these events are the desecration of the Temple in Jerusalem and the erection in it of a pagan altar in the autumn of 167 B.C. by Antiochus IV Epiphanes. The inaccurate description of the end of Antiochus' reign and his death in 11:40–45, on the other hand, suggests that the author did not know of those events, which occurred late in 164 or early in 163 B.C. The roots of the hagiographa (idealizing stories) about Daniel and his friends in chaps. 1–6 may date to an earlier time, but the entire work was given its final shape in 164 B.C.

Significance in the Biblical Tradition

In our English Bibles, Daniel is placed among the Major Prophets, following the tradition of the Greek OT. In the Hebrew Bible, Daniel stands in the third part of the canon, among the so-called Writings or wisdom books. The difference is clear, that between seer and sage. In the Greek-speaking Jewish community and in the Christian tradition generally, Daniel was seen primarily as a prophet whose chief function was to lay out the outlines of the future. However, in the Palestinian community that produced the Hebrew Bible, Daniel was understood fundamentally to be a wise man and dream interpreter.

Moreover, the ancient writers knew more about Daniel than canonical Scripture preserves. A number of Aramaic texts found among the Dead Sea Scrolls either allude to Daniel or, in the case of the so-called Prayer of Nabonidus (1QPrNab), tell a previously unknown story of a Babylonian king healed by a Jewish exorcist (see Dan. 4). In two texts the book of Daniel is amplified with the story of Susanna and the Elders, the story of Bel and the Dragon, and additions to chap. 3 called "The Prayer of Azariah and the Song of the Three Youths." One text is Theodotion, the more literal Greek translation of Daniel (ca. A.D. 180). The second text is the Septuagint (LXX), the older Greek translation (ca. 100 B.C.). In the case of Daniel, it is the Theodotion text that appears in the Greek Bible; in this one instance alone, the LXX is not the text normally found in the Greek OT. The latter reports what the three Jewish heroes said while they were strolling in the fiery furnace; the other two stories present additional material about Daniel, stressing his ability to act as a wise judge in the case of Susanna and, in Bel and the Dragon, his power over the pagan deities of Babylon. Of course, Daniel is known by the NT writers and forms a significant part of the background of the NT apocalypse (cf., e.g., Dan. 7 and Rev. 20).

Beyond this literary evidence of the book's vitality in stimulating the imagination of the late biblical writers, Daniel has had an enduring theological impact. The stories of the saints in chaps. 1–6 have contributed to the determination of Jews and Christians to lead personal lives of courage and collective lives of obedience, trusting that the cause of justice will prevail in the end. Even though it fails, as all efforts of this kind do fail, to name correctly the day and the hour of the turning of the ages, the vision of the overthrow of the little horn on the terrible fourth beast (7:8–12) has been an abiding inspiration to those who have had to face the power of tyrants while remaining confident that God supports the endurance and survival of the righteous. And finally, the gift of the kingdoms of the earth to "one like a son of man" (7:13)—identified with the people who wrote the book of Daniel in the first place, the saints of the Most High (7:18)—has encouraged believers to hope that the kingdoms of the world would one day become the kingdom of God and of God's people.

COMMENTARY

1:1–6:28
Tales from the Diaspora

1:1–21
Four Jewish Heroes Do Well in Babylon

The first story of the book of Daniel is set in the court of Nebuchadnezzar, a great Neo-Babylonian monarch who ruled 605–562 B.C. Twice in his early years—once in 597 and again in 587—this king had to besiege and capture Jerusalem to put down revolts by his Judean vassals. However, neither of these incursions occurred in the third year of Jehoiakim's reign (606 B.C.; cf. Dan. 1:1). In fact, as the more contemporary and therefore more accurate account in 2 Kings 24:1–16 shows, the Judean king who was besieged in Jerusalem was Jehoiachin, not his father Jehoiakim. Evidently such details mattered little to the storyteller: the point was to place the four noble and unblemished Jewish captives Daniel, Hananiah, Mishael, and Azariah, who were renamed Belteshazzar, Shadrach, Meshach, and Abednego respectively (v. 7), in the royal household in Babylon, at the very epicenter of the action.

The ensuing narrative unfolds in three parts. In vv. 1–7 the Jewish lads are put into a three-year instructional program in the curriculum of courtly wisdom (v. 4) under the tutelage of Ashpenaz, the "chief eunuch" (an administrative title rather than a clinical diagnosis). Not only are they to learn the "literature and language of the Babylonians" (v. 4) so that they would be competent to serve as courtiers, but they were to enjoy daily rations of the "king's delicacies and wine from his own stock" (v. 5).

To modern readers the terms sound reasonable enough, but not to the narrator and the audience of that time. The next episode of the story, vv. 8–16, makes clear that although the food and wine may have been fit for a king, they were not appropriate for devout Jewish youths who are being presented as role models. Were the food and drink bad because they were mixed with categories of foods forbidden in the Torah—blood (Gen. 9:4; Deut. 12:23), the flesh of the unclean animals such as swine (Deut. 14:3–20), an animal that had died of itself (Deut. 14:21), or wine or meat originally offered to idols (Exod. 34:15)? Were they unacceptable because they had not been prepared according to the dietary practices that came to be hallmarks of later Pharisaic Judaism? Or was Daniel simply afraid of moral defilement, of owing the king too much? The text does not say; all we know is that Daniel declines to accept the dishes from the royal table for fear of defilement. Even though the captive Judean King Jehoiachin is pictured in 2 Kings as readily accepting rations from the same source (2 Kings 25:29–30), Daniel and his friends challenge their captors to feed them nothing but vegetables and water (Dan. 1:12). If at the end of ten days their condition is deemed to be worse than that of the noble non-Jewish youths in the royal academy of wisdom, they will be willing to accept the consequences. The challenge is accepted and the lads win the right to eat only the nondefiling food.

The final scene of the story (vv. 17–21) shows Nebuchadnezzar's great satisfaction with the four Jewish youths, not on account of their healthy appearance (apparently he knew nothing of the dietary crisis and its happy resolution), but because of their superior exposition of "every matter of wisdom and insight which the king elicited from them" (v. 20). Readers learn that this superior wisdom was a gift of God (v. 17).

Ritual defilement and kosher cooking remain ambiguous aspects of the story, but this much is its moral seems clear: God can be trusted. With the gifts of good health and outstanding skill spread on record, the original audience of the book of Daniel could rest assured that God gives power to those who dare to live vigorously in the world even while they dare to maintain their sharp identity as followers of the one true God.

2:1–49
Daniel, the Dream Interpreter

In the second tale of the book, Daniel and his three friends continue to demonstrate the vitality of lives that are lived in the trust that God will vindicate courage and righteousness in the coming culmination. Classified by commentators as "a court tale of contest," this story pits Daniel against the second-rate astrologers and wizards of the Babylonian court with predictable results. After all, the latter learned their charms and tricks from their guild; in contrast, as was demonstrated in chap. 1, Daniel got his skill from God. He is a new Joseph, dream interpreter to a foreign king.

The first scene, vv. 1–16, establishes the problem of the story and the plot quickly thickens. In Hebrew Nebuchadnezzar cries, "I had a dream" (v. 3); in Aramaic his staff reply, "Tell your servants the dream and we will make [its] import known." But their confidence fades, for, as it turns out, the king has forgotten the dream. They are being commanded—on pain of death, v. 5—to produce an interpretation of something that they must first reproduce! Miserably they admit defeat, and the enraged king

orders a purge of all the wise men of Babylon. When Daniel and his friends also are threatened with the mass slaughter, Daniel takes the risk of asking for an appointment with the king "in order that he might make known the import [of the dream] to the king" (v. 16).

In this second scene of the story, Daniel and the friends huddle together in prayer to God in the hope that their lives might be spared. Their prayer is answered; the "mystery" (vv. 18–19, 27–30, 47; 4:9) is revealed. The Aramaic term *raz*, which underlies the English word "mystery," signifies the eschatological secrets the meaning of which God alone can reveal. And God does solve this mystery for Daniel, who proceeds to describe to Nebuchadnezzar the king's own dream: he saw before him a shining colossus with body parts arranged in descending order of value: a golden head, followed by a silver chest, bronze belly and thighs, and legs of iron with feet mixed with clay. This four-part statue is suddenly struck by a stone that "detached itself without the aid of any hand and struck the statue at its feet of iron and ceramic and pulverized them" (v. 34; see Lacocque, p. 45).

As was the case with Pharaoh's dreams, the meaning of the dream as now set forth by the Jewish sage (vv. 36–49) is favorable to the king and yet not without its ambiguities. The dream of the colossus proves to be an allegory of world history; it was a literary device well known to ancient readers and also one that anticipates the first apocalypse in Daniel (7:2–8). It is a history of imperialism in continuous decline. It culminates in human disaster. For his part, however, Nebuchadnezzar is safe. He is, as Daniel assures him, the golden head. Which empires are represented by the other three parts of the colossus is not made crystal clear by Daniel's interpretation. If the silver chest is the historically insignificant "Median Empire," then the bronze torso would be the Persian Empire that eventually succeeded it, and the legs of iron with feet mixed with ceramic would be the Macedonian Empire in the Middle East beginning with Alexander the Great (who completed his conquest of the Middle East in 331 B.C.), and, after his death in 323, the four successor kingdoms ruled by Alexander's generals. Of particular interest to the readers of Daniel would be the Ptolemaic kingdom in Egypt and the Seleucid dynasty of Antioch in Syria, which took turns in dominating Judah during the ensuing centuries. These, the interpretation suggests, will find themselves on shaky footings. If the dream interpretation is written from a perspective later than 252 B.C., when an abortive marriage between the Egyptian and Antiochene ruling houses qualified as "iron mixed with ceramic made from clay" (v. 43; see Lacocque, p. 46) the message to readers would be clear: when these things take place you are near the time when "the God of heaven will establish his kingdom which will never be destroyed, and the rule of which will never be left to another people" (v. 44). Then they, the wretched of the earth, the persecuted chasidim, which include the writer and the readers, will inherit the earth.

The chapter concludes with the remarkable dignification of all parties. Nebuchadnezzar accepts with grace the judgment of Daniel upon his dream and renders a brief but devout prayer to the "God of gods and Lord of kings" (v. 47). Daniel and his friends also receive new authority and stature. Above all, God is dignified by Jew and Gentile alike. Perhaps this theme comes closest to the central affirmation of the chapter—that through the faithfulness of his Jewish servants, God will one day be universally praised as the sole sovereign of the world.

3:1-30
The Three Young Men in the Fiery Furnace

The Nebuchadnezzar who was so benign and positive at the end of chap. 2 becomes in chap. 3 a tyrant in the classic sense. He is also a fool, for in the first scene of the story (vv. 1–7), he sets up a golden image (perhaps of himself) and orders everyone to worship it whenever the maestro strikes up the band (v. 5). When nearly the entire population show themselves pleased to prostrate themselves in such manner, the stage is set for conflict with the one group that is not likely to heed such demands, the obedient, God-fearing Jews.

Those who hung around the court as enforcers learn about the recalcitrance of Shadrach, Meshach, and Abednego (Daniel does not appear in this story), and they inform on the Jews to the king (vv. 8–12). Nebuchadnezzar, in a rage, calls the lads before him, threatens them with death in a crematorium, and puts to them the burning if rhetorical question (v. 15): "Who is the God who can deliver you from my hand?"

The RSV rather obscures the daring reply of the three Jews by its recourse to the indefinite phrase, "If it be so . . ." Perhaps the translators were nervous about the implications of the Aramaic, which may be translated literally: "If the God whom we serve is able to save us from the burning fiery furnace and from your hand, O king, he will do so; but even if he doesn't, let it be known to you, O king, that we will not serve your gods" (vv. 17–18). The Jews' reply suggests that they were more certain of God's absolute opposition to idolatry than they were of God's power to snatch them from the oven. But they were still willing to put fidelity to God's law

ahead of their own salvation from the fire. The kind of faith that sent the early Christian martyrs to the lions in the arena, that sustained the Jewish heroes of the Spanish Inquisition, that drove the Puritans across the sea and enabled the Quakers to stand straight with their hats on before the magistrate is prefigured in the consistency of these three lads.

In the next episode of the story (vv. 19–25) the three young men are thrown into a fire so hot that it slays the very men who cast them into it. But they get up and walk around in the company of a fourth man, whose appearance was "like a son of the gods" (v. 25). This enigmatic fourth figure was understood by early Christian interpreters to be none other than the second person of the Trinity and is depicted as such in early and medieval Christian paintings. Actually, this "one like a son of the gods" is an angelic figure, for angels play an important role in the book of Daniel, even to the point of appearing with proper names for the first time. They are never very far away from the earthly career of the saints, who in chap. 7 are after all known as "the saints of the Most High ones" (7:18).

The climax of the miracle story and the royal testimony follow in 3:26–30. Nebuchadnezzar summons the three young men out of the fiery hell in which they should surely have died (v. 26). At that climactic moment they emerge and are inspected by all the functionaries who had gathered around to watch. They are found not only to be unharmed but to lack even any smell of fire upon them. The vindication of the God of Israel is completed in the words of the pagan king Nebuchadnezzar, who in a final edict acknowledges that "there is no other god who is able to rescue like this." At the very least, this story enshrines the hope of the authors that the religion of the Jews would be tolerated in the context of foreign domination, including that of Antiochus IV Epiphanes. At the most, this story anticipates the day when God's authority will be universally accepted, even by the kings of hated enemy empires.

4:1-37
A Mad King and His Spiritual Adviser

The next story is another court tale, but hardly one of contest between Daniel and the failed wise men of Babylon (vv. 6–7). Daniel is recognized as competent to a degree beyond all others at the court. Nebuchadnezzar terms Daniel the one "in whom is the spirit of the holy gods" (vv. 8, 9) and the one "for whom no mystery (raz) is difficult." But Daniel's role is really minimal in this story. This is a story of two kings, one surrounded by earthly pomp and power, the other invisible but possessing the true heavenly power. As vv. 17, 25, and 32 show, earthly power is derivative and is simply awarded by God to those whom God chooses. In this story of two kings, the role of Daniel is to give significance to the entire experience. After his initial hymn of praise to God (vv. 1–3), Nebuchadnezzar reports to Daniel a strange dream (vv. 4–18). With some trepidation, appropriate to one who brings evil tidings to the mightiest monarch of the world (v. 19), Daniel announces the bad news and the good news that goes with it (vv. 19–27). Readers are not surprised when the entire drama of the dream comes to pass (vv. 28–33).

The king's dream begins with a picture of a marvelous tree in the midst of the earth, the world tree, which provides food for all flesh (a motif well known in ancient literature and found elsewhere in the OT; see Ezek. 17:22–24; 31:1–9; →Tree of Life, The). This signally important tree is hewn down by the order of a "watcher." To cut down the world tree is an obvious world disaster, for it eliminates the sources of nourishment and order in the midst of the earth. And yet the focus remains on the tree itself, which appears as a banded stump and suddenly turns into a man whose mind has become that of a beast (vv. 15–16). For seven times, doubtless seven years, this tragic state is to persist.

Daniel, the interpreter of the "mystery," simply identifies the great tree with Nebuchadnezzar in his flourishing heyday and the stump and the beastly minded man with the Nebuchadnezzar of the future. This terrible judgment against the king can be eased, he says, by works of righteousness. By showing mercy to the oppressed, the king is promised "a lengthening of [his] tranquility" (v. 27).

Everything happens as Daniel predicts. Nebuchadnezzar, the earthly king, affirms his sovereignty in a reasonably mild exclamation: "Is this not the great Babylon which I built for a seat of government by my mighty power and for my majestic glory?" The heavenly voice announces that this arrogation of glory has triggered the sentence of God, whereupon Nebuchadnezzar becomes the pitiful grass-eating and claw-bearing beast (v. 33) that the dream had anticipated. At the end of the seven-year period predicted, Nebuchadnezzar reverses his own self-glorification, lifts up his eyes, and, in the first flash of reason following his madness, affirms the sovereignty of the most high God (vv. 34–35) and is restored to a glory even greater than what he formerly possessed.

Readers are left with an impression that the final line of the story provides a moral: God's ways are just, and "those who walk in arrogance he is able to bring down." However, this theme is nuanced by a note sounded in the dream itself: "The Most High rules the kingdom of men,

and gives it to whom he will, and sets over it the lowliest of men" (v. 17, RSV; see also v. 25). How is Nebuchadnezzar an illustration of that point, since his lowliness is only a temporary phenomenon? Perhaps we hear in these phrases the voice of the author and the author's community, those lowly saints of the Most High (7:18) who look with eager anticipation to the coming eschatological age of righteousness in which they will bear rule. Perhaps this voice intends to sound the oft-repeated theme of Scripture that God "has put down the mighty from their thrones, and exalted those of low degree; he has filled the hungry with good things, and the rich he has sent empty away" (Luke 1:52–53, RSV).

5:1–31
The Handwriting on the Wall

The contest between Daniel and the wise men of Babylon resumes with unabated vigor in the book's fifth tale. Once again cryptic symbols and their proper interpretation are at issue; and once again only Daniel, in whom—as King Belshazzar himself acknowledges—"the spirit of the holy gods" (v. 14) resides, can interpret the symbols. The stakes are high this time too, for, as it happens, the king is brought under judgment of death by the mysterious text written upon the wall by the ghostly hand (v. 30).

The scene is set by vv. 1–4, which introduce the bawdy Belshazzar, arrogant with his thousand lords, his wives, and his concubines. To the horror of the readers, he orders his servants to bring out the sacred vessels stolen by Nebuchadnezzar "his father" from the Temple in Jerusalem; with them he and his lords toast the diverse idols of Babylon (v. 4; →Belshazzar).

The plot of the story begins to develop in vv. 5–9, when "the fingers of a man's hand appeared" and began to write mysterious graffiti on the wall. The terrified king summons his incompetent sages to help interpret the puzzle and in the process "the queen" is introduced. Because of her long memory (v. 11), one feels that she is supposed to be Belshazzar's mother or grandmother and possibly the widow of Nebuchadnezzar, rather than Belshazzar's own wife. In any case, this queen's knowledge of Daniel's interpretive skills leads to his warm welcome by the king.

Daniel unfavorably contrasts Belshazzar's arrogance and idolatry with Nebuchadnezzar's hard-won acknowledgment of the sovereignty of God (vv. 17–23), and then proceeds to threaten his very existence by reading and interpreting the four words on the wall (vv. 24–31). Modern scholars tend to see the mysterious Aramaic words as a series of coins whose relative values are determined by weight (mene = mena, value: 60; tekel = shekel, value: 1; parsin = half mena, value: 30). Some even push beyond this interpretation to find in the series an evaluation of the Neo-Babylonian monarchs after Nebuchadnezzar. But all of this is background; in the foreground of his interpretation (vv. 25–28) Daniel resorts to wordplay. He treats the three different words as passive verbs related to the following verbs: m-n-h, "numbered"; t-q-l, "weighed"; and p-r-s, "divided"; the final word is illumined by even a further pun, paras, "Persia." Under Daniel's terrible, light touch, the mystery of the divine sentence is disclosed. In the reading of the inscription and in the events that follow, the faith of the writer of Daniel and his community is driven home once again: God's sovereignty over all arrogant, human sovereignties is absolute and unchallenged. God can use lowly but faithful captives among the Jewish people to assist in the overthrow of the mightiest monarchs.

6:1–28
Daniel's Passion in the Lions' Den

The culminating tale of the first half of the book of Daniel involves not only a conflict between the ideal Jew of the Diaspora and his rivals and enemies at the court, but also a contest between principles—the irrevocable "law of the Medes and the Persians" (vv. 8, 15) and the law of God. The story culminates in the usual way with the pagan king acknowledging the universal sovereignty of the God of Israel as if in anticipation of the universal rule of the kingdom of heaven at the end of history. Since history records no "Darius the Mede," the story may refer to Darius I Hystaspes (522–486 B.C.), the Persian king who is said by the historians Herodotus and Josephus to have divided his empire into satrapies (see Dan. 6:1–2).

This tale exhibits a "chiastic" or X-like structure in which the second part reverses the order of the first. This outline may be schematized as follows:

Daniel prospers over other satraps, vv. 1–3.
 His jealous enemies set a trap, vv. 4–9.
  Darius makes a tragic decree, vv. 10–15.
   Daniel imprisoned in lions' den, vv. 16–18.
    Daniel delivered, vv. 19–22.
   Daniel released, v. 23.
  Darius traps the accusers, v. 24.
 Darius makes a decree for good, vv. 25–27.
Daniel prospers, v. 28.

The story unfolds inexorably. Daniel's piety proves to be both his danger (v. 5) and his salvation (v. 23). Rival officials swarm in to the king with a single idea in mind: to create an intolerable conflict of interest for Daniel, who can neither disobey the law of his God nor escape the inexorable law of the royal decree of

the king of the Medes and the Persians. They persuade the king—who appears here as a doddering victim of their manipulations—to make a decree that no one may beseech favor from any god or any person for thirty days except himself, Darius. And, as they anticipated, Daniel continues to pray to the God of Israel (vv. 10–13). Against his better judgment, but trapped by his own edict, the king is obliged to sentence Daniel to death by lions (v. 16).

In many respects the conclusion of this story can be described as a passion narrative hauntingly similar to the great passion account of Jesus in the synoptic Gospels. The king, like Pilate, is uneasy about condemning this man to death because he is blameless (v. 22). However, the crowd of learned doctors and important people demands that the law of the empire be followed, and the hero is condemned to death. Nonetheless, the king's conscience remains guilty about the matter. Daniel is put in the place of death, and then after a time (in his case one day, not three) he emerges alive from the pit of death because he trusted God (v. 23). A major difference, of course, is that Daniel did not die because "God sent his angel and shut the lions' mouths" (v. 22, RSV).

7:1–12:13
Dreams and Visions Recounted by Daniel

7:1–28
The Vision of "One Like a Son of Man"

7:1–8, Four Beasts from the Sea. No reader can fail to sense the radical shift that takes place as one moves from the six edifying tales of righteous Jews at work to the dream-visions of the end of history that make up the second half of the book of Daniel. Chap. 7 itself marks the move from the third-person narrations of the external history of Daniel to the first-person account of Daniel's inner life as visionary and seer. It is the most important chapter of the entire book, the fulcrum on which all the rest balances. Here the long-awaited link between the obedient behavior of the saints exemplified in the first six chapters of the book and the destiny of the faithful ones in the coming kingdom of heaven on earth is made clear.

The structure of chap. 7 may be easily recognized. Verses 1–8 contain a dream-vision of four beasts that emerge out of the sea (v. 3). This vision culminates in the appearance of an eleventh horn on the head of the fourth beast. Then, the second portion of the chapter, vv. 9–14, depicts the Day of Judgment itself and identifies the parties found wanting at this great assembly as well as those who will inherit the kingdom that shall not be destroyed (v. 14). The final scene includes an interpretation of the initial vision presented to the seer Daniel by an angel (vv. 15–28).

The dream of four great beasts arising from the sea may have its roots in cosmogonic myth; think of the chaos monsters Rahab (Job 26:12–13; Ps. 89:9–11; Isa. 51:9–10) and Leviathan (Ps. 74:13–17; Isa. 27:1). But myth has faded from its purest form here, because the beasts are historicized in Daniel's vision. The angel makes this clear in Dan. 7:17, "these four great beasts are four kings who shall arise out of the earth" (RSV). The sequence is very reminiscent of Nebuchadnezzar's dream of the statue in chap. 2, except that the beasts are arranged in order of relative danger rather than in order of intrinsic worth. Both in ancient and modern times, commentators have understood this sequence to be as follows: the lion with eagle's wings (v. 4) represents the Babylonian Empire; the bear with three ribs in its mouth (v. 5) represents the "Median Empire"; the leopard with the wings of a bird and four heads (v. 6) is Persia; and finally, the dreadful beast with no name but with great iron teeth and ten horns is the Hellenistic kingdom of Alexander the Great. Among the ten horns, an eleventh springs up that destroys others; it has eyes like those of a man and a mouth speaking "enormities" (see Lacocque, p. 135). This figure is taken by many modern commentators to be Antiochus IV Epiphanes, 175–163 B.C., the king during whose reign, in the view of the community of Daniel, the culmination of history would take place.

Early on, Jewish and Christian interpreters read the sequence as follows: the lion is Babylon; the bear is Persia; the leopard with four heads is the Hellenistic empire of Alexander and its four successor kingdoms; the dreadful beast with iron teeth is Rome. The community that brought the book of Daniel into the canon of the Hebrew Scriptures may already have made this fundamental shift in their interpretation of the animal allegory, for they surely would have known that the end of the age had failed to materialize during the reign of Antiochus IV Epiphanes. Certainly by NT times the shift had been made, for the beast in Revelation 13 is clearly a composite portrait of the four animals of Daniel 7 and its wounded head probably signified the emperor Nero (Rev. 13:3). Contemporary Jewish application of the fourth beast to the Roman Empire was known as well, as 2 Esdras 11:39–46 and 12:10–34 make clear. In his late fourth-century A.D. commentary on Daniel, Jerome argues for Rome as the fearsome fourth beast and pours opposition and hostility on the opposing view of the Neo-

platonist philosopher Porphyry, whose views on Daniel are identical with those of modern commentators.

Two things are at stake in this issue. First, if the fourth beast is Rome, then it might be possible for an interpreter to identify its various horns as kings and archfiends throughout the history of the Roman Empire and its successors, even down to modern times. One might make the eleventh horn into Charles Stuart, as his seventeenth-century English Puritan opponents did, or Adolf Hitler, or some yet unborn dictator of our own time. Second, if the fourth beast represents Rome, then the writer of Daniel 7 was truly attempting to be a prophet for the long range, for he and his community could not yet have known Rome as a real power in the Middle East of the second century B.C. (much less the sixth century B.C.!). The events of the ensuing verses in the chapter would then become events of the distant future and not events that lie close at hand, within three and a half years (v. 25) of the time of the writing of the book. The book of Daniel would then cease to be an interpretation of a current crisis as well as a call for courage in the face of an existing persecution and would be disconnected from real history. The current scholarly consensus holds that such an approach is fundamentally atypical of biblical writers, and that, whether prophets or apocalyptists, their primary task was always to try to make sense of the events facing them during their own time. Subsequent interpreters may loosen the knot that binds the text to the history in the midst of which it was written, but the writers of Daniel intended to give readers some way of making sense of the oppression and the tragedy of their own period.

7:9–14, The Judgment Scene. This passage lies at the very heart of the book of Daniel, and is probably the most important scene in the entire work in terms of its impact upon subsequent Jewish and Christian thought. In his vision, Daniel watches as "one that was ancient of days" takes his place on a throne of judgment. The throne itself is apparently a chariot with burning wheels that looked like God's earthly throne, the Ark of the covenant, seen by Ezekiel in his inaugural vision (Ezek. 1:15–28). The great heavenly books are opened and the four beasts are judged. The fourth beast, including the little horn, is slain, and the rest are held in captivity after having been stripped of their dominion. The vision of judgment concludes with an introduction of the ruler of the new age: "Behold, with clouds of heaven there came one like a son of man" (Dan. 7:13, RSV). The two Greek versions of Daniel differ on how to understand the preposition "with." As the LXX seems to understand it, the one like a son of man descends from heaven on the clouds, as if he were an angelic figure borne down from the heavenly realm to assume rule in the world. On the other hand, Theodotion translates the phrase as if the one like a son of man were coming *together with the* clouds, the implication being that he is a human being who rides up from the earth as clouds rise up from the horizon. The issue dividing these two translations is whether this king of the new age will be a deity ruling a community of deities or whether he and other humans will be exalted to play a role in the divine economy. A similar ambiguity lingers around the son of man figure elsewhere in Jewish tradition. Perhaps his distant ancestor is the Canaanite figure of young Baal who rides on the storm clouds (→ Baal). A distinctly preexistent and evidently well-known heavenly son of man is a striking character in the Jewish apocalypses 1 Enoch (see particularly 46:1–8; 48:1–10; 62:9–14) and 2 Esdras (see 11:39–40, 43–46; 12:10–11, 31–34; 13:1–3). Indeed, this preexistent heavenly figure of Jewish tradition may be the one of whom Jesus speaks in such passages as Matt. 10:23; 16:27–28; Mark 8:38; and 13:26, in which he seems to be referring to some heavenly figure who will come on clouds as the judge of the Last Day (→ Son of Man).

7:15–28, The Angelic Interpretation of the Vision. Whatever the history of the "one like the son of man" as an independent heavenly figure of Jewish apocalyptic expectation, it seems clear here that the one to whom "was given dominion and glory and kingdom . . . and his kingdom one that shall not be destroyed" (Dan. 7:14, RSV) is a human being. Indeed, he is a collective human being, namely, the saints of the Most High (vv. 18, 22, 27). That identification emerges in the exposition of the dream that Daniel receives from one of the heavenly court. Though some interpreters prefer to view the "saints" or "holy ones" as members of a category of angels called the "most high ones," a more likely identification is with a human community, namely, the community that wrote and preserved this book of Daniel. The interpreter assures this community through the writer of the book of Daniel that in a very short time—a time, two times, and half a time (v. 25)—the dominion would be taken from the hands of the tyrant and given to the saints to rule forever and ever. In short, these people are the wave of the future, and that future is at hand.

8:1–27
The Vision of the Ram and the He-Goat

The second eschatological vision (not a dream in this case) in the book of Daniel is dated two years after the first; it transports the seer to Susa, the capital of Elam, now the province of Khuzis-

tan in Iran. There Daniel sees a wild, irresistibly powerful two-horned ram charging about (vv. 3–4) until it is bested by a unicornlike he-goat (vv. 5–7). The great horn of this triumphant he-goat is broken off (v. 8) but replaced by four horns and then a fifth. The latter horn, though initially small, grows up to the "host of heaven" (vv. 9–10)—possibly the stars, or even toward the angelic army. The "prince of the host" (v. 11) is accosted by the arrogant horn and loses the worship due to him, his sanctuary, and even his "host" (v. 12). The desecration of the sanctuary, accompanied by a dread event called "the transgression that makes desolate" (v. 13, RSV), must endure for 2300 evenings and mornings, i.e., 1150 days (v. 14).

In vv. 15–27, the meaning of all this is made clear to Daniel by the angel Gabriel. His speech, given at the command of a disembodied voice (v. 16) and bracketed by severe but understandable emotional reactions on Daniel's part (vv. 17, 27), is the first anywhere in the Bible to be communicated to a mortal by an angel with a proper name of his own. Interest in angels becomes a hallmark of Jewish apocalyptic literature in its later development (see, e.g., 1 Enoch 6–9); it is perhaps surprising that of named angels we hear in Daniel only of Gabriel (here and in 9:21) and Michael (10:13; 12:1), though hosts of heavenly beings adorn the visionary scenes, and other divine interlocutors revealed truth to Daniel as well (see, e.g., all of chap. 10). Nevertheless, the appearance of angels here as independent figures marks a considerable development beyond those earlier "angels" who spoke with Moses (Exod. 3:1–6), Gideon (Judg. 6:1–24), and the parents of Samson (Judg. 13:1–20)—all of whom proved to be God himself, intervening directly in human affairs (→ Angel).

In the interpretive portion of this vision account (Dan. 8:19–26), the angel makes specific identifications. Again, the beasts become an allegory of world history—the two-horned ram is Media-Persia, and the he-goat is Alexander the Great (v. 21). The imagery of swiftness and power attests to Alexander's conquest of the Near East. From the siege and conquest of Tyre in 332 B.C. to Alexander's death in 323, only a decade passed. And, even though more than a century and a half passed from the death of Alexander (v. 8) to the persecution of the Jews by Antiochus IV Epiphanes, known cryptically as the little horn (v. 9) and the "one who understands riddles" (v. 23), the angel leaps over the years to the time that really matters. That time is the 1150 days, which is the three-plus years (vv. 14, 26) through which Daniel and his community were passing.

The Temple is the central focus of the abominations of "the time of the end" (v. 17); the king who pits himself against God's house and God's truth will "by no human hand . . . be broken." Antiochus did, of course, die, possibly late in 164 B.C., certainly by early 163 B.C. while campaigning in Persia (see 1 Macc. 6:1–16, 2 Macc. 9:1–28, both of which understand the death to be at least an indirect act of God). And the "sanctuary was restored to its rightful state" (v. 14) almost right on the 1150-day schedule. True, the ultimate solution to the evil of history did not occur, and the saints did not receive the kingdom. But a profound faith is kindled here that has always drawn Jews and Christians into the future: God will make a full end to tyranny.

9:1–27
The Meaning of the Seventy Years

Almost an extension of chap. 8, the dialogue between Daniel and Gabriel about the meaning of the passage of the years—now interlaced with an interpretation of the seventy years of the "desolations of Jerusalem" foreseen by the prophet Jeremiah (v. 2)—continues. But the dialogue must wait until Daniel has uttered a great prose prayer of penitence on behalf of his people (vv. 13–19).

This prayer, with its elements of ascription, confession, and petition, most closely resembles three other long prose prayers, Ezra 9:6–15; Neh. 1:5–11; and 9:6–37. As a group, these three may reflect the practice of penitential prayer in the Jewish community late in the OT period. The formulas of such prayers are familiar from as early as Solomon's great prayer at the dedication of the Temple (1 Kings 8:22–53). In desperate straits, the people beseech God to forgive their sins for the sake of God's own name and loving-kindness. A prophetic-like voice speaks (Dan. 9:11), identifying the tragic circumstances of the age as nothing other than the curse, the punishment for national covenant breaking (cf. Lev. 26:14–45; Deut. 28:15–68; 29:18–28). Babylonian captivity or Antiochene persecution are thus interpreted as divine retribution for sin (Dan. 9:12–13). And the people have failed to take the obvious and necessary next step: "We have not mollified the Lord." However, the means of that mollification are at hand. They are precisely such prayers of penitence. And the great Deuteronomistic tradition of restoration and renewal following repentance (see 1 Kings 8:46–53) assures that God will show mercy upon the desolate sanctuary (Dan. 9:17), especially for the sake of God's own name (v. 19; → Deuteronomist).

But now a pressing theological question asserts itself. Does the writer of Daniel think God's purpose in bringing history to its end can be changed merely by uttering human prayers? The text before us would seem to disconnect the penitential prayer from the angel's announcement of the desolator's ultimate end (v. 27), because the God-given word of interpretation went forth at the beginning of Daniel's supplication (v. 23). In no way does the divine word respond to the issues raised by the prayer. Perhaps the prayer should be viewed not as an effort to change God's mind and to hasten the divine intervention that will bring history to its climactic end, but more simply as an act of piety done for its own sake, like a sacrifice in the Temple. Perhaps the prayer relies on the faith that, as in times past, present trouble and future renewal alike are manifestations of the free but righteous will of Yahweh.

The angel Gabriel, the first angel in the Bible to be described as arriving by wings (v. 21), effortlessly expands Jeremiah's 70 years of captivity (Jer. 25:11–14) to 70 weeks of years or 70 × 70 = 490 years. The angel subdivides the 490 years to make this passage of history—which otherwise would, from an apocalyptic point of view, have been essentially meaningless—into a significant periodization of time. The 7-week or 49-year period of v. 25 refers, quite accurately, to the Babylonian exile of the Jews (587–538 B.C.). Perhaps the "anointed one" alluded to in v. 25 is Zerubbabel, the last legitimate descendant of the Davidic house (see Hag. 1:1–14; Zech. 6:9–14). Then, 62 weeks of Dan. 9:26 represent the 434 years of the Persian and Hellenistic periods. At the end of this period is a final week of 7 years. Verse 26 describes the beginning of that week with the cutting off of the last anointed one—a reference to Antiochus' deposition of the legitimate high priest Onias III in favor of his brother Jason in 175 B.C. (2 Macc. 4:8). The desolator of Dan. 9:27 is surely Antiochus, who, in Jewish eyes, "destroyed the city and the sanctuary" by profaning them. The final three and a half years of history are marked by the dominance of "the one who makes desolate," but for that one the end comes on schedule at the end of the second half of the last week. Does this mean that the writer of chap. 9 knew about the cleansing of the Temple on Kislev 25, 164 B.C. (1 Macc. 4:52–58), an event which occurred just a little more than three years after its desolation on Kislev 15, 167? Does he know about Antiochus' death shortly after that event? Perhaps so. Perhaps this standard three-and-a-half-year sequence is only a visionary guess. History may have proved to be more complicated than the writer of Daniel 9 thought. But, for the writer, Daniel's posture is the right one, nonetheless. Penitence, courage, and trust in God's ability to complete the divine purpose of redemption are the themes of the great penitential prayer of Daniel 9 through which the prophet demonstrates how to think and speak while the periods of the ages roll round.

10:1–12:13
The Great Apocalypse of Daniel

10:1–11:1, The Onset of the Vision. The location and length of this final vision in the book of Daniel, together with the lengthy preparations and ecstatic experiences that take up all of chap. 10, suggest that it is intended to be the climactic experience of the book. The scope of the vision is cosmic, including even the heavenly realm in which angels carry on their own combat (10:13, 20). The vast historical sweep in this vision comprises a history that, in the view of the writer, is not a meaningless ebb and flow of events but is a great drama of good and evil played out according to a script written in advance by God in the divine book of destiny (10:21). This ancient and, for us, difficult notion of the predetermination of history is reiterated throughout this final vision (10:14; 11:27, 35, 39). Such a concept does not seem very useful for us today who know that history is a clash of conflicting pressures and forces and includes totally unexpected developments; however, it underscores the profound conviction that God has the power to complete the divine redemptive purpose in the world and that the end of history is firmly in God's hands.

11:2–39, A Visionary Review of History. The history that the angel now recounts to Daniel, as a means of assuring him that God will not be mocked, mentions no personal names; yet, up to a certain point, it faithfully parallels certain events that transpired. The first part of the vision takes Daniel from the beginning of the Persian Empire (v. 2) up through the appearance of Alexander the Great in the east (v. 3) and his death in 323 B.C. and the division of the empire into four Hellenistic dynasties (11:4). The focus quickly falls on the Ptolemies of Egypt, known here as the kings of the south, and the Seleucids of Antioch in Syria, known as the kings of the north; and it culminates in an account of the reign of Antiochus III the Great (vv. 10–19). The second part of the review of history, vv. 20–39, is devoted entirely to the reign of Antiochus IV Epiphanes, 175–163 B.C. The command of detail in this portion of the vision underscores general scholarly agreement that the author lived during these years. The writer acknowledges the initial successes of Antiochus (v. 22) and goes on to describe his two campaigns against Egypt. The first campaign (vv. 25–28; cf. 1 Macc. 1:16–19) led, according to 2 Macc. 5:5–21, to the looting of the Temple. Perhaps this event accounts for the remark in Dan. 11:28, "but his disposition toward the holy covenant will be hostile." The second campaign is described in Dan. 11:29–39. Not only did it fail in its objective of Egyptian conquest, it led to full-scale political repression of Jewish religion and ethnic identity (cf. 1 Macc. 1:30–32). Other sources suggest that Antiochus installed a Syrian garrison in Jerusalem at this time, 167 B.C. Such action in turn led directly to the reconstitution of Jerusalem as a Greco-Syrian city and the use of the Temple as a place for worship of Baal Shamen, "lord of heaven," known in his polite guise as "the Olympian Zeus" (2 Macc. 6:2). This horrible development is described in Dan. 11:31, embedded in which is the cryptic allusion to the "abomination that makes desolate" (see also Dan. 8:13; 9:27; 12:11; 1 Macc. 1:54)—perhaps an altar devoted to the sacrifice of swine, the animal most pleasing to Baal. The text goes on to acknowledge that some resistance by "the people who know their God" developed (Dan. 11:32). This "people" is surely the community for and by whom the book of Daniel was written. They are presented here as pious and wise but also as victims of sword and flame, captivity and plunder (v. 33). The writer acknowledges that these saints "receive a little help" (v. 34). This cryptic allusion has occasioned much debate. Many hold the opinion that the "little help" refers to the heroes of 1 and 2 Maccabees, the freedom fighters led by Judah the Maccabee (in Gk. Judas Maccabeus) and his brothers. And, if the "Hasideans, mighty warriors of Israel, every one who offered himself willingly for the law" (1 Macc. 2:42), are the same observant community whose members wrote and read the book of Daniel, then they are perceived as sober allies by the zealous rebels. For their part, the *chasidim* must have viewed the political activists as champions of the right. And yet they remain only "a little help," perhaps because they went too far in their efforts to usher in a new order of justice and equity, one only God could bring about.

This section of the great vision concludes in Dan. 11:36–39 with a simple portrait of a tyrant, possibly even a mad one, willing and able to work his designs without being challenged even by the gods (v. 37) and yet unaware that his ultimate doom has been sealed in secret by the God who is the master of all of history and whose word is the last as well as the first.

11:40–12:4, A Prophecy of the Future. Up to this point, everything has taken place as "predicted"; readers therefore have confidence that the balance of the vision will also transpire. In fact, however, it does not. Verses 40–45 present Antiochus as meeting his final doom in the aftermath of a historically unknown victory over Egypt. He is pictured as dying between Jerusalem, "the glorious holy mountain" (v. 45), and the sea, when, in fact, extrabiblical records attest that Antiochus died while campaigning in

Persia. We can assume, therefore, that the writer was actually living between vv. 39 and 40, namely, after the desolation of the Temple on Kislev 15, 167 B.C. but before its restoration on Kislev 25, 164 B.C., and before the death of Antiochus, which must have taken place somewhat after that latter event, hence early in 163 B.C. As is always the case, the prophecy of the end was in error, its timing considerably off. But the Jewish and Christian communities acknowledged that fact when they admitted the book of Daniel to their canon of sacred Scripture. The canonizers knew that the end had not come on time, but they allowed the vision to remain as testimony to what they held to be fundamentally and perpetually true, namely, that God is the victor in the struggle of history.

In this process, they preserved the most important innovation contained in the book of Daniel, the notion of resurrection in 12:1–3: "and many of those who sleep in the dust of the earth shall awake, some to everlasting life, and some to shame and everlasting contempt" (12:2, RSV). Isa. 26:19 may allude to the possibility of the resurrection of the dead, but if so, it is the only other instance of the concept in the OT. "Those who are wise" (Dan. 12:3) may well refer to the chasidim of which the writer of Daniel is a part. Whether they pass over into the realm of the holy ones of God, the host of angels, is not entirely clear, though the notion that they will shine "like the stars forever and ever" might support the idea. In any case, the writer of Daniel has dared here to go further than any theological predecessor in Israel since he suggests that beyond the culmination of human history and God's victory on behalf of righteousness is a world populated by the saints themselves.

12:5–13, Conclusion. The great vision of the culmination of history is over, but the persistent question remains: "How long?" (v. 6). The traditional answer is given: "A time, two times, and half a time" (see 7:25, 9:27; the three years, two-and-a-third months [by lunar reckoning] of 8:14 is a deviation from this stereotypical response). This oblique sequence allows the author to say that by the time the Temple is desolated, the end

is imminent. No more need be said (v. 9). In the meantime, those who are righteous have an interim task, to "purify themselves and make themselves white and be refined" (v. 10).

The book concludes with what may well be two additions composed by the writer himself or by some later editor. These glosses (vv. 11–12) lengthen the time before the culmination to 1290 days and 1335 days, respectively. Perhaps they display an anxious adjustment by someone who did not experience the end on its proper timetable. Had the writer lived through the expected three-and-a-half-year period, we might assume that he would have known about the cleansing of the Temple on Kislev 25, 164 B.C. (1 Macc. 4:52) because that event would have occurred in just a little over three years from the time of its profanation. He might even have known about the death of Antiochus, which must have occurred soon after the latter date. It is odd that he made no mention of these great events! Perhaps the writer realized that the ultimate culmination of God's saving purpose, including the glorious resurrection of the righteous dead, did not belong to the simple turning of political fortune, but that it, in time and significance, lay well beyond the vicissitudes of Jewish history during the second century B.C.

Bibliography

Baldwin, J. C. *Daniel.* Tyndale Old Testament Commentaries. Downers Grove, IL: Inter-Varsity Press, 1978.

Collins, J. J. *Daniel.* The Forms of the Old Testament Literature. Grand Rapids, MI: Eerdmans, 1984.

Hanson, P. D. *The Dawn of Apocalyptic.* Philadelphia: Fortress, 1975.

Hartman, L. F., and A. DiLella. *The Book of Daniel.* Anchor Bible, 23. Garden City, NY: Doubleday, 1978.

Lacocque, A. *The Book of Daniel.* Translated by D. Pellauer. Atlanta, GA: Knox, 1979.

Porteous, N. *Daniel.* Old Testament Library. Philadelphia: Westminster, 1965.

Towner, W. S. *Daniel.* Interpretation: A Bible Commentary for Preaching and Teaching. Atlanta, GA: Knox, 1984.

HOSEA

GENE M. TUCKER

INTRODUCTION

The book of Hosea is one of the most appealing and most difficult books of the Hebrew Bible. Its powerful language, rich in evocative images and metaphors, has grasped the attention of readers from the earliest times to the present. In compelling ways the prophet employs the language and the realities of family life—husband and wife, parents and children—to communicate an understanding of the relationships past, present, and future between Yahweh and the people of Israel. Christian commentators of the late nineteenth and early twentieth centuries, in particular, considered Hosea's thought one of the high points of the OT, noting especially his stress on the love of God and the deep connections he drew between faithfulness to God and morality.

But as readers begin to explore this book, it becomes clear that understanding Hosea requires serious work. Among its difficulties are problems of text and language that occasionally make the received text virtually unreadable. The style of speech or writing sometimes appears erratic, including shifts of speaker and addressee without introduction as well as abrupt changes of mood, tone, and subject matter. Clear markers between individual units are, in most cases, absent. It is not even clear if Hosea's speeches generally were short, like those in Amos, or long, like those in Jeremiah. Some of the units are doubtless dialogues between the prophet and his addressees and, in some cases, he must be quoting the words of the people or other individuals, but in such instances one determines the speaker only with difficulty, if at all.

Nevertheless, neither the translator, the commentator, nor serious readers have the luxury of perpetually withholding judgment on the meaning of difficult lines. They need to be read and interpreted. Examination of the prophet's historical and cultural context, the literary characteristics of the book, and its message will provide a framework for addressing most of the book's difficulties.

Historical and Cultural Context

Both the general period of the prophet's activity and a number of his speeches can be dated with relative certainty. The book's superscription (1:1) locates Hosea in the reigns of certain kings of the eighth century B.C. Moreover, the book contains allusions to international affairs, some of which can be identified with events known from external sources. Other such allusions remain obscure because the names of kings are not given in these cases. Hosea clearly began his work while the dynasty of Jehu was still on the throne, that is, before the death of Jeroboam II (786–746 B.C.). Consequently, he emerged about 750 B.C. and was active right up to the fall of Samaria in 721 B.C. What seems to be one of his latest speeches (13:16) anticipates but does not attest to the fall of the city at the hands of an Assyrian army.

Other possible historical allusions include 8:4, which mentions a succession of kings; 7:3–7, which seems to refer to the assassination of an Israelite monarch; 5:8–14, which probably alludes to the Syro-Ephraimite war of 735–733 B.C.; and 13:10–11, in which the prophet attacks the way in which one king gained the throne.

Hosea was active, then, during the last, turbulent decades of the Northern Kingdom, Israel. During this period, the little state lived under the constant threat of invasion by Assyria and of conflicts with its neighbors, including Judah, the Southern Kingdom. Internally, the situation was chaotic. Following the long and relatively prosperous reign of Jeroboam II, there were constant struggles for the throne. In three decades (750–721 B.C.), Hosea would have seen no less than seven monarchs come and go.

The cultural context is just as important as the political history for understanding Hosea. He was a prophet of the Northern Kingdom, the only one whose words have come down to us in a separate book. In contrast to Judah, with its relatively stable Davidic dynasty, Israel's traditions concerning kingship involved designation by Yahweh's spirit, not just hereditary descent, and even allowed for revolt in the name of Yahweh. Moreover, geography influenced culture. Judah in the south was relatively isolated; Israel was more open to foreign trade and other contacts and thus more cosmopolitan. Israel's land was more fertile than the hill country of Judah, supporting an economy based mainly on agriculture.

In such an environment, the cults of the Canaanite gods throve. The earlier northern prophets, Elijah and Elisha, opposed the

707

prophets and priests of Baal. At the heart of the conflict were two questions: Who makes the land fertile, Yahweh or Baal? Is it possible to give allegiance to more than one deity? On these questions the earlier prophets had been unambiguous, insisting on singleness of devotion to Yahweh, who alone makes the land fertile. In spite of the apparent victory of those earlier prophets, Canaanite religion was alive in both subtle and explicit ways in Israel a century later, constituting one of the main problems that Hosea addressed.

Literary Characteristics

On the surface, the book of Hosea consists of two quite distinct parts, accounts and speeches concerning the family life of the prophet (chaps. 1–3) and a series of prophetic speeches (chaps. 4–14). The chapters concerning the prophet's family, though related to one another, are quite distinct. Chap. 1 is a third-person report of the Lord's command to Hosea to take a "wife of harlotry" and have "children of harlotry" (RSV) and of the prophet's fulfillment of the command. Chap. 2, which is connected to chap. 1 by the names of the children, provides a poetic version of a lawsuit against an unfaithful wife. Chap. 3 is the prophet's first-person account of the Lord's command to love a promiscuous woman.

The speeches in chaps. 4–6 are primarily indictments or sentences directed against the people of Israel or specific groups (such as the priests), although there are some prophecies of salvation as well. In most of these speeches, Hosea, like the other OT prophets, communicates the word of the Lord, either in direct or indirect address. More than one principle of composition seems to have been at work in the organization of this collection. On the one hand, there is a rough chronological order and, on the other hand, a theological scheme. First in chaps. 4–11 and then in chaps. 12–14 there is a move from indictment to prophecy of judgment and then to announcement of salvation.

History of Composition

The words of Hosea have come down to us as literature, in the form of written word and in a self-contained book, but they doubtless did not originate that way. Hosea, like all the other early prophets of Israel, proclaimed his message orally on a series of occasions over a period of years. Others, first disciples or supporters who had heard him and then members of later generations, committed the oral words to writing and passed them on. During this process, particularly as God's word announced by Hosea was applied to later situations, other words were added. There is not sufficient evidence to determine whether Hosea himself was involved in the process of recording what he had said, like, for example, Jeremiah, who dictated his speeches to Baruch the scribe (Jer. 36). In fact, compared with other prophetic books, Hosea provides relatively little evidence for reconstructing the stages of its history of transmission and composition.

An earlier critical view resolved some of the complexities of the book by relegating all of the positive announcements and expectations to later authors or editors. That view has by and large been rejected, but some concerns about the history of the book's composition can be resolved by appeals to diverse authorship. Certainly the first and last verses of the book were not written by Hosea; both 1:1 and 14:9 presume the existence of a written work and would have been added long after the time of Hosea. Likewise the third-person report about the prophet (1:2–9), although representing authentic tradition, does not present itself as a composition written by Hosea. There are a few other additions, including some reflecting Judean perspectives (e.g., 1:7), but most of the book stems from an early tradition about the words of Hosea.

The initial stages in the composition of the book took place amid the troubled circumstances leading to the fall of Israel. After this time, the Hosea tradition would have been transmitted in Judah. Some of the difficulties that beset readers probably stem from the differences in dialect between the Hebrew of the north and that of the south. Thus, it is not only modern interpreters who cannot understand Hosea's language fully but possibly even early Judeans as well.

Message and Significance

Finally, however, the book of Hosea is complex essentially because of the subtlety, depth, and passion of the prophet's thought. He is so deeply involved in his message that his style often lacks restraint. Unlike Amos, whose message is the almost unqualified proclamation of judgment, Hosea hears the Lord promising both disaster and salvation and even having a change of heart (11:8–9).

At the heart of Hosea's message stands his concern with the relationship between Yahweh and Israel. Depending heavily on the ancient traditions of Israel's salvation and election through the Exodus, he recalls the Lord's past and present faithfulness to the chosen people. He accuses and indicts the people not so much for specific sins, though those are noted, but for unfaithfulness. The specific form of this breach of faith is apostasy, the acceptance of other gods. From this sin all others follow, including ritual, political, and social abuses.

The unfaithfulness of Israel justifies the

announcement of judgment in the form of military defeat and destruction. Although that judgment is in accord with the law and seems absolute, Yahweh struggles within himself and then renounces the punishment of Israel (11:5–9). At points the punishment seems designed to correct Israel's ways, to reestablish the relationship with Yahweh. In this context, whether before, during, or after the punishment is renounced, Hosea proclaims Yahweh's courtship of unfaithful Israel and announces salvation. The book's last word is one of salvation. But even if this would have been the prophet's last word, it is a mistake to hear that message apart from the others of accusation, judgment, and divine struggle.

The book of Hosea is significant, first, as the only literary product of a prophet from the Northern Kingdom, Israel. It thus provides one of the major sources for understanding that nation's theology and religion. Second, both the traditions Hosea assumes and the ideas he expresses influenced later Israelite thought in decisive ways. Specifically, Hosea stands in a line that leads to the Deuteronomic thinkers responsible for the book of Deuteronomy and the Deuteronomistic History work (Deuteronomy through 2 Kings). Jeremiah is another successor to Hosea. Specific themes linking these two prophets include the emphasis on the covenant relationship between Yahweh and Israel and on the love of God. With respect to his emphasis on the love of God, it is remarkable that Hosea, though attacking Canaanite religion, introduced into biblical thought some of its language and symbolism. Through his own book and through the just-mentioned lines of tradition, Hosea has left the imagery of a God who is like a faithful husband to a people who are like a prostitute, a God who struggles over that people's future like a parent agonizing over a wayward child.

COMMENTARY

1:1–3:5

Wife and Children as Signs

In addition to the book's superscription (1:1), these chapters contain five relatively distinct units, recognizable in terms of both form and content. The first (1:2–9) and last (3:1–5) are narratives; the others are speeches of Yahweh or of the prophet on Yahweh's behalf. The central discourse (2:2–15) follows the pattern of a husband's legal case against an unfaithful wife.

Much in these chapters concerns Hosea's family life, but the fundamental message concerns the relationship between Yahweh and his unfaithful people.

In large measure because of the initial report that Yahweh commanded Hosea to "take a wife of harlotry and have children of harlotry" (1:2, RSV), these chapters have presented serious problems for interpreters and have evoked a wide range of explanations. Some early Christian and Jewish commentators took the references to Hosea's marriage and family as allegorical, thus avoiding the embarrassment that God would actually command an immoral act. Others argued that Hosea merely reports a dream or vision. Neither interpretation seems reasonable, because the accounts are written as direct reports of events.

Many modern commentators view all three chapters as biographical or autobiographical, namely, the account of how the prophet learned the love of God through his own painful marriage. "Wife of harlotry" (1:2) is taken to mean that Gomer was not a whore when Hosea married her but had such tendencies. Eventually she took a lover or lovers, but the prophet found her and bought her back (3:1–5). This reconstruction assumes that the woman of chap. 3 is the Gomer of chap. 1 and that the order of the chapters corresponds to the chronology of Hosea's life. Such may be the case, but the text itself is not so explicit.

These chapters, more likely, contain reports of symbolic actions by the prophet, actual events performed to bring the word of God to life. If one takes Hosea 1:2 seriously, the prophet knew the word of God before his marriage and before he gave his children their symbolic names. Reports of symbolic actions by prophets are quite common (2 Kings 13:14–19; Isa. 7:14; 8:1–4; Jer. 19; 32).

Hosea's marriage and family life result from his understanding of God's word and do not provide experiences that taught him what to believe or say. Gomer, as a "wife of harlotry," represented unfaithful Israel and, like most other Israelites, had participated in the Canaanite fertility cult. Hosea's message is not that his wife and family are so unusual but, to the contrary, all Israel has prostituted itself to false gods.

The order of the narratives and speeches in these chapters suggests but does not actually specify a theological as well as a chronological sequence. Thematically, the movement is from sin and accusation, to indictment and announcement of judgment, to renewal through purchase and purging, to announcement of salvation. That progression expressed the theology of the final editors of the section; whether Hosea himself saw history unfolding in such an order is unclear.

1:1, Superscription. Like the initial verses of most other prophetic books, this one serves several purposes. It identifies the prophet and locates him in a particular time, thus stressing the historical concreteness of God's word. The title of the book, "the word of the Lord that came to Hosea," makes a theological claim on behalf of the written work, namely, that it has the authority of divine revelation.

1:2–9, Wife and Children. This third-person narrative reports Yahweh's command to Hosea and the prophet's fulfillment of it. The general prescription (v. 2) includes a reason, "for the land commits great harlotry by forsaking the Lord" (RSV). The account of the command's execution occurs in three parts corresponding to the births of the three children, each of whom is given a symbolic name. Although the birth and naming of each child presents a complete message, the unit as a whole develops from accusation and threat of punishment (vv. 4–5), to the Lord's withdrawal of forgiveness (v. 6), then to the radical proclamation that the ancient covenant between Yahweh and Israel is terminated (vv. 8–9). Except for the relatively early Judean editorial addition in v. 7, the passage announces unqualified punishment upon Israel.

1:10–2:1, From Judgment to Salvation. This unit has no clear beginning or conclusion. It provides comment on the previous one, mentioning or alluding to the names of all three children and turning them from signs of judgment to symbols of hope (cf. 2:21–23). The anticipated future includes a great population in Israel (v. 10a), renewal and recognition of the covenant with Yahweh (v. 10b), the reunification of Israel and Judah under a single ruler (v. 11a), possession of the land (v. 11b), and the Lord's compassion for the people (2:1). Though standing in sharp contrast to the mood and message of 1:2–9, this unit does not deny the announcement of judgment but looks beyond it.

Certainly Hosea was capable of such a message, but it remains possible that the passage is a later addition. Hos. 1:10–2:1 presumes the completion of 1:2–9; its impersonal style is unlike what is found elsewhere in the book; and the expectations are similar to those found in exilic texts.

2:2–15, Yahweh's Wife on Trial. Thematically as well as verbally, this passage is directly related to 1:2–9. On the surface, and especially at the outset, the prophet accuses his wife of unfaithfulness. Generally, the unit follows the pattern of the legal process, moving from indictment (vv. 2, 4b–5; cf. also vv. 8, 13) to announcement of the punishment (vv. 6–13). In this process the children are called upon to argue the case (v. 2). However, the prophet in court against his wife comprises a thinly disguised metaphor for Yahweh's trial against Israel, paralleling the symbolic actions of 1:2–9. That such is the case becomes more obvious toward the end, as the "wife" is said to use her wealth for Baal (v. 8), as the accuser threatens to turn her land from rich farmland to a barren waste (v. 12), and as the hoped-for renewal of the relationship is likened to the time of the Exodus (v. 15). By v. 13 ("says the Lord"), the voice of the prophet has clearly become the voice of Yahweh.

The wife Israel is accused literally and figuratively of prostitution (vv. 2, 4, 7, 10, 13) and, more specifically, unfaithfulness to Yahweh by participating in the cult of Baal (vv. 8, 12–13) and forgetting Yahweh (v. 13). This prostitution included the failure to "know" that it was Yahweh who provided all good things (vv. 5, 8, 12). The punishment includes public ridicule (vv. 3, 10), the end of all religious practices and celebrations (v. 11), the withdrawal of grain, wine, wool, and flax (v. 9), and the destruction of vineyards and orchards (v. 12).

Nevertheless, the unit concludes on a strong note of hope, for Yahweh vows to court Israel as in the early days of their relationship (vv. 14–15). Using the warmest language of affection and alluding to the Exodus traditions, Yahweh promises to take her into the wilderness again and make a new beginning so that Israel will be responsive as she was at the first.

2:16–23, A New Covenant. Each of the two parts of this section is introduced by the same formula, "And in that day, says the Lord" (vv. 16, 21). The prophet speaks throughout on behalf of Yahweh, sometimes directly to Israel and elsewhere referring to Israel in the third person. Both parts express the unqualified good news of a renewal of God's covenant with Israel. Yahweh himself takes the initiative, and no prerequisites for the relationship are stated.

In the first unit (vv. 16–20), the prophet employs the intimate metaphor of betrothal and marriage to characterize the covenant. It is quite remarkable for the prophet to refer to the Lord as the "husband" of Israel, resorting to human experience as a way of describing the depth and intimacy of the love between God and people. But such language also includes polemic: Israel will call Yahweh "my husband" ('ishi) and not "My Baal" (ba'li), which also can mean "my husband." Obviously the prophet rejects the latter expression because it may also be read as the name of the Canaanite deity. This new covenant will include all living things, thought by many of Hosea's contemporaries to be under the control of fertility deities.

The relationship between God and people will be characterized by depth of righteousness, justice, steadfast love, mercy, and faithfulness and will endure forever. The expression that Israel "shall know the Lord" (v. 20) sums up the relationship between God and Israel.

In the second unit (vv. 21–23), Hosea again refers to the natural order to describe the mutual responsiveness in the renewed relationship between Yahweh and people. However, the names of children (1:2–9) provide the dominant metaphors. Each name is, in turn, reversed from its initial meaning as announcement of judgment to proclamation of salvation. Just as the name of the third child, "Not my people," had entailed an abrogation of the covenant, so the covenant will be renewed by using formulas of mutual loyalty, "You are my people . . . you are my God" (v. 23).

3:1–5, Yahweh's Forgiving Love. This complete and self-contained unit—only the "again" of v. 1 integrates it into the sequence of chaps. 1–3—is a prophetic, symbolic action report written in the first person. Put another way, the story of Hosea's purchase of an adulteress is not autobiography but prophetic proclamation. Generally, it proceeds according to the traditional three movements of such reports: divine instructions for the action (v. 1), fulfillment of the instructions (vv. 2–3), and interpretation of the action's meaning (vv. 4–5). However, the pattern is not followed rigidly, for the instructions already give an initial interpretation of the deed ("just as Yahweh loves the people of Israel"). Moreover, the action goes further than the divine command, for once Hosea purchases the woman he places her in isolation from all sexual contact. The interpretation (vv. 4–5) develops this particular point by arguing that the Lord will deprive the people of leaders and religious practices so that they will eventually return to their God.

The woman is not named. She may or may not be the Gomer of 1:3. Hosea 3:1–5 could be a parallel account of the initial marriage or a later event in Hosea's troubled life with his "wife of harlotry." The meaning of the symbolic action report, however, though subtle, is clear and concrete. Although Israel acts unfaithfully, Yahweh continues to love her so much that he will buy her away from her other lovers. God's love includes discipline, for he will withdraw government and religion, in effect removing the structures of civilization from the land. As a result, Israel will eventually return and seek its God directly. The concluding lines concerning "David their king" (v. 5b) probably stem from a later Judean editor.

4:1–14:9
Prophecies of Judgment and Salvation

Virtually all the material in these chapters is presented as the written form of prophetic speeches. Some, such as 4:1–3, are short and self-contained, probably corresponding, more or less, to their original oral delivery. Other units, such as 4:4–19 and 5:8–7:16, seem to have been created by those who collected and edited the words of Hosea, as they sometimes combined individual sayings into small collections or longer discourses. These chapters are by no means randomly ordered, however. First chaps. 4–11 and then chaps. 12–14 proceed from accusation and announcement of judgment to announcement of salvation.

4:1–3, Yahweh's Lawsuit. This passage, with its summons to hear and its comprehensive indictment of Israel, provides a fitting introduction to the collection of speeches in Hosea 4–14. Even more concretely than in the lawsuit against the unfaithful wife in chap. 2, this section follows the pattern of a trial. The word translated "controversy" (v. 1, RSV) is a technical term for a lawsuit. Whether the prophet is following a ritual pattern for a trial against those who break the covenant or simply using the language of ordinary courtroom procedure is not certain. After the summons, the prophet presents first a general (v. 1b) and then a specific (v. 2) indictment. The general indictment states Israel's failures; there is no "faithfulness," "kindness," or "knowledge of God," characteristics of the future covenant announced in 2:19–20. The specific indictment lists five crimes that correspond to half of the commandments in the Decalogue (Exod. 20:2–17; Deut. 5:6–21). Though there is exact verbal correspondence to the Decalogue in only the last three violations, it is clear that behind this list stands a tradition of law and covenant known to both Hosea and his Israelite audience.

Because of the ambiguity inherent in the Hebrew verb tenses, v. 3 can be read either as referring to the future, "the land shall dry up" or to the present, "the land dries up." If one accepts the former option, the speech concludes with an announcement of judgment; if the latter, the prophet is describing the effects of the people's sins. In either case, failure of the covenant relationship (v. 1b) leads to crimes against persons (v. 2), which in turn lead to the destruction and suffering of the natural order itself, including land, air, and sea and their inhabitants (v. 3).

4:4–10, Against Unfaithful Priests. This passage is the first in a series of speeches (4:4–

711

19) on the theme of corrupt worship and its effects. The language of the courtroom continues ("contend," v. 4), but now Yahweh, through the prophet, turns from the inhabitants of the land to address the priests. Such a shift of address indicates the beginning of a new unit.

Yahweh acts as both plaintiff or prosecutor and judge, moving back and forth from accusations to announcements of judgment. The priests have failed in one of their central responsibilities, teaching the law to the laity (v. 6), thus they bear responsibility for the destruction of the people. "Knowledge," a major theological term for Hosea (cf. 2:20; 4:1; 6:3), in this context refers to teaching and learning the content of the law. That the priests "feed on the sin [or sin offering] of my people" (v. 8) means they are using the corrupt sacrificial worship to satisfy themselves. In short, the priests are guilty of prostitution, namely, forsaking Yahweh (v. 10). Their punishment will fit their crimes (v. 9), including rejection by Yahweh (v. 6), destruction of their families (vv. 5b, 6b, 10a), and shame (v. 7).

4:11–14, Corrupt Worship. There is a "spirit of prostitution" (v. 12) in Israel. It is not, however, simply a matter of belief or feeling or even apathy toward God but entails certain specific actions. So, "inquire" (v. 12) is a technical term for acts of divination, the consultation of idols or other pagan cult objects to discover the future. The people sacrifice at places usually identified with Canaanite gods such as Baal (v. 13), and they participate in cultic prostitution (v. 14). Most of the passage details such sins, but it concludes with the announcement of judgment using proverbial language (v. 14b).

"Harlotry" and "to play the harlot," common terms here and throughout Hosea, do not refer to ordinary prostitution, the sale of sexual favors. Rather, they symbolize Israel's apostasy (v. 12). Verse 14 refers quite specifically to cultic prostitution, sexual acts performed as a part of the fertility cult and, therefore, constituting one form of apostasy. Cultic prostitution, like other forms of Canaanite worship, must have been a real alternative for Hosea's contemporaries. According to Deut. 23:17–18, cultic prostitution was illegal, and money earned by such prostitutes was not allowed in the Temple.

4:15–19, Shameful Worship. As the indictments of Israelite worship continue, the prophet urges Judah not to follow the example of the Northern Kingdom (v. 15). Israelites have taken up pagan practices at Canaanite places of worship (v. 13) and have corrupted rituals at the major Yahwistic centers such as Gilgal and Beth-aven (v. 15; cf. Amos 5:5). Although vv. 18–19 present major textual problems, they appear to link drunkenness with prostitution, and both with false worship.

5:1–7, Against the Leaders. This section could very well result from the combination of two originally independent prophetic addresses, vv. 1–2 and 3–7. The first part begins with Yahweh's threefold call to hear, addressed to the priests, the house of Israel—probably a group of leaders—and the king. Then comes a threefold statement of reasons for punishment, each using a hunting metaphor (vv. 1b–2a), followed by a general announcement of judgment (2b).

Verses 3–7 likewise move from accusation or reasons for punishment (vv. 3–5) to the announcement of punishment (vv. 6–7), addressed to the nation as a whole. The speaker must be the prophet, for he refers to Yahweh in the third person throughout. The reasons are the familiar indictment that Israel is guilty of prostitution and does not know Yahweh, who knows her. "To know" (vv. 3, 4) involves more than cognition; this verb characterizes the covenant relationship between God and people. Consequently, when the people do decide to seek Yahweh, they will find that he has withdrawn from them, in effect abrogating the covenant and leaving only disaster.

5:8–6:6, The Folly of War Between Israel and Judah. The historical background of this passage, which alludes to border conflicts between Israel and Judah as well as alliances with Assyria, probably is the Syro-Ephraimite war of 734 B.C. (cf. Isa. 7:1–2; 2 Kings 15:27–30). As the Assyrian army under Tiglath-pileser III began to move into Syro-Palestine, Israel and other states in the region formed an alliance against the invaders, but Judah refused to join. Israel then mounted a campaign to force Judah to join the revolt, and Judah successfully resisted.

Hosea is critical of both Judah and Israel, announcing judgment on both houses in the form of military defeat. The address begins with cries of alarm followed by an announcement of disaster against the Northern Kingdom (5:8–9). As the prophecy of punishment continues against Israel and Judah (5:10–14), Hosea alludes to the crimes of each nation: Judah's is the appropriation of Israelite territory (5:10a), and Israel's is its entangling alliances (5:13).

In 5:15 the Lord's speech continues, but now as a declaration that he will withdraw and wait for the people to turn to him in penitence. The penitential song of the people (6:1–3) uses the imagery of judgment in 5:11–14, and then, in 6:4–6, Yahweh speaks again, responding to the song. Is the people's repentance and approach to Yahweh sincere, or shallow? If one allows 6:4–6 to interpret the song of the people, it appears that their repentance is superficial, "like the dew that disappears early" (v. 4). The key to the passage, and to the question of true repentance, is 6:6. It is not in acts of worship ("sacrifice" and "burnt offerings") that true faith is recognized but in "steadfast love" and "the knowledge of God."

6:7-7:7, Sin Throughout the Land and in High Places. In this section, which probably comes from the same era as the previous one, Yahweh speaks to accuse and indict first the nation in general, including its priests (6:7-7:2), and then its leadership in particular (7:3-7). There is no prophecy of punishment as such. Except for the allegation of murder (6:9), the accusations against the people are quite general and are organized geographically by a listing of major Israelite cities ("Adam" in 6:7 is a location, not a person). Although the accusations against the leaders do not include the pronouncement of judgment, there is a description of the disasters that accompany political treachery. Hosea implies, but does not state, that the monarchy is doomed. The most fundamental sin is that, although kings fall, not one of them cries to the Lord (7:7).

7:8-16, Rebellious Israel. The first of these addresses (vv. 8-13) continues one of the themes of 5:8-6:6, the foolishness of Israel's reliance on foreign alliances instead of on Yahweh, who waits in vain for acts of loyalty and repentance so that he can "redeem" them (v. 13). The expressions "return," "seek," "call," and "cry" refer not only to a change of heart or feeling toward the Lord but also to specific actions, including public worship, prayer, and formal inquiry concerning the will of God. Because Israel turns in the wrong direction—to foreign nations rather than to Yahweh—destruction will come. According to 7:14-16, the rebellion includes relying on other gods and participating in the bloody rituals of the fertility cult (v. 14; cf. 1 Kings 18; Deut. 14:1; Lev. 19:28).

8:1-14, Israel Rejects the Good and Pays the Price. Although this chapter is probably an edited collection of originally independent units, it presents a clear and coherent summary of Hosea's accusations against Israel. It begins and ends with general and comprehensive statements of Israel's sins. The nation has broken the covenant and violated the law (v. 1). Certainly the prophet has in view the tradition of the covenant at Sinai and the laws accepted by Israel, to which he alludes frequently (cf. 2:18, 23; 4:2; 12:9; 13:4). That Israel has forgotten its maker (v. 14) is another way of saying the people have broken the covenant. This rebellion involves both political and religious activity. Israel set up kings and princes without Yahweh's approval (vv. 4a, 10b; cf. 7:3, 7; 8:10;

9:15; 10:3, 7, 15; 13:10) and tried to buy security with foreign alliances (vv. 9-10a). Religious violations include making idols (v. 4b), including the golden calf in Samaria (vv. 5-6; cf. 1 Kings 12:26-33 on such images in Dan and Bethel). Altars and sacrifices are scorned (Hos. 8:11, 13), either because the worship itself is corrupt or because the people rely on ritual instead of covenant faithfulness. Such activities can lead only to disaster, stated here both as predictable effects in the worlds of nature and of international affairs (vv. 7-8) and as God's direct intervention to destroy (vv. 5, 6, 10, 13-14).

9:1-9, Judgment on Festivals. The presence of direct address and references to specific rituals in vv. 1-6 suggest that Hosea delivered this speech to people assembled for a particular religious festival. Such a joyful festival would have involved thanksgiving and celebration of the renewal of life. There is no reason to think that the songs, prayers, libations, and sacrifices were not directed to Yahweh. Hosea, however, begins by prohibiting the celebration, accusing the people of harlotry, of forsaking their God (v. 1), and of self-serving ceremonies (v. 4). He then brings the bitter news that all such celebrations will end and Israel will go into exile to Egypt (vv. 2-3, 6).

It is not surprising that the bearer of such words encountered "great hatred" (v. 7), not only from the people in general, but also from the religious leaders (v. 8). "The prophet is a fool, the man of the spirit is mad" is probably a quotation of Hosea's opponents. Like other prophets he was able to endure such animosity because he saw himself as a "watchman" (cf. Jer. 6:17; Ezek. 3:16-21; 33:7-9) called by God to sound the necessary warnings.

9:10-17, A Sinful Past and a Barren Future. The discourse shifts from prophetic address to a speech of Yahweh that recalls the history of Israel's unfaithfulness and announces harsh judgment. Although Yahweh cared for the people in the wilderness, even there, at Baal-peor (Num. 25:1-8), they dedicated themselves to Baal. Because they turned to this fertility god, all fertility and progeny will, ironically, be taken away (Hos. 9:11-14, 16). The reference to evil in Gilgal (v. 15) may recall the importance of that place during the period of the settlement (Josh. 5:9-10), but more likely it is a condemnation of monarchy, for Saul's kingship began there (1 Sam. 11:14-15). Consequently, Yahweh will abandon Israel and turn it out of the land (Hos. 9:17).

10:1-8, Kingship and Idolatry. The passage is a summary of Israel's past, present, and future in which the sin of idolatry is linked to the monarchy (cf. 8:4–14). Mistaking the source of its prosperity, Israel expanded and depended upon its corrupt cult (10:1, 5). Even if the people reject the monarchy and profess to rely upon Yahweh, they cannot be trusted (vv. 3–4). Therefore the Lord will destroy all the places and fixtures of worship, and the king will die.

10:9–12, A Call to Repent. This is one of the few speeches in which Hosea explicitly calls for Israel to change its ways so that the people may be saved from destruction. He accuses the nation of a history of sin (v. 9), announces punishment as a means to discipline the wayward people (vv. 10–11), and appeals for acts of righteousness and repentance that will lead to salvation (v. 12).

10:13–15, Trust in Weapons Leads to War. Commencing with proverbial sayings on the inevitability of cause and effect, the prophet announces that horrible warfare will come because the people relied upon weapons, rather than, presumably, Yahweh.

11:1–11, "I Am God, Not a Human Being." In one of the most remarkable passages in all of Scripture, Yahweh meditates on his relationship to Israel and arrives at an astounding conclusion. Except for v. 10, a secondary addition, Yahweh is the speaker throughout. Although the soliloquy contains dramatic shifts in mood, tone, and contents, it is a single speech. God is pictured as ambivalent, undecided about what to do.

Beginning with the compelling metaphor of God as parent and Israel as son, vv. 1–7 proceed as a prophecy of punishment. Yahweh recalls the history of his relationship with Israel, establishing the grounds for judgment by contrasting his loving care for the people (vv. 1, 2–3) with their unfaithfulness (v. 2). Then follows the expected announcement of punishment (vv. 5–7) in the form of military defeat, exile to Egypt and Assyria, and slavery.

However, the metaphors of parent and son at the beginning have already established the basis for a different outcome. In vv. 8–9 Yahweh is heard to express doubts, to question his decision, and even to have a change of heart, deciding not to act on the basis of his legitimate anger. Yahweh's care for Israel has always been like that of a parent for a child, and his compassion goes beyond even that. Verse 9 is the heart of the soliloquy and the center of the prophet's thought. Hosea takes human metaphors for God's love as far as they will go and then stresses that the difference between God and human beings involves his capacity for radical, forgiving love.

Once the decision against judgment has been made, the announcement of salvation in vv. 10–11 appears almost anticlimactic. Verse 10 seems to be a comment on v. 11, which proclaims the return of God's people from Egypt and Assyria, reversing the announcement of v. 5.

11:12–12:14, Israel's Treachery. With accusations of betrayal and announcements of punishment, this section proceeds as if the words of chap. 11 had never been spoken. The passage is not a single speech but a collection of sayings on the themes of Israel's deceptive behavior from the beginning of its existence and the authority of the prophetic word. The accusations are argued in some detail; the announcements of judgment are quite general.

Ephraim, a designation for the Northern Kingdom deriving from the name of a prominent Israelite tribe, is accused of lies and deceit, specifically by establishing alliances with Assyria and Egypt (11:12–12:1). The concluding lines of 11:12 probably come from a Judean editor. As in 4:1–3 and 4:4–10, Yahweh initiates a lawsuit against his people (12:2–6). The indictment reaches into antiquity, citing the traditions about Israel's ancestor, Jacob. Hosea presumes that his hearers know the story of the birth of Jacob and his brother Esau (Gen. 25:21–26), his nocturnal struggle with God at the Jabbok, at which time he received the name Israel (Gen. 32:22–32), and his dream at Bethel (Gen. 28:11–17). Surprisingly, the lawsuit includes admonitions to return to God (Hos. 11:6). Verses 7–9 accuse Israel of two violations, crooked business practices and arrogance. Yahweh recalls the Exodus and threatens to return Israel to its status before it occupied the land (v. 9).

If Yahweh speaks to defend the authority of the prophetic word (vv. 10–14), Hosea's audience must have questioned it. Yahweh, not human opinion, stands behind the prophetic word and vision; even Moses was a prophet by whom the Lord brought Israel out of Egypt (v. 13). Consequently, harsh prophetic accusations against false worship cannot be challenged.

13:1–16, Death Sentence for Israel. In four loosely connected discourses, Hosea announces the end of the history of salvation because of Israel's rebellion against Yahweh. The first (vv. 1–3), a clearly structured prophecy of punishment, gives idolatry as the reason for judgment (vv. 1–2), a judgment graphically described as Israel's disappearance like a "mist" or smoke (v. 3). The second (vv. 4–8), another prophecy of punishment, indicts Israel by contrasting Yahweh's graceful care with the people's failure to remember (vv. 4–6). In a single verse (v. 4), the Lord reminds Israel of the Exodus, the covenant, and the law. The judgment will be brutal, for the same Lord who is like a husband or a parent will fall on Israel like a wild animal (vv. 7–8). The third discourse (vv. 9–11), a disputation between Yahweh and the people, attacks the institution of kingship. The final unit (vv. 12–16) is the harshest announcement of punishment in the book. Hosea provides allusions only to those sins that have led to such a divine intervention (vv. 12–13, 16a), and Yahweh questions whether or not he should turn the people over to the power of death (v. 14). But this divine deliberation does not end like the one in 11:8–9. Rejecting compassion, Yahweh proclaims the end of Israel through military catastrophe, including the death of little children and pregnant women.

14:1–8, A Call to Return and a Promise of Renewal. Mood and message shift dramatically in the book's final prophetic speeches. There are two distinct addresses, their contents and their juxtaposition reminiscent of a penitential liturgy. First the prophet himself speaks, calling Israel to return to its God (vv. 1–3). The prayer he teaches them to speak includes petitions for forgiveness, confessions of sin, and vows to reject foreign alliances and handmade gods. It concludes with an affirmation of confidence in God. Second, Yahweh himself speaks (vv. 4–8), just as the priest in such liturgies conveyed the oracle of salvation. Yahweh promises to heal the people with love and to ensure that they prosper and flourish. The concluding verse (v. 8) is a reminder that Yahweh is the one who cares for Israel.

14:9, Postscript. The style and point of view of this scribal addition to the book are similar to those of the book of Proverbs and other wisdom literature. A pious scribe recommends study of the book of Hosea to all those who are wise and would learn "the ways of the Lord." By the time this verse was added, the influence of the book of Hosea had reached far beyond eighth-century Israel.

Bibliography
Andersen, F. I., and D. N. Freedman. *Hosea: A New Translation with Introduction and Commentary.* Anchor Bible, 24. Garden City, NY: Doubleday, 1980.

Emmerson, G. I. *Hosea: An Israelite Prophet in Judean Perspective.* Journal for the Study of the Old Testament Supplement Series, no. 28. Sheffield: JSOT Press, 1984.

Mays, J. L. *Hosea.* Old Testament Library. Philadelphia: Westminster, 1969.

Ward, J. M. *Hosea: A Theological Commentary.* New York: Harper & Row, 1966.

Wolff, H. W. *Hosea.* Hermeneia. Philadelphia: Fortress, 1974.

JOEL

J. WILLIAM WHEDBEE

INTRODUCTION

Form

The Book of Joel poses a question for interpreters. Is it a prophetic liturgy secondarily expanded into an apocalyptic work? Is it a liturgy rooted in the mythic pattern of the ancient Near Eastern New Year festival? Or is it a self-conscious literary composition with a striking symmetry and unity? Most recent interpreters have argued for the unity of Joel in its canonical shape, though recognizing that special tensions exist between its historical and eschatological aspects. In particular, the entangled lines of connection between past and future are difficult to separate. What, for example, is the relationship between the past event of the locust plague and the future event of the Day of the Lord?

The superscription characterizes the work as "the word of Yahweh" (1:1), but that designation makes a claim simply for divine origin, that its message comes from God, and says nothing about the form of the book. The opening pair of imperatives ("hear . . . give ear," 1:2a), which are but the first in a series of commands (1:2–3, 5a, 8, 11, 13, 14; 2:1, 12–13, 15–17), offers the chief clue to the form of the first half of Joel: it consists principally of various sorts of calls to the community, calls centered in narration, complaint, repentance, and petition.

After the opening call to attention (1:2a), which is linked with a command to tell the news of an unprecedented event to future generations (1:2b–4), a series of calls follows: first, a call for communal complaint occasioned by a devastating locust plague (1:5–14); second, a call to sound the alarm (2:1) coupled with a description of the Day of Yahweh (2:1b–11) and concluding with a call for repentance (2:12–14); and third, an expanded summary, which ends with a climactic petition (2:15–17).

The book's decisive turning point comes in the narrative description of Yawheh's positive response to Israel's cry for help (2:18, 19a), a report that corresponds formally to the terse description of the plague of locusts (1:4). This second report introduces two series of oracles that serve as an answer to the communal complaint, not only announcing immediate relief from the plague (2:19b–27) but disclosing the constitutive events connected with the Day of Yahweh,

events that affect the destiny of Israel and the nations (2:28–3:21).

The two major parts of the book are unified by the two narrative pieces (1:4 and 2:18, 19a). These brief reports serve as linchpins for the book, holding together the series of calls (1:5–2:17), on the one hand, and the serialized oracles (2:18–3:21), on the other. Within the latter oracular announcements, two formulas of recognition are found: Israel shall know Yahweh as exclusive and unrivaled God in its midst (2:27 and 3:17). Strategically located at the end of each series of oracles, they form both climax and bridge within the oracular movement, thus offering further evidence of symmetry and unity.

Finally, impressive evidence of a unifying perspective emerges in the way the book speaks about time, a rhetoric vividly displayed in the opening call to attention, which demands a comparison of the locust plague with past events ("Has such a thing happened in your days, or in the days of your fathers?" 1:2b, RSV) and then commands the transmission of this news to future generations ("tell your children of it, and let your children tell their children, and their children another generation," 1:3, RSV). This call gives a clue to the form of the whole book: it will be a "hear and tell" show that unveils a brilliant panorama of time's imperious movement from the immediate past to the distant future. The rhetoric of temporality appears throughout the book, beginning with this opening call for evaluation of the past and transmission to the future (1:2b–3; cf. 2:2b), then centering in the announcements of the imminent Day of the Lord (1:15, 2:1b) and the consequent call for repentance in the present time ("Yet even now . . ." 2:12–14), and continuing with a series of eschatological formulas that thrust the tale into the future ("it shall come to pass afterward," 2:28a; see also 3:1a, 18a).

The Problem of Composition and the Literary and Religious Significance

The very features that unify the book efface and blur the traces of compositional history. The theory once dominant among biblical scholars of two stages of composition, which argued that a prophetic response to a locust plague was later expanded by apocalyptic editors, is now passé. Most would still allow for a complex history of the book's composition, but interpreters are increasingly content to posit a postexilic date for the final form of the book without delineating clear-cut stages of development. Even the evidence for dating is entirely circumstantial: there is no sign of a king, and the leadership is in the hands of elders; Israel is scattered among the nations (3:2); the Temple, with its priesthood and ritual, are at the center of the community's life (1:9, 13; 2:14); the community is apparently small (2:16); Phoenicians and Greeks, not Assyrians and Babylonians, are active in slave trading (3:6). All such clues point to a probable postexilic date (ca. 500–350 B.C.).

Though the exact historical context of Joel remains hidden, the religious and social settings may be sought in those circles that emphasized the prophet's role within the religious establishment. Joel appears to be a prophet who serves as a kind of director, claiming divine authority to give orders and oracles to the assembled community, including the priests. But the most profound intention of the book is to show how the prophetic poetry of the past (Joel's vital engagement with the prior prophetic tradition has long been noted, Isa. 13:6 in Joel 1:15; Amos 1:2 in Joel 3:16; Obad. 17 in Joel 2:32) illumines a new crisis—a locust plague—that is a horrifying harbinger of the Day of the Lord. The call to tell the news to future generations (1:2–3) is the watchword for a group that felt itself to be living on the eve of a new epoch. Its members possibly formed a "literary opposition" party that, in contrast to the priestly leaders, expected "new acts of Yahweh" (see Wolff).

Perhaps in the end it is the passion for understanding time that is the touchstone for the religious significance of Joel. Yet, ironically, the kind of temporality that animates Joel undercuts attempts to reconstruct the book's historical and religious context. Fragments of tradition and text become recomposed into a larger field of vision whose poetic movement, though bound by time, nonetheless restructures past, present, and future. The composition uses realistic and surrealistic images, creating a macabre montage that transfigures the unprecedented day of the locusts into the cataclysmic Day of the Lord. Ordinary time is thereby transformed and transcended.

COMMENTARY

1:1
Superscription

Composed of a formula typical for beginning a prophetic book, this verse is noteworthy for its extreme brevity (cf. Hos. 1:1; Mic. 1:1; Zeph. 1:1; Jon. 1:1). It does not record names of reigning kings or places or dates, but only the prophet's name and the name of his father. This very brevity highlights the divine origin of the prophet's message.

1:2–4
Introduction

The prophecy begins with a traditional call to attention (cf. Isa. 1:2; 28:23; Prov. 4:1), coupled with a didactic question and a command to tell later generations (1:2–3). This opening sets the fundamental tone and tempo for the whole book by anticipating a narrative mode that appears immediately in the account of different stages in a locust plague (1:4). The introduction engages the attention of the audience, ensures remembrance of the message by its repeated communication to future generations, and dramatizes the major topic, a plague of locusts, that prefigures the Day of Yahweh.

1:5–2:17
Prophetic Directions to the Community to Engage in a Complaint Ceremony

Poetic parallelism, in which new elements are added incrementally, unifies the various units that make up 1:5–2:17 (→ Poetry). Its pattern of repetition and amplification intensifies the movement and builds to a climax (see esp. 2:15–17).

1:5–20, From Convocation to Complaint.
This unit offers a stellar instance of a call for communal complaint, a well-attested genre in ancient Israel (1:5–14; cf. 2 Sam. 3:31; Isa. 23:1–14). The prophet presents an elaborate, imploring address to three specific groups most vitally affected by the locust plague (drunkards, farmers, and priests) as well as an appeal for the community to lament like a virgin bereft of her bridegroom. The sequence moves in ascending order within the communal hierarchy, beginning with drunkards and ending with priests, the last named providing the most crucial link between community and Yahweh. Such convocations in the face of national emergency were typical in Israel, but here the threat outstrips usual calamities, because the locust plague foreshadows the Day of Yahweh (1:15). The cry of woe before the "Day" forms the centerpiece, since the call to lament leads to it and the complaint (1:16–20) follows from it.

2:1–14, From Command to Sound the Alarm to Call for Repentance.
Another call uses a traditional cry of alarm before an enemy

attack (2:1; cf. Hos. 5:8; 8:1; Jer. 4:5; 6:1). The locusts of chap. 1, likened already to "a nation, powerful and without number" (1:6), now appear as a vast army, mounting a full-scale attack on Jerusalem (2:2b–9). Though there are differences between the depictions in chaps. 1 and 2, the interlocking themes and images suggest continuity, though probably not identity, between the events portrayed in these two texts. What is past in chap. 1 moves ineluctably into a futuristic key in chap. 2. The temporal perspective shifts, but the interplay and tension between past and future, between the day of the locusts and the Day of the Lord, is maintained and even emphasized. The nearness of the Day of the Lord (1:15; 2:1b) closes the gap between past and future, making the present into a narrow ledge that juts out from the concrete reality of the past plague and then drops off into the yawning darkness of the imminent Day of Yahweh.

The prophet now makes explicit Yahweh's implicit involvement with the disaster: the same God who commands sounding the alarm (2:1a) before the invading hordes identifies himself as the commander of the army (2:11). And it is the same God who then calls for repentance in the hour of crisis ("Yet even now, return to me with all your heart," 2:12). The call to repentance includes two components: the first delineates the mode of repentance (2:12,13a); the second presents the motivation for repentance (2:13b). The question, "Who knows whether he will return and repent and leave a blessing behind him?" (2:14a; cf. Jon. 3:9; 2 Sam. 12:22), is linked to the call by a play on the word "return." This "who" question, counterposed to the "Who can endure it?" of 2:11, maintains dramatic tension by highlighting the uncertainty about whether one could expect automatically a beneficent response from Yahweh.

The interrogative mood expressed by these two questions intensifies the existential dread. Israel stands isolated and vulnerable, by turns horror-stricken and hopeful; its sole resource is the covenant God whose terrifying mask conceals the deeper truth of one who "is gracious and merciful, slow to anger, and abounding in steadfast love" (2:13; cf. Exod. 34:6–7 and esp. Jon. 4:2).

2:15–17, From Expanded Summary to Climactic Petition. The final call is a striking summation of those preceding it, moving backward to echo key notes of the earlier texts (2:15a parallels 2:1a; 2:15b parallels 1:14a). The modifications and expansions of earlier motifs are designed both to emphasize the necessity for total community involvement (even babes and newlyweds must come) and to provide the petition the priests should use ("Spare thy people, O Lord, and make not thy heritage a reproach,"

2:17a). This petition concludes with a question that appeals to Yahweh's honor: "Why should they say among the peoples, 'Where is their God?' " (2:17b; cf. Pss. 79:10; 115:2), a question that brings the first major movement to a forceful climax.

2:18–3:21
The Divine Response to the Communal Complaint

2:18–19a, A Narrative Description of Yahweh's Action. These verses introduce oracles given in response to the community's penitence and petition and thereby constitute the pivot on which the book turns. The temporal horizon is now vastly expanded, moving forward in time from the immediate relief of the present emergency to the subsequent events that affect the future destiny of Israel and of the nations. The eschatological formula "And it shall come to pass afterward" (2:28) forms a break between the first and second series of oracles (2:19b–27 and 2:28–3:21 respectively). Moreover, a third reference to the nearness of the Day of the Lord (3:14b; cf. 2:1b; 1:15a) tightens the temporal gap between these two sets of oracles: the immediate relief of the plague is intimately connected with the imminent coming of the "Day," thus stressing the need to remain in a perpetual posture of vigilance and repentance.

2:19b–27, First Series of Oracles. An oracle of assurance (cf. Isa. 41:10, 13–14; 43:1–5) announces Yahweh's merciful response and reverses the effects of the plague of locusts. In the midst of language typical of this genre ("fear not," . . . "be glad and rejoice," vv. 21–23), Yahweh makes the most explicit statement of reversal: "I will restore to you the years the swarming locust has eaten, the hopper, the destroyer and the cutter, my great army which I sent among you," 2:25), a promise explicitly echoing 1:4 and 2:11. The recognition formula in 2:27 ("you shall know") forms both a climax for the first series of oracles and a bridge to the oracles that follow.

2:28–3:21, Second Series of Oracles. Joel 2:28–32 contains the promise of an outpouring of the Spirit on "all flesh" and is probably the most famous single text in Joel, since early Christians claimed that it was fulfilled on the day of Pentecost (Acts 2:17–21). Within Joel, this promise provides the first decisive sign in a series of eschatological events to come "afterward." Its significance lies in the extension of the prophetic gift to the whole community, whether old or young, male or female, slave or free, thus fulfilling the ancient Mosaic wish

(Num. 11:29) and correlating with other prophetic texts concerned with the gift of the Spirit (cf. Ezek. 36:26–27; 37:14). To be sure, the revolutionary extension of this gift is not universal; the nations will experience radical exclusion and destruction in the judgment to come (cf. the interpretations in Acts 2:16–21; Rom. 10:13).

The outpouring of the Spirit is accompanied by cosmic portents such as darkened sun and bloodied moon, phenomena traditionally associated with the coming of the "great and terrible day of the Lord" (2:30–31; cf. Isa. 13:10; Zeph. 1:15). Salvation will come to those who call upon the name of the Lord and those whom the Lord calls (2:32), a promise that maintains the delicate balance between the reciprocal "callings" of human supplicants and God.

The last subunit (3:1–21) is introduced by another typical eschatological formula, "For behold, in those days and at that time" (3:1a). It ties Israel's restoration with the divine intention to judge "all the nations" (3:1b–2). What unfolds is probably the most baroque passage in Joel, a text whose sometimes jarring changes of focus suggest a complex compositional history (e.g., many interpreters consider 3:4–8 to be a later addition). The passage fits the general category of the so-called oracles against the nations (cf. Isa. 13–23; Jer. 46–50; Obad.).

The announcement of the coming judgment incorporates a summons to battle (3:9–12), an old genre (cf. Jer. 5:10; 6:4–6; 46:3–6) that functions here ironically. The nations are called to arms, but, in fact, they are to assemble in the symbolic valley of Jehoshaphat (= "Yahweh judges") to be cut down in a bloody harvest and to be tread upon as grapes crushed in a wine vat (3:13). The entangled web of metaphors—spun out of judicial, martial, and agricultural images—creates a macabre effect. The parody at work in the scene comes out most vividly in an ironic inversion of a famous prophecy: "Beat your ploughshares into swords and your pruning hooks into spears" (3:10; cf. Isa. 2:4; Mic. 4:3). The eschatological war against the nations will be a reversal of the enemy invasion of Jerusalem (2:1–9). This section includes a promise of divine refuge for Israel in the coming storm (3:16). The second instance of the old recognition formula not only echoes 2:27 but effectively epitomizes the goal of the oracles: "you shall know that I am Yahweh your God, who dwell in Zion" (3:17a).

The book concludes with a prophecy concerning the contrasting destinies of Judah/Jerusalem and the nations (3:18–21). To some it seems anticlimactic and therefore a later addition. Yet it serves as a telling reprise for the second half of the book. The imagery of paradise regained, evoking memories of Eden (Gen. 2; Ezek. 47:1–13), does not represent a total return to a universal paradise, since the superabundant fertility of Judah has as its negative corollary the desolation of Egypt and Edom (3:18–19).

In the end, the oracles in 2:18–3:21 answer back to the opening call of the book and fill out the future dimensions of the story. Joel began with a simple summons to listen and to tell "your children and the children of your children" (1:3) in order to transmit the memory of things past as a prophetic message for things future. This memory involves both fear and hope. Moreover, the words of a portentous past are written into the Janus face of the future.

Bibliography

Ahlström, G. *Joel and the Temple Cult of Jerusalem.* Supplements to Vetus Testamentum, 21. Leiden: Brill, 1971.

Allen, L. *The Books of Joel, Obadiah, Jonah and Micah.* New International Commentary on the Old Testament. Grand Rapids, MI: Eerdmans, 1976.

Kapelrud, A. *Joel Studies.* Uppsala: Lundequistska, 1948.

Prinsloo, W. *The Theology of Joel.* Beihefte zur die alttestamentliche Wissenschaft, 163. Berlin: de Gruyter, 1985.

Wolff, H. W. *Joel and Amos.* Hermeneia. Philadelphia: Fortress, 1976.

AMOS

ROY F. MELUGIN

INTRODUCTION

The Book of Amos is a prophetic book of only nine chapters. Its central focus is the proclamation of Yahweh's judgment against Israel because some Israelites had oppressed the poor. Yahweh's burning wrath is directed against various nations but particularly against Israel because it treats people violently and unjustly. Yahweh's anger is, indeed, so hot that the downfall of Israel is imminent. Only at the end of the book can one find clearly expressed a message of hope, but that expectation seems to apply primarily to Judah rather than to the northern state of Israel, which is the major subject of the book (→ Israel). Most scholars think this proclamation of salvation for Judah is the product of literary activity much later than the time of Amos.

What little is known about this prophet must be reconstructed from the book itself. Amos came from Tekoa in Judah (1:1; cf. 7:12) and understood himself to have been commissioned by Yahweh to prophesy to Israel during the reign of Jeroboam II (ca. 786–746 B.C.). He does not seem to have been a lifelong prophet but rather a shepherd and "dresser of sycamore trees" (7:14, cf. 1:1).

Most scholars today believe that Amos communicated by spoken rather than by written words. It seems likely that others subsequently arranged the oral traditions that they had received; yet scholars are not agreed concerning the details of this process. Almost no one doubts that the book of Amos grew over time, but it remains difficult to reconstruct precisely the stages of development. It is perhaps better to begin with the book in its completed form and to interpret first of all, and perhaps primarily, the completed text.

The book of Amos consists of three major sections: an introductory superscription (1:1) and "motto" (1:2); the main body of the book (1:3–9:6); and a concluding postscript (9:7–15). The first and third sections presuppose Jerusalem as the central focus of divine activity: Uzziah, king of Judah, is listed ahead of Jeroboam, king of Israel (1:1). Yahweh roars from Jerusalem, his dwelling place (1:2). At the end of the book, the concern for the "falling booth of David" (9:11) centers upon the Jerusalemite royal dynasty; the reestablishment of the Jerusalemite political authority is the center of attention.

The main body of the book, by contrast, is notably Israelite in focus. Northern cities—Samaria, Bethel, and Gilgal—are prominent. Jeroboam, king of Israel, is the monarch against whom judgment is directed (7:9, 10–17). It is probable that the tradition's northern orientation, preserved in the second section, represents earlier stages of the tradition and that the first and third sections represent a reinterpretation of earlier Amos material to reflect the way that tradition was later read in Judah.

The structure for the main body of the book (1:3–9:6) is provided by certain "repetitional compositions," i.e., compositions whose parts exhibit great similarity in form and language: "for three transgressions of x and for four . . ." (1:3–2:16); "thus the Lord Yahweh showed me . . ." (7:1–9; 8:1–3). Between the two major "repetitional compositions" (1:3–2:16; 7:1–9:4), one finds, for the most part, poetic utterances.

The main body of the book can be divided into two major parts (1:3–4:13; 5:1–9:6). The first (1:3–4:13) begins with a "repetitional composition" of oracles against various peoples (1:3–2:16). This "repetitional composition" is followed by a group of utterances (3:1–4:12) introduced by "Hear this word . . ." (3:1). This part concludes with a hymn, which praises Yahweh for the previous words of judgment (4:13).

The second part (5:1–9:6), which, like the first, concludes with a doxology (9:5–6), also contains a "repetitional composition," a series of similarly worded vision reports (7:1–9:4). Furthermore, the second part includes a group of utterances (5:1–6:14) introduced by "Hear this word . . ." (5:1). But, unlike the first, the "repetitional composition" appears near the end of this part rather than at the beginning. Moreover, the section of text introduced by "hear this word . . ." appears at the beginning of the second part rather than in second place, as in the first part.

COMMENTARY

1:1–2

Superscription and Motto

The superscription in Amos begins with the title "the words of Amos" followed by a reference to his vocation as a shepherd, a reference to his home, and an indication of the time during which he functioned as a prophet.

The phrase "who was among the shepherds of Tekoa" is particularly significant. The book of Amos points out that Amos prophesied not as a part of lifelong profession, but rather as a "shepherd and dresser of sycamore trees," who was called by Yahweh to leave his flock and to prophesy to Israel (7:15). Indeed, the report that his home was Tekoa (1:1) indicates that his special commission to speak to Israel involved leaving familiar environs for a mission outside Judah.

Dating Amos's activity to "two years before the earthquake" corresponds to language about similar phenomena elsewhere in the book (8:8; 9:1, 5). The purpose of the superscription is to show that Amos's words were fulfilled in the earthquake that occurred subsequent to his preaching.

The "motto" (v. 2) contains language typical of theophanies (an OT theophany reports the appearance of God and its effect on the earth; → Theophany): "gives his voice" or "roars" in the thunder of a storm (Pss. 18:13; 46:6; 104:7; Isa. 30:30). The southern bias of this verse is clear: Yahweh roars from Jerusalem. Both the "motto" and the superscription, with the southern king Uzziah named ahead of Jeroboam, king of Israel, express the conviction that Amos's prophecy to Israel was the work of the God who dwells in Jerusalem.

1:3–9:6

The Main Body of the Book

This second section of the book, consisting of two major parts, revolves around the theme of God's presence. In the first part, a series of judgment speeches lays a foundation for an exhortation, namely, that the people should prepare for Yahweh to appear in their midst. The second part, building upon that exhortation, portrays Yahweh's presence as an event resulting in Israel's death.

1:3–4:13

Laying the Foundation for Yahweh's Theophany

The first part of the book's main body (1:3–4:13) opens with a lengthy section of poetry containing, at the outset, a series of oracles of judgment against various nations, including Israel (1:3–2:16). An elaboration of the judgment upon Israel follows (3:1–4:3). These judgment speeches

set the context for exhortations to enter Yahweh's presence (4:4–5) or to prepare for a theophany (4:6–12), an encounter in which Israel would have to meet its judge face to face.

This part is structured as follows:

1:3–4:12, Prophetic proclamation
  1:3–4:3, Laying the foundation for a theophany: proclamation of judgment
    1:3–2:16, Against the nations and Israel
    3:1–4:3, Further judgment on Israel
  4:4–12, Exhortations concerning entry into Yahweh's presence
4:13, Response: doxological hymn

Yahweh has sent his burning anger upon various nations and upon Israel for their crimes against humanity (1:3–4:3). His anger is still burning, and he will not "cause it [his anger] to return" (or less literally, "to cease"). His wrath, still active, will lead to military defeat, destruction by fire, and exile for those nations who have violently abused other persons. This message of judgment has a two-part structure: first, judgment against various peoples, one of which is Israel (1:3–2:16); and second, singular attention to judgment upon Israel (3:1–4:3).

1:3–2:16, Against the Nations and Israel. This "repetitional composition" contains a series of short, stereotyped oracles against various foreign peoples, concluding with oracles against Judah and Israel. They are introduced by a brief accusation and announcement of punishment: "For three crimes of x and four I will not cause it to return." (Such formulations, "graduated numerical sayings" [x + 1], are common in the biblical tradition and in the ancient Near East [e.g., Ps. 62:11–12; Job 33:14–15; Prov. 30:15–16, 21–23, 29–31]). The rationale for using "three, four" here is unclear, especially since these numbers do not correspond to the number of crimes enumerated. More certain is the nature of the crimes specified; they are all (except for Judah) violent abuses of human beings.

Yahweh's punishment for these crimes occurs in the form of his anger, which, once sent forth, will not be called back. Fire, a stereotypical expression for Yahweh's anger (Deut. 32:22; Isa. 5:24, 25; 9:19; 66:15; Jer. 15:14; 17:4), is kindled to "eat" the "strongholds" of these nations' cities, with the result that they will suffer defeat, death by the sword, and exile.

Yahweh's anger directed against his own people, namely, Judah and, especially, Israel, provides the climax in this "repetitional composition." While Judah's misdeeds are stated generally as disobedience to law and walking according to lies, the crimes of Israel involve oppression of the poor: "they sell the righteous for silver and the needy for a pair of shoes" (Amos 2:6, RSV). Such social abuses are nonetheless violations against Yahweh, for they "profane" his "holy name" and altars and desecrate his sacred house (2:7–8).

Furthermore, although Yahweh has graciously delivered Israel, the Israelites have disobeyed him. The contrast between "I" and "you" statements personalizes and, thereby, emphasizes Israel's improper response: "*I* raised up some of your sons as prophets . . . as Nazirites . . .*" (v. 11; →Nazirites); *"you* made the Nazirites drink wine . . . *you* commanded, saying, 'you must not prophesy' " (v. 12).

Because Israel has oppressed the poor, profaned Yahweh's name, abused his Nazirites, and silenced his prophets, Yahweh will punish the nation by military defeat (vv. 13–16). This defeat is expressed first by the image of an overloaded wagon that "presses down" (RSV) or "breaks open" (see Wolff 1977, p. 134) what is underneath. Then the imagery shifts to the portrayal of the fate of warriors in defeat.

3:1–4:3, Further Judgment on Israel. This compositional unit consists of the following speeches: 3:1–2, 3–8, 9–12, 13–15; 4:1–3. The focus is upon Israel—its misdeeds and the judgment upon it. The message of judgment begins with 3:1–2, which takes the form of a judgment oracle: first, there is a call to hear ("Hear this word . . ."), second, a basis or reason for judgment ("you only have I known . . ."), and third, an announcement of punishment ("therefore I will punish . . ."). Election is no guarantee of God's favor; it involves, rather, a demanding responsibility and serves as the basis for divine judgment and punishment. All else in 3:1–4:3 follows from this claim, which confronts the audience by its boldness and starkness.

What follows in 3:3–8 is an attempt by means of disputation language to support the assertion of vv. 1–2. In this disputation, Amos argues that he has spoken, not on his own, but at Yahweh's behest. The disputation begins with a series of rhetorical questions, e.g., "Do two walk together unless they have met?" The answer to this question and those that follow is obvious; each of these phenomena is the result of a "cause-and-effect" sequence. The disputation comes to resolution in v. 8. The disputation's logic depends upon the relationship between "cause" and "effect" to persuade the audience that the prophet's word of judgment is most assuredly "caused" by *Yahweh's* having spoken.

The text's imagery also helps the audience understand Amos's message. The first image conjures up in the mind something routine and nonthreatening: two do not walk together unless they have met. But the remaining questions in vv. 3–5 elicit mental pictures of life-threatening circumstances in the animal world, namely, a lion roaring over prey, a bird

falling into a trap, or a snare springing from the ground because it has caught something. The imagery has escalated from the innocuous to that of vicious threat to life. Still, no human life is yet at stake.

With Amos 3:6, human life is thrown into question: "If a trumpet is blown in a city, do not the people tremble? If evil befalls a city, has not Yahweh done it?" Now the audience is personally involved, for images of threat to human life have emerged. "Could it be *our* city in which an alarm trumpet is sounded?" Such an emotional reaction, though unstated, may well have been elicited in the audience, for Amos has already said that Yahweh will visit his chosen people's iniquity upon them (3:2) and that punishment will come in the form of military defeat (2:13–16).

The resolution in Amos 3:8 justifies the sense of foreboding conveyed in vv. 3–6: the lion *has* roared—a symbol of military attack—and the people are certainly afraid. The stage is now set for an elaboration of Yahweh's judgment.

Amos 3:9–11 presents a modified form of the prophetic oracle of judgment—with the basis for judgment in v. 10 and the announcement of judgment in v. 11. It begins with instruction to God's heralds: "proclaim to the strongholds of Ashdod . . . and say, 'Assemble on the mountains of Samaria and see the great terrors in her midst. . . .' " Yahweh's chosen in Samaria stand under judgment because of their sins, ironically subject to the scrutiny of gentile witnesses whom Yahweh has not known (cf. v. 2).

Imagery of military strength and defeat continues: Samaria's "strongholds," symbols of military might, are stocked with "violence and oppression" (v. 10). The city has hoarded violence and oppression, as if the people feared they might not have enough! Such commodities will not, however, protect them. An enemy will attack them and destroy the lofty "strongholds" (v. 11).

Amos 3:12 employs two images to elaborate the previous oracle: first, the shepherd who rescues nothing but torn animal parts from the lion, and, second, the recovery of nothing but furniture fragments from the enemy. Not only will the "strongholds" be brought low; nothing but fragments of the furnishings will be left. Still another image, that of a lion having devoured its prey (v. 12), connects animal violence to military defeat. Moreover, the lion's roaring over its prey is said to be the voice of Yahweh (v. 8). Thus the lion's attack (vv. 4, 12), the blowing of the alarm trumpet in a city (v. 6), the activity of witnesses in Yahweh's trial against Samaria (v. 9), the enemy's destruction of Samaria's mighty "strongholds" (v. 11), and the decimation of furnishings (v. 12) are all images that work together to depict the total annihilation of the city.

Amos 3:13–15 extends the portrayal of devastation. The legal language of v. 9, wherein witnesses are summoned, continues in an installation-of-witnesses speech (vv. 13–15): "Hear and testify against the house of Jacob...." The witnesses testify that the altar at Bethel will be punished and that Yahweh will destroy "houses." Destruction is not limited to the strongholds but includes also the great houses of the upper class. Moreover, there will be no refuge from the slaughter. The horns of the altar, long a place of refuge (1 Kings 1:50; 2:28), will be cut off. The last hope for escaping the catastrophe consequently vanishes.

The final result is exile (Amos 4:1–3). The wealthy women of Samaria, who have oppressed the poor, will be led away by "hooks" through the breaches in the city wall—gaps in the protective wall opened by the enemy. Not only is there destruction of strongholds, houses, furnishings, and the horns of the altar; the people are also taken into exile. Truly nothing is left.

4:4–12, Entry into Yahweh's Presence. The divine judgment proclaimed in Amos 1:3–4:3 paves the way for two exhortations concerning entry into Yahweh's presence (4:4–5, 6–12). Because Yahweh's anger has initiated judgment, Israel must prepare to confront his presence (see esp. v. 12). The first of these exhortations (vv. 4–5) is sarcastic in tone. It parodies a language summoning worshipers to enter the sanctuary and offer a sacrifice. One can imagine a summons such as "Come to Bethel and bring a sacrifice," but no religious official would have said, "Come to Bethel and transgress." Such mock encouragement must mean "Go right on sinning with your sacrifices, which you love to flaunt, so that all may see your piety! This is indeed the way to enter Yahweh's presence!"

The second exhortation (vv. 6–12) turns from sarcastic exhortation concerning Israelite behavior to a recitation of what Yahweh has done. Yahweh has sent a series of punishments in the hope that these chastisements would induce repentance, but all to no avail: "They did not return to me." So Yahweh announces judgment still to come (v. 12a) and exhorts Israel to "prepare" for a theophany (v. 12b) where they will "meet" him face to face (see Exod. 19:11, 15, 17 to observe "prepare" [RSV: "be ready"] and "meet" as terms associated with theophany).

4:13, Doxology. The doxology praises Yahweh for his creative power. It serves as a hymnic response that extols him for the preceding words of judgment (1:3–4:12).

5:1–9:6
Death and the End for Israel

This second part of the book's main body may be understood as a sequel to the exhortation to prepare for a theophany (4:12). Yahweh's arrival involves death and the end for Israel (5:1–9:6). This section is structured as follows:

5:1–9:4, Prophetic proclamation
    5:1–6:14, Utterances concerning the death of Israel
        5:1–17, The proclamation of death
        5:18–6:14, Elaboration of the proclamation of death
    7:1–9:4, Vision reports concerning the end of Israel
9:5–6, Response: doxology

5:1–17, The Proclamation of Death. This passage has two parts: vv. 1–9 and vv. 10–17. Verses 1–9 begin with a funeral lament (vv. 1–2): "Hear this word . . ." (call to hear); "fallen, no more to rise . . ." (lament proper). The prophet employs the image of a dead virgin and the genre of a funeral lament to portray a total end for Israel. For a woman to die a virgin was indeed something to bewail, as the narrative of Jephthah's daughter shows (Judg. 11:29–40). So too Israel dies, prematurely and unfulfilled, like a woman who had borne no children.

In v. 3, a word from God substantiates the lament: "The city which goes forth a thousand will have a hundred left...." The imagery is that of a military disaster; the army is virtually wiped out. The funeral lament (vv. 1–2) and the announcement of defeat in battle (v. 3) express in concrete terms a transition from power or life to impotence or death.

In vv. 4–5, however, the language shifts to an exhortation that encourages behavior leading to life ("Seek me and live") and then an admonition ("Do not seek Bethel . . ."), as well as basis for the admonition ("for Gilgal will go into exile and Bethel will become nothing").

How should one assess the transition from lament over death (vv. 1–3) to exhortation about life? First, one must recognize that the language in vv. 4–5 is ironic. A typical exhortation would not encourage persons to seek Yahweh but would promote pilgrimages to the leading Yahweh sanctuaries. Verses 4–5 are obviously a parody of conventional speech, a parody that exhorts people to avoid seeking Yahweh in the very places he is thought to be present.

Verses 6–7 form a second exhortation: "Seek Yahweh and live, lest he break out like fire . . . and it eat with no one to quench...." Destruction by fire is viewed as a creature, which has a mouth and eats. The metaphor of a devouring fire connects v. 6 to vv. 1–3. A fire that consumes is much like death in that what once was no longer is.

In v. 7, the prophet accuses people using figurative language. Justice is not literally turned to wormwood, nor is righteousness actually thrust down to the ground. But the comparison is meaningful: justice is not merely absent; it is turned into something else, something for which bitter wormwood is an appropriate metaphor. Or again, justice is not simply abandoned; it is cast down.

The doxology (vv. 8–9) continues the tone of judgment. Yahweh, who quite properly "turns" one thing into another (e.g., deep darkness into morning), is deliberately contrasted with Israel's improper "turning" of justice into wormwood. This hymn of praise sets Yahweh's behavior over against that of Israel.

Verses 10–17 are made up of three parts: vv. 10–13, 14–15, and 16–17. The repeated use of "therefore" is an important stylistic connector (vv. 11, 13, 16), as is the repetition of the verb "hate" (vv. 10, 15) and the phrase "in the gate" (vv. 10, 12, 15). The term "gate," a reference to the town gate where legal proceedings were customarily held, refers to the place and practice of justice. Indeed, justice is the basic theme of vv. 10–17.

Verses 10–12 provide the reasons for judgment, e.g., "They hate the reprover in the gate. . . ." But announcement of judgment for the future also appears: "houses of hewn stone you have built but you shall not live in them. . . ." Then, in v. 13, "therefore" appears, introducing a second assertion concerning the future: "Therefore the prudent in that time will be silent, for it is a bad time."

Three "imagined scenes" underlie vv. 10–13. The first elicits a scene in the town gate in which those who speak for justice encounter opposition from those who "hate" or "abhor" truthfulness (v. 10). Undoubtedly the former were despised by those who were using the legal process to acquire property unjustly at the expense of the poor. The second "imagined scene" brings to mind a picture of such abuse and its results. The poor are "trampled upon" (a rich figurative expression) with the result that their oppressors unjustly acquire wealth, such as houses and vineyards. Uninhabited houses and vineyards whose wine remains unimbibed provide concrete images that express the prophet's conviction that the elaborate plans to manipulate the legal system for illegitimate acquisition will result in the inability to enjoy the luxuries so painstakingly but unjustly acquired. The third "imagined scene" involves the mental picture of that day of judgment in which the "prudent" will keep silent (v. 13). Yahweh's judgment will bring such a terrible time that silence is the only wise response.

Amos 5:14–15 comprises two parts: an exhortation plus two purpose clauses (v. 14) and an exhortation plus an expression of possibility (v. 15). The tone of v. 14 appears initially to be that of a sincere exhortation. However, the end of the second purpose clause alters this tone. The addition of "as you have said" gives to the exhortation a new and mocking tone, for it pokes fun at the audience and its cheap mouthing of confidence in the divine presence as it prattles piously, "Yahweh is with us. . . ."

The final clause of the second exhortation ("perhaps Yahweh . . . will be gracious to a remnant of Joseph") reinforces the mocking tone of vv. 14–15. Such expressions were used in Israel to propose certain courses of action in the hope that the action might lead to favorable consequences (Gen. 16:2; Num. 22:6, 11; 23:3; 1 Sam. 6:5). But this particular expression of possibility (Amos 5:15b) ridicules the audience and their understanding of the significance of Yahweh's presence.

Verses 16–17 conclude the compositional unit (vv. 1–17) with an announcement of judgment. The time of judgment is portrayed as a time of mourning in cities and vineyards. Such activities might actually take place in a time of catastrophe, but the purpose of vv. 16–17 is to represent Israel's calamity by portraying it in terms of death. Thus, the end of the composition returns to the theme found at its beginning.

Verses 16–17 close with the words "for I will cross over in your midst." This assertion, namely, that Yahweh's presence will bring death, colors one's reading of the exhortation in vv. 14–15. The purpose clause, "that Yahweh . . . may be with you," can no longer be read straightforwardly. When read in the light of v. 17b, that purpose clause expresses an aim that, ironically, leads to death. The summons for people to prepare to meet their God (4:12) will come to fruition. He *will* be present—to bring death.

5:18–6:14, Elaboration on the Proclamation.

This unit is composed of two sections (5:18–27; 6:1–14). In each section a woe-utterance (5:18–20; 6:1–7) is followed by a Yahweh-speech in which the Deity says, "I hate . . ." (5:21–27; 6:8–14). Each of these two parts has its own particular emphases.

Amos 5:18–27 confronts the audience with an ironic reversal of what is normally expected. In vv. 18–20, the Day of Yahweh, contrary to popular opinion, is not a day to be desired but rather a day of darkness. Verses 21–23 also overturn ordinary expectation through Yahweh's assertion that he "hates" his worshipers' sacrifices. Israelites traditionally believed that Yahweh desires sacrifice. But here he rejects it, announcing that he wants justice and righteousness instead (v. 24).

Yahweh's hatred of Israel's sacrifices (5:21) brings to a climax a motif that begins in Amos 5:10. There the people are said to "hate" those who seek justice in the gate. Yet those who hate justice are exhorted to "hate evil," to "love good," and to establish justice in the gate (5:15) —to love what they hate and to hate what they presumably love. In 5:21–23, Yahweh proclaims his "hatred" of their sacrifices, the sacrifices they "love" to proclaim (4:4–5). Thus, Yahweh hates what Israel loves and loves what Israel hates.

Amos 6:1–14 condemns the majesty and splendor of Israel. The woe utterance (vv. 1–7) portrays leaders in positions of responsibility who in their revelry are interested only in luxury and self-indulgence but are unfortunately "not sick over the shattering of Joseph" (v. 6). Crime and punishment are ironically interrelated: those who are the "first" among the people (v. 1) will be the "first" to go into exile (v. 7). They maintain their status, even when the social order collapses.

Verses 8–14 also attack the splendor or pride of Israel. Yahweh "hates" it; therefore he will "deliver up" the city and its "fullness." Even if ten are left in one house, they too will die (vv. 9–10), and all houses will be destroyed (v. 11). The theme of Israel's pride appears also in vv. 13–14; the Israelites are proud of their military prowess. But, ironically, all their territory will be taken in a military invasion by a foreign nation.

7:1–9:4, Visions of Israel's End. This unit is made up of five vision reports (7:1–3, 4–6, 7–9; 8:1–3; 9:1–4) plus two supplements (7:10–17; 8:4–14) inserted into this vision report sequence. The first two reports narrate visions of devastating judgments against Israel in which the prophet succeeds, through intercessory prayer, in persuading Yahweh to withdraw the punishment. In the third and fourth visions, however, Yahweh announces an irrevocable judgment against Israel: "I will not again pass him by" (7:8; 8:2). The fifth vision report elaborates the message of judgment.

The vision reports develop the theme of death present in the second part of the main body (5:1–9:6). Like a wall tested by a plumb-line and found to be unfit, so Israel fails the test and therefore must, like the wall, be torn down (7:7–8). The word play (Heb. *qayitz*, "summer fruit", and *qetz*, "end") introduces a description of Israel's end (8:1–3). The final vision (9:1–4) fills out the picture of death: none escape the sword. No matter how far they flee, they cannot escape Yahweh's eyes; at his command they will die.

A supplement to the third vision (7:10–17) reports conflict between Amos and Amaziah, priest of Bethel. The book's concern over attempts to silence the prophetic word (cf. 2:11–12; 3:7–8) is at issue in this narrative. Amaziah cannot rightfully order Amos to prophesy in Judah since his commission is from Yahweh and not from Amaziah (7:12–15). Moreover, Amos is not a lifelong prophet but rather a shepherd who was given a special calling—to prophesy to Israel.

A supplement (8:4–14) to the fourth vision elaborates the message of death and mourning found in 8:3. But the judgment is radicalized. It involves more than exile, starvation, and death; there will be a famine of hearing Yahweh's creating and sustaining words.

9:5–6, Doxology. This hymn continues the language of mourning and of the shaking (rising and falling) of the earth (9:5; cf. 8:8; 9:1). The hymnist praises Yahweh, the sovereign creator, who controls the waters, moves the world, and even makes it mourn.

9:7–15
Postscript

The book ends with a reinterpretation of the message of judgment. By disputing the claim that deliverance from Egypt exempts Israel from judgment, the author claims that Yahweh will destroy "the sinful kingdom" (vv. 7–8a). This kingdom (the Israelite monarchy?) will disappear, but the "house of Jacob" will not be completely destroyed. Only sinners will die, and a remnant will survive (vv. 8b–10). Verses 11–15, undoubtedly composed during the Babylonian exile, understand the surviving remnant as linked to the renaissance of the "falling" Davidic dynasty. The ability of Jerusalemites so to reinterpret the earlier Amos tradition is a testimony to the vitality of the sacred word in shaping and reshaping faith.

Bibliography
Coote, R. B. *Amos Among the Prophets.* Philadelphia: Fortress, 1981.

Mays, J. L. *Amos: A Commentary.* Old Testament Library. Philadelphia: Westminster, 1969.

Tucker, G. "Prophetic Authenticity: A Form-Critical Study of Amos 7:10–17." *Interpretation* 27 (1973): 423–34.

Wolff, H. W. *Amos the Prophet: The Man and His Background.* Philadelphia: Fortress, 1973.

———. *Joel and Amos.* Hermeneia. Philadelphia: Fortress, 1977.

OBADIAH

MICHAEL H. FLOYD

INTRODUCTION

The Book of Obadiah is one long complex unit. But there are apparent tensions between the opening of Obadiah and the rest of the book with which any conception of its overall form must reckon.

The superscription (v. 1) identifies it as a vision, but the following subheading introduces it as a speech. The speaker is identified as Yahweh, God of Israel, but the quotation actually begins (v. 1) and ends (vv. 19–21) with someone else speaking. The subject is said to be the neighboring nation of Edom, but parts of the book concern the nations in general. These features begin to make sense since the term "vision" can refer to whatever the prophetic imagination has been divinely enabled to perceive, whether images seen (Dan. 8:1–12) or words heard (1 Sam. 3). It can also refer derivatively to a written report of such perceptions (Hab. 2:2; Jer. 36). Obadiah's inclusion of other voices besides the divine voice under the rubric of a speech of Yahweh shows that it is not, however, just such a record. The convention of reporting prophetic perceptions has been adapted to show that the text itself has divinatory significance. This document was meant to provide for its interpreters not just information about past prophecies, but also prophetic insight into the present. The whole book is a visionary word of Yahweh in this sense, though, strictly speaking, only vv. 2–18 comprise a speech of Yahweh. The incorporation of an announcement concerning the nations within an address to Edom (v. 15) is but one indication of the book's concern to integrate these two subjects. The focus is on Edom as one of the central agents, along with Israel, in a world-historical process that ultimately affects all peoples.

The book thus has integrity with respect to both form and content, but the close similarity between parts of it and parts of another anti-Edomite prophecy suggests that the author may have drawn on previously existing oracular materials (cf. vv. 1–5; Jer. 49:7, 9, 14–16). There is no consensus among modern interpreters, however, regarding any earlier stages, and since nothing biographical is known about the prophet for whom the book is named, there is no telling whether any certain parts of it or the whole should be attributed to him. In any case, the book in its final form is not so much a collection of prophecies, each occasioned by a particular event, as it is a critical reflection on

the type of historical process represented by a whole period of Israelite-Edomite relations. The book's retrospective viewpoint presupposes both the Edomites' participation in the Babylonian conquest of Jerusalem in the sixth century B.C. (Ps. 137:7) and a subsequent attack on Edom by former allies, which cannot be as precisely dated (→ Edomites; Nabatea, Nabateans). Such considerations would put the final composition sometime in the postexilic period, probably in the sixth or fifth century B.C.

Behind these events there lie memories of the Edomites' refusal to allow the Hebrew refugees led by Moses to pass through their land (Num. 20:14–21) as well as of wars in which Edom came under and broke free from the control of Israelite monarchs (2 Sam. 8:13–14; 1 Kings 11:14–22; 2 Kings 14:7, 22; 16:6; 2 Chron. 20; 21:8–10). Obadiah comes from a tradition of prophetic, anti-Edomite polemic generated by this history (e.g., Isa. 34:5–17; Jer. 49:7–22; Lam. 4:21–22; Ezek. 25:12–14, 35; Amos 1:11–12 and Mal. 1:2–4). In form, Obadiah represents the emergence of a type of divination through historiographical study, which was especially characteristic of prophecy in the postexilic period. This development is further evident in the final canonical forms of other prophetic books, as well as in the final composition of historical narratives such as the Pentateuch and the Deuteronomistic History (→ Deuteronomistic Historian; Sources of the Pentateuch).

COMMENTARY

In its opening lines (v. 1), the word on Edom identifies the reception of an oracle from Yahweh with a diplomatic communication that puts all nations on notice; then, by means of a summons to battle, all are urged to align themselves against Edom in the coming struggle. This beginning suggests that whatever Yahweh has to say about Edom will also affect the rest of the world and that policy toward this nation will somehow influence all national destinies.

The oracle's first section (vv. 2–4) begins to explain what has happened to Edom and how this affects other nations. First comes a description of the Edomites' present predicament (vv. 2–3). As a result of Yahweh's control over their affairs and as a consequence of their own self-deceptive pride, they find themselves in a despicable state. A false sense of security, engendered by the region's naturally defensible high terrain, is symptomatic of their overall hubris. Then comes an indication of what Edom's situation portends for the international order (v. 4). Even if as a world power Edom were to be this arrogant, Yahweh would bring it down just the same. (See for the symbol of the eagle, Ezek. 17:1–10; for the image of being cast down from the stars, Isa. 14:12–17.) Edom's present fate is thus both an example of what Yahweh could do to any nation and part of what he is doing in accord with his larger design for the whole world.

The main body of the oracle (vv. 5–17) has two sections. The first (vv. 5–7) develops in greater detail the description of Edom's present predicament in vv. 2–3. Edom's dire straits are further described in terms of a double cross by former allies, who in their plundering have taken more than thieves and left less than harvesters. In falling prey to such victimization, there is hardly any evidence of Edom's proverbial wisdom! (See Jer. 49:7; Bar. 3:22.) The second section (vv. 8–15) similarly fills in the description of the worldwide future implications barely outlined in v. 4. These two sections are linked by a question (vv. 8–9) that asks rhetorically whether Edom's misfortunes are not the beginning of "the Day of Yahweh," whose scenario includes the Edomites' loss of their wisdom traditions as a prelude to their utter destruction (→ Judgment, Day of).

The Edomites' impending doom thus provides the paradigmatic case for what will befall all nations on that day (v. 15). As Edom's fortunes are even now being reversed, so is the world situation about to be reversed. And the pivot on which this cosmic process turns is the sanctuary of Yahweh in Jerusalem. Its destruction is the great wrong that needs to be set right, and its restoration to holiness (v. 17a) is the focal point of the great transformation. The change begins with Edom because its participation in the destruction was most treacherous. As kindred neighbors, the Edomites should not have joined with the alien powers. Because they were so heavily implicated in Jerusalem's "day of trouble" (note the recurrence of this phrase and variations in vv. 11–14), they are the first to have the troubles of the Day of Yahweh. They now know from their former allies the same kind of treachery that Israel once knew from them, and thus "on that day" Edom will finally be consumed by Israel (v. 18). The other nations that took part in or condoned the violation of Yahweh's sanctuary will similarly find that their victory toasts have turned to drunken gulps from the cup of doom (v. 16; cf. Ps. 75:8; Isa. 51:17–23; Jer. 25:15–17). But as for Israel, whose refuge on Mount Zion was once cut off (v. 14), they will now find there a refuge from which to dispossess all those who had dispossessed them (v. 17).

The outcome of this turnabout is described in vv. 19–21: Israel will fully regain its territoriality, Edom will become subordinate to the authority that emanates from Yahweh's sanctuary in Jerusalem, and Yahweh's cosmic kingship will then be once again intact.

By referring to Israel as Jacob and to Edom as Esau, Obadiah explicitly associates its reflections on the historic animosity between these two peoples with the pentateuchal stories of the intrafamilial strife between the twin sons of Isaac and Rebekah (Gen. 25:19–33:20; note 25:30b and 32:28). Against this background it becomes evident that the book is not just nationalistic sentiment masked in religious terms. Along with Israel's sense of being divinely destined to overcome Edom (Gen. 25:23; Num. 24:18) there come several other, relatively paradoxical, realizations: the conflict with Edom is rooted in the same fratricidal tendencies as intra-Israelite conflict; Israel encounters God in crippling struggles as well as in victorious ones (Gen. 32:24–32); and God could be fully encountered through reconciliation with Edom (Gen. 33:1–17; note v. 10b). Within a mythic frame of reference, which regards Yahweh's sanctuary in Jerusalem as the sign and center of the divinely established cosmic order (Ps. 48), Obadiah makes a theological analysis of a particular type of historical situation: there can be communities with enough common interests and affinities to make them like brothers who nevertheless opportunistically relate to imperial powers so as to exploit one another. But whenever this happens, cosmic standards of justice have been violated, creating an imbalance in the world order that God will inevitably redress.

Bibliography

Bewer, J. A., et al. "Obadiah." *A Critical and Exegetical Commentary on Micah, Zephaniah, Nahum, Habakkuk, Obadiah and Joel.* International Critical Commentary. New York: Scribner's, 1911. Pp. 3–46.

Childs, B. S. *Introduction to the Old Testament as Scripture.* Philadelphia: Fortress, 1979. Chap. 23.

McCarter, P. K. "Obadiah 7 and the Fall of Edom." *Bulletin of the American Schools of Oriental Research,* 221 (1976): 87–91.

Watts, J. D. W. *The Books of Joel, Obadiah, Jonah, Nahum, Habakkuk and Zephaniah.* Cambridge Bible Commentary on the New English Bible. Cambridge: Cambridge University Press, 1975.

Wolff, H. W. *Obadiah and Jonah: A Commentary.* Translated by M. Kohl. Minneapolis, MN: Augsburg, 1986.

JONAH

TERENCE E. FRETHEIM

INTRODUCTION

The Book of Jonah probably dates from the fifth century B.C. when continuing hardships, foreign subjugation, and the nonfulfillment of exilic promises raised the issue of God's justice for Israel (cf. Mal. 2:17; 3:14–15).

The exact reference to Jonah in 1:1 roots the book in history (2 Kings 14:25), but literary features (e.g., irony, satire, hyperbole, repetition, humor, and the ending) indicate a nonhistoriographic purpose. The book is best seen as an interpretive development of these roots in the form of a short story pervasively didactic and carefully structured. Jonah himself becomes a type representing certain pious Israelites who hold a problematic theological perspective; Nineveh (cf. Nah. 3:1) is probably a cipher for the Persians (cf. Jth. 1:1). The book is a unity, as most recent scholars recognize, though the author uses many earlier motifs and traditions (cf. Gen. 18; 1 Kings 19; Jer. 18, 36; Joel 2). The book is prophetic in that it speaks a word of judgment and grace to a specific audience, evoking amendment of thought and life.

The book raises anew Abraham's question over Sodom, "Will the Judge of all the earth do right?" (Gen. 18:25), in view of Exod. 34:6, "... a God merciful and gracious, slow to anger, and abounding in steadfast love ..." (cf. Jon. 4:2). Jonah's disobedience is symptomatic of a theological view that questions the indiscriminate extension of God's mercy to the wicked, especially in light of Israel's suffering at their hands. But simple justice is not God's way; God remains free to be gracious toward those who deserve nothing but punishment. This is true for both Jonah (Israel) and Nineveh. The object of the book is theological change that would effect obedience. God's means are heuristic, and to the very end Jonah retains freedom to resist.

COMMENTARY

1:1–3, Jonah Called. Unlike other prophets who spoke oracles against the nations, Jonah is called to deliver a word of judgment to Nineveh in person. Because this means that the wicked destroyers of Jonah's homeland might repent and that God might respond in mercy rather than deserved judgment (cf. 4:2), Jonah's sense of justice is violated. Hence, to escape to a place in which God's call might be less compelling, he buys the most expensive ticket on a ship heading in the opposite direction—to Tarshish in Spain.

1:4–16, Jonah Pursued. Because Jonah's flight has an adverse effect on God's possibilities for Nineveh, God pursues the reluctant mediator of the divine word—not to visit him with wrath but to turn him around. Far from demonstrating divine omnipotence, the storm provides a new context for decision making but does not predetermine the results.

To lighten the ship, the sailors sacrifice the cargo to their gods; Jonah, however, closes his eyes to what God is about and descends into a deep sleep, a descent culminating in 2:6. Ironically, the captain reminds the prophet of his religious responsibilities, recognizing that prayer does not finally shape the divine response. When the lots pinpoint Jonah as the one who has occasioned the crisis, he is assaulted with questions. Responding incompletely, he nevertheless makes a confession that eventually moves the sailors to faith in his God, action that anticipates the Ninevites' response. But the confession does not stop the storm; in fact, the weather gets worse. What is at stake for God is Jonah's theologically informed disobedience, not his faith.

Attuned to the signs of transcendence, the sailors wonder how to stop the storm. Jonah confesses that he is the problem and asks to be thrown overboard. His sense of justice will not allow the innocent to perish for the guilty. Even more, refusing to change his convictions, which presumably would have stopped the storm, Jonah will show God what justice means; he will take upon himself the punishment he deserves. God, however, refuses to be bound by strict canons of justice and mercifully delivers Jonah by means of a fish. The sailors, meanwhile, insightfully recognizing that Jonah's death is not required, strive to return him to where he can be obedient. They finally agree to Jonah's request, reminding God that this is a divine dilemma; they should not be blamed if Jonah is innocent. The storm stops and the sailors respond as faithful Israelites would.

1:17–2:10, God's Deliverance and Jonah's Response. The use of the fish to achieve God's purposes brackets Jonah's prayer. The fish, of unknown species, is God's instrument for saving Jonah from the sea and transporting him (in three days and nights, the time it takes for a journey from the underworld) to the place where God's call can be restated. In response to the deliverance from drowning, Jonah sings a song of thanksgiving from the fish's belly. Using traditional metaphoric language (cf. Pss. 30; 42), here also used literally, he recalls his distress, lament, and descent to the doors of Sheol (the abode of the dead, located beneath the sea floor). Ironically, he contrasts himself with the pagans, failing to see that he has forsaken God as much as they. He voices the central theme of God's deliverance—ironically, for he would limit God's exercise of the mercy that saved him. The prayer reveals no real change in an otherwise pious Jonah, but God and the fish mercifully, if unceremoniously, bring the unrepentant prophet home.

3:1–10, Nineveh and God Repent. The pattern of threatened disaster followed by human and divine repentance is common in Israel's experience (cf. Joel 2) and is enunciated in Jer. 18:7–11 as available to all. Hyperbole is pervasive. Nineveh is described in terms much larger than life; archaeology knows no such incredibly large city. Despite Jonah's minimal effort, everyone in the most evil city of the age immediately repents, even the animals. Deliberately overdrawn, such details highlight the irony of the reluctant prophet's unparalleled success.

Still in need of Jonah, God repeats the call. This act protects Jonah's freedom to resist in the face of much divine activity; but this time he acquiesces. Yet, his graceless message in the shadow of his own experience of divine love and his negative response to the results of his own preaching (4:1) indicate that he goes under duress and without mercy in his heart. His unconditional message—an unprecedented countdown to doom—speaks Jonah's own mind regarding what should occur; this will serve justice.

Surprisingly, the Ninevites believed God, and it is they who spread the word throughout the city. Like the captain, the king leads his community in repentant acts (cf. Jer. 36), acknowledging that they are not salvific in themselves. Human repentance is a necessary but not sufficient factor; salvation will depend finally on the kind of God that God is. God's repentance of evil, turning from an announcement of judgment having ill effects, is finally rooted in divine love (4:2), which cannot be presumed upon by those who repent. The divine repentance shows that God is not immutable. God is affected by people's actions and will reshape plans in that light, all in the service of God's unchangeable will for salvation of as many as possible.

4:1–11, A Theological Debate. Jonah becomes very angry, strenuously objecting to God's act of salvation! He now offers his reasons for fleeing. He had feared God would let mercy override justice, even for non-Israelites (cf. Ps. 145:8–9). Jonah does not disagree with the priority of God's grace as such, but he will not be a partner to its indiscriminate exercise. God must conform to basic canons of justice in responding to human conduct. Otherwise, God is capricious and life is absurd. And so, Jonah asks God to kill him (cf. Elijah in 2 Kings); he has participated in an act of injustice, and that is worthy of the death sentence. But God again refuses to accept Jonah's challenge (cf. 1:12) and mercifully engages him in conversation. God's approach is such that Jonah is free to respond, as the question format indicates: is his anger a proper response to Nineveh's deliverance? Jonah does not respond verbally (cf. 1:6) but challenges God with the firmness of his resolve. God should take another look at the situation; Jonah will sit and wait God out.

Again there is an impasse. Rather than a baneful storm, God now sends a beneficial plant; rather than being exposed to the elements, Jonah is protected from them. Ironically, God reinforces Jonah's shade with his own construction, displaying the plenitude of divine deliverance beyond human deserving or possibility. Through this ad hoc plant God delivers the one who is angry at God for delivering others. Ironically, when Jonah sits in the shadow of God's generosity, he rejoices. Heuristically, God responds with worm and wind; the plant withers and Jonah wearies. He is given a taste of destruction. How could he want that for anybody? But Jonah again wishes for death in view of such give-and-take capriciousness; God is not just.

Now God asks: is anger a proper response to the plant's destruction? A clever question—either answer impales Jonah. If the response is negative (as it should have been), recognizing that he is not in a position to make claims regarding God's gift to him, then he would be admitting that he cannot make judgments concerning what God does with God's own creatures. But if it is affirmative (as it was), then he tacitly recognizes God's right to do what God wills regarding Nineveh, for God's claims regarding Nineveh are much greater than Jonah's regarding the plant. What Jonah (Israel) has received from God is pure gift, given apart from questions of justice, concerning which he can make no claims. Therefore, if such gifts should be lost or given to others, the question of divine fairness is inappropriate.

God's freedom to have mercy is affirmed

rather than God's compassion as such ("am I not allowed to have pity" is the sense of v. 11; cf. Matt. 20:15). Yet, God's will for all is salvation, and so one can expect that God, out of love, will be moved to compassion toward his repentant creatures, even the cows.

Bibliography

Allen, L. *The Books of Joel, Obadiah, Jonah, and Micah*. New International Commentary on the Old Testament. Grand Rapids, MI: Eerdmans, 1976.

Craghan, J. *Esther, Judith, Tobit, Jonah, Ruth*. Old Testament Message, 16. Wilmington, DE: Glazier, 1982.

Fretheim, T. *The Message of Jonah: A Theological Commentary*. Minneapolis, MN: Augsburg, 1977.

Landes, G. "Jonah, Book of." *The Interpreter's Dictionary of the Bible, Supplementary Volume*. Nashville, TN: Abingdon, 1976. Pp. 488–91.

Magonet, J. *Form and Meaning: Studies in Literary Techniques in the Book of Jonah*. Bible and Literature Series, vol. 8. Sheffield: Almond, 1983.

Wolff, H. W. *Jonah: Church in Revolt*. St. Louis, MO: Clayton, 1978.

MICAH

W. EUGENE MARCH

INTRODUCTION

The Book of Micah, the sixth of the twelve Minor Prophets, consists of a collection of prophetic materials broadly categorized as announcements of punishment and salvation. The book has two major parts, 1:2–5:15 and 6:1–7:20, preceded by a superscription (1:1). The two major parts are arranged in similar fashion, moving from accusations and announcements of destruction to pronouncements of hope and deliverance.

The superscription designates Micah of Moresheth as spokesman of the addresses collected in this book. Although Micah spoke during the reigns of Jotham, Ahaz, and Hezekiah, approximately 742 to 698 B.C., we know very little about him.

In 745 B.C. the Assyrian Empire began a period of expansion under the leadership of Tiglath-pileser III. In 721 B.C. Assyria destroyed Samaria, the capital city of Israel (→ Samaria, City of; Samaria, District of), and took captive thousands of Israelites. Judah, Micah's principal place of activity, also felt the pain of Assyrian attack (→ Judah, Kingdom of). In 713 B.C. Judah barely avoided a major confrontation with the Assyrians. Then, in 701, Assyria's Sennacherib (→ Sennacherib) launched a major onslaught. Thousands of people were slain and many more were taken captive. Jerusalem was besieged but miraculously escaped destruction.

The book of Micah is built around a core of material widely regarded as original to Micah the Moreshite and fitting the times of the Assyrian crisis (chaps. 1–3). Debate continues among commentators, however, with respect to the remainder of the book.

The book of Micah seems to have grown in two or perhaps three stages. The first stage involved the work done by the prophet Micah remembered by a group of disciples and some of Judah's leaders (cf. Jer. 26:18–19). The second phase appears to have involved people concerned with preserving collections of prophetic announcements, particularly those of Isaiah and Micah (a close affinity exists between these two books). The first and second phase of the book's development may overlap.

The third phase, however, seems to postdate the destruction of Jerusalem by the Babylonians in 587 B.C. Micah 6–7 is best understood from the perspective of the sixth or early fifth century B.C. The historical catastrophes experienced by Israel and Judah are given a theological interpretation. The justice of God has been worked. The punishment of Jacob is a sign for God's people and the nations of the world. The everlasting mercy of God will be exercised, however, to reclaim God's people as a further sign of God's intention for all humankind.

For the Christian community the book of Micah has taken on special significance. Micah 5:2–4 announces a righteous shepherd who will come forth from Bethlehem to rule on behalf of God. The Gospel of Matthew quotes Micah (Matt. 2:6) in support of the tradition that Jesus of Nazareth was born in Bethlehem.

COMMENTARY

PART ONE: 1:1–5:15

The Reign of the LORD Over the Nations

1:1, Micah, the Moreshite. The prophet is remembered as Micah of Moresheth. The name "Micah," which means "Who is like the Lord?" is a common name type in ancient Israel. Moresheth, also known as Moresheth-gath, was a small village approximately twenty-five miles southwest of Jerusalem (1:14). The village has not yet been positively identified by archaeologists. Apart from the superscription, nothing in the book of Micah gives any concrete information about the prophet. The material in the book was associated with this Micah by ancient editors. These same ancient editors dated the work of Micah to the reigns of Jotham, Ahaz, and Hezekiah. Micah is remembered in Jer. 26:18 as having uttered words of doom against Zion and Jerusalem that prompted Hezekiah to repent. The primary subjects of the oracles are the capital cities of the Northern and Southern kingdoms, Samaria and Jerusalem.

1:2–16, Mourning Inescapable Destruction. Micah's message begins with a call to all peoples to hear the Lord. Material originally much more concrete and time-bound is made applicable by later editors to a wider audience: an announcement first directed at Samaria (1:3–7) is linked with a cry of lament for Jerusalem (1:8–16). This entire text serves to set the mood for the announcement that will unfold in chaps. 1–5: the sovereign Lord addresses humanity with judgment and deliverance. The controversy God has with Israel and Judah is thus put in a worldwide context.

The Lord is described as coming forth from the holy place provoking an upheaval of nature (→Theophany). The "holy temple" (RSV) or "sacred palace" (JB) of 1:2, in view of the indictment against Jerusalem in 1:5, probably refers to God's heavenly abode (cf. Pss. 11:4; 18:7; Isa. 6:2), though the term often refers to the Temple in Jerusalem (Pss. 5:8; 65:5; 138:2). God comes forth to battle enemies (Judg. 5:4; Isa. 26:21; Ps. 68:8), but here the "foe" is God's own people.

The judgment centers on the capital of the Northern Kingdom, Samaria, and on the rampant idolatry that signals the sin of Israel. Jerusalem is also mentioned, but almost as an aside (some commentators think it is an addition). As in Hosea, the widespread presence of idols is categorized as harlotry (1:7). Destruction of all idols constitutes part of the punishment. Because Samaria sought prosperity by such harlotry, the city will be laid waste. In 722/721 B.C. the Assyrian Shalmaneser captured and destroyed Samaria.

Verses 8 and 9 link the preceding announcement of forthcoming judgment on Samaria with the following description of disaster reaching the gate of Jerusalem. The prophet laments an incurable wound inflicted on the people (1:8). The prophet's anguish is punctuated by reference to "my people" (1:9). In the language and mode of mourning ("stripped," "naked," 1:8) the prophet laments the death of his people. In the Hebrew of 1:16 a singular feminine "you," possibly Jerusalem, is enjoined to lament by shaving her head. Her "children" (RSV) or "sons" (JB) are the outlying villages, whose inhabitants have been taken away into exile.

A number of uncertainties in a poorly preserved Hebrew text result in a wide variety of translations. Nonetheless, the basic outline of 1:8–16 is clear. With numerous wordplays involving the names of the towns mentioned, a picture of mounting disaster is painted. The people of Beth-leaphrah in 1:10 are told to roll in the dust (compare the term 'aphrah with the word "dust" in Hebrew, 'apar). The Hebrew term for "steeds" (RSV) or "horse" (JB) in 1:13 also sounds like the city name "Lachish." Such style is perhaps strange to modern readers, but it effectively guides the hearer to a sense of the total destruction that is the subject of the lamentation.

Many of the places mentioned in Micah 1 cannot be identified conclusively. Those that

can lie to the southwest of Jerusalem and protect its approach routes. In 701 B.C. Sennacherib mounted an offensive against Judah from this direction. Sennacherib boasted in his annals of capturing forty-six cities, laying seige to Jerusalem, and taking away a large company of captives. This attack could well provide the historical setting for these verses.

2:1–5, Woe to Greedy Land-grabbers. Woe sayings are used frequently by the prophets to threaten the wicked by announcing imminent disaster (cf. Amos 5:18–20; 6:1–3; Isa. 5:8–24; 10:1–4). The subject here is the covetous oppression of greedy land-grabbers who ignored time-honored stipulations against treacherous dealings with neighbors (Exod. 30:17; 34:24; Lev. 6:1–5; 19:13; Prov. 14:31; 22:16). They plot ways (2:1) to acquire more land (possibly by making loans and then foreclosing). By so doing they attack the foundation of Israel's economy and society, a system based on the right of families to be free landholders obligated to no one.

The wickedness of the greedy will be their own ruin. The Lord will yoke the wicked with an evil they cannot escape (2:3). The land they so desperately desired will be taken from them (probably by conquerors). Professional mourners will sing a taunting, satirical dirge over them (2:4). Their ruin will be irreversible. They will have no one to represent them when land is reallocated after the coming judgment (2:5). The sentence of the wicked matches their crime.

This rather specific accusation seems to have been expanded later to refer to a wider audience. The terms "this breed" (JB) or "this family" (RSV) in 2:3 and "my people" in 2:4 seem to generalize the original charge. Likewise, "an evil time" and "in that day" in the same verses enable the message to be heard repeatedly in varying situations by the community that treasured the prophet's words.

2:6–11, Against False Preaching. Though the Hebrew text is problematic, the essential point is clear. Those who speak soothing lies to the people mislead them concerning the gravity of the situation. While the helpless are being deceived, defrauded, and expelled from their homes (2:8–10), the perpetrators of oppression are being assured by their "preachers" that all is well. Opposition is silenced (2:6). The false preachers wrongly use tradition to assure the people of God's patience (so Micah 2:7; cf. Exod. 34:6; Ps. 103:8; Joel 2:13).

The term sometimes translated as "preach" (RSV) can have a pejorative connotation such as "rant" or "rave." The activity described is usually associated with the speaking of prophets (Amos 7:16; Ezek. 20:46; 21:2). This passage indicates a serious controversy between the speaker and other "preachers" like that encountered earlier by Amos (Amos 3:3–8; 7:14–17) and later by Jeremiah (Jer. 28:5–9).

"This people" (2:11), a term that indicates a degree of separation between prophet and people not reflected in 1:9, wants only to hear words of blessing, promises of plenty (cf. such words in Joel 2:24; Amos 9:13–14). Though they drive widows and orphans from their homes (2:9–10), they applaud false preachers who will not tell the truth (2:11). Both people and preachers are rejected by the prophet.

2:12–13, The Gathering of Jacob. This is an enigmatic passage. Scattered "Jacob," a reference to God's people, is assured that the Lord will gather them. Such a word seems out of place in a context of accusation and announcement of impending judgment. Probably this word was added, at the time of the Babylonian attack on Jerusalem in 587 B.C. or even later. If it is original to the eighth century, it may represent a visionary hope that those taken into exile after the fall of Samaria in 722/721 B.C. will one day return.

3:1–4, Unjust Cannibals. Using the striking and shocking image of cannibalism, the prophet describes those responsible for administering justice as devouring the prophet's people (cf. 1:9). Various terms are chosen to designate these leaders: "princes," "heads," "rulers." In the villages the elders traditionally cared for matters of justice in courts convened at the town's gate. Others appointed by the king may also have had responsibility. Because they loved evil rather than good, the authorities allowed justice to fail (cf. Amos 5:10–15; Isa. 1:17, 21–23; Deut. 1:9–18).

As in preceding oracles, the punishment fits the crime. The rulers refused to hear the cries of their victims; thus, their cries for deliverance to the Lord (3:4)—in hope that they will be heard and delivered (Pss. 22:5; 107:13, 19; 142:5–6)—will be in vain (3:4). The Lord will turn away before their evil deeds (cf. Pss. 13:1; 27:9; 69:17).

3:5–8, Against Profiteering Prophets. Introducing his speech with the messenger formula "thus says the Lord," Micah levels a severe word of judgment against deceiving prophets who speak words of peace and well-being for a price. Such venal prophets will find themselves enshrouded with darkness. They will be confused, shamed, disgraced. Denied God's word, they will cover their lips in mourning (cf. Ezek. 24:17, 22).

In contrast, the speaker claims an endowment by God's spirit that guarantees a successful mission (3:8). Strength to persevere ("power," RSV) in the face of opposition is

linked with the courage ("might," RSV) that characterizes brave warriors. The capacity to recognize and act for justice completes the prophet's endowment. The wrongs of the social order are denounced for what they represent: rebellion against the will of God, sin.

3:9–12, The Inescapable Judgment. With almost the same words as in 3:1 the prophet calls the rulers and leaders of Israel to give heed. Zion and Jerusalem, chosen and protected by God, are fouled with blood and wrongdoing. Misdirected zeal to build (3:8), perhaps, has prompted illegal or unjust acquisition of land. The authorities have ignored appeals for justice and their responsibility to uphold it (Exod. 23:1–3, 6–8). Judges, priests, and prophets are all for sale.

A cardinal tenet of the "official" theology of Micah's day was that God had chosen the Davidic king and Jerusalem (→ Covenant) and would maintain and protect both forever (Pss. 46; 48; 132). Thus, leaders trust the theology and say, "Is not the Lord in our midst? Evil will not come upon us" (Micah 3:11).

The prophet, however, has a different view (3:12). Because the leaders have forsaken God's way, Jerusalem and Zion, like Samaria before (cf. 1:6), will be plowed up and become a wooded hill!

4:1–5, God Will Reign in Zion. In striking contrast to the preceding announcement, this well-known promise succinctly expresses a hope for universal peace with justice founded on the benevolent reign of the Lord. A Jerusalem based on bloody wrongdoing has no future (3:9–12). God's intention for a transforming peace will be realized for individuals and nations.

The promise includes four elements. Zion, the mount on which God's house stands, will become preeminent in the latter days (4:1). All nations will come in pilgrimage to this new center to receive divine instruction, torah, and divine adjudication of international disputes (4:2–3). There will be worldwide peace, the dismantling of the machines of war, and the construction of implements of production (4:3). Finally, all people will have the means and the security to pursue life to the fullest (4:4).

But there is no illusion. The nations do not yet act in accordance with this expectation. Nonetheless God's people affirm their intention to live on the basis of their hope in God's promise (4:5).

There is much debate about the historical setting of this famous passage and its almost identical parallel in Isa. 2:2–4. The slight differences between the two suggest that neither is related directly to the other; both are dependent on some other tradition. Perhaps those who collected and transmitted the message of

Micah included this promise because it enhanced the theological perspective they proclaimed. God's response to iniquity was judgment, but God's intention thereby was to refashion the people and establish a worldwide dominion marked by peace and justice.

4:6–8, Gathering the Survivors. These verses present two brief promises of restoration in the latter days, a theme introduced in 4:1–5. The first saying, 4:6–7, announces the gathering and return of those driven into exile by the historical disasters that have befallen Israel and Judah. The term frequently translated "lame" is used to describe Jacob in Gen. 32:31. It is used in Micah as a poetic reference to the people of Israel/Judah, to Jacob, wounded by the encounter with God. A remnant (→ Remnant) will be fashioned by God and established in Zion where God will reign. In 4:8, the second brief saying continues the theme of God's restoration of dominion at Zion (cf. 3:9–12; 4:1–5).

4:9–10, You Shall Be Rescued. This oracle of salvation is built on a contrast between present distress and future deliverance. It is the first of three sayings beginning with "now." A series of taunting questions is addressed to a singular "you," the daughter of Zion, a personification of Jerusalem (cf. 4:8, 13). The people face a time of terror. The king has perhaps died or at least lost authority. Jerusalem and her people cry out as a woman in labor (cf. Jer. 4:31; 6:24; 13:21). "Now" the people will be forced from city into open field!

The last lines of the oracle change the message to one of salvation. God will intervene to rescue the daughter of Zion. This rescue is described as "redemption," the legal process of securing the release of someone or something. God's people will be delivered from their enemies. The explicit mention of Babylon in 4:10 suggests that the relevant historical circumstance is the exile of many Judeans after Babylon destroyed Jerusalem in 587 B.C.

4:11–13, You Shall Thresh the Nations. The second "now" oracle uses language associated with threshing grain. Hostile nations, perhaps the neighboring states or some more generalized enemies of a later time, will gather to desecrate Zion (4:11). As part of God's mysterious plans, however, these enemy peoples are actually being gathered like sheaves for threshing (4:12). "Now" many are gathering against the daughter of Zion. But God will work a reversal whereby Zion will thresh those so gathered. The wealth gained as booty will be devoted to God (cf. Josh. 6:17–19; 1 Sam. 15:3). A relatively rare divine title, "Lord of all the earth" (Josh. 3:11, 13; Ps. 97:15; Zech. 4:14; 6:5), further emphasizes the visionary character of the passage.

5:1–4, God's Ruler to Come. The third "now" oracle declares that a ruler will emerge to shepherd God's people in an appropriate manner. Bethlehem, the family home of King David (cf. 2 Sam. 16:1), will be this leader's birthplace. The distress described (5:1) is perhaps related to Sennacherib's attack in 701 B.C., but the specific terminology used ("siege") suggests the Babylonian attack a century later (cf. 2 Kings 24:10; 25:21; Jer. 52:5). Christian tradition claimed this oracle in its exposition of the origins of Jesus (Matt. 2:5–6; John 7:42).

5:5–9, Rule Among Adversaries. In this unit, comprised of three originally independent sayings (5:5–6, 7, 8–9), two primary assertions are made. First, Assyria will never again dominate. Second, God's remnant (cf. 2:12; 4:6–7), God's special work, will be secure among the nations. This will come to pass at some later time when God brings about the reversal of current conditions. As the text now stands, this coming new security is linked with the appearance of the ruler celebrated in the preceding verses. The language and theme of this unit suggest a sixth- or fifth-century setting for its composition.

5:10–15, The Final Purge. The concluding oracle of chaps. 1–5 serves to recall the opening announcement of God's intention to judge Samaria, Jerusalem, and all peoples (1:2–7). An original poem built on the repetition of "I will cut off . . ." has been supplemented with the last two verses. False sources of confidence, whether military (horses and chariots) or religious (soothsayers and idols), will be destroyed. The people and the land will be purged of all that is offensive to God. The nations that will not obey or listen (cf. 1:2) will encounter God's punishment. The concluding verse uses anthropomorphic language to emphasize that God will not permit human disobedience to prevail.

PART TWO: 6:1–7:20

The Reign of the LORD Over His People

6:1–5, God's Controversy. This dramatic passage initiates the carefully arranged sequence that follows. God is portrayed as filing a lawsuit against the people (cf. Isa. 1:18–20; 3:13–15; Hos. 4:1–3, 4–6; Jer. 2:4–13). The witnesses summoned are the mountains, hills, and foundations of the earth rather than the more frequent heavens and earth (Isa. 1:2; Deut. 32:1). God speaks as both plaintiff (6:1–2) and defendant (6:3–5). This kind of address is sometimes called a covenant lawsuit and has as its background a type of international suzerainty treaty that spelled out the terms and consequences of agreements made between an overlord and vassal.

God speaks directly to "my people" and recalls the saving history in which God has repeatedly rescued and led Israel (Deut. 7:8; Josh. 24:5–11; Pss. 78:42–55; 105:26–45). In light of this history God cannot understand the people's faithlessness. God redeemed Israel so that the saving acts of God would be known and recited with praise and honor.

6:6–8, God's Requirements. In response to God's questions in the preceding verses, Micah 6:6–8 provides an acknowledgement of a need for forgiveness and reconciliation. The unidentified speaker represents those who seek instruction on the appropriate sacrifice to offer God (6:6–7). A procedure of requesting priestly clarification of such matters is the background for the passage (cf. 1 Sam. 6:2–4).

A famous summary of God's requirements then follows (6:8). God seeks the doing of justice, which involves the faithful honoring of God-established relationships (cf. Amos 5:15; Isa. 1:12–17; Jer. 7:5–6). Second, God expects the love of "kindness" (RSV), a devotion to loyalty, the practice of steadfast love (cf. Hos. 2:19; 4:1–3; 6:6). The third requirement is proper attention to God, to "walk humbly" (RSV) rather than presumptuously (cf. Prov. 11:2–3; 15:33; 18:12). This verse (6:8) is often quoted as a summation of the prophetic ethical tradition.

6:9–16, God's Intention to Punish. The central point is clear: God announces punishment because of social injustice (6:11; cf. 3:2–3, 9–11). A series of bad things will befall the people and the land (6:13–15; cf. Deut. 28:25–46). The people are accused of adopting the ways of the house of Omri, and more particularly those of Ahab (6:16), who was remembered for moral wrongdoing and encouraging idolatry (1 Kings 16:30–34; 21:1–15). This reference suggests a relatively late period when the tradition of Omri and Ahab had become a well-known symbol for wickedness (cf. 2 Kings 8:27; 21:3). The consequence of that sin will be desolation and scorn (cf. Jer. 19:8; 29:18; Lev. 26:31–33).

7:1–7, A Time of Trial. The time is a wicked time (cf. 6:10–12). As after the gleaning when nothing is left in the field, the speaker feels

alone (7:1). All of the righteous ones, the godly, have perished (7:2). The wicked join together to accomplish their goals (7:3). As a result the society breaks down completely; the relationships that make life productive and enjoyable cease (7:2, 5–6). In such a time of trial the faithful wait for deliverance (7:7). Thereby they express their confidence in God (Pss. 38:15; 42:5, 11; 43:5; 130:5–6). In the NT the coming of Jesus is seen as producing a similar crisis (Matt. 10:21, 35–39; Mark 13:12–13; Luke 12:52–53).

7:8–20, God's Forgiveness Will Prevail. The closing verses of chaps. 6–7 sound liturgical. First there is a song of trust (7:8–10) followed by a promise of restoration (7:11–13). Next is an appeal that the nations be compelled to acknowledge God (7:14–17) with a concluding song of praise, sung by the people, of the Lord's steadfast love and compassion (7:18–20). The individual poems may have been developed separately but their present arrangement seems purposeful. The judgment announced in 6:9–16 will eventually give way to vindication, restoration, and pardon (7:8–20).

In these verses, a number of allusions are somewhat unclear. The enemy remembered in 7:10 is probably Edom, which participated in the destruction of Jerusalem in 587 B.C. (cf. Obad. 10–15; Isa. 34:8–14; Ps. 137:7). In 7:11–12 a dispersed people return, apparently to Jerusalem, where the walls will be rebuilt. This text probably assumes a time in the early fifth century B.C. The text of 7:15 is difficult to understand since it remains unclear to whom the "you," "I," and "him" or "them" refer.

The concluding verses (7:18–20) are much clearer. In the language of a time-honored theological formulation, God's forgiveness is extolled (cf. Exod. 34:6–7; Pss. 86:15; 103:8–10; 145:8; Jon. 4:2; Joel 2:13; Neh. 9:14). The iniquity of God's people brought disaster. The incomparable God of forgiveness, however, will act to bring restoration as a sign of continuing faithfulness to Abraham (7:19–20).

Bibliography
Hillers, D. *Micah*. Hermeneia. Philadelphia: Fortress, 1984.

Mays, J. *Micah*. Old Testament Library. Philadelphia: Westminster, 1976.

Wolff, H. W. *Micah the Prophet*. Translated by R. D. Gehrke. Philadelphia: Fortress, 1981.

NAHUM

DUANE L. CHRISTENSEN

INTRODUCTION

The Book of Nahum is a poetic text composed for use within an ancient Israelite worship setting. Its subject is the imminent fall of Nineveh, the capital of Assyria from the time of Sennacherib (705–681 B.C.) to its destruction in 612 (→Nineveh). As an oracle against a foreign nation, its original performance was probably motivated by political aims.

No book in the Bible has been maligned as much as this one. It is frequently described as a vengeful, nationalistic expression of glee over the destruction of a bitter enemy that some would want to remove from the canon of sacred Scripture altogether. Nahum has been described as ethically and theologically deficient, even the work of a false prophet. As a result, the book has been virtually ignored in both the modern church and synagogue.

Much of this fate is, however, not deserved. Nahum is primarily a book about God's justice, not about human vengeance, hatred, and military conquest. It is best read as a complement to the book of Jonah. Whereas Nahum focuses on the "dark side" of God, Jonah portrays God's mercy and compassion toward the same wicked city. Both aspects are essential for an understanding of the divine nature. It should be noted that, though the positive side of God is muted in Nahum, it is by no means absent (see 1:3, 7).

No interpreter has understood the essential message of Nahum more clearly than Martin Luther when he wrote: "The book teaches us to trust God and to believe, especially when we despair of all human help, human powers, and counsel, that the Lord stands by those who are His own against all attacks of the enemy, be they ever so powerful" (Maier, p. 86).

A careful analysis of the poetry reveals an elegant literary structure: the book consists of two equal halves framing 2:10. Identically structured units appear in 1:4–6; 2:3–5; and 2:11–13d. The best way to explain the remarkable structural symmetry of the book is to posit musical influence. The Hebrew text of Nahum bears the mark of original musical composition and performance within an ancient Israelite liturgical setting. Hence, the hand that shaped this sophisticated work of literary art is that of an author/composer.

An opening hymn (1:1–10) sets the tone for what follows: a display of awesome power when Yahweh appears as the Divine Warrior. Nahum has taken the first half of an acrostic poem already in existence and adapted it to new ends. The resulting acrostic pattern forms a sentence that, together with the central verse of the book (2:10), summarizes his message: all will be utter desolation and ruin when Yahweh appears in judgment. Most of the book consists of a lengthy taunt song in four parts that is directed against the wicked city of Nineveh (1:15–3:19).

COMMENTARY

1:1–10
Acrostic Hymn of Theophany: Yahweh's Vindicating Wrath

In Nahum 1, an acrostic hymn based on at least the first half of the Hebrew alphabet has apparently been adapted to a new purpose, perhaps to form a cipher (code) from the sequence of letters and/or other opening elements (see van der Woude). This cipher contains a summary of the meaning of the book:

> I am the exalted Yahweh
> and (I am) in the presence of sin;
> In a flood (I am) bringing a full end
> completely.

Verse 1 contains a double title: the book of Nahum is both an "oracle" and a "book of (the) vision," the latter lending some support to the notion of a scribal cipher in vv. 2–10.

Verse 2 describes the wrath of Yahweh in terms reminiscent of ancient Canaanite poetic patterns. God is presented as "jealous" and "avenging"—terms subject to distortion in English translation. In particular, the attribution of "vengeance" to the character of Yahweh has been the source of misunderstanding. As G. E. Mendenhall has shown, the Hebrew root nqm is properly translated by terms that designate punitive vindication in a judicial sense and should not be construed as involving "malicious retaliation for inflicted wrongs." As a result, Yahweh is here depicted as a suzerain (→Covenant), one who demands the exclusive devotion of his vassals; for he is utterly intolerant of rivals.

Verse 2 is set over against vv. 9–10, both of which focus on "the dark side" of Yahweh, namely, his jealous anger that leads to punishment. Verse 3 and vv. 7–8 present the other side of Yahweh, one who is "slow to anger" (cf. Exod. 34:6–7). Nah. 1:4–6 functions as a "refrain," which may be compared with similar refrains in 2:3–5 and 2:11–13d. These verses focus on the reaction of the cosmos to the appearance of the Divine Warrior and include a number of allusions to Canaanite mythology. For example, the description of Yahweh in 1:2 contains the Hebrew names for both the Canaanite gods El and Baal. Moreover, the terms "sea" and "rivers" in 1:4 also allude to deities of the same names in Canaanite lore.

The difficulties many have found in translating 1:9–10 are lessened by dividing the poetry as the following translation does:

> What will you devise / against Yahweh? /
>   a full end / He Himself will make /
> It will not arise a second time /
>   (namely) distress /
> For / (you will be) like entangled thorns /
> And (though you are) like soddened /
>   drunkards /
> Consumed (you will be) /
>   like dry stubble / completely /

This unit is set off from what precedes it by the abrupt use of a plural opening verb ("devise") and the use of the term "completely," both as its final word and as a term constructed from the initial letter of each poetic line in the continuation of the acrostic poem. The image of a mass of sopping wet, matted thorns burning like dry stubble is striking. The fire of Yahweh knows no limitation, as the prophet Elijah demonstrated so vividly on Mount Carmel (1 Kings 18).

1:11–14
Transitional Oracles: The Defeat of Belial

Verses 11 and 14 are addressed to Nineveh on the one hand (feminine singular) and the king of Assyria on the other (masculine singular) and function as a frame surrounding an oracle introduced by the formula "Thus says Yahweh" (1:12–13). The prophetic announcement that "Belial has come forth from you" (1:11) is balanced by a word of judgment announcing the king's coming oblivion (1:14). The oracle in 1:12–13 is directed to Judah (feminine singular) announcing that when the Assyrians are cut off, Yahweh will set Judah free. Belial here, and in 1:15 below, is the personified leader of the enemy forces (→ Belial). Taken literally, the

name may mean something like "no value," "worthlessness," "confusion," or "chaos."

1:15–3:19
Taunt Song Against Nineveh

The rest of the book consists of an extended taunt song arranged in four parts, the first two of which are separated by a transitional summation of the book as a whole (2:10) and a short dirge (2:11–13), which contains within it an oracle against Nineveh introduced by the formula "utterance of Yahweh."

1:15–2:9, Taunt Song Against Nineveh: Part One. Verse 15 contains familiar words (cf. Isa. 52:7) addressed to Judah, urging her to resume normal behavior because Belial has been cut off. Nah. 2:1–2 declare to Nineveh that "a shatterer has come up against you"; for Yahweh is restoring "the majesty of Jacob." These verses are set over against a visionary description in which the citadel of Nineveh is stormed (2:6–8a). Between these two units stands a refrain (2:3–5) in which the "actual" assault on Nineveh is described graphically. This first section of the taunt song concludes with a lament portraying the plundering of the city (2:8b–9).

2:10, Summation: All Is Utter Desolation and Ruin. Nah. 2:10 is the structural center of the book. The assonance of the opening three Hebrew words is striking and yet difficult to capture in translation: perhaps "desolation and dissipation and dilapidation." The final two Hebrew words of this verse (cf. Joel 2:6) are a conundrum for virtually all translators and interpreters. The translation of K. J. Cathcart, "and the faces of all gather paleness," may well be correct.

2:11–13d, Transitional Dirge: The Lion's Den. The image of the lion is rich, both in the Bible and in Assyrian culture. The refrain parallels that in 1:4–6, where the mighty Yahweh appeared in all his wrath. The "lion of Judah" is a familiar poetic image of Yahweh (cf. Amos 3:8); but lions are also a dominant motif within Assyrian art. Here the den of the mighty Assyrian lion, who has taken so much prey, is destroyed. The unit concludes with a prophetic oracle, introduced by the familiar "utterance of Yahweh," that makes explicit the divine source of this destruction (2:13).

2:13e–3:7, Taunt Song Against Nineveh: Part Two. The final clause of 2:13, "And the voices of your messengers will be heard no more," introduces the funeral lament over the "bloody city" in 3:1. This lament is balanced structurally by a dirge in 3:7 that poses the rhetorical question, "Who will mourn Nineveh's ruin?" These bracketing verses enclose another graphic vision of bloody carnage (3:2–3; cf. 2:3–5), one set over against a prophetic oracle of judgment (3:5–6) that is introduced by the familiar "utterance of Yahweh of hosts." The imagery is repulsive: Yahweh will expose Nineveh's nakedness and pelt her with filth. At the center of this unit stands the reason for such vile judgment: Nineveh's gross harlotry (3:4).

3:8–13, Taunt Song Against Nineveh: Part Three. An opening lament (3:8) poses the rhetorical question, "Are you better than Thebes?" The destruction of Thebes at the hands of Ashurbanipal marked the zenith of Assyrian expansion and, apparently, the high point of Assyrian brutality as well. The prophetic judgment of 3:9–12 makes it clear that Assyria will experience the same fate it meted out to Thebes. This section concludes in 3:13 with an oracle of judgment in which destruction is announced using language reminiscent of ancient Near Eastern treaty curses.

3:14–19, Taunt Song Against Nineveh: Part Four. The book of Nahum ends with a remarkable funeral lament. Using bitter irony, the author urges the people to prepare for a siege by strengthening their fortifications (3:14–15). But all is in vain, as the vision of 3:16–18a makes clear. Like locusts, the leaders of Nineveh take flight, leaving the hapless king to his fate. His wound is fatal, and all who hear the report clap their hands (3:19b). The dirge concludes with a rhetorical question: "For upon whom has not come your evil unceasingly?" The only other book in the Hebrew Bible to end with a question is that of Jonah, which, curiously, also has Nineveh as its subject.

Bibliography

Cathcart, K. J. *Nahum in the Light of Northwest Semitic.* Biblica et orientalia, 26. Rome: Biblical Institute Press, 1973.

Christensen, D. L. *Transformations of the War Oracle in Old Testament Prophecy: Studies in the Oracles Against the Nations.* Missoula, MT: Scholars Press, 1975.

Maier, W. A. *The Book of Nahum: A Commentary.* St. Louis, MO: Concordia, 1959.

Mendenhall, G. E. *The Tenth Generation.* Baltimore, MD: Johns Hopkins University Press, 1973. Pp. 69–104.

Woude, A. S., van der. "The Book of Nahum: A Letter Written in Exile." *Oudtestamentische Studien* 20 (1977): 108–26.

HABAKKUK

MARVIN A. SWEENEY

INTRODUCTION

The Book of Habakkuk provides little direct historical or personal information about the prophet to whom it is attributed. He is identified twice simply as "Habakkuk the Prophet" (Hab. 1:1; 3:1), with no indication of the time in which he lived. Consequently, later nonbiblical traditions place Habakkuk in a number of historical contexts. In its title, the apocryphal Bel and the Dragon (second century B.C.) claims to be "from the Prophecy of Habakkuk, son of Jeshua of the Tribe of Levi" and identifies the prophet as a contemporary of Daniel, living during the Babylonian exile. The pseudepigraphical Lives of the Prophets (first century A.D.) follows this dating, although it identifies Habakkuk as a member of the tribe of Simeon. The midrashic work Seder 'Olam Rabbah (second–third century A.D.) claims that Habakkuk lived during the reign of King Manasseh (697–642 B.C.), whereas the Jewish mystical work Sefer ha-Zohar (ca. A.D. 1280) identifies Habakkuk as the son of the Shunammite woman whom the prophet Elisha (ninth century B.C.) restored to life (2 Kings 4:8–37).

Most modern scholars agree that reference to the rise of the Chaldeans (Hab. 1:6) and the general descriptions of distress in the land of Judah (chaps. 1–2) indicate that Habakkuk spoke during the reign of King Jehoiakim (609–598 B.C.) or perhaps during the brief reign of his son Jehoiachin (597 B.C.). Judah became a vassal state of the Chaldean or Neo-Babylonian Empire following Nebuchadnezzar's defeat of the Egyptian army at Carchemish and Hamath in 605 B.C. (→ Chaldea; Nebuchadnezzar). Jehoiakim was a loyal subject of Babylon for three years, imposing heavy taxation on the population of Judah and repressing dissent to meet the demands of the Babylonian monarch. After Jehoiakim revolted in 602 B.C., Nebuchadnezzar sent bands of raiders to harass Judah until he could mount a full-scale invasion of the land. Jehoiakim probably died during the Babylonian siege of Jerusalem in 598 B.C. Following the capitulation of the city, Nebuchadnezzar deported the new king, Jehoiachin, and leading members of Judean society to Babylon (→ Babylon). Many scholars believe that Habakkuk, a contemporary of Jeremiah, was a prophet active at the Temple of Jerusalem during these years (see Jeremiah).

The book of Habakkuk is designed to address the theological issue of theodicy, which involves justifying the righteousness of God in circumstances of great evil. The superscription in Hab. 1:1 identifies the first major section of the book (chaps. 1–2) as a "pronouncement." The word "pronouncement," frequently translated as "burden," refers to a specific type of prophetic oracle, one based on a vision or other revelatory experience that attempts to explain the manner in which God's purpose will be manifested in human affairs. It is generally spoken by a prophet in response to an inquiry or complaint concerning a particular situation. Here the pronouncement is presented in the form of a dialogue between Habakkuk and God. In the first exchange, the prophet complains that the land is in turmoil (1:2–4), but God responds that the turmoil is caused by a divine plan to establish Chaldean dominance in the world (1:5–11). Habakkuk then complains about the treachery of the Chaldeans, who have overstepped their bounds and do not acknowledge God as the source of their power (1:12–17). God's response, reported in Hab. 2:1–20, includes a vision that states the basic principle that, unlike those who are arrogant, those who are righteous will live by their steadfast faith. The lengthy elaboration of this principle in vv. 5–20 employs five "woe" oracles to predict that the Chaldeans will eventually fall victim to their excessive greed.

The second major section of the book, identified by its superscription as the "prayer" of Habakkuk (3:1), follows in Hab. 3:1–19. Many scholars have argued that this "prayer" was not an original part of the book, because it appears to be a liturgical psalm, distinct from chaps. 1–2. In the present form of the book, however, the psalm functions as the prophet's reaction to the "pronouncement" of chaps. 1–2. The psalmist petitions God to defeat an invading enemy. Using theophanic imagery, the psalmist acknowledges God's role as Master of the Universe and waits faithfully for the manifestation of God's power (→ Theophany), which will eventuate in the downfall of the Chaldeans. Consequently, the book of Habakkuk affirms the righteousness of God and anticipates the realization of the divine plan.

Habakkuk has played an important role in both Judaism and Christianity. The authors of the Dead Sea Scrolls produced a commentary on the first two chapters of the book in the first century B.C. The apostle Paul used Hab. 2:4 as a major textual basis for formulating the doctrine of "justification by faith" (Rom. 1:17; Gal. 3:11; cf. Heb. 10:38–39). Likewise, the talmudic Rabbi Simlai identified this verse as a summary of all the 613 commandments of the Torah (b. Mak. 23b–24a). In Jewish tradition, Habakkuk 3 is understood as a description of the revelation at Sinai; it is read as the prophetic portion for the second day of the festival of Shavuot (Pentecost), which commemorates the giving of the Torah at Sinai (b. Meg. 31a).

COMMENTARY

1:1–2:20

The Pronouncement of Habakkuk

Habakkuk's pronouncement represents his attempt to explain the significance of the rise of the Neo-Babylonian Empire and its domination of Judah. Although he views the Babylonians as wicked oppressors of the righteous, Habakkuk maintains that the rise of Babylon is an act of God, the true master of the world. However, greed and the failure to recognize God as the source of its power have caused Babylon to overextend its grasp in an attempt to master the entire earth. The oppressed nations will then overthrow Babylon and God's righteousness will triumph.

Habakkuk's pronouncement is presented in the form of a dialogue between the prophet and God. The prophet's understanding of Babylon's rise develops as God responds to each of Habakkuk's complaints.

1:1, The Superscription. This verse is a title for the pronouncement that follows. Not only does it identify the type of prophetic oracle employed here, it also designates Habakkuk as a "prophet." Because of this title many scholars think that Habakkuk was a professional Temple prophet.

1:2–4, Habakkuk's First Complaint. Habakkuk uses typical complaint language (cf. Job 19:1–7; Ps. 18:6, 41) to protest to God concerning the breakdown of order in the land caused by an unnamed wicked party. The identity of this "wicked" party has prompted much discussion. Some maintain that it is none other than Jehoiakim and his officials, because the prophet's description of the land's turmoil includes terminology used elsewhere to indicate

Judahite abuses of social justice (Amos 3:10; Isa. 10:1; Ps. 12:6; Prov. 16:28–29). Certainly, Jehoiakim was no stranger to the abuses of social justice, as Jeremiah's condemnation of this king demonstrates (Jer. 22:1–8, 13–19). Nevertheless, the "wicked" party should be identified as the Babylonians. In Hab. 1:4, the description of the righteous "surrounded" by the wicked employs a verb that also means "besieged," suggesting Babylon's military actions (cf. 1:10). In such circumstances, Babylonian justice (1:7) would undermine Judean law (1:4). Furthermore, Habakkuk 1:13 identifies the Babylonians as "wicked," and the "violence" of Babylon (1:9; cf. 1:8; 2:17) corresponds to Habakkuk's complaint in v. 2.

1:5–11, God's First Response. The divine response to Habakkuk's complaint states that the Chaldean's emergence depends on God's intentional activity. God identifies no specific purpose for this act, although Habakkuk's comment in v. 12 suggests that it was as judgment. After describing the might of its army, however, God defines the basic problem with Babylon, "Then they sweep through like wind, pass by, and incur guilt; their own might has become their god" (v.11). The Babylonians do not recognize that God has given them their victories.

1:12–17, Habakkuk's Second Complaint. Dissatisfied with God's response, Habakkuk renews his complaint. He begins by referring to God as creator and master of the universe. (The statement "We shall not die" is an ancient scribal emendation of the text, which originally read, "You shall not die.") Habakkuk challenges God directly in v. 13 by asking how he can tolerate the evil of Babylon's treachery against the righteous. In v. 14, he then proceeds to charge that God is directly responsible for the triumph of evil over righteousness. Using the imagery of a fisherman to describe Babylon's greed and idolatry, the prophet then asks God how long this evil will continue.

2:1–20, Habakkuk's Report of God's Second Response. Habakkuk stands watch (cf. Ezek. 3:16–21; 33:1–9) to wait for God's response to his "complaint." It begins with instructions to write down the vision that is to follow, a procedure that is known for both visions (Isa. 29:11–12) and pronouncements (Isa. 30:6–7, 8), and to wait for the time of its fulfillment. The basic principle of the vision is stated in Hab. 2:4, "Behold, his soul within him is arrogant [lit., "puffed up"], it is not upright, but the righteous shall live due to his steadfast faith." The Hebrew term translated as "steadfast faith" expresses reliability, confidence, continuity, and trust (→ Faith). Here, it refers to the confidence of the righteous in God's reliability and indicates that the righteous will continue to trust in God despite adversity. This text contrasts Babylon, puffed up by its own arrogance, with the righteous people whom it is oppressing and implies that whereas the righteous will live, Babylon will not.

Verses 5–20 elaborate the meaning of 2:1–4. Babylon is compared to a boisterous drunk who is initially inflamed by wine but who quickly fades under its influence as he drinks more and more. The insatiable greed of the drunk is illustrated by a mythological reference to Sheol or Death personified, whose appetite is never satisfied. A taunt by the nations who will rise up against Babylon then illustrates the coming downfall of the wicked empire. The taunt includes five woe oracles accusing Babylon of various crimes that will bring punishment. These include plundering (vv. 6b–8), extortion (vv. 9–11), bloodshed (vv. 12–14), degradation of people and lands (vv. 15–17), and idolatry (vv. 18–19). The statement concerning idolatry summarizes the reason that the other crimes take place and reiterates the basic problem concerning Babylon, its failure to recognize God (cf. 1:11, 16; 2:4, 13a). The section concludes with a demand for silence before the Lord (v. 20), which frequently precedes the manifestation of God's power (cf. Zeph. 1:7; Zech. 2:13; Ps. 46:10).

3:1–19
The Prayer of Habakkuk

The prayer petitions God to manifest divine power in the world so as to deliver the land from invaders (v. 16). The introductory and closing sections of this petition (vv. 2, 16–19a) bracket two sections that depict a theophany (vv. 3–6, 7–15). A theophany, a description of God's manifestation in the world, generally includes two elements, a description of his approach and descriptions of accompanying natural upheavals (cf. Deut. 33:2; Judg. 5:4–5; Mic. 1:3–4; Ps. 68:8–9). These theophanic sections express the psalmist's confidence that God will indeed intervene to defeat the invaders. In this respect, the psalmist demonstrates the steadfast faith of the righteous mentioned in Hab. 2:4.

The technical musical terms that appear in the prayer (vv. 1, 3, 9, 13, 19) suggest that it may have been employed as a liturgical psalm in the Temple at Jerusalem.

3:1, The Superscription. The psalm is named a prayer, the title given to a number of psalms that probably functioned as part of the Temple liturgy (cf. Pss. 17:1; 86:1; 90:1; 102:1;

142:1). The term "Shigionoth" is related to an Akkadian term that means "song of lament" and appears in the title of Psalm 7, a lament psalm. In its present context, the term may refer to the prophet's complaints in chaps. 1–2, indicating that the psalm is Habakkuk's reaction to God's response.

3:2, Introduction. The psalmist asks God to manifest the divine "work" in the world (cf. 1:5). Within the context of this book, such "work" would refer to the vision of Babylon's downfall (2:4–19).

3:3–6, Description of God's Approach. Here, the psalmist reports God's appearance in the world. He advances from Teman (Edom) and Paran, names that are used to refer to the region of Mount Sinai (cf. Deut. 33:2; Judg. 5:4–5).

3:7–15, Description of God's Victory. Drawing on ancient mythological traditions, the psalmist praises God for past victories. He refers to the defeat of the Midianites during the Exodus period (Num. 25; 31) and to God's defeat of the sea, the symbol of cosmic chaos, at the time of creation (cf. Ps. 104; Job 38–39). In this respect, the psalmist extols God as the master of both the natural world and the realm of human events.

3:16–19a, Conclusion. The psalmist, overwhelmed by God's majesty, expresses confidence that God will answer the petition despite the present adverse conditions. The imagery of "hinds' feet" indicates the psalmist's sense of security and trust in God (cf. Ps. 18:33).

3:19b, Instructions to the Choirmaster. This psalm is to be accompanied by stringed instruments (cf. Pss. 4:1; 6:1; 54:1; 55:1; 61:1; 67:1; 76:1; Isa. 38:20).

Bibliography
Achtemeier, E. *Nahum-Malachi*. Interpretation. Atlanta, GA: Knox, 1986.
Brownlee, W. H. *The Text of Habakkuk in the Ancient Commentary from Qumran*. Society of Biblical Literature Monograph Series, 11. Philadelphia: Society of Biblical Literature, 1959.
Gowan, D. G. *The Triumph of Faith in Habakkuk*. Atlanta, GA: Knox, 1976.
Smith, J. M. P., et al. *A Critical and Exegetical Commentary on Micah, Zephaniah, Nahum, Habakkuk, Obadiah, and Joel*. International Critical Commentary. Edinburgh: Clark, 1911.
Taylor, C. L., Jr. "Introduction and Exegesis of Habakkuk." *The Interpreter's Bible*. Edited by G. A. Buttrick, et al. Nashville, TN: Abingdon, 1956. Vol. 6, pp. 973–1003.

ZEPHANIAH

ELIZABETH ACHTEMEIER

INTRODUCTION

The Book of Zephaniah, one of the twelve Minor Prophets, is made up of nine brief prophetic oracles. They are, as a collection, introduced by a superscription (1:1) and concluded by an appendix (3:18–20). Chaps. 1 and 2 probably date from shortly after 640 B.C., while chap. 3, vv. 1–17 come from the years 612–609. The present form of the book is a unity; each oracle is linked, whether linguistically or thematically, with the one that has gone before it.

The prophet Zephaniah was active during the reign of King Josiah in Judah (1:1; 639–609 B.C.), one of the periods when Judah enjoyed independence from foreign domination. The Assyrian Empire was tottering and finally fell with the loss of its capital city to the Babylonians in 612 B.C. The Egyptian Empire did not subject Judah to its yoke until 609 B.C., when Josiah was killed in the battle of Megiddo. Thus Zephaniah's ministry occurred in a period of political renewal and territorial expansion (→ Judah, Kingdom of).

But Judah also needed a religious renewal. Assyrian domination of the kingdom during the reigns of Josiah's predecessors Manasseh (698–642 B.C.) and Amon (642–640 B.C.) had brought with it foreign customs and pagan deities. Canaanite Baal worship flourished, with its abominable practices of sacred prostitution and child sacrifice, and those prophets who objected were persecuted or killed. Josiah therefore instituted a widespread religious reform based on the book of Deuteronomy in which all worship was centralized in Jerusalem and pagan cults and priests were removed. Deuteronomy became the law of the land, and the covenant with the Lord was renewed (→ Covenant). The first two chapters of Zephaniah reflect the corruption in Judah before this reform. The last chapter reflects the reform's failure.

COMMENTARY

1:1, Superscription. We know nothing of Zephaniah other than what his book tells us. He is the one prophet for whom four generations of forebears are listed. However, the Gedaliah listed is not the governor of 1 Kings 25:22, and the Hezekiah named is probably not the king who reigned over Judah in the eighth century B.C. Zephaniah was a contemporary of Jeremiah's and, like that prophet, may have been a member of the party that championed the Deuteronomic reform of 622/21 (→ Deuteronomy).

1:2–6, The Announcement of Judgment. The book opens with a radical announcement that God's wrath will destroy the whole of creation because of the wickedness of human beings. Nothing will be left; all will be obliterated.

The judgment, however, centers on Judah. Because of its idolatry (vv. 4–5; →Baal; Milcom), syncretism (v. 5), and backsliding (v. 6), God will destroy not only Judah, but everyone. The covenant relationship between God and the people never precludes God's judgment of their sin.

1:7–13, The Indictment Against Judah. Judah's sins are enumerated. Assyrian dress and customs have corrupted the court (v. 8), violence and fraud permeate society, and pagan gods such as those that were thought to guard the thresholds of houses are worshiped (v. 9). But the primary indictment occurs in v. 12. The Judeans are compared to wine, left to thicken and spoil upon its "lees" or sediment. They do nothing to return to God, because they believe that God does nothing—either good or bad. In short, they have invented a world from which they think God's rule and action are totally absent.

Consequently, God, the Lord of nature and history and of the covenant, declares war against his people. He prepares the sacrifice, which preceded wars in the OT, and consecrates his warriors (v. 7). The coming battle is then described. Appropriately, it will begin in the commercial section of a Jerusalem that has become thoroughly secularized (vv. 10–11), but then it will spread to every part of the land (v. 13), with God searching out his apostate people to destroy them.

1:14–18, The Day of the Lord. The day of God's warfare against earth is called the "Day of the Lord," and this passage, made famous in the Roman Catholic mass and in poetry and music as the *dies irae* (Lat., "day of wrath"), describes the nature of that day. It opens with the war cry of God, the "mighty man" (v. 14), and brings total devastation. Nothing can turn it aside, neither fortification (v. 16) nor bribe (v. 18). In fulfillment of the covenant curse of Deut. 28:29, the Judeans will grope like the blind as they meet the fire of God's wrath that consumes the whole earth (vv. 17–18).

The Day of the Lord

The concept of the Day of the Lord has its roots in Israel's tribal league (1220–1000 B.C.), when it was believed that God, the Divine Warrior, fought for Israel against its enemies. On that Day, the Israelites expected God to defeat all their enemies and to exalt Israel. The prophets upset this popular idea by declaring that the imminent Day would bring God's judgment on the wicked in Israel as well, leaving only a faithful remnant (see Amos 5:18–20; Isa. 2:6–22; Ezek. 7:5–27; Joel 1:15; 2:1–11; Mal. 4:5). Thus the Day would be for Israel too a day of battle, wrath, darkness, and destruction.

2:1–4, The Call to Repentance. There is only one way Judah may be spared on the Day of the Lord, namely, by repentance. The prophet therefore calls the people to an assembly for a nationwide day of fasting and penitence. The urgency of his call is marked by the threefold "before" in v. 2. If the people will renounce their proud attempt to be their own gods and seek the Lord in humility and obedience and in that trust which is righteousness before God, they may escape the judgment (v. 3). As an illustration of the coming judgment, the destruction of the four remaining cities of the Philistine confederacy is portrayed.

2:5–15, Universal Judgment Pictured. The thought of v. 4 continues with a portrayal of the destruction of the known world, symbolized by Philistia to the west (vv. 5–7), Moab and Ammon to the east (vv. 8–11), Ethiopia inclusive of Egypt to the south (v. 12), and Assyria to the north (vv. 13–15). Judgment comes on the other nations because of their pride: pride of wealth, alluded to by the mention of greedy Canaanite traders (v. 5) and of fine cedar work (v. 14); pride of power (vv. 8, 10); and pride of self-security (v. 15). These nations and their gods will, however, finally bow before the sovereignty of God (cf. v. 11).

There will be left a remnant of Judah, however, which will then possess the territory of these former enemies (vv. 7, 9). The conditional note of 2:3 has now become a promise that there will be those who escape the judgment.

3:1–8, Woe to the Unrepentant. It has become evident, however, that most of the people in Judah will not return to their God. Zephaniah therefore pronounces a woe oracle over them, i.e., a lament for the dead.

God has tried in vain to correct his errant people. He has sent them prophets (v. 2) and illustrated his wrath by destroying nations around Judah (v. 6). Daily he has shown his covenant faithfulness by sustaining the round of nature (v. 5). God had expected Judah to perceive his ways and respond in covenant faithfulness (v. 7), but Judah had not. Its rebellion is summed up in the oppression wrought by its officials and judges (v. 3) and by the priests' and prophets' corruption of their offices (v. 4). Judah continues unashamedly in its ways (v. 5).

Yahweh's response is "therefore wait for me" (v. 8), a phrase that means "wait for my action" (cf. Isa. 40:31). The Lord will assemble all nations, including Judah, to court for trial and he will testify against them. The sentence will be death for all who have rebelled against his rule (v. 8; cf. Ezek. 20:33).

3:9–13, The New People of God. Judgment, however, is not God's final word, and so beyond his destroying work lies his work of salvation. There is a faithful remnant that has spread out into the world (see 2:7, 9). From that remnant God will make a new humanity—a new faithful people who will serve him, who will call on his name in truth (cf. 1:5; Gen. 11:1–9), and who will come to Jerusalem to worship him (vv. 9–10).

This new people will no longer make for themselves gods, no longer try to construct for themselves a world without God. Rather, in the humility appropriate to creatures before their Creator, they will depend solely on God for their lives and security, reflecting his moral character and faithfully fulfilling their covenants with their Lord and with one another. The result will be that good and peaceful life that God intended for creation in the beginning (cf. Gen. 1:31).

3:14–17, The Joy of the New Creation. The final picture presented by Zephaniah is one of unbounded joy, of the new people of God—personified by Zion—singing and shouting aloud, holding carnival, because God has removed his judgments against them and secured their lives against all enemies and evil (vv. 14–15). If God is for them, nothing and no one can be against them.

God is for them indeed. No longer does he take up his war cry against them (cf. 1:14). Rather, v. 17 reads, "he will hold his peace in his love" (cf. RSV margin). Now there is peace between earth and heaven.

Moreover, not only Israel rejoices, but God too is pictured in celebration. He has taken up his eternal dwelling place in the midst of his people (v. 15; cf. Ezek. 37:26–27). The God who created the earth and who has the power to destroy it, the God who sustains all the processes of nature and rules over every nation, the Mighty Warrior against whom nothing and no one can stand—in short, the God presented throughout the oracles of Zephaniah—that God nevertheless has great joy, and indeed exults, when he can live in covenant with faithful human beings. Such is the final message of the book of Zephaniah. Zephaniah's portrayal of such a joyful fellowship was a picture for the future presented to seventh-century-B.C. Judah; it is consonant with similar pictures in both the OT and the NT.

3:18–20, A Later Appendix. In the Hebrew text, v. 18 does not properly connect with v. 17 and is largely unintelligible. Moreover, vv. 19–20 seem to echo passages in Isaiah 56–66. These three verses are probably an expansion, added to

Zephaniah by the Deuteronomistic editors in the sixth century B.C., to make the book's message applicable to their exilic time. Verses 19–20 promise that exiled Israel will be returned to its homeland and that its fortunes will be restored before the eyes of all the world. Zephaniah's own thought that only a remnant will survive may be implied here, but these verses lack the explicit eschatological emphases found in 3:11–13, 14–17.

Bibliography

Achtemeier, E. *Nahum–Malachi*. Interpretation: A Bible Commentary for Preaching and Teaching. Atlanta, GA: Knox, 1986.

Eaton, J. H. *Obadiah, Nahum, Habakkuk, and Zephaniah*. Torch Bible Commentaries. London: SCM, 1961.

Taylor, C. L. "The Book of Zephaniah." *The Interpreter's Bible*. New York, Nashville, TN: Abingdon, 1956. Vol. 6, pp. 1005–34.

HAGGAI

PETER R. ACKROYD

INTRODUCTION

Haggai is known only from the book that bears his name, and from his appearance, with Zechariah, in one narrative in Ezra (5:1; 6:14). The name in Hebrew means "festal" or "of a festival," perhaps marking his birth on such a day, but we have no genealogy and no information other than what may be deduced from the Book of Haggai and the narrative. He is described as a prophet (1:1; Ezra 5:1), and his function as messenger of God is stressed in Hag. 1:13 ("messenger of Yahweh with the message of Yahweh" or "in the divine commission"). The background to his activity is indicated by the dates, all in the second year of Darius I of Persia (522–486 B.C.; → Darius), and by the names of the leaders Zerubbabel (→Zerubbabel) and Joshua (Jeshua), the high priest (→Jeshua). While Darius established his rule, there was a period of political upheaval. The book itself gives indications of natural disasters and of economic difficulties. Conditions for the small Judean community cannot have been easy in these years.

The structure of the book shows close links with Zechariah 1–8: the dates (Hag. 1:1, [15a]; 1:15b–2:1; 2:10, [18], 20) are similar to those in Zechariah. The chronological references (except those bracketed in the foregoing list) provide a framework to the oracles and the two small narratives in 1:12–14 and 2:11–14. In their style, these dates resemble elements in the Priestly work and in Chronicles, which suggests that in their present form they may be of later, editorial, origin. The links between the two prophetic collections suggest that this part of the "book of the twelve prophets" (see Introduction to the Prophetic Books) was shaped by one particular group in the postexilic period.

The careful structuring of the material suggests a deliberate presentation of the prophet and his part in the reestablishment of Temple and community during the early Persian period: in this, the book may be set alongside the various narratives in Ezra 1–6, to which it provides a counterpart. Though the prophetic oracles in the book reveal various facets of the prophet's activity, their presentation within an archival structure may be designed to interpret their significance rather than merely to record them. The present form of the book reflects on and expounds a prophet involved in events of lasting importance for the Jewish community,

presented here as the "remnant" (→ Remnant).

The text of Haggai is for the most part clear (the fragment of date in 1:15a may be misplaced; the reference in 2:18 is incomplete). It is often supposed that the oracles are in prose, but this does not do full justice to their strongly rhythmic quality (esp. 1:4–11; 2:3–9, 14, 21–23). The oracular style of earlier prophecy is here blended with more didactic and homiletic elements (see also Malachi), marked by repetition (note the repeated "reflect upon your way of life" or "your condition" in Hag. 1:5, 7; cf. 2:15, 18).

The limited amount of material and the difficulties of interpretation suggest that we cannot give a full picture of Haggai's message. Nor should it be assumed that Haggai and Zechariah, now so closely linked and appearing to act in unison, according to Ezra 5–6, held the same views about the nature and hopes of the community. Haggai provides one line of approach to the delicate problems of political subjection; his message is full of confidence that his people, self-centered and reluctant though they may be, respond to the prophetic summons and face a future of hope and blessing. The relation between the Temple, symbol of the divine presence, and the well-being of the people is a theme of great importance in the postexilic period for the right understanding of how the community rethought its position after the disasters of conquest and disruption.

COMMENTARY

1:1–11, Restore the Temple! These verses clearly form a unit, perhaps built up from two or three smaller sections. The date (1:1) introduces a pronouncement on the people's reluctance to restore the Temple (1:2); 1:3 introduces a further prophetic word (1:4–6). But the two sections are linked in that the quotation of the people's comment in the former is answered by the questions and challenges of the latter. Failure to restore the Temple is connected with distressing economic conditions—poor harvests and inflation. A new element in vv. 7–11 provides an elaboration of the aforementioned theme: the promise of the divine presence is set over against the

745

people's preoccupation with their own affairs and is set in contrast with a drought seen as divine judgment.

1:12–15a, The Response. Those addressed —Davidic heir and governor Zerubbabel, high priest Joshua, and the people—acknowledge the prophet's authority, their spirits divinely stirred (for the use of this expression with reference to Cyrus, see Ezra 1:1).

1:15b–2:9, The Glory of the Temple. After a new date formula, the prophet opens with an exhortation to courage, followed by an assurance of God's presence. Doubts about the temple now being restored, poor by contrast with memories of its former state (2:3–5), are answered by the promise of a divine intervention in the affairs of the world, to glorify the Temple and to make it both a center for the tribute of all nations and a pledge for the well-being of the Judean community.

2:10–19, Purity and Prosperity. There are two elements: vv. 10–14 and vv. 15–19. An inquiry regarding the nature of holiness and uncleanness (vv. 11–13) introduces a judgment on the unfitness of the people (v. 14). This unit resumes the theme of failure to restore the Temple: the people's present state is unacceptable before God. But the second element (vv. 15–19) shows that a restored Temple, glorified by his presence, assures well-being for the future. These verses contrast the past with the future and represent a further development of themes used in the opening section of the book.

2:20–23, Davidic Promise. A specific word to Zerubbabel offers him executive power from God, like the signet ring that represents royal authority (cf. 1 Kings 21:8). Both in these verses and in Hag. 2:6–7, we may see evidence of a hope for the overthrow of alien rule and a restoration of independence for Judah under a Davidic ruler, but it is possible that the conventional pictures of theophany point to divine intervention rather than political upheaval. The Persian period reveals various ways in which the Jewish community thought about its life as a subject people and about its hopes for the future.

Bibliography
Ackroyd, P. "Haggai." In *Peake's Commentary on the Bible.* Edited by M. Black and H. H. Rowley. New York: Nelson, 1962. Pp. 643–45.

Baldwin, J. *Haggai, Zechariah, Malachi.* Tyndale Old Testament Commentaries. London: Tyndale, 1972.

Mason, R. *The Books of Haggai, Zechariah, and Malachi.* Cambridge Bible Commentary on the New English Bible. Cambridge: Cambridge University Press, 1977.

Meyers, C., and E. Meyers. *Haggai, Zechariah 1–8.* Anchor Bible, 25B. Garden City, NY: Doubleday, 1987.

Petersen, D. *Haggai and Zechariah 1–8.* Old Testament Library. Philadelphia: Westminster, 1985.

ZECHARIAH

DAVID L. PETERSEN

INTRODUCTION

The Book of Zechariah has two parts. The first is 1–8, visions and oracles for the most part attributable to Zechariah, son of Berechiah, who was active as a prophet from 520 to 518 B.C. The second is 9–14, sometimes called Deutero-Zechariah, anonymous oracles that, though difficult to date, derive from a period later than that of the first section, most probably the fifth–fourth centuries B.C. Within these two units there is significant diversity. In 1–8, there are eight vision reports interspersed with speeches, and then in 9–14, two "oracles," as indicated by the superscriptions at the beginning of chaps. 9 and 12. Hence, for the final editor of Zechariah 9–14, this section appears to be made up of two primary units: chaps. 9–11 and 12–14.

Although the historical setting for the second part of the book is virtually impossible to determine, the setting for the first part is rather clear. By the mid-sixth century B.C. the Persian Empire had replaced the neo-Babylonians as the controlling power not only of Mesopotamia, but of Syro-Palestine as well (→ Babylon). Judah, which had earlier been a subdivision of the Babylonian Empire, was now a subprovincial district in the Persian Empire. Those who had been deported as captives in 595 and 587 B.C. by the Babylonians had become Persian prisoners (→ Exile).

With the advent of this new empire led by Cyrus, whom the prophet of Isaiah 40–55 labeled as a "Messiah" (Isa. 45:1), fortunes for some Israelites began to look up (→ Cyrus II). Some of those who had been deported, as well as their children born in captivity, were allowed to return to the homeland. Moreover, Persian policy, which included support for local religions, supported the restitution of the Temple in Jerusalem. There were, however, competing notions of what the rebuilt community should look like, especially about religious and political matters. During the years 520–518 B.C., Israelites, including both those who had been in exile and those who had remained in the land, were attempting to rebuild their community in and around Jerusalem. The book of Haggai attests to this process with very focused attention on the rebuilding of the Temple (→Haggai). Haggai suggests that important leadership roles during this period were held by Joshua, the high priest, and Zerubbabel, a member of the Davidic royal line

and, probably, a minor official of the Persian Empire with civil responsibilities. Zechariah 1–8, too, is designed to provide a way of thinking about the restoration time, but not in quite so concrete a way as Haggai.

Zechariah 9–14 has been dated by biblical scholars to widely varying settings, from the pre-exilic to the Greco-Roman periods. Several recent studies have suggested the fifth–fourth centuries B.C. as the most likely context. This was a time when the stability, even identity of the Judahite community was at issue. The problems of the community were so severe that the authors of 9–14 thought it necessary for Yahweh to intervene directly.

One of the paramount difficulties in discussing Deutero-Zechariah is the issue of its boundaries. Some scholars have, with good reason, suggested that Malachi is in fact part of the material added to Zechariah, making Zech. 9:1 through Mal. 3:24 a sizable block of late prophetic literature added to Zechariah 1–8. (Zech. 9:1, 12:1, and Mal. 1:1 all commence with the word "oracle.") Because of the lack of scholarly consensus about the relation of Malachi to Deutero-Zechariah, it seems appropriate to take the clue for its interpretation from the final form of that text, namely, that there are two "oracles": 9–11 and 12–14.

COMMENTARY

PART ONE: 1:1–8:23
Visions and Oracles of Restoration

1:1–6:8
Visions

There are eight visions in Zechariah 1–8. Visions are an important part of the prophetic repertoire (e.g., Amos 7:1–7; Jer. 1:11–14). However, in no other prophetic book do they make up so large a part of the prophet's proclamation. The visions in 1–8 share three essential themes: they depict activity between heaven and earth, they present a world in which things are on the move, and they provide a perspective that is universal (note the phrase "all the earth" in Zech. 1:11; 4:14). By using these themes, the visionary seems to be suggesting that Yahweh's imminent action is truly universal and that what he does will restore Judah.

1:8–17, First Vision. Zechariah beholds the divine corral where the deity's horses are at rest. The place is well watered, almost Edenic—v. 8, "near the watery deep" (RSV "in the glen"). Zechariah is disturbed to learn that things are calm since Judah still suffers the effects of defeat and exile. The horses and riders that serve as the deity's patrol report to a messenger of the Lord, who is present, that the earth is at peace (Zech. 1:11). The messenger then poses a disturbing question: "How long, O Yahweh of Hosts, before you have compassion?" This lamentlike language receives a response in the form of two oracles: Yahweh has become jealous for Israel and he will do something. A promise focusing on Temple restoration and rebuilt cities follows. This vision authorizes the prophet to proclaim that a change is about to occur for Judah and Jerusalem.

1:18–21, Second Vision. The prophet reports seeing four horns. Although the report is enigmatic, the prophet probably sees an altar that in ancient Syro-Palestine often had four corners or horns (→ Altar). However, this image is interpreted as referring to the four powers that decimated Judah. One senses here that the four horns symbolize all foreign nations. Artisans or smiths who are on the way will not reconstruct an altar but will destroy those who have destroyed Jerusalem and its altar. If the first vision promised weal to Israel, the second promises woe to foreign nations, especially those that destroyed Israel.

2:1–5, Third Vision. Here the prophet, for the first time, enters the visionary world. He meets a man who is undertaking measurements of Jerusalem, measurements that prescribe dimensions for the restored city. An angelic interpreter interrupts these proceedings and proclaims that the new Jerusalem will exist without boundaries. (Boundaries for the restored Jerusalem were, in contrast, revealed in Ezek. 40–48.) Moreover, Yahweh, symbolized by walls of fire, will protect Israel. By the end of this vision, Zechariah's reports begin to focus on Judah and Jerusalem within the universal compass established in the first two visions.

3:1–10, Fourth Vision. With the introduction of Joshua the high priest, the visionary vocabulary becomes even more specific than in earlier visions. The prophet sees the divine council, but without the Deity present. (See 1 Kings 22:19–23 for a description of the divine council in action.) Joshua is cleansed and purified, presumably so that he may undertake his priestly role. If the Temple were to be rebuilt, it

would be necessary to have the priesthood in place. Ezekiel 40–48 addresses this matter but does not suggest that the high priest has a role. For Zechariah, a high priest is necessary. This fourth vision serves to justify not only the role of high priest but a specific person to hold it.

4:1–5, 10b–14, Fifth Vision. In this vision, interrupted in the middle by an oracle (4:6–10a), Zechariah reports his vision of a golden lampstand, a type of lampstand attested to by archaeological discovery. It is not the classic Jewish menorah, but a bowl with seven pinched or indented spouts. Above it stand two trees that presumably provide the lamp with olive oil. The seven spouts symbolize Yahweh's all-searching and beneficent eyes. The two trees or "sons of oil" no doubt refer to the two leaders of the postexilic community, the civil leader and the high priest. The imagery here does not seem to be that of anointing. Rather the writer emphasizes the interrelationship between the lamp, which symbolizes the divine presence, and the trees, which symbolize human leadership in the restored community. There is something of an innate, divine-human connection as symbolized by the trees, which provide oil for the lamp, and the lamp, which provides the light for the trees. This vision suggests a rather specific form of leadership structure for the restored community, namely, civil and priestly leaders who depend upon Yahweh for their power.

5:1–4, Sixth Vision. Zechariah sees a flying scroll of huge and yet precise proportions. The divine mediator interprets it as a curse, which is a standard feature of Israel's covenant with God (→Covenant). The point of this vision is straightforward. In the restored community Yahweh will continue to punish evildoers, almost magically. This perspective alone suggests that for Zechariah the restoration would not be utopian; there would still be those who err, and they would be punished.

5:5–11, Seventh Vision. In this most bizarre of the visions, Zechariah sees a basket with lead lid and, inside, a figure personifying wickedness. This vision report has several distinctive features. It denigrates Mesopotamia, the plain of Shinar, the land toward which the basket of evil is headed. Moreover, the basket heading east allows some sort of cosmic balance to be achieved. Evil goes out of Syro-Palestine while presumably there are those loyal to Yahweh, the "good," who are moving from the east, or Mesopotamia, to Syro-Palestine.

6:1–8, Eighth Vision. In this final vision Zechariah again sees the horses, which are now joined by chariots and set before bronze mountains, nothing less than the opening to the place where God dwells. Things are now in motion, unlike the calm of the first vision. The Deity's patrol has been sent out; restoration for Judah is under way. The good news of renewal for those loyal to Yahweh has been perceived and reported by the visionary Zechariah. The visions put the events of ca. 520–518 B.C. in cosmic perspective.

1:1–8:23
Oracles

Although visions predominate in Zechariah 1–8, oracular material is prominent as well. An oracle introduces the book (1:1–6). Its language is typical of Israel's pre-exilic prophets. With this rhetoric, Zechariah is presented as an authentic prophetic voice. But these verses have a specific meaning: return, lest you suffer the disaster that befell your fathers!

Apart from the introduction, there are two basic sorts of oracles: those scattered throughout the visions, in 1:7–6:15, and those collected at the end of this section in chaps. 7–8. The first sort seem to be a response to the visions. For example, Zech. 1:14–17 specifies that the future time of weal will concentrate on Jerusalem but will as well include other cities. The oracles in Zech. 4:6–10 interpret the complex imagery of the lampstand vision by referring to specific individuals, Zerubbabel and Josiah.

When oracles do occur, there is always more than one. (Not all visions receive an oracular response.) This multiplicity of sayings attests to the rich implications of the visions, so much so that the sayings connected to one vision (e.g., 4:6–7, 8–10) often provide distinctive emphases. In this instance, the first oracle emphasizes the prominence of Zerubbabel in comparison with Joshua, and the second focuses on Zerubbabel as Temple builder.

The oracles associated with the visions seem thematically both similar to and different from those visions. They are different in the way that they emphasize the importance of the royal figure and the special place of Jerusalem in the restored polity. They concretize what was left unspecified in the visions. Nonetheless there are certain commonalities between the visions and these oracles. For example, one may note the continuity between the cosmic symbolism of the four winds in the final vision, and the notion of four winds in 2:10. Interestingly, both the visions and oracles in 1–8 share certain motifs present in the book of Isaiah, for example, the personified Zion (Isa. 4:9), cities of Judah (Isa. 4:49), and nations coming to Zion (Isa. 56:6–7).

The oracles in Zechariah 7–8 are quite different. This collection begins as a response not to vision reports but to a question posed in 7:3: should the community continue to mourn and fast? In the oracular material that follows, there

are three basic sections: 7:1–14; 8:1–17, and 8:18–23. In the first small subcollection, there is a response of sorts to the question about fasting that eventuates in a series of counterquestions, vv. 5–7, as well as more general hortatory language, vv. 8–14. Then, in the second collection, which is itself subdivided into three blocks (8:1–8, 9–13, 14–17), the reader learns that Yahweh will act on behalf of Zion and that a marvelous restoration will occur. But, as with the previous collection, the ending provides admonitory language as a prerequisite of the good times that are about to occur. The end time will not be a utopia, namely, a time without problems.

In the final collection of oracles, 8:18–23, the prophet's long-awaited answer to the query raised in 7:3 is presented: fast shall become feast. But even here there is admonition—"love truth." Then, in the final two oracles of the first part of the book, a universalistic note is struck as the importance of Jerusalem is highlighted by reference to an international pilgrimage in which many peoples will come to Zion.

Some interpreters have been tempted to think that the visions in the book of Zechariah present the primary or important material and that the oracles are of secondary importance. To suggest this would be far from the mark. In the final form of the book the oracles in chaps. 1–6 provide the exposition of the meaning of the visions, many of which seem to demand interpretation. Furthermore, chaps. 7–8 present a picture of the prophet that enlarges the one given in the visions. In the earlier section, Zechariah was a visionary, one whose work required further interpretation. In the final two chapters, he becomes oracular speaker, answering questions and commenting on topics of importance to the postexilic community. Together, chaps. 1–6 and 7–8 constitute a comprehensive picture of prophetic activity, one in which Zechariah's prophetic credentials are emphasized. This is important since some have maintained that the book of Haggai is written to defend his role as prime mover in the rebuilding of the Temple. One may suggest, by contrast, that Zechariah 1–8 justifies the full range of this prophet's activity.

PART TWO: 9:1–14:21
Oracles About the Future

9:1–11:17
First Oracle

Like the book of Amos, Zechariah 9 begins with oracles against foreign nations. Similar to Amos

749

too is the fact that in this chapter the nations are those of Syro-Palestine: Phoenicia, Syria, and Philistia. Also similar to Amos, the cities within these nations are mentioned by name. Unlike the oracles in Amos, however, there is less attention to indictment of these nations than there is to the punitive action of Yahweh. Yahweh will defeat these nations and cities, an action enabling him to be perceived as guardian of his nation. One result of this divine war will be the institution of Yahweh's kingship (9:9–13): "His kingdom shall be from sea to sea." Moreover, those who worship Yahweh are to be saved from their plight (vv. 11–13). The motif of Yahweh as divine warrior is picked up and highlighted at the end of the poem in vv. 14–15. In graphic language, we hear that those whom he is protecting will consume the blood of the slain enemy warriors. The divine war will bring fertility and prosperity (vv. 16–17). Zechariah 9 involves two essential themes: defeat and destruction for the foreign nations and return and restoration for Israel.

Theme and language change in Zechariah 10. In v. 1, the people of Yahweh are commanded to request rain. The theme of fertility connects 10:1 with 9:17. However, in 10:1, fertility is the result of a petition to Yahweh rather than the result of a successful institution of Yahweh's kingship, as it is in chap. 9. One senses a different topic in v. 2, which appears to have the form of a judgment oracle. There is an indictment in the first half of the verse, a description of improper forms of intermediation, and then in the second half, a retrospective judgment that the people (here construed in metaphoric terms as "sheep,") wander without leadership. The connecting word, "shepherd," unites vv. 2 and 3. It would seem that, in v. 2, shepherds were religious leaders, prophets, or priests, whereas in vv. 3–5, one has the impression that "shepherd" is in fact a political leader. It is not, however, easy to determine whether the leader is Israelite or foreign.

Unlike 10:1–2, which seem to be short, unrelated poems, 10:3–12 appears to be a longer and unified unit, which, apart from the negative statement in v. 3, contains significant positive statements about Israel. Verses 4–5 speak of military action, but here, unlike Zechariah 9, it is the people who fight instead of Yahweh. The allusive style uses descriptions of Israel's earlier battles, for example, the riders on horses and similar language from Exod. 15:1. Like Zechariah 9, however, this poem concerns both the Northern and the Southern kingdoms, namely, Judah and Ephraim, as was the case in Zech. 9:13. Verses 8–12 promise that Yahweh will reverse his exile of Israel by acting to bring them back. Just as the military language echoes the Red Sea events, so too the language of return

alludes to salvation at the Red Sea. Zech. 10:11 suggests that just as Israel earlier escaped from Egypt, so now they will escape from captivity in Mesopotamia. The poem puts this prophecy of military action and return in a theological perspective by concluding with a promise that their strength will be in Yahweh and they shall glory in his name.

Zechariah 11 begins with an address to yet another foreign nation, Lebanon. However, the tone of this oracle is different from the standard oracle against a nation, like the one in 9:1–8. Imperatives, e.g., "Open your doors" (11:1)—as well as literary personifications, for example, "O cypress" (11:2)—make this an unusual literary piece. What appears to be a call to obedience directed at Lebanon quickly and ironically becomes a call to self-destruction: "Open your doors, O Lebanon, that the fire may devour your cedars." This entire poem, 11:1–3, uses terms from the forest: jungle, forest, oak, tree, cypress, cedar. This vocabulary is consistent with the notion of fertility raised earlier in chaps. 9 and 10. However, since this is a poem against a foreign nation, destruction rather than the creation of fertility is the point. Direct discourse as well as the language of fertility create a literary linkage between 10:1 and 11:3.

The rest of Zechariah 11, except for the woe oracle (v. 17), is prose. Zech. 11:4–17 and 13:7–9 both speak against shepherds. Some scholars have suggested that, despite the fact 13:7–9 is poetry and 11:4–17 is, with the exception of v. 17, prose, both texts belong together as one piece, an examination of Israel's leaders. Zech. 11:4–16 is an autobiographical narrative in form. However, the identity of the individual described is as obscure as that of the shepherds or shepherd in chap. 10. Someone is charged with the responsibility of becoming a shepherd for a flock. This is, however, an unhappy task since the flock has been doomed to slaughter. Improper attention to wealth has resulted in a sentence of doom for this flock.

The autobiographic report continues and we hear that some individual, the first person "I" in vv. 7–8, does in fact assume the role of shepherd. While this ambiguous shepherd performed his role, he reports having destroyed three other shepherds. This statement suggests a context in which there is social friction within the community out of which this text has grown. As a result of these difficulties, the person who had assumed the role of shepherd declined that role, especially since he reports that the flock is in fact destined to die.

Termination of this person's role as shepherd is described in vv. 10–14, a description that, though obscure, no doubt refers to the ritual destruction of the symbols of leadership. This same individual is, in vv. 15–16, challenged to act as shepherd again. However, this time the person refuses. And then, in v. 16, the author presents the notion of a shepherd as one who will destroy.

The role of shepherd here is obviously complex. In the ancient Near East, the shepherd metaphor normally refers to the royal office—that of the king (→ Shepherd). In the postexilic era and within the Israelite context, the metaphor of shepherd might refer either to a religious or to a civil-religious leader. In any case, the tone of this prosaic section at the end of chap. 11, a section that concludes the first "oracle," is decidedly negative. The war oracle in 11:17 reemphasizes the notion of a worthless shepherd and includes formal curses upon one who exercises this role. In 13:7–9, the shepherd is clearly Yahweh's or "my shepherd." Similar to chap. 11 is the strong feeling of solidarity between the sheep/people and the shepherd/leader as well as the suffering all parties will undergo.

Interestingly, in 13:8–9, there is provision for a remnant, a group that will survive Yahweh's punishment of the shepherd and his flock. Using standard covenant language, the author proclaims that the survivors will become Yahweh's people. In contrast to these verses in Zechariah 13, however, the language about shepherds in Zechariah 11 is fundamentally negative in its view of the future. Woe overpowers a positive outlook.

12:1–14:21
Second Oracle

Unlike Zechariah 9–11 the final chapters of the book record "a word of the Lord concerning Israel." Consistent with this difference is a further distinction in literary style and theme. Whereas chaps. 9–11 were predominantly poetry, chaps. 12–14 are predominantly prose. In addition, the phrase "on that day" recurs with such regularity that these chapters appear to be made up of small fragments. (The phrase "on that day" appears in 12:3, 4, 6, 8 [2 times], 9, 11; 13:1, 2, 4; 14:4, 6, 8, 9, 13, 20). In spite of the fact that these final three chapters seem to focus on Israel, chap. 12 does begin by setting an international context for Yahweh's activity. At the outset we learned that there will be strife between those loyal to Yahweh and "all the peoples round about" (12:2). In 12:1–9, the author highlights the prominent position Jerusalem will have in the cosmic battle. There is even a hint of intra-Israelite strife (13:2). However, this issue remains muted compared to its importance in Isaiah 56–66. The Zion tradition appears in the motif of an inviolable city in which the deity lives.

The author then shifts themes and in 12:10–13:1 deals with the Davidic monarchy tradi-

tions. In so doing, he broaches the matters of earlier culpability and future possibilities. Some reference to apparent persecution and resulting mourning, as that has been caused by the Davidic house, is introduced in 12:10. However, the author foresees the possibility of cleansing for the Davidic line by Yahweh's purifying waters (13:1). This can happen, however, only after radical clan-by-clan lamentation (12:11–14).

Zech. 13:2–6 is a thematic complex on prophecy. Although Zech. 13:2 commences with reference to idols, prophecy as such, not simply false prophecy, receives strong negative judgment. It would appear that in this condemnation the writer thinks prophecy in the preclassical or classical molds is no longer to be allowed. If someone claims to be a prophet, "his father and mother who bore him, will say to him 'you shall not live.'" Whereas Zechariah 12–13 seemed to allow for continuity with earlier Israelite traditions, notably the Zion and Davidic motifs, Zech. 13:2–6 presents a counterbalance challenging the possibility of prophetic activity in the present age.

In Zechariah 14, one senses an intensification of motifs already broached in the book, e.g., military activity against Yahweh's foes. Consequently, some interpreters have viewed this chapter as apocalyptic in its orientation (→ Apocalyptic Literature). As in 12:1–13:6 the subsections of Zechariah 14 are segmented by the occurrence of the phrase "on that day." And as before conflict is understood from the very outset as part of the Day of Yahweh (14:1). The motif of despoiling predator nations attested elsewhere (Nah. 2:9; Hag. 2:7–8) initiates this culminating chapter. But then the Zion tradition reappears in the prophecy of a battle at Jerusalem in which some Yahwists will survive while others will not. The remnant motif present in Zech. 13:9 reappears in 14:2. Then in 14:4–5 the personal presence of Yahweh as warrior is depicted using traditional themes from Israel's description of theophany, namely, the appearance of the deity and the attendant disturbance of the cosmic order. Even Israelites will flee from God's terrifying presence.

The theophany will cause fantastic changes in the natural world. There will be a radically new time when human experience of this age will be abrogated—no more cold, but presumably pleasant warmth, no more night but continuous light (14:6–7; cf. Isa. 24:23). Eden-like living waters (cf. Joel 4:18) will presumably lead to marvelous fertility.

All this will result from Yahweh's kingship. Moreover, the doctrine of Deut. 6:4, that Yahweh is one, will be firmly established (Zech. 14:9). Consistent with this constancy will be the elevated place of the royal city, even as literally "the whole land" recedes and becomes a plain (cf. Isa. 40:4). Zech. 14:11 corroborates the promise of an impressive population for Jerusalem given earlier in Joel 4:20.

Zech. 14:12–15 returns to the topic of Yahweh's defeat of those who will attack Jerusalem. They will suffer from decimating plagues (14:12). Classical holy war traditions are used to describe the battle in which warriors from the same army will kill each other, a motif that, in 14:14, is reformulated to recognize the possibility of intra-Israelite conflict—"even Judah will fight against Jerusalem." The final portion of 14:14 returns to the notion of despoilation introduced in 14:1, just as 14:15 picks up on the plague motif broached in 14:12.

Zech. 14:16–21 portrays a time after the decisive military confrontation. Some from the attacking nations have survived, but now instead of attacking Jerusalem they will come on an annual pilgrimage for the Feast of Booths (14:16). There is even a punitive threat—no rain—to enforce this journey (14:17). The "family of Egypt" comes in for special attention (14:18–19). Finally, 14:20–21 provides ritual prescriptions for the celebration of that feast. Horses, bells, inscriptions, special basins, and sacrifices at the Temple will make up this remarkable ritual event. Zech. 14:20–21 implies that, by this time, the purity requisite for legitimate Yahwistic rituals will have been achieved.

There are several important themes in Deutero-Zechariah: military conflict, especially against foreign nations and with Yahweh as principal warrior; indictment of communal leaders, whether foreign or domestic, whether civil or religious; the hope of restoration for Jerusalem and those loyal to Yahweh; and the anticipation of a new time in which things will be very different and very good but still not perfect. Despite the significant literary variety present in Zechariah 9–14, there is remarkable thematic unity within these two oracles, 9–11 and 12–14. These "oracles" present the reader with two versions of Yahweh-initiated action. In 9–11 the primary tone is doom; in 12–14 it is that of promise.

The final form of Zechariah provides the reader with two literatures that have been juxtaposed and presented as one book. Despite their discrete points of origin, there are integral connections between 1–8 and 9–14. There are, of course, similarities in language, for example, "the daughter of Zion" in 2:10 and 9:9. But more importantly, both sections share important themes: the divine initiative, the cosmic scope of Yahweh's activity, and the important role of Zion in the restored community. Since such important ties link 1–8 to 9–14 and since 1–8 was composed earlier than the final chapters, it seems likely that those who wrote 9–14 knew and were influenced by 1–8. The earlier writers were concerned essentially about what was happening in their time, namely, the restoration in Judah ca. 520 B.C. The later authors focused instead on Yahweh's future action, activity that would enable the restored community to do more than just survive and bring a time when the people would receive Yahweh as king and would be his glorious people.

Bibliography

Achtemeier, E. Nahum–Malachi. Interpretation: A Bible Commentary for Preaching and Teaching. Atlanta, GA: Knox, 1986.

Baldwin, J. Haggai, Zechariah, Malachi. Tyndale Old Testament Commentaries. London: Tyndale, 1972.

Mason, R. The Books of Haggai, Zechariah and Malachi. Cambridge Bible Commentary on the New English Bible. Cambridge: Cambridge University Press, 1977.

Petersen, D. Haggai and Zechariah 1–8. Old Testament Library. Philadelphia: Westminster, 1985.

Smith, R. Micah–Malachi. Word Biblical Commentary, 32. Waco, TX: Word, 1984.

MALACHI

P Λ U L D. H A N S O N

INTRODUCTION

Literary Form

With the exception of 1:1 and 4:4–6, the Book of Malachi can be read as a compositional unity from the hand of a single author. It is held together by a common literary form, a narrative report of a dispute. Time and again, Yahweh makes an assertion, and the priests or the people respond with a query, usually implying objection to the divine pronouncement. This question leads to a clarification of the divine assertion; the intention of the divine word is elaborated and strengthened in the direction of indictment and judgment of the doubting people or of admonition.

Questions concerning authorship have revolved around the superscription in 1:1. Though some scholars take the Hebrew word mal'aki in this verse to be the personal name of the prophetic author, an alternative explanation seems preferable, namely, that the word derives from a misreading of the term "my messenger" (mal'aki) in 3:1 as a personal name designating the author. If this is the case, the book of Malachi is an anonymous composition that may have at one time circulated with two other anonymous collections, Zechariah 9–11 and Zechariah 12–14, a possibility suggested by the appearance of the same formula at the head of all three collections, "Oracle, word of Yahweh." Structurally, the book divides into six sections, 1:2–5; 1:6–2:9; 2:10–16; 2:17–3:5; 3:6–12; and 3:13–4:3.

Historical Setting

Though undated, the book of Malachi can be placed with confidence in the first half of the fifth century B.C. The high hopes connected with the era of the restored Temple reflected in the prophecies of Haggai and Zechariah clearly have been shattered. The book describes a priesthood that has degenerated into practices violating the laws regulating ritual sacrifice and that is lax in its responsibility of guiding and teaching the people. And the effects of degeneration and laxity are apparent throughout the land: people are reneging on their tithes; intermarriage is calling into question the identity of the Jewish community; and the day laborers, widows, orphans, and sojourners are suffering oppression. Nehemiah, whose activity in Judah began in 445 B.C., focused his reform efforts on ending intermarriage (Neh. 10:28–30), restoring the practices of honest tithing (10:32, 38–39) and of proper ritual (10:33–37), and ending exploitation of the poor (5:1–13). It is plausible to see Malachi as active shortly before the debut of Nehemiah. Thus, the book may be placed in the reign of Xerxes I (486–464 B.C.), when the Persians were experiencing their first stinging defeats by Greek armies. At this time, Judah was a vassal state of the Persians, living under a non-Davidic governor appointed by the Persians (Mal. 1:8), and may have been searching the international conflicts of the time for signs of divine intervention.

Socioreligious Setting

The author of Malachi writes from a perspective combining ethical norms rooted deeply in pre-exilic prophecy with concerns about proper sacrifice and exemplary conduct on the part of the priests. The object of attack is the presiding or Zadokite priesthood (→ Zadok). The attack is based on an ideal of priestly fidelity associated with God's "covenant with Levi," an archaic ideal to which certain levitical priests were appealing in their polemic against the dominant (and in their eyes defiled) priesthood. This polemic has a long prehistory reaching back to the Davidic period when the Mushite Abiathar served in the tabernacle alongside Zadok the Zadokite priest (→ Mushi). From the time of Solomon on, the Zadokites came to dominate the Temple cult, and the Mushites were restricted increasingly to outlying shrines and nontemple functions like itinerant teaching. As a result, traces of an ongoing polemic between Zadokites (or Aaronides) and Mushites can be seen in many parts of the Bible, e.g., Exodus 32, Numbers 12, 16, and 25, and Isaiah 56 and 66. The message of the book of Malachi, with its combination of ritual concerns and prophetic themes and its diatribe against the presiding Zadokite priesthood, can therefore best be understood as arising among levitical priests who feel that the present degraded state of the rival priesthood and the demoralized condition of the land substantiate their claims to legitimate priestly authority in Temple and community. Astutely, they attack the position of their rivals by pointing out how the latter's conduct directly contradicts the Priestly Blessing of Num. 6:23–27. At the same time, they substantiate their own claim to authority by appealing to the archaic blessing of Levi found in the Blessing of Moses (Deut. 33:8–11). It is likely that Malachi belongs to a late stage of protest that arose in connection with Zadokite control over the Temple rebuilding in the years 520–515 B.C. (see Isa. 56–66). The bleak conditions of Temple and community and the apparent inability of the protagonists to effect thoroughgoing reform abet the development of an apocalyptic outlook. What the righteous but disenfranchised cannot accomplish, God will accomplish in an awesome day of judgment and vindication, which will purge from the land all evil, restore a pure priesthood from the sons of Levi, and inaugurate an era of blessing.

Religious Significance

The themes of Malachi were important for a community threatened from within by moral degeneracy and cultic decay. These themes preserved classical early Yahwistic and prophetic concerns for justice and compassion. They also nurtured the integrity of a cultic and sacrificial system that played an important part socially, by undergirding the identity of the Jews within the Persian Empire, and economically, by equitably redistributing the produce of the land. Though the conditions faced by Ezra and Nehemiah suggest that the reform movement advocated in Malachi remained largely ineffectual, the book likely played a part in preparing the way for the two great reformers as they traveled from Persia to Judah on their mission of restoring stability to the land. The admonition added later to Malachi in 4:4 indicates that later readers recognized the words of Malachi to be fully in the spirit of God's commandments to Moses. Indeed, the themes of God's unchanging love and loyalty and the standards of fidelity and justice and dignity in worship that this book places before those who fear the Lord are themes whose meaning have not gone unnoticed among the spiritually sensitive down to our own time. Another theme also left its imprint on later ages, that describing the "messenger" (identified in 4:5 as Elijah) who would prepare the way for the Lord on the Day of Judgment (Mark 1:2; Matt. 11:10, 14; 17:10–13; Luke 1:17; John 1:21, 25; m. 'Ed. 8.7; Tg. Ps.-J. Exod. 40:10; Tg. Ps.-J. Deut. 30:4). The reemergence of this theme in the Gospels gives special significance to the fact that Malachi provides the link between OT and NT in most Christian Bibles.

COMMENTARY

1:2–5, The Sovereignty of God's Love. Yahweh's first word is directed to the heart of the people: "I have loved you." In the disputational style of the book, the people reply, "How have you loved us?" Yahweh's reply is based upon a comparison between two brothers, who are the eponymous ancestors of Edom and Israel. In contrast to God's love for Jacob, Esau has been the object of divine wrath. The comparison is harsh, but drives home the fact that Israel's election is based on nothing but the sovereign love of God. But why should Edom have been singled out as the example of divine curse? Though the early history of the relationship between Edom and Israel was a mixture of enmity and peaceful coexistence, the Edomites came to represent the epitome of evil when they used the Babylonian destruction of Judah and Jerusalem in 587 B.C as an opportunity to plunder the land (Lam. 4:21–22; Ps. 137:7; cf. Isa. 34:5–9; 63:1–6). Reference to Yahweh's undoing of their every effort to rebuild may be related to the pressure that was placed on Edom from the east and that culminated a century or two later in Edom's being driven into southern Judah by the Nabateans. This unit concludes by expressing a universalistic leitmotif in the book, "Yahweh is exalted beyond the border of Judah."

1:6–2:9, Faithful Priests Honor God. The unit begins with a proverbial saying, "Son honors father, and servant his master." In a double exchange with the priests, Yahweh goes on to assert that though he is father and master, the priests give him no honor, but rather despise his name by offering blemished sacrifices. We thus witness a situation in which the standards for Temple ritual set by the Torah (e.g., Deut. 15:21; 17:1; Lev. 22:17–25) are flagrantly broken. The priests no longer take the reality of God seriously, since, according to the Deuteronomic tradition here attested, the divine name is the reality of the deity manifested in the cult (Deut. 12:5, 11; 16:2, 6). The condemnation in v. 10 is harsh: no cult would be preferable to the existing one! Mal. 1:11, which has been the object of considerable debate and is often regarded as secondary, is integral to this argument, if it is read as an intentional contrast to the despicable disregard for God's reality by the priests. They are despising the God who is exalted among the nations and who is honored by every pure offering, regardless of where it is offered. This is the second instance of the book's universalistic leitmotif.

The priests are responsible for bringing blessing to the people and for leading them in the way of blessing by faithfully instructing them in the Torah. The priests have failed in both these duties (2:1–3, 8–9). Hence the disputation develops into a pronouncement of judgment: Yahweh's curse falls upon the priests, as their hereditary line is broken off, as they are rendered unfit for service by becoming defiled in a most shameful manner, with the dung of their own offerings being spread over their faces, and as people no longer honor them as teachers. The impact of this judgment is heightened by way of a contrast. Between the two prongs of the judgment Yahweh describes his "covenant with Levi," a covenant described in the Blessing of Moses (Deut. 33:8–11). When upheld, the fruits of this covenant were "life and peace," for in it the priests feared and honored the name of the Lord and through their example and teaching "turned many from iniquity."

2:10–16, Marriage Is a Covenant. The prophet addresses a larger audience as he turns to a problem threatening the very unity of the community. That unity is established upon a principle expressed in the opening prophetic question: "Do we not all have one father? Did not one God create us?" This central confession of Yahwistic faith is now being denied by the people through their marrying foreigners and thereby becoming yoked to foreign gods. The second half of this unit points out how the priests themselves again are instrumental in leading the people to unfaithfulness: though marriage is nothing less than a covenant witnessed by God, the priests are faithless to the wives of their youth. Such action notwithstanding, they are thrown into a quandary when Yahweh refuses to accept their sacrifices. "I hate divorce," Yahweh declares, and with this statement concludes a plea for marital faithfulness that goes beyond the one found in the Torah (cf. Deut. 24:1–4).

2:17–3:5, The Day of Yahweh's Cleansing. The disputation that begins this unit brings to light the perversion of values and the collapse of true faith that undermines the community's health. The people weary God by saying, "All who do evil are good in the eyes of Yahweh, and God takes delight in them," and by asking, "Where is the God of justice?" Poignantly these two sentences describe a shocking cynicism and mocking disbelief that defiantly resists prophetic critique and efforts to stir up feelings of remorse.

Before such an audience any prophet is tempted to despair. But here we find what was beginning to emerge as another response to a bleak situation, a vision of the coming of the very one the people have mocked and denied, the God of justice! God's way is prepared by mal'aki ("my messenger"). Against the background of Isa. 40:1–11, we can best picture this messenger as one of the heralds of the divine assembly, an individual charged with preparing the people for the day of Yahweh's epiphany. Proper preparation means the restoration of a sanctified cult, for the Temple is to this writer, as it was to the Deuteronomistic writers and to Ezekiel, Haggai, and Zechariah, the place of Yahweh's presence among the people. As expected in light of Mal. 2:4–7, the sanctification of the cult and the restoration of sacrifices pleasing to Yahweh would be carried out by a purified levitical priesthood (compare the messenger's purifying the sons of Levi with the seraph's purifying Isaiah as a part of the latter's commissioning in Isa. 6:6–7). Then Yahweh would appear for the great Day of Judgment and would restore the land by pronouncing judgment against all those who break the commandments. The list of offenders, namely, sorcerers, adulterers, those who swear falsely, those who oppress the day laborer, the widow, and the orphan, and those who cast aside the alien, harks back to the ideals of early Yahwism and to the stringent moral standards of the pre-exilic prophets. Just as the collapse of a moral universe was tied to a collapse of belief, so too the list of offenders is summarized by a phrase focusing on the heart of the broken covenant, those who do not fear Yahweh. A resanctified priesthood and a land purged of those defiantly breaking the covenant and its Torah—that is the vision of this unit, a vision directly addressing the problems described in the units immediately preceding and following it.

3:6–12, The Fruits of Honest Tithing. In these verses, the writer compares Yahweh's never-changing faithfulness with the perpetual apostasy of Israel. But even after this history of ingratitude and sin, the age-old invitation is extended once again: "Return to me, and I will return to you." True to the disputational style, the people try to deflect the thrust of this call to repentance by asking, "How can we return?" Their response leads into another indictment: the people are robbing Yahweh by reneging on the tithes they are committed to bring into the Temple storehouse. Yahweh's charge involves more than a gesture of piety; the Temple was the organ through which the produce of the land was redistributed, both to Temple personnel and to other groups in the land. Dereliction in fulfilling one's rightful tithe was thus tantamount to upsetting the cosmic harmony that alone could assure prosperity in the land. Once the people renew their commitment to the Temple, the cosmic harmony of which the Temple cult was the earthly center will be reestablished, and the curse visiting the land because of the people's disobedience will give way to blessing (cf. Hag. 1–2). This sentiment leads into another formulation of the universalistic leiftmotif of the book: the restoration of the tithe will redound to Yahweh's glory far beyond Judah, for all nations will witness the fruits of true worship (v. 12).

3:13–4:3, God Will Restore the Distinction Between the Righteous and the Wicked.

One last time the theme of blasphemy is revisited, as the disputation exposes the arrogant disdain of the wicked: "It is useless to serve God. . . . We shall declare the arrogant blessed. . . . Not only are evildoers successful, but when they test God, they escape punishment." This deplorable situation, similar to the one that evoked judgment in 2:17–3:5, introduces here another contrast: over against the wicked there now appear those who fear Yahweh. Though the leaders and most of the people have obliterated the distinction between righteousness and evil, that distinction is preserved before Yahweh, written in "a book of remembrance" (cf. Ps. 139:16; Dan. 12:1). On the day when Yahweh acts, the righteous will be delivered and reconstituted as Yahweh's "special possession," fulfilling an ancient promise reaching back to Yahweh's covenant with Israel at Sinai (Exod. 19:5–6). Before Yahweh's holiness, all wickedness will be burned like stubble, whereas for those who fear Yahweh the "sun of righteousness" will rise "with healing in its wings." The God-fearers are even envisioned as being drawn into the action on Yahweh's Day of Judgment, as was later the case in the sectarian writings of Qumran.

4:4–6, Closing Exhortation.

A later editor has added an appropriate exhortation, much in the style of the book of Deuteronomy, urging reverence for the Torah. Another postscript identifies the messenger of 3:1 with Elijah, the prophet who was taken up into heaven by a fiery chariot (2 Kings 2:11) and who would be instrumental in healing the foundation of Jewish community, the family, as a means of preparing a people for covenantal blessings rather than for the ban of destruction.

Bibliography

Dentan, R. C. "The Book of Malachi, Introduction and Exegesis." The Interpreter's Bible. Nashville, TN: Abingdon, 1956. Vol. 6, pp. 1117–44.

Glazier–MacDonald, B. Malachi, The Divine Messenger. Society of Biblical Literature Dissertation Series, 98. Atlanta, GA: Scholars Press, 1987.

Hanson, P. D. The People Called: The Growth of Community in the Bible. San Francisco: Harper & Row, 1986. Chap. 8.

Kaiser, W. C. Malachi: God's Unchanging Love. Grand Rapids, MI: Baker, 1984.

Mason, R. The Books of Haggai, Zechariah and Malachi. Cambridge Bible Commentary on the New English Bible. Cambridge: Cambridge University Press, 1977.

PART FOUR

THE
APOCRYPHA

INTRODUCTION TO THE APOCRYPHA

J O H N   J.   C O L L I N S

The term "apocrypha" means "hidden things," but in ecclesiastical contexts it is used to refer to those books included in the OT of the Latin Vulgate translation but not in the Hebrew Bible. Traditionally this designation has been applied to fifteen books or portions of books: 1 Esdras, 2 Esdras, Tobit, Judith, The Additions to Esther, Wisdom of Solomon, Sirach, Baruch, Letter of Jeremiah, Song of the Three Youths (including the Prayer of Azariah), Susanna, Bel and the Dragon (this and the previous two known collectively as The Additions to Daniel), Prayer of Manasseh, 1 Maccabees, and 2 Maccabees. Also included among the Apocrypha, especially in the Bibles of the Greek Orthodox and other Orthodox churches, are 3 and 4 Maccabees and Psalm 151, which are found in manuscripts of the Greek Bible (the Septuagint, LXX). The Psalms of Solomon are also found in manuscripts of the Greek Bible but have not traditionally been included in the category Apocrypha.

ORIGIN OF THE CATEGORY "APOCRYPHA"

The distinction between canonical and apocryphal writings is found clearly in 2 Esdras 14. There Ezra is inspired to dictate ninety-four books and instructs: "Make public the twenty-four books that you wrote first and let the worthy and the unworthy read them; but keep the seventy that were written last, in order to give them to the wise among your people" (2 Esd. 14:45–46). The seventy books constitute a category of esoteric literature, presumably including apocalyptic revelations such as are found in 2 Esdras itself, but the esoteric character is atypical of the traditional Apocrypha.

By the time 2 Esdras 14 was written at the end of the first century A.D., the canon of the Hebrew Bible was closed. The number of books was variously given as twenty-two or twenty-four, but the variation can be explained as a matter of counting (e.g., Jeremiah and Lamentations may be counted as one or as two; the same is true for Judges and Ruth; see Beckwith, pp. 235–73). Traditionally, the closing of the canon was associated with the so-called Council of Jamnia about A.D. 90. The tendency in some recent studies (Leiman, Beckwith) has been to push back the closing of the Hebrew canon to the pre-Christian era.

The rabbis appear to have recognized three classes of books: those that "defile the hands" (the sacred canonical Scriptures), books that

Previous page: Personification of Wisdom; detail of an illustration in a tenth-century A.D. Greek manuscript now called The Paris Psalter.

were withdrawn or stored away (Heb. *ganaz*) and whose use was subject to restrictions, and "outside books" (*separim chisonim*) whose use was forbidden. The famous rabbi Akiba is said to have specified Sirach as one of the forbidden books, but It is cited in the Talmud "much like any other biblical book" (Leiman, p. 97), so his opinion cannot have prevailed. Yet it did not "defile the hands" either (*t. Yad.* 2:13). Origen remarks that Tobit and Judith were not even among the hidden books (Gk. *apocrypha*) of the Jews (*Letter to Africanus* 13), but there is no clear evidence that there was an official list of books that were stored away.

The Greek-speaking Christian church accepted a larger collection of Jewish writings as authoritative than what was included in the Hebrew canon. The traditional explanation of this fact is that Alexandrian Judaism had a more extensive canon than its Palestinian counterpart and that the Christians adopted the canon of the Diaspora. The notion of an Alexandrian canon, however, has been discredited by the work of Sundberg, who argues that only the Torah and the Prophets were closed before A.D. 70. The Christian church, then, inherited an open canon in the area of the Writings. Whether in fact the list of canonical Writings was still fluid in Diaspora Judaism at the time of the great revolts (A.D. 66–135) is disputed (e.g., Beckwith, p. 385), but at least it was fluid in Christianity in the second and third centuries. When Melito of Sardis in the late second century A.D. was asked for "an accurate statement of the ancient books," he had to send to Palestine for an answer. His list is confined to the Hebrew canon, but without Esther. Others were more inclusive. Tertullian was aware that the book of Enoch was not in the Jewish canon; yet "since Enoch by the same scripture has also made proclamation concerning the Lord, nothing whatever must be rejected by us which pertains to us" (*On Women's Dress* 1.3). Clement of Alexandria cited Tobit, Sirach, and the Wisdom of Solomon as Scripture and Judith and 2 Maccabees as historical sources. Origen accepted Susanna as part of the text of Daniel although he knew it was not in the Hebrew, because Susanna "is found in every church of Christ." Tobit could not be used in disputation with Jews but could within the churches (*Letter to Africanus* 13).

In preparing the Latin Vulgate (A.D. 390–405), Jerome was committed to the *Hebraica veritas* (Lat., "the Hebrew truth") in canon as well as text. Yet he translated the additional books and passages too and called attention to their apocryphal status in his prefaces. The prefaces, however, were not always copied or heeded, and so the Western church came to regard all books of the Vulgate as part of Scripture. The Gelasian Decree at the end of the fifth century recognized Tobit, Judith, the Wisdom of Solomon, Sirach, and 1 and 2 Maccabees; other Apocrypha, such as Susanna, were accepted as parts of other biblical books.

The Protestant Reformers did not condemn the Apocryphal books but denied that they had divine authority or that they could be used to establish doctrine. The Council of Trent in 1546 affirmed the canonicity of the apocryphal books, with the exceptions of 1 and 2 Esdras and the Prayer of Manasseh, which were less firmly supported by tradition. These books were printed in an appendix to the NT in subsequent editions of the Vulgate. The Apocrypha were still included in the King James Version of 1611 but were omitted with increasing frequency in later printings.

The Roman Catholic church today abides by the decision of the Council of Trent on the matter of canon. Catholics sometimes refer to the disputed books as "deuterocanonical," implying that they were written later than the protocanonical OT. The Greek Orthodox church accepts, in addition, 1 Esdras, Psalm 151, the Prayer of Manasseh, and 3 Maccabees, with 4 Maccabees in an appendix. The Russian Orthodox church accepts 1 and 2 Esdras, Psalm 151, and 3 Maccabees.

THE LITERARY GENRES

The works of the Apocrypha may be classified under two broad headings: narrative texts and discursive texts. Within the category of narrative we may distinguish works of historiography (1 and 2 Maccabees), historical fiction (Judith, Tobit, 3 Maccabees), and an apocalypse (2 Esdras). Within the category of discursive writing we may distinguish sapiential writings (Sirach, Wisdom of Solomon), exhortations (4 Maccabees, Letter of Jeremiah), and prayers (Prayer of Manasseh, Prayer of Azariah).

The Narrative Works

Historiography. There has been a growing awareness in recent years that historiography is never simply a record of fact but always involves an imaginative, constructive element. The distinction between history and fiction is not an absolute one, but the terms are useful for indicating the extremes of a continuum.

The most obviously "historical" book of the Apocrypha is undoubtedly 1 Maccabees. This work was composed toward the end of the second century B.C., most probably in Hebrew. It reports the events from the outbreak of the Maccabean revolt to the end of the reign of Simon (134 B.C.) and draws on some earlier written sources (e.g., the chronicles of John Hyrcanus, 1 Macc. 16:24). It is written in a sober style, which inspires confidence in its reliability. Nonetheless, it should not be taken as an unbiased account. On the contrary, it may be viewed as political propaganda for the Hasmonean house, which is described as "the family of those men through whom deliverance was given to Israel" (5:62). Throughout, the Maccabees are presented as "pious" while their opponents are "lawless."

The ideological aspects of the narrative are especially evident in the speeches and prayers attributed to the protagonists. The deathbed speech of Mattathias serves to place the Maccabees in the tradition of the biblical heroes from Abraham to the companions of Daniel. There are frequent allusions to biblical prototypes throughout the narrative—Mattathias' first act of violence is legitimated by analogy with that of Phinehas in Num. 25:6–11. The author also inserts hymns of praise to Judas (1 Macc. 3:3–9) and Simon (14:4–15). The success of the Maccabees is attributed throughout to the power of their God (e.g., 3:19, 4:9–11). None of this is to deny the value of 1 Maccabees as a historical source, when due account is taken of its tendentious nature.

2 Maccabees is an epitome of a longer history by Jason of Cyrene, who may have been an eyewitness to the events he reports. The purpose of the abbreviator is stated explicitly in 2:25: "we have aimed to please those who wish to read, to make it easy for those who wish to memorize and to profit all readers." History, as conceived in 2 Maccabees, can accommodate heavenly apparitions and interventions (e.g., 2 Macc. 11:8). The religious character of this history is evident in the central role of the Temple (e.g., in the miraculous story of Heliodorus in chap. 3). It also serves a broader hortatory purpose, as is evident in the martyrdom of the seven brothers in 2 Maccabees 7 and in the account of the death of Antiochus Epiphanes in chap. 9. Yet, while 2 Maccabees lacks the sober tone of 1 Maccabees, it is not necessarily inferior as a historical source. It preserves a number of important documents in chap. 11 and its account of the events leading up to the Maccabean revolt is in some respects more complete and accurate than that of 1 Maccabees. It also presents an interestingly different account of the events, focusing more on Judas and neglecting his father and brothers. The deaths of the martyrs are also recognized as a factor that contributed to the Jewish victory. Consequently the history as reported in 2 Maccabees is less amenable to the propaganda of the Hasmonean house. The popularity of the books of Maccabees rests, surely, on the fact that they are our main sources for a very important episode in Jewish history.

Historical Fiction. The work known as 1 Esdras (3 Ezra in the Latin Vulgate) might also be classified as historiography, since it is primarily a variant text of the end of Chronicles, Ezra, and part of Nehemiah. It includes, however, a narrative that is not paralleled in the biblical text and belongs to another genre. This is the story of Darius' banquet in 3:1–4:63, which tells of the contest of wisdom between three courtiers in which the Jew Zerubbabel is victorious. This story belongs to a widespread genre variously identified as "court tale" because of its setting or "wisdom tale" because of its theme. Biblical examples can be found in the Joseph story in Genesis, in Esther, and Daniel 1–6. The designation "Diaspora novel" is sometimes used for the Jewish tales, but this ignores the non-Jewish examples such as the tale of Ahiqar. These tales fall into the category of historical fiction, because they describe a setting in realistic historical detail, but unlike the books of Maccabees they are scarcely constrained at all by the record or recollection of historical events. The objective of the story in 1 Esdras is to establish the superior wisdom of the Jewish youth Zerubbabel.

A number of other tales of the Apocrypha are set in the eastern Diaspora. Tobit is said to have been taken captive to Assyria in the days of Shalmaneser in 722 B.C. The book's cavalier approach to historical data is shown by the fact that the secession of the northern tribes from Jerusalem (922 B.C.) is said to have taken place when the same Tobit was a very young man. In part, the portrayal of Tobit as a suffering, righteous man is reminiscent of the prologue of Job. The folkloristic character of the story is evident in the episode concerning the evil demon Asmodeus, who slew each of a woman's seven husbands before they had been with her. It is also significant that Tobit is said to be the uncle of Ahiqar and thereby located in relation to a broader cycle of Near Eastern folklore.

We have noted already that the first six chapters of the book of Daniel are made up of court or wisdom tales. We know from the Dead Sea Scrolls that Daniel 4 was a variant of a traditional tale, of which another older variant is found in the Prayer of Nabonidus. In another Danielic composition, 4QPseudoDan, Daniel delivers a prophecy in a royal court. Two other stories are attached to the Greek version of Daniel, Bel and the Dragon and Susanna. The story of Bel and the Dragon is set in the royal court like the stories in Daniel 1–6. It also shares the motif of the lions' den with Daniel 6. In the protocanonical book, polemic against idolatry was a subordinate theme (e.g., Dan 3:18; 5:23). In the apocryphal stories, it receives the primary emphasis as Daniel unmasks the fraudulence of the gods of the Babylonians. The episode where Habbakuk is transported to Babylon by the hair of his head to feed Daniel in the lions' den is an element of fantasy that contrasts with the relatively sober canonical stories.

The story of Susanna is found after Daniel 12 in the LXX, before Daniel 1 in the translation of Theodotion. (Bel and the Dragon appears after Susanna in the LXX and after Daniel 12 in Theodotion.) The story tells how the intervention of Daniel saved the innocent Susanna from her detractors. The tale is set in Babylon but Daniel is described simply as "a young lad," not as an official in the royal court. The wisdom he exhibits recalls the judicial wisdom of Solomon in 1 Kings 3 rather than the mantic wisdom of Daniel 1–6. Daniel's role in the story is probably due to a play on his name (Heb., "my judge is God") rather than to the tradition of Daniel as a wise courtier. The story itself is a tale of parabolic reversal, in which the youthful Daniel confounds his elders and the suspect woman is proven more righteous than the judges of her people.

The book of Judith has a stronger appearance of history than either Tobit or the Danielic stories, in the sense that it claims to describe a public event of some magnitude—an invasion of Syria and Palestine by Nebuchadnezzar. The author's disregard for historical accuracy, however, is evident not only in the confused statement that Nebuchadnezzar was king of the Assyrians, but also in the assumption that the events in question take place after the return from the Exile. There is no independent record elsewhere of these events, and even the scene of the action in Judah (Bethulia) is an enigma. The very name of the protagonist, Judith (Heb., "Jewess"), suggests that she is a type figure rather than a historical individual. The story recalls the exploits of the woman Jael in Judges 4. The theological lesson, that God can destroy the most powerful enemies of Israel even by the hand of a woman, is celebrated in a hymn in chap. 16 and was probably intended to inspire Jewish resistance to foreign oppressors.

A final example of historical fiction, 3 Maccabees, is set not in the eastern Diaspora, but in Egypt during the reign of Ptolemy IV Philopator. The story involves two episodes. First there is an attempt by Ptolemy to enter the Temple of Jerusalem, which is prevented.

This episode is apparently based on the story of Heliodorus in 2 Maccabees 3. Second, there is an attempt to reduce the Egyptian Jews to the status of slaves and brand them with the emblem of Dionysus. The order is thwarted, first by lapses in the king's memory and then by the miraculous intervention of two angels. A variant account of this episode is found in Josephus *Against Apion* 2:53–55, where it is set in the reign of Ptolemy Euergetes II (Physcon). Various attempts have been made to establish the historical reliability of the story in one setting or the other. Philopator was devoted to the cult of Dionysus, and Physcon was notorious for his cruelty and was ill disposed to the Jews. At most, however, we can speak of partial historical reminiscences. The story is not a record of historical events but a fantasy of supernatural deliverance from extreme danger. The threat to the Jewish people is reminiscent of the book of Esther, and 3 Maccabees has many close parallels with the Greek translation of Esther. Like the stories of the fiery furnace and the lions' den in Daniel, it was designed to support endurance in an alien, sometimes hostile environment.

Apocalypse: 2 Esdras. 2 Esdras is a composite work. Chaps. 1 and 2 (together also called 5 Ezra) are made up of a collection of oracles with an apocalyptic vision in 2:42–48. Chaps. 15 and 16 (called 6 Ezra) are also a collection of oracles with an eschatological focus. Both of these passages are of Christian origin. The bulk of 2 Esdras however (chaps. 3–14) is taken up with a Jewish apocalypse, commonly called 4 Ezra, which dates from about A.D. 100.

2 Esdras 3–14 is an apocalypse in the sense that it is a revelation of eschatological mysteries mediated by an angel. It is a complex work made up of three dialogues (chaps. 3:1–9:25), three visions (9:26–13:58), and an epilogue. The constituent parts are held together by a narrative thread that tells of Ezra's transformation from a skeptical critic of divine justice to a receptive vehicle for divine revelation. The dialogues are reminiscent of the book of Job because of Ezra's probing questions. Interestingly, the author emphasizes that Ezra has neither ascended to heaven nor descended to hell (4:8) and so does not lay claim to the kind of apocalyptic knowledge associated with Enoch. What the dialogues establish, however, is that the problem of divine justice is insoluble without such revelation. In the transitional chapter (9:26–10:59) Ezra finds himself cast in the role of comforter; he tells the woman in his vision to "let yourself be persuaded . . . and consoled" (10:20). Thereafter he accepts his own advice, as the angel describes the fulfillment that is to come. Commentators have been troubled by the change in Ezra's attitude in the second half of the book, and some have suggested multiple authorship or that Ezra and the angel are mouthpieces for different parties. These suggestions are unnecessary if we take seriously the narrative character of the book, which invites the reader to identify with Ezra in his transition from doubt to faith.

The Discursive Writings

Sapiential Works. Pride of place among the discursive writings must go to the two great wisdom books, Sirach (or the Wisdom of Jesus the

Son of Sirach) and the Wisdom of Solomon. Sirach is the only book of the Apocrypha that may have been considered canonical by some rabbis or whose status was seriously in dispute (see Leiman, pp. 92–102). Its popularity in Christianity is reflected in its Latin name, *Liber Ecclesiasticus*, or "Church Book." The Wisdom of Solomon was the book of the Apocrypha most widely used in early Christianity, both Eastern and Western, although it was listed among the NT Scriptures, not the OT, in the Muratorian canon. It was widely accepted as Scripture by the end of the second century, but Origen says it was still disputed in the third.

While both of these books stand in the wisdom tradition and have important affinities with each other, they are still quite different in character. Sirach, sometimes called Ecclesiasticus, is essentially a collection of proverbs and maxims, after the manner of the book of Proverbs. Like Proverbs 8, it includes a poem placed on the lips of personified wisdom. Sirach makes a significant departure from Proverbs, however, when it identifies wisdom with the book of the Torah of Moses (Sir. 24:23). This identification does not restrict the range of Sirach's wisdom, but serves as a norm for the discernment of true wisdom. The sage, in Sirach's view, is one who studies the law of the Most High and is concerned with prophecies, but who also travels through foreign lands to seek the good and evil among humankind (Sir. 39). The biblical history provides a parade of exemplars of wisdom, which is reviewed in the "Praise of the Fathers" (chaps. 44–49) and marks the first attempt to integrate sacred history into a wisdom book.

Sirach is exceptional among ancient Jewish writings in that we know who wrote it and when and who translated it and when. This very specificity may well have militated against its acceptance in the canon, when the book of Daniel, which was composed at a slightly later time, could pass as a work from the age of prophecy. The fact that we know the provenance of Sirach, however, is valuable for the historian and makes Sirach useful, in a way that earlier wisdom books are not, as a witness to the society of a particular period: Jerusalem shortly before the Hellenistic reform in the early second century B.C. Sirach's posture has rightly been dubbed conservative; for him the Torah remained the norm. Yet he was far from closed-minded and his book reflects familiarity with Greek literature as well as with the biblical tradition. The encomium of the high priest Simon (chap. 50) enables us to place Sirach in the political context of the time.

The Wisdom of Solomon, in contrast, has scarcely any proverbial material and is presented as an exhortation to the rulers of the earth to "love righteousness." It is a product of the Greek-speaking Diaspora, most probably of Alexandria, and reflects a thought-world similar to that of the philosopher Philo. There is continuity with Sirach in the figure of personified wisdom (here equated with the Gk. *logos*, or "word"; 9:1–2), and also in the incorporation of biblical history in chaps. 10–19. As in Sirach, this history is a store of examples, a point that the Wisdom of Solomon underlines by omitting the names of the biblical personalities.

The most striking aspect of the Wisdom of Solomon is undoubtedly its use of Greek philosophy and in particular its acceptance of the Platonic idea of the immortality of the soul. On this point it contrasts sharply with Sirach, who held that "whether life is for ten or a hundred or a thousand years there is no inquiry about it in Hades" (Sir. 41:4). Wisdom's account of the judgment after death was also indebted to Jewish apocalyptic traditions such as we find in 1 Enoch, but the dominant tone of the work is Hellenistic. The sentiment that "a perishable body weighs down the soul" (9:15) was alien to Hebraic Judaism but had far-reaching influence on Christianity. Wisdom anticipates another doctrine of Catholic Christianity in chap. 13 where it appears to endorse the idea of revelation through nature, as Paul also does in Romans 1.

Another hymn in praise of wisdom is found in chap. 3 of the book of Baruch. This book is made up of segments of diverse origin, at least some of which were composed in Hebrew. They were appended to the book of Jeremiah in many manuscripts of the Greek Bible and are sometimes cited as part of that book. The wisdom poem is found in 3:9–4:4 and is reminiscent of that in Job 28, insofar as it emphasizes that humanity does not know the way to wisdom. Unlike Job, but like Sirach, Baruch concludes by identifying wisdom with "the book of the commandments of God" (4:1). Baruch, however, construes this identification in a way that is more nationalistic than what we find in any earlier Jewish wisdom book: "Happy are we, O Israel, for we know what is pleasing to God" (4:4).

Exhortations. We have noted already that the Wisdom of Solomon is presented as an exhortation to the kings of the earth, but the hortatory purpose of the book is pursued indirectly through reflections on the nature of wisdom and of the universe. A more direct form of exhortation is found in 4 Maccabees, which like Wisdom is a product of the Hellenistic Diaspora (possibly Antioch). The subject addressed is whether reason is sovereign over emotions. "Reason," however, is virtually equated with obedience to the law—the Jewish law in all its particularity, including dietary restrictions. Fidelity to the law is the point at issue in the stories of the Maccabean martyrs that are adduced as illustrations. The stories show that it is possible to be faithful to the full law, even in the face of torture. The reasonableness of such conduct is suggested by the hope for "a life of eternal blessedness" (17:18) and more particularly by the inherent nobility of virtue.

4 Maccabees is a rhetorical rather than philosophical work. It simply asserts that the Jewish law is in accord with reason. Granted this assumption, it is able to portray the conduct of the martyrs in terms that Greeks could respect. It is eclectic in its philosophy, with smatterings of Stoicism and Platonism. Its peculiarity lies in its combination of an uncompromising, particularistic adherence to the law and a thoroughly Hellenized consciousness, which placed a high value on philosophy even if it did not pursue it rigorously.

A very different homiletical work is found in the Letter of Jeremiah, which was most probably composed in Hebrew no later than the second century B.C. Sometimes it stands as an independent work in the manuscripts and sometimes it is attached to the book of Baruch. It is a straightforward polemic against idolatry, divided into segments by such pronouncements as "From this you will know that they are not gods; so do not fear them" (v. 23). It is devoid of any attempt to find common ground with the gentile world in the manner of Hellenistic compositions such as 4 Maccabees.

Prayers. The recitation of prayers is a characteristic feature of Jewish writings of the Hellenistic period. Sometimes prayers were added in the course of transmission of biblical books. The Hebrew book of Esther is remarkable for its lack not only of prayers but even of reference to the Deity. The Greek additions to Esther compensate for these deficiencies by placing prayers on the lips of Mordecai and Esther. They also mention that the Jews cried to God at the beginning of their problems (11:10, which comes before chap. 1 in the Gk.) and at the end Mordecai declares that "these things have come from God." The prayers of Mordecai and Esther are prayers for deliverance specific to their contexts. Esther uses the opportunity to protest that she had not eaten at Haman's table—an issue on which the Hebrew text was silent.

The Greek translation of Daniel is also embellished in chap. 3 by the addition of the prayers of Azariah and the three youths. These are traditional prayers, not specially composed for this context. The prayer of the three youths is appropriate to its context in the fiery furnace. It is a hymn reminiscent of Psalm 136 that gives thanks to the Lord for the works of creation. The Prayer of Azariah, in contrast, is a communal confession of sin, which is singularly inappropriate in the context. This type of prayer is very common in postexilic Judaism. Biblical examples can be found in Nehemiah 9 and Daniel 9 and a later example in the Qumran text "Words of the Heavenly Luminaries" (4QDibHam). Typically they contain a confession of sin, acknowledgement of God's justice, reference to the dejected state of Israel, and prayer for deliverance. They reflect an understanding of history that is characteristic of the Deuteronomistic writings. Since these prayers are widespread over a period of several centuries they were probably variations on a pattern of liturgical prayer. (Another prayer of the same type is found in Bar. 1:15–3:8, which has verbal parallels to the prayer in Daniel 9.)

The Prayer of Manasseh is an individual confession of sin that exhibits the same logic and pattern as the communal prayers. It begins by establishing the justice of God and follows with a confession of sin and plea for mercy. The inspiration for the prayer is evidently derived from 2 Chronicles 33, which tells of the repentance of Manasseh and refers to his prayer.

The book of Baruch concludes with another lengthy prayer in 4:5–5:9 that calls on Israel to take courage because God's punishment is not final. Once again, the predicament of Israel is understood as a punishment for sin, in accordance with Deuteronomistic theology. In this case, however, the emphasis is on the imminent restoration, and the language recalls Isaiah 40–55.

The book of Psalms in the LXX also includes an additional psalm, Psalm 151. A longer variant of this psalm has been found in Hebrew at Qumran. There is reason to think that the Greek Psalm 151 was a condensation of this Hebrew psalm and of another that followed it in the Qumran Psalms Scroll. The psalm is ascribed to David himself. In the Greek version it recalls the election of David and his triumph over Goliath.

This review has been confined to those prayers and psalms that are printed separately in modern editions of the Apocrypha. Prayers are scattered throughout the apocryphal books. Notable examples include the rousing prayer for divine intervention in Sirach 36, which is widely thought to be inserted out of context, and Solomon's prayer for wisdom in Wisdom of Solomon 9. The book of Tobit contains a confession of sin in chap. 3, benedictions by Tobias and Raguel in chap. 8, and a prayer of rejoicing by Tobit in chap. 13 that recalls the Song of Hannah in 1 Samuel 2. Judith has a song of victory in Judith 16 and there are laments for the desolation of Jerusalem in 1 Macc. 2:6–12; 3:45, 49–53.

OTHER EXTRACANONICAL LITERATURE

The Apocrypha can scarcely be said to be a representative collection of Jewish literature between the Bible and the Mishnah. Some major categories are underrepresented. The apocalyptic literature is represented only by 2 Esdras, which is one of the finer works of the genre, but somewhat atypical nonetheless. The Apocrypha includes no Testament as an independent work, although testaments are included in 1 Maccabees (2:49–70, testament of Mattathias) and Tobit (4:3–21, mainly moral instruction, and 14:3–11, mainly predictive). Sibylline Oracles, which flourished in Hellenistic Judaism from the second century B.C., are not represented. In general, the extensive literature dealing with eschatological prophecy was only minimally taken up. Biblical paraphrases, such as we find in *Jubilees* and *Pseudo-Philo*, are also omitted. The Dead Sea Scrolls have brought to light other genres of literature (Rules, Commentaries [*pesharim*]) that are not hinted at in this collection.

At least some books that were not finally included in the Apocrypha were sometimes regarded as authoritative in the early church. 1 *Enoch* is cited in the Letter of Jude and is probably alluded to in 1 Pet. 3:19–20 and 2 Pet. 2:4. It is cited as Scripture in the Letter of Barnabas and Tertullian argued that it should be accepted by Christians since it "made proclamation concerning the Lord" (*On Women's Dress* 1.3). *The Assumption of Moses* is also cited in Jude. Clement of Alexandria displayed familiarity with several Pseudepigrapha. Many of the Pseudepigrapha (*Jubilees*, 1 *Enoch*, *Ascension of Isaiah*) were preserved by the Ethiopian church, intermingled in the biblical manuscripts, and *Jubilees* at least was accepted as canonical (see Beckwith, pp. 478–505).

SIGNIFICANCE

The significance of this extracanonical literature is manifold. It is of great historical importance for understanding the variety within Jewish religion in the formative period of Christianity and of rabbinic Judaism. Stories and motifs from the Apocrypha have become embedded in Western culture—Handel wrote oratorios on Susanna and Judas Maccabeus. Italian and German operas were composed on the theme of Judith. Susanna, Tobit, and Judith were popular subjects for artists. A verse from 2 Esdras (6:42, which says that the waters occupy one-seventh part of the earth) is said to have inspired Columbus on his voyage of discovery (see Metzger, pp. xviii–xx).

The theological importance of the Apocrypha is considerable too. The very existence of this body of literature is a reminder that the canon, in any of its forms, is a selection from a wider corpus of traditional literature and that there was considerable fluidity on its boundaries. The recent revival of interest in the Apocrypha and Pseudepigrapha can only enrich our appreciation of the biblical heritage by helping us recover a fuller spectrum of the tradition.

Bibliography

Beckwith, R. *The Old Testament Canon of the New Testament Church.* Grand Rapids, MI: Eerdmans, 1985.

Charlesworth, J. H., ed. *The Old Testament Pseudepigrapha.* 2 vols. Garden City, NY: Doubleday, 1983, 1985.

Collins, J. J. *Between Athens and Jerusalem: Jewish Identity in the Hellenistic Diaspora.* New York: Crossroad, 1983.

———. *The Apocalyptic Imagination.* New York: Crossroad, 1984.

Leiman, S. Z. *The Canonization of Hebrew Scripture.* Hamden, CT: Archon, 1976.

Metzger, B., ed. *The Oxford Annotated Apocrypha.* Expanded edition. New York: Oxford University Press, 1977.

Nickelsburg, G. W. *Jewish Literature Between the Bible and the Mishnah.* Philadelphia: Fortress, 1981.

Sparks, H. F. D., ed. *The Apocryphal Old Testament.* Oxford: Clarendon, 1984.

Stone, M. E., ed. *Jewish Writings of the Second Temple Period.* Philadelphia: Fortress, 1984.

Sundberg, A. C. *The Old Testament of the Early Church.* Cambridge, MA: Harvard University Press, 1964.

1 ESDRAS

RALPH W. KLEIN

INTRODUCTION

The First Book of Esdras contains an alternate form of the text of 2 Chronicles 35–36, Ezra 1–10, Neh. 7:73–8:13, and an account of a contest in the court of Darius (1 Esd. 3:1–5:6) not attested elsewhere in the Bible.

The book is called Esdras *a* in the Septuagint (LXX), where it is distinguished from Esdras *b*, a literal Greek translation of the OT books of Ezra and Nehemiah. 1 Esdras is called 3 Ezra in the Latin Vulgate (Vg.), where it, the Prayer of Manasseh, and 2 Esdras (known there as 4, 5, and 6 Ezra) are printed as a supplement to the NT.

The relationship between 1 Esdras and other portions of the canon is as follows:

1 Esd. 1:1–22 = 2 Chron. 35:1–19
1 Esd. 1:23–24 = (no parallel)
1 Esd. 1:25–58 = 2 Chron. 35:20–36:21
1 Esd. 2:1–5a = 2 Chron. 36:22–23 / Ezra 1:1–3a
1 Esd. 2:5b–15 = Ezra 1:3b–11
1 Esd. 2:16–30 = Ezra 4:7–24
1 Esd. 3:1–5:6 = (no parallel)
1 Esd. 5:7–73 = Ezra 2:1–4:5
1 Esd. 6:1–9:36 = Ezra 5:1–10:44
1 Esd. 9:37–55 = Neh. 7:73–8:13a.

Except for the last section above, 1 Esdras omits everything from the book of Nehemiah. Neh. 7:73–8:13a is treated, probably correctly, as a part of the story of Ezra, without mention of Nehemiah. The major addition in 1 Esd. 3:1–5:6 recounts the wisdom of Zerubbabel and explains why Darius, the Persian king, authorized a return of the Jews from Babylon to Jerusalem and their rebuilding of the Temple, and why he supported financially and legally the postexilic religious establishment in Jerusalem. It also exalts Zerubbabel and, implicitly, the Davidic line.

Ezra 4:7–24 has been moved to a position before 1 Esd. 3:1–5:6 (at 1 Esd. 2:16–30). According to this passage, criticisms from the enemies of the Jews during the days of Artaxerxes led to the cessation of work on the Temple until the time of Darius, even though Artaxerxes ruled after Darius. 1 Esdras partially unscrambled this confusion by putting Darius' efforts to stop the Temple in 2:16–30 before his permission for Zerubbabel to rebuild the Temple in 3:1–5:6.

To some 1 Esdras represents a fragmentary copy of an earlier arrangement of the Chronicler's history. In this view all or most of 1 Chronicles 1 to 2 Chronicles 34 has been lost from the beginning of 1 Esdras and at least Neh. 8:13b–18 from the end. Recent studies, however, question whether there ever was a Chronicler's history consisting of a unified account of 1 and 2 Chronicles and Ezra (or Ezra and Nehemiah) (→ Chronicler).

Others, therefore, treat 1 Esdras as a more or less complete document that has been drawn from the materials now in 1 and 2 Chronicles, Ezra, and Nehemiah. They represent the integrity of the present book and seek to understand what its author or editor might have wanted to say by the present arrangement of materials. Tamara Eskenazi, for example, believes that the author of 1 Esdras wanted to conform the books of Ezra and Nehemiah to the ideology of the books of Chronicles by giving special emphasis to the centrality of David, the inclusive characteristics of Israel, the doctrine of retribution and the need to obey the prophets, and the Temple and its practices. Anne E. Gardner attempts to relate 1 Esdras as a complete book to the events and people of the Maccabean crisis. The reinterpretation of the death of Josiah in 1:23–24 shows that this disaster too was the result of sin and not divine caprice. The insertion of the story of the three bodyguards was to show that all the riches and power in the world are of no interest compared to rebuilding the Temple. The Temple's central importance is also emphasized by setting the beginning and ending of the book in the Temple, or at least in its vicinity.

Whether the book is a fragment or complete, whether its order represents an earlier form of the Chronicler's history or a compilation drawn from the canonical books of 2 Chronicles, Ezra, and Nehemiah, this much is certain: the addition in 1:23–24 helps to resolve the theological anomaly of Josiah's premature death, and the addition in 3:1–5:6 places great emphasis on the Davidic Zerubbabel and explains why the Persian Darius was moved to authorize the rebuilding of the Temple.

The Greek translation now contained in 1 Esdras, though relatively free, is based on an older and often shorter form of the Hebrew and Aramaic biblical text. Esdras *b* in the LXX is based on a Semitic text that closely resembles the later, Masoretic Text (MT).

COMMENTARY

(For passages with parallels elsewhere in the canon, readers are referred to the commentaries on the appropriate sections of 2 Chronicles, Ezra, and Nehemiah.)

1:1–2:30
Extracts from 2 Chronicles and Ezra

1:1–58
The Last Kings of Judah

1:1–22 (2 Chron. 35:1–19), Josiah's Passover. It is unlikely that 1 Esdras originally began at this point, since Josiah is not introduced in v. 1 as the king and no year is provided in the date formula of this verse (see 2 Chron. 34:8, where the date is given as Josiah's eighteenth year). The Levites slaughtered the Passover sacrifice as they had for the Passover of Hezekiah (2 Chron. 30:17), and the Passover was both roasted and boiled (cf. Exod. 12:8–9; Deut. 16:7). No Passover had been held like this one since the time of Samuel the prophet (1 Esd. 1:20; in 2 Kings 23:22 the last such Passover was held when the judges ruled Israel). The uniqueness of this Passover, in the opinion of the Chronicler, apparently consisted in the prominent role of the Levites.

1:23–24 (without canonical parallel), The Reason for the Fall of Israel. These verses are a supplement based on 1 Kings 13:2, 32 (a prophecy of the rise of Josiah) or 2 Kings 23:24–27. They explain that the evil of the people at the time of Josiah was so great that the judgmental words of the LORD eventually had to rise up against Israel. Without these verses some might conclude that the great piety of Josiah would have prevented the final destruction of Jerusalem that occurred a few years after his death. C. C. Torrey believes that these two verses were part of the original text of Chronicles.

1:25–33 (2 Chron. 35:20–27), The Death of Josiah. Josiah was killed in a battle with Pharaoh Neco of Egypt, near Megiddo, in 609 B.C. The Egyptian leader was on his way to the Euphrates to support the Assyrians, who had suffered a series of defeats at the hands of the Neo-Babylonian Empire. The death of Josiah at the age of forty is theologically unexplained in 2 Kings and in fact it seems to contradict the doctrine of retribution, which held that a person's fate corresponded to his or her deeds (→ Retribution). According to 2 Chron. 35:21, Neco sent messengers to Josiah warning him not to disobey the word of the LORD by opposing his march toward the Euphrates. In v. 28, 1 Esdras asserts that this word of the LORD that favored Neco was actually delivered by Jeremiah the prophet. By ignoring such a prophetic word in his attack on Neco, Josiah brought about his premature death. 1 Esdras reports that these events were recorded in the histories of the kings of Judea (cf. 2 Kings 23:28) while 2 Chron. 35:25 adds that the laments for Josiah were written in "the laments," a reference either to the biblical book of Lamentations or to some other similar collection.

1:34–58 (2 Chron. 36:1–21), The Successors of Josiah and the Destruction of Jerusalem. The names of the kings are confused in 1 Esdras: instead of the expected Jehoahaz in v. 34, the Greek text reads Jeconiah (= Jehoiachin), and instead of Jehoiachin in v. 43, the Greek text reads Jehoiakim. According to 2 Chron. 36:4 (1 Esd. 1:37 is defective), the king of Egypt made Eliakim king and then changed his name to Jehoiakim. Neco exiled Jehoahaz to Egypt according to 2 Chron. 36:4, but 1 Esdras reports in 1:38 that Jehoiakim brought Zarius (?) from Egypt.

1 Esdras 1:40 follows 2 Chron. 36:6 in reporting that Jehoiakim was taken to Babylonian exile (cf. 2 Kings 24:1, 5). 1 Esdras speaks of the king's uncleanness and impiety (v. 42), whereas 2 Chron. 36:8 mentions his abominations. Both 2 Chronicles (36:12) and 1 Esdras (1:47) criticize Zedekiah for refusing to submit to the word of the LORD delivered through Jeremiah. 1 Esdras adds that Zedekiah violated an oath sworn to Nebuchadnezzar and transgressed the laws of the LORD (v. 48).

When the Exile finally came, it lasted for seventy years, to fulfill the word of Jeremiah (v. 58; cf. Jer. 25:11; 29:10). During this time the land enjoyed its Sabbath rest in fulfillment of Lev. 26:34–35. Because the people had not made provision for proper Sabbath observance in the pre-exilic period, rest for the land was provided by the Exile. Through this Sabbath rest the word of the prophet Jeremiah has been linked to and interpreted by a passage from the Torah.

2:1–30
The Early Days of the Return

2:1–5a (2 Chron. 36:22–23; Ezra 1:1–3a), The Decree of Cyrus. The last verses of 2 Chronicles are repeated in the opening verses of Ezra. 1 Esdras does not repeat the doublet at the end of Chronicles and the beginning of Ezra, and this fact has led a number of scholars to suppose that the books of 1 and 2 Chronicles and (at least) Ezra once formed a part of the supposed Chronicler's history of Israel (see the "Introduction" above). Cyrus, under the influence of the Lord of

Israel, decreed that the Judean exiles could go home and restore the Temple to fulfill the word of Jeremiah (e.g., Jer. 51:1, 6; cf. Isa. 41:2, 25; 44:28; 45:1).

2:5b–15 (Ezra 1:3b–11), The Return Under Sheshbazzar.

After Cyrus had given permission for the return to the land of Israel and the rebuilding of the Temple, he urged that the returnees be supported with generous offerings by their neighbors. He also restored the Temple vessels, which had been captured by Nebuchadnezzar (2 Kings 24:13; 25:13–16; 2 Chron. 36:10, 18; Jer. 52:17–19), to Sheshbazzar, the governor. This restoration helped to establish continuity between the First and Second Temples, just as the new Temple was set on its old site (Ezra 6:3; 1 Esd. 6:24) and the altar on its original foundations (Ezra 3:3; 1 Esd. 5:50).

2:16–30 (Ezra 4:7–24), Letters to and from Artaxerxes.

According to Ezra 4:4–5 (1 Esd. 5:72–73), the people of the land harassed the Jews and prevented the completion of the Temple during the time of Cyrus (559–530 B.C.) and up to the second year of Darius (522–486 B.C.). The next verses, Ezra 4:6–23, justify the Jewish rejection of help from their neighbors (Ezra 4:3), since subsequent history—fifty years later—proved that the Samarians had no positive interest in the restoration of Jerusalem (→Samarians). Ezra 4:24 returns chronologically to 4:5, the cessation of work on the Temple that lasted until 520 B.C.

1 Esdras lacks an equivalent for most of the obscure Ezra 4:6, and it has moved the whole unit under discussion to a different place than it occupies in the book of Ezra. Because of the ringing endorsement of the Temple by Darius in 1 Esd. 3:1–5:6, it was necessary to put the account of Darius stopping the Temple building earlier. Thus, readers of 1 Esdras are not able to treat 1 Esd. 2:16–29 (Ezra 4:6–23) as a digression designed to show the faithless character of the Samarians. This shift in location also separates this passage from its continuation in 1 Esd. 6:1–7:9 (Ezra 5:1–6:18). Ezra 4:7–6:18 is written in Aramaic and often referred to as the Aramaic Chronicle.

Various Samarian leaders in the time of Artaxerxes I (465–424 B.C.) complained in writing to the Persian king about the rebellious character of Jerusalem. They charged that the Jews were repairing the walls of the city and laying the foundations for the Temple (2:18; "the building of the Temple is now going on," 2:20; cf. the more general "repairing the foundations" in Ezra 4:12). These activities, according to the accusers, would lead to loss of taxes for the empire and open revolt. They implored the king to check the official archives that would show that the Jews had always been rebellious and that

this troubling characteristic, in fact, had been the reason for the destruction of Jerusalem by the Babylonians. They alleged that the present rebellion would deprive the king of his Syro-Palestinian holdings.

The king's records confirmed the charges that Jerusalem had long been the home of rebels and cruel kings (2:26–27; Ezra 4:18–20). He ordered all work on the city to cease, and the Samarian officials hurried to Jerusalem with a military force and stopped the building. Hence the building of the Temple ceased until the second year of Darius, or 520 B.C. According to both 1 Esdras and Ezra, the reason for the delay in Temple building was the interference by local obstructionists, not the indifference of the restoration community, as in Haggai and Zechariah.

3:1–5:6

The Contest of the Bodyguards

3:1–17a, What One Thing Is Strongest?

King Darius prepared a great banquet for all the officials of the Persian Empire, which stretched from India to Ethiopia (cf. Esther 1:1; 8:9). While there is a hint that the king had insomnia (1 Esd. 3:3), the king is asleep during the initial contest among the bodyguards. Strangely, the bored bodyguards determined for themselves what prizes the king would award in the contest (vv. 5–7). Whoever would come up with the wisest answer about what is the strongest would receive fine clothing, a gold bed, and an exalted position as "kinsman" of the king. In his retelling of the account, first-century Jewish historian Josephus has the king himself propose the contest and promise the rewards (*Antiquities of the Jews* 11.3.2 §35).

The bodyguards decided to put their proposals under the king's pillow and to abide by the decision he and the three nobles of Persia would make. The first two bodyguards proposed wine and the king respectively as the two strongest things in all the world. The third suggested that women are the strongest, but then changed his answer to truth, since it is the victor over all things. When the king woke up and learned about the contest, he summoned all his officials and ordered the three bodyguards to explain the reasons for their opinions.

3:17b–24, The Speech of the First Bodyguard.

Each speech has a common introductory formula ("Gentlemen," followed by a rhetorical question), and each ends in a similar way ("he stopped speaking"). Wine demonstrates its strength by equally leading astray the mind of all classes in society. Wine makes

771

people forget sorrows or poverty, but it also makes people forget to be friendly. People drunk with wine fight, and when they sober up, they cannot remember what they have done. After exploring the ambiguities of wine, the wise bodyguard concludes that it must be the strongest thing, since it forces people to do the things he has just described.

4:1–12, The Speech of the Second Bodyguard. References to men as the strongest (v. 2; cf. 4:14) have led to the proposal that a speech about the strength of men has been lost. The second bodyguard concentrates primarily on the ambivalent qualities of the king. Kings get people to fight for them blindly and to turn over all their booty to the royal treasury. Soldiers hardly ever wonder whether the goal of war justifies the supreme sacrifice. Farmers too are controlled by the king, who forces them to pay taxes on their produce. The word obey is prominent in this speech (vv. 3, 5, 10, 11, 12). People fight for or farm for the king even though he is only a man (v. 6). In addition, the king eats, drinks, and sleeps, and so he is vulnerable. Yet no one attacks him or goes off to take care of his own business (v. 11). Seven times in vv. 7–9, the speaker notes that whatever the king commands, his subjects do.

4:13–41, The Speech of the Third Bodyguard. The fact that Zerubbabel suddenly appears without advance notice in v. 13 probably means that the contest among the bodyguards once served another (non-Jewish?) function before it was included in 1 Esdras. Zerubbabel first reviews the previous proposals about the king, men, and wine before turning to consider women. Since women are the originators of kings and other rulers, by giving birth to them, they are clearly superior to these political figures. Women also raise the men who plant vineyards, which in turn produce wine. Women make men's clothes and affect their reputation. Men who have accumulated all sorts of treasures drop them in open-mouthed amazement when they gaze at a beautiful woman. Men leave their parents and their native lands to live out their lives with their wives. Hence, the bodyguard argues, "women rule over you."

While soldiers are forced by the king's power to fight, men voluntarily undertake all sorts of military or dangerous adventures for the women they love. They face wild animals or even take up lives of crime so that they can lay their trophies at the feet of a woman. Many lose their minds because of women, become slaves because of them, and perish or sin because of them.

The third bodyguard, Zerubbabel, even dares to contrast the strength of women with that of King Darius. While foreign lands fear him, his concubine Apame playfully takes his crown and puts it on her head and slaps the king with her left hand. The king looks at her in open-mouthed amazement like the rich men noted above. He laughs when she laughs; when she becomes angry, he flatters her. This defense of the strength of women is an incisive critique of the second bodyguard's proposal about the strength of kings.

Just when it seems as if the case is closed— the king and his nobles look at one another, astonished at Zerubbabel's boldness and ready to make their decision (v. 33)—the third bodyguard begins to assert the superiority of truth as the strongest of all phenomena (cf. Ps. 117:2; 146:6). "Truth" may connote rightness, steadfastness, and uprightness in addition to its usual meanings. Truth is a quality of God. Earth and heaven call upon and bless truth; all the previous candidates for the strongest thing— wine, the king, women, the sons of men and their works—are deemed unrighteous or deceptive. Because of their unrighteousness people die, but truth is strong and prevails forever and ever. Truth controls the strength, kingship, power, and majesty of all the ages (1 Esd. 4:40; cf. 1 Chron. 29:11–13 and the doxological conclusion to the Lord's Prayer). Truth is an impartial judge. That is why Zerubbabel could tell the truth about the king's subordination to his concubine in 1 Esd. 4:29–32. Finally, the bodyguard prays, "Blessed be the God of truth!" (This prayer hints that God himself may even be stronger than truth; cf. also vv. 34– 35a.) The speech of the third bodyguard leads the people to acclaim his answer. The Latin rendering of their cheer—*Magna est veritas et praevalet* ("Great is truth and it will prevail")— has become a well-known proverb.

4:42–57, Zerubbabel's Prize. Darius recognized Zerubbabel as the wisest of his bodyguards and honored him as a kinsman (v. 42; cf. 3:7). Thanks to the story of the three bodyguards, Zerubbabel becomes in 1 Esdras the most important person of the restoration period. He is wise, pious, and loves the people. God gave him the wisdom that won the contest. As in Daniel, a Jew has pitted his wisdom against that of gentile rivals and has won both the contest and the king's favor. His personal success and his favor with Darius did not make him forget his duty. Zerubbabel reminded the king of vows that he and Cyrus had made to build Jerusalem, to return the ritual vessels there, and to rebuild the Temple. Though 1 Esd. 1:55 (2 Chron. 36:19) reports that the kings of the Chaldeans destroyed the Temple, v. 45 blames that action on the Edomites (cf. Ezek. 36:5; Obad. 11–14).

In his favorable reply (1 Esd. 4:47–57) Darius combined elements of the decree of Cyrus

(Ezra 1:2–4; 6:3–5), his own affirmation of this decree (Ezra 6:6–12), and Artaxerxes' authorization of Nehemiah (Neh. 2:5, 8). He granted Zerubbabel and the other returnees safe conduct, provided cedar wood from Lebanon to rebuild the Temple, and exempted the Jews from governmental searches of their houses. Darius also excused the Jews from taxes and expelled the Idumeans (Edomites) from their territory. He provided for annual grants for rebuilding the Temple and for maintaining the regular worship, perhaps hoping that sacrifices and prayers would be made for him and his sons (cf. 1 Esd. 6:31; Ezra 6:10). Like his predecessor Cyrus (Ezra 6:5), he commanded that the Temple vessels be restored. In 1 Esdras and Ezra the Temple vessels are returned also by Sheshbazzar (1 Esd. 2:14–15; Ezra 1:11; cf. 1 Esd. 6:18–19; Ezra 5:14–15), in addition to Zerubbabel. The commandment to offer seventeen daily sacrifices (1 Esd. 4:52) is unattested elsewhere in the OT.

4:58–63, The Jewish Response. Zerubbabel (called only the "young man" in v. 58) offered appropriate thanksgiving to the King of Heaven, who had granted him wisdom. When he shared the good news with other Jews in Babylon, they rejoiced for seven days, a response more enthusiastic than seems to have been the case historically.

5:1–6, The Leaders of the Return. Darius provided the caravan with a cavalry escort of one thousand and sent them off with martial music. The names in v. 5 show some confusion. Jeshua is the high priest of the early postexilic period (see Ezra 3:2). The other figure is the governor Zerubbabel. Read: "Zerubbabel, son of Shealtiel, son of Jehoiachin, of the house of David . . ." The book of Ezra makes no mention of Zerubbabel's Davidic descent, perhaps because the author was receptive to Persian domination and attached no hopes for deliverance to the house of David.

5:7–9:55

Extracts from Ezra and Nehemiah

5:7–7:15

The Rebuilding of the Temple

5:7–46 (Ezra 2:1–70; cf. Neh. 7:6–73a), The List of Those Who Returned. This list may be a composite summary of a number of returns to Palestine during the reigns of Cyrus and his successor Cambyses, though in 1 Esdras it is used to describe the return of Zerubbabel during the reign of Darius. Twelve leaders are listed in v. 8 (instead of Bigvai [RSV] read

Nahamani [cf. Neh. 7:7]). Laity are listed in 1 Esd. 5:9–23, priests in vv. 24–25, Levites and other Temple personnel in vv. 26–35, and those who could not prove their ancestry in vv. 36–40. The governor Attharias (= tirshata' of the Hebrew text [Ezra 2:63; Neh. 7:65]) seems to be falsely identified in 1 Esd. 5:40 with Nehemiah (cf. Neh. 8:9; 10:1). The list presupposes that the community in Palestine was composed almost exclusively of Jews who had been in exile (cf. Jer. 24:10), though this does not conform to historical fact.

5:47–65 (Ezra 3:1–13), The Altar and the Temple Foundation. The text of Ezra implies that the altar was set up without delay, in September, 538 B.C., though it has confused Zerubbabel with Sheshbazzar. According to the arrangement of materials in 1 Esdras, however, the altar was reestablished only in the reign of Darius (522–486 B.C.). The people celebrated the Feast of Booths (or Tabernacles), which began on the fifteenth day of the seventh month, and offered up the daily sacrifices required for this feast. Thereafter, all appointed feasts were kept (1 Esd. 5:52).

The foundation of the Temple was laid on the new moon of the second month of the second year of their return (v. 57, lacking in Ezra 3; but see 1 Esd. 5:56 and Ezra 3:8). In 1 Esdras this account must refer to 520 B.C., a date that causes difficulty in 1 Esd. 5:63, where some were still alive who had seen the First Temple that had been destroyed sixty-seven years earlier. In Ezra 3:8 the "second year" refers to the second year of the exiles' work on the house of God, not to the second year after their return from exile.

The ceremony at the beginning of the repairs on the Temple echoes that of Solomon at the dedication of the Temple (1 Kings 8; 2 Chron. 5–7) and of David at the bringing of the Ark to Jerusalem (1 Chron. 15–16). Older people, who had seen the First Temple, wept, while many others rejoiced. The Greek of 1 Esd. 5:65 suggests that people could not hear the trumpets because of the weeping of the people. The corresponding Hebrew verse (Ezra 3:13) notes that the people could not distinguish the sounds of shouts of joy from the shouts of weeping.

5:66–73 (Ezra 4:1–5), Opponents Stop the Building of the Temple. Adversaries heard the sound of the trumpets and came to find out what was going on. The Jewish leaders refused the offer of these enemies, who claimed to have been worshiping the LORD ever since Esarhaddon had brought them to Palestine. The placement of these verses in the reign of Darius by 1 Esd. 5:6 (cf. 5:47, 56, 57) causes great difficulties, since Zerubbabel and Jeshua seem to be under orders from Cyrus, the second Persian king before Darius, to rebuild the Temple. It may be that 1 Esdras originally had only a two-month interruption of work during the reign of Darius, and that the present confusion results from partial assimilation to the text of Ezra.

6:1–7:15 (Ezra 5:1–6:22), The Temple Completed. Work on the Temple resumed in the second year of Darius (6:1; this date is lacking in Ezra 5:1), thanks to the encouragement of the prophets Haggai and Zechariah and the leadership of Zerubbabel and Jeshua. Tattenai and Shetharbozenai (transcribed as Sisinnes and Sathrabuzanes in 1 Esdras), Persian officials of Coele Syria and Phoenicia (called the province "Beyond the River" in Ezra 5:3), questioned the Jews about their authorization for Temple building and demanded (1 Esd. 6:12; Ezra 5:10 "asked") a list of the leaders' names. Fortunately, they decided to bring their concerns to Darius instead of trying to stop the project. In their letter to Darius they quoted the Jews' self-defense (1 Esd. 6:13–20), in which the Jews recited the history of the Temple from its erection by Solomon to its destruction by Nebuchadnezzar and to the authorization to rebuild it by Cyrus. They claimed that the Temple vessels were given by Cyrus to their governors Sheshbazzar and Zerubbabel (6:18; Ezra 5:14 mentions only Sheshbazzar). The Persian officials concluded their letter by asking Darius if the claim of Cyrus's approval for the Temple was true.

Darius found the decree of Cyrus in Ecbatana and ordered the Persian officials not to interfere with the Temple and to allow Zerubbabel, the governor of the Jews, and his colleagues to continue (1 Esd. 6:27). The text of Ezra (6:7) does not identify the governor by name, nor does it call him the servant of the LORD (cf. also 1 Esd. 6:29; Ezra 6:8). Darius ordered financial support for the Temple and for the sacrificial service that would be carried on there. He also put any opponents of the Temple under the threat of capital punishment (1 Esd. 6:32). Verse 33 refers to the LORD who is "called upon" at the Temple; the corresponding text of Ezra (6:12) refers to God "who has caused his name to dwell there."

The Persian officials cooperated with the Jews, and the work proceeded, encouraged by Haggai and Zechariah, the command of God, and the consent of Cyrus, Darius, and Artaxerxes (1 Esd. 7:1–4). The latter king, of course, ruled long after the Temple was completed. Perhaps his provisions for the Temple at the time of Ezra led to the addition of his name here. The Temple was completed on the twenty-third (7:5; Ezra 6:15: third) day of the month Adar, in the sixth year of Darius (April 1, 515 B.C.). The twenty-third of Adar fell on a Friday; the third on a Sabbath. At the dedica-

tion the priests and Levites performed the appropriate sacrifices as prescribed in the Pentateuch (the author of 1 Chron. 23–26 attributed such prescriptions to David). 1 Esdras adds that the gatekeepers were at each gate (7:9; this reference is lacking in Ezra 6:18).

Subsequently (in the text of Ezra the language switches from Aramaic back to Hebrew at this point), the community kept the Passover and the Feast of Unleavened Bread in thanksgiving for the help given them by Darius, who here is given the unusual title of "the king of the Assyrians" (1 Esd. 7:15; Ezra 6:22). At the rededications of the Temple in the time of Hezekiah and Josiah, Passover was also observed (2 Chron. 30:13–27; 2 Chron. 35:1–19).

8:1–9:55
The Career of Ezra

8:1–67 (Ezra 7:1–8:36), Ezra's Trip to Jerusalem. Fifty-seven years later, in the seventh year of Artaxerxes (458 B.C.), Ezra, a priest and scribe, was sent to Jerusalem to investigate the situation there on the basis of the law. Ezra's priestly status is demonstrated by the genealogy in 8:1–2. The king's letter (8:9–24; the text of Ezra 7:12–26 is in Aramaic) commanded Erza to lead Jews to Jerusalem, deliver gifts to the Temple, make inquiry about how the law was being implemented in Judah and Jerusalem, and appoint judges to administer and teach the law.

Ezra expressed his thanksgiving at the beginning of a first person narrative (1 Esd. 8:25–90; Ezra 7:27–9:15). After a list of those who were ready to return with Ezra (1 Esd. 8:28–40; Ezra 8:1–14), Ezra sought to find additional priests and Levites to go with him to Jerusalem; in the book of Ezra only the absence of Levites is mentioned. Thirty-eight descendants of Levi were found, in addition to 220 Temple servants. Ezra fasted and prayed for protection but did not seek a royal escort, lest that be construed as a lack of trust in the power of the LORD. He entrusted the enormous gifts he was bringing to twelve priests, who were charged with delivering the gifts to the authorities in Jerusalem. The inflated totals—equal to the income of 100,000 to 500,000 people—may be an attempt to give glory to the Temple. The king, his officials, and all Israel had given these gifts (1 Esd. 8:55) just as they did for the construction of Solomon's Temple (1 Chron. 26:26).

With God's help Ezra's entourage arrived safe and sound in Jerusalem and turned over the gifts to two priests and two Levites. A series of animal sacrifices—12 bulls, 96 rams, 72 lambs, and 12 he-goats—may express the idea that the restoration community was "all Israel," since the numbers are all multiples of twelve.

8:68–9:36 (Ezra 9:1–10:44), A Crisis over Mixed Marriages. Ezra was informed that a number of people, including the leaders, had married foreign wives, a situation that had the potential of leading to syncretistic practices. After expressing shock and mourning for this iniquity, Ezra confessed Israel's sin throughout its history but also noted the gracious actions of God that had recently given them a root and a name. The LORD had also brought them into favor with the Persian kings who glorified the Temple of the LORD and raised Zion from desolation (1 Esd. 8:81; cf. the more modest claims in Ezra 9:9). This restored community now had violated the law and the prophets by intermarrying with the peoples of the land, and this raised the possibility that God would destroy the community without root, seed, or name.

At the suggestion of Shecaniah (Gk., Jeconiah), Ezra led the people in taking an oath to divorce their foreign wives (1 Esd. 8:91–96; Ezra 10:1–5). In response to a proclamation that threatened severe penalties, an assembly was held of all the tribes of Judah and Benjamin in Jerusalem on the twentieth day of the ninth month. The multitude listened to Ezra and agreed to divorce their foreign wives, though they asked for additional time because of the large number of people involved and the inclement weather and decided to turn the matter over to a special investigative commission. Ezra appointed the commission on the new moon of the tenth month, and it completed its work by the new moon of the first month. Thus, within a year of Ezra's departure from Babylon (1 Esd. 8:61), a purified community had been created in Jerusalem. The account closes in 8:18–36 (Ezra 10:18–44) with a list of 101 or 102 priests, Levites, and laity who had intermarried. The problem, which was primarily confined to the upper classes, involved only a very small percent of the population.

9:37–55 (Neh. 7:73–8:13a), Ezra Reads the Law. 1 Esdras appears to contain an equivalent to Neh. 7:73, the last verse of the list in Nehemiah 7. If this judgment is correct, the compiler of 1 Esdras probably knew the present arrangement of the books of Ezra and Nehemiah. Some argue that 1 Esdras did not know about Nehemiah 1–7 and that his placement of Nehemiah 8 right after Ezra 10 represents the original location for this chapter. Most are agreed that the events of Nehemiah 8 belong *historically* in the context of Ezra 10.

Ezra read the law to the assembly on the first day of the seventh month, at the east gate of the Temple. The book from which Ezra read for five to six hours (1 Esd. 9:41) was very likely some form of the Pentateuch. The people assented to the law by calling out "Amen" and by prostrating themselves on the ground. Thirteen Levites taught the law to the assembly by explaining what had been read (v. 48).

Verse 49 should be emended to read: "Ezra the chief priest and reader said to the Levites, who were teaching the multitudes . . ." The Greek text has the "governor" (*Attharatēs*) address Ezra and the Levites (cf. RSV and Neh. 8:9). Ezra assured the Levites that the day was a holy feast day, and that there was no reason to mourn since the LORD would exalt them. Inspired by what they had heard, the community prepared for a festive meal, in which those who had nothing could also share. The book of 1 Esdras breaks off in mid-sentence in 9:55, "And they came together . . ." The Hebrew text of the corresponding verse in Neh. 8:13 reads: "And on the second day the heads of the fathers' houses of all the people, with the priests and the Levites, gathered together to Ezra the scribe in order to study the words of the law." Did 1 Esdras originally end in mid-sentence, with this whole verse, or with all of Neh. 8:13–18, the account of the celebration of the Feast of Booths (Feast of Tabernacles)? According to Neh. 8:17 there had been no Feast of Booths like this since the days of Jeshua (Joshua; cf. 2 Chron. 30:26; 2 Chron. 35:18). Josephus, who follows 1 Esdras in the *Antiquities*, alludes to all of Neh. 8:13–18 (*Antiquities of the Jews* 11.5.5 §157).

Bibliography

Crenshaw, J. "The Contest of Darius' Guards." In *Images of Man and God*. Edited by David M. Gunn. Sheffield: Almond, 1981. Pp. 74–88.

Eskenazi, T. C. "The Chronicler and the Composition of 1 Esdras." *Catholic Biblical Quarterly* 48 (1986): 39–61.

Gardner, A. E. "The Purpose and Date of I Esdras." *Journal of Jewish Studies* 37 (1986): 18–27.

Myers, J. M. *I & II Esdras*. Anchor Bible, 42. Garden City, NY: Doubleday, 1974.

Nickelsburg, G. W. E. "The Bible Rewritten and Expanded." In *Jewish Writings of the Second Temple Period*. Compendia Rerum Iudaicarum ad Novum Testamentum, 2.2. Edited by M. E. Stone. Philadelphia: Fortress, 1984. Pp. 89–156.

Torrey, C. C. *Ezra Studies*. Prolegomenon by W. F. Stinespring. New York: KTAV, 1970 (1910).

2 ESDRAS

MICHAEL E. STONE
with
THEODORE A. BERGREN

INTRODUCTION

Names and Parts

A number of writings in Jewish and Christian tradition are connected with the figure of Ezra, or Esdras, as the name is rendered in Greek. In the Greek and Latin Bible manuscripts that preserve the most familiar of these works, it was customary to distinguish them by number (i.e., 1 Esdras, 2 Esdras, 3 Esdras, etc.). Unfortunately, the Septuagint (the Greek translation, LXX), the Latin Vulgate, many later Latin manuscripts, and the English editions all use different numbering systems. Complicating the situation even more is the fact that the Second Book of Esdras actually consists of three independent writings (chaps. 1–2, chaps. 3–14, chaps. 15–16). Modern biblical scholars customarily use either a system of numbering derived from the Latin Vulgate or one derived from the later Latin manuscripts. Here we will use the one derived from the Vulgate in which 1 Ezra is the canonical book of Ezra; 2 Ezra is the canonical book of Nehemiah; 3 Ezra is the book of 1 Esdras in the English Apocrypha; and 4 Ezra is the central portion of 2 Esdras (i.e., 2 Esdras 3–14). To identify the two independent writings that accompany 4 Ezra, the title 5 Ezra is used to refer to 2 Esdras 1–2, while 6 Ezra identifies 2 Esdras 15–16.

Literary Analysis and Description

5 Ezra. 5 Ezra, which was composed as an independent literary unit, is made up of two parts: a prophetic indictment of God's people (1:4–2:9) and a promise of redemption to a new people (2:10–48).

4 Ezra. 4 Ezra is an apocalypse, a form of literature in which heavenly secrets, often including information about the impending end of days, are revealed to a seer. Such revelations are frequently presented as visions, mediated by an angel (see the books of Daniel and Revelation). 4 Ezra consists of seven such visions, separated by small narrative units. The first three visions take the form of dialogues between Ezra, the pseudonymous author (→ Pseudonym), and an angel of God. The fourth is a waking experience of the heavenly Jerusalem; the fifth and sixth are symbolic dreams interpreted by an angel. The seventh vision relates Ezra's receipt of sacred scriptures from God and his transmission of them.

6 Ezra. 6 Ezra may have been written as an appendix to 4 Ezra. In literary form the work moves from prophetic prediction of eschatological woes (15:5–16:34) to exhortation of God's people (16:35–78). In content, 6 Ezra is heavily dependent upon the OT prophetic writings.

Text and Original Language

5 Ezra. 5 Ezra was probably written in Greek, although it survives only in two significantly different Latin versions.

4 Ezra. 4 Ezra is a Jewish work, originally written in Hebrew. The Hebrew original was translated into Greek and from Greek into a variety of languages by different churches: Latin, Ethiopic, Syriac, Georgian, Arabic, Armenian, and Coptic. The Hebrew and Greek versions are lost, except for a few quotations, and all modern translations of the book are based on these later "daughter" versions.

6 Ezra. Although a fragment of 6 Ezra exists in Greek, the book's probable language of composition, the work survives in full only in two Latin versions.

Historical, Social, and Religious Setting

5 Ezra. The date, place of origin, and authorship of 5 Ezra are uncertain. The contents of the book suggest, however, that it was composed during the second century A.D. by a Christian who was writing in the context of a dispute with Judaism.

4 Ezra. We can be more confident about the circumstances of the composition of 4 Ezra. The book stems from the last decade of the first century A.D. and was composed in reaction to the Roman destruction of Jerusalem in A.D. 70. Its primary concern, therefore, is to understand that traumatic event. To do this the book charts Ezra's development from distress to consolation. This development is paralleled by his growth as a visionary until, by the end of the sixth vision, he is designated a prophet. Full consolation has also brought full prophetic status. Thus another major concern of the book, the restoration of the tradition of secrets concerning the eschaton, or end-time, is made possible by Ezra's consolation.

Little is known about the social setting of the book, although it is possible to point to literary connections between 4 Ezra and other Jewish writings. Especially close are the *Syriac Apocalypse of Baruch*, which is dependent on 4 Ezra and written somewhat later, and the *Biblical Antiquities* of Pseudo-Philo, which seems to be earlier than 4 Ezra. In addition, the eagle vision of 4 Ezra (chaps. 11-12) is explicitly related to the vision of Daniel 7 (see 4 Ezra 12:11). Whether these literary relationships imply a social, historical continuity or something about the author's self-conscious sense of writing in a tradition cannot be finally established.

It is possible that the dialogues between Ezra and the angel in the first three visions reflect the conflicting viewpoints of two different groups in society. It seems more fruitful, however, to think of the conflicts in the book as reflecting the author's inner life and developing perspective. In its general views and attitudes, 4 Ezra seems to be close to rabbinic Judaism as it developed in the decades after the destruction of the Temple in A.D. 70.

6 Ezra. 6 Ezra was written to encourage a community in a time of persecution. Internal indications suggest a date in the late third century A.D. (see commentary below on 15:28-33). The work is usually regarded as a Christian composition, although Jewish authorship cannot be excluded.

Role in Religious Communities

5 Ezra. The texts of 5 and 6 Ezra were joined with 4 Ezra at some time before A.D. 800. (For the historical influence of the combined work, see commentary below under 4 Ezra.) The latter part of 5 Ezra (2:33-48) exerted a strong influence upon the liturgy of the Roman church.

4 Ezra. The role of 4 Ezra in Judaism remains largely unknown, since Jewish tradition lost it at an early date. Its wide circulation among the Christian churches indicates its popularity there. 4 Ezra was on the fringe of canonical scriptures in the Latin church down to the Council of Trent and is usually included in manuscripts of the Latin Bible (the Vulgate). Its position was similar in the Armenian church. Other churches seem to have cherished it but did not consider it fully part of Scripture. The "Prayer of Ezra" (8:20-36) had an independent life in the Latin and Syriac liturgical traditions.

6 Ezra. 6 Ezra does not seem to have had a strong influence in Jewish or Christian com-

munities. It is quoted extensively, however, by the British historian Gildas (sixth century A.D.).

COMMENTARY

PART ONE: 1:1-2:48

The Fifth Book of Ezra

A short work composed independently of 4 Ezra and 6 Ezra, 5 Ezra depicts Ezra as a prophet pronouncing judgment on God's people and announcing the transferral of God's patrimony to a new people or new "nations."

1:1-3

Ascription

The book is ascribed to "the prophet Ezra," whose priestly genealogy is traced (cf. Ezra 7:1-5; 1 Esd. 8:1-2). The designation of Ezra as "prophet" is unusual. In Ezra-Nehemiah and 1 Esdras he is described as "priest" or "scribe."

1:4-2:9

Prophetic Indictment

At God's command, Ezra indicts God's people, Israel, for their continual disobedience to the divine commandments. The present people will be abandoned, and God's inheritance will be given to a new people.

1:4-23, Historical Recital. After being commissioned by God as a prophet, Ezra recalls God's mighty acts for Israel during the Exodus. This historical review touches upon various well-known highlights of the biblical Exodus story but also includes several incidents not mentioned there (see vv. 11, 20b). Interwoven with the elements of the historical recital are rhetorical questions and statements of exasperation uttered by God (vv. 7b-9; 14b; 15b-17a; 21b), emphasizing the people's persistent unfaithfulness.

Such rehearsals of God's saving acts occur frequently in the Hebrew Bible (see, e.g., Pss. 105 and 106; Ezek. 20). This recital is especially close to the prayer in Neh. 9:6-31 (attributed to Ezra in the LXX) and to Psalm 78. In fact it may have been modeled on the latter. While the present passage serves as a prelude to God's indictment of the unfaithful people, a very different use of such a historical summary is made in 4 Ezra 3:4-27 (see commentary below).

1:24-37, Pronouncement of Judgment. On the basis of the incriminating evidence brought forward in the historical recital, God delivers an indictment against his people. He will turn and "give [his] name" to "other nations," who will be characterized by qualities of gratitude, obedience, and belief.

The simile of the hen gathering her brood and the context of vv. 30–33 have close parallels in the NT synoptic Gospels (cf. esp. Matt. 23:30–38). These parallels are interpreted by most commentators as evidence for Christian authorship of 5 Ezra.

1:38–40, Vision of the Coming People. Ezra, addressed by God as "father," is summoned by God to observe "the people coming from the east." Language and images that had earlier been used to describe the return of Israel from exile (cf. Bar. 4:36; 5:5) and the expectation of the eschatological return of the dispersed tribes of Israel (cf. 4 Ezra 13:46–47) are here applied to the new people of God. In a symbolic way the heritage of Israel is given to this people. God announces that the leaders who will be given to the people coming from the east will include the three patriarchs and the twelve minor prophets.

2:1–7, Further Pronouncement of Judgment. In a passage strongly recalling Bar. 4:11–21, Jerusalem, the "mother" of the people who have "sinned before the Lord God," bewails her children's sins. Whereas in Baruch Jerusalem sees her children returning from the east (Bar. 5:5), here Ezra is again invoked as "father" to testify against both mother and children and so bring about their destruction. This summons to Ezra (2:5–7) is often interpreted as a reference to the destruction of Jerusalem in A.D. 70 or 135.

2:8–9, Woe Against Assyria. The next section, in which God threatens Assyria with the punishment of Sodom and Gomorrah, seems incongruous in its context. It is not clear whom the author intends to identify as "Assyria."

2:10–41
Prophetic Exhortation of the New People

The focus of the book shifts from indictment of God's former people to encouragement of the newly chosen people.

2:10–14, Blessing and Instruction. God announces that his new people will inherit blessings previously reserved for Israel (vv. 10–11). That 5 Ezra is not a Jewish work in its present form is clear from this deprecatory reference to Israel. In addition, there are numerous echoes of phrases from the NT in these verses (cf. Matt. 24:22; Mark 13:37; Luke 11:9–10).

2:15–32, Exhortation of the Mother. The image of the mother, introduced in 2:2–6, is elaborated. In contrast to the previous passage, however, here the mother and her role are depicted in positive terms. The prophet encourages the mother to embrace her sons (v. 15) and, after enumerating the eschatological delights awaiting her children, informs her of her earthly, social responsibilities (vv. 20–23). The mother is reassured that when the day of tribulation comes, her children will receive "the first place in [God's] resurrection" (v. 23). The emphasis on eschatology (vv. 18–19, 24, 26–30) and resurrection (vv. 16, 23, 31) is especially pronounced.

The description of the mother in 2:15–32 is presented in deliberate contrast to that found in 2:2–6. In Bar. 4:8–35, which seems to have influenced the author of 5 Ezra, the mother in both her desolate and joyful aspects represents Jerusalem. In 5 Ezra, however, though the sorrowing mother appears to be Jerusalem, the book's Christian tenor has persuaded many commentators that the mother addressed in 2:15–32 stands for the church.

2:33–41, Encouragement of the Nations. Ezra, now speaking in the first person, states that he was commanded by God on Mount Horeb to go to Israel but was rejected. He directs to the nations who "hear and understand" a series of exhortatory, eschatologically oriented statements. The depiction of Ezra on Mount Horeb (equated in biblical tradition with Mount Sinai) suggests a typological comparison of Ezra with Moses. These figures are also compared in 4 Ezra 14:1–8 and in various rabbinic sources.

2:42–48
The Vision of Ezra

Ezra receives a vision of a tall young man distributing crowns to a surrounding multitude on Mount Zion. An angel informs Ezra that the youth is the "son of God" and the crowd, those who "confessed the name of God." The vision probably represents Jesus rewarding Christian confessors (possibly martyrs). Though it has close parallels in Revelation 7 and the early Christian work *Hermas, Similitudes* 8–9, the vision is clearly based on Jewish models, especially 4 Ezra 13.

PART TWO: 3:1–14:48
The Fourth Book of Ezra

The section 3:1–14:48, which we are referring to as 4 Ezra, is a separate work from the preceding chaps. 1–2 and the following chaps. 15–16. It focuses on the religious problems raised for Judaism by the destruction of the Temple and Jerusalem by the Romans in A.D. 70.

3:1–5:20
First Vision

The first vision is composed of four parts: an address to God, a dispute, a dialogic prediction, and a direct prediction. In the first the seer alone is the speaker; the second and third are dialogues between the seer and an angel; the fourth is set in the mouth of the angel alone.

3:1–3, Introduction. The protagonist, Ezra, is presented lying on his bed during the thirtieth year of the Babylonian exile. He is distressed by the suffering of Zion and breaks into an inspired address to God. Curiously, Ezra is identified with Salathiel (Heb. Shealtiel), perhaps Salathiel the father of Zerubbabel. See Ezra 3:2; 5:2.

3:4–36, Address. The address to God falls into two parts. The first, 3:4–27, sets forth the wondrous works of God in history, from the creation of Adam (3:5), through the saving of Noah (3:11), the election of Abraham (3:13), Exodus and Sinai (3:17–19), to David (3:23). In counterpoint to these events, the repeated sins of humankind and the punishment that God visits upon them are highlighted (3:7, 9–10, 25–27). The destruction of Jerusalem is the climax of sin and punishment. Even more significantly, throughout the address Ezra accuses God of responsibility for these events: God created; God punished; even when God gave the Law to "bring forth fruit in them," the evil inclination remained in the heart of the people "and thou didst not hinder them" (3:8, RSV).

In the Hebrew Bible such recitals of the gracious deeds of God usually precede the making or renewal of a covenant between God and Israel or form part of a legal indictment of Israel before the heavenly court for transgressing the covenant (cf. Josh. 24; Ezek. 20; Neh. 9). Here 4 Ezra strikingly inverts the biblical form and indicts God before the bar of his own justice for conducting the world unjustly. This radical position comes out of the seer's struggle to understand the seemingly incomprehensible destruction of the Temple.

4 Ezra's view that the tendency to sin was inherited from Adam by all generations is not unlike Pauline attitudes about original sin. What 4 Ezra says is inherited, however, is not sin but the weakness that enables persons to sin (3:26–27).

Following this very strong statement, a new, almost reflective tone enters (3:28–36). Ezra asks whether Babylon is any better (morally) than Zion, that it has gained dominion (3:28). Israel, whatever its sins, is still more God-fearing than other nations: "What nation has kept thy commandments so well?" (3:35, RSV). Already in the prophetic writings, although the political affliction of Israel by foreign nations was seen as the working of God, questions were raised about the moral qualities of the nations (see Isa. 10:5–19; cf. Jer. 25:8–14). Yet the justice of the punishment was not questioned by the prophets, whereas for 4 Ezra the moral faults of Babylon (Rome) raise questions about the justice of the punishment itself. Setting the theme for the dialogic dispute that follows, Ezra reproaches God who has "not shown to any one how thy way may be comprehended" (3:31, RSV). In this way the central issue of the book is posed, that of the justice of God's action toward Israel and by implication toward all humankind.

4:1–25, The Dispute. The angel Uriel appears in response to the address. He chides Ezra for wishing to understand the "way of the Most High," i.e., the working of divine providence. By use of riddle questions (4:5–8) and the striking dual parable of the forest and the sea (4:13–18) he demonstrates to Ezra that "men on earth can understand earthly things and nothing else; only those who live above the skies can understand the things above the skies" (4:21, NEB). Ezra responds that the angel has misconstrued his intent. He had only wanted to ask "why the people whom you loved has been given over to godless tribes" (4:23, RSV).

Ezra has posed a major issue. He wishes to understand the course of events as he has presented them in the preceding address. The angel does not deny the validity of his presentation but replies that this is something mortals cannot understand. Ezra responds that Uriel has avoided the question. What a strange sort of dialogue! It has no parallel in the other apocalypses, and perhaps, like much of the dialogue in the first three visions, it reflects the author's own inner conflicts.

The riddle questions here in 4:5–8 and in 5:36–37 imply a rejection of the possibility of specially revealed knowledge of heavenly secrets such as one finds in many apocalypses. In spite of this rejection of special knowledge, Ezra repeatedly formulates his quest in terms of knowing and understanding. He seeks to understand the working of God, incomprehensible to him when he considers the fate of Israel. This is a proper subject of concern to mortals, he insists, in spite of the angel's denial.

4:26–52, Dialogic Prediction. Continuing the dialogue form, the author shifts from disputatious to predictive dialogue. The angel makes certain prophetic pronouncements about which the seer poses simple questions to elicit information. Although most of the angel's responses are clear, the transition from disputation to predictive dialogue is marked by a cryptic oracular passage (4:26–32; cf. similar transitional passages in 5:41–42; 6:8–10; 7:25; 8:3). The pronouncement that "the age is hastening swiftly to its end" (4:26, RSV) is elaborated in the ensuing oracle (4:33–52), as the seer seeks more details about the prediction of the imminent end: when will this be (4:33); is human evil delaying it (4:38–39); has more time passed than is to come (4:44–46)? To these three queries the angel replies that the times are predetermined (4:34–37), that they will not be delayed (4:40–43), and that most of the times are past (4:50). The section concludes with the seer's question whether "those days" are imminent (4:51).

In this section the angel repeatedly emphasizes the idea that the future has been predetermined by God (4:36–37, 42, 50). Counterpointing this idea is a pervasive sense of urgency and haste (4:26, 33, 40–42, 51). These themes and the tension between them are central to the thought of the book. How, then, does their introduction respond to the questions the seer has posed at the end of the previous section? They clearly do not satisfy Ezra, for he returns to the same questions again in the second vision. It is as if here the angel takes up the last of Ezra's questions in 4:52 and answers it alone.

5:1–13, Direct Prediction. The next passage, spoken entirely by the angel, is very like that which concludes the second vision (6:11–29). The dominant idea is that evil will peak before the end comes. This evil, which is caused by human sin, will be characterized by disruption of social, family, and natural order. The signs, as these fierce events are called, are presented in four groups—cosmic disruption (5:4b–5), the reign of the eschatological ruler (5:6–7), chaos (5:8–9), and the loss of wisdom (5:9b–11). Such lists of signs are widespread in Jewish and Christian apocalypses, in rabbinic literature, and in the NT (e.g., Matt. 24:6–29; Mark 13:7–24; Luke 21:9–26; *1 Enoch* 99:4–9; *m. Soṭa* 9:15). They derive partly from passages in the Hebrew Bible that assume that the regularity of nature can be disturbed by human sin (e.g., Lev. 26:18–26; Deut. 11:17). Ezra is to watch for these signs that will alert him to the imminent end (4 Ezra 9:1–2). He is to fast for another seven days, after which he will hear "yet greater things than these" (5:13, RSV).

5:14–20, Conclusion. In 5:14–15 Ezra's violent physical reaction to the vision is described. Real trance experience, perhaps even that of the author, may lie behind this description. The onset of the experience was marked in 3:1–3, where Ezra is described as lying on his bed and contemplating the destruction of Zion until inspiration seizes him and he is impelled to speak.

At the very end of the vision he is approached by Palatiel, leader of the people, who is concerned for his welfare; but Ezra dismisses him.

5:21–6:34
Second Vision

The second vision is composed of four main parts exactly corresponding to the four main parts of the first vision. The same shift of speech from the seer, to dialogue, to direct angelic prediction occurs here too.

5:21–22, Introduction. The first lines conclude the narrative transition, referring back to the angelic commandment in 5:13 and the introduction to the first vision. The onset of Ezra's vision experience is described, as in 3:3.

5:23–30, Address. The first part of the address (5:23–27) is a series of comparisons, showing that there is one chosen thing of each kind. These comparisons culminate in the characterization of Israel as the elect people of God. Election is described as "love" (5:27), a theme that recurs in the disputatious dialogue that follows. God's punishment of Israel is consequently described not in the legal language of judgment, but as "hate" (5:30). In the second part of the speech (5:28–30) Ezra poses three questions. The root of his concern is once again the fate of Israel; here he poses the issue to God in terms of his love for Israel.

5:31–40, The Dispute. As on the earlier night, the angel appears and reproaches Ezra, saying, "Do you love [Israel] more than his Maker does?" (5:33, RSV). Note the prominence of the idea of love. Ezra responds, saying, "I try to understand the *ways of the Most High*" (5:34, NEB; cf. 3:31). The angel again employs riddle questions to demonstrate Ezra's inability to comprehend the way of God's governance of the world, which is also described in terms of love and judgment. Ezra accepts the limitations of his abilities and, in contrast to the first vision, here does not pose anew the questions about the fate of Zion. The angel concludes: "You cannot discover my judgment, or the goal of the love that I have promised my people" (5:40, RSV; cf. 4:21).

5:41–6:10, Dialogic Prediction. The transition from dispute to prediction is marked by a question and an oracular response (5:41–42). Verse 5:40 had hinted at the future ("goal" and "judgment"), and in 5:41 the seer asks about God's future action. Will the redemption include all generations or only those actually alive at the end (cf. 13:19–20; and see 1 Thess. 4:13–17)? The simile of the crown, used in the response (4 Ezra 5:42), clearly implies that judgment will take place in an equal fashion for all, through resurrection (cf. 5:45).

In a series of questions Ezra expresses his impatient desire to see the judgment immediately. Using the image of a womb, the angel emphasizes the fixed order of creation—as a womb cannot produce ten at once, so the earth would contradict its natural properties if it produced the allotted number of human beings simultaneously (5:46–49) and so hastened the end. Still, the angel assures him, the creation "already is aging and passing the strength of youth" (5:55, RSV). Thus Ezra learns that all will be judged equally, that judgment cannot be immediate, and that the end is fixed and unchangeable but will come soon.

In 5:56 the issue of a timetable is abandoned as Ezra desires to know "through whom you will visit your creation." The beginning of the end, he is told, will be through human agency (perhaps a reference to the Messiah), though its consummation will be through God. God's unique role is strongly supported by the series of statements in 6:1–6. God alone made the whole of creation. Even before that he planned the events of the end, and he alone will execute them. In 6:7, when Ezra asks about the division between this age and the age to come, the angel's answer is couched in symbolic terms. As Jacob's hand grasped Esau's heel (see Gen. 25:26), so nothing will intervene between the two ages.

6:11–29, Direct Prediction. By its reference to signs revealed "on a previous night" (6:12) the next section refers to the corresponding prediction passage at the end of the first vision (5:1–13). The angel warns Ezra that he will hear a loud voice that may cause the earth to shake (6:13–16). Ezra hears the divine voice (6:17), which delivers an oracle (6:18–20a) and reveals signs of the end (6:20b–28).

The heart of the passage lies in the revelation of the "end of the signs" (6:12). It is introduced by solemn events: an elaborate question, the seer's rising to his feet (he has been lying down throughout the first two visions), the shaking of the earth, and the resounding divine voice—recalling the theophanies of, e.g., Judg. 5:4; 1 Kings 19:11–12; Nah. 1:5; Ps. 18:13. A list of woes follows, describing the events that will signal the breakdown of cosmic order. Finally, in 6:26–28, redemption is briefly described. This note of hope marks the end of the first part of the book, climaxing the spiritual struggle and questioning of the first two visions.

6:30–34, Conclusion. The next verses contain the injunctions with which the second vision concludes (cf. 5:13; 9:23–25). The statement that the seer is acceptable to God (6:32b) is a new element, an innovation no doubt related to the preceding message of re-

demption. The cryptic command in 6:34 not to think vain thoughts may refer to questions and responses such as those in 4:2, 20–21 and 5:33, 40. The essential message is, Believe because of the signs, and do not ask such questions.

6:35–9:25
Third Vision

The exceptionally long third vision (longer than the first and second combined) falls into three major sections, 6:35–7:44; 7:45–8:3; and 8:4–9:25. Each of these parts is structured, basically, like the first two visions.

6:35–37, Section 1: Introduction. As in the introduction to the first two visions, the seer's troubled state of mind is described, followed by the onset of his spiritual experience and speech.

6:38–59, Section 1: Address. The address is parallel in general to the prayerful addresses that open the preceding visions. Like them, it is formulated in the second person and is divided into two parts: 6:38–54 and 6:55–59. The first part tells of the works done on the six days of creation. In the second part the implications of this recital are set forth. The creation account often draws word for word on Genesis 1. No other similar use of Genesis 1 in a prayer is known. The recital of creation is so presented as to emphasize the election of Israel (6:55–59). Several special themes are introduced: the idea of creation through divine speech (e.g., 6:38, 43), the creation of the luminaries for the service of humankind (6:45–46), the preservation of Leviathan and Behemoth (6:49–52) and their purpose in the events of the eschaton (6:52). Verses 54–59 focus the author's problem for the ensuing dispute. While 6:54 connects "the people whom you have chosen" with the creation of Adam, 6:59 asks, "Was the world really made for us? Why, then, may we not take possession of our world?" (NEB). In the first vision the problem is formulated in terms of history, moving from creation to exile. In the second vision it is put in terms of the election of Israel. The present address combines these two preoccupations; its chief subject is creation, yet its questions arise from the concept of election.

The prophecy of redemption at the end of the second vision did not satisfy the author. Now he returns to the same basic issues: Why is the fate of Israel as it is? How does that accord with divine justice and providence? A shift has taken place in the author's understanding during the first two visions and is highlighted by the fact that he does not even mention the destruction of the Temple, previously the central issue.

7:1–25, Section 1: Dispute. As in 4:1 and 5:31, the dispute opens with the appearance of an angel who commands the seer to stand, the sign of a particularly solemn context (cf. 6:13; 10:33; 14:2). The angel begins by recounting two parables and their explication (7:3–16). Both parables stress that a difficult first stage must be traversed before the spacious future is achieved. If this is a response to 6:59 ("Why, then, may we not take possession of our world?" NEB), then the world to come, not this world, is Israel's heritage. The image of the city in the second parable may suggest such a view, since a city is a common way of referring to the future world or the heavenly Jerusalem (cf. *Herm. Sim.* 9.12.5). 4 Ezra 7:15–16 implies the same conclusion, with its contrast between mortality and "the future world."

In 7:17–18 Ezra objects that although it is reasonable to ask the righteous to sustain the difficulties of this world, since they will inherit the world to come, the wicked will suffer in both worlds. The angel rebukes Ezra for thinking he understands God's justice better than God himself. The fate of the righteous and the wicked is written in the Torah (→ Torah). The wicked did not hearken (7:22), so they will be punished, and the righteous will be rewarded (7:21–25).

One problem is that although Israel is clearly under discussion up to 7:10, from there on the passage refers to the righteous and the wicked in general. Even allusions to Torah here do not unambiguously refer to Israel; in 7:11 "my statutes" seems to mean divine commands in general. The discourse shifts from Israel, via Adam's sin, to the righteous and the wicked, the reverse of the development in chap. 3.

7:26–44, Section 1: Direct Prediction.

The next passage opens with the prophetic phrase "Behold, the time will come" (7:26; cf. 5:1; 6:18) and concludes with an assertion of the special revelation made to Ezra. 4 Ezra 7:26 deliberately relates this passage to the preceding direct predictions (5:1–13; 6:11–29) and forms a complement to them, carrying the prediction on to the day of judgment. The passage is structured according to the eschatological timetable.

In this passage, as elsewhere in the book, the Messiah is called "servant" (some translations give "son," reflecting a Greek word with both meanings but a Hebrew original that meant "servant"). The messianic kingdom precedes the Day of Judgment and is limited to four hundred years, after which the Messiah will die. Unlike the fifth and sixth visions, here the Messiah plays no role in the inception of his kingdom. Following his death (which is unparalleled in other sources) the world will revert to the state before creation. Then a new world will be created, and the resurrection of the dead and judgment will take place. The picture of God on a throne rebuking the wicked

is appropriate to the representation of this judgment as a courtroom scene (cf. Dan. 7:9–14). The withdrawal of mercy, highly stressed here, is connected with the idea that judgment is perfect. Until that time, there is place for mercy; but on the Day of Judgment itself, truth alone will rule.

7:45–74, Section 2: The Dispute.

The dispute opens the second section of the vision, which concludes with 8:3. Broadly, the passage may be designated "dialogic dispute," for Ezra's questions urge his point of view against the angel's. Its major parts are Ezra's sustained address (7:45–48); the angel's response concerning the two worlds (7:49–51); a parable narrated by the angel (7:52–57); Ezra's statement of the moral of the parable (7:58), from which the angel draws the implications (7:59–61); Ezra's lament (7:62–69); the angel's final, detailed response (7:70–74).

Starting from the view that the world to come is for the righteous only (cf. 7:26–44), Ezra objects that few persons will be saved but many damned (7:45–48). Although the objection somewhat resembles that of 7:17–18, it is focused not on eschatological reward, but on the present quandary that is evident only after the revelation about reward. This quandary is the problem of the "evil heart," which now leads to the damnation of "almost all who have been created" (7:48, RSV). The angel's assertion in 7:50 implies that God values the righteous highly and that it was to reward them that he created the world to come. The parable of the precious and base metals (7:52), which is completed in 8:2–3, further suggests that God, owner of the precious, keeps them unmixed with the worthless.

In this way the angel repeats and refocuses Ezra's initial charge: indeed there are only few righteous, he asserts, but over them God rejoices. To this hard message Ezra responds with a lament, a cry of distress. He had opened the pericope with the exclamation, "Blessed are those who are alive and keep thy commandments!" (7:45, RSV). Now he closes the body of his argument and the lament with the contrasting, "And if we were not to come into judgment after death, perhaps it would have been better for us" (7:69, RSV).

The pericope concludes with the angel's carefully argued reply (7:70–75) that judgment is foreordained, human action foreseen, and its results provided for in advance; that because human beings have intelligence they exercise free will and consequently bear the results of their actions; and that this is particularly true of the requirements of Torah, which were given to humans, but which they did not observe.

7:75–99, Section 2: Dialogic Prediction.

The next pericope is composed chiefly of the

angel's sustained response to the seer's question whether after death recompense will ensue immediately (7:75). The response falls into three parts: introduction on the nature of death (7:76–78); the description of the postmortem state of the wicked (7:79–87) and the righteous (7:88–98); and a conclusion (7:99). The descriptions of the fates of the righteous and the wicked are closely parallel in their structure. They are sevenfold, corresponding, it seems, to the seven heavens. The passage is very distinctive, with a title ("Concerning death the teaching is: . . ." RSV) and a conclusion ("This is the order of the souls of the righteous, . . ." RSV).

At the time of death, which is decreed by God, the soul leaves the body and adores the glory of God (7:78). A detailed description of the state of the souls of the dead follows. This teaching is unique in ancient Jewish literature, although the idea of such a state is found elsewhere, e.g., *Testament of Abraham* A. 13–14. The view of 4 Ezra 7 is that this intermediate state comes directly after death and is itself succeeded by resurrection and judgment.

7:100–115, Section 2: Dispute. The exact point of the transitional dialogue in 7:100–101 is obscure, but it seems to be whether souls experience any interval between their death and entry into their postmortem habitations.

The elaborate formula in 7:102 introduces a major new topic. In his ongoing search for some softening of what he perceives as draconian divine judgment, Ezra moves from considering the fate of the souls after death to intercession: will there be intercession on the Day of Judgment? The angel answers with an uncompromising no. In the past, the seer protests, there has been intercession, so why not in the future (7:106–111)? If such prayer has been effective in this corrupt world, he argues (and adduces examples from Scripture to prove his point), surely it will be so in the world to come. To the contrary, the angel replies, intercession is an indication of the imperfection of this world "in which the glory of God does not abide continually" (7:112). But in the future, perfect age, there will be no intercession. This accords with the view, noted earlier in the book, that until the end humans can repent and will experience God's mercy; but at the end truth and judgment alone will prevail (7:32–38). No intercessory prayer will be possible.

7:116–8:3, Section 2: Second Dispute. The second dispute is a complex passage composed of four parts: Ezra's lament (7:116–126), the angel's response (7:127–131), an exegesis of Exod. 34:6–7 (7:132–140), and the angel's response and conclusion (8:1–3). We have characterized 7:116–126 as a lament, even though it is a series of questions. Four such passages of lament can be isolated in the first three visions: 4:12, 22–24;

5:35; 7:62–69; and 7:116–126. These laments occur when the seer despairs of achieving any resolution to his problems. Each opens with a rhetorical question about the purpose of birth and then poses the point of the seer's despair.

The angel answers in terms of free will and the responsibility of human beings for their actions (7:127–131). He implicitly rejects the idea of "original sin" that Ezra might have implied (7:118) and strongly asserts the freedom of human action and the corresponding human responsibility for this action. His position is bolstered by a quotation of Deut. 30:19, a rare use of a proof-text in our book (7:129). The response to the issue of the few and the many is not that there is some means by which the many can be saved from punishment, but that there will be more joy over the few than there will be grief over the many (7:131; cf. 7:60–61).

Just as the angel used Scripture to make his point, so Ezra cites Scripture in his prayerful response (7:132–140). In a phrase-by-phrase exegesis of Exod. 34:6–7, Ezra asserts God's mercy and compassion. (Both the selection of the passage and the method of interpretation—midrash—recall rabbinic reflection on the nature of God.) The relations implied between God and human beings are complex, but the overall point is clear, that humans can survive only because of God's mercy.

In his final response, which is also the conclusion of the second section of the vision, the angel reiterates the opening position of 7:49–61. Indeed, 8:1–3 is the conclusion of the parable that was told in 7:52–59 (8:2 should be translated "But I will explain the parable [i.e., that of 7:52–59] to you, Ezra"). This subdivision concludes, as it started, with the assertion of the inevitability of human fate. The problem of the few and the many remains unresolved.

8:4–19a, Section 3: Monologue. The monologue that opens the third section of this very long vision and the prayer (8:19b–36) are first-person addresses by Ezra that together function similarly to the speeches with which the first three visions open. In the monologue Ezra presents the issues that concern him (8:4–14) and then the questions arising from them (8:15–19a). If the creation of human beings was such a complex and wondrous procedure, Ezra asks, why does God destroy them so quickly (8:14)? This question seems universal, yet in vv. 15–18 the specific fate of Israel is to the fore; Ezra prays in Israel's behalf. Thus the issue of the few and the many, which runs through the whole second section of the third vision, is refocused in an intriguing way.

Both the content and style of this passage are so structured as to reiterate God's responsibility for creation of human beings. The tone is set gently by 8:4–5, Ezra's apostrophe to his own soul; in his address to God the theme becomes dominant (8:6–12), and it is brought to absolute explicitness by vv. 13–14. God is responsible for the creation and growth of mortals as well as for their fate. The line of argument is similar to that of 3:4–36, where God is made responsible for the course of history.

8:19b–36, Section 3: The Prayer. The prayer pronounced by Ezra forms the second part of his introductory speech. It has had a special influence in various churches, some of which transmitted it separately for liturgical use. The parallelism that is typical of biblical prayers also dominates its literary character. It is composed of an opening doxology (8:20–23), a call for attention and statement of purpose (8:24–25), and the body of the prayer, consisting of intercessory petition, confession, and grounds for petition (8:26–36). The same central elements (doxology, confession, and petition) occur in earlier prayers, especially Ezra 9, Nehemiah 9, and Daniel 9.

The thrust of the prayer is a call for divine mercy. The argument that God cannot be called "merciful" except by forgiving "us sinners, who have no just deeds to our credit" (8:32, NEB) is a reference back to the midrash on the divine attributes (7:132).

The prayer carries on the preoccupation with the issue of the few and the many, but concern for Israel, which was prominent in the address (8:15–18), now disappears. The prayer is focused on the conflict between the ideas of 8:1–3 and God's care, evident in creation.

8:37–62a, Section 3: Dispute. The next passage, a mixture of dispute and prediction, is composed of two speeches by the angel, separated by a short address by the seer. The definitive comment by the angel in v. 40 and the character of vv. 61–62 show that the end of the long third vision is approaching.

The passage plays a clear role within the overall framework of the third vision. All Ezra's attempts to find mercy for the wicked are rebuffed. Ezra, although he reflects love for humankind by his concern, in fact loves them less than God, whose love is expressed by his very joy over the righteous. Thus Ezra's argument in behalf of the wicked is misplaced, and he should rejoice, instead, over his own reward and that of those like him (8:46–49). This reward is detailed in the remarkable list in vv. 51–54.

The wicked have determined their own fate, denying God even though they knew that they must die an eternal death (8:56, 58). Their death and the corresponding life of the righteous, which is asserted in v. 46, bracket the heart of the passage. So, the problem of the few and the many has been resolved—the many perish not as God's responsibility but as their own.

The passage concludes with two classical, apocalyptic themes, the nearness of the end and the revelation of the secrets to the righteous (vv. 61–62a). Finally, Ezra seems to have accepted the angel's arguments and docilely turns in 8:63 to asking questions about the signs. His understanding has reached a new stage that makes such questions relevant.

8:62b–9:22, Section 3: Direct Prediction. The next pericope falls into four sections, with questions by the seer alternating with addresses by the angel. If we take the direct predictions at the end of the first two visions together they present events that are to occur at the time of the messianic woes and at the Day of Judgment (5:1–13; 6:11–29). Although the present passage fulfills a corresponding role at the end of the third vision, it does not add to their list of events. Instead, it focuses on the issue of when the signs will take place. This is a question that has been on the seer's mind since early in the first vision (4:33). Here Ezra is told that when he observes the predicted signs starting to happen he will know the end is near (9:1–4). The importance and use of such lists of signs is to enable those who know them to tell when the end is coming.

Verses 5–6 are somewhat obscure but seem to introduce the idea of the purposiveness of creation, or the divine intent expressed in the eschatological reward. The eschatological redemption is described only very briefly and then, in 9:10–11, the angel returns to the idea that repentance is only possible in this world. In conclusion, Ezra reasserts the position that he has held throughout this vision, but now he neither argues with God nor reproaches him (9:14–16).

The angel's final address accepts Ezra's answer and strongly reasserts the relationship between deed and reward (9:17). Disobedience is the work of humankind, not of God, who takes responsibility for the righteous and their perfection. The images used for the righteous are drawn from earlier passages in the book.

9:23–25, Section 3: Conclusion and Injunctions. In the concluding injunctions Ezra is commanded to live in an open field for seven days, eating only the flowers that grow there. At the end of that period, the angel promises, "I will come and talk with you" (v. 25).

9:26–10:59

Fourth Vision

The fourth vision is pivotal in the structure of the book and displays a major shift in the author's perceptions. It begins much like the previous three visions, but concludes with the description of a profound waking experience much different from any the seer has undergone before.

9:26–28, Introduction. A new narrative context is set by the new physical location (the field) and by the eating of the flowers. The seer's distress, inspiration, and speech are described here just as in the first three visions.

9:29–37, Address. The address is exactly parallel in function to those with which the first three visions began. A question is posed to God based on a recital of history (cf. 3:4–36; 6:38–59). God revealed himself to Israel in the wilderness and pronounced the Law (9:29–31); God's speech, quoted directly, does not occur in the Bible but is derived from 4 Ezra 3:20–22.

Here Ezra's concern is refocused. He has accepted the angel's views on divine providence and theodicy. Now anomalies about the idea of Torah become central. God gave Torah, yet left the evil inclination in the heart of the people, so the Torah was unable to produce its fruit of eternal life. These ideas, already raised tellingly in 3:19–22, are here brought up again even more acutely. The anomaly is that the eternal Torah survives the vessel that contains it.

9:38–10:4, Vision, First Part. The vision does not respond to the real problems raised in the address. The author is conscious of this, as is clear from 9:39 ("abandoning my meditations," NEB) and 10:5 ("I interrupted the train of my thoughts," NEB). Since he is a skilled writer, this discontinuity probably arose from the author's actual vision experience. That experience caused a reorientation of his perception of the world as a result of which the former issues ceased to concern him.

The passage is composed of initial description (9:38–39), Ezra's dialogue with the woman (9:40–42), and the woman's tale (9:43–10:4). She tells him that, barren for thirty years, she eventually bore a child and raised him, and that on the day of his marriage he fell down dead. She fled to the field, determined to mourn until she died. It has been suggested that this is a folktale, used by the author of 4 Ezra for his own purposes. If so, then the story is incomplete, for it has no ending, and it is well integrated into the book.

In a number of respects the figures of Ezra and the woman are parallel. Her thirty barren years can be compared with the thirty years since the fall of Jerusalem in 3:1. Her fasting, mourning, and weeping exactly parallel Ezra's in the previous part of the book.

10:5–24, Vision, Second Part. Ezra then talks to the mourning woman to comfort her

(10:5–17), and her response (10:18) is followed by his final address (10:19–24). The most important aspect of this passage is the change in Ezra's role from the one comforted to comforter. We noted above that the mourning woman took on many of the characteristics that Ezra himself, as mourner for Zion, had borne previously. Just as the woman plays Ezra's role, Ezra now takes on that of the angel. He reproves the woman (10:6), just as the angel reproved him (e.g., 4:2; 5:33). Like the angel, here Ezra implies that the woman does not see the whole picture. Moreover, there are clear parallels between the rhetorical techniques the angel used earlier and those Ezra now employs (cf. 7:54 with 10:9; 5:51–53 with 10:12–14). The author uses these literary means to mark the change in Ezra's own understanding and spiritual state.

This reversal of roles flows from Ezra's acceptance of the implications of the angel's prior teaching. Although he had, even at the end of the third vision, encountered difficulty in accepting the ideas about the few and the many, here he uses them to comfort the woman (10:10). Even further, he who had questioned God's justice consoles her, saying, "If you acknowledge the decree of God to be just, you will receive your son back in due time" (10:16, RSV). Thus Ezra consoles the woman, using the very ideas and concepts he himself has struggled to accept from the beginning of the book.

10:25–27a, Transformation. The next passage is unique in Jewish apocalyptic literature. Four stages of transformation are described: the illumination of the woman's countenance (10:25), her cry and the shaking of the earth (10:26), her transformation into a city (10:27), and Ezra's cry of terror. The city is, of course, the heavenly Jerusalem.

The most striking thing about this section is the intensity of the seer's experience. Sight, hearing, and physical orientation are disturbed until the terrified Ezra cries out for his angelic guide and loses consciousness (10:28–30). What is being described is an intense emotional experience analogous to conversion, i.e., the restructuring of personality in light of beliefs previously assented to, and an ensuing enlightenment. Each of the various elements of this experience have parallels earlier in the book (cf. 6:13–16; 7:125; see Dan. 10:6).

10:27b–37, The Appearance of the Angel. The angel appears in response to Ezra's call, just as in 5:31 and 7:1. The familiar figure of the angel connects this rather different experience to the preceding ones. The description of Ezra's faint in v. 30 and the dialogue with the angel in vv. 31–37 convey a strong sense of his inner turmoil. Ezra is commanded to stand (10:33), as he was twice previously (6:13 and 7:2). This is a sign of the particular solemnity of the revelation that is to follow (cf. 14:2).

10:38–54, The Interpretation. The central message of the vision, the restoration of Zion, is the consolation Ezra sought. The passage makes three points. First, the vision is called a revelation of secrets (10:38–39). Note how the interpretation is bracketed by references to the revelation of secrets (10:38, 55–59). Second, the interpretation proper is given, opening with a formal title (10:40) and followed by a summary of the contents of the vision (10:41–43). A detailed interpretation of most of the vision ensues: the woman is Zion; her thirty years of barrenness are the three hundred years before offerings were made in Zion; the birth of the son is Solomon's building of the city; his careful nurture is the time of Israel's habitation of the city; and his death is the destruction of Zion (10:44–48). Third, the angel explains Ezra's experience to him (10:49–54). Verse 38 tells us of Ezra's fear; v. 55 of its reversal.

In his vision Ezra sees both the woman and her transformation into a city. These two parts of the same vision differ: whereas the woman symbolizes Zion, the city *is* Zion. Both elements are seen in the vision, and both are explained in the interpretation. Moreover, the city is not said to disappear, nor is Ezra said to wake from a dream. The vision experience continues throughout.

10:55–59, Conclusion and Injunctions. Structurally, the next section resembles the conclusions of the preceding visions (encouragement, 10:55; injunctions, 10:55b–56; explanation, 10:57; and concluding injunctions, 10:58–59). The content, however, differs. Ezra is told to go in and see the building, implying that the building is still there (10:55). He is to see "as much as the eye can see" (cf. 1 Cor. 2:9), indicating special revelation of an esoteric type.

11:1–12:51

Fifth Vision

The fifth vision, a symbolic dream vision and interpretation, conveys the message of the imminent end of the hated Roman Empire and the coming of the messianic kingdom. It stands in a long tradition of political visions, the chief biblical representatives of which are Daniel 2 and 7. The interpretation of this vision is crucial for dating 4 Ezra.

11:1a, Introduction. Unlike the preceding visions, here there is no description of the seer's psychological state but only the observation that he saw a dream.

11:1b–12:3a, Vision. A long passage narrates the content of the complex symbolic dream. The dream falls into three chief parts, the description of the eagle (11:1b–35), the judgment scene (11:36–46), and the execution of the judgment (12:1–3a).

The dream is described in very great detail. Expressions like "and I looked and behold" mark the introduction of new elements and form one of the notable characteristics of the style of this passage. The various stages are (1) general description (11:1b), (2) initial stance of the eagle (11:2–4), (3) the eagle's rule over the whole earth (11:5–6), (4) preparation for the rule of the wings and the heads (11:7–9), (5) summary and observations (11:10–11), (6) rule of the wings on the right-hand side (11:12–19), (7) rule of the wings on the left-hand side (11:20–21), (8) summary (11:22–23), (9) rule of four small wings (11:24–27), (10) fate of remaining two small wings (11:28–32), (11) fate of the heads (11:33–35), (12) appearance of the lion (11:36–37), (13) indictment of the eagle (11:38–43), (14) sentencing of the eagle (11:44–46), (15) execution of the sentence (12:1–3a).

Stages 13–15 clearly represent a legal process, including the laying of specific charges, the sentencing, and the execution of the sentence. Although the animal symbolism is sustained throughout the vision, God is not included in the symbolic structure. A measure of self-involvement of the seer in the dream is found (11:36), as is usual in dreams, but there is no hint of an angelic guide or of any action attributed to the seer. This vision is much more typical of apocalypses than are those found in the preceding sections of the book.

12:3b–9, Seer's Response. Opening with an introduction (12:3b), the response passage continues with a brief soliloquy by Ezra (12:4–6; cf. 7:62) and a prayer to God (12:7–9). Like 10:25–37 and 13:13b–20, this section recounts the seer's response to the dream and his prayer for enlightenment. All three passages contain the sequential elements of fear, wonderment, and prayer. At the literary level the passage carries readers from the dream to the interpretation. The appearance of the angel, as in the sixth vision, is assumed but not described.

12:10–36, Interpretation. In the interpretation the symbols are each stated, and then their meaning is given. The introduction (12:11–12) is followed by seven stages of interpretation (12:13–34), ending with a conclusion (12:35–36). The dream is explicitly said to be of the fourth of the beasts that Daniel saw (12:11–12), referring to Daniel 7. It is extremely rare that an apocalyptic vision is set in an explicit relation to other visions. The various wings, little wings, and heads are identified as kings and rulers of an empire. The lion is the Messiah, and the destruction of the eagle is the freeing of the earth from the tyranny of that empire.

The vision is thus interpreted as a summary presentation of the history of the Roman Empire. Historical surveys of this sort are particularly prevalent in the literature of the Second Temple period (see Dan. 7; 10–12; 1 Enoch 85–90). History is presented as a schematic process. The author's interest is not merely in the abstract presentation of such a scheme but in discerning just where he stands in this process. A similar interest is betrayed in Ezra's question at the end of the third vision (8:63).

As in many apocalyptic overviews of history, the point at which the author moves from the telling of past history to real prediction may be assumed to indicate the date at which the book was written. Thus the exact identification of the wings, little wings, and heads is of great importance. The author seems to move from history to prediction in the time of the third head. The most persuasive suggestion would make the second wing Augustus and the three heads Vespasian, Titus, and Domitian. If so, the vision was written in the time of Domitian, A.D. 81–96, probably in the early 90s.

12:37–39, Conclusion and Injunctions. The next section is structurally parallel to the conclusions of the first four visions. Ezra is commanded to write the vision in a book, to hide it, and to teach it only to the truly wise (cf. Dan. 12:4). This is the first such command in 4 Ezra, and the theme is central to chap. 14. Ezra has become the recipient of secrets that are to be transmitted further.

12:40–51, Narrative Interlude. Verse 51 is properly part of the preceding section; the rest is a narrative interlude. The only other such narrative interlude is 5:16–19, which comes after the first vision. Here, the passage is composed of an introduction (12:40), the people's address to Ezra (12:41–45a), Ezra's response (12:45b–49), and a narrative conclusion (12:50).

A key to the understanding of this passage is the familiar concept "it would be better to die than live." This was Ezra's piercing cry in 4:12, and now the people pronounce it (12:44). God's spokesman, the angel, comforted Ezra in chap. 4; here Ezra comforts the people in God's name. Thus, as in the fourth vision, a reversal of roles has taken place.

Ezra is called a prophet by the people (12:42), a title that is now appropriate, since he speaks for God. This designation fits with his full assumption of the role of apocalyptic seer, already evident in the preceding pericope. He tells the people who inquire after his doings merely that he has been "praying on account of Zion." In accordance with the command to con-

ceal the secrets, Ezra does not hint at the revelation he has received.

13:1–13:58
Sixth Vision

In a dream Ezra sees a man arising from the sea and conquering his enemies. The man is interpreted as the servant who will overcome the wicked in the eschatological battle and gather the scattered tribes of Israel. The dream provides a more detailed discussion of certain things spoken of in the preceding vision. The redeemer figure is described as "man." His title and superhuman character have been compared with those of the Son of man in 1 Enoch and in the NT.

13:1, Introduction. A simple verse records Ezra's dream after seven days (cf. 12:39, 51).

13:2–13a, Dream. The narrative of the dream falls into four episodes separated by "after this, I looked and behold": the appearance of the man (13:2–4); preparations for attack and defense (13:5–7); the battle (13:8–11); and the redemption (13:12–13a). It is set in a very simple narrative framework, and its symbol structure is also simple when compared with the fifth vision.

The man appears from the sea (cf. Dan. 7:2–3). He flies on the clouds of heaven (cf. Dan. 7:13), and wherever he turns all melt. A multitude assembles to attack him, and he bestrides a mountain. They attack, but he destroys them with his fiery breath. Then a peaceful multitude assembles before him. What is notable is that the language used to describe the man's appearance and activity is suggestive of a superhuman or cosmic role. The flying on clouds, the melting of enemies, and the fiery breath are all elements usually found of God as divine warrior (cf. Pss. 18:7–15; 29:3–9).

13:13b–20a, Seer's Response. Like 12:36–39, the next passage forms a bridge between the dream and its interpretation. Ezra prays to the Most High, referring to his own worthiness. He concludes with two cries of "Alas!" based on his own understanding of the vision. Significantly, 13:20a is a reversal of what Ezra and the community had previously said, "Better my death than my life" (4:12; 12:44). Now Ezra asserts, "Better to be alive at the end than dead." An important change has taken place in his understanding.

13:20b–55, Interpretation. The angel's explanation of the dream is composed of an introduction and an answer to the seer's question (13:20b–24), the interpretation of the dream (13:25–53a), and a conclusion (13:53b–55). In this passage there is considerable repetition and lack of clarity. The man is interpreted three times (13:25–26, 32, 51–52); the sequence of events is interrupted (cf. vv. 25–26 and 32–39).

In his response (13:20b–24) to Ezra's words the angel reasserts the seer's position, using language very close to that of 9:7–8. He then proceeds to interpret the dream. The angel says that the man is the precreated Messiah who will deliver creation and rule the remnant (see 3:6; 6:6; 9:8; and 12:32 on precreation). The interpretation of the mountain is influenced by Dan. 2:34 and contradicts the vision (cf. 13:6 and 36). The fiery elements that destroy the enemies in the dream are here interpreted in legal terms.

The tight relationship between vision and interpretation observed in the fourth and fifth visions is absent. Moreover, the brief dream here contrasts with the diffuse, somewhat incoherent interpretation. A number of elements of the dream are not interpreted, while many elements of the interpretation are not hinted at in the dream. Most striking is the long description of the ten tribes (13:40–47) to which the author appends a description of the redemption of those in the land (13:48–50), a description having no basis in the vision.

The author seems to be writing an interpretation to an inherited symbol structure. This would explain the disjunction of dream and interpretation. Notably, the figure of the Messiah in the interpretation is congruent with the rest of the book, whereas the figure in the dream, with its superhuman, cosmic characteristics, draws on a different tradition with analogies elsewhere in the period of the Second Temple.

13:56–58, Conclusion and Injunctions.
The brief conclusion contains an angelic assurance, an injunction, and the promise of future revelations. The praise of Ezra's love of wisdom shows that he has reached a stage when he will be told "yet weightier and more wondrous matters."

14:1–48
Seventh Vision

The concluding vision differs from all those preceding. It is the story of a waking experience, a direct revelation from God to Ezra, culminating in the revelation of the Scriptures, both public and secret. It concludes with Ezra's translation to heaven.

14:1–2, Introduction. God calls to Ezra from a bush, using the same formula of summons and response as in the calls of Abraham, Moses, and Samuel (Gen. 22:1; Exod. 3:4; 1 Sam. 3:4–8).

14:3–18, Address. The divine address to Ezra, instructing him as to his conduct, may be divided into three parts: history of the revelation

to Moses (14:3–6), prediction (14:7–12), and final injunctions (14:13–18).

The crucial nature of this vision is highlighted by various means. The vision opens with an address by God, not by the seer. The history starts from the call of Moses and the Exodus, and climaxes with Sinai. (The direct quotation of God's speech that occurs in v. 6 is not from the Bible, but is apparently related to 14:45–46; cf. 9:31.) The theme of secret and public revelation is introduced and recurs throughout this vision (see already 12:37–38). The command to remember the "signs," "dreams," and "interpretations" (14:8) focuses all the eschatological prophecies of the book in this vision. The double prediction of Ezra's end and the end of the world (14:9–12, 16–18) heightens the sense of impending doom. This sense is reinforced by the foretelling of Ezra's ascension (14:9), by the prediction of the division of the times (14:11–12), by the announcement of the senescence of the earth and the consequent woes (14:10, 16–18a), and by the foretelling of the coming of the eagle (14:18b). The imminence of this final prophecy is marked by the expression "and now."

14:19–22, Speech. Ezra accepts the injunctions God has laid upon him, and at the end of v. 20 he poses a question to God: how will his reproof be received by those still unborn? To resolve this issue he asks for inspiration from the Holy Spirit so that he can write down "the things which were written in thy law" (14:22, RSV).

14:23–26, Injunctions. Ezra's prayer is granted, and God issues instructions to him. Ezra, to whom the scriptures will be revealed anew, is to depart for forty days, like Moses. He is to comfort the people, prepare writing tablets, and take skilled scribes with him.

14:27–36, Ezra's Speech. In accordance with the divine command Ezra addresses the people. He calls for attention (14:28), relates the historical sins of Israel that account for the present situation (14:29–33), exhorts the people and promises them reward (14:34–35), and concludes with an injunction (14:36). The formula "Hear these words, O Israel" (14:28) occurs also in 9:30 and recalls Deuteronomy. The historical recital serves to highlight God's grace and Israel's unfaithfulness, much like the use of such recitals in the Bible (e.g., Ezra 9; Neh. 9; Ps. 106; contrast the use of historical recital earlier in 4 Ezra 3). The exhortation assures the people that if only they repent, they will receive eternal life. The theme taken up is that of Torah, one that had been raised but not resolved in 9:29–37.

14:37-48, Revelation of Scriptures. The next verses describe the execution of the commands laid upon Ezra by God in 14:23-26. Ezra returns to the field with the five men (cf. v. 37). The next day he undergoes a waking experience in which he is given a goblet full of the Holy Spirit to drink. He senses the influx of inspiration, the feeling of enlightenment. He retains its content and is able to articulate it, so that the scribes can write it (14:38-41). This is a remarkable description of an experience that transcends those related previously. It not only authenticates Ezra's vision, but also explains how he could have written ninety-four books in forty days. The five scribes are also said to be inspired and to write in an unknown script. The crucial point is reached in God's instructions to Ezra concerning the disposal of the newly revealed books. Twenty-four books (one traditional reckoning of the Hebrew Bible) are to be made known publicly; the remaining seventy are to be transmitted secretly. These secret books are said to contain saving knowledge (14:47). They apparently include 4 Ezra itself, for in 12:37-38 the eagle vision is described, using the same language as is here used of the secret books. The theme of life is taken up. The scriptures are given so that "those who wish to live in the last days may live" (14:22, RSV).

In a certain way, chap. 14 is about the revelation of 4 Ezra itself. This conclusion is also indicated by the parallel between the forty days of the six previous visions and the forty days of the seventh vision. The revelation that is at the heart of this narrative is both that of the ninety-four books and that of the secrets of the times that Ezra has received. It forms a true climax to the spiritual quest and saga of Ezra's development.

The final verse (14:48) is uncertain on textual grounds, but clearly in view of 14:15 some such description of Ezra's translation is demanded.

PART THREE: 15:1-16:78

The Sixth Book of Ezra

Composed possibly as an appendix to 4 Ezra, 6 Ezra predicts and describes calamities that will soon occur on the earth and promises deliverance to those of God's people who refrain from sin.

15:1-4
The Prophetic Commission

God instructs the prophet (who is unnamed, but in the present context is to be understood as Ezra) not only to speak his prophecy but also to record it in writing.

15:5-16:34
Prediction of Worldwide Catastrophes

Through the prophet, God announces that destruction and calamities are about to take place in the world in general and in certain specific locations, as punishment for human sin. These "woes" form part of the traditional historical schema of eschatological literature: cf. 4 Ezra 5:1-13, 6:17-24, and commentary.

15:5-19, Forecasting of Calamities. After briefly reviewing the impending woes, the prophet states that these are actions of punishment by God that are brought about by iniquity on earth, especially that practiced against innocent and righteous people. The consequent tribulation will be universal (15:14) and will manifest itself in the form of violence in society. The events predicted in vv. 15-19 find parallels elsewhere in eschatological literature (cf. Mark 13 and parallels; 4 Ezra 5:1-2, 9-10; 13:30-31).

15:20-27, Condemnation of Sinners. An indictment is delivered against sinners that encompasses both rulers who persecute the righteous (15:20-21) and sinners among God's people (15:24-25). This theme of condemnation of sin is recurrent in 6 Ezra (see esp. 16:53-67, 76-78).

15:28-33, Vision of Conflict in the East. The prophet describes a vision of two military forces (each represented symbolically by an animal) engaged in battle in the east. It is generally thought that these two forces represent the troops of Odenathus of Palmyra ("the Arabian dragons," v. 29) and those of Shapur I of Persia ("the Carmonians," v. 30), which fought on the eastern borders of the Roman Empire in A.D. 260-261. If this identification is correct, it establishes the earliest possible date of composition for the work.

15:34-45, Vision of Storm Clouds. The seer proceeds to relate a symbolic vision of storm clouds that arise from various directions, come into conflict, and pour out destruction on the earth. Eventually the storm clouds reach and destroy "Babylon," almost certainly a symbolic representation of Rome (see 4 Ezra 3:28-36 and commentary above; cf. Rev. 14:8; 18:2-3). Although 6 Ezra 15:43-45 thus anticipate (as in Revelation) or describe the destruction of Rome, it is not possible to identify with precision the historical events (if any) represented in 15:34-42.

15:46-63, Condemnation of Asia. The prophecy turns to a condemnation of Asia for "shar[ing] in the glamour" (15:46, RSV) of the "hateful" Babylon (again to be identified with Rome; cf. esp. Rev. 17:3–5; 18:3). Because of its imitation of Rome's harlotry and its persecution of God's people, Asia will be totally devastated; in fact, the agents of Rome's destruction will turn back to plunder Asia (15:60). The special attention given here to the fate of Asia makes it seem possible that 6 Ezra was composed in this province.

16:1–17, The Inevitability of God's Judgment. After the prophet threatens destruction to four major parts of the Roman Empire (16:1–2), his discourse takes a more reflective turn. Employing a series of rhetorical questions set in parallel structure (16:3–11), the seer uses examples from the spheres of natural and human activity to emphasize the conclusiveness of God's judgment, once it has been set in motion (cf. Amos 3:3–8).

16:18–34, Prediction of Desolation on the Earth. The prophet envisions the initial stages of the impending catastrophes, then sketches in graphic terms the desolation that will prevail on earth in their wake. The idea of desolation as a result of God's judgment is familiar from prophetic and eschatological literature (cf. Isa. 6:11; Zeph. 3:6). In addition, various of the specific images employed here find parallels elsewhere (to 6 Ezra 16:28, cf. Amos 5:3 and Matt. 24:40–41; to 6 Ezra 16:29–31, cf. Isa. 17:6; to 6 Ezra 16:32, cf. Isa. 7:23–25).

16:35–78
Exhortation of God's People

Whereas the first major part of 6 Ezra is concerned exclusively with prediction of woes (15:5–16:34), the book's final section focuses on the exhortation of God's people. God's elect are counseled to withdraw from worldly activity and to abstain vigorously from sin, in view of the impending calamities.

16:35–52, Advice and Instruction. The prophet warns God's people of the imminence of the coming destruction and exhorts them to be like "strangers on earth" (16:40, NEB) during the time of tribulation. Every worldly activity should be undertaken as though it will not bear fruit, since in fact the land will soon be plundered and its inhabitants taken captive.

The image of childbirth in 16:38–39 is close to 4:40–42 and to 1 Thess. 5:3. Also, the literarily parallel statements that make up 16:41–47 show similarities to Deut. 28:30–33, 38–42 and 1 Cor. 7:29–31.

16:53–67, Warnings to Sinners. As was noted above (see commentary on 15:20–27), 6 Ezra features a strong polemic against sin. The present section stresses the futility of trying to hide one's sins from God. The recital of God's acts of creation in 16:55–62, intended to underscore the creator's omniscience, finds parallels in wisdom literature (cf. Job 38; Sir. 43) and in apocalyptic literature (cf. 4 Ezra 4:5–9; 1 Enoch 93:11–14).

16:68–73, Prediction of Persecution. The seer anticipates the advent of a terrible persecution against "those who fear the Lord" (16:70; cf. 15:8–10, 20–21, 52–56). This persecution will demonstrate the "tested quality" (16:73, RSV) of God's chosen people.

16:74–78, Concluding Instruction to the Elect. The prophetic discourse concludes with a reassurance of salvation to the elect and a stern warning to them not to be overcome by sin.

Bibliography

Box, G. H. "4 Ezra." In *Apocrypha and Pseudepigrapha of the Old Testament*. 2 vols. Edited by R. H. Charles. Oxford: Clarendon, 1913. Vol. 2, pp. 542–624.

Coggins, R. J., and M. A. Knibb. *The First and Second Books of Esdras*. Cambridge Bible Commentary on the New English Bible. Cambridge: Cambridge University Press, 1979.

Metzger, B. M. "The Fourth Book of Ezra." In *The Old Testament Pseudepigrapha*. 2 vols. Edited by J. H. Charlesworth. Garden City, NY: Doubleday, 1983. Vol. 1, pp. 516–59.

Myers, J. M. *I and II Esdras*. Garden City, NY: Doubleday, 1974.

Stone, M. E. "Coherence and Inconsistency in the Apocalypses: The Case of 'The End' in 4 Ezra." *Journal of Biblical Literature* 102 (1983):229–43.

——— "Reactions to Destructions of the Second Temple: Theology, Perception and Conversion." *Journal for the Study of Judaism* 12 (1981):195–204.

Thompson, A. L. *Responsibility for Evil in the Theodicy of 4 Ezra*. Missoula, MT: Scholars Press, 1977.

TOBIT

GEORGE W. E. NICKELSBURG

INTRODUCTION

Literary Analysis

Tobit as Narrative. Tobit is a piece of historical fiction set in the Assyrian captivity that recounts the sufferings of a pious Israelite and his family and God's alleviation of these troubles. From a literary point of view Tobit is a rich and complex text that eludes simple analysis. Taken as a whole, however, the work is a sophisticated and carefully crafted narrative.

Briefly, this is the plot. In spite of his faithfulness to God and his many deeds of mercy to others, Tobit suffers greatly. When he can no longer believe that God will deliver him, he prays for death. In another city, his relative Sarah also sees death as the only likely solution to her suffering. But when all appears hopeless, God sends healing by means of the angel Raphael. Parallel to the story of Tobit is the uncompleted story of Israel. Tobit's situation is paradigmatic for the exiled nation. As God has chastised Tobit, so Israel, suffering in exile, is being chastised. But God's mercy on Tobit and his family guarantees that this mercy will bring the Israelites back to their land. Since this event, described only in predictions, awaits fulfillment, one level of the double story is incomplete.

The author's mastery of narrative technique is evident at many points. The plot develops, is complicated, and is resolved in classic fashion. Parallel scenes advance the plot and develop characterization. Narrative tension is maintained by revealing to readers what the characters do not know and by moving in and out of alternating scenes with different subplots and characters. These characters are exemplary in their piety and believable in their human flaws. The protagonist, Tobit, is a complex figure. Although he epitomizes the right life and is articulate in his conviction that God rewards the righteous, he can vacillate between faith and doubt. His movement, however, from despair at the beginning to doxology at the end, offers a model and a promise for readers who can empathize with his predicament. Humor is an important component in Tobit, and one often senses the author's delight in entertaining readers. This factor notwithstanding, the book is a serious treatment of the religious problem of innocent suffering.

Other Literary Forms. Although the author writes narrative, the complex use of other literary forms enriches the work and complicates the issue of its genre. The characters express sorrow and praise in prayers and hymns written in the diction and forms of contemporary Israelite liturgical usage. Twice Tobit instructs his son in a deathbed testament. First he speaks in proverbs. Later, his prediction of future events is reminiscent of historical apocalypses, such as Daniel 7–12. God's resolution of Tobit's suffering, which dominates the narrative, is recounted in an extended angelic epiphany or appearance.

In addition to these clearly discernible forms are traces of folkloristic motifs and themes such as "The Grateful Dead" and "The Dangerous Bride." Also reflected is the traditional tale of the persecuted and vindicated courtier (Dan. 1–6, Esther, and the nonbiblical story of Ahiqar).

Religious Dimensions

The literary complexity of Tobit mirrors the richness of the book's religious expression. Fundamentally, the work makes a many-faceted statement about the interrelationships of God, humanity, and the world, and it does so through many traditional religious themes. Basic is the assertion that a providential God orchestrates the events of life and history for the benefit of Israel and the Israelites. Faithfulness to God and love toward others are rewarded.

The author's assertions about the sovereignty of God do not avoid the problematic aspects of human experience, which are explained in several ways. Evil spirits wreak havoc on the righteous and innocent. Since the righteous are not perfect, the merciful God must sometimes "scourge" or "chastise" them before providing their due rewards. The dispensing of such rewards is, moreover, no simple matter and involves a complex divine juggling act; final benefit for all requires temporary suffering for some.

A central factor in the book is the inability of human beings to perceive divine activity. This failure to understand is, in an important sense, the point of the work. God's purpose moves on in spite of human ignorance of it. Heaven's decisions and actions are hidden from human knowledge. The healing angel is

791

thought to be merely a friendly and helpful companion. A journey undertaken for one purpose has unimaginably beneficial consequences. People widely separated wrongly suppose that the worst is happening. The resolution of the plot involves a revelation—not simply of the angel's identity, but of the triumph of God's purpose and the frailness of human faith. Tobit is not an apocalyptic work. Nonetheless, in its two-storied universe, with angels and demons, its claim that God's hidden purposes are operative, and its assertion that God's triumph will be revealed, the book owes a debt to apocalyptic texts like 1 Enoch.

Although the author's eye is on the workings of the heavenly court, God intervenes on earth in human life and history. God and the angels are "with" the righteous as they live their lives and "with" Israel in its exile. Human beings are healed now, and final healing will restore the people to their land and again give them access to the sanctuary from which they apostasized.

Constitutive of the book's portrayal of God's activity on earth is its own version of the cross-cultural myth of the disguised heavenly helper. NT students will find here one prototype for the Marcan Gospel's story of Jesus, the hidden Son of God who comes to heal and combat Satan, and whose unique saving death reveals his identity.

For the author of Tobit, God's merciful, saving activity is cause for doxology, and the book is replete with hymns and hymnic language. Tobit's progress from doubt to affirmation is marked by his successive use of a prayer of lament and a hymn of praise. It is not accidental that the book itself is said to be a doxological confession of God's great and marvelous activity (12:16–22).

Social Aspects

For the author of Tobit, religion is embodied in social realities—of which we are given some tantalizing glimpses. Marriage and family are central for social stability and for Israelite national and religious identity. Of marriage customs and family obligations there are numerous hints. Proper burial of the dead is a pervasive concern. The pious life is enacted in concrete deeds of loving-kindness. Thus, the religious obligation to bring tithes and first fruits is intended to benefit others, and the rich have a special responsibility to share their wealth through the giving of alms.

For Israelites in exile the righteous life has its negative social consequences. Tobit is persecuted and ridiculed by antagonistic and unsympathetic neighbors. The importance of endogamy (i.e., marriage within one's own tribal group) must be underscored, because intermarriage and assimilation are an easy capitulation to the social pressures felt in a minority situation.

Place and Time of Writing

Tobit is thoroughly exilic in its viewpoint, and return to the land of Israel and Jerusalem is a consummation devoutly to be awaited. These factors, inextricably woven into the narrative fabric, strongly suggest that the book was written in the Diaspora (i.e., among Jews living outside the land of Palestine). A date in the third century B.C. seems likely, although the oral and folkloric roots are older.

Text

Tobit was composed in Aramaic and translated into Hebrew and Greek. The Greek was transmitted in a long form (G^2, supported by the Old Latin version) and a short form (G^1). Fragments of several Aramaic and Hebrew manuscripts from Qumran indicate that the long form is more original (although it lacks two sections found in G^1 and the Old Latin: 4:7–19; 13:6–10a). All major English editions (including the forthcoming revision of the RSV) are now based on the long form. This commentary follows that form but makes occasional reference to possible original readings in G^1 (sometimes supported by the Old Latin).

COMMENTARY

1:1–2

Superscription

The superscription describes the work as "the book of the words of Tobit"; it was written at the command of the angel Raphael (12:20) as a doxological confession of God's intervention in the lives of the protagonists. The name Tobit is a Greek form of the Hebrew name Tobi, probably short for Tobiah ("Yahweh is my good"), which in the present work is the name of Tobit's son (in Gk., Tobias). Tobit's home was in Thisbe, a city the author locates in upper Galilee. The location is the first of a number of parallels with 1 Enoch, which describes certain mythic events as taking place in the same general area (1 Enoch 13:4–10).

1:3–2:10
Tobit's Piety and Its Consequences

The narrative begins as Tobit recounts his piety and its anomalous consequences. Although he did not participate in Israel's apostasy, he and his family were taken into exile, where his pious concern cost him his job and his physical well-being.

1:3–9
Tobit in Galilee

The first person singular narrative begun here will continue until 3:7, when the story of Sarah is introduced by an anonymous third-person narrator who will recount the rest of the story. Using the idiom of the two ways (1:3; see commentary below on 4:3–19), Tobit describes himself as a righteous Israelite who devotes himself to acts of kindness for his exiled compatriots in Assyrian Nineveh.

This activity is traced back to his days in Israel, where he was an exception among the apostates in the Northern Kingdom (1:4–8). Tobit describes the prevailing situation—Jeroboam's schism and his establishment of a rival sanctuary at Dan (1 Kings 12:25–33; cf. Tob. 2:6, the quotation of Amos's oracle against Bethel). The divine establishment of the Jerusalem Temple will be emphasized in chap. 14. In the midst of Israelite apostates, Tobit is singularly faithful to the Jerusalem sanctuary, to which he makes the pilgrimages prescribed in the "eternal commandment" in the Mosaic Torah (Deut. 16:16–17). Tied to these pilgrimages are the obligations to bring first fruits and tithes: first fruits of crops (Deut. 26:1–11); tithes of herds (Lev. 27:32); first shearings (Deut. 18:4); tithes of crops (Lev. 27:30; Deut. 14:22–23); a tithe turned into money (Deut. 14:25); and the third-year tithe for the orphans, widows, and sojourners (Deut. 14:28–29). Emphasized in this recitation are the Israelites' obligations to Jerusalem and to the Aaronidic priesthood, the Levites, and the poor and deprived. Concerning the last, Tobit will say much more later.

Tobit learned the law from his grandmother. This reference to the family is the first of many. Already in the next sentence, Tobit states that he married a woman from his own kindred; in 4:12–13 he will instruct their son Tobias to do so.

1:10–2:10
Tobit's Piety in Assyria

The deportation to Assyria provides the story of Tobit with the Diaspora setting that is presumed for the rest of the narrative. As before, Tobit's piety is the author's central concern, but now this pious conduct has disastrous consequences.

1:10–15, Tobit's Success in Shalmaneser's Court. With the deportation (722 B.C.; see 2 Kings 17), Tobit takes up residence in Nineveh, the capital of Assyria, where he remains the pious exception. Tob. 1:10–13 is reminiscent of Dan. 1:8–20, where Daniel and his friends rise to prominence in a Mesopotamian court after maintaining righteous conduct in a gentile context. Other elements typical of Daniel 3 and 6 will occur in Tob. 1:16–22. Tobit's deposit of money and inability to retrieve it are crucial for the development of the plot in chaps. 4–11. That the Israelite Gabael lives in Media (as do Sarah and her family, 3:7) can be explained by 2 Kings 17:6, which locates part of the deportees in the cities of Medes.

Although the text follows the narrative in 2 Kings 17–18, its historical statements and inferences are incorrect. The succession of Assyrian kings was: Shalmaneser V, 727–722 B.C.; Sargon II, 722–705; Sennacherib, 705–681; and Esarhaddon, 681–669. Shalmaneser and Sennacherib were brothers and not father and son. Although Sargon defeated Samaria and deported the Israelites, his absence here and in the next section is probably due to the omission of his name in 2 Kings.

1:16–22, Tobit Persecuted and Restored. Events here parallel Daniel 3 and 6. The Israelite courtier is persecuted for righteous deeds and then restored to high position. Different from Daniel, the persecution and restoration of Tobit occur under successive kings, and the righteous deeds are acts of mercy, deeds of particular interest to this author. On feeding the hungry and clothing the naked, see Tob. 4:16. The concern is emphasized by the many commands to give alms (cf. 4:7–11). On burial of the dead, cf. 2:1–10; 4:3–4; 6:14; 8:12; and 14:10–13. The importance of burial is presumed in the Hebrew Bible, as it is throughout the literature of the ancient world. Exposure of bodies was especially abhorrent (cf. Deut. 28:26; 1 Kings 21:24; 2 Kings 9:30–37; Ps. 79:2–3).

Sennacherib's murder of Judeans (Tob. 1:18) is not indicated in 2 Kings 19, 2 Chronicles 32, or Isaiah 37, although his defeat is seen as divine punishment. While Sennacherib's death occurred two decades after his siege of Jerusalem, 2 Kings 19:35–37; 2 Chron. 32:20–21; and Isa. 37:37–38 suggest a much shorter period of time (here specified as forty days). Again the author of Tobit is misled. Tobit's persecution for burying the victims of the king is reminiscent of Euripides' *Antigone*.

In 1:21–22 Tobit identifies Ahiqar as his nephew. The story of Ahiqar was a popular tale about a sage in the court of Esarhaddon who was conspired against by his nephew Nadin (called Nadab in Tob. 14:10–11), condemned to death, rescued, and restored to power. The plot parallels Daniel 3 and 6. The earliest evidence for the story is fifth-century B.C. Aramaic papyrus found at the ruins of the Egyptian Jewish colony of Elephantine. Neither the manuscript nor the later versions of the text, translated into numerous other languages, indicate that Ahiqar was a Jew or a relative of someone named Tobit. The author of Tobit mentions Ahiqar again in 2:10; 11:18; and 14:10, where details of the story's plot are given. Tob. 4:17 closely parallels a proverb in 2:10 of the Syriac version of the Ahiqar story.

2:1–10, Tobit's Blindness. This scene parallels the previous one: mention of a monarch; Tobit's burial of the dead; the disastrous consequences; and reference to Ahiqar's kindness. Different from 1:16–22, the consequences of this event will require most of the rest of the book to resolve.

The incident is typical of the characterization of Tobit and portrays one of the major problems dealt with in the book. The pious Israelite suffers because he attends to the needs of others. Tobit's piety is evident in his concern to bury the Israelite and in other details. He observes the feast of Pentecost, and, more important, he wishes to share his meal with the poor (cf. 1:17; Luke 14:12–24; 16:19–31). The references to ablution are puzzling. According to Num. 19:11–19, contact with the corpse renders one unclean for seven days. The present text suggests that Tobit's ablution cleanses him, so that he can enter his house (Tob. 2:4–5). The sequence: burial, ablution, sleeping outdoors (vv. 7–9) may indicate impurity (thus G[1]), or it may simply provide narrative cause for the event that follows. The function of the reference to sunset is unclear. Does Tobit postpone the burial so that he can eat the meal on the feast day? Or has the detail been suggested by the references to sunset in Num. 19:19–22 and Amos 8:9? (See the next paragraph.)

The quotation of Amos 8:10 in Tob. 2:6 is ironic. The oracle against the sinners of Bethel, who trample on the poor and take their grain (Amos 5:11; 8:4–6) is here applied to the pious one who shares his bread with the poor. Elements in the Amos passage are woven into the narrative of Tobit: it is on a feast day (Tob. 2:1) that Tobit's joy turns to sorrow (v. 5) and mourning (v. 6). The motif of mockery will return in 3:1–15. Why does the author have his hero blinded by bird droppings? It is a cruel conclusion to the incident, and one can imagine the continued mockery. Perhaps the birds are agents of a demon like Asmodeus (3:8; cf. *Jub.* 11:11, where Satan sends ravens to devour seed; and

Mark 4:4, 15, which appears to know some such tradition). In any case, the event triggers the divinely directed scenario that is tracked through the rest of the plot. Perhaps the author asserts that God works even in cruel and evidently arbitrary circumstances. Such a point is reinforced by a comparison with Sir. 38:1–7. Although physicians are agents of divine healing, their failure will facilitate God's plans for the Tobiad family. The section ends with a motif that will recur frequently. Tobit's family grieves, because they do not know of God's eventual disposition of the case (cf. 11:17–18).

2:11–3:17
Tobit's Fate Linked to Sarah's

Tobit's reproach by Anna and his death wish are parallel to Sarah's reproach by her servants and her prayer for death. This literary diptych and its immediate sequel are the turning point in the story. The prayers are heard, but they will be answered in an unexpected way—through healing rather than death. This resolution will join two parts of the family and solve another problem for Israelites in exile—finding a suitable spouse with whom to maintain one's religious and cultural identity in a foreign land. The description of Israelites in prayer is integral to the author's view of piety, and the laments prepare for the contrasting hymn of praise in chap. 13.

2:11–3:6
Tobit Led to Seek Escape in Death

The problem of Tobit's blindness is exacerbated by a new domestic incident, which leads him to pray for death as an escape from his misery.

2:11–14, Tobit's Criticism and Anna's Reproach. The exacerbation of Tobit's troubles is tied to his concern about the righteous life, but the section is replete with irony. The prosperous, influential, and generous public servant is now dependent on his wife's earning power and the generosity of her employers. Although his deeds stemmed from his trust in God and presumed God's reward, he cannot believe that he is the recipient of the generosity of others. These reactions flesh out the characterization of a complex and believable human being. His central virtue—a concern with righteousness—is his undoing. In a state of depression because he fails to experience God's blessing for his righteous deeds, Tobit interprets an act of generosity as confirmation of his sad plight. Now he believes his wife has strayed from the straight and narrow. Concern with righteousness has become an obsession. His shaken faith in divine retribution has its corollary in his inability to trust Anna.

Her response is ironic, although its precise meaning is unclear. According to G² Tobit's criticism shows his true colors ("Now we can see what you are" 2:14 NEB). The text of G¹ looks like an ironic suggestion that Tobit is playing God, claiming to know everything (in spite of his blindness).

3:1–6, Tobit's Prayer. God's righteous judgment is the pervading theme of Tobit's prayer. In keeping with the book's double focus, this judgment is dispensed to individuals like Tobit and is evident in the nation's exile. His earlier recitation of his pious deeds notwithstanding (chaps. 1–2), Tobit does not claim perfection, but confesses "my sins and errors" (3:3). The prayer does not presume that God exacts retribution for every sin. Verse 2 balances divine justice with mercy and faithfulness. Nonetheless, the prayer recognizes God's right to exact the retribution that Tobit sees in his life. Paradoxically, Tobit parallels the punishment he perceives in his righteous life with the nation's plight, which tradition uniformly saw as just.

Tobit's petition (v. 6) expresses another paradox—faith's mixture of doubt and acceptance. As woes are compounded, Tobit can no longer believe that God will reverse these disasters. Yet he accepts the divine sovereignty that expresses itself in premature death. This acceptance is not based on a belief that such a death will be reversed through resurrection and eternal life.

3:7–15
Sarah Led to Seek Escape in Death

The swift movement from Nineveh to Ecbatana to the heavenly throne room (v. 16) and the use of temporal expressions (vv. 7, 10, 11) tighten the narrative and unify the action, but they also depict God's control over widely scattered events.

3:7–9, Sarah Reproached by Her Maids. Sarah's plight is similar to Tobit's. She is an innocent victim of circumstances beyond her control. The demonic element, perhaps suggested in 2:10, is explicit here. The reproach that Tobit felt in the disparity between his piety and his lot in life has its counterpart in the reproach of Sarah's inability to consummate her marriage and have children to continue her father's line. The motif of the demon lover was widespread. In contemporary Jewish literature it is closely paralleled in the story of watchers, angelic beings who descend from heaven to mate with human women, in 1 Enoch 6–11. Here the demon who cannot consummate his lust kills his rivals.

3:10–15, Sarah's Prayer. Sarah's response and prayer have their own nuances. Her reflections move from self-pity to filial concern. Because her contemplated suicide would grieve her father, she turns to Tobit's solution. Let God take her life. Although Sarah's prayer is similar to Tobit's, there are remarkable differences. Sarah begins with praise and never refers to God's justice. To the contrary, she protests her innocence (cf. vv. 14–15a with vv. 3, 5). Moreover, a second reference to her death is modified. If God does not see fit to let her die, then let God heed her (and remove her affliction). It is an alternative Tobit has not considered.

3:16–17
A Solution Prepared in Heaven

Prayer catalyzes the divine resolution of human problems. The introductory expression "at that very time" and the repetition of the verb "hear" connect this scene with the prayers, and the rest of the paragraph summarizes the events to come. In the heavenly throne room the seven archangels (cf. 1 Enoch 20) relay the prayers they receive (cf. Tob. 12:12, 15) and are sent to answer them. Raphael's name (Heb., "God has healed") denotes the angel's activity (cf. 1 Enoch 10:4, 7; 40:9). For a close parallel to this view of the divine throne room and the relationship between prayer and the angels' roles as intercessors and agents of deliverance cf. 1 Enoch 8–10; 40; 47; 97:5; 99:3; 100:4. The probable original wording of Tob. 3:16 and 12:12, 15, "before the glory of the Great One (Holy One)," reflects the formulas in 1 Enoch 103:1; 104:1. God's providence will result in Tobias' marriage to the woman for whom he is the most suitable husband (3:17). This providence is evident in Tobit's and Sarah's simultaneous return to the world where their prayers will be answered.

4:1–11:19
The Healing of Tobit and Sarah

Heaven has made its decision to deliver Tobit and Sarah; the enactment remains to be described. Essential to the narrative art in these chapters is a disparity between readers' knowledge of what is happening and the characters' ignorance. This disparity has its humorous side but also makes a religious statement: God's purposes are operative even when they are not perceived. The denouement will reveal this to the characters.

4:1–5:3
Tobit Prepares for His Death

Certain that his prayer will be answered, Tobit prepares for his death. He must straighten out his finances and give his son the testamentary advice typical of deathbed situations.

4:1–2, Tobit Remembers a Bank Deposit.
Human events can have a divine dimension. We may paraphrase 4:1 as follows: "As soon as God had decided to help, God jogged Tobit's memory." This recollection will trigger events that effect the healing of Tobit and Sarah and the marriage of Tobias and Sarah. Tobit's human perception is altogether different. Confronted with the certainty of his death, he wishes to secure his son's future. And so he remembers the money he deposited (1:14–15), which can lift Tobias from the family's present deprivation. He cannot suspect the outcome of Tobias' journey.

4:3–19, Tobit's Testament.
Tobit's certainty about his imminent death is evident in his testamentary instruction to Tobias. The genre is familiar from texts like Genesis 49, Deuteronomy 31–34, 1 Enoch 81–82, 91, Jubilees 21–23, the Testament of Moses, and the Testaments of the Twelve Patriarchs. (On the literary form, see the commentary below on 14:1–11.) The narrative in Tobit has already presented the exemplary biographical material typical of these texts. The context here confines itself to the kind of ethical instruction that predominates in many Jewish testaments. The focal issues are the special concerns in Tobit: proper burial (4:3–4); charitable and generous use of wealth and possessions (vv. 7–11, 14, 16–17); and endogamous marriage (vv. 12–13). This specific advice is punctuated with general instructions that use the categories of the "two ways." This section and its reprises in 12:6–10 and 14:10–11 have many parallels in Jewish wisdom literature and lend an explicitly didactic tone to the present work (→ Wisdom). The poetic parallelism in this section is not indicated in all English editions.

Typical of the testamentary form is the summoning of the son (4:3) and the command to bury. This text stresses the son's responsibility to his parents (cf. Matt. 8:21; Luke 9:59). The phrasing recalls the commandment to honor one's parents (Exod. 20:12; Deut. 5:16) and its paraphrase in Sir. 7:27. Tob. 4:3–4 reflects this author's broader interest in familial matters.

Verses 5–6 introduce the idiom of the two ways—of righteousness (or truth) and iniquity. The imagery is typical of Jewish and early Christian wisdom instruction and appears also in pagan sources. A parallel to the antithetical formulation of these verses and to 4:19 occurs in 1 Enoch 94:1–5.

A major section of text, Tob. 4:7–19, is omitted in G², but its originality is supported by its presence in G¹ and the Old Latin translation, which otherwise tends to agree with G².

The prospering of the ways of the righteous (v. 6) forms a transition to the discussion of wealth in vv. 7–11, where Tobit promises that generosity will be rewarded. Verse 7b expresses a principle of appropriate compensation ("Do not turn away your face . . . the face of God will not be turned away"). Similarly, to give alms to others is to lay up treasure for oneself (v. 9). Almsgiving was an important part of Israelite piety and expressed the biblical concern for the poor (→ Alms). The topic is integral to this book. The hero himself performed such acts of charity (1:3, 17), and his commands here provide the ethical context for Tobias' receipt of the money from Gabael in Rages (9:1–6). As Raphael and Tobit repeat later, God rewards such generous use of wealth (12:8–10; 14:11). There is irony in Tobit's observations, however. He is awaiting a premature death, which is not the proper recompense for his conduct. But for the author, who knows the outcome, the statement is true, and it will be reiterated when it is shown to be true. Tob. 4:11 suggests a parallel between almsgiving and sacrifice, which will be made explicit in 12:9. According to this view, one obtains forgiveness and atonement not only through sacrifice in the temple, but also through generous deeds. Several centuries later the idea would have a special and essential religious function for the Jews, whose Temple had been permanently destroyed.

The injunctions about wealth and possessions provide a context for NT statements on the subject, especially the wisdom material in Matt. 6:19–33; Luke 12:22–34, in passages peculiar to Luke, and in the Letter of James.

From the responsible use of wealth, Tobit returns to the topic of the family (cf. Tob. 4:3–4), here the making of a proper marriage. In one of the book's playful ironies, Tobit gives instructions that will be carried out in a way he hardly suspects. Tobias' journey to fetch the money will result in his marriage to the kind of wife Tobit has in mind. The prohibition against marriage to a foreign spouse appears already in the story of Isaac and Rebekah (Gen. 24:3), where a journey is also undertaken to find such a spouse. The concern reappears in Ezra 9–10 and Neh. 10:28–30, is emphasized in Jubilees' recasting of the Genesis narratives, and is central in Joseph and Asenath. The topic is especially relevant here in a document set in the Diaspora. Tob. 4:13 reflects the author's sociopsychological insight. In an alien culture it can be tempting for a member of the minority to marry into the majority to prove oneself better than one's compatriots. For Tobit such arrogant disdaining of one's own people leads to the destruction of the nation and religious and cultural disorder. This, rather than a notion of racial purity, is the basis for endogamy.

The proverb in v. 13b is probably traditional. Although the proverb begins with a comment on the arrogance of exogamous marriage (i.e., marriage outside the tribal unit), the next two lines discuss useless behavior and its results—loss, want, and hunger. Verse 14a complements this train of thought and may have been part of the tradition: shiftless behavior can lead to hunger; so can the withholding of wages (for the biblical command, cf. Lev. 19:13). In the context of Tobit, 4:14a is a command for the proper use of wealth, with the promise of appropriate recompense.

Verses 14b–15a are a pair of general injunctions. The first is a balanced line ("in all . . . in all") that begins like v. 12 ("watch yourself"). The second is the earliest datable formulation of the Golden Rule.

Verses 15b–17 touch on traditional topics of Jewish piety: feed the hungry, clothe the naked, give alms. The subject of food is introduced by a reference to the abuse overdrinking—also a traditional wisdom topic (cf. Prov. 23:29–35; Sir. 31:25–30; T. Judah 11–14, 16). Tob. 4:17 is one of several parallels to the story of Ahiqar (2:10 in the Syriac version of Ahiqar; see commentary above on 1:16–22). Here the point is: sustain the hungry, but if they are sinners, leave your food at the grave of the righteous dead. The ethic is startlingly narrow and the practice obscure, but the author's interest in burial is evident.

The interpretation of 4:18–19 depends on one's textual reconstruction; the omission in G^2 ends at v. 19b (" . . . the Lord gives"). In G^1 and the Old Latin seeking good counsel and the imagery of the two ways are central. Verse 19a may reflect Ps. 34:1, a psalm whose theme is relevant to the story of Tobit. The warning about nations' lack of good counsel (cf. Deut. 32:28) is pertinent in a Diaspora writing. What God gives varies according to the texts: in G^1, "all good things" (cf. Matt. 7:7–14, with many parallels to this text); in G^2, "good counsel." According to the Old Latin and G^2 in part, God exalts and brings down to Sheol. The concluding admonition parallels 1 Enoch 94:5, which also concludes a section of two ways instruction (1 Enoch 94:1–5).

4:20–5:3, Tobit's Instructions About the Money. His ethical instructions completed, Tobit takes up the subject of money in Rages (4:1–2). Still speaking in the idiom of wisdom instruction, he assures Tobias that this money will reverse their circumstances if Tobias uses it rightly (4:20–21). Tobias' response (5:1) echoes Exod. 19:8; 24:3; 7; and Josh. 1:16 and constitutes his formal acceptance of his father's Torah, on teaching. Tob. 5:3b answers Tobias' second question in v. 2b and forms a transition to the next section of the story.

5:4–22
Tobias Hires a Traveling Companion

Tobias' journey to Rages in Media requires a traveling companion. Little do Tobit and Tobias suspect that he will be an angel sent to effect God's beneficent purposes. This ignorance and the double entendres by Tobit and Raphael are the subject of considerable narrative delight.

5:4–8, Tobias Finds Raphael. The section of Tobit that is cast in the form of an angelic epiphany begins here as the angel appears to Tobias in human form. The presence of an unrecognized divine being is an ancient folkloristic motif (cf. Gen. 18). Especially close to Tobit is its use in Books 1–3 of Homer's Odyssey.

Raphael's words in 5:6 suggest that this man is a frequent traveler through Mesopotamia. In reality, Raphael alludes to his angelic journeys (cf. v. 9). The distance from Rages to Ecbatana took Alexander's army ten days' forced march.

5:9–16a, Tobit's Conversation with Raphael. The author continues the playful description of the ignorance of Tobit and Tobias over the real state of affairs. As readers know, Tobit's concern about Raphael's lineage and qualifications is beside the point.

The opening words of the conversation are psychologically loaded. Tobit reacts bitterly to the angel's common greeting "may all be well with you," and with some self-pity he likens himself to the dead man he expects to be. But Raphael means what he says and predicts an outcome that Tobit cannot comprehend.

When Tobit queries Raphael about his family, the angel futilely attempts to avoid the issue. He must lie. The discussion of Raphael's lineage is, of course, absurd, but his and his father's alleged names suggest the story's outcome (Azarias, Gk., from the Heb. for "The Lord has helped"; Ananias, Gk., from the Heb. for "the Lord has had mercy"). Tobit's desire to know the facts (Gk. alētheia) about Raphael's family is a piece of authorial irony, but it is also a theological comment: human beings can know "the truth" only when God reveals it, and human precautions are a charade when God is in charge. Both Tobit's comment on Raphael's family stock (v. 13) and his benediction on the angel (v. 16) are gratuitous.

5:16b, Tobit's Farewell. The two textual traditions narrate this section with different nuances. In G^1 there is a play on the idea of "the way." God will prosper Tobias on his journey, as God prospers the "way" of the righteous (cf. 4:19). The idea appears in G^2 in the next section. Here G^2 implies that Tobit expects to be alive when Tobias returns. In both texts Tobit's wish for an angelic guide unwittingly expresses the truth.

5:17–22, Anna's Sorrow and Tobit's Encouragement. For Anna, Tobias' departure is a cause for sorrow, and the expected monetary gain is not worth the risk. Her sensibility contrasts with Tobit's faith: an angel will accompany Tobias, his journey will prosper, and he will return safely.

6:1–17
Tobias and Raphael on the Road to Media

The journey to Media has several functions. Most obviously, it provides the geographic movement that enables Tobias to seek his financial fortune. But in God's scheme, Tobias is headed for other, unexpected goals. He will meet the woman destined to be his bride, and along the way he will acquire the magical apparatus that will facilitate the healing of Tobit and Sarah.

6:1–8, Tobias Catches a Fish. As elsewhere in the story, God intervenes directly in human events. The means for healing Tobit and Sarah literally leaps out of the water just as Tobias arrives at the riverbank. God has prepared a great fish to accomplish the divine purpose. The parallel to the Jonah story is clearer in G^1, where the fish attempts to swallow Tobias himself rather than just his foot (cf. also commentary below on 14:3b–7). An allusion to magical practice for physical cure and exorcism is evident, but the author's appraisal of it is less certain. Perhaps he makes fun of magic. In any case one wonders how Tobias can survive a journey through the Mesopotamian heat transporting the reeking organs of the fish. Although the journey is from one geographic location to another, the narrative recalls the accounts of Enoch's cosmic journeys (1 Enoch 17–36). In the company of an angel Tobias travels to a place where he sees something he does not understand. When he asks, the angel explains.

6:9–17, Raphael Promises Tobias a Bride. When Tobias and Raphael have traversed the 325 miles to the Median capital, the angel informs Tobias of the events that will take place in Ecbatana. The section serves two functions. First, it allows Tobias to protest against the dangers of marrying Sarah but then to accept Raphael's assurance of divine protection. This acceptance is remarkable since he does not know that his companion is an angel. Second, in this section Tobias receives the instructions necessary to defeat the demon.

The conversation is carefully constructed and held together by key words. The references

to "this night" emphasize how swiftly the action will move and how imminent is the danger that Tobias may perish on his wedding night. Raphael's repeated urging ("listen to me, brother") meets with resistance. Tobias has "heard" about the fate of Sarah's previous husbands, and he is "afraid" the same will happen to him. After Raphael's reassurances and the formulaic "fear not," typical of epiphanies (though Tobias does not perceive this as such), the young man acquiesces in what he has "heard" from Raphael. The angel uses several arguments. He responds to Tobias' concern that he live to bury his parents (4:3–4) by recalling Tobit's other command that he marry a woman from his family (4:12–13). In addition, the apparatus for an exorcism, combined with earnest prayer, will effect the couple's deliverance. Finally, without citing his sources, Raphael assures Tobias that Sarah is the bride eternally destined for him. Predestination is an aspect of the author's belief that God intervenes in human affairs.

7:1–9:6
The Travelers in Media: Sarah Is Healed

This lengthy section solves the second of the problems in chap. 3. Sarah is healed when Tobias and Raphael dispose of Asmodeus. Moreover, Tobias' marriage fulfills Tobit's commandment (4:12–13) and dramatizes the importance of endogamy.

7:1–8a, Tobias and Raphael Are Welcomed. Once Tobias has agreed to marry Sarah, he is anxious to be taken to her house, where he is welcomed with great emotion. As in 6:13, the author assumes that news traveled through the Mesopotamian Israelite communities. Although Tobit is "healthy and alive," Raguel finds incongruous the blindness of a man who fits the Greek ideal of goodness and nobility (the translator uses the Gk. terms *kalos* and *agathos*) and epitomizes Israelite piety (he is righteous and does deeds of mercy; cf., e.g., 1:3).

7:8b–15, The Wedding of Tobias and Sarah. Tobias wastes no time in reminding Raphael of his promise to arrange a marriage with Sarah. One did not discuss business before meals. Tobias' breach of etiquette underscores the urgency of the request. Raphael's role as marriage broker combines features from Genesis 24, where Abraham sends a servant to find a wife for Isaac, promising that an angel would accompany him (Gen. 24:7, 40).

Tobias need not worry; according to the law of levirate marriage, he is the leading candidate for Sarah's hand, a fact emphasized by the references to the law of Moses (cf. Deut. 25:5–10). The author is concerned not with descendants for the first husband, the point of levirate law, but with Sarah's status as an only child (Tob. 3:15). In this context Raguel's willingness to "tell the truth" (7:10) is praiseworthy. The author's irony appears in Raguel's statement, "Eat, drink, and be merry tonight, for there is no one else to take Sarah my daughter, except you" (v. 10). It is an ad hoc reformulation of the familiar aphorism; past events suggest that tomorrow Tobias will be dead. Tobias' single-minded determination to marry Sarah contrasts with Raguel's vacillation between the assumption that Tobias will die like the others and his hope that things will be different. This hope may reflect Raguel's evident ignorance of the demonic cause of the husbands' deaths. The brief description of the wedding ceremony sheds a little light on the details of such occasions. The document that Raguel writes is not the ketubah (Heb., a marriage contract written by the bridegroom) well known from rabbinic writings.

7:16–8:18, The Wedding Night: Healing and Joy.

With the wedding ceremony and meal finished, the moment of truth has arrived. Will the marriage be consummated, or will another bridegroom die? The mother is hopeful and quiets her daughter's sorrow with the doubly repeated "have courage" (Gk. tharsei), very likely a translation of the same Aramaic as Raphael's "fear not" (6:17).

The first part of 8:4 appears to have originally been located after v. 1. The parents bring Tobias to the wedding chamber, and then they leave and shut the door. Whether the text ever described the demon's entrance into the wedding chamber is uncertain. In any case Tobias' magical ritual and the young couple's prayer stand in the same order as in Raphael's earlier description (6:16–17).

The idea that the stench of roasted fish organs (now many days ripe) could drive off a demon was surely intended as humorous, though it may reflect some actual ritual. "Binding" is a technical term used for the incapacitating of demons. The description recalls 1 Enoch 10:4, where Raphael binds Asael hand and foot (cf. Matt. 22:13). Asmodeus' banishment to Egypt suggests that Tobit was written in a place other than in Egypt.

The prayer of Tobias and Sarah is a functional equivalent of the magical ritual. They pray for mercy (Gk. eleos, a technical term in Tobit for deliverance; see commentary below on 13:1–2) and salvation (Gk. soteria). They have already been saved from the demon; so the prayer (which fits well with other liturgical elements in Tobit) is a petition for continued blessing. Perhaps the references to the fish and the ritual go back to older folkloristic motifs that were early integrated into this story. Note-worthy in the prayer is the allusion to Genesis, not as a reference to Scripture, but as a reminder of God's will in creation.

The prayer's doxological character contrasts with Raguel's pessimistic assumption that Tobias will die. For readers the digging of the grave is a ludicrous act of unfaith that parallels some of Tobit's actions. The narration of the simultaneous contrasting events inside and outside the wedding chamber parallels chap. 3. When Raguel ascertains that Tobias is alive, he sings a hymn similar to Sarah's and Tobias' prayer.

8:19–9:6, The Wedding Feast, the Money Recovered.

Now that the bridegroom has survived the family hex, Raguel orders a sumptuous public feast. Tob. 8:21 focuses on family relationships, and Raguel's repeated "have courage, child" (in G²) parallels Edna's words to Sarah (7:18) and emphasizes Tobias' status as the family's son.

With the marriage of Tobias the nature of the journey has changed. Tobias' companion has shown his credibility and is sent on alone to fetch the money. Time is of the essence. Tobias' delay will worry his father, or perhaps his father will die before the young man returns. When Gabael arrives, he is welcomed as a member of the family (cf. 1:14), and his meeting with Tobias (9:6) closely parallels that in 7:1–8.

10:1–11:18
The Return of Tobias

This major section recounts the completion of Tobias' journey and the healing of Tobit. Thus a solution is found for the problem that led to the development of the plot.

10:1–7a, Anticipation and Apprehension at Home.

Again the author juxtaposes simultaneous contrasting scenes. Over against the joy of the wedding celebration stands the gloom of the Tobiad household. Not only are Tobit and Anna ignorant of events in Ecbatana, they assume the worst. The scene is a counterpart to 5:17–22, but the interaction between Tobit and Anna has become more bitter. The psychology is interesting. Tobit counts the days of Tobias' absence (10:1; cf. 9:4) and creates a pessimistic scenario to explain the delay. When Anna outdoes him by supposing that Tobias has died, Tobit responds with words of comfort, which Anna refuses to accept. She acts as one mourning the dead.

10:7b–11:1a, Newlyweds and Parents Bid Farewell.

Again changing scenes, the author returns to the dutiful son's concern about his father. Understandably, Raguel wants his new-found son and newly healed daughter to remain, but when he fails to delay the departure, he sends Tobias off with his bride and with a substantial dowry that is a down payment on a full inheritance (cf. Raphael's prediction, 6:11).

The scene is a counterpart to the farewell in 5:16b. In overlapping speeches Raguel and Edna offer parting words of instruction and encouragement. Central is the book's pervading concern with family, expressed with complementary sentiments. Raguel reminds Sarah that in her father-in-law's house she will be the daughter of Tobit and Anna. Edna exhorts her "son" to care for "my daughter." Both send the couple off "in peace," wishing them a safe journey, prosperity, and children that Raguel and Edna will live to see. Raguel's concluding exhortation about honoring parents may be textually out of place and may have originally been addressed to Sarah. Tobias praises God, as we have come to expect.

11:1b–4, Tobias and Raphael Arrive at Nineveh. As earlier, Raphael instructs Tobias, reminding him, as well as readers, that the fish's gall has yet to be used. A curious narrative touch is the reference to Tobias' dog, which had gone off on the journey with them (5:16, G¹; 6:1, G²) and is now mentioned again for the first time.

11:5–15a, Reunion and Healing. The author returns to Anna (cf. 10:7a), who despite her gloomy protests, is still watching the road for Tobias' return. She is her blind husband's eyes and informs him that "your son" is coming. Raphael's instructions build narrative tension. The wording of G², "he will see the light" (v. 7), suggests a wordplay, for Tobias is "the light of my eyes" (v. 14, G²; cf. Anna's expression in 10:5). Anna's readiness to die recalls the motif in 4:4. With a touch of pathos the father is depicted as stumbling out to meet his son. The healing has a magical or miraculous element; fish gall works where the physicians had failed (cf. 2:10). But plot is of importance. The physicians' failure allowed Tobit to recover his money, Sarah to be healed, and Tobias to find his destined wife. Doxology is in order, as when Sarah was healed. The motif will be expanded in chaps. 12–13. The interpretation of Tobit's experience as scourging and mercy will also recur in 13:1–2. That Tobit "sees" his son has double meaning, connoting both the son's return and Tobit's recovery of his sight. The scene has some interesting parallels (and resonances?) in Luke 15:20–24.

11:15b–18, The Parents Meet Their New Daughter. With this scene another theme is resolved. Tobit meets the wife he had hoped Tobias would find (4:12–13). Of course, he praises God on his way to meet her. The people's astonishment is a motif that will be typical of the later miracle stories in the Gospels. Tob. 11:17

again emphasizes the family. The rejoicing of the people gives the scene the character of a communal festival (cf. Esther 8:16–17). Reference to "the Jews," if original to the text, is odd in a document about a northern Israelite family (but cf. 1:3–7 and chap. 13). On Ahiqar and Nadab, see commentary above on 1:16–22.

12:1–13:18
The Aftermath of the Healing

Now that the major problems have been resolved, the author provides a final narrative twist. When Tobit and Tobias offer their helper a bonus, they discover his real identity and are told that appropriate thanks belongs to God who sent the healer. So they sing hymns of praise, and Tobit writes the doxological book we have been reading—including a hymn of praise (chap. 13).

The assertion by some scholars that chaps. 13–14 are late additions to the book is not supported by the Aramaic and Hebrew fragments from Qumran, which contain parts of both chapters.

12:1–22
The Healer Reveals Himself and Ascends

The author now concludes the angelic epiphany introduced at 3:16–17. The disguised angel reveals his true identity, Tobit and Tobias react in terror, Raphael reassures them, commissions them to a task, and then disappears.

12:1–5, Tobit Wishes to Square Accounts. The protagonists continue to act in accordance with their wrong perceptions. As Tobias' summary suggests (v. 3), Raphael has resolved all their problems and is worthy of a special reward. The 50-percent commission vastly exceeds what was implied in 5:14 but is consonant with the generosity espoused throughout the book.

12:6–10, Raphael Instructs Tobit and Tobias. Raphael's self-revelation and instructions are given privately to the men of the story and not in the presence of Anna and Sarah, who have also been beneficiaries of the angel's activities. Raphael emphasizes that proper payment is the offering of praise and thanks for God's deeds in the presence of all humanity (vv. 6–7; cf. vv. 17–18). Such public acknowledgment anticipates the universalistic note to be struck in 13:11 and 14:6–7.

The injunctions in 12:7b–10 indicate the proper use of wealth and promise blessings to the giver of alms. By the time readers come to this reprise of Tobit's testamentary instructions (4:5–11), it is clear that almsgiving does deliver from death (cf. 4:10; 14:11). The combined references to prayer, fasting (G[1], Old Latin), almsgiving, and "storing up" gold are paralleled in Matt. 6:1–21, which thus reflects its background in Jewish wisdom teaching.

12:11–21, Raphael Reveals His Identity and Ascends. Raphael reviews past events, revealing to the protagonists the divine activity of which they had been unaware. His explanation brings Tobit and Tobias up to date on what readers have known since 3:16–17 and adds a few details to that section. Raphael is one of seven angels of the presence who have special access to the divine throne room, where they relay the prayers of humanity in the form of memoranda to the heavenly King. The text of 12:13 is uncertain. According to G[1], Tobit's pious deeds were not hidden from the angelic witness. The motif of testing in G[2] suggests the same idea but may imply some divine initiative in the incident described in 2:1–10. (On Raphael's second function as divinely sent savior, or specifically, healer, see commentary above on 3:16–17.)

The form of Raphael's self-revelation, as well as the human reaction, the angelic reassurance, and the sudden disappearance, are traditional elements in the epiphany form. More often than not, such epiphanies have a commissioning function. Although that function is not central in Tobit (Raphael appears in order to heal), it is present in the command to praise God and write a doxological book (12:20; cf. Rev. 1:19) and in the fulfillment of the command (Tob. 12:22). That angels do not eat human food is a traditional idea (cf. *T. Abraham* 4, Recension A; Luke 24:36–43). The formula, "I am ascending to him who sent me" (Tob. 12:20), recalls the language of the Fourth Gospel, which shares with Tobit a common pattern of a descending and ascending Savior.

12:22, Tobit and Tobias Praise God. This verse concludes the principal narrative in the book by underscoring its doxological tone, which is punctuated by the hymn that follows.

13:1–14:1
Tobit's Hymn of Praise

Tobit's hymn partakes of two worlds. Its themes, diction, and literary form are typical of Israelite piety in the real world in which the author of Tobit and his audience lived. Indeed, it may be a reused liturgical composition. Because the hymn reflects real usage, it lends verisimilitude to the literary portrait of Tobit in the fictive setting that constitutes the hymn's second world.

Within the world of that narrative, the hymn not only serves the literary functions of characterization and plot development but also helps to express some of the author's central religious conceptions: exile and return; judgment, repentance, righteousness, and deliverance; God's sovereignty and ultimate triumph.

Between the narrative introduction (13:1) and conclusion (14:1) the hymn is framed by a pair of matched benedictions (13:1, 18). The introduction (vv. 1–2) sets the theme (divine justice and mercy), and the body of the poem is divided into two major sections addressed to the "sons of Israel" in Exile (vv. 3–7) and to Jerusalem (vv. 8–18). Pairs of opposing words ("scourge"/"have mercy"; "grieve"/"rejoice"; "scattered"/"gathered") contrast Israel's present situation in exile and its future return to Jerusalem, which are functions of God's judgment for sin and the salvation that will follow repentance.

The composition is a hymn of praise in response to God's mighty acts, a prayer of rejoicing. Its consistently optimistic tone is evident in the repetition of verbs like "praise," "exalt," "give thanks," "rejoice." Although much of the vocabulary is reminiscent of the Psalter (esp. Pss. 92–118), key themes and terminology reflect the concerns of the author and the author's time. Israel is in dispersion. The glory of Jerusalem and the Temple are eschatological or end-time realities, described in imagery derived from the Isaian tradition. God's royal rule is denoted by such titles as "King of the Ages" and "King of Heaven," which do not occur in the Psalter, but are frequent in liturgical passages in the apocalyptic literature of the Hellenistic period.

13:1–2, Introduction. An initial blessing with an explication ("I give thanks to you / Blessed are you . . . because . . .") is formulaic in prayers of this period (cf. 1QH 5:20; 10:14). The terminology in the address implies the title "King of the Ages" (cf. Tob. 13:6, 10). (On the word pair "scourge"/"have mercy," see commentary below on v. 5, where it applies to Israel, and above on 11:15a, where Tobit applies the words to his own experience.) The double theme of judgment and salvation is developed in v. 2. Sickness and healing were, in Israelite thought, a descent to and return from Hades. On the God who kills and brings to life, cf. Deut. 32:39; 1 Sam. 2:6. For the whole complex of ideas here, see Wisd. of Sol. 16:13–15; cf. also 2 Macc. 7:35, in the context of resurrection. For death, Sheol, and resurrection as metaphors for exile and return, cf. Ezekiel 37 and Bar. 2:17; 3:4–8.

13:3–7, Address to Israel in Exile. The address to "the sons of Israel" (v. 3) is presumed in this section in its use of the second person plural. This first major part of the prayer, like the second (vv. 8–18), concludes with the author speaking in the first person singular (vv. 6–7).

This section (and not least its titles for God) emphasizes the power and majesty of the Divine Judge, who has scattered Israel into exile because of their sins. As chastisement or scourging, however, this banishment is the act of the heavenly "Father" (v. 4). Israel is to acknowledge this act for what it is—in the presence of the nations—lest they conclude that their might led to the defeat of Israel (cf. Deut. 32:27–31). Semantically and conceptually, a fine line separates Israel's "confession" of God's judicial power from their "giving thanks" to God. Such thanksgiving and praise recognize that God's scourging is not ultimate punishment but paternal chastisement that will be mercifully alleviated when God gathers the scattered people. This mercy is predicated on Israel's repentance. When they "turn" back to God, then God will "turn" to them, a common prophetic theme. This crucial motif of Israel's repentance, absent in Deuteronomy 32, is present, however, in its context (Deut. 30:1–6) and appears in Jewish texts of the Hellenistic and Roman periods that employ the historical scheme found in the latter chapters of Deuteronomy.

13:8–14:1, Address to Jerusalem. This second part of the prayer complements the first. Reference is made to Israel's punishment (vv. 9, 14), Jerusalem's suffering because of the sins of its "sons" (v. 9; cf. 2 Macc. 5:19–20), and the present distress of its inhabitants (v. 10). But the text's emphasis on God's anticipated salvation is evident in the density of doxological terminology and the repeated references to joy and gladness. Since salvation presumes repentance, earlier mention of Israel's iniquities (v. 5) and the nation's status as sinners (v. 6) is replaced by reference to their new status as "the righteous" (vv. 9, 13).

Although Tobit is depicted as a Galilean and the author doubtless thinks of a Return to the whole of the land of Israel, this hymn focuses on Jerusalem as the locus of salvation. This emphasis is consonant with the account of Tobit's journeys to Jerusalem (1:5–8) and the eschatological scenario in 14:5–7. Jerusalem's importance is indicated by the fourfold use of the name (13:8, 9, 16, 17) and the shift from the plural address to the Israelites in vv. 3–7 to the singular address to Jerusalem in vv. 8–18. This mode of direct address and the concern for the deliverance of Jerusalem and its attendant joy are paralleled in the "Apostrophe to Zion" (a noncanonical poem preserved on the Qumran Cave 11 Psalms Scroll 22:1–15), Bar. 4:36–5:9, and *Psalm of Solomon* 11 (cf. also Sir. 36:1–17), which are probably remnants of a category

of literature that gave liturgical expression to Zion-centered future hope (cf. also the prayers in Dan. 9:4–19; Bar. 1:15–3:8; the Prayer of Azariah [Song of Three Youths 1–22]).

The chief source for these expressions of a hope in Zion's restoration is in the oracles of Isaiah 40–66 (esp. Isa. 54:11–14 [cf. Tob. 13:16–18] and Isa. 60:4–14 [cf. Tob. 13:11]). Thus, Tobit 13 and other contemporary texts attest a liturgical or contemplative setting for nourishing the older, unfulfilled prophetic hopes for restoration. A bolder expression of the hope for a divinely rebuilt Jerusalem appears in Rev. 21:9–27, which has also been influenced by a tradition fed by Ezekiel 40–48.

14:2–15
Death and Narrative Closure

Our story closes with the deaths of the *dramatis personae*, and the accounts serve several narrative functions. Tobit's testament contains final instructions that bring closure to aspects of the story. The land of exile will perish. The return of God's scattered people, anticipated in chap. 13, is guaranteed by the prophetic word. The command to give alms is repeated. Proper burials are carried out. Tobit's prediction about Nineveh's destruction is fulfilled.

14:2–11
Tobit's Death and Second Testament

The final chapter centers on Tobit's death. His second testament (see commentary above on 4:3–19, Tobit's first testament) has many elements typical of the genre: the protagonist's deathbed situation and his age (14:2, 3); the summoning of children and grandchildren (v. 3); eschatological prediction (vv. 4–7); ethical instructions (vv. 8–11a); death and burial (v. 11b). Two literary peculiarities of Tobit govern the shape of the testamentary form here. Tobit's ethical instructions have already been given in chap. 4, where he anticipated his death. In keeping with the author's parallelism between the individual and the nation, most of Tobit's instructions in chap. 14 constitute a prediction about Israel's future that complements the scenario in Tobit's hymn (chap. 13).

14:2–3, Tobit's Deathbed. In contrast to chap. 4, when he sorrowfully anticipated the premature death he had invoked as an escape from an unbearable life, Tobit now dies "in peace" after the full and prosperous life that has been the reward of his piety. The texts differ as to his age. Death at one hundred and fifty-eight

(G^1) seems more likely than one hundred and twelve (G^2); we would expect the pious hero to live longer than his son, who dies at the age of one hundred and twenty-seven (14:14). In keeping with earlier emphases, Tobit's life after his recovery has been marked by almsgiving and doxology. In preparation for his death, the father summons his son and grandsons (G^1, Old Latin) in order to give his testament.

14:4–7, Tobit's Testamentary Prophecy. Speaking with the insight traditionally ascribed to a deathbed situation, Tobit utters a prophecy that he supports by an appeal to "the prophets of Israel" (G^2) and the word of Nahum (G^2, which G^1 has revised to the more familiar story of Jonah [see also commentary above on 6:1–8]). The appeal to the veracity of the prophetic word (cf. 2:6) attests the authority of the prophetic corpus in the author's time.

The first event in the predictive scenario is the destruction of Nineveh (612 B.C.). Reference to the event is natural in a story set in that city, although the repeated vendetta (14:4, 10, 15) is hardly prepared for in the narrative (but cf. 1:16–20). Though apologetic in tone (prophecy has been fulfilled), it may also express the author's unhappiness with Diaspora existence.

Tobit's prediction has the expected references to the Babylonian Exile, the Return, and the building of the Second Temple. More interesting are his expectations of a glorious eschatological Temple, the Gentiles' conversion and abandoning of their idols, the return of the whole Dispersion, and the expunging of evildoers from all the earth. Certain of these elements appeared in chap. 13 and are rooted in prophetic tradition (esp. Isaiah 40–66). Close parallels in the eschatological scenarios in 1 Enoch 10–11; 90; and 91:7–9, 11–17 may attest common tradition.

14:8–11a, Tobit's Ethical Instructions. In this summary statement reference to almsgiving and doxology is an expected final emphasis. Testaments teach ethics by positive and negative example. Tobit's example, already recounted in detail, is here supplemented by a brief reference to Ahiqar and Nadab. Ahiqar's alms-giving was suggested in 2:10. The allusion to death and life, darkness and life is a reprise of 13:2.

14:11b–12a, Tobit and Anna Die and Are Buried. With Tobit's death and burial the testamentary form concludes. The glorious burials of the main characters (vv. 11–13) are a final reminder that this is a story about the wealthy. For this author the pious rich deserve such obsequies. By way of contrast cf. 1 Enoch 103:5–8 and Luke 16:19–31. Tobit's and Anna's burials resolve the concerns in 4:3–4; 6:14; 14:10.

14:12b–15, Tobias' Death. Tobias' responsibility as a son extends to the burial of his father-in-law and mother-in-law. The author brings closure to his story by associating Tobias' death not with his burial, but with his joy and his praise of God for Nineveh's destruction. This last word guarantees the fulfillment of the other predictions in Tobit's testament.

Bibliography

Doran, R. "Narrative Literature." In *Early Judaism and Its Modern Interpreters*. Edited by R. A. Kraft and G. W. E. Nickelsburg. Philadelphia: Fortress; Atlanta, GA: Scholars, 1986. Pp. 287–310.

Lindenberger, J. M. "Ahiqar." In *The Old Testament Pseudepigrapha*. Edited by J. H. Charlesworth. 2 vols. Garden City, NY: Doubleday, 1983, 1985. Vol. 2, pp. 479–507.

Nickelsburg, G. W. E. *Jewish Literature Between the Bible and the Mishnah*. Philadelphia: Fortress, 1981. Pp. 30–35.

_____. *Resurrection, Immortality, and Eternal Life in Intertestamental Judaism*. Harvard Theological Studies, 26. Cambridge, MA: Harvard University Press, 1972.

Petersen, N. R. "Tobit." In *The Books of the Bible*. Edited by B. W. Anderson. New York: Scribner, forthcoming.

Pfeiffer, R. H. *History of New Testament Times with an Introduction to the Apocrypha*. New York: Harper, 1949. Pp. 258–84.

Zimmermann, F. *The Book of Tobit*. New York: Harper, 1958.

JUDITH

L U I S   A L O N S O - S C H Ö K E L

INTRODUCTION

Historical Context

Hellenism. For the Jewish community the encounter with Hellenism, the cultural influence of Greece, was a time of challenge and crisis. Throughout its history Israel had managed to assimilate alien cultural elements: Babylonian legal tradition, Canaanite poetry, Egyptian wisdom literature, etc. Israel had been able to incorporate alien law into its own context of covenant and to reshape the narrative structure of myths to generate symbols valid for its own experience.

Apparently, the pervading presence of Hellenism after the conquest of Palestine by Alexander the Great in 332 B.C. posed a more serious challenge. Hellenism presented itself as a higher culture, with great richness and strong allure. Greek culture was not wholly bound up with traditional Greek religious thought. It was also a literature, a philosophy, and an ethics. Over the course of time a form of Judaism even developed that included Hellenistic values, showing that many Jews considered Hellenism to be reconcilable with their religious beliefs.

Antiochus IV Epiphanes. At a certain point, however, a grave crisis arose. After the death of Alexander the Great in 323 B.C., his empire was divided among his generals into Greek, Egyptian, and Syrian areas. Ptolemy and his descendants ruled in Egypt; Syria came under the control of the Seleucids. Judea and the rest of Palestine was disputed territory, subject first to the Ptolemaic kingdom (301–198 B.C.), and after 198 B.C. to the Seleucids. When Antiochus III captured the area in 198 B.C., he issued an edict that allowed the Jews free exercise of their religion and their national customs. For twenty-five years a forward-looking Jewish party developed, open to collaboration and to assimilation of Greek customs (→ Alexander; Seleucids, The).

In 175 B.C. Antiochus IV Epiphanes ascended the throne. He sought to advance the growth of Hellenism as a means of promoting cultural uniformity and stability in his empire. Though some Jews welcomed this development, others were opposed to it. When disturbances broke

out in Jerusalem in 168 B.C., Antiochus responded with a cruel persecution of the Jews of Judea. Coexistence and collaboration with Hellenism became impossible. The party that advocated collaboration was discredited. As the books of Maccabees tell, the hour had come for the passive resistance of the martyrs and the active resistance led by Judah the Maccabee (→ Maccabees).

It was against this background, that the book of Judith was composed. In it the name of the protagonist is the feminine form of the national hero's name: Judah/Judith. The book highlights fidelity to the Lord and his commandments, trust in God, and a combative attitude. The context of crisis and belligerence produced a partial and simplified vision, one with no nuances. With religious fervor, the author calls for armed resistance.

Narrative Art

With the passage of time the Jews had developed their narrative technique (also with Hellenistic influences). By the time in which Judith was written it was possible to construct an ample and well-modulated narrative emerging out of a central idea rather than a collection of loosely related episodes. Among the classical books of Israel, only the story of Joseph shows such narrative ability.

The book of Judith is a literary innovation, although not in its narrative motifs, which are traditional. The proud and aggressive ruler depicted in Judith is the successor of the character of Sennacherib in Isaiah 36–38. Over against him, the heroine is, in literary terms, a direct descendant of Jael, who slays the defeated general Sisera (Judg. 4–5). She also has some of the traits of the wise woman of 2 Samuel 20, who saves the inhabitants of the city by tossing the rebel's head to the besiegers. The alion Achior, who sings the praises of Israel in Judith 5, has his antecedents in Rahab of Jericho (Josh. 2) and in Balaam (Num. 22–24). The theme of seduction is already insinuated in the story of Jael. The head cut off and used to create confusion among the enemy is an obvious offshoot of the story of David and Goliath, except that the weak and beautiful woman takes the place of the handsome and almost weaponless shepherd boy. And the victory of a weak people through divine intervention is as traditional as one can imagine—although this time it is accomplished

"Judith" has been translated from the Spanish by Justo L. González.

804

without an angel of death, pestilence in the enemy camp, or miracles (see 2 Kings 6–7; Isa. 38).

Purpose and Function

The repetition of traditional themes is significant both as a vehicle and as part of the message. The author wishes to encourage the people by bringing to mind national memories transformed into an original and interesting story. The past is still present and may repeat itself, even while taking new forms. Judith the widow personifies the nation. She gives advice like Deborah, strikes like Jael, and sings like Miriam. The book also continues, actualizes, and enriches the great lyrical tradition of an Israel that sings of its heroes and its God.

Text

Originally written in Hebrew, the book has come down to us in an artless and literal Greek translation. Behind this translation it is sometimes possible to recreate the original Hebrew text. There does exist a translation of the Greek text into Latin (known as the Old Latin), which follows the Greek text rather closely. On the other hand, the Vulgate, the Latin translation prepared by Jerome, differs markedly from the Greek. In his "Preface to Judith" Jerome claims that he worked from an Aramaic text of Judith, which he translated in a single night. Although the Aramaic text Jerome used is no longer known, scholars think it was a rather free translation of the Greek. Thus Jerome's translation is not generally considered a valuable witness to the original form of the Hebrew text. The Vulgate (or the Aramaic text on which it was based) often seems to be trying to improve on the Greek text, although usually detracting from its vigor and enlarging on its piety.

COMMENTARY

1:1–16, A Clash of Giants. In the very first paragraph the author winks at us to let us know that the story is fictional and that we should not waste our time trying to identify its historical setting. Only by accepting the fiction will we gather the meaning. Nebuchadnezzar never ruled in Nineveh, as stated in Jth. 1:1, nor did Arpachshad rule in Ecbatana (see Gen. 10:22–24).

The first chapter depicts the clash of two mighty kings, Nebuchadnezzar and Arpachshad, and enjoys the hyperbole. The immense walls of Ecbatana are the measure of Nebuchadnezzar's victory, which in turn will be the

implicit measure of what takes place in Bethulia. Nebuchadnezzar wishes to involve all kingdoms from Persia to Egypt in his conquest of Ecbatana. But their wish for neutrality and their disrespectful attitude raise his ire.

At the end of the chapter the author drops a phrase that should be carefully read and remembered. Nebuchadnezzar, the author says, destroyed Ecbatana and "turned its beauty into shame" (1:14). Later on, the narrative will introduce another beauty that someone will seek to shame (13:16).

A respite of four months while victory is celebrated is another hyperbole by a storyteller who is in no hurry and feels no need to be conservative in numbers. Meanwhile, does the king's ire abate? No one can go unpunished who humiliates the most powerful man on earth. Is he only a man?

2:1–13, The Divine King. King Nebuchadnezzar makes decisions and issues commands like a god. The author purposely places on the lips of the king expressions that the prophets put on the lips of God—compare v. 11 with Ezek. 5:11; 7:4, 9; and 9:5, 10; and v. 12 with Isa. 46:11 and 48:15. He who originally appeared like another Sennacherib (2 Kings 18:19) now seems to aspire to a divine role—like the king in Isaiah 14. He does not swear by his god, but "as I live, and by the power of my kingdom." This oath contains a satirical allusion to the pretensions of Antiochus IV Epiphanes.

From the pinnacle of power Nebuchadnezzar moves to excessive pride. Habitual readers of the Bible know that such arrogance cannot be victorious or remain unpunished. The phrase "what I have spoken my hand will execute" (RSV) is laden with irony for wise readers, and even for some not so wise. Although we do not know the details—which keeps our interest—we do know the outcome—which calms us.

Holofernes (or, more properly, Horofernes) is a Persian name. Also Persian is the formula "preparing earth and water" (2:7). Those are two more signs of the fictional character of the story, which freely knits together diverse pieces of history: Ecbatana of Media, the Babylonian king of Assyria, Persian generals, and so forth.

2:14–3:10, Holofernes the Conqueror. The general with a Persian name is put in command of an Assyrian army. In the cryptic language of the book, Assyria stands for Syria, that is, the Seleucid kingdom. Nebuchadnezzar is Antiochus IV. Holofernes is probably Nicanor, one of Antiochus' generals, whose name means "conqueror."

The route of the campaign is not geographically logical, nor does the author pretend that it is. The purpose of the itinerary is to cover a wide expanse in a brief time. There is considerable variety—strong cities, desert bedouins, shepherds, and farmers—one could say, all of culture. The list also includes traditional names, some of which have no political significance at the time when the book was written but do have historical resonance for Jewish readers—names such as Japheth, Midian, and those of territories that had been Phoenician or Philistine.

In brief strokes the campaign places the general at the Mediterranean coast. Azotus and Ascalon, names in the ancient Philistine Pentapolis, surrender themselves and their possessions unconditionally. They could be called vassals or, even better, slaves, like the Egyptians in the time of Joseph (Gen. 47:13–26). We are reminded of Jeremiah who, during the gravest crisis in the nation's history, admonished the Judeans to "bring your necks under the yoke of the king of Babylon, and serve him and his people and live" (Jer. 27:12, RSV).

But the reaction of Holofernes goes beyond the orders he has received from the king, or at least those recorded in the narrative. His religious policy also goes beyond the intentions of those who have surrendered. Holofernes seeks to destroy the various national religions to install the sole worship of Nebuchadnezzar. At this point one hears echoes of the divine title of Antiochus IV Epiphanes, "god manifest." The contemporary implications of the preceding chapter become clearer (cf. Dan. 11:36; 2 Macc. 9:12). Chap. 3 ends with a radical option. To save their lives the peoples must surrender their freedom and even their religion. Again, compare the measures taken by Antiochus IV in 1 Maccabees 1.

Having subdued the coastal peoples, the general camps before Dothan of Judea. There his rapid advance will be stopped. He makes camp, however, with the morale of the undisputed conqueror. All he has to do is to stretch out his hand to occupy a defenseless region that he has already encircled.

4:1–15, Resistance at Bethulia. This is the point of the dramatic and unexpected contrast—unexpected, that is, for naive readers, but not unexpected for the readers who know the Bible. In an extreme situation, Judea does not surrender but rather makes ready for war. From this small territory two forces will oppose the military giant—the courage of a people and their trust in God.

The author takes time to describe the situation, still symbolically. The return from exile and a rebuilt Temple would seem to correspond to the times of Haggai and Zechariah. The high priest's name, Joakim, is a detail that seems to be taken from the book of Nehemiah (Neh. 12:10, 26). Other anachronistic elements are the extension of the land as far as Samaria, the fact that the Jews have no king, and that the supreme authority is that of the high priest, assisted by a senate. In fact the book refers to the conditions described in 1 Macc. 4:36–61 and 2 Macc. 10:1–8, where the Temple is consecrated anew after its desecration by Antiochus IV.

In the story the people fear for the Temple, since they have heard of the measures Holofernes has taken against other local religions. This concern permits the narrator to focus on the religious theme, after having given primary attention to geographical details. In effect the narrator treats the Temple as the absolute center of the country and for its inhabitants.

The people's reaction is not limited to the purely ritual and liturgical measures of sackcloth, ashes, and humble prayer. At this point the defense of the Temple also requires military measures. Prayer and preparation for war go together. Rather than the quietness required by Isa. 30:15, what is needed is an attitude like that of Neh. 4:17, where the builders of Jerusalem's walls worked with their weapons at their sides. The military preparation is described in general terms, although the description of the passes to be defended recalls the narrow passes of Megiddo. The religious preparation is prayer, expressing the people's trust.

At the end of chap. 3 we encountered for the first time the name of Judea, the scene of the rest of the book. In 4:6 we encounter that of Bethulia, the center of resistance. It would be useless to try to pinpoint the place; it has never existed on the map of Palestine. One should look rather to its symbolic meaning.

Bethulia (in Gk., *Baityloua*) is not Jerusalem, which would have been the obvious place for the confrontation (as in the time of Hezekiah and Sennacherib). Is Bethulia perhaps intended as a polemical contrast to the capital? At any rate there are other possible connotations. In 1 Chron. 4:30 there is a reference to Bethuel in the lands of Simeon. The tribe of Simeon will play an important part in the book of Judith. Moreover, Bethulia sounds like a cross between Bethel and *betulah*. Bethel was a religious capital with a tradition going back to the times of the patriarchs. *Betulah* is a Hebrew word meaning "virgin, young woman." It is a good name for a city that wishes to remain spotless. (Recall the phrase "turned its beauty into shame" in 1:14.)

5:1–21, The Foreigner's Report. The storyteller seems to enjoy keeping the reader in suspense. As if the narrative rhythm of the preceding sections were not slow enough, a lateral episode is inserted here involving a secondary character. This episode will be ably woven into the plot until its final unfolding.

At the end of his campaign Holofernes encounters his first serious resistance. He is surprised and enraged. He is surprised, according to the author's depiction, by this strange people, and as a general he feels the need for information. In the list of his questions (5:3–4) there are echoes of Num. 13:17–20 (Moses' inquiries regarding the Canaanites). The focus of the series of questions in Judith is on the different behavior of these people, for "they alone, of all who live in the west" have defied Holofernes.

Holofernes' questions are answered by Achior, the Ammonite leader. He is a character with several functions. He is an alien who will join the people of Israel, like Rahab. He is a teacher of the history and theology of Israel to foreign ears. An ally of Holofernes, he will turn against the invader. He will be the trustworthy witness at the end. Achior's summary of Israel's national history would tell nothing new to Jewish readers. The author's interest is in the point of view, for Achior is a hostile foreigner. How should foreigners look upon Jews?

The historical portion of Achior's speech is stylized and refers only to the main stages of Israel's history, giving preference to geographical movements and characterized by the absence of personal names. There is no mention of Abraham, Jacob, Moses, or David (similar to the historical sketch in Wisd. of Sol. 10). It is as if there were a choral protagonist, the people, and a transcendant one, God. From Chaldea to Mesopotamia, and then to Canaan. Pause. Deportation and repatriation. Following the narrative setting of the book, the informer stops at this point. The action of God becomes noticeable at the third stage of the people's journey. "Their God commanded them to leave their place" (5:9). It becomes more explicit at the fourth stage. God "afflicted the whole land of Egypt, . . . dried up the Red Sea, . . . and led them on to Sinai" (5:12–14). In the last two stages of deportation and repatriation God's action establishes a principle of retribution (5:17–19), thus giving the entire piece a didactic and rhetorical character.

Achior, the narrator, wishes to make Holofernes understand a principle of history and to move him to act in consequence. This will serve as a lesson to readers. Holofernes was warned but did not heed the warning. As an irony of history, he will have caused his own destruction. For Jewish readers it will also have been helpful to remind them of the principle that what is important is to be faithful to God, who will be on their side, even in times of war. In the historical process of relation with God, once the fidelity of the people is broken, the next necessary step is return. The Jews are a people who have already returned to God, a subject to which we shall return in chap. 9.

5:22–6:9, Reaction to the Speech. The reaction is quite hostile, tumultuous on the part of the soldiers, more rationally articulated by the general. The narrator shows us characters and attitudes dramatically through action. The soldiers cannot accept something that will undercut their vanity as soldiers. This trait will propel the narrative action to the final denouement. "It's their own fault," readers will comment, without the author saying so explicitly. Pride and arrogant self-confidence remind us of Sennacherib's thoughts as described in Isa. 10:8–11 and 36:18–20. Fatal blindness reminds us of Pharaoh entering the waters with his armies, going to meet death. As the saying goes, "God blinds those whom God will destroy."

On the surface the officers' words are justifiable bragging. In what they do not say, they are a lesson in theology. "They are a people with no strength or power for making war" (5:23b, RSV). Yes, because God needs no armies to grant victory. A few are enough against many. God has weapons enough. This is a constant theme in the history of Israel, since the time of the Exodus. Foreigners will not and therefore cannot understand this, even when they are told by a foreigner like themselves, Achior. As Ps. 20:7 puts it, "Some boast of chariots, and some of horses; but we boast of the name of the Lord our God" (RSV).

The speech of Holofernes in 6:2–9, beside abounding in rhetorical bragging, is an *ad hominem* response to Achior on the theological plane. Achior had not spoken of the military might of the Jews, and therefore he did not have to be refuted on that point. He had spoken highly of the conditional protection of their God. On this point a rebuttal was needed.

The general's bragging is a hyperbolic echo of his officers' cries and really addressed to them. Readers see in his words a dramatic irony awaiting the denouement. The irony will be obvious to those who hear overtones of similar attitudes (Ben-hadad in 1 Kings 20:10–11; Amaziah and Jehoash in 2 Kings 14:9–10).

The theological theme is more important. Holofernes claims exclusive deity for the king, Nebuchadnezzar, with the formula "who is God except . . . ," a phrase whose lineage is classic (Isa. 43:11; 44:6, 8; 45:5–21; 46:9; Ps. 18:31). What the Jews profess of their God, Holofernes professes of his king. Nebuchadnezzar's almost divine title is significant, "the lord of the whole earth."

Holofernes invents a refined punishment for Achior, one that combines ire and mockery. He is to share in the fate of the Jews, who are to be destroyed. This decision plays a role in the narrative, for by allowing him to keep his life temporarily, Holofernes gives him a continuing place in the story. The intended punishment also has an ironic function. Those who foresee the ultimate outcome are already laughing. Those who do not will also laugh in the end.

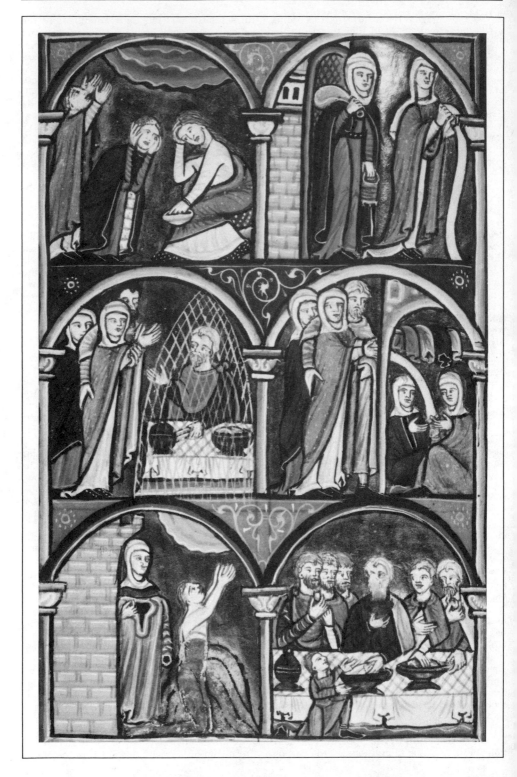

6:10–21, Achior's Lot. Achior is an Ammonite, and therefore an enemy of Israel, excluded from the sacral community (Deut. 23:3–4). Now, forced to do so by his recent master, he will join the Jewish people. Notice the movement. The soldiers lead him out of the allied pagan camp and toward Jewish territory. The Jews then introduce him into the city. Thus Achior imitates the movement of the Jews that he has just described. Leaving pagan Egypt, they enter the land of Canaan. The enemy is taking Achior to salvation. This will be his reward for having spoken truly regarding the Jews. The literary character of Achior may represent the proselytes of the time, who left paganism for a superior ethics or religion. In the narrative Achior has simply approached; he is at the gates.

Achior lying bound is like an insulting and mocking present from the besiegers. He is an important officer. He could become a spy against Holofernes. No matter. Those who are secure in their victory can afford to give the adversary some minor advantages.

The author has decided that the inhabitants of Bethulia will receive this enemy cordially and without suspicion. They believe what he tells them. The reader must simply accept things as they are told and look at the scene. Here is the Ammonite "in the midst of their people," telling them what has happened. In another scene, in 14:8, we shall hear echoes of this one, with another person "in the presence of the people." Achior then becomes a guest of Uzziah, the city magistrate. In passing, we are told that this magistrate is of the tribe of Simeon. Later we shall see the significance of this detail.

The naive credulity of the people is neutralized and even justified by their trust in God. The people of Bethulia respond with an invocation that is the basis for their petition (6:19), implying the great theological principle of Ps. 138:6, "though the Lord is high, he regards the lowly; but the haughty he knows from afar" (RSV; cf. Ps. 113:6–7). There follows a night of calling for help to the God of Israel.

The hospitality banquet and the night of prayer close the episode of Achior, which has interrupted the military action. In exchange for this delay, we have learned about life in Bethulia, which begins to take on increased importance in the narrative.

7:1–32, The Besieged City. The picture of the small city surrounded by a huge army centers all the action on one point. From a human perspective it is obvious that Holofernes will win. Theologically, we expect the Lord's victory. Readers who recall the siege of Sennacherib will expect that "the angel of the Lord" will settle the matter. Or they could look to the poetic expressions of Psalms 46 and 48, which describe God's victories. The writer chooses a different narrative line, opening new fields of action by having the general choose a different military strategy.

The new strategy is suggested by allied chiefs. The contrast with Achior is noteworthy. He had recommended no attack to avoid shame. They also recommended not attacking but rather subduing the city through thirst, so as not to face losses. When Holofernes agrees, the narrative gains time. God will not be called upon to save the city at the break of dawn.

The advice of the allied officers betrays their lack of understanding. They say that the Israelites rely "on the height of the mountains," on the topography of their land and on the strategic placement of their strongholds. They judge like the Syrians in 1 Kings 20:23. The truth of the matter is that Israel does not receive its help from the mountains but from the Lord (see Ps. 125, and 1 Kings 20:28).

The temporal structure of the new action is asymmetrically divided. On the first day (vv. 1–5) the besiegers advance. The Israelites grow concerned and set a night watch. The second day (vv. 6–19) the besiegers take the springs. The defenders are discouraged, but they call upon the Lord. After thirty-four days of continuing siege and thirst (vv. 20–29), the people demand surrender. Uzziah persuades the people to hold out for five more days (vv. 30–32). God is given a limited time for action. This turn of events opens another measure of time in the narrative, one that is narrow and tense.

Returning to the beginning of the chapter, Holofernes' new strategy revolves around the spring. This traditional detail, confirmed by archaeology (Hazor, Jerusalem, Megiddo), has a clear function in the narrative. Moreover, for readers who know biblical language, a spring is loaded with symbolic value. A never-failing spring is God for Israel (Isa. 8:6; 12:3; Jer. 2:13; Ps. 36:9); all others are "cracked cisterns" or rivers that flood and destroy.

The inhabitants of Bethulia are at first alarmed and prepare to resist the assault. Then comes the scarcity of water, which is described with overtones from Lam. 2:11, 21. The people mutiny, like the Israelites in Egypt (Exod. 5:21) or like other rebellions in the desert, when they

---

Opposite: Scenes from the story of Judith; page from an illustrated manuscript in Munich, twelfth to thirteenth centuries A.D. At top, Judith raises her hands toward heaven (perhaps praying) and covers her head with ashes before going with her maidservant to see Holofernes. At center, Judith is led before Holofernes and to his tent. The bottom scenes depict Judith bathing and Holofernes' feast.

declared that they would rather live and be slaves (Exod. 14:12). In contrast to those other rebellions, in their present mutiny against their leaders the honor of God is not denied. If the people suffer now, it is because of their past sins. They humbly accept the punishment, as Jeremiah had urged an earlier generation to do (Jer. 27:12). Intimidated by the crowd, Uzziah weakens. He gives God a deadline, which is the same as tempting God, for God will intervene "at the set time which I appoint" (Ps. 75:2, RSV) and not when the people decide.

8:1–8, The Protagonist Enters. Finally, after seven chapters full of events, the protagonist, Judith, enters. The ancients gave no titles to their books, or they simply called them by their first word. Unwarned readers have no idea at this point that the book has a feminine protagonist. That is not the case for those of us who know the title or who have read it before.

Judith enters belatedly, like a prima donna coming on stage in the second act of the opera. She is adorned with all the qualities that the author freely bestows on her. She is beautiful, rich, and devout. She is also a widow who leads an ascetic life. Her name, Judith (Heb. *yehudit*), is the feminine of Judah or Judahite (*yehudah* or *yehudi*), and she is the personification of the Jewish people. Like Uzziah, she belongs to the tribe of Simeon, probably as a reminder and contrast with Dinah, the violated sister of Simeon (see Gen. 34). She is a widow, for the Jewish nation is living at a time of grave danger and affliction, like a forlorn widow. In her faithfulness to her husband's name she embodies the nation's faithfulness to its Lord.

8:9–36, Speech and Dialogue. It is noteworthy that Judith summons the chiefs rather than attending the council. In this she acts like Deborah calling Barak (Judg. 4). From her voluntary retreat she enjoys undeniable authority. Her lengthy speech is programmatic, with prophetic accents and abundant echoes of several biblical texts. Through her mouth tradition calls on the present. Two points should be underscored. First of all, she corrects the people's interpretation that their present situation is a punishment from God. It is not so. The people are faithful to God (cf. Ps. 44:18–19), and their suffering is a test from God, such as those sent earlier to the patriarchs. It is an honor to be tested and purified by God. Second, a surrender would have enormous consequences for all Israel. Bethulia is presently holding the future of all the people, for "the temple and the altar" rest upon them.

There follows a brief and tense dialogue. The words of Uzziah are ambiguous (8:28–31). There could be a sting of irony in them, as though saying, "We know that you are intelligent, but you really do not understand. You should go back and pray, while I fulfill my oath." Or they could be sincere, coming from one who acknowledges in the wise Judith a prophetic gift like Elijah's, capable of bringing rain. In either case the oath cannot be undone.

Judith does not answer directly. She accepts the oath and the deadline, and she announces that she has a secret and personal plan. She takes full responsibility. From the chiefs she requires trust and support, with no questions asked. Here the author, who already had an ace of suspense in the deadline of five days, plays another ace by mysteriously announcing a memorable event to come.

9:1–14, Judith's Prayer. First of all, Judith prays. Compared to an average psalm, her prayer is long. In the economy of the book, it is exceedingly long. There is cause for haste; only four days are left. Yet Judith spends all this time in prayer. For her, as for the author, it is time best used.

In the prayer the space devoted to supplication is minor, while the hymnic introduction of praise is much longer. The outline is as follows: vv. 2–4, historical evocation of the God of the patriarch Simeon; vv. 5–6, God the Lord of history; v. 7, the power of the Assyrians; vv. 8–9, petition; vv. 11–12, God as Savior and Creator; and vv. 13–14, repetition and acknowledgment. Why this unequal distribution? The petition is based on and framed by the hymnic verses. Judith's action will be God's action. This action, which reaches back to the patriarchs, is foreseen and governed by God. It will be revelatory.

The meaning of the prayer is shown through a web of explicit and implicit correspondences. Explicit are the actions of the Shechemites in shaming a virgin of Israel (v. 2) and the plan of the Assyrians to shame the Temple (v. 8), and the striking of "slaves along with princes" by both Assyrians and Judith (vv. 3, 10). Implicit is Dinah as virgin and Judith as widow, both women conventionally seen as weak and defenseless before the alien. Judith represents Israel in its weakness, for she is a woman and a widow (vv. 9–10). The power of Assyria is opposed to Jewish weakness, and God takes the side of the weak (vv. 7, 11, 14). God, who acts through human means, has no parallel and is equal only to God.

By the time her prayer ends, do we know more of Judith's plan? A little more. Though Judith says nothing to the leaders of the people, thus arousing our curiosity, she has nothing to hide from God. In allowing us to listen to her private prayer, the author could let us know fully what the plan is. The narrative takes an intermediate course. We know that Judith plans to employ the seduction of her words ("by the deceit of my lips," "make my deceitful words to be their wound and stripe," vv. 10, 13, RSV). Only her words? What about her beauty? What does the reference to Dinah tell us?

The prayer partly imitates the poetic style of the Psalms, using synonyms and parallelisms. It contains quotations and echoes from the Psalms and the Prophets. Where it breaks with tradition is in its positive valuation of Simeon's vengeance, which Genesis condemns both in the narrative put in Jacob's lips and in the testament of the patriarch (Gen. 34:30 and 49:5–6). The author of our book takes the side of Simeon and Levi against Jacob. And now we see why the author decided to make the heroine a member of the diluted, if not extinct, tribe of Simeon.

10:1–23, Judith Goes to the Assyrian Camp. Finally the protagonist begins to act— but not immediately (vv. 1–10). The beautiful coquette spends part of the little time remaining in careful toilette that the author divides into nine separate actions. Now the storyteller mocks readers' haste. And we tell ourselves, "Apparently the seduction will not be merely verbal."

Judith's dress is laden with symbolic meaning when seen in the light of Isa. 52:1–2, where Jerusalem is called by God to joy and feasting. "Awake, put on your strength, ... put on your beautiful garments.... Shake yourself from the dust" (RSV). As Judith's widow's garments mourned the oppression of the people, so her joyous raiment anticipates salvation. The new action has begun. Judith's beauty will conquer, sweeping all as it passes. The narrator enjoys letting us see that beauty through the eyes of others in the story. The first of these are the leaders of Bethulia, who in their brief prayer correctly link her beauty with the glory and exaltation of Jerusalem (Jth. 10:8).

Judith's other measures are part of her secret. Why does she need to take with her clean food? To keep the laws of purity or as part of her plan? Her maid will be a silent figure, a witness, a defense, a helper. We must gaze upon Judith leaving through the eyes of the inhabitants of Bethulia—from above, wondering, worrying. With a technique like that of cinematography, changing our perspective, the storyteller lets us see her next coming toward us in the enemy guardpost. This is the beginning of the conquering advance of beauty, which contrasts with the destructive advance of Holofernes (vv. 11–19). Who will win? Judith conquers the guards (v. 14), creates a tumult among the soldiers (v. 18), overcomes the staff and the general himself (v. 23), and then falls prostrate. That beautiful face humbles itself before the general, as if beauty were rendering homage to the power of arms. Is it so? Holofernes is thinking about conquering her, and he sees her already surrendering.

It is at this point that the masterful irony of these chapters comes into play. Judith's words walk a narrow edge of ambiguity. Their interpretation will depend on the hearers' attitude. Judith appears to surrender before the defenders of Bethulia do likewise. She goes over to the enemy with very valuable information. It is a good exchange—Judith for Achior.

One has to read and reread the dialogue to grasp its ironic ambiguity. "They are about to be handed over to you," Judith says, and readers recall the five-day limit. "You have saved your life.... Do not be afraid.... He will treat you well," the soldiers reply. Their words sound almost like an oracle of salvation (cf. Isa. 42:1–7). What does it mean, for a man to treat a woman well? Admiring Judith, the soldiers speculate on the prowess of the Jewish men who "will be able to ensnare the whole world" (RSV), never suspecting that this woman is a snare.

11:1–12:20, Judith and Holofernes Face to Face. It is in this section of the narrative that the dramatic irony reaches its apex, as it develops at various levels. The irony appears in the verbal duel between the beautiful and the powerful. We have already been told that Judith is wise and able (like so many other women in the history of Israel). The action now shows the vanity and sensuality of Holofernes. The woman will use these two vices as allies in her plan. She will bait his vanity by praising his successes, promising new ones, and downplaying the role of the king. His sensuality, captivated by the display of her beauty, will be awakened with signs and gestures of acceptance, until his desire becomes passion, assured of conquest.

Vanity and sensuality are unable to see through Judith's ambiguities, for to be suspicious would be to acknowledge his own vanity and to call a halt to sensuality. Judith praises the power and wisdom of the general, and this is like a challenge. Let his sagacity unmask her; let his power overcome her. Otherwise he will be shown to be weak and naive.

Also, in a long and complicated discourse Judith leads the general along legal and religious paths that he does not understand, where he is lost. She had promised to lead him free of danger along the mountain passes. The general has to accept her guidance and be grateful for her information, while being unable to understand or criticize her. To crown it all, Judith appears with the impressive aureole of the prophet or confidante of God. Hers is a superior knowledge that all must follow.

Throughout the entire duel, like a permeating light, there is the radical polarity between man and woman and the traditional correspondence, suggested in the narrative, between a city and a woman. The general, whose king "shamed the beauty" of Ecbatana, will conquer the woman Judith before he conquers Bethulia. On her part Judith has been entering the camp, even into the commander's tent and, through his eyes, into his heart. How will this battle of love end? Love walks with death.

11:1–23, An Arcane Report. Holofernes opens

the first round of the dialogue to the greater glory of the "king of all earth," whom all either serve or will serve. He addresses the young woman with an air of protective condescension, as lord of life and death, with words that are traditionally heard from God, "Have courage and you will live." Not really knowing what he says, he adds, "tonight and from now on."

Judith responds by glorifying Holofernes, the true creator of the king's victories. With a different intention she echoes the general, calling Nebuchadnezzar "king of all the earth" and foretelling a cosmic domain for him, such as is described in Psalm 8 or in Dan. 2:38 and 4:20–22. (The author of Daniel is almost contemporary with the author of Judith.) She even dares to swear by the king's life.

After a long introduction in which she gains his goodwill, Judith begins to analyze the present situation of Bethulia. To do this she takes Achior's speech as a point of reference. This is a risky move, but the risk is controlled by astuteness. Judith quotes Achior to draw the opposite conclusion—or rather to put forth the alternative that Achior's conditional style left open. In summary, the Jews are invincible only if they obey the commandments of their God. But they are about to break them, and therefore their downfall is near.

While entangling the inexpert general in religious considerations, Judith (or rather the author) is also issuing a warning to Jews in the collaborationist party. Take care not to give way in the observance of the commandments! Whoever surrenders a wall surrenders the city. The worst of all is that this party is in control of Jerusalem (11:14–15).

In v. 16 Judith thrusts with one of her mysterious phrases aimed at the same time in two directions, at Holofernes and at readers. "God has sent me to accomplish with you things that will astonish the whole world, as many as shall hear about them" (RSV).

The following verse prepares and justifies a fundamental maneuver in her plan of action and also shows her trust in God. She concludes with a promise. She, with her own hand (neither the king nor he himself), will give the general the attributes of David, the title of shepherd and a throne in Jerusalem.

Holofernes' answer is extravagant. He will either accept Judith's God in his pantheon, or he will convert. (On this expression, "your god," see Ruth 1:16 and Dan. 2:47.) Judith will be a wife or a concubine to the king. (Or is Holofernes keeping her for himself?) The general has allowed himself to be carried away by Judith, and his tone becomes religious, even devout. His last phrase closes the passage with a sharp irony. It is as if he were saying, "Thanks to me, you will be famous in all the world." Let it be! (suggests the author). So it is! (say readers).

12:1–20, A Guest of Honor. The dialogue becomes more terse, and the setting changes. With her words Judith has built around herself a sacred aura of fascination as well as a refuge to which she can go to maneuver. She will be able to invoke religious motivations as needed, giving her freedom of movement.

In the new field, that of amorous conquest, Holofernes leads the gallant siege. First he makes a gesture of generous vanity, exquisite food on silver dishes. This offer might impress and bribe the young and hungry refugee. Judith takes shelter in the religious observances that she has so wisely discussed and declines the offer. Second, the eunuch seeks to transform Judith into "one of the daughters of the Assyrians who serve in the house of Nebuchadnezzar" (v. 13, RSV). Judith accepts with renewed ambiguity. Third, as the two sit face to face, eating and drinking, Judith's ambiguity reaches its apex.

The details underline the sensuous atmosphere that pervades the explicit words—the food, the soft fleeces on which to lie, the wine, and "her woman's finery." The language is carefully chosen, and one must listen attentively. The characters will interpret it in one way and the readers in another. While the general substitutes insinuation for direct proposition, the young woman, with feints of verbal fencing, pushes her enemy to the place where she wants him. Holofernes is too sure of himself to doubt or suspect. When she declines, he has to respect her convictions. When she does not object or agrees to a proposal, he takes the final answer for granted. The result is that the general abandons himself to her looks, to overwhelming passion, to the excitement of wine. In the end the powerful general is at the mercy of the young woman.

There are three responses by Judith that should be underlined: 12:4; 12:14; and 12:18. Each has a temporal reference. The first is to the framework of five days (of which the narrator opportunely reminds us). The other two are to the immediate present ("at once" and "today") as an exceptional occasion. Also, the term "lord" changes its meaning. The first time it refers to Judith's God. In the other two instances it could refer either to Holofernes or to the Lord.

The general's words to the eunuch Bagoas clearly express what today we would call machismo. "It will be a disgrace if we let such a woman go without enjoying her company" (v. 12, RSV). In the context of the story, such machismo fits well with the arrogance of power.

13:1–10, The Fatal Night. The dialogue ends. The action begins. It is all on Judith's part, for Holofernes lies prostrate, "overcome with wine." The narrator adds some earlier details that are necessary to have the plan work.

The servants all retire to their various tents. Outside the general's tent the maid waits. In the bedchamber the man and woman are alone. But Judith does not feel alone, for with her is the Lord whom she twice invokes, mentally and briefly.

Following the traditional models of Hebrew narrative, the action is now expressed in a series of brief strokes, with a great density of verbs, thus giving speed to the narrative. Among the details, one should note that Judith uses the enemy's own sword (like David beheading Goliath) and that she takes the canopy (a private and reserved possession) as her proof.

By the time Judith reaches the gates of Bethulia, the story could be over. At least it could for modern readers. But not for readers of those times, who wished to complete, to exploit, and above all to celebrate.

13:11–14:10, The Victorious City. At this point the narrative takes on a festive tone. Hymns and praises overshadow the action. Judith speaks three times before her fellow citizens can recover from their surprise and respond to her. Twice her words are those of a hymn. The third time they are more informative. When those in Bethulia respond, they pronounce blessings.

In the first speech (13:11), the initial words, rather than a petition, are quotations or echoes of Pss. 24:7; 118:19; and Isa. 26:2. "God is with us" is an oracular formula, reminiscent of "immanuel." In the second speech (13:14), praise continues. The previous statement spoke of "today"; the second speaks of "this night," echoing the Passover ritual (see Exod. 12:12). In this second speech Judith begins the report of the enemy's death. In the third speech (13:15–16), this statement is more informative, with exhibit of proof and an oath of innocence ("He committed no act of sin with me," RSV). Readers can imagine the effect of the head of Holofernes raised by Judith in the wavering light of the fire.

The people respond to Judith's words by praising and blessing God. The chief of the city pronounces a more elaborate blessing, including the two traditional components, "may God bless you" and "the Lord be blessed" (cf. Gen. 14:19–20). The choral "amen" of the people is the third part, which underscores the almost liturgical tone of the scene. The more informative details are interspersed in that setting.

In Jth. 14:1–4 Judith takes military command of the city. In the form of orders she foretells what will take place. The pattern of events is familiar from other biblical descriptions of the death of an enemy leader. For the hanging head, see 1 Sam. 31:9–10 (the head of Saul) and 1 Macc. 7:47 (the head of Nicanor; cf. 2 Macc. 15:30–35). For the mobilization of the Israel-

ites, see Judg. 3:26–30. And for the spoils, see, e.g., Gen. 34:27–29; 1 Sam. 17:52–54; and 2 Kings 7:14–16.

The encounter between Achior and Judith (14:5–10) closes the secondary story of the Ammonite leader. The one who had been a benevolent preacher of the history of Israel and a proselyte is now a witness. A paradoxical witness, he gives his testimony by falling on his face and losing his spirit. The deed is so great that he cannot bear it and loses his senses. When he recovers, all he can do is pronounce another benediction. He is converted and is fully incorporated into the community of Israel, even against the rules of Deut. 23:3–4. With Judith's report, which the narrator does not repeat, time is taken up until daybreak.

14:11–19, In the Assyrian Camp. The narrator knows how to exploit contrasts. To the discovery and information in Bethulia correspond the discovery and spreading of the news in the camp. To the ritual joy of the besieged corresponds the funeral rite of the besiegers. The narrator enjoys telling us how the alarm rises along the military hierarchy toward the center and the head. There it is suddenly interrupted, for the general lies headless. The author also knows how to develop the discovery and the reaction by Bagoas in a crescendo of verbs. These verbs first move forward: "went . . . knocked . . . opened . . . found." Then they stop: "cried out . . . wept . . . groaned . . . shouted . . . rent his garments." Bagoas' report is intensively emotional. But his pain and indignation are the joy of the narrator and of the readers. The Jews, Bagoas says, are slaves and traitors, and a woman from among them "has brought disgrace." The woman has conquered the man, the servant the master.

Since the author was not willing to end the story at 13:10, this would be another good ending place, with the shouts of despair of the besiegers, in contrast to their arrogant confidence in the initial chapters. But the author would rather end with a joyous tone and wishes to savor and prolong the joy of victory. Narratively, we are now descending.

15:1–13, Denouement. This chapter does not add much to the narrative. It describes the rout of the enemy, pursuit, and plunder. The author could have saved time but is caught in the very web of the narrative, like a sportscaster after a victory for the home team.

One should note for their political implications the congratulations of the high priest and of the senate. The highest authorities confirm that belligerent resistance is the correct attitude and that collaborationism is wrong. The Israelites can plunder the material goods of the enemy, but they must not accept their customs.

Not only do the authorities approve, but they also affirm that "God is well pleased." This is the ultimate referendum, which the people approve with a unanimous "amen."

Then Judith, who has acted as a prophet, an intercessor, and a strategist, takes on the role of choreographer, like Miriam (see Exod. 14–15). Finally, she takes the crown of a poet. The storyteller will not begrudge praise and makes the protagonist the author of the final hymn.

16:1–17, Canticle of Judith. Her poem is wide in scope, like the prayer in chap. 9. Its movement is majestic, with synonymous repetition and evocative, bold strokes (vv. 3, 9). The generative theme is succinctly stated in v. 6: "But the Lord Almighty has foiled them by the hand of a woman" (RSV). "The Lord" is a name that resounds seven times in the hymn. He is "omnipotent" in creation and in repeated historical events. The "them" who are foiled are now the Assyrians, the very powerful and invincible Assyrians. "By the hand of a woman" refers to an individual and recent event. God chooses the weak to overcome the strong.

The structure of the hymn is as follows: (A) vv. 1–2, introduction; vv. 3–12, historical depiction; (B) v. 13, introduction; vv. 14–15, cosmic depiction; (C) vv. 16–17, conclusion. The parallelism between historical action and cosmic action is traditional (cf. Ps. 136). The eschatological ending harkens back to the prophets.

The relationship between the historical and the cosmic goes beyond a mere parallelism or coincidence. There is a unifying dynamism. The recent history has been dramatic—aggression, extreme danger, and miraculous deliverance. Such was also the drama of creation, with its resistance and rebellion, which the Lord's power repeatedly overcomes (cf. Isa. 52:9–11). Then comes a basic contrast. While God rules over the cosmos directly, in history God prefers to act and to triumph by means of the weak, as long as they fear the Lord. Judith's mighty deed has been above all a new revelation of the Lord.

Although the psalm is full of quotations and echoes from the OT, it is still original. What follows are a few parallels to guide readers:

v. 4—Ps. 3:6; Isa. 37:24; Jer. 1:15
v. 5—2 Kings 8:12; Ps. 137:9; Nah. 3:10
v. 6—Judg. 4:9; Ps. 33:10
v. 7—Deut. 1:28; 3:11
v. 13—Exod. 15:1; Ps. 144:9
v. 14—Pss. 33:6–9; 104:30
v. 15—Pss. 46:3; 97:4–5; Mic. 1:4
v. 17—Isa. 66:24

The section of highest poetical quality is vv. 3–9. Here one finds a well-developed antithesis between the massive and overwhelming advance of Assyria and Judith's meticulous actions: a woman against an army; seduction against aggression; beauty against strength. Between the two, as a wedge, intervenes the transcendent Lord, whose extended arm Judith is (v. 6). She is exalted by contrasts of mythical or legendary flavor ("the sons of Titans, . . . tall giants," v. 7, RSV).

Verse 9 is masterful in its use of the ambivalent verbs "ravished" and "captivated," which belong to the language both of war and love, as well as by the symmetry of its poetic lines and by the surprising leap from subject to subject ("her sandal . . . her beauty . . . her sword").

The final verse is also an admonition. Empires and nations decide their own final lot, "in the day of judgment" by their attitudes toward the weak people of Israel. The psalm is followed by a processional dance (cf. Ps. 68) that leads to the Temple in Jerusalem.

16:8–25, Epilogue. It would appear that the readers of that time, or at least many of them, would wish to know what happened next. So, Judith was very rich, very famous; she had many suitors; and she did not marry. Would this disillusion readers? No. With her unbreakable fidelity to the memory of her first husband Judith symbolizes the fidelity of the people to its only Lord. From this fidelity follows a stable peace. Judith lives to be one hundred and five, fifteen years longer than Moses, five years less than Joshua. The peace she has secured lasts longer than any achieved in the times of the judges.

Bibliography

Cowley, A. E. "The Book of Judith." In *Apocrypha and Pseudepigrapha of the Old Testament.* Edited by R. H. Charles. 2 vols. Oxford: Clarendon, 1913. Vol. 1, pp. 242–67.

Craghan, J. *Esther, Judith, Tobit, Jonah, Ruth.* Old Testament Message, 16. Wilmington, DE: Glazier, 1982.

Craven, T. S. *Artistry and Faith in the Book of Judith.* Society of Biblical Literature Dissertation Series, 70. Chico, CA: Scholars Press, 1983.

Dancy, J. C. *The Shorter Books of the Apocrypha.* Cambridge Bible Commentary on the New English Bible. Cambridge: Cambridge University Press, 1972.

Enslin, M. S. *The Book of Judith.* Jewish Apocryphal Literature, 7. Leiden: Brill, 1972.

Montague, G. T. *The Books of Esther and Judith.* Pamphlet Bible Series, 21. New York: Paulist Press, 1973.

Moore, C. A. *Judith.* Anchor Bible, 40. Garden City, NY: Doubleday, 1985.

Purdie, E. *The Story of Judith in German and English Literature.* Paris: Honoré Champien, 1927.

THE ADDITIONS TO ESTHER

DAVID J. A. CLINES

INTRODUCTION

The Additions to Esther are those portions found in the Greek Bible (the Septuagint version [LXX]) that are not found in the Hebrew Bible. When Jerome (ca. A.D. 342–420) prepared the Latin (Vulgate [Vg.]) version of the Bible, being an enthusiast for the Hebrew original, he moved the passages found only in the Greek version to the end of the book, even though they belong logically at various points in the course of the narrative. When the chapter and verse numbering of the Bible was introduced (in the thirteenth century A.D.), the Additions to Esther were numbered from 10:4 onwards, the last verse of the Hebrew Esther having been 10:3. Some modern versions and editions use the letters A to F to designate these Additions. Some English versions of the Bible (e.g., RSV) print only the Additions in the Apocrypha; some (e.g., NEB), in addition to printing the Hebrew Esther in the Old Testament, also print the whole of the book of Esther, including the Additions, in the Apocrypha; and some (e.g., JB, NAB) print only one book of Esther, translating both the Hebrew text and the Greek Additions in the sequence in which they appear in the Greek Bible.

These are the six Additions:

1. A 1–17 = 11:2–12:6   Mordecai's dream and the discovery of a conspiracy

2. B 1–7 = 13:1–7   The first royal letter

3. C 1–30 = 13:8–14:19   The Prayer of Mordecai and the prayer of Esther

4. D 1–16 = 15:1–16 (= Vulgate 15:4–19)   Esther's appearance before the king

5. E 1–24 = 16:1–24   The second royal letter

6. F 1–10 = 10:4–11:1   The interpretation of Mordecai's dream; colophon

Addition F bears the verse numbers immediately following the last verse of the Hebrew Esther (10:3) because its subject matter follows on from it, though its last verse (11:1) belongs logically at the very end of the book; then the other Additions are numbered in sequence. Thus, Addition F, even though it contains what is logically the last material of the book, has the earliest chapter and verse numbers of the Additions.

The Origin of the Additions

The Additions are found only in the Greek Bible, and not in the Hebrew, but some of them seem to have existed earlier in a Hebrew or Aramaic form. This is the case with Additions A, C, D, and F, where traces of a Semitic original are still visible. Additions B and E (the royal letters), on the other hand, are obvious examples of flowery Greek rhetorical style and must have been composed originally in Greek. All the Additions are most probably Jewish in origin, especially Additions A and F, which breathe an anti-Gentile spirit. The Semitic Additions are quite likely Palestinian in origin, while the Greek Additions more probably come from a Jewish community outside Palestine, such as that in Alexandria, Egypt where the LXX version of the Bible was made.

The date of the Additions is witnessed to by the unusual colophon or concluding bibliographic notice attached to the book at 11:1 (omitted by NAB). This librarian's note records that the Greek Esther, including the Additions, was brought from Jerusalem, where it had been translated, to Egypt in the fourth year of Ptolemy and Cleopatra. The date is therefore ca. 114 B.C. (but ca. 77 or ca. 48 B.C. are also possibilities, since there was more than one Ptolemy with a wife named Cleopatra).

COMMENTARY

11:2–12:6 = A 1–17, Addition A: Mordecai's Dream and the Discovery of a Conspiracy. The Greek Esther frames the Esther story with a narrative of a dream of Mordecai at the beginning (11:5–11) and an account of its interpretation at the end (10:6–11). Though the details of the dream are somewhat cryptic, it is plain that the dream is a divine revelation. That in its turn means that the events of the Esther story, and in particular the deliverance of the Jews from danger, are seen by the Greek book as divinely foreseen and divinely engineered. The dream is made known to Mordecai a whole year before the events that begin the Hebrew story (cf. "the second year" in 11:2 = A 1 with 1:3). The Greek Esther is thus immediately different from the Hebrew version, where God is never mentioned by name, and only the coincidences of the plot and the eventual deliverance of the Jews point to the activity of God behind the scenes. Here, from the very beginning, Mordecai knows "what God had determined to do" (11:12 RSV = A 11), at least in general.

The dream also has the function of changing the Esther story from a court tale of the struggle of rival courtiers or a success story of the wit and wisdom of Jewish heroes at the Persian court into a narrative with cosmic and apocalyptic dimensions, for the conflict between the two courtiers Mordecai and Haman becomes a struggle between two mythological "dragons" (cf. Rev. 12:3). Their contest is accompanied by earthquake and universal war, all the nations rising up against the righteous.

A further function of the Addition is to enhance the importance of Mordecai as compared with Esther. Such a tendency is perhaps already observable in the Hebrew book itself, where the final note focusing on the greatness of Mordecai seems to have been added to an earlier form of the book. By comparison with the Hebrew book, where Mordecai enters the story only in his relation to Esther, in the Greek Esther he is initially the channel of divine revelation, and it is he who finally utters the authoritative interpretation of the meaning of the dream and thus of the history narrated in the book. It is true that Esther is the tiny spring that becomes a great river (11:10 = A 9; cf. 10:6 = F 3), but that hardly makes her the hero. The tendency toward making Mordecai the greater hero is even more marked in 2 Macc. 15:36 where the festival of Purim is known as "Mordecai's Day."

The second element in this first Addition (12:1–6 = A 12–17) is a slight elaboration of the brief narrative in the Hebrew book recounting Mordecai's discovery of a plot by two palace officials to assassinate the king (2:21–23). The expansion is busily functional, answering all the questions curious readers might raise about the story. Thus, how did Mordecai manage to overhear their plot? He was dozing, lit., "at rest" at the time. What made him suspect them? Their "nervousness" (see Moore, pp. 177–78). What were their names? Gabatha and Tharra. Did they confess to their crime, or were they put to death on the word of Mordecai? They confessed. What happened to Mordecai? He was promoted and rewarded.

Although the Additions seem to have been specially composed for their places in the book of Esther, they diverge at some points quite significantly from the Hebrew narrative. In this Addition, for example, Mordecai is represented at the beginning as "a great man, serving in the court of the king" (11:3 RSV = A 2), whereas in the Hebrew book it is not even certain that he is a courtier of any rank to begin with. Here, also, when Mordecai discovers the plot of the two eunuchs, it is he himself and not Esther (as in 2:22) who informs the king. Here he is rewarded immediately (12:5 = A 16), whereas in the Hebrew story it will be crucial for the plot that Mordecai has not been rewarded at the appropriate time.

13:1–7 = B 1–7, Addition B: The First Royal Letter. This elaborate and florid Addition is designed to lie between 3:13 and 3:14 of the Hebrew text. Its striking stylistic differences from the authentic Persian royal documents of the book of Ezra (4:17–22; 6:3–12; 7:12–26), for example, rule out the likelihood of its being genuine.

Addition B professes to explain from the king's point of view why the massacre of the Jews was ordered. Since it was written by a Jew, however, we may expect to observe some ironies in it. The king, for example, boasts that he is "not elated with presumption," though 1:1–8 gives the lie to that. Nor can it be unsatirical that in a decree commanding genocide he claims that he is "always acting reasonably and with kindness" (13:2 RSV = B 2). His false concern for the "tranquility" of the lives of his subjects and the stability of the kingdom (13:2, 7 = B 2, 7) is matched only by the inaccuracy of his praise of Haman as excellent in good judgment and "distinguished for his unchanging goodwill and steadfast fidelity" (13:3 RSV = B 3). We are not meant to forget that in the context (3:12) it is Haman himself who composes this royal decree, including its extravagant testimonial to Haman! The overarching irony is the bombastic and insincere style that is attributed to the Persian monarch; the author of the Addition has read the original Esther story in the right spirit (see Esther, "Commentary," 8:1–22). We observe that in this high-sounding epistle no mention is made of anything so vulgar as money. Readers will not have forgotten, however, that a very substantial bribe has been spoken of a moment ago (3:9).

There are some notable similarities between this letter and that of the letter attributed to Ptolemy Philopator in 3 Macc. 3:12–29, a Greek work of the first century B.C. The composition of speeches was of course part of the stock-in-trade of every writer trained in the Greek rhetorical schools. Our author has also drawn upon the wording of the older (Hebrew) Esther story, as, for example, in the description of the Jews as "a certain hostile people, who have laws contrary to those of every nation and continually disregard the ordinances of the kings" (13:4 RSV = B 4; cf. 3:8).

13:8–14:19 = C 1–30, Addition C: The Prayer of Mordecai and the Prayer of Esther. The prayers put in the mouths of Mordecai and Esther for divine assistance at their time of crisis follow the interchange of messages between Mordecai and Esther in chap. 4. It is usually thought that the author of these Semitic Additions (A, C, D, and E) was chiefly concerned with introducing religious language and activity into a book in which religion and the very name of God were strikingly absent. That may well be so, but there were certainly other narrative concerns as well.

In this Addition the principal interest from a narrative point of view is to explain Mordecai's unmotivated and apparently reckless behavior in refusing obeisance to Haman as prime minister of the Persian government (3:2). The Hebrew text suggested that being a Jew had something to do with Mordecai's refusal, but the connection of thought and motive in 3:4 ("for he had told them that he was a Jew," RSV) is left very indistinct. The author of this Addition wants to exculpate Mordecai of the blame candid readers of the Hebrew story might cast upon him. It was not out of insolence or pride or desire for fame that he refused to honor Haman, says this Addition; he "would have been willing to kiss the soles of his feet, to save Israel!" (13:13 RSV = C 6). Readers may well wonder why Mordecai did not take that farsighted view when invited to do obeisance to Haman in the first place, or whether Mordecai is deceiving himself somewhat. His claim that he refused to bow down to Haman to avoid "setting the glory of a human above the glory of God" (13:14 = C 7) does not ring true either, since we know that in Israelite, Persian, and Hellenistic times courtly obeisance by Jews was not frowned upon even by the most strictly religious. Mordecai here says nothing of the ethnic reason that is suggested in the reference to Haman as an Agagite in 3:1. In his prayer to God it is the strictly religious explanation that prevails.

Mordecai's self-justification aside, his prayer is a rather conventional and unremarkable piece, with overtones of many preexisting biblical models for prayer. It contains praise (13:9–11 = C 2–4), leading into self-exoneration (13:12–14 = C 5–7), followed by petition (13:15–17 = C 8–10). The prayer is indeed psychologically apt, for it represents Mordecai as deeply engaged with the struggle for power. It is no accident that he keeps on addressing God as "Lord" (Gk. kyrios), for he views God essentially as a cosmic version of the Persian emperor: "there is no one who can oppose your will" (13:9 = C 2). A consequence of this view is that any disaster that may befall the Jewish people will be God's fault, not Mordecai's, so God is asked not to neglect his people whose enemies are now plotting against them.

Esther's prayer (14:3b–19 = C 14b–30) contains its share of conventionalities, such as the confession of sin (14:6 = C 17), which is of doubtful relevance and is no less self-regarding than Mordecai's. But its markedly stronger passion redeems it from the self-righteousness of Mordecai's prayer. She first prays for her people (14:3–11 = C 16–22) and then at equal length for herself (14:12–19 = C 23–30). She vigorously defends her authentic Jewishness by affirming that she abhors the splendor of the Persian court and her own personal royal regalia, hates sleeping with an uncircumcised Gentile, and has never eaten the royal food. Her standards of Jewish separateness and food-law observance are as rigorous as Daniel's, except that this depiction seems to conflict with that of 2:9 where she is given her food allowance from the regular provision of the harem. She has not had a day's happiness from the day of her arrival at the court, she avers (14:18 = C 29). This interest in Esther's psychology, which will be more marked still in Addition D, fills an evident gap in the Hebrew story, which is singularly reticent on the characters' emotions (Haman in 5:13 is the exception that proves the rule).

15:4–19 or 15:1–16 = D 1–16, Addition D: Esther's Appearance Before the King. In the Latin (Vg.) version the next three verses (15:1–3) give the words of Mordecai's message to Esther via Hathach the eunuch (so also the Douay-Rheims version). These verses do not belong here logically, but after 4:8, where they are placed in more modern Catholic versions like JB, NAB (NAB numbers them B 8–9). In the LXX and therefore in NEB, for example, their material is incorporated in 4:8; RSV, translating only the Greek Additions, omits them entirely, and numbers the remainder of the Addition 15:1–16.

This Addition is a dramatic expansion of 5:1–2, where the story of Esther's entrance to the king's presence is told somewhat laconically, considering the danger it involves and the consequences that hang upon it. The principal interest here is a psychological one; Esther's feelings are explored with all the finesse of a popular romantic novel. Although she gives every appearance of assuredness, she is inwardly "frozen with fear" (15:5 RSV = D 5) because of the mortal danger and because of the fearsome countenance of the king. (In the spirit of the Greek Addition, the Old Latin version makes an extra addition: "He saw her as a bull at the peak of his anger, and he considered killing her; but he was uncertain, and calling out, he said, 'Who dares to enter unsummoned into the court?' ") Esther faints from terror, but the king leaps down from his throne, clasps her in his arms, and reassures her with the news that the prohibition of entry into the king's presence unbidden applies only to their subjects, not to the queen herself. The mortal danger has all been a mere matter of miscommunication!

It is characteristic of the piety of the author of the Additions that the king's crucial change of attitude is explicitly ascribed to God: "God changed the spirit of the king to gentleness" (15:8 RSV = D 8). This then becomes a turning point for the narrative as a whole, to some extent usurping the significance of the happy coincidence of the reading of the royal records in 6:1–3.

The impact of this scene on the character of Esther is no doubt to make her more of a "traditional" woman. Her beauty is particularly emphasized, and her delicacy, fearfulness, and fainting fits are contrasted with the king's masculine dignity and authority. In the Hebrew story, on the other hand, Esther conducts this scene and its sequel entirely on the basis of her wits.

16:1–24 = E 1–24, Addition E: The Second Royal Letter. This Addition is inserted after 8:12 of the Hebrew text, that is, immediately after the account of the sending out of the second decree. Its style is, if anything, even more bombastic and convoluted than that of Addition B. It is probably not out of place to detect some malice on the author's part towards Gentiles who need to cover up the truth by periphrasis. Readers may also be amused at the author's skill in composing a text explaining why the previous (unalterable) royal decree is now inoperative.

In this Addition, purporting to be a further letter from Artaxerxes, the elaborate opening (16:1b–9 = E 1b–9) sententiously observes that even those who have been most highly honored by their superiors can prove unworthy of the trust reposed in them. The king lets slip an admission that he himself has been deceived and that his methods of administering the empire stand in need of some revision (16:9 = E 9)—improbabilities in any authentic Persian document, but pardonable gibes by our Jewish author.

The crux of the matter is reached in 16:10–14, where Haman, who was always desperate to be thought an insider (5:12; 6:6–8), suffers a fate worse than death in being excoriated for un-Persian activities (he is "an alien to the Persian blood, and quite devoid of our kindliness," 16:10 RSV = E 10). Treated with exceptional generosity, considering that he is a foreigner, Haman has taken advantage of his status to plot against the Jews and thereby undermined the stability of the Persian state and left it an easy prey to the Macedonians (i.e., the Greeks, who are the Persians' traditional enemies). A more wildly improbable hypothesis is hard to imagine, but it is reasonably in keeping

with the king's lack of candor in referring to Mordecai as "our savior and perpetual benefactor" (16:13 RSV = E 13), when he had evidently forgotten all about him and had never even given him the customary reward. The author of the Addition is enjoying the irony.

From the point of view of the Jews the most important element of the letter is the advice of the king to provincial officials everywhere that "you will do well not to act upon the instructions given by Haman" (16:17 = E 17). The king distances himself from the first decree and no doubt runs counter to the convention of the unalterability of Persian law. In the Hebrew story the king evades any responsibility for devising a means of diverting the purpose of the first decree (see Esther, "Commentary," 8:7–8). The author of this Addition also has the king contradicting some details of the narrative proper, in that Haman was not impaled at the city gate but in his own courtyard, and his sons were not executed before this letter was sent (7:9–10; 9:7–10). Is this a lapse on the author's part or a hint that Artaxerxes is still not entirely in touch with events? Most surprising of all in this letter is the royal command that the festival of commemoration should be observed not just by Jews but by all the inhabitants of the empire upon pain of spear and fire. Any city or country not celebrating Purim is to be made "not only impassable for men, but also most hateful for all time to beasts and birds" (16:24 RSV = E 24). The excessiveness both of the command and of its sanctions (even in Persia it would be strange to execute anyone for not celebrating a festival!) suggests that the author is still writing in a satirical mode, as if to say: "In Persia nothing is done by halves." Even if the festival of Purim was originally a non-Jewish festival, as was probably the case, the king is not referring to anything but the Jewish festival here, for it is the commemoration of the deliverance from Haman's plan that is being demanded.

10:4–11:1 = F 1–11, Addition F: The Interpretation of Mordecai's Dream; Colophon. This sixth Addition follows from the short paragraph about Mordecai that concludes the Hebrew story (10:1–3). The Addition draws together the very beginning and very end of the Greek version of Esther.

It must be confessed that Mordecai's dream was not a remarkably coherent one. That is no doubt a permissible fault in a real dream, but this is a literary product. Should Mordecai be a dragon? How is Mordecai as dragon related to the "nation of the righteous" (11:7 = A 6)? How did the great river from a little spring deal with the dragons or with the nations prepared for war? It may be that the dream was originally a quite independent narrative having nothing to do with the story of Esther and Mordecai. It is perhaps significant that the variant Greek text of Esther (the A text) interprets the river not as Esther but as the enemies of the Jews, and actually offers an interpretation of the sun and the light as a revelation to the Jews, rather than simply failing to interpret them, as does the Greek version (the LXX). In either case the function of the dream and its interpretation in the Greek Esther is obviously both to attribute the salvation of the Jewish people to God, rather than to either of the human heroes, and to affirm that history is foreseen and directed by God.

The other interesting facet of the Addition is the explanation given of the name Purim. In the Hebrew story, there is only one "lot" (Heb. pur), which is that cast by Haman to determine the day for the extermination of the Jews (3:7). The plural word Purim, however, demands a different explanation, which the Addition duly provides. The two lots are destinies made by God, not Haman, and they are the different destinies of the gentile nations and of the Jews. By rights, this explanation of the term should have superseded that given in 3:7, and it is interesting that in the A text (though not in the LXX, i.e., the B text) that verse is omitted.

The last verse of Addition F (11:1 = F 11) is technically known as a colophon, a concluding note written either by a scribe or a librarian. Such colophons were appended to works in ancient Greek libraries, like the famous one at Alexandria, especially when the librarian had some doubts about the authenticity of the text or needed to note some details about its provenance. Here we have both the name and place of origin of the translator and the date of acquisition of one particular copy of the text that evidently became the ancestor of all other copies. The reference to the authenticity of the text suggests that there was some awareness that the text of the book of Esther had been tampered with (perhaps precisely by the inclusion of these Additions!). And the librarian's notation that the present text had been supplied by Dositheus who "said" that he was a priest and Levite and that he and his son "said" the text was genuine perhaps implies that the librarian doubted it. It was this Greek version that became the book of Esther for Christians through most of the Christian centuries; for Jews the Hebrew text of course remained the authentic Esther scroll.

Bibliography

Clines, D. J. A. The Esther Scroll: The Story of the Story. Journal for the Study of the Old Testament Supplement Series, no. 30. Sheffield: JSOT, 1984.

Gregg, J. A. F. "The Additions to Esther." In Apocrypha and Pseudepigrapha of the Old Testament. 2 vols. Edited by R. H. Charles. Oxford: Clarendon, 1913. Vol. 1, pp. 665–84.

Moore, C. A. Daniel, Esther and Jeremiah: The Additions. Anchor Bible, vol. 44. Garden City, NY: Doubleday, 1977.

WISDOM OF SOLOMON

JAMES M. REESE

INTRODUCTION

The Wisdom of Solomon produces a variety of impressions on readers. It is learned but contains simplistic arguments, traditional in content but original in form of presentation. It is hostile to pagan practices but sympathetic to certain aspects of Hellenism, that fusion of Greek and Near Eastern culture that developed in the centuries after Alexander the Great's conquests. In style it alternates between the parallelism characteristic of OT poetry and the elaborate periodic sentences found in Greek oratory. Its subject matter ranges widely over philosophical problems, ethical questions, theological doctrines, historical descriptions, psychological reflections, and scientific teaching. Because of the broad scope of the Wisdom of Solomon commentators are divided as to its date, origin, structure, unity, and even its original language.

The book receives its traditional name from the unknown author's identification of himself with King Solomon, famous for his pursuit of wisdom. The literary form and special vocabulary indicate that it is a Hellenistic school tract. Its author was a pious Jewish intellectual, an enthusiastic supporter of traditional belief, but someone also open to cultural adaptation and doctrinal progress.

Subject matter, method of developing arguments, and familiarity with the OT point to its author as a teacher of Jewish students in Alexandria. The complicated style, difficult to follow in the last section, suggests that the composition of the book extended over a period of years. Yet the large number of cross-references in the form of flashbacks favor the overall unity of this complex production. The undertaking has many marks of a work-in-progress, and the intricate syntax of the last half betrays the lack of a final revision. A single couplet (19:22) brings the book to a dramatic close.

As a unified whole the Wisdom of Solomon belongs to the literary genre of protreptic, a genre of rhetorical exhortation in Greek philosophy. The sprawling genre of protreptic met the author's needs, namely, to justify God's actions toward the Israelites, to encourage Jewish readers to love their revealed tradition, to display encyclopedic knowledge capable of impressing sophisticated readers, and to portray biblical morals as superior to Hellenistic. The case is argued with great skill by a creative use of figurative language and literary allusions. The author's skill at coining new compound words compares favorably with that of the ancient Greek playwright Aeschylus.

The opening address to "you judges of the earth" is a literary device to focus attention, but the book is directed to readers thoroughly familiar with Jewish tradition and OT writings. In fact, after the author assumes the person of King Solomon to pray to the "God of our fathers and Lord of mercy" (9:1) for the gift of Lady Wisdom, the bulk of the remaining text speaks directly to God in prayerful dialogue. This too is a literary artifice in keeping with the flexibility of a protreptic.

Structure

The flowing style and frequent asides make clear-cut divisions between major parts difficult to isolate, but the following outline preserves both the unity and the complexity of its composition.

The first part, 1:1–6:11 and 6:17–21, is an exhortation to blessed immortality. This section is a diatribe, a form of argumentative discourse developed in the Greek philosophical schools. In this diatribe the author argues that the promises of the Mosaic covenant are the heritage of those virtuous believers who trust in the Lord who led their ancestors out of Egypt. Because "righteousness is immortal" (1:15; →Righteousness), the rewards promised will be enjoyed not for a short time on earth but "in God's hand for ever" (3:1).

In the second part, 6:12–16 and 6:22–10:21, we find praises of Lady Wisdom, personified as God's throne partner. These chapters form an aporia, a statement of a philosophical problem. They begin by promising to resolve the aporia, "What is Wisdom and how does she come into being?" (6:22). The lengthy answer makes these chapters an exposition of several theological and ethical questions involved in the human quest for eternal life with God.

Warnings not to abandon divine wisdom for human folly form the third part, 11:15–16:1a. This section is another diatribe, serving to justify God's conduct toward all human sinfulness, especially that of Israel's enemies during the Exodus, an issue that will form the subject of the fourth part. (The close connection between the two parts accounts for the insertion of Part Three as an excursus after Part Four has already begun in 11:1–14.) The length, subject matter, and special purpose of Part Three all suggest that it is a major division of the Wisdom of Solomon. It performs the role of providing necessary background information.

Part Four is 11:1–14 and 16:1b–19:22, praise of God as Israel's liberator. The last part is a syncrisis, or comparison, an adaptation of a Hellenistic form in which two persons or qualities or events are compared. The author contrasts two modes of the Lord's activity. Israel's all-powerful Creator used the same natural events for the benefit of Israel and the destruction of Israel's Egyptian oppressors. This syncrisis is a skillful adaptation of the Greek genre that conveys the lesson stated in the final couplet, "In every way, Lord, you magnify and glorify your people; present at every moment in every place, you never ignore their needs" (19:22).

Setting and Purpose

The focus on the Exodus in the last half of the Wisdom of Solomon and the book's frequent allusions to the religious practices of ancient Egyptians point to Alexandria as the book's place of origin. The self-conscious literary style of the Wisdom of Solomon and the many demands that its complicated rhetorical structure place upon readers caution against seeing this work as a historical appeal to Egyptian authorities to treat the Jewish community more humanely. Its frequent references to the cruelty of ancient Egyptians and its harshness toward all forms of pagan religious practice make the Wisdom of Solomon ill suited to be a political tract in a concrete historical crisis. Its approach is not calculated to gain outside support for a cause. On the contrary, it is the kind of exhortation that appeals to the loyalty of a group questioning its own identity and direction. It is not a document that arose out of an actual persecution of Jews; its style and content point to literary activity within a rabbinical school as the setting for its composition.

The author was familiar with metropolitan culture and capable of appreciating scientific research. But what believing Jews have received from God is the value at stake. God is with them in their present situation, and so "their hope is full of immortality" (3:4). Danger comes not so much from outside political forces as from loss of faith in God and the providence guiding history (→ Providence). The large number of terms borrowed from Hellenistic anthropology, philosophy, psychology, medicine, and the popular cult of the goddess Isis point to a date near the beginning of the reign of the Roman Emperor Augustus in 28 B.C.

The unknown author argues for fresh stands on religious questions under discussion by Jewish intellectuals of that period. With vivid language the Wisdom of Solomon proclaims personal immortality for the just. In spite of difficulties and disappointments like sterility and early death, the lot of those remaining loyal to Israel's God is preferable to the path of sinners. On judgment day, by means of God's gift of "incorruptibility" (2:23; 6:19), "the just will stand with great confidence in front of those tormenting him" (5:1; → Judgment, Day of).

Religious Significance

To the large Jewish community in and around Alexandria, a city whose population the Jewish philosopher Philo put at over a million persons (*Flaccus* 43), the Wisdom of Solomon offered a formal apologia for a vigorous stance against the appeal of Hellenism. In a sense, each of its four parts could stand alone as a defense of some value of Israel's revelation.

Joined together in this sustained protreptic, these four major parts provide a powerful appeal for continued fidelity to the Mosaic covenant. How effective this exhortation proved for its original readers is not known. Nor does the NT offer any clear literary allusion to the text of the Wisdom of Solomon. Though some images and technical terms, like the "radiance" of wisdom, appear in both, the similarities are a result of themes drawn from a common religious climate.

COMMENTARY

PART ONE: 1:1–6:11; 6:17–21

Exhortation to Blessed Immortality

An extended, self-contained diatribe, 1:1–6:11 and 6:17–21, sets the tone for the entire book. Forces are at work seeking to shape human destiny, which finds its center not in this age but in eternal life. A series of vivid tableaux describes the fate of the righteous as reigning forever, safe "in the hand of God" (3:1).

From this extended appeal, the nature of the Wisdom of Solomon as an apologia (an argued defense of beliefs) is clear. Only God can draw human beings to their eternal destiny. This long diatribe prepares readers for the polemic against idolatry in Part Three. The author shows sophisticated literary skill in setting up this exhortation in the schema *a b a b a*. The first, third, and fifth developments take the form of exhortations (1:1–15; 3:1–5:1; 6:1–11). Between these appeals are inserted two descriptions: the first, of evil conduct (1:16–2:24), and the second, of God's judgment upon evil conduct (5:2–23). The appendix, 6:17–21, serves to summarize the exhortations.

1:1–15
Exhortation to Walk in Righteousness

Serving as an introduction to the entire book is an ardent appeal to "you judges of the earth," a phrase taken from the Septuagint (LXX) translation of Ps. 2:10. They are to seek righteousness (in the sense of holiness), for "righteousness is eternal" (1:15). This exhortation sets the mood in three ways: by its poetic style, by its appeal to biblical themes, and by its ethical demands. An examination of these three features will illustrate characteristics common to the entire Wisdom of Solomon.

The poetic style imitates the parallelism of Hebrew poetry, in which each line contains a complete clause (→ Poetry). The language employs figurative speech, e.g., calling God "Power" (1:3) and "Ear of Jealousy" (1:10). Biblical themes are pervasive. One searches for God "in simplicity of heart" (1:1), an expression alluding to the words of the aged David as he prayed before the assembly of Israel in 1 Chron. 29:17. And worshipers must avoid "murmuring" (1:10, 11), almost a technical term in Exodus 15–17 for scorning the God of the covenant. Failure to trust in God's care is a way to call divine punishment upon one's life (1:12–14).

By far the greatest preoccupation of this introduction is attention to ethics; it insists that God refuses worship from those who are malicious (1:3). The text does not resolve the dilemma whether ignorance opens the way to malice or whether malice is the underlying cause of ignorance (1:4–5). The introduction begins with ethical goals but then shifts attention to the pursuit of wisdom, enemy of all kinds of sin. What wisdom achieves, God accomplishes. Both search human hearts and bring secret motives to light (1:6–11).

The final verses of this opening exhortation make clear the orientation of all its parts (1:12–15). Moral integrity and righteousness are not ethical matters limited only to this life; rather, they primarily concern future life. Never does the Wisdom of Solomon isolate human destiny from God's care for creation. "For God did not make death nor does he delight in the destruction of living beings" (1:13). God's care to maintain the varieties of living species offers an insight into his loving nature.

When this divine care is directed to hu-

mans, it is not limited to protecting the species as such but offers immortality to each person. Obviously God did not "make death" (1:13), an allusion to the result of human sin described in Gen. 3:19. Thus immortality is not simply a natural quality of human souls but a dimension of "righteousness" (1:15). How God overcomes death and communicates the gift of immortality will be explained as the book unfolds (→ Immortality; Soul).

1:16–2:24
Description of Evil Conduct

Abruptly the scene changes from the royal figures addressed in 1:1–15 to a group of evildoers. Rather than describing their conduct, the author allows these opponents of God to describe their own deeds and motives. This first-person narrative conveys their arrogant cynicism, in which ill will colors their knowledge of God. In certain ways the description presents a stereotype of the Greek philosophical tradition of Epicureanism (→Epicureans). The Epicureans viewed the soul as made of subtle matter. The picture is simplistic, but it captures the feeling of despair in much Hellenistic philosophy contemporary with the author. Human life appears "short and painful" (2:1); "our end is irreversible" (2:5).

Those who hold this foolish view of life pour out a violent tirade that extends for exactly twice as many lines as were devoted to describing their miserable state (2:6–20; thirty-six lines). For them life has only two goals: to seek pleasure and to prove by their conduct that might makes right. This diatribe is a lively portrayal of the contrast between the high moral standards of Jewish society and the perceived corruption of Hellenistic permissiveness. The contrast is an implicit exaltation of the moral superiority of God's chosen people.

Some influence from OT pictures of suffering just believers, especially the suffering servant figure of Isaiah 53, colors this vivid description (→Servant). Certain church fathers saw in Wisd. of Sol. 2:12–20 a prediction of the Passion of Jesus. Other commentators viewed these verses as a Christian interpolation based on the Gospel passion narratives. But no image of a suffering "messiah" should be read into the designation of the persecuted just man as "son of God" (2:18). The salvation envisioned here is simply rescue from verbal and physical abuse. Sinners mock self-control and passive resistance as no protection against their philosophy that might makes right.

In a brief reply of nine verses the author passes judgment on Hellenistic morality, which attracted some Jewish students. Bluntly put, "They were deceived for their evil blinded them" (2:21). The battle is between the closed world of expediency that offers no hope and the "mysteries of God," which assure the "last honors of blameless souls" (2:22).

In a concluding remark (2:23–24) the author states the eschatological basis for evaluating human life: "God created human beings for incorruption, and made them as an image of his own eternity" (2:23; some ancient manuscripts and modern commentators read "nature" in place of "eternity"). This profound statement introduces a new insight into Jewish teaching by borrowing the concept of "incorruption" from Epicurean philosophy. Incorruption was a divine quality that prevented the subtle atoms of the gods from escaping their bodies; it thus assured their immortality.

By appropriating this technical term, the author is engaging in a polemic on two fronts. First, he places human immortality in the divine sphere, as an "image" of God rather than a quality inherent in human nature. Second, he affirms that eternal life is a pure divine gift designated by God to draw certain human beings into a form of communion surpassing natural powers. This carefully articulated eschatological outlook permeates the entire diatribe (→ Eschatology).

What then is death? Not part of God's plan but the result of demonic envy. These verses provide an original, creative interpretation of the fall of the man and woman of Gen. 3:1–19. The serpent is implicitly identified with the devil who induced these first mortals to challenge God and thereby lose their precious gift of "incorruption." As a result, human beings are now subject to a double death, in both the realm of nature and the sphere of eschatological destiny. This bold appropriation of Hellenistic philosophical vocabulary to articulate faith identifies the original audience of the Wisdom of Solomon as a specific group of knowledgeable Jewish intellectuals.

3:1–5:1
Exhortation to Upright Conduct

The central section of the opening diatribe is the longest and most carefully developed of its three exhortations (1:1–15; 3:1–5:1; 6:1–11). Its structure indicates that the author felt a need to justify this new eschatological perspective at length with specific examples.

3:1–12, The Contrasting Fates of the Upright and the Sinful.
The section opens with a joyful announcement of the eternal reward for "upright souls" (3:1). First, they must undergo a period of testing that baffles unbelievers. Trials are God's way of revealing who is "worthy of himself" (3:5). To be worthy of God means exactly that: victorious over death, the just enjoy life with God. The just are empowered to participate in God's lordship. In using the term "souls"

to identify the just, the text neither affirms nor denies resurrection of the body; it affirms only continuity in personal existence. "Soul" is one of the author's favorite words. Appearing over twenty-five times, it reflects the influence of Hellenistic psychology, which identified conscious activity with the spiritual principle of life.

Those who remain faithful to the Mosaic tradition will be assigned to preside over the judgment of their wicked oppressors. Once more the promise serves as an incentive to fidelity. Only those who persevere in doing what God wants "will abide with him in love," that is, enjoy divine "favor and mercy" (3:9).

A graphic contrast shows why the gloom of sinners is justified. First, they have no hope in the future because they cut themselves off from the Lord. Second, their life upon this earth is marred by disappointments in three areas: marriage, family, and posterity. These three provide the subject matter for extended reflections presented in a series of overlapping contrasts, a technique also used extensively in Part Four.

3:13–4:6, True and False Faithfulness.
The first arena for the testing of conduct by the promise of eternal life with God is fidelity in marriage. Rather than exalting physical fruitfulness as a criterion for divine approval (→ Child, Children), the author proclaims that the Lord will look for "fruit in the visitation of souls," that is, for moral integrity (3:13). The expression "visitation" to describe final judgment on life is the common OT image for God's intervention either to punish or to reward. The Wisdom of Solomon alludes here to Isa. 56:4–5 but gives it an eschatological significance. Promises of fidelity are extended so that even eunuchs, who have no hope of offspring, can hope for an honorable role in the new age. Their struggles to remain chaste are "good birth-pangs" (3:15).

The bleak picture of unfaithful marriage unions continues by identifying their offspring as bad seed, destined not only for personal doom but also to disappear without progeny. Neither will they enjoy consolation "on the day of decision" (3:18). Here final judgment is called by a Greek legal term. This is one of the many instances of the authors balancing images from Hellenistic and from Jewish traditions.

The real fruitfulness in human life is to produce virtue. "For in its recollection is immortality, because it is known in the sight of God and in the sight of human beings" (4:1). This juxtaposing is emphatic in that it provides an opportunity for the author to clarify the different effects of human and divine remembering. God's remembering triumphantly carries those who have virtue into eternal life, "crowning with victory the struggle of those who are not soiled" (4:2). This image, modeled on Greek athletic contests, is a strong plea to Jewish readers to opt for divine friendship.

Having made this urgent appeal, the author moves on to the third area where improper unions produce painful results: when children end up as accusers of their parents' sinful lives (4:4–6).

4:7–5:1, Eschatological Triumph of the Just.
A final comparison illustrates the same lesson of the superiority of upright conduct. Only those familiar with the Bible could understand the double allusion here. To the story of Enoch's being snatched from earth by God in Gen. 5:24 are joined reflections about the moral crassness of sinners based on Isa. 57:1–11.

This detailed exhortation ends with a vivid contrast between the wicked, who will wither away under the burden of their sins, and the just, who stand triumphantly at God's judgment before "those who tormented him and despised his suffering" (5:1). This picture of the just person is a good example of the author's use of inclusion or ring style, i.e., a return to the topic with which he began this exhortation (see 3:1).

5:2–23
Description of God's Judgment on Evil

The author's love of balance accounts for a second description that carefully parallels the monologue of evildoers in 2:6–20. The device of making sinners speak once more, after they have seen their error, gives this passage a special persuasive power. Having seen God vindicate the upright in the eschatological judgment, sinners repeat many of the images and examples they used in their previous mockery. This speech thus forms an ironic reprise of their earlier attack on the righteous. They voice regret that they came to understand too late. The images of a ship passing through water (5:10) and of a bird in flight leaving no trace (5:11) skillfully utilize the riddle of Prov. 30:19 to wonder at the emptiness of sin.

The author drives home what is at stake in human choices by balancing this lament of sinners over their foolish choices with another praise of the righteous. They enjoy reward "in the Lord's hand," from which they receive a royal crown (5:16). This picture recalls the book's opening address to earthly kings. But now the description of God is expanded by drawing upon the warrior imagery of Isa. 59:17. The apocalyptic elements introduced briefly here (5:16–23) anticipate the long descriptions of God using nature against sinners in Part Four.

These poetic images do not provide sufficient information to pronounce on what happens to sinners after death. The author's primary concern is to convince readers to pursue God's will so that they may join the "sons of God" or "saints" in the heavenly beatitude of God's court. At this point the text does not have to add another condemnation of sinners; they have already condemned themselves.

The length to which the author goes to picture the glorification of the upright proclaims its central role in his teaching. Obviously he deemed the lesson to be of supreme importance for Jews living in the environment of Alexandria. Unless they were committed to an eschatological view of their destiny, they would not have the depth of motivation needed to remain faithful to the God of Israel. Victory in the contest of life against forces of evil comes from the "spirit of the Powerful One," who easily sweeps away all human arrogance (5:23).

The imagery of this description comes from the popular apocalyptic movement that flourished among Jews between 200 B.C. and A.D. 200 (→ Apocalyptic Literature). Its goal was to encourage Jews, who were a subject people, and to keep alive their hope for enjoying God's covenant promises, which this author has translated into eternal rewards. Unless God acts, the sin that entered the world through "the devil's envy" (2:24) "will make the whole earth a waste" (5:23). A profound awareness of sin's destructive power penetrates the long diatribe that opens the Wisdom of Solomon. The author will now draw it to a close with an exhortation that prepares readers for Part Two.

6:1–11
Exhortation to Seek Wisdom

Once more the text addresses rulers. The terminology differs from that used in the opening admonition, in keeping with the author's attraction to synonyms. This literary fiction of an exalted audience both ties the whole section of the book together and presses home the sense of urgency marking the diatribe. The real audience is the Jewish intellectual community, which needs to be confirmed in its faith. What it needs is neither political influence nor territorial domination but "power from the Most High" (6:3).

The mood of this exhortation is somber, because the readers are being blamed for failure to "walk according to the will of God" (6:4). They are not to depend on any supposed privileges, presuming that their God, "the Lord of all does not shrink from any face" (6:7, alluding to Deut. 1:17). Rather, they must "learn wisdom," for that is the only protection against

824

"falling away," in the sense of committing apostasy, the supreme spiritual folly (6:9).

This mention of wisdom serves as a hinge enabling the author to prepare for Part Two of this protreptic, which will celebrate the mysterious Lady Wisdom. She is the one who empowers believers to receive the gift of blessed immortality, the goal of their existence.

In its opening exhortation, Wisd. of Sol. 1:6 uses the term "wisdom" to designate God as a "beneficent spirit." That experience of God must have worn thin for Jews exposed so long to the many attractions of Hellenism. This complicated diatribe urges them to open their lives once more to their mission in the world. As usual, the author blends traditional biblical teaching with technical terminology from contemporary Hellenistic culture. Greek philosophers could not even agree whether or not any kind of providence existed. Israel's God "is provident toward all" (6:7). So the author can end the first part of his work with an emphatic couplet, "Set your desire then on my discourse; long for it and you will become learned" (6:11).

6:17–21
Concluding Summary of Part One

Thoughtful touches like this summary identify the author of the Wisdom of Solomon as a teacher, unable to leave a topic without making one final connection for pupils. Even after beginning the praises of Lady Wisdom in 6:12–16, he stops to insert an extended syllogism in the style cultivated by the Stoics, namely, a sorites (→ Stoics). It celebrates practical wisdom as the crowning achievement of an upright life. The seven qualities listed as generated by loyalty in pursuing God's will restate in a succinct way those virtues that "you judges of the earth" were urged to cultivate in the opening exhortation (1:1–15). The logic is not perfect, but the thrust is meant to be more emotive than didactic.

The insertion of this summary as a kind of afterthought is one final reminder that goodwill on the part of believers is essential for participating in the moral transformation and blessed immortality that ultimately come through God's gift of Lady Wisdom.

PART TWO: 6:12–16; 6:22–10:21
Praises of Lady Wisdom, Personified as God's Throne Partner

The outstanding characteristic of Part Two is the personification of God's saving presence as the woman who shares his throne. Lady Wisdom is mentioned explicitly over twenty-five times in Part Two. The personification of wisdom appears in the OT and in other Jewish writings (e.g., Prov. 8; Sir. 24). The Wisdom of Solomon, however, makes two significant modifications to bring Lady Wisdom into closer contact with Hellenistic civilization.

First, her activities are modeled on the portrait of Isis, worshiped widely in the Aegean area and Egypt as goddess of culture and benefactor of humanity. The praises of Isis were formulated in litanies, called aretalogies, which recorded her outstanding accomplishments in promoting human culture. Original Jewish readers of this protreptic would have recognized that it was drawing upon the picture of Isis to present the Lord of Israel as ultimate benefactor of humanity by his sending of Lady Wisdom to work on behalf of members of the chosen people.

Second, the author spells out his own development as the fruit of the presence of Lady Wisdom within his body, mind, and spirit. She gave him the qualities that Hellenistic philosophers urged political leaders to cultivate in the self-help ethical manuals of that era, known as the kingship tracts. These manuals came into existence after the death of Alexander the Great when his generals set up kingdoms in the ancient Near East. They needed public support for their new style of leadership. Accordingly, they employed famous philosophers as tutors for their children to train them to be benefactors of humanity. These kingship tracts helped future kings prepare for their tasks.

Part Two of the Wisdom of Solomon deliberately mirrors contemporary Hellenistic ethical and religious documents to celebrate the God of Israel as source of those skills and talents responsible for all human growth. It is the heart of the author's apologia for biblical faith as Israel's contribution to humanity. Only by fidelity to their revelation of a superior religious tradition can Jewish intellectuals bring knowledge of the true God and of salvation to the world. The author offers new theological insights to these readers as "kings" in the sense that they have the destiny to uphold the Lord's law in the world. The sublimity of its message accounts for its ornate and scholarly style, with many plays on words and figures of speech that add to the luster of Lady Wisdom.

6:12–16, 22–25
Prologue Introducing Lady Wisdom

Suddenly, without transition, the style and imagery of the Wisdom of Solomon change. No longer is the author engaged in a diatribe to provide incentives for the cultivation of a life of holiness. Now this ideal is portrayed concretely in the activity of a "shining and spotless" woman (6:12). As God's "throne partner" she offers the gift of blessed immortality that readers have been urged to seek. Thanks to her presence, holiness is not an agonizing struggle but a joyful experience that floods the human spirit with well-being and loving communion with the Lord. The text pictures God as originating this desirable communion by dispatching Lady Wisdom to those who choose to "love" and "seek" her. These two activities were urged upon the "kings" in the opening address (cf. 1:1). The transformation that she effects is spelled out in the sorites that divides this prologue (6:17–21).

In the second half (6:22–25) of this short prologue, in which the author assumes the identity of King Solomon, he appropriates a technical expression from the Isis litanies—"I will proclaim"—to outline the program for Part Two. He will undertake a quest for answers to questions: who or what is Lady Wisdom? How did she originate? What are her secrets? The author promises a comprehensive search "from the beginning of creation" and an openness that holds back nothing of her "secrets," in contrast to the practices of contemporary mystery cults (6:22). Their mysteries could not be revealed.

The very nature of Lady Wisdom precludes such pettiness, for she has nothing to do with "pining envy." The questions raised give this second part of the book the nature of an aporia or problem composition. Questions will be answered first in the portrait of Lady Wisdom and of her gifts (7:22b–8:16) and then in the concluding ode that traces her saving influence in the world from Adam to Moses (10:1–21). In carrying out this promise the author reveals himself as a committed religious teacher who has internalized the covenant values of Israel's faith. Consequently, he prefaces his praises of Lady Wisdom with an enthusiastic description of his personal encounter with her. This description provides the setting for his theological teaching on God's providence and salvation.

7:1–22a
Autobiographical Account of an Encounter with Lady Wisdom

To enhance the credibility of his revelation about Lady Wisdom, "Solomon" explains how he began his personal relationship with her. He had no advantage because he was born a king. Hellenistic philosophers often made the point that a king is no different from any other human being. He came into this world during a "ten-month" period of time (7:2). It is no accident that the rare compound used here also occurs in a litany of Isis. One of her good works was to guard the "ten-month" pregnancies of her devotees. In fact, this autobiographical sketch is marked by over fifteen words never found in the OT, including new compounds found only in this book. By this choice of unusual words the

artful Solomon displays his familiarity with contemporary science and culture.

The point this approach makes is that under Wisdom's direction he reacted to his common condition of being subject to human weakness in an uncommon way—he prayed. He correctly reasoned that every human being needs divine help. God answered his plea in two ways: in the form of "prudence" and through the action of "Wisdom's spirit" (7:7). Young Solomon found himself with a new attitude as well as enjoying great material advantages given by Lady Wisdom.

He confesses that, ironically, he did not know that she was their "female begetter" (7:12; RSV: "mother"). This new feminine coinage is an example of a practice popular among Hellenistic writers. The author uses this same technique again, calling Lady Wisdom "female initiate" and "female selector" (8:4).

The last part of this autobiographical recollection provides insight into who Lady Wisdom is (7:14–22a). Solomon now asks God directly for accurate knowledge and a worthy attitude, because God is "guide of Wisdom and director of the wise" (7:15), phrases that recall Hellenistic titles of Isis and Hermes as guides of souls. He goes on to say in a series of seven phrases that God has already given him the whole range of human knowledge from astronomy to botany (7:17–21). Abruptly he changes direction and states boldly that all this came to him from the "craftswoman" Wisdom, a feminine form applied to her three times (7:22; 8:6; 14:2).

The surprise is that what was attributed to God is immediately assigned to Lady Wisdom without restriction. By refusing to make any clear distinction between the two, the author indicates that the identity of Lady Wisdom is an aporia, a theological problem to be probed. In one sense she cannot be separated from God as some kind of distinct entity, like the "emanations" of Hellenistic philosophical speculation. At the same time the technique of personifying this dimension of God provides a shift of perspective to generate a desire to enter into communion with the Lord. The author wishes to communicate his own "friendship with God" (7:14).

7:22b–8:16
A Portrait of Lady Wisdom and List of Her Gifts

Having provided his credentials, the self-styled King Solomon now fulfills his promise to reveal "who Wisdom is." The answer is a complex and challenging philosophical meditation.

7:22b–8:1, The Qualities and Activities of Wisdom. It begins with a list of twenty-one

826

diverse qualities that are deeply rooted in Hellenistic learning (7:22–23); ten of these terms never appear in the LXX. Lady Wisdom resembles the Stoic world spirit, which is immanent in the universe, permeating, unifying, and vivifying all. In addition, she has a transcendent spirit that communicates goodness, mercy, and loving-kindness to intelligent creatures.

Since many of these qualities were also applied to Isis in her litanies, they obviously communicated to the original audience a variety of connotations whose significance is lost on modern readers. Lady Wisdom operates universally and effectively because she acts like rays of the sun emanating from the divine glory. Her identity is further defined by five activities that make her a kind of cosmic soul (7:24–25). These actions derived primarily from contemporary speculation on the relation of divine power to human existence. Wisdom serves as mirror (7:26) to reflect qualities attributed to the divine sphere in the eclectic philosophical climate popular among the Stoics.

Lady Wisdom has transcendent features. She possesses powers belonging to Israel's Lord, the one Creator and Savior. She makes all things new. In each successive generation she enters into holy souls and prepares friends of God and prophets. She has made creatures lovable to God and never fails in her mission to transform persons (7:27–30). A striking couplet sums up her work in the world: "With force she stretches from one end of the earth to the other and rules the whole universe gently" (8:1).

In abstract terms Lady Wisdom is God's providence. But the author delivers the message of God's wisdom as empowered saving presence in a poetic language that spoke to cultured Jewish readers. This portrait instructs them that they do not have to espouse Greek ideals to find meaning in life. On the contrary, to abandon the unique Lord of the universe, who promises eternal friendship, is supreme folly.

8:2–16, Gifts Available from Wisdom.
Having fulfilled his promise to reveal who Lady Wisdom is, the author now explains her secrets in the form of gifts she has given him and offers to anyone else willing to woo her and be united with her in marriage. Here the text draws first on the language of Hellenistic mystery cults to interpret what love for Wisdom is. It explains that communion with her culminates in the so-called four cardinal virtues: prudence, justice, courage, and self-control (8:7). In a departure from the biblical practice, the text employs the technical terminology of Hellenistic ethics. Thus, justice designates what is due others, rather than the state of holiness, as in Wisd. of Sol. 1:1.

As a whole, these four virtues constitute the holiness that is "more useful in life" than anything, because they bring eternal life. For all this use of technical vocabulary, the imagery of Lady Wisdom giving birth to these virtues is a significant departure from philosophical ethics, which saw virtue as the achievement of purely human effort. Not so, insists the author. Lady Wisdom gives birth to true virtue only in hearts loyal to God.

Other gifts that Lady Wisdom brings transform her followers into seasoned and articulate "life companions," a metaphor never employed in the OT. With a certain amount of repetition, the text closes this portrait of Lady Wisdom by returning to the autobiographical style. In a carefully balanced and artistically constructed conclusion with daring sexual imagery, Solomon once more reminisces about the advantage he recognized for his kingship of a life led in intimate companionship with Lady Wisdom (8:9–16). She gave him satisfaction and superiority even over powerful kings. The lesson for readers is that they do not have to fear but can have "joy and merriment" at every moment. In terms of the literary unfolding of the book, this personal story sets the stage for the following prayer.

8:17–9:18
Prayer Begging God for Lady Wisdom

8:17–21, Introduction to the Prayer.
The solemn language introducing an intense prayer to God to be allowed to receive Lady Wisdom reflects the author's deep religious experience and his desire to convey it to young Jewish intellectuals. Its thrust is eschatological: "immortality is having Wisdom as a relative" (8:17). That emphasis does not lessen a whole range of present benefits flowing from Lady Wisdom's presence: good delights, unlimited wealth, glory.

Here appears a controversial verse that has been understood as teaching the preexistence of the soul. "I was a child of good natural condition and had received a good soul, or rather, being good I came into a spotless body" (8:19–20). In context, however, this sentence describes the author's status at the moment of his ardent prayer. As he had stated earlier, Lady Wisdom gave him "all good things" before he recognized her presence (7:11). So now he shows that, thanks to her influence, he "came into" a spotless body, in the sense of the Greek ideal of a sound mind in a sound body. Recognizing his maturity as gift, he responds by praying with his whole heart to God for Lady Wisdom.

9:1–12, Structure of the Prayer for Wisdom.
This plea is a free translation and elaboration of the famous prayer of Solomon in 1 Kings 3:6–9. It can be divided into an address to

God (9:1–3) and two parallel petitions, each joined with a motive for offering this prayer (9:4–9, 10–12). The address to "God of our fathers and Lord of mercy" directs this prayer to the author of the covenants with the patriarch Abraham and the lawgiver Moses. This is the same God who is creator and whose providence governs all.

What is new in the address is the theological insight, namely, that God created by his "word," and in particular that God established the human family by Lady Wisdom (9:1b–2a). This amounts to another way of saying what was affirmed earlier, that she is God's providence. She has a role in enabling humans to participate in her task of managing the whole universe "in holiness and uprightness" (9:3). They do so when they conduct themselves like kings by ruling over their share of creation in integrity of heart. All in all, this opening is pregnant with the author's vision of the purpose of creation.

By the loftiness and variety of the address to God, young Solomon stimulates in pious readers a sense of their importance and encourages them to resist Alexandria's metropolitan appeal. By describing Lady Wisdom in Hellenistic religious and philosophical terminology, he exalts biblical revelation above human learning.

The first petition asks God for Lady Wisdom in her capacity as "throne partner" (9:4), the bold image repeated from 6:14. This title is linked to both the goddess Isis and to Fate in Hellenistic piety. By what right does Solomon expect to receive her as gift? Not because he is a king but "because I am your servant and son of your maidservant" (9:5, an uncharacteristic direct quotation of Ps. 115:7, LXX). He supports his petition by spelling out his weaknesses in body, mind, and deed. This motive introduces the reality behind all prayer, namely, that even the most accomplished human being will be accounted as nothing without Lady Wisdom. In other words, salvation is God's free gift.

The example of his divinely imposed mission to build the Temple with its altar (9:8) may not seem relevant to a sophisticated audience. The Jerusalem Temple, however, is cited in its cosmic significance, as symbol and model of the heavenly sanctuary, where God receives adoration from the saints. Only Lady Wisdom can communicate an appreciation of that divine worship. Thus, the first petition ends by emphatically repeating her divine prerogatives (9:9).

The second petition is an elaborate plea that God send Lady Wisdom (9:10–12). It is artistically constructed in ten balanced poetic clauses expressing Solomon's absolute need for her help. She goes into labor to bring forth for him the discernment and good works practiced by his wise father, David.

9:13–18, Concluding Reflection. The prayer itself consists of only these two dynamic petitions. The remaining verses (9:13–18) form a reflection and transition. First, they recall the opening of Part Two and the promise to explain who Lady Wisdom is and what her secrets are (see 6:22–23). Then they elaborate the truths stated in the prayer itself: human beings are weak and need special protection. An allusion to Plato's teaching in *Phaedo* 81c, that the tent of the earthly body weighs down the "constantly reflecting mind," occurs in 9:15.

Once more the author cannot refrain from adding an additional comment. This takes the form of an oratorical question to emphasize the need for Lady Wisdom and God's "holy spirit" (9:17). The question is answered by a practical example of her impact. The exchange forms an appropriate summary to the aporia section of the book and acts as a hinge to Part Four: she enables mortals to exercise upright conduct on earth and to "be saved" (9:18). This is the first appearance of the verb "save" that will dominate the remainder of the work.

10:1–21
The Saving Power of Lady Wisdom

Chap. 10 has its own style and unity, characterized by two striking features. The first is the repetition of the emphatic "she" to designate Lady Wisdom six times as aiding Israel's heroes. The second literary feature is the absence of the proper name of any of these heroes. Not only does that style imply an audience familiar with the OT narratives; it also makes the patriarchs types or models to illustrate ways by which Lady Wisdom manifests her saving power.

The first beneficiary of Lady Wisdom's protection was Adam, when he abided on earth "alone," i.e., bereft of any companion. His position exemplifies the point made in the prayer that even the most illustrious mortal, the head or "father of the cosmos," is nothing without Wisdom, a lesson repeated below (10:8–9). When Adam was deceived by "the devil's envy" (2:24), she rescued him from the consequences. By way of contrast, Cain is mentioned as one who refused to heed Lady Wisdom. A poetic image identifies her as the "pilot" of Noah's ark, a title also attributed to Isis. More attention is devoted to Abraham and his brother Lot, with an allusion to the popular story about the unbelieving wife who was turned into a pillar of salt.

Only Jewish readers would recognize the allusion to Jacob's ladder of Gen. 28:12 in the reference to the "kingdom of heaven" (10:10). His piety amid a variety of hardships shows that Wisdom's help does not eliminate struggle, but she does empower the devout to overcome

(10:12). From Joseph the text skips directly to Moses, thus limiting the number of examples to seven. At this point Lady Wisdom begins to protect "a holy people and blameless posterity" (10:15), a change that prepares for the examples of Part Four. This verse also introduces two changes of style. The author goes from third-person narrative to direct address to God (10:20) and also begins to describe events in the form of a series of contrasts. The same situation that serves as a blessing on the chosen people brings destruction upon their enemies (11:5–14).

Part Two comes to a resolution appropriate for the literary problem or aporia in the author's favorite technique, a summarizing couplet: "Wisdom opened the mouths of the speechless and made the tongues of babies distinct" (10:21). These achievements point to universal harmony and integration of Jewish and Hellenistic cultures, because they were both attributed to the goddess Isis in her litanies and assigned to the messianic age in Isa. 35:6.

PART THREE: 11:15–16:1a

Warnings Not to Abandon Divine Wisdom for Human Folly

Ancient writings did not employ footnotes. One of the techniques used to supply background material was the excursus. The Wisdom of Solomon brings this technique to a high point of development by forming a diatribe out of a series of excursuses. This part of the book, therefore, is more reflective and abounds in hostile judgments against the culture that threatened to corrupt its pious readers. Part Three serves a double function. First, it is a powerful condemnation of idolatry, the chief expression of human folly. Second, it provides a reasoned defense of Judaism's monotheism. Its nature as an excursus is emphasized by its insertion within Part Four (11:1–14; 16:16–19:22), which describes God's saving activity during the Exodus. This breaking off after the first comparison drives home the truth that Israel's God dominates history. What is at stake in this diatribe is the vindication of God's way of governing the universe.

The exaltation of God's authority, addressed to human rulers in 6:1–11, prepared readers for this dissertation on divine providence. The whole development is held together by a traditional biblical theme, that God punishes idolaters by the instruments of their sin: "through those things which one uses to commit sin, through them comes punishment" (11:16). In some way God lets sinners take on the qualities of the creatures that they worship.

11:15–12:27
A Defense of God's Provident Ruling of the World

11:15–12:2, God's Restraint in Punishing Sin. The mention of thirst as punishment for the ancient Egyptians serves as occasion for inserting a long defense of God's intervention against the Egyptians who practiced animal worship, a vice mentioned three times in Part Three (11:15–26; 12:23–27; 15:14–16:1a). Perhaps to respond to criticisms of God's harsh treatment of the Egyptians as recorded in the biblical account of the Exodus, the text hastens to exempt God from any charge of vindictiveness in punishing. On the contrary, God's "all-powerful hand" (11:17), capable of meting out any mode of punishment, even to the point of creating fearful instruments of torture, always acts with love and restraint.

This highly imaginative presentation ironically offers God a whole list of possible instruments of torture that he could create on the spot. Their psychological impact would be to instill fear in the worshipers of idols. God could cause fear by calling upon Fate, the supreme power conceived in Greek religion as ruling over gods and mortals. Having mentioned the possibilities, the text shows God acting in a way completely different from Fate. As the author says to the Lord, "You have arranged all in measure and number and weight" (11:20). The text continues speaking to God about the manner in which he fulfills all his activity, showing that it achieves the Greek ideal of perfect balance and harmony.

The prayerful dialogue style gives this diatribe greater apologetic power, in that it exhibits an even deeper religious intimacy than the cult of Isis could. The Lord's covenant promises and powerful protection are always available to loyal worshipers. The reminder, "For to prevail mightily is always in your power" (11:21), is spoken to the Lord but directed to Jewish students tempted to sample Hellenistic cults. Rather than being harsh or arbitrary, the God who punished Israel's enemies in Egypt always acts as a concerned and merciful benefactor who does not have any self-interest to protect.

What Egyptians criticized as punishment had a different role. All divine conduct is a display of the truth stated above in 1:13 that God does not delight in the destruction of any living creature. "You overlook sins of mortals with a view to repentance; for you love all creatures. For you would not have fashioned anything you hated" (11:23–24). By using vocabulary similar to that in the polemic against sinners in chap. 2, the text continues the plea for fidelity to Israel's tradition. The same God who "created humans for incorruption" (2:23) did so by placing his "incorruptible spirit in all" (12:1). Because there is continuity between earthly existence and eternal life, God disciplines mortals now to engender the fidelity and righteousness that reign forever.

12:3–27, Speaking to God About Providence.

The emotional pitch of the text reaches new heights as the author enters into a series of four brief personal exchanges with God about the workings of providence. First, in a dense outpouring that has prompted modern editors to see some textual corruption, the text paradoxically reminds God that he hated the Canaanites for their magical rites of idolatry and cannibalism (12:3–11a). Knowing that they were an "accursed seed," God nevertheless eliminated them only gradually, to provide an opportunity for repentance.

Second, employing legal terminology and the technique of rhetorical questions, the text affirms strongly God's providence (12:11b–18). Infinite strength is the basis of this justice. Rather than acting in the "might makes right" manner of those who oppressed the innocent worshiper in 2:18, God always manifests honesty and fairness. In the third brief colloquy God's providence is presented as a lesson to the chosen people "that the upright person should show loving-kindness" (12:19). The lesson itself is straightforward, but its application is so obscure that it created difficulty for copyists. Such variety exists in the manuscripts that many commentators think that the original reading has been lost. They question how punishing enemies "ten thousandfold" either exhibits fairness or provides a lesson that invites Jews to expect mercy (12:22). Assuming the text is sound, we find in it the realism of the author, who here assumes a prophetic stance. The very severity of God's conduct toward the chosen people's foes is their own best hope for survival, for it is an unmistakable sign of his providence calling them to conversion.

This paradox gives rise to the fourth conversation with God, which focuses on the conduct of the Egyptians during the Exodus as illustrating the painful lesson of perceiving God's punishment too late (12:23–27). The Egyptians were the most striking example of the principle underlying Part Three: sinners are punished by the instruments of their sins. By going to the limits of idolatry in worshiping brute animals, they became so completely hardened that they could not perceive God's efforts to correct them by punishments. "And so the fullness of condemnation overwhelmed them" (12:27).

13:1–9
Why Aeon Worship Fails

Again the author's ability as teacher manifests itself in a carefully developed condemnation of idolatry. The remainder of Part Three is not limited to the ancient Egyptian foes of Israel but focuses on the idolatry of contemporary Hellenism. Chaps. 13–15 form the most methodological development of the whole exhortation as they lash out against the chief forms of idolatry in order of increasing malice.

They are written from the point of view of faith with a twofold objective: apologetic and polemic. As an apologia they confirm believers in the wisdom of worshiping the God of revelation, whose power was celebrated in Part Two. As a polemic this series of diatribes mocks what Hellenism has to offer as a source of comfort and hope. The series builds to a climax, beginning with the least offensive form of idolatry, nature worship, whose devotees were merely "foolish" (13:1). Next, those who worship carved statues are "doomed" (13:10). Worse is a person who fashions idols out of clay, "for such a one knows that he sins more than all" (15:13). Finally, "most stupid of all and more wretched than a foolish child" are those who worship brute animals, the kind of idolatry practiced by Israel's masters in Egypt (15:14).

The first of these polemics begins with a short but skillfully constructed passage against nature worship (13:1–9). Argument from analogy is used, namely, that anyone perceiving the beauty of the universe should recognize that its source must be superior and stronger and more beautiful. An objection is raised that this kind of idolatry springs from goodwill and so is excusable. But this defense is rejected on the principle that anyone capable of exploring the richness of the cosmos is easily within reach of quickly finding the Lord of all (→ Creation).

In this concluding judgment the cosmos is designated as "Aeon" (13:9; RSV: "world"), the widespread Hellenistic personification of the universe as eternal and living, without beginning, middle, or end. This argument rests upon belief that the Lord has manifested himself through creation, inviting humans to enjoy transcendent religious experience greater than the popular desire to "become Aeon," i.e., to enter into the cosmic harmony of the universe.

13:10–14:8
Condemnation of Those Who Worship Idols

The second form of idolatry condemned was more common, namely, idol worship. It is now treated at greater length and in a variety of ways

(→ Idol). First, with biting irony the text ridicules trust in idols by offering detailed descriptions of the stages involved in selecting and carving material for an idol and preventing it from falling, and then begging this helpless object for all kinds of favors (13:10–19).

Next, the description turns to the role that idols played in sea voyages (14:1–8). This is the only passage outside of Part Two that speaks of Lady Wisdom, the "craftswoman" who governs this dangerous activity. Only God's providence can lead sailors across the waves safely. The case of Noah's ark is cited as proof, although no proper name is mentioned. God acted as pilot for Noah, selected to be "the hope of the world" (14:3–6). God's protection elicits a blessing, but idols and their makers are cursed for their cruel deceptions.

14:9–15:6
A Short History of the Origin and Spread of Idolatry

14:9–21, The Euhemeristic Explanation. Probing deeper into the folly of idolatry, the author interrupts the series of illustrations by inserting an excursus within an excursus. This brief sketch of the origin and spread of idolatry heaps further scorn upon the practice. It draws upon contemporary inscriptions erected by Hellenistic kings to glorify their contributions to society. Its basis is the so-called Euhemeristic theory that gods are deified mortals. Little is known about Euhemerus, who lived about 300 B.C. The theory attributed to him developed over a period of time and existed in a variety of forms. The Wisdom of Solomon finds it useful to bolster the case against idolatry.

This historical note begins with a statement of the theme, which also serves as title for the excursus: "Equally abhorrent to God are the sacrilegious and their sacrilege; without doubt both performance and performer will be punished!" (14:9–10). This title is composed with the help of unusual terms, repeated at the end (15:6), thus setting the development apart clearly as a unit. The title also gives this survey a moralizing tone that is developed from the opening condemnation of idolaters for their misuse of God's creation. They exemplify human malice and scandal at its worst (14:11–14).

The moral depravity of idolaters is illustrated by two examples. In the first case, a father translates his untimely grief into idolatrous "mysteries and rites." In the course of time "the sacrilegious custom is observed as law" (14:15–16a). The second example began in the vanity of rulers who courted their subjects' favor by having their statues erected at advantageous locations throughout their kingdoms. The sculpture proved so attractive that

after the ruler's death his statue continued to encourage honor. This eventually led to worship in times of misfortune and oppression (14:16b–21).

14:22–31, A Vice List. The historical survey goes on to spell out the ever increasing evil consequences of idolatry in the form of a Hellenistic vice list, which describes the desolation that sin causes. Vice lists were a commonplace in contemporary Cynic-Stoic diatribes. The specific vices mentioned fit better, however, into the standard of morality urged by biblical writers. The list serves the author's purpose of illustrating that the moral life of Jewish believers was superior to that of pagans, among whom "everything is pell mell" (14:25). After describing typical sins, the list repeats in different words the underlying principle of Part Three: "For worship of unmentionable idols is source and cause and goal of all evil" (14:27).

Concluding the list is a sin that links it to the revelation of the God of Israel, perjury (14:28–31). Why accent this vice? Because perjury is a practical form of idolatry that denies God's concern for human integrity and mocks his power to bring humans to their destiny. Perjurers are the living antithesis of "the judges of the earth," addressed in the opening of the book, whose concern was to honor the Lord.

15:1–6, The Reward of Those Who Worship Israel's God. The final paragraph of this historical summary contrasts the sad story of idolatry's harm with a happy outburst praising the covenant of Israel's God, "gracious and true, slow to anger and ruling in all mercy" (15:1), for watching over the chosen people. Implied in it is praise for faithful Jews who have not let themselves be enticed by the allure of painted idols. Jewish readers could not miss the allusion to the Sinai covenant. Into the traditional covenant formula of Exod. 34:6 is inserted the Stoic term for providence, "ruling," used earlier for the work of Lady Wisdom (cf. 8:1).

This passage serves to reinforce the diatribe against idolatry by reminding readers about the gift of revelation they enjoyed. Their links to the living God differ from links to an idol. Revelation nourishes and is nourished by a hope "full of immortality" (cf. 3:4), in contrast to the empty hopes of all whose lives are involved with idols. Believers' hope rests on "knowing" the Lord who promises eternal happiness, which is the reward of virtue (cf. 4:1).

15:7–13
Condemnation of Those Making Clay Idols

The author's scorn for potters who make idols pours out in the emotional description summed up in the word he coined, translated as "perverted drudgery" (15:8), to show contempt for those who know they are "sinning beyond all others" (15:13). Such arrogance stirred the author's ire. By refusing to admit that his life is a "loan" from God and by willfully making "counterfeits" for personal gain, the maker of clay idols reveals that his own heart is made of "ashes" (15:10, a term from Isa. 44:20, LXX). His hope is as fragile as his product. The text illustrates the principle inspiring this long diatribe, that sinners are punished by the very matter of their sins.

In turning breakable clay into an "inane god," such potters chart a foolish destiny and exchange hope for eternal life into wearying toil. This example incorporates a commonplace in Greek protreptic literature, that life is a plaything of the gods, a "carnival" where fools seek profit and pleasure. Those who buy into that shallow form of life shut their hearts to the opening plea of the entire book, "Love justice" (1:1).

15:14–16:1a
Animal Worship as the Most Evil Form of Idolatry

A transitional paragraph both concludes the diatribe against idolatry and prepares to continue the comparisons based on the Exodus from Egypt. The ancient Egyptians who enslaved the Israelites deserve to be scorned as "most foolish" and "more miserable than an infant's soul" (15:14, recalling 12:24) for two reasons: they esteemed even their enemies' idols and they worshiped hostile and ugly beasts.

The first identifies the Egyptians as stupid children lacking any personal judgment. They embraced the sins and ignorance of their enemies by attributing to them superhuman powers. The second reason for calling ancient Egyptians incomparably foolish is that the brute animals they worshiped were inferior to other animals. In fact, since these beasts are the very ones cursed by God for their part in humanity's fall, they lack "both the praise of God and his blessing" (15:18–19, referring to Gen. 1:22; 3:14). This multiple folly prompted God to visit upon the ancient Egyptians punishment by means of the same type of creeping animals they worshiped (16:1a). This climactic statement completes the justification of God's conduct toward the enemies of his people. The author is now free to celebrate God's care for the chosen people during the Exodus as the final phase of his exhortation to Jewish students to remain faithful to their tradition.

PART FOUR: 11:1–14; 16:1b–19:22
Praise of God as Israel's Liberator

The subject matter of the final part of the book relates to the role of Lady Wisdom, yet forms an independent section, a literary syncrisis, i.e., a set of contrasts between the different ways God treated Israel and its enemies. The Lord, addressed throughout, is pictured as carrying out a series of dramatic interventions related to the departure of Israel from Egypt. The author freely uses data from biblical and traditional sources to construct seven contrasts.

Not only does the Lord determine the outcome, but both Egyptians and Israelites are aware of what is happening to each other. The Israelites experienced a certain degree of suffering, but it was always brief and served to teach that the Lord never abandons them. In contrast, the Egyptians are held fully responsible for their sins against God and Israel.

After the first set of contrasts Part Four is suspended to insert Part Three (11:15–16:1a), which provides a systematic theological justification for the Lord's way of acting on behalf of the chosen people during the Exodus. The syncrisis itself is too complicated to allow for an adequate apologia for God's providence, which is an integral part of the aim of the Wisdom of Solomon. Since Part Four could not achieve its goal without the systematic diatribe against idolatry, these two sections complement each other.

11:1–14, First Contrast: The Lord Offers Drink to Israel but Subjects Egyptians to Thirst. A brief introduction provides the setting for the contrasts (11:1–3). The narrator speaks directly to the Lord, with whom he recalls key moments in Israel's history. Since no proper names occur, only Jewish readers familiar with the traditions of the Exodus would be capable of following these imaginative musings that glorify the interventions of Israel's God. Often the biblical order and details are modified.

The first divine intervention comes when the Israelites wandering in the desert call upon the Lord and he supplies water "from a sharp rock" as a "remedy" for their thirst (11:4, recalling Deut. 8:15). Then follows the characteristic feature of Part Four, a description of the Lord's contrasting treatment of the hostile Egyptians with respect to water. The underlying principle governing these examples is that God is teaching and saving Israel. "For through the events that punished their enemies, through these very things they were aided in their need" (11:5).

An elaborate description, both adapting and going beyond details of the plague of the "ever-flowing river," describes the punishment of the Egyptians. They suffered not only from seeing their drinking water turned to blood but also from seeing the divine favor upon the Israelites (11:6–14; see Exod. 7:17–21). The midrashic modifications introduced are designed to appeal to Hellenistic readers. They give these contrasts an apologetic tone (→ Midrash).

Some added details come from Jewish oral tradition, but many others were no doubt simply invented by the author to embellish the description of God's favor toward the chosen people. Their great variety made the accounts difficult reading for later scribes copying new manuscripts, so that many textual variants appear in manuscripts. Variation in translations is often linked to the manuscript reading chosen by a translator.

16:1b–4, Second Contrast: The Lord Sends Strange Animals to Feed Israelites and Starve Egyptians. The book returns to the contrasts after the long diatribe against idolatry, which ends with the animal worship of the ancient Egyptians. During the Exodus both Israelites and Egyptians suffered the torment of hunger. The Lord's people, however, experienced his care in the form of an unexpected gift. He sent quail as a delicacy to nourish them. At the same time he sent upon the starving Egyptians animals so ugly that they took away all appetite. This contrast rests on an imaginative interpretation of the impact of the plague of frogs, presented as punishment for the persecution of the Israelites (see Exod. 8:2–7).

16:5–15, Third Contrast: God Exposes Both Israelites and Egyptians to Poisonous Animals but Rescues the Israelites. The two groups go through an even more severe crisis: being bitten by poisonous animals. The original Jewish readers would recognize the allusion to the bites of the fiery serpents (see Num. 21:5–9). The text stresses that the healing must be attributed not to the image of the serpent erected by Moses but to God's mercy and word. The Lord snatched believers from death—identified as both the River of Forgetfulness, Lethe, and Hades, two Hellenistic terms for the underworld—and brought them healing (16:10–13).

The contrast changes the details in the case of the Egyptians, who were plagued not by poisonous animals but by locusts (see Exod. 10:12–20). The Exodus text does not mention flies. The contrast rests almost entirely on the healing of the Israelites and draws from it praise for God as the only one who has power over "life and death" (16:13). These terms are used in the religious sense of eternal life with God or complete separation from him.

The message to be learned is succinctly summarized in the closing reminder to the Lord, "It is impossible to escape your hand" (16:15). There is a deliberate recall of the dramatic rescue of the righteous just one in Part One, snatched away from enemies to live forever confidently with the Lord (see 5:1, 15).

16:16–17:1, Fourth Contrast: The Lord Uses Creation to Destroy Egyptians and Heavenly Food to Feed Israelites. This carefully constructed central contrast, replete with literary allusions and poetic phrases, contains numerous didactic references. After describing the hardening of the Egyptians, the narration tells how they and their animals were lost in the mysterious storm in which fire and rain cooperated against them (see Exod. 9:22–25). Their punishment contrasts with the miraculous feeding of the Israelites on the "bread from heaven," the "food of angels" (16:20, recalling Ps. 77:25, LXX). This bread not only resisted changes of nature in the desert but "afforded every delight and adapted to every taste," as an expression of the Lord's surpassing "tenderness" (16:20–21). The manna's power to withstand the elements gave believers perspective on how little they suffered compared with Egyptians, whose crops were destroyed.

Rather than end the syncrisis at this point, the author generalizes with a prayerful consideration. The Lord's heavenly gift provides the model for the people's spiritual insight. Addressing the Lord directly in this syncrisis, the author is struck with religious awe that "creation opens up for the benefit of those who trust in you" and responds "to the desire of those who beg" (16:24–25). Such a display of divine love teaches believers that their real life is sustained ultimately not by creatures but by the divine "word." These favors invite them to "anticipate the rising of the sun in praising" the Lord so that dawn finds them "praying" for what they need (16:28). This responsive and confident faith community forms a strong contrast to the "hope of the ungrateful" that melts and flows off like "useless water" (16:29).

This personal outpouring reveals the motives behind the book's opening admonition, "Be concerned about the Lord in goodness and seek him in simplicity of heart" (1:1). What is at stake is fidelity to divine revelation as key to personal integrity and eternal destiny. In this religious framework the final couplet of this central contrast serves to remind readers that the ancient Egyptians were closed to God's grace: their "undisciplined souls went astray" (17:1). Rather than being like idolaters, slaves to nature or any other creature, believers reap the divine bounty lavished by God's tenderness on all creation through faith, prayer, and self-control.

833

17:2–18:4, Fifth Contrast: God Sends Darkness to Terrify Egyptians and Light to Fortify His People. The longest of the contrasts contains a lively poetic description of the terrors experienced by the Egyptians. This passage depicting their fear is difficult to understand in places because it contains unusual comparisons, plays on words, and penetrating psychological insights. More than thirty terms never found elsewhere in the LXX appear in it. The impact of the plague of darkness that engulfed not only the land but also the minds and the hearts of the Egyptians is described in striking metaphors at great length. In fact, the text devotes five times as much space to this display of divine punishment as it does to the experience of light enjoyed by the Israelites before their departure.

In theological terms, what the author contrasts are two ways in which God's "eternal providence" works (17:2; see 14:3). This providence turned the arrogant captors of the chosen people into "prisoners of darkness and captives of lingering night" behind the veil of "Forgetfulness," the river of Hades from which God protected his people (17:3; see 16:11). This vivid description portrays how the power of darkness worked on the imagination of the Egyptians to accent sights and sounds so that "they thought what they had seen was worse" than it really was (17:6). Through divine intervention those who promised to drive out all fear from Egypt themselves suffered "a timidity so sick it was laughable" (17:8).

This vivid picture leads up to a descriptive definition of fear, placed at the very center of this long development: "fear is nothing other than betrayal by the resources of the reasoning faculty, ignorance converting anticipation into the worst form of torture" (17:12–13). This psychologizing definition reflects a kind of speculation popular among contemporary Hellenistic writers, who interpreted Homeric myths and the "descents into hell" in psychological terms.

Once the definition is formulated, the author balances the description with further images of "unexpected fear" at work through dreams, which formed an "unbarred prisoner," made either by "monstrous phantoms" or by the "betrayal of the soul" (17:15). Hellenistic philosophers looked on dreams as psychological self-punishment. The author of the Wisdom of Solomon was aware of such speculation, but he viewed dreams as instruments of divine providence directing human destiny and trapping sinners in their evil choices. This approach continues his apologia for fidelity to revelation. Sin traps all classes of human beings, like farmers, shepherds, and solitary workers, in "one chain of darkness" (17:17). Their fear foreshadowed

even worse punishment at the hands of divine justice.

The short second part of this fifth contrast celebrates the blessing of freedom upon the chosen people. It came first on them in the gratitude of the Egyptians for not being wiped out when they were helpless in their prison of darkness. More importantly, God's blessing took the form of a "flaming column," the pillar of fire God prepared, along with a protecting sun, to lead them on their journey to freedom (18:1–3).

This contrast affirms once more the justice of God in punishing the Egyptians severely. They fully deserved their loss of freedom for imprisoning the Israelites, who had the mission to give "the light of the incorruptible law to the world" (18:4). This revelation recalls the longer justification of God that opened Part Three, the only other time the adjective "incorruptible" occurs in this work. There the author reminded God, "Your incorruptible spirit is upon all" (12:1).

God's all-powerful justice obliges him to demand responsible conduct from everyone. For their part, being true to themselves is the condition for recognizing both God's presence in human affairs and the law revealed to Israel as light of the world. The Egyptians fall into the same category as the wicked of Part One, who strayed from the way of truth and did not let the light of justice shine for them (see 5:6–7).

18:5–25, Sixth Contrast: The Word of the Lord Brings Death to the Egyptian Firstborn but Freedom to Israel. Mention of the law suggests Moses, the lawgiver. This contrast, which deals with the death of the firstborn of the Egyptians in the Red Sea, takes its origin from an allusion to the attempted slaughter of Moses and the actual killing of an unknown number of Israelite babies. In punishment, God destroyed not only Egyptian children but also their soldiers in the water.

That incident prompts a further elaboration, a poetic description of the first Passover feast, celebrated in Egypt as the Israelites anticipated their freedom (18:6–9). This description tends to clutter the comparison, but it also supplies elements usually included in them. First, the Israelites knew about "the destruction of the enemy," i.e., the final fate of the Egyptians. Second, it repeats the principle governing the contrasts, why God brought them about: "for by the way you punished our adversaries, you also invited us to glory" (18:8).

The destroying angel of the Exodus is portrayed as God's "all-powerful word," reaching from earth to heaven. But the Egyptians learned too late that Israel is truly "God's son" (18:10–16). The contrasting scene pictures Israel as being rescued from an "experience of death."

Without offering details the text refers to the time when Aaron, dressed in priestly robes, intervened through "prayer and the propitiation of incense" to appease God's anger (18:21; see Num. 16:46–47).

19:1–21, Seventh Contrast: The Lord Leads Israel to Safety and Destroys Its Captors. The last contrast begins by portraying one final act of malice on the part of Egyptians. In a desperate "plan of folly" they try to stop the Israelites, whom they had already agreed to let go. The point of the contrast is the way God organized Israel's escape without violating either Egypt's freedom or the laws of nature. Creation obeyed the divine "commands" to expedite Israel's marvelous journey through the sea "on a plane of green grass," skipping like lambs and praising "you, Lord, the one who rescued them" (19:5–9). God's people kept in mind the previous suffering, for them a short prelude to comfort, but for Egyptians, who "justly suffered their own evil deeds," a disaster (19:10–13).

Similarities to the central contrast appear at this point. The tone is highly emotive, with the author addressing God explicitly as "Lord," and using the second-person pronoun five times. First, the malice of the Egyptians is presented as even greater than that of the Canaanites who resisted the arriving Israelites (19:13d–17). The second, concluding description pictures the transformation of nature, repeating the miracle of the manna, now called "ambrosial food" (19:18–21; see 16:20–22).

19:22, Concluding Comment. The final couplet, addressed to the Lord, is an optimistic expression of the attitude permeating the entire protreptic: the Lord has always brought the chosen people through danger. Readers are left to draw the conclusion: to abandon the faith community is self-destruction.

Bibliography

Clark, E. G. *The Wisdom of Solomon.* Cambridge Bible Commentary on the New English Bible. Cambridge: Cambridge University Press, 1973.

Collins, J. J. "Cosmos and Salvation: Jewish Wisdom and Apocalyptic in the Hellenistic Age." *History of Religions* 17 (Nov. 1977): 121–42.

Reese, J. M. *The Book of Wisdom and the Song of Songs.* Old Testament Message. Wilmington, DE: Glazier, 1983.

_____. *Hellenistic Influences on the Book of Wisdom and Its Consequences.* Analecta Biblica 41. Rome: Biblical Institute Press, 1970.

Reider, J. *The Book of Wisdom.* New York: Harper, 1957.

Winston, D. *The Wisdom of Solomon.* Anchor Bible, 43. Garden City, NY: Doubleday, 1979.

SIRACH

JAMES L. CRENSHAW

INTRODUCTION

In most Greek manuscripts the title of this book identifies its genre and author: the Wisdom of Jesus the Son of Sirach. The Syriac text has a shorter version, the Wisdom of Bar Sira. Latin tradition drops the name and introduces descriptive categories such as "the Church Book" (Ecclesiasticus, so the Vulgate) and *Parabolae* ("Proverbs," according to Jerome, who states that a Hebrew copy had this title). On two occasions later Jewish writers introduce a citation from Sirach with the words *hammoshel 'amar* (Heb., "the Parabolist said"). At least one Jewish scholar, Saadia (d. A.D. 942), refers to Sirach as *seper musar* ("the Book of Discipline/ Instruction").

The manuscript tradition yields some confusion about the author's name and precise relationship to Sira. In all probability his name was Jeshua ben Eleazar ben Sira, the name Simon in some manuscripts having entered the text by mistake from 50:1. The "ch" ending on Sirach in the Greek manuscripts represents either a Greek *chi*, indicating an indeclinable word, or a final Hebrew *alep*. For convenience, in this commentary Ben Sira designates the author and Sirach the book.

In a way the twofold title in which literary type and authorship appear seems entirely appropriate for a book that bridges two cultures, the Hebraic and the Hellenistic. Sirach represents the culmination of Jewish wisdom literature of the sort found in the book of Proverbs (→ Wisdom). Although Sirach introduces distinctive features, specifically the integration of Israel's sacred history into the wisdom tradition, the book resembles Proverbs in all essentials. At the same time, pride of authorship deriving from the Greek culture prompted Ben Sira to identify himself rather than attribute the written product to King Solomon or to some other figure of the past.

The Historical Setting

Sirach opens with a prologue written by Ben Sira's grandson, who arrived in Egypt during the thirty-eighth year of Ptolemy Euergetes and resided there for some time before translating the book into Greek. The reference is to Ptolemy Physcon VII Euergetes II, who ruled Egypt from 170 to 164 and again from 145 to 117 B.C. Ben Sira was probably active as late as 180 and

perhaps even later. The death in 195 of the Simon whose ministry as high priest made such a lasting impression on Ben Sira reinforces this dating of Ben Sira's activity between 200 and 180 B.C.

The first twenty years of the second century B.C. inaugurated a lull before the storm brought on by the Maccabean revolt. To express gratitude for Jewish assistance in routing the Egyptian garrison in the citadel at Jerusalem in 198 B.C., the Seleucid king Antiochus III made several concessions: the royal coffers would help defray the cost of sacrifices; materials for the construction of the Temple were exempt from taxes; the people were obligated to live according to the law of their ancestors; the Senate, priests, scribes, and sacred singers were exempt from various taxes; citizens in Jerusalem were exempt from taxes for three years; and other citizens enjoyed a reduction in taxes of one-third, while slaves were emancipated. The situation changed as a result of Syria's defeat at the hands of the Romans in Magnesia in 190. Pressed for increased revenues, the Seleucid rulers rescinded the exemptions from taxes and restricted the privileges they had earlier granted to Jews.

The internal situation reflected the political climate on the larger scene. Opportunists joined forces with rulers and their challengers, hoping to be on the side of the victor. Competing families, Tobiads and Oniads, divided the people's loyalty, and the rivalry between Jews and Samaritans extended the dissension even further. The struggle between Jason and Menelaus for the office of high priest demonstrates the degree to which avarice and greed affected religious office (see 2 Macc. 4–5). Their willingness to compromise Hebrew ways in favor of Greek customs illustrates the degradation of the priesthood and explains why Ben Sira praises Simon, the father of Onias III, so lavishly. At the same time Antiochus IV Epiphanes' deposition of Onias constituted an infringement by a foreign government on the religious freedom of the Jews that precipitated open revolt. Only a few allusions in Sirach betray this volatile political atmosphere (50:25–26, a reference to Edomites, Philistines, and Samaritans; 40:25–26 and 50:1, 23–24, which possibly criticize the contenders for the high priesthood for fomenting strife and for offering money for the religious office). Perhaps the unique prayer in 36:1–17 for renewed deeds of salvation arises from Ben Sira's sense that the sacred legacy was in jeopardy at the moment.

Relation to Tradition

The translator identifies his grandfather as a student of Jewish Scriptures, which already exist in his time as three distinct entities: the Law, the Prophets, and the other books. The last division was still open, and Ben Sira fully expects his book to find a place beside the other wisdom books. In his view Israel's wisdom cast a wide net, embracing the sacred tradition as well as, presumably, the usual fare of literature such as Proverbs, Job, and Ecclesiastes. His grandson acknowledges a practical dimension of knowledge in that all instruction enables an individual to live in compliance with Jewish law. He also assumes that a translation into the adopted language of Jews in Egypt, probably at Alexandria, will facilitate obedience to the Torah.

Ben Sira's grandson also recognizes the inadequacy of his translation, conceding that things originally expressed in Hebrew have different nuances from their nearest equivalent in the Greek tongue. If this protest amounts to something more than a modest disclaimer, it suggests that the disappearance of the Hebrew text of Sirach is particularly unfortunate. Recent discoveries of considerable portions of Sirach in Hebrew have thus ushered in a new stage of research on the book, although the Greek text remains fundamental to every analysis.

According to the grandson, Ben Sira specialized in instruction and wisdom. This description accords with Ben Sira's own understanding of his vocation as a wise man and a scribe. Admittedly, the latter term occurs in a conventional text about various vocations (36:24); the oldest such text seems to be the Egyptian *Instruction of Duauf*. More reliable therefore is the self-description in 50:27, where Ben Sira characterizes his book as "instruction in understanding and knowledge," and in 51:23–30, where he implies that he administers a school (Heb. *bet hammidrash*, "house of study"). This is the first clear mention of an Israelite school, although some scholars have assumed the existence of the institution at a much earlier date on the basis of parallels with Egypt and Mesopotamia, and to some extent Ugarit; the needs of the royal court, especially with respect to diplomacy; scattered archaeological evidence in Palestinian inscriptions; and the quality of Israel's literature.

Ben Sira uses the first person freely, as does also the unknown author of Ecclesiastes, but the actual extent of autobiography remains uncertain. Much of this material belongs to literary convention, and it therefore reveals little about specific details in Ben Sira's life. Even the much discussed allusion to travel in 34:9–12 may fall into the category of literary convention, and the ambiguous allusion to deliverance from some peril associated with a journey may consequently indicate nothing about Ben Sira's travels. On the other hand, he may very well have represented his compatriots before a foreign government in the same way John and his son Eupolemus negotiated on behalf of Judea (2 Macc. 4:11) and Philo defended the Jewish cause before Caligula.

Efforts to glean information about Ben Sira's domestic situation on the basis of his harsh observations about daughters and his reference to a shrewish wife stray wide of the mark, for such descriptions belong to the traditional teachings of ancient sages. Nevertheless, Ben Sira does introduce a virulence in his observations about women that exceeds anything in Ecclesiastes, Proverbs, or Job.

It appears that Ben Sira cherished irreconcilable traditions, the prophetic and the wisdom. Believing in inspiration during his own day, he endeavored to write a book that was in the tradition of the Mosaic legislation and the prophetic corpus. For Ben Sira instruction embraced far more than the general insights, however astute, achieved by the wise. It included the specific law of Moses. The majestic hymn about wisdom in 24:1–29 thus occupies a central position in the book, for it claims the Mosaic teaching as the essence of wisdom. This may not constitute a declaration of war against the Greek understanding of knowledge as the fruit of reasoned inquiry, but the insistence that revelation lies at the heart of learning gives Judaism a distinct advantage over Hellenism in this regard.

The insistence on inspiration may actually have emerged as a response to Israel's wisdom literature, which elevates human inquiry as the fundamental mode of existence. Although the compilers of Proverbs 1–9 challenged this understanding of knowledge by inserting religious devotion into the equation, thereby insisting that the fear of the Lord was both essence and the principal element of knowledge, Ben Sira takes an even greater step. For him wisdom is identical with the Mosaic legislation at Sinai and hence a divine gift rather than a human achievement.

This integration of themes from Yahwism (Israel's specific religious traditions) and wisdom occurs throughout the book, not simply in the praise of famous men (44:1–50:21). Allusions to Israel's sacred tradition function as examples and warnings, whereas earlier teachers had restricted their material to universal experience. Ben Sira goes so far as to quote David's bold response to the divine anger: "We shall fall into the hands of the Lord, not into the hands of men; for his majesty is equal to his mercy" (2:18; cf. 2 Sam. 24:14). Elsewhere Ben

Sira alludes to pentateuchal traditions from the primeval history (Gen. 1–11) and the patriarchal narratives (Gen. 12–50). He mentions Adam (Sir. 33:10; 40:1), Eve (25:24), Lot (16:8), Sodom and Gomorrah (39:23, NEB), the fallen angels (16:7), the Flood (40:10), the Noachian covenant (17:12), the image of God (17:3), the creation account (39:16, 21), and Jacob's descendants (23:12).

Allusions to matters outside the book of Genesis also occur, such as the six hundred thousand Israelites who perished in the wilderness (16:9–10), the divine epithet "Holy One" (4:14), the Mosaic Law (24:23), Zion (36:13–15), and the tree that sweetened water (38:5). Twice Ben Sira brings together a large number of sacred themes. In 24:1–12 he refers to creation by means of a heavenly mist, the pillar of cloud symbolizing God's dwelling place, Jacob and Israel, the holy tabernacle, Jerusalem, and the special people of God; in 36:1–17 to divine signs and miracles, the reciting of God's wonders, tribes of Jacob and their inheritance, people called by God's name, Israel as God's firstborn, the city of God's sanctuary, prophecies spoken in God's name, and Aaron's blessing.

The Forms of Expression

Ben Sira's literary expression borrows heavily from Proverbs, Job, and Ecclesiastes. He offers instruction to students, using the technical language of a teacher who addresses his students as sons. Interesting variations of "my son" do occur, for example, "holy sons" (39:13), "children" (3:1), "my children" (23:7; 41:14), and "you who need instruction" (51:23). Ancient instructions typically employ imperatives, freely offering prescriptive advice reinforced with warnings and admonitions. These instructions resemble brief paragraphs on specific subjects, often set off from what follows or precedes by refrains and repeated phrases. In this regard Ben Sira develops a practice that the author of Proverbs 1–9 preferred, presumably because it gave ample opportunity to support his teachings with religious arguments.

These paragraph-length instructions cover a wide range of topics, for they aim to prepare young men for coping in society. Hence the teacher discusses everything from table manners to religious duties, always concentrating on the best way to succeed in an endeavor. Almost all Ben Sira's advice has a strong practical bent, even when the subject extends to matters like dreams (34:1–8), shame (41:17–42:8), and death (41:1–4). At times he endeavors to solve vexing theological dilemmas, such as justifying the vocation of the physician in a society that believes sickness indicates divine punishment for sin (38:1–15), and comparing the scribe's life of leisure to the drudgery of other types of work,

while at the same time recognizing the contribution that laborers make to the well-being of the community (38:24–39:11). Much of Ben Sira's energy addresses the difficult area of sexual conduct and, more generally, relations between the sexes, but he also speaks often about parental responsibilities to discipline children. These instructions strive at inculcating attitudes that issue in specific actions; they answer questions like "How should I respond to people from widely different social strata, the wealthy and paupers? What is my duty in the matter of charitable contributions? When should I speak in a public meeting?"

Sirach also has numerous truth statements, often called sentences, the other major form of expression in proverbial literature. These brief aphorisms capture what were regarded as timeless and universal truths, expressing them in a way that seizes the imagination and lingers in memory. "A rich man does wrong, and he even adds insults; a poor man suffers an injustice, and he must apologize" (13:3). "A story told at the wrong time is like music in a time of mourning, but rebuke and punishment are always wise actions" (22:6). "A new friend resembles new wine; after it has aged, one can drink it with pleasure" (9:10b). "All living beings become old like a garment, for the ancient decree reads, 'You must surely die'" (14:17).

Like teachers before him Ben Sira varies the truth statements enormously. He uses the "better than" proverb ("Better is a man's wickedness than a woman who does good; and a woman brings shame and disgrace," 42:14), the numerical proverb ("I take pleasure in three things which are beautiful in the sight of the Lord and of men: agreement between brothers, friendship among neighbors, and a wife and husband living in harmony," 25:1), and the particle of existence ("There is one who by keeping silent is deemed wise, while another is detested for talking too much; there is one who keeps silent because he has no answer, while another remains silent because he knows when to speak," 20:5–6). Ben Sira also pronounces benedictions and maledictions ("Blessed is the man who does not err with his lips and does not suffer remorse for sin," 14:1; "Woe to timid hearts and to slack hands, and to the sinner who leads a double life," 2:12), and he uses rhetorical questions freely ("What race is worthy of honor? The human race. What race is worthy of honor? Those who fear the Lord. What race is not worthy of honor? The human race. What race is not worthy of honor? Those who break the commandments," 10:19).

In these cases, Proverbs serves as Ben Sira's guide to literary expression. To some degree that is true of prayer, which achieves prominence in Sirach despite its meager role in Prov. 30:7–9. With Ben Sira the wise man becomes a worshiper, unashamedly offering prayers to the

Deity (22:27–23:6; 36:1–17). The titles with which Ben Sira addresses God emphasize majesty and intimacy: "Lord, Father and Ruler of my life" (23:1); "Lord, Father and God of my life" (23:4); "Lord, the God of all" (36:1); "the Lord, the God of the ages" (36:17). This sage lifts up his voice in hymnic praise (42:15–43:33; 51:1–12), particularly when the wonders of nature steal his imagination. For this hymnic praise the author of Job is Ben Sira's mentor, even if some of the poems in the book of Job amount to dubious praise. At least two things stand out as one surveys the wonders that Ben Sira extols: a sense of awe and a recognition that the human eye has only penetrated the surface. Moreover, Ben Sira's language waxes eloquent, especially in his use of exquisite images for freezing rain, frost, and racing clouds (in 43:14–20, pools put on ice "like a breastplate," hoarfrost becomes "pointed thorns," clouds "fly forth like birds").

Two didactic compositions resemble the hymns, although these learned meditations leave the impression of rational reflection and studious instruction (16:24–17:14; 39:12–35). These compositions explore the place of humankind in the universe and affirm a legitimate role for everything, even things that appear to be out of place in an orderly universe. Closely related to these meditations, especially in function, is the debate form, for which Ecclesiastes paved the way within Israelite wisdom literature. (This device to stave off dissent, specifically denial of divine justice, appears in Egyptian wisdom traditions as well.) Ben Sira warns against an attitude that presumes too much about God's patience, mercy, and sovereignty (5:3–6) and challenges the assumption that one can sin with impunity ("Do not say: 'I am hidden from the Lord, and who from on high will remember me? Among so many people I shall not be noticed, for what is my life in the boundless creation?' " 16:17). Here the normal form ("Do not say . . . for . . .") has given way to an elaborate rationale introduced by an expression demanding close scrutiny: "Behold!" (16:18–23).

Like Proverbs and Job, Sirach uses the hymnic form to praise wisdom (24:1–29), but he introduces altogether new concepts. Whereas wisdom in Job 28 remains inaccessible to everyone but the Lord, in Sirach she takes up residence at Jerusalem and expresses herself through the law of Moses. Proverbs 8 stresses wisdom's participation in creating and ordering the world, a theme that Ben Sira picks up and elaborates in peculiar fashion. A universal motif, creation by a mist that covers the earth, bows before particularist notions such as a dwelling in Jacob and an inheritance in Israel, a resting place in Zion among an honored people, the portion of the Lord. The erotic relationship between student and wisdom, present in Proverbs 8 and 9, achieves new expression in an acrostic poem that concludes Sirach (51:13–20, 30), an earlier form of which was discovered in Cave 11 at Qumran.

An astonishing shift takes place when Ben Sira actually sings praises of mortals (44:1–50:24). Like the formal expressions of praise called encomia in Greek culture, these walks through the gallery of biblical characters prepare the way for an effusive display of respect for the high priest in office during Ben Sira's time. The choice of heroes, highly selective, betrays a prejudice for priestly lineage and for individuals who contributed to Israel's religious establishment. Not a woman graces the pages of this account, despite the contribution of women to the religious life as recorded in sacred literature. Pride of position goes to Moses, Aaron, and Phinehas; David, Solomon, Hezekiah, Josiah, Zerubbabel, and Joshua receive praise for their part in reforming and strengthening the Temple and its service. Others who make this select list impressed Ben Sira by miraculous feats rather than by the content of their prophetic teaching. By design the personalities make an appearance according to the threefold division of the Hebrew canon: Pentateuch first, Prophets next, and the Writings last, except for an afterthought that returns to the starting point, Enoch, and works backwards to Adam.

The essential themes of the book, fear of the Lord and wisdom, interact so effectively that some question remains about which of these occupies prominence. The author of Proverbs 1–9 subjugated fear of the Lord to wisdom, relegating this religious aspect to the essence and first principle of knowledge. For Ben Sira fear of the Lord has no rival, not even from the person who acquires wisdom: "How great is he who has gained wisdom! But there is no one superior to him who fears the Lord. The fear of the Lord surpasses everything" (25:10–11). This exalted appreciation for religion leads Ben Sira to conclude that wisdom's garland and root exist in the fear of the Lord. Therefore, such religious devotion alone justifies a sense of accomplishment in Ben Sira's eyes (10:22).

Beneath these themes of true piety and the quest for knowledge lies an explosive issue that threatens to divide Ben Sira's constituency. Can one believe in divine justice? The tension between wrath and mercy lends immense pathos to the book, which virtually begins and ends with an affirmation of both concepts. Besides the traditional arguments for divine justice—God's knowledge of events before they occur, the testimony of past experience, the anticipation of an eschatological (final) redressing of all wrongs, the necessity of acknowledging the limits of human knowledge—Ben Sira introduces two new arguments, one psychological and the other metaphysical. Sinners suffer inner stress, and the universe itself fights on behalf of the virtuous. Both efforts to secure a rational theodicy, that is, a defense of the justice of God, have parallels in the Greek culture of the second century B.C. For Ben Sira, the harmony of creation manifests divine glory, a term that occupies an exalted position in the final chapters of the book.

The Larger Environment

Although Sirach resembles other Jewish literary works of the third to first century B.C., the book also has points of contact with Greek literature. Affinities with Jewish wisdom link Sirach more closely with those texts in Hebrew than with the Greek Wisdom of Solomon. Ben Sira shares a few phrases with Ecclesiastes, but he does not endorse this book's skepticism, particularly with regard to the divine-human relationship. The book of Tobit places more emphasis on specific acts of piety as an expression of loyalty to the Mosaic law, but both Tobit and Sirach freely lift their voices in prayer. Whereas Ben Sira prays for wondrous acts on God's part, Tobit both prays for and experiences divine feats. Baruch's poem on wisdom (3:9–4:4) does not integrate mythic themes about wisdom's role in creation with the idea that the concrete expression of wisdom occurs in the law. *The Testament of the Twelve Patriarchs* transcends the ritual aspects of religion to a degree that Ben Sira never achieves. The author of Wisdom of Solomon embraces Hellenistic concepts enthusiastically, whereas Ben Sira's indebtedness to the Greeks appears to be no more than unconscious breathing of the air.

Occasional parallels occur between Sirach and Greek authors (Theognis, Sophocles, Xenophon, Euripides, Hesiod, and Homer), but none of them requires actual literary dependence. The comparison of death to falling leaves in Sir. 14:18 and in Homer, a natural association of ideas, belongs to folk wisdom. The Stoic declaration, "He is the all!" occurs in Sirach, along with a host of Greek ideas and customs: a eulogy of ancestors, the notion of a rational universe, the balancing of human freedom and divine providence, dining customs, and pride of authorship. Perhaps Ben Sira's attitude toward physicians owes much to the Greek ethos. Links with Egyptian wisdom may exist, especially in the attitude to shame, the use of the bee to illustrate the importance of small things, and the comparison of the scribal profession to other types of work.

The air that Ben Sira breathed may have been Hellenized, but he does not permit it to overcome him. The Stoic ideal of world citizenship can find no toehold, for Ben Sira believes that Israel is the Lord's portion. Links with Aramean wisdom through Ahiqar, although plausible, may belong to folk tradition, e.g., references to the futility of opposing a flowing river and the revelation of character through one's clothes. Ben Sira does not openly endorse Jewish eschatological hopes, but he approaches them in fervent prayer (36:6–12). One strange allusion to the Lord's fighting on behalf of those who strive to the death for truth must have taken on new meaning during the Maccabean revolt. Earlier wisdom had no place for God as cocombatant.

Ben Sira's opponents are Jews who have surrendered their Jewish heritage, becoming indifferent to the Mosaic law and adopting a libertine life-style. They do not believe in the traditional concept of reward and retribution, hence they associate with dangerous companions. Unlike Wisdom of Solomon, Sirach directs its message to Jews and lacks any explicit attack against the dominant culture in the Mediterranean region. Ben Sira does not hate Hellenism, but he believes in the superiority of Jewish wisdom and ethics.

The Text

The Greek text survives in two forms: codices such as Sinaiticus, Vaticanus, and others; and a longer form of certain cursives (the most important of which is identified by its catalogue number, 248). The Old Latin and Vulgate used the Greek text of Sirach, which has also influenced the Syriac Peshitta to some degree (→ Texts, Versions, Manuscripts, Editions). In 1896–1900 parts of the Hebrew text dating from the ninth to twelfth centuries A.D. came to light after having disappeared for centuries. The Cairo Genizah, a medieval synagogue storage room for discarded manuscripts that was rediscovered in the nineteenth century, yielded about two-thirds of the Hebrew text (labeled A, B, C, D); another leaf (E) was discovered in 1931. Additional fragments of B and C came to light in 1958 and 1960; three years later a fragmentary scroll was discovered at Masada containing 39:27–44:17 in mutilated form. The B manuscript from Cairo closely resembles this scroll from Masada. This original Hebrew version antedates the Greek, but it has numerous errors and glosses (explanatory comments by the scribe). The freedom with which scribes rewrote this text indicates that it was not considered sacred like the books of the Hebrew canon. An interesting feature of Cairo B and E, an arrangement of the text in poetic lines, occurs also in a fragment of 6:20–31 (the ends of the lines) that was found in Cave 2 at Qumran. In all, the Cairo Genizah has yielded Sir. 3:6–16:26; 30:11–38:27; and 39:15–51:30, plus fragments of other chapters.

Although they are not usually reproduced in English translations, titles for individual sections are found in both the Greek and Hebrew texts (20:27; 23:7; 24:1; 30:1, 16, 44:1; 51:1; Heb., 31:12 = Gk. 34:12, 41:14, and 44:1). Transitions between sections also occur several times (42:25 to 43:1; 43:33 to 44:1; 49:16 to 50:1). In the Hebrew an extra psalm similar to Psalm 136 follows 51:12. The sequence from chap. 31 to 36 differs in the Hebrew, Vulgate, and Syriac from the Greek, which offers a less likely order at this point.

Sirach was not included in the Hebrew Bible, but the book was often cited until the tenth century A.D. in rabbinic circles, occasionally as sacred Scripture. Some features of the book are closer to Sadducean teaching than to Pharisaic, which may have precluded its inclusion in the canon, although its relatively late date probably explains its omission. Within the Christian church the status of Sirach has varied. The author of the Letter of James was especially fond of Sirach; and the writers of the pseudepigraphal works the *Didache*, the *Shepherd of Hermas*, and the *Letter of Barnabas* as well as Clement of Alexandria used it as a source of inspiration. The early Latin fathers included Sirach as one of the five Solomonic books; Cyprian, bishop of Carthage in the middle of the third century, affirmed the canonical status of Sirach, later proclaimed at the Council of Trent. Protestant churches do not accept Sirach as canonical, though it is valued as instructive and edifying.

COMMENTARY

The Prologue. The Greek text opens with a prologue in which the translator commends his grandfather's insights and asks for readers' indulgence in instances where the translation lacks exactness. The audience, Jews in the Diaspora, and possibly some Egyptians (unless the praise of Israel's wisdom, like Deut. 4:6, targets Jewish readers) learns that the author of the book was a teacher who read (i.e., explained) the Scriptures. These sacred texts already existed in two distinct divisions, the Law and the Prophets, plus another group, still undefined. Sirach draws inspiration from all three divisions, although it most resembles those books in the third group. Ben Sira's teachings have a practical *raison d'etre*, to enable one to observe the Mosaic law.

1:1–21, Wisdom and the Fear of the Lord. Because wisdom derives from God and is fully known only by the creator, Ben Sira endeavors to identify it by demonstrating the intimate rela-

tionship between wisdom and fear of God. Two impossible tasks emphasize wisdom's hiddenness; these resemble numerical proverbs, at least in rhetorical function. Just as none can count the sand of the sea or explore the abyss, so nobody but God possesses wisdom. Consequently, humankind ought to fear the Lord, precisely because a small measure of wisdom comes to favored creatures. Here God pours out wisdom in the same way the Holy Spirit is poured out, making the customary identification of wisdom and spirit (Wisd. of Sol. 1:4–7) doubly interesting. Ben Sira praises fear of the Lord highly: it brings joy and long life, for awe and religious devotion, the essential meaning of the concept of the fear of God, constitute both the first principle and essence of wisdom. (Although v. 21 is not present in the older Greek manuscripts, Skehan and Di Lella argue for its authenticity.)

1:22–2:6, The Necessity for Patience. The impatient individual will not acquire wisdom, whereas the humble one endures testing, fortified by hope and faithfulness, the two ingredients in the Hebrew word *'amunah*. Israelite and Egyptian wisdom literature warns against hotheaded behavior, the opposite of wise conduct, and advocates patience until the correct moment when speech achieves maximum potential. In certain circumstances good people encounter extraordinary testing, partly through the evil machinations of powerful officials but also as a means of shaping character. Ben Sira encourages fidelity in trying circumstances in the same way the Letter of James urges steadfastness (James 1:2–15), but the two authors respond differently to the question "How can I become wise?" Ben Sira advises observance of the law whereas the Letter of James suggests that one ask God for wisdom. Both authors warn against having a divided mind, for God knows the authentic character of every person. Ben Sira admirably brings together free will and divine largesse (Sir. 1:26; 2:6).

2:7–18, The Vastness of Divine Compassion. The prevalence of temptation does not necessarily imply an uncaring Deity. Ben Sira affirms the ancient credo from Exod. 34:6–7, particularly those attributes that bring comfort to the believer. As an object lesson, Ben Sira quotes David's bold response to divine displeasure (2 Sam. 24:14), thus emphasizing divine mercy equivalent to majesty. This entire section in Sirach shows rhetorical flourish and balancing of refrains grouped together in threes ("you who fear the Lord"; "who ever ... ?"; "woe to"; "those who fear the Lord"). Similarly, the assertion in Sir. 2:11 that the Lord is compassionate corresponds to 2:18, which brings together power and tenderness. The appeal to lessons from experience to reinforce God's justice ignores the force of Job's personal attack against overconfidence on the part of the wise. Nevertheless, Ben Sira could have justified his position by noting that Job ultimately experienced honor after only temporary distress.

3:1–16, Filial Duty. This reflection on the implications of the commandment to honor one's parents preserves an early example of the belief in the efficacy of good deeds, their power to offset transgression in the final reckoning. Ben Sira's observations about old age and its unwelcome features may reflect changing economic factors in Judea and the accompanying breakdown of the larger family. The earlier identification of wisdom with length of years has yielded before harsh examples of persons like Auranus whom the author of 2 Maccabees describes as advanced in years and no less advanced in folly (2 Macc. 4:40). An aged father's vanishing strength and reduced intellectual acumen offer occasions for insensitive youth to seize unprecedented authority in daily affairs, but such seemingly innocent usurpation of power has devastating consequences, particularly in destroying the offender's relationship with a higher authority, God. The same goes for those who lack respect for their mothers, whose curse the Lord reinforces.

3:17–31, Intellectual Modesty. The inquirer after knowledge needs to recognize that some things can never be discovered, for wisdom conceals itself. Nevertheless, a discerning person will ponder proverbs, seeking to learn as much as can be known. Where revealed knowledge vies with insights achieved through human effort, considerable tension results. The author of Deut. 29:29 and 30:11–14 wrestles with this problem generated by suspicion that worthwhile things require extraordinary expenditure of energy and insists that mystery remains, although God has bestowed considerable information on humankind. The manner of posing the questions reveals the presence of disconcerting claims that such revealed truth is too accessible to be truly valuable. Ben Sira confronts a similar attitude and adopts the earlier stance that God has granted adequate insights. Here is a call for intellectual humility, one that may address Greek influence among young Jews or even the philosophical quest in the Greek world.

4:1–10, Kindness to the Poor. Intellectual rigor that manifests itself in studying proverbs does not require one to withdraw from society and its deprived citizens. Ben Sira advises his students to relieve the burdens borne by the poor, for which kindness God will respond favorably. Such unfortunate individuals already have enough vexation without having to wait for a handout or having their hopes dashed by a potential benefactor who pretends not to see them. Ben Sira reproduces ancient belief that the Holy One attends to the prayer of the afflicted, which in this instance takes the form of a curse against the person who increased the poor one's burden (4:6). Potential officials are thus encouraged to use their power to improve the lot of widows and orphans, daring all the while to render verdicts in favor of the powerless rather than currying favor from the rich.

4:11–19, Wisdom's Practical Benefits. Ben Sira describes some rewards that accompany wisdom, making it worthwhile to endure initial hardship in the quest for her. Here wisdom is personified, at least as a literary figure. She leads new students along difficult paths and tests their resolve, eventually rewarding those who endure faithfully (4:17–18). This idea corresponds to the sages' teaching that the Lord disciplines those who occupy a place of favor. Wisdom bestows joy, life, honor, and divine approval. Her benefits know no limit, even outside Judea, for she enables some individuals to judge nations.

4:20–6:4, Speaking Wisely. This section deals with timidity in speech and its opposite, reckless talk. In the first instance Ben Sira considers the person who refrains from speaking when the occasion demands some comment (4:20–28). The result is concealed wisdom, hence worthless. The truly intelligent individual recognizes the right moment and seizes the opportunity to throw light on the situation. This does not mean that one must speak in every circumstance, for sometimes silence is wiser, particularly when passions run freely. Nevertheless, one should have courage to state the truth and to fight for its supremacy. Ben Sira makes an astonishing claim: that God will fight alongside you in this struggle on behalf of truth.

Rash speech comes in many forms (4:29–6:4). Ben Sira warns against freethinkers who let their lusts govern their lives, thinking wealth lasts forever. He uses an old formula of debate to withstand those practical atheists who deny God's sovereignty on the basis of delayed punishment or who presume on divine mercy in the same way a later philosopher said, "God will forgive. That's his business." Instead of these types of speech, one ought to be thoughtful and consistent, scrupulously avoiding slander and boasting. The power of speech brings honor and shame, so silence is preferable to speech unless understanding governs the tongue. Ben Sira thus carries on an ancient discussion, a favorite topic among the wise, but also one that later captured the imagination of the author of the Letter of James.

6:5–17, Friendship. Not everyone who claims to be a friend can be trusted, for some people use friendship for their own advantage, turning away when the slightest sign of adversity arises. Ben Sira recommends caution in choosing intimates, even to the point of testing potential friends. A pleasant demeanor and kind words draw others to a person, but rare indeed should be the individual who shares his or her inner secrets. The expression "one in a thousand" (6:6) occurs in Job and Ecclesiastes for a rare find; the same usage appears in Egyptian wisdom literature. Ben Sira acknowledges the fact that some so-called friends take excessive liberty, becoming overly familiar. As protection from abuse of friendship, Ben Sira advises extreme measures: remaining distant from enemies and maintaining a guard toward one's friends. The Egyptian *Instruction of Amenemope*, written for Amenemope's son Sesostris, goes even farther, discouraging trust in anyone. Sirach does not manifest such a jaundiced view; instead, it endorses friendship enthusiastically, calling a true friend an elixir of life, a shelter, and a treasure.

6:18–37, Wisdom's Unwelcome Discipline. Ancient teachers made no secret of the difficulties confronting those who wished to become learned. Here Ben Sira compares wisdom to a field in need of plowing and to a yoke that eager students place on their shoulders (6:19, 24). Behind the first metaphor lies the erotic dimension of learning, elsewhere expressed as a lover in pursuit of a beloved, especially wisdom personified as a woman who invites students to her banquet. But the image of plowing, frequently used as a euphemism for sexual relations, also seems to be associated in this instance with another metaphor, wisdom viewed as a rough path students must travel, unless the reference is to a rocky field. In any event, Ben Sira observes that the time of harvesting makes all the effort worthwhile. Then he makes an enigmatic assertion that wisdom, like her name, is carefully guarded (6:22). The meaning of this claim has escaped contemporary interpreters, unless it makes a pun on the Hebrew noun *musar* ("instruction"), which resembles a participle *musar* ("removed, withdrawn") or less likely, the noun *moser* ("bond, halter").

The second metaphor, wisdom as a yoke, suggests that it both assists in the effort to plow a field and imposes discomfort at the same time. Ben Sira urges students to accept the burden gladly, knowing that at last the yoke will transform itself into emblems of royalty. This type of language also occurs with regard to the demands of the law, which some rabbis understood as a yoke (cf. Jesus' invitation to take on his yoke, Matt. 11:29–30). Ben Sira concludes this advice with some immensely practical suggestions about being alert to hear intelligent persons dispense wisdom (6:34–37). Students are told to seek out gifted individuals and to visit them regularly. Lest this counsel be misconstrued, he adds that these enterprising students ought to remember the ultimate source of knowledge, God, and consequently to reflect often on the commandments.

7:1–17, The Fate of the Wicked. This section warns against ungodly conduct and admonishes readers to adopt habits that will not bring a punishment of fire and worms. Two features of this discussion catch the attention of modern interpreters. The first is the personification of evil, which is similar to the personification of wisdom in Proverbs 1–9. Sin has a will of its own, choosing its own companions. Hence an erotic component possibly colors the remark about sowing the furrows of injustice (7:3). The second feature involves a difference between the Greek and Hebrew versions. The addition of fire as punishment in the Greek text of 7:17 may reflect developments in thought among Jews in Alexandria about the afterlife as a time of punishment, although the same expression occurs in Isa. 66:24.

In Sir. 7:4–5 the natural movement from the Lord to an earthly ruler betrays their functional kinship in Ben Sira's mind. Nevertheless, the attitude toward official responsibility differs from earlier wisdom, which encourages persons to seek high office and to act justly in positions of leadership. The pressure on judges from foreign sources may explain Ben Sira's attitude. The subject of prayer crops up often in Sirach. Verse 14 urges perseverance and warns against verbosity in public gatherings and at prayer.

7:18–28, Domestic Advice. Except for the reference to cattle, this section focuses on intimate relationships between husbands and wives, parents and children, and owners and slaves. Ben Sira recognizes the immense worth of an intelligent and good wife, but he also knows that not every man is so fortunate. He therefore discourages anyone from remaining in a marriage that lacks affection. Ben Sira's comments about slaves reflect the biblical law allowing a Hebrew slave to go free after six years' service (Exod. 21:2; Deut. 15:12). The linguistic shift from cattle to children, although offensive to modern readers, indicates the indispensable role of domestic animals in an agricultural community. The remarks about a father's responsibility to see that his daughter finds a suitable husband shows that this important task was not taken lightly, despite Ben Sira's suspicion about the character of daughters, which manifests itself later with considerably more virulence than here. In one Hebrew manuscript (A) the father is urged to find wives for his sons while they are young, hence preventing temptation.

7:29–36, Obligations to Priests and the Poor. Ben Sira's high regard for priests finds expression here. He implores his readers to provide the necessary means of their subsistence, particularly since Mosaic law commands it. Ben Sira also encourages charitable deeds, among which he appears to include religious ritual in connection with the dead. The Greek text tones down this reference to a cult of the dead, suggesting instead that Ben Sira mentions burial rites, so important to the author of Tobit. The motive for such kindness is self-interest, both the anticipation of divine favor and the avoidance of punishment.

8:1–19, Some Things to Avoid. A sense of humor underlies the observations about old age and death, but the gravity of subject matter can scarcely be missed. Ben Sira's allusion to lack of respect for the aged reflects the conflict between the generations that became particularly harsh during this time of competing worldviews, Hebraism and Hellenism. The association of old age and death flows naturally, but Ben Sira's comments do not have the power of Ecclesiastes' poem on the same topic (Eccles. 12:1–7). The appeal to the insights acquired by those persons who have lived a long time ignores Job's attack on this traditional attitude. Ben Sira advises students to listen to sages as they talk about their lessons from experience. He thinks such attention to learned people will enable one to serve powerful officials, the goal of students in older wisdom traditions, at least in Egypt. The warning against legal disputes with individuals whose financial resources will determine the outcome demonstrates Ben Sira's practical approach to things. This cautious realism also rests behind his warning against letting down one's guard, particularly in the presence of someone who might talk too freely to others.

9:1–9, Relationships with Women. This section treats a husband's behavior toward his own wife and toward other women. Ben Sira implies that jealousy has a way of injuring the one who lacks trust; the specific background for this intriguing comment about a wife who turned the tables on her jealous husband is missing. The warning against surrendering to a woman's power occurs elsewhere in Prov. 31:3, advice from King Lemuel's mother to her son. Ben Sira's primary concern in this section is to alert students to the dangers associated with sexual laxity. His worry is essentially an economic one (cf. Deut. 22:28–29), but not entirely, for he thinks adulterous conduct brings destruc-

tion in the end. Much of this material recalls the warnings against the strange woman in the book of Proverbs. Ben Sira's observation about dining with another man's wife uses the image of leaning on the elbow, i.e., acting too familiarly (a reading preserved in codex 248).

9:10–16, Friends and Neighbors. This section returns to some of the ideas expressed in 8:1–19, almost as if to contrast faithful friends with harmful acquaintances. The statement that an old friend resembles old wine seems proverbial, but Ben Sira may have composed it himself. He reiterates the danger of ruthless and powerful companions, who make one walk as if in the presence of hidden snares. Similarly, he repeats the recommendation that students acquire wisdom from sages, adding that the subject of study should be the Mosaic law. As in 8:17–19, this unit closes with a reference to the damaging effect of the tongue, specifically from a person who reveals confidential information and/or talks too much.

9:17–10:5, On Rulers. The optimism underlying Ben Sira's statement about God's active participation in assuring that the right ruler achieves power (10:4) demonstrates the pervasive quality of traditional views, even when political circumstances seem to render them obsolete. Ben Sira affirms a benevolent providence, one that operates universally rather than merely on Israel's behalf. Still, the Greek text insists that the ruler of the whole earth shows special favor to scribes. Thus Ben Sira combines universalist and particularist thinking in a way that was typical of ancient wisdom literature. The initial comment about rulers (9:17) states that a person's skill at a particular craft manifests power over the medium, and that a ruler's persuasive speech manipulates subjects in a desired manner. Ben Sira observes that the product reveals the skill of an artisan in the same way a magistrate's language demonstrates his competence as a ruler of the people.

10:6–11:1, Pride and Honor. This section asserts that even the most powerful ruler succumbs to a horrible death, hence has no reason to be proud (10:9–10), and that human beings are both honorable and dishonorable, necessitating a decision about who deserves respect and who does not (10:19–25). Ben Sira had witnessed a transferal of power of great magnitude, the victory by Antiochus III over the Ptolemaic empire. Nevertheless, this astute observer of the political scene realizes that today's king is tomorrow's corpse. The anecdote about an illness that mystifies the physician (or that the physician makes light of, 10:9–10) may have a specific king in mind, but the point applies generally. A mighty ruler became mortally ill, inheriting unwanted vermin at death (10:11). In light of the inevitable end awaiting all mortals, every arrogant boast becomes hollow. This example of pride offers an occasion for Ben Sira to deliver a brief homily on its awful results (10:12–18). In particular, human arrogance has prompted God to intervene in the political arena, replacing proud rulers with humble ones. This motif of a topsy-turvy world occurs in Egyptian wisdom literature, but without Ben Sira's optimism that the change promises good things for society at large.

This section has a striking example of a rhetorical device whereby the same answer is solicited for opposite questions (10:19). In this way Ben Sira emphasizes differences among human beings, who are worthy of honor and contempt. This necessity for distinguishing among citizens leads to a discussion of sociological differentiations, which Ben Sira challenges. He insists that the customary honor bestowed on the rich and famous should take into account another ingredient, whether or not they fear God. This quality alone determines who deserves honor, and this means that poor people who fear God ought to be held in high esteem. This principle prompts Ben Sira to make an astonishing claim that free persons will serve intelligent slaves (10:25). Nothing suggests the actual manumission of slaves, however, for the implication is that perceptive slaves use their learning to their own advantage.

Because all human beings suffer decay, distinctions that take into account religious and intellectual qualities count most. But some persons overdo humility by depriving themselves of life's bounty, while others pretend to have plenty although lacking essential commodities. Ben Sira advocates a little common sense, while acknowledging that people usually honor the poor for their intelligence and the rich for their possessions.

11:2–28, Appearances Are Deceiving.
This section takes up the subject of deceptive appearances, insisting that intelligent persons probe beneath the surface of things to get to the heart of the matter. Good looks and expensive clothes do not make a person, and those whose appearance is less pleasing may actually be far more impressive. Ben Sira uses an illustration of the bee, which despite its smallness is responsible for the sweetest of things (11:3). An Egyptian Instruction, Papyrus Insinger, uses the same example. Anyone who takes present honors seriously forgets their fleeting nature, for God works in mysterious ways, sometimes reversing one's fortunes. For this reason one ought to refrain from judging persons in adverse circumstances. Their status could change in a moment. The

same principle applies to the prosperous, who could easily lose everything. It follows that no one's true character is manifest until the moment of death. Ben Sira therefore offers some simple advice: wait until a person's death to make a final assessment of that life (11:28). Because he does not believe in life beyond the grave, Ben Sira assumes that God will weigh one's deeds, balancing the good against the bad, and hand out reward or punishment during one's lifetime. However, this idea of a rigid accounting later came to play an important role in the Pharisaic belief in an afterlife.

In this connection Ben Sira cautions against hasty judgments deriving from an unwillingness to listen to others and to reflect on matters prior to speaking. The decisive factor in human relations is impenetrable, for it derives from the Lord who does wonders. No one can understand why one person, whom modern critics would label a workaholic, fails to amass a fortune while another, who is less capable and less industrious, achieves extraordinary success (11:11–12). Ben Sira attributes the success and failure to God's hidden action. From this source come good luck and bad, life and death, wealth and poverty. Nevertheless, Ben Sira boldly asserts that God's favor falls to the godly (11:17). Still, this practical teacher acknowledges that human beings have no assurance that a life of hard work will result in years of luxurious living, since death steals into the presence of confident individuals, mocking their unused wealth. Ben Sira's efforts to defend God's reputation for just dealings imply that a brief moment of bliss can compensate for a life of misery. His argument mixes realism and idealism; people undergoing hardship forget their better times, and those who enjoy life's bounty easily blot out all memory of earlier unhappiness. That is why the final moment looms large in Ben Sira's thinking.

11:29–14:19, On Wealth.
Although many topics surface in this long section, the unifying theme is riches. Ben Sira discusses some unfortunate character traits of many wealthy people and cautions poor people against courting the favors of the affluent. His reason is that people associate with their own kind (13:2, 15–20). Another compelling argument concerns the destructive behavior that unscrupulous persons of power display toward those whom they consider inferior. Moreover, Ben Sira insists, foolish people deny themselves many pleasures, hoping to amass a fortune and forgetting how quickly death can strike. Given the unpredictability of life, human assessments seem somewhat skewed, particularly when rich individuals can offend others and add insult to injury, whereas the poor are victimized and submit to the further indignity of offering

apologies (13:3). In connection with his comments about death Ben Sira uses a simile that must have occurred to numerous thinkers, specifically that the passing of humans resembles falling leaves. Nature's cycle takes place, with new leaves replacing old ones; in the same way, some people die and others come into being (14:18).

Ben Sira introduces an interesting criterion for deciding when to give alms. Good deeds should be targeted for devout people, inasmuch as they occupy a special place in God's eyes (12:1–7). Such thinking naturally produced the clever proverb of a later time that God loves the poor but helps the rich. This attitude does not represent a rigid rule in Ben Sira's mind. Rich persons can be scoundrels; hence ordinary citizens should not invite the wealthy into their homes. Some scheming individuals will usher in strife and dissent while pretending friendship. The real test of friendship requires adversity, for only genuine friends remain when circumstances become tough. Ben Sira mentions a metal mirror as a device for determining bogus friendship (12:10–11). This illustration may allude to the ancient idea of a magic mirror that revealed friends and enemies. Alternatively, it offers a dubious analogy that false friendships corrode just as a metal mirror does. By frequent polishing, one can prevent tarnish.

The futility of trying to be something one is not produces some fine observations. For example, whoever flirts with danger deserves no pity, and any earthen pot that foolishly strikes against a kettle can hardly expect sympathy when it shatters. Similarly, whoever grasps pitch will discover its adhesive power, and whoever lifts too heavy a weight will regret the action (13:1–2). Living creatures associate by species, so rich and poor do not belong together. The analogy is inadequate, since the two represent a single species. Nevertheless, Ben Sira presses the point. Wolves do not associate with lambs, dogs with hyenas, or wild asses with lions. All these examples serve to highlight the vulnerable status of poor people in the presence of the rich (13:15–20). If anyone accepts an invitation to dine with the wealthy, caution should prevail, and deference, but not too much—that would result in the poor person's disappearing into the woodwork. Ben Sira states a fact: the rich can do nothing wrong whereas the poor can do nothing right, at least in the estimation of the crowd, which lifts up a falling rich person but pushes down a poor one, or it listens attentively to the rich but ignores the words of the lowly (13:21–23).

Having said all this, Ben Sira refuses to condemn wealth outright, for not all riches have sin's taint. As a matter of fact, he encourages people to enjoy life's good things rather than passing the days as a miser (13:24; 14:3–16).

Here Ben Sira repeats Ecclesiastes' advice, which a later scribe turned into a commandment that all people must give an account for every good thing not enjoyed. The emphasis of this unusual ruling lies on the goodness of creation and God's desire that human beings appreciate nature's largesse. Ben Sira's motive differs significantly: death approaches, so make the most of things without incurring divine wrath. Given the complexity of these issues, Ben Sira's remark that devising proverbs requires much effort seems appropriate (13:26).

14:20–15:10, Wooing Wisdom. The happy person acquires wisdom by every available means: stalking her like game, spying on her, camping alongside the wall of her house, building a nest (according to the Hebrew text) in her branches, and enjoying her shade (14:22–27). Such an individual achieves all this by mastering the law. Wisdom's response to such ardor includes conduct appropriate to a bride and mother (15:2). She comes eagerly to meet her lover, offering bread and water. The understanding that she bestows on her husband assures prosperity, honor, and eloquence. But she withholds herself from fools and arrogant people, restricting her favors to those who practice piety, the outward expression of wisdom.

15:11–20, Freedom of Choice. The previous section concludes with an allusion to impious sinners, perhaps freethinkers. Ben Sira attempts to refute their argument that conduct is determined by external forces. He insists that everyone has free will, indeed that God created humans good but they exercised freedom and chose their evil inclination (15:14). Later rabbis developed the notion of two inclinations, an evil one and a good one. As far as Ben Sira is concerned, evil did not originate with God. Other Israelites thought differently, blaming either God or Satan. Although Ben Sira accuses humans, he assures them that God sees everything (15:18), the implication being that justice ultimately prevails.

16:1–23, Misguided Thinking. Discarding traditional Israelite attitudes toward numerous progeny, Ben Sira sees children as a blessing only if they fear God. But such bold thinking has its limits, and he rejects the opinion that one can sin with impunity because God dwells in the remote heavens. Appealing to personal experience and to biblical record (16:5–10), Ben Sira refutes the claim that an indifferent God overlooks human sin. The giants who rebelled against heaven, the inhabitants of Sodom, the Canaanites, the rebellious Israelites—they all experienced divine retribution. The same exacting punishment applies to individuals, and God's mercy matches the divine wrath. Therefore it is foolish to deny God's active distribution of justice. Ben Sira quotes two examples of such misguided thinking (16:17, 20–22), between which he reflects on the majesty of God (16:18–19).

16:24–17:14, Divine Wisdom in Creation. Traditions about creation and the Sinaitic legislation come together in this unit, which gives the impression of mathematical precision. God created the universe in perfect order; hence nothing inappropriate can occur (16:26–28). The same care went into the fashioning of human beings, to whom God gave special gifts such as divine likeness and authority over all other creatures (17:1–4). One manuscript (248) adds that God gave the five senses to humans, and to those God added a sixth (understanding) and a seventh (speech). The divine solicitude eventuated in a covenant between God and the people, who beheld the glorious majesty at Sinai and received the law (17:12–14). Curiously, only relationships between human beings are mentioned here.

17:15–18:14, The Compassionate Judge. Ben Sira endeavors to explain God's special relationship with Israel. To be sure, God watches over all people, but the care of non-Jews falls to other designated divine beings (17:17). God's attention focuses on Israel, whose deeds of charity bring immense joy but whose sins are fully known and despised. Nevertheless, God leaves open the door of repentance for fragile human beings (17:24). Unlike humans, God lives forever. The greatness and majesty of God escape detection and defy description. Ben Sira asks the same question that Psalm 8 does, "What is man?" and answers somewhere between the Psalmist's and Job's responses (18:8). Whereas the Psalmist spoke of human glory and Job of misery, Ben Sira emphasizes the brevity of life and bleak prospects in the grave, but he also highlights God's compassionate shepherding (18:9–14).

18:15–18, Kind Words. Kind words ought to accompany a gift, for they are superior to it. The implicit contradiction in a gift from one who begrudges it (18:18) recalls Ben Sira's discussion of true generosity in 14:3–10.

18:19–29, Using Caution. Wise persons use caution in all things, particularly vows, for they know how quickly fortunes change. Ben Sira reverses the usual order of the expression "from evening to morning." Ecclesiastes also admonishes its students to pay their vows promptly and urges caution in taking vows (Eccles. 5:2, 4–5).

18:30–19:12, Self-Control. This section warns against two kinds of behavior related to drinking and speech. Ben Sira opposes a lavish life-style if one cannot afford it, and he makes fun of people who cannot refrain from telling what they know. The humorous illustrations convey his point beautifully: a word about to burst one's insides, birth pangs, and an arrow in one's thigh cause great discomfort for fools (19:10–12). The association of wine and women as temptation (19:2) occurs also in Egyptian wisdom literature.

19:13–17, Rebuking Others. Because everyone offends with the tongue, intelligent people give others every opportunity to clarify what actually occurred. Four of the five verses employ anaphoristic style, repeating the phrase "Question a friend/neighbor" for rhetorical effect.

19:18–30, Wisdom and Cleverness. Israel's sages recognized that information could be put to dubious use, indeed that intelligence itself sometimes functioned in the cause of evil. Such cleverness is attributed to the serpent in Gen. 3:1 and to Jonadab who schooled Amnon in the art of seduction (2 Sam. 13:3). Because of this negative potential of wisdom, the sages were reluctant at first to attribute wisdom to God. In this unit Ben Sira brings together the basic themes of the book, wisdom and the fear of God. (Verses 18, 19, 20c, and 21 are later additions to the text.) The description of unscrupulous persons whose outward demeanor conceals inner hostility demonstrates profound psychological understanding, and the juxtaposition of a statement indicating awareness that things are not always what they seem over against a straightforward assertion that one is known by the impression made on others indicates cautious realism.

20:1–31, Guarding One's Speech. Egyptian and Israelite sages developed a highly sophisticated concept of rhetoric that consisted of timeliness, restraint, integrity, and eloquence. Knowing when to speak and when to remain silent was a mark of intelligence; in Egypt a sage was known as "a silent one." Truthfulness and persuasiveness were essential if one expected to make optimal use of the right moment for speech. The wise trained themselves to speak well in behalf of truth, but they also acknowledged that some people possessed an innate gift of eloquence. This understanding of speech and silence was more complex than it might appear, as the two sayings in Prov. 26:4–5 illustrate. They isolate instances when neither silence nor speech achieves the desired goal. Ben Sira therefore works with a revered tradition when considering the merit of speech and silence. In his view, silence in itself may derive from ineptness.

Violence in a good cause necessarily aborts, like a eunuch's desire to seduce a woman (20:4). What seems to be a bargain may cost one dearly (20:12). The meaning of this obscure saying may be that some people obtain a bargain while others pay exorbitant prices.

21:1–10, Sin's Smooth Path. This counsel to sinners has two graphic images: sin resembles a viper (21:2), and an assembly of sinners is like a bundle of tow (21:9; the Greek contains a wordplay here). Roads were not normally paved in ancient Israel, but sin's path is so smooth that its occupants slip into the grave (21:10). Ben Sira likens building a house with borrowed money to preparing one's tomb (21:8; unless the reading "for the winter" is original, which suggests stupidity in failing to gather wood).

21:11–22:18, The Wise and Foolish. The contrast between the wise and fools occurs frequently in ancient wisdom literature. Here Ben Sira gives some examples of conduct typical of each group. Their attitudes toward learning also set them apart, for the wise value education. In a sense wisdom connotes good manners, but it implies more: weighing what one hears, thinking first, then speaking, improving on maxims (21:15). In a word, the wise expand knowledge like an overflowing river (21:13). Fools are like leaking containers, retaining nothing (21:14). Hence mourning for them lasts forever as opposed to the usual seven days (Heb. *shiba'*; 22:12). It appears that Ben Sira thought one's quest for wisdom permitted the setting aside of normal etiquette (21:23; cf. 14:23). Ben Sira's remark about the birth of a daughter may derive from the fact that she cannot continue the family name, but the context implies that he has in mind the onerous task of locating a husband for the daughter (22:3–5). Instead of a fence on a hill, the image in 22:18 may be that of small pebbles on a wall, having been placed there to alert farmers when jackals threatened a crop (cf. RSV and JB).

22:19–26, Holding on to Friendship. This section returns to the subject of friendship (see 6:5–17) and presents a complementary dimension of human relationships in which the remarkable resiliency of affections comes to expression. Ben Sira recognizes that the bond uniting friends can snap when one person exceeds the limits of propriety, but he also celebrates the amazing readiness to forgive that characterizes genuine friendship. The sudden shift from third person to first in v. 25 has precedent in Ecclesiastes, where first person style dominates one particular section (Eccles. 1:12–2:26). For Ben Sira the shift may be a subtle move to emphasize the personal dimension of friendship.

22:27–23:6, A Prayer for Self-Control. This remarkable prayer asks for wisdom's harsh discipline to prevent licentious thoughts. It uses the image of a sentry on one's lips and a seal to keep harmful words at bay (22:27). The prayer also recognizes the danger of pride that encourages passionate indulgence (23:4).

23:7–15, Proper Use of Language. Two types of language bring ruin: The first, empty religious oaths and frequent reference to God, incurs divine wrath (23:9–11); the second, coarse talk, issues in public disgrace (23:13–15). Ben Sira's allusion to the inheritance of Jacob (23:12) refers to the Israelites rather than to the land promised them.

23:16–27, Fornication and Adultery. Hunger for "bread" makes fornicators incapable of refusing the offer, and they rationalize their conduct by pretending the utmost in discretion (23:18). God's eyes, brighter by far than the sun, observe the action. (Did not God see everything before creation? After creation, God still sees everything that happens.) Women who commit adultery offend God, their husbands, and children (23:23). All who behave in this manner destroy themselves.

24:1–22, Wisdom Praises Itself. Reminiscent of Prov. 8:22–9:12, this hymn draws on creation imagery (a lifegiving mist and a divine word), but it endeavors to bring together the universal and particular: wisdom exalts herself in the heavenly realm, and she receives God's command to dwell with the Jews. This exclusivism contrasts with 1 *Enoch* 42:1–2, which states that she found no dwelling place on earth but that iniquity was more successful, settling like rain or dew in the desert. Ben Sira likens wisdom to a luxuriant tree or vine, from which human beings obtain delectable fruit (24:13–22).

24:23–34, Reflection on Wisdom. Ben Sira identifies wisdom with the Mosaic law, which bestows life like the rivers of Eden. Nevertheless, the first occupant of Eden did not fully grasp her, nor has anyone done so since that early attempt (24:28). This abstracting of wisdom reflects a poignant sense of despair, which locates wisdom in creation. That experience is tempered somewhat by the claim that the Mosaic law is a concrete expression of wisdom (24:23). Ben Sira's own effort has overflowed its banks, prompting him to write a further treatise for posterity (24:30–34).

25:1–26:27, Good and Bad Wives. Two surprising comments occur in this unit. Ben Sira exalts the fear of the Lord over wisdom and attributes the instigation of evil to woman. Normally, piety served as the initial stage to wisdom; often religious expression is called the crowning achievement of knowledge. But here Ben Sira subjects wisdom to religion (25:10–11). A similar break with traditional interpretation takes place when he blames Eve for the origin of sin (25:24), for Jewish literature of this general period usually accuses Adam of introducing death. In some circles his crime consists of a refusal to repent. Ben Sira's description of two types of wives plumbs the depths of sadness and soars to lofty heights of joy. Two important manuscripts, 70 and 248, together with the Syriac add a section about an appropriate choice of a wife and about harlots. Ben Sira's characterization of loose women who drink from any spring and open their quiver for any arrow demonstrates powerful imagery as a pedagogic tool (26:12).

The best manuscripts of Sirach lack 26:19–27, which seem to reflect later sentiment, although the ideas generally agree with Ben Sira's attitude toward women. The metaphor of one's wife as a fertile field occurs widely in Israelite and non-Israelite wisdom. The book of Proverbs may have inspired these comments, but they use harsher language than their earlier counterpart.

26:28–27:15, Honesty. The merchant's profession offers an easy means of cheating the buyer, so much so that Ben Sira thinks the temptation virtually irresistible (26:29–27:1). He also believes that eloquence and clear reasoning reveal character (27:4–7).

27:16–28:26, Offenses Against Companions. Ben Sira observes that betrayal of a friend's secrets destroys the friendship forever and that the "third tongue," a technical expression for slander in rabbinic literature, ruins three people: the slanderer, the person being slandered, and whoever believes the cruel report. A tension exists here between realistic observation and religious ideology. Ben Sira's emphasis on forgiving one's neighbor for offenses has precedent in earlier wisdom literature, although the motive is not exactly altruistic. Prov. 25:21–22 recommends kind actions toward enemies and promises divine reward for this conduct. The image of "coals on the head" may derive from an Egyptian ritual of repentance. The section on actions that double back to harm the actor also has biblical and extrabiblical precedent.

29:1–20, Lending Money. Whereas Prov. 22:26 advises against surety, Ben Sira offers a cautious defense of the practice. His rationale, purely religious, implies the winning of divine favor by lending to the needy (29:9). No usury is mentioned (cf. Lev. 25:36).

29:21–28, Hospitality. In the Greco-Roman world some men dwelt in other people's houses and rendered various services in return. Ben Sira's observations imply a similar arrangement, which he compares unfavorably with humble circumstances in one's own abode.

30:1–13, On Rearing Children. Ancient sages believed in the effectiveness of the whip.

A Sumerian sage reminisces about school days and indicates that he was caned for numerous offenses. Similar texts from Egypt refer to the constant threat of physical punishment in school but promise ample rewards for the pain. The book of Proverbs also encourages vigorous discipline for disobedient children, so that the nonbiblical saying "Spare the rod and spoil the child" adequately sums up the teaching about this subject.

Ben Sira urges parents to wield a heavy hand, whipping children soundly and keeping some distance to avoid familiarity. The primary concern is the father's welfare. The Hebrew text adds a graphic image: as a python pounces on a wild beast, so crush a son's loins while he is young.

30:14–25, On Good Health. In the ancient Near East sickness posed a special intellectual problem in addition to its physical burden. Was illness a sign of divine displeasure? The simple answer, based on a concept of reward and retribution that pervaded popular belief, brought immense grief to innocent people. The book of Job wrestles with this vexing problem, although it fails to resolve the issue. Job's friends and Elihu give voice to the conventional understanding that grievous deeds alone explain the extremity of his suffering, but Job adamantly maintains innocence. In general, the book of Proverbs fueled the thinking of Job's detractors. Ben Sira has mixed feelings about the problem (cf. 38:1–15). On the one hand, with Job he realizes that not all misery comes as divine punishment. On the other hand, Ben Sira believes that wicked persons fall into God's punishing hands. Healthy persons are the richest of all individuals, but the sick bear a double burden: the illness and knowledge that God is angry toward them. After v. 24 the order of the Greek text becomes confused (30:25–33:13a and 33:13b–36:16 are transposed).

31:1–11, On Riches. To be sure, wealth has some bad side effects, but so does poverty. Pursuit of riches for their own sake brings ruin, but wealth affords noble opportunities. The Hebrew word *mamon* occurs here for "gold" (31:8), possibly for the first time.

31:12–32:13, Conduct at Meals. Like ancient Egyptian wisdom, which offers advice on etiquette at meals, Ben Sira teaches what is proper in his day. His remark about the eye in 31:13 is puzzling, but probably reflects the notion that the expression "desires of the eyes" sums up all evil. His attitude to wine (31:25–31) is more positive than that in Proverbs (cf. Prov. 23:29–35), while his comments on vomiting echo Seneca's remark that his contemporaries "vomit in order to eat and eat so as to vomit." The Greek background of Ben Sira's remarks about banquets is seen in the choice of a host to select the guest list and to say grace, as well as in the wreath of honor.

32:14–33:6, God-Fearers and Sinners. A Hebrew idiom lies behind the double imperatives in vv. 19–20, indicating a condition and its consequence. The absolute statement about the well-being of a God-fearer needs to be qualified by the realities of experience. Ben Sira's zeal for the law leads to extreme statements, like the one about the utter reliability of the sacred dice (33:3). He had complete confidence in priests who manipulated the Urim and Thummim. These rocks probably had a Hebrew *waw* or a *taw* on them. Priests asked questions with "yes" or "no" answers, continuing until two rocks with the same letter appeared.

33:7–15, Differences in Things and People. The universe consists of pairs; human beings likewise comprise camps of opposites, divinely constituted. Therefore some days are sacred, others not, and some men are chosen for the priesthood, others not. No women were among the priestly ranks; this exclusion of women reflects the attitude of the Jewish authorities toward purity and impurity.

33:16–18, Ben Sira's Personal Appeal. Acknowledging his temporal sequence at the end of inspired writers, Ben Sira claims to have excelled at wisdom and asks for a hearing from leaders. The latter is a rhetorical device in Wisdom of Solomon especially (Wisd. of Sol. 1:1; 6:1–2).

33:19–23, Financial Independence. Ben Sira offers sound advice to overly pious persons who gave all their possessions away to receive credit from God. Better wait until the hour of death, he suggests.

33:24–31, Treatment of Slaves. In the Decalogue asses, oxen, servants, and a neighbor's wife occur in the prohibition against coveting. Ben Sira also links asses and servants in this way. His remarks on slaves are in keeping with the tendency of wisdom literature to reflect the values of the reasonably well-to-do. Essentially conservative, it recommends the status quo, abhorring revolutionary periods in society. The king, although a potential threat, should be obeyed for safety's sake, if for no other reason. In Israel Solomon and Hezekiah were honored as patrons of the intelligentsia. Kings, in turn, were expected to shepherd the people (this metaphor is particularly common in Egypt). This same attitude of paternalism is reflected in the exquisite depiction of Job's happier days in Job 29–31. Ben Sira advises harsh treatment of slaves but balances his words with the reminder that they represent considerable investment (in blood, i.e., purchased with one's life substance).

34:1–8, Empty Dreams. Three means of predicting the future are rejected because they lack substance, resembling a reflection in a mirror. Ben Sira says that dreams generate excitement in senseless people. Biblical precedent for divine communication through dreams forced Ben Sira to qualify his remarks (34:6). But how could one determine the source of dreams?

The attitude toward dreams in the ancient world varied considerably. In Mesopotamia dream revelations were so common that a "science" of predicting the future arose. Specialists in interpreting dreams existed throughout the ancient Near East. The Hebrew Bible also witnesses to their presence (cf. the Joseph story and Daniel), but confusion over the source of dreams eventually led to a disparaging of this media of revelation (cf. Jeremiah's objection to dreams). The supernatural source of dreams persists in the NT (e.g., the stories about Pilate's wife and Joseph's escape from Herod's wrath).

34:9–17, The Protection of Wisdom. Travel's broadening influence compensates for risk involved in journeys away from home, and experience derived from them helps some people escape danger. Wisdom shelters the God-fearer.

34:18–35:20, Authentic Sacrifices and Prayers. Ben Sira continues the prophetic criticism of sacrifices that are not accompanied by moral rectitude. He employs a strong image: sacrifices gained from abuse of the poor are as offensive as murdering a son before his father. For Ben Sira deeds of kindness do not take the place of ritual (35:1–5). Although the law commands the offering of sacrifices, one's attitude and moral character determine God's response. Genuine repentance is essential, regardless of how frequently one fasts (34:26).

36:1–17, A Prayer for Deliverance of Jews. This fervent prayer for decisive action on God's part looks back on the Exodus and forward to the messianic era. Ben Sira notices disparity between the assurances just articulated and the dire circumstances of the Jews. He therefore pleads for God to restore them and crush the enemy. His guarded language in v. 10 may allude to Antiochus the Great. The comment about prophetic predictions (36:15) witnesses to the popular conviction that the unfulfilled oracles promising weal cannot abort. For a brief moment Ben Sira abandons the universalism of the sages altogether. It should be noted, however, that the earlier sages' generosity did not extend to the fools among them. The universalism was therefore a qualified one, moral qualities determining the assessment.

850

36:18–26, Using Discriminating Judgment. Some food tastes better than other food, and some wives are better than others. Ben Sira's observations assume the "purchase" of wives and the arrangement of marriages by fathers. The Hebrew text calls the wife her husband's best vineyard, a common image in the Bible. Despite the risk (cf. 25:16–20), Ben Sira favors marriage over the single life.

37:1–6, True and False Friends. In the context of discussing friendship Ben Sira laments the creation of the evil inclination (but cf. 15:14). The text of v. 3 is not well preserved in the Greek or Hebrew, apparently reflecting the reluctance of later readers to attribute evil to God. In later rabbinic tradition, however, God's responsibility for creating the evil inclination is freely admitted, although a corresponding good inclination is postulated. In every individual the evil inclination was said to antedate the good by a dozen years, which seemed to explain the early occurrence of folly.

37:7–15, On Advisers. Shrewd practical advice does not suffice for Ben Sira, who adds some religious observations as well. He presupposes polygamy and astrology in the comments about a rival wife (37:11) and seven watchmen (37:14). Presumably, the seven people observe the heavenly bodies in an effort to discern the future. The allusion may, however, suggest an exaggerated attempt to spot danger from human foes. The combination of self-reliance and prayer for divine leadership shows how Ben Sira lives fully in two worlds, that of secular sages and the one inhabited by deeply religious individuals. For him the insights acquired through reason, although significant, need the greater knowledge that God makes accessible to devout souls.

37:16–31, Using Intelligence for One's Well-Being. Intelligence that does not issue in beneficial actions is wasted. Ben Sira uses two illustrations, a teacher whose words offend others (37:20–21) and a person whose eating habits harm the body (37:29–31). A curious contrast occurs in this section: lone individuals vanish soon but Israel survives indefinitely (37:25). This idea represents a break with earlier wisdom tradition, which was individualistic in its teachings.

38:1–15, On Physicians. Ben Sira counters objections to doctors who, in the view of some people, interfered with divine punishment for sin. He still thinks of sickness as punishment, for he advises prayer, repentance, and sacrifice when illness strikes, and he implies that sinners will need physicians (38:15). Nevertheless, he defends the medical profession, arguing that God created medicines and that doctors solicit divine aid in the practice of their trade. The Hebrew text states that sinners act proudly before physicians, presumably disparaging their services.

38:16–23, Grief for the Dead. According to 22:12, mourning for the dead lasted seven days, but here Ben Sira advises a shorter period of grief because of its adverse physical effect. The dead person's "epitaph" is sobering: mine today, yours tomorrow (38:22). Notably, Ben Sira does not mention prayers for the dead, which later became a custom among the Jews (but cf. 7:33–34). The unusual early termination of mourning recalls David's unconventional behavior after the death of the child conceived by Bathsheba and the comment about no coming back echoes David's solemn observation that the child "will not return to me" (2 Sam. 12:23). Ben Sira's astonishing counsel to let the remembrance of the dead cease contrasts sharply with the usual attitude about the importance of a lasting remembrance. Even Ecclesiastes complains bitterly because one cannot count on a permanent reputation.

38:24–39:11, Advantages of Being a Scribe. Like the Egyptian *Instruction of Duauf*, Sirach contrasts the occupations of various craftsmen with that of scribes. Ben Sira does not disparage the contribution of artisans in society (38:32, 34); on the other hand, he holds scribes in much higher esteem because of their status as royally appointed officials and leaders in high councils. This description of a scribe's subject matter focuses on the Scriptures, but not exclusively so (39:1). Egyptian sages emphasized the lasting memorial of scribes, writings that are recited for generations; Ben Sira simply mentions the reputation that endures (39:9–11).

39:12–35, In Praise of the Creator. In his effort to respond to the vexing problem of the apparent injustice of God, Ben Sira borrows heavily from earlier wisdom literature, but he also draws on the Greek philosophical tradition. He looks to the future for final rectification, explains suffering as disciplinary, recognizes that appearances deceive, and affirms justice in the face of apparent injustice, surrendering to mystery and raising a voice of hymnic praise. But he introduces new emphases, the one psychological and the other metaphysical. Sinners experience excessive anxiety, and the universe fights on behalf of virtuous people. The latter idea of a rational order that consists of complementary pairs derives from Greek arguments for an inherent justice in the world. In vv. 26–27 Ben Sira asserts that one's inner state determines how certain things appear to that person. Wisdom of

Solomon develops this psychological idea fully, showing the devastating power of fear to turn ordinary things into objects of terror.

40:1-11, The Heavy Yoke. Ben Sira draws on a lively tradition about the miserable lot entrusted to humans. His language recalls Gen. 3:17-20, the divine curse on rebellious Adam, as well as Job's ruminations about the terrible plight of human beings (Job 7 and 14). One also hears an echo of the unflattering characterization of the human disposition that brought on the Flood (Gen. 6:5). Moreover, Ben Sira's allusion to returning to the mother of all recalls Job's reference to returning there (possibly the aforementioned maternal womb but more likely he uses a euphemism for the underworld). Whereas the earlier texts from Genesis and Job describe a universal human bondage, one in Job's case exacerbated by divine surveillance, Ben Sira thinks God's watchful care assures a measure of justice, multiplying sinners' grief sevenfold. The miserable experience of human beings, outlined in detail here, throws in relief the preceding praise of the creator.

40:12-27, Life's Positive Features. Ben Sira continues the argument that God sees and punishes evil and rewards good deeds. He also uses a rhetorical device to emphasize nine things that surpass others that are good in themselves (e.g., a friend or companion is welcome, but to be husband and wife is preferable).

40:28-41:13, On Death. The attitude toward death in various wisdom texts reflects both realism and faint hope. The latter manifests itself in feelings of consolation over a life well lived (the harvesting of golden shocks of grain) and expresses confidence in the timing of death's summons after a long, prosperous life (cf. Job 4-5). But the sages also know a darker side of death, the premature visitation by the angel of death who seizes persons unawares. An Egyptian sage states that protests at this time accomplish nothing worthwhile, for the messenger of death does not consider youth to rest outside its grip. Some individuals, like Job, actually welcomed death because of their personal suffering, while others, like Ecclesiastes, viewed the shadow of death as a grievous burden affecting every waking moment. Ben Sira's cool detachment contrasts noticeably with Job and Ecclesiastes, but he still refuses to endorse belief in life after death, which the author of Dan. 12:2 does a couple of decades later. Wisdom of Solomon welcomes the Greek notion of immortality as an answer to this problem.

41:14-42:8, Two Kinds of Shame. The Hebrew text has a title before v. 16 ("Instruction about Shame"). Ben Sira first explores some actions where shame has a proper place (41:17-23) then proceeds to name further acts that ought not to cause a sense of shame (42:1-5). The reference to an old man in 42:8a probably relates to fornication but was mistakenly read "contends with a youth." The motivation in this unit is thoroughly secular—winning popular approval (42:8b).

42:9-14, On Daughters. A father's worries over a daughter are chronicled, beginning with temptations during her tender youth and continuing after her marriage. The Hebrew text characterizes her, nonetheless, as a secret treasure. Still, the popular proverbs that conclude this section reveal a low opinion of women that often finds expression in rabbinic, Greco-Roman, and early Christian literature.

Ben Sira's Attitude Toward Women

The view of women in ancient wisdom literature is not easily assessed. The notorious "foreign woman" represents a threat to youth in Egypt and Israel, and warnings against harlots and adulteresses are ubiquitous. On the other hand, sages frequently praise wives as gifts from God, although conceding that some wives occasion much sorrow. Furthermore, wisdom assumes the form of woman, at least in Israelite metaphorical speech. But she has a counterpart—Madam Folly. The author of Ecclesiastes laments his inability to locate a single woman of worth, although he can only find one man in a thousand. In the story of the contest of Darius' pages (1 Esd. 3:1-4:41) woman is praised as the strongest thing in the world, excepting truth and its Author.

Ben Sira inherits this mixed tradition about women and contributes one new dimension, the category of evil daughters as a subject of discussion. His characterization of wicked daughters is thoroughly obscene. In addition, he introduces the adjective ra'ah (Heb., evil) in the expression "wicked woman." Although the text is disputed, he may also have made the ridiculous statement that a man's wickedness is better than a woman's goodness. Still, he recognized the value of a good wife, even while viewing her from a man's perspective. In all this, Ben Sira was a child of his time.

42:15-43:33, A Hymn in Praise of the Creator. This hymn introduces the long section in praise of the fathers, as the transition in 43:33 makes specific. Ben Sira asserts that even angels lack the ability to praise God fully, hence his own effort only scratches the surface. Yet that surface is a wondrous one, as Ben Sira illustrates with rare poetic images. The summary statement that God is "the all" does not indicate pantheism, for Ben Sira adds that the Creator is greater than the sum of the parts (43:27–28). A sense of awe permeates the language about natural phenomena (sun, moon, stars, rainbow, lightning, and dew, etc.).

44:1–50:24, Praise of the Fathers. A general introduction (44:1–15) and a specific conclusion from Ben Sira's own day (50:1–24) conclude this journey through Israel's sacred history. Although the material of the hymn is thoroughly Hebraic, the similarities with Greek encomia (rhetorical compositions in praise of heroes) are noteworthy, suggesting to some interpreters that Ben Sira models his hymn on these orations. His own special interests surface in the choice of heroes to stand out in the list and in what he recalls about some of the others. The priestly institution and its founders occupy central position, and the contribution of others to the religious establishment at Jerusalem comes into play. These include David, Solomon, Hezekiah, Josiah, Zerubbabel, Jeshua, and Simon II. The list of Israel's worthy men includes a sampling of heroes, but its exclusive nature is highlighted by the absence of women and non-Israelites. The emphasis on the miraculous carries over to what Ben Sira says about prophets, whose wondrous deeds outshone their words in his estimation.

With this hymn Ben Sira thoroughly integrates Israel's sacred history into the thought of the wise, whose literature before him does not betray the slightest hint of familiarity with Israel's special religious story. Presumably, the hymn attributes the miraculous deeds to God's gift of wisdom, which guided these men and enabled them to make a name for themselves.

The description of Simon II may function polemically, for Ben Sira seems to have witnessed the corruption of the priesthood under Jason and Menelaus. Ben Sira's choice of a starting point for the poem in 44:16 witnesses to the popularity of reflection on Enoch during the second century B.C.; the later reference to him, followed by mention of Joseph, Shem, Seth, and Adam (Israelite heroes!) has suggested to some scholars that the book is not in the form that Ben Sira planned for it. The most surprising feature of the hymn is the absence of any specific Torah or wisdom piety.

The Hymn in Praise of Israel's Heroes

Ben Sira's hymn in praise of the fathers has been described by Burton Mack as a complete reading of epic history that served as a mythic etiology for Judaism in the period of the Sec-

ond Temple. The hymn's architectonic structure is tripartite, with two transitional units:

Establishment of Covenants	I
Conquest of the Land	*Transition*
History of Prophets and Kings	II
Restoration	*Transition*
Climax (Simon II)	III

Common themes unite the figures belonging to the major units, for example, "the promise of a blessing" links together the personalities from Abraham to Jacob. The poem's encomiastic traits are emphasized. Four parts emerge from this analysis: first, prooemium or introduction (44:1–15); second, genealogy (44:16–49:16); third, narration of the subject's achievements (50:1–21); and fourth, epilogue (50:22–24). In this reading 49:14–16 serves as a bridge from the past to the present, juxtaposing Adam and Simon II in a manner that makes praise of the latter both appropriate and effective. The praise is commemorative rather than entertaining, but Ben Sira makes efficient use of various rhetorical devices that occur in Greek encomia. These include, among others, amplification by syncrisis (the juxtaposition of opposites for rhetorical effect), hyperbole, rhetorical questions, appeal to experience gained through travel, reference to the person's character and reputation for good deeds, claim that words cannot adequately describe the individual, and assertion that the person's contribution to society is unprecedented. Nevertheless, it must be acknowledged that 1 and 2 Chronicles provide many parallels to Ben Sira's use of biblical material. For example, 1 Chronicles remained silent about some undesirable conduct on David's part.

It is striking that Ben Sira completely drops Ezra from the biblical record. Explanations for the omission of Ezra vary, but three attempts to explain this anomaly merit consideration. One answer appeals to changed socioeconomic circumstances that made mixed marriage a matter of indifference in the late third and early second century B.C. In this view, Ezra's legislation about marriage with foreigners was too strict, inasmuch as it failed to take into account long-standing practice among the Jews. Therefore, embarrassment led Ben Sira to omit Ezra from the heroes deemed worthy of praise.

A second explanation concentrates on the scribal profession. The scribe in Ezra's day was narrowly and exclusively oriented toward the Mosaic law. Ben Sira understands the vocation of scribe much more broadly. The interest in the law was complemented by research in the wisdom tradition. In a sense Ben Sira transforms the office of priest-scribe into that of teacher-sage, whose authority rests ultimately on his scholarship, insights, and communicative skills.

A third response to the silence about Ezra focuses on the state of the priestly office in the period after Simon II's death. Onias III was a pious leader but lacked the qualities of bold leadership. Like Ezra, he was a political quietist. For this reason Ben Sira does not want to extol Ezra as someone whom Onias III could emulate. Instead, Ben Sira skips over Ezra and highly praises Onias' father, hoping to stimulate a desire on Onias' part to pattern his actions after his father and predecessor in the office of high priest.

Two other omissions in the hymn have occasioned some comment. Joseph does not appear in the body of the hymn, although the brief "afterthought" in 49:14–16 mentions him along with the prediluvians Shem, Seth, and Adam (Enoch appears for a second time here, but the Siriac and the Masada texts do not include him at 44:16). One possible reason for this curious situation is that Joseph's link with the northern tribes of Ephraim and Manasseh and his blessing on these sons implied a positive attitude toward the hated Samaritans. The active campaign waged by the Samaritans and the Tobiads in Transjordan against the policies of Simon II may have generated enough animosity to prompt Ben Sira's silence about Joseph. Another explanation is that Ben Sira pulled Joseph's name out of sequence to blot out any record of Joseph's role as adviser to the Pharaoh. A third answer takes its cue from the fact that Onias III switched allegiance from the Seleucids to the Ptolemies. Ben Sira does not want to give the appearance of approving this shift of loyalty. None of these answers deals with the problem adequately if the allusion to Joseph in 49:14–16 derives from Ben Sira; for this reason, as well as for its strange location, some interpreters consider these verses secondary.

Ben Sira also omits Saul, although the biblical record contains enough negative material on this tragic figure to explain his absence in the hymn. Furthermore, Ben Sira makes no secret of his hatred for the Samaritans, whom Saul would undoubtedly have recalled, and David, Saul's enemy, is Ben Sira's hero. Finally, Saul was not an example of piety for later Judeans, at least in sacred memory.

50:25–26, A Numerical Proverb. This expression of animosity toward Philistines, Edomites, and Samaritans seems out of place in the book, and it hardly expresses the universalism typical of earlier sages. Nevertheless, Ben Sira's attitude toward these neighboring peoples reflects the animosity resulting from hostile actions directed toward Judeans who returned from captivity in Babylonia and attempted to resettle in Jerusalem and its immediate vicinity. The inhabitants of Samaria are linked together with archrivals, Philistines

and Edomites. The bitterness toward all three groups resulted in military action by the Hasmonean rulers shortly after Ben Sira's day.

50:27–29, Ben Sira's Epilogue. The author identifies himself by name and commends his teachings to readers.

51:1–30, An Appendix. This appendix consists of a prayer (51:1–12), a psalm (sixteen verses in the Hebrew but missing in Greek), and an acrostic poem (51:13–30). The prayer resembles a thanksgiving psalm in which the author praises God for deliverance from some danger. The psalm in the Hebrew text is made up of numerous biblical quotations; its kinship with Psalm 136 has attracted some attention. Finally, Ben Sira describes his successful acquisition of wisdom, a motif that recurs in Wisdom of Solomon with erotic overtones (like the manuscript of Sir. 51 discovered at Qumran). The invitation to attend Ben Sira's house of instruction (Heb. *bet hammidrash*) is the first of its kind. The Hebrew text of v. 29 also mentions Ben Sira's academy (*yeshivah*). The emphasis on human learning and divine mercy in the last verses conclude the book in a way that brings together the tension throughout.

Bibliography

Alonso-Schökel, L. "The Vision of Man in Sirach 16:24–17:14." In *Israelite Wisdom*. Edited by J. Gammie et al. Missoula, MT: Scholars Press, 1978. Pp. 235–45.

Box, G. H., and W. O. E. Oesterley. "The Book of Sirach." In *The Apocrypha and Pseudepigrapha of the Old Testament in English*. 2 vols. Edited by R. H. Charles. Oxford: Clarendon, 1913. Reprint. London: Oxford University Press, 1971. Vol. 1, pp. 268–517.

Crenshaw, J. L. *Old Testament Wisdom*. Atlanta, GA: Knox, 1981.

Jacob, E. "Wisdom and Religion in Sirach." In *Israelite Wisdom*. Pp. 247–60.

Mack, B. L. *Wisdom and the Hebrew Epic*. Chicago: University of Chicago Press, 1985.

Sanders, J. T. *Ben Sira and Demotic Wisdom*. Society of Biblical Literature Monograph Series, 28. Chico, CA: Scholars Press, 1983.

Skehan, P. A., and A. A. Di Lolla. *The Wisdom of Ben Sira*. Anchor Bible, 39. Garden City, NY: Doubleday, 1987.

Snaith, J. G. *Ecclesiasticus or the Wisdom of Jesus Son of Sirach*. Cambridge Bible Commentary. Cambridge: Cambridge University Press, 1974.

von Rad, G. *Wisdom in Israel*. Nashville, TN: Abingdon, 1972.

Yadin, Y. *The Ben Sira Scroll from Masada with Introduction, Emendations and Commentary*. Jerusalem: Israel Exploration Society, 1965.

BARUCH

DANIEL J. HARRINGTON

INTRODUCTION

The Book of Baruch (sometimes also called 1 Baruch to distinguish it from the noncanonical books designated as *2 Baruch* and *3 Baruch*) is a composite work consisting of a narrative introduction (1:1–14), a prose prayer attributed to the Jewish exiles in Babylon (1:15–3:8), a poem about the elusiveness of wisdom and the identification of wisdom and the Law (3:9–4:4), and another poem in which the theological significance of Israel's exile is explained and the hope of restoration is explored (4:5–5:9).

The three major sections (1:15–3:8; 3:9–4:4; 4:5–5:9) appear to have been originally independent works. Because all three pieces were connected with Israel's experience of exile in Babylon and its hope for return to the homeland (though the connection of 3:9–4:4 with this theme is quite weak), they were joined together and given a narrative framework (1:1–14). All three pieces combine words and phrases from the Hebrew Bible (especially Dan. 9, Job 28, and Isa. 40–66) into a kind of pastiche that ends up being a new and somewhat creative composition.

Most likely, the narrative framework and the three major parts were composed in Hebrew. The evidence for this hypothesis was laid out by J. J. Kneucker in *Das Buch Baruch* (1879), in which a reconstruction of the original Hebrew text was attempted and explained in great detail. Although Kneucker convinced most scholars that 1:1–3:8 reflected a Hebrew original, there was resistance to the idea that the last two parts (3:9–4:4; 4:5–5:9) were written in Hebrew. But D. G. Burke's *Poetry of Baruch* (1982) seems to have established that those two sections also were composed in Hebrew. The criteria used in establishing Hebrew as the original language include the poetic style, the reliance on parallelism, the clarity gained by retroversion (i.e., retranslation) into Hebrew, and the occasional instances where the Greek translator may have misunderstood the Hebrew original.

Of the extant texts of the book of Baruch, the Greek translation of the lost Hebrew original is the most important. The Greek text of Baruch appears in four uncial manuscripts of the Septuagint and in thirty-four minuscule manuscripts (→ Texts, Versions, Manuscripts, Editions). There are also versions in Syriac, Latin, Coptic, Ethiopic, Arabic, and Armenian.

The alleged author of the book is Baruch the son of Neriah, the secretary and companion of Jeremiah. If Baruch was the author, he would have written in the early sixth century B.C. from Babylon. This setting, however, is universally acknowledged today to be a literary fiction, and the book of Baruch is considered an example of pseudepigraphy. The chief arguments for this position are historical and literary. Not only is there no other evidence that Baruch was in Babylon, but also there are so many mistakes and inaccuracies in the narrative framework (1:1–14) that Baruch the son of Neriah could not have been responsible for them. Furthermore, the three major parts (1:15–3:8; 3:9–4:4; 4:5–5:9) are mosaics of biblical passages (Dan. 9, Job 28, and Isa. 40–66) that were most likely not even in existence in the early sixth century B.C.

There is a wide range of opinion about when the book as a whole and its parts were composed. The spectrum of scholarly views extends from the period of the Exile to the second century A.D. Most scholars place the work in the Maccabean period (200–60 B.C.). Further precision in dating is hard to achieve, mainly because of the method of composition (a pastiche of biblical phrases) and because of the lack of clear allusions to contemporary historical events.

Although the work is set in Babylon, the fact that it appears to have been composed in Hebrew suggests that it originated in Palestine. This setting is confirmed to some extent by the narrative framework's insistence that the three major sections were intended as advice for the Jerusalem community. Nothing can be said about the identity of the author. In fact, we must reckon with the possibility of four different authors—one for each major section plus the final redactor who supplied the framework and put the parts together. Of course, we cannot rule out the possibility that one author was responsible for more than one part.

The individual parts of the book of Baruch have distinctive theologies. The exiles' prayer (1:15–3:8) admits that the Exile was the Lord's just punishment of the people on account of their sin but appeals nonetheless to the Lord's goodness and mercy as well as to his own glorification in restoring Israel. The wisdom poem (3:9–4:4) alludes to Israel's situation in exile but offers no sustained reflection on it. The wisdom poem's focus is the elusive quest for wisdom and the real opportunity for Israel to discover wisdom in God's gift of the Law. The poem of consolation (4:5–5:9) returns to the subject of exile but is primarily concerned with offering encouragement about the return from exile under the guidance of the "everlasting one." It presents the Exile as God's just punishment of Israel for its sins.

The joining of these three pieces into a whole provided a reflection on aspects of Israel's exile in Babylon and its restoration to the land. The central position given to the wisdom poem (3:9–4:4) makes the Law into the pivot for moving from the sadness and despair of exile (1:15–3:8) to the confident hope in restoration (4:5–5:9). If the redaction took place during the Maccabean period, the book of Baruch may have been part of the movement of religious restoration that accompanied the Maccabean triumph over Antiochus IV Epiphanes. Since the first part (1:15–3:8) drew extensively on Daniel 9, the final redaction probably occurred at some chronological distance from the events of the Maccabean crisis.

The Hebrew book of Baruch was not included among the canonical books in the Hebrew Bible. Its Greek version appears in many manuscripts of the Septuagint. The Council of Trent in a decree issued on 8 April 1546 listed Baruch among the canonical books of the OT as part of or closely associated with the book of Jeremiah.

COMMENTARY

1:1–14
Narrative Framework

After a prescript (1:1–2), the book sets a "historical scene" (1:3–9) and gives an instruction from the Jewish Babylonian exiles to those Jews who remain in Jerusalem (1:10–14). The prescript provides a more extended genealogy for Baruch than appears in Jer. 32:12. There is no other evidence that Baruch was in Babylon. According to Jer. 43:5–7, he accompanied Jeremiah into Egypt. The date formula "in the fifth year, on the seventh of the month" is peculiar for its omission of the name of the month. Since both Jerusalem and its Temple seem to be intact (see 1:7–14), the date formula may refer to Nebuchadnezzar's first capture of Jerusalem and deportation in 597 B.C. (see 2 Kings 24:10–17).

The historical framework (1:3–9) paints a picture of Baruch reading what follows (1:15–5:9) to the Jewish exiles under the leadership of King Jeconiah (Jehoiachin). The biblical inspiration for the scene may have been Hananiah's

prophecy in Jer. 28:1–4 and Jeremiah's letter to the exiles in Babylon in Jer. 29:1–32. The Jewish community assembled in Babylon by the otherwise unknown river Sud, as they did under Ezekiel's leadership by the river Chebar (see Ezek. 1:1). Their observance of the anniversary of the capture of Jerusalem by mourning, fasting, and praying (1:5) fits in with Jewish custom of the Second Temple period (see Zech. 7:1–7; Neh. 9:1; Ezra 8:21; Dan. 9:3). Their collection for the Jerusalem community (1:6–7) expresses a solidarity between the Babylonian exiles and Jerusalem. The high priest in Jerusalem is the otherwise unknown Jehoiakim (see 1 Chron. 6:13–15). In his first attack on Jerusalem (597 B.C.), Nebuchadnezzar had carried off vessels from the Temple (see 2 Kings 24:13). Likewise, in the second Babylonian attack (587), sacred vessels were taken and brought to Babylon (see 2 Kings 25:13–17). The reference in 1:8–9 is to a substitute set of vessels allegedly made under Zedekiah after the exile of Jehoiachin. Although there is no mention of a substitute set in 2 Kings 24:18–25:7, its existence is a logical necessity if Temple service were to continue. According to Ezra 1:7–11, the Temple vessels were returned to Jerusalem only under the Persian king Cyrus in 538 B.C.

In the instruction that accompanies the collection (1:10–14), the people first urge that the money be spent on material for sacrifices at the Jerusalem Temple (1:10). The assumption is that the Temple worship at Jerusalem continued through the Exile (see Jer. 41:5). The Jerusalem community is asked to pray for the Babylonian king and for the exiles (1:11–13). As in Dan. 5:1, Belshazzar, the son of Nabonidus, is wrongly identified as the son of Nebuchadnezzar. This positive attitude toward the Babylonian kings reflects Jeremiah's own stance (see Jer. 29:7). For the idea of the postexilic community praying for the Persian king and his sons, see Ezra 6:10. The Jerusalem community is also to pray on behalf of the Babylonian exiles (1:13). Their present suffering is interpreted as just punishment for their sins. What follows is to be read as a confession (see Lev. 5:5; 16:21; Num. 5:7) on "the day of the feast and in the days of the solemn assembly." Perhaps there is reference to the Day of Atonement or to the anniversary of Jerusalem's fall.

1:15–3:8
The Exiles' Prayer

Only at 2:11 is God addressed directly in prayer. Before 2:11 the text is a confession of Israel's sinfulness and an admission that the Exile is a just punishment (1:15–2:10). The prayer proper (2:11–35) is followed by a concluding summary

(3:1-8). The prayer starts out as a close rewriting of Daniel's confession in Dan. 9:4-19 with the help of other biblical phrases (esp. from Jeremiah). But by 2:19 the Danielic confession is left behind, because the material has been used up.

1:15-2:10, Preliminary Confession. The obvious biblical model is Dan. 9:7-8, 10-14. Nearly every word from that passage is reproduced here. Phrases from other biblical books fill out and expand the Danielic confession. The one "original" move is the identification of Israel's great sin in Bar. 2:3 as cannibalism. The beginning of the confession of sins (1:15-18) uses the vocabulary of Dan. 9:7-8, 10 (see Neh. 9:26, 32-33). The people are to proclaim that in their experience God has been shown just because their punishments resulted from their own sins. All the people of Judah and Jerusalem, especially their leaders, are accused of failing to obey God's commands.

The admission of communal guilt in Dan. 9:11 is expanded in Bar. 1:19-22 by phrases from Deuteronomy (9:7; 29:19) and Jeremiah (7:24-25; 11:4-5; 26:5; 32:30). A pattern of disobedience set in the Exodus has continued until the Exile. The curse (see Dan. 9:11) is the just outcome of this disobedience. Instead of heeding Moses and the prophets, the people served other gods and did evil. Bar. 2:1-2 is almost a verbatim quotation of Dan. 9:12-13. The mention of the incomparable evil done in Jerusalem (see Dan. 9:12) and the allusion to something written in the law of Moses (see Dan. 9:13) leads the author to identify this evil as cannibalism (Bar. 2:3; Lev. 26:29; Deut. 28:53; Jer. 19:9; Lam. 2:20; 4:10). This terrible crime is presented as the reason why Israel has been subjected to other nations and scattered in exile (2:4). Israel's low state (see Deut. 28:13) is attributed to its sin in refusing to hear the Lord's voice (2:5), once more in terms taken from Dan. 9:8, 11, 16.

The third part of the preliminary confession of guilt (2:6-10) begins as the first part did, by using the contrast between God's righteousness and Israel's shame from Dan. 9:7. Almost every other phrase is taken over directly from Dan. 9:12-14, with additional material from Jer. 7:24 in Bar. 2:8 and Dan. 9:10 in Bar. 2:10. The text confirms the righteousness of God in all the calamities that have befallen Israel and blames them all on Israel's failure to repent and its refusal to hear God's voice and to walk according to the divine commands.

2:11-35, The Prayer Proper. The first part of the prayer proper (2:11-18) appeals to God's activity in the Exodus and admits the people's sin. It urges God to look with favor on Israel for two reasons: that all the earth might know that Israel is called by the Lord's name (2:15) and that Israel may give glory to God and ascribe justice to him (2:18). These themes reappear in the concluding summary (3:6-7). Whereas up to this point God had been talked about in the third person, now with 2:11 God is addressed in the second person. The same shift occurs in Dan. 9:15. Bar. 2:11-12a follows Dan 9:15 closely, with some influence from Jer. 32:21. While Bar. 2:12b-13a corresponds to Dan. 9:16, the reason why God should turn away his wrath ("because we are left as few among the nations") has been imported from Jer. 42:2. The idea of Jerusalem and its people having become a byword among its neighbors (Dan. 9:16b) was used in Bar. 2:4. Bar. 2:14-15 begins and ends with phrases adapted from Dan. 9:17 and Dan. 9:19. The idea of God giving favor before captors appears in Gen. 39:21, and the challenge that God should save Israel so that all the earth might recognize God as Lord occurs in 2 Kings 19:19. After Bar. 2:16 combines Deut. 26:15 and Dan. 9:18, Bar. 2:17-18 contrasts the dead in Sheol who cannot honor God and testify to his justice (see Pss. 6:5; 88:11-12; Isa. 38:18) with even the weakest and frailest living person who can do so. There is probably a personification of Israel in defeat and in exile in 2:18.

The second part of the prayer proper (2:19-26) gives God's mercy as the only reason for approaching God (2:19). In failing to heed Jeremiah's call to serve the king of Babylon, Israel has brought upon itself the severe punishments that it has endured. After alluding to Dan. 9:18b in specifying God's mercy as the basis of the prayer, Bar. 2:19-20 refers back to Dan. 9:6 ("your servants the prophets") as the vehicles by which God makes known his will. God's will for Israel is expressed in Bar. 2:21-23 by a pastiche of quotations from Jer. 27:12-13; 27:9; 7:34; and 48:9. The result of Israel's refusal to serve the king of Babylon has been the desecration of the graves of Israel's ancestors (see Jer. 8:1), the exposure of their bones to heat by day and to cold by night (see Jer. 36:30), the death of the people from various causes (see Jer. 16:4; 32:36), and the desolation of the Jerusalem Temple. These punishments were the consequence of Israel's evil deeds (see Jer. 11:17). According to Bar. 2:27-35, even these punishments were part of God's goodness and mercy toward Israel. Israel should have known this from the Torah (see Deut. 31:24-25; Josh. 8:32). The alleged quotation from the Torah in Bar. 2:29-35 uses phrases from Deuteronomy (esp. 30:1-10) and Jeremiah. It attributes Israel's exile to its stubborn failure to hear God's voice (2:29-30a) and foresees Israel's repentance in the land of exile and its return to God (2:30b-33). It looks forward to resettlement in the ancestral land and great growth for the people (2:34). It concludes with God's promise of an eternal covenant with Israel according to the terms of Jer. 31:31–34 and an eternal homeland as a reversal of 1 Kings 14:15 (2:35).

3:1–8, Conclusion. The prayer ends by appealing to almighty God to hear Israel's prayer and to have mercy by remembering that hearing Israel's prayer is in God's interest. Some ideas of the prayer up to this point reappear, giving the impression that 3:1–8 was intended as a summary and conclusion. The initial approach to God in 3:1–3 contrasts God and Israel: God is almighty and lives forever, whereas Israel is mortal and lives in anguish. Again Israel admits its sin and appeals to God's mercy. The description of the exiles as "dead" in 3:4 may reflect a Greek mistranslation of the Hebrew or the idea of the exiles as spiritually dead (see Ezek. 37:1–14). "Remember," the key word of the prayer, occurs in Bar. 3:5. As in 2:11–18, God is urged to remember Israel for the sake of his own name and so that he may be glorified (3:7). The prayer ends with the plea that God take notice of Israel's plight in exile in language that alludes back to 2:4, 13, 26.

3:9–4:4
The Wisdom Poem

The setting in exile is established both in the beginning (3:10–11) and at the end (4:2–3). Almost every phrase in the poem is found elsewhere in the Hebrew Bible, though this poem does not follow one text as closely as the preceding prayer followed Daniel 9. Its major themes—the elusive character of wisdom and the identification of wisdom and the Law—appear most clearly in Job 28 and Sirach 24, respectively. The wisdom poem exhibits a chiastic structure in five parts: the first (3:9–14) and fifth (4:1–4) stanzas identify wisdom and the Law; the second (3:15–23) and fourth (3:29–38) stanzas reflect on the quest for wisdom; and the middle stanza (3:24–28) joins the two themes in an indirect way.

The poem begins in 3:9 by paralleling (and thus equating) the commandments of life (see Deut. 30:15–20) and wisdom. It proceeds in 3:10–11 to describe Israel's exile in Babylon not only as life in a foreign land but even as existence among the dead in Sheol. Israel's exile is explained in 3:12 as due to its abandoning the fountain of wisdom (see Prov. 18:4), which here must refer to God's Law, as the parallel phrase "the way of God" in 3:13 makes clear. If Israel had kept the Law, it would have dwelt in everlasting peace. The stanza ends in 3:14 with the imperative "learn" plus five "where" clauses. Wisdom, strength, knowledge, long life, and enlightenment and peace are to be found in the Law. The consequence of ignoring the fountain of wisdom has been exile and life among the dead.

Wisdom's elusive character is brought out in the second stanza (3:15–23). The treatment of this theme is reminiscent of Job 28, which contrasts the human search for and discovery of precious metals and stones and the unsuccessful human quest for wisdom. A second piece of background is supplied by the motif of personified wisdom's search for her rightful place (see Sir. 24; 1 *Enoch* 42:1–3; Wisd. of Sol. 7; Col. 1:15–20). From what follows in Bar. 3:16–23, it is clear that the double question in 3:15 about finding wisdom's place and entering its treasures or storehouses is rhetorical. Those who "play with the birds of the heaven" (3:17) are probably described in terms taken from Job 41:5. The description of those who work in silver in 3:18 may be metaphorical; that is, it may be a reference to those who scheme and are greedy for money. The judgment passed on the persons mentioned in 3:16–18 is that they have disappeared into Sheol and others have taken their places (3:19). The cycle repeats itself from generation to generation, according to 3:20–21. Failing to perceive wisdom is described there in terms of not finding the "way" of wisdom. The stanza concludes in 3:22–23 by listing peoples who have not understood wisdom's "way." It mentions two places with a reputation for wisdom: Canaan (Phoenicia; see Ezek. 28:4; Zech. 9:2), and Teman (Edom; see Jer. 49:7; Obad. 1:8–9). Then it denies that Hagar's sons (Ishmaelites; see Gen. 16, 21) found wisdom. The "merchants of Merran" may have been from Midian (see Gen. 37:28). "Storytellers" and the seekers of understanding likewise did not find wisdom.

The central stanza (3:24–28) describes the greatness of the universe created by God and denies that God gave wisdom to the "giants" of old. Since both the first and the fifth stanza identify wisdom as the Law, the third stanza is an oblique testimony to Israel's status as the elect people of God. At first glance, the reference to "the house of God" in 3:24a would seem to be the Jerusalem Temple (see Sir. 24:10–12). But because of 3:24b–25, most commentators conclude that the house of God is the entire created universe. The "giants" were born from the rebellious angels who knew the heavenly secrets and shared them with humans (see 1 *Enoch* 7). According to 3:27–28, they were not given genuine knowledge by God and so they perished.

The fourth stanza (3:29–38) takes up the theme of the elusiveness of wisdom, which was the theme of the second stanza (3:15–23). After establishing that humans cannot find and possess wisdom (3:29–31), it describes God as the wise governor of the universe (3:32–35) and as the one who gave wisdom to Israel in the form of the Law (3:36–38). The section about the failure of humans to find wisdom (3:29–31) is reminiscent not only of Job 28 but also of

Deut. 30:12–13, an indirect preparation for the later identification of wisdom and the Law. The second section (3:32–35) establishes that God alone knows wisdom (see Job 28:23–27) and describes God's governance of the universe. The reference to "light" in 3:33 may mean lightning. Throughout this section the emphasis is on the obedience of creation in carrying out God's plans. The third section (3:36–38) identifies the God who creates and governs with the God of Israel, who gave wisdom to Israel as his beloved people. In the literature of the early church, the description of wisdom in 3:38 ("Afterward she appeared upon the earth and lived among human beings") was applied to Jesus. Modern scholars have argued that the sentence was a Christian addition. It is best taken, however, as a Jewish reference to Wisdom dwelling among human beings on earth (see Prov. 8; Sir. 24, and Wisd. of Sol.).

The final stanza (4:1–4) takes up two themes from the first stanza: Israel's situation in exile and the Law as wisdom. Identifying wisdom with "the book of the commandments of God" (4:1) recalls Sir. 24:23 ("the book of the covenant of the Most High God"). The idea that one's response to God's commands leads either to life or death (4:2) echoes the phrase "the commandments of life" (3:19; see Deut. 30:15–20). The command to Jacob to turn and walk toward wisdom brings back the setting in exile and continues the "way" imagery. Bar. 4:3 may indicate that God might offer wisdom (the Law) to another nation, or it may simply refer to other nations boasting over Israel's defeat. The poem concludes by declaring Israel happy or blessed (see Matt. 5:3–12; Luke 6:20–23) because through the Law it knows what pleases God.

4:5–5:9
The Poem of Consolation

The third major piece concerns the Exile directly. It is a pastiche of biblical phrases taken chiefly from Isaiah 40–55. After an introductory exhortation to the remnant of Israel (4:5–8), the personified Jerusalem addresses the "neighbors of Zion" and the exiles (4:9–29). Then the narrator encourages Jerusalem to look toward the restoration of her children (4:30–5:9). The responsibility for the Exile is placed on God, who used that experience to punish Israel for its sins. Nevertheless, the emphasis in this poem is God's promise to restore the exiles to Jerusalem.

The poem of consolation (4:5–8) begins by calling Israel to "take courage" (see 4:21, 27). In addressing the "memorial of Israel" the author refers to the exiled remnant that keeps alive the memory of Israel. The responsibility for the Exile is placed on Israel's sins, especially in sacrificing to demons rather than to God (4:7).

Nevertheless, exile does not mean the total destruction of God's people (4:6). Israel is accused of forgetting God and of grieving Jerusalem (4:8). The second part of this charge sets the stage for Jerusalem's portrayal as a person addressing first the "neighbors of Zion" in 4:9–16 and then the exiles in 4:17–29.

Those nearby peoples who had seen Zion's capture are personified as "neighbors of Zion." In her address to them (4:9–16), Mother Jerusalem first explains the responsibility and reason for Israel's plight. Despite appearances, God is really the one who brought about the Exile. The favorite epithet for God in this part of the book is the "everlasting one" (see 4:8, 10, 14, 20, 22, 24, 35; 5:2). Jerusalem's role as a mother deprived of her sons is portrayed poignantly in 4:10–13. She is both widowed and made childless. The fault is with Israel for turning aside from God's Law. Next (4:14–16) Mother Jerusalem urges the "neighbors of Zion" to remember Israel's captivity when God brought their enemies against them. After a repetition of 4:9b, the Babylonians are described in highly negative terms taken from Deut. 28:49–50. This first address has put in proper theological perspective the major actors in the Exile: God, Israel, and the Babylonians.

The second address (4:17–29) is directed to the Jewish exiles, though the transition is made obliquely by a rhetorical question. It begins and ends with the promise that God, who brought these disasters upon Israel, will rescue it (4:18, 29). In between, the text emphasizes that God brought these calamities on Israel (see 4:25, 27) and that God will deliver Israel (see 4:21–24, 27). God is the "everlasting one" and the "holy one" (4:20, 22), who hears the people's prayers (4:27, 28). In a reversal of the language of Isa. 52:1 and 61:3, Mother Jerusalem puts on the "sackcloth of supplication" (see 4:20) to pray on behalf of her children. In Bar. 5:1, she will put on forever the beauty of the glory of God. Twice (4:21, 27) she urges her children to "take courage" and pray to God, in full confidence that her captive children will be restored to her (4:23). The "neighbors of Zion," who had seen Israel's captivity, will see its glorious restoration (4:24). The enemies of Israel will be punished (4:25). Israel itself is urged to be patient (4:25) in its exile, though the reason for the Exile is traced to its own resolve to go astray from God (4:28).

Having addressed the people in 4:5–8 and narrated Mother Jerusalem's address in 4:9–29, the poet now speaks directly to Jerusalem in 4:30–5:9. Three imperatives ("take courage" in 4:30, "look" in 4:36, and "arise" in 5:5) divide the text into stanzas. The first stanza (4:30–35) describes the fall of Babylon, the captor of Israel, as part of the consolation of Israel (see Isa. 40:11; 51:3, 12; 61:2–3). A threefold reversal of the beatitude form ("wretched will those be . . .") in 4:31–32 introduces the theme of reversal in 4:33–34. God is described as the one who "named" Jerusalem; in 5:4 the city is called "peace of righteousness and glory of godliness." According to 4:35, the "everlasting one" will bring fire on Babylon (see Isa. 34:10; Jer. 50:32; 51:30, 58), and it will become an abode for demons (see Isa. 13:21; 34:14).

The second and third stanzas presuppose the picture of Jerusalem watching the return of the exiles (see Isa. 40:9–11). Personified Jerusalem first is told (4:36–5:4) to look at her sons returning to her at God's command. For the idea of the exiles coming from "east and west" in 4:37, see Isa. 62:6–9. At 5:1–2, the "sackcloth of supplication" described in 4:20 is put off by Jerusalem and replaced by the cloak of God's righteousness and the headdress of glory (see Isa. 61:10). In doing so, she conforms to Isa. 52:1; 61:3. In 5:3–4, the motifs of God's splendor (4:24) and God's naming Jerusalem (4:30) are brought to fulfillment.

Then the personified Jerusalem (5:5–9) is told once more to look for her returning children, as in Isa. 40:9–11. Here, however, the focus is the exiles who come back. The return takes place at the command of God and under God's leadership. The exiles rejoice that God has remembered them (5:5) and are carried in glory (5:6). In fulfillment of Isa. 40:4, their way will be made straight and easy (5:7). According to 5:8, God will even make the woods and trees provide shade. A close parallel (probably dependent on Bar. 5:8) appears in *Pss. Sol.* 11:6–7. The light of God's glory (see Isa. 60:1–3) will lead Israel back, with personified Mercy and Righteousness beside him (5:9).

Bibliography

Burke, D. G. *The Poetry of Baruch.* Chico, CA: Scholars Press, 1982.

Moore, C. A. "I Baruch." In *Daniel, Esther, and Jeremiah: The Additions.* Anchor Bible, 44. Garden City, NY: Doubleday, 1977. Pp. 255–316.

Schürer, E. *The History of the Jewish People in the Age of Jesus Christ.* Vol. 3, pt. 2. New English version revised and edited by G. Vermes, F. Miller, and M. Goodman. Edinburgh: Clark, 1987. Pp. 734–43.

Tov, E. *The Book of Baruch, Also Called I Baruch (Greek and Hebrew).* Missoula, MT: Scholars Press, 1975.

Whitehouse, O. C. "I Baruch." In *The Apocrypha and Pseudepigrapha of the Old Testament.* 2 vols. Edited by R. H. Charles. Oxford: Clarendon, 1913. Vol. 1, pp. 569–95.

LETTER OF JEREMIAH

DANIEL J. HARRINGTON

INTRODUCTION

The Letter of Jeremiah purports to contain advice from Jeremiah to Jews exiled in Babylon on why they should avoid participating in non-Jewish worship. The structure of the book is set by nine refrains (vv. 16, 23, 29, 40, 44, 52, 56, 65, 69) in which the writer concludes that the pagan idols are not gods at all. After providing a historical setting in the exiled community at Babylon (vv. 1–6), the work gives ten reflections on the foolishness and uselessness of idol worship, concluding all but the last with the refrain. The reflections are repetitive and without any clear logical progression.

The work has been transmitted in Greek and in versions dependent on the Greek text, but there is a scholarly consensus, based on the style of the Greek and some probable mistranslations, that Hebrew was its original language. In the two most important Greek manuscripts of the Septuagint (Vaticanus and Alexandrinus) it appears as a separate book between Lamentations and Ezekiel. The Latin tradition attaches it to the book of Baruch, and so it is often taken as the sixth chapter of Baruch.

The scene for Jeremiah's letter is the exile of Jews in 597 B.C. under Nebuchadnezzar (see v. 2). The idea of a letter from Jeremiah to the exiled community in Babylon derived from Jeremiah 29, while the content and many of the phrases have been taken over from Jeremiah 10 and other biblical polemics against idol worship (see Pss. 115:4–8; 135:15–18; Isa. 40:18–20; 41:6–7; 46:1–7). Indeed, the work as a whole is a rewritten and expanded version of Jeremiah 10, taking its thrust from the Aramaic slogan in Jer. 10:11: "May the gods who did not make the heavens and the earth perish from the earth and from under the heavens."

The statement in v. 3 that the Babylonian exile would last "up to seven generations" (cf. Jer. 29:10, where it is supposed to last only seventy years) is sometimes taken as indicating composition late in the fourth century B.C. Since one generation lasts about forty years (see Judg. 3:11, 30), subtracting 280 years from 597 B.C. would give a date of 317 B.C. The allusion to the work in 2 Macc. 2:1–3 and the discovery of a fragment of the Greek version in a Qumran Cave 7 manuscript dated about 100 B.C. suggest the second century B.C. as the latest possible date of composition. If it was composed in Hebrew, a setting in the land of Israel and a time in which attitudes toward foreign cults were hostile (perhaps during the crisis under Antiochus IV Epiphanes) seem likely. The writer, however, is quite familiar with Babylonian customs and may have written in Babylon at an earlier time.

The Letter of Jeremiah provides a handbook of arguments why Jews should not worship foreign gods. The idols are powerless, helpless, and lifeless, without sense perception or consciousness. They are human fabrications and cannot do what the God of Israel does. They serve no purpose. Their manufacturers, priests, and devotees are shameful, deceitful, and foolish.

The Letter of Jeremiah is not considered canonical by Jews or Protestants. Catholics take it as chap. 6 of Baruch but do not use it in the current lectionary.

COMMENTARY

1–7, Historical Setting. The warnings against idolatry in Babylon are placed in the context of Jeremiah's letter to the exiles there (see Jer. 29). Since Nebuchadnezzar was not really responsible for the exile of 587 (see 2 Kings 25:11), this exile must have occurred in 597 (see 2 Kings 24:14–16). The warnings are addressed to Jews in Babylon who might be attracted to participation in foreign worship. The promise of return to Israel after "seven generations" (v. 3) can be taken as an indication of the date of the book's composition (shortly after Alexander's conquest). Or perhaps it was only a way of dealing with Jer. 29:10 ("When seventy years are completed for Babylon, I will visit you and fulfill for you my promise and bring you back to this place"), when in fact the return from exile had not been complete. When tempted to join in Babylonian worship, the exiles are urged to confess in their hearts the God of Israel, who will protect them with his angel (see Exod. 23:23; 32:34).

8–16, First Warning. Even though the idols are dressed and decorated in great splendor, they remain powerless. Made with great skill, they nevertheless cannot speak (v. 8). The gold and silver used in their crowns is taken by the priests for their own purposes and shared with

861

the temple prostitutes (vv. 9–11a). Their beautiful garments corrode, and their faces gather dust (vv. 11b–13). Even their weapons and symbols of power are useless (vv. 14–15). The conclusion is that, since the idols are not gods, the exiles should not worship them (v. 16).

17–23, Second Warning. The idols lack sense perception and consciousness. After comparing the idols to a broken dish in their uselessness (v. 17a), the Letter presents a series of pictures intended to show that they are not conscious of anyone or anything outside themselves. The feet of the worshipers raise dust up into their eyes (v. 17b). The idols are locked in like prisoners (v. 18) and cannot even see the lamps lit for them (v. 19). They are blocks of wood, and their garments are eaten by worms (v. 20). Smoke blackens their faces (v. 21), and birds and animals alight on them (v. 22). Their total lack of sensitivity proves that they are not gods and therefore deserve no fear (v. 23).

24–29, Third Warning. The idols are lifeless, helpless, and senseless. Not only would the idols' gold tarnish unless polished by a human being, but also in the process of manufacture and purchase (vv. 24–25) the idols are totally unconscious. They have to be carried, need to be set upright, and cannot right themselves (vv. 26–27). The sacrifices offered to the idols are used selfishly by the priests and their wives and are even touched by menstruating women (vv. 28–29; see Lev. 12:1–8). The lifelessness, helplessness, and senselessness of the idols proves that they are not gods and do not deserve worship (v. 29b).

30–40a, Fourth Warning. The idols do not act like God. The first part of this warning (vv. 30–33) pictures women serving meals to the idols and priests either behaving in grotesque ways or stealing clothes from the idols. The second part (vv. 34–38) focuses on their inability to achieve anything. The idols cannot pay back good or evil, set up or depose kings, give money or wealth, demand the fulfillment of vows, rescue people, and so forth. These things, of course, are done by Israel's God. The idols are no better than rocks, and there is no reason to worship them (vv. 39–40a).

40b–44, Fifth Warning. The practices connected with idol worship are foolish. The first example (v. 41) is bringing a man who cannot speak before the idol in hope of a cure when the idol itself cannot speak. How can this powerless object give power to a human being? The second example (v. 43) involves the Babylonian practice of cultic prostitution described by Herodotus in *Histories* 1.199 as the most disgraceful of the Babylonian customs. A god that would allow such a custom cannot be a real god deserving worship.

45–52, Sixth Warning. The idols are human fabrications, manufactured by mortal craftsmen who engage in a deceit (vv. 45–47). Thus when the priests futilely consult the idols in time of war, all will know that the idols were only products of human ingenuity (vv. 48–51).

53–56, Seventh Warning. The idols are powerless. They cannot do what God does—set up kings, give rain, judge, or deliver (vv. 53–54). When fire breaks out in their temple, the priests escape but the idols perish in the flames (v. 55). When a king or an enemy comes, they offer no resistance (v. 56). Since they cannot do what one would expect from God, why should anyone imagine that they are gods?

57–65, Eighth Warning. Since the idols are powerless and a god is supposed to be powerful, they are the most useless things imaginable. Their powerlessness is demonstrated by their inability to protect themselves from robbers (vv. 57–58). Persons, even inanimate objects and the forces of nature perform their assigned functions (vv. 59–63a), but idols do not perform the function of real gods (vv. 63b–65).

66–69, Ninth Warning. The theme of the uselessness of the idols is continued by showing that they do not act like gods, the sun and moon, or even wild beasts (who at least can flee danger). Since there is no evidence that the idols act like gods, therefore there is no reason to treat them like gods.

70–73, Tenth Warning. The argument is concluded by comparing the useless idols to scarecrows (see Jer. 10:5), a thorn bush, and a dead body. Just as their clothing rots, so will the idols rot. Therefore the just person who has no idols will be far from reproach.

Bibliography

Ball, C. J. "Epistle of Jeremy." In *The Apocrypha and Pseudepigrapha of the Old Testament*. 2 vols. Edited by R. H. Charles. Oxford: Clarendon, 1913. Vol. 1, pp. 596–611.

Moore, C. A. "Epistle of Jeremiah." In *Daniel, Esther, and Jeremiah: The Additions*. Anchor Bible, 44. Garden City, NY: Doubleday, 1977. Pp. 317–58.

THE ADDITIONS TO DANIEL

ROBERT DORAN

GENERAL INTRODUCTION

The Additions to Daniel consist of three extended passages not found in the Masoretic Text (MT) of Daniel, but found in the two different Greek versions of the OT, the Septuagint (LXX) and Theodotion (→ Texts, Versions, Manuscripts, Editions): the Song of the Three Youths, Susanna, and Bel and the Dragon.

The LXX places both of the narrative additions after the MT Daniel, with Bel and the Dragon standing before Susanna. Theodotion, on the other hand, attempted to integrate the additions with MT Daniel, so that the progress of Daniel from youth to old age is described. The Susanna narrative, placed before MT Daniel, shows the rise to prominence of the young Daniel; Bel and the Dragon extends the chronological sequence of MT Daniel 1–6 (which includes the reigns of Nebuchadnezzar, Belshazzar, and Darius) by adding two episodes set at the court of Cyrus.

Song of the Three Youths

INTRODUCTION

Contents

In both versions this passage lies between MT Dan. 3:23 and 3:24 and consists of three unequal parts: first, the Prayer of Azariah, the Hebrew name of Abednego (vv. 1–22); second, a short prose account of the fate of the three Jews in the furnace (vv. 23–27); third, a hymn sung by the three youths while in the furnace (vv. 28–68). The relationship between MT Dan. 3:23 and 3:24 is highly dramatic. The three Jewish youths are thrown into an incredibly hot furnace and presumably destroyed, when suddenly Nebuchadnezzar is perturbed and in astonishment claims to see four men in the fire, the fourth looking like a divine being. Nebuchadnezzar reacts to the miracle by praising the God of the Jews. The author of the Addition must have found the transition too sudden and provided the details of the miracle. As in Exodus 15, 1 Samuel 2, and elsewhere, the narrative is supplemented by poetic material. Deliverance comes in response to prayer, and deliverance demands a hymn of praise. The Addition thus emphasizes the reciprocal covenantal faithfulness of God and the three young men.

Original Language and Date

The text of the LXX and Theodotion are very similar, the major differences occurring in the narrative sections of the Addition. There are no compelling linguistic arguments for assuming the Greek to be a translation of an originally Hebrew or Aramaic text.

The Addition must have been composed before the LXX translation, which is usually dated ca. 100 B.C.

Religious Significance

That much psalmody was written in the postexilic period has been confirmed by the extensive poetic materials found among the Dead Sea Scrolls, not only the major collection of Thanksgiving Hymns (IQH), but also other fragmentary nonbiblical psalmic material, and the Prayer of Nabonidus (4QPrNab). The prayer and hymn in this Addition must be set within this context—the contents of both are commonplace for the period. The Addition emphasizes that heroes must be men of piety and that the basis of their wisdom is fear of the Lord.

COMMENTARY

1–2, Introduction. In Theodotion only Azariah says the prayer, while in the LXX all three pray. The Addition is variously prepared for in the translation of MT Dan. 3:23–24. In Theodotion no mention is made here of the death of those who threw the three youths into the furnace, but their death is mentioned in vv. 23–25 of the Addition. The LXX is closer to MT in maintaining the deaths in LXX Dan. 3:23; in vv. 23–25 of the Addition, the LXX distin-

863

guishes between those who threw the youths in the furnace and those who were stoking the fire. It is these latter who die in vv. 23–25.

3–22, The Prayer. After a brief introductory invocation (v. 3), the prayer divides into two parts: a proclamation of God's justice in punishing the sin of Israel (vv. 4–10); and a petition for mercy, a pledge of worship, and a call for God to help (vv. 11–22). Whether spoken by Azariah alone or by the three youths, the "we" of the prayer is collective: the prayer is a communal lament, recognizing the national guilt and pleading for national deliverance. The themes are traditional: confession of sin (cf. Hos. 14:2–8; Jer. 3:22b–4:2; 14:7–9); the just judgment of God (cf. Tob. 3:2–6; Add. to Esther 14:3–19); retribution against enemies (cf. Pss. 60:12; 79:12; 80:16; 83:13–18). Overall, the closest parallels are the prayers in Dan. 9:4–20 and Bar. 1:15–3:8.

Although the description of the enemies of the nation in v. 9 refers primarily to the persecution of Nebuchadnezzar that constitutes the plot of Daniel 3, ancient readers undoubtedly applied the description to the persecution of the Jews by Antiochus IV Epiphanes in 168–164 B.C.

The call for God's help is based on the covenant made to Abraham in Gen. 22:17. In contrast to the prayers in Dan. 9:4–20 and Bar. 1:15–3:8, no explicit reference is made to Moses, perhaps because the poetic contrast between the covenant promise of numerous descendants and the present smallness of the nation (vv. 13–14) most closely resembles the situation of Abraham. The substitution of a contrite soul and a humbled spirit for sacrifice in the now destroyed Temple continues the prophetic demand for proper conduct alongside the sacrificial ritual (Isa. 1:10–17; Amos 5:21–27; Ps. 51:16–17) and echoes the statements of Ben Sira that keeping the law brings atonement (Sir. 34:18–35:20).

23–27, Short Prose Interlude. Moore rightly notes that logically the angel should have cooled down the fire before Azariah began his prayer. He concludes with other scholars that this prose interlude originally introduced the following hymn of the three youths and that later the prayer of Azariah was inserted before this interlude.

28–68, The Hymn of the Three Youths. Following a brief introduction (v. 28), the hymn divides into five sections: first, a doxology to God enthroned in his heavenly temple (vv. 29–34); second, a call to praise addressed to the heavenly creatures (vv. 35–41); third, a call to praise addressed to creatures between heaven and earth (vv. 42–51); fourth, a call to praise addressed to creatures on earth (vv. 52–59); and fifth, a call to praise addressed to all humanity, particularly Israel (vv. 60–68).

The first section of the hymn is clearly distinct from the rest. It addresses God directly and, while the rest of the hymn has a repeated refrain in the second half of each verse, this section varies the refrain. There is no reason to conclude, however, that this first section was an originally independent composition. The traditional quality of the hymnic material is shown by the striking agreement between vv. 29–30 and LXX Tob. 8:5. Verse 31 refers to God's heavenly temple, as one also finds in Ps. 11:4; Hab. 2:20; and most fully in the "Songs of the Sabbath Sacrifice" from the Dead Sea Scrolls (4QShir-Shab).

The following sections of the hymn (vv. 35–68) provide close correspondences to Psalm 148. The repeated use of the same refrain in each verse is the same poetic device found in Psalm 136, and the wording of vv. 67–68 echoes Ps. 136:1–3. There is some variation in order between the LXX and Theodotion, particularly in vv. 44–51, but such is to be expected in lists of this kind. The overall progression from the heavens to earth and finally to humans remains the same, however, and follows the general order of creation in Genesis 1. The hymn then specifies the praise to be offered by Israel, and in this is similar to Sirach 24.

Susanna

INTRODUCTION

Contents

This Addition describes how the young, wise Daniel intervenes to save the beautiful Susanna who had been condemned to death for adultery on the testimony of false witnesses, elders of the Jews who had been rebuffed in their advances to her.

There are striking differences between the LXX and Theodotion in the telling of the story. Since the major English translations give only the Theodotionic version, emphasis will be placed here on providing an adequate presentation of the LXX. (For an English translation of the LXX, see Moore, pp. 99, 104, 114–15.)

First, the LXX begins at v. 5b–6 and has the quality of a superscription: "Concerning those about whom the Master said, 'Lawlessness came forth from Babylon' from elders, judges, those who seemed to guide the people; and lawsuits used come to them from other cities." Second, the conclusion to the story also differs: "Wherefore the youths are the beloved of Jacob because of their integrity. Let us take care that the youths become courageous sons. For if the youths live reverently, a spirit of understanding and insight will be in them for ever." Third, several additional sentences in Theodotion are not found in the LXX, and there is very little verbatim agreement between the two tellings.

Some of the Theodotionic additions (e.g., vv. 11, 31b, 36b, 39) simply add dramatic color. Others are more significant. While Theodotion situates the trial scene in the house of Susanna's husband, Joakim, the LXX places the trial at the synagogue of the city (v. 28), emphasizing the involvement of all the Jewish community. Such an emphasis coincides with the preference of the LXX for titles rather than proper names: Susanna in Theodotion v. 22 is the Jewess in LXX v. 22; in the body of the narrative Daniel is known as "the youth" four times in the LXX (vv. 44, 52, 55, 60), while Theodotion uses this appellation only once (v. 45); on two occasions the LXX emphasizes that the elders were judges (vv. 29, 34), where Theodotion simply designates them as elders (see Engel). This contrast between the two protagonists in the LXX is sharply sketched in a clause in v. 52, a clause not found in Theodotion, "and they led the elder to the youth," and is continued in the LXX's conclusion, where stress is placed on the importance of youths in the Jewish community. At the very spot where the Jewish community met, the synagogue, the LXX contrasts the officials of that community, the elder-judges, with the youth, and the faithful Jewess with the perverted leaders. Theodotion has softened this contrast so that it is more a story of a particular attempt by two wicked elders against an individual woman who was saved by a young man, Daniel.

Religious Significance

The narrrative can be compared to stories in other cultures concerning an innocent woman falsely accused (see Thompson, motif K2112) and a clever young man (see Thompson, motif J1140–50). The Jewish author has employed such a typology to convey his own particular message.

In the LXX version of the story the leaders of the people are contrasted with the youth to whom a spirit of insight has been given (v. 45). While Theodotion speaks of God rousing the Holy Spirit already in the youth, the LXX has an angel injecting the Spirit into the youth. The leaders of the people are viewed with suspicion. As the statement in v. 51b (found only in the LXX) indicates, one should not believe the elders simply because they are elders. Insight belongs not by right to those in authority; it is given. The conclusion, formulated to draw the moral of the story, states that the education of youths is to be carefully guarded—they will live reverently and a spirit of insight will be in them. Such a conclusion seems an attempt to assert control over the youths, for the thrust of the story itself leads in the opposite direction, to a critique of institutional authority and a distinction between institutional office and the spirit of insight.

In the Theodotionic version the description of the two evil men as members of a larger group of elders who held their position as judges for that year does away with the sharp contrast developed by the LXX. The elders are simply two wicked men who happen to be elders, not the only leaders of the community. The fuller description of Susanna and her family heightens the sense that this is a narrative about one event that occurred, not a caution against institutional office as such. Susanna becomes a model of piety in the face of coercion to act wickedly, and the story serves to explain how Daniel rose to prominence among the exiled Jewish community (v. 64).

Original Language

The Susanna narrative has not been found among the Qumran fragments of Daniel, and there are no external criteria for claiming that the Greek Susanna is a translation of a Semitic original, whether Hebrew or Aramaic. One argument for the originality of the Greek version is the existence of the puns based on Greek in vv. 54–55. But a Greek translator could have made such puns in Greek because there were puns in the Semitic original, just as English translators of the Greek text try to do. The Greek contains many Semitisms, however, and most scholars have concluded that there was an original Semitic version of the Susanna story.

A secondary question, given the differences between the LXX and Theodotion, is whether Theodotion is a revision of the LXX, or whether there were two Semitic texts, one behind the LXX and another behind Theodotion. To such questions no certain answer is possible, but the neater solution is, I believe, not to multiply nonexistant Semitic originals unless absolutely necessary.

Date and Setting

If there was an original Semitic narrative, it must predate the LXX translation of Daniel, that is, predate 100 B.C. It has been suggested that the suspicious attitude toward authority figures within the Jewish community in the LXX might provide a clue to the date. But one should remember that stories poking fun at authority figures are always popular, as are stories of beautiful virtuous maidens saved from lecherous leaders. Dating of such stories must always remain surmise.

COMMENTARY

1–6, Introduction. In the Theodotionic version, these verses introduce readers to the actors and the scene of the narrative, the house of Joakim. Joakim's wealth and prominence in the community are stressed. While Susanna receives social standing only as the wife of the rich Joakim, Theodotion emphasizes her piety and her instruction in the law of Moses.

That the LXX begins with v. 5b has been persuasively argued recently by Engel from the evidence of certain Greek manuscripts and the Syriac version. In the LXX, vv. 5b–6 act as a titular description of the narrative and underscore what was said above about the narrative as a critique of authority.

The quotation of God's word in v. 5b is problematic. It is not even certain how far the quotation extends, though the citation is probably "Lawlessness came forth from Babylon." This saying is not found in the MT or LXX, although the form of the saying is common: from x will come y, as, for example, in Isa. 2:3; 45:23; 51:4; Jer. 1:14; 23:15.

7–41
The Attempted Seduction and Trial of Susanna

The two main parts of this section in Theodotion are vv. 7–27 and vv. 28–41. In v. 7 the people leave Joakim's house; in v. 28 they return. The first part divides into three acts: vv. 7–14, the growing passion of the elders; vv. 15–18, the opportunity while Susanna wishes to bathe; vv. 19–27, the confrontation and propositioning of Susanna.

The LXX also divides into two parts, although here the division is marked not by the crowd's return to the house but by a change of scene to the synagogue of the city (v. 28b). The first part has two acts: vv. 7–10 describe the sudden infatuation of the two elders; vv. 12–28, the sexual harassment of Susanna.

7–27, The Attempted Seduction. The narrative in Theodotion develops skillfully. Readers sense how the elders' day-after-day glimpse of the beautiful Susanna strolling carefree in the lush garden gradually changes to a desire to view her and finally to passion; how that passion at first shames but then bonds them in a conspiracy for both to have their way with her. The author heightens the sensuality with the evocation of the beautiful maiden bathing in the heat of the day, a motif found in the Bathsheba incident at 2 Sam. 11:2, and the elaboration, found in Jub. 33:2 and T. Reub. 3:10–4:1, of Reuben's sleeping with Jacob's concubine Bilhah. The innocence of Susanna is underlined, as it is said twice that the elders were hidden and unseen.

The climax is the confrontation of the two elders with Susanna. Moore emphasizes that the demand of v. 20 ("Let us have you") is an "indelicate Greek expression for sexual intercourse," and the elders' coarse speech contrasts with their more dignified language before the people at vv. 37–38. The heightened psychological description in Theodotion continues as Susanna groans (v. 22). Her screams show her to be true to the Mosaic law of Deut. 22:24. The scene of the screaming maiden, the shouting elders, and the running servants occurs only in Theodotion.

The LXX narrative is more restrained and less developed as a story. Susanna is described as an elegant woman, and the names of her husband and father are given, both to increase the sense of her social propriety and to stress the impropriety of the elders as they act against "the wife of their brother of the sons of Israel" (v. 7). Their desire appears in the LXX as a result of a chance meeting, not as a gradual development. The innocence of Susanna in all this is stated—she does not know what has happened.

The scene shifts to the very next day, as the two elders try to beat each other out like two lovesick adolescents. One elder interrogates the other, and then both confess (vv. 13–14). The use of legal terminology is nicely ironic. Instead of confession leading to repentance, they bond together against the innocent woman and try to rape her. The Greek term *ekbiazesthai* in v. 19 reflects the case law of Deut. 22:25–28 and indicates how the elders are breaking the law. Susanna's speech echoes the response of Joseph to Potiphar's wife in Gen. 39:9, as well as the words of David in 2 Sam. 24:14 and the martyred brothers in 2 Maccabees 7. The emotional scene in Theodotion vv. 24–27 is missing: in the LXX the elders slink away threatening revenge for their rebuff.

28–41 (Theodotion; 28b–41, LXX), The Trial. In Theodotion the trial takes place at the house of Joakim. The inner psychology of the two elders is given, both in their vicious desire to have Susanna killed (v. 28) as well as in their desire to see her beauty (v. 32). The inner emotions of Susanna are depicted (v. 35) and also the outward show of emotion by her household (v. 33). Theodotion emphasizes the beauty of Susanna but tones down the LXX account and has only Susanna's veil lifted, as in the ordeal of the suspected adulteress in Num. 5:11–31. The ritual of the laying on of hands (v. 34) follows that of Lev. 24:14 against the man who blasphemes. The exact meaning of the ritual is debated, but the community, through the witnesses, is physically pressing the communal uncleanness that has resulted from the breakdown of social order onto the sinner and then expelling/exterminating that ritual impurity from its midst. The outward ritual act contrasts strikingly with the inner purity of Susanna. But the combined word of the elders (vv. 36–40) carries weight, and Susanna is condemned to death.

The LXX shifts the scene to the city synagogue, and the authoritative position of the two sinners is stressed. To the synagogue comes the whole household of Susanna. The refinement of Susanna contrasts with the lust of the elders who order her to be uncovered. The LXX does not specify, as does Theodotion, that this refers only to her head, and Zimmermann draws attention to the discussion of the ordeal of the suspected adulteress in m. Soṭa 1:5, where the priest was not only to loosen her hair, as in Num. 5:11–31, but to tear her garments so that he lay bare her bosom. Both ritual ordeals, however, were to apply only if there were no witnesses. In its narrative context this action of the elders serves only to shame Susanna and treat her as a harlot (Hos. 2:10; Ezek. 16:37–39) before the actual trial is over.

The LXX places the prayer of Susanna and the positive response of God before the false testimony of the elders. To a certain extent this diminishes the drama of the narrative. The false witness of the two elders in the LXX is almost self-incriminatory as they reveal themselves to be voyeurs of the alleged criminal act.

42–62

The Clever Young Man

With the condemnation pronounced against her, all seems over for Susanna. But a new actor, God, enters the scene and he uses as his agent the young man Daniel. The name Daniel, "My Judge is God" (Heb.; → Daniel), is most apt, as Daniel both defends the innocent and corrects a perversion of justice.

The method Daniel uses to uncover the truth is the separate cross-examination of witnesses. Thus the narrative contrasts the evil elders who relied on their authority with the clever judge, Daniel. Such contrast is a motif found frequently in folk literature (see Thompson, motif J1141.3; 1153).

Daniel separates himself from the previous procedure. His intervention is similar to that demanded by m. Sanh. 6:1–2 whereby, when a person is being led out to be stoned, a herald must call out his crime and request that anyone who could show the criminal's innocence step forward. Daniel himself demands a careful examination as required by Deut. 19:16–21 (cf. Deut. 13–14; 17:4). Since the community has not followed such procedure, Daniel can call them foolish, lacking Torah wisdom. The wisdom of Daniel is further demonstrated by his ability with words, as he puns the responses of the two elders (vv. 54 and 58).

The death of the elders follows the principle of retribution of Deut. 19:18–21 and is in line with what the rabbis later claim was the Pharisaic interpretation of the law, that false witnesses should be killed even if the falsely accused had not been executed. The Sadducees held a more lenient position (m. Mak. 1:6).

This section in the LXX is clearly marked off from the previous narrative by the exclamatory "And behold" as well as by the appearance of the new actor, the angel. The major differences in this passage between the two versions have already been noted in the introduction.

When Daniel interrogates the second elder, the LXX reads, "Why was your seed corrupted like that of Sidon and not of Judah?" Sidon is the son of Canaan (Gen. 10:15) and, in the Table of Nations, Sidon's descendants would seem to include Sodom and Gomorrah (Gen. 10:19).

As the LXX in v. 7 had noted the family aspect of the sin— Susanna was the wife of their brother—so at the end the LXX notes how the elders were punished as they had intended to do to their sister (v. 62). The LXX details the punishment: "They judged them to be false witnesses, led them off, and threw them into a ravine. Then the angel of the Lord threw fire through their midst." The evildoers are taken outside the city to be stoned (see m. Sanh. 6:4). The combination of stoning and fire is found also in the punishment of Achan (Josh. 7:25). Here the angel takes part in the punishment as if it were one of the community as the people are purified of the evil in their midst.

63–64

The Epilogue

Theodotion provides a happy ending, as befits the way the author has fashioned the narrative as exemplar, while the LXX draws a lesson for readers.

Bel and the Dragon

INTRODUCTION

Comparison of the Septuagint and Theodotion

Bel and the Dragon deals with the clever success of Daniel at court and with the danger that success brought him. Daniel shows his superiority by exposing as nongods what the Babylonians and their king worship—a statue of Bel and a snake/dragon.

The two Greek versions tell substantially the same story, but details vary; for example, in v. 11 in Theodotion the priests suggest the procedures to follow, while in the LXX Daniel does so. The main difference is, as noted in the General Introduction above, the way Theodotion has integrated this story with MT Daniel. The LXX begins its account as if readers knew nothing about the Daniel of this narrative: "There was a certain man, a priest whose name was Daniel, son of Abal, a confidant of the king of Babylon." These details about this Daniel do not contradict anything readers of LXX Daniel previously knew. It is surprising, however, to be given such genealogical details at the beginning of this narrative. It is as though one were introducing Daniel for the first time, a Daniel different from the Daniel of chaps. 1–12. A priest named Daniel is known to have returned from the exile in Babylon (Ezra 8:2; Neh. 10:6). As noted above, the LXX Susanna is a story of how God gives insight to youths, not a narrative showing how the young Daniel came to be well known among the people. As Susanna comes after Bel and the Dragon in the LXX, the young Daniel in the LXX would again be differentiated from the priest and confidant of the king of Babylon. These two narratives in the LXX are clearly marked off from the Daniel of MT Daniel, while Theodotion has integrated them to provide a fitting beginning and end to the career of Daniel.

Another marked difference between the two versions is the identification of the Habakkuk of the story. The Theodotionic version clearly designates him as "the prophet Habakkuk in Judea" (v. 33). There is no such identification in the LXX: Habakkuk is simply someone taking a bowl of stew and a jug of wine out to the harvesters (v. 33). The narrator does not say whether he is in Judea or in the Babylonian countryside. Theodotion has neatly tied Bel and the Dragon to biblical literature, identifying an unknown character as a known prophet.

Narrative Structure

The narrative has been nicely welded together into a single plot. The LXX and Theodotion use different connectives, but in both versions the narrative coheres. The major actors remain the same throughout—Daniel, the king, and the Babylonians. Both Bel and the snake are characterized as objects that the Babylonians worship (vv. 3, 23). After the snake is destroyed, all those from the region (LXX v. 23; Theodotion: "the Babylonians") came against Daniel to complain that the king had become a Jew, had overthrown Bel, and had killed the snake. The story of the threat to Daniel's life is thus strongly connected with the preceding narrative. The king's first confession of Bel's greatness (v. 18) and his final confession of Daniel's God (v. 41) use almost exactly the same formulas, even though LXX and Theodotion offer minor differences. This repetition is highly significant and helps unite the narrative. The LXX further connects the two episodes by the phrase "in that place" in v. 23, but also by developing the motif of eating. This motif dominates the Bel episode (vv. 7, 8, 9, 11, 15, 17, 21). In the snake episode the king claims, "You cannot say he is bronze. Look, he lives and eats and drinks." Daniel then destroys the snake by offering it fatal food (v. 23). In the Theodotionic version the connection is made through the notion of life: Daniel worships the living God (v. 5), while Bel is not a living God (v. 6); the king asserts that Daniel cannot say that the snake is not a living God (v. 24), but Daniel insists that it is his God who lives (v. 25). The links between all the episodes in both versions are so pervasive that the narrative must be seen to be a whole. Such stories, of course, could theoretically have existed independently, but there is no evidence that they did.

Structurally, the narrative has the same basic organization as that found in Daniel 6:

	Daniel	LXX
High Status of Daniel	6:1–3	1–27
Threat to Status	6:4–18	28–33
Deliverance	6:19–22	34–41
Status Restored	6:23–28	42

Both are stories of conflict, but different emphases are important. Daniel 6 pays little attention to the details of how Daniel achieved his high status, while that is precisely the emphasis in Bel and the Dragon. In this story, by using the narrative form of the success of the clever courtier the author shows how Daniel rose in status. Daniel solves two problems: if Bel does not eat, who does? Is the snake's eating and drinking a proof of divinity? In the first incident Daniel cleverly traps the priests through the use of ashes; in the second, he makes a special mixture in the form of barley cakes that he feeds to the snake, which then dies. This narrative form recalls that of Daniel 2, where Daniel rises in status through his interpretation of the king's dream (see 2:46–49). In Bel and the Dragon Daniel's rise in status is most clearly seen in the LXX, where Daniel receives control over the priests of Bel and is given the provisions normally given to the temple, no small gift. After Daniel destroys the snake, however, the description of success is not given, and immediately the narrative moves to the threat against Daniel. This sequence shows the close coherence of the narrative as a whole, which combines two genres kept distinct in the narratives of Daniel 1–6: the success of the wise courtier and the court conflict.

But this narrative really does not concern the court at all, except peripherally as Daniel is a confidant of the king. It is the Babylonians who revere Bel and the snake (vv. 3, 23) and who initiate the action against Daniel. That the narrative has its origins in a court conflict narrative, however, is betrayed by its ending. The author follows what usually happens in court conflict stories and has those who plotted Daniel's destruction thrown to the lions (v. 42). Properly, this should mean all the inhabitants of the region (LXX), all the Babylonians (Theodotion). Bel and the Dragon is not really a court conflict. It is a conflict between Daniel and the Babylonians as such.

The choice of Bel and the snake was not capricious. Bel was the titulary god of Babylon, Marduk, who is portrayed in the Enuma Elish as the one who brings order out of chaos. He battled against Tiamat, leader of the forces of chaos (→ Tiamat). Scholars have questioned whether living snakes were ever worshiped in Babylon, and some have suggested that Bel and the Dragon must have been written in Egypt against active Egyptian zoolatry. But such theories have too constrictive a view of the relationship between an author's characters and the author's historical environment. Tiamat was portrayed iconographically as a dragonlike or snakelike figure in the battle between herself and Marduk. The author of Bel and the Dragon is in fact poking fun at the two main characters of the Babylonian creation myth, the Enuma Elish. Opposed to this mythology is the God of Daniel, who created heaven and earth and who has authority over all humanity (v. 5).

Original Language and Setting

There are linguistic hints that both the LXX and Theodotion are translations of Hebrew. Moore, however, notes the difficulties of deciding between Hebrew and Aramaic and suggests that the stories were originally composed in Aramaic, but that Theodotion was based on a Hebrew translation of the Aramaic. Such a theory seems overly complex.

The story must have been written by the date of the Greek translation of Daniel (ca. 100 B.C.). Otherwise there are few clues as to the date. Conflict stories in which an oppressed people poke fun at their oppressors can arise at any time. The narrative clearly functions to bolster Jewish identity and self-esteem vis-à-vis their oppressors and symbolically destroys them. As Judea was part of the Babylonian and later Persian empires, and as officials of those empires were known in Judea, this parody could have been written anywhere in the empire.

COMMENTARY

1–2
Introduction

In the LXX stress is laid on the priesthood of Daniel, an indication that this story will be about religious competition. LXX also provides a genealogy: Daniel is the son of Abal. Scholars have tried to ascertain what the Hebrew name would be and have suggested Hebel, Abiel, or Habal.

Theodotion provides a historical introduction to the story. According to Herodotus, Cyrus was the maternal grandson of Astyages of Media, whose kingdom he took by force (Herodotus, History 1.107, 130). Cyrus issued the edict of 538 B.C. that allowed Jews to return to Jerusalem to rebuild the Temple (→ Cyrus). Theodotion emphasizes the important position of Daniel: he is distinguished above all the king's friends, as in MT Daniel 6:4.

3–22
The Idol Bel

3–7, The Problem. Herodotus (History 1.183) speaks of a golden statue of Bel in Babylon that was 18 feet high. In Bel and the Dragon, Bel's statue is of clay and bronze, two of the elements mentioned in the vision of Dan. 2:32–33. The amount of food supplied to Bel each day is immense: besides the twelve bushels of finest flour, Theodotion reads forty sheep and some fifty gallons of wine, whereas the LXX has four sheep and some fifty gallons of oil.

The contrast between the king and Daniel is set forth in v. 4. The reverence of Cyrus for Bel is known from an inscription in which Cyrus claims that Marduk (= Bel) brought him to power in Babylon; Cyrus wished to be known as "Cyrus, the king who worships you [Marduk]."

8–15, The Test. The king angrily takes the debate a perilous step further with the threat of death. Theodotion characterizes the charge against Daniel as one of blasphemy (v. 9), whereas the LXX simply states the charge that Daniel said Bel did not eat what was offered to him. The LXX has Daniel involve Bel's attendants in the threat.

At this point the stories are told differently in the LXX and Theodotion. Theodotion has the priests come forward confidently and suggest the conditions of the test, and then provides the reason for their confidence, the secret entrances. Daniel scatters the ashes in the king's presence, and so readers can already surmise what is going to happen. The suspense is taken away. In the LXX, on the other hand, Daniel tells the king to seal the doors and, without the king's knowledge, has ashes scattered on the floor. Readers wonder what will happen.

16–22, The Solution. In LXX the king's reaction to seeing the seals intact is quite understandable, as he was not privy to Daniel's stratagem. In Theodotion, to the contrary, the king behaves rather foolishly, as he should have first checked the ashes. In the LXX Daniel cleverly deduces by means of the footprints how the priests could enter and shows the secret entrances to the king, whereas Theodotion has the priests show them to the king.

In Theodotion the king kills the priests, but it is Daniel who destroys the statue of Bel and its temple. In the LXX the king hands over the priests to Daniel (as slaves?), gives Daniel the temple's provisions, and himself destroys the statue of Bel. Theodotion thus emphasizes the complete destruction of the temple and its functionaries as well as Daniel's role in it. The LXX, on the other hand, points out the financial reward of Daniel. The role of the king in the LXX is consonant with the complaint of the crowd in v. 28, whereas the one in Theodotion is at odds with it.

23–42
The Snake

23–27, The Killing of the Snake. Daniel seems to have set himself an impossible task as he proposes to kill the great snake/dragon without the help of sword (LXX: "implement of iron") or rod. Such conditions only enhance Daniel's cleverness. In the LXX the king stresses that the snake eats, so Daniel makes something for him to eat. The mixture Daniel concocts does not sound too appetizing, but as every good chef knows, presentation is everything, and Daniel displays it in the form of barley cakes. When Daniel throws them to the greedy snake, it eats and bursts apart. Daniel rubs in his success with a rhetorical question in the LXX, "It is not this that you worship, O king, is it?"

28–32, The Conflict. Daniel's success over the snake does not lead to a reward but to conflict. All the people of the country are convinced that the king has become a Jew. The king is shown in a very bad light as he caves in to the demands of the crowd. The conflict is not between Daniel and the king but has been raised to the level of Jew versus Babylonian. Daniel is put in a pit again, as in Daniel 6. The LXX specifies that the pit was for conspirators against the king. There must have been many to keep up the rations of two condemned persons per day. Theodotion stresses that food was kept from the lions so that they would devour Daniel. The LXX explicitly notes the improper behavior of the Babylonians as they are said not to want to give Daniel burial, the greatest dishonor one could show.

33–39, Salvation. The major differences in the Habakkuk episode were noted in the Introduction above. A strong argument can be made that in the LXX the Habakkuk incident is an insertion, as there is a strange repetition between v. 38 and the end of v. 39. In v. 38, after Habakkuk has brought him food, Daniel prays, "The Lord God remembered me, he who does not desert those who love him." At the end of v. 39, after Daniel has eaten and the angel has returned Habakkuk back to his place, the text reads, "The Lord God remembered Daniel." If one were to leave out the Habakkuk incident, the text would run smoothly "And Daniel was in the pit six days [v. 32b]. But the Lord God remembered Daniel [v. 39b]. Later the king went out to mourn Daniel and, peeking into the pit, he saw him sitting." One suspects that originally there was no miraculous description, simply the assertion that God remembered and saved Daniel.

Theodotion has smoothed out the story to accommodate the Habakkuk episode: there is no second mention of God's remembering Daniel. The incongruity still stands, but in both versions God's care for his followers is stressed. Theodotion simply heightens the miraculous by having the angel give Habakkuk a round-trip journey from Judea to Babylon in one day.

40–42, Conclusion. The story climaxes in the confession of the king and the restored high status of Daniel as his enemies are eaten by the still hungry lions. That Theodotion has the king confess the God of Daniel recalls the confession of Darius in Dan. 6:26. It goes further, however, in Bel and the Dragon, as the king also confesses that there is no other besides God, a clear reversal of the king's previous attachment to Bel in v. 18.

Bibliography

Davies, W. "Bel and the Dragon." In *The Apocrypha and Pseudepigrapha of the Old Testament*. 2 vols. Edited by R. H. Charles. Oxford: Clarendon, 1913. Vol. 1, pp. 652–64.

Engel, H. *Die Susanna-Erzählung* (The Susanna Narrative). Göttingen: Vandenhoeck & Ruprecht, 1985.

Moore, C. A. *Daniel, Esther, and Jeremiah: The Additions*. Anchor Bible, 44. Garden City, NY: Doubleday, 1977.

Nickelsburg, G. W. E. *Jewish Literature Between the Bible and the Mishnah*. Philadelphia: Fortress, 1981. Pp. 19–43.

Thompson, S. *Motif-index of Folk-literature*. Rev. and enl. ed. 6 vols. Bloomington, IN: Indiana University Press, 1955–58.

Zimmermann, F. "Bel and the Dragon." *Vetus Testamentum* 8 (1958): 438–40.

_____. "The Story of Susanna and Its Original Language." *Jewish Quarterly Review* 48 (1957/58): 236–41.

PRAYER OF MANASSEH

DANIEL J. HARRINGTON

INTRODUCTION

The Prayer of Manasseh contains an invocation of God (vv. 1–7), a confession of sins (vv. 8–10), and a petition for forgiveness (vv. 11–15). It uses many biblical phrases, apparently according to the Septuagint (LXX) version, and stands in line with the conventions of postexilic Jewish prayer. Its key descriptions of God as "the God of the righteous" (v. 8) and "the God of those who repent" (v. 13), while not explicitly biblical phrases, serve to capture the basic spirit of the prayer.

The Prayer of Manasseh was most likely composed in Greek. This position is supported by its author's apparent acquaintance with the LXX, the occurrence of some Greek words that are unusual in translations from the Hebrew, and a few strange Greek constructions. Several phrases, however, preserve the flavor of a Semitic composition.

Even though the work was not part of the LXX, it is customarily included in editions of the Greek Bible immediately after the Psalms and under the heading "Odes." Thus it appears in two Greek uncial manuscripts of the LXX, (Alexandrinus and Turicensis; → Texts, Versions, Manuscripts, Editions). It is also preserved in the *Apostolic Constitutions* and *Didascalia*, early church manuals from the third and fourth centuries A.D. The most important versions are the Syriac and the Latin.

Manasseh was king of Judah from 698 to 642 B.C. According to 2 Kings 21:1–18, Manasseh was a wicked king, especially because he introduced foreign cults into Jerusalem and Judah, even to the extent of setting up the graven image of Asherah in the Jerusalem Temple (see 2 Kings 21:7). He is also said to have shed much innocent blood (see 21:16). Nevertheless, Manasseh had the long reign of fifty-five years (see 21:1).

A different portrait of Manasseh appears in 2 Chron. 33:1–20. After describing the wicked deeds done by Manasseh (vv. 2–9), the Chronicler states that he was captured by the Assyrians and taken off into exile in Babylon (vv. 10–11). In his distress, Manasseh sought God's favor, humbled himself, and prayed to God. The result of his prayer was that God heard his prayer and restored him to his kingdom in Jerusalem (vv. 12–13). Then Manasseh embarked on a program of restoring proper worship to Jerusalem (vv. 14–17). The concluding summary of his life (vv. 18–20) claims that "his prayer" is written in both the "Chronicles of the Kings of Israel" and the "Chronicles of Hozai (or, the Seers)."

The Prayer of Manasseh purports to be the prayer uttered by Manasseh according to 2 Chron. 33:12–13 and preserved in two chronicles. Since the earliest evidence for the present text comes from the third century A.D., and the prayer was probably composed in Greek, we are most likely dealing with a pseudepigraphical work produced under Manasseh's name many centuries after his death. Since there are no discernible Christian elements, it was probably composed by a Greek-speaking Jew. It is not impossible, however, that a Christian author putting himself in Manasseh's position could have written this Jewish prayer. The author's use of phrases from the LXX suggests a date for the original composition around the turn of the era, though there is no further precision on this matter.

The major theological themes of the Prayer of Manasseh are the mercy of God and the power of repentance. The God of Israel's ancestors, who is also the Creator and Sustainer, is addressed as "compassionate, long-suffering, and very merciful" (v. 7). Because he repents over the evils done by human beings (v. 7), he can be said to have established repentance for sinners (v. 8) and can be addressed as the "God of those who repent" (v. 13).

Manasseh presents himself as the worst of sinners. Thus the clear message is that, if God accepts Manasseh's prayer (see 2 Chron. 33:13), repentance is possible for any sinner. God's reception of Manasseh's repentance serves to display publicly the mercy and goodness of God (see vv. 11, 14).

Although considered authoritative by Eastern Orthodox churches, the Prayer of Manasseh is not considered canonical by Jews, Protestants, or Roman Catholics. Since the Council of Trent, the Latin translation of it is placed in an appendix to the Latin Bible. The original author apparently composed it to fill the gap created by the statement in 2 Chron. 33:18–20 that Manasseh's Prayer had been preserved in two chronicles. In carrying out this exercise, he produced a prayer treasured by many readers for its theology of repentance.

COMMENTARY

1–7, Invocation. Manasseh begins the prayer by addressing God directly and reflecting on the attributes of God. The customary references to the "Lord Almighty" as Israel's God and the Creator give way to reflection on God's mercy shown in forgiving sinners. The invocation provides the reason why Manasseh may approach God with his confession. The traditional invocation of the "God of our fathers" (see Exod. 3:6, 15; 4:5; 1 Chron. 29:18) is given a twist with the phrase "and of their righteous offspring," suggesting a division within the descendants of the patriarchs between the righteous and the unrighteous (see Tob. 13:9, 13; Rom. 9:6). With his prayer, Manasseh wishes to align himself with the righteous in Israel.

The naming of God in v. 1 is followed in vv. 2–3 by an account of what God has done in creation, described in three participial clauses: "who made . . . who shackled . . . who closed . . . and sealed." The description of God's making heaven and earth (see Gen. 1:1; 2:1) is modified by the phrase "with all their order" (see Gen. 2:1, LXX). Shackling the sea (v. 3) is an act attributed to God also in Job 38:8, 10, 11 and Ps. 104:7, 9. The "abyss" is the "deep" of the creation account (see Gen. 1:2; 7:11; 8:2), the subterranean watery region beneath the earth. The agents by which God works ("by your word of command . . . by your fearsome and glorious name") presuppose the ancient Near Eastern idea of the active force of words and names.

Fear and trembling is the response to the Creator on the part of all created things (v. 4). The Semitic idiom "from the face of your power" could be translated either "because of your power" or "before whose power." In vv. 5–6 the theme of awe in response to God is developed by linking divine attributes and somewhat unusual adjectives beginning with the so-called alpha-privative (i.e., the Greek letter *alpha* used as a negative particle): the majesty of God's glory (see Ps. 144:5, 12, LXX) is unendurable; the wrath of his threat toward sinners is irresistible; and the mercy of his promise is infinite and unsearchable. The "mercy of his promise" probably refers to God's promise to forgive sinners when they repent. Thus Manasseh goes beyond the fascinating and fearsome aspect of the divine mystery and arrives at the chief theme of his prayer—God's willingness to forgive repenting sinners.

The invocation concludes in v. 7 with an appeal to God's mercy. After a series of adjectives ("compassionate, long-suffering, and very merciful") based on Joel 2:13 (LXX), Manasseh echoes the final phrase of Joel 2:13 (LXX) when he describes God as "repenting over the evils of human beings." Although in Joel the "evils" refer to the calamities that came upon Israel because of its sins, here the evils are the apostasies committed by King Manasseh (see 2 Kings 21:1–9; 2 Chron. 33:1–9). The prayer assumes that God will pardon those evil deeds in merciful response to sincere repentance. The second half of v. 7 is absent from the two Greek manuscripts. It was very likely part of the original text and lost accidentally in the textual transmission. The line serves to draw the invocation to a close and to focus on that aspect of God to which the following confession of sin and request for forgiveness of sins are directed.

8–10, Confession. Next, Manasseh accuses himself of his many sins, especially as they related to fostering foreign cults and neglecting the Jerusalem Temple (see 2 Kings 21:1–18; 2 Chron. 33:1–9). The confession proper begins in v. 8 by invoking the Lord as "the God of the righteous," an epithet without biblical foundation but one that allows Manasseh to approach God in spite of his admitted sinfulness. The God of the righteous established repentance not for the righteous patriarchs who did not sin against him but precisely for a sinner like Manasseh. The sinfulness of Manasseh is emphasized by his description of himself as "the sinner." While the Hebrew Bible does not describe the patriarchs in the same terms as Manasseh does, the portrayal of them in Genesis certainly contrasts with what is said of Manasseh in 2 Kings 21:1–9 and 2 Chron. 33:1–9. The contrast between the righteous and the sinners with respect to repentance appears in several Gospel sayings (see Mark 2:17 and parallels; Luke 15:7; 10:13). The sins of Manasseh, which are described in 2 Kings 21:1–18 and 2 Chron. 33:1–9, mainly concerned what was perceived as encouraging foreign cults and idol worship ("according to the abominable practices of the nations," see 2 Chron. 33:2).

Describing his sins as "beyond the number of the sand of the sea" (v. 9), Manasseh hesitates to approach God in prayer. The "height of heaven" refers to God's throne (see Isa. 38:14). The Syriac version adds the following to the verse: "And now Lord, I have been justly put down and deservedly afflicted." This verse allows a smoother transition to v. 10 and is probably original.

The description of Manasseh as weighed down with "many an iron chain" in v. 10 derives from 2 Chron. 33:11 ("bound him with bronze fetters"). The translation of the following phrase is problematic: whereas the RSV reads "so that I am rejected," most other translations render the phrase as a description of Manasseh's not being able to lift up his head. There is manuscript evidence for an additional phrase ("not doing your will and keeping your commandments") between "in thy sight" and "setting up abominations," but most interpreters dismiss it as a gloss.

11–15, Petition. The petition for forgiveness, for which the invocation and confession have prepared, calls upon "the God of those who repent" to forgive sins. Manasseh promises to spend all his days in praising God. Manasseh's petition for forgiveness begins in v. 11 by appealing to God's goodness. The image of bending "the knee of the heart" indicates that his prayer comes from deep within him and is made with full consciousness (see Joel 2:13: "rend your hearts and not your garments"). The petition is based on Manasseh's dramatic admission of his sinfulness in v. 12: "I have sinned, Lord, I have sinned, and I myself recognize my iniquities." This emphatic statement summarizes what has been said previously about Manasseh's sins and prepares for the prayer that follows.

The repetitive "forgive me, Lord, forgive me" in v. 13 balances "I have sinned, Lord, I have sinned" in the preceding verse. Manasseh trusts that God will not destroy him along with his iniquities, store up memory of his evils forever, or condemn him to Sheol (see Ps. 63:9). The "lowest parts of the earth" are not so much a region of torment as they are a place of separation from God (see Ps. 88:5–6). His prayer appeals to the Lord as "the God of those who repent." Like the epithet "the God of the righteous" in v. 8, it is not a biblical expression, but it does capture the spirit of Manasseh's prayer as a whole.

According to v. 14, God's answering Manasseh's prayer will be a display of the divine goodness and mercy, because all recognize Manasseh's unworthiness. The salvation envisioned by Manasseh involved release from captivity and restoration in Jerusalem (see 2 Chron. 33:12–13). Manasseh's resolve to praise God always in v. 15 probably alludes to his zeal in driving out foreign cults and restoring the worship of Yahweh after his return to Jerusalem (see 2 Chron. 33:15–17). He envisions a oneness between the worship on earth and the worship offered to God by the entire host of the heavens. The prayer ends with a doxology (see 1 Chron. 29:11) and an "Amen" (see 1 Chron. 16:36; Tob. 8:8; 1 Cor. 14:16).

Bibliography

Charlesworth, J. H. "Prayer of Manasseh." In *The Old Testament Pseudepigrapha*. 2 vols. Edited by J. H. Charlesworth. Garden City, NY: Doubleday, 1983, 1985. Vol. 2, pp. 625–37.

Ryle, H. E. "Prayer of Manasses." In *The Apocrypha and Pseudepigrapha of the Old Testament*. 2 vols. Edited by R. H. Charles. Oxford: Clarendon, 1913. Vol. 1, pp. 612–24.

1 MACCABEES

LAWRENCE H. SCHIFFMAN

INTRODUCTION

Title and Original Language

It is generally agreed that the First Book of Maccabees was originally written in Hebrew. Even though no manuscripts or fragments still exist in Hebrew, the Greek text of 1 Maccabees has the unmistakable style of a rather literal translation from the Hebrew. Moreover, the church father Origen (third century A.D.) claimed that the Hebrew title of 1 Maccabees was *Sarbethsabaniel*. This puzzling title is difficult to interpret but may be a somewhat corrupt rendering of Hebrew *sar bet 'el* ("Prince of the House of God") or of *sfar bet sabanai 'el* ("Book of the House of the Resisters of God"). Most Greek manuscripts simply term the books of 1 and 2 Maccabees *Makkabaion A* and *Makkabaion B*. By the second century A.D. *Ta Makkabaika* ("The things Maccabean" or "Maccabean Histories") was the designation for both 1 and 2 Maccabees. The early church father Clement of Alexandria (second century A.D.) termed 1 Maccabees *to Biblion ton Makkabaikon* ("The Book of Things Maccabean") and 2 Maccabees *he ton Makkabaikon epitome* ("The Epitome of Things Maccabean"). Although "Maccabee" (meaning "hammer") was originally the nickname of the hero Judah, the use of the title "Maccabean Histories" led to the custom of referring to all of the heroes of the book as "Maccabees."

Circulation

1 Maccabees was not only composed in Hebrew, but it was also written in a style imitating that of biblical historiography. Translated into Greek, 1 Maccabees was known to the first-century A.D. Jewish historian Josephus, who used it as the basis of his account in the *Antiquities of the Jews*. It is possible that the last two chapters of 1 Maccabees were not available to Josephus, since he seems to lack adequate sources for the reign of Simon. The Greek translation was included in the Hellenistic canon of the Greek-speaking Jews, and, therefore, eventually in the canon of the Christian church. In this manner it was preserved. Knowledge of this book was widespread among the church fathers. Yet the contents of 1 Maccabees began to circulate among Jews only in the Middle Ages, indirectly through the Latin translation. Our book, like 2 Maccabees, must be sharply distinguished from the medieval Jewish composition *Megillat Antiochus* ("Scroll of Antiochus") or *Megillat Hashmonim* ("Scroll of the Hasmoneans"), first mentioned by the Jewish scholar Saadia Gaon (A.D. 882–942).

Manuscript evidence for 1 Maccabees is also widespread, although the book is absent from the Codex Vaticanus. The most important manuscript witnesses are Codex Sinaiticus (fourth century A.D.), Alexandrinus (fifth century A.D.), and Venetus (eighth century A.D.).

Contents

1 Maccabees presents an account of the history of Judea from 175 to 134 B.C. It describes the background of the Maccabean revolt, the revolt itself, the exploits of Judah the Maccabee (in Gk. Judas Maccabeus), and the efforts of his brothers Jonathan and Simon to permanently reestablish Jewish nationalism and religious practice.

The author is clearly a believing Jew who emphasizes the piety of Judah's family, the Hasmoneans, and their trust in God. At the same time, he gives full credit for their success to their own sagacity and tenaciousness. The author seeks to highlight the excellence of the Hasmonean dynasty and in this respect may be seen as an official historian of the dynasty. He sees the Maccabees as emulating various biblical figures and presents a defense for the charismatic leadership the Hasmoneans provided. Judah's piety is especially emphasized in the prayers and speeches attributed to him. The author sees this family as specially selected by God to bring about the deliverance of Israel from the empire of the Seleucid kings.

Over and over the author emphasizes the antinomian character of the Jewish opponents of the Maccabees—they are "lawless men." All opponents of the Hasmoneans are seen as motivated only by the basest of motives and allied against the way of God's Torah.

Sources

Numerous documents are included in this work to prove the legitimacy of Hasmonean rule within the context of the Seleucid empire and contemporary international law. In addition, the author has included various poetic extracts that must come from poems that circulated in that period. Beyond this, the various theories regarding the sources of 1 Maccabees are speculative. (For additional discussion, *see* 2 Maccabees, "Introduction.")

The author of 1 Maccabees was certainly influenced by the style of the biblical historiographical books, especially the books of 1 and 2 Samuel. Judah's accomplishments are often described in ways evocative of the triumphs of Saul, Jonathan, and David. Like the historiographical books of the Bible, 1 Maccabees has a prominent chronological framework, though the dates are given in accord with the Seleucid era, which began with the capture of Babylon in 312 B.C. by the former general of Alexander the Great, Seleucus 1. As a source for reconstructing the events of the period, historians have generally held 1 Maccabees in high regard, considering it to be earlier and more trustworthy than 2 Maccabees. In certain respects, however, the evidence and approach of 2 Maccabees must be preferred. Specific instances will be discussed throughout the commentary. The author of 1 Maccabees appears to be quite familiar with the practices of the Seleucid empire. On the other hand, he seems to exaggerate numbers greatly and takes the opportunity, like all historians of his period, to place speeches of his own composition in the mouths of his heroes.

Date

Virtually all scholars take the view that the book had to have been written before the Roman conquest of Judea in 63 B.C., since the Romans are presented in 1 Maccabees as friends and allies of the Hasmoneans. The author's knowledge of the period of John Hyrcanus requires that he wrote not much before John's death in 104 B.C. The most probable date for the composition of 1 Maccabees, therefore, is the first decades of the first century B.C. Goldstein (pp. 62–64) dates the composition to the reign of Alexander Janneus (103–76 B.C.), but not later than 90 B.C.

Historical Background

Ptolemies and Seleucids. In the summer of 332 B.C., Palestine was conquered by Alexander the Great (356–323 B.C.). The land and people of Israel were now part of the new Hellenistic world, the cultural fusion of Greek and Near Eastern traditions that developed in the lands conquered by Alexander and held by his successors. After Alexander's death in 323 B.C., his generals, known as the *diadochi* (Gk., "successors"), were unable to maintain the unity of the kingdom. Individual generals were appointed to rule as satraps over particular areas

on the old Persian pattern but eventually came to rule in their own right. In 323 B.C., Ptolemy took control of Egypt and in 305 B.C. was officially crowned. Seleucus was made satrap of Babylon in 322 B.C. After some difficulties, he established himself and his empire on sound footing in 312 B.C. Seleucus extended his kingdom to the entire eastern part of the empire of Alexander. These two states, the Ptolemaic and the Seleucid, were destined to play a profound role in the history of Palestine in the Hellenistic era.

By 301, Ptolemy finally established his hold on Palestine, although Seleucus claimed legal title to the area. Consequently, during the third century B.C. Ptolemaic and Seleucid armies fought five times over Palestine. Despite heavy damage, the Ptolemies were able to maintain control over this territory. Ptolemaic military units were stationed throughout Palestine, and many Greek cities were established. An extensive officialdom sought to develop economic life and trade. Among the crops to be imported to Ptolemaic Egypt from Palestine and southern Syria were grain, olive oil, smoked fish, cheese, meat, dried figs, honey, and dates. Palestine also assumed importance as a crossroads for the spice trade.

At the same time, there is virtually no information from this century regarding Jewish political affairs. We do know that the high priest Onias II got into a disagreement regarding taxation with Ptolemy III Euergetes (246–221 B.C.), who was reputed to have visited the Jerusalem Temple. The result of the dispute was the imposition in 242 B.C. of the young Joseph son of Tobiah, a nephew of the high priest, as a tax collector for the entire nation. The rivalry between the Tobiad family and the Oniad high priests would eventually play a part in the attempts at radical hellenization of Judea later in the second century B.C.

In 221 B.C. the Seleucid king Antiochus III tried to invade Palestine. His initial attempts failed, but he persisted. The death of king Ptolemy IV Philopator in 204 B.C. opened the way for Antiochus III. In 201 B.C. he invaded the country again and quickly took it. By 198 the Seleucids had established firm control that would continue until the Maccabean revolt. By the time Ptolemaic rule came to an end in Palestine Hellenistic cities had been firmly established throughout the country. The process of Hellenism had sunk strong foundations that would ultimately tear the nation apart but also play a role in its renewed independence.

Hellenistic Reform and the Maccabean Revolt. Throughout the years of warfare between the Seleucids and Ptolemies, each empire had its supporters among the aristocracy of Jerusalem. When Seleucid rule finally became stablized, the pro-Ptolemaic party was left disenfranchised. After his conquest, Antiochus III affirmed the right of the Jews to live according to their ancestral laws. The gerousia (Gk.), that is, the council of elders, and the high priest Simon II, emerged as supporters of the Seleucids. But Onias III, who followed his father Simon II as high priest, changed the direction of his foreign policy and became at least a covert supporter of the Ptolemies. This, in turn, led the pro-Seleucid party to denounce him to the current Seleucid ruler, Seleucus IV. In an effort to shore up his rule, Onias went to Antioch in 175 to meet with the king.

Seleucus IV died in 175 B.C. and was succeeded by the infamous Antiochus IV Epiphanes (reigned 175–164 B.C.). Onias did not convince him of his loyalty and was forced to remain in Antioch. Onias' brother Jason then bought the right to the high-priesthood from Antiochus, as well as the right to establish in Jerusalem a gymnasium and ephebium, the central educational and cultural institutions of a Greek city. Jason thus refounded Jerusalem as a Hellenistic city, a polis. The right to live according to the Torah granted to the Judeans by Antiochus III was now rescinded. In its place, the Jews were to live under the law of the newly constituted Greek city. Among other changes, this meant that the majority of those who previously had had full rights under the laws of the Torah now found themselves as second-class citizens in an oligarchy. Athletic activities characteristic of Greek culture became prominent, and the gerousia was probably purged of those members who did not support this reform.

Jason's brand of hellenization was apparently not radical enough for some. As a member of a family that had been pro-Ptolemaic, he soon found himself opposed by the pro-Seleucid Tobiad family and by the three brothers Simon, Menelaus, and Lysimachus. The Tobiads plotted to replace Jason with Menelaus as high priest. In 172 B.C. Menelaus bought the office from Antioch. After an armed battle, Jason was forced to flee Jerusalem. Menelaus, now in control, appropriated funds from the Temple treasury to present gifts to Antiochus.

This misappropriation and his not being of the Oniad family turned the people bitterly against Menelaus. Violence broke out in Jerusalem, and Lysimachus, who had been left in control while Menelaus was in Antioch, fell in battle. Despite an appeal from representatives of the gerousia to replace Menelaus, Antiochus allowed him to continue in office, and the representatives were executed. It was not long before popular discontent would become full-scale revolt under new leaders.

During 169 B.C., when Antiochus made an ultimately unsuccessful attempt to conquer Egypt, a false rumor of his death led Jason to leave his hiding place in Transjordan and assault the city. He succeeded in driving Menelaus and his supporters into the citadel. Yet Jason was not able to reassert his rule. Apparently, popular forces arose against him, remembering that he had started the Hellenistic reform, and forced him to flee the Holy City again. Despite a slaughter by Antiochus himself, insurrection continued in Jerusalem. Antiochus' general Appollonius tried to control matters by establishing a fortress, known as the Akra, at the center of the city, but this attempt led only to further popular opposition and to massive flight of Jews from the city, some having been dispossessed to make room for the garrison he stationed there.

It is possible that at this time foreign deities were introduced into the Temple, creating further friction. Earliest attempts at organized rebellion were probably led by the Hasidim, a group of pietists who abhorred the religious compromises in Hellenistic Jerusalem. To stem the rising rebellion, Antiochus initiated the famous persecutions, which, far from being the beginning of our story, came after years of struggle and insurrection, fueled by the attempt of Hellenistic Jews to foist their way of life on the entire nation of Israel. There is no evidence at all that Antiochus pursued a policy of hellenization anywhere else in his kingdom. Rather, he took up this banner in Judea for tactical reasons. For Antiochus, the way to defeat the rebels was by an onslaught against the forces that propelled them—the Torah, the commandments, and the culture of the Jewish people.

The persecutions were enacted in the winter of 167–166 B.C. Foreign idolatrous worship and cultic prostitution were introduced into the Temple in December of 167 B.C. The God of Israel was syncretistically identified with Olympian Zeus and the Syrian god Baal-shamem. Throughout Palestine, the Sabbath and festivals were to be violated. High places were built where unclean animals were to be offered. Circumcision and observance of dietary laws were outlawed. The penalty for violations of these ordinances was death. The stage was now set for the confrontation of two opposing forces, the Jewish people and the Seleucids. The appearance of the Hasmonean (Maccabean) family would ignite the flames of full-scale revolt.

We cannot be sure if the accounts describing the beginning of the revolt are historical. Nonetheless, the refusal of Mattathias the priest of Modein and of men and women like him to succumb to the persecutions soon led many to escape to the mountains. Several thousand soon coalesced around the Hasmonean family, Judah the Maccabee and his brothers. Together with elements of the Hasidim they began to take control of villages throughout the countryside.

According to 1 Maccabees, by the time of Mattathias' death in 166/165 B.C., they had already achieved considerable success.

Under Judah the Maccabee the Jewish armies defeated successive Seleucid generals who attempted to put down the uprising. Judah soon was master of the entire country. Menelaus and the Hellenizers sought a peaceful settlement, asking that the Jews be allowed to return to their homes and that the persecution be officially suspended. The Seleucids realized the need for a political compromise. On October 15, 164 B.C., they restored the rights of the Jews as granted by Antiochus III, providing amnesty as well. While some may have taken advantage of this amnesty, the soldiers of Judah did not. In December of that year Judah and his men took Jerusalem, although the Seleucids continued to hold the Akra. On the 25th of Chislev (= December, 164) Judah purified the Temple and reorganized the sacrificial cult to conform to the Jewish tradition. This event is commemorated in the Jewish holiday of Hanukkah ("rededication"). The main objectives of the revolt, eliminating the persecutions and restoring Judaism to the nation, had been achieved.

Judah undertook wars throughout the land to defend the Jews from their pagan neighbors and at the same time to extirpate paganism from the country. After the death of Antiochus IV in 164 B.C., his son Antiochus V Eupator advanced on Judea, came to terms with Judah, and restored the rights of the Jews. Menelaus was executed by the Seleucids. In 162 B.C. Alcimus, a moderate Hellenizer, was appointed high priest, although Judah and his supporters resisted his appointment.

Alcimus sought Seleucid help to maintain his power against Judah. Fleeing to Syria, he returned with the general Bacchides. This time Judah fell in battle in 160 B.C. Judah's followers now rallied around Jonathan the Hasmonean and continued their opposition to Alcimus, to the hellenized Jews who supported him, and to their Seleucid allies. After Alcimus' death from stroke in 159, the post of high priest remained vacant for seven years. Though there was further conflict in 157, the Seleucid general Bacchides entered negotiations with Jonathan. A treaty was established, and Jonathan controlled most of Judea from a stronghold at Michmash, north of Jerusalem.

When internal affairs in Syria in 152 B.C. led to civil war between two pretenders to the throne, both sides began wooing Jonathan. Jonathan accepted the proposal of Alexander Balas, which included Jonathan's appointment

Opposite: Judah the Maccabee depicted in a twelfth-century A.D. Latin Bible now in Italy.

as high priest. Thus, on the feast of Tabernacles in 152 B.C., Jonathan appeared in the robes of the high priest. Judea was now united under the rule of the Hasmoneans. Disturbances and violence were not at an end, however. In 143 B.C. Jonathan was kidnapped and murdered by a former Seleucid ally who was made uneasy by Jonathan's growing power. Simon, Jonathan's brother, succeeded him. Simon fortified Jerusalem and secured freedom from tribute from the Seleucid ruler Demetrius II. By 142 B.C. he had driven the Seleucid garrison out of the Akra. In a public assembly in 140 B.C., Simon and his descendants were confirmed as high priest, ruler, and commander of the army. A dynasty had been established that would rule the Jewish people until the coming of the Romans in 63 B.C.

COMMENTARY

1:1–64
Background of the Revolt

1:1–10, Alexander and his Successors. The first four verses of the book briefly set the scene by tracing the origins of Hellenistic rule over the Near East. In 334 B.C. Alexander the Great set out from Pella in Macedonia on his series of conquests. The author of 1 Maccabees refers to "the land of the Kittim" as Alexander's home. The term "Kittim" originally referred to Kition on Cyprus or to the entire island. By the time of 1 Maccabees, however, the word had come to be a general term for the Aegean islands and parts of the coastline of the Mediterranean. Alexander defeated Darius III, the reigning Persian king, twice, first at Issus in 333 and then two years later at Gaugamela. By 332 Alexander had taken Palestine, and when his conquests ended, his empire stretched from Egypt to the area that is modernday Afghanistan and Pakistan.

Alexander died in Babylon on June 10, 323 B.C. Although 1 Macc. 1:6 says that he divided his kingdom among his officers before his death, in fact Alexander died without having left instructions for his succession. Struggles between rival generals resulted in the dismemberment of the empire. The emblem of kingship, the white diadem, was assumed in 306 B.C. by the generals Antigonus and Demetrius, who ruled in Greece and Asia Minor, respectively. The following year Ptolemy, who controlled Egypt, and Seleucus, who ruled Syria and the eastern part of the empire, also claimed royal status (cf. 1 Macc. 1:8–9).

1 Macc. 1:1–9 quickly skips over the century of competition between the Seleucid and Ptolemaic dynasties for control of Palestine, neglecting to mention that the Ptolemies ruled for most of that period (301–198 B.C.) until defeated at the battle of Paneas by Antiochus III ("the Great"). The interest of 1 Maccabees is in one of the sons of Antiochus III, the king Antiochus IV Epiphanes (Gk., "god manifest," or "god famous"). Verse 10 alludes to the fact that Antiochus IV had been taken as a hostage by Rome in the aftermath of the defeat of Antiochus III at the battle of Magnesia (189 B.C.). Antiochus III died in 187 and was succeeded by his son Seleucus IV. In 176 Antiochus IV was released by the Romans. After the death of Seleucus IV in 175 and the short reign of his infant son, Antiochus IV took power.

1:11–15, The Hellenistic Movement. Verses 11–15 describe the beginnings of the movement we know from other sources as the Hellenistic reform. A much more thorough account of these events is found in 2 Macc. 4:7–11. That passage tells us that Jason, the brother of the Jewish high priest, went to the king to get permission to change the legal status of Jerusalem and to reincorporate it as a Hellenistic city (*polis*), to be called Antioch. Part of the motivation must have been the economic opportunities such a reincorporation would have provided (see 1 Macc. 1:11).

The gymnasium (vv. 14–15) was the central cultural institution of Greek civilization and a prominent feature of every *polis*. In addition to physical activity and recreation, it was the place of education as well. Circumcision was known throughout the ancient world as the sign of the Jew. Nonetheless, because Greek athletics were performed in the nude, some hellenized Jews underwent epispasm, a procedure to reverse the appearance of circumcision, "the holy covenant" (RSV).

1:16–40, Antiochus IV in Egypt and Judea. Despite the account in 1 Macc. 1:16–19, which attributes the initiative to Antiochus IV, the war between Antiochus IV and Ptolemy VI Philometor (reigned 180–145 B.C.) resulted from a Ptolemaic attempt to reconquer Syria and Palestine. In 170 B.C. Antiochus routed the Egyptians. By 169 Egypt was nearly overrun and Ptolemy VI taken captive. He was, however, put back into power by Antiochus IV.

1 Macc. 1:20–64 describes Antiochus' assault on Jerusalem and the persecutions he put into effect. 1 Maccabees does not attribute a motive to Antiochus other than a passing reference to his "arrogance" and says nothing of the inner struggle between the hellenized Jews and the more traditional Jews that actually provoked the confrontation, according to 2 Maccabees 3–5. In September or October of 169 B.C. Antiochus IV sacked Jerusalem (cf. 2 Macc. 5:1, 11–26). He entered those areas of the Temple restricted to Israelites and plundered the Temple furnishings. The "curtain" (1 Macc. 1:22) is probably that separating the Holy of Holies from the sanctuary. Antiochus also took treasures that had been deposited in the Temple for safekeeping by individuals and carried out a great massacre (cf. 2 Macc. 5:12–14). 1 Macc. 1:25–28 comprises the first of a series of poetic dirges that occur in 1 Maccabees (see also 1:36–40; 2:7–13; 3:45, 50–53; 7:17; 9:21).

In about April of 167 a chief tax collector, known from 2 Macc. 5:24 to be Apollonius, "captain of the Mysians" (RSV), was sent to Judea by Antiochus. He took Jerusalem by force and then established a citadel, the Akra, which dominated Jerusalem. The exact location of the Akra is a subject of debate. This citadel was colonized by hellenized Jews, "men who were transgressors against the law" (trans. Tedesche). In 1 Macc. 1:36–40 a second dirge mourns the defilement of the sanctuary in language that recalls the destruction of the First Temple by the Babylonians in 587 (cf. Lamentations; Pss. 74; 79).

1:41–64, Antiochus' Decrees. The motivation for Antiochus' decrees outlawing local customs is explained by the author of 1 Maccabees as part of an overall policy to impose uniformity on his kingdom. Most modern scholars do not believe that Antiochus pursued such a general policy of hellenization. (For the background to Antiochus' decrees against Judaism see the Introduction and see 2 Maccabees 3–5, "Commentary.") In any event certain Jewish practices that served to separate Jews from the surrounding pagan culture were proscribed by Antiochus as punishable by death. (Goldstein is correct that Gk. *hagious*, "holy ones [i.e., priests]," in v. 46 needs to be corrected to *hagia* in accord with the Latin translation *sancta*, "holy things," i.e., sacrifices.) While some Jews acquiesced, others sought refuge. This account in 1 Macc. 1:41–53 completely ignores the internal Jewish unrest over the issue of Hellenism, described in 2 Maccabees, which seems to have led to Antiochus' decrees.

Antiochus went so far as to have an idol installed in the Temple, according to this account, on the fifteenth of Chislev, December 5, 167 B.C. The date of the twenty-fifth, given in Josephus and in 2 Macc. 1:18 and 10:5 is probably an attempt to synchronize the defilement with the rededication three years later (1 Macc. 4:52–54). Illicit sacrifices were to be offered throughout the land. The Torah, itself considered the cause of the Jewish resistance, was not to be read, and its scrolls were to be destroyed. Despite horrible tortures, Jews continued circumcision and the eating of exclusively kosher food. The mention in v. 59 of monthly offerings on the twenty-fifth of the month probably refers to observance of the king's birthday.

2:1-70
Mattathias' Revolt

2:1-28, The Rage of Mattathias. The beginning of chap. 2 introduces the Hasmonean family and describes the reaction of Mattathias and his sons to Antiochus' decrees. Mattathias and his family were among the lower clergy, priests of the clan of Joarib. As the process of hellenization advanced, they left Jerusalem and relocated in Modein (cf. 1:53). This town, seventeen miles northwest of Jerusalem in the Judean mountains, was probably the ancestral home of the family. In 2:7-14 the author puts a dirge into the mouth of Mattathias and describes the family of Mattathias as observing the traditional mourning rites (cf. Esther 4:1).

The confrontation between Mattathias and the Seleucid officials is foreshadowed in 1 Macc. 1:51-53. When the "enforcers" arrived in Modein (2:15), even the Hasmonean family was gathered among the crowd. The author accents the importance of Mattathias, placing him at center stage. Antiochus' officials offered Mattathias and his sons the status of "Friends of the King" as well as riches in return for their participation in pagan sacrifice. The Friends of the King were granted special status at court and wore distinctive purple hats and robes. Mattathias refused, but despite his eloquence, a Jew came forward to sacrifice, only to be killed by Mattathias. The author describes Mattathias as a latter-day Phineas, referring to the account of Num. 25:1-15 in which Phineas killed Zimri and Cozbi in the midst of their idolatrous sexual rites. As a result of Mattathias' actions, he and his sons fled into the mountains bordering on Samaria (cf. 2 Macc. 15:1). With this act of zeal and rage, the rebellion began.

2:29-41, Permissibility of Fighting on the Sabbath. The narrative temporarily leaves its account of Mattathias to describe an unnamed group, separate from the Hasmoneans, who also left their homes and sought refuge in the wilderness. Pursued and overtaken, this group refused to leave its camp on the Sabbath, in accord with a literalist interpretation of Exod. 16:29, nor would they fight on the holy day, even to defend themselves. Consequently, they were slaughtered when Antiochus' troops attacked on the Sabbath. The Hasmoneans emphatically decided that defensive warfare should be permitted on the Sabbath. This ruling, despite the

opposition of certain circles within Judaism, became the normative view of Jewish law.

2:42-48, The Hasidim and the Beginnings of the Revolt. Among those who joined the Hasmoneans in the early days of the revolt were a group of Hasidim, "pious ones" in Hebrew. Various attempts have been made to claim that these were an organized sect, perhaps connected with those who gave their lives in v. 38, precursors of either the Pharisees or the Essenes. None of these theories can be proven. It is best to take Hasidim as a loose term for individuals of great piety, who "volunteered in defense of the Torah" (trans. Goldstein). The initial operations of the Hasmoneans were directed against hellenizing Jews, who are called "sinners" and "lawless" (v. 44). The altars erected for their use were destroyed and they were forced to maintain the law of circumcision.

2:49-70, The Death of Mattathias. Verses 49-68 contain a "testament of Mattathias," put into his mouth by our author. Such deathbed testimonies and farewell speeches were a popular feature in ancient Jewish literature (cf. Gen. 49; Deut. 33; Josh. 23; and the pseudepigraphical composition, *The Testaments of the Twelve Patriarchs*). Mattathias recalls how the Lord stood by the great heroes of Israel, Abraham, Joseph, Phineas, Joshua, Caleb, David, Elijah, Daniel and his three companions, Hananiah, Azariah, and Mishael. He also calls on his sons, in dramatic foreshadowing, to be willing to sacrifice their lives for the covenant. Mattathias passes on the leadership of the family to Simeon, while acknowledging Judah as the military chief. Mattathias died in April of 165 B.C. (Goldstein).

3:1-9:22
Judah's Struggle for Liberation

3:1-12, Judah Defeats Apollonius. Judah succeeded his father, Mattathias (cf. 2:66). The poem in 3:3-9 tells us that Judah's earliest operations were mounted against hellenizing Jews, identified as "lawless," "evildoers," and "ungodly." Only when attacked by Apollonius (v. 10) did Judah begin to do battle with the Seleucid forces. The comment of v. 8, that "he turned away wrath from Israel," compares him with Phineas (Num. 25:11) as Mattathias was in 2:26.

Josephus suggests that Apollonius was governor of Samaria. But he may have been the collector of tribute referred to in 1:29 and identified as Apollonius in 2 Macc. 5:24. Although 1 Macc. 3:10 identifies Apollonius' troops as "Gentiles and a large force from Samaria" (RSV), it is likely that the reference is to pagan Greco-

Macedonians who then inhabited the city of Samaria and not to actual Samaritans (so Goldstein). In any event Judah was victorious in his first battle against Seleucid forces.

3:13–26, The Battle of Beth-horon. Seron, commander of Syria, decided to try his luck against Judah. He was joined by hellenizing Jews who sought to avenge Judah's earlier campaigns against them.

There were two villages, upper Beth-horon (to the southeast) and lower Beth-horon (to the northwest) on the road from Jerusalem to Lydda, between Jerusalem and Modein. The pass between them was extremely narrow (b. Sanh. 32b). Despite the fact that Judah's men were holding the higher position, they still despaired at the sight of the larger enemy forces, especially since this was only their second engagement with the Seleucids, and since they lacked adequate provisions. Judah encouraged his men, reminding them that their lives, the lives of their wives and children, and their way of life were all at stake. His comment, that "in the sight of heaven there is no difference between saving by many or by few" (3:18, RSV), recalls the words of Jonathan in 1 Sam. 14:6. The same theme is present in the story of Gideon's victory in Judges 7.

Judah fell upon the enemy suddenly and routed them, his forces killing eight hundred and putting the rest to flight westward. Josephus even reports that Seron was killed. From this time Judah was considered a force to be reckoned with.

3:27–37, Seleucid Affairs. Our author explains Antiochus' eastern campaign as resulting from the need to finance his actions against Judah's revolt. No doubt the real motivation for this campaign was to bring the eastern satrapies under control. Before he left to campaign in the east (perhaps May or June of 165) Antiochus may have established a coregency with his young son Antiochus V Eupator, appointing Lysias as guardian. Lysias, whose title of "Kinsman of the King" indicates a rank above that of "Friend of the King" (so Goldstein; cf. 2:18; 3:38), was ordered to crush the rebels. For this purpose extensive forces were deployed, although the claim that half the king's armed forces were to be dedicated to crushing Judah's insurrection at this early stage seems exaggerated.

3:38–4:25, The Battles with Nicanor and Gorgias. According to 3:38, Ptolemy son of Dorymenes, Nicanor, and Gorgias were sent to Lysias. Yet 2 Macc. 8:8–9 makes Ptolemy the one who sent Gorgias and Nicanor. These three Friends of the King were provided with large armies. The number of soldiers here (40,000 infantry and 7,000 cavalry) is probably derived

from the size of the Aramean (= Syrian) force defeated by David, according to 1 Chron. 19:18. Emmaus, where the Seleucid army camped, commanded several routes from Jerusalem to the coastal plain, yet it was exposed from the south. Expecting the immediate rout of Judah's forces, slave traders joined the camp of the Seleucid army. The additional troops who joined the Seleucid forces (1 Macc. 3:41) were, as Goldstein suggests, from Idumea and Philistia, not Syria and Philistia. The two names are written similarly in Hebrew and are easily confused.

Judah's forces assembled at Mizpah, an ancient place of prayer, where they mourned and fasted and read from the Torah. Our author inserts his fourth dirge in v. 45 (cf. 1:25–28, 36–40; 2:7–13). The exact location of Mizpah cannot be determined. It was the site of Samuel's prayer to God to enable Israel to be victorious over the Philistines (1 Sam. 7:2–14). Even without a Temple, Judah's forces put on priestly garments and offered first fruits, but they were unable to complete the rites of Nazirites since the offerings had to be made in the Jerusalem Temple. (In 1 Macc. 3:49 the translation "stirred up" in the RSV must be set aside. Tedesche translates "shaved," a part of the Nazirite rite [Num. 6:18].) After praying for deliverance, the assembly sounded the trumpets in accord with Num. 10:9.

Judah organized his army on the biblical model and then discharged the requirements of Deut. 20:1–9, the law of conscription (1 Macc. 3:55–60). Similar rites are required in the Qumran War Scroll as well. He dismissed those to be exempted and made the priest's address of encouragement. Again, he repeated his father's message (2:50) that his forces had to be ready to sacrifice their lives if necessary.

Gorgias intended to outnumber Judah's three thousand men and to take them by surprise. For this reason he had to employ hellenized Jews ("men from the Akra"), as they knew the terrain well enough to guide his troops by night. Informed of this plan, Judah slipped away and positioned his under-equipped army to attack the larger and better fortified main camp of the Seleucids (4:1–7). The speech the author attributes to Judah in vv. 8–11 recalls the deliverance of Israel at the Reed Sea (Exod. 14:10–13).

Judah's forces apparently commanded the high ground, and the Seleucids fled toward the plain as their guard posts failed to withstand the descending army of Judah (1 Macc. 4:12–15). Gazara is Gezer, where there may already have been a Seleucid stronghold to which the soldiers fled. Azotus is Ashdod and Jamnia is Yavneh. A tongue of Idumean territory may have separated Judea from the Philistine towns of Azotus and Jamnia (Goldstein), or we may read Judea for Idumea with some manuscripts (so

Tedesche). The territory of ancient Philistia was occupied by pagans in the Hellenistic period.

Gorgias' force, having failed to catch Judah's men in their camp, next appeared in the hills above their own camp, which was being burned by the Maccabean army (v. 20). They immediately fled to Philistia. Judah's men turned to the spoils and to celebrating their victory with praise of God. The refrain quoted in 4:24 ("for he is good and his mercy endures for ever," RSV) is familiar from Psalms 106; 107; 118; 136; and 1 Chron. 16:8–36 (cf. 2 Chron. 20:21).

4:26–35, The Battle with Lysias. When his men reported their failure, Lysias prepared to mount an even greater offensive. The defeat of Nicanor and Gorgias had probably taken place in summer or autumn of 165 B.C. Lysias' campaign ended in failure by late winter of 164. The dangers of an insurgency so close to the borders of the Ptolemaic empire made it worth the risk of a winter campaign. One of the reasons for advancing from the south (4:29) may have been the desire to avoid the rains. At the same time, the approach from Idumea afforded Lysias a friendly base, since the Idumeans had no sympathy for the Hasmoneans. Beth-zur, where the battle took place, was in southern Judea. Lysias chose this location since it afforded him the high ground. Judah was outnumbered, even though his army had grown substantially since the defeat of Nicanor and Gorgias.

Facing overwhelming odds, Judah prayed to God that the Seleucids be delivered into the hands of his army, just as Goliath had been handed over to David (1 Sam. 17) and the Philistines to Jonathan (1 Sam. 14:1–15). The model of those early heroes of Israel is very important to the image the author of 1 Maccabees wished to create for Judah. Judah began his prayer (1 Macc. 4:30–33) with the benediction formula, "blessed are You," which was widespread in literature of the Second Temple period (515 B.C.–A.D. 70) and which forms the basis of the Jewish liturgical system.

The battle resulted in a resounding defeat for Lysias. His decision to return home may have resulted from the news of the death of Antiochus IV and the appointment of Philip as regent for his son Antiochus V. Nonetheless, Lysias was already preparing for another engagement.

4:36–61, The Rededication of the Temple. The defeat of Lysias left the Hellenizers and Seleucids in the Akra isolated. When Judah and his men went up to the Temple they found it abandoned; the hellenized priests had probably fled to the Akra or left the city.

While some of his men fended off the troops of the Akra, Judah set out to purify the sanctuary. Only priests unblemished according to the law of Lev. 21:17–23 participated in the cleans-

ing of the sanctuary. Regarding the altar, Goldstein suggests that Judah faced a dilemma, since Deut. 12:2–4 commanded the destruction of idolatrous altars but at the same time prohibited the destruction of God's altar. What was to be done in a case in which God's altar had been defiled by idolatrous worship? Accordingly, the altar was replaced with a new one (built of unhewn stones in accord with Exod. 20:25 and Deut. 27:6), but the stones of the old altar were hidden away. The vessels, candelabrum (menorah), and incense altar had to be replaced, since Antiochus had carried them away when he first entered Jerusalem (1 Macc. 1:21–23). The burning of incense and the setting out of the loaves rendered the Temple fit for the renewal of sacrifice (4:50–51).

The first sacrificial offering was brought on the twenty-fifth of Chislev, 164 B.C. (vv. 52–53). The notion that the rededication took place on the anniversary of the day on which the Temple was defiled has given rise to the emendation of 1:54 (see commentary above on 1:54). The cornices and decorations were replaced (4:57) as they had been taken by Antiochus (1:22). The gates and doors that had been burned (4:38) were also restored. It was decreed that the festival of Hanukkah ("dedication") was to be celebrated annually as an eight-day festival.

The Mount Zion referred to in 4:60 means the Temple Mount, which needed to be fortified against the troops in the nearby Akra. It was now clear that a fortress facing Idumea was required, to prevent the Seleucids from attacking again from that direction. Hence, Beth-zur was fortified.

5:1–68, Judah Expands His Domain. The author describes Judah's early attempts to extend his territory and punish the enemies of Israel as defensive operations against gentile aggression. Akra-battene was a district in southern Samaria populated by Idumeans. The Baeanites may be the people of the city of Beon referred to in Num. 32:3, located in Transjordan. The Ammonite Timothy of 5:6, identified as a *phylarch*, Greek for a local leader, appears also in 2 Macc. 10:24–37. He is probably to be distinguished from the *strategos* named Timothy, a high official of the Seleucid empire, mentioned in 1 Macc. 5:11–44 and 2 Macc. 12:2, 10–31 (so Goldstein).

At the same time, non-Jews in surrounding locales rose up against their Jewish neighbors. Judah received pleas for help from the Jews of Gilead who had taken refuge in Dathema (1 Macc. 5:9–10) and from Galilee as well (v. 14). Gilead is the land east of the Jordan between the Yarmuk River to the north and the Arnon to the south. The location of Dathema is unknown. The Timothy who besieged the Gileadite Jews was the *strategos* by that name (see commentary above on 5:1–8). The words *en tois*

Toubiou in 5:13 have been variously understood. The RSV translates, "who were in the land of Tob," for which see Judg. 11:3. Tedesche has "who were in the village of Toubias," which his note seems to indicate is to be identified with the land of Tob. Goldstein translates "who were members of Tubias' troop," referring to a military unit under the leadership of one of the Tobiad family, a clan of hellenized Jews. If this last translation is correct, it would show that even hellenized Jews were under attack. While Judah and Jonathan went to rescue the Jews of Gilead, Simon was sent to Galilee (1 Macc. 5:17). Judah commanded those left in Judea not to do battle with the enemy; he was concerned about the risk entailed in deploying substantial forces outside of Judea. Simon was victorious and drove the pagan attackers into the city of Ptolemais, also known as Acco on the Mediterranean, north of Haifa. Unable to hold Galilee, he evacuated those Jews he had rescued (vv. 21–23).

The longer account of Judah's exploits in 5:24–54 results from his being the central hero. Indeed, v. 43 emphasizes the personal bravery of Judah, as v. 53 speaks of his kindness and concern for stragglers. Judah's attempt to avoid armed confrontation with the people of Ephron (vv. 46–51), follows the laws of Deut. 20:10–15. The exact location of most of the cities mentioned in this account cannot be established. Carnaim, known as Ashteroth-karnaim in Gen. 14:5, is north of Edrei in Transjordan. The temple of Carnaim, which Judah burns, was probably dedicated to Astarte. Raphon is in the same vicinity. Ephron is eight miles east of the Jordan, opposite Beth-shean. Judah also had to evacuate the Jews from Transjordan, since it would have been impossible to hold on to such far-flung territory. The triumphant entry of these Jews into Jerusalem described in v. 54 echoes Isa. 35:10.

Joseph and Azariah, left to command the troops in Judea, violated their instructions (1 Macc. 5:19) and marched against Jamnia (Yavneh on the Mediterranean shore). Gorgias, probably the same one mentioned in 3:38–4:25, routed their army (5:59–60). Our author gives two reasons for the rout, disobedience to commands and not being of the Hasmonean house. Here the author is emphasizing his view that the Hasmoneans were divinely chosen legitimate rulers. The Hasmonean brothers themselves continued to attain victories and to command popular support (vv. 65–66). Judah's destruction of pagan cult sites (v. 68) was part of the general Hasmonean approach to extirpating paganism from the land of Israel.

6:1–17, The Death of Antiochus IV Epiphanes.
Chronologically, 1 Macc. 6:1–17 follows 3:37. The "upper" or "inland" provinces of 6:1 are Mesopotamia and Iran. Elymais is the

region known in the Bible as Elam. No city of that name is known, however, and the precise location of Antiochus' campaign remains uncertain. Antiochus is pictured here as a temple robber, as he appears in 1:21–24. The beginning of 6:4 may be translated with the RSV, "and they withstood him in battle," or, with Goldstein, "when they stood against him for battle." Goldstein's translation allows him to conclude that no actual battle took place, but that Antiochus gave up when he saw that the inhabitants would resist.

In vv. 5–7 the text describes an envoy who related to Antiochus the events of 3:38–4:61. This account attributes the king's death to the news of the defeat in Judea. Such a sequence of events is extremely unlikely, even though Antiochus' death did occur a short time after the rededication of the Temple. Indeed, in Chislev (November/December) of 164 B.C. the news of Antiochus' death became known in Babylonia, according to an ancient clay tablet from Babylon. It is therefore not probable that events of that same month in Judea could have been known to Antiochus before he died. It is likely, therefore, that our author has presented his own interpretation of events and that the messenger is fictitious, as suggested by Goldstein.

Sensing that he was dying, Antiochus summoned the "Friends of the King," a group of courtiers (see commentary above on 2:15–28). The author has Antiochus blame his death on his despoiling of the Jerusalem Temple (cf. 1:20–24) and his attacks on Judea. The second-century B.C. Greek historian Polybius attributed Antiochus' death to his desire to plunder the temple of Artemis in Persia (*Histories* 31:9). Josephus counters Polybius' claims with the view of 1 Maccabees (*Antiquities of the Jews* 12.358–9).

The king designated Philip as regent for his young son Antiochus, electing him to bring (so Goldstein) Antiochus the diadem, robe, and signet ring, which symbolized the royal power. In so doing he displaced Lysias, whom he had entrusted with the government in his absence (3:32–36). Antiochus IV then died in early winter of 164 B.C. Lysias proved no easy match. Before Philip could assert his power, Lysias, to cement his own power over the Seleucid realm, set up Antiochus V, then nine years old, as king, giving him the title Eupator, meaning "born of a noble father."

6:18–63, The Campaign of Antiochus V Against Judea.
In 163/162 B.C., about a year after the death of Antiochus IV, spurred on perhaps by the instability attending the succession and regency of the Seleucid empire, Judah besieged the Akra. A group of pagans and hellenized Jews managed to elude the siege and approached the king, arguing that the attack on

the symbol of Seleucid hegemony over Judea and the fortification of the Temple and Beth-zur constituted an act of rebellion.

In 6:28–33 the young king is pictured as controlling affairs, although in reality power was concentrated in the hands of the regent, Lysias. The size of the forces is no doubt exaggerated here. As in Lysias' previous campaign against Judah, the approach to Beth-zur was through Idumea (see 4:29). After defending the fortress, Judah suddenly withdrew his men to Beth-zechariah, where he was soon met by the enemy. The author's description of the valiant defense of Beth-zur by the Jews in 6:31 leads us to believe that actually the Jews withdrew because they were unable to withstand the Seleucid pressure.

The detailed account of the overwhelming forces of the enemy in 6:34–41 is intended to show that it was not Judah's fault that he lost this battle. Goldstein suggests that the author took the description of the elephants from a military manual. In his view, the unfermented grape and mulberry juice stimulated the animals because of its color and taste. Elephants were commonly used in battle during the Hellenistic age, a practice apparently adopted from the Persians. Although the RSV in v. 37 says that there were "four armed men" on each elephant, that reading is based on emendation. More probable is "two" as in Tedesche and Goldstein, based on a reconstructed Hebrew original *shene shalishim*, "two riding warriors," which was easily misread as *shenayim u-sheloshim*, "thirty two," the reading in most Greek manuscripts.

After an initial success, the battle quickly went against Judah's army. His brother Eleazar, surnamed Avaran, died in battle (vv. 43–46). This tragedy may have contributed to the demoralization that caused Judah to withdraw his army.

The king was greatly aided in conquering Beth-zur by the fact that Jews were prohibited from farming the land of Israel during the Sabbatical Year (see Exod. 23:11; Lev. 25:3–7). Most probably this means that it was the year after the Sabbatical Year, at which time the lack of previous year's produce would be felt. The same problem afflicted those Jews who sought to defend the Temple against the army of Antiochus V (1 Macc. 6:51–54).

At this time, Lysias' control over the young Antiochus V was challenged by Philip. It was Philip who had actually been appointed regent by Antiochus IV on his deathbed (6:15). Lysias decided that he needed to commit his troops to the struggle against Philip for control over the empire. For this reason he sought peace in Judea (vv. 55–56).

Lysias' speech in 6:57–59 is no doubt a composition of the author. In it Lysias asserts that there is no sense in continuing the war and that the only reason the Judeans opposed the Seleucids was because the latter had prohibited the practice of Judaism. Lysias, according to our author, deliberately conceals the true reason for his desire to return to Antioch, the presence there of Philip. In a parallel in 2 Macc. 11:13 Lysias decides to make peace because he realized that God was on the side of the Hebrews.

Verses 60–61 describe the legal proceeding wherein the two sides exchanged oaths. We can imagine that this was a solemn occasion in which specific military protocol was followed. Compare the parallel description in 2 Macc. 11:13–21 and 27–33, in which the agreements take the form of a series of letters. The king's acceptance of Lysias' proposal (1 Macc. 6:61) is paralleled in a letter in 2 Macc. 11:22–26 in which Antiochus V proposes that the Jews be allowed to live according to their own laws. Only after all arrangements were concluded did the defenders of the Temple (perhaps termed Mount Zion here) withdraw from their positions.

Despite Lysias' oath of peace, Antiochus V treacherously destroyed the walls of Mount Zion (1 Macc. 6:62). Antiochus V then departed for Antioch, where he was forced to take the city by force from his erstwhile regent, Philip. His withdrawal from Jerusalem is probably to be dated to sometime in winter of 162 B.C.

7:1–25, The High-Priesthood of Alcimus.

Antiochus V and Lysias had no sooner succeeded in overcoming the challenge of Philip than they faced a more formidable opponent in Demetrius I Soter (ruled 162–150 B.C.), son of Seleucus IV Philopator (ruled 187–176 B.C.). Demetrius had been a hostage in Rome, from which he managed to escape after the death of his uncle, Antiochus IV. After establishing himself at Tripolis, in Phoenicia (Josephus *Antiquities of the Jews* 12.389; 2 Macc. 14:1), he took Antioch, and Antiochus V and Lysias were put to death. His accession is probably to be dated to October 162 B.C. (Goldstein).

The "lawless and ungodly men of Israel" (7:5, RSV) describes for the author the party of moderate Hellenizers. 2 Macc. 14:3 relates that Alcimus (whose Hebrew name was Jakim) had earlier been designated high priest. Josephus (*Antiquities of the Jews* 12.385) says that he was appointed by Lysias after the execution of Menelaus. Perhaps our passage refers to his seeking confirmation from the new ruler. Alcimus and his supporters argued that Judah and his followers had made life impossible in Judea for the supporters of the Seleucid empire.

Bacchides, whom the new king Demetrius entrusted with the task of pacifying Judea, was one of the "Friends" of King Antiochus IV (Josephus *Antiquities of the Jews* 12.393) and must have been led to support Demetrius as a result of conditions under Antiochus V and Lysias. The province "Beyond the River" (RSV) was that of Coele Syria and Phoenicia. Demetrius' own involvement in pacifying the eastern part of his empire led him to put so distinguished a leader as Bacchides in charge of affairs in Judea. Alcimus was confirmed as high priest.

Although the Hasmoneans under Judah realized the purposes of the large expeditionary force sent with Bacchides, some of the Hasidim who did not share the Hasmonean insistence on Jewish independence, but who were concerned only for religious freedom, were lulled into Bacchides' trap (1 Macc. 7:12–18). Probably the presence of the priest Alcimus convinced them that the Seleucids could be trusted. But Alcimus and Bacchides proved treacherous, arresting and executing sixty of the Hasidim. Verse 17 is an adaptation of Ps. 79:2–3 and Jer. 14:16. The story of the execution of the Hasidim is not found in the parallel account of 2 Maccabees 14.

Beth-zaith (1 Macc. 7:19) was about four miles north of Beth-zur on the road to Jerusalem. Here Bacchides again committed atrocities, denying the corpses burial (cf. v. 17). Manuscripts are divided as to whether he killed his own men who had deserted from him or some Jews who had deserted to him. If the latter, he would have killed them out of fear that they were disloyal. Despite the support Alcimus received from the Seleucid army and from the hellenizing Jews, he was unable to stabilize his power as high priest in the face of the opposition of Judah and his men.

7:26–50, The Defeat of Nicanor.

In response to the appeals of Alcimus (v. 25), King Demetrius dispatched Nicanor to assist him. The parallel account in 2 Macc. 14:18–30 suggests the possibility that there was a period of friendship between Nicanor and Judah. When Nicanor turned against him, Judah escaped. According to 1 Maccabees, however, Nicanor was treacherous from the start (vv. 26–30). Abandoning his earlier tactics of entrapment, Nicanor met Judah in battle near Capharsalama, a site for which no convincing identification has yet been made. Verse 32 is somewhat ambiguous. The version in Josephus (Antiquities of the Jews 12.405) to the effect that Nicanor was victorious and that Judah's men fled to the Akra is mistaken. The correct interpretation is that Judah was victorious and that Nicanor's men were sent scampering back to their fortress in the City of David. Otherwise, the oath of v. 35 in which Nicanor threatens to burn down the Temple would make no sense.

Nicanor's threat was made to the priests and elders who were showing him the burnt offering being made on behalf of the Seleucid king (v. 33). From the Persian period on, such offerings had been made on behalf of the king as a sign of loyalty (see Ezra 6:10). This token failed to convince Nicanor that the priests were loyal to the Seleucid empire. From the prayer the priests recited after his departure, it seems that he was correct. The first part of the poem in 1 Macc. 7:37–38 is influenced by 1 Kings 8:29–30, 43 and 9:3.

Nicanor repaired to Beth-horon, a strategic highpoint, where he met his reinforcements from Syria. Yet Judah outsmarted him by occupying Adasa, a village on the road from Jerusalem to Beth-horon, some seven miles southeast of Beth-horon. By blocking the road, Judah intended to stop Nicanor from fulfilling the oath of 1 Macc. 7:35 (Goldstein). In his prayer Judah recalls the destruction of Sennacherib's army, described in 2 Kings 19:35 (cf. 2 Macc. 15:22–24).

The battle took place in March of 161 B.C. While 1 Macc. 7:43 asserts that Nicanor was the first to fall, Josephus places the death of Nicanor later on in the battle (Antiquities of the Jews 12.409). The enemy was pursued westward, toward Gezer. The blowing of the trumpets by Judah's forces (v. 45) was intended to signal the surrounding villagers to block the path of escape of the Seleucid army so that the rout could continue. After the battle the victorious Jews cut off Nicanor's right hand as retribution for his having raised it in taking the oath to destroy the Temple (cf. 2 Macc. 15:32).

The Day of Nicanor, which was decreed as an annual festival (1 Macc. 7:49), was celebrated as a minor Jewish holiday as late as the end of the first century A.D. Fasting and mourning were forbidden on this and many other such days according to the early rabbinic text Megillat Ta'anit ("Scroll of Fasting"). The rabbis later abolished these minor commemorations in favor of Hanukkah and Purim, which remained as festivals of national deliverance.

8:1–32, Judah's Treaty with the Romans.

The account of the greatness of Rome in 8:1–16 is a collection by the pro-Roman author of information and even misinformation about the power and glory of Rome. This material is intended to justify Judah's having allied himself with a foreign nation. The author accepts the tendentious claims of the Romans that those whom they had conquered had undertaken aggression against Rome (Goldstein). The Gauls referred to in v. 2 are either those of northern Italy defeated in 190 B.C. or the Galatians of Asia Minor conquered in 189 B.C. The Carthaginian colonies in Spain were conquered in the Second Punic War (218–201 B.C.). Philip was defeated in 197 and his son Perseus, last king of Macedonia, was defeated 168 B.C. Antiochus (III) the Great was defeated by the Romans at Magnesia in 189 B.C. He was not made a prisoner as v. 7

claims, but he was forced to accept the terms of the Romans. Although India is mentioned in v. 8, it was never conquered by Antiochus III, yet he did march toward it and was widely reported to have had elephants in his forces. Media was retained by Antiochus, but Lydia had to be surrendered to the Romans along with other parts of Asia Minor, most of which were then given to Eumenes II of Pergamum. Probably vv. 9–11 are an anachronistic description of the war with the Achaean league in 146 B.C. The Roman senate did not meet daily, as v. 15 states, but usually three times each month and on festivals. It began with 120 members, and it gradually increased to approximately 300, until it was further enlarged to 600 in 81 B.C. The author apparently did not realize that there were two consuls, rather than one ruler (v. 16). The allusion to harmony in v. 16 suggests that the passage was written before the Roman civil wars.

Judah chose two ambassadors to Rome, Eupolemus and Jason. Eupolemus was the son of the same John who, according to 2 Macc. 4:11, secured royal concessions for the Jews from Antiochus III. He is perhaps to be identified with the author of the Greek work *Concerning the Kings in Judea*. Goldstein's translation "of the clan of Hakkoz" is to be preferred to the RSV's "son of Accos" in 1 Macc. 8:17. (On this priestly clan see Ezra 2:61; Neh. 7:63; cf. 1 Chron. 4:8.) Jason is otherwise unknown. The Jews continued to be taxed by the Seleucid kingdom, even after the victory of Judah over Nicanor. Further, Alcimus still remained high priest, supported by the Seleucids. It was this yoke of slavery (1 Macc. 8:18) that Judah sought to cast off by entering an alliance with the Romans. As was usual at that time, the emissaries were invited to address the senate. The claim of v. 22 that the Romans sent a bronze copy of the treaty to Jerusalem was doubted by Josephus (*Antiquities of the Jews* 12.416) in light of the usual Roman practice of depositing such bronze copies in the temple of Jupiter Capitolinus.

The text of the treaty given in 8:23–32 generally follows Roman usage except that the form had to be somewhat modified since the other party was "Judah . . . his brothers and the people of the Jews" (RSV), not a sovereign kingdom. (For a complete comparison, see Goldstein.) If the document is indeed authentic, as most historians argue, some difficulties in legal terminology have resulted from the translation of the original text from Latin into Hebrew and then in turn into the Greek translation of 1 Maccabees. The terms of the treaty are that each side promises to aid the other if attacked and not to aid the enemies of the other. Some scholars take the postscript concerning Demetrius in vv. 31–32 to be a later addition to the text (Josephus omits it).

9:1–22, The Death of Judah. Bacchides and Alcimus, the high priest, had fought in Judea already, according to 7:5–25. After the failure of Nicanor (7:39–50), Demetrius I again sent Bacchides accompanied by Alcimus to Judea, this time with "the right wing of the army," i.e., half of his infantry. From 9:4 we gather that he had some 20,000 soldiers. The route taken by the army is uncertain. One should probably read "Galilee" in v. 2 instead of "Gilgal" (so Josephus, accepted by Goldstein). There is an Arbela in Galilee but none known near Gilgal. Mesaloth probably derives from Hebrew *mesillot*, "steps," a name given to the village because of the shape of the cliffs. Yet it is difficult to see why the Seleucids would have entered Galilee and attacked one obscure village that was in difficult terrain. In any case, after taking this village and slaughtering its inhabitants, the Seleucids turned toward Jerusalem where they encamped in Nisan (March/April) of 160 B.C. They then marched to Berea, probably the modern El-Bireh, opposite Ramallah, ten miles north of Jerusalem. Meanwhile, Judah was encamped at Elasa, probably to be identified with Khirbet el-'Assi, located off the Jerusalem-Nablus road, near Ramallah, across a valley from El-Bireh. The fright and desertion of so many of Judah's soldiers presumes that the camps were located close to one another. Judah insisted on fighting the battle despite the advice of his troops. His speech in vv. 8–10 foreshadows the coming defeat.

Verse 11 is ambiguous in not specifying whether it is Judah's army or Bacchides' that marches out first. Tedesche translates literally, "The army set out from the camp and stood in battle line against them." Josephus took "the army" to be that of Bacchides who stood in battle formation arrayed against the Jews (*Antiquities of the Jews* 12.426). The second half of the verse does indeed describe a large army such as that of Bacchides, not a small band such as one that remained with Judah.

Although vastly outnumbered, the Jews initially routed the right wing of Bacchides' phalanx. The phrase "as far as Mount Azotus" (9:15, RSV) makes no geographical sense and is generally regarded as a corrupt reading. In any case, as the Jews pursued the Seleucid right wing, the left wing moved in behind Judah's forces and defeated them. Judah died on the battlefield (v. 18).

Josephus suggests that a truce allowed Jonathan and Simon to recover the body of Judah and to bury it at Modein (*Antiquities of the Jews* 12.432). Goldstein suggests that this truce may have resulted from the brothers' agreeing to call off their resistance to Alcimus. The author's attempt to model Judah's life and death after those of Israel's heroes and kings can be clearly seen in vv. 21–22. Verse 21 is influenced by 2 Sam.

1:19, David's lament for Saul and Jonathan. 1 Macc. 9:22 is an imitation of the style of royal chronicles preserved in the books of Kings (e.g., 1 Kings 11:41).

9:23–12:53
The Leadership of Jonathan

9:23–73, Jonathan's Defeat of Bacchides.

Alcimus and the pro-Seleucid Hellenistic Jews, abetted by Bacchides, quickly gained the upper hand after Judah's death. The phrases "the wicked sprouted," "and the evildoers flourished" in v. 23 are allusions to Ps. 92:7 (Goldstein). Note that the populace supported Alcimus and even cooperated in turning Judah's supporters over to the authorities. It was the cruel punishment of these heroes that must have again created the climate for revolt. It fell to Jonathan to succeed his brother and to take up the struggle against both the Seleucids and their Jewish allies (1 Macc. 9:31).

Jonathan, aware that Bacchides sought to kill him, fled with Simon and their men to the wilderness of Tekoa. Tekoa is about five miles southeast of Bethlehem, and the wilderness extended from Tekoa toward the Dead Sea. The pool where Jonathan and Simon camped may be the modern Bir ez-Za'feran, about three miles south of Tekoa, although other possibilities can be suggested. The presence of a well must have been one of the main reasons for taking refuge in this place. Verse 34, which describes Bacchides' pursuit of Jonathan, is almost certainly out of place. Its similarity to v. 43 suggests either that it originally preceded v. 43 (so Zeitlin) or, more probably, that it was a scribe's explanatory comment on v. 43, which was later copied into the manuscript at the wrong place (so Goldstein).

Jonathan sent John with the noncombatants and the baggage to ask the Nabateans if they would store their possessions (vv. 35–36). The Nabatean Arabs must have maintained some degree of freedom from the Seleucids and seemed like a reliable refuge. On the way, John and his party were intercepted by the Jambrites, an Arab tribe from Medeba some twelve miles east of the Dead Sea, and taken captive. Whether the Jambrites were also a Nabatean Arab tribe is not certain, but the author of 1 Maccabees does not associate them with the Nabateans, who are portrayed as sympathetic to the Hasmoneans (see 5:25). From 9:38 and 42 we gather that John died in the attack. We do not hear of the fate of the others.

An opportunity for revenge occurred when Jonathan and Simon heard news of a large Jambrite wedding procession from Nadabath to Medeba (vv. 37–38). Nadabath is probably to be identified with Nebo, somewhat north of

Medeba. After attacking the Jambrite wedding procession, Jonathan and his men took refuge in the swamps immediately north of the Dead Sea, on the east side of the Jordan. Bacchides and his troops crossed the Jordan on the Sabbath (reading v. 34 as an explanatory comment on v. 43; see above). They positioned themselves to the north of Jonathan facing south, so that the Jews were hemmed in by the Jordan on one side and the swamps on the north end of the Dead Sea on the other side. Jonathan's words in v. 44, "for today things are not as they were before" (RSV), is an allusion to the life-threatening situation that justified fighting on the Sabbath (cf. 2:34–41). Bacchides is pictured here as a coward who ran to take refuge in the rear when Jonathan attacked him. Jonathan and his men leapt into the Jordan and swam to the western shore, from which they made their escape. Bacchides suffered heavy casualties.

Bacchides fortified the citadel of Jerusalem (the Akra) and a string of towns to solidify his control of Judea. In all of them he built fortifications and placed garrisons that may have consisted of Jews loyal to Alcimus. The Akra was the base from which the Seleucids kept Alcimus' Hellenistic regime in power (cf. 1:29–40). It was there that Bacchides held hostages from among the aristocratic families to prevent them from throwing their lot in with Jonathan, whose exploits must have provoked widespread admiration.

According to 9:54, in May of 159 B.C. Alcimus altered the structure of the Temple, thus violating, in the author's view, the commands of the prophets Haggai, Zechariah, and Malachi, in whose time the Second Temple had been built. He attempted to tear down the barrier of the inner court. Most scholars consider this to be the wall that separated the Temple Mount from the Temple itself. Gentiles were permitted on the Temple Mount but not in the Temple itself. If so, Alcimus sought to discard the prohibition against allowing Gentiles access to the Temple. According to v. 55 he miraculously suffered a stroke and was unable to continue. Our author certainly sees this as divine intervention. Despite v. 57, which reports that Bacchides returned to Syria only after Alcimus' death, it is probable that Bacchides departed soon after completing the new fortifications, assuming Alcimus' control to have been established. In keeping with his attempt to model the history of the Hasmoneans after the early traditions of Israel, the concluding phrase of v. 57, "and the land of Judah had rest for two years" (RSV), is influenced by the language of Judg. 3:11, 30; 5:31; and 8:28.

The hellenized Jews summoned Bacchides back to Judea to deal with Jonathan and his men. Bacchides, seeking to avoid risking his forces, tried to get his allies in Judea to capture Jonathan. When the plan became known, Jonathan and his men took revenge, killing the fifty or so leaders of the pro-Seleucid party (9:61).

Bethbasi, where Jonathan and Simon assembled their forces, is to be identified with Khirbet Beit Bassa, about a mile southeast of Bethlehem. When Bacchides heard that Jonathan had fortified it, he tried unsuccessfully to conquer the town. Textual problems obscure the meaning of v. 66. The text followed by the RSV says that after leaving Simon in command at Bethbasi, Jonathan attacked two Arab tribes. Yet some manuscripts imply that he "placed in command" (so Zeitlin) these two allies in his battle against Bacchides. Goldstein similarly concludes that the text originally said that Jonathan summoned "Odomera and his brothers and the Phasironites in their encampment, so that they began to harass and attack Bacchides' troops." This view is supported also by Josephus (*Antiquities of the Jews* 13.28).

After securing the support of these nomadic tribes, Jonathan attacked Bacchides from the rear, while Simon set out to destroy the siege machines from within (v. 67). Upon defeat, Bacchides turned against the Hellenizers who had summoned him to Judea and killed many of them. He then decided to return to Syria.

As soon as Jonathan learned of Bacchides' intention to leave Judea, he proposed an exchange of prisoners and a truce (v. 70). There now ensued a long period of tranquility for Judea, some seven years until the events described in 10:69. Michmash, where Jonathan settled, is present day Mukhmas, eight miles northeast of Jerusalem. It was there that Saul and Jonathan had defeated the Philistines (1 Sam. 13:2). Jonathan the Hasmonean was not secure enough to control Jerusalem. He still had no official position and was not high priest. Judea remained a Seleucid dependency. Yet Jonathan led as a charismatic leader, much like the biblical judges, as 1 Macc. 9:73 suggests.

10:1–21, Jonathan Confirmed in Office by Alexander Balas. By 152 B.C. the hostility of Rome and of a number of petty kingdoms against Demetrius I made the time ripe for the appearance of Alexander Epiphanes, known as Alexander Balas, a pretender to the Seleucid throne. His claim to be the son of Antiochus IV Epiphanes was widely doubted in antiquity, but his attempt to gain control of the empire was abetted by the fact that Demetrius had taken to drink and had secluded himself outside Antioch. By spring or summer of 152 B.C. Alexander Balas conquered Ptolemais (Acco) on the Mediterranean seacoast. When Demetrius I began his military offensive against Alexander, he sought to make Jonathan his ally. He therefore gave Jonathan the power to raise an army and de-

livered into his hands the hostages (cf. 9:53).

Jonathan's legal recognition allowed him to take up residence in Jerusalem (10:7). The actual text of the letter from Demetrius granting these privileges to Jonathan is not preserved. Although the men in the Akra were forced to accede to this letter, they still held their position, indicating that Judea was not yet independent of Seleucid rule. The rebuilding of the walls of Jerusalem was also intended to enhance Jonathan's position, as well as to provide defense. These walls had been torn down under Lysias (see 6:62). Many of the Seleucid soldiers (see 9:52) fled, although the hellenized Jews remained in their refuge at Beth-zur (10:14).

Alexander felt constrained to better the offer of Demetrius, as he recognized the danger that an alliance of Demetrius and Jonathan would pose. In proposing to make Jonathan not only a Friend of the King (an honorary position) but also an ally, he intended to grant him some degree of autonomy. Accordingly he made him high priest (10:20), an office bestowed by the Seleucids only from the time of Antiochus IV. Indeed, the high-priesthood had been vacant since the death of Alcimus in 159 B.C. Jonathan was not of the appropriate priestly family, so that although the law of the Torah permitted him to occupy this office, his appointment was a departure from a tradition that extended from the time of Solomon up to his own day. Indeed, opposition to the Hasmonean takeover of the high-priesthood is probably the reason for the founding of the Qumran sect. The purple robe, always part of the garb of the Friends of the King, and the crown of gold were normal parts of priestly attire in the Hellenistic world. Jonathan assumed his position in 152 B.C. when he put on the Jewish high-priestly garments and celebrated the rites of the festival of Tabernacles (Sukkoth). At the same time he took advantage of his new autonomy to expand his army greatly (v. 21).

10:22–50, Demetrius I and His Defeat. Demetrius realized that he had been upstaged and sought to redress the balance by granting Jonathan even greater privileges. Since he was in fact the ruling sovereign, he was able to marshal a much more extensive list of concessions. Scholars have noted that his letter is addressed "to the nation of the Jews" (v. 25), not mentioning either Jonathan or his high-priesthood. It is possible that this was an attempt to woo the Jewish people away from Jonathan's leadership. Yet it is more likely that since he had not appointed Jonathan to his position, he preferred to make allusion simply to "the high priest" (v. 32). Demetrius ignored the agreement Jonathan had made with Alexander. The difficult syntax of this letter may be the result, if it is indeed genu-

ine, of the fact that the author of 1 Maccabees translated it from Greek into Hebrew, from which it was later retranslated in the Greek text of 1 Maccabees.

The tribute mentioned in 10:29 refers to annual payments required from communities. The salt tax and crown levies were originally in-kind payments later converted to cash payments. All three taxes were to be abolished by Demetrius. The high proportion of the taxes on the grain and fruit (one-third and one-half, respectively) make it likely that these levies had been instituted to punish Judea for having revolted. The three districts to be added to Judea were Aphairema, Lydda, and Rathamin (see 11:34). These three areas, originally transferred to Judea from Samaria by Alexander the Great, had been taken away from Judea by Antiochus IV. In 10:38 Demetrius I proposes to join them again to Judea. Samaria and Galilee are mentioned together since they constituted a single province.

The granting of special status to Jerusalem (v. 31) meant that henceforth it would not be liable to attack except as a result of aggression by its citizens. It was also to be freed from Seleucid customs duties. Demetrius was even willing to surrender control of the citadel, the Akra, to the high priest. This would have meant the end of Seleucid domination over the city, tantamount to de facto independence for the Jews and recognition of the high priest as their ruler. Jewish captives, who must have been scattered throughout the Hellenistic world in the aftermath of the Maccabean wars, were all to be set free. Moreover, beasts of burden owned by Jews were to be exempt from forced service to the government (v. 33).

Demetrius also proposed that the days surrounding Jewish festivals and the festivals themselves were to be days of customs exemption for the Jews. They would not be compelled at these times to discharge civic duties or to appear in court. The right to serve as trusted members of the armed forces was to be restored to the Jews, who, led by Jewish officers, would be allowed to observe the laws of the Torah even while serving in the Seleucid army (v. 37).

The granting of Ptolemais and its revenues to the Temple (v. 39) was an empty gesture, since it was under the control of the pretender Alexander Balas. The grant may even have been intended to punish the city for supporting Demetrius' rival. Verse 41 is ambiguous. Tedesche and the RSV take it to mean that "all the additional funds which the government officials have not paid as they did in the first years, they shall give from now on for the service of the temple" (RSV). Goldstein translates, "And if there should be any surplus which the officials in charge shall not have paid out, they shall

apply it from now on, as in former years, to the needs of the temple." The disagreement concerns the identity of the officials. The RSV (following most scholars) assumes that these are Seleucid officials who from the time of Antiochus IV ceased paying various expenses of the Temple. Goldstein takes this statement as referring to the Jewish Temple officials. He conjectures that there had been a dispute regarding funds donated by the Seleucid rulers. Excess funds had been appropriated for building purposes, although the Seleucids expected them to be used for sacrifices. This letter formally permits the procedure of reassignment that had been used by Temple officials. Further, according to most scholars, v. 42 applies to the cancellation of a levy against the Temple by the Seleucids.

The right of asylum in the sanctuary, to which v. 43 refers, did not exist for any category of criminal in biblical tradition (Exod. 21:14), let alone for debtors. Here it is extended based on Hellenistic practice. In financing the rebuilding of the Temple and the city walls (v. 45), Demetrius follows the pattern set by the Persian kings (Ezra 6:8; 7:20).

The support of Alexander Balas by the Romans, long allies of the Hasmoneans (1 Macc. 8:1–32), must have been a factor in the decision of the Jews to reject the privileges offered by Demetrius. They chose to remain loyal to Alexander, judging his alliance as more reliable. After the defeat of Alexander Balas by Ptolemy VI Philometor and the establishment of Demetrius II, son of Demetrius I, as ruler of the Seleucid kingdom (11:14–19), these same privileges were reconfirmed by Demetrius II and, this time, accepted by the Jews (11:20–37).

Manuscripts of 1 Maccabees and interpreters are divided over the sequence of events in 10:48–50. After the initial confrontation, either the army of Demetrius or that of Alexander fled with the enemy in hot pursuit. If Alexander's army was in pursuit (RSV) we can easily understand how Demetrius was lost in battle. If it was Demetrius who gained the upper hand (Goldstein), then we must assume that Alexander rallied his men and turned the battle around, at which time Demetrius fell. (For a thorough discussion, see Goldstein.) In any case, with the death of Demetrius I in the summer of 150 B.C., Alexander emerged as undisputed king of the Seleucid empire.

10:51–66, Alexander's Meeting with Jonathan. Alexander asked for the hand of Cleopatra III Thea (v. 57), daughter of Ptolemy VI Philometor. (Alexander's letter of proposal is probably the composition of the author, not an authentic document.) Ptolemy VI had supported Alexander because of his hostility to Demetrius I, caused by the latter's attempt to take Cyprus from him in 156/155 B.C. The wedding took place in summer of 150 B.C., shortly after the defeat of Demetrius I.

Jonathan, invited to the wedding, took the opportunity to ingratiate himself with Ptolemy VI and Alexander Balas by giving manifold gifts to them and their officials, the Friends of the King (vv. 59–60). The protests of some hellenized Jews were of no avail. Jonathan was treated royally and elevated to a Chief Friend of the King (cf. 10:20, where he became a Friend). He was officially designated commander and governor of the province (v. 65). Jonathan's de facto control of the province of Judea had now become de jure.

10:67–89, Jonathan's Victories.

Sometime after March of 147 B.C. Demetrius II, son of Demetrius I, attempted to recapture his kingdom from Alexander Balas. The latter had been an incompetent and unpopular king. Demetrius II had been sent by his father with a sum of money to the Greek city of Knidos, from which he set out with the help of mercenaries from Crete. Alexander returned to Antioch so as to cement his control of the Seleucid empire. In the meantime Apollonius, governor of Coele Syria (southern Syria) switched loyalties to Demetrius II, as he had originally been a supporter of Demetrius I. Camping at Jamnia (Yavneh on the Mediterranean coast) Apollonius challenged Jonathan to open combat (vv. 70–73). Jonathan, it seems, was the only local ruler to remain loyal to Alexander Balas.

Jonathan accepted the challenge together with Simon, his brother. Joppa, modern Jaffa, to the south of present day Tel Aviv, was a city on the coastal plain but adjacent to Jonathan's territory. He quickly overran the garrison of Apollonius' men.

Apollonius with his horsemen and infantry marched south through Azotus (biblical Ashdod), exposing his large force in the plain. Near Ashdod a major battle ensued, which turned out to be an ambush carefully laid by Apollonius (vv. 79–80). Jonathan's men held out until the enemy horses were exhausted. At that point Simon, whose men had been held in reserve and were fresh, quickly overwhelmed and dispersed Apollonius' forces. Jonathan pursued them to the temple of Beth-dagon, which he burned. The entire operation left Apollonius' army completely destroyed.

After hearing of his exploits at Ashdod, the people of Ashkelon quickly opened their city to Jonathan (v. 86). This foray into the coastal plain was the beginning of a process throughout the Hasmonean period of extending Jewish sovereignty to this region. Control of the coastal plain was necessary to stabilize Hasmonean rule over Palestine as a whole, as well as to make possible the economic prosperity that to

a great extent depended on Mediterranean trade. Jonathan's defeat of an ally of Demetrius II led Alexander Balas to elevate Jonathan even further, from among the Chief Friends of the King (v. 65) to the status of Kinsman (v. 89). Since he already controlled Ashdod and Ashkelon, Alexander ceded Ekron to him.

11:1–19, Ptolemy VI's Invasion.

Josephus (Antiquities of the Jews 13.103–10) suggests that Ptolemy VI Philometor entered Palestine to help his son-in-law Alexander but soon discovered that Alexander plotted to kill him. As a result he decided to switch his allegiance to Demetrius II. 1 Macc. 11:1–8 presents Ptolemy's intentions as treacherous from the start. In any case, when he arrived, aided by Alexander's welcome, Ptolemy quickly took control of the country. He kept his intentions secret, pretending to befriend Jonathan, who accompanied him as far as the Eleutherus River, present-day Nahr el-Kebir, north of Tripolis in Lebanon.

Ptolemy took his daughter from Alexander and married her to Demetrius II, justifying his actions with the claim that Alexander had plotted to kill him. The author of 1 Maccabees sees this as a false charge, simply a justification for adding Alexander's territory to the Ptolemaic holdings (v. 11). Ptolemy soon took advantage of Alexander's absence in Cilicia (v. 14) and claimed the throne of the Seleucid empire for himself as well. Josephus, however, states that it was the people of Antioch who attempted to crown Ptolemy, although Ptolemy insisted they be ruled by Demetrius II (Antiquities of the Jews 13.113–115).

According to the first-century B.C. geographer Strabo, Alexander met Ptolemy in battle on the banks of the Oinoparas River in the plain to the northeast of the city of Antioch (Geography 16.2.8). Alexander fled to the east where he met his end at the hands of an Arab sheik (11:16–17). Ptolemy's death, laconically reported in 11:18, was said by the Roman historian Livy to have occurred as a result of surgery in July of 145 B.C. (Livy Summaries 52). The native population, to ensure that their cities would not be annexed by the Ptolemaic empire, immediately rose up and slaughtered the garrisons Ptolemy had posted in Seleucid territory (vv. 3, 18). By the summer of 145 B.C. Demetrius II ruled Syria after a five-year struggle to regain the empire of his father Demetrius I.

11:20–37, Jonathan and Demetrius II.

Jonathan took advantage of the instability in the Seleucid empire to try to rid Jerusalem of the Seleucid garrison. (On the importance of control of the Akra, see the commentary above on 10:32.) Hellenistic elements in Judea appealed to Demetrius, so that Jonathan was forced to present himself at Ptolemais. There he demonstrated both his popular support and his wealth and declared his allegiance to Demetrius II. His tactics were successful, no doubt because the king was in need of such allies to consolidate his own power. He therefore confirmed the status of Jonathan as high priest and made him one of his Chief Friends, a status higher than that of Friend of the King.

The text of the letter that Demetrius issued (11:29–37) is parallel in many details to that of Demetrius I in 10:25–45, except that the mention of the Akra, which Demetrius I had offered to release (10:32), is conspicuously absent in the version of Demetrius II. From 11:41 we can gather that Jonathan had to agree at Ptolemais to lift his siege on the Akra, which he had left in place upon his departure (v. 23). The letter to Jonathan was in reality a copy of a letter Demetrius II sent to Lasthenes, chief of the mercenaries he had hired in Crete (Josephus *Antiquities of the Jews* 13.86). By now, Lasthenes had probably become Demetrius' leading minister (Goldstein). "Father" (v. 32) was an honorific title. In response to Jonathan's request (v. 28) Demetrius cedes three districts of Samaria to him (see 10:30, 38, and the commentary above). Aphairema is Ephraim; Rathamin is Ramathaim. (On the tax abatements of v. 34, see 10:29–30 and the commentary above.) Just as in 10:29, the exemption was for the Jews, designated in 11:34 as "those who offer sacrifice in Jerusalem," thus excluding the Samaritans (so Goldstein). Verses 32–36 are the text of Demetrius II's letter to Lasthenes. Verse 37 is an instruction from Demetrius to Jonathan to put a copy of his letter to Lasthenes prominently on display on the Temple Mount. The display of such decrees was common practice in the Hellenistic world.

11:38–53, Jonathan Aids Demetrius II.

Demetrius made the mistake of retiring his troops, thus creating a large group of discontented, unemployed soldiers. He retained only the mercenaries who were probably hated by the population. This set the stage for Trypho's uprising. Trypho, whose real name was Diodotus, was one of Alexander Balas's commanders at Antioch. He had been hostile to Demetrius I and II and had been involved in the attempt to crown Ptolemy VI Philometor in Antioch. By 144 B.C. he had taken the designation Trypho, "the magnificent." Then he convinced the Arab sheik raising Alexander's young son Antiochus to release the boy so that he could be crowned king. The Greco-Roman historian Diodorus gives the name of the guardian as Iamblichos, Semitic Yamliku (Diodorus *Library of History* 33.4a). This must be the origin of our author's Imalkue.

Jonathan turned now to diplomatic means to end Seleucid control of the Akra. The implication of Demetrius II's answer in vv. 42–43

was that he would relinquish control in return for Jonathan's sending him troops to help quell the incipient revolt against him in Antioch. As the rebellion increased in proportion, the king called on the Jewish soldiers (among other mercenaries), who through massive slaughter and destruction (the numbers in this passage all seem exaggerated) succeeded, at least temporarily, in keeping Demetrius in power. (See Goldstein, who supplies additional details from Josephus *Antiquities of the Jews* 13.135–41 and Diodorus *Library of History* 33.4.2–4.) Verse 53 implies that Demetrius did not turn the Akra over to Jonathan, despite his agreement (v. 42). The entire episode must have made the Jews unpopular in the Seleucid empire, since they had helped to preserve the rule of a brutal despot in the face of mass opposition. This opposition was now to lead to widespread support for Trypho.

11:54–74, Jonathan Is Again Victorious.

Antiochus VI Epiphanes must have reigned, in name, from 145 to 142 B.C. Since he was the son of Alexander Balas and Cleopatra III Thea (daughter of Ptolemy VI Philopator), he could not have been born before 149 B.C. Clearly, his rule was but a fiction to legitimize that of Trypho. Demetrius II fled to Cilicia (Josephus) or to Seleucia (Livy), in either case continuing to hold parts of the kingdom. With the help of the disaffected veterans (see commentary above on 11:38–40), Trypho took Antioch. Over Antiochus VI's seal, Trypho confirmed Jonathan's high-priesthood, including its political powers, as well as naming him to be a Friend of the King, with all the attendant privileges. Simon's territory as commander (*strategos*) extended from Tyre (the Ladder of Tyre reached from Tyre to Haifa) to Wadi el-Arish, the border of Egypt. Trypho's alliance with so strong a supporter can only be explained in light of his need for Jonathan's wealth and military power. At the same time, Jonathan's survival among all these Seleucid pretenders could only be assured by such quick changes of allegiance.

"Beyond the river" (v. 60, RSV) refers to the area known in the Persian period as the province of 'Abar Nahara, "the Trans-Euphrates province" of Syria and Phoenicia (Goldstein). There Jonathan recruited allies. He then turned to establishing control of the Mediterranean coastline (see commentary above on 10:86–89). Gaza's resistance resulted from the close relations this city enjoyed with Demetrius II. Goldstein suggests that Jonathan was *strategos* of the province of Coele Syria, but not of Phoenicia. This would explain his reaching as far as Damascus.

Supporters of Demetrius II continued their resistance, assembling a large force at Kedesh, some four miles northwest of Meron. Meanwhile Simon successfully took the fortress of Beth-zur from the hellenized Jews. Jonathan and his men camped at the Sea of Galilee. The claim that all of Jonathan's men except two fled in the face of the ambush must be exaggerated, as realized already by Josephus (*Antiquities of the Jews* 13.16), who suggested that about fifty men remained. Jonathan is here pictured as turning to prayer in the face of great danger. As the tide of battle turned, his men returned and defeated the forces of Demetrius II decisively, showing that Jonathan's prayer was answered. After this narrow escape, Jonathan returned to Jerusalem.

12:1–23, Alliances with Rome and Sparta. Because the time was propitious (Gk. *kairos*, "time," appears here in 12:1 in the sense of fortune or luck), Jonathan decided to renew the alliance with Rome (see chap. 8). The Spartans, to whom Jonathan also sent letters, had themselves demonstrated friendship to Rome. The description that follows is consistent with the diplomatic usages of the period. Jonathan's ambassadors were sent sometime between the start of the reign of Antiochus VI in 145 and the death of Jonathan in 143 B.C. As was customary, all ambassadors were allowed to address the senate. In addition, letters of safe conduct were normally granted.

What follows in 12:6–18 is the text of the letter from Jonathan to Sparta. (From v. 2 it seems that other such letters were sent to other places, but our author did not include them.) Goldstein argues at length for the authenticity of this letter. In v. 6 "the senate" (RSV) obscures the use of Greek *gerousia*, correctly rendered "the Council of Elders" (Goldstein). This is the first mention of the existence of such an institution in the Hasmonean era. Jonathan's government had been transformed from that of a rebel chieftain into an organized polity supported by a representative council. Jonathan refers to a letter (quoted in vv. 19–23) sent to Onias I, high priest from 320 to 290 B.C. (Zeitlin), or to his grandson Onias II, second half of the third century B.C. (Goldstein) by Arius I, king of Sparta in 309–265 B.C. Jonathan asks the Spartans to renew the terms of "alliance and friendship" that the original correspondence had proffered. The letter accents the renewal of the Hasmonean alliance with Rome in view of Sparta's close relations with Rome. Of the two ambassadors mentioned in v. 16, Antipater's father may be the Jason who made the first alliance with Rome in 8:17. Both men appear again in 14:22, 24 and may have been members of diplomatic families.

The letter that purports to be a copy of the one the Spartans sent to Onias I or II (v. 7) is judged by most scholars to be inauthentic, although some accept its veracity (see Goldstein for arguments in favor of its authenticity). The claim of v. 21 that the Jews and Spartans are both descended from Abraham must have come from some lost Hellenistic work. Such speculations on the kinship of nations appear in both pagan and Jewish histories of the Hellenistic era. The letter intended that the envoys who brought it would enlarge on the nature of Sparta, its culture and its people.

12:24–53, Trypho Captures Jonathan. The author returns to the narrative of chap. 11. Jonathan sought to avoid meeting the army of Demetrius II in his own territory, so he marched to the region of Hamath (modern Hama in Syria), known as the Amathitis, in the Orontes Valley. Goldstein's translation of 12:26, "were preparing to attack them," ignores the technical, military sense of Greek *tassontai*. Better is "were drawing up in formation to attack them [the Jews]" (cf. RSV; Tedesche). The enemy used a ruse to avoid Jonathan's attack and escaped across the Eleutherus river. Failing to overtake the forces of Demetrius, Jonathan attacked a local Arab tribe.

The tribe of the Zabadeans probably gave their name to Zebdani, northwest of Damascus. Jonathan had mastered an empire that in the east extended as far as that of the United Monarchy under David and Solomon. At the same time Simon was actively consolidating control of the coastal plain (vv. 33–34). Joppa (Jaffa) had apparently not been garrisoned by Jonathan after he took it (see 10:76). The area was in danger of coming under the control of Demetrius II, whose stronghold was on the coastal plain of Phoenicia.

Jonathan was constrained to consult the elders before undertaking the various projects. These elders were probably the members of the *gerousia*, the council. Jonathan's status in Antiochus VI's empire allowed him to fortify Jerusalem. He attempted to cut off the citadel (Akra), still occupied by the forces of Demetrius II, to starve the occupants out (v. 36). The wall of Jerusalem facing the Kidron Valley on the east was also repaired. Adida, which Simon fortified, is Hebrew Hadid (Ezra 2:33; Neh. 7:37), located less than four miles east-northeast of Lydda, on a hill above the plains of Judea.

Goldstein's translation, that Trypho "plotted" to become king, is to be preferred to the RSV's "attempted" (1 Macc. 12:35), since the actual murder of Antiochus VI would not take place until after that of Jonathan. Trypho intended to remove the boy king and to assume the rule of the Empire ("Asia"). Jonathan had amassed so much power that he constituted the main threat to Trypho's assumption of the Seleucid monarchy. Apparently Trypho thought he would easily lure Jonathan to Bethshan, but Jonathan came so heavily escorted that Trypho had to resort to a ruse.

Trypho offered to grant Jonathan Ptolemais, that is, Hebrew Acco. Although Demetrius I had proposed to give it to the Jews (10:39), they had rejected his entire offer. Its inhabitants had remained hostile to the Hasmoneans.

Jonathan entered Ptolemais with only a thousand men. Trypho had sent ahead orders to seize Jonathan and kill the rest. Trypho's men attempted to overtake and destroy the other two thousand of Jonathan's soldiers who had been left in Galilee, but they were able to withstand the attack. Jonathan's troops thought, however, that he had been killed, and so, on their return all Israel mourned for him. 1 Macc. 12:53 indicates that both Seleucid pretenders, Demetrius II and Trypho, were now enemies of the Jews (Zeitlin).

13:1–16:24
The Rule of Simon

13:1–30, The Death of Jonathan. The death of Jonathan left the people shocked. Simon had to rally them to stand firm against the onslaught of Trypho. It is doubtful if 13:3–6 actually preserves the words of Simon. Rather, this speech is probably from the pen of the author. Simon is pictured as presuming his brother Jonathan to be dead. In response to his address, the people declare Simon to be *hegoumenos* (Gk.), "leader, chief." Jonathan had been designated *archonta kai hegoumenon*, "ruler and leader," in 9:30.

The walls of Jerusalem, which Jonathan had started to rebuild (12:36–37), were not yet complete, so Simon hastened to finish the work (13:10–11). Simon feared that the inhabitants of Joppa (Jaffa) would defect to Trypho, opening up for him the southern coastal plain. So he sent Jonathan son of Absalom to occupy it. He may have been the brother of Mattathias son of Absalom, favorably mentioned in 11:70.

When Trypho set out to invade Judah, taking the still living Jonathan with him, Simon confronted him from the fortified town of Adida (see 12:38). Again Trypho resorted to a ruse, claiming that he was holding Jonathan for nonpayment of debt. The money he claimed must have been either an unpaid fee of some kind or a tax Jonathan had failed to collect (Goldstein). Although Simon saw through the promises of Trypho, he had little choice but to comply, fearing a loss of popular support if he did not (13:17–18).

Trypho finally was ready to face Simon in the field. Trypho's army traveled through the lowlands from the south, but Simon blocked him at every point from entering the hill country to approach Jerusalem. Adora, where Trypho tried to circle around Simon's forces, is biblical Adoraim, about six miles southwest of Hebron.

The men of the Akra were short of provisions as a result of the steps Jonathan had taken in 12:36. Their appeal to Trypho led him to finally chance cutting through, but at the last minute he was prevented by a snowstorm. Instead he turned toward Gilead where he killed Jonathan, probably out of frustration. Baskama, where he buried Jonathan, cannot be identified. It is curious that the people of the Akra, supporters of Demetrius II, turned to Trypho. If this report is accurate, it would indicate that now that Trypho had broken with Jonathan, they saw him as a potential ally.

Jonathan, who had been buried in Baskama, was disinterred and reinterred in Modein where 1 Maccabees says that Mattathias (2:70) and Judah (9:19) and, as we see, Eleazar, John, and now Jonathan were buried (13:25–30). The elaborate tomb and monument has been explained by Goldstein as including motifs common in the Hellenistic period for commemorating victory in both land and sea battles.

13:31–53, Simon Brings Independence to Judea. Trypho now felt powerful enough to have the young king Antiochus VI, probably seven years old at the time, murdered. Livy relates that Trypho arranged to have the king's surgeons kill him while supposedly operating to remove a stone. Thus in 143 or 142 B.C. Trypho crowned himself king of the Seleucid empire ("Asia"). The chaos that ensued allowed Simon to intensify his efforts to fortify Judea.

In addition, Simon was now in an enviable diplomatic position. Trypho had violated his agreements with Simon, and his military and political position was deteriorating rapidly. Demetrius II was in need of support and seemed about to emerge victorious. Simon therefore sent emissaries to Demetrius to ask for tax relief in return for his loyalty. Demetrius agreed, citing his earlier grant of privileges to the Jews (11:30–37), which he now reconfirmed. In his letter, quoted in 13:36–40, Demetrius alluded only subtly to the Hasmonean support of Trypho and Antiochus VI. Most significantly, he granted the tax exemptions.

To our author, this tax relief was tantamount to the culmination of the Hasmonean quest for freedom from foreign domination. Finally, from 142 B.C., tribute would no longer be paid to the Seleucids. Accordingly, documents would henceforth be dated according to the high-priesthood, not according to the reigns of Seleucid rulers. Simon, we may conclude, had been elected to the high-priesthood after Jonathan's death. (On the titles granted to Simon, see commentary above on 10:59–66; 11:54–59.)

Gezer (Gazara) and the Akra were the two remaining Hellenistic strongholds Simon had to conquer. (The reading "Gaza" in the Greek text of 13:43 must be corrected with Josephus.) After conquering Gezer, he set about turning it into a traditional Jewish town, expelling the Hellenistic pagans and destroying their idols, and, it seems, driving out hellenized Jews as well. He built a palace there, intending to guarantee his continued control of the region.

By 141 B.C., Jonathan's walls (12:36), as intended, had led to a serious food shortage in the Akra (13:49). Its inhabitants sued for peace and were expelled by Simon. The idols were also removed. As in the case of the conquest of Gezer, Simon and his men sang hymns of praise, probably psalms. They carried palm branches as symbols of victory. Indeed, this day was decreed a holiday and was listed in the *Megillat Ta'anit*, the Scroll of Fasting. Only later were such minor feasts abolished in favor of Hanukkah and Purim. Although Josephus claims that Simon razed the citadel, the account of 1 Maccabees is to be accepted. Our author appends the remark that by this time John Hyrcanus, Simon's son, was ready to assume a role of leadership. He was appointed as military commander (*hegoumenon*) and lived in Gezer, while Simon took up residence in the recently conquered Akra in Jerusalem.

14:1–15, The Glory of Simon. Trypho was by now extremely weak. The rising Parthian empire had by 142–141 B.C. already taken Babylonia from the Seleucids. Demetrius II marched off to oppose that threat. Our author interpreted this decision as an attempt to increase the size of his army so as to finally defeat Trypho (14:1). Arsaces VI (Mithradates I), king of Parthia in 171–138 B.C., was at this time in Hyrcania (near the Caspian Sea). He dispatched his generals, who soon took Demetrius captive. Other sources indicate that after he was exhibited as an object lesson for Parthia's subjects, Demetrius was later married to Mithradates' sister.

It is difficult to understand why a poem in praise of Simon appears at this point in the text (14:4–15). We would have expected it either at the end of chap. 13 or at the end of 14. The poem may originally have constituted the conclusion of the book, as Josephus ceases following 1 Maccabees in his account at this point. The poem praises Simon for his military exploits but, more importantly, for living in accord with the Torah and for bringing peace and prosperity to his people. In v. 15 we learn that he donated vessels to the Temple, a matter not alluded to elsewhere.

14:16–24, Alliances with Rome and Sparta. From vv. 16 and 17 it is clear that the rumors concerning Jonathan's death and Simon's accession circulated separately, so that the two events appear to have been separated by some time. In view of his still precarious position as high priest, an office in which the Seleucids had not yet confirmed him, Simon sought to gain the recognition of the allies of the Hasmoneans. Verse 18 reports that the Spartans wrote to Simon to renew the alliance previously established with the Hasmoneans (see 12:5–23). The envoys mentioned in the Spartans' letter are the very same envoys who were sent by Jonathan to Sparta and Rome in 12:16–17. Simon relied on their previous experience and their personal contacts to ensure their success. Only Numenius proceeded on to Rome. The shield of gold he presented to the Romans is said to have weighed a thousand minas, over a thousand pounds (14:24).

Goldstein, to solve a variety of chronological and textual problems, places 15:15–24 (containing the conclusion of Numenius' mission and the Roman's letter of reply) between 14:24 and 14:25. In fact, the last part of 1 Maccabees (from the end of chap. 13 on) is poorly edited, and there is no reason to expect this letter to have appeared in its proper place.

14:25–49, The Great Assembly. In gratitude for the accomplishments of Simon and his family an assembly of the Jews promulgated a document in praise of Simon that was inscribed on bronze tablets and displayed on Mount Zion. The document was dated to September 13, 140 B.C. (Goldstein). There is one textual problem in v. 28. The RSV translates "in Asaramel," taking Greek *asaramel* as a place name. The Greek word may be a rendering of a Hebrew phrase, either *hasar 'am 'el*, "the courtyard of the people of God," or *sar 'am 'el*, "prince of the people of God." Goldstein and Zeitlin prefer to assume that the text is corrupt and to translate "and prince of God's People" (Goldstein), taking this phrase as a title given to Simon alongside that of high priest. The document was proclaimed in a great assembly. While some scholars wish to see this as indicating the existence of an ongoing Sanhedrin, the occasion should be understood instead as an *ad hoc* gathering that occurred only on such major occasions as the official installation of a new high priest.

The first section of the document (vv. 29–34) recounts the glorious deeds of Simon and is in many ways a prose parallel to the poem in 14:4–15. In addition to matters already narrated in 1 Maccabees, we learn here of Simon's financial commitments to the liberation of his people. The passage stresses Simon's efforts to bring the entire country under Jewish control, not only Judea but also the border town of Beth-zur and the cities of the coastal plain.

Verse 35 states that Simon became leader and high priest before capturing the Akra (so chaps. 13–14). Indeed, this document shows that the "great assembly" that issued it was convened only to confirm the high-priesthood and temporal rule of Simon; Simon's status had already been recognized by Demetrius II (13:36) and by the people (13:42). Our text claims that Simon's alliance with Rome led Demetrius II to recognize him. Yet the order of events in 1 Maccabees would place the Roman exchange after Demetrius II's letter. It is possible that Simon had dispatched his ambassadors to Rome immediately after the death of Jonathan and that he had secured a response before Demetrius II's letter. It is also possible that our author was confused about the chronology and drew this incorrect conclusion from the information before him.

The clause contained in 14:41–45 is the resolution that follows the series of "whereas" clauses in vv. 29–40. These, therefore, are the new conditions bestowed by the assembly. Simon's high-priesthood is to be hereditary. Recognizing that he is not of the Zadokite line, the document provides that this status is to continue "until a true prophet shall arise." In addition, the document spells out his power over the Temple and the privileges to be extended to him by the people. Verse 45 concludes the document with a clause indicating the consequence of its violation. Goldstein suggests that "shall be liable to punishment" (RSV) refers to the death penalty.

In 14:46–49 the text records that both the people and Simon officially accepted these conditions. Therefore, in accord with normal legal usage of the Hellenistic period, copies of the agreement were to be provided for both sides. The copy of the document for the people was to be set up in public (perhaps in the Temple; cf. v. 27) while that for the Hasmoneans was to be deposited in the Temple archives (so Zeitlin).

15:1–14, Simon and Antiochus VII.

Antiochus VII Euergetes (reigned 138–129 B.C.) was known as "Sidetes," since he grew up at Side in Pamphylia, in southern Asia Minor. He was the son of Demetrius I and younger brother of Demetrius II. After his brother was captured by Arsaces (see 14:2–3), he attempted to gain control of the Seleucid kingdom for himself. His main obstacle was Trypho, who was still in control of much of Syria. Naturally, he turned to Simon to enlist him as an ally. The "islands of the sea," from which Antiochus wrote, is probably a reference to Rhodes, where Antiochus received news of his brother's capture, according to the ancient historian Appian (Syrian Wars 68). He confirmed all the privileges accorded to Simon by his brother Demetrius II and the other Seleucid pretenders. The granting of rights of coinage was new and meant that Simon could produce

bronze coins. This clearly represented a further step in the direction of independence. These promises, however, were apparently abrogated (see 15:28–31).

In 38 B.C. Antiochus VII arrived in the Seleucid territory. He was unable at first to make any headway until the advisers of Cleopatra III Thea, originally the wife of Alexander Balas (10:58), then of Demetrius II (11:9), advised her to throw her lot in with Antiochus VII and marry him. This alliance resulted in the mass desertion described in 15:10 (Goldstein, based on Josephus Antiquities of the Jews 13.221–222). Trypho took refuge in Dor, nine miles north of Caesarea, an ancient Phoenician port that had remained faithful to him. Antiochus VII had substantial forces, although the numbers in v. 13 are probably exaggerated. Excavations at Dor have revealed evidence of this battle. The account of this siege is continued below in v. 25.

15:15–24, Renewal of Ties with Rome.

Goldstein places this section between 14:24 and 14:25 (see commentary above on 14:24–25), and, indeed, in its present place it interrupts the description of the siege and capture of Dor. Further, the addressing of a letter to Demetrius II (15:22) can only be possible before the Romans learned of his capture by the Parthians. The consul Lucius, named as author of the letter in v. 16, has been identified by Goldstein as Lucius Caecilius Metellus, who was consul in 142. Goldstein considers this letter to be chronologically earlier than its place in the book. Zeitlin identifies the author as Lucius Calpurnius Piso, 140–139 B.C., assuming the text to be in order. In any case, this consul wrote letters to numerous kings and countries, and a copy of one such letter was delivered to Simon. The acceptance of the gold shield (see 14:24) indicated Roman willingness to renew their ties with the Hasmoneans. New to this document is the granting of the right of extradition to Simon. (For the identification of the kings and localities, see Goldstein and Zeitlin.)

15:25–16:10, Defeat of Cendebeus.

Verse 25 returns to the narration of the siege of Dor, after the interruption of vv. 15–24. Although there are some difficulties with the translation of v. 25, the verse seems to refer to a siege after the one Antiochus laid in v. 14. Simon, believing that he had entered into an alliance with Antiochus VII, attempted to come to his aid. By this time, after his marriage to Cleopatra III Thea and the attendant alliances, Antiochus no longer felt that he needed Simon, so he took a harder line. His envoy demanded the return of the Seleucid strongholds Simon had taken, seeing them as falling outside the privileges granted by Demetrius II. Further, he demanded the contraction of the Hasmonean realm to the original province of Judea, long outgrown by the exploits of Jonathan and Simon. Antiochus' true colors were shown when he demanded payment of tribute in lieu of the return of all these territories.

Athenobius, the king's envoy, delivered this message to Simon in person (v. 32). Simon argued that he had the right by law to reconquer Jewish territory and to protect his people from their enemies. For the gold and silver service that Athenobius observed, see 11:58, where Antiochus VI granted Jonathan the right to use such vessels. Simon's offer to pay only one-fifth of the tribute demanded (v. 35) left Athenobius and Antiochus VII offended.

Meanwhile, Trypho had succeeded in running the naval blockade (15:14), escaping through Ptolemais (Acco) to Orthosia, a few miles north of Tripolis. He then moved on to Apamea where he met his end, perhaps by suicide, after being besieged by Antiochus VII (Goldstein). Antiochus VII appointed Cendebeus commander of the coastal region and instructed him to invade Judea (vv. 38–39). Moving down the coast, Cendebeus first came to Jamnia (Yavneh), where he attacked the Jewish population. From there he proceeded to fortify Kedron (biblical Gederoth [Josh. 15:41], modern Katra, southeast of Ekron), using it as a guerrilla post from which to menace Judea.

John Hyrcanus, Simon's son, had been appointed commander of the army and was headquartered at Gazara (see 13:53). He must have seen firsthand the havoc wreaked by Cendebeus. Perhaps he realized that Simon's age was hindering him from taking decisive action. Simon is pictured in 16:1–3 as realizing his failing and passing this responsibility on to his sons Judah and John. The Greek text of v. 3 has Simon refer to his brother (sing.) but Tedesche and Goldstein think that the plural ("brothers") should be read.

The subject of v. 4 is ambiguous. The text says only "he selected . . ." The translators of the RSV assume that John Hyrcanus is meant. Goldstein, apparently following Josephus (*Antiquities of the Jews* 13.226–227), assumes that Simon is the subject. That assumption raises problems, since Simon had just withdrawn from command in v. 3. The wording of v. 9, however, raises problems for the assumption that John is the subject of the preceding verses. If John were the subject, v. 9 might be expected to read "Judah, his brother," whereas the text has

"Judah, the brother of John." On balance, though, John is the more likely subject. The battle described in vv. 5–10 probably took place near the brook of Ayyalon, a short distance from Modein (Goldstein). The use of cavalry by the Hasmonean forces (v. 7) is not mentioned earlier in 1 Maccabees. Placing the cavalry in the middle of his formation was certainly not a usual tactic. In any case, although Judah was wounded, the enemy was routed by the Hasmonean army.

16:11–24, The Death of Simon and Accession of John Hyrcanus. Ptolemy, Simon's son-in-law, was *strategos* of the region of Jericho. In 134 B.C. he succeeded in treacherously murdering Simon, as well as his sons Judah and Mattathias. The site of the murder, Dok, is probably to be identified with Jebel ed-Duq, near the spring 'Ain Duq, some three to four miles northwest of Jericho.

Ptolemy asked Antiochus VII to support him, offering to reduce the country to the status it held before Jonathan and Simon's military and diplomatic successes. His attempt to have John Hyrcanus assassinated was foiled, however, apparently bringing to an end the ignominious career of Ptolemy son of Abubus. The Dead Sea sect believed that the fate of Simon was a punishment for his having violated the curse against rebuilding the city of Jericho (see 4QTestim).

The author concludes in the style of the book of Kings. John ruled and served as high priest from 134 to 104 B.C. No chronicles of the high-priesthood as described in vv. 23–24 are known to have existed, although much historical material on the reign of John Hyrcanus is preserved in the writings of Josephus.

Bibliography

Bickerman, E. J. *The God of the Maccabees.* Translated by H. Moehring. Leiden: Brill, 1979.

Goldstein, J. A. *I Maccabees.* Anchor Bible, 41. Garden City, NY: Doubleday, 1983.

Hengel, M. *Judaism and Hellenism.* 2 vols. Translated by J. Bowden. Philadelphia: Fortress, 1974.

Schalit, A., ed. *The Hellenistic Age.* New Brunswick, NJ: Rutgers University Press, 1972.

Tcherikover, V. *Hellenistic Civilization and the Jews.* Translated by S. Applebaum. Philadelphia: Jewish Publication Society, 1966.

Tedesche, S., and S. Zeitlin. *The First Book of Maccabees.* New York: Harper, 1950.

2 MACCABEES

LAWRENCE H. SCHIFFMAN

INTRODUCTION

For a discussion of the name of the Second Book of Maccabees and its historical background, see 1 Maccabees, "Introduction."

Composition and Contents

2 Maccabees is an abridgment of a lost five-volume work by an otherwise unknown author, Jason of Cyrene, North Africa. Both Jason's history and the abridgment were composed in Greek, and the present book exhibits a refined rhetorical style. 2 Maccabees begins its account in the time of Seleucus IV (187–175 B.C.) and details the events leading up to the Maccabean revolt. From this book we learn of the Hellenistic reform and of the various parties of Jews whose actions ultimately led to the decrees of Antiochus IV (175–164 B.C.). 2 Maccabees then continues to recount the career of Judah the Maccabee (whose name in Gk. is Judas Maccabeus), ending after his defeat of Nicanor in 161 B.C. The entire span of the period covered by the book is approximately fifteen years.

It seems most likely that the abridger worked directly from the works of Jason of Cyrene, shortening Jason's lengthy text into this small book. Either he or a later hand added the two letters in 2 Macc. 1:1–2:18. It is difficult to judge the full extent of the work of Jason. In view of its five-volume length, it is difficult to believe that it would only have been a more detailed history of these fifteen years. It may be that the abridger selected a period of great importance to him and prepared an abridgment and adaptation of Jason's account of that period. As to the letters, there are a number of indications that they were added by a third hand, since they are not fully integrated into the text as it now stands. They may have been added in an attempt to propagate the observance of the festival of Hanukkah, which celebrated the purification of the Temple by Judah in 164 B.C. A few other additions were certainly made by either the abridger or some other editor.

Sources

2 Maccabees quotes a variety of Seleucid documents. These, presumably, were already present in the work of Jason. The quoted documents are generally regarded as authentic, even if sometimes incorrectly placed in the history. Identifying other sources used by the author is more difficult. Because of the extensive similarities between 1 and 2 Maccabees, it has been claimed that the author of 2 Maccabees used 1 Maccabees as a source, but this is unlikely. There are too many discrepancies between the two works. The possibility that both 1 and 2 Maccabees had a so-called common source raises similar problems. Although the details remain speculative, we should probably assume that some of the sources of 1 and 2 Maccabees were common, such as a biography of Judah, while other materials were distinct to each work.

Relation to 1 Maccabees

The historical periods covered by 1 and 2 Maccabees differ significantly. Both begin with the events of the Hellenistic crisis (in the 170s B.C.), but 2 Maccabees ends its account with Judah's victory over Nicanor in 161 B.C., while 1 Maccabees continues until the death of Judah's brother and successor, Simon, in 134 B.C. Although much of the account given in 2 Maccabees agrees with that of 1 Maccabees, a number of small differences exist. In particular, 2 Maccabees sometimes follows an incorrect order of events. The prime example is the placement of the rededication of the Temple after the death of Antiochus IV, when it actually occurred before. On the other hand, the account 2 Maccabees gives of the events leading up to the revolt is far more accurate and detailed than the sketchy and incorrect summary in 1 Maccabees 1.

Dating

It is generally assumed that Jason used oral reports in his history, and, therefore, that he wrote not long after 161 B.C. Goldstein, however, argues that Jason wrote in about 90 B.C. and that he sought to refute the pro-Hasmonean bias of 1 Maccabees. This theory seems overly speculative and unlikely, however. It is certain that the abridgment was made before the Roman conquest of 63 B.C. and probably before 124 B.C., since that is the date of the first letter appended to the book (2 Macc. 1:1–9).

Theology

Jason, or the summarizer, emphasizes certain religious ideas: the centrality of Temple worship, supernatural intervention in human affairs, division of body and soul, and the bodily resurrection of the pious dead. He seeks to demonstrate several times that God punishes evildoers, measure for measure, with punishments that point out the wickedness of their deeds. Because history is a manifestation of divine justice and retribution, the misfortunes of the Jewish people result from their own transgressions. Hence, the text gives a full account of the events leading up to the revolt. The punishments Israel must suffer are designed to bring it back to the right path and are a manifestation of God's love for his people.

Circulation

The first-century historian Josephus apparently did not know 2 Maccabees, as it is not used in his account in *The Antiquities of the Jews*. The book of 4 Maccabees, however, is clearly dependent on 2 Maccabees. Among the church fathers 2 Maccabees was well known, especially because of the descriptions of martyrdom that became paradigmatic for the Christian church.

COMMENTARY

1:1–2:32
Introductory Materials

1:1–9, Letter to the Jews of Egypt. Although preserved now only in a Greek translation, the letter to the Jews of Egypt was originally written in Hebrew or Aramaic. Even in translation the introductory part of the letter (vv. 1–6) reflects the standard epistolary style of Hebrew and Aramaic letters from the Hasmonean period. Verse 1, the salutation, is notable for the prominence given to Jerusalem. The series of pious prayers in vv. 2–6 are conventional good wishes, included as a formality, and should not be taken to reflect particular problems among the Egyptian Jews or subtle criticisms by the senders that the Jews of Egypt are not doing the will of God "with a strong heart and a willing spirit" (v. 3, RSV).

The letter is a specimen of a well-known type, a festal letter, sent from Jerusalem to inform Jews in outlying areas of the correct way to observe an upcoming holiday. Such documents are attested from biblical times (see 2 Chron. 30:1–9; Esther 9:20–23) through the Talmudic period (b. Sanh. 11a–b). An actual copy of such

a festal letter was recovered among the papyrus documents of the Egyptian Jewish colony of Elephantine, new modern Aswan. That letter, which was sent in 419 B.C., called on the Jews of Elephantine to observe the approaching festival of Passover.

The present letter, which is dated ca. 124 B.C. (2 Macc. 1:10), quotes an earlier festal letter (in vv. 7–9) that had been written during the reign of Demetrius II, in 143 B.C. Apparently, in 143 the Judeans had appealed to their Egyptian brethren to observe Hanukkah, and now, some twenty years later, they are again sending a festal letter to remind their coreligionists of the holiday and its significance. Verses 7–8 give a highly abbreviated version of the Maccabean crisis and its resolution. Jason, who is mentioned in v. 7 as the source of the troubles, had become high priest in 175 B.C. (His Hellenistic reform is described in 2 Macc. 4:7–22.) Jason's rebellion against "the kingdom" (1:7) probably refers to his usurpation of the high-priestly office. The burning of the gates of the Temple (v. 8) is mentioned in 1 Macc. 4:38. The shedding of "innocent blood" with which Jason is charged may refer to the murder of circumcised infants along with their mothers and other members of their families (1 Macc. 1:60–61). While Jason was not directly involved in these killings, the author of the letter traces ultimate responsibility to Jason. The author's understanding of the means by which the crisis was resolved is significant. The allusion in 2 Macc. 1:8 to the prayers of the community and God's help totally ignores the role of the Hasmoneans in overthrowing the Hellenizers. In the aftermath of the victory and the cleansing of the sanctuary, the regular sacrificial worship was restored. Verse 8b is a summary of the events described in 1 Macc. 4:36–51 and 2 Macc. 10:3. After quoting the letter of 143 B.C., the present letter goes on to call for the observance of Hanukkah (1:9). It is here designated "the feast of booths [Tabernacles, Sukkoth] in the month of Chislev [November-December]," since the first Hanukkah celebration had been celebrated in the manner of Sukkoth. The Maccabean soldiers had been unable to celebrate Sukkoth properly at its appointed time (2 Macc. 10:5–7; cf. 1 Macc. 4:52–59, where no mention of Sukkoth appears).

1:10–2:18, Second Letter to the Jews of Egypt. The salutation of the letter states that it was written by the Jews of Judea and Jerusalem, as well as the council of elders (Gk. gerousia) and Judah. Although it is undated, the letter claims to have been written shortly before the purification of the Temple, i.e., in 164 B.C. (1:18; 2:16). In fact, there is reason to believe that this letter is a much later composition. (See the lengthy argument of Goldstein, who dates the letter to 103/102 B.C.) The letter is addressed to Aristobulus, a Jewish philosopher who flourished during the time of Ptolemy VI Philometor (reigned 180–145 B.C.). There is no independent confirmation that Aristobulus served as a teacher of Ptolemy VI, though the fourth-century A.D. church historian Eusebius does preserve extracts of Aristobulus' philosophical treatise on the Torah, which he dedicated to Ptolemy VI. The letter further identifies him as a member of the family of "anointed priests," that is, of the high-priestly Oniad family. His lineage and his relationship to Ptolemy made him a key figure in the Egyptian Jewish community, and the letter was therefore addressed to him.

The letter thanks God for taking the side of the Judeans against Antiochus IV Epiphanes and for bringing about Antiochus' death at the hands of the priests of Nanea (vv. 11–17). Nanea was a goddess of Mesopotamian origin, identified by the Greeks with Aphrodite and Artemis, whose temple was in Elam. Antiochus feigned participation in a sacred marriage ritual in the hope of plundering the temple treasury. According to our letter, Nanea's priests killed Antiochus, a divine punishment for the robbery of temples. According to 1 Macc. 6:1–16 and 2 Macc. 9:1–28, Antiochus was not killed by the priests of the temple but died of illness sometime after his failed attempt to plunder the pagan temple.

This letter also seeks to enlist the Jews of Egypt in the observance of Hanukkah. It is to be celebrated "as Days of Tabernacles [booths, Sukkot] and Days of the Fire, as when Nehemiah, the builder of the Temple and the altar, brought sacrifices" (Goldstein; cf. Tedesche; RSV, which must be corrected accordingly). The author of the letter means that Hanukkah is to be celebrated in a manner like that of Sukkoth and of the Day of the Fire. Nehemiah is here given credit for what the Bible records in the name of Zerubbabel (Ezra 3:1–13). While there is some late evidence that the two figures were identified or confused with one another (see b. Sanh. 38a), Ben Sira, writing in the early second century B.C., clearly distinguishes the two men and their accomplishments (Sir. 49:11–13).

2 Macc. 1:19–35 give an account of the origin of the festival of the Day of the Fire, a celebration not mentioned in any other text. The author of the letter recounts a legend in which the priests of the First Temple hid fire from the altar in a dry well when they went into exile. (The reference to Persia [v. 19] as the place of the Jews' exile is an anachronism. Babylonia, to which the Jews had been exiled in 587 B.C., became part of the Persian Empire only in 539.) The fire, which changed to the highly flammable liquid naphtha (vv. 20, 36), was retrieved at

Nehemiah's direction and put on the altar of the newly rebuilt Second Temple. Its spontaneous combustion served to authenticate the altar and its renewed sacrificial service. Although otherwise quite unknown, the festival of the Day of the Fire was presumably commemorated by the lighting of lamps or fires. For this reason, the author of the letter uses it as a paradigm for Hanukkah. The entire story may have been influenced by familiarity with the role and transportation of sacred fires in Zoroastrianism (see Goldstein).

The author puts a prayer of supplication into the mouth of the people (vv. 24–29). Prayers of similar nature are known from the Dead Sea Scrolls and from rabbinic sources. The language of the prayer contains many biblical echoes (cf., e.g., Exod. 34:6–7; Neh. 9:31–33). Goldstein also notes that 2 Macc. 1:24–25 resembles the opening benediction of the Amidah, a traditional prayer it was obligatory for every Jew to recite. After the prayer, as the sacrifice was burning, the Levites (here called "priests") sang psalms. Verses 31–32 describe some further use of the naphtha to make fire, but unfortunately the Greek text of these verses is obscure and cannot be translated with confidence. The miraculous nature of the events is recognized by the Persian king who, himself a fire worshiper, established a shrine at that location. The author of the letter concludes with a folk etymology of the word "naphtha," claiming that it is derived from Hebrew niftar, "was exempted, freed," which he takes to mean "purified." The word actually comes from Akkadian naptu, "petroleum."

The narrative about Nehemiah and the miraculous fire provides the occasion for the author to introduce other legendary traditions associated with Jeremiah, whom the author claims was the person who ordered the fire of the altar to be taken and hidden during the Exile. The author of the letter makes repeated claims that what he says about Jeremiah is to be found in authoritative texts (2:1, 4). No other writing preserved from antiquity contains the legend of Jeremiah and the altar fire, however. Similarly, there is no other known source for the claim that Jeremiah gave the departing exiles a copy of the Torah (2:2a), although the warnings against idolatry (2:2b) are a reference to the contents of the apocryphal Letter of Jeremiah. There was an ancient tradition that Jeremiah hid the Ark of the covenant when the Babylonians sacked Jerusalem. Although the earliest version of the story is known only from the first-century B.C. Greco-Roman historian Alexander Polyhistor, he clearly derived his information from a Jewish source, perhaps Eupolemus, the author of a book entitled Concerning the Kings in Judea. This Eupolemus is perhaps the same man sent by Judah as an ambassador to Rome (see 1 Macc. 8). The claims of

2 Macc. 2:1–8, that Jeremiah also hid the tabernacle and the incense altar on Mount Nebo, near the place where Moses died, go beyond the information Alexander Polyhistor relates. All in all, 2 Macc. 1:10–2:18 reminds us that a lively literary tradition about the legendary accomplishments of various biblical figures developed during the Hellenistic period, even though most of these texts are now lost.

In 2:9–12 the author seeks to point out the parallelism between Moses' dedication of the altar and Solomon's. Both shared the miraculous, spontaneous consumption of the sacrifices, as had also occurred in the time of Nehemiah (2 Macc. 1:22). 2 Macc. 2:11, however, is enigmatic. The quoted words of Moses, which appear nowhere in Scripture, refer to a dispute between Moses and Aaron in Lev. 10:16–20 as to whether the meat of the sin offering was to be eaten by the priests. But it is not clear how Moses' words are to be related to that dispute or to the dedication ceremonies of the tabernacle and the Solomonic Temple which are the subject of vv. 9–10 and 12. The author understood 1 Kings 8:65 and 2 Chron. 7:9 to indicate that Solomon had celebrated an eight-day dedication ceremony. Goldstein is no doubt correct that our author meant in 2 Macc. 2:11 to establish that the eighth day (see Lev. 9:1) was part of the dedication ceremony. To this end he cited the requirement that the meat of the sin offering must be eaten on the eighth day as well (cf. Exod. 29:33–37). Hence the author asserts that the dedications of Moses and Solomon, like that of Judah—the festival of Hanukkah—were celebrated for eight days. He has therefore cited precedent for both aspects of Hanukkah, the use of fire, as exemplified in 1:19–36, and the eight-day period of celebration, in 2:9–12.

In the conclusion to the letter (2:13–16), Nehemiah is said to have celebrated the rededication of the Temple for eight days, a claim that cannot be paralleled from any other source. Nehemiah's founding of a library (v. 13) is also unknown. The letter informs the Jews of Egypt that Judah also collected all the sacred writings which Antiochus IV had attempted to destroy (see 1 Macc. 1:56). The materials listed in 2 Macc. 2:13 as the library of Nehemiah must, in fact, have been the contents of the protocanon reassembled by Judah. The author concludes the letter with the hope that the Jews of Egypt will join in the celebration of Hanukkah and that they will soon be gathered to the land of Israel.

2:19–32, The Abridger's Prologue. It is here with 2:19–32 that the book proper begins. The two letters (1:1–2:19) were placed at the beginning of the already complete abridgment. Since the book is an abridgment of the five-volume history by Jason of Cyrene, the author

begins with a brief description of that work, the only information regarding it that we have. Jason's history was probably written in the mid-second century B.C. At the outset the abridger makes clear that Jason's emphasis was on Judah and his exploits. The abridger claims to have altered nothing, only to have shortened the work and to have made it more accessible to general readers. Such self-serving claims are common in the introductions of classical histories and must be taken with a grain of salt.

3:1–7:42
Background of the Revolt

3:1–4:6, Onias III and Simon. The history begins with a description of the idyllic conditions prevailing during the high-priesthood of Onias III, son of Simon the Just, who was high priest before 175 B.C. Contributions to the Temple had in fact been made by the Ptolemies (during the third century B.C.) and by the Seleucid king Antiochus III (reigned 233–187 B.C.). Seleucus IV Philopator (reigned 187–175 B.C., son of Antiochus III), continued this practice. Later sources reflect a debate as to who should pay for the daily sacrifices. The Pharisees insisted that the expense be paid from public funds, while the Sadducees required that the high priest defray the expenses. In any case, all agreed that Jews had to donate the daily sacrifices, although it was permitted for non-Jews to contribute voluntary sacrifices or funds for the upkeep of the Temple. It is most probable, then, that Seleucus IV contributed to the general upkeep of the Temple.

Verses 4–7 introduce the conflict that sets in motion the plot of 2 Maccabees. Unfortunately, textual problems complicate the identification of two of the protagonists of this section. While the Greek manuscripts describe Simon as "of the tribe of Benjamin" (RSV), Latin and Armenian texts have "from the [priestly] clan of Bilgah" (Goldstein). (The clan of Bilgah was condemned by later tradition for events that took place during the Maccabean revolt [m. Sukk. 8:8, t. Sukk. 4:28].) It is impossible that Simon's brother Menelaus could have served as high priest (see 2 Macc. 4:23–24) if he were of the tribe of Benjamin, since priests had to be of the Aaronidic clan of the tribe of Levi. The reading "Bilgah" is therefore to be preferred (Tcherikover, pp. 401–402). Apollonius is understood by the Latin versions to be "son of Tharseas" (so Goldstein), although some commentators, in light of the appearance of an Apollonius son of Menestheus with the same office in 4:4 and 21, have taken the text to mean that he came from Tarsus (so RSV; Tedesche). Simon was serving as the administrator of the Temple. If he was a priest, his office was probably identical with that known in rabbinic sources as *segan ha-kohanim*, "prefect of the priests," a title for the second in command below the high priest. The quarrel between Simon and Onias III concerned the office of market supervisor, to which Simon wanted to be appointed. This official in Greek cities was responsible for inspecting the quality of merchandise, licensing merchants to sell in a particular market, and recording legal transactions. The Temple funds about which Simon informed Apollonius were those of private individuals deposited for safekeeping with the Temple. Simon argued (v. 6) that these could be appropriated without committing the horrible sacrilege of plundering a temple. Since the Seleucid kings were frequently short of money, the situation presented a tempting opportunity.

In claiming that Heliodorus' entire tour of inspection was a cloak for his plan to plunder the Temple (v. 8), the author undoubtedly reflects his own perspective more than the facts of the case. Probably Heliodorus was on a tour through the province and as part of his business in Judea intended to confiscate the money. When confronted by Heliodorus, Onias III identified a substantial sum as belonging to Hyrcanus, son of Joseph son of Tobias (v. 11). The Tobiads had been loyal to the Ptolemies until the conquest of Palestine by Antiochus III in 202–198 B.C. The other Tobiads switched allegiance to the Seleucids, while Hyrcanus took refuge in the Transjordan and remained a supporter of the Ptolemies. The fact that the Temple accepted private deposits from a sworn enemy of the Seleucid realm and that Onias III could relate this so casually led Heliodorus to move ahead with his plans.

Contrary to what Simon claimed (v. 6), the Jews saw Heliodorus' act as a sacrilege, even though the funds were those of private individuals. The sanctity of the Temple was supposed to render the deposits inviolable (v. 15). We can well imagine that many Jerusalem citizens who had their money there may have faced the prospect of economic ruin. The highly dramatic and emotional description of the people's distress in vv. 14–21 is characteristic of the author's style of history writing.

2 Macc. 3:24–29, as already observed by Bickerman (pp. 172–90), is a conflation of two different versions of how God intervened to protect his sanctuary. Verses 24–25 and 29 describe how a horse and rider, visible to everyone, attacked Heliodorus and left him and his bodyguards helpless. According to vv. 26–28, he is beaten by two young men who appear only to him, while his guards are unable to assist him. (The two young men reappear in v. 33, where they attribute Heliodorus' recovery to the intercession of Onias III.) Both of these versions have parallels in Greek literature. Apparently, the author of 2 Maccabees had two

sources before him and wove the two versions into his composition.

Modern, rationalistic commentators have suggested that Onias III may have perpetrated a ruse on Heliodorus. Others suggest that in reality some diplomatic or financial accommodation was reached. Whatever may have happened, Heliodorus was forced to retreat from his plan. God's power had been demonstrated (see vv. 37–39), and the people of Jerusalem rejoiced. Our author tells us that Heliodorus was revived through the agency of Onias, who offered what must have been a burnt offering on his behalf. Upon his recovery, Heliodorus brought a freewill offering as was permitted for non-Jews, took leave of Onias III, and returned home. There he testified to the greatness of God and his protection of Israel. The author of 2 Maccabees uses this account of Heliodorus to present the theme of the entire book: "He who has his dwelling in heaven watches over that place himself and brings it aid, and he strikes and destroys those who come to do it injury" (v. 39, RSV).

Simon, as the true instigator of Heliodorus' abortive attempt to pillage the deposits in the Temple, sought to shift the guilt to Onias III, his rival. The sympathies of the author are not in doubt. He presents Onias III in the most favorable light (vv. 1–6), undoubtedly obscuring a political situation that was in reality much more complex. Simon had a powerful ally in the person of the governor, Apollonius son of Menestheus, who is perhaps to be identified with Apollonius of Tarsus (see commentary above on 3:5). Onias found it necessary to seek a personal interview with the king. Although we do not hear further about Simon, Onias seems to have remained permanently at Antioch (see v. 33).

4:7–50, The Hellenistic Reform. Seleucus IV died on September 3, 175 B.C. The ancient historian Appian claims that he was killed in a plot hatched by Heliodorus. Whether or not Appian's information is correct, Heliodorus himself was then driven out by supporters of the successor, Antiochus IV Epiphanes. 2 Maccabees is less interested in Seleucid dynastic politics than in the change in the Jewish highpriesthood that occurred shortly after the accession of Antiochus IV. Although Onias III was still alive, his brother Jason bribed Antiochus IV not only to appoint him high priest but also to allow him to institute the Hellenistic reform that would change the legal status of Jerusalem and reconstitute it as a Greek city or *polis*. Among other things, this meant the establishment of two central public institutions, the gymnasium and the *ephebeion*. 1 Macc. 1:14 mentions only the gymnasium, an educational and athletic institution. Yet the *ephebeion* was also central to the Hellenistic way of life. (The

RSV's "a body of youth" for Greek *ephebeion* [2 Macc. 4:9] is too vague.) The *ephebeion* was an organization that provided civic, military, moral, and literary training for males within the walls of the gymnasium. Ephebic education opened to the "graduate" participation in the economic and social advantages of the Hellenistic world. In Jerusalem, the *ephebeion* was intended to engender widespread cultural change. The decision to reorganize the city of Jerusalem as a Hellenistic *polis* to be called Antioch and to enroll its citizens as Antiochenes was intended to effect the corresponding political change. Jason and his supporters sought to hellenize Jerusalem and, by extension, the entirety of Judea.

In setting up the *polis*, Jason abolished the decree of Antiochus III that had guaranteed the Jews the right to live according to the laws of the Torah and their ancestral way of life (Josephus *Antiquities of the Jews* 12.138–46). This decree had been negotiated by John, whose son Eupolemus negotiated the treaty between Judah and the Romans (1 Macc. 8:17). The gymnasium was located immediately below the *acropolis*, which may designate either the Temple Mount or the Akra, the citadel (Goldstein; see also 2 Macc. 4:14, which shows that the Temple and the gymnasium were in close proximity). In the Greek gymnasium, the exercises were performed naked, the participants wearing only the *petasos*, a broad-rimmed hat worn for protection from the sun. The report of the removal of circumcision (by epispasm) in 1 Macc. 1:15 suggests that Jewish youth also trained naked.

Although Jason is castigated by the author as wicked and as an illegitimate high priest (since Onias III was still alive and, technically, high priest), he also reports that there was considerable popular enthusiasm for Jason's reforms. Hellenism (our author is the first to use the term) must have already become influential even among elements of the priesthood well before the Hellenistic reform. The author of 2 Maccabees is fond of stating explicitly the moral lessons he wishes readers to learn from his narration. In vv. 16–17 he places the blame for the persecutions of Antiochus IV on the hellenizing tendencies of elements of the Jewish population, which he characterizes as "irreverence to the divine laws" (v. 17, RSV).

The Greek games of Tyre were held every four years, although it is not possible to identify the exact date of the games mentioned in v. 18. They were of sufficient importance for Antiochus IV to attend. The games were dedicated to the chief god of Tyre, Phoenician Melqart, who was identified with the Greek deity Hercules (or Heracles). Fees paid by participants were used for sacrifices in honor of the god. Unwilling to violate Jewish law and participate in pagan worship, even indirectly, the envoys whom Jason had sent with the money asked that their funds not be used for sacrifices but instead be applied to the building of galleys. Jewish attitudes about such matters were far from uniform. The Jewish author Eupolemus (probably to be identified with the Eupolemus mentioned in 1 Macc. 8:17 as the close associate of Judah the Maccabee and negotiator of the friendship treaty with Rome) noted with pride in his book *Concerning the Kings of Judea* that Solomon had sent a golden pillar to Hiram of Tyre "which is now set up in the temple of Zeus in Tyre." Although it is highly unlikely that there is historical substance to the claim, what is interesting is that Eupolemus evidently did not think the gift religiously improper.

In vv. 21–22 the author describes one final vignette of Jason's term as high priest, the visit of Antiochus to Jerusalem and his welcome by Jason and the city. The background to the visit is as follows.

Apollonius (cf. v. 4 and commentary) attended a royal celebration of Ptolemy VI Philometor (ruled 180–145 B.C.) that took place in about 172 B.C., when the king was fourteen years old. Cleopatra, mother of Ptolemy VI and sister of Antiochus IV, had recently died. As a result, the Ptolemaic house now had second thoughts about the peace treaty it had signed with Antiochus III in 192 B.C. This treaty had been sealed by the marriage of Cleopatra, the daughter of Antiochus III, to Ptolemy V Epiphanes. When Antiochus IV learned of this change of heart on the part of the Ptolemaic government, he moved southward, along the coastal plain (Joppa is modern Jaffa, south of Tel Aviv) to forestall any designs on Palestine that young Ptolemy VI's advisers might have. In this connection, Antiochus IV visited Jerusalem.

Three years after Jason's accession as high priest and during the same year as Antiochus' visit to Jerusalem (172 B.C.), Menelaus traveled to the king. The Greek of v. 24 is ambiguous as to whether Menelaus flattered the king or exaggerated his own importance. Like his brother Simon, he was a priest of the house of Bilgah (see commentary above on 3:4–7). In any case, he bought the high-priesthood by offering to raise the yearly tribute to 660 silver talents, a sum he was soon unable to pay. Jason's flight to Ammon (4:26) may have been to the fortress of Hyrcanus the Tobiad. Lysimachus now held the post occupied by his brother Simon in 3:4. When the commander of the Akra, who represented the interest of the Seleucid monarchy in Judea, was unable to get payment from Menelaus, the two of them were summoned before Antiochus IV. Lysimachus, the brother of Menelaus, was left in charge as Menelaus' deputy.

But the King was not in residence in Antioch, having left to put down a rebellion in

Tarsus and Mallus, cities in Cilicia, in Asia Minor. Menelaus attempted to settle his affairs with Andronicus, the official Antiochus had left in charge, by using sacred vessels to pay Andronicus the tribute he owed to Antiochus IV. Onias III, the legitimate high priest, who had been living in Antioch since 175 B.C., took himself to the temple of Apollo and Artemis, located five miles outside of Antioch at Daphne. Temples were considered places of asylum in the Hellenistic world. From there he condemned the sacrileges of Menelaus. Although Josephus offers contradictory reports (*Jewish War* 1.33; 7.423), it does indeed appear that Onias III was killed by Andronicus at the instigation of Menelaus. Yet Andronicus actually was executed by Antiochus IV for killing the child Antiochus, son of Seleucus IV. Our author may have placed Jewish affairs at center stage, and hence, misinterpreted the execution of Andronicus (cf. Goldstein). The melodramatic style of the author is again evident in his account of Antiochus' grief at Onias' murder and his rage at Andronicus (vv. 36–38). The plundering of the Temple vessels was such a great offense that it led to rioting in Jerusalem, and, eventually, to the killing of Lysimachus (v. 42).

It is not possible to tell if Menelaus was taken to trial at Tyre from Antioch or if he had already returned home before he was summoned. The accusation that Menelaus had plundered the Jerusalem Temple was put forward by members of the *gerousia*, the council of elders. Menelaus again appealed to bribery. Ptolemy son of Dorymenes, who acted on Menelaus' behalf, is probably the governor of Coele Syria and Phoenicia in 8:8. In 1 Macc. 3:38 he is chosen by Lysias to fight Judah, along with Nicanor and Gorgias. (He is probably not to be identified with Ptolemy Macron [10:12], who is reported to have been well disposed toward the Jews.) Because of the intervention of Ptolemy son of Dorymenes, Antiochus IV decided to acquit Menelaus and to execute the members of the *gerousia* who had pressed charges. The author compares the "justice" of Antiochus unfavorably with that of the Scythians, a tribe from what is now southern Russia with a reputation for excessive brutality.

5:1–27, Antiochus IV and the Desecration of the Temple.

1 Macc. 1:20 dates Antiochus' plundering of the Jerusalem Temple to 169 B.C. Yet his second campaign against Egypt, which is associated with the attack on the Temple in 2 Maccabees 5, occurred in 168 B.C. While it is possible that our author considers the entry of the Seleucid army into Palestine in 172 B.C. (4:21–22) to be the first phase of the invasion, and this to be the second, Goldstein solves the problem by translating "Antiochus made preparations for his second departure against Egypt,"

thus making possible the dating of his plundering of the Temple in 169 and the invasion in 168 B.C. The report of apparitions of troops of soldiers in the sky (vv. 2–4) is similar to the types of omens recorded by various Greco-Roman writers as preceding significant events (see Josephus *Jewish War* 6.298).

Jason, the perpetrator of the Hellenistic reform (4:7–12), had been displaced by his agent Menelaus (4:23–25) and had fled to Ammon (4:26). When he heard the false report that Antiochus IV had died, Jason took advantage of the situation to try to regain the high-priesthood (5:5–7). He must have been opposed both by the followers of Menelaus, who took refuge in the Akra, and by the nonhellenized Jews as well (Zeitlin). This opposition must have led him at some point to give up the fight and to flee again toward Ammon.

Jason was imprisoned by Aretas, the Nabatean ruler. After escaping from or being freed by Aretas, Jason made his way to Egypt, expecting that the Ptolemies would welcome an opponent of the Seleucids. In 168 B.C., as Antiochus IV prepared to invade Egypt, Jason fled to Sparta (also known as Lakedaimon), appealing to the ancient legend that claimed common kinship for the Jews and the Spartans (1 Macc. 12:7). Apparently, he did not succeed in finding refuge there. Our author reminds us (2 Macc. 5:10) that he suffered measure for measure for the transgressions he committed, a theological notion already found in 4:8. The circumstances of his death, however, are not reported.

Jason must have fled (5:7) after hearing that Antiochus IV was returning from Egypt. Antiochus IV knew that both the pro-Ptolemaic factions and the traditionalists were united against his puppet, Menelaus, so he interpreted the strife in Jerusalem as directed against him. In light of his perception that Judea had revolted, he felt legally and morally entitled to massacre and despoil the city, actions that otherwise would have been considered prohibited by law and custom. It is probable that numbers in v. 14 are exaggerated, even in light of a population estimate of 120,000 offered by Hecateus of Abdera (Josephus *Against Apion* 1.197).

By this time, Antiochus IV had liberated Menelaus from his refuge in the citadel. Menelaus then conducted the king on a tour of the Holy of Holies, within the area of the Temple non-Jews were forbidden to enter. The text of v. 16 is unfortunately corrupt, but should probably be interpreted to mean that Menelaus handed over certain sacred vessels to Antiochus.

Antiochus failed to understand that he was serving as the instrument of God's anger, which was but temporary. The idea that God used foreign kings to punish rebellious people had a long history in Israelite religion. In the eighth century B.C. the prophet Isaiah referred to Assyria and its king as "the rod of my anger" (Isa. 10:5). It is only because God was using Antiochus, the author reasons, that he did not suffer the same fate as Heliodorus (chap. 3). In 5:19–20 our author states one of his fundamental theological presuppositions. God sanctified the Temple Mount and the city of Jerusalem to raise the spiritual level of his people who dwelt in the land of Israel. Through the sanctuary they would be given the opportunity to commune with God through prayer and sacrifice. Therefore, the fate of the Temple would reflect the spiritual and religious state of the people. If they transgressed and had to be punished, the Temple might be defiled or destroyed. Yet when the people repented and returned to God, as in the days of Judah the Maccabee, the Temple would be restored to its sanctity and purity, reflecting that of the Jewish people.

Antiochus IV must have plundered both the deposits of individuals and the Temple funds belonging to the community designated for sacred purposes. He thought Judea so secure that he left various officials in Judea (5:21–23). Philip, from Phrygia in western Asia Minor, was probably appointed commander of Jerusalem and the highest Seleucid official in Judea. He appears again in 6:11 and 8:8 but is probably not the regent mentioned in 9:29. Andronicus (certainly not the one who intervened on behalf of Menelaus in 4:31–38, as he was executed) was in command over Samaria. Menelaus continued to serve as high priest.

Although the text of 5:24–26 is ambiguous, it must be Antiochus IV who sent Apollonius to Jerusalem after some two years (167 B.C.; see 1 Macc. 1:29), because disturbances against Menelaus continued in Judea. In 1 Macc. 1:29 Apollonius (whose name is not mentioned) is described as "a chief collector of tribute," no doubt a corruption of his real title of "Mysarch," commander of mercenaries from Mysia in northwestern Asia Minor. Apollonius employed a ruse, pretending to be friendly, and then attacking on the Sabbath, a fact omitted in the account in 1 Macc. 1:29–35. The account in 1 Maccabees also supplements 2 Macc. 5:26 in important ways. 1 Macc. 1:33–35 attributes the founding of the Akra, the Seleucid citadel of Jerusalem, to Apollonius' invasion.

Judah the Maccabee is described in 2 Macc. 5:27 as the earliest leader of the revolt, already beginning his guerrilla struggle at this time. Contrast the account of 1 Maccabees 2, which, besides identifying Judah's father, Mattathias, as the first to raise the banner of revolt, places the start of the revolt only after the decrees of Antiochus (1 Macc. 1:41–64; cf. 2 Macc. 6:1–11). Indeed, Judah is the central hero of 2 Maccabees, and it may be that our author wished to cast him

as aware of the dire situation even before the repressive decrees of Antiochus IV. The accounts of both 1 and 2 Maccabees contribute to a correct historical reconstruction of the events, but neither is wholly accurate. 1 Maccabees is correct in attributing to Mattathias a role in the early stages of revolt. But 1 Maccabees incorrectly sees the decrees as the cause of the revolt, whereas 2 Maccabees understands that the decrees resulted from Antiochus' desire to support the Hellenizers in the internal Jewish struggle precipitated by the Hellenistic reform.

6:1–17, The Earliest Persecutions. The agent of the king is identified in v. 1 as *geronta athenaion*, an ambiguous Greek expression that may be rendered "Geron the Athenian," "the elderly Athenaeus," or "the Athenian Elder." This agent, whatever his name, was charged with enforcing the decrees of Antiochus IV, which are themselves omitted by our text (for the decrees see 1 Macc. 1:41–50). The author of 2 Maccabees probably thought it sufficient to relate the results of the decrees (6:3–7:42). Not only were the persecutions to be directed against the Jews, but the Samaritans, still considered as Jews in the Hellenistic world, were to suffer as well. The identification of the God of Israel with Zeus was meant to transform Judaism into one of the syncretistic religions of the Greek world in which Near Eastern and Greek traditions were combined. Indeed, in the period of the Israelite monarchy, some Israelites had similarly identified the God of Israel with various local Baals (see the polemic of the prophet Hosea against such beliefs, e.g., Hos. 2:16; 5:6–7). The attributes selected for the names of the Jewish and Samaritan temples were themselves innocuous. Olympios meant "Most High" and Xenios meant "Protector of Strangers." Yet name changes would bring in their wake fundamental changes in worship and the prohibition of Jewish practice.

Sacred prostitution similar to that known from the old Canaanite cults was introduced into the Temple (v. 4). Since v. 5 refers to the offering of impure animals (including swine [1 Macc. 1:47]), it is likely that the end of 2 Macc. 6:4 should be translated with Goldstein, "and also brought forbidden things inside." This would be a reference to the introduction of the idol described in 1 Macc. 1:54. The prohibition of confessing oneself to be a Jew (2 Macc. 6:6) is taken by Goldstein as a reference to the twice daily recitation of the Shema ("Hear, O Israel"), which is already mentioned by Josephus (*Antiquities of the Jews* 4.212) and which is attributed to Second Temple times in m. *Tamid* 5:1. The cessation of the Jewish sacrifices, mentioned in 1 Macc. 1:45, is not mentioned here.

2 Macc. 6:7–9 describe various attempts to coerce the Jews to participate in non-Jewish

religious observances. The king's birthday was celebrated monthly in Hellenistic monarchies and involved sacrifices. Partaking of pagan sacrifices, however, was anathema to Jews and was prohibited by Exod. 34:15. The festival of Dionysus (Bacchus) occurred yearly, usually in the autumn around the time of the grape harvest. It was celebrated with orgiastic dancing, and the usually inebriated participants wore ivy wreaths. The beginning of 2 Macc. 6:8 may be translated "At the suggestion of Ptolemy" (RSV), referring to Ptolemy son of Dorymenes (see 4:45), although Goldstein argues for translating "on the proposal of the citizens of Ptolemais." In any case, these persecutions were extended beyond the borders of Judea to the Hellenistic cities of Syria and Palestine. The death penalty for those who refused to "hellenize" is mentioned in the decree of 1 Macc. 1:50 and in the narrative of 1 Macc. 1:57.

2 Macc. 6:10–11 briefly alludes to the killing of the women whose sons had been circumcised (cf. 1 Macc. 1:60–61) and the story of those who died in caves on the Sabbath (cf. 1 Macc. 2:29–38). Our text, however, neglects to explain that the victims would not fight on the Sabbath and, therefore, there is no mention of Mattathias' decree (1 Macc. 2:39–41). This omission fits well with the author's attribution of the initial leadership of the revolt to Judah, rather than Mattathias.

The author feels constrained to enter into the issue of theodicy (2 Macc. 6:12–17) before recounting the horrible suffering of Eleazar (6:18–31) and the mother and seven brothers (7:1–42). He proposes that God's quick punishment of the Jewish people for the sins of the Hellenists is evidence of God's mercifulness, since it prevents further transgression and punishment. In dealing with the non-Jews, God allows them to continue their misdeeds until they are worthy of complete destruction. Hence, readers should not question God's justice in chaps. 6 and 7.

6:18–31, The Martyrdom of Eleazar. The story of Eleazar (6:18–31) and the mother and seven sons (7:1–42) were independent stories of the genre of martyrdom accounts that our author incorporated into his work. Brief reference to these two stories occurs in 1 Macc. 1:62–63. In both cases the martyrdom came about because of the refusal to eat pork that was offered as a pagan sacrifice. Eleazar, one of the leading scribes, would not violate the Torah's restriction against eating pork (Lev. 11:7; Deut. 14:8) or the prohibition against eating pagan sacrifices (Exod. 34:15). Some of the hellenized Jews had respect for him and so suggested a ruse whereby he would eat kosher food, while appearing to eat the forbidden food. He judged even this a violation of the Jewish law, a position with which later rabbinic tradition agreed.

Eleazar's speech may have been composed by our author in the style of Greek historians who took the liberty of filling in such words. In any case, Eleazar argued that even if he might technically avoid violation of the law, the appearance of transgressing (Heb. *mar'it 'ayin*, a technical term in rabbinic parlance) would lead others astray and was, therefore, as serious a violation as the act itself. Further, he asserted that this violation would be punished in the hereafter, if not in this world. In v. 28 the reading "he went" must be preferred to "he was dragged," which occurs in some manuscripts, since it is clear that he voluntarily surrendered his life rather than violate the divine law.

The very same Hellenizers who had tried to save him turned against Eleazar (v. 29), probably because his heroism cast their compromise in a bad light. Goldstein contrasts this story with that of Mattathias in 1 Macc. 2:1–28. Whereas Eleazar, intending to serve as an example to his people, accepted martyrdom and did not rebel, Mattathias rose up in the same circumstances to lead his people to armed rebellion. In origin, then, the two stories presented very different ideal types, the martyr and the rebel. The author included the Eleazar story in 1 Maccabees, even though he would soon describe the rebellion of Judah and his brothers. He intended the Eleazar material as evidence of the extent of the persecution and the devotion of the Jews to their ancestral faith, not as a course of action preferable to revolt. Some Jews did believe that martyrdom alone would provoke divine intervention. Such a view is evident in the pseudepigraphical writing *The Testament of Moses*. The first edition of this work was written during the time of Antiochus' persecutions.

7:1–42, The Martyrdom of Seven Brothers and Their Mother. The story of the mother and seven sons that takes up all of chap. 7 is narrated in 2 Maccabees as another example of the horrors of Seleucid persecutions. Yet, like the story of the martyrdom of Eleazar (6:18–31), the original intent of this story may have been to counsel passive rather than active, military resistance. This story appears in various versions in ancient and medieval Jewish sources. The historicity of the story can no longer be determined in light of its appearance in the traditional form of a martyr legend. As is, the story lacks both geographical and chronological setting. Yet our author presents it among the events leading up to the revolt, indeed as a justification for taking up arms against the Seleucid rulers. The story is alluded to in 1 Macc. 1:62–63, along with that of Eleazar. Here again, the Seleucids demanded that Jews eat pork, probably from pagan sacrifices (see 2 Macc. 7:42).

The family has been arrested for the practice of Judaism and is being interrogated. Horrible tortures of the sort described in chap. 7 are indeed known from the ancient world. (After the Crusades and the Holocaust, we have no reason to doubt the terrible inhumanity our author ascribes to those who persecuted the Jews.) In v. 6 the author refers to the poem in Deuteronomy 32, identifying it by an adaptation of the words of Deut. 31:21 as "The Song Which Bore Witness Against [the Jewish People]." The highly influential poem of Deuteronomy 32 accused the Israelites of disobedience and ingratitude toward God, as a result of which God would punish his people. But eventually, as Deut. 32:6 states, "He will have compassion on his servants." By quoting this ancient poem the author uses it to interpret the Hellenistic crisis. Jason's hellenizing innovations had been identified as a sin that would provoke divine anger (2 Macc. 2:16–17). But even in the midst of the persecutions the theological model provided by Deuteronomy 32 gave grounds for hope.

While the account of the torture of the first brother asserts only the justice of God, the second brother proclaims in the Hebrew language the concept of resurrection of the dead (7:8–9). The third son adds that at the resurrection, the dismembered bodies would be restored to perfection (v. 11). The fourth asserts that he will be resurrected, but that Antiochus, because of his transgressions, would not be (v. 14). The fifth calls attention to the temporal nature of Antiochus IV's power (vv. 16–17). God, he says, will torture the king and his descendants. (The horrible death of Antiochus IV is described in 9:5–9. Antioch V Eupator, son of Antiochus IV, was killed at Demetrius I's order according to 1 Macc. 7:4.) The sixth explains to the king why it is the Jews who suffer, while he does not (vv. 18–19). The explanation consists of the traditional Jewish theodicy: the Jewish people suffer because of their sins. Yet, says the sixth boy, despite the fact that Israel deserves its fate, he, Antiochus, will be punished for "having tried to fight against God" (RSV).

As her sons are being tortured, the mother encourages them in Hebrew (vv. 21–23). Her argument is that as God created her sons originally, he will give them back their life again. Although there are similarities between the mother's language and that of Ecclesiastes (see esp. Eccles. 11:5), she shares none of Ecclesiastes' skepticism about the afterlife (Eccles. 3:19–21).

As a last resort Antiochus appeals to the seventh son with offers of reward rather than threats of punishment (2 Macc. 7:24). (On the status of Friend of the King, see 1 Maccabees, "Commentary," 2:1–28.) When the son refuses, the mother leads Antiochus to believe that she would persuade her youngest son to eat the pork. Instead, in Hebrew, she begs him to stand steadfast (vv. 27–29). We follow most commentators in seeing in v. 28 an assertion of the theory of *creatio ex nihilo*, God's creation of matter out of nothing. She tells her son: just as God created the universe out of nothing, he will again bring you back to life in the end of days. She pleads with her last surviving son to give his life, for otherwise, if he fails to sanctify the divine name (to use classical rabbinic terminology), he will not be deemed worthy of resurrection in the end of days, and she will not be reunited with him. The seventh son's final speech (vv. 30–38) recapitulates the theological assertions of his six brothers who went to their deaths before him. The author of the speech assumes the notion of a division of body and soul, both of which the youngest son is prepared to surrender rather than to violate the laws of the Torah. The boy prays that, like ancient Pharaoh, Antiochus IV will come to acknowledge the God of Israel (v. 37). His sacrifice and that of his brothers should be the last his people must suffer. The manner of the mother's death is not described. Details are supplied in a variety of later sources (see Zeitlin). Throughout the episode (cf. vv. 24, 39) the king believes he is being mocked. To the very end, even after the horrible deaths of the seven boys, he fails to perceive the steadfast faith of the Jewish people and their devotion to their God and the Torah He gave them.

8:1–9:29
Judah's Wars Against Antiochus IV

8:1–36, Judah's Early Victories. The text now returns to the story of Judah's heroism, already introduced in 5:27. Here, as there, there is no mention of Mattathias and his role (see commentary above on 5:27). 2 Macc. 8:1–8 is parallel to 1 Macc. 3:1–9. The author of 2 Maccabees also includes in v. 5 a brief reference to Judah's early victories, which are recounted in 1 Macc. 3:10–26. His earliest efforts were directed to raising an army and mounting a guerrilla struggle against the Seleucids. (On the surname Maccabeus, see 1 Maccabees, "Introduction.")

1 Macc. 3:25–4:25 parallels 2 Macc. 8:8–36. Comparisons will be noted below. 2 Maccabees is, however, unaware of the information given in 1 Macc. 3:27–37 concerning Antiochus' departure for Persia and his appointment of Lysias to oversee affairs in his absence. According to 2 Macc. 8:8 Philip (see 5:22 and commentary), governor of Judea, appealed to his immediate superior, Ptolemy (see 4:45 and commentary) for help in resisting the guerrilla attacks of Judah and his men. In 2 Maccabees, Nicanor (cf.14:12–15:37) is sent by Ptolemy, assisted by Gorgias. According to 1 Macc. 3:28 Lysias, the king's viceroy, at the command of

Antiochus IV, was to send a force to oppose Judah. Lysias appointed Ptolemy, Nicanor, and Gorgias. 2 Maccabees preserves a more reliable account here, since it is unlikely that Judea stood at the center stage of Seleucid foreign and military policy at this time. Further, in the ensuing campaign in 1 Macc. 3:40–4:25, Ptolemy does not appear. This makes sense if, in fact, he was not one of the commanders.

The financial difficulties of the Seleucid empire were proverbial (cf. 1 Macc. 3:28–31). Our author, however, is incorrect in suggesting in 2 Macc. 8:10–11 that Nicanor wanted to raise money to pay off the tribute owed to the Romans as a result of their defeat of Antiochus III in 189 B.C. In fact, this debt had already been paid off by 173 B.C., according to the Roman historian Livy. The selling of slaves was a regular part of all ancient warfare, and slave traders assembled spontaneously when needed. Our author, in his attempt to portray Seleucid persecution of the Jews, suggests that this time a special invitation was sent out by Nicanor. The cities of the seacoast were predominantly inhabited by hellenized pagans who would have been happy to share in the spoils of Seleucid campaigns against Judah.

Verses 12–23 describe the manner in which Judah, serving as a priest, fulfilled the commands for the rites of battle found in Deut. 20:1–10. This same ritual is alluded to in 1 Macc. 3:54–57. According to 1 Maccabees the preparations took place at Mizpah (1 Macc. 3:46). The report that those who were cowardly fled (2 Macc. 8:13) alludes to Deut. 20:8–9, except that in 2 Maccabees 8, those who were afraid left of their own accord, even before the ritual. The selling of property undertaken in v. 14 refers to those who had built new houses or planted new vineyards. According to Deut. 20:5–6 such soldiers should have returned home. Rather than leave their stations, however, they sold the property in question. The Maccabean fulfillment of the laws of war of Deut. 20:1–10 indicates that they did not accept the later rabbinic interpretations (m. Soṭa 8:7) that limited the application of these laws to offensive warfare of an optional character. Here we have the Maccabees fighting a defensive war of obligatory nature and still observing those rituals.

2 Macc. 8:16–20 contains the exhortation that Judah, as a priest, delivered to his army in accord with Deut. 20:2–4. He calls attention to the defilement and plundering of the Temple by Antiochus IV (2 Macc. 5:15–16; 1 Macc. 1:20–24) and the Hellenistic reform, according to which the ancestral government by the high priests, in accord with the laws of the Torah, had been replaced by the decrees of Antiochus. The mention of divine assistance against Sennacherib is a reference to the narrative of 2

Kings 18:13–19:37, which recounts Sennacherib's unsuccessful siege of Jerusalem in which 185,000 were said to have died. The other occasion to which Judah refers is nonbiblical. The Galatians were Celts who settled in large numbers in central Asia Minor in the early Hellenistic period. The reference here must be to Galatian mercenaries. Goldstein suggests that these soldiers supported Antiochus Hierax in his war with his brother Seleucus II Callius (reigned 247–226 B.C.). Some Jews must have fought on the side of Seleucus II along with the Macedonians. Although vastly outnumbered by the Galatians, the Jews and Macedonians were victorious, a triumph Judah attributes to aid from heaven.

Judah, following his interpretation of Deut. 20:9, completed the rite by appointing the provosts and dividing the men into military units (2 Macc. 8:21–22). The list of Judah's brothers is incongruent with that of 1 Macc. 2:2–5. Rather than assuming the existence of two additional brothers, as some do, we prefer to understand Joseph as a confusion for John and to read Eleazar in 2 Macc. 8:23. Eleazar's appointment "to read aloud from the holy book" (v. 23) can only be understood in light of the parallel in 1 Macc. 3:48, which describes a public reading from the Torah as part of the assembly at Mizpah. The reading is described there as for the purpose of inquiring of God and receiving oracular guidance. For the password, cf. Ps. 3:8. Passwords and slogans figure prominently in Qumran War Scroll.

The battle took place to the south of Emmaus (see 1 Macc. 3:57). 2 Macc. 8:24 reports that 9,000 enemy soldiers fell, while 1 Macc. 4:15, in the context of a detailed description of the battle, presents a more realistic figure of 3,000. It is interesting that 2 Maccabees claims that Judah's men called off their pursuit of the enemy because of the impending onset of the Sabbath (v. 26), whereas 1 Macc. 4:6–18 presents this as a tactical decision based on Judah's fear of the army of Gorgias, which had been held in reserve. The author of 2 Maccabees apparently takes the view that fighting on the Sabbath, unless it is a matter of immediate threat to life, is forbidden (cf. 1 Macc. 2:29–41). The praise and thanksgiving that the Maccabean soldiers offered (2 Macc. 8:27) must have been in the form of hymns similar to those of the Qumran War Scroll. 1 Macc. 4:24 quotes part of such a hymn that is a biblical psalmodic refrain. The reference to God in v. 27 as the one "who had preserved them to this day" has a verbal parallel in the rabbinic benediction she-heheyanu (cf. m. Ber. 9:3).

In accordance with an interpretation of Num. 31:27, half of the booty was apportioned to the soldiers who had fought and their families and half was apportioned to needy members of the community (2 Macc. 8:28). Our author departs somewhat from chronological order to relate how the spoils were divided in a similar manner after other battles (v. 30). Further, the arms were stored in caches for later use. The reference to carrying spoils to Jerusalem in v. 31 requires that we place these battles after the rededication in 10:1–8.

With 8:33–36 the scene shifts back to the victory celebration after the defeat of Nicanor. The RSV's "in the city of their fathers," i.e., Jerusalem, cannot be correct since Jerusalem was not yet conquered by Judah; it should be translated with Tedesche, "in the land of their fathers." According to 2 Macc. 8:33 Callisthenes and his followers had burned a gate in the Jerusalem Temple. In 1:8 the burning of "the gate" is attributed to Jason and his followers (cf. 1 Macc. 4:38). It is probable that Callisthenes was a hellenizing Jew who made common cause with Jason. Somehow Judah's men found them in a small house and burned them. Our author again repeats the notion that God's punishment was measure for measure. Those who had burned his house were themselves burned to death. In the same way Nicanor, who had intended to sell Jews into slavery, now fled like a runaway slave (2 Macc. 8:34), stripped of the purple broad-rimmed hat and cloak that were the usual attire of the Friends of the King. Israel's true champion and defender was its God, whose laws they followed and who protected them (v. 36).

9:1–29, Death of Antiochus IV. Some

scholars have argued that the original order of the episodes of the text has been disturbed. The problem arises from the peculiar position of 10:9 ("Such then was the end of Antiochus, who was called Epiphanes," RSV). One would expect such a statement to follow immediately after the account of Antiochus' death, which is narrated in 9:1–29. As it stands, the statement follows the episode of the purification of the Temple (10:1–8). Moreover, in the present sequence of the narrative, Antiochus IV dies before the rededication of the Temple. In 1 Maccabees the Temple is rededicated first (4:36–61), before the death of Antiochus (6:1–17). Since the chronology of 1 Maccabees seems to be correct on this point, it is reasonable to conclude that the original sequence of the narrative as composed by Jason of Cyrene placed 2 Macc. 10:1–8 after 8:36, followed by 9:1–29, and then 10:9. It is noteworthy that the sequence of events as they are now narrated in the text of 2 Maccabees follows the chronology of the second festal letter appended to the book (1:10–2:18), which gives the impression that Antiochus died before the rededication of the Temple. Thus whoever was responsible for adding the letters at the beginning of the book, whether the abridger or a later editor, was probably also responsible for changing the sequence of the events narrated.

2 Macc. 9:1–2 recounts Antiochus' failed attempt to rob a Persian temple. Persepolis, near present-day Shiraz, was the capital of Persia and was founded by Darius I. 1 Macc. 6:1 and 2 Macc. 1:13–15 say that it was the temple of Nanea in Elymais (Elam) that the king attempted to plunder. 2 Maccabees 9 is the only source that identifies Ecbatana, the royal seat of the old Median Kingdom, as the place of Antiochus IV's death. 1 Macc. 6:4 places his death on the journey from Persia back to Babylonia. According to our interpretation of 2 Macc. 8:30–32, we must assume that the abridger misunderstood the parenthetical note there about the division of the spoils of later battles and construed the battles with Timothy as having occurred immediately after the defeat of Nicanor. Therefore, when he mentioned Antiochus' anger at learning of the defeat of Nicanor, he added "and the forces of Timothy" (9:3).

On the death of Antiochus IV, cf. 1 Macc. 6:8–16. Antiochus IV's campaign in Persia and Media had been a failure. According to 2 Maccabees, he attempted to allay his frustration by attacking Jerusalem. This intention, in the view of the author, soon led to Antiochus' death. The author stresses the sufferings of the king to emphasize that he was punished by God for his deeds against the Jews (2 Macc. 9:5–10). The very torments he suffered were the same ones he had mercilessly inflicted on the Judeans. It is another instance of the author's interest in a measure-for-measure conception of justice.

In vv. 11–17 the author presents Antiochus as undergoing a deathbed repentance. He offers to reverse every course of action he has taken with respect to Jerusalem. The claims of our author regarding the king's desire to convert to Judaism raise serious doubts about the historicity of the entire account. The author seems to have begun with a narrative similar to that of 1 Macc. 6:8–16 and to have embellished it with very unlikely details designed to place Judea at the center of the affairs of the Seleucid empire and to accent the just punishments meted out by the God of Israel.

The letter that follows in vv. 18–27 is presented here as if it were written only to the Jews and as if it followed on the decisions Antiochus IV supposedly reached in vv. 11–17. Yet investigation of the letter does not bear out this conclusion. First, its contents are not a reflection of vv. 11–17. Second, critical analysis of the letter raises serious questions about its authenticity. The letter does not consistently accord with Seleucid epistolary style. The inconsistencies with vv. 11–17, however, make it unlikely that Jason of Cyrene or the abridger composed the letter. On the other hand, as it certainly is not what our author claims, we must conclude that

Jason or the abridger adapted a letter Antiochus had written to confer kingship on his son Antiochus V Eupator. This announcement would have been sent to all of the Seleucid empire and made no reference to the Jews. The letter was adapted and placed within our book as part of the tendency of the author to see Judean affairs as determining the fate of the Seleucid empire.

The "worthy Jewish citizens" of v. 19 are those who were enrolled in the *polis* of Antioch at Jerusalem, which was established as part of the Hellenistic reform (4:9). The stated purpose of the letter is to provide for an orderly succession in case of the king's death (9:21-24). Antiochus recalls the precedent of his father's similar action. Antiochus III, intending to march eastward, appointed his oldest son Antiochus, brother of Antiochus IV, as coregent and successor from 210/209 to 193/192 B.C. Seleucus IV designated from 189 to 187 B.C. Antiochus IV was well aware of the powers both within and outside of his empire waiting for his death. Among them was certainly Demetrius I, son of Seleucus IV, who was at this time a hostage in Rome. For this reason he appointed his own son, the boy Antiochus V Eupator, as his heir and coregent.

Antiochus IV died in November or December of 164 B.C. (v. 28). 1 Macc. 6:14-15 relates that the king had appointed Philip guardian of Antiochus V and had entrusted him with the regency of the kingdom. Lysias, who had been appointed to rule over the western provinces and to care for Antiochus V in the absence of Antiochus IV (1 Macc. 3:32), moved quickly to consolidate his own power and immediately proclaimed his charge sovereign (1 Macc. 6:17). Philip found it impossible to gain control and had to flee Lysias (Antiochus V was merely a figurehead at this time). He took refuge with Ptolemy VI Philometor.

10:1-8
Purification of the Temple

On the possible displacement of these verses, see commentary above on 9:1-2. 1 Macc. 4:26-35 describes Judah's battles with Lysias as preceding the rededication of the Temple. The author of 2 Maccabees places these victories after the rededication (2 Macc. 11:1-15). In so doing the author incorrectly moved them to the reign of Antiochus V (so Goldstein). In actuality these battles took place while Antiochus IV was campaigning in Persia and Media. From 2 Macc. 11:13-38 we gather that these battles ended in negotiations leading to the rescinding of the decrees of Antiochus IV. The forces still stationed in the Akra may have made Judah hesitate to capture Jerusalem and the Temple. Before long though, Judah and his men made their move and succeeded in taking control of the Temple and

rededicating it. The rededication of the Temple is narrated in 1 Macc. 4:36-60.

Greek *temenos* at the end of 2 Macc. 10:2 must be rendered "illicit shrines" with Goldstein, not "sacred precincts" with the RSV. Apparently, the Temple had been surrounded by pagan altars and shrines. Judah and his followers reinstituted the orderly conduct of the sacrificial ritual that had been suspended when the idol was brought into the Temple (1 Macc. 1:54), an event omitted in 2 Maccabees. Whereas our text says that sacrifices had been suspended for two years, 1 Macc. 1:54 and 4:52 indicate a lapse of three years. Again our author stresses that Antiochus IV and his persecutions were the instruments of God's anger, which the Jewish people had incurred because of its transgressions (v. 4).

The Temple was purified in 164 B.C. The celebration of the first Hanukkah was held in imitation of the feast of Tabernacles (Sukkoth; 2 Macc. 10:6). The *lulav* (Heb., "palm frond"), together with the willow and myrtle branches, and the *etroq* (Heb., "citron") were carried, in accordance with the traditional interpretation of Lev. 23:40. Following postbiblical custom, Judah and his followers recited the Hallel Psalms, known from later sources to be Psalms 113-118 (2 Macc. 10:7). It was decreed that Hanukkah should become a regular part of the Jewish calendar (v. 8). Although 1 Macc. 4:52-59 gives no explanation for the eight-day duration of Hanukkah, 2 Maccabees claims that the model of Sukkoth, seven days (Lev. 23:40, 42; Deut. 16:13; Num. 29:12-34) followed by the eighth day of solemn assembly (Num. 29:35-39) led to the eight-day celebration of Hanukkah. Tannaitic tradition (b. Šabb. 21b; cf. Megillat Ta'anit) relates that when the Maccabees purified the Temple, they found only one pure cruse of oil with which to light the menorah (cf. 10:3). Miraculously, it burned for eight days until additional ritually pure oil could be processed and brought to the Temple.

10:9-13:26
Judah's Wars with Antiochus V

10:9-11:15, Judah's Victories. On 10:9, see commentary above on 9:1-2. Antiochus V Eupator (reigned 164-162 B.C.) was later killed by Demetrius I (2 Macc. 14:2; 1 Macc. 7:1-4). His reign began when he was only nine years old, and his appointment of Lysias was a legal fiction. In fact, his father Antiochus IV had appointed Philip, but Lysias seized power (cf. 9:29 and commentary above), taking charge of the government and serving as "chief governor of Coele Syria and Phoenicia," a post similar to the one he had held under Antiochus IV (1 Macc. 3:32).

Ptolemy Macron (2 Macc. 10:12) was not Ptolemy son of Dorymenes mentioned in 4:45 and 8:8. The latter sought to exterminate the Jews entirely, while Ptolemy Macron was deposed because of his good relations with them. Ptolemy Macron was governor of Cyprus under Ptolemy VI Philometor. Then he transferred his allegiance to Antiochus IV, in the aftermath of the fall of Cyprus to Antiochus IV in 168 B.C. (Goldstein). At some point he was appointed governor of Coele Syria, a post Lysias took over for himself. It must have been during Ptolemy Macron's tenure that the Maccabees took control of the Temple and began to campaign against their pagan neighbors. These factors, no doubt, led Lysias to depose him. Some even accused Ptolemy of collusion or treason.

1 Macc. 5:3-5 records an abbreviated version of the same events as are narrated in 2 Macc. 10:14-23. Gorgias, the governor, was previously mentioned in 2 Macc. 8:9 as an associate of Nicanor (cf. 1 Macc. 4:1-25 where Gorgias appears as the field commander of the Seleucid army). Judah made a foray into Idumean territory that resulted in a great slaughter, although the numbers here must be exaggerated (2 Macc. 10:17). He left his brother Simon, along with Joseph (who may be his brother John; see commentary above on 8:21-23) as well as Zacchaeus (who may be the Zechariah of 1 Macc. 5:18) in command of the siege force. The incidence of treachery within Judah's forces (2 Macc. 10:20-22) is passed over in silence in the parallel account in 1 Maccabees 5.

Goldstein considers 2 Macc. 10:24-38 to be parallel to 1 Macc. 5:6-8. If so, our author has confused Yazer (in Transjordan) with Gazara (= Gezer in Judea), and this has led him to assume that the Ammonite force under Timothy had invaded Judea (cf. 1 Macc. 5:6-8; 2 Macc. 10:24, 32). Embellishments were then added to the story in 2 Maccabees concerning superhuman apparitions. Compare the earlier apparitions in 3:24-28 and 5:2-4 and the one recorded in 11:8-11. Although Jason may have been influenced by parallels from classical authors, the idea that God's heavenly armies fight with Israel is well attested in the Bible (see, e.g., Judg. 5:20; Josh. 5:13; Zech. 9:14-16). The RSV renders the beginning of 2 Macc. 10:24 as "Timothy who had been defeated by the Jews before . . . ," but Goldstein's understanding, "the first of the two by that name to be defeated by the Jews," is consistent with the existence of two Timothys (see 1 Maccabees, "Commentary," 5:1-8). The Maccabean forces performed standard biblical mourning practices, which were considered appropriate at times of national crisis. Only after praying at the base of the altar for God "to be an enemy to their enemies and an adversary to their adversaries" (cf. Exod. 23:22) did they go forth to battle.

Gazara (2 Macc. 10:32) remained in the hands of the Seleucids until it was captured by Simon in 143 or 142 B.C. (1 Macc. 13:43-48). The reference here must be to Yazer in Transjordan (see above). The report of Timothy's death makes it certain that he is not the same Timothy who appears in 2 Macc. 12:2, 18-25.

The events described in 11:1-15 have been misplaced by the author. They took place before the rededication of the Temple and the death of Antiochus IV and are parallel to 1 Macc. 4:26-35. Lysias' stated intention in 2 Macc. 11:2-3 mostly parallels his instructions from Antiochus IV in 1 Macc. 3:35-36. Yet for our author, with his mistaken chronology, the goal of Lysias was to reverse the successes of Judah and his "de-hellenization" of Jerusalem (cf. Goldstein). According to 1 Macc. 4:7 and 24, the Seleucids had already sold the high-priesthood. The levying of tribute on the Temple (2 Macc. 11:3) sounds like a euphemism for plundering it.

Verses 5-12 record 2 Maccabees' version of the battle of Beth-zur (cf. 1 Macc. 4:28-34). Beth-zur is some twenty miles south of Jerusalem on the road to Hebron. Our author pictures the Maccabees as going out to battle from Jerusalem. Here again he follows his false chronology (see above). On the apparition of the horseman, cf. 3:25 and 10:29-30.

2 Macc. 11:13-15 continues with its mistaken chronology, according to which the nine-year-old Antiochus V was already ruling (10:10). Actually, the events occurred in 164 B.C. 1 Macc. 4:35 has Lysias depart immediately to Antioch after his defeat at Beth-zur to recruit a larger army. Soon after, Judah and his men take the city of Jerusalem and rededicate the Temple (1 Macc. 4:36-61). 2 Maccabees 11, however, preserves evidence that negotiations ensued (vv. 13-38). As an analysis of the diplomatic letter quoted in vv. 16-21 indicates, these exchanges were between Lysias and Menelaus, and Judah (despite v. 15) probably played no part. Nevertheless, he took advantage of the truce to take control of Jerusalem and rededicate the Temple.

11:16-38, Letters of Lysias, Antiochus V, and the Romans.
Judah is nowhere mentioned in Lysias' letter to the Jewish people (vv. 16-21), written in 164 B.C. Most likely, this letter was written to a group of pious Jews who sought an end to the war and the persecutions, but who were not closely allied with the Maccabees. The letter may have been written as a result of the representations of the high priest Menelaus (cf. v. 29).

The second document, quoted in vv. 22-26, is a letter from Antiochus V to Lysias ("brother" is a term of endearment) and is to be dated early in 163 B.C., soon after the young king's ascension. Its actual historical context is the attempt of the king to reverse his father's mistaken policies to widen his base of support. Due to our author's incorrect dating of Lysias' campaign (see above), he relates this letter to Lysias' negotiations with the Jews in the aftermath of his defeat at Beth-zur.

The third letter (11:27–33), which is from Antiochus IV or from the young coregent Antiochus V to the *gerousia*, the Jewish council of elders, must be genuine, since no later forger would have cast Menelaus in so positive a light (v. 29). The letter proposes an amnesty for those who return home within fifteen days and desist from their military activities by March 27, 164 B.C. Further, permission is granted to the Jews to return to their ancestral laws, i.e., to reverse the effects of the Hellenistic reform. After Judah rededicated the Temple (following the correct chronology of 1 Maccabees), Menelaus must have rushed off to Antioch where he obtained this amnesty as a last-ditch attempt to preserve his own power and high-priesthood. His strategy was to separate the bulk of the pious Jews who wanted only religious freedom from the more "nationalistic" Maccabees. Menelaus' plan must have been partially successful and may have been a factor in the decline of Judah's power, which took place soon afterward.

The last letter quoted (11:34–38) purports to be from Roman envoys to the Jewish people. Although there is some reason to doubt the authenticity of this letter, the date and certain details of which are difficult to reconcile with the rest of the narrative, it was Roman policy to support Judea against the Seleucid empire. The Roman envoys requested information on the state of the negotiations so that they could help to press the case of the Jews. Despite some obscurities, the letter is probably authentic.

12:1–45, Judah Defends the Jews of Palestine.

Verse 1 is a transition necessitated by the incorrect placing of the events of chap. 11 after the rededication of the Temple. In fact, the events of 12:2 pick up immediately after 10:31. The truce of chap. 11 did in fact occur, but it preceded Judah's rededication of the Temple. The Timothy mentioned in 12:2 was commander of northern Transjordan and southern Syria (see 1 Maccabees, "Commentary," 5:1 8). Apollonius is distinguished by his patronymic ("son of Gennaeus") from others by that name who have appeared in 2 Maccabees. The other local commanders are unknown. Nicanor was not "the governor of Cyprus" (RSV; Tedesche), since Cyprus was under Ptolemaic rule until 58 B.C., but the commander of Cypriot mercenaries (Goldstein).

In the aftermath of the rededication of the Temple, the citizens of certain of the Hellenistic cities rose up against their Jewish neighbors. The inhabitants of these cities probably took Judah's rededication of the Temple as a

violation of the truce. The atrocity at Joppa in which Jewish residents of the city were lured onto boats and drowned (12:3–4; cf. 1 Macc. 5:1–2) provoked Judah to avenge their deaths. Judah's forces were able to destroy the port but could not gain entry to the city itself (2 Macc. 12:7). To prevent a similar fate from befalling the Jews of Yavneh (Jamnia), some thirty miles south, his men destroyed that harbor as well (vv. 8–9).

The background of vv. 10–12, which record Judah's alliance with an Arab tribe, may be provided by 1 Macc. 5:9–13, in which Judah received a report that the Jews of Gilead were being besieged by Timothy. On the way to Gilead, the Maccabean army defeated an Arab force and made peace with them (1 Macc. 5:24–27). The events of 1 Macc. 5:14–23 are not related in 2 Maccabees. It is difficult to determine if the omissions resulted from the work of the abridger or from the original composition of Jason of Cyrene.

Of the events of 1 Macc. 5:35–36, only the taking of Chaspho is paralleled in our account of the conquest of Caspin (2 Macc. 12:13–16). Caspin is probably present-day Khisfin, east of Lake Tiberias, near a swamp that may be the lake mentioned here. Here, according to the narrator, Judah and his soldiers, egged on by the taunts of the enemy, invoked the memory of Joshua's capture of Jericho (Josh. 6) and stormed the city, even though they lacked the usual siege equipment.

For 2 Macc. 12:17–19 cf. 1 Macc. 5:30–34, which details Judah's first encounter with Timothy. "Charax" (2 Macc. 12:17) may be either the city of Kerak, or a common noun meaning "palisaded camp." In any case, it was the center of the Toubiani, i.e., the Jews of Tob or of the Tobiad household (cf. 1 Macc. 5:13) who had always been anti-Seleucid. The author assumes that their center was still at Araq el-Emir in Transjordan, some ninety-five miles south of Caspin, but this is highly unlikely. The itinerary from Caspin to Araq el-Amir and back to Carnaim is implausible (see Goldstein).

2 Macc. 12:20–25 is parallel to 1 Macc. 5:37–43, from which we learn that the battle described here took place at Raphon. According to 2 Maccabees, Judah appointed Dositheus and Sosipater (see v. 19) over the forces besieging Timothy's stronghold. The main body of Timothy's army (the numbers are surely exaggerated here) broke ranks and fled, according to our author, because they saw a divine apparition (v. 22). The two commanders who somehow captured Timothy (v. 24) are pictured as freeing him in the hope of securing the freedom of Jewish hostages.

2 Macc. 12:26–31 is paralleled by 1 Macc. 5:44–54. Carnaim, the ancient cult site of Ashtoret (Astarte), now housed the temple of Atargatis, a goddess identified with Ashtoret in

Hellenistic times. The reference to Lysias in v. 27 is difficult to translate. We would suggest that Lysias had stationed *katoikoi* (Gk.), "military colonists," there. Again, the casualty figures must be reduced. Scythopolis (v. 29) is Beth-shan, seventy-five miles by road (but not as the crow flies) north of Jerusalem. It is noteworthy that 1 Maccabees, which has a more hostile attitude toward the Gentiles than does 2 Maccabees, does not mention the good relations between the Jews and Gentiles of Scythopolis (vv. 29-31).

For the parallel to 2 Macc. 12:32-45 see 1 Macc. 5:55-68. After the Feast of Weeks (Shavuot), the Jews again joined battle with Gorgias (cf. 2 Macc. 8:9; 10:14-15 and commentary), the governor of Idumea. Dositheos, one of the Toubiani (following Tedesche and Goldstein) was maimed in the battle, but succeeded in putting Gorgias to flight toward Marisa (Mareshah), an Idumean city in the foothills southwest of Jerusalem. Esdris (12:36) must have been mentioned earlier in a passage omitted by the abridger. He may be Azariah, probably to be identified as Eleazar, Judah's brother. Only when Judah spurred his men on with Hebrew battle cries were they finally victorious. From the parallel we gather that the events of vv. 32-35 occurred while Judah was campaigning in the north. After his return, he had to intervene to turn the tide of battle against Gorgias and the Idumeans, as described in vv. 36-37.

Adullam (v. 38) is located seven and a half miles northeast of Marisa and was still in Jewish hands. There, in preparation for the Sabbath, Judah's men performed ritual immersion, a practice apparently widespread in Second Temple times, although it never acquired the force of law. After the Sabbath, when permissible (following Goldstein's translation), the bodies were recovered and buried, as required by Jewish law. In the process, they discovered that the dead men had picked up idolatrous figurines during the battles at Yavneh (cf. 12:8-9), thus violating Deut. 7:25-26. (1 Macc. 5:67 gives a different explanation for the losses.) Judah and his men prayed to God to expiate the sin of these soldiers and collected money for an expiatory offering on their behalf. These procedures are taken by the author as indicating Judah's belief in the resurrection of the dead. In view of Lev. 4:13-21, which provides for the expiation of a sin of the entire "congregation," and the fact that the concept of expiation after death is not known in this period, Goldstein suggests that in actuality this was an offering to expiate the collective guilt of the Maccabean army. The author of 2 Maccabees reinterpreted it as indicating Judah's belief in resurrection.

13:1-26, War with Antiochus V. The background to the invasion of Judea by the young king Antiochus V Eupator in 163 B.C. (13:1-2)

must be sought in 1 Macc. 6:18-27, where Judah's siege of the Akra (the citadel of Jerusalem) and his fortification of the Temple Mount and Beth-zur are described. Upon learning these facts, Antiochus V, under the tutelage of Lysias, set out for Judea. As so often in these accounts, the numbers in 2 Macc. 13:2 and in 1 Macc. 6:30 must be scaled down.

1 Maccabees makes no mention of Menelaus' audience with the king or of the fate of Menelaus, as does 2 Macc. 13:3-8. Menelaus had been shunted aside by Judah's rededication of the Temple and therefore sought to have himself reestablished in office (Tedesche and Zeitlin assume he sought higher office). Lysias charged Menelaus (cf. 4:23-50) with being the instigator of the Hellenisitic reform and the cause of all the troubles in Judea, for which Jason was really to blame (4:7-22). As a result Menelaus was cruelly executed in Beroea, modern Aleppo. Our author again stresses the notion of measure-for-measure punishment.

Faced with Antiochus V's impending attack, Judah ordered the people to undertake a three-day fast (13:9-12; cf. Esther 4:16). Judah consulted the elders before taking the offensive (v. 13). Similarly, the king is required to consult before offensive wars in m. *Sanh.* 1:5 (with the Sanhedrin) and in the Qumran *Temple Scroll* 58:18-20 (with the high priest). According to 2 Maccabees, a preliminary skirmish took place at Modein before the main battle of Beth-zur (vv. 14-17). This preliminary skirmish is unknown in 1 Maccabees. Further, the killing of the largest elephant and subsequent death of Eleazar in 1 Macc. 6:43-46 occur in the battle of Beth-zur, whereas here parallels to those events take place in the preliminary skirmish at Modein. In 2 Maccabees the killing of the elephant is attributed to Judah himself. Either the author of 1 Maccabees has telescoped two phases of the campaign, or the author of 2 Maccabees has invented a battle to take place at the Hasmonean ancestral home, Modein (cf. 1 Macc. 2:1). The password "God's victory" is similar to the one used in 2 Macc. 8:23, "God's help." According to 2 Maccabees, the skirmish at Modein ended with a Maccabean victory.

2 Macc. 13:18-22 parallels 1 Macc. 6:31-50. The Seleucid force repeatedly assailed Beth-zur, about twenty miles southwest of Jerusalem, attempting to enter Judea from the south. According to the account of 2 Maccabees, the treason of a Jew enabled the king to negotiate a truce at Beth-zur, after which he was defeated in a skirmish (vv. 21-22). The reality is probably closer to the account of 1 Maccabees, which mentions no treason and indicates that as part of the truce the Jews had to abandon the fortress and allow the Seleucids to garrison it. The author of 2 Maccabees is either unaware of the true outcome or hesitates to admit the failures of Judah.

At this point the account in 1 Macc. 6:48, 51–54 relates the unsuccessful attempt of the Seleucids to dislodge Judah's forces from the Temple Mount. The words of 2 Macc. 13:22, "he attacked Judah's men," probably are a reference to this abortive siege. Philip, identified in 1 Macc. 6:55 as the guardian of Antiochus V (cf. 2 Macc. 9:29), was now trying to take power in Antioch. The king, therefore, sought to wind up affairs in Judea and return home to protect his throne. Consequently, the king reinstated the rights of the Jews to live according to the Torah. (Cf. the letter of Antiochus V quoted in 11:27–33.) 1 Macc. 6:55–63 presents a more realistic account, excluding the fanciful meeting with Judah (2 Macc. 13:23–24) and including the destruction of the walls of Mt. Zion by the Seleucids (1 Macc. 6:62). The appointment of the new governor and the subsequent scene at Ptolemais (Acco) appear only in 2 Macc. 13:25–26.

14:1–15:36
The Battle of Nicanor

14:1–10, The Rise of Demetrius I. 2 Macc. 14:1–15:36 is parallel to 1 Maccabees 7. Demetrius I Soter (reigned 162–150 B.C.), son of Seleucus IV Philopator, made his escape from Rome, where he was being held as a hostage, in 162 B.C. Tripoli, where Demetrius landed, is north of Sidon. He soon took control of the Seleucid empire and killed Antiochus V and Lysias (cf. 1 Macc. 7:1–4).

For 2 Macc. 14:3–10 cf. 1 Macc. 7:5–25. 1 Macc. 7:8–24 has no parallel in 2 Maccabees, as our author telescoped into one account both visits of Alcimus to Demetrius I and the campaigns of Bacchides and Nicanor. Alcimus was probably appointed to replace Menelaus by Antiochus V (Josephus *Antiquities of the Jews* 12.383–85). Upon the accession of Demetrius I, Alcimus was confirmed as high priest at his first visit, in 162 B.C. (1 Macc. 7:9). Our text is describing his second visit in 161. After his appointment, Alcimus won the confidence of the Hasidim and other pious Jews, weaning them temporarily away from the camp of Judah. But Alcimus betrayed their trust (1 Macc. 7:12–16), hence the statement of 2 Macc. 14:3 that he "had willingly defiled himself" (RSV). A priest who was implicated in murder was disqualified from service at the altar. The speech of Alcimus in vv. 6–10 is clearly the composition of our author. The RSV's "I have laid aside . . . the high priesthood" (v. 7) must rather be translated "I have been deprived of" (Goldstein; cf. Tedesche).

14:11–30, Judah's Pact with Nicanor. Paralleling 2 Macc. 14:11–15:36, 1 Macc. 7:26 reports the battle with Nicanor. Nicanor is appointed by Demetrius to reinstate Alcimus to the high-priesthood and to destroy Judah and his forces (2 Macc. 14:11–13). 1 Maccabees omits the account of 2 Macc. 14:15–17, which describes how the Jews observed mourning customs (cf. 10:25) and prayed for divine help. Expecting a full-scale attack, Judah sent a detachment with Simon to block the enemy at a village named Dessau (to be identified with Adasa, 1 Macc. 7:40–45). Simon seems to have been less than successful because the enemy surprised him.

Among the delegation that Nicanor sent to open negotiations with Judah was at least one hellenized Jew, named Mattathias (2 Macc. 14:19). Although Judah was somewhat suspicious, he entered into discussions with Nicanor (vv. 21–22). Cf. 1 Macc. 7:27–29 in which dishonest motives are imputed to Nicanor. 2 Maccabees rather blames the failure of negotiations on Alcimus (vv. 26–27).

Only 2 Maccabees stresses the friendship of Judah and Nicanor. The author credits Nicanor with encouraging Judah to settle down to marry and raise a family (vv. 23–25). Yet Nicanor's desire to have Judah constantly with him and his desire to see him tied down to house and family can be taken as a tactic designed to neutralize Judah's ability to function as a guerrilla leader. Tedesche translates v. 24 "He kept Judah under surveillance."

According to vv. 26–30 it was Alcimus who engineered the breakdown in relations between Nicanor and Judah. To advance his own interests as high priest he sought to be rid of Judah's opposition. Alcimus complained to Demetrius I that Nicanor had appointed Judah as *diadochos*, "successor" (RSV and Tedesche; Goldstein's "deputy" is not precise). Demetrius I's response produced discomfort on the part of Nicanor (v. 28), and Judah perceived it (v. 30; cf. 1 Macc. 7:30).

14:31–15:36, Judah's Final Victory. In a passage without a parallel in 2 Maccabees, 1 Macc. 7:31–32 describes a skirmish between Judah and Nicanor at Capharsalama which resulted in defeat for Nicanor and motivated his threat against the Temple (1 Macc. 7:33–38). In 2 Macc. 14:31 Nicanor is provoked when he discovers that Judah has outwitted him and gone into hiding.

The gruesome tale of martyrdom found in 2 Macc. 14:37–46 has no parallel in 1 Maccabees. It is indeed difficult to understand its place in 2 Maccabees, unless we assume that Razis knew the whereabouts of Judah. Otherwise, all it does is to demonstrate the cruel lengths to which Nicanor, now a persecutor of the Jews, would go (v. 39). Verse 46 emphasizes belief that at the time of resurrection the martyred body of Razis will be restored to wholeness (see 7:11 and commentary).

914

There is no parallel to 2 Macc. 15:1–5 in 1 Maccabees. Judah had taken refuge either within the province of Samaria or very close to the border. Nicanor's plan to attack on the Sabbath was opposed by Jews in his army (cf. 14:19 and commentary). These hellenized Jews must have been supporters of Alcimus, but even they sought to observe the Sabbath. Nicanor's haughty reply to them is seen by our author as having been his undoing (v. 5).

At this point 1 Maccabees gives the location of the battle, information either unknown to or omitted by 2 Maccabees. According to 1 Macc. 7:39–40, Nicanor positioned himself in Bethhoron and Judah in Adasa. There is no parallel in 1 Maccabees for 2 Macc. 15:6–19, Judah's preparation of his army. As he had on previous occasions (see 8:16–20), Judah followed the instructions of Deut. 20:3–4 and addressed his army with encouraging words. Judah also reminded his men that Nicanor had entered into an agreement with him which was now being violated. Finally, Judah recounted a dream or vision in which he saw Onias III (cf. 3:1–10 and commentary) and the prophet Jeremiah. Both were praying for a Maccabean victory. Jeremiah's presentation of a sword to Judah is symbolic of that victory (15:12–16). Judah's men were greatly encouraged by his exhortation, including his description of the vision. In Jerusalem, both the supporters of Judah and those of Alcimus realized that the hour of decision was at hand (v. 19).

Just before the battle was joined, Judah offered a prayer (vv. 20–24). Cf. the parallel in 1 Macc. 7:40–42, where the prayer is strikingly similar. The battle itself, which is described in 2 Macc. 15:25–30, is narrated in more detail in 1 Macc. 7:43–47. The author of 2 Maccabees emphasizes that the praises offered at the conclusion of the battle were recited in Hebrew (v. 29). He seems surprised that Judah could order the dismembering of even one so despicable as Nicanor (v. 30). 1 Macc. 7:47 does not mention Judah's role in the mutilation of Nicanor.

Judah easily advanced on Jerusalem, which was not protected by any substantial Seleucid force. He showed Nicanor's head and arm to the inhabitants of the Akra so that they would see that Nicanor was dead. Again our author emphasizes measure-for-measure punishment: the head and tongue were severed because of blasphemy, and the arm was cut off because he

had lifted it when taking an oath threatening the Temple (2 Macc. 15:32–33). 1 Macc. 7:47, conscious of the laws of ritual impurity, has the head and hand put on display just outside of Jerusalem.

It was decided to observe the commemoration of Nicanor's defeat on the thirteenth of Adar, the day before Purim or Mordecai's day (Esther 9:21), as an annual minor holiday (v. 36). As such it appears in Megillat Ta'anit. This holiday ceased to be celebrated when the minor holidays of Megillat Ta'anit were displaced by Hanukkah and Purim, which then served as the sole occasions commemorating national deliverance.

15:37–39
Epilogue by the Abridger

"And from that time the city has been in the possession of the Hebrews" (v. 37, RSV). The abridger must have written these words before the conquest of Jerusalem by Pompey in 63 B.C. Our author writes as if Judah succeeded in restoring freedom to his people, ignoring the fact that he was soon killed on the battlefield and that it took years of struggle for his brothers to achieve his goal of Jewish independence (1 Macc. 9–13). Perhaps the author realized that Judah had set in motion a struggle for religious freedom and national aspirations that would occupy the Jewish people for more than two thousand years.

Bibliography

Bickerman, E. J. *The God of the Maccabees.* Translated by H. Moehring. Leiden: Brill, 1979.

Goldstein, J. A. *II Maccabees.* Anchor Bible, 41A. Garden City, NY: Doubleday, 1983.

Hengel, M. *Judaism and Hellenism.* 2 vols. Translated by J. Bowden. Philadelphia: Fortress, 1974.

Schalit, A., ed. *The Hellenistic Age.* New Brunswick, NJ: Rutgers University Press, 1972.

Schürer, E. *The History of the Jewish People in the Age of Jesus Christ.* Vol. 1. Edited by G. Vermes, F. Millar, P. Vermes, and M. Black. Edinburgh: Clark, 1973.

Tcherikover, V. *Hellenistic Civilization and the Jews.* Translated by S. Applebaum. Philadelphia: Jewish Publication Society, 1966.

Tedesche, S., and S. Zeitlin. *The Second Book of Maccabees.* New York: Harper, 1954.

3 MACCABEES

JOHN J. COLLINS

INTRODUCTION

The Third Book of Maccabees is found in some manuscripts of the Greek Bible (Alexandrinus and Venetus, but not Vaticanus or Sinaiticus), in the Syriac Peshitta, and in the Armenian Bible (→ Texts, Versions, Manuscripts, Editions). It was not included in the Latin Vulgate and consequently not in the canon of the Roman Catholic church or in the traditional Protestant Apocrypha. It is, however, regarded as canonical in Eastern Christianity.

Despite its title, the book has nothing to do with the Maccabees. (The title was probably suggested by the fact that it follows 1 and 2 Maccabees in the manuscripts and is set in the Hellenistic period.) Instead it describes three episodes involving Ptolemy IV Philopator, king of Egypt (221–204 B.C.; → Ptolemy). The first is an introductory paragraph (1:1–5) that describes how the Ptolemy was saved from assassination at the battle of Raphia (217 B.C.) by the intervention of one Dositheus, an apostate Jew. The second, 1:6–2:24, tells of the king's unsuccessful attempt to enter the Jerusalem Temple. The third episode, which is the main body of the book (2:25–7:23), describes the Ptolemy's persecution of the Jews of Egypt.

Date

There is universal agreement that 3 Maccabees was written in Greek, most probably in Alexandria, Egypt, at some time after the battle of Raphia and before the destruction of the Jerusalem Temple (A.D. 70). Attempts to fix the date more precisely hinge on the relation of the narrative to history. The plot to assassinate the Ptolemy (1:2) is also reported by the second-century B.C. Greek historian Polybius, but not the role of the Jew Dositheus, which is reminiscent of the role of Mordecai in Esther 2:21–23. The second episode, the unsuccessful attempt to enter the Temple, has a parallel in 2 Maccabees 3 in the story of Heliodorus. A variant of the third, main episode is found in the writings of the first-century A.D. Jewish historian Josephus (*Against Apion* 2.53–55), where the Ptolemy in question is not Philopator but Ptolemy VIII Euergetes II (Physcon, 144–117 B.C.). The historical value of these accounts is assessed in different ways. Kasher claims that they are "genuinely historical" reports from the time of Philopator. A key element in his argument is the fact that Philopator is said to have attempted to enroll the Jews in the religion of the Greek god

Dionysus, a cult that this Ptolemy did, in fact, promote. Nonetheless the genre of the narrative must raise grave doubts about its historical value. It is a historical romance with strong legendary features. It is concerned with the wonderful and the miraculous and aimed at edification. Such stories may contain historical reminiscences, but their historicity is incidental and unreliable. The very fact that part of the story is variously attached to Philopator (in 3 Maccabees) and to Physcon (Josephus) shows that it became a traditional tale in which historical accuracy was not the primary concern. Tcherikover argues that the story was more likely to preserve reminiscenses of Physcon than of Philopator, but at most it would symbolize a general threat to the Jews at that time and not describe an actual event. Tcherikover, like many scholars, sets the composition of the book in the Roman period (after 30 B.C.).

There is internal evidence that the book as we have it cannot have been composed in the time of Philopator. 3 Macc. 6:6 refers to the Greek addition to the book of Daniel, and this allusion was scarcely possible before the first century B.C. Resemblances in style and language to 2 Maccabees and the *Letter of Aristeas*, a Jewish composition from the late second century B.C. (Emmet, pp. 156–57), suggest a date no earlier than the late second century B.C., while its probable dependence on Greek Esther would require a first-century B.C. date at the earliest. Tcherikover and Hadas argue more specifically for a date in the Roman period because of the statement in 2:28 that the Jews should be reduced to the popular census and slave condition. While the Greek word *laographia* simply means "census," and censuses had been taken in Ptolemaic times, the word acquired a special connotation in Roman times because of the poll tax introduced by Augustus in 24/23 B.C. This was the only *laographia* that involved a reduction of status for the Jews, because it made a clear distinction between Greeks and non-Greeks. The fact that political parity with the Alexandrians was an issue (2:30) also fits a setting in the Roman era. Kasher disputes Tcherikover's arguments in detail, but the fact remains that the *laographia* of the Roman era did affect the status of the Jews, while such a census in the time of Philopator is unattested apart from the legendary narratives of 3 Maccabees.

The different episodes of 3 Maccabees find their parallels in different sources and were probably originally independent. The decision of the author of 3 Maccabees to combine the story of the threat to the Temple with the perils of Egyptian Judaism may contain a clue to the time of composition. In *Embassy to Gaius*, the Jewish philosopher Philo describes the two dangers that confronted Judaism in the time of Caligula—the pogrom in Alexandria in A.D. 38 and the attempted violation of the Jerusalem Temple. While the stories in 3 Maccabees are traditional tales and were not composed as allegories for the Roman era, the troubles in the time of Caligula may well have been the occasion for the combination and edition of these stories in the present book. While certainty is not possible, the reign of Caligula (A.D. 37–41) provides a more plausible setting than any other that has been proposed. The objection of Anderson (p. 512) that 3 Maccabees does not read like a "crisis document" assumes that the only Jewish response to crisis in this period was the apocalyptic one (→Apocalyptic Literature). The nonapocalyptic response of 3 Maccabees reflects its distinctive social ideology and the situation of Alexandrian Judaism from which it arose.

Historical and Social Significance

The historical significance of 3 Maccabees lies not in the uncertain references about its setting but in the picture of Diaspora Judaism it presents. The Jews are loyal servants of the king but also strict observers of the law, including the distinctive dietary laws (3:3–4). While these observances provide an opportunity for their enemies, they win the respect of many, including "the Greeks," who were in no way injured and who tried to comfort the Jews (3:8–10). 3 Maccabees here distinguishes between "the Greeks" and the Alexandrian enemies of the Jews. This distinction is of dubious historical value but is also found in Philo and Josephus. The Alexandrian Jews sought the acceptance and respect of "the Greeks" and were unwilling to dignify their enemies with that name. Most fundamentally, the problems confronting the Jews in 3 Maccabees are traced to the arrogance and even madness of the king and to his bad advisers. There is no objection to pagan rule as such. In the end, when the king comes to his senses, all is well for the Jews. 3 Maccabees, then, sees persecution as an aberration that can be rectified without the removal of the pagan kingship.

Not all the hostility of 3 Maccabees is directed toward the king. The Jews who betray their religion are singled out for contempt (2:33) and eventual vengeance (7:10–16). Equality with the Alexandrians cannot be bought at the price of idolatry. Even the king acknowledges that those who "transgressed the divine commandment for their belly's sake would never be well disposed

to the king's estate either" (7:11) and gives permission that they be slaughtered.

3 Maccabees, then, attests loyalty to the letter of the law among Egyptian Jews without any of the allegorical rationalization associated with Philo or the *Letter of Aristeas*. Yet this religious particularism is maintained in the context of loyalty to the pagan rulers. Loyalty to the law is the basis of solidarity for the Jewish people in exile.

Theological Significance

Insofar as 3 Maccabees is a historical novel (a fictional tale with a realistic historical setting) it stands in a tradition that is attested in the Hebrew Bible in Esther and in Daniel 1–6. Like those stories, it is set in exile, and the Jews are exposed to danger at the whim of a gentile king. Yet the danger proves ephemeral, and the welfare of the Jews proves to be quite compatible with gentile rule. In 3 Maccabees, the removal of danger results from divine intervention in response to prayer. This is explicit in 2:21 (protection of the Temple) and again in 5:28 and 6:18. The book maintains the traditional Deuteronomic belief in retribution and makes no appeal to the ideas of immortality or afterlife that were widely accepted in Hellenistic Judaism. The fundamental faith attested by the book is in the omnipotence of God. This faith is expressed in the great prayers in chaps. 2 and 6, while the divine power is dramatized in the miraculous acts of deliverance. While 3 Maccabees lacks the philosophical depth of Philo or the Wisdom of Solomon, it is more likely to represent the faith of the rank and file of Egyptian Judaism. Its faith that God would set things right in this world was adequate for much of the history of the Diaspora, including the crisis under Caligula, but did not anticipate the disasters that would befall Egyptian Judaism in A.D. 66 and especially in A.D. 115–117 when the Alexandrian community was nearly destroyed.

The picture of Jews being rounded up for destruction (3 Macc. 4) remains, sadly, hauntingly relevant to the twentieth century.

COMMENTARY

1:1–5
The Battle of Raphia

The narrative begins abruptly with an account of Philopator's march to Raphia. The abruptness suggests that this passage was excerpted from a historical source. The main point at which 3

Maccabees differs from the account of this battle in Polybius is in the role assigned to Dositheus, who intervenes to save the king. The analogy with Mordecai in Esther 2:21–23 would seem to suggest that Dositheus is introduced as a Jewish hero, but the fact that he is explicitly said to have abandoned his religion makes this unlikely. 3 Maccabees leaves us in no doubt of its opinion of those who voluntarily forsook the law—they could not be good servants of the king and deserve death (7:11–12). There is considerable irony in the role of Dositheus. By saving Philopator's life, he indirectly causes the persecution of his people. Moreover, he causes an innocent "undistinguished person" to be killed in place of the king. Dositheus, then, is scarcely a hero. In the second century B.C., a Jew named Dositheus became a general in the army of Ptolemy Philopator (together with Onias IV, the founder of Leontopolis; Josephus *Against Apion* 2.49). "Dositheus son of Drimylus" occurs as the name of a pagan priest in a papyrus from the third century B.C., and it has even been suggested that this was, in fact, the apostate Jew (Kasher).

1:6–2:24
Philopator's Visit to Jerusalem

Philopator's visit to Jerusalem is not otherwise attested but is not implausible. He is said to have acted respectfully until he resolved to enter the Temple. We know that the Roman general Pompey did, in fact, enter the Temple in 63 B.C., but the closest parallel to 3 Maccabees is undoubtedly the story of Heliodorus in 2 Maccabees 3. In both stories a foreign dignitary attempts to enter the Jerusalem Temple over the protests of the priests. The attempt causes consternation in the whole Jewish population. Finally there is a miraculous intervention. The details of the stories are quite different: Heliodorus wants to seize the Temple treasure, Philopator merely to see the interior. There is a lengthy prayer in 3 Maccabees; in 2 Maccabees the miraculous punishment of the intruder is administered by angels, Heliodorus repents at the end; Philopator does not. The strongest case for literary dependence concerns the reaction of the Jewish populace: in both stories priests prostrate themselves, maidens who had been secluded rush outdoors, and all make supplication to God. The dramatic and emotional account is typical of Hellenistic historiography. Comparable incidents are reported by Josephus from the first century A.D., when Pilate introduced standards into Jerusalem (*Jewish War* 2.169–74; *Antiquities of the Jews* 18.55–59) and when Caligula ordered the erection of his statue in the Temple (*Jewish War* 2.184–203; *Antiquities of the Jews* 18.269–72). A noteworthy feature of the account

in 3 Maccabees is that some people propose armed resistance (1:23) but are dissuaded by "the old men and the elders." Such a division of opinion on the issue of violence was characteristic of Judaism in the first century A.D., but there was already some disagreement on the subject in the time of the Maccabees (see 1 Macc. 2).

2:1–20, The High Priest's Prayer. The high priest at the time of the battle of Raphia was Simon II, who is extolled in Sirach 50. The prayer attributed to him here resembles a type that is very widespread in postexilic Judaism and is shaped by traditional Deuteronomistic theology (Ezra 9; Neh. 9; Dan. 9; Bar. 1:15–3:8). It begins by affirming the righteousness of God and recalling his mighty deeds, including the Exodus. It also recalls the promise of 1 Kings 8 that God would heed the prayers offered in the Temple. The prayer proceeds to confess that it is "for our many and great sins" that the Jews are now troubled and concludes by asking God to blot out their sins and act "lest the transgressors boast." This prayer differs from the other Deuteronomistic prayers insofar as the distress of the Jews is not related to the exile, and there is less emphasis on the confession of sin, but the logic is the same. God is urged to act for his own sake, not because of any merit on the part of the Jews.

2:21–24, The Divine Intervention. Like Heliodorus in 2 Maccabees 3, Philopator is said to be "scourged" and knocked to the ground, although in this case there is no apparition of angels. Divine chastisements of pagan kings are often (though implausibly) reported in Jewish writings of the Hellenistic period—e.g., Nebuchadnezzar in Daniel 4 and Antiochus Epiphanes in 2 Maccabees 9. Such punishment normally leads to repentance and conversion. The dramatic conception of 3 Maccabees, however, requires that Philopator's change of heart be delayed until after his major attack on the Jews.

2:25–6:15
The Attack on Egyptian Jewry

2:25–33, The Demand Made on the Jews. The action of the king on his return to Egypt is presented as a direct result of his misadventure in Jerusalem. The proclamation "that none of those who did not sacrifice should be permitted to enter their temples" (trans. Anderson, 2:28) amounts to a proscription of Jewish synagogue worship. Moreover, the Jews are subjected to the census and reduced to a servile condition. Registration would involve branding with the emblem of Dionysus and a reduction in status. Some Jews, however, were given the option of being initiated into the mysteries of Dionysus and enjoying equal rights with the Alexandrians.

The nature and purpose of these proposals is the most controversial question in the study of 3 Maccabees. It is well known that Philopator promoted the cult of Dionysus and associated it with the royal cult. A decree preserved on papyrus provides an interesting parallel to 3 Maccabees: "By decree of the king. Persons who perform the rites of Dionysus in the interior shall sail down to Alexandria . . . and shall register themselves . . . and shall declare forthwith from what persons they have received the transmission of the sacred rites for three generations back and shall hand in the sacred book sealed up . . ." (see BGU, p. 1211). This decree shows an attempt to regulate the cult of Dionysus by registering its practitioners. A recollection of such an attempt by Philopator may underlie the narrative of 3 Maccabees.

The God of the Jews was often supposed by Greeks and Romans to be identical with Dionysus, in accordance with a common trend to identify Near Eastern gods with their more familiar Western counterparts. (Even the *Letter of Aristeas* suggests that the God of the Jews is identical with Zeus.) The identification with Dionysus is most fully argued by the Roman author Plutarch (*Table Talk* 4.6.1–2) who points to the festival of Tabernacles at the height of the vintage, Jewish ritual use of wine, and the observance of the Sabbath (Dionysus was identified with Sabazius, whose name suggested the connection with the Sabbath). During the persecution by Antiochus Epiphanes in 167 B.C., Jews were compelled to walk in the procession in honor of Dionysus, wearing wreaths of ivy (2 Macc. 6:7). It is possible that Philopator thought Judaism was a Dionysiac cult and tried to regularize its practices. 3 Maccabees, however, is our only testimony for such an action by this Ptolemy, and it is a dubious historical witness. The fact that the story contains credible historical elements does not guarantee that the main incidents happened.

The custom of branding or tattooing was associated with the cult of Dionysus from ancient times. It is likely that Philopator himself was so branded. Branding was also used to mark slaves, so that they could be captured if they ran away. 3 Maccabees appears to confuse the two kinds of branding, since the Jews are said to be reduced to servile status. The "former limited status" (2:29) probably refers to the condition of Jewish captives before their liberation by Ptolemy Philadelphus (*Let. of Arist.* 22).

The central issue in the interpretation of this passage concerns the *laographia* or census. The term could refer simply to the registration

of worshipers of Dionysus. It is probable, however, that the usage in 3 Maccabees was colored by the Roman association of a census with the poll tax, which was imposed on noncitizens (see Tcherikover, Hadas). Hence, the entire proposal of the Ptolemy is construed as an attempt to lower the status of the Jews.

The issue of citizenship is raised again by the offer of the king that those who were initiated into the mysteries would enjoy equal rights with the Alexandrians. It is not clear whether this offer is extended to all the Jews or only to a few. Underlying the episode is the dilemma of Diaspora Jews, especially in the Roman era. They aspired to equal rights with the Greeks, but citizenship would involve the worship of pagan gods in the course of civic functions. 3 Maccabees, like Philo and others, regards this price as unacceptable. There were always individual Jews who paid this price to advance their careers. (Dositheus son of Drimylus may have been such; the most famous example is Philo's nephew Tiberius Julius Alexander). 3 Maccabees not only disapproves of such people, but extols those who were willing to risk death rather than betray their religion.

3:1–10, The Slander Against the Jews. The refusal of the Jews to comply with the registration leads to an escalation of the threat. The decision to gather the Jews of the countryside to Alexandria is reminiscent of the papyrus on the cult of Dionysus, quoted above. Here, however, the purpose is not only registration but extermination. The king's resolve is supported by people who plot against the Jews. The author insists that the Jews were loyal to the king but incurred enmity because of the strangeness of their customs. The charge that Jews were disloyal because they did not worship the pagan gods is found already in the book of Daniel, but there, as in Esther, the professional rivalry of courtiers is a factor. The scandal of Jewish difference was an issue in the Diaspora. The *Letter of Aristeas* tried to overcome it by providing an allegorical interpretation of the dietary laws. There was a tradition of anti-Jewish polemic in Egypt, beginning with the Egyptian author Manetho (about 300 B.C.) and reaching a crescendo in the first century A.D. The recurring charges were "atheism" and "inhospitality" (see Josephus *Against Apion*). 3 Maccabees, like Josephus, refuses to ascribe this slander to "the Greeks." Josephus insists that the detractors are "Egyptians." 3 Maccabees calls them "foreigners" (somewhat enigmatically) and insists that "the Greeks" were well disposed to the Jews and tried to help them.

3:11–30, The Ptolemy's Decree. The remark that the Ptolemy had no regard for the power of

God suggests that he was guilty of hubris—the typical sin of tyrants in Greek tragedy on the one hand and in Hebrew tradition on the other (see the treatment of Babylon in the Prophets and of the Seleucid king Antiochus IV Epiphanes in Daniel). In his decree, Philopator places the blame on the Jews for their inhospitality at the Jerusalem Temple and their rejection of the cult of Dionysus and the offer of citizenship. The decree condemning a whole people to death seems wildly out of proportion to these charges. The threat of virtual genocide was a specter that had long haunted Diaspora Judaism, as can be seen already in the book of Esther. It had acquired some substance in the persecution of Antiochus Epiphanes (167 B.C.) and again in the pogrom in the time of Caligula (A.D. 38). While there is obvious similarity between these incidents and the anti-Semitism of modern times, it is important to bear in mind that there was no racial theory in the ancient disputes. In part, the hostility to the Jews in Egypt came from the fact that they had no sympathy with Egyptian nationalism and were all too loyal to the Roman overlords, who were thought to favor them unduly. In both ancient and modern times, however, some of the hostility came from the fact that Jews were a clearly identifiable foreign body and so an easy scapegoat on which their neighbors could vent their frustrations.

4:1–21, The Imprisonment of the Jews. The arrest of the Jews is described with considerable pathos in the emotional style of Hellenistic historiography. The use of the hippodrome anticipates the Roman use of the circus for tormenting Christians. Two anomalies in the story require comment. First, it seems that the death sentence at first only applied to the Jews from the countryside and that their kinsfolk in the city were only included because of their show of sympathy. Yet there is no apparent reason why this should have been so. Second, all those condemned to death are registered at considerable inconvenience. The registration may conceivably have been in preparation for seizing the property of the condemned, but this is not indicated here (note, however, 7:22, where the Jews recover their property according to the registration). Both these anomalies may result from the adaptation of an older story about a census, such as is described in the papyrus quoted above. That census was specifically for country folk, who were required to come to Alexandria, and the registration had a more obvious purpose.

In 3 Maccabees the registration becomes the occasion of a miracle when the paper mill and pens give out. The incident underlies the implausibility of an attempt to register the whole Jewish population of Egypt at one location. 3 Maccabees, however, construes it as "the working of invincible providence." It becomes a forewarning of the frustration of the king's further plans against the Jews.

5:1–51, The Frustration of the King's Plans. The proposed manner of execution was that the Jews be trampled by elephants who had been drugged with frankincense and wine. (The elephants are also made drunk in the parallel story in Josephus.) Intoxicating the elephants made little practical sense: war elephants were trained to kill by trampling and might be more difficult to control if they were drunk. Kasher suggests that the wine and frankincense were given as part of a Dionysiac ritual and that the execution was likewise ceremonial. The number of elephants, five hundred, is excessive: Philopator has only seventy-three elephants at the battle of Raphia. The name of the keeper of the elephants, Hermon, is reminiscent of Haman, enemy of the Jews in the book of Esther.

The story skillfully builds suspense, as the plans of the king are frustrated three times. First, the king is overcome by sleep at the appointed hour. On the second occasion he becomes forgetful of his purpose. In each case he is said to be thwarted by God, in response to the prayers of the Jews. The suspense is heightened by the prolongation of the third attempt. This time the king, who is compared to Phalaris (a sadistic tyrant of the sixth century B.C.), resolves not only to destroy the Egyptian Jews but also to attack Judea. The entry of the elephants into the hippodrome is described along with the supposed last farewells of the Jews, who fling themselves prone and cry out with a final prayer. The outcome is further delayed by the prayer of Eleazar.

6:1–15, The Prayer of Eleazar. The name Eleazar was popular in Hellenistic Judaism. It was the name of the high priest in the Letter of Aristeas (in 3 Maccabees, Eleazar is "one of the priests") and of a martyr in 2 Maccabees 6 and 4 Maccabees 5–6. Like the Maccabean martyr, this Eleazar is advanced in years. His prayer recalls previous tyrants who were humbled by God (Pharaoh in Exod. 14; Sennacherib in 2 Kings 18–19) and acts of miraculous deliverance (Daniel in Dan. 6; the three young men in Dan. 3; Jonah; the references to Daniel show the post-Maccabean date of the book). Like the earlier prayer of Simon, this one stands in the Deuteronomistic tradition, but the confession of sin is even more muted here. Eleazar asks, "If our life is forfeit by reason of irreverent deeds during our foreign sojourn, deliver us." This is the only suggestion that the persecution is a punishment for sin. God is not asked to intervene because of any merit of the Jews but lest the enemy say that God failed to deliver them. Instead, God should remember them "even in the land of their enemies." The latter phrase reflects a measure of alienation from their environment that is quite different from the perspective of Philo, who said that Jews "severally hold that land as their fatherland in which they were born and reared" (Flaccus 46).

6:16–7:23
The Deliverance of the Jews

6:16–41, The Reversal of Fortune. The story moves to its climax as the king enters the hippodrome. As in the story of Heliodorus (2 Macc. 3:26), two angels appear. It is not clear why they should not be visible to the Jews. Hadas suggests that the apparition was part of a source and that the author's own theology had no place for intermediary beings (there are no angels in the Temple incident in chap. 2). If that were so, the author could easily have omitted the angels here. The fact that they were not visible to all underlines their supernatural character. The parallel story in Josephus (Against Apion 2.53–54) also has the elephants turn on the Ptolemy's army. (Cf. Dan. 3, where the fire from the furnace burns some of the executioners, and Dan. 6, where Daniel's accusers are cast into the lions' den and devoured.)

The conversion of the king is a standard element in such stories (cf. Dan. 2–6, where pagan monarchs regularly praise the God of Daniel). Philopator passes the blame on to friends. In the stories of Daniel (3 and 6) and Esther, the primary blame clearly rests with the king's advisers, but here the Ptolemy himself had taken the initiative. In these Diaspora tales, however, it was reassuring to think that the highest authority was not itself hostile, although it might be swayed against the Jews from time to time. The establishment of a festival (3 Macc. 6:36) has an obvious precedent in Purim in the book of Esther (chap. 9). Josephus also speaks of the deliverance from the elephants as "the origin of the well-known feast which the Jews of Alexandria keep, with good reason, on this day" (Against Apion 2.55; trans. Thackery, Loeb Classical Library). Presumably there was such a feast. We do not know just what it was or how it was related to Purim.

7:1–9, Ptolemy's Letter. The letter formalizes what the king has said in chap. 6, blaming his "friends" and praising the Jews and their God. "The most high God" is a common appellation for God on the lips of Gentiles in the Hellenistic period (compare "the God of heaven" in Ezra and Nehemiah).

7:10–16, Revenge on Apostates. At the end of the book of Esther, the Jews take vengeance on

their gentile enemies and slay them by the thousand. In 3 Maccabees, these enemies get off lightly. The king accepts no blame, and, while he upbraids his "friends," he spares their lives. The vengeance of the Jews is directed toward those of their own people who voluntarily transgressed the law (even though they did so under duress). The king agrees that such people cannot be trusted, and more than three hundred of them are put to death.

The motif of the destruction of the enemy is a standard motif in stories of this kind, as a counterpart to the salvation of the righteous. In apocalyptic literature it attains a more definitive character as eternal damnation. 3 Maccabees, however, is not merely repeating the standard motif. The fact that Jews rather than Gentiles are singled out for vengeance suggests the animosity that observant Jews felt for renegades, especially in a time of crisis when the survival of the people was at stake.

7:17–23, The Departure. The story ends happily with the return of the Jews to their homes. We should note that the happy ending is "by the ordinance of the king"—there is no aspiration to independence. The festival mentioned here is presumably an extension of the one mentioned in chap. 6. The registration proves to have a providential purpose after all, as it enables the Jews to recover their possessions. The book closes appropriately with a benediction to God as "the Deliverer of Israel."

Bibliography

Ägyptische Urkunden aus den Königlichen Museen zu Berlin: Griechische Urkunden (BGU) I–VIII (1895–1933), p. 1211.

Anderson, H. "3 Maccabees." In The Old Testament Pseudepigrapha. 2 vols. Edited by J. H. Charlesworth. Garden City, NY: Doubleday, 1983, 1985. Vol. 2, pp. 509–29.

Collins, J. J. Between Athens and Jerusalem: Jewish Identity in the Hellenistic Diaspora. New York: Crossroad, 1983.

Emmet, C. W. "The Third Book of Maccabees." In The Apocrypha and Pseudepigrapha of the Old Testament. 2 vols. Edited by R. H. Charles. Oxford: Clarendon, 1913. Vol. 1, pp. 155–73.

Hadas, M. The Third and Fourth Books of Maccabees. New York: Harper, 1953.

Kasher, A. The Jews in Hellenistic and Roman Egypt. Tubingen: Mohr, 1985.

Tcherikover, V. "The Third Book of Maccabees as a Historical Source." Scripta Hierosolymnitana 7 (1961):5–6.

4 MACCABEES

STANLEY K. STOWERS

INTRODUCTION

The Fourth Book of Maccabees occurs in important manuscripts of the Greek Bible and was also circulated with the works of Flavius Josephus, the Jewish historian. In the latter it was given the apt title, "On the Sovereignty of Reason." To the eyes of modern interpreters accustomed to making a sharp theologically motivated division between "Greek" and "Jewish," the work has seemed strangely dual, even artificial. Its explicit topic is the rule of reason over the passions or emotions. The theme pervades the book and is repeated throughout (1:9, 13, 19, 30; 2:6, 24; 6:31; 7:16; 13:1; 16:1; 18:2). The topic belongs to Greek philosophy. 4 Maccabees is also about martyrs from the Maccabean conflict and expresses a kind of Judaism that partially defines itself over against the Greek way of life. Using the language and concepts of Stoicism (→ Stoics), 4 Maccabees argues that Jews can dominate their passions through reason trained and taught by the law and thus resist challenges to faithfulness even at the cost of life.

Literary Characteristics

The book is also literarily dual. Indeed the author is explicit about the work falling into two parts (3:19; cf. 1:2, 7–12). The first section, 1:1–3:18, is the discursive argument of a thesis. After an introductory narrative (3:19–4:26) that provides the dramatic setting, the second part of the work (3:19–18:24) focuses on the stories of the Maccabean martyrs: the martyrdom of Eleazar (5:1–7:23); the martyrdom of the seven brothers (8:1–14:10); and the mother of the seven (14:11–17:6). Even though the work provides substantial accounts of the martyrs' defiance and torture, it is misleading to think of the second half as essentially "historical" narratives. Argumentation and the rhetorical praise known as encomium are as important there as narrative.

The variety of generic descriptions proposed for 4 Maccabees reflects the difficulties that interpreters have experienced in providing an overall description of the work. It has most commonly been called a diatribe. Until recently scholars have usually employed "diatribe" to mean any brief popular ethical and philosophical work with dialogical characteristics. With its hypothetical objections at 1:5 and 2:24, the first part of the book, 1:1–3:18, fits this definition of the diatribe fairly well. The second part, with its long narrative sections, however, does not. Moreover, recent scholarship on the diatribe has shown that it is better defined as a type of rhetoric that has its setting in the classroom discussion of the philosophical schools. Thus while the work has some similarities to the diatribal literature, diatribe is wholly inadequate as a generic description.

Others have described 4 Maccabees as a synagogue sermon but have not provided any examples for comparison, since we know almost nothing about synagogue "preaching" in the time of 4 Maccabees. The description of 4 Maccabees in terms of the styles of oratorical praise common in Greek and Latin culture (i.e., as an encomium or panegyric) partially fits the second half of the work. There, praise of the martyrs and their virtues is a significant element. It is even possible to call the latter part of the book an *epitaphios logos* (Gk.), a commemorative funeral oration. This genre is related to panegyric, and genuine similarities to it do appear in the last chapters of 4 Maccabees.

The combination of observations that are the basis for the preceding generic descriptions are best accounted for by the techniques of the rhetorical *thesis*. The thesis is known from numerous rhetorical handbooks and student manuals known as elementary rhetorical exercises, as well as from examples of the genre and miscellaneous discussions, especially in Cicero. Theses were general theoretical and ethical questions first discussed and written about in the philosophical schools. Many of these topics were taken into the rhetorical schools where "thesis" came to mean "the investigation of a topic without reference to specific circumstances." Students were trained in how to develop theses rhetorically. Theses were contrasted with *hypotheses*, which were topics including specifics such as person, time, and place. The following are examples of theses: "whether one ought to worship God"; "whether the wise man can suffer distress"; "whether one can trust the evidence of sense perception." A thesis could be transformed into a hypothesis by adding specific circumstances and treated as a judicial case, a matter of advice, or a subject for praise or blame (i.e., treated encomiastically). Quintilian, a Roman teacher of rhetoric, gives "whether one ought to marry" as an example of a thesis that could be turned into the following hypothesis: "Should Cato have married?" (*Institutio oratoria* 3.5.8).

4 Maccabees is the rhetorical treatment of the thesis formally stated in 1:1, "whether religious reason is sovereign over the passions." In 1:1–3:18 the orator treats the subject as a typical thesis. In 3:19–18:24 the author continues to argue the thesis but fixes on the one example of the Maccabean martyrs, so that, in effect, he has added person, time, and place. The second half of the work then resembles the argument of a thesis combined with its hypothesis treated encomiastically. Thus the subject of the second half becomes "we ought to praise the martyrs if they are shown to have mastered the emotions through religious reason." This explains why 3:19–18:24 contains so many characteristics of encomium or panegyric and yet continues to argue the philosophical theses. Since the commemorative funeral oration was a speech praising dead war heroes and civic martyrs, it is not surprising that the Maccabean heroes would be praised in similar terms. Thus the common techniques of developing a thesis explain 4 Maccabees' similarities to the diatribe, panegyric, sermon, and funeral oration.

A number of commentators have thought that 4 Maccabees is the record of a speech delivered orally at a festival or occasion in honor of the martyrs. In 1:10 and 3:19 there is reference to "the present occasion." The same expression is used in funeral orations and panegyrics that were at least purportedly delivered in public. A reference to the tomb of the martyrs occurs in 17:8, and a grave site commemoration is conceivable. Students of rhetoric, however, were taught to develop hypotheses so as to portray a courtroom situation, an advisory speech to Cato, or a civic oration. Thus one can only say that 4 Maccabees literarily presents itself as an occasional oration with a live audience.

In sum, 4 Maccabees represents the perfect form for a rhetorically trained orator who is also committed to philosophy. It both rhetorically argues a philosophical thesis and develops that thesis into an encomium of those examples that are used as evidence for the thesis. The elements of encouragement and consolation in 4 Maccabees are natural to panegyric. This complex mixture of praise, moral example, and exhortation is specified in the introduction to the funeral oration in Plato's *Menexenus* (236E): "The proper speech will sufficiently praise the dead and gently exhort the living, encouraging their descendents and brethren to imitate their virtue—and to console survivors—praising the good men who in life brought joy to friends by their virtue, and gave their lives in exchange for the salvation of the living."

Authorship, Date, and Place of Origin

Although at one time 4 Maccabees was attributed to Josephus, its author is unknown. The author was almost certainly a Hellenistic Jewish man. He spoke fluent Greek and was highly trained in rhetoric. The book reflects a broad knowledge of Greek culture. He had at least a basic knowledge of Greek philosophy, namely, some form of later Stoicism. He was probably a public figure and one of the literati in some Jewish community (see 1:12). He knew Scripture, namely, the Law and the Prophets, but used Scriptural examples in a typically Greek rhetorical way. He employed the Septuagint Greek translation (LXX), and 4 Maccabees is free of Semitisms that might suggest that Greek was the author's second language. The author drew on various legends from the Maccabean period. His most important source for 4 Maccabees, however, was 2 Maccabees. The narrative portions of chaps. 3–18 are largely an expansion of 2 Maccabees 6:12–7:42.

Scholars have proposed many dates between 63 B.C. and A.D. 120 for the writing of 4 Maccabees. Since there is no clear evidence for dating, no proposal can be much more than an educated guess. The most probable suggestion would place its composition in the first century A.D. The one argument for dating that carries some weight was made by Elias Bickerman. He points to 4:2 where Apollonius is called governor of Syria, Phoenicia, and Cilicia and shows that Cilicia was only an administrative part of Syria between about A.D. 20 and 54. The administrative arrangement mentioned in 4:2, then, may be an anachronism reflecting the author's own time.

The work itself gives no evidence for place of composition. The literary setting for the martyrdoms is clearly Jerusalem. Scholars have most often proposed Alexandria and Antioch as places of composition, the former because of its famous Greek-Jewish intellectual tradition and the latter because a Christian cult of the Maccabean martyrs in Antioch seems to go back at least to the fourth century. Jerusalem or any of the Greek, Phoenician, or Jewish cities of Palestine are even more likely. Greek was a literary and administrative second language of upper-class Jews in Palestine, and Greek education continued in Jerusalem even after the Maccabean revolt. Substantial numbers of Jews who spoke Greek as a first language also lived in Palestine. Palestine and Syria together produced more Stoic teachers than any other region. Finally, however, the lack of evidence means that the author could have come from any urban setting in the Greek East with a Jewish community and could have composed the work anywhere.

Significance and Thought

To the historian of religions, 4 Maccabees is important as a witness to one way of being Jewish in a world where many types of Judaism flourished. Already in the time of the Maccabees being a Jew was, for the majority, a matter of belonging to two cultures. It was never a matter of merely choosing between Hellenism and Judaism but of continually adapting some form of Judaism to a Hellenistic world to which it already belonged. Although 4 Maccabees takes the strongest stand against compromising practices deemed essential to "the Jewish way of life," it also assumes a large area of commonality and rapprochement with "the Greek way of life." For the author this commonality surely included concrete and practical areas of social and cultural intercourse, but in 4 Maccabees it is conceived in terms of Greek philosophy.

In the world of 4 Maccabees there is a Greek way of life, a Jewish way of life, and a large area of the universally true that substantially overlaps with both ways of life. This common ground is primarily conceived in terms of human nature and worked out in psychology and ethics. The four cardinal virtues (prudence, fortitude, temperance, and justice), their subvirtues, reason, the emotions, and instincts are human. Both the Greek and Jewish ways of life aim for the virtues, although the Jewish law that produces the Jewish way of life is a superior means to them. There is no opposition between nature and the law (e.g., as human convention or supernatural) because both were ordained by God and made compatible by God. At the same time the book does not universalize the law. It is the constitution of the Jewish people.

There has been great confusion in the scholarly literature concerning the philosophical kinship of 4 Maccabees. It has been called Platonic, Aristotelian, and, most often, Stoic. Most unsatisfactory of all is the claim that it is a mishmash of philosophical commonplaces. 4 Maccabees is a rhetorical oration and not a philosophical treatise. That, however, does not mean that its philosophical thought is incoherent. In several respects its thought is definitively Stoic. This has never been clearly shown in the scholarly literature because Stoicism with its long and complex history has been treated in terms of a superficial caricature. The task is also difficult because certain types of later Stoicism adapted Platonic and Aristotelian elements into their systems and certain Platonists borrowed much from Stoics.

What is most Stoic about 4 Maccabees is the role of reason in relation to the emotions and irrational dispositions. Although all of the Hellenistic schools agreed that reason was to be master of the emotions, what this meant was developed in quite different ways and expressed in their depictions of the ideal wise man. Stoics thought that reason should thoroughly dominate the emotions. There is no room in Stoic theory for the continual and often creative struggle between the two that is characteristic of Platonism or the integration of emotion into the higher form of reason as in Aristotelian thought. The older or orthodox Stoics taught that the typical emotions of most people were diseased states of the soul that needed to be replaced by rationalized emotions. The so-called middle Stoics, especially Posidonius, taught that the emotions were innate and could not be eradicated or rationalized. They could only be tamed and mastered.

4 Maccabees stands very close to the middle Stoicism of Posidonius on several points of psychology. The emotions and dispositions are innate and cannot be eradicated but must be thoroughly subjugated by reason. The Stoic character of the work's philosophy is most clear in its depictions of the martyrs who resemble the figure of the Stoic wise man. The mother, for example, so thoroughly mastered her emotions and irrational impulses by her reasonings that she suppressed her maternal love and did not flinch or grieve when she saw her children being burned alive and dismembered. The chief virtue of the work is courage, which is defined in a typically Stoic way as endurance and constancy. The martyrs, like the wise man, know what must be endured (i.e., that which is not morally good, the emotions, and fortune). Through the power of reason they are able to endure these things. In sharp contrast to Philo's Platonic-Stoic synthesis (→ Philo) there are no traces of Platonic elements and no criticism of any Stoic doctrines in 4 Maccabees.

It is impossible to know what 4 Maccabees meant to its first readers or hearers. We can only know what it meant for the author and his implied literary audience. The latter are imagined to be Jews for whom the philosophical doctrines of 4 Maccabees are for the most part accepted as scientific knowledge. 4 Maccabees' way of arguing by means of a decisive empirical example, the endurance of the martyrs, resembles a type of "proof" for which Posidonius was famous. The work uses the thesis to define the nature of Israel's inviolable integrity as God's people. History, including the events of the Maccabean struggle, had shown that military power and political-religious institutions could not be the basis for Israel's integrity. Through the argument of its thesis concerning the endurance of the martyrs, the book seeks to show that the integrity of the whole nation can be guaranteed by the faithful sage's inner invincibility. The essential premise is that obedience to and education in the law produces virtuous character in those who are faithful. Antiochus Epiphanes violated the physical and symbolic boundaries of the nation, but he was not able to destroy the moral-religious integrity of the martyrs even though he violated their physical bodies. Therefore the soul of the nation was inviolable. 4 Maccabees answers the question, "What shall we be in order to survive?" In the form of encomium that praises the martyrs' virtues, it also contains a strong element of exhortation. What it praises, it also recommends.

The impregnable boundary may be the faithful Jew's religious reason, i.e., moral-religious character, but the faithful Jew is not merely an individual. As a member of Israel the individual bears a part of Israel's corporate responsibility to God's justice. In turn the individual can affect the whole. The martyrs in 4 Maccabees affect the whole nation in two ways. First, the example of their faithfulness had great paradigmatic power, and that helped to effect faithfulness in the rest of the nation. Second, their endurance was so meritorious that God regarded their suffering as sufficient atonement for the nation's apostasy. 4 Maccabees interprets the significance of their deaths within the tradition of "the merits of the fathers." Some individuals like Abraham and Moses were so virtuous that God henceforth blessed the whole people or all descendants on the basis of their faithfulness. Thus all Israelites receive the blessings of the covenant on the basis of God's regard for Abraham's faithfulness. So God also restored the nation's fortunes because of the Maccabean martyrs.

Apart from Christian groups, 4 Maccabees does not seem to have been known to any later types of Judaism. Christians transmitted the book, which may have been significant for early Jewish followers of Christ. Some scholars have argued that 4 Maccabees' conception of the martyrs' expiatory suffering influenced Paul's interpretation of Jesus' death. While there is virtually nothing about the atoning effect of a person's death in Jewish literature before the turn of the era, the theme is extremely important in Greek literature. Some, then, have argued that 4 Maccabees may have mediated such concepts to the earliest followers of Jesus.

This theory would also help to explain why 4 Maccabees was read as a Christian book by the later church. It was clearly important to the later church's cult and theology of martyrdom and was a force in forming that tradition. The *Martyrdom of Polycarp* (second century A.D.), the earliest piece of Christian martyr literature, seems to contain literary and conceptual echoes of 4 Maccabees. 4 Maccabees was popular among the representatives of the golden age of patristic literature in the fourth and fifth centuries. Gregory of Nazianzus, John Chrysostom, Ambrose, Augustine, and Jerome preached and wrote about the martyrs. These authors treat the Maccabean heroes as Christian protomartyrs. Thus although 4 Maccabees never achieved a canonical status in either Western or Eastern churches, it was influential especially in the latter.

COMMENTARY

1:1–12
Introduction

The introduction in 1:1–12 exhibits the advice of certain rhetoricians that writers of theses should use a special type of careful and artful introduction instead of the normal rhetorical introduction. Thus the author not only attempts to make the audience attentive but also lays out his thesis and exactly how he will treat it.

1:1–6, Statement of the Thesis. The orator announces the thesis (1:1a), urges its importance (1:1b–2), and clarifies it with a qualification (1:3–6). Modern philosophy is an academic discipline that concerns theories of knowledge and their implications. For our author and Greco-Roman culture, philosophy meant wisdom in living life. On the basis of medieval and modern assumptions about "faith and reason" interpreters have claimed that "religious reason" is an oxymoron. But with rare exceptions ancient philosophy understood reason and piety toward the gods to be integrally related. For Stoics "religion" or "piety" was one of the virtues. Like Philo and many other Jews, the writer of 4 Maccabees believed that the wisdom of philosophy found its highest expression in the teachings of the five Mosaic books of the law (see, e.g., 2:16–17). Thus the author speaks of "religious reason," probably adding "religious" to a thesis that may have already been current in the rhetorical schools.

Verse 2 not only claims importance for the thesis but also suggests the twofold treatment that the author will give to it. The rhetorical handbooks divide theses into theoretical and practical subjects. Theses were sometimes treated encomiastically, praising and recommending moral virtues. The first part of 4 Maccabees treats the thesis theoretically (1:12–3:18), while the second is encomiastic and exhortatory (3:19–18:24). Verse 2 suggests this distinction: the work will encompass both "theoretical knowledge" and praise of "practical moral thinking" (i.e., "prudence").

Verses 3–4 elaborate the thesis. The four cardinal virtues of the Platonic and Stoic schools, "rational self-restraint," "justice," "courage," as well as "practical moral thinking" in verse 2, are set against a miscellany of opposing emotions and dispositions that are all called passions (Gk. *pathē*). The word may also be properly translated as "emotions," but no modern English concept fully corresponds to the ancient idea of "passions."

Some of the rhetorical handbooks instruct authors of theses to use objections from imaginary interlocutors to sharpen the discussion and answer typical criticisms of the thesis. The objection in 1:5 is repeated in 2:24. It allows the clarification of two possible counterarguments: first, that reason cannot control emotions (i.e., passions) because it cannot even control ignorance and forgetfulness that affect the intellect itself; second, that mastery of the emotions means their elimination. The latter was a common misunderstanding of the orthodox Stoics who taught that the diseased emotions such as "irrational fear" had to be entirely eliminated and replaced with the good emotions such as "rational caution."

1:7–12, The Examples to Be Used. The second part of the introduction explains how the orator will treat the thesis in the second part of the work (3:19–18:24) by turning to the martyrs in order to illustrate it. This procedure resembles what the rhetoricians called developing a hypothesis, i.e., adding person, specific events, and place to a thesis. Verse 10 probably means that although the author could give a standard speech of formal praise of the martyrs's virtues (i.e., an encomium or panegyric), he will give an oration that commemorates dead heros. It was customary to speak of the dead as "blessed." The expression "at this time" (1:10, 3:19) may indicate that the oration was delivered at a festival commemorating the martyrdoms.

1:13–3:18
Theoretical Development of the Thesis

In 1:13–3:18 the thesis is developed with various arguments. In 1:13–30a the author follows the practice in theoretical theses of beginning with definitions and distinctions regarding the key concepts. The following section, 1:30b–3:18, provides illustrations showing that reason has mastery over each type of emotion.

1:13–30a, Definitions and Distinctions. The definition of wisdom in 1:16 may possibly have originated with the Stoics but had come to be a philosophical commonplace used by writers from various backgrounds. 4 Maccabees

has assimilated Greek ethics and psychology and yet remains definitively Jewish. It is the law, the five books of Moses, that gives content to the faculty of reason (1:17). Reason is almost the will to do God's law. The law teaches and trains the intellect (2:23; 5:24, 34; 13:24) and enables reason to develop the virtues (5:23; 13:13; cf. 11:27). The second half of 1:24 is textually problematic and the translation uncertain.

1:30b–2:23, Examples of the Power of Reason. Here the author advances examples to show how reason allows the person to master the emotions and thus obey the law. The discussion falls into three parts: reason's rule through rational self-control (1:30–2:6a); reason's rule through courage (2:6b–14); reason's rule over violent emotions through the rationally self-controlled mind (2:15–23). The most important concept in 1:30b–2:23 is "rational self-control," the most characteristically Greek virtue, which is often poorly translated as "temperance."

There are two quite different ways to translate the second part of verse 30. Hadas (similarly Anderson) renders the phrase in question, "in the case of the deeds which hamper temperance." But the following translation is equally possibly (similarly the RSV and Townsend): "by means of the restraining effects of rational self-control." The first translation has the advantage of being parallel to 1:3 and 2:6. One reason that rational self-control looms so large in 4 Maccabees is that such self-control was traditionally the habit of resisting temptations to overeat or eat the wrong kinds of foods. The Jewish food laws become the central test case in the account of the martyrdoms (1:33–34; cf. 5:16–24). Rational self-control was also the means of restraining sexual desire. The story of Joseph (2:2–3) became the example that epitomized this virtue in Jewish and early Christian literature.

In 2:6b–14 the author provides examples from the law that he treats as general humanitarian principles. In the law, lending without interest applies only to Jews (Exod. 22:25; Lev. 25:36; Deut. 23:20). Similarly, on gleaning (4 Macc. 2:9) see Lev. 19:9–10. 4 Macc. 2:9–10 shows clearly how the law provides the content for reason. Verse 14 is quite elliptical and difficult to construe precisely, although the general idea is clear (cf. Deut. 20:19–20; Exod. 23:4–5).

In discussing the hardest case of the most violent emotions (4 Macc. 2:15–23), the author will finally clarify his philosophical position on human psychology. The concepts contained in verses 21–23 are Stoic and probably come from the middle Stoicism of Panaetius and Posidonius, who emphasized that the emotions were innate and could not be eradicated. Reason's role is to subdue and master the passions completely. There is not just a standoff or creative struggle between the two parts of the soul as a Platonist might have taught. At the same time, the passions cannot be cut out. God himself created humans with passions and inclinations (2:21) that through the agency of the senses are to be ruled by the governing power of the intellect (2:22). For orthodox Stoics, the mind has no innate ideas but is consubstantial with universal divine reason. The senses work together with reason in apprehending the world empirically. Passions arise when the intellect errs about the value and nature of objects. The middle Stoics modified this position by making the passions innate. For our Jewish author the Mosaic law educates the faculty of reason and is also an object of perception. The Stoics, in one of their famous paradoxes, said that the wise man, who lives according to reason, is the only true king. He controls the only thing over which a person truly has power, the inner moral state. Our author says that the one who lives according to the law reigns over a kingdom of the virtues (2:23).

2:24–3:18, The Example of David's Thirst. Although there is no manuscript warrant, several commentators reject the phrase "those of the body" in 3:1 and replace it with the corresponding answer in 1:6. They do this because the examples of passions in 3:2–4 are not passions of the body. The author's contrast, however, is not between passions of the body and those of the soul (RSV misleadingly translates "soul" as "mind" in 3:3) but between passions of the body and those of reason. Reason is merely the governing aspect of the soul. "Passions of the reason" (2:24–3:1) refers to states of the intellect like forgetfulness, which are basically involuntary. The point then is not a contrast between soul and body but the extent to which reason controls soul-body. The author could as well have written, "those of the body and irrational aspects of the soul" in 3:1.

In introducing "desire" in 3:2, the example of King David is already in view. The Greek Bible uses "desire" of David in 2 Sam. 23:15, and desire in the focus of the story in 4 Maccabees (3:11, 12, 16). The writer already emphasized that some desires are of the body and some of the soul (1:32). The story about David illustrates both as it creatively embellishes the biblical account. The "tensing and loosing" in 3:11 reflects the Stoic explanation of the emotions. The story is yet another argument for the power of the mind when it exhibits the virtue of rational self-control (3:17; cf. 1:35; 2:16, 18; 3:19). The reason for this emphasis is clear: through this virtue a martyr can "overcome the sufferings of the body regardless of how extreme" (3:18).

In sum, 1:1–3:18 argues for the thesis in a way that stresses rational self-control over the

appetites, especially appetites of eating, and over the emotions of pain. Courage is also important. This philosophically informed orator has given a scientific explanation of the ability to endure in the face of temptation, persecution, and torture. In 3:19–18:24 he will rhetorically narrate stories that he believes profoundly prove the truth of his thesis and show that "even women and children," if they have cultivated these virtues through the law, can endure the most extreme persecution.

3:19–18:24

Development of the Thesis Through the Example of the Maccabean Martyrs

4 Macc. 3:19 is the major transition of the whole discourse. After 3:19 the style changes from the popular philosophical argumentation of a thesis to emotionally charged narratives and panegyrics. The differences, however, should not be overplayed. The first part already uses narratives about Joseph, Jacob, Moses, and David as examples, and the second part argues the thesis. The rhetorical genre of 3:19–18:24 is epideictic, the rhetoric of praise and blame customary on occasions such as weddings, funerals, commemorative celebrations, and award ceremonies. The author continues explicitly (6:31–34; 7:16–23; 13:1–7; 14:11–15:1; 16:1–4) and implicitly (throughout) to argue the thesis but also mixes argumentation with praise, or panegyric. The latter in turn is implicitly a kind of exhortation for the audience to emulate the virtues of the martyrs (see 18:1–2). The statement in 3:19 that "the proper time calls us to demonstrate the theme of rationally self-controlled reason" may refer to an occasion commemorating the martyrs at which the speech was given (cf. 1:10).

3:19–4:26

Historical Background to the Persecution

After the transitional verse 19, 3:20–4:26 provides a preface to the discussion of the martyrs. The first part (3:20–4:14) tells the story of Apollonius' attempt on the Temple treasury, and the second (4:15–26) narrates the background to Antiochus' persecutions. Here, and in the narratives that follow, the author probably drew on 2 Maccabees, but not always accurately. The author has confused "Seleucus Nicanor" (actually, Nicator) who lived ca. 358–281 B.C. with Seleucus IV Philopator (ruled 187–175 B.C.), the actual predecessor of Antiochus. Similarly, "governor of Syria, Phoenicia, and Cilicia" (4:2) is anachronistic. Cilicia was part of the province only in A.D. 20–54. Verse 5 contradicts 2 Macc. 3:7–8, where Heliodorus is put in command, not Apollonius. Such details are of little importance to the author's purposes. The orator need only provide enough narrative to make sense of the tyranny of Antiochus and his persecution of the martyrs.

Verse 15 is also inaccurate: Antiochus IV Epiphanes was not Seleucus' son but the brother of Seleucus IV Philopator. Verse 21 attributes Antiochus' attack to "divine justice" because of national apostasy from the law. The faithful endurance and deaths of the martyrs are more than isolated incidents with an exemplary personal significance in 4 Maccabees. They are an atonement and purification for the sin and apostasy under Antiochus (1:11; 17:21; 18:4). The work makes the story into a personal struggle with cosmic implications between the demonically anti-Jewish Antiochus, who is being used by God to punish and test his people, and the unlikely martyrs: an old man, seven boys, and an old woman. 4 Maccabees clearly has the struggle take place in Jerusalem, although the later church believed that the martyrdoms occurred in Antioch.

5:1–7:23
The Martyrdom of Eleazar

The section 5:1–7:23 comprises the martyrdom and eulogy of Eleazar (cf. 2 Macc. 18–31). The narratives of Eleazar's and the youths' martyrdoms have a very similar structure: the tyrant's exhortation to apostasy (5:5–13); a speech of defiance (5:14–38); torture of the hero (6:1–25); final words and death (6:26–30). In each case the narrative is followed by an encomium in praise of the martyr(s) and an appeal to their behavior as evidence for the thesis. The mother is treated differently in several respects due to the ancient hierarchical conception of gender.

5:1–4, Narrative Setting. The events unfold at a preeminent public place in Jerusalem. When Eleazar speaks, he speaks to the "people" of the city (5:15). Many Jews have already chosen apostasy by participating in the abolition of the constitution and way of life taught in the law (4:18–20). The story of Apollonius is told to show that such a thing would have been impossible if the Jewish leaders were faithful and God was with them. But now God is justly angry and sends Antiochus to punish his people (4:21). When Antiochus arrives many people bravely resist apostasy but without God's help are killed (4:24–26). In this dramatic setting, all eyes are focused on Eleazar, the boys, and the mother. In likening the

martyrdoms to an athletic contest, 17:14 describes "the world and humanity as the spectators." They are public examples and the narrative will make it clear that the fate of the nation hangs on the strength of their character.

Verse 4 introduces and characterizes Eleazar. He is a priest, skilled in the law, an old man, and a philosopher. In 2 Maccabees he is a ninety-year-old scribe. That he is a priest and known to Antiochus' court for his philosophical way of life reflects the peculiar perspective of 4 Maccabees. As a priest and expert in the law he is definitively loyal to the integrity of the Jewish nation-people-religion. As a philosopher he also lives in a larger Greek world that is partially reconcilable with Judaism. The irony of 4 Maccabees is that Greek philosophy explains how the utmost loyalty to Judaism is possible. 4 Maccabees emphasizes that each martyr faces torture and death with a disability that makes their endurance more remarkable. For Eleazar it is his old age.

5:5–13, Antiochus' Exhortation to Apostasy. Antiochus' exhortation to apostasy (5:5–13) and Eleazar's reply (5:14–38) comprise opposing philosophies. The tyrant's speech takes the form of an exhortation to adopt a certain philosophy and its way of life. His argument against Eleazar's philosophy occupies vv. 8–10. It is unjust to reject the gifts of nature such as pork; such pleasures are a good not to be rejected by those who are truly wise. The mention of pleasure and nature makes Antiochus sound vaguely Epicurean. In a way typical of Stoics and other Hellenistic schools our author has nothing positive to say about "pleasure" (see 1:20–33), even if he believes that the capacity for pleasure is inherently human.

5:14–38, Eleazar's Defiant Reply. In his reply Eleazar says that the law, in teaching "rational self-control," allows him to dominate his impulse toward pleasure (5:23). Summing up what Eleazar's case demonstrates about his thesis, the author includes the ability to dominate pleasure (6:35). Antiochus calls Eleazar to a philosophy of what is "beneficial" rather than to risk death on the basis of his philosophical doctrines (5:11). The king is enticing him to think personally and selfishly about his situation.

Eleazar, the philosopher tutored by the law, cannot reason as Antiochus urges. His defiant reply outlines the essential philosophical-religious notions of 4 Maccabees. In essence vv. 16–18 mean that Eleazar's transgression would not be a personal matter. The argument carries force if one remembers the dramatic setting. Eleazar's behavior is on display before the Jewish nation at a moment when either survival or assimilation to the Greek way of life is a real possibility. The way the nation will go depends upon whether or not the old philosopher upholds his "reputation for piety" (v. 18). In such a public situation, whether the particular transgression be minor or serious in itself, symbolically it would represent the rejection of the law (5:19–21; cf. v. 13).

The basic line of Eleazar's argument for observing the law is as follows: living by the law actually produces the virtues in us (vv. 23–24), therefore we do not eat unclean foods but believe that the law corresponds to the way that God has created us (vv. 25–27). The virtues in question are three of the four cardinal virtues generally regarded in Hellenistic culture as the mark of the wise man, plus "religion" or "piety," which was also considered an important virtue. Verses 25–26 are crucial for understanding how the author has reconciled his Greek and Jewish heritages: "Believing that God established the law, we know that the creator of the world, in giving the law, has cared for us according to nature. He has allowed us to eat the things which are well-disposed to our souls but has commanded us not to eat meats which are contrary to our souls." Now it is clear why the law produces virtues that for the author constitute the human good. God who created both the law and nature has made the teachings of the law correspond to the spiritual nature of the Jewish people. 4 Maccabees does not go on to argue that the natural constitution of all humans is created to conform to the food laws. The word translated as "well-disposed" was an extremely important concept for the Stoics. Verse 26 is reminiscent of what the Stoic Chrysippus said: "In constituting the creature, Nature made it well-disposed to itself so that it repels the harmful things and allows the things which are well-disposed" (Diogenes Laertius 7.85).

Verses 27–38 provide a rhetorical display of defiance against the tyrant. Socrates was the beginning of a long tradition of philosopher-martyrs. Under the early empire Stoics developed a reputation for opposition to tyranny. Eleazar's words are reminiscent of such Stoic defiance. Epictetus said that the tyrant could chain his leg or kill his body but never control his moral reasoning. Eleazar says the same in vv. 27–38. For 4 Maccabees, reason and the emotions are not abstract philosophical concepts. These doctrines mean that Judaism need not be subdued by a superior political power. Eleazar like the Stoic sage displays complete inner freedom. Unlike the Stoic sage he also is emboldened by belief in a future life and future retribution (5:37; cf. 13:17; 17:12).

6:1–30, The Torture and Death of Eleazar.
In the lurid description of his torture (6:1–25), Eleazar is the synthesis of a Jewish "saint" and a philosopher-martyr. He raises his eyes to heaven in the attitude of prayer and dying martyrs (6:6, 26; cf. Acts 7:55). In the language of Hellenistic moral exhortation, he is a noble athlete (4 Macc. 6:10). Athletic imagery, so important in Hellenistic moral-philosophical literature, is one of the most important figurative motifs in the work (e.g., 17:11–14). Above all, Eleazar is a model or example for his people (6:19). The narrator gives him a last chance to save himself (6:12–15), so that the old philosopher can interpret his behavior as an example (6:16–23). Within the narrative it is an example most explicitly for the youths who will follow him (6:19, 22). Eleazar's example effects a reaction of imitation beginning with the boys and their mother that will finally save the whole nation. Cynics and the later Stoics spoke frequently of the philosopher's behavior under hardship and pain as an example for imitation. The example of the perfected philosopher, the wise man, was believed to have amazing power over people's lives.

From ancient literary practice, one expects final words in a death scene (6:26–30) to express key notions for the piece of literature in question. Verses 27–29 contain concepts that are virtually without precedent in Jewish literature, including the Hebrew Bible, but that were extremely important in ancient Greek literature, especially tragedy. These also became central ideas for interpreting the meaning of Jesus' death. Eleazar could have saved himself but remains faithful to God in order to die for his people. He asks God to regard his death as a "ransom" (cf. Mark 10:45) and "purification" for the sin of his people (cf. 4 Macc. 1:11; 9:24; 12:17; 17:21–22; 18:4). In other words, Eleazar is asking God to consider his faithfulness to death as sufficient punishment for the apostasy of Israel under Antiochus. He is asking for the return of God's protecting presence as it was in the days of the Apollonius incident.

6:31–35, Eleazar's Death as Philosophical Proof.
Having depicted Eleazar's remarkable suppression of immediate self-interest for the sake of loyalty to God and the greater good of the nation, our author abruptly asserts what for him is the inescapable logic. Thus vv. 31–35 claim the narrative as "proof" of the thesis. Eleazar's self-giving is explainable by and demonstrates the governing power of reason over the irrational impulses of physical pain and the enticements of pleasure. Before amplifying Eleazar's case as proof of the thesis (7:16–23), the orator celebrates the old man in a brief encomium.

7:1–23, An Encomium and Further Argument.
The model figure for the encomium in 7:1–15 is the Stoic wise man. The metaphor of reason as pilot is common in Hellenistic philosophy, but it was the Stoics, especially in the early Roman empire, who likened the wise man

fortified with his reason to a besieged city (cf. Paul's opposition to such an attitude in 2 Cor. 10:3–6). The Stoics derived the imagery from Antisthenes who said, "Prudence is a most secure fortress which is never broken or betrayed. We ought to construct walls of defense with our own impregnable reasonings" (*Diogenes Laertius* 6.13). Instead of being compared with Stoic sages, however, Eleazar is compared to Aaron and Isaac, models of self-giving for their people through the power of reason. Eleazar himself has entered the ranks of these powerful moral examples (7:9). When the author returns to arguing his thesis (7:16–23), he raises a possible objection (7:17). What if many cannot attain the impregnable prudence that Antisthenes and our author recommend? Stoics thought that the true wise man was extremely rare and that most people did not live by reason. 4 Maccabees seems to agree. The answer to the objection seems to be that while only some will attain prudent reason, anyone who trusts in God and is devoted to his ways can fully develop his or her reason (7:18–19, 21–23). Like the Stoics, our author can say that only the wise man rules his emotions (7:23). The objection has no force for the author. Perfection is what reason and religion demand. In fact, 4 Maccabees polemicizes against Jews who would argue that torture and duress make lapses in keeping the law excusable (8:16–26). As with the philosophers, healthy reasoning is based on sure belief in true doctrines. These illustrate the author's Jewish-Stoic synthesis. Only the person who believes that they, like the patriarchs, will not die to God but live to God (7:19) and that it is blessed to suffer for the sake of virtue can attain prudent reason (7:22).

8:1–14:10
The Martyrdom of the Seven Brothers

This section, which treats the martyrdom of the seven brothers, seems to be a rhetorical expansion of 2 Macc. 7:1–38. If Eleazar's disability was old age, that of the seven brothers is youth. Stoics most often taught that children only attained the capacity for reason at age fourteen, although some held that it came earlier. It is unclear just how the author stands on this issue, except that the children are presented as exceptional because they are Jewish (e.g., 9:18). Stoics believed that children, because they were not fully rational, could only receive training; adults needed doctrines and training or in some cases doctrines alone. The youths in 4 Maccabees have received both. They were "nurtured in doctrines" (10:2), which probably include those mentioned in 7:19–22. Their victory is also attributed to the power of their reason (e.g.,

8:15). The second youngest appeals to the invincibility of "religious knowledge" (Gk., *epistēmē*) in 11:21. The narrative, however, also emphasizes their "training" (*paideia*) and "discipline" (*askēsis*), e.g., 10:10; 13:22–24.

8:1–14, Narrative Setting and Exhortation to Apostasy. Antiochus' "violent rage" (8:2) is in marked contrast to the emotional self-control of the martyrs. There are also sexual overtones to the king's admiration for the boys (8:4–5). He offers to make them friends of the king, which means employment in his government (8:5, 7). The weakness of the tyrant's philosophy and his defeat by mere boys is a major theme of 8:1–14:10. The boys conquer him by testing his arguments with reason and standing firm in their own philosophy (8:15).

8:15–9:9, False Arguments and the Brothers' Defiant Reply. False arguments that the brothers might have used but did not are given in 8:16–26. This section functions as a model of how not to think, and the orator may be polemicizing against less rigorous members of the Jewish community. Instead of excuses, the boys collectively sing out a defiant response, like a Greek dramatic chorus (9:1–9). The boys are following a long line of Jewish martyrs that includes "old men of the Hebrews" (9:6) who endured torture. By the beginning of the common era there were legendary traditions attributing martyrdom to many figures in the Hebrew Bible (cf. Heb. 11:35–37). Stoic themes reappear in 4 Macc. 9:7–8: physical suffering cannot affect the inner rational nature of the wise man; suffering is managed by the virtue of endurance. The boys can endure because they know that they will be with God and that the tyrant will be punished eternally (9:8–9).

9:10–12:19, Account of the Torture of the Seven Brothers. In a pattern that is followed with minor variation for each of the youths, the eldest son's torture, defiant words, and death is described in 9:10–25. The narration illustrates the orator's complete freedom with the account in 2 Maccabees. In the latter, the boy's tongue is cut out, he is scalped, his hands and feet cut off, and he is burned in a pan. Here he is flogged, broken on the wheel, and burned in a fire. Verse 22, "as if transformed into incorruption by the fire he endured," shares language with the Letters of Paul (Phil. 3:21; 1 Cor. 15:51–53; 2 Cor. 3:18) and certain Hellenistic philosophers. Here the reference is probably to the divine and incorruptible nature of reason and virtue rather than end-time events as in Paul. As Eleazar encouraged the boys, so the eldest son exhorts his brothers to imitate him (9:23). The third and fourth brothers will explicitly appeal to brotherhood in accepting death (10:3, 15). The narrative of the second eldest follows briefly on the first (9:26–30). The boy's insolent reply in vv. 30–32 mixes two themes: virtue is the greatest reward while vice entails the worst punishment; the judgment of divine wrath is inescapable. The latter is an important theme in both Jewish and Greek literature.

The martyrdoms of the other brothers occupy 10:1–12:19. For ancient readers, each is yet more amazing, as the boys are successively younger. The assumption is that, the younger the child, the less his reason. In the account of the third brother, only some manuscripts have 10:4, which is probably an interpolation. The third brother's "boldness" outrages the tyrant. None of the martyrs are merely loyal to their cause; they are outspoken and insolent. "Boldness" was associated especially with the speech of Cynic philosophers but was also an attribute of the Stoic wise man. The characterization of Antiochus becomes progressively more malevolent. In 10:17 he is "bloodthirsty, murderous, and completely abominable." This characterization does not square with what is known about Antiochus. The exaggerations are created to achieve a high level of pathos. The fifth brother volunteers himself for torture so that the king will receive even more punishment (11:1–3). 4 Macc. 11:7–8 are not found in some important manuscripts and may be an addition to the text.

The narrative emphasizes the youth of the sixth and seventh brothers (11:13–14; 12:1–2). The sixth proclaims that he is nevertheless equal to his older brothers in intellect (11:14). The last is so young that even the wicked king feels strong compassion for him (12:2). There are few indications, however, of their "actual" ages. In 16:9 the orator mentions that some were married and some not. The accounts of the last two emphasize with great irony the utter helplessness and defeat of the tyrant by these young boys (e.g., 11:20–27). The speech of the youngest stresses the eternal torture that the king will receive as punishment both for rejecting God's blessings and for persecuting the truly faithful (12:11–19).

The story of the seventh son breaks the tiresome pattern and concludes with a twist. Out of compassion the king sends for the mother, hoping that she will persuade her son to eat (12:6–7). The actual words of the mother are postponed (see 16:12–24, although here she is inconsistently made to encourage all of the sons), and she speaks in Hebrew so that the tyrant will not hear her exhortation to martyrdom. Feigning acceptance of the king's offer, the boy is set free and commits suicide after a defiant speech. Stoics argued that suicide was justified in cases where there was no escape from the tyranny of a despot without compromising virtue.

13:1–7, The Brothers' Example as Certain Evidence. One implication is that any Jew who is trained by the law and believes its doctrines can be fully rational and prevail over all of the nonrational impulses and dispositions of soul and body. A second implication is that the real struggle between good and evil takes place within the individual's soul. Although Antiochus is the external enemy, the real opposition to be conquered is that produced by the nonrational impulses (e.g., 13:2). This attitude is characteristically Stoic. The author believes this to be a basic teaching of the sacred Scriptures (e.g., use of David, Moses, and others as examples; "reason commended by God" in 13:3).

13:8–14:10, An Encomium and Further Argument. In 13:8–18 the author begins to praise the brothers' reason. He employs the common rhetorical device of imaginary dialogue to illustrate the thesis further. The brothers speak in turn to one another, using the typical style of moral exhortation, e.g., encouragements to virtuous behavior with reasons for such action and examples. Chap. 13:9 refers to the Daniel legend (Dan. 3) and 13:12 to Isaac who was often considered the prototype of the self-giving Israelite. In 13:19–14:1 the author provides an encomium to the brothers and brotherhood. The orator treats brotherhood as both an asset and a liability. It was a liability for the brothers because their mutual sympathy had to be overcome in order to encourage one another to accept the martyrdom (13:27). It was an asset because it made their mastery of the emotions even more remarkable, and their common brotherhood became the basis for mutual encouragement to a common cause. The Stoics showed more interest in children and "natural" familial bonds than did the other Hellenistic schools. They extensively discussed the interrelationship of natural instincts toward familial affection and "sympathy" (lit., "shared passions") and stages in the development of reason. They also discussed the rational limitations of such bonds and their relationship to socialization and moral habituation. All of these topics appear in 13:19–14:1, e.g., the physical basis for natural instincts (vv. 19–21); socialization and moral training (vv. 22, 24, 27); familial sympathy (v. 23); the rational mastery of the emotion of brotherly love (14:1). Chap. 13:27 mentions natural instincts, socialization, and moral habituation.

The orator ends his discourse on the brothers by elevating his rhetoric to a higher level of elegance and pathos in 14:2–10. He begins the section with a direct address to reason, a rhetorical device known as an apostrophe. Verse 2 echoes the Stoic paradoxes that only the wise man (i.e., fully rational person) is king and only the wise man is free. The apostrophe immediately shifts into a eulogy of the seven brothers and their brotherly harmony (vv. 3–8). "Running the course to immortality" is yet another of the numerous athletic metaphors (cf. 1 Cor. 9:24–27). The number seven was considered to have special, almost mystical, significance (4 Macc. 14:7–8). The orator concludes by addressing the audience and contrasting their mood to that of the brothers (vv. 9–10).

14:11–17:6
The Martyrdom of the Mother

2 Macc. 7:41 mentions only the mother's death. Our orator treats her torture as the climax of the story. But it is precisely because she is a striking exception to her gender that she receives the honored place. Her treatment illustrates much about the ancient construction of gender, albeit a construction modified by philosophical beliefs. If the orator presents it as amazing that boys could attain such reason and thus overcome their natural emotional bonds, it is even more amazing that a woman could do the same. Women were commonly thought to have only part of the rational capacity of men and to have much stronger passions. Cynicism and Stoicism taught that men and women had equal capacity for reason. In principle Stoics stood for sexual equality, although in practice they were inconsistent.

14:11–20, Maternal Affection. The first two verses set forth the theme: "The mind of even a woman" prevailed over the passions. Eleazar's disability was his old age, not his gender. Even though the author mentions the mother's advanced years as a disability, his emphasis is on her gender (e.g., 16:1–2). Accordingly, the orator immediately digresses into a discussion of maternal love in 14:13–20. Maternal affection is described as a very bodily and instinctual as opposed to rational disposition (14:13–19). Even birds and bees share it. Because of the great natural power of these emotions her mastery of them is the ultimate proof of the thesis (14:20; cf. 16:1–2).

15:1–32, An Encomium. The author's praise of the mother is based on a comparison between what she might have done according to her "natural" constitution and what she actually did on the basis of religious reason. At bottom, when all of the psychological mythology is stripped away, the opposition is between loyalty to her nation-culture-religion and love for her sons (15:1–2): "she loved religion more." Mothers are supposed to have stronger parental affections than fathers (vv. 4–5), and this mother loved her children more than any other woman (v. 6). Verse 5 means that because women are "weaker souls" and give birth to many children they have a more passionate nature. There was, however, more than an instinctual component to this mother's love. She also loved her sons because of their virtue (vv. 9–10).

Verses 11–28 elaborate the theme of the mother's rational mastery of maternal affection and the nature of her suffering. While Eleazar and the boys primarily endured physical suffering, the mother's suffering is a hideous affective and psychological suffering since she has to watch and commend the cruelest torture and death of her sons. The point is made in the most gruesome way (vv. 12–15, 18–21). She did not even cry. In many ways her description approaches the stereotypical characterization of Stoic *apatheia* (Gk.), lack of emotion. But she is an exception to her gender: "Religious reason gave her a man's courage" (15:23). At the same time her disability makes her endurance more noble than that of men (15:30). In vv. 25–27 the orator employs the image of casting a ballot in the council, a choice for or against argued in her heart. The orator finishes with a eulogistic flourish as he rhetorically addresses her directly as "mother of the nation" and victorious athlete (15:29). She possessed to a greater degree than men (15:30) the two most important virtues of a martyr, "constancy" and "endurance," both subcategories of courage.

16:1–11, False Arguments Considered. Verses 1–4 return to explicit argumentation of the thesis. The author regards the mother's case as the most decisive, since her maternal passions are regarded as the strongest possible. Her passions were more intense than the perils that Daniel (Dan. 6:16–18) and Mishael (i.e., Meshach, Dan. 3:19–23) faced. To heighten the emotional impact of his point, the orator employs the rhetorical technique of characterization to depict how the mother might have but did not reason (4 Macc. 16:5–11). It is an amplification through contrast (cf. 8:16–26).

16:12–17:1, The Mother's Speech to Her Sons; Her Suicide. From the contrast, 16:12–15 returns to praise of the mother. She is very much the figure of the Stoic wise man. For a dramatic conclusion the orator now introduces the delayed speech of the mother to her sons from 12:7. In 2 Maccabees the story of Eleazar is not connected with the mother and her sons as it is in 4 Maccabees 16:15. Verses 16–23 comprise her exhortation to martyrdom. The mother's speech appeals to the sense of honor and shame so important in that culture (e.g., v. 17). In 9:5–6 the sons already proclaimed it their greater duty to die, being young men. Shame and honor form a system of comparative behavior in hierarchical societies. In that culture the mother's comparison with the old man's behavior would have been a compelling argument. She again appeals to the orator's favorite examples of martyrdom, Abraham, Isaac, and the young men from Daniel. As Moses Hadas suggests, v. 18 seems to be an argument against the view expressed in 8:23 that the pleasures of life are reason to avoid martyrdom. But 16:25 does not imply the resurrection. Indeed the oration's conception of a future life is very unclear, although frequently suggested. It may be a vague immortality of the soul. In places where 2 Maccabees mentions and emphasizes the resurrection, 4 Maccabees is silent. The mother's suicide in 17:1 exhibits her modesty. The ancients considered modesty to be especially important for women. Her suicide is not mentioned in 2 Maccabees.

17:2–6, Concluding Praise of the Mother.

The section on the mother concludes with a final panegyric in 17:2–6. It stresses the unity of mother and sons in martyrdom. The reference to the stars in v. 5 may reflect the author's conception of immortality. The ancients widely believed that the stars were living beings and sometimes that the purified soul substance of the virtuous returned to them at death.

17:7–18:24
A Final Encomium

The final encomium or panegyric to the martyrs in 17:7–18:24 emphasizes the effects and benefits of their deaths. The section contains many similarities to the commemorative funeral oration that honored dead heroes of the city-state and focused civic ideology. This kind of speech was particularly important in Athens. Similarities include references to an epitaph (17:7–10); the image of the contest (17:11–16); discussion of the virtues, honor, and benefits of the heroes' sacrifice (17:17–24; 18:3–5); exhortation for the living (18:1–2); a lament (18:20–21); and a consolation (18:22–24). These elements are not put together in quite the same way as in a funeral oration, and there are important differences; but the similarities are significant. It is clear that this oration, especially if read at a commemorative event, would have performed many of the same functions as the Athenian commemorative funeral oration.

The reference to the tomb and inscription in 17:8–10 may be the rhetorical device of concrete description, as is the reference to the painting in 17:7. A number of commentators have believed that the passage indicates delivery of the oration at the tomb sites of the martyrs. The use of imaginary epitaphs in Greek literature makes a decision impossible. In Athenian funeral orations the Persian king was depicted as the cruel tyrant out to destroy the Greek way of life. The dead heroes were remembered as saviors of their people and city. The epitaph is reminiscent of these themes.

4 Macc. 17:11–16 constitute the most extend-ed and the climactic use of the athletic metaphor. The image has a different use here. Elsewhere the emphasis was on the contest between reason and the emotions and victory of reason. Here the struggle is external and public. The tyrant is the athletic opponent and the whole world and the human race the spectators. This suggests the national and international effects of the martyrs' faithful endurance that the orator will soon spell out.

The effects of the heroes' endurance and death are recounted. Perhaps surprisingly, the first effect is on the tyrant. His amazement is mentioned in 17:17 and detailed in 17:23–24. Antiochus commends the martyrs' example to his own soldiers, and they are so emboldened that they win great victories. In view of the just retribution that will be the king's ultimate fate, this benefit is an anomaly. It is well, however, to remember that our author lived in a Greek world and that he believes that integrity as a Jew and openness to Greek culture are both possible. Verse 19 is a quotation of the LXX (Greek) translation of Deut. 33:3.

Not only do the martyrs have the honor of immortality in the presence of God, but they actually saved the nation from foreign takeover (4 Macc. 17:20). On the one hand, their example of virtue enabled others to resist and demonstrated to Antiochus that he could not hellenize the nation. On the other hand, God regarded their faithful deaths as "a ransom for the sin of the nation," an "expiation" that was "through their blood." Because of their virtue God overlooked the apostasy of the nation and returned his favor. The combination of language and concepts here are most closely paralleled in early Christian texts about the effects of Jesus' death, especially Rom. 3:21–26.

Exhortation to his audience has been implicit throughout, but in 18:1–2 there is an explicit appeal to obey the law and understand the power of religious reason over the emotions. Verses 3–5 again take up the benefits effected by the martyrdoms. Verse 4 makes explicit the exemplary power of the martyrs' faithfulness to the law on the whole nation. The author perhaps suggests that Antiochus' involvement in the Parthian (i.e., Persian) War that drew him away from Judea and his ultimate failure were acts of divine punishment. Verse 5 is quite awkward, and its connection is unclear in the Greek.

Since the mother's case is treated as the climax of the story, the discourse returns to her in 18:6–18. The passage has seemed to many to be a rhetorical blunder that does not fit in the oration's conclusion. Some think it an interpolation. It does, however, draw together a picture of the piety and religious pedagogy of the family that produced seven of the eight martyrs. It particularly serves as a reflection on the power of religious education in the home. The passage is also unique in 4 Maccabees because of its many quotations from and references to Scripture. Although the style is unique, it is exactly what one would expect in a hortatory speech with the topic of childhood education.

The last four verses consist of a concluding lament (vv. 20–21) and consolation (vv. 22–24). The lament was a standard part of funeral speeches. An author influenced by later Stoicism would naturally keep grieving to a minimum. In fact, in 16:5–12 a lament was used to illustrate how the mother would have reacted if she had not been steadfast. The lament in 8:20–21 is brief and restrained. Typically, lament leads to words of consolation that point to reasons why grief should be limited. Verses 22–24 serve this purpose.

Bibliography

Anderson, H. "4 Maccabees." In *The Old Testament Pseudepigrapha*. 2 vols. Edited by J. H. Charlesworth. Garden City, NY: Doubleday, 1983, 1985. Vol. 1, pp. 531–64.

Bickerman, E. "The Date of Fourth Maccabees." *Studies in Jewish and Christian History*. Vol. 1. Leiden: Brill, 1976. Pp. 275–81.

Hadas, M. *The Third and Fourth Books of Maccabees*. New York: Harper, 1953.

Renehan, R. "The Greek Philosophic Background of Fourth Maccabees." *Rheinisches Museum für Philologie* 115 (1972): 221–38.

Townsend, R. B. "The Fourth Book of Maccabees." In *The Apocrypha and Pseudepigrapha of the Old Testament in English*. 2 vols. Edited by R. H. Charles. Oxford: Clarendon, 1913. Vol. 2, pp. 653–85.

PSALM 151

DANIEL J. HARRINGTON

INTRODUCTION

Before the discovery of the Dead Sea *Psalms Scroll* from Qumran (11QPs^a), Psalm 151 was known in its Greek version and the texts dependent on it (Syriac, Latin, Ethiopic). The Greek Psalm recounts God's choice of David (vv. 1–5) and David's victory over Goliath (vv. 6–7). David speaks in the first person, narrating events in and using phrases from 1 Samuel 16–17. Though it is easy to grasp the basic content, the Greek text sometimes gives the impression of incoherence and anticlimax. The discovery of a Hebrew version in column 28 of 11QPs^a has clarified the Greek text considerably. It is now obvious that the Greek Psalm 151 was a shortened version of two originally distinct Hebrew poems. The first of these (corresponding to vv. 1–5 of the Greek text) is fully preserved. Of the second (corresponding to vv. 6–7 of the Greek) only the first two lines remain. Both the Greek and Hebrew versions are translated in the expanded edition of the Apocrypha in the Oxford Annotated Bible (RSV). It is not possible to ascertain whether the abbreviation and the translation were done by the same person, though they may have been.

The alleged speaker of Psalm 151 is David. His use of words and phrases from 1 Samuel 16–17 indicates that the text is a poetic midrash or interpretation placed on David's lips. Since 11QPs^a can be dated through an analysis of the script to the first half of the first century A.D., the Hebrew Psalm must have been written before that time and may have been much earlier. There is nothing distinctively Essene in the text. It may have been composed before the Qumran community was founded.

The first part of the text (vv. 1–5) tells how God chose the young shepherd David to rule over his people. The emphasis on David as a musician, especially in the Hebrew version, is significant. The second part (vv. 6–7) summarizes David's victory over Goliath as the removal of Israel's shame (Gk.). In the poorly preserved Hebrew fragment the victory is associated with the power David received from his anointing. The Psalm's use of 1 Samuel 16–17 illustrates the Jewish interest in retelling the biblical story and the method of composing new poetry out of older biblical phrases.

J. A. Sanders defends 11QPs^a as reflecting an early form of the Hebrew Psalter made before the content and arrangement of the traditional canon of Psalms were fixed. Other scholars consider it a late, nonauthoritative hymnbook of both canonical and apocryphal psalms, made after the canonical Psalter had been fixed.

The Septuagint version (LXX) was known as Psalm 151 in the Syro-Hexaplar, a Syriac translation of Origen's third century A.D. critical edition of the LXX. It comes first in the group of five Syriac noncanonical psalms. Though not considered canonical in Protestant and Catholic churches (as the Greek superscription states), it appears after Psalm 150 in modern editions of the LXX.

COMMENTARY

The various versions of Psalm 151 contain different superscriptions: "A hallelujah for David the son of Jesse" (Heb.); "A thanksgiving of David" (Syriac); "This psalm was truly written by David, even though it is outside the number, when he fought alone against Goliath" (Gk.). The "number" in the Greek text refers to the canon of 150 psalms in the Hebrew Bible. The Goliath episode is described only at the end of the Greek psalm; the Hebrew Goliath psalm was separate and had its own superscription.

1–5, God's Choice of David. Psalm 151:1–5 retells the story of 1 Samuel 16 with David as the speaker. It shows how the one who was ruler over Jesse's flock became ruler over God's covenant people. The description of David in v. 1 as the youngest of Jesse's sons and a shepherd derives from 1 Sam. 16:11. The Greek version destroys the symmetry of the Hebrew text. For David's musical skill (v. 2), see 1 Sam. 16:14–23. The Greek corresponds with the beginning of the Hebrew verse except that it contains an additional verb ("fashioned") in the second member. The remainder of the Hebrew ("And I rendered glory to the Lord, I spoke in my soul. The mountains do not witness to him and the hills do not tell. The trees have cherished my words and the flock my deeds!") is absent from the Greek. The difficulty of translating and interpreting these lines has given rise to the suggestion that the picture of David here has been influenced by that of the legendary Greek musician Orpheus,

935

but the hypothesis of Orphic influence is unlikely. The Greek text of v. 3 could suggest that David's musical activity was futile since the Lord proclaims to himself. The Hebrew version shows that the text continues the reflection on praising and glorifying the all-knowing God. The omniscient God knew David as the one whom he would choose. Verses 4–5 are a poetic retelling of 1 Sam. 16:4–13. The order of events in the Greek version (anointing of David, description of his brothers) is anticlimactic. The Hebrew version maintains the proper suspense by describing first David's brothers and then God's choice of David.

6–7, David's Victory over Goliath. The first part of the Hebrew text ("The beginning of David's might after the prophet of God anointed him") is a superscription. Then David begins to narrate his battle with Goliath (see 1 Sam. 17). The Greek text is an epitome of a longer Hebrew poem. The idea of Goliath cursing by his gods appears in 1 Sam. 17:43. David's beheading of Goliath is described in 1 Sam. 17:51.

Bibliography

Charlesworth, J. H. and J. A. Sanders. "Psalm 151." In *The Old Testament Pseudepigrapha.* 2 vols. Edited by J. H. Charlesworth. Garden City, NY: Doubleday, 1983, 1985. Vol. 2, pp. 612–15.

Sanders, J. A. *The Dead Sea Psalms Scroll.* Ithaca, NY: Cornell University Press, 1967.

_____. *The Psalms Scroll of Qumran Cave 11 (11QPs^a).* Oxford: Clarendon, 1965.

PART FIVE

THE GOSPELS AND ACTS

INTRODUCTION TO THE
GOSPELS AND ACTS

NORMAN R. PETERSEN

Although the Gospels and Acts have been preserved for about two thousand years as parts of the Christian Bible, none of them was composed for the purpose of inclusion in such an anthology of texts. Each was written for quite other purposes, and each is related to other texts that were not included in the Bible. This article is devoted to a number of general issues important to readers who wish to consider the Gospels and Acts in terms of the literary and historical contexts in and for which they were written.

THE NEW TESTAMENT, ITS BOOKS, AND THEIR TITLES

Both the book known as the NT and most of the titles and authorial attributions given to its books emerged in the last half of the second century A.D. The NT is basically a selection from a much larger body of texts, many of which were written anonymously or pseudonymously by Christians of various sorts over a period of about seventy-five years, from around A.D. 50 to 125. None of the texts in the NT was written for the purpose of inclusion in the NT, the very idea of which had yet to be conceived when they were written, but were composed for specific communities and their immediate needs, much as the NT itself was created for the needs of a group of communities in the northwestern sector of the Mediterranean basin. This coalition of churches is the ancestor of the Eastern and Western (Roman) catholic or universal churches and those that came later, and its Bible was formed as a part of its own differentiation of itself from others whom it called heretics. Therefore, in order to understand the NT books in their own frames of reference, we have to consider each book as a communication between an author and an audience.

By the same historical token, it is also necessary to recognize that the titles and authorial attributions of the Gospels and Acts are neither original nor peculiar to them. The "Gospel According to" and "Acts of" titles originated at the end of the second century A.D. and were applied to other, noncanonical texts as well as the ones we have today in the NT. And from the end of the century and through the third century, numerous other "Gospels" and "Acts" were written, some similar to those in the NT and others quite different.

The titles of the canonical Gospels and Acts are related to the division of the NT into two sections, one devoted to "Gospels," the other to apostolic writings, the first of which is the book of the Acts of the Apostles. This distinction has two major consequences for subsequent readers. On the one hand, by identifying the first four books as "Gospels," the creators of the NT imputed to the four a commonality that obscures their different form and content. "Gospel" does not refer to a literary genre but to the later churches' classification of their sacred writings into "Gospels" and apostolic writings, the former having to do with Jesus and the latter with apostles.

But though each of the Gospels has to do with Jesus, it is also self-evident from them that each represents him and his significance for believers in a very different way from the others. Thus two treat him as a man born of woman (Matt.; Luke), while one represents him as a man from heaven (John). One sees him as the end-time judge who came before the end to deliver the commandments on the basis of which he will judge (Matt.), another as the God-man, belief in whose "signs" will bring, possibly spontaneously, eternal life (John). And one sees Jesus' return from heaven as in the immediate future (Mark), while others see it coming only after a delay (Matt.) or after a period of history has been completed—"the time of the Gentiles" (Luke).

In addition, by looking up the word "gospel" in a concordance one can see that only Mark may have conceived of his narrative as a Gospel (Mark 1:1), although even his use of the word is problematical because it is not clear that he means by it what Paul meant some decades previously (cf. Rom. 1:1–6; 1 Cor. 15:1–7). Matthew does not use the word in the same way as Mark, while Luke never uses the noun at all, only the verb "to proclaim [good] news." And John does not use either the noun or the verb. Historically, these four different books, rather than only one, were included in the NT to represent the diversity permissible in the catholic coalition of churches, but no sooner had this been done than their unity became focal and their differences were de-emphasized.

The second consequence of placing the four books under the heading of "Gospel" is that it obscured the fact that Luke's "Gospel" is but the first volume in a two-volume, consecutive narrative, the second half of which is in the NT called the Acts of the Apostles (cf. Luke 1:1–4; Acts 1:1–5). Whatever the reasons may have been for the ordering of the first four books, it is apparent that the position of John between Luke and Acts interrupts the literary continuity of two volumes that were composed to be read sequentially. Luke did not write a "Gospel" and "Acts"—he wrote a consecutive narrative in two parts. Indeed, when this insight is added to the foreignness of the category "Gospel" to the books subsumed under it, we can see that the creators of the NT viewed its texts in quite a different way from their authors and original readers. At least for Luke's narrative, if we only read the first volume because it is called a "Gospel," we will only be getting half of the story. We will not be able to see either where the narrative begun in the first volume ends or how its ending in the second volume informs the system of characterization, plot, and thematics that governs the whole work. But what is true of Luke-Acts is also true of

939

Matthew, Mark, and John. Each must be read in terms of its own literary character.

THE LITERARY CONTEXTS OF THE "GOSPELS" AND "ACTS"

While the NT provides its books with a context relevant to the interests of its compilers, there is a vast body of other writings that provides a context more relevant to the individual books as they were originally composed and read. It is the literary and cultural context of the times, places, and communities in and for which the books were written that informs them, not the context in and for which the later anthology was created. Just which texts are pertinent to our books depends on relations of form and content. These relations will often be referred to in the commentaries on the individual books, but for purposes of illustration a few examples are in order. The examples selected highlight both the individuality of our books and their differences from one another.

It is widely but not universally held that Matthew used Mark as a source for his narrative, indeed, as the narrative base into which he inserted a large amount of sayings material from yet other sources (see below "The Synoptic Problem"). But regardless of the question of Matthew's sources, it is important for our reading of his narrative that we see that one of the principal differences between it and Mark tends in the direction of rules for community living until Jesus' return, while Mark seems most concerned with what his readers understand about when and how the return will take place (Mark 13). Matthew represents the commandments Jesus issued for the life of believers until he returns to judge them and others. In this light, it is useful to look at other texts that are concerned with the same kinds of issues. Important are such texts as the various community rule documents found among the non-Christian Dead Sea Scrolls, Paul's extensive instructions in 1 Corinthians, the *Didache* or *Teaching of the Apostles*, a text some parts of which may be roughly contemporaneous with Matthew and now found in an anthology called *The Apostolic Fathers*, and the later apostolic constitutions and monastic rules. Like any other text, Matthew's stands on its own, but reading it in the context of these documents can help us understand how his views of Jesus and of community life differ from the views of other texts and communities. Comparison reveals not merely dependencies of one sort or another, but it also discloses the individuality of texts that are similar.

So also with John and Luke-Acts. In the case of John, it is of comparable use to look at other ancient texts treating divine beings who appear to humans in human form and disclose to them their true identity. It is useful because such disclosures are relatively rare; it is much more common to have the incognito divine beings conceal their identity for a while, as in Mark, where it is unclear whether or not he thinks of Jesus as a divine being as John and Paul do (cf. Phil. 2:6–11).

As for Luke-Acts, its author claims to be writing a historical or at least an accurate account of certain events (Luke 1:1–4; Acts 1:1–5), and therefore knowledge of other ancient history books can help us to discern what is distinctive about Luke-Acts, even how to interpret speeches he attributes to his characters. In ancient history writing it was common for authors to create the speeches felt to be appropriate to the situation, and Luke also does this. Indeed, many historical writings of his time make the same claim he does about writing an accurate account. Luke's claim must therefore be read in terms of ancient conventions, not of modern expectations. Such comparative, literary-historical observations as these indicate the value of finding the contexts appropriate to the original composition of our texts.

RELATIONS BETWEEN THE "GOSPELS"

The literary contexts in which we read the "Gospels" and "Acts" are significant for our understanding of them, but each of them also raises a number of other important issues equally and perhaps more directly pertinent. To address these issues, it is necessary to be aware of certain textual problems and the ways in which scholars have dealt with them.

We possess no original text of any NT document, only a large number of copies and quotations from writers from the second century and after. Because the copies do not always agree with one another, the discipline of text criticism evolved to try to adjudicate the different readings. Annotated editions of the Bible usually employ footnotes to show readers where the more significant differences occur, but every translation of the Bible entails decisions about numerous text-critical problems, not to mention the linguistic problems of finding adequate translations for original language words and expressions. Serious study should use at least two translations to see both how translators render the original language and how they resolve text-critical problems. Commentaries too address these issues.

While the scholarly reading of our texts produced the awareness of text-critical problems, it also discovered problems about the literary integrity of each of the texts with which we are concerned. Once an adequate text had been established, critics sought through literary-critical means to identify the linguistic, stylistic, compositional, and conceptual integrity of the texts. The results of this early literary criticism are complicated, but a few major points stand out as worthy of special attention. First, each of the five texts employs other texts as sources for its composition, and therefore all are redactions, or editions, of other texts. In the case especially of John, it also appears that someone has added or interpolated other material into John after its original sources had been edited to form an extended narrative. Second, Matthew, Mark, and Luke are so closely related as to require us to hypothesize that two of them used one of the others and probably other sources as well. The question of who used whom is the problem represented in the notion of the "Synoptic Problem." And, third, John is not related to the other three "Gospels" in the same way as the others are to each other, yet its author may have had knowledge of one or more of the others in addition to his own peculiar sources. Each of these points requires fuller

941

consideration because each has profound consequences for our reading of the texts.

Sources, Redaction, and Interpolation

Although literary critics sought to discern the integrative features of our texts, they quickly found themselves occupied with disintegrative features. Their explanation of these was that they reflected the authors' use of other texts as sources for their own. In addition to the distinctive relations between Matthew, Mark, and Luke, and between aspects of John and both Mark and Luke, Luke already self-consciously refers to his knowledge of other narratives (Luke 1:1–4). Because he does so at the beginning of Luke-Acts, his comment suggests that he knew and used other texts in the composition of both volumes. Beside his dependence on Mark or Matthew, critics have suspected sources behind at least three segments of his second volume: the Jerusalem episodes (Acts 2–5); the Antioch-oriented episodes (Acts 6:1–8:4; 11:19–30; and 12:25–15:35); and the travel narrative from 16:10 on, in which the narrator atypically speaks in the first person plural (16:10–17; 20:5–15; 21:1–18; and 27:1–28:16). Also, even though the author does not seem to have known Paul's Letters, his knowledge of such events as Paul's escape from Damascus by being lowered from a wall in a basket (Acts 9:23–25; 2 Cor. 11:32–33) suggests that he also had access to stories about Paul.

Scholars still dispute specific identifications of sources in all of our texts, but there is little disagreement about the fact that our authors used sources. This fact is perhaps more significant than the difficulty of actually pinning down a source at any given point. It is significant because it means that we cannot simply assume that our authors were either freely creative writers or eyewitness reporters. In other words, many of the words we read in our texts are words that came from other writers, not directly from our authors or from the characters our authors are writing about. But this point raises in turn the further problem of how we are to know just what the authors of our texts were trying to say in their use of other texts. Two disciplines have emerged to deal with this problem: redaction criticism and a new form of literary criticism.

Redaction or composition criticism is the other side of the coin of the source criticism that emerged out of the old literary criticism. Redaction critics seek to find the author's point from the ways he has used his sources. The method has a certain validity, but it is usually limited both by its focus on the differences between redaction and sources and by its narrow concentration on the theological motives of the author/redactor. The problem is twofold: there is disagreement about where the sources are, making the distinction between redaction and sources problematical; and it is entirely gratuitous to think that motivation is solely theological.

It was in part the result of these deficiencies that a new literary criticism was developed. Informed by modern literary criticism and narrative studies, the new criticism goes beyond redaction criticism by

1 Jesus' birth, as recounted in Luke 2:1–7; painting on a Spanish altar, twelfth century. The first two chapters of Matthew and Luke provide the only biblical accounts of Jesus' birth and early life. **2** This silk twill from the Vatican, Rome, sixth to seventh centuries, shows the angel Gabriel appearing to Mary to announce the coming birth of Jesus (see Luke 1:26–38; cf. Matt. 1:18–25 where an angel appears to Joseph). **3** The woman of Samaria at Jacob's well (see John 4:1–42); detail of an icon from a Greek collection, late sixteenth century.

1 Scenes from the parable of the
Good Samaritan (Luke 10:25–37)
are shown above the text and two
pairs of prophets on this illuminated manuscript page from the
Rossano Gospels, sixth century.
The artist has chosen in this case
to depict Jesus himself as the
Good Samaritan. Jesus is first
seen ministering to the wounded
man (*top center*) and then paying an innkeeper to care for him
(*top right*). The city of Jericho
(*top left*) balances the page. The
prophets are (*from left to right*)
David and Micah and David and
Sirach.   2 Vines and a vinedresser; detail of a Byzantine mosaic
floor from a synagogue at Beth-
shean, fifth century. Both the OT
and NT use the images of vines
and vinedressers. In John 15:1–
17, Jesus presents himself as vine
and his Father as vinedresser.
3 Jesus healing a blind man (see
Mark 10:46–52); illustration from
The Four Gospels, a twelfth-
century manuscript from a monastery on Mount Athos, Greece.

1 Jesus' last meal with his disciples (see Matt. 26:17–29; Mark 14:12–25; Luke 22:7–23) as portrayed on the Thessalonika Epitaph, fourteenth century. This meal is regarded by Christians as the basis for the sacrament of the Lord's Supper (see 1 Cor. 11:23–25). 2 The face of Jesus engraved on a Byzantine cross from Ephe-sus, tenth century. 3 Inscription from Caesarea that commemorates the erection of a building by Pontius Pilate, Roman prefect of Judea (A.D. 26–36), to honor Tiberius, Roman emperor (A.D. 14–37). 4 Jesus' crucifixion (see Matt. 27; Mark 15; Luke 23; John 19) depicted on a manuscript page from the *Gerona Beatus of* 975. Jesus hangs on the central cross, between the two criminals who were crucified with him. One soldier offers Jesus a bitter drink, while a second pierces his side. Two others prepare to break the legs of the two criminals.

1 A medieval illumination of the first Pentecost when the disciples of Jesus were "filled with the Holy Spirit" (Acts 2:4); from the Latin *Codex Monacensis*. According to the biblical narrative, the Spirit arrived with a loud wind from heaven, and tongues of fire rested on those gathered.   2 Stephen being led outside the walls of Jerusalem before being stoned (see Acts 6–7); enamel, Limoges, twelfth century.   3 Paul's encounter with Jesus on the road to Damascus (Acts 9:1–9) as portrayed on an enamel plaque from France, eleventh century.   4 Peter, as depicted in the sepulcher of the child Asellus, Rome, ca. 313.

1 A depiction of the new Jerusalem revealed to John by an angel (see Rev. 21:9–22:9); an illuminated manuscript page, shown here in part, from *The Morgan Beatus*, Spain, mid-tenth century. In the biblical account, the city is laid out as a cube with the Lord God and the Lamb as its temple. It has twelve gates (three on each of four sides), each bearing the name of one of the twelve tribes of Israel and each with an angel at it. It also has twelve foundations, each carved out of a precious stone and bearing the name of one of the twelve apostles. In this depiction, an apostle stands in each gate, beneath the disk of a particular gem. **2** John's vision of the four horsemen unleashed when the Lamb of God breaks the first four seals on a scroll (see Rev. 6:1–8); illuminated manuscript page from the *Beatus of Fernando and Sancha*, Spain, 1047. **3** An angel on an enamelled medallion from Limoges, France, second half of the thirteenth century.

1

2

3

1 The remains of Philistine
houses excavated at Ashdod. The
Philistines were a warlike people
who, with the other Sea Peoples,
migrated from the Aegean basin
to the southern coast of Palestine
in the early twelfth century B.C.
and became one of Israel's principal rivals.   **2** The Oasis Wadi
Feiran at the foot of Mount Ser-

bal, one of the highest points of
the Sinai range. This oasis is
identified by some scholars with
the biblical Rephidim, where the
Israelites stopped en route from
Egypt to the promised land and
Moses struck a rock to provide
them with water (see Exod. 17:1–
7). The exact location of Rephidim (and most other sites along

the route of the Exodus) is
uncertain.   **3** The Negeb, the
"dry, parched, south country,"
through which the Hebrews
made their first approach to the
promised land. During the period
of the monarchy, fortresses were
built in the Negeb to guard the
southern borders of Judah.

1 A shepherd's flock near Nazareth. Many prominent biblical figures were shepherds, and both OT and NT use shepherd imagery frequently. Jesus refers to himself as "the good shepherd" in John 10:1–29.　**2** A site in Jerusalem that may be the biblical pool of Bethesda (Bethzatha) where, according to John 5:2, Jesus healed a man who had been sick for thirty-eight years. The ruin was discovered by archaeologists in 1871.　**3** The shore of the Sea of Galilee between Tiberias and Capernaum. According to Matt. 4:18–22, it was along the shore of this sea that Jesus first called Peter, Andrew, James, and John to be his disciples.

1   2

3   4

1 The Nash papyrus fragment, ca. 150 B.C., containing a conflation of the text of the Ten Commandments from Exod. 20:2–17 and Deut. 5:6–21, ending with Deut. 6:4f. The Nash Papyrus was the oldest known OT manuscript prior to the discovery of the Dead Sea Scrolls.   **2** Deut. 1:20–33 written in Hebrew on a manuscript page from the British Museum Codex of the Pentateuch (ca. 950), one of the most important Masoretic manuscripts of the first five books of the Hebrew Bible.   **3** A portion of the Bodmer VII papyrus containing Jude 18–24. The collection of Bodmer papyri contain several portions of the NT, including the oldest known manuscript of Luke, 1 Peter, 2 Peter, and Jude; dated from the late second and third centuries.   **4** Manuscript page from the Gothic Codex Argenteus ("the Silver Codex") with Luke 1:6–14 written in large silver letters on purple vellum, from Ravenna, ca. 520.

going back to the old literary criticism's focus on textually integrative features. But whereas the old criticism concentrated on matters of language, linguistic style, and ideas, the new criticism is also concerned with such things as the plots of narratives, the narrator's perspective, and characterization. The new literary criticism thus builds on the old one and provides a broader base than redaction criticism for identifying the integrative features of our texts.

The problem of interpolation is yet another one readers should be aware of, because like textual variants it raises the question of which text we are to read. Interpolation entails the addition of material to an already existing text, and its presence is suspected when we come across internal contradictions or discrepancies that cannot be explained by the use of sources. When such material is placed in brackets, the text reads more coherently. Some of the best examples of interpolation are to be found in John. John 21 is a classic case of an interpolated addition because John 20:30–31 is clearly the ending of the extended narrative that precedes it; John 21 therefore continues a text that has come to an end. But interpolation is also found in other forms. In John 3:22 the narrator says that Jesus baptized people, but in 4:2 another, interpolated voice says that Jesus himself did not baptize, but only his disciples. Similarly, in John 13:36 Peter asks Jesus where he is going, but in 16:5 Jesus asks why no one asks where he is going. In John 10 too there is no little confusion engendered by the assertions that Jesus is both "the door of the sheep" (10:7b, 9) and "the good shepherd" (10:11; cf. 10:1–5). John 10:1–15 makes much more sense if 10:7b and 9 are bracketed as interpolations. Thus too in John we have to reckon with a text that has used sources (see below "John and the Synoptics") and also received interpolations. "John" is therefore two texts, one with and the other without interpolations.

The Synoptic Problem

The best way to observe the Synoptic Problem is to read Matthew, Mark, and Luke in a book in which they are printed in parallel columns. Such books are called "Gospel parallels" or "synopses," and some include John, even though it is not related to the other three in the same way that they are related to one another. Matthew, Mark, and Luke are called the "synoptic Gospels" because when read comparatively, i.e., synoptically, one can readily see detailed verbal and sequential agreements between them that can only be accounted for by hypothesizing that two of them used at least one of the others. The Synoptic Problem consists of the question, "Who used whom?" But before addressing the answers to this question, it is well to consider why the question is relevant to readers.

The close relationships between the synoptic Gospels are significant because the differences between them are often indicative of what is peculiar to each. Regardless of the answer to the question of who used whom, reading any one of them in a synopsis discloses its differences from the others. By exploring patterns of differences

943

throughout one of them, we can gain insights into its distinctive composition and message. Thus, if Matthew or Mark differs from the other in a passage they have in common, the difference in a word, a phrase, an idea, or a story is something to be explored further in each narrative. For example, if Matthew differs from Mark in his use of the word "gospel" in one place, we can turn to a concordance and find out where each of them uses the word and then check them all out in each text in our synopsis. The results are striking, as noted earlier. Similarly, it is distinctive of Mark that he characterizes Jesus' disciples as being exceedingly obtuse; they do not understand much of anything. How, viewed in a synopsis, does Matthew render the behavior of the disciples in passages he has in common with Mark? Are Matthew and Mark saying the same things about the disciples? What are they saying about them and, within the frameworks of their own narratives, why are they saying these things about them? The same kinds of questions can be asked about the characterization of Jesus.

However, this kind of comparative reading and thinking only answers the question of why synoptic relations (and editions) are important for readers, not the question of why the synoptic problem is important. The former is a literary matter, the latter a historical one, as is evident from another way of describing the problem, namely, as a question of temporal priority: who came first, who second, and who third? Priority has to do ultimately with the understanding of the history of early Christianity that results from our answer to the question of who used whom. Each text comes from a different point in time and space, and therefore the sequence in which they were written enables us to trace some of the history of the early churches. In turn, the history is important because it bears on the contexts in and for which the narratives were written. In addition, and as redaction critics have seen, if we know which text(s) a writer has used and changed, the changes and the implicit motives for them are of both literary and historical interest. Literarily, the changes and their motivation reflect one author's understanding and intent in contrast with another's. Examples of these implications of the priority of one or another of the "Gospels" can be considered after we have observed the main solutions to the Synoptic Problem. First, the proposed solutions. The following comments should be read with the help of a synopsis.

Because most introductions to the NT contain detailed discussion of the history of the Synoptic Problem, we can concentrate on the broader contours of the two main solutions, that of Matthean priority and that of Marcan priority, also known as the Two-Source or the modified Two-Source Hypothesis. Marcan priority is the most widely accepted solution, but in recent years Matthean priority has been revived by a number of scholars dissatisfied with the prevailing opinion. Importantly, however, both solutions are hypotheses, not provable solutions. For this reason, each stands or falls on its own plausibility as an answer to the question of who used whom. The accompanying diagrams represent the two solutions. The arrows on the diagrams point from the gospel or source to the one that used it.

Matthean Priority

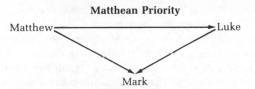

Matthean priorists argue that Matthew was the earliest Gospel, that Luke used Matthew, and that Mark used both of them, reducing their extent by abbreviating and conflating them, that is, by taking two versions of the same passage and putting them together so that portions of each are visible in Mark. For example, Matt. 13:31 has the word "parable," Luke 13:18 the word "compare," and Mark 4:30 has both words. (Note, however, that Marcan priorists can also point to conflation in the same parable, where Mark 4:32 has "shrubs," Luke 13:19 "tree," and Matt. 13:32 both words!)

Marcan Priority

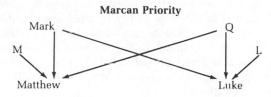

Marcan priorists, on the other hand, argue that Mark was first and that Matthew and Luke used Mark plus another source consisting largely of sayings called Q (from the first letter of *Quelle*, the German word for "source"). This is held to account for those cases where Matthew and Luke have material in common that is not in Mark or is in addition to something that Mark has in another form (the latter are called "doublets," meaning that one version comes from Mark, the other from Q). In addition, in the modified form of this hypothesis, material found only in Matthew is attributed to an M source, while material found only in Luke is attributed to an L source.

Now, Matthean priorists find Marcan priority weakened if not falsified by cases where Matthew and Luke agree with one another against Mark while allegedly following him (e.g., Matt. 13:11 and Luke 8:10 have in common "to know the secrets," while Mark 4:11 has only "the secret"). Marcan priorists respond by hypothesizing either that Matthew and Luke had different editions of Mark, or that later copyists harmonized Matthew and Luke, or that Matthew and Luke coincidentally improved Mark in the same manner. Suffice it to say, neither camp has persuaded the other. Nevertheless, the significance of the Synoptic Problem can now best be illustrated by some examples showing the literary and historical implications of the two solutions.

Regardless of which solution one prefers, it is apparent that two of the writers radically altered the earliest narrative. This is of interest for two reasons. One is that on either account the earliest narrative was not yet of such authority that it could not be significantly changed; the Jesus story had yet to become fixed and there was considerable freedom

945

available to the tellers of it. Another, more literary reason has to do with the nature of the alterations required by each solution. Thus, on Matthean priority, Luke must have destroyed everything that is characteristic of Matthew, from the turning upside down of Jesus' genealogy to the redistribution of Jesus' teachings from five major discourses to a very long journey from Galilee to Jerusalem into which many sayings of Jesus have been fitted. Similarly, Mark must have destroyed everything that is characteristic of both Matthew and Luke, especially their representation of Jesus as a teacher. Mark represents a minimal amount of Jesus' teachings and rather depicts him as more of a wonder worker (cf., e.g., Mark 1:34; 3:11–12; 5:43). From the perspective of Marcan priority, on the other hand, the last two writers appear to have been more constructive than destructive in their alterations of Mark. Matthew and Luke must have built longer narratives out of multiple sources, perhaps even offering a more accurate picture of Jesus than Mark, who lacks their strong image of Jesus as a teacher because he does not have the large number of sayings found in Q, M, and L. Matthew and Luke must have used Mark's text as their narrative base, to which each added in his own way the other sources available to him. Indeed, they have conserved their sources, whereas according to Matthean priority Luke and Mark have defaced their sources. Each solution therefore provides a very different picture of the respective authors.

The historical implications of the two solutions are much more complicated than the literary ones, because the modified Two-Source Hypothesis posits three other sources, Q, M, and L. Whereas Matthean priorists only have to identify the temporal sequence of three texts, Marcan priorists have to identify the sequence of six. Their task is therefore twice as complex, but the history they can produce will also be twice as rich. Be this as it may, some general observations can be made about the historical implications of the solutions. Perhaps the most significant issue concerns the relationship between eschatology—the expectation of an imminent end to history—and institutionalization in the early history of the churches. Did the Jesus movement begin as a loosely knit collection of people who looked for the imminent coming of the Kingdom of God, but who, as decades passed, became a structured institution with fixed beliefs and behavioral rules? Or did it begin as such an institution and from time to time produce eschatologically oriented splinter groups that reacted against institutionalization? The former picture results from the Two-Source Hypothesis, the latter follows from the hypothesis of Matthean priority. Two textual examples will suffice to show how the hypotheses produce two different historical pictures.

As noted earlier, in the so-called synoptic apocalypse (Matt. 24:1–25:46; Mark 13:1–37; Luke 21:5–38), Mark's focus is on the Kingdom's coming within the lifetime of Jesus' generation. Mark says that some people will say that the end is now, but Mark's point is that the end will not be then, but very soon afterward. Matthew, on the other hand, has in addition to Mark's material several sayings that are concerned not with the presence or nearness of the Kingdom, but with its delay (24:48; 25:5, 19). Luke too differs from Mark and Matthew and looks both backward on the destruction of Jerusalem as God's vengeance on his people and forward to a period of time before the Kingdom's coming, one he refers to as "the times of the Gentiles" (21:20–24). Thus Mark is oriented toward the Kingdom's nearness and Matthew and Luke toward its distance.

A second and not unrelated case concerns the twelve disciples. Only once do Matthew and Mark use the word "apostle" for any of the Twelve, whereas Luke not only thinks of the Twelve as twelve apostles (already in Luke 6:13), but he sees them as the apostolic leadership formed in Jerusalem at Pentecost, an event only he among early Christian writers reports (cf. Acts 1–2). Remember too that unlike Luke (and John 20) Matthew and Mark make no reference to the disciples meeting the risen Jesus in Jerusalem, let alone as forming there an apostolic institution with worldwide responsibilities. Luke-Acts is therefore highly institutional. But so, in another way, is Matthew, who presents the commandments of Jesus that are to be enforced by the church and especially by Peter (cf. Matt. 16 and 18). Mark knows nothing about either a group of twelve "apostles" or an apostolically organized worldwide institution centered in Jerusalem.

There are numerous other examples that might be added to these, but these are sufficient to show that the answer to the question of who used whom has profound consequences for our understanding both of the history of early Christianity and of the location of each of the Synoptics in that history.

John and the Synoptics

It is as evident from a reading of the four "Gospels" independently as it is from reading them in a synopsis that includes John, that John is vastly different from the Synoptics. In it, Jesus is clearly a divine being from the beginning of creation, and his human form is not his real form; in it, Jesus has a three-year career (three Passovers are mentioned, and Passover is an annual festival), not a one-year career; in it, Jesus neither exorcizes nor speaks in synoptic-like parables; in it, his deeds are signs that he has come from somewhere else and his speech, when compared to that of other actors in the story, is decidedly enigmatic; in it, Jesus appears to his disciples both in Galilee (John 21; cf. Mark 16 and Matt. 28) and in Jerusalem (John 20: cf. Luke 24 and Acts 1); and so on. John has clearly not used the Synoptics to the degree that any one of them has used any one of the others. Indeed, it appears from the peculiar designation of Jesus' wonders as "signs" that John had a source containing largely such "sign" stories, possibly including stories of Jesus' arrest, trial, death, and postresurrection appearances (cf. John 20:30–31). The question of John's relationship to the Synoptics is therefore not so much one of use as of knowledge, for John also says a number of things that are like things found in one or more of the Synoptics.

Scholars are widely divided as to the sources of John's synoptic-like knowledge, some seeing textual dependence upon Luke and/or Mark, others seeing reliance on forms of synoptic-like preliterary traditions, and yet others finding both sources possible.

Moreover, when this array of opinion is related to the distinction between sources, redaction, and interpolation in John, the points and kinds of dependency become considerably more complex. To take but four examples, we can observe that: first, John 20 agrees with Luke who, alone among the Synoptics, has Jesus appear to his disciples in Jerusalem after his resurrection, while Matthew and Mark refer to Galilee, as does John 21; second, John 13:27 agrees with Luke alone (Luke 22:3; cf. 4:13, not in John) that Satan entered Judas before he betrayed Jesus; third, in John 21:3–8, there is a story of a postresurrection wonder in which the disciples enjoy a miraculous catch of fish, while in Luke 5:1–11 a clearly related story is told in the context of Jesus' calling of his first disciples at the beginning of his career; and fourth, in John 6:1–21 are stories of Jesus' wondrous feeding of a multitude and of his walking on the lake, both of which are paralleled in the same sequence in Mark 6:30–52. Each of these cases together with others suggests that John had some knowledge of either the synoptic Gospels or traditions found in them.

The various kinds of relationships between the four Gospels thus only reinforce the conclusion drawn earlier about the apparent unity imposed upon them by their classification in the NT as "Gospels." Each text must be read as a message communicated by particular believers in particular times and places.

TRADITION HISTORY

Regardless of how one resolves the Synoptic Problem, or the problem of sources in John and Acts, it is evident from the several decades between the times when the texts were written and the times of the events recounted in them that we have to reckon with a period during which sayings and stories were orally transmitted before being written down either in our present texts or in their sources. The principal evidence for this process of oral transmission consists in multiple versions of sayings and stories that cannot well be accounted for by simply attributing them to the use of written sources. Multiple versions of many traditions are to be found both within and between the canonical Gospels, but also in noncanonical texts like the *Gospel of Thomas* and possibly the *Gospel of Peter*, where it seems likely that, regardless of their use of the canonical texts, they at points contain independent versions of traditions.

Comparative study of the multiple versions of gospel traditions has led to the conclusion that from the time of Jesus' utterance of his words and of the formation of stories about his deeds, the words and stories were transmitted orally and independently of the narrative contexts in which we now read them. Narrative contexts were first provided with the first written Gospels, whose writers drew from the available pool of individual traditions or from small collections of them, like the three seed parables in Mark 4 and the stories of Jesus' wondrous feeding and walking on the lake in John 6 and Mark 6.

One scholar described the relationship between preliterary traditions and their later narrative contexts as analogous to (traditional) pearls on a (narrative) string. This means, of course, that prior to our extended narratives there was no tradition containing an outline of Jesus' career, except for the last days of his life, for which two traditions may have provided a basis for an extended story (1 Cor. 11:23–25; 15:3–5; cf. Mark 14–16; Matt. 26–28; Luke 22–24). Interestingly enough, despite the differences between their stories of Jesus' last days, the four canonical Gospels agree most in them and differ much more widely on the chronology and topography of Jesus' preceding activities. Indeed, they differ most in the links they create between the traditions, as is immediately evident in any synopsis. But perhaps a better analogy than pearls on a string would be mosaics composed out of variously colored and shaped stones. The authors of our texts are mosaicists who fit the stones available to them into their own designs and for their own purposes.

The significance of this image for readers of our present texts is that it requires us to look at and admire the mosaics before us rather than think of the material as a window on history, through which we can see the historical Jesus doing or saying this or that. To read our texts in this historicizing way would be comparable to confusing a movie with a newscast. For example, if in reading the Sermon on the Mount in Matt. 5–7 one thinks exclusively of the historical Jesus doing and saying what is described there, rather than, in the first instance, of Matthew's depiction of this "event" as an episode within his story, one will miss *Matthew's* point. By reading Matthew's episode in a synopsis, one will quickly find out how wrong a historicizing reading is, for much of Matthew's Sermon on the Mount is also in Luke's sermon on the plain (Luke 6:20–49), much more is found elsewhere in Luke, and much of both is found independently and without such narrative contexts in the *Gospel of Thomas*. By studying the history of the traditions in the two "sermons" we can confirm the mosaic stone analogy—and go a step further to conclude that Jesus himself was not a sermonizer; the form of his speech was that of brief aphoristic and parabolic utterances. The authors created both the sermons and the image of Jesus as a sermonizer. And as for John, the discourses of Jesus are without parallel in the Synoptics and totally different from the Synoptics in content, style, and length. Study of the history of the traditions underlying our texts therefore once again directs us back to a literary appreciation of the texts.

FORM CRITICISM

Closely related to the history of traditions is the discipline of form criticism. At the same time that scholars became aware of the role of preliterary traditions, they realized that the traditions were shaped according to a limited number of formal types like aphorisms, parables, similitudes, predictions, and miracle stories. These typical forms are believed to have been the products of equally typical social situations either in the time of Jesus or that of his followers. Study of these forms or genres led, on the one hand, to formal criteria for identifying the history of individual traditions and, on the other hand, to sociological insights into the times when the traditions originated and were passed on. Form criticism is therefore a historical tool. It also has, however, certain literary dimensions.

The first form critics viewed our present texts as collections of the various types of preliterary traditions, including what they called mythic traditions like Phil. 2:6–11 and the heavenly wisdom or Sophia tradition behind John 1:1–18, both of which represent Jesus as a divine being. For form critics, the Gospels consist of the merger of traditions about the historical human being Jesus of Nazareth with a myth of a divine being, the Son of God or Word. The myths thus interpret the life of the historical Jesus as the presence in human form of a divine being. Our present texts are therefore the end products of the history of Jesus traditions. To be sure, form critics recognized that our texts were also more or less coherent narratives, but they tended to see these narrative qualities as the accidental illusion created by the juxtaposition of preliterary traditions. Our texts do not, they said, belong to the history of literature, but to the history of religion and dogma. Gospel is for them either not the designation of a literary genre or the sole genre created by early Christians, all other genres being borrowed from their cultural environment.

The literary views of form critics have not been accepted by all scholars, and some who appreciate form criticism have gone beyond it to deal with both internal literary aspects of our texts and comparative, literary-historical aspects of their similarities to other literature from antiquity, relating the texts to a variety of genres, including biography, lives of the prophets, historiography, and apocalyptic. Presently, however, there is no consensus on the generic identity of the canonical texts. Rather, the main direction of research in the Gospels and Acts is on the internal literary and narrative characteristics of the individual texts.

Bibliography

Cameron, R., ed. *The Other Gospels*. Philadelphia: Westminster, 1982.

Dibelius, M. *From Tradition to Gospel*. Translated by B. L. Woolf. New York: Scribner, 1935.

Hennecke, E., and W. Schneemelcher, eds. *New Testament Apocrypha. Vol. 1, Gospels and Related Writings*. Translated by R. McL. Wilson. Philadelphia: Westminster, 1963.

Kuemmel, W. G. *Introduction to the New Testament*. Rev. ed. Translated by H. C. Kee. Nashville, TN: Abingdon, 1975.

Mays, J. L., ed. *Interpreting the Gospels*. Philadelphia: Fortress, 1981.

Perrin, N. *What is Redaction Criticism?* Guides to Biblical Scholarship. Philadelphia: Fortress, 1969.

Petersen, N. R. *Literary Criticism for New Testament Critics*. Guides to Biblical Scholarship. Philadelphia: Fortress, 1978.

MATTHEW

REGINALD H. FULLER

INTRODUCTION

Structure

The plot or story line of the Gospel According to Matthew falls into six parts: 1:1–4:16, the person of Jesus the Messiah; 4:17–11:1, Jesus, Messiah of word and deed; 11:2–16:20, Israel's unbelief and the disciples' incipient faith; 16:21–20:34, the journey to Jerusalem; 21:1–25:46, the ministry in Jerusalem; 26:1–28:20, the Passion and resurrection.

Composition

The author of Matthew was an unknown Jewish Christian of the second generation writing around A.D. 90 in or near Antioch in Syria. The bitter criticism of the Pharisaic leaders of Jerusalem (chap. 23) and the distance from which Matthew speaks of the Jewish community ("their" synagogues, 4:23 and elsewhere) suggest that he wrote after the emergence of new rabbinic institutions at Jamnia (after A.D. 70) and that the Christian groups he was addressing were no longer part of the Jewish community. Matthew writes to provide his community with an alternative to rabbinic instruction, the Torah (→ Torah): Jesus as the founder of the true Israel (16:17–19) and the messianic expounder of the new and better righteousness (5:17–20).

Matthew's church, then, has moved away from the synagogue. As a result, it is opening itself to mission to the Gentiles (24:14; 28:19), cooperating perhaps with Jewish Christians of a different type who had long engaged in gentile mission, bringing into its fold enthusiastic prophets who neglected the ethical dimension of Christianity (7:15–20). Matthew is fighting on two fronts, against legalism on one side and antinomianism (neglect of the new righteousness) on the other. But it would be wrong to think of Matthew as primarily a polemical work. The author's purpose was pastoral, to protect his church from dangers that threatened from within.

It has often been thought that 13:52 discloses something of Matthew's background and method. He was perhaps himself trained as a "scribe for the kingdom of God." He "brought out of his treasure store things new and old," drawing upon earlier traditions and contributing new insights of his own. Among these earlier traditions was the OT, which provided him with a number of "fulfillment quotations" (see the Short Essay "Matthew's Fulfillment Citations"). Most scholars also think that he used Mark's Gospel and the lost source, commonly referred to as Q, which is reconstructed from the non-Marcan material, mainly sayings of Jesus, common to Matthew and Luke, as well as special traditions of his own, often referred to as M, (→ Synoptic Problem, The). These critical assumptions are accepted in this commentary. Note: in the commentary we shall use "stage 1" to denote authentic words of Jesus and authentic memories of his actions and incidents in his career, "stage 2" for pre-Gospel (oral) traditions, and "stage 3" for the Evangelist's redaction (i.e., material composed by the Evangelist himself; → Biblical Criticism).

Importance

There are indications, such as the Greek word *biblos*, "book," in the title and the *five* major discourses in chaps. 5–7, 10, 13, 18, and 24–25, that Matthew intended his work to serve as a foundation book for his community, like the Torah or five books of Moses in the synagogue. In fact, Matthew came to serve as the preeminent Gospel for the church as a whole. From the second century on, it is the most widely cited Gospel and the most frequently read in ancient liturgical lectionaries.

COMMENTARY

PART ONE: 1:1–4:16

The Person of Jesus the Messiah

This section forms a coherent block of material. The opening words, literally "The Book of the Genesis of Jesus Christ," could suitably cover not only the genealogy or the birth narrative but the whole of 1:1–4:16. This section shows how Jesus appeared in history, when his public ministry began in Galilee (4:12). Part One is marked off from Part Two by the words "*From then* Jesus *began* to proclaim and to say: 'turn around . . .'" and by the fact that from that verse onward Matthew closely follows Mark. The introductory section is glued together by a series of fulfillment citations marking each successive movement of the story from Bethlehem to Egypt to Nazareth to Capernaum. This section answers such questions as who Jesus was, where he came from, how he entered human history (the genealogy, 1:1–17, and again the fulfillment citations). Finally, in various ways Part One foreshadows the subsequent story of Jesus, e.g., the plot of Herod to put him to death, the homage to Jesus by the gentile magi.

1:1–17, The Genealogy. Matthew constructed this genealogy out of traditional materials to serve a Christological purpose indicated by the opening words "son of David, son of Abraham" (v. 1). Jesus emerges from Israel and fulfills the OT promise of a messianic king. The neat pattern of the genealogy (three groups of fourteen ancestors each) indicates God's carefully planned execution of his purpose. The special mention of dubious women in the genealogy (Tamar, Rahab, Ruth, and the wife of Uriah, i.e., Bathsheba) foreshadows the dubious circumstances surrounding Jesus' birth (see commentary below on 1:18–25). God worked out his purpose through scandalous or irregular unions. Readers should not be troubled by the discrepancies between Matthew's genealogy and the one provided by Luke (Luke 3:23–37). These genealogies serve not a biological but a theological purpose, and Luke's purpose is different.

1:18–25, Jesus' Conception. Annunciation stories form a regular literary genre in the Bible. They serve not to record historical fact but to interpret the role a child is destined to play in salvation history and to emphasize that that role is initiated by God. The appearance of an angel and the announcement of the child's future destiny form the core of the genre. Usually there is some impediment to the birth, e.g., sterility or old age. The situation here is that Mary has become pregnant between her betrothal and the consummation of the marriage, with the apparent suggestion of illegitimacy. In this case, the angel also serves the further purpose of inducing Joseph to adopt Jesus as his son, so that the child becomes a son of David. To the ancient world there would be no inconsistency here, for adoption provided one with ancestors as assuredly as did biological descent. The story's insistence that the conception was virginal and caused by the intervention of the Holy Spirit is not a historical statement but a Christological affirmation. It asserts that God initiated the appearance of Jesus into the world. The citation of Isa. 7:14 (Gk.) stresses not Mary's virginity but the fulfillment of the promise that God would be with his

people, a promise that received its definitive realization after Easter (28:20). The virginal conception through the Spirit has nothing to do with the preexistence and incarnation of the divine being: that is a different Christology (understanding of Jesus' identity) found in John (who does not assert Jesus' virginal conception through the Spirit) but not in Matthew.

2:1–12, The Coming of the Magi. The story of the Wise Men is like a "haggadah," i.e., a story made up from biblical materials to make a theological point (→Haggadah). Such OT passages as Num. 24:17, Ps. 72:10–11, and Isa. 60:1–7 have contributed to the composition. In fact, these texts continued to influence the tradition after Matthew's time, so suggesting that the Magi become kings as well as wise men (→Wise Men), a point Matthew himself does not make. Luke (2:15–20) also knew of a tradition of homage to the Christ child. Coupled with the memory of an unusual astral phenomenon around the time when Jesus was likely to have been born, the materials were thus at hand for the development of Matthew's story. Chap. 1 had stressed Jesus' origin in Israel. The Magi story opens the possibility of mission to the Gentiles, thereby reassuring the Jewish members of Matthew's community that the recent development of a gentile mission, however suspect to some stricter Jewish Christians, was in fact foreshadowed in Jesus' birth.

2:13–23, The Christ Child Delivered from Herod. The ground for the three scenes in this unit has been prepared in the previous unit, namely, the enquiry of the Magi at Herod's court. Scene 1 (vv. 13–15) is the flight to Egypt. Scene 2 (vv. 16–18) deals with the massacre of the children of Bethlehem. Scene 3 (vv. 19–23) narrates the return of the holy family to their homeland and their settlement in Nazareth. The three scenes are bound together by several factors. First, each move of the Christ child is undertaken by Joseph as the result of the appearance of an angel in a dream. Second, each section includes a fulfillment citation. Third, the whole narrative is governed by a certain correspondence with the story of Moses and the Exodus. These three features are integrated with Matthew's overall theological concerns. The Christ event represents the culmination of God's plan in salvation history. The whole fate of Jesus is controlled by the divine initiative. The flight into Egypt recalls the protection of the infant Moses from the plot of a wicked tyrant; the massacre of the innocents recalls the slaying of the Hebrew children by Pharaoh; the return from Egypt is explicitly linked to Israel's Exodus from Egypt. To some extent, Matthew portrays Jesus throughout the Gospel as a new Moses, the founder and lawgiver of the true Israel who in his career recapitulates the story of Moses and the Exodus.

3:1–12, The Ministry of John the Baptist.
As in the other Gospels, the ministry of Jesus is preceded by the ministry of John the Baptist. In this section Matthew follows Mark and Q but makes two important modifications to his sources. First, Matthew carefully avoids saying that John offers baptism for release from sins (cf. Mark 1:4). This is something reserved for Jesus through his sacrificial death (note the addition of "for the forgiveness of sins" in Matt. 26:28). Second, John's preaching of repentance is addressed not to the crowds (as in Luke and probably in Q) but to the Pharisees and Sadducees (→ Pharisees; Sadducees). Thus, the Baptist's preaching becomes a warning to the Judaism of Matthew's day. The adherents of the synagogue have refused to flee from the wrath of God by responding to the gospel, and God has raised up children to Abraham in the shape of the Christian church. The Stronger One who was to come after John (11–12) had by Matthew's time purged his granary in the fall of Jerusalem and is already gathering the wheat into his barn (cf. the seed parables in chap. 13) and preparing to burn the chaff with unquenchable fire.

3:13–17, Jesus' Baptism.
Matthew is following Mark, and possibly Q as well, but with a significant addition (vv. 14–15) of his own composition: Jesus came forward for baptism, and John, recognizing in him the Stronger One who was to bring a greater baptism with the Spirit and with fire, "tried to stop him." Jesus, however, insisted on going on with it; "Don't interpose, let God's plan in salvation history take its course." Upon this, John "lets it happen" (v. 15). The divine plan is that Jesus should in obedience take upon himself the role of the Son of God. With this inserted dialogue between the Baptist and Jesus, Matthew is wrestling with a problem that was embarrassing for the early church. Why was Jesus baptized by John? Does this not mean that John was the greater one? This was made specially acute because of the continuing followers of John the Baptist. The voice from heaven is not a private communication ("you are") as in Mark and Luke, but a public proclamation: "This is my Son, the Beloved One, on whom I have set my choice." The Baptist has to hear it too. And his followers must know that their master really points them to Jesus. Now in Matthew, Jesus was already announced as the messianic savior at his conception and birth. The baptism marks the point at which Jesus publicly commits himself to the role for which he had been destined at birth. The voice from heaven forms the climax of Part One.

4:1–11, The Temptation.
Matthew takes the beginning (v. 1) and the end (v. 11b) of the temptation story (→ Temptation) from Mark and uses it as a setting for the body of the story (vv. 2–11a), which he takes from Q. Following this source, Matthew binds the temptation closely to the baptism through Satan's twice-repeated address "Son of God" (first and second temptations). Its repetition after the third temptation would be inappropriate. The Spirit "snatches" Jesus away. The word translated "snatches" shows that Matthew thought of a visionary experience, like the seer in Rev. 17:3 who was also "snatched away." The three temptations come from a later stage of the Q tradition in which the title "Son of God," which was originally attached to the moment of the resurrection (Rom. 1:4), has been retrojected into the earthly life of Jesus. In form, the temptations are a scriptural "midrash" (→ Midrash) on the saying at Luke 10:18, "I had a vision of Satan having fallen like lightning from heaven." Matthew has heightened the Moses typology of the temptations by a few significant touches (cf. the flight into Egypt above, Matt. 2:13–23). Like Moses in Sinai, Jesus "fasts" (Luke: "ate nothing") for forty nights as well as days (cf. Moses in Exod. 34:28). Jesus is shown the kingdoms of the whole cosmos, like Moses, when he was shown the Promised Land from Mount Nebo (Deut. 34:1–4). This prepares the way for the Sermon on the Mount, which is to follow, and is relevant to the Matthean church's situation: the synagogue has Moses as its founder figure; the true Israel has Jesus, the giver of the messianic Torah that fulfills and supersedes the Mosaic Torah. Also, the temptations show Jesus to be the true Son of God, obeying God's command in Deuteronomy where in the wilderness, Israel, the predecessor of the post-Jamnia synagogue, had been disobedient.

4:12–16, Jesus Enters Galilee.
According to Matthew's presentation, Jesus' transfer to Galilee and the beginning of his independent ministry were occasioned by two factors: first, the baptism and temptation; second, the "delivering up" of John the Baptist. Thus, Jesus was led to move his residence from "Nazara" (sic; also Luke 4:16, which suggests that both Evangelists took this from Q) to Capernaum, which will be his base for the time being. What Matthew does not make clear is whether he thinks that Jesus returned to Nazareth after the baptism. Matthew was interested not in the precise sequence of Jesus' movements, but in the way these movements executed God's plan as announced in Scripture. The fulfillment citation in Matt. 4:15–16 closes the series that brings Jesus finally to Galilee. Its salient feature is the designation of Galilee as the "place of the Gentiles." This does

not mean that Jesus is about to embark at once on a gentile mission. In fact, Matthew will stress that Jesus' earthly mission was generally confined to Israel (10:5; 15:24). So the citation points forward to the postresurrectional commission of the disciples in Galilee (28:16–20). This will be the final outcome of the earthly ministry of Jesus. Israel will reject the message, and the good news will consequently go forth to the Gentiles. What has happened in the recent history of Matthew's church (ejection from the synagogue and subsequent mission to the Gentiles) is therefore in accord with the saving plan of God as announced in the OT.

Matthew's Fulfillment Citations

Definition. "Fulfillment citation" or "formula citation" designates those quotations of the OT that Matthew introduces with the set formula: "This was done in order that what was spoken by the prophet [name] might be fulfilled when he says . . ." There are some ten such citations in Matthew: 1:22–23 (Isa. 7:14); 2:15 (Hos. 11:1); 2:17–18 (Jer. 31:15); 2:23 (source uncertain); 4:14–16 (Isa. 9:1–2); 8:17 (Isa. 53:4); 12:17–21 (Isa. 42:1–4); 13:35 (Ps. 78:2); 21:4–5 (Isa. 62:11; Zech. 9:9); 27:9–10 (Zech. 11:12–13, but erroneously attributed to Jeremiah). There are three other citations where the formula is imperfect: 2:5–6 (Mic. 5:2); 3:3 (Isa. 40:3); 13:14–15 (Isa. 6:9–10). In 26:56 the formula occurs without a citation. The distribution of fulfillment citations is interesting. No less than seven, including the imperfect instances, occur in Part One and mark the geographical progression of the narrative. Four occur in Parts Two and Three and comment in general on Jesus' teaching and healing. Three occur in Parts Four and Five and are attached to specific incidents of the passion narrative. Five are attached to Marcan material, the rest to Matthew's special material (M). From this fact we may conclude that all of them are attached to narratives that existed prior to Matthew and that none of them formed the nucleus from which Matthew created narratives or incidents. They serve to comment on already existing traditions.
Source. There has been much discussion as to whether Matthew first selected the citations or whether they were already in use before him (perhaps in a collection of testimonia), so that Matthew drew from this source. Some of the citations in Parts Two–Five occur also outside of Matthew (e.g., Zech. 9:9 [Matt. 21:4–5] is also cited in a similar context in John 12:15) or have influenced Mark without being explicitly quoted (e.g., Isa. 6:9–10 has already influenced Mark 4:12). Thus, at least some of the citations outside of Part One were already in use prior to Mat-

thew. As for those in Part One, they are new to Matthew, with the possible exception of Isa. 7:14, which may have influenced Luke's account of the virginal conception (Luke 1:31). Thus, Matthew's policy seems to have been to make explicit those citations that had already influenced his sources and also to introduce new ones, especially in material peculiar to himself.
Text. There has been much discussion among scholars over the question of whether the fulfillment citations were taken from the Hebrew or from the Greek OT. This is a very technical and complicated question. The most probable conclusion is that where Matthew was following Mark (and Q, for that matter, although in Q there is only a general OT background, no actual use of fulfillment citations), he used the same text as his source, sometimes conforming it more closely to the Septuagint (LXX). But when introducing previously unused fulfillment citations in Part One, Matthew followed a text closer to the Hebrew text (Masoretic text, MT) or to other non-LXX texts such as the Targums (Aramaic paraphrases). What it does show is that Matthew was conservative in the use of his OT texts and that he selected from the versions available those most suitable for his purposes.
Purpose. It is generally recognized that the fulfillment citations play a central role in Matthew's theology. They are also related to the situation of his church. They show that the synagogue does not have a monopoly on the interpretation of the foundational Scriptures, that the real purpose on the OT Scriptures is to point to the Christ event, to the origin, ministry (including the preaching, teaching, and healing) of Jesus, his rejection and death. This perspective on the OT is not unique to Matthew, but Matthew worked it out most systematically in relation to the story of Jesus. The fact that the quotations come from the Prophets and the other writings, rather than from the Mosaic Torah, suggests that Matthew was writing for his own Christians. He did not write to convince the synagogue, for the Torah would have had primary authority there, and any citation from the other books alone would have carried less weight. For the Christian community, by contrast, the Prophets (and Psalms) were of paramount authority.

PART TWO: 4:17–11:1

Jesus, Messiah of Word and Deed

Having introduced Jesus in Part One as the Messiah of God, Matthew in Part Two presents him as the Messiah of word (chaps. 5–7) and of deed (8:1–9:35) and then in 9:36–11:1 extends Jesus' messianic word and work through the Twelve. Note how 4:23 and 9:35 are almost identical. These verses thus serve as an inclusio, i.e., they enclose the intervening material 4:24–9:34, which presents Jesus first as Messiah of word and then as Messiah of deed.

Matt. 4:17 (note the connecting link, "from then") marks the opening of Part Two. In it, Matthew takes over but abbreviates Mark's summary of Jesus' preaching (cf. Mark 1:14–15). This serves as a title for Parts Two and Three. The whole of Jesus' ministry is a proclamation of the kingdom of the heavens (→ Kingdom of God). Matthew nearly always uses "heavens" for God in his text: the meaning is identical. Note how the Baptist (Matt. 3:2), Jesus, and the Twelve (10:7) preach the same message. "Kingdom" means the salvation of God, deliverance from sin. This salvation will be accomplished through the cross (26:28), realized in the church, and consummated at the End (28:20).

4:18–22
The Call of the First Disciples

This unit is placed here to give Jesus an audience for the Sermon on the Mount and to allow the disciples to witness his deeds in chaps. 8 and 9 (cf. Mark 1:16–20). This experience will prepare them for their own mission in chap. 10.

5:1–2
The Setting of the Sermon on the Mount

Matthew has carefully composed this setting. Jesus "saw" the crowds. He delivered the great sermon not to the crowds directly but in their hearing. He went up into "the" mountain, i.e., the place of revelation, as Moses went up on Sinai. He sat down—the posture assumed by authorized teachers of the law (cf. 23:2). His disciples came to him: the sermon was addressed directly to them. The setting will provide an important clue when we discuss the contemporary meaning of the sermon. Finally, "he opened his mouth," a solemn phrase that tells us that Jesus is about to deliver divine revelation. Matthew's church is thus assured that this is messianic Torah, replacing the Mosaic Torah of the synagogue.

5:3–7:29
The Sermon on the Mount

The Sermon on the Mount is based on the Great Sermon of Q (cf. Luke 6:20–49). Both versions begin with the Beatitudes (→ Beatitudes), proceed to the commandment of love for the enemy, the prohibition of judgment on others, the test of true goodness (good and bad fruit), and conclude with the parable of the two houses (hearers and doers of the word). Thus, the basic structure of the sermon comes from Q. Matthew has added to the Great Sermon materials gathered from other parts of Q and from M. He has carefully organized this material in a neat structure including nine Beatitudes, six antitheses, and three works of mercy.

5:3–12, The Beatitudes. Matthew's first, fourth, fifth, and ninth Beatitudes are shared by Luke and are therefore from Q. Of these, the first three in the Lucan form (Luke 6:20–23) constitute the original stock, i.e., authentic Jesus or stage 1 material. They are brief, simple, and direct. They promise salvation to the oppressed (the poor, the hungry, and those who weep). They are addressed directly to the hearers in the second person, "Blessed are you." Between Q and Matthew's redaction the following changes have occurred: first, in conformity with Jewish Beatitudes generally, Jesus' original Beatitudes were changed into the third person plural; second, a new Beatitude of the "meek" was added to Jesus' original three Beatitudes. This is similar in kind to Jesus' Beatitudes, for it is pronounced upon the have-nots. Three more activistic Beatitudes pronounced upon the merciful, the pure in heart, and the peacemakers were also added, all of them formulated in the third person. These new Beatitudes were inspired by certain psalms and by Isa. 61:1–2.

Matthew has in turn given a more activist twist to the original Beatitudes. "Poor in spirit" (v. 3) suggests not so much economic poverty and political oppression as an interior disposition. "Mourning" (v. 4; cf. Ps. 37:11), contrasted with Luke's and Q's "weeping," suggests sorrow for one's sins and a desire for moral reformation. "Meek" (Matt. 5:5) has a more ethical nuance for Matthew (cf. 11:29; 21:5, where it is predicated of Jesus); it suggests humility and kindness. The Beatitude upon the hungry has been similarly ethicized. While "thirst" was probably added before Matthew (stage 2) the addition of "for righteousness" is undoubtedly his. Righteousness for Matthew usually means not the saving power and activity of God, as it does in Paul, but the radical demand of God to which those who have responded to Jesus' offer of salvation are obligated (cf. 5:10, 20; 6:1, 33; 21:32). With v. 7, the more activistic group of Beatitudes begins. "Merciful" means performing acts of mercy (cf. James 2:13). "Pure in heart" (Matt. 5:8; cf. Pss. 24:4; 73:1) denotes unreserved commitment to the will of God, i.e., the new righteousness. It is contrasted with the merely outward purity of the synagogue (cf. Matt. 23:25–26). "Peacemakers" (v. 9) could hardly have meant to Matthew what we mean by pacifism. In his situation it would have meant working for harmonious relations within the Christian community. This was particularly relevant in a community that included Jewish Christians of various types and recent gentile converts.

Matthew's eighth Beatitude is redactional (stage 3). It adds nothing new that is not already included in the first and ninth Beatitudes, but it does disclose important information about Matthew's church. It is addressed not to those who are being but to those *who have been* persecuted. Their persecution by the synagogue lay by now back in the past, a recent past no doubt. They had been persecuted because of their adherence to "righteousness," i.e., to the messianic Torah of Jesus rather than to the Mosaic Torah.

The ninth and final Beatitude envisages persecution as a present possibility, this time no doubt at the hands of the Romans in the time of Domitian (A.D. 81–96). Note that this Beatitude, unlike the others, contains an explicit Christology ("for my sake").

The Beatitudes contain three elements: first, the pronouncement of blessedness; second, the present attitude, state, or activity of those so pronounced; and third, the promise of salvation at the end. "Blessed" means that they already now enjoy the promise of future salvation. The future salvation is described under a number of different metaphors: possession of the kingdom of the heavens, consolation, inheritance of the land (i.e., the kingdom of God, of which the Promised Land of Canaan is a type), and satiety (i.e., the messianic banquet); the reception of "mercy" is the forgiveness of sin and final salvation; the seeing of God is not a mystic vision but saving encounter with God at the end; and the status of sonship is a life like that of angels (22:30). These promises are final rewards for radical obedience in this present age.

5:13–16, The Community as Salt and Light.

This unit serves as transition from the Beatitudes to sayings relating the new righteousness to the Torah (5:17–48). The sayings about salt and light, authentic wisdom sayings of Jesus originally addressed to his disciples, are reapplied by Matthew to his church under persecution. The church is a "contrast society," distinctive from the surrounding world, including the synagogue. Its role is to show forth what it is by its good works (v. 1, a redactional addition), to be described in the antitheses. These good works are not its own achievement, for they will lead the world to praise not the church but the heavenly Father. For the way of righteousness is both taught and made possible by Jesus.

5:17–20, The Fulfillment of the Law.

This unit serves as Matthew's introduction to the antitheses. It forms one of the most difficult yet most important passages in Matthew and one

whose meaning is most disputed among interpreters. It consists of four separate sayings, one in each verse. It will help in their interpretation if we reconstruct a possible history of the tradition behind the unit. Although the present wording of v. 17 bears the marks of Matthew's editing, the basic substance of the saying could well go back to Jesus (stage 1). In response, e.g., to the criticisms of his opponents for the breach of the Sabbath, Jesus claimed that he was fulfilling the Sabbath law, since the Sabbath rest was a symbol of the coming kingdom of God. Palestinian Jewish Christians who thought that Paul was encouraging their coreligionists in the Diaspora (→ Diaspora) to abandon the law (see Acts 21:21) took up and expanded Jesus' saying in Matt. 5:17 and expanded it with vv. 18–19 (stage 2). Jesus, they argued, never encouraged his Jewish followers to abandon circumcision or the food laws (which was true to a degree, though for Jesus the kingdom of God took priority even over the Torah). Matthew then took up these three sayings, conformed them to his own style, and added the fourth saying, v. 20 (stage 3). In doing so he sought to apply vv. 17–19 about the law to his own church, a church that contained both Palestinian and Hellenistic Jewish Christians represented by M and Mark respectively, plus recent gentile converts. For such a church the Torah was still valid, but only as reinterpreted by Jesus, as the messianic Torah, as the better righteousness that surpasses that of the synagogue (v. 20). As the antitheses will explain, the better righteousness is the Mosaic law reinterpreted as love (→ Love) or rather interpreted according to God's original intention as love. Jesus had come to reinterpret and fulfill (v. 17) the Torah. What then of every "jot and tittle" of the law (v. 18)? Did Matthew expect his Jewish Christians to continue to observe circumcision? He never says, but we may suppose that they would have continued it as Torah for them but in a spirit of tolerance toward the gentile Christians. That would mean neither forcing the rite upon them nor regarding themselves as superior to the Gentiles who did not practice it. And what of the kosher and Sabbath laws? Love perhaps required that the Gentiles eat kosher food in their table fellowship with their Jewish fellow Christians, a fellowship that would have included the Eucharist. As for the Sabbath, presumably, Jewish Christians continued to observe it on their own, while both they and the Gentiles celebrated Sundays as the fulfillment of the Sabbath. In ways like these, perhaps, Matthew's church would have implemented the teachings of vv. 18–19 in the spirit of the better righteousness of the antitheses, the Golden Rule, and the double commandment of love.

5:21–48, The Antitheses.

There are six antitheses. They all have the following form: first, thesis (citation from the old Torah); second, antithesis proper = radical reinterpretation of the Torah; third, specific illustrations of the radical command, often in picturesque terms. Three antitheses (the first, second, and fourth) are peculiar to Matthew (M); three come from Q (the third, fifth, and sixth). The latter group appears in Luke (and therefore, presumably, in Q) without the antithetical form, so the form has clearly been introduced by Matthew into the Q sayings, doubtless on the model of the antitheses in M. Does the antithetical form go back to Jesus himself? Arguably it does. The divine passive ("it was said" = "God said") is characteristic of Jesus. So too is the daring with which Jesus revises what God has said in former times, "I say to you," a way of speaking that denotes a claim to immediate and direct authority. Also the hyperbolic illustrations are characteristic of Jesus.

The antitheses fall into two groups of three (the first through the third, fourth through the sixth). They are separated structurally by the full introduction that prefaces the first and the fourth, and by the "again" that links the second group of three to the first. Further, two of the first three are based on the Ten Commandments (Exod. 20) and two of the second group on the Holiness Code (Lev. 19–20), while the respective items follow in the same order in which they occur in the OT. Matthew's aim is to provide his church with its own radicalized Torah, its own Decalogue and Holiness Code. The radicalized version of the Torah covers not only the outward behavior but also inner disposition; it claims the obedience of the whole person. Matthew sets the antitheses under the title of the "greater" or "superior righteousness" (5:20).

5:21–26, First Antithesis: On Murder. Jesus radicalized the sixth (fifth) commandment to include the prohibition of anger. Matthew appends two illustrations that give a positive force to this prohibition: believers must strive to be reconciled with their fellow believers so that the church may be a community of love. This was very relevant in a church where long-standing Jewish Christians and recent gentile converts were trying to settle down in a single community. In this antithesis, Matthew had in mind relationships within the Christian community. In the sixth and final antithesis, he will be concerned with the relationship between Christians and the outside world.

5:27–30, Second Antithesis: On Adultery. Jesus radicalized the seventh (sixth) commandment to include the prohibition of the lustful glance. Matthew adds a double saying about offenses found also in the Marcan tradition (Mark 9:43–48) that Matthew reproduces in Matt. 18:8–9. Matthew appends these extreme injunctions— to pluck out the eye, etc.—as advice in carrying out Jesus' radical command. He can hardly mean it literally: it is figurative, an expression for drastic action to avoid situations where temptation is likely. Jesus' and Matthew's basic concern is to protect the institution of marriage. Perhaps also, given Jesus' free and open treatment of women, so different from that of the rabbis, he was concerned to recognize women as persons rather than objects of male gratification.

5:31–32, Third Antithesis: On Divorce. This antithesis is tacked on to the preceding one, as is shown by its brief introduction "you have heard that . . ." and by its related subject matter. It appears to abolish rather than radicalize the Torah. This saying occurs twice in Matthew, here with a parallel at Luke 16:18 (Q) and also in Matt. 19:9 (= Mark 10:11–12). Paul also knows of Jesus' prohibition of divorce (1 Cor. 7:10–11), which gives it triple attestation. The tendency is to modify Jesus' absolute prohibition. Matthew concedes it on the ground of porneia. The traditional interpretation, "adultery," must be rejected for these reasons: first, the Greek word used is different from the word for adultery in the preceding antithesis; second, "adultery" is used where the wife's infidelity is clearly in view (John 8:3); third, the punishment for a wife's extramarital relations was stoning (Lev. 20:10; Deut. 22:22–24), and one would therefore expect the exception to be formulated as an antithesis. It has been suggested that "sexual immorality" here refers to unions with kin forbidden by the Torah (Lev. 18:6–18), contracted by pagans prior to their conversion. This would accord with the situation of Matthew's church, for such previous pagan marriages would be a problem in a Jewish church open to gentile mission.

5:33–37, Fourth Antithesis: On Oaths. This is the first of the second set of three antitheses (note "again," the full introduction as in the first antithesis and the switch from the Decalogue to the Holiness Code). The prohibition is first stated in general terms, and four specific oaths are mentioned, concluding with a positive injunction to tell the truth in all circumstances without invoking the sanction of an oath (→ Oath; cf. Lev. 19:12).

5:38–42, Fifth Antithesis: On Retaliation. The old Torah injunction was not intended to encourage revenge, but to restrict it: only an eye, not a life. Once again, the general injunction is followed by four specific examples (cf. Exod. 21:24; Lev. 24:20; Deut. 19:21).

5:43–48, Sixth Antithesis: On Love of the Enemy. The last antithesis forms a climax to the series. Here above all the "better righteousness" is expressed. The command itself is from Q (Luke 6:27–32, 35), but Matthew has reformulated it as an antithesis to Lev. 19:18. The saying is substantially authentic to Jesus. However, the command to hate the enemy occurs nowhere in the Torah, so Matthew must have a later Jewish interpretation in view such as is found at Qumran (1QS 1:9–10); Matthew is perhaps inferring from the behavior of the synagogue toward his church that such teaching was current there too.

Matthew has altered the wording of the injunction to pray: Luke (Q) has "for those who treat you wrongfully," which Matthew changes to "those who persecute you." This shows that Matthew has in mind not personal adversaries but the enemies of the church, whether Jewish or gentile, who were persecuting Christians for their faith.

Matthew has no compunction in offering a reward for the love of the enemy. The reward is that his community will become sons of God at the end (cf. the seventh Beatitude, Matt. 5:9). Love of the enemy for Matthew involves imitating the action of God in creation (v. 45) not as in Q, basing one's conduct on his mercy in offering the gift of the kingdom to sinners (Luke 6:35).

The concluding saying, "Therefore you shall be perfect as your Father, the heavenly One, is perfect" (Matt. 5:48), concludes not only the sixth Beatitude as in Luke 6:36 (which has "be merciful," referring only to the last command) but the whole series. Perfection for Matthew (cf. Matt. 19:21) means the better righteousness of 5:20 as expounded in the six antitheses, the total and unreserved obedience of the whole person. Here is another echo of the Holiness Code (Lev. 19:2), with Matthew substituting perfection for holiness. God's perfection, like his holiness in Leviticus, provides the motivation for human conduct.

6:1-18, The Deeds of Righteousness. The synagogue across the street had its own list of deeds of righteousness (almsgiving, prayer, and fasting). Matthew provides his community with the same list, but in each case the pious deed is radicalized. In this systematized form they are clearly due to Matthew. How much of the substance goes back to Jesus? On the one hand, the teaching on fasting seems to contradict Mark 2:19a. On the other hand, the picturesquely hyperbolic imagery of each of the injunctions, including that on fasting, seems characteristic of Jesus. Certainly we can accept all three injunctions as the result of his teaching. In any case, the original nucleus of the Lord's Prayer (→ Lord's Prayer, The) is authentic to Jesus (see commentary below on 6:9-15). Probably Matthew took over the three items from a written source (where they already appeared in verse form), prefaced it with an introduction that is in prose form (6:1), and inserted the Lord's Prayer (6:9-15).

6:1, Introduction. The better righteousness includes for Matthew not only a radicalization of the Decalogue and Holiness Code but also of the Jewish rules of piety that go beyond the Torah. **6:2-4, Almsgiving.** All three rules are radicalized in contrast to the behavior of the "hypo-crites," i.e., the synagogue across the street. In Greek, "hypocrite" is a neutral term meaning "actor," one who plays a role wearing a mask. Here it means those whose outward behavior stands in contrast to their inward disposition. They assume a mask of benevolence but are really concerned with their own glory and the praise of others. This will be the principal charge leveled against the Pharisees in chap. 23. Matthew again has in mind the people in the synagogue.

6:5-8, On Prayer. In Judaism, prayer was closely connected with almsgiving (e.g., Tob. 12:8). Jesus here had private prayer in view. That he did not exclude public or corporate prayer is shown by Matt. 18:19-20.

6:9-15, The Lord's Prayer. Since the Our Father interrupts the poetic structure of the three precepts, it is clearly an insertion by Matthew into his M source. It has a parallel in Luke 11:2-4, but Matthew's version is expanded. These additions are also found in Did. 8:2 and represent liturgical expansions. Jesus invited his disciples to address God as "Abba, Father," a privilege accorded to those who had responded to his message, not a right for everybody. Matthew has reverted to traditional Jewish practice by expanding it to the more fulsome "Our Father, the One in the heavens." This emphasizes God's transcendence, which Jesus himself expressed in other ways. Following the second petition, "may your reign come," Matthew has added "may your will be done, as in heaven so too on earth." This was intended to amplify and clarify the petition for the coming Reign of God; it does not really add anything new. When God's Reign comes, his will is effectively asserted on earth. The powers of evil will be overthrown and the plan of salvation accomplished. By placing the Lord's Prayer in the sermon and in the exposition of the better righteousness, Matthew probably intends the third petition to be a prayer for the fulfillment of the better righteousness through Christian obedience. In the fifth petition, Matthew reads "debts" (Luke: "sins"). Probably the tradition followed by Luke (Q or some special source) also read "debts" originally, for in Luke the ensuing clause reads "for we ourselves also forgive everyone who is indebted to us." Those who are privileged to call God "Father," i.e., the members of Matthew's community, have received forgiveness of sin. Yet they still sin daily and, therefore, need constantly to pray for forgiveness. The seventh petition should probably be translated "but deliver us from the evil one" (i.e., Satan). Like the other additions by Matthew, this does not add anything essentially new to the petition before it. The trial referred to in the sixth petition is the last great trial before the end, the time of the messianic woes, when Satan seeks to deceive the elect and tempt them to be unfaithful.

The KJV included the familiar doxology, which is absent from the more ancient texts, and therefore not original. However, according to Jewish custom, Jesus would have expected users of his prayer to ad-lib a doxology every time they said the prayer.

6:16–18, On Fasting. Prayer and fasting often went together in Jewish practice. Fasting added force to the prayer and made it more urgent. From Mark 2:18–19 it would appear that when Jesus and his disciples were on the road in Galilee they dispensed with the additional fasts of the Pharisees and of the Baptist's disciples over and above the Day of Atonement (→Atonement, Day of), which all Jews practiced. This was due to the emergency situation created by the in-breaking of God's Reign, which was like a wedding feast. It would not, however, have been inconsistent for Jesus to tell his followers *how* they were to keep the regular fast of the Day of Atonement. Such teaching would lead to the post-Easter observance in Greek-speaking communities of the "day when the bridegroom was taken from them" (Mark 2:20). Matthew omits "on that day" (9:15), so presumably Jewish Christians continued to observe Yom Kippur rather than Good Friday.

6:19–7:11, Instructions for the Community. These instructions are loosely attached to the Lord's Prayer. Verses 19–34, which contain teaching on wealth, can be connected with the petition, "Give us today enough bread for tomorrow" (v. 11). Matt. 7:1–5, on judging, may be linked to the petition on forgiveness (v. 12). Less plausibly perhaps, 7:6, on casting pearls before swine, may be tied in with 6:13, the petition for delivery from trials and evil. The longer section on prayer (7:7–11) is obviously a continuation of the teaching in 6:5–15. Most of this material is inserted by Matthew into the sermon from other parts of Q: Matt. 6:19–21 – Luke 12:33–34; Matt. 6:22–23 = Luke 11:34–36; Matt. 6:24 = Luke 16:13; Matt. 6:25–34 = Luke 12:22–31; Matt. 7:7–11 = Luke 11:9–13. Only in Matt. 7:1–5 is Matthew following the Great Sermon from Q (= Luke 6:37–38, 41–42); Matt. 7:6 is from M.

6:19–24, On Treasures. We have here three distinct sayings (vv. 19–21, 22–23, 24) that were probably independent traditions. They all have a poetic structure characteristic of Jesus. Matthew has added v. 24 from elsewhere in Q (= Luke 16:13) to the first two. This combination provides a clue to his understanding of the two sayings about the single eye: it is an eye that is exclusively fixed upon the service of God and not on material possessions. Thus, the whole unit serves to introduce the following unit on anxiety.

6:25–34, On Anxiety. It will clarify Matthew's understanding of these sayings if we reconstruct their earlier history. Stage 1: Jesus was not ad-dressing humanity in general or even Israel in particular but his disciples, those who had accepted his message of the coming Reign of God. They are to renounce their earthly callings and possessions to follow him and proclaim his message. Theirs was to be the radical obedience of itinerant charismatic preachers (cf. the rich young man, Mark 10:17–31 = Matt. 19:16–30). Stage 2: without losing the primary meaning they had for Jesus, the injunctions are now treated as conventional wisdom teaching about riches (vv. 27–29)—you don't gain anything by being anxious. Stage 3: Matthew's church no longer consisted of itinerant charismatics but was a settled community of the relatively well-to-do. Accordingly, the Evangelist prefaces the unit with the sayings on the single eye and serving two masters. Matthean Christians do not have to give up their possessions, but they must get their priorities straight. Thus, Matthew adds the word "first" to the injunction "seek God's reign" (v. 33) plus "and its [or his, God's] righteousness," the better righteousness of the antitheses and the devout precepts. It is worth noting that Matthew's Jesus addresses those "of little faith" (v. 30), a favorite designation for Matthew's church. A puny faith has many consequences; one is that it leads people to trust in uncertain riches and therefore makes them prone to anxiety.

7:1–5, On Judging. This unit represents a combination of two separate traditions. The first saying (vv. 1–2) is couched in the second person plural (you). The string of sayings that follows (vv. 3–5) is addressed to the individual (thou). This is an important clue to their meaning. Jesus prohibited his itinerant charismatics as a body from going to law courts in any circumstances. Q individualized this teaching: the post-Easter community did not condemn law courts as such but expected its members not to go to law when they had disputes with one another (cf. 1 Cor. 6:1–11). Matthew, in turn, places these injunctions in the context of the teaching on material possessions: those who get their priorities straight with regard to such possessions will never want to go to law.

7:6, On Not Desecrating the Holy. It is hard to fit this saying into what we know of the Jesus who consorted with the outcast and who healed lepers. It must be an expression of the exclusiveness of the narrowly Jewish Christian community that formulated the M tradition. How did the Evangelist himself understand it? That is even more puzzling now that his community had embarked upon a mission to the Gentiles. The *Didache* (9:5) applied the saying to the Eucharist, which is to be withheld from the profane. Given the affinities between Matthew's community and the audience for the *Didache* (they shared the Lord's Prayer and baptism in the threefold name) we may conjecture that

Matthew understood it in the same way. It is, however, difficult to relate it to the context in which Matthew has placed it.

7:7-11, Confidence in Prayer. This unit exhibits many characteristics of Jesus' speech: poetic structure, the divine passive ("it will be given to you . . . it will be opened to you," i.e., God will give . . . God will open), the picturesque illustrations (bread/stone; fish/serpent), the argument from the less to the greater ("if . . . how much more"), the realism about human nature ("you, being evil"). Above all, Jesus was absolutely certain of the goodness of God, his Abba, who was drawing near in Jesus' own ministry. It is coherent with Jesus' message that he should seek to inculcate the same confidence not in humanity in general, but specially in those who had responded to his message. The "good things" are the blessings of God's coming Reign, the things Jesus taught his disciples to pray for in the Our Father.

Q was already aware of the relation between this unit and the Our Father. In Luke 11:9-13, this teaching on prayer follows almost immediately after the Lord's Prayer (11:2-4). Jesus and Matthew have been criticized for naïveté and lack of realism. But that is because the very specific context of this teaching—its relation to the coming Reign of God—has been ignored and the promise generalized.

7:12, The Golden Rule. This saying stands on its own between the two main parts (5:17-6:18; 6:19-7:11) of the sermon and the final section (7:13-29). It harks back to the introduction of the better righteousness in 5:17-20. In Q (cf. Luke 6:31) it rounded off the command to love one's enemies. For Matthew, the better righteousness is summed up in the Golden Rule. The rule itself is not unique to Jesus. It is found in Greek and Latin literature and was adopted by Judaism from the Greco-Roman world. The early church (if not Jesus himself) then took it over from the synagogue fully aware that it was not distinctively Christian as a rule of thumb for applying the love commandment. It is often (but erroneously) claimed that elsewhere it appears only in the negative form ("Do not do to others"). Matthew has added to it v. 12c, "for this is the law and the prophets," thus showing that for him it is an aid in practicing the better righteousness that is the fulfillment of the Torah. Thus, Matthew links the Golden Rule to 5:17. And as 22:40 also shows, the quintessence of the new righteousness is the love commandment.

7:13-29, Final Injunctions. The conclusion of the Sermon on the Mount consists of four units. Each unit features a contrast: broad/narrow gate or road (vv. 13-14); good/bad fruit (vv. 15-20); lawlessness/righteousness (vv. 21-23);

house on rock/house on sand (vv. 24-27). Choices made right now determine the believers' fate at the End: "life" in v. 14 means life in the age to come; "fire" in v. 19 means the last judgment; note also "the kingdom of heaven" (v. 21) and "on that day" (vv. 22-23); the winds, rain, and overflowing rivers is imagery for the last judgment (vv. 25, 27). Matthew likes to conclude his speeches with references to the End (cf. 18:34-35; 25:31-46).

7:13-14, The Two Ways. The antithetical parallelism and rhythmic structure suggest that the basic tradition goes back to Jesus himself. This makes the form in Luke 13:23-24 an abbreviation. However, the switch from "gate" to "way" is awkward. Perhaps Matthew added the "way" to the picture (cf. 21:32; 22:16) to conform to the conventional Jewish teaching about the two ways. For Matthew the "way" is the better righteousness. Here he has in mind not the synagogue across the street but false prophets within the Christian community (see the next unit).

7:15-23, False Prophets. This unit contains two parts, a warning against false prophets (→Prophet) and the test of the prophets by their fruits. The test of fruits is from the Great Sermon in Q (Luke 6:43-44) where it had a more general application. Thus, v. 15 is the key to Matthew's intention here. His community was troubled by a problem that plagued other communities at this time, that of itinerant prophets. Various tests were offered to distinguish false from true prophets. For Paul (1 Cor. 12:3) and for the Johannine community (1 John 2:22), the test was one of orthodoxy. The *Didache* imposed a practical test: did they overstay their welcome? Matthew's test is to ask whether they practice better righteousness. We do not know exactly who these antinomian prophets were. Probably they were Greek-speaking Christians who had joined Matthew's community as a result of its recent mission to the Gentiles. This explains why Matthew deliberately omitted Mark's story of the strange exorcist (Mark 9:38-41).

7:21-23, Saying and Doing. Matthew has combined two separate units from Q (Luke 6:46 and 13:26-27) and introduced the motif of prophecy (Matt. 7:22), thus relating this unit to the preceding one and giving a more specific application of the test of fruits: they preach the better righteousness but do not practice it. As charismatics, the false prophets appeal to their miracles: Matthew tests them by their practice.

7:24-27, The Two Houses. Matthew takes over Q's conclusion to the Great Sermon (cf. Luke 6:47-49). This is an authentic Jesus parable based on Noah's Flood (cf. Matt. 24:37-39, also from Q). The Deluge is a symbol of the last judgment. Elsewhere Jesus used the last judgment in a nonparabolic context as a sanction for the decisiveness of his message (Luke 12:8-9 Q). Already in Q the application of the parable of the two houses has been modified: the believers must not only hear Jesus' message but practice his precepts. Matthew, in turn, identifies "these words of mine" (v. 26; cf. 24) with the better righteousness. This links the parable of the two houses to 5:17–20. Matthew also describes those who practice the new righteousness as "prudent" (v. 24) in their present conduct. They weigh the prospect of final judgment. Those who hear but do not translate what they have heard into practice are "foolish." Matthew will pick up the same terms, "prudent" and "foolish," in the parable of the ten maidens (25:2).

7:28–29, The Conclusion of the Sermon. Matthew has taken over the substance of this conclusion from Q (Luke 7:1) but reworded it into a formula that he will repeat with appropriate variations at the end of each of his major discourses (Matt. 11:1; 13:53; 19:1; 26:1). The mention of the "crowd" and of the "teaching" points back to 5:1 and marks off the sermon from the surrounding narrative. Also, the reference to Jesus' authority (v. 29) prepares for the ensuing section on his mighty deeds.

The Sermon on the Mount Today

Jesus addressed his radical teaching to a band of wandering charismatics who preached the impending advent of the Reign of God. They were to renounce property, lawsuits, oaths, and (apparently) either forego marriage and leave family (19:11–12) or, if married, never avail themselves of divorce and remarriage.

Already the Q tradition found it necessary, as we have seen, to modify these demands for a more settled community. Matthew was writing for a situation that had changed even more: his was a completely settled, relatively prosperous urban church. It had undergone two traumatic experiences: expulsion from the synagogue and the opening up of mission to the Gentiles. In this situation, Matthew reformulated Jesus' ethic in antithesis to the ethic of the synagogue, providing precepts of piety, seeking to make his church a community of love and reconciliation. Unfortunately, he does not seem to have thought of applying the command to love the enemy to the synagogue.

More than two centuries after the time of Matthew, the church became tolerated, and, in due course, Christianity became the official religion of the Roman Empire. When church and state entered into partnership, a double-standard ethic evolved. Only monastic communities practiced the absolute ethic of the Sermon on the Mount. Christians in the world were expected to live only according to the Decalogue. The Reformation revolted against this double standard. Right-wing Protestantism generally operated with a distinction between private and public life. Public life was governed by the rules of the Decalogue, private life by the Sermon on the Mount reduced to a matter of inner motive and disposition. Left-wing Protestantism withdrew from the world, organizing its communal life in accordance with the absolutes of the sermon.

Today we live in an increasingly secularized society. In the West, Christians still share political responsibilities with their post-Christian, secularized neighbors. In the Communist countries, Christians are excluded from political responsibilities. But on both sides of the Iron Curtain the state is almost completely secularized.

How are the teachings of the sermon applicable in this situation? The first point to note is that the sermon is addressed directly not to the world outside (represented by the crowd) but to the disciples, that is, to those who have responded to Jesus' message of the kingdom. It is totally unrealistic and impossible to expect the "world" to practice the better righteousness of the sermon. Even European states that made a public and official profession of Christian faith never lived up to the sermon. Those states professed themselves to be subject only to the standards of the Decalogue, and the established church's role was to hold the state by its proclamation to that subjection (cf. the Elizabethan *Book of Homilies*, a handbook for English preachers that became a classic). The church could never expect even the professedly Christian state to follow the better righteousness. Some remnants of this older situation survive even in the United States with its "civil religion."

With the growing secularization of both the state and society, however, the church will be challenged by the sermon to become increasingly a "contrast society"—one in which the better righteousness is practiced not just by individual Christians, but corporately by the Christian fellowship as such; this will require church discipline (cf. Matt. 18). Such a church would not be turned in upon itself: the sermon was delivered in the presence of the crowds who overheard it, and the contrast society was meant to be a light to the world and the salt of the earth. The world outside was meant to see the good works done by the contrast society and to glorify the heavenly Father.

8:1–9:35

Messiah of Deed

Chaps. 8–9 are predominantly a collection of miracle stories (→ Miracles). They are, for the most part, derived from Mark (chaps. 1–2, 4–5) and rearranged in the following sequence: (1) the healing of the leper (Matt. 8:1–4; = Mark 1:40–45); (2) the centurion's servant (Matt. 8:5–13; = Luke 7:1–10 Q); (3) Peter's mother-in-law (Matt. 8:14–15; = Mark 1:29–31); (4) summary of healings at eventide (Matt. 8:16–17; = Mark 1:32–34); (5) stilling of the storm (Matt. 8:23–27; = Mark 4:35–41); (6) the Gadarene demoniac (Matt. 8:28–34; = Mark 5:1–20); (7) the paralytic (Matt. 9:1–8; = Mark 2:1–12); (8) the ruler's daughter and the woman with the hemorrhage (Matt. 9:18–26; = Mark 5:21–43); (9) two blind men (Matt. 9:27–31); and (10) the dumb demoniac (Matt. 9:32–34). The ninth and tenth appear to be Matthew's own compositions. They are rather colorless compilations from other miracle stories. The concluding summary (9:35) corresponds to Matt. 4:23–25 and marks off the two sections that present Jesus as Messiah of word and deed.

These colorless compositions suggest that Matthew was at some pains to produce *ten* miracle stories (if we count only the specific incidents, omit summary 4, and take summary 8 as two separate stories). It has often been suggested that these ten miracles are intended to parallel the ten plagues of Egypt and are therefore part of Matthew's portrayal of Jesus as a new Moses. This is not entirely convincing, but no other plausible explanation has been offered.

There are other episodes in this section that interrupt the series of miracles. These are the would-be disciples (Matt. 8:18–22; = Luke 9:57–60 Q); the call of Matthew (Matt. 9:9–13; = Mark 2:13–17; in Mark the name is Levi; →Matthew); the question about fasting (Matt. 9:14–17; = Mark 2:18–22). These two episodes follow the healing of the paralytic in both Mark and Matthew. Matthew is combining the two themes of miracles and discipleship. Overarching these two themes is the further theme of Jesus' authority, which had been enunciated in 7:29. This combination of themes prepares readers for the commissioning of the disciples in 9:36–11:1. They will extend Jesus' messianic words and deeds further afield.

Matthew achieves his editorial purpose by providing a new context for his materials, by abbreviating his sources, by additions, and by internal modifications. We will examine the two most significant episodes in this section, namely, the stilling of the storm (8:23–27) and the paralytic (9:1–8).

8:23–27, The Stilling of the Storm. Notice the context in which Matthew has placed this episode, namely, immediately after the story of the would-be disciples. The two units are linked together by the catchword "follow." In 8:22 Jesus challenges the second would-be disciple: *"follow* me, and leave the dead to bury their

dead" (8:22). Then at the beginning of the next unit we are told that the disciples *"followed"* Jesus into the boat (8:23). This suggests that the journey across the sea is a parable for the journey of discipleship. The "little ship" (as so often in the writings of the early church fathers) is a symbol for the church. The storm, described in apocalyptic terms as an earthquake, becomes a symbol for the tribulations of Matthew's community: its expulsion from the synagogue, the trauma of the admission of Gentiles, the persecution by the Roman authorities. Matthew cuts down the story to the bare minimum, drawing our attention away from the miracle as such to its symbolic meaning. The description of the storm is abbreviated. We are simply told that Jesus was asleep (nothing about Mark's famous cushion!). The disciples address Jesus not as "Master," but as "Lord," the title of majesty by which he was known in the church. As so often in Matthew, Jesus reproaches the disciples for their "puny" faith. This is what was wrong with Matthew's church: its faith was not strong enough to face up to the apocalyptic tribulations through which it was passing. Finally, the disciples' concluding response is slightly reworded: "What kind of person is this?" Matthew thus prepares for the answer that will come in the second crossing of the lake: "God's Son" (14:33). Thus, once more the disciples in the ship symbolize Matthew's church, which confesses Jesus as the Son of God.

9:1–8, The Paralytic. Matthew reduces the story by four verses (cf. Mark 2:1–12). All non-essentials, even the elaborate demonstration of the four friends' faith, are cut out. The miracle recedes into the background and everything is concentrated on the declaration of the remission of the sick man's sins. The scribes' objection is reduced to the lapidary statement, "This fellow is blaspheming" (Matt. 9:3). Above all, the choric ending is reworded to refer not to the miracle, as in Mark 2:12, but to Jesus' pronouncement of absolution. The scribes were amazed that such authority was given to "human beings" (the same word that occurred in the choric ending of the stilling of the storm in reference to the disciples in the ship, symbolizing Matthew's church). Here is the point of Matthew's editing: Jesus' authority to remit sins devolves upon the church, as will be made clear in 18:18.

9:36–11:1

The Mission of the Twelve

Mark and Q each contained a mission of disciples during the Galilean ministry of Jesus (Mark 6:6–13; Luke 10:1–12 Q). That such a mission (perhaps even several) took place during Jesus' lifetime is probable. It has multiple attestation (Mark, Q, and perhaps M). The instruction to take the minimum of equipment is consistent with Jesus' itinerant radicalism. The terms of the commission (to preach the kingdom, rather than Jesus as the saving act of God) are pre- rather than post-Easter.

Matthew has combined material from the Marcan and Q versions of the charge. Unlike Mark, Q gives the content of the message (Matt. 10:7; = Luke 9:2).

Matthew has removed some of the sayings from the discourse about the End in Mark 13 and placed them here. He has also added sayings from M (10:5, 23). Thus he has shaped a second major discourse.

The charge consists of the following items: an exhortation to prayer for laborers for the harvest (9:36–38); the commissioning of the Twelve with a list of their names (10:1–4); instructions on the content of their message (10:5–8); directions concerning the equipment they are to take with them (10:9–10); their behavior in towns/houses (10:11–16); the prospect of persecution (10:17–25); the cost of discipleship (10:26–39); and the rewards of discipleship (10:40–42). The usual concluding formula marks the end of the discourse (11:1), thus indicating that it is the second of five major discourses.

Thus far we have seen that Matthew's primary concern is not a biography or history of Jesus but a manual for the church of his day. The puzzle of the missionary charge is that the earlier part, down to 10:23, seems irrelevant to the conditions of Matthew's community. The minimal equipment the disciples are to take with them was suited to itinerant charismatics in Palestine but hardly to the Evangelist's settled community. Even more difficult is the restriction of the mission to Israel (10:5, M), a restriction that in any case is lifted at the end of the Gospel (28:19) and from which Matthew's own community had successfully emancipated itself in its recent history. Then there is the unfulfilled promise of 10:23 (also M). Is Matthew deliberately trying to "historicize"— i.e., to reconstruct how things actually were in Jesus' time, a time very different from his own? Is Matthew just a conservative editor content simply to preserve traditions even when they have lost their relevance? Perhaps Matthew was more aware of the difference between Jesus' time and his own than modern scholars give him credit for. Perhaps he believed that this charge containing sayings that were designed for very different situations from his own still has something relevant to say. Perhaps missionaries still go out from Matthew's community, and their requirement of a minimum of baggage is meant to symbolize the urgency of the mission. Perhaps Matthew's community needs reminding that, although

they have turned toward the Gentiles, they must not give up on Israel. And what about the coming of the Son of man before the completion of the mission to Israel? Perhaps Matthew still felt that this promise provided an incentive to urgency in mission not only to Israel, but also to the Gentiles. In any case, the changes he has made make the discourse relevant to his own community. Note especially the predictions of persecution, transferred from the "little apocalypse" (Mark 13), and of division in households from Q (Luke 12:51–53). These were real experiences in Matthew's community.

PART THREE: 11:2–16:20
Israel's Unbelief and the Disciples' Incipient Faith

In Part Three, the hostility of Jesus' opponents (the Baptist movement, the Galilean cities, the relatives of Jesus) develops, and gradually Jesus extricates his disciples from Israel and welds them into a "church." This part not only intends to narrate in a historicizing way what happened in the lifetime of Jesus but to reflect the recent history of Matthew's community. This community likewise had experienced the hostility of the synagogue and had been forced to withdraw and constitute itself a distinct community with its own confession of Jesus as the Messiah (→ Messiah) and the Son of the living God (cf. 14:33; 16:16).

11:2–19
John the Baptist

The first opponents Matthew has in mind are the continuing disciples of John the Baptist. Matthew adapts four units about the Baptist from Q: the answer to John (Matt. 11:2–6; = Luke 7:18–23); Jesus' testimony about the Baptist (Matt. 11:7–11; = Luke 7:24–28); the saying about the kingdom (Matt. 11:12; = Luke 16:16) to which further sayings peculiar to Matthew are appended (Matt. 11:13–15); and finally, the parable of the children in the market place (Matt. 11:16–19; = Luke 7:31–35). As a result, Matthew has produced a minidiscourse on the Baptist. This is not one of his major discourses, for it lacks the standard concluding formula (cf. Matt. 11:1).

This minidiscourse puts the Baptist firmly in his place. He is only the forerunner of Jesus the Messiah, not the final emissary of God before the End. The message that Jesus has proclaimed (chaps. 5–7) and the works he has performed (chaps. 8–9), both of which were continued by the Twelve in chap. 10, show that Jesus is indeed the coming One to whom the Baptist has pointed (first unit). Jesus' testimony to the Baptist equates him with the return of Elijah, one who stands on the frontier of the coming Reign of God. Consequently even the most insignificant person in that kingdom is greater than John (second unit). John was like the children playing at funerals, for he preached judgment and repentance. Jesus brought the good news of the promised salvation and was like the children playing at weddings (fourth unit).

The minidiscourse is climaxed by the saying "But wisdom has been vindicated by her works" (11:19). To figure out what Matthew means by this we must look at the Lucan parallel (which is presumably identical with Q): "wisdom has been vindicated by all her children." In the Lucan or Q version, wisdom had sent a series of envoys ("children"); John the Baptist and Jesus were the last of the series. By substituting "her works" for "all her children," Matthew downgrades the Baptist. The works are exclusively the works of the Messiah (cf. Matt. 11:2), who is not just the last in the series of wisdom's envoys but the final agent of wisdom.

11:20–27
Judgment and Jubilation

After the woes on the Galilean cities (11:20–24; = Luke 10:13–15 Q), which highlight the failures in Jesus' Galilean ministry and indicate the growing opposition to his message, comes the cry of jubilation that already in Q (Luke 10:21–22) followed the woes on the cities and that initiates the process in which Jesus turns his back on unrepentant Israel and begins to form a new community of disciples. The unrepentant are ironically characterized as the "wise and understanding"; "the immature" are Jesus' disciples.

11:28–30
The Savior's Appeal

This saying is not found in Luke, but is so closely tied in location and theme to the cry of jubilation that it seems quite probable that it already stood here in Q (if not, it must be from M). Both cry and appeal present Jesus as wisdom's spokesperson. In the cry of jubilation, the Son reveals the Father (v. 27). To reveal God is the function of wisdom in the OT and in early Judaism (→Wisdom). Still more striking is the parallel between the appeal of vv. 28–30 and wisdom's invitation in Sir. 51:23–27. This helps to make sense of the appeal. On the face of it, it would seem arrogant for Jesus to invite people

to come to him, to promise them refreshment, and to claim that he himself was gentle and humble in heart (shades of Uriah Heep!) or that his yoke was kindly and his load light. But the moment we realize that it is not Jesus speaking in his own capacity but wisdom speaking through him, everything falls into place. Jesus is not personally identified with wisdom, as the prologue of John identifies him with the Logos or Word, or as the Son in that Gospel speaks of himself as a divine being who had been preexistent. Matthew knows nothing of this higher Christology.

12:1–50
Growing Hostility

At this point, Matthew returns to Mark's story line and will continue to follow it closely. He will for the most part omit only what he has already used such as the miracle stories and other incidents in chaps. 8–9 and in the appointment and mission of the Twelve in chap. 10. As before, Matthew abbreviates Mark's stories, cutting the individual units down to the bare essentials. But he also adds significant materials from other sources (Q and M). With these changes he creates a new story line, different from Mark's and serving his editorial purposes. In this section, Matthew traces the growing hostility between Jesus and his critics, a hostility that foreshadows church-synagogue relations in Matthew's own day.

12:1–8, The Plucking of the Grain. Here Matthew adds three verses (vv. 5–7) reinforcing the justification for the disciples' breach of the Sabbath. First comes a saying recalling the Stephen (→Stephen) circle's controversies over the Temple (vv. 5–6). "Something greater than the Temple" means for Matthew the presence of Jesus, who is Immanuel, God with us (cf. v. 41). Next comes the quotation from Hos. 6:6 already used in Matt. 9:13 and therefore representing Matthew's own redaction. The effect is to provide Matthew's community with further ammunition in its own controversies with the synagogue. The Sabbath is meant not for ritualistic observance but for humanitarian deeds, in other words, for the love command.

12:9–14, The Man with the Withered Hand. Matthew slightly shortens this story from Mark 3:1–6 and then adds a Q saying (Matt. 12:11–12; = Luke 14:5) together with a concluding statement (Matt. 12:12b) that summarizes teaching found elsewhere in the Gospel tradition.

12:15–21, Summary of Healings. Matthew has drastically shortened this Marcan summary (Mark 3:7–12), then added to it an extensive fulfillment citation (Matt. 12:18–21 from Isa. 42:1–4). This servant song (→Servant) expresses two important points in Matthew's theology: first, Jesus is the gentle or meek One who deals tenderly with his own (cf. Matt. 11:28–30); second, Jesus' ministry will later open up the mission to the Gentiles, which has been temporarily prohibited in the missionary charge (10:5–6).

12:22–37, The Beelzebul Controversy. In Mark this episode was simply an abstract debate between Jesus and the Pharisees. Matthew, however, prefaces it with an exorcism, following Q. The debate occurs both in Mark and Q, and Matthew, as often, conflates the two accounts. Matthew also appropriates material from elsewhere in Q about the good and bad trees (v. 33) and the saying about the idle word (vv. 36–37) either from his own version—different from Luke's—of Q or from M. The effect is to enhance the anti-Pharisaic polemic and to provide further ammunition for Matthew's controversy with the synagogue.

12:38–42, The Sign of Jonah. Following Q, Matthew places the demand for a sign immediately after the Beelzebul controversy but alters it significantly. The sign of Jonah is not just his preaching but his deliverance from the belly of the whale, seen as a type of the death and resurrection of Jesus, who is greater than Jonah. Matthew's synagogue opponents ("this generation") have been confronted by this sign, the Christian preaching of Christ crucified and risen, but have refused conversion.

12:43–45, The Return of the Evil Spirit. This came at the end of the Beelzebul controversy in Q (= Luke 11:24–26). By placing it here, Matthew makes the saying a further judgment against "this generation," i.e., the synagogue. Post-Jamnia legalism has made the last state of the house of Judaism worse than the first when it originally rejected Jesus.

12:46–50, Jesus' Earthly Family. In Mark (Mark 3:20–21, 31–35) this episode is treated in a highly negative way: Jesus' earthly family is there repudiated at the expense of his new family, the disciples. Matthew has modified this tradition. Mark had introduced the approach of Jesus' kinsfolk *before* the Beelzebul controversy: they were coming to fetch him because they thought he had gone mad. They were as opposed to Jesus as were the Pharisees. Matthew omits this earlier part. The family members approach Jesus *after* the Beelzebul section. They merely wanted to speak to him. Thus Jesus' statement about his new family loses its polemical thrust. The contrast between the two families is toned down in a manner consistent with Mary's positive role in the birth narrative.

13:1–52
The Parable Discourse

Following Mark's story line, Matthew reaches Mark's parables chapter (Mark 4:1–34). Matthew uses this material as the basis for his third major discourse, which concludes with his standard formula (Matt. 13:53). As before, Matthew adapts his Marcan materials to suit his editorial purposes. The sower and its allegorical interpretation remain almost intact, apart from stylistic alterations (13:1–9, 18–23), but the difficult intervening section about the purpose of parables is significantly modified and expanded (see below). A Q saying on the blessedness of the eyewitnesses is also inserted between the parable and its allegorical interpretation. Mark's unit on the right use of parables (Mark 4:21–25) is reduced to a single verse, since the omitted material occurs elsewhere in Matthew (Matt. 5:15; 7:2; 10:26). These omissions are curious, for Matthew is not generally averse to repeating himself, as we have seen in the case of the saying on divorce (5:31–32; 19:9). For Mark's parable of the seed growing secretly (Mark 4:26–29), Matthew substitutes the parable of the wheat and the tares (from M), to which he will later give an allegorical interpretation composed by himself (Matt. 13:36–43). He then inserts between this parable and its interpretation two further parables, namely, the mustard seed (Matt. 13:31–32 from Mark 4:30–32) and the leaven from Q (Matt. 13:33; = Luke 13:20–21), followed by Mark's concluding summary to his parable collection (Matt. 13:34; = Mark 4:33–34). At this point he inserts a fulfillment citation from Ps. 78:2 (Matt. 13:35). He then concludes the parable discourse with three further parables, the twin parables of the hidden treasure and the pearl of great price, plus the dragnet, all of them from M. Then he adds a final parabolic saying about a householder who brings out of his treasure things new and old. This provides an interesting clue to Matthew's understanding of what he was doing throughout his Gospel (see below).

In his two previous chapters, Matthew has been tracing the growing hostility of the people (representing the synagogue of Matthew's day) and the gradual emergence of the disciples as a distinct entity, foreshadowing Matthew's own church. The changes Matthew has made to his Marcan source serve these same themes.

The parables reveal the mysteries (so v. 11 in place of Mark's singular "mystery"). Mark meant by it the mystery of Jesus' messiahship. For Matthew as for Luke (Luke 8:10) what is at stake in the parables is not the messiahship of Jesus, which with the infancy narratives is known from the start, but the revealed truths about God's purpose in salvation history. For Matthew these are judgment for Israel now, salvation for the Gentiles now, and judgment of the lawless members of the church at the End. These mysteries are set out in the parable discourse. The lawless within the church are the false prophets, i.e., those condemned in the allegorical interpretation to the parable of the wheat and tares. There were doubtless people in Matthew's community who were opposed to the mission to the Gentiles and people who wanted to oust from the church those Gentiles who wanted to abandon the Torah altogether, even in its Christian interpretation. The answer is "Let both [the Jewish and Gentile Christians] grow together until harvest time" (i.e., the final judgment, Matt. 13:30). Meanwhile, Matthew's church is to remain a mixed body of wheat (those who live up to the better righteousness) and tares (those who fall short).

In this chapter, the Evangelist is acting as a scribe trained for God's Reign (v. 52) who brings out of his cupboard things new (the Matthean redaction) and old (the Jesus parables as told by himself and as preserved in the tradition).

Finally, we should note how differently Matthew portrays the disciples compared with Mark. In Mark, they constantly misunderstood Jesus (see esp. Mark 8:21), whereas in Matthew they understand all the parables without difficulty (see Matt. 13:51!). Similarly, Matthew expects his church will be able to comprehend God's purposes in salvation history once they have been explained to them, whereas it is the synagogue that will be blinded (→ Parables).

13:53–16:20
Israel's Unbelief and the Disciples' Incipient Faith

This section is based on Mark 6:1–8:30, which already had overtones of the theme Matthew develops, namely, the welding of the disciples into a community (cf. the feeding of the multitude and the dismissal of the crowd, the separation of the disciples and period of foreign travel culminating in the confession of Peter at Caesarea Philippi). However, this last episode is not so decisive for Matthew, for the disciples have already recognized Jesus as the Son of God in Matt. 14:33, while his death and resurrection had already been foretold in the Jonah saying in 12:40.

In following Mark's story line, Matthew skips from the end of the parable chapter (Mark 4:34) to the rejection at Nazareth (Mark 6:1). This is because the intervening miracles had already been used in chaps. 8–9.

13:53–58, Rejection at Nazareth. Here Matthew makes four notable changes in Mark's account. First, he speaks of "*their*" (Mark: "the")

synagogue, indicating the recent separation of synagogue and church. Second, whereas in Mark the people call Jesus "the carpenter, the son of Mary," Matthew has them ask, "Is not this the carpenter's son? Is not his mother said to be Mary?" (13:55). These changes are surprising since Mark's version would seem to be more consistent with the virginal conception, which Matthew and Luke feature but not Mark. We should recall, however, that Joseph's adoption of Jesus was important to Matthew (it made Jesus a son of David), an idea that was not inconsistent with the virginal conception since in the social world of Judaism adoption was understood quite realistically and with it went the acquisition of ancestors. The third change from Mark is that Matthew omits the reference to Jesus' relatives from the list of those who joined in rejecting him. This again is consistent with the earlier portrayal of Jesus' earthly family (see commentary above on 12:46–50). Matthew is concerned to reduce the hostility of Jesus' family toward him to an attitude of neutrality (Luke makes it positively favorable). The fourth change is that whereas Mark states that Jesus *could* do no miracle in Nazareth, Matthew simply notes that he "did" no miracle there. Matthew wants to heighten his portrait of Jesus: it was his free choice as the divine agent to do no miracles there.

Finally, it should be noted that by placing this episode immediately after the parables, with their judgment on Jesus' opponents, the impact of the rejection at Nazareth is strengthened.

14:1–2, Herod's Opinion of Jesus. This unit continues the theme of Jesus' rejection and prepares the way for the disciples' confession of him as Messiah and Son of God. Matthew drops Mark's allusion to what others are saying, and concentrates on Herod's assertion that Jesus must be the Baptist raised from the dead.

14:3–12, Herod Executes John. An abbreviated version of the Baptist's execution foreshadows the culmination of Jesus' rejection in his crucifixion.

14:13–21, First Feeding. In Mark (6:30–31) this feeding took place during the disciples' postmission retreat. Matthew places it immediately after the account of the Baptist's death: it was because Jesus heard of that that he went into retreat. Matthew has Jesus perform healings at this point. Further, he stresses the role of the disciples in distributing the provisions to the crowds (Matt. 14:19)—their function has a dignity of its own. The Evangelist also conforms the account of the blessing of the loaves to the institution narrative in the Last Supper. The loaf miracle foreshadows the church's Eucharist.

14:22–33, Walking on the Water. In Mark (6:45–52) the story of the walking (of Jesus) on the water was presented as a misunderstood epiphany. Matthew changes it by inserting a Petrine scene (14:28–32) between Jesus' self-manifestation (14:27) and the conclusion (14:33). This is the first of three such scenes involving Peter (cf. 16:17–19; 17:24–27). When Jesus says, "It is I. Have no fear!" Peter calls out from the boat, "If it's you, Lord, command me to come to you upon the waters" (14:28). Jesus thereupon invites him to come. Peter sets out but loses confidence and starts sinking, crying out, "O Lord, rescue me" (v. 30). Jesus stretches out his hand, grasps him, and reproaches him for his puny faith and for giving way to doubt. Jesus and Peter get into the boat. Instead of reacting, as in Mark, with incomprehension, the whole crew confesses Jesus as Son of God. There is a partial parallel to this scene in John 21:7–8, which suggests that it is pre-Matthew tradition and in origin a postresurrectional appearance. Peter's doubt and the disciples' confession of faith in Jesus as Son of God would fit in with an Easter setting.

As before (see commentary above on 8:23–27) the boat symbolizes Matthew's church. Here the disciples represent the church's leadership. They have been demoralized by the recent events in the community (expulsion from the synagogue; influx of Gentiles, the intrusion of false prophets). But the risen Lord is stretching out his hand to restore their morale.

14:34–36, Transition. As a transition to the discourse on purity, Matthew inserts a generalizing summary of Jesus' healings (14:34–36), an abbreviated version of Mark 6:53–56.

15:1–20, Discourse on Purity. Matthew takes up the next unit in Mark, abbreviates, rearranges, rewords it, and adds fresh material. Whereas Mark was writing for a gentile community, Matthew was writing for a community that was primarily Jewish. Consequently, he drops Mark's explanation of the purity regulations as unnecessary for his community. The clue to Matthew's other changes lies in his omission of Mark's comment "pronouncing all foods pure" (Mark 7:19). Matthew boggles at the abandonment of the kosher laws and, by adding "mouth" in 15:11 and 17, restricts the scope of Jesus' attack on the tradition of purity laws to contaminated foods. Also, by reversing the order of the discussions of hand-washing and corban (offerings dedicated to God), the Evangelist makes the gravamen of Jesus' charge against the Pharisees and scribes their neglect of the love command. Matthew further inserts a vehement attack on Jesus' opponents (vv. 12–14), who of course represent the synagogue leaders of his own day. They are blind guides who have forfeited their teaching authority. His advice is, "Ignore them!" (v. 14).

15:21–28, The Canaanite Woman. The next episode in the Marcan source is the Syrophoenician woman. Again, Matthew introduces a number of changes. The woman is now a Canaanite. The actual healing of the woman's daughter is reduced to a brief statement of the fact (v. 28c; cf. Mark 7:30). Thus, the emphasis is thrown upon Jesus' dialogues. First, there is a new preliminary dialogue between Jesus and his disciples (Matt. 15:23–24). Jesus is made to represent the earlier, strict Jewish Christian point of view that the mission was confined to the (lost) sheep of the house of Israel. Matthew assures his Jewish Christians that the difference between Jew and Gentile must be taken very seriously. (Matthew is no starry-eyed dreamer who thinks that human differences do not matter.) It is only the redeeming work of Christ and the human response of faith that can overcome that barrier. But the barrier can be overcome. That is something Matthew's Jewish Christians must now realize.

15:29–31, Summary of Healings. Matthew replaces Mark's healing of the deaf mute (Mark 7:31–37) with a generalized summary of healings. These healings take place in gentile territory. They are thus intended as a bridge between the story of the Canaanite woman and the feeding of the four thousand (15:32–39), which already in Mark was probably intended to symbolize the church's ministry to Gentiles. Note that Jesus goes up to the (sic; not "a") mountain and that he sits there. This recalls the opening of the Sermon on the Mount and the fact that Matthew intends to portray Jesus as the new Moses. Thus, he is assuring his Jewish Christians that the mission to the Gentiles has the backing of the new Moses. Also, each feeding is preceded by multiple healings (14:14).

15:32–39, Second Feeding. As in the first feeding, Matthew makes a number of minor changes from his Marcan source. These changes emphasize the role of the disciples and recall the institution of the Eucharist. This is the Eucharist for the Gentiles as the first feeding was for the Jewish Christians. Did Matthew envisage a separate Eucharist for his gentile members, such as happened at Antioch after the fracas in Paul's time (Gal. 2:11–14)? Or does the Evangelist intend to say that the Gentiles have now been admitted to the one Eucharist? Maybe the latter, for he assimilates the two feedings. The Eucharist, which had previously been confined to Jewish Christians, is now opened up to gentile converts.

16:1–4, The Demand for a Sign. In the Marcan parallel (Mark 8:12) the refusal of the sign was absolute. Here an exception is made, namely, the sign of Jonah. A cross reference to Matt. 12:38–40 is clearly intended. There we saw that the sign of Jonah was his being swallowed and regurgitated by the great fish, a type of the death and resurrection of Jesus. Matthew is continuing his anti-Pharisaic polemic. This evil generation (unbelieving Israel) had ignored that sign, and judgment had fallen upon it in the fall of Jerusalem.

16:5–12, The Leaven of the Pharisees and Sadducees. For this minidiscourse Matthew again follows Mark. But once more he has made a number of changes. For Mark's "Herod" (Mark 8:15) he substitutes "Sadducees" (cf. Matt. 16:1). This is a little surprising since Matthew was writing at a time when the Sadducees had disappeared after the Jewish war of A.D. 66–70 and were no longer a threat to Matthew's church. Maybe he sees the synagogue of his day as the heirs of all the traditions of Judaism, including that of the Temple, and it is meant as a general denunciation of the synagogue authorities of his day. The treatment of the disciples in this episode differs noticeably from that of the Marcan source. In Mark (8:17–21), the disciples fail completely to comprehend and are hardened in heart. Matthew omits most of the reproach of the disciples, leaving only the words "do you not yet understand?" and showing that they will eventually do so. Once again the real problem is the disciples' puny faith (Matthew inserts the words "O you of little faith" in 16:8). The whole passage is enigmatic, and Matthew does not seem to have made it much clearer. What have the two feedings to do with the teaching of the Pharisees and Sadducees? What teaching has Matthew in mind? Perhaps he is thinking of that exclusiveness that would deny the possibility of Jews and Gentiles sitting down at the one table, a possibility that many of Matthew's own Jewish Christians were reluctant to admit. Note that Matthew adds to Mark the assertion that the disciples did, in fact, come to understand what Jesus meant (v. 12).

16:13–20, Peter's Confession. Matthew omits the healing of the blind man at Bethesda (Mark 8:22–26). Our Evangelist has seen that for Mark this story symbolized the disciples' blindness—and Matthew's disciples are not blind, they are only deficient in faith. So Matthew passes straight from his notice about the disciples' understanding to the confession of Peter. This confession is thus seen in a highly positive light. The disciples are well on their way to understanding Jesus. The changes Matthew has made to Mark 8:27–30 are in accord with this.

The first change is to replace "me" in Jesus' opening question with "Son of man" (→ Son of man). If Son of man were a messianic title, this would make no sense. Jesus would simply be answering his own question! If, however, we understand Son of man as a self-effacing definition of Jesus' call, mission, and destiny, it does make sense. Jesus is saying to the disciples, "Given what you know about me, what you know of my calling, my activity, and the course of my ministry thus far, what is your understanding of my identity?"

We come now to the second Petrine insertion (16:16b–19). It reads: ". . . Son of the living God. In response, Jesus said to him, 'You are blessed, Simon son of Jonah, for flesh and blood did not reveal it to you but my Father, the One in the heavens. And I tell you, you are Peter (Rock), and on this Rock I will build my end-time community, and the gates of Hades will not overpower it. I will give you the keys of the Reign of the heavens, and whatever you bind on earth God will bind in the heavens, and whatever you loose on earth God will loose in the heavens.' " This passage seems to draw on traditions similar to the earlier Petrine assertion in 14:28–30. Both contain echoes of the resurrection appearance to Peter (cf. 1 Cor. 15:5; Luke 24:34; John 21:15–19). The Beatitude to Peter as the recipient of a revelation also suggests a postresurrectional encounter. It was the appearance to Peter, the first of the series, that constituted him in person as the Rock on which the church was built. Peter took the all-important step of reassembling the Twelve and thereby founding the church. "Church" means the end-time people of God, a meaning underlined by the promise that the power of death cannot overcome it. Peter too was given the power of the keys (cf. Isa. 22:15–22), the authority to bind and loose, to admit or exclude people from the community, to grant or withhold baptism.

Matthew has relocated this tradition in the earthly life of Jesus and, in doing so, transformed its meaning. The binding and loosing now refer to the authority to expound the better righteousness. (On the authority of church leadership in Matthew's community, see the Short Essay "The Church in Matthew.")

Peter's confession is not the turning point of Matthew's Gospel as it was for Mark. The disciples have already confessed Jesus as Son of God in Matt. 14:33. In Mark, Peter's confession was ignored by Jesus, who after charging him with strict silence went at once to reveal his intent to go up to Jerusalem and face death and subsequent resurrection. Matthew separates the ensuing prediction of the Passion by the words "From then." This marks not only the division between two units but also the end of the major section of his work and the beginning of a new one.

PART FOUR: 16:21–20:34

The Journey to Jerusalem

In this part, Matthew follows Mark's story line very closely, except that he makes a major division at 16:21 with the opening words "From then." Matthew is concerned with the disciples overcoming their puny faith, while Mark was concerned with their failure to understand. In fact, Matthew has his eye on the situation in his own community during the 90s of the first century. He also seeks to consolidate his community into a well-organized church, with its own standards of discipline. This concern is especially prominent in the "community discourse" of chap. 18, which is the major feature of Part Four.

16:21–23

First Passion Prediction

In Mark, the first passion prediction (Mark 8:31) was closely tied to Peter's confession and stood in sharp contrast to it: at one moment Peter confesses Jesus as Messiah, and in the next moment he deprecates Jesus' insistence that as Messiah he must suffer as the Son of man. Instead of rebuking Jesus, Peter in Matthew says, "May God in his mercy spare you this fate" (v. 22), a much milder reaction. Yet Matthew surprisingly enhances Jesus' retort: "You are a stumbling block to me" (v. 23). As will become clear later in this section, it is not that Peter misunderstands, as in Mark, but that his faith is meager: it is Peter's puny faith that is the stumbling block.

16:24–28

The Cost of Discipleship

This teaching is addressed exclusively to the disciples, not to the crowd as well (as in Mark). In Matthew, the crowd represents the synagogue across the street, and this teaching is aimed exclusively at Matthew's church. Matthew omits Mark's words "and the gospel's" from the phrase "for my sake" and drops the saying about fearless confession (Mark 8:38), thus concentrating on the theme of the last judgment when each (disciple) will be rewarded according to his or her praxis of the better righteousness (Matt. 16:27) at the coming of the Son of man. Matthew is writing for a settled community, rather than for a group of wandering charismatic preachers, which Mark still envisages. Finally, Matthew changes Mark's predication of the "coming of the kingdom in power" to a promise of the Parousia or Second Coming: "Amen, I say to you, there are some of those standing here who shall not taste of death until they see the *Son of man coming in his kingly rule*" (v. 28). Since Mat-

thew was writing at a time (around A.D. 90) when most, if not all, the original disciples would have died already and before the Parousia, we must suppose that "some" refers either to the one or two who are still surviving or, more likely, to the church of Matthew's own day. Matthew believes that the Second Coming will occur within the lifetime of a few of *his* generation: it has been postponed, but not indefinitely. And Jesus, the Son of man, will return not as their advocate (so Mark), but as the *judge* of their moral behavior. This fits in with Matthew's teaching in the parables of the tares (see above), the ten maidens, the talents, and the sheep and goats (see below).

17:1–8

The Transfiguration

As we have seen, Matthew is concerned to portray Jesus as a Moses-like figure. This motif is enhanced by the changes he makes to Mark's version of this unit (Mark 9:2–8). In Matt. 17:2 he calls attention to the *face* of Jesus: it shone like the sun (cf. Moses, Exod. 34:29–30—though the sun is not mentioned there). Matthew has used this motif from Matt. 13:43 where it describes the transfiguration of the righteous at the end. In Mark, Moses tags along with Elijah (Mark 9:4), whereas in Matthew he appears first. Later on, after the voice from heaven, Matthew adds two verses (17:6–7) describing the disciples' reaction of fear. Seeing them, Jesus approached them, touched them, and commanded them to arise and not be afraid. This latter verse is strikingly reminiscent of the resurrection appearances and suggests that the transfiguration points forward to the resurrection as well as to the Second Coming. Thus, the scene reinforces the lessons of the preceding unit about discipleship: Matthew's church is to stand under the sovereignty of the risen Lord who is the second Moses and lawgiver to his church and who will come at the end to judge that church according to its praxis of the new or better righteousness (→ Transfiguration, The).

17:9–13

Dialogue During the Descent

Most of Matthew's changes from Mark are made to improve the organization of the passage, but there is one significant change. In Mark, the disciples' reaction to the teaching about Elijah/John the Baptist is unnoticed, thus creating the impression that they failed to understand, whereas Matthew adds a verse to show that the disciples did indeed understand that Jesus was referring to John the Baptist (cf. 11:14). Their problem is not misunderstanding and perplexity, but insufficient faith.

17:14–21
The Epileptic Boy

As before (see chaps. 8–9), Matthew abbreviates this miracle story but expands the element of teaching. This he does in v. 20, which develops Matthew's favorite theme of faith: "He said to them, 'It was because of your inadequate faith [that you could not heal him].' " On the one hand, Matthew drops the poignant dialogue between Jesus and the boy's father in which the father struggles to overcome his unbelief; on the other hand, Matthew shifts the focus to the disciples' meagerness of faith and adds the saying about faith moving mountains, which occurs in Mark and Q and which Matthew typically conflates (v. 20; 21:21 = Mark 11:22–23; Luke 17:6 Q).

17:22–23
Second Passion Prediction

Matthew's changes in the actual prediction (cf. Mark 9:31) are minimal and merely stylistic. But the reaction of the disciples is altered significantly. In Mark, we are told that they failed to understand the utterance and were afraid to ask him (what it meant). In Matthew, however, they were "greatly distressed." They understood only too well: their problem once more was lack of faith.

17:24–27
The Temple Tax

This unit is peculiar to Matthew. Indeed, the style and phraseology suggest that Matthew has composed the whole unit himself. However, there are signs that he has used earlier tradition. The issue (payment of the Temple tax) could only have arisen prior to A.D. 70, for after the destruction of the Temple, the tax was diverted to the imperial treasury. Also the incident presupposes that the Christian Jews are still part of the Jewish community. The command to Peter to go fishing also recalls the tradition enshrined in Luke 5:1–11 and John 21:1–14. Matthew has inserted this unit in a context provided by Mark 9:33 (Capernaum, the house). Here Jesus, ostensibly traveling from Caesarea Philippi to Jerusalem, turns up again in Capernaum. (Jesus' itinerary is a problem for the study of Mark rather than for Matthew: Matthew is simply following his source.) We can see two reasons why Matthew should have put the episode here. First, the tax theme was already associated with Capernaum (see Matt. 9:1, 9–13 and cf. 4:13). Second, it forms a transition to the ensuing community discourse (chap. 18) since it is a rule for the life of the community. The story has a threefold structure: first, the setting—Peter and the tax collectors; second, Jesus' pronouncement;

third, the fish/coin miracle (if, indeed, it is meant to be a miracle; we are not told that it actually happened).

The point of the story lies in the pronouncement. Roman citizens were exempt from taxation; taxes were paid only by the subject peoples. The disciples are citizens of the kingdom of God and therefore (in principle) free from taxation. But to avoid scandal (cf. Paul's teaching in 1 Cor. 8 and Rom. 14) they should voluntarily comply. They should not flaunt their freedom: to pay the tax does not involve any sacrifice of principle.

18:1–35
The Community Discourse

This is the fourth of Matthew's major discourses, as indicated by the use of the concluding formula (19:1). Like the other Matthean discourses, it is compiled from three sources, namely, Mark, Q, and M. As usual, the context is provided by Mark, who in 9:33–37 records the disciples' dispute about who was the greatest among them. This provides Matthew with the opening of the discourse (Matt. 18:1–5). Matthew then combines this saying with the other Marcan saying about little children (Matt. 18:3–4; = Mark 10:15). Matthew then picks up the warning against "scandals" (offenses) from Mark 9:42–48 and reproduces it in Matt. 18:6–9. He next introduces the Q parable of the lost sheep (Matt. 18:10–14; = Luke 15:3–7), followed with the unit on reproving fellow church members (Matt. 18:15–18), the opening saying of which is from Q (Matt. 18:15; Luke 17:3). The rest of the unit (Matt. 18:16–18) is an elaboration of the first saying, perhaps from M (note in v. 17 the word "church"—Gk. *ekklēsia*—also found in the M addition to Peter's confession; see commentary above on 16:17–19). The saying about binding and loosing (18:18), which in 16:19 is applied to Peter alone, is addressed here to the disciples at large ("bind and loose" are here plurals). See also the introduction (18:1) of the discourse, which shows that it is addressed to "the disciples." Next comes the promise of Christ's presence (18:19–20) from M. The saying about reconciliation from Q (18:21–22 = Luke 17:4) serves as the introduction of the concluding parable of the unmerciful servant, which is from M and does not altogether suit the context in which Matthew has placed it, namely, of repeated forgiveness.

Some have questioned the appropriateness of the title, "Community Discourse" (alternative designations are "Community Rule" or "Church Order") on the ground that, strictly speaking, only 18:15–17 deal with church discipline and that other topics normally found in church orders are missing, such as the appointment and duties of church officers. But since most of it concerns relationships within the community, "Community Discourse" seems a fairly neutral title that does not claim too much.

In our detailed comment we shall confine ourselves to the parables and to selected sayings in the discourse (see also the Short Essay "The Church in Matthew").

18:10–14, The Parable of the Lost Sheep. Luke places this parable in quite a different context than Matthew, using it to justify Jesus' conduct in eating with the outcasts, which is probably the context in which Jesus first told it. Matthew ties it in with church discipline. The lost sheep represents erring fellow Christians. When such a one goes astray (apostatizes), the community must expend every effort to get that person back into the fold. This places a limit on the exercise of church discipline, which is dealt with in the next unit and which, as we shall see, stands in tension with the parable.

18:15–18, Church Discipline. The original Q saying (Matt. 18:15; = Luke 17:3) simply enjoined the forgiveness of an erring church member. We may suppose that Matthew is not responsible for its expansion (18:16–18) but that this had already taken place in the pre-Gospel tradition. It sets up a three-stage process for dealing with refractory members, leading, if the person remains obdurate, to final excommunication.

This drastic outcome seems inconsistent with the point made by the preceding parable of the lost sheep (18:10–14). Is the excommunicated person to be finally given up for lost? Perhaps Matthew intends the parable to modify this ruling, which he found in his strict Jewish Christian source. When persons have been finally excommunicated, the community must spare no effort to win them back.

In its earlier context in 16:19, the saying about binding and loosing referred to doctrinal decisions (see above). Here (18:18) it refers to decisions on matters of church discipline.

Matt. 18:19 is an assurance that God will answer prayer. Such assurances occur frequently in the Jesus tradition, especially in John. This assurance is, therefore, probably authentic in its basic content. It is placed here because church discipline must be exercised in the context of prayer. The promise of Christ's presence, in v. 20, is one of those Jesus sayings that, beyond all doubt, originated in post-Easter Christian prophecy. It is closely akin to the promise of the abiding presence of the risen One in Matt. 28:20, and both sayings are the fulfillment of the Immanuel quotation from Isa. 7:14 in the birth narrative (Matt. 1:23). The saying here closely parallels a rabbinic saying about the Torah: "If two or three sit together

and the words of the Law [are spoken] between them, the Divine Presence [Shekinah] rests between them" (*m. 'Abot* 3:2). How do the disciples gather "in the name of Jesus"? The rabbinic saying helps us to interpret it. The rabbis gathered to study the Torah; Matthew intends his Christians to gather to study the Torah as fulfilled by Jesus. Again, Matthew has his eye on the synagogue "across the street." They think they have the Shekinah—God's presence. Matthew assures his community that it is the risen Christ who is Immanuel, God present with the community. This promise is placed in the context of church discipline. Church discipline must be administered with the prayerful study of Jesus' teaching—as given in the discourses of Matthew's Gospel. In such a context, the decisions of the community will be legally binding.

The saying about forgiveness (Matt. 18:21–22; = Luke 17:4) is accentuated: the offended Christian must forgive the fellow believer seventy-times-seven times, i.e., with no limit. Matthew uses the saying to introduce the parable of the unforgiving servant (not very appropriately, for the point of the parable is rather different: those for whom God has forgiven so much must forgive the relatively minor offense of the erring fellow Christian). In the parable itself, the figures are exaggerated (in a manner typical of Jesus) to the point of absurdity. The exact value of ten thousand talents is uncertain, for it is always difficult to assess the value of ancient coinage. However, it gives us some idea of the amount involved to note that the revenue of Herod's kingdom came to nine hundred talents per annum. The amount owed the unforgiving servant was paltry by comparison—one hundred denarii.

Matthew intends this to be a parable of the Last Judgment—as shown by the chief character, the king, i.e., God (cf. 25:34). Forgiveness for Matthew is the quintessential expression of love (6:14–15). Love must temper even the exercise of power and discipline in the community. In the last analysis, Matthew's community lives not under the law—not even under the Torah as reinterpreted by Jesus—but because of the forgiving grace of God that becomes actual only through the cross (26:28).

The Church in Matthew

Matthew's Gospel has often been called the "ecclesiastical Gospel," for a number of reasons. Matthew is the only Gospel in which the word "church" (Gk. *ekklēsia*) occurs, once in the story of Peter's confession (16:18) and twice in the Community Discourse (18:17). Critical opinion holds that the term "church" did not figure in the teaching of the pre-Easter Jesus: the burden of his message was the coming Reign of God. But since "church" means the end-time people of God, the coming of the church was implicit in his message. After Easter the earliest community very soon (see Acts 5:11; Gal. 1:13, 22) came to understand itself to be the "church of God." Matthew or M has retrojected the word into the pre-Easter tradition.

This concern for the church is exhibited throughout Matthew. The Evangelist's understanding of the church as the true Israel is expressed in many ways: through the fulfillment citations, the treatment of Jesus as a Moses-like figure, the reinterpretation of the Torah in the Sermon on the Mount, the five major discourses corresponding to the Pentateuch, and in Jesus' extrication of the disciples from the earlier Israel and his consolidation of them into a body, which takes place from 13:54 through 19:1. But this foundation of the church is only anticipatory. Its actual foundation is not accomplished until the death and resurrection of the Messiah, when the church's mission is finally launched (28:16–20).

With all this concern for the church, Matthew shows remarkably little interest in its organization under a formal ministry. Although Peter is commissioned in chap. 16 to exercise authority to bind and loose, this authority is extended to "the disciples," i.e., to the whole community, in chap. 18. Peter, however, has certain unique functions that do not devolve on the disciples in chap. 18: he is the prime recipient of divine revelation (16:17, originally in the postresurrectional appearance to him, see above) and as such is the Rock on which the church is to be built (through Jesus' death and resurrection). These unique features are inalienable because they belong to the once-for-all events of salvation history connected with the foundation of the church. No one succeeds Peter in his church-founding functions, whereas the pastoral functions that continue in the church are apparently invested in the community as a whole. If Matthew's Gospel emanated from Antioch (→Antioch), as is widely supposed, this is all the more surprising since a generation later, by the time of Ignatius (ca. A.D. 110), Antioch had a well-organized leadership consisting of a single bishop presiding over a committee of presbyters and assisted by deacons. One would also suppose that Matthew's church, with its strong Jewish roots, already had a presbyterial organization like that of the synagogue from which it sprang (→ Presbyter, Presbytery). One must suppose that if this was so, then Matthew was anxious to portray the presbyters of his community as possessing no inherent authority of their own, but as simply the instruments through which the church exercised the authority that had devolved upon it from the apostles.

Matthew is opposed to any personal claims to authority made by whatever office bearers there may have been in his community: disciplinary decisions have to be made not autocratically but with corporate prayer and study of the teaching of Jesus (chap. 18). Office bearers must not arrogate to themselves personal honors, titles, or privileges, like the scribes and Pharisees (23:8–9): "You are not to be addressed as 'rabbi' for there is one who is your teacher, and you are all brothers and sisters. And do not call anyone your father on earth; for you have one father—the one in heaven." It is hard to suppose that there was no office of teacher (Gk. *didaskalos*, 23:8, or *kathēgētēs*, 23:10) in Matthew's community. What mattered was to distinguish between the person and the office. The office was performed by representatives of the whole community whose task was to point away from themselves to God, the only true teacher and father.

19:1–20:34
The Journey to Jerusalem

Having founded the church (in anticipation), Jesus continues his journey to Judea. He had supposedly set out for there after Peter's confession—see the "from then" in 16:21—but had stopped off at Capernaum en route.

19:1–2, Departure from Judea. Matthew notes that the crowds "followed" Jesus. The crowds are an elastic conception in Matthew. Sometimes they represent the adherents of the synagogue in Matthew's day: here they are the converts to discipleship, at least potentially. Matthew alters Mark's statement that Jesus "taught" them to Jesus "healed" them. The gift of salvation must precede teaching on the Christian way.

19:3–15, On Divorce, Celibacy, and Children. Matthew is following Mark 10:2–12, but with some noteworthy changes. First, as earlier in the discourse on purity (15:1–23), he rearranges the dialogue, placing 19:7–8 after the reference to the original law of creation (contrary to Mark 10:4–5). The effect of this change is to set up an antithesis between Jesus' teaching and that of Moses, like the antitheses of the Sermon on the Mount. Second, Matthew inserts here, as in the Sermon on the Mount (Matt. 5:32), the exceptive clause. He had already prepared the way for this in 19:3. There he changed the Pharisees' question into one with hostile intent and added to it the words "for any reason whatever." This was a matter of dispute among the Pharisees.

Finally, Matthew adds the little dialogue between the disciples and Jesus on the subject of celibacy. Celibacy is permissible for the sake of the Reign of God. This is not the ascetical celibacy of later monasticism, but a renunciation of marriage to devote oneself to the life of a wandering charismatic preacher of the coming End. Thus, eschatological celibacy is comparable to the "military celibacy" at Qumran, which envisaged a time when marriage would be renounced to engage in the final battle between the children of light and the children of darkness. We may reasonably presume that Jesus (and later Paul) practiced eschatological celibacy. For Matthew, such celibacy may be a "higher standard" (see below, next unit). As in Mark, the marriage unit is followed by the blessing of the children (vv. 13–15).

19:16–30, The Rich Young Man. Matthew had difficulty with Mark's opening of this story. This can be seen from a comparison of the two versions:

MARK	MATTHEW
"Good teacher, what shall I do to inherit eternal life?"	"Teacher, what good shall I do to possess eternal life?"
Jesus said: "Why do you call me good? No one is good, but God alone."	But he said to him, "Why do you ask me concerning the good? One is the good."

Matthew shows here the same Christological sensitivity as he showed in the baptism story (see commentary above on 3:14–15). Jesus must not be allowed to appear to deny his own goodness. Nor must he be allowed to draw too sharp a line between himself and God. In enumerating the commandments, Matthew drops "do not defraud" (Mark 10:19), which was not part of the original Decalogue. But he does add the summary of the law "you shall love the neighbor as yourself" from Lev. 19:18. Matthew is probably following the same early Christian catechism followed by Paul in Rom. 13:9, where the command to love one's neighbor similarly sums up the second table of the Decalogue. For Matthew, the love command is the quintessence of the fulfilled Torah.

Another important change is made by Matthew in 19:21:

MARK	MATTHEW
"You are lacking one thing, go, sell all you have ..."	"If you *want to be perfect* go, sell all your property ..."

This alters the whole meaning. In Mark (as for Jesus), selling all one had and giving to the poor was simply a preliminary for the life of a wandering charismatic. For Matthew, in his

settled community, voluntary poverty was a higher form of life. "Perfect" is used in a somewhat different sense from Matt. 5:48. It is a higher standard of Christian life. Commentators usually shrink from this obvious interpretation, but it seems undeniable that we have here the beginning of the double standard as it was developed later in monasticism (see the Short Essay "The Sermon on the Mount Today"). This interpretation is strengthened by its closeness to the previous unit with its teaching on celibacy. The double standard was an adjustment necessitated by the change in the church's social setting. It was the only way to preserve Jesus' requirement of the renunciation of wealth in a totally new situation.

Matthew follows Mark in appending to the story of the rich young man a dialogue between Jesus and the disciples on the danger of riches and the rewards of discipleship (Matt. 19:23–30). He stays close to Mark's wording, though with some abbreviation and stylistic improvement, until v. 28, where he inserts a new saying either from Q (cf. Luke 22:28–30) or from M. Probably Luke's form is more original and is basically an authentic Jesus saying spoken where Luke puts it, at the Last Supper. In Matthew, it is developed in accord with his interest in the picture of the Parousia: Christ will return as the Danielic Son of man and preside over the last judgment (cf. Matt. 13:36–43; 25:31–46), seated on his glorious throne (Dan. 7:9–14). "Regeneration" (Gk. *palingenesia*; → Regeneration) occurs only here in Matthew. It refers to the renewal of the world, the new heaven and earth of the end time. It is equivalent to Matthew's favorite phrase, "the consummation of the aeon" (e.g., 13:39). Since Matthew dropped "twelve" before "thrones," it would seem that he is not thinking of the Twelve but (as in chap. 18) of the whole church. The entire body of the faithful will share with the returning Son of man his function (cf. 1 Cor. 6:2–3) of judging the whole world, including Torah-Israel (the twelve tribes).

20:1–16, The Laborers in the Vineyard. At this point, Matthew inserts into Mark's outline a parable peculiar to his tradition (M). It serves to illustrate 19:30, "Many who are first shall be last, and the last first." This verse is repeated at the end of the parable (20:16) and ties in with the mention of the "first" and "last" in the body of the parable (20:8). Despite its single attestation, this is probably an authentic parable of Jesus, as is shown by the presence of a good deal of local color and by the surprise ending. In his historical situation, Jesus used the parable to interpret his conduct in eating with the outcast; for Matthew's church it would have answered Jewish Christian discomfort with the new mission to the Gentiles.

20:17–34, The Journey to Jerusalem Concluded. Matthew follows Mark fairly closely in the rest of chap. 20. The third passion prediction (20:17–19) has an abbreviated introduction (no fear or amazement of the disciples), while the question of the sons of Zebedee (vv. 20–28) is transferred to their mother. Both changes fit in with Matthew's more favorable view of the disciples compared with Mark's. Mark's healing of blind Bartimaeus becomes the healing of two anonymous blind men. Matthew has a predilection for blind healings in pairs (cf. 9:27–31). The reason for this is not clear. Possibly Matthew wishes to enhance the miraculous element. Possibly he wants to underline the truth of their confession (two witnesses!) of Jesus as the Son of David, one of his favorite Christological themes.

PART FIVE: 21:1–25:46

The Ministry in Jerusalem

Matthew follows Mark in portraying the Jerusalem ministry as Jesus' final confrontation with Torah-Israel and its final judgment. The Evangelist enhances both themes in the light of the fact that this rejection has in his own day reached a new climax with the expulsion of the Christian Jews from the synagogue.

21:1–11
The Entry into Jerusalem

Among the many changes Matthew has made to his Marcan source, three are particularly noteworthy. First, instead of an ass only, Matthew has Jesus ride on a she-ass with her colt. This is to square with the second change, the fulfillment citation in vv. 4–6 (see the Short Essay "Matthew's Fulfillment Citations"). The citation (a combination of Isa. 62:11 and Zech. 9:9) speaks of "the meek king" who comes "riding an ass and a colt, the progeny of a beast of burden." Grammatically, this is what is known as a "hendiadys," a figure of speech in which two nouns are joined with "and" represent a single noun and its modifier. The whole phrase simply means a pack donkey. Matthew, however, has chosen to take the text literally, so keen is he on the fulfillment of detail. The citation sets the keynote of Matthew's presentation of the Passion: Jesus suffers as the meek and humble king (see the Short Essay "The Passion According to Matthew"). Third, the final change occurs in the crowd's acclamation:

> Hosanna to the Son of David,
> Blessed is the One who comes in
> Yahweh's name;
> Hosanna in the heights of heaven.

Matthew has doubtless conformed the acclamation to the liturgical use of his community.

21:12–17
Cleansing of the Temple

In Mark, Jesus concludes his entry by looking around the Temple, withdrawing to Bethany for the night, and returning for the cleansing the next morning. Matthew (like Luke) wants the cleansing to be the goal and climax of the entry. Matthew omits Jesus' declaration that the Temple was to be "for all nations." The Temple had been destroyed by the time Matthew's church launched its mission to the Gentiles, so the prophecy was out of date by then.

21:18–22
Cursing of the Fig Tree

Matthew omits Mark's difficult observation, "for it was not the time for figs," because it makes the cursing unreasonable. Also by Matthew's time the "time of figs" had already passed—for the Jerusalem war of A.D. 66–70 was the final hour of decision for Israel.

21:23–27
The Question of Authority

This challenge follows immediately on the cursing of the fig tree, as in Mark 11:27–33. Matthew then reaches the point where Mark has the parable of the wicked vinedressers (Mark 12:1–12). Matthew is fond of sets of threes, so he has both prefaced and followed the vinedressers with a non-Marcan parable. Thus, the interpretation of the first and third parable depends on the interpretation of the middle parable, the vinedressers, which, as we shall see, is an allegory of salvation history.

21:28–32
Two Sons

The parable of the two sons has some similarity to Luke's story of the prodigal son, and one is tempted to suppose that it is the original form of the longer story. Matthew's short form is most likely an authentic parable of Jesus, the point of which was the contrast between the reaction of the religious authorities to his preaching and that of the outcasts. Matthew could apply the parable to the circumstances of his church without difficulty. The synagogue was like the son who said, "I go," and did not, while the gentile converts in Matthew's community were like those who said, "I will not go," but in the end did.

21:33–46
The Parable of the Wicked Vinedressers

Whatever may have been the earlier history of this parable, in Matthew and Mark it is an allegory of salvation history. The earlier servants stand for the OT prophets, and the son is equated with Jesus as the last of God's emissaries. Matthew coalesces previous emissaries into two groups, representing the Former Prophets and the Latter Prophets of the OT canon (the second group was larger than the first!), thus clarifying the allegory. Matthew notes (21:38a) that the vinedressers "recognized" the son—thus enhancing Israel's guilt. The reversal of the order in v. 39 (cast outside . . . killed) reflects the crucifixion (cf. Heb. 13:12). In Matt. 21:41, Matthew extends salvation history to cover the period since the rejection of the son: God "will destroy those wicked ones with dire punishment and will let out the vineyard to other vinedressers who will produce the fruits for him in their season." Once more Matthew portrays the traumatic experiences of his community: the disaster to Torah-Israel in A.D. 70 and the establishment of the true Israel, which practices the fulfilled Torah of the better righteousness. To drive the point home, Matthew also adds vv. 43 and 45, which repeat the point of the allegory in nonallegorical form (nation instead of vinedressers). He notes in v. 45 that Jesus' audience (the Pharisees, representing the synagogue of Matthew's time) realized that Jesus was directing the parable against them (note esp. that v. 44 is probably an early interpolation from Luke 20:18).

22:1–14
The Great Supper

The parable of the great supper has a parallel in Luke 14:15–24. Matthew's version of it, like the vineyard immediately before it, has been transformed into an allegory of salvation history. The host of the dinner party becomes a king (= God), the dinner a marriage feast for the king's son, i.e., the messianic banquet. In Matt. 22:6–7 we have a highly remarkable scenario. The invited guests murder the king's servants who come to remind them of the invitation: "The rest, seizing his servants, subjected them to abuse and killed them" (v. 6). This is followed by even more drastic action: "The king, infuriated, sent his armies, destroyed those murderers, and set fire to their city" (v. 7). All this would be quite unrealistic in a parable drawn from life, but as an allegory it makes sense: it reflects the events of the Jewish war of A.D. 66–70. Tacked in to the end is part of another parable, the man without a wedding garment (vv. 11–14). This too is quite unrealistic, for the poor man could hardly have been expected to have a wedding garment if he had just been dragged in off the street! Again, it is meant to be taken allegorically: the man represents those Gentiles who have joined Matthew's church as a result of its mission, and it is a protest against their admission on too easy terms. Some of them were sitting loose to the requirements of the Torah, and the wedding garment represents the better righteousness that is expected of all, even gentile Christians.

22:15–46
Four Conflict Stories

At v. 15, Matthew returns to Mark and presents four units in which Jesus is in conflict with his adversaries. They are the tribute money (vv. 15–22); the Sadducees' question (vv. 23–33); the great commandment (vv. 34–40); and the question about David's son (vv. 41–46). Most of Matthew's changes are stylistic, but a few betray the Evangelist's special interests. For instance, he makes the raising of the question of the tribute money a deliberate plot engineered by the Pharisees: they "took counsel to ensnare him in his talk" (v. 15). However, writing at a time when the Sadducees were no longer a threat to his community, Matthew minimizes the hostility of that confrontation. Jesus does not say to them, as in Mark, "you are badly off the tracks" (cf. v. 32 with Mark 12:27). "The Pharisees," not just a single scribe, initiate the question about the great commandment. They come together to do so, evidently with hostile intent (Matt. 22:34). And when their spokesman asks the question he is "putting him [Jesus] to the test" (v. 35). In Mark, the scribe agrees with Jesus' answer and, in fact, elaborates on it himself, whereupon Jesus compliments him for his intelligent response and assures him that he is not far from the kingdom of God (Mark 12:32–34). Matthew drops all this. It is not a friendly encounter but a hostile confrontation that brings out the main issue between church and synagogue: the fulfillment of the Torah in terms of radical love. Finally, in the unit about David's son, Matthew has Jesus address the question directly to the Pharisees while they were "gathered together" (Matt. 22:41) and emphasizes in a concluding verse (v. 46) that Jesus had effectively silenced his opponents. This statement is derived from Mark (12:34b) but shifted to this point and expanded.

23:1–36
Discourse Against the Scribes and Pharisees

Some commentators treat this discourse as part of the final apocalyptic discourse that runs

975

through the end of chap. 25 (see the concluding formula in 26:1). The objection that the scene changes in chap. 24:1 (see vv. 1 and 3) is not fatal since there is also a change of scene in the parable discourse (13:1 and 36). The change of subject matter from an attack on the Pharisees to an apocalyptic forecast is also not decisive since it would be in accord with literary convention to include a denunciation of false teachers in an apocalypse (see, e.g., Mark 13:22). At the very least, Matt. 23 serves as a bridge between the conflicts and the apocalypse. Like the other discourses, it is compiled out of materials from Mark, Q, and M. It consists of introductory warnings (vv. 1–12), of seven woes (vv. 13–33), and a prophetic oracle of judgment (vv. 34–36).

This denunciation of the Pharisees makes painful reading in the post-Holocaust era. How much of it is authentic to Jesus and how much reflects the sentiments of the post-Jamnia Matthean community? Some of the sayings, namely those from Mark and Q (23:5b = Mark 12:38b–39; [Matt. 23:14 = Mark 12:40 is absent from the best manuscripts and is clearly an interpolation]; Matt. 23:16 = Luke 6:39 Q; Matt. 23:23 = Luke 11:42 Q; Matt. 23:29–30 = Luke 11:47–48 Q) represent pre-Gospel tradition. Given this double attestation, it is difficult to eliminate *all* denunciation of the Pharisees from the authentic Jesus tradition as some are understandably trying to do since Auschwitz. What Matthew (or M before him) has done is to expand the amount of this material to enormous proportions and to cast much of it into the woe form, thus creating a much stronger impression of Jesus' anti-Pharisaism than is historically justified. We must also remember that the language of religious invective was much more virulent in those days. The synagogue liturgy in Matthew's time contained a petition that the Nazarenes (i.e., Christian Jews) might be blotted out of the book of life. It should be emphasized that Matthew himself was of course a Jew too, so he cannot be accused of anti-Semitism. This fact is only too often lost sight of completely. Lastly, Matthew is not anti-Torah. He expressly recognizes the Mosaic authority of the scribes (Matt. 23:2) and urges his church to obey their teaching. In accusing the scribes (v. 3) of saying and not doing, he evidently means they do not in their behavior obey the radically interpreted Torah as enunciated by Jesus in the Sermon on the Mount. To put it succinctly, they do not carry out the radical commandment of love.

The seventh woe (vv. 29–31) makes the point that in rejecting Jesus' teaching, the scribes and Pharisees are simply repeating what their ancestors did for the prophets. This paves the way for the wisdom oracle that predicts the persecution of the church by the synagogue (vv. 34–36 = Luke 11:49–51 Q). The persecution will be the climax of Israel's rejection of God's emissaries throughout salvation history. There are a number of interesting changes that Matthew has made to the Q form of this saying. In Luke (and almost certainly in Q), Jesus is quoting a saying of "the wisdom of God." In Matthew, it is a saying of Jesus himself. Thus, as in Matt. 11:25–30, Jesus is speaking as the personal embodiment of wisdom (= Torah). Next, Matthew defines the persecution more precisely as involving crucifixion. Torah Jews could hardly have crucified Christian Jews, for crucifixion was a Roman punishment. It must mean that they will hand the Christians over to the Roman authorities. The whole saying has been adjusted to reflect the recent experiences of Matthew's community.

23:37–39
Lament over Jerusalem

The denunciation concludes with the lament over Jerusalem (cf. Luke 13:34–35). The only major difference from Luke's version is its context. In Luke, it occurs earlier in the ministry while Jesus is still in Galilee on his way to Jerusalem. It therefore precedes the Palm Sunday entry, and the prediction "Blessed is the One who comes in the name of Yahweh" will, in Luke's perspective, be fulfilled on that occasion. In Matthew, the entry has already taken place, so the prediction can only refer to the Second Coming of Christ. Since Jerusalem will then welcome Christ at his return ("Blessed," v. 39), Matthew must mean that Israel's apostasy was not final. Jerusalem apparently will still be saved (cf. Rom. 11:26).

24:1–25:46
The Apocalyptic Discourse

As in Mark, the Jerusalem ministry ends with the so-called "little apocalypse" (→Apocalyptic Literature). Jesus is represented as predicting future history until the End. Mark knows that history down to about A.D. 68; after that it becomes vague because it still lies in what for him is the future. Matthew, writing around A.D. 90, knows what has happened since Mark, so is more definite about those events; the unknown future begins later in his version.

24:1–36, The Little Apocalypse. Matthew makes changes in Mark very cautiously, showing great respect for Mark's wording (unlike Luke, who updates the apocalypse more drastically). As a result, Matthew welds vv. 4–28 together to make a unity covering the Jewish war and the desecration of the Temple and then, at v. 29, he turns to the future: the return of Christ and the last judgment.

Matthew elaborates the description of the Second Coming in vv. 29–31. First the "sign" of the Son of man appears, preceding his actual coming (v. 30). This sign is probably the raising of the standard, as if to rally troops on the battlefield. At the appearance of this sign, all the tribes of the earth lament. Another pictorial element is the sound of the trumpet, a common feature in apocalyptic tradition (v. 31). We have already noted Matthew's love of apocalyptic embroidery (cf. 13:36–43; 16:28).

24:37–51, Parables of the End. Mark already had an appendix at the end of his apocalypse (Mark 13:28–37). It consisted of the parable of the fig tree and an exhortation to watchfulness. Matthew enlarges this appendix considerably by adding seven more parables of the End. It is worth noting that, whereas the group of parables in chaps. 21 and 22 were parables of judgment directed against the Pharisees, this group consists of parables of judgment addressed to the church.

The first of these additional parables is the Flood (Matt. 24:37–44; = Luke 17:26 Q). As Noah's Flood overtook the ungodly, so will the Second Coming be a surprise. Alone of the Evangelists, Matthew calls the Second Coming "parousia" (Matt. 24:37, 39; → Parousia), which means "arrival" and "presence."

The second parable, or rather two parabolic sayings, consists of the workers in the field and the women at the mill (vv. 40–42) with parallels in Luke 17:31, 35 Q. The third parable is the thief at night (Matt. 24:43–44; = Luke 12:39–40 Q).

The fourth parable is that of the faithful and unfaithful servants (Matt. 24:45–51; = Luke 12:41–46 Q). The point of all these parables, which are taken from the apocalyptic passages in Q, is that the Second Coming will be sudden and incalculable. Therefore, the disciples must watch for its coming at any moment.

There is some tension between the Second Coming as it is portrayed in Mark's little apocalypse and the view found in the Q passages. In Mark, the End occurs after a schedule of events leading up to it; in Q the End will be sudden and unexpected. Matthew combines the two perspectives. The known and calculable events had already occurred when Matthew wrote his Gospel. Only the Parousia was still future and would come suddenly and as a surprise.

This brings us to chap. 25 and the three great parables of the last judgment. Each of them will receive comment in turn.

25:1–13, The Ten Maidens. As it now stands, this is an allegory. The groom is the Messiah and his arrival at midnight the Parousia. The two groups of maidens stand for two different groups in the church. The ones with oil are probably those who had practiced the better righteousness of the fulfilled Torah, while those who have used up their oil will be the ones who have sat loose to the law (an-

tinomians). While this allegory is peculiar to Matthew, it has affinities with parabolic sayings elsewhere (Mark 13:33–37; Luke 12:35–38). It is tempting to suppose that Matthew (or M) has developed the allegory out of these materials with the traditional image of the Messiah as the bridegroom (Matt. 9:15).

25:14–30, The Talents. Three versions of this parable exist: the present one, Luke's (Luke 19:11–27), and a third version in the *Gospel of Thomas* (→Gospel of Thomas). Critical opinion is inclined to view Matthew's as the earliest version. However, even this form already includes secondary features: the large amounts involved (talents); an allusion to the delay in the Parousia (Matt. 25:19); a hint of the messianic banquet ("joy," vv. 21, 23); and Matthew's favorite phrases "outer darkness" and "wailing and gnashing of teeth" (cf., e.g., 22:13), all of which is apocalyptic imagery. This means that the talents, like the ten maidens, is really an allegory and has a similar meaning. The servant who buried his talent failed to pursue the better righteousness of the fulfilled Torah.

25:31–46, The Sheep and the Goats. This is neither a parable nor an allegory, but a direct description of the last judgment. However, it contains a few parabolic images with allegorical significance: shepherd, sheep, goats, and the separation of the herds to the right hand and to the left. These images may be leftovers from a genuine parable of Jesus. The shepherd is equated with a king (v. 34), the sheep with those who have fed the hungry, etc., and the goats with those who have failed to do so. Everything else is direct apocalyptic scenery: the Son of man, his angels, the gathering of all the nations, the reward and the punishment. We have noted that this cluster of parables depicts God's judgment over the church. This means that the nations will be those who have been made his disciples as a result of the church's mission (see 28:19, where the same phrase, "all the nations," occurs). Nowhere else does Matthew make it so crystal clear that the criterion to be applied to the church at the last judgment will be that of the better righteousness and that the better righteousness is the praxis of love.

Matthew concludes this discourse with his usual formula (26:1a), only this time he writes "*all* these words," i.e., all five major discourses.

PART SIX: 26:1–28:20

The Passion and Resurrection

Matthew follows Mark quite closely throughout the passion narrative and, indeed, until the

point in the empty tomb story where Mark suddenly ends. Only then does he go his own independent way.

26:1–27:66, 28:11–15, Matthew's Retelling of Mark's Story. Matthew makes stylistic improvements to Mark, as elsewhere. He also adds explanations. Pilate, we are told, is the "governor" (27:2). The high priest's name is "Caiaphas" (26:3, 57), a point on which Matthew agrees with John. Joseph of Arimathea is described as a "wealthy person" (27:57). The tomb was a new one (27:60). More significant is the addition of the formula citation in 27:9. This is about the thirty pieces of silver that Judas received for betraying Jesus (see the Short Essay "Matthew's Fulfillment Citations"). Most striking, however, are the insertions that Matthew has made at a number of points. Some of these are clearly redactional. Others seem to come from special traditions (M). The first group tends to be theologically significant, the second legendary in character.

We take the redactional additions first. In 26:1–5, Matthew rewrites the introduction to the passion narrative. First, he provides a concluding summary to the five discourses (v. 1, see above). Then in v. 2, Jesus himself (rather than the Evangelist, as in Mark) announces the approach of the Passover to his disciples and adds a new Son of man prediction to the Passion. This shows that Jesus is in control of the situation. Matthew then inserts a fuller description of the Sanhedrin's plot (→Sanhedrin). It is worth noting that Matthew recognizes that it was the high priest and elders, not the Pharisees, who were the chief instigators of Jesus' arrest. While his anti-Pharisaic concern led Matthew to exaggerate the polemic against them, he did not falsify history and make the Pharisees responsible for the crucifixion.

Next, Jesus prefaces his directions to the disciples for the Passover preparations with the words "My hour of crisis is fast approaching" (26:18), thereby showing again that he is in charge of events.

In the account of Judas's betrayal Matthew states that the authorities actually gave him thirty pieces of silver. This paves the way for the later insertion about Judas's suicide (27:3–10) and for the accompanying fulfillment citation (see above).

To the prediction of the betrayal at the Last Supper, Matthew adds 26:25, in which Jesus explicitly names Judas as the betrayer. Judas says, "Is it I, rabbi?" Note that here Judas calls

Opposite: The trial of Jesus before the Roman prefect Pontius Pilate (see Matt. 27:11–26; Mark 15:1–15; Luke 23:1–25; John 18:28–19:16) as depicted in the *Rossano Gospels* manuscript, Italy, sixth century.

Jesus rabbi (cf. v. 49), not "Lord." This shows that Judas has put himself outside the circle of the disciples who in Matthew always call him "Lord." Jesus replies, "You have said it yourself."

In the institution of the Lord's Supper (26:26–29), Matthew rewrites Mark's account to conform it with the charter narrative as it was current in his own community. Note particularly that he has added to the pronouncement over the cup the phrase "for the remission of sins" (v. 28; on the importance of this, see the commentary on 3:11, the preaching of John the Baptist above). The forgiveness of sin becomes effective only at the moment of Jesus' death. All the allusions to the saving significance of Jesus' message and activity during the ministry were conditional upon their fulfillment in his death on the cross.

Matthew makes two small but important additions to Jesus' prediction of the coming messianic banquet, which comes immediately after the words of institution: "I shall not drink *from this moment on*" and "until I drink it new *with you* in the Reign of God." These little additions make it much clearer than Mark does that, for Matthew, the death of Jesus inaugurates the Reign of God and that in it the disciples will participate in the messianic salvation.

Matthew drops the scribes from the contingent that comes to arrest Jesus (26:47), thus showing once again his respect for past history as distinct from present controversies. When Judas comes forward to identify him, Jesus urges him to get on with the job: "Do what you are here for" (v. 50), thus initiating the whole train of events. Still in charge, Jesus orders the unnamed disciple to put his sword away (v. 52).

In the procedure before the Sanhedrin, the high priest puts Jesus under oath (26:63). To the question whether he is the Messiah, Jesus replies not "I am," as in Mark, but more plausibly, "You have said it" (v. 64; i.e., "it's your word, not mine"). His reply continues with the assurance that *from now on* they will see him enthroned at God's right hand, indicating Jesus' firm confidence in his vindication by the heavenly Father. And the Evangelist introduces this statement with the word "But," thereby showing that Jesus is contradicting the high priest's attempt to embroil him in a political kind of messiahship.

There is an interesting variant reading in the account of Pilate's attempt to release Jesus under the Passover amnesty. Some ancient manuscripts read "Jesus Barabbas" (27:16–17) where the majority read simply "Barabbas." This would set up an ironic contrast between Jeshua son of Abbas (meaning "father") and Jeshua called the Messiah. Its omission in most manuscripts would be explained by the increasing reverence among Christians that led (outside Hispanic countries) to the avoidance of "Jesus" as a first name for others.

As the crucifixion squad sets out for Golgotha (27:32) and Simon of Cyrene is pressed into carrying the cross, Matthew drops Mark's note that this Simon was the father of Alexander and Rufus, presumably because they were not known in the Evangelist's church as they were in Mark's.

In the crucifixion scene (27:33–43), Matthew adds that the sour wine proffered to Jesus was laced with gall (v. 34), a detail taken from Psalm 69:21. This is in line with Matthew's fondness for fulfillment citations, although he does not actually use the citation formula here.

In the account of the mockery at the cross, Matthew adds 27:43, quoting Psalm 22:8, together with the explanation "for he said he was the Son of God." This recalls the temptation story (Matt. 4:3, 6) and so presents the crucifixion as Jesus' "last temptation." "Son of God" does not mean one who displays miraculous powers, but one completely surrendered to the will of God.

At the death of Jesus (27:45–54) "those with him" join the centurion in declaring that Jesus was "God's Son" (v. 54). This is not a confession of faith on the part of the gentile world as in Mark but, as Matthew explains, an expression of fear at the earthquake and its accompanying phenomena (see below).

In addition to these editorial modifications there are six major insertions into the passion narrative. All of them represent traditions peculiar to Matthew.

The first insert occurs at the arrest (26:52–54). When the disciple (unnamed) takes up the sword to resist, Jesus tells him to put it back in its sheath. Then comes an important Jesus saying attested only here: "Those who take up the sword shall perish by the sword." Jesus goes on to express his confidence that his Father could, if he so willed, provide legions of angels for his defense. But, Jesus says, the Scriptures must be fulfilled. This remarkable passage (different from the other inserts in that its character is not so legendary) portrays Jesus as living out the demands of the Sermon on the Mount (see 5:39). The better righteousness is not just a theory: it was fully practiced by Jesus, and, in that sense also, it was "fulfilled."

The second insert (27:3–10) concerns the suicide of Judas, a variant of the story found in Acts 1:18–19. It is a legendary explanation of the name of Akeldama ("field of blood"; → Akeldama). Matthew wishes to emphasize that Judas's end was a self-inflicted divine judgment. The accompanying fulfillment citation is the last one in Matthew and the only one added by him to the passion narrative. Matthew ascribes the citation to Jeremiah. Most of it, how-

ever, comes from Zech. 11:12–13, though there are slight reminiscences of Jer. 32:6–15 and 18:2–3. It was difficult to verify references when there were no chapter and verse numbers and when books were in scroll form.

In the third insert, Pilate's wife comes into court, warns her husband not to have anything to do "with that innocent man," and tells him of a bad dream she had had about Jesus that morning (27:19). As we recall from the birth narrative, Matthew regarded dreams as a mode of divine revelation. This insert means that for the Evangelist the doctrine of Jesus' sinlessness was not a human assessment but a matter of divine revelation.

The fourth insert is the scene in which Pilate washes his hands (27:24–25) and protests his innocence of Jesus' death. Upon this the "people" (the word [Gk. *laos*] means not just any crowd, but the holy people of God) cry out, "may his blood be on us and on our children." Here is a further attempt by Matthew to shift the blame for the death of Jesus upon Torah-Israel. This explains the disaster of A.D. 70. It does not mean that the Jews for all time are guilty of "deicide." Their judgment had already been fulfilled when Matthew wrote these words.

The fifth insert occurs at the moment of Jesus' death (27:51b–53). There was an earthquake; rocks were split, graves were opened, and many saints were raised bodily. Coming out of their tombs, they entered the holy city after Jesus' resurrection and appeared to many. This is a strange story. One wonders what the resurrected saints were doing between Good Friday and Easter. The story flatly contradicts Paul's teaching that other resurrections will occur only at the Parousia (1 Cor. 15:23). To understand it we must recall that in apocalyptic expectation the resurrection hoped for was a general one. It upset apocalyptic calculations when only one person, Jesus, was resurrected at Easter. This legend was evidently designed to stress the fact that the resurrection (→ Resurrection) is essentially a corporate event and that the resurrection of Jesus is the cause of all other resurrections, since his resurrection was the victory over death. It cannot be stressed too strongly that this legend is peculiar to Matthew and that it should be ignored in any attempt to reconstruct what happened on Good Friday.

The sixth insert is the story of the guard at the tomb. It is dispersed into three separate installments: first, 27:62–66, the posting of the guard at the request of the high priests and (note!) the Pharisees; second, 28:4, a series of remarkable events witnessed by the guards on the Sunday morning, namely, an earthquake and the appearance of an angel, which leaves the guards convulsed with fear as dead men; third, 28:11–15, the conclusion in which some members of the guard report their experiences to the high priests, who bribe them to say that Jesus' disciples had stolen the body while the guards were asleep. This story, we are told, is still current among the Jews at the time Matthew wrote.

There are a number of problems with this story. It is unlikely that the Jewish religious authorities would have gone to see Pilate during the Passover Sabbath. The reference to Jesus as an "impostor" (27:63) seems to presuppose the church's post-Easter proclamation and Israel's rejection of it. The claim that Jesus had foretold his resurrection (27:63) presupposes the development of the passion/resurrection predictions as "prophecies after the event." The request for the tomb to be sealed "till the third day" presupposes the church's Easter message and the connection of the "third day" with the empty tomb. And the resurrection is treated as an observable event rather than as a revelatory encounter and call to faith. The reference to the Pharisees' involvement in the plot, and the statement that the slanderous story was current among the Jews until Matthew's day, betrays its origin: it is an apologetic legend designed to counter the Torah-Israel's slander about the origin of the Easter faith.

28:1–8, The Empty Tomb. Matthew makes a number of striking changes from Mark's account. The purpose of the women was not to complete the burial rites (as in Mark) but simply "to see the grave." With the sealing of the tomb and the presence of the guard it would be impossible to get to the body, as the women hoped to do in Mark. We have already looked at vv. 2–3, but we should also note the descent of the angel (οἱος Mark has simply "young man"), the rolling away of the stone, and the angel sitting on it. This is the nearest that any NT writer comes to describing the actual resurrection. Earthquakes are conventional apocalyptic symbols. It shows that the resurrection is an end-time event.

In v. 7 the women carry out the command to report to the disciples. Matthew could not use Mark's conclusion, "they said nothing to anyone," as he wished to complete the Easter story with an appearance in Galilee as Mark had suggested.

28:9–10, The Appearance to the Women. Matthew evidently had access to a tradition similar to that in John 20:14–18. We cannot be certain how ancient this tradition is. There is no mention of it in the earliest list of appearances (1 Cor. 15:3–7). There are two tendencies at work: to make the male disciples witnesses of the empty tomb and to give appearances to the women at the tomb. In the earliest tradition, the women were the sole witnesses of the empty tomb (Mark 16:1–8) and Peter the sole recipient of the first appearance. This is not to say that no

woman ever saw the risen One: at the very least, women could have been among the five hundred (1 Cor. 15:6). The appearance in Matt. 28:9–10 is depicted in physical terms, a sign of later tradition (cf. Luke 24:39, 41–43; John 20:24–29). This appearance, curiously, serves no purpose except to allow the risen One to repeat the angel's charge to the women. Why then does Matthew record it? Perhaps he wants to make the women the first witnesses of the resurrection. Later tradition has called Mary Magdalene the "apostle to the apostles."

28:16–20, The Great Commission. Mark (14:28; 16:7) had pointed to an encounter between the risen One and the disciples in Galilee, but did not go on to relate this appearance. What Matthew offers here is not, strictly speaking, an appearance story. We are not told that the risen One appeared to them but simply that they "saw him" (Matt. 28:17). Nor is there anything said of his disappearing at the end. The story simply concludes with the risen One's assurance of his continuing presence. Indeed, Matthew does not seem to have taken this story from M but to have composed it by himself. But he does use pieces of earlier tradition: the doubt motif (cf. Luke 24:11; John 20:25); the commissioning, a central feature of the Easter experience; the command to baptize (this may be traditional, as is suggested by the charge to remit sins in the appearance to the Twelve as recorded in Luke 24:47 and John 20:20–23); the declaration of the risen One, that "God has handed over to me all power in heaven and upon earth" (Matt. 28:18), is based on the Son of man tradition (Dan. 7:14); the idea of a farewell charge prior to departure is a common biblical genre. Matthew probably had Moses' farewell discourse in mind (Deut. 33). Its location "on the mountain" (cf., e.g., Matt. 5:1) also reminds us of Moses.

In the actual charge, Matthew obviously betrays his hand in the command "to make disciples" (rather than "preach the good news" as in the parallel found in late manuscripts of Mark 16:15). A second sign of Matthew's hand is to be seen in the phrase "teaching them to observe all the things I have charged you." This points back to the teaching of the five discourses. The promise of the abiding presence recalls the Immanuel promise at Matt. 1:23 and its reiteration in 18:20. The abiding presence is the Matthean equivalent of the gift of the Holy Spirit, which is elsewhere associated with the resurrection appearances (Luke 24:49; John 20:22). Finally, "the consummation of the age" is a favorite expression of Matthew's, occurring five times in the Gospel. That Jesus is constantly present with his church, working through its teaching mission, is a fitting conclusion and an effective summary of the Gospel.

The Passion According to Matthew

If we wish to reconstruct what happened at the first Easter, from the plot of the Sanhedrin through the final postresurrection appearance, this can only be done through a critical analysis of all the traditions. Matthew's version is secondary and basically reproduces Mark, whose account by and large is closest to the original Jerusalem Passion narrative. In our opinion, there are only four points at which Matthew offers a valuable supplement or correction to Mark: first, the saying about those who take up the sword perishing by the sword (26:52); second, Jesus' reply to the high priest, "You've said it" (26:64); third, the name "Jesus Barabbas" (27:15, 16); and fourth, the explanation of the women's purpose on Easter morning as simply in order to see the grave (28:1). Apart from that, Matthew's additions are either theological (e.g., 27:43) or legendary (the six inserts).

The value of Matthew's passion narrative lies in the overall impression it creates. The suffering, death, and resurrection of Jesus the Messiah were so profound in meaning that each Evangelist was able to capture only a part of their total meaning. The Passions are like portraits rather than photographs, and each Evangelist contributes something to our appreciation of the story. What then is Matthew's special contribution? It lies in his presentation of Jesus' identity. For Matthew, Jesus in his Passion is the King, but the humble King. All the way through he is master of the situation. This is brought out particularly in the earlier part of the passion story, at the preparation for the Passover, at the arrest, and at the hearing before the Sanhedrin. Indeed, Jesus' answer to the high priest ("*From now on* you will see the Son of man seated at the right hand of Power") almost suggests, like John's Gospel, that the cross is the hour of glory. Almost—but not quite, for Matthew never loses sight of the fact that Jesus was the meek and humble King, as keynoted in the Palm Sunday entry (21:5). This is brought out most movingly in the mockery, where the crowd challenges him to come down from the cross and reminds him that he had said he was the Son of God. Being Son of God means, for Matthew, not triumphalist claims but the acceptance of the mission of the righteous sufferer of the Psalms, of Isaiah 53, and of Wisdom of Solomon 5. This is not a new feature in the story. It has characterized Matthew's portrait of Jesus all along, from the flight from Herod, through the baptism (with its mixed citation of Ps. 2:7 and the servant song of Isa. 42 in Matt. 3:17) and the miracle stories (note the fulfillment citation from Isa. 42 in Matt. 12:18–21). All this reaches its climax on the cross and especially in the crowd's word so impressively presented in J. S. Bach's *St. Matthew Passion* when, after the discordant turmoil of the mockery, the chorus sings in unison, "Truly this was the Son of God."

Bibliography

Brown, R. E. *The Birth of the Messiah*. Garden City, NY: Doubleday, 1977.

Davies, W. D. *The Sermon on the Mount*. Cambridge: Cambridge University Press, 1966.

Ellis, P. F. *Matthew: His Mind and His Message*. Collegeville, MN: Liturgical Press, 1974.

Jeremias, J. *The Sermon on the Mount*. Philadelphia: Fortress, 1963.

Kingsbury, J. D. *Matthew*. Proclamation Commentaries. Philadelphia: Fortress, 1977.

Meier, J. P. *The Vision of Matthew: Christ, Church and Morality in the Gospel of Matthew*. New York: Paulist Press, 1979.

Schweizer, E. *The Good News According to Matthew*. Atlanta, GA: Knox, 1975; London: SPCK, 1976.

Senior, D. *What Are They Saying About Matthew?* New York: Paulist Press, 1983.

Stanton, G. *The Interpretation of Matthew*. Issues in Religion and Theology, 3. Philadelphia: Fortress, 1983.

MARK

JOHN R. DONAHUE

INTRODUCTION

The Gospel According to Mark, the shortest of the Gospels, is generally thought to be the earliest and a source for Matthew and Luke, who incorporate it almost totally into their Gospels. It alone is called explicitly a "gospel" (Mark 1:1; 13:10; 14:9; cf. Matt. 1:1; Luke 1:1). This term is used in Second Isaiah (e.g., Isa. 40:9; 41:27; 52:7; 61:1) for the "good tidings" of God's saving action (Ps. 40:10). In secular Greek "gospel" means the good news of a significant event (e.g., the birth of the emperor) that is announced by a herald. It occurs frequently in Paul to describe the proclamation of the "Christ event," i.e., the significance that the person, life, ministry, Passion, death, resurrection, and exaltation of Jesus of Nazareth had and still has for human history and existence (1 Thess. 2:9; 1 Cor. 1:17–24; 15:1; Gal. 1:6–11; Rom. 1:16–17).

Though similar to other literary genres such as aretalogies (i.e., stories of the mighty deeds of heroic figures), lives of philosophers, martyrologies, and biblical writings such as the Elijah and Elisha cycles from 1 Kings 16 to 2 Kings 9 (→Elijah, Elisha), or the book of Daniel, the Gospel of Mark represents a wholly new genre. Its form is "kerygmatic narrative"—the presentation in story of the "good news" about and from Jesus (→ Gospel, Gospels; Kerygma).

It is customary in NT studies to distinguish three stages in the composition of the Gospels. Stage 1 consists of recollections from the historical ministry of Jesus; stage 2, oral traditions about his ministry handed down under the influence of the proclamation of the risen Lord; stage 3, the incorporation of this material along with editorial additions into the literary and theological composition of a given Evangelist. This commentary will interpret Mark's form of stage 3, i.e., how Mark's kerygmatic narrative confronts its hearers with that same challenge and offer of grace that Jesus offered to his original hearers.

Author and Setting

Like the other Gospels, the text does not identify its author, but early church tradition (beginning with Papias, ca. A.D. 120; see Eusebius *Ecclesiastical History* 3.39.15) attributed it to "Mark," a companion of Peter in Rome (1 Pet. 5:13), who is then identified with the "John Mark" of Acts 12:12, 25; 15:37–39, and the "Mark" of Philem. 24; Col. 4:10; 2 Tim. 4:1. This attribution is called into question by the apologetic desire to associate a nonapostolic Gospel with the apostle Peter, by the frequency of "Mark" as a name in the Roman Empire, and by the ancient tendency to attribute works to important figures from the past.

For the bulk of church history, principally on the authority of patristic writers (esp. Irenaeus *Against Heresies* 3.1.2) and certain internal evidence (see below), the final composition of the Gospel was situated at Rome, sometime after the martyrdom of Peter during the persecution of Nero (A.D. 64). Recently, because of the stress in Mark on Galilee as the place of the first and expected revelation of Jesus, along with its strong Palestinian coloring, its audience has been located in Galilee or southern Syria (see Marxsen).

Internal evidence from the Gospel (esp. chap. 13) offers clues to its situation and community. Like similar apocalyptic literature, Mark 13 (called often the "apocalyptic discourse"), while in the form of predictions given in the past, cryptically depicts upheavals in the lives of the readers. The civil disturbances (13:7–8) and intensity of the persecution described in 13:9–13 may reflect both Nero's persecution (A.D. 64) and the Jewish war of A.D. 66–70 (see commentary below on chap. 13).

The large number of Latinisms (Gk. terms or phrases that reflect Lat.; e.g., 5:9; 6:37; 7:4; 12:14, 42; 15:15–16, 19, 39) suggest a setting where both Latin and Greek were used. The teaching on divorce reflects Roman law (10:10–12) and the widow's offering is explained in terms of Roman coinage (12:42, lit. two coins [Gk. *lepta*] are made equivalent to the Roman *quadrans*, which equals 1/4 of a cent).

The community included large numbers of Jews. Familiarity with the Jewish Scriptures is presumed and explicit citations of and allusions to them are frequent. They are the authoritative revelation of God, and the core of Jesus' teaching is a summary from the OT (12:28–34). Yet, the OT is quoted from Greek versions, rather than translated from Hebrew; Jewish customs are explained (7:3–4); Aramaic phrases are translated (e.g., 5:41; 7:34; 14:36; 15:34), and details of Palestinian geography are vague (6:45–7:37). The Gospel contains strong attacks on Jewish laws and institutions (7:1–23; 11:15–19), and implies a mission to the Gentiles (11:17; 13:10). Most likely the community comprises Jews and gentile converts living outside of Palestine, who are breaking away from traditional Jewish observances.

The community is also most likely of lower socioeconomic status. The language of the Gospel is not elegant, literary Greek, but the spoken Greek of ordinary people with occasional Semitic influence. The rich are suspect, as are those holding positions of power (10:23–25, 42). Ordinary items such as the "pallet" (2:4, 11) and the "basket" (6:43; 8:19) are those used by the poor. Though the available evidence precludes certainty, a Jewish-Christian community at Rome shortly after A.D. 70 would be an excellent candidate for the audience of the Gospel.

Literary Characteristics

While there is no discernible written source, the Evangelist drew on early traditions (e.g., controversies of Jesus with Jewish leaders; collections of miracle stories, parables, and sayings of Jesus; and narratives of his final days in Jerusalem). Mark is, however, more than a simple collector. He leaves his distinct stamp on the Gospel, primarily by his manner of composition.

The Gospel manifests a theological conception superimposed over an original geographical framework (ministry in Galilee, beyond the confines of Galilee, journey to Jerusalem, and death in Jerusalem; cf. Acts 10:36–41). On the narrative level, events proceed to the climax in Jerusalem. The interpretive focus, however, comes in the middle. The units are structured like an arch where events on the side panels (Parts One and Two, 1:1–8:21; Parts Four and Five, 11:1–16:8) draw the onlooker to gaze to the main themes in the center (Part Three, 8:22–10:52). The structure is thus both architectonic and dramatic. As readers are drawn to the interpretive center, they are also caught up in the unfolding story of the journey of Jesus to the cross.

Mark begins with the ministry of Jesus in Galilee as the powerful Son of God who announces the kingdom, calls disciples, performs mighty works, and is acclaimed by the crowds (Parts One, Two, 1:1–8:21); he concludes with the entrance of Jesus into Jerusalem and his intensifying conflicts with Jewish leaders, leading to his crucifixion, death, and resurrection (Parts Four, Five, 11:1–16:8). In the center section (Part Three, 8:22–10:52), which is demarcated by references to "the way" (8:27; 9:33; 10:32), Jesus instructs his disciples on the meaning of his life and death (10:45), and on the cost of discipleship (carrying the cross and serving others as he did, 8:34–38; 10:42–45).

This section provides the bridge between the revelation of the powerful Son of God who in Galilee confronts the power of evil and heals the sick and the revelation of the Suffering Son of man in Jerusalem (11:1–16:8) whose blood is poured out for many (14:24; cf. 10:45).

Written in a lively, direct style, the Gospel reflects popular storytelling techniques. There is frequent use of "the historical present" (i.e., the Gk. present tense translated as past in English), which gives an "eyewitness" quality to the narrative. It is a Gospel of action where narrative (rather than the teaching of Jesus) occupies the most space, and where its different incidents (pericopes) follow in rapid succession, connected often by a simple "and." Stories of Jesus' exorcisms and healings are recounted vividly and with a detail that Matthew and Luke compress.

Frequent repetitions allow similar incidents to be presented in new guises and settings. For example, there are two narratives of calming the sea (4:35–41; 6:45–52), two feedings (6:31–44; 8:1–10), and two healings of blind beggars (8:22–26; 10:46–52). Mark also likes progressive threefold groupings, e.g., three "calls" of disciples (1:16–20; 3:13–19; 6:7–13), three passion predictions (8:31; 9:31; 10:33), and three prayers of Jesus in Gethsemane (14:32–42).

Theological Motifs

Christology. The theme of Mark's Christology, that is, his understanding of Jesus, is stated immediately: "the good news of Jesus, Messiah, Son of God" (1:1). Mark's purpose is not to prove this statement but to unfold its implications for faith and discipleship.

The titles of Jesus in Mark provide signposts along the narrative path of Mark's presentation of Jesus. Three are most important. First, Jesus is "the Christ" (i.e., Messiah, 1:1, 34 [some manuscripts], 8:29; 14:61; 15:32), used in the Bible mainly for anointed royal figures and associated with Israel's hope for a king who would restore Davidic rule (see 2 Sam. 7:12–14). It came to designate other figures (priestly or prophetic) sent to establish God's reign (→ Messiah). Second, "Son of God" (Mark 1:1, 11; 3:11; 5:7; 9:7; 14:61; 15:39) does not imply, as in later theology, "divine nature," but principally a special relationship to God. In the OT kings (Ps. 2:7), angelic beings (Job 38:7), and righteous people (Wisd. of Sol. 2:18) are "sons of God" (→ Sons of God, Children of God). Third and most importantly to Mark, Jesus is Son of man (→ Son of man). This enigmatic phrase, which in Aramaic means "human being," derives from Dan. 7:13–27, where it describes the granting of power, honor, and glory in the heavenly sphere to one like a son of man who has suffered persecution and who is identified with the "saints of the most high" (Dan. 7:18). It suggests an individual who also is representative of a larger group. Jesus as Son of man possesses power on earth (Mark 2:10, 28) will suffer, die, and be raised up (8:31; 9:9, 12, 31; 10:33, 45; 14:21, 41), and at his return as Son of man (8:38; 13:24–26; 14:62), God will save the elect and punish the wicked.

Though taking over many of these titles from his tradition, Mark reinterprets them and uses them to shape his Christology. Jesus is Son of God not simply as a figure of power (3:11; 5:7) but as the obedient son (12:6; 14:36) who suffers, dies, and is vindicated by God. The title "Son of man" (used only by Jesus) underscores the vulnerability of Jesus as well as that humanity he shares with others. It establishes rapport with readers and gives a proper understanding to Son of God.

This same Jesus who is addressed as "beloved son" by a voice from heaven (1:11; 9:7) is also very human in Mark. He shows strong emotions such as pity (1:41), violent displeasure (1:43), anger (3:5), and is moved at the suffering of others who are like sheep without a shepherd (6:34). Like the OT prophets, Jesus proclaims the need for conversion and manifests God's will through symbolic activity. Like them, he embodies the compassion of God (6:34), especially for those who are suffering or on the margin of society—lepers (1:40–45), tax collectors (2:15), and Gentiles (7:24–30).

Mark uses the perplexing "Messianic Secret" to convey a proper understanding of Jesus' life. Demons acclaim him as Son of God, but he silences them (1:24–25; 3:11–12; cf. 5:7). At other times Jesus tells people who have experienced his power to remain silent (1:34, 43–45; 3:12; 5:43; 8:30; 9:9). Two things are communicated: first, knowledge of Jesus' identity comes from suprahuman power, either that of the heavens (1:11; 9:7) or of the demons; second, proper confession of Jesus should not be made on the basis of the miracles, but only after following him to the cross. The first human in Mark who correctly addresses Jesus as Son of God is the centurion who, at the moment of Jesus' death, says, "Truly this man was the Son of God" (15:39).

Discipleship. While the Gospel of Mark is the story of Jesus, it is also the story of response to the call of Jesus. The disciples in Mark combine negative and positive traits. When Jesus calls, they follow "immediately" and they are summoned to be with him and to do the things he does: teach, heal, and cast out demons (1:16–20; 3:13–19). Jesus teaches them privately (4:34; 7:17; 9:28), gives them the "mystery of the kingdom" (4:10–12), rescues them when they are threatened by the storm, and makes them privileged witnesses to his power (4:35–41; 5:37–40).

The picture of the disciples is also one of growing estrangement from Jesus. In the first parts of the Gospel they misunderstand his miracles and teaching (4:40; 7:18; 8:16–21). In the central section (8:22–10:52) each time Jesus states that it is God's will that he suffer and die, they misunderstand (8:32–33), twice bickering over rank and prestige (9:33–34; 10:32–45). During the passion narrative, though they share a final meal with him, one disciple betrays him (14:10), others sleep during his greatest agony (14:32–42), all flee when he is arrested (14:50), and Peter denies ever knowing him (14:66–72).

This double-sided portrait of the disciples has spawned heated debate. Some argue that they represent those in the community who, fascinated by a theology of power, pride themselves in their spiritual gifts. The failure of the disciples is seen as a warning that without a theology of the cross, a triumphalist theology of glory can only end in denial and betrayal. Less harshly, others suggest that the failure of the disciples encourages those in Mark's community who have failed in the face of persecution. Though Peter denied the Lord, the early church knew him as a recipient of a resurrection appearance and as a great missionary. Jesus, who conquers death and empowers Peter to become a witness and a martyr, can conquer the weakness and betrayal of his followers (see Best, Kelber, and Weeden).

Text and Canon

Though overshadowed by Matthew and Luke, Mark's place in the canon of Scripture was not contested, and the text of the Gospel is well established since it appears in the important fourth-century manuscripts (Vaticanus, Sinaiticus, and Alexandrinus) while portions of it appear in the third-century Chester Beatty papyrus (P^{45}). The major textual problem concerns the so-called "longer ending" (Mark 16:9–20, also called the "traditional" and the "canonical" ending) that appears in a great number of ancient manuscripts and in the Greek text used for the KJV. However, earlier and more important manuscripts such as Vaticanus and Sinaiticus end at 16:8. Scholars among the patristic authors such as Eusebius and Jerome (fourth century A.D.) held that Mark ended at 16:8. Internal evidence supports this. The transition from 16:8 to the longer ending is awkward and these verses differ in language and style from the rest of the Gospel. The "longer ending" is best explained as a later attempt to soften the final words of the Gospel, "for they were afraid," and to provide it with a resurrection appearance.

COMMENTARY

PART ONE: 1:1–6:6a

Throughout Galilee Jesus Proclaims the Imminence of God's Reign in Powerful Words and Deeds

The first major phases of Jesus' activity take place mainly in Galilee and its environs. Though Mark collects here authentic recollections of the life and teaching of Jesus, he has edited and arranged them in service of his theology. In this section Jesus is very much a figure of power (1:22, 27; 2:10, 28), who summons disciples to follow him and confronts evil and sickness. His authority is established in word and deed and he is acclaimed by the crowds (e.g., 1:28, 45; 2:12). His rapid movement from place to place conveys the urgency of the gospel he proclaims.

The section is divided into a prologue (1:1–13) and two subsections (1:14–3:6; 3:7–6:6a). Each subsection begins with transitional summaries (1:14–15; 3:7–12) followed by discipleship stories (1:16–20; 3:13–20) and concludes with opposition or misunderstanding (3:6; 6:1–6a).

1:1–13
Prologue: The Beginning of the Good News

The prologue sets the stage for the public ministry of Jesus and introduces major themes of the Gospel. The superscription (1:1) announces "the beginning of the gospel" (cf. Gen. 1:1; Hos. 1:2 in LXX). "Beginning" implies not simply the start of the narrative, but that its total message is the "foundation" of that gospel that continues to be proclaimed in Mark's own time (13:10; 14:9). Mark 1:2–3, attributed to Isaiah but actually a conflation of Exod. 23:20; Mal. 3:1; and Isa. 40:3, establishes the continuity of saving history; the Gospel fulfills God's promises.

The actions and description of John (Mark 1:4–6) draw on contemporary Jewish eschatological expectations, i.e., beliefs about the "last days." John is dressed like Elijah (v. 6; see 2 Kings 1:8), who will return to prepare for the day of the Lord (Mal. 3:1; 4:5). Mark depicts John not simply as the fiery reformer preparing for the advent of this day, but as forerunner of the Messiah (Mark 9:11–13; cf. 6:15; 8:28). After a quick summary of the preaching of John (cf. Matt. 3:7–10; Luke 3:7–9) and his baptism of repentance (also practiced "in the wilderness" by the Qumran community, 1QS 3.4–5), John's ministry culminates (Mark 1:7–8) in proclaiming the advent of "the stronger one" who

will baptize in the Holy Spirit. Though Jesus does not baptize in the Gospels, an outpouring of the "spirit of holiness" was to characterize the eschatological age (Isa. 32:15–20; 1QS 4:18–21). The words and deeds of Jesus constitute a "baptism in the spirit" (→ Baptism; John the Baptist).

The second part of the prologue (Mark 1:9–13) begins with solemn biblical language, "in those days," to herald the messianic preparation of Jesus. The baptism of Jesus by John (Mark 1:9–11; Matt. 3:13–17; Luke 3:21–22; cf. John 1:29–34) conveys both the solidarity of Jesus with others so baptized (Mark 1:9), and his unique status (vv. 10–11). The opening of the heavens (cf. Isa. 64:1) and the descent of the Spirit evoke the return of the longed for prophetic spirit and the advent of the messianic age. The descent "like a dove" may reflect the Jewish comparison of the hovering spirit of Gen. 1:2 to a dove.

The high point of the baptism is the proclamation by the "voice" (a personification of God), "you are my beloved son, in whom I am well pleased" (Mark 1:11), which echoes the adoption formula of Ps. 2:7 and the choice of the servant in Isa. 42:1; 44:1. The baptism is both Jesus' messianic adoption and his commissioning as servant. The subsequent narrative will unfold how he is the "beloved son," and how his followers are to confess him as such. Both the superscription ("Son of God") and the baptism point to the Son of God on the cross (Mark 10:38–39; 15:39).

With the "testing" (more accurate than "temptation") in the wilderness (1:12–13) the messianic preparation of Jesus is complete. Like the righteous Job, Jesus is tested by Satan (Job 2:1–8). Though he will warn of Satan's power in the Gospel (Mark 4:15; 8:33), Jesus will emerge stronger than Satan (3:22–27). The "wilderness" has a double nuance as the place of the covenant betrothal between God and the chosen people (Hos. 2:14–15) and where the fidelity of the people was "tested" and found failing (Pss. 78:17–18; 106:13–33). From the wilderness also salvation will dawn for the people (Isa. 40:3; 1QS 8:12–16). Jesus as "God's son" (representing the people; see Exod. 4:22, "Israel is [God's] first-born son"; cf. Hos. 11:1) relives the testing of Israel in the wilderness but remains faithful when tested.

1:14–3:6
Initial Ministry in Galilee, Opposition from Pharisees

1:14–15, Summary of the Proclamation of Jesus. After the "handing over" (RSV, "arrest") of John, which foreshadows the fate of Jesus (8:31; 9:31; 10:33; 14:21) and of the disciples

(13:9–13), the time of preparation is complete, and in place of John's "baptism of repentance" (1:4), Jesus arrives proclaiming "the gospel of God" (v. 14), which is both the good news *from God* and *about God's* intervention in history (1 Thess. 2:3, 8–9; Rom. 1:1; 15:16). The proclamation is fourfold. First, the time (Gk. *kairos*, in the sense of time for decision) is fulfilled, recalling the apocalyptic motif that God has predetermined the stages of history. The final age has begun. Second, "The kingdom of God is at hand." "Kingdom" designates not simply the realm or place where God reigns, but better the "active ruling of God." The teaching and actions of Jesus about to unfold in the Gospel are an enactment of God's reign. This reign is "at hand," that is, imminent but not yet definitively present (Mark 9:1). Third, "Repent." The Greek *metanoia* suggests a change of heart leading to a new way of life. It also evokes the prophetic summons to conversion from evil and a turning toward God (Hos. 6:1; Isa. 1:10–20; Joel 2:12–13). Fourth, "Believe in the gospel." Repentance leads to "belief," which involves obedience to the word of God as proclaimed by Jesus and a life of discipleship.

1:16–20, The Call of the First Four Disciples. This serves as a concrete illustration of 1:14–15. All the Gospels begin with Jesus gathering disciples (lit. "learners"), which inaugurates the new eschatological community of those who will hear Jesus' word and follow in his footsteps. These calls underscore the social dimension of God's activity in Jesus. Jesus is no solitary mystic, but one who forms a community to "believe in the Gospel."

The call and commissioning narratives (1:16–20; 3:13–20; 6:7–13; cf. 2:13–14) follow a similar pattern. Unlike similar stories of the disciples of Hellenistic philosophers or Jewish rabbis in which disciples search for a teacher, here the initiative comes from Jesus (1:17; 3:13, "whom he wished"; 6:7). Those called are engaged in everyday activities (1:16; 2:14). They respond immediately (1:20; 2:14), and the summons involves personal commitment (following or "being with" Jesus, 3:13) and activity similar to that of Jesus: teaching, healing, exorcising (3:13; 6:7, 13).

1:21–45, The Inauguration of the Ministry of Jesus. Mark creates a unity (beginning and ending in Capernaum, 1:21; 2:1) of paradigmatic narratives of the public ministry of Jesus. These comprise an exorcism (1:21–28), a healing of an individual (1:29–31), group healings and exorcisms (1:32–34), a preaching tour (1:35–39), and the healing of a leper (1:40–45). The stories stress the expanding religious awe that the teaching of Jesus evokes from the crowds (1:22, 28; 37; 45) and the confrontation

with and victory over demons who recognize that Jesus is no ordinary human (1:24; 34). Here appear also the first instances of the Messianic Secret (1:34, 44), those places where Jesus enjoins silence about his identity and power.

The Miracles of Jesus in Mark

Miracle stories occupy roughly a third of the Gospel (more than the passion narrative). Mark describes the miracles of Jesus as "mighty works" (Gk. *dynameis*, 6:2; 9:39), not "signs" that authenticate the ministry of Jesus (see 8:11–13; cf. 15:29–32). From our perspective they are better called "symbols" of the power of God manifest in Jesus. This power is stronger than the forces of evil and illness and responds to the needs of suffering people. They comprise four groups: healings (1:29–31, 40–45; 2:1–12; 3:1–5; 5:25–34; 7:31–37; 8:22–26; 10:46–52); exorcisms (1:21–28; 5:1–20; 7:24–30; 9:14–27); nature miracles (4:35–41; 6:35–44; 6:45–52; 8:1–9; 11:12–14, 20–22); and one resuscitation (5:21–24, 35–43). Mark also refers to them in summaries of Jesus' ministry (1:32–34; 1:39; 3:10–12; 6:5; 6:53–56). The different groups have similar formal characteristics, which argue for oral retelling prior to Mark (→ Miracles). Similar tales of extraordinary deeds of OT prophets, Jewish rabbis, and Hellenistic heroes were common.

Mark incorporates these stories for a variety of reasons: to show Jesus as a prophet mighty in word and deed (1:27; 2:12; 6:1–6), to exalt him above other claimants to divine power (cf. 13:21–22), and to evoke wonder and awe in God's power (4:41; 7:37). By placing most of them prior to the first passion prediction (8:31–32) and the beginning of Jesus' journey to Jerusalem, Mark subjects them to the narrative paradox of his Gospel. Jesus the powerful one submits to God's will in becoming the powerless victim who is raised up by God. The resurrection is the ultimate work of power in Mark.

2:1–3:6, The Power of Jesus in Controversy with Opponents. This section contains five controversy stories, i.e., narratives culminating in a normative pronouncement, which are arranged topically, rather than historically. Though they may preserve disputes from the life of Jesus (esp. over his acceptance of tax collectors), they reflect later debates between early Christians and fellow Jews. The Pharisees (from an Aramaic word meaning "the separated ones"), who are the principal opponents here (2:16, 18, 24), constituted a popular movement (in contrast to the aristocratic Sadducees), dedicated to strict observance of the law (→ Pharisees; Sadducees).

Mark arranges these five narratives in a chiastic pattern of correspondence between the initial and final incidents to highlight the central narrative: A 2:1–12, *healing* of a paralytic; B 2:13–17, *controversy over ritual law* (i.e., not eating with unclean people); C 2:18–22, *dispute over fasting*, removal of bridegroom, contrast of old and new; B' 2:23–28, *controversy over Sabbath law*; A' 3:1–6, Sabbath *healing* of man with withered hand. This narrative unit also complements the picture of Jesus that emerged from 1:16–45. Jesus is powerful not only in the deeds of healing and exorcism, but in besting his opponents in debate. The contrast of the new and the old and the removal of the bridegroom, placed at the center, implies that Jesus' rejection of legalism and his willingness to violate the law to benefit suffering people evoked the opposition that led to his death (2:20; 3:6).

The first of these narratives (2:1–12) combines elements of two earlier narratives: the healing of a paralytic (2:1–5, 11–12) and a controversy over the power to forgive sin (2:6–10). By combining them Mark reinterprets the power of Jesus. The deeper "healing" accomplished by Jesus is release from the paralysis of sin. Since forgiveness of sin is a divine prerogative and since there are elaborate rituals of atonement, forgiveness by a word (v. 5) is tantamount to blasphemy (v. 7). The saying about the Son of man (v. 10) explains to readers that Jesus has this power as "Son of man," that is, as the one who will suffer, die, and be raised up. Mark creates a bridge between the earthly authority of Jesus and the forthcoming Passion.

The call by Jesus of a tax collector to be a disciple and Jesus' table fellowship with tax collectors (2:13–17) are based on solid historical recollection (cf. Matt. 11:19 = Luke 7:34; Luke 15:1). Jesus enacted God's offer of mercy (Mark 2:17), by associating with social and religious outcasts of his time. Tax collectors were considered dishonest and also ritually impure, because of frequent contact with Gentiles. Jesus' acceptance of them shattered fundamental religious convictions and social conventions of his contemporaries and fomented growing opposition to him (see 3:6).

The question of fasting (2:18–22) is evoked by the table setting of the previous narrative. The OT knows of both public and private fasting (Ezra 8:21–23; Zech. 7:5; Jon. 3:7–9) as a form of petitionary prayer, as a sign of mourning and repentance, and as preparation for the day of the Lord (Joel 2:14–16). The Pharisees fasted twice a week (Mark 2:18). The short parable of the bridegroom (v. 19) announces that the eschatological banquet when joy and feasting will replace fasting has begun in the ministry of Jesus. His new teaching and new practice shatters the wineskins of traditional observance. However, a time for fasting (as a sign of mourning; cf. 1 Sam. 31:13) will come when Jesus is taken away (Mark 2:20).

The final two controversies center around violations of the Sabbath law and are narrative illustrations of 2:27, "the sabbath was made for men and women, not men and women for the sabbath." Jesus first defends his disciples' violation (Exod. 34:21 prohibits "reaping" on the Sabbath) by appealing in rabbinic fashion to the precedent of David (1 Sam. 21:1–5) who violated another law by eating the consecrated "bread of the presence" (Lev. 24:5–9; Exod. 25:30) and giving it to his hungry followers. Jesus himself then violates the Sabbath rest by performing a cure. The controversies here culminate with a deepening fissure between Jesus and Jewish leaders. He is angry at their hardness of heart (cf. Mark 6:52; 8:17) and they conspire to destroy him (3:6, the first of four such references; see 11:18; 12:12; 14:1).

3:7–6:6a

Parables and Mighty Works of Jesus Cause Misunderstanding and Division

This section continues the theme of Jesus powerful in word and deed, but with escalating opposition. After a summary introduction (3:7–12) and a call narrative (3:13–19a), the first section (3:19b–4:34) comprises extensive teaching in parables (3:23; 4:2, 10, 33–34), while the second (4:35–5:43) presents four of the most dramatic "mighty works" in the Gospel. It concludes with a rejection of Jesus by his relatives (6:1–6a).

3:7–12, Summary of Activity of Jesus in Galilee. Jesus withdraws to the Sea of Galilee (from Capernaum), and crowds stream to him from a widening circle reaching beyond the confines of Palestine, anticipating his ministry there (3:7–8; cf. 7:31). He heals the sick and casts out demons who cry out, "You are the Son of God" (3:11). Mark here recapitulates the major themes of the preceding section of the Gospel: Jesus as the Messiah, powerful in word (3:8b) and deed (3:10) who, when recognized by superhuman beings (unclean spirits), enjoins secrecy. The proper meaning of Son of God (cf. 1:1, 11) remains an enigma for readers.

3:13–19, Second Call of Disciples. "He ascended the mountain" and called the disciples (3:13). This evokes Mount Sinai where Moses received the covenant that was to constitute the people of Israel (Exod. 19–34). Again the initiative is from Jesus (Mark 3:13, "he called those whom he wanted"). Lists of the Twelve appear four times in the NT (Mark 3:16–19; Matt. 10:2–4; Luke 6:14–16; Acts 1:13). The constancy of the number twelve, with variation in the names and in their order, reflects the symbolism of the twelve tribes of Israel, which Jesus now constitutes in new form. Jesus' disciples are not drawn from the educated or upper classes and include Simon "the Cananaean" (3:18, from a Semitic word meaning "zealot" [cf. Luke 6:15], i.e., a radical believer opposed to foreign rule in Palestine), as well as Judas Iscariot (mentioned last in all lists) who will betray Jesus.

3:20–35, Teaching in Parables Causes Division Among Those Who Hear Jesus.

With the constitution of the eschatological community, the next incident is a violent "clash of kingdoms" (3:20–31). It begins with Jesus at home, where some members of his family (3:21; cf. 6:1–6) think he is "out of his mind." By a literary technique used frequently (e.g., 5:21–24 [25–34] 35–43; 6:7–13 [14–29] 30–32; 14:54 [55–65] 66–72) Mark "sandwiches" (or "intercalates") one incident (the dispute on blasphemy, 3:23–34) within another (opposition from family and designation of true family of Jesus, 3:20–21, 31–34). This creates suspense (e.g., how will Jesus react to the charge of his family?) and links disparate incidents to make a unified theological statement (i.e., the divided house cannot stand, but Jesus is the stronger one who can constitute the new household of those who do God's will).

The presence of scribes "from Jerusalem" (3:22, where Jesus will ultimately suffer and die) and the serious charge of being in league with "Beelzebul," the prince of demons, heightens the opposition between Jesus and Jewish leaders. Jesus responds "in parables" (v. 23). "Parable" in Mark comprises enigmatic sayings (3:23; 4:11; 7:17) as well as longer narrative parables (4:3–9; 12:1–12). Jesus uses them both to proclaim and to defend his mission. They challenge the hearers to see themselves and God's action in a new light. The twin parables of the divided kingdom or house and the plundering of the house turn their charges back on the scribes. The exorcisms of Jesus are the plundering of Satan's house and the binding of the power of evil, by the one who emerged in the initial sections of the Gospel as the "stronger one" (1:7).

In 3:28–30, Jesus responds directly (not in parables) and harshly. Though he himself has been charged with blasphemy, his accusers commit the unforgivable sin of blasphemy against the Holy Spirit, which, in context, is the attribution to evil of a power given by God. Though all sins can be forgiven by God, the inability to distinguish good from evil makes one impervious to the presence of God.

In 3:31 the mother and brothers (and in some manuscripts, "sisters"; cf. 3:35) of Jesus (the family of 3:21) reappear and "seek" Jesus ("seek" usually has negative overtones; cf. 8:11;

11:18; 14:1). Jesus' response relativizes natural familial bonds in relationship to the "new family" created by those who do God's will. Here is an important Marcan motif. Discipleship is enlarged; neither the natural family of Jesus, nor those called to be disciples have an advantage over those who do God's will (cf. 9:38–40). Later Jesus himself will emerge as the paradigm of one who does God's will (14:36).

4:1–34, The Mystery of the Kingdom of God Given in Parables.

Along with chap. 13, Mark 4 is the longest discourse of Jesus. It continues the teaching "in parables" (3:23) as well as the motif of the division caused by Jesus. Here the mystery of the kingdom proclaimed in parables causes division between outsiders and those to whom the mystery is given (4:10–12). It is a patchwork of different material: 4:1–2, an elaborate scenic introduction; vv. 3–9, the parable of the sower; vv. 10–12, sayings on the reason for speaking in parables; vv. 13–20, the allegory of the seeds; vv. 21–25, four enigmatic sayings; vv. 26–32, two seed parables; vv. 33–34, sayings on reason for speaking in parables. A pervasive motif is that the process of growth is metaphoric of the proclamation of and response to the kingdom (cf. 1 Cor. 3:6–8; 2 Esd. 4:26–31).

The first parable (Mark 4:3–9), though called "the sower" really deals with the contrast between three failed sowings and one extravagant yield. Its hearers are caught up in the rhythm of planting and failed growth, but their expectations are shattered by the final yield. A sevenfold harvest is bountiful; thirty, sixty, and a hundredfold are unheard of. The teaching and action of Jesus is like this. The apparent rejection in the immediately preceding narratives will not prevent the hoped-for yield.

The saying of Mark 4:10–12, especially v. 12 (= Isa. 6:9–10), is one of the most controverted in NT scholarship. It implies a harsh determinism where Jesus spoke in parables in order to prevent his hearers from perceiving or understanding "lest they convert and be forgiven." (Matt. 13:13 alters Mark's "in order that" to "because.") In a deterministic worldview (like that of apocalypticism), evil that happens must have been willed in advance by God. Early Christian apologetics found in the OT a response to the rejection of Jesus. God accomplished his purpose by blinding the people as he had earlier hardened Pharaoh's heart (Exod. 4:21; 7:2–4; see also the use of Isa. 6:9–10 in Acts 28:26; John 12:40). The saying thus summarizes the *result* of the proclamation of the kingdom by Jesus and of the crucified one by the early church rather than its purpose. It also reflects the theology of Mark who uses it to interpret also the "parables" of 3:23–27. What the disciples are meant to see, which blinds outsiders, is that Jesus is the stronger one who defeats Satan. Satan can still hinder the growth of the kingdom (4:15), but the final extravagant result is assured (4:1–9).

In the allegory of the seeds (4:13–20) and the following sayings (4:21–25), Jesus instructs the audience of 4:10 on the challenge of discipleship. The three failed sowings become warnings for the pitfalls of discipleship: destruction by Satan's power (v. 15; cf. 8:31–32); initial enthusiasm, quashed by subsequent scandal (vv. 16–17; the RSV translation "fall away" is too weak)—which summarizes the action of the disciples in Mark—worldly cares, the lure of wealth, and desires for other things that "strangle the word" (vv. 18–19; cf. 10:23–25, the rich young man). The fruitful harvest (v. 20) is virtual summary of the process of conversion: hearing the word, accepting it, and bearing fruit.

The following short enigmatic sayings (4:21–25), which are found in Matthew and Luke also outside the parable discourse, are adaptations of popular proverbs to illustrate fruitful hearing (4:20). The witness of the disciples will be like a lamp (4:21; cf. Matt. 5:16); the mystery of the kingdom, though now hidden (like the identity of Jesus), will be manifest (Mark 4:22 = Luke 8:17; cf. Matt. 10:26; Luke 11:33; 12:2); the care and zeal with which they receive the word, "the measure you give," will bring extravagant results, "the measure you get" (cf. Matt. 7:2; Luke 6:38). For those who accept the word, more will be given; for those who reject it, even what they have will be lost (Matt. 13:12; cf. 25:29 = Luke 19:26; cf. 2 Esd. 7:25).

The final parables (Mark 4:26–29, 30–32), addressed to the larger audience (4:26; cf. 4:1–9) return to the growth process as a metaphor of the kingdom. Like a seed it germinates in mysterious fashion (v. 27, "he knows not how"), and has power independent of human endeavor (v. 28, "produces of itself"). Proper response to the kingdom is to be ready when the harvest is announced (v. 29; cf. 1:14–15; cf. Joel 3:13). The contrast between insignificant beginnings (the small mustard seed) and the luxuriant shrub that shelters all the birds of the air (Mark 4:32) provides an image of the contrast between Jesus with his small band of disciples and the hoped-for eschatological community (cf. Ezek. 17:22–24; Dan. 4:10–12). The conclusion (Mark 4:33–34), continues the motif of insiders and outsiders begun in 3:20. The private instruction that Jesus gives to his disciples (4:34; often in a house, 7:17; 9:28, 33; cf. 10:42) may symbolize the continued instruction of disciples within the house-churches of Mark's community.

4:35–5:43, Culmination of Mighty Works in Galilee.

This section contains dramatic exemplars of the extraordinary power of Jesus. The evils that are overcome have a cosmic and mythic power—the uncontrolled sea (4:35–41), a le-

gion of demons who inhabit the realm of the dead (5:1–20), a woman whose twelve-year illness renders her "unclean" (5:25–34; cf. Lev. 15:25–30), and the death of a young woman (Mark 5:22–24, 35–43). While the initial ministry of Jesus took place in Galilee, mainly around Capernaum on the west side of the Sea of Galilee, in 4:35–41 Jesus crosses this sea to gentile territory (the Decapolis or ten cities east of the Sea). Crossing the barrier between Jew and Gentile, symbolized by the Sea, anticipates the mission to the Gentiles that will occupy the next phase of Jesus' ministry (6:6–8:21).

The narrative of the calming of the sea (4:35–41, often called inaccurately "the walking on the water") is rich in OT allusions, where raging waters are a symbol of chaos and ominous power (Isa. 51:9–10; Ps. 89:8–10). Divine power is manifest in confining the sea within its boundaries (Gen. 1:2, 6–9) and in quelling the wind and the waves (Pss. 74:12–14; 93:3–4). Storms and raging waters also represent threats to the believer who cries out to God for deliverance (Pss. 69:1–2, 14–15; 107:23–32; cf. Mark 4:38). The narrative continues to unfold the mystery of the identity of Jesus. Like God at creation his word controls unbridled power. Like God, he rescues a beleaguered people. Though the disciples are filled with awe (which is proper to a theophany, a story of God manifesting himself; cf. Exod. 3:1–6; Isa. 6:1–5), they continue to ask who Jesus is (Mark 4:41).

The exorcism of the Gerasene demoniac (5:1–20) is one of the longest and most vivid of the NT miracles. Mark has here adapted an early folkloric narrative to his theology. (Geographical details that puzzled even ancient commentators, such as the location of Gerasa some thirty miles from the Sea of Galilee, are not important to Mark.) Just as Jesus began his ministry on Jewish soil with an exorcism (1:21–28; 1:24 and 5:7 are almost identical in Gk.), his first arrival in gentile territory (where pigs could be raised; cf. Luke 15:15) involves even more violent conflict with the power of evil. The first half describes the exorcism (5:1–13), while the second describes its effect on various people (vv. 14–20). The demoniac comes to him from the realm of the dead (v. 2; cf. Isa. 65:5, where Gentiles are a people "who sit in tombs") and his destructive power is as uncontrolled as the raging sea (Mark 5:3–5).

The narrative violates the normal pattern of exorcisms: first, meeting of demoniac and exorcist; second, silencing and expulsion of demon by exorcist; and third, departure of demon, with reaction of onlookers. Instead, on first sight (vv. 6–7) he "worships" Jesus and recognizes him as "Son of the Most High God"—a way of speaking of God characteristic of pagans (Dan. 3:26; 4:2; cf. Isa. 14:14). The exorcism (Mark 5:8) has already occurred and is mentioned almost as an afterthought. By departing from the traditional arrangement, Mark highlights the Christology of the narrative.

The expulsion of the demons into the herd of swine and their drowning in the sea initiates the purification of gentile territory. Since the unbridled power of the water has already been subjected to Jesus' power (4:35–41), it now becomes the tomb of the demons. The subsequent meeting between Jesus and the freed demoniac is also unusual in miracle stories. Rather than commanding silence, Jesus now commissions the man to proclaim, "how much the Lord has done for you and how he has had mercy on you" (5:19). He is the prototype for Mark's community of a gentile convert, freed from the domination of evil, who becomes a missionary proclaiming God's mercy.

The following two miracles, performed in a Jewish environment (5:21–22) are another instance of "sandwiching": the raising of Jairus's daughter (5:21–24a, 35–43) and the healing of a woman with a hemorrhage (5:24b–34). Both narratives have women as central characters (cf. 7:24–30) and both stress the need for faith (5:34, 36). After the initial request of Jairus, Jesus is surrounded by a crowd, while the woman who found no human assistance (vv. 25–26) approaches Jesus with belief in his power. Though the story reflects popular belief in the physical power of holy people (cf. Acts 5:15; 19:11–12), the final words of Jesus shift the emphasis to the faith of the woman. Her faith leads to salvation (liberation from evil) and health and peace (in the biblical sense of wholeness; → Peace). Like the Gerasene demoniac, she is a prototype of those who experience the benefits of the new age inaugurated by Jesus.

In 5:35–43, the narrative of Jairus's daughter resumes. Like the raising of Lazarus in John 11:1–44, the death of a loved one brings a petitioner to Jesus and becomes the occasion for presentation of Jesus' power over death. The story contrasts the turmoil of the mourners (Mark 5:38–39) with the calm assurance of Jesus (v. 39). As in the calming of the sea (4:40), faith is opposed to fear (5:36). Faith features prominently in the miracle stories (2:5; 4:40; 5:34, 36; 10:52; cf. 9:23; 11:20) where, in contrast to Hellenistic miracle accounts, it is at the beginning of the miracle rather than at its end. Mark rejects any mechanistic view that miracles give birth to faith (cf. 8:11–13; 15:32). Faith, especially as exemplified by those who carry the paralytic, the two women of Mark 5, and blind Bartimaeus, is a courageous trust in Jesus in the face of opposition. The faith the gospel demands (1:14–15) brings life and salvation.

The resuscitation is accomplished only by a word and couched in the same language the early church uses of the resurrection of Jesus (v. 41,

"rise up"; v. 42, "she arose"). Mark here reinterprets a traditional miracle in light of the resurrection faith of his church. Resurrection is victory over the power of death and the fear it injects in human life (cf. Heb. 2:14–15).

6:1–6a, The Rejection in His Own Country. Jesus' mighty works conclude with a rejection, not by opponents (cf. 3:6) but by his townspeople and relatives. The questions (vv. 2–3)—"from where do all these things come to him? What is the wisdom given him? What mighty works are wrought by his hand?"—summarize the preceding section (the words of wisdom are parables, the mighty works the three miracles) and continue the theme that those closest to Jesus are most in doubt as to his identity. Jesus responds with a proverb (confirming his reputation as one who possesses wisdom) about the frequent rejection of people by those who should know them best, which the narrator heightens by saying that Jesus "marveled at their unbelief." Unlike those in the two previous narratives whose faith brought healing and salvation, Jesus' relatives and townspeople do not allow their familiar expectations to be shattered and remain as outsiders (cf. 3:31–34).

PART TWO: 6:6b–8:21

Jesus Extends His Ministry to Jews and Gentiles Beyond Galilee

After initial narratives dealing with discipleship (6:6b–30), this section is characterized by teaching and mighty works within and beyond the confines of Galilee. It manifests a number of characteristics: sea crossings (6:45–51; 8:10, 13), movement beyond Galilee (7:31; 8:10), and doublets of significant narratives (two feedings, 6:31–44 and 8:1–9; two healings, 7:31–36 and 8:22–26; two dialogues about bread, 7:24–30 and 8:14–21). The repetitions are correlated with the geography and audience. What Jesus does for Jews in Jewish territory, he also does for Gentiles in their lands. He is a prototype for Mark's community in its mission of proclaiming the Gospel to the nations (13:10).

6:6b–13, 30
Summary of Jesus' Activity and Commission of the Twelve

This section begins with a short summary (6:6b) of Jesus' itinerant ministry and then moves to the third call and commissioning narrative (6:7–13), which intensifies the earlier calls (cf. 1:16–20; 3:7–12). Like Jesus who leaves family and home, disciples are to live a prophetic and itinerant life-style (v. 8) on the margin of society and, like him, they are to confront the power of evil and summon people to conversion.

6:14–29
Interlude: The Passion and Death of John the Baptist

This relatively long and somewhat independent narrative (the only one in Mark not about Jesus or the disciples) is interposed here by Mark (6:30 logically follows 6:13). It illustrates the risk of a prophetic life-style that confronts brutal power and prefigures the subsequent execution and arrest of Jesus. The questions of Herod in 6:14–16 reflect confusion in popular messianic expectations and anticipate similar questions in 8:27–30. The story of John the Baptist is at variance with the account of John's death by the first century Jewish historian Josephus (*Antiquities of the Jews* 18.5.1–2, §116–119) who stresses Herod's fear of John as a popular leader. The attribution of the blame for John's death to Herodias, the dance of her daughter before assembled dignitaries, and Herod's remorse give the account the flavor of a folk tale. Herod's vacillation anticipates (6:20, 26) that of Pilate (15:6–15). Both John and Jesus die because of the misuse of power by brutal but weak secular rulers (cf. Mark 10:42).

6:31–56
Jesus the Shepherd of Israel

At their return the disciples recount all that they had done and taught—the same two things that characterize Jesus' ministry—and then Jesus retires with them to a "desert place" (6:30–31). Jesus is the compassionate shepherd who feeds a pilgrim people, comes to the aid of storm-tossed disciples, and extends his ministry to the masses.

6:31–44, The Feeding of the Five Thousand. The "desert place" or wilderness (cf. 1:12) is the setting for a miraculous feeding (6:31–44; cf. 8:1–10), the only Galilean miracle of Jesus narrated in all four Gospels (see Matt. 14:13–21; 15:32–39; Luke 9:10b–17; John 6:1–13). These accounts show a double influence, from the OT narratives of the miraculous feeding of the people in the wilderness (Exod. 16:14–35; Neh. 9:15; Ps. 78:17–29, explicit in John 6:31–32), and from the Last Supper accounts of the Gospels (e.g., Mark 6:41, he blessed, broke, and gave to the disciples; cf. 14:22). They reflect the expectation of the eschatological banquet (Isa. 25:6–8), when God will feast with the elect (2 *Bar.* 29:5–8). Jesus, as the shepherd of Israel who "has compassion" on the crowd because they are like sheep without a shepherd (Num. 27:17; Ezek. 34:15), evokes God's compassion and care

in the OT (Exod. 3:7–12; Isa. 49:8–13; Ps. 23).

The narratives also draw on the double symbolism of food as teaching (Prov. 9:5; 1 Cor. 3:2; John 6:41–48) and as nourishment. Jesus first teaches the crowds many things (Mark 6:34) and then satisfies their hunger (vv. 35–44). Though the numbers (five loaves, two fish, twelve baskets, and five thousand people) are most probably symbolic, the referents are unclear. Seven, the combination of loaves and fish, frequently symbolizes adequacy or perfection; the baskets are enough for the eschatological banquet for the twelve tribes, and the five thousand people may simply be a way of exalting the miracle of Jesus over that of Elijah who feeds 100 people (2 Kings 4:42–44).

6:45–52, Sea Crossings and Healings. The following "sea miracle" (6:45–52; cf. 4:45–52) again stresses the power of Jesus over the waves and the fear of the disciples. Here added to the disciples' amazement (cf. 4:51) is the harsh view that their hearts were hardened (cf. 8:17) "because they did not understand about the loaves." The feeding (like the other mighty works of Jesus) are not simply marvels, but symbols of the new age inaugurated by Jesus, the compassionate shepherd, who comes to the aid of suffering humanity. Their enduring fear and suspicion that Jesus is a "phantom" (6:49) manifests an unconverted heart. Jesus' use of the revelational formula, "I am" (6:50; cf. 13:6; Exod. 3:13–15) turns the pericope into a veiled theophany.

6:53–56, Summary. A "Marcan summary" (cf. 1:45; 3:7–13) of the expanding extent of Jesus' mighty works (villages, cities, country) occurs in 6:53–56, and provides a transition to the stories of disputes that follow in chap. 7.

7:1–23
Jesus' New Teaching with Authority Breaks Down the Barrier Between Jew and Gentile

There is a long dispute on "clean and unclean" in 7:1–23. As a recollection of the ministry of Jesus (stage 1) this section echoes attacks on Jesus and his followers as nonobservant outsiders, and Jesus' counterrejection of legalism. Since purity regulations are not simply ritual taboos, but a means of preserving religious and ethnic identity in a hostile world, the dispute deals also with whether the community is to be exclusivist or open to "unclean" elements, e.g., Gentiles.

The controversy is divided into a dispute over clean and unclean vessels (7:1–8) and on the institution of the corban (7:9–13; see below) followed by a parabolic saying on clean and unclean (7:14–17) with a private explanation to the disciples (7:18–23; cf. 4:1–20). This defense of the neglect by his disciples of ritual practice culminates, like earlier disputes, in a pronouncement contrasting human institutions and divine precepts (cf. 2:23–28). In citing Isa. 29:13 ("this people . . . precepts of men"), Jesus recalls not only the particular verse, but other prophetic attacks on misuse of religious practices (e.g., Isa. 1:10–20; 58:1–14; Amos 5:21–24).

The distorting power of legalism is then underscored by Jesus' harsh attack on corban (7:9–13), an Aramaic term for a practice whereby children were allowed to make a financial offering to the Temple that would then absolve them from using this money to care for their parents. As in the case with ritual uncleanness, Jesus invokes the OT (Exod. 20:12; 21:17; Deut. 5:16; Lev. 20:9) against later interpretations, which are equivalent to voiding the word of God. Like the prophets Jesus here defends the vulnerable members of the community and summons people to fidelity to the Decalogue.

The saying of Mark 7:15 and its subsequent explanation (vv. 16–21) are most likely additions by the Evangelist to an earlier tradition. The rejection of particular ritual practices is now escalated to a rejection of all ritual laws. The only purity that matters is moral (i.e., interior) integrity (v. 18), which is illustrated by a rather earthy image of digestion (v. 19). Interior impurity is illustrated by a traditional list of vices that flow from the human heart (vv. 21–22; cf. Gal. 5:19–21; 1 Tim. 1:9–10; Col. 3:5–8; 1 Cor. 5:10–11). Such spiritualization of ritual law by making interior attitudes and dispositions the criteria of morality is characteristic of Judaism in a Hellenistic environment (e.g., Philo of Alexandria) as well as of early Christianity.

7:24–8:10
Jesus' Mighty Works Among Gentiles

7:24–30, The Syrophoenician Woman. As if to enforce the previous teaching, Jesus himself now enters unclean territory (Tyre, 7:24–30), where he performs his first mighty work on behalf of a gentile woman whose daughter is possessed by an unclean spirit. The brisk dialogue (vv. 26–29) contrasts with the formal confrontation with the Pharisees. Jesus seems to dismiss her initial request with a slur on the Gentiles (who were often called "dogs" by observant Jews). With rhetorical skill equal to that of Jesus in the previous pericopes, the woman turns the saying back on Jesus (v. 27), who then heals her daughter "because of what she said" (v. 29). The woman is a model of that lively and courageous faith that constitutes a proper response to Jesus.

7:31–37, The Deaf Mute. The following story, also in gentile territory, again pictures Jesus as the missionary giving hearing and speech (7:31–37). In contrast to his disciples and compatriots who hear but do not listen, the once deaf and mute Gentile becomes a herald of Jesus' mighty works (7:37).

8:1–10, The Feeding of the Four Thousand. This feeding, a virtual retelling of the earlier one, presents Jesus as one who gives sustenance to people in gentile territory. They too will be fed with the bread given to the children (see 7:27). Like the earlier story it takes place in the wilderness and reflects the language of the Lord's Supper. However, in place of the five loaves and two fish, we now have seven loaves and seven baskets, with "a few fish." As earlier, the numbers are symbolic but the referents equally uncertain. "Seven" may simply suggest a totality of gifts for the Gentiles equal to those given to the Jews. The number four thousand may be less than the earlier five thousand to indicate the precedence of Israel in salvation history (cf. Rom. 9:1–9).

8:11–21
Jesus' Actions Culminate in Opposition and Misunderstanding

Mark concludes the public manifestation of Jesus with two vignettes about two groups that have misunderstood the mighty works of Jesus throughout his ministry. In 8:11–12 the Pharisees ask for a sign from heaven (i.e., some convincing mark of divine approval). They are the opposite of those who approached Jesus simply with faith. Deeply affected by such a request (v. 12, "he sighed deeply in his spirit"), Jesus rejects their attitude, saying that no sign will be given to this generation (used in a negative sense; Matt. 16:4 reads here "an evil and adulterous" generation; cf. Mark 8:38).

The misunderstanding of the disciples is described in a particularly enigmatic narrative (8:14–21). Jesus first cautions them to beware of the "leaven" (i.e., bread as a metaphor for teaching, with the overtones of leaven as an agent of corruption) of the Pharisees and of Herod. The disciples who have only one loaf (8:14) then discuss their plight in having no bread (8:16). Jesus, strongly addressing them like the opponents in 2:8, "Why do you discuss?" (8:17), tells them that their hearts are hardened and, like the outsiders of 4:10–12, they have "eyes which do not see and ears which do not hear."

Jesus then refers back to the two multiplications of the loaves, eliciting from the disciples answers about his actions, and asks if they do not yet understand (Mark 8:19–21). The disciples never answer his question. Both the Pharisees and the disciples lack faith. The Pharisees seek for a sign; the disciples do not see beyond the actions of Jesus to the power of his person. They do not realize that the one loaf which they have with them (Jesus) is more adequate than demonstrations of power.

PART THREE: 8:22–10:52

Jesus Begins His Journey to Jerusalem Where as the Son of Man He Will Give His Life as a Ransom for Many

The centerpiece of the Gospel narrates the journey of Jesus and the disciples from the northernmost point of Palestine (Caesarea Philippi) southward to Jerusalem. References to being "on the way" (8:27; 9:33, 34; 10:17, 32, 46) punctuate the account, along with periodic geographical references (8:22, 27; 9:30, 33; 10:1, 32). Since the actual course of the journey is ill defined, "way" serves as metaphor for the way of discipleship (cf. Acts 9:2) that Jesus here teaches his disciples by word and example.

The whole section is framed by two giving-of-sight stories (8:22–26; 10:46–52) and structured around three passion predictions in the pattern: Jesus predicts his forthcoming suffering (8:31; 9:30–31; 10:32–34), followed by misunderstanding on the part of the disciples (8:32–33; 9:32; 10:35–41), which evokes further instruction by Jesus on the deeper demands of discipleship (8:34–91; 9:33–50; 10:42–45). Also, from now on there are very few miracles. Those recounted (9:14–29; 10:46–52; 11:12–14, 20) lack public acclamation and serve principally to instruct the disciples.

8:22–26
Transitional Giving-of-Sight Story

The healing of the blind man (8:22–26) at Bethsaida, a city in the north of Galilee, is important in the literary structure of the Gospel. It serves as a transition from the Galilean ministry to the journey southward to Jerusalem. More importantly, along with 10:46–52 (another healing of a blind man), it provides the frame for the important middle section where Jesus gives his disciples "insight" about his forthcoming Passion and death. After the description of the disciples themselves as blind in 8:18, the first healing, which takes place in progressive stages (8:23–25) symbolizes the progressive journey to understanding that the disciples must make. At the second healing the man given his sight

becomes a disciple who "follows on the way" (10:52). Between these stories of two blind people given sight, Jesus initiates his disciples into the mystery of the cross.

8:27–9:29
The First Passion Prediction Unit

8:27–30, The Confession of Peter. Throughout the first part of the Gospel Jesus' actions evoke questions about his identity, e.g., 1:27, "What is this . . . ?"; 4:41, "Who then is this . . . ?"; 6:2, "What is this wisdom . . . ?"; 6:14–15, the questions of Herod. Here Jesus himself poses the question "Who do men think I am?" (i.e., human beings in contrast to those with supernatural power). The disciples recount the popular opinions, but then Jesus asks their opinion. Peter, the first called, responds simply, "You are the Christ [anointed one, Messiah]," at which Jesus commands silence. In the structure of the Gospel this dialogue sets the tone for the subsequent unfolding of the proper understanding of Jesus as the Christ and the consequences of confessing him as such. For Mark's readers (and subsequent generations) the challenge facing every future believer is how properly to confess Jesus as Messiah amid conflicting claims.

8:31–33, The First Passion Prediction. The passion predictions, though in present form written from a postresurrection perspective (like the Gospel as a whole), contain a historical core. Jesus did evoke mortal opposition from segments of Jewish society and Roman leaders. The earlier fate of the prophets (2 Chron. 24:20–22; 36:15–16) and of John made him aware that he might suffer a similar fate. Like the prophets and the suffering just people of the OT (e.g., Wisd. of Sol. 2:10–20; 5:15), he hoped for vindication.

The first passion prediction plainly (Mark 8:31) indicates in what sense Jesus is the Messiah. He is such as Son of man (that human figure) who "must" suffer and be rejected by the leaders of his people. The term "must" or "it is necessary" (v. 31) offers no detailed theology of suffering, but is a concise reference to collections of OT texts cited to show that Jesus' suffering was willed by God. Coupled with the subsequent narrative of the transfiguration (9:1–8), this section (which is the approximate midpoint of the Gospel) presents a "Gospel in miniature," which reflects the pattern of rejection followed by vindication/exaltation found elsewhere in early Christian confessions (Phil. 2:5–11; cf. 1 Pet. 2:7–8) and preaching (Acts 2:22–24; 3:12–16; 4:10–12).

After his spontaneous confession (Mark 8:29), Peter's misunderstanding is surprising (8:32b). He "rebukes" Jesus—the same term used of Jesus' "rebuke" of demons (1:25). Like the relatives of 3:21, Peter may think Jesus "out of his senses." Jesus responds with an even stronger rebuke and calls Peter "Satan" (8:33). Like Satan (1:13) he attempts to turn Jesus away from God's will. Etymologically "Satan" means "adversary" and Peter is such because "he does not think the thoughts of God, but human thoughts" (v. 33).

8:34–9:1, Further Instruction on Discipleship. These sayings, often called "the cost of discipleship," are addressed to the crowd and not simply the disciples of 8:27. They unfold the most radical implications of proper confession of Jesus as Messiah. Would-be disciples must enter into that same mystery that characterized Jesus' life. Following of Jesus, denial of self-interest even to the point of losing one's life for Jesus and the Gospel (v. 35), paradoxically results in making life more secure (i.e., saving it). For a community recently exposed to the horrors of Nero's persecution, such sayings are both challenging and consoling.

The demands of discipleship are then supported by the threat of eschatological rejection of those who are ashamed of Jesus and his words (v. 38). This saying reflects current apocalyptic expectation that at the final judgment those who suffer unjustly will be vindicated and rewarded, while their persecutors will be punished (cf. Mark 13:24–27; 2 Thess. 1:4–5; Phil. 1:28; 1 Enoch 60:6; 100–101). The final saying (Mark 9:1) where Jesus says that some of his hearers will be alive when the kingdom comes in power reflects the expectation in early Christianity that the Parousia (or return) of the Lord was imminent (1 Thess. 4:15–18; 1 Cor. 7:29, 31).

9:2–13, The Transfiguration. After the prediction of the Passion and the sober demands of following Jesus, Mark presents a vision of the exaltation of the suffering Messiah (9:2–9). The term "transfigured" (v. 2) is used elsewhere of the transformation of the risen body (Phil. 3:21; 2 Cor. 3:18; cf. 1 Cor. 15:51). The account is rich in OT allusions: the appearance of the glory of the Lord to Moses on Mount Sinai after six days (Exod. 24:16–17, cf. Mark 9:2); glistening garments as a sign of the glorified state (Dan. 7:9; cf. Rev. 3:5, 4:4, 7:9; 1 Enoch 62:15–16; 2 Enoch 22:8); Elijah and Moses symbolizing the "law and the prophets" as well as two people who were taken up into God's presence (2 Kings 2:9–12; Deut. 34:6 was interpreted in postbiblical thought as the "assumption" of Moses); the cloud and the voice as symbols of God's presence (Exod. 16:10, 19:9, 16).

After the appearance of the exalted Jesus, in stylized misunderstanding, Peter (Mark 9:5) says, "It is well that we are here," and requests that they build "three booths" (a term for the dwelling of God with the people, Exod. 25:1–9; Ezek. 37:27, 43:7). The account culminates in the voice proclaiming again (Mark 9:7; cf. 1:11) that Jesus is God's beloved son, whose word is authoritative ("listen to him"). Just as at the baptism the voice from heaven sanctioned the first phase of the ministry of God's son, the more elaborate theophany of the transfiguration inaugurates the second phase (suffering and death). Jesus is God's son not only as one powerful in word and work, but in a deeper sense as the one who follows his Father's will even to the cross. Peter's unanswered request represents an attempt to rest in the glory without following the way of the cross. The narrative ends suddenly with the disappearance of the supernatural phenomenon. The disciples suddenly (9:8) see only Jesus with them. The vision and the hope it offers is no substitute for the path they must follow with Jesus, a perspective emphasized by the concluding sayings that caution secrecy until after the resurrection (9:9) and return to the theme of the deaths of John and Jesus (9:10–13).

9:14–29, The Possessed Boy. After the serene image of the transfiguration, Jesus then returns to find the disciples who earlier had cast out many demons (6:13) unable to exorcise a particularly destructive demon. Jesus attributes their inability to lack of faith (9:19, cf. 6:6) and the story becomes the occasion for instruction on faith. Jesus tells the father that "all things are possible to one who believes" (cf. 11:20–25), which evokes the prayer of the father, "Lord I believe, help my unbelief." The exorcism (9:25–27) is then recounted in more detail than normal with an overlay of resurrection language (vv. 26–27, "he is dead . . . he rose up"). Alone with the disciples Jesus tells them that such a demon can be driven out only by prayer. Whatever the original form of this vivid narrative, Mark has adapted it to his theology. The promise of glory and the coming exaltation of Jesus (the transfiguration) exist along with destructive power of evil. During Jesus' absence (which Mark's community experiences), prayer enables his followers to confront this power. The path from unbelief to belief begins with the cry, "help my unbelief." The first passion prediction unit thus concludes with a summons to faith and prayer.

9:30–50
The Second Passion Prediction Unit

9:30–32, Second Passion Prediction. The journey resumes in 9:30 followed quickly by a condensed passion prediction (the oldest form of the three), with a brief indication of the misunderstanding by the disciples (9:32). These will be followed by three collections of sayings (9:33–37, 38–41, 42–50) addressed to the disciples.

9:33–37, Dispute over the Greatest and Instruction on Service. In a pattern that will be expanded in 10:35–45, though having heard Jesus' prediction of his humiliation, the disciples argue about "who was the greatest" (9:34). Jesus' response in both word and symbol spells out the ethical implications of his example. The one who would be first must be last and servant of all (v. 35; cf. 10:45). He then takes a child, who in biblical thought is a symbol not of innocence but of powerlessness and vulnerability, and says that whoever receives the child receives him (9:36). In contrast to the disciples' concern for power, Jesus says that only those who accept the powerless and vulnerable will receive both him and God (v. 37, "the one who sent me"; cf. Matt. 25:31–46). Jesus will later say that one must actually become like the child to enter the kingdom of heaven (10:15).

9:38–50, The Unknown Exorcist and Teaching on Discipleship. The following pericope (vv. 38–41) undercuts any exclusive claim of the Twelve to divine power. Rather ironically since only a short time ago they could not exorcise (9:18), they forbid another exorcist "who was not following us" (v. 38). Jesus' reply repeats that universalistic thrust found earlier that those who are not explicitly disciples can do God's work (cf. 3:31–35).

The final section (9:42–50) collects originally independent sayings and unites them by catchwords, e.g., "scandal" (RSV, "cause to sin"; 9:42, 43, 45, 47); "salt" (9:49–50). They depict in radical images the risk of inauthentic discipleship and suggest that vying for positions of power can cause little ones (not only the powerless but those weak in faith) to "fall away" (lit. "be tripped"; the Gk. word is the root of the English "scandalize"; cf. 4:17). The seriousness of such "scandal" is supported by metaphors that suggest self-mutilation is better than losing the opportunity to enter the kingdom of God (9:47). The section concludes with a mixed metaphor of salt as accompanying Temple sacrifices ("salted with fire," Lev. 2:13; Ezek. 43:24; cf. Exod. 30:35) and as a seasoning and preservative for food. Disciples who bicker about power, rather than lead sacrificial lives, will lose their effectiveness (salt losing its saltiness). Rather they are to live in peace.

10:1–31

Interlude: Teaching to Crowds Across the Jordan

In 10:1 Jesus resumes the journey and, under the general theme of "discipleship on the way," Mark locates here the longest "ethical" section

of his Gospel (addressed to the crowds as well as to disciples). Jesus offers instruction on marriage (10:1–12), children (10:13–16), riches (10:17–27), and the rewards of discipleship (10:28–31). Since this teaching treats "domestic" issues and is located in gentile territory ("beyond the Jordan"), it addresses concerns that are alive in the "house-churches" of Mark's community. (On house-churches, see Rom. 16:5; 1 Cor. 16:19; Col. 4:15.)

10:1–12, Teaching on Divorce. To "test" Jesus, the Pharisees question his attitude toward divorce (10:1–12), an issue that divided the Pharisees themselves at the time of Jesus. His response is not simply the prohibition of divorce but a denunciation of the "hardness of heart" that opened the door to abusive divorce (v. 5). According to OT law (Deut. 24:1–4) and its application at the time of Jesus, husbands could divorce their wives on very little cause. Such practice could lead to abuse and exploitation of women. By citing the creation narratives of Genesis (esp. 1:27; 2:24) in his response, Jesus counters that the purpose of marriage was life-long mutuality and interdependence, not dominance of one party by the other. Spouses cannot treat each other as property to be discarded.

As the teaching of Jesus was handed on, it was also modified. Matthew allows divorce because of "unchastity" (5:32; 19:9; Gk. *porneia*, also interpreted as "adultery" or marriage within forbidden kinship boundaries). Paul (1 Cor. 7:12–16) allows divorce between a Christian and a pagan spouse when initiated by the latter. In Mark 10:10–11, this teaching is also adapted in two ways: first, to a Roman/Hellenistic setting where both the man (v. 11) and woman (v. 12) could initiate divorce—which a woman could not do in a Palestinian setting—and second, by explicitly prohibiting only "marrying another," it allows for divorce but without remarriage (i.e., some form of legal separation).

10:13–16, Receiving Children. The following sayings on children (10:13–16; cf. 9:33–37, 42) follow naturally after a discussion of marriage, and also may be located here because of a dispute in the early community about the baptism or admission of children. The "blessing" and "laying on of hands" (v. 16) suggest some rite of admission. Children are also without legal rights (like women under first-century divorce laws) so the two incidents reflect Jesus' concern for the powerless.

10:17–31, The Rich Young Man and Teaching on Wealth. This narrative (10:17–22) is the only instance in the Gospels where a person refuses a call to follow Jesus, and it occasions a longer discourse on wealth (10:23–31). The would-be disciple is an observant seeker after eternal life. For this Jesus "loved him," and invites him to join the circle of those first called by doing as they did (cf. 1:18; 10:28). He becomes sad since he cannot abandon his many possessions (cf. 8:36). Though there is biblical precedent for associating riches with God's blessings (e.g., Job 1:10; 42:10; Ps. 128:1–2; Isa. 3:10), the more dominant strain (taken over by Mark and expanded by Luke) is the pervasive concern for the danger of wealth. The rich are described as wise in their own eyes (Prov. 28:11) and are prone to apostasy and violence (Amos 5:4–13; Isa. 2:6–8; cf. James 5:1–6).

The subsequent sayings (Mark 10:23–25) make this clear. After the departure of the now-saddened rich young man, Jesus states, "How hard it is for the rich to enter the kingdom of God" (v. 23). They cannot make the radical sacrifice called for earlier (9:43–47). Yet even this seeming impossibility (underscored by the comparison of the camel and the eye of the needle) can yield to the power of God (cf. Gen. 18:14).

The tone of the conversation shifts with the unfinished exclamation of Peter, "We have left everything and followed you" (Mark 10:28; Matt. 19:27 completes the implicit question, by adding "What then shall we have?"). The context of Peter's exclamation is the concern of the disciples throughout this section for the rewards of discipleship, and its background is the often extravagant pictures of the future rewards of the just (1 Enoch 25:1–6, 92:3–5; 2 Esd. 7:88–99; Matt. 19:28). Jesus' response rather directs Peter to the rewards of this life. The community of disciples that will be formed by the call of Jesus will replace natural family and material possessions (Mark 10:30). Such sayings are not simply figures of speech. They here reflect the ethos of Mark's community. Early Christians, whose conversions often involved a break with their natural families, experienced new familial bonds (Acts 4:32; 1 Cor. 4:15; Rom. 16:13–17). Hospitality and mutual acceptance gave them new homes, mothers, brothers, and sisters.

Among the new family Mark omits "fathers," for in the ethos of this whole section service is to replace patriarchal power. The somewhat jarring comment that all this comes "with persecutions" mirrors actual persecutions (e.g., under Nero). Persecutions could arise also from their criticism of wealth and power, from their willingness to accept children into the community, which confronted the *patria potestas* (Lat.) or absolute power of the father in that culture, as well as from their rejection of the patriarchal structure of marriage.

10:32–45
The Third Passion Prediction Unit

The middle section of the Gospel concludes with Jesus and the disciples almost in solemn procession drawing near Jerusalem (10:32). The pattern of prediction (10:32–34) and misunderstanding (10:35–37) is elaborated by sayings of Jesus that are central to the theology of the whole Gospel (10:43–45). The misunderstandings after the prediction do not center on the problem of the suffering of Jesus as in 8:32–33, but on the implications of this for his followers. The misunderstandings are twofold: first, the request of James and John for vice-regency in the coming kingdom (10:35–40), and second, the indignation of the other disciples (10:40–42; cf. 9:34).

10:32–34, Third Passion Prediction. The third passion prediction is the most detailed of the three and a capsule summary of the passion narrative.

10:35–40, The Request of James and John. In response to the request of James and John to sit at the right and left "in glory" (i.e., when Jesus returns as judge, 8:38; 13:26), Jesus asks whether they can drink the cup he will drink and be baptized with the baptism he will be baptized with (10:38). On the narrative level this points to the forthcoming Passion, when Jesus will accept the cup that his Father offers (14:36). Since in the narrative the same disciples who protest their willingness to accept the fate of Jesus will flee at his arrest, Jesus' prediction of 10:39 ("you will drink") may be veiled allusion to the subsequent martyrdoms of James and John. In the reference to the baptism and cup, Mark's community also can reflect on their own baptisms and celebration of the Lord's Supper as a summons to follow Jesus on the way of discipleship.

10:41–45, The Indignation of the Other Disciples and Jesus' Example of True Discipleship. After the indignation of the other disciples at the request, the sayings of 10:42–45 constitute the high point of discipleship instruction of 8:22–10:52. In contrast to gentile rulers who "lord it over others," the disciples should strive to be "servants" (10:43, the Gk. term means "menial table server"), and those who wish to be "first" (like James and John) must be slaves, that is, at the beck and call of others (v. 44). The basis is that "the Son of man came not to be served but to serve and to give his life as a ransom for many" (v. 45). This saying derives its force by contrast with the first part of the Gospel where Jesus is the powerful Son of God. Power is here radically redefined in terms of self-emptying service. Behind this saying stands the figure of the Suffering Servant of Isa. 52:13–53:12 whose death brings freedom to others. "Ransom" is a technical term for the money paid to purchase freedom for a slave. Here and in 14:24, Jesus' life itself is given as such a ransom for many (cf. Rom. 3:24).

10:46–52
Transitional Giving-of-Sight Story

The healing of blind Bartimaeus at Jericho (about twenty miles northeast of Jerusalem in the Jordan Valley; cf. 1:5), along with 8:22–26, not only provides the frame for the middle section, but provides the transition to the Jerusalem ministry. Bartimaeus' cry to Jesus, "Son of David, have mercy on me" (10:47), evokes the story of David returning to claim his kingdom in Jerusalem (2 Sam. 19:31–20:3). This confession also contains the first public and unrebuked recognition of Jesus as royal Messiah. Paradoxically, Jesus, who earlier announced the imminence of God's kingdom (Mark 1:14), will reign in Jerusalem, but from the cross (15:26). After the healing, the saying of Jesus, "Your faith has saved you" (10:52), and the action of the blind man have symbolic force. The blind man who asks simply for mercy is given sight. Unlike the disciples' desire for power, which blinds them to the necessity of suffering, the faith of the blind man leads to salvation. He follows on the way as a disciple.

PART FOUR: 11:1–13:37
The Messianic Actions and Teaching of Jesus in Jerusalem

With the goal of the journey attained, Jesus now enters Jerusalem with his disciples. Where Galilee was the place of revelation of Jesus as the powerful Son of God and of his acclamation by crowds (e.g., 1:28, 45; 2:13; 3:9; 5:21; 8:1), Jerusalem quickly becomes a center of opposition (11:18, 12:12). The only mighty work of Jesus performed here is a destructive miracle (11:12–14). He calls the Temple a "den of bandits" (11:17) and engages in controversy with Temple authorities (11:27–12:38). The Jerusalem leaders are equated with the unfaithful tenants who kill the son of the owner, and the vineyard will be given "to others" (12:1–12). After leaving the Temple in 13:1, Jesus will never again enter it and utters a series of ominous prophecies against the city and Temple (13:1–27). The passion narrative unfolds in Jerusalem where the Jerusalem aristocracy in collusion with the Roman authority effect the death of Jesus (14:1–15:47). Though the resurrection is recounted in Jerusalem (16:1–8), the promised meeting between Jesus and his first followers is to take place in Galilee (16:7). The place of the first revelation becomes the center of the hoped-for appearance.

The polemic against the Jewish leaders and Jewish institutions should be evaluated in its historical and literary context. The most bitter opposition to Jesus in Mark comes not from the bulk of the people and the Pharisees but from established Temple personnel who were in league with the Romans and themselves considered illegitimate by other Jewish groups (e.g., by the Essenes). The Gospel is also written for Christians a generation after the death of Jesus, and most likely after the destruction of the Temple in A.D. 70. Different Jewish groups *and* early Christians are claiming to be authentic heirs of the traditions of Israel, and the Gospels reflect the bitterness of interreligious strife (esp. Matt. 23). Mark also reflects the apocalyptic or deterministic view of history that attributes the rejection of Jesus by his own people to God's foreordained plan.

11:1–12:44
Ministry of Jesus in Jerusalem, Conflict of Kingdoms

Though much of the material here is pre-Marcan, such as the expulsion of the buyers and sellers from the Temple (see John 2:13–22) and a collection of five controversies (11:27–33; 12:13–17, 18–27, 28–34, 35–37; cf. 2:1–3:6), the Evangelist organizes the traditions in terms of his theology. He constructs a stylized chronology of six days in Jerusalem, three prior to the passion narrative (11:1, 12, 19) and three prior to the crucifixion and burial (14:1, 12, 17; 15:42). The events of the initial days are also carefully organized. After the entry into Jerusalem and the initial opposition (11:1–26), Mark places a controversy (11:27–33) and a parable (12:1–12) at the center of the Jerusalem ministry. In these first two sections the opposition so heightens that the vineyard (heritage of Israel) will be given to others (the Jewish Christian community of Mark). In the final controversies (12:13–37) Jesus teaches about issues that are at the center of the missionary proclamation of the Gospel to the nations (Mark 13:10). After a final attack on the scribes (12:38–40) and a transitional story about a widow (12:41–44), Jesus abandons the Temple (13:1).

11:1–26, Entry into Jerusalem, Cleansing of the Temple, and Cursing of the Fig Tree. The messianic arrival at Jerusalem (11:1–11) comprises two distinct phases: the obtaining of the colt (vv. 1–6) and the acclamation of the crowd (7–11). Though often called the "triumphal entry" into Jerusalem, the acclamation of Jesus takes place prior to the actual entry (11:10), which is simply a cursory visit by Jesus and the Twelve. The narrative, dense with OT allusions, presents and reinterprets contemporary messianic expectations. The Mount of Olives (11:1) was associated with the arrival of the Messiah (Zech. 14:4; cf. Josephus *Jewish War*

2.13.5, §261–63). In contrast, however, to the militant Davidic Messiah attested in texts such as *Psalms of Solomon* 17, Jesus arrives, "humble, riding on an ass" (Zech. 9:9). While military leaders rode on horses, messengers of peace rode on donkeys. Garments were thrown on the ground to welcome an anointed king (2 Kings 9:13); the colt on which no one has ridden may recall the as yet unyoked cows that pulled the Ark (1 Sam. 6:7). In appropriating the narrative Mark stresses three things: first, Jesus as the Lord of his destiny and reliable prophet whose word is verified (Mark 11:1–8; cf. 14:12–16); second, the true understanding of Jesus' Davidic messiahship—Jesus is a peaceful Messiah who prepares for the coming of his father's kingdom (11:10); and third, the contrast between the people who acclaim Jesus (11:7–10) and the leaders who plot to kill him (11:18; 12:12).

The cursing of the fig tree (11:12–14, 20–25) and the cleansing of the Temple (11:15–19) are "intercalated" and interpret each other. The cursing of the fig tree may have developed from a parable such as Luke 13:6–9, where the unfruitful tree symbolizes an unfaithful people (Isa. 5:1–7; Jer. 8:13; Mic. 7:1) and, along with the expulsion of the buyers and sellers from the Temple, constitutes a parabolic action (familiar in the prophets, e.g., Jer. 27:2; Ezek 4:1–5:17; also connected with destruction of Jerusalem).

The enigmatic comment in Mark 11:13 that the tree is cursed for not having fruit even though "it was not the season for figs" reflects apocalyptic determinism. Paraphrased it means, "it was determined that this would not be the proper time for the Jewish leaders to bear fruit," i.e., receive Jesus. The barren tree and the mercantile Temple symbolize to Mark's community that the older religious institutions and observances are not binding (cf. 7:1–23), and they are now to see their community as a fulfillment of Isaiah's prophecy of a "house of prayer for all nations" (11:17; Isa. 56:7).

The instruction on prayer (Mark 11:21–25) evoked by Isaiah's prophecy directs the disciples' attention away from the fig tree and Temple to the challenge they face. More important than religious institution and practice is faith in God (11:22), which can accomplish the seemingly impossible (i.e., move mountains; cf. 10:27). Such faith is required in order to forgive "anyone" (v. 25) against whom you have anything. This exhortation puts into proper perspective the harsh actions and sayings of Jesus of the two previous incidents. Faith, prayer, and forgiveness are more important than complacency over the rejection of the Temple.

11:27–12:12, The Center of the Jerusalem Ministry: Jesus, the Rejected Son, Teaches with Messianic Authority. The "third entry" into Jerusalem (11:27; see 11:11, 15) is quickly followed by a "trial" of Jesus (11:28–33) over the source of his authority by the high priests, scribes, and elders (the same groups that conduct the formal trial in 15:53–65). In the Galilean controversies (2:1–3:6), the authority (2:10; 2:28) of Jesus as Son of man was established. The Jewish leaders remain blind to this authority. When challenged (11:28), Jesus responds in rabbinic fashion with a counterquestion, asking them to take a stand on the baptism of John. Caught on the horns of a dilemma (admitting John's divine authority and disbelieving him, or criticizing a popular figure) they are reduced to silence. Since John prophesied that a stronger one would come after him (1:7) and since Jesus' authority rests on divine confirmation (1:11; 9:7), Mark's readers know that the officials are implicitly indicting themselves for their rejection of Jesus.

The parable of the wicked vineyard tenants (12:1–12) forms the centerpiece of the Jerusalem ministry. *Gospel of Thomas* 65 contains a less allegorical version of the parable, omitting the reference to Isaiah 5 (as does Luke 20:9) and the beloved son (Mark 12:6). As an original parable of Jesus it could express the constant reaching out by the long-suffering God for human response in the face of continued rejection (cf. Hos. 2:2, 14–20; Jer. 3:11–14; Ezek. 16:59–63). Jesus speaks parabolically of his ministry as embodying such an offer of God's mercy to all who hear him.

Its present form manifests strong allegorical elements, such as the verbal similarity between 12:1 and Isa. 5:1–2 (where the vineyard equals the house of Israel; cf. Isa. 5:7); Mark 12:2–5, the repeated sending of servants (a term used in the OT for prophets, Jer. 7:25, 25:4; Amos 3:7; Zech. 1:6) and their violent rejection (also recalling the fate of OT prophets, 1 Kings 18:13; 22:26–27; 2 Chron. 24:20–22; 36:15–16); the final sending of the "beloved son" (Mark 12:6, a term used elsewhere for Jesus, 1:11; 9:7); and the destruction of the tenants and the transfer of the vineyard "to others" (12:9), reflecting the destruction of the Temple. The saying on the rejected stone (vv. 10–11) that becomes the cornerstone (or keystone) of a new building is added to the parable from a collection of OT "stone" texts used by early Christians as a defensive explanation for the rejection of Jesus, and to buttress their claim to be the new building (temple) of God (see Ps. 118:22; Isa. 8:14–15, 28:16; cf. Acts 4:11; 1 Pet. 2:6–8; Eph. 2:20–22).

With the aid of Isaiah 5 and the addition of "beloved son" Mark locates this allegory of the rejection of Jesus by Temple authorities at that point in the Gospel where Jesus, in conflict with Jewish authorities, is pointing to the emergence of the Christian community (the house that will be built on the cornerstone). It also answers the

999

question of Mark 11:27, "By what authority?" The authority of Jesus is that of the "beloved son" (12:6), sent from the Father, but rejected by the tenants. At the end of the parable (v. 12) the questioners from 11:27 perceive that the parable is directed against them.

12:13–34, In Controversy with Jerusalem Leaders, Jesus Offers a Compendium of Belief. The three controversies following the parable form a subunit. While the first of the five controversies (11:27–33, on authority) and the last (12:35–37) take place in the Temple, the three in 12:13–34 are not localized and are initiated in stylized fashion by the three major groups of opponents in the Gospel: Pharisees and Herodians (12:13; cf. 3:6), Sadducees (12:18), and a scribe (12:28). They deal with three issues that were paramount to Mark's community (the "others" of 12:9) in its missionary preaching to Gentiles: relation to secular authority, the meaning of resurrection, and the core of their faith, love of God and neighbor.

In the first (12:13–18) the Pharisees try to trap Jesus into taking a dangerous stand on either side of a debated issue, paying taxes to Caesar. In a theocracy, as was the ideal of Jewish society, which the Zealots of A.D. 66–70 attempted to restore, a gentile ruler could be viewed as an usurper of divine prerogatives. Paying taxes was tantamount to diminishing God's sovereignty; refusal could imply political resistance, which the Romans brutally suppressed. Just as Jesus posed a dilemma on authority to his opponents (11:29), they now retaliate in kind. The narrative depicts Jesus as victor in this contest of dilemmas (12:17, "they were amazed").

The action of Jesus (pointing to the inscription on the coin) and the saying, "return to Caesar the things of Caesar and to God the things of God," is as controverted (and misused) as any in the Gospels. While this saying (and the Gospel as a whole) never spells out just what constitute the "things of God" and "of Caesar," it *does not* relegate religion to the "spiritual" realm nor sanction the moral autonomy of the secular sphere. In the third controversy of this subunit (12:28–34) the "greatest commandment" is whole-hearted love of God and neighbor that is to permeate all of life. No human ruler shares power or demands allegiance equal to God (cf. Acts. 5:29). In its first-century context the saying of 12:17 affirms the sovereignty of God without adopting the theocratic or sectarian implications of that sovereignty (cf. Rom. 13:1–7; 1 Pet. 2:11–17).

In the following controversy (Mark 12:18–27) the mode of argument is more rabbinic, consisting of text and countertext, all taken from the Pentateuch, since the Sadducees (v.

18) gave greatest authority to the five books of Moses and (unlike the Pharisees) rejected the binding force of oral interpretations. Also in contrast to the Pharisees, they did not believe the resurrection (cf. Acts 23:8). Their objection (12:19–23) involves a rather crass interpretation of Moses' command on preserving the family line through levirate marriage (Deut. 25:5–10). Jesus attacks their attitude as unfaithful to Scripture and ignorant of God's power. Those who rise from the dead will be like the angels, spiritual beings alive in God's presence (cf. 1 Cor. 15:42–49). Jesus then cites Exod. 3:6 (the revelation of God's name to Moses) against their "scriptural proof" to argue that if God was revealed "as a God of the living" to their ancestors, these same ancestors must be alive. Mark's readers are able to find in Jesus' spiritual view of the resurrection a way to adapt their own resurrection faith to a more spiritually minded Hellenistic audience, in a manner free of crude materialistic traits (cf. 1 Cor. 15:35–38; Acts 17:32).

Unlike the previous incidents the Great Commandment (12:28–34) does not begin with a hostile question, for the scribe turns to Jesus to solve a disputed issue. Scribes and rabbis had often attempted to codify the law and summarize its more than six hundred precepts under fundamental principles. The issue here is *what* principles Jesus will choose, not whether he can do so. Asked about which commandment is "first of all," Jesus begins by quoting Deut. 6:4–5, which forms the beginning of the Jewish daily prayer, the Shema (from the Heb. verb, "hear"; → Shema). This prayer is an epitome of biblical faith and affirms the absolute sovereignty of God in all areas of life. The second commandment, also a citation of the OT (Lev. 19:18), is simply to love your neighbor as yourself.

This answer is then ratified and repeated by the scribe (Mark 12:32–33), whom Jesus states is not far from the kingdom (v. 34). The scribe in citing Hos. 6:6 confirms that such behavior is "much more" than burnt offerings and sacrifices. As the Temple will be replaced by the house of prayer (Mark 11:17) its sacrifices will be replaced by love of God and neighbor. This pericope should not be used to oppose the Christian love command to Jewish legalism. Later Jewish writings contain the command to love the neighbor (Jub. 7:20, 20:2), and urge forgiveness of enemies (Sir. 28:2; Philo On The Virtues 106–109). The praise of the scribe is Mark's way of acknowledging Christianity's debt to Judaism. Its most basic commands are the same. As with the teaching on the taxes to Caesar and the resurrection, the dual command of love offers Mark's community a way of presenting the core of their faith and heritage to outsiders.

12:35–44, The Temple Teaching of Jesus.
The explicit mention of the Temple (12:35) recalls the setting of 11:27. In three brief incidents the Marcan Jesus defines his correct messianic status and again attacks Temple authorities.

The question about David's son (12:35–37), though often listed as the final Jerusalem controversy, lacks the formal characteristics of such narratives—no question is posed by opponents and there is no counterquestion by Jesus. Rather, Jesus cites a scribal opinion that the Messiah is a Son of David, only to reject it. In view of the earlier acceptance of Son of David (10:48) as a title of Jesus, this incident is puzzling. In quoting Ps. 110:1 to show that the Messiah is David's "Lord" rather than son, the Marcan Jesus cites a psalm frequently used as a proof-text for the exaltation/resurrection of Jesus (cf. Mark 14:62; Acts. 2:34–35; 1 Cor. 15:25; Heb. 1:13). This incident reflects the theology of the Marcan church that, while affirming Jesus' Davidic origin and messianic mission, rejects popular messianic expectations and redefines them in terms of the exaltation of Jesus above his enemies.

The Temple teaching of Jesus concludes with a warning against the scribes (12:38–40), primarily for ostentatious religious practices as a pretext for injustice, "they devour the houses of widows using as a pretext lengthy prayers" (v. 39). Similar warnings are frequent in the prophetic writings (Isa. 10:1–2; Zech. 7:10; Mal. 3:5) and underscore the growing estrangement in this section between Jesus and the Jerusalem leaders.

The following incident of the widow's offering (Mark 12:41–44) continues the motif of the exploitation of widows. This destitute widow ("poor" is too weak a translation) who gives only two small coins (roughly equal to one sixty-fourth of the contemporary daily wage) does more than the rich who contribute "out of their surplus" to the Temple. She has given her whole livelihood (lit., her life). Her action has been invoked as a symbol of wholehearted discipleship, generosity, and unquestioning surrender.

The text, however, contains no explicit praise of her action—an action that seems to accomplish the very thing the scribes were accused of fostering (12:40; cf. also the criticism of corban in 7:11). Recently Jesus' statement has been interpreted as a "lament" where Jesus points to the woman as an example of the exploitation of widows (see Wright, pp. 256–65). Paraphrased it would read, "What I say is true [about the scribes]. This poor widow with nothing to spare gave everything."

Mark however adapts this "lament" to his context. The incident provides the bridge between Jesus' attacks on the Temple and its au-

thorities, Mark 11–12, and the predictions of the destruction of the Temple in Mark 13. It also prepares for the woman who anoints Jesus in Jerusalem who, like the widow, gave "what she had" (14:8; cf. 12:44) and for the discipleship of other women during the passion narrative (15:40–41, 47; 16:1–8).

13:1–37
The Apocalyptic Testament of Jesus

All four Gospels conclude the public ministry with a private address of Jesus to his disciples (Mark 13; Luke 21; Matt. 24–25; John 13–17). In Mark (followed by Matthew and Luke) the discourse contains predictions of political unrest, natural disasters, and persecution of the community—all of which culminate in cosmic upheavals that usher in the return of the Son of man. It is often called "the synoptic apocalypse" since it employs motifs and images from Jewish apocalyptic writings; like these it is "persecution literature" with a deterministic view of history (13:7, 10) that assures persecuted communities of their vindication and of God's judgment of their oppressors. Unlike much apocalyptic literature, the discourse is not in the form of a supernatural vision given a prophetic figure (e.g., Rev. 1:1, 9–10), but more akin to the *Testaments of the Twelve Patriarchs* in which, prior to his death, each of the patriarchs warns his heirs of future dangers and exhorts them to fidelity to the covenant. As a mixture of prediction and parenesis (warnings and admonitions), Mark 13 forms an "apocalyptic testament." One of the characteristics of such testaments is that, in the form of predictions from the past, the sayings address the present concerns of the community for which a document is written. Mark 13 thus becomes a key for understanding the struggles of the Marcan community.

The apocalyptic testament and the subsequent passion narrative (Mark 14–16) in effect form a dual conclusion to the public ministry of Jesus. In one, the historical Jesus is betrayed, executed, and raised up; in the other, the risen Jesus returns as glorified Son of man to gather the elect (13:24–27). Prior to the concealing of the power of Jesus in the Passion, the disciples are given a rationale for their suffering and images of hope of their vindication.

The discourse manifests a definite literary and theological structure. After an introduction in which the destruction of the Temple is predicted (13:1–4), the sufferings preceding the end time are predicted in two stages (13:5–13, 14–23). The discourse then shifts to images of their future vindication (13:24–27) and concludes with parables and exhortations to vigilance (13:28–37) addressed to the actual situation of the community. The warnings in 13:5–6, 21–23 against "deceivers," who claim to come in the name of Jesus and who work signs and wonders, suggest that the community was beset with false messiahs who interpreted the destruction of the Temple in A.D. 70 as a definite sign that the end time had arrived. By his organization of material, Mark says that all these things are simply the beginning of the woes and that the Son of man will return only "after the tribulation" (13:24). The structure undercuts any attempt to identify a particular historical event as signaling the return of Jesus.

13:1–4, The Introduction. On leaving the Temple (the setting of 12:35–44), in response to a disciple's exclamation of its beauty Jesus predicts its total destruction (13:1–2). In a change of scene (on the Mount of Olives, opposite the Temple, see Ezek. 10:18–19, 11:23; Zech. 14) the disciples then ask Jesus "when" these things will be and what "sign" will indicate they are about to unfold (Mark 13:3–4). Speculation about the signs and the temporal sequence of eschatological events is frequent in apocalyptic literature.

13:5–13, The Beginning of the Tribulation. Rather than answering the disciples' question, Jesus (vv. 5–6) warns them that deceivers claiming divine power (13:6, "I Am") will come who will lead many astray (cf. 2 Thess. 2:1–11). Wars and natural disasters are not signs, only the beginning of the "birth pangs" (Mark 13:8) of the end time.

While wars and natural disasters are familiar apocalyptic motifs as well as frequent historical occurrences in the first century, the persecutions of 13:9–13 seem to reflect real experiences of the community. A probable backdrop to these verses is the persecution under Nero (A.D. 64) as well as the civil chaos that surrounded the later years of Nero's reign and followed his death in A.D. 68. In addition to the physical horrors of Nero's persecution, the Roman historian Tacitus (ca. A.D. 56–116) records that Christians, when arrested, indicted a "vast number" of fellow Christians (Tacitus Annals 15.44). Writing from Rome at the end of the first century to warn the community at Corinth of the dangers of disharmony, Clement of Rome remarks that it was through "jealousy and envy" that the "righteous pillars" of the church were persecuted at Rome (1 Clem. 5:1–2). Clement provides evidence that discord within the Christian community contributed to the persecution. He and Tacitus support the picture of familial division and betrayal that will affect the community according to Mark 13:12–13, and that was one of the worst consequences of Nero's persecution.

These verses do not simply foretell persecution—they link together the fate of Jesus and his followers. Each is "betrayed" by those close to them (13:12; 14:10, 45) and unjustly executed by brutal civil power; in each case suffering is God's will and each is vindicated. Mark 13:9–13 does not urge passive acquiescence to persecution. Rather persecution provides the occasion when, through faithful witness, the Gospel will be proclaimed to all peoples (13:10).

13:14–23, The Desolating Sacrilege and the Great Tribulation. After the instruction on fidelity amid persecution, these verses turn again to events preceding the end, in particular the enigmatic "desolating sacrilege" (or "abomination of desolation") standing where "he" should not. More than the previous civil and natural threats, this causes tribulation such as has never occurred since the foundation of the world (13:19). Though Mark's readers seem to know the identity of the desolating sacrilege (13:14, "let the reader take note"), subsequent generations are unsure. The term derives from Dan. 9:27; 11:31; and 12:11 (cf. 1 Macc. 1:54) in reference to the desecration of the Temple by Antiochus IV who offered pagan sacrifices there (167–164 B.C.). One clue to the identity of the horror in Mark is that the neuter "sacrilege" is modified by a masculine participle, (lit.) "standing where he should not." This could well describe the entrance of the Roman general Titus into the Holy of Holies on August 9 of A.D. 70 during the final days of the Jewish war (Josephus Jewish War 6.4.7, §260; 6.6.1, §316).

For Jews and Jewish Christians the destruction of the Temple was a world-shaking event that could signal the imminent end of history (13:19–20). At this stage in the discourse (13:21–23) Mark returns to the warnings against deception that initiated the discourse. Persecution and the destruction of the Temple has spawned false messiahs and false prophets who perform "signs" and wonders (cf. Matt. 7:21–23), possibly to deceive even the elect (Mark 13:22).

13:24–37, The Return of the Son of Man. In both prediction (vv. 24–27) and parable (vv. 28–37) the Marcan Jesus offers a true eschatological scenario and describes the proper posture toward the end time. The return of the Son of man will not be concurrent with the tribulation, but "after those days" (v. 24)—thereby invalidating the claims of the false Christs. It will be accompanied by massive cosmic disturbances (vv. 24–25; cf. Isa. 13:10; 34:4; Ezek. 32:7–8; Joel 2:10, 31; 3:15) and the appearance of the Son of man on the clouds with power and glory (Mark 13:26–27; cf. 8:38–9:1; 14:62). Here is a clear allusion to the vindication and granting of power and glory to "one like a son of man" in Dan. 7:13–14, who is later equated with the "saints of the most high" who suffered persecution under Antiochus IV. Jesus as Son of man is rejected, suffers, dies, and is exalted. So too his faithful followers will be vindicated by his return—and not by the arrival of false messiahs during the tribulation.

The two concluding parables (Mark 13:28–29, 34–37) with the intervening sayings are complementary. The community is told to discern the signs of the times. Just as the budding fig tree shows that summer is near, the events predicted thus far (13:3–23) show the end is assured and near, but not here. The solemn prediction of v. 30 reflects the eschatological hope of Mark's community that Jesus' return will take place in their lifetimes (cf. 9:1).

The second parable with its introductory sayings (13:32–36) counters both undue speculation about the end and passivity. Not even Jesus knows the exact day or hour, so that his words and deeds cannot be invoked to identify any particular event with the end (vv. 32–33). The little parable of the absent master (vv. 34–36) is really an allegory of life in Mark's house-churches. Jesus is absent; each of his "servants" receives his "power" (v. 34; cf. 6:7) and each has a task (cf. 1 Cor. 12:1–12). Vigilance and fidelity (active waiting), not idle speculation, are to characterize the community (Mark 13:35–36). Jesus' final testimony gives a theology of history to his persecuted and missionary community and a promise that he is never far from them.

from the arrest, trial, and crucifixion of Jesus (here is the greatest agreement between John and the Synoptics); third, the accounts as we now have them with addition of material such as the anointing and the prayer in Gethsemane.

The passion accounts were never narrated purely for historical purposes and from their earliest stages show such strong influence of the OT that in certain places (such as the details of the crucifixion) they comprise a virtual narrative commentary (midrash) on select OT texts (e.g., Ps. 22, cited in Mark 15:24, 29, 34). Especially influential is the motif of the righteous sufferer found in the Psalms (e.g., Pss. 31:4, 11; 35:4, 11, 19–24; 38:12, 14–16) and in the Wisdom of Solomon (2:10–20; 5:1–15). Jesus, like this figure, is persecuted unjustly, suffers in silence, but is vindicated by God. Also very influential is the "servant" of the fourth servant song of Isa. 52:13–53:12 who is exalted after brutal mistreatment.

Theological concerns also shape the accounts: first, apologetic—Jesus was innocent of the charges against him and it was willed by God and predicted in Scripture that Jesus should suffer; second, soteriological—his death as ransom for many brings salvation to those who through faith accept it as an offer of God's mercy; and third, Christological—Jesus' true nature is revealed during the Passion. There is no docetic circumvention of the realism of Jesus' sufferings. Yet, the one who suffers as Son of man is also proclaimed as God's son at the very moment of his death.

PART FIVE: 14:1–16:8

The Suffering, Death, and Resurrection of the Son of Man in Jerusalem

All four Gospels conclude with a connected account of the final days of Jesus' life, his execution by Roman authorities, and the proclamation of his resurrection. No two accounts agree on all points, with the greatest discrepancy between John and the Synoptics (e.g., for John the Last Supper takes place on the "eve" of Passover; for the Synoptics, it is a Passover meal; John omits the institution of the Eucharist from his account of the Last Supper). Similarly all four accounts reflect the distinctive literary style and theological concerns of each Evangelist. Nonetheless on substantive details there is enough similarity to suggest that there were common accounts and traditions on which all the Evangelists drew.

A suggested development of the accounts is first, an early, brief kerygmatic narrative such as 1 Cor. 11:23–26 (cf. 15:3b–5) used in a liturgical setting; second, a longer account with details

14:1–52

From the Plot to Kill Jesus to the Arrest

The passion narrative comprises two major phases. In the first (14:1–52), though aware of his imminent death, Jesus is active, the teacher and leader of the disciples; in the second (14:53–15:47), Jesus is passive, moved from place to place by hostile forces, and rarely speaks.

14:1–11, The Plots Against Jesus, and the Anointing. The earlier plots against Jesus (3:6; 11:18; 12:12) now culminate in the plan of the high priests and scribes to arrest Jesus and put him to death (14:1) and in the agreement of Judas to betray him to the priests (14:10–11). According to Mark's somewhat obscure chronology (14:1, 10, 12; 15:1, 42; 16:1), the trial before Pilate (15:1–20) and the crucifixion took place on the feast of the Passover (celebrated from the evening of the 14th of Nisan to the evening of the 15th [Friday]), which was also the eve of a Sabbath (15:42; 16:1). The last meal with the disciples, followed by the betrayal, arrest, and night trial (14:12–72), took place on the evening of the 14th of Nisan (Thursday). The anointing and contract of Judas with the priests (14:1–11) should be located on the day preceding (Wednesday).

The likely independent story of a woman who anoints Jesus (14:3–9), recounted at different places in the ministry of Jesus (cf. Luke 7:36–50; John 12:1–7), is inserted between the two plots (14:1, 10) to contrast two attitudes toward the suffering Jesus, betrayal or devotion. The narrative stresses two things, the action of the woman and its interpretation (14:3, 8) and the defense by Jesus against her detractors (14:4–7).

The woman's action, "anointing" (cf. 1 Sam. 10:1; 2 Kings 9:6), constitutes an acclamation that Jesus is a royal Messiah—hence Jesus' explanation in Mark 14:8 conveys the ironic reinterpretation of messiahship characteristic of Mark (cf. 8:29–31). Her action creates an arch to the ending of the passion narrative where women accompany Jesus to the cross (15:40–41) and again propose to anoint him (16:1). The woman's action is praised by Jesus in solemn language (14:9, "Amen I say to you"). Wherever the gospel is proclaimed what she does will be spoken of "in memory of her." She confesses her faith by symbolic action and embodies those qualities of devotion, generosity, and courage that the liberating message of the gospel is to proclaim to the whole world. She and the women at the crucifixion "who followed and ministered to Jesus in Galilee" (15:41) manifest faithful discipleship when confronted by the cross, much as the chosen disciples (who flee or deny Jesus) symbolize human fragility.

Jesus' defense of her action continues the earlier attack on "religious" attitudes (14:5, giving alms to the poor) as a cloak for false religion (cf. 7:9–13; 12:38–44). When Jesus says "the poor you always have with you," he is not predicting the inevitability of poverty, but reminding his followers of the duty of Deut. 15:11, to support the poor after his death (14:7, "whenever you will, you can do good to them"). By contrast, the time when they can still serve Jesus is limited.

14:12–31, The Passover with the Disciples. Jesus' final meal with his disciples occupies an important place in the passion narrative and interprets his death. Different elements are interwoven to create a rich tapestry: the commands of Jesus regarding the arrangements for the meal (14:12–16; cf. 11:1–6); the prediction of Judas's betrayal (14:17–21); the institution of the Lord's Supper (14:22–26); and the prediction of Peter's denial (14:27–31). The actions and deeds of Jesus here tell readers the deeper meaning of the tragic events that follow. What appears simply as betrayal and execution of an innocent man is really Jesus' self-offering for many (14:24).

The narrative of the Lord's Supper is handed down in different traditions and has been influenced by the liturgical practice of the early community. Matt. 26:26–29 follows Mark, but Luke (22:14–23) and Paul (1 Cor. 11:23–25) may have independent traditions (e.g., both include the command to continue the supper, "in remembrance of me"—which Mark does not include. Common to all traditions are actions and words over bread and a cup of wine (→ Lord's Supper, The).

Though Mark portrays it as a Passover meal, essential details (such as the eating of the lamb and the account of the deliverance from Egypt) are not mentioned. His account centers on the actions and sayings of Jesus over the bread (14:22) and over the cup (14:23–25). The actions, couched in language similar to 6:41 and 8:6, are a culmination of the feeding and bread incidents in the Gospels. Jesus—who had compassion on the hungry, fed them, and offered bread to the Gentiles—is now himself the bread declared to be body that is an offering for others. The cup of blessing that Jesus gives to them and that they drink is then interpreted as "my blood" of the covenant (in some manuscripts, "new covenant"; cf. Luke 22:20; 1 Cor. 11:25; Jer. 31:31) that will be poured out "for many." The phrase recalls that the Mosaic covenant was ratified by the shedding of blood (Exod. 24:8).

The Son of man who came to serve (as Jesus does here when he gives food and drink to his followers) and to give his life as a ransom (Mark 10:45) now offers himself as a sacrificial victim. His death, like the first Passover, will effect liberation. After the "institution" the final words of Jesus (14:25) underscore that the meal is an anticipation of the eschatological banquet (that day when he will drink "the new wine in the kingdom of heaven"). He must first drink the cup of suffering (14:36) before he can celebrate the banquet hoped for by Israel when wine would flow freely and death would be conquered. Mark offers images of hope amid symbols of death and suffering.

Bracketing the supper are renewed predictions of failure by disciples, of the scattering of the sheep, and of the denial of Peter (14:27–31). Permeating these failures is a sense that all this has been willed by God (vv. 21, 27, "it is written"), which then supports the message of hope of 14:28. Jesus, who "went before" his disciples as they wandered through Galilee, will be raised up and again lead them. The prediction of denial (14:30) that is later fulfilled (14:66–72) again stresses that Jesus is a "true prophet" whose promises and predictions come to pass.

14:32–42, The Prayer in Gethsemane. Jesus, who had earlier been in control and had predicted his suffering and vindication, now begins "to become severely distressed and troubled" (v. 33), and is afflicted with a grief leading to death (v. 34). Like every human who has lived, Jesus experiences imminent death as an alien force imposed from outside, not to be loved or accepted in itself, but only in terms of some higher vision. As he spoke earlier with assurance of the power of prayer (11:24–25; cf. 14:36, "all things are possible"), he prays now that God will remove the cup of suffering (with overtones of the cup of God's wrath, Isa. 51:17, 22; Jer. 25:15; Ps. 75:7–8).

Three times (Mark 14:40, 41) he turns to those who had been his companions at a moment of God's revelation (9:2; cf. 5:37), only to find them not watching, but sleeping. He warns them to watch and pray that they may not enter into the trial (cf. Matt. 6:13; = Luke 11:4, "the Lord's Prayer"), for "the spirit is willing, but the flesh is weak" (v. 40). "Flesh" in biblical thought describes the whole person as blind to God and driven by selfish concerns (Rom. 7:5; Gal. 5:17–21); "spirit" is the person as alive to God (Rom. 8:1–17; Gal. 5:22–26). Those who through prayer do not remain open to God's presence will fail at the time of trial. Jesus who was led by the Spirit to his first trial in the wilderness (Mark 1:12–13), after prayer at Gethsemane, will remain faithful in the ultimate trial of his passion and death.

This realistic narrative conveys a message of hope to a community like Mark's that experienced suffering and persecution. This narrative neither glorifies martyrdom nor mitigates the scandal of suffering. It does present the paradox of one who, when faced by the apparent victory of sin and violence, and whose prayer was not answered, could yet address God with an affirmation of familial trust and love as *Abba* (Aramaic, "father"; cf. Gal. 4:6; Rom. 8:15). In contrast to Peter, who did not see suffering as consonant with the divine plan, Jesus accepts God's will. Like those earlier whom he called mother, sister, and brother because they did the will of God (Mark 3:31–35), he is God's son because of his obedience (cf. Heb. 5:8–9).

14:43–52, The Betrayal and Arrest. With the conclusion of his prayer, the hour has arrived (14:41); the betrayer is at hand and the arrest ensues. The designation of Judas as the betrayer (14:44) and the arrest as a whole fulfills the earlier prophecies (14:18). Betrayal by a kiss, the normal sign of respect and affection (Luke 7:38, 45; 15:20; cf. 1 Cor. 16:20) highlights the evil of Judas (Mark 14:21; cf. Prov. 27:6). After Jesus is seized, his disciples all flee (Mark 14:50).

This flight is followed by the enigmatic incident of the "youth" who is clad only in a robe and flees naked when the arresting officers try to seize him (14:51–52). Since a "youth" (same Greek term) appears at the empty tomb clad in a white robe (16:5), the two youths may symbolize the Christian initiate who strips off the old self in baptism (which in Rom. 6:1–5 is entry into the mystery of Christ's death and resurrection) and puts on a new Christian identity. "Being clothed" is a metaphor for a new mode of existence elsewhere in the NT (see Gal. 3:27; Eph. 4:24; Col. 3:10).

14:53–16:8
The "Handing Over" of Jesus to Death and to God's Power

The second half of the passion narrative completes the earlier predictions (8:31; 9:31; 10:33). Here the passive Jesus is led from accuser to accuser, abused, and finally executed. On the narrative level readers are drawn into the mystery of the suffering Messiah. However, there is another "handing over" that transpires. Dying in submission to God's will, Jesus is also handed over to God's power. The narrative does not end with the cry of agony of a dying person (15:39), but with the proclamation, "he is risen" (16:6).

The "Trials" of Jesus and the Responsibility for His Execution

Both the Jewish and Roman trials of Jesus are the subject of considerable debate, with implications for anti-Semitism throughout history. As historical sources, the Gospels themselves present problems. Only Mark (14:53–65; followed by Matt. 26:59–68) records a formal, Jewish, "night" trial with accusations, witnesses, and a sentence. Luke records a morning hearing before the Sanhedrin (Luke 22:66–71) without formal sentencing, and John has separate appearances before Annas (at night) and Caiaphas (in the morning) who conducts an interrogation (18:12–24). All the Gospels agree that the Roman prefect, Pontius Pilate (A.D. 26–36), ordered the execution (also attested by the Roman historian Tacitus, *Annals* 15.44).

Clarity about the legal situation is lacking. Jewish laws on capital trials are found in texts almost two centuries after the death of Jesus (M. *Sanh.* 4–11), so it is not known whether they reflect first-century practice. By these norms the trial in Mark is not legal, since according to the Mishnah capital trials could not be held at night or on the eve of a Sabbath or feast day (M. *Sanh.* 4:1). The sentence of death could not be pronounced on the same day as the trial (M. *Sanh.* 4:1); prior examination of witnesses, as well as independent agreement of their testimony, was required (M. *Sanh.* 4:5; cf. Deut. 19:15–18); the charge of blasphemy required the explicit pronouncing of the divine name (M. *Sanh.* 7:5); and trials were to be held in the official chamber, not in the house of the high priest (*M. Sanh.* 11:2; cf. Mark 14:54). Also uncertain is whether the Sanhedrin had the power to execute for capital offenses during Roman occupation (see John 18:31). If so, Jesus should have been stoned, which was the Jewish penalty for blasphemy.

Though reconstruction of the events would involve study of all the Gospels, Mark offers some clues to the historical situation. The public reason given in the placard on the cross (Mark 15:26), recorded in all four Gospels, was that Jesus claimed to be a king, which for the Romans was tantamount to sedition. Those crucified with Jesus are called "revolutionary bandits" (Gk. *lēstai*, 15:27; cf. 14:48). Jesus' teaching on the kingdom, his association with marginal groups in his society, and his attacks on abuses associated with the Temple made him suspect to both Romans and the Jerusalem aristocracy. Though some interrogation may have taken place before Jewish authorities, the Romans bear the responsibility for any formal trial. None of the Gospels mentions extensive participation by the Pharisees in the death of Jesus, so not all Jewish leaders, and certainly not the mass of Jewish people at the time of Jesus, rejected Jesus or were responsible for his death (→ Trial of Jesus, The).

14:53–72, The Trial Before the Sanhedrin and the Denial of Peter. Whatever historical data can be culled from Mark's version of the trial, its primary setting is within the theology of the passion narrative and of the Gospel as a whole. Mark interweaves the trial narrative (14:53, 55–65) with the story of Peter's denial (14:54, 66–72), contrasting true and false confession. In the trial itself two major theological motifs converge.

The first motif emerges from the charge that Jesus would destroy the Temple and rebuild it in three days (14:57–59; cf. 15:29–30). Criticism of a corrupt Temple was current among other Jewish groups (e.g., Essenes), and from the time of Solomon on, "temple building" was a messianic prerogative (2 Sam. 7:4–17). From 11:1 forward Mark has shown a consistent anti-Temple motif: Jesus calls the Temple a den of robbers (11:17), like the fig tree it is unfruitful, and it will be demolished so that not a stone will remain on another (13:1–4). Though "false witnesses" (14:56, 57) stem from the tradition of the trial of the righteous sufferer (Pss. 27:12; 35:11), Mark twice interprets "false" as "they did not agree" (Mark 14:56, 59). Like many actions and sayings of Jesus throughout the Gospel his Temple words are misinterpreted. However, the *content* of the charge brought by "false witnesses" is ironically true for Mark.

Jesus is the messianic temple builder who after his resurrection will form his new community, a "temple not made with hands," i.e., a "spiritual temple" (see 1 Cor. 3:16; 6:19; 1 Pet. 2:4–6).

The other major motif centers on the identity of Jesus, which has dominated the whole Gospel and now culminates in the question and answer of the high priest (Mark 14:61–62). There is a joining of titles of Jesus—"Messiah," "Son of the Blessed," "Son of man"—not found in any previous narrative. In 14:61 the high priest solemnly asks Jesus "Are you the Messiah, the Son of the Blessed One [i.e., God]?" Jesus responds (14:62) in agreement by using a formula of divine predication, "I am" (cf. 6:51; 13:6), and then redefines Son of the Blessed by reference to the Danielic Son of man (Dan. 7:13–14) and the exalted Lord of Ps. 110:1 ("seated at the right hand of power") whose glorious return will be seen by all (cf. Mark 8:38; 13:26). This response of Jesus occurs at the exact midpoint of the passion narrative and gives a proper interpretation to the following events. Jesus is Messiah and Son of God but he fulfills those roles precisely as the Son of man who has power on earth to forgive sin and heal on the Sabbath, who was yet rejected by those very authorities who question him. Yet he will return to judge his accusers (cf. 8:38–9:1; 13:26). His human vulnerability is paradoxically the path to understanding in what sense he is Son of the Blessed. Only when Jesus is understood on those terms set by God in the Gospel can proper confession of his identity take place.

Though Jesus has not technically committed blasphemy, the reaction of the Sanhedrin reveals to readers that they have paradoxically understood the true meaning of Jesus' messiahship. The trial concludes with another irony. At the very moment the Sanhedrin mocks Jesus as a false prophet (14:65), his prophecy about Peter is being fulfilled.

With the denial of Peter (14:66–72) the narrative of Peter's "following" suspended at 14:54 is now tragically resumed. Three times with an escalating intensity, Peter is charged with being a follower of Jesus (14:66, one slave girl; 14:69, the girl repeats the charge to bystanders; 14:70, all the bystanders charge him). Three times with parallel ascending vehemence Peter denies the charge (14:68, "I do not know or understand what you are saying"; 14:70, "he again denied"; 14:71, "he began to curse and swear"). The final words of him who was first called (1:16–20) and who first confessed Jesus as Messiah (8:29) are a poignant, "I do not know the person of whom you are speaking" (14:71). With the crow of the cock the prophecy is fulfilled, and Peter, recalling the words of Jesus, "breaks down and weeps."

Since "weeping" can be both a sign of repentance (2 Kings 20:4–5) and a form of prayer (Ps. 102:9; Job 16:20), the narrative points to forgiveness for Peter (see Mark 16:7).

15:1–20, The Roman Trial of Jesus. With the trial of Jesus before Pontius Pilate, the "handing over" (15:1; cf. 8:31; 9:31; 10:33) of Jesus is complete. The final day of Jesus' life (corresponding and contrasting to the initial day of his ministry in Galilee) is carefully measured by three-hour intervals according to the Roman custom (15:1, "early"; 15:25, "third hour"; 15:33, "sixth to ninth hour"; 15:42, "evening"). After the rapid pace of the Gospel where Jesus was in constant motion, the measured pace of these scenes rivets the attention of readers on the silent and suffering Jesus.

The trial before Pilate involves: accusations (15:3), an interrogation of the accused by Pilate (15:2, 4), the choice of Barabbas or Jesus (15:6–14), and the sentence (15:15) followed by the mocking (15:16–20). Before Pilate the charge is "Are you the King of the Jews?" rather than "Are you Son of the Blessed?" and the saying about the Temple is dropped. Unlike the Jewish trial (14:62), where Jesus agrees with the charge ("I am") and effectively reinterprets it ("and you will see . . ."), his response to Pilate is simply, "You have claimed this" (15:2), followed by silence when the charge is repeated. There is strong irony here. Like the demons, who earlier in Mark address Jesus as Son of God (3:11; 5:7), Pilate, who also exemplifies evil power, names Jesus as king (cf. Mark 10:42, where rulers dominate and tyrannize their subjects. Pilate was recalled to Rome in A.D. 36 for abuse of his power). Just as Jesus was Son of God, but not in the sense proclaimed by the demons, he is also king, but not in Pilate's sense. Jesus, who proclaimed the imminence of God's kingdom, is a royal Messiah who enters Jerusalem for his enthronement on the cross (15:26).

After the initial interrogation Mark recounts the choice between Barabbas and Jesus (15:6–15). Since such a custom of releasing a prisoner at Passover is not attested elsewhere, the historical foundation of this incident is uncertain. In Mark's narrative it serves to contrast the innocent Jesus with the guilty Barabbas (who committed murder in the midst of an uprising, 15:7). It also highlights the evil of the high priests (because of "envy" they handed Jesus over) who sway the crowd to choose Barabbas. There may be a subtle irony in the choice of Barabbas whose name means "Son of the Father" (Aramaic, *Abba*). Jesus, the true son of the Father, is rejected in favor of the pseudo-son. While not excusing Pilate, the narrative portrays him as capitulating to the cries of the crowd, "crucify

him"—reflecting perhaps the desire of Mark's community to mitigate the involvement of the Romans.

The mocking (15:16–20), while reflecting the Roman custom of degradation of prisoners, is also influenced by the OT (esp. Mic. 5:1, "with a rod they strike the cheek of the ruler of Israel"; cf. Isa. 50:6; 53:5). It heightens the irony of this whole section since the soldiers in hailing Jesus as king and in "worshiping him" (Mark 15:19) are paradoxically giving him that honor he will receive when God raises him up (cf. Phil. 2:5–11).

15:21–47, The Crucifixion, Death, and Burial of Jesus. The sober narrative of the crucifixion (15:21–41) masks the horror of this mode of execution. With the aid of OT allusions and quotations, the focus is shifted to its theological meaning. Like the sin offerings that are carried "out of the camp" (Lev. 16:27), Jesus is executed outside the city (cf. Heb. 13:12, "Jesus suffered outside the gate in order to sanctify the people through his own blood"). A third set of mockings occurs by the bystanders who challenge him to destroy and rebuild the Temple and come down from the cross so that they may believe (Mark 15:29–32a) and even by the "bandits" crucified with him (v. 32b). By calling their mocking "blasphemy" Mark ironically says that Jesus, who was condemned for "blasphemy," is now unwittingly hailed as the crucified God by his accusers.

The high priests similarly taunt Jesus for saving others and not himself, and say they too will believe if he comes down from the cross. In the dramatic scene of the crucified king on the cross, Mark offers a vignette of lack of belief. The bystanders and Temple officials will believe only if some dramatic miracle occurs. Jesus who earlier did no mighty work in Nazareth because of unbelief and who said earlier that one must lose a life in order to save it, is challenged at the moment of death to deny the meaning of his own life. The final paradox of this powerful scene is that, by remaining on the cross, he is both "saving himself" and "saving others" (cf. 10:45; 14:24).

The final three hours of Jesus' life are marked by apocalyptic imagery of the precreational darkness (15:33; cf. Gen. 1:2). At the ninth hour Jesus' final words, recorded by Mark in Aramaic, are an exclamation of the first verse of Psalm 22, "My God, my God, why have you forsaken me," which is then misinterpreted by the crowd as a call for Elijah. Though commentators often speak of Jesus' cry of abandonment on the cross, Psalm 22 as a whole moves from apparent despair of God's presence to a hope of vindication. Since Mark when quoting the OT normally refers to the larger context of a particular verse, readers of the Gospel are to hear Jesus' words as those of the suffering just one who dies with the hope of vindication.

With the cry and the death of Jesus two major themes of the Gospel reach their high point. The "anti-Temple" motif culminates in the splitting of the veil of the Temple (Mark 15:38). This may be the veil separating the Holy of Holies from the outer Temple or the curtain before the main entrance. Its splitting "in two from top to bottom" symbolizes that God's presence is no longer hidden. Through the death of Jesus all people now have access to God (cf. Heb. 10:19–20).

The confession of the gentile centurion, "this human being [Gk. *anthrōpos*] was truly the Son of God" (Mark 15:39), is the culmination of the Christology of the Gospel and confirms the access that the Gentiles now have to God. In contrast to the mockers who embodied false faith, the centurion symbolizes future believers who must stand before the cross and confess a crucified one to be Son of God (cf. 1 Cor. 1:18–25). Also present at Jesus' final moments are those women who had "followed" Jesus and "ministered" to him in Galilee, as well as "many others" who had come up with him to Jerusalem (Mark 15:41). Having been abandoned by his disciples, Jesus at death is accompanied by Gentiles and women—both outsiders in the eyes of the religious leaders, both to be the nucleus of the new community to be gathered by the risen Jesus.

The short narrative of the burial (15:42–47) contrasts the righteous Joseph, a respected counselor who was waiting for the kingdom of God, with the other members of the Sanhedrin. He "dares" to approach Pilate and, like the faithful disciples of John (6:29), oversees the burial of Jesus. Mark anticipates here a church composed of Jews who believed in Jesus as well as Gentiles who confess his divine sonship. The details of the burial confirm that Jesus really died (in opposition to any docetic misunderstanding) and prepare for the resurrection. After the noise and tumult of the previous hours, the day wanes with the quiet presence of the faithful women who keep watch at the tomb of Jesus (15:47).

16:1–8, The Resurrection of Jesus. The earliest tradition of the resurrection (1 Cor. 15:3b–7) affirms that Jesus died according to the Scriptures, that he was buried, and raised up on the third day. The term "raised up" is a "theological passive," meaning the same as "God raised Jesus up." In this tradition, taken over by Paul, the fact of the resurrection is followed by the appearances of Jesus to select witnesses. It contains no explicit mention of the discovery of an "empty tomb." No Gospel attempts any description of the resurrection itself

(as does the later apocryphal *Gos. Pet.* 9:35–13:57). All the Gospels, however, mention some discovery of the empty tomb and all allude to appearances (implicit in Mark, explicit in the others).

The brief Marcan resurrection narrative begins "very early" on the first day of the week (the day after the Jewish Sabbath) with the journey of three women to anoint the body of Jesus. They muse among themselves about how the stone can be removed (16:4; cf. 15:46). The stress on the large stone may be an answer to the charge that the disciples stole Jesus' body (cf. Matt. 28:11–14, where the charge is made explicit). In Mark 16:4 the women notice that the stone has been rolled away and enter the tomb. They immediately see a "young man" (cf. 14:51) clad in white and seated on the right side of the tomb. They are "amazed"—the term used often throughout the Gospel in reaction to Jesus' miracles. The core of the narrative is in the message of the young man: "You seek Jesus of Nazareth, the crucified one; he has been raised up; he is not here" (16:6). The young man then charges the women to tell "the disciples and Peter" that Jesus "is going before them" (cf. 14:28) into Galilee and there they will see him. The narrative ends with the flight of the women from the tomb, their trembling and astonishment, and their silence, "for they were afraid" (16:7–8).

The narrative of the empty tomb does not provide for Mark (or for any Gospel) a "proof" of the resurrection. Mark rejects any sign that would facilitate belief (8:12; 15:32). In the biblical world a tomb is the anteroom to the realm of the dead. The empty tomb is a symbol that by the resurrection of Jesus death has been emptied of its power (cf. Heb. 2:14). The message of the young man actually directs the attention away from the empty tomb—"he is not here"—to the proclamation "he is risen." Christian faith rests on this proclamation, not on the empty tomb.

The reaction of the women, their failure to deliver the message to the disciples, and the absence of a resurrection appearance pose many problems. Some interpret it as a final rejection of those disciples who fled and argue that even the faithful women disciples ultimately fail. This interpretation does not do justice to the force of Jesus' promise in 14:28 and to Mark's view that Jesus is the true prophet whose words will achieve their effect. The fear, wonder, and silence of the women are rather reactions that elsewhere in biblical narratives accompany theophanies and commissions given to prophets (Exod. 3:3; Isa. 6:1–5; Jer. 1:6–8; Ezek. 1:28; Luke 1:29–30). By the abrupt ending Mark also leaves his readers with a radical challenge to their faith. Belief, conversion, and discipleship do not really rest on resurrection appearances (which Mark's community of ca. A.D. 70 would not have experienced), but on the word of promise, the victory over death at that very moment when death seemed sovereign.

16:9–20
The Longer Ending of Mark

As mentioned (see above, "Introduction: Text and Canon") these verses did not constitute the earliest ending of Mark. They are a pastiche of language and motifs drawn mostly from the other Gospels or the traditions used by these Gospels. The appearance to Mary Magdalene (16:9–10, who is described here in terms found only in Luke 8:2 as "the one from whom he had cast seven demons") reflects Matt. 28:9–10 and John 20:11–18. For the subsequent appearance to two disciples "walking in the country," see Luke 24:13–35. The appearance to the Eleven at table and their commissioning (16:14–18) draws on the Gospels and Acts (Luke 24:36–49; Matt. 28:16–20; John 20:19–23; Acts 1:6–8) but elaborates the postresurrectional ministry of the disciples (not found elsewhere in the Gospels) to include speaking in tongues, handling deadly serpents and drinking any deadly thing without injury, and healing the sick.

Two of these "signs" (Mark 16:17, a term used in Mark 8:12 in a negative sense), speaking in tongues and healing, occur at Corinth (1 Cor. 12:1–11). This longer ending of Mark may stem from groups within early Christianity who prized such enthusiastic phenomena. This ending also interprets Mark in a direction in tension with the understanding of faith in the Gospel. It shows how difficult it was to accept the radical challenge to faith posed by the Gospel itself.

Bibliography
Achtemeier, P. *Mark.* Proclamation Commentaries. 2d rev. ed. Philadelphia: Fortress, 1986.
Best, E. *Following Jesus: Discipleship in the Gospel of Mark.* Journal for the Study of the New Testament Supplement Series, no. 4. Sheffield: JSOT Press, 1981.
Hurtado, L. W. *Mark.* A Good News Commentary. San Francisco: Harper & Row, 1983.
Kelber, W. *The Kingdom in Mark: A New Place and a New Time.* Philadelphia: Fortress, 1974.
Lane, W. L. *Commentary on the Gospel of Mark.* New International Commentary on the New Testament. Grand Rapids, MI: Eerdmans, 1974.
Mann, C. S. *Mark.* Anchor Bible, 27. Garden City, NY: Doubleday, 1986.
Marxsen, W. *Mark the Evangelist.* Nashville, TN: Abingdon, 1969.
Schweizer, E. *The Good News According to Mark.* Atlanta, GA: Knox, 1970.
Taylor, V. *The Gospel According to St. Mark.* London: Macmillan, 1966.
Weeden, T. *Mark: Traditions in Conflict.* Philadelphia: Fortress, 1971.
Wright, A. "The Widow's Mites." *Catholic Biblical Quarterly* 44 (1982): 256–65.

LUKE

FRED B. CRADDOCK

INTRODUCTION

Among the Gospels, the Gospel According to Luke is unique in that it has a sequel, the Acts of the Apostles. Even though the Gospel and Acts have their own separate aims, characters, geographies, histories, and stories, the companion prologues (Luke 1:1–4; Acts 1:1–2), the common literary style, the same governing themes, and the overarching theological perspectives argue persuasively that the two works are in reality one. Luke-Acts is the largest contribution by a single writer in the NT.

Quite early in the life of the church Luke and Acts were separated by the location of John's Gospel between them. Reasons are not difficult to find: Luke belongs with Matthew and Mark in the cluster called the synoptic Gospels; Acts offers a natural introduction to the Letters of Paul. However, careful readers of either Luke or Acts will want to reunite the two volumes regardless of whether Gospel or Acts is being studied. The writer has made one continuous story of the life and mission of Jesus and the life and mission of the church. The definition of the gospel as repentance and forgiveness runs throughout (Luke 24:47; Acts 2:38; 3:19; 17:30–31). The Temple, Jerusalem, Mary, and the Holy Spirit figure prominently in both volumes; Jesus' and Paul's journeys to Jerusalem and Jesus' and Stephen's deaths are companion narratives. Luke and Acts are further related as promise and fulfillment, prophecies of Jesus having their completion in the life of the church (Luke 9:22; cf. Acts 3:21; Luke 21:12–15; cf. Acts 4:3–5, 14; Luke 9:5; cf. Acts 13:51). The Gospel anticipates Acts and Acts reflects upon the Gospel. Undoubtedly, some stories Luke tells in the Gospel are framed with a story yet to come in Acts clearly in mind (See also the Introduction to the Gospels and Acts; Acts, "Introduction").

Composition of the Gospel

Authorship. The Third Gospel, like all the canonical Gospels, is anonymous. The text yields no name; neither does it provide sufficient information from which the author's name may be inferred. Still, on the basis of the text we can sketch a general portrait of the writer. We can know from the Gospel that the writer was not an eyewitness of the ministry of Jesus but records those things "delivered to us by those who from the beginning were eyewitnesses" (Luke 1:2). Perhaps the tradition is already into its second or third generation. The writer is a student of previous accounts of Jesus' life (1:1) and assumes readers are already informed in these matters. The style of the writing indicates it is the work of a person of education and taste, familiar with the methods of narrative current in that culture. The content of the Gospel also reveals a thorough knowledge of the Septuagint (LXX), a Greek translation of the Hebrew Bible widely used in synagogues in the Hellenistic world. Whether this means the author was a convert from Hellenistic Judaism or a gentile Christian is not clear. Also unclear is whether the diarylike "we" sections of Acts (16:10–17; 20:5–21:18; 27:1–28:16) are to be regarded as evidence that the writer was a traveling companion of Paul or simply making use of such a record by one who was in Paul's company. Arguments popular in the nineteenth century that medical terminology in the Gospel established the author as "Luke the beloved physician" (Col. 4:14) have since been laid to rest. The tradition that the Third Gospel was written by Luke a companion of Paul (Col. 4:14; Philem. 24; 2 Tim. 4:11) is at least as old as Irenaeus, a theologian living in Gaul about A.D. 185. At approximately the same time, confirmation of the tradition is found in Tertullian (North Africa), Clement of Alexandria (Egypt), and in a document from Italy called the "Muratorian Canon" that lists and comments on early Christian writings. In recent times, however, students of both Acts and Paul have seriously questioned whether Luke-Acts could be the work of a companion of Paul, given the differences in the presentations of Paul and his message in Paul's own writings and in Acts. Arguments over authorship have been far less heated in the last half-century, not because new evidence has appeared but because the question of authorship has been regarded as less weighty in understanding the content and accepting the authority of a biblical text.

Date and Place of Writing. The prologue to Luke speaks of dependence on eyewitnesses (1:2), so the date can be no earlier than the second generation of Christians. The author also says that many narratives about Jesus had been written previously (1:1), the Gospel of Mark most likely being among them, so this Gospel can be no earlier than Mark. Those who have argued that Luke must be dated before A.D. 64 because Luke concludes Acts with Paul still under house arrest in Rome (Acts 28:30–31) with no account of his death have mistaken the literary form for a historical record. The account of Paul's death is, in effect, implied in the farewell speech in Acts 20. Acts 28 can, therefore, close on a note of life not death, open toward the future and not closed on the past. Many have reasonably argued that Luke's record of the fall of Jerusalem (Luke 19:41–44; 21:20–24), more precisely than that of Matthew and Mark, seems to accord with the known facts of the Roman siege, and therefore Luke must be dated after A.D. 70. But how much later? That Luke knew the writings of the first-century historian Josephus and therefore must have written after A.D. 93 has never been satisfactorily established. Luke was included in Marcion's canon of Christian writings about A.D. 140. Luke seems not to have known the collected letters of Paul, which perhaps were circulating as early as the end of the first Christian century. Hence most scholars settle for a time between A.D. 80 and 90. The question of the place of writing is even more open than that of the date. Sentiment has selected Rome with Luke there with Paul, serving the apostle during his two years of house arrest. Other guesses abound, but the tradition from the time of Irenaeus (A.D. 185) is that Luke was composed in Achaea (southern Greece).

Destination and Purpose. The prologue makes it clear that the Third Gospel is addressed to a person (Theophilus) or persons already informed about the subject matter to be discussed (1:0–4). Presumably, then, the audience is Christian, and very likely gentile Christian, or at least predominantly so. The name "Theophilus" is Greek, not Hebrew. The prologue itself follows a literary tradition of the Hellenistic world. The genealogy of Jesus is traced back not to Abraham (Matt. 1:1–16), but to Adam (Luke 3:23–38). Citations from the OT are from the LXX. When following one of his sources, Mark, the author omits sections dealing with issues totally internal to Judaism—for example, the issue of ritual cleansing in Mark 7:1–23. That Luke wrote to Gentiles would also account for the substitution of Greek for Hebrew (or Aramaic) terms and names: "skull" for Golgotha, "Lord" or "teacher" for rabbi, "zealot" for Cananaean, among others. Some scholars have added to the arguments for a gentile Christian audience the fact that both Jesus' ministry and the mission of the church move favorably toward Gentiles (Luke 4:16–30; Acts 1:8; 2:39; 28:28). However, that same evidence has been used to posit the readers as Greek-speaking Jews converted to Christianity who need to understand how a movement begun in Palestine among Jews has moved into the gentile world and is becoming increasingly gentile in its membership. But even if the background of the readers is uncertain, it is clear that Luke assumes the readers respect the authority of the OT (Luke 2:22–40; 4:16–21; 16:29–31; 24:27, 44–47), and have a knowledge of it.

This Gospel, especially when joined to Acts, has provided students of it a range of defensible views as to the author's purpose, and perhaps it is an error to try to find a single intention for the book. One could conclude from the prologue that the production of many narratives (1:1) about Jesus and his followers had proven to be confusing and therefore an orderly, well-researched account would assure the readers (1:3–4). Or, perhaps the assurance Theophilus (whether the name of a person or a literary device) needed was certainty that the Christianity of his day was truly rooted in the career and teaching of Jesus. Of long standing is the view that Luke was writing an apology or defense of the Christian religion, showing the Roman world that this was no insurrectionist movement but one that deserved the respect and protection of the civil authorities. After all, Pilate had declared Jesus innocent (23:13–16) and Paul, a Roman citizen (Acts 16:37; 22:25–29), had enjoyed more the protection than the wrath of the government (Acts 23:12–35). Other scholars, taking note of the continuity Luke draws between Jesus and the law and institutions of Judaism, identify Luke's purpose as primarily that of answering such questions as: if the promises of God were to Abraham (Gen. 12:1–3), why do Jesus and his church embrace Gentiles? Has God had a change of mind? Is Israel abandoned? Did Jesus break with his heritage? Certainly Luke gives major attention to the relationship of Jesus and his followers to the law, Jerusalem, the synagogue, and the Temple. Finally, a case could be made that in Luke's time, the church was becoming established in the Roman world and aware that it now had a history. The Parousia (the return of Christ), expected by many in the first generation, had not occurred and the followers of Jesus needed a clear sense of their past in order to move into the future. Luke, say the proponents of this view, responded to that need.

Sources. When Luke speaks of having received information from "those who from the beginning were eyewitnesses and ministers of the word" (1:2; whether he is referring to one group or two is not clear), the possibility of oral sources is introduced. That Luke's research included interviews and other contacts with oral traditions is highly likely, but such sources are most difficult for readers to identify. The usual tendency has been to attribute to oral sources those portions of Luke for which no other known source exists. This material, unique to Luke, amounts to about 25 percent of the Gospel, and consists primarily of the birth stories, parables, and the resurrection narratives. Whether oral or written, this body of material is often referred to as L. From among the many narratives compiled prior to Luke (1:1), two written sources are generally recognized by students of this Gospel. One is the Gospel of Mark, whose record constitutes well over one-third of Luke. While Luke omits some sections of Mark (Mark 6:45–8:26) and inserts into the story blocks of non-Marcan material (Luke 6:20–8:3; 9:51–18:14), still it remains the case that Mark provides the basic structure for Luke. The other source has been called Q from the German word *Quelle* meaning "source," and refers to material common to Matthew and Luke but not in Mark. Examples of Q are Luke 3:7–9 and Matt. 3:7–10; Luke 4:3–12 and Matt. 4:3–10. About 25 percent of Luke is attributed to Q. In a very real sense another source for Luke was the LXX, which functioned as a literary guide and model. This is true in a general sense; for example, Luke 1:5–2:52 has the style and flavor of the LXX. But it is also true of specific stories Luke tells. For example, Mary sings (Luke 1:46–55) as Hannah sang (1 Sam. 2:1–10); Jesus in the Temple as a boy (Luke 2:41–52) is an episode inspired by the story of the boy Samuel in the Temple (1 Sam. 2–3); Jesus' raising the son of a widow at Nain (Luke 7:11–17) even draws exact phrasing from the story of Elijah and the widow's son (1 Kings 17:17–24). It remains unclear to what extent, if at all, Luke assumed his readers' knowledge of those and other such stories from the OT.

Structure and Literary Features

As stated above, Mark's Gospel provided the basic structure for Luke's. However, additions by Luke at the beginning and the ending of the story, along with noticeable modifications at the center of the Gospel, make it important for readers, even if well-acquainted with Mark, to get an overview of the structure of Luke's Gospel before beginning a detailed study of its parts. Following the prologue (1:1–4) Luke has an extended infancy and childhood narrative that includes accounts of the births of both John the Baptist and Jesus (1:5–2:52). This material is unique to Luke. Chap. 3 opens so much like the beginning of a Gospel that some scholars have theorized that this may, indeed, have been the original starting point of Luke's narrative. From 3:1 through 9:50 the setting is Galilee and the story extends from the appearance of John the Baptist to Jesus' arrival at a Samaritan village on his way to Jerusalem. A major

unit of material in the section is the Sermon on the Plain (6:20–49), Luke's version of Jesus' teachings found in Matthew's Sermon on the Mount (Matt. 5:1–7:29). In 9:51–18:14 Luke offers a special section of material often called the journey narrative because the events and teaching of this lengthy portion are hung on the image of Jesus on his way to Jerusalem. Granted, it is difficult to follow the geographical references and reconstruct the trip from Galilee to Jerusalem. However, that Jesus has "set his face to go to Jerusalem" (9:51) surfaces often in phrases such as "and as he went on his way," indicating that Luke wants all this material (some of it can be found scattered through Matthew and Mark) interpreted as falling under the shadow of Jesus' approaching death in Jerusalem. At 18:15 Luke rejoins the narratives of Matthew and Mark, approaching the city of Jerusalem in 19:11. The last major section has a Judean setting (19:28–23:56) and includes the entry into the city (19:28–44), Jesus' ministry—primarily that of teaching—within Jerusalem (19:45–21:38), and the passion story (22:1–23:56) beginning with the Last Supper and concluding with the burial. Luke concludes with the empty tomb story (24:1–12) followed by accounts of appearances of the risen Christ (24:13–53), records unlike those of Matthew and John, the other two Evangelists who relate resurrection appearances.

It is not, however, the structure of Luke's Gospel that most impresses readers, even though his infancy and resurrection narratives are certainly memorable. Rather, readers, even of a translation, know that this Gospel is the work of a consummate literary artist. Jerome recognized this fact quite early, referring to Luke as the most skilled writer among the Evangelists. Careful students will observe the points at which Luke improves upon Mark, removing redundancies, smoothing awkward lines, broadening the range of verbs to reduce monotony, and rounding off stories that seemed unfinished. But one does not have to be a careful student to appreciate the artistry of the parable of the prodigal son (15:11–32) or of the story of Jesus' appearance to two downcast disciples on the road to Emmaus (24:13–35). And reference has already been made to the unusual way Luke makes allusive use of the OT, weaving its stories and character almost unnoticed into the rich tapestry of his own telling about Jesus.

But this is not to say that Luke's primary effort is to produce an aesthetically pleasing story. After a prologue in the manner of Greek historians and an infancy narrative half-told, half-sung in the rhythm and language of the Greek OT, Luke launches what seems to be a history of Jesus and his followers. "In the fifteenth year of the reign of Tiberius Caesar, Pontius Pilate being governor of Judea" (3:1) is Luke's way of setting Jesus' career in the context of world as well as local political and religious history. This interweaving of historical figures, places and events, and the stories of Jesus and his followers continues through Acts. Luke does write as a historian. He had sources written and oral; he researched carefully; and he offers "an orderly account." Readers have a sense of chronological movement and thoroughness.

But Luke is not simply a historian. He is continuing the narrative of God's people Israel, bringing it to fulfillment in his own day in Jesus and the Christian movement. He is not just a describer; he is an advocate. He is not simply recording what happened but what really happened, introducing God as the central actor in the events that occurred. Luke is a theological historian, and a biographer as well. After all, the focus of his attention is the one character, Jesus of Nazareth. But more than a historian, more than a biographer, Luke is an Evangelist, a proclaimer of the Gospel.

The Significance of Luke for the New Testament and the Church

It is difficult to overestimate the importance of Luke's witness both for the NT of which it is a major component and for the church. However, space here permits mention of only the major contributions Luke makes to the shape and nature of the Christian tradition.

Luke is a major contributor to the church's understanding of its relation to Judaism. The issue of continuity/discontinuity was a critical one for the followers of Jesus. Paul, Matthew, John, and the author of the Letter to the Hebrews all are preoccupied with the question in different ways. Luke's accent is more on continuity than discontinuity. The story of salvation history is one narrative, not two. The Hebrew Scriptures, Jerusalem, the Temple, and the synagogue figure prominently and positively in the life of Jesus and in the Acts account of the church. This even includes Paul, the missionary to Gentiles. Many Jews reject Jesus and his message, to be sure, but God was keeping and fulfilling promises made to Abraham and his descendants.

To speak of God keeping promises is to be reminded that the central character in Luke-Acts is God. Some Christian writings are so Christocentric that in reading them one tends to forget what Luke does not forget: the story of salvation is God's story. God led Israel; God inspired prophets; God sent John the Baptist; God sent Jesus; God raised up Jesus; and God sends the Holy Spirit. God is at work through persons, nations, political leaders, laws, and institutions. Since God continues to lead and to work the divine purpose, Luke neither longs for nor calls the church back to a golden age, of Jesus or of the early church, but shows that

each time and place has its own appropriateness in the plan of God.

God, who has never been without witness in the world (Acts 14:17), is not the God only of Israel and the church but also of Adam, of all creation, and of all nations. Luke, therefore, writes not only of Jesus and the Twelve, but also of Augustus, Tiberius, and Gallio, not only of Bethlehem and Jerusalem, but also of Athens and Rome. Luke sets the Gospel in the larger history of his generation, specifying times and places. After all, as Paul says to King Agrippa, "This was not done in a corner" (Acts 26·26).

Luke alone in the NT joins historically rather than simply theologically the ministry of Jesus and the birth and spread of the church. Of the Gospels only Matthew uses the word "church" (Matt. 16:18; 18:17), but it is Luke who concludes one volume with Jesus pointing his disciples toward the church (Luke 24:49–53) and opens a second with the church being born and sent into the world (Acts 1–2). Luke's historicizing of Jesus' resurrection and ascension as two separate events has been embraced in the church's calendar with separate celebrations of Easter, Ascension Sunday, and Pentecost.

Luke offers one of the NT's definitions of the Gospel. "Repentance and forgiveness of sins should be preached in his name to all nations" (Luke 24:47). The call to repentance and the offer of forgiveness occurs more frequently in Luke than in any other NT writer. This is the message to Israel; this is the message to the nations. The cross is not a prominent feature of that proclamation. Luke's preferred way to speak of Jesus' Passion is capsuled in the expression, "Thus it is written, that the Christ should suffer and on the third day rise from the dead" (24:46). What is important to Luke is that what happened to Christ was exactly what had been prophesied in the Law, the Prophets, and the Psalms (24:44; also 24:27). In other words, God's will was and is being realized, even in Jesus' Passion. Understanding this is the removal of ignorance by repentance and the acceptance of forgiveness. Were one to use one word to describe Jesus' death in Luke's theology it would be "martyr," an example for Stephen and for all who follow in a world where the Gospel has enemies.

Luke is one of the three major witnesses in the NT to the presence and activity of the Holy Spirit, Paul and John being the other two. The commentary that follows will note how frequently and with what significance Jesus' life is characterized by the empowering presence of the Spirit and by prayer. And Jesus' last act, according to Luke, was to instruct his disciples to wait for the gift of the Spirit before they attempt to continue his work (24:49), and this they did, says Luke, waiting in Jerusalem in prayer (Acts 1).

Perhaps the characteristic of Luke's Gospel most commonly known and remarked upon is his attention to and evident concern for the oppressed and marginalized persons in society. This attention to the poor and rejected appears early in Mary's song prior to Jesus' birth (Luke 1:46–55), reappears in the favor shown to the shepherds (2:8–14), surfaces again in the social message of John the Baptist (3:10–14), is publicly announced by Jesus in his sermon in his home synagogue (4:16–21), and then becomes a refrain in his teaching (14:12–14, 21). This is not to say Jesus turned his back on the strong and prosperous. He offered his good news to religious leaders (7:36) and to the wealthy (19:1–10). In fact, some women of means helped finance Jesus' preaching missions (8:1–3). Even so, Luke's Jesus pronounces God's beatitude on the poor, the hungry, the mourners, and the excluded (6:20–23), and it is Luke's Jesus who offers to the poor, the maimed, the blind, and the lame places at the great banquet table (14:21–23).

COMMENTARY

1:1–4

The Prologue

The prologue to Luke's Gospel is without parallel in the NT, having its only similarity elsewhere in Luke at 3:1–2 and Acts 1:1–2. The Gospel of John contains a prologue, but it is a theological summary and not at all a statement of the author about sources, research, method, purpose, and addressee. Luke has employed the style of historians and technical writers of the time. This literary style is all the more noticeable since Luke shifts immediately at v. 5 to the more Semitic form, writing in the manner of the Greek OT for the entirety of the infancy narrative. For approximate parallels to Luke 1:1–4, readers are referred to the prologues to Sirach (Ecclesiasticus) and Josephus' *Jewish War* and *Antiquities of the Jews*. Even in English translation the careful construction of the prologue is evident. It consists of a single sentence, balanced between an introductory clause (protasis), "Inasmuch as many" (v. 1) and a concluding clause (apodosis), "it seemed good to me also" (v. 3, RSV). Such formal writing was a show of respect for a cultured reader, in this case Theophilus (v. 3). The expression "most excellent" is used later by Luke to refer to the Roman governor of Judea (Acts 23:26). Scholars are divided in their attempts to identify Theophilus, some taking the name as a symbol (the

word means "friend of God"), others regarding it as a real person, perhaps a Roman official who is informed about if not a convert to the Christian faith. Whether the name is a literary device or a real person, the quality of the writing is hardly of the type to have either its source or its destination in a Christian community fitting the popular image of a deprived and unlettered lot.

Since many narratives about Jesus had already been written (we know of many but we can identify only one of those known to Luke, the Gospel of Mark), it is not clear why Luke wished to add another. Perhaps the many narratives had created confusion. There is no criticism of the former accounts, but the thoroughness of Luke's research, his recording the events "in order," and his desire to give the reader certainty in matters about which the reader was already informed may combine to argue that Luke found in the earlier narratives something confusing, erroneous, or incomplete. If the reader is a Roman official who may soon make decisions affecting Christians, then getting the story straight is vitally important. Again, it is unclear whether "you have been informed" (v. 4, RSV) means having gotten information or having been instructed as a Christian. What is clear is that some time has passed since the ministry of Jesus. What Jesus said and did had already prior to Luke become a written story passed along as a tradition ("delivered" translates the special term for transmitting tradition). Now after careful research Luke joins in that transmission but prefers not to call his work a Gospel as does Mark (1:1). Rather Luke chooses a term more historical than theological: an "account." As will be seen later, he sets this account into the larger record of world history. And not only has some time passed since Jesus' ministry, but Luke assumes much more time will pass before Christ returns. One does not research and write an orderly account if one is convinced that the Day of the Lord is at hand.

1:5–2:52

The Infancy and Childhood Narrative

Both Luke and Matthew have infancy narratives but they represent quite different traditions. Some scholars have been persuaded that 3:1 was the original beginning of Luke's Gospel, the infancy stories being added later. While 3:1 is clearly a second beginning, and while interest in the circumstances of Jesus' birth probably arose some time after the resurrection (the NT records of apostolic preaching do not include references to the virgin birth), the content of 1:5–2:52 is fully consonant with the remainder of the Gospel. These early stories introduce many Lucan themes: continuity with Judaism, the line of David, God's favor on the poor and oppressed, and the importance of Jerusalem and the Temple. In fact, one could call 1:5–2:52 the Gospel in brief and not an account to satisfy questions about Jesus' origin. The style of the infancy and childhood narrative is very much that of the LXX. Not only does Luke use many allusions to the OT (Exod. 30:7; Dan. 10:7, 12; Num. 6:3; Mal. 3:1, 4–5; 2 Sam. 7:12–16; and Judg. 5:24 are but a few in chap. 1 alone), but he brings his readers into the religious world of the OT. There is no single literary genre: story, homily, poetry, song, prayer, history, and doctrine blend to welcome readers into a world where they are relaxed, oriented, at home. This literary achievement is due, in part, to Luke's allusive use of the OT, weaving the sacred past into the present story rather than quoting the OT to argue for the truth of the Christian story, as does Matthew. The readers' comfort and pleasure in 1:5–2:52 are also related to Luke's abundant use of poetry and song. Many scholars believe Luke draws upon early Christian liturgies for the songs and prayers of Mary, the angel, Zechariah, and Simeon. Luke's infancy and childhood narrative consists of two panels of material: the annunciation of the births of John the Baptist and Jesus (1:5–38), followed by a transition story, the visitation (1:39–56); and the accounts of the births of John and Jesus (1:57–2:40), followed by a transition story, the boy Jesus in the Temple (2:41–52).

1:5–56
The Annunciation of the Births of John the Baptist and Jesus

1:5–25, The Annunciation of the Birth of John the Baptist. Luke begins his narrative by setting the event in the context of contemporary history, a pattern followed through the Gospel and Acts. Herod the Great was made king by the Roman senate in 40 B.C., but his actual control began in 37 B.C. and ended with his death in 4 B.C. Luke customarily uses Judea to represent the whole of Palestine (4:44). Both Zechariah and Elizabeth were of the priestly family of Aaron, Zechariah serving at the Temple in one of the twenty-four divisions named for Aaron's twenty-four sons (1 Chron. 24:1–19). Even though they are the picture of Jewish piety, they are still childless. Elizabeth, barren in her old age, belongs to a rich tradition: Sarah, Rebekah, Rachel, wife of Manoah, and Hannah. Zechariah is on duty at the Temple for the services of morning and evening prayers when he is chosen by

lot (a method for discerning God's will, Acts 1:26) to burn the incense in the holy place where only priests could enter. There at the altar he is visited by Gabriel, one of the seven archangels of Judaism. Luke's description follows the account of Gabriel's visit to Daniel (Dan. 10): fear, the message, being stricken speechless. The angel's message is fourfold: Elizabeth will have a child to be named John (Luke 1:13); the child will give to them and to many joy and gladness (v. 14); the child will be reared in the tradition of Nazirites (v. 15; Num. 6:3; Judg. 13:2–5); and the child will minister in the spirit of Elijah who was to herald the end time and prepare Israel for it (Luke 1:16–17; Mal. 4:5). Early Christians believed Elijah would appear as forerunner of the Messiah. Unlike Matthew (Matt. 17:10–13), Luke never specifically identifies John as Elijah. Understandably, Zechariah has doubts, but for his unbelief he is stricken speechless. The worshipers outside, awaiting the overdue priest, get from him only signs and gestures but sense he has experienced God. His duty ended, Zechariah goes home and Elizabeth conceives, for which she praises God, since barrenness was not only blamed on the woman but was also viewed as a reproach from God. Zechariah is silent and Elizabeth is in hiding, creating a mood of waiting and expectation.

1:26–38, The Annunciation of the Birth of Jesus. Readers are struck by the close parallel this account bears to the preceding one: introduction of the characters, the appearance of the angel, fear, the good news, doubt, the sign, response, the angel departs. As usual, Luke dates (in the sixth month of Elizabeth's pregnancy) and locates (Nazareth was a small town of small regard, John 1:46, in south Galilee) the event to be presented. The angel's announcement of the birth comes not to the man, as in the preceding story and in Matthew's account of Jesus' birth (Matt. 1:18–25), but to the woman. Mary is a virgin, betrothed but not yet married (Luke 1:34). Betrothals, legal and binding, were usually arranged when women were quite young, still only girls. Joseph's importance is that he is of David's house and thus provides Jesus' legal connection to the throne of David (1:32; 2:4). To the angel's greeting, later scribes added "Blessed are you among women!" (RSV footnote to 1:28), perhaps a borrowing from v. 42. Throughout the annunciation and infancy stories Mary is portrayed as favored of God (v. 30), deeply thoughtful (v. 29; 2:19, 51), obedient (v. 38), believing (v. 45), worshipful (v. 46), and devoted to Jewish law and piety (2:22–51). It is little wonder that Luke names her in the company of believers when the church began (Acts 1:14). Gabriel's message to Mary is fourfold: she will have a son to be named Jesus (v. 31);

the child will be the Son of God (Ps. 2:7) and will occupy forever the throne of David (2 Sam. 7:13–16; Luke 1:32–33); the conception of the child will be effected by the overshadowing descent of God's Spirit (v. 35; Exod. 40:35; 1 Kings 8:10); as a sign of the truth of the message; and the angel informs Mary of the pregnancy of her kinswoman Elizabeth (Luke 1:36–37). Gabriel's word concludes with the message to Abraham and Sarah when they doubted the news of the birth of a child: "Is anything too hard for the Lord?" (Gen. 18:14). Mary accepts in humble obedience the word from God.

1:39–56, The Visitation. This story consists of four parts: the visit itself (vv. 39–41a); the inspired speech of Elizabeth (vv. 41b–45); the song of Mary (vv. 46–55); and Mary's return home after the visit of three months (v. 56). Since Mary accepted Gabriel's word, there is no reason to think Mary's visit was to check the truth of that word. Two women, not only kin but now drawn by a common experience, meet in an unnamed village in the hills of Judea. The one woman is old and her son will end an old era; the other is young and virgin and her son will usher in the new. Even the unborn John knows the difference and leaps in the womb when Mary enters, recalling the struggle in Rebekah's womb (Gen. 25:22). In words inspired by the Holy Spirit, Elizabeth blesses Mary as "the mother of my Lord" and as one who accepted in faith God's promise spoken by the angel. Mary's song, in response to Elizabeth and to the events that have transpired, is sometimes called the Magnificat from the opening word in the Latin translation. The song itself draws upon the song of Hannah (1 Sam. 2:1–10) with other OT allusions and phrases interspersed. Since Hannah was promised and given a child in her old age, some scholars have understood the song as having originally belonged to Elizabeth rather than Mary. In fact, some Old Latin manuscripts read "and Elizabeth said" but the earlier Greek attributes the song to Mary. Only briefly does the canticle focus upon Mary's favored place (Luke 1:48–49); the major burden of it is praise to God who has acted always in justice and mercy and will continue to do so in memory of the promise to Abraham and to his descendants forever.

Two unusual features of the song deserve attention. First, God is portrayed in terms of what God has done, because what God has done is what God will do. The past tense is commonly used in Scripture to express hope for the future. Secondly, God's justice and mercy are presented in terms of reversed fortunes for the proud and the humble, the mighty and the lowly, the rich and the poor. This pattern will reappear often in Luke; for example, recall Luke's beatitudes and woes (6:20–26) and the story of the rich man and Lazarus (16:19–31).

1:57–2:52
The Births of John and Jesus, with a Childhood Story of Jesus

1:57–80, The Birth of John the Baptist. This account consists of three parts: the birth, circumcision, and naming of the child (vv. 57–66); the inspired prophecy of Zechariah (vv. 67–79); and a summary statement about John (v. 80). As was customary, relatives and neighbors not only joined in the joy of the birth but also in the naming (Ruth 4:17). Apparently in Second-Temple Judaism the naming was linked to the circumcision, the act by which a male child was made a member of the people of God. The expectation that the boy would be named for his father was according to custom in some quarters (Tobit 1:9). That Elizabeth knew the child was to be called John may be understood as a revelation to her. That Zechariah's tongue was loosed is to be taken as miraculous, prompting him to praise God and the neighbors to be filled with fear. Throughout the hill country of Judea there is much pondering on these events, with great expectation.

Zechariah's inspired prophecy, often called the Benedictus after the first word in the Latin translation, falls into two parts: vv. 68–75 and 76–79. Resounding with OT allusions, vv. 68–75 are distinctly Jewish, similar to hymns of praise to God as deliverer (Pss. 34, 67, 103, 113) and to the thanksgiving psalms of the Dead Sea Scrolls. Jewish eschatological hopes (hopes for the end days) will be fulfilled: prophetic predictions will come to pass, the covenant with Abraham will be remembered, and all enemies will be overthrown by the "horn of salvation" (power of God, 1 Sam. 2:10; Pss. 18:2; 132:17) whom God has raised up. Luke 1:76–79, regarded by some as a Christian addition to a hymn that may have circulated among the followers of John the Baptist, specify John as the forerunner of the Messiah, drawing on Mal. 3:1–2 and 4:5–6. Malachi identifies this figure as Elijah returned. The one who will follow, bringing salvation, is characterized with lines from Isa. 9:1–2 and 42:7. Luke rounds off this story with a summary statement about John's growth, recalling Samson the Nazirite (Judg. 13:24) and Samuel (1 Sam. 2:26). When the story resumes, when John is manifest to Israel, he will come demanding the cleansing of repentance (Luke 3:3).

2:1–40, The Birth of Jesus. Again, one is struck by the close parallels in the two birth stories: joy at birth, circumcision and naming, songs of great expectation, concluding statement about the child's growth. Here, however, the style of writing is noticeably different, less like that of the OT and more like that of the remainder of the Gospel. Luke's birth story consists of five parts: the birth itself (vv. 1–7); the announcement to the shepherds (vv. 8–20); the circumcision and naming (v. 21); the purification and dedication in Jerusalem (vv. 21–38); the return to Nazareth and the summary of the child's growth (vv. 39–40).

While Matthew and Luke agree Jesus was born in Bethlehem (Matt. 2:1), their accounts of the relation of the holy family to Nazareth and to Bethlehem differ (Matt. 2:19–23). Luke says Mary and Joseph were in Bethlehem to be registered for an imperial census and taxation. Historians have been unable to confirm a universal census in the reign of Augustus (Octavius) who ruled from 27 B.C. to A.D. 14. There was a census in Palestine when Quirinius was governor of Syria (perhaps the one referred to in Acts 5:37) but that was later, about A.D. 6. Since Quirinius was a viceroy in this region earlier and since some time elapsed between enrollment and tax assessment, some scholars have argued that Luke could be generally but not exactly correct in his historical references. Luke's primary aim is to place the birth in the city of David because Jesus' continuity with the royal house of David was important for Luke's Christology, his depiction of Jesus' identity. Luke does not, however, quote the messianic prophecy about Bethlehem (Mic. 5:2) as does Matthew (2:5–6).

During this stay in Bethlehem Jesus is born and, like all newborns, is wrapped with strips of cloth to keep the body straight and assure proper growth. The guestroom was apparently occupied and hence offered no privacy, so Mary and Joseph withdrew to the stable underneath or in back of the house, perhaps in a cave. A feeding trough served as a crib. In vv. 8–20 Luke provides a scene sharply different from Matthew who sets the birth of Jesus among the wealthy and powerful (Matt. 2:1–23). The first to hear the news are the poor and lowly. The prophecy of Isa. 61:1 is being fulfilled: the poor have good news proclaimed to them. As elsewhere in these narratives, the word of God comes through an angel, a divine messenger. Luke speaks of angels as easily as he speaks of human beings. In fact, when a sign is offered as proof of the good news, it is not what moderns might regard as a sign; that is, something as extraordinary as a heavenly host. Rather the sign is as common as a baby to be found in poor circumstances, lying in a feeding trough.

Luke provides through the angel a summation of his Christology: Jesus is of the house of David (royalty), he is Savior (neither Matthew nor Mark use this title), he is Christ (Messiah), and he is Lord. This is the message about Jesus preached by the apostles (Acts 2:14–36). The content of the song by the host of heaven is not fully clear. The oldest manuscripts have as the third clause, "among people of [God's] good pleasure," i.e., "with whom he is pleased"

(RSV). Some of these were later "corrected " (by changing a single letter) to read, "among humans, good will," and that reading prevailed for centuries. The shepherds go to the city of David the shepherd, and the scene is filled with some of Luke's favorite words: wonder, pondering, making known the revelation, praising and glorifying God. The presence (glory) of God floods the story.

In the two stories that follow, the circumcision (Luke 2:21) and the purification of Mary, together with the presentation of the child (vv. 22–38), Luke offers readers several major themes important to his theology. First, Jesus is reared according to the laws of Judaism. Neither his parents nor Jesus rebelled against or rejected the law of Moses. The best of Jewish piety and obedience to Moses were observed. Five times in this section Luke speaks of actions according to the law of Moses. As for Mary's purification and the child's presentation to God, Luke interweaves the two rituals in a confusing way. According to Lev. 12:2–8, forty days after the birth of a male child the mother went through a ritual of purification, offering a lamb as a sacrifice in the Temple, or if poor, a pair of doves or pigeons. According to Exod. 13:2, 12–13, the firstborn male child belonged to God and could be redeemed (taken home) by means of an offering by the father.

A second Lucan theme lies in the setting: Jerusalem and the Temple. For Luke, the ministry of Jesus moves toward Jerusalem and the mission of the church moves out from Jerusalem. As for the Temple, Luke is alone among NT writers in his favorable view. His Gospel begins with Zechariah in the Temple and it will close with Jesus' disciples in the Temple.

A third Lucan theme is offered by old Simeon in his inspired benediction, the Nunc Dimittis (the first two words of its Latin version). Simeon, a pious man longing for "the consolation of Israel" (the messianic age), is assured by the Holy Spirit that he will live to see it. The Holy Spirit leads him to the Temple at the time of Jesus' presentation and inspires him to know the child is God's Messiah. In his inspired song, he declares Jesus to be the means of salvation for all people, Jew and Gentile. On that conviction rests Jesus' ministry and the mission of the church.

A fourth and final theme is expressed in Simeon's word to Mary (apparently this occurs in the outer court where women were allowed). Jesus will bring truth to light and will effect decision and judgment. However, in so doing he will face opposition and death. When Jesus comes to Jerusalem as an adult, the journey will be his "exodus" (Luke 9:31).

The truth of Simeon's words are confirmed by Anna, a devout woman of advanced age (2:37 may mean she is eighty-four or has been a widow eighty-four years). The two aged saints are Israel in miniature, poised in anticipation of the new. God is leading Israel to the Messiah, but the Messiah will weep over this city because it did not know the time of the messianic visitation (19:41–44). Luke rounds out the story of the Jerusalem visit: Mary and Joseph have fully kept the law, they return with Jesus to Nazareth, and the child grows in strength, wisdom, and divine favor (cf. 1:80; 1 Sam. 2:26).

2:41–52, A Childhood Story of Jesus. Anyone familiar with apocryphal stories of Jesus' childhood filled with exhibitions of the supernatural (→Apocryphal New Testament) appreciates the quiet reserve of Luke's account, the sole episode between the forty-day-old infant and the man of thirty years (3:23). The setting is again the Temple in Jerusalem. The law required pilgrimages for Passover, Pentecost, and Tabernacles (Exod. 23:14), but for those at a great distance, only Passover. Jesus is twelve and if he has already passed through the ceremony of bar mitzvah then he is a "son of the law" and obeying the command to attend Passover. When the seven-day festival ended, the pilgrims from Galilee, including Mary and Joseph, returned home. It is not surprising that a boy among friends and relatives would not be missed for a day. The reactions of the parents are natural, both in the search and in the reprimand. Jesus assumed they would know he would be in God's house (about God's business). They do not understand; Mary has even more to ponder. And what is Luke saying about Jesus? He is precocious; he knows the Scriptures and seeks deeper understanding; he is at home in the Temple; he regards God as his Father; and he obeys his parents. There is no hint of any break with Judaism. Again, Luke adds the statement of Jesus' growth, an allusion from 1 Sam. 2:26 that summarizes the development of the boy Samuel who grew up in the house of God.

3:1–4:13

Preparation for the Public Ministry of Jesus

Although 3:1 reads like the opening of a book— especially an OT prophet (e.g., Jer. 1:1; Hos. 1:1; Amos 1:1)—we found reasons above to regard the infancy narrative as an integral part of the Gospel. It is quite natural for 3:1 to have the form of a beginning since it does begin the adult and public life of Jesus. In this section Luke will present John the Baptist (3:1–20), the baptism of Jesus (3:21–22), the genealogy (3:23–38), and the temptation in the desert (4:1–13).

3:1–20, John the Baptist. Luke first identifies John by time (vv. 1–2a), place (vv. 2b–3a), and function (vv. 3b–6). Luke provides the best clear date for the ministry of John and therefore of Jesus: the fifteenth year of Tiberius would be A.D. 28–29. Pontius Pilate was prefect (technically not "governor") of Judea from 26 to 36. In addition Luke mentions three tetrarchs (a tetrarch ruled one fourth of a region): Herod Antipas and Philip were sons of Herod the Great and ruled Galilee, Perea, and the northeast areas of Ituraea and Trachonitus. Lysanias was one of several by that name who ruled Abilene, still farther to the north of Galilee. Principal religious authorities were high priests. The office was for life but the Romans appointed them as they willed. Annas served between A.D. 6 and 15. He was replaced but apparently the Jews still regarded him as high priest. His son-in-law held the office between A.D. 18 and 36. According to the Fourth Gospel, Jesus appeared before each of them at his trial (John 18:12–28). But all these rulers are but background to the coming of the word of the Lord (cf. Jer. 1:2) to John in the wilderness (desert).

The desert is not only a geographical reference; it also recalls the place of Israel's formation as God's covenant people and hence implies a return to God. John's ministry centered in the Jordan Valley where he preached a baptism of repentance for forgiveness of sins (cf. Mark 1:4). This baptism differs from proselyte baptism that was for non-Jews and Qumran baptism that was a repeated act of cleansing. Repentance and forgiveness of sins constitute the gospel for Luke (24:47).

Luke modifies his source Mark in several ways: he omits the quotation of Mal. 3:1; he extends the quotation from Isaiah 40 to include vv. 4–5 so as to present the universal reach of the gospel; and he omits the description of John's appearance as like Elijah (2 Kings 1:8) because for Luke it is Jesus who is Elijahlike.

In Luke 3:7–20 John is identified by his message. Unlike Matthew John addresses his eschatological message to the crowds. The judgment of God is not deterred by claims of privilege; lives that do not bear evidence of repentance share the fate of fruitless trees. Those who wish to avoid such a fate ask for instructions. Three groups present themselves: the crowds, tax collectors, and soldiers. The message framed for each group not only addresses the temptations peculiar to each, but provides occasion for an early glimpse of the social message of Luke and especially his attention to economic oppression and inequity.

The last portion of John's message is in response to those who would identify him as the Christ. This was a question all Gospel writers had to address because John had his disciples as did Jesus. Luke first addressed it with the leaping of John in Elizabeth's womb when Mary entered the room. John here distinguishes himself from the Christ in three ways: John is not even worthy to be a slave of the mightier One; the Christ will baptize not with water but with the Spirit and fire (anticipating Pentecost, Acts 2); and the Christ will bring judgment. Drawing on the image of spirit (wind) and fire, John likens the judgment to winnowing wheat in the wind and burning the chaff. But even judgment is good news (Luke 3:18) when repentance and forgiveness are available. For Herod Antipas, however, the clear and bold preaching of John was too indicting. Rather than responding to the message he silences the messenger. John will reappear in chap. 7, but with his imprisonment he is removed from the scene, making way for the entrance of Jesus.

3:21–22, The Baptism of Jesus.

In several respects Luke's account of Jesus' baptism differs from those of Matthew and Mark. First, there is no mention of who baptized Jesus; in the preceding verse John is shut up in prison. Second, the baptism itself is subordinated in a dependent clause in which Jesus is part of a crowd who have been baptized. Finally, Luke joins baptism to prayer. Throughout this Gospel the prayer life of Jesus receives attention. Divine participation in the event is threefold: first, heaven opens, recalling Isaiah's prayer for heaven to open and for God to come again as in the Exodus (Isa. 64:1–3). The Holy Spirit comes on Jesus and will mark all his ministry (Luke 4:14) as well as be the gift that Jesus bestows on the church (24:49; Acts 1:4–5). Second, that the Spirit assumed bodily form as a dove must be a symbolic expression asserting the clear reality of the experience, not to be confused with mere thought or feeling. And finally, divine attestation comes as a voice from heaven. The message joins Ps. 2:7, which speaks of the coronation of a king, and Isa. 42:1, which expresses God's embrace of the Suffering Servant. Here sovereignty and service are joined. The reading in some manuscripts "today I have begotten you," also drawn from Ps. 2:7, was used in the ancient church by those who argued that Jesus was adopted as Son of God at his baptism.

3:23–38, The Genealogy of Jesus.

The genealogy makes several statements important to Luke and his readers. It provides one of the two NT references to Jesus' age as an adult (John 8:57). It affirms Jesus' relation to the entire human race by tracing his line to Adam. The genealogy also establishes a point already repeatedly made by Luke, that Jesus is the son of David. It is quite clear that the family line is traced through Joseph who was legally Jesus'

father though not biologically "as was supposed" (Luke 3:23).

Anyone comparing this genealogy with Matthew's will notice Luke begins with Jesus and moves back to Adam and to God while Matthew begins with Abraham and moves forward to Jesus. Luke has more names and there are some differences. However, genealogies tended to become stylized and even symbolic. For example, Luke has eleven series of seven names, a total of seventy-seven. Many readers wonder what is achieved by tracing Jesus' family line. Does it offer an alternative way of affirming Jesus as son of God? Luke's intention is not clear. One can at least be sure of his desire to reaffirm Jesus' continuity with his Jewish heritage. What has been demonstrated by the family's piety and obedience to the law of Moses is here asserted by the genealogy.

4:1–13, The Temptation of Jesus.

Luke separates Jesus' baptism and temptation with the genealogy, but if the genealogy affirmed Jesus' continuity with his heritage, the temptation does so even more dramatically. Israel's Exodus experience of trial in the desert (Deut. 8:2) is here recapitulated in Jesus' life. The similarity between Luke's and Matthew's accounts (Matt. 4:1–11) argues conclusively for a common tradition, but readers of Luke will want to notice this version carefully so that what Luke wishes to say comes through. For example, the devil does not take Jesus up on a high mountain to show him the kingdoms of the world. Apparently Luke reserves mountains for experiences of prayer and revelation. Here the tempter provides a sudden vision. Or again, Luke has Jerusalem and the Temple the site of the final temptation. This is quite understandable since for Luke Jesus' ministry leads toward Jerusalem and the Temple, the scene of his final struggle and trial. The experience of temptation is between one full of the Holy Spirit and led by the Holy Spirit and the devil, the "slanderer," the one attempting to thwart the purposes of God. The forty days recall Israel's forty-year and forty-day experiences.

Since Jesus has yet to begin his ministry, we may surmise he is struggling with the nature and shape of his messianic role. Weakened by hunger, the first temptation is personal but also social: will this be the ministry Jesus will have? The second is political: will Jesus submit to the ruler of this world to achieve good for people in this world? The final temptation is religious: will Jesus win Jerusalem and all it symbolizes and will Jesus avoid death there by the exhibition of supernatural power? For this story to be real it must not only be assumed that what Jesus was tempted to do he could do, but also that each temptation had strong appeal. Note that one of them was even supported by

Scripture (Ps. 91:11–12). But in every case Jesus responds with Scripture (Deut. 8:3; 6:13; 6:16). The way of the Messiah is to be none of these. Luke concludes the temptations not with relief but with foreboding: "until an opportune time" (4:13). Luke anticipates the Passion, for the tempter will reenter Luke's narrative through Judas (22:3).

4:14–9:50
The Ministry of Jesus in Galilee

4:14–15
Opening Summary

Unlike Mark and Matthew, Luke does not relate Jesus' Galilean ministry to the imprisonment of John. Rather Jesus comes "in the power of the Spirit" that came upon him following baptism. Neither does Luke report Jesus preaching an eschatological message of the approaching kingdom. Instead, Luke offers the briefest sketch: Jesus teaches in the Galilean synagogues, the report of him spreads, and he is everywhere praised. Clearly Luke wants nothing substantive to be reported prior to the account of Jesus' visit in Nazareth. Although Luke 4:14–9:50 follows in general the text of Mark 1:14–9:39, some events are rearranged and, quite noticeably, Jesus' ministry according to Luke remains in Galilee. Therefore, Mark's stories of trips to peripheral regions and north to Tyre and Sidon are omitted.

4:16–30
In the Synagogue at Nazareth

Luke departs from Mark's order (this incident is much later, Mark 6:1–6), but not to say that Jesus began his ministry in Nazareth. Verses 14–15 and 23 make it clear he has already ministered elsewhere. Rather, this story is placed here programmatically, offering in miniature both the nature of Jesus' entire ministry and the fact of his rejection by his own people in view of his acceptance of and being accepted by outsiders. As Luke has repeatedly made clear, Jesus is no rebel; he lives and works within his tradition. He regularly attends the synagogue and participates as all male members were permitted to do, by reading Scripture and commenting. He follows the regular practice: stand to read, sit to comment. The passage read, Isa. 61:1–2, is his choice (Luke's quotation is in fact composite, including a line from Isa. 58:6). The closing line alludes to the joyful restoration of persons and property in the year of Jubilee (Lev. 25:8–55). Jesus offers one comment but it summarizes who he is and what he is doing. He understands himself as having received God's Spirit and ful-

filling the prophecy. The response is mixed: admiration, wondering, doubt. At this point (Luke 4:23) the encounter takes a surprisingly negative turn. Jesus quotes two proverbs: the one expressing their criticism of his not performing miracles as he did (or would do: 4:31–41) in Capernaum and the other being his response—a prophet is not acceptable at home. The tension obviously present increases sharply when Jesus defends ministry to outsiders by offering two OT stories. Both Elijah (1 Kings 17:8–14) and Elisha (2 Kings 5:1–27), prophets in Israel, took God's favor to non-Jews. To be indicted by their own Scripture was too much. In anger the Nazarenes expelled and sought to kill Jesus. Tossing a person against stones apparently was an admissible form of stoning, but this is mob, not official, action. But the trial and death are here foreshadowed. For the present, Jesus moves away from them safely. Similar incidents are common in the Fourth Gospel (John 7:30, 43–44; 8:59; 10:39). One also recalls the free movement of Elijah in the midst of enemies.

4:31–5:16
Early Popularity in Galilee

In this section Luke offers six vignettes from Jesus' ministry that indicate the range of his work—teaching, preaching, exorcising demons, healing, calling disciples—and that account for his growing popularity with the people.

4:31–37, An Exorcism in the Capernaum Synagogue. Mark 1:21–28 is followed here but with changes, such as the omission of the contrast between Jesus' teaching and that of the scribes. Capernaum lay on the north shore of the Sea of Galilee and was the center of much of Jesus' activity. The foundation of an ancient synagogue has been excavated, perhaps on the site of the one visited by Jesus (→ Capernaum). The NT assumes the active presence of evil forces in the world, and the presence of Jesus effects raging confrontations. Demons recognize Jesus as the power of God, and here a demon seeks to gain power over Jesus or at least to neutralize Jesus' advantage by the ancient practice of pronouncing an opponent's name. The battle lines are drawn, the man convulses, and the demon is exorcised. All the witnesses are amazed at the power of Jesus' word, and the news spreads rapidly. Note the focus on Jesus' word and not on the miraculous or on a ritual of exorcism (cf. v. 32; also 5:1; 8:11).

4:38–39, Healing Simon's Mother-in-Law. Luke abbreviates Mark's account (Mark 1:29–31) and alters the nature of the healing. "And he stood over her and rebuked the fever" (v. 39) is a description of an exorcism, based on the common assumption that physical illnesses were the work of evil spirits.

4:40–41, Healing the Sick at Evening. Readers can assume that this unit describes events in the same city and after sunset on the same day as the two units above. Now that the Sabbath is over, crowds gather and the sick are brought. The diseased are healed (every one of them) by laying on hands and the demon-possessed are exorcised by the strong word of rebuke. Jesus was named by a demon earlier as the Holy One of God (4:34); here he is named Christ. They recognize him who can destroy them. Jesus silences them, perhaps because he will not tolerate the confession from evil spirits, perhaps because the use of such titles would prompt misunderstandings of the nature of his mission.

4:42–44, Jesus Leaves Capernaum. Jesus moves away from the danger of popularity based on the miraculous and seeks privacy. Mark says he was praying and his disciples sought him (Mark 1:35–39). Here the crowds want him to stay. However, Jesus feels the urgency of his mission, to preach the gospel widely. Luke uses "the kingdom of God" (v. 43) for the first time here. The summary statement to the effect that Jesus was preaching in the synagogues of Judea does not mean he went to the region to the south. "Judea" in Luke can be a synonym for Palestine as a whole (1:5; Acts 10:37).

5:1–11, The Call of Disciples. Instead of Mark's early call of the first disciples (Mark 1:16–20), Luke places the call a bit later, during a preaching mission and following a miraculous catch of fish. The closest parallel is in John 21:1–8, a postresurrection story. Some scholars believe Luke's story would fit better in such a context because Peter's behavior (v. 8) would more appropriately follow his sin of denying Jesus. Understandably, the account assumes readers already know Simon, who is also called Simon Peter at v. 8. Luke's name for the Sea of Galilee is the lake of Gennesaret. Jesus presses Simon's boat into service to get away from the crowding multitude. The extraordinary catch of fish prompts in Simon fear, astonishment, and a sense of his own unworthiness to be in the presence of one of such power and knowledge. In the episode Jesus is called Master and Lord, one whose very word commanded obedience (v. 5). Although the word, "henceforth you will be catching men" (v. 10) is addressed to Simon, his partners, James and John (no mention is made of Andrew) join him in abandoning everything to become disciples of Jesus.

5:12–16, Healing a Leper. Other than altering the introduction and conclusion, Luke follows the account in Mark 1:40–45. Leprosy, a name given to a range of maladies from mildew in houses and clothes to skin diseases in hu-

mans (Lev. 13; → Leprosy), was regarded as a social disease, removing the victim from social discourse and participation in religious exercises. This man apparently violated the rules in approaching Jesus, evidence of both desperation and faith. That Jesus touched him was most unusual for he thereby entered into the man's isolation. But again, Jesus supports the law and will not be accessory to its violation. This and other acts of compassion generated great popularity and acclaim for Jesus. But Jesus is not swept away from the source of his power; he retreats to the desert for prayer. Luke's portrayal of Jesus carries this refrain.

5:17–6:11
Controversies with Pharisees

Against the backdrop of great popularity, Luke turns now to the darker side of Jesus' ministry: the stirrings of opposition and controversy. Again Luke follows Mark (2:1–3:6) but with modifications appropriate to Luke's theology and context. The issues—forgiving sin, socializing with publicans and sinners, fasting, and Sabbath observance—are offered in six stories that likely were used by the church in its debates with the synagogue.

5:17–26, The Cure of a Paralytic. Jesus' ministry has attracted not only the sick but Pharisees and teachers of the law from all parts of the country. To appreciate their presence, one must discard popular negative images of Pharisees and understand their views of law, worship, and morality (→ Pharisees). Jesus and they had much in common. The story is dramatic and complex; a man lowered through a roof (Luke says "tiles," reflecting his own urban background) is both healed and forgiven. Does this imply a relation between his illness and his spiritual state? Some scholars hold that the episode is really the joining of a healing story with a forgiveness story set within it. The awkward point lies in vv. 23–24. How can one say whether healing or forgiveness is easier and how can healing prove the authority to forgive? Forgiving sin was certainly the graver issue, for to assume a power only God possessed was blasphemy, a capital offense. The church certainly claimed that the exalted Christ, the Son of man, could forgive sin and in his name offered forgiveness. It is unclear what amazed the crowds, the healing, the pronouncement of forgiveness, or both. The conclusion is of the type that followed healings and exorcisms; forgiveness was a pronouncement and usually included in debate and opposition. No doubt the tradition carried in vv. 17–26 is a literary mix.

5:27–32, Eating with Tax Collectors and Sinners. This unit opens with the call of the man in whose home Jesus will eat with those regarded as social and religious outcasts. The man is Levi (called Matthew in the parallel Matt. 9:9; the name of Matthew occurs in the list of apostles, Luke 6:14–16 but Levi does not). His acceptance of discipleship is as complete as that of Peter, James, and John, and it is followed by a banquet at which Levi's old associates are at table with Jesus. Implied is his joy over his new life and the desire to share it (→Publicans). Eating together, an important theme in Luke-Acts, indicated total acceptance of one another. The objection of the Pharisees is directed at Jesus' disciples, showing that at issue is not a historical question about Jesus but the behavior of Christians in Luke's own day. Jesus defends himself and his church: he gives himself to those who need him. A favorite word of Luke is added to his version of the story: repentance. Repentance is both a gift and a demand of the kingdom life.

5:33–39, Concerning Fasting. Apparently this issue is also raised at Levi's house. The question is not whether fasting is right or wrong. Matthew says Jesus fasted (Matt. 4:2) and the church fasted (Matt. 6:16–18). Luke will later describe the church as fasting (Acts 13:2–3; 14:23). At issue is a matter of appropriateness. Routine fasting as the Pharisees did on Mondays and Thursdays was not an adequate reflection of God's grace and generosity toward the world. To Jesus' way of kingdom living there is an aspect of joy and thanksgiving. Weddings and banquets are proper analogies of the kingdom. Of course the Passion of Jesus evoked fasting among his followers, and until the end of days the church recalls the cross as well as Easter. Jesus tells his critics that his disciples can no more join their newfound joy to old rituals than one can tear up a new garment to patch an old, or put new wine in old skins. Christian rituals must be appropriate to the new life. Luke's concluding v. 39 is unique and unusual. Is it humor or irony? Perhaps it is a recognition that even among the new, the followers of Jesus, there remains a clinging to the old ways of Judaism.

6:1–11, Concerning the Sabbath. That there are two stories focusing on Sabbath observance may indicate the frequency with which this issue arose between church and synagogue. The first (vv. 1–5) involves a defense of Jesus' disciples, concluding with a pronouncement: "The Son of man is lord of the sabbath" (a much more Christological ending than in Mark 2:23–28). In the second (Luke 6:6–11) Jesus defends his own ministry of healing on the Sabbath. In the first the disciples are not accused of stealing; one was allowed to eat from a field while traveling (Deut. 23:25). The charge is harvesting and threshing on the Sabbath. Jesus' defense is by OT precedent (1 Sam. 21:1–

6). Apparently the point is that human need, hunger, makes a claim prior to ritual.

In the second incident, the issue is sharply set: Jesus is facing a case of need, he can do something about it, but it is the Sabbath. Mark says Jesus was angry (Mark 3:5); Luke says the Pharisees and scribes were. Jesus poses the issue so as to make inactivity before human need no option at all. The question is simply, What is one to do? Give life (good) or kill (evil)? Jesus' action is the answer: it is never the wrong day to heal and help. The angry discussion that followed anticipates the cross.

6:12–16
Choosing the Twelve Apostles

After reporting the conflicts with the Pharisees and the growing hostility toward Jesus, Luke returns to the content and spirit of 5:16: great public approval and Jesus withdrawing for times of prayer. Choosing the Twelve continues that narrative in that the apostles can help with an ever-increasing ministry and they can assure continuity when the rising fury of Jesus' opponents ends his life. Luke again reminds readers that the selection of twelve helpers was not an act to expedite matters but came after a night of prayer (cf. 3:21). And those chosen are not simply selected to be "sent out" (the verb from which the word "apostle" is derived, Mark 3:14), but they are in Luke given the name "apostles" (→Apostle). The other Gospels each use this word only once but it is more frequent in Luke (9:10; 17:5; 22:14; 24:10). One can see here an instance in which the anticipation of a second volume in which the apostles are principal figures noticeably influences Luke's Gospel narrative. As for the list of names (cf. also Mark 3:13–19; Matt. 10:1–4; Acts 1:13), Luke has Judas the son of James instead of Thaddaeus, and uses no "nicknames" such as "sons of thunder" (Mark 3:17) or "the Twin" (John 11:16). Judas Iscariot is identified by Luke alone with a rare noun for "traitor." The ancient manuscripts reflect some efforts by later scribes to standardize the list.

6:17–9:6
Ministry Between the Choosing and the Sending of the Twelve

Given the number of events and teachings between the selection of the Twelve and their being sent on a mission, we may regard this as a period of preparation for them.

6:17–49, The Sermon on the Plain. Luke has reversed the order of the call of the apostles and the healing of the crowds in Mark 3:7–19 and has shifted the setting from the sea (Mark

3:7) to a level place (Luke 6:17). Matthew places his version of this sermon after the call of four disciples and a general statement about Jesus' ministry (Matt. 4:18–25); Luke locates it after the call of twelve and a general statement about Jesus' ministry (Luke 6:12–19). In Matthew the sermon is from a mountain (Matt. 5:1); in Luke Jesus has prayed and chosen the Twelve on the mountain and now comes down to join a crowd made up of three groups: the apostles, the disciples, and the people (Luke 6:17). Luke may have in mind Jews and Gentiles by referring to both Judea and Tyre and Sidon to the north. Matthew's version is four times the length of Luke's, contains material scattered elsewhere in the Gospels, and offers interpretations within the sermon that lead many students to conclude Luke follows more closely their common source (Q). As in Matthew, Luke seems to address the sermon to Jesus' disciples (v. 20) while insisting the teachings were given in the hearing of all the people (7:1). Luke's larger audience contains those of special concern to this Evangelist: the sick and the distressed.

The sermon itself consists of five parts: blessings and woes (vv. 20–26); on love of enemies (vv. 27–36); on judging (vv. 37–42); on proof of goodness (vv. 43–46); and on hearing and doing (vv. 47–49).

6:20–26, Blessings and Woes. Unlike Matthew's nine blessings and no woes, Luke has four each, set in parallels: poor-rich, hungry-full, weeping-laughing, and rejected-accepted. By sharply contrasting life now and in the future, Luke sets the sermon in an eschatological frame of reference. This is not to say Jesus' disciples are to sit and wait for a blessed future; Christ's presence means "Today this scripture has been fulfilled" (4:21; my emphasis). A blessing is a pronouncement of God's favor, fortune, happiness, while a woe is a curse, a pronouncement of God's disfavor, disapproval, judgment (Deut. 11:26–28). As early as the Magnificat, Luke makes it clear who is recipient of God's gracious favor. Notice also the direct "you" in Luke (which does not begin in Matthew until after the Beatitudes) that implies the presence of both groups in Jesus' audience.

6:27–36, On Love of Enemies. The shifts in the Greek text from plural "you" (vv. 27–28), to singular (vv. 29–30), and back to plural (vv. 32–36), coupled with the fact that these sayings are found elsewhere in the Gospels, persuade readers that this "sermon" consists of a compilation of teachings. This unit contains two parts. The first (vv. 27–31) states the principles that Jesus' followers do not draw behavior patterns from those who victimize them (hating, cursing, abusing, striking, stealing, begging), but rather respond to others as they would wish to be treated (Luke's version of the Golden Rule; cf. Matt. 7:12). The second part (vv. 32–36) insists that neither should one's behavior be determined by one's friends. Rather, one is to imitate God, who does not reciprocate but loves even the ungrateful and selfish.

6:37–42, On Judging. Cf. Matt. 7:1–5; 15:14; 10:24–25. From what has been said above, it follows that Jesus' disciples will not judge or condemn, but give and forgive. Even the balanced justice of measure for measure is joyfully broken by the image of overflowing generosity. "Into your lap" (v. 38) refers to the large pocket formed by the fold in a robe above the belt. Verses 39–40 warn that if one learns from blind, hypocritical, and judgmental teachers, then one will become such a person. Example was a bigger factor in pedagogy then than now. Verses 41–42 use the tragicomical image of a person with a log in the eye trying to improve the condition of another with a speck in the eye.

6:43–46, On Proof of Goodness. This subunit stresses the inseparable union of what one is, what one says, and what one does. Words and deeds announce character as surely as fruit reveals the nature of a tree.

6:47–49, On Hearing and Doing. Matthew (7:24–27) and Luke draw the parable of the two builders from a common source, but Luke has adapted it for a non-Palestinian setting. The meaning is unchanged: the difference between interested auditors and obedient disciples will sooner or later become evident (James 1:22–25).

7:1–10, Healing the Centurion's Slave. Cf. Matt. 8:5–13; John 4:46–53. The centurion is a Gentile, perhaps serving under Herod Antipas or under Pilate at Caesarea. That he loved the Jewish nation and built a synagogue indicate he was a "God-fearer," one who was "at the gate" but not a convert to Judaism (cf. Cornelius, Acts 10:1–2). Unlike Matthew's account, Luke's story is of a man who never came in contact with Jesus. Two delegations, one of Jews and the other of friends, perhaps Gentiles, served as intermediaries. The image is not only of a humble, believing man, but of one who foreshadows the ingathering of Gentiles. The church later will directly take the good news to the Gentiles, but that mission has its authorization in the ministry of Jesus. Matthew uses this occasion to prophesy the time when many will come from east and west (Matt. 8:11–12), but Luke will state that later (Luke 13:28–30).

7:11–17, Raising the Widow's Son at Nain. This story is without parallel in the other Gospels but has antecedents in 1 Kings 17:17–24 and 2 Kings 4:32–37. As in 4:16–30, Luke again looks to the ministries of Elijah and Elisha to present Jesus, not only in what Jesus did but in the way the story is told. "He gave him to his mother" is verbatim from 1 Kings 17:23 in the LXX. A town southeast of Nazareth is believed by some to be the ancient Nain. Luke's "bier" or casket is likely his Greek equivalent of the Jewish stretcher on which the dead were carried outside the town for burial. The story conveys the picture of Jesus not only as compassionate, especially to women, but also as a prophet through whom the people are experiencing a divine visitation (Luke 19:44). This event also prepares readers for the witness to John about Jesus: "the dead are raised up" (7:22).

7:18–35, John the Baptist and Jesus. Cf.

Matt. 11:2–19. This unit consists of two parts: the interchange between John's disciples and Jesus (vv. 18–23) and Jesus' words concerning John (vv. 24–35). In the first part, readers have to recall 3:19–20 to know John is in prison. John had disciples; in fact, according to Acts, John's movement had extended as far as Ephesus as early as Paul (18:24–19:4). Even today a small sect in Iraq called Mandeans traces its history to John. All four Gospel writers have to deal with John, affirming his role in God's purpose while keeping him subordinate to Jesus.

John's question is essentially about Jesus' messiahship. But why the question? Is John wavering, unclear about the nature of Jesus' ministry or Jesus' failure to make claims about himself? It must be kept in mind that while John announced the coming of a stronger One, only in the Fourth Gospel does John have the revelation that the person is Jesus (John 1:24–34), though it may be implied in Matt. 3:13–14. Jesus may not fit John's image, or John may wish to prod Jesus to a public declaration. Jesus' answer, recalling Isa. 61:1–2 which Jesus read in the synagogue at Nazareth, is a description of what he is at that time doing. John, like everyone else, must draw his own conclusion, and he is blessed if he is not offended by such a Messiah.

In the second part, Jesus identifies John as a prophet fulfilling Mal. 3:1, but unlike Matthew (11:14) Luke does not say John is Elijah to come (Mal. 4:5). But for all John's greatness, this child of old parents belongs to the old age; in Jesus, child of the young virgin, God does a new thing. Luke 7:29–30 offers a parenthetical comment (so indicated in the RSV) that is perhaps the highest praise of John; that is, receiving or rejecting John's baptism was receiving or rejecting the purpose of God. Verses 31–35 are framed on two proverbs, apparently familiar in the culture, about children, some of whom are fickle and impossible to please. John's and Jesus' eating habits reflect two different life-styles and ministries but the fickle children are pleased by neither. The other children reflect their wisdom by their acceptance of John and Jesus. Those who justified God (v. 29) are justified as wise (v. 35). The focus here on eating, so important in stating who does and who does not belong to the people of God, serves well to introduce the next story.

7:36–50, Jesus Anointed by a Sinful Woman.

For Luke's story to be heard it must be separated from similar but different anointing stories in Mark 14:3–9; Matt. 26:6–13; and John 12:1–8. Luke's account involves an unnamed woman (there is no reason to assume it was Mary Magdalene, 8:2) and occurred in Galilee in the house of Simon a Pharisee. Jesus had enough in common with Pharisees for this to be no surprise, nor to be understood as a plot to trap Jesus. Since eating occurred while reclining, the woman's approach and activity were not awkward. For Simon, the act proves Jesus is no prophet since a prophet would have known her to be a sinner and would have repulsed her. But Jesus proves himself a prophet not only by his acceptance of her penitence and love but also by knowing Simon's thoughts.

The parable of the two debtors who owed, one five hundred, the other fifty denarii (a denarius was a day's wages, Matt. 20:2) points up the differences between the woman and Simon, their behaviors registering responses to forgiveness. It is somewhat surprising that Simon had not extended to Jesus the customary courtesies; this and other meals in the homes of Pharisees (Luke 11:37; 14:1) reflect tensions but not alienation and condescension.

Luke 7:47 is difficult in that Jesus seems to say the woman was forgiven much because she loved much, rather than the reverse. Surely the meaning is that she must have been forgiven much since it is evident she loves much. The conclusion of the story (vv. 49–50) could possibly have been originally in another context. After all, the issue has not been Jesus' authority to forgive sins; nor has the praiseworthy quality in the woman been her faith. It was her love that had been abundantly demonstrated.

8:1–3, Women Share in Jesus' Ministry.

Luke alone carries this note about these women, and perhaps it is placed here as a contrast to the woman in the preceding story. Joanna is mentioned here and in 24:10; Susanna, nowhere else. Mary of Magdala, prominent in the resurrection narrative, had been relieved of seven demons. Only popular legend has made her a prostitute by assimilation to the previous story. The women are said to have been healed, to have been with Jesus and the Twelve, and to have provided financial assistance. Luke's favorable reports about women began with Elizabeth and Mary and will continue through Acts.

8:4–18, The Parable of the Sower. Cf.

Mark 4:1–9; Matt. 13:10–15. Since 6:19 Luke has not followed Mark, but here he returns to that source. However, Luke leaves the setting in

Jesus' ministry quite vague and in general abbreviates the parable. The action of the sower is normal for that land in which planting preceded plowing. The parable can have the effect of instructing Jesus' followers that not all their teaching and preaching will be fruitful. It can also serve to encourage those who have looked at their failures and who have forgotten that some seed will yield abundantly. What is important is to realize this is a parable, and therefore is not a simple illustration of a point being made otherwise. Rather a parable is the message, and the message offered in such a way as to elicit listener involvement in its meaning. With parables listeners bear heavy responsibility for what is heard and understood; quite often the message is not obvious nor available to casual, unengaged listeners (→Parables). In stating the reason for speaking in parables (vv. 9–10), Luke very noticeably softens Mark 4:10–12. Luke has in mind two generally described groups: "his disciples" and "others." Since it is his disciples who ask for an explanation and yet who are the ones to whom kingdom secrets are given, we can assume an explanation will follow.

Luke omits Mark's "Lest they should turn again and be forgiven," which was Mark's way of saying that in the purposes of God lay the reasons for some not understanding Jesus' message. Matthew quotes Isa. 6:9–10 in support of this view. All the Evangelists are dealing with the fact that in the audience of Jesus (and of the church) some hear and some do not.

In the interpretation (Luke 8:11–15) the parable is made into an allegory, that is, a story in which each item in the narration is made to represent something else. Most scholars agree this interpretation represents the situation of the early church in its missionary preaching to a variety of conditions. As an "explanation" of the parable, however, the interpretation is less than clear. For example, the seed is identified as "the word of God" (an early Christian term for the gospel message) and also as the various kinds of hearers. One would have expected the hearers to be identified as different kinds of soil.

The concluding verses (16–18) consist of three separate sayings, sometimes called "floating sayings" because they are found in other contexts (Matt. 5:15; 10:26; 25:29; Luke 12:2; 19:26). The sense of the three sayings, however, is appropriate to the revealing quality of parables, in contrast to their concealing or secretive quality. Jesus came to reveal, to give light, and those who attend diligently to his words will experience increasing understanding. Others, with no more investment than spectators, will walk away empty and confused.

8:19–21, Jesus' True Family. Both Mark (3:31–35) and Matthew (12:46–50) place this

episode prior to the parable of the sower, and in Mark it occurs in a context of very tense controversy. By abbreviating the account and locating it after the parable of the sower, Luke achieves two things: any tension between Jesus and his immediate family is minimized, and the story serves to illustrate the parable: hearing and doing the word of God is the path into the fellowship created by Jesus.

8:22–25, Jesus Calms the Storm. Cf. Mark 4:35–41; Matt. 8:23–27. This story begins a series of wonders Jesus performs: stilling a storm, healing a demoniac, raising a dead girl, and healing a sick woman. If they are offered as examples of the mysteries of the kingdom, they are but loosely joined to what precedes. Luke simply says, "on one of the days" (translation mine). As usual, Luke calls Galilee a "lake"; for a non-Palestinian, "sea" meant the Mediterranean. Jesus is addressed as Master, appropriate to his action in calming the storm. The miracle is really an exorcism; the water was believed to be an abode of evil forces and a sudden storm was viewed by many as the work of demons. Jesus rebukes them as he did in other exorcisms. It is rare in the Gospels for the Twelve to be the beneficiaries of an act of Jesus' power; usually they join him in ministering to others. In their amazement they ask the question the unfolding story is answering: who is this?

8:26–39, Healing the Gerasene Demoniac. Cf. Mark 5:1–20; Matt. 8:28–34. Luke does not tell this story as lengthily and dramatically as Mark. It is Luke's one story of Jesus ministering outside Jewish territory. The manuscripts differ on the spelling of the name of the place. The account itself is of an exorcism, and though an extreme case of demon possession, the exorcism follows the usual pattern (Luke 4:31–37). The abyss was the netherworld, the abode of the dead (Rom. 10:7), of imprisoned spirits (1 Pet. 3:19), and Satan's prison (Rev. 20:3). The man who is healed (Luke's word can also mean "saved") becomes a disciple and is sent to proclaim what God has done. The story prefigures the gentile mission and gives warrant for it in Jesus' own ministry.

8:40–56, Raising Jairus's Daughter and Healing a Woman with a Hemorrhage. Cf. Mark 5:21–43; Matt. 9:18–26. Luke found these two stories already joined in Mark, who often set a story within a story. The two events have natural connections in that both involve women, both are cases of ritual uncleanness, and, in Luke, both involve "twelve years." This is the second raising of an only child in Luke (7:11–17), and the woman's touch fulfills 6:19. Jesus' word to the woman: "your faith has made you well [saved you]; go in peace" repeats his word

1025

to the sinful woman who anointed him (7:50). Whatever the condition, Jesus makes people whole again. In the account of raising Jairus's daughter, Luke introduces the inner circle (Peter, James, and John) and the desire for secrecy on the part of Jesus. Soon now Jesus will turn toward Jerusalem and death; this act of raising the dead must not confuse the public over the uses of Jesus' power in the hour of his own death. In summary, Jesus saves (8:43-48) and gives life to the dead (8:49-56).

9:1-6, Jesus Sends Out the Twelve. Cf. Mark 6:7-13; Matt. 10:1, 9-11, 14. Since the time they were chosen to be apostles (6:12-16), the Twelve have listened to and observed Jesus. Now they are in fact apostles ("those sent out"), commissioned to exorcise demons, to heal, and to preach. Like that of Jesus, their ministry will testify to the inbreaking of the kingdom and an attack on the forces of evil. For this mission Jesus gives not only authority (Mark 6:7) but also power. They do not go two by two; Luke reserves that for the seventy (10:1-12). For the journey they are to be totally dependent on God. Like the Levites they could expect hospitality and support (Num. 18:31; 1 Cor. 9:3-14). Inhospitality was not to be met with retaliation but with the simple ritual of judgment (Luke 9:5; Acts 13:51). Luke clearly has in mind the subsequent mission of the church led by the apostles, especially in the added note of universality: "preaching the gospel and healing *everywhere*" (my emphasis).

9:7-50

Forebodings and Predictions of the Passion

Even though it is not until 9:51 that Jesus turns toward Jerusalem, every unit of 9:7-50 anticipates directly or indirectly the coming Passion.

9:7-9, Herod Perplexed About Jesus. Cf. Mark 6:14-16; Matt. 14:1-2. This Herod is Antipas, son of Herod the Great and tetrarch of Galilee. The various public opinions of Jesus (repeated at 9:18-22) disturb Herod. The ministry of Jesus has now reached a center of political power, a clear prophecy of death, especially since Herod had already killed John, a fact to which Luke makes only this one reference (for the full story, see Mark 6:17-29). Herod's curiosity about Jesus will turn to desire to kill him (Luke 13:31), a desire satisfied in Jerusalem (23:6-12).

Opposite: Three disciples of Jesus portrayed on a fourteenth-century mosaic at the Kariye Church, Istanbul, Turkey.

9:10-17, Jesus Feeds the Multitude. Cf. Mark 6:30-44; Matt. 14:13-21; John 6:1-13. The apostles return; the report of their mission is brief, for the central event in which they have a part is now to be related. Only Luke identifies the place as Bethsaida (John 1:44). The feeding of the crowd is set in the context of a full ministry in Lucan terms; Jesus receives the people, he preaches, he heals, and he is concerned about lodging (only in Luke) and provisions for them. The meal itself prefigures the Lord's Supper (Luke 22:19, 24:30), both in the eucharistic language used (9:16) and in the use of the word translated "broken pieces" that came to be a term for the broken bread (*Did.* 9:3-4) of the Eucharist.

9:18-22, Peter's Confession and the First Prediction of the Passion. Cf. Mark 8:27-33; Matt. 16:13-23. Luke, like John 6:1-69, joins the feeding and Peter's confession, omitting Mark 6:45-8:26. The last geographical reference in Luke was Bethsaida and, typical of this Evangelist, Jesus is described as being in prayer. Setting the event in prayer alerts readers to its critical importance for Jesus and to the operation of God's will. The confession differs somewhat in the three Synoptics, and Luke omits the stern exchange between Jesus and Peter. Some scholars hold that Luke is thereby preserving a loftier image of Peter, but actually in Luke the entire occasion is briefer, more subdued, and wrapped in prayer. Also in Luke the charge to silence is directly tied to the prediction of the Passion, such is the force of the linkage of vv. 21 and 22 by a participle. The "must" here and elsewhere (13:33; 17:25; 22:37; 24:7, 26, 44) points to divine will.

9:23-27, The Demands of Discipleship. Cf. Mark 8:34-9:1; Matt. 16:24-28. Although the passion prediction is to the Twelve alone, the call for cross bearing is to all. Since the cross was a rather familiar instrument of death (Roman), Jesus could have spoken meaningfully of a cross prior to his own death, but Luke's readers understand their crosses after the fact of his. "Daily" alters the emphasis from martyrdom to sacrificial living. Jesus is identified as the Jewish figure "Son of man," both in suffering (v. 22), and in his return in glory from God. In v. 27, by removing "with power" (Mark 9:1), Luke could be referring to some of the disciples seeing the transfiguration or the resurrection.

9:28-36, The Transfiguration. Cf. Mark 9:2-8; Matt. 17:1-8. Luke replaces Mark's six days (Exod. 24:15-16) with eight, perhaps meaning a week later but not necessarily Sunday (sometimes called the eighth day). Again Luke says the journey was for a time of prayer, and the transfiguration occurred during prayer (recall Luke 3:21). The phrase "behold, two men" joins this story to the resurrection (24:4) and the ascension (Acts 1:10). Moses and Elijah talk with Jesus about his approaching death, or more literally, "exodus," a powerfully symbolic term. The disciples do not hear because they are asleep (cf. Luke 22:45). They wake in time to see the three glorified figures. It is the cloud, associated with the awesome presence of God (Exod. 24:15–16; Acts 1:9) that frightens the disciples. Moses and Elijah have vanished; it is Jesus, God's Chosen Son (recalling again the baptismal scene) now moving to his exodus, who is to be heard and obeyed. The silence of the disciples is appropriate.

9:37–50, Portraits of the Not-Yet-Ready Disciples. Cf. Mark 9:14–41; Matt. 17:14–23; 18:1–5. In four vignettes Luke shows the disciples unprepared for the events soon to transpire in Jerusalem. In the first (vv. 37–43a), on the day following the transfiguration, the disciples lack the power to exorcise a demon from a child. Jesus heals the boy and laments the disciples' lack of faith. How long will it take to prepare them to continue his work? In vv. 43b–45, Luke joins to these events the second prediction of the Passion. It is sharply stated, the omission of reference to the resurrection serving to emphasize his death. In v. 45 there is the mixture, not uncommon in Scripture but strange to us, of human unbelief and providential concealing of a truth. Seeing and not seeing, perceiving and not perceiving, are alike attributed to God (cf. 24:16, 31). The third vignette (9:46–48) clarifies why the disciples do not understand talk of suffering: they are concerned about greatness, with a competitive spirit. Lowliness of spirit is taught not by the example of a child but in the reception of a child, that is, in welcoming the lowliest. And finally (vv. 49–50), Jesus addresses the problem of exclusivism among his followers. Very likely Luke is addressing through words of Jesus problems that beset the church: lack of power, misunderstanding, arrogance, and exclusivism. Luke marks at 9:50 the end of the Galilean ministry; Jesus now turns with his not-yet-ready disciples toward Jerusalem.

9:51–19:28

The Journey to Jerusalem

Of this section, 9:51–18:14 is often called Luke's travel narrative, which in 18:15 rejoins Mark and Matthew. Actually, much in this section has with Matthew a common source (Q), a small portion is also in Mark, with a substantial amount peculiar to Luke. The material is arranged as a journey, with Luke on occasion reminding readers of that perspective (9:51; 13:22; 17:11) since the stories in themselves do not usually imply a journey. Some scholars hold that Luke follows the narrative of Deuteronomy, and much does fit that pattern, though not all. For example, some Elijah and Elisha echoes from 1 and 2 Kings are here also. Geographical references do not really help one reconstruct the journey, since Luke's travel narrative is more theological than geographical. Jesus moves now toward suffering; to follow him is to face the same.

9:51–62
Jesus Establishes the Nature of the Journey

The two units that open this section make clear to the disciples the nature of the way and its destination.

9:51–56, Passing Through Samaria. The journey begins with a rejection and prophesies rejection. "To be received up" refers to crucifixion, resurrection, and ascension (Acts 1:2, 11; cf. 2 Kings 2:9–11; Isa. 42:1). "Set his face" echoes Isa. 50:7, which speaks of determination in the face of opposition. Messengers are sent ahead to make preparations (anticipating Luke 22:7–13), but they meet rejection, not because Jesus is a Galilean but because he is moving on to Jerusalem. Jesus forbids any violent reaction in the manner of Elijah (2 Kings 1:9–10). Some scribes added an explanation to Luke 9:55 (see footnote on this passage in RSV). Later the Samaritans will welcome the Gospel (Acts 8:5–25).

9:57–62, Underscoring the Cost of Discipleship. Cf. Matt. 8:19–22. The three cases of would-be disciples serve to accent the demands of following Jesus whose face is set toward the cross. The call to discipleship is not set against weak and flimsy excuses but against primary personal and family obligations: attending to creature needs, filial duty, and family love. Loyalty to Jesus demands more than Elijah asked of Elisha (1 Kings 19:19–21), taking precedence over the best, not the worst, of human priorities.

10:1–24
The Mission of the Seventy

This unit consists of six subunits: the instruction of the seventy; woes upon those who reject the messengers; the return of the seventy; a thanksgiving; and a blessing.

10:1–12, The Instruction of the Seventy. This material recalls the mission of the Twelve (9:1–5; Matt. 9:37–38; 10:7–16). Traditionally Judaism spoke of seventy (some manuscripts say seventy-two) nations (Gen. 10) and Luke's sending out seventy in teams of two anticipates the mission to the nations described in Acts. The time for the mission is ripe but the resistance will be strong. However, the messengers are to be equipped only with trust in God, giving themselves to healing and preaching. They are neither to shop around for the best hospitality nor delay with conversation on the road. Whether received or rejected, their message is the same: the kingdom of God has come near. That truth is not contingent on the response. The judgment pronounced in Luke 10:12 is Jesus' comment to the messengers and not a part of their message.

10:13–16, Woes on the Impenitent. Cf. Matt. 11:21–23. Apparently Jesus had ministered in all three towns, although there is no record of his being in Chorazin (north of Capernaum). Theirs had been a privilege not shared by gentile cities and therefore, greater would be their judgment. The principle applies: to whom much is given, of them much is expected. Luke 10:16 underscores the seriousness of accepting or rejecting the disciples: treatment of them is treatment of Jesus, is treatment of God.

10:17–20, The Return of the Seventy. The report of the seventy is cast entirely in terms of exorcisms, indicating that the ministry of Jesus is gaining power over the forces of evil. The two OT allusions, the fall of Satan (Isa. 14:12) and treading on serpents and scorpions (Ps. 91:13) convey this note of victory. However, triumphalism is an inappropriate spirit among disciples; to be inscribed in God's book (Exod. 32:32–33) is the proper ground for joy.

10:21–24, A Prayer and a Blessing. Cf. Matt. 11:25–27; 13:16–17. Jesus' prayer of thanks (only Luke says Jesus rejoiced in the Holy Spirit) may have been a hymn of praise in the early church. It delights in the reversal common to much of the NT: concealed from the wise, revealed to babes. In addition, it portrays Jesus as the divine revealer, much like the figure of Wisdom in Judaism, a portrait more Johannine than Lucan. Jesus' blessing is on his disciples who are among the babes who see, a privilege the ancient leaders could only anticipate.

10:25–42
Two Stories About Seeing and Not Seeing

Having blessed his disciples for seeing, Jesus now has two encounters with persons who did not see, a lawyer and a woman named Martha. The causes of their inability to see are different and so are Jesus' remedies: in the one case, "go and do likewise"; in the other, sit still and listen. By placing these stories back to back, Luke reminds readers that the responses to Jesus' call are not the same in every case.

10:25–37, Jesus and the Lawyer. Cf. Mark 12:28–31; Matt. 22:34–40. Both Mark and Matthew have this story later, with variations in details. For Luke the story illustrates how the wise and prudent miss what babes know. The lawyer's question is about eternal life, not the greatest commandment, and he is led to answer it himself. But he cannot accept his own answer because he must press for some advantage over Jesus. To his second question Jesus offers a parable, or perhaps an example story. The story begins as a common occurrence on a dangerous road. The behavior of the priest and the Levite (a Temple assistant) is not admirable but could be explained on several grounds. The ugliness of their neglect appears sharply when, surprisingly, a Samaritan is introduced as the one unselfish, concerned, attentive, and caring to the point of delaying his own journey, expending much energy, and spending two days' wages, with the assurance of more. Ceremonially unclean, socially outcast, and religiously a heretic, the Samaritan (from the Jewish point of view) is the opposite of the lawyer as well as the priest and Levite. Jesus alters the question, Who is my neighbor? to Who proved to be a neighbor? Again the lawyer answers the question and the implications of his own answer are inescapable.

10:38–42, Jesus, Martha, and Mary. Martha and Mary appear in John's Gospel (John 11:1–12:8) and live in Bethany near Jerusalem. However, in Luke Jesus is not yet near the city. Martha's busyness indicates many guests and her work was not only hospitable but supported by laws of hospitality. Her complaint is reasonable. Jesus' response to her anxiety is not totally clear. An alternate reading to "one thing is needful" is "few things are needful, or only one." Does this mean only a few dishes, or only one dish is enough? If so, it still carries symbolic force: the greater need is spiritual food and that is the portion or "dish" that Mary had chosen.

11:1–13
Teachings on Prayer

Luke has gathered sayings of Jesus on prayer, only the parable of the friend at midnight being peculiar to Luke. Matthew has the remainder, but locates it in two places in the Sermon on the Mount (Matt. 6:9–13; 7:7–11). Luke set all these sayings in the context of Jesus' own prayer life, which prompts his disciples to ask for instruction in prayer. John had disciples who prayed and fasted (John 5:33). Luke's form of the Lord's Prayer lacks the liturgical elaborations of Matthew's and may be earlier. The shorter phrases in Luke, such as "Thy kingdom come," underline the urgent tone of the prayer. "Daily bread" is here "bread day after day" and "sins" interprets "debts." The final petition is probably eschatological: do not lead us into trial, that is, the final agony of evil before the end. The parable of the friend at midnight (Luke 11:5–8 is a bit awkward at first because it seems to focus on the one asking for bread. "Which of you" as an introduction to parables always anticipates a "No one" in response. It is soon clear that attention is on the one asleep on a mat on the floor with his children, having barred the heavy door for the night. The meaning does not lie in comparing God to a reluctant friend who helps only in response to importunity (persistence, shamelessness) but in thinking from lesser to greater. If friends respond, how much more will God. The closing verses (9–13) continue the teaching that God responds to prayer, but prayer is continual (present imperatives) asking, seeking, knocking. Even so, this persistence is in the context of a parent-child relationship that assures not only good gifts, but in this case, the highest gift: the Holy Spirit.

11:14–12:1
Conflicts and Controversies

The spirit of this section is that of controversy even though the particular issues vary: by what power Jesus exorcises demons; by what sign his power can be shown to be of God; and the hypocrisy of Jesus' critics.

11:14–28, Concerning Exorcisms. Cf. Mark 3:22–27; Matt. 12:22–30. Luke enjoys putting contrasting materials together: Holy Spirit (v. 13) and evil spirits (vv. 14–26). Following an exorcism, some marveled, some sought a sign as proof, while others charged Jesus with using the power of Beelzebul ("Baal the prince"; the Gk. text does not say Beelzebub, "Lord of the flies," 2 Kings 1:2). Jesus answers the charge with logic (Satan would not work against himself), with a comparison (How do exorcists among you cast out demons?), and a challenge (If I work by the finger of God [Exod. 8:19], then the kingdom has come). The fact is, says Jesus, Satan is being overthrown by a stronger one. But even after an evil spirit is cast out, there must be diligence or evil will return and the final condition will be even worse (cf. also Matt. 12:43–45). Luke's location of the saying about Jesus' mother (Luke 11:27–28) seems to have been influenced by Mark who locates the coming of Jesus' mother and brothers after the Beelzebul controversy (Mark 3:20–35). For Mary and for all, hearing and doing bring blessedness.

11:29–36, Concerning Signs. Cf. Matt.12:38–42; 5:15; 6:22–23. Unlike Matthew, Luke does not address Jesus' words about this evil generation to scribes and Pharisees. Also unlike Matthew, Luke's use of Jonah is not to offer a sign of the resurrection. And unlike Mark (8:12) who offers no sign, Luke offers the sign of Jonah's preaching that produced repentance. The Ninevites received from Jonah; the queen of the South received from Solomon; therefore, both will judge Jesus' audience for they refuse to receive a greater prophet than Jonah, a wiser man than Solomon. The concluding sayings on light are apparently placed here to say that to the person of integrity and openness to light, Jesus' message is clear enough and able to give the light of God to one's life.

11:37–12:1, Woes to Pharisees and Lawyers. Cf. Matt. 23:1–36, but in a different order. Luke sets these woes in the context of a meal in the home of a Pharisee, not uncommon in Luke (7:36; 14:1). Jesus had much in common with them; in fact, it was Pharisees who warned Jesus about Herod (13:31). But they differed as to what constituted the will of God. True devotion and true almsgiving are with integrity and not outward only. The three woes against these (certainly not all) Pharisees have to do with care for legal details and neglect of God's justice and love; with pride of place and attention; and with being hidden contaminators of Israel's life, like buried graves. The three woes against the lawyers (experts in Mosaic law) have to do with burdening others while claiming personal exemption; with honoring dead prophets while consenting and participating in the causes of their death; and with confusing the people both by example and teaching. Luke is thinking of the church when he adds apostles to the list of the persecuted (v. 49). "Wisdom of God" in v. 49 is in Matthew Jesus himself (Matt. 23:34; also 1 Cor. 1:24). "Required of this generation" (Luke 11:50) may refer to the fall of the nation and of Jerusalem. Luke concludes the section with two comments: one to the effect that efforts to trap Jesus continued (vv. 53–54), and the other as a word of warning to the increasing crowds concerning the harmful influence of Pharisaic hypocrisy.

12:2–13:9
Exhortations and Warnings

Luke sets these teachings in his favorite context: his disciples surrounded by a large crowd (the Gk. literally means ten thousand). His words are for his followers, but for all to hear, ponder, and if so minded, accept.

12:2–12, Call for Open Confession. Cf. Matt. 10:26–33; 12:32; 10:19. Luke draws together from Q what is scattered in Matthew. These verses participate in both present and future, both command and promise. At the end all secrets and mysteries will be revealed, and that fact necessitates full and open confession and proclamation now by those who belong to the new age. Disciples are not to be intimidated into silence, for only God is to be feared. God who cares for sparrows surely cares for those who trust. In the courts of heaven (Job 1:6–12; Isa. 40; Zech. 3) acknowledgment or denial will already have been determined on earth. Awkwardly inserted here at v. 10 is Luke's version of the sin that will not be forgiven (Mark 3:28–29; Matt. 12:32). Some early Christians took blasphemy against the Spirit to mean rejecting the inspired speech of a prophet. Here the saying seems to mean that not believing in Jesus as the Son of man on earth could be forgiven. After all, there was yet Pentecost and the call to repentance. However, if the Spirit's call to repentance and faith is dismissed as nothing, forgiveness becomes unavailable. Verses 11–12 continue the message of 2–9: under pressures religious and political, disciples are to have courage, listening to the Spirit that leads and confirms in the time of trial.

12:13–21, The Parable of the Rich Fool. This parable, found only in Luke, is prompted by a dispute between brothers over an inheritance. Apparently the regulations for such cases (Num. 27:1–11; Deut. 21:15–17) were not being followed, in the opinion of the younger brother who must wait on the older. Rather than act as judge, Jesus states a proverbial truth (Luke 12:15b) and elaborates with a parable (vv. 16–20), v. 21 being commentary on it. The parable is clear: a man is blessed with abundance and he responds with self-congratulations and conversations with himself. Family, neighbors, God: all are absent from his plans.

12:22–34, Concerning Anxiety About Things. Cf Matt. 6:25–33; 6:19–21. The injunction against anxiety is not a general one; some anxiety may be a form of care, as Paul's for the churches (2 Cor. 11:28). Here the issue is preoccupation with material things that reflects a lack of trust in God, a lack of interest in the kingdom, and a lack of generosity toward those in need. Such anxiety is not productive: can anxiety add a cubit (18 in.) to life (stature?; see footnote on this passage in RSV)? This expression may echo Ps. 39:5, a cubit meaning one more step to life's walk. Birds and flowers offer lessons in dependence on God. Anxious grasping is the pursuit of pagans who do not know that God is aware of their needs. Those who put kingdom matters first not only have their needs met but God's gifts include the kingdom as well. After all, one can even become anxious about the kingdom and forget that it is God's to give. The opposite of anxiety is that generosity that both expresses freedom and grants freedom in care for others (Luke 12:33–34).

12:35–48, Concerning Preparedness and Fidelity. Cf. Matt. 24:43–51. Having loins girded (the loose outer garment gathered up for work

or travel) and lamps burning says it in two images: prepared and awake, even if the master comes in the third watch (the Jewish night had three watches). The image of the return from a marriage feast recalls Matt. 25:1–13. Luke 12:37–38 pronounces a blessing on servants who are ready for the coming of the kingdom, or in Luke's day, for the coming of Christ. Verses 39–40 offer a brief parable of the uncertain time, the night thief being a common motif (1 Thess. 5:2–11; 2 Pet. 3:10; Rev. 3:3). However, in response to Peter's question, Jesus pronounces a blessing on that steward whose behavior is faithful apart from any calculations of the early or late arrival of the master. Ascertaining the time of the Lord's return is inadequate and inappropriate motivation for behavior. And as for leaders (those who know the master's will, Luke 12:47–48), their privileges and responsibilities are greater, but so will be their punishment for unfaithfulness.

12:49–59, Concerning the Approaching Crisis. Cf. Matt. 10:34–36; 16:2–3; 5:25–26; Mark 10:38. Probably Luke 12:49–53, 54–56, and 57–59 were not originally joined but they have enough in common to be associated here. In vv. 49–53 there are two governing images: fire, which signifies both judgment and purification, and baptism, a reference to the Passion into which Jesus soon will be plunged (Mark 10:38). Until all is accomplished Jesus is constrained, distressed, pushing against restraints. Jesus' presence is critical for the world, causing the rising and falling of many (Luke 2:34), separating doubt from faith and hence dividing households. Peace in the sense of status quo is disrupted. This has proven true historically and will be so at the end.

In 12:54–56 Jesus chastises the crowds for being clever in reading weather signs but blind to the sign from God: the presence of Jesus heralds the coming of the kingdom. In view of the nature of the present time, one should be as wise before God as before a magistrate, that is, make peace now before the judgment (vv. 57–59). In Matt. 5:25–26 this saying refers to making peace with an offending brother, but Luke sets it in the context of impending divine judgment.

13:1–9, The Call to Repentance. The material in 13:1–9 has no parallel in Mark or Matthew. It consists of two parts: vv. 1–5 and 6–9. The call for repentance, more common in Luke than other NT writers, is especially fitting here in view of the preceding teaching. Verses 1–5 contain two parallel sayings that preface calls to repentance. One has to do with Galileans, the other Jerusalemites; one deals with human evil, the other natural evil. In other words, Jesus is inclusive when he says that the desire to find direct correlations between suffering and sin are fruitless and miss the point, which is that all are sinners in need of repentance. The final blow to the idea that any person suffering must have sinned is dealt at Golgotha. As to the two tragedies mentioned, there is no other record available.

The parable of the fig tree is the closest Luke comes to the story of the cursing of the fig tree (Mark 11:12–14; Matt. 21:18–19), which he omits. Cultivating and fertilizing the tree is a symbol of God's mercy (Hos. 9:10; Isa. 5:1–7; Ezek. 17:22–24). There is still time to repent and bear fruit.

13:10–35
Tensions and Forebodings of the Passion

This section is governed by references to Jerusalem and the suffering soon to occur. Even when not named, Jerusalem casts a shadow over this material.

13:10–17, Controversy over a Sabbath Healing. This story, peculiar to Luke, recalls a similar incident in 6:6–11 at which time Jesus' opponents discussed what to do to Jesus. Here, in Luke's last reference to Jesus' appearance in a synagogue, the tension is no less great, but the dynamic is different. The synagogue ruler addresses the crowd in an indirect attack on Jesus, but it backfires: the people rejoice over what Jesus does. The controversy plays on the word "to loose" or "release." Jesus looses the woman from her infirmity (v. 12); Jesus reminds them that they loose an ox or ass on the Sabbath for watering; then why not loose this woman from Satan's bond? It is an argument from the lesser to the greater. At the end the house is divided: all those set against Jesus are shamed; all the people rejoice. Those shamed will not forget.

13:18–21, Parables of the Kingdom. Cf. Mark 4:30–32; Matt. 13:31–33. Mark has the first parable, Matthew has both, and both writers place them in a collection of parables. Luke places these two in the tension-filled journey to Jerusalem. They address the problem of discouragement and despair over apparent lack of success. The measure of kingdom work is in the result not in the small and obscure beginnings. Luke's placing the 8–10-foot mustard plant in a garden would have been rare in Palestine, most likely not his native land.

13:22–30, Strict Requirements for the Kingdom. Matthew has parallels in six different places in his Gospel. Luke reminds readers that Jesus is on his way to Jerusalem, a fact that makes the sober question appropriate. Luke often launches teachings from a problem posed

to Jesus (Luke 11:1; 12:13; 13:1, 41). The question really is the readers', who have listened to Jesus since 9:51. The teachings are obviously composite. For example, the door of 13:24 and the door of 13:25 are very different. The door into the kingdom is not only narrow but it also will close, not to be reopened for those who have no more claim than that they know Jesus socially or recall his visit to their town. Added to the pain of refusal will be the sight of a large ingathering of those who believed, including their forebears, prophets, and, surprisingly to some, Gentiles.

13:31–35, A Warning About Herod and a Lament. Verses 31–33 are only in Luke. We cannot assume the Pharisees who often had Jesus to dinner are here part of a death plot. Earlier Herod Antipas was perplexed about Jesus and wanted to see him (9:7–9). In what sense did Jesus mean Herod was a fox? In the OT a fox is destructive; among the Greeks, clever. But Herod must wait; Jesus' course is brief now but must be finished (cf. John 5:36; 17:4; 19:28; Heb. 2:10). The three days are, of course, symbolic of death and resurrection which, in God's purpose, are to be accomplished at Jerusalem. The lament over Jerusalem is in Matthew (23:37–39) at the close of Jesus' Jerusalem ministry, and by the addition "you will not see me *again*" (my emphasis) clearly refers to the Parousia. In Luke the location is awkward because Jesus has not yet gone to the city, making "how often would I have gathered you" premature. "Blessed is he who comes" (Ps. 118:26) will be shouted when he arrives in Jerusalem (Luke 19:39–44). By this early placement perhaps Luke is saying that though Israel's house is forsaken, there is yet time for repentance and for joining in the expectation of redemption. It is late but not too late.

14:1–24
Table Talk

Luke unites four disparate pieces by setting them in the context of a meal; in fact three of the four units deal with banquets. It was common in the Hellenistic world for banquets to be the setting for philosophers and teachers to offer their wisdom. But for Luke the image of Jesus at table was that of one who accepted and received all kinds of people, the proof of which was in the breaking of bread.

14:1–6, A Sabbath Healing. As already noted, it is not uncommon in Luke to see Jesus dining with Pharisees. (Concerning healings on the Sabbath and Jesus' defense of them, see commentary above on 6:6–11 and 13:10–17.) The frequency of such stories reflects the critical role of Sabbath observance in Judaism and the tension between synagogue and church over the matter. In v. 5, "a son or an ox" is more awkward than "an ass or an ox" but has the stronger manuscript support.

14:7–11, A Lesson for Guests. Jesus advises choosing the lowest place, which would avoid public embarrassment and, on occasion, provide a moment of public admiration. Such a teaching would be no more than good advice on social behavior had not Luke said Jesus spoke it as a parable (v. 7). Not etiquette but kingdom behavior is the point, as the pronouncement in v. 11 makes clear. (This pronouncement is frequent in the Gospels, Luke 18:14; Matt. 18:4; 23:12). But the ego is clever and may prompt the choice of low seats as a way to move up.

14:12–14, A Lesson for Hosts. Like the clamoring guests above, the host is caught in a cycle of self-seeking. Hosting can be a way of putting others in your debt, but why put in your debt those who cannot repay? However, in the kingdom God is host and who can repay God? Luke's list of the fringe people: the poor, maimed, lame, and blind, repeated in the next story, is his list of kingdom people. That has been clear since Mary's song (1:46–55).

14:15–24, The Parable of the Supper. Perhaps the mention of resurrection (v. 14) prompts the remark of a guest (v. 15) that in turn occasions the parable. Different versions of this parable are found in Matt. 22:1–10 and in the *Gospel of Thomas* 64 (→Gospel of Thomas). The parable assumes the custom of an invitation in advance and an invitation at the time of the meal to those who accepted the first. The excuses offered were not thin; marriage even exempted one from military duty (Deut. 20:7; 24:5), but this is no ordinary banquet competing with social and economic engagements. It is clear the parable is about the messianic banquet in the kingdom. The new invitation goes first to Luke's marginal people whom God remembers (contrast Matthew's "both bad and good"). Next the invitation widens to the outskirts of the city (Luke 14:23), probably a reference to Gentiles. In v. 24 the speaker is not the host but Jesus, speaking not to the servant (the "you" is plural) but to all.

14:25–35

Concerning Discipleship

Teachings here are paralleled in Mark and Matthew and even elsewhere in Luke. They are here gathered and addressed to the crowds; v. 25 makes clear the shift from the semiprivate material of vv. 1–24. These crowds are following Jesus but do not know he is going to his death. What he says, therefore, does not address the reluctant, as in 9:59–62, but the enthusiastic, as in 9:57. The sayings are held together by a refrain "whoever does not . . . cannot be my disci-

ple" (14:26, 27, 33). The words are stern, using the Semitic expression "hate", that is, "turn away from," "detach oneself from." Even among primary relationships Jesus demands first loyalty. The two parables, one about a farmer (a tower for watching a vineyard) and the other about a king, say to high and low, rich and poor, "Is the price of discipleship more than you are willing or able to pay?" Verses 34–35 are rather detached, paralleled at Matt. 5:13 and Mark 9:50. In this context the saying may be insisting that even an initial sincere commitment can fade if one is not careful, just as salt can lose its taste.

15:1–32

Three Parables of Joy

15:1–3, Narrative Setting. The three parables are Jesus' response to a criticism by Pharisees and scribes that he "receives sinners and eats with them." The word translated "receives" (RSV) or "welcomes" (NEB) can mean that Jesus is host to them. The issue is table fellowship and Jesus' full acceptance of sinners, as breaking bread together implied. The critics feel justified in the charge, "Behold, a glutton and a drunkard, a friend of tax collectors and sinners!" (7:34). Having three parables together is not unusual since offering material in triplets is common in Luke (9:57–62; 11:42–52; 14:18–20; 20:10–12). Matthew has a parallel (Matt. 18:12–14) to the first; the second and third are peculiar to Luke.

15:4–10, Finding the Sheep and Finding the Coin. The two parables say essentially the same thing, repetition serving to emphasize (cf. Luke 5:36–39; 14:28–32). They have the same form, "What man," "What woman," questions that always evoke the response, "No one." In Matthew a sheep "goes astray" and church leaders are instructed to find and restore such a one. In Luke the sheep is lost, as are the sinners in Jesus' presence. Ezek. 34:12 and Isa. 49:22 lie behind Luke's image of the tender shepherd. Love for the lost sheep is so strong that the ninety-nine are left in the wilderness while the search is on. Such seeking love takes great risks. The woman's ten silver coins (drachmas) represented about ten days' wages and many months of saving. She, like the shepherd, seeks diligently "until she finds it"; there is no giving up in either story. The joy of finding cannot be contained; a party is appropriate. Even Jesus' critics are invited to celebrate for such must be heaven's joy over the sinners who have come to Jesus.

15:11–32, The Loving Father. The theme of penitence in the first two parables anticipates the third, and the theme of joy (vv. 7, 10, 24, 32) binds the three together. A few points of information: according to Jewish custom, a younger son received one-third of the inheritance. Usually received at the father's death, the inheritance could be divided earlier. To feed swine was to become as a Gentile, a nobody (Lev. 11:7; Isa. 65:4; 66:17). The pods eaten were the long pods from the carob tree, eaten by animals and at times by the extremely poor. The few scholars who think Luke 15:11–32 contains what once was two parables (vv. 11–24; 25–32) miss the structure and the focus. The structure does not have two conclusions (vv. 24, 32) but one conclusion repeated, not uncommon in parables (note Matt. 25:14–30). And the focus is not the sons but the father. The father had two sons, loved two sons, went out to two sons (Luke 15:20, 28). God is a both/and, not an either/or God: to embrace sinners is not to reject Pharisees. The offense in 15:1–2, repeated at vv. 7 and 10 and voiced by the older brother is the joy, the party, the singing and dancing. Of course, let the penitent come home, but to bread and water, not grain-fed veal; to sackcloth not a new robe; to ashes not jewelry; to kneeling not dancing. Forgiveness appears to critics very much like condoning.

16:1–31
Teachings Concerning Wealth

Except for vv. 16–18, the entirety of Luke 16 is devoted to teachings about possessions, a subject of primary concern to Luke (3:10–14; 12:13–21, 32–34; Acts 2:43–6:7). The discussion is in two parts, vv. 1–15 and 19–31, each part controlled by a parable and each parable beginning "There was a rich man" (vv. 1, 19). Only v. 13 has a parallel elsewhere (Matt. 6:24).

16:1–15, Parable of the Shrewd Steward. This parable is directed to the disciples. To understand the parable it is important to separate the parable proper from comments on it. Although not unanimous, the view is widely held that the parable ends at 8a, and hence the commendation of the steward as for his prudence. What the steward had done is not clear: either he reduced the bills by subtracting his own commission (in which case he would not have been dishonest) or he permitted falsification of the amounts owed his master. The latter seems more likely. If v. 8b is commentary, then the lesson is that people of the world demonstrate an astuteness (NEB) from which children of light (1 Thess. 5:4–5) can learn. And wherein is the astuteness? Verse 9 says it lies in using possessions so as to gain rather than lose one's future. Verses 10–13 provide further commentary on wealth but not necessarily related to the parable. Each of these verses states a proverbial truth, vv. 10–12 framed on a lesser-to-greater argument, and v. 13 an either/or statement, but none of them depend

on the parable for the truth being stated. The Pharisees, here called lovers of money, were, unlike the Sadducees, generally urban and business people. Their making fun of Jesus may imply that they regarded prosperity as God's reward for righteousness (Deut. 27–28). Their self-justification may have been in the form of alms and other works of merit, but God's assessments are usually a reversal of our own.

16:16–18, Concerning the Law. Cf. Matt. 11:12–13; 5:18, 32. These sayings, differently located in Matthew, create a problem for the interpreter because they seem unrelated to the preceding or succeeding parables. Perhaps the introduction of Pharisees in vv. 14–15 prompted sayings about the law. John, whose life Luke joined to that of Jesus from birth (chaps. 1–2), was the beginning of something new (3:1–2, 18). The phrase "everyone enters it violently" (RSV) or "everyone forces his way in" (NEB) is most difficult. Luke uses the word elsewhere, with a prefix, to mean "urgently or strongly invite" (Luke 24:29; Acts 16:15). Perhaps that is the sense here, similar to compelling guests to come to the banquet (Luke 14:23). It could also refer to the large enthusiastic crowds pressing around Jesus. But even though John marks a new era there is abiding authority in the old law (16:17). However, the old must be interpreted properly, as, for example, in the case of divorce (Deut. 24:1–4). It is difficult to see any other reason for placing this teaching (Luke 16:18) here. This saying is here without context, but both Matthew (19:3–12) and Mark (10:2–12) as well as Paul (1 Cor. 7:10–16) present sayings on marriage and divorce with contexts. Luke's form of the teaching is very strict, but the other forms of this saying indicate how the church struggled with its application.

16:19–31, The Rich Man and Lazarus. The story (is it a parable, containing as it does a proper name?) of the rich man (in the Vulgate called "Dives," meaning wealthy) and Lazarus seems to bear some relationship to the story in John 11 of the raising of Lazarus from the dead. But that association concerns only the second part of this story (Luke 16:27–31) and not its first part (vv. 19–26). Some have suggested that the story's two parts are responses to two themes introduced at vv. 14–17: love of money and disregard for the law. The story itself is well traveled—versions of it are found in rabbinic as well as Egyptian literature. It reflects popular beliefs about the hereafter. Details are rich and sharp. For the rich man, dressed in robes of royalty and fine Egyptian undergarments, life is a daily feast. The poor man, clothed in running sores, squats (lies) among the dogs, famished. Both die but only the rich man is buried. Now their roles reverse (reversal of fortunes is frequent in Luke) and the change is unalterable. Up to this point all that Luke has said in warning and in instruction about material things comes vividly to mind. "Poor" is almost a synonym for "saint" as Lazarus enjoys the bliss of Abraham's bosom while the rich man lies in Hades. But in vv. 27–31 a second point vital to Luke is made. The Scriptures are sufficient for faith and when they are rejected, as the rich man has done (Mic. 2:9; Isa. 58:7), not even an event as extraordinary as a resurrection will generate belief. That proved true in the case of Jesus.

17:1–10
On Sin, Forgiveness, Faith, and Duty

These four brief teachings have no thematic unity but are joined only by a common audience: the disciples (v. 1). Some sayings attributed to Jesus are like proverbs, which have their meaning intrinsically rather than contextually. The first teaching (vv. 1–2) warns against causing any of Christ's "little ones"—that is, followers, especially new and not yet mature ones—to stumble. "Being the cause of stumbling" more accurately translates the term here than does "temptation to sin" and "cause to sin." (Cf. Mark 9:42 and Matt. 18:6–7.) This does not mean, however, that one is to avoid a brother or sister for fear of being a stumbling block. On the contrary, the second teaching (vv. 3–4) enjoins responsibility to rebuke in order to correct and to forgive, even seven times a day. A different form of vv. 3–4 is found in Matt. 18:15, 18–22. The context of the third teaching (vv. 5–6) implies that the apostles request more faith, having heard the rigorous demands of vv. 1–4. It is unclear whether Jesus' response ("Lord" is for Luke a favorite way of referring to him) is a rebuke (their faith is smaller than a mustard seed) or a word of encouragement (your own small faith will perform wonders). (Cf. Mark 11:22–23; Matt. 17:20; 21:21.) The final teaching is a parable found in Luke alone. It begins in a fashion familiar in Luke: "Will any one of you," the answer to which is "No." The servant is, in fact, a slave, serving both in the field and in the house. Even after faithful service the slave has no claim nor does he reach a point of completed duty. There is no ground for assuming reward or for boasting (Rom. 3:27); such calculations are foreign to the life of dedication. There is no joy, no laughter in the parable, but the reason may lie in the next verse: "on the way to Jerusalem."

17:11–18:30
Teachings Leading to the Final Prediction of the Passion

This section consists of events and teachings between the reminder, "on the way to Jerusa-

lem" (17:11), and the final prediction of his Passion, "Behold, we are going up to Jerusalem" (18:31). At 18:14 Luke's special section will close and at 18:15 he will rejoin the narrative of Mark.

17:11–19, The Grateful Leper. This story is only in Luke, the account in Mark 1:40–45 not being parallel here but to Luke 5:12–16. The location between Galilee and Samaria is unusual for a journey to Jerusalem that began at 9:51 passing through Samaria. Perhaps the location is used to introduce a story involving Jews and a Samaritan (17:16). Otherwise details are realistic. Lepers tended to live in groups (2 Kings 7:3), they avoided contact with nonlepers (Luke 17:12; Lev. 13:45–46; Num. 5:2), but they stayed near populated areas to beg alms. A priest had to certify healings (Lev. 14:2–32). But did the command to go to the priest include the Samaritan whose own ritual center was Mount Gerizim? And why rebuke them for not returning when they were commanded to go and in that obedience were healed (Luke 17:14)? Clearly this story follows 2 Kings 5:1–14, which is in two parts: Naaman a foreigner was healed of leprosy and then he was converted to Israel's faith. The two parts here are in vv. 11–14, the healing, and vv. 15–19, the salvation of a foreigner. The expression "Your faith has made you well" (v. 19) refers to some blessing other than healing since that was already true for all. Literally the expression is, "has saved you." The story foreshadows Acts 28:26–27 in showing faith of foreigners and the blindness of Israel. The nine, presumably Jews, are blessed and the Mosaic law is enjoined, but their response falls short of that of the Samaritan.

17:20–37, Concerning the Kingdom and the Coming Son of Man. Mark 13 and Matthew 24 combine the Parousia discourse with the prediction of the fall of Jerusalem but Luke separates them. The material here has two audiences: Pharisees ask when the kingdom will come (vv. 20–21) and Jesus speaks to his disciples about the coming of the Son of man (vv. 22–37). To understand Jesus' word to the Pharisees it is necessary to note also 19:11. There is a future coming of the kingdom, but it is also "in the midst of you." This phrase can be translated "within you" but the "you" is plural, best translated "among you," a much less subjective perspective. Jesus among them is the presence of the kingdom, but his presence is not heralded by a display of wonders.

The phrases "Lo, here it is!" or "There!" are repeated in teaching the disciples about the coming of the Son of man (v. 23; → Son of man). Jesus is identified as the Son of man who first must suffer and be rejected (v. 25). Because the church after him will suffer, the disciples will long for his coming in final deliverance. However, in their anxious expectation they are not to be fooled by the calculators of time and place. Rather that day will come with the suddenness of lightning, and at times when life seems to be proceeding normally, as in the days of Noah and Lot, when it comes, one is to give oneself to it and not try to save one's property or to escape it. Such attempts are self-defeating. After all, that event will be so decisive and final as to separate two in bed or two at work. (Notice the absence of v. 36 that some later manuscripts insert, borrowed from Matt. 24:40.) Jesus' answer to the question, Where? is as vague as his answer to the question, When? The proverb about the eagle (vulture) echoes Job 39:30. Both the where and the when of judgment will be known after it occurs, not before, as a gathering of vultures signifies a dead prey.

18:1–14, Two Parables on Prayer. These parables are in Luke alone. Both are typically Lucan in structure: an introductory statement of purpose (vv. 1, 9), with interpretive comments following the parables (vv. 6–8, 14). The first parable stresses constancy in prayer and argues from the lesser (judge) to the greater (God). Verse 8 picks up on the context (17:22–37) in which Jesus offers teachings on the coming of the Son of man. Luke's comments in vv. 6–8 assume a condition in which the faithful are persecuted, are praying for vindication, and are raising the question Israel had often asked, How long will the Lord tarry (cf. 2 Pet. 3:9)? The more pressing question is not, Will vindication come? but, Will God's people still be faithful in that day? Luke follows the parable about the prayers of the elect with one about the prayer of a sinner. Both parables are about vindication, but the word is translated "justified" (v. 14) in the second. Luke's closing comments are two: the declaration of the publican's justification (note Luke's familiar role reversal) and the pronouncement to the same effect, used in a variety of contexts (Luke 14:11; Matt. 18:4; 23:12). To regard the Pharisee as a villain and the publican as a hero is to have each get what he deserves, which misses the point: God justifies the ungodly. Equally defeating is to leave the parable thankful that one is not as the Pharisee.

18:15–17, Children and the Kingdom. Luke now returns to his Marcan source, which he left at 9:50. Unlike Mark 10:13–16 and Matt. 19:13–15, Luke calls the children "infants" and says Jesus "called them to him" (v. 16). The focus is on the children as images of discipleship and, therefore, Luke omits Jesus blessing the children as he does also Jesus' indignation with the disciples.

18:18–30, The Rich and the Kingdom. Cf. Mark 10:17–31; Matt. 19:16–30. All three Evan-

gelists agree the man was rich; Matthew says he was young (Matt. 19:20); and Luke says he was a ruler (Luke 18:18, perhaps of a synagogue), providing the composite "rich young ruler." Some details in Luke vary from Mark, but as in Mark, Jesus here rejects the designation "good." In Luke the man does not go away, and it is persons who overhear the conversation who ask, "Then who can be saved?" (v. 26). As the Pharisee in a preceding story could not trust his good deeds, this ruler cannot trust the securities of wealth. He must trust God alone. Giving his goods to the poor is not only congenial with Jesus' teachings about wealth elsewhere in Luke (and practiced in Acts) but also with the context: the next episode speaks of Jesus' death. A camel going through a needle's eye is a proverbial statement of the humanly impossible and not a description of unburdened camel crawling through a small gate. Only God can effect salvation. But to relinquish all for the sake of the kingdom is to be amply rewarded (Luke does not specify with what) both now and in the age to come.

18:31–19:28
From the Final Prediction of the Passion Until the Entry into Jerusalem

Luke continues to follow Mark, but he omits Mark's account of the request by the sons of Zebedee (Mark 10:35–45), adds the story about Zacchaeus, and offers from Q the parable of the pounds (talents, Matt. 25:14–30).

18:31–34, The Final Prediction of the Passion. Cf. Mark 10:32–34; Matt. 20:17–19. This is the third prediction of his Passion and the declaration that the journey signaled at 9:51 and discussed with Moses and Elijah on the mountain (9:31) is near completion. The Lucan theme of Jesus' Passion being the fulfillment of prophecy is stated here as elsewhere (Luke 24:25, 27, 44; Acts 3:18; 8:32–35; 13:27; 26:23). Omitted is Mark's "delivered to the chief priests and scribes" (Mark 10:33); added is the observation that the disciples did not understand (Luke 18:34). Luke's mixture of human failure and divine purpose in the expression, "This saying was hid from them" (v. 34) recalls 9:45 and anticipates 24:16. The risen Christ will open their minds to understand (24:32, 45).

18:35–43, Healing the Blind Man near Jericho. Cf. Mark 10:46–52; Matt. 20:29–34. Luke follows "this saying was hid from them" with a story that demonstrates Jesus' power to enable the blind to see. This account is, therefore, promise and prophecy of what he will do for his disciples. Luke abbreviates the story in Mark, who identifies the blind man as Bartimaeus. The blind man recognizes Jesus as Son of David, the Messiah, even though he is being rebuked by a crowd that does not see (v. 39). As announced at the outset of his ministry (4:18), Jesus opens the eyes of the blind (Isa. 35:5). The location, Jericho, and the people praising God anticipate the entry into Jerusalem.

19:1–10, Salvation Brought to Zacchaeus.
In all three synoptic Gospels Jesus approaches Jerusalem through Jericho, but only Luke has the story of Zacchaeus. It is typically Lucan in its narrative artistry and attention to detail. The structure of the story, including the criticism of Jesus, is much like that of Jesus in the home of Levi (5:27–32). As a chief tax collector (the expression occurs nowhere else in Greek literature), Zacchaeus is part of a corrupt system of economic oppression, but in response to Jesus he goes beyond the law's requirement for restitution (Exod. 22:1; Num. 5:5–7). Jesus has entered the house (Luke 19:7), but the closing remarks of Jesus are addressed to the crowd, not Zacchaeus. "This house" (v. 9) is household, the salvation of households being a common theme in Acts (10:2; 11:14; 16:15, 31; 18:8). "Son of Abraham" (Luke 19:9) is probably true genealogically and is certainly true by faith (Rom. 4:11–12; Gal. 3:9, 29). The closing pronouncement recalls the parables of Luke 15 and also the missed opportunity of the rich man in 18:18–30.

19:11–28, Parable of the Pounds.
Typically Luke prefaces the parable with an interpretive introduction (v. 11). The parable is given to correct false notions of the nature and purpose of Jesus' Jerusalem trip. The historical backdrop is that Palestinian rulers such as Archelaus did go to Rome to receive power as king but Jewish leaders protested, in that case successfully. Some scholars think Luke has combined two parables: the pounds (vv. 12–13, 15b–26), and gaining a kingdom (vv. 12, 14–15a, 27). The pounds (a mina in the Greco-Syrian monetary system was worth 100 drachmas, between 20 and 35 dollars) portion is related to Matthew's parable of the talents (Matt. 25:14–30). More likely Luke offers one story with allegorizing that fits the circumstances: Jesus went away but will return in power; some disciples are good stewards, some are not because of fearfulness; Jerusalem, which rejected his reign, was destroyed. During the prince's absence (between first and second coming) the servants were to multiply his holdings (spread the word). Of the ten, only three report: the first, second and "another," because interest can be sustained only so long. Even the fearful one should have made some gain through bankers. The exaggerated rewards highlight the point: following Jesus, especially on his way to Jerusalem, is a risk calling for courage but it will be amply rewarded. The

fearful lose out and the opponents suffer death. The closing verse (Luke 19:28) vividly portrays the one who told the parable as out in front of the crowd, going to Jerusalem and to suffering. Jerusalem is named, with all that it implied, at the beginning and ending of this parable (vv. 11, 28) and this entire section (9:51; 19:28).

19:29–21:38
The Ministry in Jerusalem

In general Luke follows Mark 11:1–13:37 here, with such changes as will be noted. Although the traditional church year compacts the Jerusalem ministry, including the Passion, into one week, Luke seems to imply a longer period (19:47; 22:53). Both Jerusalem and the Temple figure prominently in the completion of Jesus' ministry and its continuation in the mission of the church (24:44–53; Acts 1:1–14).

19:29–48
The Entry into Jerusalem

In Luke the entrance of Jesus into Jerusalem consists of three units: the entry itself, Jesus' lament over the city, and the cleansing of the Temple.

19:29–40, The Entry.
Cf. Mark 11:1–10; Matt. 21:1–9; John 12:12–16. Sending disciples ahead to make preparation recalls the beginning of the journey to Jerusalem (9:51–52). Bethany and Bethphage were villages on the eastern side of the Mount of Olives, within two miles of the city. Securing the colt is by divine knowledge and not prearrangement. The owners were probably disciples of Jesus. A king or ruler riding an ass recalls 1 Kings 1:38 and Zech. 9:9, which Matthew cites (Matt. 21:5). Putting garments along the way showed honor to a leader (2 Kings 9:13); Luke omits the use of branches. Luke alone pictures the descent from Olivet. Luke identifies the crowds as disciples, many if not all having come with him from Galilee. Jesus is praised as King but not as son of David (Luke 18:39). The Aramaic "Hosanna" is omitted from the praise that joins Ps. 118:26 and an echo of the choir's song at Luke 2:14. Verses 39–40 are in Luke alone. It is not clear why some Pharisees wanted Jesus to silence his disciples: are they registering their own unbelief or are they afraid a parade for a king could bring political retaliation? But the cosmos concurs in their praise; it cannot be stopped for truth will not remain silent (Hab. 2:11).

19:41–44, Lament over the City.
Found in Luke alone, this scene draws heavily on Jeremiah 6. The crowds have sung of peace but in

Jerusalem there will be destruction because the city is blind to its own need for repentance and forgiveness of sin, and to the fact that in Jesus God has visited the city. In vv. 43–44, Luke casts Jesus' prophecy of Jerusalem's fall in terms that describe how the Romans took the city in A.D. 70.

19:45–48, Jesus in the Temple. Cf. Mark 11:11, 15–19; Matt. 21:10–17; John 2:13–22. Luke noticeably abbreviates the account in Mark. Mal. 3:1–2 is vividly in the background. For Luke, Jesus going to the Temple is the real purpose of the journey. The Temple is cleansed for his ministry of teaching the people (v. 47), and it will be in the Temple that Jesus' disciples continue in prayer and praise following the ascension (24:53). Here in the Temple the people align themselves with Jesus but the priests, scribes, and principal men (elders who belonged to the Sanhedrin?) are offended to the point of plotting Jesus' death. Jesus' actions in the Temple, according to the synoptic Gospels, precipitated the death plots against Jesus. But for the present, his popularity protects him.

20:1–21:4
Controversies in Jerusalem

Luke follows Mark 11:27–12:44 very closely. Since the units in this section are not chronologically nor intrinsically joined, the Evangelists perhaps placed them together here to give content to the hostility against Jesus.

20:1–8, The Question of Authority. Cf. Mark 11:27–33; Matt. 21:23–27. Luke follows Mark closely but adds to Jesus' activity, "and preaching the gospel," which for Luke was repentance and forgiveness of sins. "These things" in v. 2 probably includes his message as well as cleansing the Temple and teaching there (Temple meaning the Temple precinct and not the sanctuary). "The people" are the ones favorable to Jesus, the opposite of chief priests, scribes, and elders (cf. also 19:47–48). Jesus' question about John's baptism was probably not a clever move but a repetition of an earlier affirmation: both John and Jesus were authorized of God and yet both were rejected (7:29–35). The critics say, "We do not know"; Jesus says, "Neither will I tell you."

20:9–19, The Parable of the Tenants. Cf. Mark 12:1–12; Matt. 21:33–46. Again Luke follows Mark but with modifications. The vineyard owner is gone a long time (v. 9), perhaps referring to the period prior to John. Also in Luke, only the son is killed, and that is done outside (Heb. 13:12–13), an adjustment in the story to fit the son to Jesus. The people are stunned by the word of final punishment on the tenants (Jewish leaders), sensing that they too will fall with the

nation as God gives the vineyard over to Gentiles. The vineyard was a familiar image of God's investment and expectation of return on earth (Isa. 5:1–7; Ezek. 15:1–6; 19:10–14). Luke 20:17–18, a quotation of Ps. 118:22 and an allusion to Isa. 8:14–15, join two references to the stone: in the one Jesus is the rejected but exalted one; in the other he is the key factor in God's judgment of Jerusalem. One can see that the church and Luke have modified a parable (which may have originally ended at v. 15) to include what in fact did happen both to Jesus and then to Jerusalem. Verse 19 essentially repeats the standoff between the leaders and the people reported at 19:47–48.

20:20–26, The Question of Tribute. Cf. Mark 12:13–17; Matt. 22:15–22. This is the second of three questions put to Jesus (Mark has four, including the one about the greatest commandment, 12:28–34, which Luke had earlier at 10:25–28): authority, tribute, and resurrection. Unlike Mark and Matthew who present this scene as a temptation or test of Jesus, Luke tells the story so as to stress three points. First, the questioners are spies from the priests, scribes, and elders (v. 19) who pretend to be "sincere" (RSV; NEB: "honest men"; lit., "righteous") so that they may find grounds for charging Jesus before the Roman governor (v. 20). Second, their craftiness fails in that Jesus' answer is no basis for charging him with rebellion. The answer Jesus gave left and still leaves the church with the task of discerning the lines of loyalty to God and to the state (Rom. 13:1–7; 1 Pet. 2:13–17; 1 Tim. 2:2; Tit. 3:1; Rev. 13:1–18; 18:1–24). Third, the ever-present "people" (v. 26) apparently support Jesus' answer and thus continue to be a buffer between Jesus and plotting opponents.

20:27–40, The Question Concerning the Resurrection. Cf. Mark 12:18–27; Matt. 22:23–33. The Sadducees (→ Sadducees) found authority for religion primarily in the five books of Moses in which there is no doctrine of the resurrection. Their question presupposes the levirate law of marriage (Deut. 25:5–10). Luke adds to Mark's account in vv. 35–36: the worthy are raised; they cannot die anymore; they are equal to (not "like") angels; they are children of God. Jesus' argument that the resurrection is implied even in the Mosaic books meets with the approval of overhearing scribes. The phrase "all live to him" (v. 38) infers that the resurrected life is both here and hereafter (John 11:25–26). Since Luke does not follow this with the question about the greatest commandment, the conclusion to the questioning is marked here (v. 40; Mark 12:34).

20:41–44, Jesus' Question About the Son of David. Cf. Mark 12:35–37a; Matt. 22:41–46. The question-answer period ends with Jesus asking the question. The "them" and "they" are left undefined by Luke (v. 41). The question presupposes a messianic interpretation of Ps. 110, and on the basis of it, raises the issue of the adequacy of calling the Messiah the son of David. Luke has, of course, affirmed Jesus as son of David (Luke 1:32; 3:31), but that term alone is not enough. The Christ is also like Elijah and Jonah and the Suffering Servant, but no single image says enough. And certainly "son of David" in any political sense does not.

20:45–21:4, A Warning and an Example. Cf. Mark 12:37b–44; Matt. 23:1–36. Luke has already pronounced woes on scribes and Pharisees (11:37–54); here the warning about scribes is addressed to the disciples in the presence of the larger favorable group Luke refers to as "the people." The disciples (the church) needed the warnings about ambition and greed, especially in the matter of taking over the property of widows as administrators in the faith community. Abuses due to greed sometimes plagued the church (Acts 4:32–5:11). Such love of money stood in sharp contrast to the lavish generosity of a poor widow whose only property was two lepta, coins of the least value. She trusts totally in God.

21:5–38

Jesus' Apocalyptic Discourse

Cf. Mark 13:1–37; Matt. 24:1–44. Apparently Luke has Mark 13 before him, but some modifications should be noted at the outset. The discourse is prompted by the remarks of "some" (v. 5) and not specifically by disciples. Jesus speaks in the Temple (vv. 5–7, 37–38) and not from the Mount of Olives (Mark 13:3). In fact, the Temple and "all the people" provide the favorable context of place and audience for this and all Jesus' teaching in Jerusalem. Luke's view of the Temple is a positive one in both the Gospel and Acts. The Mount of Olives was the place for lodging at night (v. 37). It should also be noted that Luke has already discussed the Parousia at 17:20–37 and therefore extracts that from present comments on the fall of Jerusalem. The discourse proper (vv. 8–36) is prompted by the prediction of the destruction of the Temple (vv. 5–7), a prediction that evokes two questions: When? What will be the sign? As to signs of the end, Luke describes three phenomena (vv. 8–11): the appearance of imposters claiming the time (Gk. *kairos*, opportune time, not *chronos*, calendar time) is here; wars, tumults, and international conflicts; and natural disasters with cosmic terror. However, it is repeatedly said that one is not to be deceived by all this; the end will not be at once. And why? There must first be a time of witnessing (vv. 12–19). This is the period of the church Luke addresses. Faithful witnesses will be brought before synagogues (fulfilled in Acts

4–5) and before governors and kings (fulfilled in Acts 24–26). In those crises they will be given a mouth and wisdom (Luke 21:15; Semitism for an appropriate message; cf. 12:11–12) that cannot be withstood (fulfilled in Acts 4:8–13; 6:10). Hatred, betrayal by friends and relatives, and death await them (Luke 21:16–17). Verse 16 makes v. 18 difficult: either v. 18 is misplaced (Luke 12:7; Matt. 10:30) or v. 16 means some will die while v. 18 promises "but not you." In any case, faithfulness is the path to life. In vv. 20–24 Luke describes the destruction of Jerusalem. Unlike Mark 13:14–20, in which the fall of the city is given an eschatological setting, Luke's account is historical and distinct from the end of the age. What Luke describes is what happened in A.D. 66–72 when Roman armies destroyed Jerusalem. "Until the times of the Gentiles are fulfilled" (v. 24) may refer to the period of the gentile mission, which went out from Jerusalem (Acts 1:8; 8:1–4). The remainder of the discourse (Luke 21:25–36) sketches what is yet to be after the time of the nations has been fulfilled. The entire cosmos will be disturbed, radically affecting human life everywhere (vv. 25–27). However, the faithful are not to be distressed but rather look up, for redemption is near. Redemption here is in the sense of rescue and not in its usual meaning of salvation by repentance and forgiveness. These verses are kin to Paul's statement on redemption in a cosmic context (Rom. 8:18–25). And as surely as one can discern the approach of summer by the leafing of a fig tree, so these signs announce the nearness of the kingdom (Luke 21:29–31). When, then, will this be? Within this generation (vv. 32–33), that is, between the period of God's punishment of Jerusalem by the Gentiles and God's judgment by the Gentiles by the appearance of the Son of man whose coming will sign the redemption of the faithful.

Luke provides his own ending to the discourse (vv. 34–36) addressing those for whom a delay in the Parousia has produced indulgence, secularism, and neglect of life before God. The end will affect everyone without exemption. However, prayerful watchfulness can have a sanctifying influence, setting one free from anxiety and the dulling influence of things. With the summary of vv. 37–38, Luke concludes the record of Jesus' public ministry.

22:1–23:56

The Passion Narrative

The passion and resurrection narratives together constitute the largest body of material in all the Gospels. These accounts may also have been the earliest to be framed into a tradition to be circulated among the churches. The central importance of this material for the church's self-understanding as well as its proclamation, liturgy, and instruction of new members is evident. The passion narrative proper begins with the Passover meal and closes with the burial of Jesus.

22:1-38
Jesus' Last Meal with His Disciples

22:1-6, The Conspiracy Against Jesus. Cf. Mark 14:1-2, 10-11; Matt. 26:1-5, 14-16. Luke fails to distinguish between Passover and the seven-day Feast of Unleavened Bread that followed (Exod. 12:6, 15; Lev. 23:5-8). The people are so favorable to Jesus they continue to be a barrier to plots to kill him. However, the initiative of one of the disciples (Luke places him among the Twelve but phrases it as though reluctantly acknowledged) provides an opportunity. But primary attention is on Satan, last seen in 4:13 leaving Jesus in the desert, to reappear at "an opportune time." That opportunity (v. 6) is now here and more trials (temptations) are to come (vv. 28, 40). Satan will work through Judas, the chief priests, and the captains (leaders among Levites, Acts 4:1; 5:24) for the betrayal (handing over, delivery) of Jesus.

22:7-13, Preparation for the Passover. Cf. Mark 14:12-16; Matt. 26:17-19. Again Luke says day of Unleavened Bread when he means Passover, as is evident in vv. 8 and 15. Luke also identifies the two disciples sent to make preparations. The event recalls preparation for the entry at 19:28-34. Not intriguing prearrangements but Jesus' prophetic knowledge is involved here. Preparation involved purchase of a slain lamb, herbs, wine, and unleavened bread.

22:14-20, Institution of the Lord's Supper. Cf. Mark 14:22-25; Matt. 26:26-29. Luke frames this scene as a classical farewell by a leader to his followers: first the meal (vv. 14-20), and then the discourse on what will soon happen and how the disciples are to conduct themselves (vv. 21-38). Unlike Mark and Matthew, the indication of the betrayer follows the institution of the Lord's Supper. Luke's account of the meal consists of two parts: vv. 15-18 and 19-20, if, indeed, vv. 19b-20 are in the original text. Most manuscripts have these verses but they are a problem because shorter readings are regarded as more original than expanded ones; vv. 19b-20 are remarkably like 1 Cor. 11:24-25; and including vv. 19b-20 gives the ritual the cup, the bread, and again the cup. (Both 1 Cor. 10:16 and the *Didache* have cup and then bread.) Quite possibly Luke has joined two traditions: vv. 15-18 tie the meal to Passover and

stress its eschatological orientation; vv. 19-20 stress sacrificial and covenant meanings. Participation meant sharing in Jesus' death as well as the future messianic meal.

22:21-38, Farewell Instruction. Luke has expanded Jesus' words at table, placing here the dispute about greatness that Mark (10:42-45) and Matthew (20:25-28) relate earlier, adding the special attention to Peter (Luke 22:31-34) and the words about two swords (vv. 35-38). Luke's location of the prophecy of betrayal underscores the possibility of falling away even among those at the covenant table. Immediately following (vv. 24-30) are Jesus' words about greatness, implying, at least, that self-exaltation is related to falling away. True exaltation is a gift of God to those who have endured Jesus' hardship, have entered into the "covenanted" (v. 29, "assigned," RSV; NEB: "vested") relation with Jesus that he had with God, and who not only share the messianic banquet, but who reign with Christ. "Judging" should be taken in the sense of leading or ruling and not of deciding the fate of others.

In v. 31, Jesus addresses all the group by the use of the plural "you," but in vv. 32-34 the conversation is between Peter and Jesus. All will be tested ("sifted," Amos 9:9), but Jesus looks to Peter to turn about, become strong, and be a source of strength for the others. The prophecy here records what, in fact, occurred: denial, abandonment, experience of the risen Christ (Luke 24:34; 1 Cor. 15:5), leadership (Acts 1:15; 2:14), prison (Acts 4:3; 12:3-5), and death (John 21:18-19). To stress the critical nature of what lies before them and Jesus (whose trial and death will fulfill Isa. 53:12), the disciples are told that present conditions demand the opposite of the days of early mission journeys when nothing was needed, all was provided (Luke 22:35). This crisis calls for full equipment for it is a time of conflict and death. Jesus uses the word "sword" symbolically, but they hear him literally. Jesus drops the subject. That they have two swords reflects the degree of their misunderstanding of Jesus' messianic role (cf. Acts 1:6).

22:39-53
The Arrest

22:39-46, At the Mount of Olives. Cf. Mark 14:26-42; Matt. 26:30-46. On this hill east of Jerusalem Jesus had been lodging at night (Luke 21:37). Luke does not call the place Gethsemane, has Jesus come to the disciples once not three times, and does not have three disciples join Jesus. All are asked to pray lest they enter into temptation. Jesus withdraws a short distance, kneels (rather than falls to the ground), and prays with anguish, struggling with the will of

God (22:42). Verses 43–44 (included in NEB; excluded in RSV, 1971 ed.) are absent from many manuscripts and are disputed. They have no parallel in Mark and Matthew, although the ministering angel (Dan. 3:25) recalls Jesus' temptation (Mark 1:13). Verse 44 pictures Jesus' anguish as being of such intensity his sweat rolled down like blood from a wound. Luke softens Mark's rebuke of the disciples and explains their sleep as due to sorrow (vv. 45–46).

22:47–53, Jesus Taken Captive. Cf. Mark 14:43–52; Matt. 26:47–56. Judas is pictured as leading the crowd and approaching Jesus to kiss him but is interrupted by Jesus (he does kiss him in Mark and Matthew). A sword (recall v. 38) is used by a disciple (Peter, John 18:10) to defend Jesus, but Jesus restores the slave's right ear (Luke 22:50) and calls a halt to the altercation. Jesus censures the leaders who have now caught him away from "the people." He taught in the daylight and they did nothing; they take him at night for they work in the power of darkness. The symbolism is quite evident.

22:54–23:25
The Trials and Sentencing

22:54–71, The Jewish Trial. Cf. Mark 14:53–72; Matt. 26:57–75. Since Jesus was taken captive by priests, Temple guards, and elders, it was natural that disposition of him begin with the Jewish authorities. However, Luke has no trial before the Sanhedrin (→ Sanhedrin) the night of the arrest, as does Mark (14:54–64), but rather, Jesus is held in custody at the high priest's house until morning (Luke 22:54, 66). Jesus does endure indignities and beating prior to his trial (vv. 63–65), the victim of insulting sport by the guards. Prior to the trial, Luke inserts Peter's denial (vv. 55–62). Peter and Jesus are at the high priest's house and the three denials occur in the courtyard, prompted by comments by a maid and two others. Peter does not invoke a curse or swear (Mark 14:71). Rather the scene carries more pathos in Luke: "And the Lord turned and looked at Peter" (v. 61). The questioning by the council (Sanhedrin) is briefer in Luke, is not led by the high priest, omits Mark's account of false witnesses and the charge that Jesus would destroy the Temple, and does not state the charge of blasphemy, though that is implied in the council's interpretation of Jesus' response to "Are you the Son of God?" Son of man and Son of God are here interchangeable (vv. 69–71). "You say that I am" is an answer that makes the council fully responsible for its interpretation and hence its actions.

23:1–25, The Roman Trial and Sentencing. Cf. Mark 15:1–15; Matt. 27:1–26. Notice that Luke does not focus on the high priest or any specific group in the Jewish trial and delivery of Jesus to Pilate; he speaks of "they" and "the whole company" (23:1, 5), stressing the guilt of Israel's leaders, in contrast to Pilate's threefold declaration of Jesus' innocence (vv. 4, 14, 22). The charge against Jesus is that he is a revolutionary, forbids taxes to Caesar (readers recall 20:25), and claims to be king (kingship is a theme Luke holds in common with John 18:29–19:22). Jesus' answer to Pilate is taken by the governor as denial (Luke 23:3–4); the same answer to the Sanhedrin was taken as admission. The summary of Jesus' activity (v. 5) introduces the word "Galilee" and gives Pilate, governor of Judea, excuse to send Jesus to Herod Antipas, tetrarch of Galilee. Earlier Luke said Herod wanted to see Jesus (9:9) and reportedly wanted to kill him (13:31–33), but here he toys with Jesus, tries to get a sign from him, makes fun of him, and returns him to Pilate (23:9–11). Their agreement that Jesus was not deserving of death (v. 15) and their cooperation in this unusual trial cemented a new relation between Pilate and Herod. Ps. 2:2 is fulfilled (Acts 4:25–28).

Luke's position on the trial of Jesus is summarized in 23:13–16: all Israel is assembled, including "the people"; Pilate tells them an examination of Jesus proves their charges wrong; Rome (Pilate and Herod) is unanimous in its judgment of Jesus' innocence; Pilate is willing to chastise Jesus and release him. But Satan had entered Judas, who led the leaders of Israel (22:47), who in turn now lead the people. Pilate repeats a third time his position and his offer. The irony of it is that the crowd asks for the release of Barabbas, a man guilty of sedition and murder, and calls for the crucifixion of one declared innocent. Some ancient manuscripts insert v. 17, a borrowing from Mark 15:6, to explain about prisoner release. Luke concludes by placing the responsibility on the Jewish crowd: Pilate granted *their* demand (v. 24); Pilate delivered Jesus *to their will* (v. 25).

23:26–56
The Crucifixion

23:26–32, The Way to the Crucifixion. Cf. Mark 15:21; Matt. 27:32. Luke alone describes the way to the place of execution. Simon of Cyrene in North Africa can be forced to carry the burden (Matt. 5:41), but here he is the symbol of the true disciple, carrying the cross "behind Jesus" (Luke 23:26). Again Luke gives favorable attention to women who alone weep over what is happening. The background is Zech. 12:10. Jesus tells them that the greater cause for tears is unbelieving Jerusalem. So terrible will be its fate that the woman without children will be fortunate, and desperate cries for shelter will go unheeded (Hos. 10:8). Jesus recites a proverb to the effect that if such crime as his death can occur now, what will be the horrors of the city's crisis? In a brief note (Luke 23:32) Luke says two others were to be crucified.

23:33–43, The Crucifixion. Cf. Mark 15:22–32; Matt. 27:33–44. Luke does not use the Aramaic "Golgotha." Jesus is crucified between the two criminals. Some manuscripts omit v. 34a but it is Lucan in that acts of ignorance can be forgiven upon repentance (Acts 3:17; 13:27; 17:30). Casting lots for his garments fulfills Ps. 22:18. At this point Luke relates the various responses to Jesus by those present. "The people" watch (v. 35); the rulers scoff, calling on Jesus for a miracle if he is indeed the Christ (v. 35); the soldiers mock him with the title "King of the Jews," offering him vinegar (vv. 36–38; cf. Ps. 69:21); and one criminal being executed rails at Jesus to save them while the other affirms Jesus' innocence (vv. 39–41). The latter shows his faith by asking to be remembered when Jesus comes in kingly power. Jesus assures him a place in Paradise (abode of the righteous, 2 Cor. 12:3; Rev. 2:7) "today"; that is, not within a twenty-four-hour period, but in the "today" of the kingdom (Luke 4:21).

23:44–49, The Death of Jesus. Cf. Mark 15:33–41; Matt. 27:45–56. Prior to Jesus' death Luke includes only two phenomena: darkness from noon until 3 p.m.; the Temple curtain between the holy place and Holy of Holies was split. This latter could mean God left the Temple, or access to God was now open, or Jesus was entering God's presence. Luke does not have the cry of dereliction or the discussion about Elijah. At the time of death, Luke says Jesus' cry was "Father, into thy hands I commit my spirit!" (v. 46, RSV). Following the death, Luke records three reponses: in the person of the centurion Rome again declares Jesus innocent; the crowds go home deeply penitent; acquaintances and the women from Galilee (8:1–3) witness his death. The women will return in Luke's narrative of the burial and resurrection.

23:50–56, The Burial of Jesus. Cf. Mark 15:42–47; Matt. 27:57–61. Joseph is identified by address, character, position, and general attitude toward Jesus and his message. His caring for the body, apparently in haste since it was late and the Sabbath was beginning (lit., "dawning"); that is, the evening star was appearing, marking the beginning of the Sabbath), has given him a favorable place in the church's memory. The women from Galilee observed the burial, prepared burial spices ahead of time, but waited in observance of the Sabbath. At death as at birth (2:21–39), Luke is careful to point out the keeping of the law.

24:1–53
The Resurrection Narrative

Although Luke's account of the empty tomb is similar to Mark's (Mark 16:1–8), this resurrection narrative as a whole is unique to Luke. All the appearances of the risen Christ are in or near Jerusalem, and they are told as occurrences of one day. Perhaps they had been so framed for the church's observance of Easter.

24:1–12, The Empty Tomb. Cf. Mark 16:1–8; Matt. 28:1–10; John 20:1–10. Luke's "they" clearly carries over from 23:56, their further identities being reserved until 24:10. Inside the tomb the perplexed women encounter two men. The reference to two men joins this text with the transfiguration (9:30) and the ascension (Acts 1:10), perhaps indicating how Luke wants the story to be understood. Since Luke repeats this empty tomb story at 24:22–24, it apparently is important to his resurrection narrative even though it is absent from the earliest account (1 Cor. 15:1–8).

Key points in Luke's story are: first, Galilee was the place of Jesus' teaching (v. 6) but is not to be, as in Mark 16:7, the site of resurrection appearances. Jerusalem will now be the center both for Christ's appearances (vv. 13–43) and for the mission of the church (vv. 44–53). Second, the women are reminded by a creedal formula of the gospel, essentially repeated at vv. 26 and 46. Third, the women are treated as disciples and not as messengers to the disciples (vv. 6–8). Fourth, the women do tell the Eleven (v. 9; "apostles," v. 10), but also "all the rest." Later Luke will say Galilean believers numbered about 120 (Acts 1:15). That the apostles did not believe the women reminds the reader what a burden a resurrection puts on faith, especially since there had not yet been an appearance. Luke 24:12, omitted in many translations, has strong manuscript support but most likely is a borrowing from John 20:3–10, and is in some tension with v. 34.

24:13–35, Appearance on the Road to Emmaus. This story, unique to Luke and comparable to the parable of the prodigal son in skill and artistry, does not appear in the early resurrection text in 1 Cor. 15:1–8, although Luke 24:34 confirms 1 Cor. 15:5. Perhaps this account was shaped with Christian worship in mind since it involves Sunday, Scripture or word, and sacrament. In the background lies Gen. 18:1–15. Emmaus has never been identified with certainty, one of the two disciples is totally unknown, and Cleopas is encountered nowhere else. In a sense, this is the church's story of encountering the living Christ. The two disciples are kept from recognizing Christ (v. 16) until their eyes are opened by witnessing to the real meaning of the Scriptures. Their recitation of what had happened concerning Jesus is basically a summary of Luke's Gospel. The disciples' recognition of Jesus, however, depends on two events: first, Jesus' interpretation of the OT Scriptures (vv. 25–27), which they were able to grasp only later (v. 32). The role of Scripture in the removal of ignorance and the generation of faith is a strong theme in Luke (16:31; 24:44–47; Acts 2:14–36). Second, Jesus reveals himself in the breaking of bread (vv. 31, 35). The language is reminiscent of that of the feeding of the multitude (9:16) and of the Last Supper (22:19). The return of the two to Jerusalem joins this story to Jesus' appearances to Peter (v. 34) and to the Eleven in the company of other disciples (vv. 36–43).

24:36–49, Appearance in Jerusalem. This narrative contains few surprises since it is framed on the same pattern as vv. 13–35: the risen Christ appears, the disciples do not recognize him, they are scolded for doubting, food is shared, Jesus opens their minds to understand Scripture, they respond in amazed joy. However in vv. 36–43 a new theme emerges: the corporeality of the risen Christ. Eating fish and offering his body for proof is an early insistence that neither is resurrection a vague Greek notion of immortality of the soul nor is the risen Christ to be separated from the historical Jesus. "See my hands and my feet" (v. 39) means the one raised is the one crucified. Verse 40, found in some manuscripts, is obviously a borrowing from John 20:20. In fact, vv. 36–43 have close affinities to John 20–21. Throughout Luke's Gospel continuity between Jesus and Judaism has been stressed. This occurs here in two ways: first, in pointing out that Jesus' Passion and resurrection are according to Jewish Scriptures (vv. 44–46); and second, in naming Jerusalem as the center from which the mission to the nations is to spread (Isa. 2:3; Acts 1:1–8). The message to be preached is that which is stated repeatedly in Luke and Acts: repentance and forgiveness of sins (Luke 24:47; Acts 2:38; 3:19; 5:31; 11:18; 17:30). To enable them for this mission they will receive power from God, the Holy Spirit, but for that power, they must wait in Jerusalem (Luke 24:49; Acts 1:4–8). In Luke's chronology, the disciples are now between Easter and Pentecost.

24:50–53, The Blessing and Departure. Luke says it was from a village near the Mount of Olives that Jesus parted from his disciples while in the act of blessing them. If v. 51b is in the original text (the evidence is divided) then his parting was his ascension. This creates a chronological problem between this account and Acts 1. Here the events are compacted into one day; Acts 1 says he appeared for forty days. Of course, parting into heaven at 24:51b does not forbid other appearances. More likely, Luke 24 compresses what is retold more extensively in Acts. The disciples return to Jerusalem as instructed and make the Temple their place of worship while awaiting the promise of power from on high.

Bibliography

Cadbury, H. J. *The Making of Luke-Acts*. New York: Macmillan, 1927.

Conzelmann, H. *The Theology of St. Luke*. New York: Harper, 1960.

Ellis, E. E. *The Gospel of Luke*. London: Oliphants, 1974.

Fitzmyer, J. A. *The Gospel According to Luke*. Anchor Bible, 28, 28A. Garden City, NY: Doubleday, 1981, 1985.

Juel, D. *Luke-Acts*. Atlanta, GA: Knox, 1983.

Keck, L. E., and J. T. Martyn, eds. *Studies in Luke-Acts*. Nashville, TN: Abingdon, 1966.

Marshall, I. H. *Commentary on Luke*. Grand Rapids, MI: Eerdmans, 1978.

Schweizer, E. *The Good News According to Luke*. Translated by D. Green. Atlanta, GA: Knox, 1984.

Talbert, C. *Reading Luke*. New York: Crossroad, 1982.

JOHN

D. MOODY SMITH

INTRODUCTION

The Gospel According to John is significantly different from the synoptic Gospels, Matthew, Mark, and Luke. Indeed, in language and theological conceptions it is much closer to the Letters of John, and this similarity is visible even in the discourses of Jesus. Yet John is also a Gospel, a narrative of the ministry and message of Jesus, and as such shares certain content and characteristics with the Synoptics.

John and the Synoptics: The Distinctive Character of the Fourth Gospel

The course of Jesus' ministry is significantly different in John in that it spans a two- or three-year period; three annual Passover festivals are mentioned (2:13; 6:4; 11:55), whereas the Synoptics speak only of the one at which Jesus met his death. Most of Jesus' ministry takes place in Judea or Jerusalem, while according to the Synoptics his public activity prior to the fateful journey to Jerusalem is in Galilee or its environs. Places and people unknown in the Synoptics play roles in John. Nicodemus, the woman of Samaria, and Lazarus are prominent figures in the Gospel of John but do not appear at all in the others. Disciples such as Thomas and Philip, who are only names in the other Gospels, ask questions or make comments in John (e.g., 14:5, 8; 20:24–29). The sheer content of John is considerably different from the Synoptics; most of what is found in John is missing from the others, and vice versa. The most notable exception to this overall difference is the narrative of Jesus' death, which runs parallel in all four Gospels. There are also similarities between John's resurrection appearance narratives and those of Matthew and Luke, which, however, differ from each other.

Jesus' miracles are narrated impressively in all the Gospels, but only in John are they called signs (e.g., 2:11), and only there are they explicitly set forth as demonstrations of Jesus' divine origin or mission (3:2). Their function is clearly to elicit faith in Jesus, although to believe that Jesus performed them is not tantamount to attaining genuine faith and understanding (3:1–12). Jesus' signs often lead to extensive discussions and debates about his identity and significance (→ Sign). In the Synoptics, on the other hand, there are, at most, brief expressions of amazement at Jesus' power on the part of the crowds.

In the synoptic Gospels, Jesus gives ethical and religious instructions that fall within the framework of Judaism. Although they contain debates over whether Jesus has violated the law, it is clear that Jesus does not think his mission and message is to abrogate the law given to Israel. In John, however, Jesus speaks of "your law" (e.g., 8:17), implying that the law belongs to an alien community, namely, the Jews, while he identifies himself with a group of disciples who have broken away to follow him. If a fundamental question in the synoptic tradition is how one should understand and respond to God's will as expressed in the law, the fundamental question of the Fourth Gospel is whether one will understand and respond to Jesus as the definitive expression of God's will or revelation.

Thus the mission and message of Jesus revolve around his self-manifestation and self-proclamation. The Kingdom of God, so prominent in the Synoptics, falls into the background as Jesus expounds and debates his own role and status. Jesus' "I am" sayings (e.g., 6:35; 8:12) are typical and distinctive of John. Although he is presented as the fulfillment of OT expectations, his messianic role goes beyond anything anticipated or adumbrated in the OT as it was read by ancient Jews. Not surprisingly, his claims evoke the sharpest dissent and dispute. The sheer content of Jesus' teaching is quite different; there is no Sermon on the Mount (or Plain), no sharp questions and injunctions, and no true parables. Even at the Last Supper and in the farewell discourses, where Jesus instructs his own disciples, his teaching has little concreteness or specificity. Rather, in a general, if moving, way he commands his disciples to love one another (13:34–35; 15:12).

The Setting and Composition of the Gospel

The dominant Christological themes of the Gospel, and particularly its controversial tone, already afford a clue to the original setting and purpose of the Gospel. In the first half (chaps. 2–12) Jesus is portrayed as constantly debating with "the Jews" about who he is and whether they should believe in him. Obviously these

Jews, and particularly the Pharisees, strongly reject and resist Jesus' claims (→ Pharisees). Yet Jesus and his disciples are acknowledged to be Jews, and throughout the Gospel many Jews are said to believe in Jesus. Apparently, the subject matter and the participants in the discussion reflect the circumstances under which the traditions behind this Gospel developed and the Gospel itself was composed.

The several references to Jews being put out of the synagogue (9:22; 12:42; 16:2) and the prominence of the Pharisees help us define more accurately the setting and the period from which John's Gospel originates (→ Synagogue). After the defeat of the Jewish revolt by the Romans in A.D. 70, Judaism underwent an internal self-assessment and retrenchment in which the party of the Pharisees played an increasingly important role. During this period measures were apparently taken to eliminate what were regarded as harmful sectarian divisions. The Twelfth Benediction of the Eighteen Benedictions used in the synagogue service pronounced a malediction upon sectarians, perhaps including Jewish Christians. The date of this benediction (perhaps ca. 80–90) is disputed, but its character is indicative of the trends of the time. Possibly some such liturgical device was used to smoke out and expel Christ-confessors from the synagogue. In any event, the fear of expulsion from the synagogue, the claims of Jesus for himself, and the sharp distinction of Jesus and his followers from the Jews bespeak a time and situation for John different from Jesus' own ministry and closer to the end of the first century. At least a part of John's purpose was to persuade followers of Jesus to leave the synagogue and join distinctively Christian communities. Quite possibly the Gospel was composed in stages or went through successive editions as the controversy developed.

On other grounds John has long been thought to be a later Gospel, and early church tradition places its writing after the other three. In the ancient church, as well as in much modern critical scholarship, it has been assumed that John wrote with knowledge of the other Gospels, although quite obviously he did not write to transmit the same material or content. John's considerable divergences from the others have recently caused this assumption to be questioned, although relatively few scholars are inclined to argue for an early date even on the basis of John's independence. Aside from the probability that it reflects a Jewish-Christian situation that developed only after A.D. 70, its retrospective and reflective character seem to bespeak a later date.

The same may be said of its religious or philosophical vocabulary or conceptuality (e.g., the role of the *logos* or Word), which has led to its being described as the most Hellenistic, and least Jewish, of the Gospels. However, such hellenization—assimilation to the high culture of the Greek-speaking world—had already occurred among contemporary Jews (e.g., Philo), particularly outside Palestine. On the other hand, the discovery of the Qumran scrolls along the shores of the Dead Sea showed that the religious vocabulary and thought-world of John was not alien to some sectarian Jews in the Holy Land itself (→ Scrolls, The Dead Sea). John's kinship with Jewish thought both in Palestine and beyond fits quite well the situation of controversy within Jewish circles that has been suggested above.

The scrolls not only opened up the possibility that John was written in Palestine or nearby but revived support for the tradition that the Fourth Gospel was, after all, the work of John, the disciple of Jesus and the son of Zebedee known from the Synoptics. That tradition was firmly established by the end of the second century, having been set forth as much as twenty-five years earlier by Bishop Irenaeus. It cannot be traced back further with any certainty, however, and several considerations militate against it, not least the slowness of the Gospel's acceptance in orthodox circles (see "The Gospel of John in the Early Church" below).

Although John the son of Zebedee, with his brother James, has a certain prominence in the other Gospels and is mentioned with Peter in Acts, he does not appear until the end of the Fourth Gospel (21:2) and then is not mentioned by name. This omission is sometimes regarded as reflecting John's personal modesty, and he is said to present himself under the guise of the Beloved Disciple, who appears only in the Fourth Gospel. Yet the Beloved Disciple is never identified as John, despite the later church tradition, although in 21:24 he is said to be responsible for the Gospel. The silence about incidents in which, according to the Synoptics, John was present (e.g., the raising of Jairus's daughter and the transfiguration) is only with difficulty explained by the modesty of a man who could refer to himself as the Beloved Disciple. The identity of the author of the Fourth Gospel remains a mystery, perhaps deliberately concealed (→ Beloved Disciple, The).

The tradition of Johannine authorship, shared by the Letters of John and Revelation, was in antiquity related to Ephesus as the place of origin of these writings (nearby Patmos for Revelation). A Church of St. John and his reputed tomb, as well as other relics, tie the Johannine literature to this ancient city of early Christian fame, where the apostle Paul also worked. Yet Ignatius, writing to the church at Ephesus before A.D. 120, fails to mention John, although he emphasizes the Ephesians' relationship with Paul. On the other hand, Acts' description of Christians in Ephesus (Acts 18:24–20:38) comports well enough with what can be inferred about Johannine origins from the Gospel, for we read of disciples of John the Baptist, disputes with Jews, the descent of the Spirit, miracles of healing, and the threat of false teaching (the theme of the Johannine Letters). Ephesus perhaps remains as good a possibility as can be proposed for the place of origin, or publication, of the Johannine writings. That the Johannine tradition originated in Palestine or Syria need not be denied (→ Ephesus).

The Gospel of John in the Early Church

If there were doubts about John's authenticity in antiquity, they quite likely had something to do with the Gospel's obvious differences from the three that had already gained wide acceptance. We hear of Christians opposed to the Fourth Gospel (e.g., Gaius of Rome), and Clement of Alexandria maintained that John was a spiritual Gospel, perhaps thereby thinking to explain its differences from the others.

Meanwhile, some Gnostic Christians, later condemned as heretical, gladly made use of the Fourth Gospel. The first known commentator on John was such a Gnostic, Heracleon, who wrote his commentary about the middle of the second century. Later, orthodox exegetes such as Irenaeus felt compelled to prove that the Gnostics were misinterpreting John and thus to save the Gospel for the church, and Origen took issue with Heracleon specifically. Nevertheless, it is not difficult to see how the Gnostics found the Fourth Gospel compatible with their emphasis upon secret knowledge as salvation and their view of Christ as more, or other, than a human being. Quite possibly, the author of 1 John, who so emphatically insists upon the materiality and tangibility of Jesus (1 John 1:1–4), intended to make clear exactly what the Word's becoming flesh (John 1:14) entailed and thus to set the interpretation of the Fourth Gospel on the right track. In any event, by the beginning of the third century John was firmly established as an authoritative Gospel, to be read alongside the other three (→ Gnosticism).

Such a reading of the Fourth Gospel is encouraged by the NT canon and has a certain theological, even literary, justification. The Jesus of John becomes united with the Jesus we know also from the synoptic Gospels, as well as the rest of the NT. This is not contrary to the intention of the evangelists, who obviously meant to write about one Jesus. Still, if John is read in this traditional way, there is a danger his distinctive witness to Jesus will fall from view. It is therefore important to ask about the contours, structure, and emphases that make this Gospel distinctive and in some ways unique. These will be our primary focus of attention.

COMMENTARY

1:1-51

Introduction

1:1-18

The Prologue

The prologue creates an aura of the cosmic and the philosophical at the outset that is resolved into the historical and the revelatory at the end, as Jesus Christ is named (1:17). Its climactic point occurs in v. 14, as the incarnation of the Word (Gk. *logos*) is announced in a passage that has become the scriptural *locus classicus* of the Christian doctrine.

The prologue also exemplifies a major problem in understanding the Fourth Gospel historically, namely, locating it within its contemporary religious and cultural context. Much of the vocabulary and piety of ancient Mediterranean religion is suggested in these few lines. At the same time, the prologue is evocative of themes from both the NT and the OT, as well as the history of ancient Judaism and Christianity.

The prologue falls into three parts, divided by the statements about John (the Baptist) in 1:6–8 and 15. The first part (vv. 1–5) deals with the cosmic, creative work of the Word and the relationship of the Word to God and creation. The second part (vv. 9–14) narrates the advent of the Word and the response evoked by it; v. 14 summarizes this advent and begins to set forth the incarnate Word's nature. For the first time the author speaks confessionally, in the first-person plural. In the third and final part (vv. 15–18) the community of disciples confesses briefly and succinctly who the Word is and what his advent means.

1:1–5, The Word in Creation. The brief opening clause, "in the beginning," immediately suggests the creation narrative of Genesis at the beginning of the Hebrew Bible. Here the Word's close association with, and participation in, God's being is clearly stated. (Yet *theos*, "God," does not have the definite article; this implies that the Word is not to be equated with the totality of God.) In Genesis, God speaks and the creation takes shape. In John, it is as if God's speaking has become reified, objectified, in the

Word. This difference is significant. The word of God or the prophetic word in the OT is almost always qualified as "the word of the LORD"; it does not have such an independent existence (→ Logos; Word).

In contemporary writers such as Philo of Alexandria (ca. 25 B.C.–A.D. 50), the great Jewish philosopher of religion, the Word had also become a semi-independent entity, mediating between God and the world. John's insistence upon the Word's role in all aspects of creation (v. 3) also parallels the creative role of Wisdom in OT and later Jewish writings (Prov. 8, Wisd. of Sol. 7). Such usage stands behind this text. By assigning the Word an indispensable role in creation, John makes clear not only that creation is good but also that in this Word creation and redemption are linked together. Salvation fulfills, rather than negates, creation.

The Word is the source of light and life for humanity (John 1:4). The latter are themes of the whole Gospel in a way the Word is not; there are subsequent references to the words of Jesus but not to Jesus as the Word. With the mention of light comes the contrast with darkness (v. 5) that is typical in the Fourth Gospel. Light and darkness are found also in the Genesis creation narrative, where they are equated with day and night (Gen. 1:3–5). In John, they have metaphysical and ethical overtones: human life is lived either in light or darkness. Or, more accurately, life means to be in the light, while to walk in darkness is death. Thus the light struggles against the darkness but is not overcome by it. The Greek verb usually translated "overcome" can also mean "comprehend," a suggestive double meaning.

1:6–8, John the Baptist. At 1:6 the focus shifts abruptly to the plane of historical events, and the style becomes more prosaic. If we already knew about John (never called "the Baptist" in the Fourth Gospel) from the Synoptics, we would envision him in the wilderness of Judea at some place near the Jordan River. Yet in this Gospel we have not yet been told where John is. Readers learn only that he was sent from God, that his name is John, and that he came (and hence was sent) to bear witness to the light (→ John the Baptist).

1:9–13, The Appearance of the Word. A further step is taken in identifying the light (v. 9). On the basis of v. 5 one would not necessarily think of the appearance of a historical personage. That the advent of a historical personage is in view, however, is clear from vv. 10–11. The Greek is not ambiguous, for the pronouns in vv. 10–11 are masculine, not neuter, as would be required if the antecedent were "light," a neuter noun in Greek. Moreover, knowledge of the Gospel, or of the Christian tradition, would render the reference in vv. 10–11 to Jesus clear enough.

The rejection referred to in v. 11 is not complete, as vv. 12–13 make plain. Although rejected by the officials of his people, Jesus is believed in by many. To receive (or accept) him is to believe in him (or "in his name"). Believers can also be described in terms of their origin or birth—with God rather than through any human or natural causation (v. 13). Nevertheless, believing is usually construed as an act of the will or a genuine decision, apart from which one's origin remains unclear.

1:14–18, Incarnation and Confession. That the Word has entered the realm of the flesh as a historical person is now made quite explicit, even though Jesus is not yet named (→ Incarnation). "Dwelt" (RSV) translates a Greek verb that implies tenting or tabernacling, evoking the motif of God's dwelling with his people, in the wilderness tabernacle and in the Temple on Mount Zion. The "we" who have seen Jesus' glory may be the whole Christian community, the circle of Jesus' disciples, or some other and smaller group. An exact identification eludes us. Near the end of the Gospel, however, those who see are clearly differentiated from all who may believe (20:29); John apparently distinguishes seeing from believing. Presumably, a group exercising authority speaks of the revelation of God, because they have actually seen the glory of Jesus the only Son and can bear witness that he is full of grace and truth.

A reference to John the Baptist (v. 15) follows the explicit mention of the incarnation (v 14), and the content of John's witness is now given (cf v. 30). The Evangelist's belief in the preexistence of Jesus is here voiced by the Baptist, who says nothing like this in other Gospel accounts. Significantly, the Baptist makes Jesus' superiority clear at the outset; no one should make any mistake about that.

Verse 16 continues the thought of v. 14 as if it had not been interrupted by the Baptist. The meaning of "fullness" is not obvious. Probably it signifies the saving gift of God (cf. Col. 1:19); "grace upon grace" would then expand upon this fullness (→ Grace). Verse 17 makes an important differentiation in that for the first time Jesus Christ is explicitly named. Conceivably, the giving of the law through Moses (v. 17a) is to be construed as grace (v. 16b) to which the grace (and truth) of Christ is now added (v. 17b). In the light of the treatment of Moses in the entire Gospel, however, v. 17 is best understood antithetically, putting Moses over against Jesus. Still the law of Moses is regarded as valid (7:51) if rightly understood (5:39), but the Jews neither understand it (5:46–47) nor obey it (7:19).

The conclusion of the prologue (1:18) rounds out its message as it refers to v. 1. That no one has seen God is a commonplace of OT theology (but cf. Exod. 24:9–11; 33:20–23; 34:6). The RSV reads "the only Son," which makes good (Johannine) sense but is not found in the oldest and best Greek manuscripts, where "only (begotten) God" is read. The latter reading is also supported by the fact that it echoes John 1:1b, where the Word is called *theos* ("God," but, as here, without the Greek article). Jesus Christ's having been in the bosom of the Father signifies his close intimacy with him. The Word Incarnate has not only seen God, he himself is *theos* and thus able to make him fully known.

At the end of the prologue one sees that it is an overture to or summation of the Gospel. Of course, the Gospel must be read, or Christian tradition known, in order to perceive this. Jesus Christ as the Word is the light who shines in darkness, who comes into the world he was instrumental in making. Rejected by his own people as a group, he was nevertheless received by individuals who believed in him, who gained the right to be children of God. As soon as the incarnation of the Word is announced, more traditionally Christian terms are employed, e.g., "grace," "glory," "truth," "only (begotten) Son," and "fullness." Finally, at the end of the prologue (v. 18), the historical revelation of God in Jesus is succinctly summed up: "He has made him known."

1:19–51
Encounter with John the Baptist and Call of the Disciples

The prologue is followed by episodes that are paralleled in the synoptic accounts; first, the witness of John (the Baptist) to Jesus (1:19–28), followed by an encounter between them (vv. 29–34). Then in a narrative comparable to but different from the call narratives of the Synoptics, Jesus gathers disciples and makes ready to begin his public activity (vv. 35–51). Unlike the Synoptics, John's Gospel has no mention of Jesus' being tempted by Satan; nor is Jesus said to open his ministry by coming forward in Galilee with a formal announcement of the approach of the Kingdom of God.

1:19–28, John the Baptist's Witness Concerning Himself. John the Baptist bears witness to Jesus before Jewish authorities, at the same time sharply delimiting his own role and thus expanding on the statement of the prologue that "he was not the light" (v. 8). He is not one of the anticipated figures of the end-time (vv. 20–21). That the "priests and Levites" are sent from Jerusalem by the Jews is significant, for the Jews, centered in Jerusalem, are the chief opponents of Jesus in John. The senders seem also to

be identified as Pharisees (v. 24), and the apparent identification of Jews and Pharisees is typical of this Gospel for which the Pharisees are representative of the Jews, particularly Jewish leadership. Perhaps the titles that John the Baptist refuses are being reserved for Jesus. When pressed, he will only claim to be a voice crying in the wilderness (v. 23; cf. Mark 1:3). Thus John the Baptist describes himself with the same Isaiah passage (Isa. 40:3) that is applied to him by Mark. He is a forerunner and witness to Jesus but claims nothing more for himself.

Having failed to elicit any useful information from John about his person, the questioners take another line (John 1:25). Using language familiar to us from the Synoptics, John exploits the question about baptism to bear witness to his role as subordinate and forerunner of Jesus (vv. 26–27). Probably to establish Jesus' superiority, the actual baptism of Jesus by John is suppressed. The scene ends abruptly with a statement locating these events as well as John's activity (v. 28). The whereabouts of Bethany beyond the Jordan, however, remains a mystery.

1:29–34, John the Baptist's Witness to Jesus. The next day (cf. vv. 35, 43) finds Jesus himself on the scene for the first time, approaching John, who identifies him in terms of his saving work (cf. v. 36). In all probability John's use of lamb imagery is to be seen against the background of the Temple sacrifice. In the Fourth Gospel, Jesus is crucified on the afternoon before Passover, as the paschal lambs are being slain (cf. 1 Cor. 5:7). The Lamb title appears only here and in 1:36 in John. The sacrificial understanding of Jesus' death is not, however, typical of the Gospel (but cf. 1 John 1:7 and Rev. 5:6–14). In referring to his earlier witness about Jesus (John 1:30; cf. v. 15), John the Baptist typifies the Gospel's retrospective stance. He now looks back on it as an event that has already transpired (vv. 31–35); only in this Gospel is John the Baptist the narrator.

The Baptist, presumably like others (v. 26), did not know Jesus, and his baptizing activity is solely a means of revealing him to Israel (v. 31). Nothing is said about repentance and forgiveness as in the Synoptics (Mark 1:4). Significantly, John the Baptist is the first to bear witness to Jesus, and he himself sees and describes the Spirit's descending and abiding upon Jesus. The Baptist thus concludes this episode by summarizing and underscoring what he has done (John 1:34); he attests that Jesus is the Son of God, rendering the definitive statement about Jesus that is attributed by the Synoptics to the voice from heaven (→ Son of God). The unique, God-directed role of the Baptist has now been heavily underscored. In the very act of bearing witness so decisively to

Jesus, John sharply defines and limits his own role.

1:35–51, The Call of Disciples. As another day's activity begins, the Baptist bears witness to two disciples (v. 36; cf. v. 29), his brief testimony evoking what was said the previous day (vv. 29–34). They follow Jesus (v. 37). Quite possibly the first of Jesus' disciples had been followers of the Baptist, as only this Gospel suggests. Although synoptic call stories occur on or near the Sea of Galilee, there is little indication of where this episode has taken place (cf. v. 28). The two disciples' brief conversation with Jesus (vv. 38–39) suggests more than it reveals. Significantly, the Evangelist translates "rabbi" (v. 38), suggesting that a non-Jewish audience is in view (cf. vv. 41, 42). There is an obvious play on seeking Jesus and staying with him (v. 39) that suggests a symbolic meaning that goes beyond location to conduct.

Subsequently, one of the disciples is identified (v. 40). That Andrew "first" found his brother Simon (Peter, v. 41) has been taken to imply that the other, unnamed disciple also found his brother. Since in the Marcan account (Mark 1:16–20) the brothers Andrew and Peter figure together with the brothers James and John, the sons of Zebedee, it has been inferred that the unnamed disciple was one of the sons of Zebedee and that he too found his brother. But such harmonization with the synoptic account hangs by the slenderest of threads. Peter, who first confesses Jesus to be the Christ in Mark (8:29; cf. Matt. 16:16) is now introduced to Jesus the Messiah (only John gives the Heb. form "Messiah"). John here stands in contrast to the Synoptics, where Jesus' identity is withheld throughout most of his public ministry. Jesus in turn calls Simon "Cephas" (in Aramaic, "Rock") or (in Gk.) "Peter" (John 1:42), just as he does in Matt. 16:18, when Peter confesses him to be the Christ (→ Peter).

Jesus' call to Philip, presumably in Galilee (John 1:43), is couched in language familiar from the Synoptics (Mark 2:14). Nathanael (John 1:45) is not named outside the Fourth Gospel (cf. 21:2). Philip's description of Jesus (1:45) is striking, for he identifies him as the Messiah announced in Scripture, indicates that he is a Galilean (Nazareth of Galilee), and calls Joseph his father. Nathanael's question about Nazareth reflects the obscurity of that small village (v. 46), and Philip's answer repeats Jesus' invitation of v. 39.

The exchange between Philip and Nathanael mirrors a characteristic theme of the Gospel: Jesus' origins are thought to explain him. But Jesus has another origin the world cannot know. Only being with Jesus provides sufficient basis to understand who he is. Nathanael's experience is immediate and decisive (vv. 47–51), as

again a characteristic motif of John's appears, namely, Jesus' omniscience or foreknowledge (vv. 47–48), which leaves Nathanael astounded (v. 48) and hardly prepared for Jesus' answer. Nathanael's confession (v. 49) is entirely appropriate, but that he stands only at the beginning of an experience of divine revelation is made clear by Jesus' rejoinder (v. 50).

Jesus' final statement details what Nathanael can expect to see (v. 51). The Greek verb and subject here suddenly become plural; more people than Nathanael will view this strange sight. Oddly, Jesus' prediction or promise is not literally fulfilled in the Gospel. Its obscurity is, however, illumined by the recognition that there is a direct reference to Jacob's dream (Gen. 28), particularly to the ascending and descending of the angels of God upon the ladder (28:12). In John 1:51, of course, they ascend and descend upon the Son of man (i.e., Jesus). (John seems to play upon an ambiguity caused by the masculine gender of the Heb. pronoun that stands for "ladder.") As Jesus evokes the imagery of the entire Genesis scene, he himself becomes the place of God's revelation and dwelling (cf. John 1:14) as ancient Bethel had been.

In these opening stories the principal traditional titles of Jesus are introduced. He is first called only "Rabbi" (teacher), then "Messiah" (Christ), "Son of God," "King of Israel," and finally "Son of man." The last is the most common appellation of Jesus in the Gospels. So, at the beginning of Jesus' public ministry in John we already gain a clear idea of who he is, as do his disciples.

2:1–12:50

Jesus' Manifestation of God's Glory Before the World

2:1–12
The Wine Miracle

Jesus' public ministry begins at a wedding feast in Cana of Galilee, a locality mentioned only in John (cf. 4:46–54), with Jesus' mother (never in John called Mary) as well as his disciples also present (cf. Mark 3:31–35; John 19:25–27). Although the imagery of a wedding (bride, bridegroom, etc.) appears in Jesus' teaching (3:29; Mark 2:19–20), only here does he attend a wedding. His participation is, moreover, extraordinary. Perhaps we are put on notice by the placing of the event on the third day (John 2:1). This seemingly odd enumeration, which does not fit the context (cf. 1:29, 35, 43), could be a way of alluding to Jesus' resurrection, a hint that the story is to be interpreted symbolically. Yet "the third day" might simply mean "three days hence."

Jesus' mother helpfully informs him that the wine has run out (v. 3), but his response seems brusque (v. 4). That Jesus' hour has not yet come is a characteristically Johannine touch (cf. 12:23). As the narrative develops, it becomes clear that "the hour" is the hour of Jesus' glorification and death. Salvation flows from the crucified, exalted Jesus. The "hour" then alludes to this saving event and suggests that Jesus' supplying wine should be understood symbolically. Moreover, in the Christian sacrament of the Lord's Supper, wine represents Jesus' blood, i.e., his death.

Although rebuffed, Jesus' mother gives instructions (1:5). The presence of six stone jars (v. 6), presumably in a home, is not explained, although their symbolic value will later become evident. As the servants obey Jesus' instructions (vv. 7–8), no miracle at all is recounted; Jesus speaks no word over the water. But such good wine is brought the steward (v. 9) that he exclaims to the bridegroom about what seems to him the reversal of ordinary practice (v. 10). The steward does not know where the wine came from (v. 9): again the motif of ignorance of Jesus' true origin. (That the servants know may suggest that they represent ministers of Jesus or the church.) The steward's words mean more than he intends. If Jesus himself is the good wine, his appearance at the culmination of salvation history is symbolized by its emergence out of the waters of Jewish purification: the last, not the first, is best.

Such a symbolic interpretation seems confirmed by the closing statement (v. 11). Jesus has performed the first of his signs, whose purpose, to indicate who he is (to manifest his glory), is now fulfilled in the disciples' response of faith. Jesus is then the new wine, perhaps embodied in the wine of the Eucharist, and his coming is an event that drastically alters the prevailing circumstances, as did the miracle of his changing water into wine.

Jesus' mother and disciples have been with him at Cana; now suddenly and inexplicably at Capernaum his brothers appear also (v. 12). They all remain there a short while, but nothing happens. Not surprisingly, modern interpreters have wondered whether we find here the remnant of a narrative framework that has been lost in later editing (see commentary below on 4:46–54).

2:13–22
The Cleansing of the Temple

Somewhat abruptly we are told that Jesus went up to Jerusalem for Passover (v. 13), the first of at least three Passovers in the Johannine narrative (cf. 6:4; 11:55). The only Passover mentioned in the other Gospels is the one at which he died (→ Passover, The).

The description of Jesus' driving the moneychangers and vendors from the Temple begins in a manner similar to the other Gospels, although there are differences in detail (e.g., Jesus' use of a whip, his direct address to those who sold pigeons). The words of Jesus and the quotation from the OT also differ. Only in John does Jesus speak of not making the Temple ("my Father's house") a house of trade (Gk. emporion; Lat. emporium; cf. Zech. 14:21) and quote Ps. 69:9. This Psalms quotation has a double sense; it not only refers to the zeal that motivated Jesus' deed but alludes to his own death (→ Temple, The).

The demand for a sign (John 2:18) is unique and typical of John (but cf. Mark 11:28). Jesus' word about destroying the temple and raising it up in three days (John 2:19) has numerous parallels (Mark 14:58 and parallels; Mark 15:29 and parallels; Acts 6:14) but not in the setting of this episode. Indeed, in other sources it is attributed to Jesus by his opponents. The question of the Jews (John 2:20) allows the narrator to inform readers of the real meaning of the saying (v. 21) and to point ahead to the disciples' future belief (v. 22). This retrospective stance, in which the author assumes the vantage point of future, postresurrection belief is typical of John (cf. 12:16). If Herod's reconstruction of the Temple (v. 20) began in 19 or 20 B.C., this event would have occurred in the year 27 or 28.

Harmonizers of the Gospels, ancient and modern, have proposed that Jesus cleansed the Temple in a similar way twice. This is possible but not likely. In all probability John has moved an event from the passion week to the beginning of the narrative. Such a move would fit his tendency to set out at the beginning matters or events that in the other Gospels take place later (e.g., the confession of Jesus as Messiah). Jesus comes to the Temple of Jerusalem, the very heart of the Israelite nation and religion, at the outset of his ministry and there confronts its authorities. Their forthcoming hostility is adumbrated, and his own death and resurrection are revealed by the testimony of Scripture and Jesus' own pronouncement.

2:23–3:21
The Discussion with Nicodemus on Birth from Above

2:23–25, Jesus' Reception at Passover.
This general, summary statement about Jesus' signs prepares us for the way in which Nicodemus will approach Jesus (3:2), as well as Jesus' cool response. Jesus' own attitude is described tersely (vv. 24–25) and grounded in the omni-

science that he frequently manifests in John (1:48; 4:39).

3:1–21, The Discussion with Nicodemus.

Nicodemus is a Pharisee and a "ruler" of the Jews, probably a member of the Sanhedrin (→ Sanhedrin). Like many figures in the Fourth Gospel, he is representative of an attitude toward Jesus, probably one known to the Evangelist (cf. 12:42). That Nicodemus says "we" suggests that he speaks for a Judaism that is open to Jesus, that is, accepts him as one (among others) sent from God. Jesus is indeed a teacher (1:38) from God, whose signs accredit his origin.

The proof of divine accreditation through signs has a venerable biblical origin and history, particularly in the Exodus narratives (Exod. 4:1–9, 17, 30). Jesus himself was perceived as a miracle worker, exorcist, and faith healer (Matt. 11:2–6; 12:28). Miracles apparently came to be expected of the promised prophet like Moses (Deut. 18:15–22), even as Moses himself had performed signs. Nicodemus' evaluation of Jesus thus seems to imply that he is such a prophetic figure.

One might have assumed that Nicodemus' acceptance of Jesus (John 3:2) would have elicited a positive response rather than what amounts to a sharp rebuke and challenge (v. 3). For the first time in John "kingdom of God" is mentioned. Whether Jesus is calling for rebirth or birth from above depends on how the Greek term *anothen* (RSV: "anew") is rendered. It means either "again" or "from above." Nicodemus understands Jesus to say "again" (v. 4), although he grossly misinterprets him as meaning physical rebirth. Jesus immediately makes clear that he speaks on a different level. Birth by water and spirit (v. 5) looks like an allusion to baptism, performed in water and, in early Christian expectation, accompanied by the gift of the Spirit. The realms of flesh and spirit (v. 6) are not to be understood generally but with reference to Christ and belief or participation in him. The flesh is the realm of unbelief, of separation from knowledge of God. That Jesus should speak as he has to one living in that realm is no marvel (v. 7). Nicodemus is called upon not to acknowledge Jesus by his old standards, but to break away from them into a new realm. Jesus' enigmatic statement about the wind or Spirit (v. 8) is bound to confound Nicodemus (v. 9). The Greek word *pneuma* can mean either, and an outsider like Nicodemus may only wonder what the blowing of the wind has to do with the working of the Spirit. The latter is not, however, erratic and arbitrary; to the believer its unaccountability signals God's grace.

Despite his initial positive reception of Jesus, Nicodemus is still in darkness (v. 10). That he is more than an individual is suggested by the following statement (v. 11) in which suddenly the verbs all become plural in Greek; heretofore they were singular. Apparently the confessing community of Jesus' disciples speaks with him to those with whom Nicodemus is aligned, the synagogue (perhaps a synagogue including members well disposed toward Jesus). Jesus' question to Nicodemus (v. 12) is proverbial and highlights the latter's ignorance. The key to the heavenly things, which Nicodemus and company do not know, is knowledge of Jesus, particularly where he is from and where he is going. Thus, in v. 13 Jesus speaks enigmatically of the ascent and descent of the Son of man, to and from heaven. Ascents to God were claimed for other personages of Judaism (e.g., Enoch, Elijah, Moses). This statement denies all such ascents to God except Jesus', and Jesus can uniquely claim to have descended from God (heaven). While Judaism could easily speak of men sent from God (1:6; 3:2) and knew of ascents to God, the claim to have descended from him was another matter. Precisely that, however, is said of Jesus.

Mention of the Son of man (v. 13) sets the stage for the further exposition of Jesus' work. Although the reference to Moses' act (vv. 14–15; cf. Num. 21:8–9) is entirely appropriate in a discussion with a teacher of Israel, from this point on Nicodemus is actually no longer in the picture; nor does Jesus seem to be the speaker. John 3:11–13 forms a bridge from their conversation into a confessional statement of the Johannine Christian community. The unmistakable reference to the crucifixion of Jesus is still, however, veiled behind the reference to Moses, whose deed is taken to be a type of Jesus'. As Moses' act saved the people from death by serpent bite, so Jesus' crucifixion saves his people from death and opens the door to eternal life.

John speaks less enigmatically in 3:16, a statement in which the gospel message is encapsulated. Here, as in v. 15, life is made contingent on faith and believing. The giving or sending of the Son is the expression of God's saving purpose; he does not intend to judge or condemn (v. 17; the same Greek verb, *krinein*, could have either meaning). The statement about the one who believes (v. 18) is straightforward and presents no problem. The one who does not believe, however, is curiously described in the Greek perfect tense as judged already (→Judgment, Day of). The Evangelist here contemplates the fact of unbelief, rejection. Such rejection is judgment for the unbeliever (v. 19) and is explained in terms of a light-darkness dualism reminiscent of the prologue (esp. vv. 5, 9). An explanation of why some avoid the light while others come to it is then given (vv. 20–21); it could mean that Jesus as light only confirms a preference for light or darkness, depending on people's previous disposition and conduct.

Faith in Jesus would then be morally predetermined. John seeks, however, to find terms adequate to explain the phenomenon of rejection and the consequent alienation of communities (church and synagogue) in which he lives or has lived. Only in such a confrontation and decision for or against Jesus may the true character of one's past, as well as the direction for the future, be seen.

3:22–36
The Second Appearance of the Baptist

3:22–24, Jesus and John Baptizing. Since Jesus is already in Jerusalem, v. 22 must mean he went into the Judean countryside. Only in John is Jesus said to have baptized (cf. 3:26; 4:1–2). Aenon (3:23) may be a derivative from a Semitic word meaning "spring." There were at least a couple of localities known as Salim, one about three miles east of biblical Shechem, the other farther north, a few miles south of Scythopolis (biblical Beth-shan). We learn also that John had not yet been arrested (v. 24; cf. Mark 1:14). This statement seems to reflect some knowledge of the synoptic account of Jesus' ministry, whether on the part of the author or a very early editor.

3:25–30, John the Baptist's Witness to Jesus. The introduction (v. 25) does not lead smoothly into the question of v. 26 but seems superfluous. One would have anticipated a dispute with disciples of Jesus if not with Jesus himself. Obviously, v. 26 refers to the opening scene (1:28). John himself is unperturbed that Jesus' baptism is attracting multitudes (3:27) and continues to bear witness to Jesus, referring to his own previous witness (v. 28; cf. 1:20, 23). The friend of the bridegroom (cf. our "best man") is obviously John the Baptist, who knows his own role in relation to Jesus' (3:29–30). He remains a faithful witness even in the face of a challenge from his own disciples. The fulfillment of joy is a mark of Jesus' eternal fellowship with his followers (15:11; 16:24; 17:13). The significance of this short episode now becomes clear: John testifies again to Jesus.

3:31–36, The Superiority of the Son. This paragraph in 3:31–36 follows logically but there is again a question about who is speaking (cf. 3:16–21). John here apparently refers to himself in the third person (v. 31b). Although there is no explicit indication of a change of speakers, vv. 31–36 (like vv. 16–21) may be understood as a kind of comment of the Evangelist upon the episode that has preceded.

The contrast (v. 31) is apparently between the Baptist and Jesus (cf. Matt. 11:11). That the witness and word of Jesus (John 3:32–34) are grounded in the Father's love (v. 35) is a way of expressing God's closeness (1:18) and unity (10:30) with Jesus. The Spirit is given by God to Jesus without measure, i.e., without limit or restriction (3:34). His giving him "all things" (v. 35) means that the Father's revelation of himself is accomplished wholly in Jesus the Son. That John the Baptist speaks of no one receiving Jesus' testimony (v. 32) and a moment later of those who do receive it (v. 36) is typical (cf. 1:10–11; 1:12–13). "God" and "Father" can be used interchangeably. Because Jesus is so frequently referred to as "Son," God is often called "Father." The Father-Son relationship symbolizes and expresses the Johannine concept of revelation. That God's revelation and salvation are now vested wholly in the Son is confirmed by the either-or alternative set out in 3:36. Belief in the Son means eternal life already. Disobedience (i.e., refusing to believe) cuts one off from life and, instead, incurs God's wrath (v. 36).

4:1–42
Jesus and the Woman of Samaria

4:1–6, Jesus at Jacob's Well. The opening sentence clearly refers to the situation described in 3:22–30 and notes Jesus' return to Galilee, a journey accomplished by going through Samaria (v. 4; → Samaria, District of). John agrees with Luke (9:52; 10:29–37; 17:11–19) in showing Jesus having contact with Samaria and the Samaritans. In neither Gospel do Samaritans fare badly. Probably Sychar (John 4:5) was at or near biblical Shechem, directly north of Jerusalem in Samaria. By Hebrew time reckoning, the sixth hour would be noon; at midday Jesus would be weary from walking. This is one of the relatively few places in John's Gospel where Jesus is allowed to show normal human frailty (cf. 11:35).

4:7–15, The Conversation. Jesus' request of the woman of Samaria is not surprising by modern standards, given the setting (v. 6), but the woman's surprise is understandable (v. 9; → Samaritans). There is, of course, no way the woman could have known the particular identity of Jesus as the bringer of salvation (v. 10). The "living water" is also running water; John typically plays upon a double meaning in Greek that cannot be duplicated in English. Jesus means salvific "living water"; the woman thinks he is speaking of ordinary "running water" in the well (cf. 3:3–4). That Jesus may be a special personage, however, is suggested by her question (4:12), which in Greek expects a negative answer: Jesus could not be greater than Jacob. Of course, Jesus is greater. Jesus now gives a more straightforward answer (vv. 13–14), revealing that the water he gives is of a radically different sort. The woman begins to understand but is apparently still thinking of the quenching of this-worldly thirst (v. 15).

The conversation embodies the typical Johannine misunderstanding in which Jesus speaks with full and authoritative knowledge (fundamentally, knowledge of who he is), while the interlocutor responds in a natural, normal but uninformed way. Even Jesus' disciples, although they are said to believe, do not fully comprehend him during his lifetime (cf. 4:32–34).

4:16–26, Jesus Reveals Himself. Jesus suddenly turns the conversation in an unexpected direction (4:16–18). His command, the woman's answer, and Jesus' rejoinder culminate in a startling revelation about herself, which she can only acknowledge as true (v. 19). Understandably, she takes Jesus to be a prophet. Her question reflects the ancient dispute and tension between Jews and Samaritans (v. 20). "This mountain" is Mount Gerizim, where the Samaritan temple had been located until its destruction by John Hyrcanus (128 B.C.). Samaritan worship, however, continued there. The question allows Jesus to contrast the old false worship, whether Jewish or Samaritan, with the new (vv. 21, 23). Worship in spirit and truth (vv. 23, 24) means, in effect, Christian worship of the God who reveals himself in Jesus, who is the truth and sends the Spirit upon his disciples after his death. Thus Jesus alludes to the hour of his death and exaltation (cf. 12:23). (There may also be a contrast with sacrificial worship.) That "the hour is coming and now is" probably means that the hour is future from the standpoint of Jesus' ministry and present to the Johannine church and readers of the Gospel.

The statement of 4:22 seems to endorse Jewish worship over Samaritan just at the point at which both are being declared no longer relevant. That salvation is from (or "of") the Jews is, at the least, an unexpected assertion in the Fourth Gospel. Because in this Gospel Samaritans are viewed more favorably than Jews, it is all the more difficult to understand why such a statement is made. Nevertheless, from the perspective of the Gospel it is correct in that Jesus is a Jew (v. 9) and represents Jewish messianic hope (1:45) rather than the Samaritan.

The woman's response to Jesus (4:25) seems to reflect Jewish messianic expectations. But perhaps she refers not to the Davidic Messiah but to a prophet like Moses (cf. Deut. 18:15–22). The Samaritans viewed themselves as the heirs of the Northern Kingdom of Israel, in which the royal line was not descended from David. Jesus replies to her by identifying and revealing himself, using the formula *ego eimi* (Gk., "It is I" or "I am"), which is characteristic of the Gospel of John (cf. 8:12). This self-revelation brings the

scene with the woman to an end, but the episode continues (→ Messiah).

4:27–30, The Woman Witnesses to the Samaritans. The disciples now return and are amazed because by conventional standards conversation between a man, much less a rabbi, and a woman was unusual. The woman, leaving her water jar (v. 28), bears witness to her people, making clear her grounds for thinking Jesus may be the Christ (v. 29). Because of her testimony, the people of the city (cf. v. 5) now come to see Jesus, but while they are on the way his disciples return to the center of the stage.

4:31–38, Jesus' Conversation with His Disciples. Jesus' disciples' entreaty (v. 31), his response, and their puzzlement (vv. 32–33) form what has become a familiar pattern (cf. 4:7–15); now Jesus' own disciples find his words a riddle and misunderstand in terms of everyday possibilities or circumstances. Jesus solves the riddle by revealing the secret of his symbolic language (v. 34): the God-given mission that is his source and sustenance. There follows a series of sayings that have as their theme, or common denominator, the harvest (vv. 35–38). Although their precise relation to the preceding conversation is not obvious, two factors help explain them. First, Jesus' own mission is, in John's thought, closely linked to his disciples' (cf. 20:21). Second, this connection now finds expression through apparently traditional sayings whose referents are no longer clear (4:35 may echo Matt. 9:37; Luke 10:2). That the harvest is not in the future, but now, is typical of John, for whom God's salvation is present in Jesus. The identification of the sower and reaper (John 4:36–37) is a problem. If they represent Jesus and the disciples, as might seem obvious, the "others" (v. 38; plural) is difficult to understand.

The passage can be fruitfully read in light of Acts 8:4–25, where Philip, who was not one of the Twelve, first preaches the gospel in Samaria. Only later do the apostles Peter and John confirm his work. If in John 4:35–38 Jesus is addressing his disciples and speaks of others who labored before them (v. 38), he may envision a similar situation.

4:39–42, The Samaritans' Belief. The Samaritans now return to the center of the narrative. Although the testimony of the woman brought many to faith (v. 39), the presence and word of Jesus himself causes more to believe and makes her testimony superfluous. That Jesus preached and made large numbers of converts in Samaria is attested by no other Gospel and is unlikely. Probably this brief narrative also reflects the mission of the early, Johannine Christians, who preached the gospel in Samaria. In John's view, firsthand experience of Jesus (vv.

40–42) is not limited to his earthly or historical presence (see 14:23; 20:29) but is fully available only after his death and exaltation. Such experiential knowledge enables one to hail him as "Savior of the world," a title used of Roman emperors.

4:43–54
The Healing of an Official's Son

4:43–46, Jesus' Return to Galilee. Jesus is still headed for Galilee (cf. 4:3) and now resumes his journey. "Two days" (v. 43) is stereotypical for a short period (cf. 4:40; 2:1). The famous saying of 4:44 is found also in the synoptic Gospels (Matt. 13:57; Mark 6:4; Luke 4:24), where it applies to Galilee or Nazareth itself (Luke 4:24); here it seems to apply to Judea. In Galilee, Jesus is welcomed according to John, although for this Gospel not Galilee but Jerusalem is the center of his activity.

4:46–54, The Healing. The reference to the earlier wine miracle of Cana (v. 46) is typical of John. The official and his mortally ill son are in Capernaum, some miles away, so that to see Jesus he must leave his son and go to Cana. In Matt. 8:5–13 and Luke 7:1–10 (Q source?) there is a story, set in Capernaum, of a Roman centurion whose servant or slave is ill. The Johannine story seems to be a variant of it, although in addition to the other differences the Q version takes place entirely in Capernaum (→ Q).

When the official approaches Jesus, he responds with what seems a negative statement (John 4:48; Mark 8:11–12), although in John's Gospel belief frequently follows upon the seeing of signs. Nevertheless the official continues to urge Jesus (John 4:49), who responds with a command that promises healing, and the official believes what Jesus has said (v. 50). The healing of the son, as it turns out, occurred just when Jesus spoke (vv. 51–53). Upon discovering this, the man (with his household) again believes, by which is now clearly meant he comes to faith in Jesus. Thus, perhaps ironically, Jesus' statement of v. 48 is fulfilled. (In the Q version, however, faith precedes the healing of the sick servant.)

5:1–47
Healing at Bethzatha and Discussion

5:1–9, The Healing. Jesus now goes up to Jerusalem to an unspecified feast. "Of the Jews" (v. 1) is superfluous except that it once again sets Jesus over against Judaism. Since Passover is anticipated in 6:4, this is presumably not a Passover feast (→ Feasts, Festivals, and Fasts).

The pool described here is probably the one unearthed by archaeologists near the Church of St. Anne north of the Temple area. The name Bethzatha (RSV) may be derived from the northern suburb of the city in which the pool was located. (Other, less likely names such as Bethesda and Bethsaida appear in some manuscripts.) The pool was, in ancient times, a kind of spa where healings were thought to take place (v. 3). Descriptions of the duration of illness are often found in healing stories (v. 5; cf. Mark 5:25); there is perhaps no symbolic significance in the number thirty-eight (but cf. Deut. 2:14). That the Johannine Jesus knows the man's condition without asking (John 5:6) is typical (cf. 1:48; 4:17–18), as is his taking or maintaining the initiative (2:4–5; 9:5–7). The man's problem in getting into the pool in time (5:7) was explained by the addition of v. 4 in early manuscripts. Typically, Jesus does not deal with that problem at all but gives a sharp command (v. 8; cf. Mark 2:9, 11). The man's healing is obviously the result of Jesus' word (cf. John 4:46–54), not of the healed person's faith (cf. Mark 5:34). Almost as an afterthought, we are told (John 5:9b) that the healing took place on a Sabbath, a common feature of Gospel healing stories (cf. 9:14; Mark 3:2) and a crucial fact in the following discussion.

5:10–18, The Persecution of Jesus. Significantly, the Jews do not question Jesus but the man healed (cf. chap. 9). When the man is accused of violating the Sabbath (v. 10), he points to the one who has healed him. But when questioned, he proves to be ignorant of Jesus, who has now withdrawn (v. 13; cf. the healed man in chap. 9). Jesus, once more taking the initiative, accosts him with a warning (5:14). The man's illness is not said to have resulted from his sin, and such a viewpoint seems to be explicitly denied in 9:2–3 (cf. Luke 13:2–3), but his destiny is still undecided (cf. John 9:38). If he then turns informer against Jesus (5:15), the latter's warning has apparently been rejected. He does, and Jesus himself is now persecuted for breaking the Sabbath (v. 16). Jesus gives his reason for working on the Sabbath in a somewhat veiled statement that seems to liken his own working to God's (v. 17). The response of the Jews is immediate and life threatening, for they take his statement to imply his equality with God. Such an offense goes far beyond Sabbath breaking, itself a capital crime (Exod. 31:14; 35:2), whether or not the Jews at this period could execute lawbreakers (cf. John 18:31). Obviously the crime of which Jesus is accused (5:18) impugns the Deity and flies in the face of Jewish monotheism; it is blasphemy (cf. Mark 14:63–64). The narrative has moved quickly from the healing of an ill man to this extreme antinomy and conflict between Jesus and the Jews, and this mortal threat to Jesus is related directly to claims made by, or for, him. The portrayal is doubtless influenced by the situation of the Johannine community (see "Introduction: The Setting and Composition of the Gospel" above).

5:19-24, The Father and Son. The basic theme of this section is the relationship of the Father and the Son as expressed in their life-giving work. Although John describes Jesus and his mission in the most exalted terms—the Father withholds nothing from the Son (vv. 19-20) —he emphasizes that the Son's authority derives wholly from the Father. The love that begins with God's revelation to and through the Son ends with the disciples' love for one another (13:34-35). The distinctive life-giving work of the Father is also accomplished by the Son, to whom judgment is wholly delegated (5:21-22). Resurrection and judgment, the hallmarks of the end of the age (i.e., eschatology), are thus the work of the Son. Those who (truly) hear the Son and believe God avoid judgment completely (cf. 3:18) and come immediately into eternal life (5:24). To reject the Son, Jesus, is to reject God (v. 23).

5:25-29, The Raising of the Dead. The thought of the preceding section moved quite naturally from the Son's relationship to the Father to eschatological salvation, resurrection and life, for the Son carries through on earth the Father's life-giving and eschatological work. Now this theme receives further treatment. Verses 26-27 reiterate vv. 21 and 22, but in v. 25 a new idea has been introduced. Clearly in v. 24 eternal life is a present possibility and possession, not something one can obtain only after death. If in v. 25 "the dead" means the spiritually dead (as in 9:39 "blind" means spiritually blind), the idea is the same as in 5:24. The phrase "is coming and now is" refers to the perspective of Jesus and that of the postresurrection church (cf. 4:23), which are here juxtaposed. In 5:28-29, however, the dead can hardly be other than the physically dead. The fact that their resurrection is anticipated ("is coming") but not present would seem to confirm this. The description of resurrection of life and judgment (v. 29) is reminiscent of Dan. 12:2. But such a distinction between those raised stands in tension with John 5:21-25, where resurrection is equated with eternal life and a resurrection of judgment would be a contradiction in terms. Verses 28-29 apparently embody a more primitive eschatology, whether the result of the evangelist's use of traditional material or of later editorial work. John brings together traditions and perspectives that are not consistent with one another (→ Eschatology; Resurrection).

5:30-47, The Testimony to Jesus. At v. 30 Jesus reiterates his relation to the Father (cf.

5:19, 26-27), for the first time introducing the category of will. The move to the theme of witness or testimony (5:31-40) follows logically. Jesus makes no claim for himself and does not testify to himself. Of course, the one who bears witness to Jesus is ultimately God (v. 32; cf. v. 37). But first Jesus mentions another witness, John the Baptist. The "you sent to John" (v. 33) equates the hearers with the Jews mentioned in 1:19, who evoke John's earlier witness. Jesus, while acknowledging John's positive importance, nevertheless puts distance between himself and his predecessor (5:34-36; cf. 3:30, 31-36). The testimony or witness of Jesus' works (5:36) naturally includes his signs but also his words and other actions. They are given Jesus by the Father as a mission to accomplish, and their accomplishment is a witness, even if his opponents do not recognize their origin.

How the Father bears witness (v. 37) is not said explicitly, but, as we have noted, Jesus' works are given him by the Father and are an aspect of his witness. The same could be said of John, a man sent from God (1:6). That Jesus' Jewish opponents had not seen God's form is perhaps a commonplace (cf. 1:18), although the claim that they had not heard his voice or had his word abiding in them (5:38) would have evoked their strong resistance. That such failure should result from their not believing Jesus adds insult to injury. Even the witness of Scripture cannot be heard unless these writings are acknowledged to bear witness to Jesus (v. 39), but the fact that they bear witness to Jesus can only be perceived in the moment one comes to Jesus (v. 40). Thus everything depends on believing or believing in Jesus.

Jesus' not receiving glory from men (v. 41) is typical of the Fourth Gospel. The succeeding statement (v. 42), while also characteristic of John's polemic, does not quite follow. Apparently it states the grounds for the opponents' rejection of Jesus and their receiving glory from one another (v. 44), although this is not made explicit here. The opponents' obduracy is then summed up (v. 43). Who is meant by "another" is unimportant. In fact, there is probably no specific referent, for Jesus here characterizes his opponents. The polemic continues in v. 44 (cf. vv. 41-42).

Finally Jesus returns to Moses, who witnesses through Scripture (cf. v. 39; 1:45) and becomes the accuser of his opponents, the Jews who think of themselves as his disciples (cf. 9:28). Belief in Jesus would follow from really believing Moses (5:46), as v. 47 reiterates. John is doubtless convinced of this; of course, the statement of vv. 46-47 reflect the beliefs of Christians. A Jew would scarcely find such clear testimony to Jesus in Scripture. There is little in the other Gospels or in early Christian literature or tradition to indicate that such issues characterized Jesus' historical ministry. The text reflects later controversies about Jesus' identity and role. In John's view, there is no neutral ground from which one may decide about Jesus, but decide one must. Such a crisis of decision is the counterpart of the Johannine dualism in which important issues are cast in terms of extreme alternatives.

6:1–71
The Feeding of Five Thousand and the Bread Discourse

Chap. 6 is a distinct literary unit, beginning with a new setting and ending with the climactic confession of Peter. Obviously, a new episode begins in chap. 7. While identifiable traditional units underlie the various narratives (e.g., the feeding of the multitude, Jesus' walking on the sea), the chapter centers on the theme of the bread that Jesus gives his disciples to eat.

6:1–15, The Feeding. Verse 1 presupposes that Jesus is in Galilee, whereas he has just previously been in Jerusalem with no indication that he was leaving. Consequently, it has been suggested that chap. 6 once stood before chap. 5, since at the end of chap. 4 Jesus is in Galilee, but no extant manuscript of the Gospel attests this order. We treat the chapters as they now stand.

The feeding of a multitude is recounted in all the synoptic Gospels (Matt. 14:13–21; Mark 6:32–44; Luke 9:10–17; cf. Mark 8:1–10; Matt. 15:32–39). It is the first in a series of events in John that has synoptic, especially Marcan, parallels in the same sequence: the feeding; Jesus' walking on the water (Mark 6:45–51; Matt. 14:22–27); a question about signs (John 6:30; Mark 8:11); a discourse on bread (John 6:31–58; cf. Mark 8:14–21; Matt. 16:5–12); Peter's confession of who Jesus is (John 6:66–71; Mark 8:27–30 and parallels). If John is not following Mark or Matthew (significant portions are missing in Luke), he knows common traditions already arranged in the same order.

As in Mark, the feeding narrative begins with Jesus' crossing the sea and the gathering of a throng (John 6:1–2). In John, only Jesus initially withdraws to a mountain (v. 3) to which he later returns (v. 15). Presumably, the feeding took place near the shore, as in the Synoptics (cf. John 6:23). John's account, although similar to the other Gospels', has distinctive features, e.g., the crowd has seen Jesus' signs (v. 2); the Passover is at hand (v. 4); Philip intercedes for the people (vv. 5–7); a young boy is the source of the loaves and fish (vv. 8–9). The account of the distribution and eating of the bread comes closest to the other Gospels, perhaps because early Christian eucharistic practice has shaped the narratives.

Accordingly, only pieces of bread are gathered after the meal (v. 13). Remarkably, all the other Gospels agree on the numbers: five thousand men, two hundred denarii worth of bread, five loaves, two fish, twelve baskets of fragments.

The reaction of the people (v. 14) is unique to John and is based on Jesus' sign (2:11, 23; 3:2; 4:19, 29, 45, 48, 53–54). He is hailed as the prophet, a typical reaction to his God-given signs (cf. 3:2). The prophet in question is in all probability the prophet like Moses predicted in Deut. 18:15–22. (Moses worked signs and wonders before Pharaoh, and through his leadership God exercised miraculous care for Israel during the Exodus from Egypt.) The perception attributed to Jesus that they were about to come and make him king (John 6:15) bespeaks a linkage between prophet and king in John's thought. The concept of messiahship in John has significant connections with prophetic, Mosaic traditions. That Jesus takes up and surpasses the work of Moses becomes a theme of the great discourse of 6:31–58.

6:16–24, Jesus' Walking on the Sea. In Matthew and Mark, as in John, Jesus' feeding of five thousand men is followed immediately by a tale of his coming to his disciples, walking across the water. But John has the disciples going from Transjordan back toward Capernaum (v. 17; cf. v. 1), the opposite direction from the Synoptics. In all of the accounts, the disciples' boat encounters strong winds, the sudden appearance of Jesus walking across the water frightens the disciples, and Jesus calms their fears, saying, "It is I" (Gk. *ego eimi*, which can also be translated "I am"; cf. vv. 41, 48, 51). In Mark and Matthew, the wind ceases when Jesus gets into the boat. In John, nothing more is said of it, but instead the immediate arrival of the boat at its destination is noted.

The awkward transitional episode (vv. 22–24) has no synoptic parallel. The people note the absence of Jesus, the one boat, and the disciples (vv. 22, 24) and correctly infer that Jesus has gone to Capernaum (vv. 24–25), although he did not embark with the disciples (v. 22). (Thus the miraculous character of Jesus' crossing is attested.) Readers are also informed of the arrival of the people who had been fed (v. 26) on the other side of the sea (v. 25). Evidently, according to the tradition John knew, the feeding took place on the eastern side of the Sea of Galilee (contrary to the Synoptics) but the discourse in Capernaum (v. 59), the center of so much of Jesus' activity according to the synoptic Gospels.

6:25–34, Bread from Heaven. With Jesus, the disciples, and the people back on the western shore of the Sea of Galilee, a long dialogue between Jesus and several groups of interlocutors now begins (6:25–59). This section sets the scene and poses the terms of the ensuing discussion and debate. Jesus typically ignores the people's question (vv. 25–26) and speaks rather to their seeking him in the first place (v. 24), revealing their deeper motivation. Jesus' injunction (v. 27) seems to presuppose that seeing signs, not eating and being filled, is a proper grounds for seeking him. The loaves they have eaten are apparently the food that perishes. Even their seeing the sign and response (vv. 14–15) must not represent the level of acceptance that Jesus requires. But Jesus holds out the possibility of their attaining a more appropriate access (v. 27). The Son of man is of course Jesus, whom God endorses as his messenger. Jesus has enjoined his hearers to labor or work (v. 27), and so their question (v. 28) is appropriate. His answer is direct and to the point (v. 29). John here adopts the terms of the great debate between Paul and his Jewish Christian opponents, faith and works, but, instead of replacing works by faith, interprets true work as faith. The people then show that they are prepared to understand that the one whom God has sent is Jesus himself, if he meets their expectations (v. 30). Their question seems to ignore the sign they have just witnessed, but it serves to indicate that what Jesus has done is not enough and to open up the necessity for further explanation of his feeding work. As a literary device it is typical of the Gospel of John.

Without waiting for Jesus' answer, the people refer to their fathers' eating the miraculous manna (Exod. 16) and quote Scripture (John 6:31). The citation is an inexact reflection of several OT passages: Exod. 16:4, 15; Num. 11:8; Neh. 9:15; Ps. 78:24; and Ps. 105:40. Nevertheless, it conveys a biblical authority that all parties to the discussion will honor. Jesus, however, offers an interpretation that differs from what he attributes to them, although they have not yet voiced it: not Moses gave, but my Father gives the bread (John 6:32). All would have agreed that it came ultimately from God, but by calling God "my Father" Jesus suggests a special role for himself in conveying that bread, while seeming to differentiate the true bread from heaven from the wilderness manna. Then Jesus subtly identifies himself with that true bread from heaven (v. 33). Thus the hearers ingenuously ask for this bread (v. 34) as the Samaritan woman asked for an unending supply of water (4:15). (The descent of the bread from heaven of course reflects the Exodus tradition that is clearly cited but may also be related to the biblical concept of the descent of wisdom, whose relationship to the Christology of the prologue has already been noted.)

6:35–51, Jesus the Bread of Life. In light of their misunderstanding (v. 34), Jesus identifies himself openly as the bread of life (v. 35) but anticipates their rejection of him (v. 36). He is obviously casting his hearers in the role of unbelieving Jews. Not surprisingly, the people who next speak are called "the Jews" (v. 41). There follows now a series of statements by Jesus (vv. 37–40) concerning his relationship to the Father and his life-giving work (cf. 3:16–21, 31–36; 5:19–24). The sure salvation of the believer is grounded in the will and gift of God, as effected in the work of Jesus, the Son.

The "murmuring" of the Jews (6:41) echoes the murmuring motif of the Exodus tradition (cf. Exod. 16:2, 8), which is the background of this entire discussion. The statement attributed to Jesus by the Jews is not an exact quotation but takes up the themes of John 6:33 and 35. Their identification of Jesus' parentage (v. 42) recalls Philip's statement to Nathanael in 1:45 (cf. Matt. 13:55; Mark 6:3). The Jews typically betray their failure to understand by attempting to explain Jesus by reference to his earthly origins (cf. John 7:40–44). Jesus' coming from God is itself the miracle. Jesus admonishes the Jews not to murmur (6:43) and explains the grounds of their unbelief (v. 44). His statements about resurrection at the last day (a familiar motif of Jewish and early Christian eschatology) recur throughout this section (vv. 39, 44, 54), reminding readers of the eschatological warrant of the truth of his words. Isaiah (54:13) is invoked as testimony that those who have actually heard the Father come to Jesus—another appeal to biblical authority (John 6:45). That no one has seen God (v. 46) is a recurring emphasis of John (cf. 1:18).

Eternal life as the consequence of belief or faith in Jesus is the central and recurring theme of the Gospel (6:47). In v. 48 we again encounter a typical Johannine "I am" (Gk. ego eimi) saying. Jesus' subsequent statements (vv. 49–51) reiterate the message of the Gospel with specific reference to the OT "text" (v. 31) and draw further implications (on v. 48, see v. 35; on v. 49, see vv. 33, 35–40). The contrast between eating the manna and eating the living and true bread is one of death and life. Finally, the life-giving bread from heaven is said to be the flesh of Jesus (v. 51). Thus the bread is now given a specific, historical, and individual identity, and this identity sets the conversation on a new track (vv. 52–58).

6:52–59, Bread and Flesh. Most of the previous discussion has dealt with the theme "bread from heaven," which is the first part of the Scripture quotation of v. 31. The latter part ("to eat") already came into view in vv. 50–51, but now the theme of eating is emphasized and explained. The question of the Jews (v. 52) leads to unequivocal assertions about the importance of eating the flesh and drinking the blood of the Son of man (vv. 53–54).

Already in 6:51 the giving of Jesus' flesh alludes to his death; in 6:52–58 that death is presupposed. Otherwise, the eating of his flesh and the drinking of his blood is unthinkable. Such a thought would in any event be abhorrent to the Jew. It becomes intelligible, however, on the basis of certain theological premises. From the death of Jesus, salvation flows (cf. 1 Cor. 15:3), and the bloodiness of his death by crucifixion suggests the inauguration of a new convenant through his sacrifice. Many interpreters see in this entire section a clear reference to the Eucharist, the sacramental meal (cf. 1 Cor. 11:23–26; Mark 14:22–25 and parallels). That John speaks of "flesh" rather than "body" sets him apart from the Synoptics and Paul; significantly he thereby takes up OT imagery ("flesh" and "blood"). Because of the richness of the sacramental allusions it is perhaps all the more puzzling that John nowhere recounts, but seems to presuppose, Jesus' institution of the Eucharist. Assuming the Eucharist is in view, participation in it, like baptism, would constitute a clear confession of faith in Jesus, a break with the synagogue, and adherence to the new community of Jesus' disciples. The rituals of worship become the dividing line between Jewish and Christian communities, as it has continued to be ever since. The notation of the geographical setting (John 6:59) brings the discourse to an end, although the following scenes obviously constitute its aftermath.

6:60–71, Further Discussion and Peter's Confession. The reaction of many disciples is understandable (v. 60), as is the subsequent withdrawal of some (v. 66). Jesus' knowledge of their thoughts is characteristic (v. 61). The apparent grounds for greater offense, the ascent of Jesus to the Father (v. 62), has, by the writing of this Gospel, already occurred (20:17).

Jesus' statement about the life-giving role of Spirit as contrasted with the flesh (6:63) constitutes a puzzle. In discounting the importance of the flesh, Jesus seems in effect to be taking back what he said in vv. 52–58 about the necessity of eating and drinking his flesh and blood. Given the conviction of the Evangelist and his community that the ascended Jesus had sent the Spirit (20:22; cf. 14:16–17), he could hardly have Jesus omit the cruciality of the Spirit's role. As it stands, however, there is a tension, perhaps best resolved by understanding that "flesh" in 6:63 has the OT sense of mortality (in contrast to the Spirit of God) and not the specific sense it acquired in vv. 53–58 in combination with "blood" (→ Flesh and Spirit). Perhaps not surprisingly, Jesus' word leads to the defection of some, which he fully foresaw (vv. 64, 65).

The withdrawal of "many" disciples (v. 66) may reflect the fact that the Gospel of John is the product of a severe conflict situation. The Twelve, however, remain faithful. In response to Jesus' question (v. 67), Peter speaks (v. 68). His role is reminiscent of, but his words unaccountably unlike, the confession in Mark 8:29 and parallels. Jesus here asks a different question, and Peter's response is initially a counterquestion. Eternal life, belief, and knowledge, all missing from the synoptic version, are concepts typical of John, but the title "Holy One of God" is strange (cf. Mark 1:24). John's version is scarcely intelligible as a rewriting of the Synoptics. The concluding reference to Judas (John 6:70–71; cf. 64) refutes any hint that Jesus has been deceived by one of his own disciples. Any such disparagement is countered by his own revelation of the satanic character of the one who was to betray him (cf. 13:2, 21–30).

7:1–52
Jesus at the Feast of Tabernacles

Chap. 7 is another discrete literary unit, with a clear beginning point at 7:1 where the locus of Jesus' activity is discussed. The episode reaches a culmination with the reappearance of Nicodemus and the official rejection of Jesus in Jerusalem. Unlike chap. 6, chap. 7 has few points of contact with the Synoptics. There is an obvious break between 7:52 and 8:12 into which the story of an adulterous woman has been inserted in later manuscripts. Chap. 7 is a carefully constructed narrative containing dialogue, but there is only a minimum of narrative framework in chap. 8.

7:1–13, Jesus' Journey to Jerusalem. The deadly intent of the Jews, first mentioned in 5:18, leads Jesus to avoid Judea, presumably because his hour has not yet arrived (cf. 2:4). Tabernacles (v. 2) is the third of the great canonical feasts, the harvest feast in early autumn (cf. 6:4; Passover falls in spring). Jesus' brothers now appear (cf. 2:12; Mark 3:31) to urge him on to Jerusalem. That Jesus had disciples there is a Johannine idea (cf. John 18:15); in the Synoptics Jesus' disciples are all Galileans. The works the brothers have in mind (7:3–4) presumably include signs. The brothers, by implying that open demonstration or proof is needed (v. 4), acknowledge they do not believe in him (v. 5). Jesus' response to them is very much like his response to his mother (2:4), for he does not move in reaction to any human initiative but only at God's command (7:8–9). As if to underscore the point, no sooner are his brothers out of the way than Jesus goes up to Jerusalem (v. 10).

The Jews who are there seeking Jesus (v. 11) are apparently hostile and to be distinguished from the crowds of people who are divided but for fear of the Jews keep quiet (vv. 12–13; on the motif of the fear of the Jews see 9:22; 12:42; cf. 20:19). The accusation that Jesus is a deceiver, leading the people astray, represents the official view of the Jewish leaders.

7:14–31, Jesus' Discourses at the Feast and Crowd Reaction.

The marveling of the Jews (v. 15) at Jesus' teaching in the Temple (cf. Mark 14:49) is based on what they know of his background; here again is the characteristic attempt to explain Jesus on the basis of inadequate knowledge of his origin (cf. John 1:46; 6:42). Jesus immediately sets matters straight (7:16). That Jesus' will is in complete harmony with God's has already been stated (6:38); now the very recognition of this fact is said to depend upon the intention to do God's will. As Jesus' unity with God is a unity of will, unity with Jesus depends on a similar unity with God's will. Jesus implicitly contrasts himself with the (unidentified) charlatan who seeks his own glory (7:18; cf. 5:43), claiming nothing for himself except that he seeks the glory of the one true God, i.e., to do his will and work.

The mention of the law of Moses (7:19) states an issue for the remainder of the chapter: who is obedient to the law? The response of the people (lit., "crowd") to Jesus' ominous question (cf. 5:18; 7:1) seems on the surface quite normal (v. 20), but as John never tires of reiterating, superficial understanding misses the point. Jesus' rejoinder (vv. 21–24) refers to the healing of 5:1–9. He then demonstrates his knowledge of the law (7:22), arguing that if circumcision is permitted on the Sabbath, making a man's whole body well ought to be permissible also (v. 23). (The fathers in v. 22 are Abraham, Isaac, and Jacob; Jesus corrects himself by indicating that circumcision is antecedent to Moses.) Thus his injunction of v. 24 does not presuppose or ask more than that the prevailing standards should be correctly applied. Jesus submits his case to the law of Moses in order that he may be proven innocent by its best standards of interpretation (cf. 7:50–51). Of course, John does not believe that Jesus is finally subordinate to Moses (cf. 5:39–47).

The Jerusalemites (7:25; cf. v. 12) are distinguishable from the Jews; their questions initially express only wonderment (v. 25) and openness to Jesus (v. 26). But finally their conclusion is negative; their statement (v. 27) corresponds to one strain of expectation according to which the Messiah would emerge out of obscurity. Again, consideration of Jesus' origins leads to erroneously negative conclusions about his role. Typically, Jesus responds with an assertion of his true origin and authority (vv. 28–29). The response to Jesus is an attempt to seize him (v. 30), which is untimely and therefore fails: Jesus' hour has not yet come. Still, many of the crowd (RSV, "people") believe because of Jesus' signs (v. 31).

7:32–52, The Official Response.

The crowd's apparent division is not shared by the officials (v. 32), however, who send out a search party to arrest Jesus. The chief priests, probably Sadducees, are allied with the Pharisees, an unlikely combination for Jesus' day (→Sadducees). The chief priests were Temple authorities then, but not the Pharisees, who came to dominance only after the Roman war (A.D. 70) when the Temple was gone. Jesus' enigmatic statement (vv. 33–34) refers to his coming death and exaltation to God. The Jews typically misunderstand (vv. 35–36) but in their misunderstanding nevertheless utter a profound truth (cf. 11:49–52). The death of Jesus will mean that his gospel will be taken to the Greeks of the Dispersion (cf. 12:20–23), that is, to the Jewish people scattered throughout the Mediterranean world. "Greeks" might mean any Gentiles (cf. Rom. 1:16), although here Greek-speaking Jews living outside the Holy Land may also be in view.

At the Feast of Tabernacles, daily libations of water were brought from the pool of Siloam (John 9:7, 11) near the foot of the Temple Mount. Possibly, when Jesus utters his pronouncement (7:37–38) on the last (seventh) day these water ceremonies are in view. His statement may be punctuated as in the RSV text or as in the RSV note; the original Greek manuscripts were without punctuation. The marginal rendering is less difficult. If it is followed, the statement of v. 38 applies to Jesus: out of his heart (Gk., "belly") the rivers of living water flow (cf. 19:34), not from the believer, as is otherwise the case. The source of the Scripture reference is unclear. The Evangelist comments (7:39) that Jesus' statement refers to the time after his crucifixion (glorification) when the Spirit, and thus the salvation given through him, would be received (cf. 16:7).

Typically, Jesus' words cause a division (7:40–43). Probably John sees Jesus as both prophet and Christ (see commentary above on 6:14–15), but the latter is the more generally acknowledged title. Those who affirm him as either are on the right track. Others challenge him on the basis of his origin (7:41b–42), for Jesus is known to come from Galilee (cf. 1:46), a supposition never contradicted in the Fourth Gospel (cf. Matt. 2:1–6; Luke 2:1–7). Jesus' earthly origins can neither discredit him nor authenticate him. Once again an attempt to seize or arrest Jesus aborts (John 7:44), presumably because his hour had not yet come.

The officers sent out to arrest (v. 32) Jesus now return, cognizant of what he has said (v. 46), and their evaluation is entirely accurate. The chief priests and Pharisees represent Jewish officialdom, but theirs is an unlikely combination. Probably the presence of the Pharisees is anachronistic and reflects the situation of Judaism in John's time (see "Introduction" above). Tellingly, only the Pharisees pose the questions in vv. 47–49. Their annoyance at their subordinates' failure to arrest Jesus is patent (v. 45), as is their impatience with these officers' awed reaction to him. The question about being led astray takes up the earlier negative opinion of Jesus (v. 12). The contemptuous description of the crowd (v. 49) may reflect learned opinion of the so-called people of the land, folk who may have been God-fearing but did not have opportunity or wherewithal to be scrupulously observant. As if to answer the question of the Pharisees (v. 48), out of the ranks of the scholars Nicodemus stands up to speak for Jesus and for a right judgment (7:24) under the law (vv. 50–51). Despite Nicodemus' standing (cf. 3:1, 10), he is derided, and his knowledge of Scripture impugned (7:52). Jesus cannot be a prophet (cf. v. 40) because he is from the wrong place.

The division over Jesus among the Jewish people falls more or less along the line between officialdom and general populace. Some of the latter may reject Jesus, but many credit him as a prophet, if not the Christ, while the leaders, particularly the Pharisees, reject his claims out of hand (cf. 12:42). He does not meet their standards. Increasingly, "Pharisees" and "Jews" will come to be used interchangeably.

7:53–8:11
The Woman Taken in Adultery

This famous story was not originally a part of the Gospel of John. The oldest manuscripts do not contain it; a few have it in other places, e.g., at the end of John or after Luke 21:38. Probably most stories of Jesus once circulated independently; this one did not find a place in John until after the Gospel was published.

8:12–59
Jesus the Light of the World: Claim and Controversy

As Jesus resumes speaking (v. 12), he now addresses the Pharisees (v. 13) or Jews (v. 22) and so, apparently, the hostile group who wanted him arrested (7:45). Although the narrative connection is not smooth, the general context of official hostility at the end of chap. 7 continues in chap. 8. This hostility is now directed to Jesus himself, who engages in vigorous and acrimonious debate with his adversaries. The debate manifests the tension between church and synagogue near the end of the first century.

8:12–20, The Light of the World. That Jesus is the light of the world has already been suggested by the prologue (1:4–5, 9). The form of Jesus' saying is, however, notable; it is an "I am" saying, typical of John (cf., e.g., 6:35; 10:7,11; 11:25). When Pharisees accuse Jesus of witnessing to himself (8:13; cf. 5:31), he insists on the truth of his testimony (v. 14), once more stating his role in terms of his origin and destiny, which his opponents repeatedly demonstrate they do not know. Jesus now stresses their ignorance, invoking their own law ("your law," 8:17) and maintaining that it vindicates his judgment, while theirs is purely human ("according to the flesh," v. 15). When Jesus calls upon the witness of his Father in accordance with the law's requirement of two witnesses, the Pharisees think that he means his earthly father. Of course, Jesus means God the Father, whom his opponents do not know.

8:21–30, Jesus' Departure. The next stage of the discussion begins with Jesus' assertion about his departure and concludes with the statement that many of his hearers believed in him (v. 30). Again the Jews misunderstand and, in asking whether he will kill himself unintentionally, inject a note of irony. Jesus will in fact die, but not as they will, in sin, that is, in unbelief (v. 24). Their unbelief is tantamount to their ignorance of Jesus' true origin, which is here contrasted with their own (v. 23). The contrast of above and below is characteristic of the dualism of John. Jesus' opponents do not know he speaks for God (v. 27). Jesus, however, points ahead to the possibility of their knowing his true identity when they have crucified him ("lifted up," v. 28), reiterating his own submission to the Father. Surprisingly, this series of exchanges seems to have a happy outcome, as many believe in him; but their belief will prove to be ephemeral.

8:31–38, The Jews Who Have Believed. There follows a discussion with Jews who have believed in him (v. 31) that quickly becomes acrimonious, as these believers fall into sharp dispute with Jesus, who soon imputes to them the intention to kill him (v. 37). The dispute becomes intelligible as the expression of extreme tension between the Johannine community and a group of Jesus' followers who wish to incorporate him into their already existing (Jewish) perspective. They deny that Jesus can invest them with a truth and give them a freedom they did not already possess in Abraham (vv. 32–33). (Such Jewish Christians survived well into the second century and beyond.) The basic question is whether or not salvation (freedom) is already given in sonship to Abraham or is available only through Christ. A similar dispute is found in Galatians 2:11–21, there cast in terms of faith (in Christ) and works (of the law). The sharp divergence of views, expressed now in terms of the Johannine dualism, is summed up in John 8:38, and from this point onward the debate concerns fatherhood.

8:39–47, Abraham's Children. The Jews continue the discussion by claiming Abraham as their father, and Jesus rejects the claim on the basis of their intent to kill him (v. 40). The Jews do not actually say they mean to kill Jesus, but their actions reveal their intentions (7:44; 8:59), despite protestations (7:20), and Jesus knows what they will do (7:19; 8:40, 44). By now there is no longer any distinction between Jews who believe and those who do not; the latter have absorbed the former.

The Jews' assertion that, as children of Abraham, they were not born of fornication (v. 41) introduces a factor not otherwise mentioned in the narrative and may suggest they think Jesus was born of fornication and is therefore discredited. Jesus' response is an absolute denial that the God who is his Father is theirs also (vv. 42–44). In a sharp display of Johannine dualism (cf. 8:23), Jesus charges that not God but the devil is their father, hence their murderous intent and malicious falsehood. The devil is the "father of lies" and stands in sharpest contrast to Jesus, who speaks (and is) the truth (v. 45). The contrast is only underscored by their attempt to convict Jesus of sin (v. 46). Their rejection of the truth is grounded in their origin, their alienation from God (v. 47).

8:48–59, Jesus Accused of Demon Possession. Although readers are prepared for the accusation that Jesus is a Samaritan (v. 48; cf. chap. 4), nothing in the Gospel suggests that Jesus is demon-possessed, a charge he flatly rejects (v. 49; but cf. Mark 3:22). In John, Jesus performs no exorcisms, perhaps because the Evangelist wants to remove this cause of suspicion. In response to the new accusations, Jesus only reiterates his close relationship to God and his promise of life (John 8:49–51). The Jews now manifest the extreme dualism underlying this debate by repeating their charge. Their question to Jesus (v. 53) is so formulated in Greek as to anticipate a negative answer; Jesus cannot be greater than Abraham. Jesus responds in turn and in kind: his claims are grounded in God's will; his opponents have no claim upon God (vv. 54–55). But while Jesus seemingly sets himself in opposition to his Jewish contemporaries he nevertheless claims the approval of Abraham, the father of the Jewish people and of their tradition (v. 56). Either Abraham was granted a vision of the future, or he was conceived of as being alive with God all along. The heated dispute ends typically, with a misunderstanding

on the part of the Jews (v. 57), an enigmatic "I am" saying of Jesus (v. 58), and a very brief narration in which the Jews demonstrate the correctness of Jesus' imputation to them of a lethal intent (v. 59).

9:1–41
The Man Born Blind

Chap. 9 is a self-contained unit, a complete episode. Typically, a miracle or sign performed by Jesus leads to a discussion and debate, which in this case reveals a good deal about the setting and purpose of the Gospel.

9:1–7, The Miracle. The initial scene (vv. 1–7) describes the miracle of Jesus' giving sight to the man blind from birth. The miracle itself is described with economy of style (vv. 1, 6–7). As much space (vv. 2–5) is devoted to the disciples' questioning the cause of the man's blindness (cf. v. 34; Luke 13:2–5), which provides the setting for God's work (cf. John 11:4). One does not wait for the Sabbath to pass to do it (9:4, 14). In view of Jesus' promise of his continued presence with the disciples after his death (chaps. 14–16), vv. 4–5 can hardly mean that the period of his saving or healing power is limited by his historical presence (cf. 14:12). In any event, Jesus indicates his intention to act without delay. His action and command (9:6–7) recall Elisha's cleansing of the leper Naaman (2 Kings 5:10; cf. also Mark 8:23). The pool of Siloam is at the foot of the hill of the old City of David, south of the Temple area. Its name, translated "sent" (RSV, 9:7), seemingly has symbolic significance (Jesus was sent from God), but that is not spelled out further.

9:8–12, The Initial Inquiry. The interchange between the man and his neighbors establishes that he is actually the one who was a blind beggar and how Jesus opened his eyes. Significantly, the once blind man knows the identity, but not the whereabouts, of Jesus (cf. 5:13).

9:13–17, A Hearing Before the Pharisees. When the man is brought before the Pharisees, the reality of the restoration of his sight is assumed (v. 13); their questioning concerns the manner of the healing and its legitimacy. Probably Jesus' making clay is regarded by some of the Pharisees as work and hence a violation of the Sabbath (v. 14). Therefore some think the miracle is illegitimate; others, impressed by his signs, do not accept this negative judgment (v. 16). The response of the blind man (v. 17) that Jesus is a prophet is entirely appropriate, since he can perform signs. The Sabbath healing is no disqualification.

9:18–23, The Parents Questioned. The Jews, not to be distinguished from the Pharisees, to make sure of the healed blind man's identity and previous condition now question the man's parents (vv. 18–19). Their response is minimally truthful but obviously evasive (vv. 20–21); they refer questions to their son.

The situation here envisioned, in which people fear disciplinary expulsion from the synagogue because of adherence to Jesus (vv. 22–23), is not unparalleled in this Gospel (12:42; 16:2; cf. Luke 6:22). Because such a situation scarcely existed in Jesus' time, efforts have been made to locate its genuine historical setting. If in the period following the Roman war (i.e., after A.D. 70) Judaism sought to retrench, excluding Christ-confessors (i.e., Christians), his parents' reaction reflects that setting. John then encourages those who believe in Jesus to confess, even at the risk of expulsion from the synagogue (John 12:42). Significantly, in the narrative, not Jesus, but his followers are threatened with such expulsion.

9:24–34, The Second Hearing. The once blind man is called in for a second, quasi-legal hearing before Jesus' accusers. It is characteristic of this man that he engages in no speculation but speaks only of his own experience (v. 25). When his adversaries begin to ask questions already addressed (v. 26; cf. v. 15), he becomes acerbic (v. 27). His obviously sarcastic question and their response (vv. 28–29) establish a stark dichotomy between Jesus' disciples and Moses', again a situation that did not arise in Jesus' day. The opponents' ignorance of Jesus' origin is typically ironic. They think it discredits Jesus; actually, they discredit themselves (v. 29). The man's rejoinder is initially biting and even humorous (v. 30). But when he utters a solemn statement in which he expresses his own (and the author's) assessment of what has transpired and who Jesus is (vv. 31–33), utter anger and rejection is then unleashed upon him (v. 34). Arrogance shines through the contemptuous question, and they cast him out of the synagogue (cf. vv. 22–23).

9:35–41, True Sight and Blindness. Now the man's knowledge of Jesus passes beyond his immediate experience of Jesus' power to an understanding of who Jesus is. He believes in Jesus the Son of man (v. 35) and worships him (v. 38); he becomes a disciple of Jesus. Jesus' statement (v. 39) has both the man and his opponents in view. The sight and blindness of which Jesus speaks are not just physical conditions. Although Jesus has restored physical sight, he obviously does not intend to blind people physically. The Pharisees' question (v. 40) also indicates the symbolic character of blindness. By claiming a sight they do not possess, they confirm their sinful status (v. 41). Their claim to sight ("we see") is implicit in their presumption in judging Jesus.

10:1–42
Jesus, the Good Shepherd

This chapter centers around the shepherd discourse (10:1–18), and the theme of shepherd and sheep continues through v. 30. Thereafter, the hostility of the Jews, who first attempt to stone Jesus (v. 31) and then to arrest him (v. 38), intensifies. The beginning has no transition or setting of the scene, but the connection with the preceding episode is also tenuous. Jesus abruptly introduces a new theme or a new set of images. The "thieves and robbers" (vv. 1, 8) may be the Pharisees of chap. 9, but the identification is not explicit.

10:1–6, The Shepherd and the Door. The "figure" (v. 6, Gk. *paroimia*) of the true shepherd contrasts him with the thief, robber, and stranger who enter the sheepfold illegitimately. The point of the passage seems clear enough, but if taken as an allegory, it is not obvious who is represented by the various figures or elements. Because Jesus later refers to himself as the good shepherd (v. 11), one identifies him also with the shepherd of v. 2. But that shepherd enters by the door, and Jesus says he is the door (v. 7). The imagery of 10:1–6 is related to the imagery of 10:7–18, but when the sections are combined, no clear picture emerges. Either the shepherd of v. 2 is not Jesus but a disciple of Jesus who leads his followers (i.e., a church), or we are dealing with two figures of speech (shepherd, door), both of which symbolize Jesus but which are not to be combined. In the former case there is a jarring effect because Jesus is the good shepherd in vv. 11 and 14.

10:7–18, Jesus as Door and Shepherd. Probably, different images are used by Jesus to describe his role: he is both door and shepherd. As door, he is the way to salvation (v. 9). Thieves and robbers now appear again (vv. 8, 10; cf. v. 1). Their identity has long mystified interpreters. The preceding chapter (esp. 9:40) suggests they are Pharisees, but this is not stated, and Pharisees otherwise do not appear. But if the imagery refers to persons known to the followers of Jesus, particularly in the community for whom John writes, the Pharisees or Jewish leaders are prime candidates. The identities of the wolf and hireling (10:12) remain as mysterious as that of the thief. The hireling's selfish motivation (v. 13) contrasts him with Jesus, whose devotion to his "sheep" (followers; vv. 14–15) is matched only by his knowledge of the Father.

Jesus' purpose, giving life, is contrasted with that of the thief (v. 10); it is fulfilled only in the laying down of his own (vv. 11–18). The wolf symbolizes the death that overtakes Jesus and threatens his sheep. The thief or hireling evades it by abandoning the sheep, but Jesus is faithful. The passage is, in effect, a meditation on Jesus' death and resurrection. His death is something he wills, not something imposed upon him (v. 18). Jesus even attributes to himself the power of his own resurrection, although its source is finally God (v. 18b). The "other sheep" (v. 16) have a referent that would have been known to the original readers; probably they symbolize gentile believers. The one shepherd and the one flock emphasize the unity of the Christian community under its Lord (cf. 17:20, 23).

Although the specific referents of this imagery may be obscure, the basic message is not. The loyalty of Jesus to his followers is underscored by his willingness to sacrifice himself for them (cf. 15:12–13), which sets him apart from other would-be shepherds or messiahs; his true disciples recognize and appreciate who he is.

10:19–21, Reactions to Jesus. The Jews' reaction to Jesus is still not uniformly hostile. While some echo the sentiments of his opponents, others draw the proper conclusions (v. 21).

10:22–30, At the Feast of Dedication. The Feast of Dedication (Hanukkah) falls in December (vv. 22–23). Solomon's portico faced east, toward Gethsemane. Despite the division of opinion (vv. 19–21), the Jews will now appear in sharp opposition to Jesus. In effect, Jesus' own brusque response (vv. 25–30) seems to put them there, for their demand (v. 24) is not hostile. His response takes up the earlier pastoral imagery and unequivocally sets the Jews apart from his followers ("sheep"). Thus the Jews are cast in the role of unbelievers, aliens to the flock (vv. 26–27) which is secure in the unity of Jesus and his Father (vv. 28–30).

10:31–39, Hostility to Jesus. The Jews' reaction (cf. 5:18), Jesus' response (10:32), and the Jews' rejoinder (v. 33) are now entirely predictable. From the standpoint of Jesus and his disciples (the Christian church), his words and deeds are given him as a commission by God. He is one with the Father. From the side of the Jews, his claim is the supreme blasphemy, the arrogation of divine prerogatives to himself (v. 33). Jesus' response takes a new turn in that he now argues on the basis of Scripture, a common court of appeal (vv. 34–38), quoting Ps. 82:6 as "your law" and taking it to be addressed to the people of Israel (John 10:35). If the people may be called gods, it cannot be blasphemy for the one whom the Father has consecrated and sent into the world to be called "Son of God." Jesus then appeals to his works (vv. 37–38; cf. v. 25) as

witnesses to him (cf. 5:36) and reasserts his unity with the Father (cf. 10:30). Again, the reaction of the Jews is predictable (v. 39).

10:40–42, Jesus' Withdrawal. This is the first of two withdrawals from public view that precede Jesus' Passion (cf. 11:54). The location of John's activity in Transjordan remains uncertain (cf. 1:28). The truth of John's witness is attested for the last time, while Jesus' own superiority is made clear (10:41). Even at this late point, people believe in Jesus (v. 42). As residents of the Transjordan they were not Judeans, perhaps not Jews.

11:1–44
The Raising of Lazarus

Chap. 11 contains two distinct, but related, incidents: the raising of Lazarus and the official Sanhedrin decision to put Jesus to death. The latter (vv. 47–53) derives from the former (vv. 45–46); because Jesus gives life, his opponents seek to deprive him of his own.

The first episode (11:1–44) is the climactic event of the public ministry of Jesus. Other Gospels narrate episodes in which Jesus restores a person to life (cf. Mark 5:35–43; Luke 7:11–17), but this story has no parallel. (A recently discovered "secret" Gospel of Mark tells a similar story in much briefer form, without naming Lazarus. It is possibly a more primitive form of John's account.)

11:1–16, The Decision to Go to Lazarus. The participants and place are identified in a curious way (vv. 1–2). Bethany is said to be the village of Mary and Martha, who have not been mentioned previously (but cf. Luke 10:38, where they are named but not their village). Mary is identified by an incident that has not yet occurred (John 12:1–8; but cf. Luke 7:37–38). The sisters' summoning Jesus (John 11:3) sets in motion a series of questions and Jesus' explanation (vv. 3–16), culminating in a journey to Bethany. Jesus makes clear the purpose of Lazarus' illness and death (vv. 4, 14–15; cf. 9:3), but he does not immediately go to Lazarus (11:6), and his delay seemingly leads to Lazarus' death (cf. vv. 21, 32). Yet Jesus is resolved to go to Judea (v. 7), despite the hostility encountered there (vv. 8, 16; cf. 10:31, 39). In response to his disciples' dismay (11:8), Jesus utters enigmatic sayings (vv. 9–10) that seem to imply that he must now act promptly (cf. 9:4–5), and he decides to go to Lazarus (11:11). That the disciples should misunderstand and require further explanation (vv. 12–15) is no surprise to readers of this Gospel. Thomas' dogged commitment and courage (v. 16) finally proves to be empty (16:32). During Jesus' ministry his disciples' belief is provisional and incomplete.

11:17–37, Conversations with the Sisters. As Jesus approaches Bethany (just to the east of Jerusalem), first Martha (vv. 20–27), then Mary (vv. 28–37), approach him in the way. Jesus' discovery that Lazarus has been dead four days (v. 17) anticipates his actual arrival at the tomb (v. 38). Jesus waited two days before starting (v. 6), and the journey apparently took a couple of days. Throughout, movement waits upon the dialogue. The Jews (v. 19) in this episode form a kind of choral background and, although they lack understanding, are not initially hostile to Jesus. The Greek *Ioudaioi*, "Jews," can be translated "Judeans," which seems appropriate here. The proximity of Jerusalem perhaps implies that the Jews are understood to be residents of the city.

Martha's statement on meeting Jesus (vv. 21–22) elicits a rejoinder (v. 23) that she misunderstands (v. 24). Jesus' word (vv. 25–26) represents a radical correction of Martha's expectation, which conforms to Jewish and much early Christian belief. Jesus, on the other hand, equates the resurrection with the life that he offers as a present reality. This is the characteristic Johannine teaching. Martha's response (v. 27) is positive but does not indicate she understands the change in eschatology Jesus has proposed.

The next scene (vv. 28–37) is virtually a doublet of the preceding, except that Mary is accompanied by the Jews (v.· 31). Mary repeats Martha's opening statement (v. 32; cf. v. 21), but here the parallel breaks off. Jesus appears deeply affected by his love for Lazarus (vv. 33–36). The scene ends as the Jews, like Martha and Mary, lament what might have been (v. 37). That they affirm Jesus' restoration of sight to the blind man and his life-giving power implies they are not enemies.

11:38–44, Lazarus Raised. When Jesus arrives at the tomb (v. 38), his conversation with Martha (vv. 39–40) confirms that Lazarus is dead and points forward to the life-restoring deed. Jesus' statement about her believing (v. 40) picks up the thread of their previous conversation (vv. 25–27), although he has not actually made the statement he attributes to himself. The raising of Lazarus will be the revelation of God's presence in Jesus and thus of his glory (cf. v. 4). The theme of the revelation of God can be stated in terms of Jesus' or God's glory (1:14). Jesus' glory or glorification is intimately associated with his death, the supreme moment of revelation (7:39; 12:23; 17:1–5). That Jesus' praying (11:41–42) is not of necessity but for others is a distinctively Johannine motif (cf. 12:30; cf. Mark 14:32–39). When Lazarus at length comes out of the tomb at Jesus' command (John 11:43), the graveclothes underscore the fact that he had died and Jesus' command to the bystanders (v.

44) that he has been made alive. Jesus' restoration of Lazarus to life is the ultimate revelation of his mission and purpose during the public ministry (cf. 5:28–29): he is the resurrection and the life.

11:45–54
The Condemnation of Jesus

Once again there is a division among the Jews (cf. 7:12–13, 43; 10:19); those who disbelieve act as informers against Jesus (11:46). The gathering of the council (Sanhedrin) against Jesus (vv. 47–53; cf. Mark 14:1–2) occurs only at this stage in John, whereas Matthew (26:59–68) and Mark (14:55–65) place it after his arrest, and it consists of a full-scale trial of Jesus. John's presentation of the dynamics of the situation may not be misleading in that Jesus was perceived by the Temple authorities as a threat to stability and therefore to their own status and privilege with the Romans (11:48). The high priest Caiaphas's (cf. Matt. 26:3) practical, self-interested advice (John 11:49–50) is at the same time a prophetic utterance of which he has no notion, foretelling the saving work of Jesus' universal mission (vv. 51–52; cf. 10:16; 17:20). The council heeds Caiaphas's advice (v. 53) and sets in motion the chain of events that will dispose of Jesus.

Jesus' withdrawal (v. 54; cf. 10:40–42) was probably for the purpose of awaiting the arrival of his hour (12:23).

11:55–12:50
Jesus' Final Jerusalem Visit and the End of His Public Ministry

11:55–57, The Expectations. The advent of the third Passover of the Gospel of John (2:13; 6:4) sets the stage for what follows, as the heightened expectancy and perplexity of the Passover pilgrims (11:56) and the hostility of Jewish officialdom (v. 57) are vividly portrayed. Only in John's Gospel are the crowds put on notice to turn Jesus in (cf. Mark 14:1–2 and parallels). From this point onward, however, there are remarkable similarities and parallels to the synoptic accounts.

12:1–8, The Anointing of Jesus. Both Matthew (26:6–13) and Mark (14:3–9) tell of a woman's anointing Jesus' head in the house of Simon the leper in Bethany within two days of Passover and after Jesus has already once entered Jerusalem. Luke (7:36–50) recounts a woman's anointing of Jesus' feet earlier in the ministry; Jesus pronounces her sins forgiven. John's placing of the incident makes the best narrative sense, for he has it occur as Jesus passes through Bethany on the way to Jerusalem at the home of Martha, Mary, and Lazarus (cf. 11:1–44). That Martha serves corresponds with Luke's characterization of her in 10:40. The words used to describe the ointment as well as its value (three hundred denarii) are virtually the same in John as in Matthew and Mark, as is Jesus' word about the poor (John 12:8). Strangely, however, John's statement about the purpose of the anointing is less clear than in the other Gospels, and there is no beautiful rounding off of the story in which Jesus says the deed will commemorate the woman (Mark 14:9). In every case (except Luke), the story portrays Jesus as being anointed for burial (John 12:7) and clearly prefigures his death.

12:9–11, The Plot Against Lazarus. The gathering of Jews around Jesus and Lazarus in Bethany gives the authorities cause to plot against Lazarus as well as Jesus. This brief scene underscores the role played by the raising of Lazarus in the authorities' decision to put Jesus to death. Possibly Lazarus here represents early Christian disciples who also came under threat because they attracted people to Jesus (16:2).

12:12–19, The Entry into Jerusalem. Like the other Gospels, John envisions a crowd coming into the city with Jesus (cf. v. 17), but there is also a crowd going out to meet him (v. 13). John's account is similar to the Synoptics', particularly in the crowd's greeting (Ps. 118:25–26; cf. Matt. 21:5 on the use of Zech. 9:9). Distinctively Johannine are the disciples' not understanding until after Jesus' glorification (John 12:16; cf. 2:17, 22), the witnessing of the crowd who had seen Lazarus raised from the dead (12:17), and the crowd's coming out to meet Jesus because of that spectacular sign (v. 18). The despair of the Pharisees (v. 19; cf. Luke 19:39) sums it up. In John's Gospel, Jesus will not leave the city again (cf. Mark 11:11). The Temple cleansing, which comes next in the Synoptics, occurred much earlier in John (2:13–22). The remainder of the chapter is distinctly Johannine, containing only a few echoes of synoptic sayings or events.

12:20–26, The Arrival of the Hour. The Greeks who approach Jesus through Philip are possibly Greek-speaking Jews. Their appearance signals the approach of Jesus' hour of glorification, i.e., his death (v. 23) and suggests the universal Christian mission that began only then. Thus this scene is, in an important sense, pivotal. The sayings of Jesus that follow (vv. 24–26) are traditional; they are found in somewhat different form in other NT writings (1 Cor. 15:36; Mark 8:34–35).

12:27–36a, The End of the Public Ministry. Jesus momentarily contemplates God's sparing him his coming death (v. 27), evoking

the entire Gethsemane scene of the synoptic Gospels (Mark 14:32–42 and parallels), otherwise not mentioned in John (but cf. Heb. 5:7). But Jesus suppresses any uncertainty: God's name will be glorified in his death (John 12:28). Although Jesus says the voice from heaven came for the crowd's benefit (v. 30), they do not understand it (v. 29). Jesus continues speaking nevertheless (vv. 31–32), and we learn (v. 33) that he has alluded to his imminent death. Jesus' announcement of his death expresses in Johannine terms its function as saving event. It is at once judgment (v. 31) and the possibility of salvation (v. 32) for all.

The crowd apparently calls Jesus "Son of man" (v. 34), although he has not used that title in the immediately preceding statement to which they refer (v. 32; but cf. v. 23). Their next question, "Who is this Son of man?" can scarcely concern his identity, since they have just used the term where Jesus used "I." (The narrator knows that "Son of man" on Jesus' lips is a form of self-reference.) The question may be about his role. They cannot credit the statement about his being lifted up (which they seem to know means crucifixion!), because the law says the Christ will abide forever. The force of their statement and questions implies that Jesus' unusual fate is tied to his use of this perplexing title, and they understand neither. Jesus cuts off further discussion with an urgent challenge to the crowd (vv. 35–36), his enigmatic statements evoking what he has previously said in 9:4 and 11:9–10. Probably Jesus refers here to the urgency of any confrontation with him, whether during his historic ministry or afterward as the gospel (good news) about him is proclaimed.

12:36b–43, Explanations of Jesus' Rejection. Jesus now withdraws. What follows is an explanation and summation of his work. Disbelief has characterized the Jewish reaction to Jesus (v. 37), and two quotations, from Isaiah 53:1 (v. 38) and 6:10 (v. 40), explain it. Both appear in other NT writings with a similar purpose (cf. Rom. 10:16; Matt. 13:14–15). John lays another explanation alongside this one, without any apparent awareness of tension. The believing authorities among the Jews who refuse to confess Jesus (John 12:42) have their priorities inverted (v. 43). Their fear of expulsion from the synagogue betrays their too high regard for human opinion.

John believed Isaiah had seen Jesus' glory; v. 41 alludes to Isaiah 6:1–3 (where John understands "Lord" to refer to Jesus), and the same narrative episode of Isaiah contains John's second quotation (12:40; Isa. 6:10). But Isaiah was not the only OT worthy to have seen Jesus Christ; the same is said of Abraham (John 8:56, 58).

12:44–50, Jesus' Summation. Jesus' public ministry ends with his final proclamation, which sums up the Johannine understanding of the Christian message. The repeated emphasis upon Jesus' complete submission and transparency to God himself is characteristic (vv. 44, 49–50), as is the claim that to believe in Jesus is to believe in God (v. 44). Jesus is light in darkness (v. 46) and eternal life to all who believe in him. He judges no one (v. 48; cf. 3:17; 8:15), yet his coming effects judgment for those who do not believe in him and therefore refuse God. What Jesus says here is not directed to his contemporaries so much as to the church and to the mission field that the Gospel has in view.

13:1–21:25

Jesus' Manifestation of God's Glory to His Disciples

With chap. 13, the second major part of the Gospel begins as Jesus is at first alone with his disciples (chaps. 13–17). When he again emerges into public view he is arrested, tried, and crucified (chaps. 18–19). But at the end, the risen Jesus is once again alone with his disciples (chaps. 20–21). Through most of this final half of the Gospel of John he directs his attention to them.

13:1–38
The Last Supper

John's account of the Last Supper (cf. Mark 14:17–25 and parallels) has no story of the preparation for the Passover meal (Mark 14:12–16 and parallels), for the last meal in the Johannine version is not the Feast of Unleavened Bread but a supper given on the preceding evening (13:1).

13:1–11, Washing the Disciples' Feet. The beginning of the meal is integrally related to Jesus' washing of the disciples' feet, an act of humble service that reverses ordinary practice and expectations. The reversal is significant, however, for Jesus' act has a symbolic meaning, portending his death. It is reported in no other Gospel and, because John omits Jesus' institution of the Lord's Supper, appears to take its place (→ Lord's Supper, The).

The introduction (vv. 1–4) moves from a statement about Jesus' full knowledge of his origin and destiny and his love for his disciples (vv. 1, 3) to a description of his preparation for a seemingly menial task (v. 4). The act itself is described with utmost economy. The confrontation with Peter (vv. 6–10) conveys its significance and meaning. In effect, Peter expresses a classical Johannine misunderstand-

ing as he refuses to allow his master to cast himself in such a humble role (vv. 6, 8). Jesus' rejoinder reveals the basis for all misunderstandings in this Gospel and points to their resolution (v. 7). The "afterward" to which he refers is not after dinner but after his glorification. Like others, the disciples cannot, during Jesus' earthly ministry, understand him. When Peter is obdurate, Jesus' threatening response (v. 8) brings him to the point of genuine understanding (v. 9), but his reaction, typically excessive, shows he still fails to comprehend. Jesus' washing of his disciples' feet means more than Peter can know. If one does not accept that service he cannot belong to Jesus (v. 8).

In view of the allusions to Jesus' approaching death at the outset of this account (vv. 1–3), it now becomes clear that the washing of the disciples' feet signifies Jesus' death on their behalf (cf. 10:11, 15; 18:12–14). This interpretation is confirmed by 13:10, particularly if the phrase "except for his feet" is omitted, as in some very ancient manuscripts. When this shorter reading is followed, the bathing of which Jesus speaks (cf. RSV) is the washing of their feet (i.e., his saving death) and no further washing, such as Peter has proposed, is necessary. Otherwise, the foot washing becomes a matter secondary to the basic purification of bathing, which is not what is intended. The scene concludes with a by now familiar explanation of Jesus' foreknowledge of his betrayal (v. 11). Many interpreters believe that John deliberately replaced the Lord's Supper with his distinctive portrayal of Jesus' washing the disciples' feet, for the words of institution interpret Jesus' death, just as the foot washing does.

13:12–20, An Interpretation of the Washing. After the foot washing, Jesus gives yet another interpretation of it (vv. 12–17). The reversal of roles that Jesus has just demonstrated should be reflected in how the disciples treat each other. The two interpretations are intimately related in John's thought: Jesus' death is an expression of his limitless, self-giving love, and he calls upon his disciples to share that same love among themselves (15:12–13; 13:34–35). Finally, Jesus once more takes account of Judas (v. 18), explains why he does so (v. 19), and makes a general statement about the relation of the apostles (ones sent), God, and himself (v. 20) that is based on a tradition known also to Matthew (10:40) and Luke (10:16).

13:21–30, Identifying the Betrayer. In John, this scene is longer and more elaborate than in any of the Synoptics. In Mark (14:17–21) and Luke (22:21–23), Judas is not explicitly named: in Matthew (26:24–25) he more or less gives himself away; but in John Judas is unmistakably identified, at least to the Beloved Disciple and to readers. In all except Luke, Jesus' opening statement (John 13:21b) is almost identical. In John, the disciples look at each other uncertainly (v. 22); as in Luke (22:23), they begin to question one another. Then begins the interplay between the Beloved Disciple, Peter, Jesus, and Judas, ending with Jesus' identifying Judas by handing him the morsel (John 13:26)— whereupon Satan enters him (v. 27)—and, in effect, sending him into the night (vv. 27, 30). John confirms, as Judas receives the morsel and departs (v. 30), that Jesus knew from the beginning that he would betray him (cf. 6:70–71).

This scene marks the first appearance of the Beloved Disciple in the Gospel (19:26–27; 20:2; 21:7, 20). He appears only in John and his identity is never revealed, although tradition since the end of the second century has identified him with John the son of Zebedee. His position nearest Jesus indicates the favor in which he was held and presumably his central role in the Johannine circle. Only the Beloved Disciple seems to be told that Judas was to betray Jesus (13:28–29; cf. 12:6). In Mark, none of the disciples would have learned the identity of the betrayer, as Luke's description of their quandary (22:23) clearly indicates.

13:31–35, The New Commandment. Following the prediction of his betrayal, Jesus speaks of his glorification, that is, his death (vv. 31–33). Through his death Jesus attains the resurrection, and God's glory can finally be seen in light of both. Everything is now said from the standpoint of the cross and resurrection; the glorified Christ speaks. The meaning of the enigmatic saying of v. 33 is from that vantage point now clear: Jesus is going to his death (cf. 7:33). This saying prepares the way for others in which Jesus will reveal how after "a little while" the disciples will see him again (14:19–20; 16:16–24).

At the point of his departure, Jesus gives his disciples a new commandment (13:34). This love commandment finds close parallels elsewhere in the NT (1 Thess. 4:9; cf. Rom. 13:9; Gal. 5:14; Mark 12:31 and parallels), and with good reason it has been taken to be an apt summary of Jesus' teaching. But in contrast to the Synoptics and Paul, who quote the command to love the neighbor from Lev. 19:18, the Johannine Jesus commands his disciples to love one another, that is, other members of the inner circle, the church. This limitation agrees with John's emphasis on the unity of the church (17:21, 23) and with his dualism. One would expect love to be directed to the circle of true disciples and not to the world (→ Love).

13:36–38, Peter's Denial Predicted. All the Gospels relate Peter's denial of Jesus (18:15–18,

25–27) and Jesus' prediction of it. In the Synoptics, the prediction occurs just prior to his agony in Gethsemane and his arrest. In John, a long discussion and discourse (chaps. 14–17) intervene, but the next distinct event thereafter is Jesus' arrest (there being no Gethsemane story in John).

14:1–17:26
The Farewell Discourses and Prayer

Chaps. 14–16 are traditionally called the farewell discourses of Jesus; chap. 17 the high-priestly prayer. Chap. 14 seems to continue the table conversation of chap. 13, however, and there is no change of setting at chap. 17. There are, nevertheless, some lines of demarcation. Plainly, Jesus begins to pray in chap. 17, and the distinctiveness of chaps. 14–17 is obvious in relation to the synoptic accounts. The events of chap. 13 have synoptic analogies and parallels through the prediction of Peter's denial (13:36–38), and these resume with the account of Jesus' arrest (18:1–11). The farewell discourses are without parallel in the other Gospels. Yet they function like the apocalyptic discourses of the Synoptics (Mark 13 and parallels) in that they tell the disciples what they may expect in the future. The synoptic apocalypses have to do with the events leading up to Christ's triumphal appearance in apocalyptic glory, while John's discourses concern his postresurrection manifestations to his disciples (14:22).

14:1–11, Jesus' Assurance and the Disciples' Questions. Jesus reassures his disciples: to believe in God is to believe in him and vice versa (v. 1)—a major theme of the entire Gospel. Jesus' statement that he is going to the Father to prepare a place for his disciples continues his answer to Peter's questions (13:36–37). Peter has rightly taken Jesus to mean that he is going to his death, but his death is also the way to the Father. How Jesus' death provides an access to himself and to God becomes a major theme of the farewell discourses. So at the outset Jesus assures his disciples they will be safe in his hands.

Despite Jesus' assurance (14:4), Thomas candidly expresses his ignorance (v. 5). Obviously, Thomas refers to the way to God; he knows of Jesus' death (11:16). Jesus answers with a ringing affirmation of his own role as the one access to the life-giving truth of God (14:6). His statement about his disciples' knowledge in v. 7 (the "you" is plural in Gk.), reveals a significant time distinction. At first he seems to imply that their failure has cut them off from God (v. 7a), but then he indicates the future state of their knowledge (v. 7b). During Jesus' ministry there are things the disciples cannot know, though they witness what Jesus says and does; but after he has departed they will truly understand how he has made God accessible to them. They will not only know him but see him.

Philip's question (v. 8) allows Jesus to reiterate and expand upon what he has just said (cf. 12:44–50). Philip's not knowing represents the disciples' inevitable ignorance at this time. In declaring that to see him is to see the Father (14:9) Jesus signals an end to the situation described in 1:18, in which no one has seen the Father (cf. 6:46; 12:45).

14:12–14, Jesus' Promise. Jesus promises his disciples that they will be empowered as well as informed (v. 12) and their prayers in his name will be answered (vv. 13–14). The qualification "in my name" is important, for it suggests the kind of prayer that will be answered, namely, one that accords with Jesus' own nature and purpose. Repeatedly in this Gospel, Jesus promises to answer his disciples' prayers (v. 14; 15:7, 16; 16:23), but assurance of answered prayer is found elsewhere in the NT as well (Matt. 7:7–11; Mark 11:24; James 1:5).

14:15–24, The Coming Counselor. Jesus' promise of his presence with his disciples is a gift, not something the disciples achieve, but it can be forfeited. Jesus demands they demonstrate their love by keeping his commandments (v. 15), that is, they are to love one another (13:34–35; 15:12).

At the same time Jesus promises them help: a Counselor (RSV), the Spirit of truth, the Holy Spirit (v. 26). (In 20:22, the risen Jesus bestows the Spirit.) "Counselor" translates *paraklētos* (Gk., "one called to the side of"), which in other contexts has legal connotations ("advocate"; cf. 1 John 2:1, where the term is used of Jesus). But this common juridical sense does not appear to be adequate to its meaning here. Jesus himself defines *paraklētos*, however, by indicating his function (see 14:15–26; 15:26; 16:7–11, 13–15). First, the Counselor underscores the distinction (dualism) between the disciples and the world (14:17). The Spirit's presence is then tantamount to the presence of Jesus, although the equation is not made explicitly (v. 18). The mysterious reference (v. 19; cf. 13:33) to Jesus' resurrection will not be lost on knowledgeable readers; Jesus points ahead to the disciples' future state and knowledge (14:20). The promise of his presence will be fulfilled for the person who keeps his commandments and therefore loves him (v. 21; cf. v. 15; → Holy Spirit, The; Paraclete).

Judas (v. 22) is not the betrayer but presumably the Judas son of James mentioned by Luke as one of the Twelve (6:16; Acts 1:13). His question allows Jesus to clarify a discrepancy between what he has just promised and other early Christian expectations (cf. 1 Thess. 4:13–17; Mark 13 and parallels). The manifestation of which Jesus speaks is not an apocalyptic, public event, but a spiritual presence contingent upon the expression of love for Jesus through keeping his word (or commandment; cf. John 14:15). Conversely, there is a threatening word to any nominal follower who does not heed Jesus: he ignores God (v. 24).

14:25–31, Jesus' Promise Repeated. Jesus now seems on the verge of taking leave of his disciples (vv. 15, 27, 30–31), although the discourses continue. Commentators have conjectured that chaps. 15–17 were interpolated, breaking an originally smooth connection between 14:31 and 18:1. Jesus repeats his promise of the Spirit (cf. 14:16–17), elaborating on its functions (v. 26), which fulfill expectations raised in 2:22; 7:39; and 12:16. "All things" surely does not mean anything conceivable but those things pertinent to Jesus' work that are necessary for disciples to know. The Fourth Gospel may itself be the literary deposit of what the Spirit-Paraclete has taught the disciples about Jesus.

In departing, Jesus bestows upon his disciples a blessing (cf. 16:33; 20:19), invoking the characteristic dualism to distinguish his peace from the world's, and again reassuring them (14:27). Jesus reiterates what he has said already (v. 28) and declares his own subordination to the Father. Once more he invokes the distinction between the time of his ministry, when he is speaking, and the time after his death when they may understand and believe (v. 29; cf. 13:19). Jesus then clearly signals the end of this conversation (14:30). The ruler of this world (Satan) is embodied in the party sent out to arrest Jesus (18:3). They, of course, do not determine Jesus' fate (cf. 7:6; 10:17–18); he does only what God commands him (14:31). Because Jesus' own command to depart is ignored until 18:1, chaps. 15–17 are often regarded as a later addition to the text.

15:1–17, The Allegory of the Vine. There now begins a long discourse of Jesus that continues uninterrupted until the disciples' question of 16:17. The fundamental point of the first part, the vine discourse, is the necessity and nature of the disciples' unity with Jesus.

15:1–8, The Vine and Branches. The metaphor of vine and branches represents the unity of Jesus and the disciples. The unity is a given, but it does not exist apart from the disciples' own participation. Jesus is both the one who commands them to abide and bear fruit and the one who enables them to do so (vv. 5–7). Their bearing of fruit is proof that they are Jesus' disciples (v. 8). In 13:34–35 Jesus has linked discipleship with mutual love; he reiterates this connection here (15:9–10, 12–14). The abiding and bearing fruit of which Jesus speaks is the mutuality of love among the disciples. The awful conse quence of not abiding in Jesus' love by express ing love for one's fellow disciple is made clear by the imagery of casting out (as distinguished from pruning) and burning (vv. 2, 6; → Vine).

The distinctive meaning of two Greek words is important. "Pruning" (Gk. *kathairein*) can also mean "cleansing"; thus fruit-bearing members of the Johannine community are cleansed so they may bear more fruit (v. 2; cf. 13:10–11). The word used of the Father's func tion in 15:1, *geōrgos* (Gk.), is the ordinary term for farmer; the RSV's "vinedresser" appropriate ly narrows the application to the vineyard but perhaps does not do justice to the fact that the *geōrgos* would be the one responsible for the vine's existence in the first place.

15:9–17, Love as Bearing Fruit. The exposition of the vine image then makes its hortatory pur pose clear (v. 12). The love of which Jesus speaks has its source in God, the Father, whose love for Jesus, the Son, finds further expression in Jesus' love for his disciples (v. 9). That love ultimately takes the form of Jesus' sacrifice of his own life (15:13; 10:11, 15). This sacrifice is the paradigm and example of the love the disci ples are to manifest for one another (15:12). Thus the disciples become Jesus' friends as they obey his command (v. 14) and share his love among themselves. Inasmuch as the death of Jesus is understood as his self-giving act and as such becomes a model for the disciples' love, Jesus is himself understood in distinctly human terms. Precisely the consciousness of the humanity of Jesus, and his death as loss, gives the love command its moral force and exem plary power.

Friendship with Jesus (v. 14) is the condi tion of receiving his revelation of God (v. 15). That the initiative and priority lies with Jesus is clear enough (v. 16); Jesus has chosen and appointed his disciples with a purpose. Their bearing fruit (v. 16) is the fulfillment of his love commandment (v. 17). It assures them of their unity with him, and thus with God, and means that their prayers will be answered (v. 16).

15:18–16:4a, The World's Hatred. The solidarity of Jesus and his disciples is now stated in a negative vein; it distinguishes them from the world, which will bear them hate. **15:18–27, The Basis of Hatred.** The world's ha tred of the community of Jesus' followers is grounded in its prior hatred of him (v. 18); that hatred will be manifest in both the crucifixion of Jesus and the persecution of his disciples. The Gospel of John arose in the context of persecu tion (v. 20). The Johannine dualism, doubtless a

reflection of that context, makes the sharpest contrast between Jesus and his disciples and the world (v. 19). In v. 20, Jesus refers to his saying of 13:16 (cf. Matt. 10:24; Luke 6:40) to explain the persecution of the disciples. Although the disciples may encounter some who will believe (15:20; cf. 17:20), the hostility of the world is emphasized, not its receptivity.

The world's hostility reflects its ignorance of Jesus' origin and commission (15:21), but the world did not become positively sinful until it rejected Jesus, God's emissary (vv. 22, 24; cf. 9:39–41). Before his coming, the world existed in darkness and death, so that he can be de scribed as its light and life (1:4–5, 9; 8:12; 11:25; 12:46). He is sent by God to effect salva tion, life, not judgment (3:17; 12:47). Neverthe less, the inevitable consequence of rejection of him is judgment, for that rejection is tan tamount to ignorance and rejection of God (15:21, 23–24). Thus John insists that genuine belief in God has now become contingent upon belief in Jesus. In v. 24b Jesus does not repre sent his opponents as having seen God (cf. 1:18) except as they have had the possibility of seeing God in him (14:9) but have rejected it. This rejection, uncanny as it is, is nevertheless the fulfillment of Scripture (15:25; Ps. 35:19; cf. Mark 4:11–12, Acts 28:26–27; Rom. 11:7–10).

Over against the sharpness of the world's re jection will stand the heavenly witness of the Counselor (*paraklētos*), the Spirit of truth (John 15:27), which Jesus will send to his disciples (i.e., the church) from the Father after his depar ture from the disciples and his return to God (cf. 16:7). This spiritual witness will be comple mented by that of the disciples, significantly described as having been with Jesus from the beginning (cf. 1 John 1:1; Acts 1:21–22). The disciples' historical witness as those who have been with Jesus from the beginning prevents revelation as a present, Spirit-inspired phe nomenon from going unchecked.

16:1–4a, The Manifestations of Hatred. Jesus explains his purpose in speaking of the world's hostility (v. 1) and then describes specific threats the community of disciples must endure (v. 2), reiterating their theological basis (v. 3). The concluding statement (v. 4; cf. v. 1) expands upon the reason for Jesus' prophecies: to prepare the disciples for persecution.

There are other references to being put out of the synagogue (9:22; 12:42); here as else where they seem to reflect the actual experi ences, as well as the fears, of the Johannine community. Whether death threats against Christians had actually been carried out is un certain. We read elsewhere in the NT of severe persecution (Gal. 1:13, 23; Acts 9:1–2; 1 Thess. 2:14–15), which at least in the case of Stephen (Acts 7:54–60) led to martyrdom. Doubtless

Jesus' death was seen by his early followers as an intimation of what they might expect, and the rise of opposition doubtless enhanced this apprehension.

16:4b–33, Jesus' Departing Words. Jesus continues to direct his disciples' attention to the future and now deals primarily with his departure and coming again to be with them. His departure is put in a new light as the necessary condition of his continued presence among them. That his presence will not be diminished, but enhanced, is a major emphasis of the Gospel. **16:4b–15, The Final Promise of the Counselor.** John's now familiar time distinction (between Jesus' earthly ministry and the postresurrection period) appears in v. 4b, where it affords a transition to Jesus' subsequent discourse. What Jesus says in v. 5 does not square with Peter's explicit question about his destination in 13:36. But Jesus seems simply to underscore the disciples' despondency to introduce the discussion that follows. The statements that have caused sorrow to fill their hearts (16:6) could be his predictions of persecution (15:18–16:4). But 16:7 suggests rather that Jesus refers also to his several previous allusions to his departure, for now he tells the disciples that because of the coming of the *paraklētos* (RSV: Counselor) it is to their advantage that he go away.

Only here (vv. 8–11) does Jesus speak of the *paraklētos* in its relation to the world rather than to the disciples. Thus the *paraklētos*, who was Counselor or Advocate for the disciples, becomes prosecuting attorney against the world. One can surmise that the Spirit will act directly to assure the disciples that God convicts and judges the world, although the world at first may not know it.

Among the disciples, the Spirit will extend the revelation Jesus has brought. This revelation is of, or about, Jesus (v. 14); but it will go beyond what Jesus was able to say before his death (vv. 12–13). Moreover, Jesus himself hints that many of the things he says will not be comprehended until after his departure (13:7). The additional revelation is from Jesus and is grounded in his ministry, but the Spirit unfolds what it means after his departure as it declares the things that are coming (v. 13), i.e., those things that have to do with the death, departure, and return of Jesus and the life of the church. **16:16–24, The Coming Joy.** Jesus repeats a mysterious saying (v. 16; cf. 7:33; 13:33; 14:19), and some of his disciples puzzle over its meaning (16:17–18). Characteristically, he knows what puzzles them (v. 19) and proceeds to unravel his own saying (vv. 19–24). Still speaking enigmatically (v. 20), he employs an analogy from common human experience (v. 21) but then makes clear he means his own departure and return

(vv. 22–23) to the postresurrection church (vv. 23–24; cf. 14:13–14). The theme of joy recurs in this discourse (16:20, 21, 22, 24); joy will characterize the disciples' life after they are united with the risen Jesus.

16:25–33, Jesus' Speech and the Disciples' Understanding. Jesus continues to speak of the postresurrection period as a time when he will speak plainly to the disciples and they will pray to the Father in his name, reiterating the themes of the reciprocity of love and of belief in his origin with God (vv. 27–28). "In figures" (vv. 25, 29) applies to how Jesus' words appear to the disciples before his glorification and the advent of the Spirit. To knowledgeable readers, Jesus already speaks plainly. The disciples seemingly understand Jesus' speech (vv. 29–30), thinking that his promise to speak plainly and not in figures (v. 25) is fulfilled. Their confession that he came from God picks up on Jesus' immediately preceding statement (v. 28) and is theologically correct. But their comprehension and implied self-satisfaction are abruptly challenged and shattered by Jesus (v. 31), who alludes to their imminent desertion of him at the moment of his trial and death (v. 32; cf. Mark 14:27; Zech. 13:7). Nevertheless, Jesus concludes his farewell discourses on an entirely positive note (John 16:33), as he points ahead to the peace that his words will provide the disciples (cf. 20:21, 26), warns them of their parlous existence in the world (cf. 15:18–19; 17:14–16), and encourages them with his triumph over the world, in which they participate if they abide in him.

17:1–26, Jesus' Prayer. Jesus' Great High-Priestly Prayer has no parallel in the other Gospels, except that in the synoptic Gospels he prays in anguish in Gethsemane; here he prays in utter serenity—but, in both cases, just before his arrest. The prayer falls into three parts, in which Jesus declares what he has accomplished (vv. 1–5), intercedes for his disciples (vv. 6–19), and broadens that intercession to include the later church (vv. 20–26). **17:1–5, Jesus' Glory.** Jesus again announces the hour has come and speaks of glorification. Several days have passed since he first did so (cf. 12:23), but theologically it is still the hour of Jesus' glorification (crucifixion); God glorifies Jesus by revealing himself in his death, and Jesus glorifies God by revealing God on the cross (17:1). Glorification in John means revelation; both are defined by Jesus' death. The power Jesus has over all humanity (v. 2, "all flesh") is the power through his death to give life to all those people God has given and will give him. Such life, defined as knowledge, is a present possibility (v. 3). Knowing God and Jesus Christ are not stages of knowledge but the same knowledge. Jesus glorifies God in revealing him to humanity, in his ministry (v. 4), and in his death and exaltation (v. 5). But Jesus' glory is not his own achievement but a primeval possession (v. 24); Jesus manifests what he already has been given. In this opening statement, Jesus sums up his ministry, his revelatory work, in characteristically Johannine terms (→ Glory).

17:6–19, Jesus' Prayer for His Disciples. As Jesus now prays for the disciples, described as the Father's gift to him (v. 6), he strongly implies divine election. Yet the statement that true followers have kept God's word hints that their own volition is meaningful. Jesus now describes them in entirely positive terms (vv. 7–8), and this description stands in contrast to his description of these same disciples just previously (16:31–32). Jesus now views them too as they are after his resurrection, when their earlier limitations have been overcome.

The remainder of Jesus' prayer for the disciples (17:9–19) deals with the world and the disciples' role and place in it. That Jesus sharply distinguishes his disciples from the world (vv. 9, 14, 16) is a typical expression of the Johannine dualism. Yet they must continue to live there (vv. 11, 15). Jesus, who had kept them safe as long as he was in the world (vv. 11, 12), as he now departs prays God to keep them "in thy name" (v. 11). Despite the world's hatred (v. 14), Jesus refuses to pray that they be taken out of the world (v. 15; the evil one is presumably Satan) but sends them into the world as the Father had sent him (v. 18). Thus the disciples too have a mission to the world (cf. 20:21), which is still intended for salvation (→ World, The).

Jesus prays that while they are in the world the disciples may be made holy (RSV: "sanctified") in the truth (17:17). "Thy word is truth" has an important, double meaning. Any Christian or Jew would quickly agree. But in Johannine terms, the word is Jesus (1:1–18), who is also the truth (1:14, 17; 14:6), so a distinctly Johannine Christian confession is concealed in this statement. At the end of this petition, Jesus says that he makes himself holy that his disciples may be made holy in truth (v. 19; cf. v. 17; the RSV translates the same Gk. word "consecrate"). The holiness of the disciples, their consecration to God, is dependent upon Jesus' holiness, as their salvation depends upon their unity with Jesus and God (v. 11; → Holiness).

17:20–26, Jesus' Prayer for the Church. Finally, Jesus prays for future believers (v. 20; cf. 20:29), for their unity with himself, the Father, and each other. This unity will serve their mission to the world (17:18, 20–21). Belief that the Father has sent Jesus (v. 21) is Christian faith (v. 8). The transmission of the glory from God, to Jesus, to the church effects this unity (v. 22) and renders believers, the church, transparent to the revelation of God. Oneness, an expression of

believers' love for one another (13:34), convinces the world of the truth of the Christian message (17:23) as it reflects God's love for Christ and his church. That love motivates and justifies the church's mission to the world (cf. 13:35).

In asking that all his disciples may ultimately be within the realm of his heavenly preexistent glory (17:24; cf. 14:2–3; 1:14), Jesus once more invokes the typical dualism in sharply distinguishing the world's ignorance from his own and his disciples' knowledge of God (17:25). Of course, there is now no knowledge of God except through belief in Jesus. As he turns to the cross (v. 26), Jesus sums up his revelatory work past and future, appropriately describing its purpose and character in terms of the realization of the love of God through Christ among his disciples.

18:1–19:42
The Passion Narrative

From the account of Jesus' arrest (18:1–11) onward, the Fourth Gospel's narrative is closely parallel to the Synoptics. Already as Jesus approaches Jerusalem, John's account begins to resemble the others. Quite possibly, the earliest Christians put together narratives of Jesus' Passion, whether in written or oral form, that antedate all the Gospels and account for the similarities between John and the Synoptics as well as the differences.

18:1–11, Jesus' Arrest. Jesus ends his final discourses with a prayer (chap. 17) and apparently only at this point leaves the site of the Last Supper (18:1) with his disciples. The garden to which Jesus and the disciples retire is not named; it is apparently Gethsemane (Matt. 26:36; Mark 14:32) on the slope of the Mount of Olives (Luke 22:39), the scene of Jesus' arrest. John characteristically emphasizes the initiative and authority of Jesus (18:4, 6, 8; cf. 10:18), who is arrested virtually at his own bidding. Only in John is Judas said to be familiar with the customary meeting place (18:2). Perhaps he betrayed this knowledge to the authorities. Only here are the Pharisees involved in Jesus' arrest (v. 3); their involvement is typical of their hostile role in John. In the Synoptics, Judas identifies Jesus with a kiss, but in John Jesus identifies himself (vv. 4–5). Although armed resistance and the cutting off of the ear of the high priest's slave is mentioned in every Gospel, only in John (v. 10) are the swordsman (Peter) and the victim (Malchus) identified by name (cf. 18:26). Jesus' authoritative command to let his disciples go free (v. 8) is interpreted as the fulfillment of his earlier word (6:39; 10:28), a culminating Johannine touch underscoring Jesus' self-sacrifice for his disciples (cf. 10:11, 15). Finally, Jesus orders an end to violent resistance (18:11; cf. Matt. 26:52–53; Luke 22:51).

18:12–27, Jesus Before the High Priest and Peter's Denial. When Jesus is taken to the high priest's house, his prediction that Peter would deny him three times is fulfilled (vv. 15–18, 25–27). In this John agrees with the other Gospels, but his account is remarkable in that it reports no nocturnal trial before the Sanhedrin (Matt. 26:59–68; Mark 14:55–65; but cf. Luke 22:66–71 where this meeting occurs on the following morning). No witnesses appear and there is no verdict (John 18:19–24). After Jesus testifies that he has always spoken quite openly, is struck by one of the attendants, and protests, he is then taken from Annas's house to Caiaphas (v. 24). John does not reproduce the more elaborate synoptic trial scene, in which Jesus was condemned for blasphemy (a charge often suggested in the Fourth Gospel).

In John, both Annas and Caiaphas are called high priest. But in vv. 13–14 (cf. 11:49) and v. 24 Caiaphas is clearly identified as high priest, and so he was, his father-in-law Annas having been deposed over a decade before Jesus' ministry began. In the narrative of vv. 15–23, however, Annas plays that role. The difficulty may be partly due to the fact that the same Greek word (*archiereus*) is sometimes used in the plural to designate "leading priests" (e.g., Mark 14:1, 10, 43, 53, 55), but some confusion remains (cf. also Luke 3:2; Acts 4:6). That in John 11:49 and 18:13 Caiaphas is described as high priest "in that year" is also odd, for it was not an annual office. Furthermore, after being told that Jesus was taken to Caiaphas (18:24) we hear nothing of what transpired there (cf. v. 28).

Peter's repeated denials of Jesus (vv. 15–18, 25–27) are related in terms similar to Mark's (14:53–54, 66–72), although there are differences of detail. For example, only John identifies one of Peter's interrogators as a kinsman of the man whose ear Peter had severed (John 18:26). Also, the cock crows immediately after Peter's final denial (v. 27), but John fails to mention Peter's weeping (Mark 14:72 and parallels).

18:28–19:16, Jesus Before Pilate. John's narration of the trial is so dramatic that it has made a lasting impression upon Christian memory and tradition, not least with respect to Pilate, who at the end appears caught between Jesus and the Jews. In the shorter synoptic version, Jesus remains silent except to respond laconically to Pilate's question of whether he may be a king (Mark 15:2 and parallels). In the Johannine, Jesus initially talks more than Pilate (18:33–38) but much less in the latter half (19:1–16), where they appear before the Jews and Pilate upbraids Jesus for not answering (19:9–10; cf. Mark 15:3–5 and parallels; →Pilate, Pontius).

18:28–38, Jesus Arraigned. Jesus is brought to Pilate at his headquarters (praetorium), the exact location of which is disputed, early in the morning. In John's account, Jesus was condemned at about noon (19:14; cf. Mark 15:25, 33–34 and parallels) on a Friday, the Day of Preparation, just before Passover, so that the Jews refuse to enter the praetorium (John 18:28). According to the unanimous testimony of the Synoptics, however, the Friday of Jesus' crucifixion followed the Passover meal, eaten the preceding evening. (Jesus was crucified on a Friday; the Gospels differ only with respect to the Jewish calendar.) The Jews have already determined that Jesus is guilty but do not answer directly Pilate's question about the charge (vv. 29–32). Obviously, they want Pilate to put Jesus to death because they have no authority to do so (v. 31). (Probably their statement to that effect reflects the actual historical situation.)

Throughout this episode Pilate moves in and out of the praetorium to question Jesus, who is inside, and then confront the Jews, who refuse to enter. Now he reenters the praetorium to question Jesus (v. 33), asking the question he puts to him in each of the other Gospels as well. Jesus' counterquestioning of Pilate and the latter's rejoinder are unique to John (vv. 34–35), as is Jesus' remarkable statement about the origin of his kingdom or kingship, with its sharp distinction between that kingship and the world. A worldly kingship would necessitate the disciples' offering physical resistance to protect Jesus from the Jews. Although Jesus was finally condemned to death and executed by Romans, in John the Jews are his mortal enemies (cf. 19:16). This state of affairs doubtless reflects the hostility between Jesus' followers and the synagogue at the time the Gospel was written. Pilate's conclusion that Jesus is, after all, a king, is met by Jesus' evasive answer (18:37), similar to his response in the Synoptics (Mark 15:2), but Jesus expands upon his unique function as witness to the truth in lines that are distinctively Johannine. Pilate's question (John 18:38) expresses his disinterest and cynicism, but it also mirrors his profound alienation from the truth.

18:39–40, Barabbas. Pilate, who would as soon be rid of the whole matter (as in Matt. 27:24, he literally washes his hands of Jesus), declares his finding that Jesus is innocent, asking the crowd whether they would have him set free (John 18:38b). Barabbas (v. 40) until this point has not been mentioned in the narrative, and no such custom as Pilate mentions (v. 39) has been documented from sources other than the Gospels. Mark (15:6–14) gives this incident in much fuller form, but the question Pilate puts to the crowd (15:9) is quite similar in John (18:39). John offers the briefest explanation of who Barabbas was; the term he uses to describe him (Gk. *lēstēs*), usually translated "robber"

(RSV), could also be applied to the kind of rebel Mark describes. The irony of the incident is obvious.

19:1–16, Jesus Condemned. At the point of the crowd's choosing Barabbas, the other Gospels have them immediately demand Jesus' crucifixion, whereupon Pilate releases Barabbas, quickly has Jesus scourged, and delivers him to be crucified (cf. Mark 15:15). In John, the trial does not end at this point, although Jesus is scourged and mocked (John 19:1–3). Pilate, who had been outside the praetorium with the Jews (18:38), evidently went inside to have Jesus scourged and now comes out again (19:4).

The trial culminates as Pilate brings Jesus out before the Jews and for the second time declares him innocent (vv. 4–5). The Jews now shout, "Crucify him!" as the crowd does in the synoptic Barabbas scene, and Pilate for the third time proclaims Jesus' innocence (v. 6; cf. Luke 23:4, 14–16, 22). When the Jews once again make their case against Jesus (John 19:7), Pilate's fears rise (v. 8). Apparently, he stands in awe of Jesus, as his question may imply (v. 9); his reaction follows from the Jews' assertion that Jesus has made himself Son of God. Jesus' silence in response to Pilate's question (v. 9) evokes a motif of the synoptic trial scene (Mark 15:4); at this stage the Johannine Jesus is scarcely prepared to explain his origins to the same Pilate who has asked cynically about truth (John 18:38). Pilate's assumptions about who has power and what power is stand in sharp contrast to Jesus' knowledge (19:10–11). Jesus knows the truth that Pilate cannot begin to understand. But even here John makes clear that Pilate is relatively innocent in comparison with Judas or, more probably, the Jews (v. 11).

Pilate's final effort to release Jesus puts his loyalty to Caesar in question (v. 12). John more than once suggests that Jesus' fate is intertwined with Jewish-Roman relations (cf. 11:48) and that Jewish leaders intend to sacrifice Jesus to Roman authority so they may continue to stand in its good graces. In Luke (23:2) Jesus' Jewish accusers represent him as politically subversive. Here the Jews suggest that Jesus is somehow a threat to Roman power, but at the same time they must know he is not. He is rather a threat to their own religious authority.

The ensuing scene (John 19:13–16) continues the byplay between Pilate and the Jews that will lead to Jesus' condemnation. The location of the pavement (v. 13) has been identified by some archaeologists, but the identification remains disputed (→ Gabbatha). Both the day and the hour (v. 14) differ from the Synoptics, in which Jesus is condemned and crucified on the morning of the first day of the feast (cf. Mark 15:25). Pilate's "Here is your King" evokes his earlier "Here is the man" (John 19:5). Jesus is king of the Jews; the implication is that Pilate will no longer take responsibility for him. The chief priests then finally disavow Jesus in proclaiming their loyalty to Caesar alone (v. 15). There is a fine irony here as the chief priests disavow not only Jesus but any king other than the Roman emperor. If, as is likely, the Gospel was written after the disastrous end of the Roman war (A.D. 70), there is a double irony. The war that was fought in the name of the lordship of God alone ended with the unequivocal assertion of the lordship of Caesar. Thus the prophecy of the chief priests would be entirely accurate. The scene concludes with Jesus' apparently being handed over to the chief priests for crucifixion (v. 16). That the Romans actually carried out the execution is clear enough (v. 15; cf. vv. 19, 23), but that John should portray Jesus as being delivered to the Jews is entirely appropriate in this Gospel (cf. 18:36) for they have been Jesus' mortal enemies all along.

The question of the role of the Jews in the death of Jesus demands that two points should now be made. First, Jesus was, in fact, executed by the Romans. Nevertheless, some priestly authorities, who served at the pleasure of the Romans, may have had an interest in Jesus' demise; that, in fact, is what the Gospel of John suggests (11:48; 19:15). Second, the extension of this guilt to Pharisees and Jews generally is unjustifiable. By "Pharisees" (and "Jews") John means not just the contemporaries of Jesus (much less all Jews); he has in view certain members of the leadership of the synagogue of his own day, with which he sees himself and his church in mortal conflict. It is the dark side of the Gospel of John that allows the broader implications to be drawn. Certainly the Evangelist could not have foreseen the awful implications and effects of his words as they have resounded through the centuries.

19:17–30, The Execution of Jesus. The crucifixion and death of Jesus is described in as few words in John as in the other Gospels. In general, the Gospels do not draw out or dramatize Jesus' death, nor do they dwell upon its horror. Crucifixion was a common form of capital punishment in the Roman world (→ Cross).

In John, Jesus carries his own cross, as was customary (cf. Mark 15:21 and parallels), to the place of his execution, Golgotha (John 19:17). Its site may now be marked by the Church of the Holy Sepulchre. According to all the Gospels, Jesus was crucified between two other condemned criminals (v. 18), and his cross bore a title that (again according to custom) named the charge on which he had been condemned (v. 19). Only in John do we read that the title was written in three languages (v. 20) and that the chief priests wanted it changed to indicate that Jesus only claimed to be king of the Jews (vv. 21–22). As they had put pressure on Pilate, they now get the back of Pilate's hand; this wretched criminal can be their king. John alone cites Ps. 22:18 on the dividing of Jesus' garments (John 19:23–24).

All the Gospels state that several women witnessed Jesus' crucifixion, although his disciples had fled at his arrest. All except Luke note that Mary Magdalene was one of them. The distinctive feature of John's account is the presence of the mother of Jesus and the Beloved Disciple at the cross. Jesus' words to his mother and to his disciple are clear enough in meaning (vv. 26, 27); whether they are to be understood literally or symbolically is the question. Christian interpretation has often seen the church symbolized in Jesus' mother, but the literal interpretation has persisted to the extent that in Ephesus, the traditional site of the grave of the apostle John, there is also a tomb venerated as Mary's.

Jesus' death is narrated much more briefly than in the Synoptics. There is no mocking of Jesus on the cross (Mark 15:29–32 and parallels); no cry of dereliction (Mark 15:34; cf. v. 37); no rending of the veil of the Temple at Jesus' death (Mark 15:38 and parallels); and no word from the centurion (Mark 15:39 and parallels). Jesus' thirsting (John 19:28) allows Scripture to be fulfilled (Ps. 69:21); as in the other Gospels he is given vinegar to drink (John 19:29). In John he says simply, "It is finished" (v. 30), and expires; the Greek phrase could be translated, "He gave over the Spirit." We have been led to expect that the glorified Jesus would send the Spirit. Jesus' earthly life and his revelatory work is complete (cf. 17:4). The hour has fully come.

19:31–37, The Piercing of His Side. This incident, found in no other Gospel, depends upon John's unique chronology in which Jesus dies before the beginning of Passover (v. 31). Breaking the legs of a crucified man was an act of mercy that hastened death by rendering the victim unable to maintain himself erect so that he could breathe. Thus because Jesus was found dead, his legs were not broken but his side pierced (vv. 33–34). The piercing causes an efflux of water and blood, which is attested by an eyewitness. The Scriptures are fulfilled (vv. 36–37). The first quotation is from Exod. 12:46 or Num. 9:12, both of which refer to the Passover lamb. (A similar passage in Ps. 34:20 refers to the righteous man.) In John 1:29 and 36, Jesus is called the Lamb of God. The second quotation is from Zech. 12:10, which speaks of the mourning of Jerusalem for him whom they have pierced (cf. Rev. 1:7). If the context of that passage is in view, it is appropriate, for Jerusalem has just caused Jesus to be pierced.

The witness (John 19:35) is likely the Beloved Disciple, who is said to have been present at the cross (v. 26) and in 21:24 also is extolled as a reliable witness. The blood and water came to have great symbolic value for Christians as signifying the Eucharist and baptism, whether or not that meaning was understood or intended originally, and commentators have pointed to a seemingly related passage in 1 John 5:6–8. The blood and water would thus symbolize the salvation wrought through the death of Jesus, particularly as it was represented in the earliest sacraments.

19:38–42, The Burial. According to all Gospel accounts, Jesus was buried by Joseph of Arimathea, variously described in the Gospels as a prominent person and an adherent of Jesus. He is not otherwise mentioned. That Joseph went to Pilate secretly because of fear of the Jews is, typically, said only by John (v. 38). Also only in John, Nicodemus joins him, bringing a large mixture of spices for anointing Jesus' body (v. 39) for burial. The Synoptics do not recount such a preparation (v. 40), for at least according to Mark and Luke the women who discovered the tomb empty intended to anoint Jesus' body. John alone notes that Jesus was interred in a garden tomb near where he had been crucified (vv. 41–42), supporting the tradition of the Church of the Holy Sepulchre, which commemorates the site of the crucifixion as well as the tomb of Jesus.

20:1–31
Empty Tomb and Resurrection Appearances

20:1–10, The Empty Tomb. The common factor in all accounts is that Mary Magdalene goes to the tomb early on Sunday morning and finds it empty (→ Mary). In John, Mary Magdalene alone makes the discovery; she conveys the news to Peter and the Beloved Disciple, who quickly go to the tomb and confirm it (vv. 3–10). The Beloved Disciple, as usual, outdoes Peter by arriving first at the tomb; he sees the discarded graveclothes (vv. 4–5) but allows Peter to enter first and see also (v. 6). Perhaps significantly, only the Beloved Disciple is said to believe (v. 8; cf. 13:21–30). That neither yet knew the Scripture predicting Jesus' resurrection (20:9; cf. 1 Cor. 15:4) underscores the unanticipated character of the discovery. The disciples return home (John 20:10) as Mary apparently stands outside the tomb weeping (v. 11), creating the impression that they go past her without sharing the good news. The poor transition and lack of attestation in other Gospels raises the question of whether the episode of Peter and the Beloved Disciple is a later insertion into a traditional text. But most ancient manuscripts of Luke contain a summary of this account or the nucleus from which it grew (Luke 24:12). Notably, Luke does not mention the Beloved Disciple but only

Peter, who leaves the tomb in a state of wonderment. Moreover, Luke 24:24 refers to such a visit to the tomb by disciples, who obviously did not attain faith. In light of this, John's reference to only the Beloved Disciple's belief (John 20:8) becomes more significant; it is somehow exceptional.

20:11–18, Mary at the Tomb. Mary, left weeping outside the tomb (v. 11), now looks inside and sees the angels mentioned in the other accounts. They ask her why she is weeping and receive an answer of unparalleled poignancy (v. 13). Then in a brief but artfully narrated scene (vv. 14–18) Mary sees and recognizes Jesus, having at first mistaken him for the gardener. This scene is paralleled only in Matt. 28:9–10, which briefly recounts how the two women, including Mary Magdalene, encounter the risen Jesus as they depart from the tomb. Both stories conclude with Jesus' instructions to deliver a message to "my brethren." In John, Jesus instructs Mary not to hold him because he has not yet ascended, although he is ascending (v. 17; cf. Matt. 28:9). Subsequent Johannine resurrection narratives are presumably to be understood as manifestations of the ascended Jesus.

20:19–29, Appearances to the Twelve and to Thomas. The resurrection scenes of chap. 20 culminate in a pair of appearances of the risen Lord to his disciples on successive Sunday evenings and find a parallel in Luke 24:36–43. In both the Lucan and the Johannine scenes, the risen Jesus' demonstration of his identity with the crucified is a dominant motif. Yet John omits Jesus' striking demonstration of his corporeal reality, namely, the eating of broiled fish. In John, the ascended, exalted Jesus appears to his disciples through closed doors (20:19, 26) and is scarcely a normal, physical presence.

The disciples must protect themselves from those Jews who have also been enemies of Jesus (v. 19). Jesus appears suddenly and mysteriously. He establishes his identity with the disciples, who are obviously convinced (v. 20), sends them to continue his mission to the world (v. 21; cf. 17:18), and equips them with his Spirit (20:22), the fulfillment of earlier promises (cf. 14:16; 16:7, 13–14). This scene marks the beginning of the church as a body inspired by the Spirit of Jesus and dedicated to the spreading of the gospel (cf. Acts 2).

Thomas' skeptical reaction to the other disciples' report of their encounter with Jesus (John 20:24–25) sets the stage for Jesus' next appearance (v. 26) and secures his own reputation as the proverbial doubting Thomas. When Jesus reappears and offers him the proof he has been seeking (v. 27), Thomas may not actually touch Jesus, although he confesses him as Lord and God (v. 28). Jesus' invitation to Thomas to touch him probably means that he has now ascended (cf. v. 17). (The ascended Jesus sends the Spirit in Acts.) Jesus' final word to Thomas puts even seeing Jesus, much less touching him, in proper perspective (v. 29), as Jesus in effect pronounces a blessing upon the church of the future for which he has already prayed (17:20).

20:30–31, The Purpose of the Gospel. The Evangelist's summation sounds like the conclusion of the book, although no manuscript lacking chap. 21 survives. Appropriately the purpose of the narrative is now stated. The theological themes of the Gospel are brought to a culmination in chap. 20, as is the literary development. Chap. 21 deals with other issues.

21:1–25
The Epilogue; Jesus' Appearance to Peter and Others by the Sea

Generally regarded as an appendix, or at best an epilogue, chap. 21 ties up neatly questions having to do with people somehow important to the Johannine community, particularly Peter and the Beloved Disciple. Whether chap. 21 was written by the same author who composed chaps. 1–20 is a debated question. The style and vocabulary, the interest in Peter, and the final appearance of the Beloved Disciple mark it as Johannine, that is, as a product of the same circles that produced chaps. 1–20. The chapter has two parts: vv. 1–14, an account of an appearance of the risen Jesus to seven disciples by the Sea of Tiberias (or Galilee); vv. 15–25, a long conversation between Jesus and Peter that continues in the same setting and concludes with an appearance of the Beloved Disciple.

21:1–14, The Appearance by the Sea. This resurrection story is unparalleled in the canonical Gospels. The closest parallel is Luke 5:1–11, a call story, in which the disciples are fishing on the Sea of Galilee (Gennesaret), Simon Peter figures prominently, and Jesus guides the disciples to make a large catch of fish. That the Lucan and Johannine stories are variants of the same tradition remains a possibility, especially in view of their apparent similarity of purpose as well as content: Jesus commissions, or recommissions, his disciples. Luke may have placed an original resurrection narrative at the outset of Jesus' ministry. The other Gospel call stories are entirely different. Interestingly, only here in John do the disciples of Jesus appear as fishermen, their vocation in the other Gospels.

This scene is said to be the third appearance of the risen Jesus to his disciples (John 21:14). Apparently, the appearance to Mary Magdalene (20:14–18) is excluded in the count, presumably because she is not a disciple. But the behavior of the disciples, before and at the appearance of Jesus, does not accord with the presumption that they know he has risen from the dead. Peter and company are returning to their previous occupation (21:3); they are astounded to see Jesus (v. 7). The story has all the marks of an initial appearance to these disciples.

The meal scene in vv. 9–13 has eucharistic overtones, although there is no wine and no eucharistic celebration that we know of involved fish. At least one of the Lucan resurrection appearances takes place at a meal (Luke 24:30; cf. 41–43). The meaning of the number of fish (153) remains a mystery. That the disciples do not dare question Jesus but know their host is the Lord (v. 12) allows a dimension of mystery to hang over the whole narrative to the end.

21:15–25, Peter and the Beloved Disciple.
The interchange between Jesus and Peter continues the same scene; the others fade into the background. Obviously, Jesus' questioning of Peter (vv. 15–17) allows Peter to reestablish himself. The exact meaning of Jesus' initial question (v. 15) is uncertain, because we cannot know precisely the antecedent of "these." We are not even certain whether "these" are the objects of Peter's love or others who also love Jesus. Nevertheless, Jesus clearly calls on Peter to validate his affirmations of love by feeding or tending Jesus' sheep or lambs, that is, his flock. Peter is thus cast in the role of church leader, pastor (i.e., one who tends a flock). Jesus' words about Peter's fate (vv. 18–19) provide the earliest hint we have of the martyrdom of Peter, which was in later tradition associated with Rome.

The final episode of the Gospel concerns the Beloved Disciple (vv. 20–24), who appears (v. 20) but does not speak. Peter's question (v. 21) probably reflects tension in the early church between circles loyal to him (cf. 1 Cor. 1:12) and those who looked to the Beloved Disciple. Jesus' response to Peter rejects that rivalry as of no concern to himself and indicates that it is no proper concern of Peter's (v. 22). The writer then notes a common misinterpretation of Jesus' statement about the Beloved Dis-

ciple and corrects it by reference to what Jesus actually said (v. 23). Probably the death of the Beloved Disciple before Jesus' return had caused some consternation. This disciple is identified not only as the true witness (cf. 19:35) but also as the author (or at least the source) of this Gospel. It has frequently been deduced, in light of church tradition, that the Beloved Disciple was John the son of Zebedee (cf. 21:2). There are, however, problems with this identification (see Introduction above). At the very least, however, this passage evinces a strong interest in the eyewitness testimony on which the Gospel is based. In the final statement (v. 25) we see a reflection of the earlier colophon (20:30–31).

Bibliography
Barrett, C. K. *The Gospel According to St. John: An Introduction with Commentary and Notes on the Greek Text*, 2d. ed. Philadelphia: Westminster, 1978.

Brown, R. E. *The Gospel According to John.* Anchor Bible 29, 29A. Garden City, NY: Doubleday, 1966, 1970.

_____. *The Community of the Beloved Disciple.* New York: Paulist Press, 1979.

Bultmann, R. *The Gospel of John: A Commentary.* Translated by G. R. Beasley-Murray et al. Philadelphia: Westminster, 1971.

Culpepper, R. A. *Anatomy of the Fourth Gospel: A Study in Literary Design.* Philadelphia: Fortress, 1983.

Kysar, R. *The Fourth Evangelist and His Gospel: An Examination of Contemporary Scholarship.* Minneapolis, MN: Augsburg, 1975.

Lindars, B. *The Gospel of John.* New Century Bible. Grand Rapids, MI: Eerdmans, 1972.

Martyn, J. L. *History and Theology in the Fourth Gospel.* 2d rev. ed. Nashville, TN: Abingdon, 1979.

Smith, D. M. "Johannine Christianity: Some Reflections on its Character and Delineation." *New Testament Studies* 21 (1975):222–48.

_____. *Johannine Christianity.* Columbia, SC: University of South Carolina Press, 1984. Pp. 1–36.

_____. *John*, 2d ed. Proclamation Commentaries. Philadelphia: Fortress, 1986.

ACTS

CARL R. HOLLADAY

INTRODUCTION

Authorship

In spite of the ancient, well-established tradition that the third Gospel and the Acts of the Apostles were written by Luke the physician, Paul's traveling companion and close associate (Philem. 24; Col. 4:14; 2 Tim. 4:11), both works are anonymous. Neither the name "Luke" nor an unnamed "physician-disciple" is even mentioned in either writing.

Both works are linked together by their common addressee, Theophilus (Luke 1:1–4; Acts 1:1–2). The similarity of their language and style, as well as their unified literary and theological purposes, leave little doubt that they derive from the same author—possibly, but not certainly, Luke.

Date

At the earliest, Acts cannot have been written prior to the latest firm chronological marker recorded in the book—Festus's appointment as procurator (24:27), which, on the basis of independent sources, appears to have occurred between A.D. 55 and 59. At the latest, it cannot have been written after the mid-second century, when it begins to be alluded to or quoted by other authors. It is commonly dated in the last quarter of the first century, after the destruction of Jerusalem in A.D. 70 (which the Gospel appears to presuppose already; cf. Luke 21:20–24).

Literary Features

Genre. Since Acts is the second part of a two-volume work, the critical task is to identify appropriately the genre of Luke-Acts. The best internal clue is provided in Luke's own preface (Luke 1:1), which suggests that the work be classified simply as a "narrative." The story that unfolds exhibits biographical, historical, theological, sermonic, and apologetic elements, yet no one of these adequately captures the full range of the work. Rather, Luke-Acts should be understood as a narrative with different dimensions and multiple purposes.

Both its form and content suggest that the work was intended to be read as the continuation of the OT biblical story. The narrative throughout confirms what the preface states:

the story is told to strengthen faith (Luke 1:4). Consequently, it should be read as an *edifying narrative* intended to inform, reinforce, and render more credible faith where it already exists and probably to create and instill faith where it does not exist.

Structure. In one sense, Acts seems organized around geographical concentric circles (1:8), in which the progress of "the Word" is traced from Jerusalem (chaps. 1–7), throughout Judea and Samaria (chaps. 8–12), and finally to "the end of the earth," probably Rome (chaps. 13–28).

In another sense, the work comprises two parts: chaps. 1–12, which present the church's beginning in Palestine and its supplanting traditional Judaism as the new locus of God's presence within Israel; and chaps. 13–28, which tell how the gospel moves westward and how God's promises are extended fully to the Gentiles. Each section has its central figure: Peter in the first and Paul in the second.

Other Features. One conspicuous feature is the *summaries* provided throughout the work. There are both fairly extensive summaries (2:42–47; 4:32–35; 5:12–16) and briefer statements documenting the numerical growth and spread of the church (2:41, 47; 4:4; 5:14; 6:7; 9:31, 42; 11:21, 24; 12:24; 14:1, 16:5; 19:20; 28:31).

Related to this is the use of *typical examples*, a literary technique through which Luke depicts a single character or event to illustrate what occurred typically. The healing of the lame man (3:1–11) may be regarded as typical of the many "signs and wonders" performed by the apostles (5:12). Barnabas' generosity is presented as a concrete example that typified the many property owners who sold their possessions (4:34–37). The episodes reported in detail during Paul's preaching mission at Philippi (16:11–40) serve to illustrate typical features of his preaching among Gentiles. His vindication before Gallio (18:12–17) concretely illustrates the way Roman authorities typically treated Christian missionaries.

One of the most striking features of Acts is the number of *speeches* contained in the book and the amount of space they occupy—roughly 20 percent of the entire narrative. They occur throughout the work, in each of its major sections, exhibiting different types: missionary speeches directed to Jews (2:14–36; 3:12–26; 13:16–41; 28:25–28) and Gentiles (10:34–43;

14:15–17; 17:22–31); various defense speeches by Peter (4:8–12, 19b–20; 5:29b–32), Stephen (7:2–53, 56, 59b, 60b), and Paul (22:1, 3–21; 23:1, 3, 5, 6b; 24:10–21; 25:8, 10–11; 26:2–23, 25–27, 29; 28:17–20); "church speeches," Christians speaking to other Christians (1:16–22; 11:5–17; 15:7–21; 21:20–25), especially Paul's "pastoral homily," or farewell address, to the Ephesian elders (20:18–35); and speeches by outsiders (5:35–39; 19:25–28, 35–40; 24:2–8; 25:14–21, 24–27). In addition, numerous prayers and conversations are reported throughout the work. By providing various types of speeches fitted to the characters and the occasion, Luke is following a practice well established among ancient authors—Jewish, Greek, and Roman.

Language and Style. Luke's language and style reflect the Hellenistic Greek typically used in literary circles of his day. While it has much in common with popular, spoken speech, it is generally more polished, and intentionally so. With his considerable vocabulary and sophisticated use of language, Luke compares favorably with contemporary classical authors, such as Xenophon. Both his language and style are heavily influenced by the Greek OT, in which he is thoroughly steeped, and this distinguishes him sharply from his Greco-Roman counterparts.

His attention to literary style can be seen in his fondness for numerous rhetorical devices, such as the well-established Greek form of emphasis by understatement (12:18; 14:28; 17:4, 12; 19:11, 23–24; 20:12; 21:39; 27:20; 28:2). His skillful use of language is also seen in the way he effectively creates literary mood or captures the atmosphere of particular occasions, whether it be the primitive religious environment of Lystra (14:8–18) or Malta (28:1–10) or a poignant farewell (20:36–37). It is also seen in his ability to write in different literary styles. In describing the earliest period of the church (chaps. 1–12), he uses an archaic, biblical style that echoes the language of the Greek OT. This helps establish the close identity between his account and the biblical story he seeks to continue. Or, he can write in a more "modern" Greek style, especially on occasions where he needs to capture the mood of a contemporary setting, such as Athens (chap. 17), Ephesus (chap. 19), or a trial scene before Romans in Caesarea (chaps. 24–26).

Links Between Acts and Luke

Perhaps the best introduction to Acts is a thorough, attentive reading of the Gospel of Luke. To be sure, Acts can be read—and historically has been read—independently of Luke's Gospel, for in one sense the story it tells is self-contained. Yet, when read in the light of Luke's Gospel, certain aspects of Acts that otherwise might remain obscure become understandable.

There are, first of all, continuous themes that run through both volumes. The "kingdom of God," which is mentioned over thirty times in the Gospel (e.g., Luke 4:43; 6:20; 8:1, 10; 9:2, 11, 27, 60, 62; 10:9, 11; 13:18, 20, 28–29; 16:16; 17:20–21; 19:11; 21:31; 22:16, 18; 23:51), continues to be preached in Acts (1:3; 8:12; 14:22; 19:8; 20:25; 28:23, 31). Jesus' insistence that his suffering, death, and resurrection were "divine necessities" (Luke 9:22; 18:31–33; 24:7, 26, 44–46; also 9:31, 44; 13:33; 17:25) is a prominent theme in the apostolic preaching in Acts (3:18; 17:3; 26:23; also 8:32–35). The very visible role played by the Holy Spirit in the life and ministry of Jesus (e.g., Luke 1:35; 2:26–27; 4:1, 14, 18–21) continues in Acts, where the Spirit "comes upon" the church, especially at critical moments (1:5; 2:1–4; 8:15; 10:44–48; 11:15–17; 19:6), but also motivates the church's prophets to speak and act (Acts 4:8; 6:3, 5; 7:55; 8:26, 29, 39; 10:19; 11:12; 13:2; 16:6–7; 19:21; 20:23; 21:4, 11).

Throughout Luke-Acts there is also a consistent emphasis on the proper use of possessions. Luke's Gospel not only records Jesus' instructions about almsgiving (3:11; 6:30; 11:41; 12:33–34; 14:14; 18:22; 19:8), it also presents many parables of Jesus where the proper attitude toward possessions is a central feature (Luke 10:29–37; 15:11–32; 16:1–9, 19–31; 19:11–27) and incidents in Jesus' ministry where discipleship is defined in terms of this question (10:38–42; 18:18–30; 19:1–10; 21:1–4). Acts continues this emphasis in its depiction of the church's generosity and willingness to dispose of its goods to assist the needy (2:44–45; 4:32–34). It also highlights the actions of generous individuals, such as Barnabas (4:36–37), Dorcas (9:36–43), and Paul (20:33–35), and churches, such as Antioch (11:29–30). It also provides negative examples to reinforce the point (1:16–19; 5:1–11; 8:20–24; 24:26).

Certain events or actions depicted in Acts are either already anticipated in Luke's Gospel or explicitly predicted: the apostles as Christ's duly appointed witnesses (Acts 1:8; 5:32; 10:41; cf. Luke 24:48); rejoicing while suffering on behalf of Christ (Acts 5:41; cf. Luke 6:23); the appropriate behavior of missionaries in the face of rejection (Acts 13:51; 18:6; cf. Luke 9:5; 10:10–11); the appropriate way to bear witness when brought before various officials (Acts 4:8–12; 5:27–32; 7:54–60; 22:1–21; 24:10–21; 25:8, 10–11; 26:1–23; cf. Luke 12:11–12; 21:12–14); offering the gospel to Jews first, and when rejected, then to Gentiles (Acts 13:46–48; 18:6; 28:23–28; cf. Luke 14:15–24; also 2:32, 34); Jesus' promise that repentance and forgiveness of sins would be preached universally (Acts 2:38; 3:19; 5:31; 11:18; 17:30–31; cf. Luke 24:47; also 1:77; 3:3).

In some instances, Luke's Gospel illuminates more fully persons or events in Acts: the ministry and preaching of John the Baptist (Acts 1:4–5; 11:16; 13:24–25; 18:25; 19:3–4; cf. Luke 3:1–22, esp. vv. 15–17); Jesus' ministry (Acts 2:22–24; 10:36–40; amplified by the entire Gospel of Luke), especially certain images or scriptures used of Christ, such as God's prophet (Acts 3:22; 7:37; cf. Luke 24:19) or the rejected stone (Acts 4:11; Luke 20:17–18).

Certain incidents in Acts are depicted in ways that parallel similar incidents in the Gospel: the healing of paralyzed persons (Acts 3:1–11; 9:32–35; cf. Luke 5:17–26); raising persons from the dead (Acts 9:36–43; 20:7–12; Luke 7:11–17; 8:40–56); exorcisms (Acts 5:16; 8:7; 19:11–16; cf. Luke 4:31–37); healing persons with fever (Acts 28:8; cf. Luke 4:38–39). In some respects, Paul's final trip to Jerusalem and his trial echo the Lucan account of Jesus' Passion: the crowds' responses (Acts 21:36; 22:22; cf. Luke 23:18); Paul's being "handed over by Jews to Gentiles" (Acts 21:11; 28:17; cf. Luke 18:32; 24:6–7); his own declarations of innocence (22:25; 23:1; 24:12–13, 16, 19–20; 25:8, 10–11; 26:21–23; 28:17–19), confirmed numerous times by Jewish and Roman officials (23:9, 29; 25:18, 25–26; 26:31–32; on Jesus' innocence, cf. Luke 23:4, 13–15, 22, 41, 47; also Acts 4:27, 30; 7:52; 22:14).

See also Luke.

COMMENTARY

1:1–26

Between Easter and Pentecost

1:1–8

Jesus' Story Continued

From the outset, Acts is connected with the third Gospel, Luke's "first volume" that gives a comprehensive account of Jesus' deeds and words until he was "taken up," or ascended into heaven (Luke 24:51). Their common addressee is Theophilus (Luke 1:1–4), otherwise unmentioned in the NT.

Whereas Luke 24 confines Christ's appearances to a single day (Easter Sunday), this period is now extended to "forty days" (Acts 1:3). His activity included "many proofs," presumably signs and wonders, various appearances to the apostles, and instructions (v. 3), which are summarized in Luke 24:44–49. The continua-

tion of the kingdom of God is anticipated in the Gospel (Luke 22:16, 18, esp. vv. 28–30). Precisely what the kingdom signified remained unclear, as the apostles' question (Acts 1:6) shows.

During a meal (v. 4), Jesus enjoins the apostles to remain in Jerusalem, echoing his earlier instruction that their prophetic witness to him would begin from Jerusalem (Luke 24:47). John the Baptist had anticipated that his form of baptism would be superseded by a more impressive form of immersion administered by the Messiah in which persons would be suffused with God's Spirit (Acts 1:5) and confronted with the fire of God's judgment (Luke 3:16).

At perhaps another gathering (Acts 1:6), the apostles ask when Christ would "restore the kingdom to Israel." His response (v. 7) exposes their misunderstanding. Entering God's kingdom is not a matter of knowing when to mark the calendar but of awaiting and receiving God's promised Spirit. The geographical scheme (v. 8) provides the organizing framework for the rest of the narrative (see Introduction).

1:9–12

Ascension

Christ's ascension has already been anticipated (Luke 9:51; Acts 1:2) but now is amplified in greater detail. Compared with the rest of the NT, Luke attaches greater significance to it as a separate event (cf. Mark 16:19; John 3:13; 6:62; 20:17; Eph. 4:8–10; 1 Tim. 3:16). In Luke 24:51, one textual tradition records Christ's ascension on Easter Sunday, whereas here it occurs forty days later (Acts 1:3). By placing the ascension on the Mount of Olives (v. 12), Luke continues his pattern of locating the post-Easter appearances in close proximity to Jerusalem (Luke 24:13, 28, 33, 47, 50, 52).

Luke's portrait is slightly reminiscent of Elijah's ascension (2 Kings 2:11), though closer to the extrabiblical tradition depicting the end of Moses' life as a disappearance into a cloud (Josephus *Antiquities of the Jews* 4.326). His promised return in similar fashion (Acts 1:11) recalls Jesus' own earlier prediction of the Son of man's return (Luke 21:27; cf. Dan. 7:13–14).

The ascension occurs in the company of the apostles (Acts 1:2, 9), who thereby become eyewitnesses (cf. 1:22). In keeping with OT criteria for certified testimony (Deut. 19:15), Luke typically provides two witnesses who interpret the event's significance (Luke 24:4). Their "white robes" probably attest their extraordinary status (cf. Luke 24:4; John 20:12). By emphasizing the manner rather than the time of Jesus' return, Luke redirects the church's attention away from end-time speculation (Acts 1:7).

1:13–26
Replacing Judas

The Twelve are named earlier (Luke 6:13–16). Heading this list are Peter and John, who figure prominently in the succeeding narrative (Acts 3:1, 11; 8:14). James's death is later recorded (12:2). Omitting Judas Iscariot now confirms his expulsion from the apostolic circle and prepares readers for his replacement (1:15–26). To this point, readers know only of Judas's betrayal (Luke 22:47–53), not his fate.

Joining the apostles are "the women," probably those from Galilee named earlier who had been healed by Jesus, supported him financially (Luke 8:2–3), witnessed the crucifixion (Luke 23:49), and first bore witness of the resurrection to disbelieving apostles (Luke 23:55–56; 24:1–11). The family of Jesus has also been introduced earlier (Luke 8:19–21), and Luke treats them favorably, especially Mary (Luke 1–2). Elsewhere, they are portrayed as embarrassed and skeptical (Mark 3:21; John 7:5; though cf. John 2:1, 12; 19:25). Here, his family are among the nucleus of the faithful.

In keeping with Jesus' earlier promise that the Twelve would enjoy special status in his coming kingdom (Luke 22:28–30), the sacred circle must be reconstituted. Accordingly, both the death of Judas and the choice of his successor are interpreted as "divine necessities" foretold in Scripture (Acts 1:16, 20). Specifying the number as 120 (v. 15; cf. "many others," Luke 8:3) indicates a sizeable pool of candidates from which successors to Judas could be found.

Two OT citations figure centrally in this first speech by Peter (Acts 1:16–22).

In Ps. 69:25 the psalmist's enemies are cursed to live deserted and lonely. In Acts 1:20a, Judas is apparently regarded as such an enemy because his "small farm" (v. 18) had turned out to be a "desolate habitation." The Lucan accent falls on the tragic circumstances of Judas's death. His is the awful fate of those who attempt to thwart God's plan (cf. 5:1–11; 12:1–23). Matthew's account provides a sharp contrast: a remorseful Judas hangs himself (Matt. 27:3–10).

How he died is uncertain. "Falling headlong" (Acts 1:18) may suggest an accidental fall from a building or even a suicidal leap. The alternative reading, "swelling up," perhaps suggests some physical malady. In either case, the pit of his stomach burst, and his blood gave the field its name, Akeldama (v. 19).

The second OT citation (Ps. 109:8; Acts

1:20b) originally called for the seizure of the enemy's goods. In its altered form here, it provides the rationale for choosing Judas' successor. The chief qualification for the replacement is continuous participation in the historical ministry to Jesus from the time of John the Baptist until the ascension (v. 22). The essential apostolic function was to be a "witness to his resurrection" (v. 22; Luke 24:45–48; Acts 2:32; 3:15; 4:33; 5:32; 10:41; 13:31). The two candidates, Joseph Barsabbas and Matthias, are otherwise unmentioned in the NT. The final choice was by casting lots, but the decision was clearly God's (v. 24).

2:1–8:3
Beginning of the Church and Spread of the Gospel in Jerusalem

2:1–47
Inauguration of the Messianic Community on Pentecost

2:1–4, The Coming of the Spirit on Pentecost. Promises made earlier by John the Baptist (Luke 3:16) and the risen Lord (Luke 24:49; Acts 1:8) are now fulfilled. Among NT writers, only Luke sets the church's beginning on the day of Pentecost, fifty days after Passover (Luke 22:1; Lev. 23:15–21). His adopting the tradition of a forty-day period of post-Easter appearances required at least this much time (Acts 1:3). The nucleus of the messianic community certainly included the apostles to whom Christ had promised the Spirit (1:8) and conceivably the 120 disciples (1:15). The Spirit's arrival is presented in a way that anticipates the prophecy in 2:19: the loud wind from heaven serves as a "wonder in the heaven above," while the tongues of fire resting on those gathered become "signs on the earth beneath." "Wind and fire" may recall a similar extraordinary appearance of the Lord to Elijah (1 Kings 29:11–13). All of those gathered, whether the Twelve or 120, were "filled with the Holy Spirit" (Acts 2:4), the first of several such occurrences involving both individuals and groups in Acts (4:8, 31; 8:17; 10:44–47; 11:15; 13:9, 52; 19:1–6). What distinguishes this particular infusion of the Spirit is that the recipients speak "in other tongues," i.e., foreign languages (cf. 1:6, 8, 11). The phenomenon is repeated at the conversion of Cornelius (10:46).

2:5–13, The Worldwide Audience. The crowd attracted by this cacophony of sounds are Jews "living in" Jerusalem, not pilgrims from the Diaspora. They are struck by the speakers' distinctive Galilean accent (v. 7; cf. 1:11), yet they comprehend what is being said in their respective native dialects (vv. 6, 8, 11). The magnitude of the miracle is underscored as they list

---

Opposite: In the excavated ruins of Ephesus this peristyle offers a view of Ionian columns that once stood before a Greek council chamber; first century B.C. Ephesus, which became the fourth largest city in the Roman Empire in the first century A.D., was the site of Paul's mission described in Acts 18:24–19:41.

the nations from which they have emigrated (vv. 9–11). With its emphasis on universal understanding, the account is sometimes read as a reversal of the universal confusion of Babel (Gen. 11:1–9). More likely, Luke wants to stress that the Jewish community which first hears the gospel at Pentecost is genuinely universal in scope, hence representative of world Jewry. His narrative description here anticipates the promise in Peter's speech that "all flesh" (Acts 2:17; also v. 21) would receive God's Spirit.

2:14–36, Peter's Sermon. Among Peter's several speeches in Acts (3:12–26; 4:8–12, 19b–20; 5:29–32; 10:34–43), this sermon has special importance. Like Jesus at his Nazareth inaugural (Luke 4:16–30), Peter is introduced as an interpreter of OT Scripture. He now begins to unfold publicly the secrets of Scripture interpretation expounded by the risen Lord to the apostles on Easter (Luke 24:44–48). The sermon introduces major Lucan themes developed throughout the book, e.g., outpouring of God's Spirit (Acts 2:17, 18; cf. 10:45), universality of the gospel (2:17, 21; cf. 2:39; 13:47–48), authenticating signs and wonders (2:19; cf. 2:43; 4:30; 5:12; 6:8; 8:13), and salvation in the name of the Lord (2:21; cf. 2:39; 4:12).

In the first part (2:14–21), Peter interprets the events of Pentecost as fulfilling Joel 2:28–32. What was expected "in the last days" (Isa. 2:2) has now come to pass: a dramatic effusion of God's Spirit experienced by men and women, young and old, accompanied by signs and wonders, both visible and audible, with truly cosmic impact. This interruption of the normal course of events is seen as a prelude to "the day of the Lord," when history would end, and a time when people would call out to the Lord for salvation.

In the second part (Acts 2:22–36), Peter explains Jesus' death and resurrection in light of two Davidic psalms: 16:8–11 and 110:1. His introduction to this part summarizes the essential features of the Jesus story that have been rehearsed at length in the Gospel: a ministry empowered by God, death by human hands yet according to God's will, resurrection by God (Acts 2:22–24). Rather than proving these claims, Peter assumes them throughout the sermon. These things the apostles have witnessed (v. 32).

In Ps. 16:8–11, as Peter reads it, David acknowledged a "Lord" who would not be abandoned to the corruption of death in Hades (Acts 2:27). Since David both died and was buried, Peter concludes that he cannot have been speaking of himself but that he must have envisioned some later figure who would escape death. Peter insists that this could only have been Jesus, who had been raised (v. 31). Peter cites Ps. 110:1, also attributed to David, as evidence that he envisioned his "Lord" sitting at

God's right hand, exalted in a position of victory over his enemies (Acts 2:34–36). Once again, Peter disqualifies David as the "exalted Lord" mentioned in the psalm since he "did not ascend into the heavens" (v. 34). By the process of elimination, Peter identifies the risen Jesus as the only legitimate candidate to whom these two psalms could intelligibly refer. Consequently, the exalted terms of the psalms, notably God's "Holy One" (v. 27) and "Lord" (v. 25), Peter applies to the crucified Jesus (v. 36). The risen Lord now is seen as the one who pours out the divine Spirit at this inaugural event (v. 33).

2:37–41, Response to Peter's Sermon. Peter's preaching strikes a responsive chord and turns the crowds into willing inquirers. The cry for salvation will be heard again (16:30; 22:10; cf. Luke 3:10, 12).

The call to repentance and the promise of forgiven sins echoes the preaching of John the Baptist (Luke 3:3, 8; cf. 5:32) and fulfills the promise of the risen Lord (Luke 24:47). The baptism Peter requires is distinguished from John's baptism by being "in the name of Jesus Christ" (cf. Acts 19:5). The formula may suggest that Jesus' name was pronounced over them at their baptism.

Along with the forgiveness of sins, the hearers receive (a measure of) what the risen Lord had received from the Father (Acts 2:33) and given to the apostles (1:4): the Holy Spirit as God's gift to the obedient (5:32). This promise of the Holy Spirit is first extended to the Jerusalem Jews assembled on Pentecost—"you and your children" and either to their chronologically distant descendants or to their geographically remote countrymen, the Jews in the Diaspora—"all that are far off." The latter expression can denote Gentiles (cf. 22:21; Eph. 2:13) but appears not to do so here. "With many other words" (Acts 2:40) indicates that Luke has provided only a summary of Peter's sermon.

2:42–47, Profile of the Early Church. Initially, the movement's success is marked with specific, impressively large numbers (2:41). Eventually, this will give way to further growth and expansion as indicated in periodic summaries (see Introduction).

This idealized portrait of the church emphasizes aspects of religious community valued in both Jewish and Greco-Roman society: daily devotion to both public and private religious activities (vv. 42, 46), awesome respect in the presence of divine power (v. 43), internal harmony and community solidarity expressed in concrete concern for each other (v. 44), and generosity (v. 45).

The voluntary sharing of possessions among members of the community distinguishes the early church (v. 44; cf. 4:32). Along with almsgiving and showing hospitality, Luke presents it as one way to use possessions responsibly (see Introduction).

3:1–4:31
Prophetic Witness in the Temple

This section exhibits a typical Lucan literary pattern: prophetic deed (3:1–11), prophetic word (3:12–26), resistance (4:1–12), divine vindication (4:13–31).

3:1–11, The Lame Man Healed. This episode has the typical features of a well-formed miracle story: setting (v. 1); description of malady or afflicted person (vv. 2–3); encounter between healer(s) and afflicted person (vv. 4–5); description of the healing miracle, consisting of healing word (v. 6), healing gesture (v. 7a), and act of healing (v. 7b); visible proof of healing (v. 8); and effects on audience or observers (vv. 9–11). Comparatively elaborate (cf. 9:32–35) and graphic in detail, it prompts Peter's sermon (3:11–12) and figures centrally in his subsequent defense (4:7, 9–10, 14, 16, 22). The portrait of the lame man is not complete until his age is finally reported as over forty years (4:22).

The prophetic deed occurs at the hands of the apostolic pair Peter and John (cf. 1:3; 4:19; 8:14–17; also Luke 22:8), but the central character here (Acts 3:6–7) and later (chaps. 3–5) is clearly Peter.

Details of time and place are given. The healing occurs at "the hour of prayer, the ninth hour"—one of the three periods of daily prayer (Dan. 6:10; Ps. 55:17) in midafternoon, coinciding with the Tamid, or daily whole offering, which was made throughout the year, twice a day, morning and evening, i.e., afternoon (Exod. 29:38–42; Num. 28:1–8; m. Pesaḥ. 5:1; m. Tamid 4:1; Josephus Antiquities of the Jews 3.237; 14.65). The scene for this episode, as for the events recorded in chaps. 3–5, is the Temple area, significant because of how Luke portrays the church as supplanting the Temple and its leadership. The Beautiful Gate was perhaps located on the eastern side of the Temple.

The man is healed in the "name of Jesus of Nazareth," whose power Peter later proclaims and defends (Acts 3:16; 4:10). The healing power is mediated through physical contact (cf. Mark 5:27–28, 30; Acts 5:15; 19:12). The effects are visible through the man's leaping and shouting praise (cf. Isa. 35:6). Wonder and amazement are responses appropriate to dramatic displays of divine power (cf. Luke 4:36; 5:9, 26).

3:12–26, Peter's Sermon in the Temple. Set within the precincts of the Temple, the sermon drives home a fundamental point: the very God whom the Jews had come to worship in the Temple (v. 13) has been at work in their midst but in a new way. The sermon throughout accents the activity of God—what God foretold in the prophets and fulfilled (vv. 18, 21), God's covenant with Abraham (v. 25), God's promise of a new prophet like Moses (v. 22; cf. Deut. 18:15–16), God's reversing the misdeeds of those responsible for Jesus' death (Acts 3:15, 26), God's glorification of his servant Jesus through the healing of the lame man (v. 13), God's eventual sending of his appointed Christ and the accompanying "times of refreshing" (vv. 19–21). The people of Israel are clearly being confronted with their own God, history, Scriptures, and legacy—in their own Temple—and are being asked to include the healing of the lame man, and by extension, the work of Jesus as part of their sacred story.

Even though God is the primary subject of the sermon, special emphasis falls on the trial of Jesus, with human misguidedness rhetorically juxtaposed with divine intervention (vv. 13–15; cf. Luke 23–24). Jesus is identified as God's servant (Acts 3:13, 26; cf. 4:27, 30; also Matt. 12:18), the fulfillment of the servant songs of Isaiah (Isa. 42:1; 52:13; 53:11). The designation "holy and righteous one" (Acts 3:14) doubtless recalls the Lucan passion narrative, with its particular stress on Jesus' innocence (cf. Luke 23:4, 13–15, 22, 41, 47; cf. Acts 4:27, 30; 7:52; 22:14). He is the "author" or pioneer of (resurrection) "life" (Acts 3:15), because through his resurrection he broke through for the first time to a new, unprecedented form of life (cf. 5:31; also Heb. 2:10; 12:2). The "prophet like Moses" image (Acts 3:22–23; cf. 7:37) makes more precise the recurrent depiction of Jesus as prophet in the Gospel (cf. Luke 4:16–30; 7:16; 13:33; 24:19).

The "times of refreshing" (RSV, Acts 3:19) may reflect the Jewish expectation that a period of relief from tribulations and woes would accompany the Messiah's final coming. Repentance and conversion are expected to trigger the Lord's final coming (cf. 2 Pet. 3:11–13; also Rom. 11:25–32). Meanwhile, Jesus as God's appointed Christ remains in heaven until God finally restores all things, as the prophets promised (Acts 3:21). The language recalls those in exile longing to be restored to their homeland by God.

4:1–4, Peter and John Arrested. Initial resistance comes from Temple authorities, Jesus' earlier antagonists (Luke 22:4, 52). A prominent source of resistance, now and in the second arrest (Acts 5:17), are the Sadducees, who had opposed Jesus (Luke 20:27–40) and later oppose Paul (Acts 23:6–10). Since they denied resurrection in principle (23:8), they specifically contest the apostles' claim that resurrection had begun with Jesus (4:2). Even though overnight custody is a relatively mild restraining action (v. 3; cf. 5:18; 12:1), it fulfills Jesus' prediction (Luke

21:12). Still, the gospel meets with significant numerical success (Acts 4:4).

4:5–22, Peter and John Before the Council. Naming members of the high-priestly family underscores the intimidating stature of the assembled Temple authorities. Annas and Caiaphas are introduced earlier as a reference point for the ministry of John the Baptist (Luke 3:2) but are unmentioned in Luke's passion narrative (cf. Matt. 26:3, 57; John 18:13–14, 24, 28; cf. 11:49). Though Annas is called high priest (Acts 4:6), he actually presided ca. A.D. 6–14. His son-in-law Caiaphas, who officiated ca. A.D. 17–36, would have been high priest during this time.

Like Jesus (Luke 20:1–8), Peter and John are challenged by the Temple authorities who inquire specifically about the lame man (Acts 4:7). As before, Peter is the principal spokesperson (v. 8), whose testimony is prompted by the Holy Spirit, in keeping with Jesus' promise (Luke 12:11–12). Salvation, understood doubly as the power to make well and to forgive sins (cf. Luke 4:18–19; 7:21–23), is now located exclusively in Jesus and his effectual name (Acts 4:12; cf. 2:21; 3:6, 16). With Jesus specifically identified as the stone rejected by Zion's builders but elevated preeminently (Ps. 118:22), readers now understand fully the parable of the vineyard (Luke 20:9–18; cf. 1 Pet. 2:4, 6–8).

The council (Acts 4:15) of authorities who had been Jesus' antagonists (Luke 22:66–23:16) are struck by Peter's unusual boldness (Acts 4:8–12). Similar forthrightness, which derives from the Spirit (Luke 12:11–12; Acts 4:8, 31), will continue to characterize their preaching (4:29) and later that of Paul (9:27–29; 13:46; 14:3; 19:8; 26:26; 28:31; cf. also 18:26).

The council also marvels that they were "unlettered," i.e., not literate as the result of formal schooling, and "outsiders," i.e., nonprofessionals (4:13). How the council identifies them with Jesus is uncertain; perhaps through their Galilean accent (cf. 1:11; 2:7; also Luke 22:59).

With the healed man standing in their midst as undeniable proof of the apostles' power, the council is stymied (Acts 4:16). Their inability to confute this visible sign of apostolic power renders true the earlier prediction of Jesus (Luke 21:15; also Acts 6:10). Their injunction (4:18) is two-pronged: neither to speak, i.e., heal anymore by pronouncing the name of Jesus (3:6), nor teach, i.e., preach publicly a message under his authority or with him as its subject (as, e.g., 3:12–26; 4:8–12). This second ban is later recalled explicitly (5:28).

Peter and John respond defiantly (4:19–20). They are compelled to speak what they have seen and heard, presumably the "deeds and words" of Jesus recorded in the Gospel (1:1; cf.

10:39; also 26:15) but most notably the Passion and resurrection (Luke 24:48; Acts 1:8, 22).

By reporting their release by the council (Acts 4:21), Luke notes the absence of any legal case against them. This action by a Jewish council signifies vindication by God, who becomes the object of widespread praise (v. 21).

4:23–31, Praying Confidently. The apostles' release is celebrated among "their own," perhaps the other apostles, more probably the small circle of disciples earlier depicted as a community of prayer (1:14; 2:42; cf. 6:4). Like Peter's earlier speeches (2:14–36; 3:12–26), the friends' prayer interprets aspects of Jesus' life as explicitly fulfilling Scripture. Its centerpiece is Ps. 2:1–2, which mentions adversaries of "the Lord" (Yahweh) and "his Anointed" (Gk. *Christos*). Luke interpreted the latter as a sure reference to Jesus, anointed with God's Spirit at his baptism (Luke 3:22; cf. 4:1, 14; Acts 10:38), hence becoming "beloved Son," or, as here, "God's holy child" (4:27).

The exact identification of the adversaries mentioned in the psalm (vv. 25–26) is difficult. As "Gentiles," the Romans are clearly implicated (Luke 23:36; cf. 23:11). The "peoples" are understood as Israel (Acts 4:27), consistent with Luke's depiction of "the [Jewish] people" as active conspirators (Luke 23:13; Acts 2:23; 3:13–14). The "kings of the earth" may refer to Herod, and "rulers" to Pilate, although Luke normally uses "rulers" to designate Jewish leaders (Luke 23:13, 35; 24:20; Acts 3:17; cf. 4:5, 8).

Here Acts looks back to the Gospel and provides a fresh interpretation of Jesus' Passion. This may help explain why Luke alone of the four Gospels includes Herod Antipas as a participant in the passion narrative, indeed connects him directly with Pontius Pilate (Luke 23:6–16).

The prayer's primary subject is God, who is addressed as Creator, and therefore Sovereign (Acts 4:24) who foretold these events (through David). Enemy actions against Jesus are placed under God's sovereignty (v. 28; cf. 2:23; Luke 22:22). This reassures the church that the resistance it now experiences is analogous to what Jesus experienced. Like Jesus, the church can expect to be vindicated by God, who is asked to empower the apostolic servants boldly to "speak the word," i.e., preach the gospel (cf. Acts 8:25; 11:19; 16:6, 32; cf. Phil. 1:14).

The prayer calls for the preached word to be accompanied by healing and "signs and wonders" in the name of Jesus (Acts 4:30), but these are seen as performed directly by "God's hand," not through human "power or piety" (cf. 3:12). This explains all the more why the council's injunction against such deeds is futile (4:7, 17–18)—it is an attempt to obstruct God's own work—and also why the apostolic witness cannot be suppressed (4:20).

God answers their prayer by providing visible signs: a quaking house and being filled with the Spirit. What was requested in prayer—boldness to preach—comes to pass, thus providing an instance of promise fulfillment within the story itself (v. 31).

4:32–5:11
Using Possessions

Luke's focus on apostolic activity in 3:1–4:31 resumes in 5:12, but this section focuses on a wider circle—the "company of believers" (v. 32)—and how God's presence is felt within the community through the proper and improper use of possessions.

4:32–37, Sharing Possessions: Barnabas. With "everything in common," the community fulfills the Hellenistic ideal of friendship expressed in sharing possessions. By selling property to care for its poor, it embodies the ideal Israel (Deut. 15:4; Lev. 25:35–38).

This generalized portrait of community generosity and submission to apostolic authority is rendered concrete in the actions of a single property owner, the Levite Joseph. The name given him by the apostles, Barnabas, is his more usual NT designation and serves to distinguish him from Joseph Barsabbas (Acts 1:23). Precisely how, if at all, the name means "son of encouragement" is unclear (→ Barnabas).

5:1–11, Hoarding Possessions: Ananias and Sapphira. This negative counterpart to the story of Barnabas is partially influenced by the OT story of Achan, whose deceitful misappropriation of sacred possessions adversely affected Israel and resulted in radical exclusion from the community: the death of him and his family (Josh. 7:16–26).

The story continues to portray the church as a Spirit-filled community (Acts 4:31), Peter as a powerful prophetic figure, and is designed to elicit proper respect for the holy among the church itself, as well as outsiders (5:5, 11). Peter's enhanced prophetic status is reflected in his knowledge of Ananias' misdeed (v. 3) and the lethal force of his indictment of Sapphira (v. 9).

Precisely how and why they were at fault should be noted. The narrative implies that property owners could sell their possessions without thereby committing themselves to the community ideal of sharing everything in common (v. 4; cf. Deut. 23:21–23; though cf. Acts 4:32, 34). Their fatal mistake was in their failure

to recognize the church as a Spirit-filled community and in failing to see that deceiving the church—and themselves—was tantamount to deceiving the Spirit. The couple's misuse of possessions is attributed to satanic force (5:3), paralleling Judas's misdeed (Luke 22:3; cf. John 13:2, 27).

5:12–42
Further Prophetic Witness in the Temple

5:12–16, Apostolic Signs and Wonders in the Temple. This summary shifts the action back to the apostles and, in fullfillment of the prayer of 4:29–30 (also 2:19), portrays their ministry of signs and wonders as stunningly successful. The locus of activity is still the Temple, "Solomon's portico" (5:12; cf. 3:11; also John 10:23), although the marvelous effects of their activity now extend into the streets, even to "towns around Jerusalem" (Acts 5:16).

This summary extends spatial limits, but numerical limits as well. No numbers are given (cf. 2:41; 4:4), but the size of the group multiplies, encompassing women (mentioned as a group for the first time) as well as men (5:14). The generalized picture of apostolic activity is once again focused in the person of Peter, whose shadow even has therapeutic power (v. 15). Somewhat similar is the healing power of Jesus' clothing (Mark 6:56; suprisingly omitted by Luke; though cf. Luke 6:18–19) and cloths touched by Paul (19:12).

5:17–26, Apostles Arrested. In response to increased apostolic successes, a second resistance occurs. Again, the high priest (v. 17), presumably Annas (4:6), and the Sadducees form the core of opposition (4:1), prompted by jealousy (cf. 13:45; 17:5). The restraining action is more intense than previously: all the apostles, not just Peter and John, are placed in a public prison, or, perhaps, are imprisoned publicly (5:18).

The release is proportionately more dramatic and is the first of three instances in Acts when a prison miraculously opens (cf. 12:6–11; 16:25–27). It is achieved by an "angel of the Lord" (i.e., God; cf. Exod. 3:2), who makes the first of several appearances in the Acts narrative (7:30; 8:26; 10:3; 12:7, 11, 23; 27:23; cf. Luke 1:11; 2:9; for OT angels in deliverance roles, cf. Dan. 3:28; 6:22). The effect is heightened by the subsequent description in Acts 5:23. Moreover, the angel countermands the council's earlier injunction (4:18) and commissions the apostles to return to the Temple and teach "all the words of this life" (5:20), i.e., resurrection life pioneered by Christ (cf. 3:15; also John 6:68; Phil. 2:16). The apostles comply, both with the angel's command and the earlier prayer (Acts 4:29). Ironically, the miraculous release of the apostles is achieved by an angel, whose existence the Sadducees deny (23:8).

The authorities assembled to hear the case were introduced earlier (5:22; 4:5–6). The council (cf. 4:15) and "all the senate of the children of Israel" (5:21) are probably the same body (cf. Exod. 12:21; also 1 Macc. 12:6; 2 Macc. 1:10; Josephus *Antiquities of the Jews* 13.166). The dialogue in Acts 5:23–26 heightens the drama, portraying the council as comically helpless. The rhetorical flourish in v. 24b, in which the officers "wonder what this might come to," provides on the lips of an outsider an unintentional prophetic insight of the outcome of future events; similarly, Gamaliel's words in 5:38–39.

5:27–32, Apostles' Defense. Though it is the apostles who are brought before the council and presented as making their collective defense (vv. 27, 29), Peter remains prominent (v. 29). The high priest's accusation (v. 28) recalls the council's earlier injunction (4:18), although the blood-guilt motif (5:28) is new (cf. 18:6; Matt. 27:25). It presupposes the earlier sermon summaries that directly accuse the Jewish people (Acts 2:23; 3:14–15) and leaders (4:10). Strictly speaking, it only implicates the high priests and the council, who are being addressed here.

The apostolic response opens by noting the moral obligation of obeying God rather than humans (5:29; cf. 4:19). The words are reminiscent of Socrates' defense before the men of Athens, "I shall obey the god rather than you" (Plato *Apology* 29D). Presupposed is the divine command of the angel (Acts 5:20–21) but earlier mandates as well (Luke 24:45–49; Acts 1:8; 4:29). The apostles have seen what their opponents have failed to see—that God has been at work in recent events (3:12, 16).

The defense summary (5:30–32) encapsulates major elements of early Christian preaching: God's raising Christ (3:15; 4:10; 10:40; 13:30, 37); Christ's death by "hanging on a tree" (Acts 10:39; Gal. 3:13; cf. Deut. 21:22–23); God's exaltation of Christ (Acts 2:33), identified, as earlier, as "pioneer (of life) and savior" (cf. 3:15); call for repentance (2:38; 3:19; 11:18; 26:20); and offer of forgiveness of sins (Luke 24:47; Acts 2:38; 3:19; 10:43; 13:38). God's role as primary agent is again stressed (5:30–31; cf. 3:12–26). Through divine reversal, God has righted their misdeed. The concluding motif is the double witness of the apostles and the Holy Spirit (5:32; Luke 24:48; Acts 1:8; cf. John 15:26–27), a gift to the obedient (Acts 2:38; also John 7:39).

5:33–42, Apostles Vindicated: Gamaliel. The council's violent urge to kill the apostles (v.

33) foreshadows its later reaction to Stephen (7:54; cf. 23:10). Vindication of the apostles comes through Gamaliel who urges caution (5:35; → Gamaliel [2]). Aligning Gamaliel with the Christian movement typically pits a sympathetic Pharisaic position against adversarial Sadducees (cf. 23:6–10; also 4:1; 5:17; Luke 20:27–40). Citing two examples of misspent leadership—Theudas (Acts 5:36) and Judas the Galilean (v. 37)—he proposes a hands-off policy (v. 38a; → Judas [7]; Theudas; Zealot). He warns his colleagues against becoming "God-fighters" (vv. 38b–39). Through this sympathetic outsider, Luke expresses his own viewpoint: to oppose the Christian movement is to oppose God. All such efforts are ill-fated (e.g., Herod, 12:22–23).

By accepting the advice of Gamaliel, the council vindicates the apostles. The punishment of beating (5:40; cf. 16:22–23; 22:19; 2 Cor. 11:24) is more severe than the earlier threat (4:21) but conforms to Jesus' promise (Luke 21:12; esp. Mark 13:9; Matt. 24:17). The prohibition to speak in the name of Jesus is repeated (4:18). The apostolic response was to rejoice in the face of persecution (Luke 6:23; cf. Matt. 5:12; also 1 Pet. 4:13; 2 Thess. 1:4), considering it honorable to suffer for the name (Acts 9:16; 15:26; 21:13). In defiant disobedience, they resume daily teaching and preaching (5:42; cf. 5:21; Luke 20:1).

6:1–8:3
Prophetic Witness Extends Beyond the Apostles: Stephen

The scope of the narrative now widens beyond the apostles and Temple. The next episode serves to introduce the next two major figures in the narrative—Stephen (6:8–8:1; also 11:19; 22:20) and Philip (8:5–40; also 21:8). A third new figure, Saul (9:1–30), is introduced in connection with Stephen (7:58–8:3). Peter reemerges as a major figure in 9:32–12:25.

6:1–7, Choosing Seven Apostolic Assistants. The previously unified community (2:42–47; 4:32) experiences its first friction, the exact nature of which depends on properly identifying the disputing parties as well as their underlying differences (→ Greeks; Hebrews; Hellenists). The neglect of the widows (6:1; cf. 1 Tim. 5:9–16) possibly resulted from ideological differences between the Aramaic-speaking Hebrew Christians who supervised the daily distribution of assistance (4:35) and the Greek-speaking Hellenistic Christians.

As a solution, the church (identified here for the first time as "disciples," 6:1, 2, 7) selects (vv. 3, 5) from their number seven men, who are installed by the apostles (vv. 3, 6), designated only here in Acts as "the twelve" (v. 2; cf. 1:26; 2:14; but cf. Luke 6:13; 8:1; 9:1, 12; 18:31; 22:3, 30, 47; also 1 Cor. 15:5, 7, 9). Their ordination to special service occurs by apostolic "laying on of hands" (Acts 6:6; cf. 13:3; 1 Tim. 4:14; 5:22; 2 Tim. 1:6; Heb. 6:2), a ritual act with OT precedent (Num. 8:10; 27:18, 23; Deut. 34:9), also employed in connection with baptism (Acts 8:17–19; 19:6) and healing (9:17; 28:8; cf. 5:12; 14:3; 19:11; also Luke 4:40; 13:13; Matt. 9:18; 19:13; Mark 6:5; 7:32; 8:23, 25; 16:18). The story, or process, reflects OT influence (Exod. 18:17–23; Num. 11:1–25; 27:15–23).

This group, which became known as "the seven" (Acts 21:8), is not here designated "deacons" (cf. Phil. 1:1; 1 Tim. 3:8–13). The two whose service is described further—Stephen and Philip—are distinguished by their prophetic deeds and words (cf. Acts 6:8, 10; 8:5–7, 13; 21:8). This is appropriate since their qualifications, apart from being well respected (cf. 16:2; 22:12; 1 Tim. 3:7, 10) and wise, included being Spirit-filled (Acts 6:3, 5; cf. 11:24; 13:52; also Luke 4:1; cf. Exod. 31:3; 35:31). "Full of faith" (Acts 6:5) may mean wonder-working faith (cf. Matt. 17:20; 21:21; Mark 11:22–23; also 1 Cor. 12:9; 13:2).

Their seven Greek names need not imply that they were native Greeks. Specifying that the Antiochian Nicolaus had become a convert to Judaism (Acts 6:5; cf. 13:43; also 2:10) suggests that the others were native Jews.

The successful resolution of the dispute is indicated by the impressive growth (6:7), especially the conversion of "a great many priests," a first. Luke thereby underscores Christianity's deepening penetration, and displacement, of the central Jewish institution—the Temple.

6:8–15, Stephen's Arrest. Resistance to Christianity now extends beyond Sadducees and Temple authorities (4:1; 5:17) to include Diaspora Jews resident in Jerusalem (6:9) and, for the first time, "the [Jewish] people" (v. 12). Whether Stephen's opponents should be envisioned as a single synagogue with different constituencies (Freedmen, Cyrenians, Alexandrians, Cilicians, Asians) or, more likely, as two separate groups—African Jews who comprised "the synagogue of freedmen" and Asian Jews—their loyalty was to the Jerusalem Temple and the Mosaic law. They see Stephen as a threat to both (v. 11). The second group later opposes Paul on the same grounds (21:27; cf. 25:8).

Unable to confute the prophetic deeds and words of the Spirit-filled Stephen (6:8, 10; cf. Luke 21:15), they resort to false witnesses and contrived charges that link Stephen's preaching to Jesus (Acts 6:13–14). Luke's account of Jesus' trial before the Sanhedrin (Luke 22:66–71) omits reference to false witnesses and their charge that he would destroy the Temple and rebuild it in three days (Matt. 26:59–61; Mark 14:55–58; cf. John 2:19–22; also Matt. 27:40; Mark 15:29).

7:1–53, Stephen's Sermon. The sermon surveys Israel's history in broad sweep, highlighting three figures: Abraham (vv. 2–8), Joseph (vv. 9–16), and especially Moses (vv. 17–43). It then treats the tabernacle/Temple (vv. 44–50) and concludes by assailing the hearers for identifying with Israel's heritage of resistance (vv. 51–53).

The historical survey is reminiscent of OT historical summaries that rehearse God's dealings with Israel (Josh. 24:1–15; Neh. 9:6–38; Jth. 5:5–21; Pss. 78, 105, 106, 135, 136). If anything, it reflects more the censorious spirit of Psalms 78 and 106, which stress Israel's persistent, cyclical disobedience throughout its history, than it does the more positive, doxological spirit of Psalm 105, which recalls God's gracious care and deliverance of Israel.

With its explicit OT quotations (Amos 5:25–27 in Acts 7:42–43; Isa. 66:1–2 in vv. 49–50), frequent OT phrases, references, and allusions, the speech has a thoroughly biblical ring. The hearers are being confronted with their own story told in the words of Scripture, although the treatment of events is selective rather than comprehensive.

In treating Abraham, Stephen omits most of the material in Gen. 12:10–16:16 and 18:1–23:20, most notably his severest test of faith, the offering of Isaac (Gen. 22). He essentially skips Isaac (Acts 7:8; Gen. 21, 24, 26) and includes Jacob (Acts 7:8; Gen. 25:19–34; chaps. 27–36) in the more important treatment of Joseph (Acts 7:9–18). He gives disproportionate attention to Moses' birth and youth (vv. 20–22), his slaying of the Egyptian (vv. 23–29), and his call (vv. 30–34), all of which summarize Exod. 1:1–4:17. He telescopes the rest of Exodus through Deuteronomy in a single section (Acts 7:35–41), major focus of which is Israel's rejection of Moses and God's consequent rejection of Israel. The giving of the law, which is prominently treated in Exod. 19–20, is mentioned only briefly (Acts 7:38).

At this point, the historical survey ceases rather abruptly, as Stephen introduces a fresh topic: the Temple. This part of the speech is less interested in historical coverage than it is in the tabernacle/Temple theme. He concludes with a trenchant critique of the Temple, citing Isa. 66:1–2 to show that no handmade building is adequate to house God.

In spite of its thoroughly biblical ring and the way in which it confronts Stephen's "brethren and fathers" (Acts 7:2) with their own story, there are some points of tension with the OT. For example, it places Abraham's call, which

Genesis locates in Haran *after* the death of his father Terah (Gen. 11:31–12:3), much earlier "in Mesopotamia, before he lived in Haran" (Acts 7:2–3). His report of Abraham's purchasing a tomb in Shechem from the sons of Hamor (v. 16) conflates Abraham's purchase of the cave of Machpelah from the Hittites for a burial place (Gen. 23; 50:13) with Jacob's purchase of a piece of land near the city of Shechem from the sons of Hamor (Gen. 33:19; Josh. 24:32).

The speech may be read as a unified defense that develops three interrelated themes: God's dwelling place; promise-fulfillment; and Israel's rejection of God's duly appointed emissaries.

Stephen insists that, as early as Abraham, Israel is promised a place to worship God (Acts 7:7b; Exod. 3:12), the land of promise (Acts 7:4). Though removed to Egypt to live as aliens in a "land belonging to others" (vv. 6, 9–15), all the patriarchs were returned for burial in the promised land (v. 16). Still, "as the time of the promise drew near" (v. 17), the people of promise remained in Egypt until God commissioned Moses to deliver them (v. 34). They spurned Moses' leadership and "in their hearts turned to Egypt" (v. 39), thus refusing the chance to obtain their promised "place." Consequently, they would be exiled again "beyond Babylon" (v. 43). Eventually, the patriarchs transferred the "tent of witness" from the wilderness to the promised land (vv. 44–45), whereupon David and Solomon sought to establish a more permanent "dwelling place for the God of Jacob" (v. 46). Contrary to the prophetic word (Isa. 66:1–2), they mistakenly thought God's presence could be confined to a handmade house. Consequently, even with the Jerusalem Temple, God's initial promise (Acts 7:7b) remained unfulfilled (vv. 49–50). The "place" where God's Spirit resides, and where the presence of God is dramatically at work, is no longer the Temple but the newly constituted messianic community, which finally fulfills God's original promise.

Although the rejection theme emerges only in the latter part of the speech, and especially with reference to Moses, it is introduced earlier. The jealous patriarchs are censured for selling Joseph, only to have their misdeed reversed by divine intervention (v. 9). But it was Moses, above all, whose leadership was rejected by "his brethren, the sons of Israel" (v. 23). First, they refused to accept his God-sent deliverance of a fellow Israelite (vv. 25–28), which led to his exile in Midian. Second, they rejected him as the God-sent "ruler and deliverer" (v. 35) who would bring them to the land of promise, and this in spite of stunning displays of God's presence through him: wonders and signs in Egypt, deliverance through the Red Sea, receiving the law at Sinai (vv. 35–38). Instead, they "thrust him aside" (v. 39), turned their hearts toward Egypt, and became idolaters (vv. 40–41). Consequently, God rejected them, turning them over to their idolatrous instincts (vv. 42–43). The speech is informed by the conviction that Moses prefigures Christ. Read against the background of the rest of Luke-Acts, the speech presents the career of Moses, and Israel's reaction to him, in ways that parallel the Christ story (v. 37; cf. 3:22–23; Luke 24:19).

The rejection theme reaches its climax in the concluding indictment (Acts 7:51–53). With vivid metaphors drawn from their own past, the hearers are characterized as "stiffnecked" (Exod. 33:3, 5) and "uncircumcised in heart and ears" (Lev. 26:41; Deut. 10:16; Ezek. 44:7; Jer. 6:10; 9:26). They are assailed as historically having resisted God's Holy Spirit (cf. Isa. 63:10) and standing in the succession of their predecessors who persecuted and killed the prophets (cf. 1 Kings 19:10, 14; 2 Chron. 24:20–22; 36:16; Neh. 9:26; Jer. 26:20–23; also Jer. 2:30). Stephen's indictment here echoes Jesus' earlier accusation (Luke 11:47–51). The hearers are implicated in the betrayal and death of the innocent prophet Jesus, the "Righteous One" (cf. Acts 3:14).

7:54—8:3, Stephen's Death and Its Impact. Resistance to prophetic words (6:10; 7:2–53) and deeds (6:8) now intensifies as the council, which earlier could only threaten, imprison, and wish to kill (5:33), finally does kill. Stephen's final accusation sends them into teeth-gritting rage (7:54; Ps. 35:16; 37:12; 112:10; Job 16:9; Lam. 2:16). In stark contrast, a Spirit-filled Stephen (Acts 7:55; also 6:3, 5) behaves like a prophet: he gazes into heaven to see God's glory (Isa. 6:1; John 12:41). He now vividly sees what Jesus had promised this same council would occur—the Son of man exalted to God's right hand (Luke 22:69), albeit standing (Dan. 7:13) rather than seated (Ps. 110:1). In reporting to the council what he sees (Acts 7:56), he both confesses and proclaims (for the first time) the risen Lord.

These same words attest the innocence of God's "Righteous One" whom they have slain (v. 52) and thereby convict the hearers. By rejecting yet another of God's prophets, the new Moses of whom their own law spoke (v. 37; Deut. 18:15), they stand under God's judgment and the threat of another expulsion from God's presence (Acts 7:42–43; cf. 3:23).

This unusual form of proclamation is met with mob violence (7:57) and a rejection that recalls Jesus' own rejection at Nazareth (Luke 4:29; cf. Job 16:10). The council's actions conform to the biblical prescription for dealing with blasphemers: death by stoning outside the city (Lev. 24:13–16; Num. 15:32–36; cf. Heb.

13:12–13), with witnesses going first (Deut. 17:2–7).

Once again, the crazed mob's frenzy contrasts with the prophet's calm confidence. Stephen's death is sketched in terms that recall Jesus' own Passion. It is the death of another innocent prophet. Like Jesus, Stephen utters a prayer of confidence rephrasing Ps. 31:5 (Acts 7:59; Luke 23:46) and finally "in a loud voice" (Luke 23:46) offers a prayer of forgiveness for his enemies (Acts 7:60; Luke 23:34).

The death of Stephen also functions to introduce Saul (Acts 7:58; 8:1, 3), who gradually enters the story (9:1–30; 11:25, 30; 12:25) and emerges as the major figure in chaps. 13–28. His participation in Stephen's death becomes a major reference point for Luke (Acts 9:1, 21; 22:4, 20; 26:9–11; cf. 1 Cor. 15:9; Phil. 3:6; Gal. 1:13, 23).

Stephen's death becomes pivotal in the narrative and marks a major transition. The "great persecution" (Acts 8:1) now widens the circle of resistance beyond Temple authorities and Jerusalem residents (chaps. 3–5; 6:12). Its salutary effect is to scatter the church throughout Judea and Samaria, in keeping with Jesus' mandate (1:8). Imagined here is a single, shared community of believers, now expelled from Jerusalem. The apostles, however, remain behind to authenticate the gospel as it spreads beyond Jerusalem (8:1; cf. 8:14; 11:1, 22).

8:4–12:25

The Gospel Spreads Outside Jerusalem to Judea, Samaria, Galilee, and the Coastland

8:4–40
Prophetic Witness of Philip

8:4–8, Philip Preaches in Samaria. A new phase opens as the gospel moves beyond Jerusalem and Judea to Samaria (1:8; 8:25). The major figure in this expansion is Philip, earlier introduced as one of "the seven" (6:5), later identified as an "evangelist" living in Caesarea (21:8; → Philip [8]). The "city of Samaria" where he proclaimed Christ may have been either Sebaste or Shechem (→ Samaria, District of). This region, earlier unreceptive to Jesus' mission (Luke 9:52–56; though cf. John 4), "gives heed" (cf. Acts 8:10; 16:14; also Heb. 2:1), thereby fulfilling the prophetic hope that "peoples from afar" would hearken to the word of God (Isa. 49:1). Power to exorcise unclean spirits, earlier demonstrated by Jesus (Luke 4:31–37; 8:26–33) now extends beyond the apostles (Acts 5:16) to Philip, as does the power to

heal the lame (Luke 5:18–26; Acts 3:1–11; cf. 9:32–34). God's reign, begun with Jesus (Luke 4:18–19; 7:22–23), continues through Philip's prophetic words and deeds (Acts 8:6).

8:9–13, Simon the Magician Converted. This first encounter with magic (cf. 13:6–12; 19:18–19) exemplifies both the gospel's triumph over popular religion and the corrupting power of greed (8:18–24). Luke emphasizes Simon's Samaritan connection (v. 9), his presumptuous claim to be "somebody great," or perhaps a "great magician" (v. 9b; cf. 5:36; 12:22–23), his unquestioned success among the Samaritans, who apparently ascribed him divine status (8:10–11; → Simon Magus).

Simon's miracle-working prowess, however, is surpassed by Philip's two-pronged ministry of preaching and healing. In preaching the kingdom of God, he continues the theme sounded by the risen Lord (1:3), the first to do so explicitly in Acts (see Introduction). Preaching "the name of Jesus" doubtless signifies the "signs and great miracles" Philip performed (8:13; also vv. 6–7). Incredibly, and impressively, "even Simon" converts (v. 13).

8:14–25, Apostles Confirm the Samaritan Mission. Even though God's power has been demonstrated through Philip's prophetic words and deeds (vv. 6–7) and has triumphed over Samaria's own hero Simon, apostolic authentication is still required (v. 14). The apostles who remained behind in Jerusalem (8:1) continue to serve as the vital link with the risen Lord (1:15–26). Their role is to validate authentic expressions of the Spirit when it moves out into new areas (cf. Acts 11:1, 22). As before, the apostolic circle is represented by the two emissaries Peter and John (8:14; cf. 3:1, 11; 4:13, 19), but Peter is clearly the spokesperson. Philip disappears from the Simon story, as it becomes a confrontation between Peter and a half-converted magician (cf. 5:1–11). Though Peter's Pentecost promise (2:38) appeared to imply a simultaneous bestowal of forgiveness and receipt of the Holy Spirit, here the two benefits are separated by a considerable lapse of time (cf. 10:44–48; 19:5–6).

Luke especially highlights the behavior of Simon. The genuineness of his full conversion is presupposed (8:13). Yet, like his Christian predecessors Ananias and Sapphira (5:1–11), he misconstrues the true nature of the Spirit and thereby the gospel. He mistakenly thinks, first, that the power to transmit the Spirit can be given to anyone indiscriminately, especially outside the apostolic circle, and second, that it can be bought (8:18) and, presumably, sold (v. 19). Peter's rebuke (vv. 20–23) takes the form of a curse, ironically almost magical in form if not in effect. The tone is solemnly biblical (cf. Deut. 12:12;

14:27, 29; Ps. 78:37; Deut. 29:18; Lam. 3:15; Isa. 58:6).

The possibility of repentance is real (though cf. Heb. 6:4–6). Simon's prayer for forgiveness (Acts 8:24) has the imploring tones of Pharaoh's confession and prayer before Moses and Aaron (Exod. 9:28; 10:17) and for this reason may be as halfhearted. Once the apostles confirm Philip's work, they themselves preach among the Samaritans (Acts 8:25).

8:26–40, Ethiopian Official Converted. In this story, the gospel continues its geographical spread beyond Judea and Samaria to the more distant coastland region, including Gaza (v. 26), and finally Azotus (Ashdod) and Caesarea (v. 40). In effect, however, the gospel has spread even farther—to the outer reaches of Ethiopia (v. 27), where the first known black Christian returned rejoicing in his newfound faith (v. 39).

If the previous story featured Philip's prophetic deeds (vv. 6–7, 13), this one features his prophetic words. His preaching of Christ (vv. 5, 12) is now seen to include Scripture interpretation as a prominent element. Like the risen Lord and his predecessors Peter (chaps. 2–5) and Stephen (chap. 7), his task is properly to interpret Scripture as it relates to Christ (Luke 24:27).

The episode further extends Luke's promise fulfillment program as yet another passage of Scripture is applied to Jesus (Acts 8:32–33). For the first time in Luke-Acts (and as a rare NT instance), Jesus' death is interpreted in light of Isa. 53:7–8: Jesus the suffering servant is denied justice in his death ("humiliation") yet vindicated in his resurrection ("life . . . taken up from the earth"). This interpretation continues the Lucan emphasis on Jesus' death as that of an innocent prophet (cf. Acts 3:14).

The story is presented as an extraordinary encounter in which God is the primary actor. From beginning to end, Philip is prompted by divine impulse (8:26, 29, 39), as later happens when the Spirit launches new initiatives (cf. 10:19; 11:12; 13:2; 16:6–10). Like his prophetic predecessors Elijah and Ezekiel, he moves at the behest of the angel of the Lord (8:26; 2 Kings 1:15) or of the Spirit, who even transfers him physically to a new locale for further mission (Acts 8:39; cf. 1 Kings 18:12; 2 Kings 2:16; Ezek. 3:14; 8:3; 11:1, 24). With such thoroughgoing, explicit divine confirmation, further apostolic confirmation would be redundant (cf. Acts 8:14–17).

The eunuch's conversion (unlike Simon's) is fully exemplary and illustrates the gospel's power to reach even the remotest regions and include outsiders (Luke 1:79). Ethiopia's remoteness and invincibility were legendary (cf. Isa. 18:1–2; Zeph. 2:12; cf. Ps. 68:31; Zeph. 3:10).

If the term "eunuch" is understood in its technical sense as a castrated male, his status as an outsider is further indicated (Deut. 23:1). It may, however, be an official title having nothing to do with his physical condition, thus indicating the social respectability of his position as the queen's minister of finance.

His inclusion within the people of God here appears to fulfill the prophetic hope that foreigners and eunuchs would eventually participate fully in the worship of God (Isa. 56:3–7). Yet, significantly, the foreigner who was previously attracted to Israel and its house of worship (1 Kings 8:41–43) is now attracted by their successor—"the good news of Jesus" (v. 35).

9:1–31
The Gospel Spreads to Damascus: Saul of Tarsus

This episode advances the Lucan narrative in two ways. First, it establishes the extraordinary nature of Saul's call, thereby certifying God's duly appointed prophet to the Gentiles who later emerges as the central figure in the church's mission (chaps. 13–28). Second, it extends the story geographically, documenting the church's spread from the coastlands (8:40) to northernmost Syria—Damascus (9:2, 3, 8, 10, 19, 22, 27), where the gospel had already taken root (v. 19b). The Damascus congregation is probably to be understood as an offshoot of the dispersion resulting from the Jerusalem persecution (8:1).

9:1–19a, Saul's Call. The story has two parts: first, Saul's encounter with the risen Lord (vv. 1–9), and second, Ananias's vision and ordination of Saul (vv. 10–19a). This narrative account is supplemented in certain ways by the two later accounts that occur in Paul's defense speeches (22:3–21; 26:2–23; also cf. Gal. 1:13–17).

Luke's portrait of Saul as the church's archenemy continues (cf. Acts 7:58; 8:1, 3), though his resistance now intensifies. His reach now extends beyond Judea (8:3) to the "synagogues at Damascus" (9:2), which are under Jerusalem's jurisdiction. The narrative implies that the intended victims are Jewish Christians who still attend synagogue.

This scene resembles other ancient accounts where enemies of God's cause through divine intervention are dramatically halted and "converted" into God's proponents (cf. 2 Macc. 3:24–40; 4 Macc. 4:1–14). The encounter is presented as a truly extraordinary reversal of events through direct, divine intervention. The blinding light appearing suddenly from heaven signifies God's dramatic interruption (Acts 9:3; cf. 22:6; 26:13). Although Saul does not "see" anyone (nor do his companions, 9:7), clearly the risen Lord "appeared" to him, presumably in a vision (v. 17; 22:14; 26:16; cf. 1 Cor. 9:1; 15:8; 2 Cor. 4:6; Gal. 1:16).

More important here than what is seen is what is heard: a prophetic call. A heavenly voice speaks to Saul using a form of double address found in earlier divine commissions (Gen. 46:2; Exod. 3:4; 1 Sam. 3:4; also cf. Luke 8:24; 10:41; 22:31). The voice indicts by interpreting Saul's activity with reference to the new reality of Christ's resurrection: to persecute (reject) Christians is to persecute (reject) Christ (Acts 9:5; Luke 10:16). The voice attests that Jesus, once rejected but now risen and vindicated, continues to be active in history. Earlier he had exerted healing power (Acts 3:16); now he exerts power to call new prophets.

The presence of witnesses, who also heard the voice (v. 7; though, cf. 22:9), confirms the reality of the occurrence. They correspond to the company of Israel who can attest the reality of God's revelation to Moses (Deut. 4:12; also cf. Wisd. of Sol. 18:1; Dan. 10:7).

It is Ananias, the Jewish Christian disciple from Damascus (cf. Acts 22:12), who experiences an explicitly defined vision (9:10), the first of several in Acts (10:3, 17, 19; 11:5; 12:9; 16:9–10; 18:9; 22:17; 23:11; 27:23; cf. Matt. 17:9). The risen Lord also speaks to him, directing his actions from heaven. In the dialogue, the Lord reveals Saul's whereabouts (Acts 9:11), predicts what is to occur (v. 12), but most importantly, encapsulates his commission to Saul (vv. 15–16).

These words summarize Luke's theological understanding of Paul as God's "chosen instrument" (cf. 22:15; Rom. 1:5; Gal. 1:15–16) and preview Paul's role later in the narrative. His chief contribution to the church's mission will be to carry the Lord's name "before the Gentiles" (Acts 13:46–49; 15:3–4, 12; 22:21; 26:16–18; 28:25–29). Yet he will also witness to the name "before kings" (25:13, 23; 26:1; 27:24; cf. Luke 12:11), as well as before "the sons of Israel" (e.g., Acts 9:19–22; 13:5, 16–41). Like the prophets (7:52), he will also suffer (9:23, 29; 13:45, 50; 14:19; 16:19–40; 19:23–41; 21:11, 27–36; 22:22; 23:10, 12–15, 27; 24:23; 25:3; 26:21; 28:17). In doing so, he follows his apostolic predecessors (5:41; cf. 15:26). In this latter respect, Luke's narrative portrait is confirmed by Paul's Letters (1 Cor. 4:9–13; 2 Cor. 6:4–10; 11:23–29).

With his deepest fears allayed by the Lord's command, Ananias obediently proceeds to ordain God's designee (Acts 9:17–19a). By laying his hands on Saul, he bestows God's healing power and restores his sight (vv. 12, 17). The reality of the healing is attested by the scales falling from his eyes (v. 18; cf. Tob. 11:12–13). Possibly, his restored sight is to be understood as the visible sign of the Spirit's presence (Acts 9:17), elsewhere manifested through speaking in tongues (cf. 2:1–4; 10:46; 19:6). His baptism removes the guilt resulting from his previous misdeeds (cf. 22:16).

9:19b–31, Saul in Damascus and Jerusalem. Saul immediately begins to carry out his divinely appointed role of preaching to the "sons of Israel" (v. 15; cf. vv. 20, 22, 27–29). Typically, prophetic proclamation is met with resistance that entailed suffering (v. 16; cf. vv. 21, 23, 29; cf. Luke 13:33–34; Acts 7:51–52). Thus this brief description of Saul's activity, first in Damascus (9:19b–25) and subsequently in Jerusalem (vv. 26–29), itself becomes a fulfillment of the Lord's words to Ananias (vv. 15–16).

The portrait of Paul that emerges here is a miniature of the portrait that unfolds later in the narrative: Paul preaching Jesus as Son of God (v. 20), the Christ (v. 22), and Lord (v. 29) —central themes of his missionary preaching (cf., e.g., 13:33; 17:3; 18:5)—to the Jews in their synagogues (9:20, 28; 13:14), creating controversy and meeting resistance (9:21; 13:45–46, 50; 14:2, 4–5, 19), even to the point of threats against his life (9:23–24, 29; 14:19; 20:3, 19), yet always dramatically delivered or vindicated (9:25, 27, 30; 14:19–20). Already readers sense the manifest destiny of this divinely commissioned prophet, that all efforts to obstruct his path will be unsuccessful, that he has God's favor and protection, that he will finally emerge triumphant (28:31). His miraculous escape from Damascus, unforgettably depicted (9:23–25; cf. 2 Cor. 11:32–33; cf. Josh. 2:15), recalls earlier vain attempts to restrain the apostles (cf. Acts 5:17–26; also 12:6–11).

Saul's immediate removal to Jerusalem (also 22:17–21; 26:20), his acceptance by the apostles through Barnabas' generous commendation, and his assimilation into the Jerusalem church (9:26–29) reflect the Lucan tendency to align Paul closely with Jerusalem (cf. 11:27–30; 15:2–30; 21:17–26). The Pauline Letters, by contrast, reflect Paul's opposite tendency—to stress his independence of Jerusalem (Gal. 1–2); in fact, Paul denies having been known by sight "by churches of Christ in Judea" (Gal. 1:22).

His opponents in Jerusalem are the Hellenists (Acts 9:29), possibly the same group who opposed Stephen (6:9). Later, Asian Jews figure prominently in opposing Paul in Jerusalem (21:27). Once again, efforts to kill him prove futile (9:29–30). Saved by the Jerusalem church, he is removed to Tarsus, his hometown (21:39; 22:3), where he remains until Barnabas fetches him (11:25).

Typically, Luke concludes the section with a summary that idealizes, generalizes, and marks a transition (9:31; cf. 2:47). With the Palestinian church (Judea, Samaria, Galilee) experiencing harmony, strength, religious devotion, and a quantifiable measure of the Spirit, Luke is now ready to describe a new stage in the church's mission. Geographically, the scene shifts to the coastlands, first Lydda and Joppa (9:32–43), then to Caesarea (chs. 10–11). The focus shifts back to Peter, who dominates the next three chapters. Most important, Gentiles officially enter the story through the figure of Cornelius.

9:32–11:30
Prophetic Ministry of Peter in Judea and the Coastland: Apostolic Witness to the Gentiles

9:32–43, Peter's Healing Aeneas and Raising Tabitha. Peter is reintroduced into the story through two "prophetic deeds": healing a paralytic and restoring to life a Christian woman renowned for her generosity. Both acts are reminiscent of Jesus' own activity (Luke 5:17–26; 7:11–17; 8:40–56). They show that Jesus is actually (still) at work through Peter (Acts 9:34; cf. 3:16; 4:10). The effects of Jesus' power are visible: in both instances, people "turn to the Lord" (9:35, 42), i.e., the Lord Jesus. This wording, as opposed to "turn to God" (cf. 14:15; 15:19; 26:20) probably implies that they were Jews (though cf. 11:21).

The latter story also echoes Elijah's raising the widow's son (1 Kings 17:17–24) and Elisha's raising the Shunammite woman's son (2 Kings 4:8–37). It thus casts Peter more firmly in an OT prophetic mold (cf. Luke 7:11–30).

Both stories are unusual in that both the afflicted persons are named: Aeneas and Dorcas. As before (when Barnabas exemplifies the church's widespread generosity, Acts 4:32–37), Luke renders generalized activity more specifically by using named instances (cf. 8:7; 9:31).

These two stories also document the further spread of the gospel. Before the pivotal Cornelius story is told, Luke will have described the spread of the gospel from Jerusalem through Judea, Samaria, and Galilee all the way northward to Damascus (9:10, 19) and now westward to Lydda and Joppa, where there are already "saints" (vv. 32, 41) and disciples (vv. 36, 38), but where additional conversions occur (vv. 35, 42). Moreover, Peter's (and therefore the apostles') influence and authority are seen to extend beyond Jerusalem to the coastlands (v. 32). In terms of the story line, Peter is now in place in Joppa (v. 43) awaiting his summons by Cornelius (10:5).

10:1–8, Cornelius' Vision. Luke's portrait of Cornelius is a model of compactness: an introductory cameo portrait (vv. 1–2) that comes to life in the narrative itself (vv. 3–8; → Caesarea). He is undeniably Gentile, a point repeatedly emphasized (10:22, 28, 35, 45; also 11:1, 3, 17–18) and on which the story hinges. Yet, he is a Gentile utterly devoted to Judaism (Rom. 2:28–29).

As a "God-fearer" (Acts 10:2, 22; cf. 13:16, 26; → Proselyte), his religious devotion is exemplified by his almsgiving and prayer, activities highly prized by Jews (Tob. 12:8; Matt. 6:2–6; 1 Pet. 4:7–9)—and by Luke (on almsgiving, see Introduction; on prayer, cf. Luke 3:21; 5:16; 6:12, 28; 9:18, 28–29; 11:1–13; 18:1–14). Though a Gentile, he has supported Jewish causes financially (Acts 10:2, "people" = Jews; cf. 10:22; also Luke 7:5). Not surprisingly, the vision occurs while he—a Gentile—observes a Jewish hour of prayer (Acts 10:3, 30; see commentary above on 3:1–11). Nor is it a prayer before deaf ears. God has accepted his exemplary service as a fitting sacrifice (10:4; cf. Lev. 2:2, 9, 16; also Tob. 12:12). Not only does he pray to God, but, completely in character, he obeys God—fully and promptly (Acts 10:7–8, 33).

10:9–16, Peter's Vision. The scene shifts from Caesarea to Joppa, and the action centers on Peter (9:43). Once again, prayer provides the setting for a vision (10:9; cf. 10:3; see commentary above on 3:1–11). All the marks of a divine revelation are present: Peter in a trance, not asleep in a dream; a "rift in the sky" (v. 11, NEB; cf. 7:56; Luke 3:21; Mark 1:10; Matt. 3:16; also John 1:51; Rev. 19:11), and a heavenly voice (Acts 10:13, 15).

The image of "great sheet of sail-cloth . . . slung by the four corners" (v. 11, NEB) is both unusual and without obvious literary parallels. The list of animals (v. 12) perhaps recalls OT lists (Gen. 1:24; 6:20; also Rom. 1:23). The divine injunction to Peter (Acts 10:13) is puzzling, unless only unclean animals are imagined in the sheet or the command is understood to apply only to unclean animals. Either way, its force is clear to Peter. With horror reminiscent of Ezekiel's (Ezek. 4:13–14), he recoils at the very thought of violating scriptural food laws (Acts 10:14; Lev. 11; Deut. 14; → Animals). The divine corrective (Acts 10:15) is sometimes understood to reflect Jesus' relaxed reinterpretation of Jewish food laws (Matt. 15:1–20; Mark 7:1–23; also Rom. 14:14). It may, however, be an appeal to the primordial period, when all creatures were "good" (Gen. 1:31; Sir. 39:33–35; also 1 Tim. 4:4). The threefold occurrence (Acts 10:16), after which the sheet ascends, attests its undeniability.

10:17–23a, Peter Receives Cornelius' Messengers. The vision so radically challenges Peter's worldview that he is genuinely perplexed (vv. 17, 19; cf. Luke 9:7; 24:4; Acts 2:12; 5:24). Even his movement to receive the delegation must be prompted by the Spirit (10:19; 11:12)—another instance where the gospel is edged along by divine impulse (8:29; 13:2; 15:28). Like Cornelius, Peter is compliant (10:21). The messengers summarize the earlier narrative but introduce the note that Peter will preach to Cornelius (v. 22). This paves the way for the sermon (10:34–43). By inviting them in as his guests (v. 23a), Peter is already acknowledging the truth of the vision and providing grounds for the later criticism (11:3).

10:23b–33, Peter and Cornelius Meet. Since they are acting at God's behest, the combined delegation leaves "the next day" (v. 23b) and travels to Caesarea, the scene of the next several events (vv. 24–48). Joining Peter are Jewish Christians from Joppa (v. 23b; cf. 9:41–42), later numbered as six (11:12), who become crucial witnesses to the conversion of the Gentiles (10:45) and confirm Peter's account at Jerusalem. The cluster of friends and family gathered by Cornelius (vv. 24, 27) becomes the nucleus of the Caesarean church (cf. 12:19; 18:22; 21:8, 16). His deference to Peter (10:25), by which he acknowledges God's messenger as well as confirms the truth of his earlier vision (vv. 5–6), also further illustrates his piety. It also allows Luke another opportunity to distinguish between divine power and human agent (cf. 3:12; 14:15; also Rev. 19:10; Wisd. of Sol. 7:1–6). Both Peter and Cornelius are responding, in their respective ways, to the same divine impulse.

10:34–43, Peter's Sermon. Whereas earlier sermons feature OT promise fulfillment and Israelite history (chaps. 2, 3, 7), this one is distinguished by its introductory statement about God's impartiality (vv. 34–35; cf. Deut. 10:17; 2 Chron. 19:7; Job 34:19; Sir. 35:12–13; Rom. 2:11; Gal. 2:6; Eph. 6:9; Col. 3:25) and its concentrated summary of the Jesus story (Acts 10:36–42), an admirable distillation of Luke's Gospel. Prophetic witness to Jesus is mentioned only briefly at the end (v. 43).

Like earlier sermons (see commentary above on 3:12–26), its chief subject is God—God's nature and what God has done through Christ. Its essential message to Gentiles is that Jesus is God's story continued. God sent, even "preached," the good news of Jesus (10:36); Jesus' anointing by God (at his baptism; v. 38; Luke 3:21–22), and being empowered by God's Spirit (cf. Luke 4:1, 14–21); his alliance with God demonstrated by his "good deeds" of healing (Acts 10:38; cf. 2:22); God righted the wrong of his death by raising him (10:40; cf. 2:24, 32; 3:15) and revealing him alive (10:41; Luke 24:13–53; Acts 1:3–11); he is ordained by God as the ultimate judge (10:42; cf. 17:31); and the story continues to be told through God-appointed witnesses under divine mandate (10:41–42; cf. Luke 24:48–49; Acts 1:8). The God to whom Gentiles, like Cornelius, are already attracted has been at work visibly and audibly through Jesus and is now being heard

in the apostolic witness. By acknowledging Jesus as God's Anointed, they will be acknowledging truly the God they already "fear" (10:2, 22).

Admittedly, God's story has Jewish roots. Jesus was attested by the prophets (v. 43) and introduced first to Israel (v. 36; cf. 13:26). His sphere of activity was "the country of the Jews [Galilee] and Jerusalem" (10:39). Yet, he is no local, national deity but has universal appeal as "Lord of all" (v. 36b). Eventually he is destined to be universal judge of the "living and dead" (v. 42). Forgiveness is now universally available (v. 43).

One important new element in this sermon is the emphasis on the God who does not "play favorites" (v. 34, JB, NEB). In Jesus is now realized God's intended vision of a humanity "without distinctions" (cf. 11:12). God fully accepts Gentiles and Jews on equal terms, and such labels as "clean"/"unclean" no longer apply (cf. 10:28); indeed, they no longer can exist. Not only can all persons be accepted by God; they can fully accept each other in ordinary social relationships, such as table fellowship (10:23; 11:3).

10:44–48, Gentiles Accepted. In this sequel, their favorable response to Peter's preaching is indicated: "hearing the word" (v. 44; 11:1; cf., e.g., 2:41; 4:4; 8:14) and "extolling God" (10:46). But especially stressed is how God takes the initiative in letting the Holy Spirit "fall" upon the Gentiles, even during Peter's sermon (v. 44), as he "began to speak," as he later reports (11:15). Clearly, God used this as an occasion to bestow the "gift of the Spirit" to the Gentiles in a manner comparable to Pentecost (11:17; cf. 2:4). Accordingly, Peter challenges anyone present to deny them water baptism, the ordinary initiation rite admitting them to Christian fellowship (10:47). Since there were no dissenters, he commands them to be baptized "in the name of Jesus Christ" (v. 48), thus acknowledging Jesus' universal lordship. His remaining with them "for some days" indicates his full acceptance of them (v. 48b; cf. John 4:40).

11:1–18, Peter Answers Jerusalem Critics. The final scene shifts to Judea, specifically Jerusalem, where the (other) apostles reside (cf. 8:1). As before, the apostles' authority to confirm legitimate expressions of the gospel is implied (8:14; cf. 11:22). Accordingly, Peter's defense of his actions occurs before them at Jerusalem. His critics are "those of the circumcision" (11:2; NEB: "those of Jewish birth"; JB: "Jews"; cf. 15:1, 5; Gal. 2:12), presumably a subgroup of Jewish Christians ("Judean brethren," Acts 11:1) who thought Gentiles should be circumcised. They appear to have criticized, first, his going to Gentiles, i.e., launching a mission to

Gentiles, and second, his eating with Gentiles, i.e., engaging in table fellowship with them (v. 3), which, according to Peter's own testimony, was prohibited (10:28).

Peter's response is to rehearse "in order" (v. 4) what had transpired. His remarks in vv. 5–16 provide a condensed account of what has already been described in 10:9–48. Repeating it underscores the signal importance of this episode, although some new details emerge. Peter's reminiscence of the risen Lord's promise (11:16; cf. 1:5; cf. Luke 3:16) is significant because it shows that the event is a fulfillment of a promise made by Jesus himself. He insists that the Gentiles had experienced precisely what the apostles had experienced at Pentecost (11:17; 10:47). Accordingly, God not only approved, but initiated, his going to the Gentiles and associating with them. Failure to recognize this, even more, refusal to act accordingly, would be tantamount to opposing God (11:15), about which readers have already been cautioned (cf. 5:3, 38–39).

The only proper response, as to Peter's earlier challenge (10:47), is silence. Accordingly, Peter's critics, and presumably the apostles and Judean Christians, "glorified God" (11:18; cf. 13:47–48). Their final concession aptly summarizes the whole preceding story: from start to finish, it has been the work of God (11:18; cf. 26:20). God moved the crucial players—Cornelius and Peter—into action, brought them together "in God's sight" (10:33), unleashed the Spirit through the preached Word, provided undeniable proof of divine presence and confirmation, and now silences the critics.

11:19–30, Christianity at Antioch. Having reported the gospel's success in Caesarea, Luke now documents the church's further geographical extension: northward up the coast to Phoenicia, notably Tyre (21:3–4) and Sidon (27:3), northwest to Cyprus (13:4–12), finally (and most impressively), some three hundred miles farther north to Syrian Antioch, the third largest city of the Roman Empire (→Antioch). His real concern is to sketch the beginnings of gentile Christianity at Antioch, which figures prominently later (13:1; 14:26–28; 15:22–35, 40; 18:22; cf. Gal. 2:11). He also uses this occasion to relate Barnabas and Saul to the earliest stages of gentile Christianity, thereby preparing them, especially Paul, for their leading role in missionizing Gentiles (Acts 13–28).

The gospel's thrust into these regions is attributed to those Jewish Christians who fled Jerusalem because of the persecution prompted by Stephen's controversial preaching and death (8:1–4). While the majority seem to have preached exclusively to Jews, a courageous minority ("some," 11:20) of Diaspora Jews from Cyprus and Cyrene took the bold step of preaching to Greeks, i.e, Gentiles. The unspo-

ken assumption is that they did so without requiring circumcision (cf. 15:1, 5). They thus put into practice generally what Peter had done specifically with Cornelius—and without divine prompting!

Even though this outreach effort occurs independently of the Jerusalem church, and without apostolic initiative, it has numerical success, which is attributed to the "hand of the Lord" (11:21; cf. Luke 1:66; 2 Sam. 3:12). Since preaching to Gentiles had been accepted in principle by the Jerusalem church (11:18), it commissions not an apostle, but Barnabas, who is nevertheless duly qualified (v. 24; cf. 4:36–37), to confirm the effort as legitimate (11:22). He sees what was already clear to the Antioch church—evidence of God's grace (v. 23). True to his name ("son of exhortation," 4:36; 9:27), he strengthens the church (cf. 13:43; 14:22). This apparently results in a second wave of conversions (11:24).

So impressive was the strength of this mission that Barnabas fetches Saul from Tarsus (where the narrative had left him earlier, 9:30; though cf. Gal. 2:1) to assist in establishing gentile Christianity at Antioch (Acts 11:26). Their year-long joint ministry succeeds in producing results conspicuous enough to require coining the new name "Christians" (v. 26; 26:28; 1 Pet. 4:16). The designation was perhaps given by outsiders as a way of distinguishing them from the Jewish community or even identifying them as a subset of Jews with specific loyalty to "Christ" (→ Christian).

In displaying generosity comparable to that of the Jerusalem church (Acts 11:27–30; 2:44; 4:32–37), gentile Christianity is seen to be equally legitimate. Typically in Luke, the proper disposition of one's possessions signals authentic faith (see Introduction).

It is difficult to correlate this trip by Paul to Jerusalem with his own chronology sketched in Gal. 1:11–2:14 (→ Paul).

12:1–25
Gospel Resisted and Vindicated in Jerusalem

12:1–5, Herod's Resistance. The gospel now meets its most intense opposition yet reported by Luke. Previously, resistance has come from religious authorities (4:1–3, 5–6; 5:17–18, 21–28, 33–42; 6:12–15; 7:54–8:3; 9:1); now the lead is taken by the chief regional civil authority (→ Agrippa I).

The form of opposition intensifies. Previously, Stephen had died violently at the hands of religious authorities (7:54–60); now, Agrippa takes more widespread action against "some who belonged to the church" (12:1). By decapitating James, he strikes at Jesus' innermost circle of apostles (→James [1]). The pleasure taken by the Jews at this action (v. 3) also represents an intensification. Until now, no blanket resistance from "the Jews" has occurred (though cf. 6:12). The core of opposition has largely been Jewish leaders, mainly Sadducees. Clearly, what Agrippa did to James he now intends to do to Peter; hence, the unusually "earnest prayer" of the Jerusalem church (12:5; cf. Jth. 4:8–15).

12:6–11, Vindication: Peter's Release. But just as the resistance intensifies, so does the form of divine vindication. The elaborate, detailed description of the security measures taken against Peter merely underscore the point. Overnight custody (4:3) and a "common prison" (5:18) now give way to a prison guarded by four squads of soldiers (12:4) and Peter chained not to the usual one guard but to a soldier on each side (v. 6). The greater the attempt to restrain God's messenger, the more dramatic the escape (vv. 7, 11). As if there were any doubt, Peter's words interpret these events for readers: rescue has come at the hands of God (v. 11). Foiled are God's opponents: Herod and the Jewish people (v. 11b). Once again, God's cause has been vindicated (cf. Dan. 3:28; also Exod. 18:4).

12:12–19, Proof of Vindication. God's vindication of Peter (and therefore the gospel) is first confirmed within the Christian community. The comic scene of the terrified girl fleeing in disbelief while Peter calmly keeps knocking (vv. 12–17) not only shows that his release was attested by witnesses—the "many gathered" (v. 12) and eventually "James [Jesus' brother] and the brethren" (v. 17; → James [3])—but also serves to reiterate the main theme: divine deliverance (v. 17).

Second, Peter's escape is confirmed publicly. The soldiers' inability to find him confirms the miracle, as does Herod's execution of them for negligence (vv. 18–19).

12:20–25, Divine Reversal. The final proof of divine vindication is Agrippa's death (vv. 20–23). More important than identifying the actual occasion mentioned in v. 20 is to note the manner and stated cause of death. Like Josephus (*Antiquities of the Jews* 19.343–52), Luke stresses its suddenness, but his horribly graphic description (v. 23b) serves to place Agrippa among the pitiable company of those who have vainly—and naively—sought to obstruct the ways of God (2 Macc. 9:5–9; Jth. 16:17). Josephus also mentions the popular acclamation of his divinity, but Luke establishes the causal connection. Not content to resist God, Agrippa competed with God. In doing so, he had met the fate Ezekiel promised Tyre (Ezek. 28:1–10). This ultimate presumption was his fatal mistake; hence, his ignominious death. As pre-

dicted, arrogant rulers would be brought low (Luke 1:52).

With such a defiant opponent vanquished, Luke needed only to observe briefly the steady, unobstructed growth of the gospel (Acts 12:24). Another ironic reversal has occurred: the killer king himself died; his innocent victim, the church, "grew and multiplied." With this last opposition movement foiled, God's messengers, Saul and Barnabas, move about freely and boldly, now in place for an even more dramatic push beyond Palestine to Asia Minor (v. 25).

13:1–28:31

The Gospel Spreads Westward "To the Ends of the Earth": Paul's Mission

13:1–14:28

Beginning of the Pauline Mission: Preaching in Cyprus and Eastern Asia Minor

Even though a major new phase of the church's westward expansion is being depicted here, the story is told in ways reminiscent of earlier chapters. Once again, a duly selected, divinely appointed pair of named individuals bears witness to the gospel (cf. Luke 10:1). Peter and John now have their counterparts in Paul and Barnabas. Just as Peter emerged as the dominant spokesperson in the earlier narrative, now it is Paul who does so.

13:1–3, Antioch: Commissioning Barnabas and Saul. Readers are already prepared to expect the church at Syrian Antioch to be a vital mission center (11:19–26). Its renown is indicated by the list of five named prophets and teachers associated with it (13:1).

Presumably through one of these prophets, the Spirit commissions Barnabas and Saul for their divinely appointed vocation (v. 2; cf. Rom. 1:1; Gal. 1:15). The very words of the commission, as well as the subsequent reference to the Spirit's explicit role (cf. Acts 13:4), indicate that the mission occurs at God's initiative, not merely because of human deliberation and planning. This is reinforced by noting the sacred setting in which the commission occurs (worshiping, fasting, and prayer).

13:4–12, Cyprus. Even though Barnabas and Saul preach to Jews in the synagogues of Salamis, on the eastern edge of Cyprus, the central event occurs at the opposite end of the island in the capital city of Paphos (→ Cyprus).

The prophetic deed reported is a confrontation between Paul and the Jewish magician

Bar-Jesus, whose Aramaic name was Elymas (v. 8). The latter's status as a false prophet (v. 6; cf. Matt. 7:15; 24:11, 24; 2 Pet. 2:1; 1 John 4:1; Rev. 16:13; 20:10) is confirmed by his efforts to obstruct the true word of God (Acts 13:8). Luke's designation of him as "magician" (v. 6; Gk. *magos*) is uncomplimentary, given the generally negative biblical attitude toward magic (cf. Deut. 18:10–12; Isa. 8:19; 44:25; 47:12–15; → Magic and Divination).

Paul's unusually harsh condemnation of Bar-Jesus (Acts 13:10) recalls biblical images (cf. Sir. 1:30; 19:26; Jer. 5:27). The emphasis on perverting God's straight paths also echoes the OT (Prov. 10:9; Hos. 14:9) and may recall the preaching of John the Baptist (Luke 3:5). The words with which Paul inflicts blindness on him also echo biblical imagery (Acts 13:11; cf. Judg. 2:15; 1 Sam. 12:15). Perhaps aware that Paul's actions will appear unjustifiably inhumane, Luke stresses that he was acting under the impulse of the Holy Spirit (Acts 13:9) and thus as God's agent against the devil's surrogate (v. 10). Also, noting the punishment's temporary status (v. 11) softens the effect.

The immediate effect of Paul's action is salutary: the proconsul believed (v. 12). This may suggest that Bar-Jesus's efforts to counter Paul's preaching involved magical deeds; hence, Luke would be portraying Paul as a more effective miracle worker. The direct correlation here between miracle and faith is comparable to that found in the Fourth Gospel (cf. John 2:11).

This story has parallels to that of Simon Magus in Acts 8. It shows the gospel's superior power over popular forms of magic as well as its power to attract an intelligent Roman official. Consequently, Rome is presented as sympathetic to the Christian movement. At the same time, Paul gains status as a miracle worker fully on par with Peter (3:1–11; 5:12–16; 9:32–43).

13:13–52, Pisidian Antioch. Here Paul's prophetic word (vv. 16b–43) is met with a divided response: Jews resist and Gentiles accept (vv. 44–52). The synagogue at Pisidian Antioch, located in Galatia, the heart of Asia Minor, some one hundred miles northeast of Perga, provides the setting for Paul's extensively reported sermon, or "prophetic word." Going first to the synagogue becomes Paul's typical missionary practice (v. 14; 14:1; 16:13; 17:1–2, 10, 17; 18:4, 19; 19:8). The sermon, identified as a "word of exhortation" (13:15; cf. 15:32; Heb. 13:22), is given in response to the invitation of the rulers of the synagogue. Paul's mode of delivery (Acts 13:16) suggests a Greco-Roman oratorical style (cf. 21:40; 26:1).

Paul's sermon here is roughly equivalent in length to Peter's Pentecost sermon (2:14–36),

and both are half the length of Stephen's speech (7:2–53). While Peter's Pentecost address consists more of explicit scriptural exposition (Joel 2; Pss. 16 and 110) than does Paul's synagogue sermon here, both culminate in preaching about Jesus, with notable emphasis on his death and resurrection. This latter feature is less prominent in Stephen's address. Paul's synagogue sermon resembles Stephen's speech, however, in the way it initially rehearses Israel's history, albeit in drastically summarized form. Though there is some overlap, it begins about where Stephen's speech leaves off—with Moses. This suggests that Luke is using sermons delivered on different occasions to unfold different stages or aspects of the Christian proclamation.

Broadly speaking, the sermon comprises two parts. First, there is a summary of Israel's history from the time of the Exodus until David (Acts 13:17–22), roughly a third of the speech. Then, the explicitly Christian story begins (vv. 23–41), with Christ introduced as David's posterity (v. 23; cf. 2:30; Rom. 1:3; Matt. 1:1; John 7:42). The outline then follows a more conventional pattern, similar to Peter's Cornelius sermon (Acts 10:34–43). The preaching of John the Baptist is an essential chapter in the story (13:24–25; cf. Luke 3:1–22, esp. 3:16; 16:16; Acts 1:22; 10:37; also John 1:20), which serves as the crucial middle link between David and Christ. A definite structural break occurs at Acts 13:26, with the repeated address introducing the second main part (cf. v. 16).

With no specific attention given to the life and ministry of Jesus (cf. 2:22; 10:36–39), the sermon moves directly to Jesus' Passion (vv. 27–29), with emphasis on the following elements: failure of the Jerusalem inhabitants and the Jewish rulers to recognize Jesus as the fulfillment of the prophets (v. 27; 3:21–25; 10:43; on the motif of the Jews' ignorance, cf. 3:17; also 17:30; 1 Cor. 2:8), which resulted in Jesus' trial (Acts 13:27); Jesus' innocence (v. 28; see commentary above on 3:14); Pilate's role (v. 28; Luke 23:1–25; see commentary above on 4:27); Jesus' death on a tree and burial (Acts 13:29); God's raising him (v. 30; see commentary above on 5:30); and his postresurrection appearances "for many days" (cf. 1:3; Luke 24:13–53) in Jerusalem to his Galilean followers, thereby qualifying them as witnesses (cf. Acts 1:8; also 10:39). Special emphasis is given to promise fulfillment (13:32–33) by interpreting his resurrection with reference to Psalms 2 and 16 (Acts 13:33–37). The form of argument is similar to that used by Peter in 2:24–36.

The sermon concludes with an offer of forgiveness of sins (13:38; cf. 2:38; 3:19; 5:31; 10:43; Luke 24:47) and freedom from the Mosaic law (Acts 13:39). With this latter motif, Luke gives the sermon a distinctive Pauline ring (cf. Rom. 3:28; 8:3; Gal. 3:23–25; 4:21–5:4), thereby preparing for the subsequent controversy created by the Pauline gospel (esp. Acts 15; cf. 15:1, 5; 21:20–26). This dual offer of good news is punctuated by a final prophetic threat (13:41) drawn from Hab. 1:5, which anticipates the Jews' rejection. Its harshness is reminiscent of Stephen's concluding accusation (Acts 7:51–53) and anticipates the note on which the Pauline mission ends (28:26–29).

The initial response to the sermon is positive, among both "Jews and devout converts to Judaism" (13:43). Opposition a week later comes from Jews, presumably members of the synagogue, whose jealousy is prompted by the unusually large response of the "whole city" (v. 44). By resisting, they fulfill Paul's prophetic anticipation of their inability to see God at work in their very presence (v. 41). Accordingly, it provides Paul and Barnabas an opportunity to state formally their principle of preaching first to the Jews, according to "divine necessity" (v. 46; 3:26; Rom. 1:16). Equally important, their rejection provides explicit justification for the gentile mission, which is also understood as direct fulfillment of the biblical promise (Acts 13:47; Isa. 49:6) as well as the full realization of Simeon's earlier vision (Luke 2:32). Thus, both the Jewish resistance and the gentile mission are presented as instances of biblical promise fulfillment.

Ironically, Paul's sermon in the synagogue becomes the occasion for the Gentiles' hearty reception and the spread of the gospel through the entire region (Acts 13:48–49). The Jews' expulsion of Paul and Barnabas from the city and the latter's corresponding response conform with Jesus' own predictions and instructions concerning appropriate missionary behavior (v. 51; cf. Luke 9:5; 10:11; also 18:6). Divine approval of the Pauline mission to the Gentiles, and thus disapproval of the Jewish resistance, is indicated by the presence of joy and the Holy Spirit among the disciples (Acts 13:52).

14:1–7, Iconium. This brief description of the Pauline mission in Iconium serves as a bridge between events described at Antioch and Lystra. The account is a generalizing summary of a mission that lasted "a long time" (v. 3), accompanied by the usual two-pronged witness of prophetic words and deeds (v. 3). Even though memorable events might have occurred during this time, none is singled out.

Luke uses Iconium to illustrate what must have happened typically in Diaspora cities that contained Jewish communities. First, as long as it could be judged on its own merits and without interference, Paul's preaching in the synagogue convinced both Jews and God-fearing Greeks who attended the synagogue. Second, resistance came from both Jews and Gentiles (unattached to the synagogue) within the city, but the real source of such resistance could be traced to the "unbelieving Jews" (v. 2). Third, in spite of such resistance, the gospel could be proclaimed boldly and attested by signs and wonders, both to great and visible effect (v. 3). Fourth, the gospel always stayed ahead of the resistance. Efforts to suppress the gospel, however hostile or threatening (v. 5), were unsuccessful in arresting the apostolic witness.

14:8–20, Lystra and Derbe. The Pauline mission now goes to a thoroughly gentile setting. Lystra has no Jews (hence no synagogue) except those who come from elsewhere (v. 19). Paul speaks not in a synagogue but openly, probably in the village street (v. 9). Every detail of the account contributes to this masterfully composed portrait of a rural, pagan village.

As usual, Luke depicts Christian witness by using the twofold structure of prophetic deed and word (cf. 3:1–26): first, a tightly composed miracle story (14:8–10; on the literary form, see commentary above on 3:1–11) that causes misunderstanding and provides the occasion for clarification (14:11–14); second, a sermon (summary) that corrects the misunderstanding and in doing so offers a new worldview through the gospel (vv. 15–17).

The story shows how Luke understood the Pauline mission to have occurred typically in a popular pagan setting. "Signs and wonders" are given a prominent role, but their significance must be properly understood and interpreted. As before, Luke insists that such power derives not from humans but from God (cf. 3:12). By employing a local Phrygian legend relating how Zeus and Hermes appeared in the human forms of Philemon and Baucis (Ovid *Metamorphoses* 8.611–725), Luke portrays the innocent misconstrual of divine power. Barnabas and Paul's emphatic disclaimer (14:14), combined with their insistence on being fully human (v. 15; cf. 10:26; Rev. 19:10; also James 5:17; Wisd. of Sol. 7:1–6; 4 Macc. 12:13; though cf. Acts 28:6), corrects this misimpression. It also shifts the accent to the true object of human worship—the Creator God.

The sermon summary (Acts 14:15–17) encapsulates essential features of early Christian missionary preaching to pagans: turning from "vain things," i.e., polytheism (v. 15; cf. Gal. 4:8–9) and turning to "a living God" (cf. 1 Thess. 1:9–10; Acts 15:19; 26:20). The main element of proclamation is God as Creator (Acts 14:15), a central feature of the biblical understanding of God (see commentary above on 4:24), yet also acknowledged among Gentiles. A theology of "natural revelation" is

1097

expressed in the conviction that in nature God has been revealed visibly to all persons as the Creator and Sustainer of human life (14:17; cf. Lev. 26:4; Jer. 5:24; Ps. 145:15; 147:8). These themes are amplified later in the Athens sermon, which introduces specific claims about Christ not mentioned here (Acts 17:22–31).

As usual, both acceptance and rejection occur. Whereas the locals are enthusiastic (14:18), resistance comes from outsiders—neighboring Jews who attempt to silence the gospel (v. 19). But the gospel is vindicated when Paul recovers from "death" (v. 19) with astonishing speed, and the mission continues unabated (v. 20).

14:21–28, Return to Syrian Antioch. The return trip is not narrated in detail but is used to introduce another important element of the Pauline mission—consolidating newly founded mission churches by providing further teaching and some organizational structure. The "strengthening" (v. 22) may be understood as an essential feature of early Christian mission (cf. 11:23; 13:43; 15:32, 41; 16:5; 18:23) and doubtless included general Christian exhortation, much of which is preserved in the Pauline Letters. But here its specific purpose is to brace the churches for continued hostility they would experience in the absence of their founding missionaries. This too seems to have been standard fare (cf. 1 Thess. 3:3; 2 Thess. 1:5–8). Jesus had envisioned as much (Luke 6:22–23; 10:16; 12:4–7, 11–12).

The organizational "strengthening" consisted in appointing leaders in each congregation. Here they are designated as "elders" (Acts 14:23), a leadership structure found in other congregations (cf. 20:17–35; also Titus 1:5; 1 Tim. 4:14; 5:17, 19; perhaps Phil. 1:1), possibly following the Jerusalem organizational model (cf. Acts 11:30; 15:2, 4, 6, 22, 23; 16:4; 21:18). "Elders" are noticeably unmentioned in the undisputed Pauline Letters.

In his carefully worded description of the return to Syrian Antioch, Luke gives special emphasis to God's role in the Pauline mission to the Gentiles. By reporting "what God had done with them" (14:27; cf. 15:4, 12; 21:19) and the "door of faith" (v. 27; 1 Cor. 16:9; 2 Cor. 2:12; Col. 4:3; Rev. 3:8) opened by God to the Gentiles (Acts 14:27; 2:17; 10:45; 11:1, 18; 13:47–48; 15:7, 12), Paul and Barnabas merely echo what Luke has repeatedly reported throughout chaps. 13–14: the primary actor in the whole mission has been God who, through the Spirit, has initiated, motivated, and sustained this mission. This explains why it has been a series of successes. A considerable length of time (14:28) is envisioned between the end of this first Pauline mission and the controversy it creates, reported in chap. 15.

15:1–35
The Jerusalem Council Resolves the Status of Gentiles

With the initial success of the gentile mission, it now becomes appropriate for Luke to address the network of questions created by an emerging gentile Christian church. If Gentiles increasingly become Christians, are they to be regarded as full equals with Jewish Christians before God? Are they not obligated to "keep the law of Moses" (v. 5)? In particular, must they not undergo circumcision, the one ritual act that symbolizes full admission to the people of God? By extension, are they not obligated then to live by the law? In a word, must not Gentiles become Jews, at least in some minimal sense, to be truly saved?

The seriousness of these questions for Luke is seen by the way he reports the Jerusalem meeting. By treating it at this juncture in the narrative, he acknowledges its importance as a watershed event.

15:1–5, Convening the Council. The reasons requiring such a called meeting of the Jerusalem authorities are carefully outlined. The disputing parties are clearly identified, and the heat of the debate noted (v. 2). It is a genuine threat within the life of the church requiring the attention of both the entire Jerusalem (Judean) church (vv. 4, 12, 22) and the highest echelons of its leaders ("apostles and elders" are mentioned five times in the chapter—vv. 2, 4, 6, 22, 23; also 16:4).

The picture is further filled out by the parade of distinguished figures, including Barnabas, Paul, Peter, James the Lord's brother, Judas Barsabbas, and Silas (→ James [3]; Judas [12]; Silas, Silvanus). Peter represents the "old guard," the apostles who figure as the prominent leadership structure in chaps. 1–14 and who disappear after chap. 15 (though cf. 16:4). James, by contrast, represents the "new guard," the elders who figure as the prominent leadership structure in chaps. 16–28 (cf. 21:18).

Luke reports two speeches, one by Peter (15:7–11), the other by James (vv. 13–21), and the contents of the agreement, formally stated in a letter (vv. 23–29). No extensive report by Barnabas and Paul is given (v. 12) since their activity reported in chaps. 13–14 is still fresh in the readers' minds.

15:6–11, Peter's Speech. His remarks reiterate three points already registered in the Cornelius episode (chaps. 10–11): first, the decision to preach to the Gentiles was God's choice not his (15:7; 10:19–20; 11:12); second, visible evidence of God's approval occurred in giving the Gentiles the Holy Spirit "just as he did to us"

(15:8; 10:44–47; 11:15–17); third, since God has "cleansed" the Gentiles, the distinction between "clean" (Jews) and "unclean" (Gentiles) no longer holds (15:9; 10:9–16, 28–29; 11:4–10, 12; cf. Rom. 10:12). His conclusion: Gentiles had been admitted by divine not human initiative. To have refused admission to Gentiles would have been to "withstand God" (Acts 11:17).

To these retrospective observations, Peter adds two new considerations, both having a distinctive Pauline ring: first, even our Jewish predecessors found the law burdensome and impossible to keep (v. 10; 13:39; Gal. 5:1; also Matt. 23:4), and second, there is only one way of salvation—"through the grace of the Lord Jesus" (Acts 15:11; cf. Rom. 3:24; 5:1–2; Gal. 2:15–16; Eph. 2:5, 8).

15:12–21, James's Speech. After Peter's remarks calm the assembly, Barnabas and Paul report "God's activity" through them among the Gentiles (v. 12; cf. Acts 14:27; 21:19). Then follows James's speech, which makes two contributions to the debate, both new. First, he provides scriptural warrant for the gentile mission, thus to what Peter started (chaps. 10–11) and what Paul and Barnabas continued (chaps. 13–14). Arguing from the Greek version of Amos 9:11–12, supplemented by Jer. 12:15 and Isa. 45:21 (Acts 15:16–18), James insists that the gentile mission was God's ancient intention, not a novel idea (v. 17).

James's second contribution was to propose a concrete solution: Gentiles should adhere to a fourfold set of prohibitions outlined in Scripture (vv. 19–20). These included abstinence from, first, pollutions of idols (Exod. 34:15–16; Lev. 17:8–9; cf. 1 Cor. 10:7, 14), including eating sacrificial meat offered to idols (Acts 15:29; 21:25; 1 Cor. 8:1–13; Rev. 2:14, 20; 4 Macc. 5:2); second, sexual immorality, specifically prohibited types of marriages (Lev. 18:1–30; 1 Cor. 6:18; 10:8); third, strangled animals, that is, those not ritually slaughtered (Gen. 9:4; Lev. 17:13; 19:26; Deut. 12:16, 23–28; 15:23); and fourth, eating animal blood (Gen. 9:4; Lev. 3:17; 17:10–14). The order of the prohibitions is not uniform (compare Acts 15:20 with v. 29 = Acts 21:25), and some ancient manuscripts omit the third prohibition since presumably it was included in the fourth.

The genius of this proposal is that these are the strictures the OT itself places on "strangers among the Jews" (Lev. 17:8, 10–13; 18:26), i.e., Gentiles. The implication is that circumcision was meant only for Jews in the first place, not Gentiles. Accordingly, gentile acceptance of these prohibitions would be fully in keeping with the Mosaic Scriptures that have been read weekly in the synagogue "from early generations" (Acts 15:21). James's proposal thus commends itself because it is scriptural in the strictest sense—it binds on Gentiles what God through Scripture had bound, and that alone, and it succeeds in waiving circumcision as a requirement for Gentiles. It thus allows Gentiles "to keep the law of Moses" (v. 5) in God's intended sense, not in the narrow sense insisted on by the "particularist" Jewish Christian Pharisees (v. 5).

15:22–29, Letter of Accord. The letter embodying this agreement repeats (for emphasis) the fourfold prohibitions (v. 29). It also indicates the scope of Jerusalem's influence over Antioch, Syria, and Cilicia (v. 23). The primary addressee was, of course, Syrian Antioch, where the problem especially had surfaced, probably because of its reputation for being the stronghold of the gentile mission (11:20–26) and for sponsoring the Pauline mission to eastern Asia Minor (13:1–3; 14:26–28). The letter also characterizes the "particularists" as a minority who had acted without due authorization from the highest authorities (15:24; cf. vv. 1, 5). In addition, it reaffirms the work of Barnabas and Paul, indeed heroizes them (v. 26), and acknowledges the importance of Antioch by sending two highly respected men, Judas Barsabbas and Silas (v. 22), to vouch for the authenticity of the agreement.

15:30–35, Joy at Antioch. Luke's report of the sequel closes this controversy. The authorized delegation before a formally assembled Antiochian congregation presents the letter, which is received joyously (v. 31)—the typical Lucan response to genuine instances of the Spirit's work (8.8, 13.52, 15.3; cf. 5:41; 8:39; 16:34). The former acrimony (15:2) is past, and Judas and Silas are returned "in peace" to Jerusalem (v. 34). The letter thus not only brought peace and joy to Antioch, it sealed harmonious relationships between Antioch and Jerusalem. This leaves Paul and Barnabas in Antioch continuing in their ministry of preaching and teaching, in position to begin the next stage of the mission, which ironically begins not with peace but with a sharp contention between these two intimate co-workers.

15:36–21:14
Paul's Mission in the Aegean

The Pauline mission now moves westward to the area of the Aegean, first focusing on mainland Greece (Macedonia and Achaia) and later on western Asia Minor, mainly Ephesus. Considered as a single "panel" of material, this section illustrates Luke's capacity for selective treatment of representative events, as well as his ability to give a comprehensive picture over a broad geographical sweep.

1099

15:36–41, Paul's Split with Barnabas. The next major phase begins not with a long-term vision for a Pauline mission to Europe but with a modest proposal to visit the churches recently established in eastern Asia Minor (v. 36). Only en route, and through divine intervention (16:6–10), do such plans develop. Luke thereby continues to emphasize that Paul's mission to the Gentiles is God's doing, not Paul's.

From other sources, it is well known that Paul and Barnabas came down on separate sides of a critical question of principle and that this occurred at Antioch (Gal. 2:1–13). This incident goes unmentioned in Acts. Luke rather explains their split as the result of a "sharp contention" over the suitability of John Mark as a mission companion. It now becomes clear why Luke earlier mentioned his departure (Acts 13:5, 13).

16:1–5, Strengthening Churches in Eastern Asia Minor. Mentioning Timothy here serves to introduce a well-known Pauline co-worker, who perhaps was converted by Paul on his initial visit to Lystra (14:6–19; cf. 1 Cor. 4:17) and who figures prominently in the Aegean mission, usually in the shadow of Silas (Acts 17:14–15; 18:5; though cf. 19:22; 20:4; → Timothy [2]).

But more than introducing a new face in the narrative, Luke is here explaining and thereby defending Paul's decision to circumcise Timothy. By showing that this action enhanced Paul's and Timothy's credibility among Jews (perhaps Jewish Christians) in the region, Luke is presenting Paul as sensitive to Jewish concerns (cf. 21:17–26; 22:3; 24:14).

At the same time, however, Paul delivers the Jerusalem "decisions" to his mission churches at Derbe, Lystra, and probably Pisidian Antioch (16:4). Since they were initially addressed to a more limited circle (15:23), Luke indicates the wider scope of the decisions. He thus places Paul's earlier gentile mission under the authority of Jerusalem's church leaders (not merely the church at Syrian Antioch), thereby emphasizing even more its full legitimacy.

16:6–10, A New Mission Emerges. In the lengthy journey westward to regions well beyond Paul's earlier stated goal (15:36), Luke depicts the emergence of a new, previously unplanned European mission as the triumph of divine over human initiative. Paul's "best laid plans" are twice overruled as first the "Holy Spirit," then "Jesus' Spirit" redraws the itinerary (vv. 6–7). At Troas, a third, even more dramatic intervention occurs in the form of a vision (dream?) beckoning Paul to Macedonia (v. 9). The Spirit's earlier messages might have come through the prophetic voice of Silas, but not this one. So direct and visibly clear was it that Paul could only conclude that Macedonia was God

calling (v. 10). Not one to disobey heavenly visions (9:4–9; 26:19), Paul complies promptly, like Peter, whom the Spirit had also directed into uncharted waters (10:19–23; 11:12).

The surprising shift to the first-person plural (16:10) introduces the first of four "we" passages in Acts (16:10–17; 20:5–15; 21:1–18; 27:1–28:16). These intriguing references may signify that the author of these sections here joins Paul's entourage and thus writes from the perspective of an eyewitness. By extension, this same traveling companion may very well have written the entire book, enhancing his overall credibility by subtle, occasional references to what he saw and experienced personally. Or, these sections may be travel diaries from an unnamed traveling companion, employed by the author, though loosely edited. Tradition has seen behind the "we" a reference to "Luke the physician," elsewhere mentioned as Paul's companion during his imprisonments (Col. 4:14; Philem. 24; 2 Tim. 4:11). The change may be purely stylistic, however, yielding no concrete historical information either about Paul's traveling companions, eyewitnesses to these events, or the authorship of these sections and the book as a whole.

16:11–40, Philippi. Paul's company responds promptly to the heavenly vision, wasting no time making the trip from Troas to Philippi in two days (v. 11). Identifying Philippi as "the principal city of that particular district of Macedonia" (v. 12, JB), one way of rendering a difficult textual problem) shows it to be the intended fulfillment of the Troas vision (→ Philippi). Luke thus gives it extended treatment. With memorable dramatic style, he skillfully sketches several representative episodes from Paul's several days there. Readers are able to see "a day in the life" of Paul the missionary to the Gentiles.

Since it is the first major stop of the European mission, Luke takes pains to underscore the thoroughly gentile setting. At the outset, he notes the city's status as a "Roman colony" (v. 12), thereby preparing readers for the narrative's preoccupation with things Roman (vv. 21, 37–39). Roman officials play prominent roles, and Luke uses proper technical terms to describe them (vv. 20, 22, 35, 36, 38). The gentile complexion of the city is reinforced by its minimal Jewish presence. Unlike most other cities visited by Paul, it has only a "place of prayer" (v. 13), which was located over a mile outside the city gate.

Other touches of local color capture the mood of a gentile city. The slave girl's "spirit of divination" is literally "spirit of Python" (v. 16), which readers would recognize as the serpent at the oracle of Delphi. The transparent profit motive of the girl's owners is also exposed in a manner typical of pagan social critics.

Five episodes are reported: (1) the conversion of Lydia (vv. 13–15), (2) Paul's confrontation with the possessed slave girl (vv. 16–18), (3) the Romans' hostility (vv. 19–24), (4) the conversion of the jailer (vv. 25–34), and (5) Paul's vindication (vv. 35–40). Each scene has its own purpose in the narrative.

The opening scene demonstrates Paul's consistent practice of going to the Jews first, for both theological and practical reasons (13:46; cf. Rom. 1:16–17). Once again, it is a gentile "worshiper of God" who is the most responsive (Acts 10:2, 22; 13:43; 17:4; 18:7). Her high socioeconomic status is suggested by her occupation (→ Purple) but also because both her name and hometown are given—the only person so identified in the narrative. Her conversion is prompted directly by the Lord (16:14; cf. Luke 24:45). After her baptism, she becomes the model of hospitality—an indication of her true discipleship (cf. Luke 19:1–10). Her home becomes the mission base for the Philippian church, which provides long-term support for the Pauline mission (cf. Acts 16:15, 40; Phil. 4:15–18).

The encounter with the slave girl has its counterpart in earlier instances where the gospel confronted Jewish magic (Acts 8:9–24; 13:8–12). Now it is pagan magic, a first. The girl's oracular utterance (16:17) is accurate and prescient: these men actually are obedient servants of God (v. 10) and will proclaim the "way of salvation" to the jailer (v. 31). Paul's exorcism of the spirit of Python, performed "in the name of Jesus" (and after the manner of Jesus; cf. Luke 4:35, 41; cf. Mark 1:25, 34; Luke 8:29; cf. Mark 5:8) is instant, indicating that the power of the risen Lord continues to work in Paul as it did through the apostles earlier (cf. Acts 3:6, 12, 16; 4:10).

The repercussions of Paul's actions are significant in that they reveal, for the first time, Roman resistance to the Christian movement. Precisely what illegal "customs" (16:21) they were thought to be advocating is not clear—probably overt proselytizing of Roman citizens. Their disturbance of the peace was serious enough to cause the Roman magistrates to inflict physical punishment (vv. 22–23; cf. 2 Cor. 11:25; cf. 1 Thess. 2:2).

The midnight prison scene resembles earlier episodes where Peter and the apostles are imprisoned (Acts 4:3; 5:17–21; 12:3–11). Similar divine intervention occurs: an earthquake that opens the prison doors and loosens chains (16:26). But unlike previous episodes, this is no escape miracle per se. Though illustrating God's power to thwart enemy attempts to suppress the gospel, it mainly serves as the backdrop for a conversion story. Edifying elements decorate the story. Imprisoned messengers of God show faith in adversity by praising God in song and prayer, thereby preaching to the other

prisoners (cf. T. Jos. 8:4–5; also Dan. 6:10–13). But the central figure is the jailer, whose cry for salvation echoes earlier cries (Luke 3:10, 12; Acts 2:37; cf. 22:10).

The jailer's conversion is compactly but fully depicted. He hears the Christian proclamation of the "word of the Lord" (16:32; cf. 4:29, 31; 8:25; 11:19; 13:46; 14:25; 16:6; Phil. 1:14; Heb. 13:7), demonstrates his penitence by washing Paul and Silas's stripes (cf. Luke 3:8; Acts 26:20), is immediately baptized along with his family (cf. 11:14; 16:15; 18:8; also John 4:53; 1 Cor. 1:16), demonstrates the genuineness of his discipleship by extending hospitality (as Lydia had done), and gives sure proof of the Spirit's presence by "rejoicing" with his household (cf. Acts 8:39; see commentary above on 15:31). Luke perhaps indicates his Christian status by portraying his newly acquired religious vocabulary—he extends the biblical greeting of peace (16:36; 1 Sam. 1:17; 20:42; 2 Sam. 15:9; 2 Kings 5:19; Jth. 8:35; Mark 5:34; Luke 7:50; James 2:16).

The final scene (Acts 16:35–40) illustrates Luke's consistent interest in vindicating the cause of the gospel. While it is the Romans who take hostile action against God's messengers (vv. 22–24), it is also the Romans who finally quail before a defiant Paul, indeed apologize and humbly ask him to leave their city! A final visit to Lydia's house suggests that Paul leaves behind a small band of committed converts, "the brethren," living under the patronage of this well-to-do Roman merchant (v. 40).

17:1–15, Thessalonica and Beroea. The ninety-five-mile journey from Philippi to Thessalonica, the capital of the province of Macedonia (→ Thessalonica), led along the Via Egnatia, which ran east-west across Macedonia from Dyrrhachium and Apollonia on the Adriatic Coast through Thrace to Byzantium. Paul's practice of going first to the synagogue by now is "customary" (see commentary above on 13:14). Specially noted is the length of his preaching ("three sabbaths," probably consecutive, v. 2), but also that Paul's argument was "from the Scriptures" (v. 2). For the first time, Paul's preaching is said to focus specifically on the necessity of Christ's suffering and resurrection (v. 3; cf. 26:23; see Introduction). This aligns Paul's preaching even more directly with the early apostolic preaching as well as the preaching of Jesus himself.

The meager response by the Jews to Paul's preaching sharply contrasts with that of the "God-fearers" and leading women (v. 4). But Luke gives even greater emphasis to the negative, "jealous" response by the Jews (v. 5; cf. 5:17; 13:45; also 7:9) and the episode involving Jason, the only "event" in either Thessalonica or Beroea Luke describes in any detail (17:5–9). It shows that in Europe, as in Asia Minor (chaps.

13–14), the real source of opposition to the gentile mission came from the Jewish synagogues, not from Roman officials.

Luke uses the episode to introduce two charges leveled by Jews (and perhaps pagans) against Christians. The first charge, "they have turned the world upside down" (RSV, 17:6), refers not to the astonishing rapidity with which the movement has spread but to its rather consistent tendency to upset the peace (16:20; 24:5, 12). The second charge implied that Christianity was a political threat because of claims about Jesus' kingship (17:7; cf. Luke 1:32–33; 19:38; 23:2–4, 37–38; on "kingdom of God," see Introduction). Especially sensitive to the potentially serious implications of such charges, Luke reports the Romans' refusal to take action, thus vindicating the church (Acts 17:9; cf. 18:12–17).

Even when the Thessalonian Jews follow the scent to Beroea and there resort to similar tactics (17:13; cf. 14:19), they are thwarted once again. The ever vigilant "brethren" protect Paul and manage his escape, thus enabling the gospel always to stay one step ahead of its opponents (17:10, 14–15; cf. 9:25; 20:3; 23:16–35). Resistance to the gospel is seen to be an exercise in futility.

In treating Beroea (17:10–14), Luke does more than continue the travel narrative. By juxtaposing Beroea with Thessalonica, he compares two different responses to Paul's gospel and thereby scores an important theological point. He first depicts the impressive response to Paul's preaching in Beroea by both Jews and Greeks (vv. 11–12). Even in the midst of the gentile mission, Jews respond positively to Paul's gospel when they are "open-minded" (JB, v. 11; preferable to RSV: "noble" and NEB: "civil"), perhaps serious-minded, and willing to "examine the Scriptures daily." Luke's fundamental point is that Jews' responsiveness to the gospel is in direct proportion to their willingness to give Scriptures a fair hearing and close scrutiny and to have them properly "opened" by Christian interpreters (Luke 24:27, 32, 45; Acts 8:35).

17:16–34, Athens. In Luke's overall literary strategy for depicting the Pauline mission in Europe, Athens provides the occasion for summarizing Paul's missionary preaching to Gentiles. This section supplements the Lystra episode (14:8–20), which shows Paul engaging popular pagan religion and only briefly outlines his preaching.

Luke sets the stage for Paul's sermon with a well-drawn description, lively with movement and dialogue, intended to capture fully the spirit of the intellectual and cultural center of Greece (vv. 16–21; → Athens). Paul's preaching in the synagogue to "Jews and God-fearers" is

introduced but dropped immediately (v. 17). Paul engages well-known schools of popular philosophy (vv. 17-18; → Epicureans; Stoics). The caricature "babbler" (v. 18), literally "seed-picker" (Gk. *spermologos*), marks Paul as a social type well known in antiquity—the wandering philosopher/preacher who, like a bird picking up seeds, collects philosophical terms here and there and uses them in his street diatribes with little or no grasp of their meaning (Demosthenes 18.127; Dio Chrysostom *Oration* 32.9). Less scornful was the suggestion that he might be preaching "foreign divinities," a charge similarly leveled against Socrates (Plato *Apology* 24B, 26B), whose memory Luke's description recalls. Noting that Paul preached "Jesus and the resurrection" (v. 18) not only helps account for their charge—they perhaps misunderstood "resurrection" (Gk. *anastasis*) as a goddess alongside Jesus—but also identifies the unnamed "man" later in the sermon (v. 31).

Luke continues to portray the ethos of Athens as Paul is led away to the Areopagus (v. 19). Whether it should be understood as a formal council or a place for uninterrupted conversation is uncertain (→ Areopagus).

Paul's sermon (vv. 22–31) is carefully linked to the Lucan setting and as carefully composed for maximum rhetorical effect, fit for a standing Greek orator (v. 22). It is addressed to the same audience as Socrates' "men of Athens" (v. 22; cf., e.g., Plato *Apology* 17A). Paul's mention of their being "very religious" (v. 22) appropriately acknowledges their renowned esteem for things divine. Concrete proof was provided by their "many objects of worship" (v. 23; cf. Wisd. of Sol. 14:20; 15:17), most notably the inscription "To an unknown god," which suggests there is one they had missed. Even though no inscription with precisely this wording is known from ancient architecture or literature, pagans acknowledged the existence of unknown gods. As an introductory theme, linking the setting to the sermon, the "unknown god" provides an effective strategy for introducing Christian preaching without offending pagan sensibilities.

Like the Lystran sermon (Acts 14:15–17), this sermon differs markedly from the other missionary sermons in Acts. There is neither reference to Israel's history nor any mention of the life, ministry, teachings, and Passion of Christ. Only at the end does it become explicitly Christian with a brief, unnamed reference to the "man" whom God raised from the dead and appointed universal judge (17:31).

Nevertheless, the sermon is anchored firmly in the biblical tradition, specifically in its presentation of God as Creator and, therefore, universal Sovereign of heaven and earth (see commentary above on 4:24). In this respect, it resonates with an equally well ingrained tradition of Greek religious-philosophical thought.

Two conclusions are drawn from this basic theological claim: first, humanly constructed shrines are inadequate to house this cosmic Creator (17:24; cf. 7:48–50), and second, sacrifices served up by human hands, with their attendant altars and images, are inappropriate for a self-sufficient God (17:25; cf. Ps. 50:12–14).

Besides "the world," God had created humanity as well (Acts 17:26–28). This contention is informed by both biblical and nonbiblical understandings of creation. Tracing the nations to "one" (person, v. 26; perhaps "stock," NEB) doubtless recalls the biblical story of Adam (Gen. 1:26–28; also Gen. 10). The ordering of "allotted periods" (probably seasons rather than historical epochs; cf. Gen. 1:14; Ps. 74:17; Wisd. of Sol. 7:18) and establishing (geographical) "boundaries" defining where nations live (cf. Deut. 32:8; also Ps. 74:17) also reflects a biblical outlook, yet not exclusively.

The more important point, however, is the corollary that humans are living beings created to "seek and discover God" (Acts 17:27–28; Deut. 4:29; Isa. 55:6; Wisd. of Sol. 13:6–7). Because of God's proximity to "each one of us," both spatially and historically (Acts 17:27; Ps. 145:18; Jer. 23:23–24; Dio Chrysostom *Oration* 12.28), "finding God" is no remote possibility. Yet neither is the discovery of God inevitable, something that happens automatically.

The claim that human beings are inseparably related to God their Creator is explicitly supported by quotations from pagan poets. The first, which is usually attributed to the sixth-century B.C. Greek philosopher-poet Epimenides, reverses the usual pantheistic Stoic assertion of divine immanence, namely, that God "is in" everything, and asserts that those who are given life by God necessarily find their life in God. Creatures are indissolubly linked with their Creator, utterly dependent on God for life, movement, and breath (v. 28). The second quotation, more certainly attributed to Aratus, the third-century B.C. Cicilian poet, draws the defensible conclusion that God's creatures are also God's "offspring" (v. 28b). The relationship, then, is not simply that of Creator and creature, but Parent and child. So far, biblical and nonbiblical religious traditions have converged in a unified understanding of God as Creator and its implications.

Next, the sermon explicitly addresses the question of how appropriate lifeless images are for the worship of a living Creator (v. 29). Although it is informed here by biblical traditions that eschew idol worship (Deut. 4:28; Isa. 40:18–20), its tone is less polemical (cf. Wisd. of Sol. 13–15; → Idol). Even some pagan critiques of idol worship were harsher. Absent is the satirical description of the woodworker or stonemason who crafts an idol and prays to it,

only to be met with stone silence (cf. Isa. 44:9–20; Wisd. of Sol. 13:10–14:7). Rather, a gentler point is made: artistic images, as aesthetically pleasing as they might be, inadequately represent Deity because they are humanly imagined and crafted, not divinely created: how can that which we fashion adequately represent the One who fashioned us?

At this point, the sermon takes a sharp turn away from the common ground established between biblical and pagan religion. Even so, image worship is attributed to "ignorance" (Acts 17:30; cf. 3:17; 13:27; Luke 23:34). God is said to "overlook" such previously misguided efforts (Sir. 28:7; cf. Rom. 1:20–23). What is now required is a fundamental change—universal repentance, which would be reflected in a more enlightened form of worship appropriate to a sovereign deity. Previously, Christian preaching has called for repentance especially on the part of Jews (Acts 2:38; 3:19; 5:31; esp. 20:21). Now a similar reorientation is being required for Gentiles as well (cf. 26:20; 1 Thess. 1:9–10; though cf. Acts 11:18).

Only now does the sermon become explicitly Christian, as Paul introduces the notion of God's universal judgment, which also reflects a biblical perspective (Acts 17:31; Ps. 9:7–8; 96:11–13; 98:8–9; also Acts 10:42; Rom. 2:16; 14:9–10; 2 Tim. 4:1; 1 Pet. 4:5). The "fixed day" renders the OT notion of the coming "day of the Lord" (Obad. 15; Amos 5:18–20; Joel 1:15; Zeph. 1:14–18; Isa. 24:21; → Judgment, Day of).

But why does the sermon take this turn before a gentile audience? Perhaps it is the theme of "universal righteousness," or "universal justice," which Luke hopes Greeks will find appealing. Retributive justice is assured because the living God has already reversed one injustice by raising Jesus from the dead (cf. Acts 3:14–15). Moreover, such justice is most likely to be mediated to the rest of humanity not through lifeless idols but through the "man" who is now alive, like God, Jesus.

The conclusion to Paul's sermon is conspicuously abrupt (17:32–34), though not unexpected, given Luke's earlier description of the setting. The light response (v. 34) included two named individuals, Dionysius and Damaris, who for some reason do not qualify for the honored status of "first converts of Achaia" (1 Cor. 16:15).

18:1–17, Corinth. Just as Philippi, Thessalonica, Beroea, and Athens have served to illustrate different aspects of Paul's missionary practice and preaching in the European mission, Corinth presents still another situation. Certain features are familiar, e.g., preaching in the synagogue first to Jews (and Greek God-fearers), then turning to Gentiles. But the total configuration is distinctively new.

Here, Luke shows, first, how Paul, assisted by co-workers, establishes the "word of God" (v. 11) in a major Greco-Roman urban center (→ Corinth); second, how he justifies directing his mission in this city away from Jews and primarily toward Gentiles; and third, how Christianity, after "settling in" to a community and then being formally charged by Jews with being illegal, is officially vindicated before Roman authorities.

Unlike other founding visits, both before and after, a vital role is played by named co-workers (v. 2; → Aquila; Prisca, Priscilla). Though described as *Jews* expelled from Rome by Claudius (ca. A.D. 49), quite possibly these Diaspora Jews were already Christians who figured in "disturbances [made] at the instigation of Chrestus" (Suetonius *Claudius* 25) in Rome involving Jews and (Jewish) Christians. Their initial association with Paul at Corinth was professional, perhaps as members of the same "leather-workers guild." During this initial period, Paul was only able to preach in the synagogue "every sabbath," presumably because during the week he actively worked at his trade. This previously unmentioned feature of his missionary practice is later stressed by Luke (20:34); it had been emphasized by Paul himself (1 Thess. 2:9; 1 Cor. 4:12; also 2 Thess. 3:7–9).

The arrival of Silas and Timothy from Macedonia marks a new stage (Acts 18:5). They increased the work force and possibly brought financial contributions from Philippi (Phil. 4:15–16; 2 Cor. 11:7–9), which enabled Paul to be "occupied [full-time] with preaching" (Acts 18:5). More explicit claims about Christ result in intense Jewish resistance not unlike previous occasions (v. 6; 13:45; 17:5, 13). This results in Paul's formal repudiation of the Jews, both by symbolic gesture (18:6; cf. Neh. 5:13; also Acts 13:51; Luke 9:5; 10:11) and solemn, biblical pronouncement of their guilt (2 Sam. 1:16; 14:9; Jer. 51:35; Ezek. 33:4–6; cf. Matt. 23:34–35; 27:25; Acts 5:28), his innocence (Acts 20:26; cf. Matt. 27:24; Sus. 46), and the legitimacy of directing his mission toward Gentiles (Acts 13:46–47; 28:28; cf. Rom. 1:16; 11:11).

The move from the synagogue next door to the house of the gentile God-fearer Titius Justus symbolizes the beginning of the gentile mission proper (Acts 18:7). Reporting the conversion of the prominent synagogue official (v. 8) may be intended to show that in direct competition with the synagogue, Paul's mission was still effective, even among Jews. In any event, the number of gentile converts ("Corinthians") swelled (v. 8).

But what happens when the church takes root in a place and becomes more highly visible, when outsiders, especially Roman officials, recognize it as something distinct from the synagogue? Might it lose its legal status and social acceptability? Would such long-term success provoke the authorities to take countermeasures against it, even suppress it? To such fears, Christ's nighttime vision to Paul appears to be addressed (vv. 9–10). As had his prophetic predecessors (Josh. 1:9; Isa. 41:10; 43:5; Jer. 1:8, 19), Paul receives divine assurance. He is urged to be fearless in proclaiming God's message and is assured of God's presence and his own personal safety. Paul's full compliance is indicated by his staying an unusually long time (eighteen months, Acts 18:11). This also confirms the truth of Christ's promise. The length of stay attests that "many people" (v. 10) did respond.

Paul's vindication before Gallio (vv. 12–17) is presented as the climax of Paul's stay in Corinth, occurring after the impressive growth of the gospel from meager beginnings has been carefully documented (→ Gallio). This episode shows that even if Christianity begins, grows, and flourishes in a Roman city like Corinth, and even if Jews bring formal charges against it before a Roman tribunal, it will elicit "no attention" from Rome. No Roman laws are being violated; only Jewish laws are being debated. By his silence Gallio approves.

18:18–23, Moving Toward Ephesus. The main function of this section is transitional, serving to get Paul from Corinth to Ephesus. With no formal ending to a "missionary journey," as previously (e.g., 14:26–28), or well-advertised beginning for a "third journey" (e.g., 15:36–41), this section should be read as a continuation of Paul's mission to Gentiles in the Aegean.

At the Corinthian suburb of Cenchreae, Paul (possibly Aquila) fulfills a Nazirite vow (though shaving the head normally occurred at the end rather than the beginning of such vows; cf. Num. 6:1–21, esp. v. 5; → Nazirites). Thereby Luke demonstrates Paul's continued fidelity to his Jewish heritage, which becomes important later (cf. Acts 20:16; 21:20–26).

Landing at Caesarea, some three hundred miles south of Antioch, remains puzzling, as does the unusually vague reference to "going up and greeting the church" (18:22). Probably the Jerusalem church is meant, although conceivably it could be the Caesarean church. Finally, having reached his home base Antioch (cf. 13:1–3; 14:24–28; 15:36–41), his departure is rather straightforward and perfunctory (18:23). Such inattention to details suggests that Luke did not intend to signal the end of one phase of Paul's mission and the formal beginning of another.

18:24–19:41, The Pauline Mission in Ephesus. The account of activities in Ephesus consists of six parts: (1) Apollos's conversion

(18:24–28); (2) Paul's baptizing twelve disciples (19:1–7); (3) establishing an effective mission in Ephesus for Asia (19:8–10); (4) Paul's prophetic deeds and the gospel's triumph over pagan magic (19:11–20); (5) Paul's plans to go to Rome (19:21–22); and (6) the gospel confronting pagan religion: Christ and Artemis (19:23–41).

Apollos's conversion occurs before Paul's arrival in Ephesus, but it is achieved by Priscilla and Aquila, duly certified members of the Pauline circle. It thus becomes the first episode of the Pauline mission at Ephesus (18:24–28).

There obviously existed a Christian community (v. 27) at Ephesus prior to, and therefore independent of, Paul (unless 18:18 intends to portray Paul as the founder of the Ephesian church). From somewhere—probably Alexandria (Egyptian Christianity is otherwise untreated by Luke; though cf. 6:9), less likely from Christians already resident in Ephesus—Apollos had been "instructed in the way of the Lord" (i.e., Jesus; 18:25; cf. 9:22; 22:4; 24:14, 22; → Apollos).

This episode illustrates how the early church, Pauline Christianity in particular, dealt with cases of imperfect knowledge, or how independent streams of Christianity were brought into the mainstream of apostolic Christianity. In this instance, the issue was an inadequate understanding of Christian baptism.

Luke also uses the Apollos episode to show how a Pauline church enters its second phase under the leadership of another teacher. A Christian teacher duly corrected by members of the Pauline circle is thus recommended by letter (18:27; cf. 2 Cor. 3:1–2; also Rom. 16:1; Col. 4:10) to another church, and Paul's successor continues to do precisely what Paul himself did when he was there (Acts 18:28).

Coupled with the Apollos confirmation is the episode involving twelve disciples of John (19:1–7), which presents a new situation. When Paul arrives at Ephesus, he finds those who are already "disciples"—probably Christians, assuming Luke uses the term consistently (v. 1; e.g., 19:9, 30; also 11:26). Yet their (Christian?) discipleship is lacking in one vital respect. They are completely ignorant of the Holy Spirit, the sure sign in Luke-Acts of full-fledged forms of Christianity (cf. Luke 3:16; Acts 1:4–5; 11:16; 13:52). They had, however, received John's baptism (19:3), although where, how, and by whom are not stated. Apollos perhaps? This suggests the existence of "Baptist sects" and the continuing influence of John's movement outside Palestine long after the death of Jesus.

The inclusion of this episode shows what Paul did to incorporate quasi-Christian groups into the church's mainstream. Just as their predecessors who were also "firsts," albeit in different ways, had done, they receive, first, baptism "in the name of Jesus" (v. 5; signifying fully

their shift of loyalty from John to Jesus) and, second, apostolic (or equivalent) confirmation by the bestowal of the Holy Spirit (v. 6), visibly evidenced, usually through speaking in tongues and prophesying (2:4, 38–39; 8:14–19; 10:44–48; 11:15).

Establishing an effective Pauline mission in Ephesus (19:8–10) follows a familiar pattern with some new features. For the first time, the content of Paul's synagogue preaching is said to focus on the "kingdom of God" (v. 8), already hinted at earlier (14:22), and repeated later (20:25; 28:23, 31; see Introduction). This links Paul still further with his predecessors (8:12) but, more importantly, with Christ (1:3; also Luke 4:43). Also striking is the duration of his ministry possibly in a public hall (→ Tyrannus, Hall of)—two years, the longest yet, and when combined with the earlier three months (Acts 19:8), can be rounded off to a three-year stay in Ephesus (20:31). Accordingly, Paul's mission radiates beyond a single city to an entire region (cf. 13:49), reaching both Jews and Greeks throughout Asia, i.e., western Asia Minor. Included would be cities of known Pauline connections: Colossae, Laodicea, and Hierapolis (Col. 4:13–17). Luke thereby shows Paul's ever-widening influence.

Luke highlights Paul's healing "powers" as an integral part of his two-year ministry (Acts 19:11–12; cf. 2 Cor. 12:12). While he has earlier performed "prophetic deeds" (Acts 13:9–12; 14:3, 8–10; 16:16–18), what now occurs is clearly "extraordinary": healing and exorcising through both direct (laying on hands) and indirect contact (19:11–12). This picture of unhindered healing power casts him even more firmly in the mold of the apostles (5:12–16) and Jesus himself (Luke 4:31–41; esp. Luke 8:43–45; cf. Mark 5:27; Matt. 9:20–22; also Mark 6:53–56; Matt. 14:34–36).

Paul's reputation as an exorcist is further enhanced as he is pitted against seven "itinerant Jewish exorcists" (Acts 19:13–17). Oddly, however, Paul does not actually exorcise the man's evil spirit (cf. Luke 4:33–37; Mark 1:23–28). Rather, the Jewish exorcists themselves acknowledge Paul's unquestioned power over the demonic order (Acts 19:13). The evil spirit then utters a confession that simultaneously qualifies Paul and disqualifies them as rightful colleagues of Jesus (v. 15). As proof, one man singlehandedly whips seven, which apparently serves to demonstrate the superiority of Paul's "power" to that of his seven Jewish competitors (cf. Luke 11:21–23). The episode ends with the point clearly made: the power of "the name of the Lord Jesus" is mediated exclusively through Paul, who brooks no rivals (cf. Luke 9:49–50; Mark 9:38–41).

Paul's own demonstrated power (Acts 19:11–12) and his proven superiority over his Jewish rivals (vv. 13–16) have a twofold effect: increased respect among the wider public (v. 17) and strengthening of the Christian community (vv. 18–20). The impressive triumph over magical practices, clearly banned in the OT (Deut. 18:10–14), Luke depicts as a purge *within the Christian community*. Those who were already "believers" now "confess" (their sins? cf. Acts 8:22–23) and publicly abandon all vestiges of pagan practices. Thereby Luke shows that Christian communities are formed gradually, not instantly. Properly purified, as before in the case of Ananias and Sapphira (5:1–16), the church experiences new growth and strength (19:20).

The mention of Paul's travel plans (vv. 21–22) signals a break in Luke's account of Ephesus. Events just described have firmly established Pauline Christianity at Ephesus. This is indicated by the summary in v. 20 and by Paul's willingness to think now of churches previously established, indeed to dispatch two co-workers to Macedonia (v. 22), but especially to look ahead, for the first time, beyond Jerusalem to Rome (v. 21). In his own words, Paul says now what was hinted earlier (9:15; also 1:8) and becomes evident later. It is a divine necessity for his mission to the Gentiles to culminate in Rome (cf. 23:11; 25:12). Luke now begins to set the stage for chaps. 21–28.

In light of Paul's statements in his letters about his mission stay at Ephesus (1 Cor. 15:32; 16:8) and Asia (2 Cor. 1:8–10, 15–17), and what is known (or reconstructed) more generally about his activities during this period, this brief Lucan interlude, as indeed the whole account of his stay in Ephesus, contains some puzzling omissions.

The final episode at Ephesus—the riot in the 24,000-seat theater prompted by the complaints of Demetrius the silversmith—serves as Luke's most detailed encounter between the gospel and pagan religion (Acts 19:23–41).

The scene depicted here is much bolder than the previous episodes where the gospel has engaged pagan culture and religion. If Paul showed polite deference to pagan religion in Athens (17:16–31), the implications of "the Way" (19:23) are now more emphatically stated: manufactured gods are not gods (v. 26). Paul no longer deftly introduces "the unknown god" but now directly confronts the world-renowned goddess Artemis (v. 27). Just as Luke has portrayed Paul's growing influence in the city and region (19:10, 17), so now the Pauline gospel becomes a major challenge to both the religion and economy of an entire city and region (vv. 26–27). In Corinth, Paul had been challenged before city officials, but the event was not widely publicized (18:12–17). Now Paul becomes a public figure, the friend of prominent regional officials (19:31), whose mission causes "no

small stir" (v. 23) throughout the city, indeed threatens the city's peaceful reputation (v. 40). Generally, Luke's description of the episode realistically captures certain features of social, commercial, and religious life in Ephesus (→ Artemis of the Ephesians; Ephesus).

Perhaps the most remarkable feature of Luke's account is the way he achieves his literary purpose through the words uttered by the two most prominent pagan spokespersons: the silversmith Demetrius (vv. 25–27) and the town clerk (vv. 35–40). Through Demetrius, Luke depicts the widespread and penetrating effect of the Pauline mission (v. 26). However meager the results of his preaching might have been in Athens (17:32–34), he has now succeeded in turning "a considerable number of people" away from the worship of gods (19:26). So successful has Paul's preaching been that now "Asia and the whole world" (v. 27) can consider Christ as a genuine alternative to Artemis.

Through the words of the town clerk (vv. 35–40), Luke defends the Christian cause. He exonerates Paul (i.e., his co-workers) as being "neither sacrilegious nor blasphemers of our goddess" (v. 37). Just as Jews earlier had been able to coexist with Romans by demonstrating a more tolerant attitude toward pagan cults (see Josephus *Against Apion* 2.237; *Antiquities of the Jews* 4.207), so now Luke similarly depicts "the Way." For all the impact Paul's mission has made on the city and region, it cannot be shown that it has been done in a way that dishonors pagan religion! Because the charges against Christians are unfounded and because Demetrius and the townspeople have failed to use proper legal channels, the real threat to peace and stability is the Ephesians themselves, perhaps the Jews, but not the Christians (Acts 19:40–41).

20:1–38, Concluding the Aegean Mission.

As planned (19:21), Paul travels to Macedonia (20:1) and Achaia (here Hellas, or Greece, v. 2), thereby adhering to his pattern of visiting recently established churches (14:21–23; 15:36), probably Philippi, Thessalonica, Beroea, perhaps Athens. The three-month stay in Greece (20:3) almost certainly occurred in Corinth, where continued Jewish resistance can easily be imagined (18:6, 12–17) and where he could catch a ship to Syria. This is a plausible time and place for his writing Romans (cf. Rom. 15:22–29; 16:1–23). Once again a Jewish plot is averted (Acts 9:23–25; cf. 20:19; 23:12–35; 2 Cor. 11:26), this time by returning overland through Macedonia.

Paul's increasing circle of co-workers (Acts 20:4) now includes persons representing various regions of his gentile mission. Puzzling is the omission of representatives of Achaia (Corinth, Athens). These seven (though perhaps only the two Asians) proceeded to Troas, while Paul and whoever is included in the "us" (v. 5) remained at Philippi, possibly so he could observe the seven-day period of Passover, thereby indicating further his continued fidelity to Jewish traditions (v. 6; cf. 18:18; 21:23–26). The mention of Passover dates Paul's stay in Philippi in the spring.

The seven-day stay at Troas (20:7–12) is notable for its description of an early Christian worship service "on the first of the week" (cf. 1 Cor. 16:2; Rev. 1:10; also Luke 24:1; Mark 16:1; Matt. 28:1), which likely ran from Saturday (so NEB; though conceivably Sunday, depending on whether Luke used a Jewish or Roman form of reckoning time) evening through daybreak (Acts 20:11). Worship in this Pauline mission church is portrayed as having three central elements: preaching (vv. 7, 11), healing (vv. 8–10), and breaking bread, i.e., the Lord's Supper (vv. 7, 11; cf. 2:42, 46; 1 Cor. 11:17–32). Luke shows Paul's mission churches conforming to the earlier apostolic pattern (Acts 2:42, 46). Raising Eutychus (vv. 9–12) also documents Paul's prophetic powers (cf. 1 Kings 17:21–22; 2 Kings 4:33–35) and his equal status with both Jesus (Luke 8:49–56; Mark 5:35–43; Matt. 9:18–26) and Peter (Acts 9:36–43). It also shows how his miraculous "powers" directly benefit the Christian community (cf. 19:11–12).

Paul's continued travels (20:13–16) are rehearsed primarily to get him to Miletus (v. 15), the site of his last sermon as a missionary in the Aegean. Apparently, he is still accompanied by the retinue described in v. 4; also the "we" section resumes, having broken off temporarily in v. 7 (cf. 16:10). Luke especially explains that Paul chose to bypass Ephesus not because it still posed a threat (2 Cor. 1:8–10; 1 Cor. 15:30–32) but to save time in reaching Jerusalem. By mentioning Pentecost, Luke again may be stressing Paul's faithfulness to his Jewish heritage (cf. Acts 18:18; 20:6; also 21:23–26).

Together with his synagogue sermon to Jews (13:16–41) and the Areopagus sermon to Gentiles (17:22–31), Paul's sermon to the Ephesian elders at Miletus (20:17–38) completes the cycle of speeches recorded by Luke in chaps. 13–20. The only sermon by Paul addressed specifically to the church (through the elders), this "pastoral homily" rounds out Luke's portrait of Paul as missionary preacher and church minister. Here Luke unfolds Paul's theology of ministry.

The sermon forms a natural conclusion to his Ephesian ministry (Acts 18:24–19:41), where Luke especially has stressed pastoral aspects of Paul's ministry: perfecting quasi-Christians through additional teaching (19:1–7; also

18:24–28); preaching (19:8–10); his ministry of healing, competing with other miracle workers, and the complete elimination of pagan, magical practices from the church (19:11–20); developing further mission plans (19:21–22); and fully engaging the social, economic, and political life of the city and region (19:23–41). His pastoral role continued as he strengthened other churches (20:1–6) and attended to matters of worship (20:7–12).

The sermon and occasion also reflect the earlier picture of governance by "elders" (Gk. *presbyteroi*) within Pauline churches (14:21–23), although here the "presbyters" (v. 17) also bear the title "bishops" (Gk. *episkopoi*, v. 28; cf. Phil. 1:1; 1 Tim. 3:1–2; Tit. 1:7; 1 Pet. 5:2).

In form, the speech is a farewell sermon, addressed primarily to the Ephesian elders and church, who do not expect to see Paul again (Acts 20:25, 38). His "departure" (v. 29) refers ostensibly to his departing Ephesus (21:1) but clearly means his death (20:24; 21:13; cf. 2 Tim. 4:6; Phil. 2:17). Thus Luke has Paul here bidding farewell to all his mission churches and the church at large.

Woven into his "testament" are the standard themes of such addresses (cf. John 14–17; 2 Timothy): anticipations of his "departure" and the circumstances surrounding it (Acts 20:25, 29); review (and defense) of past conduct (vv. 18–21, 26–27, 31, 33–34); preview of the future, immediate (vv. 22–24) and long term, including the predicted threat of heresies (vv. 29–30); "passing the torch," or preparing for his departure by advising his successors (vv. 28, 31–32). The legacy of exemplary conduct and the call to imitation, important ingredients of testaments, are heard throughout (esp. v. 35; cf. 1 Cor. 4:16; 11:1; 2 Tim. 1:8, 13–14; 3:10–17).

The speech encapsulates various features of Paul's ministry unfolded in the previous narrative. It also echoes sentiments expressed in Paul's own writings, which suggests that Luke has sought to capture the essence and tone of Paul's understanding of his own apostolic ministry.

One new element is the prospect of false teachers who would threaten Paul's legacy (Acts 20:28–30). They are depicted as wolves, a common epithet for heretics (Matt. 7:15; 10:16; John 10:12; also Did. 16:3; Ign. Phld. 2:2; 2 Clem. 5:2–4). Bishops as shepherds recalls OT images (Ezek. 34:1–31; Jer. 23:1–4; Zech. 10:3; 11:16–17) and later becomes standard Christian parlance (1 Pet. 5:1–4; John 21:15–17). He cautions against both external and internal threats (cf. 1 John 2:19). This threat of heresy echoes other NT sentiments, especially in the pastoral Letters (1 Tim. 1:3–7, 19–20; 4:1–3, 7; 2 Tim. 2:14–18, 23–26; 3:1–9; 4:3–4; Titus 1:13–16; 3:9–10), and may envision quasi-Gnostic teachings encountered by the church in Luke's own time during the late first century A.D. (→ Gnosticism).

The speech throughout underscores Paul's orthodoxy and fidelity to the apostolic preaching. The essential features of his preaching and teaching are in line with that of his apostolic predecessors (Acts 20:21, 25, 32). Especially significant is Paul's concluding reference to the saying of Jesus (v. 35), unrecorded in any of the canonical Gospels, calling for responsible care for the weak (cf. Rom. 15:1; Gal. 2:10). Paul is thus portrayed as faithful to the mission of Jesus (Luke 4:18–21), who himself commissioned Paul (Acts 20:24). Having preached and ministered in ways reminiscent of Jesus, he now bequeaths Jesus' teachings to his churches. He is a faithful and humble servant of the Lord (i.e., Jesus; v. 19; cf. Col. 3:24).

By placing Paul's "farewell address" here, Luke tacitly acknowledges awareness of Paul's death. Consequently, it need not be reported at the conclusion of the narrative (28:31). It also prepares the way for the final stage of the story— Paul's "afflictions and imprisonment" in Jerusalem (20:23; 21:11, 33), unfolding of which thereby becomes a fulfillment of the Spirit's own predictions. Coming at the end of this major period of Paul's mission in the Aegean, the sermon also becomes Luke's most compactly stated apology for his own hero and his best defense of Paul's conduct as missionary and church minister.

21:1–14, Journey to Jerusalem. Paul's next major destination is Jerusalem (cf. 19:21), where the next series of events occurs (21:15–23:30). His journey there from Ephesus is swift. This third "we" section (21:1–18; cf. 16:10) reads like a travel diary: ports of call, lengths of stay, names of hosts, and travel details about ships and the traveling party are given.

Luke uses this travel narrative to introduce some other Christian communities at Tyre (21:4), Ptolemais (v. 7), Caesarea (v. 16). Perceptive readers already might have expected to find followers of Jesus at Tyre (11:19; also Luke 6:17; 10:13–14) and Caesarea (Acts 8:40; 10:1–11:18; 12:19; 18:22). But more than simply describing an itinerary, Luke demonstrates Paul's acceptance by Palestinian churches that he himself had not established.

In the Caesarean scene (21:8–14), Luke achieves several things. First, he links Paul even more firmly with Judean Christianity. He is welcomed by "one of the seven" (v. 8), an apostolic appointee with early ties to Jerusalem whose evangelistic work had received full apostolic confirmation (8:4–40).

Second, he prepares readers for what follows immediately—Paul's arrest and imprisonment. Heretofore, Paul's mission has experienced no significant setback. At each turn, Paul

narrowly escaped being caught (9:23–25; 14:19–20; 16:35–40; 17:10; 19:30–31; 20:3, 19). This time he will not. Consequently, Luke introduces the Judean prophet Agabus (cf. 11:27–28), who performs a symbolic gesture reminiscent of the OT prophets (21:11; Isa. 20:2–6; Jer. 13:1–14). Speaking for the Holy Spirit, he also predicts that Paul's real nemesis would be "the Jews at Jerusalem"; that he would be "bound," i.e., imprisoned; and that the Jews would "deliver him over to the Gentiles," i.e., the Romans. As the Lucan narrative unfolds, each turns out to be accurate.

Third, Luke is possibly beginning his portrayal of the "passion of Paul." In one sense, Paul's journey to Jerusalem is a miniature of the much longer travel narrative in Luke's Gospel in which Jesus journeys from his Galilean mission field to his ultimate destination in Jerusalem (Luke 9:51–19:44). Certain elements of the Caesarean scene suggest some parallels between Paul and Jesus (see Introduction). Paul resolutely travels to Jerusalem (Acts 21:12–13; cf. Luke 9:51–53; 13:22; 17:11; 18:31–33; 19:11, 28), willing even to meet the fate expected of God's faithful prophets—death in Jerusalem (Acts 21:13; 20:24; Luke 13:33–34). His destiny is finally interpreted as conforming to "the will of the Lord" (Acts 21:14), even though, unlike Gethsemane, it is his companions who concede this, not Paul himself (Luke 22:42). Luke leaves little doubt, however, that Paul's going to Jerusalem, and what happens there, are divinely willed (Acts 9:15; 19:21; 23:11).

21:15–23:30
Paul in Jerusalem

21:15–26, Paul's Arrival in Jerusalem. Paul is welcomed by the Jerusalem church ("brethren," v. 17), which includes the Cypriot Mnason, one of the "earliest disciples" (v. 16), perhaps an early associate of Barnabas (4:36–37). Since Paul's last official visit to Jerusalem (15:2–4; though cf. 18:22), the leadership structure has changed. The Jerusalem elders, who earlier shared in the leadership with the apostles (15:2, 4, 6, 22, 23; 16:4), now stand alone (21:18; though cf. 11:30), probably presided over by James, the Lord's brother (21:18; cf. 12:17; 15:13–21; 1 Cor. 15:7; Gal. 1:19; 2:9, 12; also Mark 6:3; Matt. 13:55).

Paul's return is reminiscent of his earlier return to Antioch (Acts 14:24–28) and his report at the Jerusalem conference (15:4, 12), where he depicted the gentile mission as "God's doing" (21:19; cf. 9:15). His detailed report is enthusiastically received by the Jerusalem church leaders who "glorify God" (21:20). This is the typical response in Luke-Acts acknowledging that God incontestably has been at work (Luke 2:20; 5:25–

26; 7:16; 13:13; 17:15; 18:43; 23:47; Acts 4:21; 11:18). God's full approval of the Pauline mission is thus explicitly acknowledged by the Jerusalem church.

In their "speech" (21:20-25), they report the dissatisfaction of "many thousands" of Jewish Christians, probably still in Judea, perhaps especially in Jerusalem (v. 24), who are still "zealous for the law" (v. 20).

Since Luke is here introducing a new element of opposition to Paul and his mission, their precise objection should be noted. They do not object to the policy of admitting Gentiles into the church (as was once the case, 11:2-3) or to the terms for admitting them or having fellowship with them (15:1, 5). This has been settled (15:19-21, 23-29), and the terms of the Jerusalem conference are fully acceptable to them (21:25).

Instead, they are worried about the implications of Paul's teaching for those Christians who wish to remain faithful to their Jewish way of life. They fear Paul as a threat to the continued vitality of Jewish Christianity, especially in the Diaspora, and therefore in their own region. These "Torah-zealous" Jewish Christians are not trying to make gentile Christianity Jewish; they are trying to keep Jewish Christianity from becoming gentile.

Since Luke has not yet addressed these questions in his narrative, he carefully states the objections of Paul's detractors. Their general complaint (v. 21) is that Paul is teaching "apostasy from Moses" to "Jews among the Gentiles" (probably Jews living in the Diaspora). Specifically, they fear that Jews who become Christians, in Paul's view, are no longer obliged, first, to practice circumcision, and second, to "observe the [Jewish] customs." And, given Paul's own stated views about "justification apart from the law (of Moses)" (Rom. 3:21-22; 10:4; Gal. 3:23-25) and circumcision (Rom. 2:25-29; 4:9-12; 1 Cor. 7:17-19), it is not difficult to see how their perceptions might have developed.

It now becomes clear why Luke earlier reported Paul's decision to circumcise Timothy (Acts 16:3). He wished to show that circumcision is still appropriate, if not obligatory, for Jews, even in the Diaspora. Also by depicting Paul as consistently sensitive to Jewish concerns and faithfully observing Jewish customs, such as the Nazirite vow (18:18), Passover (20:6), and Pentecost (20:16), Luke has shown that even a Jew in the Diaspora "keeps the customs." In the preceding narrative, Luke has already answered these objections in advance!

Yet proof that Paul "lives in observance of the law" (21:24) is needed for this group of concerned Jewish Christians in Jerusalem. The proposed solution is some public display of Paul's fidelity to Judaism. Paul is asked to assist four Jews (doubtless Jewish Christians) who had

taken a Nazirite vow (vv. 23-24; cf. Num. 6:1-21). To complete the vow, expensive sacrifices had to be offered (Num. 6:14-17), and Paul is asked to underwrite their expenses (v. 24). This would demonstrate not only that he thinks it appropriate for his fellow Jewish Christians to "keep the customs," even as he himself had done (18:18), but also display his generosity.

But more than this, he is asked to purify himself along with them (21:24, 26). It appears that Paul is being asked to enter into the vow with the four men, but apparently this would have required a minimum thirty-day period (m. Nazir 1:3), which Luke's seven-day period of fulfillment would not allow (vv. 26-27). In fact, the biblical instructions for the Nazirite vow do not entail an "ordinary" seven-day period of purification prior to the completion of the vow, as Luke's account seems to suggest (vv. 26-27). What may be unstated in Luke's account is that the four men, in some way, had become defiled through association or contact with a corpse and that they are now in the process of fulfilling the requisite seven-day purification period (cf. Num. 6:6-12; 19:11-12).

21:27-40, Paul's Arrest in Jerusalem. Luke now describes a second source of resistance in Jerusalem to Paul—non-Christian Jews. Agabus has already predicted that "the Jews at Jerusalem" would finally "bind" Paul (21:11). Eventually, this turns out to be the case, but the real source of opposition is traced to "the Jews from Asia" (v. 27; cf. 6:9), probably Ephesus, since they recognized "Trophimus the Ephesian" (21:29; cf. 20:4; 2 Tim. 4:20). Complaints similar to those leveled against Stephen (Acts 6:13), and in a sense against Jesus himself (cf. Mark 14:58; Matt. 26:61; Mark 15:29; Matt. 27:40), are now leveled against Paul (Acts 21:28; cf. 18:13; 25:8). As one who is allegedly anti-Jewish, antilaw, anti-Temple, Paul is charged with being a threat to "everyone everywhere"—a universal menace (21:28).

Luke emphasizes that the Asian Jews *mistakenly* thought Paul had taken the gentile Trophimus into the Temple (v. 29). Their charge is thus unfounded. Nevertheless, they succeed in inciting the entire city against him. They act with a frenzied violence already encountered in Acts (5:33; 7:54, 57-58), and their murderous intentions are underscored (21:31; cf. 23:27). The mob's cry, "Kill him!" (21:36), echoes similar shouts against Jesus (Luke 23:18; cf. John 19:15). This is perhaps another stroke in the Lucan portrait of Paul's "passion."

As certainly as "the Jews" try to kill Paul, the Romans (again) come to his rescue (Acts 21:31-36; cf. 19:31). This is to be a recurrent theme of the final chapters of Acts. Even so, it is a Roman who orders Paul bound "with two chains" (21:33; cf. 12:6), thereby fulfilling

Agabus' prophecy (21:11). From this point on in Acts Paul remains imprisoned.

The interchange between Paul and the tribune (vv. 37–39), which sets the stage for Paul's first defense speech (22:1–21), provides Luke an occasion to distinguish Paul from an Egyptian who, during the procuratorship of Felix (ca. A.D. 52–59), led four thousand terrorists (Lat. *sicarii*, lit., "dagger men"; →Assassins) on a revolutionary mission against the Romans (21:38). Such a figure is described in some detail (though with some differences) by Josephus (*Jewish War* 2.254–65; also *Antiquities of the Jews* 20.169–172).

22:1–21, Paul's Defense Before the Temple Crowd.

The need for such a defense, or "apology" (Gk. *apologia*; also 25:16; cf. 19:33; 24:10; 25:8; 26:1–2; 26:24; also 1 Cor. 9:3; Phil. 1:7, 16; 2 Tim. 4:16; 1 Pet. 3:15) was anticipated by Jesus, who saw such occasions as opportunities not only to answer charges but to bear positive witness for the faith (Luke 12:11; 21:14). This speech sets the tone for the remainder of Acts, which becomes Luke's defense of Paul. So important is this apologetic theme for Luke that Paul's defense is repeated, albeit in different versions, twice in the following narrative (Acts 24:10–21; 26:2–23).

There is considerable overlap between what Paul reports in this speech (22:3–16) and what Luke has already related in his earlier narrative (9:3–19), though some new details emerge.

One major difference is that Ananias plays a more prominent role in chap. 9. His interchanges with the Lord carry the narrative (9:10–16). The Lord's commission of Paul is actually delivered to Ananias, not to Paul himself (9:15–16). In chap. 22, by contrast, Ananias plays a less central role (vv. 12–16). He restores Paul's sight, then directly delivers to Paul God's commission, which has several noteworthy features.

In chap. 22 God is defined in strongly biblical tones: the God who commissioned Moses at Sinai is now the God who commissions Paul (v. 14; Exod. 3:15–16). His "appointment" by God is reminiscent of earlier prophetic appointments (Jer. 1:4–5; Gal. 1:15–16; cf. Acts 26:16). The divine appointment entailed the ability to "discern God's will" and also see "the Just One" (in the Damascus road vision) and hear his voice. God, therefore, intended for Paul to be confronted by the Innocent Christ (cf. Luke 23:47; Acts 3:14; 7:52) and to receive his commission directly from Jesus. Thereby he becomes a duly qualified "witness" (22:15; cf., e.g., Luke 24:48; Acts 1:8; 2:32; 3:15) able to testify both to the risen Christ whom he has seen and proclaim what he has heard (4:20).

Response to his prophetic call is to be immediate, requiring the removal of his former sins (of persecution) by baptismal washing

(22:16; cf. 1 Cor. 6:11; Eph. 5:26; Titus 3:5; Heb. 10:22; 2 Pet. 1:9; also Ezek. 16:9). His baptismal initiation is like that of earlier predecessors: it was in "the name of Jesus Christ" (2:38). It now entailed "calling on his name" (22:16), which meant acknowledging loyalty to Christ primarily through formal confession but likely through prayer as well (cf. 2:21 [= Joel 2:32]; 9:14, 21; Rom. 10:12–13; 1 Cor. 1:2; 2 Tim. 2:22; also Ps. 99:6).

Two new elements are the brief rehearsal of Paul's past (Acts 22:3) and the vision in the Temple at Jerusalem (vv. 17–21). As to the former, these opening words repeat what Paul has told the tribune privately (21:39) but do so with a well-established formula for describing one's life story: born, reared, and educated (22:3; cf. Acts 7:20–22). The formula suggests that Paul probably spent the first three years of his life in his birthplace Tarsus in Cilicia but early moved to Jerusalem where he was "reared" by his family and then "educated" under Gamaliel (cf. 5:34–39). As such, he becomes a Jerusalemite, formally educated to adhere strictly and zealously to the sacred traditions of the fathers (cf. Gal. 1:14; Phil. 3:5–6; also Rom. 10:2). This opening self-portrait responds effectively to two of the charges leveled against Paul (Acts 21:28): his past record is one of utmost respect for both the Jewish people and their law.

As to the latter, Paul's speech is consistent in reporting an immediate return to Jerusalem (9:26; cf. Gal. 1:17–18). His receiving a vision in the Temple while "in a trance" (Acts 22:17; cf. 10:10; 11:5) has all the characteristics of a prophetic call (Isa. 6:1–13). But it is a call not from God, but Jesus himself. In sharp contrast to the commission mediated by Ananias, in which God appointed Paul to be a witness "to all men" (Acts 22:15), it is now Jesus who sends Paul away from Jerusalem (v. 18) exclusively to Gentiles (v. 21). With a reluctance reminiscent of Moses and other hesitant prophets (Exod. 4:10–17), Paul recalls his participation in the death of Stephen and his subsequent terroristic acts (Acts 7:54–8:3), but to no avail. He is clearly Jesus' chosen prophet to the Gentiles.

This Temple vision is perhaps Luke's response to the third charge that Paul is "against this place" (21:28). On the contrary, the Temple serves as the place where his prophetic service to God actually begins, as did Isaiah's.

Jesus' prediction of the (Jerusalem) Jews' rejection (22:18) apparently prompts the interruption, in a manner similar to the Stephen speech (7:51–8:1). Earlier Luke reported resistance among the Hellenists to Paul's preaching in Jerusalem (9:28–29) but not the wholesale Jewish obduracy implied here. Even so, Jesus' parable of the banquet (Luke 14:16–24) has prepared the way for this theme that becomes something of a commonplace in Acts (cf. 28:24–29).

Chaps. 13–20 have consistently demonstrated the resistance, for the most part, by Diaspora Jews to Paul; chap. 21 has shown widespread resistance among Jerusalem Jews (so 21:11).

22:22–29, Paul the Roman Citizen.

Luke depicts the aftermath of the speech in his typical manner: Paul is rescued from the fury of the Jews by a Roman (cf. 18:12–17). Through brief but lively dialogue, the tables are turned as the Roman centurion finally defers to the Roman Paul. The central issue is Roman citizenship (22:25, 29; cf. 16:37, 38; 23:27). Bought citizenship bows before natural born citizenship (22:28). Once again, the enemies quake in fear before the freeborn Roman citizen Paul (v. 29: cf. 16:38). Luke also emphasizes the Romans' inability to obtain any clear evidence against Paul: he is innocent (cf. Acts 23:1, 28–29; 24:22; 25:25, 26; see Introduction).

22:30–23:11, Paul Before the Sanhedrin.

In appearing before the Sanhedrin, Paul's visibility before "Jews at Jerusalem" increases. Accordingly, Luke portrays Paul as a figure of increasing significance in the life of Jerusalem Jewry.

The curious exchange between Paul and Ananias (23:1–5) contrasts the high priest's disobedience of the law with Paul's complete fidelity to the law. Ananias's unexplained action in striking Paul is seen to be in direct violation of the biblical prescriptions for impartial judgment (Lev. 19:15; Deut. 1:16–17; 19:16–19). By contrast, Paul both quotes the law (Exod. 22:28) and expresses willingness to live by it. Ananias's external, visible actions have exposed the superficial whitewash of his own Jewish loyalty (cf. Ezek. 13:10–16; also Matt. 23:27). Whether Luke knows that Ananias later died a violent death at the hands of a mob (Josephus Jewish War 2.441–42), and therefore has Paul uttering a prophetic death threat, is less certain (→ Ananias [3]).

As was the case with Peter earlier, the Sanhedrin hearing serves as a forum in which Christianity is heard—and vindicated (Acts 5:27–42). In spite of significantly different proceedings that are reported, in both cases, Pharisees emerge as allies of Christians. The "scribes of the Pharisees' party" who declare Paul innocent of any wrongdoing (23:9), and wonder whether he might truly be an agent of some divine messenger, are echoing the cautious advice of Gamaliel (5:38–39).

Luke continues his earlier agenda in depicting Christianity and Pharisaism as natural allies, hence the direct continuity between the Pharisaic branch of Judaism and Christianity. The link is expressed directly in Paul's own testimony: he is (now) a Pharisee, with a Pharisaic heritage (23:6). His Pharisaic loyalty is a present commitment, not a recently jettisoned stage of his religious past (cf. Phil. 3:5–9). His Christian proclamation of a risen Lord, and by implication, of a risen humanity (Acts 23:6), represents a particular, but defensible, form of Pharisaic theology. Belief in the risen Messiah represents the continuation of God's promises to Israel.

As the debate in the Sanhedrin unfolds, Luke distinguishes the Sadducees from "mainline Jews." He portrays them as skeptics who deny the existence of spirits or angels (v. 8), both of which are central features of the biblical witness (→ Sadducees; Pharisees).

That Paul emerges from the Sanhedrin vindicated is seen in the night vision of Jesus (v. 11), who reconfirms the validity of his testimony before the council and now also confirms his mission plans formulated earlier in Ephesus (19:21). It is one of many Lucan "promises" made within the narrative that is later fulfilled (28:23).

23:12–30, Plot Against Paul and His Planned Transfer to Caesarea.

This third plot by "the Jews" against Paul (cf. 9:23; 20:3; also 9:23; 20:19) is by far the most meticulously planned and elaborately described; it includes over forty conspirators (23:13, 21), a full-fast oath (vv. 12, 14, 21), conspiracy with the "chief priests and elders" (v. 14; 25:15; also 4:23; 22:30; 25:2), and repeated references to their determination to kill Paul (23:12, 14, 15, 21, 27).

Following the typical Lucan pattern, intensified efforts to resist the gospel are met with even more dramatic forms of deliverance (see commentary above on 5:17–26). In this case, the plot is aborted by the combined efforts of a lad (23:18), identified as Paul's nephew (v. 16), and a friendly Roman tribune who is finally willing to deploy half the city's garrison to foil the plot (vv. 23–24).

The proper interpretation of these events for readers is provided in the letter from the tribune to the governor (vv. 26–30). Even though the tribune's recounting of the events in the Temple courtyard (21:30–36) is bent in his own favor (23:27), all the important (Lucan) elements of the story are included: (1) primary responsibility for the hostile actions against Paul lies with "the Jews" (v. 27; 9:23, 29; 21:11, 27, 36); (2) Roman soldiers have shown proper respect for a Roman citizen—Romans as allies of Christians (22:24–29; also 16:38–39; 18:12–17); (3) Romans have followed proper procedures, attempting to determine precisely the nature of the charges against the accused (23:28; 22:24, 30; 25:26) and ordering his accusers to face him directly (23:30; Deut. 19:16–19); (4) it is essentially an internal conflict within Judaism concerning "questions of their law" (Acts 18:14–15; 25:18–20)—Christians are to be seen as continuous with Judaism and therefore entitled to Roman rights extended to Jews; and (5) unqualified declaration of Paul's innocence, certainly with respect to a capital offense (23:29; see Introduction).

23:31–26:32
Paul in Caesarea

The remainder of Paul's stay in Palestine occurs in Caesarea, the seat of Roman government in Palestine. This section unfolds Paul's various appearances before increasingly important Roman officials: Felix (24:1–27), Festus (25:1–27), and Agrippa (26:1–32).

23:31–35, Paul's Transfer to Caesarea. The tribune's plans as outlined earlier (vv. 23–24) are carried out. Especially noted is Paul's safe delivery to the care of Felix, who follows carefully defined protocol in ascertaining Paul's provincial home and waiting for his accusers to present their case against Paul (vv. 34–35).

24:1–27, Paul's Defense Before Felix. This episode goes well beyond Paul's appearance before Gallio (18:12–17), where the Jews' charges are repeated (18:13) and Gallio formally responds (18:14–15). Here there is a formal statement of the accusations against Paul by a prosecutor, Tertullus (24:2–8), and an equally formal response by Paul (vv. 10–21). Both speeches exhibit rhetorical polish, and legal technical terminology is used throughout the scene. Luke has sought to capture the atmosphere of a formal hearing before a high-ranking Roman official.

Tertullus' speech serves to state, in proper form, the Jews' case against Paul. The opening *ad hominem* characterization of Paul as a "plague-spot" ("perfect pest," NEB, JB) depicting him as a danger to the public good (cf. 1 Macc. 15:21) may also suggest that he is churlish or foolish (1 Sam. 25:17, 25). More to the point is the charge that he is seditious, a "fomenter of discord" (NEB; lit., "inciting riots"; cf. Acts 19:40), who causes dissensions (23:7, 10) wherever he goes among Jews "throughout the world" (cf. 16:20; 17:6)—a universal threat to Roman peace and stability. "Ringleader of the sect of the Nazarenes" probably depicts him as the instigator of a new religion, since "sect" (Gk. *hairesis*) here carries an unfavorable connotation (cf. 24:14; 28:22) absent elsewhere (5:17; 15:5; 26:5). The portrait of him as an outsider, a Jewish renegade, continues in the final charge that he "profaned the Temple" (cf. 21:28; 25:8; also 6:13; Luke 21:6). He is thus presented as insensitive to the customs and institutions of a well-established, legally protected religion.

Paul's response (24:10–21) is an adroitly crafted "defense" (v. 10). His polite deference to Felix (v. 10), which contrasts sharply with

Tertullus's ingratiating introduction (vv. 2–4), scores points with informed readers who know Felix's scandalous reputation (Tacitus *Histories* 5.9; *Annals* 12.54; Josephus *Antiquities of the Jews* 20.137–44, 162–63; →Felix, Antonius). Moreover, by limiting his remarks to his conduct in Jerusalem, Paul shrewdly redefines the charge.

But the more important element of Paul's defense is his consistent claim to be an utterly loyal Jew. He refuses to concede that he is the spokesman for a new religion. What his enemies mistakenly call a "sect" is better understood as "the Way" (v. 14). Even though "the Way" is being used here in a highly technical sense to describe the Jesus movement (9:2; 18:26; 19:9, 23; 22:4; 24:22), it nevertheless has a certain resonance with an OT expectation for the truly obedient people of God (cf. Exod. 32:8; Deut. 5:33; 9:12, 16; 11:28; 31:29). Consequently, as Paul's preferred term for the movement with which he gladly identifies himself, it more closely aligns him with the biblical tradition.

In spite of his participation in "the Way" he still speaks of his "forefathers' God," expressed here in a thoroughly gentile form (cf. 4 Macc. 12:17; Sophocles *Antigone* 838), which nevertheless is authentically biblical in tone (Exod. 3:6, 13). Moreover, his loyalty to the entire Scripture remains unshaken (Acts 24:14; also 26:22; 28:23). This has just been demonstrated in his interchange with Ananias (23:1–5) but amply attested in the earlier narrative.

He also adheres to what Scripture teaches (however minimally): the resurrection (24:15, 21; Isa. 26:19; Dan. 12:2–3; →Resurrection). His faith in this "hope" is not an unorthodox position but one "these [Jews] themselves accept" (Acts 24:15). By implication, Paul is aligning himself here with the Pharisees (23:8) and against the Sadducees (cf. Luke 20:27–40), thereby suggesting that the former (like himself) represent mainline Judaism.

Yet another line of defense is his self-portrait as a devout pilgrim who came to Jerusalem neither to preach, nor to cause riots, but to worship (v. 11). His almsgiving (v. 17) could only be construed as evidence of his loyalty to Scripture and tradition (Ps. 112:9; Isa. 58:6–8; Prov. 14:21, 31) as well as his commitment to help the weak (Acts 20:35). What is striking here is that these funds are for his "nation" (24:17), which would suggest donations to Jews generally. Conceivably, this is a reference to the Pauline relief fund for the poor Jewish Christians in Jerusalem (1 Cor. 16:1–4; 2 Cor. 8:3–6; Gal. 2:10; Rom. 15:25–28, 31), but if so it is an unusual way of putting it. His mention of "offerings" is intended to recall his participation with the four men who had a vow (21:23–27).

While Felix does not decide formally in Paul's favor, neither does he sustain Tertullus' charges. That his was not an uninformed decision is indicated by his having "a rather accurate knowledge of the Way" (24:22). By not losing, Paul wins. This is also reflected in the relative freedom he enjoys as a prisoner (v. 23).

The final meeting between Paul and Felix (vv. 24–27) portrays a shift in Luke's portrait of Felix. Paul the defender now becomes Paul the preacher. Accompanied by his Jewish wife, Drusilla, the youngest daughter of Agrippa I, Felix takes the initiative in summoning Paul. Luke shows the gospel actually attracting another Roman official (cf. 13:7–12).

Luke presents Felix as a case of failed faith, seen especially in his expressed hope for a bribe (24:26; cf. v. 17). Like others in Luke-Acts who finally are excluded from service in the kingdom (ruler, Luke 18:18–30; Ananias and Sapphira, Acts 5:1–11; Judas, 1:15–20), Felix's love for money wins out over his love for the virtues.

The final stroke in Luke's portrait of Felix is his currying favor with the Jews, which resulted in his decision to leave Paul in prison. His action closely approximates that of Pilate (Luke 23:18–25). "Two years" (Acts 24:27) probably describes the length of Paul's imprisonment rather than the duration of Felix's reign.

25:1–27, Paul Before Festus. The next stage of the proceedings takes place before Porcius Festus, who succeeded Felix as procurator between A.D. 55 and 59 (→ Festus, Porcius).

These two stages present an interesting contrast in terms of central characters. Earlier Paul spoke on his own behalf to a virtually silent Roman procurator. Now the Roman procurator speaks—and acts—on Paul's behalf, while Paul remains in the background.

The hearing before Festus serves several purposes for Luke. First, it continues the Lucan portrait of the Jerusalem Jews as Paul's arch-enemies. Luke reinforces the point by repeatedly identifying these enemies of Paul (vv. 2, 5, 7, 15). By the end of this section, the geographical extent of the Jewish resistance has widened to Caesarea as "the whole Jewish people demand his death" (v. 24). If anything, this stage reveals intensified Jewish resistance to Paul. They insist that a newly appointed procurator press the case against Paul (vv. 1–5). Their urge to kill Paul is undiminished as the cries of the Jerusalem mob are still echoing two years later (21:27, 36; 22:22–23). Presumably, their full-fast oath is still in effect (23:12–15)! Oblivious to due process (25:15–16), they are still willing to lodge serious charges unsubstantiated by hard evidence (vv. 7, 18, 26).

Second, the Festus stage describes the circumstances that enabled Paul finally to reach Rome. More specifically, it explains why Paul appealed to Caesar. Luke places squarely on the shoulders of Festus the responsibility for continuing Paul's trial. As procurator, he could have rendered a final verdict after having heard both sides in a specially called hearing. Yet, like his predecessor, Felix (24:27), he yielded to Jewish pressure (25:9). Indirectly, then, Luke suggests that Paul's hopes for justice are jeopardized by the Jews.

Many historical questions about Paul's appeal to Caesar remain unanswered. Yet from the standpoint of Luke's narrative, the significance of this episode is clear. His brief defense remarks (vv. 8, 10–11) serve Luke's purpose in several ways. Paul's threefold denial (v. 8) effectively summarizes previous charges against him. He is not against the Temple (21:28; 24:7), the law of the Jews (21:21; 23:5; 24:14–16; perhaps 18:13), or Caesar (16:21, 38–39; perhaps 18:13). The last named charge is a freshly formulated reference to sedition (24:5). Once again, Paul responds to charges made earlier in the narrative by the Jerusalem crowds (21:28) and Tertullus (24:5–7).

His second set of remarks (25:10–11) reveals a resolute Paul, sure of his rights, unwilling to be intimidated by Roman officials who themselves are willing to bend to political pressure (cf. 16:35–40). Perhaps most importantly, it allows him to state formally his appeal to Caesar (25:11). Since this is the legal mechanism through which God's plan for Paul to reach Rome is made possible, it is the most critical element. In confirming Paul's appeal (v. 12), Festus unwittingly makes possible Paul's earlier formulated mission plans (19:21) and officially confirms what God has already told Paul privately (23:11).

Third, the Festus stage reinforces Luke's portrait of Rome as sympathetic to Christianity. Except for his willingness to bend to Jewish pressure and thereby continue Paul's trial (25:9), Festus is presented throughout this section quite favorably. He emerges as a model of efficiency (v. 5), a governor who is both cautious and objective in his judgment (v. 18), scrupulously respecting Roman procedures (vv. 9, 16).

With his character duly certified by Luke, Festus serves as an important pagan witness who testifies in Paul's behalf. In both of his "speeches," he sounds the same theme. His considered judgment is that Paul's accusers have vastly overstated the seriousness of his offense (v. 18). Echoing the earlier verdict of Gallio (18:14–15), Festus sees Paul's case as an internal dispute within Judaism, "their own religion" (25:19). By placing Paul and the Jews in the same camp, he confirms Paul's own defense before the Sanhedrin (23:6–10) and his subsequent defense before Felix (24:10–21): he is not an outsider trying to be contentious; he is an insider trying to be heard.

Festus also introduces the distinctive feature of Paul's position vis-à-vis other Jews: the Easter faith—"one Jesus, who had died, is now alive" (v. 19). This conviction Paul had placed on the public record in his defense before the Jerusalem crowd, although not in this form (cf. esp. 22:6–11). Yet neither before the Sanhedrin (23:1–10) nor before Felix (24:1–27) had Paul or any of his detractors raised this point.

Festus's words (25:19) characterize exactly the secular observer puzzled by both the heat and fog of religious debate. Yet in his own odd way, Festus sees the central issue: Paul trying to convince his fellow Israelites that the risen Lord is the promised fulfillment of their (and Paul's) own Scriptures, history, tradition, and theology. It is another instance where an outsider sees the truth more clearly than Paul's opponents do (cf. 5:38–39).

In his second speech, Festus is even more emphatic. Now he is able to respond to the petition of the "whole Jewish people" (25:24). Their judgment is that Paul should die (v. 24). His verdict, by contrast, is that Paul has "done nothing deserving death" (v. 25). With this unqualified declaration of Paul's innocence, he reiterates earlier declarations by Paul himself (see Introduction). Festus's repeated stress on the need for having substantiated charges (vv. 26–27) makes essentially the same point: the absence of evidence underscores his innocence.

Fourth, the Festus stage also serves to introduce King Agrippa, the final and most important dignitary before whom Paul formally appears (vv. 13, 23–27; → Agrippa II; Bernice), thus preparing for Paul's grandest defense speech (26:2–23). As the first "king" (repeatedly identified as such by Luke, cf. 26:13, 14, 24, 26; 26:2, 7, 13, 19, 26, 27, 30) encountered by Paul, Agrippa represents the fulfillment of God's purpose for him (9:15). The other "king," of course, before whom Paul was destined to carry Jesus' name, was Caesar himself. Unlike Agrippa, he never makes an appearance in the Acts narrative, but he is already introduced, however subtly (25:8, 10, 11, 12, 21, 25, 26).

26:1–23, Paul's Defense Before Agrippa.

Paul's final "apology" is suitably crafted for the occasion. The distinguished audience and setting lend an air of expectancy to the occasion (25:23).

Even though it overlaps his earlier defense speeches (22:1–21; 24:10–21) and Luke's narrative account of his "conversion" (9:1–19), this speech has a distinctive flavor and profile. Once again, it touches on Paul's early life but identifies him exclusively with Jerusalem, no longer with the Diaspora (26:4; cf. 22:3). By underscoring his Pharisaic heritage (26:5; 22:3;

23:6), he becomes a credible defender of the resurrection faith, an important opening motif (26:7–8) and the climactic note on which the speech is interrupted (v. 23). This too has been a recurrent theme of his earlier defenses (23:6; 24:15, 21).

His life as a persecutor remains a central element (26:9–11; 7:58; 8:1–3; 9:1–2; 22:4–5), although both the force and extent of his persecution are now stated more strongly: not simply a consenting bystander to Stephen's death (8:1; 22:20) but now casting his vote in the death sentence of *many* Jerusalem Christians (26:10); no longer the single city of Damascus (9:2–3; 22:5–6) but "foreign *cities*" (26:11).

The Damascus road encounter with the risen Lord still remains the moment of dramatic reversal (vv. 12–18; cf. 9:3–9; 22:6–11), but it too has enhanced features. The "great light" (22:6; cf. 9:3) now becomes "a light brighter than the sun" (26:13). It no longer encompasses Paul alone (9:3; 22:6) but his companions (26:13). Consequently, they all fall to the ground (v. 14), not just Paul alone (9:4; 22:7).

The language of the risen Lord is now identified as Aramaic (26:14), which was already evident by the way he addressed "Saul" (9:4; 22:7). Surprisingly, he challenges Paul's obstinance by using a common Greek proverb (26:14; cf. Euripides *Bacchae* 794–95; Julian *Orations* 8.246b).

Paul receives his divine commission as part of the Damascus road encounter. There are no instructions to proceed to Damascus (22:10–11; cf. 9:8–9), nor is God's mediator Ananias even mentioned (9:10–19; 22:12–16). The risen Lord commissions him directly *on the road*, in a manner reminiscent of prophetic calls (26:16; cf. Ezek. 2:1, 3). He is directly appointed as a "servant and witness" (Acts 26:16; cf. 22:15) of what he has just seen but also of future divine revelations (16:9–10; 18:9; 22:17–21; 23:11; 27:23). Like the prophets (Jer. 1:7–8, 19), he is promised divine protection from the (Jewish) people (Acts 26:17; cf. 9:23–25, 30; 14:19; 17:10, 14; 18:12–17; 20:3; 21:30–36; 22:22–29; 23:12–35) and from the Gentiles (16:19–40; 19:23–41).

His mission efforts are bifocal: to both Jews and Gentiles (cf. 9:15; 22:15) but apparently with special attention to Gentiles (22:18–21). Again his task is stated as a prophetic commission: to open the Gentiles' eyes (26:18; Isa. 42:6–7, 16), turning them from darkness to light (cf. Isa. 9:2; Eph. 5:8; Col. 1:12–13; 1 Pet. 2:9), from Satan to God (cf. 2 Cor. 4:4; Eph. 2:2), extending them forgiveness of sins (Acts 26:18; cf. 10:43; also to Jews: Luke 1:77; 3:3; 24:47; Acts 2:38; 5:31; 13:38) and a portion of the inheritance reserved for God's holy ones (26:18; cf. 20:32; also Col. 1:12).

Unlike previous defense speeches, Paul proceeds to tell Agrippa how he executed these divine orders. The conduct that has brought him before Agrippa is the result of obeying a compelling heavenly vision (Acts 26:19). Since his commission was two-pronged, he proceeded to preach to Jews first: in Damascus (9:19–22), Jerusalem (9:26–30; 22:17–21; cf. Rom. 15:19), then throughout all Judea (Acts 26:20; though, previously unrecorded in Acts). Second, he preached to Gentiles, calling them to repent (v. 20; cf. 11:18; 17:30; 20:21) and "turn to [faith in the one] God" (26:20; cf. 14:15; 15:19; cf. 1 Thess. 1:9). Requiring deeds exemplifying repentance is a new element, reminiscent of John's preaching (cf. Luke 3:7–9; Matt. 3:7–10).

The previous narrative has also shown how his mission efforts consistently met Jewish resistance, which was especially typified by the Temple incident (Acts 26:21; cf. 21:30–31). Yet his presence before Agrippa attested the fulfillment of the promise of divine protection (v. 17), enabling him to carry out his commission as a witness (v. 16).

The speech's climax (vv. 22–23) compactly summarizes his earlier sermons (13:16–41; 14:15–17; 17:22–31) and preaching activity that has been reported extensively in the previous narrative. Basic to all his preaching has been his unshaken belief in "Moses and the prophets" (26:22; cf. 24:14) and the "promises made by God to our fathers" (26:6; Luke 24:27, 44; Acts 3:18; 28:23). Luke has consistently portrayed Paul as "arguing from the Scriptures" (e.g., 17:2), insisting that the story of Jesus is the continuation of Israel's story.

The specific focus for which Paul has claimed fulfillment of the divine promise is the suffering and death of Christ (26:23). Since this was promised, it was a "divine must" (see Introduction). But coupled with this was the Easter faith: Christ as the first to rise from the dead (26:23; 1 Cor. 15:20; Col. 1:18). As the first to experience resurrection life, he was thereby proclaimed as the "pioneer of life" (Acts 3:15). In his exalted status, the risen Lord (through Paul) has proclaimed light to both Jews and Gentiles (26:23; cf. 2 Tim. 1:10; also Matt. 4:16).

In describing what he himself has done he has presented what Agrippa and his audience should do. The defense has become a sermon.

26:24–32, Paul Vindicated. Typically, Paul's sermon is interrupted at its climactic point (cf. 17:32; 22:22). The effects of the sermon are dramatized by the contrasting responses of Festus and Agrippa. As a pagan, Festus regards belief in resurrection as incredible and Paul as deranged (26:24; cf. 12:15; John 10:20; Wisd. of Sol. 5:4). By attributing Paul's madness to "great learning," Festus unwittingly vouches for Paul and disqualifies himself (and other pagans) from rendering a proper judgment on the matter.

Agrippa, by contrast, more nearly resembles Felix in making overtures, however tentatively, toward the faith (24:22–27). While Luke never explicitly identifies Agrippa as Jewish, Paul's remarks subtly imply what readers know (26:26–27; 23:3). One who assuredly "believes the prophets" (26:27) is expected to see the clear force of Paul's argument that Christ is the fulfillment of God's biblical promise. Especially crucial is Paul's insistence to Agrippa that "these things were not done in a corner" (v. 26). As Luke's narrative has shown, the story of "the Way" has occurred in the public domain, on the stage of world history.

Whether Agrippa's response (v. 28) is to be understood as playful irony or as a serious declaration of Paul's persuasiveness, it is far short of outright rejection, much less condemnation of Paul. His final verdict is an unqualified vindication of Paul (v. 32; see Introduction). Even though Paul's speech has confirmed what Festus has already declared (25:25), it is also a subtle reminder that Festus's proposal to continue the trial was ill-advised and unjustified (25:9).

27:1–28:15
Paul's Journey to Rome

This fourth "we" section most likely is based (partially or wholly) on a travel journal to which editorial additions (vv. 9–11, 21–26, 33–36, 38) have been made (cf. 16:10). One of its distinctive features is a detailed itinerary of ports of call and geographical reference points and the mention of other place names relating to the voyage (→ Trade and Transportation). Luke unfolds the journey to Rome in well-defined sections, each contributing in its own way to an overall heroic depiction of Paul, God's duly appointed servant and witness (26:16), who makes his "triumphal entry" into Rome.

27:1–8, Getting Under Way. The decision to sail for Italy from Caesarea begins to carry out concretely Festus's earlier declaration (25:12). The mission's importance is reflected in naming the Roman centurion, Julius, and his Augustan cohort, possibly the same cohort stationed in Syria during the first century A.D. The Thessalonian Aristarchus (v. 2) is doubtless Paul's earlier traveling co-worker (19:29; 20:4; cf. Philem. 24; Col. 4:10).

Julius's kindness toward Paul (Acts 27:3) characterizes the Romans' favorable treatment generally (cf. 27:43; also 21:31–32; 22:24–30; 24:23) and typifies the hospitality extended to Paul throughout the trip (28:2, 7, 14–16). The Sidon "friends" (27:3), possibly a technical designation for Christians (cf. Luke 12:4; John 15:14–15; 3 John 15), may have been members of the Phoenician Christian community (cf. Acts 11:19; 21:3–5; also Luke 6:17; 10:13–14).

The journey northwestward from Sidon leads east of Cyprus, then westward along the southern coast of Asia Minor, past Cilicia and Pamphylia, areas well known to Paul (Cilicia: Acts 21:39; 22:3; 23:34; also 9:11; cf. Gal. 1:21; also Acts 15:41; Pamphylia: 13:13; 14:24; 15:38), to Myra, the chief city of the southwestern Asia Minor district of Lycia. Changing to one of the Egyptian grain ships bound from Alexandria to Italy that regularly stopped at Myra, they sail westward to Cnidus on the southwestern tip of Asia Minor, then southward, probably along the southern coast of Crete, past Salmone, on its northeastern tip, finally to Fair Havens, on the south-central coast of Crete. The nearby city of Lasea marked the point where the coast turns sharply north, thus exposing ships to direct winds from the sea.

27:9–12, Paul's First Prophetic Word. The travelogue is now interrupted by deliberations among the principal figures on the voyage (v. 11). The "fast" that had already occurred (v. 9) is likely a reference to the Jewish Day of Atonement (Lev. 16:29–31; 23:27–32), which fell on the tenth of Tishri (September/October). Ancient nautical wisdom regarded sea voyages after mid-September as dangerous and any between mid-November and mid-March as extremely inadvisable. Given the previous delays and difficulties already experienced, Paul predicts disastrous results if the voyage continues (Acts 27:10). The majority overrule Paul, however, deciding that the more western Cretan harbor of Phoenix is the preferable place to winter.

27:13–20, Getting Off Course in the Storm. As they sail from Fair Havens along the southern coast of Crete toward Phoenix, the northeast wind (→ Euroclydon) blowing from the coast onto the sea blows the ship off course, south of the small island of Cauda, off the southwest coast of Crete. The sailors' emergency measures include securing the small lifeboat and "undergirding" the ship. The exact nature of the latter operation is unclear. Their fear is that the ship would eventually be driven southwest to the northern coast of Africa into the hazardous bays of Greater and Lesser Syrtis (cf. Josephus *Jewish War* 2.381). The continuation of the storm into the next day causes them to begin throwing off miscellaneous equipment (vv. 18–19; cf. Jon. 1:5). Covered by the storm and blocked off from daylight, the ship loses its course completely and drifts in the Mediterranean (Acts 27:20).

The essential function of this section is to confirm the accuracy of Paul's earlier warning (v. 10), at least partially. The narrative has already demonstrated the loss of much cargo, and the threatened loss of ship and lives (v. 20).

27:21–26, Paul's Second Speech. Here Paul the prophet speaks, insisting that his previous caution has now proved true (v. 21 fulfills v. 10). Though revising his earlier prediction slightly, he is nevertheless specific as he predicts, first, no loss of life, only the ship—fulfilled in vv. 41–44; second, his successful arrival in Rome to stand before Caesar—fulfilled in 28:14, 16; third, the safety of the passengers—fulfilled in vv. 33–38, 44; and fourth, their eventual arrival at an island—fulfilled, beginning in vv. 27–32, finally in 28:1.

His vision of "God's angel" is reminiscent of earlier divine interventions during crises (18:9; 23:11; also 16:9–10). Before a pagan audience, his report also becomes an occasion for confessing "the God to whom I belong and whom I worship" (27:23; cf. Gen. 50:19; also Acts 24:14). Besides allaying Paul's fears, the divine voice confirms Festus's earlier declaration (25:12) and provides incidental Lucan testimony that Paul actually appeared before Caesar's tribunal, which is otherwise not reported later in the narrative.

27:27–32, Approaching Land. Paul's prophecy immediately begins to be fulfilled in this section when, after fourteen days, the ship approaches land. The episode raises some questions, e.g., whether the sailors' attempt to get into the lifeboat to secure the anchors from the bow represents defensible nautical practice or whether their action is properly interpreted as an escape attempt. The episode serves primarily to confirm the truth of Paul's earlier remarks (v. 22). It thus becomes the occasion for another prophetic pronouncement illustrating the umbrella of divine protection extended by Paul.

27:33–38, Paul's Third Speech. The ship's passengers now become Paul's sole responsibility. Using a familiar biblical proverb (v. 34; 1 Sam. 14:45; 2 Sam. 14:11; 1 Kings 1:52) that echoes the words of Jesus (cf. Luke 12:7; 21:18), he reaffirms his prophetic promise that none of them would be lost. Even though there are slight echoes of Jesus' eucharistic meal (cf. Luke 22:19), this should be seen as an ordinary meal before which a devout Jew offers thanks (cf. Luke 9:16; cf. John 6:11).

The effectiveness of Paul's words and actions is indicated by Luke's noting the total number of passengers as 276 (or 76, according to one textual tradition). It is not an unlikely number considering the passenger loads known from other ancient sources (cf. Josephus *Life* 15).

27:39–44, Getting to Shore. Paul's prediction is more fully realized as they now spot land (v. 39; cf. v. 26). The detailed description of the ship's striking a "shoal" (v. 41), thereby being shattered to pieces, confirms another Pauline prediction (v. 22). Some swam, others clung to pieces of the shattered ship (or perhaps to the shoulders of those who could swim), with the result that "all were saved" (v. 44).

28:1–10, Paul at Malta. Their safe arrival at Malta itself finally fulfills Paul's earlier prediction (27:26). The two incidents at Malta continue Luke's heroic portrait of Paul. On the ship, his prophetic word has proved true; on the island, his divine protection is acknowledged and his prophetic deeds are demonstrated.

Luke supplies the proper interpretation of these events through the naive reaction of the Maltese natives (v. 4), who are convinced that Paul has been protected by Dike, the Greek personification of justice. They rightly recognize that Paul has been "allowed to live." Luke has already made clear, however, that it is not by the gods of pagan religion but by the God to whom Paul belongs and whom he loyally serves (27:23–24, 35; cf. 24:14–16; 26:6–8). Surprisingly, Luke allows their testimony about Paul's being a "god" to stand without any disclaimer (28:6; cf. 14:12–18; also 10:25–26). Paul's surviving a poisonous snakebite places him under the divine protection Jesus promised to his missionaries (Luke 10:19; cf. Mark 16:18).

Paul's prophetic deeds are demonstrated concretely in his healing the father of Publius, the island chief (28:8; cf. Luke 4:38–39). Through his healing hands continues to run the power of Jesus attested throughout Luke-Acts (Luke 4:40; 13:13; Acts 5:12; 9:17; 14:3; 19:11). Typically, what happens to one happens to all (Luke 4:40–41; Acts 5:12–16; also Luke 8:1–3); consequently, the whole island benefits. Their "many gifts" (Acts 28:10) serve to confirm the reality of Paul's prophetic deeds.

28:11–15, Completing the Journey to Rome. In this final stage of the journey Paul proceeds with remarkable freedom. No mention is made of his armed guard or even of other prisoners. The image of Paul the prisoner gives way to that of Paul the missionary being given a hero's welcome by Christian communities in Italy. By reporting the existence of "brethren" at Puteoli (vv. 13–14), a major Italian port city, and in Rome itself (v. 15), Luke fully acknowledges that Christianity has preceded Paul in reaching Italy. Thus Luke does not present Paul as the founder of Italian Christianity (cf. Rom. 1:8–15). His primary interest, at this point, is to show that just as Paul had earlier been welcomed openly, and therefore accepted, by churches he himself had not established (Acts 21:1–14), so now he is fully recognized by western Christians as God's "servant and witness."

28:16–31
Paul in Rome

The primary focus of Paul's activity in Rome is on his dealings with the Roman Jewish community. Two stages are reported: defense (vv. 17–22) and proclamation (vv. 23–29). The subsequent two-year period represents a definite shift to the much broader ministry of Paul, the vindicated apostle (vv. 30–31).

28:16–22, Meeting with Jewish Leaders in Rome. Lodging in an inn under the protection of a single soldier (v. 16), Paul has considerable freedom, which allows him to summon local Jewish leaders (v. 17; cf. Luke 19:47; Acts 25:2). His "speech" to them (28:17–20) is a highly abbreviated account of previous charges made against him (21:20–21, 28; 23:26–30; 24:2–9; 25:7, 15–21, 24–27) and his previous defenses at his various trials (22:1–21; 23:6–10; 24:10–21; 25:8, 10–11; 26:2–23). In spite of its brevity, it does provide some new features. His insistence that the Romans actually had wanted to release him (28:18) represents their intentions more explicitly than previously reported. His appeal to Caesar is now justified as a response to the Jews' objections (v. 19). This renders more explicit the reason for Festus's suggested change of venue (25:9). Certain themes, however, recur: he insists that he is completely innocent (28:17–19; see Introduction) and a legitimate spokesperson for "the hope of Israel" (v. 20; cf. 23:6; 24:15, 21; 26:6–7).

In reporting that the Jewish leaders have received neither written reports from Judea nor oral reports from their fellow Jewish "brethren" (28:21; note title of address in v. 17), Luke is suggesting that whatever Jewish opposition has occurred against Paul is localized in the eastern Mediterranean, namely, Asia Minor (21:27), but especially Jerusalem (21:11, 27–36; 22:22–23; 23:1–10, 27; 24:9; 25:2, 5, 7, 15) and perhaps Caesarea (25:24). The Roman Jews have only general information about "this sect" (28:22; cf. 24:5, 14) and are willing to listen to Paul as its representative spokesperson. They stand before Paul as objective, receptive listeners, as eager to listen to new viewpoints as the Athenians were (17:22–23).

28:23–29, Preaching to Roman Jews. Obviously unable to go to one of the several synagogues in Rome at this time, as was his usual practice, Paul summons the Jewish community to his lodging, and they come in "great numbers" (v. 23). The brief outline of his testimony to them represents a digest of Paul's previously reported preaching before Jewish audiences. Once again, it conforms fully to the apostolic preaching of his predecessors, both Jesus and especially Peter: the breaking in of God's new reign (see Introduction) in the person of Jesus (the entire Gospel of Luke; also Acts 2:22–24; 10:36–41; 17:3; 18:5), both of which represent the fulfillment of God's promise in Scripture (Luke 24:27, 44; Acts 2:25–36; 3:18; 10:43; 24:14; 26:22).

Their mixed response is reminiscent of earlier occasions when Paul preached to Jewish audiences (28:24–25; 13:43; 14:4; 17:4, 11; 18:4–8; 19:10). Even though "some were convinced" (28:24), not all were, and this failure to achieve broad acceptance is regarded, oddly enough, as wholesale rejection. By interpreting their response as the very obduracy for which Israel is condemned in Isa. 6:9–10, Luke (through Paul) places them outside the pale of the Christian mission. The most receptive hearing for "God's salvation" is to be found among Gentiles (Acts 28:29). What had happened in Asia Minor (13:46–48) and Greece (18:5–6) is now repeated in Italy, thus becoming a universal pattern.

Even though this explicit use of Isa. 6:9–10 occurs only in the context of Paul's preaching to Roman Jews, its placement at the end of the narrative is significant. It applies retrospectively, strongly indicting Jewish resistance generally. It most likely reflects Luke's own situation and final assessment. In contrast to Romans 9–11, where Paul envisions an eventual conversion of Israel, Luke sees the Christian mission to Jews as finished, probably hopeless, with the church's only real hope lying with its mission to Gentiles.

28:30–31, Paul Vindicated. The rather abrupt ending of Acts leaves tantalizing questions unanswered. Luke has already anticipated some of these questions in his previous narra-

tive. He implies that Paul did appear before Caesar's tribunal (27:24) and finally died a martyr (20:25, 38; 21:13; 25:11). Reporting the full details of either of these events, which he doubtless knew, is less relevant to his purpose than the final picture he sketches of Paul, which has two fundamental elements: first, the fulfillment of the divine purpose in Paul, who as "chosen instrument" carries God's name to "all who came to him," most likely, Gentiles; and second, the full vindication of Paul and "the Way," both of whom have proceeded and flourished throughout the narrative under Roman protection and are left to proceed "boldly and unhindered." In the end, the gospel turns out to be irrepressible.

Bibliography

Aune, D. E. *The New Testament in Its Literary Environment.* Philadelphia: Westminster, 1987. Chaps. 3–4.

Cadbury, H. J. *The Making of Luke-Acts.* London: SPCK, 1958.

Conzelmann, H. *A Commentary on the Acts of the Apostles.* Philadelphia: Fortress, 1987.

Foakes-Jackson, F. J., and K. Lake. *The Beginnings of Christianity. Part I: The Acts of the Apostles.* 5 vols. London: Macmillan, 1920–33. Reprint. Grand Rapids, MI: Baker, 1979.

Haenchen, E. *The Acts of the Apostles: A Commentary.* Philadelphia: Westminster, 1971.

Johnson, L. T. *Luke-Acts: A Story of Prophet and People.* Chicago: Franciscan Herald, 1981.

Juel, D. *Luke-Acts: The Promise of History.* Atlanta, GA: Knox, 1983.

Keck, L. E., and J. L. Martyn, eds. *Studies in Luke-Acts: Studies Presented in Honor of Paul Schubert.* 2d ed. Philadelphia: Fortress, 1980.

PART SIX

THE
PAULINE
LETTERS

INTRODUCTION TO THE PAULINE LETTERS

ROBERT JEWETT

INTRODUCTION

A distinctive feature of early Christianity is that so many of its sacred writings originated as letters. All but five of the twenty-seven books in the NT are either in the form of letters or contain significant epistolary components. Letters also predominate in the writings of the apostolic fathers, the successors of the apostles. This curious feature, which sets Christianity off from other religions of the ancient world, particularly from its origins in Judaism, is due primarily to the influence of the apostle Paul. His letters, originally written to troubled congregations too distant to visit at the moment, provided the model for other writings that eventually became part of the Christian Bible.

NEW TESTAMENT LETTERS IN THE LIGHT OF ANCIENT LETTER WRITING

A large number of ancient letters have been brought to light by modern research, providing a vivid sense of how they functioned as means of communication. Several thousand papyri of private, business, and bureaucratic correspondence have been discovered in the arid regions of the Mediterranean world. Other letters have been preserved in governmental documentary collections, inscriptions, and quotations in Greco-Roman literature. Many elegant letters by classical writers and church fathers are also available for comparison.

On the basis of these examples, and the discussions of ancient epistolary theorists, it is possible to summarize the way letters were approached in the Greco-Roman world. They were understood as conversations between persons separated by distance. The writer was thought to be present to his or her readers within the letter itself, which was supposed to bear the marks of the personality and social status of the writer. Distinctions were often made between official and personal letters, but the sense of conversation at a distance surfaces even in philosophical letters and bureaucratic correspondence. The broad functions of maintaining contact between sender and recipients, imparting information, and conveying requests or commands appear to link all of these letters with those found in the NT.

A number of epistolary conventions found in the NT are typical of Greco-Roman letters. The standard opening of a letter was "sender to recipient, greeting." This was often followed by a prayer or wish for the health of the recipient and an assurance of the writer's well-being. Expressions of joy or sorrow at news received are frequently part of the epistolary opening. The closing of a letter usually consisted of a health wish and a formula of farewell. These opening and closing formulas served to communicate the desired relationship between the sender and recipient. The selection of particular formulas reveals whether a particular letter is between equals, from a superior to a subordinate, or from a subordinate to a superior.

The openings of NT Letters are clearly adapted from Greco-Roman models. The sender and addressee are incorporated in the opening sentence (e.g., 1 Thess. 1:1; 1 Cor. 1:1–2) in a typical manner. That Paul frequently introduces himself as the "apostle of Jesus Christ" signals that his letters have elements of official and authoritative communication, comparable in some regards to letters from philosophers to their disciples. The recipients are identified as churches, saints, or brethren, which conveys a religiously egalitarian, collective ethos unlike that of philosophical letters. The salutations also express the early Christian ethos: "Grace to you and peace from God our Father and Lord Jesus Christ" (1 Cor. 1:3; cf. 2 Cor. 1:2; Phil. 1:2). Compared with the opening greetings of typical letters in the ancient world, such salutations remind recipients of the participation in the new age of Christ shared by them and the writer. An even more elaborate adaptation is visible in the Christian transformation of the Greco-Roman thanksgiving. In the place of a relatively simple formula like, "I thank the god Serapis for the safe journey . . . ," Paul's thanksgivings are lengthened and filled with new theological content. In Phil. 1:3–11; 2 Cor. 1:3–7; and 2 Thess. 1:2–10, for example, the agenda of the Letter and a kind of table of contents are contained in the thanksgiving. In the case of 1 Thess. 1:2–3:13 the main argument of the Letter appears to be included in the thanksgiving, the extraordinary length of which is unparalled in ancient or modern epistolography.

The body of a NT Letter typically opens with a disclosure formula such as "I want you to know, brethren . . ." (Phil. 1:12; cf. 1 Cor. 1:10; 2 Cor. 1:8). With the exception of the term "brethren," such formulas are typical of Greco-Roman letters. The typical formulas for closing the body of a letter, expressing the desire to be "favored" by compliance with the request, are replaced by more elaborate, charismatic formulas (formulas that wish a spiritual gift for the addressees), for example, "Yes, brother, I want some benefit from you in the Lord. Refresh my heart in Christ" (Philem. 20). Often the body of a NT Letter closes with a homiletic benediction that sums up the foregoing argument and expresses a charismatic realization of divine presence and power (Rom. 15:13; Phil. 4:7; 1 Thess. 3:11–13; 2 Thess. 2:16). Another component sometimes found in the body of Pauline Letters is the travelogue, often expressing what has been called the "apostolic parousia," the spiritual presence of the apostle in the Letter (Gal. 1:18–2:21; 2 Cor. 1:15–2:13; 1 Thess. 2:17–3:10).

Unclear in epistolary theory is the relation of hortatory material to the body of a typical NT Letter. The tendency to perceive exhortative sections as separate from the theological "body" fails to account for the argumentative coherence of Letters like Romans or Hebrews. Typical opening formulas mark such parenetic sections (Rom. 12:1; Phil. 3:1; 1 Thess. 4:1) and in some instances the "now concerning" formula of Greco-Roman business letters is employed (1 Cor. 7:1; 7:25; 8:1; 2 Thess. 2:1). Research on the parenetic sections of NT Letters has also suggested the use of standardized *topoi* (Gk. "topics") from popular Greco-Roman, Jewish, or early Christian ethical instruction (e.g., Rom. 13:1–7; 1 Thess. 4:9–5:11; 2 Thess. 2:3–12). Parenetic sections of NT Letters are sometimes concluded with homiletic benedictions (e.g., 1 Thess. 5:23; 2 Thess. 3:16). At many such points a powerful sense of spiritual solidarity between writers and recipients of early Christian letters was expressed. Having initially experienced apostolic letters as means of divine encouragement, it was natural for the church to use them in later settings to reinforce the shared values of the community.

The epistolary categories that have been developed in the research of the past fifty years are admittedly modern and somewhat abstract. They derive from extensive studies of common letters, business letters, governmental correspondence, philosophical letters, and other materials from the Greco-Roman world. The inability of such categories to explain fully the organization of the body of Pauline Letters, in particular, has stimulated the rise of rhetorical analyses. The current stage of scholarly discussion centers on the relation between the epistolary types found in ancient handbooks, the rhetorical categories found in rhetorical treatises, and epistolographic categories such as "body" or "parenesis."

RHETORICAL FEATURES OF NEW TESTAMENT LETTERS

Ancient rhetorical theory was oriented primarily to the spoken word. Although rhetoricians taught their students how to write standard letters, often following the models of standard types or classical examples, they did not classify such letters under the three types of rhetoric. Modern researchers have attempted to fill this gap by classifying letters according to their epistolary type and associating them with the genres of judicial, deliberative, and demonstrative rhetoric. Among the twenty to forty types of letters listed in ancient epistolary handbooks, it is possible to identify accusing and apologetic types as fitting the judicial genre, praising and blaming types under the demonstrative category, and advising and consoling types as deliberative. No such classification is fully satisfactory, however, because exhortative materials are found in both the demonstrative and deliberative genres. Moreover, many letters in actuality are mixed types, and many pieces of literature, oratory, and epistolary discourse contain elements of more than one rhetorical genre.

Despite the difficulties in classification, there is no doubt that some NT Letters are masterpieces that conform to the highest standards of Greco-Roman rhetoric. A case has been made that Galatians fits the judicial genre as a letter of the apologetic type. The material in 2 Cor. 10–13 is an ironic apologetic letter type of the same genre. Romans appears to be a diplomatic letter with elements of popular philosophical diatribe and parenetic letter types, all of which would place it within the demonstrative genre of rhetoric. 1 Thessalonians is also demonstrative, concentrating on praise and blame with prominent emphasis on thanksgiving to God. It fits the epistolary type of the praising or thankful letter. Philemon and 2 Thessalonians are examples of deliberative rhetoric, providing advice concerning an action to be taken in the future with the traditional motifs of honor and advantage. While 2 Thessalonians would be an example of the denying or reproving letter type, Philemon appears to fit the supplicatory or advisory type.

The organization of these letters follows the guidelines of the Greek and Latin rhetorical handbooks concerning the creation of persuasive discourse. While embodying the highest standards of rhetoric in avoiding slavish conformity to standard formulas, these letters are creative vehicles of persuasion that would have been easily understood by first-century readers and hearers. For instance, the introductory section of a Pauline Letter functions as an *exordium*, the classical opening of formal discourse that establishes rapport with the audience and states the issue to be discussed (e.g., 1 Thess. 1:1–5; Rom. 1:1–12; Philem. 4–7). A *narratio*, or narration of events relevant for the issue at hand, is found in places like Gal. 1:12–2:14; Rom. 1:13–15; and 2 Cor. 2:12–13; 7:5–7. In the case of 1 Thessalonians it is possible to understand a substantial part of the extended thanksgiving as a narration of the grounds for giving thanks to God for salvation already experienced (1 Thess. 1:6–3:13). In Romans we find a formal *partitio*, a statement of the thesis of the entire letter in 1:16–17 (cf. also 2 Thess. 2:1–2). In Gal. 2:15–21 there is a well-developed *propositio*, a formal statement of the points of agreement and disagreement between Paul and the church (cf. also 2 Cor. 2:16c–17).

The main body of most Pauline Letters consists of a series of well-organized proofs that deal with theological, ethical, and organizational issues in the churches. The form of argument is heavily Jewish in its orientation, using scriptural examples and quotations. Common experiences and beliefs within the Christian community are used to support certain forms of belief and behavior and reject others. Occasionally Paul resorts to typical Greco-Roman forms of argument from natural law, household codes of behavior, or examples from everyday experience. Despite their unusual content, these proofs match Greco-Roman standards of organizing discourse. For instance, Galatians contains six interrelated proofs (Gal. 3:1–5; 3:6–14; 3:15–18; 3:26–4:11; 4:12–20; 4:21–31), followed by an exhortative proof that argues against accepting the Jewish law and following lures of the flesh (5:1–6:10). 2 Thessalonians contains two proofs concerning the issue of the second coming of Jesus Christ (2 Thess. 2:3–12; 2:13–3:5) that precisely match the topics listed in the *partitio* of 2:1–2. The most elaborate and formal proofs in the Pauline Letters are found in Romans. The first proof (Rom. 1:18–4:25) serves to confirm the thesis dealing with the power of the gospel concerning divine righteousness in 1:16–17 while the next three proofs (5:1–8:39; 9:1–11:36; 12:1–15:13) amplify the implications of the thesis for the Roman house-churches and the proposed mission to be shared with them. Each of these closely related proofs is organized in ten well-developed paragraphs, reflecting careful planning, a high level of rhetorical finesse, and a desire to find common ground with Jewish Christians for whom series of ten had theological significance. Even the most formal Pauline proof was designed for a specific audience and situation, with a concern to maintain or develop the relationship between sender and recipient that was characteristic of letters throughout the ancient world.

The conclusions of Paul's Letters contain elements characteristic of the *peroratio* of Greco-Roman rhetoric. Perorations contained recapitulations of the preceding argument and emotional appeals to support the viewpoint of the speaker or writer. It is possible to construe the conclusion of Romans (15:14–16:27) as an elaborate peroration of this type, reviewing the argument of the Letter and appealing for cooperation with Paul's missionary plans. Smaller examples of perorations have been identified in Philem. 17–22; 1 Thess. 5:23–28; and 2 Thess. 3:16–18. These are distinctively epistolary perorations, with closing greetings, final admonitions sometimes written in Paul's own hand, and requests to extend the fellowship of the holy kiss. The intense sense of commonality within the Christian communities and between them and Paul is powerfully expressed in these concluding sections of Pauline Letters, full of emotional appeals for unity and integrity.

THE ORIGINAL FUNCTION OF NEW TESTAMENT LETTERS

Most NT Letters related directly to the problems of individual congregations and to the relationships between them and the sender. The Letters are written by authoritative persons such as Paul, who founded most of the congregations he addressed. Similarly, the Johannine Letters are written by a congregational leader who calls himself "the Elder" (2 John 1:1; 3 John 1:10). A certain John, otherwise unidentified, writes to enclaves of his adherents in the seven churches of Asia (Rev. 1:4–3:22). It is likely that Hebrews, James, 1 and 2 Peter, and Jude were also perceived by their original recipients to come from founders or spiritual advisers of churches.

Despite differences in the definition of the term, NT Letters are apostolic. They express the authority of leaders perceived to be foundational for the communities being addressed. In this regard, the NT Letters are comparable to philosophical letters designed to exhort individuals to follow wise examples in response to particular situations. Senders of such letters serve as wise guides to less mature students or friends; their example is to be emulated in the quest for sound character and appropriate self-knowledge. Such letters are similar to NT writings in many ways. Still, the nature of the relationship between Paul and his recipients differed both in rationale and context from philosophical relationships. The recipients of NT Letters are groups rather than individuals; even in the case of Philemon, the Letter is also addressed to other leaders of the house-church as well as to "the church in your house" (Philem. 2). There is a peculiar combination of authority and equality between senders and recipients in most of these Letters, which contrasts not only with philosophical letters but also with other epistolary materials in the ancient world, which was highly sensitive to status differences.

Perhaps the most significant distinguishing mark is that Christian Letters express the ethos of groups and leaders that together had experienced conversion to a form of sectarian consciousness that differed substantially from the surrounding society. The intensity of their sense of internal solidarity and of their separation from a world perceived to be controlled by evil principalities and powers comes to powerful expression in epistolary materials, which were uniquely suited for maintaining distinctive relationships and conveying important information. Thus not only the formal development but also the peculiar content of these Letters display unusual features when compared with other materials in the Greco-Roman world.

THE CREATION AND INITIAL CIRCULATION OF NEW TESTAMENT LETTERS

Although no original copies are available to us, there is no doubt that the initial stage of NT Letters consisted for the most part of dictated material written by reed pens on papyrus rolls for the use of a specific congregation. On the basis of thousands of examples in the ancient world, it is clear that letters were typically written on papyrus sheets that had been pasted in series and rolled up in the form of a scroll. Scribes would cut off enough to write their particular letter, drafting their material on the inside of the scroll so that delivery instructions could be placed on the outside. The technical difficulty of working on the uneven surface of papyrus required the assistance of scribes, whose names occasionally surface in NT writings: Tertius in Rom. 16:22; Silvanus in 1 Pet. 5:12; perhaps Timothy or Silvanus in 1 Thess. 1:1. That Paul dictated his letters is also proven by the closing greeting in his own handwriting (1 Cor. 16:21; 2 Thess. 3:17), whose difference in size and elegance from the rest of the Letter is referred to in Gal. 6:11.

The original circulation of NT Letters was by messenger. The postal system of the Roman Empire was restricted to governmental agents, so private correspondence had to be sent by couriers or trusted travelers. There are many indications that messengers were often entrusted not only with the letter to be delivered but also with an intimate knowledge of its background. Since epistolary communication renders any immediate dialogue between sender and recipient impossible, emissaries often supplied this vital function. Delicate details concerning the business or controversy under discussion were often left to the trusted emissary, and in some instances the customary address was omitted on the premise that the emissary would supply the appropriate greetings. This may explain why a letter like Hebrews lacks an epistolary opening, while containing a normal epistolary closing. The expectation of a crucial role for the letter carrier may also explain the peculiar wording of Phil. 3:1, which implies that extensive admonitions have been entrusted to the emissary, to which Paul simply adds a confirmatory note. There are clear indications that knowledgeable Christian leaders carried letters to specific congregations, and were thus entrusted with the task of interpreting their message and adjudicating the disputes at hand. Phoebe is recommended as a reliable Christian leader in Rom. 16:1–2; it is generally assumed that she brought the Letter to Rome, and there is every likelihood that she was its first interpreter. Stephanas and his associates are affirmed at the end of 1 Corinthians as being privy to Paul's mind and spirit, adequately representing the congregation to him and in turn recommended as authoritative when they return to Corinth with Paul's Letter (1 Cor. 16:15–18). Titus is recommended in 2 Cor. 8:16–23 in terms that make clear that he not only bears the Letter concerning the Jerusalem offering but also will carry out the delicate negotiations with the congregation concerning its collection and delivery.

The original Pauline Letters were experienced by congregations in oral form, read aloud before the assembled church by messengers or scribes. This procedure, which would have been typical for the ancient world in which silent reading was unknown, is presupposed by the wording of Col. 4:16, "And when this letter has been read among you, have it read also in the church of the Laodiceans; and see that you read also the letter from Laodicea" (cf. 1 Thess. 5:27). This means that the rhetorical impact of NT Letters was oral; for the church as a whole, such reading of letters sounded like spoken discourse, in which an authoritative person like Paul was present in a manner that could be even more impressive than when he was actually physically present in the assembly (cf. 2 Cor. 10:10–11). The authority and eloquence of the professional scribe, messenger, or church leader reading the letter would inevitably become blended with that of the author of the letter. The author was thought to be present in spirit during the reading (1 Cor. 5:4). And unlike modern experience with NT Letters, in which small sections are read aloud or silently, the early church would have experienced even the longest Letters in one sitting. It is therefore understandable, given our more recent discoveries of the rhetorical coherence and power of this material, that such public readings would convey communication of considerable persuasiveness. The original audiences to whom the Letters were addressed would have felt in direct communication with the absent sender; the so-called apostolic parousia, or presence of the apostle in the experience of hearing the letter, is an appropriate category for this culturally conditioned attitude toward epistolary communication.

All of the evidence points to the conclusion that these occasional letters were intended for the use of specific local congregations facing particular issues that were not necessarily present in other congregations. A review of the original Pauline Letters will provide a sense of the unique congregational situations to which they were addressed as well as clues to their later publication as books.

The earliest Pauline Letter was written ca. A.D. 50 to the church at Thessalonica in response to a collapse of morale due to the unexpected death of congregational members (1 Thess. 4:13–18) and the onset of persecution (1 Thess. 3:3–10). Some interpreters think that the Thessalonian Christians had misinterpreted Paul's proclamation of the last days as though their conditions were already present and would eliminate suffering. Some of the radicals had abandoned their occupations (1 Thess. 5:14) and others were questioning the traditional marriage ethic as inappropriate for the millennial age (1 Thess. 4:1–8). Other interpreters reconstruct the setting in a different way (see the commentary on 1 Thessalonians). Although there is disagreement about the authenticity of 2 Thessalonians, it was likely written by Paul soon after the first Letter to counter a serious misunderstanding. The radicals had intensified their activities and actually called on the first Letter as proof that the millennium had arrived (2 Thess. 2:2). The second Letter to the Thessalonians reiterates Paul's futuristic eschatology and repudiates the misunderstanding of 1 Thessalonians. Both Letters are tightly organized and closely related to a peculiar set of congregational circumstances not replicated elsewhere in early Christianity, so far as we know. There is no reason to suspect that either Letter circulated widely out of its initial geographic area prior to the publication of the Pauline Letter corpus.

Galatians was written ca. A.D. 53 to a gentile Christian congregation that had accepted the message of anti-Pauline agitators who promoted circumcision (Gal. 6:12–13) and the adherence to Jewish festivals (Gal. 4:8–10). The congregation was also having difficulty living in the new age without falling victim to libertinism (Gal. 5:13–6:10). The argument concerning salvation by faith alone that Paul developed in response to this situation gained fundamental importance for the later church, but there are no clear quotations or allusions to Galatians until the middle of the second century in the writing of Justin and Marcion. Here again one gains the impression of a letter that was not circulated apart from the Pauline Letter collection.

A similar impression of highly occasional letters that attracted little interest beyond their initial audience emerges from a consideration of Philippians and Philemon. Paul's Letter to the Philippians, probably dispatched from an Ephesian imprisonment in A.D. 54–55, contains obscure references that would have been clearly understood by the original audience but baffling to outsiders. In addition to the "same things" in Phil. 3:1, there is an awkward transition from a benediction in 4:7 to a kind of peroration in 4:8–9 and then to a peculiar thank you note in 4:10–20. The Letter changes subjects rapidly from a discussion of enemies of Paul's imprisonment (1:12–30) to a criticism of congregational arrogance (2:1–18) to a consideration of the travels of Paul's associates (2:19–30). A harsh critique of libertinists (3:17–21) follows hard on an equally vehement attack on Judaizers (3:2–16), followed by an appeal for the cessation of conflict between two congregational leaders (4:2–3). Several division hypotheses have been proposed by modern researchers to eliminate these problems, none of which is more satisfactory than the canonical Letter as it stands, which appears to contain all of the elements announced in the thanksgiving in 1:3–11.

In contrast there is no doubt about the integrity of Philemon, probably written from another imprisonment in A.D. 55–56. We now understand this Letter as a subtle and profound appeal for the voluntary manumission of a runaway slave by the name of Onesimus, but for first-century congregations, unaware of the circumstances, it was little understood. While Philemon is only obliquely visible in early Christian writings, Philippians was used quite extensively by Polycarp (ca. A.D. 69–155) in his Letter to the Philippians. This seems to fit the pattern of the other letters being used for some decades primarily in the area of their initial address.

When we come to Romans and the Corinthian correspondence, a contrasting picture of extensive circulation emerges. Surveys of literary allusions and quotations indicate that 1 Corinthians was the most widely dispersed and frequently used of the Pauline Letters through the second century, with Romans following close behind. It seems consistent that these Letters also display the clearest indications of redactional activity. Texts for both Romans and 1 Corinthians have variations in their addresses indicating they were adapted for generalized use. A number of different versions of Romans circulated independently in the early church, reflected in the tangled textual history of Romans 14–16. Some passages, like Rom. 16:17–20; 1 Cor. 14:33b–36; and 2 Cor. 6:14–7:1, seem to conflict either with their immediate contexts or with things said elsewhere in the same letters. Many scholars therefore regard these passages as interpolations added by later hands to the original letters. Other apparent discrepancies, such as the differences of tone and apparent situation between 2 Cor. 1:1–2:13 and 2 Cor. 10:1–13:14 and the duplication of purpose between 2 Corinthians 8 and 9, suggest to many scholars that parts of several letters may have been combined to create the two large books we now have. Thus the Letters to Romans and Corinthians and possibly others come to us in an edited form.

THE TRANSITION FROM OCCASIONAL LETTERS TO PUBLISHED BOOKS

With the exception of the detail from Col. 4:16, cited above, there is no clear proof that Pauline Letters were used by congregations outside of the immediate area to which they were originally addressed before ca. A.D. 90. The transition from the initial period of local circulation in the 50s to the wider distribution of NT Letters toward the end of the first century is shrouded in darkness. A crucial event in this period was likely the redaction and publication of the Corinthian correspondence. Some scholars have speculated that this editing and publishing activity may have been carried out by "conservative" members of the Pauline school, to counter interpretations of Paul's letters by others that they deemed improper. If so, this "orthodox" edition of the Corinthian correspondence must have occurred in the early 90s, prior to citations from 1 Corinthians in 1 Clement, which was written in the late first or early second century A.D.

Even if the precise details of this reconstruction are incorrect, it remains likely that the transition from occasional apostolic letters to authoritative apostolic books began with the redaction, publication, and distribution of several Pauline Letters to serve ecclesiastical purposes. After the circulation of 1 Corinthians and the various efforts to do the same with Romans, other Pauline materials began to make their appearance. The pastoral Letters were created toward the end of the century, bearing the marks of the same conservative outlook evident in the redaction of the Corinthian correspondence. It appears likely that the early collections of Pauline Letters contained seven to ten letters arranged according to length, with the two Corinthian and Thessalonian Letters occasionally counted as single letters. Ultimately the Pastorals, Colossians, Hebrews, and Ephesians were included to bring the total up to thirteen. Given the derivative quality of Ephesians in particular, its role as a kind of introduction to some early form of the Pauline Letter corpus remains an intriguing speculation. That some collection of Paul's letters was extant at the turn of the century is evident from 2 Pet. 3:16. The ten-letter collection published by Marcion in the middle of the second century, with Galatians in the lead position, remains a unique variation.

The wider distribution of the Pauline Letters appears to have stimulated the creation and distribution of their critical counterparts: 2 Peter, Jude, James, the Johannine Letters, and Revelation. When the Pauline Letters were later located in a canon where they were preceded by the Book of Acts and followed by the general Letters and Revelation, the potentially dangerous and sometimes incomprehensible material could function as sacred writ. It is interesting to observe, however, that this did not take place until advances in the manufacture of larger codices (books with leaves, as opposed to scrolls) allowed material as large as the NT to be included in a single book. Within this context, each writing was able to function as a book within a comprehensive and authoritative book, capable of communicating to churches far from the locale or time of their original provenance.

Bibliography

Gamble, H. *The New Testament Canon: Its Making and Meaning.* Philadelphia: Fortress, 1985.

Jewett, R. "The Redaction of 1 Corinthians and the Trajectory of the Pauline School." *Journal of the American Academy of Religion Supplement* 46 (1978): 389–44.

———. *The Thessalonian Correspondence: Pauline Rhetoric and Millenarian Piety.* Philadelphia: Fortress, 1986.

Roetzel, C. J. *The Letters of Paul: Conversations in Context.* Atlanta, GA: Knox, 1975.

Stowers, S. K. *Letter Writing in Greco-Roman Antiquity.* Philadelphia: Westminster, 1986.

White, J. L. *Light from Ancient Letters.* Philadelphia: Fortress, 1986.

ROMANS

PAUL W. MEYER

INTRODUCTION

General Features

The position of the Letter of Paul to the Romans as the first Letter in the NT is due to the simple fact that the earliest collections of Paul's Letters were arranged in order of decreasing length and Romans is the longest. Its resulting place has been oddly appropriate, however, since it is also the most deliberate and reflective of Paul's Letters and its influence on Christian theology the greatest. The sixteenth-century reformer Philipp Melanchthon called it a "compendium of Christian doctrine" and it has in fact functioned as such for most of its long history. Its contents seem at first sight to conform to this assessment. In all other cases, Paul's Letters clearly served as surrogates for his personal presence as an apostle and leader in situations of crisis that developed in churches he himself had founded. In those other Letters Paul writes because he has to, to protect, correct, or strengthen some aspect of the gospel in the life of a particular congregation that is under risk. Romans appears to be an exception to this pattern. It is addressed to a church Paul did not establish. It does not seem to arise from an occasion that has been forced on him. There is no defense of himself, as in Galatians or 1 and 2 Corinthians, and no counterattack on those who have assaulted him or tried to seduce his converts. Instead, the argument of the Letter proceeds by a serial treatment of interlocking and perennial themes, often in sections that stand out as independent literary "blocks." Indeed, one of the challenges in the reading of Romans is to see how these sections were intended to fit together as parts of a coherent whole.

These themes, furthermore, do not seem to be peculiar to Romans; there are very few of them that do not echo passages in the other Letters. Some examples are the failure of the world to know God on his own terms (Rom. 1:18–32; 1 Cor. 1:18–25); justification by faith rather than by works of the law (Rom. 3; Gal. 3; 4; Phil. 3); Abraham (Rom. 4; Gal. 3); Adam and Christ (Rom. 5:12–21; 1 Cor. 15:21–22, 45–49); the church as the body of Christ (Rom. 12; 1 Cor. 12). There are exceptions. Conspicuous by its absence from Romans is any discussion of the nature of Paul's apostleship, any defense of his credentials or cataloging of the trials he has endured to authenticate his ministry. That these are missing appears to be a function of the absence of polemic. Conversely, one major theme that is treated at length and with passion in Romans but has no parallel in the other Letters is the discussion of the past and future destiny of Israel and its relation to the gospel (Rom. 9–11).

If Romans is the first of Paul's Letters in the order of the NT books, it is the last of his undoubted Letters to have been written (→ Paul). The themes Romans shares with the other Letters always come up elsewhere in situations of conflict or uncertainty that elicit Paul's discussion of them. But in Romans they are elaborated as part of a longer argument he has himself initiated, in deliberate and self-conscious progression. Many of its turning points are clearly marked by literary conventions (Rom. 1:8; 12:1–2; 16:1), anticipated objections and queries (3:1; 4:1, 9; 6:1), short summations (6:11; 7:12; 15:5–6), rhetorical climaxes (8:37–39; 11:28–32), and the insertion of liturgical fragments (4:25; 9:5; 11:33–36). It seems that the historical concreteness of those earlier crises and conflicts has receded and been displaced by a more deliberate accounting of what Paul has come to regard as crucial and definitive in his total work as an apostle; he appears to transcend at least to some extent the particular situations he has lived through and make available for a new audience the fruits of his experience. As a result, there has always been a powerful temptation to read Romans as a "compendium of Christian doctrine," or a systematic statement of Paul's theology.

Yet there are three important reasons for not resting with such an appraisal. For one thing, it is clear from the other Letters that Romans simply does not embrace everything that was important, even necessary, in Paul's own understanding of Christian faith and life (one may mention especially the Lord's Supper, 1 Cor. 11:23–26, and the resurrection, 1 Cor. 15:3–8, 12–19). In the second place, no part of the NT was composed simply as a presentation of its author's ideas, divorced from specific human occasions and needs. One should hesitate a long time before making Romans an exception to this rule and sundering it from early Christian history. Above all, Romans itself contains the most important evidence to help us understand its place in that history.

Occasion and Purpose

The most direct evidence for the occasion of Romans appears in the personal remarks Paul makes in the opening and closing sections of the Letter. In 1:10–15 it is clear that he is preparing the way for carrying out a long-cherished plan to visit the church at Rome, a visit he hopes will be of mutual benefit. In 15:14–33 he is much more specific. He feels he has no more "space" to carry on his mission to the Gentiles in the eastern Mediterranean and wants to extend it to the west and to Spain, and to be "sped on his way" (15:24) there by the church at Rome, to be supported by them in this enterprise. Since Paul hopes for such help from a church he did not himself establish, one motive for writing is clearly implied: he wants to present this church with an authentic representation of his message to gain its trust and backing. Before he can come to Rome, however, Paul has to make one last trip to Jerusalem to deliver the collection of money he has raised for the Jewish Christians there (→ Contribution for the Saints). This fixes the date and place for the writing of Romans fairly well, that is, during his last stay in Greece prior to his final trip to Jerusalem (at the point in the narrative of Acts represented by Acts 20:3), and probably from Corinth (Rom. 16:23 mentions "Gaius, my host," and Gaius is one of the few persons Paul admits to having baptized in Corinth, 1 Cor. 1:14). The time is probably the winter of A.D. 55 or 56. This generally undisputed dating of Romans has a significant bearing on the Letter's content. Its composition comes after the writing of Galatians and all the letters to Corinth (whatever their number), after the resolution of the Corinthian crisis, and probably also after the writing of Philippians.

If this gives us time and place, it does not yet yield a very convincing account of Paul's purpose in writing. Why should a letter aimed at gaining trust and recognition deal with just the themes we have identified? Romans is much more than a neutral exposition of admirable ideas, however coherent. It is an argument with thrust and edge; it seeks to overcome resistance and counter objections. One may easily imagine that agitators and enemies from Paul's earlier conflicts over his mission to Gentiles have had some influence in Rome that he would have been anxious to neutralize before his visit, especially if the church in the capital city was linked to the synagogue community there. (Rom. 3:7–8 shows in passing that Paul is aware of charges that have circulated against him.) We have very little knowledge of the actual composition of the church in Rome. But the evidence from Paul's Letter itself is perplexing. He seems to address the church clearly at certain points as gentile (1:13; 11:13), at others as Jewish in background (2:17; 3:9). He seems to draw his justification for writing to the Romans and his right to be heard by them from his being an apostle to the Gentiles (1:13–14) and on their being a gentile Christian community. Yet he does not incorporate into this Letter some of the themes and preoccupations most characteristic of gentile urban Christianity as these had emerged in Corinth. Instead, the argument itself is cast in profoundly Jewish terms: its controlling vocabulary, its appeals to authority and tradition, the values invoked, the techniques employed in interpreting Scripture, the things taken for granted in the minds of its readers.

The puzzle is compounded when one notes that Paul's missionary strategy included a "principle of noninterference," i.e., a resolve not to pursue his missionary activity where others had begun theirs. This resolve is clearly stated in Rom. 15:20–21; it appears earlier in 2 Cor. 10:15–16. It is an understandable policy in the light of the division of labor agreed on at the Jerusalem conference (Gal. 2:7–9) and is certainly congruent with the affectionate possessiveness Paul felt toward his own churches (e.g., Gal. 4:19–20; 2 Cor 3:1–3; 11:1–3). But how is it then that we find him writing to Rome at all? Is his departure from this principle adequately explained by his need of support from Rome for his mission to Spain? Answers to these questions have been sought by attempting to reconstruct in more detail the circumstances in which Romans was written.

These attempts have generally moved in one of two directions. The first may be called the "Roman exile hypothesis." On his first arrival in Corinth about A.D. 50, Paul made contact with a Jewish couple, Prisca and Aquila, who had recently come from Rome "because Claudius had ordered all the Jews to leave" that city (Acts 18:2–3; → Aquila; Prisca, Priscilla). Apparently they were already Christian converts by that time. The Roman biographer Suetonius, in his *Life of Claudius* (25), gives the reason for the emperor's edict (A.D. 49) in words generally taken to refer to disturbances in the Roman Jewish community over the messiahship of Jesus. We may conclude that the church had been started in Rome by A.D. 49, and that it was sufficiently Jewish in composition to have come under Claudius' ban, though presumably an indeterminate gentile Christian component would have been allowed to remain in the capital. When the ban was lifted in A.D. 54 after Claudius' death, a good part, perhaps a majority, of the Christian community was allowed to return after its five-year exile. Enormous problems of reconciliation would have resulted. The situation faced earlier

ROM

by Paul in Antioch (Gal. 2:11–14) would have become an acute local Roman problem, but with a reverse twist: now it would not be the Jewish Christians who had to accept former Gentiles into the community, but the other way around. Gentile Christians would need to be reminded of their debt to their Jewish heritage (Paul seems in fact to do just this in Rom. 11:18) and to be urged to be more tolerant of Jewish religious practices (cf. 14:3, 5–6, 14). For many scholars just such a situation is reflected in Paul's exhortations in the concluding chapters of Romans, thus confirming the exile hypothesis.

Yet this proposal does not answer all questions. The last chapters of Romans do more than simply reverse the arguments of Galatians to apply them to an inverse situation. The contrast between the "weak" and the "strong" (Rom. 15:1) appears to have developed not out of the Galatian debate but out of the distinction made in 1 Cor. 8:7–13 between the "weak" and "those who have knowledge." While this distinction is now subtly but firmly linked to the themes of Israel's history among the Gentiles and God's faithfulness (Rom. 15:7–12), a thread that runs through the body of the Letter, the connection appears contrived. Paul is very careful in Romans not to take sides; he no longer uses himself as a model (cf. Gal. 6:14; 1 Cor. 9:15–23; 10:32–33; 11:1) but points more directly to Christ (Rom. 15:3, 7). In short, Paul's exhortations do not seem to address concrete problems so much as they present paradigms of Christian behavior generated out of his experiences in both Galatia and Corinth. But most important, all the previous bulk of Romans, the profoundly Jewish appeal of the argument, is not adequately accounted for by reconstructing a situation in which it is gentile Christians who are being called upon to welcome back their exiled Jewish Christian associates.

Thus there has been another major attempt to reconstruct the occasion of Romans, which we may call the "Jerusalem crisis hypothesis." It is not time and place of writing that are in doubt, but Paul's motives, the circumstances that impelled him to write this Letter. Proponents of this view point particularly to Rom. 15:30–33, where Paul's anxiety over the outcome of his impending visit to Jerusalem is clearly expressed. That anxiety is in proportion to the importance attached by Paul to the money he has collected for the Jerusalem church and is about to deliver. The collection exemplified and actualized the unity of a church composed of both Jews and Gentiles that had been the issue at the apostolic conference in Jerusalem (Gal. 2:1–10) and that constitutes one of the running themes of Romans (cf. Rom. 1:16; 9:24; 15:7–12). With it, in Paul's view, the "truth of the gospel" stood or fell (Gal. 2:5). Whether

Paul's whole career had been worthwhile or futile depended in turn on Jerusalem's recognition of that truth (Gal. 2:2). His anxiety therefore is not limited to what might occur in Jerusalem; it is at least in part an anxiety to be rightly understood in Rome not only so that he might have the Roman Christians as allies but also that his entire mission should not be misunderstood as the irrelevant experiment of a free-lancer. The situation that occasioned Romans in this view is a crisis that lies before Paul in Jerusalem. The resources for facing it lie in his exposition of the gospel as its apostle. As a matter of fact, the themes of Romans fall rather precisely under two headings: first, the results of the controversies in Galatia, Corinth, and Philippi, now reflected upon in their interconnections and with more distance (Abraham and his promise, the Mosaic law, justification, spiritual gifts, unity and diversity in the church, eating and drinking in a religious context), and second, just those convictions Paul was going to have to defend in Jerusalem (the faithfulness and impartiality of God, the equal accountability of Jew and Gentile before God [chaps. 1–2], the equal right of Gentile and Jew as offspring of the one Abraham "who is the father of us all" [chaps. 3–4], the terms on which true obedience to God is possible [chaps. 5–8], the meaning of Israel for the life of the church [chaps. 9–11], the equal freedom and responsibility of Jewish and gentile Christian in the everyday life of the community in the world [chaps. 12–15]).

Such a reconstruction of the setting for Romans has the advantage of making historically intelligible the composition of this Letter with its undeniable thematic and reflective character. Deeply rooted in the history of Paul's relations with his congregations, it is the rendering of an account of his gospel, its fundamental warrants, the major misunderstandings to which it is susceptible, its consequences, and above all the continuities and differences between it and the Judaism out of which Paul had come.

Significance

While some find one more compelling than the other, the "Roman exile" and the "Jerusalem crisis" hypotheses are not, strictly speaking, mutually exclusive. What they have most notably in common is the perception that the relation of the infant Christian movement to Judaism, a complex mix of both continuity and innovation as in the case of most significant new departures in religious tradition, is a fundamental motif of the Letter. Being himself a participant in this transition, i.e., being himself profoundly Jewish and Christian, Paul could not deal with the issues confronting him on either hypothesis—or on both—without involving his own religious identity. The "adversary," the debating partner, in Romans is not some enemy or some heresy; it is not gentile Christianity, of which Paul is rather the advocate; nor is it Judaism, as though this were a rejected alternative left behind. It is instead in large measure the Hellenistic Jew that Paul himself was: a religious person in his highest aspirations, in his self-esteem but also his devotion to God, in his full knowledge of what God requires of human beings, in his loyalty to the Jewish Torah—yet one who despite all these virtues does not realize how religious life has been poisoned and perverted by the power of sin and needs to be shown how God has provided in his Son Jesus Christ a way of obtaining that integrity, that "righteousness," in one's relationship to God that has always eluded religious people. The expository argument that results and that forms the substance of Romans has played an immeasurable role in the centuries since, most especially in two ways: first, in helping to shape the Christian community's understanding of its relationship to the Hebrew Scriptures and to Judaism, both its debt and its distinctiveness; and second, in restoring and clarifying a sense of direction and identity in Christian reflection in times of great contention and change, such as the Pelagian controversy in the fifth century, the emergence of Protestantism in the sixteenth, and the breakdown of liberal optimism in the twentieth. These two ways in which Romans has functioned are intimately connected and are, one might say, but two sides of its significance.

The other Letters of Paul have undergone various levels of editing in the process of circulation and canonization in order to make and keep available for subsequent generations what they initially intended and contributed in their original, contingently historical settings. Romans has been comparatively free of such modification. Its authenticity is not debated. Serious questions about its integrity, i.e., whether it left the apostle's hand in the form in which we have it, are confined to chap 16. The situation in which it was composed near the end of Paul's career called forth a type of argument that transcended that situation from the beginning by its comprehensiveness and because of the perennial nature of the issues of religious identity and integrity it addresses. Thus, even though it cannot be fully understood in isolation from the other Letters that follow it in the canon, Romans has not unjustly been perceived as comprising the heart of the apostle's legacy to the Christian church.

COMMENTARY

1:1–17

Introduction

1:1–7, Salutation. Paul begins by using the conventional opening pattern of Hellenistic letters: "A (writer) to B (addressee): greeting" (cf. James 1:1; Acts 15:23). But this structural skeleton admits, and even invites, augmentation in a variety of ways. First, the greeting at the end (v. 7b) is modified under the influence of the Jewish "peace" greeting (also used in letters, cf. Dan. 4:1; 2 Macc. 1:1) and of Christian liturgical practice. Paul expects his letters to be read in public assembly. Second, descriptive modifiers are attached to the designations of both sender and recipients, allowing Paul to present his credentials and at the same time to coordinate to his own calling "as an apostle" (v. 1) that of his readers "as saints" (v. 7). This last term is explained by the addition of "beloved by God" (v. 7) and "belonging to Jesus Christ" (v. 6) and is the closest equivalent in Paul's vocabulary to the later term "Christian." That is a reminder that all Paul's extant Letters are written "within the family" to sustain, encourage, or correct people who are assumed to be baptized. God's calling initiative binds writer and recipients together, though it also distinguishes Paul by assigning him his own role as an "apostle," an envoy commissioned for a particular purpose. That is Paul's principal credential: he "has" authority because he himself stands under it. The purpose of his calling is to serve "God's gospel," a message anticipated in the writings of the Jewish prophets that formed part of the Scriptures of the early Christian community from the beginning. As the subsequent argument will elaborate, this message has its roots in the continuity of God's past relationship to his people but has its goal in eliciting trust and obedience among non-Jewish peoples as well.

In the third place, Paul augments his salutation most strikingly in Romans by noting the content of God's gospel; it "concerns his Son . . . Jesus Christ our Lord." Two parallel relative clauses further identifying this Son in vv. 3b–4 show linguistic and formal signs of being a pre-Pauline creedal fragment and are of great interest for the light they shed on the early development of Christology (Christian understanding of Jesus' nature):

[his Son]
who was descended from the seed of David
according to the flesh,
who was appointed Son of God with power
according to the spirit of holiness by [or
from] the resurrection of the dead.

This couplet is best explained as having originated from the combination of two strains of early Christian affirmation about Jesus. First, while it appears nowhere else in Paul, the origin of the Messiah from the royal line of David was one of the constants in Jewish messianic expectation based on 2 Sam. 7:11b–16 and is found in the NT in the infancy narratives of Matthew and Luke (Matt. 1:1; Luke 1:27; 2:4; cf. Mark 10:47 and parallels; Mark 12:35 and parallels; Matt. 9:27; 12:23; 15:22; 21:9, 15; John 7:42; Rev. 5:5; 22:16). Second, another tradition developed from the confession that with the resurrection Jesus was exalted to become the Son of God or the Messiah. This tradition made use of Ps. 2:7 and Ps. 110:1 and appears in its simplest form in Acts. 2:36; 5:30–31; and 13:33. Such an understanding of "Son of God" as a titular office or role to which Jesus was "appointed" at a given moment in time is also without parallel in Paul. The two traditions, one oriented more around the earthly life of Jesus as a descendant of David, the other centered in the preaching of God's resurrection of the crucified Jesus, seem to have developed at first as alternative ways of affirming Jesus to be the bearer and fulfiller of Jewish messianic hopes. In the couplet above quoted by Paul, the two traditions (which appear together again in looser order in 2 Tim. 2:8) have been clamped together by means of the word pair "flesh" and "spirit" (→ Flesh and Spirit). These terms appear in other early creedal or hymnic passages to distinguish the earthly sphere of reality (without morally pejorative connotations) and the transcendent realm of divine power (1 Tim. 3:16; 1 Pet. 3:18; 4:6; cf. John 3:6; 6:63). Combined in this way, the two sets of messianic ideas are no longer parallel but have become sequential, creating narrative movement in the creedal pattern: the earthly life of the descendant of David is a first stage followed by the postresurrection reign of the Son of God installed in divine power. An important later development is then clearly observable in Ignatius' letters (Ign. Eph. 7:2; 18:2; 20:2; Ign. Smyrn. 1:1–2): the two sets of messianic categories are again brought into parallelism but now, under the influence of the virgin birth tradition and to meet a new polemic situation, the link with the resurrection is broken and both are connected with the birth of Jesus to affirm a double origin of his person, one human and one divine. With that a major step is taken toward the patristic doctrine of the two natures of Christ. This is to go far beyond the meaning of the present passage in Rom. 1:3b–4, but it indicates the historical significance of the creedal fragment Paul quotes (→ Messiah; Son of God; Virgin Birth).

In this context the quotation is an important part of Paul's initial move to establish the common ground of a shared faith with his unknown readers. Both the title "Son of God" and the mention of the resurrection, understood as God's vindication and authorization of Jesus "in power," show that what is decisive for Paul about Jesus of Nazareth is God's identification with him. The close operating association that results is central to Paul's Christology, appears in the liturgical blessing with which the salutation ends (v. 7b), and is seen in the way Paul embarks on his next paragraph, in which he prays to God "through Jesus Christ."

1:8–15, Thanksgiving. Another standard practice in Hellenistic letter writing was to begin with a prayer of thanksgiving for the favorable circumstances of recipient or writer or both. Paul often gives thanks for the faith of his readers, not only because he understands it to be symptomatic of God's working but also because in his world confession is a public act with repercussions for the further spread of the gospel, not simply a private faith. In the present passage, the thanksgiving quickly merges after v. 8 into statements about Paul's desire to visit Rome (see above "Introduction: The Occasion and Purpose of Romans"). At the end (vv. 14–15) he explicitly traces this desire to the higher duty that governs his life and authorizes his mission; he is "one under obligation" to all alike. To register the universal range of that imperative he abandons for a moment (and only here in his Letters) his customary division of humankind into Jew and non-Jew that always has a religious dimension and adopts the cultural and linguistic designations "Hellene" (to which the Romans would have counted themselves) and "barbarian," "learned and simple" (NEB). Paul's thanksgivings often serve to signal certain concerns or themes of the subsequent letter bodies, and this deliberate point that his gospel pertains to all without regard to social standing and privilege confirms that pattern.

1:16–17, Statement of the Theme. In close logical continuity with the preceding, Paul asserts, "For I am not put to shame by the gospel." This somewhat surprising expression has little to do with moral disgrace or with personal pride. In the Septuagint (LXX), "to be put to shame" is to have a hope or expectation disappointed, a confidence proven to be misplaced (cf. Ps. 119:6; Isa. 54:4). Its opposite, as here, is to have the base on which one rests one's life turn out to warrant the trust placed in it. Paul can "have complete confidence in the gospel" (TEV) because it is God's effective way of working for human salvation. In itself that does not yet state an issue that is subject to debate. But with vv. 16–17, which bring the thanksgiving to its conclusion, Paul takes one further step. Because the content of the gospel is God's Son (vv.

1134

3–4), God's way of providing salvation pertains from now on to all who believe, Jew and Greek alike, and it involves a fresh revelation of "the righteousness of God" on these new terms. As a matter of fact, the ensuing argument of the Letter elaborates this last step and in so doing rejects certain alternative understandings of salvation (see 3:21–26). Verses 16–17 thus function as a statement of the theme of the Letter.

It is characteristic that Paul ends this introductory statement by appealing (for confirmation) to an OT text (Hab. 2:4) that brings together the three major terms "righteousness," "faith," and "life" (or salvation). But the sense in which Paul understands it is not immediately apparent. It differs in detail from both the Masoretic Text (MT) and the LXX. More important, the phrase "by faith" can be construed to modify either the subject, "the righteous person," or the verb, "shall live." A widely held view, choosing the first possibility, concludes that chaps. 1–4 of the Letter describe "the person who is righteous by faith," while chaps. 5–8 show how such a person "shall live." That would suggest that Paul simply accepts the premise that righteousness is a condition of salvation and that the issue in Romans concerns only the terms on which that righteousness is to be attained. That is probably much too simple. In the actual course of the Letter all three of the major terms of this text undergo basic redefinition and turn out to have more than one level of meaning. For example, while Paul is certainly concerned with human believing, his Greek term for "faith," as in the LXX version of Hab. 2:4, is also used for the faithfulness of God on which human trusting rests. It appears wiser, therefore, not to press this key "title" verse too hard at this point but to allow Paul's own line of thought to disclose his understanding of it.

1:18–11:36

The Central Argument

Rom. 1:18–11:36 forms a first major whole in the composition of Romans; chaps. 12–16 draw important consequences for the readers, but move at another level and incorporate materials of a quite different nature. One should avoid characterizing the first as "theological" or "dogmatic" and the second as "ethical" or "didactic," for in both parts Paul uses theological arguments of many kinds to inform, instruct, and guide his readers. Yet this first part of the body of the Letter forms the base and must be taken on its own terms.

1:18–3:20

Preparatory Considerations

A clear indication of the deliberate nature of Romans in comparison with his other Letters is that Paul does not move directly to the central content of his gospel. After the opening address, Jesus Christ is not mentioned until 3:21–26. Instead, Paul carefully prepares his readers and provides a context for his exposition in two ways. First, every interpretation of the meaning of Jesus Christ for human beings implies a certain understanding of the world, a diagnosis of the human condition to which that interpretation is addressed. Since 3:24–25 speak of "redemption in Christ Jesus" and of God's provision of a "means for dealing with sin," this preceding analysis involves mounting a "charge that all human beings, both Jews and Greeks, are under sin" (3:9), demonstrating the world's need for God's saving action. Paul does not leave the diagnosis to be inferred; he develops it at some length. A careful reading of this preparatory argument is thus crucial to a correct perception of his intentions later. Second, more importantly, if the exposition is to be persuasive and convincing, this diagnosis of the human predicament must also come to terms with the perceptions religious people have already formed about it. The tendency of religious moralists, in their scrutiny of the world about them, is to exempt themselves from their own negative judgments upon others. But since Paul wants to set forth the gospel as God's way of working for the salvation of all persons without distinction, he must also demonstrate that all stand on the same footing before God. This requires him to question certain typical and recurrent religious assumptions about God and about the terms on which salvation and life are bestowed on human beings. These two strategies of preparation are intimately intertwined in these first three chapters.

1:18–32, The Operation of God's Wrath in the World. Somewhat surprisingly, the point at which Paul begins is not human activity but God's. The word "sin" does not appear until 3:9. In striking parallelism to his claim that in the gospel God's righteousness is revealed (1:17), he asserts that on the wider stage of the world apart from the gospel what is being disclosed is God's wrath in action upon and against human beings who suppress God's truth. Paul is quite specific about that suppression. Human beings have had every opportunity to know God, indeed they have known God. Nevertheless, "in spite of knowing God, they did not honor him as God or give thanks to him" (v. 21). That is the central failure; everything else is a consequence of that. To be sure, it is a failure of human beings; they are responsible and indeed without excuse. But in presenting those consequences of their behavior, Paul insists three times (vv. 24, 26, 28) that it is God who has been at work.

Several features of this rehearsal call for attention. The first is the very notion of "the wrath of God." While the wrath of the gods plays a role in many religions, in Israelite thought it had come to be understood as God's response to human provocation that violates the divine holiness and majesty (cf. 1 Sam. 5:6; 6:9; 2 Sam. 6:7). Following the trend of postbiblical Judaism, the NT writers tend to avoid terms for divine anger and rage that occur in Greek literature, to play down the elements of passion and arbitrariness, and to link the term "wrath" with God's impartial and just judgment, his zeal for righting the wrongs that have afflicted his creation (cf. such quite different texts as 1 Enoch 91:7 and Wisd. of Sol. 5:17–20; → Wrath). The interpretation of "the wrath of God" is subject to two tendencies. One is to construe it as an impersonal process of moral retribution built into the very structure of the world, a cosmic nemesis, to sunder it from belief in a living God. The other is to overpersonalize it and to dismiss it as too human language for God. But recognition of the background to Paul's use of this phrase in apocalyptic and wisdom traditions as represented by 1 Enoch and the Wisdom of Solomon makes clear that his intent is not to trivialize the distance between the human and the divine but to sharpen the sense for God's transcendent presence in the face of, and in spite of, human suppression of his truth. The revelation of God's wrath is here the reverse side of the manifestation of his righteousness; it is God's divinity asserting itself where it is not recognized by human beings. Paul does not suggest that the revelation of God's wrath is in any way the content of the gospel. Nor does he suggest that God's wrath is revealed to some (the ungodly) while his righteousness is revealed to others (the godly), as though God had different "faces" for different classes of people. The scope of Paul's canvas has no limits; in speaking of both sorts of revelation, he has all humankind in view. And there is no suggestion that the revelation of God's wrath belongs only to a bygone era, that it has been replaced by a revelation of God's righteousness, as though the two "faces" of God succeed each other. The revelation of God's righteousness in the gospel does not take place against the backdrop of the absence of God from a world that has repudiated him; its other side is God's reacting presence in a world over which he remains in charge even when it defies him.

The second feature of this depiction of God's wrath is the way in which it is executed. The passage has many similarities to the literature of Hellenistic Judaism, especially Wisdom

of Solomon 11–15. In keeping with that tradition, there is a kind of ironic appropriateness to the reversals that follow upon human behavior "in order that they might learn that a person is punished by those very things by which one sins" (Wisd. of Sol. 11:16): failure to perceive God's power and deity with the "mind" brings a darkening of the mind (Rom. 1:20–21); those who claim to be wise turn out to be fools (v. 22); disregard for the creator obliterates the distinction between creator and creature and produces confusion about what befits nature and what violates it (vv. 25–26). The climax is reached in a traditional and artfully patterned "vice list" (vv. 29–31), the force of which derives from its cumulative impact in portraying an ordered world that has turned to moral chaos. Three times (vv. 23, 25, 26) human beings are said to have "exchanged" or "substituted" one reality for another, and three times (vv. 24, 26, 28) God is said to have given them up or "delivered them over" to the consequences of their own action. The language Paul uses, especially in depicting the power of human sensuality in vv. 26–27 (v. 27, "they were burned out by lust"), conveys the strong impression of a resulting impairment and perversion. This is not the outburst of an offended Victorian, though Paul does break off in v. 25 to utter a liturgical prayer at the thought of worshiping God's creature in place of the creator. It is the response of a representative Hellenistic Jew to the spectacle of God's grand creation, which includes human sexuality, deformed. There is a moral dimension to this distortion, as the vice list shows, but the depiction itself is surprisingly free from moralizing. Idolatry and the abuse of sexual distinctions are not here the objects or cause of God's wrath but the symptoms of its operation, examples of the disorders that result from the root failure to honor God or give thanks to him. The worst distortions are those of human religious practice. "One does not thumb one's nose at God" (Gal. 6:7b); suppressions of his truth produce corresponding negative realities to press with a new fatefulness upon the human race and shape its world. That is how a wrath traditionally associated with God's final judgment is already now being disclosed.

A third significant feature of this sober assessment of the world's condition is that the argument presupposes throughout that God is indeed known from his works, his deity manifest in his handiwork. Here too Paul shows his roots in a Hellenistic Judaism flavored with the language of Stoicism (cf. Wisd. of Sol. 13:1–9). But he emphasizes the initiative of God in making himself known (Rom. 1:19b) and universalizes access to this knowledge. The knowledge of God is not the special attainment of an intellectual elite, nor is godlessness the result of ignorance. This knowledge is not only open to all, it is given to all, "with the result that they are (all) without excuse" (v. 20b). Paul does not suggest that God is by nature or in principle unknowable, nor does he propose that what the world worships as an "unknown God" the Christian gospel now makes known (cf. the Lucan representation of Paul on the Areopagus, Acts 17:23). He does not, like the author of the Fourth Gospel, claim that no one has ever seen or known God and that the point of Christ's coming was to make him known (John 1:18). The foundation lines of Paul's argument are laid down differently: God has been known, yet he has not been recognized or honored as God. Such an argument requires one to think of the knowledge of God on two levels: God is known, yet remains unknown; not necessarily unknown but actually unknown—and that paradox is the paradox of human sinfulness itself, which is not necessary but actually universal. That the manifest God should remain without the recognition and obedience due him is the fundamental perversion of the relationship between creator and creature that draws every other kind of distortion in its wake.

We may for a moment anticipate Paul's later argument: the knowledge of God at this deeper level of recognition and honor, which otherwise is never actual because of the power of sin, is reached when the defeat of sin's power in Christ makes available a new life of obedience and righteousness. The whole argument of Romans may be summed up as an exposition of God's way of rectifying, setting right, that flawed relationship by his Son, Jesus (to whom Paul refers in his earliest Letter as "the one who delivers us from the impending wrath," 1 Thess. 1:10). In the present section, some consequences of that failure of human beings to honor God are in abuse of their bodies (Rom. 1:24), a distorted form of worship (v. 25), and a "reprobate mind," i.e., one no longer capable of discerning good and evil (v. 28). After the conclusion of this whole argument, as Paul opens the other major division of his Letter, he appeals to his readers to make their own that new life Christ has brought: ". . . present your bodies as a living sacrifice . . . which is your appropriate worship . . . be transformed by the renewal of your mind so that you may discern what the will of God is" (12:1–2).

2:1–16, Moral and Religious Persons Before an Impartial God.
So far Paul has not needed to name those he has been describing for he has been referring to all inhabitants of God's creation. There has been one specification in 1:18: God's wrath is "against all ungodliness and wickedness on the part of those who by their wickedness suppress the truth." Now it is the inevitable reaction of all moral and religious people, all those who would agree with the preceding diagnosis of the world's condition, to suppose that these words exempt them from the wrath of God. The clear and simple purpose of this next section is to close off that imagined escape.

The first six verses make this apparent. It is a mistake to picture Paul as a prosecutor indicting first the Gentile (in chap. 1) and now the Jew (in chap. 2). Rom. 3:9 may state his conclusion, but it does not describe his method. He does not now "prove" that religious moralists (there is no direct focus on the Jew until v. 17) in fact do the same things that they condemn in others. He simply assumes that they do (v. 1c). The moralist knows perfectly well the terms of God's judgment (v. 2, anticipated in 1:32). That is not the point. It is the presumption of those who put themselves on God's side in passing judgment, their illusory notion that they are exempt from judgment (v. 3), and the resulting "contempt" (v. 4) for a divine goodness and patience that ought to lead them to repentance, that is "storing up" God's wrath against them (→ Judgment, Day of). For their denial of their own accountability to God is simply their form of a knowledge of God that fails to "honor God or give thanks to him" (1:21). In its place, in vv. 6–11, Paul rings the changes on God's impartial judgment; all persons without exemption, "the Jew first and also the Greek," stand on the same footing before God and must face the consequences of their actions, whether for good or ill. Just how axiomatic this impartiality of God is for Paul is shown by the form in which Ps. 62:12 is echoed in v. 6, as an adjectival clause, almost an epithet for God. Paul's main point here stands firmly in the prophetic tradition; Amos (9:10), Micah (2:6–7), and Jeremiah (2:35; 14:13–16) all had to counter the tendency of religious people to turn trust in God into a self-immunization from his judgment, a shield behind which to evade accountability.

Just as Amos's oracles begin with the nations around Israel's periphery only to zero in on his own people (Amos 1:2–2:16), so Paul's argument quickly becomes more specific. Since he has referred now "to the Jew first and also the Greek" (resuming Rom. 1:16), the last verses of this section (2:12–16) press the point of their equal standing before God in terms of the one thing that most conspicuously divides them. Twice in one verse (v. 14) the Gentiles are defined as those who do not have the (Mosaic) law. The point of the verse is not to say that somehow Gentiles too have that law. What v. 12 states negatively, that the absence or presence of the law makes no difference in the consequences of human sinning, vv. 13–14 put positively: performance counts, and non-Jews who do "the things of the law" on their own, without being enjoined by the Mosaic law (this is the natural sense in Greek of the phrase "by nature"), do not need the Mosaic law when they come before God as their judge. Their conscience and the very existence of their moral disputations demonstrate their accountability for their own deeds (→ Conscience). Paul carefully avoids saying that the law itself is "written on their hearts," which to a Jew could only mean the end-time realization of perfect obedience on the part of God's people (cf. Jer. 31:33).

2:17-29, The Jew Before an Impartial God.

If the point that no one is exempt from accountability to God is to be carried through all the way, it must be made with explicit reference to the exemplary religious person. So Paul, in one of the most dramatically rhetorical passages in all his Letters, addresses the Jew directly in the second person singular—not because the Jew is the enemy or guilty of violation of God's law, but just because this person represents the very best in Paul's religious world, indeed the highest claims of his own religious tradition. Verses 17–21a are a single sentence, in which Paul itemizes a whole series of convictions that both reflected and shaped the Jewish sense of identity and of mission in the world during the intertestamental period. It is easy to translate with a sarcastic tone, but Paul has a sure eye for Jewish self-respect and pride, and the argument turns on that, not on Paul's demeaning his own tradition. The prerogatives of Judaism listed here (cf. Rom. 9:4–5 for a less polemic enumeration) revolve around possession of the law as the hallmark of distinction from the non-Jewish world and are climaxed in v. 20b in the strikingly Hellenistic phrase, "possessing in the law the very embodiment of knowledge and truth," i.e., the answer to all human inquiry and searching. This possession notwithstanding, the rhetorical denouement at the end puts four ironic questions, two of which directly echo the Decalogue, challenging the Jew to answer to the same divine interrogation that every religious person is inclined to proclaim to the surrounding world. Using in v. 24 a text from Isa. 52:5 that referred to the scorn of the Babylonians for the apparent weakness of the God of the Israelite exiles in their midst, Paul turns to charge that the goal of every serious religious person, to bring honor to God, is in fact subverted into its opposite by those who presume to judge the world but themselves evade accountability to God by taking their prerogatives as surrogates for obedience.

Returning in vv. 25–29 to his more sober argumentative style, Paul singles out circumcision, the most vivid symbol of individual participation in the covenant in the Hellenistic period, to make the point that all the formal tokens of religious identity depend for their meaning and validity on actual obedience, thus putting Jew and non-Jew once again on exactly the same footing before an impartial God. In

the last two verses, far from obliterating the identity of the Jew, Paul proceeds to redefine and reclaim it by contrasting what is public and secret, flesh and heart, letter and spirit. (This last contrast, repeated in Rom. 7:6 and 2 Cor. 3:6, has become a major idiom of theological language.) Genuine religious identity (including that of the Jew in the first instance) is at once authentically human and immune to human manipulation, hidden except to God. Its ultimate approbation depends on the God who judges truly, not on human appraisal. This radical appeal from all outward criteria to an inner religious integrity known and determined by God alone is a positive ingredient in Paul's preparatory argument in Rom. 1:18– 3:20, apart from which his negative indictment (3:9) cannot be rightly understood. It taps the deep lode of the OT prophets' critique of religion and is reminiscent of the sharp juxtaposition in the Sermon on the Mount between the visible marks of piety and what is recognized by "your Father who sees in secret" (Matt. 6:4, 6, 18).

3:1-8, Two Objections Anticipated.

A characteristic feature of Paul's didactic style is exemplified in this section. Not only does he directly address an imagined interlocutor in the second person, as in 2:17–24 he anticipates responses and answers them, thus ensuring that his own major conclusions are not misunderstood. Whereas in his other Letters such dialogic interchange remains occasional, it is an index to the deliberate quality of the presentation in Romans that such rhetorical questions and replies mark stages in the argument and provide clues to the structuring of the Letter (cf. 3:9; 6:1, 15; 7:7, 13; 9:14; 11:1, 11).

As is often the case, the first question (3:1) arises with unrelenting logic out of the preceding section: if that religious integrity that really counts before God has no connection with religious distinctions, what is the point of being a Jew? The question is only partially answered. The Jew has an "advantage" but it consists in the initiative and faithfulness of God, which does not depend on human fidelity. The answer is only partial because the question still lurks whether, in treating Jew and non-Jew on equal terms, God has not himself broken faith with the "direct utterances" he has entrusted to the Jews. That momentous issue, the connection between God's faithfulness and Israel's past election and future destiny, is suppressed here for full discussion in chaps. 9–11. Deferring that side of God's faithfulness, Paul focuses for the moment on God's truth and righteousness instead. One who genuinely honors God will desire, in the words of the central penitential psalm of the Hebrew Scriptures (Ps. 51:4) that God be "justified [i.e., acknowledged to be right] whenever he speaks and be vindicated whenever he enters into court proceedings with his people." Justification, on its first appearance in Romans, is not the justification of human beings but the vindication of God himself in the face of a world that fails to honor him as God and in the face of evasive religious substitutes for obedience.

This reply only hastens the second objection in vv. 5–8; if God is vindicated no matter what the infidelities of human beings, what grounds are there for condemnation or wrath at all? Paul responds by turning the train of thought in the opposite direction: the certainty that God is the judge of the world makes such a protestation ridiculous. But the question only takes new forms. God's prerogative to judge may stand, but what about his integrity and the moral consequences? Wickedness and sin seem no longer to mean anything. Why not conclude "let us do evil that good may come"? For a moment the curtain is lifted on personal charges that have been leveled against Paul. But once again no real answer is provided (until, in this case, 6:1–7:6), for a proper rejoinder cannot come until Paul has begun his positive account of justification. Until then, there is only a rough dismissal: people who talk like that deserve what they get.

3:9–20, The Solidarity of Jew and Gentile Under the Power of Sin and Before the Law. Having for the moment set these objections to one side, Paul returns to his main line of thought to draw up his indictment. There is some subtlety to the way he resumes the question of the Jew's "advantage" in v. 9. At first he seems flatly to take back what he had granted in v. 2. But he has been very careful so far—and remains so throughout Romans—not simply to obliterate the distinction between Jew and Gentile even though he insists that they stand as equals before God. It is the last point that now comes emphatically to the fore. Whatever the "advantage," it makes no difference in this: all human beings, both Jews and Greeks, are "under sin." This first mention of "sin" in Romans personifies it as an oppressing power, setting a pattern that holds for the rest of the Letter. The "evidence" to verify the charge is not merely empirical; it is certified by Scripture, here cited in a carefully constructed collage of passages from the Psalms and Isaiah that declares first the nonexistence of a single righteous person and then catalogues the symptoms of human debasement in speech and action. At the end, Paul makes sure there is no room left for religious self-exemption. The "law" (which here includes the passages just cited from Psalms and Isaiah and thus stands for the whole of the Hebrew Scriptures, as in 1 Cor. 14:21) makes this declaration "to those who are covered by the law," the Jews as well as Gentiles. It follows that the whole world is not only answerable to God but indictable. Something of Paul's distinctive

view of the Mosaic law emerges when he goes a step further to declare this silencing of every self-defense to be the very purpose of that law, a statement for which no Jewish parallel is known. The psalmist, calling on God for deliverance, had cried (Ps. 143:1c–2, LXX):

> In thy righteousness, hear me!
> Enter not into judgment with thy servant;
> for no one living shall be found
>   righteous before thee.

By adding to that last line the expression "by works of the law," Paul had already in Gal. 2:16 constructed a motto, which he now repeats (v. 20a). The true religious integrity that enables authentic obedience, but which all humankind lacks, cannot itself be produced by performing any deeds enjoined by the law. That would amount to self-salvation. It is precluded by the power of sin, which renders the law impotent to produce the obedience it calls for (cf. Rom. 8:3–4; Gal. 3:21b). Instead, "all that law does is to tell us what is sinful" (JB).

3:21–8:39
The Justification of the Unrighteous

The right knowledge of God that truly honors God as God and gives thanks to him, the proper relationship of creature to creator, and the genuine integrity that issues in true obedience are all wanting because of the power of sin. That void cannot be filled by human effort to live by the Mosaic law. Only a fresh initiative on God's part can recover for all human life a right relationship to him, the power of a new beginning, a restored integrity, and a hope for a future share in God's own glory. That this fresh initiative for the salvation of all has been effectively taken in Jesus Christ is the heart of Paul's gospel (1:16), and it is to the positive exposition of that claim that he turns at this point and for the remainder of his Letter. Such a comprehensive claim requires an appropriately rich language. In Paul's usage, the controlling terms are "righteousness" and "justification"—first of God and then of human beings. This creates some problems of understanding for modern readers, but the first solution, as in every instance of listening to another person, is to follow his own explanatory line of thought, for these are not the only words or concepts Paul uses. Each subsequent unit of Romans adds another dimension to Paul's presentation of his gospel and so refines his use of these terms.

3:21–26, The Death of Jesus Christ as the Revelation of God's Righteousness. The most important step Paul takes in this introductory passage is to locate God's fresh saving initiative in the death of Jesus on the cross, the first mention of Christ in the argument of the Letter. What is significant about Jesus here is not his teaching, his preaching or expectation of the kingdom of God, or his moral behavior, but his death. The righteousness of God now manifest apart from law is thus not first of all a divine attribute or a human moral quality bestowed by God and exemplified in Jesus' life, but God's delivering activity in the death of Jesus. Not until later does Paul elaborate his own understanding of the way this death alters the human situation. For the moment he simply accepts and uses in v. 25 what appears to be an early summary Jewish-Christian liturgical statement of the meaning of Jesus' death in terms drawn from the OT institution of sacrifice. It refers to that death as an "expiation," a place or means of removing or covering sin. Since the Greek word behind this expression is used in the LXX (e.g., Exod. 25:17) for the "mercy seat," the slab on top of the Ark of the covenant that was sprinkled with the blood of the sin offering on the Day of Atonement, this liturgical language may have been composed originally to affirm that Jesus' death surpasses and replaces the atonement ritual of the Jewish Temple (cf. Heb. 9). But the reference to the Temple may not be so direct; the same Greek term is used for the vicarious atoning effect of the deaths of the Jewish martyrs in the early Hasmonean revolt (4 Macc. 17:22; →Maccabees). In either case, Jesus' death is understood in terms of the atoning efficacy of the blood of a sacrificed life, i.e., its power to remove not only the consciousness of sin on the part of those involved but also its objective consequences in the world, to break the guilt-punishment sequence that follows violations of God's will (→Atonement; Expiation). Even elsewhere Paul does not develop such sacrificial ideas, though he frequently betrays their presence in his Christian traditions (cf. 1 Cor. 15:3; Gal. 1:4). Here he uses this traditional language to make a number of points that further his present argument.

The first is to emphasize God's own initiative in freely providing a solution to the problem described in the preceding chapters. The undeserved quality of this deliverance as a "free gift," prompted by God's own graciousness ("his grace" is not the gift itself but the generosity that produces it), will be developed further in Rom. 5:1–11. Here Paul calls it "redemption," using a figure of speech for salvation that still has some of the financial overtones of its everyday sense (cf. 1 Cor. 6:20; 7:23; →Redemption). But the emphasis is on its releasing effect. There is no suggestion whatsoever of compulsion on God to pay a price to anyone other than himself. What God has undertaken, in the formula Paul quotes, is "expiation," a means for dealing with human sin, and not "propitiation," a means for meeting God's

wrath by offering something to appease it. In all Paul's references to atonement, Christ was crucified "for us," never for God; always as a gift, never as punishment.

That leads to the second point. Paul does not play God's graciousness off against his righteousness. Instead, God's gift in the death of Jesus is itself a manifestation of God's righteousness apart from the Mosaic law. In clear continuity with the OT, especially the Psalms and Second Isaiah (Isa. 40–55), the righteousness of God is in the first place his saving action in coming to the aid of his people, his "deliverance" (e.g., Isa. 46:13; Pss. 31:1; 143:1). But vv. 25b–26, resuming a note struck in 3:3–4, show that Paul understands righteousness to refer also to a quality of integrity and consistency on God's part. God cannot go back on himself; his faithfulness to his own covenant commitments means that the working of his wrath, which abandons human beings to the consequences of their actions (and which Paul never equates with his righteousness), cannot be the last word. Even patience and forbearance cannot, for by themselves they would mean God's capitulation in the end to the disorder and distortion in his creation. Justification cannot mean simply acceptance and amnesty, though it includes these. God's claim over his own creation must finally be demonstrated by renewing its right relation to him and in this way restoring to it its own integrity and order. What justification, as this bestowal of a new righteousness and obedience, means for human beings will be discussed in Rom. 6:1–7:6. But in the meantime what is demonstrated in Christ's death is God's own integrity precisely in his acting to restore integrity to every person whose righteousness comes by faith in Jesus.

That faith is the third point. Four times in this paragraph Paul has inserted references to faith or believing (twice in v. 22; vv. 25, 26). Just what faith is like will become clear from the example of Abraham in chap. 4. But if a true relationship to God cannot be brought about by human action, faith cannot mean some prerequisite condition to be fulfilled by human beings before God can act. It is not human performance at all (4:4–5). It describes, in deliberate contrast to the law, the terms on which God's rectifying action is taken. These terms are that Jew and non-Jew alike trust God, i.e., rely completely for the renewal of life on his act in Christ, just as Paul has staked his own life on the gospel (1:16). Only these terms put all human beings on the same footing before God.

3:27–31, Jew and Gentile Before an Impartially Justifying God. This section presses the previous point about faith in two ways. First, God's generous provision of a way out of the human predicament absolutely precludes the "boasting" that was detailed at some length in chap. 2, that vaunting of the advantage or position of one group over against another that evades accountability to God, violates his impartiality, and denies the dependence of all on him for life. In explaining why this is so, Paul repeats in positive form (v. 28) the motto that was stated negatively in 3:20. The Mosaic law, by requiring certain behavior, appears to encourage "boasting" by suggesting that such behavior does not depend on a right relationship to God but can create it in the first place. Over against this Paul sets "the law of faith" (v. 27c), an expression without parallel in his Letters but similar to "the law of the spirit of life" in 8:2 and "the law of Christ" in Gal. 6:2. Contrary to appearance, the Mosaic law presumes complete trust in God and reliance on his prior salvation, and so does preclude this "boasting." In both Hebrew and Greek, one word for "faith" denotes both God's trustworthiness and reliability and the trust and reliance on him that is the appropriate human counterpart made possible by God's own faithfulness. This kind of trust is not a prerequisite for a healthy relationship to God; it is that right relationship. That is why faith is almost always mentioned when Paul writes about justification.

Second, v. 29 makes clear that behind these opposite and incompatible aspects or effects of law, one producing "boasting" and the other excluding it in favor of trust, is the fundamental issue of God himself. Every human claim to special position or advantage before God denies that all stand on an equal footing in relation to him. By making God the patron of this or that constituency, it carries with it the implicit denial that God is the God of all human beings. But that, Paul points out, contradicts the central watchword of Judaism that God is one (Deut. 6:4; → Shema). This creed requires one to embrace instead Paul's central claim that Jew and non-Jew alike are rightly related to God on the same terms. It is striking that in repeating that claim, while he denies any difference in standing, Paul still carefully refuses to obliterate the distinction itself between Jew and Gentile. Nor, he adds, does his argument signal a dismissal of the Mosaic law. Instead, "we confirm the law." Only the later stages of Paul's argument can fill out what he means by that.

4:1–25, Abraham: The Paradigm of Justification and of Faith.
At one level Paul understands his gospel to "confirm" the law (3:31) by the general congruity with the OT that he now proceeds to demonstrate with the example of Abraham. But this is a very loose sort of confirmation, requiring Paul to return to the specific issue of law later. Actually the appeal he now

makes to the OT confirms his gospel, and therein lies its significance. The credibility of his own position is at stake. Since he had contended that this new demonstration of God's righteousness apart from the law was attested already in "the law and the prophets" (3:21), a whole range of claims made in 3:21–30 has to be made good with scriptural arguments if they are to stand. One of the most important premises shared by the early Christian communities with their Jewish antecedents was that Scripture provides reliable access to God's truth. Paul would really have to abandon his gospel if such verification were not available. The appeal to Scripture is thus a form of appeal to God himself to substantiate his message. Paul can claim a hearing from an unknown congregation only because he stands himself under the authorization that Scripture provides (cf. commentary above on 1:1–7), and this explains why OT quotations form such a conspicuous part of Romans. The methods by which Paul constructs these arguments are of course those of first-century Judaism; its study and use of Scripture is on the one hand itself a tradition in which he stands and from which he draws. On the other hand, his recourse to Scripture, exactly like every use of tradition throughout human history, is a selective process in which his own priorities and perspectives become evident. By appealing, one might say, over the head of Moses, the lawgiver, to Abraham, the recipient of the promise, Paul signals his own understanding of what is pivotal in his own Jewish tradition and reclaims it to authenticate his gospel for his readers. Even this appeal to Abraham is selective. The traditions about the patriarch appear to have been extraordinarily varied in Paul's time. Abraham was a heroic figure whose story could be used to support a variety of ends. This can be seen within the NT itself. In James 2:21–24, the same verse Paul cites (Gen. 15:6) is quoted, but because it is read in the light of Abraham's offering of his son Isaac (Gen. 22:2, 9), the conclusion drawn from it is exactly contrary to Paul's. So it might seem that Paul's appeal to Scripture is circular in nature, drawing out of it only what his gospel has already determined he will find in it. But that suspicion attaches to any use of the past. The integrity of the appeal can be ascertained only be examining its inner logic in each particular instance.

In chap. 4, this invoking of Abraham proceeds in several clearly recognizable steps. In the first (vv. 2–8), Abraham, whose status in the collective memory as a paragon of rectitude is beyond question, confirms what Paul has just written in 3:27–28: boasting is precluded if a right relationship to God is determined by faith. Verses 4–5 state the mutually exclusive alternatives that shape the argument: justification is either earned or it is a matter of grace; it rests either on achievement or on trust in a God who justifies the ungodly. The place of "grace" in the contrast of v. 4 is taken by "trust" in that of v. 5. And the text of Gen. 15:6 clearly states that it was Abraham's believing God that God "regarded" as righteousness. Even Abraham was dependent on a God who "justifies the ungodly," who does not merely confirm the virtues of good people but takes the initiative in restoring a world that cannot save itself. Is that so clear if Abraham was such an exemplary figure? Was Abraham ungodly? To close that loophole, Paul applies two well-established procedures of early rabbinic exegesis, adducing a second text that repeats some wording of the first, and supporting a text from the law (the Pentateuch) with another from the prophets or the Psalms. Here it is the traditional penitential Ps. 32:1–2a that fills the breach, for it shows that "reckoning righteousness" is the equivalent of "not reckoning sin," i.e., forgiveness. Abraham, the model of religious probity, was as dependent on God's gracious initiative as David, the paradigmatic repentant sinner (assumed to be the author of that psalm). This yoking of Psalm 32 with the Genesis text intercepts such a use of the latter as is made in James 2. So the precedent of Abraham confirms that God's justifying proceeds on the basis of trust in his undeserved graciousness and leaves no room for "boasting."

The second step (vv. 9–12) rests on chronological sequence: God's consideration of Abraham's faith as righteousness precedes his covenant with Abraham and Abraham's circumcision (Gen. 17:1–27). The outward marks of Abraham the prototype Jew are therefore secondary to the faith that makes him a "true Jew" (cf. 2:28–29). Another side of Abraham, his role as ancestor, like the blessing of the Psalm just quoted, turns out to embrace all who believe without circumcision. Even in the relation of his physical descendants to him, the controlling factor in his patriarchal function is trust in God, theirs and his. So the precedent of Abraham also confirms that the terms of faith established by God for justification apart from the law mean that Jew and non-Jew stand on the same footing before an impartial God. In saying so, Paul again carefully avoids, this time only by tortured Greek syntax, a simple denial of the distinction between them (cf. 3:30).

In vv. 13–17 a third side of this powerfully symbolic figure Abraham emerges: he was the recipient of God's promise for the future. In Gen. 15:4–5 this promise was for an heir and descendants (Rom. 4:18); in Gen. 17:6–7 it was for many nations among these descendants (Rom. 4:17); by Paul's own time (Sir. 44:21) the tradition had expanded it into an end-time promise of inheriting the whole world (Rom. 4:13), a code word for all the benefits that the descendants of the patriarch might hope for. Paul's point now is that the transmission of this legacy is determined not by law but by "the righteousness of faith." This expression, used only here in Paul's Letters, directly echoes v. 11 in Greek: it is "the righteousness that was attributed to the faith [Abraham had] in the uncircumcised state" he was in when he believed. One might expect Paul to use a chronological argument again (Abraham preceded Moses), but his own reason in v. 14 is more forceful: "If the heirs are those whom the law defines as heirs, then faith is empty and this promise has been voided." The issue is not what human beings do at all, whether they adhere to the law or whether they believe (as a substitute achievement). What is at stake is the competence to determine who the heirs are. Clearly that capability does not belong to the law, whose effect is rather to evoke wrath by marking human conduct as transgression and so to disqualify people from the inheritance (v. 15; cf. 3:20, 31; 5:13, 20). (These accumulating side remarks about the law will require special treatment. See commentary below on 7:7–12.) The terms that do define the transmission are faith (God's trustworthiness and human reliance upon God) and promise, for that is the only way in which the legacy can remain a matter of God's undeserved graciousness and so be guaranteed to all the descendants of Abraham impartially in the inclusive patriarchal role that the promise itself assigned to him (Rom. 4:17a).

In these three ways Abraham confirms the gospel's description of God's justification of the unrighteous. He not only provides the illustrative example; he furnishes the determining precedent for the way in which God deals with human beings. God has not changed between Abraham and Christ. In Christ he has done what Abraham trusted him to do. So Abraham's precedent helps interpret what God has done in Christ. Verse 17 restores this focus on Abraham's God, who not only justifies the ungodly but also gives life to the dead and calls into being the things that are not. That places justification as a life-giving act in an all-embracing context. God is the creator of life at the world's beginning, the one who restores order and integrity to life in the world's dissolutions, the one who bestows eternal life at the world's end.

But what about faith? Having so far provided the paradigm for God's action in justification, Abraham now provides also the model for human believing (vv. 18–22). Faith is not some internal condition in contrast to external acts, nor intellectual assent to propositional truths. It is not anything Abraham "does" (vv. 4–5). Instead, it is his unwavering reliance in hope on God's promise to him. It is to live by another, by what God has done and will do. Verses 19–21 play on the words: instead of being "disabled" at the contemplation of his own and Sarah's bankruptcy of life, Abraham was "empowered" by his confidence in God's "power" to carry out what he had promised, and he gave glory to God.

Verses 23–25 supply the bottom line. Abandoning his descriptive third-person language, Paul for the first time since his opening address shifts to a first-person plural style that signals the confessional stance of the Christian community. Abraham's God, who gives life to the dead, is the God who "raised Jesus our Lord from the dead"; Abraham's justification lies in store for those who trust in this God. The text of Gen. 15:6, which has echoed throughout this chapter, was ultimately written for them. Paul ends by quoting another short two-part Christological formula (v. 25; cf. 1:3–4): "[Jesus], who was delivered over [to death] because of our trespasses and raised for our justification." By employing parallel passive verbs, for both of which God is the implied active agent, the formula unites Jesus' death and resurrection as inseparable parts of a single action by God, one addressed to the expiation and forgiveness of sin, the other to the renewal of life. That justification is the term for the latter brings this whole first part of Paul's argument to a fitting conclusion and prepares the way for the next chapters.

Distinctive Words and Themes in Romans 5–8

From the next section through chap. 8 an undeniable shift takes place, but it is important to note carefully what is altered and what is not. The change of style observed in 4:23–25 continues through chap. 8 except for a brief return to the more objective third person in the second section (5:12–21). Some dominant vocabulary changes. After the first two verses of chap. 5, "faith" and "to believe/trust" are scarcely used, whereas "death" and "life," "to die" and "to live" frequently appear. The "righteousness of God" is not mentioned again until 10:3. "Jew" and "Greek" disappear, along with mention of God's impartiality and faithfulness, until after chap. 8. Clearly there is a move away from the relationship of Christianity to Judaism and its traditions; only two brief quotations from the OT occur (7:7 and 8:36) and exegetical arguments like those of chaps. 3 and 4 drop out until chap. 9. Instead there is a greater focus upon the Christian community and its experience, except again for that block in 5:12–21.

New theological terms appear, such as "enmity" and "reconciliation," "slavery" and

"freedom," "adoption" and "peace." God's love and the (Holy) Spirit enter the discussion for the first time (and together, 5:5). Yet all this does not mean that the treatment of the justification of the unrighteous has been abandoned. Indeed in some respects it has become more focused: the forensic language of indictment and acquittal becomes more specific than it has ever been so far (5:13–14, 18–19; 7:1–3; 8:1, 3, 31–34); in just these passages Paul provides his own most telling reformulations of justification. Furthermore, if "righteousness" is now no longer "the righteousness of God," its new referent is the quality of rectitude and integrity in human life that belongs with obedience to God; it has a new synonym in "consecration" (or "sanctification"), a term that establishes a link in Greek with the word "saints" Paul had used in his address for "Christians" (1:7; 6:19, 22; cf. 1 Cor. 1:30; → Sanctification).

Law and sin continue to receive detailed attention, especially their relation to each other (5:20–21; 7:1–25). But above all, chaps. 5–8 (5:12–21 is now not an exception) continue the connection made in 3:25 to the death of Jesus and elaborate, first from one side and then another, Paul's understanding of its meaning and consequences for all human beings as well as for baptized Christians. The clue provided in 4:25 turns out to be the right one to follow: the "justification of the unrighteous" means for Paul not only forgiveness and acquittal but God's gift in Jesus Christ of a reordered life and hope as well. It is the burden of chaps. 5–8 to set forth this side of Paul's gospel, without any fundamental change of subject.

5:1–11, Justification Interpreted as Reconciliation: The Death of Jesus Christ as the Basis of Confidence and Hope. In this section readers encounter a variety of new ideas for the first time in Romans; the task is to ascertain their relationship to each other and to what has preceded. Paul begins by saying that justification results in peace in one's relationship to God. Verses 8 and 10 show that peace here is the removal of enmity toward God by the reconciliation effected in Jesus' death. It is not God who is reconciled but human beings, because the enmity is not God's; it is human opposition and resistance to God (Rom. 8:7–8; → Reconciliation). The removal of this barrier opens up access to "this grace" (v. 2), which is not a human condition but the undeserved graciousness on God's part that has been a key element in Paul's earlier argument (3:24; 4:4, 16). It may be "the sphere of God's grace, where we now stand" (NEB), for Paul later declares that his readers are "under grace" (6:14). In the present context, however, it seems to be that graciousness by which men and women are sustained through the trials of life, for to hold firm or fast under stress is the usual meaning of the everyday word "to stand" in Paul's Letters. But the most significant connection with the earlier chapters is concealed in many English translations, perhaps unavoidably. Both at the beginning of this section and at the end, Paul speaks of "rejoicing" (ASV, RSV, TEV), "glorying" (KJV), or "exulting" (NEB). The Greek root is the same one translated up to this point in the Letter as "boasting" (2:17, 23; 3:27; 4:2), for Paul has been describing that self-protective, unrepentant, and presumptuous confidence in God that is a recurring trait of religious people but that is irreconcilable with trust. Against that illegitimate confidence, Paul now sets a legitimate sort of "joyful trust in God through our Lord Jesus Christ" (v. 11, JB). What makes possible the change from one to the other is God's undeserved justification of the unrighteous in Jesus' death because it eliminates the need for that instinctive self-defensiveness before God that Paul calls "enmity." Verses 3 and 4 contain a rhetorical sequence (cf. 8:29–30; 10:14) that draws attention to this life as one of suffering, testing, and patient perseverance. The point is that this legitimate confidence provides staying power through the afflictions of life because it enables those who enjoy it to be "looking forward to God's glory" (JB). And this hope does not "put to shame," it does not in the end expose those who entertain it to the embarrassment of having followed a false hope (cf. Paul's own statement in 1:16). Why not? Because God has already demonstrated his love for human beings in Jesus' death (v. 8). In the meantime, Paul declares that God's love has been "poured out" in human hearts (v. 5), a striking statement found nowhere else in the Bible. Once (Sir. 18:11) it is God's mercy that is poured out; frequently it is his wrath; but the conventional language is that God pours out his Spirit (cf. the narrative of Pentecost, Acts 2:17, citing Joel 2:28). Since v. 8 makes clear that "love of God" here means God's love for human beings, not their love for God, Paul is equating the sustaining assurance of God's demonstration of his love in the death of Jesus with the life-giving power of the Spirit, which is God's own recreating presence with human beings in the world in spite of its afflictions and threats.

Just how the death of Jesus provides such supportive assurance for the future is spelled out in two steps in the second half of this section (vv. 6–10). First, Paul contrasts the death of Jesus with the rare but not impossible heroic death of an individual on behalf of another righteous person or in the name of "the good," some commanding cause like that perhaps of the Jewish martyrs in the Hasmonean revolt, an

event that shaped the consciousness of many Jews under Roman rule in Paul's time. Jesus' death is totally different. Its force as a sustaining demonstration of God's love stems from its having occurred at just such a time as conventional religion would least expect it of God, on behalf of those who in no way deserve it—in short, from its being an act of Abraham's God who "justifies the ungodly" (4:5). Second, by using a standard rabbinic method of inferring a more comprehensive conclusion that is implied in what has already been stated, Paul argues that this given present reality of justification and reconciliation in the death of God's Son makes further salvation by his life "much more certain." So justification is the granting of life in an uncertain world by extending hope and certainty, the certain hope of sharing in the life of Christ for all those who have shared in his death by receiving its benefits of reconciliation.

By filling out in this way the import of Jesus' death for human life, Paul has anticipated dominant themes of chap. 8: present affliction and future hope, enmity and peace, the sustaining power of God's love and of the presence of the Spirit. These are all treated more fully in that climax to his presentation of the justification of the unrighteous. Thus the beginning of chap. 5 and the end of chap. 8 form a bracket marking these chapters as a major whole, distinct in content as well as style (see "Distinctive Words and Themes in Romans 5–8" preceding the commentary above on 5:1–11). The interpreter needs to ask how each subsequent section advances Paul's thought.

5:12–21, Justification Interpreted as Acquittal and Life: The Universal Reign of Grace in Place of the Universal Reign of Sin. Paul himself provides the best summary of this section in an earlier Letter: "For just as in Adam all die, so also in Christ all shall be made alive" (1 Cor. 15:22). A parallelism is drawn between Adam, the biblical progenitor of the human race (Gen. 1:1–2:46; →Adam; Human Being), and Christ. Each is the first of many. Each is also a single individual who represents all others and whose actions determine and affect all others. (Throughout these verses, "the many" and "all people" are simply interchangeable expressions, according to a well-established Semitic and biblical usage; cf., e.g., Isa. 53:6, 12c.) Thus each is perceived as a universal and all-inclusive figure, not only a predecessor but a prototype of all humanity. Yet these two act and affect others in exactly opposite ways so that they are symbolic of antithetical powers and realities of worldwide scope: disobedience and obedience, condemnation and acquittal, sin and righteousness, death and life. All of history is embraced in the cosmic conflict between these powers, a major sign of Paul's indebtedness to the apocalyptic tradition in Judaism (→ Apocalyptic Literature).

The section falls naturally into three parts. The first is vv. 12–14. A full and balanced statement of the analogy between Adam and Christ is not reached until vv. 18–19. But Paul begins to set out the correlation on its negative side in v. 12. Without speculating on the origin of sin and evil, he simply takes for granted the biblical depiction of the original disobedience of Adam and Eve in Gen. 3 (→ Fall, The), with its correlate that death is the consequence of sin (Gen. 2:17; 3:19), in order to affirm the universal penetration of sin and death through Adam to the whole human race. Because the Vulgate (Vg.) Latin translation of v. 12c could be understood as "one man [Adam] ... in whom all sinned," the verse has served for centuries as the main Pauline proof-text for the notion of genetically transmitted sin, but a more natural translation is, "because all sinned." This results in an apparent contradiction, but the verse summarizes a characteristic understanding in Judaism of sin as at once guilt and fate, both an individual responsibility and a destiny that overpowers each person (as in Paul's discussion of God's wrath in 1:18–32; cf. Wisd. of Sol. 1:13; 2:23; Sir. 25:24; 2 Apoc. Bar. 54:15; → Sin). It is to this second aspect that Paul turns first. In the period between Adam and Moses, "in the absence of law," sin was "not counted," i.e., each individual was not held responsible for sin. Nonetheless everyone died, showing clearly the fateful reign of death over all as a result of Adam's action, even over those who had not committed the same kind of explicit transgression of a command as Adam's. In thus determining the fate of others, Adam prefigured Christ. In so distinguishing the period prior to Moses, Paul already has in mind what he refers to later (v. 20) as the "intrusion" of the law.

Verses 15–17 form the second part of the section. Having just touched on the similarity that coordinates the two figures, Paul in these verses underlines the differences between the two sides of the typology. The correlation is decidedly unbalanced, both quantitatively and qualitatively. Death proceeded from a single act, but the gift of life began with a multitude of trespasses. There is a lavish profuseness, an "abounding" surplus on the side of God's gift that explicitly recalls the "much more" of 5:9–10. Paul's vocabulary clearly indicates that he now has in view the situation after Moses, created by the coming of the law. On the one side, trespass, judgment, condemnation, and death emphasize in juridical language the deserved guilt and responsibility of every sinner. On the other side, the language of free gift, grace, extravagant generosity, and life emphasizes the displacement of what is due to all sinners by a totally undeserved gift in God's act of justification (mentioned in v. 16).

Verses 18–21 form the final part of the section. With these verses a difficult train of thought emerges into the clear. Over against the trespass of the one is set "the righteous act" or, better, "the justifyinge" (Tyndale's translation, 1535) of the other (v. 18). Opposite Adam's disobedience, by which all "were constituted sinners," there is Jesus Christ's obedience, by which all "shall be constituted righteous." The restatement of 1 Cor. 15:22 is complete, but it is cast now in the language of justification. Jesus' "obedience," mentioned for the first time in v. 19, is a new explanation for the way in which his whole life, but especially his death, saves others, namely by reversing the effect of Adam's disobedience. This is an independent, alternative interpretation of Jesus' death, alongside "expiation" (3:25), "God's love for us while we were still sinners" (5:8), and "reconciliation" (5:10), and should not be submerged into the notion of atonement. (This use of obedience to explain Jesus' death, and the life that preceded it, appears elsewhere in Paul's Letters only in Phil. 2:8; cf. Heb. 5:8. The idea, though not the word, is much more common in the Gospels, e.g., Matt. 3:15; Mark 14:36 and parallels; John 4:34; 6:38.)

In sum, apart from the law, sin and death (from Adam) and righteousness and life (from Christ) would be similar impersonal and inexorable destinies inflicted upon all people by virtue of the solidarity of all, first with Adam and then with Christ. But Paul returns (v. 20) to that watershed, the "intrusion" of the Mosaic law between Adam and Christ (vv. 13–14). The law adds to trespass the "sting" of condemnation (1 Cor. 15:56; Rom. 4:15). Now that sin is "counted" (v. 13), magnified and deepened by the addition of guilt, death is more than a neutral destiny; it is deserved by all. But by the very same token, now that sin is counted against everyone, life has become something more than a neutral destiny; it is the free and undeserved gift of a gracious God. It has become the overflowing abundance of grace (v. 20). Verse 21 sums up what Paul has said about the law in a remarkable sentence: the purpose of God, served by its "intrusion" on the human scene, is that just as death has been the symptom of the reign of sin as a power over human lives, so righteousness (justification) might become the symptom of the new reign of grace. Just as the law turned the reign of death in Adam (v. 14) into the reign of sin, so that same law has turned the reign of life in Christ (v. 17) into the reign of grace.

It is not the purpose of this section to weigh determinism and free will, a problem that is simply not on Paul's horizon. Chap. 6 will show very clearly that he treats his Christian readers as responsible moral agents. The issue is the universal and pervasive tyranny of sin as a power, and Paul's gospel of an overwhelming liberating power of a grace that has replaced it (cf. 6:14). This section is still about the justification of the unrighteous. It does not just describe justification as the bestowal of life in place of death (5:1–12 does that in its own way). It does not merely portray the cosmic and universal scope of justification over against the universality of death (though it does also do that). It underlines the character of justification as an act of God's undeserved graciousness, elaborating the note struck first in 3:24 and then again in 4:4, 16; 5:2—and does this in such a way as to make the Mosaic law contribute to its grace character.

6:1–7:6, Justification as the Gift of a Reordered Life.

Paul has just made the astonishing claim that one of God's purposes with the Mosaic law was to use its "increase" of sin's power over men and women to augment and reinforce grace. If that is so, one must necessarily ask the question of 6:1: "Are we to continue in sin in order that grace might increase?" Paul's imagined interlocutor has already raised this question as part of an objection pertaining to God's own moral integrity in 3:5–8. It now serves as the transition to another facet of justification. But one should pause for a moment to reflect on its significance. Rom. 3:8 shows its personal importance for Paul, as a charge leveled against him by opponents who presumably thought his teaching undermined the Jewish law and invited irresponsible license in human behavior (cf. Acts 21:21). But the theological importance of the question "Why not sin?" lies in the fact that it is inevitably and regularly raised whenever the claim is made, as here, that human perversity cannot decisively frustrate God's benevolent purpose. Such a claim has always seemed to deny the reality and seriousness of sin, as Rom. 3:5–7 exemplifies. Throughout Christian history, the universal scope that Paul has clearly attributed to grace by pitting it against the worldwide grip of sin and death in 5:12–21 has seemed to undermine everything he set forth in the early chapters about human accountability to God for moral behavior. Every radical message of grace stirs the ghost of libertinism to life. For just that reason, in Rom. 6:1–7:6 Paul does not simply turn aside from his main argument temporarily to put down a local objection. Rather, his answer forms another carefully constructed stage in his presentation of the justification of the unrighteous. Chap. 5 showed that righteousness, the rectitude and integrity restored to human life in its relation to God through the death of Jesus, is "a matter of *grace*" (4:16, my emphasis). It shows God's love for human beings while they are still sinners (5:8); it is an undeserved gift, manifesting the lavish profuseness of God's

generosity (5:17, 20). But in the present section Paul turns the argument in the opposite direction, answering the question of 6:1 by showing that God's grace involves for its recipients a new *righteousness*, a reordering and integrity that preclude an undisturbed continuation of life's previous patterns.

This sudden reversal has seemed to many interpreters to suggest a shift of audience, as though Paul were turning from the Jewish Christian members of the Roman church to the gentile Christians, correcting first the presumed legalistic tendencies of the former and now the libertarian proclivities of the latter. Such a reading gains a certain plausibility from the clear evidence that Paul had previously encountered both of these perennial religious tendencies in the churches he had founded, the one most conspicuously in Galatia and the other in Corinth. But one should avoid projecting stereotypes from his earlier correspondence onto the reading of Romans. There is little support from Paul's argument up to this point for such a hypothetical division. On the contrary, the early emphasis on God's impartiality, the tight construction of his case, and its internal continuities suggest that in this Letter, just because of diverse reactions to his preaching, Paul is fashioning a theological position that will effectively counter both tendencies at the same time. His instrument for doing this is a broad and flexible doctrine of justification that includes both God's free and undeserved initiative in the face of all kinds of conditions that legalism tries to set, and the restoration of integrity to human lives in the face of the moral chaos that libertinism breeds. The resulting exposition here in Romans has always resisted the artificial separation of justification and sanctification, of "forensic" and "sacramental" grace, of "imputed" and "infused" righteousness that the confessional debates of Christian history have produced and tended to impose on these chapters. It is just this separation that results in a corresponding literary isolation of chaps. 6–8 from chaps. 1–5, as though they were not written to the same audience. But this division should be resisted. If the formal instrument Paul uses is now the language of justification, the material heart of his theological position is his interpretation of the death and resurrection of Jesus. It was from this single vantage point that he had argued in both Galatia and Corinth. This remains the case here. As each stage in Romans, from 3:25 on, has involved recourse to the death and resurrection of Jesus as the decisive clue to God's nature and action, so this new section contains Paul's reflections on some hitherto unmentioned facets of the meaning of that event.

There are three stages to the argument of 6:1–7:6, so clearly distinguished as to amount to three separate answers to the question "Why not continue in sin?" The connection with 5:12–21 remains close, for the answers Paul now gives employ the polarities of sin and grace, death and life, disobedience and obedience that were set up by contrasting Adam and Christ.

6:1–14, Through Death to Life. The first answer to the question is that justification is a new life of righteousness because it is a death to sin. In 5:12–21, Christ was seen to be not an isolated individual but a figure who includes and represents others in such a way that he determines their circumstances and their lives; a solidarity or correspondence exists between them and him. Now Paul develops that idea. He takes it for granted that all his readers have been baptized, and that they understand this baptism to have been a baptism "into Christ's death." He does not here say that baptism created that solidarity (though it is possible to read Gal. 3:27 and 1 Cor. 12:13 as saying so), but as a "burial with Christ" (v. 4) it presupposes such solidarity and shows that it is now a solidarity in death. For his readers too a death has taken place that is irrevocable and involves the ending of each person's whole past way of life (v. 6). This is what precludes "continuing in sin."

This argument deserves a brief closer look. Paul's assumption that his readers will recognize the reference to baptism is an important indication that pre-Pauline development in Christian teaching about baptism revolved around the meaning of Jesus' death and included some kind of transfer of the benefits of that death to the baptized convert (→ Baptism). Second, the argument rests on a very basic understanding Paul has of Jesus Christ as a representative figure, a rich idea capable of being nuanced in a variety of ways quite apart from baptism. In the discussion of Adam and Christ, it is apocalyptic and universal in its symbolic scope, embracing primeval beginnings and end time, the "first" and the "last Adam" (cf. 1 Cor. 15:45). But there is also a cultic and sacrificial representation, in which Jesus died "for" others (Rom. 3:24–25; 5:6, 8, and many other passages). And there is the more legal and political kind of representation, in which one person's actions commit and oblige others, as when someone has power of attorney for another. These are all intimately connected in Paul's Christology, as one can see in one of his clearest formulations of the idea of representation, 2 Cor. 5:14–15 (". . . one has died on behalf of all; therefore all have died"). What happens to Christ happens to all those who are "in him." The phrase "in Christ Jesus" that runs through Paul's Letters (occurring in our section at 6:11 and 23, the two major dividing points) rests on this base perception, not on "mystical" ideas that have been anachronistically attributed to him.

Paul now refines this conception of Jesus Christ as a representative figure by drawing on the temporal sequence of Jesus' death and resurrection, as recounted in early liturgical summaries (beside Rom. 4:25, cf. 1 Cor. 15:3–4; 1 Thess. 4:14; Phil. 2:8–9; 2 Cor. 5:15; Rom. 8:34a). The adding of this new ingredient leads to various statements in Paul's theology about dying and rising, or suffering and living, "with Christ" (e.g., 1 Thess. 4:14; Gal. 2:19–20; Phil. 3:10–11, 21; 2 Cor. 4:10–11; 7:3; 13:4). In the present context this establishes a connection between the Christian's past and future: "For if we have been united with him in a death like his, we shall certainly be united with him in a resurrection like his" (v. 5, RSV). The solidarity that already exists between Christ and the individual in death must be followed by a solidarity in life as well. Since the latter still lies in the future, this solidarity has become a shared destiny. Verse 8 repeats this result as a flat indicative assertion about the future resurrection (like 1 Cor. 15:22). But significantly, here in v. 4 this future indicative is deflected into a statement of God's purpose for men and women in the present: "the reason why we were buried with him through this 'baptism into death' is that, just as Christ was raised from the dead through the Father's glory, we also might [now] live a new life." What shall be, already ought to be; hope and ethical obligation are simply two sides of the same future given to each individual in Christ. Verse 11 draws the bottom line: "So you also should consider yourselves to be dead to sin and alive to God in Christ Jesus." That is why one should not "continue in sin."

Verses 12–14 press this conclusion home with general exhortations that return to the terms with which chap. 5 had ended: the reign of sin and the reign of grace as two contrary authority structures. One has displaced the other, and the Christian's allegiances are to be shaped accordingly. What is remarkable about these verses is the view of the human self implicit in the injunctions. "Mortal bodies" (v. 12), "members," and "selves" (v. 13) are interchangeable terms. Bodily existence, even though still subject to death, is an aspect of the self that one has at one's disposal, as an "implement" (v. 13) to be put in the service of a transcending allegiance (cf. 1 Cor. 6:15). The self is not an end to itself; its end has been given to it in Christ.

6:15–23, Through Slavery to Freedom. The second answer to the question "Why not sin?" is that justification is a new life of righteousness because it is a being set free from the power of sin, but paradoxically it can have that quality only insofar as it is also a being brought into servitude to righteousness. Whereas the first answer was cast in terms of life and death, the categories now shift to freedom and bondage. But the most striking feature of this second answer is that it exists at all. Once one accepts Paul's premise, the destiny-creating role of Jesus as the Christ, the logic of his first reply would seem to be impregnable. Why then does he have to repeat the question once again in v. 15 and mount a second answer in these new terms? Verse 16 provides the clue by clarifying the issue of allegiance Paul raised in vv. 12–14. He does not think of human beings as autonomous creatures, or of freedom as a condition devoid of all commitment or obligation beyond oneself. No person can serve two masters, to be sure; but Paul presupposes that everyone has some "master," some controlling allegiance. The question is not whether life has such a point of orientation but which one it is, and what the outcome or goal is to which it ultimately leads. He sees the self faced with two basic alternatives, either to live in the service of sin as a power, the end result being death, or to live in service of righteousness, the end result being life. By v. 22 it is clear that the latter is a life lived for God. But at the beginning, in v. 16, he seems to put it rather clumsily when he speaks of obedience "to obedience" as the opposite of obedience "to sin"; this awkwardness only shows that in the back of his mind is the contrast between obedience and the lack of commitment altogether, the total absence of a sense of obligation that lies behind the question "Why not sin?" Verse 16 shows why the language of slavery is appropriate, for here again (cf. 5:12) Paul balances the fatefulness of human life with its freedom. People make choices, but these have lasting consequences from which one cannot escape. And in moral decisions, the constraints within which one has to live have many of their roots in fateful choices one has already freely made. So slavery to sin was a kind of "freedom with respect to righteousness" (v. 20) and freedom from sin is to be found only in a "slavery" to righteousness and to God. Paul seems to be fully aware of the scandalous incongruity of calling redemption and justification "slavery" (v. 19), but he retains the language nonetheless. Freedom, by itself, is not the answer to human existence; it is ambivalent, and its profounder dimensions open up only when one asks "Freedom from what, and for what?" and "Slavery to what?" Then the issue turns to what is being served, what allegiance is operative in every "slavery" or "freedom." As for his Christian readers, their conversion and baptism is clearly for Paul a point at which a transfer of allegiance and obligation has taken place, not because they were free to make it but because it has been made for them by God. They have "been committed" (passive) to a new pattern of living, yet they have concurred in it themselves "from the heart" (v. 17)—the same combination of fatefulness and freedom as before, but now in a liberating direction that restores human integrity ("righteousness"). That is the second reason

one should not "continue in sin" (→ Liberty). (It is instructive to compare Paul's understanding of fate and freedom with that of contemporary Stoicism; → Stoics.)

Why was the first answer, which drew upon Christian baptism to characterize the Christian life as an irrevocable death to a past way of life, inadequate? It is hard not to conclude that the explanation lies in Paul's own experience in Corinth, where his invitation to "consider oneself dead to sin and alive to God in Christ Jesus" (Rom. 6:11) had simply incited a libertinist absolutizing of freedom (→ Corinthians, The First Letter of Paul to the). A profounder exploration of human freedom and its ambivalences is required if the recipients are to remain accountable to the God who gave it and are to "honor God as God and give thanks to him" (Rom. 1:21). That is what made it necessary for Paul to add Rom. 6:12–21.

7:1–6, Through Acquittal to Commitment. This third section in Paul's answer to the question "Why not sin?" consists essentially of a legal detail that provides, when applied to the Christian life, an example and conclusion for both of the first two sections. The chosen example transcends parochial usage and applies as easily to Greek and Roman society as to Jewish (and to the twentieth century as easily as to the first). Considered by itself, the illustration (vv. 1–3) is one of the clearest definitions of justification in all of Paul's Letters, for it exemplifies the way in which a person is put into a completely altered situation by the death of someone else. The extent of the change is apparent from the fact that for a married woman exactly the same action (living with another man) brings in its train the damning epithet of an adulteress before her husband's death, but has no such effect after he dies. In the latter case, the marriage legislation is still in force; it has not been abrogated. Paul is very careful not to suggest that it has, saying rather curiously that "she has been vacated from the law" (v. 2b) rather than that the law has been voided. But the law's power to condemn her has been broken. Her deliverance from this power, simply by virtue of a death having occurred, is the point. All seems clear: the woman is the Christian set free by the death of Christ from the law's condemnation. But then the application in vv. 4–6 scrambles this neat analogy: the former husband is now the law, and it does not die; Christ, far from dying, has become the new husband to which the Christian is now free to belong; and the effect of the death is not only to end a period of captivity but to legitimate a new relationship of commitment and productive loyalty. This reconstruction of the analogy is not the product of confusion but stems directly from the movement of Paul's thought from 6:1 on, which it in turn exposes to clear view. The

Christian life is not merely a liberation, but is like ending one marriage and beginning a new one. Like the sequence of cross and resurrection adduced at the beginning (6:5, 6, 8, 10), solidarity with Christ (in his "body," 7:4a) brings a past quality of life and service to an end and opens a new one for the future. Resuming the contrasting terms he had last used in 2:29 to distinguish the outward aspects of religion that are subject to manipulation and abuse from genuine religious integrity, Paul labels the old relationship "letter" and the new, "Spirit."

7:7–25, A Backward Look: The Power of Sin to Use the Law to Effect Death. In the course of Paul's presentation of justification, a great deal has been said about sin. Paul has always used the singular of the noun (except in 4:7, an OT quotation, and 7:5, where the plural functions as a modifier of "passions"). Almost personified, it has turned out to reign and have dominion (6:14). Death is the symptom of its rule (5:21), the daily ration it distributes to its subjects (6:23). Yet its power is curiously dependent on the Mosaic law, apart from which it lies dormant (7:8b, resuming 4:15b and 5:13b). Only the law confers upon the married woman's act of living with another man the result of condemnation (7:2–3). The law magnifies sin (5:20) and accords sin its power (cf. 1 Cor. 15:56). Indeed, so closely have the functions of sin and the law meshed in Paul's reflections that death to the law (7:4) is required if one is to escape the power of sin. What in chap. 6 was a "dying to sin" (v. 10) has been replaced in the marriage illustration by "dying to the law" (7:4, 6). Correspondingly, what 6:18 referred to as "being set free from sin" has turned in 7:6 to "being exempted, vacated, from the law." It is hardly a surprise that the same logical necessity that produced the question of 6:1 now gives rise to 7:7: "what follows, then? That 'the Law is equivalent to sin'? Never!" (Moffatt's translation). When such questions have appeared earlier (in 3:1, 9, 27; 4:1, 9; and most notably in 6:1, 15), they have introduced clarifications and eliminated misunderstanding, but they have always advanced the discussion to new stages as well. That is the case here, but since the rest of chap. 7 clearly falls into two parts, each should be taken in turn.

Verses 7–12 form the first part. The inferential conjunction at the beginning of v. 12 shows that a first conclusion is being drawn to support the emphatic denial of v. 7. The Mosaic law is not the origin of sin; it is not to be confused with sin; it remains God's good and holy law. Yet law does in fact play a role in relation to sin: it identifies sin and makes it known. (Verse 7b explicitly resumes the point Paul had made in 3:20b, after affirming that the law impartially silences every attempt to evade indict-

ment.) What law supplies, however, is no merely cerebral information about sin, nor does it bestow psychological enticement on evil by the mere act of forbidding it. As the experience of the Decalogue's prohibition of inordinate desire shows (in selecting just this one of the Ten Commandments, Paul may also have the story of the Fall in mind; cf. Gen. 3:6), it produces the very thing it is supposed to prevent. Just therein lies the exoneration of God's law; it has been captured and used by sin. The most striking feature of these verses is that, even though a question concerning law is being addressed here at the outset, the real subject whose activity is recounted through the rest of chap. 7 is sin. This is the power whose sinister rule has provided the foil for the reign of grace and the justification of the unrighteous in one form or another from 5:12 on. Just as in 5:12–21, its operation is chronicled in terms of the opposites, death and life. Continuing in the vivid first person singular adopted in v. 7, Paul goes on: "In the absence of law" (v. 8b, a striking resumption of 5:13), sin was "dead," i.e., dormant, and he was alive. But when the law "came on the scene" (v. 9, an echo of 5:20), sin "sprang to life" (NEB) and Paul died (v. 10). The climax is reached in vv. 10b–11: "the very commandment that was supposed to lead to life turned out for me to lead to death; for sin, by taking advantage of me through that commandment, tricked me and by using it killed me."

The clear force of these words gives pause. The law held out the promise of life. Paul's phrasing here is carefully ambivalent. He does not say whether the arousing of such a hope was an intended function of the law in God's good purpose, frustrated by sin (as suggested by Rom. 2:13; 8:3a; and the quotations of Lev. 18:5 in Rom. 10:5 and Gal. 3:12); or whether it was a misunderstanding to expect life from it, a result of sin's deceitful use of the law (as seems required by Gal. 3:21b and Rom. 9:31–32; 10:2). The law, in scope and function, has many facets. In any case, the purpose of the law is not the first issue. It is enough that experience discovers that God's law in fact turns out to serve the strategies and ends of sin. Its result is not life but death, the symptom of sin's rule. There is not one syllable to suggest that this result is limited to those who have transgressed the law. Sin's deceit lies in its taking advantage of just those religious aspirations that make a person look to the law for life. By using the law precisely where it is honored and treasured and even obeyed, it destroys the integrity of a person's relation to God, corrodes trust and replaces it with a defensive posture no longer gratefully dependent on God nor unreservedly accountable to him.

Paul recounts this capture of the law and of the self by sin in the past tense and with the first-person singular "I." It is a mistake to read this as a personal autobiography and so to wring from it details of Paul's early life. Rom. 3:7; 1 Cor. 6:15; 10:29–30; 13:1–3, 11; 14:11, 14, 15; and especially Gal. 2:18–21 amply exhibit his penchant for casting his analyses of fundamental religious experience into the exemplary "I" of the born teacher. The past tenses depict the "history" of sin on the same epic scale as in 5:12–14, 18–21. But the settings of Gal. 2:18–21 and Phil. 3:8–14 in the manifestly autobiographical contexts that precede these passages show that it would be equally mistaken to abstract Paul's description of sin from his personal discovery of its power to pervert devout allegiance to the Mosaic law. One can as little do that here as one can sanitize his perception of Jewish religious self-awareness in 2:17–29 from his own profound personal participation in it.

Verses 13–25 form the second part of the remainder of chap. 7. As 6:15 repeated the question of 6:1 in order to advance the train of thought to another level, so 7:13 renews the question of 7:7 and repeats the emphatic assertion that it was sin that was responsible for bringing about death. But there is a difference. "The law" has been replaced by "the good." While this certainly has to do with God's law, the goodness of which Paul has just upheld, the reference now is to the good that the law held out "to me" in its promise of life (as in 7:10), thus preparing for the following verses. In addition, two parallel purpose clauses now make clear that even in sin's use of it, the law remains God's instrument. The end result fits into God's purpose for the law, namely to disclose the true nature of sin and show how "incomparably sinful" it really is. Continuing his intimately illustrative use of "I," but shifting to the present tense to emphasize its recurring pattern, Paul turns to analyze more carefully the experience in which the religious self encounters this power of sin.

Paul shifts from the contrasting words "life" and "death" he used in vv. 7–12 to a closely related but quite different pair, "good" and "evil." (The same sort of shift occurs between the two stages of his argument in chap. 6.) This pair, in turn, is joined to contrasting verbs, and these contrasts carry the argument. This is clear in vv. 18–19: "For I know that the good does not dwell in me, that is in my flesh. For to will the good is within my reach, but to produce it, to carry it out, is not. For what I do is not the good that I intend [desire, and prefer]; instead, what I actually accomplish is the very thing I do not intend [do not want, and wish to avoid]." Good and evil in this context are not abstract moral labels. They develop v. 13, where "that which is the good" is closely allied with the life promised "to me" by the

law. The attraction of the law is that it seems to lead to the life that the religious person wants and desires above all else, the more so if it is God's holy, just, and good commandment. (In 12:2, Paul will equate "the good" with the will of God.) Paul is here touching on the deepest nerve of the Jew's allegiance to the Mosaic law. This is why the person who lives by the law, and not just under it, "delights" in God's law (v. 22, a clear echo of the psalmist's praise of the law; cf. Ps. 1:2). Of course this is "moral" in a profound sense, for in religion at its best, represented for Paul by Judaism, the desire to attain life and the desire to do the good that God commands are fully joined. This willing and desiring are the more pressing the more one realizes that the good that amounts to life does not dwell within the native resources of the self taken on its own ("my flesh," v. 18).

But now, Paul goes on, this self that wants life and wills the good makes an astonishing discovery. What it does, creates, produces, and brings into being (the changes are rung on three overlapping Greek verbs) by its actions is not the intended good but exactly what it thought it could avoid by the law (exactly like the Decalogue's prohibition in vv. 7–8). The early chapters of Romans make clear enough what this means: the loss of inner integrity and of trusting reliance on God, the resulting claim to special standing that exempts one from accountability, the denial that all stand on the same footing before the same God, leads *every* religious person to abuse God's goodness and end up blaspheming his name. Verse 15 now gets its full force: "I don't understand the results of my own action!" One is compelled to paraphrase: "I know the law is good; the trouble cannot lie there. Indeed, it can't be I that am acting any longer; another power resides in me to which I am sold as a slave" (vv. 14, 17). To go a step further: "as a person wishing to do the good, I discover that God's own law, used by sin, has become a qualitatively different law, contrary to the one I adhere to in my sincere intentions. It has taken over my members, those aspects of myself by which my service and allegiance are implemented and which should be at the disposal of my own will (cf. Rom. 6:12–13), and put them at the disposal of sin. The result is that I am a prisoner of war; when I want to do the good, evil is what comes out" (vv. 21–23). "Thank God that because of Jesus Christ our Lord this demonic power is not ultimate" (v. 25a).

This passage has been a battleground for debate almost since it was written. That is because it seems to lend itself to a wide variety of applications. What is needed is to take it on its own terms as far as possible, in its literary context in Romans, and in its religious and historical context in Paul's world. It is frequently understood as describing the common frustration produced by the discrepancy between ideal intentions and actual human performance, or between reason and desire (formulated, for example, in Ovid's *Metamorphoses* 7, 18–21). This reading assigns the performance to the "flesh" as a lower self and the good intentions to an inner nature untouched by sin and results in a dualistic conflict between passion and reason in the understanding of the self that is foreign to Paul. Such dualism is suggested by v. 25b, which is Paul's terse summary; but it is refuted by his analysis, in which the "inmost self" and "flesh" are not different selves at different levels but two aspects of the one person who is "sold under sin," his sincere desire and his helpless vulnerability. What v. 15 describes is not the failure to produce results but the same bewilderment over the actual results of one's action that Paul spoke of in v. 10. Again, the experience that is detailed in this whole passage 7:7–25 is not the despair felt by a Martin Luther over his inability to live up to a demanding code; Phil. 3:4–7 shows conclusively how different Paul's self-perception is. Nor is it the exposure felt by an Augustine at the discovery that he had oriented his life's striving around an attractive but inferior surrogate for God's highest good. It is the much more shocking encounter with sin's power to use genuine devotion to the true God, channeled through adherence to God's own law, to bring about exactly the opposite of what one has hoped for: a perverted relationship to God in place of an authentic one, evil in place of the good, death in place of life. That yields a far more sinister perception of evil operating at the very center of religious life to debase it and turn it into slavery. It is this slavery from which Paul gratefully acknowledges having been set free by Christ. Rom. 7:7–25 is a backward look at "the old life of the letter" (7:6).

Finally, debate has raged over whether Paul is describing his experience as a Jew or as a Christian. That is the wrong question. There is for Paul one God of all human beings (3:29–30), and one authentic relationship to him for all, the trust exemplified by Abraham (chap. 4). All serious religious devotion is subject to being taken captive by sin and subverted into distrust and defiance of God. Of course one cannot abstract Paul's experience of that distortion from his experience with the Mosaic law. But he makes no suggestion that sin respects any boundary between Judaism and Christianity or any other religion, and his other Letters show that he knew quite well that the best intentions of Christians are subject to the same falsification. Throughout all his Letters, his gospel is that God has taken the initiative in his Son to break that power and set things right—for Jew and non-Jew alike. God's justification in Christ

of the undeserving is what confers integrity on human religion.

8:1–17, A Forward Look: The Power of the Spirit to Effect Life for Righteousness.

To move to the other side of the contrast of 7:6, Paul first restates the change effected "in Christ Jesus" (for the meaning of this phrase, see commentary above on 6:1–14). There is "no condemnation"; the power of the law to condemn has been decisively broken (the resumption of 5:16 and 7:3 is unmistakable). "The law of sin and death" (v. 2) is a shorthand summary of 7:7–25; it is the Mosaic law used by sin in such a way as to cause death. The parallel phrase, "the law of the Spirit of life," is clearly intended as a rhetorical counterpart and suggests that life is the result when the same law is used by God's Spirit, his life-giving presence and power, instead of by sin. Like the expression "law of faith" in 3:27, it joins what Paul often sets in tension; only the context can supply its meaning. But that context is clear enough. The law itself is not demonic; to link law with Spirit instead of sin is the logical sequel to the argument of chap. 6 that freedom in Christ is aimed at the reshaping of human life, both individual and corporate, according to the good that God wills for it. Verses 3–4 supply the grounding for this new connection by declaring that this was the whole purpose behind God's "sending of his own Son." This reference to Jesus is cast in formal language closely paralleling Gal. 4:4–5. It emphasizes first the complete entry of God's Son into the human condition. Paul is not worried about the "sinlessness" of Jesus, Heb. 4:15, because he conceives of sin as a power, not as defilement or guilt. Without fully entering the domain of that power, "flesh," the Son could not have broken it. The fundamental contrast in the whole passage is between the inability and weakness on the one hand of the law to renew and reorder life so long as sin is in control, and the effectual life-giving power of God's own presence in the Spirit on the other. The outcome is to open the way for the fulfillment of God's holy and just commandment. Only on these terms can Paul come back to the starting point of his Letter, an impartial God whose righteousness is to be vindicated and acknowledged (3:4) if the relationship of creature to creator is to have integrity and God is to be "honored as God and given thanks" (1:21–25).

Verses 5–8 elaborate briefly on the contrast between "flesh" and "Spirit" as these affect human beings. Each is a reality transcending the individual, but each is also a "mind-set" that involves a deliberate choice of values and human effort toward a goal. (How Paul conceives of such a "mind-set" is most clearly illumined by Phil. 2:1–13 and the "Christ hymn," vv. 6–11, cited there as its source and norm.)

Above all, each is most basically a relationship to God. The one, flesh, is a regression to the deadly "enmity" and defiance that preceded reconciliation (cf. 5:10). The other, Spirit, is God's life-giving presence and power. It is renewing because it creates a new mind-set that is not inimical to God, that submits to God's law without the distrust that corrupts obedience into self-defensiveness, and that no longer allows God's law to be used as an instrument for holding one in its power.

If these definitions of flesh and Spirit suggest that human choices are the ultimate determinants of human destiny, vv. 9–11 quickly correct that impression by returning to God's primal life-bestowing act in the resurrection of Jesus (cf. 6:1–14). What is most striking about these verses is the free interchangeability of a whole series of phrases: "belonging to Christ" (v. 9b), "being in the Spirit" (v. 9a), "God's Spirit dwelling in you" (vv. 9a, 11b), "Christ's Spirit" (v. 9b), "Christ in you" (v. 10), and "the Spirit of the one who raised Jesus from the dead" (v. 11). Each interprets the others and is interpreted by them. God is the one who gives life to the dead (4:17); he has raised Jesus from the dead. The Spirit is not the possession of some elite group within the church. It is another word for God's life-giving power present through Jesus to all that belong to him, active already in their lives in spite of the mortality that still belongs to the body, working toward righteousness and undergirding the promise that the Son's identification with them will issue ultimately in their sharing in his resurrection (cf. 6:5, 8). The Spirit is not only a mind-set; nor is it merely the external power by which God raised Jesus from the dead. It is also the power of the risen Jesus to take men and women into his power and reshape life to make it well pleasing to God—thus doing what the law could not do and reversing the power of sin. That is why Paul could call the gospel "the power of God for salvation to all who rely on him, the Jew first and also the Greek" (1:16).

Verses 12–17 bring this unit to a close in two ways. First, Paul draws the consequences for his readers in a direct call for their response that reminds one of the challenge of the Deuteronomic covenant: "See, I have set before you this day life and good, death and evil" (Deut. 30:15, RSV)—only here death and life are correlated to the conflicting claims of flesh and Spirit upon the self for its "deeds done in the body" (v. 13b; cf. 2 Cor. 5:10; → Body). But second, Paul reminds his readers that, as in Deuteronomy, such a call only follows a change of allegiance and direction already made for them. Obedience is not finally the work of the self but the result of the Spirit's leading. The Spirit produces an authentic filial relationship to God in place of slavery and verifies that gift by enabling people to address God with the intimate term "Father" (→ Adoption). The Aramaic word "Abba" suggests a liturgical acclamation of God in the mutually supportive and confirming worship of the gathered community and not simply the intimacy of private prayer. (This whole series of new terms occurs also in Gal. 4:6–7 and seems to have formed a single cluster in Paul's preaching.) It is noteworthy that the full-fledged opposite of slavery, "freedom," is reserved by Paul for future salvation (v. 21). In the meantime (v. 17), the legal image of an "heir," one whose entitlement is firmly established even though actual possession remains outstanding, offers a way to affirm the certainty of the new life in the Spirit despite its provisional and unseen aspects, and to link it to the still unrealized future consummation of God's deliverance (→ Inheritance). Both certainty and hope are based once again on that central element in Paul's gospel, the inclusion of all in the one destiny of Jesus Christ: ". . . if it is in fact true that we share his suffering in order to share also his glory" (v. 17).

8:18–30, Justification as the Gift of Hope in a Still Unredeemed World.

Paul now returns to the afflicted and precarious quality of life mentioned in 5:3–4. The credibility of his many intervening affirmations is threatened by the falsifying power of the actual experience of transiency and suffering, the footprints of death's continuing presence. Careful readers will have noted that Paul has never denied that presence, even in the last section (8:10a). Death is still "the last enemy" (1 Cor. 15:26). This is exactly why the death of Jesus remains so central to Paul's gospel. The indisputable reality of death in human life is also the most public feature of Jesus' life. His destiny-creating role as the Christ rests on his prior identification with the human condition (5:5, 8; 8:3; cf. Gal. 4:4–5). Only the irreversible sequence of Jesus' own crucifixion and resurrection clamps life to this death, discloses God to be "the one who gives life to the dead" (Rom. 4:17, 24), and enables Paul to speak of life as a final destiny. For human beings, Paul is always careful to say, the culmination of that destiny remains future (cf. 5:10, 17; 6:5, 8; 8:11). "It is in this hope that we have been saved" (8:24, the only place in Paul's undisputed Letters where he uses the verb "to save" in the past tense). This insistence on the futurity of salvation is undoubtedly a residue of Paul's past experiences with the excessive enthusiasm of Christian perfectionism, against which he repeatedly drew the cruciform shape of his own life as an apostle and as a model for authentic life in others (cf. esp. 1 Cor. 4:8–13; 2 Cor. 4:7–12; Phil. 3:12–16, 20–21). But here, as in so many other instances, a strategy in his churches became also an emphasis in his theology; the hard realism of this distinction between present and future reinforces the correspondence between Christ's life and those who are "in him," so that present affliction verifies the truth of the gospel instead of refuting it (e.g., 1 Cor. 1:26–2:5; 2 Cor. 4:7; 6:3–10; 11:23; 13:3–4; Gal. 5:11; 6:17; Phil. 1:14). In both 8:17 and 8:29, Paul returns to this basic pattern of Christ's life; in between, as he moves to a first climax of his Letter, this line of thought is elaborated in three progressive stages.

First, in vv. 19–22 the whole of creation is included in the same sequence. This is the only place in the NT where the natural world is singled out for attention, but the passage draws directly on the firm understanding of the affinity between human beings and God's total creation, of which they are a part, that runs through the OT and apocalyptic literature. (Its opposite, an essential incongruity between human beings and their world, appears in many forms of dualism in the Hellenistic world; →Gnosticism.) Frequently in Jewish writings God's end-time redemption includes the renewal of creation (e.g., Isa. 11:6–9; 65:17, 25; 66:22; 1 Enoch 91:16; Jub. 1:29); an extension of this idea traces the ills and woes of the nonhuman world to the defilement and curse of human sin (e.g., Isa. 24:1–6, 18–23; Jer. 4:19–26; Ezek. 32:6–8; with specific reference to Adam's transgression, 2 Esd. 7:11). The pangs of childbirth (Rom. 8:22) are conventional imagery for the cosmic woes accompanying God's judgment (Isa. 13:8; cf. 1 Thess. 5:3), the coming of the new age (1 Enoch 62:4) or the messiah (1QH 3:7–10); they are a fitting metaphor here for the universally shared pain that looks forward to new life (cf. John 16:21–22). Paul does not romanticize nature, nor does he treat it with contempt. The world's futility and "decay" (i.e., its vulnerability to the ravages of time), two of its most characteristic marks to Hellenistic thinking, are not the result of anything it has done; there is no "fall" of creation. Rather, they are part of the created order and fall under God's own "expectation that the creation itself will be set free" to share in the glorious liberty of God's children (Rom. 8:20–21), so bearing their own testimony to God's transcending future (→ Eschatology; Regeneration).

Second, against any pious illusions about being "children of God," vv. 23–25 reassert that it is "not only creation but also the very ones who have the Spirit as a first fruits" (a harvest metaphor for the advance portion that serves as surety for what is to follow) who participate in this urgent longing. The gift of the Spirit is not a partial resurrection, or a certificate of exemption from the world's sufferings. As surety, it confirms the gap between present and future, but at the same time sustains the expectation and turns it into a certain hope. (As v. 24 demonstrates, "hope" in Paul's Letters means both the act of expecting and the reality hoped for; → Hope.) Hope is not a poor substitute for possession, but enhances it. As certainty about God's future, it makes meaningful connection between God's salvation and the miserable realities of the present world. What can be seen in this life remains changeable and transitory, and bears the marks of death (2 Cor. 4:16–18 is Paul's own best commentary). To identify God's end with that would be to defraud faith. Instead, hope is what gives faith patience and enables it to endure in its reliance on God (v. 25).

Third, "in the same way, the Spirit also stands by to assist us in our weakness" (v. 26). The imagery is that of a heavenly court (cf. vv. 33–34), in which the "inexpressible yearnings" of both creation and community are taken up and presented on their behalf to God. Paul is drawing on a tradition that perceives God's Spirit as an advocate or defender for God's people; it appears also in the "Paraclete" sayings of the Gospel of John (→ Paraclete) and in sayings in the synoptic Gospels (Matthew, Mark, and Luke) that promise the Spirit's aid to the beleaguered community in times of persecution and trial (Mark 13:11; Matt. 10:19–20; Luke 21:15). Human beings are not left to their own resources, even to the inadequacies of their praying, to bear the burdens of this time, for the Spirit's intercession is authorized by God himself, "the searcher of human hearts" (Ps. 7:9; Jer. 17:10; cf. Ps. 139:1). Apart from this context, the assertion of v. 28 must sound superficial; in this context, it summarizes what has gone before. The ultimate assurance that "all [these] things" eventually do lead to the good that God wills lies in his unfailing assistance to "those who love him," which Paul at once defines as those whom God has called into this new relationship (cf. 1 Cor. 2:9; 8:3). A final rhetorical sequence of clauses stresses this divine purpose. Into it Paul inserts (v. 29b) another reminder of the Son: the branding mark of his life's pattern, in which glory and salvation come only by way of the cross, is what restores to human life the "image" the Creator had first willed to impress upon it (Gen. 1:27; cf. Phil. 3:21; 2 Cor. 4:4; → Image of God).

8:31–39, Justification as Vindication by the Love of God in Christ. Finally Paul returns to the love of God, which 5:5–8 has identified as the ultimate basis for hope and for that kind of confidence in God that has integrity. But he does not name love until v. 35. What God's sacrifice of his own Son (the language echoes Abraham's "not sparing" Isaac, Gen. 22:16) proves first is that God is "for us" rather than "against us." That does not mean that he is "on our side" (JB) on every human issue. But it is the very heart of Paul's teaching on justification.

The love of God does not mean a transmutation of earthly life into heavenly. It leaves history intact, with its choices, for which people and nations must still answer to God (cf. 2 Cor. 5:10). Human beings still have blood on their hands, often in the name of religion. But the ultimate accuser in the heavenly court is now the one who has taken their side in Christ Jesus. Paul is back at his starting point in 3:23–24. The rest of this section unfolds that assurance with the help of two carefully constructed rhetorical lists: one (v. 35) a sevenfold recapitulation of Paul's own personal hardships as a paradigm of the Christian life, the other (vv. 38–39) a tenfold catalogue of transpersonal powers that seem to threaten God's intent. In between, v. 36 (unfortunately often passed over in the liturgical use of this passage) makes the first appeal for confirmation to the OT since chap. 4. Ps. 44:22, originally a cry to God lamenting the assaults of Israel's enemies, now universalized as an apocalyptic truism that God's faithful are always exposed to violent death, becomes Scripture's own reminder that tribulation is a sure mark of belonging to God. The love of the Christ (v. 35) is in the last analysis the love of the eternal and omnipotent God himself (v. 39); that is the meaning for this life of calling Jesus of Nazareth, crucified and raised, "Christ Jesus our Lord."

9:1–11:36
The Faithfulness of God

In 3:1–8, Paul had anticipated two serious objections to his argument. His exposition of the justification of the unrighteous in subsequent chapters has answered the second objection: that Paul is denying the realities of sin and human accountability, ignoring the moral consequences of God's graciousness, and casting doubt on God's own integrity. But the first objection remains unfinished business still clamoring for attention. Paul's early insistence on God's impartiality (2:6–29) had provoked the question, "Does the Jew have any 'advantage,' any privilege that others do not also have?" (3:1). In replying affirmatively, Paul pointed to the "direct utterances" entrusted by God to the Jews, referred cryptically to the faithfulness of God that does not depend on human fidelity, and then switched the emphasis to God's truth and righteousness. Even that answer he seemed to take back in 3:9, although from 1:16 on he has always been careful not to obliterate the distinction between Jew and non-Jew (1:16; 2:9–10; 3:1, 30; 4:11–12).

However, far from going away, the question has in the meantime only become more acute. On Paul's own terms, the gospel of God's gracious initiative for the deliverance of all in the death of Jesus has put Jew and non-Jew on the same footing before God (3:22b–23, 30) and even provided the non-Jew with equal access to what Paul located at the very core of Jewish identity, God's promise to Abraham and Abraham's trust in that promise (chap. 4). Favoritism can never be claimed from God, as though God were the patron of one client people alone, for that would violate Judaism's central creed that God is one (3:29–30).

But what then becomes of God's faithfulness, that very reliability on which human trust, beginning with Abraham's, can alone depend? What about those "direct utterances" and God's calling of a people as his own, for which again Abraham is the prototype? Has God broken faith with his word, and with himself? What is at stake is not only the reality and future of Israel; it is above all a question about the God who has acted in Jesus Christ. That is why the argument of chaps. 1–8 is unfinished. In this connection God's "faithfulness" has several levels of meaning. His trustworthiness is his power to do what he has promised (as in 4:20–21). But it involves also his constancy, the changelessness of his purpose. And another side of his reliability is the consistency with which he deals with different groups of people, i.e., the very impartiality that raised the question in the first place. In the end, these are all aspects of God's righteousness.

These are the questions Paul addresses in the next three chapters. After a brief introduction, he proceeds in three major steps, though each section has some clear subdivisions.

9:1–5, Personal Introduction: The "Advantages" of Israel. In these intimate opening remarks, it is not at first apparent what Paul is talking about. He is affirming under oath his deeply pained concern for the Jewish people in whom his own natural and historical roots are set. He makes no charges; there is not a syllable of reproach or blame. Yet, in a manner reminiscent of Moses' impossible offer of his own life to atone for the worshipers of the golden calf (Exod. 32:31–32), Paul entertains the fleeting thought of being accursed and cut off from Christ, something just declared impossible (8:35, 39), in their place—as if they are under a ban or spell. But he turns that thought aside (until 9:31–32) and instead enumerates all the "advantages" (3:1) of the "Israelites." This new name replaces "the Jew(s)" in these three chapters (except 9:24 and 10:12, where Paul needs the pairing of Jew and non-Jew) and is a calculated recall of Judaism's roots in the patriarchal history (Gen. 32:28; →Israel: The Idea of Israel). The list itself rehearses the major tokens of the Jewish people's covenant relationship with God, the earthly branding marks of God's election—not the least of which is being the cradle of the Messiah. The thought moves Paul to a Jewish formula of thanksgiving and praise to "the God who is over all" (v. 5b) and who is the real subject of chaps. 9–11. (Although some translations punctuate so as to make the formula refer to Christ, this fits neither the context nor Paul's Christology; cf. 1 Cor. 15:28.)

9:6–29, Israel's Election as God's Free Initiative to Create a People.

In this first major section Paul reviews certain aspects of election in the patriarchal story in order to refute the suggestion that God's word has failed (v. 6). The first reason it has not is that God's past activity has been completely consistent with his justification of the unrighteous. Put another way, several of the points Paul has made in chaps. 1–4 about the standing of human beings before God in his future judgment he now confirms by turning 180 degrees to look at Israel's past history. It is most important to note that throughout this first section it is God's nature and activity that are being described; there is absolutely no attack on the Judaism of Paul's own time or censure of Israel in the past. This review embraces three points.

First, in vv. 6–13, in a remarkable resumption of his earlier redefinition of the authentic Jew (2:28–29) and of the authentic Abraham (cf. commentary above on 4:9–12), Paul now redefines Israel in such a way as to distinguish the "children of God" and "of the promise" (v. 8) from the simply physical posterity of Abraham. One should take some care in interpreting Paul. He is not trying to make room for believing Gentiles among Abraham's children (as he was in 4:9–12), much less suggesting a "spiritualized" definition of the Jewish people as a pretext for substituting the church for Israel (that would reduce vv. 1–3 to posturing). Nor is he dismissing the earthly and historic continuity of the Jewish people as inauthentic; he is not abstracting an "essential" Israel from its history. Rather, in that history itself, as every Jew would agree, the descendants of Abraham through Ishmael (Gen. 25:12–18; cf. Jub. 15:28–30; 20:11–13; → Ishmaelites) and through Esau (Gen. 36:1–8; → Edom) were not included in "Israel." (For debate in Paul's time about the identity of the true Israel, → Apocalyptic Judaism.) Historical Israel itself is determined by "promise" rather than by "flesh" (these terms are functioning here exactly as "spirit" and "letter" did in 2:29). Of course Isaac and Ishmael, one born to Abraham's wife Sarah and the other to his maidservant Hagar, were not equals. So to make the point clear, Paul comes down one generation to the twin sons of Rebecca (OT, Rebekah), "conceived from the same conjugal act with one man, Isaac" (v. 10). Here the determination of authentic Israel takes place "when they were not yet born and when they had not yet done anything good or bad, in order that God's elective intention might remain unchanged (i.e., consistent), dependent not on

works but on the one who calls" (vv. 11–12a). The point is clinched, in rabbinic fashion, with one text from the law and one from the prophets (vv. 12b–13). Election, which means the calling into being of a people, exactly like the justification of the unrighteous, is God's free act, a gift, not something due (4:4); it results from the perduring intention of God that operates "by election" (v. 11b). This is Abraham's God "who gives life to the dead and calls into being the things that are not" (4:17).

Second, vv. 14–24 reflect on "But Esau I hated." The last OT text cited in v. 13 from Mal. 1:2–3 creates a new problem. One may soften the language (since Hebrew has no comparative adverbs, there are OT texts in which "to hate" simply means "to love less": Gen. 29:30–31; Deut. 21:15; cf. Luke 14:26), but there is no doubt about God's deliberate aversion in that context in Malachi and throughout Israel's history. That raises the issue of "injustice," the negative form of favoritism, on God's part. At first Paul seems merely to continue his preceding line when he adds the two counterpoised figures of Moses and Pharaoh. Verse 16 is a manifest reinforcement of v. 11: "So it all depends not on the person who wills, nor on the person who exerts himself, but on the God who shows mercy." But v. 17 shows that Paul's shift to (Moses and) Pharaoh introduces a new dimension: God is not guided by random or arbitrary whim but by a clear purpose to assert his power and presence in human affairs. In that connection Paul introduces the image of the potter and his clay. Many readers, taking the side of the questioners in v. 19 and thinking only of the passive plasticity of the clay in the potter's hands, have taken offense at what they regard as this picture of an impersonal, unfeeling, and despotic God. It is imperative to consult the prophetic sources from which Paul is drawing this reply (Jer. 18:6; Isa. 29:16; but esp. Isa. 45:9–13). The point is not the power of the potter but his "right" (v. 21, RSV) to fashion each vessel for a function and to determine the use of each. A machine stamping out identical pots is "impersonal." In Isaiah 45, the context concerns God's "raising up in righteousness" (v. 13) his "anointed," the Persian emperor Cyrus. The even more ludicrous parallel to the clay calling the potter to account is the helpless newborn infant holding its parents answerable for the procreative act that called it into being, as personal a caricature as one could wish. But the potter's example fits Paul's needs better than the infant's because, as vv. 21–23 make quite clear, his point is God's intention to fashion different instruments and use them in different ways—a latitude so far not yet achieved by human reproduction. Neither rigid determinism nor arbitrary caprice, but creative and purposive divine freedom lie at the heart of

Paul's understanding of election (→ Election; Predestination). Corroboration for this comes in the difficult vv. 22–23. Paul's syntax is severely elliptical; v. 24 also is not a complete sentence, but it is clearly the goal toward which vv. 22–23 move. God is not simply like a potter. The purpose clauses with which both verses begin are parallel: God wishes to make himself known, first by showing his wrath and "what he can do" (a striking phrase; cf. its opposite in 8:3) by patiently enduring, i.e., by not destroying, "vessels of wrath fashioned for destruction," and then by making known "the wealth of his glory" on "vessels of mercy" prepared for that use. "Vessel" in Greek normally also means an "instrument" or piece of gear in the hands of someone (Paul himself is a "chosen instrument," lit., a "vessel of election," for God in Acts 9:15). The harshness of this language results from combining terms from the imagery of the potter with God's wrath and mercy. Paul does not identify the "vessels of wrath designed for destruction" with Jews and the "vessels of mercy" with Gentiles, much less Christians. Such a correlation can be produced only by bringing elements of chap. 11, which is a different argument, up into chap. 9. These phrases refer to figures in Israel's own history, Pharaoh and Moses respectively. Verses 22–23 thus reproduce in inverted order the juxtaposition of vv. 15–17 in order to reach toward the goal of v. 24, God's intent to create "us" as a people "not only from Jews but also from Gentiles," both of whom are included under "vessels of mercy." This reappearance of the word pair "Jew and Gentile" and the confessional "us," both totally new elements in chap. 9, brings Paul back to the main track of his exposition of God's righteousness. Thus the juxtaposition in vv. 22–23 is not contradictory but progressive, remarkably like the parallel revelation of God's wrath and his righteousness with which Paul began the whole letter in 1:17–18. These are two "sides" or "faces" of God, but they are never in equilibrium and do not result in a schizophrenic duality of purpose in God himself. The hardening of Pharaoh served the deliverance of Israel under Moses, just as the revelation of wrath serves the manifestation of God's righteousness, or the "increase" of sin by the law serves the aggrandizement of grace (5:20). There is no inconsistency between God's behavior in Israel's creation and the justification of the undeserving that creates a new people from both Jew and non-Jew.

Third, vv. 25–29 buttress v. 24 with scriptural warrants in reverse order, first for the non-Jews (from Hosea), then for the Jews (from Isaiah), but in such a way that each passage also applies to both groups. The Hosea text (vv. 25–26) is a lucid and forceful equation of calling and election with God's undeserved love; its application to the inclusion of the non-Jews in what was originally Israel's election drives home God's consistency in his covenant love on which all alike depend. The text from "Isaiah," actually from a variety of prophetic passages, returns to God's reliability in the election of authentic Israel. "Remnant" in v. 27, like "seed" in v. 29, refers to that authentic line of descent from Abraham described positively in vv. 6–13 (it is not used reductively; there is no "only" in the Greek of v. 27; see commentary below on 11:1–6). The emphasis falls on the last line, which sums up Paul's answer to the question of v. 6 whether "the word of God has failed": no, "the elect strain that is called in Isaac (v. 7) shall be saved; the Lord will carry out his word on the earth conclusively and with dispatch" (v. 28). A final quotation from Isaiah (v. 29) serves as a thanksgiving: apart from that constancy of God that has operated in Israel's election, we would (all) be like Sodom and Gomorrah, the OT prototypes of annihilation.

9:30–10:21, God's Faithfulness in the Apparent Breakdown of Election. As often before (4:1; 6:1, 15; 7:7; 8:31; 9:14), a new stage in Paul's reflection is opened with the rhetorical question, "What then shall we say?" This time, however, the words that follow are Paul's own answer and not an erroneous deduction he aims to refute. Verses 30b–33 leave behind the preceding account of God's role in the story of Israel's election and focus on the present status of that complex plot. Now for the first time Paul's readers get a clear glimpse of the reason for his pain in 9:2. For present circumstances are a baffling inversion of everything any participant in that story would have expected. In the language of the racecourse, Gentiles who were not even trying to reach God's righteousness have arrived at that goal on the proper terms of trust in God; Israel, on the other hand, pursuing a law that held out the promise of righteousness, has failed to reach even that law. By referring to the Mosaic law here not as a possession distinguishing Jew from Gentile (cf. 2:14, 20) but as Israel's unattained goal, Paul must have in mind something like that "law of faith" that precludes boasting in 3:27 (cf. commentary above on 3:27–31), the Mosaic law as presuming trust in God for its authentic obedience (2:25–29). Of course Paul is contrasting the acceptance of "God's gospel" (1:1) among his Gentile converts and the resistance his preaching has encountered among his own people. But beneath those surface reactions lies a deeper enigma. Something has gone seriously wrong (9:32), because Israel's pursuit of the goal was not carried out in trust but on the supposition that righteousness can come from performance of deeds enjoined by the law (i.e., in violation of the basic axiom under which Paul had begun his whole description of justification, 3:20). "The one who trusts in him [God] will not be put to shame." That assurance had been laid down by God as a foundation stone in Zion (Isa. 28:16), but it has become a rock of stumbling, as the Lord of hosts said he would himself become to those who refuse his message (Isa. 8:14), and Israel has stumbled on that rock (Rom. 9:32). This is Paul's own people, and this is the reason for his anguish.

On the basis of Ps. 118:22, Christianity after Paul developed a complex tapestry of OT "stone" passages to apply to Christ (1 Pet. 2:6–8; Matt. 21:42; Mark 12:10; Luke 20:17; Acts 4:11; Eph. 2:20; cf. Luke 2:34), so Paul's later readers have understandably assumed that the "stone" of v. 33 refers to Christ. But there is no use of Psalm 118 here and no preparation for such a direct allusion. Instead, Paul seems to understand the second line of the quotation, to which he returns in 10:11, as the inscription on the stone or the "rock" itself (cf. the punctuation of Isa. 28:16, RSV). In any case, this v. 33 must count as one of the most remarkable of Paul's OT quotations because of what it attributes to God: placing in the midst of his people a base of security that is at the same time an obstacle over which they will stumble (→Stumbling Block). Such an obstacle confronts those who encounter it with alternatives; yet their reactions only disclose things about themselves over which they have no control. This figure of speech thus combines the same fatefulness and freedom that have appeared in Paul's earlier analyses (Rom. 1:21–23; 5:12; 6:17; 8:12–14). God's action is not unlike that law that was supposed to lead to life but in fact led to death, a result not outside God's purpose (7:10, 13b), or God's use of "an instrument of wrath" like Pharaoh on the way to disclosing his mercy in Moses. Such a perception of God recognizes in Israel's history what Paul has come in other ways to see about God from his disclosure of his power and wisdom in the offensive message of a crucified Messiah (cf. Paul's use of the figure of the stumbling block in 1 Cor. 1:18, 21–24).

The rest of this section (chap. 10) explores these two sides of the strange reversal of 9:30–31. First, leaving the Gentiles aside, Paul first (10:1–17) concentrates on Israel's own responsibility for the current state of affairs. After a renewed personal testimony, he repeats (vv. 1–4) what has gone wrong, using the language of justification instead of his racecourse imagery; genuine zeal for God has been turned into disobedience and a pursuit of righteousness aborted into a search for "one's own" rather than God's (cf. Phil. 2:9). This diagnosis of Israel parallels precisely what Paul wrote about religious moralists in Rom. 2:1–5 and addressed to "the Jew" in 2:17–24. It should not have turned out so, for the real goal of the law as reached in

Christ is to lead to righteousness for everyone who trusts in God (10:4; Paul's Greek word "end," like the English, can mean either "cessation" as in Luke 1:33, or "goal" as in Rom. 6:21–22; both Paul's usage elsewhere and the racecourse motif here support the latter choice. But this is one of the most debated of Pauline texts). Verses 5–13 supply the scriptural backing. Here Paul follows an established rabbinic procedure for dealing with apparently contradictory biblical texts, as in Gal. 3:10–12. The law ("Moses," Rom. 10:5) does indeed invite one to establish a "righteousness of one's own" that will divide Jew from non-Jew and make life dependent on performance. On that invitation Israel "stumbled." But the same law, when one reads Deut. 30:12–14 prefixed by Deut. 9:4, forbids presuming to do for oneself what God has already done (in Christ). The message about trusting in God, "which we preach," is already located "near at hand" by Scripture, in the mouth by which human beings confess, and in the heart by which they rely upon, what God has done, and this is illustrated by two elementary Christian creeds (Rom. 10:9). That is how righteousness is attained and salvation is found, not in one's own deeds. In the words of that foundation stone that God has himself placed in Zion (9:33), to which Paul now returns (10:11), "everyone who trusts in God will be vindicated." Paul adds the word "everyone" to that text of Isa. 28:16. By what right? Because Joel 2:32 does just that (Rom. 10:13). Just as there was no distinction between Jew and Greek in the matter of sin's power (3:22b), so there is no distinction between them before the riches of one and the same God, who is Lord of all (cf. 9:5b). As in many of Paul's quotations from the OT, "Lord" stands for the name of God himself in 10:12 and does not refer separately to Christ (→ Tetragrammaton). But this fusing of the text from Deut. 30:12–14 with Paul's own "message about faith which we preach" (v. 8b), so clearly carried out by his inserting explanatory comments into that text in vv. 6–8, is both result and confirmation of his perception of complete continuity and consistency between the God of Israel and the Father of Jesus Christ. To exhibit that consistency, which is God's faithfulness, is Paul's aim in these chapters. If not all have obeyed the good news (v. 16), all the conditions for its reception have been provided by God; the bearers of his message were hailed already in Isaiah's time (vv. 14–15). Trust is created by that message and that message comes (now) through the preaching of what God has done in Christ (v. 17).

Second, in vv. 18–21, the Gentiles come back into view as Paul returns from Israel's role to God's in that enigmatic reversal of 9:30–33. Can it be that Israel did not hear or understand? The next three OT texts (10:18–20) indicate that it did indeed hear, as the earlier vv.

15–16 had confirmed, but that something else was going on. The second passage (v. 19, quoting Deut. 32:21) comes from the context of Israel's defection to idolatry in the wilderness (1 Cor. 10:7, 22 show that Paul read Deut. 32:21 in the light of Exod. 32:6 and is probably thinking of the golden calf; cf. commentary above on 9:3). It was Israel's known provocation of God that elicited his return threat to provoke them with a "nonpeople" and a "foolish nation." Paul understands that as applying now to the unforeseen success of the Gentiles in reaching the goal that Israel has missed (9:30), as is clear from his third citation in 10:20. In deliberately showing himself to people who were not even trying to find him, and who had no comprehension of God's purposes ("a nation devoid of understanding" is an ironic echo of a Jewish label for Gentiles, cf. 2:20), God was not only pursuing his justification of the undeserving; he was goading his own people and showing his attachment to them (this striking motif will be resumed in 11:11, 14). Was that a breakdown in God's election? On the contrary, as Isaiah said, God has never ceased to reach out to Israel, even in the midst of her defiance (10:21).

11:1–36, The Impartiality of God's Faithfulness. In this final chapter, Paul closes in on his goal, pulling the pieces together now in a series of concluding steps, for which he provides the familiar rhetorical markers.
11:1–10, A Remnant Continues. The last part of chap. 10 still leaves a question. God's word to Israel has not failed. Israel, descended through Jacob, yet defined by promise and not by the outward criterion of physical descent, called into being by the God who shows mercy (9:6–13, 16), is an actual people, not a fancy constructed out of future promises. If it has missed God's intent for it by a wide margin, and if God himself has had some hand in its doing so (9:31–33; 10:19), does it not follow that God has repudiated his own people? In reply, Paul uses the OT concept of the "remnant" (→Remnant). Like many other religious terms, this notion can be nuanced in different ways. Sometimes it refers to all the residue of God's people surviving a time of judgment and catastrophe; it then is used to emphasize its continuity and miraculous preservation. Paul understood the term in this inclusive sense when quoting Isa. 10:22 in Rom. 9:27, namely as a synonym of "seed" in 9:29 (RSV: "children") and 9:8 (RSV: "descendants"). But "remnant" may also be used exclusively to identify an "elite" minority within a larger whole, distinguished by special fidelity or piety; the Qumran community understood itself as such a faithful remnant (→ Scrolls, The Dead Sea). That Paul uses it in an exclusive sense here is clear from his differentiating "the elect" and

"the rest" (clearly not those included in the "remnant") in v. 7, and from the analogy he draws with the seven thousand in the days of Elijah (1 Kings 19:10, 14, 18). The difference in nuance is important. In chap. 9 Paul was distinguishing all of authentic Israel from that which was, even for Jewish perceptions, not Israel. Now he is drawing a distinction within Israel. In this meaning of "remnant," the promissory assurance that the preservation of a part gives for the future of the whole is the key. The "oracle" (v. 4, NEB) to Elijah was God's own pledge then, as it is to Paul now, that God has not abandoned his people (v. 2). Paul, however, goes out of his way (vv. 5–6) to emphasize that this continuity-providing remnant is "a matter of the election of grace" (cf. 9:11–12), the product of that undeserved creative love of God that produced a Jacob alongside of Esau, and not the result of one group's being any better or deserving than the rest of Israel. Who is that remnant? There is nothing in the text to suggest that Paul is thinking of Christians. The empirical evidence he adduces is simply his own person, not by virtue of his Christian faith, which he does not mention (that would make it a "work" in the sense of v. 6), but in his unassailable flesh and blood identity as an Israelite (v. 1), a part of Israel's whole (9:1–5). Undoubtedly Paul does not feel himself alone; he does not liken himself to Elijah in that respect. But it remains a fact that he does not appeal directly to Christ here for assurance about Israel's future but to the pledge of Israel's (and his) God. While he uses the distinction between Jew and non-Jew, he simply does not draw any lines anywhere in chaps. 9–11 between authentic Jews and authentic Christians (cf. 9:24), just as he perceives no split in himself —or in God.

A remnant of Israel, represented by Paul, did then arrive at that goal mentioned in 9:31, but (all) the rest did not. With two more texts (vv. 8–9), the first of them a complex mix of phrases from Deuteronomy and Isaiah, Paul not only documents the majority's lasting misunderstanding and blindness, but explains the painful reality of it as a deliberate deed of God. Such use of these passages belongs to a broad early Christian tradition of appeal to OT texts on God's causing blindness and misunderstanding in Israel, in order to explain the painful riddle of Jewish repudiation of the gospel (cf. the use of Isa. 6:9–11 in Matt. 13:14–15; Mark 4:12; Luke 8:10; John 12:40; Acts 28:26–27). Paul's point, however, is a continuation of Rom. 9:33 and 10:18–21: to show God's continuing presence and purpose with Israel, and so to refute the suggestion that he has abandoned it. This becomes clear in the next step.
11:11–16, The Part is Surety for the Whole. These verses should not be divided; they belong together in both thematic content and purpose.

Verse 13a ("I am talking to you Gentiles") does not mark a change of audience; that largely gentile Christian audience has been the same from 9:1 on. But Paul deliberately calls its attention to itself to accentuate these verses. If God is responsible for Israel's blindness, the question is still, has God become Israel's enemy and destroyer? "Have they faltered only finally to fall? Absolutely not! On the contrary, through their false step, salvation has been extended to the Gentiles in order to incite Israel to jealousy." Here is a double claim about God: first, that Israel's closure to God's righteousness (10:3) serves God's purpose to bestow his riches impartially upon all (10:12) and thus to extend his salvation to non-Jews; but second, that in that very action, by provoking them to anger over these outsiders (10:19), God's own "jealousy" or zeal for Israel, his undeterrable possessive claim on it, and his faithfulness to it, is operating to awaken and recall it. Paul's own calling as an "apostle to the Gentiles" (cf. 1:5) is in service to this God, so that ultimately it coincides with his own deepest desire for his kinfolk, his "flesh" (v. 14), and one loyalty cannot be played off against the other. So the beneficiaries of God's hostile treatment of Israel are the non-Jews, and the beneficiary of God's reconciliation of the world is Israel. Verses 12 and 15 are parallel and play on linguistic contrast: if Israel's "diminution" enriches the world, what will its "plenitude" produce (v. 12)? If its "being spurned" causes reconciliation, what will its "being embraced" bring about (v. 15)? The above two claims about God are so fused in Paul's mind that both these verses are ambivalent; one cannot really tell whether in describing God's ultimate benefit, "life from the dead," he means its accrual to Jew or Gentile. The distinction has evaporated in the text. Both are equally indebted to the same life-giving God (cf. 4:12). And the part is surety for the whole: the remnant, for the indivisible whole of Israel; the Jew Paul, for his "flesh"; Israel, for God's whole creation. Significantly, Paul ends (v. 16) with two OT figures for the consecrating effect of the part upon the whole, the dedicatory cereal offering for the whole harvest (Num. 15:17–21; → Heave Offering) and the root and the branch (→Branch). One might suppose that he has only the remnant and the whole of Israel in mind with these allusions, but the next verses, into which the second figure leads, demonstrate conclusively the universal scope of their application.

11:17–24, The Metaphor of the Olive Tree. Despite all the horticultural objections that have been raised about it, the theological point of Paul's metaphor of the olive tree is lucid and forceful (he concedes in v. 24 that it runs "contrary to nature"; → Olive). Directed to the non-Jews (v. 13), it makes clear, first, that salvation is available for them only in continuity with

Israel's history and in dependence on Israel's God. The root is now Israel and the branches are the Jews and the rest of humankind. Everything Paul has said in Romans about God's justification of the unrighteous in Jesus Christ is empty unless this means a restored relationship to the God of Abraham, Isaac, and Jacob. It makes clear, second, that Jew and Gentile are alike utterly dependent on the creative freedom of this God to cut out and to graft in, to bestow life on his own terms where it is wholly undeserved, both "according to nature" and "contrary to nature" (v. 24). This leaves no room for either pride ("Do not become high-minded, but stand in awe," v. 20) or contempt ("God has the power to graft them back in," v. 33). God's freedom keeps the frontiers open for his mercy rather than closed; Paul is rejecting at every point that rigid determinism of conventional religion that divides humankind into the saved and the damned. And the illustration makes clear, third, that trust in this God is the issue for men and women, for Jew (v. 23) and for non-Jew (v. 20). The precipitous severity of God and his kindness are correlated to unbelief and faith. But it is God, in his goodness and righteousness, who determines these reversals; no one can manipulate him, and any attempt to do so is a violation of trust.

The chapter ends with three distinct conclusions.

11:25–27, Prophetic Conclusion. The first answers the question about Israel's destiny and ends chap. 11. Using the term "mystery" in a meaning shaped by the apocalyptic tradition to refer to God's ultimate purposes for his world, hidden from human perception but disclosed on God's own terms (cf. Dan. 2:27–28; 1 Enoch 9:6; 63:3; → Mystery: In the OT and Judaism), Paul takes the stand of a prophet. Part of Israel has been "hardened" for the sake of all non-Jewish peoples, but "in this way" (v. 26) all Israel will be saved. The end-time miracle will consist in the justification of God's own people as ungodly (4:4), when God will "remove ungodliness from Jacob." Paul's supporting text in vv. 26–27 is a remarkable combination of Isa. 27:9; 59:20; and Jer. 31:33. In this deliverance, the two sides of God's righteousness (Rom. 3:26) will again be evident: in not tolerating ungodliness, God is "himself righteous," but by bringing the Deliverer from Zion who will establish Israel's righteousness, God is also "the one who makes righteous those who are righteous by trust." Paul does not here call for Jewish conversion to Christianity or a separate Christian mission to the Jewish people. The mystery of Judaism's refusal of the gospel is an aspect of its misunderstanding of its own tradition and of the "near word" of Deuteronomy that called for faith (chap. 10), even its misunderstanding of God. But there is no break in the Jews' relationship to God, just as no Gentile is outside God's election love (9:25–26). From the very beginning of the Letter, Paul has set forth the meaning of Christ not as an alternative or rival to God for the affections and trust of human beings, but as God's way of restoring integrity to the relationship of all, both Jew and Greek, to himself. The final salvation of all Israel is God's own "mystery," but the certainty of it, and the terms on which it must take place, like those of all God's world, are disclosed in God's revelation of his righteousness in Jesus Christ (see commentary above on 3:21–26).

11:28–32, Logical Conclusion. To this certainty and these terms Paul returns in a second conclusion, crowning the whole of chaps. 9–11, in which he speaks as a rhetorician and teacher. The tightly structured dialectic summarizes his argument:

A. "In relation to the gospel, they are [God's] enemies on your account;

B. In relation to election, they are [his] beloved on account of the patriarchs.

   C. For the gifts and calling of God cannot be rescinded.

A'. For just as you once disobeyed God but now have obtained mercy through their disobedience,

B'. So they too now have disobeyed the mercy extended to you, in order that they might themselves also now be recipients of mercy.

   C'. For God has consigned all human beings to disobedience in order to bestow mercy on all."

Line C (v. 29) reaffirms God's election and his faithfulness to his promises, the point of chap. 9. Line C' (v. 32) reaffirms God's impartiality, the point made by Paul in chaps. 2–4 that raised the issue of Israel and required the writing of chaps. 9–11. The two are not in conflict. God's justification of the undeserving embraces all human beings on equal terms, but this "universalism" is one that confronts them all with both judgment and mercy (cf. 5:12–21).

11:33–36, Liturgical Conclusion. In this third conclusion, Paul takes the stance of the worshiper and uses an early Christian hymn. Its triadic structure is clear. Verse 33 is made up of three exclamatory lines: the first praises God's wealth, wisdom, and knowledge, three very Hellenistic religious categories; the other two repeat the exclamation in terms of the Hebraic notions of God's judgments and ways. Verse 34 consists of three rhetorical questions, all drawn from OT poetic and wisdom passages, that resume in inverse order the three concepts of the first line. The implied answer to each "Who?" is "No one but God himself!" Verse 36 concludes with a couplet: the first line is a profoundly Hellenistic formula for God's omnipotence and transcendence (cf. 1 Cor. 8:6; Col. 1:16; Heb. 2:10); the last is a conventional biblical doxology. Such praise of the God who transcends human understanding can easily slip into resignation and despair (cf. 2 Apoc. Bar. 14:8–11). God remains beyond human manipulation. Still, authentic faith and obedience, and the undergirding hope of salvation, do not rest on God's withholding himself but on his making himself known, on his own terms, as a God who can be trusted. This is the God Paul praises at the conclusion of his argument.

12:1–15:13

The Community Exhortation

With 12:1 the nature and tone of the Letter shift unmistakably to ethical and practical exhortation. Romans shares with other NT Letters, not only those written by Paul, the tendency to gather such material at the end (cf. 1 Thess. 4–5; Phil. 4; Gal. 5–6; Col. 3–4; Eph. 4–6; even such documents as Hebrews and 1 Peter, which incorporate hortatory passages throughout, follow this pattern in their conclusions: Heb. 13 and 1 Pet. 5). This tendency of the Letters reflects both the influence of Jewish and Hellenistic sermonic traditions on their composition and the personal experiences of their writers as leaders in their communities and participants in their worship assemblies, where such exhortation took place (and where Paul expects his Letters to be read). Thus it is not surprising to find Paul incorporating into these final chapters of Romans material that bears many marks of traditional catechetical instruction and shows clear parallels with other Letters, his own and others'. Yet Paul is never a slave to the conventions he follows, and it is important to reflect briefly on the inner connection between his use of this material and the argument of the first part of the Letter.

Romans is peculiarly instructive because the concluding exhortations of this Letter do not emerge from Paul's own personal familiarity with the church as its founder, nor are they a response to its appeals to him for guidance. The central argument itself has shown that no sharp separation is possible between Paul's "theology" and his "ethics." His exposition of the gospel as a revelation of God's righteousness, God's gracious initiative to restore integrity to the relationships of human beings to himself and to each other, has involved release from the patterns and condemnation of the past, the renewal of commitment, and the reordering of life in this world (cf. esp. commentary above on 6:1–7:6). That exposition can certainly gain now in both intelligibility and persuasiveness by the addition of concrete advice and counsel, but it is not the case that the truth of the argument depends on the exhortation or that the revelation of God's righteousness remains somehow defective or inconclusive until Paul's gospel is "applied" by its hearers to the practice of living. His position has clearly been that the human situation and the behavior it calls for have been defined by the death and resurrection of Christ, not the other way around. The "indicative" of his gospel entails and creates an "imperative" that the exhortations can now in one sense only elaborate and clarify. But it also does not follow, on the other hand, that these concluding chapters remain essentially dispensable embellishments to his argument and, because they utilize tradition, contain no proper concerns and reflections of Paul's own. A closer look at these chapters will refute such a conclusion, but the earlier argument itself prepares the way. For in it, and especially in the diagnosis of human religious failure that accompanies Paul's exposition of God's righteousness all along, Paul nowhere represents his readers as morally disengaged or indifferent. The fundamental malaise is a distortion that the religious zeal of morally serious people has introduced into their relationship to God; the symptom of sin's power is not sloth but the breeding of just those results that an active religious commitment is seeking to prevent (cf. 2:1–24; 7:7–25; 10:1–4; 11:17–24). The human problem is not lack of religion but religion that lacks trust (faith) and for that reason does not honor God as God or give thanks to him (1:21; 3:27–30; 9:32), that misunderstands and resists God (8:5–8; 10:3). This means that the point of chaps. 12–15 is quite different from what modern readers, looking for religious encouragement in a "secular" world, may be inclined to hear. The function of these chapters is not to incite or inspire "religious" behavior or supply a moral dimension to life, as though these were missing; the world of Paul and his readers is full of both. Rather, what his readers now need are guidelines to help discern and promote integrity in a religious life that has been distorted, corrections to religious motivations that will bring these into line with the righteousness of faith, criteria for conduct suitable to the imperatives enunciated earlier (e.g., in 6:11, 12–14; 8:12). The revelation of God's righteousness does not remain defective, but the shaping of human lives to its patterns remains incomplete, an unfinished goal of the apostle's calling (1:5), and as indispensable a part of his gospel as the still unlived future conferred by the sharing of Christ's destiny (cf. commentary above on 6:1–11).

12:1–13:14
Basic Exhortations

The exhortations appear to fall into two groups: chaps. 12–13 contain elemental appeals not related to a community problem under debate; chaps. 14–15, specific overtures occasioned by the major issue that called forth the writing of Romans, the coexistence of Jews and non-Jews in one religious fellowship (Paul does not use the word "church" at all in Romans until chap. 16).

12:1–2, Transitional Introduction. Paul's opening words set the tone. "I appeal to you" (RSV) means much more than a request; a summons and an encouragement is now being extended, in a deliberate reprise of Paul's diagnosis of human disorder at the beginning of the Letter (see the concluding remark on 1:18–32 in commentary above). Embracing all human life under the metaphor of an archetypal cultic act, Paul urges his readers, on the basis of God's "compassion," to offer their "bodies," i.e., their selves as these are at their discretion for allegiance and action (cf. 6:12–13, 19), to God as a "sacrifice" that will be at once animated by the life God has bestowed, dedicated to his purposes, and acceptable to him. Approbation by God is the ultimate sanction for every cultic action, but Paul adds another. Using a Stoic term for what is peculiarly human both in distinction from the animal or material world and in affiliation with the divine (and translated variously as "reasonable," KJV, or "spiritual," RSV), Paul declares such dedication of themselves to be the authentic worship appropriate to a reordered human life. Such reordering is to consist now of their distancing themselves from the patterns and priorities of "this [present] age" (the expression appears here for the first time in Romans; cf. Gal. 1:4; 1 Cor. 2:6–8; 3:18; 2 Cor. 4:4) for the sake of the renovation that the gospel provides (cf. Rom. 6:4; 7:6; the transformation language used by Paul for this change recalls Rom. 8:29; cf. 1 Cor. 15:49; 2 Cor. 3:18; Phil. 3:21). Its signal manifestation will be a renewed "mind" possessing once more the lost capacity to "discern what the will of God is" (v. 2; cf. 1:21) and so to distinguish good and evil. The absence of casuistry or legalism from these verses only enhances the urgency of this call to individual accountability to God.

12:3–8, The Use of Diverse Gifts in One Community. A close comparison of this passage with 1 Cor. 12:4–31, especially vv. 4–11, is instructive. Paul's Corinthian crisis had demonstrated the destructive effects wrought on the cohesion and harmony of a congregation when the religious standings of competitive individuals are linked to the inevitable variations in human talents and gifts. So Paul's first call is for a tempering of conceit in one's "mind-set" (cf. 8:5–8) in favor of a more sober self-assessment "according to the measuring standard of faith God has provided to each" (v. 3). It is faith, to which all have equal access, that puts all on the same footing before God (cf. 3:22, 27, 30). All members are, like the apostle himself, beneficiaries of the one graciousness of God ("the grace given," vv. 3 and 6, appears to be a distinctively Pauline formula; cf. Rom. 15:15; 1 Cor. 3:10; Gal. 2:9). But this one grace produces "different gifts" (v. 6) that so enable the exercise of diverse functions within the group that the gifts are identified only by listing the functions (vv. 6–8; unlike 1 Cor. 12:28, this list contains no ordered ranking, for Paul is no longer disputing the Corinthians' priorities). The one grace is God's; the various gifts are human faculties (despite the formulaic expression, it is not until after Paul's time, in Eph. 3:2, 7, 8, that these two are so identified that the grace becomes itself the possessed human gift). Unlike 1 Corinthians, nothing in Paul's language here connects these gifts with the Spirit or traces the creation of this diversity to the Spirit (cf. 1 Cor. 12:11); what is retained from the Corinthian experience is the solution to the threat posed by pluralism and diversity but not the originating occasion for it in the Corinthians' glorification of ecstatic spiritual phenomena such as glossolalia (speaking in tongues). Corresponding to this relationship of the many gifts to the one grace from which they derive is the parallel relation of the many members to the "one body in Christ" (v. 5), in the service of which the many gifts are to be employed. As in 1 Corinthians this social metaphor, widely used in the ancient world, of the body as a complex organism of many members, is used to reconcile diversity and unity in the community, though Paul does not here use the expression "the body of Christ" (in Rom. 7:4 it denoted the solidarity of individuals with Christ in his destiny-creating role). Thus diversities are acknowledged but stripped of their divisive power by being subordinated to the interpretive norm of "faith." Each person is to exercise his or her own gift in recognition of its source and in a manner appropriate to its function for the whole; the gift itself has created the responsibility and supplies the norm for its right use.

12:9–21, Relations to Fellow Human Beings. Since in 1 Cor. 12:31 Paul turns from the variety of gifts to focus on love, v. 9a, "Let love be without dissimulation," has seemed to form a topic sentence for the next section. One may recognize a certain controlling position for this first admonition, but the section itself scarcely offers a coherent exposition of love comparable

to 1 Corinthians 13. The unit provides instead, in both syntax and content, a clear example of traditional catechetical admonition: short injunctions arranged in no obvious pattern, at best in small groupings linked by key terms or catchwords (cf. 1 Thess. 5:12–22; Heb. 13:1–17). Verses 9–13 appear to focus on relationships within the community and vv. 14–21 on external ones, but even this distinction is tenuous. More illuminating is the sudden increase of echoes and reminiscences of identifiable traditions: of the Jesus tradition in v. 14 (Matt. 5:44), or vv. 17 and 21 (Matt. 5:39); of Deut. 32:35 in v. 19b; of Jewish wisdom traditions in v. 15 (Sir. 7:34), v. 16 (Prov. 3:7), v. 17 (Prov. 3:4, LXX), and v. 20 (Prov. 25:21–22). This helps interpret the difficult v. 20b: in a certain Egyptian ritual, a basin of burning charcoal carried on the head was a token of penitence (cf. 2 Esd. 16:53). Thus in vv. 17–21 a clear thematic unity emerges to be summed up in the last verse (which also resumes v. 9b): the tempering of violence and revenge in hostile human relationships is less an act of human love (v. 9a) then it is the fruit of a trust that has learned to rely on God's impartial love for all (cf. Matt. 5:43–48). Human relations are nourished by security, not anxiety; the issue for Paul throughout Romans has been to identify authentic security and confidence in place of its illusory perversions (cf. Rom. 5:1–11 and see commentary above on that passage).

13:1–7, Relations to Those in Authority. Because of the many and controversial uses to which this section has been put since it was written, it is especially important to try to read it in its context in Romans and in Paul's world. A series of observations may be useful.

First, in this context the passage does not offer a comprehensive theoretical treatment of "the state" but simply guidance in relation to the specific and individual bearers of imperial authority, including the never popular collectors of taxes (v. 6); the last verse embraces a variety of civil obligations. That Christians would one day themselves exercise such authority is simply not envisaged. There is nothing specifically Christian about the appeal and no distinction is drawn between Christian and non-Christian members of the social order; that simply underscores one intent of the passage: to urge on Paul's readers the fulfillment of their civil obligations, not just the pleasant ones, and to forestall any reading of his earlier plea "not to be conformed to this present age" (12:2) as an exemption from them. Paul's language accords with this; the words "servant" (v. 4, twice) and "officers" (v. 6, JB) are standard secular terms for public functionaries and any religious connotation comes only from the attached possessive, "God's."

Second, the Greek verb used in the opening imperative belongs to the basic vocabulary of NT hortatory tradition; its root stem denotes "order" ("be subordinate to"), and it is used in this tradition to invite and summon participation in an order presumed to be hierarchical in nature, whether political (1 Pet. 2:13; Titus 3:1), or familial (of wives, Col. 3:18; Eph. 5:22, 24; 1 Pet. 3:1, 5; Titus 2:5; of household slaves, 1 Pet. 2:18; Titus 2:9). The verb is not a simple synonym for "obey"; it is never used in these NT codes of household obligations for the obedience of children to parents. Here in Rom. 13:1–2, Paul's own use of three additional Greek cognates derived from the same stem (translated "instituted," "rebels," and "institution" by the NEB) shows he is deliberately appropriating this denotation of "order," which earlier in Romans embraces the natural creation (8:20; cf. 1 Cor. 15:27–28). At the same time, Paul's use of this verb in 8:7 and 10:3 demonstrates that this subordination involves for him the recognition or acknowledgment that inspires voluntary submission. (Vivid corroboration is provided by 1 Cor. 16:15b–16, where his appeal to "be subject" is grounded in recognition of the role played by leaders, probably including women, who have dedicated or "submitted" themselves to ministry; this "order" within the religious community, 1 Cor. 14:32, 40, is closely related to its health and "peace," for God himself is not a God of anarchy, 1 Cor. 14:33.)

Third, this (necessarily) hierarchical conception of order has two implications that connect the passage with well-established traditions and so shed further light on its meaning. One is that all authority is derivative and ultimately dependent on God's authorization and sufferance, a deep-seated Jewish conviction documented in the OT prophets (Isa. 41:1–4; 45:1–3; Dan. 2:21), wisdom literature (Prov. 8:15; Sir. 10:4; 17:17; Wisd. of Sol. 6:1–3) and apocalyptic (1 Enoch 46:5; 2 Apoc. Bar. 82:9; cf. also Let. Arist. 196, 219, 224). This firm certainty, given its most vivid NT formulation in John 19:11, underlies both Rom. 13:1–7 and Revelation 13 (a passage that does not share Paul's present benign perspective on Roman imperial power and so is often too simply played off against Rom. 13). Contrary to the use often made of Rom. 13:1b to absolutize political authority, this perception binds all earthly power to God's ultimate sovereignty and thus limits and relativizes the former, just as the OT claim that the earth is the Lord's desacralizes the earth's seasons and fertility and prohibits their religious veneration (cf. 1 Cor. 10:26; Ps. 50:7–15; Hos. 2:8). Closely allied with this view of authority as derivative is the Hellenistic Jewish premise, plainly underlying vv. 3–4, that the purpose of civil authority is to reward and encourage good conduct as well as to punish and inhibit evil (cf. 1 Pet. 2:14; Let. Arist. 280, 291–92); the passage is thus informed less by a naive indulgence toward political power than by a traditional view of its noble ends that is neither contemptuous of authority as such nor extravagant in its esteem for it. This explains v. 5b, which introduces the sanction of conscience; these civil obligations are to be honored on the basis of one's prior cognizance of good and evil and one's own responsibility to the good. Beyond this, questions of illegitimate authority or the abuse of power are simply not raised; the passage shares with Mark 12:17; Matt. 22:21; Luke 20:25 a basic assent to the legitimacy of Roman power.

Fourth, this passage is distinguished from its parallels in 1 Pet. 2:13–14; 1 Tim. 2:1–2; Titus 3:1, first, by Paul's warning against resistance or "defiance of order" (v. 2) and second, by a striking emphasis on "fear" of authority (vv. 3a, 3b, 4). What is meant is a proper and deserved fear, since the authority itself is assumed to be legitimate, and the aim is to counsel a way to avoid such "fear," not to aggravate it. Just these distinctive features of the passage have invited later political use of it to force submission to the holders of power, but they actually show that Paul is interested in stabilizing the attitudes of religious subjects toward existing bearers of authority. In Paul's world the tendency of religious movements was to clothe imperial power with the absolutes of either the divine (→ Augustus; Rome: Augustus) or the demonic (cf. Rev. 13), to heighten fear, and especially in some Jewish circles to spill over into active political resistance (→Zealot). While Paul may have thought to quiet some particular political tendency in Rome such as the "tumults" that led Claudius to expel the Jews from Rome shortly before (see above "Introduction: The Occasion and Purpose of Romans"), his overriding aim is to encourage the fulfillment of social obligations in a context of trust in God and recognition of his prevailing sovereignty and order. This is consistent with both Paul's preceding counsel against resorting to revenge (12:19–21) and his subsequent pointer to God's approaching salvation as reason for sobriety in daily conduct (13:12–13).

13:8–10, Love as the Fulfillment of the Mosaic Law.
Verse 8a links this new paragraph both with the preceding, by repeating v. 7a in negative form, and with 12:9–13, by resuming its leading injunction to love. But the major contribution of this unit in the context of Romans as a whole lies in its interpretation of the law. The one continuing obligation of the Christian life that is never paid off is "the debt of mutual love" (v. 8a, JB). The reason for this is not that the law remains unfulfilled or only partially fulfilled (in all of Paul's argument in Romans with respect to justification and the law,

the issue has never revolved upon the degree to which the law is fulfilled or not). Instead, the reason is simply the law's abiding claim: one who loves "the other person" (v. 8b), the "next person" in one's daily contact (v. 10, almost universally translated "neighbor"), "has fulfilled the law" (v. 8b)—a gnomic statement of principle that defines what it is that the Mosaic law truly requires in human relations and what brings it to its "fulfillment" (v. 10b). Human relations are in view; the four commandments Paul cites (in the order of the LXX in Deut. 5:17–18, as in Luke 18:20; James 2:11) are limited to the so-called "second table" of the Decalogue, those negative commands that shield human life from violation, but he makes clear that "any other [such] commandment" (v. 9) is included in the representation of these four. All are "summed up" in the command to love one's neighbor as oneself (Lev. 19:18; cf. Gal. 5:14). While similar attempts to summarize the law are found in contemporary Judaism (→ Commandment; Golden Rule), Paul's straightforward use of Lev. 19:18 as the summary seems to derive from the Jesus tradition (Matt. 22:34–40; Mark 12:28–34; Luke 10:25–28; cf. Matt. 7:12). On the other hand, there is no hint here of the "double commandment" of Jesus, which pairs love of neighbor to love of God. In Paul's Letters "love of God" is always God's own love; human love for God is mentioned only in Rom. 8:28; 1 Cor. 2:9; and 8:3, in all three instances only to be overshadowed by human debt to God's generosity and initiative. For Paul the more appropriate human response to God's love and compassion (Rom. 12:1) is honor and thanksgiving (1:21) and trust (4:20–21) in God on the one hand, and, on the other, this love toward neighbor that is nothing else than the reordering of human life in accordance with God's will (12:2). For this is the substance of the law, the never ending claim of God on human life embodied in God's "holy, just, and good commandment" (7:12) that Paul's gospel never undermines but only confirms (3:31b; cf. 8:4).

13:11–14, Living for God's Coming Day. A final section concludes these basic exhortations and forms a closing bracket to 12:1–2. Where Paul had begun by urging his readers to abandon the patterns of "this [present] age" (12:2), he now asks for conduct appropriate to God's certain and approaching salvation. This orientation to the future and a host of new images characteristic of NT catechetical and hortatory traditions give the section a unity and flavor of its own. The "day" of God's wrath and judgment (2:5, 16), often spoken of as "darkness" (beginning with the prophetic tradition; cf. Amos 5:18), is now the day of God's coming salvation and stands as the polar opposite to the darkness of this world. (It is usually referred to by Paul as

"the day of the Lord" or "of Jesus Christ"; cf. 1 Cor. 1:8; 5:5; 2 Cor. 1:14; Phil. 1:6, 10; 2:16; 1 Thess. 5:2; contrast 2 Cor. 6:2.) Such religious use of the opposites "light" and "darkness" is so widespread in the ancient world that it cannot be identified with any one tradition; Paul's clear dualistic use here is reminiscent of 1 Thess. 5:4–8 (see also Eph. 5:7–14; John 3:19–21; 12:35–36). When this antithesis is linked to the verbal imagery of "throwing off" and "putting on" attire (sometimes martial) and to the moral contrasts between indecency and propriety and the ethical metaphors of drunkenness and sobriety, the result is a telling hortatory fusion of images deeply rooted in the Greek religious and moral world with a Jewish apocalyptic sense of temporal urgency (cf. Col. 3:8, 10, 12; Eph. 4:22, 24; 6:11, 13–17). The final imperative to "put on the Lord Jesus Christ" (v. 14a) locates this homiletic-didactic language in the setting of early Christian baptism (cf. Gal. 3:27): if baptism attests to the individual's identification with the life pattern of Jesus (Rom. 6:1–11), and this "image" is the destiny set for each by the Creator (8:29), the companion ethical catechism will consist at its heart in the appeal to "assume" and embrace that image and live by it. For that is where each person's future lies, not with "the flesh" and the "desires" it serves (v. 14b).

14:1–15:13
Specific Exhortations

This second set of appeals forms the final block of material in the Letter body of Romans. At this point and until he resumes some of the conventions of the Letter conclusion in 15:14–16:27, Paul no longer makes use of the Christian catechetical or even quasi-liturgical traditions so apparent in 12:1–13:14. The lively dialogical style of his earlier chapters is recaptured. His characteristic mode of citing OT Scripture, with an introductory formula to ground an argument instead of by mere allusion, reappears (14:11; 15:3; cf. also 12:19); the catena of quotations in 15:9–12 exactly imitates the sequences of 9:25–29 and 10:18–21. Earlier in the Letter, as the argument moved away from the relationship of Jew and Gentile and the deliberate appropriation of such Jewish traditions as those surrounding Abraham, the scriptural quotations themselves almost disappeared (the exceptions in 7:7 and 8:36 are all the more noteworthy); these citations return in thick abundance with the subject of Israel and the Gentiles in chaps. 9–11. It is scarcely accidental that the earlier pattern of biblical documentation should reassert itself just as Paul's exhortations now converge on the specific issue of solidarity of Jew and Gentile within the Christian community. Finally, whereas the basic exhortations of 12:1–13:14 contain only two references to Christ (12:5 and

13:14), this new division is replete with them. The second of those previous two, the concluding baptismal reminder of 13:14, supplies a leitmotiv for these specific exhortations, and Paul's climactic appeal in 15:7 finds its leading warrant in a solemn Christological dictum on the significance of Christ for both Jew and Gentile. In all these respects, the Paul of the main argument of Romans reemerges from his more comprehensive appeals to press his controlling preoccupation with the unity of Jew and Gentile, i.e., all human beings, before the saving power of God. This section, once again, falls naturally into three parts.

14:1–12, Jewish and Non-Jewish Observance Before an Impartial Lord. Paul's terminology bears careful observation. The person who is "weak in faith" (14:1) is one who does not "have the confidence to eat everything" (v. 2), but Paul does not put a premium on the degree of such confidence each one is able to demonstrate (he does not call anyone "strong" until 15:1; see commentary below on 15:1). Instead, it is apparent that differences of religious observance in matters of diet and holy days are under discussion because they occasion reciprocal disdain and contempt within the community (v. 3). The recurring tensions created between Jewish and gentile converts to the Christian movement by such differences in daily religious routines constitute a running theme through the NT (e.g., Mark 2:13–17, 18–20, 23–28 and parallels; Acts 10:9–16; 11:11–18; 15:6–11; Gal. 2:11–14), testimony to the long struggle to find effective bonds to transcend pluralistic practice. At first the issue in Romans 14 does not look like one created by this difference between Jew and non-Jew. Abstaining from meat and alcohol (vv. 2 and 21) are not themselves characteristic Jewish observances. They could become so because Jews (and Jewish Christians) would prefer abstinence to partaking of either in the urban settings of the empire in which both were regularly dedicated to pagan gods before being sold in the market (→Food Offered to Idols). So one is tempted to read Romans 14 in the same terms as Paul's advice to the Corinthians (1 Cor. 8:1–13; 10:12–33). But closer reading demonstrates that Paul is modulating his Corinthian experience to fit the argument of Romans (cf. commentary above on 12:3–8). At every point here the issue is the redefinition of values (cf. 12:2), and never, as in 1 Corinthians, the use or abuse of Christian freedom (the words "freedom," "conscience," and "knowledge," so central to 1 Cor. 8 and 10, never occur in Rom. 14:1–15:13; cf. 15:14).

Paul's fundamental appeal is to "accept" (JB, NEB), to take to oneself and into one's own community, the person of contrasting, even opposite, religious practice (14:1 and 15:7); his desire is to break the cycle of mutual condemnation that regularly results from religious zeal when it is lacking in trust or faith (14:3–4). A person's "standing" (v. 4), that intangible worth so fatefully linked to public religious identity and usage, is determined by the Lord to whom each belongs—a direct practical application of what Paul wrote in 2:28–29. The confidence that counts is not the confidence to eat everything but the certainty that comes from integrity in each person's life-embracing relation to the Lord, whatever the practice that accompanies it, and it was to establish that integrity that Christ's death and resurrection took place (v. 9). Jew and Gentile stand on an equal footing before God, alike dependent upon his vindication of all human religious practice (v. 4b; cf. concluding remark on 7:13–25 in commentary above), alike beholden to his gift of life to all through their inclusion in Christ's own pattern of death and life (v. 9; cf. 4:25; 5:18; 6:10–11; 8:11; 2 Cor. 5:15), and alike accountable to the God they must all eventually recognize (vv. 10b–12; cf. 2:6; 3:4, 19).

14:13–23, A Definition of "Right" and "Wrong." In this paragraph Paul clarifies the issues raised by eating and drinking in a religious context. Verse 13 plays on different nuances of the verb "to judge": one sense is to assess the worth of a fellow human being; another is to arrive at the settling of one's own values, the criteria by which those assessments of others are made. What is at stake is what one holds to be "the good" (v. 16; cf. 12:2b) or "right" and "wrong" (vv. 20b, 21a, RSV). These, along with their equivalents in the ritual law of the OT, "clean" and "unclean," are measured first by what violates the personal integrity and religious conviction of the fellow human being "for whom Christ died" (vv. 13–16). In v. 15 sparing such "injury" (RSV) to the other is the specific form of "accepting" (14:1) the religiously different person; it is a concrete instance of "loving one's neighbor as oneself" (13:9). Verses 17–19 generalize this process of definition by appealing to more conventional qualities associated with the kingdom of God, to what is "well-pleasing" to God or passes the test of human experience, and to what contributes to the common good. But vv. 20–23 return to the narrower subject at hand. Freedom is not the issue. Conceding to the one side that food does not defile (v. 20b; cf. v. 14; Mark 7:19), Paul nevertheless restates his earlier test, whether an action violates or reverses "the work of God" (v. 20a; cf. 15b). It is wrong for one to eat when one really believes one should not (vv. 20c and 23a), and right to abstain when not to do so would strike at the sensibilities of others (v. 21). The foundation of right action in every case is a right relationship to God, of trust (vv. 22a and 23). In the only use Paul makes in his Letters of the common ancient beatitude form (Rom. 4:7–8 is an OT quotation; → Beatitudes), he pronounces that person blessed whose standing before God is not itself at stake in decisions about right and wrong (v. 22b), for whom that anxiety-producing link between diet and salvation has been subordinated to secure trust in God—a kind of ultimate practical application of the Letter's argument concerning justification.

15:1–13, Christ the Paradigm for Jew and Gentile. Those who are "strong" and secure in the sense just referred to, Paul goes on, have an obligation not simply to put up with the failings of the less strong but to support them (cf. Gal. 6:2). This is the only time Paul ever distinguishes some Christians from others as "strong" (a word not used in 1 Cor. 8–10; cf. 2 Cor. 13:9), and he includes himself among its referents. But he does so only to elucidate such "strength" with the model of Christ; Christ is the suffering righteous one of Ps. 69:9, who remained obedient while enduring the ultimate derision that could be carried out in the name of religion. (For the role of Ps. 69 in the passion narrative, cf. Mark 15:23, 36 and parallels; John 2:17; 15:25.) This is the Christ Paul's readers are to "put on" (13:14). Such commitment to "please" the other rather than oneself requires the endurance and encouraging support that come from God (v. 5a; cf. 5:3–5), that give life a dimension of hope, and that the Scriptures just quoted are intended to provide (v. 4).

In vv. 7–13, a passage strikingly resumptive of chaps. 9–11, the precipitating dietary occasion for friction between Jew and non-Jew vanishes completely before the vision of God's end-time purpose that they be joined in his praise. Once again, the vision is grounded in God's defining act in Christ (vv. 8–9), whose whole life was an act of "service": first to the Jews as a surety of God's truth and faithfulness (cf. 3:4), by confirming God's promises to the patriarchs; and then to the non-Jews, as a demonstration of God's mercy, by including them in the praise of Israel's God. That this "power of God that leads to salvation for everyone who relies on him, the Jew first and also the Greek" (1:16) should continue to fill and enrich the lives of his readers is the real substance of the petition with which Paul brings the body of his Letter to its close (v. 13).

15:14–16:27
Conclusion

15:14–33, Paul's Ministry and His Plans. Resuming now the personal conversation with his readers that was broken off in 1:15, Paul speaks again of his desire to extend his work to Spain with the support and understanding of the Roman Christians. Since he was not the founder of the Roman community, both tact and the compulsions of his own self-understanding lead him to speak in vv. 14–21 of his own ministry to the Gentiles in order to explain his imposing himself on the Romans. Of special interest is the priestly metaphor in which he casts his role (v. 16); by his bringing them into the range of "God's agenda," the Gentiles are themselves Paul's "offering" to God, and so provide the grounds for his "self-esteem" (v. 17; cf. 11:13). Yet he will claim nothing apart from Christ's own action through him to bring about obedience among the Gentiles (vv. 18–19; cf. 1:5). Thus his work merges into Christ's own inclusion of the non-Jew in God's salvation (cf. 1:16). This explains why Paul lays such store by not interfering in the labors of other (Jewish-Christian?) missionaries, a policy that seems to go back to his agreement with Peter and the other apostles in Jerusalem (Gal. 2:7–8) and which he justifies by applying to himself words from the servant songs of Second Isaiah (v. 21; cf. 2 Cor. 10:15–16; Isa. 52:15b; Rom. 10:20; →Isaiah, The Book of: The Songs of the Servant of the Lord). Paradoxically, just this practice explains his turning to a congregation someone else has founded for help in extending his own mission into untraveled territory beyond (vv. 22–24). In the meantime, however, Paul has to make a last trip to Jerusalem to deliver the monetary offering to which he committed himself at that Jerusalem conference and which symbolized for him the realization of one community from both Jews and Gentiles, a central theme of his Letter (cf. 9:24; 15:8–12). Paul's plea to the Romans for their prayers in his support (vv. 30–33) betrays both the significance he attached to this trip and the anxiety he felt over its outcome.

16:1–27, Personal Greetings and Benediction. The concluding chapter comprises several items more or less typical of conventional letter closings. Some of them raise questions about the original termination of Romans.

Verses 1–2 contain a recommendation of Phoebe, possibly as the bearer of Paul's Letter to Rome. (For such recommendations, cf. Acts 18:27; 1 Cor. 16:15–17.)

Verses 3–16 add personal greetings to a large number of acquaintances, of which twenty-six are identified by name. Since so many greetings in a Letter to a church Paul has not founded or visited are surprising, and since there is evidence that Romans did at some time circulate without chap. 16 (see below), it has been suspected that this chapter was originally sent as a separate recommendation of Phoebe to a church much better known to Paul, such as Ephesus. However, chap. 16 in its present form could not have comprised an independent letter. The first two persons named, Prisca and Aquila, are known to have been in Rome earlier (Acts 18:2–3); they and others known to Paul may have returned to Rome after the lifting of Claudius' ban (see above "Introduction: The Occasion and Purpose of Romans"). It would have served Paul's interests directly to name as many individual contacts in the Roman community as he possibly could, implicitly commending them to the rest as advocates for his cause.

Verses 17–20a warn against false teachers. Their tone contrasts sharply with 15:14–32. The language is Pauline, but the content is reminiscent of Paul's earlier references to opponents (2 Cor. 11:12–15; Phil. 3:18–19; Gal. 5:11; 6:17; Rom. 3:8). Paul may be hoping to inoculate his readers in advance against possible similar opposition in the future. Ironically, these verses can be taken to refer to some more real and present danger in Rome that Paul knew about only if chap. 15 was composed largely with the impending situation in Jerusalem in mind rather than some crisis in Rome, i.e., if Romans as a whole is best explained by the "Jerusalem crisis hypothesis" (see above "Introduction").

Verses 21–23 convey greetings from Paul's associates. Paul often adds general greetings from the place of writing (1 Cor. 16:19–20; 2 Cor. 13:13; Phil. 4:21), sometimes from named persons (1 Cor. 16:19; Philem. 23–24; cf. Col. 4:10–14). The names given in v. 21 are especially intriguing. Timothy is Paul's oft mentioned associate; Lucius (the Latin form of the Greek abbreviated name Luke) may be the Lucius of Cyrene of Acts 13:1; Jason may be the Thessalonian host of Acts 17:5–9, and Sosipater is very likely the Sopater of Beroea of Acts 20:4. Thus v. 21 may be a list of the delegates who are with Paul at the time of writing Romans, preparing for the trip to Jerusalem with the collection.

Verses 25–27 constitute a formal and liturgical doxology. Both content and style are more characteristic of letters written later by Paul's followers than of Paul in his undisputed Letters (Eph. 3:20–21; 1 Tim. 1:17; cf. Jude 24–25). Since v. 26 does contain echoes of Rom. 1:2, 5, this doxology may have been composed just for this Letter, as a more stately conclusion for public reading. This is the more likely to have occurred if Romans circulated in truncated versions without Paul's own conclusion. The evidence for this, in turn, is provided by the appearance of vv. 25–27 at different points in Greek mss., even though chaps. 15–16 or 16 still always follow in extant copies: after 14:23 (the majority of late mss.); after 15:33 (one important papyrus ms. of about A.D. 200 or 250); here at the end of chap. 16 (the strongest early attestation); and sometimes in more than one, or none, of these places. This evidence has encouraged some scholars to suspect that all of chap. 16 was originally addressed elsewhere (cf. commentary above on vv. 3–16), but the same evidence also suggests that both shorter versions of the Letter were produced intentionally at a later time in connection with its wider liturgical and public use.

Verse 20b, which also appears in many mss. at different places, sometimes more than once, is Paul's own benediction, originally located as v. 24 after v. 23.

Bibliography

Achtemeier, P. J. *Romans.* Interpretation: A Bible Commentary for Preaching and Teaching. Atlanta, GA: Knox, 1985.

Barrett, C. K. *A Commentary on the Epistle to the Romans.* New York: Harper, 1957.

Cranfield, C. E. B. *A Critical and Exegetical Commentary on the Epistle to the Romans.* 2 vols. Edinburgh: Clark, 1975–79.

_____. *Romans: A Shorter Commentary.* Grand Rapids, MI: Eerdmans, 1985.

Dahl, N. A. *Studies in Paul.* Minneapolis, MN: Augsburg, 1977.

Donfried, K. P., ed. *The Romans Debate.* Minneapolis, MN: Augsburg, 1977.

Godsey, J. D. "The Interpretation of Romans in the History of the Christian Faith." *Interpretation* 34 (1980):3–16.

Käsemann, E. *Commentary on Romans.* Grand Rapids, MI: Eerdmans, 1980.

_____. *Perspectives on Paul.* Philadelphia: Fortress, 1971.

1 CORINTHIANS

ELISABETH SCHÜSSLER FIORENZA

INTRODUCTION

Literary Function and Form

Acts 18:1–18 provides some background information about the origin of the Christian community in Corinth. Coming from Athens Paul had met in Corinth the missionary pair Prisca and Aquila, who had been expelled from Rome under Claudius (A.D. 49). Paul joins them not only in their workshop as a leatherworker but also in their missionary endeavors. Although Paul stresses that he has baptized the household of Stephanas, the first Christian in Achaia, he does not say that the community originated with them. Rather the house-church of Prisca and Aquila was the originating center of the Corinthian community of Christians. According to Acts Paul remained in Corinth for one and a half years and was accused of violating the Jewish law of worship and was brought before the proconsul Gallio, probably in the fall of A.D. 51 or spring of 52. Apollos, an Alexandrian Jew who was instructed by Prisca and Aquila in Ephesus (Acts 18:24–28), continued the mission in Corinth after Paul's departure. (→Apollos; Chronology, New Testament; Gallio; Paul).

According to 1 Cor. 5:9 Paul is not writing to Corinth for the first time. He sends what we know as the First Letter of Paul to the Corinthians from Ephesus in part because his previous letter has been misunderstood and in part because new problems have arisen, about which the community had written to him. Although both letters preceding our canonical 1 Corinthians are lost, the passing reference to them allows us to understand this Letter as a part of an ongoing rhetorical discussion between Paul and the community in Corinth. We know from 2 Corinthians, however, that the community was not always a compliant partner in this exchange (see 2 Corinthians).

1 Corinthians conforms to the general structure of Pauline Letters. It begins with greetings followed by a thanksgiving (1:1–9) and ends with greetings (16:20–24) influenced by early Christian liturgical language. The main body of the Letter consists of Paul's response to written questions and oral information. Some scholars have sought to explain breaks, inconsistencies, and shifts in the Letter by supposing that a later editor compiled it from several sources.

However, the majority of scholars consider the Letter to be for the most part originally written as we have it now, although some suggest that, e.g., 11:2–16; chap. 13; and 14:34–35 are later additions. The authenticity of the Letter as a Letter of Paul's is undisputed. Most scholars put its probable date around A.D. 54.

Interpretational Approaches

The majority of exegetes no longer read the Letter as a doctrinal tractate but as a practical-theological response to historically particular issues. The Corinthian community appears to have been involved in much discussion and to have sought Paul's advice—and perhaps that of others—about moral sexual behavior, marriage, celibacy and divorce, slavery and litigations, right order and conduct of women and men, prophets and ecstatics in the communal assembly, the eating of food sacrificed to idols (→Food Offered to Idols), the immortality of the soul, and the resurrection of the dead.

An interpretation of 1 Corinthians as a practical-theological address is not possible without reconstructing its historical, social, and ecclesial "world." Since the Letter is part of an ongoing rhetorical dialogue, the interpretation of Paul's rhetoric as well as the reconstruction of its historical function depends as much on the historical-theological imagination of interpreters as on their exegetical, historical, and literary skills. Three major approaches to such an historical reconstruction can be distinguished, though they are not mutually exclusive.

The first school of interpretation surmises that underlying most of the difficulties in Corinth was a certain type of theological symbol and belief system or, better, spirituality. It probably claimed the original preaching of Prisca, Apollos, or even Paul himself as its inspiration and legitimation. This spirituality of the "strong" or of Paul's "opponents"—characterizations that never appear in the Letter—is qualified alternately as enlightened libertinism, spiritualistic asceticism, or unrestrained enthusiasm. The Corinthians who, like Paul, claim to be Spirit-empowered persons, are therefore understood as advocating incipient Gnosticism (→ Gnosticism).

More recently scholars have stressed Jewish Hellenistic wisdom theology as the speculative theological context of the Corinthians' praxis.

The Corinthians believed that they possessed divine *sophia* (Gk., "wisdom") and therefore called themselves pneumatics, "spiritual persons." Since in Hellenistic thought spirit is considered to be a heavenly substance that endows persons with a new nature, the Corinthians could have claimed such "spiritual" status of perfection. Once transformed into a new being the spiritual person no longer belongs to the sphere of the "flesh" but to the heavenly realm.

This notion that the higher soul or mind is the true self that belongs to the heavenly sphere of the Spirit is believed to have led to the conviction that the body's domain is the "flesh," the corruptible, material, and mortal reality from which the true self must be liberated. This notion of salvation has implications not only for personal moral behavior but also for relationships to less spiritually endowed members of the community. The ability to speak in tongues might have been for them a clear sign of such spiritual endowment and may have caused them to consider other Christians as inferior because they could not speak the "tongues of angels" (→ Tongues, Speaking with).

Paul in turn is assumed to argue against such an individualistic and enthusiastic spirituality by underscoring a communal and eschatological perspective. Against the Corinthians' understanding of transformation and perfection in the Spirit, Paul points out that they have not yet achieved final salvation and resurrection. Against their illusory claims to have become immortal by partaking already now in the divine heavenly sphere of the Spirit, Paul insists that they are still under the power of sin and death and that the resurrection is not yet achieved in baptism but only in an event of the future. In the interim time Christians must live out the "already and not yet" under the symbol of the crucified Christ (→ Eschatology).

This first interpretative approach, however, can be criticized for concentrating too narrowly on ideological issues and for reading the text too much in terms of a later belief system. It thus focuses on individual anthropology rather than on ecclesiological self-understanding. It conceptualizes the Corinthian situation too much in terms of confessional strife between opposing theologies and contending groups (→ Flesh and Spirit; Wisdom).

The second approach therefore maintains that the problems addressed by Paul should be understood as arising from the interaction of the Corinthian Christians with their own culture and religion in which they are still deeply rooted, although they have consciously distanced themselves from it. Most of the difficulties in Corinth can be understood in terms of this interface between missionary community

and pagan society. It is not necessary or even helpful for the reconstruction of the historical-pastoral context of 1 Corinthians to postulate an antagonistic front of spiritual enthusiasts or Gnostics as a unified theological opposition.

Located on a narrow peninsula, Corinth was a natural trading center between East and West. Its commercial growth gave birth to a flourishing industry that was essentially based on slavery. As a cosmopolitan city it is a good example for the urban character of Hellenistic society and for Roman colonialism. The citizens of Corinth were not only Romans and Greeks but also Jews and Orientals from Syria, Egypt, and Asia Minor. Each of these groups imported its own religious beliefs, customs, and rituals. Thus religious syncretism was widespread in Corinth but not more than in any other Hellenistic city of the time.

Corinth was called the city of Aphrodite; its temple of Apollo was most impressive in its monumental size, and the temple of Asclepius attracted many who sought healing. In the center of the city one could find temples of Hera, Octavia, Venus, Fortuna, Hermes, Heracles, and Poseidon. Oriental cults attracted many. In the second century the Latin novelist Apuleius describes an initiation rite of the Isis cult in Cenchreae, the seaport of Corinth. Just north of the Gulf of Corinth the Pythia and her prophets mediated divine revelation. Prophecy, speaking in tongues, and ecstasy were highly valued experiences of the time. Public feasts and private meals of associations and clubs were celebrated in the name of the gods. It was virtually impossible to avoid eating meat that had been sacrificed to the gods either at public festivals or at private business or funeral banquets in temple dining rooms and homes (→ Corinth).

The key symbol in Paul's response is that of the body: the body of the individual, the body of Jesus Christ, and the church as the body of Christ. Paul's concern with the body expresses his concern with the religious boundaries between the Christian community and its pagan society. Since segments of the missionary movement in the Greco-Roman cities had relinquished definite rituals and purity regulations, they had also relinquished an effective means to maintain their special identity as a religious group in a syncretistic religious environment. Paul's emphasis on the holiness of the Christian community as body of Christ and temple is an attempt to strengthen group identity in terms of sexual morality (see Galatians, The Letter of Paul to the).

A third interpretative emphasis seeks to elaborate not only the religious but also the sociohistorical context of 1 Corinthians in terms of the social organization and ecclesial self-understanding of the early Christian missionary movement. Traveling missionaries and house-churches were central for this movement, which depended on social mobility and patronage. Like Judaism and other oriental religions so the Christian gospel was spread by traveling business- and tradespeople like Prisca or Paul. Such traveling missionaries brought a variety of theological understandings to the churches in the Greco-Roman cities and fostered communication among them.

The house-church was the beginning of the local church in a certain city and district and became a crystallizing center for converts who still belonged to pagan households. The existence of house-churches presupposes that some citizens joined the Christian movement who were able to provide space and economic support for the *ekklēsia* (Gk., "assembly," "church") in their houses. Such converts often came from the ranks of "god-fearers" already sympathetic to Judaism. The large number of women among these leading converts is astonishing (→ Church; Proselyte).

As Christianity spread in a city, several house-churches were founded and their interaction with each other could lead to tension and dissension especially at occasions when the whole *ekklēsia* of a city assembled. The tensions in Corinth testify to this. They had their roots not only in the breaking down of ritual or religious boundaries between Jews and Gentiles, but also in the breaking down of established social boundaries between freeborn and slaves, or between different national or ethnic groups. Although some private associations and cultic groups also admitted poor people, slaves, persons with different ethnic backgrounds, or wives to membership, they generally were more socially homogeneous than the Christian house-churches, which admitted persons irrespective of their status in patriarchal household and society to full membership.

The experience of such socially mixed communities is sustained in the theological self-understanding of the Christian missionary movement. The pre-Pauline baptismal formula quoted in Gal. 3:28 proclaims that all social and religious status prerogatives and discriminations are abolished in the new kinship relations of God's children, the sisters and brothers in Christ. The house-church did not adopt the patriarchal status differences and dominance-submission relationships typical of the Greco-Roman patriarchal household (Lat. *familia*). The early Christian missionary movement was therefore not a well-integrated part of its patriarchal society but stood in tension with it. Since customary behavior rules no longer applied, the *ekklēsia-in-house* had to find new ways and modes of living together. Many of the Corinthian problems reflect an attempt to practice such a new social-ecclesial self-understanding.

Significance of 1 Corinthians

1 Corinthians is a rich resource of historical and theological information about the early Christian missionary movement in the urban centers of the Greco-Roman world. It allows us a glimpse of a local community struggling to put into practice its theological and communal self-understanding. The reconstruction of this self-understanding and of the socioreligious context of the Letter, however, depends on one's interpretational emphasis and hermeneutic approach (→ Hermeneutics).

However, the significance of the Letter as a major source of our knowledge about the community of Corinth and the early Christian missionary movement is jeopardized when commentators value Paul's response over and above the theological self-understanding and practice of the community. In doing so, they risk dissolving the distinction between the rhetorical situation as construed by Paul and the actual historical situation in Corinth. Whereas exegetes today presuppose the canonical authority of Paul and therefore give priority to his theological authority and rhetorical response, such claims to authority for Paul cannot be maintained for the historical situation. Rather than seeing Paul as the sole authoritative pastor, the following commentary seeks to achieve a balance; value is set on the Corinthian community in order to be able to understand Paul as one partner, although in retrospect a very significant one, in the theological discourse of the early Christian missionary movement.

COMMENTARY

1:1-9

Opening

The introductions to all of Paul's Letters adopt the basic conventions of Greek letter writing. In each Letter—with the exception of Galatians—address or greeting is followed by a thanksgiving or blessing.

1:1-3, Greeting. This address reflects the conventional epistolary pattern, "A to B, greeting," but, as in all the Pauline Letters, the formula undergoes expansion. Paul mentions as co-sender of the letter Sosthenes, who might be the same as the ruler of the synagogue in Corinth mentioned in Acts 18:17. Sosthenes is introduced with the title "brother," which might characterize him as a missionary co-worker of Paul's. However, Paul underlines his own authority by stressing that he was called by the will of God to be an apostle of Jesus Christ.

The recipients of the Letter are more extensively characterized. They are the church (ekklēsia, the "assembly" of decision-making citizens) of God in Corinth. In Jesus Christ they are, as those sanctified, separated from the world. Just as Paul is by divine call apostle, so they are made holy together with all those who call on the name of Jesus Christ who is the Kyrios (Gk., "Lord") of all Christians. Confession of Jesus as Kyrios and the call to holiness are common characteristics of all baptized wherever they live.

While a Greek correspondent would have concluded the address with a "greeting," and a Jewish writer would have wished peace, Paul combines both forms, but replaces the simple "greeting" (Gk. chairein) with the theological term "grace" (Gk. charis). Both, grace and peace, describe God's eschatological salvation available through Jesus Christ.

1:4–9, Thanksgiving. Paul's thanksgiving reflects the Christian standing and situation of his readers and anticipates some of the major topics of the Letter. It also functions as transition to the first major section, 1:10–4:21. God's grace is manifest in the giftedness of the community, which is rich in every respect, especially in speech and knowledge. The proclamation of Christ was confirmed among them so that they do not lack in any spiritual gift during the end-time waiting for the Parousia of Christ (→ Parousia).

The thanksgiving concludes with the promise that God will sustain the Corinthian Christians, strong and irreproachable, until the Judgment Day and with the assurance that the God who has called them into partnership or association with Jesus Christ is faithful and reliable.

1:10–4:21

Corinthian Self-Understanding and Pauline Authority

This section is crucial for the understanding of the whole Letter, since in a rhetorical discourse the problem or issue at stake is stated in the beginning. This section raises two issues: the question of the authority of different apostolic leaders and that of their preaching.

1:10–17

The Problem

Paul has heard from the associates of Chloe—who might also have been delegated to carry the official letter of the community—that divisions and disagreements exist in the community. It is Paul (v. 12) who interprets this to mean that different groups are claiming different apostles —Peter, Apollos, Paul—as their leaders. Exegetes are divided on whether there was also a "Christ group" in Corinth or whether Paul adds this fourth group as an ironic characterization of their claims.

If such a Christ group existed, they might have insisted on the sole authority of Christ and thereby relativized the authority of all the apostles. Or they could have stressed the political messiahship of Jesus, just as the Cephas group might have argued for the foundational character of Simon Peter and the Apollos group could have emphasized the eloquence and wisdom theology of Apollos. Paul's response that begins in v. 13 indicates that the first is more likely.

By insisting that Christ is not divided and by rejecting sharply all prerogatives that his own followers might have claimed on the grounds that he baptized them, Paul seems at first glance to confirm the position of the Christ group. However, he disparages their claims to stress the importance of his proclamation. He was sent by Christ to proclaim the gospel, but not with rhetorical skill lest the cross of Christ should be nullified. Whereas the Christ group might have insisted that they were independent of the apostles because they were baptized into the name of Christ, Paul reminds them that they are also dependent on him because he proclaimed to them the gospel of Christ's death and resurrection.

1:18–2:16

Discourse on Divine Wisdom

The discourse or homily on divine wisdom can be divided again into two corresponding sections, 1:18–2:5 and 2:6–16, which are related to each other as antitheses.

1:18–2:5, The Wisdom of God and the Wisdom of the World. This section is full of antithetical statements and revolves around the contrast between wisdom and folly or between the wisdom of this world and the wisdom of God. Its conceptual framework is Jewish wisdom theology rather than incipient Gnosticism.

In 1:18–25 Paul develops the message of Christ crucified in terms of wisdom theology. God has turned the wisdom of this world—which is pursued by the wise, the scribe, and the interpreter of this age—into folly because it did not enable them to know God and to understand the significance of the cross. For Greeks who seek philosophy and mysteries and for Jews who ask for messianic signs and miracles, the proclamation of Christ crucified is a scandal and folly. But for those who are called, be they Jews or Gentiles, the wisdom of this age is set aside and superseded by Christ, the Messiah, who is God's power and God's wisdom. This thesis is developed in two steps. At first glance this whole discourse on *sophia* (Gk., "wisdom") seems to interrupt Paul's defense of his authority, but the point of the following two subsections, which are the climax of the whole, indicates that this is not the case.

In 1:26–31 Paul elaborates the significance of the identification of Christ crucified with divine wisdom in terms of the Christian community. Whereas vv. 26–29 express the self-understanding of the community as the new creation, vv. 30–31 argue that God has called those who are nothing so that no one can boast before God. If anyone wants to boast they should boast in Christ, who has become for them wisdom, righteousness, sanctification, and redemption.

1 Cor. 2:1–5 explains that Paul deliberately did not use eloquent words of human wisdom and rhetorical persuasion in Corinth. Here Paul sets up a strong contrast between one sort of authentication and another. He employs a technical rhetorical term ("demonstration," Gk. *apodeixis*) to show that his preaching in weakness is legitimated by God's power—a proof that is vastly superior to the proof of external manifestations such as eloquence. Although Paul ostensibly discredits oratory and rhetoric, he himself utilizes rhetorical convention to make his point.

2:6–16, Wisdom for the Perfect or Mature. In vv. 6–16 Paul appears to shift gears suddenly when he speaks of a hidden wisdom that is revealed to the perfect or the Spirit-filled. Since he shifts here from the pronoun "I," used in the preceding and following sections, to "we," exegetes have suggested that this section is an insertion of preformed tradition that is non-Christian or an adaptation to the Gnostic language of his opponents. However, such an assumption is not justified, because the rhetoric of the whole section revolves around "I" (Paul), "you" (Corinthians), and "we" (apostles and missionaries). It is therefore Paul and not his "Gnostic" opponents who introduces the distinction between two classes of Christians for the sake of his argument in 3:1–17.

Verses 6–9 introduce the mystery of the hidden *sophia* of God. Paul's use of the expression "wisdom" shifts here from eloquence and the content of teaching to that of personified *Sophia* or Wisdom. In Jewish-Hellenistic wisdom literature the wise and perfect, in contrast

to the foolish and babes, enjoyed the intimate relationship with divine *Sophia* who was the agent of creation and salvation. Paul identifies the divine figure of *Sophia* with Christ crucified. If the rulers of this world had recognized the *Sophia*-Christ they would not have crucified this Lord of Glory. These rulers can be understood either as the human religious or political powers responsible for Jesus' crucifixion, as supernatural demonic powers dominating the present world order, or as a combination of both. To underline this great mystery of *Sophia*, Paul concludes with a quotation from Scripture (v. 9), though it is not found in our present canon. God has prepared such treasures of *Sophia* as the human mind has never conceived of for those who love God.

This true meaning of *Sophia* was, however, revealed through the Spirit of God (2:10–16). Paul elaborates this with reference to common human experience. Just as only our self-consciousness is aware of our innermost truth, so only the divine Spirit knows the innermost reality of God, which appears to be identical with the mystery of *Sophia*. Therefore one cannot speak of such truth in words taught by human wisdom but only in words taught by the Spirit that comes from God. But only those who are pneumatics ("spirituals") can receive the gifts of the Spirit; unspiritual, immature persons cannot discern spiritual truth. Those who are pneumatics judge everything but they cannot be investigated and evaluated by anyone. The whole argument concludes with the assertion that Paul (and other apostles or Christians) are such pneumatics who have the mind of Christ.

3:1–23
Application to the Corinthian Situation

This section functions as proof in the rhetorical argument of 1:10–4:21. After a transitional introduction (vv. 1–4) follow the proofs that are structured in three parts: vv. 5–9 discuss Paul's relationship to Apollos and their work in Corinth; vv. 10–15 shift from the image of the community as a missionary field to that of the community as building; and vv. 16–17 appeal to the community to realize their holiness, which shifts the image from building to temple.

Verses 1–4 connect the preceding discourse on hidden Wisdom, divine Spirit, and pneumatics with the rhetorical problem that has occasioned Paul's response. Paul who commands a wisdom unknown to the Corinthians could not speak to them as to pneumatics because their divisions, jealousy, and strife prove that they not only were but still are immature babes in Christ who can only digest infant food. If they claim to belong to different apostles and leaders (1:12) then they behave in mere human (fleshly), not spiritual, ways.

The rhetorical questions that open the first subsection (3:5–9) underline the absurdity of the Corinthians' attempt to compare different apostles and teachers. Although Paul recognizes some distinction between himself and Apollos, he insists that his and Apollos' mission are directed toward the same goal. Paul who planted and Apollos who watered are equal because it is God who gives growth and will pay the wages. Paul and Apollos are God's servants and co-workers who were mediators of the community's faith. The Corinthians are as God's field or building, the objects of missionary work.

The shift from the image of field to that of building in v. 9b, moreover, implies a shift in emphasis in 3:10–15. While the previous section rejects any comparison between Paul and Apollos, this subsection insists that there must be consistency between Paul's original preaching, which laid the foundation, and any subsequent preaching, which must build upon Paul's proclamation of Jesus Christ. Paul drives home this point by bringing the situation of the Corinthian community into eschatological perspective. The fire of divine judgment will reveal whether such subsequent "construction" coheres with the foundation laid by Paul. Thus in a subtle way, Paul makes the work of other missionaries theologically dependent on his own.

The rhetorical introduction to vv. 16–17, "do you not know?" recalls previous instruction. The metaphor of the temple is here applied to the community as a whole and thus emphasizes the unity of the community. To continue quarrels and dissension would mean to destroy the temple of God.

The argument of Paul climaxes in the peroration or summation in 3:18–23. In vv. 18–20a the argument returns to the thematic statement on *sophia*/wisdom in 1:18–20, whereas vv. 21b–23 recapitulate the theme of boasting and party divisions. This subsection makes clear that both topics are intimately intertwined. Paul concludes with a well-known philosophic (Stoic) maxim: "All things belong to the wise" but reformulates it as "all things are yours." By reversing the "party slogans," he insists that Paul, Apollos, Cephas, world, life, death, present, and future belong to the Corinthians but that they in turn "are Christ's and Christ is God's." The same subordination of Christ to God is also found in 15:28.

4:1–21
Paul's Authority

The relationship of chap. 4 to 1:10–3:23 is difficult. The chapter is usually seen as an application or as an appendix to the introductory section. However, if this section is understood as an apologetic argument in defense of Paul, then chap. 4 can be seen as the climax of this argument. In v. 6 Paul himself seems to indicate this.

Verses 1–13 suggest that the Corinthian community had attempted to evaluate Paul. Verses 1–2 sum up the preceding argument and articulate the standards of how Paul and his co-missionaries should be regarded. They are characterized as assistants or secretaries of Christ and managers or stewards of God's mysteries, administrative titles used for offices in religious associations and in civic service. What is required of such administrators is that they be reliable or trustworthy.

However, Paul does not argue that this criterion should also be used for evaluating him and his work. He eschews any evaluation and control and warns the Corinthians not to judge him prematurely. The only competent board to judge him is the eschatological tribunal. Since judgment is the prerogative of God it cannot be presumed by the Corinthian community.

Verse 6 is difficult to understand but seems to make most sense if seen as a conclusion to vv. 1–5 as well as an introduction to the following subsection. Paul has deliberately applied the preceding argument to himself and Apollos so that through their example the Corinthians might learn their lesson not to pass judgment. Although it is almost impossible to know the meaning of the expression "Nothing beyond what is written," the overall intention is clear: the Corinthians should not become inflated with self-importance by favoring one apostle over the other.

The three rhetorical questions of v. 7 are followed by three ironical exclamations in v. 8a that are corrected in v. 8b. The image of the life of the apostle as a spectacle (v. 9) is elaborated in the ironic antitheses of vv. 10–13, which utilize the form of catalogs of adverse circumstances. Rather than develop theological arguments for his own position Paul seeks to undermine that of the Corinthians through sarcastic paradoxes, ironic exaggeration, and rhetorical insinuation. The Corinthians are pictured as being in full possession of riches, satisfaction, and ruling power, as wise, strong, and honored. In contrast to them, the apostles are likened to criminals sentenced to death, to fools for Christ's sake; they are weak and despised, hungry and thirsty, ill-clad, homeless, working with their own hands, reviled, persecuted, slandered, the refuse and scum of the world. To take these exaggerated and ironic antitheses as historical information on the actual situation in Corinth would mean seriously to misconstrue the rhetoric of Paul (→ Apostle).

In 4:14–21 Paul changes tone and argument. He insists that his purpose is not to shame the Corinthians but to admonish them. This adoption of a conciliatory attitude is possible because of a shift in argument. In the preceding section he had insisted that all apostles and missionaries were equally servants of Christ and God and that therefore the Corinthians should not choose one over the other. Now he argues that, although they may have a myriad of tutors or "schoolmasters" in Christ, they have only one spiritual father—Paul, who begot them, i.e., whose missionary work converted them.

The Corinthians should imitate Paul's example and his teaching. Timothy has been sent to them because he exhibits what it means to be a "faithful child" of Paul and is fit to remind them of his teachings. However, they should not mistake this to mean that Paul himself would not come or even suspect that he will not appear in person because he feels inferior to other teachers. To the contrary, Paul threatens, he might come sooner than they think. He will then find out whether those who are arrogant are not merely eloquent but have power as well. He grounds his judgment in the nature of the reign of God, which consists not in eloquence but in power. Paul's final rhetorical question underlines his claim to unique authority and power for punishing or rewarding his offspring. It is up to the Corinthians whether he will come with a rod or in love and gentleness.

5:1–7:40
How to Live the Baptismal Self-Understanding

It is debated whether chaps. 5–6 are the conclusion of the first part of the Letter responding to oral information or whether they are a transition to the second part in which Paul answers written inquiries. Chap. 7 is then understood as the opening of the second part of the Letter since there Paul explicitly addresses issues about which the Corinthians had written.

However, the three chapters not only form a thematic unity but might also be a response to a previous letter of Paul. While chaps. 5 and 6 explicitly correct a misunderstanding of this previous letter (5:9), 7:1–11:1 addresses questions that could have been occasioned by it. Scholars have suggested that 2 Cor. 6:14–7:1 might be a surviving fragment of the previous letter since it prohibits association with immoral persons (cf. 1 Cor. 5), likens the individual member of the community to the temple of God (cf. 1 Cor. 6), probably refers to intermarriage with unbelievers (cf. 1 Cor. 7), and raises the question of idols (cf. 1 Cor. 8–10).

5:1–6:20
Insiders and Outsiders

5:1–13, Association with Immoral Members. Verses 1–5 chastise the community for not expelling a man living with his stepmother (who probably was not a Christian because she is not criticized). Since such a marriage was forbidden not only by Jewish but also by Roman law, it is possible that the couple was not married but only cohabited. Paul considers this to be a case of gross immorality. Therefore, he argues, the Corinthians should be filled with a sense of sadness rather than pride about it. They should expel the man from the community as Paul has already done, even though he is absent from the community. Paul's frustration indicates that he could not intervene directly and expel the sinner on his own authority, because only the assembled community had the right to make this decision.

However, determining the meaning of v. 5 is difficult. Paul's concern is primarily for the purity of the community and not so much for the fate of the offender. Expelled from the church the offender will be subjected to the vicissitudes of life, to suffering and death, the domain of Satan, which he has to suffer by himself without communal support so that he may be saved at the last day. Paul's reasoning for this excommunication had a disastrous effect in later centuries when the church had the power to sentence sinners, heretics, and witches to torture and death to save their souls.

However, it must be asked why the Corinthians had not acted on their own, if the case was so clear-cut? Why were they proud of such immoral behavior that was offensive even to pagans? The attitude of the Corinthians becomes understandable when we recall that according to rabbinic teachings the proselyte is like a new-born child. This notion is reflected in 4:15, where Paul insists that he has begotten the Corinthians through the gospel. In 2 Cor. 5:17 Paul speaks of those "who are in Christ" as "a new creation."

Connected with this understanding of conversion was the Jewish belief that the convert's previous social relations no longer exist. Therefore, in principle the rules of incest and marriage no longer apply. However, to avoid public scandal the rabbis modified this principle to be applied only in accordance with pagan laws. If this is the theological context of the situation in Corinth, then it is understandable why the Corinthians not only tolerated this relationship but saw it as a realization of their new life in Christ to which the restrictions of Greco-Roman law no longer applied. Verses 6–8 allude to this belief but reinterpret it. Rather than being a sign of the new life and freedom, this scandalous practice is a remnant of the old age. This is illustrated in v. 6 by a proverb about leaven that is similar to the English saying, "A rotten apple spoils the whole barrel."

Verses 7–8 connect this proverbial saying with the Jewish Passover ritual. In the Jewish religion leaven is the symbol of all that is unclean and evil and therefore must scrupulously be removed from all houses before the Passover feast. Similarly the Corinthians must remove the leaven of sin so that they will be like the batch of unleavened dough that they actually are. Their feast has already begun because their paschal lamb, Christ, has already been slain. Therefore, they should cleanse their house from the old leaven of malice and evil to celebrate the feast with the unleavened bread of sincerity and truth. In sum, vv. 6–8 are a further theological justification for Paul's demand to expel the man living with his stepmother.

Verses 9–13 indicate that this case of immorality was based on a misunderstanding of an earlier letter that Paul had written to the community in Corinth. Just as 2 Cor. 6:14 insists, "Do not be mismatched with unbelievers. For what partnership have righteousness and iniquity?" so Paul had instructed the Corinthians, "Do not associate with immoral persons" (v. 9). The Corinthians had understood this to mean not to associate with non-Christians. The boundaries establishing Christian identity were drawn between those who were members of the community and those outside of it.

In vv. 10–11 Paul clarifies his position by explaining that he did not have in mind the immoral persons of this world, for then Christians would have to move out of the world. What he actually had meant was not to associate with immoral Christians. Paul derives his characterization of the immoral person in vv. 10–11 from the traditional catalog of vices that was commonplace in popular philosophy and had already been appropriated by Hellenistic Judaism. The recognition of the formal character of such lists of vices and virtues prohibits our reading them as referring to actual problems in Corinth. Such lists are used to typify universal moral values. Here the catalog of vices is used to illustrate Paul's point that the Corinthians should not associate or have any social interaction (not even to eat) with Christians who are publicly known for their moral failure.

Verses 12–13 refer to 5:1–5 and close the argument for expelling the immoral man from the community. Paul insists that neither he himself nor the community is competent to judge outsiders. It is God who will judge those who are outside, but it is the task of the community to pass judgment on those who are inside. Paul thus maintains the dualistic distinction between outsider and insider, but he extends it to members within the community. However, Paul does not appeal to any community leaders to pass such judgment. It is the whole community that is exhorted to exercise its authority of judgment and to exclude the wicked person from its midst (Deut. 17:7, Septuagint).

6:1–11, Call to Judgment and Lawsuits Before Outsiders. Again this section can be divided into two subsections. Verses 1–8 deal with lawsuits among Christians, while vv. 9–11 contain an expanded list of vices.

Verses 1–8 are linked to the preceding section through their focus on judging and judgment. The content of the section is clear. Christians who have legal disputes and grievances against each other are going before pagan courts rather than letting God's people settle the matter. Paul argues that the community should settle its own legal cases because, as they well know, the saints (i.e., Christians) will judge not only the world but also angels. On the whole it would be better not to have lawsuits at all. Rather than to do wrong and to rob one another they should prefer to suffer wrong and let themselves be defrauded.

While Paul's argument is clear, the matter under discussion is far from being evident. The topic of this section seems to interrupt Paul's elaborations on matters of sexuality and immorality that are taken up again in 6:12–20. If 6:1–11 is read in close connection with chap. 5 then Paul would be criticizing once more the hesitancy of the community to pass judgment on other Christians. If the passage is seen in light of 6:20–7:40 then it can be surmised that the Corinthian lawsuits were caused by legal problems connected with institutional marriage. Such legal disputes could pertain, for example, to questions of dowry, divorce settlements, or inheritance. The Corinthians might not have considered them as "religious" problems to be adjudicated by the community, since according to Roman law marriage was constituted by legal contract rather than religious rite.

Verses 9–11 contain primarily traditional materials. The catalog of vices is introduced and concluded with the traditional Christian eschatological formula "to inherit the reign of God" (cf. Gal. 5:21). The list of vices is broadly the same as the one in 5:11 but underlines the sins of sexual immorality by adding "adulterers" and by specifying both the effeminate male prostitute and his partner who hires him to satisfy sexual needs. The two terms used here for homosexuality, which are absent from the list in Galatians, specify a special form of pederasty that was generally disapproved of in Greco-Roman and Jewish literature.

However, Paul is not interested in the specific items on the list but rather clearly shows an interest in increasing them to have a cumulative effect. Whereas 5:10 has four items (the immoral, the greedy, robbers, idolaters), 5:11 adds two (revilers and drunkards) and 6:9 expands the list with four (adulterers, effeminates, homosexuals, thieves) for a total of ten vices. While it goes without saying that Paul disapproves of all these activities, in the context of the Letter he is clearly concerned with heterosexual sins and marriage difficulties.

Verse 11 concludes the section with a reference to the early Christian baptismal tradition. The traditional pattern "once ... but now" describes baptism as the moment of change from a former life to a new existence. Before their baptism in the name of Jesus Christ some of the Corinthians practiced one or the other of these vices. But now by the Spirit of God they are cleansed from sin, dedicated to God, and put in right relation with God.

6:12–20, Glorify God in Your Bodies. This is a transitional section that concludes the argument of 5:1–6:11 and at the same time introduces the theme of 7:1–40. Both 6:12–20 and 7:1–40 articulate problems of holiness/purity and sexuality from the perspective of the male members of the community.

It is debated whether in this section Paul cites a general principle that he himself recognizes but modifies, or whether he quotes slogans or statements of the Corinthians against which he argues. If the former is the case, then Paul agrees with the general principle "I am allowed to do anything" or "I am free to do anything" but qualifies it in terms of his own theology. He applies this basic principle to two areas: food and prostitution. The body differs from the belly because it is destined for resurrection. If the latter is the case then Paul quotes at least three slogans: "I am free to do anything" (v. 12), "Foods are for the belly and the belly for foods but God will destroy both" (v. 13), and "Every sin which someone may commit is outside the body" (v. 18b). Paul then qualifies the first slogan in a twofold way: yes, all things are lawful, but not everything is good or of benefit to me; yes, but I shall not be ruled by anything or anyone. He also agrees with the second slogan but insists that the body is not to be used for sexual immorality but for serving the *Kyrios* who provides for the body. It is God who has raised Christ and who also will raise us.

Paul continues the argument with two rhetorical questions that are also a statement: you know that your bodies are members of Christ and therefore should never be made members of a prostitute. Similarly, you know that someone who joins himself to a prostitute becomes one flesh with her, whereas those who join themselves to the Resurrected One become one spirit with Christ.

Paul does not argue here that the believer's union with the body of Christ prohibits intercourse. He assumes rather, in order to make his point, that intercourse with a prostitute is wrong but that sex is permitted in marriage. Being incorporated into Christ in baptism makes one a member of the body of Christ, the church, and at the same time one spirit with the Resurrected One. However, it is not likely that Paul refers here to an actual problem in the Corinthian community. Rather it is safe to assume that he gives an extreme example to make his point.

Finally, Paul admonishes, "Have nothing to do with immorality." Over and against the third slogan he maintains that sins of sexual immorality are sins against one's own body. He again underlines this with a rhetorical question in diatribe style that is really an assertion: surely, you know that your bodies are a temple of the Holy Spirit. Paul understands the Christian community as the temple, more specifically the sanctuary, of the Holy Spirit (3:16), and the individual is seen as the constituent part of it. His primary concern is with the holiness and purity of the church, which is threatened with the defilement of sexual immorality.

The whole argument climaxes in the statement that the Corinthians do not belong to themselves but to God. They have been bought for God as slaves are bought by a slaveowner. Therefore their freedom is limited. Those who have been redeemed through the death of Christ must bring honor to God in and with their bodies.

In chaps. 5 and 6 Paul explains his teaching on the distinctiveness of the Christian community and the boundaries between the church, as the temple of the Spirit, and those who are outside of it. Whereas the Corinthians understood him to draw sharp boundaries in terms of membership, Paul explains that he does so in terms of impurity, which he practically identifies with sexual immorality. Just as Jewish moral traditions of the Diaspora, in order to underline the distinction between Israel and the nations, stressed that sexual immorality is the result of idolatry, so too Paul insists that holiness and purity in terms of sexual morality are the distinctive marks of the Christian community.

7:1–40

Problems Arising from the Baptismal Formula of Galatians 3:28

After having addressed issues arising from the misunderstanding of his previous teachings, Paul now responds to questions about which the Corinthians had written (v. 7a). The formula "now concerning ..." also occurs in 7:25; 8:1, 4; 12:1; and 16:1, 12. It does not structure the Letter but indicates whenever Paul explicitly refers to matters about which the Corinthian community had inquired.

Although all problems in chap. 7 seem to refer to marriage and the relationship between the sexes, Paul's reference to circumcision/uncircumcision and to slave/free in 7:17–24 indicates that the early Christian baptismal formula quoted in Gal. 3:28 provides the underpinning of the whole section. If the third pair—no longer male and female—declares with reference to Gen. 1:27 that patriarchal marriage and the procreative relationship between the sexes are no longer constitutive for the new community in Christ, then the extensive discussion of issues related to marriage becomes understandable.

Should married Christians continue or abstain from sexual intercourse? Should unmarried people get married? What is to be done if one's marriage partner is an unbeliever, either Jew or pagan? What should women do who are virgins or widows? Should one remain in an oppressive marriage relationship? Such questions can be seen as practical problems arising from the attempt to live the social relationships professed at one's baptism, although Gal. 3:28c is never explicitly mentioned in chap. 7.

The first section (vv. 1–16) addresses the question of sexual relations in marriage and of a life free of marriage (7:1–9) on the one hand, and the problem of divorce (7:10–16) on the other.

7:1–9, Sexual Abstinence. It is debated whether the statement "it is advantageous or beneficial not to touch a woman" (formulated from a male perspective!) in 7:1b is a response of Paul to a Corinthian question, whether it is a Corinthian maxim that Paul quotes with approval, or whether it is a Corinthian slogan against which Paul argues. However, the argument in vv. 2–9 seems to indicate that Paul addresses here a Corinthian question by introducing qualifications. It is clear from the climax of the argument in vv. 7–9 that Paul himself lived a life of sexual asceticism and that he valued this "charisma" highly. However, he insists, marriage is a necessity if one cannot live the asexual life demanded by freedom from the marriage bond. Those who are tempted should not abstain from intercourse. Both partners have the mutual obligation to marital intercourse, except for some limited celibate periods set aside by mutual agreement for worship. As was the practice in other oriental cults, so also Paul recognizes temporary ritual chastity.

Exegetes have pointed out how Paul carefully repeats every injunction in 7:1–5 to make sure that husband and wife have equal conjugal obligations and rights. However, Paul stresses this interdependence only for sexual and not for all marriage relationships. Moreover,

he sees marital intercourse only as a remedy for uncontrolled sexual passion. Finally, the argument does not take into account the unequal status of men and women in a patriarchal society.

7:10–16, Marriage and Divorce. While Paul counsels those who are not bound by marriage to remain free, he commands the married not to separate. However, despite this instruction of the Lord, wives—who are mentioned first and with more emphasis in 7:10–11—still have the possibility of freeing themselves from the marriage bond. If they do so, however, they must remain in this marriage-free state. They may return to their husbands but may not marry someone else.

A somewhat different problem is raised with respect to marriages between Christians and "unbelievers." In 6:12–20, Paul had asked, "Do you not know that your bodies are members of Christ?" and insisted that therefore they should not be made members of a prostitute. Likewise, Christians in mixed marriages could have asked: "Can I as a 'member of Christ' continue to have sexual intercourse with someone who does not belong to the body of Christ? Do I thereby become conformed to my partner's pagan existence and lose my standing in Christ?" In addition, as we have seen in chap. 5, Jewish and Christian missionary theology held that converts have become a new creation. They were considered to be like newborn children. Therefore the Corinthians might have believed that baptism into Christ dissolved all previous marriage bonds.

In response to this problem Paul insists that because of the missionary situation (God has called us to peace), the decision to continue or not to continue the marriage relationship should be left to the unbelieving partner but not to the Christian. If the unbeliever wants to stay married the Christian partner can consider the marriage bond as reconstituted "by intercourse" and the children of such a marriage are holy and legitimate. However, Paul's insistence that because of missionary reasons the unbelieving partner had the final decision resulted in many more difficulties for women than for men, since men were entitled by law to control the religious practices of the members of their households. Insofar as Paul sacrifices the right of the Christian partner to determine her or his marital status, he made it impossible for Christian women to divorce their non-Christian husbands, a legal option that often resulted in greater religious and social freedom, especially for economically self-sufficient women.

7:17–24, Baptismal Calling and Its Social Consequences. Exegetes misread Paul's maxim in v. 17 when they translate it as an injunc-

tion to remain in the social state in which one was called. To the contrary, Paul clearly does not advise former Jews or Gentiles to remain in the religious and social situation and state in which they were when they became Christians. Rather he insists that the religious and physical sign of initiation into Judaism (circumcision) is no longer of any social or theological significance for Christians.

Similarly the advice to slaves cannot mean that they should remain in the social situation in which they were called. Although many exegetes understand 7:21 to mean that they should remain slaves if they have the possibility to become free, the injunction of v. 23, "You were bought with a price, do not become slaves of people," prohibits such an interpretation. Paul's advice in v. 21 seems best understood as: if you still must live in the bondage of slavery, with no possibility of being freed, even though you were called to freedom, do not worry about it. However, if you have the opportunity to be set free, by all means, use this possibility and live according to your calling to freedom. Those of you who were slaves when called are now freedwomen and freedmen of the Kyrios, just as those of you who were free-born have now a master in Jesus Christ.

Both freeborn and slave women and men are equals in the Christian community because they have one Kyrios. Regardless of one's social status, however, the decisive thing is to continue in the calling to freedom that one has heard and entered into in baptism. Although Paul refers here only in passing to the first two pairs of the baptismal formula Gal. 3:28, these references indicate that the questions of the Corinthian community were related to their baptismal self-understanding.

7:25–40, Freedom from Marriage. Paul's theological advice with respect to marriage is basically similar to the advice given to slaves. It is quite possible to live a Christian life as a married person, if that was the state in which one lived when one became a Christian, although Paul himself prefers the marriage-free Christian life over the married state. This comes to the fore throughout the whole chapter but especially in his advice to the "unmarried," that is, to those who are unmarried or divorced as well as those who are engaged to be married. Engagement is probably the best explanation for the thorny problem of vv. 32–35. If sexual desire compels them, they should get married. However, it is better not to marry and to remain in the marriage-free state. If the unmarried and the widows cannot exercise self-control, they should marry in the church; but in Paul's opinion they would be happier if they were to remain free from the constraints of patriarchal marriage.

Although exegetes have much debated the meaning of "virgins" in vv. 36–38, they have seldom pointed out that Paul's advice to remain free from the marriage bond was against Augustan Roman marriage legislation. These laws levied sanctions and taxes on bachelors and required the widowed and divorced to remarry within a year if they were not over fifty years of age, and therefore entailed conflicts for the Christian community in its interaction with Greco-Roman society. However, Paul's theological argument, that those who marry are "divided" and not equally dedicated to Christian affairs, disqualified married people theologically as less engaged Christians and missionaries. It posited a rift between the married woman concerned with worldly affairs and how to please her husband, on the one hand, and, on the other hand, the marriage-free woman who was concerned with the affairs of the Kyrios as to how to be holy in body and spirit. One can only wonder how Paul could have espoused such a theology, when he had Prisca as his friend and knew missionary couples who were counterexamples to his theological reasoning.

8:1–11:1
Limitations of Christian Freedom and Power

1 Cor. 8:1 introduces the main topic of the section 8:1–11:1. It refers to the argument made by the Corinthians for a Christian's freedom to eat food sacrificed to idols. The same topic is taken up again in chap. 10. However, while 8:1–13 and 10:23–11:1 speak of things sacrificed to idols, 10:1–22 seems to address idolatry and the sacramentality of the meat itself. It has therefore been conjectured that they belong to different Letters of Paul or that Paul himself changed his position on the question of eating sacrificial meat. However, it is more likely that in chap. 8 Paul takes up the arguments of the Corinthians and seeks to modify them, while in chap. 10 he explicates his own position. Some exegetes have also regarded chap. 9 as virtually unrelated to the discussion on meat sacrificed to idols. However, chap. 9 is best understood as a rhetorical digression supporting the overall argument of 8:1–11:1.

8:1–13
Concerning Food Sacrificed to Idols

The central question of chap. 8, whether Christians are permitted to eat food sacrificed to idols, is clearly stated in 8:1 and repeated in 8:4. For a newly converted Christian in Greco-Roman cities this was not so much a religious as a social problem, since meat offered for sale and served at family celebrations, at gatherings of private associations and clubs, or at public festivals had passed in one form or another through religious rites.

Because Jews believed that it was idolatrous to eat such meat, they obtained the privilege to slaughter their animals and sell their own meat to Jews. However, it was almost impossible for newly converted Christians who were not Jewish to avoid the social occasions at which such food was offered. Moreover, for many poor citizens the meat served at public feasts was probably the only meat available to them, since meat was very expensive.

Members of the Corinthian community seem to have argued that they could consume such sacrificial food, because they all had the religious insight and knowledge that an idol has no real existence because there is no God but one (v. 4). This is explicated in vv. 5–6: whatever divine heavenly or demonic beings may exist, for Christians there is only one God whom they recognize as the creator God and whom they serve. Moreover, Christians acknowledge only one Kyrios Jesus Christ who is the agent of creation and redemption. In other words, the Corinthians' authority to eat sacrificial food was not engendered by their contempt for the body or Gnostic enthusiasm, but it was rooted in their understanding of religious equality (we all have knowledge) and their monotheistic theology.

Paul's response in chap. 8 seeks to qualify these assertions in two ways. In vv. 1b–3 he contrasts their emancipatory theological knowledge, which according to him leads to an inflated self-understanding, with his own theological key concept agapē (Gk., "love") that builds up the community. What is important is not that one has achieved some religious insight and knowledge, but that one loves God and therefore is known by God.

More significant is Paul's second modification. In v. 7 he denies that all Christians have received such emancipatory knowledge of God. Some recently converted members of the community who have eaten such food all their lives believing in the gods to whom it was sacrificed might not have ceased to believe in the divine reality behind the sacrificial meat. They are "weak" in awareness and faith.

Paul agrees with the theological contention that the eating of such food is social and not religious. No religious advantage or disadvantage is engendered by eating or by abstaining from such food. However, such religious freedom to eat or not to eat sacrificial food must not be allowed to become a stumbling block to a "weak" member of the community who still be-

lieves in the numinous and sacral quality of such food. Such persons might be encouraged by the pneumatics' example to dine with friends in pagan temples and thereby act against their conscience. Thus unwittingly those with religious insight and theological knowledge might lead "weaker" Christians to sin by wounding their conscience and thereby sin against Christ. However, Paul does not refer to an actual group of so-called "weak" Christians but only seeks to draw out the possible implications and consequences of the Corinthians' theological praxis. To do so he must declare some members of the community as "weak" or deficient. According to Paul not all Christians have arrived at the emancipatory theological knowledge that monotheism denies the existence of all other gods.

In conclusion, Paul asserts that rather than offending other Christians he prefers not to eat meat at all. This last argument indicates that not the wealthier but the impoverished Christians who normally could not afford meat might have insisted that on theological grounds they could eat such meat at pagan festivities. Since he cannot counter their argument theologically, he denies that all members of the community have arrived at such theological insight and he presents a hypothetical case to illustrate his point. While Corinthian Christians insist that all have theological knowledge, freedom, and power, Paul argues that some have a weak theological consciousness and are lacking such knowledge, freedom, and authority. Therefore the Corinthians should follow his example and not eat meat at all rather than incur possible offense. However, whereas Paul and other well-to-do Christians might have had the means and possibility to obtain kosher meat, Paul's argument makes it impossible for poor Christians to participate in pagan festivals, the rare occasions when they could eat meat at all.

9:1–27
Apostolic Self-Limitation

The rhetorical digression 9:1–27 on the rights and freedom of an apostle is not so much a defense of Paul's conduct as it is an argument, using Paul as an example, for a restricted use of power and renunciation of rights in free service.

Verses 1–14 consist of a series of rhetorical questions that center around the example of Paul. Since they require an affirmative answer, the section does not represent a defense of Paul's apostleship, although many commentaries read it in this way. Rather, it is an elucidation of Paul's apostolic freedom and power for the purpose of stressing his freely chosen self-limitation.

The argument actually begins with 8:13, since chapter divisions are secondary, and the rhetorical questions in vv. 1–2 continue the theme of Paul's personal example. They indicate his apostolic freedom and experience and cite the Corinthians as proof of his apostleship. Verse 3 is transitional and draws the parallel between "how Paul defends himself against his own critics" and the situation of the so-called "strong" in Corinth whose behavior has drawn criticism from some segments of the community.

Verses 4–14 then elaborate positively Paul's apostolic rights and claims. This section consists of twelve rhetorical questions that state the obvious. These questions present ten arguments for his rights to food and drink, to be accompanied by a woman missionary, not to have to work for his living, and to be supported by the community. Whereas in v. 7 Paul refers to the everyday examples of the soldier, the farmer, and the shepherd to argue for his right to financial aid, in vv. 9–10 he uses proof-texts from Scripture (Deut. 25:4; Sir. 6:19).

Verse 12a positively sets forth the purpose of the argument in vv. 4–14. After having established his rightful apostolic claims, Paul asserts that he has not made use of his rights but has put up with everything to avoid placing obstacles in the way of the gospel. The latter refers to a major theme in chaps. 8 and 10 that Christians should not put a stumbling block before other Christians (8:9) or scandalize them (8:13), but they should do everything not to be offensive (10:32). The rhetorical question "Do you not know?" in v. 13 assumes that the Corinthians will agree with Paul's claim that apostolic workers have a right to financial support.

Verses 15–18 return to v. 12b and discontinue the form of rhetorical questions in order to restate Paul's own practice. Paul insists that he does not write about his renunciation of apostolic rights to claim them now. Paul has never accepted financial support from the Corinthian community and he is not going to change this now. Rather his primary concern and boast remains the gospel of Christ and its unhindered path through the whole world. His "necessity" or "compulsion" as well as his freely chosen action both concern the overarching needs of his work for the gospel.

Verses 19–23 are rhetorically well crafted. The seven independent clauses are followed by dependent clauses, five of which contain the phrase "in order to win over," i.e., convert to the Christian message. These verses illustrate the principle underlying Paul's apostolic practice. He does everything "for the gospel's sake" (v. 23). Although Paul has freedom and authority he has become a slave to the needs of all persons and has accommodated himself to various groups for the sake of his missionary work. He does not defend his practice, but he presents it as a personal example that the Corinthians should imitate.

Verses 24–27 shift back to the use of analogy, which was prevalent in vv. 4–14. Just as athletes do, so also Christians must submit to strict training and discipline if they want to be victorious. In v. 26 Paul switches from the image of runners to that of boxers who harden their bodies and bring them under control by enduring hard blows and bruises in order not to be disqualified from the contest. Whereas some of the Corinthians understood their new life in the Spirit as one of empowerment and freedom, Paul uses the images of slavery and athletic endeavor to illustrate the great effort that is required, even from apostles, in order not to be "disqualified" or to place a stumbling block in the way of the gospel. This section functions as a transition to the argument in 10:1–13.

10:1–11:1
Warning Against a Relapse into Idolatry

This chapter continues to support Paul's argument in the form of examples. It begins with an epistolary adaptation of a homily on Israel in the wilderness (10:1–13), then draws out the implications for the issue at hand with reference to the Eucharist (10:14–22), and ends with a series of injunctions and rules that are introduced by Paul's modification of a Corinthian maxim (10:23–11:1).

10:1–13, The Example of Israel. 1 Cor. 10:1–13 forms a literary unit that is divided in half by the contrast between "all of the Israelites" who have experienced God's gift of salvation (10:1–5) and "some of them" who rebelled against God (10:6–11). The five positive and five negative examples are concluded with warnings against temptations (10:12–13). Some of the tensions of this section in its present context are best understood if we recognize that this homily was composed prior to its utilization by Paul. This traditional Exodus pattern—a list of God's salvific acts followed by a list of sins culminating in warnings to the contemporary audience—is found not only in various texts of the Hebrew Bible (esp. the Song of Moses in Deut. 32) and Jewish literature but also in NT writings such as Hebrews or Jude 5.

Chap. 10:1–5 is a midrashic (→ Midrash) elaboration of God's gracious acts for Israel connected with the Exodus and the sojourn in the desert. Similar elaborations of the Exodus miracles (the cloud-pillar, the Red Sea crossing, the manna, and the water from the rock) are also found in Psalms 78; 106; Neh. 9:9–21; Wisdom of Solomon 11–19; and apocalyptic literature. The clause "and the rock was Christ" is a Pauline addition, and the baptism into Moses is probably a Christian construction analogous to the baptism into Christ.

These five positive examples are followed in vv. 6–10 by five negative examples of the Exodus generation—craving evil things, idolatry, immorality, testing the Lord, and grumbling or malcontentedness—of which four are allusions to texts in Numbers. However, one of them, idolatry, is introduced as a direct quotation from Exod. 32:6. Since the question of idolatry is at the center of Paul's discussion in chap. 10, it is likely that Paul himself has added this scriptural reference.

10:14–22, Implications. The general warnings and prohibitions in vv. 12–13, which are the climax of the traditional homily, are specified by Paul in terms of idolatry or participation in pagan cultic events (v. 14). The exclusive religious maxim "avoid any worship of idols," which was characteristic of Judaism and hard for pagans in the Greco-Roman world to understand, remained in force for Pauline Christianity. It is followed by an appeal to evaluate for themselves Paul's arguments supporting the prohibition of any participation in pagan cultic events (v. 15).

Paul supports this injunction in 10:16–21 with three examples of cultic meal associations (Gk. *koinōnia*): Christian sharing of the eucharistic meal (vv. 16–17), Jewish eating of what is sacrificed in the Temple (v. 18), and participation in pagan cultic meals (vv. 19–21). Verse 22 draws the conclusion for the whole section. The organizing key concept of the argument in 10:14–21 is that of *koinōnia*, which in Hellenistic and Jewish writings of the time has the basic meaning of a relationship in which two or more individuals have a joint interest in someone or something. It describes the relationship that individuals find in their worship of a god or gods whom they have in common. The common point of comparison in all three examples is the eating of a cultic meal that results in *koinōnia*.

Utilizing a pre-Pauline early Christian eucharistic formula in v. 16, Paul argues in vv. 17–22 that just as sacrifice and cultic meals, whether Jewish or pagan, establish a community of allegiance, so does the participation in the cup of the *Kyrios* and in the one bread establish a special religious worshiping community, the one body of Christ. The death of Christ established a new covenant relationship between God and Christians as well as among those in Christ. This is a relationship with mutual loyalties and obligations. Although the participation in pagan cultic meals does not establish a special relationship with the god of a cult, since idols do not have a real existence, it does establish such an alliance community with demons.

The conclusion drawn in v. 21 is unambiguous: the character of the Christian community is exclusive not because of some magical conflict but because Christian and pagan meals establish different communities of allegiance. Such an insistence on religious exclusivism was uncommon in Greco-Roman paganism. The two rhetorical questions in v. 22 assume a negative answer. They draw on Deut. 32:21, the Song of Moses, where God says, "They have moved me to jealousy with 'no-gods' and provoked me to anger with their vanities."

Christians in Corinth seem to have felt that they could join in pagan cultic meals not only because these were highly social in character but also because they knew that idols were unreal (cf. 8:4–6). However, Paul's religious exclusivism demands that they not be involved in cultic meals associated with other religious communities. Christians must not participate in dinner parties given by their neighbors in a pagan shrine. His position allows for no compromise in the instance of quasi-religious meals in pagan cultic places.

10:23–11:1, Injunctions. After having insisted that eating at pagan sacrificial feasts is strictly forbidden, Paul returns in 10:23 to a Corinthian maxim "all things are permitted" (cf. 6:12) in order to qualify it. Then in v. 24 Paul introduces a maxim of his own: Christians should never look out only for their own interests, but they must always consider the good of others. Verses 25–27 discuss two special cases of permissible eating: Christians are allowed to eat meat sold in the markets (v. 25) as well as meat served by a host (v. 27). However, in vv. 28–30 Paul qualifies his permission by insisting that even in these cases the possible harm to others must be taken into account. In 10:31–11:1 Paul develops interrelated principles for eating in particular, and guidelines for Christian behavior in general. Persons who seek to "glorify God" will not cause others to stumble but act for others' benefit, rather than solely in their own self-interest. Paul's own attempts to "please everyone" and "not to seek his own advantage" are both an example that Christians should follow and a motive for action: "Imitate me just as I imitate Christ."

11:2–14:40

Communal Worship and Spiritual Gifts

Interpreters debate whether chap. 11 begins a new section, whether this chapter concludes the preceding section, or whether it is an independent textual unit. This debate indicates that chap. 11 forms an important link between the preceding and the following parts of the Letter. Whereas 11:2–16 (A) points forward to the discussion of spiritual gifts and their exercise in chaps. 12 and 14 (A'), 11:17–34 (B) connects back to the discussion of the Lord's Supper in 10:14–22. The whole section 11:2–14:40 thus follows the A B A' pattern and is composed as a thematic inclusion that begins and ends with the discussion of women's behavior in the worship assembly of the community. It shows that women as well as men have received the gifts of the Spirit and pray, prophesy, and ask questions in the public assembly of the community. The contrast between 11:2 and 11:17 indicates that in 11:2–16 Paul is not referring to any particular abuse.

11:2–16
Women Prophets

We no longer are able to decide with certainty what custom or style Paul wants to introduce here. Generally exegetes have conjectured that Paul is insisting that the pneumatic women leaders wear the veil according to oriental custom. However, such an understanding cannot explain why it was dishonorable for men to wear a head covering, since Jewish priests were required to do so (Ezek. 44:18). Therefore, exegetes have more recently suggested that vv. 4 and 14 prohibit men to wear long hair (Ezek. 44:20), since this caused suspicion of effeminacy and homosexuality. If, however, the text does not prohibit a "head covering" for men but refers to hairstyle, then the same must be assumed for women. Women prophets and pneumatics are admonished to wear their hair bound up like a crown rather than unbound, since this was in Greco-Roman understanding a sign of frenzy and in Jewish understanding a sign of adultery (Num. 5:18). Disheveled hair was as disgraceful for a woman as for her head to be shaven. However, whatever custom or hairstyle Paul seeks to advocate, it must not be overlooked that he does not prohibit women from publicly praying and prophesying.

More problematic are the theological arguments that Paul adduces for his injunction. Verses 3–9 consist of a midrash on Gen. 2:18–23 followed by a concluding statement in v. 10 that refers to the presence of angels in the worship assembly. Verse 3 introduces a new theological understanding ("but I want you to know") that establishes a patriarchal (head) or ontological (source) chain of authority—God, Christ, man, woman—a descending hierarchy in which each preceding member stands above the following. Similarly, Paul can declare that man is created to be the image and glory of God, while woman is the glory of man and hair is the glory of woman (v. 15). However, the

midrashic argument in vv. 7–9 does not deny woman the "image of God" status but focuses on "glory."

In vv. 11–12, Paul concedes that women and men are interdependent and that "in the Kyrios" women are not different from men. Therefore to make his point Paul resorts in vv. 13–15 to the philosophic argument "from nature" that was widely used for insisting on the subordination of freeborn women because of their "natural" differences. Finally, Paul concludes this mixture of biblical and philosophical arguments with an authoritarian assertion in v. 16, probably because he senses that his theological argument is not very convincing.

11:17–34
Divisions at the Eucharist

While Paul praises the community in Corinth for having kept the traditions with respect to public praying and prophesying of women and men, he severely reprimands their behavior at the eucharistic meal. He mentions first the divisions and groupings among them (vv. 17–19) and he goes on to criticize them for not eating "the supper of the Kyrios" when coming together. Instead of waiting for each other they eat their "own meal" so that one remains hungry and the other gets drunk (v. 21). This accusation is followed by two rhetorical questions in v. 22 and a quotation of early Christian eucharistic tradition in vv. 23–26.

Verses 17–23 clearly speak of social class distinctions. Those who humiliate the poor and despise the "ekklēsia of God" are sufficiently wealthy to own houses (vv. 22 and 34) where they can satisfy their hunger. The rhetorical question "Do you not have houses . . . ?" is best understood in the sense that Paul wants to insist that actual eating and drinking of a meal should take place in private homes and not in the ritual meal celebration of the community. In his critique of the Corinthian community Paul underlines the contrast between one's own selfish, individualistic meal and the "Lord's Supper," between one's own satisfaction and the hunger and thirst of the poor in the community. However, Paul's advice to "eat at home" does not overcome this opposition but transposes it into the division between ordinary, noncultic eating and drinking and ritual or sacramental eating and drinking, between an ordinary meal and the "Lord's Supper" (v. 34).

In quoting the tradition about the Last Supper of Jesus, Paul indicates that according to this tradition the actual meal, the eating and drinking together, was an integral part of the eucharistic celebration. The breaking of the bread and the sharing of the cup mark the beginning and end of a meal that is celebrated in remembrance of Jesus. Since the traditional material probably ended with v. 25, it is probably Paul who added a further sentence underlining the connection between the proclamation of Christ's death and his eschatological return (v. 26). Paul thus sounds an eschatological warning.

That the eschatological judgment is already upon some of the Corinthians is demonstrated by illness and death in the community. Those who eat and drink without discerning the body, i.e., the Christian community constituted by breaking the *one bread* (cf. 10:17; Rom. 12:5), expose themselves to judgment. The community gathered around the table of the *Kyrios* must overcome its divisions. Otherwise it makes itself guilty and answerable for profaning the life and death of its Lord (vv. 27–32). To achieve such unity Paul is prepared to sacrifice the actual sharing of a meal. He does so to preserve the ritual exchange of bread and wine as a cultic symbol of unity (vv. 33–34). In conclusion Paul writes that the "other things" brought to his attention are of minor importance, so that they can wait until after his arrival in Corinth (v. 34c).

12:1–31
The Gifts of the Spirit

After the introduction in 12:1–3 follows first a section on the variety of spiritual gifts (12:4–11) and then one on the one body of Christ (12:12–27). The concluding remarks in 12:28–31 return to the topic of the variety of gifts.

12:1–3, Introduction. In v. 1 Paul returns to the questions raised in the letter from the Corinthians. From vv. 2–3 it can be inferred that the Corinthians had asked how they should test pneumatics for the gifts of the Spirit. This was a very pressing question in early Christianity and various criteria are articulated in early Christian writings. Paul refers first to the Corinthians' religious experiences and spiritual impulses when they were still pagan (v. 2). Then in v. 3 he articulates a Christological criterion: no utterance inspired by the Spirit can curse Jesus. It is not very likely that either in synagogue worship or in Christian assemblies those inspired would have shouted curses against Jesus. Rather, it is more probable that Paul construes an extreme case in order to underline his positive criterion: every inspired word is identical with the Christian confession "Jesus is *Kyrios*."

12:4–11, 28–31, The Variety of Spiritual Gifts. Although there is only one positive criterion for testing those who claim the gifts of the Holy Spirit, Paul insists that there are many spiritual gifts. The section 12:4–11 is a thought unit that begins (v. 4) and ends (v. 11) with the assertion that the variety of gifts is inspired by

one and the same Spirit. Paul seems not to be concerned primarily about the unity of the community but intends to stress the diversity and multiplicity of spiritual expressions and actions. Such a variety of spiritual endowment is given to everyone for the "common good" (v. 7).

This diversity of spiritual gifts is elaborated with the enumeration of the workings of the Spirit in vv. 8–10. Each of the three lists of spiritual gifts in 12:8–10; 12:28; and 12:29–30 varies, but in all three lists speaking in tongues and its interpretation come last. Since in the second list "apostles" comes first, Paul seems to put first what is most important to him and mentions the least important last. Paul does not disqualify and repudiate speaking in tongues but he ranks it as the lowest of spiritual endowments. His concluding admonition to seek the "higher gifts" indicates that he is interested in establishing a hierarchy of gifts (v. 31).

12:12–27, The Body of Christ. To underline that members of the community have different gifts and functions Paul introduces the fable of the body that was widespread in antiquity. He applies, however, the image of the one body with its many different members at first not to the church but to Christ. Since Paul understands the church to be "the body of Christ" (v. 27), he can speak of Christ as a corporate figure with many diverse members. Through baptism in the one Spirit Christians have become one body or corporation. In this one but spiritually diversified community religious and social status stratifications no longer exist. Jews and Greeks as well as slaves and free, they all have received the one Spirit. It is often observed that in v. 13 Paul does not quote the third pair of the pre-Pauline baptismal formula in Gal. 3:28 "neither male and female," and it is suggested that he omits it because of the problems women had caused in Corinth (cf. 11:2–16 and 14:33b–36). However, such an interpretation overlooks the fact that here Paul does not use the negative form of the baptismal confession but states it positively. To add "men and women" was either redundant or, if "neither male and female" in Gal. 3:28 is best understood as "husband and wife," outright wrong.

After having stressed the oneness of the Spirit and of the body of Christ, Paul in vv. 14–20 elaborates that the individual members of the community have their own proper function and that these functions are not the same or interchangeable. If it is true that not all members of the human body can be eyes or ears, then it is also true of the Christian community that it needs many diverse gifts but still remains one and the same body.

In vv. 21–27 Paul offers a somewhat different accent. Just as the different members of the body are interdependent and need each other so also do Christians. Those who have the gift of tongues, for instance, cannot say to those with the gift of prophecy that they have no need for them. Moreover, those members of the body who are considered to be weaker or to have a more dishonorable function were given by God special attention and honor. Therefore, the diverse members of the body of Christ should not be divided but should care for each other. Because of their organic interdependence, all members of the body suffer if one is injured just as all rejoice if one receives glory. It is clear from vv. 26 and 27 that Paul uses the image and analogy of the physical body and its members to hammer home that Christians are interdependent and constitute a synergetic community, the one body of Christ. They have received diverse gifts from the one Spirit and therefore have different functions. The whole argument ends effectively in vv. 29–30 with seven rhetorical questions, each one demanding a negative answer. Not only are there different gifts but also different functions and ministries that must be used for "the common good."

13:1–14:1a
In Praise of Agapē Love

This chapter is of high literary quality. It has a rhythmic prose structure consisting of three sections: vv. 1–3 contrast love with other spiritual gifts, vv. 4–7 spell out what love does, and vv. 8–13 elaborate the permanence of love. Since this "hymn to love" is very well composed, it might have been written separately and inserted as a rhetorical digression at this point.

1 Cor. 13:1–3 repeats three times the refrain, "If I have . . . but not love, I am. . . ." This section contrasts love with the spiritual gifts of speaking in tongues, prophecy, knowledge of mysteries, miracle-working faith, almsgiving, and self-sacrifice to assert the superiority of love.

Verses 4–7 describe the workings of love in three steps. First, we have two positive descriptions of love as patient and kind. Paul then elaborates in eight negatives what love is not. It is not jealous, boastful, arrogant, rude, irritable, or resentful, nor does it insist on its own way or rejoice at wrong. Finally, v. 7 states five positive ways in which love acts. Love joins in rejoicing at truth, supports, believes, hopes, and endures all things.

1 Cor. 13:8–14:1a returns to the theme of the superiority of love but explicates the contrast between love and spiritual gifts as the contrast between permanence and transience. Whereas the spiritual gifts that are partial or incomplete will pass away when the complete wholeness comes, love will not. The contrast is between partial and complete, not between perfect and imperfect. Since the Greek word for "whole, perfect" also can mean "mature," the following reference to childhood-adulthood is an illustration of it. The spiritual gifts, valuable in themselves, will be left behind when the eschatological wholeness that is love arrives (v. 11). Such an eschatological tension is suggested by the contrast between now and then in v. 12. Mirrors or looking glasses were produced in Corinth. They were made of polished bronze or silver and therefore gave a dim, distorted reflection. Paul compares such an "imperfect reflection" with the face-to-face vision of divine reality that will do away with our present imperfect human way of knowing. In the interim time, however, when speaking in tongues and other prophetic gifts are incomplete, three gifts remain: faith, hope, and love, but love stands supreme as the most excellent gift. Therefore, the whole praise of agapē climaxes in the exhortation "make love your aim" (14:1a), which is at the same time a transition to the next section.

14:1b–40
Spiritual Gifts: Prophecy and Speaking in Tongues

With 14:1b Paul returns to the topic of the gifts of the Spirit (cf. 12:31). He does not want to be misunderstood in the sense that Christians ought not to strive for the gifts of the Spirit. After having lauded the primacy of love he gives now first place to prophecy. This emphasis on "seek to prophesy" functions as an inclusion (vv. 1b and 30) that holds the whole chapter together. The chapter can be divided into five subsections (14:1b–5, 6–12, 13–19, 20–25, 26–36), and it concludes with a summary statement in 14:37–40.

The first section, 14:1b–5, formulates communicability as a criterion for the evaluation of the spiritual gifts of speaking in tongues and prophecy. Although Paul wishes that all could speak in tongues, he values prophecy higher because it contributes more to the building up of the community. Those who speak in tongues have received this gift for their own spiritual uplift, whereas those who prophesy edify, comfort, and teach the whole assembly. Because of its communal, communicative character, Paul accords prophetic speaking first place.

After Paul has made his basic point in the preceding section he now illustrates it in 14:6–12 with three examples why speech must be intelligible. As a first example Paul points to himself, arguing that the Corinthians would not benefit if he were to speak in tongues only. Then he refers to musical instruments. Nobody will be able to recognize the tune that is played on the harp and the flute or to follow the call of the bugle if individual notes are not played distinctly. Finally, he uses foreign languages as an illustration. If people do not know each other's language they remain strangers. The whole section concludes with the exhortation to strive for those spiritual gifts that contribute to the building up of community.

Verses 13–19 explicate some consequences for those who speak in tongues. If someone speaks in tongues, that person should also pray for the gift of interpretation. Three conclusions are drawn for Christian praying and worship. First, prayer should not only be ecstatic but also should be fruitful for mind or reason. Further, the community is forced into the role of "the outsider" by such ecstatic prayer, because it does not know when to respond and ratify such prayer. Finally, Paul refers again to his own example. Although he speaks more in tongues than any of the Corinthians, he prefers to say five understandable words of instruction rather than thousands of words in tongues no one can understand.

The section 14:20–25 draws out the implications for the missionary situation. After an exhortation to be mature in intelligence but mere infants in wickedness, Paul quotes Scripture (Isa. 28:11–12) in support of his argument that tongues are ineffective as a means of missionary communication. Trance and ecstatic speech serve as a sign of spiritual endowment for unbelievers but not for those who have faith, whereas prophecy is proof of spiritual status for believers but not for unbelievers. Moreover, if all in the Christian assembly would speak in tongues and an unbelieving outsider would happen to come to their meeting, such a person would judge them to be frenzied soothsayers. Prophecy, to the contrary, is able to convict and judge such unbelieving outsiders as well as to lay their innermost thoughts open so that they will worship, recognizing God among the assembled community.

The general statement in v. 26 introduces a new section (14:26–36) in which Paul applies the insights articulated in the previous discussion to the Corinthian situation. It sums up in a general maxim Paul's instruction: everything in the ecclesial assembly should happen for edification. The whole section is clearly structured. It articulates rules for people who speak in tongues (vv. 27–28), prophets (vv. 29–33), and women or wives (vv. 34–36) that are similar in form. General sentences of regulation (vv. 27, 29, 34) are complemented by sentences that concretize them (vv. 28, 30, 35).

The last two regulations are structurally different insofar as they are expanded with supporting reasons for the regulation (vv. 31–32, 34a, 35b). Moreover, it is debated whether the general sentence in v. 29 is the heading for

both, or whether it applies only to the second regulation. The third regulation ends with a double rhetorical question that at the same time concludes all three examples. Such a structural analysis indicates that vv. 34–36 are not a secondary interpolation of the post-Pauline school but structurally well integrated in its present context.

The first regulation (vv. 27–28) insists that speaking in tongues should be done in good order and be accompanied by interpretation. If no one is around to interpret then speakers in tongues "should be silent in the assembly" and use their gift privately for their own edification.

The second regulation (vv. 29–33) demands that not more than two or three prophets should speak at the same time and should let the others weigh their prophetic message. If another prophet receives a revelation then the first prophetic speaker "should be silent." Two reasons are given. First, prophetic speaking needs to be done in good order so that all can profit from it. Second, prophetic inspirations are to be controlled by the prophets because God is a God of peace and not of confusion.

The third regulation is the most debated because it is not quite clear what special case is in mind. Is silence demanded from all women in the assembly, does it apply to the special case of women glossolalists and prophets, or are women prevented from evaluating the prophets' message? Since the Greek term for woman can be translated as "woman" or as "wife" it is also not clear whether the regulation applies only to a special class of women. However, what is clear is that silence is demanded in a special case. Just as people who speak in tongues, women and men, and prophets, women and men, are told to be silent in certain circumstances, so wives are admonished to silence, for as v. 35 suggests, the regulation applies not to all women members of the community, or even to all women endowed with spiritual gifts, but to wives.

Moreover, the text does not refer to speaking in tongues, to prophetic speaking, or to critical evaluation, but to speaking in the *ekklēsia*, the public assembly. Verse 34b is then best understood to express the Greco-Roman sentiment and legal regulations for the subordination of wives and against public speeches and demonstrations by matrons. Finally, the prohibition does not apply in general to any speaking of wives but only to their raising of questions and entering into discussions in the public assembly of the community. The concluding rhetorical questions in v. 36 indicate that Paul does not expect that this injunction will be accepted without protest by the Corinthian community, which knows of wives as leading Christian missionaries.

This is also evident from Paul's appeal to the authority of the *Kyrios* in v. 37 and his threat in v. 38. Verses 39–40 reiterate Paul's main point in chap. 14: the Corinthians should strive for the spiritual gift of prophecy and not prevent speaking in tongues. Paul's major concern is thereby decency and order.

15:1–57
About the Resurrection

A structural narrative analysis of 1 Cor. 15 indicates that it is a unit of thought held together in the form of an inclusion (vv. 1–2 and v. 58: "brothers [and sisters]/in vain"). Verses 1–11 form the basis of the argumentation. Verses 12–34 address the argument of "some" in the community that there is no resurrection of the dead but a resurrection of living people only, whereas vv. 35–57 discuss the question in which form the dead are to be resurrected—a problem raised by "someone" whom Paul calls a fool.

15:1–11, Foundation of Paul's Argument. In this section Paul seeks to establish that he is a member of the apostolic circle and shares in its authority. This argumentative unit, which forms an inclusion (vv. 1–2 and v. 11: preached/believed), can be divided into three sections.

First, in vv. 1–2 Paul draws attention to the gospel that he preached in Corinth, that they have received, by which they live, and through which they are saved if they hold firmly to it. However, Paul is uncertain whether their faith was genuine (v. 3).

Second, in vv. 3–8 Paul reiterates the gospel that he has preached to them by quoting (cf. 11:23) a traditional creedal formula in vv. 3b–5 that he expands in vv. 6–8. This traditional gospel stresses that Christ died, was buried, was raised, and was made visible or appeared. The statement that "he appeared" occurs actually or by implication six times. Whereas Paul rhetorically states that he is the last one of those who have experienced a resurrection appearance, the structure of the text marks Christ's appearance to Paul as the climax of the whole series. This is developed in the third unit (vv. 9–11). Paul rhetorically asserts that he is the least of the apostles. At the same time he makes clear that he is the most dedicated and hardest working of all the apostles. Yet, he plays this down by pointing to the grace of God. Paul thus seeks to show that he is a member of the apostolic "we-group" to whom the kerygma is entrusted (→ Kerygma).

15:12–34, The Argument of "Some." This segment proceeds in three steps. First, vv. 12–19 address the argument of some who say "There is no resurrection of the dead." They are contrast-

ed with the apostles who proclaim Christ as raised from the dead. It is debated whether the "some" denied the resurrection of the dead as such or only the resurrection of those who have died before the Parousia (glorious return) of Christ. However, if there is no resurrection of the dead (v. 12) four conclusions must be drawn: (1) Christ has not been raised (vv. 13, 16); (2) Paul's preaching is misleading and nullified (vv. 14, 15); (3) the faith of the Corinthians is in vain, they are still in their sins and deserve pity (vv. 14, 17, 19); and (4) those who have died in Christ have perished (v. 18). Whereas in Corinth both the kerygma "Christ was raised" and the statement "There is no [general] resurrection from the dead" could be held alongside each other, Paul relates them as statements exclusive of each other by adding "from the dead" to the traditional kerygma.

Second, after having pointed out the fatal consequences of this opinion for the dead and the living, Paul positively develops what the resurrection of Christ means (vv. 20–28). Christ is the "first fruit of those who have fallen asleep." Christ's resurrection as the first in a whole series is constitutive for all those following (vv. 20–22). Verse 23 establishes the temporal order of the eschatological events that are elaborated in vv. 24–28: first, Christ's resurrection and enthronement, then the resurrection of the dead at his Parousia, and finally, after having overcome all domination and evil powers, Christ will give up reign and power to God who will be "all in all." The resurrection of Christ and that of the dead are not independent theological data but are integrated as an indissoluble causal and temporal whole in the salvific plan of God for the world.

Third, vv. 29–34 are a chain of argumentation that takes up a position similar to vv. 12–19. In four rhetorical questions Paul appeals to the affective side of his readers by pointing to the futility of their and his actions if there were no resurrection of the dead. The first two rhetorical questions refer to the practice of the Corinthians to undergo baptism vicariously for their dead in the hope of saving them (v. 29). More than thirty interpretations have been proposed to explain this practice, but none is satisfactory. Paul does not question the merits of it but refers to it to elucidate his point.

The last two rhetorical questions refer to the futility of Paul's missionary sufferings and underline once more the absurdity of Christian life-style and practice if the dead are not raised (vv. 30–32). The whole series of *ad hominem* arguments concludes with two very sharp admonitions: "do not be deceived" and "become sober and do not sin!"

15:35–57, The Argument of "Some One." Adopting the style of the diatribe discussion

Paul posits a fictitious objector. The whole argument proceeds in two steps.

First, vv. 35–49 are subdivided by "so" into a comparison or simile (vv. 36–41) and an application (vv. 42–49) that seeks to reply to the objection of "some one" who might argue that if the dead are raised then they must have bodies. How and with what kind of body will the dead be raised (v. 35)? Paul's response first reminds the readers of the differences and commonalities between the seed and plant. Many different plants come from seeds that look very much alike. There are many different kinds of "flesh" (v. 39), of "body" (v. 40a), and of "glory" (vv. 40b–41). Just as the "bare kernel" of wheat and other grain is contrasted with the "future body" (vv. 37–38), so the "earthly bodies or flesh" of humans, animals, birds, and fish are contrasted with the qualitatively different "heavenly bodies or glory" of sun, moon, and stars (vv. 39–41). We sow "the bare kernel" that dies, but it is made alive again by God in its "new body," the fruit.

Verses 42–44 apply this insight in four antithetical parallelisms to the "resurrection of the dead." The two verbs "sown" and "raised" that are repeated four times speak of two successive events. The present body, which is characterized as perishable, dishonorable, weak, and physical, will be changed into the resurrected body characterized as imperishable, glorious, powerful, and spiritual. This argument is bolstered by a reference to Scripture. According to Philo (a first-century Jewish writer), the "first Adam" was made in the image of God (Gen. 1:27), while the second was made of dust and endowed with a "living soul" (Gen. 2:7). Paul corrects this sequence—by stating that the "spiritual" Adam, Christ, did not come first but the one of dust—to adapt the text to his argument for successive, qualitatively different stages. Just as we participate in the nature and image of the first Adam made of dust, so will we share in the nature and image of the final Adam, the life-giving Spirit.

Second, vv. 50–58 emphasize the need for transformation. Whereas the preceding section consisted of antithetical statements, this concluding section begins with a direct address. Having shown that it is possible to conceive of a resurrection body Paul now declares that a body different from our present one is necessary for the resurrection status. Such a qualitatively different body is no longer subject to the power of death. Whereas in baptism believers have been freed from the power of sin and of the law, in the Parousia they will be freed from the power of death. Therefore, Paul breaks out into a thanksgiving to God who gives final victory over death through Jesus Christ. Paul ends this chapter with an admonition to the Corinthian Christians to be steadfast in the gospel (v. 58), undertaking the work of Christ in the knowledge that their labors are not futile.

16:1–24

Conclusion

This last portion of the Letter contains a mixture of information and exhortations as well as personal plans and greetings. It refers twice to issues raised by the community (vv. 1 and 12) and underlines the importance of Stephanas and his missionary co-workers. On the whole, this conclusion to the Letter permits us to glimpse the everyday life of a Christian community in the missionary movement of the first century A.D.

16:1–4, About the Collection. These instructions seek to organize the collection for the church in Jerusalem. The Corinthians ought to put aside something every week so that Paul, when he arrives, can send those who are elected and accredited by the community to bring the collection to Jerusalem. Only if the community considers it advisable will Paul accompany them. Paul seems to be very cautious, possibly to avoid the accusation that he might misuse some of the funds.

16:5–14, Travel Plans. Paul first elaborates his own travel plans (vv. 5–9). He intends to stay a longer time in Corinth but has to go first to Macedonia and Ephesus where he has many enemies. Then he reminds the community again (cf. 4:17) that Timothy will arrive before him and that they should respect him and put him at ease (vv. 10–11).

Verse 12, about Apollos, is the last explicit reference to an inquiry from Corinth. Paul concedes that he was not able to persuade Apollos to visit now. He will come when an opportunity arises. Verses 13–14 add an exhortation to be watchful, courageous, firm, strong, and to do everything in love.

16:15–19, The House of Stephanas. Paul is glad about the arrival of Stephanas, Fortunatus, and Achaicus, who have come from Corinth. The household of Stephanas was the first converted in Achaia and they have devoted themselves to communal ministry. Paul seeks to underline their authority when he admonishes the Corinthians to "subordinate" themselves to them and every missionary co-worker of Paul.

16:20–24, Greetings. After having sent greetings from all the churches of Asia, from the

1188

missionary pair Aquila and Prisca (usually mentioned first!) and their house-church, and from all Christians (v. 20), Paul writes greetings with his own hand (v. 21) after having dictated the rest of the Letter. He admonishes the Corinthians to greet each other with a holy kiss (v. 20b) and concludes with a blessing (vv. 23–24). Before this final blessing he introduces two formulas derived from the earliest Christian liturgy: the anathema for anyone who does not love Christ or God and the Aramaic invocation *maranatha*, which can be rendered either as "Our *Kyrios* come" or "Our *Kyrios* has come." Unusual in this Letter ending is the addition of "love" to the wish of grace. Thus Paul underlines once more his major concern.

Bibliography

Barrett, C. K. *The First Epistle to the Corinthians.* Harper's New Testament Commentaries. New York: Harper & Row, 1968.

Bratcher, R. G. *A Translator's Guide to Paul's First Letter to the Corinthians.* London and New York: United Bible Societies, 1982.

Conzelmann, H. *1 Corinthians.* Translated by J. W. Leitch. Hermeneia. Philadelphia: Fortress, 1975.

Hurd, J. C. *The Origin of 1 Corinthians.* 2d ed. Macon, GA: Mercer University Press, 1983.

Meeks, W. A. *The First Urban Christians: The Social World of the Apostle Paul.* New Haven, CT: Yale University Press, 1983.

Murphy-O'Connor, J. *1 Corinthians.* New Testament Message, 10. Wilmington, DE: Glazier, 1979.

_____. *St. Paul's Corinth: Texts and Archaeology.* Wilmington, DE: Glazier, 1983.

Talbert, C. H. *Reading Corinthians: A Literary and Theological Commentary on 1 and 2 Corinthians.* New York: Crossroad, 1987.

Theissen, G. *The Social Setting of Pauline Christianity: Essays on Corinth.* Edited, translated and with an Introduction by J. H. Schütz. Philadelphia: Fortress, 1982.

2 CORINTHIANS

VICTOR PAUL FURNISH

INTRODUCTION

Literary Form and Structure

2 Corinthians is generally similar in form and structure to the other Pauline Letters. After the opening address (1:1–2) and blessing (1:3–11), an extended central section takes up various matters of concern to the writer and his readers (1:12–13:10), and following this there are some concluding admonitions (13:11–13) and an apostolic benediction (13:14).

Certain peculiarities and difficulties become apparent, however, as soon as one attempts a more detailed structural analysis of the body of the letter. First, it is not immediately clear how the lengthy discussion of apostleship in 2:14–7:4 is related to the references to Paul's visit in Macedonia that precede and follow it in 2:12–13 and 7:5–7. Second, the form, style, and content of the admonitions in 6:14–7:1 are not easy to reconcile with the rest of the Letter or with other Pauline exhortations. Third, there is a certain redundancy in the discussion of the collection for the church in Jerusalem (chaps. 8 and 9). And finally, the expressions of frustration and the sometimes scathing rhetoric of 10:1–13:10 are quite unexpected after the expressions of confidence and the tactful, carefully reasoned remarks in chaps. 1–9.

These and related difficulties have led many interpreters to conclude that our canonical 2 Corinthians is actually a combination of materials drawn from two or more originally independent Pauline letters, put together by an early editor, who perhaps also added some non-Pauline material. Thus, some read chaps. 1–9 and chaps. 10–13 as two separate letters (e.g., Barrett, Furnish, Martin), while others find as many as five or six letters represented here (e.g., Betz, who identifies five: 1:1–2:13 + 7:5–16 + 13:11–14; 2:14–6:13 + 7:2–4; chap. 8; chap. 9; and 10:1–13:10). Although a few have argued that 6:14–7:1 is a fragment of yet another Pauline letter, the majority of scholars either leave it in place or else regard it as non-Pauline material inserted by a later editor. Some commentators, however (e.g., Hughes), believe that all of these so-called "partition theories" are unwarranted and unnecessary; and indeed there is no specific evidence that 2 Corinthians was known in the early church in any other form than the one we have. Nevertheless, as will become apparent below in the comments on various specific passages, many of the obscuri-

ties and difficulties of this Letter would be cleared up if in fact a very early editor of the apostle's letters is responsible for the form in which it was received into the church's canon.

That various literary genres and rhetorical styles have been identified within 2 Corinthians is not in itself an argument for its composite nature, but in certain instances it may lend support to one or another of the partition hypotheses. Thus, while 2 Corinthians as a whole certainly belongs to the epistolary genre (→ Letter), chaps. 8 and 9 have been identified more particularly as "administrative letters" (see Betz, esp. pp. 129–40) and 2:24–6:13 + 7:2–4 and chaps. 10–13 as "apologetic" letters (see Betz, p. 143). Various styles are also evident in 2 Corinthians. For example, the style in 2:14–7:16 as a whole tends to be that of a teacher, while that of chaps. 10–13 is emphatically disputatious (exhibiting such literary devices as irony, parody, and self-display, often used by Greco-Roman writers against their opponents); and at certain points the style is specifically expository, as in 3:7–18 where, in the course of his discussion, the apostle offers an interpretation of Exodus 34.

As dependent as Paul is on various rhetorical conventions of his day, his own sense of apostolic vocation and specifically his sense of apostolic responsibility for the Christians of Corinth have also influenced the form and style of 2 Corinthians (however many letters it represents). To understand Paul's apostolic concerns here, one must obtain as clear a picture as the evidence will allow of the circumstances that prompted him to write as he does and of the full extent of his Corinthian correspondence.

The Five Letters to Corinth

Despite the headings under which they have been handed down in the canon, "1 Corinthians" and "2 Corinthians" are not, respectively, the apostle's first and second letters to the Corinthian congregation. We know that our "1 Corinthians" is at least the second letter, because in 1 Cor. 5:9–11 Paul refers to an earlier communication he says had been misunderstood. This earlier letter, probably the first he wrote to the Corinthians, seems not to have survived, although a few interpreters have sought to identify 2 Cor. 6:14–7:1 as a fragment of it. There is no way of determining where it was sent from, but it must have been written sometime in the period between the conclusion of the apostle's first visit (A.D. 51 or 52) and the writing of 1 Corinthians (the First Letter of Paul to the; see 1 Corinthians, "Introduction"; → Corinthians).

In 2 Corinthians Paul refers to a letter he wrote "out of an exceedingly troubled, anguished heart . . . through many tears" (2 Cor. 2:4; cf. vv. 3, 9). A few interpreters continue to hold to the traditional view that this "tearful letter" is canonical 1 Corinthians, but a larger number believe that the difficulties with this identification are virtually insurmountable. Accordingly, many have argued that most of the tearful letter is preserved in chaps. 10–13 of 2 Corinthians, while others think it more likely that it has not survived at all, even in part.

How many letters did Paul write to Corinth beyond these three? The answer to this depends upon one's view of 2 Corinthians—whether it is a single letter or a composite of two or more and, if it is a composite, how many separate letters it represents. The analysis preferred in this commentary identifies parts of only two letters in 2 Corinthians, written in the following sequence: (1) chaps. 1–9 (or, perhaps, chaps. 1–8 with chap. 9 as a separate note) and (2) chaps. 10–13. One can better understand the occasion and purpose of each of these when they are set within the broader context of Paul's Corinthian ministry as a whole.

Paul's Corinthian Ministry

Various reconstructions of the course of Paul's Corinthian ministry are possible. The following outline of his dealings with the congregation prior to the writing of 2 Corinthians should be compared with different, but equally plausible reconstructions offered by other interpreters.

The apostle's initial visit to Corinth (1 Cor. 2:1–5), during at least part of which his associates Silvanus and Timothy were also present (2 Cor. 1:19), probably took place early in the year A.D. 50 or 51. By the time he departed—according to Acts 18:11, some eighteen months later—he had succeeded in establishing a congregation in this important city (→ Corinth).

The letter mentioned in 1 Cor. 5:9–11, written sometime after 51 or 52, counseled the congregation to tolerate no immorality in its midst; but at least some of the Corinthians misunderstood this to mean that they should separate themselves even from non-Christians. This may be designated Letter A.

In response to a letter from the Corinthians and to reports of troubles within their congregation, Paul sent Timothy, probably by way of Macedonia, to remind them of the gospel by and to which they had been converted (1 Cor. 4:17; 16:10–11). Our 1 Corinthians was apparently sent simultaneously (perhaps in 54 or

55), although the apostle expected that it would be received in advance of Timothy's arrival. In this letter, which would be Letter B, the apostle answers a number of questions posed by the Corinthians, offers additional instruction, and requests a warm welcome for Timothy.

Subsequent to Timothy's mission, Paul himself evidently paid a brief "emergency visit" to the congregation, although the evidence for this is only circumstantial. First, the references in 2 Cor. 12:14 and 13:1 to an impending "third" visit presume that Paul has been in Corinth on some occasion since the eighteen-month visit during which the church was founded. And second, the statement in 2 Cor. 2:1 that he had decided against paying the congregation "another sorrowful visit" presumes that one visit had in fact been "sorrowful." Since nothing that is said in 1 Corinthians suggests that Paul would have described his first visit this way, it is probable that a second visit is in view. From what is said in 2 Cor. 2:2–11 and then later in 7:12 it appears that this second visit was unpleasant because the apostle had been grievously offended by some fellow Christian.

One may plausibly suppose that the tearful letter (2 Cor. 2:4) was written in the wake of the traumatic experience of Paul's second visit. To judge from the remarks in 2 Cor. 2:2–11 and 7:5–12, in this letter Paul chastised the congregation for not supporting him and for not disciplining the person who had offended him. This would be Letter C.

The tearful letter may have been carried to Corinth by Titus, one of Paul's associates. In any event, Titus arrived in time to observe the effectiveness of that letter in moving the congregation to repent and to renew its allegiance to Paul and his gospel (2 Cor. 7:7).

Titus's subsequent report to Paul, delivered at a meeting somewhere in Macedonia, was a great relief to the apostle (2 Cor. 7:5–7, 13–16). It would appear from what is said in 2 Cor. 8:6, 16–24 that Titus was then sent to Corinth a second time, perhaps almost immediately, to further the cause of the Pauline collection for Jerusalem. In this instance he was accompanied by two others (whose names are not given).

Chapters 1–9

If one identifies chaps. 10–13 with the tearful letter mentioned in 2 Cor. 2:4, then chaps. 1–9 (or some portion of them) may be described as "a letter of reconciliation" written after the problems addressed in chaps. 10–13 had been successfully resolved. A number of interpreters hold to this view. Others, however, argue that chaps. 1–9 must have been written before chaps. 10–13. If this is the case, then chaps. 10–13 cannot be identified with the tearful letter, and the situation in Corinth must have deteriorated markedly after chaps. 1–9 were written.

The second of these two views is the one adopted in this commentary. Thus, chaps. 1–9 would constitute the apostle's fourth letter to Corinth, *Letter D*. It was occasioned by Titus's report that Paul's tearful letter of reprimand has been effective: the congregation now regrets that it had failed to support Paul in his confrontation with an offending brother and has taken strong disciplinary action against him. Cheered by this good news, the apostle writes to assure the Corinthians of his confidence in them and takes the opportunity to renew his earlier appeal (see 1 Cor. 16:1–4) that they make a contribution to the fund he has promised to collect for the Christians of Jerusalem (see Gal. 2:1–10).

It would appear, however, that Titus had also brought word about certain persons who, having intruded themselves into the Corinthian congregation, were seeking to undermine Paul's authority. Thus, Letter D is also, in part, Paul's response to insinuations that his apostleship is not completely legitimate and that he has not been entirely straightforward in his dealings with the Corinthians.

This letter was written from Macedonia (2 Cor. 7:5) and was probably delivered to the congregation by Titus on the occasion of his second visit (2 Cor. 8:16–17). It can be dated approximately to 55 or 56, some five years after the founding of the congregation.

Chapters 10–13

It is probable that these chapters, which represent the last of Paul's extant letters to Corinth—thus, *Letter E*—were also written in Macedonia, but some months after Letter D. During these months the anti-Pauline movement in the city must have made substantial headway, because in this letter the apostle does not hesitate to express his outrage at those who, in his view, would deceive and exploit his congregation. The Corinthians are urged to reject the false charges with which they have vilified Paul and the false claims with which they have tried to establish their own authority in place of his.

In this letter Paul indicates that he will soon be coming to Corinth again (his third visit, 2 Cor. 12:14; 13:1), and in anticipation of that he warns the congregation that he is prepared to deal harshly with any who have not heeded his appeals. The most striking feature of the letter is a lengthy section in which, writing as "a fool," the apostle mocks the pretentious boasting of his opponents—he boasts not of his superior religious status and attainments as they do, but of his weakness and suffering (2 Cor. 11:1–12:13).

Paul's Letter to the Romans, probably written from Corinth, provides indirect evidence that Letter E had the desired results and that the apostle was generally well received when he visited Corinth for the third (and last) time. He informs the Romans that he is presently en route to Jerusalem with the collection, to which the Christians of Macedonia and Achaia have contributed (Rom. 15:25–26). Since Corinth was the capital city of Achaia, it would appear that the Corinthians were among the contributors to the fund. If so, then one must suppose that they had once again acknowledged the legitimacy of Paul's apostleship and their own status as a congregation under his direction.

Significance of the Letters

The two letters that constitute canonical 2 Corinthians are important both historically and theologically. Historically, they are major sources of our knowledge about one of Paul's most prominent congregations and about the challenges and issues he faced as a missionary and pastoral leader. They allow glimpses of how he was perceived by his harshest critics and, more directly, of how he wished to be perceived. They add greatly to our understanding of the importance he assigned to his collection for Jerusalem and to the administration of that, of the opposition with which he was frequently confronted, of how he dealt with controversy, and of the way he employed the services of his co-workers Timothy and Titus.

Although "doctrinal" matters are not taken up for their own sake, these two letters are no less rich in theological insight than in historical information. Common to them both is Paul's insistence that his readers must understand apostleship and evaluate anyone who professes to be an apostle only with reference to the gospel. In reflecting on the meaning of that gospel, he is led to remark on such fundamental matters as the relationship of the new covenant to the old, the significance of Christ's death, the new creation, the Spirit, how God's power is manifest in weakness, and how the believer's life is both graced by God's love and claimed for obedience to God.

COMMENTARY

1:1–11

Letter Opening

Paul observes the ancient conventions of letter writing by opening with an address, followed by a paragraph complimenting his readers.

1:1–2, Address. The letter is being sent not only to the congregation in Corinth, but also to Christians who live elsewhere in Achaia, the Roman province of which Corinth was the capital. Timothy, apparently with Paul in Macedonia, is mentioned because he endorses what the letter contains, not because he participated in the actual writing of it.

1:3–11, Blessing. In his other Letters, Paul writes of his "thanksgiving" to God for the congregation he is addressing (e.g., 1 Cor. 1:4–9). While that element is not lacking here (2 Cor. 1:11), the emphasis is on God's having comforted both the apostle and the Corinthians in the midst of afflictions (v. 11). In particular, Paul expresses his gratitude at having been delivered from a life-threatening situation in Asia (vv. 8–11). The reference may be to some experience in Ephesus, the Asian capital (see 1 Cor. 15:32; 16:8–9; see Philippians, "Introduction").

1:12–13:10

Letter Body

If, as seems probable, 2 Corinthians is a composite of at least two originally independent letters, the body of the letter introduced by 1:1–11 would be much less extensive. According to one hypothesis (see Betz), it would include only 1:12–2:13 and 7:5–16; according to another (see Furnish), it would extend at least through chap. 8 and perhaps through chap. 9.

1:12–2:13

Assurances of Concern

There are at least some in Corinth who suspect that Paul has not dealt with their congregation in an entirely straightforward manner. The opening paragraphs are designed to allay these suspicions.

1:12–14, Introductory Plea. The apostle urges his readers to be open to his explanations of actions that may have seemed thoughtless, or worse. His own conscience is clear, for he is confident that he has been guided by God's grace, "not by any ordinary wisdom" (v. 12).

1:15–17, About the Visits. At the time he wrote 1 Corinthians, Paul was planning to spend the winter in Ephesus and then, after Pentecost, to go to Macedonia. From there he intended to proceed to Corinth and then, should it be necessary, to accompany the delegation that was to deliver the money his congregations had con-

tributed for the Christians in Jerusalem (1 Cor. 16:1–9). Apparently, however, he has twice changed his plans since then, to the consternation of some people in Corinth. The first change was to allow him two visits to Corinth, one before and another following his time in Macedonia (2 Cor. 1:15–16). But that plan too was somehow changed, so that now he must respond to suggestions that he is acting irresponsibly, and perhaps even opportunistically (1:17).

1:18–22, God's Faithfulness. Paul first defends the changes in his plans by reminding his readers of the faithfulness of the God whom he serves and that all of God's promises will ultimately be fulfilled in Jesus Christ. The Corinthians themselves affirm this whenever they join in the "Amen" of Christian worship (v. 20), and through the Spirit given at their baptism they have already experienced the reality of it (v. 22).

1:23–2:11, The "Sorrowful Visit." In particular, the Corinthians are to understand that Paul canceled a projected visit because he wanted to spare them another like the one that he describes here as "sorrowful" (2:1). What little can be known about that earlier (second) visit has to be pieced together from the present passage and the comments in 7:8–12. The apostle seems to have had some nasty encounter with a member of the congregation, an experience that was all the more painful for Paul because the congregation neither rallied to his support nor reprimanded the offending brother. Subsequently, rather than return to Corinth as planned, he sent a letter that had been written "through many tears" (2:3–4) and that caused the Corinthians, at last, to take disciplinary action (see 7:8–12; the letter is probably lost, although some would find the largest part of it preserved in chaps. 10–13). Now, having learned that his adversary has been banished from the congregation, Paul advises that he be forgiven and restored to fellowship (2:5–11); the apostle's interest is not in retaliation, but in reconciliation.

2:12–13, Coming to Macedonia. Paul wants the Corinthians to know that he is now in Macedonia because of his concern about them. So anxious was he for news from Corinth, that when Titus failed to arrive in Troas with a report from there, the apostle hurried on to meet him in Macedonia. Now their meeting has taken place, and it is from Titus that Paul has learned about the good effect of the tearful letter (2:3–4; 7:6–7). Many interpreters believe that 2:13 was followed originally by 7:5, since the meeting with Titus is also in view in 7:5–16 and the discussion in 2:14–7:4 seems to have a different focus.

1193

2:14–5:19
Comments on Apostleship

Paul's concern here is evident, whether one reads his comments in the context of 2 Corinthians as a whole (believing it to be a single letter), in the context of chaps. 1–9 (believing these chapters to be a separate letter), or in the context of 2:14–7:4 only (believing this section to be a separate letter). He wants the Corinthians to understand what distinguishes the true apostle, a subject made all the more urgent because questions are being raised in Corinth about his own apostolic standing. (Since the theme of reconciliation is present in the appeal of 5:20 as well as in the affirmations of 5:18–19, most commentaries do not separate these verses, even for the purpose of analysis.)

2:14–3:6, Spreading the Gospel. A striking image for apostolic service is implicit in the exclamation of 2:14a, "Thanks be to God, who in Christ always puts us on display,... " In the Greek term translated by the last four words, Paul's readers would have recognized an allusion to the Roman "triumphs," elaborate processions sponsored by the emperor to celebrate particularly important military victories. Since the ones "on display" were the prisoners of war, paraded in chains through the streets, it must be with them and not with their triumphant captors that one is to identify the apostles. The indignities and adversities that apostles experience serve to advance the gospel (vv. 14b–16), because through them the saving death of Jesus is given a presence in the world (see 4:7–12). Sharply contrasting views are held by those referred to in 2:17a and 3:1, would-be apostles who are compared to hucksters peddling their wares in the marketplace. Paul does not require the kind of testimonial letters they carry; there is no better evidence of the authenticity of his gospel and the legitimacy of his apostleship than the existence of a church in Corinth, established through his ministry (3:2–3). The "new" and "spiritual" covenant served by his ministry (3:6; cf. Jer. 31:31–34) is the topic in 2 Cor. 3:7–18.

3:7–18, The Ministry of the New Covenant. The contrast between "the letter" that "kills" and "the Spirit" that "gives life" (3:6; cf. v. 3) is now developed (for the imagery, see esp. Exod. 31:18; Ezek. 11:19–20; 36:26–27). The story of Moses' descent from Mt. Sinai (Exod. 34:29–35) figures prominently here, and some interpreters hold that Paul is setting his reading of the passage over against that offered by those in Corinth who have challenged his apostolic credentials. His chief intention, however, is to explain why his is the ministry of a *new* cov-

enant (2 Cor. 3:6). He identifies the old covenant (v. 14) with the law chiseled on the stone tablets that Moses received on Sinai (v. 7), and he characterizes it as leading to condemnation (v. 9). Those who serve the law are therefore engaged in a "ministry of death" (v. 7). This old covenant is replaced by the gospel of Christ (v. 14), which leads to life. Those who, like Paul, serve this gospel are engaged in "the ministry of the Spirit" (v. 7) and "of righteousness" (v. 9). In vv. 12–13 the covering that Moses placed over his face (see Exod. 34:33–35) is interpreted as evidence that the old covenant has been annulled, and in vv. 14–15 it becomes a metaphor for the spiritual blindness of those who remain bound to the law. When one "turns to the Lord" in faith, however, one is freed from the law, for "where the Spirit of the Lord is, is freedom" (vv. 16–17; cf. Rom. 7:6; 8:2–8, 14–16; Gal. 4:21–5:14). The "image" in whom the Lord's glory is brilliantly mirrored (2 Cor. 3:18a) is Christ (see 4:4), and it is into the new life bestowed in him that those who see with the eyes of faith "are being transformed" (v. 18b).

4:1–6, "Jesus Christ as Lord." Paul's emphasis here on the candor and forthrightness with which he conducts his ministry (vv. 1–4) may be prompted by his concern about rival apostles in Corinth. They may have charged him with acting in underhanded ways, even misrepresenting the gospel; or he may be insinuating that they do. Moreover, unlike them he does not center his message on himself; rather, he preaches nothing but "Jesus Christ as Lord" (v. 5, echoing the early creedal affirmation, "Jesus is Lord," Rom. 10:9; 1 Cor. 12:3; Phil. 2:10–11). Indeed, the Corinthians are to understand that Paul considers himself their "slave" (cf. 2 Cor. 1:24; 12:15), quite unlike his competitors whom he will later accuse of exploiting the congregation (11:20). The readers themselves can confirm this, for it is by Paul's preaching that the light of the gospel has dawned in their lives (v. 6, with an allusion to Gen. 1:3; cf. 2 Cor. 4:4).

4:7, A Treasure in Clay Pots. Like clay pots, those who bear the gospel treasure are fragile and vulnerable, that through them God's transcendent power might be evident. The truth of this must have been recently reinforced for Paul when, overcome with a sense of helplessness in the face of some mortal danger in Asia, he was led to a profound experience of God's power (see 1:8–11). This same paradox is involved in his understanding of the gospel itself, which he identifies with God's power for salvation (Rom. 1:16) as well as with Jesus' death on the cross (1 Cor. 1:17–2:5). While the world regards the cross as a sign of weakness, Paul can identify it with God's saving power, because he associates that power with God's love and interprets Jesus' death as the definitive instance of that love (Rom. 5:6–11; cf. 2 Cor. 5:14). These ideas underlie everything that Paul has to say about apostleship in 2 Corinthians.

4:8–15, Apostolic Tribulations. In support of the point in v. 7, Paul offers a list of typical apostolic tribulations (vv. 8–9; cf. 6:4c–5; 11:23b–29; 12:10; Rom. 8:35; 1 Cor. 4:9–13) he then interprets as manifestations of Jesus' death and resurrection life (2 Cor. 4:10–15). Through the sufferings visited upon the apostles as they spend themselves for others (vv. 12, 15; cf. 12:15), the saving power of selfless, serving love is made concretely present in the world. In vv. 13–14, quoting Scripture (Ps. 115:1 in the Septuagint [LXX] Greek version; cf. 116:10 in the English), Paul emphasizes the apostles' resolve to bring faith to expression whatever the personal costs, for theirs is a confidence founded in the power of God. This view of weakness and sufferings as integral to an authentic apostolic witness sets Paul far apart from his rivals, who regard these as signs of religious inferiority, brazenly (note 10:12; 11:21b) claiming apostolic authority for themselves by reason of ethnic origin (11:22), religious superiority (e.g., 10:10; 11:23a), and rhetorical skills (11:5–6).

4:16–5:1, Boldness Despite Mortality. Resuming the affirmation of 4:1 (see also 3:4, 12; 4:13), Paul declares that despite adversities (4:8–9) and the certainty of death (5:1), true apostles boldly continue their service of the gospel. The "outer person" is one's mortal existence, which inevitably passes away; the "inner person" is one's identity as a child of God, and that is constantly being reaffirmed (4:16). One need not suppose, as many interpreters have, that the apostle's recent brush with death in Asia (see 1:8) has caused him to abandon his earlier expectation that he would live until Christ's return (see 1 Thess. 4:15, 17). It is less likely that his remarks here are prompted by threats to his life than by threats to his apostolic standing in Corinth. In 2 Cor. 4:16–5:10 he seems to be responding to charges that if he were a legitimate apostle, he would not have to endure so many sufferings and hardships. Yet as he proceeds, he broadens his comments to apply to all believers: the whole community of faith may take heart in the confidence that the reality of God transcends what can be seen and experienced in this life (4:17–18), and that beyond the common human experience of death, there is life with God (5:1).

5:2–5, The Sighing of the Spirit. As in Rom. 8:18–27, with which these verses should be compared, the human longing for release from the burden of mortality is associated with the presence of the Spirit, God's "down payment" on the eternal life for which one is destined (2 Cor. 5:5). There is an awkward mixing of metaphors here as the image of a heavenly dwelling (5:1, 2) is replaced by the image of clothing (5:2–4), but both images point to the life with God that transcends mortal existence.

5:6–10, "At Home" with the Lord. As long as believers are "at home in the body" (bearing the burdens of mortal existence, vv. 2–4), they are in one sense "away from [their] home with the Lord" (v. 6). But when their conduct is guided by their faith in God's reality rather than by things or circumstances that have only the appearance of reality, they live in the confidence that even in this mortal life they belong to the Lord (vv. 7–9). Thus, believers are ultimately accountable to Christ for how they conduct themselves here and now (v. 10).

5:11–15, Living for Christ. The rivals to whom Paul had indirectly referred at the beginning of his discussion of apostleship (2:17; 3:1) are once again in view in vv. 11–13. They have commended themselves to the Corinthians by boasting of "what is outward" (public displays of ecstasy); Paul, however, wants his readers to consider only what his preaching of the gospel has meant for them (cf. 3:2–3). True apostles are not authenticated by their religious experiences, however impressive those may be, but by "what is within"—by their devotion to those to whom they have been sent with the gospel (v. 13). To support this point, Paul invokes a familiar creedal affirmation about Christ's death (vv. 14–15; cf. esp. 1 Cor. 15:3). The love bestowed in Christ's death "controls us" (RSV) in that it lays claim to the life of every human being (2 Cor. 5:14). Those who respond in faith "live no longer to themselves," but for Christ (v. 15). In accepting life as a gift, they have been delivered from preoccupation with their own needs and self-centered goals (cf. Rom. 6:5–11) and have been freed for the service of others (cf. Rom. 14:15–18).

5:16–19, The Ministry of Reconciliation. In charging that Paul does not have the appearance, skills, or social status and that he cannot claim the achievements or religious experiences of a true apostle, his critics have shown that they judge others "from a human point of view" (v. 16a, RSV), with reference to worldly standards. Paul rejects these standards, reminding his readers that he and they, as believers, no longer regard Christ as the world does (v. 16b). Indeed, those who are "in Christ" participate in a whole "new creation" (v. 17), a radically transformed order where Christ's love, instituted through the cross, is to govern all perception and every action (v. 14; cf. Gal. 6:14–15). The apostle closely associates this new creation with the reconciliation of the world and of all people to God (2 Cor. 5:18–19). Here he calls once more (cf. vv. 14–15) upon a traditional formulation (v. 19ab; cf. Eph. 2:13–16; Col. 1:19–20), his own interpretation of which is evident in 2 Cor. 5:18–19c. "The ministry of reconciliation" (v. 18) is to be understood as that for which Christ's love claims the whole believing community, and "the word of reconciliation" (v. 19c) is the gospel itself, God's saving power made present through the cross.

5:20–7:3
Appeals About Reconciliation

The comments about reconciliation in 5:18–19 lead directly to the appeal of 5:20, and many commentators treat 5:18–21 (or, more inclusively, 5:16–6:2) as a closely knit unit. However, the shift from exposition in 2:14–5:19 to appeals in 5:20–9:15 is important.

5:20–6:2, Be Reconciled to God. Because they can affirm the reality of God's reconciling love in Christ, believers are both obliged and enabled to "be reconciled to God" (5:20). Here as elsewhere in the Pauline Letters, the appeal is based upon a preceding affirmation. These two together, the indicative and the imperative, constitute the "word of reconciliation" (5:19c), which the apostles and all believers, like ambassadors, have been commissioned to bear. There is nothing conditional about God's love; it is present (6:1–2, quoting Isa. 49:8) whether one acknowledges it and responds to it or not. But since love is not coercive (cf. 1 Cor. 13:5), apart from one's response its transforming power cannot have concrete effect. The statement that Christ was "made to be sin" so that others "might become the righteousness of God" (5:21) echoes traditional Christian teaching (cf., e.g., Rom. 8:3; Gal. 3:13; 1 Pet. 2:24) and assigns to Christ a role not unlike that accorded to the suffering servant of God in Isaiah 53 (see esp. Isa. 53:4–9).

6:3–10, An Apostolic Resumé. The self-recommendation in these verses (see v. 4) is intended to support the appeals of 5:20–6:2, but it is very different from the kind of self-recommendation for which Paul has criticized certain rival apostles (see esp. the commentary on 2:14–3:6 and 5:11–15). Although he reminds the Corinthians that his ministry has been conducted with integrity and knowledge and in the power of God (6:6–7), he claims for himself no heroic achievements or awesome religious experiences. Instead, he writes primarily of the

sufferings and indignities that he has to bear in the course of his apostolic labors (vv. 4c–5, 8–10; cf. 4:8–9).

6:11–7:3, Be Reconciled to Your Apostle. The appeals in 6:11–13 and 7:2–3 are related closely to those of 5:20–6:2, even though different words are used. If the Corinthians are truly open to the reconciling love of God, then they will surely want to be as accepting of the apostle from whom they have received "the word of reconciliation" as he is of them. The admonitions of 6:14–7:1, which charge Christians to separate themselves from "unbelievers" (6:14), are supported by a series of citations from Scripture in 6:16c–18; Lev. 26:12 (v. 16c); Isa. 52:11 (v. 17ab); Ezek. 20:34 (v. 17c); and 2 Sam. 7:14 (v. 18). These particular texts are not found elsewhere in Paul's Letters, the exclusivism that is urged in 6:14–7:1 is not typical of the apostle's thought (cf., e.g., 1 Cor. 5:9–10), the summary exhortation in 7:1 stands in tension with Paul's emphasis on the *gift* of righteousness, and there are numerous parallels between the teachings of these verses and those of the Jewish sectarian community at Qumran (→ Scrolls, The Dead Sea). It is possible, as many interpreters hold, that 6:14–7:1 were added by a later editor or, as others have suggested, that Paul himself has incorporated some preformulated material here. Whatever the case, these admonitions disrupt the primary appeals of 6:11–13 and 7:2–3, and it is difficult to understand why a later editor, or Paul himself, would have included them in this context.

7:4–9:15
Appeals About the Collection for Jerusalem

The apostle's extended expressions of confidence in his Corinthian congregation (7:4–16) help to support the preceding appeals about reconciliation (5:20–6:13; 7:2–3) and, even more importantly, prepare for subsequent appeals on behalf of his collection for the church in Jerusalem (chaps. 8 and 9).

7:4–16, Paul's Confidence in His Congregation. Many interpreters regard 7:5 as the apostle's resumption of his comments about a meeting with Titus in Macedonia started but not finished in 2:12–13. If this is correct, then 7:4 should be read more closely with 7:2–3 than with 7:5. The alternative is to read 7:4 as the topic sentence for the expressions of confidence that dominate the remainder of chap. 7, since several of the key words in v. 4 recur in vv. 5–16, and taken together vv. 4 and 16 neatly frame the whole section. In vv. 5–7 Paul emphasizes that Titus's report from Corinth had brought him great comfort, and in vv. 8–13a he indicates that it is, specifically, the Corinthians' response to the tearful letter (2:3–4) that brings him joy (see 1:23–2:11 and the commentary). That letter has made them realize that the injury done to Paul by a member of their congregation affected them all, and it prompted them, finally, to discipline the wayward brother. While the letter may have seemed overly harsh to some, they should know that it was written not out of personal pique, but for the sake of the congregation—to allow it to rediscover the reality of its commitment to Paul and his gospel (vv. 12–13a). The comments about Titus's confidence in the Corinthians (vv. 13b–15) not only allow Paul to reiterate his own (v. 16), but also anticipate Titus's imminent return to the congregation on behalf of the Jerusalem fund (see 8:6, 16–21). This will only be Titus's second visit to Corinth, since prior to the visit from which he has just returned he knew the congregation only by reputation (v. 14).

8:1–6, Titus's Return. Paul's campaign for the Jerusalem fund had been initiated in Corinth sometime prior to the writing of 1 Corinthians (see 1 Cor. 16:1–4), but the Corinthians have still not fulfilled their obligation to it (see 2 Cor. 8:10)—evidently because of questions about Paul's authority and, in particular, because of suspicions about his motives (see esp. 12:14–18). In the wake of the apostle's tearful letter, however (see above on 7:4–16), Titus was able to reinstitute the collection project in Corinth, and he is now being sent back to complete it (v. 6). Clearly, Paul hopes that the Corinthians will be encouraged to cooperate when they realize that the churches of Macedonia (which would include those in Philippi and Thessalonica) have insisted on making generous contributions, despite their meagre resources (vv. 1–5).

8:7–15, A Matter of Equality. Alluding to the Macedonian contribution to his fund for Jerusalem, Paul urges the Corinthians to make good on the contribution that they themselves have long before pledged but never fulfilled (vv. 7–8). To support this appeal he reminds them of Christ: who "became poor though he was rich, so that you, by means of his poverty, might become rich" (v. 9). Here the apostle has rephrased a traditional affirmation present in another form in Phil. 2:6–11 (cf. 1 Tim. 3:16): the preexistent Christ laid aside what he could rightfully claim as his own and for the sake of others became incarnate and obedient unto death. It is not Christ's *example* that Paul would have the Corinthians ponder, as if their giving is to be guided by some ascetic principle (e.g., "Give up everything for others, as Christ has given up everything for you"); they are asked only to contribute *insofar as they are able*, out of their "surplus" (v. 14; cf. Mark 12:43–44). It

is, rather, the principle of "equality" that is held before them (2 Cor. 8:13–15, with a citation [v. 15] of the Greek version of Exod. 16:18). They are to reflect on what it means to have been graced and claimed by Christ's love (see 5:14–15) and to have been drawn thereby into a "partnership" (8:4; RSV: a "taking part"; cf. Acts 4:36–37) of caring and sharing with all others for whom Christ died (see 1 Cor. 8:11; Rom. 14:15)—be they Jew or Gentile (→ Contribution for the Saints).

8:16–24, Commendation of Titus and the Brothers. The Corinthians are assured that Titus is returning to their congregation not just because Paul has urged him to (8:6), but because Titus himself is eager to see them again (vv. 16–17; see 7:13b–16). Accompanying him are two men whose names Paul does not provide and whose identities are probably beyond recovery (vv. 18–22, 23). One of them is referred to as "our brother" and is described in a way which suggests that he must be a regular and devoted member of Paul's apostolic entourage (v. 22). The first man Paul mentions, however, is clearly regarded as filling a more important role on this particular mission. Although he is widely known among the churches because of his "work for the gospel" (v. 18), he is evidently not one of Paul's associates; note "*that* brother" in v. 18 (RSV: "the brother") in contrast to "*our* brother" in v. 22. Moreover, he has been appointed by the churches, not by Paul himself, to oversee the administration of the collection for Jerusalem (v. 19). The Corinthians are to think of this brother as a kind of independent auditor, a person who will be able to certify that the funds that have been contributed for the saints in Jerusalem have not been misappropriated (vv. 20–21; see also 12:14–18 and commentary). It is not significant that the roles of the two brothers are no longer distinguished in v. 23, because the one concern in vv. 23–24 is to urge that all three men be warmly received in Corinth and that the congregation be responsive to their appeal for money.

9:1–5, A Further Appeal on Behalf of the Collection. Some interpreters believe that these verses introduce the subject of the collection for a second time (cf. 8:1–6), and that chaps. 8 and 9 must therefore represent two originally independent letters, chap. 8 directed to Christians in Corinth proper and chap. 9 intended for Christians elsewhere in the province of Achaia (see esp. Betz). However, it is also possible to read 9:1–5 as extending and supporting the commendations in 8:16–24 (note esp. vv. 3, 5); and the very general remarks in 9:6–15 can be viewed as a suitable conclusion for the whole of 8:1–9:5. In 9:1–4 Paul mentions the Macedonian churches for the second time in these two chapters (see 8:1–5), but now he refers to what they have been told about the Corinthians' commitment to the collection, not to their own generosity in contributing to it. One may presume that "the brothers" referred to in 9:3, 5 are the three men previously mentioned—Titus as well as his two unnamed companions (see 8:16–24). Paul trusts that by the time he himself gets to Corinth, this delegation will have in hand a contribution for Jerusalem and that the Corinthians will view it as a genuine gift (cf. 8:3), not as something that has been extorted from them (9:5).

9:6–10, On Giving Generously. In concluding his appeal on behalf of the collection for Jerusalem, the apostle emphasizes, first, that one can give generously because it is God who supplies the means. The conviction that one will reap what one sows (v. 6; cf. Gal. 6:7–9) pervades the wisdom tradition (e.g., Job 4:8; Prov. 11:18, 24; 22:8; Sir. 7:3), and the idea that "God loves a cheerful giver" (2 Cor. 9:7) derives from an addition to Prov. 22:8 that stands only in the Greek version ("God blesses a cheerful and giving man"). Although Paul assures the Corinthians that God will provide abundantly for their needs (2 Cor. 9:8), his point is not that God will enable them to attain the ancient (and modern) ideal of economic self-sufficiency. Rather, God will supply their needs so that they may in turn supply the needs of others. In v. 9 the Greek version of Ps. 112:9 is cited in support of this. If the apostle understands "his righteousness" as God's (rather than the righteousness of one who helps the needy), then he may be suggesting that every charitable act is an expression of that divine righteousness to which those who give aid are themselves eternally indebted. There are allusions to two further passages from the Greek Bible in v. 10 (Isa. 55:10; Hos. 10:12).

9:11–15, A Ministry of Praise. In v. 11 the underlying theme of vv. 6–10 is recapitulated and extended. Those who give generously are enriched by God so that they may give still more (v. 11a) with the consequence that their increasing generosity redounds to God's glory (v. 11b). From this it is clear that Paul's conception of charitable giving has not been shaped by his commitment to some general philanthropic ideal. It has been shaped instead by his conviction that every human being is ultimately dependent upon and accountable to God and that God is praised as the neighbor is affirmed and served in love (see, e.g., Rom. 15:2–6). Thus, the Corinthians should realize that contributing to the fund for Jerusalem is an important sign of their obedience to the gospel of Christ and that the thanksgivings of the beneficiaries are not really for their human benefactors, but for the greater glory of God (2 Cor. 9:12–13). The gift for

which Paul gives thanks in a final acclamation of praise (v. 15) is "the surpassing grace of God," which will be in evidence when his congregation fulfills its pledge to the collection (v. 14), as he is now confident that it will.

Were Chapters 10–13 Originally a Separate Letter?

Many interpreters believe that chaps. 10–13 could not have been part of the same letter as chaps. 1–9. In particular, beginning with chap. 10 the generally confident and conciliatory tone of chaps. 1–9 (see esp. 7:4–16) gives way to anxious pleading, an often awkward defensiveness, and numerous sharp attacks on rival apostles who are perceived to be undermining Paul's Corinthian ministry. Moreover, while it is clear that Titus has made only one visit to the Corinthian congregation prior to the writing of chaps. 1–9 (see commentary on 7:4–16), he has evidently been there twice by the time chaps. 10–13 are written (see commentary on 12:14–18).

It is frequently held that the last four chapters of 2 Corinthians are to be identified with the tearful letter mentioned in 2:3–4, 9. This is an attractive hypothesis, not only because it relieves one of having to posit a letter of which no part remains, but also because certain remarks in chaps. 10–13 seem to correspond to several of the things that Paul says, in retrospect, about why he wrote the tearful letter. He says, e.g., that he had written it for the Corinthians' own good (2:3; see 13:2, 10), out of his love for their congregation (2:4; see 11:11; 12:15), and to win their obedience (2:9; see 10:6). If the tearful letter (or part of it) is preserved in chaps. 10–13, then these chapters would have been written prior to chaps. 1–9, and the conciliatory tone of chaps. 1–9 would reflect Paul's confidence that the issues that had prompted the writing of the tearful letter have been largely resolved.

The identification of chaps. 10–13 with the tearful letter is, however, extremely problematic. First, if, as the evidence seems to suggest, chaps. 1–9 were written before chaps. 10–13 (see commentary on 12:14–18), then chaps. 10–13 cannot possibly be identified with the letter mentioned in 2:4. But even if one allows that chaps. 10–13 could have been written before chaps. 1–9, other difficulties remain. Second, although a major concern in the tearful letter was the case of a Corinthian brother who had somehow offended Paul (2:3–11; 7:8–12), one reads nothing at all about this matter in chaps. 10–13. Third, when the apostle describes what his tearful letter has achieved (7:5–12), there is not even an indirect reference to the subject that dominates chaps. 10–13, the threat to the

Corinthians' faith and to Paul's status that is posed by certain rival apostles. And finally, while the tearful letter had been written so that the apostle would not have to pay a personal visit to his congregation (1:23–2:4), chaps. 10–13 were written so that an impending visit would be more productive (10:2; 12:14, 20–21; 13:1–2, 10).

It is probable, then, that canonical 2 Corinthians is constituted of two originally separate letters, with chaps. 1–9 representing the earlier (Letter D) and chaps. 10–13 representing the later (Letter E). During the months that separated the writing of these two letters, the influence of the rival apostles over the Corinthian congregation must have greatly increased. This would explain why in chaps. 10–13 Paul seems to be almost at his wit's end in knowing how to deal with a congregation in which he had expressed a great deal of confidence not long before.

It is impossible to know exactly why, when, or by whom these two letters were combined, although it must have been sometime after Paul's death and probably by someone who wished to give the apostle's letters a broader distribution. The ending of Letter D and the beginning of Letter E seem not to have survived, either because they were lost before the two were combined, or because they were deleted as superfluous during the editorial process.

10:1–18
An Appeal for Obedience

The apostle plans to arrive in Corinth soon (e.g., 12:14), and everything in chaps. 10–13 is written in anticipation of that visit (13:10), including the comprehensive appeal of 10:1–6. This appeal is supported, first, by the apostle's insistence that he will not fail to deal with those who oppose him (vv. 2–6), and then, more extensively, by some remarks about his apostolic authority (vv. 7–11) and jurisdiction (vv. 12–18).

10:1–6, No Worldly War. Paul's appeal is issued on the basis of "the gentleness and kindness of Christ" (v. 1a). This is probably not a reference to Jesus' earthly character and conduct, but to the whole saving event of Christ's incarnation and obedience unto death, his becoming "poor" for the sake of others (cf. 8:9; Phil. 2:6–11). It is significant that the Corinthians are not summoned to be obedient to Paul or to some particular teaching. The appeal is for their "obedience to Christ" (2 Cor. 10:5), doubtless to be understood in the most fundamental sense as "faith's obedience" (Rom. 1:5) to the gospel (Rom. 10:16; cf. 15:18). Since Paul is aware of the accusation that he is more im-

pressive in his letters than he is in person (2 Cor. 10:1b, alluding to the criticism that will be quoted in v. 10), he insists that he is not going to be intimidated by any who oppose him or who reject his appeal (vv. 2, 4b, 6). Their charge that he conducts his ministry "according to worldly standards" (v. 2) may be based on his continuing work as a craftsman in order to support himself (see 11:7–11), as well as on his reluctance to boast of special charismatic powers or religious experiences (see 5:11–13; 12:1–10). In responding to the charge, Paul makes use of several military images (vv. 3–6); this may suggest just how embattled he is feeling. Although his campaign for the gospel necessarily takes place "in the world," he maintains that he does not wage it "according to worldly standards" (v. 3). Indeed, because his campaign for the gospel is no worldly war, he must use unconventional "weapons"— weapons he is confident are powerful enough to bring victory (vv. 4, 5). The conviction that lies behind the affirmation of v. 3 is characteristically Pauline: believers can and must live out their faith "in the world" without surrendering to the world's values and claims (variously expressed in Rom. 12:1–2; 1 Cor. 7:29–31; Phil. 3:19–20).

10:7–11, The Question of Authority. Since Paul's critics in Corinth have challenged his apostolic status, he follows the appeal of vv. 1–6 with some comments about his authority, taking care to emphasize that it is a gift from the Lord and is to be used constructively, not as a means of intimidation (vv. 8–9). Two of the charges made against him by the rival apostles are simply denied. First, their vaunted relationship to Christ—perhaps they had known Jesus personally or claim to have had some extraordinary vision of the resurrected Lord—is in no way superior to his own (v. 7b). Second, it is completely untrue that his "demanding and impressive" letters are only bluff, for he will be quite able to translate his words into action when he is with them in person (vv. 10–11). He is probably perceived as "weak" because he seems to lack the charismatic powers about which his rivals boast (see 5:11–13) and perhaps also because he has not asked the Corinthians to underwrite his personal expenses, something to which legitimate apostles are entitled (see 11:7–11; 1 Cor. 9:3–18). His public speaking is regarded as "contemptible" and uninspired because it is not embellished with the rhetorical flourishes and adornments so much in vogue (cf. 2 Cor. 11:6).

10:12–18, The Question of Jurisdiction. Paul's defense of his apostolic authority continues here, but now he is more aggressive in bringing charges against his rivals. When he declares that he does not have the audacity to claim the same status as they (v. 12a), the irony is clear, for he regards them as "false apostles" who serve Satan rather than Christ (11:13–15)! Moreover, their pretentious flaunting of letters of recommendation (see 3:1b) shows their ignorance of the fact that only God's recommendation really counts (vv. 12b, 17–18); one may compare what Paul says about the source of his apostolic authority in 3:4–6. (The scriptural quotation in v. 17 is a very free adaptation of the Greek version of Jer. 9:24.) Problems of translation cloud the exact meaning of 2 Cor. 10:13–16, but Paul's general concern is clear. Christians who boast of a status and authority superior to his have appeared on the scene in Corinth, intruding themselves into the congregation that he has founded and seeking to take it over. Paul's protest in vv. 13–14 reflects the principle that he applies to his own ministry (expressly stated in Rom. 15:20–21): apostles are commissioned to carry the gospel where it has not yet been preached, not where someone else has already laid a foundation. It also reflects his conviction that, as the "father" of the Corinthian congregation, he stands in a unique and continuing relationship to it (1 Cor. 4:14–16). Paul's competitors must be disputing both of these points.

11:1–12:13
"Fool's Speech"

The necessity to defend his apostolic status and authority has forced Paul into an awkward position, because he might be perceived to be doing the same kind of boasting for which he criticizes his rivals (e.g., 5:12; 11:12). That he is quite aware of this danger is evident from his remarks in 10:7–18 and especially from the self-consciousness with which he composes this part of his letter. The description of this as a "fool's speech" derives from the apostle's introduction of it as "a little bit of foolishness" (11:1) and from his comment at the end, "I have been a fool!" (12:11). He characterizes it this way partly because he knows that one should boast only of the Lord (10:17–18), but also because he boasts about things of which others would be ashamed. One may read 11:1–21a as an extended introduction to the speech, 11:21b–12:10 as the speech proper, and 12:11–13 as an epilogue.

11:1–4, The Endangered Bride.
Paul begs his readers to put up with some foolish boasting (v. 1), which he justifies by emphasizing how concerned he is about them (vv. 2–4). Indicating that his care for them is akin to God's concern for Israel, he depicts himself as a father (cf. 1 Cor. 4:14–15) and the Corinthians as his daughter who is being given in marriage (2 Cor. 11:2). Just as a Jewish father's responsibility was to guard his daughter's virginity between the time

of her betrothal and the consummation of her marriage, so the apostle's task is to keep his congregation from harm until the close of history when Christ returns to claim his own. (The church is also depicted as Christ's bride in Eph. 5:23–32; Rev. 19:7–9; 21:2; but the idea that lies behind this passage is best seen in Phil. 1:9–11.) Specifically, the Corinthians are in danger of being seduced by persons who would lure them away from Paul's gospel and thus from their original commitment to Christ (2 Cor. 11:3–4). There is perhaps an allusion in v. 3 to a Jewish legend that identified the serpent of Genesis 3 with Satan and implied a sexual seduction of Eve. From v. 4 one learns that Paul's rivals have "come" to Corinth from elsewhere and that they are winning a following for a gospel that is different from his.

11:5–15, The False Apostles.
Some interpreters (e.g., Barrett) argue that the ironic title "superapostles" (v. 5; see also 12:11) is used of the leaders of the church in Jerusalem, by whom Paul's competitors claim to have been authorized for a ministry in Corinth. Others (e.g., Furnish) regard it as a reference to the rival apostles themselves, who pretentiously claim a status superior to Paul's. It is certain that these rivals are the "false apostles" mentioned later, whom Paul further describes as Satan's ministers disguised as ministers of Christ (vv. 13–15). The remark in v. 6 suggests that Paul's style as a public speaker is being compared unfavorably with theirs, probably because it lacks the rhetorical ornamentation cultivated by popular orators; and this unadorned style is perhaps being used as evidence that he also lacks the special knowledge one should expect an apostle to have. Paul's refusal to let the Corinthians help with his personal expenses (see 1 Cor. 9:12b, 15–18) has been offered as further evidence of his inferior status, and the apostle responds to this in 2 Cor. 11:7–11. His critics must have argued that if Paul's apostleship were valid he would not demean himself by continuing to work as a common craftsman, since he knows that apostles are entitled to support by their churches (v. 7; see 1 Cor. 9:4–12a, 13–14). In response, Paul urges the Corinthians to regard his conduct as demonstrating a genuine concern not to burden them with his own needs (vv. 8–11).

11:16–21a, Tolerating Fools.
The apostle continues to beg his readers' indulgence for the boasting he is about to do (v. 16 repeats the plea of v. 1), concedes that it is foolish (v. 17), and explains that the circumstances have forced him to it (v. 18). But since the Corinthians, "being wise," have already "put up with fools" (v. 19), even allowing themselves to be exploited by them (v. 20), they will surely grant Paul this favor. The targets of Paul's sarcasm are his rivals

and, even more directly, the congregation to which they have gained access. The further sarcastic gibe in v. 21a anticipates the strange theme of the apostle's boasting, his "weakness."

11:21b–33, Paul's Ministerial Credentials. As he begins his foolish boasting, the apostle insists that his ethnic and religious heritage is no less Jewish than that of his rivals (v. 22; cf. esp. Phil. 3:5), and that his credentials as a minister of Christ are in fact superior to theirs (2 Cor. 11:23a). To document the latter he provides a long list of the hardships and deprivations that he has suffered as an apostle (vv. 23b–29; cf. the similar catalogs in 4:8–9; 6:4c–5; 12:10; Rom. 8:35; 1 Cor. 4:9–13). It is important to notice, however, that he offers these as signs of his weakness (2 Cor. 11:29a, 30), not to boast of the courage and strength with which he has endured them. The same understanding of the apostolic office that he had enunciated in 4:7–15 is present here: in the apostle's sufferings the death and resurrection life of Jesus are made visible and thus the transcendent power of God is proclaimed. The "labor(s)" mentioned in vv. 23b, 27 refer to Paul's arduous work as a craftsman, as do the deprivations listed in v. 27. Some of the other tribulations he catalogs may correlate with events narrated in Acts, e.g., "imprisonments" (v. 23b; cf. Acts 16:23–40), "beatings" (vv. 23b, 24–25a; cf. Acts 16:22; cf. 1 Thess. 2:2), a stoning (v. 25b; cf. Acts 14:19), and "danger from Gentiles" (v. 26; cf. Acts 19:23–41). The account of Paul's narrow escape from Damascus (vv. 32–33) is also recounted in Acts 9:23–25, but in a significantly different context. In Acts, the story is offered as one of several illustrations of Paul's courage and ability to overcome adversity. Here, the apostle himself includes it as one more example of his weakness and vulnerability.

12:1–4, A Journey to Paradise. Turning to the subject of "visions and revelations granted by the Lord," the apostle reluctantly continues his foolish boasting (v. 1). That he refers to himself in the third person (vv. 2–4) suggests how uncomfortable he is talking about his own religious experiences. The specific subject of his boast is an ecstatic episode in which he had been transported to Paradise, which he locates in the third heaven. (This is not an account of Paul's apostolic call, or "conversion"; for this see esp. Gal. 1:15–16.) Numerous ancient reports of such experiences survive, but this one differs in that it provides little information about what happened and is not employed for any special edifying purpose. Whether the apostle's journey took place "in the body" or apart from it he does not know and seems not to care; there is no hint of anything that he may have seen; and what he heard he is not allowed to

disclose. Paul's intention is evidently to caricature the private religious experiences of which his rivals boast, thus emphasizing that they are of no value for an apostle's proper work—which is to advance the gospel and to serve those who receive it (see 5:12–13).

12:5–10, An Oracle from the Lord. Here the apostle abandons the fool's role that he has been playing in 11:21b–12:4. He could boast, as his rivals do, of impressive religious connections, experiences, and achievements, but he chooses instead to speak only of his weaknesses (vv. 5–7a). Indeed, he regards the "thorn" that he bears in his flesh as a proper reminder that he should not be too elated by the ecstatic experiences that have been his (v. 7b). Paul nowhere specifies the nature of this satanic impediment, but it was probably some kind of physical ailment, not seriously disabling, but certainly bothersome enough to prompt him to pray for divine healing. When the Lord finally responded to his petitions for relief, however, it was not with a cure but with an oracle: "My grace is enough for you; for power is made fully present in weakness" (vv. 8–9a). What this oracle promises is not a cure, but that God's power will sustain the apostle in the midst of his weakness and misery. In this oracle the gospel itself is conveyed, the word of the cross (see 4:7–15 and commentary). Clearly then, "the power of Christ" to which Paul refers in his own comment on the oracle (vv. 9b) is the power of God's saving and sustaining love that is present in Christ's death. The hardship list of v. 10b recapitulates the much longer catalog in 11:23b–29, and the declaration, "When I am weak, then I am strong" (v. 10b, RSV) reiterates the message of the oracle in v. 9a; the power of the crucified Christ is disclosed in Paul's weaknesses, and in the adversities he bears as an apostle.

12:11–13, Epilogue. Looking back over the whole of 11:1–12:10, Paul emphasizes once more that this foolish boasting has been forced upon him by the "superapostles" (see 11:5 and commentary), and that he is in no respect inferior to them (v. 11). He too has performed the healings and other signs that the Corinthians have been led to expect of a true apostle (v. 12), although he does not belabor this point. From the way he refers to these in other Letters (notably Rom. 15:18–19; Gal. 3:1–5), it is clear that he regards his preaching of the gospel, not his performance of wondrous deeds, as the truly definitive evidence of apostleship. The remark in 2 Cor. 12:13 is made in view of the Corinthians' suspicion that Paul has not asked them for support because he did not have that right (see commentary on 11:7–11), and the irony of the remark and of the apostle's plea for pardon is explained by his conviction that his competitors have in fact exploited the congregation (11:20).

12:14–13:10
Disavowals and Warnings

The appeal for obedience that is introduced in 10:1–18 and supported by the fool's speech of 11:1–12:13 is now resumed and further supported. Paul makes a few additional remarks in his own defense and, in prospect of his impending third visit, urges the Corinthians to help make it a constructive one.

12:14–18, The Allegation of Fraud. During Paul's initial visit to Corinth a congregation had been founded, and on his second visit he had had a nasty confrontation with one of its members. Now that a third visit is at hand, he wants the Corinthians to know that he will continue to care for his own personal needs while he is with them (see 11:7–11); rather than claiming anything of theirs, he will give himself to them in love (vv. 14–15; cf. 5:14–15; 8:9). The charge of deceit to which the apostle refers in v. 16 probably grows out of the suspicion that at least some of the money that he is soliciting for Jerusalem (see chaps. 8, 9) will be kept back for himself. In rebuttal, Paul refers to the exemplary way that his two representatives, Titus and the unnamed "brother" of 8:22, had conducted themselves when in Corinth on behalf of the collection (vv. 17–18; the "famous" brother of 8:18–19 was not Paul's representative). Because it is probable that the visit by Titus *anticipated* in chap. 8 is the same one on which Paul *looks back* here in chap. 12, a number of interpreters conclude that chaps. 1–9 were written before chaps. 10–13.

12:19–21, About Improper Behavior. The apostle assures his readers that the present letter is written out of a genuine concern for them, not just to refute the charges of his critics (v. 19). Specifically, he is worried that he may find such immorality among them when he arrives that he will be reduced to mourning for their errant ways (vv. 20–21). He must also surely realize that if the present disorder continues, his apostolic authority and credibility will be further diminished.

13:1–4, Warning. On his second, unhappy visit to Corinth (see 2:1), Paul had apparently issued a warning to those who had brought him to grief; now, in a second warning, he assures the Corinthians that he will show no leniency toward anyone whom he may find still unrepentant when he visits for the third time (vv. 1–2). Paul is therefore confident that he has satisfied the scriptural rule about multiple "witnesses" (v. 1; see Deut. 19:15; Matt. 18:16), which Jews

of his day understood to require the fair warning of wrongdoers. Since his readers, probably at the behest of the rival apostles, have asked for "proof" that Paul is really a spokesman for Christ, they will surely have it if he is forced to take disciplinary action when he comes (2 Cor. 13:3). The affirmation about Christ's death and resurrection in v. 4a, which is in accord with early creedal formulations (e.g., Rom. 1:4; 6:4; 1 Cor. 6:14; cf. Phil. 3:10), gives weight to the warning of vv. 2–3 and prompts the statement of v. 4b. Because one encounters in the apostle's weaknesses the death of Jesus, one also encounters there the resurrection power of God (cf. 12:9; see also 4:7–15 and commentary).

13:5–9, Admonition. Those Corinthians who have been persuaded that they ought to demand proof of Paul's apostleship (v. 3; cf. 10:7) should really be examining the authenticity of their own Christian existence (v. 5). If their faith passes the test, then Paul's apostleship will pass the test too (vv. 6–7), because it is through his ministry that they have been brought to the gospel ("the truth," v. 8) and nurtured in it. Thus, the apostle is able to rejoice in his weaknesses, insofar as the power of the cross that is disclosed in them finds expression in the faith and obedience of his congregation (v. 9).

13:10, The Purpose of the Letter. Paul has planned for the Corinthians' contribution to the Jerusalem fund to be ready for him when he arrives for his third visit (see 9:3–5). However, with that visit now at hand (12:14; 13:1), his relationship to the congregation has become so problematic that he must wonder whether the Corinthians will make any contribution at all. By writing this letter he hopes to improve the situation so that his forthcoming visit can be a constructive and productive one. (This purpose is in accord with the contents of chaps. 10–13, but not with those of chaps. 1–9; see "Introduction".) There is indirect evidence that this letter achieved its purpose. In Romans, probably written during his third visit to Corinth, Paul reports that the Christians of Macedonia and Achaia (of which Corinth was the provincial capital) "have chosen to make a generous contribution to the poor among God's holy people at Jerusalem" (15:25–26, NJB).

13:11–14
Letter Closing

If parts of two or more originally independent letters have been incorporated into 2 Corinthians, then one cannot be completely sure which of them was concluded by these verses. (The numbering of these verses varies slightly among modern editions and translations, some of which count them as 11–13.)

13:11–13, Final Admonitions and Greetings. The succinct appeals of v. 11 are comparable to those in Rom. 12:9–13; 1 Cor. 16:13–15; and 1 Thess. 5:12–22. Whether the kind of "holy kiss" mentioned in 2 Cor. 13:12 was already part of the church's liturgy in Paul's day is uncertain, but it is in any case a symbolic expression of the sense of Christian community that the apostle hopes his readers have not lost. "The saints" whose greetings he conveys (v. 13) are probably the members of the congregation in the particular Macedonian city from which he is writing (perhaps Thessalonica or Beroea).

13:14, Benediction. Because the benedictions that close the other Pauline Letters are shorter, some interpreters attribute this one to a later editor. Its contents, however, are thoroughly Pauline.

Bibliography

Barrett, C. K. *A Commentary on the Second Epistle to the Corinthians.* Harper's New Testament Commentaries. New York: Harper & Row, 1973.

Betz, H. D. *2 Corinthians 8 and 9: A Commentary on Two Administrative Letters of the Apostle Paul.* Edited by G. W. MacRae. Hermeneia. Philadelphia: Fortress, 1985.

Bruce, F. F. *1 and 2 Corinthians.* New Century Bible. Grand Rapids, MI: Eerdmans, 1971.

Bultmann, R. *The Second Letter to the Corinthians.* Original German Edition edited by E. Dinkler. Translated by R. A. Harrisville. Minneapolis, MN: Augsburg, 1985.

Furnish, V. P. *II Corinthians.* Anchor Bible, 32A. Garden City, NY: Doubleday, 1984.

Georgi, D. *The Opponents of Paul in Second Corinthians.* Philadelphia: Fortress, 1986.

Hughes, P. E. *Paul's Second Epistle to the Corinthians. The English Text with Introduction, Exposition and Notes.* New International Commentary on the New Testament. Grand Rapids, MI: Eerdmans, 1962.

Martin, R. P. *2 Corinthians.* Word Biblical Commentary, 40. Waco, TX: Word, 1986.

GALATIANS

WILLIAM BAIRD

INTRODUCTION

Among the writings of Paul, none is more important or more difficult than the Letter of Paul to the Galatians. This Letter presents important features of Paul's life and announces significant doctrines. Yet questions about the historical setting of the Letter cannot be answered with certainty. About two issues, however, interpreters can be confident: first, Paul is the author (1:1; 6:11); and second, the Letter is a unity, written in its present form as a single document.

Although the Letter is addressed to "the churches of Galatia," the exact location of these churches is disputed. The original kingdom of the Galatians was in the north-central area of Asia Minor, but in 25 B.C. the Romans reorganized this region to include in the province of Galatia areas to the south (→ Galatia). According to the south Galatian or "province" theory, the churches addressed in Galatians are churches of this southern region—churches established during the so-called "first missionary journey" of Paul (Acts 13:4–14:28). Paul normally refers to regions according to their provincial designation (1 Cor. 16:19; 2 Cor. 8:1).

According to the north Galatian or "territorial" theory, the churches addressed in the Letter are churches in the original territory of Galatia. The Acts of the Apostles includes no account of a mission to this region, but Acts 16:6 may imply a trip to the northern territory. After describing a visit to Derbe and Lystra, the author notes that Paul and his companions traveled through "the Phrygian and Galatian regions." Thus, a visit to the region of Galatia appears to be distinguished from and later than the visit to the cities of the south. In Gal. 3:1, Paul addresses his readers as "foolish Galatians." Although this designation would be appropriate for the ethnic Galatians of the north, it scarcely fits the residents of the south (see Acts 14:11). Paul does not always refer to regions by their provincial name (Gal. 1:17). According to most scholars, the north Galatian theory is to be preferred.

As to the social and religious makeup of the Galatian churches, most of the members were Gentiles. Paul's mission is primarily directed toward non-Jews (1:16; 2:2, 7–9), and the issue of circumcision, crucial to the Letter, would hardly be a question for Jewish converts. When

Paul implies that his readers had not known God (4:9), he probably refers to their previous life in paganism. Nevertheless, some of the Galatian Christians may have been Jews or persons who had had contact with the synagogue. This is suggested by the type of scriptural argument Paul employs in chaps. 3 and 4. As in other Pauline churches, members of the congregations were probably drawn from a variety of social and economic classes (see 3:28).

The date and place of writing are debated. Some suppose that Galatians was written early in Paul's career. Actually a very early date is excluded, since the Letter was not written until at least fourteen years after Paul's conversion (see 2:1). Those who favor an early date usually adopt the south Galatian theory and identify the Jerusalem visit of 2:1–10 with that of Acts 11:30. According to this view, the Jerusalem visit of Acts 15:4–29 took place after Galatians had been written. More likely, Acts 15 and Galatians 2 refer to the same event—the Jerusalem conference. Assuming the north Galatian theory and interpreting 4:13 to imply two visits to Galatia prior to the Letter, the second visit would have been the one mentioned in Acts 18:23 (the first, in Acts 16:6) where Paul is on the way to his Ephesian ministry. Paul's charge that the Galatians have "so quickly turned away" (1:6) suggests that not much time has elapsed since his last visit. Thus, Galatians was probably written from Ephesus in about A.D. 55.

In the Letter, Paul attacks a group that is troubling the Galatian churches (1:7; 5:12). He charges them with perverting the gospel (1:7–9) by insisting that the Galatians be circumcised (5:2; 6:12–13) and keep the law (3:2–5; 5:4–6). Concerning the identity of these troublemakers, three main theories have been advanced: first, they are Judaizers or Jewish Christians who believe gentile converts must keep the Jewish law; second, they are libertine spiritualists or Gnostics who advocate ethical license (→ Gnosticism); third, there are two groups causing trouble in Galatia (Judaizers and libertines). Some variation of the first theory is probably best: the troublemakers are Jewish Christians who have invaded the Galatian churches from outside with the intention of correcting Paul's truncated gospel. They believe the people of God need an identity that is shaped according to Jewish rites and practices.

The purpose of Galatians is to counter the activity of these troublemakers. Paul's primary concern is to "re-present" "the truth of the gospel" (2:5, 14)—the good news that God has acted in Christ to redeem all people (4:4). This action conveys the Spirit that is received by faith and not by works of the law (3:2). The identity of the people of God is found in a new creation (6:15) that shatters the old distinctions—a new identity in Jesus Christ (3:28).

In general, Galatians conforms to the pattern of ancient letters (→ Epistle). It opens with a salutation (1:1–5) and ends with a conclusion written in the author's own hand (6:11–18). The conventional paragraph of thanksgiving ("I give thanks," 1 Cor. 1:4) is replaced by an expression of dismay and anathema ("I am amazed," 1:6). Recent research has attempted to analyze the body of Galatians according to patterns of classical rhetoric. However, Paul appears to use a variety of rhetorical expressions to develop the main lines of his message: an autobiographical narrative (1:11–2:21); his central argument (3:1–4:31); and a final exhortation and instruction (5:1–6:10).

COMMENTARY

1:1–10
Introduction to the Letter

1:1–5, Salutation. Paul opens his Letters according to the ancient pattern: the author introduces himself or herself; the recipients of the letter are named; and a greeting is expressed. Paul stresses his role as an "apostle" (see Rom. 1:1–6; → Apostle). The term refers to a person who has been sent with a commission. Paul clarifies his office by a double denial: he is not an apostle "from human beings" or "through a human being." Instead, his apostleship is "through Jesus Christ and God"; God is the source and Christ is the agent of his call (Gal. 1:15–16; 1 Cor. 1:1). About Christ, Paul adds a phrase from an early Christian confession: God "raised him from the dead." Paul also includes in his address the co-workers "who are with me."

The Letter is being sent "to the churches of Galatia"—the only Pauline Letter addressed to a group of congregations in a region larger than a single city. To them he sends his typical greeting, "grace and peace," which combines Greek and Hebrew expressions. This greeting is expanded to include another confessional statement about Christ: he is the one "who gave himself for our sins" (see Rom. 5:8; 1 Cor. 15:3) and "rescued us from the present evil age."

Paul believed the world was under the control of evil forces (2 Cor. 4:4; Rom. 8:38), but with the coming of Christ the new age had already dawned (→ Eschatology).

1:6–10, The Situation in Galatia. At this point, Paul would normally present a paragraph of thanksgiving (Rom. 1:8–15). Instead, he offers a statement of dismay: "I am astonished." Paul is astonished that the Galatians are so quickly deserting the one who called them, that is, God (see Gal. 5:8; Rom. 8:30; 1 Cor. 1:9). The Galatians are turning to another gospel (see 2 Cor. 11:4), although there is no other. The troublemakers are perverting the gospel by insisting that it include the demand to keep the law and be circumcised. However, to conceive of the gospel as a collection of rules and rites is not simply to distort it, it is to destroy it.

The problem is the gospel, not the preacher. Even if Paul himself (a divinely appointed apostle) or an angel (a messenger from heaven) should preach another gospel, let that one be "accursed"—a word that describes something dedicated to God for destruction (see Josh. 6:17). The true gospel is the one that Paul had preached and the Galatians received—the good news disclosed in Christ (Gal. 3:1). Although the gospel can be preached in a variety of ways (see 1 Cor. 1:23; 2 Cor. 4:5; Phil. 1:15–18), there is only one gospel.

Paul's concern is to please God, not people (1 Thess. 2:4–5). The troublemakers may suppose that his law-free gospel is trimmed to fit his hearers (see 1 Cor. 9:20–21). But as Paul says, "I do everything for the sake of the gospel" (1 Cor. 9:23). His loyalty to God is seen in his obedience; he is a slave of Christ (Rom. 1:1; Phil. 1:1).

1:11–2:21
An Autobiographical Narrative: Paul's Loyalty to the Gospel

1:11–17, The Gospel Received by Revelation. Paul's gospel is not a human gospel. He neither received it from a human being, nor was he taught it. Instead, he received the gospel through a revelation of Christ—a revelation whose content is Christ. Proof that God has acted is seen in the transformation of Paul. His former life was devoted to Judaism (see Phil. 3:4–6). He had been a persecutor of the church (see 1 Cor. 15:9). Paul's zeal led him to oppose the followers of Jesus as apostates who preached a crucified Messiah (1 Cor. 1:23). Moreover, Paul had advanced in Judaism beyond many of his own age among his people, since he was so zealous for the law and the traditions.

The source of Paul's gospel is God—"the one who had set me apart from my mother's womb." Before Paul could act, God had acted

—an action by grace. This way of describing the revelation is reminiscent of the call of the prophets (Jer. 1:5) and indicates that Paul is primarily depicting a commission rather than a conversion. However, his reference to "my former life-style in Judaism" (Gal. 1:13) indicates that a conversion was involved. Paul's sparse description stands in contrast to the detailed accounts of the Acts of the Apostles (9:3–9; 22:6–11; 26:12–18). Paul simply declares that God's Son had been revealed to him (1 Cor. 9:1; 15:8). The purpose of this revelation was that Paul should preach Christ to the Gentiles; the revelation was also commission.

Immediately after the event, Paul did not confer with "flesh and blood," that is, with any human being. In particular, he did not go to Jerusalem to consult with those who had previously been appointed apostles. Paul went away instead to Arabia, or Nabatea, the area to the south and east of Damascus. Although it is sometimes supposed that Paul went there to meditate, it is more likely that he began to preach (see 2 Cor. 11:32–33)—prior to any contact with the Jerusalem authorities.

1:18–24, A Brief Visit to Jerusalem. After three years, Paul did go to Jerusalem. He went on his own initiative for the purpose of making the acquaintance of Cephas. Cephas, the Aramaic for Peter (i.e., "rock"), was leader of the Jerusalem church. Paul stayed in Jerusalem only fifteen days and, while there, saw none of the other apostles except James. This is the same visit described in Acts 9:26–30. James is the brother of Jesus (Mark 6:3) who was later to become the leader of the church (Gal. 2:9, 12; see Acts 15:13; 21:18). Paul confirms the truth of his narrative by swearing an oath (see 1 Thess. 2:5; 2 Cor. 1:23; 11:31; Matt. 5:34).

Next, Paul travels to the regions of Syria and Cilicia. In Cilicia is Paul's hometown, Tarsus (see Acts 9:30; 21:39; 22:3), and in Syria is Antioch where he carried on a ministry (Acts 11:26; 13:1–2; Gal. 2:11–14). In this period, Paul claims that he was still not known by sight to the churches in Judea. Nevertheless, they knew Paul by reputation. He quotes them as saying that the former persecutor is now preaching "the faith" (see 3:23). The words of the Judean believers imply that his radical transformation could only have been accomplished by the action of God. Consequently, the Judeans give praise to God because of Paul.

2:1–10, The Jerusalem Conference. After fourteen years, Paul again visits Jerusalem. This interval is most likely the time since Paul's last visit (1:18–19), although it could be fourteen years since his conversion. The conference described here is the same as the one depicted in Acts 15:4–21. Paul says he made this trip "ac-

cording to revelation," that is, according to the will of God. In a private meeting with the leaders of the church, he presented the gospel that he had been preaching. When he says "lest I . . . had been running in vain" (Gal. 2:2) he does not intend to suggest that the Jerusalem leaders were to pass judgment on his gospel—the message that he had received by revelation (1:15–16). The gospel is not negotiable. The issue is the practice of the mission—the way the mission is functioning in the Pauline churches (see 1 Thess. 3:5). About this, the leaders of the church —as Paul shows in Gal. 2:11–21—could exercise a disruptive force. They, not the gospel, are being judged.

Along with Barnabas, Paul brought Titus, an uncircumcised Greek Christian. Titus was proof that a Gentile could be a member of the people of God without being circumcised. Into the conference slipped some "false Christians" (v. 4) who wanted to enslave Paul by demanding the circumcision of Titus. Paul resolutely refused, so that the "truth of the gospel" might be maintained for the Galatians (and other gentile converts). To turn a ritual into a demand is to destroy the gospel (see 1:7).

Next Paul summarizes the deliberations of the leaders. In v. 6 he describes them as "those who are reputed to be somebody" (see v. 2), and in v. 9 he calls them "pillars" of the church (see Rev. 3:12). Although these terms are not derogatory in themselves, they are given a disparaging meaning when Paul observes that the leaders' reputation means nothing to him or to God (v. 6). These leaders demanded no additional requirements for Paul's mission; they recognized that he had been entrusted with the gospel to the Gentiles just as Peter (or Cephas) had to the Jews. The reference to "the gospel to the uncircumcised" and the gospel "to the circumcised" does not imply two different gospels; the one gospel is preached to two different groups.

As sign of this agreement, the Jerusalem leaders extended to Paul and Barnabas the "right hand of fellowship" (v. 9)—a practice signifying friendship and accord. The leaders are named, with James first, probably because he had become the leader of the church in the city (see Acts 15:13–19) just as Cephas (Peter) had been the leader of the mission outside of Jerusalem (see Acts 9:32–43). Although they made no demands, the leaders did make a request: that Paul collect an offering for the economically deprived of the Jerusalem congregation—something he was eager to do (see 1 Cor. 16:1–4; 2 Cor. 8:1–9:15; Rom. 15:25–28).

2:11–21, Confrontation in Antioch. After the conference, Cephas (Peter) visited Antioch. Here a church had been founded where Gentiles had been accepted into the life of the Christian community (Acts 11:19–26; → Antioch). When

Cephas arrived, he participated in the meals of the congregation—meals where Jewish and gentile converts ate together without regard to Jewish food laws. Later, when some emissaries of James arrived, Cephas withdrew, because he feared the partisans of circumcision. The latter are probably to be identified with the "false Christians" of Gal. 2:4, while the unnamed people from James were probably more moderate. They recognized the Jerusalem agreement, but believed the people of God needed an identity that would set them apart from the pagans. Following the lead of Cephas, the rest of the Jews of the Antioch church joined in his hypocrisy—a kind of playacting rather than honesty. Barnabas, Paul's associate in gentile mission (Acts 13:1–14:18; 15:35–16:4), was "carried away," too.

Paul opposed Cephas "to his face" (Gal. 2:11) in front of the church. According to Paul, Cephas and the others were not conforming to "the truth of the gospel." Paul quotes his indictment of Cephas, but the extent of the quotation cannot be ascertained. Verse 14 is certainly part of the quotation, since Paul spoke directly to Cephas in second-person singular. When Paul said that Cephas lived like a Gentile, he referred to Cephas's original conduct in Antioch. When Paul charged Cephas with compelling the Gentiles to live like Jews, he implied that Cephas's withdrawal was equivalent to requiring the Gentiles to keep Jewish rules in order to participate in the community.

In vv. 15–17, Paul continues to address the Jews (and perhaps Cephas) as his use of "we" indicates. We, he says, are Jews by nature (born and reared as Jews) and not gentile sinners, that is, those who do not have the law (see Rom. 2:14; 1 Cor. 9:21). Yet we Jewish Christians know that a person is not brought into right relationship with God by "works of the law" but by faith in Christ. "From the works of the law, no one will be declared righteous" (a loose quotation of Ps. 143:2). When Paul says that the Jews, in being justified, are found to be sinners, he means that the fact that righteousness is by faith has the effect of putting Jews, like Gentiles, outside the law (Gal. 2:15). This action, which identifies the Jews as sinners, however, does not mean that Christ is a minister of sin, since the Jews (before faith) were already in actuality sinners in need of God's grace (see Rom. 2:17–24).

In Gal. 2:18–21, Paul changes from "we" to "I." To rebuild what he once destroyed would be to return to the works of the law. But Paul cannot do this, since he has died to the law (Rom. 7:1–4). This death has been accomplished by unity with Christ—a unity signified by baptism (Gal. 3:27; Rom. 6:3–10). Through faith, Paul has shared in the crucifixion and resurrection, so that the living Christ is present in him (see Phil. 1:21). In his old body ("in the flesh"), Paul has a new identity. He lives by faith in the Son of God who loved him (see Rom. 5:6–8; 2 Cor. 5:14) and gave himself as a redemptive sacrifice (see Rom. 3:24–25). This assertion of Paul confirms the grace of God—that redemption is a gift. But to claim that righteousness comes through the law is to make Christ's death unnecessary.

3:1–4:31
Paul's Argument: The Gospel Has Superseded the Law

3:1–5, An Appeal to the Experience of the Galatians. Paul begins his argument by reminding the Galatians of their original Christian experience. "Foolish Galatians," he calls them (see Luke 24:25), for they have been hypnotized by the troublemakers (Gal. 1:6–9). Before their eyes, the crucified Christ was openly portrayed. Preaching the gospel is "re-presentation" of Christ (1:16; 1 Cor. 2:2).

About this experience Paul asks whether the Galatians received the Spirit by doing the law ("works of the law") or by accepting the gospel ("the hearing of faith"; see Rom. 10:17). Paul assumes that the Spirit is the gift commonly received by believers (1 Cor. 2:12; →Holy Spirit, The). For Paul, the Spirit signifies the presence of the living Christ (Rom. 8:9–11). Thus, the Galatians began their experience with the Spirit, but they are ending in the flesh—seen in their interest in circumcision (see Rom. 2:28). To engage in this retrogression is to admit that all they have experienced adds up to nothing. Instead, their experience, evident in spiritual gifts (1 Cor. 12:8–11), should have proved that God had been at work—before the troublemakers arrived.

3:6–18, Arguments from Scripture. Paul begins by quoting Gen. 15:6. God promised Abraham that he would be the father of many descendants. In response, Abraham "had faith in God and it was counted to him for righteousness." Abraham was declared to be right with God solely on the basis of faith. Interpreting the text, Paul concludes that it is through faith that people become descendants of Abraham. The argument is supported by a reference to Gen. 12:3 together with Gen. 18:18, which says that in Abraham all the nations (Gentiles) will be blessed. By faith people share the blessing of Abraham. In announcing this, Scripture preached the gospel beforehand in Abraham.

Gen. 12:3, however, notes that some people will be cursed. This suggests another text, Deut. 27:26, that pronounces a curse on all who do not keep all the commands. According to Paul's argument in Gal. 2:16, one cannot be justified by works, and the law shows that those who fail to keep all the commandments are transgressors, under the curse that the law decrees. However, the law affirms a better way: "The person who is righteous by faith shall live" (Hab. 2:4; see Rom. 1:17), so that the notion that one can get right with God by works of the law is denied. Nevertheless, Scripture can be read from the viewpoint of works, not from the perspective "of faith" (Gal. 3:12). Paul illustrates this by citing Lev. 18:5, which says that those who keep the law "shall live" (v. 12). Yet, as Paul has argued in v. 10, it is impossible to keep the law, and those who fail to obey all its commands do not receive life.

Throughout this section Paul follows rabbinic methods of interpretation and in v. 13 makes use of a device whereby the appearance of the same word relates two texts. Thus the term "curse" in Deut. 27:26 recalls Deut. 21:23: "Cursed is everyone who hangs on a tree." For Paul, this text can be applied to Christ, who in his crucifixion is identified with sinful humanity (2 Cor. 5:21), becoming a curse for us. Christ, by this action, redeemed us from the curse that the law pronounced. Redemption is a deed whereby freedom (e.g., for a slave) is purchased at cost (Rom. 3:24; 1 Cor. 6:19–20; →Redemption). Through Christ's identification with us, we are identified with Abraham (see Gal. 3:16) so that we are not cursed, but share the blessing: the promise of the Spirit (v. 2).

Next (vv. 15–18) Paul argues from a human analogy. He notes that once a will has been ratified it cannot be changed. In the same way, the law that did not come until 430 years (Exod. 12:40) after the promise cannot nullify the covenant previously ratified by God. Focusing on a fine point, Paul observes that the promise was extended to Abraham's "offspring" (singular) not "offsprings" (plural). This suggests that the true descendant of Abraham is Christ. Thus the inheritance cannot be through the law, but through the promise.

3:19–29, The Giving of the Law and the Coming of Faith.

Since the law cannot supersede the promise, for what purpose was it given? It was added "because of transgressions," that is, to increase trespasses (Rom. 5:20)—to show that sin is against the will of God (see Rom. 7:13). Moreover, the law was temporary (in force until the true offspring should come) and inferior—given by angels through an intermediary. The notion that the giving of the law took place in the presence of angels is suggested by the Greek version of Deut. 33:2 (see Acts 7:53; Heb. 2:2). The intermediary is Moses, and the presence of an intermediary shows that the revelation was not direct (God is one).

Is this inferior law against the promises? In spite of evidence to the contrary, Paul declares a resounding "No." The law serves a different purpose in the economy of God. It cannot do what the promise does: give life (see Rom. 7:10). Instead, the law imprisons people under the power of sin (Rom. 3:9) until the time when the promise may be received through faith.

Before Christ came (Gal. 4:4), the law functioned as the household slave who supervised the discipline of the child. But now that faith has come, we are no longer under this slave, but have become children of God through faith in Christ (4:5–7; Rom. 8:14)—full members in the household of God. Paul reminds the Galatians that they had been united with Christ (Gal. 2:20)—a unity signified by baptism (Rom. 6:3–7; 1 Cor. 12:13). Just as believers put on clothing after baptism, so they are clothed with Christ. This dramatic sign is (unlike circumcision that was for men only) open to all; it proves that the old distinctions have ceased to count. In Christ there is neither Jew nor Greek (religious discrimination; Rom. 3:22–23; 10:12), slave nor free (social discrimination; 1 Cor. 7:22; Philem. 16), male nor female (sex discrimination; see, however, 1 Cor. 11:2–16; 14:34–35). All are one in their new identity in Christ. Thus the believers belong to Christ (the one offspring) and inherit the promise spoken to Abraham.

4:1–11, Slavery and Adoption.

To advance his argument, Paul takes up another analogy. A child, before becoming of age, is no better off than a slave in the household. Until the time appointed by the father, the child is under guardians and managers. Similarly, as long as we were children (before faith came; 3:23), we were enslaved to the elemental powers of the world. Paul, like many of his contemporaries, believed the world was under the control of evil forces (see 2 Cor. 4:4; Rom. 8:38). To be under their power meant to be slaves of sin (Gal. 3:22).

At the time appointed by God (see Rom. 5:6; 1 Cor. 10:11), God sent forth the Son of God. For Paul, the title "Son" stresses the close relationship between Christ and God (see Rom. 5:10; 8:32). Two things are said about the Son: first, he was born of woman, that is, identified with humanity (see Job 14:1; Matt. 11:11; Luke 7:28); second, he was born under the law, that is, identified with those under sin (Gal. 3:22). The sending of the Son has a dual purpose: to redeem or secure freedom for those under the law (3:13) and to make possible gentile adoption into the household of faith (see Rom. 8:14–17). Proof that these purposes have been accomplished is seen in the reception of the Spirit (Gal. 3:2) whereby the Galatians can cry "Abba"—an Aramaic term of direct address to God (see Mark 14:36; Rom. 8:15). Addressing God in this way shows that the Galatians are not slaves but heirs.

In Gal. 4:8, Paul refers again to the situation before faith—to the time when they did not know God (see 1 Thess. 1:9) and were enslaved to the false gods of pagan polytheism (1 Cor. 8:5; 10:20). Rather than knowing God (as an object; see Rom. 11:33–36), they "are known by God"; God had first known and chosen them (see Rom. 8:29–30; 1 Cor. 8:3; 13:12). In view of the resulting relationship with God, why, Paul asks, would the Galatians want to return to the previous situation—to slavery under the powerless and worthless elemental forces (Gal. 4:3)?

Thus Paul presents a startling argument: to submit to the law is to return to the situation of paganism. Apart from the gospel, Jews and Gentiles alike are under the power of sin (3:22). Evidence of this slavery can be seen in the Galatian concern to observe the rituals of the Jewish calendar—matters that are of no importance for the believer (see Rom. 14:5–6). Paul despairs, wondering if his ministry on behalf of the Galatians has been in vain.

4:12–20, Paul's Personal Appeal. Paul says, "Become as I am, as I became as you." He wants them to identify with his faithfulness to the gospel (see 1 Cor. 4:16; 11:1), just as he identified with them during his ministry (see 1 Thess. 2:8; 1 Cor. 9:21). Then the Galatians did Paul no wrong; rather, they graciously received him. Apparently Paul stopped in Galatia to recover from a physical malady. This illness is usually interpreted as the "thorn in the flesh" of 2 Cor. 12:7–10, and details from Galatians are used to identify the ailment. Whatever it was, the Galatians did not respond with scorn or loathing; they received Paul as a heavenly messenger, as Christ himself (see Gal. 3:1). At that time, they deserved a blessing, for they were ready to give Paul one of their most precious possessions: their eyes.

Now the situation has changed. Anticipating their response to this Letter, Paul asks, "Have I become your enemy by telling you the truth?" (see 2 Cor. 12:15). The troublemakers, on the other hand, try to exploit their relationship with the Galatians. They eagerly court the Galatians, but actually want to shut them out—out of the relation of friendship to Paul, out of participation in the community of promise. In his final appeal, Paul speaks as a loving mother (see 1 Thess. 2:7) who is suffering the pains of labor, awaiting their birth as mature Christians. Paul wishes he could be present in person so as to change his tone rather than use the harsh words of this Letter.

4:21–31, The Allegory of the Two Sons. Next, Paul presents a concluding argument from Scripture. He addresses the Galatians as "those who desire to be under the law" (see 3:23; 4:5), that is, to yield to the teaching of the troublemakers. Then he asks, "Do you hear what the law says?" To answer the question, he refers to narratives from Genesis (chaps. 16, 17, and 21) about the two sons of Abraham. One of these was Ishmael (whom Paul never names), the son of the slave woman Hagar. The other was Isaac, the son of the free woman Sarah (also unnamed). These sons are contrasted in the manner of their birth. The son of the slave was born "according to the flesh" (i.e., in the ordinary way), the son of the free woman, "through the promise" (see Gal. 3:16, 29).

Interpreting the story as an allegory, Paul says the women symbolize two covenants (→ Covenant). The slave woman, Hagar (the name is similar to Semitic words meaning "mountain"), represents the covenant at Sinai—the covenant of the law that is observed in "the present Jerusalem" (Gal. 4:25). The children of this covenant are born into slavery under the law (3:23; 5:1). The second covenant (see 1 Cor. 11:25; 2 Cor. 3:6) is represented by the heavenly Jerusalem (see Heb. 12:22; Rev. 3:12; 21:2) that embodies the freedom Christians already enjoy (see Phil. 3:20). According to Paul, this city is "our mother"—it stands for the new covenant whereby people become children of Abraham through faith (Gal. 3:7).

Paul expands the allegory (4:27) by quoting from Isa. 54:1. In its original setting this text contrasted the barren woman (the city of Jerusalem during the Exile) with the woman who has a husband (the city before the Exile) to show that after the return from exile Jerusalem would be more fruitful and joyful than ever. Paul identifies the barren woman as Sarah, the heavenly Jerusalem, the mother of Isaac. Thus, "you" (the gentile Christians of Galatia) are like Isaac, children of promise (see Gal. 3:29)—children not of the slave but of the free woman (4:31).

When Paul says the child of the flesh persecuted the child of the Spirit he may have in mind an interpretation of Gen. 21:9 whereby the child of Hagar taunts the child of Sarah. When he notes that "it is so now," Paul is thinking of Jewish persecution of Christians that he has known as both perpetrator (Gal. 1:13; 1 Cor. 15:9) and victim (2 Cor. 11:24). The quotation from Gen. 21:10 indicates that the troublemakers should be thrown out of the Galatian churches (see Gal. 1:8–9).

5:1–6:10
Final Exhortation and Instruction

5:1–12, Freedom and the Slavery of Circumcision. On the basis of the previous argument, Paul makes a final plea and presents additional instructions. He declares that Christ has set the Galatians free for the purpose of freedom. They should stand fast in their loyalty to the gospel and resist the efforts of the troublemakers. They should not be enslaved again to the law, nor submit to the demand for circumcision. Although Paul has not mentioned it in his earlier argument, circumcision, which was noted in his narrative (2:3, 12), is clearly a major issue in the Galatian controversy.

If the Galatians have themselves circumcised, serious consequences would follow. For one, Christ would be of no benefit; if salvation requires this work of the law, Christ, who is the true ground of salvation, "died for nothing" (2:21). Also, those who receive circumcision are obligated to keep the whole law (see Rom. 2:25), that is, they put themselves under a requirement that cannot be fulfilled (Gal. 3:10; 6:13). Those who are seeking justification in this way are separated from Christ; they have fallen from grace (2:21; → Grace).

The true way to righteousness is through the Spirit, which the Galatians have received by faith (3:2). The Spirit is the down payment on life in the future (2 Cor. 1:22) and the basis for the hope of acquittal in the final judgment (see Rom. 2:5). From the perspective of faith in Christ, circumcision is a matter of indifference (Gal. 6:15; 1 Cor. 7:19). What matters is faith coming to expression in love—not a required ritual, but a way of life (see Gal. 5:14, 22).

The Galatians had once been on the right track (3:3)—they were running well (a metaphor from athletics, see 1 Cor. 9:24)—but someone got in their way. The persuasion to swerve from the truth of the gospel (Gal. 2:5, 14) did not come from God who called them (1:6), but from the troublemakers. Their influence has started to permeate the congregations, for, as a proverb says, "A little yeast spreads to the whole loaf" (1 Cor. 5:6); evil is contagious.

In spite of some defectors, Paul is confident that most of the Galatians will follow his admonition. As to the one troubling you (Paul is probably speaking hypothetically, not about a particular individual; see Gal. 1:9), such a one deserves condemnation rather than acquittal in the future judgment (see 1:8–9). Apparently, some have charged that Paul, as in his earlier zeal for the traditions (1:14), is still preaching circumcision (see 1 Cor. 9:20; Acts 16:3). Yet, if Paul were still advocating this Jewish ritual, why is he being persecuted by the Jews? (2 Cor. 11:24). He utters a harsh outburst against the agitators, "Would that those who are troubling you would castrate themselves."

5:13–26, Freedom and the Discipline of the Spirit. After reminding the Galatians that they were called to freedom, Paul warns them not to let their liberty become a "base of operations" (a military term) for the flesh. Perhaps the troublemakers have charged that Paul's message of freedom fosters immorality. As vv. 15 and 26 indicate, however, the trouble that they

have instigated has resulted in behavioral problems within the Galatian congregations. To correct these, Paul urges his readers to serve one another through love. The whole law is fulfilled in one command: "love your neighbor" (Lev. 19:18; Rom. 13:9)—the true way to keep the law. Proof that the Galatians need the command is presented in 5:15: they are acting like wild animals.

Paul urges them to walk by the Spirit so that they will not fulfill the desire of the flesh. The term "walk" is used to describe a style of life. The desire of the flesh represents the effort to order life according to material things. Spirit and flesh are opposing powers, and the conflict between the two results in moral paralysis: "you are not able to do what you will" (v. 17; see Rom. 7:15–23). In contrast to the external demands of law, the discipline of the Spirit is inward—the discipline of freedom (see 2 Cor. 3:17).

In 5:19–23, Paul presents conventional ethical formulas: vice and virtue lists. Teachers of ethics in Paul's day liked to enumerate features of bad and good conduct (see Rom. 1:29–31; 1 Cor. 6:9–10). Paul's vice list ("the works of the flesh") is not restricted to sexual immorality (the so-called "sins of the flesh"), but includes such "spiritual" evils as enmity, jealousy, anger, and selfishness. Paul had warned the Galatians about these evils before. People who do such things will not inherit the "kingdom" (see 1 Cor. 6:10)—a term that refers to participation in the future reign of God (see 1 Cor. 15:24, 50).

The fruit of the Spirit is spontaneous. Though Paul includes such typical Greek virtues as humility and self-control, items in his list have theological significance: "peace," for example, depicts the new relationship that the believer has with God (Rom. 5:1). Love is the fundamental force of the entire ethic. Its deeds have nothing to do with law (Gal. 5:23); love cannot be commanded or judged by law. Those who belong to Christ can produce the fruit of the Spirit and avoid the works of the flesh because they have been crucified with Christ (2:20)—the old self has been put to death (see Rom. 6:5–6). Paul concludes with a statement of the indicative and the imperative. "If we live by the Spirit" (indicative), "let us walk by the Spirit" (imperative); Christians should live in response to the new being that they have received.

6:1–10, Practical Instruction to the Churches. After the heated controversy of the previous chapters, this advice seems ordinary. Yet, Paul wants to show that the mundane life of the church continues. Making use of familiar proverbs, he gives practical instruction on how Christians can live by the Spirit (5:25). If one of the members is caught in a trespass (perhaps a legal violation), those who live by the Spirit ought to restore that person to the community in an attitude of gentleness (one fruit of the Spirit; 5:23). Remember, Paul warns, every one of you (he uses the singular) is subject to temptation. Since all believers endure difficulties, they ought to "bear one another's burdens" (6:2). This sort of concern fulfills the law of Christ—the law of love (5:14) that has nothing to do with legal requirements (see 5:23).

Although believers are under obligation to others, they are also responsible for themselves. They must avoid arrogance (5:26), supposing that they are something when they are nothing (2 Cor. 12:11). Each one should examine one's own work to see if there is any ground for boasting (see Rom. 15:17). Everyone should carry one's own "load" (a word that can mean "cargo" or "weight"). At the same time, those who are taught should share provisions with those who teach the gospel (see 1 Cor. 9:4, 14).

In 6:7, Paul quotes a familiar proverb: "Whatever one sows, one will also reap." This saying is found in Greek and Jewish writings, but Paul gives it meaning in the context of his larger argument. To sow to the flesh means to do the works of the flesh (5:19–21); to reap corruption means to effect destruction and death (see Rom. 6:23; 8:13). To sow to the Spirit means to produce the fruit of the Spirit (5:22–23); to reap eternal life means to assure participation in the coming kingdom of God (5:21). This cause-and-effect relationship should encourage people not to grow weary in doing good, for at the proper time the outcome will be realized. In the time that remains, Christians should do good to all people (see Rom. 12:18), but especially to "the household of faith"—the members of the church.

6:11–18
Conclusion of the Letter

Paul normally dictated his letters and added the final greeting in his own hand (1 Cor. 16:21). The "large letters" may be for emphasis. Before concluding, Paul launches a final attack on the troublemakers. They want to make a good showing by forcing the Galatians to be circumcised. In the flesh of these Gentiles, the agitators think they can exhibit a basis for boasting in their own accomplishments. This action could also serve to protect them from zealous Jews. Apparently some Jews are persecuting their compatriots who are lax in their association with the uncircumcised (see Gal. 5:11). For all their devotion

to the law, the troublemakers do not keep the commandments themselves (see 5:3).

In contrast, Paul intends never to boast in his own accomplishments, but solely in the cross of Christ. This is a strange sort of boasting, since the crucifixion is a scandal (5:11; 1 Cor. 1:23). Through crucifixion with Christ (Gal. 2:20), the world has been crucified to Paul; the world, which is a power over against God (1 Cor. 2:12; 3:19), has no hold on the apostle. At the same time, Paul has been crucified to the world; his old self, trapped in the flesh, has been put to death (Gal. 5:24).

In 6:15, Paul repeats the principle stated in 5:6: circumcision is a matter of indifference. Although neither circumcision nor uncircumcision counts for anything, what counts is the new creation (2 Cor. 5:17). This new being that the believers have received in Christ becomes a rule or standard for life—like the Spirit, a new indicative (see Gal. 5:25). Those who obey the indicative—who walk according to the rule—shall receive peace (Rom. 5:1) and mercy (Rom. 11:31–32). They are those who by faith have come to be a part of God's people—"the Israel of God" (Gal. 6:16).

In a final assertion of freedom, Paul exclaims, "Henceforth let no one trouble me!" Instead of the mark of circumcision, he bears the brand-marks of slavery to Jesus—the visible scars of persecution (2 Cor. 11:23–25). Paul's benediction is similar to those with which he concludes other Letters (see Phil. 4:23; Philem. 25). He hopes the Galatians will say "Amen" in response to the reading of the Letter.

Bibliography

Betz, H. D. Galatians: A Commentary on Paul's Letter to the Churches in Galatia. Hermeneia. Philadelphia: Fortress, 1979.

Bruce, F. F. The Epistle to the Galatians: A Commentary on the Greek Text. The New International Greek Commentary. Grand Rapids, MI: Eerdmans, 1982.

Burton, E. D. A Critical and Exegetical Commentary on the Epistle to the Galatians. International Critical Commentary. Edinburgh: Clark, 1921.

Ebeling, G. The Truth of the Gospel: An Exposition of Galatians. Philadelphia: Fortress, 1984.

Howard, G. Paul: Crisis in Galatia. A Study in Early Christian Theology. Society for New Testament Studies Monograph Series, 35. London and New York: Cambridge University Press, 1979.

EPHESIANS

NILS ALSTRUP DAHL

INTRODUCTION

Transmission

The title "To the Ephesians" is first attested by Irenaeus, ca. A.D. 180. A generation earlier, however, Marcion had edited a collection of Paul's letters that used the title "To the Laodiceans" for Ephesians. Probably the famous heretic took the title from a still earlier edition that he used. It is likely, therefore, that the Letter of Paul to the Ephesians circulated separately as a "general letter" from Paul before it became part of a collection and was supplied with a title and later with a local address in the prescript (1:1).

Literary Genre

The Letter to the Ephesians contains remarkably few references to specific persons, places, events, or controversial issues. It might be destined for any group of gentile Christians who did not know Paul personally. The Letter praises God for his blessing in Christ, extols God's great power and rich mercy, and reminds former Gentiles of the privileges that God has granted to them as well as to the Jews, with whom they have been united. On this basis the addressees are admonished to live up to their calling and avoid gentile vices, but Ephesians does not contain deliberations about more or less advisable courses of action. The author does not engage in dialogue with the addressees or debate with opponents but unfolds themes with which the audience ought to be familiar. The style is both elevated and peculiar (see esp. 1:3–14).

Several scholars have suggested that in spite of the epistolary form Ephesians is best understood as a summary of Paul's teachings (perhaps a "testament"; →Testament [3]), as a theological treatise or a meditation upon the theme "Christ and the Church," as a baptismal homily, or as an introduction to Paul's collected letters. Not all of these suggestions are mutually exclusive. A letter might substitute for a public speech as well as for personal conversation, and in antiquity the art of letter writing could be considered part of the art of persuasion (rhetoric). The rhetoric of Ephesians is a variant of the demonstrative (or "epideictic") genre, which was used, for example, to praise the excellence of a god, an out-standing person, a virtue, or a city and its laws. Ephesians demonstrates the magnitude of God's benefactions. However, it does also have the purpose of a letter—to overcome distance and establish and cultivate contact between sender and addressees. As in 1 Thessalonians—where everything is much more specific—information and reminders are placed within a framework of thanksgiving and intercession, and a background section is followed by appeals. The addressees are asked to reciprocate the apostle's concern for them (Eph. 3:13; 6:19–20).

Setting

Taken at face value, Ephesians is a letter from Paul destined for one or several churches within the field of his mission to the Gentiles but not founded by the apostle himself. Being under arrest, he was not able to visit them, so he sent Tychicus, who was to supplement the letter with oral information (see 1:15–16; 3:1–2; 6:20–22). Apparently on the same mission, Tychicus was also to visit Colossae, accompanied by the runaway slave Onesimus (Col. 4:7–9). Most defenders of Pauline authenticity conclude that Ephesians is a circular letter, destined for Laodicea and Hierapolis, perhaps also for other churches that Tychicus was to visit. The complex relationship among Ephesians, Colossians, and the Letter to Philemon may then be explained by the assumption that the imprisoned apostle commissioned one of his assistants to write to Colossae and another to write a circular letter.

An increasing number of exegetes, Roman Catholics as well as Protestants, find it more likely that Ephesians is a pseudonymous letter, written some time after the death of Paul. The Letter presupposes a setting in which Christians who ought to have been mature were exposed to a variety of false doctrines (4:13–16). The admission of Gentiles on equal terms with the Jews is no longer a controversial issue but is presented as a revealed mystery of which Paul was the mediator (2:11–3:13). Scholars who agree on a post-Pauline origin still evaluate Ephesians in divergent ways, e.g., as a faithful reproduction of Paul's theology, as a partial distortion of his "theology of the cross," or as an inspired reinterpretation that legitimates the later development of the church and its orders. The following exposition presumes that the anonymous author was a personal disciple of Paul, possibly a Jew, who wrote a letter in Paul's name to make Paul present to Christians who were separated from the apostle in time rather than space. At a time when Christianity in Asia Minor was threatened by fragmentation and the Pauline heritage was in danger of being lost, Ephesians calls Christians back to the basis of their own existence, Paul's gospel and mission to the Gentiles, and their own baptism.

COMMENTARY

1:1–2
Salutation

Ephesians, like Romans, mentions only Paul as the sender. Otherwise the form of the salutation has a normal Pauline form except for the address. The early manuscripts do not mention any location; the insertion of "in Ephesus" before "and faithful/believers" is secondary and clumsy (see RSV note). A local address must either have been absent from the beginning or omitted before Ephesians was incorporated in any collection of the Pauline Letters. There is some evidence that Romans was converted into a general Letter by omission of "in Rome" in Rom. 1:7 and 15 and deletion of chaps. 15–16. In the case of Ephesians it is more likely that the desire to have a letter from Paul to all Christians may have provided a reason for the composition of the entire Letter. A letter that concludes with a wish of peace to "all who love our Lord Jesus" may well have begun with a salutation of "the saints who are also faithful."

1:3–14
Introductory Praise of God

Not only Ephesians but also 2 Corinthians and 1 Peter begin by a "benediction" that praises "the God and Father of our Lord Jesus Christ." In contemporary Judaism, regular prayers usually had the form of "benedictions" that opened and/or concluded with the formula, "Blessed (be) He" or "Blessed (be) Thou." Brief benedictions were also to be uttered on special occasions, e.g., at the reception of news or at happy encounters (thus already Gen. 24:27). This practice forms the background for the occasional use of a benediction at the opening of a letter (cf. 1 Kings 5:7; 2 Chron. 2:11–12). A blessing of this type may praise God for what he has done for the speaking person (2 Cor. 1:3–11, cf., e.g., 1 Sam. 25:32–34, 39). If God is praised for what he has done for the other person(s), the benediction serves as a solemn, originally courtly, form of

congratulation (e.g., Gen. 14:20; 1 Kings 10:9; Ruth 4:14). In praising God, 1 Peter praises Christians happy in spite of their sufferings (1:3–12, cf. 3:14; 4:14). Ephesians praises God for what he has done "in Christ" for all Christians (Eph. 1:3–12), congratulating the gentile addressees who have become partakers of all God's blessings.

The theme of the benediction is that God is to be blessed because he has "blessed us with all kinds of spiritual blessings" (Eph. 1:3). The theme is unfolded in a long series of clauses and phrases attached to one another, sometimes loosely, in consecutive subordination, without any full stop in the Greek text. The text is a unified whole. God is the acting subject, Christ the mediator of God's action and of the benefits Christians have received and possess in Christ. The emphasis gradually shifts from the acts of God to the experience of believers, but there is no argument that moves straight forward. The progress is circular, moving backward and forward from God's benefactions in Christ to the eternal decision of God's will and to God's ultimate purpose. Transitions from one circuit to the next are marked by repetition of the formula "in Christ" or variants at the end or at the beginning of the subsections (1:3, 4–6, 7–10, 11–12, 13–14).

Not only Colossians and other Pauline Letters but also Jewish hymns and prayers provide parallels to the phraseology and some of the themes, but only to a minor degree to the style of the benediction. It has been suggested that the opening benedictions of Ephesians and 1 Peter were modeled upon benedictions used in connection with baptism. This may possibly apply to some parts of the text, but the author of Ephesians has composed the benediction and not quoted an already existing hymn.

1:3, Heavenly Blessings. The blessings for which God is praised are not earthly (as in Deut. 28:2–13) but "spiritual blessings in the heavenly heights." We may picture them as stored in heaven until they were bestowed in Christ. As the text proceeds it mentions various aspects of these blessings: adoption as God's sons (Eph. 1:5, cf. Gal. 4:5; 2 Cor. 6:18), rich grace, redemption and forgiveness through the death of Christ (Eph. 1:6–8, cf. Col. 1:14; Rom. 3:24–25), and also wisdom and insight, as God has revealed his secret plan for the entire universe (Eph. 1:8–10, cf. Dan. 2:20–23). In Christ the chosen ones have become God's own lot (Eph. 1:11–12; cf. JB, TEV). The combination of more or less familiar words and themes have a cumulative effect that evokes emotive as well as doctrinal associations.

1:4–6, Election in Christ. The correspondence between God's intention and action was a common theme (cf. Num. 23:19 and, e.g., Rom. 8:28–30). In Ephesians the idea of predestination is given a special form: already before the origins of the world God has in Christ chosen those whom he would bless in Christ (1:3–4, cf. 1:9; 3:12). This presupposes not only that Christ was in the beginning "with God" (John 1:1), but also that he was designated from the beginning to be the mediator of the blessings God had prepared for his chosen ones (cf. 1 Pet. 1:18–19; 2 Tim. 1:9–10). The correspondence between what God has decided and what he performs is restated in Eph. 1:5, 9–10, and in v. 11, where God is referred to as the one who performs all that his will has decided. The audience is to be assured that God, who in Christ has already done what he intended, will bring his action to completion.

1:7–12, Purpose and Consequences. The most comprehensive statement of God's purpose pertains to God's plan for "all things," the universe of heavenly powers and human beings (1:9–10). The main verb in v. 10 normally means to sum up or recapitulate a complex discourse in a brief summary (cf. Rom. 13:10). The verb may, however, have been taken to mean "to bring to a head" and associated with the metaphoric use of "head" (of a body; see 2 Esdras 12:17–18, NEB). The general idea in Eph. 1:9–10 is therefore likely to be that God's secret plan for "the fullness of time" was to bring the entire history of the universe to its completion in Christ, who is himself the supreme head (cf. 1:20–23; 4:15–16). By the unification of Gentiles and Israelites in the church, God has realized an essential part of this plan (cf. 2:11–22; 3:5–12).

In a similar way, God's final goal for his chosen ones is in line with what he has already done for them. God has chosen them "to be holy and without fault before him" (1:4, TEV; cf. 5:27; Col. 1:22). In Eph. 1:11–12 the Greek syntax is less than clear and translations vary. The unit may best be understood as a somewhat overloaded summary statement: "In Christ we have been singled out, as we were predestined (already before the completion of God's design for the universe) . . . , that—to the praise of God's glory—we should be the ones who have hope in Christ" (v. 10). The entire benediction concludes with two statements of goal and consequence. The first has been interpreted in several ways (see, e.g., KJV, RSV). As Ephesians often connects nearly synonymous words, the intended meaning may be that God's goal was "to redeem and secure us for himself." The ultimate goal is the praise of God's glory. Like God's grace and benefactions (v. 6) and the existence of a community that already has hope in Christ (v. 12), even the inclusion of Gentiles (v. 14) aims at the glorification of God.

1:13–14, The Seal of the Spirit. After the summary statement in vv. 11–12 the gentile addressees are reminded of what happened when they first heard the gospel and responded with faith: they were "sealed" with the Holy Spirit. At the time Ephesians was written, the gift of the Spirit appears to have become an integral part of baptismal theology and ritual, more than an actual experience as it was at the beginning of the Christian mission to the Gentiles (Acts 10:44–48; 15:7–9; Gal. 3:2, 5). Even in Ephesians, however, the "seal of the Spirit" is considered a stamp God has put on those who belong to him and are under his protection and a first installment of their inheritance (cf. 2 Cor. 1:21–22; Eph. 4:30). The gentile addressees are to be assured that God's promise pertains to them and that they have a full share in all of God's blessings in Christ.

The entire benediction performs what it says and praises God by rehearsing his benefactions. Striking a note of congratulation, it reminds the addressees of the many things for which they ought to praise God. Indirectly it also admonishes them to conduct their lives in such a way that God may be glorified by their existence. The benediction is an "exordium" or prologue to the Letter; a more precise statement of the theme is part of the intercession that follows (1:18–19).

1:15–2:22
Intercession, Theme, and Exposition

As in most Letters of Paul, an assertion of thanksgiving and prayer expresses the sender's appreciation of and concern for the addressees. The prayer report is elaborated in a way that prepares for the theme(s) and the main content of the Letter (cf. Rom. 1:9–17; Col. 1:9–12). In the characteristic style of Ephesians a beginning exposition is attached to the thematic formulations of Eph. 1:18–19.

1:15–16, Thanksgiving. As a consequence of the preceding praise of God the thanksgiving is brief and has an unusual form. Nearly all editors and translators accept the text of 1:15 in the majority of Greek manuscripts, according to which Paul gives thanks because he has heard about "the faith . . . and the love" of the addressees, as in Col. 1:4. The words "the love," however, are not present in the earliest and generally best manuscripts, text of which may be translated: "because I have heard about the faith that is yours, in the Lord Jesus, and that also pertains to all the saints." This would make sense in a letter that is destined for a general audience.

1:17–19, Intercession. The prayer for inspired wisdom and revealed knowledge combines several current phrases (see, e.g., Wisd. of Sol. 7:7). Three indirect questions specify the content of knowledge for which Paul is reported to pray and that the letter seeks to convey (Eph. 1:18–19). The call of God, which has given hope to Gentiles without hope, is the main theme (see 4:1, 4). The clauses in 18b and 19 state subthemes that are treated in reverse order, the manifestation of God's sovereign might in Christ (1:20–23), his power at work among the believers (2:1–10), and the "glory of God's inheritance"—which Gentiles now share with "the saints" (2:11–22; 3:6). The prayer is not for esoteric revelations but for a deeper understanding of the common Christian faith.

1:20–23, The Enthronement of Christ. The resurrection and heavenly enthronement of Christ provide the evidence of God's might. The imagery is drawn from a common Christological use of Ps. 110:1 (i.e., use of the text to express and support the Christian understanding of Jesus, e.g., Rom. 8:34; Acts 2:32–35), combined with Ps. 8:6 (as in 1 Pet. 3:22). The language is hymnic and does not distinguish between the enthronement of Christ and the future subjection of his "enemies" and of "all things" (unlike 1 Cor. 15:22–28; Heb. 2:5–9; 10:12–13). Ephesians does, however, make another distinction. Christ is enthroned in the high heavens, above all known and unknown powers in the universe. They are subjected to him, and he is exalted as "head above all" (like God, 1 Chron. 29:11), but God has given him to the church, and it is the church, not the universe, that is the body and "fullness" of Christ, "who himself receives the entire fullness of God" (NEB) or "fills the universe in all its parts" (e.g., NEB note, KJV), as God does (Jer. 23:24, see also Eph. 4:9).

2:1–10, Made Alive with Christ. The text turns to the work of God's power among those who believe (cf. 1:19). In the Greek text the sentence that begins with "And you" (v. 1) is never completed. With "us" as the object, the intended sentence is resumed and expanded in 2:4–7, where the core is formulated in loose analogy with and dependence upon what is said about God's work in Christ (1:20): "But God . . . has made us (who were dead) alive and made us sit with him on thrones in the high heavens." The cause of the irregular syntax in vv. 1–3 is that the portrayal of former Gentiles as "dead in transgressions and sins" has been expanded into a generalized description of the human predicament apart from Christ. Together with later insertions and comments this contributes to a multifaceted set of contrasts: God's rich mercy and power to make the dead alive over against death in sins; heavenly seats of honor together with Christ instead of existence in the atmosphere below the moon, where the devil holds

sway; evidence of God's superabundant grace in ages to come in contrast to conformity to the age of this world. Not only former Gentiles, but all who have a share in the salvation in Christ deserved wrath because of what they did, like those who are still outsiders—but God has loved them with great love.

The assertion that Christians have already been saved, raised, and enthroned with Christ goes beyond what Paul says (e.g. Rom. 5:9–10; 6:1–11); not even Colossians (2:11–14; 3:2–4) offers full parallels. Ephesians may draw upon the language of hymns that praised God as if his mighty work of salvation had already been completed. Appended comments, however, interpret the realized salvation in Pauline terms: "by grace, through faith . . . not because of works, lest anybody should boast" (Eph. 2:5b, 8–9). A contrast between two ways of life, in sins or in good works prepared by God, encloses the subsection and brings the prayer report to a delayed conclusion (2:2–3, 10; cf. Phil. 1:9–11; Col. 1:9–10).

The World and the Church

Popularized science of Hellenistic culture, especially astronomy, has left some traces upon the way in which Ephesians talks about the world or the universe ("all things," e.g., 1:10; 3:9). The "air" is the atmosphere between the earth and the lowest of the celestial spheres that surround it (2:2; 4:9). The symbolic reference to four immeasurable dimensions presupposes that the universe itself is spherical; its height reaches up to the zenith, its invisible depth down to the nadir (3:18). The spheres were generally supposed to be the habitat of powers (stars, subordinate gods, and demons—or, in Judaism, angels) who operated in nature and influenced events on earth. The use of abstract nouns to designate the cosmic powers is attested in some Pseudepigrapha and early Christian and Gnostic writings (→ Gnosticism; Pseudepigrapha). Ephesians shows no interest in their specific classes and functions (see 1:20; cf. Rom. 8:38–39; Col. 1:16). A phrase that rarely occurs outside Ephesians, "in the heavenly places" ("realms" or "heights") indicates their location in the universe (Eph. 3:10; 6:12). The same poetic circumlocution "in (the) heaven(s)" can, however, also be used about the heavenly throne of God and Christ outside the world of space and time (1:20; cf. 1:4; 2:6).

The explicit association of the cosmic powers with the devil is unusual but corresponds with a more general evaluation of "this world" as "darkness" (6:11–12; cf. 2:1–3; 4:17–19; 5:8–12). However, dualistic trends, i.e., the tendency to depict the whole universe as divided radically between good and evil powers, are counterbalanced by a strong emphasis upon the sovereignty of God, the Creator and Father of all (e.g. 3:9, 14–15; 4:6). Ephesians makes no attempt to explain the origins of evil but insists that God has proved his sovereign might by enthroning the risen Christ above the universe and all powers within it (1:19–22; 4:10). As Christ is the "head above all," his body, the church, is like a world, a renewed universe whose organic cohesion and growth depends upon its relation to the heavenly head (1:22–23; 4:7–16; see also Col. 1:17–18; 2:10, 19). God's eternal but secret design for his creation was put into effect when Christ unified Israelites and Gentiles in one body, and through the church the "richly variegated wisdom" of God's governance was made known to the powers who acted as rulers over various segments of a divided world (Eph. 3:4–11; cf. 1:9–11; 2:14–18).

In the world the cosmic powers still act as hostile forces, allied with the devil. Christians have to stand firm and fight them (6:10–17). In union with Christ, however, they have already risen above the world in which they still face trials and tribulations. The cosmological imagery has in Ephesians become a vehicle to communicate Paul's conviction that no power whatsoever can "separate us from the love of God in Christ Jesus our Lord" (see Rom. 8:31–39). In the historical context it must also have had the same implications as the explicit warnings in Colossians (Col. 2:4–3:4): efforts to escape the world and ascend to heaven by means of ascetic practices and visionary experiences are both futile and unnecessary. By the grace of God the members of the church have already been freed from bondage and enthroned in heaven as associates of Christ. What matters is that they do not relapse into the vices that are still in full swing in the outside world but do those good works for which they have been created, and that they relate to one another in such a way that the body of Christ and all its members will grow up toward Christ, in truth and in love. (→ Angel; Church; Demon; Devil; Heaven; Power; Stars; World, the)

2:11–22, Reminder: Alienation and Reconciliation.

As in 2:1–10 the former Gentiles are reminded of what they once were and what they now have become (cf. 5:8 and, e.g., Col. 1:21–22; Titus 3:3–7). The core sentence is v. 13: "But now, in Christ Jesus, you who once were far off have come near by the (atoning) blood of Christ." The terms "far off" and "near" allude to Isa. 57:19 but are, as in Jewish usage, applied respectively to those who lack and those who have full legal and religious rights as the people of God. The opening and concluding sentences deal with the former and the present status of uncircumcised Gentiles (Eph. 2:11–12, 19–22). They were once foreigners with no share in the privileges of Israel (cf. Rom. 9:5), but now they are "fellow citizens of the saints," not merely aliens with limited rights. A cluster of loaded metaphors, God's city, household, building, and temple, center around the identification of Christ as the *cornerstone* and the apostles and prophets as the foundation laid in Zion (Isa. 28:16; cf. 1 Pet. 2:4–10). The upbuilding of the entire structure depends upon Christ in the same way as the growth of the body (Eph. 2:19; cf. 4:16; Col. 2:19).

A middle segment, Eph. 2:14–18, explains how Christ through his atoning death brought about the transfer from "far off" to "near by." The text has a poetic flavor and alludes to the messenger of peace in Isa. 52:7 as well as to the peace for the far and the near in Isa. 57:19. Christ is himself identified with the peace he has brought and announced. This peace means unification of the Jewish and non-Jewish parts of humanity, creation of "one new human being," reconciliation of both parts with one another and with God "in one body," and free access to the Father "in one Spirit."

Ephesians maintains that to overcome duality Christ abrogated "the law of commandments" and broke down the "dividing wall" of hostility. The metaphor may allude to a cosmic wall around God's heavenly abode (e.g., 1 Enoch 14) but also to the wall that barred the access of foreigners to the Temple (see Acts 21:27–30; cf. Ezek. 44:20; 44:5–9). Ephesians, moreover, gives a negative twist to the notion that the commandments provided "walls" that protected the purity of Israel (*Let. Arist.* 139–42) and regards the Law as a set of rules for communal life and worship that alienated Gentiles and caused hostility but were unable to reconcile sinners with God. (For a somewhat similar view see Heb. 7:18–19; 9:1–10).

The reminder in Eph. 2:11–22 is, like the entire Letter, addressed to Christian Gentiles who have been united with the original heirs of God's promise without becoming Jews (see 3:6). The text does, however, presuppose that both parts of humanity were in need of peace and reconciliation through the cross of Christ. The distinction between "the uncircumcision" (RSV, lit., "foreskin") and circumcision "in the flesh, made by hands" (v. 11) has become obsolete as Christ has inaugurated a new age in which both parts have access to the Father in one Spirit and are built up to be the temple where God dwells in the Spirit. As Gentiles within the church in this context are regarded as representatives of the entire non-Jewish world, the Jews in the church may represent all Israel, as in Romans 11. Ephesians, however, never mentions the fact that some Jews rejected

Christ, nor does it say anything about how the addressees relate, or ought to relate, to Jews in their own midst or in Jerusalem. The author's concern is, apparently, the roots and origin of the church in Israel more than the actual relationship between Christians and Jews.

3:1–21
Paul's Ministry and Intercession

3:1–13, Information About the Sender.
In Ephesians this information is inserted between the beginning and the continuation of a renewed assertion of intercession (3:1, 14–21). The report tells no news; it is a retrospective summary that portrays Paul as mediator of the formerly hidden but now revealed mystery of Christ (cf. Col. 1:25–29; 2 Tim. 1:8–11; Rom. 16:25–27, and already 1 Cor. 2:6–16; 4:1). The first of two circular moves, from Paul to the mystery and back, draws attention to the special revelation granted to Paul and to his insight into the mystery that was revealed to "the holy apostles and prophets" (Eph. 3:2–7). The second move emphasizes that Paul, by the grace of God, became an active agent of revelation. His ministry to the Gentiles made the Creator's secret plan, to include the Gentiles as "fellow heirs" and members of the body of Christ, public knowledge, available to heavenly powers as well as to human beings (3:8–13, see also 2:11–22; 3:6). Several features of this stylized portrait are already present in the undisputed Letters of Paul (see 1 Cor. 1; 5:1–11; Gal. 1.11–16; 2:7–9). In a special way, however, it emphasizes that all gentile Christians owe their existence as members of the church to Paul's work as the agent of the revealed mystery of Christ.

3:14–19, The Intercession Resumed and Concluded.
The prayer is that God through his Spirit will give strength at the inner center, that Christ may be present through faith, and love be a firm foundation, so that the believers have the disposition that is necessary if they are to obtain true knowledge and reach the ultimate goal. In Jewish tradition, the immeasurable vastness of the world often illustrated the limitations of human understanding (e.g., Job 11:7–10). God, however, might reveal all mysteries of the world to a man of God like Moses (e.g., 2 Apoc. Bar. 59:4–11). Ephesians uses comprehension of the dimensions of the universe as a rhetorical preamble to prepare for the climax of the prayer: "That you may have power . . . to know the love of Christ that surpasses knowledge" (Eph. 3:19, RSV).

3:20–21, Doxology.
A formula celebrating God's glory brings the intercession and the whole first part of the Letter to an appropriate conclusion. The form "To him who is able to . . . be glory" occurs also in Rom. 16:25–27 and Jude 24–25. In Ephesians God's immense power is a recurrent theme (see 1:11, 19).

4:1–16
Basic Appeal and Incentives

4:1–6, Worthy of the Calling.
A polite but urgent appeal marks the transition to the second main part of the Letter (cf. Rom. 12:1; Philem. 8). The basic request, that those who are called by God should live up to their calling, corresponds to the thematic formulation in Eph. 1:18 and covers all the exhortations in 4:1–6:20. The first specification is that those who have received one common hope must conduct their lives and relate to one another in such a way that the given unity is preserved: "one Spirit and one body" (4:1–4). The very carefully arranged correlation of "one" and "all" in vv. 5–6 has antecedents in a common Greek tradition that could be adapted to Jewish monotheism and to Christian faith (see 1 Cor. 8:6; Heb. 2:10–11; Rom. 11:36). In the context of Ephesians the formula expounds the basis of the unity that has to be preserved. The appended description in Eph. 4:7–16 as well as echoes from the preceding (see esp. 2:14, 16, 18) confirm that the purpose of the exhortations is not merely to tell Christians what they ought to do but also, or even more, to motivate them to live up to their calling.

4:7–16, Unity in Diversity.
The explanation supporting the appeal treats the theme of one body with many parts in a way that is both similar to and different from Rom. 12:3–8 and 1 Cor. 12:6–30. The ascended Christ is identified as the giver of diverse measures of grace. The quotation of and comments upon Ps. 68:18 in Eph. 4:8–11 presuppose an alteration of the text from "he took . . ." to "he gave gifts." The free rendering goes back to a Jewish tradition that applied the passage to Moses, who ascended to heaven (according to this tradition) to receive the Torah and give gifts. Ephesians combines a Christological interpretation of the passage with the representation of the ascended Christ as the supreme head. The "gifts" of Christ are not identified with spiritual gifts in general (in spite of v. 8) but with persons who were assigned to preach the gospel and/or to take care of the congregations. As a result, modern commentators have debated the extent to which Ephesians presupposes and legitimates an institutionalized ministry. In the context, however, the interest centers on the workers' common task, to build up the church and ward off all kinds of false teaching, so that the entire body of Christ and all its members may grow up in harmony and reach full maturity (vv. 12–16; see Short Essay "The World and the Church" above).

4:17–24
Two Ways of Life

A stern warning (vv. 17–19) and a positive reminder (vv. 20–24) introduce the series of negative and positive prescriptions in 4:25–30.

4:17–19, No Longer Like the Gentiles. The stereotyped, dark picture of Gentiles is reminiscent of Rom. 1:21–32, but it is used in a traditional way as a warning not to act as idolatrous people do (see, e.g., Lev. 19:1–4; 1 Pet. 1:14). Their ignorance of the true God has resulted in the loss of moral sensitivity and decency. In practice this led to a combination of what were considered typical pagan vices: impurity in contrast to holiness and unfair gain at the expense of others (not merely greed; see also 5:3–5).

4:20–24, The Old and the New Human Being. The addressees should not relapse into their former way of life because they did "learn Christ" when they received the gospel and were instructed to "put off the old . . . and put on the new human being." The teaching is probably a summary of baptismal instruction (see Col. 3:9–11; Gal. 3:17–18; cf. Col. 2:11–12; Rom. 6:3–6). Familiarity with current interpretations of Genesis 1–3 and with Pauline teaching would enrich readers' understanding of the symbolism (see, e.g., Rom. 5:12–21; 8:29; 13:12, 14; 1 Cor. 15:44–49, 53–54). Ephesians, however, uses the reminder about the meaning of baptism in a hortatory context and insists that the initiation has to be followed up by an ongoing inner renewal (4:23; cf. 3:16–17).

4:25–5:20
Negative and Positive Admonitions

Diverse rules of conduct are loosely interconnected, as often in moral exhortations. Some formulations go back to the OT (e.g., Zech. 8:16; Ps. 4:4); many are taken over from catechetical instruction and/or from Colossians (e.g., Gal. 5:19–21; 1 Thess. 4:11; Col. 3:5–17; 4:5). Ephesians, however, tends to formulate the traditional topics after a pattern, main characteristics of which are use of second-person plural forms, coordination of negative and positive imperatives, and appended or inserted reasons for the warnings and recommendations (see Eph. 4:25–32; 5:3–12, 15–18). The sequence also shows careful composition. The first series of admonitions (4:25–32) is linked to the preceding reminder (vv. 20–24) and spells out what Christians should already know. They should be imitators of God, in whose image "the new human being" was created (5:1–2). The strict warnings in 5:3–14 elaborate the theme "no longer like the Gentiles" (4:17), and a final series (5:15–20) provides a gradual transition to the directives for wives and husbands.

Familiar precepts are reformulated to stimulate and motivate former Gentiles to behave as new and continuously renewed persons. Their words, actions, and reactions should not harm but benefit those who are fellow members of the one body. Christ's saving grace, love, and sacrifice provide the model for mutual forgiveness and love. Anger and pernicious speech may bedevil the fellowship; pagan immorality and self-interest contaminate the "children of light." The stern warnings against association with immoral outsiders may seem to recommend the kind of isolation that the Essenes practice (→ Essenes), but they are not meant to be strict rules of sectarian discipline (cf. 1 Cor. 5:9–10). Both the injunction to bring to light the shameful "works of darkness" and, in the present context, the quotation from an unknown source in Eph. 5:14 presuppose social contacts that may result in the conversion of outsiders. Among insiders and outsiders alike, Christians should not behave like ignorant pagans but be wise, able to discern what is the will of God (5:15–17; see also 5:10; Rom. 12:2; Col. 4:5–6). Sober but filled with the Spirit, they are to give thanks in their common worship and also, in continuation of Jewish custom, in daily life (see also Eph. 5:4; Col. 3:16–17; 1 Thess. 5:18).

5:21–6:9
Domestic Duties

As in the shorter and earlier code in Col. 3:18–4:1, the rules are arranged in three pairs: wives and husbands, children and fathers, slaves and masters—an order that can be traced back to Aristotle and that has left traces in many later treatments of what a good household should be like. The earliest Christian examples address each group separately (see also 1 Pet. 2:18–3:7).

5:21, Introductory Statement. In Ephesians the introductory formulation "subject to one another" (Eph. 5:21) further modifies the common tendency to make the master of the house responsible for the good order of the entire household.

5:22–33, Wives and Husbands. The extended treatment moves repeatedly back and forth from wives and husbands to the relationship between Christ and the church, which is seen as the model for human marriage in two ways: first, the husband is the head of his wife (cf. 1 Cor. 11:3) as Christ is the head of the church (see Eph. 1:22–23); second, Christ loved and gave himself up for the church, his bride (5:25–27; cf. Ezek. 16:8–14; 2 Cor. 11:2; Rev. 21:9). The two sets of metaphors are fused in Eph. 5:28–33 by means of a subtle combination of Gen. 2:24, "the two shall be one flesh," and the commandment of love in Lev. 19:18, which is paraphrased by "love their own bodies," "his own flesh," and "as himself." Christ's unification with the church, his bride and his body, is the "great mystery" contained in Gen. 2:24 (see also 2:23). The emphatic formula "I for my part" (Eph. 5:32, NEB) implies a contrast with another interpretation, most likely one arguing that union with Christ excluded human marriage—not only relations with a prostitute, as Paul argued in 1 Cor. 6:15–17. For early Christianity, celibacy or abstinence was the main alternative to the inherited household ethos that the disclosure of the "great mystery" in Ephesians both upholds and modifies.

6:1–4, Children and Parents. The Alexandrian Jewish author Philo had already connected the commandment to honor one's parents with general rules of household duties. The rule for fathers in Eph. 6:4 is the part of the code that most easily can be used to support authoritarian paternalism, but it may refer to "education" rather than strict "discipline."

6:5–9, Slaves and Masters. The presence of slaves in Christian households is not felt as a problem by the author, but Ephesians stresses that slaves and masters have reciprocal duties and the same impartial Lord in heaven. In comparison with Pauline texts like 1 Cor. 7:20–24, 29–31; Gal. 3:28; and Philemon, however, the household rules in Ephesians are evidence of an increasing closeness to generally accepted standards.

6:10–20
Final Exhortations

Exhortations to be strong, stand firm, and be awake, and to pray and make intercession, especially for the sender, conclude the main part of the letter (cf. 1 Cor. 16:13; Col. 4:2–3). The elaborated admonition to "put on the whole armor of God" resumes the theme of Eph. 4:24 in a new form. Most of the weapon metaphors go back to the OT (see Isa. 11:5; 59:16–17; Wisd. of Sol. 5:16; cf. Isa. 52:7), but they may have been used in catechetical traditions (see Rom. 13:12; 1 Thess. 5:8). The "weapons" are not simply human virtues but rather effects of God's own might, which provides protection in the fight against the invisible powers that cause tribulations and temptations. Equipped with the "gospel of peace" and the "sword of the Spirit," Christians are also to engage actively in the cosmic battle.

6:21–24
Epistolary Conclusion

The commendation of Tychicus, who is to carry the letter and supplement it with oral reports, is formulated by analogy with Col. 4:7–9 but omits the reference to Onesimus. Wishes of peace and grace are Pauline variants of the customary greetings at the end of a letter. The formulation is unusual, however. Verse 23 seems to make "the grace" contingent upon the attitude of the addressees (cf. Gal. 6:16), perhaps an indication that the author feared that not all Christians would heed the reminders and admonitions of his "letter from Paul."

Bibliography

Bruce, F. F. *The Epistles to the Colossians, to Philemon, and to the Ephesians.* New International Commentary on the New Testament. Grand Rapids, MI: Eerdmans, 1984.

Efird, J. M. *Christ, the Church, and the End: Studies in Colossians and Ephesians.* Valley Forge, PA: Judson, 1980.

Mitton, C. L. *Ephesians.* New Century Bible. Greenwood, SC: Attic Press, 1976.

Patzia, A. G. *Colossians, Philemon, Ephesians.* Good News Commentary. San Francisco: Harper & Row, 1984.

Sampley, J. P. "And the two shall become one flesh": A Study of Traditions in Eph. 5:21–33. Society for New Testament Studies Monograph Series, 16. London and New York: Cambridge University Press, 1971.

Sampley, J. P., et al. *Ephesians, Colossians, 2 Thessalonians, The Pastoral Epistles.* Proclamation Commentaries. Philadelphia: Fortress, 1978.

Taylor, W. F., and J. H. P. Reumann. *Ephesians, Colossians.* Augsburg Commentary on the New Testament. Minneapolis, MN: Augsburg, 1985.

PHILIPPIANS

RONALD F. HOCK

INTRODUCTION

The city of Philippi in northeastern Macedonia was named for Philip II, king of Macedonia (359–336 B.C.) and father of Alexander the Great. By the second and first centuries B.C., however, Roman influence became dominant; the city was connected to Italy by the road known as the Via Egnatia, settled on several occasions with Roman veterans, and reorganized as a Roman colony (Colonia Julia Augusta Philippensis) complete with Roman gods and Roman law (→ Philippi).

About A.D. 50 the apostle Paul, accompanied by Silas and Timothy, left Asia Minor for Europe and landed at Neapolis, where they picked up the Via Egnatia and traveled on to Philippi (Acts 16:11–12). Acts has a vivid, if episodic, account of the founding of the Philippian church: conversations with Lydia, the purple dealer, at a Jewish prayer meeting outside the city led to her conversion and offer of hospitality (vv. 13–15); they encountered a prophetess, which led to a dispute with her masters and ended with the beating and imprisonment of Paul and Silas (vv. 16–24); there was an earthquake and resulting confusion at the prison, which led to the conversion of the jailor (vv. 25–34); the local authorities made a formal apology for having beaten Paul, a Roman citizen (vv. 35–39); and they departed from the city (v. 40).

Paul's Letters confirm few of these details, although the beating and imprisonment are alluded to in 1 Thess. 2:2 and Phil. 1:30. Paul's silence, however, does not invalidate the Acts account. Indeed, the many Roman features—the designation "colony" (Acts 16:12), the Roman terms for local authorities (vv. 20, 35), the prohibition of unapproved religions within the city (vv. 13, 21), the appeal to rights of Roman citizens (v. 37)—lend it considerable plausibility.

In the Letter of Paul to the Philippians there is a further echo of Roman custom that Acts does not mention. There was a special relationship between Paul and the Philippians, a relationship that existed, Paul says, "from the first day" (Phil. 1:5; 4:15). Paul describes it in language reminiscent of a Roman legal "partnership," in which partners contributed toward some goal, in this case the advancement of the gospel (1:5, 7; 4:15). This partnership expressed itself in repeated, if irregular, gifts from the Philippians to Paul (4:10, 15).

Consequently, contact with the Philippian church continued after Paul's departure. In fact, shortly afterward the Philippians sent Paul gifts twice at Thessalonica (Phil. 4:16) and later at Corinth (2 Cor. 11:9). Added to these visits by Philippians are others by Paul or Timothy to Philippi (Acts 19:22; 20:1–4). Hence, we can suppose a lengthy and close relationship as background for the Letter to the Philippians, written when Paul is in prison (Phil. 1:7) and has received yet another gift (4:18).

Philippians belongs to that group of Letters including Romans, 1–2 Corinthians, Galatians, 1 Thessalonians, and Philemon whose Pauline authorship no one doubts. Within this group Philippians ranks fifth in length (1730 words).

Two issues in particular have been raised regarding Philippians: its literary integrity and its dating and placement. Some scholars, noting the sharp change in tone at 3:1–4:1, the delay in thanking the Philippians for their gift until 4:10–20, and a reference in the Letter of Polycarp (a second-century bishop of Smyrna) to letters of Paul to Philippi (Pol. Phil. 3:2) have proposed that the canonical Letter is a composite of two or three separate letters. This proposal, however, has convinced few scholars. Hence the following comments assume the Letter's literary integrity.

The second issue is much harder to decide. Traditionally, Philippians has been placed during Paul's Roman imprisonment in the early 60s (cf. Acts 28:14–31), suggested, no doubt, by references to the praetorian guard (Phil. 1:13) and the household of Caesar (4:22). Scholars, however, note that these references do not point exclusively to Rome and that a Roman imprisonment is problematic on other grounds. Consequently, they have proposed other locations, such as the imprisonment at Caesarea in Judea in the late 50s, known from Acts 23:33–26:32. Or, knowing that Paul was imprisoned in several other, if unspecified, places (2 Cor. 11:23), they have conjectured an Ephesian imprisonment in the mid-50s on the basis of Paul's reference to fighting with beasts at Ephesus (1 Cor. 15:32). Still, neither of these locations is without its problems, so that the matter is really at an impasse.

COMMENTARY

1:1–11
The Opening of the Letter

1:1–2, Salutation. Paul follows letter-writing conventions of his day when he opens this Letter with the names of senders and recipients (v. 1) as well as with his greetings (v. 2). The conventional formula, however, was brief: A to B, greetings. Paul expanded this formula, and though his expansion here is not as great as in Rom. 1:1–7 and Gal. 1:1–5, it is still distinctive. For example, Timothy appears as co-sender, not in itself peculiar, as he is listed in the salutations of 2 Corinthians, Philemon, and 1 Thessalonians, but in the first two he has a subordinate role as "brother" to Paul (2 Cor. 1:1; Philem. 1) and in the third he comes after Silvanus (1 Thess.1:1). In the salutation of Philippians, however, Timothy alone is co-sender and is Paul's equal, since both are "slaves of Christ Jesus" (1:1). Timothy's unique status here accords with his close relationship to Paul as his "son" (2:22) and with his genuine concern for the Philippians (2:19–20). This concern had arisen from Timothy's presence at the founding of the Philippian church (cf. Acts 16:1, 11–40) as well as from subsequent visits (cf. Acts 19:22; 20:1–4), and it explains Paul's intention to send him in particular on a future visit (Phil. 2:19–24).

Paul's use of the designation "slave" is also unusual (cf. Rom. 1:1). His usual self-designation is "apostle" (so Rom. 1:1; Cor. 1:1; 2 Cor. 1:1; Gal. 1:1), and its absence here is probably because Paul's relations with the Philippians were such that he hardly had to assert his authority; by contrast, there were challenges to his apostleship at Corinth and in Galatia. In any case, the term "slave" is significant in that Paul elsewhere uses slave imagery of himself and Timothy (Phil. 2:22) and of the Philippians (2:12) and often speaks metaphorically of Jesus as "master" (2:11; cf. 1:2; 3:8, 20; 4:5, 23).

The description of the recipients is distinctive in that only here are certain "overseers" (Gk. episkopoi) and "aides" (diakonoi) referred to (1:1). Their precise role is difficult to determine, but they were no doubt leaders and perhaps had some role in the gift (see 4:10–20).

Finally, instead of the conventional "greetings" (cf. Acts 15:23) Paul expands: "Grace to you and peace from God, our father, and the master, Jesus Christ" (Phil. 1:2), a fixed formula in Paul (Rom. 1:7; 1 Cor. 1:3; 2 Cor. 1:2; Philem. 3).

1:3–11, Thanksgiving. This section opens with "I give thanks to my God . . . ," a formulaic expression that is typical of Paul's Letters (Rom. 1:8; 1 Cor. 1:4; 1 Thess. 1:2; Philem. 4) and paralleled to some extent in ancient letters generally. This thanksgiving is noteworthy in several respects. For example, one phrase in Phil. 1:3 is ambiguous, capable of being rendered "whenever I remember you" or "whenever you remember me." If the latter is correct, then we have an appropriately early, if veiled, note of thanks for the Philippians' gift. One objection to the Letter's integrity would thus be removed.

The remainder of the thanksgiving is clear enough, elaborating on Paul's gratitude from several angles. Thus, besides the "when" of his thanksgiving (v. 3), there is also the "how"—his thanksgiving is made "with joy" (v. 4), an emotion that characterizes the tone of the Letter as a whole—and the "why," namely, Paul's formal partnership (v. 5). Accordingly, Paul's pause to express his intense feelings for the Philippians—they are "in his heart" and he "yearns" to see them (vv. 7–8)—is understandable, particularly so in his own difficult circumstances of being "in chains" and having to defend himself (v. 7). Finally, Paul gives the content of his prayers: that the Philippians' love for one another abound more and more, and especially in that knowledge that helps them to distinguish what is right and so makes them pure and blameless on the day of Christ that will redound to the glory and praise of God (vv. 9–11).

1:12–4:20
The Body of the Letter

1:12–26, Paul's Circumstances. The words "I want you to know . . ." (v. 12) are a conventional formula for signaling the body of a letter and so point to the letter's purpose. That purpose was to inform the Philippians of Paul's circumstances as a prisoner. He does not at first speak about his personal prospects. Instead he dwells on the prospects for the gospel, and in this matter he has reason for joy (v. 18). His being a prisoner has turned out surprisingly for the advancement of the gospel (v. 12): first, Paul's chains have made Christ known throughout the praetorian guard and beyond (v. 13), and second, his chains have emboldened other Christians to speak the word fearlessly (v. 14). Paul admits that not all these Christians are preaching out of the best motives (v. 15). In fact, some are doing so out of rivalry, supposing that they are thereby causing Paul's chains to pinch even more (vv. 16–17). Nevertheless, Christ is being preached, making Paul joyful (v. 18).

Paul's own prospects are less sure. He is confident of his own eventual salvation, but in the short run life and death seem equally possible as the outcome of his trial (v. 19). This uncertainty prompts Paul to reflect on the desirability of

living or dying, and, as Paul himself admits, he is hard pressed to choose between the two (vv. 20–23). For Paul personally death is preferable because then he will be with Christ (v. 24), but for the Philippians his living seems to him to be more essential—even fated (v. 25). Hence Paul looks forward to living, even visiting the Philippians, and so to helping them in their advancement and joy in the faith (v. 25). The repetition of the word "advancement" (cf. v. 12) gives closure to this section, and the reference to joy (cf. v. 18) underscores the tone of the Letter which was set in 1:4.

1:27–2:18, The Philippian Situation. This section flows easily from the previous one, for already in 1:24 Paul began to turn his thoughts away from his own situation to that of the Philippians. And their lot is not an easy one either; they have not merely to believe in Christ, but also to suffer for Christ (v. 29). Accordingly, if they are going to live worthy of the gospel, they must, Paul says, stand firm and united (v. 27). This advice is couched in athletic imagery: they are to compete together with one soul (v. 27), not be startled by their opponents (v. 28), and see their lives as Christians as a contest (v. 29). The identity of the opponents (v. 28) is uncertain. They may be traveling Christian missionaries with a different understanding of the faith or, more likely, people at Philippi who are causing problems for the church.

In 2:1–4 Paul continues his call for unity, though now in the language of partnership (cf. 1:5: the Philippians are "to be of one mind," 2:2). In addition, he counsels against factiousness and glory seeking and instead encourages humility or deference toward others (vv. 3–4), a quality especially evident in Christ, which prompts Paul to digress long enough to cite a hymnic tribute to Christ as once slave but now master (vv. 5–11).

2:6–11, The Christ Hymn

No passage of Philippians has attracted as much scholarly attention as this hymn. This attention is explained in part by the various lexical, grammatical, and exegetical problems in these verses but especially by the very importance of the hymn as one of the earliest witnesses to Christological reflection, i.e., reflection on the nature and mission of Jesus. The hymn was first recognized as such over sixty

Opposite: The Via Egnatia near Philippi, Greece. It was its position on the Via Egnatia, the Roman road connecting Byzantium with ports leading to Italy, which brought Philippi to prominence.

years ago, and scholars continue to debate such matters as the hymn's author, structure, redaction, background, setting, and meaning.

Although some scholars still hold to Pauline authorship, the presence of non-Pauline words or emphases points to someone other than Paul, although it is uncertain whether that person was a Jewish Christian or one more influenced by Greco-Roman culture. Likewise, the structure of the hymn is uncertain; an original form of two (vv. 6–8, 9–11), three (vv. 6–7a, 7b–8, 9–11), or more stanzas has been proposed. Complicating the matter is the question of how much Paul may have modified the hymn. Thus the phrase "even death on a cross" (v. 8) is often regarded as an addition by Paul, and some scholars would add "those in heaven, on earth, and under the earth" (v. 10).

The conceptual background of the hymn is variously explained by looking to the OT (esp. the Suffering Servant of Isaiah), to intertestamental Jewish writings and their concern with wisdom and the righteous sufferer, or to redeemer figures of Gnostic speculations. This background debate is the most hotly contested and is far from decided.

On the matter of setting, however, scholars tend to agree that the hymn was regularly used in Christian liturgy. Indeed, we can picture the singers of the hymn bowing on cue at the phrase "at the name 'Jesus' " (v. 10) as they confessed "Jesus Christ is Lord" (v. 11)—perhaps during baptism or at the Eucharist.

With all this uncertainty surrounding the hymn it is not surprising that its meaning is debated too, although at a general level it is clear that the author has taken the principal facts of the gospel, Christ's death and resurrection (cf. 1 Cor. 15:3–5), and interpreted them in terms of humiliation (vv. 6–8) and exaltation (vv. 9–11), of being enslaved (v. 7) and made master (v. 11).

In its present context in Philippians the hymn serves several purposes. It serves Paul's exhortation to humility (v. 3) by grounding it in Christ's having humbled himself (v. 8), and it gives emphasis to the slave-master theme announced at 1:1–2.

In 2:12–18 Paul resumes his exhortation with an eye to the Philippians' salvation (v. 12), their divine assistance in this (v. 13) and their harmonious conduct that sets them off from the world (v. 15); therefore, Paul will have reason to boast at the day of Christ (v. 16), which prompts again the theme of joy (vv. 17–18).

2:19–3:1a, Visits to the Philippians. Paul turns his thoughts from the day of Christ to the more immediate future and specifically to his plans to send Timothy (vv. 19–23), Epaphroditus (vv. 25–30), and perhaps himself (v. 24). Announcements of visits by Paul or his associates are typical of his Letters (e.g., Rom. 15:22–29; 1 Cor. 4:17–21).

Paul speaks of Timothy's visit first, but it is Epaphroditus who will leave first, as is clear from Paul's "hopes" of sending Timothy (Phil. 2:19, 23) but the "necessity" of sending Epaphroditus back (v. 25). Consequently, it was Epaphroditus who would have carried the letter to Philippi. What we know of him derives only from this Letter: he was a Philippian Christian who had been commissioned to deliver the gift to Paul (4:18). What made his return necessary was his distress that news had reached Philippi of his near fatal illness (vv. 26–27). Hence when he recovered, Paul hastily sent him back, though not without warm praise for having risked his life in completing his commission (vv. 28–30). His return will be another occasion for joy (vv. 28–29).

Timothy's visit will follow. Paul wants to know more about the situation at Philippi, and Timothy will report back, but Paul does not want to send him until he can say something specific about his own predicament as a prisoner (v. 23). In the meantime Paul prepares for that visit by lavishing on Timothy warm praise, especially for his genuine concern for the Philippians (vv. 20–22). Finally, Paul hints again at his own possible visit (v. 24; cf. 1:26, 27; 2:12).

3:1b–4:1, Paul's Warning and Theological Defense.

At this point the tone and style shift abruptly from joy and exhortation to warning and theological argument. The shift has prompted some to suspect the Letter's integrity, but such abruptness is not uncommon (e.g., 1 Thess. 2:14–16).

The warning is brief: watch out for the dogs; watch out for evil workers; watch out for the program of mutilation (Phil. 3:2). The identity of these "dogs" is not clear, but their vaunting of Jewish credentials (cf. vv. 3–4) and the term "evil workers," which recalls a similar epithet in 2 Cor. 11:13, point to the same (or similar) groups of missionaries Paul had opposed in Corinth and in Galatia. The people are probably not identical to the "opponents" referred to earlier (cf. Phil. 1:28). In any case, this threat allows Paul to set out his own theology by means of assertion, differentiation, and qualification.

In 3:3–11 Paul first asserts that he and his followers represent the true circumcision (in contrast to physical circumcision, which he calls "mutilation" in v. 2), in that he advocates a spiritual worship and a boasting in Christ, not in the flesh (v. 3). Then he explains his views by differentiating them from those of the rival missionaries (vv. 4–11). Paul claims that he has not made a virtue out of necessity, as it were, since he also could boast "in the flesh," as the following biographical statements make clear: circumcised on the eighth day (cf. Gen. 17:12; Lev. 12:3), belonging to the people of Israel and the tribe of Benjamin (cf. Rom. 11:1), a Hebrew born of Hebrews (a difficult phrase, referring either to his pure ethnic stock or to his Jewish culture), a Pharisee according to law (cf. Gal. 1:14), a persecutor of the church out of zeal (cf. 1 Cor. 15:9; Gal. 1:13–14), and blameless in the eyes of the law (Phil. 3:4–6).

Precisely these sorts of boasts, Paul says, now count as nothing because of Christ. The imagery here is economic: what Paul once counted as "profit" or "gain" he now regards as "loss" (vv. 7–8). Indeed, only his master Christ now counts as "gain," so Paul's hope is only in that righteousness which comes from God through faith in Christ's death and resurrection and involves sharing that death and attaining resurrection from the dead (vv. 9–11).

In vv. 12–16 there are so many problems in the manuscript evidence, the words, and the grammar that the exact meaning is hard to determine. Nevertheless, it is clear that Paul is qualifying what he has just said: "Not that I have already received or am already perfect" (v. 12). Instead, using athletic imagery, he says that if he has not attained he is still pursuing the "prize" of the higher calling of God in Christ (v. 14), and that he expects the Philippians to have the same attitude (vv. 15–16).

This higher calling is then contrasted with the earthly things that occupy the thoughts of those whose god is the belly and who glory in their shame (v. 19). Just who these "enemies of the cross of Christ" (v. 18) are is again not clear. But since they apparently indulge the flesh rather than boast in it, they are probably not the missionaries of vv. 2–3; thus they represent a third group endangering the Philippians (1:28). In any case, Paul urges the Philippians to imitate him (v. 17), since their true country is not on earth but in heaven (v. 20). Christological and eschatological formulas follow (v. 21), and the section concludes on the familiar note of joy (4:1).

4:2–9, Specific Exhortations.

The hortatory tone that Paul used in the closing verses of the last, largely theological, section (cf. 3:15–17; 4:1) is again dominant, although now the exhortation is intended for specific individuals. Two women, named Euodia and Syntyche, are urged to be of the same mind (v. 3). The nature of their dispute is lost to us, but the phrase "be of the same mind" recalls that of 2:2 ("be of one mind") and thus links up with the partnership theme (1:5). And Paul calls the women his "fellow athletes in the gospel" (4:3). Accordingly, he may be exhorting them to subordinate their personal disagreement to the broader interests of the partnership to advance the gospel (cf. 1:5). Paul then asks another individual, known only as "yokefellow," to intercede for him in this matter (4:3). The attempt to identify this person has led to many conjectures: Epaphroditus, Timothy, Silvanus, Luke, even Lydia. But we simply do not know.

In 4:4, however, the exhortations become general. There is the now familiar call to be joyful (v. 4). But especially noteworthy here is the rhetorically effective use of repetition and variation that make the concluding exhortation memorable: "Whatever is true, whatever is revered, whatever is just, whatever is pure, whatever is amiable, whatever is reputable, if there is any virtue, if there is any praise—think about these things" (v. 8). These qualities are probably those Paul had in mind but did not specify earlier when he prayed for the Philippians to "approve what really matters" (1:10).

4:10–20, Paul's Thanks for the Philippians' Gift. Earlier in the Letter Paul had occasion to allude to the gift of the Philippians (esp. 2:30; cf. 1:3). Now, however, he takes up the matter directly. And what strikes readers beyond Paul's genuine gratitude is the delicacy of his wording. He alternates between assertion and qualification so as not to be misunderstood.

The section begins on a note of joy, the joy that the Philippians had at length revived their thoughts about him as evidenced by the gift (v. 10). But to avoid the appearance of criticizing them for not thinking about him more often, Paul adds the qualification "but you did not have any opportunity" to do so (v. 10). Then Paul hastens to avoid the counterimpression that he is dependent on them. He is, he claims, "self-sufficient," a term borrowed from popular philosophy (v. 11), for he is equally able to handle abundance and want (v. 12). But then to avoid slighting the gift Paul adds: "Nevertheless, you have done what is right in sharing my affliction" (v. 14).

At this point Paul expands on the gift and the Philippians' relationship with him. He recalls the partnership that he has with them alone in giving and receiving and refers specifically to earlier gifts at Thessalonica (vv. 15–16). But then comes another qualification: "Not that I am seeking the gift . . ." (v. 17). And finally there is a formal acknowledgment, couched first in the language of business: "I am in receipt of everything from you through Epaphroditus" (v. 18). Paul does not specify, but the gift presumably included food and clothing, perhaps writing materials. In any case the section closes with religious language as Paul then refers to the gift as a fragrant offering, an acceptable sacrifice (v. 18). A prayer for the Philippians' needs to be met (v. 19) and a doxology (v. 20) round out the section, and the body of the Letter.

4:21–23
The Closing of the Letter

4:21–22, Greetings. Typical of ancient letters generally and of Paul's Letters in particular are final greetings. The greetings in Romans are very extensive (Rom. 16:3–16), but they are clearly exceptional. Usually the exchange of greetings is brief, as here (see also 1 Cor. 16:19–21; 2 Cor. 13:12; 1 Thess. 5:26–27; Philem. 23–24). Of special note are the greetings from the "household of Caesar" (Phil. 4:22), a phrase that refers not to the imperial family itself but to the slaves, freedmen, and other members of the emperor's staff, and not only in Rome but everywhere imperial administration was conducted. Specifically, those sending greetings may have had some connection with a Roman colony like Philippi or may have been the soldiers guarding Paul (cf. 1:13).

4:23, Final Prayer. This Letter closes on a liturgical note, as do all Paul's Letters. Indeed, the benediction here is identical to that in Philemon 25 (cf. Gal. 6:18; 1 Thess. 5:28).

Bibliography

Collange, J.-F. *The Epistle of Saint Paul to the Philippians*. London: Epworth, 1979.

Kümmel, W. G. *Introduction to the New Testament*. 2d ed. Nashville: Abingdon, 1975. Pp. 320–35.

Martin, R. P. *Carmen Christi: Philippians 2:5–11 in Recent Interpretation and in the Setting of Early Christian Worship*. Rev. ed. Grand Rapids, MI: Eerdmans, 1983.

———. *Philippians*. New Century Bible Commentary. Grand Rapids, MI: Eerdmans, 1983.

Sampley, J. P. *Pauline Partnership in Christ: Christian Community and Commitment in Light of Roman Law*. Philadelphia: Fortress, 1980.

COLOSSIANS

J. CHRISTIAAN BEKER

INTRODUCTION

Authorship

The church in Colossae was not founded by Paul but by Epaphras, a disciple of the apostle (1:7–8; 4:12–13). The Letter of Paul to the Colossians makes clear that the Colossians "have not seen my face" (2:1) and that Paul has only received reports about them from Epaphras (1:4, 7, 8). Colossae was a city in Asia Minor, located in the valley of the Lycus River. Originally an important trading center, it was soon overshadowed by its neighboring cities, Hierapolis and Laodicea (4:13, 15–16), and disappears from history after it was hit by an earthquake in ca. A.D. 60 (→ Colossae).

The Letter to the Colossians presents itself as a letter written by Paul while he was in prison (1:24; 4:3, 10, 18). However, the language and style of the Letter strongly suggest its post-Pauline origin. The peculiarities of language and style cannot simply be explained by appealing to the special situation that Paul faces in his debate with the Colossian heretics, especially because Paul's typical vocabulary is absent—terms such as "righteousness," "justification," "freedom," "law," "believe," and "justify," which are regularly used by him in polemical situations.

Colossians was most likely written by a pupil of Paul's who wanted to make sure that after Paul's death his apostolic authority and presence were continued in Paul's missionary territory in Asia Minor.

Thus he writes a Pauline letter, very much in the manner of Paul when he could not be personally present in his churches (1:9; 2:1; 4:7, 8, 18). The author shows acquaintance with some of Paul's letters, especially with Romans—cf. the similarity between Rom. 6:1–11 and Col. 2:11–13; 3:5–11—although Paul's Letter to Philemon is the only one on which the author is directly dependent (cf. the list of Paul's co-workers [Philem. 23, 24] in 4:10–17).

The Colossian Heresy

The Letter presupposes a crisis situation in the Colossian church. False Christian teachers have infiltrated the predominantly gentile Christian community and threaten to subvert its loyalty to Christ. The situation is formally analogous to that in Galatia, where Paul also had to insist on an exclusive commitment of the Galatians to "Christ alone" against Christian teachers who deemed it necessary to supplement the confession to Christ with obedience to the Jewish Torah. However, although both Galatians and Colossians focus on the exclusivity of Christ over against supplemental religious practices, the heretical front in the two Letters is quite dissimilar. To be sure, Colossians gives us no precise picture of the heretics' teaching. Still, references to it in 2:6–23 suggest a blending of various religious elements: asceticism and moral rigorism combine with features of esoteric rites similar to those practiced by mystery religions. This type of syncretism was characteristic of the Phrygian region of Asia Minor, where Colossae, Hierapolis, and Laodicea were located.

Scholars have traced Phrygian syncretism from the third century B.C. to the Christian movement called Montanism in the second century A.D. Its ascetic features are mentioned in 2:16, 18, 21–23: "food," "drink" (2:16); "self-abasement" (2:18); "do not handle, do not taste, do not touch" (2:21); and "rigor of devotion, self-abasement, severity to the body" (2:23). Moreover, asceticism is combined not only with "mystery" elements but also with other kinds of observance: "angel worship" (2:18); "visions" (2:18); "festival" (2:16); "new moon" (2:16); and "Sabbath" (2:16).

Thus, it seems likely that certain Jewish-Hellenistic features formed part of the syncretistic mix, although it is difficult to be precise on this point. There is no polemic against the Torah in Colossians. Moreover, the worship of angels (2:18) militates against a Jewish provenance of the Colossian heresy. The connections that have been made between Colossians and Qumran with respect to "angelic communion" are too speculative to be convincing. It is quite possible that the observance of the calendar is not due to Jewish practices, but to the influence of the moon-god, Men, who was popular in the Colossian region.

The Letter refers as well to "the elements of the world" (Gk. *ta stoicheia tou kosmou;* 2:8, 20). Although the precise meaning of this phrase is unclear, it certainly refers to an aspect of the Colossian heresy. Two possible interpretations suggest themselves: the author either lifts the term from the vocabulary of the heretics or he coins it himself as an antiheretical slogan.

COMMENTARY

1:1-8
Introduction

After a greeting in Paul's customary style (1:1–2), the thanksgiving clause (1:3–8) underscores two issues. First, the author gives thanks for the faithful reception of the gospel in the Colossian community as preached to them by Paul's disciple, Epaphras, and he stresses with a triadic formula the faith, love, and hope of the Colossians. Second, the author "Paul" emphasizes the worldwide impact of the gospel (1:6) so as to remind the local church about its ecumenical stature.

1:9-2:23
The Didactic Section

The paragraphs 1:9–2:5 form one sequential unit and constitute the foundation for the antiheretical polemic of 2:6–23. Thus 1:9 marks the beginning of the didactic section.

1:9-14, The Intercession and Thanksgiving. The intercession (1:9–11) is intimately connected to the general thanksgiving (1:12–14) by means of a participial clause ("giving thanks," 1:12). The thanksgiving makes frequent use of traditional Christian material. It employs in both vv. 13 and 14 a liturgical baptismal formula (cf. the shift from "you" in v. 12 to "us" and "we" in vv. 13 and 14). Baptismal language is present as well in the opposition of the two dominions, "darkness" and "the kingdom"—a transfer caused by the punctual act of God's saving deliverance in Christ (as shown by the tense of the Gk. verbs in v. 13). Moreover, the unusual phrase "his beloved Son" (v. 13) is reminiscent of baptismal phraseology (Mark 1:11; cf. 9:7; 12:6; Eph. 1:6); so is the interpretation of "redemption" as "forgiveness of sins" (Col. 1:14; cf. Acts 2:38; 10:43, 47; Mark 1:4).

1:15-20, The Christ Hymn. The author has used a Christian hymn known in the Colossian community in the service of his antiheretical polemic. (For similar early Christian poems about Jesus, cf. John 1:1–18 and Phil. 2:6–11.)

The hymn consists of two strophes or stanzas (vv. 15–18a; vv. 18b–20) and celebrates Christ as the unique mediator of creation (vv. 15–18a) and of redemption (vv. 18b–20). The hymn strongly affirms the reality of the created world: the figure of wisdom—celebrated in Prov. 8:22–31 as the mediator of creation—is here transferred to Christ: "in him," "through him," and "for him," "all things" (or "the universe") "were created" (v. 16).

By tracing the manner in which the author edits the traditional hymn, we ascertain how he desires it to be understood. He not only inserts the words "the church" in v. 18a and the phrase "that in everything he might become preeminent" in v. 18b, but he also adds the words "by the blood of his cross" to the clause "making peace whether on earth or in heaven" in v. 20. By means of these insertions the author wants to correct the exclusive reference of the hymn to Christ's exaltation, as well as the purely cosmic meaning of the phrase "the head of the body" (v. 18). Therefore, the author stresses Christ not only as the head of the church (v. 18a) but also as the crucified savior (v. 20). Moreover, the insertion in v. 18 amends the static quality of the hymn by giving it a dynamic referent toward the historical future.

1:21-23, The New Status of Christians. The author's interpretation of the Christ hymn must be understood not only in terms of these inserts into the hymn itself but also in terms of the framework in which he places the hymn. The author corrects not only the static character of the hymn but also supplements it with direct applications to the human plight and its need for salvation. He does so not only by referring to readers' baptisms and the forgiveness of their sins in 1:12–14 but also by reminding them of their new status in Christ (vv. 21–23).

1:24-2:5, Paul's Ministry. This section celebrates not only the worldwide significance of Paul's apostolate but also his sufferings for the cause of the gospel. Verse 23 sets the stage for the subsequent paragraphs: "the gospel —which has been preached to every creature under heaven and of which I, Paul, became a minister." Paul's image is painted in universal colors just as "the gospel" (1:5) is for the author identical with the Pauline gospel. Paul is not only the apostle par excellence whose authority equals that of the gospel (vv. 23–29) but also the martyr who incarnates in his ministry "the afflictions of Christ" (v. 24) and who is now imprisoned for the sake of the gospel (1:23; 4:3, 10, 18; cf. Eph. 6:20).

2:6-23, The Antiheretical Polemic. This unit constitutes the center of the Letter: the argument intertwines confessional statements with antiheretical polemic. The section must be subdivided into three paragraphs: first, a Christian imperative (vv. 6, 7); second, the indicative of God's victory in Christ (vv. 8–15); third, the futility of the heretical demands (vv. 16–23).

The key to the argument can be summarized as "Christ alone": Christ represents not only the total fullness of God, but also the all-sufficient fullness of life and salvation for Christians (v. 10; cf. vv. 11–15, 17, 19). The

1227

"Pauline" gospel does not proclaim a deficient Christology (an understanding of Jesus' identity)—as the heretics charge. Rather, the heretics' insistence on supplementing Christ with other divine agencies constitutes a betrayal of the triumph of Christ, because those supplements to the gospel honor, in fact, those angelic powers and principalities that Christ has annulled in his death and resurrection (v. 15). And if "Christ alone" is the exclusive basis of Christian life, the worship of powers in addition to Christ manifests a religious anxiety and uncertainty on the part of Christians that contradicts the joyful thanksgiving (1:11b, 12; 3:15) and knowledge and wisdom (1:10, 28; 2:3; 3:16) of Christian life.

Therefore, imperatives of exclusive commitment to Christ abound in this section (cf. vv. 6, 8, 16, 18; cf. also the question of v. 20). These imperatives are not legalistic demands for perfection. Rather these demands flow naturally from the pure gift of God's liberating act in Christ.

Thus, it is clear that the section 1:9–2:23 constitutes the basic didactic and thematic unit of the Letter. It consists of two interrelated parts: the Christian foundation for the antiheretical argument (1:9–2:5) and the basic antiheretical argument itself (2:6–23).

3:1–4:6
The Exhortation

Whereas the didactic section (1:9–2:23) focuses on "the presence of the reality of Christ," the theme of the following section (3:1–4:6) is "the reality of Christ in Christian life." This type of unit scholars often call parenesis (a term in Greek rhetoric for moral advice and exhortation).

3:1–4, The Risen Christ and the Christian Life. The unit opens with a transitional paragraph (3:1–4) that connects 1:9–2:23 with the more specific mandates of 3:5–4:6. The opening phrase "If then you have been raised with Christ" (3:1a) is parallel to the phrase "If with Christ you have died" (2:20; cf. its repetition in 3:3) and follows from it, so that it seems that 2:20–3:4 forms a coherent unit. Nevertheless, the exhortations of 3:1a–2 ("seek the things that are above" [v. 1a]; "set your mind on things that are above, not on things that are on earth" [v. 2], which will be explicated in 3:5–17, transcend with their general ethical thrust the specificity of the antiheretical polemic of 2:20–23. Therefore, it is preferable to view 3:1–4 as the beginning of a new section, which provides the Christological foundation for the imperatives of 3:1a, 2 and of 3:5–17.

The section 3:1–4 shows that—notwithstanding the Letter's emphasis on the already accomplished "risen" status of Christians with Christ (2:12; 3:1) and notwithstanding its exhortation "to seek the things that are above" (v. 1) and "to set your minds not on things that are on earth" (v. 2)—the author does not contemplate a spiritualistic flight from the world. Rather, he insists on Christian life within the boundaries and conditions of this world. Indeed, the household code of 3:18–4:1 emphasizes orderly relations of Christians in church and world—in marriage, family, and work. Moreover, although the author interprets the resurrection of Christians with Christ as an already accomplished fact (2:11–12; 3:1), the author points in 3:3–4 to Christian life as an historical pilgrimage and not as a static "heavenly" condition. The author stresses that the present life of Christians "in Christ" (2:10) is nevertheless a "hidden life" that must await its full manifestation at the Parousia, the end-time appearance of Christ when Christians will be joined to him in glory (v. 4).

3:5–17, Mandate for a New Morality. The unit 3:5–17 draws specific exhortations from the Christological indicatives of 3:1, 3, 4 and, therefore, fills out the content of v. 2 ("set your minds on things that are above, not on things that are on earth").

3:5–11, The Old Morality. Imperatives abound in this section (vv. 5, 8, 9, 12, 15 twice, 16; cf. also the participles that have the force of imperatives in vv. 13 twice, 14, 16 twice, 17). The author reminds his readers of the numerous sins associated with "the old nature" (v. 9) and points to the new reality of Christian life in which all people are equal in Christ (v. 11).

3:12–14, The New Morality. The author complements the essentially negative exhortations of 3:5–11 with a list of Christian virtues in 3:12–14, climaxing with his striking definition of love as "the bond of perfection" (v. 14).

He parallels the double series of five vices in vv. 5 and 8 (pagan sins of the past in v. 5; ecclesial sins as present temptations in v. 8) with a series of five virtues in v. 12—all of which, it should be noticed, refer to interhuman social relations.

3:15–17, The New Worship. The section closes with what reads like a Pauline Letter ending: a wish for peace, emphasizing communal worship and a Christian life-style, framed by a twofold stress on thankfulness (vv. 15–17).

3:18–4:6, The Household Codes. The household code explicates the basic principle of 3:17: "And whatever you do, in word or deed, do everything in the name of the Lord Jesus, giving thanks to God the Father through him." In other words, the author has applied a household code—current in Hellenistic-Roman culture to regulate relations within the family between husbands, wives, children, and slaves —to the *church* as the new "house of God" (cf. the development of this notion in Eph. 2:19–20). The author adds an exhortation to the Colossians to pray for themselves and for the mission of the imprisoned apostle (4:2–6).

4:7–18
Final Greetings

The Letter ends with personal information to be communicated by the conveyors of the Letter, Tychicus and Onesimus (vv. 7–9), and with greetings of Paul's co-workers (vv. 10–18; a list of six names almost identical with the list of Philem. 23–24).

Bibliography

Crouch, J. E. *The Origin and Intention of the Colossian Haustafel.* Forschungen zur Religion und Literatur des Alten und Neuen Testaments, 109. Göttingen: Vandenhoeck & Ruprecht, 1972.

de Boer, M. "Images of Paul in the Post-Apostolic Period." *Catholic Biblical Quarterly* 42 (1980): 359–80.

Francis, F. O., and W. A. Meeks. *Conflict at Colossae.* Missoula, MT: Scholars Press, 1975.

Lightfoot, J. B. *St. Paul's Epistles to the Colossians and to Philemon.* Grand Rapids, MI: Zondervan, 1959. Originally published in 1876.

Lohse, E. *Colossians and Philemon.* Hermeneia. Philadelphia: Fortress, 1971.

Moule, C. F. D. *The Epistles of Paul the Apostle to the Colossians and to Philemon.* Cambridge: Cambridge University Press, 1957.

1 THESSALONIANS

PHEME PERKINS

INTRODUCTION

The First Letter of Paul to the Thessalonians is probably the earliest of Paul's Letters (A.D. 50 or 51). Thessalonica was one of the two most important trading centers in Roman Greece. It had a harbor on the Thermic Gulf, lay near the midpoint of the Via Egnatia, and was the terminus of the road leading up to the Danube. Although it was the Roman capital of Macedonia, Thessalonica remained a free Greek city with its own council and coinage (→ Thessalonica).

Paul had founded the church there after preaching in Philippi (2:2). Acts 17:1–10 pictures a relatively brief mission in Thessalonica, which was centered in the Jewish community. Conflict led to rioting and accusations before the city officials, politarchs (Acts 17:6; a term peculiar to Thessalonica), that Paul was causing trouble by preaching another king than Caesar. 1 Thessalonians suggests Paul stayed in the city for a longer period of time, since he was able to practice his trade (2:9) and had received financial help from Philippi ninety-five miles away (Phil. 4:16). Paul writes to a church composed of gentile converts (1 Thess. 1:9–10; 2:14?), a fact that coincides with Paul's assertion that his mission was to the Gentiles (Gal. 2:9). If Acts is correct at least in reporting that Paul was suddenly forced out of the city, the concern evident in 1 Thess. 2:17–18 may be due to Paul's unexpected departure. Unable to return (due to health? cf. 2 Cor. 12:7), Paul sent Timothy north from Athens (1 Thess. 3:1–3). Timothy has rejoined Paul (at Corinth? cf. Acts 18:5) with a good report about the church. 1 Thessalonians is written in response. Paul does not refer to churches founded after Thessalonica, so it would appear that the Letter was written within some months of Paul's departure from Thessalonica.

1 Thessalonians follows the conventional pattern of Paul's Letters: (a) greetings, from the apostle and associates (1:1); (b) thanksgiving (1:2–10); (c) Letter body, with eschatological conclusion (2:1–3:13); (d) exhortations (4:1–5:24); (e) final blessing and greetings (5:25–28). The Letter's peculiar elements may be related to its setting. Paul does not identify himself with a formulaic phrase indicating his apostolic role and carries elements of thanksgiving through the body of the Letter (2:13; 3:7–10).

The text of 1 Thessalonians presents impor-tant variants in 2:7 and 3:2. In 1 Thess. 2:7 a number of early Greek manuscripts read nēpi-oi, "babes," in the phrase "we were babes among you." Others have the word ēpioi, "gentle," which only occurs elsewhere in the NT in 2 Tim. 2:24. Since Paul uses nēpioi elsewhere in his Letters, the reading ēpioi, "gentle," though less frequently attested would seem to be preferred. A reading with "gentle" also suits the imagery Paul is using in this verse. In 1 Thess. 3:2, Timothy is variously described as "God's fellow worker," "God's servant," and in an attempt to harmonize the divergent readings as "God's servant and our fellow worker." The expression "God's fellow servant," though less frequently attested than "God's servant" seems to be the one that causes the most difficulty and underlies the compound phrase. Paul does refer to himself and Apollos as "God's fellow workers" in 1 Cor. 3:9. Therefore, that reading may be preferred.

The most difficult textual question in 1 Thessalonians does not derive from divergent readings in the manuscripts but from the suggestions of modern scholars that 2:13–16 are a later interpolation into the Letter. The passage evokes thanksgiving for the Thessalonians' reception of Paul's preaching and then launches into a harsh condemnation of the "Jews" as Jesus killers, as enemies of God and God's prophets and apostles, and as experiencing God's wrath. Although Paul can speak of his own sufferings at the hands of both Jews and Gentiles (e.g., 2 Cor. 11:26; Rom. 15:31) and has just suffered at Philippi (1 Thess. 2:2), the vindictive tone of this passage is not characteristic of the apostle. Paul's earlier reference to the exemplary imitation of the apostle by the Thessalonians when they received the gospel message in affliction (1:6) has already treated the general subject of this passage. The harsh treatment of the "Jews" in this passage, some scholars argue, would be less surprising in a Christian writing after the destruction of Jerusalem in A.D. 70 (e.g., Matt. 21:33–46). Some scholars have argued for a non-Pauline interpolation here on the basis of computer analyses of the language of this section. They indicate that the section reflects an amalgamation of different Pauline expressions. Scholars who continue to treat this passage as part of the original Letter insist that it reflects Paul's response to a particular group of persecutors familiar to himself and the audience.

COMMENTARY

1:1–10
Greetings and Thanksgiving

1:1, Greetings. Paul includes his co-workers, Timothy and Silvanus, as senders of the Letter. Timothy has just returned from Thessalonica. Acts 17:4 mentions Silas (= Silvanus) as Paul's assistant in the Thessalonian mission. The greeting combines the conventional Greek expression "grace" with the Jewish "peace."

1:2–10, Thanksgiving. The expanded thanksgiving for the recipients is a Pauline innovation in the letter form, which commonly began with a more abbreviated and formal wish for the well-being of the recipient and sometimes mentioned that of the sender. Paul's thanksgivings often single out themes to be developed in the Letter. Here we find Paul emphasizing the faith, love, and hope of the Thessalonians (v. 3). That God has chosen them is evident not only in the success of Paul's preaching but also in their willingness to provide an example for other churches by rejoicing when their conversion entailed suffering. In that way they can claim to imitate both the apostle and the Lord (vv. 5–7). It may be that the Philippians who sent Paul aid at Philippi were responsible for spreading the story of the Thessalonians' conversion in the rest of Greece. Paul appears to have taught his converts that suffering was to be expected as a normal part of Christian life (e.g., Rom. 5:3; 12:12; Phil. 4:14). Since Christians know that they are "imitating" the apostle in suffering, suffering does not count against their conviction that they are beloved and chosen by God.

1 Thess. 1:9b–10 concludes the thanksgiving with an early creedal formula that expresses the meaning of conversion for gentile converts. They turn away from idols to the true God (cf. Gal. 4:9; 2 Cor. 3:16, in an OT citation; Acts 3:19; 9:35; 11:21), and they await Jesus' coming from heaven at the judgment. Because they have turned to serving the true God, the Thessalonians will not face the wrath of God, which would come against all those non-Jews who "do not know God" (cf. Rom. 1:18–32). Since this sentence is not Pauline in its phrasing, it was probably a formula that was commonly used in the early Christian mission to the Gentiles.

2:1–3:13
Paul's Ministry in Thessalonica

2:1–12, Paul's Example in Thessalonica. Paul reminds his readers of the example he had set in preaching among them. He uses the imag-

ery of a philosophic preacher, whose concern is to nurture the souls of human beings and turn them away from slavery to false opinions, values, and passions to the truth. Paul also wants to remind the Thessalonians that his mission was different from other popular preachers who might flatter and manipulate their audiences to make money from such preaching. Paul preaches the gospel he has been given by God in the face of great opposition and hardship (vv. 1–5).

Paul uses the images of a nurse (v. 7) and a father (vv. 11–12) to describe his work among the Thessalonians. These images were frequently used by philosophers of Paul's day to show how the true philosopher would vary his style of speech from harsh scolding to gentle encouragement and consolation as the needs of the audience changed. Paul has intensified these images in two ways. He describes himself as a gentle nurse taking care of her own children, not merely someone else's. Before he introduces the image of "father," Paul makes it clear that his love for the Thessalonians goes so far that he is willing to share not just the gospel but "our own selves." Paul shares himself by laboring at his trade rather than requiring the congregation to support him (vv. 8–9). Paul concludes with the kinds of speech he had used in encouraging the Thessalonians to live lives worthy of God (vv. 11–12). In addition to such preaching, Paul's own life and conduct, which is "holy, righteous, and blameless" (v. 10), is meant to be an example followed by his converts (e.g., 1:6).

2:13–16, Excursus on Persecution. Some scholars think that this sharp condemnation of "the Jews" as Jesus killers and opponents of God was added to the Letter by a later disciple of Paul (see "Introduction" above). However, Paul does refer to his own efforts, before his conversion, to wipe out the followers of Jesus (Gal. 1:13; 1 Cor. 15:9). He distinguishes the "remnant," both Jewish and gentile believers, from the "vessels of wrath" upon whom the Lord's sentence will be like that against Sodom and Gomorrah (Rom. 9:22–29). He refers to the "remnant" that was not guilty of "killing the prophets" in Elijah's time (Rom. 11:3, citing 1 Kings 19:10). Paul also refers to Jewish unbelief making them "enemies of God" for the sake of the Gentiles who have come to believe (Rom. 11:28). Elsewhere Paul speaks of Judaizing Christians as "enemies of the cross of Christ" and predicts the destruction that awaits them (Phil. 3:18–19). In that context he contrasts such false believers with those to whom he writes. They are exhorted to imitate the apostle, who shares Christ's sufferings, so that they will share the same glorious transformation into Christ (Phil. 3:10–11, 17, 20–21). It is possible to see this section as an interruption in the train of thought of the Letter, perhaps provoked by a particular incident the Thessalonians had endured (1 Thess. 2:14).

The expression in 1 Thess. 2:16b is very close to one used in the conclusion to an account of the many sins of the Shechemites in *T. Levi* 6:11 (→Pseudepigrapha). It may have been an established expression for divine retribution against notorious sinners that did not require a reference to a specific event. Other scholars, who consider the rest of the section Pauline, think that this phrase was added by a later scribe, alluding to the destruction of Jerusalem.

2:17–20, Paul's Desire to See the Thessalonians. Paul returns to his account of the affectionate relationship between himself and the church. The Greek word *aporphanizō,* "made orphans" (RSV: "were bereft," v. 17), can refer to parents who have lost children or vice versa. Since Paul speaks of Satan as the cause of his chronic illness (2 Cor. 12:7), that may have been the reason he was unable to journey back to Thessalonica. Paul's concern for the well-being of the community is not merely grounded in affection, he also considers his churches to be the "evidence" that he has carried out the mission God gave him, which will be presented at the judgment (1 Thess. 2:19–20).

3:1–5, Timothy Is Sent to Thessalonica. Paul sends his trusted associate Timothy (cf. 1 Cor. 4:17; 16:10–11; Phil. 2:19–23) to strengthen and encourage the church. He is concerned that trials may have "disturbed" the community (1 Thess. 3:3). Rather than upset the church, the coming of such trials should confirm Paul's preaching, since he predicted that they would be the destiny of Christians. Nevertheless, they could have served as Satan's way of undermining their faith and destroying Paul's mission.

3:6–10, Timothy's Report on the Church. According to Acts 18:5, Timothy met Paul in Corinth. There he delivered a glowing report about the faith and love of the Thessalonians. They return Paul's feelings of affection. As a result Paul is comforted in his own afflictions (cf. Rom. 1:12; 2 Cor. 7:4, 13; Philem. 7).

3:11–13, Paul's Prayer for the Thessalonians. Paul expresses his thanksgiving and joy in prayer for his converts and expresses his hope of being reunited with them. While the previous section has emphasized their faith, these verses shift to love and holiness. The love that they have seen in the apostle is to extend not only to fellow Christians but to all people (v. 12). Love is the basis of that holiness which will make the Christians acceptable to God in the judgment (cf. love as fulfillment of the law in Gal. 5:14; Rom.

13:10). This emphasis on love and holiness (cf. 1 Thess. 2:10; 4:3, 7; 5:23) forms the transition to the hortatory part of the Letter.

4:1–12
Live a Life of Holiness

4:1–8, Holiness and Sexuality. 1 Thess. 4:1–12 expands on themes taken from a tradition of interpreting the laws in Leviticus 17–26 in Hellenistic Judaism. Parallels to this material are found in 1 Pet. 1:1–2:3, 11–12. "Holiness" is an attribute that distinguishes the elect community from the world around it. Paul has already taught them that Christian life requires abandoning the sexual immorality and lust that Jewish moralists associated with the pagan world (e.g., Wisd. of Sol. 14–15). Paul uses the peculiar word *skeuos* (Gk., "vessel") in v. 4 to refer to the wife (cf. 1 Pet. 3:7). It is not clear whether the advice to "take a vessel in holiness and honor" simply means that Christians should marry (e.g., 1 Cor. 7:2) or whether it also refers to teaching about sexual conduct within marriage (e.g., 1 Cor. 7:3–5). Pagan moralists often insisted that even within marriage sexuality should remain subject to reason. Marriage was not to be an occasion for "lust." 1 Thess. 4:6 enjoins that no one wrong his brother "in this thing/business." If the context of the passage is still sexuality, then the offense would appear to be adultery. Other exegetes rely on the fact that the Greek word *pragma* can also mean "business" and that the verb for "defraud," *pleonektein,* also appears in commercial contexts. They argue that Paul has shifted to speak about relationships of the small traders at Thessalonica. (1 Cor. 6 combines issues of lawsuits between Christians and the sexual immorality of visiting prostitutes.)

4:9–12, Mutual Love. When Paul returns to the theme of mutual love, he encourages the Thessalonians to live a life of "quietness," "minding one's own affairs," following the apostle's example by working with their hands so as to command respect and depend on no one. Many of these themes can be traced in pagan moralists. Some of the social ideals of a group of mutual friends who live quietly and are not dependent on others were particularly evident in the Epicurean groups (→ Epicureans). Along with the love that is to be directed to those outside the group (3:12), these verses show us the early church seeking to map out its place in the social world of the Greco-Roman cities. But Christian love is not motivated by the utilitarian desire for a pleasant life expressed in Epicureanism. Instead, Paul coins the expression "*theodidaktos*" (Gk., "taught of God") to emphasize its divine origin.

4:13–5:11
The Coming of the Lord

4:13–18, Hope for the Dead. Paul now turns to the third virtue he mentioned in 1:3, hope. He adopts the philosophic idea of a "letter of consolation" to Christian use. Such writings often parallel the language of epitaphs. Death is described as sleep; the deceased has been snatched from the world of the living; grief should be moderated by the recognition that nothing from this world can touch the dead. At the same time, the living are reminded that they will soon join those who have died. A few scholars think that the persecutions mentioned in 1 Thessalonians led to the death of members of the community. The Thessalonians may have thought that the dead had lost the possibility of salvation when the Lord returns (v. 15).

Paul's Christian "consolation" expands the basic belief that the Lord has been raised (v. 14; cf. 1:10) with an apocalyptic tradition derived from Jesus (vv. 16–17ab; cf. Dan. 7:13; Mark 13:26–27; Matt. 24:31; 1 Cor. 15:52). Paul's formulation of this tradition reverses the pessimistic language of pagan epitaphs. They spoke of the dead being "snatched" from life. Paul speaks of the living being "snatched" to join the Lord and the deceased members of the community who have gone before them (1 Thess. 4:17). What Paul intends by this image is not clear: do the risen Christians then descend to earth with the Lord or are they taken into heaven? Elsewhere Paul speaks of those alive at the Parousia—the glorious return of Jesus—being instantaneously transformed (1 Cor. 15:51–53). Here, he may be thinking of the image of the crowd going out to welcome a royal dignitary at his "appearance" (Gk. *parousia*).

5:1–11, When Will the Day of the Lord Come? Paul continues to remind the Thessalonians about the coming of the Lord with a collection of images that were common in early Christian apocalyptic literature. Although he believes that the Lord will return soon, the tradition of the Lord's coming like a "thief in the night" (cf. Luke 12:39–40; Matt. 24:43; Rev. 3:3; 16:15; 2 Pet. 3:10) makes it impossible to calculate "when" the Lord is to return. The Day is as inevitable as labor pains (cf. Jer. 6:24; 22:23; Mic. 4:9; 1 Enoch 62:4; Mark 13:8) even though the people are thinking that all is peaceful and secure (cf. Jer. 6:14; 8:11; Ezek. 13:10; Mic. 3:9–11). The true Christian response is to always be "ready" (cf. Mark 13:32–35; Matt. 24:42–43). The contrast between "sons of light" and "sons of darkness" is used to distinguish those who lived according to God's will from those who do not.

The image of putting on military armor comes from Isa. 59:17. There God puts on the breastplate of righteousness and the helmet of salvation as he is about to come in judgment (cf. Wisd. of Sol. 5:17–20). Paul has adapted this image to the three virtues: faith, love, and hope. The reminder that our destiny is to be "with the Lord" and the call to encourage one another (1 Thess. 4:9–11) pick up the conclusion to the previous section (4:17c–18).

5:12–28
Community Life

5:12–22, Relationships with Others. Paul now returns to the more general theme of the relationships that should characterize the "holiness" of a Christian community. Many of these themes will be repeated in other Pauline exhortations such as Rom. 12:3–18: respect leaders (1 Thess. 5:12–13a; Rom. 12:3–8); be at peace (1 Thess. 5:13b; Rom. 12:18); help the weak (1 Thess. 5:14b; Rom. 14:1); do not repay evil for evil but do good to all (1 Thess. 5:15; Rom. 12:17a); rejoice (1 Thess. 5:16; Rom. 12:12a); pray unceasingly, give thanks (1 Thess. 5:17–18; Rom. 12:12c; cf. Eph. 5:20); do not quench the Spirit (1 Thess. 5:19; Rom. 12:11b); do not despise prophecy but test it (1 Thess. 5:20–21a; prophecy as a gift in the church, Rom. 12:6); and hold to the good and avoid evil (1 Thess. 5:21b–22; Rom. 12:9b). The only unusual element in this exhortation is admonishing the *ataktos* (1 Thess. 5:14a). The Greek word appears in papyri with the sense of loafing around when one ought to be working. This verse would seem to repeat Paul's admonition of 4:11 that Christians ought to work for their living and not be dependent upon others (e.g., wealthy patrons).

5:23–28, Final Prayer and Greetings. The Letter concludes with Paul's final prayer that God will keep the community in holiness until the coming of the Lord (vv. 23–24). The Thessalonians are to reciprocate by praying for the apostle (v. 25). This Letter is to be read at the meetings of the community (vv. 26–27).

Bibliography

Best, E. *The First and Second Epistles to the Thessalonians.* New York: Harper & Row, 1972.

Bruce, F. F. *1 and 2 Thessalonians.* Word Biblical Commentary, 45. Waco, TX: Word, 1982.

Malherbe, A. J. *Paul and the Thessalonians: The Philosophic Tradition of Pastoral Care.* Philadelphia: Fortress, 1987.

Marshall, I. H. *1 and 2 Thessalonians.* New Century Bible Commentary. Grand Rapids, MI: Eerdmans, 1983.

Reese, J. M. *1 and 2 Thessalonians.* New Testament Message, 16. Wilmington, DE: Glazier, 1979.

2 THESSALONIANS

PHEME PERKINS

INTRODUCTION

The Second Letter of Paul to the Thessalonians is written to deal with two problems that have arisen in the church: first, misinterpretations of teachings that claim to be Pauline and yet insist that "the day of the Lord has come" (2:2), and second, the conduct of persons who reject Paul's teaching about working and living quietly (3:6–12). Both of these themes were addressed in the parenesis of 1 Thessalonians (1 Thess. 4:13–5:11, on the day of the Lord; 4:11 and 5:14, on working and not living "idly"). In addition, the church continues to suffer tribulations (2 Thess. 1:5–10; cf. 1 Thess. 1:6; 2:14–16), which may contribute to the confusion about Paul's teaching.

Although 2 Thessalonians elaborates on themes from 1 Thessalonians and concludes with a sharp assertion of Pauline authenticity (3:17), a number of scholars doubt that Paul himself composed the Letter. When Paul refers to his own writing elsewhere, he does so in a disciplinary context (Gal. 6:11; 1 Cor. 16:21) or a contractual one (Philem. 19), not as a sign of authenticity. The opening greeting, 2 Thess. 1:1–2, is almost identical with 1 Thess. 1:1, something not found elsewhere in Paul's Letters. The insertion of teaching on tribulation and divine vengeance in the thanksgiving is peculiar (contrast its location in 1 Thess. 2:13–16). 2 Thessalonians treats faith and love in the thanksgiving but omits hope. The expression "steadfastness of hope in our Lord Jesus Christ" from 1 Thess. 1:3 appears to be rendered "steadfastness of Christ" in 2 Thess. 3:5. Comparing the two Letters, one also finds a dominant theme of the first, personal affection between the apostle and the church, missing from the second. The themes of imitation and holiness appear only briefly (2 Thess. 2:13; 3:7). Yet, they were repeated in the earlier exhortation. We have further evidence for a link between confusion over the coming of the Lord and misinterpretation of Pauline letters in 2 Pet. 3:15–17. There interpretation of Paul's letters is associated with interpretation of "other scriptures." 2 Thessalonians seems to reflect a somewhat earlier situation. People are making false claims about letters and other "words" said to come from the apostle, but Paul's letters do not yet form an independent group of authoritative writings. 2 Thessalonians is presented as an authoritative teaching of Paul in its own right.

There are three major textual variants in 2 Thessalonians. In many manuscripts 2 Thess. 2:3 reads "man of sin" instead of "man of lawlessness." That reading may have arisen out of an attempt to clarify the apocalyptic idea of rebellion against God implied in the expression "lawlessness." 2 Thess. 2:13 has variant readings attached to the expression "God chose you." Some manuscripts have "as first fruits"; others "from the beginning." Modern editors and translators remain divided over which reading is preferred. Either could be Pauline. Often "as first fruits" (= "first converts") is rejected because it does not make sense in the context. 2 Thess. 3:16 reads "in every way" in some manuscripts and "in every place" in others. Creating the parallel "time/place" by dropping a consonant would appear to account for the second reading.

COMMENTARY

1:1–12
Greetings and Thanksgiving

1:1–2, Greetings. 2 Thessalonians copies the greeting of 1 Thess. 1:1 with the substitution of "our" for "the" in the phrase "in God our Father" and a repetition of the modifying phrase from the first clause to bring the grace and peace clause into balance.

1:3–12, Thanksgiving. The thanksgiving consists in a single sentence, which can be divided into three sections: vv. 3–4, 5–10, and 11–12. Verses 3–4 give thanks for the growth of faith and love in persecution. The references to faith, love, and steadfastness recall 1 Thess. 1:3. The afflictions that made the community an example for all the churches in Macedonia and Achaia (1 Thess. 1:8–9) have become the content of the apostle's boast "in the churches" (v. 4).

Verses 5–10 describe God's judgment against persecutors. The author turns to an apocalyptic theology of divine vengeance to show that persecutions are a "sign" (RSV: "evidence") that those who suffer are actually God's elect. According to this view, afflictions suffered by the righteous blot out their transgressions. The righteous will not have to suffer at the judgment. Therefore Israel's afflictions are seen as a sign of God's election (e.g., *Pss. Sol.* 13:9–10; 2 Macc. 6:12–16; *2 Apoc. Bar.* 13:3–10; 78:5). The present sufferings of the elect are immaterial compared to the judgment that awaits those who do not know God and those who are disobedient to the gospel when the Lord (= Jesus) comes to exercise divine judgment (2 Thess. 1:7–10). Presumably the second group, those disobedient to the gospel, refers to persons who persecute the Christians instead of being converted by their preaching (cf. Rom. 10:16). The first group is described using typical Jewish phrasing for Gentiles in contrast to Jews (e.g., Ps. 79:6; Jer. 10:25, Septuagint [LXX]) or Christians (1 Thess. 4:5). These verses echo OT judgment language (e.g., Isa. 2:10–11, 17, 20).

2 Thess. 2:11–12 contains a prayer for the Thessalonians. After the digression on divine punishment and reward, the author returns to a prayer that the congregation will be among the elect (cf. v. 5). The Lord is glorified by the present faithfulness of the community (cf. Isa. 66:5).

2:1–12
The Day of the Lord

2:1–2, False Teaching About the Parousia. 2 Thessalonians indicates that the source of confusion about the Parousia—the glorious return of Jesus—lies in prophetic oracles, words, or letters from Paul that are being used to support the claim that the Day of the Lord has come. If the letter being falsely interpreted was 1 Thessalonians, the false view would have to account for the fact that Christians had not been snatched up to be with the Lord (1 Thess. 4:17).

2:3–9, The Coming of the Lawless One. 2 Thessalonians appeals to an apocalyptic tradition about the last days to show that the claim the Day of the Lord has come is false. Apostasy is frequently listed as one of the evils of the end time (e.g., *Jub.* 23:14–21; 2 Esd. 5:1–12; 1QpHab 2:1–3). Rebellion against God is epitomized in a mysterious figure, "the man of lawlessness, son of destruction" (2 Thess. 2:3), who may be a heavenly figure or a human being who is a satanic figure (cf. Zech. 3:1, Satan is opposed to God; "son of Gehenna" appears in Matt. 23:15; and the Essenes designate those dominated by the angel of darkness as "sons of the pit," 1QS 9:16, 22; CD 6:15; 13:14). Satanic overtones of self-exaltation are attached to human rulers in Jer. 46:2–26; Ezek. 28:1–10; Dan. 11:21–45 (see also Rev. 13:1–18).

2 Thess. 2:5–7 breaks into the exposition of end-time events with the claim that Paul had taught the Thessalonians about the *katechon* (Gk.), the person or thing restraining the "man of lawlessness." The apocalyptic scenario of divine retribution introduced in 1:5–9 makes it likely that God's divine plan is the ultimate source of "restraint." However, since the "restrainer" operates while "lawlessness" is still at work in the present (perhaps in the persecution of the righteous? 2 Thess. 2:7), it is possible that the author has some present manifestation of evil in mind as well. The conditions attached to removal of the restraint in v. 7 are unclear.

Verses 8–9 return to describing the end time. Jesus' Parousia is a final battle in which the lawless one is destroyed (cf. 1 Cor. 15:24–28). But he is not destoyed until he has exercised the function of the false prophet of the end time and led many astray (cf. Mark 13:22; Matt. 24:24; Rev. 13:13–14).

2:10–12, Condemnation of the Unrighteous. The apocalyptic revelation concludes with a final condemnation of unbelievers (vv. 10, 12, where "the truth" means the truth of the gospel; cf. 1:8, 10). Ultimately, even the delusion of the unbeliever is rooted in God's act, an appropriate punishment for those who have turned away from God (Rom. 1:24–28; 9:14–29).

2:13–17
Salvation for the Elect

2:13–14, Thanksgiving for God's Call. The return to a second thanksgiving echos 1 Thessalonians. Instead of "beloved by God" (1 Thess. 1:4), the author uses "beloved by the Lord" (2 Thess. 2:13). If the text originally read "from the beginning," the author is speaking of God's election as an act that takes place from the beginning of time (e.g., Gal. 1:15, on Paul's calling before he was born), not simply the beginning of Paul's ministry. God's election is not complete until the elect have received salvation.

2:15–17, Stand Fast in the Tradition. The exhortation to hold fast to true Pauline tradition is followed by a prayer similar to 1 Thess. 3:2b, 8, 11–13, but stripped of the personal references in 1 Thessalonians.

3:1–5
Prayer for Steadfastness

3:1–2, Prayer for the Apostle. The request for prayer on behalf of the apostle picks up 1 Thess. 5:25. But the picture of apostolic life as constant danger from evil persons has been drawn in general terms (cf. Isa. 25:4; Jer. 15:21) and lacks the concreteness of such references elsewhere in Paul (e.g., Phil. 1:24).

3:3–5, Prayer for the Thessalonians. Once again the author prays that the audience will remain steadfast in what they have been taught (cf. 2:17) and that the Lord will protect them from the attempts of Satan to destroy their faith (cf. 2:9; 1 Thess. 2:18; 3:5).

3:6–18
Instructions to the Community

3:6–12, Against Idle Persons. The author turns to the requirement that Christians imitate Paul (1 Thess. 1:6) to address the problem created by those who refuse to follow Paul's instructions to work, live in a quiet, peaceful way, and avoid "idleness" (1 Thess. 1:6; 2:7–9; 3:4; 4:10–12; 5:14). It appears that these people are burdening other Christians for their support (2 Thess. 3:8, 10; cf. Prov. 10:4).

3:13–15, Against Associating with the Idle. The author reaffirms Christian concern for "doing good" to others. But charity is not to include fellow Christians who will not live according to the rule established by the apostle. Some exegetes think that though these people are not excluded from the Christian community (cf. Matt. 18:15–17; 1 Cor. 5:3–5), they may have been barred from the community meals (see the temporary exclusion of a member of the Corinthian community in 2 Cor. 2:5–11).

3:16–18, Final Blessing. The final prayer and wish for peace (cf. 1 Thess. 5:23, 28) frames a reminder of the apostolic authority of the teaching contained in the Letter. Once again the personal element, greetings to the congregation (1 Thess. 5:26), is missing from 2 Thessalonians. Paul's presence to his churches is carried by the genuine apostolic teaching in his Letters.

Bibliography

See 1 Thessalonians, "Bibliography."

1, 2 TIMOTHY AND TITUS

RALPH P. MARTIN

INTRODUCTION

The First and Second Letters to Timothy and the Letter to Titus are commonly referred to as the "Pastoral Letters" because they provide readers with insight into Paul's role—whether direct or (more likely) as understood by his followers—as pastor of pastors, a leader who provided for continuing leadership in the churches.

Authorship and Setting

The matters of authorship and setting are interwoven. The Letters are addressed to Paul's faithful travel companions, Timothy and Titus, who have been allotted special spheres of labor: Timothy to the Macedonian churches and Titus in the church at Corinth. It is not surprising that both men received, according to these Letters, positions of pastoral leadership in the Pauline churches, at Ephesus and Crete respectively, and that Paul would wish to write to them in a way that fitted their needs as church "officials," offering directives for the congregations on such matters as controlling, guiding, and instructing new members. False ideas had entered on the scene and are menacing, so the two pastors are called to be alert and active in repelling them.

Nevertheless, the question has been much debated whether Paul actually wrote these letters or whether a later writer employed Paul's name to give credibility and authority to what he put down in writing, presumably believing that he was representing the apostle's mind for a later generation. An intermediate position, much ventilated in recent decades, is that a member of Paul's school used Paul's fragmentary materials, especially to do with travel plans and personal matters (2 Tim. 3:10–11; 4:9–18), around which he wove these Letters to relate Paul's teaching, as he understood it, to a fresh set of circumstances that arose after Paul's martyrdom in A.D. 65.

Several reasons are offered by those who deny these Letters were written by Paul himself. First, some of the language, both in style and content, stands at odds with what we find in the accepted Letters of Paul. Other literary features are the heavy style, the insertion of hymnic and confessional passages (e.g., 1 Tim. 3:16; 2 Tim. 2:11–13), and the recital of ethical lists of virtues and vices (1 Tim. 1:9–10; 3:2–3; 6:11; Titus 1:7–

8), along with the lengthy regulations given to control the selection and appointment of church leaders.

Conscious of these objections, some scholars (e.g., Kelly) have submitted that the differences in style and content, including the variations of titles ascribed to Christ and the heavy emphasis on ethical seriousness, can all be attributed to the use of a secretary whom Paul employed. Paul dictated the main themes to be inserted but left it to his amanuensis or secretary to fill out the Letter in the way he saw fit; hence the exceptional style and addition of non-Pauline language.

Second, the type of ministry outlined in these Letters, notably 1 Timothy 3, has been seen as pointing to a development of the Pauline model in a later decade, when the church moved to the pattern of a single leader in charge. On the other side, it has been argued that the model of ministry in these Letters is based on the OT Judaic pattern rather than the situation of a fully institutionalized church that we see in 1 Clement (A.D. 95) and Ignatius (ca. A.D. 110).

Third, the false teaching opposed by the writer has similarly been interpreted in different ways. The nineteenth-century Tübingen school—which proposed a theory of early Christian development based on continual conflict—confidently appealed to 1 Tim. 6:20 as a sign that the Pastorals were written to counteract the influence of Marcion (ca. A.D. 140), a teacher deemed heretical and who wrote a book titled *Antitheses*, "Contradictions"—the very term used in this text.

But it is extremely unlikely that the Pastorals are so late, since the false ideas are not those of the second century and share a more Jewish character (1 Tim. 1:4; cf. 4:7; Titus 3:9; 2 Tim. 4:4). Decisively, the persecutions envisioned in these Letters predate the imperial policy of hostility that may have begun as early as the emperor Domitian (ca. A.D. 90).

Message

The uncertainty of being able to locate these short letters in any given period makes interpretation hazardous. But certain broad conclusions are possible. These Letters reflect the beginnings of the "institutional church," with a growing organizational fixity and accommodation to this world's life. Hence the ethical admonitions are slanted, and orders of ministry, with rudimentary creeds and confessions, are part of the church's essence. The writer sends a clear signal via Timothy and Titus to the churches to remain faithful to the Pauline gospel in the face of gnosticizing (→ Gnosticism) threats, and this call is one of holding fast to the "deposit" of apostolic teaching. Yet there is also a sensed danger of formalism and a dead orthodoxy. So the writer recalls Paul's teaching and warns against mere creedalism (2 Tim. 3:5).

COMMENTARY

1 TIMOTHY

1:1–2, Greeting. Unlike the Pauline Letters (except Gal.) there is no thanksgiving. Paul's authority as an "apostle" is appealed to, and Timothy is called "my true child in faith" (similar to 1 Cor. 4:17).

1:3–7, Warnings against False Teachers. Paul's visit to Macedonia (a frequently mentioned area of the Pauline mission) and Timothy's base in Ephesus (like Paul's in 1 Cor. 16:8–9) are made the setting for an attack on "teachers of the law" (1 Tim. 1:7) whose influence is being felt in the Asian congregations in the writer's day. These people are guilty of "teaching a different doctrine" from the apostolic gospel. The teaching was evidently a type of Jewish Gnosticism brought over into the church, since the teachers are still regarded as associated with the Christian communities (see Dibelius). Their interest centered in a speculative treatment of the OT linked with an elaborate cosmological theory by which the origin of the universe was explained (see 4:7; Titus 1:14; 3:9).

1:8–11, Comment on the Law. The designation of the errorists as would-be "teachers of the law" leads to an interlude on the role of the law, presumably the Jewish moral code embodied in the Decalogue (Exod. 20:2–17). Building on Paul's statement in Rom. 7:16 that the law is good, the argument moves in a new direction and equates law keeping with acceptable social behavior. The negative aspect is that the moral law curbs immoral practices, recited from some current vice list, typical of those commonly condemned by pagan moral philosophers as well as by Jewish and Christian writers (e.g., Rom. 1:29–30). The standard in this text is Paul's gospel entrusted to him (1 Tim. 1:11; 2 Tim. 1:11–14). The reference to "sound [lit., healthy, wholesome] teaching" paves the way for later texts in these letters that make a lot of this idea (2 Tim. 4:3; Titus 1:9; 2:1; cf. 1 Tim. 6:3; 2 Tim. 1:13; Titus 1:13; 2:8).

1:12–17, Paul's Life Story in Review. In autobiographical language (as in Gal. 1:13–16; 1 Cor. 15:9–11) but with the colors painted in more sombre shades (cf. Phil. 3:5–11), the "conversion and call" of Saul of Tarsus are set forth. Formerly he was opposed to all Christians stood for and was their active enemy (cf. Acts 26:11). Now, thanks to God's mercy, he is a recipient of divine grace to forgive and remake his past ways. The explanation lies not only in such Pauline terms as "grace," "faith," "love" (1 Tim. 1:14) but in the concession that he acted out of "ignorance."

The introductory phrase, "The saying can be trusted" (v. 15), occurs five times in the pastoral Letters. Here it introduces a piece of teaching about Christ's saving activity, needed to account for Paul's experience of God's grace and pardon (v. 16). Such an autobiographical episode is based on Paul as "an illustration" of the gospel attached to his name. The fitting response to Paul's gospel is doxology (v. 17), patterned on Jewish prayer-speech. Hence "Amen" invites the readers' reaction of assent.

1:18–20, The Charge Renewed. "This command" (v. 18) looks back to vv. 3 and 5 where Timothy is counseled to check false teachers in Ephesus. They are named as Hymenaeus and Alexander, who are identified presumably because they were known to have been Paul's opponents in his day. It is possible that the latter person reappears in 2 Tim. 4:14, just as Hymenaeus does in 2 Tim. 2:17. Paul is said to have dealt drastically with them by consigning them to Satan, the great enemy of the church (cf. 1 Cor. 5:5 and the stories in Acts 5:1–11; 13:5–11). Some type of excommunication is in view but with a remedial purpose. The two uses of "faith" (v. 19) suggest they are guilty of a double fault: they have turned from active trust in God, to which Timothy is called as he seeks to keep his conscience clear, and they have departed ruinously from "the faith," the Pauline gospel. By contrast, some "prophetic word" uttered by a charismatically gifted person (1 Cor. 14:29–33) had pointed Paul to him (cf. Acts 13:1–3; see Barrett; see also Acts 16:1–3).

2:1–7, Instruction in Public Prayer. In the opening of chap. 2 we are possibly reading parts of an early manual of church order based on the rubric of 3:15 (similar to 1 Clem. 59–61). The repetition of "all" (in 1 Tim. 2:1, 4, 6) sounds a note of polemic against the exclusivist tendency among the gnosticizing opponents. "Kings" refers to the Roman emperors and their provincial officials, "all who are set over us" (cf. Rom. 13:1–7; 1 Pet. 2:13–14; Pol. Phil. 12:3). The desire is for good government, religious toleration and tranquil times (see 1 Clem. 61:1–3) to enable Christians to practice their religion and uphold high moral values. God's design has provided a universal gospel by the gift of Christ who "gave himself as a ransom [as in Mark 10:45] for all" (1 Tim. 2:6). The worldwide note goes back to Isa. 45:21, 22, an OT testimony that may be alluded to in a cryptic Greek expression (1 Tim. 2:6; lit., "the witness in its own times," i.e., fulfilling God's promises in his own good time; so NEB, Hanson). Of this saving plan Paul is the appointed exponent, with his mission to the non-Jewish world now a fact of history (see Rom. 15:15–29).

2:8–15, Women's Role. Public praying is recommended, in an echo of Mal. 1:11. The domestic code that gives guidance to the women members regarding hairstyle and dress is akin to 1 Pet. 3:3–5 but with a sharper point put on the need for "good deeds," a term found in Eph. 2:10. The writer's interest is in the practice of religion, where evidently the women were vulnerable to being led astray (see esp. 1 Tim. 5:3–16; 2 Tim. 3:6–9). This background (also to be seen in 1 Cor. 14:34–35) may account for the apparent antifeminist tones of the following section. Women are cautioned not to aspire to be teachers because, first, they are open to being led astray, as Eve was; here Jewish ideas are pressed into service, as in 2 Cor. 11:2, 3; and second, their salvation lies in honoring the place the code gives them as homemakers and mothers. The text places a high value on marriage and procreation against a Gnostic low regard for both (1 Tim. 4:3; Irenaeus *Against Heresies* 1.24.2: "marriage and bearing children are of Satan"). There is some evidence of a women's prophetic movement in Asia, which these Letters seek to check (see MacDonald).

3:1–7, Credentials for Overseers. Another "faithful saying" prefaces the double profile that follows. First to be introduced are *episkopoi* (Gk.), lit. "overseers," who are usually equated with "elders," as in Acts 20:17, 28; Titus 1:6–9 with its parallel requirements; and 1 Pet. 5:1–2. The key idea is supervision, and qualifications for this "noble task" are listed. The three most significant are, first, blameless character, both inside (1 Tim. 3:2) and outside church life (v. 7); second, sound marriage and family life (vv. 2, 4–5: "the husband of one wife" is ambiguous, but it probably means fidelity within the married state); third, ability as a teacher (v. 2), implying maturity and experience (v. 6).

3:8–13, Credentials for Deacons. The other office mentioned is that of deacon, a general term meaning "every kind of service in the

propagation of the gospel" (see Kelly); and Timothy himself is called a deacon in this way (4:6). The character references are parallel with the earlier list of 3:1–7 but with two important exceptions: first, there is a probationary time (v. 10) requiring the deacons to be tested as they prepare to be promoted (v. 13); second, it is not clear whether "their wives" (TEV; RSV has "the women," but the Greek has no article) refers to deacons' spouses (so also NEB, NIV) or, more likely with most commentators except Hanson, "women deacons" such as Phoebe (Rom. 16:1) or the women helpers of Paul at Philippi (Phil. 4:2–3). The introductory "in the same way" (1 Tim. 3:11) as in v. 8 leads us to expect a fresh category, i.e., deaconesses.

3:14–16, The Church as God's House and Its Head. Expanding a metaphor found in 1 Cor. 3:9 and 11, the teaching characterizes the church as "the pillar and mainstay of the truth," i.e., the bulwark of Pauline "orthodoxy." Then comes a hymnic confession, comprising three matching couplets to form a "song of the incarnation" (→ Incarnation) in six lines marked by both rhythm and rhyme in the original. Each couplet brings together the earthly and the heavenly and demonstrates how Christ is the great unifier who has reconciled the world in an achievement that is prolonged in the church's mission in history.

4:1–16, More Warnings and Encouragements. It is natural that, after a statement of "the secret of our religion" (3:16), the errors of false teachers should be exposed. Some church members have evidently fallen victim to a gnosticizing insistence that marriage is evil and abstinence from food is the way to perfection. The basis for this claim was a belief that Christians were already living a heavenly existence (2 Tim. 2:17–18) that denied sexual differences and refused bodily appetites. On the contrary, God's creation is good (Gen. 1:31) and food is his gift (Ps. 24:1, which may be the "word of God" of 1 Tim. 4:5) to be enjoyed (so 6:17; see 1 Cor. 10:23–32, highlighting thankfulness as our response that consecrates all workaday activity).

Timothy is now summoned to fulfill his office as a "noble servant of Christ Jesus" (1 Tim. 4:6). The idioms are athletic but also drawn from the calling of the Stoic ideal person, Christianized to promote "the practice of religion" (vv. 7–8). Genuine self-control is set over against the spurious regimen in 4:1–3; interpreters have noted links with Colossians 2:16–23. A fragment of "personal conversation" between Paul and the then youthful Timothy may be seen in 1 Tim. 4:12–16. It is an intensely warm paragraph with Paul's language evident in v. 12. Timothy's call to service is traced to a *charisma*

(Gk., "gift") that came via the prophetic sign (see 1:18) and the approval of the elders whose hands were placed on him (cf. Num. 27:18–23) as a mark of either a transference of authority or a recognition that he was already gifted by the Spirit. Contrast 2 Tim. 1:6, which speaks only of Paul's imposition of hands.

The function Timothy discharges is that of an "apostolic and prophetic teacher" (to quote *Mart. Pol.* 16). Pastoral and liturgical responsibilities include the public reading of Scripture (1 Tim. 4:13); proclamation that seems to be tied to the exposition of scriptural words with a dash of "exhortation"; and teaching that emphasizes the catechetical training of believers. Timothy must also practice his faith in devoted living, so that his "progress" (v. 15) needs to outstrip the advance of false teachings (see 2 Tim. 2:16; 3:9). Only along the path of patient duty lies his and his hearers' "salvation."

5:1–6:2, Pastoral Duties. This is a lengthy section devoted to a recital of many-sided needs in the pastoral sphere. First, the "older man" (Gk. *presbyteros*) is a generic description, not used of a church officer. Such a one is to be treated respectfully by the younger leader (4:12). The "older women" (5:2) are to receive similar regard, while relations with the "younger women" are to be honorable.

Second, this leads on to the case of "widows" to whom more attention is given than to any other social group, mainly (we may infer) because they were a source of trouble. The problem may be explained by the survival needs of women who lacked support in days before welfare or Social Security. So the injunction to "honor" those genuinely bereft means "support financially" (v. 3) by enrolling them on this list (v. 9). But there is a lower age-limit in v. 9 (set at sixty years, which is when a person became "old" in antiquity) and a moral test (v. 10). Otherwise the widow is the responsibility of her family (vv. 4–8), and widows in their prime and who are sexually active should be counseled to marry (v. 11) and establish family life (v. 14; Titus 2:4–5) as a precaution against filling their idle days with tale-bearing pursuits, including the use of incantations and falling into prostitution (vv. 12–13, 15; see Hanson; MacDonald; → Women).

Believers must, where they can, help one another directly and not leave "the church" to assume the cost of the really needy.

Third, elders who exercise a leadership role, perhaps by presiding at the Eucharist, and who in particular are engaged in preaching and teaching merit special distinction (vv. 17–18). Citing Deut. 25:4 and a "saying of Jesus" taken from the Gospel tradition (Luke 10:7; Matt. 10:10), the rule is that such men are deserving of an honorarium or even a set salary.

Fourth, it is necessary also to exercise discipline among the leadership. Timothy is to address boldly those who are persistent sinners once he is satisfied that the charge is well supported (an OT precaution taken from Deut. 17:6, 19:15; cf. Matt. 18:16; 2 Cor. 13:1). He is to be wary of receiving them back into office (1 Tim. 5:21–22; this laying on of hands is a sign of readmission). Even if he errs in his disciplinary decisions, at God's judgment all will be put right (vv. 24–25). His motives should be "pure" (v. 22) but not based on a wrongheaded asceticism that forbade wine (v. 23) to be used medicinally to aid his weak constitution that would be aggravated by his having to deal with offenders (see 4:12).

Fifth, another troublesome area is the relation between masters and slaves in the congregation (6:1–2). Here (as in Titus 2:9, 10) the slaves have duties to perform while little is said of what the slave owners should do (cf. Col. 4:1; Eph. 6:9).

6:3–10, The Theme of Denunciation Renewed. A new factor is introduced with the caution that, first, the opponents are motivated by love of money (v. 5), presumably by charging gullible people for their teaching but maybe by embezzlement of church funds; and second, Timothy must steer clear of such practices (v. 11) since all life is transitory (v. 7) and he should be "content" (cf. Phil. 4:11) with the basic necessities of sustenance and shelter (1 Tim. 6:8). To forget this Christian teaching, which goes back to the gospel tradition (Matt. 6:25–33; Luke 12:22–31, "the sound words" of v. 3), is to be exposed to temptation that can lead to ruin, both material and spiritual (v. 9). The warning is confirmed by the moral commonplace that covetousness, here called "love of money," is evil.

6:11–16, Timothy's Calling. Timothy's pursuit is rather to be the virtues that make for the gaining of eternal life (vv. 11–12). The imagery is athletic as he is summoned to a "noble contest" (v. 12), which looks back to either the commencement of his Christian life at baptism when he made a "noble confession" (v. 12) or the ordination charge he received at the outset of his service. In creedal language, v. 13 recalls Jesus' own "noble confession" and dates his "witnessing" in "the time of Pontius Pilate" (cf. John 18:28–38). Similarly, the later Creed would locate this turning point of salvation history "under Pontius Pilate." The "command" (v. 14) is better understood as his ordination vow rather than a baptismal pledge. Timothy's fidelity is again contrasted to current ideas, namely, the imperial cult that claimed the Roman emperor as "sovereign lord" (as in Rev. 17:14; 19:16). On the contrary, only God is to be so honored (as in

1 Tim. 1:17), since God is immortal and majestic. Yet his nature is seen in our Lord Jesus Christ whose "appearing" is expected in his own time (2 Tim. 4:1, 8; Titus 2:13).

6:17–19, An Interlude. This short section emphasizes how fleeting is earthly wealth in contrast to the possession of "life indeed" (v. 19), i.e., eternal life.

6:20–21, Timothy's Final Recall. This is an epitome of the entire Letter, with its twin ideas: Timothy's task is to guard the deposit of Paul's teaching and not get sidetracked into the error at Ephesus that is no better than "empty noise" and vain disputation; those who have fallen for gnosticizing ideas, such as the men in 1:19–20, have lost their way (1:6).

2 TIMOTHY

1:1–2, Greeting. As with 1 Timothy, the names are placed first, with emphasis on Paul's role as a divinely authorized apostle entrusted with the message. Timothy is his "dear child," which has a warmer tone than 1 Tim. 1:1.

1:3–8, Timothy's Calling. Paul's ancestry (Rom. 9:3–5; Phil. 3:4–6) is given to recall Timothy's pedigree of Christian faith (Acts 16:1–3). Paul's close relationship is marked by his prayers, and Timothy's "tears" (see Acts 20:37) testify to a filial bond. This detail is added to stress how needful it is for Paul's gospel to be maintained in the church by those who have received "the gift" of ordained ministry in the Pauline succession (2 Tim. 1:6). Some expressive terms of exhortation are interesting: "stir up anew," lit., "fan into a flame" (v. 6); pastors like Timothy should not show a "cowardly spirit" (v. 7); like Paul (Rom. 1:16; Phil. 1:20) they should not be "ashamed" of (by disowning) the Lord or the apostolic message, even if it entails suffering for the gospel.

1:9–14, Patterns of Paul's Ministry. The theme is the gospel of Paul, of which he is praised as "herald, apostle, and teacher" (v. 11). The saving activity of God in election and his calling men and women in grace is celebrated (vv. 9–10; cf. Eph. 1:3–10). The focus of this piece of creedal statement is the "appearing," i.e., incarnation (see 1 Tim. 3:16) of his son, "our savior Christ Jesus." The salvific work is described in stately terms, e.g., rendering death ineffectual and casting light on "life and immortality," that is, immortal existence beyond death, which is a divine gift (1 Tim. 1:17; 6:16). Paul is known to have been loyal to this message leading to a martyr's death, but what God has

entrusted to him has been preserved intact in the church of the writer's day and remains to be handed on (2 Tim. 1:14; 2:1–2).

1:15–18, Warnings and Example. But Paul's work is under attack. There has been a slide into gnosticizing error (2:16–18) in the Asian province (1:15). Yet all is not lost while there is the memory of Onesiphorus (also preserved in the apocryphal *Acts of Paul and Thecla*; this story tells how he acted as Paul's host at Iconium) and his sacrificial ministry (vv. 17–18) to encourage the followers of the great apostle.

2:1–7, Ministry: Responsibility and Rewards. Timothy is advised to ensure a succession of authentic teaching (vv. 1–2; cf. *1 Clem.* 44) and is promised a just reward for his labors. That reward is probably to include a remuneration (based on 1 Cor. 9:7, echoed in 1 Tim. 5:17–18) as well as the prospect of an eternal inheritance (in 2 Tim. 2:10, "with eternal glory"). But there are qualifications to be met. The Christian minister is like a soldier on active service (vv. 3–4) and should avoid distraction (contrast Paul's waiver in 1 Cor. 9:12; 2 Cor. 12:13). The image of the athlete illustrates how rigorous training and self-discipline (as in 1 Tim. 4:7, 16) are needful. The working farmer is entitled to his first share of the harvest—a clear sign that some financial compensation for the ordained ministry is in view.

2:8–26, Ministry: Its Theme and a Call to Steadfastness. As often in the pastoral Letters, some practical advice is reinforced by a quotation of traditional material. The background here is Paul's fidelity to the gospel—drawn from Rom. 1:3–4 with its twin ideas of Jesus' messiahship ("the seed [family] of David") and resurrection (2 Tim. 2:8). Such loyalty was maintained at considerable cost (v. 9). So a "song of the martyrs" (vv. 11–13) is altogether appropriate. Couched in a series of "if . . . then" statements to form a quartet of hymnic lines, the verses are full of Paul's theology (patterned on Phil. 1:12–28; see Hanson) pressed into service for a new situation. The setting is the dismal situation of apostasy (in 1:15, shortly to be identified, 2:17–18). Readers are reminded that loyalty to one's baptismal profession (v. 11; Rom. 6:1–11; cf. Col. 2:20; 3:1) does not go unrewarded (Rom. 8:17; Pol. *Phil.* 5:2), even if unworthy church leaders abandon the Pauline faith (2 Tim. 2:12) and the believer's allegiance is sorely strained (v. 13).

So Timothy is to pass on this clarion call, to avoid mere "verbal disputes" (1 Tim. 6:4, 20) and to be a true Paulinist (2 Tim. 2:15, a worker unashamed of his job and Paul's gospel; Rom. 1:16). The term "worker" often has a bad sense in Paul: see 2 Cor. 11:13 and Phil. 3:2. Here its positive meaning is emphasized by reference to v. 6: the farmer who works hard by driving a straight plow. The opponents as "evil workers" are unmasked (vv. 16–17); here alone in these Letters is the alien teaching precisely identified (see Kelly). The writer exposes some kind of teaching regarding a baptismal resurrection, akin to 1 Cor. 4:8; 15:12, with the corollary that baptism ushered believers into a haven of spiritual existence that exempted them from moral restraints and canceled any future hope of resurrection. The best parallel verse is in the newly discovered *Gnostic Treatise on Resurrection* from the Nag Hammadi library (→ Nag Hammadi): "As the apostle said . . . we have suffered with him, and arisen with him and ascended into heaven with him. This is the spiritual resurrection which swallows . . . [the] resurrection of the flesh." On Hymenaeus, see 1 Tim. 1:20 for his excommunication. The second-century *Acts of Paul* associates this teaching with Demas and Hermogenes (see 2 Tim. 4:10 for the former name; 1:15 for the latter).

The antidote lies in the assurance that God's church will abide, even though some leaders defect and some members at Ephesus are seduced. The proof-text of Isa. 28:16 is joined to Num. 16:5 to indicate this confidence. Then comes a warning, based on Isa. 52:11, to steer clear of evil influences (2 Tim. 2:20–21) and to dedicate one's energies to more profitable exercises (vv. 22, 23). A final contrast is drawn between the true "servant of the Lord," mirrored in Timothy and the teachers, referred to in v. 16. Whether there is hope for them is uncertain, since v. 26 is a teaser and its meaning depends on how "held captive" by him and set free "to do his will" are related. The pronouns are different, but they can well refer to the devil. If so, the element of contingency in "perhaps God may give them a change of mind" underlines the pessimism. But the true Pauline remnant is secure (v. 19).

3:1–9, Last Days and Present Duties. The summons to "understand this" in the light of impending "hard times" (v. 1) is intended to put Timothy and—through him—the present readers on the alert. A set of powerful contrasts follows (vv. 2–5), fashioned according to the Jewish idea of a testamentary warning, i.e., the writer contemplates the immediate future in the light of his own demise (see 4:1–8). The vice list is based on Rom. 1:29–31, which is an indictment of pagan morals, but the style here is much more formal and intended to be remembered. The contrast "outward form of religion" versus "inward dynamic" (2 Tim. 3:5) shows how a lax spirit has invaded the church. There are leaders whom Timothy must identify and oppose (vv. 5–6a). Their baneful influence is seen in the fascination they exercise over

"weak women" who have become exposed to male solicitation (v. 6b). The resistance shown to Paul's strict moral code (called "the knowledge of the truth," v. 7) is illustrated by what happened to Moses, whose authority was opposed by Egyptian magicians (Exod. 7–9). But the fate of the opponents at Ephesus will be just as certain as that of those in Egypt (2 Tim. 3:9). Timothy's stance as Paul's representative must be firm: "avoid such persons" (v. 5b).

3:10–17, Paul's Example and Influence. Timothy has much to encourage him in his stand. We note three factors. First, the tradition based on Acts 13–14 is evidently well known in the Asian churches. Strangely, the incidents of the apostle's sufferings and loyalty to the truth are taken from these sections of Acts that precede Paul's meeting with Timothy, yet the latter is intended to recall them (2 Tim. 3:10–11). The chief point, however, is that Paul, like the righteous psalmist (in Ps. 34:19), was rescued and saw the results of his courage. Second, all who remain firm must expect to encounter hostility, often coming from religious leaders like those who practice evil arts (2 Tim. 3:13). Third, the Pauline church rests on a firm foundation in "holy Scripture," which Paul had made his court of appeal (Rom. 15:4). Early influence in Timothy, traced back to his home life (see 2 Tim. 1:5), included a knowledge of the Greek OT, which is divinely authoritative chiefly because it leads to Christ and has become an indispensable tool in the equipment of Christian leaders (3:15–17). The allusion here to Scripture's authority is made polemically, i.e., in defense of Pauline "orthodoxy," which alone claims to understand its meaning over against "heretical" usage.

4:1–8, Paul's Testament Continued. The verb "I solemnly charge you" is a term commonly used of a "last will and testament," and here it has that flavor in the light of Paul's impending martyrdom (vv. 6–8). The invoking of divine names (v. 1) adds an extra seriousness, as does the eschatological reminder of Christ's "appearing" in final glory. In the light of such a setting, the appeal "proclaim the [Pauline] message" is reinforced, especially as Timothy's commission stands in opposition to the false teachers' work, now an evident reality that Paul is said to have foreseen. The opponents (of v. 3) trade on human love of novelty, called here "getting their ears tickled" (see 1 Tim. 1:4; Titus 1:14 for their "myths"). More seriously, Paul's gospel is under fire.

2 Tim. 4:6–8 is a noble statement celebrating Paul the martyr. The language draws on Phil. 2:12–30, especially 2:17 for the rare verb "to be offered up as a libation." Since such an offering to the gods often preceded a sea journey, commenced by the ship's weighing

anchor, Spicq thinks that "my departure" has this reference; but in Phil. 1:23 the corresponding verb "to depart" is used, with no nautical allusion. The prospect of death looms large, and Paul's reward at the final day is a spur to faithful Christian service.

4:9–22, Personal Details. Various names are introduced to give Pauline reminiscences of colleagues in the Ephesian ministry (Acts 19, 20; Col. 4:7, 10–18; Philem. 24). There is one who left Paul's side to return home (Demas, 2 Tim. 4:9) and one who, in the tradition of Acts 15:37–39, had previously abandoned Paul and who now came back to his side (John Mark, 2 Tim. 4:11). Tychicus is a well-known apostolic colleague and courier of Paul (Col. 4:7; cf. Eph. 6:21; see also Titus 3:12), sent to Ephesus. References to Paul's clothing and the call for "scrolls," that is, the parchments (the OT in Greek; → Writing), add a lifelike touch to the narrative of his confinement. He has already been faced with the "preliminary inquiry" (2 Tim. 4:16) with no hope of acquittal. His rescue (v. 17) is traced to divine action in an idiom drawn from Ps. 22:22. The prospect, however, is ultimate martyrdom, to be celebrated with a doxology. The final greetings (2 Tim. 4:19–22) serve only to underscore the good standing of the great apostle whose legacy his followers want to preserve in the church.

TITUS

1:1–4, Greetings. This opening section of salutation in the name of Paul to his colleague Titus is the fullest and richest (in theological terms) of the three pastoral Letters. Above all, he and Titus share a "common faith," i.e., the faith of the universal church (Spicq), since Paul is the epitome of divine truth.

1:5–9, Credentials for Leaders. Titus, who had a special relationship to Corinth (see 2 Cor. 2:13; 7:6–16; 8:16–24; 12:18), is now settled at Crete, where Pauline Christianity is evidently established. There is need to consolidate the work by appointing church leaders ("elders" in Titus 1:5–6 are further described in vv. 7–9 under the title of "overseers," akin to 1 Tim. 3:1–7; see also 2 Tim. 2:24–26). These leaders are to have suitable qualifications, with pride of place in all the lists given to ability in teaching Paul's gospel (Titus 1:9). Personal habits (sobriety, not greed) and good family order are commended.

1:10–16, False Teachers To Be Opposed. Those who resist Paul's gospel are identified as Jewish Christian Gnosticizers (see 1 Tim. 1:4–7), called "the circumcision" (Titus 1:10) and advocates of "Jewish myths" (v. 14), i.e., the

notion of angelic intermediaries, like the ideas in Col. 2:8, 18, 22 (so Dibelius). Also, as at Colossae, there is a strong ascetic movement based on Jewish food laws (Titus 1:15), which this text rigorously opposes by adapting probably Paul's stand on the side of the "strong" in Rom. 14:20 (see Barrett) and at Corinth (1 Cor. 8) and maybe by reaching back to the gospel tradition (Mark 7:15, 19). The combined effect of error in doctrine (Titus 1:11) and an unhealthy rejection of God's provision in food has led to disturbance of Christian family life (v. 11; cf. 2 Tim. 3:6) and the presence of teachers who seek to get rich ("base gain," v. 11; "by their actions they disown the claim to know God," v. 16) by living off the congregation. Their greed, it is said, is a local trait, since Cretans are reported to be perverse, according to the poetic tag quoted from Epimenides, a Cretan teacher, about 500 B.C. The false claim that the tomb of Zeus was in Crete is known to (and condemned by) Callimachus, 305–240 B.C., who insists that the king of the gods cannot die.

2:1–10, A Social Code. In a way already followed in the Letters of Timothy (1 Tim. 3; 4; 5; 2 Tim. 2:22) the various members of the social order in the church are admonished. The difference is that here it is not office holders who are in view but diverse age and social groups, especially slaves (Titus 2:9–10; 3:1). The same virtues, however, are urged on professing believers, with chief emphasis placed on self-restraint (2:2, 4, 6) and respect for those in a "higher" social bracket. Self-control is seen in the call to temperance (v. 3) and submission (v. 5). Young wives are urged to be "good workers at home" in opposition to the tendency visible in 1 Tim. 5:13. Titus too is counseled to be a model leader (Titus 2:1, 7, 15), rich in "noble deeds" (as in 1 Tim. 4:11–12; 1 Pet. 5:1–5). The overall motive is to commend the Christian message and way of life to the pagan society (Titus 2:5, 10).

2:11–3:15, Final Instructions. It is helpful to consider first the two sections 2:11–14; 3:4–7, which are probably drawn from a baptismal liturgy that celebrates the new life in the church, thanks to the saving acts of God in Jesus Christ by the Spirit (an implicit trinitarian statement). The opening verb (in 2:11) marks this fragment as an "appearance" theology, which is picked up at 3:4: "the kindness of God . . . appeared." See 1 Tim. 3:16 for a similar idiom. God's grace moves believers to renounce their former impiety (Titus 3:3) and live a wholesome life (2:12; the adverbs here may well sum up in a nutshell the moral ethos of the pastoral Letters). Christians reflect on God's deliverance from evil (2:14) and their entrance on a purified life-style, marked by "good deeds" (2:14; see Eph. 2:10).

The language of Titus 2:13 is notoriously difficult, but some recent scholars have adopted an older suggestion made by F. J. A. Hort: "glory" is explained by what follows, i.e., the appearing in God's glory is in the person of the savior Christ Jesus (as in 2 Cor. 4:6 in the Pauline tradition; see Hanson for details). The turning point in human experience is located at baptism (Titus 3:5), which marked a rebirth and a renewal by the Spirit (the idiom is more Johannine— John 3:3–7—than Pauline, in spite of the "justification" language). The baptismal reminder is evidently drawing on a "mixed" tradition, including a (Johannine) polemic against the prevailing cult of emperor worship. A lot of the terms used are paralleled in Domitian's claim to be "lord and god," e.g., "appearing," "savior," "great God," "kindness," "philanthropy" (Titus 3:4).

Disturbances in congregational life are to be put down in an authoritative way (Titus 2:15; cf. 1 Cor. 7:6, but the peril of wrongheaded teaching may account for the shift). Yet Titus as a leader is to use discretion in handling obstinate "heretics," which is the Greek term used for persons who cause "divisions" (Titus 3:9–11). The setting is evidently a group in the church that is anti-Pauline (cf. 1 Tim. 1:4; 6:4; 2 Tim. 2:23).

By contrast, the author recalls the contact Paul had with well-known colleagues such as Tychicus (see commentary above on 2 Tim. 4:12) or Apollos (1 Cor., Acts) as well as lesser known names (Artemas, Zenas "the lawyer," who may have aided Paul in his encounter with the Roman authorities; they are otherwise quite unknown in the NT). These are the persons who represent the gospel as Paul's faithful helpers; and all "who love us in the faith" (Titus 3:15) are likewise added testimony to Paul's apostolic standing that needs to be asserted in the teeth of heretical teaching.

Bibliography

Barrett, C. K. *The Pastoral Epistles in the New English Bible*. New Clarendon Bible. Oxford: Clarendon, 1963.

Dibelius, M. *The Pastoral Epistles: A Commentary on the Pastoral Epistles*. Revised by H. Conzelmann. Translated by P. Buttolph and A. Yarbro. Hermeneia. Philadelphia: Fortress, 1972.

Easton, B. S. *The Pastoral Epistles: Introduction, Translation, Commentary and Word Studies*. New York: Scribner, 1947.

Hanson, A. T. *The Pastoral Letters*. New Century Bible. Grand Rapids, MI: Eerdmans, 1982.

Kelly, J. N. D. *A Commentary on the Pastoral Epistles: I Timothy, II Timothy, Titus*. Harper's New Testament Commentaries. New York: Harper & Row, 1964.

MacDonald, D. R. *The Legend and the Apostle*. Philadelphia: Westminster, 1983.

Spicq, C. *Saint Paul: Les épîtres pastorales*. Etudes bibliques. Paris: Gabalda, 1969.

PHILEMON

NORMAN R. PETERSEN

INTRODUCTION

We do not know exactly when or where the Letter of Paul to Philemon was written or where Philemon lived (Colossae? see Col. 4:9, 12, 17), but the Letter itself presupposes a story that is basic for our understanding of it. This story consists of the events Paul refers to in the Letter: Philemon incurs a debt to Paul (his conversion? v. 19b); Paul is imprisoned (v. 9; cf. vv. 1, 10, 13, 23); the slave Onesimus runs away from his master Philemon and incurs a debt to him (v. 15; cf. vv. 11–13, 18–19a); Onesimus is converted by an imprisoned Paul (v. 10; cf. v. 13); Paul hears a report of Philemon's love and faith (vv. 4–7); Paul sends Onesimus back to Philemon (v. 12), and he sends a Letter of appeal to Philemon, guaranteeing repayment of Onesimus' debt but also calling in Philemon's debt to him (vv. 17–19); Onesimus and the Letter arrive at Philemon's house (implied); Philemon responds to Paul's appeal (vv. 20–21); and Philemon and the church that meets at his house anticipate a visit by Paul (v. 22).

At issue both in Paul's writing of the Letter and in the decision with which it confronts Philemon is the social and symbolic integrity of the new family of brothers and sisters, the church. Philemon is a master in the world and a brother in the church, and now his slave has become his brother. In Col. 3:22–4:1 and Eph. 6:5–9, Letters that Paul may not have written, the question such relations pose is viewed in terms of how masters and slaves in the church are to relate to one another; the answer is that masters must be just and slaves obedient. In his Letter to Philemon Paul does not offer this answer. Indeed, he seems to envision a different question: whether or not a brother can be a master to a brother not only in the church, but also in the world. Paul urges Philemon to receive Onesimus as he would receive Paul himself, his partner (v. 17), fellow worker (v. 1), and brother (vv. 7, 20), namely, as an equal, not as an inferior. Verses 16 and 21 suggest further that Paul envisions a change in their worldly statuses as well. Paul expects that Philemon will not only "obey" his appeal to receive Onesimus as a brother, but also do even more than Paul has explicitly asked, possibly even terminate their master-slave relationship by freeing Onesimus.

Because Paul has no legal right to demand this, and because he sees this relationship as a problem in the church, his desires and motives are couched in the most careful rhetoric. He begins (vv. 4–7) with praise for Philemon's demonstrations of faith and love and for refreshing the hearts of the saints, the members of his church. Paul too acts out of love when he declares that for love's sake he is appealing to Philemon rather than commanding him, as he has the authority in Christ to do (vv. 8–10). The situation requires (v. 8) an act by Philemon that Paul could command, but Paul chooses rather to appeal for Philemon's act of goodness as a matter of consent rather than of compulsion (v. 14). However, once Paul has indicated his authority in the matter, Philemon cannot forget it, and neither does Paul. In verse 21 he throws his previous caution to the winds and expresses his confidence not in Philemon's free consent, as though to an appeal, but in his obedience, as though to the command that Paul did not give.

That the matter at stake is significant enough for Paul both to choose his words carefully and then to shift his tone so dramatically is further reflected in his placing of the seemingly personal matter in a public light. The Letter is addressed to the whole congregation that meets in Philemon's house (vv. 1b–2 and the plural "you" in vv. 22b, 25), and Paul suggests that a half-dozen other fellow workers with him are aware of what is going on (vv. 1a, 23–24). In this way, Paul exerts considerable social pressure on Philemon in addition to his own apostolic influence.

The magnitude of the problem derives from the possibility that Philemon's failure to receive his brother as a brother would threaten the very essence of what it means to be a brother (or sister), which every believer is by virtue of having become a child or son of God at baptism ("son of God" is for Paul an asexual notion—there is no male or female; cf. Gal. 3:26–4:7; 1 Cor. 7). Philemon's failure to respond affirmatively to Paul's appeal would result not only in a breach in the social and symbolic fabric of the brother-and-sisterhood, but also in Philemon's demonstration that he is neither a brother nor a son of God. It is in this light that we must view Paul's announced visit, for he will have to treat Philemon's response in terms of its implications for the brotherhood.

COMMENTARY

1–3, Opening. The address (vv. 1–2) and greetings (v. 3) are typical of Paul's Letters, except that here he identifies himself as a prisoner of or for Jesus Christ (cf. vv. 9, 13). It is not known where he was imprisoned, but because Archippus, Epaphras, and Onesimus are elsewhere identified as residents of Colossae (Col. 4:9, 12, 17), this may be the place to which the Letter was sent. Philemon is the host of a house-church that, according to contemporary architectural patterns, would have been limited to fifteen to thirty members. The letter is addressed to the whole church, although Paul speaks almost exclusively to Philemon ("you" in vv. 22b and 25 is in the plural). "Fellow workers" and "fellow soldiers" represent a relationship of responsibility to and with Paul, either as associates in his travels, like Timothy, or as residential functionaries like Philemon and Stephanas (cf. 1 Cor. 16:15–18). "Brother" and "sister" (Philem. 1, 2, 7, 16, 20), on the other hand, are sibling identities all believers enjoy by virtue of their being "children" or "sons of God" the Father (v. 3), which they become initially at baptism (Rom. 8:12–17; Gal. 3:26–4:7) and fully at the imminent return of Christ, when they will enter into the kingdom of God. Similarly, "Lord" means "master," and therefore believers are also equals as slaves of God or Christ, whom God has appointed master of all believers (Rom. 6:15–23; 1 Cor. 1:2; 8:5–6; Phil. 2:1–22). These identifications are significant because they are the basis for Paul's dealings with the worldly master and slave, Philemon and Onesimus. In opposition to this worldly relationship Paul concentrates on the ultimate identity of all believers as children of God and, therefore, as brothers and sisters to one another. For Paul the very form of human existence is that of enslavement (to sin working through the mortal, perishable, and sexually inclined flesh), but for believers this form is in the process of being transformed into the imperishable and asexual form of the sons of God, of whom Christ is the firstborn (Rom. 8:12–30; 1 Cor. 15; 2 Cor. 3:17–5:10; Phil. 3:20–21). Although still in human form, the believer's status as a "slave" is through Christ's death transferred from sin to Christ himself as Lord or master (1 Cor. 6:19–20; 7:21–23; cf. Rom. 3:24; Gal. 3:13, where "redemption" is a purchase from enslavement). Consequently, if one is not a brother to a brother, one's status as a child of God is in jeopardy, both in the church and therefore also in the kingdom of God.

4–7, Thanksgiving. The brief thanksgiving is also typical of Paul's Letters. In them, he establishes a basis for his subsequent appeals or exhortations by referring to his past relationship with the addressees and including a statement of his knowledge about their faith and love. Here, the thanksgiving is structured as a chiasm, that is, ideas, words, phrases, or images are repeated, with variations, in reverse order, e.g., A B B' A'. He refers first to Philemon's love (A) and then to his faith (B; v. 5), and then continues by speaking further first of Philemon's acts of faith (B'; v. 6) and then of his acts of love (A'; v. 7) that have refreshed the hearts of the saints. The translation of v. 6 is difficult, but the knowledge Paul hopes Philemon's faith will promote consists of what it means to be a son of God and a slave of Christ (see commentary above on vv. 1–3). The thanksgiving therefore expresses approval of Philemon's past behavior in Christ, but it also provides a strategic lever for Paul to secure a continuation of that behavior.

8–22, Appeal. Following his thanksgivings Paul usually makes appeals for specific future behavior on the part of his addressees. These sections can be long or short, depending largely on the number of topics addressed (cf. 1 Thess. 4–6; 1 Cor. 1–16!). This Letter is distinctive because in vv. 8–10 Paul discloses that his language of appeal is a loving mask for his authority to command. His disclosure here is related both to his focus on acts of love in his thanksgiving and to his desire also to have Philemon act out of love rather than from his own position of authority over Onesimus. Paul's mode of relating to Philemon thus becomes a model for Philemon in his relationship with Onesimus. "Love" is that familial quality of relations that builds up those who are party to the relationship (cf. 1 Cor. 8:1b; 10:23–24; 13:4–7). Thus, in the only topic of this Letter, Paul says that "for love's sake" he appeals to Philemon concerning his (Paul's) child, Onesimus (vv. 9–10). However, it is only after considerable rhetorical delay that Paul finally gets to the point of his appeal: "receive him as you would receive me" (v. 17). Both the delay before the point and what follows it in vv. 18–22 must be appreciated if we are to understand just what this appeal entails. Two compositional aspects of the appeal section are in this respect significant.

The first is what appears to be another chiasm. In v. 8, Paul refers to his authority to command (A) Philemon in the matter at issue, but in vv. 9–10 he indicates his preference rather to make an appeal (B). Then, in v. 14 Philemon's response is described as one of consent (B') out of his own free will, as to an appeal, not one of compulsion or of necessity, as to a command. However, at the end of the appeal section in v. 21, Paul refers to Philemon's response as an act of obedience (A'), as though to a command. Related to this chiastic unit is a sequence of terms that climax with the reference to obedience. Verse 8 indicates that there is but one fitting response (what is "required") to the problem. The problem is like a puzzle missing one piece, and only one will fit. If what is required is that Philemon be a brother to Onesimus (vv. 15–17), the absence of this "piece" is a threat to the brotherhood, the "puzzle." In v. 14, this missing piece is referred to as yet another act of goodness by Philemon. But in v. 21 it appears that Paul does not completely trust Philemon's choice of pieces, for here he speaks of his act as one of obedience. Despite the early rhetoric of appeal and consent, obedience is the last word. This strange shift is further reflected in the second compositional aspect of vv. 8–22.

Although no translation can fail to convey the turn in Paul's appeal when he takes stylus in hand (v. 19), none has fully captured the series of contrasts or alternative expressions represented in the Greek text of vv. 8–16. These serve to delay the appeal proper until v. 17. The series is as follows:

vv. 8–9a	bold enough to command	I prefer for love's sake to appeal
9b	old man/ ambassador	a prisoner for Christ Jesus
10	my son	whom I fathered
11	formerly useless	now useful
12–13	whom I sent to you	whom I wanted to keep with me
14	not by necessity	but by free will
15	he was parted from you for a while	that you might have him forever
16a	not as a slave	but as a beloved brother
16b	especially to me	but how much more to you
16c	both in the flesh	and in the Lord

This series, and even more so the Greek grammatical constructions, show just how carefully Paul composed this part of his appeal. The list enables us to decide between "old man" and "ambassador" for the ambiguous word in v. 9b. "Old man" is not a proper contrast with "a prisoner for Christ Jesus," especially when "ambassador" is so closely related to Paul's authority to command and to his metaphorical fatherhood (see also 2 Cor. 5:20; Eph. 6:20; and the more

common pairing of "Apostle and slave of Christ Jesus" in Rom. 1:1; Gal. 1:1, 10). "Ambassador" is a metaphor for Paul's apostolic role, in which capacity he has the authority to command. More significant for the Letter and its appeal, however, is the rhetorical and compositional difference between vv. 8–16 and vv. 18–22.

After Paul expresses his appeal in v. 17, he adds the promissory note in v. 18, endorses the note, and then shifts his tone entirely, as though at that moment he decided that appealing was inadequate. Thus, having guaranteed payment of Onesimus' debt with his note he proceeds to call in Philemon's debt to him (v. 19b). Presumably, Paul converted (fathered) Philemon; hence Philemon owes him his self or life, i.e., his position as a son of God. Paul then emphatically declares that he wants some joy from Philemon in the Lord and, echoing the reference in v. 7 to Philemon's refreshing of the hearts of the saints, he summons Philemon to refresh his heart too (v. 20). But v. 21 also hearkens back to the command in v. 8, for now Paul expresses his confidence in Philemon's obedience—and more. Then, in a gesture that is now as much a stick as a carrot, Paul tells Philemon to prepare a room for him, because he hopes that through the church's prayers he will soon be able to visit them all (v. 22). This visit is ominous because it will bring a response to Philemon's handling of his debt to Paul. The price he will have to pay and the veiled point of Paul's appeal are identical.

In part, both the price and the point entail Philemon's receiving of his slave as a brother. But this begs the question of how Philemon can remain master over his newborn brother. That this question pervades the Letter is suggested by its cautious yet reckless rhetoric. And it is further suggested both by Paul's reference to Philemon doing "even more" than is "requested" of him, and by Paul's assertion that Onesimus is a brother "both in the flesh and in the Lord." Is the giving up of the worldly role of his brother's master a part of the price—and the appeal? Does Paul want him to free his slave? If not, Paul would have shaped his appeal differently, like the authors of Col. 3:22–4:1 and Eph. 6:5–9. Alternatively, if Philemon does not pay the price Paul expects, will he not pay another price in the loss of his status as a brother—and son of God? Philemon's choice is between being a master and being a son of God.

23–25, Close. The concluding greetings and blessings are again typical of Paul's Letters, although here the list of fellow workers sending their greetings also contributes to the pressure on Philemon for they are, as it were, witnesses.

1247

Bibliography

Bruce, F. F. *The Epistles to the Colossians, to Philemon, and to the Ephesians*. The New International Commentary on the New Testament. Grand Rapids, MI: Eerdmans, 1984.

Church, F. F. "Rhetorical Structure and Design in Paul's Letter to Philemon." *Harvard Theological Review* 71 (1978): 17–31.

Lohse, E. *Colossians and Philemon*. Translated by W. R. Poehlmann and R. J. Karris. Hermeneia. Philadelphia: Fortress, 1971.

Moule, C. F. D. *The Epistles to the Colossians and to Philemon*. The Cambridge Greek Testament Commentary. Cambridge: Cambridge University Press, 1977.

Petersen, N. R. *Rediscovering Paul: Philemon and the Sociology of Paul's Narrative World*. Philadelphia: Fortress, 1985.

PART SEVEN

THE GENERAL LETTERS TO THE CHURCHES

INTRODUCTION TO THE
GENERAL LETTERS
TO THE CHURCHES

PHEME PERKINS

The Pauline Letters made the apostolic letter a mode of authoritative teaching in early Christianity. Of the remaining writings of the NT, some are genuine letters between two parties like 2 and 3 John. But a number of writings are not "letters" in that sense. They are sermons like Hebrews or general works of instruction like James or even heavenly revelations like Revelation. But the importance of the apostolic letter as a form of instruction is evident in these writings because they often include letterlike openings or closings, or employ themes that were developed in the Pauline letter tradition. For example, 2 Thess. 2:2 indicates that differences in interpreting apostolic teaching had to be resolved. A similar problem forms the "occasion" of writing in 2 Pet. 3:15–16. The author refers to the earlier "apostolic" letter 1 Peter (3:1). But 2 Peter is concerned with misinterpretation of Paul. This example shows that the authority of the Pauline Letters lies behind the writing of letters in the name of other apostles.

The importance of the "apostolic letter" was probably responsible for the inclusion in the canon of two brief letters from a teacher in the Johannine churches, who speaks of himself as "the elder" (2 John 1; 3 John 1). 1 John, a didactic treatise against a dissident group, is not cast as a "letter" at all. Nevertheless 1 John is commonly spoken of as a "letter." Some scholars think that it was sent along with 2 John, which contains specific instructions to exclude the dissidents from the community. Indirect influence of the letter genre may be detected in the emphasis upon writing to the addressees (e.g., 1 John 1:4; 2:12; 5:13).

Although the Pauline correspondence appears to have been the paradigm for apostolic letters, 2 and 3 John may be independent of its influence. A private letter, 3 John uses conventional formulas to express a wish for the "health" of the recipient (v. 2), while 2 John has a Christianized prayer for "grace, mercy, and peace" (v. 3). Its phrasing probably reflects the expectation that 2 John is to be read to the church as was the case with Pauline Letters. Both conclude with conventional expressions of the unsatisfactory character of written communication and the hope for a personal visit (2 John 12; 3 John 13–14). The Johannine Letters, like their Pauline counterparts, presuppose a situation in which churches sharing a common heritage are linked together by written communications from authoritative teachers in the tradition.

Previous page: Head of an angel; detail of a mosaic in the Church of St. Catherine, Sinai, sixth century.

Such letters were often carried by associates, whose faithfulness is attested by the author (3 John 12).

Unlike the Pauline tradition, the Johannine tradition appears to have kept the didactic treatise separate from the "letter." Paul had adapted the letter to serve as a vehicle of community instruction by substituting extensive thanksgivings for the conventional epistolary wishes for the health of the recipient. He cites from Scripture and traditional hymns and creeds and expands the body of the letter with theological and ethical instruction (→ Letter). Since the other writings in this group have used the "letter" as frame for didactic writing, the Pauline pattern appears to have been the decisive influence on their development. (See Introduction to the Pauline Letters.)

THE PAULINE PARADIGM

To see what the Pauline Letters have contributed to these works, we need to compare them with the pattern established in the Pauline letter tradition. The writings in this group lack the personal immediacy of the Pauline correspondence. Among the didactic works, only 1 Peter has all the parts of a typical letter: address and opening greeting (1:1–2); thanksgiving (1:3–9); body (1:10–5:11), which is divided into a theological reflection on Christian identity (1:10–2:10) and extensive ethical teaching (2:11–5:11); closing (5:12–14), which includes reference to a secretary and final greetings. These divisions correspond to the pattern established by the Pauline correspondence.

Another feature of Paul's Letters that survives only in the Petrine Letters is the use of "apostolic example" in exhortation. Paul links apostolic suffering with the example of Christ and calls upon his audience to "imitate" him (e.g., Phil. 3:12–17). 2 Peter, which is a "testament" (→ Testament), exhorts its readers to remember what they have learned after the author dies (1:12–15). 1 Pet. 5:1 links the author with the elders of the Christian community as a "fellow elder." 1 Peter emphasizes the example of the suffering of Christ as an example for Christians who must expect to suffer for their Christian faith (2:21–23; 3:17–18; 4:1–2, 13).

Although 1 and 2 Peter, James, and Jude are "pseudonymous" in the sense that they do not appear to have been composed by the apostles who are claimed as their author, they show none of the interest in expanding on the life or teaching of the fictive author that one finds elsewhere in pseudonymous writings (→ Apocryphal New Testament; Pseudepigrapha). 1, 2, 3 John and Revelation do not claim to be by a fictive author but were later all attributed to the apostle John (→ John the Apostle).

Address and Greeting

The Pauline address and greeting frequently attach the designation "apostle," often with further qualification, to the sender's name; other attributes may be attached to the naming of the addressees, and the greeting concludes by invoking grace and peace on the recipients. 1

Pet. 1:1–2 resembles this form. However, the addressees are not members of a specific community but the "exiles of the Diaspora in Pontus, Galatia, Cappadocia, Asia and Bithynia." In other words, the Letter is a general one to Christians in Roman Asia Minor (see Color Map 12; → Provinces). Rev. 1:4 picks the seven churches in Asia as addressees. James 1:1 omits any specific geographical designation and simply refers to the "twelve tribes in the Diaspora." It also uses a secular expression "greeting" rather than the "grace and peace" form. James has the title "servant/slave" instead of "apostle." 2 Pet. 1:1 combines "apostle" and "servant" (also found in Rom. 1:1), but later 2 Peter speaks of the "apostles" as persons from the past (3:2). That Letter lacks any geographic designation. It is addressed to all believers. Jude 1 also speaks to all believers. The sender is identified as "servant" and as "brother of James." Its greeting takes the form of a wish for "mercy, peace, and love." Although not part of the epistolary introduction, Rev. 1:1 speaks of what is to follow as a revelation from God through Jesus, the revealing angel, and "his servant, John" to "his servants." Thus the use of "servant" in these writings probably represents a common speech pattern in many of the churches of Asia Minor.

The greeting and address sections of these Letters do not create a fictive setting in which the "apostle" is presumed to be speaking. Instead, they show a desire to universalize apostolic teaching for all faithful believers. The situation is quite different in the nonepistolary treatise, 1 John. There the author seeks to establish himself and those who receive his teaching as the only legitimate heirs of a tradition that goes back to Jesus (1 John 1:1–5).

Thanksgiving

Most of the Pauline Letters contain a thanksgiving that echoes some of the themes in the Letter that follows. This part of the paradigm appears only in 1 Pet. 1:3–9. As in the Pauline examples, the thanksgiving concludes with a reference to the reward awaiting faithful Christians in the last days.

Body of the Letter

With the exception of 2 and 3 John, the "body" in each of these examples comprises material that has been cast as a didactic treatise, a sermonic exhortation, or an apocalypse. The personal references, requests, and commands typical of the letter are missing. Hebrews even claims to be a "discourse" (5:11; 6:1; 13:22). 2 Pet. 1:12–14 establishes what follows as the "testament" of the dying apostle. Rev. 1:1 speaks of the work as a "revelation" (→ Revelation). The "letter" forms a subsidiary section in which a heavenly message is directed from the Lord to the "angels" of the churches (Rev. 1:4–6; 1:9–3:22). These "messages" are prophetic warnings to the churches to remain faithful. The promises for those who are found faithful at the judgment are reflected in the visions of Revelation 19. Since Revelation uses symbolism from the letters later in the book, there is no reason to think that the epistolary section was ever independent of the apocalypse as a whole. The "letters" of Revelation are part of the "prophetic book" (22:6–19) and carry with them the aura of being "heavenly" letters rather than mere human communications. The nearest analogy to such a letter in the Pauline corpus is Galatians, which carries conditions of curse and blessing for its recipients.

In some cases the body of the Pauline Letter begins with a theological section, which is followed by exhortation directed to the community (e.g., Rom. 1–11; 12–15; Gal. 1–4; 5–6). Some of the treatises in this group follow a similar pattern. 1 Peter begins with a reflection on the significance of baptism for the new identity of Christians (1:10– 2:10) and then turns to ethical instruction (2:11–5:11). Although most of the work is general exhortation, James concludes with rules for relationships within the community (5:12–20). A similar turn toward community rules is evident in the epilogue of 1 John (5:13–21). Similarly, Hebrews brings its discourse to a close with exhortation to the community (13:1–17). Jude 20–23 is a generalized example of such a conclusion.

Closing

The letter closing in the Pauline corpus includes a final benediction and greetings from the apostle and his associates (or the writer of the letter) to the addressees. Jude has a final doxology (vv. 24–25) but no greetings. A very brief expression of praise addressed to Christ concludes 2 Peter (3:18b). James lacks a formal closing. 1 Peter follows its doxology (5:11) with greetings from the writer of the letter, Silvanus (5:12), and an associate of the author, Mark (5:13). Both names could also refer to persons who had been part of the Pauline mission. A Mark is referred to in the conclusion of Philemon (v. 24; also Col. 4:10; → Mark). Silvanus (Silas) is mentioned as co-sender in 1 Thess. 1:1 (and 2 Thess. 1:1). He worked with Paul and Timothy at Corinth (2 Cor. 1:19) and is an important figure in the Pauline mission in Acts (15:22–41; 18:18; → Silas, Silvanus). Here these figures, presumably well known to the Christians in Asia Minor, are part of the church at Rome (the Babylon of 1 Pet. 5:13).

The claim that Hebrews is a letter rests solely on its conclusion. After a brief allusion to the possibility that the anonymous author might be "restored" to the addressees, which may be related to the travel plans at the conclusion of Pauline Letters (Heb. 13:18–19; cf. Philem. 22), a lengthy benediction (Heb. 13:20–21) is followed by a brief appeal and greetings (13:22–25). A familiar figure from the Pauline mission, Timothy, is mentioned as having been released (v. 23; → Timothy). The author links his return to the addressees with that of Timothy. The originating community is then identified vaguely as "those from Italy," perhaps referring to Christians outside Rome (v. 24). Although such allusions were later used to link this writing with Paul, the author views himself and his audience as members of a later generation (2:3–4). Some exegetes think that Heb. 13:22– 25 was added to the discourse when it was copied for general circulation.

EXHORTATION

The occasion and content of each of these writings are treated in the commentaries in this volume. Here we turn to the type of moral exhortation found in these writings to see how it compares with patterns established in the Pauline tradition. Studies of the form and use of moral exhortation in Paul's Letters suggest seven areas of comparison: (1) indications of the tradition as one known to the audience; (2) type of material designated as known by the audience; (3) statements of general applicability such as expectations of suffering and the moralist's commonplace of "knowing and not doing"; (4) paradigms of virtue and vice; (5) indications of personal relationship such as teacher/student (father/son) or a sage about to die or depart; (6) refashioning of character through gaining control of passions or statements of motive for doing so; and (7) legitimation of a new "social world," a new vision of reality in which Christians live. This vision may be legitimated by appeal to the authority of law or Scripture or by contrast with other social groups.

Tradition as Known to the Audience

The addressees may be presumed to be familiar with the traditions of a writing either because they are generally accepted in the community, such as those from the OT, or have been previously taught by the author.

Hebrews warns its readers against "drifting away" (2:1). The moral commonplace of "babes" who still need milk, in contrast to the mature who can understand the more profound teaching of the writer, is another way of reminding the readers of what they should know (5:11–6:12). They are exhorted to persevere and to recover their initial enthusiasm (10:23–25, 32–39). The ethical exhortation in Hebrews reflects established community patterns, though the doctrinal reflections that explain the superiority of Christ the heavenly high priest seem to represent new teaching for the "mature."

1 John emphasizes the fact that both the doctrinal and ethical teaching of the author (1:1, 5; 2:7, 21–24; 3:11) correspond with what the community has known "from the beginning" (cf. 2 John 5). The dissidents are thus condemned as persons who have departed from the community and its tradition.

1 Peter opens with extensive allusions to the baptismal transformation of the recipients that is the basis of what is presumed to be known by the audience (1:18). 2 Peter has the author reminding the audience of what they have been taught (1:12–13; 3:1), teaching grounded in the revelation received at the transfiguration and in a true understanding of prophecy (1:16–21). As in 1 John, those who teach otherwise can only be destroying the tradition and themselves (2 Pet. 2:1–3, 10–21).

James joins proverblike sayings and discourse material in its exhortation. The proverbial form of much of the exhortation suggests that it is known to all persons as "wisdom." Questions used to introduce sayings perform a similar function (e.g., 2:5, 25; 3:12; 4:1, 4).

Jude enlists the audience in the struggle for a common faith (vv. 3, 5, 17) that could be perverted by the false teaching and passion-ridden life of those who neglect it (vv. 4, 6, 12–13, 15–16, 19).

Revelation also exhorts its audience to "remember" a faithfulness and love that was in danger of being lost (Rev. 2:5, 13, 19 [despite greater love in the present, the teaching of a false prophetess could destroy the community]; 3:1–3, 15).

Types of Tradition That Are "Known"

All of the NT authors invoke passages from the OT as traditional hortatory material. Jude introduces warnings from Jewish Pseudepigrapha (1 Enoch in vv. 6–15 and As. Mos. in v. 9). 2 Peter incorporates much of Jude in its apocalyptic affirmation of judgment, though the author may change the application of particular examples, omit particular parts of an example, or shift the order to coincide with the OT (cf. Jude 6–12 and 2 Pet. 2:1–17).

Other traditional material includes ethical and philosophic commonplaces from Hellenistic, Jewish, and popular philosophic preaching. Hebrews combines the fiery image of apocalyptic judgment with the platonizing vision of the true heavenly sanctuary in which nothing can be shaken (e.g., 12:18–29). The characterization of God in James 1:17 points toward a similar background, as do the references to the cycle of nature and the paradox of human ability to tame animals while unable to master passion in 3:6–8. 1 Pet. 2:18–3:7 represents Christian adaptation of the ethos of the "household code" (cf. Col. 3:18–4:1; Eph. 5:21–6:9). 2 Peter opens with a lengthy salutation cast in the terminology of Hellenistic moral teaching (1:3–11). The description of the true prophetic word inspired and properly understood through operations of the divine Spirit acting like a lamp or morning star of 2 Pet. 1.19–21 has parallels in Philo (On Noah's Work as a Planter 117; Change of Names 203; Who Is the Heir of Divine Things? 89; 259).

2 Peter adapted material from Jude without designating it as such. 2 Pet. 3:15–16 indicates that Paul's letters enjoyed authoritative status within the community. And 2 Pet. 3:1 shows that 1 Peter was also known to the addressees. Some exegetes find the references to the transfiguration (2 Pet. 1:16–18) an indication that written gospel traditions also belonged to the authoritative tradition of the community. 1 Pet. 3:18–22 speaks of the story of Jesus as the foundation for the Christian willingness to suffer. Hebrews also contains allusions to the story of Jesus' suffering and exaltation (5:7–9; 13:12–13). Although both authors could be dependent upon oral tradition, their way of speaking about Jesus' exemplary life suggests some underlying narrative account of Jesus' suffering and not merely a reference to formulas used in preaching. The testimony of "Spirit, water, and blood" in 1 John 5:6–8 may be linked to the addition of "blood and water" to that community's passion story in John 19:34–35.

James contains a number of parallels to sayings of Jesus, though they are never designated as such (e.g., James 1:5 and Matt. 7:7; James 1:17 and Matt. 7:11; James 2:5 and Matt. 5:3, 5; 11:5; James 2:8 and Matt.

22:39–40; James 4:3 and Matt. 7:7–8; James 12:39; 5:12 and Matt. 5:34–37). James never invokes Jesus in its exhortation.

General Moral Commonplaces

James employs the ethical commonplace of knowing and not doing (1:22–27; 2:14–17; 3:1, 13; 4:17). But by far the most pervasive commonplace in this group of writings is the need for Christians to endure or persevere. Endurance may be required because of sufferings to which the community is subjected as in 1 Peter (e.g., 1:5–9; 4:1–6, 12–13, 16–18; 5:6–10). But it is also the requirement of an ongoing life of holiness in this world (James 1:2–4, 12–15; 5:7–11; Heb. 12:1–10), which has to be revived when a community has lost its initial enthusiasm.

Paradigms of Virtue and Vice

We have already seen that 1 Peter and Hebrews use the suffering of Christ as an example for the Christian life. The "victory" sayings in Revelation (2:7, 11, 17, 26–28; 3:5, 12, 21) not only direct readers to the visions of final fulfillment at the end of the book; they also recall the opening vision of the glorious Son of man as the one who has conquered death (1:5, 17). OT figures are extensively used as examples in exhortation. They appear in all the writings of this group except 2 and 3 John, which are private letters (e.g., Heb. 11; James 2:21–25; 5:11; 1 Pet. 3:5–6; 2 Pet. 2:5–10; 1 John 3:12–15; Jude 5–7, 11; Rev. 2:14, 20).

Language of Personal Relationship

While asymmetrical relationships such as teacher/student or parent/child are the common pattern in hortatory discourse, these writings almost always use the language of parity, of common standing between the author and addressees. References to the addressees as "brothers" or "beloved" predominate. 1 John also employs the language of "children," which had apparently become a common community designation in the Johannine churches (e.g., 3:1–2; 2:12–14, 18, 28). The father in relation to whom the Johannine Christians are "children" is God, not the author of the Letter (e.g., 1 John 2:21–25). The author of 1 Peter is a "fellow elder" to the elders of the community (5:1). 2 Peter writes to those who have received a "faith equal to ours" (1:1) and Jude to those who share a common faith and salvation (v. 3) and who also look back to the "predictions of the apostles of our Lord Jesus Christ" (v. 17). The prophet of Revelation is one who has shared with his fellow Christians suffering, the kingdom, and endurance (1:9). Thus, the primary relationship that governs exhortation in these writings is the mutual instruction of "beloved brothers," "children of God," partners in a common faith and hope. It is not grounded in a disparity of age, education, or office. Nor do we find even that "apostolic authority" that Paul sometimes invokes in his letters (e.g., 1 Cor. 4:14–21; 2 Cor. 13:10).

Refashioning Character

The persistent emphasis upon controlling the passions links Christian moral exhortation to the concern with reshaping the behavior and character of persons (e.g., James 4:1–12; 2 Pet. 1:4). The exhortations to mutual love also fall in this category (e.g., James 2:8–17; 4:11–12; 5:9; Heb. 13:1–2; 1 Pet. 4:8; 2 Pet. 1:7; 1 John 2:7–11; 3:11–18; 2 John 5; 3 John 5–6; Rev. 2:19). The most extensive imagery of reshaping character appears in 1 Peter, since the author stresses the radical transition from death, disobedience, slavery to passion, impurity, and the like to their opposites through the addressees' "rebirth" as Christians (e.g., 1:2–4, 14, 18–23; 4:6; 2:10).

Legitimating a Social World

The emphasis on reversal in 1 Peter is correlated with the expectation that the mere fact of being identified as a Christian could lead to scorn, harassment, or persecution from neighbors or former associates. Christians must maintain exemplary conduct (e.g., 1 Pet. 2:12; 3:13–16; 4:3–5, 16). Opposition from outsiders may have helped to solidify the boundaries of the Christian community. Hebrews suggests that its audience had more enthusiasm in the early days that required suffering and sacrifice than it does at present (Heb. 10:32–39). It is not clear whether the Letter's doctrinal argument for the superiority of Christ's sacrifice over Jewish worship is also directed at legitimating its vision of Christian salvation against the influence of Christians maintaining close ties with Judaism (e.g., 13:9–16). James does not link the general "trials" suffered by Christians with any particular group. Discrepancies between wealth and poverty create problems within the community (e.g., James 1:9–11; 2:1–7; 4:13–17) as well as from without (2:6–7; 5:1–6).

1 John (also 2 John) and 2 Peter confront a different problem of legitimation: division within the Christian community. In 1 John, the author writes against the Christological teaching and ethical perfectionism of a dissident group that has separated itself from the communities to which his addressees belong (e.g., 2:18–25; 4:1–6). The love command that shapes the ethical tradition of the community is invoked to show that such persons must be "children of the devil" (1 John 3:1–10). Despite their claims, they have no share in the salvation that comes to those who remain in fellowship with the author. 2 Peter castigates as false prophets persons who deny the traditional preaching about the judgment (2:1–3; 3:1–5). They are still within the community to which he writes and make their case by appeal to Paul's letters. Although Jude 4 refers to some who have gained admission to the community and who would destroy the faith, the tract is so general in its condemnation that it may not have any particular group in mind. The concluding exhortation simply takes the division between "worldly people, devoid of Spirit" and Christians as an occasion to remind the audience not to weaken its efforts toward holiness (Jude 17–23).

Revelation suggests problems of legitimation that stem from pressures within and outside of the community. In addition to those who have lost their initial fervor, the letters refer to false prophets (Rev. 2:12–29) and condemn some who "claim to be Jews but are not" (2:9; 3:9). From outside, the churches face the possibility of persecution (1:9, the visionary has been exiled; 2:10, 13). The issue of wealth and accommodation to the mores of the larger society is raised in connection with the church at Laodicea (Rev. 3:15–18). Revelation 18 contains a condemnation of the wealth from the east on which Rome had built its empire. The visions of the beast suggest that some Christians stood to suffer economic loss and persecution because they would not participate in the social forms of ruler worship (Rev. 13:3, 8, 12, 16–17). Some scholars have suggested that these various pressures represent a single crisis: the possibility that Christians would accommodate their behavior to the larger pagan culture to avoid economic loss, persecution, and in some cases death. The intensity of the argument in Revelation against accommodation suggests that the false prophets may have provided a rationale for doing so. Traditions like 1 Pet. 2:13–17 circulated in Asia Minor. They taught Christians to be subject to human institutions and to honor the emperor. (1 Peter assumes that Christians will still face hostility from outsiders.) But Revelation sees such accommodation as a satanic plot that will lose the community its salvation.

With varying degrees of intensity the expectation of divine judgment plays an important role in legitimating the worldview of the churches. Christians find themselves a minority whose views are in opposition to the larger world. The expected reversal at the judgment is more than a reward for good behavior. It represents a "remaking" of the order of things according to the Christian vision. Consequently, while judgment language may simply serve to remind the audience to remain faithful in Hebrews and James, it plays an important role in reasserting the community of the persecuted Christian minority in 1 Peter and Revelation. For 1 John it provides an explanation for the divisions that have arisen within the church: they are manifestations of the "Antichrist." Jude and 2 Peter suggest that "delay of the Parousia [the second coming of Christ]" is just as much a threat to the foundations of the community as persecution. In very different ways, then, these writings show us the churches of Asia Minor struggling to maintain their traditions and shape Christian identity at the end of the first century.

Bibliography

Doty, W. G. *Letters in Primitive Christianity*. Philadelphia: Fortress, 1973.

Feine, P., J. Behm, and W. G. Kummel. *Introduction to the New Testament*. Nashville: Abingdon, 1966. Pp. 176–77, 258–333.

Meeks, W. A. *The Moral World of the First Christians*. Philadelphia: Westminster, 1986.

Stowers, S. K. *Letter-Writing in Greco-Roman Antiquity*. Philadelphia: Westminster, 1986.

White, J. L. "St. Paul and the Apostolic Letter Tradition." *Catholic Biblical Quarterly* 45 (1983): 433–44.

HEBREWS

H A R O L D   W.   A T T R I D G E

INTRODUCTION

The work known as the Letter to the Hebrews was not originally a letter; nor were its addressees likely to have been "Hebrews." Though often thought to be Paul, the identity of the author is unknown. The opinion that it was a Pauline composition was held in Alexandria from the second century on, although prominent figures such as Origen recognized difficulties with that attribution. His remark that "only God knows" who really wrote the piece is often cited. In the Latin West there were, at first, doubts about Pauline authorship. Tertullian, for instance, considered Barnabas the author. By the fourth century the Eastern opinion came to be accepted in the West, and Pauline authorship remained unquestioned until the Renaissance and Reformation, when stylistic considerations again caused doubts. Luther, and many scholars since, suggested Apollos as the author. Numerous other candidates have been advanced, including Prisca and Aquila, Silas, and Jude. None is satisfactory, and Origen's judgment is fully warranted.

The general range within which Hebrews was written runs from about A.D. 60 to about 95. The earlier date is suggested by the author's reference to himself and his community as second-generation Christians (2:3–4). The advanced state of the traditions used in the text, especially its Christology (the way it identifies Jesus), also presupposes some time for development. Few critics date Hebrews any earlier than 60. The upper end of the date range is often anchored in the use of Hebrews by 1 Clement. Although that use is at times doubted, it is obvious, especially in 1 Clement 36. That letter from the leadership of the Roman church to Corinth is normally dated to A.D. 95–96, although that date is hardly secure, and the work could have been written any time between A.D. 75 and 120. This provides an upper end for the date of Hebrews of about A.D. 110.

The range might be compressed further by internal considerations. Many critics argue that Hebrews was written prior to A.D. 70 because it refers to the Jewish temple worship as a present reality and does not mention the destruction of the Temple, but neither argument is probative. Both Jewish and Christian authors writing after 70 refer to the Temple in present terms. More important, Hebrews is not interested in the actual cult of the Herodian Temple but in the depiction of the cult of the desert tabernacle. The author uses that scriptural picture as part of his constructive Christology, not as an apologist or polemicist, and the basis of his argument is exegesis, not history.

The reference to Timothy in 13:23, if to Paul's collaborator, could push the upper end of the date range down to the midnineties, since it is unlikely that Timothy would have been alive, well, and ready to travel much later.

The genre of the work is problematic because it ends with standard epistolary formulas but lacks an initial address and greetings. Components of the text exhibit significant formal patterns useful for determining the overall genre. A section such as 3:1–4:13 is a virtually self-contained homily, with an introduction (3:1–6), citation of Scripture (3:7–11), exposition leading up to an exhortation (3:12–4:11), and conclusion with a rhetorical flourish (4:12–13). The same pattern prevails in 8:1–10:18. An introduction sets certain themes (8:1–6). A scriptural quotation introduces certain complementary notions (8:7–13). A complex comment on these themes follows (9:1–10:10). A reprise of the lesson, referring back to the scriptural text, concludes the section (10:11–18). Elements of this sermonlike pattern are found in other parts of the Letter as well, but they are most obvious in these chapters. The document as a whole is as much a scripturally based homily as are its component parts, and its self-description as a "word of exhortation" (13:22) is apt. The conclusion suggests that the exhortation was sent to a congregation at some distance from its author.

The designation of the addressees as "Hebrews" seems to be a later scribal inference based on the contents of the text. Many commentators, both patristic and modern, have followed the title's lead, assuming that, because of its concern with Jewish institutions and traditions, the work was addressed to Jews or to Jewish Christians. Identification of the addressees is correlated with hypotheses about the aims of the text. If written to Jews, Hebrews might be designed as an invitation to accept the Christian confession. If to Jewish Christians, it might aim to prevent a relapse to the ancestral religion. Both construals of the addressees and the aim of the work have been defended, but neither is persuasive. The obvious familiarity with Jewish institutions and exegetical traditions is indicative of the author's background but says little about his audience. Other Jewish Christians, such as Paul, address predominantly gentile communities, e.g., Galatia and Corinth, with sophisticated exegetical arguments and appeals to Jewish traditions. The intended audience of this text may also have been gentile.

While the ethnic origin of the intended readers is unclear, Hebrews does give some data about them. They had been Christians for some time (5:12) and, because of that commitment, had experienced persecution (10:32–34), which is expected to continue (12:3–13; 13:3). Part of Hebrews' function is to inspire the faithful endurance necessary to meet such threats. Of equal importance, the community seems to be undergoing a crisis of confidence. Some have been neglecting the community assembly (10:25). Such behavior may be a reaction to outside threats or even to the attractions of traditional Judaism, but it could equally well derive from a waning enthusiasm with complex causes. It is also not clear how well informed our author was about these causes. He senses, however, the possibility of apostasy and wants to prevent it by rekindling faith.

The attempt to rekindle the faith of a community faced with pressure from its environment and with internal fatigue is conducted in two ways. The author appeals directly to the addressees in a series of warnings (6:4–12; 10:26–31; 12:15–16) and exhortations. The thrust of these exhortations is summarized in 4:14–15. The addressees are urged to hold what they have, especially their "confession" of Christ. They are also called to movement of various kinds. At times the movement, based on cultic imagery, is one of approach to God (4:16; 10:19–22). At other times it is movement onward (6:1) or outward (11:15; 13:13) to the world in loving service. Such hortatory imagery is concretized in the appeals to specific virtues, especially to fidelity (chap. 11) and endurance (12:1–13).

The hortatory or parenetic program of Hebrews is grounded in Christological exposition. The author begins with traditional affirmations in chaps. 1 and 2, introduces in 5:6–10 an exegetical base for further reflection by his fresh interpretation of a text, then proceeds in the central expository section (7:1–10:18) to develop a new presentation of Christ's person and work. That presentation affirms both the heavenly character and full humanity of the Son. At the same time, it shows how his sacrificial death is existentially relevant for the addressees because it inaugurated a new covenantal relationship with God. It is the virtues of that covenant relationship that the addressees are called upon to display. They are assured that they can be faithful and hopeful, for Christ is their example and his exaltation is a surety for their own.

COMMENTARY

1:1–4

Exordium

The first four verses of Hebrews constitute a single complex or periodic sentence, a structure favored in artistic Greek prose. The sentence is embellished with many figures of speech, such as alliteration, assonance, and chiasm, which are characteristic of Hebrews' rhetorical artistry.

The function of an exordium is to encapsulate the major themes of a work, and these verses succeed admirably. Verses 1 and 2 highlight the theme of God's speech, and Hebrews will constantly revert to God's word in Scripture as the foundation and source of its theological reflection. At the same time, that scriptural word must be understood in the light of God's speech "in these last days," "through a Son," and belief in Christ regularly provides the framework for interpretation of scriptural texts. The contrast in these verses between prophets and Son also indicates the sort of argumentation dominating Hebrews that will regularly compare old and new divine dispensations and argue that the new is absolutely superior to the old.

While vv. 1–2 indicate something of the form of what is to come, v. 3 gives an important indication of its content. With its balanced clauses, participial style, and semitizing Greek, the verse has plausibly been identified as a fragment of a hymn celebrating Christ's preexistence, incarnation, and exaltation much like Phil. 2:6–11 or Col. 1:15–18. As in those hymns, the Christological pattern derives from the Jewish wisdom tradition, a derivation confirmed by the quotation of images ("effulgence of his glory and imprint of his being") drawn from Wisd. of Sol. 7:25. The hymn closes with an allusion ("he took a seat at the right hand") to Ps. 110:1, a key text for early Christian descriptions of the exaltation of Christ and an important text for the whole of Hebrews.

The imagery of the transitional Heb. 1:4, portraying Christ as superior to the angels and having a special name, is a standard part of exaltation scenes (Phil. 2:10–11; Eph. 1:20–22; 1 Pet. 3:22). Mention of the angels also serves as a sort of rubric superficially uniting the next two chapters.

1:5–2:18
Christ Exalted and Humiliated

The first major movement of the text reemphasizes traditional affirmations about Christ. It does so in two neatly balanced and formally distinct halves, separated by a brief exhortation.

1:5–14
A Scriptural Catena

Catenas ("chains") or florilegia ("bouquets") of scriptural texts testifying to a certain belief are known from first-century Jewish sources. Christians too apparently made such collections to support their belief that Jesus was the Messiah. Hebrews incorporates one such collection, perhaps with some modifications. Some of the texts cited here, such as Ps. 2:7 in Heb. 1:5 or Ps. 110:1 in Heb. 1:13, appear elsewhere as testimonies to Christ's exaltation. Others, such as Ps. 45:6–7 in Heb. 1:8–9 and Ps. 102:25–27 in Heb. 1:10–12, are unique to this collection. Many of these texts are originally royal psalms, celebrating the coronation (Pss. 2, 110) or the royal virtues (Ps. 45) of an Israelite king. Taken from context, they are understood to be oracles addressed to Christ. In the original catena, all of the texts were probably taken to refer to the exaltation. Our author apparently construed them within the framework of the Christology of the preexistent Christ, as the reference to the "introduction of the firstborn into the world" in Heb. 1:6 suggests. However the catena's Christological story was construed, it functions as a whole to highlight the heavenly character of Christ, to the point that a scriptural address to God is understood of Christ (vv. 8–9). Because of his status as Son, Christ is superior to the angels.

2:1–4
A Parenetic Interlude

The first hortatory passage draws an *a fortiori* inference from Christ's superiority over the angels. If the message that they helped to deliver needed to be taken seriously, how much more so ought the addressees heed the message delivered by the Son. Elaborate theories about the aims of Hebrews have been unnecessarily developed on the basis of the comparison with angels. The comparison, based on the traditional exaltation schema, serves the immediate function of grounding this appeal to heed the salvific message, while, in the Christological development, it dramatically affirms the heavenly dimension of Christ. Apart from the allusion to angels at 2:16, which serves to structure the work, the angels largely disappear from the text.

2:5–18
Humiliation Before Exaltation

The second half of the first movement in the text strongly affirms the reality of the Son's incarnation. The argument proceeds in two segments, an exegesis of a psalm, then a more imagistic presentation of Christ's salvific action.

2:5–9, Exposition of Psalm 8:4–6. The psalm is superficially linked to the previous discussion of Christ and angels with the note (v. 5) that eschatological (end-time) sovereignty is granted to someone other than angels. The text is introduced with an indefinite allusion to its speaker, common in first-century exegetical works. The psalm originally celebrated the glorious status of human beings, made "little lower than the angels" and for that reason "crowned with honor and glory." Our author takes the "man" and "son of man" not as references to humanity generally, but as a cipher for Christ. Whether he did so on the basis of some "Son of man" or "New Adam" Christology is irrelevant. Then, in his exegetical comment (vv. 8b–9), he drives a wedge between what had originally been clauses in synonymous parallelism and takes the "subjection below angels" as a reference to Christ's incarnation and death, which preceded his "coronation" or exaltation.

2:10–18, Reflection on the Incarnation. Another bit of probably traditional Christological speculation emphasizes both the reality of Christ's humanity and the salvific purpose of his Passion. The imagery throughout is striking. God, in drawing many of his children to heavenly glory, "perfects" the one who leads them on their way to salvation (v. 10). That perfection is achieved through suffering (v. 10) and through doing battle with the diabolical forces that hold sway over death (v. 14). Salvation involves, first of all, liberation from the fear of death (v. 15) by one who "grabs hold of" human beings (v. 16). Such imagery stems from Greco-Roman heroic myths describing the descent into Hades of figures such as Heracles, who released death's captives and led them back to life. These ancient myths were reinterpreted in philosophical and literary sources as paradigms of liberation from the fear of death. The early affirmation of Christ's exaltation has obviously been reinterpreted in an environment where such myths and their interpretations were current.

In this pericope, the author modifies the traditional mythologically tinged portrait of Christ's salvific action by suggesting that the incarnation has a specifically ecclesial focus and that salvation is the result of divine election, not simply the natural affinity of savior and saved hinted at in v. 11. In vv. 12–13, he cites Ps. 22:22 and Isa. 8:17–18 as sayings of the incarnate Christ, who thus professes his intent to announce God's name in the "midst of the assembly [or church]" and who displays his faith or trust in God along with "the children God has given" him.

The pericope, and the first major movement of Hebrews, concludes (vv. 17–18) with a summary about Jesus, using for the first time in the text the title of high priest. Within the NT this title is used of Christ only in Hebrews, but it was probably not our author's invention. Like virtually everything else in the first two chapters, it is probably part of the Christological tradition of the community addressed. The attributes of Christ as high priest, faithful and merciful (v. 17), as well as the portrait of his activity, aiding those who are undergoing the trials he himself had to face (v. 18), are also probably parts of a traditional portrait. A large part of the author's Christological creativity will consist in emphasizing a different dimension of Christ's priesthood.

is greater than the house he constructs, and God is the builder of all. The last phrase evokes the Christology of the exordium without explicitly identifying Christ and God. The argument proceeds (v. 5) exegetically. According to Num. 12:7, Moses is a faithful "servant," clearly an honorific epithet. Hebrews, however, using a technique similar to that of 2:5–9, reverses the significance of the epithet and uses it to contrast Moses with Christ, who, as Son, is "over" not "in" God's house and is, therefore, superior to Moses, the servant.

Hebrews moves to parenesis by playing (v. 6) on the term "house(hold)." The addressees are members of the house over which Christ presides, but that membership is conditional, dependent on maintaining "boldness" and "hope's boast." Both motifs will recur in later exhortations.

The homily will focus on Ps. 95:7–11, introduced, as are several other scriptural citations, with reference to the Holy Spirit (Heb. 3:7). The text (vv. 7–11) follows fairly closely the Septuagint (LXX) version of the psalm.

3:1–5:10
Faith and the Merciful High Priest

The next major movement of Hebrews falls into two halves, each of which develops a motif drawn from the epithets of Christ in 2:17. The first segment (3:1–4:13) consists of a self-contained, exegetical homily warning against faithlessness. While chaps. 1 and 2 laid the groundwork for the doctrinal development of Hebrews, this homily prepares for the fuller parenetic treatment of faith in chap. 11. The second half of this movement (4:14–5:10) returns to the Christological theme, reinforcing the perspective of chap. 2 but introducing a new element, Ps. 110:4, which will form the basis of the subsequent Christological exposition.

3:1–11
Introduction and Scriptural Citation

The author introduces his homily with a comparison between Christ and Moses. As in the comparison between Christ and the angels, there is no hint of polemic. The comparison again shows the superlative status of Christ, even more faithful than the greatest hero of ancient Israel. At the same time, it prepares for the content of the exegetical homily, which will focus on the generation of Israelites led by Moses. The superiority of Christ to Moses is demonstrated from Scripture. The fact that Moses was "faithful" is derived from Num. 12:7, alluded to in Heb. 2:2. That text had spoken of Moses being faithful in God's "house" or "household." That term introduces an illustrative analogy (vv. 3–4) to the effect that a builder

3:12–4:11
Exposition of Psalm 95

The exposition falls into three distinct segments, each of which cites a verse of the psalm and appeals to other scriptural texts or data for interpretive help. The first segment (3:12–19) warns against faithless disobedience. The second (4:1–5) redefines a key term in the psalm. The last (4:6–11) makes a parenetic application.

3:12–19, A Warning Example. The appeal to the Israelites of the desert generation as a warning example is common in Jewish homiletics and is paralleled in Paul's admonition in 1 Corinthians 10. The beginning (Heb. 3:12) and ending (v. 19) of this section indicate that the object of the warning is "faithlessness." The author urges his audience to actualize the psalm's call by encouraging one another (v. 13) in their own "today." The content of their encouragement follows after a parenthetical remark (v. 14) and consists in the call not to have hard hearts (v. 15).

The exposition initially hinges on several wordplays. Faithlessness (Gk. *apistia*) is linked first (v. 12) with "apostasy" (*apostēnai*). Then both are contrasted with what the addressed are parenthetically (v. 14) urged to maintain, their "initial reality" (*hypostasis*). That term, which appears here, in 1:3, and in 11:1, is often mistranslated. The philosophical connotations, obvious in 1:3, are probably operative here as well, although somewhat paradoxically; for how can reality have a beginning? That seeming paradox is at the heart of the subtle conceptual play that our author will make in his central exposition (7:1–10:18).

1262

The exposition proceeds (vv. 16–18) with a portrait of the failure of the Israelites drawn largely from Numbers 14, stressing the connection of sin (Heb. 3:17), disobedience (v. 18), and faithlessness (v. 19). The warning, however, remains on a general level. At the same time, the author notes the fact, implied by the psalm, that the desert generation, because of its failure, could not enter God's "rest" or "resting place."

4:1–5, The Nature of the Rest. On the presumption that the psalm is addressed to the "today" of the audience, its implicit promise of a "rest" must remain open (v. 1) and available for those who, unlike the ancient Israelites (v. 2), have faithfully heard God's word (v. 3). The next exegetical move is to explain how such a rest is possible. The move is necessary because the term "rest" in the psalm referred to the "resting place" of Canaan, the goal of the wandering Israelites. Hebrews interprets by use of an argument known in rabbinic exegesis as a *gezera shawa* (Heb.), wherein a word in one text is explained by its obvious meaning in another. The argument in vv. 3–5, which works only on the basis of the Greek OT, stipulates that the meaning of "rest" in Psalm 95 is given by the use of a similar word, "[God] rested," in Gen. 2:2. There "rest" refers to the place or state that God entered after completing the works of creation. The same heavenly "rest" awaits faithful Christians.

4:6–11, The Contemporary Call. The promise to obtain a share in God's "rest" was not fulfilled in the conquest of Canaan under Joshua. Otherwise, Hebrews argues, David, the presumed author of the psalm, would not have spoken in his day of a possibility of entering God's "rest." That possibility is now defined with the evocative term "Sabbath festivity" (v. 9) because it is a share in the condition of the primordial Sabbath. The exposition concludes with a summons to strive to participate in this heavenly salvation by avoiding the failure of the Exodus generation (v. 11).

4:12–13
A Rhapsody on God's Word

The homily had demonstrated the contemporary relevance of one segment of God's ancient speech. A rhetorical flourish highlights the point with vivid imagery. God's speech is compared to a sword that can pierce the innermost depths of the human person (v. 12). That piercing has a discerning or judgmental function and the note of judgment is reemphasized as the imagery shifts (v. 13). Before God's word nothing is hidden, but all is "naked and laid bare." This rare term probably evokes the image of a sacrificial victim whose neck is bared to the priest's

knife. "God's word" here means God himself, by metonymy—as when we say "the White House" meaning the President or "the Throne" meaning the Queen. The flourish concludes on an ambiguous note, in a phrase meaning either "our discourse is about him" or "to him we have to render an account." Such ambiguity is typical of our author and the ominous note of the second sense prepares for some of his stern warnings.

4:14–16
Transitional Parenesis

The author draws implications from the preceding exposition, many themes of which find echoes here. At the same time he prepares for what follows. Particularly worthy of note are the two elements of the parenesis. The addressees are urged to "hold fast" to their confession, an element of which was, no doubt, the affirmation of "Jesus, the son of God" (v. 14). They are also urged to "approach," a term probably drawn from the cultic sphere, to the "throne," where they can find mercy and help from a sympathetic high priest (vv. 15–16).

5:1–10
The Sympathetic High Priest

5:1–4, High-Priestly Qualifications. The development of the high priest Christology proceeds with a brief reflection on the qualifications for ordinary human high priests. They serve as mediators between God and humanity by offering sacrifices for sins (5:1). They "moderate their emotions" toward those who sin in ignorance, since they themselves are beset with weakness (v. 2) and must offer sacrifices for themselves as well as the people (v. 3). Finally, they are "called by God," as was the first high priest, Aaron. These idealized qualifications are shaped by what the author knows of his true high priest and are designed to intimate both similarities and differences, many of which will become apparent only as the exposition develops.

5:5–10, Christ as High Priest. The author first (vv. 5–6) applies to Christ the notion of the divine election, noting that the one who called him Son, in the words of Ps. 2:7, also addressed to him Ps. 110:4, "You are a priest forever, according to the order of Melchizedek." Ps. 2:7, cited in Heb. 1:5, is a common early Christian exaltation text, as is the first verse of Psalm 110, cited in Heb. 1:13. Ps. 110:4, however, is not cited elsewhere in early Christian sources independent of Hebrews. Its use by our author is no doubt part of his creative reinterpretation of Christological traditions and is the foundation of the exposition in chap. 7.

The final verses of the pericope reemphasize the full humanity of the true high priest by virtue of which he can be the sympathetic heavenly intercessor. Heb. 5:7 portrays Christ in anguished prayer, being heard by God because of his "reverence," or "godly fear." The portrait is vaguely reminiscent of Gethsemane but cannot be a simple allusion to the Gospel accounts since there Christ's request that the "cup pass from him" is not granted. The portrait rather relies on qualities of pious prayer, as developed in the Psalms and in contemporary Jewish sources. Coupled with that portrait is a proverbial expression (v. 8), long familiar to the Greek tradition, that one learns from suffering. What Christ learns is obedience, not because he was disobedient, but because learning had a saving function. That function is vaguely intimated in the language of v. 9. Through his educative suffering, Christ was "perfected" as a "cause of eternal salvation." The central chapters will give these lapidary formulas more definite content. The pericope closes with the novel language of the "priesthood according to Melchizedek."

5:11–6:20

Preliminary Exhortation

The author dramatically delays the development of his novel Christological insights and turns to exhortation. He first challenges his addressees to follow his "difficult discourse" (5:11–6:3); then offers balanced words of warning and encouragement (6:4–12); and finally undergirds the encouragement with a reflection on the certainty of God's promises (6:13–19).

5:11–6:3
A Challenge to the Addressees

With provocative irony the author tells his addressees that they are not ready for his advanced teaching but are "sluggish in their hearing" (5:11). To push his point he deploys commonplace Hellenistic educational images (vv. 12–14), used with their normal metaphorical referents as a new metaphor for Christian doctrine. The addressees are like babes who can only take the milk of rudimentary education, here symbolizing basic exegesis (5:12) and elementary catechesis (6:1–2). They are not yet adults who can digest the solid food of ethical doctrine (5:13); they have not yet engaged in the rigorous athletic exercise of ethical discernment (5:14). That stage of advanced learning symbolizes the author's own "difficult discourse" (5:11).

The ironic quality of the challenge is apparent in the summons (6:1) not to rehearse basic Christian teaching, elements of which are enumerated in vv. 1–2, but to move on to "maturity." The author promises such movement "with God's assistance" (v. 3).

6:4–12
Warning and Encouragement

6:4–6, The Warning. The first of Hebrews' three major monitory passages is its most stern. A series of common images for religious experience recalls the conversion to a new life (vv. 4–5). These images contrast with the action of apostasy, depicted as crucifying and mocking the Son of God (v. 6). Our author declares the impossibility of "renewing unto repentance" those who have had the experience of the spirit and then fallen away. Many unconvincing attempts have been made to ameliorate the severity of the warning. Like many other early Christians, our author is a rigorist who does not maintain the possibility of repentance for apostasy. He does not, however, accuse his addressees of the sin but intimates that, if they do not "progress toward maturity," they could be heading toward danger.

6:7–8, An Illustration. Between warning and encouragement comes a brief agricultural image contrasting a fruitful field blessed by God (v. 7) with a field of thorns and thistles destined to be burned (v. 8). The images relate, in inverse or chiastic order, to the hypothetical situation of apostates and his addressees. The fire to which the second field is destined is, at the level of the image, a farmer's clearing technique, but it conjures up ominous scenes of eschatological punishment.

6:9–12, Encouragement. The hypothetical character of the warning now becomes clear. The author believes that the positive part of his illustration, which "pertains to salvation," applies to his addressees (v. 9). He recalls, in a general way, their service and love (v. 10) and exhorts them to maintain their hope (v. 11). In chap. 10 he will give more details of their previous behavior. Now he simply notes that he encourages them so that they will not be what he had ironically called them at 5:11, "sluggish." Instead, they will display the faith and endurance of those who inherited the promises of old (v. 12).

6:13–20
God's Promise and Oath

The importance of hope and the certainty that grounds it has been a subordinate theme running through Hebrews. It achieves somewhat clearer profile in this brief scriptural meditation that supports the preceding word of encouragement. The argument relies on common Jewish traditions about the immutability of God's promises and the significance of his scriptural oaths. The whole pericope prepares for discussion in 7:20–25 of the oath that supports God's designation of a priest "according to the order of Melchizedek."

The reflection begins (vv. 13–14) with a reference to God's oath to Abraham in Gen. 22:16–17, then uses a human analogy to indicate the function of the oath, to provide extra certainty to human recipients of a promise (vv. 16–17). Encouraged by "two unchangeable things," presumably God's unspecified promise and his confirming oath, the addressees can hold on to hope (v. 18).

The whole parenetic pericope concludes, as it had begun in 5:11–14, with an oddly mixed metaphor. Hope is likened, as commonly in Greek literature, to an anchor (v. 19), but the anchor is not only an image of stability. It also "enters within the veil." The metaphor for hope is thus affected by the ultimate source on which hope is based, Jesus, the "forerunner." The abruptly introduced image of the veil, which separates the inner and outer sanctuaries of the tabernacle, prepares for the imagery that will dominate chaps. 8–10. The author picks up the thread of the Christological development with another allusion to Ps. 110:4.

7:1–10:25
The Exposition on Christ as High Priest

The central movement of Hebrews falls into two balanced segments. The first (7:1–28) explores the significance of Ps. 110:4 and ultimately reaffirms in a striking way the emphasis of Hebrews 1 on the heavenly quality of Christ. The second (8:1–10:19) both reaffirms the reality of the incarnation, as in chap. 2, and indicates how Christ's high-priestly act is, and must be, at once heavenly and earthly.

7:1–28
Christ and Melchizedek

Formally, the chapter constitutes an exegetical discussion of Ps. 110:4 based upon the only other OT text that mentions Melchizedek, Gen. 14:17–20. This exegesis, emphasizing the heavenly character of Christ's priesthood, may have been inspired by the abundant contemporary speculation on Melchizedek as a heavenly figure, examples of which are found in the Alexandrian Jewish writer Philo, at Qumran, and in Gnostic sources. Whatever the inspiration, Hebrews is quite restrained in its comments on Melchizedek, utilizing only what is necessary to make the Christological point.

7:1–3, Introduction. The exposition begins with a selective citation of Gen. 14:17–20 (Heb. 7:1–2a), followed by well-known, but erroneous, etymological interpretations of the name Melchizedek (→ Melchizedek) and of the city over which he ruled (v. 2). From the pregnant silence of Scripture is deduced Melchizedek's status as "fatherless, motherless, without genealogy" (v. 3). The most important deduction in this rhetorically elaborate series is the eternal character of Melchizedek's priesthood. The basic point of the whole chapter is that in designating Christ as "high priest according to the order of Melchizedek," Scripture affirms that he is the high priest of an eternal, spiritual order.

7:4–10, Melchizedek and the Levites. Before making the main Christological point, the author adduces an admittedly (v. 9) playful exegetical argument to demonstrate the superiority of Melchizedek and, by implication, Christ to the levitical priests (→ Levites) of the OT. His argument is based on the fact that the law (Num. 18:21) stipulates that priests who are descendants of Levi are to take tithes from the rest of the people (Heb. 7:5). Genesis 14 indicates that Melchizedek, who has no levitical genealogy, took a tithe from their ancestor. Moreover, Melchizedek blessed Abraham (Heb. 7:6), indicating, by virtue of a general principle formulated for the occasion (v. 7), that Melchizedek is superior to Abraham. By implication, Melchizedek received a tithe from the tithers through their ancestor (vv. 9–10) and is superior to them.

7:11–19, The Implications of a New Priest. The argument becomes more serious as the author explores the implications of Ps. 110:4, taken as a promise of a new, nonlevitical priesthood. Some apologetic considerations may underlie the argument at this point. According to accepted Christian traditions, Jesus was a Judahite and therefore could not have been a priest because of the scriptural requirements of levitical descent (Heb. 7:13–14). Ps. 110:4, with its reference to a nonlevitical priest, might have been used to justify Christ's priestly title, but Hebrews does not make that simple point. Rather, the introduction of a nonlevitical priest must mean that the whole law is altered (Heb. 7:11–12). The "likeness of Melchizedek" indicates what this alteration involves (v. 15). As the argument from silence in v. 3 had suggested, Christ's priesthood does not have to do with the realm of flesh but with the "indissoluble life" of the spirit (v. 16). The failure of the law, which necessitated its change, is indicated in the note that it did not bring "perfection" (vv. 11, 19). Chaps. 8–10 will indicate what this perfection is and how it relates to the perfection attributed to Christ.

7:20–25, The Confirming Oath. The significance of the discussion at 6:13–17 now becomes apparent. Ps. 110:4 contains, besides its reference to an eternal priesthood, a case of God swearing, which further distinguishes the priesthood of Christ from that of the Levites (Heb. 7:20–21). The point is made only as a preparation for the characteristically abrupt introduction of a new theme, the "covenant" of which Jesus is the surety or guarantor (v. 22). Like the allusion to "perfection" in the previous pericope, this new theme will be developed in the following exposition. For the moment the author notes the difference between human priests who, by the law of fleshly succession, are continually replaced (v. 23) and the Son who lives forever as intercessor (vv. 24–25). The picture reaffirms a dimension of Christ's heavenly priesthood that had appeared previously (2:17–18) and that was probably part of the Christological tradition.

7:26–28, Conclusion. A rhapsodic finale, formally similar to the remarks on God's word (4:12–13) concludes this exposition. Verse 26 stresses the heavenly character of Christ. The remaining verses summarize the contrast that has developed through the chapter. The note that Christ does not need to sacrifice for himself as do ordinary high priests (v. 27) recalls the qualifications of high priests in 5:3. The contrast between the mortal priests whom the law appoints and the "Son perfected forever" appointed by the divine oath (v. 28) summarizes the major contrast of the previous pericope. These summary verses frame a reference, the first since the exordium, to Christ's principal priestly act, his once-for-all self-sacrifice for sin, the subject of the following exposition.

8:1–10:18
Christ's Sacrifice and the New Covenant

As noted in the Introduction, this section of Hebrews, much like 3:1–4:11, is in a homiletic form. At a superficial level, the exposition presents two biblical models for understanding Christ's death. One is the action of the high priest on the Day of Atonement. Christ's death is thus seen as the truly atoning sacrifice (→Atonement). At the same time, it is seen to be a covenant-inaugurating sacrifice. At a more formal level, the exposition develops not through detailed exegesis but by reflecting on certain key antitheses: earth-heaven, old-new, external-interior. The pericope will ultimately show how Christ's sacrificial death is the meeting point wherein these oppositions are mediated and overcome.

8:1–6, Introduction: The Heavenly Tabernacle. The "summary" of what has been said (v. 1) alludes once again to Ps. 110:1. Christ, seated at God's right hand, has been shown in the previous chapter to be a heavenly "liturgist." He must, therefore, function in the "true" or heavenly temple (Heb. 8:2), and, like any high priest, he must have something to offer (v. 3). The distinction between earthly and heavenly sanctuaries is then highlighted. On earth, where Christ could not have been a priest (v. 4), the sacred ministers serve at what is only a "shadowy copy" of the true temple (v. 5a). The dichotomy between a heavenly realm of truth and a "shadowy" earthly copy employs platonic language, but the notion of a heavenly temple is a traditional Jewish one. It is based on ancient Near Eastern ideas that lie behind the scriptural verse, Exod. 25:40, cited in Heb. 8:5b. In Jewish apocalypses, such as 1 Enoch or 2 Esdras, there are frequent depictions of a heavenly or eschatological temple. Among more hellenized Jews such as Philo, the heavenly temple becomes a more "spiritual" reality. Indications of a similar understanding will emerge as the exposition proceeds. The introduction concludes with a reference to the theme of the covenant, hinted at in 7:22. The superiority of Christ's liturgy is correlated with the superiority of the promises of the covenant of which he is mediator.

8:7–13, The Promised New Covenant. A lengthy quotation of Jer. 31:31–34, following the LXX fairly closely, performs two functions, much as the catena in chap. 1 both introduced a parenetic remark and served to develop the Christology. As the introductory and concluding verses (vv. 7, 13) suggest, the passage demonstrates that the old covenant was defective and in need of replacement. More importantly, it indicates what are the "greater promises" (v. 6) on which the new covenant is based. The author shows what he takes these promises to be by the repeated citation of part of the passage at the conclusion of the exposition (10:16–17). The new covenant is an interior one of the heart and mind, and under it sins are effectively forgiven.

9:1–10, The Old, Earthly Cult. The exposition develops in five balanced segments. The first describes the "regulations for worship and the worldly sanctuary" of the old covenant (v. 1). These topics are treated in inverse order. A brief inventory of the outer (v. 2) and inner (vv. 3–5) portions of the tabernacle is based principally on the accounts in Exodus 25–26. Some details have been modified, such as placement of an incense altar in the inner portion of the tabernacle (Heb. 9:4), a notion probably based on extrabiblical traditions. Less easily explained is the reversal of the conventional names for the outer and inner portions of the tabernacle found in some manuscripts and probably the original reading. Whatever the reason for it, our author regularly calls the inner portion not the "Holy of Holies" but simply the "Holies" (here regularly translated "sanctuary").

The latter half of the pericope (vv. 6–10) focuses on the main "regulation for worship" on which the Christological portrait turns. As Leviticus 16 stipulates, entry into the sanctuary is reserved for the high priest alone, only once a year, on the Day of Atonement, when he sprinkles the "mercy seat" with the blood of sacrificial animals (Heb. 9:6–7). This arrangement is immediately (v. 8) taken to be indicative of the imperfection of the old cult in which access to the sanctuary where God dwells is blocked. Hebrews will later (10:19–20) note that with the new covenant direct access to God is made possible. For the moment the author notes that the old cult is simply a "parable" or symbol for the present (v. 9a). In its imperfection it is, however, a negative image of the present. In itself, the old cult consists of actions that cannot cleanse conscience (v. 9b), cannot, that is, touch the realm of the spirit because they only affect external things and are thus regulations dealing with the flesh (v. 10). The same implicit spirit-flesh dichotomy deployed in the critique of the law at 7:16 resurfaces and unites, while it interprets, the antitheses of heaven-earth, internal-external. The worldly cult and its regulations remain "until a time of correction" (v. 10), which is not some future event but the inauguration of a new covenant by Christ.

9:11–14, The New, Heavenly Cult. The second segment of the exposition describes the heavenly liturgy. Verse 11 sets the scene in the "more perfect" tabernacle "not of this creation." Fanciful allegorical interpretations of this verse, applying it to Christ's body—physical, glorified, sacramental, or ecclesiastical—are unwarranted. The author simply exploits the mythic picture of a heavenly temple to suggest that Christ's exaltation, his "passage through the heavens" (4:14), was the point at which his sacrifice was consummated, just as the sacrifice of the Day of Atonement is consummated when the high priest sprinkles the blood on the mercy seat. Christ's sacrifice, however, involved not animals' blood but his own (v. 12). How such blood is sprinkled in heaven remains for the moment a mystery, but our author does indicate that he views all of this highly realistic imagery as a metaphor when he indicates that the sacrifice of Christ was effected "through eternal spirit" (v. 14). Unlike the sacrifices of the old, earthly cult, which only cleanse the flesh (v. 13), the sacrifice of the new, heavenly cult operates on the spiritual level, affecting "conscience" or the consciousness of sin (v. 14).

9:15–22, The New Covenant. The third and central segment of the exposition apparently interrupts the picture of the "heavenly liturgy," but the interruption is a crucial move in the development of the exposition. The theme of a "promised inheritance" that has run through the text (1:14; 4:1; 6:12; 8:6) is now united with the notion of the covenant (v. 15; → Covenant). The connection is made through a wordplay on the Greek term diathēkē, which can mean both "will or testament" and "contract or covenant." The first sense clearly operates in vv. 16–17, which argue that the death of a testator is necessary for a diathēkē to come into force. The facetious character of the argument becomes apparent as the author turns (v. 18) to the first diathēkē or covenant, which cannot be assimilated to the model of a will. The point of comparison is that the first covenant also involved a sacrifice and purificatory sprinkling of blood, as is demonstrated with allusions (Heb. 9:19, 21) to Exodus 24 and citation (Heb. 9:20) of Exod. 24:8. The pericope thus demonstrates that real bloodshed is a requirement for the inauguration of a covenant and that the covenant is the vehicle for the attainment of the divine promises.

9:23–28, The New, Heavenly Cult. The fourth segment of the exposition, thematically corresponding to the second, reverts to the realm where Christ's sacrifice is seen to have been consummated, "heaven itself" (v. 24), a connection influenced by platonic designations of the ideal world. What is supposed to transpire in this realm is thus the ideal counterpart of the purification of cultic paraphernalia just described (9:13, 19–22). This heavenly cleansing, like the "tabernacle not of this creation," has occasioned much scholarly speculation, but our author has already indicated the referent of the imagery. The spiritual realities cleansed by Christ's sacrifice are the consciences of believers.

At this point no interpretation of the imagery of heavenly cleansing is offered. Instead, Hebrews insists on the uniqueness of Christ's sacrifice, as opposed to the multiplicity of the old cultic sacrifices (vv. 25–26). The same antithesis of one and many that first appeared in the exordium reemerges and serves as another device to interpret the fundamental antitheses of the exposition.

The preference for unity over multiplicity is another platonic theme, but the unity involved here is not a metaphysical one. Rather, it is the uniqueness of an action that takes place "at the end of the ages" (v. 26) and that is but the first stage in an eschatological drama, the last act of which is yet to be played (v. 28). The glance at the eschaton (end) signals a shift in the basic antitheses to be effected in the next pericope. At the same time, it heralds an eschatological motif that will develop in the final chapters.

10:1-10, The New, Earthly-Heavenly Sacrifice. The fifth segment of the exposition formally balances the first, turning from heaven back to earth. Here the play on the antitheses in the exposition reaches its dramatic climax. The introductory verse gives a first indication of the decisive play. The law is said to be but a "shadow of the good things to come," that is, with the inauguration of the new covenant. It is not the "very image" of those realities. The reference to "shadow" recalls the description of the earthly sanctuary in 8:5, but it is here used within a temporal, not spatial dichotomy. The term "image" is used not in its most obvious sense of a copy, but in a technical philosophical usage attested among contemporary Platonists, in the sense of the ideal form. The author of Hebrews, however, uses this platonic term not of a metaphysical reality but of a historical event. The next remarks (vv. 2–4) repeat the familiar criticism of the "shadow" or old cult, which could not cleanse conscience. The multiplicity of its activity attests to its impotence and signals the fact that it could only recall sins (v. 3). Here a commonplace of Jewish homiletics is turned into a critique. The grounds for the inefficacy of the cult are again located in the unworthy means by which it attempts atonement (v. 4).

The latter half of the pericope returns to the sacrifice of the new order. The argument hinges on a scriptural citation, Ps. 40:6–8, which, like the texts cited in Heb. 2:12–13, is taken to be a word of Christ. The introduction to the citation (v. 5) significantly situates the utterance at the point where Christ "enters the cosmos." Hebrews has previously focused on the movement of Christ into the heavenly sanctuary and the realm of the spirit. Moreover, the cosmos, as the realm of the flesh, has previously been depicted as inimical to the realm of the spirit (9:1–10) where the true sacrifice takes place (9:11–14).

The original psalm had read "ears you have hollowed out for me." Hebrews, following the LXX, reads (v. 5), instead, "a body you have prepared for me." This is one of the two elements of the text on which the following interpretive comment focuses and the basis on which the "cosmos" is revalued. The second significant element appears at the end of the citation (v. 7) where the speaker says that he came, as the "scroll of the book" testifies, "to do your will, O God."

An interpretive comment sets up an opposition between the two modes of sacrifice mentioned in the psalm, the external "sacrifices, offerings, holocausts, and sin offerings," i.e., the whole old cultic system, on the one hand (v. 8), and "doing God's will" (v. 9) on the other. The note that the speaker abrogates the former and establishes the latter indicates how the author understands Christ's sacrifice and the imagery that he has been using to describe it. That sacrifice is an act of conformity to the will of God, hence, internal and spiritual. At the same time it is bodily, hence, earthly. Because it is both at once, it is the sort of act that can fittingly inaugurate the new covenant promised in Jeremiah. All of this is summarized in a solemnly triumphant finale (v. 10). "We are sanctified" and thereby receive one promise of the new covenant "by that will" of God to which Jesus Christ conformed himself in the "sacrifice of his body," which is the reality that casts its shadow backward on the law and which is absolutely "once-for-all," unique.

10:11–18, Concluding Flourish. As the earlier embedded homily concluded with a festive reflection on God's word (4:12–13), the central exposition concludes with a summary of the effects of Christ's sacrifice. The language of vv. 11 and 12 is familiar from the exposition and includes an allusion (vv. 12b–13) to Ps. 110:1, the first since Heb. 8:1. The reference to "subjection of the enemies" recalls the first citation of the text (1:13) and points again to the eschatological consummation of Christ's mission. But the most important inference to be drawn from the sacrifice relates to what has already been accomplished, the "perfection" of those who are being sanctified (v. 14). As the critique of the old cult at 10:1–2 indicated, "perfection," as applied to believers, refers to the cleansing of their conscience, the qualification which makes them fit to worship God in truth (9:14). The category thus functions rather like Paul's language of "justification." A second citation (vv. 16–17) of a portion of Jeremiah (Jer. 31:33–34) highlights the major themes of the exposition, an interior or spiritual covenant and effective forgiveness of sin. The concluding tag (Heb. 10:18) points once again to the abrogation of the old cultic order.

10:19-25
Transitional Parenesis

With language similar to the transitional parenesis of 4:14–16, the author begins to draw implications from his Christological exposition. His initial comment (vv. 19–21) restates the objective situation on which exhortation is based, that Christians have a "new and living way through the veil." That veil, an image from the tabernacle's design first met at 6:19, is here surprisingly equated with Christ's flesh. That paradoxical equation follows naturally from the revaluation of the cosmic and bodily spheres effected in 10:1–10. If flesh had been something barring access to God, Christ's flesh, offered on the cross, is the point at which access to God is made available. The following series of exhortations highlights the cardinal virtues of faith, hope, and love while making more specific recommendations to take baptism seriously (v. 22), to hold on to the confession (v. 23), and to persevere in fellowship (vv. 24–25), all in the eschatological perspective of the coming "day."

10:26–12:13
Exhortation to Faith and Endurance

The next major movement of Hebrews is parenetic. Like the central expository section, it is introduced with a word of warning and encouragement (10:26–39). Then the addressees are urged to have faith in a lengthy encomium on that virtue (chap. 11). The list of exemplars of faith culminates in a portrait of Christ that also introduces an explicit call to endurance (12:1–13).

10:26–39
Preliminary Exhortation

10:26–31, A Renewed Warning. As in chap. 6, the author issues a stern warning against apostasy, grounded in the principle enunciated at 10:18, that there remains no sacrifice for sin after the death of Christ. To make the point the author uses an *a fortiori* argument like that of 2:1–4. The capital punishment for abrogating the Law of Moses, as stipulated in Deut. 17:6, provides the point of comparison with the situation of the addressees. How much more serious will be the situation of those who reject the new covenant (Heb. 10:29)? The warning concludes with scriptural verses and the author's own ominous epigrammatic remark (v. 31), all of which emphasize divine judgment.

10:32–39, New Encouragement. In Hebrews' parenetic program encouragement regularly follows and complements warning. Here encouragement consists of a recollection of past persecution successfully endured. The author mentions the direct personal indignities and deprivations that his addressees experienced but calls special attention to the ways in which they offered mutual support in time of need (vv. 33–34). An important aim of the concluding parenetic chapters is to reinforce such a sense of community.

The recollection leads to an explicit call for "boldness" (v. 35) based on "endurance" (v. 36) and "faith" (v. 39), the two virtues highlighted in what follows. Between the two is set

a composite scriptural quotation. A phrase from Isa. 26:20 in the LXX, "yet a very little while," suggests again the eschatological perspective within which the parenesis develops. The remark of Hab. 2:3–4, well known from Paul's discussion of faith (Rom. 1:17; Gal. 3:11), that the righteous will live by faith, directly introduces the discussion of that virtue.

11:1–40
An Encomium on Faith

This famous chapter, although incorporating features of other genres, is best described as an encomium on faith, much like the encomium on wisdom in Wisdom of Solomon 10. Like that text, it relies on examples drawn from the history of Israel. These examples also serve as models of faith and help to define it. Faith emerges as a both cognitive and affective quality, belief in certain fundamental truths about and fidelity to God. Faith, moreover, is seen to be involved in the two sorts of behavior recommended in the parenesis, steadfastness in the face of persecution and movement onward and outward to a heavenly goal.

11:1–7, Faith from Creation to Noah. The initial definition of faith (v. 1), formally paralleled in many philosophical texts, is condensed and evocative. It is the "reality of things hoped for" in the sense that through it hopes are attained. The term for "reality" is the same one used at 1:3 and 3:14 and has the same objective connotations. Faith is also the "proof of things unseen," that is, the quality by which humans are put in touch with the unseen realities of God and by which they attain things unseen in the present.

Using the figure called anaphora, in which successive clauses begin with the same element, examples of faith are now cataloged, beginning (v. 3) with the faith that believers have in creation and extending through the fidelity of the protomartyr Abel, Enoch, the propositional content of whose faith is specified (v. 6), and Noah who by his faith achieved deliverance.

11:8–12, The Faith of Abraham and Sarah. Attention is focused on the patriarchs, first because they accepted the status of aliens even within their promised land based upon their expectation of a divinely prepared "city" (vv. 7–10). Then Abraham, along with Sarah, is seen to have been enabled to achieve the impossible through faith (vv. 11–12).

11:13–16, A Reflection on the Patriarchs' Faith. The author interrupts the catalog to expand on the image of the patriarchs as "wander-

1269

ing people of God." What motivated their quest was the desire for a better, that is, heavenly homeland or divine "city," not simply a new earthly dwelling place. This reflection recalls the interpretation of the term "rest" from Psalm 95 in Heb. 4 and anticipates the image of the heavenly Jerusalem in 12:18–24.

11:17–22, Faith from Abraham to Joseph. The historical catalog resumes with an allusion to the *Aqedah* (Heb.), the "binding of Isaac" in Genesis 22, taken to be an example of belief in the resurrection (vv. 17–18), and then the blessings bestowed by Isaac and Jacob on their descendants. These acts, like Joseph's request to have his bones buried in Israel, all attest the hopeful expectation that is part of faith.

11:23–31, Faith from Moses to the Conquest. Both Moses' parents and Moses himself display fidelity to God in the face of royal opposition. Moses' faith leads him to accept persecution and, in a mysterious anticipation of chap. 12, "the reproach of Christ" (v. 26). Faith, founded in a vision of the unseen God (v. 27), also enabled Moses to depart from Egypt, as Abraham had departed from Haran. Similar salvific faith inspired his followers (vv. 29–31).

11:32–40, Later Examples of Faith. At this point Hebrews abandons the device of anaphora and conveys a sense of the abundance of examples of faith primarily by asyndeton or the avoidance of conjunctions. The names of some judges as well as David and Samuel introduce a list of their typical accomplishments (vv. 32–35a). There follows a list of persecutions endured (vv. 35b–38). The encomium concludes with a note that these examples of faith did not attain the promise now available to the addressees.

12:1–13
Christ, Faith, and Endurance
Another little homily, combining the virtues mentioned at 10:36–39, completes this parenetic movement.

12:1–3, The Perfect Paradigm, Christ. The homily is introduced with a portrait of Christ the "athlete." The imagery is commonplace in Hellenistic and early Christian parenesis. Here the race that Christ and the addressees run in a stadium filled with the heroes of the past is a race of faith. Victory in the race is assured because Christ, the "leader (or inaugurator) and perfecter" of faith, has already run the course and won the prize through his endurance of the cross. The author calls his addressees to follow the example and imitate through endurance the faith of Christ.

12:4–13, Suffering and Education. The call to endure is supported by a reflection on the proverbial theme of educative suffering mentioned earlier (5:8) in connection with Christ. The theme is now (vv. 5–6) developed through citation of Prov. 3:11–12 and an exposition of its theme of beneficial paternal discipline. This theme was an old response of the wisdom tradition to the problem of theodicy (defending the justice of God in the face of evil); here it is used for parenetic ends. The homily concludes (Heb. 12:12–13), as it began, with athletic imagery and a call to brace for the race.

12:14–13:21
Life in View of the End
The final parenetic movement reinforces the eschatological perspectives of the text while emphasizing the implications to be drawn from Christ's sacrificial act.

12:14–29
Warning and Hope
12:14–17, A Final Warning. A shift from the athletic imagery of the homily appears in the call to pursue peace and sanctification (v. 14). This is followed by the last severe warning of the dangers of apostasy, consisting of a citation of Deut. 29:18 and an interpretation of that text's image of the "root of bitterness" in terms of the biblical character Esau, who lost his inheritance. The addressees should avoid making a similar mistake with their promised heavenly inheritance.

12:18–24, Earthly Sinai and Heavenly Zion. As earlier warnings had been followed by encouragement, the threat is balanced by a characterization of the addressees' situation in a set of contrasting images. A description (vv. 18–21) of the awesome theophany at Sinai inspired by Exodus 19 and appealing to Deut. 9:19 is juxtaposed with a picture of the "heavenly Jerusalem" (Heb. 12:22–24). The basic image, foreshadowed in the references to the city in chap. 11, is derived from Jewish apocalyptic traditions, but it is given particularly joyous connotations. The reference to the divine judge (v. 23) is balanced by the mention of the mediator of a new covenant, whose atoning blood cries out in a better fashion than that of Abel (v. 24).

12:25–29, The End in View. Words of warning and hope are again intermingled. On the one hand, it is impossible to escape the heavenly judge who will shake the foundations of created reality (vv. 25–26a). The addressees, on the other hand, can take consolation in that they already have possession of something unshakable, a "kingdom" through which they can offer fitting service to God, who is, as Deut. 4:24 intimates, "a consuming fire."

13:1–21
Final Recommendations and Rhetorical Conclusion

The stylistic shift to specific recommendations has occasionally led to unnecessary theories that the chapter is a secondary addition. It appropriately concludes the text.

13:1–6, Loving Service. The author rapidly advocates rather common virtues of brotherly love, hospitality, charity to prisoners (recalling 10:34), chastity, simplicity, and reliance upon God, described in Ps. 118:6 (LXX) as the psalmist's "helper."

13:7–17, True Worship. Within the framework of appeals involving the community's leaders (vv. 7, 17) comes a description of what true Christian worship involves. It is founded on the eternal Christ (v. 8) and modeled on his sacrifice, which differs radically from the old cult (vv. 9–11). Christ died a shameful death "outside the gate" to sanctify his people. Christians should follow his example, accepting reproach (v. 13) and offering only sacrifices of praise and good works (vv. 15–16). This rejection of cult in favor of loving service is a direct corollary of the revaluation of the "cosmos" in 10:1–10.

13:18–21, Finale. Personal requests, a benediction, praying for the addressees to be strengthened, and a doxology bring the text proper to its end.

13:22–25
Epistolary Conclusion

The final verses with their personal greetings and gracious farewell were probably appended to the work when it was actually sent to its addressees. There is no reason to suspect that anyone but the unknown author penned them.

Bibliography
Bruce, F. F. *The Epistle to the Hebrews.* Grand Rapids, MI: Eerdmans, 1964.

Hughes, P. E. *A Commentary on the Epistle to the Hebrews.* Grand Rapids, MI: Eerdmans, 1977.

Käsemann, E. *The Wandering People of God: An Investigation of the Letter to the Hebrews.* Minneapolis, MN: Augsburg, 1984.

Kobelski, P. J. *Melchizedek and Melchiresha[c].* Catholic Biblical Quarterly Monograph Series, 10. Washington: Catholic Biblical Association, 1981.

Peterson, D. *Hebrews and Perfection: An Examination of the Concept of Perfection in the Epistle to the Hebrews.* Society for New Testament Studies Monograph Series 47. Cambridge: Cambridge University Press, 1982.

Thompson, J. *The Beginnings of Christian Philosophy.* Catholic Biblical Quarterly Monograph Series, 13. Washington: Catholic Biblical Association, 1982.

Williamson, R. *Philo and the Epistle to the Hebrews.* Arbeiten zur Literatur und Geschichte des hellenistischen Judentums, 4. Leiden: Brill, 1970.

JAMES

LUKE T. JOHNSON

INTRODUCTION

The Letter of James is moral exhortation in the form of a general letter, from whose contents we learn little about its intended readers. The greeting, "to the twelve tribes in the Diaspora" (1:1), could indicate a Jewish-Christian audience but need not. Likewise, the practices condemned and the attitudes enjoined do not allow the depiction of a specific community or its problems. Neither are we certain whether the author is James the brother of the Lord or a pseudepigrapher, whether the writing is among the earliest or latest in the NT collection.

The teaching of James is general rather than particular, traditional more than novel, moral rather than theological. The dominant mood of its verbs is the imperative. The goal of the writing is not so much right thinking as right acting. The fundamental contrast is between verbal profession and action; when James contrasts "faith" and "works" (2:14), he sets empty belief in opposition to lived practice.

James's perspective is theocentric rather than Christocentric. Jesus' name occurs only twice (1:1; 2:1), and the messianic convictions concerning Jesus' death and resurrection are lacking. On the other hand, James knows and makes use of Jesus' sayings (cf. 1:6; 2:8; 5:12).

His perspective is theocentric because explicit statements about the God who creates, calls, blesses, and judges support James's moral exhortations. His theological outlook is most clearly expressed in 3:13–4:10. He sees two measures for human behavior: the measure of God who creates all things and the measure of "the world" that resists God's claim on creation. James calls adherence to these measures "friendship." One can either be a "friend of the world" or a "friend of God" and act accordingly. James's specific interest is the "double-minded person" (1:8; 4:8), who wants to live by both measures at once, confessing commitment to God, but contradicting it in action. James exhorts his readers to action consonant with conviction.

James is remarkable for its positive appropriation of Torah, whose separate aspects it mediates to the messianic community (→ Torah). The short exhortations concerned with practical behavior resemble and incorporate elements of the wisdom tradition. Since wisdom is by nature cosmopolitan, James shows traces of Hellenistic moral philosophy as well as

of the biblical books of Proverbs and Ecclesiastes. James also contemporizes the voice of the prophets. His attack on oppression echoes the accents of Isaiah and Amos (5:1–6). James also affirms the Law, calling it the "Law of Liberty" (2:12). He does not mean ritual observances but the moral teaching of Torah, summarized by the Decalogue and the "law of love" (Lev. 19:18; cf. 2:8–11). James elaborates this commandment in the light of Lev. 19:11–19 and Jesus' words.

The literary structure of James is not obvious. The only epistolary element is the greeting. Chap. 1 consists entirely of short commands and aphorisms with little apparent connectedness. These are followed by a series of short essays employing the lively oral style of Hellenistic teaching called the diatribe. The essays are in turn interspersed with other short commandments (cf. 4:11; 5:9, 12). Elaborate structural analyses are unconvincing, but neither is James simply a careless pastiche. The themes broached by way of aphorism in chap. 1 are elaborated in the essays, so that the opening exhortations serve as a prologue and table of contents.

James claims neither novelty nor depth. But no reader can mistake its lively voice or moral passion. Traditional teaching is given vibrancy in this exhortation to practical faith and active love.

COMMENTARY

1:2–27, Opening Exhortations. Without any real transition from the greeting, James launches a series of admonitions. Each takes the form of a second-person (1:2, 16, 19, 21, 22) or third-person (1:4, 5, 6, 7, 9, 13, 19) imperative. Some of the commands are accompanied by explanatory statements ("for"), which provide the exhortation's warrant (e.g., 1:6, 11, 13, 20, 24). This part of James strongly resembles such collections as Proverbs, especially since the instructions represent reminders of already well-understood norms (1:3, 20).

As in other collections of traditional wisdom, the discrete sayings lack obvious thematic connections. Attempts at contextual analysis are therefore hazardous. Thus, although "testing" appears both in 1:2 and in 1:12–14, it is not clear that the term means the same thing in both places. In 1:2, it refers to external testing, as in persecution; in 1:14, it seems to mean internal "temptation." The real thematic links are to be found not between these aphorisms themselves but between each of them and the later essays. The place to find a comment on the "endurance of testing" of 1:2, for example, is in 5:7–11.

Despite the disjointedness of the opening section, three of James's characteristic concerns emerge clearly. Each of them involves a contrast. The first contrast is between two measures, God and the world opposed to God. The outlook of the world is duplicitous and envious. In contrast, God gives with simplicity and without rebuke (1:5). God can be defined, in fact, as the giver of every good and perfect gift (1:17). Worldly desire conceives sin, and sin when it reaches term gives birth to death (1:15). In contrast, God gives genuine birth to humans by his word of truth and makes them the first fruits of his creatures (1:18). This "implanted word" is able, in turn, to save their souls, if they receive it in meekness (1:21).

The second contrast is between the attitudes and behavior consistent with each measure. To live by God's word of truth means putting aside anger in favor of meekness, since "anger does not accomplish God's righteousness" (1:20). It means regarding poverty and wealth in ways shocking to a world that uses them as the means of testing worth; before God, "the poor brother boasts in his exaltation, and the rich man in his humiliation" (1:9–10). It means being driven not by evil desires (1:14), but by the wisdom that comes from God in response to the prayer of faith (1:5–6). Most paradoxically, it means counting trials "all joy" (1:2)—an attitude available only to those whose Messiah had sanctified suffering and thereby transformed the norms for human worth.

The third and most characteristic contrast is between the sham religiosity of word or appearance and a devotion "pure and stainless before God," which is honest speech and care for the dispossessed (1:26). These are the attitudes and actions that keep one "unstained from the world" (1:27). For James, it is not the learning but the doing of wisdom that counts. His readers are to be "doers of the word and not hearers only" (1:22). Genuine blessedness comes from the "doing of a deed," which is the aim of all moral instruction (1:22–25). The double-minded person (1:8) who would profess without practicing is told emphatically to avoid self-deception (1:16). Unless religion involves effective action in the world, it is "useless" (1:26).

2:1–13, The Law of God's Kingdom. The first of James's essays extends to 2:26 but can

conveniently be divided at 2:13. The literary conventions of the diatribe are used vigorously throughout the next three chapters. Note in this section the direct address to the reader (2:1, 5), the vivid imaginary dialogue (2:3), and rhetorical questions (2:4, 5, 6, 7). James sketches a situation in which readers fail to live by their convictions (2:1–7). He then develops more fully the measure by which they ought to live (2:8–13).

Since James writes for a general audience, it is unlikely that he criticizes the practice of a particular community when he describes an assembly in which rich and poor are treated so differently. In fact, the precise nature of the assembly itself is unclear. The word "gathering" (Gk. synagōgē, "synagogue") in 2:2 could refer to the Christian worship service. But James's subsequent argument suggests that this assembly is the occasion for community judicial decisions. We know that some Christian communities took over from Judaism the office of local presbyters who handled finances and settled internal disputes (cf. 1 Cor. 6:1–8; 1 Tim. 5:17–25). Whatever the social setting, James condemns the blatant discrimination practiced within it: members of the assembly give precedence to the rich and slight the poor (2:3).

James's objection has two bases. First, a bias toward the rich contradicts the original experience of the members of the Christian community. In their lives it was the rich who oppressed them by dragging them into court and who scorned their religion (2:6–7). By so doing, the rich acted consistently by their measure of reality. But James's readers had been given another measure. God had chosen the poor in the world's estimation to be "rich with respect to faith, and heirs of the kingdom" (2:5). How could an assembly gathered under God's rule act in accord with the world's measure?

James's second objection is that their "respect for appearances" has led them to betray their faith in Jesus Christ (2:1). He accuses them of being, as a result, judges with evil designs (2:4). His language deliberately evokes the ancient practice of community judgment in Israel (cf. Ruth 4:1–8); its constant principle was that decisions must be made "without partiality" (Deut. 1:17; Lev. 19:15; 1 Tim. 5:21). Judges were not to be swayed by appearances but by the merits of a case. But if the rich are given special places in the assembly simply because of their lordly appearance, the community is corrupting its judgment. That is plain enough. How is it also betraying its faith in Jesus?

It betrays *faith* first of all, because the very basis for the community's existence is God's choice of the poor, so that they are "rich in faith." The community should have the same preference for the poor that God has shown.

Their behavior betrays their loyalty to Jesus as well, since he had identified the love of neighbor as central to Torah: "You shall love your neighbor as yourself" (cf. Mark 12:30–31). James calls this the "royal law," or better, the "law of the kingdom" into which God has called them (2:8).

James finds that Torah itself provides specific guidelines for the fulfillment of the law of love, first in the Decalogue (2:11; cf. Rom. 13:8–10), but also in the prescriptions of Leviticus. Thus, James sees in Lev. 19:15, right before the commandment to love the neighbor, a prohibition of partiality in judgment. This is the first of several times that James uses all of Lev. 19:11–19 to articulate the meaning of love for the neighbor (4:11; 5:4, 9, 12, 19). When he says, therefore, that one does well to fulfill "the whole law" (2:10) and to do so "according to the scripture" (2:8), he is serious on both counts.

In 2:12–13, James gives a concise summary of his points and a transition to the next section: the law of love is one of "freedom" since it inhibits only harmful activity and enables authentic human existence; life according to its measure does not oppress but liberates others—thus there can be no discrimination on the basis of power or possessions; and finally, this way of life is according to God's measure, which is one of mercy, not condemnation.

2:14–26, Living Faith and Love.

James's characteristic emphasis on behavior consistent with conviction (cf. 1:22, 26) is now made explicit. The "usefulness" of theory is always a moralist's concern. For James, the contrast is between a faith that is merely verbal and one that shows its "life" in action.

The diatribal style is again heavily used in this section, as James employs a fictional dialogue with an imagined interlocutor (2:18–23). The dialogue is propelled by rhetorical questions (2:14, 19, 20, 21), an apostrophe (2:20), and even a pun: faith without works (Gk. erga) is empty (Gk. argē).

James's argument begins with an example drawn from life (2:14–17). His point is simple: words without actions are futile. A needy brother or sister (2:15) cannot be helped either by a blessing or a benevolent attitude (2:16), but only by the concrete actions that incarnate them. Deeds rather than speech carry conviction. The example is framed in 2:14 and 2:17 by its specific application: faith without deeds is "dead."

The last phrase of 2:17, "faith simply by itself" provides an important clue to James's understanding. In the ensuing dialogue, he pillories one who equates faith with "right belief" as though it were simply confession or an assent of the intellect, rather than essentially a re-

sponse to God made up of loyalty, trust, endurance, and obedience. Thus his response to a person who "has faith" of the confessional sort is ironic: "you do well" (2:19). In fact, such belief is meaningless, since it is compatible with a life hostile to God. Even demons confess truly that "God is One"—and shudder (2:19). For James, authentic faith is simply faith enacted.

In 1:25, James told his readers to gaze into the "perfect law of freedom" so they could learn to be "doers of the word." Now he draws from Torah the first two of his four exemplars, each of whom models some aspect of active faith in God (cf. also 5:11, 17). In Abraham's offering of his son Isaac (Gen. 22:9, 12), faith came to perfection in action (2:21). James does not say that deeds add something to a "saving" faith, but that Abraham's action was the intrinsic expression of faith itself, as essential to its life as the soul is to the body's (2:26). In a compressed formula, he asserts that "faith co-works the works," and it is faith itself that he says comes to maturity (2:22; cf. 1:4).

Like Paul in Gal. 3:6, James cites Gen. 15:6 to show that Abraham was declared righteous for his faith (2:23), but he adds his distinctive identification of those who live by God's measure: Abraham was called "friend of God" (cf. 4:4). And as James explicitly mentions the "sister" in need (2:15), so he adds the female example of Rahab, whose hospitality to Israel's spies enacted her implicit response of faith in Israel's God (2:25; cf. Josh. 2:9–13).

Some readers find James to be at odds with the Paul of Galatians. But Paul would surely agree that what matters is "faith being worked out by love" (Gal. 5:6). Their focuses, to be sure, are quite different. James is not debating the theological grounds for salvation. He advocates a "true religion," which he understands as effective action for others in the world.

Here is the deeper resonance to the choices of Abraham and Rahab as examples. In Jewish lore, they stand as models for hospitality. James began this discussion with a call to just such "acts of mercy" (2:13) as feeding, clothing, and sheltering the needy (2:16). These fit his definition of religion as "visiting orphans and widows in their affliction" (1:27). Only this kind of faith keeps one "unstained from the world."

3:1–12, The Control of Speech.

There are two possible literary transitions to this essay on speech (the metonym for which is "the tongue"). The first is the mechanical word linkage provided by "body," which is found in 2:26 and twice more in 3:2–3. The second and more likely is the completion of James's definition of religion (1:26–27). In the previous essay he dealt with "visiting orphans and widows"; now he can address "controlling the tongue" (cf. 1:26). The essay also picks up from the aphorism of 1:19: "Let everyone be quick to hear but slow to speak," and provides, in turn, a transition to James's discussion of true wisdom (3:13), for the connection between wisdom and taciturnity was, in the ancient world, truly proverbial (cf. Prov. 17:28; Sir. 5:13).

If in the previous sections James appeared as a close reader of Torah and his exhortations as midrashic (→ Midrash), here he shows his Hellenistic side. The miniature essay on the tongue (3:3–8) touches on many of the standard elements in the discussion of human speech by Greek moralists.

Thus, it is commonplace to assert the difficulty of controlling ("bridling") the tongue with the analogy of bridling a horse (3:3). The analogy also suggests the power of the tongue, since to control it is to guide a great beast. Another standard comparison: the tongue is to the body as a rudder is to a ship. So also the tongue can "boast of great things, though small." The boast is not challenged; James recognizes the power of speech. A third comparison follows, this time to a small fire that enflames a whole forest (3:5). James develops the image by declaring, "the tongue is a fire" (3:6), and spiraling hyperbolically to its being a "world of evil" and "lit from hell and igniting the whole cycle of becoming" (3:6). Finally, he repeats the impossibility of truly controlling speech. In contrast to the domestication of all creation, human speech itself remains "an evil upheaval, a cup of deadly poison" (3:7–8).

However lively in expression, such points can be found in Hellenistic discussions. James gives a special edge to the topic, however, by the way he frames it. In 3:1–2, he directs these remarks to those who would be teachers in the messianic community, cautioning them about that role, for "we shall receive a greater judgment" (3:1). If proper speech is difficult for anyone, it is a particular peril for those who make a profession of it. But if one does not fail in speech, then one is truly perfect (3:2; cf. 1:4). At the least, James gives eloquent witness to speech as the primary symbol of human existence.

Even more strikingly, he concludes the essay with his usual contrast between God's measure and that of the world, stressing the impossibility of living by both at once. He condemns the contradiction inherent in blessing God (in prayer) and also cursing humans (3:9). Such behavior is contradictory because humans are made "according to the image of God" (3:9). To combine such forms of speech is like trying to get both sweet and brackish water from the same source or figs from an olive tree; it's not done (3:10–11). As he did in 2:1–26, James links fidelity to God with loyalty to humans. Just as people should be "single-minded" in their adherence to God's word,

so should their speech be "single-minded" toward each other.

3:13–4:10, Friendship with God. The heart of James's writing and the key to its understanding are found in 3:13–4:10. This self-contained literary unit brings together a number of themes adumbrated in chap. 1. It also provides the explicit conceptual framework that shapes James's teaching as a whole.

We meet here again the double-minded person (1:8; 4:8) contrasted to the simple and generous God (1:5, 17; 4:6); the reversal worked by God so that the proud are lowered and the humble are raised (1:9–10; 4:6–10); and a wisdom from God opposed to a wisdom against God (1:5; 3:15). In a word, James puts before his readers the choice between two measures and demands of them a choice: will it be God or the world?

The contemporary editions and translations that divide this section at 3:18 do so mistakenly, for 3:13–4:10 stands as a literary whole. In form, it is a call to conversion. James sets up an indictment in 3:13–4:6, to which a plea for repentance responds in 4:7–10.

The charge to repent is stylistically simple, consisting of ten imperatives, three of them accompanied by emphatic reassurances (4:7, 8, 10). These verses deliberately echo the language of repentance found in the prophets (e.g., LXX Hos. 5:5; Ezek. 36:25; Amos 9:5). The indictment is literarily more complex, alternating rhetorical questions (3:13; 4:1, 2, 4, 5) and antithetical propositions (3:14–17; 4:2–3, 4, 6). Its climax is the apostrophe and rhetorical questions of 4:4–5.

Within this literary structure, James establishes thematic unity by using the conventional Hellenistic discussion of the vice of envy. Not only do terms for envy recur in 3:14, 16; 4:2; and climactically in 4:5, but many other expressions otherwise strangely combined make sense here because of their traditional association with that vice. Thus, envy is usually considered a misanthropic vice particularly given to bitterness and rivalry (3:14). It leads to social upheaval (3:16), wars (4:1), and above all murder (4:2). Why does envy have such associations? Because it is based on a perception of reality that equates having with being. Humans are therefore in competition for existence and worth. If one has more, then another must have less and be less. The logic of such competition leads to murder, the physical removal of rivals.

James places this analysis of envy within an explicitly religious framework. The perception generating envy is a wisdom "from below" (lit., "earthly," 3:15), which is essentially opposed to the "wisdom from above" (3:15). The source of each wisdom is clear. That from below fittingly comes from the devil (3:15; 4:7), for in the biblical tradition the devil represents envy (cf. Wisd. of Sol. 2:24). He operates in the realm of the human mind (Gk. *psychē*, 3:15). The wisdom from above comes from God, and operates in the spirit (Gk. *pneuma*) God made to dwell in humans (4:5). In contrast to the envious devil, God gives without rebuke (1:5), indeed overflows in generosity: "He gives more gift" (4:6).

Each measure has its appropriate behavioral expression. The wisdom from below leads to "lying against the truth" (3:14) and "every foul deed" (3:16). It can lead, in fact, to the distortion of religion itself, in a self-deception (cf. 1:26) that tries to manipulate even God in prayer (4:3).

In contrast, the wisdom from God leads to "noble behavior" (3:13), to peaceful and merciful attitudes, and to "good fruits" (3:17). As envy leads to wars and murder (4:1–2), so the "fruit of righteousness is sown in peace by those who do peace" (3:18).

James concludes his indictment by asserting the absolute incompatibility of these ways of life. One cannot be at the same time a "friend of the world" and "a friend of God" (4:4). In the Hellenistic language of friendship, to be friends meant having a spiritual affinity, a deeply shared unity, to be, in effect, "one soul." A "friend of the world" therefore is one who sees things by the measure of earthly wisdom. These James calls "adulterers," using Torah's term for those breaking covenant with God (cf. Hos. 3:1; Ezek. 16:38). They have established themselves as enemies of God (4:4).

James's specific target here as throughout the Letter is the double-minded person who wants to be "friends with everyone," to live by both measures at once. James's indictment demands of this person action consonant with knowledge: "do you not *know*?" (4:4). He demands a "cleansing of the hands and purifying of the heart," which means becoming single-minded rather than double-minded, living by God's standard rather than the world's.

In his final exhortations, James makes several remarkable statements concerning the relationship between God and human beings. By turning to God, the evil spirit can be resisted and made to flee (4:7); God can then be approached by humans. More surprisingly, God responds to such initiative and draws near (4:8). Indeed, God answers those who humble themselves before him, giving them gifts and "raising them up" (4:6, 7, 10; cf. 1:9).

4:11–17, Against Arrogance. After the coherence of the previous section, the final part of James again appears as disjointed. A freestanding commandment with its warrant (4:11–12) is followed by two condemnatory paragraphs (4:13–17; 5:1–6), each beginning with "come

now" (4:13; 5:1). These attacks lead to positive instructions concerning external affliction (5:7–11) and internal edification (5:12–20).

Although it is not immediately evident how warnings against slander, heedlessness, and oppression should connect to James's call to conversion in 3:13–4:10, all three can be understood as manifestations of *arrogance*, the self-aggrandizing and hostile attitude that for James epitomizes the measure of the world opposed to God: "God resists the arrogant but gives gifts to the humble" (4:6; cf. Prov. 3:34).

The prohibition of 4:11 addresses once more the use of the tongue, a persistent preoccupation of the Letter (cf. 1:19, 26; 2:12, 16–17; 3:2, 9–10). Here James condemns slander. The Greek expression can mean any loud or boisterous speech, but in Scripture the term is associated with secret and hostile speech against another (cf. Pss. 50:20; 101:5; Wisd. of Sol. 1:11) and appears as such in NT vice lists (cf. Rom. 1:30; 2 Cor. 12:20).

By repeating the word "brother" three times in a single verse (4:11), James emphasizes the disruption caused the community by such malevolent speech. But in 4:12, his language shifts slightly: "Who are you to judge your neighbor?" The change of terms leads us to James's distinctive understanding of this vice. First, slander is an offense against the law of the kingdom (2:8), which is love for the neighbor. As we have observed, James reads Lev. 19:18 in its original context, and in Lev. 19:16 there is the clear prohibition of slander against the neighbor. James also uncovers the spiritual implications of slander. To speak against another maliciously and in secret always involves a negative judgment of the other, indeed a condemnation, that arrogantly assumes a superiority over the other.

James pushes beyond ethical churlishness to religious sin. The slanderer also asserts a superiority to the Law, which explicitly forbids slander, and in effect assumes the role of judge over the Law. In so doing, the slanderer asserts superiority to the Lawgiver and thus has become "not the doer of the Law but its judge" (4:11). James decisively crushes this pretension by reasserting faith's most fundamental conviction: there is only One Lawgiver and One Judge, and they are the same. James states the infinite distance between this Lord and human arrogance: only one of them is "able to give life and to destroy it."

That reminder provides the transition to the condemnation in 4:13–17. Arrogance is now expressed by the blithe and heedless confidence that human calculation can actually secure the future and that life consists in the "buying and getting" of business (4:13). James mocks such self-delusion. Humans cannot secure even their tomorrow, much less their "next year" (4:14).

The lives of humans are literally not in their own control. If they lived by God's measure, they would recognize the utter contingency of their existence and projects (cf. 1:9–11), for only by the will of God can they live or do anything at all (4:15). Their presumption that God is irrelevant to their life and has no claim on their world is evil boasting, a pride based only in empty arrogance (4:16).

The final line of this section (4:17) seems oddly placed. What does the sin of omission have to do with slander and pretension? Not much that is obvious, but James uses it as a transition to the next form of arrogance, which sins by the omission of elementary social justice: the oppression practiced by the rich (5:1–6).

5:1–11, Persecution and Patience. This section falls neatly into two corresponding parts. In 5:1–6, James prophetically condemns the rich who oppress and murder innocent people. In 5:7–11, he exhorts "the brethren" to attitudes appropriate for the context of persecution. The paragraphs are linked thematically by the judgment of God (5:1, 3, 7–8), which appears as a threat to the oppressors and a comfort to the oppressed.

Is James attacking wealthy members of the messianic community? It seems unlikely. That there were wealthier members among his readers seems probable from 1:9; 2:12; and even 4:13, but here the rich are the outsiders, who, according to 2:6, oppress members of the community and bring them to court.

James does not condemn wealth as such but the greed and injustice involved in creating it. The "measure of the world," which equates being and having, here finds perfect expression. The oppressors seek to become "more" by robbing workers of their fair wages (5:4). Such defrauding of the laborer is also explicitly condemned by Lev. 19:13, which James understands as an elaboration of the law of love. He adopts the voice of Amos and Isaiah in castigating these breakers of covenant. In 4:1–2 we saw that envy led to murder. The withholding of wages gradually kills, and James makes the accusation directly: "you have murdered the just man" (5:6).

Against the wisdom of the world, which legitimates the survival of the savage, James places the coming judgment of God. In his call to conversion, he had told the double-minded to "be miserable and cry out" as a sign of repentance (4:8–9). Here the same terms are used as signs of the punishment coming on the oppressors (5:1). The rich consider that they have secured their life, but instead they have "piled up treasure for the last days," by which James means a wealth of punishment. Their possessions will rot and rust as they will themselves

(5:3). In a vivid twist of sacrificial imagery, James calls them calves fattened for the day of slaughter (5:5). Because they have abused laws to do injustice, God will judge them, for he keeps covenant even when humans do not: "the cries of the laborers have reached the ears of the Lord of hosts" (5:4).

What attitudes should those who undergo oppression have? James exhorts them to patience. Instead of the usual term denoting "endurance," however, (as in 1:3–4), he twice uses an expression typically used in the Bible of judges: they are to be "long-suffering." James means by this that they are not to anticipate the judgment of God, either by violently resisting their oppressors (5:6) or (in a response natural among the oppressed) turning on each other with bitterness and reproach (5:9; cf. Lev. 19:18a).

Instead they are to "fix their hearts" on God, remaining faithful to the one who called them (5:8). They can in fact do this because the judgment of God is both certain and soon: "The judge is standing at the gates" (5:9). James's language here suggests that he means specifically the return of Jesus as judge (cf. 1 Thess. 3:13; 1 Cor. 15:23; Matt. 24:3).

As James proposed Abraham and Rahab as examples of faith active in deeds, so he presents Job as the paradigm of faith enduring affliction. Job represents "the prophets" who both suffered and showed long-suffering. James clearly implies that the "merciful and compassionate" God rewards such endurance: "You have seen the purpose of the Lord" (5:11).

5:12–20, Life in the Community. The Letter concludes with a number of separate exhortations whose organizing principle is life together in the church, with a specific focus on the sort of speech that should obtain in the messianic community. James thereby provides the positive ideal of speech, which he regards as essential to authentic religion (1:26).

He insists in the first place on plain speech without the taking of oaths (5:12). Here is one of the clearest instances of a commandment deriving from the sayings of Jesus (cf. Matt. 5:33–37) as well as from Torah (cf. Lev. 19:12). The phrase "lest you fall under judgment" indicates as well that such speaking is in fulfillment of the law of liberty (cf. also 2:12–13; 4:11; 5:9) and also connects this command to the discussion of the Lord's judgment in 5:7–11.

The messianic community is also one constituted by prayer. A paean to prayer in every circumstance, joyful or sorrowful, is found in 5:13–18. James's readers are thereby reminded that their lives are bound by more than mutual affection, above all by their shared relationship with God. The community is therefore to respond to threats of sickness or sin by gathering in prayer.

When someone is physically ill, the elders of the church come together in prayer for the sick person. When James adds, "The prayer of faith will save the sick person and the Lord will raise him up" (5:15), his language almost certainly recalls the healing stories of the synoptic tradition (cf., e.g., Mark 2:9; 3:3; 5:41). The community is threatened even more powerfully by the sins of its members. The confessing of sins, therefore, accompanied by prayers for each other, not only restores the deviant individual to spiritual health, but it also heals the community as such (5:16). To show the power of such prayer, James cites the last of his exemplars from Torah. The prophet Elijah, "though only a human being like us," accomplished wonders by the "prayer of faith" (5:17–18; see 1 Kings 17:1; 18:42–45).

James's final exhortation is not accidentally chosen. The community that lives by the word of truth (1:18) and has received with meekness the implanted word of God (1:21) must work together against individual and communal self-deception and deviation (5:19; cf. 1:13, 16, 23, 26; 2:20). Mutual correction and exhortation are therefore expressions of love for the neighbor (cf. Lev. 19:17). At the end, James exhorts all his readers to do for each other what he has been trying to do for them.

Bibliography

Dibelius, M. *James: A Commentary on the Epistle of James.* Revised by H. Greeven. Edited by H. Koester. Translated by M. Williams. Hermeneia. Philadelphia: Fortress, 1976.

Johnson, L. T. "Friendship with the World/Friendship with God: A Study of Discipleship in James." In *Discipleship in the New Testament.* Edited by F. Segovia. Philadelphia: Fortress, 1985. Pp. 166–83.

Laws, S. *A Commentary on the Epistle of James.* Harper's New Testament Commentaries. San Francisco: Harper & Row, 1980.

Mayor, J. B. *The Epistle of St. James.* 3d ed. London: Macmillan, 1910.

1 PETER

PAUL J. ACHTEMEIER

INTRODUCTION

The First Letter of Peter is addressed to Christians in five of the Roman provinces that occupied the area of modern Turkey. Its language reveals that its author was an educated person, acquainted with the theological terminology reflected in Paul's Letters, who knew the situation in Asia Minor in the last years of the first century A.D., some years after the traditional date for Peter's martyrdom in A.D. 64. For that reason, many scholars question its authorship by the disciple Peter. In addition, the names Silvanus (→ Silvanus; 5:12) and Mark (→ Mark; 5:13) are more closely associated in the NT with Paul (Mark: Philem. 24; 2 Tim. 4:11; Col. 4:10; Acts 12:25; 15:37–39; Silvanus: 2 Cor. 1:19; 1 Thess. 1:1; 2 Thess. 1:1) than with Peter, as is the area to which the Letter is addressed. In the only first-person reference by the author to himself, the term used is "elder" (1 Pet. 5:1), a term not associated with Peter, and the additional reference to himself as "a witness of the sufferings of Christ" cannot refer to a historical situation, since Peter was not present at the crucifixion of Jesus, according to the unanimous tradition in the Gospels. Nor can the reference to Silvanus in 5:12 as one "through whom" the letter was written indicate a letter dictated to Silvanus by Peter, since the Greek phrase "by someone" refers to the person who delivered the letter, as in Acts 15:23, not the one who wrote it; reference to such a scribe takes a different form, as in Rom. 16:22. The reference to Mark as "my son" (1 Pet. 5:13) does not refer to physical relationship any more than does the reference to Silvanus as "faithful brother" (5:12). "The elect one in Babylon" (5:13; RSV: "She who is in Babylon, who is likewise chosen") refers not to Peter's wife but to the church from which the letter is being sent (the word for "church" in Greek is feminine in gender). None of these details therefore refers to the historical Peter's actual family situation.

The reference to Babylon is probably a cryptic name for Rome (→ Rome; see Rev. 18), continuing the metaphor of Christians as the chosen people now living as exiles in the world, as did the Jews when they were exiled to Babylon (see 1 Pet. 1:1; 2:11). Historic Babylon at this time was only a small, insignificant village; there is no indication that the historical Peter (→ Peter) ever visited it.

References to a situation of suffering (e.g., 1:6; 2:20; 3:14; 4:1, 12–13; 5:9) need not assume an official, empire-wide Roman persecution (→ Persecution) of Christians. The fact that Christians no longer participated in the many religious festivals celebrated in the Hellenistic world (see 4:4) is enough to account for the sporadic outbreaks of persecution suffered by followers of Christ that are reflected in this Letter. The fact that the readers' identification as Christians was enough to provoke suffering (4:16) indicates a time late in the first century A.D., by which time Roman authorities had discovered that Christians were not, as they had earlier assumed, a sect within Judaism.

The purpose of the Letter is to comfort Christians who, because of their new situation, are no longer acceptable to their cultural world. A number of metaphors are used to portray that situation: they are like exiles or aliens (1:1; 2:11), like slaves (2:18–25) or wives (3:1–6), who in that culture had few legal rights. Again, they are like newborn infants (2:2) who through baptism (1:2) have a new hope and a new inheritance (1:4); they are like priests in a new sanctuary (2:4–8), like stones in a new building (2:5), like a new people chosen by God (2:10). They are like workers setting about a task (1:13), like soldiers armed for conflict (4:1). In a variety of ways, therefore, the author seeks to encourage readers who, because of their new situation as believers, can no longer participate in their culture as they once did (4:3) and who must now suffer the same rejection Christ did (2:21) and for many of the same reasons (3:17–18; 4:1). Yet that new situation is of such surpassing value that the future recompense is worth the present, temporary discomfort (1:6; 4:7–8, 13–14; 5:10).

The dominant motif of 1 Peter is therefore the contrast between what the readers had once been and what they have now become because of their obedience to Christ. It is the author's message that the new situation is worth any suffering it may require.

In summary, 1 Peter is a general letter, probably written from Rome around the end of the first century, by follower(s) of the apostle Peter, who wished to convey to besieged gentile Christians in Asia Minor the encouragement and comfort contained in the gospel Peter preached during his years as a missionary to the Jews (Gal. 2:7–8). Couched in traditional theological terms familiar to its readers, the Letter sought to add the authority of the apostle Peter to the faith of those who lived in a traditionally Pauline missionary area.

COMMENTARY

PART ONE: 1:1—2:3

A New Person in Christ and How to React

1:1–2

Salutation

This is the nuts and bolts of the Letter: from whom, to whom, and why. The form is common to the Hellenistic world: A to B, greetings, followed by a wish or a prayer for prosperity or good health. Typically for NT Letters—especially Paul's—this format is adapted to Christian use (→Salutations). In a pun on the normal word for "greetings" (Gk. *chairein*), the author substitutes the word for "grace" (Gk. *charis*), and to it is added the word "peace" (Heb. *shalom*), rich in its connotations of order and wholeness. Those to whom the Letter is written are also addressed in analogy to OT terms: "exiles of the Diaspora" recalls the events that scattered Jews over the face of the inhabited Western world, forcing them to live in cultures alien to their religion (→ Exile; Diaspora). This use is clearly analogical, since those addressed are Gentiles, as the rest of the Letter makes clear. Yet their fate is not due to historical accident. They are what they are by the direct purpose of God: set aside by his Spirit to follow his Son and to be baptized into him. The similarity to Matt. 28:19—make disciples (here: obey); baptize (here: sprinkled with his blood) in the name of the Trinity (here: Father, Spirit, Jesus Christ)—shows the extent to which our author relies on familiar Christian tradition. Those addressed live in the northern half of Asia Minor; two of the "provinces" were also visited by Paul (Galatia, Asia). The names do not conform entirely to Roman provincial boundaries; by this time Pontus and Bithynia had become one province. The area intended is clear, however, as is the purpose: to address people of the northern half of Asia Minor who, by God's will, had become obedient to Jesus Christ. Given their situation, they will surely need God's grace and peace!

1:3–12

The Christian's New Situation

The author begins the body of the Letter with a summary of the points to be made in the remainder of the discussion. Hence this passage serves as an introduction to the entire Letter.

1:3–9, Newness in Christ. Newness in Christ describes the readers' situation, and the author now turns to address that point. The metaphors pile one upon another—their situation is so new only analogy can describe it. Their future is one so new for human beings that only a second birth can be compared to it, with its new life and its new inheritance (vv. 3–4). Their future is so precious only gold can be compared to it, though like gold they will be tested by fire (vv. 6–7). Their reaction to Christ is so solid and joyful that only the importance of the outcome of history itself can begin to do it justice (vv. 5, 8–9). Trusting in someone they have not seen; rejoicing in a future that contains fiery testing; loving someone who has placed them before an unknown future, helpless as babes—is that not irrational, even foolish? No, because such actions are based on Christ's victory over death (v. 3b) and the promise that God will guard and uphold them in that new life (v. 5) until they reach the promised salvation (v. 9). Here is the paradox of Christian existence: joy in the face of suffering; assurance of deliverance in the midst of persecution; complete reliance not on what is visible but on the unseen God. The rest of the Letter simply expounds those basic insights.

1:10–12, Long Ago Foretold. That the readers are not subject to the whims of fate or the accidental forces of history is clear from the fact that what is now happening was foretold long ago, thus demonstrating that God remains in control of events. But more, the time in which the readers live is the climax of history. OT prophets inquired about it, and even angels longed to catch a glimpse of it. That prophets could foresee the future was due to the presence with them of the Christ who has now been revealed (v. 11). Small wonder that those early Christians had little trouble finding a witness to Christ in the Hebrew Scriptures. The very spirit of Christ had been at work in them!

1:13–2:3

How to React

The gifts of God are never without corresponding responsibility; that is now the theme to which our author turns.

1:13–16, To New Life. Roll up the sleeves of your mind! No time now to sit. The task is clear: conform your life, once lived totally apart from God (v. 14), to the new situation in which you find yourself (v. 15). One must now be set aside —the meaning of "holy"—for God's purposes. One is to pattern one's behavior according to God's priorities (v. 16).

1:17–21, To Old Life. If one is to respond appropriately to the new life, one can do it only by abandoning the old one. Again, the metaphors tumble over one another. Like exiles whose own values are constantly threatened by the culture in which they are forced to live, Christians must hold fast to God's priorities (v. 17; see 1:1; 2:11; 4:3–4). Like captives freed because their ransom has been paid, Christians are free from the shackles that bound them to their old and futile ways (1:18; see 4:2, 6). Like people for whom a sacrifice has been made to God, and a most precious sacrifice—his own son—Christians who now know the goal of history (1:20) look to their own future with a confidence inspired by God's son risen from the dead (vv. 19, 21; see 1:3).

1:22–2:3, To the Christian Community. New times demand new companions who share in the new situation. So with Christians. New creatures born of God's own creative word (see Gen. 1:1; John 1:1), Christians are to cling to one another as to members of their own family (1 Pet. 1:22). That is what the church is meant to be. That fellowship alone abides, though all else fails (vv. 24–25).

The author returns to the first metaphor: newborn babes (2:2; see 1:3). Abandoning the evil and futile practices of their former lives (2:1), Christians are now to seek, indeed yearn for, that living and abiding word of God that conveys his love and his kindness in the same way that a baby yearns for its mother's milk. That nourishment, that word, is what sustains the Christians in their new life; it alone sustains them, and it is all they need.

PART TWO: 2:4–3:12

A New People in Christ and How to React

The author turns, in this second major part of the Letter, to a consideration of how Christians as a group should react to their new life and their new situation. In the first part, that new life was considered from the perspective of the individual; here it is considered from the viewpoint of that new individual in a new community, namely, the community of fellow Christians. The transition from consideration of the new life from an individual to a communal perspective was begun in 1:22–2:3, which thus served both as a conclusion to the first part and an introduction to the second.

2:4–10

A New People, Strange to Others

Typically for our author, themes announced in the opening verses now receive further exposi-

tion. Both the newness (see 1:3; 2:2) and the resulting strangeness of Christ's new people (see 1:1, 17) are taken up again in these verses, and additional insights are given.

What was discussed in 2:1–3 under the metaphor of new birth is now considered under the metaphors of a new building (vv. 4–8) and a new people (vv. 9–10).

The whole of the author's discourse on a new people is woven from threads taken from the OT; Christ's spirit was already present with the writers of the OT, informing them about the future (see 1:10–11).

The theme of the verses is given in 2:4: Christ, though precious to God, is also rejected by some human beings. Christ is the living stone because he is risen from the dead; he is the cornerstone (see v. 6) for those who build their lives on trust in him, and in that way also share his risen life (v. 5a). The community is not passive, however, as a building is; its members are to be active in their Christian life, serving God as did the priests of old (v. 5b).

The enigma of the rejection of God's own cornerstone is considered in vv. 7–9. Our author is no ethereal optimist, giving sugarcoated palliatives and refusing to look facts in the face. People do reject Christ—his crucifixion alone demonstrates that fact—but that rejection does not diminish Christ, it diminishes those who reject him. Even the OT knew that would happen, as the next two quotations demonstrate. The stumbling, the rejection occurs because people do not accept God's creative word incarnate in Christ (cf. 1:2, where accepting Christ is identified as obedience). Yet just as obedience occurred in accordance with God's will, so does the disobedience (2:8b). One should not make too much of that statement, as though every individual's fate were sealed from the beginning. Rather, the statement grows out of the question whether those who oppose God can also thwart his gracious plan for the redemption of sinful humanity. Such is not the case, and the import of this phrase is that nothing occurs that is beyond the power and purview of God. God remains in control of his world, and even rejection of his Son cannot stay his primary purpose of salvation. The same problem is raised in Rom. 9:19–26 and is answered there and in 11:25–26: God's final goal is salvation for human beings. The presence in Rom. 9:33, and here in v. 6, of a quotation from Isa. 28:16 shows both authors are pursuing the same line of thought. The question apparently was a common one for early Christians. The emphasis in this passage is not on those who disobey, however. Rather, it is on those who obey, as 1 Pet. 2:9–10 makes clear. Here again, our author takes over a whole collection of phrases used to describe Israel as God's chosen people and applies them here to Christians whose fellowship now comprises both

Jews and Gentiles. The emphasis is again on the contrast between then and now and, hence, on the newness of the Christians' present situation.

2:11–3:7
How to React to the World

So new is the Christians' situation, in fact, that they must learn a whole new set of reactions to the world with which they had once been so familiar. Those reactions are introduced (vv. 11–12) and discussed by means of three examples: the conduct of citizens, of slaves, and of wives and husbands.

2:11–12, Introduction. Once more, the metaphor of exiles and aliens occurs (see 1:1, 17), describing the relationship of Christians to their own culture: they are now strangers in the midst of what once was familiar. Viewed as evildoers, Christians must by their good conduct give the lie to such accusations.

2:13–17, As Good Citizens. To be a good citizen in the Roman Empire meant to obey its laws and the edicts of its rulers (see Rom. 13:1–7). Being good Christians means to live as decent citizens do. The need for Christians to abstain from unacceptable cultural practices (see 1 Pet. 4:3) will excite enough criticism; no need to make it worse with acts unbecoming decent folk. Christians must live in such a way that accusations against them are shown to be foolish chatter based on ignorance.

2:18–25, As Good Slaves. The same point is made using slaves as the example. Slaves, like Christians, undergo punishment; if it is undeserved and quietly borne, it has God's approval, but only then. Evil slaves, like evil Christians, only get what they deserve when they are punished. The pattern from which that kind of insight is derived is Jesus himself. His conduct during his Passion shows how Christians are to react in a similar situation of hostility. Once astray, they are now under the Shepherd's care and must act accordingly (v. 25).

3:1–7, As Good Wives and Husbands. The point is made again, now using wives as an example. Though legally subject to others (once father, now husband), good wives nevertheless even in such a situation lead exemplary lives. The good wife pays attention not to outward show but to inward virtue; similarly, Christians are to pay attention not to outward show but to their inward faith, so that as true children of Sarah they do what is right and do not let others terrify them into doing what is wrong (v. 6). The good husband shows tender concern for his wife; similarly, Christians are to show concern for one another so that God will listen to their petitions to him (v. 7). In this way, three classes of people (slaves, wives, husbands) among the many to be found within the Christian community (also masters, children, rich, and poor, to name a few) serve not only as the objects of ethical advice in their own right but also as examples of the way all Christians are to act within the potentially hostile culture that surrounds them.

3:8–12
How to React in the Christian Fellowship

Typically for our author, the conclusion of the previous passage (v. 7) introduces the next. In sentiments reminiscent of Paul (see Rom. 12:9–21), Christians are advised how they are to treat one another. Here the example is the Christian fellowship itself. All of the points implied in the three examples (citizen, slave, wife, and husband) are here made explicit in relation to the conduct of Christians toward one another. The vocation of the Christian is precisely to act in the ways outlined in earlier passages; that is the way to find favor with God (v. 9). It will occasion no surprise that our author finds confirmation from the OT, this time from Ps. 34:12–16: the spirit of Christ present to those authors (see 1 Pet. 1:10–12) led them to write things that are as valid now regarding Christ as they were then regarding Israel.

PART THREE: 3:13–5:14
A Fate of Suffering in Christ and How to React

Having advised his readers how to react individually to their new situation and then collectively, our author now once again makes explicit what has been implied to this point: the new life, because it follows the suffering Christ, will inevitably be one of suffering. Following a goodness so new that to those who oppose it it appears as evil, Christians prepare themselves for a new life now and for the new future still to come.

3:13–22
Christ's Fate Has Historic Importance

The universality of Christ's importance is now illustrated by the fact that not only for the living, but also for the dead Christ's example in suffering and his message of God's mercy are of ultimate significance.

3:13–17, Christ's Earthly Fate. Like a musician creating a symphony, our author resumes themes enunciated earlier (see 1:6; 2:12, 15, 19–20; 3:9) and continues to develop them. What happened to Christ is here presumed, rather than made explicit, and the implications of Christ's life for the Christian's life are then enunciated.

The bold affirmation that none will harm those zealous for what is right (v. 13) must immediately be modified in the light of reality. In fact, many—including Christ!—who are zealous for what is right do suffer (v. 14), yet in spite of that one is not to fear. Christ's lordship is all-important, and not even suffering is to deter the Christian from confessing it (v. 15a). One must always be ready to let others know why one does what one does in light of Christ's lordship (v. 15b), but it must never be done arrogantly or with condescension. Most important of all, Christians must never give others a justifiable reason to accuse them of evil. If Christians are innocent of the evil with which they are charged, that fact will come to light, and then those who think following Christ leads to evil will to their shame discover their error (v. 16). If suffering is inevitable, however, let it be wrongly afflicted despite one's good behavior, rather than rightly inflicted because of one's wrong behavior (v. 17).

Beneath the surface of this discussion lies the realization that human culture is so irreversibly opposed to God that it can only make a false judgment about the acts of those who seek to obey God by following Christ. That point will become explicit in 4:1–4, but it already plays its role in this discussion of the suffering inflicted on faithful Christians.

3:18–22, Christ's Supernatural Task. The reason for preferring unjust to just suffering lies in the fate of Christ; v. 18 makes that explicit. Yet Christ's death had more significance than for the living only; it had significance even for those who are lying in the bonds of death. Volumes have been written in the attempt to understand the exact nuances of v. 19 and the earlier traditions that may underlie the verse. Yet in this context of the meaning of Christ's fate, it seems to point to the fact that not even death prior to the appearance of Christ could separate the ungodly from Christ's proclamation of God's redemption and mercy. Such an understanding is confirmed in 4:6, which is a further commentary on this passage. Further, tradition held that those of Noah's generation were the most evil people who ever lived; after all, they caused God to flood the earth. Yet even they heard Christ's words of mercy!

And Noah? He and his companions in the ark were delivered from a sin-corrupted world into a renewed and cleansed creation by means of the waters of the flood (3:20). Similarly, Christians are delivered by the water of baptism from a sin-corrupted existence to a renewed and cleansed life in Christ (v. 21). That has been our author's point from the beginning (see 1:3–4). Baptismal water therefore symbolizes not a washing of bodily dirt but a spiritual cleansing through the power of Christ's victory over death (see Rom. 6:1–11 for a similar view of the meaning of baptism). It is to that victorious Christ that baptism links us, to that Christ who now rules over all creation by the authority of God himself. No wonder our author thinks temporary suffering is a small price to pay for so great a privilege.

4:1–11
A New Life Now and a New Time Coming

This passage, with its continuing discussion of the significance of Christ's sacrificial death, resumes the thought of 3:18. We find here the clearest statement in the Letter about the current situation of the readers in relation to their cultural environment. The verses also offer hope for a time when that painful relationship will end.

4:1–6, A New Life Now. What the new life Christians enjoy by reason of baptism into Christ means for their life among their former friends and within their culture is made clear in these verses. Where once Christians participated in the general activities of their surrounding culture (v. 3), they now no longer do so. They are, as Christians, like strangers in a strange land, in which they must live as cultural nonconformists in a time highly suspicious of any nonconformity. That is the situation that the metaphors of "exiles" and "aliens" are intended to illumine, just as are the metaphors of "slaves" and "wives." We are not to understand that the Christians were actually exiles or aliens in Asia Minor, any more than they were all actually slaves or women. The point is simply that because the Christians' new values did not permit them to participate in the social and religious customs of their culture as they once had, they would now have no more legal status or protection than that enjoyed by resident aliens or people exiled from their native lands (a common enough fate in the Roman world). For that reason they would also be hated, and that hatred would occasionally express itself in sporadic persecution (1:6 reflects the potential for persecutions to break out at any time; 4:12 reflects the actuality of persecutions that have broken out). But such persecutions were occasional and local and were based on cultural hostility rather than on some official, empire-wide persecution of all Christians everywhere.

Because such a Christian attitude of nonconformity was made necessary by the fate of
Christ himself, such suffering meant deliverance from a life of enmity to God (sin) and
hence was worth any price (vv. 1–2).

Suffering was, therefore, not a regrettable accident but a virtual necessity; until society itself
was transformed, Christians could expect the
same hostility to be directed against them that
was directed against Christ. Yet the society that
caused such suffering would also have to give
account of itself before God for its rejection of
the good news about Christ (v. 5), as will all,
both living and dead, who have heard that good
news (v. 6).

4:7–11, A New Time Coming. That time of
accounting, and of the transforming of society,
was not far off; of that our author was convinced
(v. 7). Yet incredibly—and here is the key to why
suffering was worth the cost—that new time
coming could already be enjoyed now, in the
Christian fellowship. The way Christians now
acted and were to act toward one another was
simply a foreshadowing of that time when all of
society would be transformed by the visible rule
of God. Mutual love (v. 8), ungrudging hospitality (v. 9), activity carried on for the benefit of
others, as befits God's grace (vv. 10–11a)—that
and more would be the order of the day in that
new, transformed society. It was just that grace
that Christ had revealed, and hence, in the end,
all that was done would glorify that Christ and
the God who sent him (v. 11b).

4:12–19
How to React in the World

The very different lives Christians live, not conformed to the world but transformed by Christ
(see Rom. 12:2), inevitably provoke hostility and
sporadic outbreaks of persecution against them.
Yet that reaction of the world should not occasion surprise (1 Pet. 4:12) but rather rejoicing (v.
13)! Such suffering is part of the redemptive
suffering of Christ; to be reproached for following him is to share in the grace his suffering
occasioned (vv. 14, 16). But again the familiar
warning: don't think just because you are a
Christian, any suffering you must endure automatically displays such grace. If you suffer for
evil acts, such suffering has nothing to do with
Christ (v. 15; see 2:16, 20; 3:17).

There is another reason why suffering can
be a source of rejoicing, however, and that is
because our author is convinced that such suffering is the beginning of the final judgment, a
judgment that will begin, just as did salvation,
with the household of God (4:17). Thus, the
apparent victory of non-Christians over the
Christian fellowship should not cause those
"victors" to rejoice but to reflect: if those who

followed God's will are subject to such suffering, what will be the fate of those who did not
follow his will (vv. 17–18)?

The result: those who suffer as Christians are
not to succumb to the temptation to strike back
or engage in compensatory evil. Rather, as did
Christ, they are to entrust their fate to their creator (see 2:23), who will be faithful to his promise
of redemption given in Christ (v. 19).

5:1–11
How to React in the Christian
Fellowship

Following a pattern exhibited throughout the
Letter, our author, having told his readers the
nature of the new life they have assumed, now
tells them how to react to that strange newness
both in the world and in the Christian fellowship. To be at home in the new life means to
be accepted into the Christian community that
has accepted that new life and to be rejected by
the society at large that has rejected it. That is
the basic insight our author has been following
in the whole Letter.

**5:1–6, How Leaders and Followers Are to
React.** The author here identifies himself as a
fellow "elder" (v. 1), but it is not clear whether
that has a literal meaning (old man) or is symbolic (leader), since there is a reference to "younger
people" in v. 5. While "elder" is a known early
Christian title for leaders, "younger people" is
not normally used as a synonym for "followers,"
i.e., those that are not leaders. Whatever one
may decide on that issue, however, it is clear
that elders do play a leadership role here (vv.
2–3), whether by virtue of age or bestowal of that
office by the congregation.

The author further characterizes himself as
a witness to the sufferings of Christ (v. 1), yet
that may mean not so much the suffering Christ
underwent as it means the suffering those undergo who belong to Christ. Since suffering
here is coupled with the glory that is yet to
come, a coupling we saw in 4:13 where it
specifically referred to the suffering undergone
by those who follow Christ, that is probably
what is meant here. Thus the author means to
say that he, like his readers, has both seen suffering and, as a member of the Christian community, has shared in the glory that will finally
be made visible when the present age ends.

While separate advice is given to both "older" and "younger" Christians in this passage,
the point is the same: they are not to be overbear-
ing toward one another. They must wear humility like a garment, which is present wherever its
wearer is (v. 5). While it is not explicit, it is
likely that the example of Christ remains in the
author's mind. Elders are to exercise their leadership with the same selflessness that character-

ized Christ's own life and death. Verse 6 serves as the climax of the advice to both old and young: live now in the humility being imposed on you by a hostile culture because you do God's will, because in due time God will transform his world, and then the whole of human society will reflect the way Christians now act toward one another and even toward those who persecuted them.

5:7–11, How Members Are to React. The author ends his Letter to his beleaguered readers with some final words on how members of the household of faith are to live their lives in their hostile world. They are to be under no illusions: their opposition is satanic and would, if it could, destroy them (v. 8). But because their confidence is in God, they need have no anxiety on that score. If God is for them, no opposition can be of ultimate significance (v. 7; cf. Rom. 8:31). Temptations to give in to the demands of their culture are therefore to be resisted, even when that means suffering, because such suffering is the universal badge of the true followers of Christ (1 Pet. 5:9). Yet more, such suffering is temporary, because God's plan for his world includes a final restoration in which Christ's followers will have a glorious part. With such a future in store, God will surely not abandon them in their present difficulties (v. 10). For that reason, the only proper response of those who follow Christ, whether or not they must undergo suffering, is one of praise to the God whose gracious and redemptive dominion over all his creation will finally be revealed (v. 11).

5:12–14
Closing Greetings

It was often the custom of people who wrote letters like this to conclude with a passage in their own handwriting (see Gal. 6:11–18; 1 Cor. 16:21–23; Col. 4:18; 2 Thess. 3:17–18; perhaps also Philem. 19). Whether that is the case here

or not we are not told, but our author does conclude his Letter in the fashion typical for that time. Silvanus is the one who delivered rather than who wrote the letter (see the Introduction).

The author characterizes what is contained in the Letter as "God's true grace," something he has both declared and about which he has exhorted. Grace is thus both a gift and a responsibility, something reflected in this Letter that has regularly alternated declarations of God's grace with advice on the proper ways to respond to the new situation in which that grace has placed the follower of Christ. It is that grace, which includes both gift and responsibility, in which the readers are urged to stand fast. (On the likely symbolic rather than literal meaning of Babylon, see the Introduction.) Later tradition associated the Mark who wrote the Gospel bearing that name with Peter in Rome; verse 13b probably is an early form of that tradition. The Christian kiss was a regular form of showing familial intimacy among members of the household of faith (e.g., 1 Cor. 16:20; 2 Cor. 13:12; 1 Thess. 5:26). What could be a more appropriate ending to this Letter to the beleaguered followers of Christ than the wish for peace, both now in the midst of their suffering and in God's promised new world when all suffering will be a thing of the past.

Bibliography

Beare, F. W. *The First Epistle of Peter.* 3d ed. Oxford: Blackwell, 1970.

Best, E. *1 Peter.* New Century Bible. Grand Rapids, MI: Eerdmans, 1982.

Cranfield, C. E. B. *The First Epistle of Peter.* London: SCM, 1954.

Elliott, J. H. *A Home for the Homeless: A Sociological Exegesis of 1 Peter, Its Situation and Strategy.* Philadelphia: Fortress, 1981.

Selwyn, E. G. *The First Epistle of St. Peter.* New York: Macmillan, 1955.

2 PETER

RICHARD J. BAUCKHAM

INTRODUCTION

The structure of the Second Letter of Peter can be analyzed as follows:

1:1–2, Address and greeting
T^1 1:3–11, Theme: A summary of Peter's message
T^2 1:12–15, Occasion: Peter's testament
A^1 1:16–19, First apologetic section
A^2 1:20–21, Second apologetic section
T^3 2:1–3a, Peter's prediction of false teachers
A^3 2:3b–10a, Third apologetic section
E^1 2:10b–22, Denunciation of the opponents
T^4 3:1–4, Peter's prediction of scoffers
A^4 3:5–10, Fourth apologetic section
E^2 3:11–16, Exhortation
3:17–18, Conclusion

2 Peter belongs not only to the literary genre of letter but also to that of "testament" (→ Testament [3]). Four passages in particular (T^1–T^4 above) are in testament style and identify 2 Peter as Peter's testament, in which, foreseeing his death, he makes provision for his teaching (1:3–11) to be remembered (1:12–15) and predicts the coming of false teachers after his death (2:1–3a; 3:1–4). Around these testamentary passages are arranged a series of apologetic passages (A^1–A^4) in which Peter's teaching is defended against the objections of the false teachers. Two exhortations (E^1, E^2) contrast the libertine behavior of the opponents (2:10b–22) with the holy conduct expected of the readers (3:11–16).

In Jewish usage the testament was a *fictional* genre, used to attribute material to OT figures. It is therefore likely that 2 Peter is also a pseudonymous work, attributed to Peter after his death. This presumption is confirmed by the fact that, whereas the testamentary passages predict the coming of the false teachers (2:1–3a; 3:1–4), in the apologetic passages they are referred to in the present tense (2:10b–22; 3:5, 9, 16). Clearly they are the author's contemporaries with whom he is conducting a current debate. His juxtaposition of future- and present-tense references to them conveys the message: these apostolic prophecies are now being fulfilled. But, in that case, his fiction is meant to be a transparent one.

These literary considerations and the probable date of 2 Peter (see commentary below on

3:1–4) make Petrine authorship very improbable. The real author's reason for writing a testament of Peter lies in his wish to defend the apostolic message in the postapostolic period against opponents who held that, in important respects, it was now discredited. He wished to claim no authority of his own but to vindicate the continuing normative authority of the apostles' teaching. His choice of Peter as pseudonym may imply that his letter was sent out by the Roman church, which remembered Peter as its most prestigious leader.

The two features of the opponents' teaching that dominate the author's debate with them are eschatological skepticism (i.e., skepticism about things expected to occur at "the end") and moral libertinism. Probably their aim was to free Christianity of elements derived from its Jewish background that were proving an embarrassment in a pagan cultural environment: its apocalyptic eschatology, which was alien to Hellenistic thinking and particularly problematic when the Parousia—the glorious return of Jesus—failed to occur (3:4), and its ethical rigorism, which made life difficult for Christians in the context of pagan society's greater permissiveness. Against them the author holds that the future hope for divine judgment and salvation and the ethical motivation it provides are essential features of normative apostolic teaching that must be maintained.

2 Peter faces the twin problems of Christianity's transition from a Jewish to a Hellenistic environment and from the apostolic to the postapostolic age. In response it asserts the normativeness of apostolic teaching, not woodenly repeated, but interpreted for a new situation. Thus the Christian message undergoes in 2 Peter a significant degree of translation into Hellenistic cultural terms (see commentary below on 1:3–11), but at the same time the author resists an extreme hellenization, such as the opponents advocated, in which essential elements of the apostolic message were lost. To preserve the ethical demand and the future hope of the gospel, he reasserts the Jewish apocalyptic perspective of primitive Christianity. In its striking combination of Hellenistic religious language and apocalyptic eschatology, 2 Peter provides a model for the church's perennial task of retaining the gospel's essential content while giving it meaningful expression in new cultural contexts.

COMMENTARY

1:1–2, Address and Greeting. The address introduces at once a major concern of the Letter: to communicate apostolic teaching to a post-apostolic age. It compares the faith of the apostles ("ours") and that of the (postapostolic) readers to point out that the latter are at no disadvantage.

1:3–11, A Summary of Peter's Message. This passage is a summary of Peter's definitive teaching as it is to be remembered after his death. It follows a standard sermon pattern in three parts: first, a reference to God's saving activity in the past (vv. 3–4); second, ethical exhortation, based on the first part and with the third in view (vv. 5–10); and third, the promise of eschatological salvation (v. 11). The main point is that Christians must confirm their calling through moral effort if they are to inherit the promises of eschatological salvation. This is therefore a positive statement of the two aspects of apostolic teaching—the future hope and the ethical motivation it provides—which the rest of 2 Peter is to defend against the eschatological skepticism and moral libertinism of the opponents.

Despite the insistence in vv. 5–10 that faith must have moral results and that Christ's promises have ethical conditions, the author is clear that salvation is not a human achievement. It is the grace of God that makes moral progress possible (vv. 3, 8), while final salvation will not be a *quid pro quo* but the lavish provision of the divine generosity (v. 11).

This passage is also notable for its translation of the apostolic message into the language of Hellenistic religion. The author is concerned with making contact with the moral ideals and religious aspirations of his cultural context but at the same time avoiding the loss of real Christian substance in which the extreme hellenization of the gospel by his opponents resulted. Hence, the Christian hope is stated in strongly Hellenistic terms in v. 4b, as escape from mortality through sharing the immortality of the gods, but this description is balanced by the more traditional one in v. 11 and especially by the cosmic eschatology of chap. 3. The author does not allow a merely individual and spiritual immortality to replace the apocalyptic hope for the triumph of God's righteousness in world history (cf. 3:13).

Hellenistic terminology is also prominent in the list of virtues in 1:5–7. But while in this way acknowledging that some of the ethical ideals of paganism are also Christian, the author gives them a decisively Christian context by means of the first and last items. Christian faith is the root from which all virtues grow, and Christian love is the crowning virtue to which all the others must contribute.

1:12–15, Peter's Testament. Echoing the standard language of the testament genre, the author presents 2 Peter as a testament written to provide a permanent reminder of Peter's teaching.

1:16–19, First Apologetic Section. Here the author begins his defense of Peter's teaching by replying to the first of the objections leveled against it by the opponents. The objection (implied by the denial of it in v. 16) was that when the apostles preached the future coming of Jesus as judge and king, their message was not based on divine revelation but was a "myth" in the sense of a human invention. The author has two replies to this charge. First, in vv. 16b–18, he appeals to the transfiguration, of which the apostles were eyewitnesses. He sees it as God's appointment of Jesus to be the messianic king of Psalm 2, proclaimed Son of God (Ps. 2:7) on the holy mountain (Ps. 2:6) with the task of subduing the world to God's rule (Ps. 2:8–9). Thus the apostles saw Jesus divinely appointed to the office that he will exercise at his coming in glory. Second, the apostles' preaching of the Parousia was also reliably based on OT prophecy (2 Pet. 1:19).

1:20–21, Second Apologetic Section. A second objection, which would undermine the author's appeal to OT prophecy, must now be met. The opponents denied the divine origin of the prophetic writings, claiming that although the prophets may have received signs, dreams, and visions, their prophecies were their own human interpretations of these, not God-given interpretations. (This is probably the view that is contradicted in the difficult v. 20b.) The author's reply insists on the divine inspiration of the prophets' words.

2:1–3a, Peter's Prediction of False Teachers. The author now introduces the opponents explicitly by means of Peter's prophecy of them. His principal accusation against them is that they disown their Master, Jesus, by flouting his moral authority. Evidently their teaching encouraged immoral behavior by denying eschatological judgment: ironically, they are thereby incurring judgment at the imminent Parousia (v. 1b).

2:3b–10a, Third Apologetic Section. The opponents scoffed at the idea of future judgment at the Parousia. Divine judgment never happens, they said. It must be taking time off or taking a nap (v. 3b). To refute this claim, the author cites well-known OT examples of divine judgment: the judgment of the fallen angels (following current Jewish exegesis of Gen. 6:1–6), the Flood, and the destruction of Sodom and Gomorrah.

These instances establish the general rule that God punishes the wicked (2 Pet. 2:9b), but they are also typological prophecies of the judgment to come. Hence, the universal character of the Flood (v. 5) and the burning of Sodom and Gomorrah (v. 6) are mentioned, since they foreshadow the universal judgment by fire in the future (3:7, 10).

The examples also show that God delivers the righteous when he judges the wicked (2:9a), and so Noah and Lot are models of faithful Christians who will be delivered from the eschatological judgment. Both were committed to righteousness in situations ripe for judgment (the details in vv. 5, 7–8 derive from Jewish exegetical tradition). What enables such people to persist in righteousness is the hope for deliverance when God's righteousness prevails. In the same way, the hope of the Parousia should sustain 2 Peter's readers in the practice of righteousness.

In this passage, the author begins to use the Letter of Jude as a source (cf. Jude 6–8). He continues to do so down to 3:3 but adapts the material to meet the needs of argument against a different kind of false teaching.

2:10b–22, Denunciation of the Opponents. Here the author exposes the sins of his opponents with considerable rhetorical effect. They are not well-meaning Christians who fall into sin through ignorance and weakness; they are brazen, deliberate sinners who think themselves above moral constraints. They treat the powers of evil with contempt (v. 10b), heedless of the danger of falling into their grip. They openly indulge in all manner of sensuality and turn even the church's fellowship meals into occasions for self-indulgence, so that the author punningly calls these "love-feasts" (Gk. *agapai*) "deceits" (*apatai*: v. 13b; cf. Jude 12). But by means of two comparisons he shows the attitudes of the opponents to be sheer stupidity that will lead to their condemnation at the judgment they deny. He compares them with irrational animals, whose natural destiny is to be slaughtered (2 Pet. 2:12), and with the OT prophet Balaam, whose greed for financial reward blinded his judgment, so that he was foolish enough to think he could oppose God's will with impunity (vv. 15–16; cf. Num. 22). In his case even an irrational animal knew better!

The opponents were teachers who compounded their guilt by leading others astray, especially recent converts (2 Pet. 2:18), attracted by the potent promise of "freedom" (v. 19) —i.e., freedom from fear of divine judgment and hence from moral constraint. But the opponents cannot give the freedom they promise because they themselves are slaves to sin and its destructive power (v. 19b). Whereas real liberation comes through subjection to God's will, the freedom from divine authority of which the false teachers boast turns out to be mere subjection to evil. So, as teachers, they are like dry wells and quickly disappearing haze, which seem to offer refreshment but soon disappoint (v. 17a).

Verses 20–22 stress the seriousness of moral apostasy. Like the man in Jesus' story (Matt. 12:43–45), to which v. 20b alludes, Christians who return to the immorality of their pagan past are in a worse state than before their conversion, because then they sinned in ignorance, whereas now they sin against the light and with contempt for grace.

3:1–4, Peter's Prediction of Scoffers. By mentioning 1 Peter and echoing 2 Pet. 1:12–15, 3:1–2 return to testament style and introduce a second prediction by Peter, which portrays the opponents as skeptics who mock divine revelation. They claim that the prophecy of the Parousia, which had been expected within the lifetime of the first generation of Christians ("the fathers"), has proved illusory now that that generation has passed away (v. 4). This objection provides the best indication we have of the date of 2 Peter, since it probably reflects a problem that would have arisen about A.D. 80–90 but that seems to have been quickly forgotten and is never mentioned in the literature of the second century. But the eschatological skepticism of the opponents did not result solely from the nonfulfillment of the Parousia prophecy; the last phrase of v. 4 suggests that this only confirmed their rationalistic assumption that divine interventions in history do not happen.

3:5–10, Fourth Apologetic Section. The author makes two replies to the scoffers' objection in v. 4. The first (vv. 5–7) counters the rationalistic assumption in v. 4b by arguing that the continuance of the world as a stable habitation for humanity is not to be taken for granted but depends on the will of the Creator. The picture in vv. 5–6 is of the universe brought into existence out of the waters of chaos (Gen. 1:2, 6–7, 9) and then at the time of the Flood submerged again (cf. Gen. 7:11). Since there has been one universal judgment, by water, the prophecy of another, by fire, is credible (2 Pet. 3:7). The author envisages world history in three periods, divided by the two great cosmic cataclysms of the Flood (cf. 2:5) and the eschatological conflagration. But his interest in these is more moral than cosmological. It is the fire of divine judgment that will burn up the sky and expose the evil world to God's judgment (v. 10) so that the new world of righteousness may be established (v. 13). The ideas and imagery derive from Jewish apocalyptic, whose relevance the author is keen to assert against the extreme hellenization of the gospel by his opponents.

The second reply (vv. 8–9) meets the problem of the delay of the Parousia (v. 4a) with arguments already traditional in Jewish apocalyptic. In v. 8, God's eternal perspective on history is contrasted with the short-term expectations of human beings. To say that God is "late" in fulfilling his promises (v. 9) is to judge by impatient human standards. Moreover, the delay is no cause for complaint but a sign of God's grace by which he bears with sinners in hope of their repentance. But so that sinners should not be able to presume on God's forbearance, delaying repentance, the author then stresses that the Parousia will come unexpectedly, like a burglar at night (v. 10; cf. Matt. 24:43–44; 1 Thess. 5:2).

3:11–16, Exhortation. Just as the opponents' eschatological skepticism was the corollary of their libertinism, so the readers' hope of the Parousia should have as its corollary a life of righteousness. The key lies in v. 13: in the new world, unlike the present one, Righteousness (personified) will be at home. So those who hope to live there must become righteous (vv. 11, 14) and thus fulfill God's purpose in delaying the Parousia (v. 15a).

Since Paul's Letters to the churches to which 2 Peter was written were already being treated as Scripture (v. 16b), the author wishes to point out that his teaching is in harmony with Paul's. The opponents' misinterpretation of Paul (v. 16) could mean that they claimed Paul's support for their antinomian view of Christian freedom or that they held Paul's expectation of the Parousia to be disproved.

3:17–18, Conclusion. The testamentary convention—that Peter is forewarning of false teachers to come—reappears in this closing summary of the Letter's message.

Bibliography

Bauckham, R. J. *Jude, 2 Peter.* Word Biblical Commentary, 50. Waco, TX: Word, 1983.

_____. "2 Peter: An Account of Research." *Aufstieg und Niedergang der römischen Welt* II/25/4. Berlin: de Gruyter, 1986.

Fornberg, T. *An Early Church in a Pluralistic Society.* Lund: Gleerup, 1977.

Käsemann, E. "An Apologia for Primitive Christian Eschatology." *Essays on New Testament Themes.* Studies in Biblical Theology, 41. London: SCM, 1964. Pp. 169–95.

Neyrey, J. H. "The Form and Background of the Polemic in 2 Peter." *Journal of Biblical Literature* 99 (1980): 407–31.

1, 2, 3 JOHN

R. ALAN CULPEPPER

INTRODUCTION

The First, Second, and Third Letters of John open a window on one period in the life of the Johannine community, Christian groups that earlier had produced the Gospel of John. Indeed, interpretation of these writings depends in large measure on reconstructing their historical context from the sparse clues they supply. A major question concerns the relationship between the Johannine Letters and the Gospel of John. While some interpreters argue that one or all of the Letters precede the composition of the Gospel of John, most Johannine scholars now date the Letters after the Gospel or late in the extended period of its composition. A date about A.D. 100 is therefore preferred for the Letters. The three Letters are also usually attributed to one author, who may or may not have been the final editor of the Gospel.

The principal factor in the setting of the Letters appears in 1 John 2:19—the Johannine community was split; some of its members had left it. 1 John was written to the remaining members of the community to encourage them to remain faithful and to warn them against the errors of the opponents who had left the community.

1 John neither begins nor ends like a letter, presumably because it was not sent to another town but intended to be read locally. It is also anonymous, though there is no convincing evidence for assigning it to any figure other than the "elder" (Gk. *presbyteros*) of 2 John 1 and 3 John 1 (→ Presbyter, Presbytery).

Apparently both the elder and his opponents held to a common tradition. 1 John offers an interpretation of this tradition and calls the community to hold to the teaching it had received, but it does not quote the Gospel of John or refer to the Beloved Disciple (→ Beloved Disciple). One explanation for the absence of such an appeal is that the opponents claimed these authorities also.

The issues in the debate between the elder and the opponents are suggested by emphases in the Letters themselves. Whereas the Gospel was written "in order that you may believe that Jesus is the Christ, the Son of God" (John 20:31), 1 John insists that one must confess that Jesus Christ has come in *flesh* (4:2). 2 John 7 identifies the deceivers as those who do not confess "Jesus Christ come [having come or coming] in *flesh*." From this emphasis on the incarna-

tion, we may assume that the opponents held to the divinity of the Christ but either denied or diminished the significance of his humanity. Their view may be an early indication of Docetism, the heresy that emerged in the second century claiming that Jesus only *seemed* to be human.

In response, the elder reaffirmed the importance of the confession that the Christ came in flesh. The allusion to "water and blood" (1 John 5:6) may also be a reassertion of the importance of the death of Jesus. The opponents evidently placed so much emphasis on the coming of Jesus as the heavenly revealer (a key motif in the Fourth Gospel) that his death was no longer important for salvation. The elder consequently reasserted the importance of the humanity of Jesus and the saving significance of his death.

Similar inferences yield other points of difference between the two factions. The elder appealed to the community's hope for the future. Although both factions held that believers have crossed over from death into life (1 John 3:14), the elder contended that the future coming requires that believers purify themselves and be righteous (3:2, 7).

The ethical teachings of the Gospel of John do not include anything like the richness of the Sermon on the Mount. Consequently, the elder repeatedly called for observance of the new commandment, love for one another, and for living "just as" Jesus lived (1 John 2:6, 18, 27; 3:2, 3, 7, 12; 4:17; 2 John 4, 6; 3 John 2, 3). In the view of the elder, the opponents had violated this community ethic by leaving the community; they had shown that they did not love the brethren. Those who remained, he exhorted, should continue to be faithful both to the tradition they had received "from the beginning" and to the community ethic of love for one another.

2 John and 3 John were probably written at about the same time as 1 John, but they are letters to sister churches. 2 John is addressed to "the elect lady and her children," while 3 John is addressed to Gaius, a member of a congregation that had received travelers sent by the elder. From these letters we gain further information regarding steps the elder was taking to prevent the dissension from spreading to other congregations in the constellation of Johannine churches.

The Johannine Letters continue to have value for both historical and theological reasons. Because they cast light on a chapter in the history of the Johannine community, the Letters allow us to read the Gospel of John with greater insight. They expose both the strengths and weaknesses of Johannine theology and record the problems to which that theology was vulnerable. As a collection and individually, the Letters also provide a tragic reflection on the hostility and distortions that are created by schisms and divisions within the church. Their greatest value, therefore, may be realized as a by-product of their original purpose: they may help the church to recognize the destructive effects of divisions within the Christian community.

COMMENTARY

1 JOHN

1:1-4
The Prologue: The Word of Life

The opening words of 1 John announce that "the word of life" has been manifest. The message of life is grounded in the life of Jesus, God's son, who revealed the nature of eternal life, that life of another aeon that God's children now share. The prologue, therefore, introduces many of the Letter's major concerns: the reality of the incarnation, the nature of the life revealed by Jesus, and the importance of participation in the community if one is to share in that life.

Numerous outlines with varying numbers of divisions have been suggested for 1 John. The structure followed here is based on the repetition of the statement "God is ..." three times in the Letter: "God is light" (1:5), "He is righteous" (2:29), and "God is love" (4:8). 1 John then demands that these qualities must dominate the lives of believers, i.e., God's children, just as they were manifested by Jesus. Raymond E. Brown, in his definitive commentary on the Letters, proposes a structure that highlights the repetition of "This is the Gospel" (lit., "message") in 1:5 and 3:11. The structure of the Letter is all the more difficult to define in outline form because of its use of transitional verses and paragraphs that may be placed with either the preceding or the following verses (e.g., 2:28; 4:1-6).

1:5-2:27
Light Among God's Children

If God is light, then God's children must walk (or live) in light. The issue is not the nature of God but the opponents' claim that they had a unique relationship with God. In response, the elder charges that their claims are false because they do not live in purity (i.e., light) or practice love for other believers. Their departure from the community proves that they were not really a part of it. Since they do not belong to the people of God, they are of the world; they belong to darkness, evil, and falsehood.

1:5-2:2, The Incompatibility of Light and Sin. Because there is no darkness in God, there can be no sin in God's people. This axiom, which the opponents would have accepted also, does not mean that believers cannot sin, however.

1 John 1:6-2:2 is composed of six "if, then" statements. Three expose the errors of the opponents by quoting their slogans, characterizing their way of life, and asserting the consequences of their inconsistency. Since the author three times repeats the formula, "if we say ..." (vv. 6, 8, 10), the opponents and perhaps some who remained within the community were apparently making assertions like: "we have fellowship with him" (v. 6); "we have no sin" (v. 8); and "we have never sinned" (v. 10). Those who live in sin cannot claim fellowship with God, however, because he is light. Moreover, if we say we have no sin we deceive ourselves and make God a liar.

On the other hand, the other three conditional sentences (1:7, 9; 2:1-2) offer assurances for those who recognize the presence of sin in their lives and confess it to God. Jesus Christ is now an advocate before the Father for those who confess their sin (→ Paraclete). The importance of the death of Jesus as an expiation for sin is also reasserted, not only for the community but for the whole world (→ Expiation).

2:3-11, Love as a Test of Knowledge. Just as the previous section quotes the sayings of the opponents using the formula, "if we say ... ," three further claims are introduced in this section by means of the phrase, "the one who claims": "the one who claims, 'I know him' " (2:4); "the one who claims to abide in him" (2:6); and "the one who claims to be in the light" (2:9).

John 17:3 defines eternal life as knowing God. The notion that knowledge of God could bring a person salvation or deliverance from this world was prevalent in ancient religions. Undoubtedly both the elder and those who had left the community claimed that they knew God. The elder demands, however, that knowledge of God must be confirmed by how one lives and suggests two tests: keeping God's commandments (1 John 2:3) and living "just as" Jesus lived (2:6). These tests recall the new commandment, "that you love one another *just as* I loved you" (John 13:34). What love for a brother or sister requires is defined later (1 John 3:17–18). Here, love is associated with light. Hate—the only alternative to love in Johannine thought—is a sign that one is walking in darkness. And in God there is no darkness at all (1:5).

2:12–17, Conflict with the World. The presence of light in the Christian community that is surrounded by a world characterized by darkness points metaphorically to the conflict between the two. The elder, therefore, assures the community that it was already victorious and forbade any compromise with the world. Here, *the world* is used not in a neutral sense to designate the created order but as a reference to all that lies under the power of evil (5:19; → World, The).

Verses 12–14 express assurance of victory over evil in two poetic stanzas (12–13; 14). Three groups are addressed in each stanza: children, fathers, and young men. The change to the past tense in v. 14 is only a stylistic variation and does not refer to some previous communication. As C. H. Dodd notes, the assurances to each of the groups are equally true for all believers. The Johannine writings call all believers "children of God," and the terms "fathers" and "young men" probably derive from references such as Jer. 31:34 and Joel 2:28.

Since the world is irreconcilably opposed to the community of believers, the elder admonishes the faithful that they cannot love the world and love God also. One love comes from evil ("the world") and is passing away; the other comes from God and abides forever.

2:18–27, Conflict Within the Community. The conflict with the world had invaded the community, however. Some had left the community, and these the elder calls "antichrists" (→Antichrist, The). The appearance of such foes signaled the arrival of the "last hour"—a term found only in 1 John 2:18 in the NT. The elder did not need to explain the circumstances of the schism because members of the community already knew about it. We may infer, however, that the dispute was primarily about how Jesus was to be understood, as outlined in the Introduction.

Three emphatic addresses, "(and) you" (2:20, 24, 27), provide the structure for this section. Since some of those who remained may have considered joining the other faction, the elder assures them, "you have an anointing," by which he probably meant the Holy Spirit. They know the truth already, but the Antichrist is the Liar, the one who denies the Christ. The

opponents, however, had been a part of the community, so the issue must be a specific confession of Christ, as suggested by 1 John 4:2. Yet, the elder warns that those who do not confess the Son do not have the Father either. He appeals, therefore, for the community to abide in the tradition they had received from the beginning and not to depart from it, following those who had left the community. They already had the promise of eternal life. They did not need a new teaching; they needed only to abide in the teaching they had already received from the Holy Spirit through the tradition of the community.

2:28–4:6
Righteousness Among God's Children

Because the conflict with the world had entered the community, the Johannine Christians needed guidance in distinguishing their opponents. Three related sections follow: the first deals with the hope of the righteous (2:28–3:10), the second with the love command (3:11–24), and the third with tests of the two spirits (4:1–6). The conflict that had engulfed the community was no less than a conflict between the children of God and the children of the devil. The elder shared the common assumption that the child would be like the parent. The children of God will see God, but they must be righteous, even as God is righteous. While the children of the devil continue in sin and lawlessness, the Johannine Christians cannot sin because they have been born of God.

Maintaining the command to love others within the community was a crucial test of one's faith. Like Cain, the children of the devil had no love for their brothers or sisters and did not share with those in need.

A different spirit was working within each faction of the divided community. The elder, therefore, charges the faithful to test the spirits both by what they said and by who followed them.

2:28–3:10, The Hope of the Righteous. The anointing received by the faithful brings both assurance and the requirement of righteousness. Because God is righteous, all who are "born of him"—a favorite Johannine description for the gift of eternal life that reorients the lives of the faithful—must be righteous also. The elder reasserts the hope of the coming of God at the end of time (→ Parousia). Human life will reach its ultimate fulfillment when the faithful see God and find that they are like him. This hope, however, also requires that the faithful purify themselves so that they will be ready to see God (see Matt. 5:8).

In Johannine thought sin and righteousness

are opposites, like light and darkness or truth and falsehood. Each characterizes a way of life. Sin, above all, is characterized not as immorality but as unbelief (see John 16:8–9). The believers, therefore, cannot sin. One of the enigmas of 1 John is the relationship between 3:6, 9 and 1:8, 10. The former verses indicate that the believer cannot sin, while the latter claim that one who denies sin is deceived and makes God a liar. The alternative in chap. 3, however, is between "doing sin" (3:4, 8, 9) and "doing righteousness" (3:7, 10). The elder recognizes that believers sin also (1 John 1:8, 10), but demands that the faithful lead lives characterized by righteousness. The child must —and inevitably will—be like the parent, according to the elder. Believers will be righteous, like God; and those who do not belong to the community of the faithful will be like their father, the devil (see John 8:44).

3:11–24, The Love of the Righteous. The clearest sign of sin is the lack of love. The opponents have shown that they do not love the community, the elder charges, because they departed from it. The Johannine love command is significantly more restricted than that of the Sermon on the Mount, which commands love for one's enemies (Matt. 5:44). The new commandment required love for "one another," which was interpreted to mean love for others within the Christian community.

Those who did not love their Christian brothers and sisters, the elder charges, were like Cain, who killed his brother. Those who live by this command, however, have already crossed over from death into life. Such love is therefore an essential quality of that life that God gives to his own. That love is most clearly manifest in Jesus' act of laying down his life for his own. Believers, therefore, ought to live "just as" Jesus did. Specifically, the love command requires that one who sees a brother or sister in need will share with the one in need. Love is not just a feeling, therefore; it is the way the faithful live.

1 John 3:19–21 is open to multiple interpretations. The elder's concern seems to be the confidence that believers may have in God. Some interpreters take these verses as a warning that God's judgment will be even greater than our judgment on ourselves. The tone of the verses, however, is one of assurance rather than warning. Our hearts may know our shortcomings, but God knows all things. Moreover, the faithful may be confident before God because they keep his commands.

His commands, of course, are twofold: believe (John 14:1), and love one another (John 13:34; 15:12; 1 John 2:7–11; 3:11, 16–18; 4:7–21). Both the keeping of these commands and the presence of the Spirit confirm one's place within the new covenant.

4:1–6, The Two Spirits. The reference to the Spirit in 3:24 introduces the need to distinguish between the work of two spirits: the spirit of truth and the spirit of deception. 1 John extends the dualism of John's worldview by reference to the two spirits, but parallels can be found in the Qumran scrolls and elsewhere. By saying that false prophets have "gone out" into the world (4:1), the elder is probably alluding to those who had gone out from the community (2:19).

One test to distinguish truth from deception is that of content (see Deut. 13:1–5). The elder adds to the required confession the affirmation that Jesus Christ came "in flesh" (cf. John 20:31). The opponents who had gone out from the community apparently either denied that the divine Word could become human or else they diminished the significance of his humanity in their effort to exalt his divinity. This error led to the heresy known as Docetism, the view that Jesus only *seemed* to be human. In contrast, 1 John demands full recognition of Jesus' humanity.

The second test of the spirits is that of response. The children of God respond to the divine Spirit, while the world responds to the spirit of deception. It may be, therefore, that the opponents were actually winning more converts than were the faithful who remained with the elder.

4:7–5:12
Love Among God's Children

The twin commands to believe and to love one another are linked in 3:23. Now each is considered again in major sections that bring the themes of the Letter to their fullest expression. Earlier sections admonish the community that just as God is light (1:5) and righteous (2:29), so the people of God must be free from sin. This section develops the essential link between God's love and the love of Christians for one another. 1 John 4:7–21 ranks along with 1 Corinthians 13 as one of the finest statements in the NT on the experience and nature of divine love within the human community. As in other parts of the Letter, transitional units (e.g., 5:1–4; 5:13) form links with both the preceding and the following verses. 1 John 5:1–4 affirms that those who keep the love commandment have been born of God. They have both God's testimony and the life that God gives to his children (5:5–12).

4:7–21, The True Nature of Love. The love command was treated earlier in 2:7–11 and 3:11, 16–18. Now the elder delivers his climactic statement on the subject. The short, simple clauses of vv. 7–10 are almost poetic. Because love emanates from God's essential nature and because God's children live in response to their intimate relationship with him, love must characterize the Christian community. Again, the elder is not speaking of love in general, as though anyone who loves another human being belongs to God. He still has in mind the "new command" that Jesus' followers love one another.

Those who live by this community ethic demonstrate that they already share in that life of unending fellowship with God. Those who do not love (i.e., the opponents) show that they have not come to know God. Verse 9 echoes John 3:16, and 4:11–16a comments on each part of the verse. Love comes not from the best of the human spirit but from the character of God, and especially in God's sending his Son as an expiation for sin (2:2; 4:10). No one has seen God, but God's love is brought to its fulfillment and completion in the community of believers. Through the witness of the Beloved Disciple, the community has seen the Son and can bear witness to him through its confession.

The experience of the abiding presence of the Spirit confirms the community's knowledge of God. By living in response to God's self-revelation in Jesus, the community of believers experiences the fullness of God's love and the ultimate purpose of life. The fulfillment of God's love for us in our relationships with others results in a communion with God that not only brings his love to completion but also casts out fear of the future.

The beginning of v. 18 is marked variously in different manuscripts, but most translations place the beginning at "there is no fear in love" (RSV). One who knows God's love does not need to fear God's judgment. The elder may be responding to the charges of the opponents, who apparently dismissed the future judgment because they had already "crossed from death into life" (3:14). While reasserting the importance of the command to love, the elder maintains the reality of the future judgment also—but protects himself from the charge that he fears the judgment because he does not know God's love.

Returning to the command to love, the elder concludes this section by pointing again to the contradiction involved in saying that one loves God when one does not show love for brothers and sisters in the Christian community.

5:1–12, The True Nature of Faith. The verb "believe" reappears in 5:1 (see 3:23), introducing a section that describes how love leads to the victory of faith. The structure of this section is indicated by the three references to "the one who believes" (5:1, 5, 10) and the three pronouncements: "this is the victory" (5:4), "this is the testimony" (5:9, 11), and "this is the life" (5:11). By linking the twin commands, to believe and to love, to the content of true belief and the experience of that life that is God's gift, the elder brings his themes to a climax.

Previously, each use of the verb "to be born" referred to the believer; the same seems to be true in 5:1 also. The one who loves the parent loves the child. Although the child may be understood as a reference to either Jesus or the believer, the latter is more likely. 1 John 5:1 restates the principle behind 4:20: one cannot love God if one has no love for God's children.

Love of God requires keeping both of the Johannine commandments (believe, love). The community's faith is also its victory over the world because the world under the power of evil seeks to destroy both the community's faith and its ethic of love.

The victor, therefore, is the one who maintains the faith. The content of true faith is then specified: faith in Jesus, the son of God, who came through water and blood. The latter phrase is probably an affirmation of the true humanity of Jesus in both his incarnation and his death. Both were significant for the elder's understanding of salvation. The opponents, on the other hand, apparently diminished the significance of Jesus' death because of their emphasis on his role as the heavenly revealer. To the water and the blood, which were soon associated with baptism and the Lord's Supper, the elder added a third witness that confirms the first two: the Spirit.

An insertion at the end of v. 7, originating in Latin manuscripts from the fourth century, the so-called Johannine Comma, adds: "in heaven: Father, Word, and Holy Spirit; and these three are one; and there are three who testify on earth." This gloss, apparently motivated by early trinitarian debates, is not found in any Greek manuscript before the fifteenth century.

Through the water, the blood, and the Spirit, God has borne witness to his Son; and his testimony is greater than any human testimony. Just as the body of the Letter begins with an affirmation of the message the community had received (1:5), so it ends with a declaration of the testimony it has experienced (5:11). God's testimony, however, is received only by faith. Those who respond to his revelation in Jesus with authentic faith are given life in his Son.

5:13–21
The Epilogue

In the conclusion the elder restates his purpose for writing (5:13) and instructs the community regarding: the confidence they can have in prayer (vv. 14–15), whom to pray for (vv. 16–17), and the confidence they can have because of their faith (vv. 18–20). The Letter concludes with a warning about idolatry (v. 21).

Verse 13 is reminiscent of both 1:4 and the purpose statement in the Gospel (John 20:31). Since the Letter is addressed to believers, the emphasis is on knowing the life they already have. If the faithful recognize that they already have eternal life, they will not be swayed by the appeals made by the opponents.

The elder's faithful adherents can also have confidence in prayer. When believers are so responsive to the guidance of the spirit of truth that their prayers accord with God's will, God hears their prayers and grants their requests.

This general assurance regarding confidence in prayer leads to the troublesome question of prayer for one who is sinning. Again, the syntax is not altogether clear. Who gives life, the one who prays or God? Ultimately, of course, only God can give life. The distinction is not so much between types of sin as between persons for whom one should pray. Since sin was understood by the Johannine Christians fundamentally as unbelief (John 16:9), in the context of 1 John the deadly sin must be refusal to confess Jesus. Specifically, those who commit the deadly sin are those who refuse to confess Jesus having come in flesh (4:2), as the elder required. All sin threatens the life of God's children, and must be confessed (see 1:6–2:2), so one should pray for fellow Christians. Drawing a hard line, however, the elder forbids prayer for the opponents who withdrew from the community.

The Letter closes with a reminder of the certainties to which the faithful may cling. We know: the believer does not sin (see 3:6, 9) and Jesus Christ protects believers; we are God's, while the world is under the power of evil; and the son of God has come to reveal God to us and to give us eternal life. The closing warning against idolatry, while seemingly out of place, may be taken as a final warning against the false teachings of the community's opponents.

2 JOHN

This short Letter was probably written by the author of 1 John and about the same time as the longer Letter. Echoes of words and phrases from 1 John can be found in 2 John, but the sequence of the writing of the two Letters is debated. 1 John, which does not begin like a letter, was evidently written to the remnant of the central Johannine community. 2 and 3 John, which follow a more typical letter form, were written to churches or individuals in churches that were closely associated with the elder's congregation.

The elder does not identify the recipient by name, nor apparently is there any need to identify himself by name. The emphases on truth and love in the opening verses implicitly speak of faithfulness to the tradition received and defended by the elder and other followers of the Beloved Disciple.

The greeting, with the distinctive term "mercy," is similar to the greeting in 1 Tim. 1:2 and 2 Tim. 1:2. The elder rejoices at the faithfulness of fellow believers from the sister church and appeals for continued fraternal relations as they continue to practice the love required by the new commandment. The need for fraternal relations was all the more necessary since the deceivers (i.e., the elder's opponents) had gone out from the community. The error of their teaching was that they did not confess that Jesus Christ had come (or perhaps that he was coming) in flesh. The participle is in the present tense (lit., "coming"), but most interpreters hear v. 7 as an echo of 1 John 4:2.

The elder's real concern is that the false teaching and dissension that plagued his congregation not spread to the sister church. To prevent this from happening he lays down the principle that one who abides in the teaching of Christ (received through the Johannine school) has fellowship with God. One who departs from this teaching, or goes beyond it, should not be received by the church. By refusing to extend hospitality to those who spread false teaching, the church could protect itself from the opponents who had gone out from the elder's congregation.

The Letter closes with an expression of desire to visit the sister church and fraternal greetings from the "children" of their "elect sister."

3 JOHN

The primary difficulty in interpreting this short letter from the elder to Gaius, the beloved, is deciphering the relationships among the individuals who are named (Gaius, Diotrephes, Demetrius) and the elder. The elder did not have to explain these relationships to Gaius, so they remain unclear to later readers.

A plausible reconstruction of the situation yields the following picture. Diotrephes emerges as the leader of a church within the orbit of Johannine Christianity. His role may not yet have been formalized as that of a bishop, however, and nothing is said of his relationship to other churches. In an effort either to protect his authority or to protect the church from false teachings, Diotrephes had been rejecting the emissaries sent by the elder, speaking against them, and threatening to exclude from the church anyone who would receive them. Ironically, Diotrephes seems to have taken the same measures that the elder urged in 2 John as means for stopping the spread of the false teachings of the opponents. Perhaps because he could not tell one itinerant teacher or evangelist from another, Diotrephes forbade extending hospitality to any itinerant.

Gaius, however, had been cooperating with the elder and extending hospitality to those he sent. The elder wrote 3 John, therefore, to appeal for Gaius to continue to provide hospitality to the Johannine "brothers" and to warn him about Diotrephes. Whether Gaius was a member of the church over which Diotrephes had extended his authority is unclear.

The elder also commended Demetrius as one whose testimony was true. Indeed, it is likely that Demetrius was the bearer of this letter.

Like 2 John, the Letter closes with the hope that the elder will soon be able to visit the recipient. Greetings are sent from "the friends," which was evidently used along with "brothers" and "beloved" as a term of address for fellow Johannine Christians (see John 3:29; 11:11; 15:13–15).

Bibliography

Brown, R. E. *The Epistles of John.* Anchor Bible, 30. Garden City, NY: Doubleday, 1982.

Culpepper, R. A. *1 John, 2 John, 3 John.* Knox Preaching Guides. Atlanta, GA: Knox, 1985.

Dodd, C. H. *The Johannine Epistles.* Moffatt Commentaries. London: Hodder and Stoughton, 1946.

Houlden, J. L. *The Johannine Epistles.* Harper's New Testament Commentaries. New York: Harper & Row, 1973.

Smalley, S. S. *1, 2, 3 John.* Word Biblical Commentary, 51. Waco, TX: Word, 1984.

JUDE

RICHARD J. BAUCKHAM

INTRODUCTION

Form and Structure

The structure of the Letter of Jude can be analyzed as follows:

1–2, Address and greeting
3–4, Occasion and theme
  A 3, The appeal to contend for the faith
  B 4, The background to the appeal: The false teachers, their character and judgment
5–23, Body of the Letter
  B' 5–19, The background: A commentary on four prophecies of the doom of the ungodly
    5–7, 8–10, 9, Three OT types and interpretation including Michael and the devil
    11, 12–13, Three more OT types and interpretation
    14–15, 16, The prophecy of Enoch and interpretation
    17–18, 19, The prophecy of the apostles and interpretation
  A' 20–23, The appeal
24–25, Concluding doxology

It is important to notice that the initial statement of the theme of the Letter (vv. 3–4) contains two parts (A and B) that correspond, in reverse order, to the two parts of the body of the Letter (B' and A'). The main purpose of the Letter is the appeal "to contend for the faith" that is announced in v. 3 and spelled out in vv. 20–23. But v. 4 explains that this appeal is necessary because the readers are in danger of being misled by false teachers. The claim in v. 4 that these teachers are people whose ungodly behavior has already been condemned by God is then substantiated by the exegetical section (B'), which argues that these are the people to whom the scriptural types and judgments refer.

Section B' is a carefully composed piece of scriptural commentary, which resembles the commentaries on Scripture found among the Dead Sea Scrolls in two ways: its underlying assumption, that OT Scripture is prophetic of the last times in which the author and his readers live, and its exegetical method, which treats figures mentioned in Scripture as "types" that will be fulfilled when their counterparts appear at the end of days. It consists of a series of four main "texts" (vv. 5–7, 11, 14–15, 17–18)

and comments on each (vv. 8–10, 12–13, 16, 19). The first two "texts" are in fact summary references to OT figures; the third and fourth are quotations not from the OT but from the apocryphal apocalypse known to us as 1 Enoch and from a prophecy of the apostles. But all are treated as texts on which commentary is given. In each case the transition from "text" to commentary is marked by a reference to "these men," indicating that Jude's opponents are the people to whom the "text" refers, and by a transition from the past or future tense to the present tense, indicating that the type or prophecy is now being fulfilled. In one case a secondary text is introduced to help the commentary on the main "text" (v. 9).

The Opponents

Jude's opponents were a group of itinerant charismatics. The one thing that is clear about their teaching is that they were antinomians, who understood the grace of God in Christ (v. 4) as a deliverance from all moral constraint. Evidently they claimed to have received this teaching in visions ("dreamings," v. 8) and saw themselves and their followers as the truly spiritual people (v. 19), free from external moral authority. Against them Jude insists on the seriousness of God's moral requirements, which will take effect in the judgment of willful transgressors at the Parousia (the glorious return of Christ).

Provenance and Authorship

Several features of the Letter indicate its origin in Palestinian Jewish Christianity. Jude, unlike most NT authors, habitually uses the OT in Hebrew rather than the Septuagint Greek. His exegetical methods, his apocalyptic outlook, and the high value he attaches to apocryphal works of Jewish apocalyptic origin are all characteristic of Jewish Christian circles in Palestine, which understood Jesus and the gospel in terms of Jewish apocalyptic expectations (→ Eschatology).

The character of the Letter is therefore entirely consistent with its attribution to Judas the brother of Jesus. There is no clear evidence of date, but an earlier rather than a later date is probable, and it may in fact be one of the earliest books in the NT. Its special value is that it offers a glimpse into those original Palestinian

Christian circles in which Jesus' own blood relations were leaders.

COMMENTARY

1–2, Address and Greeting. James the brother of the Lord was the only man in the early church who could be called simply "James" without ambiguity. So by calling himself "brother of James," the author identifies himself as Judas the brother of Jesus (Mark 6:3).

3–4, Occasion and Theme. Jude's Letter is not the extended discussion of Christian salvation he had intended to write, but a more *ad hoc* response to the news that these churches have been "infiltrated" by a group of prophets who take Christian freedom to mean freedom from moral restraint. Jude says that by rejecting Christ's moral demands they are disowning him as Master. But such people are one of the prophesied dangers of the last times. Their immoral behavior and coming judgment have been prophesied, as Jude will show in vv. 5–19. In the face of such danger, Jude's readers need to fight for the gospel ("the faith") as it was taught them ("the saints") by the apostles who founded their churches: what this "fight" involves will be explained in vv. 20–23.

5–10, Three Old Testament Types. Three classic examples of those who incur divine judgment are given: the whole generation of Israel exterminated in the wilderness after the Exodus (Num. 14), the angels who left their heavenly position in order to mate with women (Gen. 6:1–4, as interpreted in the apocryphal account *1 Enoch* 6–19), and the Sodomites, whose sin is here condemned not as homosexual rape but as an attempt at sexual relations with angels (Gen. 19:4–11). The point in the last two cases is the outrageous transgression of the moral order of creation. The particular point in the first case is that the Lord's own people, who have experienced salvation, are not immune from judgment if they repudiate his lordship.

Jude's opponents are like these types (v. 8) in that they indulge in sexual immorality, repudiating the Lord's commandments, and like the Sodomites insult angels ("the glorious ones"). Probably they disparaged the angels in their role as guardians of the moral order. Jude expands on this charge of slandering angels by contrasting their behavior with that of the archangel Michael in an apocryphal account of the burial of Moses (v. 9). In this story the devil accused Moses of murder. Michael, acting as advocate for Moses and in this role "disputing with the devil," knew that the charge was a slander but "did not presume to condemn the devil for slander." Instead he referred the matter to the divine Judge who alone has authority to rule on an accusation brought under the Law. By contrast the false teachers presume to reject, on their own authority, the charges that the angels, as spokesmen for the Law, bring against them. They do so because they claim to be above such accusations, subject to no moral authority. Given Jude's readers' knowledge of the story, v. 9 exposes the spiritual conceit of the opponents, whose attitude to the angels reveals a resistance to all moral authority, even God's.

11–13, Three More Old Testament Types. Jude's opponents are typified not just as people who practice immorality (as in vv. 5–10) but also as teachers and corrupters of others. The OT figures are recalled as portrayed in Jewish tradition: Cain, the first heretic; Balaam, the prophet who, in his greed for financial gain, gave the advice that led Israel into apostasy (Num. 25:1–4; 31:16); and Korah, the archetypal schismatic, who led others in contesting Moses' authority and the divine origin of certain laws.

Verse 12a should be translated, "These are the people who feast with you at your fellowship meals, without reverence, like dangerous reefs." It is in the context of the fellowship meals (Gk. *agapē*) that the false teachers deliver their prophetic oracles that entice people into immorality. Their proximity is therefore as dangerous as that of a reef to a ship. They claim to be shepherds of the flock, but the only people they actually look after are themselves, by requiring the church to support them.

The four metaphors from nature (vv. 12b–13) are examples of nature failing to follow the laws ordained for it. Apocalyptic writers expected such lawlessness in nature in the last days (cf. *1 Enoch* 80:2–6): to Jude it suggests the lawlessness of the false teachers of the last days. The point of the first two metaphors is that, although the false teachers claim great value for their teaching, in fact they are of no benefit to anyone. Worse, they are positively harmful (like the filth cast up by the sea). Finally, like stars that go astray from their courses, misleading those who look to them for guidance, they will be extinguished in the underworld.

14–16, The Prophecy of Enoch. With its emphatic repetition of "ungodly," this text hammers home the message of the whole exegetical section (vv. 5–19): those who indulge in ungodly conduct, as the false teachers do, are those on whom judgment will fall at the Parousia. (By inserting "the Lord" into the quotation Jude refers it to the Lord Jesus.)

This quotation from the apocalypse of Enoch (1 Enoch 1:9), along with allusions elsewhere in his Letter, shows that Jude held it in high regard, as many Jews did. But since he pairs this quotation with another nonscriptural prophecy (v. 18), he need not have regarded it as part of the canon. The text and its application (v. 16) stress the arrogant *words* in which the false teachers reject God's will in order to follow their own.

17–19, The Prophecy of the Apostles. Jude complements Enoch's ancient prophecy with a modern one, which was part of the teaching his readers received from the apostles who founded their churches. Verse 19 indicates that the false teachers gathered an elitist faction who claimed the same kind of charismatic status as themselves. But their behavior is clearly inspired not by the Spirit but by their own natural instincts.

20–23, The Appeal. Here Jude reaches the main point of his Letter: given the danger posed by the false teachers, his readers are to "carry on the fight for the faith" (v. 3). Four injunctions summarize Christian living (vv. 20–21): first, the church's life must be built on the foundation of the gospel, with its moral imperative. Second, prayer in the Spirit exemplifies the true charismatic nature of the church. Third, readers must keep their place in God's love by obeying him. Fourth, they must live in hope of the Lord's coming to bring final salvation to those who remain faithful. In these ways they can resist the influence of antinomian teaching and stay on the path of positive Christian obedience.

Verses 22–23 explain how they are to behave toward the false teachers and those influenced by them. The text is very uncertain, but the general advice is clear: to exercise Christian love, but only in conjunction with great care to avoid the contaminating effect of the opponents' influence. But in his awareness of the danger they pose, Jude by no means gives up hope for their reclamation.

24–25, Closing Doxology. The first part of this magnificent doxology is in effect a confident prayer that God will preserve the readers from the spiritual disaster with which the false teaching threatens them and bring them to the destiny he intends for them, when they will be presented as perfect sacrifices in his heavenly temple. Jude's concern to combat the false teaching is finally aimed at this goal: that the church should be fit to be offered to God's glory.

Bibliography
Bauckham, R. J. *Jude, 2 Peter.* Word Biblical Commentary, 50. Waco, TX: Word, 1983.

———. "Jude: An Account of Research." *Aufstieg und Niedergang der römischen Welt* II/25/4. Berlin: de Gruyter, 1986.

Ellis, E. E. "Prophecy and Hermeneutic in Jude." *Prophecy and Hermeneutic in Early Christianity.* Tübingen: Mohr, 1978.

Sidebottom, E. M. *James, Jude, 2 Peter.* New Century Bible Commentary. Grand Rapids, MI: Eerdmans, 1982.

REVELATION

DAVID E. AUNE

INTRODUCTION

Author and Date

The author of the Revelation to John says that his name is "John" (1:4, 9; 22:8), that he is a "servant" of God (1:1; an OT title of honor) and a "brother" of those he addresses (1:9). He was probably well known to them, making further identification unnecessary. When he describes Revelation as a "prophetic book" (1:3; 22:7, 10, 18, 19), he indirectly claims the status of a prophet. He may have belonged to a circle of prophets (cf. 22:9, 16). He was acquainted with the condition of each of the seven churches (cf. 2:1–3:20), possibly the result of an earlier itinerant prophetic ministry. The author's familiarity with the OT and the presence of numerous Semitisms make it certain that he was a Jewish Christian who may have been an apocalyptist before his conversion (→ Eschatology). There is a possibility that he was a refugee from Palestine in the aftermath of the first Jewish revolt (A.D. 66–73). After the middle of the second century it was widely believed that the apostle John, the son of Zebedee, wrote Revelation (Justin *Dialogue* 81.4; Irenaeus *Against Heresies* 4.20.11). Yet the author never calls himself an apostle and even refers to the twelve apostles as past founders (21:14). No internal evidence suggests any connection between the author and an apostle of the same name.

Since the late second century A.D., the prevailing opinion has been that Revelation was written toward the end of the reign of the Roman emperor Domitian (A.D. 81–96), i.e., ca. A.D. 95 (Irenaeus *Against Heresies* 5.30.3). Later Christian writers regarded Domitian as the sponsor of a major persecution of the church (Eusebius *Ecclesiastical History* 3.17). However, there is no evidence that the Roman government *officially* persecuted Christians between A.D. 64 (the persecution under Nero) and A.D. 250 (the persecution under Decius). Nevertheless, other factors indicate that Revelation was written toward the end of the first century: first, the use of the code name "Babylon" (Rev. 17:5) as a reference to Rome would only be probable after A.D. 70; second, the twelve apostles are referred to as revered founders of the past (Rev. 21:14); third, Revelation refers to the rumors of Nero's return that circulated from A.D. 68 to the end of the century (Rev. 13:3; 17:10–11).

Occasion and Purpose

John wrote to a group of seven Anatolian churches that were apparently experiencing persecution by Roman authorities. One Christian had already been publicly executed (2:13), possibly more (6:9–11; 20:4), and John expected that others probably would be (2:10; 6:11). Was the situation so grim or did John paint an overly pessimistic picture? Though there was no official Roman campaign against Christians between A.D. 64 and 250, sporadic persecutions certainly occurred. Following the Neronian persecution, being a Christian was tantamount to being part of a criminal conspiracy, and Christians (unlike other religious groups) were punished simply for being Christians (Tacitus *Annals* 15.44.5; Pliny *Letters* 10.96.2–3). Their crime was an unwillingness to worship any God but their own, an exclusiveness the Greeks labeled "atheism." The refusal to sacrifice to pagan gods and on behalf of deified emperors was perceived as a threat to the harmonious relationship between people and the gods. Whether Christians were persecuted or not depended on the zeal of the provincial governor and (perhaps more importantly) public opinion. The legal basis for charges against Christians in Roman law was simply a voluntary prosecutor (Lat. *delator*, "informer"), the charge of being a Christian, and a provincial governor willing to punish people on that charge.

One major purpose of Revelation, therefore, was to offer comfort and encouragement to persecuted Christians. John accomplished this in two ways: by revealing the blessed future state of Christians who are faithful to the testimony of Jesus even at the cost of their own lives and by assuring the readers of the inevitability and imminence of the divine punishment of their persecutors. John's revelatory message also condemned all types of cultural accommodation between Christians and their pagan environment.

Literary Form

Revelation is an "apocalypse," a type of revelatory literature consisting of an extended vision report mediated by a supernatural revealer and disclosing heavenly secrets or information about the end of the world. Many apocalypses originated within Judaism from ca. 200 B.C. to ca. A.D. 100 (→Apocalyptic Literature). Some of the literary features of apocalypses include pseudonymity, historical reviews presented as predictions of the future, reports of dreams or visions, bizarre imagery, dialogues between the revealer and the author, and an emphasis on the imminence of the end. Revelation, however, is not pseudonymous nor does it contain historical reviews.

Interpreting Revelation

Revelation is the book in the NT that modern Western readers find the most foreign. Ancient Jewish and Christian apocalyptic literature is highly symbolic; often the symbolism is bizarre. In Revelation, for example, the Lamb looks as though it has been killed and has seven horns and seven eyes (5:6); the beast from the sea has seven heads and ten horns (13:1). The contrast between such grotesque images and reality suggests that such visions have symbolic or mythopoetic significance. Yet apocalyptic language is not a code that can be broken down into a table of equivalents. The special genius of apocalyptic is its ability to universalize the harsh realities of particular historical situations by transposing them into a new key using archaic symbols of conflict and victory, suffering and vindication. Thus the beast from the sea represents Rome—yet more than Rome. More accurately it represents an antagonistic role in the cosmic drama currently played by Rome but previously played by others. Revelation is a literary classic, therefore, because it not only encapsulates human experience but it gives that experience a transcultural yet Christian significance.

Literary Analysis

The literary analysis of Revelation is problematic because of the juxtaposition of tightly organized sections of material with more loosely constructed "digressions." The author favored the number seven (symbolizing completeness), which he used fifty-four times. He also used groupings of seven (heptads) as a structural device. Four extensive sections of Revelation are arranged in heptads: seven proclamations (2:1–3:20), seven seals (6:1–8:5), seven trumpets (8:8–11:18), and seven bowls (15:1–16:21). John also inserted three extensive sections of visions consisting of six digressions. The first two sections are 7:1–17 (the sealing of the 144,000), inserted between the opening of the sixth and seventh seals, and 10:1–11:14 (two digressions: John's renewed commission; the two prophetic witnesses), inserted between the sixth and seventh trumpets.

These two insertions both expand the effects of the sixth set of plagues and delay the onset of the seventh. The third insertion, 12:1–14:20, consists of three digressions that introduce the major actors in the eschatological drama and concludes with the final judgment at the Parousia.

Revelation consists of two major sections framed by a prologue and an epilogue. The prologue is limited to 1:1–8, and 22:6–21 constitutes the epilogue. The two main sections of Revelation are strikingly unequal in size. The first section deals with Christ's proclamations to the seven churches (2:1–3:20), introduced by John's visionary commission (1:9–20). In turn, Rev. 1:9–3:21 introduces the main part of the work in 4:1–22:5. The structure of this main part of Revelation is the most problematic. One major problem is deciding whether various sections recapitulate or repeat the eschatological events narrated in later sections. For example, are the similarities between the plagues unleashed by the seven trumpets and seven bowls alternate ways of describing the same events? It is more likely that the author intends to create a unique chronological synthesis of eschatological events. Most of Revelation consists of a single extensive vision report (1:9–22:9). The author has imposed an artificial literary unity on many separate textual units by linking them together in an apparent chronological order using phrases such as "after these things" and (more frequently) "then I saw." This technique fosters the impression that the visions are narrated in the order in which the author received them. Further, the author has used an "encompassing" technique, for the seventh seal encompasses the effects of the seven trumpets and seven bowls, while the seventh trumpet encompasses the effects of the seven bowls. That suggests that the author intended to present the complex events of the end (4:1–22:9) in chronological order (the only exception is the three digressions inserted between 11:18 and 15:1). However, this appearance of chronological order does not exclude the likelihood that the sources the author used (e.g., the trumpet and bowl visions) might in fact have described similar events using varied apocalyptic imagery. These considerations suggest the following outline for Revelation:

1:1–8, Prologue
1:9–20, John's commissioning vision
2:1–3:22, Christ addresses the seven churches
　2:1–7, To Ephesus
　2:8–11, To Smyrna
　2:12–17, To Pergamum
　2:18–29, To Thyatira
　3:1–6, To Sardis
　3:7–13, To Philadelphia
　3:14–22, To Laodicea
4:1–22:9, From tribulation to glory

COMMENTARY

1:1–8

Prologue

The prologue consists of six literary units clearly separate from the continuous narrative beginning in v. 9. The numerous thematic and verbal parallels between vv. 1–8 and the epilogue (22:6–21) suggest that these two sections frame the entire book. The first sentence in Revelation functions, like the initial sentences in many ancient books, as the author's own descriptive title (vv. 1–2). The term "revelation" in 1:1 refers not to the literary form of Revelation, but rather to the revelatory experience of the author. The title provides divine authority

for the entire book by giving the stages by which the revelation was mediated to John: God gave it to Jesus Christ who transmitted it through his angel to his servant John for the benefit of the servants of God, i.e., the seven churches. The mention of a *single* angel as the revelatory agent between Jesus Christ and John (cf. 22:6, 8) suggests that John had but one angelic tour guide responsible for mediating supernatural visions to him. Yet this fact is only mentioned in the prologue and epilogue and is contradicted by the main part of the book in which a variety of otherworldly beings guide John and speak to him. John's qualifications not only include the fact that he is a channel for divine revelation but also that he himself has faithfully borne witness to the word of God and to the testimony of Jesus (1:2b).

The first of seven beatitudes is placed here (v. 3; cf. 14:13; 16:15; 19:9; 20:6; 22:7, 14). John's preference for the number seven as both a symbolic number and an organizational principle suggests that the inclusion of precisely *seven* beatitudes, though unnumbered, is not accidental. This pronouncement of blessing upon readers and upon those who both hear and obey (repeated in 22:7) is probably based on the practice of beginning or concluding readings or presentations of the words of God with various "read and keep" or "hear and obey" formulas (Matt. 7:24, 26; John 12:47; *Herm. Vis.* 5:5; *2 Clem.* 19:1–3). John intended his composition to be read aloud before Christian congregations (Rev. 1:3) and perhaps used an epistolary framework for that reason (cf. 1 Thess. 5:27; Col. 4:16). Since he calls his book "the words of this prophecy" (NIV), and the prophetic books of the OT followed the reading from the Torah in synagogues, John compares his book positively with the Hebrew Scriptures.

Revelation is the only Jewish or Christian apocalypse that is framed as a *letter*, with an epistolary prescript in 1:4–5a and a concluding postscript in 22:21. Hellenistic epistolary prescriptions typically consisted of three elements: the superscription (sender), the adscription (addressee), and the salutation. "Grace to you and peace" is a Christian salutation first appearing in Paul's letters (→ Letter; Salutations). The elaborate salutation in 1:4–5a is a Johannine expansion of the traditional salutation. The phrase "from him who is and who was and who is to come" (v. 4; cf. 1:8; 11:17; 16:5) alludes to the Septuagint (LXX) version of Exod. 3:14, in which the divine name "Yahweh" is interpreted to mean "the one who is." This name was familiar in Hellenistic Judaism in both Egypt and Anatolia, though in early Christian texts it is found only in Revelation. Just as Moses is told by God to tell the people that "the one who is" had sent him, so John legitimizes his prophetic status and book by claiming that it was inspired by "the one who is."

The doxology of Rev. 1:5b–6 immediately follows the epistolary prescript of vv. 4–5a, an unusual epistolary pattern paralleled only in Galatians 1:3–4. Doxologies normally consist of three elements: "to whom / be the glory [Gk. *doxa*] / forever. Amen" (Rev. 4:9; 5:13b–14; 7:12). Each element can be variously expanded. Here "him" (God) is modified by several verbal forms describing in temporal sequence the redemptive action of God through Christ: he has *loved* us, *freed* us from our sins, and *made* us a kingdom, priests.

Rev. 1:7–8 is an example of an "amplified oracle," i.e., a prophetic saying appended to another one to expand or interpret it (for other examples cf. 13:9; 14:13; 16:15). Christian prophetic pronouncements could receive a responsory "amen" (1 Cor. 14:16) and were subject to evaluation and interpretation (1 Cor. 14:29). John's inclusion of these oracles underlines his prophetic ministry. Here the first oracle predicts the Parousia (Gk., "coming") of Christ as a cosmic event witnessed by everyone and anticipates the distress and fear of unbelievers about to experience judgment (cf. Rev. 19:11–16). The second oracle begins with the affirmative response "Even so. Amen" (1:7b), it is attributed to the "Lord God," and it contains three "I am" predications. First, the divine name "Alpha and Omega" (cf. "First and Last," 1:17) was drawn from Hellenistic revelatory magic where it abbreviated the seven Greek vowels, which were widely believed to constitute a name of the highest God. Second, "the one who is and who was and who is to come" combines Jewish and Hellenistic divine names. Third, "the Almighty" is borrowed from Judaism. In the highly stratified society of John's day, deities and rulers were accorded strings of extravagant titles. One of John's strategies for underlining the majesty and power of God and Christ in contrast to Satan and the earthly rulers in league with him is the use of titles of dignity drawn from various sources (cf. 1:17–18; 19:11–16).

1:9–20

John's Commissioning Vision

John's divine commission narrated in 1:9–20 introduces not only the proclamations to the seven churches dictated by the exalted Christ (2:1–3:22) but the main part of Revelation as well (4:1–22:5). This is a commission for a *particular task* (i.e., to write what he will see and hear), not an inaugural vision calling him to the prophetic vocation (cf. Exod. 3:1–12; Isa. 6:1–13; Ezek. 1:1–3:11; similar commands to write down the substance of revelatory visions are found in 2 Esd. 14; *Herm. Vis.* 2.4.3; 5.5–7; and *Herm. Sim.* 9.33.1). The purpose of this visionary commission to write is to provide divine legitimation for a controversial message.

The circumstances surrounding John's visionary experience are briefly recounted in Rev. 1:9–10. He received the vision on Patmos, a tiny island (five miles wide by eight miles long) in the Aegean Sea about sixty miles southwest of Ephesus. He was there "on account of the word of God and the testimony of Jesus," i.e., probably he had been sentenced to exile because he was a Christian (a view first mentioned ca. A.D. 190 by Clement of Alexandria, *The Rich Man's Salvation* 42), though there is no evidence that Patmos was a Roman penal colony. Exile (which had several voluntary and involuntary forms) was a relatively lenient form of punishment in Roman jurisprudence usually reserved for people of wealth and position (part of a pervasive legal double standard). The vision occurred on the "Lord's day" (probably Sunday, the Christian day of worship commemorating the Lord's resurrection) when John was suddenly "in the Spirit," i.e., in a trance (cf. Acts 11:5; 22:17). Prophesying was an activity often exercised in worship services (1 Cor. 14:26–33; *Did.* 10:7; *Herm. Mand.* 11).

The vision itself (Rev. 1:11–20) consists of an epiphany of the heavenly Christ appearing to John on earth, introduced (v. 11) and concluded (v. 19) by commands that John write what he *sees* (and hears) in a book for the seven churches. Supernatural commands to write the substance of a divine revelation, occasionally found in Judaism (cf. Isa. 30:8; 2 Esd. 14) are common in Greco-Roman literature (e.g., Aelius Aristides *Orations* 48.2; Callimachus *Aetia* 1.1.21–22; Plato *Phaedo* 4.60E–61B). After hearing a loud voice behind him commanding him to write (Rev. 1:11), John turns around. He first sees seven golden lampstands, and in their midst stood "one like a son of man" with white hair, eyes like fire, feet like polished bronze, and a voice like the roar of "rushing waters" (NIV). He held seven stars in his right hand, a sharp sword issued from his mouth, and his face shone as the sun. John responds in a manner typical for recipients of such vision reports: he falls down paralyzed with fear (Dan. 8:17; 10:9–11; 1 Enoch 14:14; 2 Enoch 1:7). The awesome figure urges John not to be afraid and identifies himself with a series of descriptive phrases indicating that he is none other than the exalted Christ. In Rev. 1:17b–18, he describes himself with several divine titles, refers to his death and resurrection, and claims to possess the keys to death and Hades. According to the ancient mythical view, both heaven and the underworld were linked to this world by doors or gates (cf. 4:1). In Hellenistic Anatolia, the ancient goddess Hekate was accorded universal sovereignty as mistress of the cosmos and was thought to possess the keys to Hades. John, therefore, por-

1303

trays Christ as usurping the authority of Hekate as well as every other natural or supernatural authority.

The entire vision is a pastiche of language from Jewish epiphanies ("appearances" of divine beings on earth). John's main source of imagery for this epiphany is Dan. 10:5–14 (describing the angel Gabriel), supplemented by features from the description of God in Dan. 7:9 (hair white like wool) and from the mysterious figure in Dan. 7:13 ("one like a son of man"). In Jewish literature, similar epiphanic language is found in *Joseph and Aseneth* (*Jos. Asen.*) 14.8–11; *Apoc. Zeph.* 6:11–14. Similar descriptions of divine beings seen in epiphanies are found in Greek sources (Homer *Iliad* 8.41–44; 13.22–25; Callimachus *Hymn to Apollo* 2.3). The author uses various visual and verbal attributes from the vision in the descriptions of Christ that form the introduction to each of the seven letters, thereby linking Rev. 2:1–3:22 to the introductory commission vision. The entire scene has enough similarities to various OT epiphanies to make it entirely plausible to readers familiar with that background. The metaphorical character of what John sees is made obvious in v. 20, where the seven stars are interpreted as the seven angels of the churches and the seven lampstands as the seven churches themselves. The seven lampstands suggest the seven-branch golden menorah of the tabernacle and Temple (Exod. 25:31–40) seen in Zechariah's vision (Zech. 4:1–2), which today is the religious symbol of Judaism.

2:1–3:22

Christ Addresses the Seven Churches

The seven proclamations, written by John for their present context, have a strong emphasis on the behavior expected of the addressees and a specific relevance for each community's concrete situation. Often inaccurately characterized as letters, the seven proclamations are actually prophetic messages in the form of ancient royal or imperial *edicts* (public proclamations of laws or policies enacted by a ruler possessing the requisite authority), an appropriate form of expression for the exalted Christ who is depicted as both king and priest in John's vision (1:9–20). Each of the proclamations exhibits a similar

Opposite: The cosmic events described in Rev. 6:12–17 are portrayed on this illuminated manuscript page from *The Morgan Beatus*, Spain, mid-tenth century. Following an earthquake, the unjust cower in caves (*at bottom*), fearing the judgment of God. The heavenly throne of God is at top, and the darkened sun and reddened moon are at center.

structure: first, an introduction (containing the addressee, the phrase "thus says" [RSV: "the words of"], and phrases identifying the sender); second, a central section introduced by "I know" and that includes recognition and praise for past behavior, censure, and admonitions for change; and third, a double conclusion with a call for vigilance and an exhortation to conquer.

No one knows why John wrote just to these seven churches, particularly when there were many other important Christian congregations in Asia Minor (e.g., Magnesia, Tralles, and Hierapolis). By the late second century the seven churches addressed by John were understood as symbolizing the universal church. According to the Muratorian Canon (the oldest list of NT books, ca. A.D. 180): "John also, though he wrote in the Apocalypse to seven churches, nevertheless speaks to them all." All seven were within one hundred miles of Ephesus in the Roman proconsular province of Asia and possibly formed a circuit for itinerant Christian prophets and teachers. After the fall of Jerusalem following the first Jewish revolt of A.D. 66–73, Anatolia had become one of the most important geographical centers of Christianity, with a population of perhaps eighty thousand Christians by the end of the century.

Each of the seven proclamations is addressed to the "angel" of that community. Since John elsewhere consistently uses the Greek term *aggelos* ("angel," "messenger") of supernatural beings subordinate to God, it is likely that the term has that meaning here. Various scholars have argued that the term "angel" actually refers to a local leader such as the bishop. Or, translated "messenger," it may refer to representatives John sent to the churches with copies of his circular apocalypse. Yet the idea that each church is represented in the heavenly world by an angelic figure who somehow personifies that church, though unparalleled, is apparently John's meaning.

2:1–7, To Ephesus. Ephesus was the most illustrious city of Asia Minor, a center of travel, trade, and commerce, and the seat of the Roman provincial governor. It had a population of ca. 225,000 and was a center of the imperial cult boasting four imperial temples. During the reign of Domitian, Ephesus became the "warden" (Gk. *neokoros*) of the imperial temple in Asia. Since the mid-first century, Ephesus had also been an important Christian center (Acts 18–20; 1 Cor. 15:32; 16:8). The Ephesian church receives a generally positive evaluation (Rev. 2:2–3). They have worked hard and have patiently endured persecution and ostracism, the focus of a great deal of late first-century Christian exhortation (cf. James 1:2–4; Pet. 1:6–7; 2:11–18). They are a pure church uncorrupted by false apostles whom they have tested and unmasked (Rev. 2:2). During this period the testing of itinerant apostles and prophets becomes a widespread necessity (*Did.* 11–13). In such an atmosphere the legitimacy of John's credentials was of critical importance. The term "apostle" (meaning "emissary") was applied to itinerant missionaries in early Christianity. Christian communities were scattered throughout the ancient world and linked by traveling Christians (including apostles, prophets, and teachers) dependent on local hospitality (3 John 5–8). Like other religious movements, Christianity had its share of charlatans (*Herm. Man.* 11.12; *Did.* 11.6). The Ephesians are particularly commended for opposing the Nicolaitans (see commentary below on Rev. 2:12–17), possibly identical with the "evil men" and false apostles of 2:2. The Nicolaitans are mentioned by several early Christian writers (Irenaeus *Against Heresies* 1.26.3; 3.11.1; Hippolytus *Refutation of All Heresies* 7.36.3) and improbably traced to Nicolas of Antioch (Acts 6:5). The Ephesians are faulted for abandoning the love they had at first (Rev. 2:5). They are exhorted to remember their previous condition and with that in mind to repent and behave as they once did. If they fail to do so, Christ threatens to "come" to them (not in the Parousia but in an act of temporal judgment; cf. 2:16) and blot their community out of existence. These remarks suggest that second-generation Christians may have developed a comfortable accommodation with the pagan world that John, an intolerant separatist, opposed.

One part of the two-part conclusion of each of the proclamations is the formula "He who has ears, let him hear / what the Spirit says to the churches" (v. 7a). In OT prophetic oracles, the recipients are frequently enjoined to "Hear the word of Yahweh!" (1 Kings 22:19; Amos 7:16; Jer. 42:15). The first part of this saying is found in various formulations seven times in the sayings of Jesus in the synoptic Gospels (e.g., Mark 4:9, 23). The formula was closely associated with the sayings of Jesus and thus an appropriate concluding refrain for prophetic messages from the heavenly Christ.

The reward for conquering (a military metaphor) mentioned in the second part of the conclusion (Rev. 2:7b) is the privilege of eating the fruit of the tree of life in the paradise of God (22:1, 19), a metaphor for eternal life (Gen. 3:22–24). The tree or plant of life, first mentioned in the OT in Gen. 2:9 (paired with the fatal tree of the knowledge of good and evil), was a familiar theme throughout the ancient Near East, particularly in early Judaism (*T. Levi* 18:10–11; 2 Esd. 8:52; 4 *Bar.* 9:16).

2:8–11, To Smyrna. Smyrna, a city with excellent harbor facilities, prosperous in both Hellenistic and Roman times, lay forty miles north of Ephesus, its major rival. Smyrna became a

center for the imperial cult when, in competition with eleven other cities, it was granted the right to have a temple to Tiberius, Livia, and the senate in A.D. 29 (Tacitus *Annals* 4.55–56). A temple to *dea Roma* (Lat., "the goddess Rome") was dedicated before the mid-second century B.C. This community, which apparently had few if any wealthy members (Rev. 2:9), had experienced severe persecution as the apparent result of Jewish "slander." They are not *real* Jews, claims John, but a synagogue of Satan. This implies that Christians are the *true* Israel (a widespread Christian view; cf. Gal. 6:16; Phil. 3:3). The term "slander" here in all likelihood refers to the Jewish role in denouncing Christians to Roman authorities. Since Jews had a special status exempting them from certain cultic obligations, Jewish Christians could take advantage of those benefits by claiming to be Jews. In Bithynia, ca. A.D. 110, there is evidence that pagan *delatores* (Lat., "accusers" in criminal proceedings) denounced Christians to the authorities (Pliny *Letters* 10.96). The possibility that some Christians will soon be imprisoned (Rev. 2:10) indicates the seriousness of the situation. Roman prisons were used for just three reasons: to compel obedience to a magistrate's order, to confine the accused until trial, or for detainment until execution. Antipas has already been publicly executed (2:13), and he was probably not alone (6:9–11; 11:7; 20:4). The reward for faithfulness is the "crown (or more accurately, 'wreath') of life," a metaphor for eternal life (2:10b). In the Greek world, wreaths were used as prizes in athletic contests and were buried with the dead symbolizing their victories in life. The "wreath of life" is not drawn from military imagery, however, for neither the Greeks nor the Romans ever gave posthumous military decorations. In v. 11 the victorious Christian is promised exemption from the second death (see commentary below on 20:14).

2:12–17, To Pergamum. Pergamum, "the most renowned of Asia" (Pliny *Natural History* 5.126), was located sixty-eight miles north of Smyrna and had an estimated population of 120,000. Pergamum was the site of an enormous altar of Zeus now displayed in reconstructed form in the Pergamon Museum in East Berlin. As the site of the first and most important temple to the deified Augustus, Pergamum was an important center for the imperial cult. "Satan's throne" (v. 13) may refer to this center of imperial worship or, less likely, to the great altar of Zeus or possibly to the seat of judgment used by Roman magistrates. The Pergamene Christians are commended for their steadfastness in the face of persecution. Antipas, mentioned only here in early Christian literature, was very likely executed for failing to sacrifice to the gods on behalf of deified emperors. He is called "my faithful witness" (NIV); the Greek term for "witness" is *martys,* a term that shortly came to include the idea of dying for the faith. Nevertheless the church is censured for tolerating some who hold the teaching of Balaam involving eating food sacrificed to idols and practicing immorality. In early Judaism and early Christianity, heresy was not so much "heterodoxy" (deviant opinions or doctrines) as "heteropraxy" (deviate practices); idolatry and immorality were thought closely associated. Balaam was a non-Israelite diviner whose contact with Israel is described in Numbers 22-24 and who was regarded as instrumental in leading Israel into idolatrous and immoral practices (Num. 25:1-5; 31:16). In later Jewish tradition, Balaam is regarded as a paradigmatic false prophet (Philo *Life of Moses* 1.263-304; Josephus *Antiquities of the Jews* 4.126-30). The practice of eating food sacrificed to idols was problematic for both Jews and Christians. Ancients rarely ate meat, and when they did it was usually part of public or private religious celebrations in which the edible parts of sacrificial animals were eaten. Such meat was taboo for Jews (4 *Macc.* 5:2-3; *m.* '*Abod. Zar.* 2.3), a prohibition often enforced by Jewish Christians (Acts 15:29), though Paul was equivocal on the subject (1 Cor. 8:4-13; 10:14-11:1). The Nicolaitans (Rev. 2:15), often thought to be Gnostics, are accused of teaching sexual immorality and eating meat offered to idols, both libertine practices. However, Gnostic texts encourage neither libertine sexual promiscuity nor the eating of sacrificial meat. The Pergamene Christians are urged to repent, otherwise Christ threatens to come to them in judgment (cf. 2:5). Those who conquer are promised hidden manna and a white stone with a new name inscribed on it. "Manna" (a Heb. term meaning "what is it?") was the name for miraculous "bread" supplied to the Israelites by God (Exod. 16:1-36; →Manna). Jews expected God to repeat that miracle in the last days (John 6:31-34; 2 *Apoc. Bar.* 29:8). Manna is therefore another metaphor for eternal life (as in John 6:49-51). The significance of the white stone is disputed.

2:18-29, To Thyatira. Thyatira was located forty-five miles southeast of Pergamum. The church is commended for its faith, service, and patient endurance like the Ephesian church (2:2-3). Unlike the latter, the Thyatirans' present spiritual condition is judged healthier than formerly (v. 19). Like the Pergamenes, they are denounced for tolerating heretics (vv. 20-23). An unnamed woman prophet nicknamed "Jezebel" teaches Christians to indulge in sexual promiscuity and eat sacrificial meat (see commentary above on 2:12-17). The similarity between "Jezebel's" program and that of the Nicolaitans (cf. 2:14-15) suggests

that she is one of their local leaders. The statement "I gave her time to repent" (v. 21) probably refers to an earlier prophetic judgment speech delivered by John or a member of his prophetic circle. The threat that "Jezebel" and her circle will become sick and suffer tribulation and even death (vv. 22-23) is perhaps the kind of judgment implied in earlier references to the "coming" of Christ (2:5, 16). Physical illness among Christians could be construed as divine punishment for sin (1 Cor. 11:29-30). Jezebel is the name of the infamous foreign wife of king Ahab of Israel, whose checkered career is recounted in 1 Kings 16:28-19:3 and 2 Kings 9:22, 30-37. With a corps of 850 prophets of Baal (1 Kings 18:19), she opposed true prophets of Yahweh (1 Kings 18:4) and introduced "harlotries and sorceries" to Israel. The Thyatiran "Jezebel" possibly used her prophetic gift for legitimating the deviant practices of which she is accused in v. 20. Philo warned his readers against would-be prophets who might lead people to adopt pagan practices (*Special Laws* 1.315-16). Verses 24-25 specifically address those in the church who are not followers of "Jezebel" and who have not learned "the deep things of Satan," a possible reference to the "profound" teachings of "Jezebel." John may be parodying a motto of "Jezebel" by substituting the word "Satan" for "God" (cf. 1 Cor. 2:10). In Rev. 2:26-27, the one who conquers is promised a delegated share of Christ's sovereign rule (cf. 5:10; 20:4; 22:5; cf. 2 Tim. 2:12).

3:1-6, To Sardis. Sardis, forty miles southeast of Thyatira and forty-five miles east of Smyrna, was one of the more illustrious cities of ancient Anatolia and a major rival of Ephesus and Smyrna, boasting a temple to Augustus. The earthquake of A.D. 17 destroyed much of the Hellenistic city (Tacitus *Annals* 2.47), which was rebuilt with aid from the emperors Tiberius and Claudius. During the Imperial period, her population ranged between 60,000 and 100,000 inhabitants. Recent archaeological exploration has uncovered one of the largest ancient synagogues yet known, accommodating about 1,000 people, reflecting the presence of a large, wealthy, and influential Jewish community.

Christ is described as he "who has the seven spirits of God and the seven stars" (3:1, alluding to 1:16-20). The spirits represent angels (cf. 4:5; 5:6; 8:2), a metaphor derived from Zechariah 4. This church receives primarily censure; only a minority of Christians "have not soiled their garments" (Rev. 3:4). Christ knows their true spiritual condition. Though they appear hale and hearty to others, they are actually on the point of spiritual death (v. 1b). They are encouraged to wake up and change their ways before it is too late (v. 2). In the NT, watchfulness is an indispensable characteristic of the people of God in view of the imminence of the end (Mark 13:33-37; Matt. 25:13). If they fail to awake and repent, Christ threatens to come unexpectedly, like a thief (Rev. 3:3), an allusion to a saying of Jesus also preserved in Matt. 24:42-44 and Luke 12:39-40 (cf. Rev. 16:15). The saying has three distinctive motifs: the exhortation to watch, the metaphor of the thief (first occurring in 1 Thess. 5:2 and later in 2 Pet. 3:10) and the unexpected time of arrival. Only in Rev. 3:5 and 16:15 is the thief identified with Christ. Those who conquer will be rewarded with white garments (3:4b-5a), probably not so much an allusion to the flourishing local garment industry as a metaphor of ritual, moral, and spiritual purity. White garments were worn on religious festivals and when performing cultic acts such as sacrifice and by victorious Roman generals when celebrating triumphs in Rome. Further, their names will not be blotted out of the book of life, another metaphor for eternal life. Athens and other Greek cities had the custom of erasing from the rolls the names of citizens executed by the state (Dio Chrystom *Discourse* 31.84-85; Xenophon *Hellenica* 2.3.51). Having one's name written in the book of life thus suggests heavenly citizenship (Heb. 12:23; cf. Phil. 3:20; 1 Pet. 1:17). The idea of a "book of life" (frequently mentioned; cf. Rev. 13:8; 17:8; 20:15; 21:27) from which one's name could be erased is common in Judaism (Exod. 32:32-33; *Jub.* 30:20-22; *Jos. Asen.* 15:4[3]). Christ's promise to confess the victorious Christian's name before the Father and his angels alludes to a saying of Jesus found in the Q tradition (Matt. 10:32 = Luke 12:8) and in Mark 8:38 = Luke 9:26, though John was probably dependent on oral rather than written tradition.

3:7-13, To Philadelphia. Philadelphia, located thirty miles southeast of Sardis, suffered extensive damage in the earthquake of A.D. 17 (Tacitus *Annals* 2.47.3-4), though lesser quakes occurred frequently (Strabo 12.8.18). Heavily dependent on viticulture because of a rich volcanic soil (Strabo 13.4.11), the city was radically affected by Domitian's edict of A.D. 92 ordering half the provincial vineyards cut down and replanted. Alluding to Isa. 22:22, Christ is designated as he "who has the key of David, who opens and no one shall shut, who shuts and no one opens" (Rev. 3:7), probably referring to his power to admit or bar people from the heavenly kingdom (cf. Matt. 16:19). The exalted Christ has set an "open door" before the Philadelphian Christians (Rev. 3:8), a metaphor referring to their "reserved seats" in the eschatological kingdom. The Christian community appears to be relatively small and poor, but it has nevertheless remained steadfast in its faith (v. 8). There was apparently a Jewish synagogue there (v. 9), and

Philadelphian Christians had probably suffered from accusations by Jews before Roman authorities as in Smyrna (v. 9). Because they have kept the testimony of Jesus by patiently enduring persecution, they will be kept from "the hour of trial which is coming on the whole world" (v. 10). This refers to the coming eschatological period of tribulation (9:3-21) from which they will be protected (7:1-8; cf. the final petition in the Lord's Prayer, Matt. 6:13 = Luke 11:4). "Those who dwell upon the earth" (Rev. 3:10) are unbelievers (cf. 6:10; 8:13; 11:10; 13:8, 14; 17:8) who repeatedly refuse to repent in spite of the eschatological plagues unleashed by God (e.g., 9:20-21; 16:9, 11). Christ's promise to come soon (3:11) should be understood not as a coming in judgment (as in 2:5, 16; 3:3), but as the Parousia, in which he comes to deliver his people (14:14-16; 22:7, 20). Those who conquer will be made pillars in the temple of God (3:12), a feature suggesting that the new Jerusalem is a metaphor for the Christian community. Revelation is a book filled with graffiti; conquering Christians will have inscribed on them the names of God, the city of God, and the new Jerusalem (v. 12), varied metaphors indicating eschatological salvation. Reference to the new Jerusalem descending from heaven anticipates the more detailed description in 21:2-22:5.

3:14-22, To Laodicea. Laodicea, forty miles southeast of Philadelphia, was destroyed in an earthquake in A.D. 60 (*Sib. Or.* 5.290-91) and was subsequently rebuilt (*Sib. Or.* 4.107-8). An imperial temple was constructed after the quake. It was the most important city in the Lycus valley where two other cities also contained Christian communities, Hierapolis and Colossae (Col. 4:13). The region had a large Jewish population (Cicero *Pro Flacco* 28.68; Josephus *Antiquities of the Jews* 12.147-53). The community is condemned for being neither cold nor hot, but lukewarm (Rev. 3:15-16). This metaphor for ineffectiveness has been linked to the region's water supply. The "hot" springs of Hierapolis were famous for their medicinal properties, and the "cold" waters of Colossae were prized for their purity. The tepid waters of Laodicea, however, were both abundant and bad. Though the church thinks itself rich and lacking nothing, it is actually "wretched, pitiable, poor, blind and naked" (v. 17). To remedy this deplorable spiritual state, they require "gold" refined by the fires of testing and patient endurance, "white garments" of purity, and "eye salve" to restore their sight (v. 18). Laodicea was in fact the site of a medical school and a local pharmaceutical industry with a secret recipe for an effective eye salve. The famous metaphor of Christ standing at the door and knocking (v. 20) has been explained as an allusion to Song of Sg. 5:2 or a modified saying of

Jesus (Luke 12:35–38; cf. Mark 13:33–37). Greco-Roman revelatory magic had a special procedure for enlisting the services of a *paredros daimōn*, "assisting divinity" (Gk.), that involved preparing a meal and sharing it with the god, a procedure parodied here where the risen Jesus alone controls the situation, not the practitioner. The victorious Christians will be able to sit with Christ upon his throne, just as he sat upon the throne of his Father (Rev. 3:21), another reference to sharing Christ's reign (cf. 2:26–27).

4:1–22:9

From Tribulation to Glory

A new stage of John's revelatory vision begins in 4:1, where the scene shifts from earth to heaven. Most of the following (4:1–19:10) focuses on the terrible eschatological tribulations that will occur before the Parousia.

4:1–7:17
The Six Seals

Even though the first major section of the main part of Revelation includes primarily 4:1–8:1, it cannot be strictly limited to this passage since the roll with seven seals contains the entire course of eschatological events through 22:9.

4:1–5:14, The Heavenly Throne Room. A heavenly throne room scene introduces each of the three heptads of seals, trumpets, and bowls (4:1–5:14; 8:1–5; 15:1–8), anchoring each series of events in the sovereignty of God, who controls history. This first throne room scene is the longest and most detailed. The author must orient readers to the inhabitants and activities that will be repeated or amplified in later scenes. John sees an open door in heaven and the voice that he heard behind him (1:10), i.e., the exalted Christ, invites him to "come up hither" where future events will be revealed to him. Just as ancient cosmology conceptualized a door or gates connecting earth with the underworld (cf. 1:18), the notion of a door separating earth from heaven was also common. The related motifs of the heavenly door, the invitation to enter, and a vision of the throne room of God constitute a commonplace in ancient revelatory literature (cf. 1 Enoch 14:8–25; T. Levi. 2:6; 5:1). At once, John is "in the Spirit" (Rev. 2:2; cf. 1:9), a trance-like state necessary for a visionary ascent to heaven. Immediately he finds himself present as an observer in the heavenly throne room. Throughout the ancient world, high gods (the Greek Zeus, the Roman Jupiter, the Babylonian Marduk, and the Israelite Yahweh) were conceptualized as great kings dwelling in magnificent heavenly palaces with innumerable

supernatural courtiers. Occasionally OT prophets are depicted as making visionary ascents to the heavenly court where, by eavesdropping on the proceedings, they learn what will later transpire on earth (1 Kings 22:17–23; Isa. 6:1–7; Zech. 3:1–5; cf. Jer. 23:18). John's description, dependent on Ezek. 1:4–28, generally tallies with traditional Jewish conceptions of heaven. John first sees the magnificent throne of the God but avoids attempting to describe God himself (Rev. 4:3; cf. 22:4). The cosmic symbolism of the circle is reflected in the encircling rainbow "round" the throne (4:3), the four living creatures encircling the throne (v. 6), the circle of twenty-four elders (v. 4), all encircled by an innumerable multitude of angels (5:11). God, at the center of all, is the ultimate cosmic reality. The thunder and lightning emanating from the throne (v. 5) suggests the Sinai theophany (Exod. 19:16–18; 20:18–20; cf. Isa. 29:6). The four living creatures described in Rev. 4:6–8 (cf. Ezek. 1:5–25; Isa. 6:2), symbolize the omniscience of God. After Irenaeus (ca. A.D. 180) the four creatures came to symbolize the four Gospels (Mark is the lion, Luke the ox, Matthew the man, and John the eagle). The ensemble worn by twenty-four elders, white garments and gold wreaths, was customary for embassies and suppliants to Hellenistic kings and Roman emperors. The number twenty-four, found only here in Revelation, symbolizes the complete people of God (twelve Israelite tribes plus twelve apostles). The seven torches of fire (Rev. 4:5) are based on the menorah of the tabernacle and Temple (cf. Zech. 4:1–10), and the "sea of glass" (Rev. 4:6) may represent the transcendence of God, his separation from the created order.

Following the description of the serene magnificence of the throne room of God and the worship perpetually offered to God by heavenly beings (4:1–11), John's attention is drawn to a scroll with seven seals in the right hand of God (5:1), who is remarkably passive throughout the scene. A brief drama then unfolds in which someone is sought who is worthy to break the seals and open the scroll (vv. 2–4). One function of the heavenly council motif is the commissioning of an emissary (cf. Isa. 6:8: "Who can we send?"; 1 Kings 22:20: "Who will entice Ahab?"; cf. Rev. 5:2: "Who is worthy to open the scroll?"). John weeps when no one is found, dramatizing Israel's past messianic expectation. One of the elders tells John that the Lion of the tribe of Judah (Gen. 49:9), the Root of David (Isa. 11:1, 10), i.e., the Messiah, has conquered and is therefore qualified (Rev. 5:5). Yet John sees not a lion but a lamb looking as though it had been slain (v. 6). The striking contrast between the two images suggests the contrast between the type of warrior messiah expected by first-century Judaism and Jesus' role as a suffering servant (cf. Matt.

11:2–6 = Luke 7:18–23). The term "lamb" (occurring twenty-nine times in Revelation) alludes to the sacrificial death of Jesus under the image of the Passover lamb (cf. 1 Cor. 5:7; 1 Pet. 1:19; John 1:29). What is the significance of the scroll and why is the Lamb alone able to open it? The scroll represents the final stage in God's predetermined redemptive purpose for the world, to be realized between the exaltation of Christ, following his death and resurrection, and the final inauguration of the eternal reign of God; that is, it symbolizes the entire eschatological program narrated in Revelation. The antiphonal hymns of Rev. 5:9–14 celebrate the worthiness of the Lamb whose death has provided salvation for people of every nation. Though the Lamb has already been exalted to the throne of God and shares his rule, God's plan remains incomplete unless he (the only qualified emissary of God) receives full power and authority (symbolized by the scroll) to achieve the final eschatological victory.

Hymns in Revelation

An important feature of the heavenly throne room ceremonial in Revelation is the presence of sixteen hymns or hymnlike compositions at various points in the narrative. These hymns are arranged as two single hymns (15:3–4; 12:10–12), and seven antiphonal units (4:8–11; 5:9–14; 7:9–12; 11:15–18; 16:5–7; 19:1–4, 5–8). John has not quoted or modified traditional Christian hymns but has composed them himself, making use of traditional Jewish and Christian liturgical elements (e.g., hallelujah, amen, the sanctus [4:8], doxologies [5:13; 7:10, 12; 19:1], and acclamations [4:11; 5:9, 12]). The OT occasionally mentions the heavenly liturgy sung to God by angelic beings (Isa. 6:3; Ps. 103:20), a conception elaborated in Jewish apocalypses and testaments (2 Enoch 18:8–9; T. Job 51:1–4; 52:12). Yet apart from the sanctus, such songs are rarely reproduced (cf. Apoc. Abr. 17:6–21). The Romans (borrowing Hellenistic kingship traditions) developed an elaborate imperial court ceremonial that included the singing of hymns and the shouting of acclamations to the emperor (Dio Cassius 59.24.5; Suetonius Nero 20.3). Alone among apocalyptic writers, John has combined Jewish traditions of the heavenly liturgy with aspects of Roman court ceremonial and used hymns as a narrative device to interpret the significance of eschatological events.

6:1–17, The First Six Seals. The breaking of each of the first six seals by the Lamb unleashes a series of tribulations that preview the trumpet and bowl judgments. Most of the seals represent typical Jewish and early Christian conceptions of the final tribulations (cf. Mark 13:3–8, 24–27, and parallels). The opening of the first four seals sends out four horsemen (adapted from Zech. 1:8–11; 6:1–8), each inflicting a particular kind of judgment on humanity: irresistible conquest, war and bloodshed, famine, disease and death. With the opening of the fifth seal, John sees the souls of martyrs beneath the altar crying out for justice; they are told to wait until their number is completed (Rev. 6:9–11; cf. 7:1–8). The opening of the sixth seal is followed by a series of cosmic disturbances: a great earthquake (a phenomenon all too familiar to the province of Asia), a solar eclipse, the moon turns red, stars fall to earth (cf. Mark 13:24–25; Matt. 24:29), the sky vanishes, and every mountain and island is moved. These terrible catastrophes move unbelievers of every social station to fear the judgment of God and the Lamb, for, they say (Rev. 6:17), who can stand before the day of their wrath? While the last judgment appears to be inaugurated by the opening of the sixth seal, the eschatological program of Revelation still requires the trumpet and bowl plagues.

7:1–17, First Digression: The Sealing of the 144,000. The question of 6:17 provides an introduction to 7:1–17, a digression dealing with how the "servants of God" (7:3) will fare during the coming catastrophes. A twofold answer is provided in 7:1–17. First (vv. 1–8), the effects of the plagues on Christians are delayed while 144,000 servants of God (prospective martyrs) are sealed on their foreheads, 12,000 from each of the twelve tribes of Israel. This throng of 144,000 constitutes the martyr-witness cadre of the church (cf. 14:1; 15:1–2). Their sealing does not protect them against death at the hands of Roman authorities but against the plagues aimed at unbelievers. The motif of immunity derives from the tradition that the Exodus plagues harmed only Egyptians, not Israelites (Exod. 8:22; 9:4–7, 26; 10:23; Philo Life of Moses 1.143–46). Second (Rev. 7:9–17), John receives a visionary preview of an innumerable host (Gen. 15:5) representing all of the people of God (Rev. 7:9). Unlike the 144,000 martyrs, other Christians will perish in the "great tribulation" (v. 14) but will enjoy an eternal state of blessedness with the dawn of the everlasting kingdom (cf. 21:1–5).

8:1–11:14

The Seventh Seal and the Six Trumpets

8:1, The Seventh Seal. The opening of the seventh seal, unlike the first six, results in an anticlimactic period of silence in heaven, perhaps representing the primeval silence of the seventh day of creation. The sealed scroll has now been completely opened, and the remainder of Revelation follows the script it contains, beginning with the trumpet judgments.

8:2–5, The Altar of Incense. As in the other heptads, the opening scene is in heaven. An angel stands at the heavenly altar before the throne of God where the prayers of Christians (no doubt for deliverance and justice) are like smoke mingled with incense rising up before God. The censer filled with fire from the altar that the angel casts down to the earth symbolizes the punishment of humanity that will follow the blowing of each of the trumpets.

8:6–9:21, The First Six Trumpets. The narrative of the seven trumpet judgments, like that of the seven bowls of God's wrath (15:1–16:21), is an eschatological application of the ten plagues of Egypt (Exod. 7–12). Though the Egyptian plagues were a recurring theme in early Jewish literature, they are rarely interpreted *eschatologically* (an exception: *Apoc. Abr.* 30). The preliminary character of the judgments unleashed by the seven trumpets is obvious since only *one-third* of the targeted persons or things are affected. Two-thirds of the natural and human world thus survive for the final round of bowl tribulations. This pattern is unique in Jewish apocalypses and is the author's way of accommodating a trebling of the final punishments. The tribulations unleashed by the seven trumpets are as follows: (1) hail, fire, and blood fall; a third of the earth is burned (Rev. 8:7; cf. the seventh plague of Exod. 9:22–25 and the fourth and seventh bowls in Rev. 16:8–9, 19–21); (2) a great mountain pollutes the sea with blood, destroying a third of sea creatures and ships (Rev. 8:8–9; cf. first plague of Exod. 7:20–21 and the second bowl in Rev. 16:3); (3) a star named Wormwood (named for its poisonous effect, since no actual star had that name) falls on a third of the rivers and springs, poisoning them (Rev. 8:10–11; no model in Exod. 7–12 or counterpart in Rev. 15–16); (4) one-third of the sun, moon, and stars become darkened (Rev. 8:12; similar to the ninth plague of Exod. 10:21 and the fifth bowl-plague in Rev. 16:10); the final three trumpets form a group of three woes announced in 8:13 (cf. 9:12; 11:14); (5) the fifth trumpet causes a star to fall from heaven to earth (Satan, cf. 12:9), which releases a plague of locusts from the bottomless pit who harm only those lacking God's seal (9:1–12; cf. the eighth plague of locusts in Exod. 10:4–20; no counterpart in Rev. 15–16); (6) the four angels bound at the Euphrates River, symbolizing four nations, kill one-third of humankind (Rev. 9:13–19; similar to punishment of the sixth bowl in Rev. 16:12). John concludes by observing that the

plagues did not cause unbelievers to repent of their idolatry and immorality (9:20–21). Does this mean that these punishments were intended to serve as a deterrent? Since John's narratives of the trumpet and bowl plagues do not mention repentance as their purpose, references to the failure of people to repent (9:20–21; 16:9, 11) may indicate that John has used Jewish sources that originally emphasized repentance. Of course, repentance was not the purpose of the original Exodus plagues even though Pharaoh's failure to repent is mentioned (Exod. 7:3–4a; 10:1). The failure to repent is a motif derived from Exod. 7–12.

10:1–11, Second Digression: The Angel and the Little Scroll. Following the sixth trumpet (9:13–21), John inserts two digressions (10:1–11; 11:1–14) that expand on the effects of the sixth trumpet (11:14 mentions that the second woe = sixth trumpet has passed) and dramatically delay the blowing of the seventh in 11:15–18 (just as 7:1–17 delays opening the seventh seal in 8:1). John sees a majestic angel whom he describes with imagery like that used to describe visions of God. The angel holds a small scroll, reminding us of the sealed scroll in chap. 5. The angel swears a powerful oath by the creator of heaven, earth, and the sea (and what is in them), which he enacts by touching all three elements (10:5–6). The substance of this oath is the prophecy that there will be no further delay but that when the seventh trumpet sounds the mystery of God predicted by the prophets will be fulfilled (v. 7). The term "mystery" is a technical apocalyptic term meaning divinely concealed information about the end of the age now disclosed to the inspired insight of a prophet or apocalyptist (1 Enoch 103:2; 1QpHab 7:5; 1 Cor. 15:51; Rom. 11:25–26). When John takes the scroll from the angel (Rev. 10:8), he is told to eat it (v. 9). This prophetic symbolic action is modeled after Ezek. 2:8–3:3, where the episode dramatizes Ezekiel's prophetic call (Ezek. 1:1–3:27). The scroll symbolizes the prophetic word within Ezekiel (cf. Ezek. 3:1) and in Rev. 10:10–11. As soon as John has eaten the scroll he is told (v. 11), "You must *again* prophesy about many peoples and nations and tongues and kings." This renewed commission reveals John's prophetic consciousness, a commission primarily applicable to the impending judgments of the seven bowls that John will describe.

11:1–14, Third Digression: The Two Prophetic Witnesses. This section narrates the mission of two mysterious eschatological prophetic witnesses. Their ministry, logically following John's renewed prophetic commission in 10:8–11, dramatizes testimony borne by John and his prophetic colleagues. John has probably

1311

fused two earlier Jewish oracles (11:1–2 and vv. 3–13), connected only by the mention of the holy city (vv. 2, 8). In vv. 1–2, John is given a measuring stick and told to measure the temple of God, the altar, and the worshipers (a symbol of protection). Is John referring to a literal or a symbolic temple? Since the Herodian Temple was destroyed when Jerusalem fell in A.D. 70, vv. 1–2 may preserve an oracle uttered by a Jewish prophet in besieged Jerusalem late in the war, hoping that the Temple would be preserved (Josephus Jewish War 6.286). The temple and altar probably represent the people of God, while the outer court is the unbelieving world. This entire section is not a vision that John sees but a meditation on the theme of the two witnesses. The pagan domination over the holy city will be for forty-two months (Rev. 11:2); the prophetic witness will be active for 1,260 days (v. 3). Both figures are derived from the "time, two times, and half a time" (i.e., three and one-half years) of Dan. 7:25, symbolizing a limited period of time.

The second oracle (Rev. 11:3–13) focuses on the ministry of the two prophetic witnesses abruptly concluded by the appearance of an eschatological adversary. The passage begins with an allusion to the two olive trees and the two (instead of seven) lamps of Zech. 4:1–14; the olive trees represent Zerubbabel the claimant to the Davidic throne and Joshua the high priest (Zechariah based his hopes for the restoration of Judah on them). The description of the witnesses draws from traditional Jewish conceptions of Enoch, Elijah, and Moses, all taken up alive into heaven like the two witnesses (v. 12). They have the power to perform punitive miracles; they can destroy their opponents with fire and cause drought (like Elijah; cf. 2 Kings 1:9–16; 1 Kings 17:1) and smite the earth with plagues (like Moses; cf. Exod. 7–10). Strangely, the *content* of their message is not mentioned. They are often interpreted as Elijah and Moses (whose eschatological return was expected; cf. Mal. 4:5–6; Deut. 18:15–18, though not in tandem) or Enoch and Elijah (*Apoc. Elijah* 4:7–19). Yet they do not embody two specific eschatological figures (since they are identical in every respect) but represent the prophetic witness of the Christian church. The number *two* emphasizes the reliability of their testimony (Num. 35:30; Deut. 19:15; John 8:13–18). When the brief period of their immunity is over, they will be killed by the beast from the bottomless pit (Rev. 11:7; i.e., the beast of 13:1 and 17:8). The scene of their prophetic activity and the place where their unburied bodies lie is in "the great city," certainly Jerusalem, prophetically called "Sodom" and "Egypt," where Christ was crucified, yet actually representative of the world that has rejected the gospel and slain its messengers. Suffering and martyrdom were

closely associated with the prophetic role in early Judaism (Neh. 9:26; 1 Thess. 2:15; Matt. 23:34–36 = Luke 11:49–51; Acts 7:52).

11:15–16:16
The Seventh Trumpet and the Six Bowls

Intercalated between the blowing of the seventh trumpet (11:15–18) and the narrative of the six bowls (15:1–16:16) are three separate visionary "digressions" that together form a continuous eschatological narrative (12:1–14:20).

11:15–18, The Seventh Trumpet. The seventh trumpet appears to inaugurate the eschaton, for an unidentified heavenly voice announces: "the kingdom of the world has become the kingdom of our Lord and of his Christ" (v. 15). Yet, as in the case of the sixth seal (6:12–17), this is another preliminary anticipation.

11:19–12:17, Fourth Digression: Satan and the Messiah. In 11:19, the heavenly temple is opened to the accompaniment of atmospheric and seismic phenomena associated with an epiphany (cf. 8:5, which introduces the series of seven trumpets). John has used both Hellenistic and Jewish traditions in composing this chapter. The myth of the eschatological battle between Michael and the dragon (12:7–9) is inserted into the myth of the woman who bears a child and is attacked by a great red dragon (12:1–6, 13–17). The myth of the woman, the child, and the dragon (12:1–6, 13–17) can be read in several ways. In a Christian context, it is natural to understand the woman of vv. 1–6 as Mary and the child as Jesus. Yet in vv. 13–17, where "the rest of her offspring" (v. 17) are mentioned, she seems to personify Zion or the church, while her persecuted offspring represent Christians. The child is clearly the Messiah, described as "one who is to rule all the nations with a rod of iron" (v. 5, alluding to Ps. 2:9). The fact that the child was "caught up" to God and to his throne (Rev. 12:5) suggests the ascension of the resurrected Jesus. This ascension motif and the yet unrealized messianic rule of the child presuppose the Christian view of *two* comings of Christ, whereas Judaism expected just *one* coming of the Messiah. John has rewritten a Hellenistic version of the combat myth found throughout the ancient world. The particular myth John used is the Greek Leto-Apollo-Python myth. The goddess Leto, pregnant with Apollo, was pursued by the dragon Python. Leto fled to a distant island and eventually gave birth to Apollo who, when just four days old, killed Python. To his adaptation of the myth of Leto-Apollo-Python, John has prefixed a description of the two myth-images that served as a catalyst for his juxtaposition of two mythic traditions. A woman appears in heaven (v. 1) followed by the appearance of a great red dragon, her antagonist (v. 3). The woman is presented in astral imagery (clothed with the sun, the moon under her feet, and wearing the crown of the Zodiac) as the queen of the cosmos (v. 1). Artemis, Hekate, and Isis were similarly described. The dragon (alias the devil, the ancient serpent, and Satan, v. 12), the primary antagonist of God, first appears at this point in John's eschatological drama (v. 3). The ascension of the child in v. 5 is described using the rapture motif commonly found in Greek myths involving deification through ascension to heaven.

The myth of the heavenly battle in which Michael defeats and expels Satan and his angels (vv. 7–9; a variant version is reflected in Rev. 9:1; cf. 1 Enoch 90:21) is always a primordial rather than an eschatological event in Jewish thought (2 Enoch 29:4–5; Adam and Eve 12–16; cf. Isa. 14:12–15). Yet Satan's eschatological fall to earth is closely paralleled in the only vision of Jesus preserved in Gospel tradition: "And he said to them [seventy disciples], 'I saw Satan fall like lightning from heaven' " (Luke 10:18, RSV). The fact that Michael is the one who defeats Satan, not the Messiah as in Christian tradition, underscores the Jewish character of Rev. 12:7–9. John's elaborate identification of the dragon in v. 9 further suggests his modification of a Jewish source.

13:1–18, Fifth Digression: The Two Beasts. Here John introduces the dragon's two earthly allies, the beast from the sea and the beast from the land who, with the dragon, constitute an unholy eschatological trinity. Many versions of a primal myth of combat between the great gods and a sea dragon or similar monsters circulated in the ancient world. The Greeks told stories about the conflict between Zeus and Typhon, Apollo and Python, the Babylonians about Marduk and Tiamat, and the Israelites about Yahweh and Rahab (Isa. 51:9–10; Ps. 89:10) or Leviathan (Ps. 74:13–14). According to Jewish primeval mythology, God created two sea monsters on the fifth day of creation, Leviathan and Behemoth (Gen. 1:21; cf. 2 Esd. 6:49–52). The female monster Leviathan was confined to the sea (Apoc. Abr. 21:4) while her male counterpart, Behemoth, was confined to the desert (1 Enoch 60:7–9). In Rev. 13, John exhibits his familiarity with the expectation that after the Messiah is revealed, Behemoth will appear from his place and Leviathan will ascend from the sea (2 Apoc. Bar. 29:3). John sees the first beast (the female Leviathan) rise from the "sea" (representing the abyss or bottomless pit [cf. Rev. 11:7] and symbolizing evil and chaos). Blasphemous names are written on its seven heads, and dia-

dems adorn each of its ten horns (Rev. 13:1). The appearance of the beast (v. 2) combines several features of the four separate beasts from the sea described in Dan. 7:2–7. The great harlot sits on this beast (Rev. 17:3), whose seven heads stand both for Rome's seven hills and for its seven kings (17:9–10). Horns symbolize power, and the ten diadems suggest universal sovereignty that parodies the rule of Christ (19:12). This beast personifies human opposition to God as represented by the Roman Empire. In Judaism, the sea monster came to represent oppressive foreign nations (Dan. 7:1–8), and occasionally the chaos monsters Rahab or Leviathan represented Egypt (Ps. 74:14; 87:4; Isa. 30:7; Ezek. 29:3). Since this beast has the throne and power of the dragon (Rev. 13:2b), it functions as Satan's earthly representative and as a parody of Christ. The worship that is given to this beast (v. 4) was that connected with the imperial cult. The "blasphemous names" referred to in v. 1 may refer to the honorific titles (such as "lord" and "god") applied to living emperors. One of the beast's seven heads, though fatally wounded, is miraculously healed (v. 3), parodying the death and resurrection of Christ and a possible reference to the legend of Nero's return (Sib. Or. 3.63–74; 4.119–24; 5.33–34). Nero committed suicide on June 9, 68, but few saw his corpse or witnessed his burial. Though hated in Italy, he was popular in the eastern provinces. From A.D. 68 to 88, at least three Nero impersonators appeared. The fact that this beast warred against the saints and conquered them (Rev. 13:7) refers to those such as Antipas who had been executed for refusing to sacrifice in connection with the imperial cult (2:13; cf. 6:9–11; 20:4).

The second beast from the earth (the male Behemoth) had two horns like a lamb, and it spoke like a dragon, obviously a wolf in sheep's clothing (13:11). Later referred to as the "false prophet" (16:13; 19:20; 20:10), it acts as the agent and promoter of the first beast, orchestrating and enforcing its universal worship (13:12). The second beast performs deceptive miracles, persuading people to fashion a cult statue of the beast that has the power of speech (vv. 13–15). Christian eschatology anticipated eschatological "false Christs" and "false prophets" who would perform miracles (cf. Mark 13:22; Matt. 24:24; 2 Thess. 2:9). Religious fraud was common in the ancient world, though it is unknown in connection with the imperial cult. The second beast represents a local authority concerned with the worship of the first beast, probably the priesthood of the imperial cult, the most important cult in the province of Asia. The foundation of the provincial cult of Domitian at Ephesus late in the first century (involving the obligatory participation of the entire province of Asia) provided a climate in which enormous pressures were placed on Christians to be loyal citizens and participate in the imperial cult. Sacrifices and prayers were not ordinarily directed to the emperor but to the gods on his behalf, yet Christians generally refused to make any kind of sacrifices. Emperors were not officially regarded as gods until they were posthumously pronounced *divus* (Lat., "divine") by the Roman senate, though Gaius (A.D. 37–41) and Domitian (A.D. 81–96) are exceptions. In the eastern provinces, however, they were often accorded cults while living. The second beast compels everyone to be marked on the right hand and forehead with the name of the beast; unbelievers and lapsed Christians thus form an identifiable group in contrast to faithful Christians marked with God's seal (Rev. 7:2–8). The coded name of the first beast is 666, a number that is the total of the numerical value of the letters spelling "Nero Caesar" in Aramaic, John's native language.

14:1–20, Sixth Digression: Three Visions of Victory. John now reports a more comforting series of victory visions. First (vv. 1–5), he sees on Mount Zion the Lamb with the throng of 144,000 faithful martyrs who have the names of Christ and God written on their foreheads (cf. 7:4–8). This group of celibate males (v. 4) is the "first fruits" of the people of God who will share Christ's millennial reign (19:4–6). Their sexual purity represents separation from all forms of sin and idolatry; they are males because they are depicted as victorious soldiers. OT prerequisites for participation in holy wars included the preservation of ritual purity through sexual abstinence (Deut. 23:9–10). This holy war theology was understood eschatologically by the Essenes, who kept themselves in a state of continual ritual purity in readiness for the imminent eschatological conflict.

The second vision (Rev. 14:6–12) consists of three angelic announcements, the proclamation of the gospel to all humanity intended to elicit repentance (vv. 6–7), the announcement of "Babylon's" fall (v. 8, anticipating chap. 18), and a warning of the terrible consequences for those who worship the beast and its image and who bear the name of the beast (vv. 9–11).

The third vision (vv. 13–20), begins with two complementary prophetic sayings articulating the theme of vv. 14–20: Christians who die in the Lord are blessed (v. 13). John envisions the final judgment (vv. 14–20; later described in 19:11–16), based on Joel 3:13, as a twofold harvest, one of grain (Rev. 14:14–16), the other of grapes (vv. 17–20). Harvest was a frequent Jewish metaphor for the last judgment (Isa. 27:12; Joel 3:13; 2 Esd. 4:26–32). Christ, described as the "son of man" of Dan. 7:13–14 (cf. Rev. 1:13), reaps the earth with his sickle. Though the Parousia is not described with tradi-

tional Christian imagery (e.g., 1 Thess. 4:15–17), the grain harvest represents the gathering of Christians (Matt. 24:31), while the vintage harvest (Rev. 14:17–20) refers to the judgment of the ungodly (Isa. 63:1–6; cf. Rev. 19:15b).

15:1–16:16, The First Six Bowls. John introduces this third heptad by reporting another sign in heaven (cf. 12:1, 3): seven angels with the seven last plagues. The introductory throne room scene depicts those who had conquered the beast standing beside the sea of glass with harps and singing the song of Moses and the Lamb (vv. 2–3). The Pentateuch records two songs of Moses, a victory song following the Exodus (Exod. 15:1–18) and his swan song (Deut. 32:1–43). Though Rev. 15:3b–4 alludes to *both*, the theme of a new and final Exodus predominates. Seven angels emerge from the heavenly tabernacle (the heavenly model for the portable sanctuary used by Israel before the building of Solomon's Temple; cf. Exod. 25–27; Heb. 8:2–5) and receive seven bowls or cups filled with the wrath of God (Rev. 15:7), an OT judgment metaphor (Isa. 51:17–23). The plagues enumerated in Revelation 16 include (1) the plague of sores or boils (v. 2; the sixth plague in Exod. 9:9); (2) the sea turns to blood, killing all sea animals (Rev. 16:3); (3) the rivers and wells become blood (v. 4; both resemble the first plague in Exod. 7:20–21); (4) the sun scorches people (Rev. 16:8–9; partially resembling the heavenly fire of the seventh plague in Exod. 9:22–24); (5) the throne and kingdom of the beast are blanketed with darkness (Rev. 16:10; the ninth plague of Exod. 10:21); (6) the Euphrates dries up (Rev. 16:12; no counterpart in Exodus); (7) great earthquakes, the great cities collapse, the islands and mountains disappear, huge hailstones fall (vv. 18–21; similar to the hail of the seventh plague in Exod. 9:22).

16:17–19:10
The Seventh Bowl and the Punishment of Babylon

Babylon was a great and ancient Mesopotamian city of interest to Judaism chiefly because the short-lived Neo-Babylonian Empire (605–539 B.C.) captured Jerusalem and destroyed Solomon's Temple (586 B.C.). In the OT it became a symbol for the current superpower. In Revelation and other Jewish and Christian literature written after A.D. 70, "Babylon" became a cryptic name for Rome (*Sib. Or.* 5:143, 159; 1 Pet. 5:13; cf. Eusebius *Ecclesiastical History* 4.23.11). Like Babylon before, Rome had captured Jerusalem and destroyed the Herodian Temple in A.D. 70.

16:17–21, The Seventh Bowl. The pouring out of the seventh bowl represents the climax of the seals, trumpets, and bowls, the final plagues sent by God to afflict humanity (15:1). God himself proclaims "It is done!" (16:17). As part of this last plague "God remembered great Babylon" (v. 19), an editorial link by John to indicate that the seventh bowl includes the judgment of Babylon (17:1–19:10).

17:1–18, The Great Harlot. This visionary episode is unique in Revelation for, unlike the other vision sequences, it describes a static scene, or tableau. This vision of "Babylon" belongs to a Hellenistic literary genre called *ekphrasis*, i.e., a "detailed description" of a work of art. Though the works of art on which the description is based have perished (probably marble bas-reliefs), copies have survived on ancient coins. These coins, some minted during the reign of Vespasian, depict *dea Roma* (Lat., "the goddess Rome") seated on Rome's seven hills with the river god Tiber reclining at the right and the she-wolf with Romulus and Remus at the lower left. Some coin types reduce the Tiber to wavy lines below the seven hills. The goddess Dea Roma was particularly popular in Anatolia from the mid-second century B.C. on. John used this popular depiction of the glory of Rome as a means for vilifying Rome and contrasting her with the new Jerusalem.

John ties the new vision to the previous section (15:1–16:21) by having a bowl angel show him the judgment of the great harlot seated on many waters (17:1–2). Carried away by the Spirit, John sees a woman sitting on a scarlet beast full of blasphemous names with seven heads and ten horns (v. 3), the beast from the sea (13:1). This woman, decked out like a successful prostitute (Athens is said to dress as tentatiously like a prostitute in Plutarch *Pericles* 12.2), holds a golden cup filled with impurities (Rev. 17:4). On her forehead is written "a name of mystery" (RSV), "Babylon the Great, Mother of Harlots and of Earth's Abominations" (v. 5). What does this "mysterious" name mean? The tutelary deity of Rome had a secret name (Plutarch *Roman Questions* 61). Servius suggested that Rome's name was concealed to prevent the deity from being invoked to leave the city. The secret name of Rome was popularly thought to be "Amor" ("love"), the Latin name for Rome, "Roma," spelled backwards. Perhaps aware of this tradition, John depicts Rome as a prostitute, i.e., the antithesis of love. The angel explains that the beast "was, and is not, and is to come" (Rev. 17:8), suggesting both the Nero legend (13:3) and parodying the God who "is, was, and is to come" (1:4, 8; 4:8). The woman herself represents "the great city" dominating the world, i.e., Rome (17:18). Yet in v. 9, the angel interprets the seven heads as the seven mountains on which the woman sits, i.e., the traditional seven hills on which Rome was situated. The seven hills, however, are really

seven kings; five have fallen, one is, and the other has not yet come (v. 10). There has been endless speculation about the identity of these kings. If the seventh king is Nero (who when he returns will be the eighth, v. 11), who are the previous six? Nero was the sixth emperor (counting Julius Caesar), and Domitian the twelfth; no matter how the names of the emperors are juggled around, they do not neatly fit John's scheme of seven. That suggests that the number seven is simply a schematic representation for the complete number of Roman emperors. Actually, according to tradition, Rome did have seven kings during the Roman monarchy (753–509 B.C.). The symbolic significance of the number seven led to the widespread belief among both Romans and Etruscans that the period of kings had been destined to conclude with the seventh king of the seventh *saeculum* (Lat., "generation," "reign"). The ten horns (v. 10) are ten client kings of Rome who are of "one mind" (RSV) or "one accord," an ancient technical term for the kind of concord within a city and unanimity among nations brought about by the benevolence of the gods (in this case ordained by God, 17:17). These client kings, therefore, are not coerced into an alliance with Rome but are in full agreement with it. Their united forces will unsuccessfully war against the Lamb, who will conquer them (v. 14; cf. 19:19–20). The angel interprets the waters (the Tiber) under the harlot as representative of all humanity over which Rome has temporary control (v. 15). In vv. 16–17 a coalition of ten kings allied with the beast will attack and destroy the harlot. The Nero legends anticipated the return of Nero from the east with a great army to destroy his enemies in Rome (*Sib. Or.* 4.138–39; 5.93–110, 361–85). During the period of the late republic (133–41 B.C.), Rome experienced almost continual internal disorder brought on by a relatively independent army of professional soldiers under the control of strong leaders, some of whom captured the city. When Sulla captured Rome in 82 B.C., he had thousands of his opponents murdered. With the recent instability of the year of the three emperors (A.D. 68–69), the vengeance on Rome associated with Nero's return had ample historical precedent.

18:1–19:8, Reactions to Babylon's Fall. Chap. 18 is a pastiche of five different types of poetic compositions all focusing on the fall of Babylon. The first section, vv. 1–3, though often referred to as a dirge or lament, is actually a prophetic taunt song. Taunt songs were used by OT prophets for deriding the enemies of Israel and announcing their downfall (Isa. 23–24, 47; Jer. 50–51; Ezek. 26–27). This taunt consists first of an angelic announcement anticipating the fall of Babylon (Rev. 18:1–3). The opening words, "Fallen, fallen is Babylon the Great" (cf. 14:8) are derived from Isa. 21:9. There, as here, the statement is a prophetic anticipation of a future event that will surely come to pass.

Rev. 18:4–8, attributed to a "heavenly voice," refers to the *future* fall of Babylon. It conforms to a particular prophetic form, the *summons to flight*, consisting of an initial summons to flee followed by a threat of judgment. The form is often found in the writing prophets, particularly Jeremiah and often in connection with fleeing from Babylon (e.g., Jer. 50:8–10; 51:6–10; Isa. 48:20–22; 52:11–12). The form is also found in Christian prophecies (Mark 13:14–20). The command "Come out of her!" (Rev. 18:4) is followed by an encouragement to repay Rome double for her deeds (v. 6). The reason for leaving is because of the imminent arrival of plagues associated with the seventh bowl (v. 8).

In vv. 9–20, John has incorporated three dirges attributed to those sympathetic to Babylon (those enriched by their dealings with the city), kings (vv. 9–10), merchants (vv. 11–17a; cf. Ezek. 27:12–24), and the merchant marine (Rev. 18:17b–19). Each brief threnody or dirge is introduced with "Alas! alas!" (vv. 10, 16, 19) and concludes with the slightly varied refrain that Babylon's destruction has been accomplished in "one hour" (vv. 10b, 17a, 19b). Modeled after Ezek. 26–28, these dirges conclude with a cry of joy in Rev. 18:20. Rome is presented in vv. 11–14 using the common image of the central world market first found in Isocrates (*Panegyricus* 42; cf. Strabo 17.1.13). The extensive Roman trade in rare commodities was proverbial.

An angel then throws a millstone into the sea symbolizing the downfall of "Babylon" (Rev. 18:21–24). This action contains features typical of the "reports of prophetic symbolic actions" found in OT prophets (e.g., 1 Kings 22:11; 2 Kings 13:14–19). Here in the setting of apocalyptic prophecy an angel rather than a prophet performs the action, which John has modeled after a similar action reported in Jer. 51:63–64 where Jeremiah tells a messenger to throw a stone into the Euphrates, symbolizing Babylon who will sink to rise no more.

The throne room scene in Rev. 19:1–8 is the fifth and last poetic section in this passage. The first antiphonal hymn celebrates the judgment of "Babylon" as an accomplished fact, the subject of the angelic disclosure according to 17:1. This section contains four hymns arranged in two antiphonal strophes: first, 19:1b–2 / 19:3; second, 19:5b / 19:6b–8. In turn, vv. 5b–8 constitute an antiphonal response to vv. 1b–4. The term "hallelujah" (a Hebrew liturgical formula meaning "praise Yahweh," found only here in the NT) is used three times to introduce three of the hymns (vv. 1, 3, 6) and as an antiphonal response in v. 4b. The song of great heavenly multitude (v. 1), probably angelic beings (cf. 5:11), like the angelic taunt of 18:1–3, focuses on the judgment of "Babylon" (and the vindication of the martyrs) as an accomplished fact (vv. 1b–4). The entire scene closely resembles the heavenly liturgy of 5:11–14 (cf. 14:1–3; 15:2–4). An unidentified voice from the throne provides the cue for all of God's servants to praise him (v. 5), introducing a second set of hymns celebrating the fact that God "reigns" (RSV), better translated "has established his reign." The eschatological perspective of this hymn is that the kingdom of God is fully present. The hymn also celebrates the imminent union of Christ with his people using the metaphor of marriage, with the Lamb as the bridegroom and the church as his bride (cf. Eph. 5:21–32; 2 Cor. 11:2).

19:9–10, Conclusion. This brief section, which forms a conclusion to 17:1–19:8, bears several verbal and thematic similarities with 22:6–9. In both, an angel commissions John to write, a beatitude is pronounced, and John is discouraged from worshiping the angelic revealer. The angelic claim that "these are the true words of God" (v. 9b) refers to the entire section 17:1–19:8.

19:11–21:8
The Judgment of God's Adversaries

John has emphasized the structural and thematic importance of 19:11–21:8 by framing it between a pair of angelic revelations (17:1–19:10 and 21:9–22:9) that begin and end with numerous verbal and thematic similarities. Both use female imagery; Babylon the harlot is the central concern of 17:1–19:10, while the Bride, the new Jerusalem, is the focus of 21:9–22:9.

19:11–20:3, The Victorious Parousia. From the vantage point of earth, John sees the heavens opened (a theme associated with divine revelation and equivalent to the open door in heaven in 4:1; cf. Ezek. 1:1; Mark 1:10; Acts 7:56). Christ rides forth as a divine warrior leading the heavenly armies against the beast, the false prophet, and the dragon who are defeated and punished in the reverse order of their appearance in Revelation 12–13. Though this scene depicts the Parousia (fulfilling Rev. 1:7), the traditional Christian Parousia imagery is missing (cf. 1 Thess. 4:15–17; Mark 13:27; Matt. 24:31). The reason is twofold: first, the emphasis here is on the *judicial* function of the Parousia (as in 2 Thess. 1:5–10; 2 Pet. 3:8–13), and second, in Revelation the eternal messianic kingdom is placed on a renovated earth so that Christ comes to his people on earth rather than transferring them to heaven. In describing Christ as a victorious warrior, John piles up descriptive epithets and attributes in a manner similar to the Patmos vision in Rev. 1:9–20. Christ's many diadems (19:12) symbolize his sovereignty as "King of kings and Lord of lords" (v. 16). He alone knows his secret name, corresponding to Rome's secret name (17:5). The single allusion to his redeeming death is his robe, which has been dipped in blood (cf. 1:5; 5:9; 7:14; 12:11). His public name is "The Word of God" (19:13; cf. John 1:1–3; 1 John 1:1). An angel announces the imminent destruction of the earthly opponents of God (Rev. 19:17–18) followed by a brief narrative of the decisive defeat of the beast and the slaughter of his client kings and their armies by the armies of Christ. After the beast and the false prophet are captured, they are consigned to the eternal torment of the lake of fire (vv. 19–21). Since the beast and his allies have already destroyed "Babylon" in accordance with God's will (17:16–17), this victory must represent the conquest and destruction of the remaining opponents of God and the Lamb (but cf. 20:7–9). The "lake of fire," mentioned six times in Revelation 20–21, has no close parallels in Jewish eschatology, though fire itself is often connected with eschatological punishment. The next to last stage in the conquest of evil is the confinement of Satan (identified by his several aliases as in 12:9) by an angel to the bottomless pit (the abyss, whence he came) for a thousand years (20:1–3). In Jewish legend, the free rein that he and his angels have exercised on earth must end by God's eschatological intervention (1 Enoch 10; 54:6; 69:27–28; cf. Isa. 24:21–22).

20:4–6, The Millennial Kingdom.
During the temporary restraint of Satan (20:1–3), the martyrs alone are raised in the first resurrection (20:5) and reign with Christ on earth for a thousand years (cf. 2:26–27; 7:15–17; 14:1 5). Satan is later released for a limited period (20:3; Jewish eschatology knows no such temporary release of Satan). The notion of a temporary messianic kingdom became a subject for speculation within Judaism after A.D. 70. 2 Esdras 7:26–29 anticipates an intermediate messianic kingdom lasting four hundred years (after which the Messiah dies), while an indefinite period is mentioned in 2 Apoc. Bar. 40:3 (cf. 2 Esd. 12:34; 1 Cor. 15:24–28). Various rabbinic sages reportedly proposed that the messianic kingdom would last from forty to seven thousand years. What is the function of such a temporary messianic kingdom? It reconciles the expectation of a messianic kingdom with the notion of the final realization of the eternal reign of God. Jewish messianic expectation was based on the hope of the restoration of the house of David (cf. Pss. Sol. 17). Yet Jewish eschatological expectation tended to focus not on the restoration of a dynasty, but on a single messianic king sent by God (hence a dispensable theocratic symbol) to restore the fortunes of Israel. A messianic interregnum, therefore, functions as an anticipation of the perfect and eternal theocratic state that will exist when primordial conditions are reinstated forever. Since the Messiah was not a supernatural being in Jewish thought, he must eventually die (as in 2 Esd. 7:29). Yet for Christians, the messianic kingdom could obviously not end that way. As early as Paul, the messianic kingdom of Christ, after an indefinite period, concludes when Christ transfers his sovereignty to God (1 Cor. 15:24–28). To accommodate such a provisional state, John has awkwardly duplicated the final eschatological events and inserted the temporary millennial kingdom in the middle. He narrates two final wars (Rev. 19:11–21; 20:7–10), two victories over Satan (20:1–3; 20:10); two resurrections (20:4–6; 20:12–13); two judgment scenes (20:4; 20:12–13); and two states of blessedness (20:4; 20:12).

20:7–15, The Release and Defeat of Satan.
After Satan's release, he gathers armies from the nations of the earth for a last hopeless attempt to destroy the millennial kingdom on Mount Zion (20:7–9; cf. 14:1–5). Gog and Magog, derived from Ezekiel 38–39, are generic names for nations hostile to Israel who unsuccessfully attempt to annihilate the people of God. Yet they will be decisively defeated by judgments from heaven (Ezek. 38:22). Since the names Gog and Magog occur only rarely in Jewish apocalypses, John depends directly on Ezekiel. After Satan's defeat he, like the beast and false prophet before him, is perpetually confined to the lake of fire (Rev. 20:10).

The final judgment is depicted in vv. 11–15 in traditional eschatological imagery (1 Enoch 90:20–27). The second resurrection, implied but unmentioned, enables the rest of the dead (martyrs alone experience the first resurrection), both righteous and wicked, to stand before the throne of God awaiting his verdict. Into this traditional scene of the opening of two sets of books, John has inserted a reference to the book of life (Rev. 20:12; cf. 13:8; 17:8; 21:27). The metaphor of two sets of heavenly tablets or books on which righteous and wicked deeds are recorded for reference on the day of judgment was common in early Judaism.

21:1–8, The New Heavens and the New Earth.
John then sees a new heaven and a new earth that have replaced their earlier counterparts that have "passed away" (21:1; cf. 20:11). It is strange that such a cosmic cataclysm is passed over with just two oblique references. The eventual destruction of heaven and earth is part of Christian tradition (Matt. 5:18 = Luke 16:17; 2 Pet. 3:10–13). The descent of the new Jerusalem is accompanied by the commentary that God now dwells with humankind and all death and suffering are now eliminated from

human experience (Rev. 21:3–4) with the reinstatement of primordial conditions. In some strands of Jewish eschatology the heavenly Jerusalem replaces the earthly Jerusalem (2 Esd. 7:26; 10:41–44).

The climactic statement of God found in Rev. 21:5–8 summarizes the central message of Revelation. The reliability of the message is guaranteed by the speaker, God himself, the Alpha and the Omega (cf. 1:8) and the Beginning and the End (a widespread Hellenistic divine title emphasizing cosmic sovereignty and lordship). God's message is that those who conquer, i.e., hold fast to the word of God and the testimony of Jesus, will be children of God and enjoy eternal blessedness; those who do not renounce their sinful ways will be punished with eternal torment. God's role in Revelation is similar to popular conceptions of the emperor's primary function: to dispense justice by punishing the disobedient and rewarding the obedient.

21:9–22:9
The New Jerusalem

Here, as in 17:1, a bowl angel invites John to see a special sight, the Bride, the wife of the Lamb, i.e., the new Jerusalem (the people of God under the metaphor of a city), the antithesis of the great harlot of Babylon. The new Jerusalem that John sees descending from heaven is then described in numerous details indicating that it symbolizes the people of God (21:9–22:5). The twelve gates bear the names of the twelve Israelite tribes (cf. Ezek. 48:30–34). In Rev. 21:15–21, John's angelic guide measures the city, whose length, width, and height is twelve thousand stadia (at 187 meters per stadion, the city would be an enormous cube 1,367 miles on each side). The eschatological temple described in Ezek. 42:16–20 is square, in contrast to Solomon's rectangular Temple (1 Kings 6:2), though its innermost room was cubical (1 Kings 6:20). Poetic descriptions of the future Jerusalem describe it as constructed of precious stones (Isa. 54:11–12; Tob. 13:16–17). The precious stones adorning the new Jerusalem contrast with the jewels worn by the great harlot (Rev. 17:4). Each of the twelve foundations of the city bears the name of one of the twelve apostles (Rev. 21:14) and consists of a single enormous precious stone (vv. 19–20). The names of these stones correspond to those mounted on the breastplate of the Israelite high priest (Exod. 28:17–20; 39:10–13). The identity of the new Jerusalem with the church suggests that the twelve stones symbolize the priestly status of the people of God (Rev. 1:6; 5:10; 20:6).

In 22:1–6, John sees aspects of the city based on traditional Jewish conceptions of the three central features of Eden: the throne of God, the river, and the fruitful tree of life (1

Enoch 25:1–7; 2 Enoch 8:1–8). The term "paradise" (meaning "garden" or "park") was used for the earthly Eden and for heaven (Jub. 4:23; 2 Enoch 8:3, 5, 6 [long]; 8:1, 3, 8 [short]; Luke 23:43). In Jewish legends, Adam lived in paradise (the third heaven, 2 Cor. 12:3–4; 2 Enoch 8:1) and was expelled to earth for his disobedience. The eschatological restoration of primal Edenic conditions found in the OT prophets (Isa. 11:6–9; 65:17–25) became an important theme in apocalyptic thought. According to Rev. 2:7, the tree of life grows in paradise. The traditional river flowing out of Eden (Gen. 2:10) has become the river of life, and the trees of life grow on both banks of the river (inspired by Ezek. 47:1–12). The final goal of salvation is now realized (Rev. 22:3–5). The servants of God are finally able to see him (ordinarily unachievable; cf. Exod. 33:17–20; John 1:18), which means that they share his holiness and righteousness. His name is on their foreheads because they belong to him forever. In fulfillment of the promise made in Rev. 3:21, they will reign with him forever (22:5). Only the 144,000 martyrs shared the earlier millennial reign with Christ (20:4).

22:6–21
Epilogue

Rev. 22:6–9 is a transitional passage that both functions as a conclusion to the larger angelic revelation in 21:9–22:5 (which is parallel to the earlier angelic revelation in 17:1–19:9) and as a conclusion to the entire work. The numerous parallels to 1:1–8 indicate that 22:6–21 does indeed function as an epilogue. John follows the literary conventions concluding Jewish apocalypses by emphasizing the truth and importance of his revelatory message and by referring to how this prophetic book should be used. When he claims that "I John am he who heard and saw these things" (v. 8), he is using a common ancient witness formula emphasizing the reliability of the eyes and ears in gathering direct personal knowledge. Most Jewish apocalypses feign antiquity and so mention the problem of preserving their message for the last days (Dan. 8:26; 12:4, 9; 1 Enoch 1:2). John wrote for his own time so the work must not be sealed until the end but immediately published since the end is near (Rev. 22:10). The staccato quality of 22:12–17 corresponds to 1:1–8. Two complementary prophetic oracles with Jesus as the speaker are quoted in 22:12–13. The reference to his imminent coming (v. 12) is complemented by his claim to be the Alpha and Omega (v. 13; cf. 1:7–8). The seventh and last beatitude of 22:14 pronounces a salvific blessing on those who have washed their robes (cf. 7:14; 16:15), i.e., have been redeemed by the blood of the Lamb and so have access to the new Jerusalem, from which sinners are excluded (cf. 21:8, 27). Another saying of Jesus is cited in 22:16: "I Jesus have sent my angel to you [plural, i.e., the hearers]"; it functions to guarantee the authenticity and authority of the revelation granted to John for the churches. In v. 16b, Jesus identifies himself as the root and offspring of David (emphasizing his messianic status; cf. Isa. 11:1, 10) and as the bright morning star (symbolizing universal sovereignty). The invitation of the Spirit and Bride (i.e., the people of God) to "come" is not addressed to Jesus but invites readers to share in the redemption and the salvation that only the faithful will experience.

The final paragraph in vv. 18–20 contains the author's attempt to safeguard his revelation by pronouncing conditional curses on those daring to add or subtract anything from his book (cf. 1 Enoch 104:10–13). The integrity formula, "do not add, do not delete," was used widely throughout the ancient world in histories to guarantee the accurate use of sources, in treaties to protect their integrity, and in revelatory literature to claim completeness. The penalty for tampering with the text of Revelation is either to experience the plagues described in the book or to be barred from the holy city. Jesus, who testified to the truth of John's revelation, promises "Surely I am coming soon," to which John responds "Amen. Come Lord Jesus!" (v. 20). This concluding prayer probably translates the ancient Aramaic eucharistic formula *marana tha* ("our Lord, come!") found in 1 Cor. 16:22 and *Did.* 10:6. The promise of the imminent Parousia is reiterated several times throughout Revelation (cf. Rev. 3:11; 16:15; 22:7).

Bibliography

Beasley-Murray, G. R. *The Book of Revelation.* New Century Bible Commentary. Rev. ed. Grand Rapids, MI: Eerdmans, 1978.

Caird, G. B. *A Commentary on the Revelation of St. John the Divine.* New York: Harper & Row, 1966.

Collins, A. Y., ed. *Early Christian Apocalypticism: Genre and Social Setting.* Semeia, 36. Atlanta: Scholars Press, 1986.

Collins, J. J., ed. *Apocalypse: The Morphology of a Genre.* Semeia, 14. Missoula, MT: Scholars Press, 1979.

Hemer, C. J. *The Letters to the Seven Churches of Asia in Their Local Setting.* Journal for the Study of the New Testament Supplement Series, no. 11. Sheffield: JSOT Press, 1986.

PHOTOGRAPH CREDITS

Black-and-white photographs. 1: Reproduced by Permission of the British Library Board, London; *18:* Musée du Louvre, Paris/Photo by Cliché des Musées Nationaux; *42:* Synagogue of Capernaum/Erich Lessing Culture and Fine Arts Archives (hereafter E. Lessing); *73:* Reproduced through the courtesy of the Michigan-Princeton-Alexandria Expedition to Mount Sinai (hereafter M-P-A Expedition); *124:* Kunsthistorisches Museum, Vienna/E. Lessing; *202:* Reproduced by Permission of the British Library Board, London; *264:* Bild-Archiv der Österreichischen Nationalbibliothek, Vienna/Lichtbildwerkstätte Alpenland; *332:* British Museum, London/E. Lessing; *390:* Edition Leipzig/Frank Speckhals; *395:* M-P-A Expedition; *440:* Bibliothèque Nationale, Paris/E. Lessing; *498:* Reproduced by Permission of the British Library Board, London; *529:* M-P-A Expedition; *568:* British Museum, London/E. Lessing; *626:* Staatliche Museum zu Berlin/E. Lessing; *757:* Bibliothèque Nationale, Paris; *808:* Bayerische Staatsbibliothek, Munich, nr. 13157; *878:* Biblioteca Guarneriana of San Daniele del Friuli, Italy; *937:* M-P-A Expedition; *978:* Cathedral of Rossano, Italy/Scala/Art Resource, New York; *1026:* Kariye Church, Istanbul/E. Lessing; *1080:* E. Lessing; *1119:* M-P-A Expedition; *1178:* E. Lessing; *1222:* E. Lessing; *1249:* M-P-A Expedition; *1304:* © The Pierpont Morgan Library, New York, 1988, M. 644, fol. 112.

Color photographs following page 462. A1: 1. Library of the Cathedral, Gerona, Spain/E. Lessing; 2. Armenian Patriarchate, Jerusalem/David Harris; 3. Reproduced by Permission of the British Library Board, London. *A2:* 1. Museum of Damascus, Syria/E. Lessing; 2. Museum of Aleppo (Halab), Syria/E. Lessing; 3. Tomb of Mennah, Thebes, Egypt/E. Lessing; 4. Bild-Archiv der Österreichischen Nationalbibliothek, Vienna. *A3:* 1. The John Ryland University Library of Manchester; 2. Tomb of Rekhmere, Thebes, Egypt/E. Lessing; 3. Egyptian Museum, Leiden, The Netherlands/E. Lessing; 4. From Erwin R. Goodenough, *Jewish Symbols in the Greco-Roman Period,* Bollingen Series XXXVII, Vol. 11: *Symbolism in the Dura Synagogue.* Copyright © 1964 by Princeton University Press. Photographs by Fred Anderegg. Plate XII Reprinted by permission of Princeton University Press. *A4:* 1. Biblioteca Apostolica Vaticana, Rome/Archivio Fotografico; 2. Rock-

efeller Archaeological Museum, Jerusalem/E. Lessing; 3. Bibliothèque Nationale, Paris. *A5:* 1. Bibliothèque Nationale, Paris; 2. Reproduced by Permission of the British Library Board, London; 3. Musée du Louvre, Department of Oriental Antiquities, Paris/E. Lessing. *A6:* 1. Museum of Aleppo (Haleb), Syria/E. Lessing; 2. Musée du Louvre, Department of Oriental Antiquities, Paris/E. Lessing; 3a, 3b. From Erwin R. Goodenough, *Jewish Symbols in the Greco-Roman Period,* Bollingen Series XXXVII, Vol. 11: *Symbolism in the Dura Synagogue.* Copyright © 1964 by Princeton University Press. Photographs by Fred Anderegg. Plate XXI reprinted by permission of Princeton University Press. *A7:* 1. Colegiata de San Isidoro, Archivo Biblioteca Museos, Léon, Spain/ARXIU MAS; 2. Musée du Louvre, Paris/E. Lessing. *A8:* 1. Instituto Poligrafico e Zecca dello Stato, Rome; 2. Bibliothèque Nationale, Paris; 3. Israel Museum, Jerusalem; 4. Reifenberg Collection, Israel Museum, Jerusalem/E. Lessing.

Color photographs following page 942. B1: 1. Museum of Catalan Art, Barcelona, Spain/Scala/Art Resource, New York; 2. Biblioteca Apoltolica Vaticana, Rome/Archivio Fotografico; 3. Collection Paul Canellopoulos, Athens/E. Lessing. *B2:* 1. Cathedral of Rossano, Italy/Scala/Art Resource, New York; 2. Zev Radovan, Jerusalem; 3. National Library, Athens/E. Lessing. *B3:* 1. Byzantium Museum, Athens/E. Lessing; 2. Kunsthistorisches Museum, Vienna/E. Lessing; 3. Collection of I.D.A.M., Israel Museum, Jerusalem/E. Lessing; 4. Cathedral of Gerona, Spain/ARXIU MAS. *B4:* 1. Bayerische Staatsbibliothek, Munich; 2. Tresor de l'Eglise, Gimel-les-Cascades, France/E. Lessing; 3. Musée des Beaux Arts, Lyons, France/E. Lessing; 4. Museo Lateranense, Rome/E. Lessing. *B5:* 1. © The Pierpont Morgan Library, New York, 1988, M. 644, fol. 222v; 2. Biblioteca Nacional, Madrid/ARXIU MAS; 3. Municipal Museum, Limoges, France/E. Lessing. *B6:* 1. E. Lessing; 2. E. Lessing; 3. E. Lessing. *B7:* 1. E. Lessing; 2. E. Lessing; 3. E. Lessing. *B8:* 1. Cambridge University Library, Cambridge; 2. Reproduced by Permission of the British Library Board, London; 3. Fondation Martin Bodmer, Bibliotheca Bodmeriana, Cologny-Genève, Switzerland; 4. Univeristet Biblioteket, Uppsala, Sweden.

INDEX TO COLOR MAPS

This index lists geographical names found on the color maps at the back of this book. The number(s) of the map(s) on which the name appears is listed first, followed by the key, or grid reference (a letter-figure combination that refers to the letters and figures at the margins of the map). Places whose names changed over time are identified by a "see also" reference. For example, the entry for Azotus indicates it can be found on Map 11 in location B5, and on Map 13 in location A5, and readers are referred to Ashdod, its alternate name.

Mittani, 1, D2
Mitylene, 16, D2
Mizpah, 5, 7, 9, B4; 11, C4
Moab, 2, D3; 3, C5; 4, C4; 5, C6; 6, C3; 7, 9, C5–D5
Modein, 11, B4
Moeris, lake, 2, A4
Moesia, 12, D2; 16, C1
Moladah, 9, B6
Moresheth-gath, 7, B5
Moschi, people, 8, C1
Musa, Gebel, 2, C5
Mycenaean-Minoan Domain, 1, A2
Myra, 16, E3
Mysia, 16, D1

Nabatea, 12, E3; 13, 15, D6
Nabateans, people, 9, B6–C6; 11, D6; 16, F4
Nahariyeh, 7, B2
Nain, 13, 15, C3
Nairi, 6, D1
Naphtali, tribe, 3, C2
Narbata (Narbatah), 9, 11, 13, B3
Narbo, 12, B2
Narbonensis, 12, B2
Nazareth, 13, 15, B3
Neapolis (in Macedonia), 16, C1
Neballat, 9, B4
Nebo, 9, B5
Nebo, Mount, 2, D3; 3, D4; 5, 7, C5
Negeb, 2, C3; 3, B6; 5, 7, A6
Netophah, 9, B5
Nicaea, 10, F2; 16, D1
Nicomedia, 16, E1
Nicopolis (in Achaia), 16, C2
Nicopolis (in Palestine), 13, B5. See also Emmaus
Nile, river, 1, 6, D4; 6, C3; 10, B3; 12, E4
Nile Delta, 2, A3
Nimrud, 6, E2. See also Calah
Nineveh, 1, 6, D2; 8, C2
Nippur, 1, 6, E3; 8, D3
Nisibis, 6, D2; 8, C2
No. See Thebes
Nob, 7, B4
Noph, 1, B3. See also Memphis
Noricum, 12, C2
North Wall, First and Second (in Jerusalem), 14, B2–C2, B1–C1
Numidia, 12, B3
Nuzi, 1, E2

Olbia, 10, B1
Olives, Mount of (in Jerusalem), 14, E2
On, 1, B3; 6, C3. See also Heliopolis
Ono, 9, B4
Opis, 8, D2
Ortona, 16, A1
Ostia, 16, A1
Oxus, river, 8, F1; 10, E2

Paddan-aram, 1, D2

Paestum, 16, A1
Pamphylia, 12, E3; 16, E2
Paneas, 11, D1; 13, C2. See also Caesarea Philippi
Paneas, region, 13, C1
Pannonia, 12, C2
Panticapaeum, 10, B1
Paphlagonia, 16, E1
Paphos, 16, E3
Paran, Wilderness of, 2, B3
Parsa, 8, D3. See also Persepolis
Parthia, 8, E2; 10, D2
Parthian Empire, 12, F3
Pasargadae, 8, E3
Patara, 16, D3
Pattala, 10, F3
Pella (in Macedonia), 10, A1
Pella (in Palestine), 9, 11, 13, 15, C3
Pelusium, 2, 8, 10, B3; 6, C3; 16, E4
Penuel, 5, 7, C4
Perea, 13, 15, C4; 16, E2
Pergamum, 12, 16, D2
Persepolis, 8, E3; 10, D3
Persian Gulf, 1, F4; 8, 10, D3. See also Lower Sea
Persis, 8, E3; 10, D3
Pessinus, 16, E2
Pharathon, 11, C4
Phasael, tower (in Jerusalem), 14, B2
Phasaelis, 13, C4
Phaselis, 6, B2
Phasis, 8, C1
Philadelphia, 11, D4; 15, D5. See also Rabbah
Philistia, 4, B4; 5, 7, A5; 11, A5–B4
Philistines, people, 3, A5
Philoteria, 11, C2
Phoenicia, 4, 5, 13, B2–C1; 6, C2; 7, B1–C1; 11, C1–C2
Phoenix, 16, C3
Phrygia, 6, B1; 16, E2
Pibeseth, 2, A4
Pisidia, 16, E2
Pithom, 2, A4
Polemon, Kingdom of, 16, F1
Pontus, 12, E2; 16, E1
Prophthasia, 10, E3
Propontis, 16, D1
Pteria, 8, B1
Ptolemais, 11, 13, 15, B2. See also Acco
Punon, 2, D4; 4, C5
Pura, 8, F3; 10, E3
Puteoli, 16, A1
Pyramids, Great, 2, A4

Qarnini, 7, C2
Qarqar, 6, C2
Qumran, 11, 13, 15, C5

Raamses, 2, A3
Rabbah, 2, D3; 3, 5, 7, 9, D4; 4, C4. See also Philadelphia
Raetia, 12, C2
Ragaba, 11, D3
Ramah, 5, 7, B4; 9, C4

Ramathaim, 11, B4
Ramath-mizpeh, 3, D4
Ramoth-Gilead, 3, 5, 7, D3; 4, C3
Raphana, 13, 15, D2
Raphia, 2, 6, C3; 4, B4; 5, 7, A5; 9, 11, A6
Red Sea, 1, 6, 8, C4; 2, C6–D6; 10, B4; 12, E4
Rehob, 3, C2
Rephidim, 2, C5
Reuben, tribe, 3, C5
Rha, river, 12, F1
Rhagae, 8, 10, D2
Rhegium, 16, A2
Rhine, river, 12, C1
Rhodes, island, 1, 6, 8, B2; 16, D3
Riblah, 8, C2
Rimmon, 7, C4
Rome, 12, C2; 16, A1
Royal Portico (in Jerusalem), 14, C2
Rubicon, river, 12, C2
Rumah, 5, B2

Sais, 6, 8, B3
Saka (Scythians), people, 8, 10, F1
Salamis, 16, F3
Salecah, 4, D3
Salim, 13, 15, C4
Salmone, Cape, 16, D3
Salonae, 12, C2
Salt Sea, 2, D3; 3, 5, 7, 9, 11, C5; 4, C4. See also Dead Sea
Samaga, 11, D4
Samal, 6, D2
Samaria, 5, 7, 9, B3; 6, 11, C3. See also Sebaste
Samaria, region, 11, C3; 13, 15, B4
Samarkand (Maracanda), 10, F2
Samerina, 7, B4–C3
Samos, island, 6, B1; 16, D2
Samothrace, island, 16, C1
Sangarius, river, 1, B1; 16, E1
Sardinia, island, 12, B2
Sardis, 6, B1; 8, B2; 10, A2; 16, D2
Sarepta, 13, C1; 15, B1
Sarmatia, 12, D1–E1
Scythians, people, 8, D1; 10, B1, F1
Scythopolis, 11, 13, 15, C3. See also Beth-shan
Sebaste, 13, 15, B4. See also Samaria
Second Quarter (in Jerusalem), 14, C2
Sela, 2, D4; 4, C5; 6, C3
Seleucia, 11, D2; 16, F2
Sepphoris, 11, C2; 13, C3; 15, B3
Serabit-el-Khadem (Dophkah), 2, B5
Serpent's Pool (in Jerusalem), 14, B3
Sevan, Lake, 6, E1

Map 1

The Ancient World
at the Time of the Patriarchs

⇒ Possible Route of Abraham and the
Patriarchs (Early 2nd Millennium B.C.)

━━ Areas of influence of major
powers about 1350 B.C.

0 50 100 150 200 250Mls
0 100 200 300 400Kms

© Copyright HAMMOND INCORPORATED, Maplewood, N.J.

Caspian Sea

Persian Gulf
(Lower Sea)

Dilmun?

MEDIA

Mt. Ararat

Cyrus

Araxes

L. Urmia

Tepe Giyan

Ecbatana

ELAM

Susa

ZAGROS MOUNTAINS

GUTIUM

URARTU

L. Van

HURRIANS (HORITES)

ASSYRIA

Nuzi

Arbela

Tepe Gawra

Tell Leilan

Tell Brak

Nineveh

Calah

Asshur

Jarmo

Eshnunna

Akkad

Agade?

Sippar

Cuthah

Babylon

Nippur

BABYLONIA

KASSITES

Isin

Lagash

Sumer

Erech

Ur

Eridu

Tigris

Euphrates

MITANNI

Harran

Paddan-aram

Tell Halaf

Mari

Tadmor

KASHKA

HITTITE EMPIRE (HATTI)

Hattusas

Alaca Hüyük

Boghazköy

Mazuwatt

Kanish

L. Tuz

Kizzuwatne

Taurus Mts.

Carchemish

Alalakh

Ebla

Hamath

Kadesh

Haleb

Damascus

KEDAR

ASSUWA

Troy

Hermos

Sardis

Ephesus

Miletus

ARZAWA

Beycesultan

LUKKA

Meandros

Rhodes

Knossos

MINOAN DOMAIN

CAPHTOR
(Crete)

MYCENAEAN DOMAIN

ALASHIYA,
KITTIM
(Cyprus)

Ugarit

Arvad

Gebal

Sidon

Tyre

Dor

Hazor

Megiddo

Joppa

Gaza

Shechem

Jerusalem

Hebron

Beer-sheba

Jericho

Kadesh-barnea

MIDIAN

Dumah

Tema

Dedan

Mediterranean Sea
(Great or Upper Sea)

Red Sea

CANAAN

Sinai

EGYPT

Avaris
(Zoan)

Lower Egypt

On

Memphis
(Noph)

Heracleopolis

Hermopolis

Akhetaton
(Tell el-Amarna)

Abydos

Nile

Libyan Desert

The Exodus

Map 2

Possible route of the Exodus
Unsuccessful invasion of Canaan
Trade routes

0   20   40   60   80   100 Mls
0   40   80   120   160 Kms
© Copyright HAMMOND INCORPORATED, Maplewood, N. J.

The Great Sea
(Mediterranean Sea)

LEBANON

Gebal
Berytus
Sidon
Damasc
Tyre

BASH

Acco   Hazor   Asht
Mt. Carmel   Madon
Dor   Megiddo   Edrei
Taanach   Beth-shan
Shechem   Jabbok
Aphek
Joppa   Shiloh   AMMON
Bethel   Rabb
Gezer   Jericho
Ashdod   Hesh
Ashkelon   Jerusalem   Mt. Ne
Gaza   Eglon?   Lachish   Salt   Dibor
Debir?   Hebron   Sea   Arnon
Arad   Zoar   MOAB
L. Sirbon   Raphia   Kir-haresteth
Brook of Egypt   Beer-sheba   Horman   Zered
Pelusium   Negeb   Ije-abarim
(Sin)   The Way of the Sea   Wilderness   Bozrah
Tanis   Baal-   of   Zin   Punon
Raamses   zephon   Zilu   Sela
Goshen   Wilderness of Shur   Gebel Halal   Kadesh-barnea   Gebel Harun
Pibeseth   Pithom   L. Timsah
(Bubastis)   Succoth   The Way to Shur
EGYPT   Bitter   Wilderness   of   Paran   Ezion-geber
Heliopolis   Lakes   Wilderness   LAND
(On)   Mitla   of
Great   Pass   Sinai
Pyramids   Memphis   Etham   Peninsula   OF
(Noph)   Marah?   Wilderness
L.   Elim?   of   MIDIAN
Moeris   Dophkah?   Sin   Hazeroth?
Crocodilopolis   (Serabit-el Khadem)   Kibroth-
Alush?   hattaavah?
Heracleopolis   Rephidim?   Taberah?
Mt. Sinai   Red
(Gebel Musa)   Sea
Akhetaton (Tell el-Amarna)

Nile Delta
Nile
(Gulf of Suez)
(Gulf of Aqaba)
The King's Highway

Map 3

Settlement in Canaan and the Tribal Areas
(ca. Mid-Eleventh Century B.C.)

◇◇◇◇ Area settled by Israelites

JUDAH Twelve Israelite tribes

━━━━ Tribal boundary

┅┅┅┅ Approximate tribal boundary

Gezer Unconquered Canaanite city
(according to Judges 1)

▪ City of Refuge

```
0      10     20     30    40 Mls
0        20         40      60 Kms
```

© Copyright HAMMOND INCORPORATED, Maplewood, N.J.

The Great Sea

SIDONIANS

MT. LEBANON

HIVITES

ARAMEANS

MT. HERMON

Damascus

Sidon

Ahlab

Tyre

Kanah

Beth-shemesh?

DAN Dan (Laish)

BASHAN

Achzib

Kedesh

Yiron

Merom

Beth-
anah?

Hazor

Acco

NAPHTALI

Ashtaroth

Aphek

Rehob

Hannathon

ASHER

ZEBULUN

Gath-hepher

Sea of
Chinnereth

Golan

Edrei

Achshaph?

Helkath?

Shimron

Iphon

Mt. Tabor

ISSACHAR

Jezreel

Havvoth-jair

Ramoth-
gilead

Dor

Megiddo

Taanach

Beth-shan

GILEAD

Dothan

Ibleam

Jabesh-gilead?

Hepher

MANASSEH

Plain of Sharon

Tirzah

Zaphon?

Succoth

Mt. Ebal

Mt. Gerizim

Shechem

Mahanaim

Jabbok

AMMON

Aphek

Tappuah

Michmethath

Shiloh

Adam

Ramah

Mizpeh?

Joppa

EPHRAIM

GAD

Jazer

Rabbah

Gath

Bethel

Ai

Gilgal

Gezer

Shaalbim

Gibeon

Jericho

Heshbon

Ekron

Sorek

DAN

Ajalon

BENJAMIN

Bezer

Ashdod

Zorah

Jebus
(Jerusalem)

Mt. Nebo

Beth-shemesh

Medeba

Ashkelon

Libnah

Adullam

REUBEN

PHILISTINES

Gath?

Beth-zur

Salt

Gaza

Eglon?

Lachish

Hebron

Dibon

Aroer

Gerar

JUDAH

CALEB

Ziph

Debir?

Sea

Arnon

Ziklag?

Arad?

MOAB

Sharuhen

Besor

Beer-sheba

Hormah

SIMEON

Kir-hareseth

Negeb

Zoar

Tamar

Zered

River of Eygpt

EDOM

The Empire of David and Solomon

(ca. 1000-924 B.C.)

Map 4

Boundary of the empire at its greatest extent

Territory conquered by David

⊡ Fortified places of Solomon

⚒ Copper mining centers

0 10 25 50 75 Mls
0 20 40 60 80 100 120 Kms

© Copyright HAMMOND INCORPORATED, Maplewood, N.J.

— The Great Sea
(Mediterranean Sea)

Hamath

Arvad

Kadesh
Zedad
Hazar-e

ARAM — ZOBAH
Lebo-hamath

Gebal
Berothai

Berytus

BETH-REHOB

Sidon
Damascus

ARAM — DAMASCUS

Tyre
Abel
Dan
Kedesh
Hazor
MT. HERMON
MAACAH
ARGOB
Ashtaroth

Acco
Cabul
GESHUR

Mt. Carmel

Dor
Megiddo
Taanach
Mt. Gilboa
Jezreel
Beth-shan
TOB
Edrei
Ramoth-gilead
Salecah

Hepher

Shechem
Succoth
Mahanaim?

Joppa
ISRAEL
Jordan
Baalath?
Gezer
Beth-horon
Bethel
Rabbah
AMMON

Ashdod
Gibeah
Jericho
Heshbon

Ashkelon
Gath?
Beth-shemesh
Jerusalem
Medeba

Gaza
Lachish
Hebron
Salt
Sea
Aroer

PHILISTIA
Ziklag?

Raphia
Gerar
Beer-sheba
Arad
MOAB

JUDAH
Tamar
Kir-hareseth

AMALEK
Bozrah

Kadesh-barnea
Punon

River of Egypt

EDOM

Sela

Sinai

Arabah

Ezion-geber

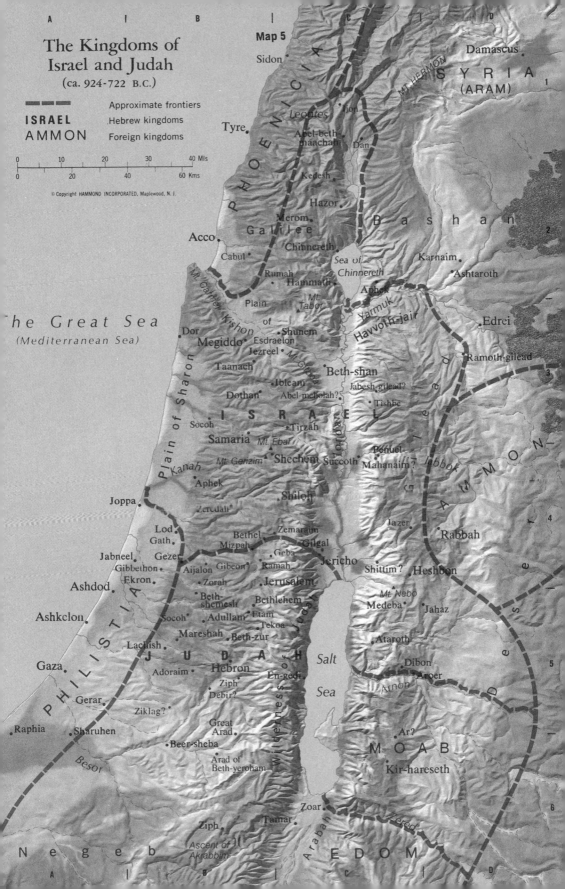

A   I   B   I   C   D

The Kingdoms of Israel and Judah
(ca. 924-722 B.C.)

Map 5

– – – – Approximate frontiers

ISRAEL   Hebrew kingdoms

AMMON   Foreign kingdoms

0   10   20   30   40 Mls
0   20   40   60 Kms

© Copyright HAMMOND INCORPORATED, Maplewood, N.J.

Damascus

Sidon

Leontes

Mt. HERMON

SYRIA (ARAM)

1

P H O E N I C I A

Tyre

Abel-beth-maachah

Ijon

Dan

Kedesh

Hazor

Merom

Galilee

B a s h a n

Acco

Chinnereth

Cabul

Rumah

Sea of Chinnereth

Karnaim

Ashtaroth

2

The Great Sea
(Mediterranean Sea)

Hammath

Plain

Mt. Tabor

Aphek

Yarmuk

Havvoth-jair

Edrei

Mt. Carmel

Kishon

of

Shunem

Esdraelon

Dor

Megiddo

Jezreel

Taanach

Mt. Gilboa

Beth-shan

Jabesh-gilead?

Ramoth-gilead

3

Ibleam

Abel-meholah?

Tishbe

Dothan

I S R A E L

Plain of Sharon

Socoh

Tirzah

Samaria

Mt. Ebal

Penuel

Mahanaim?

Succoth

Kanah

Mt. Gerizim

Shechem

A M M O N

Jabbok

Aphek

Shiloh

Zeredah

Joppa

Jazer

Rabbah

4

Lod

Bethel

Zemaraim

Gath

Mizpah

Gilgal

Gibeon?

Jabneel

Gezer

Geba

Jericho

Gibbethon

Aijalon

Ramah

Shittim?

Heshbon

Ekron

Zorah

Jerusalem

Ashdod

Beth-shemesh

Bethlehem

Mt. Nebo

Medeba

Jahaz

Ashkelon

Socoh

Adullam

Etam

Tekoa

Mareshah

Beth-zur

Ataroth

Lachish

J U D A H

Dibon

Aroer

5

Gaza

Adoraim

Hebron

En-gedi

Salt Sea

Arnon

Gerar

Ziph

Debir?

Ziklag?

Great Arad

Wilderness of Judah

Ar?

M O A B

Raphia

Sharuhen

Beer-sheba

Kir-hareseth

Arad of Beth-yeroham

P H I L I S T I A

Besor

Zoar

Ziph

Tamar

Zered

N e g e b

Ascent of Akrabbim

Araban

E D O M

A   I   B   I   C   D

Map 6

The Assyrian Empire

- - - - Assyrian empire—ca. 824 B.C.
───── Assyrian empire—ca. 640 B.C.
Cyrene Greek colonies underlined in red

0 50 100 150 200 250 300 350 MIs
0 100 200 300 400 500 Km

Caspian Sea

Lower (Eastern) Sea

MADAI

Ecbatana

ELAM

Susa (Shushan)

CHALDEANS

BABYLONIA

Sippar
Cutah
Babylon
Borsippa
Nippur
Larsa
Erech
Ur

Diyala

Tigris

Euphrates

Anat

EMPIRE

URARTU

Mt. Ararat
L. Van
L. Sevan

Cyrus
Araxes

Minni

L. Urmia

ARARAT

ZIKIRTU
Turushpa
Lake Nairi

Dur Sharrukin
Nineveh
Calah (Nimrud)
Asshur
Arbela

Nisibis
Gozan

Habor

Meliṭene

Tadmor

Haran
Tll Barsib
Carchemish
Aleppo

Samal
Arpad

Qarqar
Hamath

SYRIA

Damascus

KEDAR

ARIBI
(ARABS)

Dumah

Tema

Dedan

TUBAL

Kanish

Tyras

CILICIA
Tarsus

CIMMERIANS (GOMER)

PHRYGIA
Gordion
L. Tuz
Ancyra

MESHECH

LYDIA
Sardis

Astacus
Ancyra

TAURUS MTS.

Arvad

Cyprus

Sidon
Tyre

PHOENICIA
AMMON

Samaria
Jerusalem
JUDAH
Eltekeh trib. to Assyria
Raphia MOAB
Pelusium EDOM
Sela

Red Sea

ISRAEL

EGYPT
to Assyria 671-651 B.C.

Sais
Tanis
On
Bubastis
Memphis
Heracleopolis
Hermopolis
Siut
Abydos

Thebes

Nile

LIBYANS

Oasis of Siwa

Libyan Desert

GREEK CITY STATES

Abydos
Cyzicus
Lesbos
Euboea
Chios
Athens
Samos
Corinth
Miletus
Sparta
Rhodes

Aegean Sea

Crete

Phaselis

Upper (Western) Sea

Cyrene

Judah After the
Fall of Israel
(722-586 B.C.)

Map 7

- – – – Approximate frontiers
- **AMMON** Independent kingdoms
- DU'RU Assyrian provinces

0   10   20   30   40 Mis
0   20   40   60 Kms

© Copyright MCMLXXVIII HAMMOND INCORPORATED, Maplewood, N.J.

Damascus

**DIMAŠQI
(ARAM)**

Sidon

Leontes

Ijon

Tyre
(free city)

Abel-beth-
maachah

Dan

Kedesh

Achzib

Hazor

Nahariyeh

Acco

Chinnereth

QARNINI

Sea of
Chinnereth

Karnaim

Ashtaroth

Jotbah

Aphek

HAURINA

the Great Sea

(Mediterranean Sea)

Mt. Carmel

Mt.
Tabor

Shunem

Yarmuk

Dor

Megiddo

Jezreel

Ramoth-gilead

Taanach

Beth-shan

Jabesh-gilead?

Ibleam

Dothan

Tirzah

Samaria

Mt. Ebal

Shechem

Succoth

Penuel

Mahanaim?

Jabbok

Mt.
Gerizim

Kanah

Shiloh

Aphek

AMMON

Joppa

Bene-berak

Jazer

Rabbah

Beth-dagon

Lod

Rimmon

Gath

Bethel

Aiath

Gilgal

Shittim?

Eltekah?

Mizpah

Geba

Jericho

Jabneel

Gezer

Gibeon

Ramah

Elealeh

Ajalon

Gibeah

Anathoth

Sibmah

Heshbon

Gibbe-
thon

Jerusalem

Nob

Ashdod

Ekron

Mt. Nebo

Timnah

Beth-
shemesh

Bethlehem

Medeba

Jahaz

Azekah

Ashkelon

Moresheth-
gath

Adullam

Tekoa

Ataroth

Gath?

Mareshah

Beth-zur

Dibon

Aroer

Lachish

Arnon

Gaza

Salt

Adoraim

Hebron

En-gedi

Sea

Gerar

Bethel-ezel

Ziph

MOAB

Debir?

Ar?

Ziklag?

Great
Arad

Raphia

Sharuhen

Beer-sheba

Kir-hareseth
(Kir, Kir-heres)

Arad of
Beth-yeroham?

EGYPT

Besor

Negeb

Tamar

Zoar

Zered

EDOM

Map 8

Great Empires of the Sixth Century B.C.

Political boundaries of major powers ca. 560 B.C.
Limits of the Persian empire ca. 500 B.C.
Persian royal road

0   100 200 300 400 500 Mls
0   200 400 600 800 Kms

© Copyright HAMMOND INCORPORATED, Maplewood, N.J.

SAKA

Cyropolis

F Iaxartes

CHORASMIA

SOGDIANA

Bactra

BACTRIA

Aral Sea

Oxus

MARGUS

Margiana

ARACHOSIA

ARIA

Caspian Sea

Hadranta

Rhagae

DRANGIANA

PARTHIA

GEDROSIA

Pura

MAKA

CARMANIA

PERSIS

Yzd

Gabae

Pasargadae

Persepolis (Parsa)

MEDIA (559-550 B.C.)

ELAM

SUSIANA

Susa

Behistun

Rhagae

Persian Gulf

Gerrha

Erythraean Sea

MEDIA

ASSYRIA

Nineveh

Aoshur

Arbela

Opis

Babylon

BABYLONIA

Nippur

Erech

Ur

Sippar

Tigris

Euphrates

Anat

Harran

Nisibis

Carchemish

URARTU

MOSCHI

SCYTHIANS

KINGDOM OF LYDIA

Sardis

Ephesus

Miletus

Xanthus

LYDIA

(670-546 B.C.)

Sinope

Phasis

Trapezus

Black Sea

Byzantium

Apollonia

Chersonesus

THRACE

MACEDONIA

GREECE

Athens

Sparta

Marathon

Rhodes

Crete

Cyrene

CYRENE

Mediterranean Sea

LIBYA

Temple of Amon (Siwa)

KINGDOM OF EGYPT

(663-525 B.C.)

Sais

Memphis

Pelusium

Gaza

JUDAH

Jerusalem

Megiddo

Tyre

Gebal

Arvad

Damascus

Tadmor

Riblah

Hamath

Thapsacus

NEW BABYLONIAN EMPIRE

(625-529 B.C.)

Dumah

ARABS

Tema

Dedan

Elath

Red Sea

Thebes

Syene (Elephantine)

Nile

ETHIOPIA (CUSH)

Libyan Desert

Danube

Ister

Cyprus (trib. to Egypt 569-525 B.C.)

The Return from Exile
(Late Sixth Century B.C.)

Map 9

- ⚉ Satrapy capital
- ⊙ Provincial capitals
- ▢ District capitals
- • Towns

→ Possible route of
returning exiles

0 5 10 15 20 25 30 35 40 Mls
0 10 20 30 40 50 60 Kms

© Copyright HAMMOND INCORPORATED, Maplewood, N.J.

SIDON

Damascus

from Babylon

Mt. HERMON

DAMASCUS

Tyre

TYRE

Kedesh

Hazor

KARNAIM

Achzib

ACHZIB

Acco

ACCO

Karnaim

Lake
Gennesaret

Beth-
yerah

Yarmuk

HAURAN

The Great Sea

Dor

Mt. Carmel

DOR

Plain of Sharon

Strato's
Tower

Narbatah

Beth-shan

Pella

Jordan

GILEAD

(Mediterranean Sea)

Samaria

Gerasa

Mt. Ebal

Mt. Gerizim

Shechem

Jabbok

Apollonia

SAMARIA

Accrabbah

Aphek

Shiloh

Joppa

?

Ono

Neballat

Lod

Hadid

Beeroth

Bethel

Ai

Rabbah

Gittaim

Lower

Beth-horon

Mizpah

Ramah

Beth-gilgal

Tyre of Tobiah

Jamnia

Gezer

Gibeon

Geba

Jericho

AMMON

Kiriath-jearim

Anathoth

Beth-haccherem

Jerusalem

Heshbon

Ashdod

Zanoah

JUDAH

(YAHUD)

Bethlehem

Medeba

Azekah

Adullam

Netophah

Ashkelon

Keilah

Tekoa

Mareshah

Nebo

Beth-zur

Salt
Sea

Lachish

Gaza

Hebron

En-gedi

Arnon

Gerar

Ziklag?

MOAB

En-rimmon

IDUMEA

Raphia

Beer-sheba

Jeshua?

Moladah

(EDOMITES)

Beth-pelet?

NABATEAN   ARABS

ASHDOD

Map 10

The Empire of Alexander

Limits of Alexander's empire 323 B.C.

CYPRUS Allied states and client kingdoms
dependent on Alexander

Alexander's route

Major Battles

• Cities founded by Alexander.

----- Nearchus' voyage

0 100 200 300 400 500
0 200 400 600 800

© Copyright HAMMOND INCORPORATED, Maplewood, N.J.

Arabian Sea

Aral Sea

Caspian Sea

Black Sea

Aegean Sea

Mediterranean Sea

Red Sea

Persian Gulf

Indus

SCYTHIANS

MASSAGETAE

CHORASMIA

SOGDIANA

BACTRIA

ARIA

ARACHOSIA

GEDROSIA

CARMANIA

PERSIS

PARTHIA

MEDIA

SUSIANA

BABYLONIA

ARMENIA

ARABIA

ASIA MINOR

THRACE

MACEDONIA

EPIRUS

HELLAS

BITHYNIA

CYRENAICA

LIBYA

EGYPT

ETHIOPIA (CUSH)

Libyan Desert

Alexander died at Babylon in June 323 B.C.

Probable ancient coastline

Pattala

Nicaea

Bucephala

Taxila

Alexandria

Alexandria Arachosiorum (Kandahar)

Prophthasia

Alexandria Areion (Herat)

Bactra

Alexandria ad Caucasum

Maracanda

Alexandria Eschate

Oxus

Jaxartes

Hydaspes (Jhelum)

Hyphasis (Beas)

Pura

Alexandria

Harmozia

Persepolis

Pasargadae

Susa

Ecbatana

Rhagae

Caspian Gates

Hecatompylus

Gaugamela

Arbela

Tigris

Euphrates

Babylon

Thapsacus

Damascus

Jerusalem

Sidon

Tyre

Gaza

Pelusium

Memphis

Alexandria

Nile

Thebes

Syene

Oracle of Amon

Cyrene

Crete

Sparta

Athens

Ephesus

Sardis

Halicarnassus

Miletus

Gordion

Ancyra

Issus

Tarsus

Granicus

Ilium

Trapezus

Sinope

Olbia

Panticapaeum

Pella

Danube

Ister

331

333

332

331

330

330

329

328

328

327

326

325

325-24

324

323

331

Palestine
Under the Maccabees

- - - **Boundary of Judea before the uprising, 166 B.C.**

1 **Conquests under Jonathan, 160-142 B.C.**

2 **Conquests under Simon, 142-134 B.C.**

3 **Conquests under John Hyrcanus, 134-104 B.C.**

4 **Conquests under Aristobulus I, 104-103 B.C.**

5 **Conquests under Alexander Jannaeus, 103-76 B.C.**

Maccabean domain at maximum extent

0   5   10   15   20   25   30   35 Mls
0   10   20   30   40   50 Kms

© Copyright HAMMOND INCORPORATED, Maplewood, N.J.

Map 11

A   B   C   D

Tyre
Ladder of Tyre
Paneas
Gadasa (Kadesh)
Hazor
Seleucia
GAULANITIS
Ptolemais (Acco)
Gamala
Lake Gennesaret
Carnaim
Arbela
GALILEE
Hippos
Dion
Sepphoris
Philoteria
Gaba
Mt. Tabor
Abila
Gadara
Dora
Ephron
Narbata
Scythopolis
Bethsean
Pella
Gerasa
SAMARIA
Samaria
Amathus
Ragaba
Strato's Tower
Capharsaba
Sichem
Mt. Gerizim
Apollonia
Pharathon
Alexandrium
TOBIADS
Joppa
Ramathaim
Gedor
Beth-dagon
Adida (Hadid)
Timnah
Aphairema
Tyrus
Philadelphia (Rabbah)
Free city state
Lydda (Lod)
Gophna
Bethel
Dok
Jamnia (Jabneh)
Modein
Jericho
Samega
Beth-horon
Elasa
Mizpah
Michmash
Gazara (Gezer)
Caphar-salama
Adasa
Heshbon
Emmaus
Azotus (Ashdod)
Cedron
Jerusalem
Qumran
Medeba
Ekron
JUDEA
Hyrcania
Ascalon
Free city state
Beth-zacharias?
Bethbasi
Machaerus
Marisa (Mareshah)
Adullam
Tekoa
Adora
Beth-zur
Anthedon
Hebron
Gaza
IDUMEA
En-gedi
Salt Sea
Masada
Arad
Raphia
Beer-sheba
Characmoba
Zoara
AKRABATTENE

The Great Sea (Mediterranean Sea)

Plain of Sharon

Plain of Esdraelon

Jordan

NABATEANS

The Roman World

Limits of direct Roman rule
or political influence at the
birth of Jesus

- - - - Provincial or state boundaries

SYRIA Roman provinces

LYCIA Client kingdoms or states

0   100 200 300 400 500 Mls
0 200 400 600 800 Kms

© Copyright HAMMOND INCORPORATED, Maplewood, N.J.

Map 12

Caspian Sea

Rha (Volga)

Phasis

COLCHIS

ARMENIA

Artaxata

PARTHIAN EMPIRE

Ctesiphon

Arabia

Red Sea

Sarmatia

BOSPORUS KDM.

Black Sea

Trapezus

Sinope

PONTUS

Amisia

CAPPADOCIA

COMMAGENE

SYRIA

Antioch

Tarsus

CILICIA

NABATAEA

KDM. OF HEROD

Jerusalem

EGYPT

Memphis

Nile

Thebes

Germania Magna

Albis (Elbe)

Lost by Rome in A.D. 9

Rhine

Augusta Trevorum

CARPATHIANS

Dacia

Ister (Danube)

Danube

NORICUM

PANNONIA

RAETIA

ILLYRICUM

Salonae

MOESIA

THRACE

Byzantium

MACEDONIA

Thessalonica

BITHYNIA & PONTUS

Nicaea

GALATIA

ASIA

Pergamum

Ephesus

LYCIA & PAMPHYLIA

CYPRUS

ACHAIA

Athens

Corinth

Aegean Sea

CRETA

Cyrene

Internum

Alexandria

CYRENAICA

Atlantic Ocean

Britannia

Lutetia

LUGDUNENSIS

Lugdunum

BELGICA

Gaul

AQUITANIA

Burdigala

NARBONENSIS

Narbo

Hispania

TARRACONENSIS

Tarraco

Caesaraugusta

Emerita Augusta

LUSITANIA

BAETICA

Corduba

Tingis

Rubicon

Rome

CORSICA

SARDINIA

Caralis

SICILIA

Syracuse

Tarentum

Sea of Adria

Carthage

Caesarea

Cirta

NUMIDIA

MAURETANIA

Mare (Mediterranean Sea)

Leptis Magna

AFRICA

Mare Internum (Mediterranean Sea)

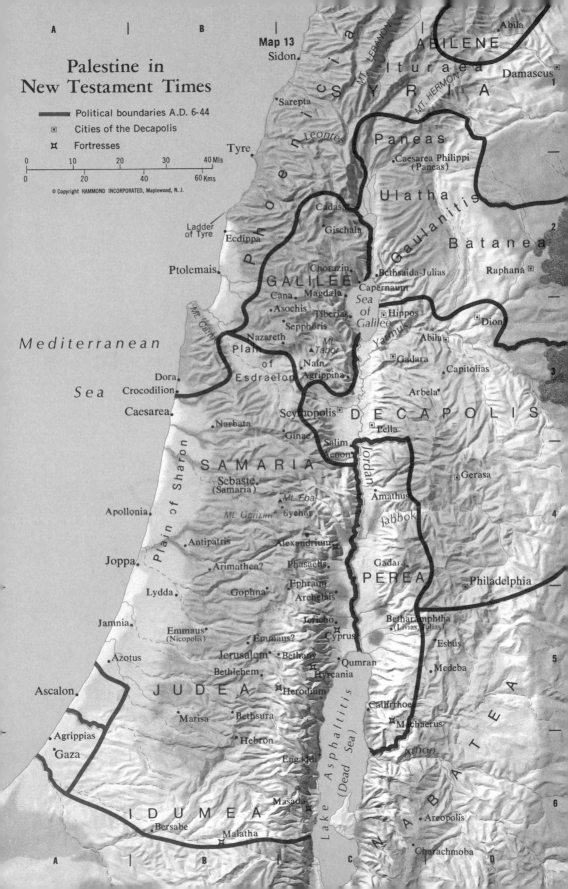

Palestine in New Testament Times

Map 13

━━━ Political boundaries A.D. 6-44
⊡ Cities of the Decapolis
⋈ Fortresses

0 10 20 30 40 Mls
0   20   40   60 Kms

© Copyright HAMMOND INCORPORATED, Maplewood, N.J.

Mediterranean

Sea

ABILENE

Abila

Ituraea

S Y R I A

Sidon

Mt. LEBANON

Mt. HERMON

Damascus

Sarepta

Leontes

Paneas

Caesarea Philippi
(Paneas)

Tyre

Ladder
of Tyre

Ecdippa

Cadasa

Gischala

Ptolemais

Chorazin

Ulatha

Bethsaida-Julias

Raphana ⊡

G A L I L E E

Cana Magdala

Capernaum

Sea
of
Galilee

Hippos ⊡

Dion ⊡

Asochis

Tiberias

Sepphoris

Nazareth

Mt. Carmel

Mt. Tabor

Yarmuk

Abila

Nain

Agrippina

Gadara ⊡

Capitolias

Dora

Crocodilion

Plain
of
Esdraelon

Arbela

Caesarea

Narbata

Scythopolis ⊡

D E C A P O L I S

Pella

Ginae

Salim
Aenon

S A M A R I A

Sebaste
(Samaria)

Jordan

Gerasa ⊡

Mt. Ebal

Apollonia

Mt. Gerizim Sychar

Jabbok

Amathus

Antipatris

Alexandrium ⋈

Gadara

Joppa

Arimathea?

Phasaelis

P E R E A

Philadelphia

Lydda

Gophna

Ephraim

Archelais

Jamnia

Emmaus
(Nicopolis)

Emmaus?

Jericho

Cyprus ⋈

Betharamphtha
(Livias-Julias)

Azotus

Jerusalem

Bethany

Qumran

Esbus

Bethlehem

Hyrcania ⋈

Medeba

Ascalon

Herodium ⋈

Callirrhoe

J U D E A

Marisa

Bethsura

Agrippias

Hebron

Machaerus ⋈

Gaza

Engaddi

Arnon

Lake
Asphaltitis
(Dead Sea)

N A B A T E A

Masada ⋈

I D U M E A

Areopolis

Bersabe

Malatha ⋈

Charachmoba

Phoenicia

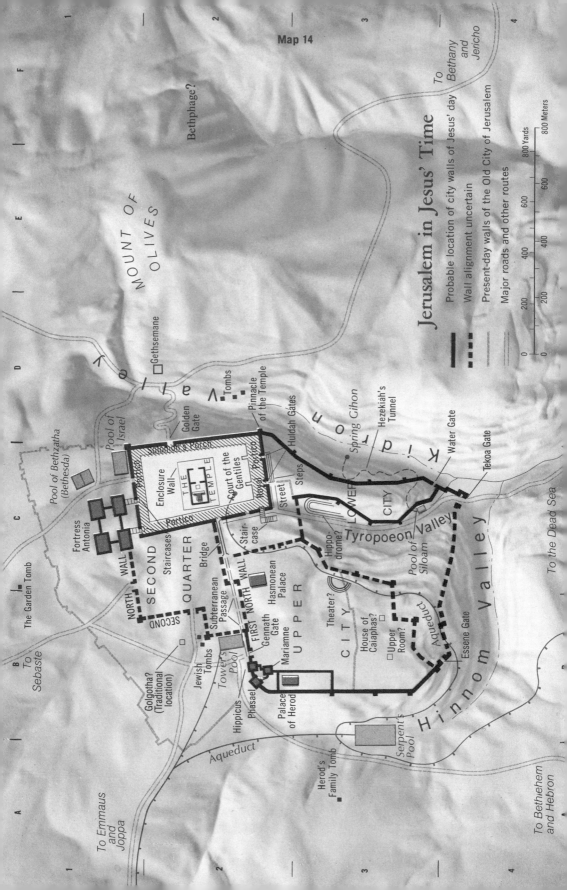

Map 14

Jerusalem in Jesus' Time

Probable location of city walls of Jesus' day
Wall alignment uncertain
Present-day walls of the Old City of Jerusalem
Major roads and other routes

800 Yards
800 Meters

600
600

400
400

200
200

0
0

To Bethany and Jericho

Bethphage?

MOUNT OF OLIVES

Gethsemane

Kidron Valley

Tombs

Pinnacle of the Temple

Golden Gate

Pool of Israel

Solomon's Porch

Spring Gihon

Huldah Gates

Hezekiah's Tunnel

Water Gate

Tekoa Gate

Portico
Portico
Enclosure Wall
THE TEMPLE
Court of the Gentiles
Royal Portico
Portico

Steps

Street

Staircase

LOWER CITY

Pool of Bethzatha (Bethesda)

Fortress Antonia

Staircases

Bridge

Subterranean Passage

SECOND QUARTER

NORTH WALL

SECOND NORTH WALL

Hippo-drome?

Tyropoeon Valley

Pool of Siloam

The Garden Tomb

FIRST NORTH WALL

Gennath Gate

Hasmonean Palace

Theater?

House of Caiaphas?

Upper Room?

Aqueduct

Essene Gate

Hinnom Valley

To the Dead Sea

Mariamne

UPPER CITY

Jewish Tombs

Tower's Pool

Golgotha? (Traditional location)

Hippicus

Phasael

Palace of Herod

To Sebaste

To Emmaus and Joppa

Aqueduct

Herod's Family Tomb

Serpent's Pool

To Bethlehem and Hebron

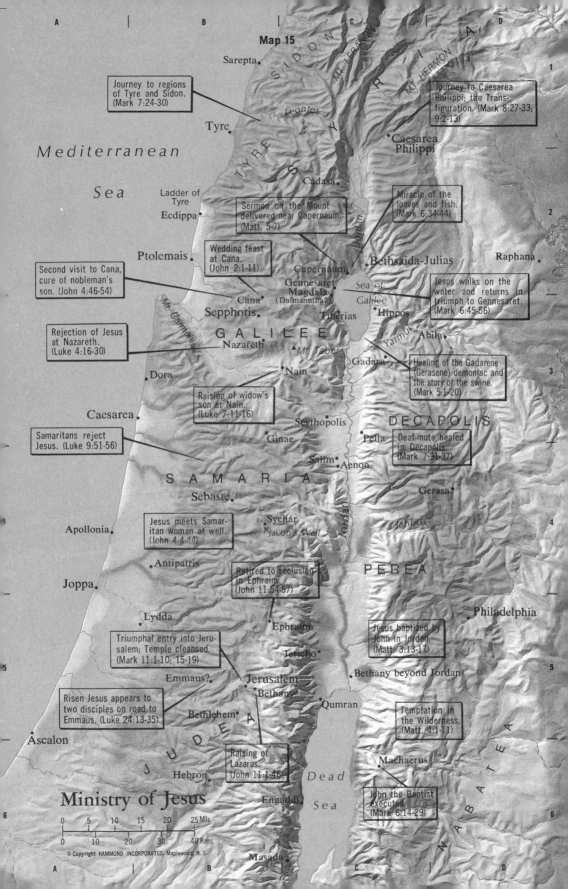

Map 15

A · B · C · D

SIDON · MT. LEBANON · S Y R I A

1

Sarepta

MT. HERMON

Leontes

Tyre

Journey to regions of Tyre and Sidon. (Mark 7:24-30)

Journey to Caesarea Philippi; the Transfiguration. (Mark 8:27-33; 9:2-13)

Caesarea Philippi

Mediterranean

Sea

2

Cadasa

Ladder of Tyre

Ecdippa

Sermon on the Mount delivered near Capernaum. (Matt. 5-7)

Miracle of the loaves and fish. (Mark 6:34-44)

Jordan

Ptolemais

Wedding feast at Cana. (John 2:1-11)

Capernaum

Bethsaida-Julias

Raphana

Second visit to Cana, cure of nobleman's son. (John 4:46-54)

Gennesaret

Magdala (Dalmanutha?)

Jesus walks on the water and returns in triumph to Gennesaret. (Mark 6:45-56)

Cana

Sea of Galilee

Mt. Carmel

Sepphoris

G A L I L E E

Tiberias

Hippos

3

Rejection of Jesus at Nazareth. (Luke 4:16-30)

Nazareth

▲ Mt. Tabor

Yarmuk

Abila

Dora

Nain

Gadara

Healing of the Gadarene (Gerasene) demoniac and the story of the swine. (Mark 5:1-20)

Raising of widow's son at Nain. (Luke 7:11-16)

Caesarea

Scythopolis

D E C A P O L I S

Samaritans reject Jesus. (Luke 9:51-56)

Ginae

Pella

Deaf-mute healed in Decapolis. (Mark 7:31-37)

4

S A M A R I A

Salim

Aenon

Gerasa

Sebaste

Jabbok

Apollonia

Jesus meets Samaritan woman at well. (John 4:4-44)

Sychar

Jacob's Well

P E R E A

Antipatris

Joppa

Retired to seclusion in Ephraim. (John 11:54-57)

Philadelphia

5

Lydda

Ephraim

Jesus baptized by John in Jordan. (Matt. 3:13-17)

Triumphal entry into Jerusalem; Temple cleansed. (Mark 11:1-10; 15-19)

Jericho

Jordan

Emmaus?

Jerusalem

Bethany beyond Jordan

Risen Jesus appears to two disciples on road to Emmaus. (Luke 24:13-35)

Bethany

Temptation in the Wilderness. (Matt. 4:1-11)

Bethlehem

Qumran

Ascalon

J U D E A

Raising of Lazarus. (John 11:1-46)

Machaerus

N A B A T E A

Hebron

Dead

John the Baptist executed. (Mark 6:14-29)

Ministry of Jesus

Engaddi

Sea

6

0 5 10 15 20 25 Mls

0 10 20 30 40 Kms

© Copyright HAMMOND INCORPORATED, Maplewood, N.J.

Masada

A · B · C · D

The Journeys of Paul
According to the Book of Acts

- — — First missionary journey
- ——— Second missionary journey
- ——— Third missionary journey
- ——— Paul's journey to Rome
- — Provincial boundaries in the Roman Empire ca. A.D. 60

300 Mls

500 Kms

© Copyright HAMMOND INCORPORATED, Maplewood, N.J.

Map 16

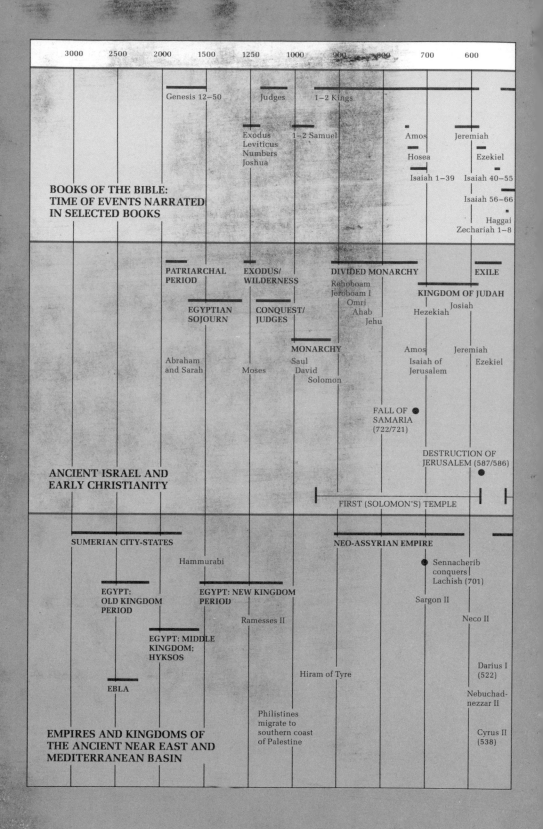

3000	2500	2000	1500	1250	1000	900	800	700	600

**BOOKS OF THE BIBLE:
TIME OF EVENTS NARRATED
IN SELECTED BOOKS**

Genesis 12–50

Judges

1–2 Kings

Exodus
Leviticus
Numbers
Joshua

1–2 Samuel

Amos

Jeremiah

Hosea

Ezekiel

Isaiah 1–39

Isaiah 40–55

Isaiah 56–66

Haggai
Zechariah 1–8

**ANCIENT ISRAEL AND
EARLY CHRISTIANITY**

**PATRIARCHAL
PERIOD**

**EXODUS/
WILDERNESS**

DIVIDED MONARCHY

EXILE

Rehoboam
Jeroboam I
Omri
Ahab
Jehu

KINGDOM OF JUDAH

Josiah

Hezekiah

**EGYPTIAN
SOJOURN**

**CONQUEST/
JUDGES**

MONARCHY

Abraham
and Sarah

Moses

Saul
David
Solomon

Amos
Isaiah of
Jerusalem

Jeremiah
Ezekiel

FALL OF ●
SAMARIA
(722/721)

DESTRUCTION OF
JERUSALEM (587/586)
●

FIRST (SOLOMON'S) TEMPLE

**EMPIRES AND KINGDOMS OF
THE ANCIENT NEAR EAST AND
MEDITERRANEAN BASIN**

SUMERIAN CITY-STATES

NEO-ASSYRIAN EMPIRE

Hammurabi

● Sennacherib
conquers
Lachish (701)

**EGYPT:
OLD KINGDOM
PERIOD**

**EGYPT: NEW KINGDOM
PERIOD**

Sargon II

Neco II

Ramesses II

**EGYPT: MIDDLE
KINGDOM;
HYKSOS**

Darius I
(522)

Hiram of Tyre

Nebuchad-
nezzar II

EBLA

Philistines
migrate to
southern coast
of Palestine

Cyrus II
(538)